PRAISE
THE BANTAM NEW COLLEGE ITALIAN AND ENGLISH DICTIONARY

". . . thorough, accurate, well-organized, clear, and up to date . . . Relevant to the student's contemporary life . . . It is bound to become a mainstay in the field."
—Albert N. Mancini, Professor of Romance Languages, The Ohio State University

---

"Both the method and the execution seem to me excellent . . . It would be impossible to find elsewhere as good a dictionary of this size."
—Beatrice Corrigan, Professor Emeritus, Editor, University of Toronto Press

---

"Apart from its accurate philological approach, its most useful grammatical apparatus, and other singular features, this concise dictionary is the first which is based primarily on *American* English usage . . . It contains numerous up-to-date colloquial and technical terms which cannot be found in any other similar dictionary."
—M. Ricciardelli, Professor of Italian and Comparative Literatures, Editor of *Forum Italicum*

Comprehensive, authoritative, and completely modern, **THE BANTAM NEW COLLEGE ITALIAN AND ENGLISH DICTIONARY** is a landmark in foreign language reference works.

THE BANTAM NEW COLLEGE DICTIONARY SERIES

Robert C. Melzi, Author

ROBERT C. MELZI, D. in L., A.M., Ph.D., was trained in Italy, at the University of Padua, and in the United States, at the University of Pennsylvania. He has done extensive linguistic research, traveling frequently to his native country. Now professor of Romance Languages at Widener College, he has contributed articles and reviews to many learned journals, is the author of *Castelvetro's Annotations to the Inferno,* The Hague and Paris, 1966 (Castelvetro was one of Italy's foremost philologists), and is an associate editor of *The Scribner-Bantam English Dictionary* (Scribner's, 1977; Bantam Books, 1979). Professor Melzi is a Cavaliere in the Order of Solidarity of the Republic of Italy.

Edwin B. Williams, General Editor

EDWIN B. WILLIAMS (1891–1975), A.B., A.M., Ph.D., Doct. d'Univ., LL.D., L.H.D., was chairman of the Department of Romance Languages, dean of the Graduate School, and provost of the University of Pennsylvania. He was a member of the American Philosophical Society and the Hispanic Society of America. Among his many lexicographical works are *The Williams Spanish and English Dictionary* (Scribner's, formerly Holt) and *The Bantam New College Spanish and English Dictionary.* He created and coordinated the Bantam series of original dictionaries—English, French, German, Italian, Latin, and Spanish. The University of Pennsylvania named "Williams Hall" in honor of Edwin B. Williams and his wife, Leonore, and is establishing the "Williams Chair in Lexicography," as the first chair in lexicography in an English-speaking country.

THE BANTAM NEW COLLEGE
ITALIAN & ENGLISH DICTIONARY

ROBERT C. MELZI, Ph.D.
Widener College, Philadelphia

BANTAM BOOKS
TORONTO · NEW YORK · LONDON · SYDNEY

THE BANTAM NEW COLLEGE
ITALIAN & ENGLISH DICTIONARY
A Bantam Book / April 1976
2nd printing ...... January 1978 4th printing .... April 1980
3rd printing .... February 1979 5th printing .... May 1981

ISBN 0-553-20267-7

Published simultaneously in the United States and Canada

Bantam Books are published by Bantam Books, Inc. Its trademark, consisting of the words "Bantam Books" and the portrayal of a bantam, is Registered in U.S. Patent and Trademark Office and in other countries. Marca Registrada. Bantam Books, Inc., 666 Fifth Avenue, New York, New York 10103.

PRINTED IN THE UNITED STATES OF AMERICA

14 13 12 11 10 9 8 7

CONTENTS

PREFACE

Inasmuch as the basic function of a bilingual dictionary is to provide semantic equivalences, syntactical constructions are shown in both the source and the target languages on both sides of the Dictionary. In performing this function, a bilingual dictionary must fulfill six purposes. That is, an Italian and English dictionary must provide (1) Italian words which an English-speaking person wishes to use in speaking and writing (by means of the English-Italian part), (2) English meanings of Italian words which an English-speaking person encounters in listening and reading (by means of the Italian-English part), (3) the spelling, pronunciation, and inflection of Italian words and the gender of Italian nouns which an English-speaking person needs in order to use Italian words correctly (by means of the Italian-English part), (4) English words which an Italian-speaking person wishes to use in speaking and writing (by means of the Italian-English part), (5) Italian meanings of English words which an Italian-speaking person encounters in listening and reading (by means of the English-Italian part), and (6) the spelling, pronunciation, and inflection of English words which an Italian-speaking person needs in order to use English words correctly (by means of the English-Italian part).

It may seem logical to provide the pronunciation and inflection of English words and the pronunciation and inflection of Italian words and the gender of Italian nouns where these words appear as target words inasmuch as target words, according to (1) and (4) above, are sought for the purpose of speaking and writing. Thus the user would find not only the words he seeks but all the information he needs about them in one and the same place. But this technique is impractical because target words are not alphabetized and could, therefore, be found only by the roundabout and uncertain way of seeking them through their translations in

PREFAZIONE

Dato che la funzione principale di un dizionario bilingue è quella di fornire all'utente equivalenze semantiche, le costruzioni sintattiche sono indicate in entrambe le lingue, quella di partenza e quella di arrivo, in entrambe le parti del Dizionario. Per compiere questa funzione, un dizionario bilingue deve raggiungere sei scopi differenti. Cioè, un dizionario italiano e inglese deve fornire (1) nella parte inglese-italiano, le parole italiane che la persona anglofona vuole adoperare parlando e scrivendo l'italiano; (2) nella parte italiano-inglese, il significato in inglese delle parole italiane che tale persona oda nella lingua parlata o legga in libri o giornali; (3) nella parte italiano-inglese, l'ortografia, la pronunzia, la flessione delle parole italiane e il genere dei nomi italiani che la persona anglofona deve conoscere per servirsi correttamente della lingua italiana; (4) nella parte italiano-inglese, le parole inglesi che la persona italofona vuole adoperare parlando o scrivendo l'inglese; (5) nella parte inglese-italiano, il significato in italiano delle parole inglesi che tale persona oda nella lingua parlata o legga in libri o giornali; (6) nella parte inglese-italiano, l'ortografia, la pronunzia figurata e la flessione delle parole inglesi che la persona italofona deve conoscere per servirsi correttamente della lingua inglese.

A prima vista potrebbe sembrare logico che la pronunzia e la flessione delle parole inglesi e la pronunzia e la flessione delle parole italiane e il genere dei nomi italiani fossero indicati dove queste parole si trovano nella lingua d'arrivo, dato che le parole della lingua d'arrivo, secondo i punti (1) e (4) enunciati più sopra, sono consultate da coloro che vogliono parlare e scrivere in lingua straniera. In questa maniera l'utente troverebbe non solo le parole che cerca, ma tutte le informazioni che gli sono necessarie, nello stesso luogo. Questa tecnica, peraltro, non è pratica poiché le parole della lingua d'arrivo non si trovano in ordine

the other part of the dictionary. And this would be particularly inconvenient for persons using the dictionary for purposes (2) and (5) above. It is much more convenient to provide immediate alphabetized access to pronunciation and inflection where the words appear as source words.

alfabetico e potrebbero quindi essere trovate solo in maniera complicata nella parte opposta del dizionario. E ciò sarebbe specialmente scomodo per coloro che usano il dizionario per gli scopi (2) e (5) menzionati più sopra. È molto più semplice aggiungere la pronunzia e la flessione nella serie alfabetica in cui le parole si trovano nella loro lingua di partenza.

Since Italian is an almost perfectly phonetic language, IPA transcription of Italian words has been omitted. The only elements of pronunciation not shown by standard spelling are the values of tonic **e** and **o** (§1; pp. 3, 4) the stress of words stressed on the third syllable from the end (§3,3; p. 5), the value of intervocalic **s** when unvoiced, and the values of **z** and **zz** when voiced (§1; p. 4); these are shown in the entry words themselves.

Dato che l'italiano è una lingua quasi perfettamente fonetica, non si è data la trascrizione delle parole italiane nell'alfabeto dell'Associazione Fonetica Internazionale. Considerando che l'ortografia comune non mostra il vario timbro della **e** (§1, p. 3) e della **o** (§1, p. 4) quando esse sono toniche, l'accento delle parole sdrucciole (§3,3, p. 5), la pronunzia della **s** sorda (§1, p. 4) e la pronunzia delle **z** e **zz** sonore (§1, p. 4), si è data tale informazione nell'esponente stesso.

All words are treated in a fixed order according to the parts of speech and the functions of verbs, as follows: adjective, article, substantive, pronoun, adverb, preposition, conjunction, transitive verb, intransitive verb, reflexive verb, auxiliary verb, impersonal verb, interjection.

Ogni singola voce è trattata secondo uno schema fisso che si riferisce alle parti del discorso o alle funzioni del verbo, nel seguente ordine: aggettivo, articolo, sostantivo, pronome, avverbio, preposizione, congiunzione, verbo transitivo, verbo intransitivo, verbo riflessivo, verbo ausiliare, verbo impersonale e interiezione.

Meanings with labels come after more general meanings. Labels (printed in roman and in parentheses) refer to the preceding entry or phrase (printed in boldface).

I significati accompagnati da sigle si trovano dopo quelli di accezione più generale. Tali sigle (che sono sempre stampate in carattere romano e in parentesi) si riferiscono all'esponente precedente, stampato in grassetto, o alla frase precedente, ugualmente stampata in grassetto.

In view of the fact that the users of this Italian and English bilingual dictionary are for the most part English-speaking people, definitions and discriminations are provided in English. They are printed in italics and in parentheses and refer to the English word which they particularize:

Dato che gli utenti di questo dizionario bilingue italiano e inglese sono per lo più anglofoni, definizioni e locuzioni esplicative sono apportate in inglese. Sono stampate in corsivo e in parentesi e si riferiscono sempre alla parola inglese il cui significato cercano di spiegare:

porter ['portər] *s* (*doorman*) portiere *m;* (*man who carries luggage*) facchino; . . .
órdine *m* order; . . . series (*e.g., of years*); college (*e.g., of surgeons*); . . .

English adjectives are always translated by the Italian masculine form

Gli aggettivi inglesi sono sempre tradotti in maschile italiano, anche se il

regardless of whether the translation of the exemplary noun modified would be masculine or feminine:

nome che qualificano sia un femminile italiano:

tough [tʌf] *adj* duro; . . . ; (*luck*) cattivo; . . .

In order to facilitate the finding of the meaning and use sought for, changes within a vocabulary entry in part of speech and function of verb, in irregular inflection, in the use of an initial capital, in the gender of Italian nouns, and in the pronunciation of English words are marked with parallels: ||, instead of the usual semicolons.

Per facilitare l'uso del Dizionario, i raggruppamenti sono stati fatti secondo le parti del discorso, la funzione del verbo, la flessione irregolare, l'uso della maiuscola iniziale, il genere dei nomi italiani e la pronunzia delle parole inglesi e sono separati da sbarrette verticali: ||, invece del punto e virgola che è stato generalmente usato.

Since vocabulary entries are not determined on the basis of etymology, homographs are included in a single entry. When the pronunciation of an English homograph changes, this is shown in the proper place after parallels:

Dato che gli esponenti in questo Dizionario non sono stati selezionati su base etimologica, tutti gli omografi sono inclusi sotto il medesimo esponente. Il cambio di pronunzia di un omografo inglese è indicato al posto adatto dopo sbarrette verticali:

frequent [ˈfrikwənt] *adj* frequente || [frɪˈkwent] or [ˈfrikwənt] *tr* . . .

However, when the pronunciation of an Italian homograph changes, the words are entered separately:

Però, quando la pronunzia di un omografo italiano cambia, si hanno esponenti separati:

retina *f* small net
rètina *f* (anat) retina
tóc·co -ca (-chi -che) *adj* . . . || *m* touch; . . .
tòc·co *m* **(-chi)** chunk, piece; . . .

Periods are omitted after labels and grammatical abbreviations and at the end of vocabulary entries.

Il punto è stato omesso dopo sigle, abbreviazioni grammaticali, ed alla fine di ogni articolo.

Proper nouns are listed in their alphabetical position in the main body of the Dictionary. Thus **Svezia** and **svedese** do not have to be looked up in two different sections of the book. And all subentries are listed in strictly alphabetical order.

Tutti i nomi propri sono posti nella loro posizione alfabetica nel corpo del Dizionario: quindi **Svezia** e **svedese** non si trovano in sezioni separate di questo libro. Per la medesima ragione di semplicità d'uso, le parole e frasi contenute sotto ogni esponente sono poste in ordine alfabetico.

The gender of Italian nouns is shown on both sides of the Dictionary, except that the gender of masculine nouns ending in **-o**, feminine nouns ending in **-a** and **-ione**, masculine nouns modified by an adjective ending in **-o**, and feminine nouns modified by an adjective

Il genere dei nomi italiani è indicato in entrambe le parti del Dizionario, eccezion fatta nella parte inglese-italiano, per le parole maschili che terminano in **-o**, per le parole femminili che terminano in **-a** e in **-ione**, per i nomi maschili accompagnati da un

ending in **-a** is not shown on the English-Italian side.

aggettivo che termina in **-o** e per i nomi femminili accompagnati da un aggettivo che termina in **-a**.

The feminine form of an Italian adjective used as a noun (or an Italian feminine noun having identical spelling with the feminine form of an adjective) which falls alphabetically in a separate position from the adjective is treated in that position and is listed again as a cross reference under the adjective:

Quando un nome femminile italiano ha la medesima grafia della forma femminile di un aggettivo o quando tale forma femminile di aggettivo è usata come nome, lo si trova elencato nella sua posizione alfabetica come nome e poi di nuovo come rinvio interno sotto l'aggettivo:

nòta *f* mark, score, . . .
nò•to -ta *adj* . . . || *m* . . . || *f* see **nota**

The centered period is used in vocabulary entries of inflected words to mark off, according to standard orthographic principles in the two languages, the final syllable that has to be detached before the syllable showing the inflection is added:

Qualora l'esponente italiano o inglese sia un vocabolo a flessione, un punto leggermente elevato sopra il rigo è stato usato per separare, secondo le regole ortografiche di ciascuna delle due lingue, la sillaba finale che dev'essere rimossa prima che la nuova desinenza di flessione possa essere attaccata al corpo dell'esponente, per es.:

vèc•chio -chia (-chi -chie) *adj* . . .
put•ty ['pʌti] *s* **(-ties)** . . . || *v* (*pret & pp* **-tied**) . . .
hap•py ['hæpi] *adj* **(-pier; -piest)** . . .

If the entry word cannot be divided by a centered period the full form is given in parentheses:

Se l'esponente non può essere scisso a mezzo del suddetto punto, la forma completa è indicata in parentesi:

mouse [maʊs] *s* **(mice** [maɪs]) . . .
mouth [maʊθ] *s* **(mouths** [maʊðz]) . . .
die [daɪ] *s* **(dice** [daɪs]) . . . || *s* **(dies)** . . . || *v* (*pret & pp* **died;** *ger* **dying)** *intr* . . .

Many Italian verbs which take an indirect object have, as their equivalent, English verbs which take a direct object. This is shown on both sides of this Dictionary by the insertion of (with *dat*) after the Italian verb, e.g.,

Molti verbi italiani che reggono un oggetto indiretto hanno come equivalenti inglesi verbi che reggono un oggetto diretto. Questa equivalenza è indicata in entrambe le parti del Dizionario con l'aggiunta di (with *dat*) dopo il verbo italiano, per es.:

ubbidire §176 *intr* . . . ; (with *dat*) to obey
obey [o'be] *tr* ubbidire (with *dat*)

On the Italian-English side inflection is shown by: a) numbers that refer to the grammatical tables of articles, pronouns, etc., and to the tables of model verbs; they are placed before the abbreviation indicating the part of speech:

Nella parte italiano-inglese la flessione si indica: a) con numeri che si riferiscono alle tavole grammaticali degli articoli, dei pronomi, ecc., e alle tavole dei verbi modello; questi numeri sono posti innanzi all'abbreviazione indicante la parte del discorso:

mì•o -a §6 *adj & pron poss*
lui §5 *pron pers*
congiùngere §183 *tr & ref*

b) the first person singular of the present indicative of verbs in which the stess falls on either an **e** or an **o** not stressed in the infinitive or on the third syllable from the end, whatever the vowel may be:

b) con la prima persona singolare del presente dell'indicativo dei verbi non sdruccioli all'infinito in cui l'accento tonico cade o su una **e** o su una **o**, o su qualsiasi vocale di una parola sdrucciola:

ritornare (ritórno) *tr* . . .
visitare (vìsito) *tr* . . .

c) the feminine endings of all adjectives which end in **-o**:

c) con la desinenza femminile di tutti gli aggettivi che terminano in **-o** nel maschile:

laborió•so -sa [s] *adj* . . .

d) the plural endings of nouns and adjectives which are formed irregularly:

d) con la desinenza plurale dei nomi e aggettivi che si formano in maniera irregolare:

bràc•cio *m* **(-cia** *fpl***)** . . . || *m* **(-ci)** . . .
cit•tà *f* **(-tà)** . . .
dià•rio -ria (-ri -rie) *adj* . . . || *m* . . . || *f* . . .
fotogram•ma *m* **(-mi)** . . .
fràn•gia *f* **(-ge)** . . .
laburi•sta (-sti -ste) *adj* . . . || *mf* . . .
la•go *m* **(-ghi)** . . .
òr•co *m* **(-chi)** . . .
òtti•co -ca (-ci -che) *adj* . . . || *m* . . . || *f* . . .

e) the full plural forms of all nouns that cannot be divided by a center period or whose plural cannot be shown by such division:

e) con la completa forma plurale di quei nomi che non possono essere scissi col suddetto punto o che hanno mutamenti interni:

re *m* **(re)** . . .
caporeparto *m* **(capireparto)** . . .

I wish to express my gratitude to many persons who helped me in the production of this book and particularly to Dr. Edwin B. Williams who, ever since graduate school, has been a constant inspiration and who has established the principles upon which this book was compiled, to my wife and children, who patiently aided and abetted me through ten years of research and compilation, to Richard J. Nelson, Sebastiano DiBlasi, Walter D. Glanze, and to Giacomo De Voto, Miro Dogliotti, and Michele Ricciardelli.

Labels and abbreviations

Sigle ed abbreviazioni

abbr abbreviation—abbreviazione
(acronym) word formed from the initial letters or syllables of a series of words—parola costituita dalle lettere o sillabe iniziali di una serie di parole
adj adjective—aggettivo
adv adverb—avverbio
(aer) aeronautics—aeronautica
(agr) agriculture—agricoltura
(alg) algebra—algebra
(anat) anatomy—anatomia
(archaic) arcaico
(archeol) archeology—archeologia
(archit) architecture—architettura
(arith) arithmetic—aritmetica
art article—articolo
(astr) astronomy—astronomia
(astrol) astrology—astrologia
(aut) automobile—automobile
aux auxiliary verb—verbo ausiliare
(bact) bacteriology—batteriologia
(baseball) baseball
(basketball) pallacanestro
(bb) bookbinding—legatoria
(Bib) Biblical—biblico
(billiards) biliardo
(biochem) biochemistry—biochimica
(biol) biology—biologia
(bot) botany—botanica
(bowling) bowling
(boxing) pugilato
(bridge) bridge
(Brit) British—britannico
(cards) carte da gioco
(carp) carpentry—falegnameria
(checkers) gioco della dama
(chem) chemistry—chimica
(chess) scacchi
(coll) colloquial—familiare
(com) commercial—commerciale
comb form elemento di parola composta
comp comparative—comparativo
cond conditional—condizionale
conj conjunction—congiunzione
(cricket) cricket
(culin) cooking—cucina
dat dative—dativo
def definite—determinativo, definito
dem demonstrative—dimostrativo
(dentistry) medicina dentaria
(dial) dialectal—dialettale
(dipl) diplomacy—diplomazia
(disparaging) sprezzante
(eccl) ecclesiastical—ecclesiastico
(econ) economics—economia
(educ) education—istruzione
e.g., or *e.g.*, per esempio
(elec) electricity—elettricità
(electron) electronics—elettronica
(ent) entomology—entomologia
(equit) horseback riding—equitazione
f feminine noun—nome femminile
(fa) fine arts—belle arti
fem feminine—femminile
(fencing) scherma
(fig) figurative—figurato
(fin) financial—finanziario
(football) football americano
fpl feminine noun plural—nome femminile plurale
fut future—futuro
(geog) geography—geografia
(geol) geology—geologia
(geom) geometry—geometria
ger gerund—gerundio
(golf) golf
(gram) grammar—grammatica
(herald) heraldry—araldica
(hist) history—storia
(hort) horticulture—orticoltura
(hunt) hunting—caccia
(ichth) ichthyology—ittiologia
i.e., cioè
imperf imperfect—imperfetto
impers impersonal verb—verbo impersonale
impv imperative—imperativo
ind indicative—indicativo
indef indefinite—indefinito, indeterminativo
inf infinitive—infinito
(ins) insurance—assicurazione
interj interjection—interiezione
interr interrogative—interrogativo
intr intransitive verb—verbo intransitivo
invar invariable—invariabile
(Italian cards) carte italiane
(jewelry) gioielleria
(joc) jocular—faceto
(journ) journalism—giornalismo
(law) diritto, legge
(letterword) word in the form of an abbreviation which is pronounced by sounding the names of its letters in

succession and which functions as a part of speech—parola in forma di abbreviazione che si ottiene pronunziando consecutivamente la denominazione di ciascuna lettera e che funziona come parte del discorso
(lexicography) lessicografia
(ling) linguistics—linguistica
(lit) literary—letterario
(log) logic—logica
m masculine noun—nome maschile
(mach) machinery—macchinario
masc masculine—maschile
(math) mathematics—matematica
(mech) mechanics—meccanica
(med) medicine—medicina
(metallurgy) metallurgia
(meteor) meteorology—meteorologia
mf masculine or feminine noun according to sex—nome maschile o nome femminile secondo il sesso
m & f see below between (mythol) and (naut)
(mil) military—militare
(min) mining—lavorazione delle miniere
(mov) moving pictures—cinematografo
mpl masculine noun plural—nome maschile plurale
(mus) music—musica
(mythol) mythology—mitologia
m & f masculine and feminine noun without regard to sex—nome maschile e femminile senza distinzione di sesso
(naut) nautical—nautico
(nav) naval—navale
neut neuter—neutro
num number—numero
(obs) obsolete—in disuso
(obstet) obstetrics—ostetricia
(opt) optics—ottica
(orn) ornithology—ornitologia
(painting) pittura
(pathol) pathology—patologia
(pej) pejorative—peggiorativo
perf perfect—perfetto, passato
pers personal—personale; person—persona
(pharm) pharmacy—farmacia
(philately) filatelia
(philol) philology—filologia
(philos) philosophy—filosofia
(phonet) phonetics—fonetica
(phot) photography—fotografia
(phys) physics—fisica
(physiol) physiology—fisiologia
pl plural—plurale
(poet) poetical—poetico
(poker) poker
(pol) politics—politica
pp past participle—participio passato
poss possessive—possessivo
pref prefix—prefisso
prep preposition—preposizione
prep phrase prepositional phrase—frase preposizionale
pres present—presente
pret preterit—passato remoto
pron pronoun—pronome
(pros) prosody—prosodia
(psychoanal) psychoanalysis—psicanalisi
(psychol) psychology—psicologia
(psychopath) psychopathology—psicopatologia
qlco or *qlco* qualcosa—something
qlcu or *qlcu* qualcuno—someone
(racing) corse
(rad) radio—radio
ref reflexive verb—verbo riflessivo o pronominale
rel relative—relativo
(rel) religion—religione
(rhet) rhetoric—retorica
(rok) rocketry—studio dei razzi
(rowing) canottaggio
(rr) railroad—ferrovia
(rugby) rugby
s substantive—sostantivo
(scornful) sprezzante
(Scot) Scottish—scozzese
(sculp) sculpture—scultura
(sew) sewing—cucito
sg singular—singolare
(slang) gergo
s.o. or *s.o.* someone—qualcuno
(soccer) calcio
spl substantive plural—sostantivo plurale
(sports) sport
ssg substantive singular—sostantivo singolare
s.th or *s.th* something—qualcosa
subj subjunctive—congiuntivo
suf suffix—suffisso
super superlative—superlativo
(surg) surgery—chirurgia
(surv) surveying—agrimensura, topografia
(taur) bullfighting—tauromachia
(telg) telegraphy—telegrafia
(telp) telephone—telefonia
(telv) television—televisione
(tennis) tennis
(tex) textile—tessile
(theat) theater—teatro
(theol) theology—teologia
tr transitive verb—verbo transitivo
(trademark) marchio di fabbrica
(typ) printing—tipografia
(U.S.A.) S.U.A.
v verb—verbo
var variant—variante
(vet) veterinary medicine—medicina veterinaria
(vulg) vulgar—volgare, ordinario
(wrestling) lotta
(zool) zoology—zoologia

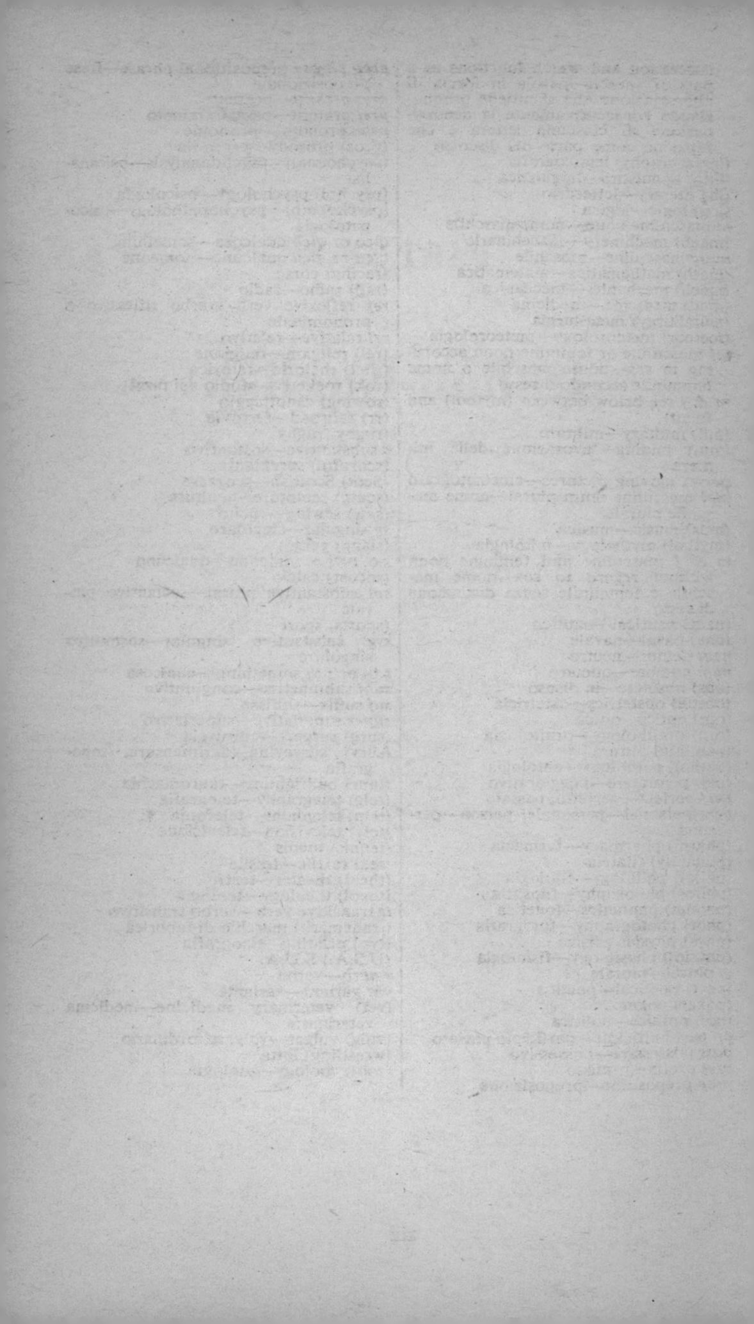

PART ONE

Italian-English

Italian Spelling and Pronunciation

§1. The Italian Alphabet. 1. The twenty-one letters of the Italian alphabet are listed below with their names and their sounds in terms of approximate equivalent English sounds. Their gender is masculine or feminine.

LETTER	NAME	APPROXIMATE SOUND
a	a	Like *a* in English *father*, e.g., **facile, padre.**
b	bi	Like *b* in English *boat*, e.g., **bello, abate.**
c	ci	When followed by **e** or **i**, like *ch* in English *cherry*, e.g., **cento, cinque;** if the **i** is unstressed and followed by another vowel, its sound is not heard, e.g., **ciarla, cieco.** When followed by **a, o, u,** or a consonant, like *c* in English *cook*, e.g., **casa, come, cura, credere.** The digraph **ch,** which is used before **e** and **i,** has likewise the sound of *c* in English *cook*, e.g., **chiesa, perché.**
d	di	Like *d* in English *dance*, e.g., **dare, madre.**
e	e	Has two sounds. One like *a* in English *make*, shown on stressed syllables in this DICTIONARY by the acute accent, e.g., **séra, trénta;** and one like *e* in English *met*, shown on stressed syllables in this DICTIONARY by the grave accent, e.g., **fèrro, fèsta.**
f	effe	Like *f* in English *fool*, e.g., **farina, efelide.**
g	gi	When followed by **e** or **i,** like *g* in English *general*, e.g., **gelato, ginnasta;** if the **i** is unstressed and followed by another vowel, its sound is not heard, e.g., **giallo, giorno.** When followed by **a, o, u,** or a consonant, like *g* in English *go*, e.g., **gamba, goccia, gusto, grado.** The digraph **gh,** which is used before **e** and **i,** has likewise the sound of *g* in English *go*, e.g., **gherone, ghisa.** When the combination **gli** (a) is a form of the definite article or the personal pronoun, (b) is final in a word, or (c) is intervocalic, it has the sound of Castilian *ll*, which is somewhat like *lli* in English *million*, e.g., (a) **gli uomini, gli ho parlato ieri,** (b) **battagli,** (c) **figlio, migliore.** When it is (a) initial (except in the word **gli,** above), (b) preceded by a consonant, or (c) followed by a consonant, it is pronounced like *gli* in English *negligence*, e.g., (a) **glioma,** (b) **ganglio,** (c) **negligenza.** The combination **gl** followed by **a, e, o,** or **u** is pronounced like *gl* in English *globe*, e.g., **glabro, gleba, globo, gluteo, inglese, poliglotto.** The digraph **gn** has the sound of Castilian *ñ*, which is somewhat like *ni* in English *onion*, e.g., **signore, gnocco.**
h	acca	Always silent, e.g., **ah, hanno.** See **ch** under **c** above and **gh** under **g** above.
i	i	Like *i* in English *machine*, e.g., **piccolo, sigla.** When unstressed and followed by another vowel, like *y* in English *yes*, e.g., **piatto, piede, fiore, fiume.** For **i** in **ci,** see **c** above, in **gi,** see **g** above, and in **sci,** see **s** below.

LETTER	NAME	APPROXIMATE SOUND
l	elle	Like *l* in English *lamb,* e.g., **labbro, lacrima.**
m	emme	Like *m* in English *money,* e.g., **mano, come.**
n	enne	Like *n* in English *net,* e.g., **nome, cane.**
o	o	Has two sounds. One like *o* in English *note,* shown on stressed syllables in this DICTIONARY by the acute accent, e.g., **dópo, sóle;** and one like *ou* in English *ought,* shown on stressed syllables in this DICTIONARY by the grave accent, e.g., **còsa, dònna.**
p	pi	Like *p* in English *pot,* e.g., **passo, carpa.**
q	cu	This letter is always followed by the letter **u** and the combination has the sound of *qu* in English *quart,* e.g., **quanto, questo.**
r	erre	Like *r* in English *rubber,* with a slight trill, e.g., **roba, carta.**
s	esse	Has two sounds. When initial and followed by a vowel, when preceded by a consonant and followed by a vowel, and when followed by **c** [k] **f, p, q,** or **t,** like *s* in English *see,* e.g., **sale, falso, scappare, spazio, stoffa;** and when standing between two vowels and when followed by **b, d, g** [g], **l, m, n, r** or **v,** like *z* in English *zero,* e.g., **paese, sbaglio, svenire.** However, **s** standing between two vowels in some words and initial **s** followed by **b, d, g** [g], **l, m, n, r,** or **v** in some foreign borrowings are pronounced like *s* in *see,* e.g., **casa*, tesa, smoking, slam** In this DICTIONARY this is indicated by the insertion of [s] immediately after the entry word. However, when initial **s** stands between two vowels in a compound, its pronunciation remains that of initial **s,** e.g., **autoservizio** and this is not indicated. The digraph **sc,** when followed by **e** or **i** has the sound of *sh* in English *shall,* e.g., **scelta, scimmia;** if the **i** is unstressed and followed by another vowel, its sound is not heard, e.g., **sciame, sciopero.** The trigraph **sch** has the sound of *sc* in English *scope,* e.g., **scherzo, schiavo.**
t	ti	Like *t* in English *table,* e.g., **terra, pasto.**
u	u	Like *u* in English *rule,* e.g., **luna, mulo.** When followed by a vowel, like *w* in English *was,* e.g., **quanto, guerra, nuovo.**
v	vu	Like *v* in English *vain,* e.g., **vita, uva.**
z	zeta	Has two sounds. One like *ts* in English *nuts,* e.g., **grazia, zucchero;** and one like *dz* in English *adze,* e.g., **zero, mezzo.** In this DICTIONARY the sound of *dz* in *adze* is indicated by the insertion of [dz] immediately after the entry word. If the sound is long, [ddzz] is inserted

* Intervocalic **s** is generally voiced in the north of Italy.

2. The following five letters are found in borrowings from other languages.

LETTER	NAME	EXAMPLES
j	i lunga	**jazz, jingo**
k	cappa	**kiosco, kodak**
w	doppia vu	**water-polo, whisky**
x	ics	**xenofobo, xilofono**
y	ìpsilon	**yacht, yoghurt**

3. Consonants written double are longer than consonants written single, that is, it takes a longer time to pronounce them, e.g., **camino** *chimney* and **cam-**

mino *road,* **capello** *hair* and **cappello** *hat.* Special attention is called to the following double consonants: **cc** followed by **e** or **i** has the sound of *ch ch* in English *beach chair,* that is, a lengthened *ch* (not the sound of *ks*), *e.g.,* **accento; cch** has the sound of *kk* in English *bookkeeper,* e.g., **becchino; cq** has the sound of *kk* in English *bookkeeper,* e.g., **acqua; gg** followed by **e** or **i** has the sound of *ge j* in English *carriage joiner,* e.g., **peggio; ggh** has the sound of *g g* in English *tag game,* e.g., **agghindare.**

§2. Division of Syllables. In the application of the following rules for the syllabic division of words, the digraphs **ch, gh, gl, gn,** and **sc** count as single consonants.

(a) When a single consonant stands between two vowels it belongs to the following syllable, e.g., **ca·sa, fu·mo, ami·che, la·ghi, fi·glio, biso·gno, la·sciare.**

(b) When a consonant group consisting of two consonants of which the second is **l** or **r** stands between two vowels, the group belongs to the following syllable, e.g., **nu·cleo, so·brio, qua·dro.**

(c) When a consonant group consisting of two or more consonants of which the first or the second is **s** stands between two vowels, that part of the group beginning with **s** belongs to the following syllable, e.g., **ta·sca, bo·schi, fine·stra, super·sti·zione, sub·strato.**

(d) When a consonant group consisting of two or three consonants of which the first is **l, m, n,** or **r** stands between two vowels, the **l, m, n,** or **r** belongs to the preceding syllable, the other consonant or consonants to the following syllable, e.g., **al·bero, am·pio, prin·cipe, mor·te, in·flazione, com·pleto.**

(e) When a double consonant stands between two vowels or between a vowel and **l** or **r,** the first belongs to the preceding syllable, the second to the following syllable, e.g., **bab·bo, caval·lo, an·no, car·ro, mez·zo, sup·plica, lab·bro, quat·tro.**

§3. Stress and Accent Marks. 1. Whenever stress is shown as part of regular spelling, it is shown on **a, i,** and **u** by the grave accent mark, e.g., **libertà, giovedì, gioventù,** on close **e** and **o** by the acute accent mark, e.g., **perché,** and on open **e** and **o** by the grave accent mark, e.g., **caffè, parlò.** This occurs (a) in words ending in a stressed vowel, as in the above examples, (b) in stressed monosyllables in which the vocalic element is a diphthong of which the first letter is unstressed **i** or **u,** e.g., **già, più, può,** and (c) on the stressed monosyllable of any pair of monosyllables of which one is stressed and the other unstressed, in order to distinguish one from the other, e.g., **dà** *he gives* and **da** *from,* **è** *is* and **e** *and,* **sé** *himself* and **se** *if,* **sì** *yes* and **si** *himself.*

2. Whenever stress is not shown as part of regular spelling, it is often difficult to determine where it falls.

(a) In words of two syllables, the stress falls on the syllable next to the last, e.g., **ca'sa, mu'ro, ter'ra.** If the syllable next to the last contains a diphthong, that is, a combination of a strong vowel (**a, e,** or **o**) and a weak vowel (**i** or **u**), the strong vowel is stressed, regardless of which vowel comes first, e.g., **da'ino, ero'ico, ne'utro, fia'to, dua'le, sie'pe, fio're, buo'no.**

(b) In words of more than two syllables, the stress may fall on the syllable next to the last, e.g., **anda'ta, canzo'ne, pasto're** or on a preceding syllable, e.g., **fis'sile, gon'dola, man'dorla.** In these positions also the stressed syllable may contain a diphthong, e.g., **inca'uto, idra'ulico, fio'cina.**

(c) If a weak vowel in juxtaposition with a strong vowel is stressed, the two vowels constitute two separate syllables, e.g., **abba·i'no, ero·i'na, pa·u'ra, miri'ade, vi'a.**

(d) Two strong vowels in juxtaposition constitute two separate syllables, e.g., **pa·e'se, aure'ola, ide'a, oce'ano.**

(e) Two weak vowels in juxtaposition generally constitute a diphthong in which the first vowel is stressed in some words, e.g., **flu'ido** and the second vowel in others, e.g., **piu'ma.**

(f) If a word ends in a diphthong, the diphthong is stressed, e.g., **marina'i, parla'i, ero'i.**

3. In this DICTIONARY, stress is understood or shown on all words that do not bear an accent mark as part of regular spelling according to the following principles. In the application of these principles, individual vowels and not diphthongs are counted as units. In some words in which it is not necessary to show stress, an accent mark is used to show the quality of the stressed vowels **e** and **o.**

As in regular Italian spelling, stress is shown on **a, i,** and **u** by the grave accent mark, on close **e** and **o** by the acute accent mark, and on open **e** and **o** by the grave accent mark.

(a) It is understood that in words of more than one syllable in which no accent mark is shown, the stress falls on the vowel next to the last, e.g., **casa,**

fiato, duale, abbaino, paura. In such words as **sièpe, fióre, buòno, paése, fluènte, eròe, nói, pòi,** the accent mark is used to show the quality of the vowel.

(b) An accent mark is placed on the stressed vowel if the word is stressed on the third vowel from the end, e.g., **mùsica, sìmbolo, dàino, incàuto, marinàio, contìnuo, infànzia.** If this vowel is **e** or **o,** the acute or grave accent mark must correspond to the quality of the vowel, e.g., **fiòcina, rómpere, nèutro, eròico, assèdio, filatóio.**

(c) Contrary to the above-mentioned principle of counting vowels, an accent mark is placed on the strong vowel of a final diphthong, e.g., **marinài, assài.**

(d) Contrary to the above-mentioned principle of counting vowels, an accent mark is placed on the **i** of final **ia, ie, ii,** and **io,** e.g., **farmacìa, scìa, farmacìe, mormorìi, gorgoglìo, fìo.**

(e) An accent mark is placed on some borrowings ending in a consonant, e.g., **hàrem, revòlver.**

(f) The loss of the last vowel or last syllable of a word does not alter the position of the stress of the word, e.g., **la maggior parte, in alcun modo, fan bene.**

§4. The Definite Article and Combinations with Prepositions.

		MASC	MASC	MASC	FEM	FEM
		BEFORE CONSONANT	BEFORE s IMPURE OR z[1]	BEFORE VOWEL	BEFORE CONSONANT	BEFORE VOWEL
	SG	il	lo	l'	la	l'
	PL	i	gli	gli[2]	le	le[3]
WITH a	SG	al	allo	all'	alla	all'
	PL	ai	agli	agli[2]	alle	alle[3]
WITH di	SG	del	dello	dell'	della	dell'
	PL	dei	degli	degli[2]	delle	delle[3]
WITH con	SG	col	collo	coll'	colla	coll'
	PL	coi	cogli	cogli[2]	colle	colle[3]
WITH da	SG	dal	dallo	dall'	dalla	dall'
	PL	dai	dagli	dagli[2]	dalle	dalle[3]
WITH in	SG	nel	nello	nell'	nella	nell'
	PL	nei	negli	negli[2]	nelle	nelle[3]
WITH su	SG	sul	sullo	sull'	sulla	sull'
	PL	sui	sugli	sugli[3]	sulle	sulle[3]

[1] Other letters and groups of letters, which occur in a few words, are **gn, pn, ps, sc, x,** and **i** before a vowel, sometimes spelled **j** or **y.**

[2] These forms may drop the **i** before words beginning with **i,** e.g., **gl'inglesi.**

[3] The **e** of these forms is not elided, e.g., **le erbe.**

§5. Personal and Reflexive Pronouns.

PERSONS	SUBJECT	PERSONAL DIRECT OBJECT	PERSONAL INDIRECT OBJECT	REFLEX. & RECIPROCAL DIRECT & INDIRECT OBJECT	PERSONAL PREPOSITIONAL OBJECT	REFLEX. & RECIPROCAL PREPOSITIONAL OBJECT
SG						
1	**io** *I*	**mi** *me*	**mi** *to me*	**mi** *myself; to myself*	**me** *me*	**me** *myself*
2	**tu** *you*	**ti** *you*	**ti** *to you*	**ti** *yourself; to yourself*	**te** *you*	**te** *yourself*
3 MASC	**egli, lui** *he*	**lo** *him* or *it*	**gli** *to him*	**si** *himself; to himself*	**lui** *him*	**sé** *himself*
3 FEM	**lei, essa** *she*	**la** *her* or *it*	**le** *to her*	**si** *herself; to herself*	**lei, essa** *her*	**sé** *herself*
2 FORMAL	**Lei** *you*	**La** *you*	**Le** *to you*	**si** *yourself; to yourself*	**Lei** *you*	**sé** *yourself*
PL						
1	**noi** *we*	**ci** *us*	**ci** *to us*	**ci** *ourselves; to ourselves; each other; to each other*	**noi** *us*	**noi** *ourselves; each other*
2	**voi** *you*	**vi** *you*	**vi** *to you*	**vi** *yourself; yourselves; to yourself; to yourselves; each other; to each other*	**voi** *you*	**voi** *yourself; yourselves; each other*
3 MASC	**loro, essi** *they*	**li** *them*	**loro** *to them*	**si** *themselves; to themselves; each other; to each other*	**loro, essi** *them*	**sé** *themselves; each other*
3 FEM	**loro, esse** *they*	**le** *them*	**loro** *to them*	**si** *themselves; to themselves; each other; to each other*	**loro, esse** *them*	**sé** *themselves; each other*
2 FORMAL	**Loro** *you*	**Li** / **Le** } *you*	**Loro** *to you*	**si** *yourselves; to yourselves; each other; to each other*	**Loro** *you*	**sé** *yourselves; each other*

ci and **vi** both mean also *here, there, to it, in it, to them, in them, about it.*
ne means *of, from,* or *with him, her, it, them; some, any; from here, from there, thence, about it.*

meco *with me,* **teco** *with you,* and **seco** *with him, with himself; with her, with herself; with you, with yourself, with yourselves; with them, with themselves; with each other* may be used instead of **con me, con te,** and **con sé** respectively.

COMBINATION OF DIRECT AND INDIRECT OBJECT

PERSONS		PERSONS	
1 SG **&** **3** SG	**me lo** / **me la** *him, her, it to me*	**1** PL **&** **3** SG	**ce lo** / **ce la** *him, her, it to us*
1 SG **&** **3** PL	**me li** / **me le** *them to me*	**1** PL **&** **3** PL	**ce li** / **ce le** *them to us*
2 SG **&** **3** SG	**te lo** / **te la** *him, her, it to you*	**2** PL **&** **3** SG	**ve lo** / **ve la** *him, her, it to you*
2 SG **&** **3** PL	**te li** / **te le** *them to you*	**2** PL **&** **3** PL	**ve li** / **ve le** *them to you*
3 SG **&** **3** SG	**glielo** *him, her, it to him* / **gliela** *him, her, it to her*	**3** SG **&** **3** PL	**lo** / **la** VERB **loro** *him, her, it to them*
3 SG **&** **3** PL	**glieli** *them to him* / **gliele** *them to her*	**3** PL **&** **3** PL	**li** / **le** VERB **loro** *them to them*
2 SG FORMAL **&** **3** SG	**Glielo** / **Gliela** *him, her, it to you*	**3** SG **&** **2** PL FORMAL	**lo** / **la** VERB **Loro** *him, her, it to you*
2 SG FORMAL **&** **3** PL	**Glieli** / **Gliele** *them to you*	**3** PL **&** **2** PL FORMAL	**li** / **le** VERB **Loro** *them to you*

The form **si** (third singular and plural reflexive and reciprocal indirect object) changes to **se** before one of the direct objects **lo, la, li,** and **le,** and before **ne, e.g., se lo mette** he puts it on; **se n'è andato** he went away.

In combinations, **ne** occupies the same position as **lo, la, li,** and **le,** e.g., **me ne,** and forms one word with **gli,** namely, **gliene.**

§6 Possessive Adjectives and Pronouns

PERSON, NUMBER & SEX OF POSSESSOR	GENDER & NUMBER OF POSSESSIVE ADJECTIVE OR PRONOUN ACCORDING TO THE GENDER & NUMBER OF THE PERSON OR THING POSSESSED				MEANING OF ADJECTIVE	MEANING OF PRONOUN
SG	MSG	MPL	FSG	FPL		
1	**il mio**	**i miei**	**la mia**	**le mie**	*my*	*mine*
2	**il tuo**	**i tuoi**	**la tua**	**le tue**	*your*	*yours*
3 MASC	**il suo**	**i suoi**	**la sua**	**le sue**	*his*	*his*
3 FEM	**il suo**	**i suoi**	**la sua**	**le sue**	*her*	*hers*
3 NEUT	**il suo**	**i suoi**	**la sua**	**le sue**	*its*	*its*
2 FORMAL	**il Suo**	**i Suoi**	**la Sua**	**le Sue**	*your*	*yours*
PL						
1	**il nostro**	**i nostri**	**la nostra**	**le nostre**	*our*	*ours*
2	**il vostro**	**i vostri**	**la vostra**	**le vostre**	*your*	*yours*
3	**il loro**	**i loro**	**la loro**	**le loro**	*their*	*theirs*
2 FORMAL	**il Loro**	**i Loro**	**la Loro**	**le Loro**	*your*	*yours*

The definite article, shown here, is not generally used (a) in direct address, e.g., **mio caro amico** *my dear friend,* (b) after the verb **essere**, e.g., **la casa è nostra** *the house is ours,* and (c) when a singular form modifies the name of a relative, e.g., **sua sorella** *his sister.*
With forms of the indefinite article, the possessive adjective, whether standing before or after the noun, is translated by *of* plus the possessive pronoun, e.g., **un amico mio** *a friend of mine;* **una sua zia** *an aunt of his* (or *of hers*).
The forms of the possessive pronouns also have the force of nouns, e.g., **il mio** *my property, my belongings;* **i suoi** *his people, relatives, followers, troops, retinue,* etc.; **la mia** *my letter;* **la sua** *his opinion.*

§7. The Demonstrative Adjective.

	MASC	MASC	MASC	FEM	FEM
	BEFORE CONSONANT	BEFORE s IMPURE OR z (see note 1, p. 7)	BEFORE VOWEL	BEFORE CONSONANT	BEFORE VOWEL
SG	**quel** *that*	**quello**	**quell'**	**quella**	**quell'**
PL	**quei** *those*	**quegli**	**quegli**	**quelle**	**quelle**
SG	**questo** *this*	**questo**	**questo** or **quest'**	**questa**	**questa** or **quest'**
PL	**questi** *these*	**questi**	**questi**	**queste**	**queste**

§8. The Demonstrative Pronoun.

	MASC	FEM	MASC
SG	**quello** *that one*	**quella**	**quegli** *that one; the former*
PL	**quelli** *those*	**quelle**	
SG	**questo** *this one*	**questa**	**questi** *this one; the latter*
PL	**questi** *these*	**queste**	

The demonstrative pronoun **quello** is often followed by **che, di,** or **da** and the masculine singular form may be shortened to **quel** before these words.

SG	**colui** *that one*	**colei**
PL	**coloro** *those*	**coloro**
SG	**costui** *this one*	**costei**
PL	**costoro** *these*	**costoro**

code•sto -sta -sti -ste and **cote•sto -sta -sti -ste** are demonstrative adjectives and demonstrative pronouns and mean *that* (*of yours*).

§9. Indefinite Article and Numeral Adjective.

MASC	MASC	MASC	FEM	FEM
BEFORE CONSONANT	BEFORE S IMPURE OR Z (see note 1, p. 7)	BEFORE VOWEL	BEFORE CONSONANT	BEFORE VOWEL
un *a, an; one*	**uno**	**un**	**una**	**un'**

§10. Indefinite Pronoun uno.

MASC	FEM
uno *one*	**una**

§11. Correlative Indefinite Pronoun.

	MASC	FEM
SG	**l'uno . . . l'altro** *one . . . the other*	**l'una . . . l'altra**
PL	**gli uni . . . gli altri** *some . . . the others*	**le une . . . le altre**

§12. Reciprocal Indefinite Pronoun.

	MASC	FEM
SG	**l'un l'altro** *each other, one another*	**l'una l'altra**
PL	**gli uni gli altri**	**le une le altre**

Table of Regular Endings of Italian Verbs

The stem to which the endings of the gerund, past participle, present participle, imperative, present indicative, present subjunctive, imperfect indicative, preterit indicative, and imperfect subjunctive are attached is obtained by dropping the ending of the infinitive, viz., **-are, -ere, -ire.**

The stem to which the endings of the future indicative and present conditional are attached is obtained by dropping the **-e** of the ending of the infinitive of all conjugations and changing the **a** of the ending of the infinitive of the first conjugation to **e.**

The letters before the names of some of the tenses of this table correspond to the designation of the tenses shown on the following page.

Letters printed in italics have a written accent that is not part of the regular spelling.

TENSE	FIRST CONJUGATION	SECOND CONJUGATION	THIRD CONJUGATION
inf	**-are**	**-*é*re** (or **´ere**)	**-ire**
ger	-ando	-*è*ndo	-*è*ndo
pp	-ato	-uto	-ito
pres part	-ante	-*è*nte	-*è*nte
(a) *impv*	-a -ate	-i -*é*te	-i -ite
(b) *pres ind*	-o -i -a -iamo -ate -ano	-o -i -e -iamo -*é*te -ono	-o -i -e -iamo -ite -ono
(c) *pres subj*	-i -i -i -iamo -iate -ino	-a -a -a -iamo -iate -ano	-a -a -a -iamo -iate -ano
(d) *imperf ind*	-avo -avi -ava -avamo -avate -*à*vano	-*é*vo -*é*vi -*é*va -evamo -evate -*é*vano	-ivo -ivi -iva -ivamo -ivate -*ì*vano
(e) *pret ind*	-*à*i -asti -*ò* -ammo -aste -*à*rono	-*é*i -*é*sti -*è* -*é*mmo -*é*ste -*é*rono	-*ì*i -isti -ì -immo -iste -*ì*rono
imperf subj	-assi -assi -asse -*à*ssimo -aste -*à*ssero	-*é*ssi -*é*ssi -*é*sse -*é*ssimo -*é*ste -*é*ssero	-issi -issi -isse -*ì*ssimo -iste -*ì*ssero
(f) *fut ind*	-er-*ò* -er-*à*i -er-à -er-*é*mo -er-*é*te -er-anno	-*ò* -*à*i -à -*é*mo -*é*te -anno	-*ò* -*à*i -à -*é*mo -*é*te -anno

TENSE	FIRST CONJUGATION	SECOND CONJUGATION	THIRD CONJUGATION
pres cond	-er-èi -er-ésti -er-èbbe -er-émmo -er-éste -er-èbbero	-èi -ésti -èbbe -émmo -éste -èbbero	-èi -ésti -èbbe -émmo -éste -èbbero

MODEL VERBS
ORDER OF TENSES

(a) imperative
(b) present indicative
(c) present subjunctive
(d) imperfect indicative
(e) preterit indicative
(f) future indicative

In addition to the infinitive, gerund, and past participle, which are shown in line one of these tables, all simple tenses are shown if they contain at least one irregular form, except (1) the present conditional, which is always formed on the stem of the future indicative, (2) the imperfect subjunctive, which is always formed on the stem of the *2nd sg* of the preterit indicative, and (3) the present participle, which is generally formed by changing the final **-do** of the gerund to **-te** (exceptions being shown in parentheses after the gerund).

Letters printed in italics have a written accent that is not part of the regular spelling.

§100 ACCÈDERE—accedèndo—acceduto
(e) accedètti *or* acced*é*i *or* accèssi; acced*é*sti; accedètte *or* accedé *or* accèsse; acced*é*mmo; acced*é*ste; accedèttero *or* acced*é*rono *or* accèssero

§101 ACCÈNDERE—accendèndo—acc*é*so
(e) acc*é*si, accend*é*sti, acc*é*se, accend*é*mmo, accend*é*ste, acc*é*sero

§102 ADDURRE—adducèndo—add*ó*tto
(b) adduco, adduci, adduce, adduciamo, adduc*é*te, add*ù*cono
(c) adduca, adduca, adduca, adduciamo, adduciate, add*ù*cano
(d) adduc*é*vo, adduc*é*vi, adduc*é*va, adducevamo, adducevate, adduc*é*vano
(e) addussi, adduc*é*sti, addusse, adduc*é*mmo, adduc*é*ste, add*ù*ssero

§103 AFFÌGGERE—affiggèndo—affisso
(e) affissi, affigg*é*sti, affisse, affigg*é*mmo, affigg*é*ste, aff*ì*ssero

§104 **AFFLÌGGERE**—affliggèndo—afflitto
(e) afflissi, affliggésti, afflisse, affliggémmo, affliggéste, afflìssero

§105 **ALLÙDERE**—alludèndo—alluso
(e) allusi, alludésti, alluse, alludémmo, alludéste, allùsero

§106 **ANDARE**—andando—andato
(a) va *or* va' *or* vai, andate
(b) vò *or* vado, vai, va, andiamo, andate, vanno
(c) vada, vada, vada, andiamo, andiate, vàdano
(f) andrò, andrài, andrà, andrémo, andréte, andranno

§107 **ANNÈTTERE**—annettèndo—annèsso or **annéttere,** annetténdo, annésso
(e) annettéi *or* annèssi *or* annéssi; annettésti; annetté *or* annèsse *or* annésse; annettémmo; annettéste; annettérono *or* annèssero *or* annéssero

§108 **APPARIRE**—apparèndo—apparso
(a) apparisci *or* appari; apparite
(b) apparisco *or* appàio; apparisci *or* appari; apparisce *or* appare; appariamo; apparite; apparìscono *or* appàiono
(c) apparisca *or* appàia; apparisca *or* appàia; apparisca *or* appàia; appariamo; appariate; apparìscano *or* appàiano
(e) apparvi *or* apparìi *or* apparsi; appariste; apparve *or* apparì *or* apparse; apparimmo; appariste; appàrvero *or* apparìrono *or* appàrsero

§109 **APPÈNDERE**—appendèndo—appéso
(e) appési, appendésti, appése, appendémmo, appendéste, appésero

§110 **APRIRE**—aprèndo—apèrto
(e) aprìi *or* apèrsi; apristi; aprì *or* apèrse; aprimmo; apriste; aprìrono *or* apèrsero

§111 **ÀRDERE**—ardèndo—arso
(e) arsi, ardésti, arse, ardémmo, ardéste, àrsero

§112 **ASPÈRGERE**—aspergèndo—aspèrso
(e) aspèrsi, aspergésti, aspèrse, aspergémmo, aspergéste, aspèrsero

§113 **ASSÌDERE**—assidèndo—assiso
(e) assisi, assidésti, assise, assidémmo, assidéste, assìsero

§114 **ASSÌSTERE**—assistèndo—assistito
(e) assistéi *or* assistètti; assistésti; assisté *or* assistètte; assistémmo; assistéste; assistérono *or* assistèttero

§115 **ASSÒLVERE**—assolvèndo—assòlto *or* assoluto
(e) assolvéi *or* assolvètti *or* assòlsi; assolvésti; assolvé *or* assolvètte *or* assòlse; assolvémmo; assolvéste; assolvérono *or* assolvèttero *or* assòlsero

§116 **ASSÙMERE**—assumèndo—assunto
(e) assunsi, assumésti, assunse, assumémmo, assuméste, assùnsero

§117 **ASSÙRGERE**—assurgèndo—assurto
(e) assursi, assurgésti, assurse, assurgémmo, assurgéste, assùrsero

§118 **AVÈRE**—avèndo—avuto
(a) abbi, abbiate
(b) ho, hai, ha, abbiamo, avete, hanno
(c) àbbia, àbbia, àbbia, abbiamo, abbiate, àbbiano
(e) èbbi, avésti, èbbe, avémmo, avéste, èbbero
(f) avrò, avrài, avrà, avrémo, avréte, avranno

§119 **AVVIARE**—avviando—avviato
(b) avvìo, avvìi, avvìa, avviamo, avviate, avvìano
(c) avvìi, avvìi, avvìi, avviamo, avviate, avvìino

§120 **BÉRE**—bevèndo—bevuto
(a) bévi, bevéte
(b) bévo, bévi, béve, beviamo, bevéte, bévono
(c) béva, béva, béva, beviamo, beviate, bévano
(d) bevévo, bevévi, bevéva, bevevamo, bevevate, bevévano
(e) bévvi *or* bevéi *or* bevètti; bevésti, bévve *or* bevé *or* bevètte; bevémmo; bevéste; bévvero *or* bevérono *or* bevèttero
(f) berrò, berrài, berrà, berrémo, berréte, berranno

§121 **CADÉRE**—cadèndo—caduto
(e) caddi, cadésti, cadde, cadémmo, cadéste, càddero
(f) cadrò, cadrài, cadrà, cadrémo, cadréte, cadranno

§122 **CECARE**—cecando—cecato
(a) cièca *or* cèca; cecate
(b) cièco *or* cèco; cièchi *or* cèchi; cièca *or* cèca; cechiamo; cecate; ciècano *or* cècano
(c) cièchi *or* cèchi; cièchi *or* cèchi; cièchi *or* cèchi; cechiamo; cechiate; cièchino *or* cèchino
(f) cecherò, cecherài, cecherà, cecherémo, cecheréte, cecheranno

§123 **CÈDERE**—cedèndo—ceduto
(e) cedéi *or* cedètti; cedésti; cedé *or* cedètte; cedémmo; cedéste; cedérono *or* cedèttero

§124 **CHIÈDERE**—chiedèndo—chièsto
(e) chièsi, chiedésti, chièse, chiedémmo, chiedéste, chièsero

§125 **CHIÙDERE**—chiudèndo—chiuso
(e) chiusi, chiudésti, chiuse, chiudémmo, chiudéste, chiùsero

§126 **CÌNGERE**—cingèndo—cinto
(e) cinsi, cingésti, cinse, cingémmo, cingéste, cìnsero

§127 **CÒGLIERE**—coglièndo—còlto
(a) cògli, cogliéte
(b) còlgo, cògli, còglie, cogliamo, cogliéte, còlgono
(c) còlga, còlga, còlga, cogliamo, cogliate, còlgano
(e) còlsi, cogliésti, còlse, cogliémmo, cogliéste, còlsero

§128 **COMINCIARE**—cominciando—cominciato
(b) comìncio, cominci, comìncia, cominciamo, cominciate, comìnciano
(c) cominci, cominci, cominci, cominciamo, cominciate, comìncino
(f) comincerò, comincerài, comincerà, cominceremo, comincerete, cominceranno

§129 **COMPÈTERE**—competèndo—*pp* missing

§130 **CÒMPIERE**—compièndo—compiuto
(a) cómpi, compite
(b) cómpio, cómpi, cómpie, compiamo, compite, cómpiono
(c) cómpia, cómpia, cómpia, compiamo, compiate, cómpiano
(d) compivo, compivi, compiva, compivamo, compivate, compìvano
(e) compiéi *or* compìi; compiésti *or* compisti; compié *or* compì; compiémmo *or* compimmo; compiéste *or* compiste; compiérono *or* compìrono

§131 **COMPRÌMERE**—comprimèndo—comprèsso
(e) comprèssi, comprimésti, comprèsse, comprimémmo, compriméste, comprèssero

§132 **CONCÈDERE**—concedèndo—concèsso
(e) concedéi *or* concèssi *or* concedètti; concedésti; concedé *or* concèsse *or* concedètte; concedémmo; concedéste; concedérono *or* concèssero *or* concedèttero

§133 **CONCÈRNERE**—concernèndo—*pp* missing
(e) concernéi *or* concernètti; concernésti; concerné *or* concernètte; concernémmo; concernéste; concernérono *or* concernèttero

§134 **CONÓSCERE**—conoscèndo—conosciuto
(e) conóbbi, conoscésti, conóbbe, conoscémmo, conoscéste, conóbbero

§135 **CONQUÌDERE**—conquidèndo—conquiso
(e) conquisi, conquidésti, conquise, conquidémmo, conquidéste, conquìsero

§136 **CONSÙMERE**—*ger* missing—consunto
(a) missing
(b) missing
(c) missing
(d) missing
(e) consunsi, consunse, consùnsero
(f) missing

§137 **CONVÈRGERE**—convergèndo—convèrso
(e) convèrsi *or* convergéi; convergésti; convèrse *or* convergé; convergémmo; convergéste; convèrsero *or* convergérono

§138 **CONVERTIRE**—convertèndo—convertito
(e) convertìi *or* convèrsi; convertisti; convertì or convèrse; convertimmo; convertiste; convertìrono *or* convèrsero

§139 **CÓRRERE**—corrèndo—córso
(e) córsi, corrésti, córse, corrémmo, corréste, córsero

§140 **COSTRUIRE**—costruèndo—costruito
(a) costruisci, costruite
(b) costruisco, costruisci, costruisce, costruiamo, costruite, costruìscono
(c) costruisca, costruisca, costruisca, costruiamo, costruiate, costruìscano
(e) costruìi *or* costrussi; costruisti; costruì *or* costrusse; costruimmo; costruiste; costruìrono *or* costrùssero

§141 **CRÉDERE**—credèndo—creduto
(e) credéi *or* credètti; credésti; credé *or* credètte; credémmo; credéste; credérono *or* credèttero

§142 **CRÉSCERE**—crescèndo—cresciuto
(e) crébbi, crescésti, crébbe, crescémmo, crescéste, crébbero

§143 **CUCIRE**—cucèndo—cucito
(b) cùcio, cuci, cuce, cuciamo, cucite, cùciono
(c) cùcia, cùcia, cùcia, cuciamo, cuciate, cùciano

§144a **CUÒCERE**—cuocèndo *or* cocèndo (cocènte)—còtto *or* cociuto

(a) cuòci, cocéte
(b) cuòcio, cuòci, cuòce, cociamo, cocéte, cuòciono
(c) cuòcia, cuòcia, cuòcia, cociamo, cociate, cuòciano
(d) cocévo, cocévi, cocéva, cocevamo, cocevate, cocévano
(e) còssi, cocésti, còsse, cocémmo, cocéste, còssero
(f) cocerò, cocerài, cocerà, cocerémo, coceréte, coceranno

§144b **DARE**—dando—dato
(a) dà *or* dài *or* da'; date
(b) dò *or* dò; dài; dà; diamo; date; danno
(c) dìa, dìa, dìa, diamo, diate, dìano
(e) dièdi *or* dètti; désti; dière *or* dètte *or* diè; démmo; déste; dièdero *or* dèttero
(f) darò, darài, darà, darémo, daréte, daranno

§145 **DECÌDERE**—decidèndo—deciso
(e) decisi, decidésti, decise, decidémmo, decidéste, decìsero

§146 **DELÌNQUERE**—delinquèndo—*pp* missing
(a) missing
(c) missing
(e) missing

§147 **DEVÒLVERE**—devolvèndo—devoluto
(e) devolvéi *or* devolvètti; devolvésti; devolvé *or* devolvètte; devolvémmo; devolvéste; devolvérono *or* devolvèttero

§148 **DIFÈNDERE**—difendèndo—diféso
(e) difési, difendésti, difése, difendémmo, difendéste, difésero

§149 **DILÌGERE**—diligèndo—dilètto
(a) missing
(b) missing
(c) missing
(d) missing
(e) dilèssi, diligésti, dilèsse, diligémmo, diligéste, dilèssero
(f) missing

§150 **DIPÈNDERE**—dipendèndo—dipéso
(e) dipési, dipendésti, dipése, dipendémmo, dipendéste, dipésero

§151 **DIRE**—dicèndo—détto
(a) di' *or* dì; dite
(b) dico, dici, dice, diciamo, dite, dìcono
(c) dica, dica, dica, diciamo, diciate, dìcano
(d) dicévo, dicévi, dicéva, dicevamo, dicevate, dicévano
(e) dissi, dicésti, disse, dicémmo, dicéste, dìssero
(f) dirò, dirài, dirà, dirémo, diréte, diranno

§152 **DIRÌGERE**—dirigèndo—dirètto
(e) dirèssi, dirigésti, dirèsse, dirigémmo, dirigéste, dirèssero

§153 **DISCÈRNERE**—discernèndo—*pp* missing
(e) discernéi; discernésti; discerné *or* discernètte; discernémmo; discernéste; discernérono *or* discernèttero

§154 **DISCÙTERE**—discutèndo—discusso
(e) discussi, discutésti, discusse, discutémmo, discutéste, discùssero

§155 **DISSÒLVERE**—dissolvèndo—dissòlto
(e) dissòlsi *or* dissolvéi *or* dissolvètti; dissolvésti; dissòlse *or* dissolvé *or* dissolvètte; dissolvémmo; dissolvéste; dissòlsero *or* dissolvérono *or* dissolvèttero

§156 **DISTÌNGUERE**—distinguèndo—distinto
(e) distinsi, distinguésti, distinse, distinguémmo, distinguéste, distìnsero

§157 **DIVÈRGERE**—divergèndo—*pp* missing
(e) obsolete

§158 **DIVÌDERE**—dividèndo—diviso
(e) divísi, dividésti, divise, dividémmo, dividéste, divìsero

§159 **DOLÉRE**—dolèndo—doluto
(a) duòli, doléte
(b) dòlgo, duòli, duòle, doliamo, doléte, dòlgono
(c) dòlga, dòlga, dòlga, doliamo, doliate, dòlgano
(e) dòlsi, dolésti, dòlse, dolémmo, doléste, dòlsero
(f) dorrò, dorrài, dorrà, dorrémo, dorréte, dorranno

§160 **DOVÉRE**—dovèndo—dovuto
(b) dèbbo *or* dèvo; dèvi; dève; dobbiamo; dovéte; dèbbono *or* dèvono
(c) dèva *or* dèbba; dèva *or* dèbba; dèva *or* dèbba; dobbiamo; dobbiate; dèvano *or* dèbbano
(e) dovéi *or* dovètti; dovésti; dové *or* dovètte; dovémmo; dovéste; dovérono *or* dovèttero

§161 **ELÌDERE**—elidèndo—eliso
(e) elisi, elidésti, elise, elidémmo, elidéste, elìsero

§162 **EMÈRGERE**—emergèndo—emèrso
(e) emèrsi, emergésti, emèrse, emergémmo, emergéste, emèrsero

§163 **ÉMPIERE & EMPIRE**—empièndo—empito *or* empiuto
(a) émpi, empite

(b) *é*mpio, *é*mpi, *é*mpie, empiamo, empite, *é*mpiono
(c) *é*mpia, *é*mpia, *é*mpia, empiamo, empiate, *é*mpiano
(d) empivo, empivi, empiva, empivamo, empivate, em-pìvano
(e) empi*é*i *or* empìi; empi*é*sti; *or* empisti; empié *or* empì; empi*é*mmo *or* empimmo; empi*é*ste *or* empiste; empi*é*rono *or* empìrono
(f) empirò, empir*à*i, empirà, empir*é*mo, empir*é*te, em-piranno

§164 ÈRGERE—ergèndo—èrto
(e) èrsi, erg*é*sti, èrse, erg*é*mmo, erg*é*ste, èrsero

§165 ESÌGERE—esigèndo—esatto
(e) esig*é*i *or* esigètti; esig*é*sti; esigé *or* esigètte; esig*é*mmo; esig*é*ste; esig*é*rono *or* esigèttero

§166 ESÌMERE—esimèndo—*pp* missing
(e) esim*é*i *or* esimètti; esim*é*sti; esim*é* *or* esimètte; esim*é*mmo; esim*é*ste; esim*é*rono *or* esimèttero

§167 ESPÀNDERE—espandèndo—espanso
(e) espand*é*i *or* espandètti *or* espansi; espand*é*sti; espandé *or* espandètte *or* espanse; espand*é*mmo; espand*é*ste; espand*é*rono *or* espandèttero *or* esp*à*nsero

§168 ESPÈLLERE—espellèndo—espulso
(e) espulsi, espell*é*sti, espulse, espell*é*mmo, espell*é*ste, esp*ù*lsero

§169 ESPLÒDERE—esplodèndo—espl*ò*so
(e) espl*ò*si, esplod*é*sti, espl*ò*se, esplod*é*mmo, esplod*é*ste, espl*ò*sero

§170 ÈSSERE—essèndo—stato
(a) sii, siate
(b) s*ó*no, sèi, è, siamo, siète, s*ó*no
(c) sìa, sìa, sìa, siamo, siate, sìano
(d) èro, èri, èra, eravamo, eravate, èrano
(e) fui, f*ó*sti, fu, fummo, f*ó*ste, f*ù*rono
(f) sarò, sar*à*i, sarà, sar*é*mo, sar*é*te, saranno

§171 ESTÒLLERE—estollèndo—*pp* missing
(e) missing

§172 EVÀDERE—evadèndo—evaso
(e) evasi, evad*é*sti, evase, evad*é*mmo, evad*é*ste, ev*à*sero

§173 FARE—facèndo—fatto
(a) fa *or* fài *or* fa'; fate

(b) fàccio *or* fò; fài; fa; facciamo; fate; fanno
(c) fàccia, fàccia, fàccia, facciamo, facciate; fàcciano
(d) facévo, facévi, facéva, facevamo, facevate, facévano
(e) féci, facésti, féce, facémmo, facéste, fécero
(f) farò, farài, farà, farémo, faréte, faranno

§174 **FÈNDERE**—fendèndo—fenduto *or* fésso
(e) fendéi *or* fendètti; fendésti; fendé *or* fendètte; fendémmo; fendéste; fendérono *or* fendèttero

§175 **FÈRVERE**—fervèndo—*pp* missing
(e) fervéi *or* fervètti; fervésti; fervé *or* fervètte; fervémmo; fervéste; fervérono *or* fervèttero

§176 **FINIRE**—finèndo—finito
(a) finisci, finite
(b) finisco, finisci, finisce, finiamo, finite, finìscono
(c) finisca, finisca, finisca, finiamo, finiate, finìscano

§177 **FLÈTTERE**—flettèndo—flèsso
(e) flettéi *or* flèssi; flettésti; fletté *or* flèsse; flettémmo; flettéste; flettérono *or* flèssero

§178 **FÓNDERE**—fondèndo—fuso
(e) fusi, fondésti, fuse, fondémmo, fondéste, fùsero

§179 **FRÀNGERE**—frangèndo—franto
(e) fransi, frangésti, franse, frangémmo, frangéste, frànsero

§180 **FRÌGGERE**—friggèndo—fritto
(e) frissi, friggésti, frisse, friggémmo, friggéste, frìssero

§181 **GIACÉRE**—giacèndo—giaciuto
(b) giàccio; giaci; giace; giacciamo *or* giaciamo; giacete; giàcciono
(c) giàccia, giàccia, giàccia, giacciamo, giacciate, giàcciano
(e) giàcqui, giacésti, giàcque, giacémmo, giacéste, giàcquero

§182 **GIOCARE**—giocando—giocato
(a) giuòca *or* giòca; giocate
(b) giuòco *or* giòco; giuòchi *or* giòchi; giuòca *or* giòca; giochiamo; giocate; giuòcano *or* giòcano
(c) giuòchi *or* giòchi; giuòchi *or* giòchi; giuòchi *or* giòchi; giochiamo; giochiate; giuòchino *or* giòchino
(f) giocherò, giocherài, giocherà, giocherémo, giocheréte, giocheranno

§183 **GIÙNGERE**—giungèndo—giunto
(e) giunsi, giungésti, giunse, giungémmo, giungéste, giùnsero

§184 **GODÉRE**—godèndo—goduto
(e) godéi *or* godètti; godésti; godé *or* godètte; godémmo; godéste; godérono *or* godèttero
(f) godrò, godrài, godrà, godrémo, godréte, godranno

§185 **IMBÉVERE**—imbevèndo—imbevuto
(e) imbévvi, imbevésti, imbévve, imbevémmo, imbevéste, imbévvero

§186 **INCÓMBERE**—incombèndo—*pp* missing
(e) incombéi *or* incombètti; incombésti; incombé *or* incombètte; incombémmo; incombéste; incombérono *or* incombèttero

§187 **INDÙLGERE**—indulgèndo—indulto
(e) indulsi, indulgésti, indulse, indulgémmo, indulgéste, indùlsero

§188a **INFERIRE**—inferèndo—inferito *or* infèrto
(a) inferisci, inferite
(b) inferisco, inferisci, inferisce, inferiamo, inferite, inferìscono
(c) inferisca, inferisca, inferisca, inferiamo, inferiate, inferìscano
(e) inferìi *or* infèrsi; inferisti; inferì *or* infèrse; inferimmo; inferiste; inferìrono *or* infèrsero

§188b **INSTARE**—instando—*pp* missing

§189 **INTRÌDERE**—intridèndo—intriso
(e) intrisi, intridésti, intrise, intridémmo, intridéste, intrìsero

§190 **INTRÙDERE**—intrudèndo—intruso
(e) intrusi, intrudésti, intruse, intrudémmo, intrudéste, intrùsero

§191 **IRE**—*ger* missing—ito
(a) *sg* missing, ite
(b) missing
(c) missing
(d) ivo, ivi, iva, ivamo, ivate, ìvano
(e) *1st sg* missing, isti, *3rd sg* missing, *1st pl* missing, iste, ìrono

§192 **LÈDERE**—ledèndo—léso *or* lèso
(e) lési, ledésti, lése, ledémmo, ledéste, lésero

§193 **LÈGGERE**—leggèndo—lètto
(e) lèssi, leggésti, lèsse, leggémmo, leggéste, lèssero

§194 LIQUEFARE—liquefacèndo—liquefatto
(a) liquefà, liquefate
(b) liquefò or liquefàccio; liquefài; liquefà liquefacciamo; liquefate; liquefanno
(c) liquefàccia, liquefàccia, liquefàccia, liquefacciamo, liquefacciate, liquefàcciano
(d) liquefacévo, liquefacévi, liquefacéva, liquefacevamo, liquefacevate, liquefacévano
(e) liqueféci, liquefacésti, liqueféce, liquefacémmo, liquefacéste, liqueféccero
(f) liquefarò, liquefarài, liquefarà, liquefarémo, liquefaréte, liquefaranno

§195 MALEDIRE—maledicèndo—maledétto
(a) maledici, maledite
(b) maledico, maledici, maledice, malediciamo, maledite, maledìcono
(c) maledica, maledica, maledica, malediciamo, malediciate, maledìcano
(d) maledicévo *or* maledivo; maledicévi *or* maledivi; maledicéva *or* malediva; maledicevamo *or* maledivamo; maledicevate *or* maledivate; maledicévano *or* maledìvano
(e) maledìi *or* maledissi; maledisti *or* maledicésti; maledì *or* maledisse; maledimmo *or* maledicémmo; malediste *or* maledicéste; maledìrono *or* maledìssero
(f) maledirò, maledirài, maledirà, maledirémo, malediréte, malediranno

§196 MALVOLÉRE—*ger* missing—malvoluto
(a) missing
(b) missing
(c) missing
(d) missing
(e) missing
(f) missing

§197 MANCARE—mancando—mancato
(b) manco, manchi, manca, manchiamo, mancate, màncano
(c) manchi, manchi, manchi, manchiamo, manchiate, mànchino
(f) mancherò, mancherài, mancherà, mancherémo, mancheréte, mancheranno

§198 MÉTTERE—mettèndo—mésso
(e) misi, mettésti, mise, mettémmo, mettéste, mìsero

§199 MÌNGERE—mingèndo—minto
(e) minsi, mingésti, minse, mingémmo, mingéste, mìnsero

§200 **MÒRDERE**—mordèndo—mɔ̀rso
(e) mɔ̀rsi, mordésti, mɔ̀rse, mordémmo, mordéste, mɔ̀rsero

§201 **MORIRE**—morèndo—mɔ̀rto
(a) muɔ̀ri, morite
(b) muɔ̀io, muɔ̀ri, muɔ̀re, moriamo, morite, muɔ̀iono
(c) muɔ̀ia. muɔ̀ia, muɔ̀ia, moriamo, moriate, muɔ̀iano
(f) morrò *or* morirò; morrài *or* morirài; morrà *or* morirà; morrémo *or* morirémo; morréte *or* moriréte; morranno *or* moriranno

§202 **MUÒVERE**—muovèndo *or* movèndo (movènte)—mɔ̀sso
(a) muɔ̀vi, movéte
(b) muɔ̀vo, muɔ̀vi, muɔ̀ve, moviamo, movéte, muɔ̀vono
(c) muɔ̀va, muɔ̀va, muɔ̀va, moviamo, moviate, muɔ̀vano
(d) movévo, movévi, movéva, movevamo, movevate, movévano
(e) mɔ̀ssi, movésti, mɔ̀sse, movémmo, movéste, mɔ̀ssero
(f) moverò, moverài, moverà, moverémo, moveréte, moveranno

§203 **NÀSCERE**—nascèndo—nato
(e) nàcqui, nascésti, nàcque, nascémmo, nascéste, nàcquero

§204 **NASCÓNDERE**—nascondèndo—nascósto
(e) nascósi, nascondésti, nascóse, nascondémmo, nascondéste, nascósero

§205 **NEGLÌGERE**—negligèndo—neglètto
(a) missing
(b) missing
(c) missing
(e) neglèssi, negligésti, neglèsse, negligémmo, negligéste, neglèssero

§206 **NUÒCERE**—nuocèndo—nociuto
(a) nuɔ̀ci, nocéte
(b) nuɔ̀ccio *or* nɔ̀ccio; nuɔ̀ci; nuɔ̀ce; nociamo; nocéte; nuɔ̀cciono *or* nɔ̀cciono
(c) nɔ̀ccia, nɔ̀ccia, nɔ̀ccia, nociamo, nociate, nɔ̀cciano
(d) nocévo, nocévi, nocéva, nocevamo, nocevate, nocévano
(e) nɔ̀cqui, nocésti, nɔ̀cque, nocémmo, nocéste, nɔ̀cquero
(f) nocerò, nocerài, nocerà, nocerémo, noceréte, noceranno

§207 **OFFRIRE**—offrèndo (offerènte)—offèrto
(e) offrìi *or* offèrsi; offristi; offrì *or* offérse; offrimmo; offriste; offrìrono *or* offèrsero

§208 **OTTÙNDERE**—ottundèndo—ottuso
(e) ottusi, ottundésti, ottuse, ottundémmo, ottundéste, ottùsero

§209 **PAGARE**—pagando—pagato
(b) pago, paghi, paga, paghiamo, pagate, p*à*gano
(c) paghi, paghi, paghi, paghiamo, paghiate, p*à*ghino
(f) pagherò, pagher*à*i, pagherà, pagher*é*mo, pagher*é*te, pagheranno

§210 **PARÉRE**—parèndo (parvènte)—parso
(a) missing
(b) p*à*io; pari; pare; pariamo *or* paiamo; par*é*te; p*à*iono
(c) p*à*ia; p*à*ia; p*à*ia; pariamo *or* paiamo; pariate *or* paiate; p*à*iano
(e) parvi, par*é*sti, parve, par*é*mmo, par*é*ste, p*à*rvero
(f) parrò, parr*à*i, parrà, parr*é*mo, parr*é*te, parranno

§211 **PÀSCERE**—pascèndo—pasciuto
(a) pasc*é*i *or* pascètti; pasc*é*sti; pascé *or* pascètte; pasc*é*mmo; pasc*é*ste; pasc*é*rono *or* pascèttero

§212 **PÈRDERE**—perdèndo—pèrso *or* perduto
(e) perd*é*i *or* pèrsi *or* perdètti; perd*é*sti; perd*é*, *or* pèrse *or* perdètte; perd*é*mmo; perd*é*ste; perd*é*rono *or* pèrsero *or* perdèttero

§213 **PERSUADÉRE**—persuadèndo—persuaso
(e) persuasi, persuad*é*sti, persuase, persuad*é*mmo, persuad*é*ste, persu*à*sero

§214 **PIACÉRE**—piacèndo—piaciuto
(b) pi*à*ccio, piaci, piace, piacciamo, piac*é*te, pi*à*cciono
(c) pi*à*ccia, pi*à*ccia, pi*à*ccia, piacciamo, piacciate, pi*à*cciano
(e) pi*à*cqui, piac*é*sti, pi*à*cque, piac*é*mmo, piac*é*ste, pi*à*cquero

§215 **PIÀNGERE**—piangèndo—pianto
(e) piansi, piang*é*sti, pianse, piang*é*mmo, piang*é*ste, pi*à*nsero

§216 **PIÒVERE**—piovèndo—piovuto
(e) pi*ò*vvi, piov*é*sti, pi*ò*vve, piov*é*mmo, piov*é*ste, pi*ò*vvero

§217 **PÒRGERE**—porgèndo—p*ò*rto
(e) p*ò*rsi, porg*é*sti, p*ò*rse, porg*é*mmo, porg*é*ste, p*ò*rsero

§218 **PÓRRE**—ponèndo—p*ó*sto
(a) p*ó*ni, pon*é*te
(b) p*ó*ngo, p*ó*ni, p*ó*ne, poniamo, pon*é*te, p*ó*ngono
(c) p*ó*nga, p*ó*nga, p*ó*nga, poniamo, poniate, p*ó*ngano
(d) pon*é*vo, pon*é*vi, pon*é*va, ponevamo, ponevate, pon*é*vano
(e) p*ó*si, pon*é*sti, p*ó*se, pon*é*mmo, pon*é*ste, p*ó*sero

§219 **POTÉRE**—potèndo (potènte *or* possènte)—potuto
(a) missing
(b) p*ò*sso, pu*ò*i, può, possiamo, pot*é*te, p*ò*ssono

(c) pòssa, pòssa, pòssa, possiamo, possiate, pòssano
(e) potéi *or* potètti; potésti, poté *or* potètte; potémmo; potéste; potérono *or* potèttero
(f) potrò, potrài, potrà, potrémo, potréte, potranno

§220 **PRÈNDERE**—prendèndo—préso
(e) prési, prendésti, prése, prendémmo, prendéste, présero

§221 **PROVVEDÉRE**—provvedèndo—provveduto *or* provvisto
(e) provvidi, provvedésti, provvide, provvedémmo, provvedéste, provvìdero

§222 **PRÙDERE**—prudèndo—*pp* missing
(e) *1st sg* missing; *2nd sg* missing; prudé *or* prudètte; *1st pl* missing; *2nd pl* missing; prudérono *or* prudèttero

§223 **RÀDERE**—radèndo—raso
(e) rasi, radésti, rase, radémmo, radéste, ràsero

§224 **REDÌGERE**—redigèndo—redatto
(e) redassi, redigésti, redasse, redigémmo, redigéste, redàssero

§225 **REDÌMERE**—redimèndo—redènto
(e) redènsi, redimésti, redènse, redimémmo, rediméste, redènsero

§226 **RÈGGERE**—reggèndo—rètto
(e) rèssi, reggésti, rèsse, reggémmo, reggéste, rèssero

§227 **RÈNDERE**—rendèndo—réso
(e) rési *or* rendéi *or* rendètti; rendésti; rése *or* rendé *or* rendètte; rendémmo; rendéste; résero *or* rendérono *or* rendèttero

§228 **RETROCÈDERE**—retrocedèndo—retrocèsso *or* retroceduto
(e) retrocèssi *or* retrocedéi *or* retrocedètti; retrocedésti; retrocèsse *or* retrocedé *or* retrocedètte; retrocedémmo; retrocedéste; retrocèssero *or* retrocedérono *or* retrocedèttero

§229 **RIAVÉRE**—riavèndo—riavuto
(a) riabbi, riabbiate
(b) riò, riài, rià, riabbiamo, riavéte, rianno
(c) riàbbia, riàbbia, riàbbia, riabbiamo, riabbiate, riàbbiano
(e) rièbbi, riavésti, rièbbe, riavémmo, riavéste, rièbbero
(f) riavrò, riavrài, riavrà, riavrémo, riavréte, riavranno

§230 **RIDARE**—ridando—ridato
(a) ridài *or* ridà; ridate
(b) ridò, ridài, ridà, ridiamo, ridate, ridanno
(c) ridìa, ridìa, ridìa, ridiamo, ridiate, ridìano

(e) ridièdi *or* ridètti; ridésti; ridiède *or* ridètte; ridémmo; ridéste; ridièdero *or* ridèttero
(f) ridarò, ridarài, ridarà, ridarémo, ridaréte, ridaranno

§231 **RÌDERE**—ridèndo—riso
(e) risi, ridésti, rise, ridémmo, ridéste, rìsero

§232 **RIFLÈTTERE**—riflettèndo—riflèsso *or* riflettuto

§233 **RIFÙLGERE**—rifulgèndo—rifulso
(e) rifulsi, rifulgésti, rifulse rifulgémmo, rifulgéste, rifùlsero

§234 **RILÙCERE**—rilucèndo—*pp* missing

§235 **RIMANÉRE**—rimanèndo—rimasto
(b) rimango, rimani, rimane, rimaniamo, rimanéte, rimàngono
(c) rimanga, rimanga, rimanga, rimaniamo, rimaniate, rimàngano
(e) rimasi, rimanésti, rimase, rimanémmo, rimanéste, rimàsero
(f) rimarrò, rimarrài, rimarrà, rimarrémo, rimarréte, rimarranno

§236 **RINCORARE**—rincorando—rincorato
(a) rincuòra, rincorate
(b) rincuòro, rincuòri, rincuòra, rincoriamo, rincorate, rincuòrano
(c) rincuòri, rincuòri, rincuòri, rincoriamo, rincoriate, rincuòrino

§237 **RISOLARE**—risolando—risolato
(a) risuòla, risolate
(b) risuòlo, risuòli, risuòla, risoliamo, risolate, risuòlano
(c) risuòli, risuòli, risuòli, risoliamo, risoliate, risuòlino

§238 **RISPÓNDERE**—rispondèndo—rispósto
(e) rispósi, rispondésti, rispóse, rispondémmo, rispondéste, rispósero

§239 **RÓDERE**—rodèndo—róso
(e) rósi, rodésti, róse, rodémmo, rodéste, rósero

§240 **RÓMPERE**—rompèndo—rótto
(e) ruppi, rompésti, ruppe, rompémmo, rompéste, rùppero

§241 **ROTARE**—rotando—rotato
(a) ruòta, rotate
(b) ruòto, ruòti, ruòta, rotiamo, rotate, ruòtano
(c) ruòti, ruòti, ruòti, rotiamo, rotiate, ruòtino

§242 **SALIRE**—salèndo—salito
(b) salgo, sali, sale, saliamo, salite, sàlgono
(c) salga, salga, salga, saliamo, saliate, sàlgano

§243 **SAPÉRE**—sapèndo (sapiènte)—saputo
(a) sappi, sappiate
(b) sò, sai, sa, sappiamo, sapéte, sanno
(c) sàppia, sàppia, sàppia, sappiamo, sappiate, sàppiano
(e) sèppi, sapésti, sèppe, sapémmo, sapéste, sèppero
(f) saprò, saprài, saprà, saprémo, sapréte, sapranno

§244 **SCÉGLIERE**—sceglièndo—scélto
(a) scégli, scegliéte
(b) scélgo, scégli, scéglie, scegliamo, scegliéte, scélgono
(c) scélga, scélga, scélga, scegliamo, scegliate, scélgano
(e) scélsi, scegliésti, scélse, scegliémmo, scegliéste, scélsero

§245 **SCÉNDERE**—scendèndo—scéso
(e) scési, scendésti, scése, scendémmo, scendéste, scésero

§246 **SCÈRNERE**—scernèndo—*pp* missing
(e) scernéi *or* scernètti; scernésti; scerné *or* scernètte; scernémmo; scernéste; scernérono *or* scernèttero

§247 **SCÌNDERE**—scindèndo—scisso
(e) scissi, scindésti, scisse, scindémmo, scindéste, scìssero

§248 **SCOIARE**—scoiando—scoiato
(a) scuòia, scoiate
(b) scuòio, scuòi, scuòia, scoiamo, scoiate, scuòiano
(c) scuòi, scuòi, scuòi, scoiamo, scoiate, scuòino

§249 **SCÒRGERE**—scorgèndo—scòrto
(e) scòrsi, scorgésti, scòrse, scorgémmo, scorgéste, scòrsero

§250 **SCRÌVERE**—scrivèndo—scritto
(e) scrissi, scrivésti, scrisse, scrivémmo, scrivéste, scrìssero

§251 **SCUÒTERE**—scotèndo—scòsso
(a) scuòti, scotéte
(b) scuòto, scuòti, scuòte, scotiamo, scotéte, scuòtono
(c) scuòta, scuòta, scuòta, scotiamo, scotiate, scuòtano
(d) scotévo, scotévi, scotéva, scotevamo, scotevate, scotévano
(e) scòssi, scotésti, scòsse, scotémmo, scotéste, scòssero

§252 **SEDÉRE**—sedéndo—seduto
(a) sièdi, sedéte
(b) sièdo *or* sèggo; sièdi; siède; sediamo; sedéte; sièdono *or* sèggono
(c) sièda *or* sègga; sièda *or* sègga; sièda *or* sègga; sediamo; sediate; sièdano *or* sèggano
(e) sedéi *or* sedètti; sedésti; sedé *or* sedètte; sedémmo; sedéste; sedérono *or* sedèttero

§253 **SEPPELLIRE**—seppellèndo—sepólto *or* seppellito
(a) seppellisci, seppellite
(b) seppellisco, seppellisci, seppellisce, seppelliamo, seppellite, seppellìscono
(c) seppellisca, seppellisca, seppellisca, seppelliamo, seppelliate, seppellìscano

§254 **SODDISFARE**—soddisfacèndo—soddisfatto
(a) soddisfa *or* soddisfài *or* soddisfa'
(b) soddisfàccio *or* soddisfò *or* soddisfo; soddisfài *or* soddisfi; soddisfà *or* soddisfa; soddisfacciamo; soddisfate; soddisfanno *or* soddìsfano
(c) soddisfàccia *or* soddisfi; soddisfàccia *or* soddisfi; soddisfàccia *or* soddisfi; soddisfacciamo; soddisfacciate; soddisfàcciano *or* soddìsfino
(d) soddisfacévo, soddisfacévi, soddisfacéva, soddisfacevamo, soddisfacevate, soddisfacévano
(e) soddisféci, soddisfacésti, soddisféce, soddisfacémmo, soddisfacéste, soddisfécero
(f) soddisfarò, soddisfarài, soddisfarà, soddisfarémo, soddisfaréte, soddisfaranno

§255 **SOLÉRE**—solèndo—sòlito
(a) missing
(b) sòglio, suòli, suòle, sogliamo, soléte, sògliono
(c) sòglia, sòglia, sòglia, sogliamo, sogliate, sògliano
(e) missing
(f) missing

§256 **SÒLVERE**—solvèndo—soluto
(e) solvéi *or* solvètti; solvésti; solvé *or* solvètte; solvémmo; solvéste; solvérono *or* solvèttero

§257 **SONARE**—sonando—sonato
(a) suòna, sonate
(b) suòno, suòni, suòna, soniamo, sonate, suònano
(c) suòni, suòni, suòni, soniamo, soniate, suònino

§258 **SÓRGERE**—sorgèndo—sórto
(e) sórsi, sorgésti, sórse, sorgémmo, sorgéste, sórsero

§259 **SOSPÈNDERE**—sospendèndo—sospéso
(e) sospési, sospendésti, sospése, sospendémmo, sospendéste, sospésero

§260 **SPÀNDERE**—spandèndo—spanto
(e) spandéi *or* spandètti *or* spansi; spandésti; spandé *or* spandètte *or* spanse; spandémmo; spandéste; spandérono *or* spandèttero *or* spànsero

§261 **SPÀRGERE**—spargèndo—sparso
(e) sparsi, spargésti, sparse, spargémmo, spargéste, spàrsero

§262 **SPÈGNERE**—spegnèndo—spènto
(b) spéngo *or* spèngo; spégni *or* spègni; spégne *or* spègne; spegniamo; spegnéte; spéngono *or* spèngono
(c) spénga *or* spènga; spénga *or* spènga; spénga *or* spènga; spegniamo; spegniate; spéngano *or* spèngano
(e) spènsi, spegnésti, spènse, spegnémmo, spegnéste, spènsero

§263 **STARE**—stando—stato
(a) sta *or* stai *or* sta'; state
(b) stò, stài, sta, stiamo, state, stanno
(c) stìa, stìa, stìa, stiamo, stiate, stìano
(e) stètti, stésti, stètte, stémmo, stéste, stèttero
(f) starò, starài, starà, starémo, staréte, staranno

§264 **STRÌDERE**—stridèndo—*pp* missing
(e) stridéi *or* stridètti; stridésti; stridé *or* stridètte; stridémmo; stridéste; stridérono *or* stridèttero

§265 **STRÌNGERE**—stringèndo—strétto
(e) strinsi, stringésti, strinse, stringémmo, stringéste, strìnsero

§266 **STRÙGGERE**—struggèndo—strutto
(e) strussi, struggésti, strusse, struggémmo, struggéste, strùssero

§267 **SVÈLLERE**—svellèndo—svèlto
(b) svèllo *or* svèlgo; svèlli; svèlle; svelliamo; svelléte; svèllono *or* svèlgono
(c) svèlla *or* svèlga; svèlla *or* svèlga; svèlla *or* svèlga; svelliamo; svelliate; svèllano *or* svèlgano
(e) svèlsi, svellésti, svèlse, svellémmo, svelléste, svèlsero

§268 **TACÉRE**—tacèndo—taciuto
(b) tàccio, taci, tace, taciamo, tacéte, tàcciono
(c) tàccia, tàccia, tàccia, taciamo, taciate, tàcciano
(e) tàcqui, tacésti, tàcque, tacémmo, tacéste, tàcquero

§269 **TÀNGERE**—tangèndo—pp missing
(a) missing
(b) *1st sg* missing; *2nd sg* missing; tange; *1st pl* missing; *2nd pl* missing; tàngono
(c) *1st sg* missing; *2nd sg* missing; tanga; *1st pl* missing; *2nd pl* missing; tàngano
(d) *1st sg* missing; *2nd sg* missing; tangéva; *1st pl* missing; *2nd pl* missing; tangévano
(e) missing
(f) *1st sg* missing; *2nd sg* missing; tangerà; *1st pl* missing; *2nd pl* missing; tangeranno

§270 **TÈNDERE**—tendèndo—téso
(e) tési, tendésti, tése, tendémmo, tendéste, tésero

§271 **TENÉRE**—tenèndo—tenuto
(a) tièni, tenéte
(b) tèngo, tièni, tiène, teniamo, tenéte, tèngono
(c) tènga, tènga, tènga, teniamo, teniate, tèngano
(e) ténni, tenésti, ténne, tenémmo, tenéste, ténnero
(f) terrò, terrài, terrà, terrémo, terréte, terranno

§272 **TÒRCERE**—torcèndo—tòrto
(e) tòrsi, torcésti, tòrse, torcémmo, torcéste, tòrsero

§273 **TRARRE**—traèndo—tratto
(a) tràì, traéte
(b) traggo, tràì, trae, traiamo, traéte, tràggono
(c) tragga, tragga, tragga, traiamo, traiate, tràggano
(d) traévo, traévi, traéva, traevamo, traevate, traévano
(e) trassi, traésti, trasse, traémmo, traéste, tràssero

§274 **UCCÌDERE**—uccidèndo—ucciso
(e) uccisi, uccidésti, uccise, uccidémmo, uccidéste, uccìsero

§275 **UDIRE**—udèndo *or* udièndo—udito
(a) òdi, udite
(b) òdo, òdi, òde, udiamo, udite, òdono
(c) òda, òda, òda, udiamo, udiate, òdano
(f) udirò *or* udrò; udirài *or* udrài; udirà *or* udrà; udirémo *or* udrémo; udiréte *or* udréte; udiranno *or* udranno

§276 **ÙRGERE**—urgèndo—*pp* missing
(a) missing
(e) missing

§277 **USCIRE**—uscèndo—uscito
(a) èsci, uscite
(b) èsco, èsci, èsce, usciamo, uscite, èscono
(c) èsca, èsca, èsca, usciamo, usciate, èscano

§278 **VALÉRE**—valèndo—valso
(b) valgo, vali, vale, valiamo, valéte, vàlgono
(c) valga, valga, valga, valiamo, valiate, vàlgano
(e) valsi, valésti, valse, valémmo, valéste, vàlsero
(f) varrò, varrài, varrà, varrémo, varréte, varranno

§279 **VEDÉRE**—vedèndo—veduto *or* visto
(e) vidi, vedésti, vide, vedémmo, vedéste, vìdero
(f) vedrò, vedrài, vedrà, vedrémo, vedréte, vedranno

§280 **VEGLIARE**—vegliando—vegliato
(b) véglio, végli, véglia, vegliamo, vegliate, végliano
(c) végli, végli, végli, vegliamo, vegliate, véglino

§281 **VÉNDERE**—vendèndo—venduto
(e) vendéi *or* vendètti; vendésti; vendé *or* vendètte; vendémmo; vendéste; vendérono *or* vendèttero

§282 **VENIRE**—venèndo (veniènte)—venuto
(a) vièni, venite
(b) vèngo, vièni, viène, veniamo, venite, vèngono
(c) vènga, vènga, vènga, veniamo, veniate, vèngano
(e) vénni, venisti, vénne, venimmo, veniste, vénnero
(f) verrò, verrài, verrà, verrémo, verréte, verranno

§283 **VÈRTERE**—vertèndo—*pp* missing

§284 **VÌGERE**—vigèndo—*pp* missing
(a) missing
(b) *1st sg* missing; *2nd sg* missing; vige; *1st pl* missing; *2d pl* missing; vìgono
(c) *1st sg* missing; *2d sg* missing; viga; *1st pl* missing; *2d pl* missing; vìgano
(d) *1st sg* missing; *2d sg* missing; vigéva; *1st pl* missing; *2d pl* missing; vigévano
(e) missing

§285 **VÌNCERE**—vincèndo—vinto
(e) vinsi, vincésti, vinse, vincémmo, vincéste, vìnsero

§286 **VÌVERE**—vivèndo—vissuto
(e) vissi, vivésti, visse, vivémmo, vivéste, vìssero
(f) vivrò, vivrài, vivrà, vivrémo, vivréte, vivranno

§287 **VIZIARE**—viziando—viziato
(b) vìzio, vizi, vìzia, viziamo, viziate, vìziano
(c) vizi, vizi, vizi, viziamo, viziate, vìzino

§288 **VOLÉRE**—volèndo—voluto
(a) vògli, vogliate
(b) vòglio, vuòi, vuòle, vogliamo, voléte, vògliono
(c) vòglia, vòglia, vòglia, vogliamo, vogliate, vògliano
(e) vòlli, volésti, vòlle, volémmo, voléste, vòllero
(f) vorrò, vorrài, vorrà, vorrémo, vorréte, vorranno

§289 **VÒLGERE**—volgèndo—vòlto
(e) vòlsi, volgésti, vòlse, volgémmo, volgéste, vòlsero

§290 **VOLTEGGIARE**—volteggiando—volteggiato
(b) voltéggio, voltéggi, voltéggia, volteggiamo, volteggiate, voltéggiano
(c) voltéggi, voltéggi, voltéggi, volteggiamo, volteggiate, voltéggino
(f) volteggerò, volteggerài, volteggerà, volteggerémo, volteggeréte, volteggeranno

A

A, a [ɑ] *m & f* first letter of the Italian alphabet
a *prep* (**ad** in front of a vowel) to, e.g., **diede il libro a Giovanni** he gave the book to John; in, e.g., **a Milano** in Milan; at, e.g., **a casa** at home; within, e.g., **a tre miglia da qui** within three miles from here; on, e.g., **portare una catena al collo** to wear a chain on one's neck; e.g., **al sabato** on Saturdays; for, e.g., **a vita** for life; by, e.g., **fatto a mano** made by hand; with, e.g., **una gonna a pieghe** a skirt with pleats; as, e.g., **eleggere a presidente** to elect as chairman; into, e.g., **fu gettato a mare** he was thrown into the sea; of, e.g., **un quarto alle due** fifteen minutes of two
àba•co *m* (**-chi**) (archit) abacus
abate *m* abbot
abbacchiare §287 *tr* to knock down (*e.g., olives*); to sell too cheap || *ref* to lose courage; to be dejected
abbacchia•to -ta *adj* (coll) dejected
abbàc•chio *m* (**-chi**) baby lamb (*slaughtered*)
abbacinare (abbàcino) *tr* to dazzle; to deceive
abbadéssa *f* var of **badessa**
abbagliante *adj* dazzling || *m* (aut) bright light, high beam
abbagliare §280 *tr* to dazzle; to deceive; to blind (*with the lights of a car*)
abbà•glio *m* (**-gli**) error; **prendere abbaglio** to make a mistake
abbaiaménto *m* bark (*of dog*)
abbaiare §287 *intr* to bark; to yelp
abbaino *m* dormer window; skylight; attic
abbambinare *tr* to walk (*a heavy piece of furniture*)
abbandonare (abbandóno) *tr* to abandon; to give up; to let go (*e.g., the reins*); to let fall; (sports) to withdraw from || *ref* to yield; to lose courage
abbandóno *m* abandon, abandonment; desertion; neglect; relaxation; renunciation (*of a right*); cession (*of property*); withdrawal (*from a fight*)
abbarbicare §197 **(abbàrbico)** *intr & ref* to cling; to hold on
abbassalin•gua *m* (**-gua**) tongue depressor
abbassaménto *m* lowering; reduction; drop, fall
abbassare *tr* to lower; to dim (*lights*); to turn (*the radio*) lower; **abbassare le armi** to surrender; **abbassare la cresta** to yield || *ref* to lower oneself; to drop
abbas•so *m* (**-so**) angry shout (*of a crowd*) || *adv* down, below; downstairs || *interj* down with!
abbastanza *adj invar* enough || *adv* enough; rather, fairly
abbàttere *tr* to demolish; to fell; to shoot down; to refute (*an argument*); to depress || *ref* to be depressed, be downcast
abbattiménto *m* demolition; felling; shooting down; chill; (fig) depression; **abbattimento alla base** (econ) basic exemption (*from taxes*)
abbattu•to -ta *adj* dejected, downcast || *f* clearing (*of trees*)
abbazìa *f* abbey; abbacy
abbecedà•rio *m* (**-ri**) speller, primer
abbelliménto *m* embellishment, ornamentation
abbellire §176 *tr* to embellish, adorn; to landscape
abbeverare (abbévero) *tr* to water (*animals*) || *ref* to quench one's thirst
abbevera•tóio *m* (**-tói**) watering trough
abbìc•cì *m* (**-cì**) alphabet; speller, primer; ABC's, rudiments
abbiènte *adj* well-to-do || *m*—**gli abbienti** the haves; **gli abbienti e nullatenenti** the haves and the have-nots
abbiettézza or **abiettézza** *f* abjectness, baseness
abbièt•to -ta or **abièt•to -ta** *adj* abject, base, low
abbiezióne or **abiezióne** *f* wretchedness, baseness
abbigliaménto *m* attire, wear
abbigliare §280 *tr & ref* to dress; to dress up
abbinaménto *m* coupling; merger
abbinare *tr* to couple; to join, merge
abbindolare (abbìndolo) *tr* to dupe, deceive
abbiosciare §128 *ref* to fall down; to lose heart, be downcast
abbisognare (abbisógno) *intr* to be in need
abboccaménto *m* interview, conversation
abboccare §197 **(abbócco)** *tr* to swallow (*the hook*); to fit (*pipes*) || *intr* to bite (*said of fish*); to fall; to fit (*said of pipes*) || *ref* to confer
abbocca•to -ta *adj* palatable; slightly sweet (*wine*)
abbonacciare §128 *ref* to calm down, abate (*said of weather*)
abbonaménto *m* subscription; **abbonamento postale** mailing permit
abbonare (abbòno) *tr* to take out a subscription for (*s.o.*) || *ref* to subscribe || §257 *tr* to remit (*a debt*); to forgive
abbona•to -ta *mf* subscriber; commuter
abbondante *adj* abundant, plentiful; heavy (*rain*)
abbondanza *f* abundance, plenty
abbondare (abbóndo) *intr* (ESSERE & AVERE) to abound; to exceed; **abbondare di** or **in** to abound in
abbonire §176 *tr* to calm; to placate || *ref* to calm down
abbordàbile *adj* accessible, approachable; negotiable (*curve*)

abbordàg·gio *m* **(-gi)** boarding (*of an enemy ship*); **andare all'abbordaggio di** to board
abbordare (abbórdo) *tr* to board (*an enemy ship*); to negotiate (*a curve*); to face (*a problem*); (fig) to buttonhole
abborracciare §128 *tr* to botch, bungle
abborracciatura *f* botch, bungle
abbottonare (abbottóno) *tr* to button ‖ *ref* (coll) to keep to oneself
abbottonatura *f* buttoning; row of buttons
abbozzare (abbòzzo) *tr* to sketch; to hew (*e.g., a statue*); (naut) to tie up ‖ *intr* (coll) to take it
abbòzzo *m* sketch, draft
abbracciabò·sco *m* **(-schi)** (bot) woodbine
abbracciare *m* embrace, embracing ‖ §128 *tr* to embrace, hug; to seize (*an opportunity*); to become converted to (*e.g., Christianity*); to enter (*a profession*); to span, encompass ‖ *ref* to cling; to embrace one another
abbràc·cio *m* **(-ci)** embrace, hug
abbrancare §197 *tr* to grab; to herd ‖ *ref* to cling; to join a herd
abbreviaménto *m* abbreviation, shortening
abbreviare §287 **(abbrèvio)** *tr* to abbreviate, shorten, abridge
abbreviatura *f* shortening, abridgment
abbreviazióne *f* abbreviation
abbrivo or **abbrivio** *m* headway (*of a ship*); **prendere l'abbrivio** to gather momentum
abbronzante [dz] *adj* suntanning ‖ *m* suntan lotion
abbronzare [dz] **(abbrónzo)** *tr & ref* to bronze; to tan
abbronza·to -ta [dz] *adj* tanned, suntanned
abbronzatura [dz] *f* tan, suntan
abbruciacchiare §287 *tr* to singe
abbrunare *tr* to brown; to hang crepe on ‖ *ref* to wear mourning
abbrunire §176 *tr* to turn brown; to tan; to burnish
abbrustolire §176 *tr* to toast; to singe ‖ *ref* to tan; to become sunburned
abbrutiménto *m* degradation, brutishness
abbrutire §176 *tr* to degrade; to brutalize ‖ *intr & ref* to become brutalized
abbuiare §287 *tr* to darken; to hush up, hide ‖ *ref* to grow dark; to become gloomy ‖ *impers*—**abbuia** it's growing dark
abbuòno *m* allowance, discount; handicap (*in racing*)
abburattaménto *m* sifting
abburattare *tr* to sift, bolt
abdicare §197 **(àbdico)** *tr & intr* to abdicate; **abdicare a** to give up, renounce; to abdicate (*e.g., the throne*)
abdicazióne *f* abdication
aberrare (abèrro) *intr* to deviate
aberrazióne *f* aberration
abéte *m* fir
abetina *f* forest of fir trees
abiàti·co *m* **(-ci)** (coll) grandson
abièt·to -ta *adj* abject, base, low
abigeato *m* (law) cattle rustling
àbile *adj* able, clever, capable; (mil) fit
abili·tà *f* **(tà)** ability, skill
abilitare (abìlito) *tr* to certify (*e.g., a teacher*); to qualify, license
abilita·to -ta *adj* certified (*teacher*)
abilitazióne *f* qualification; certification (*of teachers*)
abissale *adj* abysmal
Abissìnia, l' *f* Abyssinia
abissi·no -na *adj & mf* Abyssinian
abisso *m* abyss; fountain (*of knowledge*); slough (*of degradation*)
abitàbile *adj* inhabitable
abitàcolo *m* (aer) cockpit; (aut) cab, interior; (naut) compass bowl; **abitacolo elettabile** (aer) ejection capsule
abitante *mf* inhabitant; resident
abitare (àbito) *tr* to inhabit; to occupy ‖ *intr* to dwell, live, reside
abitati·vo -va *adj* living, e.g., **condizioni abitative** living conditions
abita·to -ta *adj* inhabited, populated ‖ *m* built-up area
abita·tóre -trice *mf* dweller
abitazióne *f* dwelling; housing
àbito *m* suit (*for men*); dress (*for women*); garb, attire; habit; **abiti** clothes; **abito da ballo** evening gown; **abito da cerimonia** formal dress; **abito da inverno** winter suit; winter clothes; **levarsi l'abito** to doff the cassock; **prender l'abito** to enter the Church
abituale *adj* habitual
abituare (abìtuo) *tr* to accustom ‖ *ref* to grow accustomed
abitudinà·rio -ria *adj* **(-ri -rie)** set in his ways
abitùdine *f* habit, custom
abituro *m* (poet) shanty, hut
abiura *f* abjuration
abiurare *tr* to abjure
ablati·vo -va *adj & m* ablative
ablazióne *f* (med) removal; (geol) erosion
abluzióne *f* ablution
abnegare §209 **(abnégo & abnègo)** *tr* to renounce, abnegate
abnegazióne *f* abnegation, self-denial
abnòrme *adj* abnormal
abolire §176 *tr* to abolish
abolizióne *f* abolition
abominàbile *adj* abominable
abominare (abòmino) *tr* to abominate, detest
abominazióne *f* abomination
abominévole *adj* abominable
aborige·no -na *adj* aboriginal ‖ *m* aborigine; **aborigeni** aborigines
aborrire §176 & **(abòrro)** *tr* to abhor, loathe ‖ *intr*—**aborrire da** to shun, shrink from
abortire §176 *intr* to abort
abòrto *m* abortion, miscarriage; **aborto di natura** monstrosity
abrasióne *f* abrasion; erosion
abrasi·vo -va *adj & m* abrasive
abrogare §209 **(àbrogo)** *tr* to abrogate
abrogazióne *f* abrogation

abruzzése *adj* of the Abruzzi || *mf* person of the Abruzzi || *m* dialect of the Abruzzi
àbside *f* (archit) apse
abusare *intr*—**abusare di** to go to excesses in (*e.g., smoking*); to take advantage of; to impose on
abusi•vo -va *adj* illegal, abusive; unwarranted
abuso *m* abuse, excess
acà•cia *f* (**-cie**) acacia
acanto *m* acanthus
àcaro *m* (ent) acarus, mite, tick; **acaro della scabbia** itch mite
ac•ca *m* & *f* (**-ca** or **-che**) h (*letter*); **non valere un'acca** (coll) to not be worth a fig
accadèmia *f* academy
accadèmi•co -ca (**-ci -che**) *adj* academic || *mf* academician
accadére §121 *intr* (ESSERE) to happen, occur
accadu•to -ta *adj* happened, occurred || *m* fact, event; what has taken place
accagliare §280 *tr*, *intr* (ESSERE) & *ref* to curdle, coagulate
accalappiaca•ni *m* (**-ni**) dogcatcher
accalappiare §287 *tr* to catch (*a dog*); to snare; (fig) to fool
accalcare §197 *tr* to crowd || *ref* to throng
accaldare *ref* to get hot; to become flushed
accalda•to -ta *adj* hot; perspired
accalorare (**accalóro**) *tr* to excite || *ref* to get excited
accalora•to -ta *adj* excited, animated
accampaménto *m* encampment, camp; camping
accampare *tr* to encamp; to advance, lay (*a claim*) || *ref* to camp, encamp
accaniménto *m* animosity, bitterness; obstinacy, stubbornness
accanire §176 *ref* to persist; to work doggedly; **accanirsi contro** to harass
accani•to -ta *adj* obstinate, persistent; furious; fierce, ruthless, bitter (*fight*)
accanto *adv* near, nearby; **accanto a** near
accantonaménto *m* tabling (*e.g., of a discussion*); reserve (*of money*); (mil) billeting; (sports) camping
accantonare (**accantóno**) *tr* to set aside (*money*); (mil) to billet
accaparraménto *m* cornering (*of market*)
accaparrare *tr* to corner (*merchandise*); to hoard; to put a down payment on (*e.g., a house*); (coll) to gain (*somebody's affection*)
accaparra•tóre -trice *mf* monopolizer; hoarder
accapigliare §280 *ref* to pull each other's hair; to scuffle; to come to blows
accapo or **a capo** *m* paragraph
accappa•tóio *m* (**-tói**) bathrobe
accapponare (**accappóno**) *tr* to castrate (*a rooster*) || *ref* to wrinkle; **mi si accappona la pelle** I get gooseflesh
accarezzare (**accarézzo**) *tr* to caress, fondle; to pet; to nurture (*e.g., a hope*); **accarezzare le spalle di** to strike; to club
accartocciare §128 (**accartòccio**) *tr* to wrap up in a cone || *ref* to curl up
accartoccia•to -ta *adj* curled up
accasare [s] *tr* & *ref* to marry
accasciaménto *m* dejection
accasciare §128 *tr* to weaken, enfeeble; to depress || *ref* to weaken; to lose heart
accasermare [s] (**accasèrmo**) *tr* to quarter, billet
accatastare *tr* to register (*real estate*); to pile, heap up
accattabri•ghe *mf* (**-ghe**) quarrelsome person, scrapper
accattare *tr* to beg for; to borrow (*e.g., ideas*) || *intr* to beg
accattonàg•gio *m* (**-gi**) begging, mendicancy
accattó•ne -na *mf* mendicant, beggar
accavalcare §197 *tr* to straddle; to go over
accavalciare §128 *tr* to bestride
accavallare *tr* to superimpose; to cross (*one's legs*) || *ref* to pour forward, run high (*said of waves*)
accecaménto *m* blinding
accecare §122 *tr* to blind; to countersink || *intr* (ESSERE) to become blind || *ref* to blind oneself
acceca•tóio *m* (**-tói**) countersink
accèdere §100 *intr* (ESSERE) to enter, approach; to accede
acceleraménto *m* acceleration
accelerare (**accèlero**) *tr* & *intr* to accelerate
accelera•to -ta *adj* accelerated; intensive (*course*); local (*train*) || *m* local train
acceleratóre *m* accelerator
accelerazióne *f* acceleration
accèndere §101 *tr* to kindle; to turn on (*e.g., the light*); to light (*e.g., a match, a cigar*) || *ref* to catch fire; to become lit; **accendersi in viso** to become flushed
accendisìgaro *m* lighter
accendi•tóio *m* (**-tói**) candle lighter
accenditóre *m* lighter
accennare (**accénno**) *tr* to nod; to point at; to sketch || *intr* to refer; to hint
accénno *m* nod; sign; allusion
accensióne *f* lighting, kindling; (aut) ignition; (law) contraction (*of a debt*); **accensione improvvisa** spontaneous combustion
accentare (**accènto**) *tr* to accent
accènto *m* accent; stress; (poet) accent (*word*); **accento tonico** stress accent
accentraménto *m* centralization
accentrare (**accèntro**) *tr* to concentrate, centralize
accentuare (**accèntuo**) *tr* to accentuate || *ref* to become aggravated
accentuazióne *f* accentuation
accerchiaménto *m* encirclement
accerchiare §287 (**accérchio**) *tr* to encircle, surround
accertàbile *adj* verifiable
accertaménto *m* ascertainment, verification; determination (*e.g., of taxes*)

accertare (accèrto) *tr* to assure; to ascertain, verify; to determine (*the tax due*) || *ref* to make sure
accé·so -sa [s] *adj* lit; turned on; on (*e.g., radio*); excited, aroused; bright (*color*)
accessìbile *adj* accessible; moderate (*price*)
accessióne *f* accession
accèsso *m* access, approach; admittance, entry; fit (*of anger, of coughing*)
accessò·rio -ria (-ri -rie) *adj* accessory || *m* accessory; (mach) accessory, attachment
accétta *f* hatchet, axe, cleaver; **tagliato con l'accetta** rough-hewn
accettàbile *adj* acceptable
accettare (accètto) *tr* to accept
accettazióne *f* acceptance; receiving room; (econ) acceptance
accèt·to -ta *adj* agreeable; welcome; **male accetto** unwelcome
accezióne *f* meaning, acceptation
acchiappafarfal·le *m* (**-le**) butterfly net
acchiappamó·sche *m* (**-sche**) fly catcher
acchiappare *tr* to grab, seize; (coll) to catch in the act
acchito *m* (billiards) break; **di primo acchito** at first
acciaccare §197 *tr* to crush; to trample upon; (coll) to lay low (*e.g., by illness*)
acciac·co *m* (**-chi**) illness, infirmity, ailment
acciaiare §287 *tr* to convert into steel; to strengthen with steel
acciaierìa *f* steel mill, steelworks
ac·ciàio *m* (**-ciài**) steel; **acciaio inossidabile** stainless steel
acciaiòlo *m* whetstone
acciambellare (acciambèllo) *tr* to shape in the form of a doughnut || *ref* to curl up
acciarino *m* flintlock; linchpin; (nav) war nose (*of a torpedo*)
accidèmpoli *interj* (slang) darn it!
accidentale *adj* accidental
accidenta·to -ta *adj* paralyzed; uneven, rough (*road*); broken (*ground*)
accidènte *m* accident; crack-up; (coll) paralytic stroke; (coll) hoot, fig; (coll) pest, menace (*child*); (mus) accidental; **accidenti!** (coll) darn!, damn!; **correre come un accidente** to run like the devil; **mandare un accidente a** to wish ill luck to; **per accidente** perchance
accìdia *f* sloth
accidió·so -sa [s] *adj* slothful
accigliare §280 *ref* to frown, knit one's brow
accìngere §126 *ref*—**accingersi a** to get ready to
-àccio -àccia *suf adj & mf* (**-acci -acce**) no good, e.g., **gentaccia** no good people; good-for-nothing, e.g., **ragazzaccio** good-for-nothing boy
acciò or **acciocché** *conj* (poet) so that
acciottolare (acciòttolo) *tr* to pave with cobblestones
acciottola·to -ta *adj* cobblestone || *m* cobblestone pavement

acciottolì·o *m* (**-i**) clatter (*e.g., of dishes*)
accipìcchia *interj* (coll) darn it!
acciuffare *tr* to seize, grab, pinch (*a thief*)
acciu·ga *f* (**-ghe**) anchovy
acclamare *tr* to acclaim || *intr* to voice one's approval
acclamazióne *f* acclamation
acclimatare (acclìmato) *tr & ref* to acclimate
acclimatazióne *f* acclimatation
acclive *adj* (poet) steep
acclivi·tà *f* (**-tà**) acclivity
acclùdere §105 *tr* to enclose
acclu·so -sa *adj* enclosed
accoccare §197 **(accòcco & accócco)** *tr* (poet) to nock (*the arrow*)
accoccolare (accòccolo) *ref* to squat down
accodare (accódo) *tr* to line up || *ref* to line up, queue
accogliènte *adj* cozy, hospitable, inviting
accogliènza *f* reception, welcome
accògliere §127 *tr* to receive; to welcome; to grant (*a request*) || *ref* (poet) to gather
accoglitrice *f* receptionist
accòlito *m* acolyte, altar boy; follower
accollare (accòllo) *tr* to overload (*a cart*); **accollare qlco a qlcu** to charge s.o. with s.th || *intr* to go up to the neck (*said of a dress*) || *ref* to assume, take upon oneself
accolla·to -ta *adj* high-necked (*dress*); high-cut (*shoes*) || *f* accolade
accollatura *f* neck, neckhole
accòlta *f* (poet) gathering
accoltellare (accoltèllo) *tr* to knife
accomandante *m* limited partner
accomandatà·rio *m* (**-ri**) (law) general partner
accomàndita *f* (law) limited partnership
accomiatare *tr* to dismiss || *ref* to take leave
accomodaménto *m* arrangement; compromise; settlement
accomodante *adj* accommodating, obliging
accomodare (accòmodo) *tr* to arrange; to fix; to settle || *intr* to be convenient || *ref* to adapt oneself; to agree; to sit down; **si accomodi** have a seat, make yourself comfortable
accomodatura *f* arrangement; repair
accompagnaménto *m* retinue; cortege; (mus) accompaniment; (law) writ of mandamus; (mil) softening-up (*by gunfire*)
accompagnare *tr* to accompany; to escort; to follow; to match || *ref*—**accompagnarsi a** or **con** to join
accompagna·tóre -trice *mf* escort; guide; (mus) accompanist
accomunare *tr* to mingle, mix; to unite, associate; to share
acconciaménto *m* arrangement
acconciare §128 **(accóncio)** *tr* to prepare for use; to arrange; to set (*e.g., the hair*) || *ref* to adorn oneself; to dress one's hair; to adapt oneself
acconcia·tóre -trice *mf* hairdresser

acconciatura *f* hairdo; headdress
accón·cio -cia *adj* (**-ci -ce**) proper, fitting
accondiscendènte *adj* acquiescing, acquiescent
accondiscendènza *f* acquiescence
accondiscéndere §245 *intr* to acquiesce, consent; to yield
acconsentire (**acconsènto**) *intr* to consent, acquiesce
acconsenziènte *adj* consenting, acquiescing
accontentare (**accontènto**) *tr* to satisfy, please || *ref* to be satisfied, be pleased
accónto *m* installment
accoppare (**accòppo**) *tr* (coll) to kill; (coll) to beat to death || *ref* (coll) to get killed
accoppiaménto *m* pairing; mating; (mach) parallel operation
accoppiare §287 (**accòppio**) *tr* to couple, pair, cross (*e.g., animals*) || *ref* to mate, copulate
accoppiata *f* daily double (*in races*)
accoraménto *m* sadness, sorrow
accorare (**accòro**) *tr* to stab to death; to sadden || *ref* to sadden, grieve
accora·to -ta *adj* saddened, grieving
accorciare §128 (**accórcio**) *tr & ref* to shorten; to shrink
accorciatura *f* shortening; shrinking
accordare (**accòrdo**) *tr* to harmonize (*colors*); to reconcile (*people*); to tune up; to grant; (gram) to make agree || *ref* to agree; to match
accorda·to -ta *adj* tuned up || *m* (econ) credit limit
accorda·tóre -trice *mf* (mus) tuner
accordatura *f* tuning
accòrdo *m* agreement, accordance; (law) mutual consent; (mus) harmony; **d'accordo** O.K., agreed; **d'accordo con** in accord with; **di comune accordo** with one accord; **essere d'accordo** to agree; **mettersi d'accordo** to come to an agreement
accòrgere §249 *ref* to perceive, notice; **accorgersi di** to become aware of, realize; **senza accorgersi** inadvertently
accorgiménto *m* smartness; device, trick
accórrere §139 *intr* (ESSERE) to run up, rush up
accortézza *f* alertness; shrewdness, perspicacity
accòr·to -ta *adj* alert; shrewd, perspicacious
accosciare §128 (**accòscio**) *ref* to squat
accostàbile *adj* approachable
accostaménto *m* approach; combination (*e.g., of colors*)
accostare (**accòsto**) *tr* to approach; to bring near; to leave (*a door*) ajar || *intr* to be near; to cling, adhere; (naut) to come alongside; (naut) to maneuver alongside a pier; (naut) to change direction, haul || *ref* to approach, come near; to cling (*e.g., to a faith*)
accosta·to -ta *adj* ajar
accò·sto -sta *adj* (coll) near || *m* approach; help || **accosto** *adv* near; **accosto a** near, close to
accovacciare §128 *ref* to crouch
accovonare (**accovóno**) *tr* to sheave
accozzàglia *f* hodgepodge; motley crowd
accozzare (**accòzzo**) *tr* to jumble up; to collect, gather (*people*) together || *ref* to collect, congregate
accòzzo *m* jumble, medley
accreditàbile *adj* chargeable (*e.g., account*); creditable
accreditaménto *m* crediting
accreditare (**accrédito**) *tr* to credit, believe; to accredit (*an ambassador*); to credit (*one's account*)
accredita·to -ta *adj* confirmed (*news*); accredited
accréscere §142 *tr & ref* to increase
accresciménto *m* increase
accucciare §128 *ref* to curl up (*said of dogs*)
accudire §176 *tr* (coll) to attend (*a sick person*) || *intr*—**accudire a** to take care of
acculturazióne *f* acculturation
accumulare (**accùmulo**) *tr, intr & ref* to accumulate; to gather
accumulatóre *m* storage battery
accumulazióne *f* accumulation
accuratézza *f* care, carefulness
accura·to -ta *adj* careful, painstaking
accusa *f* accusation, charge; **pubblica accusa** (law) public prosecutor
accusare *tr* to accuse, charge; to betray; to acknowledge (*receipt*); (cards) to declare, bid
accusati·vo -va *adj & m* accusative
accusa·to -ta *adj* accused || *mf* defendant
accusató·re -trice *mf* accuser; **pubblico accusatore** (law) public prosecutor, district attorney
accusatò·rio -ria *adj* (**-ri -rie**) accusatory, accusing
acèfa·lo -la *adj* headless; without the first page (*said of a manuscript*)
acèr·bo -ba *adj* unripe, green, sour
àcero *m* maple tree, sugar maple
acèrri·mo -ma *adj* bitter, fierce
acetato *m* acetate
acèti·co -ca *adj* (**-ci -che**) acetic
acetificare §197 (**acetìfico**) *tr* to acetify
acetilène *m* acetylene
acéto *m* vinegar; **aceto aromatico** aromatic spirits; **sotto aceto** pickled
acetóne *m* acetone
acetósa [s] *f* (bot) sorrel
acetosèlla [s] *f* wood sorrel
acetó·so -sa [s] *adj* vinegarish || *f* see **acetosa**
Acherónte *m* Acheron
Achille *m* Achilles
acidificare §197 (**acidìfico**) *tr* to acidify
acidi·tà *f* (**-tà**) acidity; **acidità di stomaco** heartburn
àci·do -da *adj* acid, sour || *m* acid; **sapere d'acido** to taste sour
acìdu·lo -la *adj* acidulous
àcino *m* berry (*of grapes*); bead (*of rosary*)
acme *f* acme; crisis
acne *f* acne

acònito *m* (bot) monkshood
àcqua *f* water; rain; purity (*e.g., of a diamond*); **acqua a catinelle** pouring rain; **acqua alta** high water; **acqua corrente** running water; **acqua dolce** fresh water; drinking water; **acqua in bocca!** mum's the word!; **acqua morta** stagnant water; **acqua ossigenata** hydrogen peroxide; **acqua potabile** drinking water; **acqua salata** salt water; **acqua viva** spring; **all'acqua di rose** very mild; **avere l'acqua alla gola** to be in dire straits; **della più bell'acqua** of the first water; **fare acqua** to leak (*said of a boat*); **fare un buco nell'acqua** to waste one's efforts; **portare acqua al mare** to carry coals to Newcastle; **prendere l'acqua** to get wet; **sott'acqua** (fig) underhand; **tirare l'acqua al proprio mulino** to be grist to one's mill; **versare acqua in un cesto** to waste one's efforts
acquafòrte *f* (**acquefòrti**) etching
acquaforti•sta *mf* (**-sti -ste**) etcher
ac•quàio -quàia (**-quài -quàie**) *adj* watering (*trough*) || *m* sink
acquaiò•lo -la *adj* water || *m* water carrier; (sports) water boy
acquamarina *f* (**acquemarine**) aquamarine
acquaplano *m* aquaplane
acquaràgia *f* turpentine
acquarèllo *m* var of **acquerello**
acquà•rio *m* (**-ri**) aquarium || **Acquario** *m* (astr) Aquarius
acquartierare (**acquartièro**) *tr* (mil) to quarter || *ref* to be quartered
acquasanta *f* holy water
acquasantièra *f* (eccl) stoup
acquàti•co -ca *adj* (**-ci -che**) aquatic, water
acquattare *ref* to crouch, squat
acquavite *f* brandy; liquor, rum
acquazzóne *m* downpour, heavy shower
acquedótto *m* aqueduct
àcque•o -a *adj* aqueous, watery
acquerelli•sta *mf* (**-sti -ste**) watercolorist
acquerèllo *m* watercolor; watered-down wine
acquerùgiola *f* fine drizzle
acquiescènte *adj* acquiescent
acquietare (**acquièto**) *tr* to pacify, placate || *ref* to quiet down
acquirènte *mf* buyer, purchaser; **il miglior acquirente** the highest bidder
acquisire §176 *tr* to acquire
acquisi•tóre -trice *mf* salesperson, agent || *m* salesman || *f* saleswoman
acquistare *tr* to purchase, buy; to acquire; to gain (*e.g., ground*) || *intr* to improve
acquisto *m* buy, purchase; acquisition
acquitrino *m* marsh
acquitrinó•so -sa [s] *adj* marshy
acquolina *f*—**far venire l'acquolina in bocca a** to make one's mouth water
acquó•so -sa [s] *adj* watery
acre *adj* sour; pungent; acrid; bitter (*words*)
acrèdine *f* acrimony, sourness
acrimònia *f* acrimony
acro *m* acre
acròba•ta *mf* (**-ti -te**) acrobat
acrobàti•co -ca (**-ci -che**) *adj* acrobatic || *f* acrobatics
acrobatismo *m* acrobatics
acrobazìa *f* acrobatics; stunt, feat
acrocòro *m* plateau
acrònimo *m* acronym
acròpo•li *f* (**-li**) acropolis
acròsti•co *m* (**-ci**) acrostic
acuire §176 *tr* to sharpen, whet
acuità *f* acuity
acùle•o *m* (**-i**) quill; prickle, thorn; stinger (*of an insect*)
acume *m* acumen
acuminare (**acùmino**) *tr* to sharpen, whet
acumina•to -ta *adj* pointed, sharp
acùsti•co -ca (**-ci -che**) *adj* acoustic(al) || *f* acoustics
acutézza *f* acuteness, sharpness
acutizzare [ddzz] *tr & ref* to sharpen
acu•to -ta *adj* acute, sharp || *m* high note
ad *prep* var of **a** before words beginning with a vowel
adagiare §290 *tr* to lay down gently; to lower gently || *ref* to lie down; to stretch out
adà•gio *m* (**-gi**) adage; (mus) adagio || *adv* slowly; gently; (mus) adagio
Adamo *m* Adam
adattàbile *adj* adaptable
adattaménto *m* adaptation; adaptability
adattare *tr* to adapt, fit || *ref* to adapt oneself; to become adapted; **adattarsi a** to go with; to match; to be becoming to
adat•to -ta *adj* suitable, adequate
addebitaménto *m* debiting
addebitare (**addébito**) *tr* to debit; **addebitare una spesa a qlcu** to debit s.o. with an expense
addébito *m* charge; (com) debit; **elevare l'addebito di qlco a qlcu** (law) to charge s.o. with s.th
addènda *mpl* addenda
addèndo *m* (math) addend
addensare (**addènso**) *tr* to thicken || *ref* to thicken; to gather, throng
addentare (**addènto**) *tr* to bite || *ref* (mach) to mesh
addentatura *f* bite; (carp) tongue (*of tongue and groove*)
addentella•to -ta *adj* toothed, notched || *m* chance, occasion; (archit) toothing
addentrare (**addéntro**) *tr* to penetrate || *ref* to penetrate; to proceed
addéntro *adv* inside; **addentro in** into; inside of
addestraménto *m* training
addestrare (**addèstro**) *tr & ref* to train
addestra•tóre -trice *mf* trainer
addét•to -ta *adj* assigned; attached; pertaining || *m* attaché; **addetto stampa** press secretary
addì *adv* the (+ *a certain date*), e.g., **addì 27 gennaio** the 27th of January
addiàc•cio *m* (**-ci**) sheepfold; bivouac
addiètro *m* (naut) stern; **per l'addietro** in the past || *adv* behind; ago; **dare**

addietro to back up; **lasciarsi addietro** to delay; **tempo addietro** some time ago; **tirarsi addietro** to back away
addì·o *m* (-i) farewell; **dare l'addio** to say good-bye; **dare l'estremo addio** to pay one's last respects; **fare gli addii** to say good-bye || *interj* farewell!, good-bye!
addire §151 *tr* (poet) to consecrate || *ref* to be suitable, be becoming; **addirsi a** to be becoming to
addirittura *adv* directly; even, without hesitation; absolutely, positively
addirizzare *tr* to straighten up; **addirizzare le gambe ai cani** to try the impossible
additare *tr* to point out
additi·vo -va *adj & m* additive
addivenire §282 *intr* (ESSERE)—**addivenire a** to come to, reach (*e.g., an agreement*)
addizionale *adj* additional || *f* supplementary tax
addizionare (addizióno) *tr & intr* to add
addizionatrice *f* adding machine
addizióne *f* addition
addobbaménto *m* adornment, decoration
addobbare (addòbbo) *tr* to adorn, bedeck, decorate
addobba·tóre -trice *mf* decorator
addòbbo *m* adornment, decoration; hangings (*in a church*)
addocilire §176 *tr* to soften up
addolcire §176 *tr* to sweeten; to calm down || *ref* to mellow, soften
addolorare (addolóro) *tr & ref* to grieve; **addolorarsi per** to grieve over, lament
addolora·to -ta *adj* sorrowful || **l'Addolorata** *f* (eccl) Our Lady of Sorrows
addòme *m* abdomen
addomesticàbile *adj* tamable
addomesticaménto *m* taming
addomesticare §197 **(addomèstico)** *tr* to tame; to accustom || *ref* to become accustomed
addomestica·to -ta *adj* tame, domesticated
addominale *adj* abdominal
addormentare (addorménto) *tr* to put to sleep; to numb || *ref* to fall asleep; to be asleep (*said of a limb*)
addormenta·to -ta *adj* asleep; numbed
addossare (addòsso) *tr* to put on; **addossare qlco a qlco** to lean s.th against s.th; **addossare qlco a qlcu** to put s.th on s.o.; (fig) to entrust s.o. with s.th || *ref* to take upon oneself; to crowd together; **addossarsi a** to lean against; to crowd
addossa·to -ta *adj* leaning
addòsso *adv* on; on oneself, on one's back; about oneself; **addosso a** on, upon; against; **avere la sfortuna addosso** to be always unlucky; **dare addosso a qlcu** to assail s.o.; **levarsi d'addosso** to get rid of; **levarsi i panni d'addosso** to take the shirt off one's back
addót·to -ta *adj* adduced, alleged
addottorare (addottóro) *tr* to confer the doctor's degree on || *ref* to receive the doctor's degree
addurre §102 *tr* to adduce; to allege; (poet) to bring
Ade *m* Hades
adeguare (adéguo) *tr* to equalize; to bring in line || *ref* to conform, adapt oneself
adegua·to -ta *adj* adequate
adeguazióne *f* equalization
adémpiere §163 *tr* to fulfill, accomplish || *ref* to come true
adempiménto *m* fulfillment, discharge (*of one's duty*)
adempire §176 *tr* to fulfill, accomplish || *ref* to come true
adenòide *adj* adenoid || **adenoidi** *fpl* adenoids
adèpto *m* follower; initiate
aderènte *adj* adherent || *mf* adherent, supporter
aderènza *f* adherence; (mach) friction; (pathol) adhesion; **aderenze** connections
aderire §176 *intr* to adhere; to stick; **aderire a** to grant (*e.g., a request*); to concur with; to subscribe to
adescare §197 **(adésco)** *tr* to lure, bait, entice; (mach) to prime (*a pump*)
adesióne *f* adhesion; support; (phys) adherence
adesi·vo -va *adj & m* adhesive
adèsso *adv* now, just now; **da adesso in poi** from now on; **per adesso** for the time being
adiacènte *adj* adjacent
adiacènza *f* adjacency; **adiacenze** vicinity
adianto *m* (bot) maidenhair
adibire §176 *tr* to assign; to use
àdipe *m* fat
adipó·so -sa [s] *adj* adipose
adirare *ref* to get angry
adira·to -ta *adj* angry, mad
adire §176 *tr* to apply to (*the court*); to enter into possession of (*an inheritance*)
adocchiare §287 **(adòcchio)** *tr* to eye; to ogle; to spot
adolescènte *adj & mf* adolescent
adolescènza *f* adolescence
adombrare (adómbro) *tr* to shade; to hide, veil || *ref* to shy (*said of a horse*); (fig) to take umbrage
Adóne *m* Adonis
adontare (adónto) *tr* (obs) to offend || *ref* to take offense
adoperare (adòpero & adópero) *tr* to use, employ || *ref* to exert oneself; to do one's best
adoràbile *adj* adorable
adorare (adóro) *tr* to adore; to worship || *intr* (archaic) to pray
adora·tóre -trice *mf* worshiper || *m* (joc) admirer, suitor
adorazióne *f* adoration, worship
adornare (adórno) *tr* to adorn || *ref* to bedeck oneself
adór·no -na *adj* adorned, bedecked; (poet) fine, beautiful
adottante *mf* (law) adopter

adottare (adòtto) *tr* to adopt
adotti•vo -va *adj* adoptive; foster (*child*)
adozióne *f* adoption
Adriàti•co -ca *adj* **(-ci -che)** Adriatic || **Adriatico** *m* Adriatic
adulare (àdulo) *tr* to flatter; to fawn on
adula•tóre -trice *mf* flatterer
adulatò•rio -ria *adj* **(-ri -rie)** flattering; fawning
adulazióne *f* adulation; fawning
adulterante *adj* & *m* adulterant
adulteri•no -na *adj* bastard; adulterated
adultè•rio *m* **(-ri)** adultery
adùlte•ro -ra *adj* adulterous || *m* adulterer || *f* adulteress
adul•to -ta *adj* & *mf* adult
adunanza *f* assembly
adunare *tr* & *ref* to assemble, gather
adunata *f* reunion, meeting; (mil) muster
adun•co -ca *adj* **(-chi -che)** hooked, crooked
adunghiare §287 *tr* (poet) to claw
adu•sto -sta *adj* skinny; (poet) burnt
aerare (àero) *tr* to air, ventilate
aerazióne *f* aeration; airing
aère•o -a *adj* aerial; air; overhead; high, lofty; airy, fanciful || *m* airplane; (rad & telv) aerial
aerobrigata *f* (mil) wing
aerocistèrna *f* (aer) tanker
aerodinàmi•co -ca (-ci -che) *adj* aerodynamic(al); streamlined || *f* aerodynamics
aeròdromo *m* airfield, airdrome
aerofaro *m* airport beacon
aerofotogram•ma *m* **(-mi)** aerial photograph
aerogiro *m* helicopter
aerògrafo *m* spray gun (*for painting*)
aerolìnea *f* airline; **aerolinea principale** trunkline
aeròlito *m* aerolite, meteorite
aeromarìtti•mo -ma *adj* air-sea
aeròmetro *m* aerometer
aeromòbile *m* aircraft; **aeromobile senza pilota** drone, pilotless aircraft
aeromodellismo *m* model-airplane building
aeromodelli•sta *mf* **(-sti -ste)** model-airplane builder
aeromodèllo *m* model airplane
aeromotóre *m* windmill; aircraft motor
aeronàu•ta *m* **(-ti)** aeronaut
aeronàuti•co -ca (-ci -che) *adj* aeronautic(al) || *f* aeronautics
aeronave *f* airship, aircraft
aeroplano *m* airplane
aeropòrto *m* airport, airfield
aeroportuale *adj* airport
aerorazzo [ddzz] *m* rocket spaceship
aerorimèssa *f* hangar
aerosbar•co *m* **(-chi)** landing of airborne troops
aeroservì•zio [s] *m* **(-zi)** air service
aerosilurante [s] *f* torpedo plane
aerosiluro [s] *m* aerial torpedo
aerosòl [s] *m* aerosol
aerosostenta•to -ta [s] *adj* airborne
aerospaziale *adj* aerospace
aerospà•zio *m* **(-zi)** aerospace
aerostàti•co -ca (-ci -che) *adj* aerostatic(al) || *f* aerostatics
aeròstato *m* aerostat
aerostazióne *f* air terminal
aerotas•sì *m* **(-sì)** taxiplane
aerotrasportare (aerotraspòrto) *tr* to airlift
aerotrasporta•to -ta *adj* airlifted; airborne
aerovìa *f* (aer) beam (*course indicated by a radio beam*); (aer) air lane
afa *f* sultriness; **fare afa a** (coll) to be a pain in the neck to
afèresi *f* apheresis
affàbile *adj* affable, agreeable
affaccendare (affaccèndo) *tr* to busy || *ref* to busy oneself, bustle
affaccenda•to -ta *adj* busy, bustling; occupied with busywork
affacciare §128 *tr* to show or display at the window; to bring forward (*e.g., an objection*); to raise (*a doubt*) || *ref* to show oneself (*at the door or window*); to present itself (*said of a doubt*)
affaccia•to -ta *adj* facing
affagottare (affagòtto) *tr* to bundle || *ref* to bundle up; to dress sloppily
affamare *tr* to starve
affama•to -ta *adj* starved, ravenous || *mf* starveling; hungry person; wretch
affannare *tr* to worry, to afflict || *intr* to pant; to be out of breath || *ref* to worry; to bustle around
affanna•to -ta *adj* panting; out of breath; worried
affanno *m* shortness of breath; grief, sorrow
affannó•so -sa [s] *adj* panting; wearisome
affardellare (affardèllo) *tr* to bundle together; (mil) to pack
affare *m* affair, matter; business; condition, quality; deal; **affari** business; **affari esteri** foreign affairs; **un buon affare** a good deal; a bargain
affarismo *m* sharp business practice
affari•sta *mf* **(-sti -ste)** unscrupulous operator
affarìsti•co -ca *adj* **(-ci -che)** sharp
affascinante *adj* fascinating, charming
affascinare (affàscino) *tr* to fascinate, charm; to seduce; to spellbind || **(affascino)** *tr* to bundle, to sheave
affascina•tóre -trice *adj* fascinating, charming || *mf* charmer, spellbinder
affastellare (affastèllo) *tr* to fagot (*twigs*): to sheave, bundle (*e.g., hay*); to pile, heap (*wood, crops, etc*); (fig) to jumble up
affaticare §197 *tr* to fatigue, tire, weary || *ref* to get tired; to weary; to toil
affatica•to -ta *adj* weary, tired
affatto *adv* quite, entirely; **niente affatto** not at all; **non . . . affatto** not at all
affatturare *tr* to bewitch; to adulterate (*e.g., food*)
affermare (afférmo) *tr* to affirm, assert || *intr* to nod assent || *ref* to take hold (*said, e.g., of a new product*)
affermati•vo -va *adj* & *f* affirmative
affermazióne *f* affirmation; assertion,

statement; success (*e.g., of a new product*); (sports) victory

afferrare (affèrro) *tr* to grab, grasp; to catch, nab || *ref* to cling

affettare (affétto) *tr* to slice; to cut up || **(affètto)** *tr* to affect

affetta·to -ta *adj* affected || *m* cold cuts

affettatrice *f* slicing machine

affettazióne *f* affectation

affetti·vo -va *adj* emotional

affèt·to -ta *adj* afflicted, burdened || *m* affection, love; feeling

affettuosi·tà [s] *f* (-tà) love, affection

affettuó·so -sa [s] *adj* affectionate, loving, tender

affezionare (affezióno) *tr* to inspire affection in || *ref*—**affezionarsi a** to become fond of

affeziona·to -ta *adj* affectionate, loving; **Suo affezionatissimo** best regards; **tuo affezionatissimo** love, as ever

affezióne *f* affection

affiancare §197 *tr* to place next; to favor, help; (mil) to flank

affiataménto *m* harmony; teamwork

affiatare *tr* to harmonize

affibbiare §287 *tr* to buckle, fasten; to deliver (*a blow*); to play (*a trick*); to slap (*a fine*)

affidaménto *m* consignment, delivery; trust, confidence; **dare affidamento** to be trustworthy; **fare affidamento su** to rely upon

affidare *tr* to entrust; to commit (*to memory*); **affidare qlco a qlcu** to entrust s.o with s.th || *ref* to trust; **affidarsi a** to trust in

affievoliménto *m* weakening

affievolire §176 *tr* to weaken || *ref* to grow weaker

affiggere §103 *tr* to post; to fix (*one's eyes or glance*) || *ref* to gaze, stare

affigliare §280 *tr & ref* var of **affiliare**

affilacoltèl·li *m* (-li) steel (*for sharpening knives*)

affilara·sóio *m* (-sói) strop

affilare *tr* to sharpen, hone, whet; to make thin || *ref* to become thin

affila·to -ta *adj* sharp, sharpened; thin || *f* sharpening

affila·tóio *m* (-tói) sharpener

affilatrice *f* grindstone

affiliare §287 *tr* to affiliate || *ref* to become affiliated; **affiliarsi a** to become a member of

affilia·to -ta *adj* affiliated || *mf* affiliate; foster child; member of a secret society

affiliazióne *f* affiliation

affinare *tr* to sharpen; to refine, purify; to improve (*e.g., one's style*) || *ref* to improve

affinché *conj* so that, in order that; **affinché non** lest

affine *adj* akin, related; similar || *mf* in-law || *m* kinsman || *f* kinswoman || *adv*—**affine di** in order to

affini·tà *f* (-tà) affinity

affiochire §176 *tr* to make hoarse; to weaken || *ref* to become hoarse; to grow dim (*said of a candle*)

affioraménto *m* surfacing; (min) outcrop

affiorare (affióro) *intr* to surface, emerge; to appear, to show

affissare *tr* (poet) to fix || *ref* to concentrate; (poet) to gaze

affissióne *f* posting, bill posting

affis·so -sa *adj* fixed; posted || *m* bill, poster; door or window; (gram) affix

affittacàme·re *m* (-re) landlord || *f* landlady

affittanza *f* rent

affittare *tr* to rent || *ref*—**si affitta** for rent

affitto *m* rent, rental; **dare in affitto** to rent (*to grant by lease*); **prendere in affitto** to rent (*to take by lease*)

affittuà·rio -ria *mf* (-ri -rie) renter; tenant

affliggènte *adj* tormenting, distressing

affliggere §104 *tr* to afflict, distress || *ref* to grieve

afflit·to -ta *adj* afflicted, grieving || *mf* afflicted person, wretch

afflizióne *f* affliction, distress

afflosciare §128 **(afflòscio)** *tr* to cause to sag; to weaken || *ref* to droop; to sag; to be deflated; to faint

affloscire §176 *tr & ref* var of **afflosciare**

affluènte *adj & m* confluent

affluènza *f* confluence; abundance; crowd

affluire §176 *intr* (ESSERE) to flow (*said of river*); to flock (*said of people*); to pour in (*said of earnings*)

afflusso *m* flow

affogaménto *m* drowning

affogare §209 **(affógo)** *tr* to drown; to smother || *intr* (ESSERE) to drown

affoga·to -ta *adj* drowned; poached (*egg*)

affollaménto *m* crowd, throng

affollare (affóllo & affòllo) *tr* to crowd; to overcome || *ref* to crowd

affolla·to -ta *adj* crowded

affondaménto *m* sinking

affondami·ne *m* (-ne) mine layer

affondare (affóndo) *tr* to sink; to stick || *ref* to sink

affondata *f* (aer) nosedive

affóndo *m* (fencing) lunge || *adv* deeply

afforestare (afforèsto) *tr* to reforest

affossare (affòsso) *tr* to ditch; (fig) to table (*e.g., a proposal*); to hollow out || *ref* to become sunken or hollow (*said, e.g., of cheeks*)

affossatóre *m* ditchdigger; gravedigger

affrancare §197 *tr* to set free; to free; to redeem (*a property*); to stamp || *ref* to free oneself; to take heart

affrancatrice *f* postage meter

affrancatura *f* stamp, stamping

affràngere §179 *tr* to weary; (obs) to break down (*the spirit*)

affran·to -ta *adj* weary; broken down, broken-hearted

affratellaménto *m* fraternization

affratellare (affratèllo) *tr* to bind in brotherly love || *ref* to fraternize

affrescare §197 **(affrésco)** *tr* to fresco; to paint in fresco

affré•sco *m* (-schi) fresco
affrettare (**affrétto**) *tr & ref* to hurry, hasten
affretta• to -ta *adj* hurried
affrontare (**affrónto**) *tr* to face, confront || *ref* to meet in combat; to come to blows
affronta•to -ta *adj*—**affrontati** (herald) combattant
affrónto *m* affront, offense
affumicare §197 (**affùmico**) *tr* to smoke; to blacken; to smoke out; to smoke (*meat or fish*)
affumica•to -ta *adj* smoked; dark (*glasses*)
affusolare [s] (**affùsolo**) *tr & ref* to taper
affusola•to -ta [s] *adj* tapered; slender
affusto *m* gun carriage
afga•no -na *adj & mf* Afghan
àfo•no -na *adj* voiceless
aforì•sma *m* (-smi) aphorism
afó•so -sa [s] *adj* sultry
Africa, l' *f* Africa
africa•no -na *adj & mf* African
afrodisìa•co -ca *adj & m* (-ci -che) aphrodisiac
afta *m* mouth ulcer; **afta epizootica** (vet) foot-and-mouth disease
àgata *f* agate || **Agata** *f* Agatha
agènda *f* notebook; agenda
agènte *adj* active || *m* agent; broker; merchant; officer; **agente delle tasse** tax collector; **agente di cambio** stockbroker; money changer; **agente di commercio** broker, commission merchant; **agente di custodia** jailer; **agente di polizia** police officer, policeman; **agente di spionaggio** informer; **agente provocatore** agent provocateur
agenzìa *f* agency; office, branch; **agenzia immobiliare** real-estate office
agevolare (**agévolo**) *tr* to facilitate, help
agevolazióne *f* facility; **agevolazione di pagamento** easy terms
agévole *adj* easy
agevolézza *f* facility
aggallare *intr* to come to the surface
agganciaménto *m* docking (*in space*); (rr) coupling
agganciare §128 *tr* to hook; (rr) to couple; (mil) to engage (*the enemy*)
aggàn•cio *m* (-ci) docking (*in space*); (rr) coupling
aggég•gio *m* (-gi) gadget
aggettivale *adj* adjectival
aggettivo *m* adjective
agghiacciaménto *m* freezing
agghiacciante *adj* hair-raising, frightful
agghiacciare §128 *tr* to freeze || *ref* to freeze; to be horrified
agghiaccia•to -ta *adj* frozen, icy
agghindare *tr & ref* to preen, primp
àg•gio *m* (-gi) agio; **fare aggio** to be at a premium
aggiogare §209 (**aggiógo**) *tr* to yoke
aggiornaménto *m* adjournment (*e.g., of a meeting*); bringing up to date
aggiornare (**aggiórno**) *tr* to bring up to date; to adjourn || *ref* to keep up with the times
aggiraménto *m* surrounding, outflanking
aggirare *tr* to surround, outflank; to swindle || *ref* to roam, wander; **aggirarsi su** to approximate; to be almost
aggiudicare §197 (**aggiùdico**) *tr* to adjudicate, award || *ref* to win
aggiudicazióne *f* adjudication, award
aggiùngere §183 *tr* to add; to join, connect || *ref* to be added; to join
aggiunta *f* addition
aggiuntare *tr* to attach, join
aggiun•to -ta *adj & m* associate, assistant, deputy || *f* see **aggiunta**
aggiustàbile *adj* repairable
aggiustaménto *m* settlement; adjustment; (mil) correction (*of fire*)
aggiustare *tr* to fix, repair; to adjust; (mil) to correct (*cannon fire*); **aggiustare per le feste** (coll) to fix; (coll) to give a good beating to || *ref* (archaic) to come closer; (coll) to manage; (coll) to come to an agreement
aggiusta•tóre -trice *mf* repairer, fixer || *m* repairman
aggiustatura *f* fixing, repairing, repair
agglomerare (**agglòmero**) *tr & ref* to pile up; to crowd together
agglomerato *m* built-up area; **agglomerato urbano** urban center
agglutinare (**agglùtino**) *tr & ref* to agglutinate
agglutinazióne *f* agglutination
aggobbire §176 *tr* to bend, bend over || *intr* (ESSERE) *& ref* to hunch over
aggomitolare (**aggomìtolo**) *tr* to coil || *ref* to curl up
aggradare *intr* (with *dat*) (poet) to please; **come Le aggrada** as you please
aggradire §176 *tr* to appreciate || *intr* (poet) (with *dat*) to please
aggraffare *tr* to hook; to grab; to join (*metal sheets*) with a double seam; to stitch, staple
aggraffatrice *f* folding machine; (mach) can sealer
aggranchire §176 *tr* to benumb; to deaden, stupefy || *intr* to become numb
aggrappare *tr* to grab; to clamp || *ref* to cling
aggravaménto *m* aggravation
aggravante *adj* (law) aggravating (*circumstances*)
aggravare *tr* to aggravate; to overload (*e.g., one's stomach*) || *ref* to get worse
aggrà•vio *m* (-vi) burden (*e.g., of taxes*); **fare aggravio a qlcu di qlco** to impute s.th to s.o.
aggraziare §287 *tr* to embellish; to render graceful || *ref* to win, gain; to ingratiate oneself
aggrazia•to -ta *adj* graceful; polite
aggredire §176 *tr* to assail, attack, assault
aggregare §209 (**aggrègo**) *tr & ref* to join, unite
aggrega•to -ta *adj* adjunct || *m* aggregation
aggressióne *f* aggression

aggressi•vo -va *adj* aggressive || *m* (mil) poison gas
aggressóre *m* aggressor
aggricciare §128 *tr* to wrinkle; (slang) to knit (*e.g., the brow*) || *ref* (poet) to shiver
aggrinzare *tr & ref* to wrinkle
aggrinzire §176 *tr & ref* var of **aggrinzare**
aggrondare (**aggróndo**) *tr* to knit (*the brow*)
aggrottare (**aggròtto**) *tr* to knit (*the brow*)
aggrovigliare §280 *tr* to tangle, entangle || *ref* to become entangled
aggrumare *tr & ref* to clot; to coagulate
aggruppare *tr* to group
agguagliare §280 *tr* to level; to equalize; to compare
agguantare *tr* to grab; to nab; (coll) to hit; **agguantare per il collo** to grab by the neck || *ref*—**agguantarsi a** to get hold of
agguato *m* ambush; **cadere in un agguato** to fall into a trap; **stare in agguato** to wait in ambush
agguerrire §176 *tr* to train for war; to inure to war; to inure
aghétto *m* shoestring; (mil) lanyard
agiatézza *f* comfort, wealth; **vivere nell'agiatezza** to live in comfort
agia•to -ta *adj* well-to-do, comfortable
àgile *adj* agile, nimble; prompt
agili•tà *f* (**-tà**) agility, nimbleness; promptness
à•gio *m* (**-gi**) comfort; opportunity; ease; **agi** conveniences, comforts; **a Suo agio** at your convenience; **aver agio** to have time; **stare a proprio agio** to feel at ease; to be comfortable; **vivere negli agi** to live comfortably
agiografia *f* hagiography
agiògrafo *m* hagiographer
agire §176 *intr* to act; to work; (theat) to act, perform
agitare (**àgito**) *tr* to agitate, shake; to stir; to stir up; to discuss (*e.g., a problem*) || *ref* to toss; to shake; to stir; to get excited
agita•to -ta *adj* rough, choppy (*sea*); troubled, upset || *mf* violently insane person
agita•tóre -trice *mf* agitator || *m* shaker
agitazióne *f* agitation
agli §4
agliàce•o -a *adj* garlicky
à•glio *m* (**-gli**) garlic
agnellino *m* little lamb, lambkin
agnèllo *m* lamb
agnizióne *f* recognition
agnòsti•co -ca *adj & mf* (**-ci -che**) agnostic
a•go *m* (**-ghi**) needle; pointer (*of scales*); stem (*of valve*)
agognare (**agógno**) *tr* to covet
agóne *m* contest; arena
agonìa *f* agony, death struggle; anguish
agonìsti•co -ca *adj* (**-ci -che**) competitive, aggressive (*spirit*); athletic (*competition*) || *f* athletics
agonizzare [ddzz] *intr* to agonize, be in agony; (fig) to die out
agopuntura *f* acupuncture
ago•ràio *m* (**-rài**) needle case
agosta•no -na *adj* August, e.g., **pomeriggio agostano** August afternoon
agostinia•no -na *adj & m* Augustinian
agósto *m* August
agrà•rio -ria (**-ri -rie**) *adj & m* agrarian || *m* landlord || *f* agriculture
agrèste *adj* country
agrìco•lo -la *adj* agricultural
agricoltóre *m* farmer; agriculturist
agricoltura *f* agriculture
agrifò•glio *m* (**-gli**) holly
agrimensóre *m* surveyor
agrimensura *f* surveying
a•gro -gra *adj* sour, bitter || *m* citrus juice; sourness, bitterness; surrounding country
agrodólce *adj* sweet and sour; (fig) acidulous (*tone*)
agronomìa *f* agronomy
agrònomo *m* agronomist
agrume *m* citrus (*tree and fruit*); **agrumi** citrus fruit
agucchiare §287 *intr* to knit or sew idly
agùglia *f* spire; top; (ichth) gar; (poet) eagle; (obs) needle
aguzzare *tr* to sharpen; to whet (*the appetite*)
aguzzino [ddzz] *m* slave driver; jailer
aguz•zo -za *adj* sharp, pointed
ah *interj* ah!, aha!; ha!
ahi *interj* ouch!
ahimè *interj* alas!
àia *f* yard, barnyard; threshing floor; governess || **L'Aia** *f* the Hague
Aiace *m* Ajax
àio *m* (**ài**) tutor
aiòla *f* lawn; flower bed
àire *m* push; short run (*preparing for a jump*); **dare l'aire a** to start off; **prendere l'aire** to take off
airóne *m* heron
aitante *adj* robust, stalwart
aiuòla *f* (poet) var of **aiola**
aiutante *adj* helping || *mf* assistant || *m* (mil) adjutant; **aiutante di campo** aide-de-camp; **aiutante di sanità** orderly
aiutare *tr* to help || *ref* to strive; to help oneself; to help one another
aiutato *m* first assistant (*e.g., of a surgeon*)
aiuto *m* aid, help; assistant; first assistant (*of a surgeon*)
aizzare (**aìzzo**) *tr* to incite, to incite to riot; to sic (*a dog*)
al §4
a•la *f* (**-li & -le**) wing; sail, vane (*of windmill*); blade (*e.g., of fan*); brim (*of hat*); (football) end; **ala a freccia** backswept wing; **ala di popolo** throng; **fare ala a** to line up along
alabarda *f* halberd
alabardière *m* halberdier
alabastri•no -na *adj* alabaster; white as alabaster
alabastro *m* alabaster
àlacre *adj* eager, lively
alacrità *f* alacrity

alàg·gio *m* (**-gi**) hauling, towing
alamaro *m* braid, gimp
alambic·co *m* (**-chi**) still
alano *m* Great Dane
alare *adj* wing (*e.g., span*) || *m* andiron || *tr* to haul
Alasca, l' *f* Alaska
ala·to -ta *adj* winged, sublime
alba *f* dawn, daybreak
albagìa *f* haughtiness
albanése [s] *adj & mf* Albanian
Albanìa, l' *f* Albania
àlbatro *m* (orn) albatross
albeggiaménto *m* dawning
albeggiare §290 (**albéggio**) *intr* (ESSERE) to dawn; (poet) to sparkle (*said, e.g., of ice*) || *impers* (ESSERE)—**albeggia** the day dawns
alberare (**àlbero**) *tr* to plant (*trees*); to reforest; to hoist (*a mast*); to mast (*a ship*)
albera·to -ta *adj* tree-lined; (naut) masted
alberèllo *m* small tree; apothecary's jar
albergare §209 (**albèrgo**) *tr* to lodge; to put up at a hotel; (fig) to harbor || *intr* to lodge; to put up
alberga·tóre -trice *mf* hotelkeeper
alberghiè·ro -ra *adj* hotel
albèr·go *m* (**-ghi**) hotel; refuge; hospitality; **albergo diurno** day hostel; **albergo per la gioventù** youth hostel
àlbero *m* tree; poplar; (mach) shaft; (naut) mast; **albero a camme** (aut) camshaft; **albero a gomito** (aut) crankshaft; **albero di distribuzione** (aut) camshaft; **albero di Natale** Christmas tree; **albero di trasmissione** (aut) transmission; **albero genealogico** family tree
albicòc·ca *f* (**-che**) apricot
albicòc·co *m* (**-chi**) apricot tree
al·bo -ba *adj* (poet) white || *m* album; bulletin board; (law) roll; comic book; **albo d'onore** honor roll || *f* see **alba**
albóre *m* (poet) whiteness; (poet) dawn
album *m* (**album**) album, scrapbook
albume *m* albumen
albumina *f* albumin
àlca·li *m* (**-li**) alkali
alcali·no -na *adj* alkaline
alce *m* moose; elk
alchìmia *f* alchemy
alchimi·sta *m* (**-sti**) alchemist
alcióne *m* halcyon
alciò·nio -nia *adj* (**-ni -nie**) halcyon
àlco·le *m* alcohol
alcolici·tà *f* (**-tà**) alcoholic content
alcòli·co -ca *adj* (**-ci -che**) alcoholic || *m* alcoholic beverage
alcolismo *m* alcoholism
alcolizzare [ddzz] *tr* to intoxicate || *ref* to become intoxicated
alcolizza·to -ta [ddzz] *adj* intoxicated || *mf* alcoholic
alcool *m* (**alcool**) var of **alcole**
alcoolici·tà *f* (**-tà**) var of **alcolicità**
alcoòli·co -ca (**-ci -che**) *adj & m* var of **alcolico**
alcoolismo *m* var of **alcolismo**
alcoolizzare [ddzz] *tr* var of **alcolizzare**
alcoolizza·to -ta [ddzz] *adj & mf* var of **alcolizzato**
alcòva *f* bedroom; bed; alcove
alcunché *pron* something, anything
alcù·no -na *adj & pron* some; **alcu·ni -ne** some; quite a few, several, a good many
aldilà *m* life beyond, afterlife
àlea *f* chance, hazard; **correre l'alea** to try one's luck
aleggiare §290 (**aléggio**) *intr* to flutter; to flap the wings; to hover
aleróne *m* var of **alettone**
alesàg·gio *m* (**-gi**) (mach) bore
alesare (**alèso**) *tr* (mach) to bore
alesatóre *m* reamer
alesatrice *s* boring machine
Alessandria d'Egitto *f* Alexandria
alessandri·no -na *adj & mf* Alexandrian || *m* Alexandrine (*verse*)
Alessandro *m* Alexander; **Alessandro Magno** Alexander the Great
alétta *f* small wing; fin (*of fish*); (aer) tab; **aletta di compensazione** trim tab; **aletta parasole** (aut) sun visor
alettóne *m* (aer) aileron, flap
Aleuti·no -na *adj*—**Isole Aleutine** Aleutian Islands
al·fa *m* (**-fa**) alpha || *f* esparto
alfabèti·co -ca *adj* (**-ci -che**) alphabetical
alfabetizzazióne [ddzz] *f* teaching to read; learning to read
alfabèto *m* alphabet; code (*e.g., Morse*)
alfière *m* flagbearer, standardbearer; (chess) bishop
alfine *adv* finally, at last
al·ga *f* (**-ghe**) alga; **alga marina** seaweed
àlgebra *f* algebra
algèbri·co -ca *adj* (**-ci -che**) algebraic
Algèri *f* Algiers
Algerìa, l' *f* Algeria
algeri·no -na *adj & mf* Algerian
aliante *m* (aer) glider
alianti·sta *mf* (**-sti -ste**) glider pilot
àli·bi *m* (**-bi**) alibi
alice *f* anchovy
alienàbile *adj* alienable
alienare (**alièno**) *tr* to alienate; to transfer, convey || *ref*—**alienarsi dalla ragione** to go out of one's mind
aliena·to -ta *adj* alienated || *mf* insane person; dispossessed person
alienazióne *f* alienation
alieni·sta *mf* (**-sti -ste**) alienist
alièno -na *adj* disinclined; (poet) foreign, alien
alimentare *adj* alimentary || **alimentari** *mpl* food, foodstuff || *v* (**aliménto**) *tr* to feed; to fuel
alimentari·sta *m* (**-sti**) food merchant; food-industry worker
alimenta·tóre -trice *mf* stoker || *m* (mach) stoker, feeder
alimentazióne *f* nourishment; feeding; (mil) loading; **alimentazione artificiale** intravenous feeding
aliménto *m* food, nourishment; feed; **alimenti** alimony (*maintenance*)
alimònia *f* alimony
alìnea *f* (law) paragraph, section

alìquota *f* share; parcel, quota
aliscafo *m* hydrofoil
alisè•o -a *adj* trade (*wind*) || *m* trade wind
alitare (àlito) *intr* to breathe; to blow gently; **non alitare** to not breathe a word
àlito *m* breath; (fig) breeze
alìvo•lo -la *adj* (poet) winged; (fig) swift
alla §4
allacciaménto *m* binding; connection, linking
allacciare §128 *tr* to bind, tie; to connect; to buckle; (fig) to deceive
allacciatura *f* lacing; buckling
allagare §209 *tr* to flood, overflow
allampana•to -ta *adj* tall and lean, lanky
allargare §209 *tr* to broaden, widen; **allargare la mano** to be lenient; to be liberal; **allargare il freno** to give free rein || *ref* to widen, spread out; **mi si allarga il cuore** I feel relieved
allargatura *f* widening
allarmante *adj* alarming
allarmare *tr* to alarm || *ref* to worry, become alarmed
allarme *m* alarm; **allarme aereo** air-raid warning; **cessato allarme** all clear; **falso allarme** false alarm; **stare in allarme** to be alarmed
allascare §197 *tr* (naut) to ease, slacken (*a rope*)
allato *adv* (poet) near; **allato a** near; beside; in comparison with
allattaménto *m* nursing, feeding; **allattamento artificiale** bottle feeding
allattare *tr* to nurse (*at the breast*); to feed (*with a bottle*)
alle §4
alleanza *f* alliance
alleare (allèo) *tr* to ally || *ref* to become allied; to be connected
allea•to -ta *adj* allied || *mf* ally
allegare §209 **(allégo)** *tr* to enclose; to adduce; to allege; **allegare i denti** to set the teeth on edge || *intr* (hort) to ripen
allega•to -ta *adj* enclosed || *m* enclosure
alleggeriménto *m* lightening, easing
alleggerire §176 *tr* to lighten; to alleviate || *ref* to put on lighter clothes; **alleggerirsi di** (naut) to jettison
allegorìa *f* allegory
allegòri•co -ca *adj* (**-ci -che**) allegorical
allegraménte *adv* cheerfully, merrily; thoughtlessly
allegrézza *f* joy, cheerfulness
allegrìa *f* cheer, gaiety; **stare in allegria** to be merry || *interj* good cheer!
allé•gro -gra *adj* cheerful, merry, gay || *m* (mus) allegro
allelùia *m* hallelujah
allenaménto *m* training
allenare (alléno) *tr & ref* to train
allena•tóre -trice *adj* training || *mf* trainer, coach
allentare (allènto) *tr* to loosen, slacken; to mitigate; (coll) to deliver (*a blow*); **essere allentato** to have a hernia || *ref* to slow up; to loosen up; to diminish
allergìa *f* allergy
allèrgi•co -ca *adj* (**-ci -che**) allergic
allérta *f* alert || *adv* alert, on the alert
allessare (allésso) *tr* to boil
allés•so -sa *adj* boiled || *m* boiled meat, boiled beef
allestire §176 *tr* to prepare, make ready; to rig (*e.g., a ship*); to produce (*e.g., a play*)
allettaménto *m* allure, fascination
allettante *adj* alluring, enticing
allettare (allètto) *tr* to allure, entice; to confine to bed; to bend (*plants*) to the ground || *ref* to be confined to bed
allevaménto *m* raising, breeding; flock
allevare (allèvo) *tr* to raise, breed; to rear
alleva•tóre -trice *mf* raiser, breeder
alleviare §287 **(allèvio)** *tr* to alleviate, lighten
allibire §176 *intr* (ESSERE) to turn pale; to be astonished, be dismayed
allibraménto *m* registration, entry; booking (*of bets*)
allibrare *tr* to register, enter; to book (*a bet*) on a horse
allibratóre *m* bookmaker (*at races*)
allietare (allièto) *tr* to cheer, enliven
alliè•vo -va *mf* pupil, student; follower, disciple || *m* trainee; **allievo ufficiale** cadet
alligatóre *m* alligator
allignare *intr* to take root; to do well, prosper
allineaménto *m* alignment; falling in line
allineare (allìneo) *tr* to align; (typ) to justify || *ref* to align oneself, be aligned
allinea•to -ta *adj* aligned; **non allineato** nonaligned, uncommitted
allitterazióne *f* alliteration
allo §4
allòc•co *m* (**-chi**) horned owl; (fig) dolt, nincompoop
allocu•tóre -trice *mf* (poet) speaker
allocuzióne *f* (poet) speech, address
allòdola *f* lark, skylark
allogare §209 **(allògo)** *tr* to place; to let, lease; to find employment for; to invest (*money*); to marry off (*a daughter*)
allòge•no -na *adj* minority || *mf* member of an ethnic minority
alloggiaménto *m* (mil) lodging, quarters; (carp, mach) housing
alloggiare §290 **(allòggio)** *tr* to lodge, put up || *intr* to lodge, stay
allòg•gio *m* (**-gi**) lodging, living quarters; accommodations
allontanaménto *m* removal; estrangement
allontanare *tr* to remove; to send away; to exonerate; to dismiss; to alienate || *ref* to go away; to withdraw; to become estranged
allóra *adj* then || *adv* then; at that time; in that case; **da allora** ever since; **da allora in poi** from that time on; **fino allora** until then; **per allora** at that time

allorché *conj* when
allòro *m* laurel; **riposare sugli allori** to rest on one's laurels
allorquando *conj* (poet) when
àlluce *m* big toe
allucinante *adj* hallucinating; dazzling; deceptive
allucinare (**allùcino**) *tr* to hallucinate; to dazzle; to deceive
allucinazióne *f* hallucination
allùdere §105 *intr* to allude
allume *m* alum
alluminare (**allùmino**) *tr* to illuminate (*a manuscript*); (poet) to light
allumìnio *m* aluminum
allunàg·gio *m* (**-gi**) lunar landing; **allunaggio morbido** soft lunar landing
allunare *intr* to land on the moon
allunga *f* (mach) adapter
allungàbile *adj* extensible; extension (*table*)
allungaménto *m* lengthening
allungare §209 *tr* to lengthen; to stretch out (*e.g., the hand*); to dilute (*e.g., wine*); (coll) to deliver (*e.g., a slap*); (sports) to pass (*the ball*); **allungare il collo** to crane the neck; **allungare il passo** to walk faster || *ref* to grow longer; to stretch; to grow taller
allun·go *m* (**-ghi**) (sports) sprint; (sports) forward pass
allusióne *f* allusion
alluvióne *m* flood
almanaccare §197 *tr* to dream of || *intr* to dream, muse
almanac·co *m* (**-chi**) almanac
alméno *adv* at least; if only
alno *m* (bot) alder
àloe *m* & *f* aloe
alògeno *m* halogen
alogenuro *m* halide
alóne *m* halo
alòsa *f* (ichth) shad
alpacca *f* German silver
alpe *f* high mountain, alp || **le Alpi** the Alps
alpèstre *adj* mountainous; (fig) uncouth
alpigia·no -na *adj* mountain, mountainous; (fig) uncouth || *mf* mountaineer
alpinismo *m* mountain climbing
alpini·sta *mf* (**-sti -ste**) mountain climber
alpinìsti·co -ca *adj* (**-ci -che**) mountain-climbing
alpi·no -na *adj* alpine; Alpine || *m* alpine soldier
alquan·to -ta *adj* & *pron* some; **alquanti -te** some; quite a few, several, a good many || **alquanto** *adv* somewhat, rather
Alsàzia, l' *f* Alsace
alsazia·no -na *adj* & *mf* Alsacian
alt *m* (**alt**) halt, stop || *interj* halt!, stop!
altaléna *f* seesaw; swing; (fig) ups and downs; **altalena a bilico** seesaw; **altalena sospesa** swing
altalenare (**altaléno**) *intr* to seesaw; to swing
altana *f* roof terrace
altare *m* altar
altarino *m* small altar; **svelare gli altarini** (joc) to expose the skeleton in the closet
altèa *f* marsh mallow
alterare (**àltero**) *tr* to alter; to falsify; to adulterate; to anger || *ref* to alter; to become adulterated; to get angry
altera·to -ta *adj* altered; adulterated; feverish; angry
alterazióne *f* change, alteration; adulteration; slight fever
altercare §197 (**altèrco**) *intr* to dispute, quarrel
altèr·co *m* (**-chi**) altercation; **venire a un alterco** to get into a quarrel
alterìgia *f* haughtiness
alternare (**altèrno**) *tr* & *ref* to alternate
alternati·vo -va *adj* alternating || *f* alternative; choice
alterna·to -ta *adj* alternate; alternating (*current*)
alternatóre *m* (elec) alternator
altèr·no -na *adj* alternate
altè·ro -ra *adj* proud, haughty
altézza *f* height; width (*of cloth*); depth (*of water*); pitch (*of sound*); (astr, geom) altitude; (fig) loftiness, nobility; (naut) latitude; (typ) size; **essere all'altezza di** to be up to, be equal to; (naut) to be off || **Altezza** *f* Highness
altezzó·so -sa [s] *adj* haughty
altic·cio -cia *adj* (**-ci -ce**) tipsy
altìmetro *m* altimeter
altipiano *m* var of **altopiano**
altisonante [s] *adj* high-sounding
altissi·mo -ma *adj* very high, highest || **l'Altissimo** *m* the Most High
altitùdine *f* altitude
al·to -ta *adj* high; tall; wide (*cloth*); deep (*water*); upper; full (*day*); late (*e.g., Easter*); deep (*sleep*); early (*Middle Ages*); loud (*voice*); lofty (*peak*) || *m* top; upper part; high quarters; **alti e bassi** ups and downs; **fare alto e basso** to be the undisputed boss; **guardare qlcu dall'alto in basso** to look down one's nose at s.o.; **in alto** up || **alto** *adv* up
altofórno *m* (**altifórni**) blast furnace
altoloca·to -ta *adj* high-placed, high-ranking
altoparlante *m* loudspeaker
altopiano *m* (**altipiani**) plateau
altrettan·to -ta *adj* & *pron* as much; the same; **altrettan·ti -te** as many || **altrettanto** *adv* as much; the same
altri *indef pron invar* someone; someone else; **non altri che** no one else but
altrièri *m* & *adv* day before yesterday
altriménti *adv* otherwise
al·tro -tra *adj* other; next (*world*); **altro ieri** day before yesterday; **chi altro?** who else?; **domani l'altro** the day after tomorrow; **fra l'altro** among other things; **ieri l'altro** the day before yesterday; **l'altro anno** last year; **l'altro giorno** the other day; **noi altri** we; **qualcun altro** somebody else; anybody else; **quest'altro (giorno, mese, anno)** next (day, month, year) || *pron* other; anything

else; **altro che!** why yes! || **l'altro** §11 *correlative indef pron* || **l'altro** §12 *reciprocal pron*
altrónde *adv* (poet) somewhere else; **d'altronde** besides; on the other hand
altróve *adv* elsewhere, somewhere else
altrui *adj invar* somebody else's, other people's || *pron invar* somebody else || *m*—**l'altrui** what belongs to someone else
altrui·sta (-sti -ste) *adj* altruistic || *mf* altruist
altura *f* height; (naut) high seas
alun·no -na *mf* pupil, student
alveare *m* beehive
àlveo *m* bed (*of a river*)
alvèolo *m* alveolus; socket (*of tooth*); cell (*of honeycomb*)
alzabandiè·ra *m* **(-ra)** raising of the flag
alzacristal·li *m* **(-li)** (aut) crank (*to raise a window*)
alzàia *f* tow line; towpath
alzare *tr* to lift, raise; to cut (*cards*); to shrug (*one's shoulders*); to set (*sail*); **alzare al cielo** to praise to the sky; **alzare i tacchi** to show a clean pair of heels; **alzare la cresta** to get cocky || *ref* to rise; to get up; **alzarsi in piedi** to stand up
alzata *f* raising, lifting; shrugging (*of shoulders*); standing up; riser (*of step*); three-tier candy tray; **alzata di scudi** rebellion; **alzata di testa** whim, caprice
alzavàlvo·le *m* **(-le)** (aut) valve lifter
alzo *m* gunsight
amàbile *adj* amiable; sweetish (*wine*)
amabili·tà *f* **(-tà)** amiability, kindness
ama·ca *f* **(-che)** hammock
amàlga·ma *m* **(-mi)** amalgam
amalgamare (amàlgamo) *tr* to amalgamate || *ref* to amalgamate; to blend
amalgamazióne *f* amalgamation
amante *adj* loving, fond || *m* lover || *f* mistress
amanuènse *m* amanuensis, scribe
amare *tr* to love; to like || *ref* to love one another
amareggiare §290 **(amaréggio)** *tr* to make bitter; to sadden || *ref* to become bitter; to sadden
amarèna *f* sour cherry
amarétto *m* macaroon
amarézza *f* bitterness
ama·ro -ra *adj* bitter || *m* bitters; bitterness
amarógno·lo -la *adj* bitterish
amarra *f* (naut) hawser
amarrare *tr & intr* var of **ammarrare**
ama·tóre -trice *mf* lover; amateur
amató·rio -ria *adj* **(-ri -rie)** amatory, of love
amàzzone [ddzz] *f* horsewoman; female jockey; (obs) riding habit; **cavalcare all'amazzone** to ride sidesaddle || **Amazzone** *f* (myth) Amazon
ambage *f* winding path; **ambagi** circumlocutions; **senz'ambagi** without beating about the bush
ambascerìa *f* embassy
ambà·scia *f* **(-sce)** shortness of breath; grief, sorrow
ambasciata *f* embassy; ambassadorship; errand, mission
ambasciatóre *m* ambassador
ambasciatrice *f* ambassadress
ambedùe *adj invar*—**ambedue i** or **le** both || *pron invar* both
ambiare §287 *intr* to amble, pace (*said of a horse*)
ambiatura *f* pacing (*said of a horse*)
ambidè·stro -stra *adj* ambidextrous
ambidùe *adj & pron invar* var of **ambedue**
ambientare (ambiènto) *tr* to accustom; to place (*a story in a certain period*) || *ref* to get accustomed to one's surroundings; to orient oneself
ambienta·tóre -trice *mf* interior decorator; (theat) decorator
ambiènte *adj* room, e.g., **temperatura ambiente** room temperature || *m* environment; habitat; milieu; room; **trovarsi fuori del proprio ambiente** to be out of one's element
ambigui·tà *f* **(-tà)** ambiguity
ambì·guo -gua *adj* ambiguous
àm·bio *m* **(-bi)** amble, pacing
ambire §176 *tr* to be eager for || *intr* to be ambitious; **ambire a** to be ambitious for
àmbito *m* range, circle; (mus) range; **nell'ambito di** within
ambizióne *f* ambition
ambizióso -sa [s] *adj* ambitious || *mf* ambitious person
ambo or **am·bi -be** *adj pl*—**ambo i, ambo le, ambi i, ambe le** both
ambosèssi *adj invar* of both sexes, e.g., **giovani ambosessi** young people of both sexes
ambra *f* amber; **ambra grigia** ambergris
ambròsia *f* ambrosia; (bot) ragweed
ambulante *adj* itinerant; circulating; ambulant || *m* mail car
ambulanza *f* ambulance
ambulare (àmbulo) *intr* (coll) to ambulate
ambulatòrio -ria (-ri -rie) *adj* ambulatory || *m* clinic, first-aid department
Amburgo *m* Hamburg
amèba *f* amoeba
a·men *m* **(-men)** amen || *interj* amen!
ameni·tà *f* **(-tà)** *f* amenity; pleasantry
amèno -na *adj* pleasant, agreeable; amusing (*fellow*)
Amèrica, l' *f* America; **l'America del Nord** North America; **l'America del Sud** South America
americana *f* bicycle race between pairs
americanismo *m* Americanism
americanizzare [ddzz] *tr* to Americanize || *ref* to become Americanized
america·no -na *adj & mf* American || *m* vermouth with bitters || *f* see **americana**
ametista *f* amethyst
amianto *m* asbestos
amicale *adj* (poet) friendly
amichévole *adj* friendly; (sports) noncompetitive
amicìzia *f* friendship; **stringere amicizia con** to make friends with

ami•co -ca (-ci -che) *adj* friendly || *mf* friend; beloved || *m* boy friend; lover, paramour; **amico del cuore** bosom friend || *f* girl friend; mistress
amidàce•o -a *adj* starchy
amidatura *f* starching
àmido *m* starch
Amlèto *m* Hamlet
ammaccare §197 *tr* to crush; to pound; to bruise; to dent
ammaccatura *f* bruise; dent
ammaestraménto *m* instruction, teaching; training
ammaestrare (ammaèstro & ammaéstro) *tr* to teach, to educate; to train (*animals*)
ammainare (ammàino) *tr* to lower (*e.g., a flag*)
ammalare *intr* (ESSERE) to fall ill || *ref* to fall ill; **ammalarsi di** to come down with
ammala•to -ta *adj* ill, sick || *mf* patient
ammaliare §287 *tr* to cast a spell on; to charm, enchant, fascinate; to bewitch
ammalia•tóre -trice *adj* charming, enchanting || *mf* charmer || *m* enchanter, sorcerer || *f* enchantress, sorceress
amman•co *m* **(-chi)** shortage
ammanettare (ammanétto) *tr* to handcuff
ammaniglia•to -ta *adj* shackled; (fig) closely bound, closely tied
ammannare *tr* to sheave (*grain*)
ammannire §176 *tr* to prepare (*a dish*); to dish up (*a meal*)
ammansare *tr & ref* var of **ammansire**
ammansa•tóre -trice *mf* (poet) tamer
ammansire §176 *tr* to tame; to calm || *ref* to become tamed; to calm down
ammantare *tr* to mantle, clothe; to cover; to hide (*the truth*)
ammanto *m* mantle, cloak; (fig) authority
ammaràg•gio *m* **(-gi)** landing on water; splashdown (*of a space vehicle*)
ammaraménto *m* var of **ammaraggio**
ammarare *intr* (aer) to land on water; (rok) to splash down
ammarrare *tr* (naut) to moor
ammassare *tr* to amass || *ref* to crowd, throng
ammasso *m* heap, pile; cluster (*of stars*); government stockpile
ammattiménto *m* worry, nuisance
ammattire §176 *intr* (ESSERE) to go crazy; **fare ammattire** to drive crazy
ammattonare (ammattóno) *tr* to floor with bricks
ammattona•to -ta *adj* floored with bricks || *m* brick floor; bricklaying
ammazzare *tr* to kill || *ref* to kill oneself; to get killed
ammazzasèt•te *m* **(-te)** braggart
ammazza•tóio *m* **(-tói)** slaughterhouse
ammènda *f* fine; satisfaction (*for injury*); **fare ammenda** to make amends
ammendaménto *m* emendation: improvement (*of land*)
ammendare (ammèndo) *tr* to emendate; to improve (*land*)
ammennìcolo *m* excuse; trifle; **ammennicoli** extras
ammés•so -sa *adj* admitted; **ammesso che** supposing that; **ammesso e non concesso** for the sáke of argument
amméttere §198 *tr* to admit; to accept, suppose
ammezzare [ddzz] **(ammèzzo)** *tr* to leave half-finished (*a piece of work*); to fill halfway; to empty halfway
ammezzato [ddzz] *m* mezzanine
ammiccare §197 *intr* to wink; to cock one's eye
amministrare *tr* to administer, manage
amministra•tóre -trice *mf* administrator, manager; **amministratore delegato** chairman of the board
amministraziòne *f* administration, management: **ordinaria amministrazione** run-of-the-mill business
ammiràbile *adj* admirable
ammiràglia *f* (nav) flagship
ammiragliato *m* admiralty
ammirà•glio *m* **(-gli)** admiral; **ammiraglio d'armata** admiral; **ammiraglio di divisione** rear admiral; **ammiraglio di squadra** vice admiral; **grande ammiraglio** admiral of the fleet
ammirare *tr* to admire || *intr* to wonder
ammirati•vo -va *adj* admiring; exclamation (*mark*)
ammira•tóre -trice *mf* admirer || *m* suitor
ammiraziòne *f* admiration
ammirévole *adj* admirable
ammissìbile *adj* admissible; permissible
ammissióne *f* admission; (mach) intake; **ammissione comune** consensus
ammobiliaménto *m* furnishing; furniture
ammobiliare §287 *tr* to furnish
ammodernare (ammodèrno) *tr* to modernize
ammòdo *adj invar* well-mannered, polite || *adv* properly
ammogliare §280 **(ammóglio)** *tr* to marry, give in marriage || *ref* to marry, get married
ammoglia•to *adj* married || *m* married man
ammollare (ammòllo) *tr* to soften; to soak; to slacken (*e.g., a hawser*); to deliver (*a slap*) || *ref* to get soaked
ammollire §176 *tr* to soften; to weaken || *ref* to soften; to mellow
ammonìaca *f* ammonia
ammoniménto *m* warning
ammonire §176 *tr* to admonish, reprimand
ammoni•tóre -trice *adj* warning
ammoniziòne *f* admonition, warning
ammontare *m* amount, total || *v* **(ammónto)** *tr* to pile up || *intr* (ESSERE) to amount
ammonticchiare §287 *tr* to pile up, heap up
ammorbare (ammòrbo) *tr* to infect, contaminate
ammorbidènte *m* softener
ammorbidire §176 *tr* to soften; to mitigate || *ref* to soften
ammortaménto *m* amortization; payment, redemption (*of a loan*)

ammortare (ammòrto) *tr* to amortize
ammortire §176 *tr* to deaden; to weaken, soften
ammortizzaménto [ddzz] *m* amortization, amortizement
ammortizzare [ddzz] *tr* to amortize; (aut) to absorb (*shocks*)
ammortizzatóre [ddzz] *m* (aut) shock absorber
ammosciare §128 **(ammóscio)** *tr, intr & ref* var of **ammoscire**
ammoscia·to -ta *adj* (coll) downcast
ammoscire §176 *tr* to make sag; to make flabby || *intr & ref* to sag; to become flabby; to droop
ammucchiare §287 *tr* to heap up, pile up || *ref* to crowd together
ammuffire §176 *intr* (ESSERE) to become moldy
ammusare *tr & intr* to nuzzle
ammutinaménto *m* mutiny, riot
ammutinare (ammùtino & ammutino) *tr* to incite to riot || *ref* to mutiny
ammutinato *m* mutineer
ammutolire §176 *intr* (ESSERE) to become silent; to be dumfounded
amnesìa *f* amnesia
amnistìa *f* amnesty
amnistiare §287 or §119 *tr* to amnesty
amo *m* hook; **abboccare all'amo** to bite, to swallow the hook
amorale *adj* immoral; amoral
amorali·tà *f* **(-tà)** immorality; amorality
amóre *m* love; eagerness; **amor proprio** amour-propre, self-esteem; **con amore** with pleasure; **d'amore e d'accordo** in perfect agreement; **fare all'amore** to make love; **fare l'amore** to flirt; **per amor del cielo** for heaven's sake; **per amore di** for the sake of; **un amore di bambino** a charming child; **un amore di cappello** a darling hat
amoreggiare §290 **(amoréggio)** *intr* to flirt; to play around
amorévole *adj* loving; kindly
amòr·fo -fa *adj* amorphous; safety (*match*)
amorino *m* cupid; cute child; love seat; (bot) mignonette
amoró·so -sa [s] *adj* loving; kindly; amorous; love (*e.g., life*) || *mf* lover || *m* fiancé || *f* fiancée
amovìbile *adj* removable
amperàg·gio *m* **(-gi)** amperage
ampère *m* ampere
amperòmetro *m* ammeter
amperóra *m* ampere-hour
ampiézza *f* width, breadth; trajectory (*of a missile*); amplitude; **ampiezza di vedute** open-mindedness
àm·pio -pia *adj* **(-pi -pie)** ample; wide; roomy
amplèsso *m* (poet) embrace
ampliaménto *m* amplification, extension
ampliare §287 *tr* to enlarge, widen || *ref* to widen
amplificare §197 **(amplìfico)** *tr* to amplify; to widen; to exaggerate
amplifica·tóre *m* (rad & telv) amplifier
amplificazióne *f* amplification
amplitùdine *f* amplitude
ampólla *f* cruet; (eccl) ampulla
ampollièra *f* cruet stand
ampollosi·tà [s] *f* **(-tà)** grandiloquence, turgidity
ampolló·so -sa [s] *adj* grandiloquent, turgid
amputare (àmputo) *tr* to amputate
amputazióne *f* amputation
amulèto *m* amulet, charm
anabbagliante *m* (aut) low beam; **anabbaglianti** (aut) dimmers
anacàr·dio *m* **(-di)** cashew
ànace *m* var of **anice**
anacorè·ta *m* **(-ti)** anchorite, hermit
anacronismo *m* anachronism
anacronìsti·co -ca *adj* **(-ci -che)** anachronistic(al)
anàgrafe *m* bureau of vital statistics; registry of births, deaths, and marriages
anagram·ma *m* **(-mi)** anagram
analcòli·co -ca (-ci -che) *adj* nonalcoholic; soft (*drink*) || *m* soft drink
analfabè·ta *mf* **(-ti -te)** illiterate
analfabèti·co -ca *adj* **(-ci -che)** unalphabetized, unalphabetic
analfabetismo *m* illiteracy
analgèsi·co -ca *adj & m* **(-ci -che)** analgesic
anàli·si *f* **(-si)** analysis; breakdown; **analisi grammaticale** parsing; **analisi dell'urina** urinalysis
anali·sta *mf* **(-sti -ste)** analyst; **analista finanziario** financial analyst; **analista tempi e metodi** efficiency expert, efficiency engineer
analìti·co -ca *adj* **(-ci -che)** analytic(al)
analizzare [ddzz] *tr* to analyze; to assay (*ores*); (telv) to scan
analogìa *f* analogy
anàlo·go -ga *adj* **(-ghi -ghe)** analogous; similar
anamnè·si *f* **(-si)** (med) case history
ananasso *m* pineapple
anarchìa *f* anarchy
anàrchi·co -ca (-ci -che) *adj* anarchical || *m* anarchist
anatè·ma or **anàte·ma** *m* **(-mi)** anathema
anatomìa *f* anatomy
anatòmi·co -ca *adj* **(-ci -che)** anatomic(al)
ànatra *f* duck; drake
anatròccolo *m* duckling
an·ca *f* **(-che)** hip; (coll) thigh (*e.g., of a chicken*); **dare d'anche** to run away; **menare anca** to walk
ancèlla *f* maidservant
ancestrale *adj* ancestral
anche *adv* also, too; even; (poet) yet; **anche a** + *inf* even if + *ind*
anchilosare (anchilòso) *tr* to paralyze || *ref* to become paralyzed
anchilòsto·ma *m* **(-mi)** hookworm
àn·cia *f* **(-ce)** (mus) reed
ancillare *adj* servant
ancòra *adv* still, yet; again; more e.g., **ancora cinque minuti** five minutes more
àncora *f* anchor; keeper (*of magnet*); armature (*of buzzer or electric bell*); **ancora di salvezza** last hope; **gettar l'ancora** to cast anchor; **salpare** or **levar l'ancora** to weigh anchor
ancoràg·gio *m* **(-gi)** anchorage, berth

ancorare (**àncoro**) *tr* to anchor; to tie (*e.g., a currency to gold*) || *ref* to anchor; to hold fast
ancorché *conj* although
andalu•so -sa *adj & mf* Andalusian
andaménto *m* course, progress
andante *adj* ordinary, common; continuous
andare *m* going; gait; **a lungo andare** in the long run || §106 *intr* (ESSERE) to go; to spread (*said of news*); to be (*e.g., proud*); to work (*said of machinery*); (with *dat*) to fit, e.g., **quel vestito non gli va** that suit does not fit him; (with *dat*) to please, e.g. **quel vestito non le va** that dress does not please her; **andare a cavallo** to go horseback riding; **andare a finire** to wind up; **andare a male** to spoil; **andare a picco** to sink; **andare d'accordo** to agree; **andare in cerca di** to seek; **andare in macchina** to be in press; **andare in onda** (rad & telv) to go on the air; **andare per i vent'anni** to be bordering on twenty years; **andare pazzo per** to be crazy about; **andare soldato** to be drafted; **andare via** to go away; **come va?** how are things?; **mi va il vino dolce** I like sweet wine; **ne va della vita** life is at stake; **va da sé** it goes without saying || *ref*—**andarsene** to go away, leave
anda•to -ta *adj* gone, past; finished; (coll) spoiled (*e.g., meat*) || *f* going; journey, trip; **a lunga andata** in the long run; **andata e ritorno** round trip; **dare l'andata a** to give the go-ahead to
andatura *f* gait; pace; **fare l'andatura** to set the pace
andazzo *m* bad practice, bad habit; fad
Ande, le the Andes
andicappare *tr* to handicap
andi•no -na *adj* Andean
andirivìè•ni *m* (**-ni**) coming and going; maze; ado
àndito *m* corridor, hallway
andróne *m* hall, lobby
aneddòti•co -ca *adj* (**-ci -che**) anecdotal
anèddoto *m* anecdote
anelante *adj* panting
anelare (**anèlo**) *tr* to long for || *intr* to yearn; (poet) to pant
anèlito *m* last breath; yearning; (poet) panting; **mandare l'ultimo anelito** to breathe one's last
anellino *m* ringlet
anèllo *m* ring; link (*of a chain*); traffic circle; segment (*of a worm*); (sports) track; **ad anello** ring-shaped; **anello di congiunzione** (fig) link; **anello di fidanzamento** engagement ring || **anella** *fpl* (poet) ringlets; (archaic) rings
anemìa *f* anemia
anèmi•co -ca *adj* (**-ci -che**) anemic
anestesìa *f* anesthesia
anestesi•sta *mf* (**-sti -ste**) anesthetist
anestèti•co -ca *adj & m* (**-ci -che**) anesthetic
anestetizzare [ddzz] *tr* to anesthetize
aneuri•sma *m* (**-smi**) aneurysm
anfì•bio -bia (**-bi -bie**) *adj* amphibian; (fig) ambiguous || *m* amphibian
anfiteatro *m* amphitheater
anfitrióne *m* (lit) generous host
anfratto *m* ravine; narrow, winding, rugged spot
anfrattuosi•tà [s] *f* (**-tà**) rough broken ground; winding, rough spot
anfrattuó•so -sa [s] *adj* winding, rough, craggy
angariare §287 *tr* to pester, oppress
angèli•co -ca *adj* (**-ci -che**) angelic(al)
àngelo *m* angel; **angelo custode** guardian angel
angherìa *f* vexation; outrage; imposition
angina *f* quinsy; **angina pectoris** angina pectoris
angipòrto *m* blind alley; narrow lane
anglica•no -na *adj & mf* Anglican
anglicismo *m* Anglicism
anglicizzare [ddzz] *tr* to Anglicize || *ref* to become Anglicized
anglòfo•no -na *adj* English-speaking || *m* English-speaking person
anglosàssone *adj & mf* Anglo-Saxon
angolare *adj* angular; corner (*stone*) || *m* angle iron || *v* (**àngolo**) *tr* to take an angle shot of; (sports) to kick (*the ball*) into the corner of the goal
angolazióne *f* (mov) angle shot
angolièra *f* corner shelving; corner cupboard
àngolo *m* angle; corner
angoló•so -sa [s] *adj* angular
àngora *f* Angora cat; Angora goat
angò•scia *f* (**-sce**) anxiety, distress, anguish
angosciare §128 (**angòscio**) *tr* to distress
angoscia•to -ta *adj* tormented, distressed
angosció•so -sa [s] *adj* agonizing
anguilla *f* eel
anguillé•sco -sca *adj* (**-schi -sche**) as slippery as an eel
angùria *f* watermelon
angùstia *f* narrowness; scarcity; **stare in angustia** to be worried
angustiare §287 *tr* to distress, grieve || *ref* to worry
angu•sto -sta *adj* narrow
ànice *m* anise
anicino *m* anise cookie
anidride *f* anhydride
àni•dro -dra *adj* anhydrous
anilina *f* aniline
ànima *f* soul; life (*e.g., of the party*); core; kernel; bore (*of gun*); mold (*of button*); mind; enthusiasm; pith (*of fruit*); sounding post (*of violin*); web (*of rail*); **anima dannata** evil counselor; **anima mia!** darling!; **anima nera** villain; **anima viva** living soul; **buon'anima** late, e.g., **mio padre, buon'anima** my late father; **dannare l'anima** to lose patience; **la buon'anima di** the late; **rompere l'anima a** to annoy
animale *adj* animal; (poet) of the soul; (poet) animate || *m* animal; (fig) boor, lout

animalé·sco -sca *adj* **(-schi -sche)** animal, bestial
animare (ànimo) *tr* to animate, to enliven; to promote || *ref* to become lively or heated
anima·to -ta *adj* animated (*cartoon*); animated, lively; animal
anima·tóre -trice *adj* animating || *m* moving spirit; (mov) animator
animazióne *f* animation
animèlla *f* sweetbread
ànimo *m* mind; heart, affection; courage; **aprire l'animo** to open one's heart; **avere in animo di** to have a mind to; **mal animo** ill will; **mettersi l'animo in pace** to resign oneself; **perdersi d'animo** to lose heart; **serbare nell'animo** to keep in mind
animosi·tà [s] *f* **(-tà)** animosity, ill will
animó·so -sa [s] *adj* bold; spirited (*animal*); hostile
anióne *m* anion
anisétta *f* anisette
ànitra *f* var of **anatra**
anitròccolo *m* var of **anatroccolo**
annacquare (annàcquo) *tr* to water; to water down
annaffiare §287 *tr* to sprinkle; to water (*wine*)
annaffia·tóio *m* **(-tói)** sprinkling can
annaffia·tóre -trice *adj* watering, sprinkling
annali *mpl* annals *spl*
annaspare *tr* to reel || *intr* to gesticulate; to grope; to flounder
annata *f* year; year's activity; year's rent; year's issues (*of a magazine*)
annebbiare §287 **(annébbio)** *tr* to befog; to dim || *ref* to become foggy; to become dim
annegaménto *m* drowning
annegare §209 **(annégo)** *tr* & *intr* (ESSERE) to drown
anneriménto *m* blackening
annerire §176 *tr* to blacken || *ref* to turn black
annessióne *f* annexation
annès·so -sa *adj* united, attached || *m* annex; **con tutti gli annessi e connessi** everything included
annèttere §107 *tr* to annex; to attach, enclose; to unite; to ascribe (*importance*)
annichilante *adj* annihilating; devastating (*e.g., reply*)
annichilare (annìchilo) *tr* to annihilate || *ref* to destroy oneself; (fig) to humble oneself
annichilire §176 *tr* & *ref* var of **annichilare**
annidare *tr* to nest; (fig) to nourish, cherish || *ref* to nest; to hide; (fig) to settle
annientaménto *m* annihilation
annientare (anniènto) *tr* to annihilate; to knock down, demolish; (fig) to crush || *ref* to humble oneself
anniversà·rio -ria *adj* & *m* **(-ri -rie)** anniversary
anno *m* year; **anno bisestile** leap year; **anno luce** light-year; **anno nuovo** New Year; **anno scolastico** school year; **avere . . . anni** to be . . . years old; **l'anno che viene** next year; **l'anno corrente** this year; **quest'altr'anno** next year; **un anno dopo l'altro** year in, year out
annobilire §176 *tr* to ennoble
annodare (annòdo) *tr* to knot, tie; (fig) to tie up || *ref* to get entangled
annoiare §287 **(annòio)** *tr* to bore || *ref* to become bored
annòna *f* food; food-control agency
annonà·rio -ria *adj* **(-ri -rie)** food; rationing (*card*)
annó·so -sa [s] *adj* old, aged
annotare (annòto) *tr* to jot down; to chalk up; to annotate; to comment
annotazióne *f* note; notation, annotation
annottare (annòtta) *impers* (ESSERE) & *ref* to grow dark, e.g., **si annotta** it's growing dark; **è annottato** it grew dark
annoverare (annòvero) *tr* to count, number
annuale *adj* annual || *m* anniversary
annuà·rio *m* **(-ri)** annual, yearbook
annuire §176 *intr* to nod assent; to consent
annullaménto *m* nullification, annulment
annullare *tr* to annul, nullify, cancel; to call off || *ref* to cancel one another
annunciare §128 *tr* var of **annunziare**
Annunciazióne *f* Annunciation
annunziare §287 *tr* to announce; (fig) to forecast, foreshadow
annunzia·tóre -trice *mf* announcer, newscaster
annùn·zio *m* **(-zi)** announcement, notice; **annunzio economico** classified ad; **annunzio pubblicitario** advertisement; **annunzio pubblicitario radiofonico** (rad) commercial
ànnu·o -a *adj* yearly, annual
annusare [s] *tr* to smell; to snuff (*tobacco*)
annuvolaménto *m* cloudiness
annuvolare (annùvolo) *tr* to cloud, becloud || *ref* to become cloudy; to turn somber
anòdi·no -na *adj* pain-relieving; ineffective; weak, colorless (*person*)
ànodo *m* anode
anomalìa *f* anomaly
anòma·lo -la *adj* anomalous
anonimìa *f* anonymity
anòni·mo -ma *adj* anonymous || *m* anonymous author; **serbare l'anonimo** to preserve one's anonymity
anormale *adj* abnormal || *m* queer fellow
anormali·tà *f* **(-tà)** abnormality
ansa *f* handle (*of vase*); pretext; bend (*of a river*)
ansante *adj* panting
ansare *intr* to pant
ànsia *f* anxiety; **essere in ansia** to be worried
ansie·tà *f* **(-tà)** anxiety
ansimare (ànsimo) *intr* to pant
ansió·so -sa [s] *adj* anxious
antagonismo *m* antagonism

antagoni•sta (**-sti -ste**) *adj* antagonistic || *mf* antagonist, opponent
antagonìsti•co -ca *adj* (**-ci -che**) antagonistic
antàrti•co -ca *adj* (**-ci -che**) antarctic || **Antartico** *m* Antarctic
antecedènte *adj* preceding || *m* antecedent
antecedènza *f* antecedence
antecessóre *m* predecessor
antefatto *m* background, antecedents
anteguèr•ra (**-ra**) *adj* prewar || *m* prewar period
anteluca•no -na *adj* (poet) predawn
antenato *m* ancestor
anténna *f* lance; (naut) yard; (rad & telv) aerial, antenna; (zool) antenna
antepórre §218 *tr* to prefer; to place before
anteprima *f* (mov & theat) preview
anterióre *adj* fore, front; previous; earlier
antesignano [s] *m* forerunner
anti- *pref adj* anti-, e.g., **anticomunistico** anticommunist; un-, e.g., **antieconomico** uneconomical || *pref mf* anti-, e.g., **anticomunista** anticommunist
antiabbagliante *adj* antiglare || *m* low beam
antiàci•do -da *adj* & *m* antacid
antiaère•o -a *adj* antiaircraft || *f* antiaircraft defense
antibattèri•co -ca (**-ci -che**) *adj* antibacterial || *m* bactericide
antibiòti•co -ca *adj* & *m* (**-ci -che**) antibiotic
anticà•glia *f* (**-glie**) antique, curio; rubbish, junk
anticàmera *f* waiting room, anteroom; **fare anticamera** to cool one's heels
anticarro *adj invar* antitank
antichi•tà *f* (**-tà**) antiquity; **antichità** *fpl* antiques
anticipare (**anticipo**) *tr* to advance; to speed up; to pay in advance; to leak (*news*); to expect, anticipate || *intr* to be early
anticipa•to -ta *adj* in advance (*e.g., payment*)
anticipazióne *f* advance; collateral loan; expectation, anticipation
antìcipo *m* advance; loan (*on accounts receivable*); **in anticipo** in advance
anti•co -ca *adj* (**-chi -che**) antique, ancient, old; **all'antica** in the old-fashioned manner; **gli antichi** the ancients; the forefathers; **in antico** in olden times
anticoncezionale *adj* & *f* contraceptive
anticonformi•sta *mf* (**-sti -ste**) nonconformist
anticonformìsti•co -ca *adj* (**-ci -che**) unconventional
anticongelante *adj* & *m* antifreeze
anticongiunturale *adj* crisis, emergency
anticòrpo *m* antibody
anticristo *m* Antichrist
antidatare *tr* to predate
antiderapante *adj* nonskid
antidetonante *adj* antiknock || *m* antiknock compound
antidiluvia•no -na *adj* antediluvian
antìdoto *m* antidote
antievanescènza *f* (rad) antifading device
antifecondati•vo -va *adj* & *m* contraceptive
antìfona *f* antiphon; **capire l'antifona** (fig) to get the message
antifurto *adj invar* antitheft || *m* antitheft device
antigàs *adj invar* gas (*e.g., mask*)
antigièni•co -ca *adj* (**-ci -che**) unsanitary
antìlope *f* antelope
antimeridia•no -na *adj* antemeridian, A.M.
antimìssile *adj invar* antimissile
antimònio *m* antimony
antincèndio *adj invar* fire-fighting; fire, e.g., **scala antincendio** fire escape
antinéb•bia *adj invar* fog || *m* (**-bia**) fog light
antinéve *adj invar* snow, e.g., **catena antineve** snow chain
antiorà•rio -ria *adj* (**-ri -rie**) counterclockwise
antipatìa *f* antipathy, dislike
antipàti•co -ca *adj* (**-ci -che**) antipathetic; disagreeable; uncongenial
antipièga *adj invar* crease-resistant, wrinkle-proof
antipodi *mpl* antipodes
antipòlio *adj invar* polio (*e.g., vaccine*)
antipòrta *f* stormdoor; corridor
antiquà•rio -ria (**-ri -rie**) *adj* antiquarian || *m* antiquary, antiquarian
antiqua•to -ta *adj* obsolete; antiquated
antireligió•so -sa [s] *adj* antireligious, irreligious
antirùggine *adj invar* antirust
antirumóre *adj invar* antinoise
antisala [s] *f* anteroom, waiting room
antisassi [s] *adj invar* protecting against falling stones
antischiavi•sta *adj* & *mf* (**-sti -ste**) abolitionist
antisemi•ta [s] (**-ti -te**) *adj* anti-Semitic || *mf* anti-Semite
antisemìti•co -ca [s] *adj* (**-ci -che**) anti-Semitic
antisemitismo [s] *m* anti-Semitism
antisètti•co -ca [s] *adj* & *m* (**-ci -che**) antiseptic
antisociale [s] *adj* antisocial
antisóle [s] *adj invar* sun (*glasses*); suntan (*lotion*)
antisommergìbile [s] *adj* antisubmarine
antistatale *adj* antigovernment
antitàrmi•co -ca *adj* (**-ci -che**) mothproof
antitèmpo *adv* early, prematurely
antìte•si *f* (**-si**) antithesis
antitèti•co -ca *adj* (**-ci -che**) antithetic(al)
antitossina *f* antitoxin
antiuòmo *adj invar* (mil) antipersonnel
antivigìlia *f*—**l'antivigilia di** two days before
antologìa *f* anthology
antònimo *m* antonym
antrace *m* anthrax
antracite *f* anthracite

antro *m* cave; den, hovel
antròpi•co -ca *adj* (-**ci -che**) human
antropofagìa *f* cannibalism
antropòfa•go -ga (-**gi -ghe**) *adj* cannibalistic || *m* cannibal
antropòide *adj* anthropoid
antropologìa *f* anthropology
antropomòrfi•co -ca *adj* (-**ci -che**) anthropomorphic
antropomòr•fo -fa *adj* see **scimmia**
anulare *adj* ring-shaped, annular || *m* ring finger
Anvèrsa *f* Antwerp
anzi *adv* on the contrary, rather; **anzi che no** rather || *prep* (poet) before
anziani•tà *f* (-**tà**) seniority
anzia•no -na *adj* old, elderly; senior || *m* senior
anziché *conj* rather than
anzidét•to -ta *adj* aforesaid
anzitutto *adv* above all, first of all
apatìa *f* apathy
apàti•co -ca *adj* (-**ci -che**) apathetic
ape *f* bee; **ape operaia** worker; **ape regina** queen bee
aperitivo *m* apéritif
apèr•to -ta *adj* open; frank, candid || *m* open space; **all'aperto** in the open
apertura *f* opening; aperture; approach; **ad apertura di libro** at sight; **apertura alare** (*of a bird*) wingspread; (aer) wingspan
apià•rio *m* (-**ri**) apiary
àpice *m* apex, top; climax
apicol•tóre -trice *mf* beekeeper, apiarist
apicoltura *f* beekeeping, apiculture
Apocalisse *f* Apocalypse, Revelation
apocalìtti•co -ca *adj* (-**ci -che**) apocalyptic(al)
apòcri•fo -fa *adj* apocryphal
apofonìa *f* ablaut
apogèo *m* apogee
apòlide *adj* stateless || *m* man without a country
apolìti•co -ca *adj* (-**ci -che**) nonpolitical, nonpartisan
apologè•ta *m* (-**ti**) apologist
apologèti•co -ca *adj* (-**ci -che**) apologetic
apologìa *f* apology
apòlo•go *m* (-**ghi**) apologue
apoplessìa *f* apoplexy
apoplètti•co -ca *adj & m* (-**ci -che**) apoplectic
apostasìa *f* apostasy
apòsta•ta *mf* (-**ti -te**) apostate
apostolato *m* apostolate
apostòli•co -ca *adj* (-**ci -che**) apostolic(al)
apòstolo *m* apostle
apostrofare (**apòstrofo**) *tr* to write with an apostrophe; to apostrophize
apòstrofe *f* apostrophe (*to a person*)
apòstrofo *m* (gram) apostrophe
apoteò•si *f* (-**si**) apotheosis
appagare §209 *tr* to satisfy, gratify || *ref*—**appagarsi di** to be content with
appaiare §287 *tr* to pair, couple; to match || *ref* to match (*said, e.g., of colors*)
appallottolare (**appallòttolo**) *tr* to crumple into a ball || *ref* to become lumpy
appaltare *tr* to contract for
appalta•tóre -trice *mf* contractor
appalto *m* contract; state monopoly; **appalto di sali e tabacchi** tobacco shop
appannàg•gio *m* (-**gi**) appanage; (fig) prerogative
appannare *tr* to tarnish; to befog, becloud || *ref* to become clouded (*said, e.g., of one's eyesight*)
apparato *m* decoration; display; appliance; leadership (*of political party*); (rad, telv) set
apparecchiare §287 (**apparécchio**) *tr* to prepare; to set (*the table*) || *ref* to get ready
apparecchiatura *f* sizing (*of paper; of a wall*); preparation (*of a canvas*); apparatus
apparéc•chio *m* (-**chi**) apparatus; sizing; preparation; gadget; (rad, telv) set; airplane; **apparecchio da caccia** fighter plane; **apparecchio telefonico** telephone
apparentare (**apparènto**) *tr* to tie, unite (*through marriage*) || *ref* to become related; to become intimate; (pol) to form a coalition
apparènte *adj* apparent, seeming
apparènza *f* appearance; **in apparenza** seemingly
apparigliare §280 *tr* to pair, team (*horses*)
apparire §108 *intr* (ESSERE) to appear, seem; to look
appariscènte *adj* showy, flashy, gaudy
apparizióne *f* apparition; appearance
appartaménto *m* apartment
appartare *tr* to set aside || *ref* to withdraw, retire
apparta•to -ta *adj* secluded, solitary
appartenènza *f* belonging, membership; **appartenenze** accessories; annexes
appartenére §271 *intr* (ESSERE & AVERE) to belong; to pertain || *impers* (ESSERE & AVERE)—**appartiene a** it behooves, it is up to
appassionaménto *m* excitement, interest, enthusiasm
appassionare (**appassióno**) *tr* to move; to interest; to excite || *ref* to be deeply interested
appassiona•to -ta *adj* impassioned; deep, ardent || *m* fan, amateur
appassire §176 *intr* (ESSERE) to wilt, wither; to decay; to dry up (*said, e.g., of grapes*)
appellare (**appèllo**) *tr* (law) to appeal; (poet) to call || *ref* to appeal; **appellarsi da** or **contro** (law) to appeal
appèllo *m* call, roll call; **fare appello a** to summon (*e.g., one's strength*); **fare l'appello** to call the roll; **mancare all'appello** to be absent
appéna *adv* hardly, scarcely; only; just || *conj* as soon as; **non appena** as soon as, no sooner
appèndere §109 *tr* to hang
appendice *f* appendix; feuilleton
appendicectomìa *f* appendectomy

appendicite *f* appendicitis
Appennino, l' *m* the Appennines
appesantire [s] §176 *tr* to make heavy; to burden, overwhelm || *ref* to get heavy; to get fat
appestare (appèsto) *tr* to infect; to stink up
appesta·to -ta *adj* plague-ridden || *m* plague victim
appetire §176 *tr* to crave, long for || *intr* (ESSERE & AVERE) to be appetizing
appetito *m* appetite
appetitó·so -sa [s] *adj* appetizing, tempting
appètto *adv* opposite; **appetto a** opposite; in comparison with
appezzaménto *m* plot, parcel (*of land*)
appianare *tr* to smooth, level; to settle (*a dispute*); to get around (*a difficulty*)
appiana·tóio *m* (**-tói**) road grader
appiattare *tr & ref* to hide
appiattiménto *m* leveling; equalization
appiattire §176 *tr & ref* to flatten, to level
appiccare §197 *tr* to hang; **appiccare il fuoco a** to set on fire; **appiccare una lite** to pick a fight
appicciare §128 *tr* (coll) to string together; (coll) to kindle, light
appiccicare §197 (**appìccico**) *tr* to stick, glue; **appiccicare uno schiaffo a** to slap || *ref* to stick, adhere
appiccicatic·cio -cia *adj* (**-ci -ce**) sticky
appic·co *m* (**-chi**) grip; steep wall (*of mountain*); (fig) pretext
appiè *adv*—**appiè di** at the foot of; at the bottom of
appiedare (appièdo) *tr* to order (*a cavalryman*) off a horse; to order (*e.g., troops*) off a vehicle; to force out of a car (*said, e.g., of motor trouble*)
appièno *adv* (poet) fully
appigionare (appigióno) *tr* to rent || *ref*—**appigionasi** for rent
appigiónasi [s] *m* for-rent sign
appigliare §280 *ref* to cling, adhere; **appigliarsi a un pretesto** to seize a pretext
appì·glio *m* (**-gli**) grip; (fig) pretext
appiómbo *m* perpendicular || *adv* plumb, perpendicularly
appioppare (appiòppo) *tr* to plant with poplar trees; to tie (*a vine*) to a poplar tree; (coll) to deliver (*a blow*); (coll) to pass off (*e.g., inferior goods*)
appisolare (appìsolo) *ref* to snooze, doze
applaudire §176 & (**applàudo**) *tr* to applaud || *intr* to applaud, clap the hands; (with *dat*) to applaud
applàuso *m* applause; **applausi** applause
applicàbile *adj* applicable
applicare §197 (**àpplico**) *tr* to apply; to attach; to give (*e.g., a slap*); to put into effect (*a law*); to assign || *ref* to apply oneself
applica·to -ta *adj* applied; appliqué || *m* clerk
applicazióne *f* application; appliqué
applique *m* (elec) wall fixture
appoggiaca·po *m* (**-po**) headrest; tidy (*on back of chair*)
appoggiagómi·ti *m* (**-ti**) elbowrest
appoggiama·no *m* (**-no**) mahlstick
appoggiare §290 (**appòggio**) *tr* to lean; to rest; to prop, support; to raise (*the tone of voice*); to give (*a slap*); to second (*a motion*); (fig) to back, support || *intr* to lean; to rest || *ref*—**appoggiarsi a** or **su** to lean on
appoggia·tóio *m* (**-tói**) support, rest; banister
appoggiatura *f* (mus) grace note
appòg·gio *m* (**-gi**) support, prop; backer; backing, support; grip; (mach) bearing
appollaiare §287 *ref* to roost
appórre §218 *tr* to affix, append
apportare (appòrto) *tr* to cause; to presage; (poet) to carry
appòrto *m* carrying; contribution; (law) share
appositaménte *adv* expressely, on purpose
appòsi·to -ta *adj* proper, fitting
apposizióne *f* apposition
appòsta *adj invar* suitable || *adv* on purpose, expressly, intentionally
appostaménto *m* ambush
appostare (appòsto) *tr* to ambush || *ref* to lie in ambush
apprèndere §220 *tr* to learn || *ref* (poet) to take hold
apprendi·sta *mf* (**-sti -ste**) apprentice
apprendistato *m* apprenticeship
apprensióne *f* apprehension, fear
apprensi·vo -va *adj* apprehensive
appressare (apprèsso) *tr* (poet) to approach || *ref* to come near
appresso *adj invar* next, following || *adv* near; later on; **appresso a** near; after
apprestare (apprèsto) *tr* to prepare; to supply, provide (*e.g., help*) || *ref* to prepare, get ready
apprettare (apprètto) *tr* to dress (*leather*); to size (*cloth*)
apprètto *m* tan (*for leather*); sizing (*for cloth*)
apprezzàbile *adj* appreciable
apprezzaménto *m* appreciation; estimation
apprezzare (apprèzzo) *tr* to appreciate
apprezza·to -ta *adj* esteemed
appròc·cio *m* (**-ci**) approach; **approcci** advances
approdare (appròdo) *intr* (ESSERE & AVERE) to land; (with *dat*) (poet) to benefit; **approdare a** to come to
appròdo *m* landing
approfittare *intr*—**approfittare di** to capitalize on || *ref*—**approfittarsi di** to take advantage of
approfondire §176 *tr* to make deep; to study thoroughly || *ref*—**approfondirsi in** to go deep into
approntare (appróntο) *tr* to prepare, make ready
appropriare §287 (**appròprio**) *tr* to adapt; to bestow || *ref*—**appropriarsi a** to befit; **appropriarsi di** to appropriate; to embezzle

appropria•to -ta *adj* appropriate
appropriazióne *f* appropriation; **appropriazione indebita** fraudulent conversion, embezzlement
approssimare (appròssimo) *tr* to bring near || *ref* to approach, come near
approssimati•vo -va *adj* approximate
approssimazióne *f* approximation
approvàbile *adj* laudable
approvare (appròvo) *tr* to approve, countenance; to subscribe to (*an opinion*); to pass (*a student; a law*); to confirm
approvazióne *f* approval; confirmation; passage (*of a law*)
approvvigionaménto *m* supply
approvvigionare (approvvigióno) *tr* to supply || *ref* to be supplied
appuntaménto *m* appointment; date; **appuntamento amoroso** assignation
appuntare *tr* to sharpen; to fasten, pin; to stick (*a pin*) in; to point; to jot down, take note of; to prick up (*one's ears*); (fig) to reproach || *ref* to be turned; to aim
appunta•to -ta *adj* sharpened || *m* corporal (*of Italian police*)
appuntellare (appuntèllo) *tr* to shore up, prop up
appuntellatura *f* shoring up, propping up
appuntino *adv* precisely, meticulously
appuntire §176 *tr* to sharpen
appunti•to -ta *adj* sharp, pointed
appunto *m* note; blame, charge; **muovere un appunto a** to blame; **per l'appunto** just, precisely || *adv* exactly, precisely
appurare *tr* to ascertain
appuzzare *tr* to befoul, pollute
apribotti•glie *m* (**-glie**) bottle opener
apri•co -ca *adj* (**-chi -che**) (poet) sunny, bright
aprile *m* April
apripi•sta *m* (**-sta**) blade (*of bulldozer*); bulldozer
aprire §110 *tr* to open; to turn on; to dig (*e.g., a grave*) || *ref* to open; to clear up (*said of the weather*); **aprirsi con** to open one's heart to; **aprirsi il varco tra** to press through
apriscàto•le *m* (**-le**) can opener
aquà•rio *m* (**-ri**) aquarium || **Aquario** *m* (astr) Aquarius
aquàti•co -ca *adj* (**-ci -che**) aquatic
àquila *f* eagle; genius
aquili•no -na *adj* aquiline
aquilóne *m* north wind; kite
aquilòtto *m* eaglet; cadet (*in Italian Air Force Academy*)
Aquinate, l' *m* Saint Thomas Aquinas
ara *f* (poet) altar; are (*100 square meters*)
arabé•sca *f* (**-sche**) (mus) arabesque
arabesca•to -ta *adj* arabesque
arabé•sco -sca (-schi -sche) *adj* arabesque || *m* arabesque; doodle || *f* see **arabesca**
Aràbia, l' *f* Arabia
aràbi•co -ca *adj* (**-ci -che**) Arabic
aràbile *adj* tillable
àra•bo -ba *adj* Arabic, Arabian || *mf* Arab (*person*) || *m* Arabic (*language*)
aràchide *f* peanut (*vine*)
aragonése [s] *adj & mf* Aragonese
aragósta *f* (*Palinurus vulgaris*) lobster
aràldi•co -ca (-ci -che) *adj* heraldic || *f* heraldry
araldo *m* herald
arancéto *m* orange grove
aràn•cia *f* (**-ce**) orange
aranciata *f* orangeade
aràn•cio *adj invar* orange (*in color*) || *m* (**-ci**) orange tree
arancióne *adj & m* orange (*color*)
arare *tr* to plow; (naut) to drag (*the anchor*)
aratro *m* plow
arazzo *m* tapestry, arras
arbitràg•gio *m* (**-gi**) (sports) umpiring; (com) arbitrage
arbitrale *adj* judge's, umpire's
arbitrare (àrbitro) *tr* to umpire, referee || *intr* to arbitrate || *ref*—**arbitrarsi di** to take the liberty to
arbitrà•rio -ria *adj* (**-ri -rie**) arbitrary; wanton
arbitrato *m* arbitration
arbì•trio *m* (**-tri**) will; abuse, violation; **libero arbitrio** free will
àrbitro *m* arbiter; judge, referee, umpire
arboscèllo *m* small tree
arbusto *m* shrub, bush
ar•ca *f* (**-che**) sarcophagus; ark; chest; **arca di Noè** Noah's Ark; **arca di scienza** (fig) fountain of knowledge
àrcade *adj & m* Arcadian
Arcàdia *f* Arcadia, Arcady
arcài•co -ca *adj* (**-ci -che**) archaic
arcaismo *m* archaism
arcàngelo *m* archangel
arca•no -na *adj* mysterious, arcane || *m* mystery
arcata *f* arch; arcade
archeologìa *f* archaeology
archeològi•co -ca *adj* (**-ci -che**) archaeological
archeòlo•go -ga *mf* (**-gi -ghe**) archaeologist
archètipo *m* archetype
archétto *m* (archit) small arch; (elec) trolley pole; (mus) bow
archi- *pref adj* archi-, e.g., **architettonico** architectonic || *pref m & f* archi-, e.g., **architettura** architecture
archibù•gio *m* (**-gi**) harquebus
Archimède *m* Archimedes
architettare (architétto) *tr* to plan (*a building*); (fig) to contrive, plot
architétto *m* architect
architettòni•co -ca *adj* (**-ci -che**) architectural
architettura *f* architecture
architetturale *adj* architectural
architrave *m* architrave; doorhead, lintel
archiviare §287 *tr* to file; to lay aside, shelve; (law) to throw out
archì•vio *m* (**-vi**) archives; record office; chancery, public records
archivi•sta *mf* (**-sti -ste**) archivist, file clerk

arci- *pref adj* archi-, e.g., **arcivescovile** archiepiscopal || *pref m & f* arch-, e.g., **arciprete** archpriest
arcicontèn•to -ta *adj* (coll) very glad
arcidiàcono *m* archdeacon
arcidu•ca *m* **(-chi)** archduke
arciduchéssa *f* archduchess
arcière *m* archer, bowman
arci•gno -gna *adj* gruff, surly
arcióne *m* saddlebow; **montare in arcioni** to mount, to mount a horse
arcipèla•go *m* **(-ghi)** archipelago
arciprète *m* archpriest; dean
arcivescovado *m* archbishopric
arcivéscovo *m* archbishop
ar•co *m* **(-chi)** bow; (archit) arch; (geom, elec) arc; **arco rampante** flying buttress
arcobaléno *m* rainbow
arco•làio *m* **(-lài)** reel; **girare come un arcolaio** to spin like a top
arcuare **(àrcuo)** *tr* to arch; to bend; to camber
arcua•to -ta *adj* bent, curved; bow (*e.g., legs*); **avere le gambe arcuate** to be bowlegged
ardènte *adj* burning; hot; ardent, impassioned
àrdere §111 *tr* to burn || *intr* to burn; to be in full swing (*said, e.g., of a war*)
ardèsia *f* slate
ardiménto *m* boldness, daring
ardire *m* boldness; presumption, impudence || §176 *intr*—**ardire** + *inf* or **ardire di** + *inf* to dare to + *inf*
arditézza *f* daring; temerity
ardi•to -ta *adj* daring; rash || *m* (hist) shock trooper
ardóre *m* intense heat; ardor
àr•duo -dua *adj* arduous
àrea *f* area, surface; group, camp; **area arretrata** backward area
àrem *m* **(àrem)** harem
arèna *f* arena; **scendere nell'arena** to throw one's hat in the ring
aréna *f* sand
arenare **(aréno)** *intr* (ESSERE) & *ref* to run aground
arenària *f* sandstone
arén•go *m* **(-ghi)** (hist) town meeting
arenile *m* sandy beach
arenó•so -sa [s] *adj* sandy
areòmetro *m* hydrometer
aeronàuti•co -ca *adj & f* **(-ci -che)** var of **aeronautico**
areoplano *m* var of **aeroplano**
areopòrto *m* var of **aeroporto**
areòstato *m* var of **aerostato**
àrgano *m* winch; (naut) capstan
argentare **(argènto)** *tr* to silver; to silver-plate; to back (*a mirror*) with foil
argenta•to -ta *adj* silver; silvery; silver-plated
argentatura *f* silver plating; silver plate; foil (*of mirror*)
argènte•o -a *adj* silver, silvery
argenterìa *f* silverware
argentière *m* silversmith; jeweler
argenti•no -na *adj* silver, silvery; Argentine || *mf* Argentine || *f* high-necked sweater || **l'Argentina** *f* Argentina
argènto *m* silver; (archaic) money; **argenti** silverware; **argento vivo** quicksilver
argentóne *m* German silver
argilla *f* clay
argilló•so -sa [s] *adj* clayey
arginare **(àrgino)** *tr* to dam, dike; to hold back, check
àrgine *m* embankment, dam; (fig) defense
ar•go *m* **(-ghi)** (chem) argon; (orn) grouse || **Argo** *m* Argus
argomentare **(argoménto)** *tr & intr* to argue
argomentazióne *f* argumentation, discussion
argoménto *m* argument; pretext; subject; **fuori dell'argomento** beside the point
argonàu•ta *m* **(-ti)** Argonaut
arguire §176 *tr* to deduce, infer; (archaic) to denote
argutézza *f* wit; witty remark
argu•to -ta *adj* keen, acute; witty
argùzia *f* keenness; wit
ària *f* air; climate; look; mien; aria, tune; poem; **all'aria aperta** in the open air; **a mezz'aria** in midair; halfway; **andare all'aria** to fail; **aria condizionata** air conditioning; **avere l'aria di** to seem to; to look like; **dare aria a** to air; **in aria** in the air; **tira un'aria pericolosa** a mean wind is blowing
aria•no -na *adj & mf* Aryan
aridi•tà *f* **(-tà)** dryness, aridity; dearth
àri•do -da *adj* arid, dry, barren; (fig) dry
arieggiare §290 **(ariéggio)** *tr* to air; to imitate || *ref*—**arieggiarsi a** to give oneself the airs of
arlète *m* ram; (mil) battering ram || **Ariete** *m* (astr) Aries
ariétta *s* breeze; (mus) short aria
arin•ga *f* **(-ghe)** herring; **aringa affumicata** kippered herring, kipper
arin•go *m* **(-ghi)** assembly; field; joust; **scendere nell'aringo** to throw one's hat in the ring
arió•so -sa [s] *adj* airy, breezy; (fig) of wide scope
àrista *f* loin of pork
arista *f* (bot) awn
aristocràti•co -ca **(-ci -che)** *adj* aristocratic || *mf* aristocrat
aristocrazìa *f* aristocracy
Aristòtele *m* Aristotle
aristotèli•co -ca *adj & m* **(-ci -che)** Aristotelian
aritmèti•co -ca **(-ci -che)** *adj* arithmetical || *m* arithmetician || *f* arithmetic
arlecchino *adj invar* harlequin; fiesta (*e.g., dishes*) || **Arlecchino** *m* Harlequin
ar•ma *f* **(-mi)** arm, weapon; (fig) army; (mil) corps, service; **alle prime armi** at the beginning; **arma bianca** steel blade; **arma da taglio** cutting weapon; **arma delle trasmissioni** signal corps
armacòllo *m*—**ad armacollo** slung across the shoulders (*said of a rifle*)
armà•dio *m* **(-di)** cabinet; closet; **armadio a muro** built-in closet; **armadio**

d'angolo corner cupboard; **armadio farmaceutico** medicine cabinet; **armadio guardaroba** armoire
armaiòlo *m* gunsmith
armamentà•rio *m* **(-ri)** outfit, set (*of tools*)
armaménto *m* armament; crew; gun crew; crew (*of rowboat*); outfit, equipment
armare *tr* to arm; to dub (*s.o. a knight*); to outfit, commission (*a ship*); to cock (*a gun*); to brace, shore up (*a building*); (rr) to furnish with track || *ref* to arm oneself; to outfit oneself
arma•to -ta *adj* armed; reinforced (*concrete*) || *m* soldier || *f* army; navy; fleet; (nav) task force
arma•tóre -trice *adj* outfitting || *m* shipowner; (min) carpenter; (rr) trackwalker
armatura *f* armor; scaffold; framework, support; reinforcement (*for concrete*); (elec) plate (*of condenser*)
armeggiare §290 **(arméggio)** *intr* to fumble, fool around; to scheme; (archaic) to handle arms; (archaic) to joust
armeggì•o *m* **(-i)** fooling around; scheming, intriguing
armè•no -na *adj* & *mf* Armenian
arménto *m* herd
armerìa *f* armory
armière *m* (aer) gunner
armìge•ro -ra *adj* warlike, bellicose || *m* warrior; bodyguard
armistiziale *adj* armistice
armistì•zio *m* **(-zi)** *m* armistice
armonìa *f* harmony; **in armonia con** according to
armòni•co -ca (-ci -che) *adj* harmonic; resonant; harmonious || *f* harmonica; **armonica a bocca** mouth organ
armonió•so -sa [s] *adj* harmonious
armonizzare [ddzz] *tr* & *intr* to harmonize
arnése [s] *m* tool, implement; garb, dress; (coll) gadget; **bene in arnese** well-heeled; **male in arnese** down at the heels
àrnia *f* beehive
arò•ma *m* **(-mi)** aroma, odor; zest
aromàti•co -ca *adj* **(-ci -che)** aromatic
aromatizzare [ddzz] *tr* to flavor; to spice
arpa *f* harp
arpeggiare §290 **(arpéggio)** *intr* to play arpeggios; to play a harp; to strum
arpég•gio *m* **(-gi)** arpeggio
arpìa *f* Harpy; (coll) harpy
arpionare (arpióno) *tr* to harpoon
arpióne *m* hinge (*of door*); hook; harpoon; spike (*for mountain climbing*)
arpionismo *m* ratchet
arpi•sta *mf* **(-sti -ste)** harpist
arrabattare *ref* to exert oneself, to strive, to endeavor
arrabbiare §287 *intr* (ESSERE) to go mad (*said of dogs*) || *ref* to become angry (*said of people*)
arrabbia•to -ta *adj* mad (*dog*); angry; obstinate; confirmed
arrabbiatura *f* rage; **prendersi un'arrabbiatura** to burn up (*with rage*)
arraffare *tr* to snatch
arrampicare §197 **(arràmpico)** *ref* to climb, climb up
arrampicata *f* climbing
arrampica•tóre -trice *mf* climber; mountain climber; **arrampicatore sociale** social climber
arrancare §197 *intr* to hobble, limp; to struggle, work hard; to row hard
arrangiaménto *m* agreement; (mus) arrangement
arrangiare §290 *tr* to arrange; to fix; (coll) to steal || *ref* to manage, get along
arrecare §197 **(arrèco)** *tr* to cause; to carry, deliver
arredaménto *m* furnishing; furnishings; equipment
arredare (arrèdo) *tr* to furnish; to equip
arreda•tóre -trice *mf* interior decorator; upholsterer; (mov) property man
arrèdo *m* furnishings, furniture; piece of furniture; **arredi sacri** church supplies
arrembàg•gio *m* **(-gi)** boarding (*of a ship*)
arrenare (arréno) *tr* to sand
arrèndere §227 *tr* (archaic) to surrender || *ref* to surrender; **arrendersi a discrezione** to surrender unconditionally
arrendévole *adj* yielding, compliant, flexible
arrendevolézza *f* suppleness; compliance
arrestare (arrèsto) *tr* to stop; to arrest || *ref* to stop, stay
arrèsto *m* arrest; stop; pause; (mach) stop, catch; **arresti** (mil) house arrest; **in stato d'arresto** under arrest
arretrare (arrètro) *tr* to withdraw || *intr* (ESSERE & AVERE) & *ref* to withdraw
arretra•to -ta *adj* withdrawn; backward; back (*issue*); overdue || **arretrati** *mpl* arrears
arricchiménto *m* enrichment
arricchire §176 *tr* to enrich || *intr* (ESSERE) & *ref* to get rich
arricchi•to -ta *mf* nouveau riche
arricciacapél•li *m* **(-li)** curler
arricciare §128 *tr* to curl; to wrinkle; to screw up (*one's nose*); **arricciare il pelo** to bristle (*said of a person*); to bristle up (*said of an animal*) || *ref* to curl up
arriccia•to -ta *adj* curled up || *m* first coat (*of cement*)
arricciatura *f* curling (*of hair*); pleating (*of a skirt*); kink (*in a rope*)
arridere §231 *tr* (poet) to grant || *intr* to smile
arrin•ga *f* **(-ghe)** harangue; (law) lawyer's plea
arringare §209 *tr* to harangue; (law) to plead
arrischiare §287 *tr* to endanger; to risk || *ref* to dare, venture
arrischia•to -ta *adj* risky; daring
arrivare *tr* to reach || *intr* (ESSERE) to arrive; to happen; to get along, be

successful; **arrivare a** to reach; to succeed in
arriva•to -ta *adj* arrived; successful; **ben arrivato** welcome
arrivedér•ci *m* (**-ci**) good-bye || *interj* good-bye!, so long!
arrivedérla *interj* good-bye!
arrivismo *m* social climbing, ruthless ambition
arrivi•sta *mf* (**-sti -ste**) social climber
arrivo *m* arrival; (sports) goal line; (sports) finishing line
arroccare §197 (**arrócco**) *tr* to put (*e.g., flax*) on the distaff || §197 (**arròcco**) *tr* to shelter; (chess) to castle || *ref* to seek shelter; (chess) to castle
arròc•co *m* (**-chi**) castling
arrochire §176 *tr* to make hoarse || *intr* (ESSERE) to become hoarse
arrogante *adj* arrogant, insolent
arroganza *f* arrogance, insolence
arrogare §209 (**arrògo**) *tr*—**arrogare a sé** to arrogate to oneself || *ref* to arrogate to oneself
arrolare §237 *tr* var of **arruolare**
arrossare (**arrósso**) *tr* to redden
arrossire §176 *intr* (ESSERE) to blush; to change color
arrostire §176 *tr* to roast; to toast; **arrostire allo spiedo** to barbecue on the spit || *intr* (ESSERE) & *ref* to roast
arrò•sto *m* (**-sto & -sti**) roast
arrotare (**arròto**) *tr* to grind, hone; to smooth; to strike, run over; to grit (*one's teeth*) || *ref* to grind (*to work hard*); to sideswipe
arrotatrice *f* floor sander
arrotatura *f* sharpening
arrotino *m* grinder
arrotolare (**arròtolo**) *tr* to roll
arrotondaménto *m* rounding; rounding out; increase (*in salary*)
arrotondare (**arrotóndo**) *tr* to make round; to round out; to supplement (*a salary*) || *ref* to round out, become plump
arrovellare (**arrovèllo**) *tr* to vex || *ref* to become angry; to strive, endeavor; **arrovellarsi il cervello** to rack one's brains
arroventare (**arrovènto**) *tr* to make red-hot || *ref* to become red-hot
arroventire §176 *tr* & *ref* var of **arroventare**
arruffapòpo•li *m* (**-li**) rabble-rouser
arruffare *tr* to tangle; to muss, rumple; to confuse
arruf•fio *m* (**-fii**) tangle; confusion, mess
arruffó•ne -na *mf* blunderer; swindler
arrugginire §176 *tr, intr* (ESSERE) & *ref* to rust
arruolaménto *m* enlistment; draft
arruolare (**arruòlo**) *tr* to recruit; to draft || *ref* to enlist
arruvidire §176 *tr* to make rough, roughen || *intr* (ESSERE) to become rough
arsenale *m* arsenal; navy yard
arsèni•co -ca (**-ci -che**) *adj* arsenic, arsenical || *m* arsenic
ar•so -sa *adj* burnt; dry, parched; **arso di** consumed with
arsura *f* sultriness; dryness
arte *f* art; ability; guile; **ad arte** on purpose; **arti e mestieri** arts and crafts
artefare §173 *tr* to adulterate
artefat•to -ta *adj* adulterated; artificial
artéfice *m* craftsman; creator
artèria *f* artery
arterioscleròsi *m* arteriosclerosis
arterió•so -sa [s] *adj* arterial
artesia•no -na *adj* artesian
àrti•co -ca *adj* (**-ci -che**) arctic || **Artico** *m* Arctic
articolare *adj* articular || *v* (**articolo**) *tr* & *ref* to articulate
articola•to -ta *adj* articulated; articulate; (gram) combined; jagged (*coastline*)
articolazióne *f* articulation
articoli•sta *mf* (**-sti -ste**) columnist; feature writer
artìcolo *m* article; item; paragraph; **articolo di fondo** editorial; **articolo di spalla** comment
artificiale *adj* artificial
artificière *m* pyrotechnist; (mil) demolition expert
artifi•cio *m* (**-ci**) artifice; sophistication, affectation; **artificio d'illuminazione** (mil) flare
artificiosi•tà [s] *f* (**-tà**) artfulness, craftiness; artificiality
artifició•so -sa [s] *adj* artful, crafty; artificial, affected
artigianato *m* craftsmanship
artigia•no -na *adj* of craftsmen || *m* craftsman
artigliare §280 *tr* (poet) to claw
artiglière *m* artilleryman
artiglieria *f* artillery; **artiglieria a cavallo** mounted artillery
arti•glio *m* (**-gli**) claw; **cadere negli artigli di** to fall into the clutches of
arti•sta *mf* (**-sti -ste**) artist; actor
artìsti•co -ca *adj* (**-ci -che**) artistic
ar•to -ta *adj* (poet) narrow || *m* limb
artrite *f* arthritis
artrìti•co -ca *adj* & *mf* (**-ci -che**) arthritic
arturia•no -na *adj* Arthurian
arzigogolare [dz] (**arzigògolo**) *intr* to muse; to cavil
arzigògolo [dz] *m* fantasy; cavil
arzil•lo -la [dz] *adj* lively, sprightly; (coll) sparkling (*wine*)
arzin•ga *f* (**-ghe**) tong (*of a blacksmith*)
asbèsto *m* asbestos
ascèlla *f* armpit
ascendènte *adj* ascendant || *m* upper hand, ascendancy; **ascendenti** forefathers
ascendènza *f* ancestry, lineage
ascéndere §245 *tr* to climb || *intr* (ESSERE & AVERE) to ascend, climb
ascensionale *adj* rising; lifting
ascensióne *f* ascent, climb || **Ascensione** *f* Ascension, Ascension Day
ascensóre *m* elevator
ascésa [s] *f* ascent
ascèsso *m* abscess
ascè•ta *mf* (**-ti -te**) ascetic
ascèti•co -ca *adj* (**-ci -che**) ascetic
ascetismo *m* asceticism
à•scia *f* (**-sce**) adze

asciugacapél·li *m* (**-li**) hair drier
asciugamano *m* towel; **asciugamano spugna** Turkish towel
asciugante *adj* drying; blotting; soaking || *m* dryer
asciugare §209 *tr* to dry, dry up; to wipe; to drain (*e.g., a glass of wine*) || *ref* to dry oneself; to dry, dry up
asciuga·tóio *m* (**-tói**) towel; bath towel
asciugatrice *f* dryer
asciut·to -ta *adj* dry; skinny; blunt (*in speech*) || *m* dry land; dry climate; **all'asciutto** pennyless
ascoltare (**ascólto**) *tr* to listen to || *intr* to listen
ascolta·tóre -trice *mf* listener
ascólto *m* listening; **stare in ascolto** to listen
ascòrbi·co -ca *adj* (**-ci -che**) ascorbic
ascrit·to -ta *adj* ascribed; belonging || *m* member
ascrìvere §250 *tr* to inscribe, register; to ascribe, attribute
ascultare *tr* to sound (*s.o.'s chest*)
asèpsi [s] *f* asepsis
asètti·co -ca [s] *adj* (**-ci -che**) aseptic
asfaltare *tr* to tar, pave
asfalto *m* asphalt
asfissìa *f* asphyxia
asfissiante *adj* asphyxiating; poison (*gas*); boring
asfissiare §287 *tr* to asphyxiate; to bore || *intr* (ESSERE) to be asphyxiated
asfodèlo *m* asphodel
Àsia, l' *f* Asia; **l'Asia Minore** Asia Minor
asiàti·co -ca *adj* & *mf* (**-ci -che**) Asian, Asiatic
asilo *m* shelter; asylum; home; **asilo di mendicità** poorhouse; **asilo infantile** kindergarten; **asilo per i vecchi** old-age home, nursing home
asimmetrìa [s] *f* asymmetry
asimmètri·co -ca [s] *adj* (**-ci -che**) asymmetric(al)
asinàggine [s] *f* stupidity, asininity
asi·nàio [s] *m* (**-nài**) donkey driver
asinata [s] *f* stupidity, folly
asinerìa [s] *f* asininity
asiné·sco -sca [s] *adj* (**-schi -sche**) asinine
asini·no -na [s] *adj* asinine
àsino [s] *m* ass, donkey; **fare l'asino a** (slang) to play up to; **qui casca l'asino** here is the rub
asma *f* asthma
asmàti·co -ca *adj* & *mf* (**-ci -che**) asthmatic
àsola *f* buttonhole; buttonhole hem
aspàra·go *m* (**-gi**) asparagus; piece of asparagus; **asparagi** asparagus (*as food*)
aspèrgere §112 *tr* to sprinkle
aspersióne *f* aspersing, sprinkling
aspettare (**aspètto**) *tr* to wait for, await; to expect; **aspettare al varco** to be on the lookout for || *intr* to wait; **fare aspettare** to keep waiting || *ref* to expect
aspettativa *f* expectancy, expectation; leave of absence without pay
aspètto *m* waiting; aspect, look; **al primo aspetto** at first sight
àspide *m* asp
aspirante *adj* suction (*pump*) || *m* aspirant; applicant, candidate; suitor; upperclassman (*in naval academy*)
aspirapólve·re *m* (**-re**) vacuum cleaner
aspirare *tr* to inhale, breathe in; to suck (*e.g., air*); (phonet) to aspirate || *intr* to aspire
aspiratóre *m* exhaust fan
aspirazióne *f* aspiration; (aut) intake
aspirina *f* aspirin
aspo *m* reel
asportàbile *adj* removable
asportare (**aspòrto**) *tr* to remove, take away
asportazióne *f* removal
asprézza *f* sourness; roughness, harshness
a·spro -spra *adj* sour; rough, harsh
assaggiare §290 *tr* to taste; to sample, test; **assaggiare il terreno** (fig) to see how the land lies
assaggia·tóre -trice *mf* taster
assàg·gio *m* (**-gi**) taste, sample; tasting; test, trial
assài *adj invar* a lot of || *m* much || *adv* enough; fairly; very
assale *m* axle
assalire §242 *tr* to attack, assail; (fig) to seize
assali·tóre -trice *mf* assailant
assaltare *tr* to assault; **assaltare a mano armata** to stick up
assalto *m* assault, attack; (law) battery; **cogliere d'assalto** to catch unawares; **prendere d'assalto** to assault
assaporare (**assapóro**) *tr* to taste; to relish, enjoy
assassinare *tr* to assassinate; (fig) to murder
assassì·nio *m* (**-ni**) assassination, murder
assassi·no -na *adj* murderous || *mf* assassin, murderer
asse *m* axle; shaft, spindle; (geom, phys) axis; **asse ereditario** estate; **asse stradale** median strip || *f* plank; **asse da stiro** ironing board
assecondare (**assecóndo**) *tr* to help; to second; to uphold
assediante *adj* besieging || *m* besieger
assediare §287 (**assèdio**) *tr* to lay siege to, besiege
assè·dio *m* (**-di**) siege; **assedio economico** economic sanctions; **cingere d'assedio** to besiege
assegnaménto *m* awarding; allowance; faith, reliance; **fare assegnamento su** to rely upon
assegnare (**asségno**) *tr* to assign; to prescribe; to distribute; to award
assegnatà·rio -ria *mf* (**-ri -rie**) assignee
assegnazióne *f* assignment; awarding
asségno *m* allowance; check; **assegni** fringe benefits; **assegni familiari** family allowance; **assegno a copertura garantita** certified check; **assegno a vuoto** worthless check; **assegno di studio** (educ) stipend; **assegno turistico** traveler's check; **assegno vademecum** certified check; **contro assegno** C.O.D.

assemblàg·gio *m* (**-gi**) (mach) assembling, assembly
assemblèa *f* assembly
assembraménto *m* gathering
assembrare (**assémbro**) *tr* & *ref* to gather
assennatézza *f* good judgment, discretion
assenna·to -ta *adj* sensible, prudent
assènso *m* approval, consent
assentare (**assènto**) *ref* to be absent, to absent oneself
assènte *adj* absent || *mf* absentee
assenteìsmo *m* absenteeism
assentire (**assènto**) *tr* (poet) to grant || *intr* to assent, acquiesce; **assentire con un cenno** to nod assent
assènza *f* absence
assenziènte *adj* consenting, approving
assèn·zio *m* (**-zi**) absinthe; (bot) wormwood
asserire §176 *tr* to affirm, assert
asserragliare §280 *tr* to barricade || *ref* to barricade oneself
assèrto *m* (poet) assertion
asser·tóre -trice *mf* advocate, supporter
asserviménto *m* enslavement
asservire §176 *tr* to enslave; to subjugate
asserzióne *f* assertion
assessóre *m* councilman; alderman
assestaménto *m* arrangement; settling (*of a building*)
assestare (**assèsto**) *tr* to arrange; to adapt, regulate; to deliver, deal (*a blow*) || *ref* to become organized; to settle (*said of a building*)
assesta·to -ta *adj* sensible, prudent
assetare (**asséto**) *tr* to make thirsty; (fig) to inflame
asseta·to -ta *adj* thirsty; parched; eager || *mf* thirsty person
assettare (**assètto**) *tr* to tidy, straighten up || *ref* to straighten oneself up
assetta·to -ta *adj* tidy
assètto *m* arrangement; order; (naut) trim; **assetto longitudinale** (aer) pitch, attitude; **in assetto di guerra** ready for war; **male in assetto** in poor shape
asseverare (**assèvero**) *tr* to asseverate, assert
assicèlla *f* roofing board, lath; batten
assicuràbile *adj* insurable
assicurare *tr* to assure; to insure; to protect; to fasten; to deliver (*e.g., a thief*) || *ref* to make sure; to take out insurance
assicura·to -ta *adj* & *mf* insured || *f* insured letter
assicura·tóre -trice *mf* insurer
assicurazióne *f* assurance; insurance; **assicurazione contro gli infortuni sul lavoro** workman's compensation insurance; **assicurazione contro i danni** casualty insurance; **assicurazione incendio** fire insurance; **assicurazione infortuni** accident insurance; **assicurazione per la vecchiaia** old age insurance; **assicurazione sociale** social security; **assicurazione sulla vita** life insurance
assideraménto *m* freezing; frostbite
assiderare (**assìdero**) *ref* to freeze; to become frostbitten
assìdere §113 *ref* (poet) to take one's seat (*e.g., on the throne*)
assì·duo -dua *adj* assiduous, diligent
assième *m* ensemble || *adv* together; **assieme a** together with
assiepare (**assièpo**) *tr* & *ref* to crowd
assillante *adj* disturbing, troublesome
assillare *tr* to beset, trouble
assillo *m* gadfly; (fig) stimulus, goad
assimilare (**assìmilo**) *tr* to assimilate; to compare
assimilazióne *f* assimilation
assiòlo *m* horned owl
assiò·ma *m* (**-mi**) axiom
assiomàti·co -ca *adj* (**-ci -che**) axiomatic
assi·ro -ra *adj* & *mf* Assyrian
assisa *f* (poet) uniform, livery; (geol) layer; (archaic) duty, tax; **assise** criminal court; assembly, session; (hist) assises
assistènte *mf* assistant; **assistente sanitario** practical nurse; **assistente sociale** social worker || *m*—**assistente al lavoro** foreman || *f*—**assistente di volo** (aer) hostess
assistènza *f* assistance, help; intervention; **assistenza pubblica** relief
assistenziale *adj* welfare, charity
assìstere §114 *tr* to assist, help || *intr*—**assistere a** to attend, be present at
assito *m* flooring, boarding
assiuòlo *m* var of **assiolo**
asso *m* ace; **asso del volante** speed king; **piantare in asso** to walk out on
associare §128 (**assòcio**) *tr* to associate; **associare alle carceri** to take to prison || *ref* to associate; to become a member; to subscribe; to participate
associa·to -ta *adj* associate || *mf* associate, partner
associazióne *f* association; union; subscription; membership
assodare (**assòdo**) *tr* to solidify; to strengthen; to ascertain || *ref* to solidify; to strengthen
assoggettare (**assoggètto**) *tr* to subject, subdue || *ref* to submit
assola·to -ta *adj* sunny, exposed to the sun
assolcare §197 (**assólco**) *tr* to furrow
assoldare (**assòldo**) *tr* to hire, recruit
assólo *m* (mus) solo
assolutismo *m* absolutism
assolutìsti·co -ca *adj* (**-ci -che**) absolutist, despotic
assolu·to -ta *adj* & *m* absolute
assoluzióne *f* absolution
assòlvere §115 *tr* to absolve; to fulfill
assomigliare §280 *tr* to compare; to make similar, make equal || *intr* (ESSERE & AVERE) (with *dat*) to resemble, to look like; to be like || *ref* to resemble each other, look alike; **assomigliarsi a** to resemble
assommare (**assómmo**) *tr* to add; to be the epitome of; (archaic) to complete || *intr* (ESSERE) to amount
assonna·to -ta *adj* sleepy
assopire §176 *tr* to lull to sleep; to

soothe || *ref* to drowse, to nod; to calm down
assorbènte *adj* absorbent || *m* sanitary napkin
assorbiménto *m* absorption
assorbire §176 & (**assòrbo**) *tr* to absorb
assorbi•to -ta *adj* absorbed; **assorbito da** consumed with
assordare (**assórdo**) *tr* to deafen || *ref* to become deaf; to dim; to lessen
assortiménto *m* assortment; **avere in assortimento** (com) to carry, stock
assortire §176 *tr* to assort, sort out; to stock
assorti•to -ta *adj* assorted; **bene assortito** well matched
assòr•to -ta *adj* engrossed, absorbed
assottigliare §280 *tr* to thin; to sharpen; to reduce || *ref* to grow thinner
assuefare §173 *tr* to accustom || *ref* to become accustomed
assuefazióne *f* habit, custom
assùmere §116 *tr* to assume; to hire; to raise, elevate; (law) to accept in evidence
Assunta *f* Assumption
assunto *m* thesis, argument; (poet) task
assun•tóre -trice *mf* contractor
assunzióne *f* assumption; hiring; (law) examination || **Assunzione** *f* Assumption
assurdi•tà *f* (-**tà**) absurdity
assur•do -da *adj* absurd || *m* absurdity
assùrgere §117 *intr* (ESSERE) (poet) to rise
asta *f* staff; rod; arm (*e.g., of scale*); lance; leg (*of compass*); stroke (*in handwriting*); shaft (*of arrow*); auction; (naut) boom; (naut) mast; (elec) trolley pole; **a mezz'asta** half-mast; **vendere all'asta** to auction, auction off
astante *mf* bystander || *m* physician on duty (*in a hospital*)
astanterìa *f* receiving ward
astato *m* (chem) astatine
astè•mio -mia *adj* abstemious, temperate || *mf* teetotaler
astenére §271 *ref* to abstain
astensióne *f* abstension
astenuto *m* person who abstains from voting; abstention (*vote withheld*)
astèrgere §164 (*pp* **astèrso**) *tr* to wipe
asteri•sco *m* (-**schi**) asterisk
asticciòla *f* penholder; rib (*of umbrella*); temple (*of eyeglasses*)
àstice *m* (*Hommarus vulgaris*) lobster
asticèlla *f* (sports) bar
astinènte *adj* abstinent
astinènza *f* abstinence
à•stio *m* (-**sti**) grudge, rancor
astió•so -sa [s] *adj* full of malice, spiteful
astóre *m* goshawk
astràgalo *m* astragalus, anklebone
astrakàn *m* Persian lamb
astrarre §273 *tr* to abstract || *intr*—**astrarre da** to leave aside, overlook
astrat•to -ta *adj* abstract || *m* abstract
astrazióne *f* abstraction
astringènte *adj* & *m* astringent
-astro -astra *suf adj* -ish, e.g., **verdastro** greenish || *suf mf* -aster, e.g., **poetastro** poetaster
astro *m* star, heavenly body; (bot) aster; (fig) star
astrologìa *f* astrology
astrològi•co -ca *adj* (-**ci -che**) astrological
astròlo•go *m* (-**gi** or -**ghi**) astrologer
astronàu•ta *mf* (-**ti -te**) astronaut
astronàuti•co -ca (-**ci -che**) *adj* astronautic(al) || *f* astronautics
astronautizzare [ddzz] *intr* (ESSERE) to be an astronaut
astronave *f* spaceship, spacecraft
astronomìa *f* astronomy
astrònomo *m* astronomer
astronòmi•co -ca *adj* (-**ci -che**) astronomic(al)
astruserìa *f* abstruseness
astrusi•tà *f* (-**tà**) abstruseness
astru•so -sa *adj* abstruse
astùc•cio *m* (-**ci**) case, box
astu•to -ta *adj* astute, crafty
astùzia *f* astuteness, craftiness
àta•vo -va *mf* ancestor
ateismo *m* atheism
atei•sta *mf* (-**sti -ste**) atheist
Atène *f* Athens
atenèo *m* athenaeum; university
ateniése [s] *adj* & *mf* Athenian
àte•o -a *adj* atheistic || *mf* atheist
atlante *m* atlas || **Atlante** *m* Atlas
atlànti•co -ca *adj* (-**ci -che**) Atlantic || **Atlantico** *m* Atlantic
atlè•ta *mf* (-**ti -te**) athlete
atletéssa *f* female athlete
atlèti•co -ca (-**ci -che**) *adj* athletic || *f* athletics; **atletica leggera** track and field
atmosfèra *f* atmosphere
atmosfèri•co -ca *adj* (-**ci -che**) atmospheric
atòllo *m* atoll
atòmi•co -ca *adj* (-**ci -che**) atomic; (coll) stunning
atomizzare [ddzz] *tr* to atomize
atomizzatóre [ddzz] *m* atomizer
àtomo *m* atom
atòni•co -ca *adj* (-**ci -che**) (pathol) weak
àto•no -na *adj* (gram) atonic
atout *m* (**atouts**) trump
à•trio *m* (-**tri**) entrance hall, lobby
atróce *adj* atrocious
atroci•tà *f* (-**tà**) atrocity
atrofia *f* atrophy
atròfi•co -ca *adj* (-**ci -che**) atrophied
atrofizzare [ddzz] *tr* & *ref* to atrophy
attaccabottó•ni *mf* (-**ni**) bore, pest, buttonholer
attaccabri•ghe *mf* (-**ghe**) (coll) quarrelsome person, scrapper
attaccaménto *m* attachment, affection
attaccapan•ni *m* (-**ni**) coathanger
attaccare §197 *tr* to attach; to bind, unite; to sew on; to stick; to hitch (*a horse*); to hang; to attack; to strike up (*a conversation*); to begin; to communicate (*a disease*); **attaccare un bottone a** (fig) to buttonhole || *intr* to stick; to gain a foothold, take root; to begin || *ref* to stick; to

cling; to spread (*said of a disease*); (fig) to become attached
attaccatìc·cio -cia *adj* (**-ci -ce**) sticky
attacchino *m* billposter
attac·co *m* (**-chi**) attachment; onslaught; fastening; beginning; seizure (*e.g., of epilepsy*); spell (*e.g., of coughing*); (elec) plug; (rad) jack; (sports) forward line; **attacco cardiaco** heart attack
attagliare §280 *ref*—**attagliarsi a** to fit, become
attanagliare §280 *tr* to grip; to seize; to hold (*e.g., with tongs*)
attardare *ref* to tarry, delay
attecchire §176 *intr* to take root; to take hold
atteggiaménto *m* attitude
atteggiare §290 (**attéggio**) *tr* to compose (*e.g., one's face*); to place || *ref* to pose; to strike an attitude
attempa·to -ta *adj* elderly
attendaménto *m* camping; jamboree (*of Boy Scouts*)
attendare (**attèndo**) *ref* to encamp; to pitch one's tent
attendènte *m* (mil) orderly
attèndere §270 *tr* to await; (archaic) to keep; **attendere l'ora propizia** to bide one's time || *intr*—**attendere a** to attend to
attendìbile *adj* reliable
attendismo *m* wait-and-see attitude
attendi·sta (**-sti -ste**) *adj* wait-and-see || *mf* fence-sitter
attenére §271 *tr* (poet) to keep (*a promise*) || *intr*—**attenere** (with *dat*) to concern, e.g., **ciò non gli attiene** this does not concern him || *ref*—**attenersi a** to conform to
attentare (**attènto**) *intr*—**attentare a** to attempt (*s.o.'s life*) || *ref* to make an attempt, dare
attentato *m* attempt
attenta·tóre -trice *mf* would-be murderer; attacker
attèn·ti *m* (**-ti**) attention || *interj* (mil) attention!
attèn·to -ta *adj* attentive; careful
attenuare (**attènuo**) *tr* to extenuate, play down; to attenuate; to mitigate
attenzióne *f* attention; **fare attenzione** to take care; **prestare attenzione** to pay attention
atterràg·gio *m* (**-gi**) landing; **atterraggio di fortuna** emergency landing; **atterraggio senza carrello** crash-landing
atterraménto *m* landing; pinning, pin (*in wrestling*); (boxing) knocking down; **atterramento frenato** (aer) arrested landing
atterrare (**attèrro**) *tr* to fell; to knock down; to pin (*in wrestling*); (fig) to humiliate || *intr* to land; **atterrare scassando** or **atterrare senza carrello** to crash-land
atterrire §176 *tr* to frighten, terrify || *ref* to become frightened
atté·so -sa [s] *adj* awaited, expected; **atteso che** considering that || *f* waiting; expectation; **in attesa (di)** waiting (for)
attestare (**attèsto**) *tr* to certify, attest; to prove; to join; (mil) to deploy || *ref* (mil) to take a stand
attestato *m* certificate
attestazióne *f* testimony; affidavit; attestation, proof
àtti·co -ca (**-ci -che**) *adj & mf* Attic || *m* attic
attì·guo -gua *adj* adjacent, contiguous
attillare *tr & ref* to preen
attilla·to -ta *adj* tight, close-fitting; tidy, all dressed up
àttimo *m* moment, split second; **di attimo in attimo** any moment
attinènte *adj* related, pertinent
attinènza *f* relation; **attinenze** appurtenances; annexes
attìngere §126 *tr* to draw (*water*); to get; (poet) to attain (*e.g., glory*)
attingi·tóio *m* (**-tói**) ladle
attirare *tr* to draw, attract
attitùdine *f* aptitude; attitude
attivare *tr* to activate; to expedite
attivazióne *f* activation; reassessment
attivi·tà *f* (**-tà**) activity; **attività** *fpl* assets
atti·vo -va *adj* active; profit-making || *m* assets
attizzare *tr* to stir, poke (*a fire*); (fig) to stir up
attizza·tóio *m* (**-tói**) poker
at·to -ta *adj* apt, fit || *m* act, action; gesture; (law) instrument; **all'atto pratico** in reality; **atti** proceedings (*of a learned society*); **atti notarili** legal proceedings; **atto di nascita** birth certificate; **fare atto di presenza** to put in a brief formal appearance; **atto di vendita** bill of sale; **nell'atto o sull'atto** in the act
attòni·to -ta *adj* astonished
attorcigliare §280 *tr* to twist || *ref* to wind; to coil up
attóre *m* actor; (law) plaintiff; **attore giovane** (theat) juvenile; **primo attore** (theat) lead
attorniare §287 (**attórnio**) *tr* to surround; (fig) to dupe
attórno *adv* around; **andare attorno** to walk around; **attorno a** around, near; **darsi d'attorno** to busy oneself; **levarsi qlcu d'attorno** to get rid of s.o.
attortigliare §280 *tr* to twist || *ref* to wind; to coil up
attraccare §197 *tr & intr* to moor, dock
attrac·co *m* (**-chi**) mooring, docking
attraènte *adj* attractive
attrarre §273 *tr* to attract, draw
attratti·vo -va *adj* attractive; alluring || *f* attraction, charm
attraversaménto *m* crossing; **attraversamento pedonale** pedestrian crossing
attraversare (**attravèrso**) *tr* to cross; to go through; to thwart; **attraversare il passo a** to stand in the way of
attravèrso *adv* across; crosswise; **andare attraverso** to go down the wrong way (*said of food or drink*); (fig) to go wrong; **attraverso a** through, across || *prep* through, across
attrazióne *f* attraction
attrezzare (**attrézzo**) *tr* to outfit, equip

attrezzatura *f* outfit; gear, equipment; **attrezzatura di una nave** rigging; **attrezzature** facilities
attrezzi·sta (**-sti -ste**) *mf* gymnast || *m* toolmaker; (theat) property man
attrézzo *m* tool, utensil; **attrezzi** gymnastic equipment
attribuire §176 *tr* to award; to attribute; **attribuire qlco a qlcu** to credit s.o. with s.th || *ref* to ascribe to oneself, claim for oneself
attributo *m* attribute
attribuzióne *f* attribution
attrice *f* actress; (law) plaintiff; **prima attrice** (theat) lead
attristare *tr* (poet) to sadden || *ref* to become sad
attri·to -ta *adj* worn, worn-out || *m* attrition; disagreement
attruppare *tr* to band, group || *ref* to mill about, throng
attuàbile *adj* feasible
attuale *adj* present; present-day, current
attuali·tà *f* (**-tà**) timeliness; reality; **attualità** *fpl* current events; **di viva attualità** newsworthy; timely; in the news
attualizzare [ddzz] *tr* to bring up to date || *ref* to become a reality
attuare (**àttuo**) *tr* to carry out, make come true || *ref* to come true
attuà·rio -ria (**-ri -rie**) *adj* (hist) transport (*e.g., ship*) || *m* actuary
attuazióne *f* realization
attutire §176 *tr* to mitigate; to deaden (*a sound, a blow*) || *ref* to diminish (*said of a sound*)
audace *adj* audacious
audàcia *f* audacity
audiofrequènza *f* audio frequency
audiovisi·vo -va *adj* audio-visual
auditi·vo -va *adj* var of **uditivo**
auditóre *m* var of **uditore**
auditò·rio *m* (**-ri**) auditorium
audizióne *f* program; audition; (law) hearing
àuge *f* acme; **essere in auge** to enjoy a great reputation; to be in vogue; to be on top of the world
augurale *adj* well-wishing; salutatory
augurare (**àuguro**) *tr* to wish; to bid (*good day*) || *intr* to augur || *ref* to hope; to expect
àugure *m* augur
augù·rio *m* (**-ri**) wish; augury, omen
augustè·o -a *adj* Augustan
augu·sto -sta *adj* august, venerable
àula *f* hall; classroom; (poet) chamber (*of a palace*)
àuli·co -ca *adj* (**-ci -che**) courtly; noble, elevated
aumentare (**auménto**) *tr* to augment, increase || *intr* (ESSERE) to increase, rise
auménto *m* increase
àura *f* (poet) breeze; (poet) breath
àure·o -a *adj* golden, gold
aurèola *f* halo
auricolare *adj* ear; first-hand || *m* (telp) receiver; (rad) earphone
auròra *f* dawn; (fig) aurora
ausiliare *adj* auxiliary || *m* collaborator, helper
ausilià·rio -ria (**-ri -rie**) *adj* auxiliary; (mil) supply || *m* helper; (mil) reserve officer || *f* female member of the armed forces
ausì·lio *m* (**-li**) (poet) help
auspicare §197 (**àuspico**) *tr* to wish, augur
àuspice *m* sponsor; (hist) augur
auspì·cio *m* (**-ci**) sponsorship; (hist, poet) augury, omen; **sotto gli auspici di** under the auspices of
austeri·tà *f* (**-tà**) austerity
austè·ro -ra *adj* austere
australe *adj* austral, southern
Austràlia, l' *f* Australia
australia·no -na *adj & mf* Australian
Austria, l' *f* Austria
austrìa·co -ca *adj & mf* (**-ci -che**) Austrian
autarchìa *f* autarky; autonomy (*of an administration*)
autàrchi·co -ca *adj* (**-ci -che**) autonomous, independent
autènti·ca *f* (**-che**) authentication of a signature or a document
autenticare §197 (**autèntico**) *tr* to authenticate
autentici·tà *f* (**-tà**) authenticity
autènti·co -ca (**-ci -che**) *adj* authentic, genuine || *f* see **autentica**
autière *m* (mil) driver
auti·sta *mf* (**-sti -ste**) (aut) driver
au·to *f* (**-to**) auto
autoabbronzante [dz] *adj* tanning || *m* tanning lotion
autoaffondaménto *m* scuttling
autoambulanza *f* ambulance
autobiografìa *f* autobiography
autobiogràfi·co -ca *adj* (**-ci -che**) autobiographical
autoblinda·to -ta *adj* armored
autoblin·do *m* (**-do**) armored car
autobótte *f* tank truck
àuto·bus *m* (**-bus**) bus
autocarro *m* truck, motor truck
autocèntro *m* (mil) motor pool
autocistèrna *f* tank truck
autocivétta *f* unmarked police car
autocolónna *f* row of cars
autocombustióne *f* spontaneous combustion
autocontròllo *m* self-control
autocorrièra *f* intercity bus, highway bus
autocrazìa *f* autocracy
autocrìti·ca *f* (**-che**) self-criticism
autòcto·no -na *adj* autochthonous, independent
autodecisióne *m* free will
autodeterminazióne *f* self-determination
autodidat·ta *mf* (**-ti -te**) self-taught person
autodidàtti·co -ca *adj* (**-ci -che**) self-instructional
autodifésa [s] *f* self-defense
autodisciplina *f* self-discipline
autòdrómo *m* automobile race track
autoemotè·ca *f* (**-che**) bloodmobile
autofilettante *adj* self-threading
autofurgóne *m* van; **autofurgone cellu-**

lare police van; **autofurgone funebre** hearse
autogiro *m* autogyro
autogovèrno *m* self-government
autògra•fo -fa *adj* autographic(al) || *m* autograph
auto•grù *f* (**-grù**) tow truck
autolesioni•sta *mf* (**-sti -ste**) person who wounds himself to avoid the draft or collect insurance
autoletti•ga *f* (**-ghe**) ambulance
autolibro *m* bookmobile
autolìnea *f* bus line
autò•ma *m* (**-mi**) automaton, robot
automàti•co -ca (**-ci -che**) *adj* automatic || *m* snap
automatizzare [ddzz] *tr* to automate
automazióne *f* automation
automèzzo [ddzz] *m* motor vehicle
automòbile *f* automobile, car; **automobile da corsa** racing car; **automobile di serie** stock car; **automobile fuori serie** custom-made car
automobilismo *m* motoring
automobili•sta *mf* (**-sti -ste**) motorist
automobilìsti•co -ca *adj* (**-ci -che**) car, automobile
automo•tóre -trice *adj* self-propelled || *f* (rr) automotive rail car
autonolég•gio *m* (**-gi**) car rental agency
autonomìa *f* autonomy; (aer, naut) cruising radius
autonomi•sta *adj* (**-sti -ste**) autonomous
autòno•mo -ma *adj* autonomous, independent
autoparchég•gio *m* (**-gi**) parking; parking lot
autopar•co *m* (**-chi**) parking; parking lot
autopiano *m* player piano
autopilò•ta *m* (**-ti**) (aer) automatic pilot
autopómpa *f* fire engine
autopsìa *f* autopsy
autorà•dio *f* (**-dio**) car radio
autóre *m* author; perpetrator; creator, maker
autoreattóre *m* ramjet engine
autorespiratóre *m* aqualung
autorévole *adj* authoritative
autorimessa *f* garage
autori•tà *f* (**-tà**) authority
autorità•rio -ria *adj* (**-ri -rie**) authoritarian
autoritratto *m* self-portrait
autorizzare [ddzz] *tr* to authorize
autorizzazióne [ddzz] *f* authorization
autoscala *f* hook and ladder; ladder (*of hook and ladder*)
autoscuòla *f* driving school
autoservì•zio *m* (**-zi**) bus service, bus line; self-service
autosilo *m* parking garage
autostazióne *f* bus station
autostèllo *m* roadside motel
auto•stòp *m* (**-stòp**) hitchhiking; **fare l'autostop** to hitchhike
autostoppi•sta *mf* (**-sti -ste**) hitchhiker
autostrada *f* highway, turnpike
autosufficiènte *adj* self-sufficient
autote•làio *m* (**-lài**) (aut) frame
autotrasportare (**autotraspòrto**) *tr* to truck
autotrasportatóre *m* trucker
autotreni•sta *m* (**-sti**) truck driver, teamster
autotrèno *m* tractor trailer
autoveìcolo *m* motor vehicle
autovettura *f* car, automobile
autrice *f* authoress
autunnale *adj* autumnal, fall
autunno *m* autumn, fall
avallare *tr* to endorse (*a promissory note*); to guarantee
avallo *m* endorsement (*of a promissory note*)
avambràc•cio *m* (**-ci**) forearm
avampósto *m* outpost
avancàrica *f*—**ad avancarica** muzzle-loading
avanguàrdia *f* vanguard; avant-garde
avanguardismo *m* avant-garde
avanguardi•sta *m* (**-sti**) avant-gardist; (hist) member of Fascist youth organization
avannòtto *m* small fry (*young fresh-water fish*)
avanti *adj* preceding || *m* forward || *adv* forward, ahead; **andare avanti** to proceed, to go ahead; **andare avanti negli anni** to be up in years; **avanti a** in front of; **avanti che** rather than; **avanti di** before; **essere avanti** to be advanced (*in work or study*); **in avanti** ahead || *prep*—**avanti Cristo** before Christ; **avanti giorno** before daybreak || *interj* come in!
avantièri *adv* day before yesterday
avantrèno *m* (aut) front-axle assembly; (mil) limber
avanzaménto *m* advancement
avanzare *tr* to advance; to overcome; to be creditor for, e.g., **avanza cento dollari da suo fratello** he is his brother's creditor for one hundred dollars; to save || *intr* (mil) to advance || *intr* (ESSERE) to advance; to stick out; to be abundant; to be left over, e.g., **avanzano due polpette** two meatballs are left over; **avanzare negli anni** to grow older || *ref* to advance, come forward
avanza•to -ta *adj* advanced; progressive || *f* (mil) advance
avanzo *m* remainder; **avanzi** remains
avarìa *f* damage, breakdown; (naut) average
avariare §287 *tr* to damage, spoil || *intr* to spoil
avaria•to -ta *adj* damaged, spoiled
avarìzia *f* avarice, greed
ava•ro -ra *adj* avaricious, stingy || *mf* miser
avellana *f* filbert
avellano *m* filbert tree
avèllo *m* (poet) tomb
avéna *f* oats
avére *m* belongings, property; assets, credit; amount due || §118 *tr* to have; to hold; to wear; to receive, get; to stand (*a chance*); to be, e.g., **avere . . . anni** to be . . . years old; **avere caldo** to be hot; to be warm; **avere fame** to be hungry; **avere freddo** to be cold; **avere fretta** to be in a hurry;

avere paura to be afraid; **avere ragione** to be right; **avere sete** to be thirsty; **avere sonno** to be sleepy; **avere torto** to be wrong; **avere vergogna** to be ashamed; **avere voglia di** to be anxious to; **avere qlco da** + *inf* to have s.th to + *inf*, e.g., **ho molto lavoro da fare** I have a lot of work to do; **averla con** to be angry at; **non avere niente a che fare con** to have nothing to do with || *impers*—**v'ha** there is || *aux* to have, e.g., **ha letto il giornale** he has read the newspaper; **avere da** + *inf* to have to + *inf*, e.g., **avevo da lavorare** I had to work; to be to + *inf*, e.g., **ha da venire alle cinque** he is to arrive at five o'clock
avià·rio -ria (**-ri -rie**) *adj* bird || *m* aviary
avia·tóre -trice *mf* aviator || *f* aviatrix
aviazióne *f* aviation
avicoltóre *m* bird raiser; poultry farmer
avidi·tà *f* (**-tà**) avidity, greediness
àvi·do -da *adj* avid, greedy
avière *m* airman
aviogètto *m* jet plane
aviolìnea *f* airline
aviopista *f* (aer) airstrip
avioriméssa *f* (aer) hangar
aviotrasporta·to -ta *adj* airborne
avi·to -ta *adj* ancestral
a·vo -va *mf* grandparent; ancestor || *m* grandfather || *f* grandmother
avocare §197 (**àvoco**) *tr* to demand (*jurisdiction*); to expropriate
avò·rio *m* (**-ri**) ivory
avul·so -sa *adj* (poet) torn, uprooted; (poet) separated
avvalére §278 *ref*—**avvalersi di** to avail oneself of
avvallaménto *m* sinking, settling
avvallare *tr* (poet) to lower (*e.g., one's eyes*) || *ref* to sink; (lit) to humiliate oneself
avvalorare (**avvalóro**) *tr* to strengthen, confirm || *ref* to gain strength
avvampare *tr* (poet) to inflame || *intr* (ESSERE) to burn
avvantaggiare §290 *tr* to be profitable to; to benefit || *ref* to profit; **avvantaggiarsi su** to overcome; to beat
avvedére §279 *ref*—**avvedersi di** to notice, become aware of
avvedutézza *f* discernment; shrewdness
avvedu·to -ta *adj* prudent; shrewd; **fare qlcu avveduto di** to inform s.o. of
avvelenaménto *m* poisoning
avvelenare (**avveléno**) *tr* to poison || *ref* to take poison; to be poisoned
avveniménto *m* happening, event
avvenire *adj invar* future, to come || *m* future; **in avvenire** in the future || §282 *intr* (ESSERE) to happen, occur; **avvenga quel che vuole** come what may
avventare (**avvènto**) *tr* to hurl; to deliver (*a blow*); to venture (*an opinion*) || *ref* to throw oneself
avventatézza *f* thoughtlessness, heedlessness
avventa·to -ta *adj* thoughtless, heedless; **all'avventata** heedlessly
avventì·zio -zia *adj* (**-zi -zie**) outside, exterior; temporary, occasional
avvènto *m* advent; elevation, rise
avven·tóre -tóra *mf* customer, consumer
avventura *f* adventure
avventuriè·ro -ra *adj* adventurous || *m* adventurer || *f* adventuress
avventuró·so -sa [s] *adj* adventurous, adventuresome
avverare (**avvéro**) *tr* to make true || *ref* to come true
avvèr·bio *m* (**-bi**) adverb
avversà·rio -ria (**-ri -rie**) *adj* opposing, contrary || *mf* adversary, opponent
avversióne *f* aversion
avversi·tà *f* (**-tà**) adversity
avvèr·so -sa *adj* adverse; (obs) opposite || **avverso** *prep* (law) against
avvertènza *f* prudence, caution; advice; **avvertenze** instructions, directions
avvertiménto *m* caution, warning; advice
avvertire (**avvèrto**) *tr* to caution, warn; to notice
avvezzare (**avvézzo**) *tr* to accustom; to inure; to train; **avvezzar male** to spoil || *ref* to get accustomed
avvéz·zo -za *adj* accustomed
avviaménto *m* starting; introduction; trade school; good shape (*of a business*); (mach) starting; (typ) adjustment (*of printing press*)
avviare §119 *tr* to start, set in motion; to introduce; to initiate; to begin || *ref* to set out
avvia·to -ta *adj* going, thriving (*concern*)
avvicendaménto *m* alteration, rotation (*of crops*)
avvicendare (**avvicèndo**) *tr* & *ref* to alternate
avvicinaménto *m* approach; rapprochement
avvicinare *tr* to bring near or closer; to approach, go or come near to || *ref* to approach, come near; **avvicinarsi a** to come closer, approach
avviliménto *m* discouragment, dejection
avvilire §176 *tr* to degrade; to deject || *ref* to become dejected, become discouraged
avviluppare *tr* to entangle, snarl; to wrap
avvinazza·to -ta *adj* & *mf* drunk
avvincènte *adj* fascinating
avvìncere §285 *tr* to fascinate, charm; (poet) to twine
avvinghiare §287 *tr* to claw; to clasp, clutch || *ref* to grip one another
avvì·o *m* (**-i**) beginning
avvisàglia *f* skirmish; **prime avvisaglie** onset; first signs
avvisare *tr* to inform, advise; (archaic) to observe, notice
avvisa·tóre -trice *mf* announcer, messenger || *m* alarm; (theat) callboy; **avvisatore acustico** (aut) horn; **avvisatore d'incendio** fire alarm
avviso *m* advise; notice, poster; opinion; **avviso di chiamata alle armi**

notice of induction; **sull'avviso** on one's guard
avvistare *tr* to sight
avvitaménto *m* (aer) tailspin
avvitare *tr* to screw; to fasten || *ref* (aer) to go into a tailspin
avviticchiare §287 *tr* to entwine || *ref* to cling
avvivare *tr* to revive; to stir up
avvizzire §176 *tr* & *intr* (ESSERE) to wither
avvocatéssa *f* woman lawyer
avvocato *m* lawyer, attorney
avvocatura *f* law, legal profession
avvòlgere §289 *tr* to wind; to wrap up; to spread over, surround || *ref* to wind around; to wrap oneself up
avvolgiménto *m* winding; wrapping; (elec) coil; (mil) envelopment
avvol·tóio *m* (-tói) vulture
avvoltolare (**avvòltolo**) *tr* to roll up || *ref* to roll around, wallow
azièndа [dz] *f* business, firm
azionare (**azióno**) *tr* to start; to drive, propel
azionà·rio -ria *adj* (-ri -rie) (com) stock
azióne *f* action, act; (law) suit; (com) share (*of stock*); **azione legale** prosecution; **azione privilegiata** preferred stock
azioni·sta *mf* (-sti -ste) stockholder, shareholder
azòto [dz] *m* nitrogen
azoturo [dz] *m* nitride
aztè·co -ca *adj* & *mf* (-chi -che) Aztec
azzannare *tr* to seize with the fangs
azzardare [ddzz] *tr* to risk; to advance || *ref* to dare
azzarda·to -ta [ddzz] *adj* daring
azzardo [ddzz] *m* chance, hazard
azzardó·so -sa [ddzz] [s] *adj* hazardous, risky
azzeccagarbu·gli *m* (-gli) shyster
azzeccare §197 (**azzécco**) *tr* to hit; to deliver; to pass off (*counterfeit money*); **azzeccarla** (coll) to hit the mark
azzimare [ddzz] (**àzzimo**) *tr* & *ref* to spruce up
àzzi·mo -ma [ddzz] *adj* unleavened (*bread*)
azzittare & **azzittire** §176 *tr* to hush || *ref* to keep quiet
azzoppare (**azzòppo**) *tr* to cripple || *ref* to become lame or crippled
Azzòrre [ddzz] *fpl* Azores
azzuffare *ref* to come to blows; to scuffle
azzur·ro -ra [ddzz] *adj* blue || *m* blue; Italian athlete (*in international competition*)
azzurrógno·lo -la [ddzz] *adj* bluish

B

B, b [bi] *m* & *f* second letter of the Italian alphabet
ba·bàu *m* (-bàu) bogey, bugbear
babbè·o -a *adj* foolish || *mf* fool
babbo *m* (coll) daddy, father
babbù·cia *f* (-ce) babouche; bedroom slipper
babbuino *m* baboon
babèle *f* babel || **Babele** *f* Babel
babilònia *f* confusion || **Babilònia** *f* Babylon
babórdo *m* (naut) port
bacare §197 *ref* to become worm-eaten
baca·to -ta *adj* worm-eaten; rotten
bac·ca *f* (-che) berry
bacca·là *m* (-là) dried codfish; (coll) skinny person; (coll) lummox
baccalaureato *m* baccalaureate, bachelor's degree
baccanale *m* bacchanal
baccano *m* noise, hubbub; **fare baccano** to carry on
baccante *f* bacchant
baccellière *m* (hist) bachelor
baccèllo *m* pod
baccellóne *m* simpleton, fool
bacchétta *f* rod, wand, baton; **bacchetta magica** magic wand; **bacchette del tamburo** drumsticks
bacchétto *m* stick; handle (*of a whip*)
bacchettó·ne -na *mf* bigot
bàcchi·co -ca *adj* (-ci -che) Bacchic
Bacco *m* Baccus
bachè·ca *f* (-che) showcase
bachelite *f* bakelite
bacheròzzo *m* worm; earthworm; (coll) cockroach
bachicoltura *f* silkworm raising
baciama·no *m* (-ni) kissing of the hand
baciapi·le *mf* (-le) bigot
baciare §128 *tr* to kiss; **baciare la polvere** to bite the dust || *ref* to kiss one another
bacia·to -ta *adj* kissed; rhymed (*couplet*)
bacile *m* basin
bacillo *m* bacillus
bacinèlla *f* small basin; (phot) tray
bacino *m* basin; reservoir; cove; (anat) pelvis; **bacino carbonifero** coal field; **bacino di carenaggio** drydock; **bacino fluviale** river basin
bà·cio *m* (-ci) kiss; **a bacio** with a northern exposure
baciucchiare §287 *tr* to keep on kissing || *ref* to pet
ba·co *m* (-chi) worm; **baco da seta** silkworm
bacuc·co -ca *adj* (-chi -che)—**vecchio bacucco** dotard
bada *f*—**tenere a bada** to stave off; to delay
badare *tr* to tend, take care of || *intr* to attend; to take care; to pay attention; **badare a** to mind; to watch

over; to attend to; **badare alla salute** to take care of one's health
badéssa *f* abbess
badìa *f* abbey
badilata *f* shovelful
badile *m* shovel
baffo *m* whiskers; whisker; **baffi** mustache; whiskers; **baffo di gatto** (rad) cat's whiskers; **leccarsi i baffi** to lick one's chops; **sotto i baffi** up one's sleeve
baga·gliàio *m* (**-gliài**) (rr) baggage car; (rr) baggage room; (aut) baggage rack
bagaglièra *f* baggage room
bagaglière *m* baggage master
bagà·glio *m* (**-gli**) baggage, luggage; (*of knowledge*) fund
bagagli·sta *m* (**-sti**) porter (*in a hotel*)
bagarinàg·gio *m* (**-gi**) profiteering; (theat) scalping
bagarino *m* profiteer; scalper
bagà·scia *f* (**-sce**) harlot, prostitute
bagattèlla *f* trifle, bauble
baggiano *m* nitwit, simpleton
bà·glio *m* (**-gli**) (naut) beam
baglióre *m* shine, gleam
bagnante *mf* bather, swimmer; vacationer at the seashore
bagnare *tr* to bathe; to wet; to soak; to water, sprinkle; to moisten; (fig) to celebrate || *ref* to bathe; to wet one another
bagnaròla *f* (coll) bathtub
bagnasciu·ga *f* (**-ghe**) (naut) waterline
bagnino *m* lifeguard
bagno *m* bath; bathroom; bathtub; **bagno di luce** diathermy; **bagno di schiuma** bubble bath; **bagno di sole** sun bath; **bagno di vapore** steam bath; **bagno turco** Turkish bath; **essere in un bagno di sudore** to be soaked with perspiration; **fare il bagno** to take a bath
bagnomarìa *m* (**bagnimarìa**) double boiler; bain-marie; **a bagnomaria** in a double boiler
bagórdo *m* carousal, revelry; **far bagordi** to carouse, revel
bàio bàia (**bài bàle**) *adj* & *m* bay || *f* bay; jest; trifle; **dare la baia a** to make fun of, tease
baionétta *f* bayonet; **baionetta in canna** with fixed bayonet
bàita *f* mountain hut
balaustrata *f* balustrade
balaùstro *m* baluster
balbettaménto *m* stammering
balbettare (**balbétto**) *tr* to stammer; to speak poorly (*a foreign language*) || *intr* to stammer; to babble (*said of a baby*)
balbettì·o *m* (**-i**) babble (*of a baby*); stammering
balbùzie *f* stammering
balbuziènte *adj* stammering || *mf* stammerer
Balcani, i the Balkans
balcàni·co -ca *adj* (**-ci -che**) Balkan
balconata *f* balcony; (theat) upper gallery
balcóne *m* balcony
baldacchino *m* canopy, baldachin
baldanza *f* boldness; aplomb, assurance
baldanzó·so -sa [s] *adj* bold; self-assured
bal·do -da *adj* bold; self-assured
baldòria *f* carousal, revelry; **fare baldoria** to carouse, revel
baldrac·ca *f* (**-che**) harlot, prostitute
baléna *f* whale
balenare (**baléno**) *intr* to stagger || *intr* (ESSERE) to flash, e.g., **gli balena un pensiero** a thought flashes through his mind || *impers* (ESSERE)—**balena,** it is lightning
balenièra *f* whaler, whaleboat
baléno *m* flash; flash of lightning; **in un baleno** in a flash
balenòttera *f* rorqual
balèstra *f* crossbow; (aut) spring, leaf spring
balestrière *m* crossbowman
bàlia *f* wet nurse; **balia asciutta** dry nurse; **prendere a balia** to wet-nurse
balìa *f* power; **in balia di** at the mercy of
balìsti·co -ca (**-ci -che**) *adj* ballistic || *f* ballistics
balla *f* bale; (vulg) lie
ballàbile *adj* dance || *m* dance tune
ballare *tr* to dance || *intr* to dance; to shake; to be loose; to wobble (*said, e.g., of a chair*)
ballata *f* ballad; (mus) ballade
balla·tóio *m* (**-tói**) gallery; perch (*in birdcage*)
balleri·no -na *adj* dancing || *m* ballet dancer; dancer; dancing partner || *f* dancing girl; ballerina; chorus girl; ballet slipper; (orn) wagtail
balletto *m* ballet; chorus
ballo *m* dance; chorus; ball; stake; **ballo di San Vito** Saint Vitus's dance; **ballo in maschera** masked ball; **in ballo** at stake; in question; **tirare in ballo** to drag in
ballonzolare (**ballónzolo**) *intr* to hop around
ballottàg·gio *m* (**-gi**) runoff
ballottare (**ballòtto**) *tr* to ballot (*e.g., a candidate*)
balneare *adj* bathing; water, watering
baloccare §197 (**balòcco**) *tr* to amuse with toys || *ref* to play; to trifle, to fool around
balòc·co *m* (**-chi**) toy; hobby
balordàggine *f* silliness
balór·do -da *adj* silly, foolish
balsàmi·co -ca *adj* (**-ci -che**) balmy; antiseptic
balsamina *f* balsam
bàlsamo *m* balm, balsam
bàlti·co -ca *adj* (**-ci -che**) Baltic
baluardo *m* bastion, bulwark
baluginare (**balùgino**) *intr* (ESSERE) to flicker; to flash (*through one's mind*)
balza *f* crag, cliff; flounce (*on dress*); fringe (*on curtains, bedspreads, etc.*)
balza·no -na *adj* white-footed (*horse*); odd, funny || *f* flounce; fringe; white mark (*on horse's foot*)
balzare *tr* to throw (*a rider; said of a horse*) || *intr* (ESSERE) to jump, leap;

to bounce; **balzare in mente a** to suddenly dawn on
balzellare (balzèllo) *intr* to hop
balzèllo *m* hop; tribute; tax; toll; **stare a balzello** to lie in wait
balzellóni *adv*—**a balzelloni** leaping, skipping
balzo *m* leap; bounce; **pigliare la palla al balzo** to take time by the forelock
bambàgia *f* cotton wool
bambinàggine *f* childishness
bambinàia *f* nursemaid; **bambinaia ad ore** baby sitter
bambiné•sco -sca *adj* (**-schi -sche**) childish
bambi•no -na *adj* childish || *mf* child
bambòc•cio *m* (**-ci**) fat baby; doll; rag doll
bàmbola *f* doll; **bambola di pezza** rag-doll
bam•bù *m* (**-bù**) bamboo
banale *adj* banal, commonplace
banali•tà *f* (**-tà**) banality, commonplaceness, triviality
banana *f* banana; hair with curls shaped as rolls
bananièra *f* banana boat
banano *m* banana plant
ban•ca *f* (**-che**) bank; embankment
bancàbile *adj* negotiable
bancarèlla *f* cart, pushcart; stall
bancà•rio -ria (**-ri -rie**) *adj* bank, banking || *m* bank clerk
bancarótta *f* bankruptcy; **fare bancarotta** to go bankrupt
banchettare (banchétto) *intr* to feast, banquet
banchétto *m* banquet
banchière *m* banker
banchina *f* garden bench; bicycle path; sidewalk; shoulder (*of highway*); dock, pier; (rr) platform; (mil) banquette
ban•co *m* (**-chi**) bench; seat; bank; witness stand; school (*of fish*); **banco di coralli** coral reef; **banco di ghiaccio** ice pack; **banco di nebbia** fog bank; **banco di prova** (mach) bench; **banco di sabbia** sandbar; **banco d'ostriche** oyster bed; **banco lotto** lottery office
bancogiro *m* (com) transfer of funds
bancóne *m* counter; bench
banconòta *f* banknote
banda *f* band; **andare alla banda** (naut) to list; **da ogni banda** from every side; **mettere da banda** to put aside
bandèlla *f* hinge (*of door or window*); hinged leaf (*of table*)
banderuòla *f* banderole; weather vane
bandièra *f* flag; banner; **battere la bandiera (e.g., italiana)** to fly the (*e.g Italian*) flag; **mutar bandiera** to change sides
bandierare (bandièro) *tr* (aer) to feather
bandire §176 *tr* to announce (*e.g., a competitive examination*); to banish
bandìsti•co -ca *adj* (**-ci -che**) (mus) band
bandi•to -ta *adj* announced; open (*house*) || *m* bandit || *f* preserve (*for hunting or fishing*)
bandi•tóre -trice *mf* town crier; auctioneer; barker
bando *m* announcement; banishment; **bandi matrimoniali** (eccl) banns; **mandare in bando** to exile, banish
bandolièra *f* bandoleer; **a bandoliera** slung across the shoulders
bàndolo *m* end of a skein; **perdere il bandolo** to lose the thread (*e.g., of a story*)
bara *f* bier, coffin
barac•ca *f* (**-che**) hut, cabin; (fig) household; **fare baracca** to carouse around
baracca•to -ta *adj* lodged in a hut or a cabin; slum (*e.g., section*) || *m* dweller in a hut or a cabin; slum dweller
baraccóne *m* big circus tent
baraónda *f* hubbub; mess
barare *intr* to cheat (*e.g., at cards*)
bàratro *m* abyss, chasm
barattare *tr* to barter; **barattare le carte in mano a uno** to distort someone's words; **barattar parole** to chat, talk || *intr* to barter
barattière *m* grafter
baratto *m* barter
baràttolo *m* can, canister, jar
barba *f* beard; whiskers; barb, vane (*of feather*); (naut) line; **barba a punta** imperial, goatee; **fare la barba (a)** to shave; **farla in barba a qlcu** to act in spite of s.o.; to dupe s.o.; **mettere barbe** to take root; **radersi la barba** to shave
barbabiètola *f* beet; sugar beet
barbafòrte *m* horseradish
barbagian•ni *m* (**-ni**) owl; (fig) jackass
barbà•glio *m* (**-gli**) glitter, dazzle
barbaré•sco -sca (**-schi -sche**) *adj* Barbary || *m* inhabitant of the Barbary States
barbàri•co -ca *adj* (**-ci -che**) barbaric
barbà•rie *f* (**-rie**) barbarism, barbarity
barbarismo *m* barbarism
bàrba•ro -ra *adj* barbarous, barbaric || *m* barbarian
barbazzale *m* curb (*of bit*)
Barberìa, la Barbary States
barbétta *f* fetlock (*tuft of hair on horse*); goatee; (mil) barbette; (naut) painter
barbière *m* barber
barbierìa *f* barbershop
barbi•glio *m* (**-gli**) barb (*of arrow*)
barbi•no -na *adj* shoddy; botched; stingy
bàr•bio *m* (**-bi**) (ichth) barbel
barbiturato *m* barbiturate
barbitùri•co -ca (**-ci -che**) *adj* barbituric || *m* barbiturate
barbo *m* var of **barbio**
barbò•gio -gia *adj* (**-gi -gie**) senile
barbóne *m* long beard, thick beard; poodle; (coll) bum, hobo
barbó-so -sa [s] *adj* boring
barbugliare §280 *tr* to stutter (*e.g., a word*) || *intr* to stutter; to bubble, gurgle
barbu•to -ta *adj* bearded
bar•ca *f* (**-che**) boat; heap; (fig) family

affairs; **barca a motore** motorboat; **barca da pesca** fishing boat; **barca a remi** rowboat
barcàc•cia *f* (**-ce**) (theat) stage box
barcaiòlo *m* boatman
barcamenare (**barcaméno**) *ref* to manage, get along
barcarizzo *m* (naut) gangway
barcaròla *f* barcarole
barcata *f* boatful
barchéssa *f* tool shed
barchétta *f* small boat; (naut) log chip
barcollare (**barcòllo**) *intr* to totter, stagger
barcollóni *adv* staggering, tottering
barcóne *m* barge
bardare *tr* to harness || *ref* to get dressed
bardatura *f* harnessing; harness
bardo *m* bard
bardòsso *m* —**a bardosso** (archaic) bareback
barèlla *f* stretcher
barellare (**barèllo**) *tr* to carry on a stretcher || *intr* to totter, stagger
barenatura *f* (mach) boring
bargèllo *m* (hist) chief of police; (hist) police headquarters
bargì•glio *m* (**-gli**) wattle
baricèntro *m* center of gravity; (fig) essence, gist
barile *m* barrel, cask
barilòtto *m* keg
bàrio *m* barium
bari•sta *mf* (**-sti -ste**) bartender, barkeeper || *m* barman || *f* barmaid
baritonale *adj* baritone
barito•no -na *adj* barytone || *m* baritone
barlume *m* glimmer, gleam
baro *m* cheat, cardsharp
baròc•co -ca *adj & m* (**-chi -che**) baroque
baròmetro *m* barometer
barόne *m* baron
baronéssa *f* baroness
barra *f* bar; link; rod; sandbar; **andare alla barra** to plead a case; **barra del timone** (naut) tiller; **barra di torsione** (aut) torsion bar; **barra spaziatrice** space bar (*of typewriter*)
barrare *tr* to cross, draw lines across (*a check*)
barrétta *f* bar (*e.g., of chocolate*)
barricare §197 (**bàrrico**) *tr* to barricade || *ref* to barricade oneself
barricata *f* barricade
barrièra *f* barrier; bar; **barriera corallina** barrier reef
barrire §176 *intr* to trumpet (*said of elephant*)
barrito *m* trumpeting, cry of an elephant
barroc•ciàio *m* (**-ciài**) cart driver
barròc•cio *m* (**-ci**) cart
baruffa *f* fight, quarrel
barzellétta [dz] *f* joke
basale *adj* basal
basalto *m* basalt
basaménto *m* foundation (*of building*); baseboard; base (*of column*)
basare *tr* to base || *ref*—**basarsi su** to be based on; to rest on
ba•sco -sca *adj & mf* (**-schi -sche**) Basque
bascula *f* balance, scale
base *f* base, foundation; (fig) basis; **a base di** composed of, made of; **base navale** naval base, naval station; **in base a** according to
basétta *f* sideburns
bàsi•co -ca *adj* (**-ci -che**) (chem) basic
basilare *adj* basic, fundamental
Basilèa *f* Basel
basìli•ca *f* (**-che**) basilica
basìli•co *m* (**-ci**) basil
basilissa *f* (fig) queen bee
bàsolo *m* large paving stone
bassacórte *f* barnyard
bassézza *f* baseness
bas•so -sa *adj* low; shallow; late (*e.g., date*); (fig) base, vile; **basso di statura** short || *m* bottom; hovel (*in Naples*); (mus) basso || **basso** *adv* low; down; **a basso, da basso** or **in basso** downstairs
bassofóndo *m* (**bassifóndi**) (naut) shallows, shallow water; **bassifondi** underworld, slums
bassopiano *m* lowland
bassorilièvo *m* bas-relief
bassòt•to -ta *adj* stocky || *m* basset hound
bassotuba *m* bass horn
bassura *f* lowland; (fig) baseness
basta *f* hem; basting (*with long stitches*) || *interj* enough!
bastante *adj* sufficient, adequate; comfortable (*income*)
bastar•do -da *adj* bastard; irregular || *m* bastard
bastare *intr* to suffice, be enough; **basta!** enough!; **basta che** + *subj* as long as + *ind;* **bastare a sé stesso** to be self-sufficient; **non basta che** + *subj* not only + *ind*
bastévole *adj* sufficient
bastiménto *m* ship; shipload
bastióne *m* bastion; (fig) defense, rampart
basto *m* packsaddle; (fig) burden
bastonare (**bastóno**) *tr* to club, cudgel; **bastonare di santa ragione** to give a good thrashing to
bastonata *f* clubbing, cudgeling; **darsi bastonate da orbi** to thrash one another soundly
bastoncino *m* small stick; roll; (anat) rod
bastóne *m* stick, cane; pole; club; baton; staff; French bread; **bastone a leva** crowbar; **bastone animato** sword cane; **bastone da golf** club; **bastone da montagna** alpenstock; **bastone da passeggio** walking stick; **bastone da sci** ski pole; **bastoni** suit in Neapolitan cards corresponding to clubs; **mettere il bastone tra le ruote** to throw a monkey wrench into the machinery
batàc•chio *m* (**-chi**) clapper (*of bell*); cudgel
batata *f* sweet potato

batisfèra *f* bathysphere
batista *f* batiste, cambric
batòsta *f* blow; (fig) blow
bàtrace or **batrace** *m* batrachian
battà·glia *f* (**-glie**) battle; campaign
battagliare §280 *intr* to fight
battagliè·ro -ra *adj* fighting, warlike
battà·glio *m* (**-gli**) clapper (*of bell*); knocker
battaglióne *m* battalion
battèllo *m* boat; **battello di salvataggio** lifeboat; **battello pneumatico** rubber raft
battènte *m* leaf (*e.g., of door*); knocker; tapper (*of alarm clock*)
bàttere *m*—**in un batter d'occhio** in the twinkling of an eye || *tr* to beat; to hit; to strike; to strike (*the hour; said of a clock*); to click (*teeth, heels*); to clap (*hands*); to stamp (*one's foot*); to mint (*coins*); to fly (*a flag*); to beat (*time*); to scour (*the countryside*); to flap (*the wings*); (sports) to bat; (sports) to kick (*a penalty*); **battere a macchina** to type; **battere il naso in** to chance upon; **battere la fiacca** to goof off; **battere la grancassa per** to ballyhoo; **battere la strada** to be a streetwalker; **senza batter ciglio** without batting an eye || *intr* (ESSERE) to beat down (*said, e.g., of rain*); to beat (*said of the heart*); to chatter (*said of teeth*); to knock (*at the door*); **battere in ritirata** to beat a retreat; **battere in testa** (aut) to knock
batterìa *f* battery; set (*of utensils*); (sports) heat
batterici·da (**-di -de**) *adj* bactericidal || *m* bactericide
battèri·co -ca *adj* (**-ci -che**) bacterial
battè·rio *m* (**-ri**) bacterium
batteriologìa *f* bacteriology
batteriòlo·go -ga *mf* (**-gi -ghe**) bacteriologist
batteri·sta *mf* (**-sti -ste**) jazz drummer
battesimale *adj* baptismal
battésimo *m* baptism; **tenere a battesimo** to christen
battezzare (**battézzo**) [ddzz] *tr* to christen || *ref* to receive baptism; to assume the name of
battibaléno *m*—**in un battibaleno** in the twinkling of an eye
battibéc·co *m* (**-chi**) squabble
batticuòre *m* palpitation; (fig) trepidation
battilò·ro *m* (**-ro**) goldsmith; silversmith
battimano *m* applause
battimuro *m*—**giocare a battimuro** to pitch pennies (against a wall)
battipalo *m* pile driver
battipan·ni *m* (**-ni**) clothes beater
battira·me *m* (**-me**) coppersmith
battiscó·pa *m* (**-pa**) washboard, baseboard
batti-sta *adj & mf* (**-sti -ste**) Baptist
battistèro *m* baptistry
battistra·da *m* (**-da**) outrider; (sports) leader; (aut) tread
battitappéto *m* carpet sweeper
bàttito *m* beating; palpitation; ticking; wink; pitter-patter (*of rain*)
batti·tóio *m* (**-tói**) leaf (*e.g., of door*); casement; cotton beater
battitóre *m* (hunt) beater; (baseball) batter
battitrice *f* threshing machine
battitura *f* thrashing, whipping; threshing (*e.g., of wheat*)
battu·to -ta *adj* beaten; hammered || *m* pavement || *f* beat; stroke, keystroke; meter (*in poetry*); witticism, quip; (hunt) battue; (mus) bar; (tennis) service; (theat) line; (theat) cue; **battuta d'aspetto** (mus) pause; **dare la battuta** to give the cue
batùffolo *m* wad; (fig) bundle
baule *m* trunk; **baule armadio** wardrobe trunk; **fare i bauli** to be on one's way; **fare il baule** to pack one's trunk
baulétto *m* small trunk; handbag; jewel case
bava *f* slobber; foam, froth; burr (*on metal edge*); **avere la bava alla bocca** to be frothing at the mouth; **bava di vento** breath of air, soft breeze
bavaglino *m* bib
bavà·glio *m* (**-gli**) gag
bavarése [s] *adj & mf* Bavarian || *f* Bavarian cream; chocolate cream
bàvero *m* collar
bavièra *f* beaver (*of helmet*) || **la Baviera** Bavaria
bavó·so -sa [s] *adj* slobbering, slobbery
bazza [ddzz] *f* protruding chin; windfall
bazzana [ddzz] *f* sheepskin
bazzècola [ddzz] *f* trifle, bauble
bazzicare §197 (**bàzzico**) *tr* to frequent
bazzòt·to -ta [ddzz] *adj* soft-boiled; uncertain (*weather*)
beare (**bèo**) *tr* to delight || *ref* to be delighted, be enraptured
beatificare §197 (**beatìfico**) *tr* to beatify
beatitùdine *f* beatitude, bliss
bea·to -ta *adj* blissful, happy; blessed || *mf* blessed
be·bè *m* (**-bè**) baby
beccàc·cia *f* (**-ce**) woodcock
beccaccino *m* snipe
beccafi·co *m* (**-chi**) figpecker, beccafico
bec·càio *m* (**-cài**) butcher
beccamòr·ti *m* (**-ti**) gravedigger
beccare §197 (**bécco**) *tr* to peck; to pick; (coll) to catch || *ref* to peck one another; to quarrel
beccata *f* peck
beccheggiare §290 (**becchéggio**) *intr* (naut) to pitch
becchég·gio *m* (**-gi**) (naut) pitching
beccherìa *f* butcher shop
becchime *m* food for poultry
becchino *m* gravedigger
béc·co *m* (**-chi**) beak, bill; tip, point; nozzle (*e.g., of teapot*); billy goat; (vulg) cuckold; **bagnarsi il becco** (joc) to wet one's whistle; **mettere il becco in** (coll; joc) to stick one's nose into; **non avere il becco di un quattrino** to not have a red cent
beccùc·cio *m* (**-ci**) small bill; lip, spout
beccuzzare *tr* to peck || *ref* to bill (*said of doves*)

béce·ro -ra *adj* (coll) boorish || *m* (coll) boor
beduì·no -na *adj & m* Bedouin
befana *f* (coll) Epiphany; old hag
bèffa *f* jest, mockery; **farsi beffa di** to make fun of
beffar·do -da *adj* mocking
beffare (bèffo) *tr* to mock, deride || *ref* —**beffarsi di** to make fun of
beffeggiare §290 (befféggio) *tr* to scoff at, deride
bè·ga *f* **(-ghe)** quarrel; trouble
beghina *f* Beguine; bigoted woman
begònia *f* begonia
bèl *adj* apocopated form of **bello,** used only before masculine singular nouns beginning with a consonant except impure **s, z, gn, ps,** and **x,** e.g., **bel ragazzo**
belare (bèlo) *tr* to croon || *intr* to bleat, baa; to moan
belato *m* bleat, baa
bèl·ga *adj & mf* **(-gi -ghe)** Belgian
Bèlgio, il Belgium
bèll' *adj* apocopated form of **bello,** used only before singular nouns of both genders beginning with a vowel, e.g., **bell'amico; bell'epoca**
bèlla *adj fem* of **bello** || *f* belle; girlfriend; final draft; (sports) final game; (sports) rubber match; **alla bell'e meglio** the best one could; **bella di notte** (bot) four-o'clock
belladònna *f* belladonna
bellétto *m* rouge, makeup
bellézza *f* beauty; **che bellezza!** how lovely!; **la bellezza di** as much as
bellici·sta *adj* **(-sti -ste)** bellicose
bèlli·co -ca *adj* **(-ci -che)** war, warlike
bellicó·so -sa [s] *adj* bellicose
belligerante *adj & m* belligerent
belligeranza *f* belligerence
bellimbusto *m* fop, dandy, beau
bèl·lo -la (declined like **quello §7**) *adj* beautiful; lovely; handsome; good-looking; pleasing; fine; quite a, e.g., **una bella cifra** quite a sum; fair; pretty; **bell'e fatto** ready-made; taken care of; **farla bella** to start trouble; (coll) to do it, e.g., **l'hai fatta bella** you've done it; **farsi bello** to dress up; **farsi bello di** to appropriate || *m* beauty; beautiful; climax; fine weather; beau; **il bello è** the funny thing is; **sul più bello** just then; **sul più bello che** just when || *f* see **bella** || **bello** *adv*—**bel bello** slowly
bellospìrito *m* **(begli spiriti)** wit, bel-esprit
bellui·no -na *adj* wild, fierce
bellumóre *m* **(begli umori)** jolly fellow
bel·tà *f* **(-tà)** beauty (*woman*); (lit) beauty
bélva *f* wild beast
belvedére *adj* (rr) observation (*car*) || *m* belvedere; (naut) topgallant
Belzebù *m* Beelzebub
bemòlle *m* (mus) flat
benama·to -ta *adj* beloved
benarriva·to -ta *adj* welcome
benché *conj* although, albeit
bènda *f* bandage; band; blindfold; **benda gessata** cast, surgical dressing
bendàg·gio *m* **(-gi)** bandage
bendare (bèndo) *tr* to bandage; **bendare gli occhi a** to blindfold
bendispó·sto -sta *adj* well-disposed
bène *adj* well; well-born || *m* goal, aim; good; love; sake; **bene dell'anima** profound affection; **beni** (econ) assets, goods; **beni di consumo** consumer goods; **beni immobili** real estate; **beni mobili** personal property, chattels; **beni rifugio** hedge (*e.g., against inflation*); **è un bene** it is a blessing; **fare del bene** to do good; **per il Suo bene** for your sake; **voler bene a** to love, like; to care for || *adv* well; all right; properly; **ben bene** quite carefully; **star bene** to be well; **va bene** O.K., all right
benedetti·no -na *adj & m* Benedictine
benedét·to -ta *adj* blessed; holy
benedire §195 *tr* to bless; to praise; **andare a farsi benedire** (coll) to go to wrack and ruin; **mandare a farsi benedire** (coll) to get rid of, dump
benedizióne *f* benediction; boon
beneduca·to -ta *adj* well-behaved
benefattóre *m* benefactor
benefattrice *f* benefactress
beneficare §197 (benèfico) *tr* to benefit, help
beneficènza *f* welfare; charity, beneficence
beneficiale *adj* beneficial
beneficiare §128 *intr* to benefit
beneficià·rio -ria *adj & mf* **(-ri -rie)** beneficiary
beneficiata *f* benefit performance; streak of good luck; streak of bad luck
benefi·cio *m* **(-ci)** benefice; profit; favor; benefit
benèfi·co -ca *adj* **(-ci -che)** beneficial; beneficent
benemerènte *adj* deserving, well-deserving
benemèri·to -ta *adj* worthy, deserving || *m*—**benemerito della patria** national hero || *f*—**la Benemerita** the Carabinieri
beneplàcito *m* approval, consent; **a beneplacito di** at the pleasure of
benèssere *m* well-being, comfort; prosperity
benestante *adj* well-to-do || *mf* well-to-do person
benestare *m* approval; prosperity; **dare il benestare a** to approve
benevolènte *adj* benevolent
benevolènza *f* benevolence
benèvo·lo -la *adj* well-meaning; benevolent
benfat·to -ta *adj* well-done; well-favored; shapely
benga·la *m* **(-li & -la)** fireworks
benga·li *adj & m* **(-li)** Bengalese
beniami·no -na *mf* favorite child; favorite
benigni·tà *f* **(-tà)** benignity; graciousness; mildness (*of climate*)

beni·gno -gna *adj* benign; gracious; mild (*climate*)
benintenziona·to -ta *adj* well-meaning
benintéso [s] *adv* of course, naturally
bènna *f* bucket, scoop (*e.g., of dredge*)
benna·to -ta *adj* (lit) well-born
benpensante *m* sensible person; conformist
benportante *adj* well-preserved
benservito *m* testimonial, recommendation; **dare il benservito a** to dismiss, fire
bensì *adv* indeed || *conj* but
bentorna·to -ta *adj & m* welcome || *interj* welcome back!
benvenu·to -ta *adj & m* welcome; **dare il benvenuto a** to welcome
benvi·sto -sta *adj* well-thought-of
benvolére *tr*—**farsi benvolere da qlcu** to enter the good graces of s.o.; **prendere a benvolere qlcu** to be well-disposed toward s.o.
benvolu·to -ta *adj* liked, loved
benzina *f* gasoline, gas; benzine; **far benzina** (coll) to get gas
benzi·nàio *m* (**-nài**) gasoline dealer; gas-station attendant
benzòlo *m* benzene
beóne *m* drunkard, toper
bequadro *m* (mus) natural
berciare §128 (**bèrcio**) *intr* (coll) to yell
bére *m* drink, drinking || §120 *tr* to drink; (fig) to swallow; **bere come una spugna** to drink like a fish; **darla a bere** to make believe
bergamòt·to -ta *adj* bergamot || *m* bergamot orange || *f* bergamot pear
berillio *m* beryllium
berlina *f* pillory; berlin, coach; (aut) sedan; **mettere alla berlina** to pillory
berlinése [s] *adj* Berlin || *mf* Berliner
Berlino *m* Berlin
bermuda *mpl* Bermuda shorts || **le Bermude** Bermuda
bernòccolo *m* bump, protuberance; (fig) knack
berrétta *f* biretta
berrétto *m* cap; **berretto a sonagli** cap and bells; **berretto da notte** nightcap; **berretto goliardico** student cap
bersagliare §280 *tr* to harass, pursue; to bomb, bombard
bersà·glio *m* (**-gli**) target; butt (*of a joke*); target (*of criticism*)
bèrta *f* pile driver; **dar la berta a** to ridicule
bertùc·cia *f* (**-ce**) Barbary ape; **fare la bertuccia di** to ape
bestémmia *f* blasphemy
bestemmiare §287 (**bestémmio**) *tr* to blaspheme, curse
bestemmia·tóre -trice *adj* blasphemous || *mf* blasphemer
béstia *f* beast, animal; **andare in bestia** to fly into a rage; **bestia da soma** beast of burden; **bestia nera** pet aversion, bête noire; **bestie grosse** cattle
bestiale *adj* beastly, bestial
bestiali·tà *f* (**-tà**) beastliness; blunder
bestiame *m* livestock; **bestiame da cortile** barnyard animals; **bestiame grosso** cattle
bestino *m* gamy odor; stench of perspiration
bestiòla *f* tiny animal; pet
bestsèl·ler *m* (**-ler**) best seller
Betlèmme *f* Bethlehem
betonièra *f* cement mixer
béttola *f* tavern
bettolière *m* tavern keeper
bettònica *f* betony; **conosciuto più della bettonica** very well-known
betulla *f* birch
bèuta *f* flask
bevanda *f* drink, beverage
beveràg·gio *m* (**-gi**) beverage, potion
bevìbile *adj* drinkable
bevi·tóre -trice *mf* drinker
bevuta *f* drink, drinking
bezzicare §197 (**bézzico**) *tr* to peck; to vex || *ref* to fight one another
biacca *f* white lead
biada *f* feed; **biade** harvest
bianca·stro -stra *adj* whitish
biancherìa *f* laundry; linen; underwear; **biancheria da letto** bed linen; **biancheria da tavola** table linen; **biancheria di bucato** freshly laundered clothes; **biancheria intima** underclothes
bianchézza *f* whiteness
bianchire §176 *tr* to blanch; to bleach; to polish
bian·co -ca (**-chi -che**) *adj* white; clean; **bianco come un cencio lavato** as white as a ghost || *m* white; **dare il bianco a** to whitewash; **in bianco** blank (*paper*); **mangiare in bianco** to eat a bland or non-spicy diet; **ricamare in bianco** to embroider
biancóre *m* whiteness
biancospino *m* hawthorn
biascicare §197 (**biàscico**) *tr* to chew with difficulty; to peck at (*one's food*); to mumble
biasimare (**biàsimo**) *tr* to blame
biasimévole *adj* blamable, censurable
biàsimo *m* blame, censure; **dare una nota di biasimo a** to censure
biauricolare *adj* binaural
Bìbbia *f* Bible
bibe·rón *m* (**-rón**) nursing bottle
bìbita *f* soft drink
bìbli·co -ca *adj* (**-ci -che**) Biblical
bìblio·bus *m* (**-bus**) bookmobile
bibliòfi·lo -la *mf* bibliophile
bibliografia *f* bibliography
bibliotè·ca *f* (**-che**) library; bookshelf, stack; collection (*of books*); **biblioteca ambulante** walking encyclopedia
bibliotecà·rio -ria *mf* (**-ri -rie**) librarian
bìbu·lo -la *adj* absorbent (*e.g., paper*)
bi·ca *f* (**-che**) pile of sheaves
bicarbonato *m* bicarbonate; **bicarbonato di soda** bicarbonate of soda, baking soda
bicchierata *f* glassful; wine party
bicchière *m* glass
bicchierino *m* small glass, liquor glass; **bicchierino da rosolio** whiskey glass, jigger
biciclétta *f* bicycle
bicilìndri·co -ca *adj* (**-ci -che**) two-cylinder

bicìpite *adj* two-headed || *m* biceps
bicòc•ca *f* **(-che)** castle built on a hill; shanty, hut
bicolóre *adj* two-color
bicòrno *m* two-cornered hat
bidèllo *m* school janitor, caretaker
bidènte *m* two-pronged pitchfork
bidimensionale *adj* two-dimensional
bidóne *m* can (*for milk*); drum (*for gasoline or oil*); jalopy; (slang) fraud
bidon•ville *f* **(-ville)** shantytown
biè•co -ca *adj* **(-chi -che)** awry; sullen; cross; fierce; **guardar bieco** to look askance (at)
bièlla *f* connecting rod
biennale *adj* biennial || *f* biennial show
biènne *adj* biennial
bièn•nio *m* **(-ni)** biennium
bièto1a *f* Swiss chard
biétta *f* wedge, chock; (naut) batten
bifase *adj* diphase
biffa *f* (surv) rod
biffare *tr* to cross out; (surv) to level
bìfi•do -da *adj* bifurcate
bifocale *adj* bifocal
bifól•co *m* **(-chi)** ox driver; clodhopper, boor
biforcaménto *m* bifurcation
biforcare §197 **(bifórco)** *tr* to bifurcate
biforcazióne *f* bifurcation, branching off; fork (*of a road*)
biforcu•to -ta *adj* forked; cloven (*e.g., hoof*)
bifrónte *adj* two-faced
bi•ga *f* **(-ghe)** chariot
bigamìa *f* bigamy
bìga•mo -ma *adj* bigamous || *mf* bigamist
bighellonare (bighellóno) *intr* to idle, dawdle, dally
bighelló•ne -na *mf* idler, dawdler
bigino *m* (slang) pony (*used to cheat*)
bì•gio -gia *adj* **(-gi -gie)** gray, grayish; (fig) undecided
bigiotterìa *f* costume jewelry; costume jewelry store
bigliardo *m* billiards
bigliet•tàio *m* **(-tài)** ticket agent; (rr) conductor
bigliettería *f* ticket office; (theat) box office
bigliétto *m* note; card; ticket; **biglietto d'abbonamento** commutation ticket; season ticket; **biglietto d'andata e ritorno** round-trip ticket; **biglietto di banca** banknote; **biglietto di lotteria** lottery ticket, chance; **biglietto d'invito** invitation; **biglietto di visita** calling card; business card; **biglietto di Stato** banknote; **mezzo biglietto** half fare
bigné *m* **(bigné)** puff, creampuff
bigodino *m* curler; roller
bigón•cia *f* **(-ce)** vat; bucket; **a bigonce** abundantly
bigón•cio *m* **(-ci)** vat; tub; (theat) ticket box (*for stubs*)
bigottismo *m* bigotry
bigòt•to -ta *adj* bigoted || *mf* bigot
bilàn•cia *f* **(-ce)** balance, scale; **bilancia commerciale** balance of trade; **bilancia dei pagamenti** balance of payments || **Bilancia** *f* (astr) Libra
bilanciare §128 *tr & ref* to balance
bilancière *m* balance; balance wheel; rope-walker's balancing rod
bilàn•cio *m* **(-ci)** balance; **bilancio consuntivo** balance sheet; **bilancio preventivo** budget; **fare il bilancio** to balance; to strike a balance
bile *f* bile; **rodersi dalla bile** to burn with anger
bìlia *f* billiard ball; marble; (billiards) pocket
biliardino *m* pocket billiards; pinball machine
biliardo *m* billiards
biliare *adj* bile; gall (*stone*)
bìli•co *m* **(-chi)** balance, equipoise; **in bilico** in balance; **tenere in bilico** to balance
bilìngue *adj* bilingual
bilióne *m* billion; trillion (Brit)
bilió•so -sa [s] *adj* bilious
bim•bo -ba *mf* child
bimensile *adj* bimonthly
bimèstre *m* period of two months
bimotóre *adj* twin-engine || *m* twin-engine plane
binà•rio -ria (-ri -rie) *adj* binary || *m* (rr) track; **binario morto** (rr) siding; **uscire dai binari** (rr) to run off the track; (fig) to go astray
bina•to -ta *adj* binary; twin (*e.g., guns*)
binda *f* (aut) jack
binòcolo *m* binoculars; **binocolo da teatro** opera glasses
binò•mio -mia (-mi -mie) *adj* binomial || *m* binomial; couple, pair
bìoccolo *m* wad (*of cotton*); flake (*of snow*); flock (*of wool*)
biochìmi•co -ca (-ci -che) *adj* biochemical || *m* biochemist || *f* biochemistry
biodegradàbile *adj* biodegradable
biofisica *f* biophysics
biografìa *f* biography
biogràfi•co -ca *adj* **(-ci -che)** biographic(al)
biògra•fo -fa *mf* biographer
biologìa *f* biology
biòlo•go *m* **(-gi)** biologist
biondeggiare §290 **(biondéggio)** *intr* to be or become blond; to ripen (*said of grain*)
bión•do -da *adj* blond, fair || *m* blond; blondness || *f* blonde
biopsìa *f* biopsy
biòssido *m* dioxide
bipartìti•co -ca *adj* **(-ci -che)** two-party, bipartisan
biparti•to -ta *adj* bipartite || *m* two-party government
bìpede *adj & m* biped
bipènne *f* double-bitted ax
biplano *m* biplane
bipósto *adj invar* having seats for two || *m* two-seater
birba *f* rascal, rogue
birbante *m* scoundrel, rascal; (joc) madcap, wild young fellow
birbanterìa *f* knavery; trick
birbonata *f* trick

birbó·ne -na *adj* wicked || *mf* rascal, rogue, scoundrel
bireattóre *m* twin jet
birichinata *f* prank
birichi·no -na *adj* prankish; spirited || *mf* rogue; urchin
birillo *m* pin; **birilli** ninepins; tenpins
Birmània, la Burma
birra *f* beer; **birra chiara** light beer; **birra scura** dark beer
bir·ràio *m* **(-ràì)** brewer; beer distributor
birrerìa *f* brewery; tavern; beer saloon
bis *adj invar*—**treno bis** (rr) second section || *m* **(bis)** encore || *interj* encore!
bisàc·cia *f* **(-ce)** knapsack; saddlebag; bag (*of mendicant friar*)
Bisànzio *m* Bysantium
bisa·vo -va *mf* great-grandparent; ancestor || *m* great-grandfather || *f* great-grandmother
bisbèti·co -ca (-ci -che) *adj* shrewish; crotchety; cantankerous || *f* (fig) shrew
bisbigliare §280 *tr & intr* to whisper
bisbì·glio *m* **(-gli)** whisper
bisbòccia *f*—**fare bisboccia** to revel
bisboccióne *m* reveler
bis·ca *f* **(-che)** gambling house
Biscàglia *f* Biscay, e.g., **Baia di Biscaglia** Bay of Biscay; **la Biscaglia** Biscay
biscaglina *f* (naut) Jacob's ladder
biscazzière *m* gaming-house operator; habitué of a gaming house; marker (*at billiards*)
bìschero *m* (mus) peg
bì·scia *f* **(-sce)** snake; **biscia d'acqua** water snake
biscottare (biscòtto) *tr* to toast
biscotterìa *f* cookie factory; cookie store
biscottièra *f* cookie jar
biscottifì·cio *m* **(-ci)** cookie factory
biscòt·to -ta *adj* twice-baked || *m* cookie
biscròma *f* (mus) demisemiquaver
bisdòsso *m*—**a bisdosso** bareback
bisecare [s] §197 **(bìseco)** *tr* to bisect
bisènso [s] *m* double meaning
bisessuale [s] *adj* bisexual
bisestile *adj* leap (*year*)
bisettimanale [s] *adj* biweekly
bisettrice [s] *f* bisector
bisezióne [s] *f* bisection
bisìlla·bo -ba [s] *adj* disyllabic
bislac·co -ca *adj* **(-chi -che)** queer, extravagant
bislun·go -ga *adj* **(-ghi -ghe)** oblong
bismuto *m* bismuth
bisnòn·no -na *mf* great-grandparent; **bisnonni** ancestors || *m* great-grandfather || *f* great-grandmother
bisógna *f* (lit) task, job
bisognare (bisógna) *intr* (with *dat*) to need, e.g., **gli bisognavano tre litri di benzina** he needed three liters of gasoline || *impers*—**bisogna** + *inf* it is necessary to, e.g., **bisogna partire** it is necessary to leave; **bisogna che** + *subj* must, to have to, e.g., **bisogna che me ne vada** I must go, I have to go; **bisognando** if need be; **non bisogna** one should not; **più che non bisogna** more than necessary
bisognévole *adj* needy
bisógno *m* need; want, lack; **aver bisogno di** to need; **c'è bisogno di** there is need of; **se ci fosse bisogno** if need be
bisognó·so -sa *adj* needy || **i bisognosi** the needy
bisolfato [s] *m* bisulfate
bisolfito [s] *m* bisulfite
bisolfuro [s] *m* bisulfide
bisónte *m* bison
bistec·ca *f* **(-che)** beefsteak, steak; **bistecca al sangue** rare steak
bisticciare §128 *intr & ref* to quarrel, bicker
bistìc·cio *m* **(-ci)** quarrel, bickering; play on words, pun
bistrattare *tr* to mistreat
bìstu·ri *m* **(-ri)** bistouri, surgical knife
bisul·co -ca [s] *adj* **(-chi -che)** cloven
bisun·to -ta *adj* greasy
bitagliènte *adj* double-edged
bitórzolo *m* wart (*on humans, plants, or animals*); pimple (*on human face*)
bitta *f* (naut) bollard
bitume *m* bitumen, asphalt
bituminó·so -sa [s] *adj* bituminous
bivaccare §197 *intr* to bivouac; to spend the night
bivac·co *m* **(-chi)** bivouac
bì·vio *m* **(-vi)** fork (*of road*); **essere al bivio** (fig) to be at the crossroads
bizanti·no -na [dz] *adj* Byzantine
bizza [ddzz] *f* tantrum; **fare le bizze** to go into a tantrum
bizzarrìa [ddzz] *f* extravagance, oddity
bizzar·ro -ra [ddzz] *adj* bizarre, odd; skittish (*e.g., horse*)
bizzèffe [ddzz] *adv*— **a bizzeffe** plenty, in abundance
bizzó·so -sa [ddzz] [s] *adj* irritable
blandire §176 *tr* to blandish, coax; to soothe, mitigate
blandìzie *fpl* blandishment
blan·do -da *adj* bland
blasfemare (blasfèmo) *tr & intr* to blaspheme
blasfè·mo -ma *adj* blasphemous
blasona·to -ta *adj* emblazoned
blasóne *m* coat of arms, blazon
blaterare (blàtero) *intr* to babble
blatta *f* water bug, cockroach
blenoraggìa *f* gonorrhea
blè·so -sa *adj* lisping
blindàg·gio *m* **(-gi)** armor
blindare *tr* to armor
bloccare §197 **(blòcco)** *tr* to block; to blockade; to stop; to jam; to close up; to freeze (*e.g., prices*); (sports) to block || *intr*—**bloccare su** to vote as a block for || *ref* to stop
blòc·co *m* **(-chi)** block; blockade; notebook, pad; freezing (*e.g., of wages*); **in blocco** in bulk
bloc-notes *m* **(-notes)** notebook
blu *adj invar & m* blue
blua·stro -stra *adj* bluish
bluffare *intr* to bluff
blusa *f* blouse; smock

bò•a *m* (**-a**) boa || *f* buoy
boà•rio -ria *adj* (**-ri -rie**) cattle
boa•ro -ra *adj* ox || *m* stable boy
boato *m* roar; **boato sonico** sonic boom
bobina *f* spool (*of thread*); coil (*of wire*); reel (*of movie film; of magnetic tape*); roll (*of film*); cylinder, bobbin; (elec) coil; **bobina d'accensione** spark coil
bóc•ca *f* (**-che**) mouth; nozzle; muzzle (*of gun*); pit (*of the stomach*); opening; straits; pass; **a bocca aperta** agape; **bocca da fuoco** cannon; **di buona bocca** easily pleased; **in bocca al lupo!** good luck!; **per bocca** orally; **rimanere a bocca asciutta** to be foiled; to be left high and dry; **tieni la bocca chiusa!** shut up!
boccaccé•sco -sca *adj* (**-schi -sche**) written by or in the style of Boccaccio; bawdy, licentious
boccàc•cia *f* (**-ce**) ugly mouth; grimace; **fare le boccacce** to make faces
boccà•glio *m* (**-gli**) nozzle (*of hose or pipe*); mouthpiece (*of megaphone*)
boccale *adj* oral || *m* jug, tankard
boccapòrto *m* hatch; port; mouth (*of oven or furnace*); **chiudere i boccaporti** to batten the hatches
boccascè•na *m* (**-na**) proscenium, front (*of stage*)
boccata *f* mouthful; **andare a prendere una boccata d'aria** to go out for a breath of fresh air
boccétta *f* small bottle, vial; small billiard ball
boccheggiante *adj* gasping; moribund
boccheggiare **§290** (**bocchéggio**) *intr* to gasp
bocchétta *f* nozzle (*of sprinkling can*); mouthpiece (*of wind instrument*); opening (*of drainage or ventilation system*); **bocchetta stradale** manhole
bocchino *m* cigarette holder; mouthpiece (*of cigarette or of musical instrument*)
bòc•cia *f* (**-ce**) decanter; ball (*for bowling*); **bocce** bowls
bocciare **§128** (**bòccio**) *tr* to score (*at bowling*); to reject (*a proposal*); to flunk (*a student*)
bocciatura *f* failure
boccino *m* jack (*at bowls*)
bocciòlo *m* bud
bóccola *f* buckle; earring; (mach) bushing
bocconcino *m* morsel; (culin) stew
boccóne *m* mouthful; piece; morsel; **buttar giù un boccone amaro** to swallow a bitter pill; **levarsi il boccone di bocca** to take the bread out of one's mouth (to help someone); **mangiare un boccone** to have a bite || **bocconi** *adv* flat on one's face
boè•mo -ma *adj* & *mf* Bohemian
boè•ro -ra *adj* & *m* Boer
bofonchiare **§287** (**bofónchio**) *intr* to snort, grumble
bò•ia *m* (**-ia**) hangman, executioner
boiata *f* (slang) infamy; (slang) trash
boicottàg•gio *m* (**-gi**) boycott
boicottare (**boicòtto**) *tr* to boycott
bòl•gia *f* (**-ge**) pit (*in hell*)
bólide *m* (astr) bolide, fireball; (aut) racer; (joc) lummox; **andare come un bolide** to go like a flash
bolina *f* (naut) bowline; **di bolina** (naut) close-hauled
bolivia•no -na *adj* & *mf* Bolivian
bólla *f* bubble; blister; ticket; **bolla di consegna** receipt; **bolla di spedizione** delivery ticket; **bolla di sapone** soap bubble; **bolla papale** papal bull
bollare (**bóllo**) *tr* to stamp; to brand
bolla•to -ta *adj* stamped; sealed
bollatura *f* stamp; brand; postage
bollènte *adj* boiling, scalding hot
bollétta *f* ticket; receipt; bill; **essere in bolletta** (coll) to be broke
bollettà•rio *m* (**-ri**) receipt book
bollettino *m* bulletin; receipt; **bollettino dei prezzi correnti** price list; **bollettino di versamento** (com) deposit ticket; **bollettino meteorologico** weather forecast
bollire (**bóllo**) *tr* & *intr* to boil
bolli•to -ta *adj* boiled || *m* boiled beef
bollitura *f* boiling
bóllo *m* mark, cancellation; revenue stamp; postmark; seal; **bollo a freddo** seal (*embossed*); **bollo postale** cancellation, postmark
bollóre *m* boiling; sultriness; (fig) passion, excitement; **alzare il bollore** to begin to boil
bolló•so -sa [s] *adj* blistery
bolscevi•co -ca *adj* & *mf* (**-chi -che**) Bolshevik
bolscevismo *m* Bolshevism
ból•so -sa *adj* broken-winded (*horse*); asthmatic
bòma *f* (naut) boom
bómba *f* bomb; bubble gum; fireworks; (aer) double loop; (journ) scandal; **bomba a idrogeno** hydrogen bomb; **bomba a mano** hand grenade; **bomba antisommergibile** depth charge; **bomba a orologeria** time bomb; **bomba atomica** atom bomb; **bomba H** (*acca*) H bomb; **tornare a bomba** (fig) to get back to the point
bombàggio *m* swelling (*of a spoiled can of food*)
bombardaménto *m* bombing, bombardment
bombardare *tr* to bomb, bombard; to besiege (*with questions*)
bombardière *m* (aer) bomber; (mil) artilleryman
bombétta *f* derby (*hat*)
bómbola *f* bottle, cylinder; **bombola d'ossigeno** oxygen tank
bombonièra *f* candy box
bomprèsso *m* (naut) bowsprit
bonàc•cia *f* (**-ce**) calm; calm sea; (fig) normalcy; (com) stagnation
bonacció•ne -na *adj* good-hearted, good-natured
bonarie•tà *f* (**-tà**) kindheartedness, good nature
bonà•rio -ria *adj* (**-ri -rie**) kindhearted, good-natured
boncinèllo *m* hasp
bonìfi•ca *f* (**-che**) reclamation; re-

claimed land; improvement (*e.g., of morals*); clearing of mines; (metallurgy) hardening and tempering
bonificare §197 (**bonìfico**) *tr* to reclaim; to discount, make a reduction of; to clear of mines
bonìfi•co *m* (**-ci**) discount
bonomìa *f* good nature; simple-heartedness
bon•tà *f* (**-tà**) goodness; kindness; **avere la bontà di** to be kind enough to; **bontà mia (sua, etc.)** through my (his, her, etc.) kindness; **per mia (sua, etc.) bontà** through my (his, her, etc.) efforts
bòra *f* northeast wind
borace *m* borax
borbogliare §280 (**borbóglio**) *intr* to gurgle; to rumble
borbòni•co -ca (-ci -che) *adj* Bourbon || *m* Bourbonist
borbottare (**borbòtto**) *tr* to mutter || *intr* to mutter; to gurgle; to rumble (*said, e.g., of thunder*)
borbottì•o *m* (**-i**) mutter; gurgle; rumble
bòrchia *f* upholsterer's nail; boss, stud
bordare (**bórdo**) *tr* to border, hem
bordata *f* (naut) tack; (nav) broadside
bordatura *f* border, hem
bordeggiare §290 (**bordéggio**) *intr* (naut) to tack
bordèllo *m* brothel
borde•rò *m* (**-rò**) list; note; (theat) box office, receipts
bórdo *m* side (*of ship*); border, hem; edge, rim; (naut) tack; (naut) board; **a bordo** on board; **a bordo di** on board; on, in; **bordo d'entrata** (aer) leading edge; **bordo d'uscita** (aer) trailing edge; **d'alto bordo** (naut) big, sea-going; (fig) high-toned; **virare di bordo** (naut) to change course
bordóne *m* staff; bass stop (*of organ*); drone (*of insect*); **tener bordone a** (mus) to accompany; (fig) to hold the bag for
bordura *f* hem, edge; rim
boreale *adj* northern, boreal
borgata *f* hamlet, village
borghése [s] *adj* middle-class || *mf* bourgeois, person of the middle class; civilian; **in borghese** in civilian clothes; in plainclothes
borghesìa *f* bourgeosie, middle class; **alta borghesia** upper middle class
bór•go *m* (**-ghi**) borough; small town; suburb
borgógna *m* Burgundy (*wine*) || **la Borgogna** Burgundy
borgognóne *m* iceberg
borgomastro *m* burgomaster
bòria *f* haughtiness, vainglory
bòri•co -ca *adj* (**-ci -che**) boric
borió•so -sa [s] *adj* haughty, puffed-up; blustery
bòro *m* boron
borotal•co *m* (**-chi**) talcum powder
bórra *f* flock (*for pillows*); (fig) rubbish, filler
borràc•cia *f* (**-ce**) canteen (*e.g., for carrying water*)
bórro *m* gully
bórsa *f* bag; pouch; bourse, exchange; (sports) purse; **borsa da viaggio** traveling bag; **borsa dell'acqua** hot-water bag; **borsa della spesa** shopping bag; **borsa di ghiaccio** ice bag; **borsa di studio** scholarship; **borsa merci** commodity exchange; **borsa nera** black market; **borsa valori** stock exchange; **essere di borsa larga** to be generous; **o la borsa o la vita!** your money or your life!; **pagare di borsa propria** to pay out of one's own pocket
borsaiòlo *m* pickpocket
borsanéra *f* black market
borsaneri•sta *mf* (**-sti -ste**) black marketeer
borseggiare §290 (**borséggio**) *tr* to pick the pocket of; to rob
borseggia•tóre -trice *mf* pickpocket
borség•gio *m* (**-gi**) theft
borsellino *m* purse
borsétta *f* handbag, pocketbook
borsétto *m* man's purse
borsi•sta *mf* (**-sti -ste**) recipient of a scholarship; stockbroker
borsìsti•co -ca *adj* (**-ci -che**) stock-exchange
borsite *f* bursitis
boscàglia *f* thicket, underbrush
boscaiòlo *m* woodcutter
boscheréc•cio -cia *adj* (**-ci -ce**) wood, woodland; rustic; pastoral
boschétto *m* coppice, copse
boschi•vo -va *adj* wooded, wood
bò•sco *m* (**-schi**) woods, forest; **bosco ceduo** or **da taglio** tree farm
boscó•so -sa [s] *adj* wooded, woody
bòsforo *m* (lit) straits || **Bosforo** *m* Bosphorus
bòsso *m* boxwood
bòssolo *m* box; cartridge case
botàni•co -ca (-ci -che) *adj* botanic(al) || *m* botanist || *f* botany
bòtola *f* trap door
bòtolo *m* small snarling dog
bòtta *f* hit; bump; rumble (*e.g., of an explosion*); thrust, lunging (*in fencing*); (fig) disaster; **botta dritta** (fencing) lunge; **botta e risposta** give-and-take; **botte da orbi** severe beating
bot•tàio *m* (**-tài**) cooper
bótte *f* barrel, cask, casket
botté•ga *f* (**-ghe**) store, shop; **chiudere bottega** to close up shop
botte•gàio -gàia (-gài -gàie) *adj* store, shop || *mf* storekeeper, shopkeeper
botteghino *m* box office; lottery agency
bottìglia *f* bottle; **bottiglia Molotov** Molotov cocktail
bottiglierìa *f* wine store, liquor store
bottino *m* booty, spoil; capture; cesspool; sewage
bòtto *m* hit, bump; explosion; noise; toll (*of bell*); **di botto** all of a sudden
bottoncino *m* small button; cuff button; **bottoncino di rosa** rosebud
bottóne *m* button; stud; bud; **attaccare un bottone a** (fig) to buttonhole; **botton d'oro** (bot) buttercup; **bottone automatico** snap; **bottone della**

luce (elec) pushbutton; **bottoni gemelli** cuff links; **bottoni gustativi** taste buds
bottonièra *f* row of buttons; buttonhole; (elec) panel (*with buttons*)
bova•ro -ra *adj & m* var of **boaro**
bovile *m* ox stable
bovi•no -na *adj* cattle, cow; bovine || *m* bovine
box *m* (**box**) locker (*e.g., in a station*); box stall (*for a horse*); pit (*in auto racing*); garage (*on the ground floor of a split-level*); play pen
boxare (**bòxo**) *intr* to box
boxe *f* boxing
bòzza *f* stud, boss; bump (*caused by blow*); rough copy, draft; **bozze** (typ) galleys, galley proof
bozzèllo *m* (mach) block and tackle
bozzétto *m* sketch
bòzzolo *m* cocoon; lump (*of flour*)
bra•ca *f* (**-che**) safety belt; (naut) sling; **brache** (archaic) breeches; (joc) trousers
braccare §197 *tr* to stalk; to hunt out
braccétto—a braccetto arm in arm
bracciale *m* armlet, armband; arm rest
braccialétto *m* bracelet
bracciante *m* laborer
bracciata *f* armful; stroke (*in swimming*); **bracciata a rana** breaststroke; **bracciata sul dorso** backstroke
bràc•cio *m* (**-cia** *fpl*) arm (*of body*); unit of length (*about 60 centimeters*); **a braccia aperte** with open arms; **avere le braccia legate** to have one's hands tied; **braccia** laborers; **braccio destro** right-hand man; **braccio di ferro** Indian wrestling; **fare a braccio di ferro** to play at Indian wrestling; **sentirsi cascare le braccia** to lose courage || *m* (**-ci**) arm (*e.g., of sea, chair, lamp, etc.*); beam (*of balance*); **braccio diretto** cutoff (*of river*)
bracciòlo *m* arm; arm rest; banister
brac•co *m* (**-chi**) hound, beagle
bracconàg•gio *m* (**-gi**) poaching
bracconière *m* poacher
brace *f* embers; (coll) charcoal; **farsi di brace** to blush
brachétta *f* flap (*of trousers*); (bb) joint; **brachette** shorts
brachière *m* truss (*for hernia*)
bracière *m* brazier
braciòla *f* chop, cutlet
bra•do -da *adj* wild, untamed
bra•go *m* (**-ghi**) (lit) mud, slime
brama *f* ardent desire; covetousness; longing
bramare *tr* to desire intensely; to covet; to long for
bramino *m* Brahmin
bramire §176 *intr* to roar; to bell (*said of a deer*)
bramito *m* bell (*of deer*)
bramosìa [s] *f* covetousness; greed
bramó•so -sa [s] *adj* (lit) covetous, greedy
bran•ca *f* (**-che**) branch (*of tree*); flight (*of stairs*); **branche** (poet) clutches
brànchia *f* gill
brancicare §197 (**bràncico**) *tr* to finger, handle || *intr* to grope
bran•co *m* (**-chi**) flock, herd; (pej) crowd
brancolare (**bràncolo**) *intr* to grope
branda *f* cot
brandèllo *m* tatter, shred
brandire §176 *tr* to brandish
brando *m* (lit) sword
brano *m* shred, bit; excerpt; **cadere a brani** to fall apart; **fare a brani** to tear apart
brasare *tr* to braze (*to solder with brass*); (culin) to braise
brasile *m* brazil (*nut*) || **il Brasile** Brazil
brasilia•no -na *adj & mf* Brazilian
bravàc•cio *m* (**-ci**) braggart, swaggerer
bravare *tr* to challenge; to threaten || *intr* to brag
bravata *f* swagger, bluster; boast; stunt
bra•vo -va *adj* good, able; honest; goodhearted; brave; **alla brava** rapidly; **bravo ragazzo** good boy; **fare il bravo** to boast, be a braggart || *m* mercenary soldier; bravo, hired assassin || **bravo!** *interj* well done!, bravo!
bravura *f* ability; bravery; bravura
brèc•cia *f* (**-ce**) breach, gap; crushed stone
brefotrò•fio *m* (**-fi**) foundling hospital
Bretagna, la Britanny
bretèlla *f* suspenders; strap, shoulder strap
brètone *adj* Breton; Arthurian
brève *adj* brief, short; **in breve** in a nutshell; **per farla breve** in short || *m* (eccl) brief || *adv* (lit) in short
brevettare (**brevétto**) *tr* to patent
brevétto *m* patent; (aer) license; (obs) commission
brevià•rio *m* (**-ri**) compendium; handbook, vade mecum; (eccl) breviary
brevi•tà *f* (**-tà**) brevity
brézza [ddzz] *f* breeze
brezzare (**brézzo**) [ddzz] *tr* to winnow || *intr* to blow gently
bricchétta *f* briquet
bric•co *m* (**-chi**) kettle, pot
bricconata *f* rascality
briccó•ne -na *mf* rascal
bricconerìa *f* rascality
brìciola *f* crumb; **ridurre in briciole** to crumb, crumble
brìciolo *m* bit, fragment; (fig) least bit; **andare in bricioli** to crumble; **mandare in bricioli** to crumble
bri•ga *f* (**-ghe**) worry, trouble, **attaccar briga** to pick a fight; **darsi la briga di** to worry about; **trovarsi in una briga** to be in trouble
brigadière *m* noncommissioned officer (*in carabinieri*); (hist) brigadier
brigantàg•gio *m* (**-gi**) brigandage
brigante *m* brigand
brigantino *m* (naut) brig, brigantine; **brigantino goletta** (naut) brigantine
brigare §209 *tr* to plot; to scheme to get || *intr* to plot, scheme
brigata *f* company; (mil) brigade
brì•glia *f* (**-glie**) bridle; harness (*for holding baby*); (naut) bobstay; **a briglia sciolta** at full speed; **tirare le briglie a** to bridle
brillante *adj* brilliant || *m* cut diamond

brillare *tr* to husk, hull (*rice*); to explode (*e.g., a mine*) || *intr* to shine, sparkle; **far brillare** to explode, blow up
brillì·o *m* (**-i**) shine, sparkle
bril·lo -la *adj* tipsy
brina *f* frost
brinare *tr* to frost; to turn (*e.g., hair*) gray || *impers* (ESSERE)—**è brinato** there was frost; **brina** there is frost
brinata *f* frost
brindare *intr* to toast; **brindare alla salute di** to toast
brìndisi *m* (**-si**) toast; pledge; **fare un brindisi a** to toast
bri·o *m* (**-i**) sprightliness, liveliness, verve, spirit
briò·scia *f* (**-sce**) brioche
briò·so -sa [s] *adj* sprightly, lively
briscola *f* briscola (*game*); trump (*card*)
britànni·co -ca *adj* (**-ci -che**) British, Britannic
britan·no -na *adj* British || *mf* Briton
brìvido *m* shake, shiver; thrill; **brivido di freddo** chill, shiver
brizzola·to -ta *adj* grizzled
bròc·ca *f* (**-che**) pitcher; pitcherful; shoot, bud; hobnail
broccatèllo *m* brocatel
broccato *m* brocade
bròc·co *m* (**-chi**) twig; shoot; center pin (*of shield or target*); (coll) nag; **dar nel brocco** to hit the bull's eye
bròccolo *m* (bot) broccoli; **broccoli** broccoli (*as food*)
bròda *f* slop, thin or tasteless soup; mud
brodàglia *f* slop
brodétto *m* fish soup
bròdo *m* broth; **andar in brodo di giuggiole** (fig) to swoon with joy; **brodo in dadi** cube bouillon; **brodo ristretto** consommé
brodó·so -sa [s] *adj* thin, watery (*soup*)
brogliàc·cio *m* (**-ci**) (com) daybook, first draft; (naut) first draft of logbook
brò·glio *m* (**-gli**) plot, intrigue; maneuver; **broglio elettorale** political maneuver
bròlo *m* (archaic) garden; (lit) garland
bromìdri·co -ca *adj* (**-ci -che**) hydrobromic
bròmo *m* bromine
bromuro *m* bromide
bronchite *f* bronchitis
brón·cio *m* (**-ci**) pout, pouting; **fare il broncio** to sulk; **tenere il broncio a** to harbor a grudge against
brón·co *m* (**-chi**) bronchial tube; thorny branch; ramification (*of antlers*)
brontolare (**bróntolo**) *tr* to grumble (*to express with a grumble*); to grumble at || *intr* to grumble, mutter; to rumble; to gurgle (*said of water*)
brontolì·o *m* (**-i**) grumble, mutter; rumble; gurgle
brontoló·ne -na *mf* grumbler; curmudgeon
bronzare [dz] (**brónzo**) *tr* to bronze
brónze·o -a [dz] *adj* bronze; tanned
bronzina [dz] *f* little bell; (mach) bearing; (mach) bushing
brónzo [dz] *m* bronze
brossura *f* brochure; **in brossura** paperback
brucare §197 *tr* to browse, graze
bruciacchiare §287 *tr* to singe
bruciante *adj* burning
bruciapélo *m*—**a bruciapelo** point-blank
bruciare §128 *tr* to burn; to burn down; to singe; to scorch; to cauterize (*a wound*); (sports) to overcome with a burst of speed; **bruciare le tappe** to go straight ahead; to press on || *intr* (ESSERE) to burn; to smart, sting || *ref* to burn (*e.g., one's fingers*); to get burnt; to blow (*one's brains*) out; to burn out (*said of an electric light or fuse*); **bruciarsi i vascelli alle spalle** to burn one's bridges behind one
bruciatìc·cio *m* (**-ci**) burnt material; **sapere di bruciaticcio** to taste burnt
brucia·to -ta *adj* burnt; burnt out || *m* burnt taste or smell || *f* roast chestnut
bruciatóre *m* burner; heater; **bruciatore a gas** gas burner; **bruciatore a nafta** oil burner
bruciatori·sta *m* (**-sti**) oil burner mechanic
bruciatura *f* burn
brucióre *m* burning; burn; inflammation; **bruciore agli occhi** eye inflammation; **bruciore di stomaco** heartburn
bru·co *m* (**-chi**) caterpillar; worm
brùffolo *m* (coll) small boil
brughièra *f* waste land; heath
brulicare §197 (**brùlico**) *intr* to crawl; to swarm (*e.g., with bees*); to teem (*with people*)
brulichì·o *m* (**-i**) crawling; swarming; teeming
brul·lo -la *adj* barren, bare
bruma *f* shipworm; (lit) fog; (lit) winter
bruna·stro -stra *adj* brownish
brunire §176 *tr* to burnish
bru·no -na *adj* brown; dark (*bread; complexion*) || *m* brown; dark; brunet; **vestire a bruno** to dress in black || *f* brunette
bru·sca *f* (**-sche**) horse brush; **con le brusche** curtly
bruschézza *f* brusqueness
bruschino *m* scrub brush
bru·sco -sca (**-schi -sche**) *adj* sour; curt, gruff; sharp (*weather*); dangerous; sudden || *m* twig || *f* see **brusca**
brùscolo *m* speck, mote; **fare di un bruscolo una trave** to make a mountain out of a molehill
brusì·o *m* (**-i**) buzz, buzzing; (fig) whispering (*gossip*)
brutale *adj* brutal
brutali·tà *f* (**-tà**) brutality
brutalizzare [ddzz] *tr* to brutalize
bru·to -ta *adj & m* brute
brutta *f* rough copy
bruttare *tr* (lit) to soil
bruttézza *f* ugliness; (fig) lowliness
brut·to -ta *adj* ugly, homely; foul (*weather*); bad (*news*); **alle brutte** at the worst; **con le brutte** harshly; **farla brutta a** to play a mean trick on;

guardare brutto to look irritated; **vedersela brutta** to foresee trouble || *m* worst; bad weather || *f* see **brutta**
bruttura *f* ugliness
bùbbola *f* lie; trifle
bùbbolo *m* jingle bell (*on horse*)
bubbòni•co -ca *adj* (**-ci -che**) bubonic
bu•ca *f* (**-che**) hole; pit; hollow; **buca cieca** trap (*for hunting*); **buca del biliardo** pocket; **buca delle lettere** mailbox; **buca del suggeritore** prompter's box; **buca sepolcrale** grave
bucané•ve *m* (**-ve**) snowdrop
bucanière *m* buccaneer
bucare §197 *tr* to pierce; to prick; to puncture (*a tire*)
bucato *m* wash; laundry; **di bucato** freshly laundered; **fare il bucato in famiglia** (fig) to not air one's family affairs, to not wash one's dirty linen in public
bucatura *f* piercing; puncturing; puncture; **bucatura di una gomma** flat tire
bùc•cia *f* (**-ce**) rind, peel; skin (*of a person; of fruit and vegetables*); tender bark; **fare le bucce a** (coll) to thwart, frustrate
bucherellare (bucherèllo) *tr* to riddle
bu•co *m* (**-chi**) hole; **fare un buco nell'acqua** to fail miserably
bucòli•co -ca *adj* (**-ci -che**) bucolic, pastoral
Budda *m* Buddha
buddismo *m* Buddhism
buddi•sta *mf* (**-sti -ste**) Buddhist
budèl•lo *m* (**-la** *fpl*) bowel; **budella** bowels; guts || *m* (**-li**) casing (*for salami*); pipe; blind alley
budino *m* pudding
bùe *m* (**buòi**) ox (*for draft*); steer (*for meat*); **bue muschiato** musk ox
bùfalo *m* buffalo
bufèra *f* storm; **bufera di neve** snowstorm; **bufera di pioggia** rainstorm; **bufera di vento** windstorm
buffa *f* cowl; gust of wind; (archaic) trick, jest
buffare *tr* to huff (*at checkers*) || *intr* to joke; (archaic) to blow
buffetterìa *f* (mil) accouterments
buffétto *m* tap, slight blow
buf•fo -fa *adj* funny, comical || *m* gust of wind; comic || *f* see **buffa**
buffonata *f* buffoonery; antics
buffóne *m* buffoon, clown; (hist) jester; **buffone di corte** court jester
buffonerìa *f* buffoonery
buffoné•sco -sca *adj* (**-schi -sche**) clownish
bugìa *f* lie; candlestick; **bugia ufficiosa** white lie
bugiar•do -da *adj* lying, false || *mf* liar
bugigàttolo *m* cubbyhole
bugna *f* ashlar; (naut) clew
bugnato *m* ashlar; (archit) boss
bù•io -ia (*pl* **-i -ie**) *adj* dark || *m* darkness; **buio pesto** pitch dark
bulbo *m* bulb
bùlga•ro -ra *adj & mf* Bulgarian || *m* Russian leather
bulinare *tr* to engrave
bulino *m* burin
bullétta *f* tack
bullonare (bullóno) *tr* to bolt
bullóne *m* bolt
buon *adj* apocopated form of **buono,** used before masculine singular nouns except those beginning with impure **s, z, gn, ps,** and **x**
buon' *adj* apocopated form of **buona** used before feminine singular nouns beginning with a vowel, e.g., **buon'ora**
buonagràzia *f* (**buonegràzie**) courtesy, good manners; **con Sua buonagrazia** with your permission
buonamano *f* (**buonemani**) tip, gratuity
buonànima *f* departed; **la buonanima di** the late lamented
buonavò•glia *m* (**-glia**) intern (*in a hospital*); (coll) lazybones || *f* good will
buoncostume *m* morals
buongu•stàio *m* (**-stài**) gourmet; connoisseur
buò•no -na *adj* good; kind; high (*society*); cheap (*price*); **alla buona** plainly; without ceremony; **buono a nulla** good-for-nothing; **con le buone** kindly, gently; **che Dio la mandi buona a** may God be kind with; **essere in buona con** to be on good terms with || *m* good person; bond; ticket; **buono a nulla** ne'er-do-well; **buono del tesoro** government bond; **buono di consegna** delivery order; **buono premio** trading stamp
buonsènso *m* common sense
buontempó•ne -na *adj* jolly || *m* playboy || *f* fun-loving girl; playgirl
buonumóre *m* good humor, good cheer
buonuscita *f* indemnity, bonus; severance pay
burattare *tr* to sift
buratti•nàio *m* (**-nài**) puppeteer; puppet maker
burattinata *f* clowning
burattino *m* puppet
buratto *m* sifter, sifting machine
burbanza *f* haughtiness, arrogance
burbanzó•so -sa [s] *adj* haughty, arrogant
bùrbe•ro -ra *adj* gruff, surly
bùr•chio *m* (**-chi**) (naut) lighter
burgun•do -da *adj & mf* Burgundian
burla *f* joke, jest; prank; **mettere in burla** to ridicule; **fuori di burla** joking aside
burlare *tr* to ridicule || *intr* to be joking || *ref*—**burlarsi di** to make fun of
burlé•sco -sca (**-schi -sche**) *adj* funny; mocking; burlesque; jocose || *m* burlesque; mock-heroic
burlétta *f* joke, jest; **mettere in burletta** to ridicule
burló•ne -na *mf* joker, jester
burócrate *m* bureaucrat
burocràti•co -ca *adj* (**-ci -che**) bureaucratic; clerical (*error*)
burocrazìa *f* bureaucracy; red tape
burra•sca *f* (**-sche**) storm
burrascó•so -sa [s] *adj* stormy
burrièra *f* butter dish
burrifi•cio *m* (**-ci**) butter factory, dairy
burro *m* butter
burróne *m* canyon, ravine
burró•so -sa [s] *adj* buttery

buscare §197 *tr* to get; to catch || *intr* to be damaged || *ref*—**buscarsi un malanno** to catch a cold
busécchia *f* casing (*for sausage*)
busillis *m*—**qui sta il busillis** here's the rub, that's the trouble
bussa *f* hit, blow; **venire alle busse** to come to blows
bussare *intr* to knock; **bussare a quattrini** (fig) to hit somebody for a loan
bussata *f* knock (*at the door*)
bussa·tòio *m* (**-tòi**) knocker
bùssola *f* sedan chair; door; revolving door; swinging door; ballot box; (mach) bushing; (aer & naut) compass; **perdere la bussola** to lose one's bearings
bussolòtto *m* dice box
busta *f* envelope; briefcase; **busta a finestrella** window envelope; **busta primo giorno** first-day cover; **in busta a parte** under separate cover
bustapa·ga *f* (**-ga**) pay envelope
bustarèlla *f* bribery; kickback
bustina *f* powder, dose; small envelope; (mil) cap, fatigue cap
busto *m* chest, trunk; bust; corset
butirró·so -sa [s] *adj* buttery
buttafuò·ri *m* (**-ri**) bouncer (*in a night club*); (theat) callboy; (naut) outrigger
buttare *tr* to throw; to waste (*e.g., time*); to give off (*e.g., smoke*); **buttar giù** to demolish; to swallow; (fig) to discredit; to jot down; **buttar via** to throw away; to cast aside || *intr* to secrete, ooze || *ref* to throw oneself; to let oneself fall; **buttarsi giù** (fig) to become downcast
butterare (**bùttero**) *tr* to pock, pit
bùttero *m* pockmark; cowboy
buzzo [ddzz] *m* (vulg) belly; **di buzzo buono** with energy; willingly

C

C, c [tʃi] *m & f* third letter of the Italian alphabet
càbala *f* cabala; cabal, intrigue
cabina *f* cabin, stateroom; car, cage (*of elevator*); cockpit (*of airplane*); booth (*of telephone*); cab (*of locomotive*)
cablàg·gio *m* (**-gi**) (elec) cable (*in auto or radio*)
cablare *tr* to cable
cablografare (**cablògrafo**) *tr* to cable
cablogram·ma *m* (**-mi**) cablegram, cable
cabotàg·gio *m* (**-gi**) coasting trade, coastal traffic
cabrare *intr* to zoom
cabrata *f* zoom
cacào *m* cocoa
cacasènno *m* (slang) wiseacre
cacatò·a *m* (**-a**) cockatoo
càc·cia *m* (**-cia**) pursuit plane, fighter; (nav) destroyer || *f* chase, hunt; pursuit; **caccia alle streghe** witch hunt
cacciagióne *f* small game; venison; kill (*e.g., of game birds*)
cacciapiè·tre *m* (**-tre**) (rr) cowcatcher
cacciare §128 *tr* to hunt; to chase; to rout; to send out; to stick, thrust; to utter (*e.g., a cry*); **cacciar fuori** to pull out; **cacciar via** to chase away || *ref* to hide; to intrude; to get; to wind up; to thrust oneself; **cacciarsi negli affari di** to butt into the affairs of
cacciasommergìbi·li *m* (**-li**) subchaser, submarine chaser
cacciata *f* hunting party; expulsion
cacciatóra *f* hunting jacket; **alla cacciatora** (culin) stewed with herbs
cacciatóre *m* hunter; (aer) fighter pilot; **cacciatore di frodo** poacher; **cacciatore di teste** headhunter
cacciatorpedinie̊·re *m* (**-re**) destroyer
cacciatrice *f* huntress
cacciavi·te *m* (**-te**) screwdriver
càccola *f* gum (*on edge of eyelid*); (slang) snot
caccoló·so -sa [s] *adj* gummy (*eyelid*); (slang) snotty
ca·chi (**-chi**) *adj* khaki || *m* Japanese persimmon; khaki
cacic·co *m* (**-chi**) Indian chief; boss (*in Latin America*)
cà·cio *m* (**-ci**) cheese; **come il cacio sui maccheroni** (coll) at the right moment
cacofóni·co -ca *adj* (**-ci -che**) cacophonous
cac·tus *m* (**-tus**) cactus
cadau·no -na *adj* each || *pron* each one
cadàvere *m* corpse, cadaver
cadavèri·co -ca *adj* (**-ci -che**) cadaverous
cadènte *adj* falling (*star*); rickety (*house*); run-down, decrepit (*person*)
cadènza *f* cadence, rhythm; accent (*peculiar to a region*)
cadére §121 *intr* (ESSERE) to fall; to sink; to slough (*said, e.g., of crust*); to fail; (gram) to end; **cadere a proposito** to come in handy; to come at the right moment; **cadere dalle nuvole** to be dumfounded
cadétto *m* cadet
càdmio *m* cadmium
caducità *f* transiency, brevity
cadu·co -ca *adj* (**-ci -che**) fleeting; deciduous
cadu·no -na *adj & pron* var of **cadauno**
cadu·to -ta *adj* fallen; lost, gone astray; **i caduti** the fallen, the dead || *f* fall; crash (*of stock market*); slump (*of prices*)
caf·fè *m* (**-fè**) coffee; café
caffeina *f* caffeine
caffetteria *f* cafeteria
caffettièra *f* coffeepot

cafó·ne -na *adj* loud, gaudy || *m* boor, lout
cagionare (cagióno) *tr* to cause, produce
cagióne *f* cause, reason; **a cagione di** because of
cagionévole *adj* sickly, delicate
cagliare §280 *tr, intr* (ESSERE) & *ref* to curdle, curd
cagliata *f* curd
cà·glio *m* **(-gli)** rennet
cagna *f* bitch
cagnara *f* barking (*of dogs*); uproar, confusion
cagné·sco -sca (-schi -sche) *adj* dog-like, doggish || *m*—**guardare in cagnesco** to look askance at; **stare in cagnesco con** to be angry with
Caino *m* Cain
Càiro, il Cairo
cala *f* cove; (naut) hold
calabrése [s] *adj* & *mf* Calabrian
calabróne *m* hornet
calafatare *tr* (naut) to caulk
cala·màio *m* **(-mài)** inkwell
calamaro *m* squid
calamita *f* magnet; (*mineral*) loadstone; (fig) magnet, attraction
calami·tà *f* **(-tà)** calamity, disaster
calamitare *tr* to magnetize
calamitó·so -sa [s] *adj* calamitous
càlamo *m* reed, quill
calandra *f* calender; (aut) grille
calandrare *tr* to calender
calante *adj* waning (*moon*)
calàp·pio *m* **(-pi)** snare; noose
calapran·zi *m* **(-zi)** dumbwaiter
calare *tr* to lower; to strike (*sails*) || *intr* (ESSERE) to fall, sag (*said, e.g., of prices*); to grow shorter (*said of days*); to come down; to shrink (*said, e.g., of meat*); to lose weight; to set (*said, e.g., of the sun*); to wane (*said of the moon*); (mus) to drop in pitch || *ref* to let oneself down; to dive
calata *f* lowering; descent; invasion; fall; wharf; (coll) intonation; **calata del sole** sunset
cal·ca *f* **(-che)** crowd, throng
calca·gno *m* **(-gni)** heel || *m* **(-gna** *fpl*) (fig) heel; **alle calcagna di** at the heels of
calcare *m* limestone || §197 *tr* to trample; to trace (*on paper*); to tread (*the boards*); to emphasize; **calcare la mano** to exaggerate; **calcare le orme di** to follow in the footsteps of
calce *m*—**in calce** at the foot of the page; **in calce a** at the foot of || *f* lime; **calce viva** quicklime
calcedònio *m* chalcedony
calcestruzzo *m* concrete
calciare §128 *tr* & *intr* to kick
calciatóre *m* soccer player; football player
calcificare §197 **(calcìfico)** *tr* & *ref* to calcify
calcificazióne *f* calcification
calcina *f* mortar; lime
calcinàc·cio *m* **(-ci)** flake of plaster; **calcinacci** ruins, rubble
calci·nàio *m* **(-nài)** lime pit
calcinare *tr* to calcine; to lime (*e.g., a field*)
càl·cio *m* **(-ci)** kick; soccer; calcium; (*e.g., of rifle*) butt; **calcio d'inizio** (sports) kickoff
calciocianamide *m* calcium cyanamide
cal·co *m* **(-chi)** tracing; cast; imprint
calcografia *f* copper engraving
calcolare (càlcolo) *tr* to calculate; to estimate, reckon; to compute; to consider
calcola·tóre -trice *adj* calculating || *m* calculator; computer; schemer || *f* calculating machine, adding machine
càlcolo *m* calculation; estimate; planning; calculus; (pathol) calculus, stone; **calcolo biliare** gallstone; **calcolo errato** miscalculation; **fare calcolo su** to count upon
calcolò·si *f* **(-si)** (pathol) stones
calcomanìa *f* decalcomania
caldàia *f* boiler
cal·dàio *m* **(-dài)** cauldron, boiler
caldalléssa *f* boiled chestnut
caldana *f* flush
caldano *m* brazier
caldarròsta *f* roast chestnut
caldeggiare §290 **(caldéggio)** *tr* to favor, support; to recommend
calde·ràio *m* **(-rài)** coppersmith; boilermaker
calderóne *m* cauldron
cal·do -da *adj* warm; hot; rich (*voice*); **caldo, caldo** quite recent || *m* heat; warmth; **aver caldo** to be warm (*said of people*); to be hot (*said of people*); **fa caldo** it is warm; it is hot; **non mi fa nè caldo nè freddo** it leaves me cold, it does not move me
calefazióne *f* heating
caleidoscò·pio *m* **(-pi)** kaleidoscope
calendà·rio *m* **(-ri)** calendar
calènde *fpl*—**calende greche** Greek calends
calendimàggio *m* May Day
calèsse *m* buggy, gig
calére *impers*—**non mi cale** (lit) I don't care
calettare (calétto) *tr* to dovetail, mortise || *intr* to fit
calibrare (càlibro) *tr* to gauge, calibrate
càlibro *m* caliber; (mach) callipers; (fig) quality, importance
càlice *m* wine cup; (bot) calyx; (eccl) chalice
cali·cò *m* **(-cò)** calico
califfo *m* caliph
calìgine *f* fog, mist; (fig) darkness
caliginó·so -sa [s] *adj* foggy, misty; (fig) dark, gloomy
calla *f*—**calla dei fioristi** calla lily
calle *f* lane, alley
callifu·go *m* **(-ghi)** corn remedy
calligrafia *f* penmanship; handwriting
calli·sta *mf* **(-sti -ste)** chiropodist
callo *m* corn; callus; **fare il callo a** to get used to; **pestare i calli a qlcu** to step on s.o.'s feet
callosi·tà [s] *f* **(-tà)** callosity; callus
calló·so -sa [s] *adj* corny; callous; hard
calma *f* calm, tranquillity

calmante *adj* sedative, calming, soothing || *m* sedative
calmare *tr* to calm, soothe, appease || *ref* to calm down; to subside, abate
calmierare (calmièro) *tr* to fix the price of
calmière *m* ceiling price; price control
cal·mo -ma *adj* calm, quiet, still || *f* see **calma**
calo *m* decrease; shrinkage
calomelano *m* calomel
calóre *m* heat; warmth; fervor, ardor; (pathol) rash, inflammation; (vet) rut, mating season
caloria *f* calorie
calòri·co -ca *adj* **(-ci -che)** caloric
calorìfero *m* heater, radiator
caloró·so -sa [s] *adj* warm; hot; cordial; heated
calò·scia *f* **(-sce)** var of **galoscia**
calòtta *f* skullcap; case (*e.g., of watch*); (aut) hubcap; (mach) cap; **calotta cranica** skull
calpestare (calpésto) *tr* to trample
calpestì·o *m* **(-ì)** trampling
calùgine *f* down (*of bird*)
calùnnia *f* calumny, slander
calunniare §287 *tr* to calumniate, slander
calunnia·tóre -trice *mf* slanderer
calunnió·so -sa [s] *adj* slanderous
Calvàrio *m* (Bib) Calvary
calvìzie *f* baldness
cal·vo -va *adj* bald
calza *f* sock; stocking; wick; **calza da donna** stocking; **calze** hose, hosiery; **fare la calza** to knit
calzamàglia *f* tights
calzare *m* footwear || *tr* to wear, put on (*shoes, gloves, or socks*) || *intr* to fit (*said of any garment*); to suit
calzascar·pe *m* **(-pe)** shoehorn
calza·tóio *m* **(-tói)** shoehorn
calzatura *f* footwear; **calzature** footwear
calzaturière *m* shoe manufacturer
calzaturiè·ro -ra *adj* shoe (*e.g., industry*) || *m* shoe worker
calzaturifi·cio *m* **(-ci)** shoe factory
calzeròtto *m* woolen sock
calzet·tàio *m* **(-tài)** hosier
calzettóne *m* knee-high woolen sock (*for mountain boots*)
calzifi·cio *m* **(-ci)** hosiery mill
calzino *m* sock; **calzini corti** socks; half hose; **calzini lunghi** knee-high socks
calzo·làio *m* **(-lài)** shoemaker; cobbler
calzolerìa *f* shoemaker's shop; shoe store
calzoncini *mpl* shorts
calzóne *m* trouser leg; **calzoni** trousers, pants; slacks; **calzoni a zampe d'elefante** bell-bottom trousers, flares
camaleònte *m* chameleon
camarilla *f* cabal, clique
cambiadi·schi *m* **(-schi)** record changer
cambiale *f* promissory note, IOU
cambiaménto *m* change, modification
cambiare §287 *tr* to change, exchange; to shift (*gears*) || *intr* to change, switch || *ref* to change (*clothing*); **cambiarsi in** to turn into
cambiavalu·te *m* **(-te)** moneychanger
càm·bio *m* **(-bi)** change; switch; rate of exchange; (mil) relief; **cambio a cloche** shift lever, stick; **cambio di velocità** gearshift; **in cambio di** in exchange for, in place of
cambrètta *f* staple (*to hold a wire*)
cam·brì *m* **(-brì)** cambric
cambusa *f* (naut) galley
cambusière *m* steward
càmera *f* room; bedroom; chamber; **camera ardente** funeral parlor; **Camera dei comuni** House of Commons; **Camera dei deputati** House of Representatives; **camera d'aria** inner tube; **camera di sicurezza** detention cell; vault (*of bank*)
camera·ta *m* **(-ti)** friend, comrade || *f* dormitory; barracks; roomful (*of students or soldiers*)
cameratismo *m* comradeship
camerièra *f* waitress; maid, chambermaid
camerière *m* waiter; steward; valet
camerino *m* small room; toilet, lavatory; (nav) noncommissioned officer's quarters; (theat) dressing room
càmice *m* gown (*of physician*); smock (*of painter*); (eccl) alb
camicerìa *f* shirt store; shirt factory
camicétta *f* blouse
camìcia *f* shirt; casing, jacket (*e.g., of boiler*); lining (*e.g., of furnace*); vest (*of sailor*); folder; **camicia da giorno** chemise; **camicia da notte** nightgown; **camicia di forza** strait jacket; **camicia di maglia** coat of mail; **camicia nera** black shirt (*Fascist*); **camicia rossa** red shirt (*Garibaldine*); **dare la camicia** to give the shirt off one's back; **essere nato con la camicia** to be born with a silver spoon in one's mouth; **perdere la camicia** to lose one's shirt
cami·ciàio -ciàia *mf* **(-ciài -ciàie)** shirtmaker, haberdasher
camiciòla *f* sport shirt; undershirt; T-shirt; (obs) vest
camiciòtto *m* smock (*of mechanic*); jumper; sport shirt
caminétto *m* small fireplace; fireplace
camino *m* fireplace; chimney, smokestack; shaft (*in mountain*); mouth (*of volcano*); (naut) funnel
cà·mion *m* **(-mion)** truck
camionale *f* highway
camioncino *m* small truck; panel truck, pickup truck
camionétta *f* small truck; van (*e.g., of police*)
camioni·sta *m* **(-sti)** truckdriver, teamster
camma *f* (mach) cam; (mach) wiper
cammellière *m* camel driver
cammèllo *m* camel
cammèo *m* cameo
camminaménto *m* (mil) communication trench
camminare *intr* to walk; to go, run
camminata *f* walk; gait; (obs) hall with fireplace
cammina·tóre -trice *mf* walker; runner

cammino *m* road, way, route; path (*e.g., of the moon*); course; journey; **cammin facendo** on the way; **cammino battuto** beaten path; **cammino coperto** (mil) covered way; **mettersi in cammino** to set out, start out
camomilla *f* camomile
camòrra *f* underworld
camò•scio *m* (**-sci**) chamois
campagna *f* country; countryside; country property; season (*for harvesting*); campaign; **andare in campagna** to go on vacation (in the country)
campagnò•lo -la *adj* country, rural ‖ *mf* peasant
campale *adj* field (*artillery*); pitched, decisive (*battle*)
campana *f* bell; bell glass, bell jar; lamp shade; (archit) bell; **a campana** bell-bottomed; **campana a martello** alarm bell, tocsin; **campana di vetro** bell glass; **campana pneumatica** caisson
campanàc•cio *m* (**-ci**) cowbell
campanaro *m* bell ringer; (archaic) bell founder
campanèlla *f* small bell; door knocker; curtain ring; (bot) bluebell
campanèllo *m* bell; small bell; doorbell, chimes; **campanello d'allarme** alarm bell
campanile *m* steeple, belfry; native city or town
campanilismo *m* parochialism
campano *m* cowbell
campare *tr* to keep alive; to save; to bring out the details of ‖ *intr* (ESSERE) to live; to survive; **si campa** one ekes out a living
campa•to -ta *adj*—**campato in aria** without any foundation ‖ *f* span
campeggiare §290 (**campéggio**) *intr* to camp, encamp; to stand out
campeggia•tóre -trice *mf* camper
campég•gio *m* (**-gi**) camping, outing; campground; (bot) logwood
campeggi•sta *mf* (**-sti -ste**) camper
campèstre *adj* field, country; (sports) cross-country
campidò•glio *m* (**-gli**) capitol ‖ **Campidoglio** *m* Capitoline (*hill*); Capitol (*temple*)
campionare (**campióno**) *tr* to sample
campionà•rio -ria (**-ri -rie**) *adj* of samples; trade (*exposition*) ‖ *m* sample book, catalogue, pattern book
campionato *m* championship, title
campióne *m* champion; sample; specimen; standard; **campione senza valore** uninsured parcel, sample post
campionéssa *f* championess
campionissimo *m* world champion, ace
campo *m* field; camp; ground; tennis court; golf course; center (*e.g., for refugees*); **campo addestramento** training camp; **campo d'aviazione** airfield, airport; **campo di battaglia** battlefield; **campo petrolifero** oil field; **lasciare il campo** to retreat; **mettere in campo** to bring up, adduce; **piantare il campo** to pitch camp

camposanto *m* cemetery, churchyard
camuffare *tr* to disguise, mask; to camouflage ‖ *ref* to disguise oneself
camu•so -sa *adj* snub-nosed
Canadà, il Canada
canadése [s] *adj & mf* Canadian
canàglia *f* scoundrel; rabble
canagliata *f* knavery, mean trick
canale *m* canal; irrigation ditch; network (*of communications*); pipe, drain; (anat) duct, tract; (rad, telv) channel; (theat) aisle; **Canale della Manica** English Channel; **Canale di Panama** Panama Canal; **Canale di Suez** Suez Canal
canalizzare [ddzz] *tr* to channel; to install pipes in; (elec) to wire
canalizzazióne [ddzz] *f* channeling; piping; ductwork; (elec) wiring
canalóne *m* ravine
cànapa *f* hemp
cana•pè *m* (**-pè**) sofa, couch; (culin) canapé
cànapo *m* rope, cable
Canàrie, le the Canaries
canarino *m* canary
cancàn *m* noise, racket
cancellare (**cancèllo**) *tr* to cancel, erase; to obliterate; to write off (*a debt*); to scratch (*a horse*) ‖ *ref* to vanish, fade
cancellata *f* railing
cancellatura *f* erasure
cancellazióne *f* cancellation; erasure (*of a tape*)
cancelleria *f* chancellery; stationery
cancellière *m* chancellor; court clerk; registrar, recorder
cancèllo *m* gate, railing, grating
canceró•so -sa [s] *adj* cancerous ‖ *mf* cancer victim
cànchero *m* trouble; troublesome person; (coll) cancer
cancrèna *f* gangrene; **andare in cancrena** to become gangrenous
cancrenó•so -sa [s] *adj* gangrenous
cancro *m* cancer; (bot) canker ‖ **Cancro** *m* (astr) Cancer
candeggiante *adj* bleaching ‖ *m* bleaching agent, bleach
candeggiare §290 (**candéggio**) *tr* to bleach
candeggina *f* bleach
candég•gio *m* (**-gi**) bleaching
candéla *f* candle; candlestick; candlepower; (aut) spark plug; **studiare a lume di candela** to burn the midnight oil; **tenere la candela a** to favor the love affair of
candelabro *m* candelabrum
candelière *m* candlestick
candelòra *f* Candlemas
candelòtto *m* big wax candle; **candelotto lacrimogeno** tear-gas canister
candida•to -ta *mf* candidate
candidatura *f* candidature, candidacy
càndi•do -da *adj* white; candid
candire §176 *tr* to candy
candi•to -ta *adj* candied ‖ *m* candied fruit
candóre *m* whiteness; candor
cane *m* dog; hound; hammer, cock (*of gun*); ham actor; **cane barbone**

poodle; **cane bastardo** mongrel; **cane da ferma** setter; **cane da guardia** watchdog; **cane da presa** retriever; **cane da punta** pointer; **cane grosso** big shot; **cane guida per ciechi** seeing eye dog; **cane sciolto** (pol) lone wolf; **come un cane** all alone; **come un cane in chiesa** as an unwelcome guest; **da cani** poorly; **menare il can per l'aia** to beat around the bush; **non c'è un cane** there is nobody there; **raddrizzare le gambe ai cani** to perform an impossible task
canèstro *m* basket
cànfora *f* camphor
cangiante *adj* changeable (*color*); changing, iridescent
canguro *m* kangaroo
canìcola *f* dog days
canile *m* doghouse, kennel
canino *adj* canine || *m* canine tooth
canìzie *f* gray hair; head of gray hair; old age
canna *f* cane, reed; rod (*for fishing or measuring*); pipe (*of organ*); barrel (*of gun*); **canna da zucchero** sugar cane; **canna di caduta** disposal chute; **canna fumaria** chimney; **canna della gola** (coll) windpipe
cannèlla *f* small tube; tap (*of barrel*); cinnamon
cannèllo *m* pipe, tube; stick (*e.g., of licorice*); (chem) pipette; **cannello ossiacetilenico** acetylene torch; **cannello ossidrico** oxyhydrogen blowpipe
cannellóni *mpl* cannelloni
cannéto *m* cane field
cannìbale *m* cannibal
cannìc·cio *m* (**-ci**) wicker frame; shade made out of rushes
cannocchiale *m* spyglass; **cannocchiale astronomico** telescope
cannonata *f* cannonade, cannon shot; (slang) hit
cannoncino *m* small gun; **cannoncino antiaereo** antiaircraft gun
cannóne *m* gun, cannon; pipe, stovepipe; box pleat; shin (*of cattle*); **è un cannone** (coll) he's the tops
cannoneggiare §290 (**cannonéggio**) *tr* to cannonade, shell
cannonièra *f* gunboat
cannonière *m* gunner, artilleryman; kicker (*in soccer*)
cannùc·cia *f* (**-ce**) reed; thin tube; stem (*e.g., of pipe*); straw (*for drinking*); (chem) pipette
canòa *f* canoe; launch
canòcchia *f* mantis shrimp
cànone *m* canon; rule; rent; fee, charge (*for use of radio*)
canonicato *m* canonry
canòni·co -ca (**-ci -che**) *adj* canonical, canon (*law*) || *m* canon; priest || *f* parsonage, rectory
canonizzare [ddzz] *tr* to canonize
canò·ro -ra *adj* song (*bird*); melodious
canottàg·gio *m* (**-gi**) boating, rowing
canottièra *f* undershirt, T-shirt; skimmer, boater
canottière *m* oarsman
canòtto *m* skiff, scull, shell
canovàc·cio *m* (**-ci**) dishcloth; embroidery cloth; plot (*of novel or play*)
cantàbile *adj* singable; songlike; cantabile || *m* song
cantamban·co *m* (**-chi**) jongleur, wandering minstrel; mountebank
cantante *adj* singing, song || *mf* singer
cantare *m* song; chant; laisse, epic strophe || *tr* to sing; to chant || *intr* to sing; to chant; (coll) to squeal
cantàride *f* Spanish fly
càntaro *m* urn
cantastò·rie *mf* (**-rie**) minstrel
canta·tóre -trice *adj* singing || *mf* singer
cantau·tóre -trice *mf* singer composer
canterano *m* chest of drawers
canterellare (**canterèllo**) *tr & intr* to sing in a low voice, hum
canteri·no -na *adj* singing, warbling; decoy (*bird*) || *mf* songster, singer
càntero *m* urinal
canticchiare §287 *tr & intr* to hum
cànti·co *m* (**-ci**) canticle
cantière *m* shipyard, dockyard; navy yard; undertaking, work in progress; **avere in cantiere** to have in hand, be working at; **cantiere edile** building site; builder's yard
cantilèna *f* singsong; **la stessa cantilena** the same old tune
cantimban·co *m* (**-chi**) var of **cantambanco**
cantina *f* cellar; wine cellar; wine shop, canteen
cantinière *m* cellarman; butler; wineshop keeper; sommelier
canto *m* song, singing; chant; canto; crow (*of rooster*); chirping (*of grasshopper*); corner, edge; (mus) voice part; **canto del cigno** swan song; **dal canto mio** for my part; **d'altro canto** on the other hand; **da un canto** on the one hand
cantonata *f* corner (*of street*); **prendere una cantonata** to make a blunder
cantóne *m* corner (*of room or building*); canton
cantonièra *f* corner cupboard; (rr) section worker's house
cantonière *m* road laborer; (rr) section hand
cantóre *m* choir singer; cantor; (poet) singer
cantùc·cio *m* (**-ci**) nook, niche
canutézza *f* hoariness
canutìglia *f* gold thread
canu·to -ta *adj* gray-haired; white-haired; (poet) white
canzonare (**canzóno**) *tr* to mock, ridicule
canzonatò·rio -ria *adj* (**-ri -rie**) mocking
canzonatura *f* mockery, gibe
canzóne *f* song; canzone
canzonétta *f* canzonet; popular song
canzonetti·sta *mf* (**-sti -ste**) singer (*e.g., in a nightclub*) || *m* songster || *f* songstress
canzonière *m* songbook; collection of poems; song writer
caolino *m* kaolin

caos *m* chaos
caòti•co -ca *adj* (**-ci -che**) caotic
capace *adj* capacious; capable, intelligent; legally qualified; **capace di** with a capacity of (*e.g., fifty people*); **essere capace di** to be able to; **fare capace di** to convince of
capaci•tà *f* (**-tà**) capacity; capability
capacitare (**capàcito**) *tr* to persuade || *ref* to become convinced
capanna *f* hut, cabin; thatched cottage; bathhouse
capannèllo *m* group, crowd
capanno *m* hunting box; cabana, bathhouse
capannóne *m* large shed; hangar
caparbiàggine *f* var of **caparbietà**
caparbie•tà *f* (**-tà**) obstinacy, stubborness
capàr•bio -bia *adj* (**-bi -bie**) stubborn, hard-headed
caparra *f* down payment, deposit; performance bond
capatina *f* short visit
capeggiare §290 (**capéggio**) *tr* to lead
capeggia•tóre -trice *mf* leader
capellini *mpl* small vermicelli
capéllo *m* hair; **averne fin sopra i capelli** to have one's fill; **capelli** hair; **capelli a spazzola** crew cut; **c'è mancato un capello che** + *subj* he came close to + *ger*; **far rizzare i capelli a qlcu** to make s.o.'s hair stand on end
capellóne *m* hippie, beatnik
capellu•to -ta *adj* hairy; long-haired
capelvènere *m* maidenhair
capèstro *m* halter; gallows
capezzale *m* bolster; (fig) bedside
capézzolo *m* nipple, teat; udder
capidò•glio *m* (**-gli**) var of **capodoglio**
capiènza *f* capacity (*e.g., of bus*)
capigliatura *f* head of hair
capillare *adj* capillary; (fig) far-reaching
capinéra *f* (orn) blackcap
capintè•sta *m* (**-sta**) boss; (sports) head, leader
capire §176 *tr* to understand; **capire a volo** to grasp immediately || *intr*—**non capire dalla contentezza** to be bursting with joy || *ref* to understand each other; to agree
capitale *adj* capital; mortal (*sin*) || *m* capital; principal; **capitale sociale** capital stock || *f* capital (*of country*)
capitalismo *m* capitalism
capitali•sta *mf* (**-sti -ste**) capitalist
capitalisti•co -ca *adj* (**-ci -che**) capitalistic
capitalizzare [ddzz] *tr* to capitalize; to compound (*interest*)
capitana *f* flagship
capitanare *tr* to lead, captain
capitanerìa *f* (hist) captaincy; **capitaneria di porto** harbor-master's office; coast guard office; port authority's office
capitano *m* captain; skipper, master (*of ship*); commander (*in air force*); **capitano di corvetta** or **capitano di fregata** (nav) lieutenant commander; **capitano di gran cabotaggio** master; **capitano di lungo corso** master; **capitano di porto** harbor master; **capitano di vascello** (nav) commander
capitare (**càpito**) *intr* (ESSERE) to arrive; to happen, occur; to happen to get, e.g., **capitò a casa mia alle tre** he happened to get to my house at three; **capitare bene** to be lucky; **dove capita** at random
capitazióne *f* poll tax
capitèllo *m* (archit) capital; (bb) headband
capitolare *adj* & *m* capitular || *v* (**capìtolo**) *intr* to capitulate, surrender
capitolato *m* (com) specifications
capitolazióne *f* capitulation
capìtolo *m* chapter; article, paragraph (*of contract*)
capitombolare (**capitómbolo**) *intr* to tumble
capitómbolo *m* tumble; **fare un capitombolo** (fig) to collapse
capitóne *m* big eel
capitozzare (**capitòzzo**) *tr* to poll (*a tree*)
capo *m* head; chief; boss, leader; top; (geog) cape; (nav) chief petty officer; **a capo scoperto** bareheaded; **capo d'accusa** (law) charge; **capo del governo** prime minister; **capo dello stato** president, chief of state; **capo di vestiario** garment; **capo scarico** scatterbrain; **col capo nel sacco** (fig) heedlessly; **da capo** all over (again); **fare capo a** to flow into; **in capo a** at the end of (*e.g., one month*); **in capo al mondo** at the end of the world; **per sommi capi** briefly; **rompersi il capo** to rack one's brain; **scoprirsi il capo** to take one's hat off; **senza capo né coda** without rhyme or reason; **venire a capo di** to come to the end of
capobanda *m* (**capibanda**) bandmaster; ringleader
capocamerière *m* headwaiter
capocannonière *m* (**capicannonièri**) petty gunnery officer; (soccer) leader in number of goals
capòcchia *f* head (*e.g., of a match*)
capòc•cia *m* (**-ci** & **-cia**) head of household; foreman, boss (*e.g., of road-workers or farmers*)
capocòmi•co *m* (**-ci**) head of dramatic company
capocòr•da *m* (**capicòrda**) (elec) binding post, terminal
capocrònaca *m* (**capicrònaca**) leading article
capocronista *m* (**capicronisti**) city editor
capocuòco *m* (**capocuòchi** & **capicuòchi**) chef
capodanno *m* (**capodanni** & **capi d'anno**) New Year's Day
capodò•glio *m* (**-gli**) sperm whale
capofàbbrica *m* (**capifàbbrica**) foreman, superintendent
capofabbricato *m* (**capifabbricato**) air-raid warden

capofamìglia *m* (**capifamìglia**) head of the family
capofila *m* (**capifila**) head of a line || *f* (**capofila**) head of a line
capofitto *adj invar*—**a capofitto** headlong
capogiro *m* vertigo, dizziness; **da capogiro** dizzying, e.g., **prezzi da capogiro** dizzying prices
capolavó•ro *m* (**-ri**) masterpiece
capolèttera *m* (**capilèttera**) letterhead; (typ) first large bold letter of a paragraph
capolìnea *m* (**capilìnea**) terminal, terminus
capolino *m*—**fare capolino** to peep
capolista *m* (**capilista**) first (*of a list*); (sports) leader || *f* (**capolista**) first (*of a list*)
capoluò•go *m* (**-ghi**) capital (*of province*); county seat
capomacchini•sta *m* (**-sti**) chief engineer
capomastro *m* (**capomastri** & **capimastri**) foreman; building contractor
capomùsica *m* (**capimùsica**) bandmaster
capoofficina *m* (**capiofficina**) superintendent (*of shop*)
capopàgina *m* (**capipàgina**) heading (*of newspaper*)
capopèzzo *m* (**capipèzzo**) gunnery sergeant
capopòpolo *m* (**capipòpolo**) demagogue
caporale *m* corporal
caporeparto *m* (**capireparto**) department manager, floor walker; shop foreman
caporióne *m* ringleader
caposaldo *m* (**capisaldi**) (fig) main point, basis; (mil) stronghold; (surv) datum
caposezióne *m* (**capisezióne**) department head
caposquadra *m* (**capisquadra**) group leader; (sports) team captain
capostazióne *m* (**capistazióne**) station master
capostìpite *m* founder (*of family*); prototype, archetype
capotaménto *m* var of **cappottamento**
capotare (**capòto**) *intr* var of **cappottare**
capotasto *m* nut (*of violin*)
capotàvola *m* (**capitàvola**) head of the table, honored guest
capòte *f* (aut) top
capotrèno *m* (**capitrèno** & **capotrèni**) (rr) conductor
capottaménto *m* var of **cappottamento**
capottare (**capòtto**) *intr* var of **cappottare**
capoufficio *m* (**capiufficio**) office manager
capovèrso *m* paragraph; (typ) indentation
capovòlgere §289 *tr* to overturn; (fig) to upset || *ref* to overturn; (fig) to be or become reversed
capovolgiménto *m* upset; (fig) reversal
capovòlta *f* overturn; turn (*in swimming*)
cappa *f* cape, cloak; mantle; letter K; shroud (*of clouds*); (naut) trysail; **cappa del cielo** vault of heaven; **navigare alla cappa** (naut) to lay to
cappèlla *f* chapel; **cappella mortuaria** undertaker's parlor || **Cappella Sistina** Sistine Chapel
cappel•làio *m* (**-lài**) hatter, hat maker or dealer
cappellano *m* chaplain
cappellata *f* hatful
cappellerìa *f* hat store
cappellièra *f* hatbox
cappèllo *m* hat; bonnet; cap (*of mushroom*); head (*of nail*); cowl (*of chimney*); preamble (*of newspaper article*); **cappello a cencio** slouch hat; **cappello a cilindro** top hat; **cappello a cono** dunce cap; **cappello a due punte** cocked hat; **cappello a tre punte** three-cornered hat; **cappello del lume** lampshade; **cappello di feltro** felt hat; **cappello di paglia** straw hat; **cappello floscio** fedora; **fare di cappello** to take one's hat off; **prendere cappello** to take offense
cappellóne *adj invar* Western (*movie*) || *m* big hat; (coll) recruit; (mov) Western character
càppero *m* (bot) caper; **capperi!** (coll) wow!
càp•pio *m* (**-pi**) bow; noose; loop
capponàia *f* chicken coop
cappóne *m* capon
cappòtta *f* cape; navy coat; hood (*of car*)
cappottaménto *m* upset, rolling over
cappottare (**cappòtto**) *intr* to upset, roll over
cappottatura *f* (aer) cowl
cappòtto *m* overcoat; lurch (*at the close of game*); (cards) slam; **cappotto da mezza stagione** lightweight coat
cappuccino *m* espresso with cream; Capuchin (*friar*)
Cappuccétto *m*—**Cappuccetto Rosso** Little Red Ridinghood
cappùc•cio *m* (**-ci**) hood, cowl; cabbage; cap (*of fountain pen*)
capra *f* goat; nanny goat; tripod
ca•pràio -pràia *mf* (**-prài -pràie**) goatherd
caprét•to -ta *mf* kid
capriata *f* truss (*to support roof*)
caprìc•cio *m* (**-ci**) whim, fancy, caprice; tantrum; flirting; (mus) capriccio
capricció•so -sa [s] *adj* whimsical, capricious; naughty; fanciful, bizarre
Capricòrno *m* (astr) Capricorn
caprifò•glio *m* (**-gli**) honeysuckle
caprimul•go *m* (**-gi**) (orn) goatsucker
capri•no -na *adj* goatlike, goatish || *m* smell of goat
capriòla *f* female roe deer; caper, somersault; **fare capriole** to cut capers, to caper
capriòlo *m* roe deer; roebuck
capro *m* he-goat, billy goat; **capro espiatorio** scapegoat
capróne *m* he-goat, billy goat
càpsula *f* capsule; percussion cap; cap (*of bottle*); (rok) capsule
captare *tr* to captivate; to catch, inter-

cept; to harness (*a waterfall*); (rad, telv) to pick up (*a signal*)
captazióne *f* undue influence (*to secure an inheritance*)
capzió•so -sa [s] *adj* insidious, treacherous
carabàttola *f* (coll) trifle
carabina *f* carbine
carabinière *m* carabineer; Italian military policeman, carabiniere; (*hist*) cavalryman
caracollare (caracòllo) *intr* to caracole, caper; (coll) to trot along
caracòllo *m* caracole, caper
caraffa *f* carafe, decanter
caràmbola *f* carom
carambolare (caràmbolo) *intr* to carom
caramèlla *f* piece of hard candy; taffy; (coll) monocle; **caramelle** hard candy
caramellare (caramèllo) *tr* to caramel; to candy
caramèllo *m* caramel (*burnt sugar*)
caraménte *adv* affectionately
carati•sta *m* (**-sti**) shareholder (*in ship or business*)
carato *m* carat; share (*of ship*)
caràttere *m* character; type; handwriting; characteristic; disposition; **carattere corsivo** (typ) italic; **carattere maiuscolo** capital; **carattere minuscolo** small letter, lower case; **carattere neretto** or **grassetto** (typ) boldface
caratteri•sta *m* (**-sti**) character actor ‖ *f* (**-ste**) character actress
caratteristi•co -ca (-ci -che) *adj* & *f* characteristic
caratterizzare [ddzz] *tr* to characterize
caratura *f* share (*in business or ship*)
cara•vàn *m* (**-vàn**) trailer, mobile home
caravanserrà•glio *m* (**-gli**) caravansary
caravèlla *f* caravel; carpenter's glue
carbo•nàio -nàia (-nài -nàie) *adj* coal ‖ *m* coal man, coal dealer ‖ *f* charcoal pit; coalbin, bunker; coal yard
carbonato *m* carbonate
carbón•chio *m* (**-chi**) (agr) smut (*on wheat*); (jewelry) carbuncle
carboncino *m* charcoal (*pencil and drawing*)
carbóne *m* coal; charcoal; carbon (*of arc light or primary battery*); **carbone bianco** hydroelectric power; **carbone dolce** charcoal; **carbone fossile** coal; **fare carbone** to coal
carbòni•co -ca *adj* (**-ci -che**) carbonic
carbonièra *f* coal yard; (naut) collier; (rr) tender
carbonile *m* (naut) bunker
carbònio *m* (chem) carbon
carbonizzare [ddzz] *tr* to carbonize; to char
carbùncolo *m* boil, carbuncle; (archaic) ruby
carburante *m* fuel
carburatóre *m* carburetor
carburazióne *f* (aut) mixture
carburo *m* carbide
carcassa *f* carcass; framework; (aut) jalopy; (fig) wreck
carcerare (càrcero) *tr* to jail
carcerà•rio -ria *adj* (**-ri -rie**) jail, prison
carcera•to -ta *adj* imprisoned ‖ *mf* prisoner
càrce•re *m* (**-ri** *fpl*) jail, prison
carcerière *m* jailer, prison guard
carciòfo *m* artichoke
cardàni•co -ca *adj* (**-ci -che**) universal (*e.g., joint*)
cardano *m* universal joint
cardatrice *f* carding machine
cardellino *m* goldfinch
cardìa•co -ca (-ci -che) *adj* heart, cardiac ‖ *m* heart patient
cardinale *adj* cardinal ‖ *m* (eccl, orn) cardinal
cardinalì•zio -zia *adj* (**-zi -zie**) cardinal, cardinal's
càrdine *m* hinge; (fig) pivot, mainstay (*e.g., of theory*)
càr•dio *m* (**-di**) cockle (*mollusk*)
cardiochirurgìa *f* heart surgery
cardiogram•ma *m* (**-mi**) cardiogram
cardiòlo•go *m* (**-gi**) cardiologist
cardiopalmo *m* tachycardia
cardiopatìa *f* heart disease
cardo *m* (bot) thistle; (bot) cardoon
carèna *f* ship's bottom; (aer) outer cover (*of airship*); (bot) rib
carenàg•gio *m* (**-gi**) careening a ship; careen
carenare (carèno) *tr* to careen (*a ship*)
carenatura *f* streamlining; **carenatura di fusoliera** (aer) turtleback
carènza *f* lack, want
carestìa *f* famine; scarcity (*e.g., of manpower*)
carézza *f* caress; **fare una carezza a** to caress
carezzare (carézzo) *tr* to caress
carezzévole *adj* caressing, fondling; sweet, suave; blandishing
cariare §287 *tr* to cause (*a tooth*) to decay; to corrode ‖ *ref* to decay; to rot
carïàtide *f* caryatid
caria•to -ta *adj* decayed
càri•ca *f* (**-che**) office, appointment; charge; (fig) insistence
caricaménto *m* loading
caricare §197 **(càrico)** *tr* to load; to burden; to wind (*a watch*); to fill (*a pipe*); to charge (*a battery*); to deepen (*a color*); **caricare la mano** to exceed; **caricare le dosi** to exaggerate ‖ *ref* to burden oneself
carica•to -ta *adj* exaggerated, affected
carica•tóre -trice *adj* loading ‖ *m* clip, magazine (*for rifle*); loader (*of gun*); cassette (*of tape recorder*); charger (*of battery*); longshoreman; (phot) cartridge, cassette
caricatura *f* caricature, cartoon; **mettere in caricatura** to ridicule
caricaturi•sta *mf* (**-sti -ste**) cartoonist, caricaturist
càrice *m* (bot) sedge
càri•co -ca (-chi -che) *adj* loaded; burdened; vivid (*color*); strong (*tea*); charged (*battery*) ‖ *m* loading; load, burden; charge; cargo ‖ *f* see **carica**
càrie *f* caries, decay
cari•no -na *adj* nice, pretty, cute; **questa è carina!** this is funny!

cari·tà *f* **(-tà)** charity; alms; (poet) love; **per carità** please
caritatévole *adj* charitable
caritati·vo -va *adj* (obs) charitable
carlin·ga *f* **(-ghe)** fuselage
Carlo *m* Charles
Carlomagno *m* Charlemagne
carlóna *f*—**alla carlona** carelessly, haphazardly
carlòtta *f* charlotte || **Carlotta** Charlotte
carme *m* poem, lyric poem
carmì·nio *m* **(-ni)** carmine
carnagióne *f* complexion
car·nàio *m* **(-nài)** carnage; slaughter house; mass of humanity
carnale *adj* carnal, sensual; full (*e.g., brother, cousin*)
carname *m* carrion
carne *f* flesh; meat; **bene in carne** plump; **carne da macello** cannon fodder; **carne suina** pork; **carne viva** open wound; **essere solo carne ed ossa** to be nothing but skin and bones; **in carne ed ossa** in person, in the flesh; **troppa carne al fuoco** too many irons in the fire
carnéfice *m* executioner
carneficina *f* slaughter, carnage
càrne·o -a *adj* fleshy, meaty; flesh-colored
carnet *m* **(carnet)** notebook; checkbook; backlog
carnevale *m* carnival
carnièra *f* hunting jacket; gamebag
carnière *m* gamebag
carnìvo·ro -ra *adj* carnivorous || *mpl* carnivores; Carnivora
carnò·so -sa [s] *adj* fleshy
ca·ro -ra *adj* dear (*beloved; high in price*) || **caro** *adv* dear || *m* high price; beloved; **i miei cari** my parents; my relatives; my friends
carógna *f* carcass; cad, rotter; **carogne** carrion
carosèllo *m* tournament; carousel, merry-go-round
caròta *f* carrot; (fig) lie
caròtide *f* carotid artery
carovana *f* caravan; group, crowd; union of longshoremen; apprenticeship; (naut, nav) convoy; **far carovana** to join a tour; **fare la carovana** to be an apprentice
carovaniè·ro -ra *adj* caravan || *f* desert trail
carovi·ta *m* **(-ta)** high cost of living; cost-of-living increase
carovìve·ri *m* **(-ri)** high cost of living; cost-of-living increase
carpa *f* (ichth) carp
carpentière *m* carpenter
carpire §176 *tr* to snatch, seize; to extract, worm (*a secret*)
carpóni *adv* on all fours; **avanzare carponi** to crawl
carradóre *m* cart maker, wheelwright
car·ràio -ràia (-rài -ràie) *adj* passable for vehicles || *f* cart road
carrarèc·cia *f* **(-ce)** country road; rut
carreggiata *f* paved road; track (*of vehicles*); (fig) right path
carrellare (carrèllo) *intr* (mov, telv) to dolly
carrellata *f* (mov) dolly shot, tracking shot
carrèllo *m* car (*for narrow-gauge track*); carriage (*of typewriter*); cart (*for shopping*); (aer) landing gear; (mach, rr) truck; (mov, telv) dolly; **carrello d'atterraggio** (aer) undercarriage, landing gear; **carrello elevatore** fork-lift truck
carrétta *f* cart; tramp steamer
carrettata *f* cartful; **a carrettate** abundantly
carrettière *m* cart driver, drayman; teamster
carrétto *m* small cart; **carretto a mano** pushcart
carriàg·gio *m* **(-gi)** wagon; **carriaggi** (mil) baggage train
carrièra *f* career; **di gran carriera** at top speed
carrieri·sta *mf* **(-sti -ste)** unscrupulous go-getter
carriòla *f* wheelbarrow
carro *m* wagon; cart; wagonload; cartload; carload; (rr) car; (astr) Plough; (poet) chariot; **carri armati** (mil) armor; **carro allegorico** float (*in a pageant*); **carro armato** (mil) tank; **carro attrezzi** (aut) tow truck, wrecker; **carro bestiame** (rr) cattle car; **carro botte** or **carro cisterna** (aut) tank truck; (rr) tank car; **carro di Tespi** traveling show; **carro funebre** hearse; **carro gru** (rr) wrecking crane; **carro marsupio** (rr) double decker (*used to transport automobiles*); **carro merci** (rr) freight car; **Gran Carro** (astr) Big Dipper; **mettere il carro innanzi ai buoi** to put the cart before the horse; **Piccolo Carro** (astr) Little Dipper || *m* **(carra** *fpl*) carload; wagonload; cartload
carròzza *f* wagon carriage; **carrozza letti** (rr) sleeping car; **carrozza ristorante** (rr) dining car; **carrozza salone** (rr) club car; **con la carrozza di S. Francesco** on shank's mare; **signori, in carrozza!** (rr) all aboard!
carrozzàbile *adj* open to vehicular traffic || *f* road open to vehicular traffic
carrozzèlla *f* small wagon; baby carriage; wheelchair; hackney
carrozzino *m* baby carriage; sidecar
carrozzóne *m* wagon; hearse; caravan (*e.g., of gypsies*); (rr) car
carruba *f* carob
carrubo *m* carob tree
carrùcola *f* pulley
carta *f* paper; document (*e.g., of identification*); **alla carta** à la carte; **carta assorbente** blotter; **carta astronomica** astronomical map; **carta bianca** carte blanche; **carta bollata** stamped paper (*for official documents*); **carta carbone** carbon paper; **carta catramata** tar paper; **carta da disegno** drawing paper; **carta da gioco** playing card; **carta da giornale** newsprint; **carta da imballaggio** or **da impacco** wrapping paper; **carta da lettera** or **da lettere** writing paper; **carta geografica** map, chart; **carta igienica** toilet paper; **carta oleata** wax paper; **carta torna**

sole litmus paper; **carta velina** India paper; tissue paper; **carta vetrata** sandpaper; **carte** papers, writings; **carte francesi** cards in the four suits spades, hearts, diamonds, and clubs; **carte napoletane** cards in the four suits gold coins, cups, swords, and clubs; **fare le carte** to shuffle the cards; **fare le carte a qlcu** to tell s.o.'s fortune with cards
cartacarbóne *f* **(cartecarbóne)** carbon paper
cartàc•cia *f* **(-ce)** waste paper
cartàce•o -a *adj* **(-i -e)** paper
Cartàgine *f* Carthage
car•tàio *m* **(-tài)** papermaker; paper dealer; (cards) dealer
cartamonéta *f* paper money
cartapècora *f* parchment
cartapésta *f* papier-mâché
cartà•rio -ria *adj* **(-ri -rie)** paper
cartastràccia *f* **(cartestracce)** wrapping paper; wastepaper
cartég•gio *m* **(-gi)** correspondence; (aer, naut) reckoning
cartèlla *f* lottery ticket; card (*e.g., of bingo*); page of manuscript; Manila folder; schoolbag; briefcase; binding (*of book*); **cartella clinica** clinical chart; **cartella di rendita** government bond; **cartella esattoriale** tax bill; **cartella fondiaria** bond certificate
cartellino *m* label; nameplate (*on door*); file; (sports) contract; **cartellino di presenza** timecard; **cartellino signaletico** criminal record
cartèllo *m* poster; sign (*on store*); (com) cartel, trust; **cartello di sfida** challenge; **cartello stradale** traffic sign
cartellóne *m* show bill, theater poster; bill (*for advertising*); **tenere il cartellone** to find public favor, make a hit, be the rage
car•ter *m* **(-ter)** chain guard (*of bicycle*); (aut) crankcase
cartièra *f* papermill
cartilàgine *f* cartilage, gristle
cartina *f* dose; cigarette paper; small map
cartòc•cio *m* **(-ci)** paper cone; charge (*of gun*); cornhusk; (archit) scroll
cartògrafo *m* cartographer
carto•làio *m* **(-lài)** stationer
cartolerìa *f* stationery store
cartolina *f* card, post card; **cartolina precetto** induction notice
cartomante *mf* fortuneteller
cartoncino *m* light cardboard, calling card; **cartoncino natalizio** Christmas card
cartóne *m* cardboard, carton; **cartone animato** (mov) animated cartoon
cartùc•cia *f* **(-ce)** cartridge; shot, shell; **mezza cartuccia** (fig) half pint
cartuccièra *f* cartridge belt
casa [s] *f* house; dwelling; home; household; **andare a casa** to go home; **casa base** (baseball) home base; **casa colonica** farm house; **casa da gioco** gambling house; **casa del diavolo** faraway place; **casa di bambole** playhouse, doll's house; **casa di correzione** reform school; **casa di cura** sanatorium, private clinic; **casa di riposo** convalescent home, nursing home; **casa di spedizione** shipping agency; **casa di tolleranza** bawdyhouse; **casa madre** home office, headquarters; **esser di casa** to be intimate; **fuori casa** (sports) away; **in casa** (sports) home; **metter su casa** to set up housekeeping; **sentirsi a casa** to feel at home; **stare a casa** to stay at home; **star di casa** to dwell, live
casac•ca *f* **(-che)** coat; **voltar casacca** to be a turncoat
casàccio *m*—**a casaccio** at random; heedlessly
casalin•go -ga (-ghi -ghe) [s] *adj* home, domestic; stay-at-home; homey; home-made || **casalinghi** *mpl* household articles || *f* housewife
casamatta [s] *f* casemate, bunker
casaménto [s] *m* apartment house, tenement; tenants
casata [s] *f* house, lineage
casato [s] *m* birth, family; (obs) family name
cascame *m* waste; remnants (*e.g., of silk*)
cascante *adj* flabby, loose; (poet) languid, dull
cascare §197 *intr* (ESSERE) to fall, droop; to fit (*said of clothes*); **cascare dalla noia** to be bored to death; **cascare dal sonno** to be overwhelmed with sleep; **cascare diritto** to escape unscathed; **non casca il mondo** the world is not coming to an end
cascata *f* fall, waterfall; necklace (*e.g., of pearls*); **a cascata** flood of, e.g., **telefonate a cascata** flood of telephone calls || **le Cascate del Niagara** Niagara Falls
cascina *f* farm house; dairy barn
ca•sco *m* **(-schi)** helmet, crash helmet; electric hairdrier; cluster (*e.g., of bananas*)
caseggiato [s] *m* built-up zone; block, row of houses; apartment house
caseifì•cio *m* **(-ci)** dairy, creamery, cheese factory
casèlla [s] *f* pigeonhole; square (*of paper*); **casella postale** post-office box
casellante [s] *mf* gatekeeper || *m* (rr) trackwalker
casellà•rio [s] *m* **(-ri)** filing cabinet; row of post-office boxes; **casellario giudiziale** criminal file
casèllo [s] *m* tollgate (*on turnpike*); (rr) trackwalker's house
casèrma *f* barracks; fire station
casino [s] *m* country house; clubhouse; (slang) whorehouse; (slang) noise, racket
casìsti•ca *f* **(-che)** case study; (eccl) casuistry
caso *m* case; chance; fate; vicissitude; opportunity; **a caso** inadvertently; **al caso** eventually; **caso fortuito** (law) act of God; **caso mai** assuming that, in the event that; **è il caso** it is the moment; **far caso a qlco** to notice s.th; **in ogni caso** in any event; **mettere il caso che** suppose; **mi fa caso** I am surprised; **non fare caso a** to

make nothing of, pay no attention to; **per caso** perchance
casolare [s] *m* hut, hovel; isolated farmhouse
casòtto [s] *m* cabana, bathhouse; sentry box
Càspio *adj* Caspian
càspita *interj* you don't say!
cassa *f* box; chest; case; stock (*of rifle*); cash; cash register; desk (*e.g., in hotel*); check-out (*in a supermarket*); **a pronta cassa** by cash; **cassa acustica** loudspeaker; **cassa di risparmio** savings bank; **cassa malattia** health insurance; **cassa rurale** farmers' credit cooperative; **in cassa** in hand (*said of money*)
cassafórma *f* (**casseforme**) (archit) form (*for cement*)
cassafòrte *f* (**cassefòrti**) safe
cassapanca *f* (**cassapanche** & **cassepanche**) wooden chest
cassare *tr* to erase, cancel; to cross off; (law) to annull
cassata *f* Neapolitan ice cream with soft core; Sicilian cake
cassazióne *f* annulment, abolition; cancellation
casserétto *m* (naut) poop
càssero *m* (naut) quarterdeck; **cassero di poppa** (naut) cockpit
casseruòla *f* saucepan
cassétta *f* small box; coach box; (theat) box office; **cassetta dei ferri** workbox; **cassetta delle lettere** mail box; **cassetta di cottura** dish warmer; **cassetta di sicurezza** safe-deposit box; **cassetta per ugnature** miter box
cassettièra *f* chest of drawers
cassétto *m* drawer; **cassetto di distribuzione** (mach) slide valve
cassettóne *m* chest of drawers; (archit) coffer, caisson
cassiè•re -ra *mf* cashier; teller
cassóne *m* large case, large box; chest; caisson (*for underwater construction*); body (*of truck*); (mil) caisson
cassonétto *m* cornice
cast *m* cast (*of actors*)
casta *f* caste
castagna *f* chestnut; **castagna d'India** horse chestnut
castagnéto *m* chestnut grove
castagno *m* chestnut tree; chestnut (*lumber*); **castagno d'India** horse chestnut tree
casta•no -na *adj* chestnut (*color*)
castellana *f* chatelaine
castellano *m* lord of the castle, squire
castellétto *m* scaffold; (min) gallows, headframe
castèl•lo *m* castle; works (*e.g., of watch*); scaffold; jungle gym; hydraulic boom, bucket lift (*on truck*); (naut) forecastle; **castello di menzogne** pack of lies; **castello in aria** castle in Spain ‖ *m* (**-la** *fpl*) (archaic) castle
castigare §209 *tr* to punish; (poet) to correct, castigate
castigatézza *f* purity (*e.g., of style*)
castiga•to -ta *adj* decent, modest; pure (*language*)
Castìglia, la Castile
castiglia•no -na *adj* & *mf* Castilian
casti•go *m* (**-ghi**) punishment; (fig) scourge; **mettere in castigo** (coll) to punish
casti•tà *f* (**-tà**) chastity; (fig) purity
ca•sto -sta *adj* chaste; pure, elegant (*language or style*)
castóne *m* setting (*of stone*)
castòro *m* beaver
castrare *tr* to castrate; to spay; (fig) to expurgate
castra•to -ta *adj* castrated; spayed; (fig) effeminate ‖ *m* mutton (of castrated sheep); eunuch
castróne *m* wether (*sheep*); gelding (*horse*); (fig) nincompoop
castronerìa *f* (vulg) stupidity
casuale *adj* fortuitous, casual; sundry (*e.g., expenses*)
casuali•tà *f* (**-tà**) chance, accident
casùpola [s] *f* hut, hovel
catacli•sma *m* (**-smi**) cataclysm
catacómba *f* catacomb
catafal•co *m* (**-chi**) catafalque
catafàscio *adv*—**a catafascio** topsy-turvy
catalès•si *f* (**-si**) catalepsy
catàli•si *f* (**-si**) catalysis
catalizza•tóre -trice [ddzz] *adj* catalytic ‖ *m* catalyst
catalogare §209 (**catàlogo**) *tr* to catalogue
catàlo•go *m* (**-ghi**) catalogue
catapècchia *f* hovel
catapla•sma *m* (**-smi**) poultice, plaster; (fig) bore
catapulta *f* catapult
catapultare *tr* to catapult
cataratta *f* cataract; sluice (*of canal*)
catarro *m* catarrh
catar•si *f* (**-si**) catharsis
catàrti•co -ca *adj* (**-ci -che**) cathartic
catasta *f* pile, heap
catastale *adj* land (*office*)
catasto *m* real-estate register; land office
catàstrofe *f* catastrophe; wreck
catastròfi•co -ca *adj* (**-ci -che**) catastrophic
catechismo *m* catechism
catechizzare [ddzz] *tr* to catechize
categorìa *f* category; weight (*in boxing*); (sports) class
categòri•co -ca *adj* (**-ci -che**) categorical; classified (*telephone directory*)
caténa *f* chain; range (*of mountains*); (archit) tie beam; **catene da neve** tire chains; **mordere la catena** to champ the bit
catenàc•cio *m* (**-ci**) bolt; (fig) jalopy; (journ) giant-size headline
catenèlla *f* chain
cateratta *f* var of **cataratta**
catèrva *f* great quantity, large number
catetère *m* catheter
cateterizzare [ddzz] *tr* to catheterize
catinèlla *f* water basin; **pióvere a catinelle** (coll) to rain cats and dogs
catino *m* basin
càtodo *m* cathode
Catóne *m* Cato; **Catone il Maggiore** Cato the Elder
catòr•cio *m* (**-ci**) (coll) piece of junk

catramare *tr* to tar
catramatrice *f* asphalt-paving machine
catrame *m* tar, coal tar
càttedra *f* desk (*of teacher*); chair, professorship
cattedrale *adj* & *f* cathedral
cattedràti·co -ca (-ci -che) *adj* pedantic || *m* professor
catte·gù *m* **(-gù)** catgut
cattivare *tr* to captivate
cattivèria *f* wickedness; piece of wickedness
cattivi·tà *f* **(-tà)** captivity
catti·vo -va *adj* bad; wicked; vicious (*animal*); worthless; poor (*reputation; condition*); nasty; naughty; (archaic) cowardly || *mf* wicked person || *m* bad taste; **sapere di cattivo** to taste bad
cattolicità *f* catholicity
cattòli·co -ca (-ci -che) *adj* catholic || *adj* & *mf* Catholic
cattura *f* capture, seizure; arrest
catturare *tr* to capture, seize; to arrest
caucàsi·co -ca *adj* & *mf* **(-ci -che)** Caucasian
caucciù *m* **(caucciù)** rubber
càusa *f* cause, motive; fault; lawsuit, action; **a causa di** on account of; **causa civile** civil suit; **causa penale** criminal suit; **fare causa** to take legal action; **intentare causa a** to bring suit against
causale *adj* causal || *f* cause
causare (càuso) *tr* to cause
causìdi·co *m* **(-ci)** amicus curiae; (joc) pettifogger
càusti·co -ca *adj* **(-ci -che)** caustic
cautèla *f* caution; precaution, care
cautelare *adj* guaranteeing, protecting || *v* **(cautèlo)** *tr* to guarantee, protect || *ref* to take precautions
cauterizzare [ddzz] *tr* to cauterize
càu·to -ta *adj* cautious, prudent; cagey
cauzióne *f* security, bail; **dare cauzione** to give bail
cava *f* quarry; cave; (fig) mine
cavadènti *m* **(-ti)** (coll) tooth puller, poor dentist
cavagno *m* (coll) basket
cavalcare §197 *tr* to ride; to cross over (*e.g., a river*) || *intr* to ride; **cavalcare a bisdosso** to ride bareback; **cavalcare all'amazzone** to ride sidesaddle
cavalcata *f* ride; cavalcade
cavalcatura *f* mount
cavalca·vìa *m* **(-vìa)** bridge (*between two buildings*); overpass
cavalcióni *adj*—**a cavalcioni (di)** astride
cavalierato *m* knighthood
cavalière *m* rider (*on horseback*); knight; cavalier; chevalier; **a cavaliere** astride; **cavaliere d'industria** adventurer; **cavaliere errante** knight errant; **essere a cavaliere di** to overlook (*e.g., a valley*); to stretch over (*e.g., two centuries*)
cavalla *f* mare
cavalleggièro *m* cavalryman
cavalleré·sco -sca *adj* **(-schi -sche)** chivalrous, knightly
cavallerìa *f* cavalry; chivalry, knighthood; (fig) chivalry
cavallerizza *f* manège, riding school; horsemanship; horsewoman
cavallerizzo *m* horseman; riding master
cavallétta *f* grasshopper
cavallétto *m* tripod; easel; trestle (*of ski lift*); scaffold (*e.g., of stonemason*); sawhorse, sawbuck
cavalli·no -na *adj* horse, horse-like || *m* foal, colt || *f* foal, filly; **correre la cavallina** to be on the loose; to sow one's wild oats
cavallo *m* horse; knight (*in chess*); crotch (*of pants*); **a cavallo** on horseback; **a cavallo di** astride; **andare col cavallo di San Francesco** to ride shank's mare; **cavallo a dondolo** hobbyhorse; **cavallo di battaglia** battle horse; (fig) specialty, forte; **cavallo da corsa** race horse; **cavallo da tiro** draft horse; **cavallo di Frisia** cheval-de-frise; **cavallo di ritorno** confirmed news; **cavallo vapore** metric horsepower; **essere a cavallo** (fig) to have turned the corner
cavallóne *m* big horse; billow
cavallùc·cio *m* **(-ci)** little horse; **a cavalluccio** on one's shoulders; **cavalluccio marino** (ichth) sea horse
cavare *tr* to dig; to extract (*e.g., a tooth*); to pull out (*e.g., money*); to draw; **cavare il cuore a qlcu** to move s.o. to compassion; **cavare una spina dal cuore a qlcu** to ease so.o.'s mind || *ref* to take off (*e.g., one's hat*); **cavarsela** to overcome an obstacle; to get out of trouble; **cavarsi la camicia di dosso** to give the shirt off one's back; **cavarsi la fame** to eat one's fill; **cavarsi la voglia** to satisfy one's wishes
cavastiva·li *m* **(-li)** bootjack
cavatap·pi *m* **(-pi)** corkscrew
cavaturàccio·li *m* **(-li)** corkscrew
cavèrna *f* cave, cavern
cavernó·so -sa [s] *adj* cavernous; deep (*voice*)
cavézza *f* halter; (fig) check
càvia *f* guinea pig; **cavia umana** (fig) guinea pig
caviale *m* caviar
cavìc·chio *m* **(-chi)** peg
cavì·glia *f* **(-glie)** ankle; bolt; pin, dowel, peg
caviglièra *f* ankle support
cavillare *intr* to cavil, quibble
cavillo *m* quibble
cavilló·so -sa [s] *adj* quibbling, captious
cavi·tà *f* **(-tà)** cavity
ca·vo -va *adj* hollow || *m* hollow; cable; trough (*between two waves*); (naut) hawser; **cavo di rimorchio** towline; **cavo telefonico** telephone cable || *f* see **cava**
cavolfióre *m* cauliflower
càvolo *m* cabbage; **cavolo di Bruxelles** Brussels sprouts (*food*); (bot) Brussels sprout; **non capire un cavolo** (vulg) to not understand a blessed thing
cazzòtto *m* (vulg) punch, sock
cazzuòla *f* trowel

ce §5
cecare §122 *tr* to blind
cèc·ca *f* (**-che**) magpie; **fare cecca** to misfire
cecchino *m* sniper
céce *m* chiekpea
ceci·tà *f* (**-tà**) blindness
cè·co -ca *adj & mf* (**-chi -che**) Czech
Cecoslovàcchia, la Czechoslovakia
cecoslovac·co -ca *adj & mf* (**-chi -che**) Czechoslovak
cèdere §123 *tr* to cede; to give up; to sell at cost; **cedere il passo** to let s.o. through; **cedere la strada** to yield the right of way; **non cederla** to be second to none || *intr* to give in, yield; to give way, succumb; to sag
cedévole *adj* yielding; soft; pliable
cedìglia *f* cedilla
cediménto *m* cave-in; (fig) yielding
cèdola *f* slip; coupon
cedri·no -na *adj* citron; citron-like; cedar, cedar-like
cédro *m* (*Citrus medica*) citron; (*Cedrus*) cedar; **cedro del Libano** cedar of Lebanon
CEE *m* (letterword) (**Comunità Economica Europea**) EEC (*European Economic Community - Common Market*)
cefalèa *f* slight headache; headache
cèfalo *m* (ichth) mullet
cèffo *m* snout; (pej) face; **brutto ceffo** ugly mug
ceffóne *m* slap in the face
celare (**cèlo**) *tr* to hide, conceal
cela·to -ta *adj* hidden || *f* sallet
celebèrri·mo -ma *adj* very famous, renowned
celebrare (**cèlebro**) *tr & intr* to celebrate
celebrazióne *f* celebration
cèlebre *adj* famous, renowned, celebrated
celebri·tà *f* (**-tà**) celebrity
cèlere *adj* swift, rapid; express (*train*); short, quick; prompt || **Celere** *f* special police
celeri·tà *f* (**-tà**) swiftness, rapidity; speed (*e.g., of a machine gun*)
celèste *adj* heavenly, celestial; blue, sky-blue || *m* blue, sky blue; **celesti** heavenly spirits; (mythol) gods
celestiale *adj* celestial, heavenly
cèlia *f* jest; **mettere in celia** to deride; **per celia** in jest
celiare §287 (**cèlio**) *intr* to jest, joke
celibatà·rio -ria (**-ri -rie**) *adj* single || *m* old bachelor
celibato *m* celibacy; bachelorhood
cèlibe *adj* single, unmarried || *m* bachelor
cèlla *f* cell; **cella frigorifera** walk-in refrigerator; **cella campanaria** belfry
cèllofan or **cellofàn** *m* cellophane
cèllula *f* cell; **cellula fotoelettrica** photoelectric cell
cellulare *adj* cellular; ventilated (*fabric*); solitary (*confinement*)
celluloìde *f* celluloid
celluló·so -sa [s] *adj* cell-like, cellular || *f* cellulose
cèl·ta *mf* (**-ti -te**) Celt
cèlti·co -ca *adj* (**-ci -che**) Celtic; venereal (*disease*)
cementare (**ceménto**) *tr* to cement
ceménto *m* cement, concrete; **cemento armato** reinforced concrete
céna *f* supper; **Ultima Cena** Last Supper
cenàcolo *m* cenacle
cenare (**céno**) *intr* to sup, have supper
cenciaiò·lo -la *mf* ragpicker
cén·cio *m* (**-ci**) rag, duster (*for cleaning*)
cenció·so -sa [s] *adj* tattered, ragged
cénere *adj* ashen || *f* ash; cinder; **andare in cenere** to go up in smoke; **ceneri** ashes (*of a person*); **ridurre in cenere** to burn to ashes || **le Ceneri** Ash Wednesday
cenerèntola *f* (fig) Cinderella || **Cenerèntola** *f* Cinderella (*of the fable*)
cén·gia *f* (**-ge**) ledge (*of a mountain*)
cénno *m* sign; wave (*with hand*); nod; wag; wink; gesture; hint; notice; **ai cenni di** at the orders of; **fare cenno a** or **di** to mention; **fare cenno di no** to shake one's head; **fare cenno di sì** to nod assent
cenò·bio *m* (**-bi**) monastery
cenobi·ta *m* (**-ti**) monk, cenobite
censiménto *m* census
censire §176 *tr* to take the census of
cènso *m* wealth, income; census (*in ancient Rome*)
censóre *m* censor; faultfinder; (educ) proctor
censuà·rio -ria (**-ri -rie**) *adj* income; tax (*register*) || *m* taxpayer
censura *f* censure; censorship; faultfinding
censurare *tr* to censure; to criticize, find fault with
centàuro *m* centaur
centellinare *tr* to sip; to take a nip of
centellino *m* sip, nip
centenà·rio -ria (**-ri -rie**) *adj & mf* centenary, centennial || *m* centenary, centennial (*anniversary*)
centèsi·mo -ma *adj* hundredth || *m* hundredth; centime; cent; penny
centìgrado *m* centigrade
centigrammo *m* centigram
centìmetro *m* centimeter; tape measure
cèntina *f* (archit) centering; (aer) rib
centi·nàio *m* hundred; **un centinaio di** about a hundred || *m* (**-nàia** *fpl*)—**a centinaia** by the hundreds
cènto *adj, m & pron* a hundred, one hundred; **per cento** per cent
centomila *adj, m & pron* a hundred thousand, one hundred thousand
centóne *m* cento
centopiè·di *m* (**-di**) centipede
centrale *adj* central || *f* headquarters, home office; powerhouse, generating station; telephone exchange; **centrale di conversione** (elec) transformer station; **centrale telefonica** central
centralini·sta *mf* (**-sti -ste**) telephone operator
centralino *m* telephone exchange
centralizzare [ddzz] *tr* to centralize
centrare (**cèntro**) *tr* to center; to hit the center of

centrattac·co *m* (**-chi**) (sports) center forward
centrìfu·go -ga *adj* (**-ghi -ghe**) centrifugal || *f* centrifuge
centrino *m* centerpiece
centrìpe·to -ta *adj* centripetal
centri·sta *mf* (**-sti -ste**) (pol) centrist
cèntro *m* center; **al centro** downtown: **far centro** to hit the mark
centrocampo *m* (soccer) midfield
centuplicare §197 (**centùplico**) *tr* to multiply a hundredfold
cèntu·plo -pla *adj* & *m* hundredfold
céppo *m* trunk, stump; log; block (*for beheading*); brake shoe; stock (*of anchor*); **ceppi** stocks, fetters || **il Ceppo** (coll) Christmas
céra *f* wax; face, aspect, air, look; **di cera** waxen; pale; **cera da scarpe** shoe polish; **avere buona cera** to look well; **fare buona cera a** to welcome
ceralac·ca *f* (**-che**) sealing wax
ceràmi·co -ca (**-ci -che**) *adj* ceramic || *f* ceramics
cerare (**céro**) *tr* to wax
Cèrbero *m* Cerberus
cerbiatto *m* fawn
cerbottana *f* blowgun, peashooter
cer·ca *f* (**-che**) search, quest; **in cerca di** in search of
cercare §197 (**cérco**) *tr* to seek, look for; to desire, yearn for; **cercare il pelo nell'uovo** to be a faultfinder, to nitpick || *intr* to try
cerca·tóre -trice *adj* seeking || *mf* seeker; mendicant || *m* prospector
cérchia *f* coterie; compass, limits (*of a wall*); circle (*of friends*)
cerchiare §287 (**cérchio**) *tr* to hoop (*a barrel*); to circle, encircle
cér·chio *m* (**-chi**) circle; hoop; loop; **fare il cerchio della morte** (aer) to loop the loop; **in cerchio** in a circle || *m* (**-chia** *fpl*) (archaic) circle
cerchióne *m* rim; tire (*of metal*)
cereale *adj* & *m* cereal
cerebrale *adj* cerebral
cère·o -a *adj* waxen; wax-colored, pale
cerfò·glio *m* (**-gli**) chervil
cerimònia *f* ceremony; **fare cerimonie** to stand on ceremony; to make a fuss
cerimoniale *adj* & *m* ceremonial
cerimonière *m* master of ceremonies (*at court*)
cerimonió·so -sa [s] *adj* ceremonious
cerino *m* wax match; taper
cernéc·chio *m* (**-chi**) tuft (*of hair*)
cernièra *f* hinge; clasp (*of handbag*); **a cerniera** hinged; **cerniera lampo** zipper
cèrnita *f* sorting, selection, grading
céro *m* church candle; **offrire un cero** to light a candle
ceróne *m* make-up (*of actor*)
ceròtto *m* adhesive tape; (fig) bore; **cerotto per i calli** corn plaster
certame *m* (poet) combat; competition, contest (*of poets*)
certézza *f* certitude, assurance, conviction, certainty
certificare §197 (**certìfico**) *tr* to certify, certificate
certificato *m* certificate
cèr·to -ta *adj* such, some; convinced; certain; real, positive || *m* certainty; **di certo** or **per certo** for certain || **certi** *pron* some || **certo** *adv* undoubtedly
certósa *f* Carthusian monastery, charterhouse
certosi·no *m* Carthusian monk; chartreuse (*liquor*); **da certosino** with great patience
certu·no -na *adj* (obs) some || **certuni** *pron* some
cerùle·o -a *adj* cerulean
cerume *m* ear wax
cervellétto *m* cerebellum
cervelli·no -na *adj* & *mf* scatterbrain
cervèllo *m* (**cervèlli** & **cervèlla** *fpl*) brain; head; mind; **dare al cervello** to go to one's head
cervellòti·co -ca *adj* (**-ci -che**) queer, extravagant
cervice *f* (anat) cervix; (poet) nape of the neck
cervië·ro -ra *adj* lynx-like; || *m* lynx
cervi·no -na *adj* deer-like || **Cervino** *m* Matterhorn
cèrvo *m* deer; (ent) stag beetle; **cervo volante** kite
Cèsare *m* Caesar
cesàre·o -a *adj* Caesarean; (poet) courtly
cesellare (**cesèllo**) *tr* to chase, chisel; to carve, engrave; to polish (*e.g., a poem*)
cesella·tóre -trice *mf* chaser, engraver, chiseler
cesellatura *f* chasing, engraving; polished writing
cesèllo *m* burin, graver
cesóia *f* shears, metal shears; **cesoie** shears (*for gardening*)
cesoiatrice *f* shearing machine
cèspite *m* source (*of income*); (poet) tuft
céspo *m* tuft
cespù·glio *m* (**-gli**) bush, shrub, thicket
cèssa *f*—**senza cessa** without letup
cessare (**cèsso**) *tr* to stop, interrupt || *intr* to cease, stop; **cessare di** + *inf* to stop + *ger*
cessazióne *f* cessation, discontinuance; **cessazione d'esercizio** going out of business
cessionà·rio *m* (**-ri**) assignee
cèsso *m* (vulg) privy, outhouse
césta *f* basket, hamper
cestinare *tr* to throw into the wastebasket; to reject (*a book, article, etc.*)
césto *m* basket; tuft; head (*e.g., of lettuce*)
cesura *f* caesura
cetàceo *m* cetacean
cèto *m* class; **ceto medio** middle class
cétra *f* lyre; cither; inspiration
cetriolino *m* gherkin
cetriòlo *m* cucumber; (fig) dolt
che *adj* what; which; what a, e.g., **che bella giornata!** what a beautiful day! || *pron interr* what || *pron rel* who; whom; that; which; (coll) in which || *m*—**essere un gran che** to be a big

shot, to be somebody || *adv* how, e.g., **che bello!** how nice!; **non . . . che** only, e.g., **non venne che Luigi** only Luigi came; no one but, e.g., **non restò che mio cugino** no one but my cousin stayed || *conj* that; (*after comparatives*) than, as
ché *adv* (coll) why || *conj* (coll) because; (coll) so that
checché *pron* (lit) whatever, no matter what
checchessìa *pron* (lit) anything, everything
chèla *f* claw
che•pì *m* (-**pì**) kepi
cherubino *m* cherub
chetare (chéto) *tr* to quiet; to placate || *ref* to quiet down, become quiet
chetichèlla *f*—**alla chetichella** surreptitiously, stealthily
ché•to -ta *adj* quiet, still
chi *pron interr* who; whom || *pron rel* who; whom; **chi . . . chi** some . . . some
chiàcchiera *f* chatter, idle talk; gossip; glibness; **fare quattro chiacchiere** to have a chat
chiacchierare (chiàcchiero) *intr* to chat; to gossip
chiacchierata *f* talk, chat; **fare una chiacchierata** to visit
chiacchieri•no -na *adj* talkative, loquacious
chiacchierì•o *m* (-**i**) chattering, jabbering (*of a crowd*)
chiacchieró•ne -na *adj* talkative, loquacious || *mf* chatterbox
chiama *f* roll call; **fare la chiama** to call the roll; **mancare alla chiama** to be absent at the roll call
chiamare *tr* to call; to hail (*a cab*); to invoke, call upon; **chiamare al telefono** to call up; **esser chiamato a** to have the vocation for || *ref* to be named; **si chiama Giovanni** his name is John
chiamata *f* call; (law) designation (*of an heir*); (telp) ring; (theat) curtain call; (typ) catchword
chiappa *f* (vulg) buttock; (slang) catch (*e.g., of fish*)
chiarét•to -ta *adj & m* claret
chiarézza *f* clarity, clearness
chiarificare §197 (**chiarìfico**) *tr* to clarify
chiarificazióne *f* clarification
chiariménto *m* explanation
chiarire §176 *tr* to clear up, explain; to unravel || *intr* (ESSERE) to clear, become clear || *ref* to make oneself clear; to assure oneself
chia•ro -ra *adj* clear; bright; light (*color*); honest; clear-cut; plain (*language*); illustrious, famous || *m* light; bright color; brightness; **chiaro di luna** moonlight; **con questi chiari di luna** in these troubled times; **mettere in chiaro** to clarify, explain || **chiaro** *adv* plainly; **chiaro e tondo** bluntly, frankly
chiaróre *m* light, glimmer
chiaroveggènte *adj & mf* clairvoyant
chiaroveggènza *f* clairvoyance
chiassata *f* uproar, disturbance, racket; noisy scene
chiasso *m* noise; uproar; alley; **far chiasso** to cause a sensation
chiassó•so -sa [s] *adj* noisy; gaudy
chiatta *f* barge; pontoon
chiavarda *f* bolt
chiave *f* key; wrench; (archit) keystone; (mus) clef; **avere le chiavi di** to own; **chiave a rollino** adjustable wrench; **chiave a tubo** socket wrench; **chiave di volta** keystone; **chiave inglese** monkey wrench; **fuori chiave** off key; **sotto chiave** under lock and key
chiavétta *f* key; cock; cotter pin
chiàvi•ca *f* (-**che**) sewer
chiavistèllo *m* bolt
chiazza *f* spot, blotch
chiazzare *tr* to spot, blotch; to mottle
chiazza•to -ta *adj* spotted, mottled
chic•ca *f* (-**che**) sweet, candy
chìcchera *f* cup
chicchessìa *pron indef* anyone, anybody
chicchirichì *m* cock-a-doodle-doo
chic•co *m* (-**chi**) grain, seed; bead (*of rosary*); bean (*of coffee*); **chicco di grandine** hailstone; **chicco d'uva** grape
chièdere §124 *tr* to ask; to ask for; to beg (*pardon*); to require; to sue (*for damages or peace*); **chiedere a qlcu di** + *inf* to ask s.o. to + *inf*; **chiedere in prestito** to borrow; **chiedere qlco a qlcu** to ask s.o. for s.th || *ref* to wonder
chiéri•ca *f* (-**che**) tonsure; priesthood
chiéri•co *m* (-**ci**) clergyman; altar boy; (archaic) clerk
chièsa *f* church
chiesuòla *f* small church; clique, set (*e.g., of artists*); (naut) binnacle
chì•glia *f* (-**glie**) keel; **chiglia mobile** (naut) centerboard
chilo *m* kilo, kilogram; **fare il chilo** to take a siesta
chilociclo *m* kilocycle
chilogrammo *m* kilogram
chilohèrtz *m* kilohertz
chilometràg•gio *m* (-**gi**) distance in kilometers
chilomètri•co -ca *adj* (-**ci -che**) kilometric; interminable (*e.g., speech*)
chilòmetro *m* kilometer
chilo•watt *m* (-**watt**) kilowatt
chimèra *f* chimera; daydream, utopia
chimèri•co -ca *adj* (-**ci -che**) chimerical
chìmi•co -ca (-**ci -che**) *adj* chemical || *m* chemist || *f* chemistry
chimòno *m* kimono
china *f* slope, decline; India ink; cinchona
chinare *tr* to bend; to lower (*one's eyes*); **chinare il capo** to nod assent; **chinare la fronte** to yield, give in || *ref* to bend, stoop
china•to -ta *adj* bent, lowered; bitter; with quinine, e.g., **vino chinato** wine with quinine
chincàglie *fpl* notions, knicknacks, sundries

chincaglière *m* notions or knicknack dealer
chincaglierìa *f* knicknack; **chincaglierie** knicknacks, notions
chinina *f* quinine (*alkaloid*)
chinino *m* quinine (*salt of the alkaloid*)
chi·no -na *adj* bent, lowered || *f* see **china**
chiòc·cia *f* (**-ce**) brooding hen
chiocciare §128 (**chiòccio**) *intr* to cluck; to sit, brood; to crouch
chiocciata *f* brood
chiòc·cio -cia (**-ci -ce**) *adj* hoarse || *f* see **chioccia**
chiòcciola *f* snail; (anat) cochlea; (mach) nut
chioccolì·o *m* (**-i**) cackle (*of hen*); gurgle (*of water*)
chiodare (**chiòdo**) *tr* to nail
chioda·to -ta *adj* nailed shut; hobnailed
chiòdo *m* nail; spike; obsession; craze; (coll) debt; **chiodi** climbing irons; **chiodo a espansione** expansion bolt; **chiodo da cavallo** horseshoe nail; **chiodo di garofano** clove; **chiodo ribattino** rivet
chiòma *f* hair; mane; foliage; (astr) coma
chioma·to -ta *adj* hairy, long-haired; leafy
chiòsa *f* gloss
chiosare (**chiòso**) *tr* to gloss, comment on
chiò·sco *m* (**-schi**) kiosk, stand, newsstand; pavilion, bandstand
chiòstra *f* circular range (*of mountains*); (poet) enclosure; (poet) set (*of teeth*); (poet) zone, region
chiòstro *m* cloister
chiòt·to -ta *adj* quiet, still; **chiotto chiotto** still as a mouse
chiromante *mf* palmist
chiromanzìa *f* palmistry
chiropràtica *f* chiropractice
chirurgìa *f* surgery
chirùrgi·co -ca *adj* (**-ci -che**) surgical
chirur·go *m* (**-ghi & -gi**) surgeon
chissà *adv* maybe
chitarra *f* guitar; **chitarra hawaiana** ukulele
chitarri·sta *mf* (**-sti -ste**) guitar player
chiùdere §125 *tr* to shut, close; to lock; to turn off; to fasten; to block (*a road*); to fence in; to nail shut (*a box*); to strike (*a balance*); to conclude, wind up; **chiudere a chiave** to lock; **chiudere bottega** to go out of business; **chiudere il becco** (slang) to shut up || *intr* to shut, close; to lock || *ref* to shut, close; to lock; to withdraw; to cloud over
chiùnque *pron indef invar* anybody, anyone || *pron rel invar* whoever, whomever; anyone who, anyone whom
chiurlo *m* (orn) curlew
chiusa [s] *f* fence; lock (*of canal*); end, conclusion (*e.g., of letter*)
chiusino [s] *m* manhole
chiu·so -sa [s] *adj* shut, closed, locked; stuffy (*air*); high-bodiced (*dress*); close (*vowel*) || *m* enclosure, corral; close || *f* see **chiusa**
chiusura [s] *f* closing, end; fastener; lock; **chiusura lampo** zipper, slide fastener
ci §5
ciabatta *f* slipper; old shoe
ciabat·tàio *m* (**-tài**) cobbler
ciabattare *intr* to shuffle along
ciabattino *m* cobbler, shoemaker
ciàc *f* (mov) clappers
cialda *f* wafer; thin waffle
cialdóne *m* cone (*for ice cream*)
cialtró·ne -na *mf* rogue, scoundrel; slovenly person
ciambèlla *f* doughnut; **ciambella di salvataggio** life saver
ciambellano *m* chamberlain
ciampicare §197 (**ciàmpico**) *intr* to stumble along
ciana *f* (slang) fishwife
cianamide *f* cyanamide
ciàn·cia *f* (**-ce**) chatter, prattle, idle gossip
cianciare §128 (**ciàncio**) *intr* to chatter, prattle
cianciafrùscola *f* trifle, bagatelle
cianfrusà·glia *f* (**-glie**) trifle, trinket; rubbish, trash, junk
cianìdri·co -ca *adj* (**-ci -che**) hydrocyanic
cianògeno *m* cyanogen
cianuro *m* cyanide
ciao *interj* (coll) hi!, hello!; (coll) goodbye!, so long!
ciarla *f* chatter, prattle, idle talk; gossip
ciarlare *intr* to chatter, prattle
ciarlatanata *f* charlatanism, quackery
ciarlataneria *f* charlatanism
ciarlatané·sco -sca *adj* (**-schi -sche**) charlatan
ciarlatano *m* charlatan, quack
ciarliè·ro -ra *adj* talkative, garrulous
ciarpame *m* rubbish, junk
ciaschedu·no -na *adj indef* each || *pron indef* each one, everyone
ciascu·no -na *adj indef* each || *pron indef* each one, everyone
cibare *tr & ref* to feed
cibà·rio -ria (**-ri -rie**) *adj* alimentary || **cibarie** *fpl* foodstuffs, victuals
cibo *m* food; meal; (fig) dish
cicala *f* cicada; grasshopper; locust; (fig) chatterbox; (naut) anchor ring
cicalare *intr* to prattle, babble; to chatter
cicaléc·cio *m* (**-ci**) prattle, babble; chatter
cicatrice *f* scar
cicatrizzare [ddzz] *tr* to heal (*a wound*) || *intr* (ESSERE) & *ref* to heal, scar
cicatrizzazióne [ddzz] *f* closing, healing (*of a wound*)
cic·ca *f* (**-che**) butt (*of cigar or cigarette*); (slang) chewing gum
ciccare §197 *intr* to chew tobacco; (coll) to boil with anger
cicchettare (**cicchétto**) *tr* (slang) to prime (*a carburetor*); (slang) to dress down, reprimand || *intr* to tipple
cicchétto *m* nip (*of liquor*); (slang) dressing down

cìc•cia *f* (**-ce**) (joc) flesh; (joc) fat
cicció•ne -na *mf* fatty
ciceróne *m* guide || **Cicerone** *m* Cicero
ciclàbile *adj* open to bicycles; bicycle, e.g., **pista ciclabile** bicycle trail
cìcli•co -ca *adj* (**-ci -che**) cyclic(al)
cicli•sta *mf* (**-sti -ste**) cyclist, bicyclist
ciclo *m* cycle; (coll) bicycle; **ciclo operativo** (econ) turnover
ciclomotóre *m* motorbike
ciclomotori•sta *mf* (**-sti -ste**) driver of motorbike
ciclóne *m* cyclone
ciclòpe *m* cyclops
ciclòpi•co -ca *adj* (**-ci -che**) cyclopean, gigantic
ciclopista *f* bicycle trail
ciclostilare *tr* to mimeograph
ciclostile or **ciclostilo** *m* mimeograph
ciclotróne *m* cyclotron
cicógna *f* stork
cicòria *f* chicory; endive
cicuta *f* hemlock
cìe•co -ca (**-chi -che**) *adj* blind; **alla cieca** blindly || *mf* blind person || *m* blind man; **i ciechi** the blind
cièlo *m* sky; heaven; weather, climate; roof (*e.g., of wagon*); **a ciel sereno** in the open air; **cielo a pecorelle** mackerel or fleecy sky; **dal cielo** from above; **non stare né in cielo né in terra** to be utterly absurd; **per amor del cielo** for heaven's sake; **portare al cielo** to praise to the skies; **santo cielo!** good heavens!; **volesse il cielo che . . . !** would that . . . !
cifra *f* number, figure; Arabic numeral; sum, total; digit; initial, monogram; cipher, code; **cifra d'affari** amount of business, turnover; **cifra tonda** round number
cifrare *tr* to cipher, code; to embroider (*a monogram*)
cifrà•rio *m* (**-ri**) code, cipher
cì•glio *m* (**-glia** *fpl*) eyelash; eyebrow; **a ciglio asciutto** with dry eyes; **ciglia** (zool) cilia; **senza batter ciglio** without batting an eye || *m* (**-gli**) (fig) edge, brow
ciglióne *m* bank, embankment
cigno *m* swan; cob
cigolante *adj* creaky, squeaky
cigolare (**cìgolo**) *intr* to squeak, creak
cigolì•o *m* (**-i**) squeak, creak
Cile, il Chile
cilécca *f*—**fare cilecca** to misfire
cileccare §197 (**cilécco**) *intr* to goof, blunder; to fail
cilè•no -na *adj & mf* Chilean
cilè•stro -stra *adj* (poet) azure, blue
cilì•cio *m* (**-ci**) sackcloth
ciliè•gia *f* (**-gie & -ge**) cherry
ciliè•gio *m* (**-gi**) cherry tree
cilindrare *tr* to calender (*e.g., paper*); to roll (*a road*)
cilindrata *f* (aut) cylinder capacity, piston displacement
cilìndri•co -ca *adj* (**-ci -che**) cylindric(al)
cilindro *m* cylinder; top hat; roll, roller
cima *f* top, summit; tip (*e.g., of a pole*); peak (*of mountain*); edge, end; rope, cable; head (*e.g., of lettuce*); (coll) genius; **da cima a fondo** from top to bottom
cimare *tr* to cut the tip off; to shear; (agr) to prune
cimasa *f* (archit) coping
cìmbalo *m* gong; (obs) cymbal; **in cimbali** tipsy; in a tizzy
cimè•lio *m* (**-li**) relic, souvenir, memento
cimentare (**ciménto**) *tr* to risk (*e.g., one's life*); to provoke; (archaic) to assay || *ref* to expose oneself; to venture
ciménto *m* risk, danger; (archaic) assay
cìmice *f* bug; bedbug; (coll) thumbtack
cimièro *m* crest; (poet) helmet
ciminièra *f* chimney (*of factory*); smokestack (*of locomotive*); funnel (*of steamship*)
cimitèro *m* cemetery, graveyard; (fig) ghosttown
cimósa [s] or **cimóssa** *f* selvage; blackboard eraser
cimurro *m* distemper; (joc) cold
Cina, la China
cinabro *m* cinnabar; crimson; red ink
cìn•cia *f* (**-ce**) titmouse
cinciallégra *f* great titmouse
cincilla *f* chinchilla
cincischiare §287 *tr* to shred; to wrinkle, crease; to waste (*time*); to mumble (*words*) || *intr* to wrinkle, crease
cine *m* (coll) cinema
cineamatóre *m* amateur movie maker
cine•asta *m* (**-sti**) motion-picture producer; movie fan; movie actor || *f* movie actress
cinecàmera *f* movie camera
cinedilettante *mf* amateur movie maker
cinegiornale *m* newsreel
cinelàndia *f* movieland
cìne•ma *m* (**-ma**) movies; movie house
cinematografare (**cinematògrafo**) *tr* to film, shoot
cinematografia *f* cinema, motion pictures, movie industry
cinematogràfi•co -ca *adj* (**-ci -che**) movie, motion-picture; movie-like
cinematògrafo *m* motion picture; movie theater; (fig) hubbub; (fig) funny sight
cineparchég•gio *m* (**-gi**) drive-in movie
cinepar•co *m* (**-chi**) drive-in movie
cineprésa [s] *f* movie camera
cinère•o -a *adj* ashen
cinescò•pio *m* (**-pi**) kinescope, TV tube
cinése [s] *adj & mf* Chinese
cineteatro *m* movie house; **cineteatro all'aperto** outdoor movie
cinetè•ca *f* (**-che**) film library
cinèti•co -ca (**-ci -che**) *adj* kinetic || *f* kinetics
cingallégra *f* var of **cinciallegra**
cìngere §126 *tr* to surround; to gird (*e.g., the head*); to gird on (*e.g., the sword*); **cingere cavaliere** to dub a knight; **cingere d'assedio** to besiege
cìnghia *f* belt, strap; **tirare la cinghia** to tighten one's belt
cinghiale *m* wild boar
cinghiata *f* lash
cingola•to -ta *adj* track-driven, caterpillar

cìngolo *m* endless metal belt, track; girdle, belt (*of a priest*)
cinguettare (**cinguétto**) *intr* to chirp, twitter; to babble
cinguettì•o *m* (**-i**) chirp, twitter; (fig) babble
cìni•co -ca (**-ci -che**) *adj* cynical || *m* cynic
cinìglia *f* chenille
cinismo *m* cynicism
cinòfilo *m* dog lover
cinquanta *adj, m & pron* fifty
cinquantenà•rio -ria (**-ri -rie**) *adj* fifty-year-old; occurring every fifty years || *m* fiftieth anniversary
cinquantènne *adj* fifty-year-old || *mf* fifty-year-old person
cinquantèn•nio *m* (**-ni**) period of fifty years, half century
cinquantèsi•mo -ma *adj, m & pron* fiftieth
cinquantina *f* about fifty; **sulla cinquantina** about fifty years old
cìnque *adj & pron* five; **le cinque** five o'clock || *m* five; fifth (*in dates*)
cinquecenté•sco -sca *adj* (**-schi -sche**) sixteenth-century
cinquecènto *adj, m & pron* five hundred || *f* small car || **il Cinquecento** the sixteenth century
cinquina *f* set of five; five numbers (*drawn at Italian lotto*); (mil) pay
cinta *f* fence, wall; circuit, enclosure; circumference (*of a city*)
cintare *tr* to surround; to fence in; to hold (*in wrestling*)
cin•to -ta *adj* surrounded, girded || *m* belt; girdle; **cinto erniario** truss || *f* see **cinta**
cìntola *f* waist; belt; **con le mani alla cintola** idling, loafing
cintura *f* belt; waist; waistband; lock (*in wrestling*); **cintura di salvataggio** life preserver; **cintura di sicurezza** safety belt
cinturare *tr* to surround
cinturino *m* strap (*of watch or shoes*); hem (*e.g., of cuffs*)
cinturóne *m* belt; Sam Browne belt
ciò *pron* this; that; **a ciò** for that purpose; **a ciò che** so that; **ciò nondimeno** or **ciò nonostante** though, nevertheless; **con tutto ciò** in spite of everything; **per ciò** therefore
ciòc•ca *f* (**-che**) lock (*of hair*); cluster (*e.g., of cherries*)
ciòc•co *m* (**-chi**) log; **dormire come un ciocco** to sleep like a log
cioccolata *adj invar* chocolate || *f* chocolate (*beverage*)
cioccolatino *m* chocolate candy
cioccolato *m* chocolate; **cioccolato al latte** milk chocolate
cioè *adv* that is to say, namely; to wit; rather
ciondolare (**cióndolo**) *tr* to dangle || *intr* to dawdle; to stroll, saunter
cióndolo *m* pendant, charm
ciondolóne *m* idler || *adv* dangling
ciòtola *f* bowl
ciòttolo *m* pebble, small stone; cobblestone
ciottoló•so -sa [s] *adj* pebbly
cip *m* (**cip**) chip (*in gambling*)
cipì•glio *m* (**-gli**) frown
cipólla *f* onion; bulb (*e.g., of a lamp*); nozzle (*of sprinkling can*)
cippo *m* column; bench mark
ciprèsso *m* cypress
cìpria *f* face powder; **cipria compatta** compact
ciprìo•ta *adj & mf* (**-ti -te**) Cypriot
Cipro *m* Cyprus
circa *adv* about, nearly || *prep* concerning, regarding, as to
cir•co *m* (**-chi**) circus; **circo equestre** circus; **circo glaciale** cirque; **circo lunare** walled plain
circolante *adj* circulating; lending (*library*) || *m* available cash (*of a corporation*)
circolare *adj* circular; cashier's (*check*) || *f* circular (*letter*); (rr) beltline || *v* (**cìrcolo**) *intr* to circulate
circolazióne *f* circulation; traffic; currency; **circolazione sanguigna** bloodstream; circulation of blood
cìrcolo *m* circle; circulation (*of blood*); reception (*e.g., at court*); club, set, group
circoncìdere §145 *tr* to circumcise
circoncisióne *f* circumcision
circonci•so -sa *adj* circumcised
circondare (**circóndo**) *tr* to surround, encircle; to overwhelm (*e.g., with kindness*) || *ref* to surround oneself; to be surrounded
circondà•rio *m* (**-ri**) district; surrounding territory
circonduzióne *f* rotation (*e.g., of the body in calisthenics*)
circonferènza *f* circumference
circonflès•so -sa *adj* circumflex
circonlocuzióne *f* circumlocution
circonvallazióne *f* city-line road; (rr) beltline
circonvenire §282 *tr* to circumvent; to outwit
circonvenzióne *f* circumvention
circonvici•no -na *adj* neighboring, nearby
circoscrit•to -ta *adj* circumscribed
circoscrìvere §250 *tr* to circumscribe
circoscrizióne *f* district; circuit
circospèt•to -ta *adj* circumspect, cautious
circospezióne *f* circumspection
circostante *adj* neighboring, surrounding, nearby || **circostanti** *mpl* neighbors; bystanders, onlookers
circostanza *f* circumstance
circonstanziale *adj* circumstantial
circostanziare §287 *tr* to describe in detail; to circumstanciate
circostanzia•to -ta *adj* detailed, circumstantial
circuire §176 *tr* to circumvent
circùito *m* circuit; race (*of automobiles or bicycles*); **circuito stampato** (rad, telv) printed circuit
circumnavigare §209 (**circumnàvigo**) *tr* to circumnavigate
circumnavigazióne *f* circumnavigation
cirìlli•co -ca *adj* (**-ci -che**) Cyrillic

Ciro *m* Cyrus
cirro *m* cirrus
cirrò•si *f* (**-si**) cirrhosis
cispa *f* gum (*on edge of eyelids*)
cisposità [s] *f* gum; gumminess
cispó•so -sa [s] *adj* gummy
ciste *f* cyst
cistèrna *f* cistern; tank
cisti *f* cyst
cistifèllea *f* gall bladder
citante *mf* (law) plaintiff
citare *tr* to cite, quote; to mention; (law) to summon, subpoena
citazióne *f* citation, quotation; mention; (law) summons, subpoena; (mil) commendation
citillo *m* (zool) gopher
citòfono *m* intercom
citostàti•co -ca *adj* (**-ci -che**) (biochem) cancer-inhibiting
citrato *m* citrate
cìtri•co -ca *adj* (**-ci -che**) citric
citrul•lo -la *adj* simple, foolish || *mf* simpleton, fool
cit•tà *f* (**-tà**) city, town || **Città del Capo** Cape Town; **Città del Messico** Mexico City; **Città del Vaticano** Vatican City; **città fungo** boom town
cittadèlla *f* citadel
cittadinanza *f* citizenship
cittadi•no -na *adj* city, town, civic || *mf* citizen; city dweller, urbanite || *m* townsman
ciù•co *m* (**-chi**) (coll) donkey, ass
ciuffo *m* lock, forelock; tuft; (bot) tassel
ciuffolòtto *m* (orn) bullfinch
ciurlare *intr*—**ciurlare nel manico** to play fast and loose
ciurma *f* crew, gang, mob
ciurmare *tr* (archaic) to charm; (archaic) to trick, inveigle
ciurmatóre *m* swindler, charlatan
civétta *f* barn owl, little owl; unmarked police car; ship used as decoy; (fig) coquette, flirt
civettare (**civétto**) *intr* to flirt
civetterìa *f* coquettishness, coquetry
civettuò•lo la *adj* coquettish; attractive
cìvi•co -ca *adj* (**-ci -che**) civic; town, city
civile *adj* civil; civilian || *mf* civilian
civili•sta *mf* (**-sti -ste**) attorney, solicitor
civilizzare [ddzz] *tr* to civilize || *ref* to become civilized
civilizzazióne [ddzz] *f* civilizing (*e.g., of barbarians*); civilization
civil•tà *f* (**-tà**) civilization; civility
civismo *m* good citizenship
clac•son *m* (**-son**) horn (*of a car*)
claire *f* (**claire**) grating (*in front of a store window*)
clamóre *m* clamor, uproar
clamoró•so -sa [s] *adj* noisy; clamorous
clan *m* (**clan**) clan; clique
clandesti•no -na *adj* clandestine
clangóre *m* clangor, clang
clarinetti•sta *mf* (**-sti -ste**) clarinet player
clarinétto *m* clarinet
clarino *m* clarion
classe *f* class
classicheggiante *adj* classicistic
classicismo *m* classicism
classici•sta *mf* (**-sti -ste**) classicist
classici•tà *f* (**-tà**) classical spirit; classical antiquity
clàssi•co -ca (**-ci -che**) *adj* classic(al) || *m* classic
classìfi•ca *f* (**-che**) rank, rating (*in competitive testing*); classification; (sports) rating
classificare §197 (**classìfico**) *tr* to classify; to rate, rank || *ref* to score
classificazióne *f* classification
claudicante *adj* lame, limping
claudicare §197 (**clàudico**) *intr* to limp
clauné•sco -sca *adj* (**-schi -sche**) clownish
clàusola *f* provision, proviso; clause; close, conclusion (*e.g., of a speech*); **clausola rossa** instructions for payment (*in bank-credit documents*); **clausola verde** shipping instructions (*in bank-credit documents*)
clausura *f* (eccl) seclusion; (fig) secluded place
clava *f* club, bludgeon
clavicémbalo *m* harpsicord
clavìcola *f* clavicle, collarbone
clematide *f* clematis
clemènte *adj* clement, indulgent; mild (*climate*)
clemènza *f* clemency; mildness
cleptòmane *adj & mf* kleptomaniac
clericale *adj* clerical || *m* clericalist
clericalismo *m* clericalism
clèro *m* clergy
clessidra *f* water clock; sandglass
clicchettì•o *m* (**-i**) clicking, click-clack (*e.g., of a typewriter*)
cli•ché *m* (**-ché**) cliché; stereotype (*plate*)
cliènte *m* client, customer, patron
clientèla *f* clientele, customers; practice (*of a professional man*)
cli•ma *m* (**-mi**) climate
climatèri•co -ca *adj* (**-ci -che**) climacteric; crucial
climatè•rio *m* (**-ri**) climacteric; crucial period
climàti•co -ca *adj* (**-ci -che**) climatic
climatizzazióne [ddzz] *f* air conditioning
clìni•co -ca (**-ci -che**) *adj* clinic || *m* clinician; highly skilled physician || *f* clinic; private hospital
cli•sma *m* (**-smi**) enema
clistère *m* enema; **clistere a pera** fountain syringe
cloa•ca *f* (**-che**) sewer
cloche *f* (**cloche**) woman's wide-brimmed hat; (aer) stick; (aut) floor gearshift
clorare (**clòro**) *tr* to chlorinate
clorato *m* chlorate
cloridri•co -ca *adj* (**-ci -che**) hydrochloric
clòro *m* chlorine
clorofilla *f* chlorophyll
clorofòr•mio *m* (**-mi**) chloroform
cloroformizzare [ddzz] *tr* to chloroform
cloruro *m* chloride

coabitare (coàbito) *intr* to live together; to cohabit
coabitazióne *f* sharing (*of an apartment*)
coaccusa·to -ta *adj* jointly accused || *m* codefendant
coacèrvo *m* accumulation (*e.g., of interest*)
coadiutóre *m* coadjutor
coadiuvante *adj* helping || *m* helper
coadiuvare (coàdiuvo) *tr* to assist, advise
coagulare (coàgulo) *tr & ref* to coagulate, clot
coagulazióne *f* coagulation, clotting
coàgulo *m* clot
coalescènza *f* coalescence
coalizióne *f* coalition
coalizzare [ddzz] *tr & ref* to unite, rally
coartare *tr* to coerce, force
coartazióne *f* coercion, forcing
coatti·vo -va *adj* forceful, compelling
coat·to -ta *adj* coercive
coautóre *m* coauthor
coazióne *f* coercion
cobalto *m* cobalt
cocaina *f* cocaine
cocainòmane *mf* cocaine addict
coc·ca *f* (**-che**) notch (*of arrow*); corner, edge (*e.g., of a handkerchief*); three-mast galley
coccarda *f* cockade
cocchière *m* coachman, cab driver
còc·chio *m* (**-chi**) coach; chariot
cocchiume *m* bung
còc·cia *f* (**-ce**) sword guard; (coll) head, noggin
còccige *m* coccyx
coccinèlla *f* ladybug
cocciniglia *f* cochineal
còc·cio *m* (**-ci**) earthenware; broken piece of pottery
cocciutàggine *m* stubborness
cocciu·to -ta *adj* stubborn
còc·co *m* (**-chi**) coconut (*tree and nut*); (bact) coccus; (coll) egg; (coll) darling, favorite
cocco·dè *m* (**-dè**) cackle
coccodrillo *m* crocodile
còccola *f* berry (*of cypress*); darling girl
coccolare (còccolo) *tr* to fondle, cuddle || *ref* to nestle, cuddle up; to bask
còcco·lo -la *adj* (coll) nice, darling || *m* darling boy || *f* see **coccola**
coccolóne or **coccolóni** *adv* squatting
cocènte *adj* burning
cocktail *m* (**cocktail**) cocktail; cocktail party
còclea *f* dredge; (anat) cochlea
cocómero *m* watermelon; (coll) simpleton
cocorita *f* parakeet
cocuzza *f* (coll) pumpkin; (coll) head, noggin
cocùzzolo *m* crown (*of hat*); peak (*of mountain*)
códa *f* tail; train (*of skirt*); pigtail (*of hair*); **coda di paglia** (coll) uneasy conscience; **con la coda dell'occhio** out of the corner of the eye; **con la coda tra le gambe** with its tail between its legs; (fig) crestfallen; **di coda** last; **fare la coda** to stand in line; **in coda** in a row; at the tail end
codardìa *f* (lit) cowardice
codar·do -da *adj* cowardly || *mf* coward
codazzo *m* (pej) trail (*of people*)
codeina *f* codein
codé·sto -sta §7 *adj* || §8 *pron*
còdice *m* code; codex; **codice della strada** traffic laws; **codice di avviamento postale** zip code
codicillo *m* codicil
codificare §197 **(codìfico)** *tr* to codify
codi·no -na *adj* reactionary; conformist || *m* pigtail (*of a man*); (fig) reactionary; conformist || *f* small tail
códolo *m* tang, shank (*e.g., of knife*); handle (*of spoon or knife*); head (*of violin*)
coeducazióne *f* coeducation
coefficiènte *m* coefficient
coerciti·vo -va *adj* coercive
coercizióne *f* coercion
coerède *mf* coheir
coerènte *adj* coherent; consistent
coerènza *f* coherence; consistency
coesióne *f* cohesion
coesistènza *f* coexistence
coesìstere §114 *intr* to coexist
coesi·vo -va *adj* cohesive
coetàne·o -a *adj & m* contemporary
coè·vo -va *adj* contemporaneous, coeval
cofanétto *m* small chest, small coffer
còfano *m* chest, coffer; box, case (*for ammunition*); (aut) hood
còffa *f* masthead, crow's-nest
cofirmatà·rio -ria *adj & mf* (**-ri -rie**) cosigner
cogitabón·do -da *adj* (poet & joc) thoughtful, meditative
cogitare (cògito) *tr & intr* (poet & joc) to cogitate
cógli §4
cògliere §127 *tr* to gather; to hit (*the target*); to pluck (*flowers*); to grab, seize; (fig) to guess; **cogliere in flagrante** to catch in the act; **cogliere la palla al balzo** to seize time by the forelock; **cogliere nel giusto** to hit the nail on the head; **cogliere qlcu alla sprovvista** to catch s.o. napping; **cogliere sul fatto** to catch in the act
coglióne *m* (vulg) testicle; (vulg) simpleton, fool
coglionerìa *f* (vulg) great stupidity
cognata *f* sister-in-law
cognato *m* brother-in-law
cògni·to -ta *adj* (poet & law) well-known
cognizióne *f* cognition, knowledge
cognóme *m* surname, family name
coguaro *m* cougar
cói §4
coibènte *adj* nonconducting || *m* nonconductor
coincidènza *f* coincidence; harmony, identity; transfer (*from one streetcar or bus to another*); (rr) connection
coincìdere §145 *intr* to coincide
coinquilino *m* fellow tenant
cointeressare (cointerèsso) *tr* to give a share (*of profit*) to

cointeressa·to -ta *adj* jointly interested || *mf* party having a joint interest
cointeressènza *f* interest, share
coinvòlgere §289 *tr* to involve
còito *m* coitus, intercourse
cól §4
colà *adv* over there
colabròdo *m* colander, strainer
colàg·gio *m* (**-gi**) loss, leak
colapa·sta *m* (**-sta**) colander
colare (**cólo**) *tr* to filter, strain; to sift (*wheat*); to cast (*metals*); **colare a picco** to sink || *intr* to leak, drip; to flow (*said of blood*); **colare a picco** to sink
colata *f* casting (*of metal*); stream of lava; slide (*of snow or rocks*)
colatic·cio *m* (**-ci**) drip, dripping
cola·tóio *m* (**-tói**) colander, strainer
colazióne *f* breakfast; lunch; **colazione al sacco** picnic; **prima colazione** breakfast; **seconda colazione** lunch
colbac·co *m* (**-chi**) busby
colèi §8 *pron dem*
colèn·do -da *adj* (archaic) honorable
colè·ra *m* (**-ra**) cholera
colesterina *f* cholesterol
colì·brì *m* (**-brì**) hummingbird
còli·co -ca *adj* & *f* (**-ci -che**) colic
colino *m* strainer
cólla §4
còlla *f* glue; paste; **colla di pesce** isinglass
collaborare (**collàboro**) *intr* to collaborate; to contribute (*to newspaper or magazine*)
collaboratóre *m* collaborator; contributor (*to newspaper or magazine*)
collaborazióne *f* collaboration
collaborazioni·sta *mf* (**-sti -ste**) collaborationist
collana *f* necklace; series, collection (*of literary works*)
collante *adj* & *m* adhesive
collare *m* collar || *v* (**còllo**) *tr* to lift or lower (*with a rope*)
collasso *m* collapse
collaterale *adj* & *m* collateral
collaudare (**collàudo**) *tr* to test; to approve; to pass
collauda·tóre -trice *mf* tester
collàudo *m* test
collazionare (**collazióno**) *tr* to collate
cólle §4
còlle *m* hill; low peak; mountain pass
collè·ga *mf* (**-ghi -ghe**) colleague, associate
collegaménto *m* connection, telephone connection; contact; (mil) liaison
collegare §209 (**collégo**) *tr* to join, connect || *intr* to agree, be in harmony || *ref* to become allied; to make contact, make connection (*e.g., by phone*)
collegiale *adj* collegiate || *mf* boarding-school student
collegiata *f* collegiate church
collè·gio *m* (**-gi**) college (*e.g., of surgeons*); boarding school, academy
còllera *f* anger, wrath; **montare in collera** to become angry
collèri·co -ca *adj* (**-ci -che**) hot-tempered, choleric
collètta *f* collection; collect (*in church*)
collettivismo *m* collectivism
collettivi·tà *f* (**-tà**) collectivity, community
colletti·vo -va *adj* collective || *m* party worker (*of leftist party*)
collétto *m* collar; flank (*of a tooth*)
collet·tóre -trice *adj* connecting; collecting (*pipe*) || *m* collector; tax collector; manifold; (elec) commutator (*of D.C. device*); (elec) collector (*of A.C. device*); **collettore d'ammissione** intake manifold; **collettore di scarico** exhaust manifold
collettorìa *f* tax office; small post office
collezionare (**collezióno**) *tr* to collect (*e.g., stamps*)
collezióne *f* collection; collection, series (*of literary works*)
collezioni·sta *mf* (**-sti -ste**) collector
collìdere §135 *intr* to collide
collimare *tr* to point (*a telescope*) || *intr* to coincide, match; to dovetail
collina *f* hill; **in collina** in the hill country
collinó·so -sa [s] *adj* hilly
collì·rio *m* (**-ri**) eyewash
collisióne *f* collision; (fig) conflict: **entrare in collisione** to collide
cóllo §4
còllo *m* neck; piece (*of baggage*); package, parcel; **al collo** in a sling; (fig) downhill; **collo del piede** instep; **collo d'oca** crankshaft; **in collo** in one's arms (*said of a baby*)
collocaménto *m* placement, employment; **collocamento a riposo** retirement; **collocamento in aspettativa** leave of absence without pay; **collocamento in malattia** sick leave
collocare §197 (**còlloco**) *tr* to place; to find employment for; to sell; **collocare a riposo** to retire; **collocare in aspettativa** to give a leave of absence without pay to; **collocare in malattia** to grant sick leave to
collocazióne *f* location (*of a book in a library*); catalogue card
colloidale *adj* colloidal
collòide *m* colloid
colloquiale *adj* colloquial
collò·quio *m* (**-qui**) talk, conference; colloquy; colloquium, symposium
colló·so -sa [s] *adj* gluey, sticky
collotòrto *m* (**collitòrti**) bigot, hypocrite
collòttola *f* nape or scruff of the neck
collùdere §105 *intr* to be in collusion
collusióne *f* collusion
colluttó·rio *m* (**-ri**) mouthwash
colluttare *intr* to scuffle, fight
colluttazióne *f* scuffle, fight
cólma *f* high-water level (*during high tide*)
colmare (**cólmo**) *tr* to fill, fill up; to fill in (*with dirt*); to overwhelm; **colmare una lacuna** to bridge a gap
colmata *f* silting; reclaimed land; sand bank
cól·mo -ma *adj* full, filled up || *m* top, peak, summit; (archit) ridgepole; (fig) acme; **al colmo di** at the height

of; **è il colmo** that's the limit || *f* see **colma**
colofóne *m* colophon
colofònia *f* rosin
colombàia *f* dovecot
colombèlla *f* ingenue; **a colombella** vertically
colóm•bo -ba *mf* pigeon, dove || **Colombo** *m* Columbus
colònia *f* colony; cologne; settlement; summer camp; **colonia penale** penal colony; penitentiary || **Colonia** *f* Cologne
coloniale *adj* colonial || *m* colonial; colonist; **coloniali** imported foods
colòni•co -ca *adj* (**-ci -che**) farm (*e.g., house*)
colonizzare [ddzz] *tr* to colonize; to settle
colonizzazióne [ddzz] *f* colonization
colonna *f* column; row; **colonna sonora** sound track; **Colonne d'Ercole** Pillars of Hercules
colonnato *m* colonnade
colonnèllo *m* colonel
colonnétta *f* small column; gasoline pump
colò•no -na *mf* sharecropper; colonist; settler; (poet) farmer
colorante *adj* coloring || *m* dye; stain
colorare (**colóro**) *tr & ref* to color; to stain
colora•to -ta *adj* colored; stained (*glass*)
colorazióne *f* coloring
colóre *m* color; paint; suit (*of cards*); flush (*at poker*); shade; character (*of a deal*); **di colore** colored (*man*); **farne di tutti i colori** to be up to all kinds of deviltry; **farsi di tutti i colori** to change countenance
colorifi•cio *m* (**-ci**) paint factory; dye factory
colorire §176 *tr* to color
colori•to -ta *adj* colored, flushed; expressive || *m* color, complexion; (fig) expression
coloritura *f* coloring; characteristic; political complexion
colóro §8
colossale *adj* colossal
Colossèo *m* Coliseum
colòsso *m* colossus
cólpa *f* fault; sin; guilt; (law) injury; **avere la colpa** to be guilty; to be wrong; **essere in colpa** to be guilty
colpévole *adj* guilty || *mf* guilty person, culprit
colpevoli•sta *mf* (**-sti -ste**) person who prejudges s.o. guilty
colpire §176 *tr* to hit, strike; to harm; to impress; **colpire nel segno** to hit the mark
cólpo *m* hit, blow; strike; tip, rap; knock; shot; round (*of gun*); cut, slash (*of knife*); thrust (*e.g., of spear*); lash (*of animal's tail*); toot (*of car's horn*); **andare a colpo sicuro** to know where to hit; **colpo apoplettico** stroke; **colpo da maestro** master stroke; **colpo d'aria** draft; **colpo d'ariete** water hammer; **colpo di fortuna** stroke of luck; **colpo di fulmine** love at first sight; **colpo di grazia** coup de grâce; **colpo di mano** surprise attack; **colpo di scena** dramatic turn of events; **colpo di sole** sunstroke; **colpo di spugna** wiping the slate clean; **colpo di stato** coup d'état; **colpo di telefono** telephone call; **colpo di testa** sudden decision, inconsiderate action; **colpo di vento** gust of wind; **colpo d'occhio** view; glance, look; **di colpo** at once; **fallire il colpo** to miss the mark; **fare colpo** to make a hit; **sul colpo** then and there; **tutto in un colpo** all at once
colpó•so -sa [s] *adj* unpremeditated; involuntary (*e.g., manslaughter*)
coltèlla *f* butcher knife; (elec) knife switch
coltellàc•cio *m* (**-ci**) hunting knife; butcher knife; (naut) studding sail
coltellata *f* stab, gash, slash; **fare a coltellate** to fight with knives
coltelleria *f* cutlery
coltelli•nàio *m* (**-nài**) cutler
coltèllo *m* knife; **a coltello** edgewise (*said of bricks*); **avere il coltello per il manico** to have the upper hand; **coltello a serramanico** switchblade knife; pocketknife
coltivare *tr* to cultivate
coltiva•to -ta *adj* cultivated
coltivatóre *m* farmer
coltivazióne *f* cultivation
cól•to -ta *adj* cultivated; learned (*word*) || *m* garden; (archaic) worship
cóltre *f* blanket; comforter; (fig) pall; **coltri** bedclothes
coltróne *m* quilt
coltura *f* cultivation; crop; culture (*e.g., of silkworms, bacteria*)
colubrina *f* culverin
colùi §8 *pron dem*
comandaménto *m* commandment
comandante *m* commanding officer; commandant; (nav) captain; **comandante del porto** harbor master; **comandante in seconda** (naut) first mate
comandare *tr* to command, order; to direct (*employees*); to register (*a letter*); (mach) to regulate; (mach) to control; (poet) to overlook, command the view of (*e.g., a valley*); **comandare a bacchetta** to command in a dictatorial manner || *intr* to command; **comandi!** (mil) at your orders!
comando *m* command, order
comare *f* godmother; (coll) friend, neighbor; (coll) gossip
combaciare §128 *tr* (archaic) to gather || *intr* to fit closely together; to tally, dovetail; to coincide
combattènte *adj* fighting || *m* combatant
combàttere *tr & intr* to combat || *ref* to fight one another
combattiménto *m* combat; fight; battle; **fuori combattimento** knockout, K.O.; **fuori combattimento tecnico** technical knockout, T.K.O.; **mettere fuori combattimento** to knock out; (fig) to weaken

combatti·vo -va *adj* pugnacious, combative
combattu·to -ta *adj* heated (*discussion*); overcome (*by doubt*); torn (*between two opposing feelings*)
combinare *tr* to combine; to match (*e.g., colors*); to organize || *intr* to agree; **combinare a** to succeed in || *ref* to agree; to chance, happen; to combine
combinazióne *f* combination; chance; coverall (*for mechanics or flyers*)
combrìccola *f* gang
combustibile *adj* combustible || *m* fuel, combustible
combustióne *f* combustion; (poet) upheaval
combutta *f* gang, band; **essere in combutta** to be in cahoots
cóme *m* manner, way; **il come e il perchè** the why and the wherefore || *adv* as; like; as for; how; **come mai?** why?; **e come!** and how!; **ma come?** what?, how is it? || *conj* as; as soon as; while; how; because; since; **come se** as if
comecché *conj* (lit) although; (poet) wherever
comedóne *m* blackhead
cométa *f* comet
comici·tà *f* (-tà) comicalness
còmi·co -ca (-ci -che) *adj* comic(al) || *m* comic; author of comedies; comic actor
comignolo *m* chimney pot; ridge (*of roof*)
cominciare §128 *tr & intr* to begin, start, commence
comitato *m* committee
comitiva *f* group, party; (poet) retinue
comì·zio *m* **(-zi)** (pol) meeting, rally; (hist) comitia
còm·ma *m* **(-mi)** paragraph, article (*of law or decree*)
commèdia *f* comedy; play, drama; (fig) farce; **commedia di carattere** comedy of character; **commedia d'intreccio** comedy of intrigue; **far la commedia** to pretend, feign; **finire in commedia** to end ludicrously; **finire la commedia** to stop faking
commediante *mf* actor; comedian (*amusing person*); (fig) hypocrite
commediògra·fo -fa *mf* playwright, comedian
commemorare (commèmoro) *tr* to commemorate
commemorati·vo -va *adj* commemorative, memorial
commemorazióne *f* commemoration
commènda *f* commandership (*of an order*); (eccl) commendam
commendàbile *adj* commendable
commendare (commèndo) *tr* (lit) to commend, praise; (obs) to entrust
commendati·zio -zia (-zi -zie) *adj* introductory || *f* letter of introduction; recommendation
commendatóre *m* commander (*of an order*)
commendévole *adj* commendable
commensale *mf* guest; table companion
commensurare (commènsuro & commensuro) *tr* to compare; to proportion, prorate
commentare (comménto) *tr* to comment, comment on
commentà·rio *m* **(-ri)** commentary; diary, journal
commenta·tóre -trice *mf* commentator
comménto *m* comment; **fare commenti** to criticize; **non far commenti!** don't waste your time talking!
commerciàbile *adj* marketable
commerciale *adj* commercial; common, ordinary
commerciali·sta *mf* **(-sti -ste)** business-administration major; attorney specializing in commercial law
commerciante *mf* merchant, dealer
commerciare §128 **(commèrcio)** *tr* to deal in; to buy and sell || *intr* to deal
commèr·cio *m* **(-ci)** commerce, trade; illegal traffic; (poet) intercourse; **commercio all'ingrosso** wholesale (trade); **commercio al minuto** retail (trade); **fuori commercio** not for sale; **in commercio** for sale
commés·so -sa *adj* committed || *mf* clerk (*in a store*) || *m* salesman; clerk (*in a court*); janitor (*in a school*); **commesso viaggiatore** traveling salesman || *f* saleslady; order (*of merchandise*)
commestibile *adj* edible || **commestibili** *mpl* staples, groceries; foodstuffs
comméttere §198 *tr* to join, connect; to commit; to charge, commission; to peg; (poet) to entrust || *intr* to join, fit
commettitura *f* joint, seam
commiato *m* leave; **dare commiato a** to dismiss; **prender commiato** to take one's leave
commilitóne *m* comrade, comrade in arms
comminare *tr* (law) to determine, fix (*a penalty*)
comminatò·rio -ria *adj* threatening
commiserare (commìsero) *tr* to pity, feel sorry for
commiserazióne *f* commiseration
commissariale *adj* commissioner's, e.g., **funzioni commissariali** commissioner's functions; commissar's functions
commissariato *m* commissary; inspector's office
commissà·rio *m* **(-ri)** commissary; inspector; commissioner; **commissario del popolo** commissar; **commissario di bordo** purser; **commissario di pubblica sicurezza** police inspector; **commissario tecnico** (sports) soccer commissioner
commissionare (commissióno) *tr* to commission, order
commissionà·rio -ria (-ri -rie) *adj* commission || *m* commission merchant
commissióne *f* commission, agency; order (*of merchandise*); committee; errand; commitment (*of an act*)
commisurare *tr* to proportion (*e.g., crime to punishment*)
committènte *mf* buyer, customer

commodòro *m* commodore
commòs·so -sa *adj* moved; moving
commovènte *adj* moving, touching
commozióne *f* commotion; emotion; **commozione cerebrale** (pathol) concussion
commuòvere §202 *tr* to move; to touch; to stir || *ref* to be moved; to be touched
commutare *tr* to commute; to switch || *ref* to turn
commuta·tóre -trice *adj* commutative || *m* (elec) change-over switch; (elec) commutator (*switch*); (telp) plugboard || *f* converter
commutatori·sta *mf* (**-sti -ste**) (telp) operator
commutazióne *f* commutation; (telp) selection; (elec) switchover
co·mò *m* (**-mò**) chest; chest of drawers
còmoda *f* commode
comodare (**còmodo**) *tr* to lend || *intr* (with *dat*) to please, e.g., **non le comoda** it doesn't please her
comodino *m* night table; (theat) bit player; **fare il comodino a** (coll) to follow sheepishly
comodi·tà *f* (**-tà**) comfort; convenience; opportunity
còmo·do -da *adj* comfortable; convenient; easy; loose-fitting; calm || *m* convenience; ease; advantage; comfort; opportunity; **a Suo comodo** at your convenience; **comodo di cassa** credit (*at the bank*); **con comodo** without hurrying; **fare comodo** to come in handy; (with *dat*) to please, e.g., **non gli fa comodo** it doesn't please him; **fare il proprio comodo** to think only of oneself; **stia comodo!** make yourself at home! || *f* see **comoda**
compaesa·no -na *mf* fellow citizen || *m* fellow countryman || *f* fellow countrywoman
compàgine *f* strict union; connection; assemblage; (fig) cohesion
compagna *f* companion, mate; (archaic) company
compagnìa *f* company; **Compagnia di Gesù** Society of Jesus; **compagnia stabile** (theat) stock company
compa·gno -gna *adj* like, similar || *m* fellow; companion, comrade; mate; partner; **compagno d'armi** comrade in arms; **compagno di viaggio** fellow traveler || *f* see **compagna**
companàti·co *m* (**-ci**) food to eat with bread
comparàbile *adj* comparable
comparati·vo -va *adj & m* comparative
compara·to -ta *adj* comparative
comparazióne *f* comparison
compare *m* godfather; best man (*at wedding*); fellow; confederate
comparire §108 *intr* to appear; to be known; to cut a figure
comparizióne *f* appearance (*in court*)
comparsa *f* appearance; (theat) extra, supernumerary; (law) petition, brief; **far comparsa** to cut a figure
compartecipare (**compartécipo**) *intr* to share
compartecipazióne *f* sharing; **compartecipazione agli utili** profit sharing
compartécipe *adj* sharing
compartiménto *m* circle, clique; district; (naut, rr) compartment
compartire §176 & (**comparto**) *tr* to divide up, distribute
compassa·to -ta *adj* measured; stiff, formal; reserved; self-controlled
compassionare (**compassióno**) *tr* to pity
compassióne *f* compassion, pity
compassionévole *adj* compassionate; pitiful
compasso *m* compass; **compasso a grossezza** calipers
compatìbile *adj* excusable; compatible
compatiménto *m* compassion; condescension
compatire §176 *tr* to pity; to forgive, overlook; to bear with; **farsi compatire** to become an object of ridicule || *intr* to pity
compatriò·ta *mf* (**-ti -te**) compatriot
compattézza *f* compactness
compat·to -ta *adj* compact, tight
compendiare §287 (**compèndio**) *tr* to epitomize, summarize
compèn·dio *m* (**-di**) compendium, summary; **fare un compendio di** to abstract
compendió·so -sa [s] *adj* compendious, brief, succinct
compenetràbile *adj* penetrable
compenetrabilità *f* penetrability
compenetrare (**compènetro**) *tr* to penetrate; to permeate; to pervade || *ref* to be overcome; **compenetrarsi di** to be conscious of
compensare (**compènso**) *tr* to compensate, pay; to balance, offset; to clear (*checks*)
compensa·to -ta *adj* compensated; laminated || *m* laminate; plywood
compensazióne *f* compensation; offset; (com) clearing (*of checks*)
compènso *m* reward; retribution, pay; **in compenso** on the other hand
cómpera *f* var of **compra**
comperare (**cómpero**) *tr & intr* var of **comprare**
competènte *adj* competent
competènza *f* competence; jurisdiction; **competenze** honoraria
compètere §129 *intr* to compete; to concern; to have jurisdiction
competiti·vo -va *adj* competitive
competi·tóre -trice *mf* competitor, contender
competizióne *f* competition, contest
compiacènte *adj* complaisant, obliging
compiacènza *f* complaisance, kindness; pleasure
compiacére §214 *tr* to gratify || *intr* (with *dat*) to please, e.g., **non posso compiacere a tutti** I cannot please everybody || *ref* to be pleased; **compiacersi con** to congratulate; **compiacersi di** to be kind enough to
compiaciménto *m* pleasure; congratulation; approval

compiaciu·to -ta *adj* pleased, satisfied
compiàngere §215 *tr* to pity || *ref* to feel sorry
compian·to -ta *adj* lamented (*departed person*) || *m* sympathy; (poet) sorrow; (poet) lament
compiegare §209 (compiègo) *tr* to enclose (*in a letter*)
cómpiere §130 *tr* to complete, finish; to fulfill, accomplish; **compiere . . . anni** to be . . . years old; **compiere gli anni** to have a birthday || *ref* to happen; to come true
compilare *tr* to compile
compila·tóre -trice *mf* compiler
compilazióne *f* compilation
compiménto *m* fulfillment, accomplishment
compire §176 *tr* to complete, finish; to fulfill, accomplish; **per compir l'opera** as if it weren't enough || *ref* to happen; to come true
compitare (cómpito) *tr* to syllabify; to read poorly; to spell, spell letter by letter
compitazióne *f* spelling letter by letter
compitézza *f* courtesy, politeness
cómpito *m* task; exercise; homework
compi·to -ta *adj* courteous, polite; (poet) adequate
compiu·to -ta *adj* accomplished
compleanno *m* birthday; **buon compleanno** happy birthday
complementare *adj* complementary; additional (*tax*) || *f* graduated income tax
compleménto *m* complement; (mil, nav) reserve
complessióne *f* build, physique
complessi·tà *f* (-tà) complexity
complessi·vo -va *adj* total, aggregate
complès·so -sa *adj* complex, complicated; compound (*fracture*) || *m* whole; complex; **in complesso** in general
completare (complèto) *tr* to complete, carry through; to supplement, round off
complè·to -ta *adj* complete, full; overall, thoroughgoing; **al completo** full (*e.g., bus*) || *m* set (*of matching items*); suit of clothes; **completo femminile** lady's tailor-made suit; **completo maschile** suit
complicare §197 (còmplico) *tr* to complicate || *ref* to become complicated
complica·to -ta *adj* complicated, complex
complicazióne *f* complication
còmplice *mf* accomplice, accessory
complici·tà *f* (-tà) complicity
complimentare (compliménto) *tr* to compliment || *ref*—**complimentarsi con** to congratulate
compliménto *m* compliment; congratulation; favor; **complimenti** regards; **complimenti!** congratulations!; **fare complimenti** to stand on ceremony; **senza complimenti** without ceremony; without any further ado
complimentó·so -sa [s] *adj* ceremonious; complimentary
complottare (complòtto) *intr* to plot
complòtto *m* plot, machination
compluù·vio *m* (-vi) valley (*of roof*)
componènte *adj* component || *mf* member || *m* component (*component part*) || *f* component (*force*)
componìbile *adj* sectional (*e.g., bookcase*)
componiménto *m* composition, settlement (*of a dispute*)
compórre §218 *tr* to compose; to arrange; to settle (*a quarrel*); to lay out (*a corpse*); (typ) to set
comportaménto *m* behavior
comportare (compòrto) *tr* to allow, tolerate; to entail || *ref* to behave; to handle (*said, e.g., of a motor*); **comportarsi male** to misbehave
compòrto *m* (com) delay
compòsi·to -ta *adj* composite || **composite** *fpl* (bot) Compositae
composi·tóio *m* (-tói) (typ) composing stick
composi·tóre -trice *mf* compositor, typesetter; composer || *f* typesetting machine
composizióne *f* composition; settlement
compósta *f* compote; **composta di frutta** stewed fruit
compostézza *f* neatness, tidiness; good behavior; orderliness
compostièra *f* compote, compotier
compó·sto -sta *adj* compound; neat, tidy; well-behaved || *m* compound || *f* see **composta**
cómpra *f* purchase; shopping; **compre** shopping
comprare (cómpro) *tr* to buy, purchase; to buy off || *intr* to buy, shop; to trade
compra·tóre -trice *mf* buyer, purchaser
compravéndere §281 *tr* to make a deal in, to transfer (*e.g., a house*)
compravéndita *f* transaction; transfer (*e.g., of real estate*)
comprèndere §220 *tr* to comprehend, include, comprise; to overwhelm; to understand; to forgive
comprendò·nio *m* (-ni) (joc) understanding
comprensìbile *adj* understandable, comprehensible
comprensióne *f* comprehension, understanding
comprensi·vo -va *adj* comprehensive; understanding
comprensò·rio *m* (-ri) land to be reclaimed; area, zone, e.g., **comprensorio turistico** tourist area
comprè·so -sa [s] *adj* comprised, included; understood; deeply touched; immersed
comprèssa *f* compress
compressióne *f* compression
comprès·so -sa *adj* compressed; (fig) repressed; (aut) supercharged || *f* see **compressa**
compressóre *m* compressor; **compressore stradale** road roller
comprimà·rio *m* (-ri) (med) associate chief of staff; (theat) second lead

comprìmere §131 *tr* to compress; to repress, restrain; to tamp
compromés•so -sa *adj* jeopardized, in danger || *m* compromise; referral (*to arbitration*)
comprometttènte *adj* compromising
comprométtere §198 *tr* to compromise; to endanger; to involve, commit; (law) to refer (*to arbitration*)
comproprie•tà *f* (**-tà**) joint ownership
comproprietà•rio -ria *mf* (**-ri -rie**) joint owner
compròva *f* confirmation
comprovare (compròvo) *tr* to confirm; to circumstantiate
compulsare *tr* to consult, peruse; to summon (*to appear in court*)
compulsi•vo -va *adj* compulsive
compun•to -ta *adj* contrite, repentant
compunzióne *f* compunction
computàbile *adj* computable
computare (còmputo) *tr* to compute
computi•sta *mf* (**-sti -ste**) bookkeeper
computisterìa *f* bookkeeping
còmputo *m* computation, reckoning
comunale *adj* municipal, town (*e.g., hall*); community-owned; (poet) common
comunanza *f* community; **in comunanza** in common
comune *adj* common || *m* normalcy; commune, municipality, town; town hall; (hist) guild; (nav) common seaman; **in comune** in common || *f* commune (*in communist countries*); (theat) main stage entrance; **andare per la comune** to follow the crowd; **per la comune** commonly
comunèlla *f* cabal, clique; passkey (*in a hotel*); (law) mutual insurance (*of cattlemen*); **fare comunella con** to consort with
comunicàbile *adj* communicable
comunicante *adj* communicant; communicating || *m* priest who gives communion
comunicare §197 (**comùnico**) *tr* to communicate; to administer communion to || *intr* to communicate || *ref* to spread; to receive communion, to commune
comunicati•vo -va *adj* communicable, spreading; communicative
comunicato *m* communiqué; **comunicato commerciale** advertisement, ad; **comunicato stampa** press release
comunicazióne *f* communication; statement; (telp) connection; **comunicazioni** communications
comunióne *f* community; (law) community property || **Comunione** *f* Communion
comunismo *m* communism
comuni•sta (-sti -ste) *adj* communist || *mf* communist; (law) joint tenant
comunìsti•co -ca *adj* (**-ci -che**) communistic
comuni•tà *f* (**-tà**) community
comunità•rio -ria *adj* (**-ri -rie**) community, e.g., **interessi comunitari** community interests
comùnque *adv* however, nevertheless || *conj* however, no matter how
cón §4 *prep* with; by (*e.g., boat*); **con** + *art* + *inf* by + *ger*, e.g., **col leggere** by reading
conato *m* effort, attempt
cón•ca *f* (**-che**) washbowl, washbasin; copper water jug; valley, hollow; (poet) shell; **conca idraulica** drydock
concatenaménto *m* (poet) concatenation
concatenare (concatèno) *tr* to link || *ref* to unfold, ensue
concatenazióne *f* concatenation
concàusa *f* joint cause; (law) aggravation
cònca•vo -va *adj* concave; hollow || *m* hollow
concèdere §132 *tr* to grant, concede; to stretch (*a point*) || *ref* to let oneself go, give oneself over
concènto *m* harmony; (fig) agreement
concentraménto *m* concentration
concentrare (concèntro) *tr* to concentrate; to center || *ref* to concentrate, focus; to center
concentra•to -ta *adj* concentrated; condensed (*e.g., milk*) || *m* purée (*e.g., of tomatoes*)
concentrazióne *f* concentration; (chem) condensation
concèntri•co -ca *adj* (**-ci -che**) concentric
concepìbile *adj* conceivable
concepiménto *m* conception; (fig) formulation
concepire §176 *tr* to conceive; (fig) to nurture
concerìa *f* tannery
concèrnere §133 *tr* to concern
concertare (concèrto) *tr* to scheme, concert; (mus) to orchestrate, arrange || *ref* to agree
concerta•to -ta *adj* agreed upon; (mus) with accompaniment || *m* ensemble (*of orchestra, soloists, and chorus*)
concerta•tóre -trice *mf* arranger || *m* plotter, schemer
concertazióne *f* (mus) arrangement
concerti•sta *mf* (**-sti -ste**) concert performer, soloist
concèrto *m* concert; concerto; (fig) choir
concessionà•rio *m* (**-ri**) sole agent, concessionaire; dealer; lessee (*of business establishment*)
concessióne *f* concession; dealership; admission
concessi•vo -va *adj* concessive
concès•so -sa *adj* granted, admitting
concètto *m* concept; opinion
concettó•so -sa [s] *adj* concise; full of ideas; full of conceits
concettuale *adj* conceptual
concezióne *f* conception; formulation
conchìglia *f* shell, conch; (sports) jock guard, protective cup
conchiùdere §125 *tr, intr & ref* var of **conclùdere**
cón•cia *f* (**-ce**) tanning
conciapèl•li *m* (**-li**) tanner
conciare §128 (**cóncio**) *tr* to tan; to cure (*e.g., tobacco*); to arrange; to

straighten up; to reduce; to cut (*a precious stone*); **conciare per le feste** (coll) to give a good beating to || *ref* to get messed up, get dirty
conciatét·ti *m* (-ti) roofer
conciató·re -trice *mf* tanner
conciliàbile *adj* reconcilable
conciliàbolo *m* conventicle, secret meeting
conciliante *adj* conciliatory
conciliare *adj* council || *m* member of an ecclesiastical council || §287 *tr* to conciliate, reconcile; to settle (*a fine*); to promote (*e.g., sleep*); to obtain (*a favor*) || *ref* to become reconciled
concilia·tóre -trice *adj* conciliatory || *mf* conciliator, peacemaker || *m* justice of the peace
conciliazióne *f* conciliation || **la Conciliazione** the Concordat (*of 1929 between Italy and the Vatican*)
concì·lio *m* (-li) council; church council
concimàia *f* manure pit
concimare *tr* to manure
concimazióne *f* spreading of manure; chemical fertilization
concime *m* manure; fertilizer
cón·cio -cia (-ci -ce) *adj* tanned || *m* ashlar; dung, manure; (archaic) agreement; **concio di scoria** cinder block || *f* see **concia**
conciofossecosaché *conj* (archaic) since
concionare (concióno) *intr* (archaic) to harangue
concióne *f* (archaic) harangue; (archaic) assembly
conciossiacosaché *conj* (archaic) since
concisióne *f* concision, brevity
conci·so -sa *adj* concise, brief
concistòro *m* consistory; (fig) assembly
concitare (còncito) *tr* to excite, stir up
concita·to -ta *adj* excited; (poet) decisive
concitazióne *f* impetus; excitement
concittadi·no -na *mf* fellow citizen
conclave *m* conclave
conclùdere §105 *tr* to conclude || *intr* to conclude; to be convincing || *ref* to conclude, end; **concludersi con** to end with; to result in
conclusionale *adj* (law) summary
conclusióne *f* conclusion; **conclusioni** (law) summation
conclusi·vo -va *adj* conclusive
conclu·so -sa *adj* concluded; terminated; (poet) closed
concomitante *adj* concomitant
concordanza *f* concordance, agreement; (gram) concord; **concordanze** concordance (*e.g., to the Bible*)
concordare (concòrdo) *tr* to agree on; to make agree || *intr* & *ref* to come to an agreement
concordato *m* agreement; concordat; settlement (*with creditors*)
concòrde *adj* in agreement
concòrdia *f* concord, harmony
concorrènte *adj* competitive || *m* (com) competitor; (sports) contestant
concorrènza *f* competition
concorrenziale *adj* competitive (*e.g., price*)
concórrere §139 *intr* to converge; to concur; to compete
concórso *m* attendance; concurrence; combination (*of circumstances*); competition; competitive examination; contest; **concorso di bellezza** beauty contest; **concorso di pubblico** turnout; **fuori concorso** not entering the competition; in a class by itself
concretare (concrèto) *tr* to realize (*e.g., a dream*); to conclude, accomplish || *ref* to come true
concretézza *f* concreteness, consistency
concrè·to -ta *adj* concrete, real; practical || *m* practical matter; **in concreto** really, in reality
concubina *f* concubine
concubinàg·gio *m* (-gi) concubinage
concubinato *m* var of **concubinaggio**
conculcare §197 *tr* (lit) to trample under foot; (lit) to violate
concupire §176 *tr* (poet) to lust for
concupiscènza *f* concupiscence, lust
concussióne *f* extortion, shakedown; **concussione cerebrale** (pathol) concussion
condanna *f* conviction; sentence; (fig) blame, condemnation
condannare *tr* to condemn; to find guilty, convict; to sentence; to damn (*to eternal punishment*); to declare incurable; to wall up
condanna·to -ta *adj* condemned || *m* convict
condensare (condènso) *tr* & *ref* to condense
condensa·to -ta *adj* condensed (*e.g., milk*)
condensatóre *m* condenser
condensazióne *f* condensation
condiménto *m* condiment, seasoning
condire §176 *tr* to season
condiret·tóre -trice *mf* associate manager
condiscendènte *adj* condescending
condiscendènza *f* condescension
condiscéndere §245 *intr* to condescend
condiscépo·lo -la *mf* schoolmate, school companion
condividere §158 *tr* to share
condizionale *adj* & *m* conditional || *f* (law) suspended sentence
condizionare (condizióno) *tr* to condition; to treat (*to prevent spoilage*)
condizionatóre *m* air conditioner
condizióne *f* condition; term (*of sale*); **a condizione che** provided that; **condizioni** condition, shape (*e.g., of a shipment*); **essere in condizione di** to be in a position to
condoglianza *f* condolence; **fare le condoglianze a** to extend one's sympathy to
condolére §159 *ref* to condole
condomì·nio *m* (-ni) condominium
condòmi·no -na *mf* joint owner (*of real estate*)
condonare (condóno) *tr* to condone; to remit
condóno *m* pardon, parole
condót·to -ta *adj* country (*doctor*) || *m* duct, canal; conduit || *f* behavior,

conduct; district (*of country doctor*); transportation; pipeline; (theat) baggage; **condotta forzata** flume
conducènte *m* driver; bus driver; motorman
condù•plex *mf* (**-plex**) (telp) party-line user
condurre §102 *tr* to lead; to drive (*a car*); to round up (*cattle*); to pipe (*e.g., gas*); to conduct; to trace (*a line*); to take; to bring; to manage; **condurre a termine** to bring to fruition, realize || *intr* to lead || *ref* to behave; to betake oneself, go; **condursi a** (poet) to be reduced to (*e.g., poverty*)
conduttivi•tà *f* (**-tà**) conductivity
condutti•vo -va *adj* conductive
condut•tóre -trice *adj* guiding, leading || *m* operator (*of a bus*); driver (*of a car*); (rr) engineer; (rr) ticket collector; (phys) conductor
conduttura *f* conduit, pipeline
conduzióne *f* conduction; leasing
conestàbile *m* constable (*keeper of a castle*)
confabulare (**confàbulo**) *intr* to confabulate, commune; to connive, scheme
confacènte *adj* suitable, appropriate; helpful
confare §173 *ref*—**confarsi a** to agree with, e.g., **le uova non gli si confanno** eggs do not agree with him
confederare (**confèdero**) *tr & ref* to confederate
confedera•to -ta *adj & m* confederate
confederazióne *f* confederation
conferènza *f* conference; lecture; **conferenza illustrata** chalk talk; **conferenza stampa** press conference
conferenziè•re -ra *mf* speaker, lecturer
conferiménto *m* conferring, bestowal
conferire §176 *tr* to confer, bestow; to add; to contribute || *intr* to confer; to contribute; **conferire alla salute** to be healthful
conférma *f* confirmation; **a conferma di** (com) in reply to, confirming
confermare (**confermo**) *tr* to confirm; to verify; to retain (*in office*) || *ref* to become more sure of oneself; to prove to be; to remain (*in the conclusion of a letter*)
confessare (**confèsso**) *tr & ref* to confess
confessionale *adj* confessional; church; church-related, parochial (*e.g., school*) || *m* confessional
confessióne *f* confession
confès•so -sa *adj* acknowledged, self-admitted; **confesso e comunicato** having made one's confession and taken communion
confessóre *m* confessor
confetteria *f* candy store, confectioner's shop
confettièra *f* candy box
confettière *m* candy maker; candy dealer, confectioner
confètto *m* sugar-covered nut, sweetmeat; losenge, drop
confettura *f* candy; preserves, jam; **confetture** confectionery
confezionare (**confezióno**) *tr* to make; to tailor (*a suit*)
confezióne *f* preparation, manufacturing; packaging; **confezioni** ready-made clothes
confezioni•sta *mf* (**-sti -ste**) ready-made clothier
conficcare §197 *tr* to drive (*a nail*); to thrust (*a knife*) || *ref* to become embedded
confidare *tr* to trust (*a secret*) || *intr* to trust || *ref* to confide
confidènte *adj* confident || *mf* confident; informer
confidènza *f* confidence; secret; familiarity
confidenziale *adj* confidential; friendly
configgere §104 *tr* to plunge, thrust
configurazióne *f* configuration
confinante *adj* bordering || *mf* neighbor
confinare *tr* to exile; to confine || *intr* to border
confinà•rio -ria *adj* (**-ri -rie**) border (*e.g., zone*)
Confindùstria *f* (acronym) **Confederazione Nazionale degli Industriali** National Confederation of Industrialists
confine *m* border, boundary line; boundary mark, landmark
confino *m* exile (*in a different town*)
confi•sca *f* (**-sche**) confiscation
confiscare §197 *tr* to confiscate
confit•to -ta *adj* nailed; bound; tied; **confitto in croce** nailed to the cross
conflagrazióne *f* conflagration
conflitto *m* conflict
conflittualità *f* confrontation; belligerent attitude
confluènte *m* confluent
confluènza *f* confluence
confluire §176 *intr* to flow together, join; to converge
confóndere §178 *tr* to confuse; to overwhelm (*with kindness*); to humiliate; **confondere con** to mistake for || *ref* to mix; to become confused
conformare (**confórmo**) *tr* to shape; to conform || *ref* to conform
conformazióne *f* conformation
confórme *adj* faithful, exact; in agreement; true (*copy*)
conformeménte *adv* in conformity
conformi•sta *mf* (**-sti -ste**) conformist
conformi•tà *f* (**-tà**) conformity; **in conformità di** in conformity with, in accord with
confortante *adj* comforting
confortare (**confòrto**) *tr* to comfort
confortévole *adj* comforting, consoling; comfortable
confòrto *m* comfort, solace; convenience; corroboration; **conforti religiosi** last rites
confratèllo *m* brother, confrere
confratèrnita *f* brotherhood
confricare §197 *tr* to rub
confrontare (**confrónto**) *tr* to compare, confront; to consult || *intr* to correspond

confrónto *m* comparison; (law) cross examination; **a confronto di** or **in confronto a** in comparison with; with regard to
confusaménte *adv* vaguely, hazily
confusionale *adj* confusing; confused
confusionà·rio -ria (-ri -rie) *adj* blundering; scatterbrain || *mf* blunderer; scatterbrain
confusióne *f* confusion, disorder; noise; error; embarrassment; shambles
confu·so -sa *adj* confused, mixed; vague, hazy; **in confuso** indistinctly
confutare (cònfuto) *tr* to confute
confutazióne *f* confutation
congedare (congèdo) *tr* to dismiss; to let (*a tenant*) go; (mil) to discharge || *ref* to take leave
congeda·to -ta *adj* discharged || *m* discharged soldier
congèdo *m* dismissal; leave; permission to leave; (mil) discharge; envoy, envoi; **congedo per motivi di salute** sick leave; **dare il congedo a** to discharge; **prender congedo** to take leave
congegnare (congégno) *tr* to assemble (*machinery*); to contrive, cook up
congégno *m* contrivance, gadget; mechanism; design (*of a play*)
congelaménto *m* freezing; frostbite
congelare (congèlo) *tr & ref* to freeze, congeal
congela·tóre -trice *adj* freezing || *m* freezer; freezer unit; freezing compartment (*of a refrigerator*)
congènere *adj* similar, alike
congeniale *adj* congenial
congèni·to -ta *adj* congenital
congèrie *f* congeries
congestionare (congestióno) *tr* to congest
congestióne *f* congestion
congettura *f* conjecture
congetturare *tr* to conjecture
congiùngere §183 *tr & ref* to unite, join
congiuntiva *f* (anat) conjunctiva
congiuntivite *f* (pathol) conjunctivitis
congiunti·vo -va *adj* conjunctive; subjunctive || *m* subjunctive || *f* see **congiuntiva**
congiun·to -ta *adj* joined; joint || *m* relative
congiuntura *f* juncture; joint; circumstance, situation; **bassa congiuntura** (econ) unfavorable circumstance; (econ) crisis
congiunzióne *f* conjunction
congiura *f* conspiracy, plot
congiurare *intr* to conspire, plot
congiura·to -ta *adj & m* conspirator
conglobare (conglòbo) *tr* to lump together
conglomerare (conglòmero) *tr & ref* to pile up, conglomerate
conglomera·to -ta *adj & m* conglomerate
congratulare (congràtulo) *intr* to rejoice || *ref*—**congratularsi con** to congratulate
congratulazióne *f* congratulation
congrèga *f* gang; cabal; religious brotherhood
congregare §209 **(congrègo)** *tr & ref* to congregate
congregazióne *f* congregation
congressi·sta *mf* **(-sti -ste)** delegate || *m* congressman || *f* congresswoman
congrèsso *m* congress, assembly; conference; convention
congruènte *adj* congruous
congruènza *f* congruence
còn·gruo -grua *adj* congruous; congruent
conguagliare §280 *tr* to adjust; to make up (*what is owed*)
conguà·glio *m* **(-gli)** balance; adjustment (*of wages*)
coniare §287 **(cònio)** *tr* to mint, coin
coniatura *f* mintage, coinage
còni·co -ca (-ci -che) *adj* conic(al) || *f* conic section
conìfera *f* conifer
coniglièra *f* warren, rabbit hutch
conì·glio *m* **(-gli)** rabbit
cò·nio *m* **(-ni)** die (*to mint coins*); mintage; wedge; **dello stesso conio** (fig) of the same feather; **di nuovo conio** newly-minted; new-fangled
coniugale *adj* conjugal
coniugare §209 **(còniugo)** *tr* to conjugate || *ref* to marry, get married
coniuga·to -ta *adj* coupled, paired || *mf* spouse, consort
coniugazióne *f* conjugation
còniuge *mf* spouse; **coniugi** *mpl* husband and wife
connaturale *adj* inborn, innate
connatura·to -ta *adj* deep-seated, deep-rooted; congenital
connazionale *mf* fellow countryman
connessióne *f* connection
connés·so -sa & connès·so -sa *adj* connected, tied
connéttere & connèttere §107 *tr* to connect, link || *ref* to refer
connetti·vo -va *adj* connective
connivènte *adj* conniving
connivènza *f* connivance
connotare (connòto) *tr* to connote
connotato *m* personal characteristic
connù·bio *m* **(-bi)** wedding, union
còno *m* cone
conòcchia *f* distaff
conoscènte *mf* acquaintance
conoscènza *f* knowledge; acquaintance; understanding; consciousness; **conoscenza di causa** full knowledge; **essere a conoscenza di** to be acquainted with; **prendere conoscenza di** to take cognizance of
conóscere §134 *tr* to know; to recognize; **conoscere i propri polli** to know one's onions; **conoscere per filo e per segno** to know thoroughly; **conoscere ragioni** to listen to reason; **darsi a conoscere** to make oneself known; to reveal oneself || *intr* to reason || *ref* to acknowledge oneself to be; to know one another
conoscìbile *adj* knowable
conosci·tóre -trice *mf* connoisseur, expert
conosciu·to -ta *adj* known, well-known; proven
conquìdere §135 *tr* (poet) to conquer

conquista *f* conquest
conquistare *tr* to conquer, win
conquista•tóre -trice *adj* conquering || *m* conqueror; lady killer
consacrare *tr* to consecrate || *ref* to dedicate oneself
consacrazióne *f* consecration
consanguineità *f* consanguinity
consanguìne•o -a *adj* consanguineous; **fratello consanguineo** half brother on the father's side || *m* kin
consapévole *adj* aware, conscious
consapevolézza *f* awareness, consciousness
còn•scio -scia *adj* (**-sci -sce**) conscious
consecuti•vo -va *adj* consecutive
conségna *f* delivery; (mil) order; (mil) confinement (*to barracks*); **in consegna** (com) on consignment
consegnare (**conségno**) *tr* to deliver; to entrust; (mil) to confine (*to barracks*)
consegnatà•rio *m* (**-ri**) consignee
conseguènte *adj* consequent; consistent; **conseguente a** resulting from; consistent with
conseguènza *f* consequence; consistency; **in conseguenza di** as a result of
conseguìbile *adj* attainable
conseguiménto *m* attainment
conseguire (**conséguo**) *tr* to attain; to obtain || *intr* to ensue, result
consènso *m* consent, approval; consensus
consensuale *adj* mutual-consent (*e.g., agreement*)
consentiménto *m* consent
consentire (**consènto**) *tr* to allow, permit || *intr* to agree, consent; to yield; to admit
consenziènte *adj* consenting
consèr•to -ta *adj* intertwined; folded (*arms*); **di conserto** in agreement
consèrva *f* preserve; purée (*e.g., of tomatoes*); tank (*for water*); sauce (*e.g., of cranberries*); **conserve alimentari** canned goods; **di conserva** together, in a group; **far conserva di** to preserve
conservare (**consèrvo**) *tr* to preserve; to keep; to cure (*e.g., meat*); to cherish (*a memory*) || *ref* to keep; to remain; to keep in good health
conservati•vo -va *adj* preserving; conservative || *m* conservative
conserva•tóre -trice *adj* preserving; conservative || *mf* keeper, curator; conservative
conservatorìa *f* registrar's office (*in a court house*)
conservatò•rio *m* (**-ri**) conservatory; girl's boarding school (*run by nuns*)
conservatorismo *m* conservatism
conservazióne *f* conservation; preservation; self-preservation; canning
consèsso *m* assembly
consideràbile *adj* considerable; large, important
considerare (**consìdero**) *tr* to consider; to rate; (law) to provide for
considera•to -ta *adj* considered; **considerato che** considering that, since; **tutto considerato** all in all, considering
considerazióne *f* consideration
considerévole *adj* considerable
consigliare *adj* council, councilmanic || §280 *tr* to advise, counsel || *ref* to consult
consigliè•re -ra *mf* counselor, advisor || *m* chancellor (*of embassy*); councilman; **consigliere delegato** chairman of the board
consì•glio *m* (**-gli**) advice, counsel; will (*of God*); decision, idea; council; **consiglio d'amministrazione** (com) board of directors; **consiglio dei ministri** cabinet; **consiglio municipale** city council; **l'eterno consiglio** the will of God; **venire a più miti consigli** to become more reasonable
consìmile *adj* similar
consistènte *adj* consistent, solid; trustworthy
consistènza *f* consistency, resistance; foundation, grounds
consìstere §114 *intr* to consist; **consistere in** to consist of
consociare §128 (**consòcio**) *tr* to syndicate, unite
consocia•to -ta *adj* syndicated, united
consociazióne *f* syndicate, association, group
consò•cio -cia *mf* (**-ci -cie**) fellow shareholder; associate, partner
consolare *adj* consular || *v* (**consólo**) *tr* to console, cheer, comfort || *ref* to rejoice; to take comfort
consolato *m* consulate
consola•tóre -trice *adj* comforting || *mf* comforter
consolazióne *f* consolation
cònsole *m* consul
consò•le *f* (**-le**) console
consòlida *f*—**consolida maggiore** comfrey; **consolida reale** field larkspur
consolidaménto *m* consolidation
consolidare (**consòlido**) *tr* to consolidate || *ref* to consolidate; to harden
consolida•to -ta *adj* consolidated; joint (*e.g., balance sheet*); hardened || *m* funded public debt; government bonds
consonante *adj* & *f* consonant
consonànti•co -ca *adj* (**-ci -che**) consonant
consonanza *f* consonance; agreement; (mus) harmony
cònso•no -na *adj* consonant
consorèlla *adj* sister (*e.g., company*) || *f* sister of charity; sister branch; sister firm
consòrte *adj* (poet) equally fortunate; (poet) united || *mf* consort, mate, spouse
consorterìa *f* political clique
consòr•zio *m* (**-zi**) syndicate, consortium; (poet) society
constare (**cònsto**) *intr* to consist || *impers* to be known; to be proved; to understand, e.g., **gli consta che Lei ha torto** he understands that you are wrong
constatare (**constato** & **cònstato**) *tr* to verify, ascertain, establish

constatazióne *f* ascertainment, verification
consuè·to -ta *adj* usual, customary; **consueto a** accustomed to, used to || *m* manner, custom; **di consueto** generally
consuetudinà·rio -ria *adj* (**-ri -rie**) customary; common (*law*)
consuetùdine *f* custom; common law; (poet) familiarity
consulènte *adj* advising, consulting || *mf* adviser, expert
consulènza *f* expert advice
consulta *f* council
consultare *tr* to consult || *ref* to take counsel; to counsel with one another; **consultarsi con** to take counsel with
consultazióne *f* consultation; reference; **consultazione popolare** referendum
consulti·vo -va *adj* advisory
consulto *m* consultation (*of physicians*); legal conference
consul·tóre -trice *mf* adviser, expert || *m* councilman
consultò·rio *m* (**-ri**) clinic, dispensary
consumare *tr* to consume; to perform, to consummate || *ref* to be consumed, to waste away
consuma·to -ta *adj* consummate, accomplished; consummated (*marriage*); consumed, worn out
consuma·tóre -trice *adj* consuming || *mf* consumer; customer (*of a restaurant*)
consumazióne *f* consummation (*e.g., of a crime*); consumption (*of food*); food or drink
consumismo *m* consumerism
consumo *m* consumption; wear
consunti·vo -va *adj* end-of-year (*e.g., report*); (econ) consumption || *m* balance sheet
consun·to -ta *adj* worn-out
consunzióne *f* consumption
contàbile *adj* bookkeeping || *mf* accountant; bookkeeper, clerk; **esperto contabile** certified public accountant
contabili·tà *f* (**-tà**) accounting, bookkeeping; accounts
contachilòme·tri *m* (**-tri**) odometer; (coll) speedometer
contadiné·sco -sca *adj* (**-schi -sche**) farm, farmer; rustic
contadi·no -na *adj* rustic || *mf* peasant, farmer
contado *m* country, countryside
contagiare §290 *tr* to infect
contà·gio *m* (**-gi**) contagion
contagió·so -sa [s] *adj* contagious
contagi·ri *m* (**-ri**) tachometer
contagóc·ce *m* (**-ce**) dropper, eyedropper
contaminare (**contàmino**) *tr* to contaminate; to pollute
contaminazióne *f* contamination; pollution
contante *adj & m* cash; **in contanti** cash
contare (**cónto**) *tr* to count; to limit; to regard, value; to propose; **contarle grosse** (coll) to tell tall tales || *intr* to count; **contare su** to count on
contasecón·di *m* (**-di**) watch with second hand
conta·to -ta *adj* limited; numbered (*e.g., days*)
conta·tóre -trice *adj* counting || *mf* counter || *m* meter; **contatore dell'acqua** water meter; **contatore della luce** electric meter
contattare *tr* to contact
contatto *m* contact
cónte *m* count
contèa *f* county
conteggiare §290 (**contéggio**) *tr* to charge (*e.g., a bill*) || *intr* to count
contég·gio *m* (**-gi**) reckoning, calculation; (sports) count; **conteggio alla rovescia** countdown
contégno *m* behavior; reserve, reserved attitude; air
contegnó·so -sa [s] *adj* reserved, dignified
contemperare (**contèmpero**) *tr* to adapt; to mitigate, moderate
contemplare (**contèmplo**) *tr* to contemplate
contemplati·vo -va *adj* contemplative
contemplazióne *f* contemplation
contèmpo *m*—**nel contempo** meanwhile
contemporaneaménte *adv* at the same time
contemporàne·o -a *adj* contemporaneous || *mf* contemporary
contendènte *adj* fighting || *m* contender, fighter; (law) contestant
contèndere §270 *tr* to contest, oppose || *intr* to contend, fight || *ref* to fight
contenére §271 *tr* to contain || *ref* to restrain oneself; to behave
conteniménto *m* containment
contenitóre *m* container
contentare (**contènto**) *tr* to satisfy, content || *ref* to be satisfied
contentézza *f* gladness, contentedness, contentment
contentino *m* gratuity, makeweight, gift to a customer
contèn·to -ta *adj* contented, glad, happy; satisfied || *m* (poet) happiness, contentedness
contenuto *m* content; contents
contenzióne *f* contention
contenzióso [s] *m* legal matter; legal department (*of a corporation*)
conterìe *fpl* beads, sequins
conterrà·neo -nea *adj* from the same country || *m* fellow countryman || *f* fellow countrywoman
conté·so -sa [s] *adj* coveted || *f* contest; dispute; **venire a contesa** to dispute
contéssa *f* countess
contestare (**contèsto**) *tr* to serve (*e.g., a summons*); to deny; to challenge, contest; **contestare qlco a qlcu** to charge s.o. with s.th
contestazióne *f* notification, summons; dispute, confrontation; challenge
contè·sto -sta *adj* (poet) intertwined || *m* context
conti·guo -gua *adj* contiguous
continentale *adj* continental
continènte *adj & m* continent
continènza *f* continence
contingentaménto *m* import quota
contingentare (**contingènto**) *tr* to assign a quota to (*imports*)

contingènte *adj* possible, contingent; (obs) due || *m* contingent; import quota; **contingente di leva** draft quota
contingènza *f* contingency
continuare (**contìnuo**) *tr* to continue || *intr* to last, continue; **continuare a** + *inf* to keep on + *ger*
continuazióne *f* continuation
continuì·tà *f* (-**tà**) continuity
contì·nuo -nua *adj* continuous; direct (*current*); **di continuo** continuously
cón·to -ta *adj* (archaic) well-known; (poet) gentle; (poet) narrated || *m* figuring; account; bill, invoice; check (*in a restaurant*); opinion; worth, value; **a conti fatti** everything considered; **chiedere conto di** to call to account; **conto all'indietro** countdown; **di conto** valuable; **estratto conto** (com) statement; **fare conto di** + *inf* to intend to + *inf*; **fare conto su** to count on; **fare di conto** to count; **fare i conti senza l'oste** to reckon without one's host; **il conto non torna** the sums do not jibe; **in conto** on account; **in conto di** in one's position as; **per conto di** in the name of; **per conto mio** as far as I am concerned; **render conto di** to give an account of; **rendersi conto di** to realize, be aware of; **tener conto di** to reckon with; **tener di conto** to treat with care; **torna conto** it is worthwhile
contòrcere §272 *tr* to twist || *ref* to writhe
contorciménto *m* contortion, writhing
contornare (**contórno**) *tr* to surround
contórno *m* outline; contour; circle (*of people*); side dish (*of vegetables*)
contorsióne *f* contorsion; gyration (*e.g., of a dancer*); squirm
contòr·to -ta *adj* twisted (*e.g., face*)
contrabbandare *tr* to smuggle
contrabbandiè·re -ra *adj* smuggling || *mf* smuggler; bootlegger
contrabbando *m* contraband; smuggling; **di contrabbando** by smuggling; (fig) without paying
contrabbasso *m* contrabass, bass viol
contraccambiare §287 *tr* to reciprocate, return || *intr* to reciprocate
contraccàm·bio *m* (-**bi**) exchange; **in contraccambio di** in exchange for, in return for
contraccólpo *m* shock, rebound; recoil (*of a rifle*); backlash (*of a machine*)
contrada *f* road; (poet) region
contraddire §151 (*impv sg* **contraddici**) *tr* to contradict || *ref* to contradict oneself; to contradict one another
contraddistinguere §156 *tr* to earmark || *ref* to stand out
contraddittò·rio -ria (-ri -rie) *adj* contradictory; incoherent || *m* open discussion, debate
contraddizióne *f* contradiction
contraènte *adj* contracting; acting || *mf* contractor (*person who makes a contract*); (law) party
contraère·o -a *adj* antiaircraft
contraffare §173 *tr* to counterfeit; to fake, sham || *intr* (archaic) to disobey || *ref* to camouflage oneself, disguise oneself
contraffat·to -ta *adj* counterfeit; adulterated; apocryphal
contraffat·tóre -trice *mf* counterfeiter; falsifier
contraffazióne *f* forgery; fake; imitation; piracy (*of book*); mockery (*of justice*)
contraffòrte *m* spur (*of mountain*); crossbar (*to secure door*); (archit) buttress
contraggènio *m*—**a contraggenio** against one's will
contral·to (-**to**) *adj* alto || *m* contralto (*voice*) || *f* contralto (*singer*)
contrammiralà·glio *m* (-**gli**) rear admiral
contrappasso *m* retributive justice
contrappesare [s] (**contrappéso**) *tr* to counterweight, counterbalance
contrappéso [s] *m* counterweight, counterpoise
contrappórre §218 *tr* to oppose; to compare || *ref*—**contrapporsi a** to oppose
contrappó·sto -sta *adj* opposing || *m* opposite, antithesis
contrappunto *m* counterpoint
contrare (**cóntro**) *tr* (boxing) to counter; (bridge) to double
contrariare §287 *tr* to oppose, counter; to thwart; to contradict; to bother, vex
contrarie·tà *f* (-**tà**) contrariety, vexation; setback
contrà·rio -ria (-ri -rie) *adj* contrary, opposite || *m* opposite; **al contrario** on the contrary; **al contrario di** unlike; **avere qlco in contrario** to have some objection, object
contrarre §273 *tr* & *ref* to contract
contrassegnare (**contrasségno**) *tr* to earmark, mark
contrasségno *m* earmark; proof
contrastare *tr* to oppose; to obstruct; to prevent || *intr* to contrast; to disagree; (poet) to quarrel || *ref* to contend
contrasto *m* contrast; fight, dispute; (telv) contrast knob
contrattàbile *adj* negotiable
contrattaccare §197 *tr* to counterattack
contrattac·co *m* (-**chi**) counterattack
contrattare *tr* to contract for, negotiate a deal for || *intr* to bargain
contrattèmpo *m* mishap
contrat·to -ta *adj* contracted || *m* contract
contrattuale *adj* contractual
contravveléno *m* antidote
contravvenire §282 *intr* (with *dat*) to contravene; **contravvenire a** to infringe upon
contravvenzióne *f* violation; ticket, fine; **in contravvenzione** in the wrong; **intimare una contravvenzione a** to give a ticket to
contrazióne *f* contraction
contribuènte *mf* taxpayer
contribuire §176 *intr* to contribute
contributo *m* contribution
contribu·tóre -trice *mf* contributor

contribuzióne *f* contribution
contristare *tr & ref* to sadden
contri·to -ta *adj* contrite
contrizióne *f* contrition
cóntro *m* con, contrary opinion || *adv* —**contro di** against, versus; **dar contro a** to oppose; **di contro** opposite, facing; **per contro** on the other hand || *prep* against, versus; at; **contro pagamento** upon payment; **contro vento** into the wind; **contro voglia** unwillingly
controbàttere *tr* (mil) to counterattack; (fig) to contest
controbilanciare §128 *tr* to counterpoise, counterbalance
controcanto *m* (mus) counterpoint
controcarro *adj invar* antitank
controchìglia *f* keelson
controcorrènte *f* countercurrent; undertow; (fig) undercurrent || *adv* upstream
controdado *m* lock nut
controffensiva *f* counteroffensive
controfigura *f* (mov) stand-in; (mov) stuntman
controfilo *m*—**a controfilo** against the grain
controfinèstra *f* storm window
cóntrofirma *f* countersign
controfirmare *tr* to countersign
controfòdera *f* inner facing (*of a suit, between lining and cloth*)
controfuò·co *m* (**-chi**) backfire (*to check the advance of a forest fire*)
controindicare §197 (**controìndico**) *tr* to contraindicate
controllare (**contròllo**) *tr* to control, check || *ref* to control oneself
contròllo *m* control, check; restraint; (rad, telv) knob
controllóre *m* (com) comptroller; (rr) ticket collector, conductor
controluce *f* picture taken against the light || *adv* against the light
contromano *adv* against traffic
contromar·ca *f* (**-che**) check, stub (*e.g., of ticket*)
contromàr·cia *f* (**-ce**) countermarch; (aut) reverse, reverse gear
contromezzana [ddzz] *f* (naut) topsail
contronòta *f* countermanding note
contropalo *m* strut
controparte *f* (law) opponent
contropedale *m* foot brake (*of a bicycle*)
contropélo *m* close shave (*in the opposite direction of hair's growth*) || *adv* against the grain; the wrong way (*said of the hair*); against the nap; **accarezzare contropelo** to stroke the wrong way
contropiède *m* counterattack; **cogliere in contropiede** to catch off balance
contropòrta *f* storm door
controproducènte *adj* counterproductive, self-defeating
contropropósta *f* counterproposition
contropròva *f* proof; second balloting
contrórdine *m* countermand
controrèplica *f* retort; (law) rejoinder
controrifórma *f* Counter Reformation
controrivoluzióne *f* counterrevolution
controsènso *m* nonsense; mistranslation
controspallina *f* (mil) epaulet
controspionàg·gio *m* (**-gi**) counterespionage
controvalóre *m* equivalent
controvènto *m* (archit) strut; (archit) crossbrace || *adv* windward
controvèrsia *f* controversy
controvèr·so -sa *adj* controversial, moot
controvòglia *adv* unwillingly
contumace *adj* (archaic) contumacious; (law) absent from court; (law) guilty of nonappearance
contumàcia *f* quarantine; (archaic) contumacy; (law) nonappearance; **in contumacia** (law) in absentia
contumèlia *f* contumely
contundènte *adj* blunt
conturbante *adj* disturbing, upsetting
conturbare *tr* to disturb, upset || *ref* to become perturbed
contusióne *f* bruise, contusion
contu·so -sa *adj* bruised
contuttoché *conj* although
contuttociò *conj* although
convalescènte *adj* convalescent
convalescènza *f* convalescence
convalescenzià·rio *m* (**-ri**) convalescent home
convàlida *f* validation; confirmation
convalidare (**convàlido**) *tr* to validate; to confirm; to strengthen (*e.g., a suspicion*)
convégno *m* meeting, convention
conveniènte *adj* convenient; adequate; useful; profitable (*business*); cheap, reasonable
conveniènza *f* convenience; suitability, fitness; propriety; profit; **convenienze** conventions
convenire §282 *tr* to fix (*e.g., a price*); (law) to summon || *intr* (ESSERE) to convene; to agree; to fit, be appropriate; (poet) to flow together || *ref* to be proper; (with *dat*) to behoove, befit, e.g., **gli si conviene** it behooves him || *impers*—**conviene** it is necessary
convènto *m* convent; monastery
convenu·to -ta *adj* agreed upon || *m* agreement; (law) defendant; **convenuti** conventioners, delegates
convenzionale *adj* conventional
convenzióne *f* convention
convergènte *adj* converging, convergent
convergènza *f* convergence
convèrgere §137 *intr* to converge
convèrsa *f* lay sister; flashing (*on a roof*)
conversare (**convèrso**) *intr* to converse
conversazióne *f* conversation
conversióne *f* conversion; change of heart; (mil) wheeling
convèrso *m* lay brother
convertibile *adj* convertible || *m* (aer) fighter-bomber || *f* (aut) convertible
convertibili·tà *f* (**-tà**) convertibility
convertire §138 *tr* to convert, change; to translate || *ref* to convert, change; (poet) to address oneself

converti•to -ta *adj* converted || *mf* convert
convertitóre *m* converter
convès•so -sa *adj* convex
convincènte *adj* convincing
convìncere §285 *tr* to convince; to convict || *ref* to become convinced
convinciménto *m* conviction
convin•to -ta *adj* convinced, confirmed; convicted
convinzióne *f* conviction
convita•to -ta *adj* invited || *mf* guest (*at a banquet*)
convito *m* banquet
convitto *m* boarding school
convit•tóre -trice *mf* boarding-school student
convivènte *adj* living together
convivènza *f* living together; **convivenza illecita** cohabitation; **convivenza umana** human society
convìvere §286 *intr* to live together; to cohabit
conviviale *adj* convivial
convì•vio *m* (**-vi**) banquet
convocare §197 (**cònvoco**) *tr* to summon, convoke; to convene
convocazióne *f* convocation
convogliare §280 (**convòglio**) *tr* to convoy, escort; to convey, carry
convò•glio *m* (**-gli**) convoy; cortege; (rr) train
convolare (**convólo**) *intr*—**convolare a nozze** to get married
convòlvolo *m* (bot) morning-glory
convulsióne *f* convulsion
convul•so -sa *adj* convulsive; convulsed; choppy (*style*)
coonestare (**coonèsto**) *tr* to justify, palliate
cooperare (**coòpero**) *intr* to cooperate
cooperati•vo -va *adj & f* cooperative
coopera•tóre -trice *adj* coadjutant, cooperating || *m* coadjutor
cooperazióne *f* cooperation
coordinaménto *m* coordination
coordinare (**coórdino**) *tr* to coordinate; to collect (*ideas*)
coordinati•vo -va *adj* (gram) coordinate
coordina•to -ta *adj & f* coordinate
coordinazióne *f* coordination
coòrte *f* cohort
copèr•chio *m* (**-chi**) lid, cover; top (*of box*)
copertina *f* small blanket, child's blanket; cover (*of book*)
copèr•to -ta *adj* covered; protected; cloudy; obscure || *m* cover; shelter; **al coperto** under cover; indoors; secure || *f* blanket, cover; seat cover; case, sheath; (naut) deck; **coperta da viaggio** steamer rug, lap robe; **far coperta a** to cover up for
copertóne *m* canvas; casing, shoe (*of tire*); **copertone cinturato** belted tire
copertura *f* covering; cover; coverage; whitewash; (boxing) defensive stance; (archit) roof
còpia *f* copy; (poet) abundance; (archaic) opportunity; **brutta copia** first draft; **copia a carbone** carbon copy; **copia dattiloscritta** typescript; **per copia conforme** certified copy (*formula appearing on a document*)
copialètte•re *m* (**-re**) letter file; copying press
copiare §287 (**còpio**) *tr* to copy
copiati•vo -va *adj* indelible; copying
copiatura *f* copying; copy; plagiarism
copìglia *f* cotterpin
copilò•ta *mf* (**-ti -te**) copilot
copióne *m* (theat) script
copiosi•tà [s] *f* (**-tà**) copiousness
copió•so -sa [s] *adj* copious
copi•sta *mf* (**-sti -ste**) scribe; copyist
copisterìa *f* copying office; public typing office
còppa *f* cup, goblet; bowl; pan (*of balance*); trophy; (aut) crankcase; (aut) housing; **coppe** suit of Neapolitan cards corresponding to hearts
coppàia *f* chuck (*of lathe*)
còppia *f* couple; pair; **a coppie** two by two; **far coppia fissa** to go steady
coppière *m* cupbearer
coppìglia *f* var of **copiglia**
cóppo *m* earthenware jar (*for oil*); **roof** tile
copribu•sto *m* (**-sto**) bodice
copricapo *m* headgear
copricaté•na *m* (**-na**) chain guard (*on bicycle or motorcycle*)
coprifuò•co *m* (**-chi**) curfew
coprinu•ca *m* (**-ca**) havelock
coprire §110 *tr* to cover; to occupy (*a position*); to coat (*e.g., a wall*); to drown (*a noise*) || *ref* to cover oneself; (econ) to hedge
copriteiè•ra *m* (**-ra**) cozy
coprivivan•de *m* (**-de**) dish cover
cò•pto -pta *adj* Coptic || *mf* Copt
còpula *f* copulation; (gram) copula
coque *f* see **uovo**
coràg•gio *m* (**-gi**) courage; effrontery; (obs) heart; **fare coraggio a** to hearten, encourage; **prendere il coraggio a quattro mani** to screw up one's courage
coraggió•so -sa [s] *adj* courageous
corale *adj* choral; (archaic) cordial; (fig) unanimous || *m* chorale
coralli•no -na *adj* coral
corallo *m* coral
corame *m* engraved leather
coramèlla *f* razor strop
Corano *m* Koran
corata *f* haslet
coratèlla *f* giblets
corazza *f* breastplate, cuirass; shoulder pad (*in football*); armor plate; carapace, shell
corazzare *tr* to armor || *ref* to armor, protect oneself
corazza•to -ta *adj* armor-plated, armored; plated; protected || *f* battleship, dreadnought
corazzière *m* cuirassier; mounted carabineer
còrba *f* basket
corbellerìa *f* (coll) blunder
corbèllo *m* basket; basketful
corbézzolo *m* (bot) arbutus; **corbezzoli!** gosh!
còrda *f* rope; tightrope; string (*of an*

instrument); chord; woof; cord; plumbline; **dare la corda a** to wind (*a clock*); **essere con la corda al collo** to have a rope around one's neck; **mostrare la corda** to be threadbare; **tagliare la corda** to take off, leave; **tenere sulla corda** to keep in suspense
cordame *m* cordage
cordata *f* group of climbers tied together
cordellina *f* (mil) braided cord, braid; (mil) lanyard
cordiale *adj & m* cordial
cordiali·tà *f* (-tà) cordiality
cordièra *f* (mus) tailpiece
cordò·glio *m* (-gli) sorrow, grief
cordonata *f* gradient
cordóne *m* cordon; (anat, elec) cord; curbstone; **cordone litorale** sandbar; **cordone sanitario** sanitary cordon
corèa *f* St. Vitus's dance ‖ **Corea** *f* Korea
corea·no -na *adj & mf* Korean
coréggia *f* leather strap
coreografia *f* choreography
coreògrafo *m* choreographer
coriàce·o -a *adj* tough, leathery
coriàndolo *m* (bot) coriander; **coriandoli** confetti
coricare §197 (**còrico**) *tr* to put to bed ‖ *ref* to lie down, go to bed
corindóne *m* corundum
corìn·zio -zia *adj & mf* (**-zi -zie**) Corinthian
cori·sta *mf* (**-sti -ste**) choir singer, choirmaster ‖ *m* chorus man; (mus) tuning fork; (mus) pitch pipe
corìza [dz] or **corizza** [ddzz] *f* coryza
cormorano *m* cormorant
cornàcchia *f* rook, crow
cornamusa *f* bagpipe
cornata *f* butt; hook, goring (*by bull*)
còrne·o -a *adj* horn, horn-like ‖ *f* cornea
cornétta *f* (mus) cornet; (mus) cornet player; (telp) receiver; (hist) pennon (*of cavalry*)
cornétto *m* little horn; amulet (*in shape of horn*); crescent (*bread*); ear trumpet
cornice *f* cornice; frame; (typ) box; (archit) pediment
cornicióne *m* (archit) ledge; (archit) cornice
cornificare §197 (**cornìfico**) *tr* (joc) to cuckold
corniòla *f* carnelian
còrniola *f* (bot) dogberry
còrniolo *m* (bot) dogwood
còrno *m* horn; wing (*of army*); edge, end; (mus) horn; **corno da caccia** hunting horn; **corno da scarpe** shoe horn; **corno dell'abbondanza** horn of plenty; **corno dogale** (hist) Doge's hat; **corno inglese** (mus) English horn; **non capire un corno** to not understand a blessed thing; **non valere un corno** to not be worth a fig; **un corno!** (slang) heck no! ‖ *m* (**còrna** *fpl*) horn (*of animal*); **alzare le corna** to raise one's head; to become rambunctious; **dire corna di** to speak evil of; **fare le corna** to make horns, to touch wood (*to ward off the evil eye*); **mettere le corna a** to cuckold (*one's husband*); to be unfaithful to (*one's wife*); **portare le corna** to be cuckolded; **rompersi le corna** to get the worst of it
cornu·to -ta *adj* horny; horn-shaped; (vulg) cuckolded
còro *m* choir; chorus; chancel
corollà·rio *m* (**-ri**) corollary
coróna *f* crown; coronet; wreath, garland; range (*of mountains*); collection (*e.g., of sonnets*); stem (*of watch*); felloe (*of wheel*); (astr) corona; (rel) string (*of beads*); (mus) pause; **fare corona a** to surround
coronaménto *m* crowning; (archit) capstone; (naut) taffrail
coronare (**coróno**) *tr* to crown; to top, surmount
coronà·rio -ria *adj* (**-ri -rie**) coronary; (hist) rewarded with a garland
corpétto *m* baby's shirt; waistcoat, vest
corpino *m* bodice; vest
còrpo *m* body; substance; staff (*of teachers*); (mil) corps; (typ) em quad; **a corpo a corpo** hand-to-hand (*fight*); (sports) in a clinch; **a corpo morto** heavily; doggedly; **andare di corpo** to have a bowel movement; **avere in corpo** (fig) to have inside; **corpo del reato** corpus delicti; **corpo di Bacco!** good Heavens!; **corpo di ballo** ballet; **corpo di commissariato** (mil) supply corps; **corpo di guardia** guard, guardhouse; **corpo semplice** (chem) simple substance; **prendere corpo** to materialize
corporale *adj* bodily, body ‖ *m* (eccl) corporal, Communion cloth
corporativismo *m* corporatism (*e.g., of Fascist Italy*)
corporati·vo -va *adj* corporative, corporate
corpora·to -ta *adj* corporate
corporatura *f* size, build
corporazióne *f* corporation
corpòre·o -a *adj* corporeal
corpó·so -sa [s] *adj* heavy-bodied
corpulèn·to -ta *adj* corpulent
corpùscolo *m* particle; (phys) corpuscle
Corpus Dòmini *m* (eccl) Corpus Christi
corredare (**corrèdo**) *tr* to provide, furnish; to annotate, accompany
corredino *m* layette
corrèdo *m* trousseau; outfit, garb; actor's kit; furniture; equipment; apparatus (*e.g., footnotes*)
corrèggere §226 *tr* to correct; to straighten (*e.g., a road*); to rewrite, revise (*news*); to touch up the flavor of ‖ *ref* to reform
corrég·gia *f* (**-ge**) leather strap
corregionale *adj* fellow ‖ *mf* person of the same section of the country
correità *f* complicity
correlare (**corrèlo**) *tr* to correlate
correlati·vo -va *adj* correlative
correla·tóre -trice *mf* second reader (*of a doctoral dissertation*)

correlazióne *f* correlation; (gram) sequence
corrènte *adj* current; running; fluent; recurring; run-of-the-mill || *m*—**essere al corrente di** to be acquainted with; to be abreast of; **mettere al corrente di** to acquaint with || *f* current; draft (*of air*); stream (*of water*); mass (*of lava*); (elec) current; (fig) tide; **contro corrente** upstream; **corrente alternata** (elec) alternating current; **corrente continua** (elec) direct current; **corrente di rete** (elec) house current
córrere §139 *tr* to travel; to run (*a risk; a race*); **correre la cavallina** to sow one's wild oats || *intr* (ESSERE & AVERE) to run; to speed; to race; to flow; to fly (*said of time*); to elapse; to be (*e.g., the year 1820*); to be current (*said of coins*); to spread (*said of gossip*); to mature (*said of interest*); to intervene (*said of distance*); to have dealings; **ci corre!** there is quite a difference!; **ci corre poco che cadesse** he narrowly escaped falling; **correre a gambe levate** to run at breakneck speed; **corre l'uso** it is the fashion; **corrono parole grosse** they are having words; **non corre buon sangue fra loro** there is bad blood between them
corresponsàbile *adj* jointly responsible
corresponsióne *f* payment; (fig) gratitude
correttézza *f* correctness
corretti•vo -va *adj* corrective || *m* flavoring
corrèt•to -ta *adj* correct; flavored; spiked
corret•tóre -trice *mf* corrector; **correttore di bozze** proofreader
correzionale *adj* correctional
correzióne *f* correction
còrri còrri *m* rush
corri•dóio *m* (**-dói**) corridor; hallway; (tennis) alley; (theat) aisle
corridóre *adj* running || *m* racer; runner (*in baseball*)
corrièra *f* mail coach; bus
corrière *m* courier; mail; carrier (*of merchandise*)
corrispetti•vo -va *adj* equivalent, proportionate || *m* requital, compensation
corrispondènte *adj* corresponding, equivalent || *mf* correspondent
corrispondènza *f* correspondence
corrispóndere §238 *tr* to pay, compensate || *intr* to correspond
corri•vo -va *adj* rash; indulgent
corroborante *adj* corroborating || *m* tonic
corroborare (**corròboro**) *tr* to corroborate; to invigorate
corroborazióne *f* corroboration
corródere §239 *tr* to corrode; to erode
corrómpere §240 *tr* to spoil; to corrupt; to suborn || *ref* to putrefy, rot
corrosióne *f* corrosion
corrosi•vo -va *adj* & *m* corrosive
corró•so -sa *adj* corroded; eroded
corrót•to -ta *adj* corrupted, corrupt; putrefied, rotten || *m* (archaic) lament
corrucciare §128 *tr* to anger, vex || *ref* to get angry
corrùc•cio *m* (**-ci**) anger, vexation
corrugaménto *m* wrinkling; (geol) fold
corrugare §209 *tr* to wrinkle, knit (*one's brow*) || *ref* to frown
corruscare §197 *intr* (poet) to shine
corruttèla *f* corruption
corruttìbile *adj* corruptible
corrut•tóre -trice *adj* corrupting, depraving || *m* seducer; briber
corruzióne *f* corruption; putrefaction, decomposition
córsa *f* race; run; trip; fare; (mach) stroke; (hist) privateering; **a tutta corsa** at full speed; **corsa al galoppo** flat race; **corsa al trotto** harness racing; **corsa semplice** one-way ticket; **corse** horse racing; **da corsa** race, for racing, e.g., **cavallo da corsa** race horse; **di corsa** running, in a hurry; **fare una corsa** to run an errand; **prendere la corsa** to begin to run
corsalétto *m* corselet
corsa•ro -ra *adj* privateering || *m* privateer, corsair, pirate
corsétto *m* corset
corsìa *f* aisle; ward (*in hospital*); runner (*of carpet*); lane (*of highway*); **corsia d'accesso** entrance lane; **corsia d'uscita** exit lane
Còrsica, la Corsica
corsivi•sta *mf* (**-sti -ste**) (journ) political writer
corsi•vo -va *adj* cursive; (poet) running; (poet) current || *m* cursive handwriting; (typ) italics
córso *m* course; navigation (*by sea*); path (*of stars*); parade; large street; boulevard; tender (*of currency*); current rate, current price (*of stock at the exchange*); **corso d'acqua** watercourse; **fuori corso** (*coin*) no longer in circulation; **in corso** in circulation; in progress; **in corso di** in the course of; **in corso di stampa** in press
còr•so -sa *adj* & *mf* Corsican
cor•sóio -sóia (**-sói -sóie**) *adj* running (*knot*); (mach) on rollers || *m* slide (*of slide rule*); (mach) slide
córte *f* court; **corte bandita** open house; **Corte d'appello** appellate court; **Corte di cassazione** Supreme Court; **fare la corte a** to pay court to, woo
cortéc•cia *f* (**-ce**) bark; crust (*of bread*); (fig) appearance; (anat) cortex
corteggiaménto *m* courtship
corteggiatóre *m* wooer, suitor
cortég•gio *m* (**-gi**) retinue; cortege
cortèo *m* procession; parade; funeral train; wedding party
cortése *adj* courteous, polite; (lit) liberal; (poet & hist) courtly
cortesìa *f* courtesy, politeness; (lit) liberality; (poet & hist) courtliness; **per cortesia** please
còrtice *f* cortex
cortigia•no -na *adj* flattering; courtly || *mf* courtier; flatterer || *f* courtesan
cortile *m* courtyard; barnyard

cortina *f* curtain; **cortina di ferro** iron curtain; **cortina di fumo** smoke screen; **oltre cortina** behind the iron curtain
cortisóne *m* cortisone
cór·to -ta *adj* short; close (*haircut*); **alle corte** in short; **essere a corto di** to be short of; **per farla corta** in short
cortocircùito *m* short circuit
cortometràg·gio *m* (**-gi**) (mov) short
cor·vè *f* (**-vè**) tiresome task, drudgery; **corvè di cucina** kitchen police
corvétta *f* corvette
corvi·no -na *adj* raven-black
còrvo *m* raven; crow
còsa [s] *f* thing; **belle cose!** or **buone cose!** regards!; **che cosa** what; **cosa da nulla** a mere trifle, nothing at all; **cos'ha?** what's the matter with you (him, her)?; **cosa pubblica** commonweal; **cosa strana** no wonder; **cose** belongings; **per la qual cosa** wherefore; **per prima cosa** first of all; **sopra ogni cosa** above all; **tante belle cose!** best regards!; **una cosa** something; **una cosa nuova** a piece of news
cosac·co -ca (-chi -che) *adj* Cossack's ‖ *mf* Cossack
cò·scia *f* (**-sce**) thigh; haunch; leg (*of gun*); (archit) abutment; **coscia di montone** leg of lamb
cosciènte *adj* conscious; sensible; aware
cosciènza *f* conscience; consciousness; conscientiousness; awareness
coscienzió·so -sa [s] *adj* conscientious
cosciòtto *m* leg; leg of lamb
coscrit·to -ta *adj* conscript ‖ *m* conscript, recruit, draftee
coscrìvere §250 *tr* to conscript
coscrizióne *f* conscription, draft
così [s] *adj invar*—**un così... or un... così** such a ‖ *adv* thus; like this; so; **così . . . come** as . . . as; **così così** so so; **e così via** and so on, and so forth; **per così dire** so to speak
cosicché [s] *conj* so that
cosiddét·to -ta [s] *adj* so-called
cosiffat·to -ta [s] *adj* such, similar
cosino [s] *m* (coll) little fellow
cosmèti·co -ca *adj & m* (**-ci -che**) cosmetic
còsmi·co -ca *adj* (**-ci -che**) cosmic; outer (*space*)
còsmo *m* cosmos; outer space
cosmòdromo *m* space center
cosmologìa *f* cosmology
cosmonàu·ta *mf* (**-ti -te**) cosmonaut, astronaut
cosmopoli·ta *adj & mf* (**-ti -te**) cosmopolitan
còso [s] *m* (coll) thing, what-d'you-call-it
cospàrgere §261 *tr* to spread; to sprinkle
cospèrgere §112 *tr* (poet) to wet, sprinkle
cospètto *m* presence; **al cospetto di** in the presence of
cospì·cuo -cua *adj* distinguished, outstanding; huge, immense; (poet) conspicuous
cospirare *intr* to conspire, plot
cospira·tóre -trice *mf* conspirator
cospirazióne *f* conspiracy, plot
còsta *f* side; rib; coast, seashore; slope; welt (*along seam*); wale (*in fabric*); (naut) frame
costà *adv* there; over there
costaggiù *adj* down there
costante *adj & f* constant
Costantinòpoli *f* Constantinople
costanza *f* constancy ‖ **Costanza** *f* Constance
costare (còsto) *intr* (ESSERE) to cost; to be expensive; **costare caro** to cost dear; **costare un occhio della testa** to cost a fortune
costarica·no -na or **costaricènse** *adj & mf* Costa Rican
costassù *adv* up there
costata *f* rib roast; side
costeggiare §290 (**costéggio**) *tr* to sail along; to run along; to border on ‖ *intr* to coast
costèi §8 *pron dem*
costellare (costèllo) *tr* to stud, star
costellazióne *f* constellation
costernare (costèrno) *tr* to dismay, cause consternation to
costernazióne *f* consternation
costì *adv* there
costiè·ro -ra *adj* coast, coastal; offshore ‖ *f* coastline; gentle slope
costipare *tr* to constipate; to heap, pile ‖ *ref* to become constipated
costipazióne *f* constipation
costituènte *adj* constituent; constituting ‖ *m* member of constituent assembly; (chem) constituent
costituire §176 *tr* to constitute; to form ‖ *ref* to form; to become; to appoint oneself; to give oneself up (*to justice*); **costituirsi in giudizio** (law) to sue (*in civil court*); **costituirsi parte civile** (law) to appear as a plaintiff (*in civil court*)
costituto *m* (law) pact, agreement; (naut) master's declaration (*to health authorities*)
costituzionale *adj* constitutional
costituzióne *f* constitution; charter; composition; (law) appearance; surrender (*to justice*)
còsto *m* cost; **a costo di** at the price of; **ad ogni costo** at any cost; **a nessun costo** by no means; **a tutti i costi** at any cost, in any event; **costo della vita** cost of living; **sotto costo** below cost
còstola *f* rib; spine (*of book*); back (*of knife*); **avere qlcu alle costole** to have s.o. at one's heels; **rompere le costole a** (fig) to break the bones of; **stare alle costole di** to be at the back of
costolétta *f* chop, cutlet
costolóne *m* (archit) groin
costóro §8 *pron dem*
costó·so -sa [s] *adj* costly
costrìngere §265 *tr* to force, constrain; (poet) to compress
costritti·vo -va *adj* constrictive
costrizióne *f* constriction
costruire §140 *tr* to construct, build

costrut·to -ta *adj* constructed || *m* profit; sense; (gram) construction; **dov'è il costrutto?** what's the point?
costruttóre *m* builder
costruzióne *f* construction; building
costùi §8 *pron dem*
costumanza *f* custom
costumare *intr* (+ *inf*) to be in the habit of (+ *ger*) || *intr* (ESSERE) to be the custom; to be in use
costumatézza *f* good manners
costuma·to -ta *adj* polite, well-bred
costume *m* custom, manner; costume, dress; bathing suit
costumi·sta *mf* (**-sti -ste**) (theat) costumer
costura *f* seam
cotale *adj & pron* such || *adv* (archaic) thus
cotan·to -ta *adj & pron* (poet) so much || **cotanto** *adv* (poet) such a long time
còte *f* flint
coténna *f* pigskin; rind; (coll) hide, skin
coté·sto -sta §7 *adj dem* || §8 *pron dem*
cóti·ca *f* (**-che**) (coll) hide, skin (*of porker*)
cotógna *f* quince (*fruit*)
cotognata *f* quince jam
cotógno *m* quince (*tree*)
cotolétta *f* chop, cutlet
cotóne *m* cotton; thread; **cotone fulminante** guncotton; **cotone idrofilo** absorbent cotton; **cotone silicato** mineral wool
cotonière *m* cotton manufacturer
cotonniè·ro -ra *adj* cotton || *mf* cotton worker
cotonifi·cio *m adj* (**-ci**) cotton mill
cotonó·so -sa [s] *adj* cotton; cottony
còtta *f* cooking; baking; drying (*of bricks*); (sports) exhaustion; (coll) drunkenness; (joc) infatuation, love; (eccl) surplice; **cotta d'armi** coat of mail
cottimi·sta *mf* (**-sti -ste**) pieceworker
còttimo *m* piecework
còt·to -ta *adj* cooked; baked; burnt; suntanned; (joc) half-baked; (joc) in love; (sports) exhausted || *m* brick || *f* see **cotta**
cottura *f* cooking; **a punto di cottura** (culin) done just right
coutènte *mf* (law) joint user; (telp) party-line user
cóva *f* brooding; nest
covare (cóvo) *tr* to brood, to hatch; to harbor or nurse (*an enmity*); to nurture (*a disease*); **covare con gli occhi** to look fondly at; **covare le lenzuola** to loll around || *intr* to smolder (*said of fire or passion*)
covata *f* brood, covey
covile *m* doghouse; den
cóvo *m* shelter; den, lair; **farsi il covo** (fig) to gather a nestegg; **uscire dal covo** to stick one's nose out of the house
covóne *m* sheaf; cock (*of hay*)
còzza *f* cockle
cozzare (còzzo) *tr* to hit; to butt (*one's head*) || *intr* to butt; (fig) to clash; **cozzare contro** to bump into || *ref* to hit one another; to fight
còzzo *m* butt; clash, conflict
crac *m* crash
crampo *m* cramp
cràni·co -ca *adj* (**-ci -che**) cranial
crà·nio *m* (**-ni**) cranium, skull
cràpula *f* excess (*in eating and drinking*)
cras·so -sa *adj* crass, gross; large (*intestine*)
cratère *m* crater; bomb crater
cràuti *mpl* sauerkraut
cravatta *f* tie, necktie; **cravatta a farfalla** bow tie; **fare cravatte** to be a usurer
creanza *f* politeness; **buona creanza** good manners
creare (crèo) *tr* to create; to name, elect
creati·vo -va *adj* creative
crea·to -ta *adj* created || *m* creation, universe
crea·tóre -trice *adj* creative || *mf* creator
creatura *f* creature; baby; **povera creatura!** poor thing!
creazióne *f* creation; (poet) election
credènte *adj* believing || *mf* believer
credènza *f* credence, faith, belief; sideboard, buffet; (coll) credit
credenziale *f* letter of credit; **credenziali** credentials
credenzière *m* butler
crédere §141 *tr* to believe; to think; **lo credo bene!** I should say so! || *intr* to believe; to trust; **credere a** to believe in; **credere in Dio** to believe in God || *ref* to believe oneself to be
credìbile *adj* credible
credibilità *f* credibility
crédito *m* credit
credi·tóre -trice *mf* creditor
crèdo *m* credo, creed
credulità *f* credulity
crèdu·lo -la *adj* credulous
crèma *f* cream; custard; **crema da scarpe** shoe polish; **crema di bellezza** beauty cream; **crema di pomodoro** cream of tomato soup; **crema evanescente** vanishing cream; **crema per barba** shaving cream
cremaglièra *f* rack; cogway, cograil
cremare (crèmo) *tr* to cremate
crema·tóio *m* (**-tói**) crematory
cremató·rio *m* (**-ri**) crematory
cremazióne *f* cremation
cremerìa *f* creamery
crèmisi *adj & m* crimson
Cremlino *m* Kremlin
cremlinologìa *f* Kremlinology
cremortàrtaro *m* cream of tartar
cremó·so -sa [s] *adj* creamy
crèn *m* horseradish
creolina *f* creolin
crèo·lo -la *adj & mf* Creole
creosòto *m* creosote
crèpa *f* crack, crevice; rift
crepàc·cio *m* (**-ci**) crevasse; fissure
crepacuòre *m* heartbreak
crepapància *m*—**mangiare a crepapancia** to burst from eating too much
crepapèlle *m*—**ridere a crepapelle** to split one's sides laughing

crepare (**crèpo**) *intr* to burst; to crack; to chip; (slang) to croak; **crepare dalla sete** to die of thirst; **crepare dalle risa** to die laughing; **crepare d'invidia** to be green with envy
crepitare (**crèpito**) *intr* to crackle (*said of fire or weapons*); to rustle (*said of leaves*)
crepiti·o *m* (**-i**) crackle; rustle; pitter-patter (*of rain*)
crepuscolare *adj* twilight; (fig) dim
crepùscolo *m* twilight
crescènte *adj* rising, growing; crescent (*moon*) || *m* (astr & heral) crescent
crescènza *f* growth
créscere §142 *tr* to grow, raise; to increase || *intr* (ESSERE) to grow; to increase; to rise (*said, e.g., of prices*); to wax (*said of the moon*); **farsi crescere** to grow (*a beard*)
crescióne *m* watercress
créscita *f* growth; outgrowth; rise (*of water*)
crèsima *f* confirmation
cresimare (**crèsimo**) *tr* to confirm
Crèso *m* (mythol) Croesus
cré·spo -spa *adj* crispy, kinky; (archaic) wrinkled || *m* crepe || *f* wrinkle; ruffle
crésta *f* comb (*of chicken*); crest; **abbassare la cresta** to come down a peg or two; **alzare la cresta** to become insolent
crestàia *f* (coll) milliner
créta *f* clay
cretése [s] *adj & mf* Cretan
cretinerìa *f* idiocy
creti·no -na *adj & mf* idiot, cretin
cribro *m* (poet) sieve
cric·ca *f* (**-che**) clique, gang; group; crevice
cric·co *m* (**-chi**) (aut) jack
cricéto *m* hamster
cri cri *m* chirping (*of crickets*)
criminale *adj* criminal; (law) penal || *mf* criminal
criminali·sta *mf* (**-sti -ste**) penal lawyer, criminal lawyer
criminalità *f* criminality
crìmine *m* crime
criminologìa *f* criminology
criminòlo·go *m* (**-gi**) criminologist
criminó·so -sa [s] *adj* criminal
crinale *adj* (poet) hair || *m* ridge (*of mountains*)
crine *m* horsehair; (poet) hair; (poet) sunbeam
crinièra *f* mane
crinolina *f* crinoline
cripta *f* crypt
criptocomuni·sta *mf* (**-sti -ste**) fellow traveler
crisàlide *f* chrysalis
crisantèmo *m* chrysanthemum
cri·si *f* (**-si**) crisis; shortage (*of houses*); attack (*e.g., of fever*); outburst (*of tears*); (econ) slump; **crisi ancillare** or **domestica** servant problem; **in crisi** in difficulties
cristallerìa *f* glassware; crystal service; glassware shop; glassworks
cristallièra *f* china closet
cristalli·no -na *adj* crystalline || *m* crystalline lens
cristallizzare [ddzz] *tr & ref* to crystallize
cristallo *m* crystal; glass; pane (*of glass*); windshield; **cristallo di rocca** rock crystal; **cristallo di sicurezza** (aut) safety glass
cristianaménte *adv* in a Christian manner, like a Christian; (coll) decently; **morire cristianamente** to die in the faith
cristianésimo *m* Christianity
cristianità *f* Christendom
cristia·no -na *adj & mf* Christian
Cristo *m* Christ; **avanti Cristo** before Christ (B.C.); **dopo Cristo** after Christ (A.D.); **un povero cristo** (slang) a poor guy
critè·rio *m* (**-ri**) criterion; judgment
crìti·ca *f* (**-che**) criticism; critique; slur
criticare §197 (**crìtico**) *tr* to criticize, censure; to find fault with
crìti·co -ca (**-ci -che**) *adj* critical || *mf* critic; (coll) faultfinder || *f* see **critica**
crittografìa *f* cryptography
crittogram·ma *m* (**-mi**) cryptogram
crivellare (**crivèllo**) *tr* to riddle
crivèllo *m* sieve, riddle
croa·to -ta *adj & mf* Croatian
Croàzia, la Croatia
croccante *adj* crisp, crunchy || *m* almond brittle, peanut brittle
crocchétta *f* croquette
cròcchia *f* chignon, topknot
crocchiare §287 (**cròcchio**) *intr* to crackle; to sound cracked or broken; to cluck (*said of a hen*); to crack (*said of joints*)
cròc·chio *m* (**-chi**) group (*of people*); **far crocchio** to gather around
cróce *f* cross; x (*mark made by illiterate person*); tail (*of coin*); (fig) trial; **Croce del Sud** Southern Cross; **croce di Malta** Maltese cross; **Croce Rossa** Red Cross; **croce uncinata** swastika; **fare una croce sopra** to forget about; **gettare la croce addosso** (fig) to put the blame on; **mettere in croce** to crucify
crocefisso *m* crucifix
crocerossina *f* Red Cross worker
croceségno *m* cross, x (*mark made instead of signature*)
crocétta *f* (naut) crosstree
croce·vìa *m* (**-vìa**) crossroads, intersection
crocia·to -ta *adj* crossed; crusading; see **parola** || *m* crusader || *f* crusade
crocièra *f* cruise; (archit) cross (*vault*); (mach) cross (*of universal joint*)
crocière *m* (orn) crossbill
crocifiggere §104 *tr* to crucify
crocifissióne *f* crucifixion
crocifis·so -sa *adj* crucified || *m* crucifix
crò·co *m* (**-chi**) crocus
crogiolare (**crògiolo**) *tr* to cook on a low fire; to simmer; to temper (*glass*) || *ref* to bask; to snuggle (*e.g., in bed*)
crògiolo *m* cooking on a low fire; simmering; tempering (*of glass*)
crogiòlo *m* crucible; (fig) melting pot
crollare (**cròllo**) *tr* to shake (*e.g., one's head*) || *intr* (ESSERE) to fall down, collapse || *ref* to shake

cròllo *m* shake; fall, collapse
cròma *f* (mus) quaver
cromare (**cròmo**) *tr* to plate with chromium
croma·to -ta *adj* chromium-plated; chrome || *m* chrome yellow
cromatura *f* chromium plating
cròmo *m* chrome, chromium
cromosfèra *f* chromosphere
cromosò·ma [s] *m* (**-mi**) chromosome
cròna·ca *f* (**-che**) chronicle; report, news; **cronaca bianca** news of the day; **cronaca giudiziaria** court news; **cronaca mondana** social column; **cronaca nera** police and accident report; **cronaca rosa** wedding column; stork news
cròni·co -ca (**-ci -che**) *adj* chronic || *mf* incurable
croni·sta *mf* (**-sti -ste**) reporter; chronicler
cronistòria *f* chronicle
cronologìa *f* chronology
cronològi·co -ca *adj* (**-ci -che**) chronologic(al)
cronometrare (**cronòmetro**) *tr* to time
cronomètri·co -ca *adj* (**-ci -che**) chronometric(al); split-second
cronometri·sta *m* (**-sti**) (sports) timekeeper
cronòmetro *m* stopwatch; chronometer
crosciare §128 (**cròscio**) *tr* (archaic) to heave, throw || *intr* to rustle (*said of dry leaves*); to pitter-patter (*said of rain*)
cròsta *f* crust; bark (*of tree*); scab; slough; shell (*of crustacean*); poor painting
crostàceo *m* crustacean
crostata *f* pie
crostino *m* toast
crostó·so -sa [s] *adj* crusty
croupier *m* (**croupier**) croupier
crucciare §128 *tr* to worry, vex; to chagrin || *ref* to worry; to become angry
cruccia·to -ta *adj* afflicted; worried; angry; chagrined
crùc·cio *m* (**-ci**) sorrow; (obs) anger; **darsi cruccio** to fret
cruciale *adj* crucial
crucivèr·ba *m* (**-ba**) crossword puzzle
crudèle *adj* cruel
crudel·tà *f* (**-tà**) cruelty
crudézza *f* crudity; harshness
cru·do -da *adj* raw; rare (*meat*); (poet) cruel
cruèn·to -ta *adj* (lit) bloody
crumiro *m* scab (*in strikes*)
cruna *f* eye (*of a needle*)
cru·sca *f* (**-sche**) bran; (coll) freckles
cruscante *adj* Della-Cruscan; affected || *m* member of the Accademia della Crusca
cruschèllo *m* middlings
cruscòtto *m* (aut) dashboard; (aer) instrument panel
cuba·no -na *adj* & *mf* Cuban
cubatura *f* volume
cùbi·co -ca *adj* (**-ci -che**) cubic; cube (*root*)
cubitale *adj* very large (*handwriting or type*)
cùbito *m* cubit; (poet) elbow
cubo *m* cube
cuccagna *f* plenty; windfall; Cockaigne
cuccétta *f* berth
cucchiàia *f* large spoon; ladle; trowel; bucket (*of power shovel*); **cucchiaia bucata** skimmer
cucchiaiàta *f* spoonful; tablespoonful
cucchiaino *m* teaspoon; teaspoonful; spoon (*lure*)
cuc·chiàio *m* (**-chiài**) spoon; spoonful; tablespoon; **cucchiaio da minestra** soupspoon
cucchiaióne *m* ladle
cùc·cia *f* (**-ce**) dog's bed; **a cuccia!** lie down!
cucciare §128 *intr* (ESSERE) & *ref* to lie down (*said of a dog*)
cucciolata *f* litter (*e.g., of puppies*)
cùcciolo *m* puppy; cub; (fig) greenhorn
cuc·co *m* (**-chi**) cuckoo; simpleton; darling (*child*)
cuccuru·cù *m* (**-cù**) cock-a-doodle-doo
cucina *f* kitchen; cuisine; kitchen range; **cucina componibile** kitchen with sectional cabinets; **cucina economica** kitchen range; **fare da cucina** to prepare a meal
cucinare *tr* to cook; (fig) to fix
cucinétta *f* kitchenette
cuciniè·re -ra *mf* cook
cucire §143 *tr* to sew; to stitch || *ref*—**cucirsi la bocca** to keep one's mouth shut
cucirino *m* sewing thread
cuci·tóre -trice *adj* sewing || *mf* sewing machine operator || *f* seamstress; sewing machine (*for bookbinding*); **cucitrice a grappe** stapler
cuci·to -ta *adj* sewn || *m* sewing; needle work
cucitura *f* seam; sewing; stitches
cu·cù *m* (**-cù**) cuckoo
cuculo or **cùculo** *m* cuckoo
cùffia *f* bonnet (*for baby*); coif; (rad) headset; (telp) headpiece; (theat) prompter's box
cugi·no -na *mf* cousin
cui *pron invar* whose; to which; whom; which; of whom; of which; **per cui** (coll) therefore
culatta *f* breech (*of a gun*)
culinà·rio -ria (**-ri -rie**) *adj* culinary || *f* gastronomy
culla *f* cradle
cullare *tr* to rock (*a baby*); (fig) to delude || *ref* to have delusions
culminante *adj* highest; culminating
culminare (**cùlmino**) *intr* to culminate
cùlmine *m* top, summit
culo *m* (vulg) behind; (slang) bottom (*of glass or bottle*): **culi di bicchiere** (coll) fake diamonds
cul·to -ta *adj* cultivated; learned (*e.g., word*) || *m* cult, worship
cul·tóre -trice *mf* devotee
cultura *f* culture; **cultura fisica** physical culture
culturale *adj* cultural
cumino *m* (bot) caraway seed; (bot) cumin
cumulati·vo -va *adj* cumulative

cùmulo *m* heap, pile; concurrence (*of penal sentences*); cumulus
cuna *f* cradle
cùneo *m* wedge; chock; (archit) voussoir
cunétta *f* ditch; gutter
cunìcolo *m* small tunnel; burrow
cuòcere §144a *tr* to cook; to bake (*bricks*); to burn, dry up; (fig) to stew || *intr* to cook; to burn; to dry up; (with *dat*) to grieve, to pain
cuò•co -ca *mf* (**-chi -che**) cook
cuòio *m* (**cuòi**) leather; **avere il cuoio duro** to have a tough hide; **cuoio capelluto** scalp || *m* (**cuoia** *fpl*) (archaic) leather; **tirare le cuoia** (slang) to croak, to kick the bucket
cuòre *m* heart; **avere il cuore da coniglio** to be chicken-hearted; **avere il cuore da leone** to be lion-hearted; **cuori** (cards) hearts; **di cuore** gladly; heartily; **fare cuore a** to encourage; **stare a cuore** to be important
cupidìgia *f* cupidity, greed, covetousness
Cupido *m* Cupid
cùpi•do -da *adj* greedy, covetous
cu•po -pa *adj* dark; deep (*color, voice*); sad, gloomy
cùpola *f* dome, cupola; crown (*of hat*)
cura *f* care; interest; cure; ministry; (poet) anxiety; **a cura di** edited by (*e.g., text*)
curare *tr* to take care of; to heed || *intr* to see to it || *ref* to take care of oneself; to care; to deign; **curarsi di** to care for
curatèla *f* (law) guardianship
curati•vo -va *adj* curative
cura•to -ta *adj* cured; healed || *m* curate
cura•tóre -trice *mf* curator; trustee; editor (*of critical edition*); receiver (*in bankruptcy*)
curculióne *m* (ent) weevil
cur•do -da *adj & mf* Kurd
cùria *f* curia; bar
curiale *adj* curia; legal
curialé•sco -sca *adj* (**-schi -sche**) hair-splitting, legalistic
curiosare [s] (**curióso**) *intr* to pry around, snoop; to browse around
curiosi•tà [s] *f* (**-tà**) curiosity; whim; curio
curió•so -sa [s] *adj* curious; bizarre, quaint
curro *m* roller
cursóre *m* process server; court messenger; slide (*of slide ruler*)
curva *f* curve, bend; sweep; **curva di livello** contour line
curvare *tr* to curve, bend; **curvare la fronte** to bow down, yield || *intr* to curve (*said of a road*); to take a curve, negotiate a curve || *ref* to curve, bend; to bow; to become bent; to warp
curvatura *f* curving, bending; warp; stoop, curvature; camber
cur•vo -va *adj* bent, curved || *f* see **curva**
cuscinétto *m* small pillow; pad (*for ink*); buffer (*zone*); (mach) bearing; **cuscinetto a rulli** roller bearing; **cuscinetto a sfere** ball bearing
cuscino *m* pillow; cushion
cùspide *f* point (*e.g., of arrow*); (archit) steeple
custòde *adj* guardian (*angel*) || *m* custodian; janitor; warden; guard; (coll) policeman, cop
custòdia *f* safekeeping, custody; case (*e.g., of violin*); trust; (mach) housing
custodire §176 *tr* to keep; to protect, guard; to be in charge of (*prisoners*); to take care of; to cherish (*a memory*)
cutàne•o -a *adj* cutaneous
cute *f* (anat) skin
cuticagna *f* (joc) nape of the neck
cutìcola *f* epidermis; cuticle; dentine
cutireazióne *f* skin test (*for allergic reactions*)
cutréttola *f* (orn) wagtail

D

D, d [di] *m & f* fourth letter of the Italian alphabet
da *prep* from; to; at; on; through; between; since; with; by, e.g., **è stato arrestato dalla polizia** he was arrested by the police; worth, e.g., **un libro da mille lire** a book worth a thousand lire; worthy of, e.g., **azione da gentiluomo** action worthy of a gentleman; at the house, office, shop, etc., of, e.g., **dal pittore** at the house of the painter; **da Giovanni** at John's; **dall'avvocato** at the lawyer's office; **d'altro lato** on the other hand; **d'ora in poi** from now on
dabbasso *adv* downstairs; down below
dabbenàggine *f* simplicity, foolishness
dabbène *adj invar* honest, upright, e.g., **un uomo dabbene** an honest man; simple, foolish, e.g., **un dabben uomo** a Simple Simon
daccanto *adv* near, nearby
daccapo *adv* again, all over again; **andar daccapo** to begin a new paragraph; **daccapo a piedi** from top to bottom
dacché *conj* since
dado *m* cube; pedestal (*of column*); (mach) nut; (mach) die (*to cut threads*); **dadi** dice; **giocare ai dadi** to shoot craps; **il dado è tratto** the die is cast
daffare *m* things to do; bustle; **darsi daffare** to bustle, bustle about
da•ga *f* (**-ghe**) dagger
dagli §4 || *interj*—**dagli al ladro!** stop thief!; **e dagli!** cut it out!
dài §4

dài·no -na *mf* fallow deer || *m* fallow deer; buckskin
dal §4
dàlia *f* dahlia
dalla §4
dallato *adv* aside; sideways
dalle §4
dalli *interj*—**dalli al ladro!** stop thief!; **e dalli!** cut it out!
dallo §4
dàlma·ta *adj & mf* (**-ti -te**) Dalmatian
Dalmàzia, la Dalmatia
daltòni·co -ca *adj* (**-ci -che**) color-blind
daltonismo *m* color blindness
dama *f* lady; dancing partner; checkers; **andare a dama** (checkers) to be crowned; **dama di compagnia** companion; **dama di corte** lady-in-waiting
damare *tr* (checkers) to crown
damascare §197 *tr* to damask
damaschinare *tr* to damascene
dama·sco *m* (**-schi**) damask || **Damasco** *f* Damascus
damerino *m* fop, dandy
damigèlla *f* (lit) damsel; (orn) demoiselle; **damigella d'onore** bridesmaid
damigiana *f* demijohn
danaro *m* var of **denaro**
danaró·so -sa [s] *adj* wealthy, rich
dande *fpl* leading strings
danése [s] *adj* Danish || *mf* Dane || *m* Danish (*language*); Great Dane
Danimarca, la Denmark
dannare *tr* to damn; to bedevil || *ref* to be damned; to fret
danna·to -ta *adj* damned; wicked; terrible (*e.g., fear*) || *m* damned soul
dannazióne *f* damnation
danneggiare §290 (**dannéggio**) *tr* to damage; to injure, impair
danneggia·to -ta *adj* damaged; injured, impaired || *mf* victim
danno *m* damage; injury; (ins) loss; **chiedere i danni** to ask for indemnification; **far danni a** to damage; **rifare i danni a** to indemnify; **tuo danno** so much the worse for you
dannó·so -sa [s] *adj* damaging, harmful
dante *m*—**pelle di dante** buckskin
danté·sco -sca *adj* (**-schi -sche**) Dantean, Dantesque
danti·sta *mf* (**-sti -ste**) Dante scholar
Danùbio *m* Danube
danza *f* dance; dancing
danzare *tr & intr* to dance
danza·tóre -trice *mf* dancer
dappertutto *adv* everywhere
dappiè *adv*—**dappiè di** at the foot of
dappiù *adv*—**dappiù di** more than
dappòco *adj invar* worthless
dappòi *adv* (obs) afterwards, after
dapprèsso *adv* near, nearby, close
dapprima *adv* first, in the first place
dapprincìpio *adv* first, in the beginning; over again
dardeggiare §290 (**dardéggio**) *tr* to hurl darts at; to beat down on; to look daggers at || *intr* to hurl darts; to beat down
dardo *m* dart, arrow; tip (*of blowtorch*)
da·re *m* (**-re**) (com) debit; **dare e avere** debit and credit || §144b *tr* to give; to set (*fire*); to hand over; to lay down (*one's life*); to render (*e.g., unto Caesar*); to give away (*a bride*); to take (*an examination*); to tender (*one's resignation*); to say (*good night*); to shed (*tears*); **dare acqua a** to water; **dare alla luce** to give birth to; to bring out (*e.g., a book*); **dare aria a** to air; **dare . . . anni a qlcu** to think that s.o. is . . . years old; **dare a ridire** to give rise to complaint; **dare da intendere** to lead to believe; **dare fastidio a** to bother, annoy; **dare fondo a** to use up; **dare gli otto giorni a** to dismiss, fire; **dare il benvenuto a** to welcome; **dare il via a** to start (*e.g., a race*); **dare la colpa a** to declare guilty; to put the blame on; **dare la mano a** to shake hands with; **dare l'assalto a** to assault; **dare luogo a** to give rise to; **dare noia a** to bother; **dare per certo a** to assure; **dare ragione a** to agree with; **dare torto a** to disagree with; **dare via** to give away || *intr* to burst; to begin; to beat down (*said of the sun*); **dare a** to verge on; to face, overlook; **dare addosso a** to attack, persecute; **dare ai** or **sui nervi di** to irritate, irk; **dare alla testa a** to go to one's head, e.g., **il vino gli dà alla testa** wine goes to his head; **dare contro a** to disagree with; **dare del ladro a** to call (s.o.) a thief; **dare del Lei a** to address formally; **dare del tu a** to address familiarly; **dare di volta il cervello a** to go raving mad, e.g., **gli ha dato di volta il cervello** he went raving mad; **dare giù** to abate; **dare in** to hit; **dare in affitto** to rent, lease; **dare nell'occhio** to attract attention; to hit the eye; **dare nel segno** to hit the target || *ref* to put on, e.g., **darsi la cipria** to put powder on; **darsela a gambe** to take to one's heels; **darsela per intesa** to become convinced; to take for granted; **darsele** to strike one another; **darsi a** to give oneself over to; **darsi delle arie** to put on airs; **darsi il vanto di** to boast of; **darsi un bacio** to kiss one another; **darsi la mano** to shake hands; **darsi la morte** to commit suicide; **darsi pace** to resign oneself; **darsi pensiero** to worry; **darsi per malato** to declare oneself ill; to fall ill; **darsi per vinto** to give in, submit; **può darsi** it's possible, maybe; **si dà il caso** it happens
dàrsena *f* dock; basin
data *f* date; deal (*of cards*); **a . . . data** (com) . . . days hence, on or before . . . days; **di fresca data** new (*e.g., friend*); **di vecchia data** old (*e.g., friend*)
datare *tr* to date || *intr*—**a datare da** beginning with
datà·rio *m* (**-ri**) date stamp
dati·vo -va *adj & m* dative
da·to -ta *adj* inclined, bent; addicted; given; appointed (*date*); **dato e non concesso** assumed for the sake of

argument; **dato che** since || *m* datum || *f* see **data**
da·tóre -trice *mf* giver, donor; **datore di lavoro** employer; **datore di sangue** blood donor; **datori di lavoro** management
dàttero *m* date; (zool) date shell
dattilografare (dattilògrafo) *tr* to typewrite, type
dattilografìa *f* typewriting
dattilògra·fo -fa *mf* typist
dattiloscopìa *f* examination of fingerprints
dattiloscrit·to -ta *adj* typewritten || *m* typescript
dattórno *adv* near, nearby; **darsi dattorno** to strive; **stare dattorno a** to cling to; **togliersi dattorno qlcu** to get rid of s.o.
davanti *adj invar* fore, front || **davan·ti** *m* (**-ti**) front, face || *adv* ahead, in front; **davanti a** in front of; **levarsi davanti a qlcu** to get out of someone's way; **passare davanti a** to pass, outstrip
davanzale *m* window sill
davanzo *adv* more than enough
davvéro *adv* indeed; **dire davvero** to speak in earnest
daziare §287 *tr* to levy a duty on
dà·zio *m* (**-zi**) duty, custom; custom office
dèa *f* goddess
debellare (debèllo) *tr* (lit) to crush
debilitare (debìlito) *tr* to debilitate
debilitazióne *f* debilitation
débi·to -ta *adj* due || *m* debit; debt; **debito pubblico** national debt
debi·tóre -trice *mf* debtor
débole *adj* weak; faint; gentle (*sex*); **debole di mente** feeble-minded || *m* weakness, weak point; weakness, foible; weakling
debolézza *f* weakness, debility
debordare (debórdo) *intr* (ESSERE & AVERE) to overflow
debòscia *f* debauchery
deboscia·to -ta *adj* debauched || *mf* debauchee
debuttante *adj* beginning || *mf* beginner || *f* debutante
debuttare *intr* to come out, make one's debut; (theat) to perform for the first time; (theat) to open
debutto *m* debut; (theat) opening night, opening
dècade *f* ten; period of ten days; (mil) ten days' pay
decadènte *adj & m* decadent
decadènza *f* decadence; lapse (*of insurance policy*); (law) forfeiture
decadére §121 *intr* (ESSERE) to decline; to lose one's standing; (ins) to lapse; **decadere da** (law) to forfeit
decadiménto *m* decadence; (law) forfeiture
decadu·to -ta *adj* fallen upon hard times
decaffeinizzare [ddzz] *tr* to decaffeinate
decalcificatóre *m* water softener
decalcomanìa *f* decalcomania
decàlo·go *m* (**-ghi**) decalogue
decampare *intr* to decamp; **decampare da** to abandon (*a plan*)
decano *m* dean
decantare *tr* to praise, extol; to decant; (lit) to purify || *intr* to undergo decantation
decapàggio *m* (metallurgy) pickling
decapitare (decàpito) *tr* to behead, decapitate
decapitazióne *f* beheading
decappottàbile *adj & f* (aut) convertible
decèdere §123 *intr* (ESSERE) to die; to decease
decelerare (decèlero) *tr & intr* to decelerate
decennale *adj & m* decennial
decènne *adj & mf* ten-year-old
decèn·nio *m* (**-ni**) decade
decènte *adj* decent; proper
decentralizzare [ddzz] *tr* to decentralize
decentrare (decèntro) *tr* to decentralize
decènza *f* decency; propriety
decèsso *m* decease, demise
decìdere §145 *tr* to decide; to persuade || *intr & ref* to decide; **deciditi!** make up your mind!
decifràbile *adj* decipherable
decifrare *tr* to decipher, decode; (fig) to puzzle out (*e.g., somebody's intentions*); (mus) to sight-read
dècima *f* tithe
decimale *adj & m* decimal
decimare (dècimo) *tr* to decimate
decìmetro *m* decimeter; **doppio decimetro** ruler
dèci·mo -ma *adj, m & pron* tenth || *f* see **decima**
decisionale *adj* decision-making
decisióne *f* decision
decisi·vo -va *adj* decisive, conclusive
deci·so -sa *adj* determined, resolute; appointed (*time*)
declamare *tr* to declaim || *intr* to declaim; to inveigh
declamazióne *f* declamation
declaratò·rio -ria *adj* (**-ri -rie**) declarative
declinare *tr* to decline; to declare, show; (gram) to decline; (lit) to bend || *intr* to set (*said, e.g., of a star*); to slope; to diminish
declinazióne *f* declination; (gram) declension
declino *m* decline
declì·vio *m* (**-vi**) declivity, slope
decollàg·gio *m* (**-gi**) take-off; lift-off
decollare (decòllo) *tr* to decapitate || *intr* (aer) to take off; (rok) to lift off
decòllo *m* take-off; lift-off
decolorante *adj* bleaching || *m* bleach
decompórre §218 *tr, intr & ref* to decompose
decomposizióne *f* decomposition
decompressióne *f* decompression
decongelare (decongèlo) *tr* to thaw; (com) to unfreeze
decontaminare (decontàmino) *tr* to decontaminate
decorare (decòro) *tr* to decorate
decorati·vo -va *adj* decorative
decora·tóre -trice *mf* decorator

decorazióne *f* decoration
decòro *m* decorum, propriety; decor; dignity; decoration
decoró·so -sa [s] *adj* fitting, decorous, proper; dignified
decorrènza *f* beginning, effective date; lapse
decórrere §139 *intr* (ESSERE) to elapse; to begin; (lit) to run; **a decorrere da** effective, beginning with
decór·so -sa *adj* past || *m* period, span; course; development; **nel decorso di** in the course of
decòt·to -ta *adj* (com) insolvent || *m* decoction
decozióne *f* (com) insolvency
decrèpi·to -ta *adj* decrepit
decréscere §142 *intr* (ESSERE) to decrease
decretare (decréto) *tr* to decree
decréto *m* decree; **decreto legge** decree law
decùbito *m* recumbency
decuplicare §197 **(decùplico)** *tr* to multiply tenfold
dècu·plo -pla *adj* tenfold || *m* tenfold part
decurtare *tr* to diminish, decrease
decurtazióne *f* decrease
dèda·lo -la *adj* (lit) ingenious || *m* maze, labyrinth
dèdi·ca *f* **(-che)** dedication; inscription (*in a book*)
dedicare §197 **(dèdico)** *tr* to dedicate; to inscribe (*a book*) || *ref* to devote oneself
dèdi·to -ta *adj* devoted; addicted
dedizióne *f* devotion; (obs) surrender
dedurre §102 *tr* to deduce; to deduct; to derive; (hist) to found (*a colony*)
deduzióne *f* deduction
defalcàbile *adj* deductible
defalcare §197 *tr* to deduct, withhold
defal·co *m* **(-chi)** deduction, withholding
defecare §197 **(defèco)** *tr* (chem) to purify || *intr* to defecate
defenestrare (defenèstro) *tr* to throw out of the window; (fig) to fire; (pol) to unseat
defenestrazióne *f* defenestration; (fig) firing, dismissal
deferènte *adj* deferential; (anat) deferent
deferènza *f* deference
deferire §176 *tr* to submit; (law) to commit; **deferire il giuramento a qlcu** to put s.o. under oath || *intr* to defer
defezionare (defezióno) *intr* to desert, defect
defezióne *f* defection
deficiènte *adj* deficient, lacking || *mf* idiot
deficiènza *f* deficiency; idiocy
dèfi·cit *m* **(-cit)** deficit
deficità·rio -ria *adj* **(-ri -rie)** lacking; deficit (*e.g., budget*)
defilare *tr* to defilade || *ref* to protect oneself
deofinìbile *adj* definable
definire §176 *tr* to define; to settle (*an argument*)
definiti·vo -va *adj* definitive; **in definitiva** after all
defini·to -ta *adj* definite
definizióne *f* definition; settlement (*of an argument*)
deflagrare *intr* to burst into flame; (fig) to burst out
deflazionare (deflazióno) *tr* (com) to deflate
deflazióne *f* deflation
deflèttere §177 *intr* to deflect
deflettóre *m* (aut) vent window; (mach) baffle
deflorare (deflòro) *tr* to deflower
defluire §176 *intr* (ESSERE) to flow down; (fig) to pour out
deflusso *m* flow; outflow, outpour; ebbtide
deformare (defórmo) *tr* to deform; to cripple; to alter (*a word*)
defórme *adj* deformed, crippled
deformi·tà *f* **(-tà)** deformity
defraudare (defràudo) *tr* to defraud, bilk
defun·to -ta *adj* dead; deceased; defunct; late || *mf* dead person, deceased || *m* deceased; **i defunti** the deceased
degenerare (degènero) *intr* (ESSERE & AVERE) to degenerate; to worsen
degenera·to -ta *adj* degenerate, perverted || *mf* degenerate, pervert
degenerazióne *f* degeneracy, degeneration
degènere *adj* degenerate
degènte *adj* bedridden; hospitalized || *mf* patient; inpatient
degènza *f* confinement; hospitalization
dégli §4
deglutire §176 *tr* to swallow
degnare (dégno) *tr* to honor || *ref* to deign, condescend
degnazióne *f* condescension
dé·gno -gna *adj* worthy; **degno di nota** noteworthy
degradante *adj* degrading
degradare *tr* to degrade; to downgrade; (mil) to break || *ref* to become degraded
degradazióne *f* degradation
degustare *tr* to taste
degustazióne *f* tasting
dèh *interj* oh!
déi §4
deiezióne *f* excrement; (geol) detritus
deificare §197 **(deìfico)** *tr* to deify
dei·tà *f* **(-tà)** deity
dél §4
dela·tóre -trice *mf* informer
delazióne *f* informing; (law) administration of an oath
dèle·ga *f* **(-ghe)** proxy, power of attorney
delegare §209 **(dèlego)** *tr* to delegate
delega·to -ta *adj* delegated || *m* delegate; (eccl) legate
delegazióne *f* delegation
deletè·rio -ria *adj* **(-ri -rie)** deleterious
delfino *m* dolphin; (hist) dauphin
delibare *tr* to relish; to touch on; to ratify (*a foreign decree*)

delibazióne *f* ratification (*of a foreign decree*)
deliberare (delìbero) *tr* to deliberate; to decide; to award (*at auction*) || *intr* to deliberate
delibera·to -ta *adj* deliberate; resolved
deliberazióne *f* deliberation; decision
delicatézza *f* delicacy; gentleness; tactfulness; luxury
delica·to -ta *adj* delicate; gentle; tactful
delimitare (delìmito) *tr* to delimit
delineare (delìneo) *tr* to outline, sketch || *ref* to take shape; to appear
delinquènte *m* criminal
delinquènza *f* delinquency; **delinquenza minorile** juvenile delinquency
delìnquere §146 *intr* to commit a crime
delì·quio *m* **(-qui)** fainting spell, swoon; **cadere in deliquio** to faint
delirare *intr* to be delirious; to rave; (lit) to stray
delì·rio *m* **(-ri)** delirium; frenzy; **andare in delirio** to go wild; **cadere in delirio** to become delirious
delitto *m* crime
delittuó·so -sa [s] *adj* criminal
delìzia *f* delight; (hort) Delicious (*variety of apple*)
deliziare §287 *tr & ref* to delight
delizió·so -sa [s] *adj* delicious; delightful
délla §4
délle §4
déllo §4
dèl·ta *m* **(-ta)** delta
delucidare (delùcido) *tr* to elucidate; to remove the sheen from
delucidazióne *f* elucidation; removal of sheen
delùdere §105 *tr* to disappoint; to deceive; to foil
delusióne *f* disappointment; deception
delu·so -sa *adj* disappointed; deceived
demagnetizzare [ddzz] *tr* to demagnetize
demagogìa *f* demagogy
demagò·go *m* **(-ghi)** demagogue
demandare *tr* (law) to commit
demà·nio *m* **(-ni)** state land, state property
demarcare §197 *tr* to demarcate
demarcazióne *f* demarcation
demènte *adj* demented, crazy; idiotic || *mf* insane person; idiot
demènza *f* insanity, madness; idiocy
demèrito *m* demerit
demilitarizzare [ddzz] *tr* to demilitarize
democràti·co -ca (-ci -che) *adj* democratic || *mf* democrat
democrazìa *f* democracy || **Democrazia Cristiana** Christian Democratic Party
democristia·no -na *adj* Christian Democratic || *mf* Christian Democrat
demogràfi·co -ca *adj* **(-ci -che)** demographic
demolire §176 *tr* to demolish
demoli·tóre -trice *adj* wrecking; destructive || *mf* wrecker
demolizióne *f* demolition
dèmone *m* demon
demonìa·co -ca *adj* **(-ci -che)** fiendish; demoniacal
demò·nio *m* **(-ni)** demon; **avere il demonio addosso** to be full of the devil
demoralizzare [ddzz] *tr* to demoralize || *ref* to become demoralized
demoralizza·to -ta [ddzz] *adj* demoralized, dejected
denaro *m* money; denier (*of nylon thread*); **avere il denaro contato** to be short of money; **denari** suit of Neapolitan cards corresponding to diamonds
denatura·to -ta *adj* denatured
denegare §209 **(dènego** or **denégo)** *tr* to deny
denigrare *tr* to denigrate; to backbite
denominare (denòmino) *tr* to call, designate
denomina·tóre -trice *adj* designating || *m* denominator
denominazióne *f* denomination; designation
denotare (denòto) *tr* to denote
densi·tà *f* **(-tà)** density
dèn·so -sa *adj* dense, thick
dentale *adj & f* dental
dentare (dènto) *tr* to notch, scallop || *intr* to teethe
dentaruòlo *m* teething ring
denta·to -ta *adj* toothed
dentatura *f* set of teeth; teeth (*of gear*)
dènte *m* tooth; peak (*of mountain*); pang (*of jealousy*); fluke (*of anchor*); prong (*of fork*); **battere i denti** to shiver; **dente canino** canine tooth; **dente del giudizio** wisdom tooth; **dente di latte** baby tooth; **dente di leone** (bot) dandelion; **mettere i denti** to teethe
dentellare (dentèllo) *tr* to notch, scallop; to perforate (*stamps*)
dentellatura *f* notch; perforation (*of postage stamps*); (archit) denticulation
dentèllo *m* notch, scallop; lace; (archit) dentil
dentièra *f* denture, plate; cog
dentifrì·cio -cia (-ci -cie) *adj* tooth || *m* dentifrice
denti·sta *mf* **(-sti -ste)** dentist
dentizióne *f* teething
déntro *adv* inside, in; **dentro di** inside of; within; **essere dentro** (coll) to be behind bars; **in dentro** inward || *prep* inside of
denuclearizzare [ddzz] *tr* to denuclearize
denudare *tr* to denude; to strip; (lit) to unveil
denunciare §128 *tr* var of **denunziare**
denùnzia *f* denunciation; announcement; report
denunziare §287 *tr* to denounce; to accuse; to announce; to report
denutri·to -ta *adj* undernourished
denutrizióne *f* undernourishment
deodorante *adj & m* deodorant
deodorare (deodóro) *tr* to deodorize
depauperare (depàupero) *tr* to impoverish
depennare (depénno) *tr* to strike out, expunge
deperìbile *adj* perishable

deperiménto *m* deterioration; decline
deperire §176 *intr* (ESSERE) to deteriorate; to perish; to decay
depilatò·rio -ria *adj & m* (**-ri -rie**) depilatory
deplorare (**deplòro**) *tr* to deplore; to reproach
deplorévole *adj* deplorable; reproachable
depolarizzare [ddzz] *tr* to depolarize
depórre §218 *tr* to lay; to lay down (*crown, arms*); to depose (*e.g., a king*); to take off (*clothes*); to give up (*hope*); to renounce; **deporre l'abito talare** to doff the cassock
deportare (**depòrto**) *tr* to deport
deporta·to -ta *adj* deported || *mf* deportee
deportazióne *f* deportation
depositare (**depòsito**) *tr* to deposit; to register, check || *intr* to settle (*said, e.g., of sand*)
deposità·rio -ria (**-ri -rie**) *adj* deposit || *mf* depositary
depòsito *m* deposit; checking (*e.g., of a suitcase*); registration; heap (*e.g., of refuse*); warehouse; morgue; receiving ward; (mil) depot; **deposito bagagli** baggage room
deposizióne *f* deposition; Descent from the Cross
deprava·to -ta *adj* depraved
depravazióne *f* depravation
deprecare §197 (**deprèco**) *tr* to deprecate
depredare (**deprèdo**) *tr* to plunder
depredazióne *f* depredation
depressióne *f* depression
deprès·so -sa *adj* depressed
deprezzaménto *m* depreciation
deprezzare (**deprèzzo**) *tr* to depreciate; to underestimate || *intr* (ESSERE) to depreciate
deprimènte *adj* depressing
deprìmere §131 *tr* to humble, discourage; to depress
depurare *tr* to purify
deputare (**dèputo**) *tr* to deputize, delegate
deputa·to -ta *mf* deputy, delegate; representative
deputazióne *f* deputation, delegation
deragliaménto *m* derailment
deragliare §280 *intr* to be derailed, to run off the track
derapàg·gio *m* (**-gi**) skidding
derapare *intr* to skid
derelit·to -ta *adj & mf* derelict
derelizióne *f* dereliction
dereta·no -na *adj & m* posterior
derìdere §231 *tr* to deride, mock
derisióne *f* derision, ridicule
derisò·rio -ria *adj* (**-ri -rie**) derisory, derisive
deriva *f* (aer) vertical stabilizer; (aer, naut) leeway; (naut) drift; **alla deriva** adrift
derivare *tr* to derive; to branch off (*e.g., a canal*) || *intr* (ESSERE) to be derived, arise; to drift
deriva·to -ta *adj* derivative || *m* derivative (*word*) || *f* (math) derivative
derivazióne *f* derivation; (elec) shunt; (telp) extension
dermatòlo·go *m* (**-gi**) dermatologist
dermòide *f* imitation leather
dèro·ga *f* (**-ghe**) exception; **in deroga a** deviating from
derogare §209 (**dèrogo**) *intr* to transgress; **derogare a** to deviate from
derrata *f* foodstuff; **derrate** foodstuff, produce
derubare *tr* to rob
dèr·vis *m* (**-vis**) or **dervì·scio** *m* (**-sci**) dervish
desalazióne [s] *f* desalinization
desalificare [s] §197 (**desalìfico**) *tr* to desalt
dé·sco *m* (**-schi**) dinner table; meal
descritti·vo -va *adj* descriptive
descrìvere §250 *tr* to describe
descrizióne *f* description
desegregazióne [s] *f* desegregation
desensibilizzare [s] [ddzz] *tr* to desensitize
desèrti·co -ca *adj* (**-ci -che**) desert, wild
desèr·to -ta *adj* deserted; **andare deserto** to be unattended || *m* desert
desideràbile [s] *adj* desirable
desiderare (**desìdero**) [s] *tr* to desire; **farsi desiderare** to make oneself scarce; to be dilatory
desidè·rio [s] *m* (**-ri**) desire; craving; lust; **lasciar desiderio di sé** to be greatly missed
desideró·so -sa [s] *adj* desirous
designare [s] *tr* to designate
designazióne [s] *f* designation
desinare *m* dinner || *intr* to dine
desinènza *f* (gram) ending
desì·o *m* (**-i**) (lit) desire
desìstere [s] §114 *intr* to desist
desolante *adj* distressing
desolare (**dèsolo**) *tr* to distress; (lit) to devastate
desola·to -ta *adj* desolate; distressed
desolazióne *f* desolation; distress
dèspo·ta *m* (**-ti**) despot
despòti·co -ca *adj* (**-ci -che**) var of **dispotico**
despotismo *m* var of **dispotismo**
des·sèrt *m* (**-sèrt**) dessert
destare (**désto**) *tr* to awaken; to stir up || *ref* to wake up
destinare *tr* to destine; to assign; to address
destinatà·rio -ria *mf* (**-ri -rie**) consignee; addressee
destinazióne *f* destination; assignment
destino *m* destiny; (com) destination
destituire §176 *tr* to demote; to dismiss; to deprive
destituzióne *f* demotion; dismissal
dé·sto -sta *adj* awake; (fig) wide-awake
dèstra *f* right, right hand
destreggiare §290 (**destréggio**) *intr* to maneuver || *ref* to manage shrewdly
destrézza *f* skill, dexterity
destrière or **destrièro** *m* (lit) steed
dè·stro -stra *adj* right; skillful || *f* see **destra**
destròr·so -sa *adj* clockwise; righthand; (bot) dextrorse
destròsio *m* dextrose

desùmere [s] §116 *tr* to obtain; to infer
detecti•ve *m* (-ve) detective
detèc•tor *m* (**-tor**) (rad) detector
detenére §271 *tr* to hold; to detain
deten•tóre -trice *mf* holder; receiver (*of stolen goods*)
detenu•to -ta *mf* prisoner
detenzióne *f* illegal possession; detention
detergènte *adj & m* detergent
detèrgere §164 (*pp* **detèrso**) *tr* to cleanse; to wipe
deterioràbile *adj* perishable
deteriorare (**deterióro**) *tr* to spoil ‖ *intr* (ESSERE) *& ref* to deteriorate, spoil
determinare (**detèrmino**) *tr* to determine; to fix; to decide; to cause ‖ *ref* to decide; to happen
determinatézza *f* determination; precision
determinati•vo -va *adj* (gram) definite
determina•to -ta *adj* given; resolved, determined
determinazióne *f* determination
deterrènte *adj & m* deterrent
detersi•vo -va *adj* cleansing ‖ *m* cleanser; detergent
detestàbile *adj* detestable
detestare (**detèsto**) *tr* to detest
detettóre *m* detector; **detettore di bugie** lie detector
detonare (**detòno**) *intr* to explode, detonate
detonatóre *m* blasting cap, detonator
detonazióne *f* detonation; report
detrarre §273 *tr* to take away; (lit) to detract
detrat•tóre -trice *mf* detractor
detrazióne *f* detraction; deduction
detriménto *m* detriment
detrito *m* debris; detritus; (fig) outcast, outlaw
detronizzare [ddzz] *tr* to dethrone
détta *f*—**a detta di** according to
dettagliante *m* retailer
dettagliare §280 *tr* to tell in detail; to itemize; to retail ‖ *intr*—**pregasi dettagliare** please send detailed information
dettà•glio *m* (**-gli**) detail; retail
dettame *m* (lit) law, norm
dettare (**détto**) *tr* to dictate; (lit) to compose, write; **dettar legge** to impose one's will
dettato *m* dictation; (lit) style
dettatura *f* dictation
dét•to -ta *adj* called, named; **detto (e) fatto** no sooner said than done ‖ *m* saying ‖ *f* see **detta**
deturpare *tr* to disfigure, mar
deturpazióne *f* disfigurement, disfiguration
devalutazióne *f* devaluation
devastare *tr* to devastate, lay waste; (fig) to disfigure
devasta•tóre -trice *adj* devastating ‖ *m* devastator
devastazióne *f* devastation
deviaménto *m* switching; derailment; (fig) straying
deviare §119 *tr* to turn aside; to lead astray; (rr) to switch; (rr) to derail ‖ *intr* to deviate; to wander; to go astray; (rr) to run off the track
deviatóre *m* (rr) switchman; (elec) two-way switch
deviazióne *f* deviation; detour; curvature (*of the spine*); (phys) declination; (phys) deflection; (rr) switching
deviazionismo *m* deviationism
deviazioni•sta *mf* (**-sti -ste**) deviationist
devoluzióne *f* transfer
devòlvere §147 *tr* to transfer ‖ *intr & ref* (lit) to roll down
devò•to -ta *adj* devoted; devout, pious ‖ *m* devout person; worshiper
devozióne *f* devotion
di §4 *prep* of; in, e.g., **la più bella della famiglia** the prettiest one in the family; (*with definite article*) some, e.g., **mi occorrono dei fiammiferi** I need some matches; than, e.g., **più veloce del baleno** faster than lightning; from, e.g., **è di Milano** he is from Milan; off, e.g., **smontare di sella** to get off the saddle; about, e.g., **discutere di politica** to talk about politics; with, e.g., **ornare di fiori** to adorn with flowers; made of, e.g., **una casa di mattoni** a house made of bricks; by, e.g., **di notte** by night; for, e.g., **amor di patria** love for one's country; worth, e.g., **casa di dieci milioni** house worth ten million; in the amount of, e.g., **multa di mille lire** fine in the amount of one thousand lire; son of, e.g., **Carlo Giovannini di Filippo** Carlo Giovannini son of Philip; daughter of, e.g., **Anna Ponti di Antonio** Anna Ponti daughter of Anthony; **di corsa** running; **di gran lunga** greatly; by far; **di . . . in** from . . . to; **di là da** beyond; **di nascosto** stealthily; **di qua da** on this side of; **di quando in quando** from time to time; **di tre metri** three meters long or wide or high
dì *m* (**dì**) day; **a dì** (e.g., **ventisei**) this (e.g., twenty-sixth) day; **conciare per il dì delle feste** (coll) to beat up
diabète *m* diabetes
diabèti•co -ca *adj & mf* (**-ci -che**) diabetic
diabòli•co -ca *adj* (**-ci -che**) diabolic(al)
diàcono *m* deacon
diadè•ma *m* (**-mi**) diadem (*of king*); tiara (*of lady*)
diàfa•no -na *adj* diaphanous
diafonìa *f* (telp) cross talk
diafram•ma *m* (**-mi**) diaphragm; (fig) partition
diàgno•si *f* (**-si**) diagnosis
diagnosticare §197 (**diagnòstico**) *tr* to diagnose
diagonale *adj & f* diagonal
diagram•ma *m* (**-mi**) diagram; chart
diagrammare *tr* to diagram
dialettale *adj* dialectal
dialètti•co -ca (**-ci -che**) *adj* dialectic(al) ‖ *m* dialectician ‖ *f* dialectic; (philos) dialectics
dialètto *m* dialect
dialettòfo•no -na *adj* dialect-speaking ‖ *m* dialect-speaking person

dialogare §209 **(diàlogo)** *intr* to carry on a dialogue
dialoga·to -ta *adj* written in the form of a dialogue || *m* dialogue
diàlo·go *m* **(-ghi)** dialogue
diamante *m* diamond; **diamante taglia-vetro** glass cutter
diametrale *adj* diametric(al)
diàmetro *m* diameter
diàmine *interj* good heavens!; the devil!; sure!
diana *f* (mil) reveille || **Diana** *f* Diana
dianzi *adv* (lit) a short while ago
diàpa·son *m* **(-son)** (mus) pitch; (mus) tuning fork
diapositiva *f* (phot) slide, transparency
dià·rio -ria (-ri -rie) *adj* daily || *m* diary; journal; **diario scolastico** homework book || *f* per diem
diarrèa *f* diarrhea
diascò·pio *m* **(-pi)** slide projector
diaspro *m* jasper
diàstole *f* diastole
diatermìa *f* diathermy
diatriba *f* diatribe
diavolàc·cio *m* **(-ci)** devil; **buon diavolaccio** good fellow
diavolerìa *f* deviltry; devilment; evil plot
diavolè·rio *m* **(-ri)** hubbub, uproar
diavoléto *m* hubbub, uproar
diavolétto *m* little devil, imp
diàvolo *m* devil; **avere il diavolo in corpo** to be nervous; **avere un diavolo per capello** to be in a horrible mood; **buon diavolo** good fellow; **essere come il diavolo e l'acqua santa** to be at opposite poles; **fare il diavolo a quattro** to make a racket; to try very hard
dibàttere *tr* to debate || *ref* to struggle; to writhe
dibattiménto *m* debate; (law) pleading, trial
dibàttito *m* debate
dicastèro *m* department, ministry
dicèmbre *m* December
dicerìa *f* rumor, gossip
dichiarare *tr* to declare, state; to find (*guilty*); to proclaim; to nominate, name || *ref* to declare oneself to be; to declare one's love; to plead (*e.g., guilty*)
dichiarazióne *f* declaration; avowal (*of love*); return (*of income tax*); **dichiarazioni** representations
diciannòve *adj* & *pron* nineteen; **le diciannove** seven P.M. || *m* nineteen; nineteenth (*in dates*)
diciannovèsi·mo -ma *adj, m* & *pron* nineteenth
diciassètte *adj* & *pron* seventeen; **le diciassette** five P.M. || *m* seventeen; seventeenth (*in dates*)
diciassettèsi·mo -ma *adj, m* & *pron* seventeenth
diciottèsi·mo -ma *adj, m* & *pron* eighteenth
diciòtto *adj* & *pron* eighteen; **le diciotto** six P.M. || *m* eighteen; eighteenth (*in dates*)
dici·tóre -trice *mf* reciter
dicitura *f* caption, legend; (lit) wording, language
dicotomìa *f* dichotomy
didascalìa *f* note, notice; caption; legend (*e.g., on coin*); (mov) subtitle
didascàli·co -ca *adj* **(-ci -che)** didactic
didàtti·co -ca (-ci -che) *adj* didactic; elementary school (*director, principal*) || *f* didactics
didéntro *m* (coll) inside
didiètro *m* behind; back (*of house*) || *adv* behind
dièci *adj* & *pron* ten; **le dieci** ten o'clock || *m* ten; tenth (*in dates*)
diecimila *adj, m* & *pron* ten thousand
diecina *f* about ten
dière·si *f* **(-si)** dieresis
diè·sis *m* **(-sis)** (mus) sharp
dièta *f* diet; **dieta idrica** fluid diet
dietèti·co -ca (-ci -che) *adj* dietetic || *f* dietetics
dieti·sta *mf* **(-sti -ste)** dietitian
dièt̀ro *adj invar* back, rear || *m* back, rear || *adv* back, behind; **dal di dietro** from behind; **di dietro** hind (*legs*); back (*side*); behind, back (*e.g., of cupboard*) || *prep* behind; beyond; after; upon; **dietro a** behind; beyond; after; according to; **dietro consegna** on delivery; **dietro domanda** upon application; **dietro versamento** upon payment; **essere dietro a** to be in the process of
dietrofrónt *m* (mil) about face
difatti *adv* indeed
difèndere §148 *tr* to defend, protect || *ref* to protect oneself; (coll) to get along
difensi·vo -va *adj* & *f* defensive
difen·sóre -sóra or **difenditrice** *adj* defense || *mf* defender
difésa [s] *f* defense; bulwark; protection; **legittima difesa** self-defense; **pigliare le difese di** to defend, back up; **venire in difesa di** to go to the defense of
difettare (difètto) *intr* to be lacking; to be defective; **difettare di** to lack
difetti·vo -va *adj* defective
difètto *m* lack; blemish; fault; defect; **essere in difetto** to be at fault; **far difetto a** to lack, e.g., **gli fa difetto il denaro** he lacks money
difettó·so -sa [s] *adj* defective
diffamare *tr* to defame, slander
diffama·tóre -trice *mf* defamer, slanderer
diffamazióne *f* defamation, slander
differènte *adj* different
differènza *f* difference; spread; variance; **a differenza di** unlike; **c'è una bella differenza** it's a horse of another color
differenziale *adj* & *m* differential
differenziare §287 **(differènzio)** *tr* to differentiate
differiménto *m* deferment
differire §176 *tr* to postpone, defer || *intr* to be different; to differ
difficile *adj* hard, difficult; awkward (*situation*); hard-to-please; unlikely

|| *mf* hard-to-please person || *m*—**fare il difficile** to be hard to please; **qui sta il difficile!** here's the trouble!
difficol·tà *f* (**-tà**) difficulty; defect; obstacle; objection
difficoltó·so -sa [s] *adj* difficult, troublesome; fastidious
diffida *f* notice; warning
diffidare *tr* to give notice to; to warn || *intr* to mistrust
diffidènte *adj* distrustful
diffidènza *f* mistrust
diffóndere §178 *tr* to spread; to circulate; to broadcast || *ref* to spread; to dwell at length
diffórme *adj* unlike; (obs) deformed
diffrazióne *f* diffraction
diffusióne *f* spreading; circulation (*of a newspaper*); diffusion; (rad) broadcast
diffu·so -sa *adj* diffuse; widespread
diffusóre *m* diffuser (*to soften light*); baffle (*of loudspeaker*); (mach) choke
difilato *adv* forthwith, right away
difrónte *adj invar* in front
difterite *f* diphtheria
di·ga *f* (**-ghe**) dike; dam
digerènte *adj* alimentary (*canal*), digestive (*tube*)
digerìbile *adj* digestible
digerire §176 *tr* to digest; to tolerate, stand
digestióne *f* digestion
digesti·vo -va *adj* digestive
digèsto *m* digest
digitale *adj* digital || *f* (bot) digitalis
digitalina *f* (pharm) digitalin
digiunare *intr* to fast
digiu·no -na *adj* without food; deprived; **digiuno di cognizioni** ignorant; **tenere digiuno** to keep in ignorance || *m* fast; **a digiuno** on an empty stomach; **fare digiuno** to fast
digni·tà *f* (**-tà**) dignity; **dignità** *fpl* dignitaries
dignità·rio *m* (**-ri**) dignitary
dignitó·so -sa [s] *adj* dignified
digradare *tr* to shade (*colors*) || *intr* to slope; to fade
digredire §176 *intr* to digress
digressióne *f* digression
digrignare *tr* to show (*one's or its teeth*); to grit (*one's teeth*)
digrossare (**digròsso**) *tr* to rough-hew; to whittle down; (fig) to refine || *ref* to become refined
diguazzare *tr* to beat (*a liquid*) || *intr* to wallow; to splash
dilagare §209 *intr* to flood, to overflow; to spread abroad
dilaniare §287 *tr* to tear to pieces || *ref* to slander one another
dilapidare (**dilàpido**) *tr* to squander
dilatare *tr* to expand; to dilate || *ref* to expand; to spread
dilatazióne *f* expansion; dilation
dilatò·rio -ria *adj* (**-rî -rie**) delaying; dilatory
dilavare *tr* to wash away, erode
dilava·to -ta *adj* dull, flat; wan
dilazionare (**dilazióno**) *tr* to delay, put off; (com) to extend
dilazióne *f* delay; (com) extension
dileggiare §290 (**diléggio**) *tr* to mock
dilég·gio *m* (**-gi**) mockery, scoffing; **mettere in dileggio** to scoff at
dileguare (**diléguo**) *tr* to scatter || *intr* (ESSERE) to disappear, vanish; to melt
dilèm·ma *m* (**-mi**) dilemma
dilettante *mf* amateur; dilettante
dilettanté·sco -sca *adj* (**-schi -sche**) amateurish
dilettare (**dilètto**) *tr* to delight || *ref* to delight; **dilettarsi a** + *inf* to delight in + *ger*; **dilettarsi di** to pursue as a hobby, e.g., **si diletta di pittura** he pursues painting as a hobby
dilettévole *adj* delectable, delightful
dilèt·to -ta *adj* beloved || *m* loved one; pleasure; hobby
diligènte *adj* diligent
diligènza *f* diligence; stagecoach
dilucidare (**dilùcido**) *tr* to elucidate
diluire §176 *tr* to dilute
dilungare §209 *tr* (archaic) to stretch || *ref* to expatiate; to be ahead by several lengths (*said of a race horse*)
dilungo *m*—**a un dilungo** more or less
diluviare §287 *tr* to devour || *intr* (ESSERE & AVERE) to rain (*said, e.g., of bullets*) || *impers* (ESSERE)—**diluvia** it is pouring
dilù·vio *m* (**-vi**) deluge, flood; **diluvio universale** Flood
dimagrante *adj* reducing
dimagrare *tr* to thin down || *intr* (ESSERE) to become thin; to lose weight; to become exhausted (*said of land*); (fig) to become meager
dimagrire §176 *intr* (ESSERE) to become thin; to lose weight, reduce
dimanda *f* var of **domanda**
dimane *adv* (coll) tomorrow
dimani *m & adv* var of **domani**
dimenare (**diméno**) *tr* to wag (*the tail*); to beat (*eggs*); to wave (*one's arms*); to stir up (*a question*) || *ref* to toss; to busy oneself
dimensióne *f* dimension; (fig) nature
dimenticanza *f* oversight, neglect; **andare in dimenticanza** to be forgotten
dimenticare §197 (**diméntico**) *tr* to forget; to forgive || *ref* to forget; **dimenticarsi di** to forget; to neglect
dimenticatóio *m*—**mettere nel dimenticatoio** (coll) to forget
diménti·co -ca *adj* (**-chi -che**) forgetful; neglectful
dimés·so -sa *adj* humble, modest (*demeanor*); low (*voice*); shabby (*clothes*)
dimestichézza *f* familiarity
diméttere §198 *tr* to dismiss; to release || *ref* to resign
dimezzare [ddzz] (**dimèzzo**) *tr* to halve
diminuire §176 *tr* to lessen, reduce; to lower (*prices*) || *intr* (ESSERE) to diminish
diminuti·vo -va *adj & m* diminutive
diminuzióne *f* diminution
dimissionare (**dimissióno**) *tr* to dismiss, discharge || *ref* to resign
dimissionà·rio -ria *adj* (**-ri -rie**) resigning, outgoing

dimissióne *f* resignation; **dare le dimissioni** to resign

dimól·to -ta *adj & m* (coll) much ‖ **dimolto** *adv* (coll) much

dimòra *f* stay; residence; (lit) delay; **mettere a dimora** to install; to plant (*trees*); **senza dimora** (lit) without delay; **senza fissa dimora** vagrant

dimorare (dimòro) *intr* to stay; to reside; (lit) to delay

dimostràbile *adj* demonstrable

dimostrante *m* demonstrator

dimostrare (dimóstro) *tr* to demonstrate; to register (*e.g., anger*); **dimostrare trent'anni** to look thirty ‖ *intr* to demonstrate ‖ *ref* to prove oneself to be

dimostrati·vo -va *adj* demonstrative; (mil) diverting

dimostra·tóre -trice *mf* demonstrator

dimostrazióne *f* demonstration

dinàmi·co -ca (-ci -che) *adj* dynamic ‖ *f* dynamics

dinamismo *m* dynamism

dinamite *f* dynamite

dìna·mo *f* (**-mo**) generator, dynamo

dinanzi *adj invar* front, e.g., **la porta dinanzi** the front door; preceding, e.g., **il mese dinanzi** the preceding month ‖ *adv* ahead; beforehand; (lit) before; **dinanzi a** before, in front of

dina·sta *m* (**-sti**) dynast

dinastìa *f* dynasty

dinàsti·co -ca *adj* (**-ci -che**) dynastic

dindo *m* (coll) turkey

dindòn *m* ding-dong ‖ *interj* ding-dong!

dinièg·o *m* (**-ghi**) denial

dinoccola·to -ta *adj* gangling; clumsy (*gait*)

dinosàuro [s] *m* dinosaur

dintórno *m*—**dintorni** surroundings, neighborhood ‖ *adv* around; **dintorno a** around

dì·o -a *adj* (**-i -e**) (poet) godly ‖ *m* (**dèi**) god; **gli dei** the gods ‖ **Dio** *m* God; **che Dio la manda** cats and dogs (*said of rain*); **come Dio volle** at long last; **come Dio vuole** botched (*piece of work*); **Dio ci scampi!** God forbid!; **Dio santo!** good heavens!; **grazie a Dio** God willing; thank God; **voglia Dio** God grant

diòce·si *f* (**-si**) diocese

dìodo *m* (electron) diode

diomedèa *f* (orn) albatross

diottrìa *f* (opt) diopter

dipanare *tr* to unravel, unwind

dipartiménto *m* department

dipartire §176 *tr* (archaic) to divide ‖ *intr* (**diparto**) (ESSERE) & *ref* (lit) to depart

dipartita *f* (lit) departure; (lit) demise

dipendènte *adj* dependent ‖ *mf* employee

dipendènza *f* dependence; employment; annex; (com) branch; **in dipendenza di** as a consequence of

dipèndere §150 *intr* (ESSERE) to depend; **dipendere da** to depend on

dipìngere §126 *tr* to paint; **dipingere a olio** to paint in oils; **dipingere a tempera** to distemper ‖ *ref* to paint oneself; to put make-up on; to appear, e.g., **gli si dipinse in volto la paura** fear appeared on his face

dipin·to -ta *adj* painted ‖ *m* painting, picture

diplò·ma *m* (**-mi**) diploma, certificate

diplomare (diplòmo) *tr* to grant a degree to; to graduate ‖ *ref* to receive a degree; to graduate

diplomàti·co -ca (-ci -che) *adj* diplomatic; true, faithful (*copy*) ‖ *m* diplomat ‖ *f* diplomatics

diploma·to -ta *adj* graduated ‖ *mf* graduate ‖ *m* alumnus ‖ *f* alumna

diplomazìa *f* diplomacy

dipòi *adv* after, thereafter

diportare (dipòrto) *ref* (lit) to behave; (obs) to have a good time

dipòrto *m* recreation; (obs) sport; **andare a diporto** to go on an outing; to go for a walk

diprèsso *adv*—**a un dipresso** about, approximately

diradare *tr* to thin out (*vegetation*); to disperse; to space out (*one's visits*) ‖ *intr* (ESSERE) & *ref* to diminish; to disperse

diramare *tr* to prune; to circulate (*notices*); to issue (*a communiqué*) ‖ *ref* to branch out; to spread

diramazióne *f* branch; ramification; issuance

dire *m* talk; **per sentito dire** by hearsay; **stando al dire** according to his words ‖ §151 *tr & intr* to say; to tell; to call (*e.g., s.o. a genius*); to talk; **detto (e) fatto** no sooner said than done; **dica pure!** go ahead!; speak up!; **dire bene di** to speak well of; **dire di no** to say no; **dire di sì** to say yes; **direi quasi** I dare say; **dire la sua** to have one's say; **dire male di** to speak ill of; **dirla grossa** to make a blunder; to tell a tall tale; **dirlo chiaro e tondo** to speak bluntly; **dirne un sacco e una sporta a** to pour insults upon; **è tutto dire** that's all; **non c'è che dire** it's a fact; **non fo per dire** I do not want to boast; **per così dire** so to speak; **per meglio dire** rather; **trovarci a dire** to find fault with; **trovare da dire con** to have words with; **voler ben dire** to be sure; **voler dire** to mean ‖ *ref*—**dirsela con** to connive with; **si dice** it is said

dirètro *m & adv* (archaic) behind, back

direttìssima *f* (rr) high-speed line; **per direttissima** straight up (*in mountain climbing*)

direttìssimo *m* express train

diretti·vo -va *adj* managerial ‖ *m* board of directors ‖ *f* directive; direction; guideline

dirèt·to -ta *adj* direct; **diretto a** addressed to; directed at; bound for ‖ *m* through train

diret·tóre -trice *mf* manager; principal ‖ *m* director; **direttore di macchina** (naut, nav) chief engineer; **direttore di tiro** (nav) gunnery officer; **direttore di un giornale** editor; **direttore d'or-**

chestra orchestra leader; **direttore responsabile** publisher; **direttore tecnico** (sports) manager || *f* see **direttrice**
direttò·rio -ria (-ri -rie) *adj* directorial || *m* directory
direttrice *adj fem* directing; guiding; front (*wheels*) || *f* directress; line of action
direzionale *adj* directional; managerial
direzióne *f* direction; management; run (*of events*)
dirigènte *adj* leading; managerial || *m* employer; boss; leader; executive
dirìgere §152 *tr* to direct; to turn; to lead || *ref* to address oneself; **dirigersi verso** to head for
dirigìbile *adj & m* dirigible
dirimpètto *adj invar & adv* opposite; **dirimpetto a** opposite to; in comparison with
dirit·to -ta *adj* straight; right; unswerving; (coll) smart || *m* law; obverse, face (*of coin*); fee, dues; (fin) right; **a buon diritto** rightly so; **di diritto** by law; **diritti d'autore** copyright; **diritti di segreteria** registration fee; **diritti doganali** customs duty; **diritti speciali di prelievo** (econ) special drawing rights; **diritto canonico** canon law; **diritto consuetudinario** common law; **diritto internazionale** international law; **in diritto** according to law || *f* right, right hand || **diritto** *adv* straight; **tirare diritto** to go straight ahead
dirittura *f* direction; uprightness; (sports) straightaway, home stretch
dirizzóne *m* blunder
diroccare §197 **(diròcco)** *tr* to knock down || *intr* (ESSERE) (archaic) to fall down
dirocca·to -ta *adj* dilapidated, rickety
dirompènte *adj* fragmentation (*bomb*)
dirottaménto *m* hijacking; skyjacking (*of an airplane*)
dirottare (dirótto) *tr* to detour (*traffic*); to hijack (*e.g., a ship*); to skyjack (*an airplane*) || *intr* to change course
dirottatóre *m* hijacker; skyjacker (*of a plane*)
diròt·to -ta *adj* copious, heavy (*rain, tears*); (lit) craggy; **a dirotto** cats and dogs (*said of rain*)
dirozzare [ddzz] **(dirózzo)** *tr* to rough-hew; to refine || *ref* to become polished
dirugginire §176 *tr* to take the rust off; to limber up; to gnash (*one's teeth*); to clear (*one's mind*)
dirupa·to -ta *adj* rocky, craggy
dirupo *m* rock; crag, cliff
disabbigliare §280 *tr & ref* to undress, disrobe
disabita·to -ta *adj* uninhabited
disabituare (disabìtuo) *tr* to disaccustom || *ref* to become unaccustomed
disaccenta·to -ta *adj* unaccented
disaccòrdo *m* disagreement
disadat·to -ta *adj* unfit
disadór·no -na *adj* unadorned, bare
disaffezionare (disaffezióno) *tr* to alienate the affection of; to estrange || *ref* to become estranged
disaffezióne *f* dislike
disagévole *adj* troublesome, uncomfortable
disagiare §290 *tr* to trouble, inconvenience
disagia·to -ta *adj* uncomfortable; needy
disà·gio *m* (-gi) discomfort; need
disalberare (disàlbero) *tr* to dismast
disambienta·to -ta *adj* bewildered, strange
disàmina *f* examination, scrutiny
disaminare (disàmino) *tr* to scrutinize; to weigh
disamorare (disamóro) *tr* to alienate the affection of; to estrange || *ref* to become estranged
disancorare (disàncoro) *intr* to weigh anchor; to leave port || *ref* to weigh anchor; (fig) to free oneself
disanimare (disànimo) *tr* to dishearten
disappetènza *f* loss of appetite
disapprovare (disappròvo) *tr* to disapprove
disapprovazióne *f* disapproval
disappunto *m* disappointment
disarcionare (disarcióno) *tr* to unsaddle, unhorse; to kick out
disarmare *tr* to disarm; to dismantle (*a scaffold*); to ship (*oars*); (naut) to unrig || *ref* to disarm; (fig) to give up
disarma·to -ta *adj* unarmed, defenseless
disarmo *m* disarmament; dismantling; unrigging
disarmonìa *f* discord; contrast
disarmòni·co -ca *adj* (-ci -che) discordant
disarticolare (disartìcolo) *tr* to limber up; to disjoint || *ref* to become dislocated
disassociare §128 **(disassòcio)** *tr* to dissociate
disastra·to -ta *adj* damaged || *mf* victim
disastro *m* disaster, calamity; wreck
disastró·so -sa [s] *adj* disastrous
disattèn·to -ta *adj* inattentive; careless
disattenzióne *f* inattention; carelessness
disattivare *tr* to deactivate (*e.g., a mine*)
disavanzo *m* (com) deficit
disavvedu·to -ta *adj* heedless
disavventura *f* misfortune
disavvertènza *f* inadvertence
disavvezzare (disavvézzo) *tr* to break (*s.o.*) of a habit || *ref*—**disavvezzarsi da** to give up or lose the habit of
disavvéz·zo -za *adj* unaccustomed
disbórso *m* disbursement, outlay
disboscare §197 **(disbòsco)** *tr* to deforest
disbrigare §209 *tr* to dispatch || *ref* to extricate oneself
disbri·go *m* (-ghi) prompt execution, dispatch
discacciare §128 *tr* (lit) to chase away
discanto *m* (mus) harmonizing
discàpito *m* damage; **tornare a discapito di** to be detrimental to
discàri·ca *f* (-che) discharge (*e.g., of pollutants*); dumping (*of refuse*); unloading (*of a ship*)

discàri·co *m* (**-chi**) exculpation; **a discarico di** in defense of
discatóre *m* hockey player; discus thrower
discendènte *adj* descending; sloping; down (*train*) || *mf* descendant
discendènza *f* descent; pedigree
discéndere §245 *tr* to go down || *intr* (ESSERE & AVERE) to descend, go down; to slope; to fall (*said, e.g., of thermometer*); to get off; **discendere in picchiata** (aer) to nose-dive
discènte *mf* student, pupil
discépo·lo -la *mf* disciple
discèrnere §153 *tr* to discern
discernìbile *adj* discernible
discerniménto *m* discernment
discésa [s] *f* descent; slope; drop
discettare (**discètto**) *tr* (lit) to discuss
dischiodare (**dischiòdo**) *tr* to take the nails out of
dischiùdere §125 *tr* to open; to reveal
discin·to -ta *adj* scantily dressed; untidy; in disarray
discioglìere §127 *tr* to dissolve, melt; (lit) to untie || *ref* to dissolve, melt
disciplina *f* discipline; whip, scourge
disciplinare *adj* disciplinary || *m* regulation || *tr* to discipline
disciplina·to -ta *adj* obedient
di·sco *m* (**-schi**) disk; (phonograph) record; bob (*of pendulum*); (ice hockey) puck; (sports) discus; (rr) signal; (pharm) tablet; **disco combinatore** (telp) dial; **disco microsolco** microgroove record; **disco volante** flying saucer
discòfilo *m* record lover
discòide *m* (pharm) tablet, pill
dìsco·lo -la *adj* undisciplined, wild || *m* rogue, rascal
discolorare (**discolóro**) *tr* to discolor || *ref* to pale
discolorazióne *f* discoloration; paleness
discólpa *f* defense
discolpare (**discólpo**) *tr* to defend
disconnèttere §107 *tr* to disconnect
disconóscere §134 *tr* to ignore, to disregard; to be ungrateful for
discontinuare (**discontìnuo**) *tr* to perform sporadically || *intr* to lose continuity
disconti·nuo -nua *adj* uneven
disconvenire §282 *intr* (ESSERE) (lit) to disagree || *impers* (ESSERE) (lit) to be improper
discoprire §110 (**discòpro**) *tr* to discover
discordante *adj* discordant
discordare (**discòrdo**) *intr* (ESSERE) to disagree, differ
discòrde *adj* discordant; opposing
discòrdia *f* discord, dissension
discórrere §139 *intr* to talk, chat; (coll) to keep company; **discorrere del più e del meno** to make small talk; **e via discorrendo** and so forth
discórso *m* discourse; conversation; speech; **pochi discorsi!** (coll) cut it out!
discostare (**discòsto**) *tr* to remove || *ref* to withdraw; to differ
discò·sto -sta *adj* distant || **discosto** *adv* far
discotè·ca *f* (**-che**) record library; discotheque
discreditare (**discrédito**) *tr* to discredit
discrédito *m* discredit
discrepanza *f* discrepancy
discretaménte *adv* rather; fairly well
discré·to -ta *adj* discreet; fairly large; fair
discrezióne *f* discretion
discriminante *adj* discriminatory; extenuating || *m* (math) discriminant
discriminare (**discrìmino**) *tr* to discriminate; to extenuate
discriminazióne *f* discrimination
discussióne *f* discussion; argument
discus·so -sa *adj* controversial
discùtere §154 *tr* to discuss || *intr* to discuss; to argue
discutìbile *adj* moot, debatable
disdegnare (**disdégno**) *tr* to disdain, scorn || *ref* (obs) to be angry
disdégno *m* disdain, scorn
disdegnó·so -sa [s] *adj* disdainful
disdétta *f* ill luck; (law) notice
disdicévole *adj* unbecoming, unseemly
disdire §151 *tr* to retract; to belie; to cancel; to countermand; to terminate the contract of || *ref* to retract; **disdire a** to be unbecoming to
disdòro *m* shame; **tornare a disdoro di** to bring shame on
disegnare [s] (**diségno**) *tr* to draw; to sketch; to design; (obs) to elect
disegna·tóre -trice [s] *mf* cartoonist; designer || *m* draftsman
diségno [s] *m* drawing; sketch; outline; plan; design; **disegno animato** (mov) cartoon; **disegno di legge** (law) bill
disellare [s] (**disèllo**) *tr* var of **dissellare**
diserbante *adj* weed-killing || *m* weed-killer
diseredare (**diserèdo**) *tr* to disinherit
diseredа·to -ta *adj* disinherited || **i diseredati** the underprivileged
disertare (**disèrto**) *tr* to desert; (lit) to lay waste || *intr* to desert
disertóre *m* deserter
diserzióne *f* desertion
disfaciménto *m* disintegration
disfare §173 *tr* to undo; to defeat; to melt; to unknit; to break up (*housekeeping*); **disfare il letto** to remove the bedclothes || *ref* to spoil (*said, e.g., of meat*); **disfarsi di** to get rid of
disfatta *f* defeat
disfattismo *m* defeatism
disfatti·sta *mf* (**-sti -ste**) defeatist
disfat·to -ta *adj* undone; defeated; melted; broken up; ravaged || *f* see **disfatta**
disfida *f* (lit) challenge
disfunzióne *f* malfunction
disgelare (**disgèlo**) *tr* & *intr* to thaw
disgèlo *m* thaw
disgiùngere §183 *tr* & *ref* to separate
disgiunti·vo -va *adj* disjunctive
disgràzia *f* disfavor; bad luck, misfortune; accident; **per disgrazia** unfortunately

disgrazia•to -ta *adj* unlucky; wretched
disgregaménto *m* disintegration
disgregare §209 (**disgrègo**) *tr & ref* to disintegrate
disgregazióne *f* disintegration
disguido *m* miscarriage, missending (*of a letter*)
disgustare *tr* to disgust, sicken || *ref* to become disgusted, sicken; to have a falling-out, to part company
disgusto *m* disgust, repugnance
disgustó•so -sa [s] *adj* disgusting
disidratare *tr* to dehydrate
disìlla•bo -ba *adj* disyllabic || *m* disyllable
disillùdere §105 *tr* to delude, deceive || *ref* to become disillusioned
disillusióne *f* disillusion
disimboscare §197 (**disimbòsco**) *tr* to put back in circulation
disimparare *tr* to unlearn, forget
disimpegnare (**disimpégno**) *tr* to release; to free, to open; to loosen; to redeem (*a pledge*); to clear; to perform || *ref* to succeed
disimpégno *m* release; redemption; performance; disengagement; **di disimpegno** for every day (*e.g., a suit*); main (*e.g., hallway*)
disimpiè•go *m* (**-ghi**) unemployment; (mil) withdrawal
disincagliare §280 *tr* to set afloat; (fig) to disentangle
disincantare *tr* disenchant
disinfestare (**disinfèsto**) *tr* to exterminate
disinfestazióne *f* extermination
disinfettante *adj & m* disinfectant
disinfettare (**disinfètto**) *tr* to disinfect
disingannare *tr* to disillusion || *ref* to become disillusioned
disinganno *m* disillusion
disinnescare §197 (**disinnésco**) *tr* to defuse
disinnestare (**disinnèsto**) *tr* to disconnect; to throw out, disengage
disinserire §176 *tr* (elec) to disconnect; (aut) to disengage
disintasare [s] *tr* to unclog
disintegrare (**disìntegro**) *tr & ref* to disintegrate
disintegrazióne *f* disintegration
disinteressare (**disinterèsso**) *tr* to make (*s.o.*) lose interest || *ref* to lose interest; to take no interest
disinteressa•to -ta *adj* selfless, unselfish
disinterèsse *m* disinterest; unselfishness
disintossicare §197 (**disintòssico**) *tr* to free of poison; (fig) to clean the air in || *ref* to shake the drug habit
disinvòl•to -ta *adj* free and easy; fresh, forward
disinvoltura *f* naturalness, ease of manners, offhandedness; freshness; impudence
disì•o *m* (**-i**) (poet) desire
disistima *f* scorn, low regard, disesteem
disistimare *tr* to scorn, hold in low regard
dislivèllo *m* difference of level; disparity
dislocaménto *m* transfer of troops; (naut) displacement
dislocare §197 (**dislòco**) *tr* to transfer (*troops*); to post (*sentries*); (naut) to displace
dislocazióne *f* (mil) transfer; (geog, naut, psychol) displacement
dismisura *f* excess; **a dismisura** excessively
disobbedire §176 *intr* var of **disubbidire**
disobbligare §209 (**disòbbligo**) *tr* to free from an obligation || *ref* to repay a favor
disoccupa•to -ta *adj* unemployed, jobless; idle; unoccupied || *m* unemployed person; **i disoccupati** the jobless
disoccupazióne *f* unemployment
disone•stà *f* (**-stà**) dishonesty; shamelessness
disonè•sto -sta *adj* dishonest; shameless; immoral
disonorante *adj* disgraceful
disonorare (**disonóro**) *tr* to dishonor, disgrace; to seduce
disonóre *m* dishonor, shame
disonorévole *adj* dishonorable; shameful
disoppilare (**disòppilo**) *tr* to clear of obstructions
disópra *adj invar* upper || *m* (**disópra**) upper part, top; **prendere il disopra** to have the upper hand || *adv* above; **al disopra di** above
disordinare (**disórdino**) *tr* to cancel, countermand; to confuse; to mess up || *intr* to indulge || *ref* to become disorganized
disordina•to -ta *adj* confused; messy; untidy; intemperate
disórdine *m* confusion; mess; disarray; disorder; intemperance
disorganizzare [ddzz] *tr* to disorganize; to disrupt
disorganizzazióne [ddzz] *f* disorganization, disorder; disruption
disorientaménto *m* disorientation; confusion, bewilderment
disorientare (**disorièento**) *tr* to cause (*s.o.*) to lose his way; to confuse; to disorient || *ref* to be bewildered; to lose one's bearings
disorienta•to -ta *adj* disoriented; confused, bewildered; lost, astray
disormeggiare §290 (**disorméggio**) *tr* to unmoor
disossare (**disòsso**) *tr* to bone || *ref* (lit) to lose weight
disótto [s] *adj invar* below || *m* (**disótto**) lower part, bottom || *adv* below; **al disotto di** below, underneath
disotturare *tr* to unclog
dispàc•cio *m* (**-ci**) dispatch; urgent letter; **dispaccio telegrafico** telegram
dispara•to -ta *adj* disparate
disparére *m* disagreement
dispari *adj invar* odd, uneven
dispari•tà *f* (**-tà**) disparity
dispàrte *adv*—**in disparte** apart, aside; **starsene in disparte** to keep aloof
dispèn•dio *m* (**-di**) expenditure; waste
dispendió•so -sa [s] *adj* expensive; wasteful

dispènsa *f* cupboard; pantry; distribution; number (*of magazine*); installment (*of book*); dispensation; (naut) storeroom; (coll) store
dispensare (**dispènso**) *tr* to exempt, free; to distribute || *ref*—**dispensarsi da** to get out of
dispensà·rio *m* (**-ri**) dispensary
dispensa·tóre -trice *mf* dispenser
dispensiè·re -ra *mf* dispenser || *m* steward
dispepsìa *f* dyspepsia
dispèpti·co -ca *adj* & *mf* (**-ci -che**) dyspeptic
disperare (**dispèro**) *intr* to despair; **fare disperare** to drive crazy || *ref* to despair
dispera·to -ta *adj* hopeless || *m* poor wretch; **come un disperato** desperately || *f*—**alla disperata** with all one's might
disperazióne *f* desperation, despair
dispèrdere §212 *tr* to scatter; to waste || *ref* to disperse; (fig) to waste one's energies
dispersióne *f* dispersion; loss; (elec) leakage
dispersività *f* tendency toward disorganization
dispersi·vo -va *adj* dispersive; disorganized
dispèr·so -sa *adj* scattered; lost; dispersed; missing in action
dispersóre *m* (elec) leakage conductor
dispètto *m* spite; (lit) haughtiness; **a dispetto di** in spite of; **far dispetto a** to provoke
dispettó·so -sa [s] *adj* pestiferous; spiteful, resentful
dispiacènte *adj* sorry; distressing
dispiacére *m* sorrow, displeasure || §214 *intr* (ESSERE) to be displeasing; to be sorry, e.g., **mi dispiace** I am sorry; (with *dat*) to displease; (with *dat*) to dislike, e.g., **le mie parole gli dispiacciono** he dislikes my words; **Le dispiace?** would you please?; **se non Le dispiace** if you don't mind
dispiegare §209 (**dispiègo**) *tr* to manifest; (lit) to unfurl || *ref* to spread out; to flow out
displù·vio *m* (**-vi**) divide, watershed; ridge (*of roof*)
disponìbile *adj* available; open-minded
disponibili·tà *f* (**-tà**) availability; inactive status; **disponibilità** *fpl* available funds
dispórre §218 *tr* to dispose; to prepare || *intr* to provide; to dispose; **disporre di** to have (*available*) || *ref* to get ready
dispositivo *m* gadget; device; (mil) deployment
disposizióne *f* arrangement; inclination, disposition; disposal; instruction; (law) provision
dispó·sto -sta *adj* arranged; disposed; provided; willing; **ben disposto** disposed || *m* (law) proviso
dispòti·co -ca *adj* (**-ci -che**) despotic
dispotismo *m* despotism
dispregiati·vo -va *adj* disparaging; (gram) pejorative
disprè·gio *m* (**-gi**) contempt; disrepute
disprezzàbile *adj* contemptible; negligible
disprezzare (**disprèzzo**) *tr* to despise
disprèzzo *m* contempt, scorn
dìsputa *f* dispute; debate
disputàbile *adj* debatable
disputare (**dìsputo**) *tr* to contest; to discuss; to vie for (*victory*) || *intr* to dispute, debate; to vie || *ref* to vie for
disqualificare §197 (**disqualìfico**) *tr* to disqualify
disquisizióne *f* disquisition
dissacrare *tr* to desecrate
dissacrazióne *f* desecration
dissaldare *tr* to unsolder
dissanguare (**dissànguo**) *tr* to bleed || *ref* to bleed; to ruin oneself
dissangua·to -ta *adj* bled white; **morire dissanguato** to bleed to death
dissapóre *m* disagreement
disseccare §197 (**dissécco**) *tr* to dry || *ref* to dry; to dry up
disselciare §128 (**dissélcio**) *tr* to remove the cobblestones from
dissellare (**dissèllo**) *tr* to unsaddle
disseminare (**dissémino**) *tr* to disseminate; to scatter
dissenna·to -ta *adj* foolish, unwise; crazy, mad
dissensióne *f* dissension
dissènso *m* dissent; disagreement
dissenterìa *f* dysentery
dissentire (**dissènto**) *intr* to dissent
dissenziènte *adj* dissenting || *mf* dissenter
disseppellire §176 *tr* to exhume
dissertare (**dissèrto**) *intr* to discourse
dissertazióne *f* dissertation
disservì·zio *m* (**-zi**) poor service
dissestare (**dissèsto**) *tr* to unsettle; to disarrange
dissesta·to -ta *adj* financially embarrassed; mentally deranged
dissèsto *m* financial embarrassment; mental derangement
dissetante *adj* thirst-quenching
dissetare (**disséto**) *tr* to quench the thirst of || *ref* to quench one's thirst
dissezióne *f* dissection
dissidènte *adj* & *m* dissident
dissidènza *f* dissent
dissì·dio *m* (**-di**) dissent; disagreement
dissigillare *tr* to unseal || *ref* (lit) to melt
dissìmile *adj* unlike
dissimulare (**dissìmulo**) *tr* to dissimulate, disguise || *intr* to dissimulate
dissimulazióne *f* dissimulation
dissipare (**dìssipo**) *tr* to dissipate; to squander; to clear up (*a doubt*) || *ref* to dissipate
dissipa·to -ta *adj* & *mf* profligate
dissipa·tóre -trice *mf* squanderer
dissipazióne *f* dissipation
dissociare §128 (**dissòcio**) *tr* to dissociate, disassociate || *ref* to dissociate or disassociate oneself
dissociazióne *f* dissociation

dissodare (dissòdo) *tr* to cultivate
dissolutézza *f* profligacy
dissolu·to -ta *adj & mf* profligate
dissoluzióne *f* dissolution
dissolvènza *f* (mov) fade-out; **dissolvenza incrociata** (mov) lap dissolve
dissòlvere §155 *tr* to dissolve; to clear up (*a doubt*); (obs) to untie || *ref* to dissolve
dissomiglianza *f* dissimilarity
dissonanza *f* dissonance
dissotterrare (dissottèrro) *tr* to exhume; to unearth
dissuadére §213 *tr* to dissuade
dissuè·to -ta *adj* (lit) unaccustomed
dissuggellare (dissuggèllo) *tr* to unseal
distaccaménto *m* (mil) detachment
distaccare §197 *tr* to detach; to remove; to transfer; to outdistance || *ref* to stand out; to withdraw, become separated
distacca·to -ta *adj* detached; branch (*office*)
distac·co *m* (**-chi**) detachment; separation; (sports) spread (*in points*)
distante *adj* distant; aloof; different || *adv* far away
distanza *f* distance; **mantenere le distanze** to keep one's distance; **tenere a distanza** to keep at arm's length
distanziare §287 *tr* to outdistance
distare *intr* to be distant
distèndere §270 *tr* to stretch; to spread; to unfurl; to relax; to knock down; to write || *ref* to stretch; to spread out; to relax
distensióne *f* relaxation; relaxation of tension
disté·so -sa [s] *adj* stretched out; full (*voice*); lank (*hair*) || *m*—**per disteso** in full || *f* expanse; row; **a distesa** with full voice; at full peal
distillare *tr* to distill; to exude; to pour; to trickle || *intr* (ESSERE) to trickle || *ref*—**distillarsi il cervello** to rack one's brain
distilla·to -ta *adj* distilled || *m* distillate
distilla·tóre -trice *mf* distiller || *m* still
distillerìa *f* distillery
distinguìbile *adj* distinguishable
distìnguere §156 *tr* to distinguish; to make out; to tell (*one thing from another*); to divide
distinta *f* note, list; **distinta di versamento** deposit slip
distintaménte *adj* distinctly; sincerely yours
distinti·vo -va *adj* distinctive || *m* emblem, insignia, badge
distin·to -ta *adj* distinct; distinguished; sincere (*greetings*); reserved (*seat*); **Distinto Signor . . .** (*on an envelope*) Mr. . . . || *f* see **distinta**
distinzióne *f* distinction
distògliere §127 *tr* to dissuade; to deter; to distract; to turn (*one's eyes*) away
distòrcere §272 *tr* to distort; to twist || *ref* to become distorted; to sprain (*e.g., one's ankle*)
distorsióne *f* distortion; sprain; **distorsione acustica** wow
distrarre §273 *tr* to distract; to divert; to amuse; to pull (*a muscle*) || *ref* to become distracted; to relax
distrat·to -ta *adj* absent-minded
distrazióne *f* absent-mindedness; distraction; diversion (*of money*); pull (*of muscle*)
distrét·to -ta *adj* (obs) close; (obs) hard-pressed || *m* district; precinct (*e.g., of police*); circuit (*of court*); ward (*in city*); **distretto militare** draft board; **distretto postale** postal zone || *f* stricture; necessity
distrettuale *adj* district
distribuire §176 *tr* to distribute; to pass out; to allot; to deploy (*troops*); (theat) to cast (*roles*); (mov) to release; (mil) to issue (*e.g., clothing*)
distribu·tóre -trice *adj* distributing, dispensing || *mf* distributor, dispenser || *m* distributor; **distributore automatico** vending machine; **distributore di benzina** gasoline pump
distribuzióne *f* distribution; issue; delivery; (aut) timing gears; (mov) release; (fig) dispensation
districare §197 *tr* to unravel || *ref* to extricate oneself
distrofia *f* dystrophy
distrùggere §266 *tr* to destroy; to ruin
distrutti·vo -va *adj* destructive
distruzióne *f* destruction
disturbare *tr* to disturb, bother; **disturbo?** may I come in? || *ref* to bother; to go out of one's way
disturba·tóre -trice *mf* disturber; **disturbatore della quiete pubblica** disturber of the peace
disturbo *m* trouble, bother; disturbance; (rad) interference; **disturbi atmosferici** static, atmospherics; **togliere il disturbo a** to take leave of
disubbidiènte *adj* disobedient
disubbidiènza *f* disobedience
disubbidire §176 *intr* to disobey; (with *dat*) to disobey
disuguaglianza *f* inequality; disparity
disuguale *adj* uneven; unequal
disuma·no -na *adj* inhumane; unbearable
disunióne *f* disunion
disunire §176 *tr* to disunite
disusa·to -ta *adj* obsolete, out of use
disuso *m* disuse; **in disuso** obsolete
disùtile *adj* useless; burdensome || *m* worthless fellow; (com) loss
disvì·o *m* (**-i**) miscarriage, missending (*of a letter*)
ditale *m* thimble; fingerstall
ditata *f* poke with a finger; finger mark; dab (*with a finger*)
dito *m* (**dita** *fpl*) finger; toe; **avere le dita d'oro** to have a magic touch; **dita della mano** fingers; **dita del piede** toes; **legarsela al dito** to never forget || *m* (**diti**) finger, e.g., **dito indice** index finger; **dito anulare** ring finger; **dito medio** middle finger; **dito mignolo** little finger; **dito pollice** thumb
ditta *f* firm, house; office
dittàfono *m* intercom; dictaphone
dittatóre *m* dictator

dittatura *f* dictatorship
dittongare §209 (**dittòngo**) *tr* to diphthongize
dittòn•go *m* (**-ghi**) diphthong
diurèti•co -ca *adj* & *m* (**-ci -che**) diuretic
diur•no -na *adj* daily; daytime || *f* (theat) matinée
diutur•no -na *adj* long-lasting
diva *f* diva; (mov) star; (lit) goddess
divagare §209 *tr* to amuse; to distract || *intr* to digress || *ref* to relax
divagazióne *f* distraction; digression; relaxation
divampare *intr* (ESSERE & AVERE) to blaze, flare
divano *m* divan; couch, sofa
divaricare §197 (**divàrico**) *tr* to spread (*one's legs*); to open up (*an incision*)
divà•rio *m* (**-ri**) difference
divèllere §267 *tr* to eradicate, uproot
diveni•re *m* (**-re**) (philos) becoming || §282 *intr* (ESSERE) (lit) to become; (archaic) to come
diventare (**divènto**) *intr* (ESSERE) to become; **diventare di tutti i colori** to blush; to be embarrassed; **diventare grande** to grow up; **diventare matto** to go mad; **diventare pallido** to turn pale; **diventare piccolo** to grow smaller; **diventare rosso** to blush
divèr•bio *m* (**-bi**) argument; **venire a diverbio** to have an altercation
divergènza *f* divergency
divèrgere §157 *intr* to diverge
diversificare §197 (**diversìfico**) *tr* to diversify || *ref* to be diversified; to differ
diversióne *f* diversion
diversi•tà *f* (**-tà**) diversity
diversi•vo -va *adj* diverting || *m* diversion
diver•so -sa *adj* different; **diver•si -se** several, e.g., **diverse ragazze** several girls || **diver•si -se** *pron* several
divertènte *adj* diverting, amusing
divertiménto *m* amusement, pastime; fun; (mus) divertimento
divertire (**divèrto**) *tr* to amuse, entertain; (lit) to turn aside || *ref* to have fun, enjoy oneself; (lit) to go away
diverti•to -ta *adj* amused; amusing
divétta *f* starlet
divezzare (**divézzo**) *tr* to wean || *ref*—**divezzarsi da** to get out of the habit of
dividèndo *m* dividend
dividere §158 *tr* to divide; to partition; to split; to share in (*e.g., s.o.'s grief*) || *ref* to be divided; to become separated; **dividersi fra** to divide one's time between
divièto *m* prohibition; **divieto d'affissione** post no bills; **divieto di parcheggio** no parking; **divieto di sosta** no stopping; **divieto di svolta** no turns; **divieto di transito** no thoroughfare
divinare *tr* (lit) to divine
divina•tóre -trice *adj* divining || *m* diviner
divinazióne *f* divination
divincolare (**divìncolo**) *tr* & *ref* to wriggle
divini•tà *f* (**-tà**) divinity
divinizzare [ddzz] *tr* to deify
divi•no -na *adj* divine
divisa *f* uniform; motto; part (*in hair*); **divise** foreign exchange
divisare *tr* (lit) to intend
divisìbile *adj* divisible
divisióne *f* division; partition; (sports) league
divisionismo *m* (painting) divisionism; (pol) separatism
divismo *m* (mov) star system; (mov) adulation of stars
divisóre *m* (math) divisor
divisò•rio -ria (**-ri -rie**) *adj* dividing || *m* partition; (math) divisor
di•vo -va *adj* (lit) divine || *m* (theat, mov) star; (lit) god || *f* see **diva**
divolgare §209 (**divólgo**) *tr* & *ref* var of **divulgare**
divorare (**divóro**) *tr* to devour; to gulp down; to consume; **divorare la via** to burn up the road
divora•tóre -trice *adj* consuming || *mf* consumer (*e.g., of food, books*)
divorziare §287 (**divòrzio**) *intr* to become divorced; **divorziare da** to divorce
divorzia•to -ta *adj* divorced || *m* divorcé || *f* divorcée
divòr•zio *m* (**-zi**) divorce
divulgare §209 *tr* to divulge; to publicize; to popularize || *ref* to spread; to become popular
divulga•tóre -trice *adj* popularizing || *mf* popularizer; **divulgatore di calunnie** scandalmonger; **divulgatore di notizie** telltale
divulgazióne *f* publicizing; popularization
divulsióne *f* (surg) dilation
diziona•rio *m* (**-ri**) dictionary; **dizionario geografico** gazetteer
dizióne *f* diction; reading (*of poetry*)
do [dɔ] *m* (**do**) (mus) do; (mus) C
dóc•cia *f* (**-ce**) shower; gutter (*on roof*); spout; (fig) dash of cold water; **fare la doccia** to take a shower
docciare §128 (**dóccio**) *tr*, *intr* (ESSERE) & *ref* to shower
doccióne *m* trough, gutter; gargoyle
docènte *adj* teaching || *m* teacher; **libero docente** certified university teacher
docènza *f* teaching post; **libera docenza** lectureship
dòcile *adj* docile; tame; amenable (*person*); workable (*material*)
documentare (**documénto**) *tr* to document || *ref* to gather information
documentà•rio -ria *adj* & *m* (**-ri -rie**) documentary
documénto *m* document; paper; **documenti di bordo** ship's papers
dodecafonìa *f* twelve-tone system
dodecasìlla•bo -ba *adj* twelve-syllable, dodecasyllable
dodicèsi•mo -ma *adj*, *m* & *pron* twelfth
dódici *adj* & *pron* twelve; **le dodici**

twelve o'clock || *m* twelve; twelfth (*in dates*)
dó·ga *f* (**-ghe**) stave
dogale *adj* (hist) of the doge
dogana *f* duty; customs; custom house
doganière *m* customs officer
dòge *m* (hist) doge
dò·glia *f* (**-glie**) (lit) pain, pang; **doglie** labor pains
dò·glio *m* (**-gli**) barrel; (lit) large jar
dogliò·so -sa [s] *adj* (lit) sorrowful
dòg·ma *m* (**-mi**) dogma
dogmàti·co -ca (**-ci -che**) *adj* dogmatic || *mf* dogmatist
dogmatismo *m* dogmatism
dólce *adj* sweet; soft; gentle; fresh (*water*); mild (*climate*); delicate (*feet*); **dolce far niente** sweet idleness || *m* sweet; sweet dish; **dolci** candy
dolceama·ro -ra *adj* bittersweet
dolcézza *f* sweetness; mildness; gentleness
dolcia·stro -stra *adj* sweetish
dolcière *m* candy maker; pastry baker
dolcificare §197 (**dolcìfico**) *tr* to sweeten
dolciume *m* sweet; **dolciumi** candy
dolènte *adj* aching; sorrowful; sorry
dolére §159 *intr* (ESSERE & AVERE) to ache, e.g., **gli dolgono i denti** his teeth ache || *ref* to grieve || *impers* (ESSERE) to be sorry, e.g., **mi duole che Lei non possa venire** I am sorry that you won't be able to come
dolicònice *m* bobolink
dòllaro *m* dollar
dòlo *m* fraud, malice, guile
dolomite *f* dolomite || **Dolomiti** *fpl* Dolomites
dolorante *adj* aching
dolorare (**dolóro**) *intr* (lit) to ache
dolóre *m* ache; sorrow; contrition
doloró·so -sa [s] *adj* painful; sorrowful
doló·so -sa [s] *adj* intentional, fraudulent; (law) felonious
domàbile *adj* tamable
domanda *f* question; application; appeal; (econ) demand; **domanda suggestiva** (com) leading question; **fare una domanda** to ask a question
domandare *tr* to ask; to ask for; **domandare la parola** to ask for the floor || *intr* to inquire || *ref* to wonder; (lit) to be called
doma·ni *m* (**-ni**) tomorrow || *adv* tomorrow; **a domani** until tomorrow; **domani a otto** a week from tomorrow; **domani l'altro** the day after tomorrow
domare (**dómo**) *tr* to tame; to extinguish; to quell
doma·tóre -trice *mf* tamer
domattina *adv* tomorrow morning
doméni·ca *f* (**-che**) Sunday
domenicale *adj* Sunday (*e.g., rest*)
domenica·no -na *adj* & *m* Dominican (*e.g., order*)
domesticare §197 (**domèstico**) *tr* to domesticate
domèsti·co -ca (**-ci -che**) *adj* family; household; familiar; domestic || *mf* domestic, servant || *f* maid; **alla domestica** family style; **domestica a mezzo servizio** part-time domestic
domiciliare *adj* house || §287 *tr* (com) to draw || *ref* to dwell; to settle
domicilia·to -ta *adj* residing
domicì·lio *m* (**-li**) domicile, residence; principal office; **domicilio coatto** imprisonment; **franco domicilio** free delivery
dominare (**dòmino**) *tr* to dominate, rule; to master; to overlook || *intr* to prevail; to reign || *ref* to control oneself
domina·tóre -trice *mf* ruler
dominazióne *f* domination; rule
domineddìo *m invar* (coll) the Lord God
dominica·no -na *adj* & *mf* Dominican (*e.g., Republic*)
domì·nio *m* (**-ni**) dominion; domain
dòmi·no *m* (**-no**) domino (*cloak*); dominoes (*game*)
dòn *m* (used only before singular Christian name) don (*Spanish title*); Don (*priest*); uncle (*familiar title of elderly man*)
donare (**dóno**) *tr* to donate; to give as a present || *intr*—**donare a** to be becoming to
dona·tóre -trice *mf* donor; **donatore di sangue** blood donor
donazióne *f* gift, donation
donchisciotté·sco -sca *adj* (**-schi -sche**) quixotic
dónde *adv* wherefrom, whence
dondolare (**dóndolo**) *tr* to swing, rock || *ref* to swing, rock; to loaf around
dondolì·o *m* (**-i**) swinging, rocking
dóndolo *m*—**a dondolo** rocking (*chair, horse*); **andare a dondolo** to loaf around
dondoló·ne -na *mf* idler, loafer
dongiovan·ni *m* (**-ni**) Don Juan
dònna *f* woman; ladyship; (lit) lady; (coll) Mrs.; (coll) maid; (cards) queen; **da donna** woman's, e.g., **scarpe da donna** woman's shoes; **donna cannone** fat lady (*of circus*); **donna di casa** housewife; **Nostra Donna** Our Lady
donnaiòlo *m* ladies' man, philanderer
donné·sco -sca *adj* (**-schi -sche**) womanly, feminine
dònnola *f* weasel
dóno *m* gift; **in dono** as a gift
donzèlla [dz] *f* (lit) damsel
donzèllo [dz] *m* (coll) doorman; (lit) page
dópo *adv* afterwards, later; **dopo che** after; **dopo di** after || *prep* after; **dopo** + *pp* after having + *pp*
dopobar·ba *adj invar* after-shaving || *m* (**-ba**) after-shaving lotion
dopodomani *m* & *adv* the day after tomorrow
dopoguèr·ra *m* (**-ra**) postwar era
dopolavóro *m* government office designed to organize workers' leisure time
dopopranzo *m* afternoon || *adv* in the afternoon
doppiàg·gio *m* (**-gi**) (mov) dubbing

doppiare §287 (**dóppio**) *tr* to double; (mov) to dub
doppière *m* candelabrum
doppiétta *f* double-barreled shotgun; (aut) double shift
doppiézza *f* duplicity
dóp·pio -pia (**-pi -pie**) *adj* double; coupled; double-dealing || *adv* twice, twofold || *m* double; twice as much; (tennis) doubles; (theat) understudy
doppióne *m* duplicate; (philol) doublet
doppiopèt·to *adj invar* double-breasted || *m* (**-to**) double-breasted suit
dorare (**dòro**) *tr* to gild; (culin) to brown; **dorare la pillola** to sugar-coat the pill
dora·to -ta *adj* gilt, golden
doratura *f* gilding
dormicchiare §287 *intr* to doze
dormiènte *adj* sleeping || *mf* sleeper
dormiglió·ne -na *mf* sleepyhead
dormire (**dòrmo**) *tr* & *intr* to sleep; **dormire a occhi aperti** to be overcome with sleep; **dormire della grossa** to sleep profoundly; **dormire tra due guanciali** to be safe and secure
dormita *f* long sleep; **fare una bella dormita** to have a long sleep
dormitò·rio *m* (**-ri**) dormitory
dormivé·glia *m* (**-glia**) drowsiness
dorsale *adj* dorsal; back (*bone*) || *m* head (*of bed*); back (*of chair*) || *f* (geog) ridge
dòrso *m* back; (sports) backstroke
dosàg·gio *m* (**-gi**) dosage
dosare (**dòso**) *tr* to dose
dosatura *f* dosage
dòse *f* dose
dòsso *m* back; (lit) summit; **levarsi di dosso** to take off; **mettersi in dosso** to put on
dotare (**dòto**) *tr* to provide with a dowry; to endow; to bless
dotazióne *f* dowry; endowment; supply
dòte *f* dowry; gift; endowment
dòt·to -ta *adj* learned, erudite || *m* scholar; (anat) duct
dottorale *adj* doctoral
dottó·re -réssa *mf* doctor
dottrina *f* doctrine; Christian doctrine
dóve *m* where; **per ogni dove** everywhere || *adv* where; **da dove** or **di dove** from where; which way; **fin dove** up to what point; **per dove** which way || *conj* where; whereas
dovére *m* duty, obligation; homework; **a dovere** properly; **doveri** regards; **farsi un dovere di** to feel duty-bound to; **mettere qlcu a dovere** to put s.o. in his place; **più del dovere** more than one should; **sentirsi in dovere di** to feel duty-bound to || §160 *tr* & *intr* to owe || *aux* (ESSERE & AVERE) must, e.g., **deve farlo** you must do it; to have to, e.g., **dovei partire** I had to leave; ought to, e.g., **dovrebbe lucidare la macchina** he ought to polish the car; should, e.g., **dovresti immaginarti** you should imagine; to be to, e.g., **il treno doveva arrivare alle sei** the train was to arrive at six; to be supposed to, e.g., **deve aver fatto un lungo viaggio** he is supposed to have taken a long journey
doveró·so -sa [s] *adj* proper, right
dovìzia *f* (lit) abundance, wealth
dovunque *adv* wherever, anywhere; everywhere
dovu·to -ta *adj* & *m* due
dozzina [ddzz] *f* dozen; room and board; **da** or **di dozzina** common, ordinary; **tenere a dozzina** to board
dozzinale [ddzz] *adj* common, ordinary
dozzinante [ddzz] *mf* boarder
dra·ga *f* (**-ghe**) dredge
dragàg·gio *m* (**-gi**) dredging
dragami·ne *m* (**-ne**) minesweeper
dragare §209 *tr* to dredge
dràglia *f* (naut) stay
dra·go *m* (**-ghi**) dragon; **drago volante** kite
dragóna *f* sword strap
dragoncèllo *m* (bot) tarragon
dragóne *m* dragon; dragoon
dram·ma *m* (**-mi**) drama, play; **dramma musicale** (hist) melodrama || *f* drachma; dram
drammàti·co -ca (**-ci -che**) *adj* dramatic || *f* drama, dramatic art
drammatizzare [ddzz] *tr* to dramatize
drammatur·go *m* (**-ghi**) playwright, dramatist
drappég·gio *m* (**-gi**) drape; pleats
drappeggiare §290 (**drappéggio**) *tr* to drape || *ref* to be draped
drappèlla *f* pennon (*on bugler's trumpet*)
drappèllo *m* squad, platoon
drapperìa *f* dry goods; dry-goods store
drappo *m* cloth, silk cloth; (billiards) green cloth, baize
dràsti·co -ca *adj* (**-ci -che**) drastic
drenàg·gio *m* (**-gi**) drainage
drenare (**drèno**) *tr* to drain
dressàg·gio *m* (**-gi**) *m* training (*of animals*)
dribblare *tr* & *intr* (sports) to dribble
drit·to -ta *adj* straight; (lit) correct; **dritto come un fuso** straight as a ramrod || *m* (fig) old fox || *f* right; (naut) starboard
drizza *f* (naut) halyard
drizzare *tr* to straighten; to address; to erect; to cock (*the head*); to direct (*a blow*); **drizzare le gambe ai cani** to do the impossible; **drizzare le orecchie** to prick up one's ears || *intr* (naut) to hoist the halyard || *ref* to stand erect
drò·ga *f* (**-ghe**) drug; spice; seasoning
drogare §209 (**drògo**) *tr* to drug; to spice, season
drogherìa *f* grocery (store)
droghière *m* grocer
dromedà·rio *m* (**-ri**) dromedary
dru·do -da *adj* (archaic) faithful; (lit) strong || *m* (obs) vassal; (lit) lover
drùi·da *m* (**-di**) druid
drupa *f* (bot) drupe, stone fruit
duale *adj* & *m* dual
dualismo *m* dualism
duali·tà *f* duality
dùb·bio -bia (**-bi -bie**) *adj* doubtful || *m* doubt; misgiving; **mettere in dub-**

bio to question; to risk; **senza dubbio** no doubt
dubbió·so -sa [s] *adj* dubious; doubtful; (lit) dangerous
dubitare (dùbito) *intr* to doubt; to suspect; **dubitare di** to mistrust; to doubt; **non dubitare!** don't worry!
du·ca *m* **(-chi)** duke; (lit) leader
ducato *m* duchy; ducat
duce *m* leader; duce
duchéssa *f* duchess
duchessina *f* young duchess
duchino *m* young duke
due *adj & pron* two; **le due** two o'clock || *m* two; second (*in dates*) || *f*—**fra le due** between two alternatives
duecenté·sco -sca *adj* **(-schi -sche)** thirteenth-century
duecentèsi·mo -ma *adj, m & pron* two hundredth
duecènto *adj, m & pron* two hundred || **il Duecento** the thirteenth century
duellante *adj* dueling || *m* duelist
duellare (duèllo) *intr* to duel
duèllo *m* duel; contest; debate; **sfidare a duello** to challenge to a duel
duemila *adj, m & pron* two thousand || **Duemila** *m* twenty-first century
duepèz·zi *m* **(-zi)** two-piece bathing suit
duétto *m* (mus) duet
dulcamara *f* (bot) bittersweet
dulcina *f* artificial sweetening
duna *f* dune
dunque *m*—**venire al dunque** to come to the point || *adv* then || *conj* therefore, hence || *interj* well!
duodèno *m* (anat) duodenum
duòlo *m* (lit) grief
duòmo *m* cathedral; dome (*e.g., of a boiler*)
du·plex *m* **(-plex)** (telp) party line
duplicare §197 **(dùplico)** *tr* to duplicate
duplica·to -ta *adj & m* duplicate
duplicatóre *m* duplicator
dùplice *adj* twofold, double || *f* (racing) daily double
duplici·tà *f* **(-tà)** duplicity
duràbile *adj* durable, lasting
duràci·no -na *adj* clingstone || *f* clingstone peach
durallumìnio *m* duralumin
durare *tr* to endure, bear || *intr* to last; **durare a** + *inf* to keep on + *ger*; **durare in carica** to remain in office
durata *f* duration; lasting quality; **di lunga durata** long-lasting
durante *prep* during; throughout
duratu·ro -ra *adj* enduring, lasting
durévole *adj* lasting, durable
durézza *f* hardness; toughness; rigidity
du·ro -ra *adj* hard; hard-boiled (*egg*); durum (*wheat*); tough (*skin*); harsh; (phonet) voiceless || *m* hard part; hard floor; hard soil; **il duro sta che . . .** the trouble is that . . . ; **tener duro** to hold out
duróne *m* callousness, callosity
dùttile *adj* ductile; tractable

E

E, e [e] *m & f* fifth letter of the Italian alphabet
e *conj* and
ebani·sta *m* **(-sti)** cabinetmaker
ebanisterìa *f* cabinetmaking; cabinetmaker's shop
ebanite *f* ebonite, vulcanite
èbano *m* ebony
ebbène *interj* well!
ebbrézza *f* intoxication, drunkenness
èb·bro -bra *adj* intoxicated || *mf* drunk
ebdomadà·rio -ria *adj & m* **(-ri -rie)** weekly
èbete *adj* stupid, dull, dumb
ebollizióne *f* boil, boiling
ebrài·co -ca (-ci -che) *adj* Hebrew, Hebraic || *m* Hebrew (*language*)
ebrè·o -a *adj & mf* Hebrew || *m* Hebrew (*language*); Jew; **ebreo errante** Wandering Jew
è·bro -bra *adj & mf* var of **ebbro**
ebùrne·o -a *adj* (lit) ivory
ecatòmbe *f* hecatomb, slaughter
eccedènte *adj* exceeding || *m* excess
eccedènza *f* excess, surplus
eccèdere §123 *tr* to exceed || *intr* to go too far
eccellènte *adj* excellent
eccellènza *f* excellence || **Eccellenza** *f* Excellency
eccèllere §162 *intr* (ESSERE) to excel
eccèl·so -sa *adj* unexcelled; very high || —**l'Eccelso** *m* the Most High
eccentrici·tà *f* **(-tà)** eccentricity
eccèntri·co -ca (-ci -che) *adj* eccentric; suburban || *mf* vaudeville performer || *m* (mach) eccentric
eccepìbile *adj* objectionable
eccepire §176 *tr* (law) to take exception to || *intr* (law) to object
eccessi·vo -va *adj* excessive; overweening (*opinion*)
eccèsso *m* excess; **all'eccesso** excessively; **andare agli eccessi** to go to extremes; **dare in eccessi** to fly into a rage; **eccesso di peso** excess weight
eccètera *adv* and so forth, et cetera
eccètto *prep* except, but; **eccetto che** except that; unless
eccettuare (eccèttuo) *tr* to except
eccettua·to -ta *adj* excepted || **eccettuato** *prep* except
eccezionale *adj* exceptional
eccezióne *f* exception; objection; **ad eccezione di** with the exception of; **d'eccezione** extraordinary; **sollevare un'eccezione** (law) to take exception
ecchimò·si *f* **(-si)** bruise
eccì·dio *m* **(-di)** massacre
eccitàbile *adj* excitable

eccitaménto *m* instigation; excitement
eccitante *adj* stimulating || *m* stimulant
eccitare (**èccito**) *tr* to excite || *ref* to become excited or aroused; (sports) to warm up
eccitazióne *f* excitement; (elec) excitation
ecclesiàsti•co -ca (**-ci -che**) *adj* ecclesiastical || *m* clergyman
ècco *tr invar* here is (are), there is (are); **ecco che** here, e.g., **ecco che viene** here he comes; **eccoci** here we are; **ecco fatto** that's it; **eccola** here she is; here it is; **eccomi** here I am; **eccone** here are some || *intr invar* here I am; here it is; **quand'ecco** suddenly || *interj* look!
eccóme *interj* and how!, indeed!
echeggiare §290 (**echéggio**) *intr* (ESSERE & AVERE) to echo
eclètti•co -ca *adj* & *mf* (**-ci -che**) eclectic
eclissare *tr* to eclipse || *ref* to be eclipsed; (coll) to vanish, sneak away
eclis•si *f* (**-si**) eclipse
eclìtti•ca *f* (**-che**) ecliptic
èclo•ga *f* (**-ghe**) var of **egloga**
è•co *m* & *f* (**-chi** *mpl*) echo; **far eco a** to echo
ecogoniòmetro *m* sonar
ecologìa *f* ecology
economato *m* comptroller's or administrator's office
economìa *f* administration; management; economy; economics; **economia aziendale** business management; **economia di mercato** free enterprise; **economia domestica** home economics; **economia politica** political economy; economics; **economie** savings; **fare economia** to save
econòmi•co -ca *adj* (**-ci -che**) economic(al); cheap
economi•sta *mf* (**-sti -ste**) economist
economizzare [ddzz] *tr* & *intr* to economize, save
ecòno•mo -ma *adj* thrifty || *m* comptroller; administrator
ecosistè•ma [s] *m* (**-mi**) ecosystem
ecumèni•co -ca *adj* (**-ci -che**) ecumenical
eczè•ma [dz] *m* (**-mi**) eczema
édera *f* ivy
edìcola *f* shrine; newsstand
edificante *adj* edifying
edificare §197 (**edìfico**) *tr* to build; to edify || *intr* to build
edifica•tóre -trice *adj* building || *mf* builder
edificazióne *f* building; edification
edifi•cio *m* (**-ci**) building, edifice; pack (*e.g., of lies*); structure
edile *adj* building, construction || *m* builder, construction worker
edilì•zio -zia (**-zi -zie**) *adj* building, construction || *f* building trade
edìpi•co -ca *adj* (**-ci -che**) Oedipus (*e.g., complex*)
Edipo *m* Oedipus
èdi•to -ta *adj* published
edi•tóre -trice *adj* publishing || *mf* publisher; editor (*e.g., of a text*)
editorìa *f* publishing; publishers
editoriale *adj* editorial; publishing || *m* editorial
editoriali•sta *mf* (**-sti -ste**) editorial writer
editto *m* edict
edizióne *f* edition; performance; (fig) vintage
edonismo *m* hedonism
edoni•sta *mf* (**-sti -ste**) hedonist
edòt•to -ta *adj* (lit) informed, acquainted; **rendere qlcu edotto su qlco** (lit) to inform s.o. of s.th
edredóne *m* eider, eider duck
educanda *f* boarding-school girl; convent-school girl
educandato *m* (convent) boarding school for girls
educare §197 (**èduco**) *tr* to educate; to rear, bring up; to train; to accustom, inure; (lit) to grow
educati•vo -va *adj* educational
educa•to -ta *adj* educated; polite, well-bred
educa•tóre -trice *mf* educator
educazióne *f* education; breeding, manners; **educazione civica** civics
edule *adj* edible
efèbo *m* (coll) sissy
efèlide *f* freckle
effeminatézza *f* effeminacy
effemina•to -ta *adj* effeminate; frivolous
efferatézza *f* savagery
effervescènte *adj* effervescent
effervescènza *f* effervescence
effettivaménte *adv* really
effetti•vo -va *adj* real, true; effective; full (*e.g., member*); regular (*e.g., army officer*) || *m* effective; total amount; (mil) manpower
effètto *m* effect, result; (com) promissory note; (billiards) English; (sports) spin; **a questo effetto** for this purpose; **effetti** effects, belongings; **effetto di luce** play of light; **effetto ottico** optical illusion; **fare effetto** to make a sensation; **fare l'effetto di** to give the impression of; **in effetto** in fact; **mandare a effetto** to carry out; **porre in effetto** to put into effect
effettuàbile *adj* feasible
effettuare (**effèttuo**) *tr* to bring about; to contrive; to actuate; **effettuare (una corsa, un servizio)** to run, e.g., **l'autobus effettua una corsa ogni mezz'ora** the bus runs every half hour
efficace *adj* effective; forceful (*writer*)
efficà•cia *f* (**-cie**) effectiveness, efficacy; (law) validity
efficiènte *adj* efficient
efficiènza *f* efficiency; **in piena efficienza** in full working order; in top condition
effigiare §290 *tr* to portray, represent
effi•gie *f* (**-gie** or **-gi**) effigy; image
effìme•ro -ra *adj* ephemeral
efflusso *m* flow, outflow
efflù•vio *m* (**-vi**) effluvium; emanation (*e.g., of light*)
effrazióne *f* (law) burglary
effusióne *f* effusion; outflow; shedding (*of blood*); effusiveness
egemonìa *f* hegemony

egè·o -a *adj* Aegean
ègida *f* aegis
Egitto, l' *m* Egypt
egizia·no -na *adj & mf* Egyptian
eglantina *f* sweetbrier
eglefino *m* haddock
égli §5 *pron pers* he
èglo·ga *f* (**-ghe**) eclogue
egocèntri·co -ca *adj & mf* (**-ci -che**) egocentric
egoismo *m* egoism, selfishness
egoi·sta (**-sti -ste**) *adj* selfish || *mf* egoist
egoìsti·co -ca *adj* (**-ci -che**) egoistic(al)
egotismo *m* egotism
egoti·sta (**-sti -ste**) *adj* egotistic || *mf* egotist
egrè·gio -gia *adj* (**-gi -gie**) (lit) outstanding; **Egregio Signore** Mr. (*before a man's name in an address on a letter*); Dear Sir
eguaglianza *f* equality
eguale *adj* var of **uguale**
egualità·rio -ria *adj & m* (**-ri -rie**) equalitarian
éhi *interj* hey!
éi *pron* (lit) he; (archaic) they
eiaculazióne *f* ejaculation
eiettàbile *adj* ejection (*seat*)
eiezióne *f* ejection
él *pron* (archaic) he
elaborare (**elàboro**) *tr* to elaborate; to digest; to secrete
elabora·to -ta *adj* elaborate || *m* written exercise
elaboratóre *m* computer
elaborazióne *f* elaboration; data processing
elargire §176 *tr* to donate
elargizióne *f* donation
elastici·tà *f* (**-tà**) elasticity; agility; (com) oscillation; (com) range
elàsti·co -ca (**-ci -che**) *adj* elastic || *m* rubber band; bedspring
élce *m & f* holm oak
elefante *m* elephant; **elefante marino** sea elephant
elefantéssa *f* female elephant
elegante *adj* elegant, fashionable
elegantó·ne -na *mf* fashion plate || *m* dandy, dude
eleganza *f* elegance, stylishness
elèggere §193 *tr* to elect
eleggìbile *adj* eligible
elegìa *f* elegy
elegìa·co -ca *adj* elegiac
elementare *adj* elementary || **elementari** *fpl* elementary schools
eleménto *m* element; rudiment; member; cell (*of battery*); **elementi** personnel, e.g., **elementi femminili** female personnel
elemòsina *f* alms; (eccl) collection; **chiedere l'elemosina** to beg; **vivere d'elemosina** to live on charity
elemosinare (**elemòsino**) *intr* to beg
Èlena *f* Helen
elencare §197 (**elènco**) *tr* to list; to enumerate
elèn·co *m* (**-chi**) list; **elenco telefonico** telephone directory
eletti·vo -va *adj* elective
elèt·to -ta *adj* elect; distinguished (*audience*); precious (*metal*); chosen (*people*) || *mf* elect
elettorato *m* electorate, constituency
elet·tóre -trice *mf* voter; elector
elettràuto *m* automobile electrician; automotive electric shop
elettrici·sta *mf* (**-sti -ste**) electrician
elettrici·tà *f* (**-tà**) electricity
elèttri·co -ca (**-ci -che**) *adj* electrical || *m* electrical worker
elettrificare §197 (**elettrìfico**) *tr* to electrify
elettrizzare [ddzz] *tr* to electrify (*e.g., a person*) || *ref* to become electrified
elèttro *m* amber
elettrocalamita *f* electromagnet
elettrocardiògrafo *m* electrocardiograph
elettrocardiogram·ma *m* (**-mi**) electrocardiogram
elettrodinàmi·co -ca (**-ci -che**) *adj* electrodynamic || *f* electrodynamics
elèttrodo *m* electrode
elettrodomèsti·co -ca (**-ci -che**) *adj* electric household || *m* electric household appliance
elettroesecuzióne *f* electrocution
elettròge·no -na *adj* generating (*unit*)
elettròli·si *f* (**-si**) electrolysis
elettrolìti·co -ca *adj* (**-ci -che**) electrolytic
elettròlito *m* electrolyte
elettromagnèti·co -ca *adj* (**-ci -che**) electromagnetic
elettromo·tóre -trice *adj* electromotive || *m* electric motor || *f* electric train; electric railcar
elettróne *m* electron
elettróni·co -ca (**-ci -che**) *adj* electronic || *f* electronics
elettropómpa *f* electric pump
elettrosquasso *m* electroshock
elettrostàti·co -ca (**-ci -che**) *adj* electrostatic || *f* electrostatics
elettrotècni·co -ca (**-ci -che**) *adj* electrotechnical || *m* electrician; electrical engineer || *f* electrical engineering
elettrotrèno *m* electric train
elevaménto *m* elevation
elevare (**èlevo & elèvo**) *tr* to lift, elevate; (math) to raise || *ref* to rise
elevatézza *f* loftiness, dignity
eleva·to -ta *adj* high, lofty
eleva·tóre -trice *adj* elevating || *m* elevator
elevazióne *f* elevation; (sports) jump; (math) raising
elezióne *f* election; choice
èlfo *m* elf
èli·ca *f* (**-che**) propeller; (geom) helix
elicoidale *adj* helicoidal
elicòttero *m* helicopter
elidere §161 *tr* to annul; to elide || *ref* to neutralize one another
eliminare (**elimino**) *tr* to eliminate
eliminatò·rio -ria (**-ri -rie**) *adj* eliminating || *f* (sports) heat
eliminazióne *f* elimination; extermination
èlio- *comb form adj* helio-, e.g., **eliocentrico** heliocentric || *comb form*

m & f helio-, e.g., **elioterapia** heliotherapy
èlio *m* helium
eliocèntri·co -ca *adj* (**-ci -che**) heliocentric
eliògrafo *m* heliograph
elioteràpi·co -ca *adj* (**-ci -che**) sunshine (*treatment*); sunbathing (*establishment*)
eliotrò·pio *m* (**-pi**) heliotrope; bloodstone
elipòrto *m* heliport
elisabettia·no -na *adj* Elizabethan
elì·sio -sia *adj* (**-si -sie**) Elysian
elisióne *f* elision
eli·sir *m* (**-sir**) elixir
èlitra *f* elytron, shard
élla *pron* (lit) she ‖ **Ella** *pron* (lit) you
ellèboro *m* hellebore
ellèni·co -ca *adj* (**-ci -che**) Hellenic
ellìsse *f* ellipse
ellis·si *f* (**-si**) (gram) ellipsis
ellìtti·co -ca *adj* (**-ci -che**) elliptical
-èllo -èlla *suf adj* little, e.g., **poverello** poor little
elmétto *m* helmet; tin hat
élmo *m* helmet
elogiare §290 (**elògio**) *tr* to praise
elò·gio *m* (**-gi**) praise, encomium; write-up; **elogio funebre** eulogy
eloquènte *adj* eloquent
eloquènza *f* eloquence
elò·quio *m* (**-qui**) (lit) speech, diction
élsa *f* hilt
elucidare (**elùcido**) *tr* to elucidate
elùdere §105 *tr* to elude, evade
elusi·vo -va *adj* elusive
elvèti·co -ca *adj & mf* (**-ci -che**) Helvetian
elzevi·ro -ra [dz] *adj* Elzevir ‖ *m* Elzevir book; (journ) literary article
emacia·to -ta *adj* emaciated, lean
emanare *tr* to send forth; to issue ‖ *intr* (ESSERE) to emanate; to come forth
emanazióne *f* emanation; issuance
emancipare (**emàncipo**) *tr* to emancipate ‖ *ref* to become emancipated
emancipazióne *f* emancipation
emarginare (**emàrgino**) *tr* to note in the margin; (fig) to put aside, neglect
emarginato *m* marginal note
emàti·co -ca *adj* (**-ci -che**) blood, hematic
ematite *f* hematite
embar·go *m* (**-ghi**) embargo
emblè·ma *m* (**-mi**) emblem
emblemàti·co -ca *adj* (**-ci -che**) emblematic
embolìa *f* embolism
èmbrice *m* flat roof tile; shingle
embriologìa *f* embryology
embrionale *adj* embryonic
embrióne *m* embryo
emendaménto *m* emendation (*of a text*); amendment (*to a law*)
emendare (**emèndo**) *tr* to correct; to emend; to amend (*a law*) ‖ *ref* to reform
emergènza *f* emergence; emergency
emèrgere §162 *intr* (ESSERE) to emerge; to surface (*said of a submarine*); to loom; to stand out
emèri·to -ta *adj* emeritus (*professor*); famous
emerotè·ca *f* (**-che**) periodical library
emersióne *f* emersion; surfacing
emèr·so -sa *adj* emergent
emèti·co -ca *adj & m* (**-ci -che**) emetic
eméttere §198 *tr* to emit, send forth; to utter (*a statement*); (com) to issue
emiciclo *m* hemicycle; floor (*of legislative body*)
emicrània *f* migraine, headache
emigrante *adj & mf* emigrant
emigrare *intr* (ESSERE & AVERE) to emigrate
emigra·to -ta *adj & mf* emigrant
emigrazióne *f* emigration; migration (*e.g., of birds*)
eminènte *adj* eminent
eminènza *f* eminence; (eccl) Eminence
emisfèro *m* hemisphere
emissà·rio *m* (**-ri**) emissary; outlet (*river or lake*); drain
emissióne *f* emission; issuance; (rad) broadcast
emistì·chio *m* (**-chi**) hemistich
emittènte *adj* emitting; issuing; (rad) broadcasting ‖ *f* (rad) transmitting set; broadcasting station
emofilìa *f* hemophilia
emoglobina *f* hemoglobin
emolliènte *adj & m* emollient
emoluménto *m* fee, emolument
emorragìa *f* hemorrhage
emorròidi *fpl* hemorrhoids, piles
emostàti·co -ca (**-ci -che**) *adj* hemostatic ‖ *m* hemostat
emotè·ca *f* (**-che**) blood bank
emotivi·tà *f* (**-tà**) emotionalism
emoti·vo -va *adj* emotional ‖ *mf* emotional person
emottisi *f* (pathol) hemoptysis
emozionante *adj* emotional, moving
emozionare (**emozióno**) *tr* to move, stir; to thrill
emozióne *f* emotion
empiastro *m* var of **impiastro**
émpiere §163 *tr & ref* var of **empire**
empie·tà *f* (**-tà**) impiety; cruelty
ém·pio -pia *adj* (**-pi -pie**) impious; pitiless, wicked
empire §163 *tr* to fill; (lit) to fulfill; **empire qlcu di insulti** to heap insults on s.o. ‖ *ref* to get full
empìre·o -a *adj* heavenly, sublime ‖ *m* empyrean
empìri·co -ca (**-ci -che**) *adj* empirical ‖ *mf* empiricist
empirismo *m* empiricism
empiri·sta *mf* (**-sti -ste**) empiricist
émpito *m* (lit) rush; fury
empò·rio *m* (**-ri**) emporium, mart
emulare (**èmulo**) *tr* to emulate
emulazióne *f* emulation, rivalry; (law) evil intent
èmu·lo -la *adj* emulous ‖ *mf* emulator
emulsionare (**emulsióno**) *tr* to emulsify
emulsióne *f* emulsion
encefalite *f* encephalitis
encìcli·ca *f* (**-che**) encyclical
enciclopedìa *f* encyclopedia

enciclopèdi•co -ca *adj* **(-ci -che)** encyclopedic
enclave *f* enclave
enclìti•co -ca *adj & f* **(-ci -che)** enclitic
encomiàbile *adj* praiseworthy
encomiare §287 **(encòmio)** *tr* to praise
encò•mio *m* **(-mi)** encomium, praise
endecasìlla•bo -ba *adj* hendecasyllabic || *m* hendecasyllable
endemìa *f* endemic
endèmi•co -ca *adj* **(-ci -che)** endemic
èndice *m* nest egg; (obs) souvenir
endocàr•dio *m* **(-di)** (anat) endocardium
endocarpo *m* (bot) endocarp
endòcri•no -na *adj* endocrine
endourba•no -na *adj* inner-city
endovenó•so -sa [s] *adj* intravenous
energèti•co -ca (-ci -che) *adj* energy (*e.g., crisis*); (med) tonic || *m* (med) tonic
energìa *f* energy, power
enèrgi•co -ca *adj* **(-ci -che)** energetic
energùme•no -na *mf* wild or mad person
ènfa•si *f* **(-si)** emphasis; forcefulness
enfàti•co -ca *adj* **(-ci -che)** emphatic
enfiare §287 **(énfio)** *tr & ref* to swell
enfisè•ma *m* **(-mi)** emphysema
enfitèu•si *f* **(-si)** lease (*of land*)
enig•ma *m* **(-mi)** enigma, riddle, puzzle
enigmàti•co -ca *adj* **(-ci -che)** enigmatic, puzzling
-ènne *suf adj* -year-old, e.g., **ragazzo diciassettenne** seventeen-year-old boy || *suf mf* -year-old person, e.g., **diciassettenne** seventeen-year-old person
ennèsi•mo -ma *adj* nth
-èn•nio *suf m* **(-ni)** period of . . . years, e.g., **ventennio** period of twenty years
enòlo•go -ga *mf* **(-gi -ghe)** oenologist
enórme *adj* enormous
enormeménte *adv* enormously
enormi•tà *f* **(-tà)** enormity; outrage; absurdity
Enrico *m* Henry
ènte *m* being; entity; corporation; agency, body
enterocli•sma *m* **(-smi)** enema
enti•tà *f* **(-tà)** entity; value, importance
entomologìa *f* entomology
entram•bi -be *adj*—**entrambi i** both || *pron* both
entrante *adj* next (*e.g., week*)
entrare (éntro) *intr* (ESSERE) to enter; to go (*said of numbers*); to get (*into one's head*); **entrarci** to make it, e.g., **con questi soldi non c'entro** I can't make it with this money; **entrarci come i cavoli a merenda** to be completely out of line; **entrare a** to begin to; **entrare in** to enter (*e.g., a room*); to fit in; to go in (*said of a number*); to get into (*one's head*); **entrare in amore** to be in heat (*said of animals*); **entrare in ballo** to come into play; **entrare in carica** to take up one's duties; **entrare in collera** to get angry; **entrare in collisione** to collide; **entrare in contatto** to establish contact; **entrare in gioco** to come into play; **entrare in guerra** to go to war; **entrare in società** to make one's debut; **entrare nella parte di** (theat) to play the role of; **entrare in vigore** to become effective; **Lei non c'entra** this is none of your business; **questo non c'entra** this is beside the point
entrata *f* entry; entrance; **entrata di favore** (theat) complimentary ticket; **entrate** income
entratura *f* entry; entrance; assumption (*of a position*); familiarity
éntro *adv* inside || *prep* within; **entro di** within, inside of
entrobórdo *m* inboard motorboat
entrotèrra *f* inland, hinterland
entusiasmare *tr* to carry away, enthuse || *ref* to be carried away, to become enthused
entusiasmo *m* enthusiasm
entusia•sta (-sti -ste) *adj* enthusiastic || *mf* enthusiast, devotee
entusiàsti•co -ca *adj* **(-ci -che)** enthusiastic
enucleare (enùcleo) *tr* to elucidate; (surg) to remove
enumerare (enùmero) *tr* to enumerate
enumerazióne *f* enumeration
enunciare §128 *tr* to enunciate, state
enunciati•vo -va *adj* (gram) declarative
enunciazióne *f* enunciation, statement
enzi•ma [dz] *m* **(-mi)** enzyme
èpa *f* (lit) belly, paunch
epàti•co -ca *adj* **(-ci -che)** hepatic, liver
epatite *f* (pathol) hepatitis
epènte•si *f* **(-si)** epenthesis
eperlano *m* (ichth) smelt
èpi•co -ca *adj & f* **(-ci -che)** epic
epicurè•o -a *adj & m* epicurean
epidemìa *f* epidemic
epidèmi•co -ca *adj* **(-ci -che)** epidemic(al)
epidèrmi•co -ca *adj* **(-ci -che)** epidermal; (fig) superficial, skin-deep
epidèrmide *f* epidermis
Epifanìa *f* Epiphany
epiglòttide *f* (anat) epiglottis
epìgono *m* follower; descendant
epìgrafe *f* epigraph
epigram•ma *m* **(-mi)** epigram
epigrammàti•co -ca *adj* **(-ci -che)** epigrammatic
epilessìa *f* (pathol) epilepsy
epilètti•co -ca *adj & m* **(-ci -che)** epileptic
epìlo•go *m* **(-ghi)** epilogue; conclusion
episcopale *adj* episcopal
episcopalia•no -na *adj & mf* Episcopalian
episcopato *m* episcopate, bishopric
episòdi•co -ca *adj* **(-ci -che)** episodic
episò•dio *m* **(-di)** episode
epìstola *f* epistle
epistolà•rio *m* **(-ri)** letters, correspondence
epitàf•fio *m* **(-fi)** epitaph
epitè•lio *m* **(-li)** epithelium
epìteto *m* epithet; insult
epitomare (epìtomo) *tr* to epitomize
epìtome *f* epitome
èpo•ca *f* **(-che)** epoch; period; moment; **fare epoca** to be epoch-making
epopèa *f* epic
eppure *conj* yet, and yet
epsomite *f* Epsom salt

epurare *tr* to cleanse; to purge
epurazióne *f* purification; purge
equànime *adj* calm, composed; impartial
equanimità *f* equanimity; impartiality
equatóre *m* equator
equatoriale *adj & m* equatorial
equazióne *f* equation
equèstre *adj* equestrian
equilàte•ro -ra *adj* equilateral
equilibrare *tr* to balance; (aer) to trim || *ref* to balance one another
equilibra•to -ta *adj* level-headed
equilibra•tóre -trice *adj* stabilizing || *m* (aer) horizontal stabilizer
equilì•brio *m* **(-bri)** equilibrium, balance; (fig) proportion; **equilibrio politico** balance of power
equilibri•sta *mf* **(-sti -ste)** acrobat, equilibrist
equi•no -na *adj & m* equine
equinoziale *adj* equinoctial
equinò•zio *m* **(-zi)** equinox
equipaggiaménto *m* equipment, outfit
equipaggiare §290 *tr* to equip, outfit; (naut) to fit out; (naut) to man
equipàg•gio *m* **(-gi)** equipage; (naut) crew, complement; (sports) team; (rowing) crew
equiparare *tr* to equalize (*e.g., salaries*)
équipe *f* team
equipollènte *adj* equivalent
equi•tà *f* **(-tà)** equity, fair-mindedness
equitazióne *f* horsemanship
equivalènte *adj & m* equivalent
equivalére §278 *intr* (ESSERE & AVERE) —**equivalere a** to be equivalent to || *ref* to be equal
equivocare §197 **(equivoco)** *intr*—**equivocare su** to mistake, misunderstand
equìvo•co -ca (-ci -che) *adj* equivocal; ambiguous || *m* misunderstanding
è•quo -qua *adj* equitable, fair
èra *f* era, age; **era spaziale** space age
erà•rio *m* **(-ri)** treasury
èrba *f* grass; **erba limoncina** lemon verbena; **erba medica** alfalfa; **erbe** vegetables; **erbe aromatiche** herbs; **far l'erba** to cut the grass; **in erba** (fig) budding; **metter a erba** to put to pasture
erbàc•cia *f* **(-ce)** weed
erbaggi *mpl* vegetables
erbaiò•lo -la *mf* fresh vegetable retailer
erbici•da *m* **(-di)** weed-killer
erbivéndo•lo -la *mf* fresh fruit and vegetable retailer
erbivo•ro -ra *adj* herbivorous
erbori•sta *mf* **(-sti -ste)** herbalist
erbó•so -sa [s] *adj* grassy
Èrcole *m* Hercules
ercùle•o -a *adj* Herculean
erède *m* heir || *f* heiress
eredi•tà *f* **(-tà)** inheritance; heredity
ereditare (erèdito) *tr* to inherit
eredità•rio -ria *adj* **(-ri -rie)** hereditary; crown (*prince*)
ereditièra *f* heiress
eremi•ta *m* **(-ti)** hermit
eremitàg•gio *m* **(-gi)** hermitage
èremo *m* hermitage
eresìa *f* heresy
eresiar•ca *m* **(-chi)** heretic
erèti•co -ca (-ci -che) *adj* heretical || *mf* heretic
erèt•to -ta *adj* erect, straight
erezióne *f* erection
ergastola•no -na *mf* lifer
ergàstolo *m* life imprisonment; prison for persons sentenced to life imprisonment
èrgere §164 *tr* (lit) to erect; (lit) to lift || *ref* to rise (*said, e.g., of a mountain*)
èrgo *m invar*—**venire all'ergo** to come to a conclusion || *adv* thus, hence
èri•ca *f* **(-che)** heather
erìgere §152 *tr* to erect, build || *ref* to rise; **erigersi a** to set oneself up as
eritrè•o -a *adj & mf* Eritrean
ermafrodi•to -ta *adj & m* hermafrodite
ermellino *m* ermine
ermèti•co -ca *adj* **(-ci -che)** airtight; watertight; hermetic
èrnia *f* hernia; **ernia del disco** (pathol) herniated disk
eródere §239 *tr* to erode
eròe *m* hero
erogare §209 **(èrogo)** *tr* to distribute; to bestow
erogazióne *f* distribution; bestowal
eròi•co -ca *adj* **(-ci -che)** heroic
eroicòmi•co -ca *adj* **(-ci -che)** mock-heroic
eroìna *f* heroine; (pharm) heroin
eroismo *m* heroism
erómpere §240 *intr* to erupt, burst out
erosióne *f* erosion
eròti•co -ca *adj* **(-ci -che)** erotic
erotismo *m* eroticism
èrpete *m* (pathol) herpes, shingles
erpicare §197 **(érpico)** *tr* to harrow
érpice *m* harrow
errabón•do -da *adj* (lit) wandering
errante *adj* errant; wandering
errare (èrro) *intr* to wander; to err; (lit) to stray
erra•to -ta *adj* mistaken, wrong
erròne•o -a *adj* erroneous
erróre *m* error, mistake; fault; (lit) wandering; **errore di lingua** slip of the tongue; **errore di scrittura** slip of the pen; **errore di stampa** misprint; **errore giudiziario** miscarriage of justice; **salvo errore od omissione** barring error or omission
ér•to -ta *adj* arduous, steep; erect || *f* arduous ascent; **all'erta** on the alert
erudire §176 *tr* to educate, instruct
erudi•to -ta *adj* erudite, learned || *m* scholar, savant
erudizióne *f* erudition, learning
eruttare *tr* to belch forth (*e.g., lava*); to utter (*obscenities*) || *intr* to belch
erutti•vo -va *adj* eruptive
eruzióne *f* eruption
esacerbare (esacèrbo) *tr* to embitter; to exacerbate || *ref* to become embittered
esagerare (esàgero) *tr & intr* to exaggerate
esagera•to -ta *adj* exaggerated, excessive || *mf* exaggerator
esagerazióne *f* exaggeration

esagitare (esàgito) *tr* to perturb
esàgono *m* hexagon
esalare *tr* to exhale; **esalare l'ultimo respiro** to breathe one's last || *intr* to spread (*said of odors*)
esalazióne *f* exhalation; fume, vapor
esaltare *tr* to exalt; to excite || *ref* to glorify oneself; to become excited
esalta•to -ta *adj* frenzied, excited || *mf* hothead
esame *m* examination; checkup, test; **dare gli esami** to take an examination; **esame attitudinale** aptitude test; **esame del sangue** blood test; **esame di riparazione** make-up test; **fare gli esami** to prepare a test (*for a student*); **prendere in esame** to take in consideration
esàmetro *m* hexameter
esaminan•do -da *mf* candidate; examinee
esaminare (esàmino) *tr* to examine; to test
esamina•tóre -trice *mf* examiner
esàngue *adj* bloodless; (fig) pale
esànime *adj* lifeless
esasperante *adj* exasperating
esasperare (esàspero) *tr* to exasperate || *ref* to become exasperated
esasperazióne *f* exasperation
esattézza *f* exactness; punctuality
esat•to -ta *adj* exact; punctual
esattóre *m* tax collector; bill collector
esattorìa *f* tax collector's office; bill collector's office
esaudire §176 *tr* to grant
esauriènte *adj* exhaustive; convincing
esauriménto *m* depletion (*e.g., of merchandise*); (pathol) exhaustion; (naut) drainage
esaurire §176 *tr* to exhaust; to play out (*e.g., a hooked fish*); to use up || *ref* to be exhausted; to be depleted; to be sold out
esauri•to -ta *adj* exhausted; depleted; sold out; out of print
esau•sto -sta *adj* exhausted; empty
esautorare (esàutoro) *tr* to deprive of authority; to discredit (*a theory*)
esazióne *f* exaction; collection
é•sca *f* (**-sche**) bait; punk (*for lighting fireworks*); tinder (*for lighting powder*): **dare esca a** to foment
escandescènza *f*—**dare in escandescenze** to fly off the handle
escava•tóre -trice *mf* excavator, digger || *m* excavator; **escavatore a vapore** steam shovel || *f* (mach) excavator
escavazióne *f* excavation
eschimése [s] *adj & mf* Eskimo
esclamare *tr & intr* to exclaim
esclamati•vo -va *adj* exclamatory; exclamation (*mark*)
esclùdere §105 *tr* to exclude; to keep or shut out
esclusióne *f* exclusion; **a esclusione di** with the exception of
esclusiva *f* sole right, monopoly; (journ) scoop
esclusivi•sta (-sti -ste) *adj* clannish; bigoted || *mf* bigot; (com) sole agent
esclusi•vo -va *adj* exclusive; intolerant, bigoted || *f* see **esclusiva**
esclu•so -sa *adj* excluded, excepted
escogitare (escògito) *tr* to think up, invent; to think out
escoriare §287 **(escòrio)** *tr & ref* to skin
escoriazióne *f* abrasion
escreménto *m* excrement
escrescènza *f* excrescence
escrè•to -ta *adj* excreted || *m* excreta
escursióne *f* excursion; (mach) sweep; (mil) transfer; **escursione termica** (meteor) temperature range
escursioni•sta *mf* **(-sti -ste)** excursionist, sightseer
escussióne *f* (law) examination, cross-examination
esecrare (esècro) *tr* to execrate
esecrazióne *f* execration
esecuti•vo -va *adj & m* executive
esecu•tóre -trice *mf* (mus) performer || *m* executor; **esecutore di giustizia** executioner || *f* executrix
esecuzióne *f* accomplishment, completion; performance; execution; **esecuzione capitale** capital punishment
esegè•si *f* **(-si)** exegesis
eseguire (eséguo) & §176 *tr* to execute, carry out; to perform
esèm•pio *m* **(-pi)** example; **a mo' d'esempio** as an illustration; **dare il buon esempio** to set a good example; **per esempio** for instance
esemplare *adj* exemplary || *m* copy; specimen || *v* **(esèmplo)** *tr* (lit) to copy
esemplificare §197 **(esemplìfico)** *tr* to exemplify
esentare (esènto) *tr* to exempt
esènte *adj* exempt, free
esenzióne *f* exemption
esèquie *fpl* obsequies, funeral rites
esercènte *adj* practicing || *mf* dealer, merchant
esercire §176 *tr* to practice; to run (*a store*)
esercitare (esèrcito) *tr* to exercise; to tax (*e.g., s.o.'s patience*); to practice, ply (*a trade*); to wield (*e.g., power*) || *ref* to practice
esercitazióne *f* exercise, training; **esercitazioni militari** drilling
esèrcito *m* army; (fig) flock; **Esercito della Salvezza** Salvation Army
eserci•zio *m* **(-zi)** exercise; practice; training; homework; occupation; drill; **d'esercizio** (com) administrative (*expenses*); **esercizio finanziario** fiscal year; **esercizio provvisorio** (law) emergency appropriation; **esercizio pubblico** establishment open to the public; **esercizio spirituale** (eccl) retreat
esibire §176 *tr* to exhibit || *ref* to show oneself, appear; **esibirsi di** to offer to
esibizióne *f* exhibition
esigènte *adj* demanding, exigent
esigènza *f* demand, requirement, exigency
esìgere §165 *tr* to demand; to require; to exact; to collect
esigìbile *adj* due; collectable
esigui•tà *f* **(-tà)** meagerness, scantiness
esì•guo -gua *adj* meager, scanty

esilarante *adj* exhilarating; laughing (*gas*)
esilarare (**esìlaro**) *tr* to amuse || *ref* to be amused
èsile *adj* slender, thin; weak
esiliare §287 *tr* to exile || *ref* to go into exile; to withdraw
esilia•to -ta *adj* exiled || *m* exile (*person*)
esì•lio *m* (**-lî**) exile, banishment
esìmere §166 *tr* to exempt || *ref*—**esimersi da** to avoid (*an obligation*)
esì•mio -mia *adj* (**-mi -mie**) distinguished, eminent
-èsi•mo -ma *suf adj & pron* -eth, e.g., **ventesimo** twentieth; -th, e.g., **diciannovesimo** nineteenth
esistènte *adj* existent; extant
esistènza *f* existence
esistenzialismo *m* existentialism
esìstere §114 *intr* (ESSERE) to exist
esitante *adj* hesitant
esitare (**èsito**) *tr* to retail || *intr* to hesitate; (med) to resolve itself
esitazióne *f* hesitation; haw (*in speech*)
èsito *m* result, outcome; sale; outlet; (philol) late form; **dare esito a** (com) to reply
esiziale *adj* ruinous, fatal
èsodo *m* exodus, flight
esòfa•go *m* (**-gi**) esophagus
esonerare (**esònero**) *tr* to exempt, release
esònero *m* exemption, release
Esòpo *m* Aesop
esorbitante *adj* exorbitant
esorbitare (**esòrbito**) *intr*—**esorbitare da** to go beyond
esorcismo *m* exorcism
esorcizzare [ddzz] *tr* to exorcise
esordiènte *adj* beginning, budding || *mf* beginner || *f* debutante
esòr•dio *m* (**-di**) beginning
esordire §176 *intr* to make a start; (theat) to debut; (theat) to open
esortare (**esòrto**) *tr* to exhort
esortazióne *f* exhortation
esò•so -sa *adj* greedy, avaricious; hateful; exorbitant (*price*)
esòti•co -ca *adj* (**-ci -che**) exotic
esotismo *m* exoticism; borrowing (*from a foreign language*)
espàndere §167 *tr* to expand || *ref* to spread out; to confide
espansióne *f* expansion; effusiveness
espansionismo *m* expansionism
espansivi•tà *f* (**-tà**) effusiveness
espansi•vo -va *adj* expansive; effusive
espan•so -sa *adj* flared; expanded, dilated
espatriare §287 *intr* to emigrate
espà•trio *m* (**-tri**) emigration
espediènte *m* expedient, makeshift; ruse; **vivere di espedienti** to live by one's wits
espedire §176 *tr* to expedite || *ref*—**espedirsi di** to get rid of
espèllere §168 *tr* to expel, eject
esperiènza *f* experience; experiment
esperiménto *m* experiment; test
espèr•to -ta *adj & m* expert
espettorare (**espèttoro**) *tr & intr* to expectorate

espiare §119 *tr* to expiate; to placate (*the gods*); **espiare una pena** to serve a sentence
espiató•rio -ria *adj* (**-ri -rie**) expiatory
espiazióne *f* expiation
espirare *tr & intr* to breath out, to exhale
espirazióne *f* exhaling
espletare (**esplèto**) *tr* to dispatch, complete
esplicare §197 (**èsplico**) *tr* to carry out; (lit) to explain
esplicati•vo -va *adj* explanatory
esplìci•to -ta *adj* explicit
esplòdere §169 *tr* to shoot; to fire (*a shot*) || *intr* (ESSERE & AVERE) to explode; to burst forth
esploditóre *m* blasting machine
esplorare (**esplòro**) *tr* to explore; to search, probe; (telv) to scan
esplora•tóre -trice *mf* explorer || *m* (nav) gunboat; **giovane esploratore** boy scout
esplorazióne *f* exploration; (telv) scanning
esplosióne *f* explosion, blast; (fig) outburst
esplosi•vo -va *adj & m* explosive
esponènte *adj* (typ) superior || *m* spokesman; dictionary entry; catchword (*of dictionary*); (math) exponent; (naut) net weight
espórre §218 *tr* to expose, show; to expound; to abandon (*a baby*); to lay out (*a corpse*); to lay open (*to danger*) || *intr* to show, exhibit || *ref* to expose oneself
esportare (**espòrto**) *tr* to export
esporta•tóre -trice *mf* exporter
esportazióne *f* export, exportation
esposìmetro *m* exposure meter
esposi•tóre -trice *mf* commentator; exhibitor
esposizióne *f* exposition; abandonment (*of a baby*); exhibit, fair; line (*of credit*); exposure (*of a house*); (phot) exposure
espó•sto -sta *adj* exposed; aforementioned || *m* petition, brief; foundling
espressióne *f* expression; feeling
espressi•vo -va *adj* expressive
esprès•so -sa *adj* manifest; express; prepared on the spot || *m* espresso; messenger; special-delivery letter; special-delivery stamp
esprìmere §131 *tr* to express; to convey (*an opinion*); (lit) to squeeze || *ref* to express oneself
espropriare §287 (**espròprio**) *tr* to expropriate || *ref* to deprive onself; **espropriarsi di** to divest oneself of
espròprio *m* (**-pri**) expropriation
espugnare *tr* to take by storm
espulsióne *f* expulsion; (mach) ejection
espulsóre *m* ejector
espurgare §209 *tr* to expurgate
éssa §5 *pron pers* she; it
ésse §5 *pron pers* they
essènza *f* essence
essenziale *adj* essential || *m* main point
èssere *m* being; existence; condition; (coll) character; **in essere** in good shape || §170 *intr* (ESSERE) to be;

c'è there is; **ci sono** there are; **ci sono!** I get it!; **come sarebbe a dire?** what do you mean?; **come se nulla fosse** as if nothing had happened; **esserci** to have arrived, to be there; **essere di** to belong to; **essere per** to be about to; **può essere** maybe; **sarà** maybe; **sia . . . sia** both . . . and; whether . . . or || *aux* (ESSERE) (to form passive) to be, e.g., **fu investito da un tassametro** he was run over by a taxi; (to form the compound tenses of certain intransitive verbs and all reflexive verbs) to have, e.g., **sono arrivati** they have arrived; **mi sono appena alzato** I have just got up || *impers* (ESSERE) to be, e.g., **è giusto** it is fair

éssi §5 *pron pers* they
essiccare §197 *tr* to dry || *ref* to dry up
essicca•tóio *m* (**-tói**) drier
essiccazióne *f* drying
èsso §5 *pron pers* he; it; **chi per esso** his representative
essudare *intr* to exude
èst *m* east
èsta•si *f* (**-si**) ecstasy; **andare in estasi** to become enraptured
estasiare §287 *tr* to enrapture, delight || *ref* to become enraptured
estate *f* summer
estàti•co -ca *adj* (**-ci -che**) ecstatic, enraptured
estemporàne•o -a *adj* extemporaneous
estèndere §270 *tr* to extend; to broaden (*e.g., one's knowledge*); to draw up (*a document*) || *ref* to extend
estensìbile *adj* applicable; **inviare saluti estensibili a** to send greetings to be extended to (*e.g., another person*)
estensióne *f* extension; extent; expanse (*e.g., of water*); (mus) compass, range
estensi•vo -va *adj* extensive
estèn•so -sa *adj*—**per estenso** fully
estensóre *adj* extensible || *m* compiler (*e.g., of a dictionary*); (sports) exerciser, chest expander
estenuante *adj* exhausting
estenuare (**estènuo**) *tr* to exhaust || *ref* to become exhausted
esterióre *adj* exterior || *m* outside appearance
esteriori•tà *f* (**-tà**) appearance
esternare (**estèrno**) *tr* to reveal, manifest || *ref* to confide
estèr•no -na *adj* external; outside; day (*student*) || *m* exterior, outside; (baseball) outfielder; **all'esterno** outside; **in esterno** (mov) on location
èste•ro -ra *adj* foreign || *m* foreign countries; **all'estero** abroad
esterrefat•to -ta *adj* terrified
esté•so -sa [s] *adj* extended, wide; **per esteso** in full
estè•ta *mf* (**-ti -te**) aesthete
estèti•co -ca (**-ci -che**) *adj* aesthetic || *f* aesthetics
esteti•sta *mf* (**-sti -ste**) beautician
estima•tóre -trice *mf* appraiser; admirer
èstimo *m* appraisal; assessment
estìnguere §156 *tr* to extinguish; to quench (*thirst*); to pay off (*a debt*) || *ref* to die out
estinguìbile *adj* extinguishable; payable
estin•to -ta *adj* extinguished; extinct || *m* deceased, dead person
estintóre *m* fire extinguisher
estirpare *tr* to uproot; to eradicate; to pull (*a tooth*)
estirpa•tóre -trice *mf* eradicator || *m* (agr) weeder
estivare *tr & intr* to summer
esti•vo -va *adj* summer; summery
estòllere §171 *tr* to extol
èstone *adj & mf* Estonian
estòrcere §272 *tr* to extort; **estorcere qlco a qlcu** to extort s.th from s.o.
estorsióne *f* extortion
estradare *tr* (law) to extradite
estradizióne *f* extradition
estràne•o -a *adj* extraneous, foreign; aloof || *mf* outsider
estrapolare (**estràpolo**) *tr* to extrapolate
estrarre §273 *tr* to extract, draw; to pull (*a tooth*)
estrat•to -ta *adj* extracted || *m* extract; abstract; certified copy; (typ) offprint; **estratto conto** bank statement; **estratto dell'atto di nascita** copy of one's birth certificate
estrazióne *f* extraction; drawing (*of lottery*)
estrèma *f* (sports) wing, end
estremi•sta *adj & mf* (**-sti -ste**) extremist
estremi•tà *f* (**-tà**) end; tip, top; extremity; **le estremità** the extremities
estrè•mo -ma *adj* extreme; **esalare l'estremo respiro** to breath one's last || *m* extremity; end, extreme; **essere agli estremi** to be near the end; **estremi** essentials || *f* see **estrema**
estrìnse•co -ca *adj* (**-ci -che**) extrinsic
èstro *m* horsefly; whim, fancy; inspiration; **estro venereo** heat (*of female animal*)
estrométtere §198 *tr* to oust, expel
estró•so -sa [s] *adj* fanciful, whimsical; inspired
estrovèr•so -sa or **estroverti•to -ta** *adj & mf* extrovert
estrùdere §190 *tr* to extrude
estuà•rio *m* (**-ri**) estuary
esuberante *adj* exuberant; buoyant
esuberanza *f* exuberance; buoyancy; **a esuberanza** abundantly
esulare (**èsulo**) *intr* (ESSERE & AVERE) to go into exile; **esulare da** to be alien to
esulcerare (**esùlcero**) *tr* to ulcerate on the surface; (fig) to exacerbate
esulcerazióne *f* superficial ulceration; (fig) exasperation, exacerbation
èsule *mf* exile (*person*)
esultante *adj* exultant, jubilant
esultare *intr* to exult
esumare *tr* to exhume; to revive (*e.g., a custom*)
esumazióne *f* exhumation; revival
e•tà *f* (**-tà**) age; **che età ha?** how old is he (or she)?; **ha la sua età** he (or she) is no longer a youngster; **l'età di mezzo** Middle Ages; **maggiore età** majority; **mezza età** middle age; **minore età** minority
etamine *f* cheesecloth
ètere *m* ether

etère·o -a *adj* ethereal
eternare (etèrno) *tr* to immortalize || *ref* to become immortal
eterni·tà *f* **(-tà)** eternity
etèr·no -na *adj* eternal, everlasting || *m* eternity; **in eterno** forever
eterodòs·so -sa *adj* heterodox
eterogène·o -a *adj* heterogeneous
èti·ca *f* **(-che)** ethics
etichétta *f* label; card (*e.g., of a library*); etiquette; **etichetta gommata** sticker
etichettare (etichétto) *tr* to label
èti·co -ca (-ci -che) *adj* ethical; consumptive || *m* consumptive || *f* see **etica**
etile *m* ethyl
etilène *m* ethylene
etìli·co -ca *adj* **(-ci -che)** ethyl
ètimo *m* etymon
etimologìa *f* etymology
etìope *adj* & *mf* Ethiopian
Etiòpia, l' *f* Ethiopia
etiòpi·co -ca *adj* **(-ci -che)** Ethiopian
etisìa *f* tuberculosis
ètni·co -ca *adj* **(-ci -che)** ethnic(al)
etnografìa *f* ethnography
etnologìa *f* ethnology
etru·sco -sca *adj* & *mf* **(-schi -sche)** Etruscan
ettàgono *m* heptagon
èttaro *m* hectare
ètte *m* (coll) particle, jot, whit, tittle
ètto or **ettogrammo** *m* hectogram
-étto -étta *suf adj* rather, e.g., **piccoletto** rather small; -ish, e.g., **rotondetto** roundish
ettòlitro *m* hectoliter
eucalipto *m* eucalyptus
eucaristìa *f* Eucharist
eufemismo *m* euphemism
eufonìa *f* euphony
eufòni·co -ca *adj* **(-ci -che)** euphonic
euforìa *f* euphoria
eufòri·co -ca *adj* **(-ci -che)** euphoric
eufuismo *m* euphuism
eugenèti·co -ca (-ci -che) *adj* eugenic || *f* eugenics
eunu·co *m* **(-chi)** eunuch
europè·o -a *adj* & *mf* European
Euròpa, l' *f* Europe
eurovisióne *f* European television chain
eutanasìa *f* euthanasia
Èva *f* Eve
evacuaménto *m* evacuation
evacuare (evàcuo) *tr* to evacuate || *intr* to evacuate; to have a bowel movement
evacuazióne *f* evacuation; bowel movement
evàdere §172 *tr* to evade; to complete (*a deal*); to answer (*a letter*); to execute (*orders*) || *intr* (ESSERE) to flee, escape
evanescènza *f* evanescence; (rad) fading
evanescènte *adj* evanescent; vanishing
evangèli·co -ca *adj* **(-ci -che)** evangelic (al)
evangeli·sta *m* **(-sti)** evangelist
evangelizzare [ddzz] *tr* to evangelize; to campaign for; to subject to political propaganda
evaporare (evapóro) *tr* & *intr* to evaporate
evaporatóre *m* evaporator; humidifier
evaporazióne *f* evaporation
evasióne *f* evasion, escape; (com) reply; **dare evasione a** to complete (*an administrative matter*)
evasi·vo -va *adj* evasive
eva·so -sa *adj* escaped || *m* escapee
evasóre *m* tax dodger
eveniènza *f* eventuality, contingency; **nell'evenienza che** in the event (that); **per ogni evenienza** just in case
evènto *m* event; **eventi correnti** current events; **fausto** or **lieto evento** happy event
eventuale *adj* contingent
eventuali·tà *f* **(-tà)** eventuality
eversi·vo -va *adj* upsetting; destructive
evidènte *adj* evident; clear
evidènza *f* evidence; clearness; **mettersi in evidenza** to make oneself conspicuous; **tenere in evidenza** (com) to keep active
evirare *tr* to emasculate
evitare (èvito) *tr* to avoid, shun; **evitare qlco a qlcu** to spare s.o. s.th, to save s.o. from s.th
èvo *m* age, era; **evo antico** ancient times; **evo moderno** modern times; **medio evo** Middle Ages
evocare §197 **(èvoco)** *tr* to evoke
evoluire §176 *intr* (aer, nav) to maneuver
evolu·to -ta *adj* developed; progressive; modern
evoluzióne *f* evolution
evòlvere §115 *tr* to develop || *ref* to evolve
evvi·va *m* **(-va)** cheer || *interj* long live!, hurrah for!
èx *adj invar* ex-, e.g., **la sua ex moglie** his ex-wife; ex, e.g., **ex dividendo** ex dividend
ex li·bris *m* **(-bris)** bookplate
extraconiugale *adj* extramarital
extraeuropè·o -a *adj* non-European
ex vó·to *m* **(-to)** votive offering
eziologìa *f* etiology

F

F, f ['effe] *m* & *f* sixth letter of the Italian alphabet
fa *m* **(fa)** (mus) F, fa
fabbisógno *m invar* need; requirement
fàbbri·ca *f* **(-che)** building, construction; factory, plant
fabbricante *mf* builder, manufacturer
fabbricare §197 **(fàbbrico)** *tr* to manufacture; to fabricate
fabbrica·to -ta *adj* built || *m* building
fabbricazióne *f* building; erection; manufacturing; fabrication (*invention*)

fabbro *m* blacksmith; locksmith; (fig) master; **fabbro ferraio** blacksmith
faccènda *f* business, matter; **faccende domestiche** household chores
faccendiè·re -ra *mf* operator, schemer
faccétta *f* small face; face, facet
facchinàg·gio *m* (**-gi**) porterage; (fig) drudgery
facchino *m* porter; **lavorare come un facchino** to work like a slave
fàc·cia *f* (**-ce**) face; countenance; **avere la faccia di** to have the gall to; **di faccia a** opposite; **faccia da galeotto** (coll) gallows bird; **faccia tosta** cheek, gall; **in faccia a** in front of
facciale *adj* facial
facciata *f* façade; page; (fig) surface appearance
face *f* (lit) torch
facè·to -ta *adj* facetious
facèzia *f* pleasantry, banter; **scambiar facezie** to banter with each other
fachiro *m* fakir
fàcile *adj* easy; inclined; loose (*morals*); glib (*tongue*); **è facile** it is probable || *m* something easy
facili·tà *f* (**-tà**) facility, ease; inclination; **facilità di pagamento** easy payments, easy terms; **facilità di parola** glibness
facilitare (**facìlito**) *tr* to facilitate; to grant (*credit*); to give (*easy terms*)
facilitazióne *f* facilitation; easy terms; cut rate
facinoró·so -sa [s] *adj* criminal || *m* hoodlum, thug
facoltà *f* (**-tà**) faculty; power; school (*of a university*); **facoltà** *fpl* means, wealth
facoltati·vo -va *adj* optional
facoltó·so -sa [s] *adj* wealthy, affluent
facóndia *f* loquacity, gift of gab
facón·do -da *adj* loquacious
facsìmi·le *m* (**-le**) facsimile
faènza *f* faïence || **Faenza** *f* Faenza
fàg·gio *m* (**-gi**) (bot) beech
fagia·no -na *mf* pheasant
fagiolino *m* string bean
fagiòlo *m* bean; (coll) sophomore; **andare a fagiolo a** (coll) to fit perfectly; **fagiolo bianco** lima bean
fà·glia *f* (**-glie**) (geol) fault
fagòtto *m* bundle; (mus) bassoon; **far fagotto** (coll) to pack up
fàida *f* vengeance, vendetta
faìna *f* stone marten
falange *f* phalanx
fal·bo -ba *adj* tawny
falcata *f* step, stride; bucking
falce *f* scythe; crescent (*of moon*); **falce messoria** sickle
falcétto *m* sickle
falciare §128 *tr* to mow
falcia·tóre -trice *mf* mower || *f* mowing machine
falcidiare §287 *tr* to reduce; to cut down
fal·co *m* (**-chi**) hawk; **falco pescatore** osprey
falcóne *m* falcon
falconerìa *f* falconry
falconière *m* falconer
falda *f* band, strip; flake (*of snow*); gable (*of roof*); brim (*of hat*); foot (*of mountain*); slab (*of stone*); waist plate (*of armor*); hem (*of suit*); flounce (*of dress*); layer (*of rock*); flap, coattail; **falda della camicia** shirttail; **falde** straps (*to hold a baby*); **mettersi in falde** to wear tails
falegname *m* carpenter; cabinetmaker
falegnamerìa *f* carpentry; cabinetmaking; carpenter shop; woodworker shop
falèna *f* moth
falla *f* hole, leak; (archaic) fault
fallace *adj* fallacious, deceptive
fallà·cia *f* (**-cie**) fallacy
fallare *intr & ref* (lit) to be mistaken
fallìbile *adj* fallible
fallimentare *adj* bankrupt; ruinous
falliménto *m* bankruptcy; (fig) collapse, failure
fallire §176 *tr* to miss (*the target*) || *intr* (ESSERE) to go bankrupt; to fail || *intr* (AVERE) (lit) to be mistaken
falli·to -ta *adj & mf* bankrupt
fallo *m* error, fault; sin; flaw; phallus; (sports) penalty; (sports) foul; **cadere in fallo** to make the wrong move; to be mistaken; **cogliere in fallo** to catch in the act; **far fallo a** to fail, e.g., **gli faccio fallo** I fail him; **senza fallo** without fail
fa·lò *m* (**-lò**) bonfire
falpa·là *f* (**-là**) flounce, furbelow
falsare *tr* to falsify, alter; (lit) to forge
falsari·ga *f* (**-ghe**) guideline (*for writing*); model, pattern; **seguire la falsariga di** to follow in the footsteps of
falsà·rio *m* (**-ri**) forger; counterfeiter
falsétto *m* falsetto
falsificare §197 (**falsìfico**) to falsify; to forge, fake
falsificazióne *f* falsification; forgery; misrepresentation
falsi·tà *f* (**-tà**) falsehood; falsity
fal·so -sa *adj* false; wrong (*step*); assumed (*name*); bogus, counterfeit, fake (*money*); phony || *m* falsehood; perjury; forgery; **commettere un falso** to perjure oneself; to commit forgery; **giurare il falso** to bear false witness; to perjure oneself
fama *f* fame; reputation; **cattiva fama** notoriety
fame *f* hunger; dearth; **aver fame** to be hungry; **avere una fame da lupo** to be as hungry as a wolf, to be as hungry as a bear; **morire di fame** to starve to death; to be ravenous
famèli·co -ca *adj* (**-ci -che**) starving, famished
famigera·to -ta *adj* notorious
famìglia *f* family; community; **di famiglia** intimate; **in famiglia** at home
famì·glio *m* (**-gli**) beadle, usher; hired man
familiare *adj* family; familiar, intimate; homelike || *m* member of the family
familiari·tà *f* (**-tà**) familiarity; **avere familiarità con** to be familiar with

familiarizzare [ddzz] *tr* to familiarize
famó•so -sa [s] *adj* famous, illustrious
fanale *m* lamp, lantern; (rr) headlight; **fanale di coda** taillight
fanalino *m* small light; (aut) parking light; (aut) tail light
fanàti•co -ca (-ci -che) *adj* fanatic, fanatical || *mf* fanatic
fanatismo *m* fanaticism
fanatizzare [ddzz] *tr* to make a fanatic of
fanciulla *f* girl; spinster; bride
fanciullè•sco -sca *adj* **(-schi -sche)** childish; children's
fanciullézza *f* childhood; (fig) infancy
fanciulo•lo -la *adj* childish; childlike || *mf* child || *m* boy || *f* see **fanciulla**
fandònia *f* fib, tale, yarn
fanèllo *m* (orn) linnet; (orn) finch
fanfara *f* military band; fanfare
fanfaróne *m* braggart
fangatura *f* mud bath
fanghìglia *f* mud, slush
fan•go *m* **(-ghi)** mud; **fare i fanghi** to take mud baths
fangó•so -sa [s] *adj* muddy
fannullo•ne -na *mf* idler, loafer
fanóne *m* whalebone
fantaccino *m* infantryman, foot soldier
fantascientìfi•co -ca *adj* **(-ci -che)** science-fiction
fantascienza *f* science fiction
fantasìa *f* fantasy, fancy, whim; (mus) fantasia; **di fantasia** fancy
fantasió•so -sa [s] *adj* fanciful; imaginative
fanta•sma *m* **(-smi)** ghost, spirit; phantom; **fantasma poetico** poetic fancy
fantasticare §197 **(fantàstico)** *tr* to imagine, dream up || *intr* to daydream
fantasticherìa *f* imagination, daydreaming
fantàsti•co -ca *adj* **(-ci -che)** fantastic || **fantastico** *interj* unbelievable!
fante *m* infantryman, foot soldier; (cards) jack; (obs) youth
fanterìa *f* infantry
fanté•sca *f* **(-sche)** (joc, lit) housemaid
fantino *m* jockey
fantòc•cio *m* **(-ci)** puppet
fantomàti•co -ca *adj* **(-ci -che)** ghostly; mysterious
farabutto *m* scoundrel, heel
faraóna *f* guinea fowl
faraóne *m* Pharaoh; (cards) faro
farcire §176 *tr* to stuff
fardèllo *m* bundle; burden; **far fardello** to pack one's bags
fare *m* doing; break (*of day*); way (*of acting*); **sul far della sera** at nightfall || §173 *tr* to do; to make; to work; to take (*e.g., a walk, a step*); to give (*a sigh*); to deal (*cards*); to suffer (*hunger*); to lead (*a good or bad life*); to render (*service*); to log (*e.g., 15 m.p.h.*); to be, e.g., **tre volte tre fa nove** three times three is nine; to build (*e.g., a house*); to put together (*a collection*); to prepare (*dinner*); to say, utter (*a word*); to have (*a dream*); to give (*fruit*); to pay (*attention*); to play (*a role*); to stir up (*pity*); to mention (*a name*); **fare il** (or **la**) to be a (*e.g., carpenter*); **fare** + *inf* to have + *inf*, e.g., **gli ho fatto . . .** I had him . . . ; to make + *inf*, e.g., **il medico mi fece . . .** the doctor made me . . .; to have + *pp*, e.g., **farò fare . . .** I shall have . . . done; **fare acqua** to leak, to take in water; to get a supply of water; (coll) to urinate; **fare a metà** to divide in half; **fare a pugni** to come to blows; **fare a tempo** to be on time; **fare benzina** to buy gasoline; **fare caldo a** to keep warm, e.g., **questa coperta gli fa caldo** this blanket keeps him warm; **fare carbone** to coal; **fare . . . che** to have been . . . since, e.g., **fanno tre mesi che siamo in questa città** it has been three months since we have been in this city; **fare che** + *subj* to see to it that + *ind*, e.g., **faccia che comincino a lavorare subito** see to it that they begin to work at once; **fare colpo** to make an impression; **fare corona a** to crown; **fare cuore a** to encourage; **fare del male a** to harm; **fare di** + *inf* to see to it that + *ind;* **fare di tutto** to do one's best; **fare festa a** to cheer; **fare fiasco** to fail; **fare finta di** to pretend to; **fare fronte a** to face, meet; **fare fuoco su** to fire upon; **fare il gioco di** to play into the hands of; **fare il pappagallo** to parrot, ape; **fare il pieno** to fill up (*with gasoline*); **fare la bocca a** to get used to; **fare la calza** to knit; **fare la coda** to queue up, line up; **fare la festa a** to kill; **fare la guardia** to stand guard; **fare la mano a** to get used to; **fare le cose in famiglia** to wash one's dirty linen at home; **fare le cose in grande stile** to splurge; **fare legna** to gather firewood; **fare l'occhio** to become accustomed; **fare mente** to pay attention; **fare onore a** to do honor to; **fare paura a** to frighten; **fare sangue** to bleed; **fare sapere a qlcu** to let s.o. know; **fare scalo** (aer, naut) to make a call; **fare sì che** to act in such a way that; to see to it that; **fare silenzio** to keep silent; **fare specie a** to amaze, e.g., **il tuo comportamento gli fa specie** your behavior amazes him; **fare tesoro di** to prize; **fare una bella figura** to look good; to make a fine appearance; **fare una mala figura** to look bad; to make a bad showing; **fare una malattia** (coll) to get sick; **fare vela** to set sail; **fare venire** to send for; **fare vigilia** to fast; **farla corta** to cut it short; **farla franca** to get off scot-free; **farla grossa** to commit a blunder; **farla in barba a** to outwit; **farne di cotte e di crude, farne di tutti i colori,** or **farne più di Carlo in Francia** to engage in all sorts of mischief; to paint the town red; **non fare che** + *ind* to do nothing but + *inf* || *intr*—**averla a che fare con** to have words with; to have to

deal with; **fare a coltellate** to have a fight with knives; **fare a girotondo** to play ring-around-the-rosy; **fare al caso di** to fit; to suit; **fare a meno di** to do without; **fare da** to serve as, e.g., **fare da cuscino** to serve as a pillow; **fare da cena** to fix dinner; **fare di cappello** to take one's hat off; **fare presto** to hurry; **fare per** to be just the thing for; **fare tardi** to be late || *ref* to become; to cut (*e.g., one's hair*); to move, e.g., **farsi in là** to move farther; **farsi avanti** to come forward; **farsi beffe di** to make fun of; **farsi bello** to bedeck oneself; to dress up; **farsi bello di** to boast about; to appropriate; **farsi gioco di** to make fun of; **farsi le labbra** to put lipstick on; **farsi strada** to make one's way; **farsi una ragione di** to rationalize, explain to oneself; **farsi un baffo** to not give a hoot; **si fa giorno** it is getting light; **si fa tardi** it is getting late || *impers*—**che tempo fa?** what's the weather like?; **fa** ago, e.g., **alcune settimane fa** a few weeks ago; **fa estate** it is like summer; **fa fino** it is smart; **fa freddo** it is cold; **fa luna** there is moonlight, the moon is out; **fa nebbia** it is foggy; **fa notte** it is nighttime; it is dark; it is getting dark; **fa sole** it is sunny, the sun is out; **fa tipo** or **fa tono!** that's classy!; **non fa nulla** it doesn't matter, never mind

farètra *f* quiver

farfalla *f* butterfly; bow tie; (mach) butterfly valve; (coll) promissory note

farfallóne *m* large butterfly; blunder; Don Juan

farfugliare §280 *intr* to mumble, mutter

farina *f* flour; **farina d'avena** oatmeal; **farina di legno** sawdust; **farina di ossa** bone meal; **farina gialla** yellow corn meal

farinàce•o -a *adj* farinaceous || **farinacei** *mpl* flour-yielding cereals

farinata *f* porridge

faringe *f* pharynx

faringite *f* pharingitis

farinó•so -sa [s] *adj* floury; powdery (*snow*); crumbly, friable

farisèo *m* Pharisee; (fig) pharisee

farmacèuti•co -ca *adj* (**-ci -che**) pharmaceutical, drug

farmacìa *f* pharmacy; drugstore; medicine cabinet; **farmacia di guardia** or **di turno** drugstore open all night and Sunday

farmaci•sta *mf* (**-sti -ste**) pharmacist, druggist

fàrma•co *m* (**-ci** or **-chi**) remedy, medicine

farneticare §197 (**farnètico**) *intr* to rave

farnèti•co -ca (**-chi -che**) *adj* raving || *m* delirium; craze

faro *m* lighthouse, beacon; (aut) headlight; **faro retromarcia** (aut) back-up light

farràgine *f* hodgepodge

farraginó•so -sa [s] *adj* confused, mixed

farsa *f* farce; burlesque

farsè•sco -sca *adj* (**-schi -sche**) farcical, ludicrous

farsétto *m* sweater; (hist) doublet

fascétta *f* girdle; band; wrapper; clamp; **fascetta editoriale** advertising band (*of book*)

fà•scia *f* (**-sce**) band; belt; bandage; newspaper wrapper; **fascia del cappello** hatband; **fascia di garza** gauze bandage; **fascia elastica** abdominal supporter; (aut) piston ring; **fasce del neonato** swaddling clothes; **in fasce** newborn; **sotto fascia** in a wrapper

fasciame *m* (naut) planking; (naut) plating

fasciare §128 to bind; to bandage; to wrap; to surround

fasciatura *f* bandaging, dressing

fascìcolo *m* number, issue; pamphlet; file, dossier; (bb) fasciculus

fascina *f* fagot

fascina•tóre -trice *mf* charmer

fàscino *m* fascination, charm

fà•scio *m* (**-sci**) bundle; sheaf; bunch (*of flowers*); pencil or beam (*of rays*); fascist party

fascismo *m* fascism

fasci•sta *adj* & *mf* (**-sti -ste**) fascist

fase *f* phase, stage; (aut) cycle; (astr, elec, mach) phase

fastèllo *m* bundle, fagot

fasti *mpl* records, annals; notable events; (hist) Roman calendar

fastì•dio *m* (**-di**) annoyance; (coll) loathing, nausea; **avere in fastidio** to loathe; **dar fastidio a** to annoy; **fastidi** troubles, worries

fastidió•so -sa [s] *adj* annoying, irksome; irritable; (obs) disgusting

fastì•gio *m* (**-gi**) top, summit

fa•sto -sta *adj* (lit) propitious || *m invar* pomp, display || *mpl* see **fasti**

fastó•so -sa [s] *adj* pompous, ostentatious

fata *f* fairy; **buona fata** fairy godmother; **Fata Morgana** Fata Morgana (*mirage; Morgan le Fay*)

fatale *adj* fatal; inevitable; irresistible (*woman*)

fatalismo *m* fatalism

fatali•sta *mf* (**-sti -ste**) fatalist

fatali•tà *f* (**-tà**) fatality, fate

fatalóna *f* vamp

fata•to -ta *adj* fairy, enchanted; (lit) predestined

fati•ca *f* (**-che**) fatigue, weariness; labor; **a fatica** with difficulty; **da fatica** draft (*e.g., horse*); of burden (*beast*); **durar fatica a** + *inf* to have trouble in + *ger*

faticare §197 *intr* to toil; **faticare a** to be hardly able to

faticó•so -sa [s] *adj* burdensome, heavy; (lit) weary

fatìdi•co -ca *adj* (**-ci -che**) fatal

fato *m* fate, destiny

fatta *f* kind, sort; **essere sulla fatta di** to be on the trail of

fattàc•cio *m* (**-ci**) (coll) crime

fattézze *fpl* features

fattìbile *adj* feasible, possible
fattispècie *f*—**nella fattispecie** in this particular case
fat·to -ta *adj* made, e.g., **fatto a mano** handmade; broad (*daylight*); deep (*night*); ready-made (*e.g., suit*); **ben fatto** well-done; shapely; **esser fatto per** to be cut out for; **fatto di** made of; **venir fatto a** to happen, chance, e.g., **gli venne fatto d'incontrarmi** he happened to meet me || *m* fact; act, deed; feat; action; business, affair; **badare ai fatti propri** to mind one's own business; **cogliere sul fatto** to catch in the act; **dire a qlcu il fatto suo** to give s.o. a piece of one's mind; **fatto compiuto** fait accompli; **fatto d'arme** feat of arms; **fatto si è** the fact remains that; **in fatto di** concerning; as of; **sapere il fatto proprio** to know one's business; **venire al fatto** to come to the point || *f* see **fatta**
fat·tóre -tóra or **-toréssa** *mf* farm manager || *m* maker; factor; steward || *f* stewardess; manager's wife
fattorìa *f* farm; stewardship
fattorino *m* delivery boy, messenger boy; conductor (*of streetcar*)
fattrice *f* (zool) dam
fattucchiè·re -ra *mf* magician || *m* sorcerer || *f* sorceress, witch
fattura *f* preparation; workmanship; bill, invoice; (coll) witchcraft; (lit) creature
fatturare *tr* to adulterate; to invoice, bill
fattura·to -ta *adj* adulterated || *m* (com) turnover
fatturi·sta *mf* (**-sti -ste**) billing clerk
fà·tuo -tua *adj* fatuous
fàuci *fpl* jaws; (fig) mouth
fàuna *f* fauna
fàuno *m* faun
fàu·sto -sta *adj* propitious, lucky
fau·tóre -trice *mf* supporter, promoter
fava *f* broad bean; **pigliare due piccioni con una fava** to catch two birds with one stone
favèlla *f* speech; (lit) tongue
favilla *f* spark; **far** or **mandare faville** to sparkle
favo *m* honeycomb
fàvola *f* fable; tale; **favola del paese** talk of the town
favoló·so -sa [s] *adj* fabulous; mythical
favóre *m* favor; help; cover (*e.g., of night*); **a favore di** for the benefit of; **di favore** special (*price*); complimentary (*ticket*); **favore politico** patronage; **per favore** please; **per favore di** courtesy of
favoreggiaménto *m* abetting, support
favoreggiare §290 (**favoréggio**) *tr* to abet, support
favoreggia·tóre -trice *mf* abettor, supporter, backer
favorévole *adj* favorable; propitious
favorire §176 *tr* to favor; to accept; to oblige, accommodate; **favorire qlcu di qlco** to oblige s.o. with s.th; **favorisca** + *inf* please + *inf*, be kind enough to + *inf;* **favorisca alla cassa** please pay the cashier; **favorisca uscire!** please leave!; **tanto per favorire** just to keep you company; **vuol favorire?** won't you please join us (*at a meal*)?; please help yourself!
favorita *f* royal mistress
favoritismo *m* favoritism
favori·to -ta *adj* & *mf* favorite || *m* protegé; **favoriti** sideburns || *f* see **favorita**
fazióne *f* faction; **essere di fazione** to be on guard duty
fazió·so -sa [s] *adj* factious || *m* partisan
fazzolétto *m* handkerchief; **fazzoletto da collo** neckerchief
fé *f* var of **fede**
feb·bràio *m* (**-bràì**) February
fèbbre *f* fever; fever blister; **febbre da cavallo** (coll) very high fever; **febbre da fieno** hay fever; **febbre dell'oro** gold fever
febbricitante *adj* feverish
febbrile *adj* feverish
Fèbo *m* Phoebus
féc·cia *f* (**-ce**) dregs; (fig) dregs (*of society*); **fino alla feccia** to the bitter end
fèci *fpl* feces
fècola *f* starch
fecondare (**fecóndo**) *tr* to fecundate
fecondazióne *f* fecundation; **fecondazione artificiale** artificial insemination
fecondi·tà *f* (**-tà**) fecundity
fecón·do -da *adj* fecund, prolific
féde *f* faith; certificate; wedding ring; faithfulness; **far fede** to bear witness; **in fede di che** in testimony whereof; **in fede mia!** upon my word! **prestar fede a** to put one's faith in; **tener fede alla parola data** to keep one's word
fedecommésso *m* fideicommissum; trusteeship
fedéle *adj* faithful, devoted || *mf* faithful person; **i fedeli** the faithful
fedel·tà *f* (**-tà**) faithfulness, allegiance; fidelity; **ad alta fedeltà** hi-fi
fèdera *f* pillowcase
federale *adj* federal
federali·sta *mf* (**-sti -ste**) federalist
federati·vo -va *adj* federative
federa·to -ta *adj* federate, federated
federazióne *f* federation; (sports) league
Federico *m* Frederick
fedìfra·go -ga *adj* (**-ghi -ghe**) unfaithful, treacherous
fedina *f* police record; **avere la fedina sporca** to have a bad record; **fedine** sideburns
fégato *m* liver; courage; **fegato d'oca** pâté de foie gras; **rodersi il fegato** to be consumed with rage
félce *f* fern
feldspato *m* feldspar
felice *adj* happy; blissful; glad; felicitous
felici·tà *f* (**-tà**) happiness; bliss
felicitare (**felìcito**) *tr* to make happy; **che Dio vi feliciti!** God bless you! ||

ref to rejoice; **felicitarsi con qlcu per qlco** to congratulate s.o. for or on s.th
felicitazióne *f* congratulation
feli·no -na *adj & m* feline
fellóne *m* (lit) traitor
félpa *f* plush
felpa·to -ta *adj* covered with plush; soft (*e.g., step*)
féltro *m* felt; felt hat
felu·ca *f* (**-che**) two-cornered hat; (naut) felucca
fémmina *adj & f* female
femminile *adj* feminine, female || *m* feminine gender
femminili·tà *f* (**-tà**) femininity, womanliness
femminismo *m* feminism
fèmore *m* femur; thighbone
fendènte *m* slash with a sword
fèndere §174 *tr* to split, cleave; to plow (*water*); to rend (*air*); to make one's way through (*a crowd*) || *ref* to split; to come apart
fenditura *f* split, breach, fissure
fenice *f* phoenix
fenì·cio -cia (**-ci -cie**) *adj & mf* Phoenician || **la Fenicia** Phoenicia
fèni·co -ca *adj* (**-ci -che**) carbolic
fenicòttero *m* flamingo
fenòlo *m* phenol
fenomenale *adj* phenomenal
fenòmeno *m* phenomenon; freak, monster; **essere un fenomeno** to be unbelievable
ferace *adj* (lit) fertile
ferale *adj* (lit) mortal, deadly
fèretro *m* bier, coffin
feriale *adj* working (*day*); weekday
fèrie *fpl* vacation; **ferie retribuite** vacation with pay
ferire §176 *tr* to wound; to strike; **senza colpo ferire** without striking a blow || *ref* to wound oneself
ferì·to -ta *adj* wounded, injured || *m* wounded person; injured person; **i feriti** the wounded; the injured || *f* wound, injury
feritóia *f* loophole; embrasure
feri·tóre -trice *mf* assailant
férma *f* setting (*of setter or pointer*); (mil) service; (mil) enlistment
fermacarro *m* (rr) buffer
fermacar·te *m* (**-te**) paperweight; large paper clip
fermacravat·ta *m* (**-ta**) tiepin
fermà·glio *m* (**-gli**) clasp; buckle; clip; brooch
fermare (**férmo**) *tr* to stop; to pay (*attention*); to fasten; to close, shut; to detain (*in police station*); to set (*game*); to reserve (*seats*) || *ref* to stop; to stay
fermata *f* stop; **fermata a richiesta** or **facoltativa** stop on signal
fermentare (**ferménto**) *tr & intr* to ferment
fermentazióne *f* fermentation
ferménto *m* ferment
ferméżza *f* firmness; steadfastness
fér·mo -ma *adj* firm; stopped; quiet (*water*); (fig) steadfast; **fermo in posta** general delivery; **fermo restando che** seeing that; **stare fermo** to be quiet || *m* stop; detention; **mettere il fermo a** to stop (*a check*)
fermopòsta *m* general delivery || *adv* care of general delivery
feróce *adj* fierce; wild
ferò·cia *f* (**-cie**) ferocity, ferociousness, fierceness
feròdo *m* (aut) brake lining
ferragósto *m* Assumption; mid-August holiday
ferrame *m* ironware
ferramén·to *m* (**-ti**) iron or metal bracket; iron or metal trimming || *m* (**-ta** *fpl*)—**ferramenta** hardware
ferrare (**fèrro**) *tr* to shoe (*a horse*); to hoop (*a barrel*)
ferra·to -ta *adj* iron; ironclad; shod (*horse*); spiked (*shoe*); well-versed || *f* pressing, ironing; mark or burn (*caused by ironing*); (coll) iron grate
ferravèc·chio *m* (**-chi**) scrap-iron dealer, junkman
fèrre·o -a *adj* iron; ironclad
ferrièra *f* ironworks; (obs) iron mine
fèrro *m* iron; tool; anchor; sword; **ai ferri** on the grill, broiled (*e.g., steak*); **essere sotto i ferri del chirurgo** to go under the knife; **ferri** shackles; **ferri del mestiere** tools of the trade; **ferro battuto** wrought iron; **ferro da arricciare** curling iron; **ferro da calza** knitting needle; **ferro da cavallo** horseshoe; **ferro da stiro** iron, flatiron; **ferro fuso** cast iron; **ferro grezzo** pig iron; **mettere a ferro e fuoco** to put to fire and sword; **venire ai ferri corti** to get into close quarters
ferromodellismo *m* hobby of model railroads
ferrotranvièri *mpl* transport workers
ferrovìa *f* railroad; **ferrovia a dentiera** rack railway; **ferrovia sopraelevata** elevated railroad
ferrovià·rio -ria *adj* (**-ri -rie**) railroad
ferrovière *m* railroader
fèrtile *adj* fertile
fertilizzante [ddzz] *adj* fertilizing || *m* fertilizer
fertilizzare [ddzz] *tr* to fertilize
fervènte *adj* fervent
fèrvere §175 *intr* to be fervent; to rage (*said, e.g., of a battle*); to go full blast
fèrvi·do -da *adj* fervent
fervóre *m* fervor; (fig) heat
fervorino *m* lecture, sermon
fesserìa *f* (slang) stupidity, nonsense; (slang) trifle
fés·so -sa *adj* cracked; cleft; (slang) dumb || *m* (lit) cranny; **fare fesso qlcu** (slang) to play s.o. for a sucker
fessura *f* crack; cranny
fèsta *f* feast; holiday; birthday; saint's day; **a festa** festively; **buone feste!** happy holiday!; **conciare per le feste** to drub the daylights out of; **fare festa a** to welcome; **fare le feste** to spend the holidays; **far festa** to celebrate; to take the day off; **far la festa**

a to do in, kill; **festa del ceppo** Christmas; **festa da ballo** or **danzante** dancing party; **festa della mamma** Mother's Day; **festa del papà** Father's Day; **festa di precetto** (eccl) day of obligation; **festa nazionale** national holiday; **mezza festa** half holiday
festante *adj* cheerful
festeggiaménto *m* celebration
festeggiare §290 **(festéggio)** *tr* to celebrate, fete; to cheer
festi•no -na *adj* (lit) rapid ‖ *m* party
festivi•tà *f* **(-tà)** festivity
festi•vo -va *adj* festive, holiday
festóne *m* festoon
festó•so -sa [s] *adj* cheerful, merry
festu•ca *f* **(-che)** straw; (fig) mote
fetènte *adj* stinking; stink (*bomb*) ‖ *mf* (fig) stinker, louse
fetìc•cio *m* **(-ci)** fetish
feticismo *m* fetishism
fèti•do -da *adj* stinking, fetid
fèto *m* fetus
fetóre *m* stench
fétta *f* slice; **tagliare a fette** to slice
fettina *f* thin slice; twist (*of lemon*); **fettina di vitello** veal cutlet
fettùc•cia *f* **(-ce)** tape, ribbon
fettuccine *fpl* noodles
feudale *adj* feudal
feudalismo *m* feudalism
feudatà•rio -ria (-ri -rie) *adj* feudatory ‖ *m* feudal vassal
fèudo *m* fief
fiaba *f* fairy tale; tale, yarn
fiacca *f* tiredness; sluggishness; **batter la fiacca** to loaf, to goof off
fiaccare §197 *tr* to weaken; to weary; to break ‖ *ref* to weaken; to break (*e.g., one's neck*)
fiacche•ràio *m* **(-ràl)** (coll) hackman, cabman
fiacchézza *f* weakness; sluggishness
fiac•co -ca *adj* **(-chi -che)** weak; sluggish; slack ‖ *f* see **fiacca**
fiàccola *f* torch; **fiaccola della discordia** firebrand
fiaccolata *f* torchlight procession
fiala *f* vial, phial
fiamma *f* flame; blaze; (mil) insignia; (nav) pennant; **alla fiamma** (culin) flaming; **dare alle fiamme** to set on fire; **diventare di fiamma** to blush; **in fiamme** afire
fiammante *adj* blazing; **nuovo fiammante** brand-new
fiammata *f* blaze; flare-up
fiammeggiante *adj* flaming, blazing; (archit) flamboyant
fiammeggiare §290 **(fiamméggio)** *tr* to singe ‖ *intr* to flame, blaze
fiammìfero *m* match
fiammin•go -ga (-ghi -ghe) *adj* Flemish; Dutch (*e.g., master*) ‖ *mf* Fleming ‖ *m* Flemish (*language*); (orn) flamingo
fiancata *f* blow with one's hip; dig, sarcastic remark; side, flank; (nav) broadside
fiancheggiare §290 **(fianchéggio)** *tr* to flank; to border (*a road*); to support
fiancheggia•tóre -trice *mf* supporter, backer
fian•co *m* **(-chi)** flank, side; hip; **di fianco** sideways; **fianco a fianco** side by side; **fianco destr'!** (mil) right face!; **fianco destro** (naut) starboard; **fianco sinistr'!** (mil) left face!; **fianco sinistro** (naut) port; **prestare il fianco a** to leave oneself wide open to; **tenersi i fianchi dal ridere** to split one's sides laughing
Fiandre, le *fpl* Flanders
fia•sca *f* **(-sche)** flask
fiaschetterìa *f* tavern, wine shop
fia•sco *m* **(-schi)** straw-covered wine bottle; flask; fiasco
fiata *f* (archaic) time
fiatare *intr* to breathe; **senza fiatare** without breathing a word
fiato *m* breath; (archaic) stench; **avere il fiato grosso** to be out of breath; **bere d'un fiato** to gulp down; **col fiato sospeso** holding one's breath; **dare fiato a** to blow, sound (*a trumpet*); **d'un fiato** or **in un fiato** without interruption; in one gulp; **fiati** (mus) winds; **senza fiato** out of breath
fiatóne *m*—**avere il fiatone** to be out of breath
fìbbia *f* clasp, buckle
fibra *f* fiber
fibró•so -sa [s] *adj* fibrous
ficcana•so [s] *mf* **(-si** *mpl* **-so** *fpl*) (coll) busybody, meddler; nosy person
ficcare §197 *tr* to stick; to drive (*e.g., a nail*); to push; **ficcare gli occhi addosso a** to gaze at, stare at; **ficcare il naso negli affari degli altri** to poke one's nose in other people's business ‖ *ref* to hide; to butt in; to get involved
fi•co *m* **(-chi)** fig; fig tree
ficodìndia *m* (*pl* **fichidindia**) prickly pear
fidanzaménto *m* engagement, betrothal
fidanzare *tr* to betroth ‖ *ref* to become engaged
fidanza•to -ta *adj* engaged ‖ *m* fiancé ‖ *f* fiancée
fidare *tr* to entrust ‖ *intr* to trust ‖ *ref* to have confidence; **fidarsi a** (coll) to dare to; **fidarsi di** to trust, rely on
fida•to -ta *adj* trustworthy, reliable
fi•do -da *adj* (lit) faithful, trusted ‖ *m* loyal follower; credit; **far fido** to extend credit
fidùcia *f* faith, confidence; (com) credit; **di fiducia** trustworthy
fiducià•rio -ria (-ri -rie) *adj* fiduciary ‖ *mf* fiduciary, trustee
fidució•so -sa [s] *adj* confident, hopeful
fièle *m invar* gall, bile; acrimony
fienile *m* hayloft
fièno *m* hay
fierìsti•co -ca *adj* **(-ci -che)** of a fair, e.g., **attività fieristica** activity of a fair
fiè•ro -ra *adj* fierce; dignified; proud ‖ *f* fair; exhibit; wild beast

fièvole *adj* feeble, weak
fifa *f* (coll) scare; **avere la fifa** (coll) to be chicken; **avere una fifa blu** (coll) to be scared stiff
fifó·ne -na *mf* (coll) scaredy-cat
figgere §104 *tr* (lit) to drive, thrust || *ref*—**figgersi in capo** to get into one's head
figlia *f* daughter; (com) stub; **figlia consanguinea** stepdaughter on the father's side
figliare §280 *tr & intr* to whelp (*said of animals*)
figlia·stro -stra *mf* stepchild || *m* stepson || *f* stepdaughter
figliata *f* litter (*e.g., of pigs*)
fi·glio -glia *mf* child, offspring || *m* son; **figli** children; **figlio consanguineo** stepson on the father's side || *f* see **figlia**
figliòc·cio -cia (-ci -ce) *mf* godchild || *m* godson || *f* goddaughter
figliolanza *f* children, offspring
figliò·lo -la *mf* child || *m* son, boy || *f* daughter, girl
figura *f* figure; illustration; figurehead; face card; **far bella figura** to make a good showing; **far cattiva figura** to make a poor showing; **far figura** to look good; **figura retorica** figure of speech
figurante *mf* (theat) extra, super
figurare *tr* to feign; to represent || *intr* to figure; to appear; to make a good showing || *ref* to imagine; **si figuri!** imagine!
figurati·vo -va *adj* (fa) figurative
figura·to -ta *adj* figurative (*speech*); transcribed (*pronunciation*); illustrated (*book*)
figurina *f* figurine; card, picture (*of a series of athletes or entertainment celebrities*)
figurini·sta *mf* **(-sti -ste)** dress designer; costume designer
figurino *m* fashion plate; fashion magazine
figuro *m* scoundrel; gangster
figuróne *m*—**fare un figurone** to make a very good showing
fila *f* row; file, line; series; **di fila** in a row; **fare la fila** to wait in line; **file** ranks
filàc·cia *f* **(-ce)** lint
filaccicó·so -sa [s] or **filacció·so -sa** [s] *adj* thready, stringy
filaménto *m* filament
filamentó·so -sa [s] *adj* thready, stringy; thread-like
filanda *f* spinning mill; silk spinning mill
filante *adj* spinning; shooting (*star*); thready; flowing (*e.g., line*)
filantropìa *f* philanthropy
filantròpi·co -ca *adj* **(-ci -che)** philanthropic
filàntro·po -pa *mf* philanthropist
filare *m* row, line || *tr* to spin; to drip, ooze; to rest on (*one's oars*); to make (*e.g., ten knots*); (naut) to pay out; (mus) to hold (*a note*); **filare l'amore** to be in love || *intr* to spin (*said of a spider*); to rope, thread (*said of wine or syrup*); to make sense; to drip; **fare filare dritto qlcu** to keep s.o. in line; **filare a** to do (*e.g., twenty miles an hour*); **filare all'inglese** to take French leave; **fila via!** (coll) get out!
filarmòni·co -ca (-ci -che) *adj* philharmonic || *f* philharmonic society
filastròc·ca *f* **(-che)** rigmarole; nursery rhyme
filatelìa *f* philately
filatèli·co -ca (-ci -che) *adj* philatelic(al) || *mf* philatelist
fila·to -ta *adj* spun; well-constructed (*speech*) || *m* yarn
fila·tóio *m* **(-tói)** spinning wheel
filatura *f* spinning; spinning mill
filettare (filétto) *tr* to fillet; (mach) to thread
filettatura *f* stripe (*on a cap*); (mach) thread
filétto *m* fillet; stripe; snaffle (*on a horse's bit*); fine stroke (*in handwriting*); (mach) thread; (typ) ornamental line, headband; (typ) rule
filiale *adj* filial || *f* branch office
filiazióne *f* filiation
filibustière *m* filibuster, buccaneer; adventurer
filièra *f* (mach) drawplate; (mach) die (*to cut threads*)
filigrana *f* filigree; watermark (*in paper*)
filippi·no -na *adj* Philippine || *m* Filipino || **le Filippine** the Philippines
Filippo *m* Philip
filistè·o -a *adj & m* philistine; Philistine
Fillide *f* Phyllis
film *m* **(film)** film; movie, motion picture; **film parlato** or **sonoro** talking picture
filmare *tr* to film
filmina *f* filmstrip
filmìsti·co -ca *adj* **(-ci -che)** movie, motion-picture
filmotè·ca *f* **(-che)** film library
fi·lo *m* **(-li)** thread; wire; yarn; blade (*of grass*); breath (*of air*); string (*of pearls*); edge (*of razor*); **dare del filo da torcere** to cause trouble; **essere ridotto a un filo** to be only skin and bones; **fil di voce** thin voice; **filo a piombo** plumb line; **filo d'acqua** thin stream; **filo della schiena** or **delle reni** spine; **filo spinato** barbed wire; **passare a fil di spada** to put to the sword; **per filo e per segno** in detail; from beginning to end; **senza fili** wireless; **stare a filo** to stand upright; **tenere i fili** (fig) to pull wires; **tenere in filo** to keep in line; **un filo di** a bit of || *m* **(-la** *fpl*) string (*e.g., of cooked cheese*); (archaic) file, row
filo·bus *m* **(-bus)** trolley bus
filodiffusióne *f* wired wireless; cable TV
filodrammàti·co -ca *adj & mf* **(-ci -che)** (theat) amateur
filogovernati·vo -va *adj* on the government side
filologìa *f* philology
filòlo·go -ga (-gi -ghe) *adj* philologic(al) || *m* philologist
filóne *m* vein (*of ore*); ripple (*of a cur-*

rent); stream; loaf (*of bread*); (lit) mainstream; **filone d'oro** gold lode
filó•so -sa [s] *adj* stringy
filosofia *f* philosophy
filosòfi•co -ca *adj* (**-ci -che**) philosophic(al)
filòso•fo -fa *mf* philosopher
filovia *f* trolley bus line
filtrare *tr* to filter; to percolate (*coffee*) || *intr* to filter, permeate
filtrazióne *f* filtering, filtration
filtro *m* filter; philter
filugèllo *m* silkworm
filza *f* string (*of pearls*); series (*of errors*); row; dossier, file; basting (*of dress*)
finale *adj* final, last; consumer (*goods*) || *m* end, ending; (mus) finale; (sports) finish || *f* end, ending; (sports) finals
finali•sta *mf* (**-sti -ste**) finalist
finali•tà *f* (**-tà**) end, purpose
finanche *adv* even
finanza *f* finance
finanziaménto *m* financing
finanziare §287 *tr* to finance
finanzià•rio -ria (**-ri -rie**) *adj* finance, financial || *f* (com) holding company
finanzia•tóre -trice *mf* financial backer
finanzièra *f* frock coat; **alla finanziera** with giblet gravy
finanzière *m* financier; (coll) customs officer
fin•ca *f* (**-che**) column, row (*of ledger*)
finché *conj* until, as long as; **finché non** until
fine *adj* fine, thin; choice, nice || *m* end, purpose; conclusion; (lit) limit, border; **a fin di bene** to good purpose, for the best; **secondo fine** ulterior motive || *f* end, conclusion; **condurre a fine** to bring to fruition; **fine di settimana** weekend; **in fin dei conti** after all; **senza fine** endless
fine-settima•na *m* or *f* (**-na**) weekend
finèstra *f* window; (lit) gash, wound; **finestra a gangheri** casement window; **finestra a ghigliottina** sash window; **finestra panoramica** picture window; **finestre** (lit) eyes
finestrino *m* (aut, rr) window
finézza *f* thinness; delicacy; finesse; kindness
fingere §126 *tr* to feign, pretend; (lit) to invent || *intr* to feign, pretend || *ref* to pretend to be
finiménto *m* finishing touch; **finimenti** harness
finimóndo *m* fracas, uproar
finire §176 *tr* to end; to put an end to; **finiscila!** cut it out! || *intr* (ESSERE) to end, to be over; to abut; to wind up; **finire con** + *inf* to wind up + *ger*; **finire di** + *inf* to finish + *ger*, e.g., **ho finito di farmi la barba** I have finished shaving
fini•to -ta *adj* finished; accomplished; finite; exhausted; **aver finito** to be through; **falla finita!** cut it out!; **farla finita con** to be through with; **farla finita con la vita** to end one's life
finitura *f* finish, finishing touch
finlandése [s] *adj* Finnish || *mf* Finlander, Finn || *m* Finnish (*language*)
Finlàndia, la Finland
finni•co -ca *adj* & *mf* (**-ci -che**) Finnic
fi•no -na *adj* fine, thin; refined; pure; sheer; **fare fino** (coll) to be refined || *adv* even; **fin a quando?** till when?; **fin da domani** beginning tomorrow; **fin da ora** beginning right now; **fin dove?** how far?; **fin in cima** up to the top; **fino a** until; down to; up to; as far as; **fin qui** up to now; up to this point
finòc•chio *m* (**-chi**) fennel; (vulg) fairy, queer
finóra *adv* up to now, heretofore
finta *f* pretense; fly (*of trousers*); (sports) feint; **far finta di** + *inf* to pretend to + *inf*, to feign + *ger*
fintantoché *conj* until
fin•to -ta *adj* false (*teeth*); fake; fictitious; sham (*battle*) || *mf* hypocrite || *f* see **finta**
finzióne *f* pretense; fiction; figment
fio *m*—**pagare il fio** to pay the piper; **pagare il fio di** to pay the penalty for
fioccare §197 (**fiòcco**) *intr* (ESSERE) to fall (*said of snow*); to flow (*said, e.g., of complaints*) || *impers* (ESSERE) —**fiocca** it is snowing
fiòc•co *m* (**-chi**) bow, knot; flake (*of snow*); flock, tuft (*of wool*); (naut) jib; **coi fiocchi** excellent; made to perfection; **fiocco pallone** (naut) spinnaker
fioccó•so -sa [s] *adj* flaky
fiòcina *f* harpoon
fiò•co -ca *adj* (**-chi -che**) feeble, faint
fiónda *f* sling; slingshot
fio•ràio -ràia (**-ràî -ràie**) *mf* florist || *f* flower girl
fiorami *mpl*—**a fiorami** with flower design
fiordaliso *m* fleur-de-lis; (bot) iris; (lit) lily
fiòrdo *m* fjord
fióre *m* flower; prime (*of life*); best, pick; bloom; **a fior d'acqua** on the surface; skimming the water; **a fior di labbra** in a low tone, sottovoce; **a fior di pelle** skin-deep, superficial; **fior di** (coll) a lot of; **fiore di latte** cream; **fiori** (cards) clubs; **primo fiore** down (*soft hairy growth*)
fiorènte *adj* flourishing, thriving
fiorenti•no -na *adj* & *mf* Florentine
fiorettare (**fiorétto**) *tr* (fig) to overembellish
fiorétto *m* little flower; choice, pick; overembellishment; choice passage (*from life of saint*); foil; button of foil
fioricoltóre *m* var of **floricoltore**
fioricoltura *f* var of **floricoltura**
fiorino *m* florin
fiorire §176 *tr* to cause to flower; to adorn with flowers || *intr* (ESSERE) to flower, bloom; to flourish; to break out (*said of skin eruption*); to get moldy
fiori•sta *mf* (**-sti -ste**) florist
fiori•to -ta *adj* flowering; flowery;

mottled; moldy; studded (*e.g., with errors*)
fioritura *f* flowering; flourish; mold; (pathol) eruption
fiorrancino *m* (orn) kinglet, firecrest
fiorràn•cio *m* (**-ci**) marigold
fiòtto *m* gush, surge; (obs) wave
Firènze *f* Florence
firma *f* signature; power of attorney; good reputation; (mil) enlisted man; **buona firma** famous writer; **farci la firma** (coll) to accept quite willingly; **firma di favore** guarantor's signature
firmaiòlo *m* (mil) enlisted man
firmaménto *m* firmament
firmare *tr* to sign
firmatà•rio -ria (-ri -rie) *adj* signatory ‖ *mf* signer, signatory
fisarmòni•ca *f* (**-che**) accordion
fiscale *adj* fiscal, tax
fischiare §287 *tr* to whistle; to boo ‖ *intr* to whistle; to ring (*said of ears*); to blow (*said, e.g., of a factory whistle*)
fischiettare (**fischiétto**) *tr & intr* to whistle
fischiétto *m* whistle (*instrument*)
fi•schio *m* (**-schi**) whistle; hiss, boo; blow (*of whistle*); ringing (*in the ears*)
fi•sciù *m* (**-sciù**) kerchief, fichu
fisco *m invar* treasury; internal revenue service
fisi•co -ca (-ci -che) *adj* physical; bodily ‖ *m* physicist; physique; (obs) physician ‖ *f* physics
fisima *f* whim, fancy, caprice
fisiologìa *f* physiology
fisiològi•co -ca *adj* (**-ci -che**) physiological
fisionomìa or **fisonomìa** *f* physiognomy; countenance, face; appearance
fisionomi•sta *mf* (**-sti -ste**) person good at faces; physiognomist
fi•so -sa *adj* (lit) fixed
fissàg•gio *m* (**-gi**) (phot) fixing
fissare *tr* to fix; to fasten; to gaze at; to reserve; to hire; **fissare lo sguardo** to gaze ‖ *ref* to gaze, stare; to become obsessed; to settle down
fissati•vo -va *adj* fixing
fissa•to -ta *adj* fixed; (coll) cracked ‖ *mf* (coll) crackpot
fissa•tóre -trice *adj* (phot) fixing ‖ *m* fixer; **fissatore per capelli** hair spray; hair dressing
fissazióne *f* fixation; fixed idea
fissile *adj* fissionable
fissionàbile *adj* fissionable
fissióne *f* fission
fis•so -sa *adj* fixed; regular ‖ *m* pay
fistola *f* (pathol) fistula; (lit) pipe
fitta *f* pang, stitch; crowd; great amount; (coll) blow; (obs) quagmire
fittàvolo *m* tenant farmer
fittì•zio -zia *adj* (**-zi -zie**) fictitious
fit•to -ta *adj* fixed, dug in; thick, dense; pitch (*dark*) ‖ *m* thick; rent; tenancy ‖ *f* see **fitta**
fittóne *m* (bot) taproot
fiuma•no -na *adj* river; from Fiume ‖ *m* person from Fiume ‖ *f* flood, stream
fiumara *f* torrent
fiume *m* river; **a fiumi** like a river
fiutare *tr* to snuff, sniff; to smell
fiutata *f* snuff, sniff
fiuto *m* sense of smell; snuff; flair
flàcci•do -da *adj* flabby
flacóne *m* flacon
flagellare (**flagèllo**) *tr* to scourge, lash, flagellate
flagèllo *m* whip, scourge; pest, plague; (coll) mess
flagrante *adj* flagrant; **in flagrante** (**delitto**) in the act
flan *m* (**flan**) pudding; (typ) mat
flanèlla *f* flannel
flàn•gia *f* (**-ge**) flange
flato *m* gas, flatus
flatulènza *f* flatulence
flautino *m* flageolet
flauti•sta *mf* (**-sti -ste**) flutist
flàuto *m* flute; **flauto diritto** or **dolce** (mus) recorder
fla•vo -va *adj* (lit) blond, golden
flèbile *adj* mournful
flebite *f* phlebitis
flèmma *f* apathy; coolness; phlegm
flemmàti•co -ca *adj* (**-ci -che**) phlegmatic(al)
flessìbile *adj* flexible, pliable
flessióne *f* bending; (com) fall, drop; (gram) inflection
flessuó•so -sa [s] *adj* lithe, willowy; winding; flowing (*style*)
flèttere §177 *tr* to flex; (gram) to inflect
flirtare *intr* to flirt
flòra *f* flora
floreale *adj* floral
floricoltóre *m* floriculturist
floricoltura *f* floriculture
flòri•do -da *adj* florid; flourishing
flò•scio -scia *adj* (**-sci -sce**) flabby; soft (*hat*)
flòtta *f* fleet
flottante *adj* floating ‖ *m* (com) floating stock
flottare (**flòtto**) *tr & intr* to float
flottiglia *f* flottilla
fluènte *adj* flowing
fluidità *f* fluidity
flùi•do -da *adj & m* fluid; fluent (*style*)
fluire §176 *intr* (ESSERE) to flow; to pour
fluitazióne *f* log driving
fluorescènte *adj* fluorescent
fluorescènza *f* fluorescence
fluorìdri•co -ca *adj* (**-ci -che**) hydrofluoric
fluorite *f* fluor, fluorite
fluorizzazióne [ddzz] *f* fluoridation
fluòro *m* fluorine
fluoruro *m* fluoride
flusso *m* flow; flood (*of tide*); high tide; (pathol) flow (*e.g., of blood*); (phys) flux
flutto *m* (lit) wave
fluttuare (**flùttuo**) *intr* to fluctuate; to bob, toss; to waver; to surge, stream
fluviale *adj* fluvial, river
fobìa *f* phobia
fò•ca *f* (**-che**) seal; sealskin
focàc•cia *f* (**-ce**) flat, rounded loaf; cake
focaccina *f* bun

fo•càia *adj fem* (**-càie**) flint
focale *adj* focal
fóce *f* mouth (*of river*)
focèna *f* porpoise
fochi•sta *m* (**-sti**) fireman, stoker; fireworks manufacturer
foco•làio *m* (**-lài**) (pathol) focus; (fig) hotbed
focolare *m* hearth; firebox; fireside, home
focó•so -sa [s] *adj* fiery, high-spirited
fòdera *f* lining (*of suit*); cover, case
foderare (**fòdero**) *tr* to line; to cover
fòdero *m* sheath, scabbard; raft
fó•ga *f* (**-ghe**) ardor, impetus
fòg•gia *f* (**-ge**) fashion, shape; **a foggia di** shaped like
foggiare §290 (**fòggio**) *tr* to shape, fashion
fòglia *f* leaf; petal; foil (*of gold*); **mangiare la foglia** (fig) to get wise, catch on
fogliame *m* foliage
fò•glio *m* (**-gli**) sheet; bill, banknote; folio; newspaper; permit; **foglio d'avviso** notice; **foglio di congedo** (mil) discharge; **foglio d'iscrizione** application; **foglio di via** (mil) travel orders; **foglio modello** blank form; **foglio rosa** (aut) permit; **foglio volante** flier, handbill
fógna *f* sewer, drain
fognatura *f* sewerage
fòla *f* tale, fable
fola•ga *f* (**-ghe**) (zool) coot
folata *f* gust; (lit) flight (*of birds*)
folclóre *m* folklore
folgorante *adj* striking; flashing; meteoric (*career*)
folgorare (**fólgoro**) *tr* to strike (with lightning) || *intr* to flash by || *impers* —**folgora** it is thundering
fólgore *m* (lit) thunderbolt || *f* flash of lightning; thunderbolt
fólla *f* crowd; (fig) flock
follare (**fóllo**) *tr* to full
fòlle *adj* mad, crazy; (aut) neutral; (mach) loose (*pulley*)
folleggiare §290 (**folléggio**) *intr* to act foolishly; to frolic
folleménte *adv* desperately, madly
follétto *m* elf; little imp
follìa *f* madness, lunacy; folly; **alla follia** madly; **far follie per** to be crazy about
follìcolo *m* follicle
fól•to -ta *adj* thick; beetle (*brow*); deep (*night*) || *m* depth (*e.g., of the night*); thick (*e.g., of the battle*)
fomentare (**foménto**) *tr* to foment
fòmite *m* (lit) instigation; impetus
fónda *f* anchorage; lowland; saddlebag; **alla fonda** at anchor
fónda•co *m* (**-chi**) (hist) warehouse
fondale *m* depth (*of river, sea*); (theat) backdrop
fondamentale *adj* fundamental, basic
fondamén•to *m* (**-ti**) ground, foundation; basis; **fare fondamento su** to count on; **fondamenti** elements; **senza fondamento** baseless; without getting anywhere || *m* (**-ta** *fpl*)—**fondamenta** foundations (*of a building*)
fondare (**fóndo**) *tr* to found; to build; to charter || *ref*—**fondarsi su** to rely on; to be based upon
fondatézza *f* basis, ground, foundation
fonda•to -ta *adj* well-founded
fonda•tóre -trice *mf* founder
fondazióne *f* foundation
fondèllo *m* bottom, base
fondènte *m* flux
fóndere §178 *tr* to smelt; to melt; to blow (*a fuse*); to cast (*a statue*); to blend (*colors*) || *intr* to melt; to blend || *ref* to melt; to blend; to burn out
fonderìa *f* foundry
fondià•rio -ria (**-ri -rie**) *adj* real-estate, land || *f* real-estate tax
fondina *f* holster; (coll) soup dish
fondi•sta *mf* (**-sti -ste**) editorialist; (sports) long-distance runner
fóndita *f* (typ) font
fonditóre *m* smelter, founder
fón•do -da *adj* deep || *m* bottom; fund; innermost nature; seat; end; background; land, property; **a doppio fondo** with a false bottom; **a fondo** thoroughly; **a fondo perduto** as an outright grant; **dar fondo** (naut) to cast anchor; **dar fondo a** to exhaust; **di fondo** (journ) editorial; (sports) long-distance; **fondi** funds; lees; **fondi di bottega** remnants; **fondi di caffè** coffee grounds; **fondo comune d'investimento** mutual fund; **fondo d'ammortamento** sinking fund; **fondo di beneficenza** community chest; **fondo tinta** foundation (*in make-up*); **in fondo** in the end; at the bottom; after all
fonè•ma *m* (**-mi**) phoneme
fonèti•co -ca (**-ci -che**) *adj* phonetic || *f* phonetics
fonògeno *m* pickup (*of record player*)
fonògrafo *m* phonograph, Gramophone
fonogram•ma *m* (**-mi**) telegram delivered by telephone
fonologìa *f* phonology
fonorivelatóre *m* pickup (*of record player*)
fonovalìgia *f* portable phonograph
fontana *f* fountain; spring; source
fónte *m* (lit) spring, source; **fonte battesimale** font || *f* spring; fountain; source; **da fonte autorevole** on good authority
foraggiare §290 *tr* to subsidize || *intr* to forage
foràg•gio *m* (**-gi**) forage, provender, fodder
foràne•o -a *adj* rural; outer; (naut) outer (*dock*)
forare (**fóro**) *tr* to pierce; to bore; to puncture || *intr* to have a flat tire || *ref* to be punctured
foratura *f* puncture
fòrbice *f*—**a forbice** (sports) scissors (*e.g., kick*); **forbici** scissors; clippers; **forbici per le unghie** nail clippers
forbire §176 *tr* to wipe; to polish; to shine
fór•ca *f* (**-che**) fork; pitchfork; gallows; mountain pass; **fare la forca a qlcu** (slang) to betray s.o.; (slang) to do s.o. dirt; **fatto a forca** V-shaped

forcèlla *f* fork (*of bicycle or motorcycle*); mountain pass; fork-shaped pole; hairpin; cradle (*of handset*); (coll) wishbone (*of chicken*)
forchétta *f* fork; (coll) wishbone (*of chicken*); **alla forchetta** (culin) cold (*e.g., lunch*)
forchettata *f* forkful; blow with a fork
forchettóne *m* carving fork
forcina *f* hairpin
fòrcipe *m* forceps
forcóne *m* pitchfork
forellino *m* pinhole
forèsta *f* forest
forestale *adj* forest, park
foresterìa *f* guest quarters (*in college or monastery*)
forestierismo *m* borrowing (*from another language*)
forestiè·ro -ra *adj* foreign || *mf* foreigner; stranger; outsider
forfettà·rio -ria *adj* (**-ri -rie**) job, e.g., **contratto forfettario** job contract; all-inclusive, e.g., **combinazione forfettaria** all-inclusive price agreement
fórfora *f* dandruff
fòr·gia *f* (**-ge**) forge; smithy
forgiare §290 (**fòrgio**) *tr* to forge
foriè·ro -ra *adj* forerunning || *mf* forerunner, harbinger
fórma *f* shape; form; mold (*e.g., for cakes*); wheel (*of cheese*); (typ) form; **forma da cappelli** hat block; **forma da scarpe** shoe tree; shoe last (*used by shoemaker*); **forme** shape, body; good manners; **salvare le forme** to save face
formaggièra *f* dish for grated cheese
formàg·gio *m* (**-gi**) cheese
formaldèide *f* formaldehyde
formale *adj* formal; prim
formalismo *m* formality
formali·tà *f* (**-tà**) formality
formalizzare [ddzz] *tr* to scandalize || *ref* to be shocked
formare (**fórmo**) *tr & ref* to form
forma·to -ta *adj* formed || *m* format
formazióne *f* formation
fòrmica *f* (trademark) Formica
formì·ca *f* (**-che**) ant
formi·càio *m* (**-cài**) anthill; (fig) swarm
formichière *m* anteater
formicolare (**formìcolo**) *intr* to swarm; to crawl || *intr* (ESSERE) to creep (*said, e.g., of a leg*)
formicolì·o *m* (**-i**) swarm; creeping sensation, numbness
formidàbile *adj* formidable
formó·so -sa [s] *adj* shapely, buxom
fòrmula *f* formula; (aut) category, class; **formula dubitativa** (law) lack of evidence; **formula piena** (law) acquittal
formulare (**fòrmulo**) *tr* to formulate
formulà·rio *m* (**-ri**) formulary; form
fornace *f* furnace, kiln
for·nàio -nàia *mf* (**-nài -nàie**) baker
fornèllo *m* stove, range; (*of boiler*) firebox; bowl (*of pipe*); (min) shaft; **fornello a gas** gas range; **fornello a spirito** kerosene stove; chafing dish
fornire §176 *tr* to furnish, supply
forni·tóre -trice *mf* supplier, purveyor
fornitura *f* supply; order; delivery
fórno *m* oven; furnace; kiln; bakery; (theat) empty house; **al forno** or **in forno** baked; **alto forno** blast furnace; **forno crematorio** crematorium; **far forno** (theat) to play before an empty house
fóro *m* hole
fòro *m* forum; (law) bar
forosétta [s] *f* (lit) peasant girl
fórse *m* doubt; **mettere in forse** to endanger; to put in doubt || *adv* perhaps, maybe
forsenna·to -ta *adj* mad, insane || *mf* lunatic
fòrte *adj* strong; firm; bad (*cold*); fat, hefty; fast (*color*); offensive (*joke*); hard (*smoker*); main (*dish*); (lit) thick || *m* strong person; fortress; bulk, main body; forte; (lit) thick; **sapere di forte** to have a strong flavor; **farsi forte** to bear up; **farsi forte di** to appropriate, use; to be cocksure of || *adv* hard, strong; much; loud; openly; a lot; fast; swiftly
fortézza *f* fortress; strength; fortitude
fortificare §197 (**fortìfico**) *tr* to fortify || *ref* to be strengthened; to dig in
fortificazióne *f* fortification
fortino *m* blockhouse, redoubt
fortùi·to -ta *adj* fortuitous
fortuna *f* fortune; luck; good luck; fate, destiny; (lit) storm; **avere fortuna** to be lucky; to be a hit; **buona fortuna!** good luck!; **di fortuna** makeshift, emergency; **non aver la fortuna di** to not be fortunate enough to; **per fortuna** luckily
fortunale *m* storm, tempest
fortuna·to -ta *adj* fortunate, lucky
fortunó·so -sa [s] *adj* eventful
forùncolo *m* boil; pimple
forviare §119 *tr* to mislead, lead astray || *intr* to go astray
fòrza *f* strength; force; power; police; (phys) force; **a forza di** by dint of; **a tutta forza** at full speed; **bassa forza** (mil) enlisted personnel; **di forza** by force; **di prima forza** first-rate; **far forza a** to encourage; to force; **fare forza a sé stesso** to restrain oneself; **forza!** courage!; **forza di corpo** (typ) height-to-paper; **forza maggiore** force majeure, act of God; **forza muscolare** brawn; **forza pubblica** police; **forza viva** kinetic energy; **per forza** of course; under duress
forzare (**fòrzo**) *tr* to force; to strain; to rape; to tamper with (*a lock*); **forzare il passo** to hasten one's step; **forzare la consegna** (mil) to violate orders
forza·to -ta *adj* forced; force (*e.g., feed*) || *m* convict
forzière *m* chest, coffer
forzó·so -sa [s] *adj* compulsory; imposed by law
forzu·to -ta *adj* husky, robust
foschìa *f* smog; mist; haze

fó·sco -sca *adj* **(-schi -sche)** dark; gloomy; misty
fosfato *m* phosphate
fosforeggiare §290 **(fosforéggio)** *intr* to phosphoresce; to glow
fosforescènte *adj* phosphorescent
fòsforo *m* phosphorus
fòssa *f* grave; hollow; hole, ditch; moat; pit; den (*of lions*); **fossa biologica** sewage-treatment plant; **fossa di riparazione** (aut) pit; **fossa settica** septic tank
fossato *m* ditch; moat
fossétta *f* dimple
fòssile *adj* & *m* fossil
fossilizzare [ddzz] *tr* to fossilize ‖ *ref* to become fossilized
fòsso *m* ditch; moat
fò·to *f* **(-to)** photo
fotocòpia *f* photocopy
fotocopiare §287 **(fotocòpio)** *tr* to photocopy
fotoelèttri·co -ca (-ci -che) *adj* photoelectric ‖ *f* (mil) searchlight
fotogèni·co -ca *adj* **(-ci -che)** photogenic
fotogiornale *m* pictorial magazine
fotografare (fotògrafo) *tr* to photograph
fotografìa *f* photography; photograph
fotogràfi·co -ca *adj* **(-ci -che)** photographic
fotògrafo *m* photographer
fotogram·ma *m* **(-mi)** (phot) frame
fotoincisióne *f* photoengraving
fotolampo *m* flashlight
fotòmetro *m* exposure meter
fotomontàg·gio *m* **(-gi)** photomontage
fototubo *m* phototube
fra *m invar* brother, e.g., **fra Cristoforo** Brother Christopher ‖ *prep* among; between; in, within
frac *m* **(frac)** swallow-tailed coat
fracassare *tr* to crash, smash ‖ *ref* to crash
fracasso *m* crash; uproar; (coll) slew
fràdi·cio -cia (-ci -cie) *adj* rotten; soaked ‖ *m* rotten part; decay; wet ground
fràgile *adj* fragile; brittle; frail
fragilità *f* fragility, frailty
fràgola *f* strawberry
fragóre *m* din; peal; roar
fragoró·so -sa [s] *adj* noisy
fragrante *adj* fragrant
fraintèndere §270 *tr* to misunderstand
frammassóne *m* Freemason
frammassonerìa *f* Freemasonry
frammentare (frammménto) *tr* to fragment
frammentà·rio -ria *adj* **(-ri -rie)** fragmentary
framménto *m* fragment
framméttere §198 *tr* to interpose ‖ *ref* to meddle; **frammettersi in** to intrude in, to butt into
frammèzzo [ddzz] *adv* in the middle ‖ *prep* in the midst of
frammischiare §287 *tr* to mix ‖ *ref* to concern oneself
frana *f* landslide; (fig) collapse
franare *intr* to slide; to collapse
francesca·no -na *adj* & *mf* Franciscan
francé·sco -sca (-schi -sche) *adj* (archaic) French ‖ **Francesco** *m* Francis ‖ **Francesca** *f* Frances
francése *adj* French ‖ *m* French (*language*); Frenchman (*person*); **i francesi** the French ‖ *f* Frenchwoman
francesismo *m* gallicism
francesizzare [ddzz] *tr* to Frenchify
franchézza *f* frankness
franchì·gia *f* **(-gie)** franchise; exemption; deductible insurance; (naut) shore leave; **franchigia postale** franking privilege
Frància, la France
fran·co -ca (-chi -che) *adj* free; frank; Frankish; **farla franca** to get off scot free; **franco di porto** prepaid, postpaid; **franco domicilio** home delivery, free delivery ‖ *m* franc ‖ **Franco** *m* Frank
francobóllo *m* postage stamp, stamp
frangènte *m* breaker, surf; **essere nei frangenti** to be in bad straits
fràngere §179 *tr* to crush; (lit) to break ‖ *ref* to break, comb (*said of waves*)
frangétta *f* bangs
fràn·gia *f* **(-ge)** fringe; embellishment; shoreline; bangs; **frangia di corallo** coral reef
frangìbile *adj* breakable
frangiflut·ti *m* **(-ti)** breakwater
frangi·vènto *m* **(-vènto)** windbreak
frangizòl·le *m* **(-le)** disc harrow
Frankfur·ter *m* **(-ter)** hot dog
fran·tóio *m* **(-tói)** crusher; **frantoio a mascelle** jawbreaker
frantumare *tr* to crush; to break to pieces ‖ *ref* to be crushed; to go to pieces
frantume *m* fragment; **andare in frantumi** to go to pieces
frappé *m* **(frappé)** shake; frappé; **frappé alla menta** mint julep; **frappé di latte** milk shake
frappórre §218 *tr* to interpose ‖ *ref* to interfere; to intervene
frasà·rio *m* **(-ri)** language, speech
fra·sca *f* **(-sche)** branch; bush; ornament; whim; frivolous woman, flirt
frase *f* sentence; (mus) phrase; **frase fatta** cliché; **frase idiomatica** idiom; **frasi** words; **frasi di commiserazione** condolences
fraseggiare §290 **(fraséggio)** *intr* to use phrasing; to use big words; (mus) to phrase
fraseologìa *f* phraseology
fràssino *m* ash tree
frastagliare §280 *tr* to cut out (*e.g., paper*)
frastaglia·to -ta *adj* indented, jagged; ornamented
frastornare (frastórno) *tr* to disturb; (lit) to prevent
frastuòno *m* din, roar
frate *m* friar, monk, brother
fratellanza *f* brotherhood
fratellastro *m* stepbrother; half brother
fratèllo *m* brother; **fratelli** brothers and sisters; **fratello consanguineo** half brother on the father's side; **fratello**

di latte foster brother; **fratello gemello** twin
fraterni·tà *f* (-tà) fraternity
fraternizzare [ddzz] *intr* to fraternize
fratèr·no -na *adj* fraternal, brotherly
fratrici·da (**-di -de**) *adj* fratricidal || *mf* fratricide
fratricì·dio *m* (**-di**) fratricide
fratta *f* brushwood; (coll) hedge
frattàglie *fpl* giblets, chitterlings, offal
frattanto *adv* meantime, meanwhile
frattèmpo *m*—**nel frattempo** meanwhile
frattura *f* fracture; break; breach
fratturare *tr & ref* to fracture, break
fraudolènto *adj* fraudulent
frazionare (**frazióno**) *tr* to fractionate; to break up
frazionà·rio -ria *adj* (**-ri -rie**) fractional
frazióne *f* fraction; hamlet; (eccl) breaking of the host
fréc·cia *f* (**-ce**) arrow, bolt; steeple, spire; clock (*on hosiery*); (archit) rise; (fig) aspersion; **freccia consensiva** arrow (*on traffic light*); **freccia direzionale** (aut) turn signal
frecciata *f* arrow shot; taunt, gibe; **dare una frecciata a** to hit for a loan
freddare (**fréddo**) *tr* to chill; to kill
freddézza *f* chill; cold, coldness; coolness, cold shoulder; sang-froid
fréd·do -da *adj* cold; cool, chilly; frigid || *m* cold, cold weather; chill; **a freddo** cold; cooly; **avere freddo** to be cold (*said of people*); **fare freddo** to be cold (*said of weather*); **freddo cane** biting cold; **sentire freddo** to feel cold; **sudare freddo** to be in a cold sweat
freddoló·so -sa [s] *adj* chilly (*person*)
freddura *f* joke, pun; cold weather
fredduri·sta *mf* (**-sti -ste**) punster
fregagióne *f* rubbing, rubdown, massage
fregare §209 (**frégo**) *tr* to rub; to strike (*a match*); (slang) to steal; (slang) to cheat, dupe; (vulg) to make love with || *ref* to rub (*e.g., one's hands*); **fregarsene di** (vulg) to not give a hoot about
fregata *f* rubbing; (nav) frigate; (orn) frigate bird; (slang) cheating
fregatura *f* (slang) cheating; (slang) hitch, halt
fregiare §290 (**frégio**) *tr* to decorate; to fret
fré·gio *m* (**-gi**) decoration; insignia (*on cap of officer*); (archit) frieze
fré·go *m* (**-ghi**) line, stroke
frégola *f* rut, heat; (slang) mania, craze
fremènte *adj* throbbing; thrilling
frèmere §123 *tr* (lit) to beg insistently || *intr* to throb; to be thrilled; to shake, tremble, rustle; to shudder (*with horror*); (fig) to boil; (fig) to fret
frèmito *m* throb; thrill; shudder; roar; quiver
frenare (**fréno**) *tr* to brake, stop; to bridle (*a horse*); to curb (*passions*); to restrain (*e.g., laughter*); **frenare la corsa** to slow down || *intr* to put the brakes on || *ref* to control oneself
frenatóre *m* (rr) brakeman
frenesìa *f* frenzy; (fig) craze, fever; (lit) thought
frenèti·co -ca *adj* (**-ci -che**) frenzied; frantic; crazy, enthusiastic
fréno *m* bit, bridle; brake; (fig) check; (mach) lock; **freno ad aria compressa** air brake; **mordere il freno** to champ the bit; **senza freno** wild, unbridled; **tenere a freno** to keep in check
frenologìa *f* phrenology
frequentare (**frequènto**) *tr* to frequent; to attend || *intr* to associate
frequenta·tóre -trice *mf* patron, customer; frequenter, habitué
frequènte *adj* frequent; rapid (*pulse*); (lit) crowded
frequènza *f* frequency; attendance; **frequenza ultraelevata** ultrahigh frequency
frèsa *f* milling cutter; burr (*of dentist's drill*)
fresatrice *f* milling machine
fresatura *f* (mach) milling
freschézza *f* freshness; coolness
fré·sco -sca (**-schi -sche**) *adj* fresh; cool; **fresco di malattia** just recovered; **fresco di stampa** fresh off the press; **fresco di studi** fresh out of school; **star fresco** to be in a fix; to be all wrong || *m* cool weather; tropical fabric; **di fresco** recently; **fare fresco** to be cool (*said of weather*); **mettere al fresco** (coll) to put in the clink; **per il fresco** in cool weather
frescó·ne -na *mf* (slang) dumbell
frescura *f* coolness, freshness
frétta *f* hurry, haste; **avere fretta** to be in a hurry; **in fretta** in a hurry; **in fretta e furia** in a rush
frettazzo *m* plasterer's wooden trowel; steel brush
frettoló·so -sa [s] *adj* hurried, hasty
freudismo *m* Freudianism
friàbile *adj* friable, crumbly
friabilità *f* friableness
fricassèa *f* fricassee
frìggere §180 *tr* to fry; **mandare qlcu a farsi friggere** to tell s.o. to go to the devil || *intr* to fry; to sizzle; to fret
friggitorìa *f* fried-food shop
frigidézza *f* frigidity
frigidi·tà *f* (**-tà**) coldness; frigidity
frìgi·do -da *adj* cold; frigid
frì·gio -gia *adj* (**-gi -gie**) Phrygian
frignare *intr* to whimper
frigorìfe·ro -ra *adj* refrigerating || *m* refrigerator; (journ) morgue
fringuèl·lo -la *mf* chaffinch, finch
frinire §176 *intr* to chirp
frisata *f* gunnel
frittata *f* omelet; **fare la frittata** (coll) to make a mess of it
frittèlla *f* fritter; pancake; (coll) grease spot
frit·to -ta *adj* fried; cooked, ruined || *m* fry, fried platter
frittura *f* frying; fry, fried platter
frivolézza *f* frivolity
frìvo·lo -la *adj* frivolous; flighty
frizionare (**frizióno**) *tr* to massage

frizióne *f* friction; massage; (aut) clutch
frizzante [ddzz] *adj* crisp, brisk (*weather*); sparkling (*wine*)
frizzare [ddzz] *intr* to tingle; to sparkle, fizz (*said of wine*); (fig) to sting
frizzo [ddzz] *m* jest, witticism; gibe, dig
frodare (**fròdo**) *tr* to cheat, swindle
fròde *f* fraud; **frode fiscale** tax evasion or fraud
fròdo *m invar* customs evasion; **di frodo** smuggled
frò·gia *f* (**-ge** or **-gie**) nostril (*of horse*)
fròl·lo -la *adj* high (*meat*); soft, tender; (fig) weak
frónda *f* branch, bough; political opposition; **fronde** foliage; ornaments
frondó·so -sa [s] *adj* leafy
frontale *adj* front; frontal
frónte *m* (mil, pol) front; **far fronte a** to face; to face up to; to meet (*expenses*); **tenere fronte a** to face, resist || *f* forehead, brow; countenance; title page; headline; (fig) face; **a fronte** opposite, facing; **a fronte di** (com) in reference to; **dietro front!** (mil) about face!; **di fronte a** in the face of; facing; **di fronte a tutti** in plain view; **fronte destr'!** (mil) right face!; **mettere a fronte** to compare; **tenere a fronte** to have in front of one's eyes
fronteggiare §290 (**frontéggio**) *tr* to face, front || *ref* to face one another
frontespì·zio *m* (**-zi**) title page
frontièra *f* border, frontier
frontóne *m* (archit) pediment; (archit) gable
frónzolo *m* bauble, gewgaw; **fronzoli** finery, frippery
fròtta *f* crowd; swarm; flock
fròttola *f* fib; popular poem; **frottole** humbug
frugale *adj* frugal (*meal; life*); temperate (*in eating or drinking*)
frugare §209 *tr* to rummage through; to search (*a person*) || *intr* to rummage, poke around
frùgo·lo -la *mf* restless child, imp
fruire §176 *tr* to enjoy || *intr*—**fruire di** to enjoy
fruitóre *m* user
frullare *tr* to beat, whip || *intr* to flutter; to spin; **frullare per il capo a** to get into the head of, e.g., **cosa gli è frullato per il capo?** what got into his head?
frulla·to -ta *adj* whipped || *m* shake (*drink*)
frullatóre *m* electric beater
frullino *m* egg beater
fruménto *m* wheat
frumentóne *m* corn
frusciare §128 *intr* to rustle
fruscì·o *m* (**-i**) rustle, rustling
frusta *f* whip; egg beater
frustare *tr* to whip, lash; (fig) to censure; (coll) to wear out (*clothes*)
frustata *f* lash; (fig) censure
frustino *m* whip, crop
fru·sto -sta *adj* worn out, threadbare || *f* see **frusta**
frustrare *tr* to frustrate, baffle; to discomfit
frut·ta *f* (**-ta** & **-te**) fruit; **essere alle frutta** to be at the end of the meal, to be having one's dessert
fruttare *tr* & *intr* to yield
fruttéto *m* orchard
frutticoltóre *m* fruit grower
fruttièra *f* fruit dish
fruttìfe·ro -ra *adj* fruit-bearing; fruitful, profitable; (lit) fecund
fruttificare §197 (**fruttìfico**) *intr* to fructify; to yield
fruttivéndo·lo -la *mf* fruit dealer
frutto *m* fruit; **frutti di mare** shellfish; **mettere a frutto** to make yield
fruttuó·so -sa [s] *adj* fruitful, profitable
fu *adj invar* late (*deceased*); son of the late . . . ; daughter of the late . . .
fucilare *tr* to shoot
fucilata *f* rifle shot
fucilazióne *f* execution by a firing squad
fucile *m* rifle, gun; **fucile ad aria compressa** air gun; **fucile da caccia** shotgun; **un buon fucile** a good shot
fucilerìa *f* fusillade
fucilière *m* rifleman
fucina *f* forge, smithy
fu·co *m* (**-chi**) (bot) rockweed; (zool) drone
fùcsia *f* fuchsia
fu·ga *f* (**-ghe**) flight; leak; row (*e.g., of rooms*); spurt (*in bicycle race*); (mus) fugue; **di fuga** hastily; **prendere la fuga** to take flight; **volgere in fuga** to put to flight; to take flight
fugace *adj* passing, fleeting
fugare §209 *tr* (lit) to avoid; (lit) to put to flight; (lit) to dispel
fuggènte *adj* passing, fleeting
fuggévole *adj* fleeting
fuggia·sco -sca (**-schi -sche**) *adj* fleeing, fugitive || *mf* fugitive; refugee
fuggi fug·gi *m* (**-gi**) stampede
fuggire *tr* to flee; to avoid || *intr* (ESSERE) to flee, run away; (sports) to take the lead; **fuggire a** to flee from
fuggiti·vo -va *adj* & *mf* fugitive
fulcro *m* fulcrum; (fig) pivot
fulgènte *adj* (lit) resplendent
fùlgi·do -da *adj* resplendent
fulgóre *m* resplendency, radiance
fuliggine *f* soot
fuligginó·so -sa [s] *adj* sooty
fulmicotóne *m* guncotton
fulminante *adj* crushing (*illness*); withering (*look*); explosive || *m* exploding cap; (coll) match
fulminare (**fùlmino**) *tr* to strike by lightning; to strike down; to confound, dumfound || *ref* (elec) to burn out, to blow out || *impers* (ESSERE)—**fulmina** it is lightning
fùlmine *m* lightning, thunderbolt; **fulmine a ciel sereno** bolt out of the blue
fulmìne·o -a *adj* swift, instant
ful·vo -va *adj* tawny
fumaiòlo *m* chimney; smokestack; (naut) funnel

fumante *adj* smoking; steaming; dusty
fumare *tr* to smoke; (lit) to exhale || *intr* to smoke; to steam; to fume; **fumare come un turco** to smoke like a chimney
fumata *f* smoking; smoke signal; **fare una fumata** to have a smoke
fuma·tóre -trice *mf* smoker
fumetti·sta *mf* (**-sti -ste**) cartoonist
fumétto *m* cartoon; **fumetti** comics
fumigare §209 (**fùmigo**) *tr* (obs) to fumigate || *intr* to steam, smoke
fumigazióne *f* fumigation
fumi·sta *m* (**-sti**) heater man; joker, hoaxer
fumisterìa *f* fondness for practical jokes; bamboozling
fumo *m* smoke; vapor, steam; smoking; (coll) hot air; **andare in fumo** to go up in smoke; **fumi** vapors, fumes; **mandare in fumo** to squander; to thwart; **sapere di fumo** to taste smoky; **vedere qlcu come il fumo negli occhi** to not be able to stand s.o.; **vender fumo** to peddle influence
fumòge·no -na *adj* smoke, e.g., **cortina fumogena** smoke curtain
fumó·so -sa [s] *adj* smoky; obscure
funambolismo *m* tightrope walking; (fig) acrobatics
funàmbo·lo -la *mf* tightrope walker; (fig) acrobat
fune *f* rope, cable; **fune portante** suspension cable
fùnebre *adj* funeral; funereal, gloomy
funerale *adj & m* funeral
funerà·rio -ria *adj* (**-ri -rie**) funeral
funère·o -a *adj* funereal; funeral
funestare (**funèsto**) *tr* to afflict
funè·sto -sta *adj* baleful; mournful
fungàia *f* mushroom farm; mushroom bed; flock, swarm
fùngere §183 *intr*—**fungere da** to act as
fun·go *m* (**-ghi**) mushroom; fungus; **fungo atomico** mushroom cloud; **venir su come i funghi** to mushroom
fungó·so -sa [s] *adj* fungous
funicolare *adj* cable, cable-driven || *f* funicular railway
funivìa *f* cableway
funzionale *adj* functional
funzionalità *f* functionalism
funzionaménto *m* working order; functioning
funzionare (**funzióno**) *intr* to work; to function; **funzionare da** to act as
funzionà·rio -ria *mf* (**-ri -rie**) functionary, official; public official
funzióne *f* function; office; duty; (eccl) service; **facente funzione** acting; **mettere in funzione** to make (*s.th*) work
fuò·co *m* (**-chi**) fire; burner (*of gas range*); focus; (fig) home; (lit) thunderbolt; **al fuoco!** fire! (*warning*); **andare per il fuoco** (culin) to boil over; **cuocere a fuoco lento** (culin) to simmer; **dar fuoco a** to set fire to; **di fuoco** fiery; blushing; **far fuoco** to fire; **fuochi artificiali** fireworks; **fuoco di fila** enfilade; **fuoco!** (mil) fire!; **fuoco di paglia** (fig) flash in the pan; **fuoco di segnalazione** flare; **fuoco fatuo** will-o'-the-wisp; **fuoco incrociato** cross fire; **fuoco nutrito** drumfire; **mettere a fuoco** to focus; **mettere una mano sul fuoco** to be absolutely sure, to swear by it
fuorché *prep* except; **fuorché di** except to
fuòri *adv* outside, out; aside; e.g., **lasciar fuori** to leave aside; **andar di fuori** (culin) to boil over; **dar fuori** to do away with; to squander; **di fuori** outside; **far fuori** to publish; **fuori di** out of; outside of; beyond (*a doubt*); off (*the road*); beside (*oneself*); **fuori d'uso** out of style; obsolete; **il di fuori** the outside; **in fuori** protruding; forward; **mettere fuori** to throw out; to spread; to exhibit || *prep* beyond; out of; outside; **fuori commercio** not for sale; **fuori concorso** in a class by itself (himself, etc.); **fuori luogo** untimely, out of place; **fuori (di) mano** far away; solitary; **fuori testo** inserted, tipped in
fuoribór·do *m* (**-do**) outboard; outboard motor
fuoricombattimén·to (**-to**) *adj* knocked out || *m* knockout
fuorigiò·co *m* (**-co**) (sports) offside
fuorilég·ge *mf* (**-ge**) outlaw
fuorisè·rie (**-rie**) *adj* custom-built || *m & f* custom model || *f* custom-built car
fuoristra·da *m* (**-da**) land rover
fuoriusci·to -ta *adj* exiled || *mf* political exile || *f* leak; flow; protrusion
fuorvia·to -ta *adj* mislead, misguided
furbacchió·ne -na *mf* slippery person
furberìa *f* slyness, cunning
fur·bo -ba *adj* sly, cunning || *mf* knave; **furbo di tre cotte** slicker
furènte *adj* furious
furerìa *f* (mil) company headquarters
furétto *m* ferret
furfante *m* sharper, scoundrel
furfanterìa *f* rascality
furgoncino *m* small delivery van
furgóne *m* truck; patrol wagon; hearse; **furgone cellulare** prison van
furgoni·sta *mf* (**-sti -ste**) truck driver, teamster
fùria *f* fury; strength, violence; hurry; **a furia di** by dint of; **con furia** in a hurry; **far furia a** to urge; **montare in furia** to go berserk; to fly off the handle
furibón·do -da *adj* furious, wild
furière *m* soldier attached to company headquarters
furió·so -sa [s] *adj* furious; fierce; mad
furóre *m* furor, frenzy; violence; longing; **far furore** to be a hit, to be all the rage
furoreggiare §290 (**furoréggio**) *intr* to be a hit, be all the rage
furti·vo -va *adj* stealthy; furtive; stolen (*e.g., goods*)
furto *m* theft; stolen goods; **di furto** stealthily; **furto con scasso** burglary
fusa [s] *fpl*—**fare le fusa** to purr
fuscèllo *m* twig
fusciac·ca *f* (**-che**) sash (*around the waist*)

fusèllo [s] *m* spindle; axle, shaft

fusìbile *adj* fusible || *m* (elec) fuse

fusióne *f* fusion; melting; merger; blending (*of colors*)

fu·so -sa *adj* melted; molten

fuso [s] *m* spindle; shank (*of anchor*); shaft (*of column*); (aut) axle; **fuso orario** time zone

fusolièra *f* (aer) fuselage

fustagno *m* fustian

fustàia *f* adult forest, full-grown forest

fustèlla *f* (perforating) punch; (pharm) price stub

fustigare §209 (**fùstigo**) *tr* to whip

fusto *m* trunk (*of tree*); stalk; stem (*of key*); beam (*of balance*); butt (*of gun*); trunk, body; frame (*of armchair*); tank (*for holding liquids*); drum (*metal receptacle*); holding stick (*of umbrella*); shaft (*of column*); **d'alto fusto** full-grown (*tree*)

fùtile *adj* futile, trifling

futilità *f* futility

futurismo *m* futurism

futuri·sta *mf* (**-sti -ste**) futurist

futu·ro -ra *adj* & *m* future

G

G, g [dʒi] *m* & *f* seventh letter of the Italian alphabet

gabardi·ne *f* (**-ne**) gabardine; gabardine raincoat or topcoat

gabbamón·do *m* (**-do**) cheat, sharper

gabbanèlla *f* gown (*of physician or patient*); robe

gabbano *m* cloak; frock; **mutare gabbano** to be a turncoat

gabbare *tr* to dupe, cheat || *ref*—**gabbarsi di** to make fun of

gàbbia *f* cage; ox muzzle; dock (*in courtroom*); (mach) housing; (naut) top; (naut) topsail; **gabbia d'imballaggio** crate; **gabbia toracica** rib cage

gabbiano *m* sea gull

gabbo *m*—**farsi gabbo di** to make fun of; **prendere a gabbo** to make light of

gabèlla *f* (obs) customs, duty

gabellare (**gabèllo**) *tr* to palm off; to swallow (*e.g., a tall story*); (obs) to tax

gabinétto *m* office (*of doctor, dentist, lawyer*); cabinet; chamber (*of judge*); toilet; closet; laboratory; **gabinetto da bagno** bathroom; **gabinetto di decenza** toilet, bathroom

ga·gà *m* (**gà**) fop, dandy; lounge lizard

gaggìa *f* acacia

gagliardétto *m* pennon; pennant

gagliardìa *f* (lit) vigor; (lit) prowess

gagliar·do -da *adj* vigorous; stalwart; hearty (*e.g., voice*)

gagliòf·fo -fa *adj* loutish; rascal || *mf* lout; rascal

gaiézza *f* gaiety, vivacity

gàio gàia *adj* (**gài gàie**) gay, vivacious

gala *m* & *f* gala; gala affair; **di gala** formal; **mettersi in gala** to dress up || *f* frill; bow tie (*for formal attire*); (naut) bunting

galalite *f* casein plastic, galalith

galante *adj* gallant, courtly; amorous; pretty, graceful

galanterìa *f* gallantry, courtliness

galantuò·mo *m* (**-mini**) honest man; (coll) my good fellow

galàssia *f* galaxy

galatèo *m* good manners

galèna *f* (min) galena

galeóne *m* galleon

galeòt·to -ta *adj* (archaic) intermediary (*in love affairs*) || *m* galley slave; convict; (archaic) procurer

galèra *f* galley; forced labor

gali·lèo -lèa (**-lèi -lèe**) *adj* & *m* Galilean

galla *f* (bot) gall; (pathol) blister; **a galla** afloat; **tenersi a galla** (fig) to keep alive; to manage; **venire a galla** to come to the surface

galleggiante *adj* floating || *m* float

galleggiare §290 (**galléggio**) *intr* to float

gallerìa *f* tunnel; gallery; balcony; mall, arcade; wind tunnel

Galles, il Wales

gallése [s] *adj* Welsh || *m* Welshman; Welsh (*language*) || *f* Welsh woman

gallétta *f* cracker; hardtack; (naut) ball on top of flagpole

gallétto *m* cockerel; (fig) gallant; (fig) whippersnapper; (mach) wing nut; **fare il galletto** to swagger

gàlli·co -ca *adj* & *m* (**-ci -che**) Gallic

gallina *f* hen; **gallina faraona** guinea fowl

gal·lo -la *adj* Gallic; (sports) Bantam (*weight*) || *m* rooster, cock; weathercock; Gaul; Gallic (*language*); **fare il gallo** to strut; **gallo cedrone** wood grouse; **gallo d'India** turkey

gallòc·cia *f* (**-ce**) (naut) cleat

gallóne *m* braid; stripe; chevron; gallon

galoppare (**galòppo**) *intr* to gallop; (fig) to rush around

galoppata *f* gallop

galoppa·tóio *m* (**-tói**) bridle path

galoppino *m* errand boy; **galoppino elettorale** ward heeler

galòppo *m* gallop; **andare al piccolo galoppo** to canter; **di gran galoppo** at full speed; **piccolo galoppo** canter

galò·scia *f* (**-sce**) overshoe, rubber

galvanizzare [ddzz] *tr* to electroplate; (fig) to galvanize

galvanoplàsti·ca *f* (**-che**) electroplating

gamba *f* leg; stem; (aer) shock strut; **a gambe all'aria** upside down; **a gambe levate** at top speed; upside down; **darsela a gambe** to take to one's heels; **essere in gamba** to be in good shape; to be on the ball; **essere male in gamba** to be in bad shape; **gamba di legno** peg leg; **gambe a ciambella** bowlegs; **le gambe mi fanno giacomo** my knees shake;

prendere qlcu sotto gamba to make light of s.o.; raddrizzare le gambe ai cani to try the impossible
gambale *m* legging, gaiter; boot last; leg (*of boot*)
gamberétto *m* shrimp
gàmbero *m* (*Astacus, Cambarus*) crawfish
gambétto *m* stumble; trip; (chess) gambit
gambo *m* stem
gamèlla *f* (mil) mess kit, mess tin
gamma *f* gamut; range; **gamma d'onda** (rad) wave band
ganà•scia *f* (**-sce**) jaw; (aut) brake shoe; **mangiare a quattro ganasce** to eat like a horse
gàn•cio *m* (**-ci**) hook; clasp; hanger
gan•ga *f* (**-ghe**) gang; (min) gangue
gànghero *m* hinge; clasp; **uscire dai gangheri** to fly off the handle
gàn•glio *m* (**-gli**) ganglion
ganzo [dz] *m* (slang) lover; (coll) slicker
gara *f* competition, match; **fare a gara** to compete; **gara d'appalto** competitive bidding
garagi•sta *m* (**-sti**) garage man
garante *adj* responsible || *m* guarantor; **farsi garante per** to vouch for
garantire §176 *tr* to guarantee; to secure (*a mortgage*)
garanti•to -ta *adj* guaranteed, warranted; downright, absolute (*liar*)
garanzìa *f* guarantee, warranty; insurance, assurance
garbare *tr* (naut) to shape (*a hull*) || *intr* (ESSERE) (with *dat*) to like, e.g., **non gli garbano le Sue parole** he does not like your words
garbatézza *f* politeness, courtesy
garba•to -ta *adj* polite, courteous
garbo *m* politeness, good manners; gesture; act; shape (*of a hull*); good cut (*of clothes*); elegance (*in painting or writing*); **a garbo** correctly
garbù•glio *m* (**-gli**) tangle, confusion; mess
gardènia *f* gardenia
gareggiare §290 (**garéggio**) *intr* to compete, vie
garétta *f* var of **garitta**
garétto *m* var of **garretto**
garganèlla *f*—**bere a garganella** to gulp down
gargarismo *m* gargling; gargle
gargarizzare [ddzz] *intr & ref* to gargle
gargaròzzo *m* throat, gullet
garitta *f* railroad-crossing box; (mil) sentry box; (rr) brakeman's box
garòfano *m* carnation, pink
garrése [s] *m* withers
garrétto *m* ankle (*of man*); hock (*of horse*)
garrire §176 *intr* to chirp, twitter; to flap; (archaic) to quarrel
garrito *m* chirp, twitter
garròtta *f* garrote
gàrru•lo -la *adj* garrulous
garza [dz] *f* gauze
garzonato [dz] *m* apprenticeship
garzó•ne -na [dz] *mf* helper || *m* helper, boy; apprentice; (archaic) bachelor; **garzone di stalla** stablebo[y]
gas *m* (**gas**) gas; gasoline; **gas asfissiante** poison gas; **gas delle miniere** firedamp; **gas esilarante** laughing gas; **gas illuminante** illuminating gas; **gas lacrimogeno** tear gas
gasdótto *m* gas pipeline
gasificare §197 (**gasìfico**) *tr* var of **gassificare**
gasòlio *m* Diesel oil
gasòmetro *m* var of **gassometro**
gassificare §197 (**gassìfico**) *tr* to gasify
gassi•sta *m* (**-sti**) gasworker; gas fitter; gas-meter reader
gassòmetro *m* gasholder, gas tank
gassó•so -sa [s] *adj* gaseous, gassy || *f* soda, pop
gastronomìa *f* gastronomy
gatta *f* she-cat, tabby; **comprare la gatta nel sacco** to buy a pig in a poke; **gatta ci cova** something is rotten in Denmark; **pigliare una gatta da pelare** to take on a heavy burden, to get a tiger by the tail
gattabùia *f* (coll) clink, lockup
gattamòrta *f* (**gattemòrte**) hypocrite
gattino *m* kitten; (bot) catkin
gat•to -ta *mf* cat || *m* tomcat; tamper pile driver; **gatto a nove code** cat o'-nine-tails; **gatto soriano** tortoise-shell cat; **quattro gatti** a handful of people || *f* see **gatta**
gattóni *adv* on all fours
gattopardo *m* (zool) serval; **gattopardo americano** ocelot
gattùc•cio *m* (**-ci**) compass saw; (ichth) small dotted dogfish
gaudènte *adj* jovial || *m* bon vivant
gàu•dio *m* (**-di**) joy, happiness
gavazzare *intr* (lit) to revel
gavétta *f* mess kit, mess gear; **venire dalla gavetta** to come up through the ranks
gavitèllo *m* buoy
gazza [ddzz] *f* magpie
gazzarra [ddzz] *f* racket, uproar
gazzèlla [ddzz] *f* gazelle
gazzétta [ddzz] *f* newspaper; gazette; newsmonger, gossip; **Gazzetta Ufficiale** Official Gazette (*in Italy*); Congressional Record (*U.S.A.*)
gazzettino [ddzz] *m* small newspaper; column, e.g., **gazzettino rosa** social column; newsmonger, gossip
gazzósa [ddzz] *f* var of **gassosa**
gèl *m* gel
gelare (**gèlo**) *tr* to freeze; to nip || *intr* (ESSERE) & *ref* to freeze || *imper* (ESSERE & AVERE)—**gela** it is freezin[g]
gelata *f* frost
gela•tàio -tàia *mf* (**-tài -tàie**) ice-cream dealer
gelaterìa *f* ice-cream parlor
gelatièra *f* ice-cream freezer
gelatière *m* ice-cream dealer
gelatina *f* gelatin; jelly; **gelatina di frutta** fruit jelly; gum drop
gelatinizzare [ddzz] *tr & ref* to gelatinize; to jell
gela•to -ta *adj* frozen || *m* ice cream

gelato da passeggio ice cream on a stick, popsicle
gèli·do -da *adj* icy, ice-cold
gèlo *m* frost; ice; cold; **diventare di gelo** to remain dumfounded; **farsi di gelo** to be cold or aloof; **sentirsi il gelo addosso** to get a chill
gelóne *m* chilblain
gelosìa [s] *f* jealousy; great care; shutter
geló·so -sa [s] *adj* jealous; solicitous
gèlso *m* mulberry
gelsomino *m* jasmine
gemebón·do -da *adj* (lit) moaning
gemellàggio *m* sisterhood (*of two cities*)
gemèl·lo -la *adj* twin; sister (*ship*) || *mf* twin || **gemelli** *mpl* cufflinks || **Gemelli** *mpl* (astr) Gemini
gèmere §123 *tr* (lit) to lament || *intr* (ESSERE & AVERE) to moan, groan; to suffer; to squeak (*said of a wheel*); to ooze; to coo (*said of a dove*)
gèmito *m* moan; howl (*of wind*)
gèmma *f* gem; (bot) bud
gemma·to -ta *adj* gemmate; jeweled
gendarme *m* gendarme, policeman
genealogìa *f* genealogy
generalato *m* generalship
generale *adj* general || *m* general; **generale d'armata** (mil) general; **generale di brigata** brigadier general; **generale di corpo d'armata** lieutenant general; **generale di divisione** major general || *f* (mil) assembly; **stare sulle generali** to speak in vague generalities
generali·tà *f* (-tà) generality; majority; **generalità** *fpl* personal data
generalizzare [ddzz] *tr* to generalize; to bring into general use || *intr* to generalize, deal in generalities
generare (**gènero**) *tr* to beget; to generate || *ref* to occur
genera·tóre -trice *adj* generating || *m* generator || *f* generatrix
generazióne *f* generation
gènere *m* genus; kind, type; genre; (gram) gender; **del genere** similar, alike; **farne di ogni genere** to commit all sorts of mischief; **genere umano** mankind; **generi alimentari** foodstuffs; **generi diversi** sundries, assorted articles; **in genere** generally
genèri·co -ca (**-ci -che**) *adj* generic; vague; all-round; general (*e.g., practitioner*) || *mf* (theat) actor playing bit parts || *m* vagueness, imprecision
gènero *m* son-in-law
generosi·tà [s] *f* (-tà) generosity
generó·so -sa [s] *adj* generous; rich (*wine*)
gène·si *f* (**-si**) genesis || **il Genesi** Genesis
genèti·co -ca (**-ci -che**) *adj* genetic(al) || *f* genetics
genetlìa·co -ca (**-ci -che**) *adj* birth || *m* birthday
gengiva *f* (anat) gum
genìa *f* set, gang; (lit) breed
geniale *adj* clever; genial; inspired, genius-like
geniali·tà *f* (-tà) cleverness, ingeniousness; genius; (lit) geniality
genière *m* (mil) engineer
gè·nio *m* (**-ni**) genius; (mil) corps of engineers; **andare a genio** (with *dat*) to like, e.g., **la musica moderna non gli va a genio** he does not like modern music; **fare qlco di genio** to do s.th willingly
genitale *adj* genital || **genitali** *mpl* genitals
geniti·vo -va *adj & m* genitive
geni·tóre -trice *mf* parent
gen·nàio *m* (**-nài**) January
genocìdio *m* genocide
Gènova *f* Genoa
genovése [s] *adj & mf* Genoese
gentàglia *f* riffraff, rabble, scum
gènte *adj* (archaic) gentle || *f* people; nation; family; (nav) crew; **gente d'arme** soldiers; **gente di mal affare** riffraff; **gente di mare** sailors
gentildònna *f* gentlewoman
gentile *adj* gentle; nice; genteel || **Gentili** *mpl* heathen
gentilézza *f* gentleness; kindness; **per gentilezza** kindly, please
gentilì·zio -zia *adj* (**-zi -zie**) of noble family; (lit) ancestral
gentiluò·mo *m* (**-mini**) gentleman, nobleman
genuflèttere §177 *ref* to kneel down
genui·no -na *adj* genuine
genziana *f* gentian
geofisi·co -ca (**-ci -che**) *adj* geophysical || *f* geophysics
geografìa *f* geography
geogràfi·co -ca *adj* (**-ci -che**) geographic(al)
geògra·fo -fa *mf* geographer
geologìa *f* geology
geòlo·go -ga *mf* (**-gi -ghe**) geologist
geòme·tra *m* (**-tri**) geometrician; land surveyor
geometrìa *f* geometry
gerà·nio *m* (**-ni**) geranium
gerar·ca *m* (**-chi**) leader
gerarchìa *f* hierarchy
geràrchi·co -ca *adj* (**-ci -che**) hierarchical; **per via gerarchica** through proper channels
Geremìa *f* Jeremiah
geremìade *f* jeremiad
gerènte *m* manager, director; **gerente responsabile** (journ) managing editor
gèr·go *m* (**-ghi**) jargon
geriatrìa *f* geriatrics
Gèrico *f* Jericho
gèrla *f* pannier (*carried on the back*)
Germània, la Germany
germàni·co -ca *adj* (**-ci -che**) Germanic
germànio *m* germanium
germanizzare [ddzz] *tr* to Germanize
germa·no -na *adj* german, e.g., **fratello germano** brother-german; Germanic || *m* (lit) brother-german; **germano nero** (orn) coot; **germano reale** (orn) mallard
gèrme *m* germ; (lit) offspring
germici·da (**-di**) *adj* germicidal || *m* germicide

germinare (**gèrmino**) *intr* (ESSERE & AVERE) to germinate
germogliare §280 (**germóglio**) *tr* to put forth || *intr* (ESSERE & AVERE) to bud, sprout
germó·glio *m* (**-gli**) bud, sprout
geroglìfi·co -ca *adj* & *m* (**-ci -che**) hieroglyphic
Geròlamo *m* Jerome
gerontocò·mio *m* (**-mi**) or **gerotrò·fio** *m* (**-fi**) old people's home, nursing home
gerùn·dio *m* (**-di**) gerund
Gerusalèmme *f* Jerusalem
gessare (**gèsso**) *tr* to plaster; to lime (*a field*)
gèsso *m* gypsum; plaster; chalk; (sculp) plaster cast
gessó·so -sa [s] *adj* plastery, chalky; chalklike
gèsta *f* (archaic) army; **gesta** *fpl* deeds, exploits
gestante *f* pregnant woman
gestazióne *f* gestation
gesticolare (**gestìcolo**) *intr* to gesticulate
gestióne *f* management, operation; data processing
gestire §176 *tr* to manage, operate || *intr* to gesticulate; (theat) to make gestures
gèsto *m* gesture; attitude; act, deed
ge·stóre -strice *mf* manager, operator; **gestore di stazione** (rr) station agent
gestualità *f* bodily movements (*e.g., of an actor*)
Gesù *m* Jesus; **Gesù Cristo** Jesus Christ
gesui·ta *m* (**-ti**) Jesuit
gesuìti·co -ca *adj* (**-ci -che**) Jesuitic(al)
gettare (**gètto**) *tr* to throw; to cast; to pour; to lay (*e.g., a floor*); to send forth; to yield; to broadcast (*seed*); to risk (*one's life*); **gettare la colpa addosso a qlcu** to lay the blame on s.o.; **gettare le armi** to lay down one's arms; **gettar giù** to fell, knock down; **gettar sangue** to bleed || *ref* to throw oneself; to plunge; to flow, empty (*said of a river*)
gettata *f* pour, pouring; jetty; shoot, sprout; cast; range (*of a gun*); **gettata cardiaca** (med) rate of flow of blood
gèttito *m* yield; waste; **far gettito di** to waste
gètto *m* throw; gush; shoot, sprout; cast; precast concrete slab; (aer) jet; **a getto** (aer) jet; **a getto continuo** continuously; **di getto** spontaneously; **far getto di** to waste; **primo getto** first draft
gettonare (**gettóno**) *tr* (coll) to call up from a pay station; (coll) to make the selection of (*a record in a juke-box*)
gettóne *m* counter, token; attendance fee; (cards) chip
gettopropulsióne *f* jet propulsion
ghepardo *m* cheetah
ghép·pio *m* (**-pi**) kestrel
gherì·glio *m* (**-gli**) kernel, meat (*of nut*)
gherlino *m* (naut) warp, line
gherminèlla *f* trick, sleight of hand; trickery
ghermire §176 *tr* to claw; to seize
gheróne *m* gusset
ghétta *f* gaiter; **ghette** spats
ghétto *m* ghetto
ghiacciàia *f* icebox, cooler
ghiac·ciàio *m* (**-ciài**) glacier; **ghiacciaio continentale** polar cap
ghiacciare §128 *tr* to freeze || *intr* (ESSERE) to freeze || *impers* (ESSERE) —**ghiaccia** it is freezing
ghiaccia·to -ta *adj* iced; ice-cold; frozen || *f* flavored crushed ice
ghiàc·cio -cia (**-ci -ce**) *adj* icy, ice-cold || *m* ice; **ghiaccio secco** dry ice
ghiacciò·lo -la *adj* crumbly, breakable || *m* icicle; popsicle
ghiàia *f* gravel, crushed stone
ghianda *f* fringe (*on a curtain*); (bot) acorn; **ghiande** mast (*for swine*)
ghiandàia *f* (orn) jay
ghiàndola *f* gland
ghibelli·no -na *adj* & *m* Ghibelline
ghièra *f* ferrule; ring
ghigliottina *f* guillotine; **a ghigliottina** sash (*window*)
ghigliottinare *tr* to guillotine
ghigna *f* (coll) grimace
ghignare *intr* to grimace; to sneer
ghigno *m* sneer, smirk; grin
ghinèa *f* guinea
ghìngheri *m invar*—**in ghingheri** dressed up
ghiót·to -ta *adj* fond; gluttonous; eager; dainty (*food*) || *f* (culin) dripping pan
ghiottó·ne -na *mf* glutton; (zool) glutton, wolverine
ghiottonerìa *f* gluttony; tidbit; (fig) rarity
ghiòzzo [ddzz] *m* dolt; (ichth) gudgeon
ghirba *f* jar; (coll) skin, life
ghiribizzo [ddzz] *m* (coll) whim, caprice
ghirigòro *m* doodle, curlicue
ghirlanda *f* garland, wreath
ghiro *m* dormouse; **dormire come un ghiro** to sleep like a log
ghisa *f* cast iron
già *adv* already; once upon a time; formerly || *interj* indeed!
giac·ca *f* (**-che**) jacket, coat; **giacca a due petti** double-breasted coat; **giacca a vento** windbreaker
giacché *conj* since
giacènte *adj* lying; idle (*capital*); unclaimed (*letter*); in abeyance
giacènza *f* lying; stay, abeyance; **giacenze di capitali** idle capital; **giacenze di magazzino** unsold stock of merchandise
giacére §181 *intr* (ESSERE) to lie; to be in abeyance; (lit) to be prostrate
giacì·glio *m* (**-gli**) pallet, cot
giaciménto *m* field, bed; **giacimento petrolifero** oil field
giacinto *m* hyacinth
Giàcomo *m* James
giaculatòria *f* ejaculation (*prayer*); litany (*monotonous account*); curse
giada *f* jade
giaggiòlo *m* (bot) iris

giaguaro *m* jaguar
giaiétto *m* jet (*black coal*)
gialappa *f* (pharm) jalap
gialla·stro -stra *adj* yellowish
gial·lo -la *adj* yellow; detective (*book or picture*); white (*with fear*) || *m* yellow; detective story, whodunit; suspense movie; **giallo dell'uovo** egg yolk
giamaica·no -na *adj & mf* Jamaican
giàmbi·co -ca *adj* (**-ci -che**) iambic
giambo *m* iamb
giammài *adv* never
giansenismo *m* Jansenism
Giappóne, il Japan
giapponése [s] *adj & mf* Japanese
giara *f* crock, jar
giardinàg·gio *m* (**-gi**) gardening
giardinétta *f* station wagon
giardiniè·re -ra *mf* gardener || *f* jardiniere; mixed pickles; mixed salad; wagonette; station wagon
giardino *m* garden; **giardino d'infanzia** kindergarten; **giardino pensile** roof garden; **giardino zoologico** zoological garden
giarrettièra *f* garter
Giasóne *m* Jason
giavanése [s] *adj & mf* Javanese
giavellòtto *m* javelin
gibbó·so -sa [s] *adj* gibbous, humped; humpbacked; rough (*ground*)
gibèrna *f* cartridge box; cartridge belt
gi·bus *m* (**-bus**) opera hat
gi·ga *f* (**-ghe**) gigue, jig
gigante *adj & m* giant
gigantè·sco -sca *adj* (**-schi -sche**) gigantic
gigantéssa *f* giantess
gigióne *m* ham actor
gì·glio *m* (**-gli**) Madonna lily; fleur-de-lys
gilda *f* guild
gi·lè *f* (**-lè**) vest, waistcoat
gimnòto *m* electric eel
ginecologìa *f* gynecology
ginecòlo·go -ga *mf* (**-gi -ghe**) gynecologist
gine·pràio *m* (**-pràì**) juniper thicket; (fig) mess
ginépro *m* juniper
ginèstra *f* (bot) Spanish broom
Ginèvra *f* Geneva
ginevri·no -na *adj & mf* Genevan
gingillare *ref* to trifle; to idle
gingillo *m* trifle, bauble
ginnà·sio *m* (**-si**) secondary school; gymnasium
ginna·sta *mf* (**-sti -ste**) gymnast
ginnàsti·co -ca (**-ci -che**) *adj* gymnastic || *f* gymnastics; **ginnastica a corpo libero** or **ginnastica da camera** calisthenics
gìnni·co -ca *adj* (**-ci -che**) gymnastic
ginocchiata *f* blow with the knee; blow on the knee
ginocchièra *f* kneepad; elastic bandage (*for knee*); kneepiece (*of armor*)
ginòc·chio *m* (**-chi**) knee; **avere il ginocchio valgo** to be bowlegged; **avere il ginocchio varo** to be knock-kneed; **in ginocchio** on one's knees || *m* (**-chia** *fpl*) knee; **fino alle ginocchia** knee-deep; **gettarsi alle ginocchia di** to go down on one's knees to; **mettere qlcu in ginocchio** to bring s.o. to his knees
ginocchióni *adv* on one's knees
giocare §182 *tr* to play; to stake, bet, risk, gamble; to make a fool of || *intr* to play; to gamble; to circulate (*said of air*); (fig) to play a role; **giocare a** to play; to wager; **giocare a mosca cieca** to play blindman's buff; **giocare con** to risk; **giocare d'armi** to fence; **giocare d'azzardo** to gamble; **giocare di** to use (*e.g., one's wits*); **giocare di gomiti** to elbow one's way; **giocare di mano** to steal; **giocare sulle parole** to play on words; to pun || *ref* to risk (*e.g., one's life*); to gamble away
giocata *f* wager, stake; game, play
gioca·tóre -trice *mf* player; gambler; speculator
giocàttolo *m* toy, plaything
giocherellare (giocherèllo) *intr* to play, trifle
giochétto *m* children's game; child's play; dirty trick
giò·co *m* (**-chi**) game; gambling; play; wager, stake; set; joke; (cards) hand; **entrare in gioco** to come into play; **fare gioco a** to come in handy to; **fare il doppio gioco** to be guilty of duplicity; **fare il gioco di** to play into the hands of; **giochi di equilibrio** balancing act; **gioco da ragazzi** child's play; **gioco d'azzardo** gambling; game of chance; **gioco dei bussolotti** (fig) jugglery; **gioco di destrezza** game of skill; **gioco di parole** play on words, pun; **gioco di prestigio** sleight of hand; **gioco di società** parlor game; **metter in gioco** to risk; to stake; **per gioco** for fun; **prendersi gioco di** to make fun of
giocofòrza *m*—**è giocoforza** + *inf* it is necessary + *inf*
giocolière *m* juggler
giocón·do -da *adj* merry, joyful
giocó·so -sa [s] *adj* jocose, jolly
giogàia *f* dewlap; chain of mountains
gió·go *m* (**-ghi**) yoke; beam (*of balance*); rounded peak; pass
giòia *f* joy, happiness; darling; jewel; **darsi alla pazza gioia** to have a wild time
gioielleria *f* jewelry; jewelry store
gioiellière *m* jeweler
gioièllo *m* jewel
gioió·so -sa [s] *adj* joyful
gioire §176 (*pres part* missing) *intr* to rejoice
Giòna *m* Jonas
Giordània, la Jordan (*country*)
giorda·no -na *adj & mf* Jordanian || **Giordano** *m* Jordan (*river*)
Giórgio *m* George
giorna·làio -làia *mf* (**-lài -làie**) newsdealer
giornale *m* newspaper; magazine; (com) journal; **giornale di bordo** log, logbook; **giornale murale** poster; **giornale radio** newscast

giornaliè·ro -ra *adj* daily || *mf* day laborer
giornalismo *m* journalism
giornali·sta *mf* (**-sti -ste**) journalist; **giornalista pubblicista** free-lance writer || *m* newspaperman || *f* newspaperwoman
giornalménte *adv* daily
giornata *f* day; day's work; birthday; pay, salary; battle; day's march; **giornata campale** pitched battle; **giornata della mamma** Mother's Day; **giornata lavorativa** workday; **vivere alla giornata** to live from hand to mouth
giórno *m* day; **a giorni** within the next few days; **a giorni . . . a giorni** some days . . . others; **a giorno** open, openwork (*needlework*); full (*light*); **ai giorni nostri** nowadays; **al giorno d'oggi** nowadays; **buon giorno** good day; good morning; good-bye; **dare gli otto giorni a** to dismiss, fire; **di ogni giorno** everyday (*e.g., clothes*); **essere a giorno** to be up to date; **giorno dei morti** All Souls' Day; **giorno di lavoro** workday; **giorno di paga** payday; **giorno fatto** broad daylight; **giorno feriale** weekday; **giorno festivo** holiday; **mettere a giorno** to bring up to date; **otto giorni oggi** one week from today; **passare un brutto giorno** to have a bad time; **un giorno o l'altro** one of these days
giòstra *f* joust; merry-go-round
giostrare (**giòstro**) *intr* to joust; to get along, manage; to idle, loiter
Giosuè *m* Joshua
Giotté·sco -sca *adj* (**-schi -sche**) of the school of Giotto
giovaménto *m* benefit, advantage
gióvane *adj* young; youthful; fresh (*e.g., cheese*); Younger, e.g., **Plinio il Giovane** Pliny the Younger || *m* young man; boy, apprentice; **i giovani** the young || *f* young woman
giovanile *adj* youthful
Giovanni *m* John; **Giovanni Battista** John the Baptist
giovanòtta *f* young woman
giovanòtto *m* young man; (coll) bachelor
giovare (**gióvo**) *tr* (lit) to help || *intr* (with *dat*) to help, to be of use to || *ref* to avail oneself || *impers* (ESSERE) —**non giova** it's no use
Giòve *m* Jupiter
giove·dì *m* (**-dì**) Thursday; **giovedì santo** Maundy Thursday
giovèn·ca *f* (**-che**) heifer
gioventù *f* youth
giovévole *adj* helpful, beneficial
gioviale *adj* jovial
giovinézza *f* youth
gip *f* (**gip**) jeep
gippóne *m* large jeep, panel truck
giràbile *adj* endorsable
giradi·schi *m* (**-schi**) record player
giradito *m* (pathol) felon
giraffa *f* giraffe; (mov, telv) boom, crane
girafilièra *f* diestock
giramà·schio *m* (**-schi**) tap wrench
giraménto *m*—**giramento di testa** vertigo, dizziness
giramón·do *m* (**-do**) globetrotter
giràndola *f* girandole; pinwheel; (fig) weathercock
girandolare (**giràndolo**) *intr* to stroll, saunter
girante *mf* endorser || *f* blade (*e.g., of fan*)
girare *tr* to turn; to tour; to go around, travel over; to switch (*the conversation*); to film, shoot; to transfer (*a phone call*); to endorse; (mil) to surround || *intr* to turn; to circulate; to spin (*said of one's head*) || *ref* to turn; to toss and turn
girarrósto *m* turnspit; **girarrosto a motore** rotisserie
girasóle *m* sunflower
girata *f* turn; walk, ramble; (com) endorsement; (cards) deal; (coll) tongue-lashing
giratà·rio -ria *mf* (**-ri -rie**) endorsee
giravòlta *f* turn, pirouette; bend; sudden change of mind
girellare (**girèllo**) *intr* to stroll, wander around
girèllo *m* rump; go-cart, walker
girévole *adj* revolving
girino *m* tadpole; bicycle rider competing on the Tour of Italy
giro *m* periphery; turn, revolution; ride; size (*of hat*); edge (*of glass*); round (*of a doctor*); (sports) tour; (sports) lap; (com) transfer; (cards) hand; (theat) tour; **a giro di posta** by return mail; **andare in giro** to poke along; **giro collo** neckline; **giro d'affari** volume of business, turnover; **giro di parole** circumlocution; **fare il giro di** to tour; **mettere in giro** to spread (*news, gossip*); **nel giro di** within (*a period*); **prendere in giro** to poke fun at
girobùssola *f* gyrocompass
girondolare (**giróndolo**) *intr* var of **girandolare**
giróne *m* (sports) conference; (sports) division; (sports) league; (archaic) circle
gironzolare [dz] (**girónzolo**) *intr* to stroll, saunter
giropilò·ta *m* (**-ti**) gyropilot
girosco·pio *m* (**-pi**) gyroscope
girotóndo *m* ring-around-a-rosy
giròtta *f* weather vane
girovagare §209 (**giròvago**) *intr* to roam, wander
giròva·go -ga (**-ghi -ghe**) *adj* wandering; strolling (*player*) || *m* vagrant, hobo
gita *f* trip, excursion, outing
gita·no -na *adj* & *mf* Gypsy
gitante *mf* excursionist, vacationist
gittata *f* range (*of gun*)
giù *adv* down; **andar giù** to go down; to deteriorate; to get worse; **buttar giù** to throw down; (culin) to start to cook, e.g., **buttar giù gli spaghetti** to start to cook the spaghetti; (fig) to jot down; **da . . . in giù** for the past . . . ; **dar giù** to look worse (*said*

of a sick person); **esser giù** to be downcast; **giù di lì** thereabouts; **in giù** down; downstream; **mandar giù** to swallow; **non andar giù** to not be able to stomach or swallow, e.g., **non gli vanno giù i bugiardi** he cannot stomach liars; **venire giù** to come down; to crumble; to collapse
giubba *f* coat, jacket; mane
giubbétto *m* small coat; bodice; jerkin
giubbòtto *m* jacket (*e.g., of a motorcyclist*); **giubbotto salvagente** (aer, naut) life jacket
giubilare (**giùbilo**) *tr* to retire, to pension || *intr* to rejoice
giubilèo *m* jubilee
giùbilo *m* jubilation, exultation
giuda *m* Judas || **Giuda** *m* Judas
giudài•co -ca *adj* (**-ci -che**) Judaic
giudaismo *m* Judaism
giudè•o -a *adj* Judean; Jewish || *mf* Judean; Jew
giudicare §197 (**giùdico**) *tr* to judge; to find (*e.g., s.o. innocent*); to try (*a case*) || *intr* to judge, deem
giudicato *m* (hist) Sardinian region; **passare in giudicato** (law) to become final
giùdice *m* judge; magistrate, justice; **giudice conciliatore** justice of the peace; **giudice popolare** member of the jury
giudizià•rio -ria *adj* (**-ri -rie**) judicial, judiciary
giudì•zio *m* (**-zi**) judgment; wisdom; trial; sentence; **giudizio di Dio** (hist) ordeal; **giudizio finale** Last Judgment; **metter giudizio** to mend one's ways
giudizió•so -sa [s] *adj* judicious, wise
giùggiola *f* jujube; (joc) trifle; **andare in brodo di giuggiole** to swoon, become ecstatic
giugno *m* June
giugulare *adj* jugular || *v* (**giùgolo**) *tr* to cut the throat of
giulèbbe *m* julep
giuliana *f* (culin) julienne || **Giuliana** Juliana
giuli•vo -va *adj* gay
giullare *m* jongleur; (pej) mountebank
giumén•to -ta *mf* beast of burden || *f* female saddle horse
giun•ca *f* (**-che**) (naut) junk
giunchìglia *f* (bot) jonquil
giun•co *m* (**-chi**) (bot) rush
giùngere §183 *tr* to join (*e.g., one's hands*) || *intr* (ESSERE) to arrive; **giungere a** or **in** to arrive at, reach; **giungere a** + *inf* to succeed in + *ger;* **mi giunge nuovo** it's news to me
giungla *f* jungle
Giunóne *f* Juno
giunòni•co -ca *adj* (**-ci -che**) Junoesque
giunta *f* addition; makeweight; strip (*of cloth*); junta; committee; **di prima giunta** at the very beginning; **per giunta** in addition
giuntare *tr* to join
giuntatrice *f* (mov) splicer
giunto *m* (mach) joint, coupling; **giunto a sfere** ball-and-socket joint; **giunto cardanico** universal joint
giuntura or **giunzióne** *f* joint; juncture, seam
giuò•co *m* (**-chi**) var of **gioco**
giuraménto *m* oath; **deferire il giuramento a** to put under oath
giurare *tr* to swear, pledge || *intr* to swear
giura•to -ta *adj* sworn || *m* juror
giurìa *f* committee; jury
giurìdi•co -ca *adj* (**-ci -che**) juridical
giurisdizióne *f* jurisdiction
giurisprudènza *f* jurisprudence
giuri•sta *mf* (**-sti -ste**) jurist
Giusèppe *m* Joseph
Giuseppina *f* Josephine
giusta *prep* according to; in accordance with
giustappórre §218 *tr* to juxtapose
giustézza *f* correctness, justness; (typ) measure
giustificàbile *adj* justifiable
giustificare §197 (**giustìfico**) *tr* to justify || *ref* to excuse oneself
giustificazióne *f* justification
giustìzia *f* justice; **far giustizia a** to execute; **farsi giustizia da sé** to take the law into one's own hands; **render giustizia a** to do justice to
giustiziare §287 *tr* to execute
giustizière *m* executioner; (obs) judge
giu•sto -sta *adj* just; opportune || *m* just man; just price; rights, due || **giusto** *adv* just, justly
gla•bro -bra *adj* smooth (*face*)
glaciale *adj* glacial; (fig) icy
gladiatóre *m* gladiator
gladiòlo *m* gladiolus
glàndola *f* var of **ghiandola**
glassa *f* glaze, icing
glassare *tr* to glaze, ice
glèba *f* clod, lump of earth
gli §4 *art* || §5 *pers pron*
glicerina *f* glycerin
glìcine *m* wistaria
gliéla; gliéle; gliéli; gliélo; gliéne §5
globale *adj* total, aggregate
glòbo *m* globe; **globo oculare** eyeball
globulare *adj* globular, global
glòbulo *m* globule; (physiol) corpuscle
gloglottare (**gloglòtto**) *intr* to gobble; to gurgle
gloglottì•o *m* (**-i**) gobble, gobbling; gurgle
glòria *f* glory
gloriare §287 (**glòrio**) *tr* (lit) to exalt || *ref* to boast; to glory
glorificare §197 (**glorìfico**) *tr* to glorify
glorió•so -sa [s] *adj* glorious; proud
glòssa *f* gloss
glossà•rio *m* (**-ri**) glossary
glòttide *f* glottis
glottòlo•go -ga *mf* (**-gi -ghe**) linguist
glucòsio *m* glucose
glùtine *m* gluten
gnòc•co *m* (**-chi**) potato dumpling
gnòmo *m* gnome
gnòrri *m invar*—**fare lo gnorri** to feign ignorance
gòb•bo -ba *adj* hunchbacked || *mf*

hunchback || *f* hump; hunch; hump (*of gibbous moon*); hook (*of nose*)
góc·cia *f* (**-ce**) drop; bead; **avere la goccia al naso** to have a runny nose; **goccia d'acqua** raindrop
góc·cio *m* (**-ci**) drop, swallow
gócciola *f* drop; bead
gocciolare (**gócciolo**) *tr & intr* to drip
gocciola·tóio *m* (**-tói**) dripstone
goccioli·o *m* (**-i**) drip, trickle
godére §184 *tr* to enjoy || *intr* to take pleasure; to revel; to profit || *ref* to enjoy; **godersela** to have a good time
godìbile *adj* enjoyable
godiménto *m* enjoyment, pleasure
goffàggine *f* clumsiness
gòf·fo -fa *adj* awkward; ill-fitting
gógna *f* pillory; **mettere alla gogna** to pillory
góla *f* throat; neck; gluttony; gorge (*of mountain*); mouth (*of cannon*); flue (*of chimney*); (archit) ogee; **far gola a** to tempt; **mentire per la gola** to lie shamelessly; **tornare a gola** to repeat (*said of food*)
golétta *f* neck (*of shirt*); (naut) schooner
gòlf *m* (**gòlf**) sweater, cardigan; (sports) golf
gólfo *m* gulf; **golfo mistico** orchestra pit || **Golfo Persico** Persian Gulf
Gòlgota, il Golgotha
goliardo *m* goliard; university student
golosi·tà [s] *f* (**-tà**) gluttony; tidbit
goló·so -sa [s] *adj* gluttonous; appetizing
gómena *f* hawser
gomitata *f* blow with the elbow; nudge
gómito *m* elbow; bend; **alzare il gomito** to crook the elbow; **dare di gomito a** to nudge
gomìtolo *m* skein, clew
gómma *f* gum; rubber; eraser; tire; **bucare una gomma** to have a flat tire; **gomma arabica** gum arabic; **gomma a terra** flat tire; **gomma da masticare** chewing gum; **gomma lacca** shellac
gommapiuma *f* foam rubber
gomma·to -ta *adj* gummed; with tires
gommatura *f* gumming; (aut) tires
gommi·sta *m* (**-sti**) tire dealer; tire repairman
gommó·so -sa [s] *adj* gummy
góndola *f* gondola; (aer) pod
gonfalóne *m* gonfalon
gonfiare §287 (**gónfio**) *tr* to inflate, blow up; to bloat; to swell; to exaggerate; to puff up || *intr* (ESSERE) to swell || *ref* to swell; to puff up; to bulge, balloon
gonfiatura *f* inflation; exaggeration
gonfiézza *f* swelling; grandiloquence
gón·fio -fia (**-fi -fie**) *adj* inflated, swollen; conceited || *m* swelling, bulge
gonfióre *m* swelling
gongolare (**góngolo**) *intr* to rejoice; to be elated
goniòmetro *m* goniometer; protractor
gònna *f* skirt; **gonna pantaloni** culottes
gonnèlla *f* skirt; (fig) petticoat
gonnellino *m* kilt; ballerina skirt
gón·zo -za [dz] *mf* simpleton, fool
gòra *f* millpond; marsh; (coll) spot
górbia *f* tip (*of umbrella*)
gorgheggiare §290 (**gorghéggio**) *tr & intr* to warble; to trill
gorghég·gio *m* (**-gi**) warbling; trill
gór·go *m* (**-ghi**) whirlpool; (lit) river
gorgogliare §280 (**gorgóglio**) *intr* to gurgle
gorgó·glio *m* (**-gli**) gurgle
gorgogli·o *m* (**-i**) gurgling
goril·la *m* (**-la**) gorilla
gòta *f* cheek; (lit) side
gòti·co -ca *adj & m* (**-ci -che**) Gothic
Gòto *m* Goth
gótta *f* (pathol) gout
gottazza *f* (naut) scoop
gottó·so -sa [s] *adj* gouty
governale *m* fin (*of bomb*); (obs) rudder
governante *adj* governing || *m* ruler || *f* governess; housekeeper
governare (**govèrno**) *tr* to rule, govern; to steer (*a ship*); to tend (*animals*); to wash and dry (*dishes*); to run (*e.g., a bank*) || *intr* to steer
governati·vo -va *adj* government
govèrno *m* government; tending (*e.g., of animals*); running (*of household*); cleaning (*of house*); blending (*of wine*); (archaic) steering
gózzo *m* crop, craw (*of bird*); (pathol) goiter
gozzovigliare §280 *intr* to go on a spree
gracchiare §287 *intr* to caw
gràc·chio *m* (**-chi**) caw; (orn) chough
gracidare (**gràcido**) *intr* to croak; to honk (*said, e.g., of a goose*)
gràcile *adj* weak, frail; thin, delicate
gradasso *m* swaggerer, braggadocio
grada·to -ta *adj* graded; gradual
gradazióne *f* gradation; alcoholic proof; **gradazione vocalica** (phonet) ablaut
gradévole *adj* pleasant
gradiménto *m* pleasure; acceptance (*of a product*); liking
gradinata *f* steps; tier (*of seats*)
gradino *m* step; (fig) stepping stone
gradire §176 *tr* to like; to welcome
gradi·to -ta *adj* agreeable; welcome (*guest*); kind (*letter*)
grado *m* degree; rank; (nav) rating; (archaic) step; **a buon grado o a mal grado** willy-nilly; **a grado a grado** little by little; **a Suo grado** according to your wishes; **di buon grado** willingly; **di secondo grado** secondary (*school*); **essere in grado di** to be in a position to; **saper grado a** (lit) to be grateful to
graduale *adj & m* gradual
graduare (**gràduo**) *tr* to graduate
gradua·to -ta *adj* graduated || *m* noncommissioned officer
graduatòria *f* ranking; rank
graffa *f* clamp; brace, bracket
graffiare §287 *tr* to scratch; (coll) to swipe
graffiétto *m* tiny scratch; marking gage
gràf·fio *m* (**-fi**) scratch
grafia *f* writing, spelling; (gram) graph

gràfi·co -ca (-ci -che) *adj* graphic || *m* graph, diagram; designer (*for printing industry*); member of printers' union || *f* graphic arts
grafite *f* graphite
grafologìa *f* graphology
gragnòla *f* hail
gramàglia *f* crepe; widow's weeds; **in gramaglie** in mourning
gramigna *f* couch grass; weed
grammàti·co -ca (-ci -che) *adj* grammatical || *m* grammarian || *f* grammar
grammo *m* gram
grammofòni·co -ca *adj* **(-ci -che)** phonograph, recording
grammòfono *m* phonograph, record player
gra·mo -ma *adj* poor, sad; wretched, miserable; frail, sickly
gran *adj* apocopated form of **grande**, used before singular and plural nouns beginning with a consonant sound other than *gn, pn, ps,* impure *s, x,* and *z*
gra·na *m* **(-na)** Parmesan cheese || *f* **(-ne)** cochineal; grain (*of wood, metal, etc*); (slang) dough; (coll) trouble
granàglie *fpl* grain, cereals
gra·nàio *m* **(-nài)** granary, barn
granata *adj invar & m* garnet (*color*) || *f* pomegranate (*fruit*); garnet; broom; grenade
granatière *m* grenadier
granatina *f* grenadine
Gran Bretagna, la Great Britain
grancassa *f* bass drum
grancèvola *f* spider crab
gràn·chio *m* **(-chi)** crab; claw (*of hammer*); (coll) cramp; **prendere un granchio** to make a blunder
grandangolare *adj* wide-angle
grande *adj* big, large; great; tall; high (*mass; voice*); long (*time*); capital (*letter*); full (*speed*); grown-up || *m* grownup; grandeur; grandee; **fare il grande** to show off; **i grandi** the great; **in grande** on a large scale; lavishly
grandézza *f* size; enormity; greatness; quantity; **in grandezza naturale** life-size; **grandezze** ostentatiousness
grandezzó·so -sa [s] *adj* ostentatious
grandiloquènza *f* grandiloquence
grandinare (gràndino) *tr* (obs) to hail || *intr* to hail || *impers* (ESSERE & AVERE)—**grandina** it is hailing
grandinata *f* hailstorm
gràndine *f* hail
grandiosi·tà [s] *f* **(-tà)** grandeur, magnificence
grandió·so -sa [s] *adj* grandiose, grand
grandu·ca *m* **(-chi)** grand duke
granduchéssa *f* grand duchess
granèllo *m* grain, seed; speck
grànfia *f* clutch
granìco·lo -la *adj* grain, wheat
granire §176 *tr* to grain; to stipple; (mus) to make (*the notes*) clear-cut || *intr* to teethe
granita *f* sherbet, water ice
granito *m* granite
granitura *f* knurl, milled edge
grano *m* wheat; grain of wheat; grain; speck; **grano duro** durum wheat; **grano saraceno** buckwheat; **grano turco** corn
granturco *m* corn
granulare *adj* granular || *v* **(grànulo)** *tr* to granulate
granulatóre *m* crusher
grànulo *m* granule, pellet, bud
granuló·so -sa [s] *adj* granular; lumpy; gritty; friable, crumbly
grappa *f* eau de vie; clamp, brace
grappétta *f* staple; crampon
grappino *m* (naut) grapnel
gràppolo *m* bunch, cluster
grassàg·gio *m* **(-gi)** (aut) lubrication
grassatóre *m* highwayman
grassazióne *f* holdup
grassétto *m* boldface
grassézza *f* fatness; richness
gras·so -sa *adj* fat; rich; greasy; risqué || *m* fat, suet; grease; shortening
grassòc·cio -cia *adj* **(-ci -ce)** pudgy, plump
grata *f* grate, grating
gratèlla *f* strainer; sieve; broiler
gratìc·cia *f* **(-ce)** (theat) gridiron
gratìc·cio *m* **(-ci)** lattice, trellis
gratìcola *f* gridiron; grating; graticule
gratìfi·ca *f* **(-che)** bonus
gratificare §197 **(gratìfico)** *tr* to give a bonus to; (fig) to pelt (*with insults*)
gratificazióne *f* bonus
gratis *adv* gratis, free, for nothing
gratitùdine *f* gratitude
gra·to -ta *adj* grateful, appreciative || *f* see **grata**
grattacapo *m* trouble, worry
grattacièlo *m* skyscraper
grattare *tr* to scratch; to scrape; to grate; (slang) to snitch || *intr* to scratch; to grate
grattùgia *f* grater
grattugiare §290 *tr* to grate
gratùi·to -ta *adj* gratuitous, free
gravame *m* burden; tax; (law) appeal; **fare gravame a qlcu di qlco** to impute s.th to s.o.
gravare *tr* to burden, oppress; (obs) to seize || *intr* (ESSERE & AVERE) to weigh; to lie; to be sorry, e.g., **gli grava d'avermi disturbato** he is sorry to have bothered me || *ref*—**gravarsi di** to take upon oneself
grave *adj* heavy; burdensome; grave, serious || *m* (phys) body; **stare sul grave** to put on airs
graveolènte *adj* stinking
gravézza *f* heaviness; burden; oppression; (obs) taxation
gravidanza *f* pregnancy
gràvi·do -da *adj* pregnant; fraught
gravi·tà *f* **(-tà)** gravity
gravitare (gràvito) *intr* to gravitate; to weigh, lie
gravitazióne *f* gravitation
gravó·so -sa [s] *adj* heavy; hard, burdensome; oppressive
gràzia *f* grace; pardon, mercy; delicacy; kindness; **di grazia!** please!;

essere nelle grazie di qlcu to be in s.o.'s good graces; **fare grazia di qlco a qlcu** to spare s.o. s.th; **grazia di Dio** abundance, bounty; **grazie!** thank you!; **grazie tante!** thanks a lot!; **in grazia di** thanks to; **male grazie** bad manners; **per grazie** as a favor; **render grazia a** to thank; **saper grazia a** to be thankful to

graziare §287 *tr* to pardon; **graziare qlcu di qlco** to grant s.th to s.o.

grazió•so -sa [s] *adj* graceful, pretty; gracious; (lit) free, gratuitous

Grècia, la Greece

grè•co -ca (-ci -che) *adj & mf* Greek || *f* fret, fretwork; bullion (*on Italian general's hat*); tunic

gregà•rio -ria (-ri -rie) *adj* gregarious || *m* private; follower

grég•ge *m* **(-gi** or **-ge** *fpl*) flock, herd

grég•gio -gia (-gi -ge) *adj* coarse; raw, unrefined || *m* crude oil

gregoria•no -na *adj* Gregorian

grembiale *m* var of **grembiule**

grembiule *m* apron; frock; smock

grembiulino *m* pinafore

grèmbo *m* lap; womb; bosom

gremire §176 *tr* to crowd || *ref* to become crowded

gremi•to -ta *adj* overcrowded

gréppia *f* manger, crib

gréto *m* dry gravel bed of a river

grettézza *f* stinginess; narrow-mindedness

grét•to -ta *adj* stingy; narrow-minded

grève *adj* heavy; uncouth; (lit) grievous

gréz•zo -za [ddzz] *adj* raw, crude; coarse

gridare *tr* to cry out; to cry for (*help*); (coll) to scold || *intr* to cry out, shout

grido *m* cry (*of animal*) || *m* (**grida** *fpl*) cry; scream; shout; yell; fame; **di grido** famous; **grido di guerra** war cry; **ultimo grido** latest fashion

grifa•gno -gna *adj* rapacious, fierce

griffa *f* hobnail; (mov, phot) sprocket

grifo *m* snout (*of pig*); (pej) snoot; (lit) griffin

grifóne *m* vulture; (mythol) griffin

grigia•stro -stra *adj* grayish

grì•gio -gia *adj & m* **(-gi -gie)** grey

grigiovérde *adj invar* olive-drab || *m* olive-drab uniform

grìglia *f* gridiron, broiler; grate, grille; (elec) grid (*of vacuum tube*)

grillare *tr* to grill, broil || *intr* to sizzle; to bubble (*said of fermenting wine*); to have a sudden whim

grillétto *m* trigger

grillo *m* cricket; whim, fancy

grimaldèllo *m* picklock

grìnfia *f* claw, clutch; **grinfie** clutches

grinta *f* grim or forbidding face

grinza *f* wrinkle; crease; **non fare una grinza** to be perfect

grinzó•so -sa [s] *adj* wrinkled; creased

grippare *intr & ref* to bind, jam

grisèlla *f* (naut) ratline

gri•sou *m* **(-sou)** firedamp

grissino *m* breadstick

Groenlàndia, la Greenland

grómma *f* incrustation, deposit

grónda *f* eaves; slope (*of ground*)

grondàia *f* gutter (*of roof*)

grondare (**gróndo**) *tr* to drip || *intr* (ESSERE) to ooze (*said, e.g., of perspiration*); to drip; **grondare di sangue** to stream with blood

gròppa *f* back (*of animal*); top (*of mountain*); **restare sulla groppa a** to be stuck with, e.g., **gli sono restati sulla groppa cento esemplari** he is stuck with one hundred copies

groppata *f* bucking (*of horse*)

gróppo *m* knot, tangle; lump (*in throat*); squall

groppóne *m* back, rump

gròssa *f* gross; **dormire della grossa** to sleep like a log

grossézza *f* bigness; thickness; density; swelling (*of river*); (fig) coarseness; **grossezza d'udito** hardness of hearing

grossi•sta *mf* **(-sti -ste)** wholesaler

gròs•so -sa *adj* big, large; thick; heavy (*seas*); swollen (*river*); hard (*breathing*); offensive (*words*); coarse (*e.g., salt*); pregnant; deep (*voice*); (coll) important; **alla grossa** approximately; **di grosso** a lot, very much; **dirla grossa** to talk nonsense; **farla grossa** to make a blunder; **grosso d'udito** hard of hearing; **in grosso** wholesale; **spararle grosse** to tell tall tales || *m* bulk; main body (*e.g., of an army*) || *f* see **grossa**

grossola•no -na *adj* coarse; boorish, uncouth; big (*blunder*)

gròtta *f* grotto; (coll) inn

grotté•sco -sca (-schi -sche) *adj & m* grotesque || *f* (hist) grotesque painting

grovièra *f* Gruyère cheese

grovì•glio *m* **(-gli)** tangle, snarl

gru *f* **(gru)** (orn, mach) crane

grùc•cia *f* **(-ce)** crutch; clothes hanger; (obs) wooden leg

grufolare (**grùfolo**) *intr* to nuzzle || *ref* to wallow (*in mud*)

grugnire §176 *tr & intr* to grunt

grugnito *m* grunt

grugno *m* snout; (pej) snoot; **fare il grugno** to sulk

grui•sta *m* **(-sti)** crane operator

grullerìa *f* foolishness

grul•lo -la *adj* silly, simple

gruma *f* deposit, incrustation

grumo *m* lump; clot

grùmolo *m* heart (*e.g., of lettuce*); small lump

grumó•so -sa [s] *adj* lumpy; incrusted, scaly

gruppo *m* group; main body (*e.g., of runners*); club; **gruppo elettrogeno** generating unit; **gruppo motore** (aut) power plant

grùzzolo *m* hoard, pile; **farsi il gruzzolo** to feather one's nest

guadagnare *tr* to earn; to win; to gain; to pick up (*speed*); to reach (*port*) || *intr* to win; to look better || *ref* to win; to win over; **guadagnarsi il pane** or **la vita** to earn one's living

guadagno *m* earnings; profit; **a basso**

guadagno (rad, telv) low-gain; **ad alto guadagno** (rad, telv) high-gain
guadare *tr* to wade, ford
guado *m* ford; (bot) woad; **passare a guado** to ford
guài *interj* woe!
guaina *f* case; scabbard, sheath; corset; (aut) seat cover
guàio *m* (**guài**) trouble || *interj* see **guài**
guaire §176 *intr* to yelp; to whine
guaito *m* yelp, whine
gualcire §176 *tr* to crumple
gualdrappa *f* saddlecloth
Gualtièro *m* Walter
guàn•cia *f* (**-ce**) cheek; moldboard; cheek side (*of gunstock*)
guanciale *m* pillow; **dormire tra due guanciali** to sleep safe and sound
guan•tàio -tàia *mf* (**-tài -tàie**) glove maker; glove merchant
guanterìa *f* glove factory
guantièra *f* glove case; tray
guanto *m* glove; **gettare il guanto** to fling down the gauntlet; **raccogliere il guanto** to take up the gauntlet; **trattare con i guanti gialli** to handle with kid gloves
guantóne *m* big glove; **guantoni da pugilato** boxing gloves
guardabarriè•re *m* (**-re**) (rr) gatekeeper, crossing watchman
guardabò•schi *m* (**-schi**) forester
guardacàc•cia *m* (**-cia**) gamekeeper
guardacò•ste *m* (**-ste**) coast guard; coast-guard cutter
guardafi•li *m* (**-li**) (elec) lineman
guardalì•nee *m* (**-nee**) (rr) trackwalker; (sports) linesman
guardama•no *m* (**-no**) guard (*of sabre or rifle*); work glove; (naut) handrail
guardaportó•ne *m* (**-ne**) doorman
guardare *tr* to look at; to protect, watch; to pay attention to; to face, overlook; (obs) to keep to (*one's bed*); (obs) to keep (*a holiday*); **guardare a vista** to keep under close watch; **guardare dall'alto in basso** to look down one's nose at; **guardare di sotto in su** to leer at || *intr* to look; to pay attention; **Dio guardi!** God forbid!; **guardare a** to face (*said, e.g., of a room*); **guardare di non** + *inf* to be careful not to + *inf;* **guardare in faccia** to face (*e.g., danger*); **stare a guardare** to keep on the sidelines || *ref* to look at one another; to look at oneself; **guardarsi da** to keep from; to guard against
guardarò•ba *m* (**-ba**) wardrobe; linen closet; checkroom, cloakroom
guardarobiè•re -ra *mf* checkroom attendant || *f* hatcheck girl
guardasigil•li *m* (**-li**) minister of justice (*in Italy*); (Brit) Lord Privy Seal; (U.S.A.) attorney general; (hist) keeper of the seals
guardaspal•le *m* (**-le**) bodyguard
guardata *f* quick look, glance
guarda•vìa *m* (**-vìa**) guardrail; median strip
guàrdia *f* watch; guard; top water level; flyleaf; **di guardia** on duty; **fare la guardia a** to watch; **guardia campestre** forester; **guardia carceraria** prison guard; **guardia del corpo** guard, body guard; **guardia di finanza** customs officer; **guardia d'onore** honor guard; **guardia forestale** forester; park guard; **guardia giurata** private policeman; **guardia medica** emergency clinic; **guardia municipale** police officer; **guardia notturna** night watch; **mettere qlcu in guardia** to warn s.o.; **montare la guardia** to be on guard duty, keep guard; **stare in guardia** to be on one's guard
guardiamari•na *m* (**-na**) (nav) ensign
guardiano *m* keeper; warden; watchdog; (eccl) superior; **guardiano notturno** night watchman
guardina *f* lockup; **in guardina** in jail
guardinfante *m* bustle (*worn under the back of a woman's skirt*)
guardin•go -ga *adj* (**-ghi -ghe**) wary
guàrdolo *m* welt (*in shoe*)
guardóne *m* peeping tom
guarentì•gia *f* (**-gie**) guarantee
guarìbile *adj* curable
guarigióne *f* cure, recovery
guarire §176 *tr* to cure; to heal || *intr* (ESSERE) to recover; to heal
guaritóre *m* healer; quack
guarnigióne *f* (mil) garrison
guarnire §176 *tr* to equip; to rig; to trim; (naut) to rig; (culin) to garnish || *intr* to add beauty
guarnizióne *f* decoration; trimming; lining; (culin) garniture; (mach) gasket; (mach) washer
Guascógna, la Gascony
guascó•ne -na *adj & mf* Gascon
guastafè•ste *mf* (**-ste**) kill-joy
guastare *tr* to ruin, spoil; to undo; to wreck; (obs) to lay waste; **guastare le uova nel paniere a** to spoil the plans of || *ref* to spoil; to worsen (*said, e.g., of the weather*); (mach) to break down; **guastarsi con qlcu** to quarrel with s.o.; **guastarsi il sangue** to blow one's top
guastatóre *m* commando
gua•sto -sta *adj* ruined, spoiled; wrecked || *m* breakdown; corruption; discord
guatare *tr* (lit) to look askance or with fear at
Guayana, la Guyana
guazza *f* dew
guazzabù•glio *m* (**-gli**) muddle, mess
guazzare *tr* to make (*an animal*) wade in a river || *intr* to wallow
guazzétto *m* stew, ragout
guazzo *m* puddle, pool; gouache
guèl•fo -fa *adj & mf* Guelph
guèr•cio -cia (**-ci -ce**) *adj* cross-eyed; one-eyed; almost blind || *mf* cross-eyed person; one-eyed person
guèrra *f* war; warfare; **guerra a coltello** internecine feud; **guerra di Troia** Trojan war; **guerra fredda** cold war; **guerra lampo** blitzkrieg; **guerra mondiale** world war

guerrafon·dàio -dàia (-dài -dàie) *adj* warmongering || *mf* warmonger
guerreggiare §290 **(guerréggio)** *tr* to fight, war against || *intr* to fight || *ref* to make war on one another
guerré·sco -sca *adj* **(-schi -sche)** warlike
guerriè·ro -ra *adj* war, warlike || *mf* fighter || *m* warrior
guerrìglia *f* guerrilla
guerriglièro *m* guerrilla (*soldier*)
gufo *m* misanthrope; (orn) horned owl
gùglia *f* spire; peak
gugliata *f* needleful
Guglièlmo *m* William
guida *f* guide; guidance; driving; runner (*rug*); guidebook; manual (*of instruction*); (aut) steering; **guida a destra** right-hand drive; **guide** reins (*of horse*); (mach) slide
guidaiòlo *m* leader (*among animals*)
guidare *tr* to guide, lead; to steer; to drive || *intr* to drive || *ref* to restrain oneself
guida·tóre -trice *mf* driver
guiderdóne *m* (lit) premium, prize
guidóne *m* pennant, pennon
guidoslitta *f* bobsled
guidovìa *f* ski lift
Guinèa, la Guinea
guinzà·glio *m* **(-gli)** leash; (fig) **fetter,** shackle
guisa *f* way, manner; **in guisa che** so that; **in guisa di** under the guise of
guit·to -ta *adj* miserly, niggardly || *m* strolling player
guizzare *intr* to dart; to wriggle; to flash (*said of lightning*); (naut) to yaw || *intr* (ESSERE) to slip away
guizzo *m* dart; wriggle; flash
gù·scio *m* **(-sci)** shell; pod (*of pea*); tick (*of mattress*); **guscio di noce** nutshell; **guscio d'uovo** eggshell
gustare *tr* to taste; to relish || *intr* (ESSERE & AVERE) to please; to like, e.g., **gli gustano le gite in barca** he likes boat rides
gusto *m* taste; pleasure, fun; whim; style; **di cattivo gusto** tasteless; **di gusto** gladly, with gusto; **prendere gusto per** to take a liking for; **prendersi il gusto di** to relish; **provar gusto** to have fun
gustó·so -sa [s] *adj* tasty
guttapèrca *f* gutta-percha
gutturale *adj* & *f* guttural

H

H, h ['ɑkkɑ] *m* & *f* eighth letter of the Italian alphabet
handicappare *tr* var of **andicappare**
hangar *m* **(hangar)** hangar
havaia·no -na *adj* & *mf* Hawaiian
henné *m* henna
hertz *m* hertz
hertzia·no -na *adj* Hertzian
hi-fi *f* (coll) hi-fi
hockei·sta *m* **(-sti)** hockey player
hollywoodia·no -na *adj* Hollywood, Hollywood-like
hurrà *interj* hurrah!

I

I, i, [i] *m* & *f* ninth letter of the Italian alphabet
i §4 *def art* the
iarda *f* yard
iato *m* hiatus
iattanza *f* boasting, bragging
iattura *f* misfortune, calamity
ibèri·co -ca *adj* **(-ci -che)** Iberian
ibernare (ibèrno) *intr* to hibernate
ibi·sco *m* **(-schi)** hibiscus
ibridare (ìbrido) *tr* & *intr* to hybridize
ibri·do -da *adj* & *m* hybrid
icàsti·co -ca *adj* **(-ci -che)** figurative; realistic
-ìccio -ìccia *suf adj* -ish, e.g., **gialliccio** yellowish
iconocla·sta *mf* **(-sti -ste)** iconoclast
iconografìa *f* iconography
iconoscò·pio *m* **(-pi)** iconoscope
iddì·o *m* **(-i)** god || **Iddio** *m* God
idèa *f* idea; goal, purpose; bit, touch; **avere idea di** to have a mind to; **dare l'idea di** to seem; **farsi un'idea di** to grasp the notion of; **idea fissa** fixed idea; **neanche per idea** not in the least
ideale *adj* & *m* ideal
idealismo *m* idealism
ideali·sta *mf* **(-sti -ste)** idealist
idealìsti·co -ca *adj* **(-ci -che)** idealistic
idealizzare [ddzz] *tr* to idealize
ideare (idèo) *tr* to conceive
idea·tóre -trice *mf* inventor
idem *adv* ditto
idènti·co -ca *adj* **(-ci -che)** identical
identificare §197 **(identìfico)** *tr* to identify || *ref* to resemble each other; **identificarsi con** to identify with
identificazióne *f* identification
identi·tà *f* **(-tà)** identity
ideologìa *f* ideology
idi *mpl* & *fpl* ides
idillìa·co -ca *adj* **(-ci -che)** idyllic
idìl·lio *m* **(-li)** idyll; romance
idiò·ma *m* **(-mi)** language, idiom
idiomàti·co -ca *adj* **(-ci -che)** idiomatic

idiosincrasìa *f* aversion; (med) idiosyncrasy
idiò·ta (-ti -te) *adj* idiotic || *mf* idiot
idiotismo *m* idiom; idiocy
idiozìa *f* idiocy
idolatrare *tr & intr* to idolize
idolatrìa *f* idolatry
ìdolo *m* idol
idonei·tà *f* **(-tà)** fitness, aptitude; qualification
idòne·o -a *adj* fit; qualified; opportune
idra *f* hydra
idrante *m* hydrant, fireplug
idratante *adj* moisturizing
idratare *tr & ref* to hydrate
idrato *m* hydrate
idràuli·co -ca (-ci -che) *adj* hydraulic || *m* plumber || *f* hydraulics
ìdri·co -ca *adj* **(-ci -che)** water, e.g., **forza idrica** water power
idrocarburo *m* hydrocarbon
idroelèttri·co -ca *adj* **(-ci -che)** hydroelectric
idròfi·lo -la *adj* absorbent
idrofobìa *f* hydrophobia, rabies
idròfo·bo -ba *adj* hydrophobic, rabid
idròfu·go -ga *adj* **(-ghi -ghe)** waterproof
idrogenare (idrògeno) *tr* to hydrogenate
idrògeno *m* hydrogen
idròpi·co -ca (-ci -che) *adj* dropsical || *mf* patient suffering from dropsy
idropisìa *f* dropsy
idroplano *m* hydroplane (*boat*)
idropòrto *m* seaplane airport
idrorepellènte *adj* water-repellent
idroscalo *m* seaplane airport
idro·scì *m* **(-scì)** water ski
idroscivolante *m* (naut) hydroplane
idrosilurante *m* torpedo plane
idròssido *m* hydroxide
idroterapìa *f* hydrotherapy
idrovìa *f* inland waterway
idrovolante *m* seaplane, hydroplane
idròvo·ro -ra *adj* suction (*pump*) || *f* suction pump
ièna *f* hyena
ièri *m & adv* yesterday; **ieri l'altro** the day before yesterday; **ieri notte** last night; **ieri sera** last evening, last night, yesterday evening
ietta·tóre -trice *mf* hoodoo
iettatura *f* evil eye; bad luck, jinx
igiène *f* hygiene; sanitation
igièni·co -ca *adj* **(-ci -che)** hygienic, sanitary
igname *m* yam
igna·ro -ra *adj* unaware; inexperienced
igna·vo -va *adj* (lit) slothful
ignizióne *f* ignition
ignòbile *adj* (lit) ignoble
ignomìnia *f* ignominy; outrage
ignominió·so -sa [s] *adj* ignominious
ignorante *adj* ignorant; illiterate || *mf* ignoramus
ignoranza *f* ignorance
ignorare (ignòro) *tr* to not know; to ignore
ignò·to -ta *adj & m* unknown
ignu·do -da *adj* (lit) naked || *m* (lit) naked person
il §4 *def art* the
ilare *adj* cheerful
ilari·tà *f* **(-tà)** cheerfulness; laughter
ìlice *f* (lit) ilex, holm oak
ìlio *m* (anat) ilium
illanguidire §176 *tr* to weaken || *intr* (ESSERE) to get weak
illazióne *f* inference
illéci·to -ta *adj* illicit, unlawful || *m* unlawful act
illegale *adj* illegal
illeggiadrire §176 *tr* to embellish
illeggìbile *adj* illegible
illegìtti·mo -ma *adj* illegitimate
illé·so -sa *adj* unhurt, unharmed
illettera·to -ta *adj & mf* illiterate
illiba·to -ta *adj* spotless, pure
illimita·to -ta *adj* unlimited
illìri·co -ca *adj* **(-ci -che)** Illyrian
illògi·co -ca *adj* **(-ci -che)** illogical
illùdere §105 *tr* to delude
illuminare (illùmino) *tr* to illuminate; to brighten; to enlighten || *ref* to grow bright
illumina·to -ta *adj* illuminated; enlightened; educated
illuminazióne *f* illumination; enlightenment
illuminismo *m* Age of Enlightenment
illusióne *f* illusion; delusion; **farsi illusioni** to indulge in wishful thinking
illusionismo *m* sleight of hand; magic
illusioni·sta *mf* **(-sti -ste)** magician
illu·so -sa *adj* deluded || *mf* deluded person
illusò·rio -ria *adj* **(-ri -rie)** illusory, illusive
illustrare *tr* to illustrate; to explain, elucidate || *ref* to become famous
illustra·to -ta *adj* illustrated, pictorial
illustra·tóre -trice *mf* illustrator
illustrazióne *f* illustration; illustrious person
illustre *adj* illustrious, famous
illustrìssi·mo -ma *adj* distinguished; honorable; **Illustrissimo Signore** Dear Sir; Mr. (*addressing a letter*)
imbacuccare §197 *tr & ref* to muffle up; to wrap up
imbaldanzire §176 *tr* to embolden || *intr* (ESSERE) *& ref* to grow bold
imballàg·gio *m* **(-gi)** wrapping, packaging
imballare *tr* to wrap up, package; to bale; to race (*the motor*); **imballare in una gabbia** to crate || *ref* to race (*said of a motor*)
imballa·tóre -trice *mf* packer
imballo *m* packing; packaging, wrapping; racing (*of motor*)
imbalsamare (imbàlsamo) *tr* to embalm; to stuff (*animals*)
imbambola·to -ta *adj* gazing, staring; stunned, dumfounded; sleepy-eyed; sluggish
imbandierare (imbandièro) *tr* to bedeck with flags
imbandire §176 *tr* to prepare (*food, a meal, a table*) lavishly
imbarazzante *adj* embarrassing, awkward
imbarazzare *tr* to embarrass; to encumber, hamper; to upset (*the stomach*)

imbarazza·to -ta *adj* embarrassed, perplexed; upset (*stomach*); ill-at-ease
imbarazzo *m* embarrassment; annoyance; **imbarazzo di stomaco** upset stomach
imbarbarire §176 *tr & ref* to make barbarous; to corrupt (*a language*)
imbarcadèro *m* landing pier
imbarcare §197 *tr* to ship; to load, embark; to ship (*water*) || *ref* to sail; to embark; to curve (*said of furniture*)
imbarca·tóio *m* (**-tói**) landing pier
imbarcazióne *f* boat; **imbarcazione di salvataggio** lifeboat
imbar·co *m* (**-chi**) embarkation; port of embarkation
imbardare *intr & ref* (aer) to yaw; (aut) to swerve, lurch
imbardata *f* (aer) yaw; (aut) swerve, lurch
imbarilare *tr* to barrel
imbastardire §176 *tr* to corrupt || *ref* to become corrupt
imbastire §176 *tr* (sew) to baste; (fig) to sketch out
imbastitura *f* (sew) basting
imbàttere *ref*—**imbattersi bene** to be lucky; **imbattersi in** to come across; **imbattersi male** to have bad luck
imbattìbile *adj* unbeatable
imbavagliare §280 *tr* to gag
imbeccare §197 (**imbécco**) *tr* to feed (*a fledgling*); (fig) to prompt
imbeccata *f* beakful; (fig) prompting
imbecillàggine *f* imbecility
imbecille *adj & mf* imbecile
imbecilli·tà *f* (**-tà**) imbecility
imbèlle *adj* unwarlike; cowardly
imbellettare (**imbellétto**) *tr* to apply rouge to, apply make-up on || *ref* to put on make-up
imbellire §176 *tr* to embellish
imbèrbe *adj* beardless; callow
imbestialire §176 *tr* to enrage || *intr* (ESSERE) *& ref* to become enraged
imbévere §185 *tr* to soak; to soak up; to imbue || *ref* to become soaked; to become imbued
imbiancare §197 *tr* to whiten; to bleach; to whitewash || *intr* (ESSERE) *& ref* to turn white (*said, e.g., of hair*); to clear up (*said of weather*)
imbiancatura *f* bleaching (*of laundry*); whitening; whitewashing
imbianchiménto *m* bleaching
imbianchino *m* whitewasher; house painter; (pej) dauber
imbianchire §176 *tr* to whiten; to bleach || *ref* to turn white
imbiondire §176 *tr* to bleach (*hair*) || *intr* to become blond; to ripen (*said of wheat*)
imbizzarrire [ddzz] *intr* (ESSERE) *& ref* to become skittish (*said of a horse*); to become infuriated
imbizzire [ddzz] §176 *intr* (ESSERE) to get angry
imboccare §197 (**imbócco**) *tr* to feed by mouth; to put (*an instrument*) in one's mouth; to take, enter (*a road*); to prompt || *intr* (ESSERE) to flow; to open (*said of a road*); (mach) to fit
imboccatura *f* entrance (*of street*); inlet; opening, top (*e.g., of bottle*); bit (*of bridle*); (mus) mouthpiece; **avere l'imboccatura a** to be experienced in
imbóc·co *m* (**-chi**) entrance; inlet; opening
imboniménto *m* claptrap
imbonire §176 *tr* to lure, entice (*s.o. to buy or enter*)
imbonitóre *m* barker
imborghesire §176 *tr* to render middle-class || *intr* (ESSERE) to become middle-class
imboscare §197 (**imbòsco**) *tr* to hide; to hide (*s.o.*) underground || *ref* to shirk; to be a slacker
imbosca·to -ta *adj* (mil) shirking, draft-dodging || *m* (mil) slacker; (mil) goldbrick || *f* ambush; **tendere un'imboscata** to set an ambush
imboscatóre *m* accomplice of a draft dodger; hoarder (*of scarce items*)
imboschire §176 *tr* to forest
imbottare (**imbótto**) *tr* to barrel
imbottigliare §280 *tr* to bottle; to bottle up || *ref* to get bottled up (*said of traffic*)
imbottire §176 *tr* to pad, fill; to stuff; to pad (*a speech*)
imbottita *f* bedspread, quilt
imbottitura *f* padding
imbra·ca *f* (**-che**) breeching strap (*of harness*); safety belt; (naut) sling
imbracare §197 *tr* to sling
imbracciare §128 *tr* to fasten (*shield*); to level (*gun*)
imbrancare §197 *tr & ref* to herd
imbrattacar·te *mf* (**-te**) scribbler
imbrattamu·ri *mf* (**-ri**) dauber
imbrattare *tr* to soil, dirty; to smudge, smear
imbrattaté·le *mf* (**-le**) dauber
imbratto *m* dirt; smudge, smear; daub; scribble; swill
imbrigliare §280 *tr* to bridle
imbroccare §197 (**imbròcco**) *tr* to hit (*the target*); to guess right
imbrodare (**imbròdo**) *tr* to soil
imbrogliare §280 (**imbròglio**) *tr* to cheat; to mix up; to tangle; to confuse; **imbrogliare le vele** (naut) to take in the reef || *ref* to get tangled up; to get confused; to turn bad (*said of weather*)
imbrò·glio *m* (**-gli**) cheat; tangle; (naut) reef; **cacciarsi in un imbroglio** to get involved in a mess
imbroglió·ne -na *mf* swindler
imbronciare §128 (**imbróncio**) *intr* (ESSERE) *& ref* to pout, sulk || *ref* to lower (*said of the weather*)
imbroncia·to -ta *adj* sulky, surly; cloudy, overcast
imbrunire *m*—**sull'imbrunire** at nightfall || §176 *intr* (ESSERE) to turn brown || *impers* (ESSERE)—**imbrunisce** it is growing dark
imbruttire §176 *tr* to mar; to make ugly || *intr* (ESSERE) *& ref* to grow ugly
imbucare §197 *tr* to mail; to put in a hole || *ref* to hide

imburrare *tr* to butter
imbuto *m* funnel
imène *m* (anat) hymen, maidenhead
imitare (**ìmito**) *tr* to imitate
imita•tóre -trice *mf* imitator; (theat) mimic
imitazióne *f* imitation
immacola•to -ta *adj* immaculate
immagazzinare [ddzz] *tr* to store, store up
immaginare (**immàgino**) *tr* to imagine; to guess; to invent || *ref*—**si immagini!** of course!; not at all!
immaginà•rio -ria *adj* (**-ri -rie**) imaginary
immaginativa *f* imagination
immaginazióne *f* imagination
immàgine *f* image; picture
immaginó•so -sa [s] *adj* imaginative
immalinconire §176 *tr* to sadden || *intr* (ESSERE) & *ref* to become melancholy
immancàbile *adj* unfailing; certain
immane *adj* monstruous; gigantic
immangiàbile *adj* uneatable, inedible
immantinènte *adv* (lit) immediately
immarcescìbile *adj* incorruptible
immateriale *adj* immaterial
immatricolare (**immatrìcolo**) *tr* to matriculate
immatricolazióne *f* matriculation
immatu•ro -ra *adj* immature; premature
immedesimare (**immedésimo**) *tr* to identify; to blend || *ref* to identify oneself
immediataménte *adv* immediately
immediatézza *f* immediacy
immedia•to -ta *adj* immediate
immemoràbile *adj* immemorial
immèmore *adj* forgetful
immèn•so -sa *adj* immense, huge
immèrgere §162 *tr* to immerse; to plunge || *ref* to plunge; to become absorbed
immerita•to -ta *adj* undeserved
immeritévole *adj* undeserving
immersióne *f* immersion; submersion (*of a submarine*); (naut) draft
imméttere §198 *tr* to let in; **immettere qlcu nel possesso di** (law) to grant s.o. possession of
immigrante *adj* & *mf* immigrant
immigrare *intr* (ESSERE) to immigrate
immigrazióne *f* immigration; (biol) migration
imminènte *adj* imminent
imminènza *f* imminence
immischiare §287 *tr* to involve || *ref* to meddle; to become involved
immiserire §176 *tr* to impoverish || *intr* (ESSERE) & *ref* to become impoverished; to become debased
immissà•rio *m* (**-ri**) tributary
immissióne *f* letting in, introduction; intake; insertion (*in lunar orbit*)
immòbile *adj* motionless, immobile; real (*property*) || **immobili** *mpl* real estate
immobiliare *adj* real, e.g., **proprietà immobiliare** real estate; real-estate, e.g., **imposta immobiliare** real-estate tax
immobilizzare [ddzz] *tr* to immobilize; to pin down; to tie up (*capital*)
immodè•sto -sta *adj* indecent; immodest
immolare (**immòlo**) *tr* to immolate
immondézza *f* filth; impurity
immondez•zàio *m* (**-zài**) rubbish heap, dump; garbage can
immondìzia *f* trash; garbage; filth
immón•do -da *adj* filthy, dirty; unclean
immorale *adj* immoral
immorali•tà *f* (**-tà**) immorality
immortalare *tr* to immortalize
immortale *adj* immortal
immortalità *f* immortality
immò•to -ta *adj* (lit) motionless
immune *adj* immune
immunizzare [ddzz] *tr* to immunize
immutàbile *adj* immutable
immuta•to -ta *adj* unchanged
ì•mo -ma *adj* (lit) bottom, lowest || *m* (lit) bottom; (lit) depth
impaccare §197 *tr* to pack, wrap up
impacchettare (**impacchétto**) *tr* to pack, bundle
impacciare §128 *tr* to hamper; to embarrass || *ref* to meddle
impaccia•to -ta *adj* hampered; clumsy
impàc•cio *m* (**-ci**) embarrassment; hindrance; trouble; **essere d'impaccio** to be in the way
impac•co *m* (**-chi**) wrapping; (med) compress
impadronire §176 *ref*—**impadronirsi di** to seize; to take possession of; to master (*a language*)
impagàbile *adj* invaluable, priceless
impaginare (**impàgino**) *tr* (typ) to make up (*in pages*), paginate
impaginato *m* (typ) page proof
impagliare §280 *tr* to cane (*a chair*); to stuff (*an animal; a doll*); to pack in straw
impalare *tr* to impale; to tie to a pole or stake || *ref* to stiffen up
impala•to -ta *adj* stiff, rigid
impalcatura *f* scaffold; frame, framework
impallidire §176 *intr* to turn pale; to blanch; to grow dim (*said of a star*); (fig) to wane
impalmare *tr* (lit) to wed
impalpàbile *adj* impalpable
impaludare *tr* to make swampy or marshy || *intr* to become marshy
impanare *tr* to bread; to thread (*a screw*) || *intr* to screw in
impaniare §287 *tr* to trap, ensnare || *ref* to fall into the trap
impantanare *tr* to turn into a swamp || *ref* to get stuck, to sink (*in vice*)
impaperare (**impàpero**) *ref* to fluff, make a slip
impappinare *tr* to confuse || *ref* to blunder; to stammer
imparare *tr* to learn; **imparare a memoria** to learn by heart || *intr* **imparare a** to learn to, to learn how to
impareggiàbile *adj* peerless, unmatched
imparentare (**imparènto**) *tr* to bring into the family || *ref*—**imparentarsi con** to marry into
impari *adj* odd, uneven
imparrucca•to -ta *adj* bewigged
impartire §176 *tr* to impart
imparziale *adj* impartial

impasse *f* blind alley; deadlock; (cards) finesse
impassìbile *adj* impassible, impassive
impastare *tr* to knead; to mix; to smear with paste
impasta•to -ta *adj* kneaded; smeared; **impastato di** tainted with; overwhelmed with (*sleep*)
impasto *m* paste; pastiche
impastoiare §287 (**impastóio**) *tr* to fetter, hamstring
impataccare §197 *tr* to besmear, soil
impattare *tr* to even up; to tie (*a game*); **impattarla con** to tie (*a person*)
impatto *m* impact
impaurire §176 *tr* to scare || *ref* to get scared
impàvi•do -da *adj* fearless
impazièn te *adj* impatient
impazientire §176 *intr* (ESSERE) & *ref* to get impatient
impazièn za *f* impatience
impazzare *intr* (ESSERE) to be wild with excitement; to go mad; (culin) to curdle
impazzata *f*—**all'impazzata** at top speed; berserk
impazzire §176 *intr* (ESSERE) to go crazy; **fare impazzire** to drive crazy
impeccàbile *adj* impeccable
impeciare §128 (**impécio**) *tr* to tar
impedènza *f* impedance
impediménto *m* hindrance, obstacle, impediment
impedire §176 *tr* to impede, hinder; to obstruct || *intr* to prevent; **impedire** (with *dat*) **di** + *inf* or **che** + *subj* to prevent from + *ger*
impegnare (**impégno**) *tr* to pawn; to reserve (*a room*); to engage (*the enemy*); to keep occupied; to pledge || *ref* to obligate oneself; to go all out; to become entangled
impegnati•vo -va *adj* demanding (*activity*); binding (*promise*)
impegna•to -ta *adj* pawned; pledged; occupied; committed
impégno *m* commitment; obligation; task; zeal; **senza impegno** without promising
impegolare (**impégolo**) *tr* to tar || *ref* to become entangled
impelagare §209 (**impèlago**) *ref* to bog down; to become entangled
impellicciare §128 *tr* to fur; to veneer
impenetràbile *adj* impenetrable
impenitènte *adj* impenitent; confirmed
impennàg•gio *m* (**-gi**) (aer) empennage
impennare (**impénno**) *tr* to feather; (fig) to give wings to || *ref* to rear (*said of a horse*); to take umbrage; (aer) to zoom
impennata *f* rearing (*of horse*); (aer) zoom
impensàbile *adj* unthinkable
impensa•to -ta *adj* unexpected
impensierire §176 *tr* & *ref* to worry
imperante *adj* prevailing
imperare (**impèro**) *intr* to rule, reign; to prevail; **imperare su** to rule over
imperati•vo -va *adj* & *m* imperative
imperatóre *m* emperor
imperatrice *f* empress
impercettìbile *adj* imperceptible
imperdonàbile *adj* unforgivable
imperfèt•to -ta *adj* & *m* imperfect
imperfezióne *f* imperfection
imperiale *adj* imperial || *m* upper deck (*of bus or coach*); **imperiali** imperial troops
imperiali•sta *adj* & *mf* (**-sti -ste**) imperialist
impè•rio *m* (**-ri**) empire; rule
imperió•so -sa [s] *adj* imperious; imperative
imperi•to -ta *adj* (lit) inexperienced
imperitu•ro -ra *adj* immortal; everlasting, imperishable
imperìzia *f* inexperience
imperlare (**impèrlo**) *tr* to bead; to cover with beads (*of perspiration*)
impermalire §176 *tr* to provoke || *ref* to become provoked
impermeàbile *adj* waterproof || *m* raincoat
imperniare §287 (**impèrnio**) *tr* to pivot; (fig) to base
impèro *adj invar* Empire || *m* empire; control, sway
imperscrutàbile *adj* inscrutable
impersonale *adj* impersonal
impersonare (**impersóno**) *tr* to impersonate || *ref*—**impersonarsi in** to be the embodiment of; (theat) to impersonate
impertèrri•to -ta *adj* undaunted
impertinènte *adj* impertinent, pert
impertinènza *f* impertinence
imperturbàbile *adj* imperturbable
imperturba•to -ta *adj* unperturbed
imperversare (**impervèrso**) *intr* to storm, rage; to be the rage
impèr•vio -via *adj* (**-vi -vie**) impassable
ìmpeto *m* impetus; onslaught; violence; outburst; **d'impeto** rashly
impetrare (**impètro**) *tr* to beg for; to obtain by entreaty || *intr* (ESSERE) (lit) to turn to stone
impetti•to -ta *adj* puffed up with pride
impetuó•so -sa [s] *adj* impetuous
impiallacciare §128 *tr* to veneer
impiallacciatura *f* veneer, veneering
impiantare *tr* to install (*a machine*); to set up (*a business*); to open (*an account*)
impiantito *m* floor, flooring
impianto *m* installation; plant; system
impiastrare *tr* to plaster; to dirty
impiastricciare §128 *tr* to plaster; to daub; to soil
impiastro *m* (med) plaster; (fig) bore
impiccagióne *f* hanging
impiccare §197 *tr* to hang
impicciare §128 *tr* to hinder; to bother || *ref* to meddle, butt in; **impicciarsi degli affari propri** to mind one's own business
impìc•cio *m* (**-ci**) hindrance; trouble; **essere d'impiccio** to be in the way
impicció•ne -na *mf* meddler
impiccolire §176 *tr* to reduce in size || *ref* to shrink in size
impiegare §209 (**impiègo**) *tr* to employ;

to use; to devote (*one's energies*); to spend (*time*); to invest (*capital*); to take (*time*) || *ref* to have a job
impiegatì·zio -zia *adj* (**-zi -zie**) employee, white-collar
impiega·to -ta *mf* employee; clerk
impiè·go *m* (**-ghi**) employment; use; job; place of business; investment
impietosire [s] §176 *tr* to move to pity || *ref* to be moved to pity
impietrire §176 *tr, intr* (ESSERE) & *ref* to turn to stone
impigliare §280 *tr* to entangle || *ref* to become entangled
impigrire §176 *tr* to make lazy || *intr* (ESSERE) & *ref* to get lazy
impinguare (**impìnguo**) *tr* & *ref* to fatten
impinzare *tr* to stuff || *ref* to stuff oneself; **impinzarsi il cervello** to stuff one's brain (*with knowledge*)
impiombare (**impiómbo**) *tr* to lead; to plumb, seal with lead; to fill (*a tooth*); (naut) to splice (*a cable*)
impiombatura *f* seal; filling (*of tooth*); (naut) splicing
impipare *ref*—**impiparsi di** (slang) to not give a hoot about
implacàbile *adj* implacable
implicare §197 (**ìmplico**) *tr* to implicate; to imply
implìci·to -ta *adj* implicit, implied
implorare (**implòro**) *tr* to implore
implume *adj* unfledged, featherless
impolìti·co -ca *adj* (**-ci -che**) unpolitical; impolitic, injudicious
impollinare (**impòllino**) *tr* to pollinate
impoltronire §176 *tr* to make lazy || *ref* to get lazy
impolverare (**impólvero**) *tr* to cover with dust || *ref* to get covered with dust
impomatare *tr* to pomade; to smear with pomade
imponderàbile *adj* imponderable; weightless
imponderabilità *f* imponderability; weightlessness
imponènte *adj* imposing; stately
imponìbile *adj* taxable || *m* taxable income
impopolare *adj* unpopular
impopolarità *f* unpopularity
impórre §218 *tr* to place, put; to impose; to order; to compel; to give (*a name*) || *intr* (ESSERE) to be imposing; (with *dat*) to order, command || *ref* to command respect; to win favor; to be necessary
importante *adj* important; sizable || *m* important thing
importanza *f* importance; size; **darsi importanza** to assume an air of importance
importare (**impòrto**) *tr* to import; to imply; to involve || *intr* (ESSERE) to be of consequence || *impers* (ESSERE) —**importa** it matters; **non importa** never mind
importa·tóre -trice *mf* importer
importazióne *f* importation; import
impòrto *m* amount
importunare *tr* to bother, importune
importu·no -na *adj* importunate, bothersome || *mf* bore
imposizióne *f* imposition; giving (*of a name*); order, command; taxation
impossessare (**impossèsso**) *ref*—**impossessarsi di** to seize; to master (*a language*)
impossìbile *adj* & *m* impossible
impossibili·tà *f* (**-tà**) impossibility
impossibilitare (**impossibìlito**) *tr* to make impossible; to make unable or incapable
impossibilita·to -ta *adj* unable
impòsta *f* tax; shutter; (archit) impost; **imposta complementare** surtax; **imposta sul valore aggiunto** value-added tax
impostare (**impòsto**) *tr* to start, begin; to state (*a problem*); to mail; to lay (*a stone*); to open (*an account*); to attune (*one's voice*); to lay the keel of (*a ship*) || *ref* to take one's position, get ready
impostazióne *f* beginning, starting; laying; mail, mailing; (com) posting
impo·stóre -stóra *mf* impostor
impostura *f* imposture
impotènte *adj* weak; impotent
impotènza *f* impotence
impoveriménto *m* impoverishment
impoverire §176 *tr* to impoverish || *intr* (ESSERE) & *ref* to become impoverished
impraticàbile *adj* impracticable; impassable
impratichire §176 *tr* to train, familiarize || *ref* to become familiar (*e.g., with a task*)
imprecare §197 (**imprèco**) *tr* to wish (*e.g., s.o.'s death*) || *intr* to curse
imprecazióne *f* imprecation, curse
imprecisàbile *adj* undefinable
imprecisióne *f* inexactness, inaccuracy
impreci·so -sa *adj* vague, inexact
impregnare (**imprégno**) *tr* to impregnate
impremedita·to -ta *adj* unpremeditated
imprendìbile *adj* impregnable
imprendi·tóre -trice *mf* contractor || *m*—**imprenditore di pompe funebri** undertaker
imprenditoriale *adj* managerial
imprepara·to -ta *adj* unprepared
impreparazióne *f* unpreparedness
imprésa [s] *f* enterprise; undertaking; achievement; firm, concern; (theat) management; **impresa (di) pompe funebri** undertaking establishment
impresà·rio [s] *m* (**-ri**) manager; (theat) impresario
imprescindìbile *adj* essential, indispensable; unavoidable
impresentàbile *adj* unpresentable
impressionàbile *adj* impressionable
impressionante *adj* striking, impressive; frightening
impressionare (**impressióno**) *tr* to impress; (phot) to expose || *ref* to become frightened; (phot) to be exposed
impressióne *f* impression
imprestare (**imprèsto**) *tr* (coll) to lend

imprèstito *m* (philol) borrowing
imprevedìbile *adj* unforeseeable
imprevedu•to -ta *adj* unforeseen
imprevidènte *adj* improvident
imprevi•sto -sta *adj* unforeseen, unexpected || **imprevisti** *mpl* unforeseen events
imprigionare (**imprigióno**) *tr* to imprison
imprìmere §131 *tr* to impress; to imprint; to impart (*e.g., motion*)
improbàbile *adj* improbable, unlikely
ìmpro•bo -ba *adj* dishonest; laborious
improdutti•vo -va *adj* unproductive
imprónta *f* print, imprint; mark; **impronta digitale** fingerprint
improntare (**imprónto**) *tr* to impress, imprint; to mark
improntitùdine *f* audacity, impudence
impronunziàbile *adj* unpronounceable
impropè•rio *m* (**-ri**) insult
improprie•tà *f* (**-tà**) impropriety; error
impprò•prio -pria *adj* (**-pri -prie**) improper, inappropriate; (math) improper
improrogàbile *adj* unextendible
impròvvi•do -da *adj* improvident
improvvisare *tr* to improvise || *ref* to suddenly decide to become
improvvisa•to -ta *adj* improvised; impromptu || *f* surprise; surprise party
improvvisazióne *f* improvisation
improvvi•so -sa *adj* sudden || *m* (mus) impromptu; **all'improvviso** or **d'improvviso** suddenly
imprudènte *adj* imprudent; rash
imprudènza *f* imprudence; rashness
impudènte *adj* shameless; brazen; impudent
impudènza *f* shamelessness; impudence
impudicìzia *f* immodesty
impudi•co -ca *adj* (**-chi -che**) immodest, indecent
impugnare *tr* to grip, seize; to take up (*arms*); to impugn, contest
impugnatura *f* handle; grip, hold; hilt, haft
impulsi•vo -va *adj* impulsive
impulso *m* impulse; **dare impulso a** to promote, foment
impuneménte *adv* with impunity
impunità *f* impunity
impuni•to -ta *adj* unpunished
impuntare *intr* to stumble, trip; to stutter || *ref* to stutter; to balk; to be stubborn; **impuntarsi a** or **di** + *inf* to stubbornly insist on + *ger*
impuntigliare §280 *ref* to persist, insist
impuntire §176 *tr* to tuft (*e.g., a pillow*)
impuntura *f* backstitch
impuri•tà *f* (**-tà**) impurity; unchastity
impu•ro -ra *adj* impure; unchaste
imputàbile *adj* attributable
imputare (**ìmputo**) *tr* to impute; to charge, accuse; (com) to post
imputa•to -ta *mf* accused, defendant
imputazióne *f* imputation; charge, accusation; (com) posting
imputridire §176 *tr* & *intr* (ESSERE) to rot
in *prep* in; at; into; to; on, upon; through; during; married to, e.g., **Maria Roberti in Bianchi** Marie Roberti married to Bianchi; as, e.g., **in premio** as a prize; by, e.g., **in automobile** by car; of, e.g., **studente in legge** student of law; **essere in quattro** to be four; **in alto** up; **in breve** soon; in a word; **in giù** down; **in là** there; **in qua** here; **in realtà** really; **in seguito a** because of
-ina *suf fem* about, e.g., **cinquantina** about fifty
inabbordàbile *adj* unapproachable
inàbile *adj* unfit; ineligible; awkward
inabili•tà *f* (**-tà**) unfitness; awkwardness; inability
inabilitare (**inabìlito**) *tr* to incapacitate; to render unfit; to disqualify
inabilitazióne *f* disqualification
inabissare *tr* to plunge || *ref* to sink
inabitàbile *adj* uninhabitable
inabita•to -ta *adj* uninhabited
inaccessìbile *adj* inaccessible; unfathomable
inaccettàbile *adj* unacceptable
inacerbire §176 *tr* to exacerbate || *ref* to grow bitter
inacidire §176 *tr* & *ref* to sour
inadattàbile *adj* unadaptable; maladjusted
inadat•to -ta *adj* inadequate
inadegua•to -ta *adj* inadequate
inadempiènte *adj* not fulfilling; **inadempiente agli obblighi di leva** draft-dodging
inafferràbile *adj* that cannot be caught or captured; incomprehensible; elusive
inalare *tr* to inhale
inalatóre *m* inhaler
inalberare (**inàlbero**) *tr* to hoist || *ref* to rear; to fly into a rage
inalteràbile *adj* unalterable
inamidare (**inàmido**) *tr* to starch
inamida•to -ta *adj* starched; pompous, starchy
inammissìbile *adj* inadmissible
inamovìbile *adj* irremovable
inamovibili•tà *f* (**-tà**) irremovability; tenure
inane *adj* inane; futile
inanella•to -ta *adj* curly; beringed
inanima•to -ta *adj* inanimate; lifeless
inanizióne *f* starvation
inappagàbile *adj* unquenchable
inappaga•to -ta *adj* unsatisfied
inappellàbile *adj* definitive, final
inappetènza *f* lack of appetite
inapprezzàbile *adj* inappreciable, imperceptible; inestimable
inappuntàbile *adj* faultless, impeccable
inarcare §197 *tr* to arch; to raise (*one's eyebrows*)
inargentare (**inargènto**) *tr* to silver
inaridire §176 *tr* to dry; to parch || *ref* to dry up
inarrestàbile *adj* irresistible
inarrivàbile *adj* unattainable; inimitable
inarticola•to -ta *adj* indistinct, inarticulate
inascolta•to -ta *adj* unheeded
inaspetta•to -ta *adj* unexpected
inaspriménto *m* exacerbation

inasprire §176 *tr* to aggravate || *ref* to sour; to become embittered; to become sharper; to become fierce or furious
inastare *tr* to hoist (*flag*); to fix (*bayonets*)
inattaccàbile *adj* unattackable; unassailable; **inattacabile da** resistant to
inattendìbile *adj* unreliable
inattè·so -sa [s] *adj* unexpected
inatti·vo -ta *adj* inactive
inaudi·to -ta *adj* unheard-of
inaugurale *adj* inaugural; maiden (*voyage*)
inaugurare (**inàuguro**) *tr* to inaugurate; to usher in (*the New Year*); to open (*e.g., an exhibit*); to unveil (*a statue*); to sport for the first time
inaugurazióne *f* inauguration
inauspica·to -ta *adj* (lit) inauspicious
inavvedu·to -ta *adj* careless, rash
inavvertènza *f* inadvertence, oversight
inavverti·to -ta *adj* unnoticed; inadvertent, thoughtless
inazióne *f* inaction
incagliare §280 *tr* to hamper; to run aground || *intr* (ESSERE) & *ref* to run aground; (fig) to get stuck
incà·glio *m* (**-gli**) running aground; hindrance, obstacle
incalcinare *tr* to whitewash; to lime (*a field*)
incalcolàbile *adj* incalculable
incallire §176 *tr* to make callous || *intr* (ESSERE) to become callous; to become inured
incalli·to -ta *adj* callous; inveterate
incalzante *adj* pressing
incalzare *tr* to press, pursue || *intr* to be imminent; to be pressing || *ref* to follow one another in rapid succession
incamerare (**incàmero**) *tr* to confiscate
incamminare *tr* to launch; to guide, direct || *ref* to set out; to be on one's way
incanagli·to -ta *adj* vile, despicable
incanalare *tr* to channel || *ref* to flow
incancrenire §176 *tr* to affect with gangrene || *ref* to become gangrenous; (fig) to become callous
incandescènte *adj* incandescent; (fig) red-hot
incandescènza *f* incandescence
incannare *tr* to reel, wind
incantare *tr* to bewitch; to auction off || *ref* to become enraptured; to be spellbound; to jam, get stuck (*said of machinery*)
incanta·tóre -trice *adj* enchanting || *m* enchanter || *f* enchantress
incantésimo *m* enchantment, spell
incantévole *adj* enchanting, charming
incanto *m* enchantment; bewitchery; auction; **d'incanto** marvelously well
incanutire §176 *tr, intr* (ESSERE) & *ref* to turn gray-headed, to turn gray (*said of a person*)
incanuti·to -ta *adj* hoary
incapace *adj* incapable; (law) incompetent || *mf* oaf; (law) incompetent
incapaci·tà *f* (**-tà**) incapacity; (law) incompetence
incaparbire §176 *intr* (ESSERE) & *ref* to be obstinate; to be determined
incaponire §176 *ref* to get stubborn; to be determined
incappare *intr* (ESSERE) to stumble
incappottare (**incappòtto**) *tr* to cover with a coat || *ref* to wrap oneself in a coat
incappucciare §128 *tr* to cover with a hood
incapricciare §128 *ref*—**incapricciarsi di** to take a fancy to; to become infatuated with
incapsulare (**incàpsulo**) *tr* to encapsulate; to cap
incarcerare (**incàrcero**) *tr* to jail, incarcerate; (fig) to confine
incaricare §197 (**incàrico**) *tr* to charge || *ref*—**incaricarsi di** to take charge of; to take care of
incarica·to -ta *adj* in charge; visiting (*professor*) || *mf* deputy; **incaricato d'affari** chargé d'affaires
incàri·co *m* (**-chi**) task; appointment, position; **per incarico di** on behalf of
incarnare *tr* to incarnate, embody
incarna·to -ta *adj* incarnate || *m* pink complexion
incarnazióne *f* incarnation
incarnire §176 *intr* (ESSERE) & *ref* to grow in (*said of a toenail*)
incarni·to -ta *adj* ingrown (*toenail*)
incartaménto *m* file, dossier
incartapecori·to -ta *adj* shriveled up
incartare *tr* to wrap up (*in paper*)
incasellare [s] (**incasèllo**) *tr* to file; to sort out
incasellatóre [s] *m* post-office file clerk
incassare *tr* to box up; to put (*a watch*) in a case; to mortise (*a lock*); to channel (*a river*); to cash (*a check*); (fig) to take (*e.g., blows*) || *intr* to fit; to take it
incasso *m* receipts
incastellatura *f* scaffolding
incastonare (**incastóno**) *tr* to set, mount (*a gem*); **incastonare citazioni in un discorso** to stud a speech with quotations
incastrare *tr* to insert; to mortise; (fig) to corner || *intr* to fit || *ref* to fit; to become imbedded; to telescope (*said, e.g., of a train in a collision*)
incastro *m* joint; insertion; (carp) tenon; (carp) mortise
incatenare (**incaténo**) *tr* to chain, put in chains; to tie down, restrain
incatramare *tr* to tar
incàu·to -ta *adj* unwary, careless
incavallatura *f* truss (*to support roof*)
incavare *tr* to hollow out; to groove
incava·to -ta *adj* hollow
incavatura *f* hollow
incavicchiare §287 *tr* to peg
incavigliare §280 *tr* to peg
incavo *m* hollow; cavity; **incavo dell'ascella** armpit
incazzottare (**incazzòtto**) *tr* (naut) to furl

incèdere *m* stately walk || §123 *intr* to walk stately
incendiare §287 (**incèndio**) *tr* to set on fire; (fig) to inflame || *ref* to catch fire
incendià·rio -ria *adj & mf* (**-ri -rie**) incendiary
incèn·dio *m* (**-di**) fire; **incendio doloso** arson
incenerire §176 *tr* to reduce to ashes; to wither (*e.g., with a look*) || *ref* to turn to ashes
inceneritóre *m* incinerator
incensare (**incènso**) *tr* (eccl) to incense; (fig) to flatter
incensa·tóre -trice *mf* incense burner; (fig) flatterer
incensière *m* incense burner
incènso *m* incense
incensura·to -ta *adj* uncensured; (law) having no previous record
incentivo *m* incentive
inceppare (**incéppo**) *tr* to hinder; to shackle || *ref* to jam (*said of firearm*)
incerare (**incéro**) *tr* to wax
incerata *f* oilcloth; (naut) raincoat
incernierare (**incernièro**) *tr* to hinge
incertézza *f* uncertainty, incertitude
incèr·to -ta *adj* uncertain; irresolute || *m* uncertainty; **incerti** extras; **incerti del mestiere** cares of office, occupational annoyances, occupational hazards
incespicare §197 (**incéspico**) *intr* to stumble
incessàbile *adj* (lit) ceaseless
incessante *adj* unceasing, incessant
incèsto *m* incest
incestuó·so -sa [s] *adj* incestuous
incètta *f* cornering (*of market*)
incettare (**incètto**) *tr* to corner (*market*)
incetta·tóre -trice *mf* monopolizer
inchiavardare *tr* to key, bolt
inchièsta *f* probe, inquest; (journ) inquiry
inchinare *tr* to bend; to bow (*the head*) || *intr* (lit) to go down (*said of stars*) || *ref* to bow; to yield
inchi·no -na *adj* bent; bowing || *m* bow; curtsy
inchiodare (**inchiòdo**) *tr* to nail; to spike; to rivet; to tie, bind; to stop (*a car*) suddenly; to transfix || *ref* to freeze (*said, e.g., of brakes*); (fig) to be tied down; (fig) to go into debt
inchiostrare (**inchiòstro**) *tr* (typ) to ink
inchiòstro *m* ink; **inchiostro di china** India ink, Chinese ink
inciampare *intr* to trip, stumble
inciampo *m* stumbling block, obstacle; **essere d'inciampo a** to be in the way of
incidentale *adj* incidental
incidènte *adj* incidental || *m* incident; accident; argument, question
incidènza *f* incidence
incidere §145 *tr* to engrave; to cut; to record (*a record, a tape; a song*); **incidere all'acqua forte** to etch || *intr*—**incidere su** to weigh heavily on (*expenses, a budget*); to leave a mark on
incinerazióne *f* incineration; cremation
incinta *adj fem* pregnant
incipiènte *adj* incipient
incipriare §287 *tr* to powder || *ref* to powder oneself
incirca *adv* about; **all'incirca** more or less
incisióne *f* engraving; cutting (*of a record*); recording (*of a tape; of a song*); incision; **incisione all'acquaforte** etching
incisi·vo -va *adj* incisive; sharp (*photograph* || *m* incisor
inciso *m* (gram) parenthetical clause; (mus) theme; **per inciso** incidentally
incisóre *m* engraver, etcher
incitare *tr* to incite, provoke
incivile *adj* uncivilized; uncouth
incivilire §176 *tr* to civilize || *ref* to become civilized
inclemènte *adj* inclement, harsh
inclemènza *f* inclemency, harshness
inclinare *tr* to tilt; to bow, bend; to incline || *intr* (fig) to lean || *ref* to bend
inclinazióne *f* inclination; slope; **inclinazione laterale** (aer) bank; **inclinazione magnetica** magnetic dip
incline *adj* inclined
incli·to -ta *adj* famous; noble
inclùdere §105 *tr* to enclose, include
inclusi·vo -va *adj* including; **inclusivo di** including
inclu·so -sa *adj* enclosed; included; inclusive || *f* enclosed letter
incoerènte *adj* incoherent
incògliere §127 *tr* (lit) to catch in the act || *intr*—**incogliere a** to happen to
incògni·to -ta *adj* unknown || *m* incognito; unknown; **in incognito** incognito || *f* (math) unknown quantity; (fig) puzzle
incollare (**incòllo**) *tr* to glue, paste; to size (*paper*) || *intr* to stick || *ref* to stick; to take on one's shoulders
incollatura *f* neck (*of horse*); glueing, sticking
incollerire §176 *intr & ref* to get angry
incolloca·to -ta *adj* unemployed
incolonnare (**incolónno**) *tr* to set up in columns
incolonnatóre *m* tabulator
incolóre *adj* colorless
incolpàbile *adj* blamable; (lit) guiltless
incolpare (**incólpo**) *tr*—**incolpare di** to charge with
incól·to -ta *adj* uncultivated; unkempt
incòlume *adj* unharmed, unhurt
incolumità *f* safety, security
incombènte *adj* (*danger*) impending; (*duty*) incumbent
incombènza *f* task, charge, incumbency
incómbere §186 *intr* (ESSERE) to be impending; to be incumbent
incombustibile *adj* incombustible
incominciare §128 *tr & intr* (ESSERE) to begin
incommensuràbile *adj* immeasurable; (math) incommensurable
incomodare (**incòmodo**) *tr* to bother, disturb || *ref* to bother; **non s'incomodi!** don't bother!
incòmo·do -da *adj* bothersome, inconvenient || *m* inconvenience; ailment;

levare l'incomodo a to get out of the way of
incomparàbile *adj* incomparable
incompatìbile *adj* incompatible; unforgivable
incompetènte *adj & mf* incompetent
incompiu•to -ta *adj* unfinished
incomplè•to -ta *adj* incomplete
incompó•sto -sta *adj* untidy; unkempt; unbecoming (*behavior*)
incomprensìbile *adj* incomprehensible
incomprensióne *f* lack of understanding
incompré•so -sa [s] *adj* misunderstood
incomprimìbile *adj* irrepressible; incompressible
inconcepìbile *adj* inconceivable
inconciliàbile *adj* irreconcilable
inconcludènte *adj* inconclusive; insignificant
inconcus•so -sa *adj* (lit) unshaken
incondiziona•to -ta *adj* unconditional
inconfessàbile *adj* unspeakable, vile
inconfessa•to -ta *adj* unavowed
inconfondìbile *adj* unmistakable
inconfutàbile *adj* irrefutable
incongruènte *adj* inconsistent
incòn•gruo -grua *adj* incongruous
inconoscìbile *adj* unknowable
inconsapèvole *adj* unaware, unconscious
incòn•scio -scia *adj & m* (-sci -sce) unconscious
inconseguènte *adj* inconsistent, inconsequential
inconsidera•to -ta *adj* inconsiderate
inconsistènte *adj* flimsy; inconsistent
inconsistènza *f* flimsiness; inconsistency
inconsolàbile *adj* inconsolable
inconsuè•to -ta *adj* unusual
inconsul•to -ta *adj* ill-advised, rash
incontamina•to -ta *adj* uncontaminated
incontenìbile *adj* irrepressible
incontentàbile *adj* insatiable; hard to please; exacting
incontinènza *f* incontinence
incontrare (incóntro) *tr* to meet; to encounter, meet with || *intr* (ESSERE) to catch on (*said, e.g., of fashions*) || *ref* to meet; to agree || *impers* (ESSERE) to happen
incontrastàbile *adj* indisputable
incontrasta•to -ta *adj* undisputed
incóntro *m* meeting; encounter; success; meet; game, fight, match; occasion, opportunity; **all'incontro** on the other hand; opposite; **andare incontro a** to go towards; to go to meet; to face; to meet (*expenses*); to accommodate; **farsi incontro a** to advance toward
incontrollàbile *adj* uncontrollable
incontrolla•to -ta *adj* unchecked
incontrovertìbile *adj* incontrovertible
inconveniènte *adj* inconvenient || *m* inconvenience, disadvantage
incoraggiante *adj* encouraging
incoraggiare §290 *tr* to encourage
incorare §257 **(incuòro)** *tr* to hearten
incordare (incòrdo) *tr* to string (*e.g., a racket*); to tie up (*with a cord*) || *ref* to stiffen (*said of a muscle*)
incornare (incòrno) *tr* (taur) to gore
incorniciare §128 *tr* to frame; (journ) to border; (slang) to cuckold
incoronare (incoróno) *tr* to crown
incoronazióne *f* coronation
incorporàbile *adj* absorbable; adaptable
incorporare (incòrporo) *tr* to incorporate; to absorb || *ref* to incorporate
incorpòre•o -a *adj* incorporeal
incorreggìbile *adj* incorrigible
incórrere §139 *intr* (ESSERE)—**incorrere in** to incur
incorrót•to -ta *adj* uncorrupt
incosciènte *adj* unconscious; unaware; irresponsible || *mf* irresponsible person
incosciènza *f* unconsciousness; irresponsibility; madness
incostante *adj* inconstant, fickle
incredìbile *adj* incredible, unbelievable
incrèdu•lo -la *adj* incredulous || *mf* disbeliever; doubter
incrementare (increménto) *tr* to increase, boost
increménto *m* increase, increment, boost
incresció•so -sa [s] *adj* disagreeable, unpleasant
increspare (incréspo) *tr* to ripple; to wrinkle; to knit (*the brow*); to pleat || *ref* to ripple
incretinire §176 *tr* to make stupid; (fig) to deafen || *intr* (ESSERE) to become stupid; to lose one's mind
incriminare (incrìmino) *tr* to incriminate
incrinare *tr* to flaw; to ruin
incrinatura *f* crack, flaw
incrociare §128 **(incrócio)** *tr* to cross || *intr* (naut) to cruise || *ref* to cross one another; to interbreed
incrociatóre *m* (nav) cruiser
incró•cio *m* (-ci) crossing; cross; crossroads; crossbreed
incrollàbile *adj* unshakable
incrostare (incròsto) *tr* to incrust; to inlay (*e.g., with mosaic*) || *ref* to become incrusted
incrostazióne *f* incrustation
incrudelire §176 *tr* to enrage || *intr* to commit cruelties || *intr* (ESSERE) to become cruel; **incrudelire su** to commit cruelties upon
incruèn•to -ta *adj* bloodless
incubare (ìncubo & incubo) *tr* to incubate
incubatrice *f* incubator; brooder
incubazióne *f* incubation; **in incubazione** brewing (*said of an infectious disease*)
ìncubo *m* nightmare
incùdine *f* anvil; **essere tra l'incudine e il martello** to be between the devil and the deep blue sea
inculcare §197 *tr* to inculcate
incunàbolo *m* incunabulum
incuneare (incùneo) *tr & ref* to wedge
incuràbile *adj & mf* incurable
incurante *adj* careless, indifferent
incùria *f* malpractice; neglect
incuriosire [s] §176 *tr* to intrigue || *ref* to be intrigued
incursióne *f* incursion; **incursione aerea** air raid

incurvare *tr* to bend; (lit) to lower || *intr* (ESSERE) & *ref* to bend; to warp
incurvatura *f* bend, curve
incustodi·to -ta *adj* unguarded, unwatched
incùtere §154 *tr* to inspire; **incutere terrore a** to strike with terror
ìndaco *adj* & *m* indigo
indaffara·to -ta *adj* busy
indagare §209 *tr* & *intr* to investigate; **indagare su** to investigate
indaga·tóre -trice *adj* probing, searching || *mf* investigator
indàgine *f* investigation, inquiry
indarno *adv* (lit) in vain
indebitare (indébito) *tr* to burden with debts || *ref* to run into debt
indebita·to -ta *adj* indebted
indébi·to -ta *adj* undue; unjust; fraudulent (*conversion*) || *m* what one does not owe; excess payment
indeboliménto *m* weakening
indebolire §176 *tr, intr* (ESSERE) & *ref* to weaken
indecènte *adj* indecent
indecènza *f* indecency; outrage
indecifràbile *adj* indecipherable
indecisióne *f* indecision
indeci·so -sa *adj* uncertain; undecided; indecisive
indecoró·so -sa [s] *adj* indecorous, unseemly
indefès·so -sa *adj* indefatigable
indefinìbile *adj* indefinable
indefini·to -ta *adj* indefinite; undefined
indegni·tà *f* (-tà) indignity
indé·gno -gna *adj* unworthy; disgraceful
indelèbile *adj* indelible
indelica·to -ta *adj* indelicate
indemagliàbile *adj* runproof
indemonia·to -ta *adj* possessed by the devil; restless
indènne *adj* undamaged, unscathed; **tener indenne** to guarantee against harm or damage
indenni·tà *f* (-tà) indemnity; indemnification; **indennità di carica** special emolument; bonus; **indennità di carovita** cost-of-living allowance; **indennità di preavviso** severance pay; **indennità di trasfèrta** per diem
indennizzare [ddzz] *tr* to indemnify
indennizzo [ddzz] *m* indemnification; indemnity
inderogàbile *adj* inescapable
indescrivìbile *adj* indescribable
indesideràbile *adj* undesirable
indesidera·to -ta *adj* unwished-for; undesirable
indeterminati·vo -va *adj* indefinite
indetermina·to -ta *adj* indeterminate; (gram) indefinite
indi *adv* (lit) then; (lit) thence; **da indi innanzi** (lit) from that moment on
India, l' *f* India; **le Indie Occidentali** the West Indies; **le Indie Orientali** the East Indies
india·no -na *adj* & *mf* Indian; **fare l'indiano** to feign ignorance || *f* printed calico
indiavola·to -ta *adj* devilish, fierce; impish (*child*)
indicare §197 **(ìndico)** *tr* to indicate; to show
indicati·vo -va *adj* & *m* indicative
indica·to -ta *adj* appropriate, fitting; recommended, advisable
indica·tóre -trice *adj* indicating, pointing || *m* indicator; **indicatore di direzione** (aut) turn signal; **indicatore di livello** gauge; **indicatore di pressione** pressure gauge; **indicatore di velocità** (aut) speedometer; **indicatore stradale** road sign; **indicatore telefonico** telephone directory
indicazióne *f* indication; direction; **indicazioni per l'uso** instructions
ìndice *m* index finger; pointer, gauge; indicator; sign, indication; index; (typ) fist; **indice delle materie** table of contents || **Indice** *m* Index; **mettere all'Indice** to put on the Index; to ban, index
indicìbile *adj* inexpressible, unspeakable
indietreggiare §290 **(indietréggio)** *intr* (ESSERE & AVERE) to withdraw
indiètro *adv* back; behind; **all'indietro** backwards; **dare indietro** to return, give back; **domandare indietro** to ask back; **essere indietro** to be slow (*said of a watch*); to be behind; to be backward, be slow; **tirarsi indietro** to withdraw; to step back
indifendìbile *adj* indefensible
indifé·so -sa [s] *adj* defenseless
indifferènte *adj* indifferent; **essere indifferente a** to be the same to; **lasciare indifferente** to leave cold
indifferènza *f* indifference
indìge·no -na *adj* indigenous || *m* native
indigènte *adj* indigent, poor
indigestìbile *adj* indigestible
indigestióne *f* indigestion
indigè·sto -sta *adj* indigestible; (fig) dull, boring
indignare *tr* to anger, shock || *ref* to be aroused, be indignant
indigna·to -ta *adj* indignant, outraged
indignazióne *f* indignation
indigni·tà *f* (-tà) indignity
indimenticàbile *adj* unforgettable
indipendènte *adj* & *m* independent
indipendènza *f* independence
indire §151 *tr* to announce publicly; (lit) to declare (*war*)
indirèt·to -ta *adj* indirect
indirizzare *tr* to direct; to address
indirizzà·rio *m* (-ri) mailing list
indirizzo *m* address; direction
indiscernìbile *adj* indiscernible
indisciplina *f* lack of discipline
indisciplina·to -ta *adj* undisciplined
indiscré·to -ta *adj* indiscreet; tactless
indiscrezióne *f* indiscretion; gossip; news leak
indiscus·so -sa *adj* unquestioned
indiscutìbile *adj* indisputable
indispensàbile *adj* indispensable || *m* essential
indispettire §176 *tr* to annoy || *ref* to get annoyed
indisponènte *adj* vexing, irritating

indispórre §218 *tr* to indispose; to disgust
indisposizióne *f* indisposition
indispó·sto -sta *adj* indisposed
indissolùbile *adj* indissoluble
indistin·to -ta *adj* indistinct
indistruttìbile *adj* indestructible
indisturba·to -ta *adj* undisturbed
indìvia *f* endive
individuàbile *adj* distinguishable
individuale *adj* individual
individuali·tà *f* (-tà) individuality
individuare (**indivìduo**) *tr* to individuate; to outline; to single out
indivìduo *m* individual; fellow
indivisìbile *adj* indivisible
indivi·so -sa *adj* undivided
indiziare §287 *tr* to cast suspicion on
indizià·rio -ria *adj* (**-ri -rie**) circumstancial
indì·zio *m* (**-zi**) clue; token; symptom
indòcile *adj* indocile, unteachable
Indocina, l' *f* Indochina
indocinése [s] *adj & mf* Indochinese
indoeuropè·o -a *adj & m* Indo-European
indolcire §176 *tr* to sweeten ‖ *ref* to become sweet
indole *f* temper, disposition; nature
indolènte *adj* indolent
indolenziménto *m* soreness, stiffness; numbness
indolenzire §176 *tr* to make sore or stiff; to benumb ‖ *ref* to become sore or stiff
indolenzi·to -ta *adj* sore, stiff; numb
indolóre *adj* painless
indomàbile *adj* indomitable
indoma·ni *m* (**-ni**) morrow, next day; **l'indomani di . . .** the day after . . .
indoma·to -ta *adj* (lit) indomitable, untamed
indòmi·to -ta *adj* (lit) indomitable, untamed
Indonèsia l' *f* Indonesia
indonesia·no -na *adj & mf* Indonesian
indorare (**indòro**) *tr* to gild; (culin) to brown; (fig) to sugar-coat
indoratura *f* gilding
indossare (**indòsso**) *tr* to wear; to put on
indossatrice *f* mannequin, model
indòsso *adv* on, on one's back; **avere indosso** to have on, wear
Indostàn, l' *m* Hindustan
indosta·no -na *adj & mf* Hindustani
indòtto *m* (elec) armature (*of motor*)
indottrinare *tr* to indoctrinate
indovinare *tr* to guess; **indovinarla** to guess right; **non indovinarne una** to never hit the mark
indovina·to -ta *adj* felicitous
indovinèllo *m* puzzle, riddle
indovi·no -na *mf* soothsayer, fortuneteller
indù *adj invar & mf* Hindu
indùb·bio -bia *adj* (**-bi -bie**) undoubted, undisputed
indubita·to -ta *adj* undeniable
indugiare §290 *tr* to delay ‖ *intr* to linger; to hesitate ‖ *ref* to linger
indù·gio *m* (**-gi**) delay; **rompere gli indugi** to come to a decision; **senza ulteriore indugio** without further delay
indulgènte *adj* indulgent
indulgènza *f* indulgence
indùlgere §187 *tr* to grant; to forgive ‖ *intr* to be indulgent; **indulgere a** to indulge; to yield to
indulto *m* (law) pardon
induménto *m* garment; **indumenti intimi** undergarments, unmentionables
indurire §176 *tr* to harden ‖ *intr* (ESSERE) to harden; to get stiff
indurre §102 *tr* to induce
indùstria *f* industry; **grande industria** heavy industry
industriale *adj* industrial ‖ *m* industrialist
industrializzare [ddzz] *tr* to industrialize
industriare §287 *ref* to try, try hard; **industriarsi a** or **per** + *inf* to try to + *inf*, to do one's best to + *inf*
industrió·so -sa [s] *adj* industrious
indut·tóre -trice *adj* inducing, provoking ‖ *m* (elec) field (*of motor*)
induzióne *f* induction
inebetire §176 *tr* to dull; to stun ‖ *intr* (ESSERE) & *ref* to become dull; to be stunned
inebriare §287 (**inèbrio**) *tr* to intoxicate ‖ *ref* to get drunk
inebriante *adj* intoxicating
ineccepìbile *adj* unexceptionable
inèdia *f* starvation, inanition; boredom
inèdi·to -ta *adj* unpublished; new, novel
ineduca·to -ta *adj* uneducated; ill-mannered
ineffàbile *adj* ineffable
inefficace *adj* ineffectual, ineffective
inefficàcia *f* inefficacy
inefficiènte *adj* inefficient
ineguale *adj* unequal; uneven
inelegante *adj* inelegant; shabby
ineleggìbile *adj* ineligible
ineluttàbile *adj* inevitable, inescapable
inenarràbile *adj* unspeakable
inerènte *adj* inherent
inèrme *adj* unarmed, defenseless
inerpicare §197 (**inérpico**) *ref* to clamber
inèrte *adj* inert
inèrzia *f* inertia; inactivity
inesattézza *f* inaccuracy
inesat·to -ta *adj* inaccurate, inexact; uncollected
inesaudi·to -ta *adj* unanswered
inesaurìbile *adj* inexhaustible
inescusàbile *adj* inexcusable
inesigìbile *adj* uncollectable
inesistènte *adj* inexistent
inesoràbile *adj* inexorable
inesperiènza *f* inexperience
inespèr·to -ta *adj* inexperienced; unskilled
inesplicàbile *adj* inexplicable
inesplica·to -ta *adj* unexplained
inesplora·to -ta *adj* unexplored
inesplò·so -sa *adj* unexploded
inespressi·vo -va *adj* inexpressive
inesprimìbile *adj* inexpressible

inespugnàbile *adj* impregnable; incorruptible
inespugna•to -ta *adj* unconquered
inestimàbile *adj* priceless, invaluable
inestinguìbile *adj* inextinguishable
inestirpàbile *adj* ineradicable
inestricàbile *adj* inextricable
inèt•to -ta *adj* inept
ineva•so -sa *adj* unfinished (*business*); unanswered (*mail*)
inevitàbile *adj* unavoidable, inevitable
inèzia *f* trifle, bagatelle
infagottare (infagòtto) *tr* & *ref* to bundle up
infallìbile *adj* infallible
infamante *adj* shameful, disgraceful
infamare *tr* to disgrace; to slander
infame *adj* infamous; villainous; (coll) horrible || *mf* villain
infàmia *f* infamy; (coll) botch, bungle
infangare §209 *tr* to splash with mud; (fig) to stain, spot
infante *adj* & *mf* infant, baby || *m* infante || *f* infanta
infantile *adj* infantile, childish
infànzia *f* infancy, childhood
infarcire §176 *tr* to cram; (culin) to stuff
infarinare *tr* to sprinkle with flour; to powder; (fig) to cram || *ref* to be covered with flour
infarinatura *f* sprinkling with flour; (fig) smattering
infastidire §176 *tr* to annoy || *ref* to be annoyed, lose one's patience
infaticàbile *adj* indefatigable, tireless
infatti *adv* indeed; really
infatuare (infàtuo) *tr* to infatuate || *ref* to become infatuated
infatua•to -ta *adj* infatuated
infàu•sto -sta *adj* unlucky, fatal
infecón•do -da *adj* barren
infedéle *adj* unfaithful; inaccurate || *mf* infidel
infedel•tà *f* (-tà) unfaithfulness; inaccuracy; infidelity
infelice *adj* unhappy, unfortunate; unfavorable || *mf* wretch
infelici•tà *f* (-tà) unhappiness
inferióre *adj* inferior; lower; **inferiore a** lower than; less than; smaller than
inferiorità *f* inferiority
inferire §188a *tr* to inflict; to infer; (naut) to bend (*a sail*)
infermare (infèrmo) *tr* (lit) to weaken || *intr* (ESSERE) to get sick
infermerìa *f* infirmary
infermiè•re -ra *adj* nursing || *m* male nurse || *f* nurse; **infermiera diplomata** trained nurse
infermierìsti•co -ca *adj* (-ci -che) nursing
infermi•tà *f* (-tà) infirmity
infér•mo -ma *adj* infirm; sick || *m* patient
infernale *adj* infernal
infèr•no -na *adj* (lit) lower (*region*) || *m* hell; inferno
inferocire §176 *tr* to infuriate || *intr*—**inferocire su** to be pitiless to || *intr* (ESSERE) to become infuriated
inferriata *f* grating, grill
infervorare (infèrvoro & infervóro) *tr* to excite, stir up || *ref* to get excited; to become absorbed
infestare (infèsto) *tr* to infest
infettare (infètto) *tr* to infect
infetti•vo -va *adj* infectious
infèt•to -ta *adj* infected; corrupted
infezióne *f* infection
infiacchire §176 *tr* to weaken || *intr* (ESSERE) & *ref* to grow weak
infiammàbile *adj* inflammable
infiammare *tr* to inflame; to ignite || *ref* to catch fire, ignite
infiamma•to -ta *adj* burning; aflame; inflamed, excited
infiammazióne *f* inflammation
infi•do -da *adj* untrustworthy
infierire §176 *intr* to become cruel; to be merciless to; to rage (*said, e.g., of a disease*)
infievolire §176 *tr* to weaken
infìggere §103 *tr* to thrust, stick, sink || *ref*—**infiggersi in** to creep in; to work in
infilare *tr* to thread (*a needle*); to insert (*a key*); to transfix (*with a sword*); to put on (*e.g., a coat*); to pull on (*one's pants*); to slip on (*a dress*); to slip (*e.g., one's arm into a sleeve*); to string (*beads*); to hit (*the target*); to take (*a road*); to enter through (*a door*); **infilare l'uscio** to slip away; **infilarle tutte** to succeed all the time; **non infilarne mai una** to never succeed || *ref* to slip; to sink; to slide (*e.g., through a crowd*)
infilata *f* row; string (*e.g., of insults*); (mil) enfilade; **d'infilata** lengthwise
infiltrare *ref* to infiltrate; to seep; (fig) to creep
infilzare *tr* to pierce; to string; (sew) to baste
infilzata *f* string (*of pearls, of lies, etc.*)
ìnfi•mo -ma *adj* lowest, bottom
infine *adv* finally
infingar•do -da *adj* lazy, slothful
infini•tà *f* (-tà) infinity
infinitèsi•mo -ma *adj* & *m* infinitesimal
infiniti•vo -va *adj* (gram) infinitive
infini•to -ta *adj* infinite || *m* infinite; infinity; (gram) infinitive; (math) infinity; **all'infinito** ad infinitum
infino *adv* (lit)—**infino a** until; as far as; **infino a che** as long as
infinocchiare §287 **(infinòcchio)** *tr* (coll) to fool, bamboozle
infioccare §197 **(infiòcco)** *tr* to adorn with tassels
infiorare (infióro) *tr* to adorn with flowers; (fig) to sprinkle; (fig) to embellish || *ref* to be covered with flowers
infiorescènza *f* inflorescence
infirmare *tr* to weaken; to invalidate
infischiare §287 *ref*—**infischiarsi di** to not care a hoot about
infisso *m* frame (*e.g., of door*); fixture
infittire §176 *tr, intr* (ESSERE) & *ref* to thicken
inflazionare (inflazióno) *tr* to inflate
inflazióne *f* inflation
inflessìbile *adj* inflexible

inflessióne *f* inflection
inflèttere §177 *tr* (lit) to inflect
inflìggere §104 *tr* to inflict
influènte *adj* influential
influènza *f* influence; (pathol) influenza
influenzare (influènzo) *tr* to influence, sway
influire §176 *intr* to have an influence; **influire su** to influence || *intr* (ESSERE) —**influire in** to flow into
influsso *m* influence; (lit) plague
infocare §182 *tr* to make glow with heat || *ref* to catch fire; to get excited
infoca·to -ta *adj* red-hot; sultry
infognare (infógno) *ref* (coll) to sink (*e.g., in vice*); (coll) to get stuck (*e.g., in debt*)
infoltire §176 *tr* & *intr* (ESSERE) to thicken
infonda·to -ta *adj* unfounded, groundless
infóndere §178 *tr* to infuse, instill
inforcare §197 **(infórco)** *tr* to pitch (*hay*); to bestride; to mount (*a horse or bicycle*); to put on (*one's eyeglasses*)
inforcatura *f* pitching with a fork; crotch
informare (infórmo) *tr* to inform; (fig) to mold || *ref* to conform; to inquire; **informarsi da** to seek or get information from; **informarsi di** or **su** to inquire about; to find out about
informati·vo -va *adj* informative, informational
informa·tóre -trice *adj* underlying || *mf* informer; (journ) reporter || *m* informant (*of a foreign language*)
informazióne *f* piece of information; **chiedere informazioni sul conto di** to inquire about; **informazioni** information
infórme *adj* shapeless
informicolire §176 *ref* to tingle; **informicolirsi a** to go to sleep, *e.g.,* **gli si è informicolita la gamba** his leg went to sleep
infornare (infórno) *tr* to put in the oven; to bake
infornata *f* batch (*of bread*); (coll) flock
infortunare *ref* to get hurt
infortuna·to -ta *adj* injured || *mf* casualty, victim
infortù·nio *m* (**-ni**) accident, mishap; **infortunio sul lavoro** job-connected injury
infossare (infòsso) *tr* to bury || *ref* to cave in, settle; to become sunken (*said of eyes or cheeks*)
infracidare (infràcido) *tr* var of **infradiciare**
infracidire §176 *intr* to rot
infradiciare §128 **(infràdicio)** *tr* to drench || *ref* to get drenched; to rot (*said of fruit*)
inframmettènza *f* interference, meddling
inframméttere §198 *tr* to interpose || *ref* to meddle, interfere
inframmezzare [ddzz] **(inframmèzzo)** *tr* to intersperse
infràngere §179 *tr* & *ref* to break
infrangìbile *adj* unbreakable
infran·to -ta *adj* broken, shattered
infraró·so -sa *adj* & *m* infrared
infrascrit·to -ta *adj* mentioned below
infrastruttura *f* underpinning; infrastructure; (rr) roadbed
infrazióne *f* infraction, breach
infreddatura *f* mild cold
infreddolire §176 *ref* to feel cold, to be chilled
infrenàbile *adj* irrepressible
infrequènte *adj* infrequent
infrollire §176 *tr* to make (*meat*) high || *intr* (ESSERE) & *ref* to get high (*said of meat*); (fig) to soften
infruttuó·so -sa [s] *adj* unprofitable
infuòri *adv* out; **all'infuori** outward; **all'infuori di** except
infuriare §287 *tr* to infuriate, enrage || *intr* to get blustery; to rage || *intr* (ESSERE) to lose one's temper
infusióne *f* infusion; sprinkling (*of holy water*)
infuso *m* infusion
ingabbiare §287 *tr* to cage; to jail; to corner; to build the framework of
ingabbiatura *f* frame, framework
ingaggiare §290 *tr* to hire; to engage || *ref* to sign up; to get tangled up
ingàg·gio *m* (**-gi**) engagement; (sports) bonus (*for signing up*)
ingagliardire §176 *tr* to strengthen || *ref* to become strong
ingannare *tr* to deceive; to cheat; to elude; to beguile || *ref* to be mistaken
inganna·tóre -trice *adj* deceptive || *mf* impostor
ingannévole *adj* deceitful; deceptive
inganno *m* deception; illusion
ingarbugliare §280 *tr* to entangle; to jumble || *ref* to get mixed up; to become embroiled
ingegnare (ingégno) *ref* to manage; to scheme
ingegnère *m* engineer
ingegnerìa *f* engineering; **ingegneria civile** civil engineering; **ingegneria meccanica** mechanical engineering
ingégno *m* brain, intelligence; talent; genius; expediency; (lit) machinery
ingegnosità [s] *f* ingeniousness
ingegnó·so -sa [s] *adj* ingenious; euphuistic
ingelosire [s] §176 *tr* to make jealous || *intr* (ESSERE) & *ref* to become jealous
ingemmare (ingèmmo) *tr* to adorn or stud with gems
ingenerare (ingènero) *tr* to engender
ingèni·to -ta *adj* inborn
ingènte *adj* huge, vast
ingentilire §176 *tr* to refine
ingenui·tà *f* (**-tà**) ingenuousness; ingenuous act
ingè·nuo -nua *adj* ingenuous, artless || *m* (theat) artless character || *f* (theat) ingénue
ingerènza *f* interference
ingerire §176 *tr* to ingest, swallow || *ref* to meddle

ingessare (**ingèsso**) *tr* to put in a plaster cast; to plaster up
ingessatura *f* (surg) plaster cast
inghiaiare **§287** *tr* to gravel, cover with gravel
Inghilterra, l' *f* England; **la Nuova Inghilterra** New England
inghiottire (**inghiótto**) & **§176** *tr* to swallow; to swallow up; to pocket (*one's pride*)
inghirlandare *tr* to bedeck with garlands; (lit) to encircle
ingiallire **§176** *tr* & *intr* (ESSERE) to turn yellow
ingigantire **§176** *tr* to exaggerate || *intr* (ESSERE) to grow larger, increase
inginocchiare **§287** (**inginòcchio**) *ref* to kneel down
inginocchia·tóio *m* (**-tói**) prie-dieu
ingioiellare (**ingioièllo**) *tr* to bejewel; (fig) to stud
ingiù *adv* down; **all'ingiù** downwards
ingiùngere **§183** *tr* to order, command || *intr* (with *dat*) to order, command, e.g., **il giudice ingiunse all'imputato di rispondere** the judge ordered the accused to answer
ingiunzióne *f* order; (law) injunction
ingiùria *f* insult, abuse; damage, wear
ingiuriare **§287** *tr* to insult
ingiurió·so -sa [s] *adj* insulting
ingiustificàbile *adj* unjustifiable
ingiustifica·to -ta *adj* unjustified
ingiustìzia *f* injustice
ingiu·sto -sta *adj* unjust, unfair || *m* unjust person
inglése [s] *adj* English; **all'inglese** in the English fashion; **andarsene all'inglese** to take French leave || *m* Englishman; English (*language*) || *f* Englishwoman
ingoiare **§287** (**ingóio**) *tr* to swallow; to gulp down; **ingoiare un rospo** (fig) to swallow one's pride
ingolfare (**ingólfo**) *tr* (aut) to flood || *ref* to form a gulf; to get involved; (aut) to flood
ingollare (**ingóllo**) *tr* to swallow, gulp down
ingolosire [s] **§176** *tr* to make the mouth of (*s.o.*) water || *intr* (ESSERE) & *ref* to have a craving
ingombrante *adj* cumbersome
ingombrare (**ingómbro**) *tr* to clutter
ingóm·bro -bra *adj* encumbered, cluttered || *m* encumbrance; **essere d'ingombro** to be in the way
ingommare (**ingómmo**) *tr* to glue
ingordìgia *f* greed
ingór·do -da *adj* greedy, covetous
ingorgare **§209** (**ingórgo**) *ref* to get clogged up
ingór·go *m* (**-ghi**) blocking, congestion; **ingorgo stradale** traffic jam
ingovernàbile *adj* uncontrollable
ingozzare (**ingózzo**) *tr* to gobble, gulp down; to swallow; to cram (*e.g., a goose for fattening*)
ingranàg·gio *m* (**-gi**) gear, gearwheel; (fig) meshes; **ingranaggio di distribuzione** (aut) timing gear; **ingranaggio elicoidale** worm gear
ingranare *tr* to engage (*a gear*); **ingranare la marcia** to throw into gear || *intr* to be in gear; to succeed
ingrandiménto *m* enlargement; increase
ingrandire **§176** *tr* to enlarge; to increase; || *intr* (ESSERE) & *ref* to increase, get larger
ingrassare *tr* to fatten; to lubricate || *intr* (ESSERE) & *ref* to get fat; to get rich
ingrassa·tóre -trice *mf* greaser, lubricator || *f* grease gun; lubricating machine
ingratitùdine *f* ingratitude
ingra·to -ta *adj* ungrateful; thankless || *mf* ingrate
ingraziare **§287** *ref* to ingratiate oneself with
ingrediènte *m* ingredient
ingrèsso *m* entrance; admittance, entry; **ingressi** hallway furniture; **primo ingresso** debut
ingrossaménto *m* enlargement; swelling
ingrossare (**ingròsso**) *tr* to enlarge; to swell; to make bigger; to dull (*the mind*); to raise (*one's voice*) || *intr* (ESSERE) & *ref* to swell; to thicken; to become fat; to become pregnant; to become important
ingròsso *m*—**all'ingrosso** wholesale; approximately, more or less
ingrullire **§176** *tr* to drive crazy || *intr* (ESSERE) & *ref* to become silly; **fare ingrullire** to drive crazy
inguadàbile *adj* not fordable
inguainare (**inguaìno**) *tr* to sheathe
ingualcìbile *adj* wrinkle-free, wrinkleproof
inguanta·to -ta *adj* with gloves on; **con le mani inguantate** with gloves on
inguarìbile *adj* incurable
inguine *f* (anat) groin
ingurgitare (**ingùrgito**) *tr* to swallow, gulp down
inibire **§176** *tr* to inhibit
inibi·tóre -trice *adj* inhibiting || *m* inhibitor
inidòne·o -a *adj* unfit, unqualified
iniettare (**inièttо**) *tr* to inject || *ref* to become bloodshot; **iniettarsi di sangue** to become bloodshot
iniezióne *f* injection
inimicare **§197** *tr* to make an enemy of; to alienate || *ref*—**inimicarsi con** to fall out with
inimicìzia *f* enmity
inimitàbile *adj* inimitable, matchless
ininterrót·to -ta *adj* uninterrupted
iniqui·tà *f* (**-tà**) injustice; iniquity
inì·quo -qua *adj* unjust; wicked
iniziale *adj* & *f* initial
iniziare **§287** *tr* to initiate || *ref* to begin
iniziativa *f* initiative; sponsorship; **iniziativa privata** private enterprise
inizia·tóre -trice *adj* initiating || *mf* initiator, promoter
iniziazióne *f* initiation
inì·zio *m* (**-zi**) beginning, start
innaffiare **§287** *tr* var of **annaffiare**
innaffia·tóio *m* (**-tói**) var of **annaffiatoio**
innalzaménto *m* elevation

innalzare *tr* to raise; to elevate; **innalzare al cielo** to praise to the sky || *ref* to rise; to tower
innamorare (**innamóro**) *tr* to charm, fascinate; to inspire with love || *ref* to fall in love
innamora·to -ta *adj* in love, enamored; fond || *mf* sweetheart || *m* boyfriend || *f* girl friend
innanzi *adj invar* previous, prior (*e.g., day*) || *adv* ahead, before; **innanzi a** in front of; **innanzi di** + *inf* before + *ger;* **mettere innanzi** to prefer; to place before; to advance (*an excuse*); **per l'innanzi** before, in the past; **tirare innanzi** to get along || *prep* before; above; **innanzi tempo** ahead of time; **innanzi tutto** above all
innà·rio *m* (**-ri**) hymnal
inna·to -ta *adj* inborn, innate
innegàbile *adj* undeniable
inneggiare §290 (**innéggio**) *intr*—**inneggiare a** to sing the praises of
innervosire [s] §176 *tr* to make nervous
innescare §197 (**innésco**) *tr* to bait (*a hook*); to prime (*a bomb*)
inné·sco *m* (**-schi**) primer; detonator
innestare (**innèsto**) *tr* (hort & surg) to graft; (surg) to implant; (med) to inoculate (*a vaccine*); (mach) to engage; (elec) to plug in (*e.g., a plug*); **innestare la marcia** (aut) to throw into gear || *ref* to be grafted; **innestarsi in** to merge with; **innestarsi su** to connect with
innèsto *m* (hort & surg) graft; (surg) implant; (med) inoculation; (mach) engagement; (mach) coupling; (elec) plug
inno *m* hymn; **inno nazionale** national anthem
innocènte *adj* innocent || *m* innocent; **innocenti** foundlings
innocènza *f* innocence
innò·cuo -cua *adj* innocuous, harmless
innominàbile *adj* unmentionable
innomina·to -ta *adj* unnamed
innovare (**innòvo**) *tr* to innovate
innovazióne *f* innovation
innumerévole *adj* countless, innumerable
-ino -ina *suf adj* little, e.g., **poverino** poor little; hailing from, e.g., **fiorentino** hailing from Florence, Florentine || *suf f* see **-ina**
inoccupa·to -ta *adj* unoccupied || *m* person looking for his first job
inoculare (**inòculo**) *tr* to inoculate
inoculazióne *f* inoculation
inodó·ro -ra *adj* odorless
inoffensi·vo -va *adj* inoffensive
inoltrare (**inóltro**) *tr* (com) to forward (*e.g., a request*) || *ref* to advance
inóltre *adv* besides, in addition
inóltro *m* (com) forwarding
inondare (**inóndo**) *tr* to inundate, flood; to swamp
inondazióne *f* flood, inundation
inoperosità [s] *f* idleness
inoperó·so -sa [s] *adj* idle
inopina·to -ta *adj* (lit) unexpected
inopportu·no -na *adj* inopportune, untimely
inoppugnàbile *adj* incontestable; indisputable
inorgàni·co -ca *adj* (**-ci -che**) inorganic
inorgoglire §176 *tr* to make proud || *intr* (ESSERE) & *ref* to grow proud
inorridire §176 *tr* to horrify || *intr* (ESSERE) to be horrified
inospitale *adj* inhospitable
inosservante *adj* unobservant
inosserva·to -ta *adj* unnoticed; unperceived
inossidàbile *adj* stainless
inquadrare *tr* to frame; to arrange
inquadratura *f* framing; (mov, phot) frame
inqualificàbile *adj* unspeakable
inquietante *adj* disquieting
inquietare (**inquièto**) *tr* to worry || *ref* to worry; to get angry
inquiè·to -ta *adj* worried; restless; angry; (lit) stormy
inquietùdine *f* worry; restlessness; preoccupation
inquili·no -na *mf* tenant
inquinaménto *m* pollution
inquinare *tr* to pollute
inquirènte *adj* investigating
inquisi·tóre -trice *adj* inquiring || *m* inquisitor
inquisizióne *f* inquisition
insabbiare §287 *tr* to cover with sand; to pigeonhole; to shelve || *ref* to get covered with sand; to bury oneself in sand; to get stuck
insaccare §197 *tr* to bag; to stuff (*e.g., salami*); (mil) to hem in; (fig) to bundle up; (coll) to gulp down || *ref* to be packed in; to crumple up; to disappear behind a thick bank of clouds (*said, e.g., of the sun*)
insaccato *m* participant in a sack race; **insaccati** cold cuts, lunch meat
insalata *f* salad; (fig) mess
insalatièra *f* salad bowl
insalubre *adj* unhealthy
insaluta·to -ta *adj* unsaluted; **andarsene insalutato ospite** to take French leave
insanàbile *adj* incurable; implacable
insanguinare (**insànguino**) *tr* to bloody; to cover with blood; to bathe in blood
insa·no -na *adj* insane
insaponare (**insapóno**) *tr* to soap; to lather; (fig) to soft-soap
insaporire §176 *tr* to flavor || *intr* (ESSERE) to become tasty
insaputa *f*—**all'insaputa di** without the knowledge of, unbeknown to
insaziàbile *adj* insatiable
insazia·to -ta *adj* insatiate, unsatisfied
inscatolare (**inscàtolo**) *tr* to can
inscenare (**inscèno**) *tr* to stage
inscindìbile *adj* inseparable
inscrìvere §250 *tr* (geom) to inscribe
inscrutàbile *adj* inscrutable
inscurire §176 *tr, intr* (ESSERE) & *ref* to darken
insecchire §176 *tr* to dry || *intr* (ESSERE) & *ref* to dry up

insediaménto *m* installation (*into an office*); assumption (*of an office*)
insediare §287 (**insèdio**) *tr* to install || *ref* to be installed; to take one's seat; to settle
inségna *f* badge, insignia, emblem; ensign, flag; coat of arms; motto; sign (*e.g., on a restaurant*); traffic sign
insegnaménto *m* education, instruction
insegnante *adj* teaching || *mf* teacher
insegnare (**inségno**) *tr* to teach; to show || *intr* to teach
inseguiménto *m* pursuit
inseguire (**inséguo**) *tr* to pursue, chase; to chase after
insellare (**insèllo**) *tr* to saddle; to put on (*e.g., one's glasses*); to bend
insellatura *f* saddling; bending
insenatura *f* inlet, cove
insensatézza *f* nonsense, folly
insensa•to -ta *adj* nonsensical, foolish || *mf* scatterbrain
insensìbile *adj* insensible; unresponsive; insensitive
inseparàbile *adj* inseparable || *m* (orn) lovebird
insepól•to -ta *adj* unburied
inserire §176 *tr* to insert; to plug in || *ref* to slip in; to butt in
inseri•tóre -trice *adj* (elec) connecting || *m* (elec) connector, plug || *f* sorter (*of punch cards*)
insèrto *m* file, folder; insert; spliced film
inservìbile *adj* useless, worthless
inserviènte *m* attendant, porter; (eccl) server
inserzionare (**inserzióno**) *intr* to advertise
inserzióne *f* insertion; advertisement
inserzioni•sta (**-sti -ste**) *adj* advertising || *mf* advertiser
insettici•da *adj & m* (**-di -de**) insecticide
insettìfu•go *m* (**-ghi**) insect repellent
insètto *m* insect; **insetti** vermin
insìdia *f* trap, ambush; **insidie** lure
insidiare §287 *tr* to ensnare; to try to trap; to try to seduce; to attempt (*someone's life*)
insidió•so -sa [s] *adj* insidious
insième *m* whole, entirety; harmony; ensemble; set; **d'insieme** general, comprehensive; **nell'insieme** as a whole || *adv* together
insigne *adj* famous; notable; arrant (*knave*)
insignificante *adj* insignificant; petty
insignire §176 *tr* to decorate; **insignire qlcu di un titolo** to bestow a title upon s.o.
insignorire §176 *tr* (lit) to invest with a fief || *intr* (ESSERE) to enrich oneself || *ref* to enrich oneself; **insignorirsi di** to seize; to take possession of
insilare *tr* to silo, ensile
insilato *m* ensilage
insincè•ro -ra *adj* insincere
insindacàbile *adj* final, indisputable
insino *adv* (lit)—**insino a** until; as far as; **insino a che** as long as
insinuante *adj* insinuating
insinuare (**insìnuo**) *tr* to stick, thrust; to insinuate; (law) to register || *ref* to creep, filter; to ingratiate oneself; **insinuarsi in** to worm one's way into
insinuazióne *f* insinuation, hint
insìpi•do -da *adj* insipid, vapid
insistènte *adj* insistent
insìstere §114 *intr* to insist
insi•to -ta *adj* inborn, inherent
insociévole *adj* unsociable
insoddisfat•to -ta *adj* dissatisfied
insofferènte *adj* intolerant
insoffrìbile *adj* unbearable, insufferable
insolazióne *f* sunning; sun bath; sunstroke; sunny exposure
insolènte *adj* insolent
insolentire §176 *tr* to insult, abuse || *intr* to be insolent
insolènza *f* insolence; insult
insòli•to -ta *adj* unusual
insolùbile *adj* insoluble
insolu•to -ta *adj* unsolved; not dissolved; unpaid
insolvènza *f* insolvency
insolvìbile *adj* insolvent; bad (*debt*)
insómma *adv* in conclusion || *interj* well!
insommergìbile *adj* unsinkable
insondàbile *adj* unfathomable
insònne *adj* sleepless
insònnia *f* insomnia
insonnoli•to -ta *adj* sleepy, drowsy
insonorizzazióne [ddzz] *f* soundproofing
insopportàbile *adj* unbearable
insorgènte *adj* appearing || *mf* insurgent
insorgènza *f* appearance (*of illness*)
insórgere §258 *intr* (ESSERE) to rise up, revolt; to appear
insormontàbile *adj* unsurmountable, insurmountable
insór•to -ta *adj & m* insurgent
insospettàbile *adj* above suspicion; unexpected
insospetta•to -ta *adj* not suspect; unexpected
insospettire §176 *tr* to make suspicious || *intr* (ESSERE) & *ref* to become suspicious
insostenìbile *adj* indefensible; unbearable
insostituìbile *adj* irreplaceable
insozzare (**insózzo**) *tr* to soil, sully
inspera•to -ta *adj* unexpected; unhoped-for
inspiegàbile *adj* unexplainable
inspirare *tr* to inhale, breathe in
inspirazióne *f* inhalation
instàbile *adj* unstable
installare *tr* to install; to set up, settle; to induct (*in an office*) || *ref* to settle
installatóre *m* plumber; erector
installazióne *f* installation; plumbing
instancàbile *adj* untiring
instante *adj* insistent; impending || *m* petitioner
instare (*pp* missing) *intr* to insist; to threaten, be imminent
instaurare (**instàuro**) *tr* to establish
instaurazióne *f* establishment
instigare §209 *tr* var of **istigare**
instillare *tr* var of **istillare**
instituire §176 *tr* var of **istituire**

instruire §176 *tr* var of **istruire**
instrumento *m* var of **istrumento**
instupidire §176 *tr* var of **istupidire**
insù *adv* up; **all'insù** up
insubordina•to -ta *adj* insubordinate
insuccèsso *m* failure
insudiciare §128 (**insùdicio**) *tr* to soil, dirty; to sully || *ref* to get dirty
insufficiènte *adj* insufficient; failing (*in school*)
insufficiènza *f* insufficiency; failure (*in school*)
insulare *adj* insular
insulina *f* insulin
insulsàggine *f* silliness, nonsense
insul•so -sa *adj* insipid; simple, silly
insultante *adj* insulting
insultare *tr* to insult || *intr* (with *dat*) to insult
insulto *m* insult; (pathol) attack
insuperàbile *adj* insuperable; unparalleled
insupera•to -ta *adj* unsurpassed
insuperbire §176 *tr, intr* (ESSERE) & *ref* to swell with pride
insurrezióne *f* insurrection
insussistènte *adj* nonexistent, unfounded
intabarrare *tr* to wrap up
intaccare §197 *tr* to notch; to corrode; to scratch; to attack (*said of a disease*); to damage (*e.g., a reputation*); to cut into (*capital*) || *intr* to stutter
intaccatura *f* notch; (carp) mortise
intagliare §280 *tr* to carve; to engrave
intà•glio *m* (**-gli**) carving; intaglio
intanare *ref* to hide
intangìbile *adj* intangible; inviolable
intanto *adv* meanwhile; (coll) yet; (coll) finally; **intanto che** while; **per intanto** at present; in the meantime
intarsiare §287 *tr* to inlay; (fig) to stud
intarsia•to -ta *adj* inlaid
intàr•sio *m* (**-si**) inlay; inlaid work
intasare [s] *tr* to clog; to tie up (*traffic*); to stop up || *ref* to be clogged up; to be tied up; to be stopped up (*said of nose*)
intascare §197 *tr* to pocket
intat•to -ta *adj* intact, untouched
intavolare (**intàvolo**) *tr* to start (*a conversation*); to broach (*a subject*); to launch (*negotiations*)
intavolato *m* boarding, planking
integèrri•mo -ma *adj* of the utmost honesty
integrale *adj* integral; whole; wholewheat (*bread*); built-in || *m* integral
integralismo *m* policy of the complete absorption of the body politic by an ideology
integrante *adj* constituent, integral
integrare (**ìntegro**) *tr* to integrate || *ref* to complement each other
integrazióne *f* integration
integrità *f* integrity
ìnte•gro -gra *adj* whole, complete; honest, upright; intact
intelaiatura *f* frame; framework
intellètto *m* intellect, mind; understanding
intellettuale *adj* & *mf* intellectual
intellettuali•tà *f* (**-tà**) intellectuality; intelligentsia
intellettualòide *mf* highbrow
intelligènte *adj* intelligent; clever
intelligènza *f* intelligence; understanding; **essere d'intelligenza con** to be in collusion with
intellighènzia *f* intelligentsia
intelligìbile *adj* intelligible
intemera•to -ta *adj* pure, spotless || *f* reprimand, scolding; long, boring speech
intemperante *adj* intemperate
intemperanza *f* intemperance
intempèrie *fpl* inclement weather
intempesti•vo -va *adj* untimely
intendènte *m* district director; **intendente di finanza** director of customs office; **intendente militare** commissary, quartermaster
intendènza *f* office of the district director; intendance; **intendenza militare** quartermaster corps
intèndere §270 *tr* to understand; to hear; to intend; to turn (*e.g., one's eyes*); to mean; **dare ad intendere a** to lead (*s.o.*) to believe (*s.th*); **far intendere** to give to understand; **farsi intendere** to force obedience; to make oneself understood; **intender dire che** to hear that; **intendere a rovescio** to misunderstand; **intendere a volo** to catch on quickly (to); **intendere ragione** to listen to reason; **lasciare intendere** to give to understand || *intr* to aim (*toward a goal*) || *ref* to come to an agreement; **intendersela con** to be in collusion with; to have an affair with; **intendersi di** to be a good judge of; to be an expert in
intendiménto *m* understanding, comprehension; aim, goal
intendi•tóre -trice *mf* connoisseur, expert; **a buon intenditore poche parole** a word to the wise is sufficient
intenerire §176 *tr* to soften; (fig) to move || *ref* to soften; (fig) to be moved
intensificare §197 (**intensìfico**) *tr* & *ref* to intensify
intensi•tà *f* (**-tà**) intensity
intensi•vo -va *adj* intensive
intèn•so -sa *adj* intense
intentare (**intènto**) *tr* (law) to bring (*action*)
intenta•to -ta *adj* unattempted
intèn•to -ta *adj* intent || *m* intent, goal; **coll'intento di** with the purpose of
intenzionale *adj* intentional
intenziona•to -ta *adj*—**bene intenzionato** well-meaning; **essere intenzionato di** to intend to
intenzióne *f* intention; purpose; **con intenzione** on purpose
intepidire §176 *tr* & *ref* var of **intiepidire**
interbase *f* (baseball) shortstop
intercalare *m* refrain; pet word or phrase || *tr* to intercalate; to inset
intercalazióne *f* intercalation; inset
intercapèdine *f* air space
intercèdere §123 *tr* to seek, get (*a par-*

don for s.o.) || *intr* to intercede || *intr* (ESSERE)—**intercedere tra** to intervene or elapse between; to extend between; to exist between
intercettare (**intercètto**) *tr* to intercept; to tap (*a phone*)
intercetta·tóre -trice *mf* interceptor
intercettóre *m* (aer) interceptor
intercomunale *adj* long-distance (*call*)
intercórrere §139 *intr* (ESSERE) to elapse; to happen; to be, to stand
interdét·to -ta *adj* dumfounded; forbidden || *m* interdict; (coll) dumbell
interdire §151 *tr* to prohibit; (eccl) to interdict; (law) to disqualify
interessaménto *m* interest, concern
interessante *adj* interesting; **in stato interessante** in the family way
interessare (**interèsso**) *tr* to interest; to concern || *intr* to be of interest || *ref*—**interessarsi a** to take an interest in; **interessarsi di** to concern oneself with
interessa·to -ta *adj* interested; selfish || *m* interested party
interèsse *m* interest; self-interest
interessènza *f* (com) share, interest
interferènza *f* interference
interferire §176 *intr* to interfere
interfogliare §280 (**interfòglio**) *tr* to interleave
interiezióne *f* interjection
interinato *m* temporary office or tenure
interi·no -na *adj* acting || *m* temporary appointee
interióra *fpl* entrails
interióre *adj* interior || **interiori** *mpl* entrails
interlìnea *f* interlining; (typ) leading
interlineare *adj* interlinear || *v* (**interlìneo**) *tr* (typ) to lead
interlocu·tóre -trice *mf* participant (*in a discussion*); person speaking
interloquire §176 *intr* to take part in a discussion; to chime in
interlù·dio *m* (**-di**) interlude
intermedià·rio -ria (**-ri -rie**) *adj* & *mf* intermediary || *m* middleman
intermè·dio -dia (**-di -die**) *adj* intermediate || *mf* supervisor
intermèzzo [ddzz] *m* intermezzo; entr'acte; interval
interminàbile *adj* interminable, endless
intermissióne *f* intermission
intermittènte *adj* intermittent
internaménto *m* internment
internare (**intèrno**) *tr* to intern; to confine; to commit (*an insane person*) || *ref* to go deep (*into a problem*)
interna·to -ta *adj* interned || *m* internee; inmate; boarder; boarding school
internazionale *adj* international
internazionalizzare [ddzz] *tr* to internationalize
interni·sta *mf* (**-sti -ste**) internist
intèr·no -na *adj* inside, internal; inland; interior; boarding (*student*) || *m* inside; interior; (med) intern; lining (*of coat*); **all'interno** inside; **interni** (mov) indoor shots || **gli Interni** the Italian Ministry of Internal Affairs
inté·ro -ra *adj* entire, whole; full (*price*); (lit) upright, honest || *m* whole; **per intero** completely
interpellare (**interpèllo**) *tr* to interpellate; to question; to consult
interpetrare (**intèrpetro**) *tr* var of **interpretare**
interplanetà·rio -ria *adj* (**-ri -rie**) interplanetary
interpolare (**intèrpolo**) *tr* to interpolate
interpolazióne *f* interpolation
interpónte *m* (naut) between-deck
interpórre §218 *tr* to interpose || *ref* to intervene
interpretare (**intèrpreto**) *tr* to interpret
interpretazióne *f* interpretation
intèrprete *mf* interpreter
interpunzióne *f* punctuation
interrare (**intèrro**) *tr* to bury, inter; to fill in (*e.g., a marsh*) || *ref* to become silted
interra·to -ta *adj* underground; **piano interrato** basement
interrogare §209 (**intèrrogo**) *tr* to question; to interrogate
interrogati·vo -va *adj* interrogative || *m* why; question
interrogatò·rio -ria (**-ri -rie**) *adj* questioning || *m* (law) interrogatory; **interrogatorio di terzo grado** third degree
interrogazióne *f* interrogation; quiz, examination; **interrogazione retorica** rhetorical question
interrómpere §240 *tr* to interrupt
interruttóre *m* (elec) switch; **interruttore di linea** (elec) controller
interruzióne *f* interruption
interscàm·bio *m* (**-bi**) interchange
interscolàsti·co -ca *adj* (**-ci -che**) interscholastic; intercollegiate
intersecare §197 (**intèrseco**) *tr* & *ref* to intersect
intersezióne *f* intersection
interstellare *adj* interstellar
interstì·zio *m* (**-zi**) interstice
interurba·no -na *adj* interurban, intercity; (telp) long-distance || *f* (telp) long-distance call
intervallo *m* interval; pause; (educ) recess; (theat) intermission
intervenire §282 *intr* (ESSERE) to intervene; (surg) to operate; **intervenire a** to take part in
interventi·sta *mf* (**-sti -ste**) interventionist
intervènto *m* intervention; attendance; (surg) operation
intervenzióne *f* intervention
intervista *f* interview; **fare un'intervista a** to interview
intervistare *tr* to interview
inté·so -sa [s] *adj* understood; intended, designed; **bene inteso** of course; **non darsene per inteso** to not pay attention; **rimanere inteso** to agree || *f* understanding, agreement; entente
intèssere (**intèsso**) *tr* to interweave; to wreathe (*a garland*)
intestardire §176 *ref* to get obstinate; to be determined

intestare (**intèsto**) *tr* to caption; to label; (typ) to head (*a page*); **intestare qlco a qlcu** to register s.th in the name of s.o.; **intestare una fattura a** to issue a bill in the name of || *ref* to become obstinate; to take it into one's head
intesta·to -ta *adj* headed; registered (*stock*); obstinate; (law) intestate
intestazióne *f* heading; registration (*of stock*)
intestinale *adj* intestinal
intesti·no -na *adj* & *m* intestine; **intestino crasso** large intestine; **intestino tenue** small intestine
intiepidire §176 *tr* & *ref* to warm up; to cool off
intiè·ro -ra *adj* & *m* var of **intero**
intimare (**ìntimo** & **intimo**) *tr* to intimate; to order, command; to declare (*war*); to impose (*a fine*); (law) to enjoin
intimazióne *f* intimation; order; (law) injunction
intimidazióne *f* intimidation
intimidire §176 *tr* to intimidate; to threaten || *ref* to become bashful
intimi·tà *f* (**-tà**) intimacy; privacy
ìnti·mo -ma *adj* intimate; inmost; **biancheria intima** underwear, lingerie || *m* intimate friend; depth (*of one's heart*)
intimorire §176 *tr* to frighten
intingere §126 *tr* to dip || *intr*—**intingere in** to dip in || *ref*—**intingersi in un affare** to have a finger in the pie
intingolo *m* sauce, gravy; fancy dish
intirizzire [ddzz] §176 *tr* to benumb || *intr* (ESSERE) & *ref* to become numb or stiff; to become stiff and frostbitten
intirizzi·to -ta [ddzz] *adj* numb
intisichire §176 *tr* to make tubercular; (fig) to weaken || *intr* (ESSERE) to become tubercular; to wither
intitolare (**intìtolo**) *tr* to title; to dedicate || *ref* to be named; to assume the title of
intoccàbile *adj* & *m* untouchable
intolleràbile *adj* intolerable
intollerante *adj* intolerant
intonacare §197 (**intònaco**) *tr* to plaster; to whitewash; to cover (*e.g., with tar*) || *ref*—**intonacarsi la faccia** (joc) to put on one's warpaint
intòna·co *m* (**-chi**) plaster; roughcast
intonare (**intòno**) *tr* to intone; to harmonize; (mus) to tune || *ref* to harmonize, go
intonazióne *f* intonation; harmony
intòn·so -sa *adj* uncut; (lit) unsheared
intontire §176 *tr* to stun || *intr* (ESSERE) & *ref* to become stunned
intoppare (**intòppo**) *tr* to stumble upon || *intr* (ESSERE) & *ref* to stumble
intòppo *m* obstacle, hindrance
intorbidare (**intórbido**) *tr* to cloud; to muddy; to obfuscate; to upset (*friendship*); to stir up (*passions*) || *ref* to become cloudy or muddy; to become obfuscated
intorbidire §176 *tr* & *ref* to cloud; to muddy
intormentire §176 *tr* to benumb || *intr* (ESSERE) to become numb
intórno *adv* around, about; **all'intorno** all around; **intorno a** around; about; **levarsi qlcu d'intorno** to get rid of s.o.
intorpidire §176 *tr* to benumb || *ref* to become numb
intossicare §197 (**intòssico**) *tr* to poison, intoxicate
intossicazióne *f* poisoning, intoxication
intraducìbile *adj* untranslatable; inexpressible
intrafèrro *m* spark gap; air gap
intralciare §128 *tr* to hamper; to intertwine || *ref* to become hampered
intràl·cio *m* (**-ci**) hindrance; **essere d'intralcio** to be in the way; **intralcio del traffico** traffic congestion
intralicciatura *f* lattice truss (*of high-tension tower*)
intrallazzare *intr* to deal in the black market
intrallazza·tóre -trice *mf* black marketeer
intrallazzo *m* black-market dealing; kickback
intramezzare [ddzz] (**intramèzzo**) *tr* to alternate
intramontàbile *adj* undying, immortal
intransigènte *adj* & *mf* intransigent, die-hard
intransitàbile *adj* impassable
intransiti·vo -va *adj* intransitive
intrappolare (**intràppolo**) *tr* to entrap
intraprendènte *adj* enterprising
intraprendènza *f* enterprise, initiative
intraprèndere §220 *tr* to undertake
intrattàbile *adj* unmanageable, intractable
intrattenére §271 *tr* to entertain || *ref* to linger; **intrattenersi su** to dwell upon
intrattenimento *m* entertainment
intravedére §279 *tr* to glimpse, catch a glimpse of; to foresee
intravenó·so -sa [s] *adj* intravenous
intrecciare §128 (**intréccio**) *tr* to braid; to twine; to cross (*one's fingers*); (fig) to weave; to begin (*a dance*) || *ref* to become embroiled; to become intertwined; to crisscross
intréc·cio *m* (**-ci**) knitting; intertwining; plot (*of novel*); (theat) intrigue
intrepidézza *f* intrepidness, intrepidity
intrèpi·do -da *adj* intrepid
intricare §197 *tr* (lit) to entangle
intrica·to -ta *adj* tangled; intricate
intri·co *m* (**-chi**) tangle, jumble
intrìdere §189 *tr* to soak; to knead
intrigante *adj* intriguing || *mf* schemer
intrigare §209 *tr* to tangle || *intr* to intrigue || *ref* (coll) to meddle
intri·go *m* (**-ghi**) intrigue; trouble
intrìnse·co -ca (**-ci -che**) *adj* intrinsic; intimate || *m* intimate nature, core
intri·so -sa *adj* soaked || *m* mash
intristire §176 *intr* (ESSERE) to wither; to waste away

introdót•to -ta *adj* introduced; well-known; knowledgeable, expert
introdurre §102 *tr* to introduce; to insert; to open (*a speech*); to show in || *ref* to slip in
introdutti•vo -va *adj* introductory
introduzióne *f* introduction
introitare (**intròito**) *tr* to collect, take in
intròito *m* receipts, collection; (eccl) introit
introméttere §198 *tr* to insert; to introduce; to involve || *ref* to meddle; to pry
intromissióne *f* meddling; intrusion; intervention
intronare (**intròno**) *tr* to deafen; to stun
intronizzare [ddzz] *tr* to enthrone
introspetti•vo -va *adj* introspective
introspezióne *f* introspection
introvàbile *adj* unobtainable; inaccessible
introvèr•so -sa *adj* & *mf* introvert
intrùdere §190 *tr* (lit) to slip in || *ref* to intrude; to trespass
intrufolare (**intrùfolo**) *tr* (coll) to slip (*e.g., one's hand into somebody's pocket*) || *ref* to slip in, intrude
intrù•glio *m* (**-gli**) concoction, brew; hodgepodge; imbroglio; mess
intrusióne *f* intrusion
intru•so -sa *adj* intrusive || *mf* intruder
intuire §176 *tr* to know by intuition; to guess; to sense
intuiti•vo -va *adj* intuitive; obvious
intùito *m* intuition; insight
intuizióne *f* intuition
inturgidire §176 *intr* (ESSERE) & *ref* to swell
inuma•no -na *adj* inhuman; inhumane
inumare *tr* to bury, inhume
inumazióne *f* burial, inhumation
inumidire §176 *tr* to moisten || *ref* to get wet
inurbaménto *m* migration to the city
inurba•no -na *adj* uncouth, unmannerly
inurbare *ref* to move into the city; to become citified
inusa•to -ta *adj* unused; unusual
inusita•to -ta *adj* unusual; out-of-the-way
inùtile *adj* useless; worthless
inutilizzàbile [ddzz] *adj* unusable
inutilizzare [ddzz] *tr* to waste (*e.g., time*)
inutilizza•to -ta [ddzz] *adj* unused
inutilménte *adv* needlessly, to no purpose || *interj* no use!
invadènte *adj* meddlesome, intrusive
invàdere §172 *tr* to invade; to encroach on; to spread over; to overcome
invaghire §176 *tr* to charm || *ref* to fall in love
invalére §278 *intr* (ESSERE) to become established; to prevail
invalicàbile *adj* impassable, unsurmountable
invalidàbile *adj* voidable
invalidaménto *m* invalidity; invalidation
invalidare (**invàlido**) *tr* to void, invalidate; to negate (*e.g., evidence*)
invalidi•tà *f* (**-tà**) invalidity; invalidation; sickness, disability
invàli•do -da *adj* void, invalid; sick, disabled || *m* disabled person; invalid
inval•so -sa *adj* prevailing
invano *adv* in vain, vainly
invariàbile *adj* invariable
invaria•to -ta *adj* unchanging; unchanged
invasare *tr* to pot (*a plant*); to fill up (*a reservoir*); to possess, obsess
invasa•to -ta *adj* possessed, obsessed
invasióne *f* invasion
inva•so -sa *adj* invaded || *m* potting (*of plant*); capacity (*of reservoir*)
inva•sóre -ditrice *adj* invading || *m* invader
invecchiaménto *m* aging
invecchiare §287 (**invècchio**) *tr* & *intr* (ESSERE) to age
invéce *adv* on the contrary, instead; **invece di** instead of
inveire §176 *intr* to inveigh, rail
invelenire §176 *tr* to envenom; to embitter || *intr* (ESSERE) & *ref* to grow bitter
invendìbile *adj* unsalable
invendica•to -ta *adj* unavenged
invendu•to -ta *adj* unsold
inventare (**invènto**) *tr* to invent
inventariare §287 *tr* to inventory
inventà•rio *m* (**-ri**) inventory
inventi•vo -va *adj* inventive || *f* inventiveness
inven•tóre -trice *adj* inventive || *mf* inventor
invenzióne *f* invention; (lit) find
inverdire §176 *intr* (ESSERE) to turn green
inverecóndia *f* immodesty
inverecón•do -da *adj* immodest
invernale *adj* winter; wintry
inverniciare §128 *tr* to paint; to varnish
invèrno *m* winter
invéro *adv* (lit) truly, indeed
inverosimiglianza [s] *f* unlikelihood
inverosìmile [s] *adj* unlikely
inversióne *f* inversion
invèr•so -sa *adj* inverse, opposite; (coll) cross || *m* inverse
inversóre *m* inverter; **inversore di spinta** (aer) thrust reverser
invertebra•to -ta *adj* & *m* invertebrate
invertire §176 & (**invèrto**) *tr* to invert; to reverse
inverti•to -ta *adj* inverted || *m* invert
investigare §209 (**invèstigo**) *tr* to investigate
investiga•tóre -trice *adj* investigating || *mf* investigator; detective
investigazióne *f* investigation
investiménto *m* investment; collision
investire (**invèsto**) *tr* to invest; to collide with; **investire di insulti** to cover with insults || *ref*—**investirsi di** to become conscious of (*e.g., one's authority*); (theat) to become identified with (*a character*)
investi•tóre -trice *mf* investor
investitura *f* investiture
invetera•to -ta *adj* inveterate, confirmed

invetria·to -ta *adj* glazed || *f* window; window pane
invettiva *f* invective
inviare §119 *tr* to send
invia·to -ta *mf* envoy; correspondent
invìdia *f* envy
invidiàbile *adj* enviable
invidiare §287 *tr* to envy; to begrudge; **non aver niente da invidiare a** to be just as good as
invidió·so -sa [s] *adj* envious
invigorire §176 *tr* to strengthen, invigorate || *intr* (ESSERE) & *ref* to grow stronger
invilire §176 *tr* to dishearten; to vilify; to lower (*prices*) || *intr* (ESSERE) & *ref* to lose heart; to lose one's reputation
inviluppare *tr* to envelop; to wrap up
invincìbile *adj* invincible
invì·o *m* (-i) dispatch; shipment; remittance; envoy (*of a poem*)
inviolàbile *adj* inviolable
inviperire §176 *ref* to become enraged
invischiare §287 *tr* to smear with birdlime; to ensnare || *ref* to become ensnared
invisìbile *adj* invisible
invi·so -sa *adj* disliked, hated
invitante *adj* attractive, inviting
invitare *tr* to invite; to summon; (cards) to bid; (cards) to open; (mach) to screw (*e.g., a light bulb*) in; to screw (*e.g., a lid*) on
invita·to -ta *adj* invited || *m* guest
invito *m* invitation; inducement; bottom of stairway; (cards) opening
invit·to -ta *adj* unvanquished
invocare §197 (**invòco**) *tr* to invoke
invocazióne *f* invocation
invogliare §280 (**invòglio**) *tr* to induce, entice || *ref* to yearn, long
involare (**invólo**) *tr* to steal; to abduct || *intr* (ESSERE) (aer) to take off || *ref* to disappear; to fly away
invòlgere §289 *tr* to wrap, envelop; to involve || *ref* to become entangled
invólo *m* (aer) take-off
involontà·rio -ria *adj* (-ri -rie) involuntary
invòlto *m* bundle; wrapper
invòlucro *m* wrapping; shell (*of boiler*); (aer) envelope
involu·to -ta *adj* (fig) involved; (lit) enveloped
invòlvere §147 (*pret* missing; *pp* also **invòlto**) *tr* (lit) to envelop
invulneràbile *adj* invulnerable
inzaccherare (**inzàcchero**) *tr* to bespatter
inzeppare (**inzéppo**) *tr* to cram, stuff
inzuccherare (**inzùcchero**) *tr* to sweeten
inzuppare *tr* to soak || *ref* to get drenched
ìo *m* ego; self || §5 *pron pers*
iòdio *m* iodine
iodìdri·co -ca *adj* (-ci -che) hydriodic
ioduro *m* iodide
iògurt *m* yogurt
iò·le *f* (-le) (naut) yawl; (sports) shell
ióne *m* ion
iòni·co -ca *adj* & *m* (-ci -che) Ionic
ionizzare [ddzz] *tr* to ionize
iòsa [s] *f*—**a iosa** in abundance
iperacidità *f* hyperacidity
ipèrbole *f* (geom) hyperbola; (rhet) hyperbole
iperbòli·co -ca *adj* (-ci -che) hyperbolic(al)
ipereccita·to -ta *adj* overexcited
ipermercato *m* shopping center
ipersensìbile *adj* hypersensitive; supersensitive
ipersostentatóre *m* landing flap
ipertensióne *f* hypertension
ipnò·si *f* (-si) hypnosis
ipnòti·co -ca *adj* & *m* (-ci -che) hypnotic
ipnotismo *m* hypnotism
ipnotizzare [ddzz] *tr* to hypnotize
ipnotizza·tóre -trice [ddzz] *adj* hypnotizing || *m* hypnotizer
ipocondrìa·co -ca *adj* & *mf* (-ci -che) hypochondriac
ipocrisìa *f* hypocrisy
ipòcri·ta (-ti -te) *adj* hypocritical || *mf* hypocrite
ipodèrmi·co -ca *adj* (-ci -che) hypodermic
iposolfito [s] *m* hyposulfite
ipotè·ca *f* (-che) mortgage
ipotecare §197 (**ipotèco**) *tr* to mortgage
ipotecà·rio -ria *adj* (-ri -rie) mortgage
ipotenusa *f* hypotenuse
ipòte·si *f* (-si) hypothesis; **nella miglior delle ipotesi** at best; **nell'ipotesi che** in the event; **per ipotesi** by supposition
ipotèti·co -ca *adj* (-ci -che) hypothetic(al)
ipotizzare [ddzz] *tr* to hypothesize
ìppi·co -ca (-ci -che) *adj* horse, horse-racing || *f* horse racing
ippocampo *m* sea horse
ippocastano *m* horse chestnut tree
ippòdromo *m* race track
ippoglòsso *m* (ichth) halibut
ippopòtamo *m* hippopotamus
iprite *f* mustard gas
ira *f* wrath, anger, ire
irachè·no -na *adj* & *mf* Iraqi
iracóndia *f* wrath, anger
iracón·do -da *adj* wrathful
irania·no -na *adj* & *mf* Iranian
irascìbile *adj* irascible
ira·to -ta *adj* irate, angry
ire §191 *intr* (ESSERE) (lit) to go
irida·to -ta *adj* rainbow-hued || *m* world bicycle champion
ìride *f* rainbow; (anat, bot) iris
Irlanda, l' *f* Ireland
irlandése [s] *adj* Irish || *m* Irishman; Irish (*language*) || *f* Irishwoman
ironìa *f* irony
iròni·co -ca *adj* (-ci -che) ironic(al)
iró·so -sa [s] *adj* angry, wrathful
irradiare §287 *tr* to illuminate; to irradiate, radiate; to brighten; (rad) to broadcast || *intr* to radiate || *ref* to radiate; to spread
irraggiare §290 *tr* to illuminate; to irradiate, radiate, beam; to brighten; (rad) to broadcast || *intr* to radiate || *ref* to radiate; to spread

irraggiungìbile *adj* unattainable
irragionévole *adj* unreasonable
irrancidire §176 *intr* (ESSERE) & *ref* to get rancid
irrazionale *adj* irrational
irreale *adj* unreal
irreconciliàbile *adj* irreconcilable
irrecuperàbile *adj* irretrievable, irrecoverable
irredentismo *m* irredentism
irredenti•sta *mf* (**-sti -ste**) irredentist
irredèn•to -ta *adj* not yet redeemed
irredimìbile *adj* irredeemable
irrefrenàbile *adj* unrestrainable
irrefutàbile *adj* irrefutable
irregimentare (irregiménto) *tr* to regiment
irregolare *adj* irregular
irregolari•tà *f* (**-tà**) irregularity
irreligió•so -sa [s] *adj* irreligious
irremovìbile *adj* irremovable; obstinate
irreparàbile *adj* irreparable; unavoidable
irreperìbile *adj* not to be found; unaccounted for (*e.g., soldier*)
irreprensìbile *adj* irreproachable
irreprimìbile *adj* irrepressible
irrequiè•to -ta *adj* restless, restive
irresistìbile [s] *adj* irresistible
irresolùbile [s] *adj* unbreakable (*bond; contract*); insoluble; unsolvable
irresolu•to -ta [s] *adj* irresolute
irrespiràbile *adj* unbreathable
irresponsàbile *adj* irresponsible
irrestringìbile *adj* unshrinkable
irretire §176 *tr* to ensnare, entrap
irrevocàbile *adj* irrevocable
irriconoscìbile *adj* unrecognizable
irriducìbile *adj* irreducible; stubborn
irriflessi•vo -va *adj* thoughtless, rash
irrigare §209 *tr* to irrigate
irrigazióne *f* irrigation
irrigidire §176 *tr* to chill || *intr* & *ref* to stiffen, harden; to get cool
irrì•guo -gua *adj* well-watered; irrigating
irrilevante *adj* irrelevant
irrilevanza *f* irrelevance
irrimediàbile *adj* irremediable
irripetìbile *adj* unrepeatable
irrisióne *f* (lit) derision, mockery
irrisò•rio -ria *adj* (**-ri -rie**) mocking; paltry
irritàbile *adj* peevish; irritable
irritante *adj* irritating || *m* irritant
irritare (ìrrito) *tr* to irritate; to anger; to chafe || *ref* to become irritated
irritazióne *f* irritation
irriverènte *adj* irreverent
irrobustire §176 *tr* & *ref* to strengthen
irrómpere §240 (*pp* missing) *intr* to burst
irrorare (irròro) *tr* to sprinkle; to bathe, wet; to spray
irroratrice *f* sprayer; **irroratrice a zaino** portable sprayer
irruènte *adj* impetuous, rash
irruzióne *f* foray, raid; irruption
irsu•to -ta *adj* hairy, bristling
ir•to -ta *adj* prickly; shaggy (*hair*); **irto di** bristling with
iscrìvere §250 *tr* to inscribe; to register || *ref* to register; to sign up
iscrizióne *f* inscription; registration
Islam, l' *m* Islam
Islanda, l' *f* Iceland
islandése [s] *adj* Icelandic || *mf* Icelander || *m* Icelandic (*language*)
ìsola *f* island; block; **isola spartitraffico** traffic island
isolaménto *m* isolation; (elec) insulation
isola•no -na *adj* island || *mf* islander
isolante *adj* insulating || *m* (elec) insulation
isolare (ìsolo) *tr* to isolate; (elec) to insulate || *ref* to keep apart
isola•to -ta *adj* isolated; (elec) insulated || *m* city block; (sports) independent
isolatóre *m* (elec) insulator
isolazionismo *m* isolationism
isolazioni•sta *mf* (**-sti -ste**) isolationist
isolétta *f* isle
isòscele *adj* isosceles
isòto•po -pa *adj* isotopic || *m* isotope
ispani•sta *mf* (**-sti -ste**) Hispanist
ispa•no -na *adj* Hispanic
ispanoamerica•no -na *adj* & *mf* Spanish-American
ispessire §176 *tr* & *ref* to thicken
ispettorato *m* inspectorship
ispet•tóre -trice *mf* inspector; **ispettore di produzione** (mov) production manager
ispezionare (ispezióno) *tr* to inspect
ispezióne *f* inspection
ìspi•do -da *adj* bristly
ispirare *tr* to inspire || *ref* to be inspired
ispirazióne *f* inspiration
Israèle *m* Israel
israelia•no -na *adj* & *mf* Israeli
israeli•ta *adj* & *mf* (**-ti -te**) Israelite
issare *tr* to hoist
issòpo *m* hyssop
istallare *tr* & *ref* var of **installare**
istantàne•o -a *adj* instantaneous || *f* snapshot
istante *m* instant, moment; petitioner
istanza *f* petition; request, application; (law) instance; **in ultima istanza** as a final decision
istèri•co -ca (-ci -che) *adj* hysteric(al) || *mf* hysteric
isterilire §176 *tr* to make barren || *ref* to become barren
isterismo *m* hysteria, hysterics
istigare §209 *tr* to instigate, prompt
istiga•tóre -trice *mf* instigator
istillare *tr* to instill, implant; **istillare il collirio negli occhi** to put drops in the eyes
istinti•vo -va *adj* instinctive
istinto *m* instinct
istituire §176 *tr* to institute, found; (lit) to decide
istituto *m* institute; institution; bank; **istituto di bellezza** beauty parlor
istitu•tóre -trice *mf* founder; teacher, instructor || *m* tutor || *f* governess; nurse
istituzionalizzare [ddzz] *tr* to institutionalize
istituzióne *f* institution
istmo *m* isthmus
istologìa *f* histology

istoriare §287 **(istòrio)** *tr* to adorn with historical figures
istradare *tr* to direct || *ref* to wend one's way
ìstrice *m & f* (European) porcupine
istrióne *m* ham actor; buffoon
istriòni•co -ca *adj* **(-ci -che)** histrionic
istrionismo *m* histrionics
istruire §176 *tr* to instruct; to train; (law) to draw up, prepare (*a case*) || *ref* to learn
istrui•to -ta *adj* learned, educated
istruménto *m* (law) instrument
istrutti•vo -va *adj* instructive
istrut•tóre -trice *mf* instructor; (sports) coach
istruttò•rio -ria (-ri -rie) *adj* investigating, preliminary || *f* (law) preliminary investigation
istruzióne *f* instruction; (law) preliminary investigation; **istruzioni** instructions; directions
istupidire §176 *tr* to make dull; to stupefy
Itàlia, l' *f* Italy
italia•no -na *adj & mf* Italian
itàli•co -ca *adj* **(-ci -che)** italic; Italic; (lit) Italian || *m* italics
italòfo•no -na *adj* Italian-speaking || *m* Italian-speaking person
itinerante *adj* itinerant
itinerà•rio *m* **(-ri)** itinerary
ittèri•co -ca *adj* **(-ci -che)** jaundiced
itterìzia *f* jaundice
ittiologìa *f* ichthiology
Iugoslàvia, la Yugoslavia
iugosla•vo -va *adj & mf* Yugoslav
iugulare *adj & tr* var of **giugulare**
iuta *f* jute
ivi *adv* (lit) there

J
K
L

L, l ['elle] *m & f* tenth letter of the Italian alphabet
la §4 *def art* the || *m* (mus) la, A; **dare il la** to set the tone || §5 *pers pron*
là *adv* there; **al di là da venire** to come, future; **al di là (di)** beyond; **andare di là** to go in the next room; **andare troppo in là** to go too far; **farsi in là** to move aside; **in là con gli anni** advanced in years; **l'al di là** the life beyond; **più in là** further; **più in là di** beyond; **va' là!** come on!
lab•bro *m* **(-bri)** edge (*of wound*); (lit) lip || *m* **(-bra** *fpl*) lip; **labbro leporino** harelip
labiale *adj & f* labial
làbile *adj* (coll) weak; (lit) fleeting
labiolettura *f* lip reading
labirinto *m* labyrinth, maze
laboratò•rio *m* **(-ri)** laboratory; workshop; **laboratorio linguistico** language laboratory
laborió•so -sa [s] *adj* hard-working, laborious; labored (*e.g., digestion*)
laburi•sta (-sti -ste) *adj* Labour || *mf* Labourite
lac•ca *f* **(-che)** lacquer
laccare §197 *tr* to lacquer; to japan; to polish (*nails*)
lac•chè *m* **(-chè)** lackey
lac•cio *m* **(-ci)** lasso; snare; noose; string; (fig) bond; **laccio delle scarpe** shoelace; **laccio emostatico** tourniquet
lacciòlo *m* snare
lacerare (làcero) *tr* to lacerate; to tear || *ref* to tear
làce•ro -ra *adj* torn; tattered
lacèrto *m* (lit) shred of flesh; (lit) biceps
lacòni•co -ca *adj* **(-ci -che)** laconic
làcrima *f* tear; drop
lacrimare (làcrimo) *tr* (lit) to weep over || *intr* to water (*said of the eyes*); (lit) to weep
lacrima•to -ta *adj* (lit) lamented
lacrimévole *adj* pitiful
lacrimòge•no -na *adj* tear (*e.g., gas*)
lacrimó•so -sa [s] *adj* teary, watery (*eyes*); tearful; lachrymose
lacuna *f* gap, lacuna; blank (*in one's mind*); **colmare una lacuna** to bridge a gap
lacustre *adj* lake
laddóve *conj* while, whereas
ladré•sco -sca *adj* **(-schi -sche)** thievish
la•dro -dra *adj* thieving; foul (*weather*); bewitching (*eyes*) || *mf* thief; **ladro di strada** highwayman || *f* inside pocket (*of suit*)
ladróne *m* thief; highwayman; **ladrone di mare** pirate
ladrùncolo *m* petty thief, pilferer
laggiù *adv* down there
lagnanza *f* complaint
lagnare *ref* to complain; to moan
lagno *m* complaint, lament
la•go *m* **(-ghi)** lake; pool (*of blood*)
làgrima *f* var of **lacrima**
laguna *f* lagoon
lai *m* **(lai)** lay; **lai** *mpl* (lit) lamentations
laicato *m* laity
lài•co -ca (-ci -che) *adj* lay || *m* layman
lài•do -da *adj* foul; obscene
la•ma *m* **(-ma)** llama; lama || *f* **(-me)** blade (*of knife*); marsh; (lit) lowland
lambiccare §197 *tr* to distill || *ref* to strive; **lambiccarsi il cervello** to rack one's brains
lambic•co *m* **(-chi)** still
lambire §176 *tr* to lap; to graze, to touch lightly
lamèlla *f* thin sheet
lamentare (laménto) *tr* to bemoan, lament || *ref* to moan; to complain
lamentazióne *f* lamentation

lamentévole *adj* plaintive; lamentable
laménto *m* complaint, lament; moan
lamentó·so -sa [s] *adj* plaintive, doleful
lamétta *f* razor blade
lamièra *f* plate; armor plate
lamierino *m* sheet metal, lamina
làmina *f* sheet, lamina
laminare (**làmino**) *tr* to laminate; to roll (*steel*)
lamina·tóio *m* (**-tói**) rolling mill
làmpada *f* lamp, light; **lampada al neon** neon lamp; **lampada a petrolio** oil lamp; **lampada a stelo** pole lamp; **lampada di sicurezza** (min) safety lamp; **lampada fluorescente** fluorescent lamp; **lampada lampo** (phot) flash bulb
lampadà·rio *m* (**-ri**) chandelier
lampadina *f* bulb; **lampadina tascabile** flashlight
lampante *adj* shiny; clear; lamp (*oil*)
lampeggiare §290 (**lampéggio**) *tr* (lit) to flash (*a smile*) || *intr* to flash; (aut) to blink; (coll) to flash the turn signals || *impers* (ESSERE & AVERE)—**lampeggia** it lightens, it is lightning
lampeggiatóre *m* (aut) turn signal; (phot) flashlight
lampio·nàio *m* (**-nài**) lamplighter
lampióne *m* street lamp
lampìride *f* glowworm
lampo *m* lightning; flash of lightning; (fig) flash
lampóne *m* raspberry
lana *f* wool; **buona lana** (coll) rogue, rascal; **lana d'acciaio** steel wool; **lana di vetro** fiberglass, glass wool
lancétta *f* lancet; hand (*of watch*); pointer (*of instrument*)
làn·cia *f* (**-ce**) lance, spear; nozzle (*of fire hose*); launch; **lancia di salvataggio** lifeboat
lanciabóm·be *m* (**-be**) trench mortar
lanciafiam·me *m* (**-me**) flamethrower
lanciamìssi·li (**-li**) *adj* missile-launching || *m* missile launcher
lanciaraz·zi [ddzz] *m* (**-zi**) rocket launcher
lanciare §128 *tr* to throw, hurl; to drop (*from an airplane*); to launch (*e.g., an advertising campaign*) || *ref* to hurl oneself; (rok) to blast off; **lanciarsi col paracadute** to parachute, bail out
lanciasilu·ri *m* (**-ri**) torpedo tube
lancia·to -ta *adj* hurled, flung; flying, e.g., **partenza lanciata** flying start
lancia·tóre -trice *mf* hurler, thrower; (baseball) pitcher
lancière *m* lancer
lancinante *adj* piercing
làn·cio *m* (**-ci**) throw; publicity campaign; (aer) drop; (aer) release (*of bombs*); (baseball) pitch; (rok) launch; **lancio del peso** shot put
landa *f* moor; wasteland
lanerìe *fpl* woolens
languidézza *f* languidness, languor
làngui·do -da *adj* languid; sad (*eyes*)
languire (**lànguo**) & §176 *intr* to languish
languóre *m* languor; languishing; weakness; tenderness
laniè·ro -ra *adj* wool (*industry*)
lanifì·cio *m* (**-ci**) woolen mill
lanó·so -sa [s] *adj* woolly; kinky (*hair*); bushy (*face*)
lantèrna *f* lantern
lanùgine *f* down
lanzichenéc·co *m* (**-chi**) landsknecht
laónde *conj* (lit) wherefore
laotia·no -na *adj* & *mf* Laotian
lapalissia·no -na *adj* self-evident
lapidare (**làpido**) *tr* to stone (to death); (fig) to pick to pieces
làpide *f* stone tablet; tombstone
lapillo *m* lapillus
là·pis *m* (**-pis**) pencil
lappare *intr* to lap
làppola *f* (bot) burdock; (bot) bur
lappóne *adj* Lappish || *mf* Lapp || *m* Lapp (*language*)
Lappónia, la Lapland
lardellare (**lardèllo**) *tr* to lard; to stuff with bacon
lardo *m* lard; **nuotare nel lardo** to live on easy street
largheggiare §290 (**larghéggio**) *intr* to be liberal; to be lavish
larghézza *f* width; liberality; abundance; **larghezza di vedute** broad-mindedness
largire §176 *tr* (lit) to bestow liberally
largizióne *f* bestowal; donation
lar·go -ga (**-ghi -ghe**) *adj* broad, wide; ample; liberal; abundant; (phonet) open; **prenderla larga** to keep away || *m* width; open sea; square; (mus) largo; **al largo di** (naut) off; **fare largo a** to open the way to; **farsi largo** to elbow one's way; **prendere il largo** to run away; (naut) to put to sea; **tenersi al largo** to keep at a distance || *f*—**alla larga!** keep away! || **largo** *adv*—**girare largo** to keep away
làrice *m* larch
laringe *f* larynx
laringite *f* laryngitis
laringoia·tra *mf* (**-tri -tre**) laryngologist
laringoscò·pio *m* (**-pi**) laryngoscope
larva *f* (ent) larva; (lit) ghost; (lit) skeleton; (lit) sham
lasagne *fpl* lasagne
lasciapassa·re *m* (**-re**) safe-conduct; permit
lasciare §128 *tr* to leave; to let; to let go of; **lasciar cadere** to drop; **lasciarci le penne** (coll) to die; (coll) to be skinned alive; **lasciar correre** to let go; **lasciar detto** to leave word; **lasciar fare** to leave alone; **lasciare in pace** to leave alone; **lasciare libero** to let go; **lasciare scritto** to leave in writing || *ref* to abandon oneself; to abandon one another
làscito *m* (law) bequest
lascìvia *f* lasciviousness
lascì·vo -va *adj* lascivious
lassati·vo -va *adj* mildly laxative || *m* mild laxative
lassismo *m* laxity
las·so -sa *adj* lax || *m* lasso; **lasso di tempo** period of time
lassù *adv* up there, up above
lastra *f* slab; paving stone; (phot)

plate; exposed X-ray film; **farsi le lastre** (coll) to be X-rayed
lastricare §197 (**làstrico**) *tr* to pave
lastricato *m* paving, pavement
làstri·co *m* (**-ci** or **-chi**) pavement; roadway; **ridursi sul lastrico** to fall into abject poverty
lastróne *m* slab; plate glass
latènte *adj* latent
laterale *adj* lateral ‖ *m* (soccer) halfback
laterì·zio -zia (**-zi -zie**) *adj* brick ‖ **laterizi** *mpl* bricks, tiles
làtice *m* latex
latifondi·sta *mf* (**-sti -ste**) rich landowner
latifóndo *m* large landed estate
lati·no -na *adj* Latin; lateen (*sail*) ‖ *m* Latin
latitante *adj* hiding ‖ *mf* fugitive
latitanza *f* flight from justice
latitùdine *f* latitude
la·to -ta *adj* wide; broad (*meaning*) ‖ *m* side; **d'altro lato** on the other hand
la·tóre -trice *mf* bearer
latrare *intr* to bark
latrato *m* bark
latrina *f* toilet, lavatory, washroom
latta *f* tin; can
lattàia *f* milkmaid
lat·tàio *m* (**-tài**) milkman, dairyman
lattante *adj* & *m* suckling
latte *m* milk; **latte detergente** cleansing cream; **latte di gallina** flip; (bot) star-of-Bethlehem; **latte in polvere** powdered milk; **latte magro** or **scremato** skim milk
lattemièle *m* whipped cream
làtte·o -a *adj* milky
latterìa *f* dairy; creamery
làttice *m* var of **latice**
latticèllo *m* buttermilk
latticì·nio *m* (**-ni**) dairy product
lattiginó·so -sa [s] *adj* milky
lattonière *m* tinsmith
lattu·ga *f* (**-ghe**) lettuce; head of lettuce; frill
làudano *m* paregoric, laudanum
laudati·vo -va *adj* laudatory
làurea *f* wreath; doctorate; doctoral examination
laurean·do -da *mf* candidate for the doctorate
laureare (**làureo**) *tr* to confer the doctorate on; to award (*s.o.*) the title of; (lit) to wreathe ‖ *ref* to receive the doctorate; (sports) to get the tile of
laurea·to -ta *adj* laureate ‖ *m* alumnus, graduate
làuro *m* laurel
làu·to -ta *adj* sumptuous, rich
lava *f* lava
lavabianche·rìa *f* (**-rìa**) washing machine
lavàbile *adj* washable
lavabo *m* washstand; lavatory
lavacristallo *m* windshield washer
lavacro *m* washing; font; purification; **santo lavacro** baptism
lavàg·gio *m* (**-gi**) washing; **lavaggio a secco** dry cleaning; **lavaggio del cervello** brainwashing
lavagna *f* slate; blackboard; **lavagna di panno** felt board; **lavagna luminosa** overhead projector
lavama·no *m* (**-no**) washstand
lavanda *f* washing; pumping (*of stomach*); lavender
lavandàia *f* laundrywoman; **lavandaia stiratrice** laundress (*woman who washes and irons*)
lavan·dàio *m* (**-dài**) laundryman; **lavandaio stiratore** launderer
lavanderìa *f* laundry; **lavanderia a gettone** laundromat; **lavanderia a secco** dry-cleaning establishment
lavandino *m* sink
lavapiat·ti *mf* (**-ti**) dishwasher (*person*)
lavare *tr* to wash; to cleanse; **lavare a secco** to dry-clean; **lavare il capo a** to scold ‖ *ref* to wash oneself; **lavarsi le mani** to wash one's hands
lavastovì·glie *mf* (**-glie**) dishwasher ‖ *m* & *f* dishwasher (*machine*)
lavata *f* washing; **lavata di capo** scolding
lavativo *m* (coll) enema; (coll) bore; (coll) goldbricker
lava·tóio *m* (**-tói**) laundry room; washtub
lava·tóre -trice *mf* washer ‖ *m* washerman; (mach) purifier ‖ *f* washerwoman; washing machine
lavatura *f* washing; **lavatura a secco** dry cleaning; **lavatura di piatti** dishwater; washing of dishes; (fig) watery soup
lavèllo *m* wash basin; sink
lavoràbile *adj* workable
lavorante *mf* helper, apprentice
lavorare (**lavóro**) *tr* to work; to till ‖ *intr* to work; to perform; to be busy; to trade; **lavorare ai ferri** to knit; **lavorare di fantasia** to daydream; **lavorare di ganasce** to eat voraciously; **lavorare di gomiti** to elbow one's way; **lavorare di mano** to pilfer; **lavorare di traforo** to work with a jig saw
lavorati·vo -va *adj* working; workable
lavora·to -ta *adj* wrought; tilled
lavora·tóre -trice *mf* worker ‖ *m* workman; workingman ‖ *f* workingwoman
lavorazióne *f* working; manufacturing; tilling
lavorì·o *m* (**-ì**) bustle; steady work; scheming
lavóro *m* work; labor; steady work; homework; piece of work; (coll) trouble; **a lavori ultimati** when the work is finished; **lavori forzati** hard labor; **lavori in economia** time and material contract work; **lavori teatrali** theatrical productions; **lavoro a cottimo** piecework; **lavoro a maglia** knitting; **lavoro di cucito** needlework; **mettere al lavoro** to press into service
lazzarétto [ddzz] *m* lazaretto
lazzaróne [ddzz] *m* cad; (coll) goldbricker
le §4 *def art* the ‖ §5 *pers pron*
leale *adj* loyal; sincere
leali·sta *mf* (**-sti -ste**) loyalist
leal·tà *f* (**-tà**) loyalty; sincerity

lébbra *f* leprosy
lebbró•so -sa [s] *adj* leprous || *mf* leper
lécca-léc•ca *m* (**-ca**) (coll) lollypop
leccapiat•ti *m* (**-ti**) glutton; sponger
leccapiè•di *mf* (**-di**) bootlicker
leccarda *f* dripping pan
leccare §197 (**lécco**) *tr* to lick; to fawn on; (fig) to polish || *ref* to make oneself up
lecca•to -ta *adj* affected; polished || *f* licking
léc•cio *m* (**-ci**) holm oak
leccornìa *f* dainty morsel, delicacy
léci•to -ta *adj* licit, permissible; **mi sia lecito** may I || *m* right
lèdere §192 *tr* to damage, injure
lé•ga *f* (**-ghe**) league; alloy; **di bassa lega** poor, in poor taste; **fare lega** to unite
legale *adj* legal; lawyer's; official || *m* lawyer
legali•tà *f* (**-tà**) legality, lawfulness
legalità•rio -ria *adj* (**-ri -rie**) (pol) observing the rule of law
legalizzare [ddzz] *tr* to legalize; to authenticate
legame *m* bond; connection; relationship
legaménto *m* tie, bond; ligament; (phonet) liaison
legare §209 (**légo**) *tr* to tie; to bind; to unite; to set (*a stone*); to bequeath; to alloy; (bb) to bind || *intr* to bond; to mix (*said of metals*); to go together || *ref* to unite; **legarsela al dito** to never forget
legatà•rio -ria *mf* (**-ri -rie**) legatee
lega•to -ta *adj* muscle-bound || *m* legate; bequest; (mus) legato
lega•tóre -trice *mf* bookbinder
legatorìa *f* bookbindery
legatura *f* typing; binding; ligature; bookbinding; (mus) tie
legazióne *f* legation
légge *f* law; act; **dettar legge** to lay down the law; **è fuori della legge** he is an outlaw; **legge stralcio** emergency law
leggènda *f* legend; story, tall tale; (journ) caption
leggendà•rio -ria *adj* (**-ri -rie**) legendary
lèggere §193 *tr, intr & ref* to read
leggerézza *f* lightness; nimbleness; thoughtlessness; fickleness
leggè•ro -ra *adj* light; nimble; thoughtless; slight; fickle; **alla leggera** lightly || **leggero** *adv* lightly
leggia•dro -dra *adj* graceful, lovely
leggìbile *adj* legible, readable
leggì•o *m* (**-i**) lectern; music stand
legiferare (**legìfero**) *intr* to legislate
legionà•rio -ria *adj & m* (**-ri -rie**) legionary
legióne *f* legion
legislati•vo -va *adj* legislative
legisla•tóre -trice *mf* legislator
legislatura *f* legislature
legittimare (**legìttimo**) *tr* to legitimize
legittimi•tà *f* (**-tà**) legitimacy
legìtti•mo -ma *adj* legitimate; pure; just, right || *f* (law) legitim
lé•gna *f* (**-gna & -gne**) firewood; (fig) fuel
legnàia *f* woodpile; woodshed
legname *m* timber, lumber
legnata *f* clubbing, thrashing
légno *m* wood; stick; ship; coach; timber; **legno compensato** plywood; **legno dolce** softwood; **legno forte** hardwood
legnòlo *m* ply (*e.g., of a cable*)
legnó•so -sa [s] *adj* wooden; tough (*meat*); dry (*style*)
legu•lèio *m* (**-lèi**) pettifogger
legume *m* legume; **legumi** vegetables; legumes
leguminósa [s] *f* leguminous plant; **leguminose** legumes
lèi §5 *pron pers;* **dare del Lei a** to address formally
lémbo *m* edge, border; patch (*of land*)
lèm•ma *m* (**-mi**) entry (*in a dictionary*)
lèmme lèmme *adv* (coll) slowly
léna *f* energy; enthusiasm; (lit) breath
lèndine *m* nit
lène *adj* (lit) light, soft, gentle; (phonet) voiced
lenire §176 *tr* to soothe, assuage
lenóne *m* panderer, procurer
lenóna *f* procuress
lènte *f* lens; bob, pendulum bob; **lente d'ingrandimento** magnifying glass; **lenti** glasses
lentézza *f* slowness
lentìcchia *f* lentil
lentìggine *f* freckle
lentigginó•so -sa [s] *adj* freckly
lèn•to -ta *adj* slow; slack; (lit) loose (*hair*); (lit) loose-fitting (*garment*) || **lento** *adv* slowly
lènza *f* fishline
lenzuò•lo *m* (**-li**) sheet; (fig) blanket; **lenzuolo a due piazze** double sheet; **lenzuolo funebre** winding sheet, shroud || *m* (**-la** *fpl*) sheet; **lenzuola** pair of sheets (*in a bed*)
leoncino *m* lion cub
leóne *m* lion; **leone d'America** cougar; **leone marino** sea lion || **Leone** *m* (astr) Leo
leonéssa *f* lioness
leopardo *m* leopard
lepidézza *f* wit; witticism
lèpi•do -da *adj* witty, facetious
lepisma *f* (ent) silverfish
lèpre *adj invar* rendezvous, **e.g., razzo lepre** rendezvous rocket || *f* hare
lepròtto *m* leveret, young hare
lèr•cio -cia *adj* (**-ci -ce**) filthy
lerciume *m* filth, dirt
lèsbi•co -ca (**-ci -che**) *adj & mf* Lesbian || *f* Lesbian (*female homosexual*)
lésina *f* awl; stinginess; miser
lesinare (**lésino & lèsino**) *tr* to begrudge || *intr* to be miserly
lesionare (**lesióno**) *tr* to damage; to crack open
lesióne *f* damage; injury; lesion
lé•so -sa *adj* damaged; injured
lessare (**lésso**) *tr* to boil
lessicale *adj* lexical
lèssi•co *m* (**-ci**) lexicon
lessicografìa *f* lexicography
lessicogràfi•co -ca *adj* (**-ci -che**) lexicographic(al)
lessicògrafo *m* lexicographer

lessicologìa *f* lexicology
lés•so -sa *adj* boiled || *m* boiled meat; soup meat
lè•sto -sta *adj* swift; nimble; quick; **alla lesta** hastily; **lesto di lingua** ready-tongued; **lesto di mano** light-fingered
lestofante *m* swindler
letale *adj* lethal, deadly
leta•màio *m* **(-mài)** dunghill
letame *m* manure, dung
letàrgi•co -ca *adj* **(-ci -che)** lethargic
letar•go *m* **(-ghi)** lethargy; hibernation
letìzia *f* happiness, joy
lèttera *f* letter; **alla lettera** literally; **lettera morta** unheeded, e.g., **le sue parole rimasero lettera morta** his words remained unheeded; **lettere** literature; **lettere credenziali** credentials; **scrivere in tutte lettere** to spell out
letterale *adj* literal
letterà•rio -ria *adj* **(-ri -rie)** literary; learned (*word*)
lettera•to -ta *adj* literary; literate || *m* man of letters; (coll) literate, learned person
letteratura *f* literature
lettièra *f* litter, bedding
letti•ga *f* **(-ghe)** sedan chair; stretcher
lètto *m* bed; bedding; **di primo letto** born of the first marriage; **letti gemelli** twin beds; **letto a castello** bunk bed; **letto a due piazze** double bed; **letto a scomparsa** Murphy bed; **letto a una piazza** single bed; **letto bastardo** oversize bed; **letto caldo** hotbed; **letto di morte** deathbed; **letto operatorio** operating table
lèttone or **lettóne** *adj* Lettish || *mf* Lett || *m* Lett, Lettish (*language*)
Lettónia, La Latvia
let•tóre -trice *mf* reader; lecturer; meter reader || *m* reader (*e.g., for microfilm*); **lettore perforatore** reader (*of punch cards*)
lettura *f* reading; lecture; **lettura del pensiero** mind reading
letturi•sta *m* **(-sti)** meter reader
leucemìa *f* leukemia
leucorrèa *f* leucorrhea
lèva *f* lever; (mil) draft; (mil) class; **essere di leva** to be of draft age; **fare leva su** to use (*s.o.'s emotions*)
levachio•di *m* **(-di)** claw hammer
levante *adj* rising || *m* east; Levant
levanti•no -na *adj & mf* Levantine
levare (lèvo) *tr* to lift, raise; to weigh (*anchor*); to pull (*a tooth*); to break (*camp*); to collect (*mail*); to remove, take away; to subtract; **levare alle stelle** to praise to the sky; **levare il disturbo a** to take leave of || *ref* to arise; to get up; to take off; to satisfy (*e.g., one's hunger*); to rise (*said of wind*); **levarsi dai piedi** to get out of the way; **levarsi dai piedi** or **di mezzo qlcu** to get rid of s.o.
levata *f* rise; reveille; collection (*of mail*); withdrawal (*of merchandise from warehouse*); **levata di scudi** uprising
levatàc•cia *f* **(-ce)** getting up at an impossible hour; **ho dovuto fare una levataccia** I had to get up way too early
leva•tóio -tóia *adj* **(-tói -tóie)—ponte levatoio** drawbridge
levatrice *f* midwife
levatura *f* intellectual breadth
leviatano *m* leviathan
levigare §209 (lèvigo) *tr* to polish
levigatrice *f* sander; buffer
levi•tà *f* **(-tà)** (lit) levity
levitazióne *f* levitation
levrière *m* greyhound
lezióne *f* lesson; lecture; reading
lezió•so -sa [s] *adj* affected, mincing
lézzo [ddzz] *m* stench; filth
li *def art masc plur* (obs) the; **li tre novembre** the third of November (*in official documents*) || §5 *pers pron*
lì *adv* there; **di lì** that way; **di lì a un anno** a year hence; **essere lì lì per** to be about to; **fin lì** up to that point; **giù di lì** more or less; **lì per lì** on the spot
libanése [s] *adj & mf* Lebanese
Lìbano, il Lebanon
libare *tr* to toast; to taste || *intr* to toast
libazióne *f* libation
libbra *f* pound
libéc•cio *m* **(-ci)** southwest wind
libèllo *m* libel; (law) brief
libèllula *f* dragonfly
liberale *adj & m* liberal
liberali•tà *f* **(-tà)** liberality
liberare (lìbero) *tr* to free; to pay in full for; to open into (*said, e.g., of a hall opening into a room*); to clear, empty (*a room*) || *ref*—**liberarsi da** or **di** to get rid of
libera•tóre -trice *adj* liberating || *mf* liberator
liberismo *m* free trade
lìbe•ro -ra *adj* free; vacant; without a revenue stamp (*document*); open (*syllable; heart*); outspoken
liber•tà *f* **(-tà)** freedom; release (*e.g., from mortgage*); **libertà provvisoria** bail, parole; **libertà vigilata** probation; **mettersi in libertà** to put comfortable house clothes on; **rimettere in libertà** to set free
liberti•no -na *adj & mf* libertine
Lìbia, la Libya
lìbi•co -ca *adj & mf* **(-ci -che)** Libyan
libìdine *f* lust; greed
libidinó•so -sa [s] *adj* lustful
libido *f* libido
li•bràio *m* **(-brài)** bookseller
librare *ref* to balance; to soar; (aer) to glide
libratóre *m* (aer) glider
librerìa *f* bookstore; library (*room*); bookshelf; book collection
libré•sco -sca *adj* **(-schi -sche)** bookish
librétto *m* booklet; card; (mus) libretto; **libretto di banca** passbook; **libretto degli assegni** checkbook; **libretto di circolazione** car registration; **libretto ferroviario** railroad pass; **libretto di risparmio** passbook (*of savings bank*)
libro *m* book; ledger; register (*e.g., of births*); **a libro** folding; **libro di**

bordo log; **libro in brossura** paperback; **libro mastro** ledger; **libro paga** (com) payroll
liceale *adj* high-school || *mf* high-school student
licènza *f* permit; license; diploma; (mil) leave; **con licenza parlando!** excuse my language!; **dar licenza a** to dismiss; **prender licenza da** to take leave of
licenziaménto *m* dismissal; **licenziamento in tronco** firing on the spot
licenziare §287 **(licènzio)** *tr* to dismiss; to O.K. (*a book to be published*); to graduate || *ref* to take leave; to give notice, resign; to graduate
licenzió·so -sa [s] *adj* licentious
licèo *m* high school; lycée
lichène *m* lichen
licitazióne *f* auction; (bridge) bidding
lido *m* shore; sand bar
liè·to -ta *adj* glad; blessed (*event*)
liève *adj* light; slight
lievitare (lièvito) *tr* to leaven || *intr* (ESSERE & AVERE) to rise; to ferment
lièvito *m* yeast; leaven; **lievito in polvere** baking powder
li·gio -gia *adj* (**-gi -gie**) devoted
lignàg·gio *m* (**-gi**) ancestry, lineage
ligustro *m* privet
lil·la (-la) *adj invar & m* lilac
lillipuzia·no -na *adj & mf* Lilliputian
lima *f* file; **lima per le unghie** nail file
limacció·so -sa [s] *adj* miry, muddy
limare *tr* to file; to polish (*e.g., a speech*); to gnaw, plague
limatura *f* filing; filings
limbo *m* (lit) edge; (fig) limbo || **Limbo** *m* (theol) Limbo
limétta *f* nail file; (bot) lime
limitare *m* threshold || *v* **(lìmito)** *tr* to limit; to bound
limitazióne *f* limitation
lìmite *m* limit; boundary; check; (soccer) penalty line; **limite di carico** maximum weight; **limite di età** retirement age; **limite di velocità** speed limit; **senza limiti** limitless
limìtro·fo -fa *adj* neighboring (*country*)
limo *m* mud, mire
limonare (limóno) *intr* (coll) to spoon
limonata *f* lemonade; (med) citrate of magnesia
limóne *m* lemon tree; lemon
limó·so -sa [s] *adj* slimy
lìmpi·do -da *adj* limpid, clear
lince *f* lynx, wildcat
linciàg·gio *m* (**-gi**) lynching
linciare §128 *tr* to lynch
lin·do -da *adj* neat; clean
lìnea *f* line; degree (*of temperature*); **conservare la linea** to keep one's figure; **in linea** abreast; (telp) connected; **in linea d'aria** as the crow flies; **linea del fuoco** firing line; **linea del cambiamento di data** international date line; **linea di circonvallazione** (rr) beltline; **linea di condotta** policy; **linea di partenza** starting line; **linea laterale** (sports) side line
lineaménti *mpl* lineaments; elements
lineare *adj* linear || *v* **(lìneo)** *tr* to delineate
lineétta *f* dash; hyphen
linfa *f* (anat) lymph; (bot) sap; **dar linfa** (bot) to bleed
lingòtto *m* (metallurgy) pig, ingot; **lingotto d'oro** bullion
lìngua *f* tongue; language; strip (*of land*); **essere di due lingue** to speak with a forked tongue; **in lingua** in the correct language; **lingua di gatto** ladyfinger; **lingua lunga** backbiter; **lingua sciolta** glib tongue; **mala lingua** wicked tongue
linguacciu·to -ta *adj* talkative; sharp-tongued
linguàg·gio *m* (**-gi**) language
linguèlla *f* (philately) gummed strip
linguétta *f* tongue (*of shoe*); (mach) pin; (mus) reed
linguìsti·co -ca (-ci -che) *adj* linguistic || *f* linguistics
linifi·cio *m* (**-ci**) flax-spinning mill
liniménto *m* liniment
lino *m* flax; linen
linósa [s] *f* flaxseed, linseed
linotipi·sta *mf* (**-sti -ste**) linotypist
liocòrno *m* unicorn
liofilizzare [ddzz] *tr* to freeze-dry
liquefare §194 *tr & ref* to liquefy
liquefazióne *f* liquefaction
liquidare (lìquido) *tr* to liquidate; to close out; to dismiss; to settle
liquidazióne *f* liquidation; clearance; **liquidazione del danno** (ins) adjustment
liquidità *f* liquidity
lìqui·do -da *adj* liquid; (com) due || *m* liquid; cash || *f* liquid
liqui·gàs *m* (**-gàs**) liquid gas
liquirìzia *f* licorice
liquóre *m* liqueur; (pharm) liquor
liquori·sta *mf* (**-sti -ste**) liqueur manufacturer or dealer
lira *f* lira; pound; (mus) lyre || **Lira** *f* (astr) Lyra
lìri·co -ca (-ci -che) *adj* lyric; (mus) operatic || *m* lyric poet || *f* lyric; lyric poetry; opera
lirismo *m* lyricism
Lisbóna *f* Lisbon
li·sca *f* (**-sche**) fishbone; lisp
lisciare §128 *tr* to smooth; **lisciare il pelo a** to butter up, flatter; to beat up || *ref* to preen
li·scio -scia *adj* (**-sci -sce**) smooth; straight (*drink*); black (*coffee*); **passarla liscia** to get away scot-free
liscìvia *f* lye; bleach
lisciviatrice *f* washing machine
li·so -sa *adj* worn-out, threadbare
lista *f* list; strip, band; stripe; **lista delle spese** shopping list; **lista delle vivande** bill of fare; **lista elettorale** slate (*of candidates*)
listare *tr* to border; to stripe
listèllo *m* lath; (archit) listel
listino *m* price list; market quotation
litanìa *f* litany
lite *f* quarrel; lawsuit
litigante *adj* quarreling || *mf* quarreler; (law) litigant

litigare §209 (**lìtigo**) *tr*—**litigare qlco a qlcu** to fight with s.o. for s.th || *intr* to quarrel; to litigate || *ref*—**litigarsi qlco** to strive for s.th
litì•gio *m* (**-gi**) quarrel, litigation
litigió•so -sa [s] *adj* quarrelsome
lìtio *m* lithium
litografìa *f* lithography
litògrafo *m* lithographer
litorale *adj* littoral || *m* seashore, coastline
litro *m* liter
Lituània, la Lithuania
litua•no -na *adj & mf* Lithuanian || *m* Lithuanian (*language*)
liturgìa *f* liturgy
litùrgi•co -ca *adj* (**-ci -che**) liturgical
liu•tàio *m* (**-tài**) lute maker
liuto *m* lute
livèlla *f* level; **livella a bolla d'aria** spirit level
livellaménto *m* leveling; equalization
livellare (**livèllo**) *tr* to level; to equalize; to survey || *intr* (ESSERE) *& ref* to become level
livella•tóre -trice *adj* leveling || *mf* surveyor || *f* bulldozer
livellazióne *f* leveling
livèllo *m* level; **livello delle acque** sea level
lìvi•do -da *adj* livid, black-and-blue || *m* bruise
lividóre *m* bruise
livóre *m* grudge; hatred
Livórno *f* Leghorn
livrèa *f* livery
lizza *f* tilting ground; **entrare in lizza** to enter the lists
lo §4 *def art* the || §5 *pers pron*
lòb•bia *m & f* (**-bia** *mpl & fpl*) homburg
lòbo *m* lobe
locale *adj* local || *m* room; place (*of business*); (naut) compartment; **locale notturno** night spot
locali•tà *f* (**-tà**) locality, spot
localizzare [ddzz] *tr* to localize; to locate || *ref* to become localized
localizzazióne [ddzz] *f* localization; **localizzazione dei guasti** troubleshooting
locanda *f* inn
locandiè•re -ra *mf* innkeeper
locandina *f* playbill; flyer; small poster
locare §197 (**lòco**) *tr* to rent, lease
locatà•rio -ria *mf* (**-ri -rie**) lessee, renter
loca•tóre -trice *mf* lessor
locazióne *f* rent; lease; **dare in locazione** to rent
locomotiva *f* locomotive, engine
locomo•tóre -trice *adj* locomotive || *m & f* (rr) electric locomotive
locomotori•sta *m* (**-sti**) (rr) engineer
locomozióne *f* locomotion; transportation
lòculo *m* burial niche
locusta *f* locust
locuzióne *f* locution, expression; phrase; idiom
lodàbile *adj* praiseworthy
lodare (**lòdo**) *tr* to praise || *ref* to praise oneself, brag; **lodarsi di** (poet) to be pleased with
lodati•vo -va *adj* laudatory
lòde *f* praise; **con la lode** cum laude; **con lode** plus (*on a report card*)
lodévole *adj* praiseworthy, commendable
lòdo *m* arbitration
logaritmo *m* logarithm
lòg•gia *f* (**-ge**) lodge; (archit) loggia
loggióne *m* (theat) upper gallery
lògi•co -ca (**-ci -che**) *adj* logical; **esser logico** to think logically || *m* logician || *f* logic
logisti•co -ca (**-ci -che**) *adj* logistic || *f* logistics
lò•glio *m* (**-gli**) cockle
logoraménto *m* wear; attrition
logorare (**lógoro**) *tr* to wear out; to fray || *ref* to wear away; to become threadbare
logorì•o *m* (**-i**) wear and tear
lógo•ro -ra *adj* worn out; threadbare
lòlla *f* chaff
lombàggine *f* lumbago
lombar•do -da *adj & mf* Lombard
lombata *f* loin, sirloin
lómbo *m* loin; hip; (lit) ancestry
lombri•co *m* (**-chi**) earthworm
londinése [s] *adj* London || *mf* Londoner
Londra *f* London
longànime *adj* patient, forbearing
longanimi•tà *f* (**-tà**) patience, forbearance
longevità *f* longevity
longè•vo -va *adj* long-lived
longherina *f* beam, girder
longheróne *m* (aer) longeron; (**aer**) spar; (aut) main frame member
longitùdine *f* longitude
longobar•do -da *adj & mf* Lombard
lontananza *f* distance
lonta•no -na *adj* distant, remote; vague; indirect || *m* (lit) far-away place || *f*—**alla lontana** from a distance; vaguely; distant (*e.g., relative*) || **lontano** *adv* far; **da lontano** from afar; **lontano da** away from; far from; **rifarsi da lontano** to start from the very beginning
lóntra *f* otter
lónza *f* pork loin; (poet) leopard
lòppa *f* chaff; skin (*of plant*); slag, dross
loquace *adj* loquacious; (fig) eloquent
loquèla *f* (lit) tongue; (lit) style
lordare (**lórdo**) *tr* to soil, dirty
lór•do -da *adj* soiled, dirty; gross (*weight*)
lordume *m* dirt, filth
lordura *f* dirt, filth; soil
lóro §5 *pron pers* || §6 *adj poss & pron*
losan•ga *f* (**-ghe**) rhombus; (herald) lozenge
ló•sco -sca *adj* (**-schi -sche**) squint-eyed; cross-eyed; (fig) shady
lóto *m* mud
lòto *m* lotus
lòtta *f* fight; struggle; wrestling; **essere in lotta** to be at war; **lotta libera** catch-as-catch-can
lottare (**lòtto**) *intr* to fight; to quarrel; to struggle; to wrestle

lotta•tóre -trice *mf* fighter; wrestler
lotterìa *f* lottery
lottizzare [ddzz] *tr* to divide into lots
lòtto *m* lotto; parcel, lot
lozióne *f* lotion
lùbri•co -ca *adj* **(-ci -che)** lewd; (lit) slippery
lubrificante *adj & m* lubricant
lubrificare §197 **(lubrìfico)** *tr* to lubricate
lucchétto *m* padlock
luccicare §197 **(lùccico)** *intr* to sparkle; to shine
luccichì•o *m* **(-i)** glittering; shining; sparkle
luccicóne *m* big tear
lùc•cio *m* **(-ci)** pike
lùcciola *f* firefly; usherette (*in movie*); **prendere lucciole per lanterne** to make a blunder; to be seeing things
luce *f* light; sunlight; opening; glass (*of mirror*); leaf (*e.g., of door*); (archit) span; (coll) electricity; **alla luce del sole** in plain view; **fare luce** to shed light; **luce degli occhi** eyesight; **luce del giorno** daylight; **luce della luna** moonlight; **luce di arresto** (aut) stoplight; **luce di incrocio** (aut) dimmer, low beam; **luce di posizione** (aut) parking light; **luce di profondità** (aut) high beam; **luci** (poet) eyes; **luci della ribalta** (fig) stage, boards; **mettere alla luce** to give birth to; **mettere in luce** to reveal; to publish; **venire alla luce** to be born; to come to light
lucènte *adj* shiny, shining
lucentézza *f* brightness; sheen
lucèrna *f* lamp; light; **lucerne (lit) eyes** || **Lucerna** *f* Lucerne
lucernà•rio *m* **(-ri)** skylight
lucèrtola *f* lizard
lucherino *m* (orn) siskin
Lucìa *f* Lucy
lucidare (lùcido) *tr* to shine, polish; to trace (*a figure*)
lucida•tóre -trice *mf* polisher (*person*) || *f* (mach) floor polisher
lucidatura *f* polish; tracing (*on paper*)
lucidi•tà *f* **(-tà)** polish; lucidity
lùci•do -da *adj* bright; lucid || *m* shine; tracing; **lucido per le scarpe** shoe polish
lucìfe•ro -ra *adj* (poet) light-bringing || **Lucifero** *m* Lucifer, morning star
lucìgnolo *m* wick
lucrare *tr* to win, acquire
lucrati•vo -va *adj* lucrative
lucro *m* gain, earnings, lucre; **lucro cessante** (law) loss of earnings
lucró•so -sa [s] *adj* lucrative
ludì•brio *m* **(-bri)** mockery; laughingstock
lù•glio *m* **(-gli)** July
lùgubre *adj* gloomy, dismal
lui §5 *pron pers*
luìgi *m* louis || **Luigi** *m* Louis
luma•ca *f* **(-che)** snail
lume *m* light; lamp; **lume degli occhi** eyesight; **lume delle stelle** starlight; **lumi** eyesight; **lumi di luna** hard times; **perdere il lume degli occhi** to lose one's self-control; **reggere il lume a** to close one's eyes to; **studiare al lume di candela** to burn the midnight oil
lumeggiare §290 **(luméggio)** *tr* to illuminate, to shed light on
lumicino *m* faint light; **essere al lumicino** to be on one's last legs
luminare *m* star; luminary
luminària *f* illumination
lumino *m* night light; votive light; rush light
luminó•so -sa [s] *adj* luminous; bright (*idea*)
luna *f* moon; **andare a lune** to be fickle; **avere la luna di traverso** to be in a bad mood; **luna calante** waning moon; **luna crescente** crescent moon; **luna di miele** honeymoon
lunare *adj* lunar, moon
lunària *f* (min) moonstone; (bot) honesty
lunà•rio *m* **(-ri)** almanac; **sbarcare il lunario** to live from hand to mouth
lunàti•co -ca *adj* **(-ci -che)** moody; whimsical
lune•dì *m* **(-dì)** Monday
lunétta *f* lunette; fanlight
lunga *f*—**alla lunga** in the long run; **alla più lunga** at the latest; **andare per le lunghe** to last a long time, drag on; **di gran lunga** by far; **farla lunga** to dillydally
lungàggine *f* delay, procrastination
lunghézza *f* length; **lunghezza d'onda** wave length; **prendere la lunghezza di** to measure
lungi *adv* (lit) far
lungimirante *adj* (fig) far-sighted
lun•go -ga (-ghi -ghe) *adj* long; sharp (*tongue*); nimble (*fingers*); tall; thin (*soup*); (coll) slow; **a lungo** for a long time; at length; **a lungo andare** in the long run; **lungo disteso** sprawling || *m* length; **in lungo e in largo** far and wide; **per il lungo** lengthwise || *f* see **lunga** || **lungo** *prep* along; during
lungofiume *m* river road
lungola•go *m* **(-ghi)** lakeshore road
lungomare *m* seashore road
lungometràg•gio *m* **(-gi)** full-length movie, feature film
lunòtto *m* (aut) rear window
luò•go *m* **(-ghi)** place; passage; site; (geom) locus; **aver luogo** to take place; **aver luogo in** to be laid in (*e.g., a certain place*); **dar luogo a** to give rise to; **del luogo** local; **far luogo** to make room; **fuori luogo** inopportune(ly); **in alto luogo** high-placed; **in luogo di** instead of; **luogo comune** commonplace; **luogo di decenza** toilet; **luogo di nascita** birthplace; **luogo di pena** penitentiary; **non luogo a procedere** (law) no ground for prosecution; (law) nolle prosequi; **sul luogo** on the spot; on the premises
luogotenènte *m* lieutenant
lupa *f* she-wolf
lupanare *m* (lit) brothel

lupé·sco -sca *adj* **(-schi -sche)** wolfish
lupétto *m* young wolf; cub (*in Boy Scouts*)
lupinèlla *f* sainfoin
lupi·no -na *adj* wolfish
lu·po -pa *mf* wolf; **lupo cerviero** lynx; **lupo di mare** seadog; **lupo mannaro** werewolf || *f* see **lupa**
lùppolo *m* hops
lùri·do -da *adj* filthy, dirty
lusco *m*—**tra il lusco e il brusco** at twilight
lusin·ga *f* **(-ghe)** flattery; illusion
lusingare §209 *tr* to flatter || *ref* to be flattered; to hope
lusinghiè·ro -ra *adj* flattering; promising
lussare *tr* to dislocate
lussazióne *f* dislocation
lusso *m* luxury; **di lusso** de luxe; **lusso di** abundance of
lussuó·so -sa [s] *adj* luxurious, sumptuous
lussureggiante *adj* luxuriant
lussùria *f* lust
lussurió·so -sa [s] *adj* lustful, lecherous
lustrare *tr* to polish, shine; to lick (*s.o.'s boots*) || *intr* to shine, be shiny
lustrascar·pe *m* **(-pe)** bootblack
lustrino *m* sequin; tinsel
lu·stro -stra *adj* shiny, polished || *m* shine, polish; period of five years; **dare il lustro a** to shine, polish
lutto *m* mourning; bereavement; **a lutto** black-edged (*e.g., stationery*); **lutto stretto** deep mourning
luttuó·so -sa [s] *adj* mournful

M

M, m [ˈɛmme] *m & f* eleventh letter of the Italian alphabet
ma *m* but; **ma e se** ifs and buts || *conj* but; yet || *interj* who knows?; too bad!
màca·bro -bra *adj* macabre
maca·co *m* **(-chi)** macaque; (fig) dumbbell
macadàm *m* macadam
macadamizzare [ddzz] *tr* to macadamize
mac·ca *f* **(-che)** abundance; **a macca** (coll) abundantly; (coll) without paying
maccarèllo *m* mackerel
maccheróni *mpl* macaroni
màcchia *f* spot, stain; brushwood; thicket; (fig) blot; **alla macchia** clandestinely; (painting) done in pointillism; **darsi alla macchia** to join the underground; to escape the law; **macchia solare** sunspot; **senza macchia** spotless
macchiare §287 *tr* to stain, soil || *ref* to become stained; **macchiarsi d'infamia** to soil one's reputation
macchiétta *f* caricature; comedian; **fare la macchietta di** to impersonate, to parody
macchiettare (macchiétto) *tr* to speckle
macchietti·sta *mf* **(-sti -ste)** cartoonist; comedian; impersonator
màcchina *f* machine; engine; car, automobile; machination; **andare in macchina** to go to press; **fatto a macchina** machine-made; **macchina da presa** (mov) camera; **macchina da proiezione** projector; **macchina fotografica** camera; **macchina per** or **da cucire** sewing machine; **macchina per** or **da scrivere** typewriter; **scrivere a macchina** to typewrite
macchinale *adj* mechanical
macchinare (màcchino) *tr* to plot
macchinà·rio *m* **(-ri)** machinery
macchinazióne *f* machination
macchinétta *f* gadget; **macchinetta del caffé** coffee maker
macchini·sta *m* **(-sti)** engineer; (theat) stagehand
macchinó·so -sa [s] *adj* heavy, ponderous; complicated
macedònia *f* fruit salad, fruit cup
macel·làio *m* **(-lài)** butcher
macellare (macèllo) *tr* to butcher
macellerìa *f* butcher shop
macèllo *m* slaughterhouse; butchering; carnage; disaster
macerare (màcero) *tr* to soak; to mortify (*the flesh*) || *ref* to waste away
macèria *f* low wall; **macerie** ruins
màce·ro -ra *adj* emaciated; skinny || *m* soaking vat (*for papermaking*)
machiavèlli·co -ca *adj* **(-ci -che)** Machiavellian
macigno *m* boulder
macilèn·to -ta *adj* emaciated, pale, wan
màcina *f* millstone; (coll) grind
macinacaf·fè *m* **(-fè)** coffee grinder
macinapé·pe *m* **(-pe)** pepper mill
macinare (màcino) *tr* to grind, mill; to burn up (*e.g., the road*)
macina·to -ta *adj* ground || *m* grindings; ground meat || *f* grinding
macinino *m* grinder; (coll) jalopy
mà·cis *m & f* **(-cis)** mace (*spice*)
maciste *m* strong man (*in circus*)
maciullare *tr* to brake (*flax or hemp*); to crush
macrocòsmo *m* macrocosm
màdia *f* bread bin; kneading trough
màdi·do -da *adj* wet, perspiring
madònna *f* lady || **Madonna** *f* Madonna
madornale *adj* huge; gross (*error*)
madre *f* mother; stub; mold; **madre nubile** unwed mother
madreggiare §290 **(madréggio)** *intr* to take after one's mother
madrelìngua *f* mother tongue
madrepàtria *f* mother country
madrepèrla *f* mother-of-pearl
madresélva *f* (coll) honeysuckle

madrevite *f* (mach) nut; die; **madrevite ad alette** wing nut
madrigna *f* stepmother
madrina *f* godmother; **madrina di guerra** war mother
mae·stà *f* (**-stà**) majesty; **lesa maestà** lese majesty
maestó·so -sa [s] *adj* majestic, stately
maèstra *f* teacher; (fig) master; **maestra giardiniera** kindergarten teacher
maestrale *m* northwest wind (*in Mediterranean*)
maestranze *fpl* workmen
maestrìa *f* skill, mastery
maè·stro -stra *adj* masterly; main ‖ *m* teacher; master; instructor; northwester (*in Mediterranean*); **maestro di cappella** choirmaster ‖ *f* see **maestra**
mafió·so -sa [s] *adj* Mafia ‖ *mf* member of the Mafia; gaudy dresser
ma·ga *f* (**-ghe**) sorceress
magagna *f* fault, weak spot
magagna·to -ta *adj* spoiled (*fruit*)
magari *adv* even, maybe ‖ *conj* even if ‖ *interj* would that . . . !
magazzinàg·gio [ddzz] *m* (**-gi**) storage
magazzinié·re -ra [ddzz] *mf* stockroom attendant ‖ *m* warehouseman
magazzino [ddzz] *m* warehouse; store; inventory; (phot, journ) magazine; **grandi magazzini** department store
maggése [s] *adj* May ‖ *m* (agr) fallow
màg·gio *m* (**-gi**) May; May Day
maggiolino *m* cockchafer
maggiorana *f* sweet marjoram
maggioranza *f* majority
maggiorare (**maggióro**) *tr* to increase
maggiorazióne *f* increase, appreciation
maggiordòmo *m* butler; majordomo
maggióre *adj* bigger, greater; major; main; higher (*bidder*); older, elder; (mil) master (*e.g., sergeant*); biggest, greatest; highest; oldest, eldest; **andare per la maggiore** to be all the rage; **maggiore età** majority ‖ *m* (mil) major; oldest one; **maggiori** ancestors
maggiorènne *adj* of age ‖ *mf* grown-up, adult
maggiorènte *mf* notable
maggiori·tà *f* (**-tà**) (mil) C.O.'s office
maggiorità·rio -ria *adj* (**-ri -rie**) majority
magìa *f* magic
màgi·co -ca *adj* (**-ci -che**) magic
Magi *mpl* Magi, Wise Men
magióne *f* (lit) home, dwelling
magistèro *m* education, teaching; mastery; (chem) precipitation
magistrale *adj* teacher's; masterly ‖ *f* teacher's college
magistrato *m* magistrate
magistratura *f* judiciary
màglia *f* knitting; stitch; link; undershirt; sports shirt; (hist) mail; (fig) web; **lavorare a maglia** to knit
maglierìa *f* knitting mill; yarn shop; knitwear store
magliétta *f* polo shirt, T-shirt; buckle (*to secure rifle strap*); picture hook; buttonhole
maglifi·cio *m* (**-ci**) knitwear factory
mà·glio *m* (**-gli**) sledge hammer; mallet; drop hammer
maglióne *m* heavy sweater, jersey
magnàni·mo -ma *adj* magnanimous
magnano *m* (coll) locksmith
magnate *m* (lit) magnate, tycoon
magnèsio *m* magnesium
magnète *m* magnet; magneto
magnèti·co -ca *adj* (**-ci -che**) magnetic
magnetismo *m* magnetism
magnetite *f* loadstone
magnetizzare [ddzz] *tr* to magnetize
magnetòfono *m* tape recorder
magnificare §197 (**magnìfico**) *tr* to extol, praise; to magnify (*to exaggerate*)
magnificènza *f* magnificence
magnìfi·co -ca *adj* (**-ci -che**) magnificent; munificent; wonderful, splendid
ma·gno -gna *adj* (lit) great; the Great, e.g., **Alessandro Magno** Alexander the Great
magnòlia *f* magnolia
ma·go *m* (**-ghi**) magician; wizard
magóne *m* (coll) gizzard; (coll) grief; **avere il magone** (coll) to be in the dumps
magra *f* low water; (fig) dearth, want
magrézza *f* leanness; scarcity
ma·gro -gra *adj* lean, thin; meager ‖ *m* lean meat; meatless day ‖ *f* see **magra**
mài *adv* never; ever; **non . . . mai** never, not ever; **come mai?** how come?
maia·le -la *mf* pig; hog ‖ *m* pork ‖ *f* sow
maialé·sco -sca *adj* (**-schi -sche**) piggish
maiòli·ca *f* (**-che**) majolica
maionése [s] *f* mayonnaise
mà·is *m* (**-is**) corn, maize
maiuscolétto *m* (typ) small capital
maiùsco·lo -la *adj* capital ‖ *m*—**scrivere in maiuscolo** to capitalize ‖ *f* capital letter
Malacca, la Malay Peninsula
malaccèt·to -ta *adj* unwelcome
malaccòr·to -ta *adj* imprudent; awkward
malacreanza *f* (**malecreanze**) instance of bad manners; **malecreanze** bad manners
malafatta *f* (**malefatte**) defect; **malefatte** evildoings
malaféde *f* (**maleféd**i) bad faith
malaffare *m*—**donna di malaffare** prostitute; **gente di malaffare** underworld
malagévole *adj* rough (*road*); hard (*work*)
malagràzia *f* (**malegràzie**) rudeness, uncouthness
malalìngua *f* (**malelìngue**) slanderer, backbiter
malanda·to -ta *adj* run-down; shabby
malandri·no -na *adj* dishonest; bewitching (*eyes*) ‖ *m* highwayman
malànimo *m* ill will; **di malanimo** reluctantly
malanno *m* misfortune; illness; (joc) menace
malaparata *f* (coll) danger, dangerous situation
malapéna *f*—**a malapena** hardly

malària *f* malaria
malatìc·cio -cia *adj* (**-ci -ce**) sickly
mala·to -ta *adj* sick, ill; **essere malato agli occhi** to have sore eyes; **fare il malato** to play sick || *mf* patient; **i malati** the sick
malattìa *f* sickness; illness; disease; **malattie del lavoro** occupational diseases
malaugura·to -ta *adj* unfortunate; ill-omened
malaugù·rio *m* (**-ri**) ill omen
malavita *f* underworld
malavòglia *f* (**malevòglie**) unwillingness; **di malavoglia** reluctantly
malcapita·to -ta *adj* unlucky || *m* unlucky person
malcàu·to -ta *adj* rash, heedless
malcón·cio -cia *adj* (**-ci -ce**) battered
malcontèn·to -ta *adj* dissatisfied, malcontent || *mf* malcontent || *m* dissatisfaction
malcostume *m* immorality; bad practice
malcrea·to -ta *adj* ill-bred
maldè·stro -stra *adj* clumsy, awkward
maldicènte *adj* gossipy, slanderous || *mf* gossip, slanderer, backbiter
maldicènza *f* gossip, slander
male *m* evil; ill; trouble; **andare a male** to go to pot; **aversela a male** to take offense; **di male in peggio** from bad to worse, worse and worse; **fare del male** to do ill; **fare male** to be in error; **fare male a** to hurt; **farsi male** to get hurt; to hurt oneself; **far venire il mal di mare a** to make seasick; (fig) to nauseate; **Lei fa male** you should not; **mal d'aereo** airsickness; **mal di capo** headache; **mal di cuore** heart disease; **mal di denti** toothache; **mal di gola** sore throat; **mal di mare** sea-sickness; **mal di montagna** mountain sickness; **mal di pancia** bellyache; **mal di schiena** backache; **mandare a male** to spoil; **mettere male** to sow discord; **prendere a male** to take amiss; **voler male a** to bear a grudge against || *adv* badly, poorly; **male educato** ill-bred; **meno male!** fortunately!; **restar male** to be disappointed; **sentirsi male** to feel sick; **stare male** to be ill; **star male a** to not fit, e.g., **questo vestito gli sta male** this suit does not fit him; **veder male qlco** to disapprove of s.th; **veder male qlcu** to dislike s.o.
maledettaménte *adv* (coll) damned
maledét·to -ta *adj* cursed, damned
maledire §195 *tr* to curse
maledizióne *f* malediction, curse || *interj* damn it!, confound it!
maleduca·to -ta *adj* ill-bred || *mf* boor
malefatta *f* var of **malafatta**
malefì·cio *m* (**-ci**) curse, spell; witchcraft; wickedness
malèfi·co -ca *adj* (**-ci -che**) maleficent
maleolènte *adj* (lit) malodorous
malèrba *f* weed, weeds
malése *adj* & *mf* Malay
Malésia, la Malaysia
malèssere *m* malaise; uneasiness; worry
malevolènza *f* malevolence; malice
malèvo·lo -la *adj* malevolent; malicious
malfama·to -ta *adj* ill-famed; notorious
malfat·to -ta *adj* botched; misshapen || *m* misdeed
malfat·tóre -trice *mf* malefactor
malfér·mo -ma *adj* wobbly, unsteady
malfi·do -da *adj* untrustworthy
malgarbo *m* bad manners, rudeness
malgovèrno *m* misrule; mismanagement; neglect
malgrado *prep* in spite of; **mio malgrado** in spite of me || *conj* although
malìa *f* spell, charm
maliar·do -da *adj* enchanting, charming || *mf* magician || *f* enchantress, witch
malignare *intr* to gossip
maligni·tà *f* (**-tà**) maliciousness; malevolence; malignancy
mali·gno -gna *adj* malicious, evil; unhealthy; malignant || **il Maligno** the Evil One
malinconìa *f* melancholy; melancholia
malincòni·co -ca *adj* (**-ci -che**) melancholy, wistful
malincuòre *m*—**a malincuore** unwillingly, against one's will
malintenziona·to -ta *adj* evil-minded || *mf* evildoer
malinté·so -sa [s] *adj* misunderstood; misapplied || *m* misunderstanding
malió·so -sa [s] *adj* malicious; cunning; mischievous; bewitching
malìzia *f* malice; trick; mischief
malizió·so -sa [s] *adj* malicious; clever, artful; mischievous
malleàbile *adj* malleable; manageable
malleva·dóre -drice *mf* guarantor
malleverìa *f* surety
mallo *m* hull, husk
mallòppo *m* bundle; (aer) trail cable; (coll) lump (*in one's throat*); (slang) swag, booty
malmenare (**malméno**) *tr* to manhandle
malmés·so -sa *adj* shabby, seedy; tasteless
malna·to -ta *adj* uncouth; unfortunate; harmful
malnutri·to -ta *adj* undernourished
malnutrizióne *f* malnutrition
ma·lo -la *adj* (lit) bad
malòc·chio *m* (**-chi**) evil eye
malóra *f* ruin; **mandare in malora** to ruin; **va in malora!** go to the devil!
malóre *m* malaise; fainting spell
malpràti·co -ca *adj* (**-ci -che**) inexperienced
malsa·no -na *adj* unhealthy; unsound
malsicu·ro -ra *adj* unsafe; insecure
malta *f* mortar; plaster; (obs) mud
maltèmpo *m* bad weather
malto *m* malt
maltòlto *m* ill-gotten gains
maltrattaménto *m* mistreatment
maltrattare *tr* to mistreat, maltreat
malumóre *m* bad humor; **di malumore** in a bad mood
malva *f* mallow
malvà·gio -gia (**-gi -gie**) *adj* wicked || *mf* wicked person || **il Malvagio** the Evil One

malversare (malvèrso) *tr* to embezzle; to misappropriate
malversazióne *f* embezzlement; misappropriation
malvesti·to -ta *adj* shabby, seedy
malvi·sto -sta *adj* disliked; unpopular
malvivènte *mf* criminal; (lit) profligate
malvolentièri *adv* unwillingly
malvolére *m* malevolence; indolence || §196 *tr* to dislike
mamma *f* mother, mom; (lit) breast; **mamma mia** dear me!
mammaluc·co *m* (**-chi**) simpleton
mammèlla *f* breast; udder
mammìfe·ro -ra *adj* mammalian || *m* mammal
màmmola *f* violet; (fig) shrinking violet
mam·mùt *m* (**-mut**) mammoth
manata *f* slap; handful; **dare una manata a** to slap
man·ca *f* (**-che**) left hand, left
mancante *adj* missing, lacking; unaccounted for
mancanza *f* lack; absence; defect; mistake; **in mancanza di** for lack of
mancare §197 *tr* to miss || *intr* (AVERE) to be at fault; **mancare a** to break (*e.g., one's word*); **mancare di** to be wanting; to lack; **mancare di parola** to break one's word || *intr* (ESSERE) to fail (*said, e.g., of electric power*); to be lacking, e.g., **manca il sale nell'arrosto** salt is lacking in the roast; to be missing; to be absent, e.g., **mancano tre soci** three members are absent; to be, e.g., **mancano dieci minuti alle quattro** it is ten minutes to four; (with *dat*) to lack, e.g., **gli mancano le forze** he lacks the strength; to miss, e.g., **mi manca la sua compagnia** I miss his company; **mancare a** to be absent from (*e.g., the roll call*); to be . . . from, e.g., **mancano dieci chilometri all'arrivo** we are ten kilometers from the journey's end; **mancare ai vivi** (lit) to pass away; **sentirsi mancare** to feel faint || *impers*—**mancare poco che** + *subj* to narrowly miss + *ger*, e.g., **ci mancò poco che fosse investito da un'automobile** he narrowly missed being hit by a car; **non ci mancherebbe altro!** that would be the last straw!, I should say not!
manca·to -ta *adj* unsuccessful; missed (*opportunity*); abortive (*attempt*), e.g., **omicidio mancato** abortive attempt to murder; manqué, e.g., **un poeta mancato** a poet manqué
manchévole *adj* faulty
manchevolézza *f* fault, shortcoming
màn·cia *f* (**-ce**) tip, gratuity; **mancia competente** reward
manciata *f* handful
manci·no -na *adj* left-handed; underhanded || *mf* left-handed person || *f* left hand, left; (mach) floating crane
man·co -ca (-chi -che) *adj* left; (lit) sinister, ill-omened; (lit) lacking || *m* (lit) lack; **senza manco** (coll) without fail || **manco** *adv*—**manco male!** (coll) at least!; **manco per idea!** (coll) not at all! || *f* see **manca**
mandaménto *m* jurisdiction
mandante *m* (law) principal
mandare *tr* to send; to condemn (*to death*); to commit (*to memory*); to send forth (*e.g., smoke, buds*); to operate (*a machine*); **che Dio ce la mandi buona!** may God help us!; **mandare ad effetto** to carry out; **mandare all'altro mondo** to dispatch, kill; **mandare a monte** to ruin; **mandare a picco** to sink; **mandare a quel paese** to send to the devil; **mandare a spasso** to fire, dismiss; to get rid of; **mandar giù** to swallow; **mandare in malora** to ruin; **mandare in pezzi** to break to pieces; **mandare per le lunghe** to delay || *intr*—**mandare a chiamare** to send for; **mandare a dire** to send word
mandarino *m* mandarin; (*Citrus nobilis*) tangerine; (*Citrus reticulata*) mandarin orange
mandata *f* sending; delivery (*of merchandise*); group; gang (*e.g., of thieves*); turn (*of key*); **chiudere a doppia mandata** to double-lock
mandatà·rio *m* (**-ri**) mandatary, trustee
mandato *m* mandate; order; **mandato di cattura** arrest warrant; **mandato di comparizione** subpoena; **mandato di perquisizione** search warrant
mandìbola *f* jaw
mandolino *m* mandolin
màndorla *f* almond; kernel (*of fruit*)
mandorla·to -ta *adj* almond || *m* nougat
màndorlo *m* almond tree
mandràgola *f* mandrake
màndria *f* herd
mandriano *m* herdsman
mandrillo *m* mandrill
mandrino *m* (mach) mandrel; (mach) driftpin
mandritta *f*—**a mandritta** to the right
mane *f*—**da mane a sera** from morning till night
maneggévole *adj* usable; manageable; accessible to small craft (*sea*)
maneggiare §290 (**manéggio**) *tr* to work (*e.g., clay*); to handle; to wield (*a sword*); to knead (*dough*); to manage; (equit) to train
manég·gio *m* (**-gi**) handling; intrigue; horsemanship; management; riding school; manège
mané·sco -sca *adj* (**-schi -sche**) ready-fisted; hand (*e.g., weapons*)
manétta *f* throttle (*on a motorcycle*); **manette** handcuffs, manacles
manfòrte *f*—**dar manforte a** to help
manganèllo *m* bludgeon, cudgel
manganése [s] *m* manganese
màngano *m* calender; mangle
mangeréc·cio -cia *adj* (**-ci -ce**) edible
mangerìa *f* graft, peculation
mangiàbile *adj* edible
mangiana·stri *m* (**-stri**) tape recorder
mangia-pane *m* (**-pane**) idler
mangia·prèti *m* (**-prèti**) priest hater
mangiare *m* eating; food || *v* §290 *tr*

to eat; to bite, gnaw; to erode; to embezzle, graft; (cards, chess) to take; **mangiar la foglia** to get wise || *intr* to eat; **mangiare alle spalle di qlcu** to eat at the expense of s.o. || *ref* to eat up; **mangiarsi il fegato** to be green with envy; **mangiarsi la parola** to break one's promise; **mangiarsi le unghie** to bite one's nails; **mangiarsi una promessa** to break one's promise

mangiasòldi *adj invar* money-eating, e.g., **macchina mangiasoldi** money-eating contraption

mangiata *f* (coll) fill, hearty meal, bellyful

mangiatóia *f* manger, crib

mangia•tóre -trice *mf* eater

mangime *m* fodder; feed; poultry feed

mangimìsti•co -ca *adj* (**-ci -che**) feed, e.g., **attrezzature mangimistiche** feed machinery

mangió•ne -na *mf* great eater, glutton

mangiucchiare §287 (**mangiùcchio**) *tr* to nibble

mangusta *f* mongoose

manìa *f* mania, craze; complex; whim; **mania di grandezza** delusions of grandeur

manìa•co -ca (**-ci -che**) *adj* maniacal; enthusiastic || *m* maniac; fan, enthusiast

màni•ca *f* (**-che**) sleeve; hose; (coll) crowd, bunch; **essere di manica larga** to be broad-minded; **essere nelle maniche di qlcu** to be in the favor of s.o.; **è un altro paio di maniche** this is a horse of another color; **in maniche di camicia** in shirt sleeves; **manica a vento** air sleeve, windsock; **manica per l'acqua** hose || **la Manica** the English Channel

manicarétto *m* dainty, delicacy

manichino *m* mannequin; cuff; (obs) handcuff; **fare il manichino** to model

màni•co *m* (**-chi & -ci**) handle; stock (*of rifle*); shaft (*of golf club*); stem (*of spoon*); (mus) neck; **manico di scopa** broomstick

manicò•mio *m* (**-mi**) insane asylum, madhouse

manicòtto *m* muff; (mach) collar; (mach) nipple; (mach) sleeve

manicu•re *mf* (**-re**) manicure, manicurist (*person*) || *f* (**-re**) manicure (*treatment*)

manicuri•sta *mf* (**-sti -ste**) manicurist

manièra *f* manner, fashion, way; **belle maniere** good manners; **di maniera** (lit, painting) Manneristic; **di maniera che** so that; **in nessuna maniera** by no means; **maniere** bad manners

maniera•to -ta *adj* mannered, affected; genteel

maniè•ro -ra *adj* tame, gentle || *m* manor house, mansion || *f* see **maniera**

manieró•so -sa [s] *adj* genteel; mannered

manifattura *f* manufacture; factory; product; ready-made wear

manifestare (**manifèsto**) *tr* to manifest || *intr* to demonstrate || *ref* to turn out to be

manifestazióne *f* manifestation; **demonstration**

manifestino *m* leaflet, handbill

manifè•sto -sta *adj* manifest, clear || *m* poster, placard; manifest; (pol) manifesto; **manifesto di carico** (naut) manifest

manìglia *f* handle; knob; (naut) link (*of chain*)

manigóldo *m* criminal; scoundrel

manipolare (**manìpolo**) *tr* to concoct; to adulterate; (telg) to transmit

manipola•tóre -trice *mf* schemer || *m* telegraph key

manìpolo *m* sheaf; (eccl; hist) maniple; (fig) handful

maniscal•co *m* (**-chi**) blacksmith

manna *f* manna; godsend

mannàia *f* axe; knife (*of guillotine*)

mano *f* hand; way (*in traffic*); coat (*of paint*); (lit) handful; (fig) finger; fingertip; **alla mano** plain, affable; **a mani nude** barehanded; **a mano** by hand; **a mano a mano** little by little; **a mano armata** armed (*e.g., robbery*); at gunpoint; **andare contro mano** to buck traffic; **a quattro mani** four-handed; **avere le mani bucate** to be a spendthrift; **avere le mani in pasta** to have one's fingers in the pie; **avere le mani lunghe** to be light-fingered; **battere le mani** to clap; **con le mani in mano** idle; **dare la mano a** to shake hands with; **dare man forte a** to help; **dare una mano** to pitch in; **dare una mano a** to lend a hand to; **di lunga mano** beforehand; **essere colto con le mani nel sacco** to be caught red-handed; **essere svelto di mano** to be light-fingered; **far man bassa (su)** to plunder; **fuori mano** out of the way; **mani di burro** butterfingers; **mani in alto!** hands up!; **man mano (che)** as; **mettere mano a** to begin; **mettere le mani sul fuoco** to guarantee; to swear; **per mano di** at the hands of; **prendere la mano** to balk; to get out of hand; **tenere la mano a** to abet; **venire alle mani** to come to blows

manodòpera *f* labor, manpower; **manodopera qualificata** skilled labor

manòmetro *m* manometer

manométtere §198 *tr* to tamper with

manomissióne *f* tampering

manomòrta *f* (law) mortmain

manòpola *f* mitten; handgrip; strap (*to hold on to*); (rad, telv) knob; (hist) gauntlet

manoscrit•to -ta *adj & m* manuscript

manoscrìvere §250 *intr* to write in one's own handwriting

manovale *m* laborer, helper; hod carrier

manovèlla *f* handle, crank; lever

manòvra *f* maneuver; (rr) shifting; **fare manovra** to maneuver; (rr) to shift

manovrare (**manòvro**) *tr* to maneuver; to handle, drive; (rr) to shift || *intr* to maneuver; (rr) to shunt, shift; (fig) to plot

manovratóre *m* motorman; driver; (rr) brakeman; (rr) flagman
manrovè·scio *m* (**-sci**) backhanded slap
mansalva *f*—**rubare a mansalva** to help oneself freely (*e.g., to the till*)
mansarda *f* mansard
mansióne *f* duty, function
mansuè·to -ta *adj* tame; meek
mansuetùdine *f* tameness; meekness
mantèlla *f* coat; (mil) cape
mantellina *f* (mil) cape
mantèllo *m* woman's coat; coat (*of animal*); (fig) cloak; (mil) cape; (mach) casing
mantenére §271 *tr* to keep; to maintain; to hold (*e.g., a position*) || *ref* to stay alive; to last; to remain, stay, continue
manteniménto *m* keeping; maintenance
mantenu·to -ta *adj* kept || *m* gigolo || *f* kept woman
màntice *m* bellows; folding top (*of carriage*); (aut) convertible top
manto *m* mantle; coat; cloak
Màntova *f* Mantua
mantovana *f* valance
manuale *adj & m* manual
manualizzare [ddzz] *tr* to make (*e.g., a machine*) hand-operated; to include in a manual; to prepare a manual of
manù·brio *m* (**-bri**) handlebar; handle; dumbbell
manufat·to -ta *adj* manufactured || *m* manufactured product; manufacture
manutèngolo *m* accomplice
manutenzióne *f* maintenance, upkeep
manza [dz] *f* heifer
manzo [dz] *m* steer; beef
maometta·no -na *adj & mf* Mahometan, Mohammedan
maomettismo *m* Mahometanism, Mohammedanism
Maométto *m* Mahomet
maóna *f* barge
mappa *f* map; bit (*of key*)
mappamóndo *m* globe; map of the world
marachèlla *f* mischief
maramèo *m*—**fare marameo** to thumb one's nose
mara·sma *m* (**-smi**) utter confusion; (pathol) decreptitude, feebleness
maratóna *f* marathon
maratonè·ta *m* (**-ti**) Marathon runner
mar·ca *f* (**-che**) mark, label; make, brand; token; ticket; (hist, geog) march; **di marca** of quality; **marca da bollo** revenue stamp; **marca di fabbrica** trademark
marcare §197 *tr* to mark; to label; to brand; to keep the score of; to score (*e.g., a goal*); to accentuate
marcatèm·po *m* (**-po**) timekeeper
marca·to -ta *adj* marked, pronounced
marchésa *f* marchioness, marquise
marchése *m* marquess, marquis
marchia·no -na *adj* gross (*error*)
marchiare §287 *tr* to brand
màr·chio *m* (**-chi**) brand; initials; characteristic; trademark
màr·cia *f* (**-ce**) march; operation; pus; (aut) gear, speed; (mil) hike; (sports) walk; **far marcia indietro** to back up; (naut) to back water; **marcia indietro** (aut) reverse; **marcia nuziale** wedding march
marciapiède *m* sidewalk; (rr) platform
marciare §128 *intr* to march; (mil) to advance; (sports) to walk; (coll) to function; **far marciare qlcu** to keep s.o. in line
màr·cio -cia (**-ci -ce**) *adj* rotten; infected; corrupt || *m* rotten part; decayed part; corruption || *f* see **marcia**
marcire §176 *intr* (ESSERE) to rot
marciume *m* rot; pus; decay
mar·co *m* (**-chi**) mark
marconigram·ma *m* (**-mi**) radiogram
marconi·sta *mf* (**-sti -ste**) radio operator
mare *m* sea; bunch, heap; **al mare** at the seashore; **alto mare** high sea; **fa mare** the sea is rough; **gettare a mare** to throw overboard; **mare grosso** rough sea; **mare territoriale** territorial waters; **promettere mari e monti** to promise the moon; **tenere il mare** to be seaworthy
marèa *f* tide; sea (*e.g., of mud*); **alta marea** high tide; **bassa marea** low tide; **marea di quadratura** neap tide; **marea di sizigia** spring tide
mareggiata *f* coastal storm
maremòto *m* seaquake
mareògrafo *m* tide-level gauge
maresciallo *m* marshall; warrant officer
marétta *f* choppy sea; instability
margarina *f* margarine
margherita *f* daisy; **margherite** beads
marginale *adj* marginal
marginatóre *m* margin stop (*of typewriter*); (typ) try square
màrgine *m* margin; edge; **margine a scaletta** thumb index
marijuana *f* marijuana, marihuana
marina *f* seashore; seascape; navy; **marina mercantile** merchant marine
mari·nàio *m* (**-nài**) seaman, sailor
marinara *f* middy blouse
marinare *tr* to marinate; **marinare la scuola** to cut school, play truant
marinaré·sco -sca *adj* (**-schi -sche**) sailor, seamanlike
marina·ro -ra *adj* sea, sailor; seamanlike; nautical || *m* (coll) sailor || *f* see **marinara**
mari·no -na *adj* marine, nautical || *f* see **marina**
mariòlo *m* rascal
marionétta *f* puppet, marionette
maritale *adj* marital
maritare *tr* to marry || *ref* to get married
marito *m* husband
marìtti·mo -ma *adj* maritime, sea || *m* merchant seaman
marmàglia *f* riffraff, rabble
marmellata *f* jam, preserves; **marmellata di arancia** orange marmalade
marmi·sta *m* (**-sti**) marble worker; marble cutter
marmitta *f* pot, kettle; (aut) muffler
marmittóne *m* (coll) sad sack
marmo *m* marble
marmòc·chio *m* (**-chi**) brat

marmòre·o -a *adj* marble

marmorizzare [ddzz] *tr* to marble

marmòtta *f* marmot; woodchuck; (fig) sluggard; (rr) switch signal

marmottina *f* salesman's sample case

marna *f* marl

marnare *tr* to marl

marocchi·no -na *adj & mf* Moroccan || *m* morocco leather

Maròcco, il Morocco

maróso [s] *m* billow, surge

marra *f* hoe; fluke (*of anchor*)

marrano *m* Marrano; (fig) scoundrel; (lit) traitor

marronata *f* (coll) blunder, boner

marróne *adj invar* maroon, tan || *m* chestnut; (coll) blunder

Marsiglia *f* Marseille

marsigliése [s] *adj* Marseilles || *m* native or inhabitant of Marseilles || *f* Marseillaise

marsina *f* swallow-tailed coat

Marte *m* Mars

marte·dì *m* (**-dì**) Tuesday; **martedì grasso** Shrove Tuesday

martellare (**martèllo**) *tr* to hammer; to pester (*with questions*) || *intr* to throb; (fig) to insist

martellata *f* hammer blow

martellétto *m* hammer (*of piano or bell*); lever (*of typewriter*)

martèllo *m* hammer; **martello dell'uscio** knocker; **martello perforatore** jackhammer

martinétto *m* jack; **martinetto a vite** screw jack

martingala *f* half belt (*sewn in back of sports jacket*); martingale (*of harness*)

martinic·ca *f* (**-che**) wagon brake

martìn pescatóre *m* kingfisher

màrtire *m* martyr

marti·rio *m* (**-ri**) martyrdom

martirizzare [ddzz] *tr* to martyrize

màrtora *f* marten

martoriare §287 (**martòrio**) *tr* to torment

marxi·sta *adj & mf* (**-sti -ste**) Marxist

marzapane *m* marzipan

marziale *adj* martial

marzia·no -na *adj & mf* Martian

marzo *m* March

mas *m* (**mas**) torpedo boat

mascalzóne *m* cad, rascal

mascèlla *f* jaw; jawbone

màschera *mf* usher || *f* mask; masque; **maschera antigas** gas mask; **maschera di bellezza** beauty pack; **maschera respiratoria** oxygen mask; **maschera subacquea** diving helmet

mascheraménto *m* camouflage

mascherare (**màschero**) *tr, intr & ref* to mask; to camouflage

mascherata *f* masquerade

mascherina *f* little mask, loup; tip (*of shoe*); (aut) grille; (phot) mask

maschiare §287 *tr* (mach) to tap

maschiétta *f* tomboy; **alla maschietta** bobbed (*hair*); **tagliare i capelli alla maschietta** to bob the hair

maschiétto *m* baby boy; pintle

maschile *adj* masculine; manly; **men's;** male (*sex*); boys' (*school*) || *m* masculine

mà·schio -schia *adj* manly, virile; male || *m* male; keep, donjon; tenon; (mach) tap; (carp) tongue

mascolinizzare [ddzz] *tr* to make masculine or mannish || *ref* to act like a man

mascoli·no -na *adj* masculine; mannish (*woman*)

masnada *f* mob, gang; (obs) group

masnadière *m* highwayman

massa *f* mass; body (*of water*); (elec) ground; **mettere a massa** (elec) to ground; **in massa** in a body; **massa ereditaria** (law) estate

massacrante *adj* killing, fatiguing

massacrare *tr* to massacre; to ruin; to wear out, fatigue

massacro *m* massacre

massaggiare §290 *tr* to massage

massaggiatóre *m* masseur

massaggiatrice *f* masseuse

massàg·gio *m* (**-gi**) massage

massàia *f* housewife

massèllo *m* block (*of stone*); (metallurgy) pig, ingot

masserìa *f* farm

masserìzie *fpl* household goods

massicciata *f* roadbed; (rr) ballast

massìc·cio -cia (**-ci -ce**) *adj* massive; bulky; heavy; (fig) gross || *m* massif

màssi·mo -ma *adj* maximum; top || *m* maximum; limit; **al massimo** at the most || *f* maxim; maximum temperature

massi·vo -va *adj* massive

masso *m* rock, boulder

Massóne *m* Mason

Massonerìa *f* Masonry

mastèllo *m* washtub

masticare §197 (**màstico**) *tr* to chew, masticate; to mumble (*words*); to speak (*a language*) poorly; **masticare amaro** to grumble

masticazióne *f* mastication

màstice *m* mastic; glue; putty

mastino *m* mastiff

mastodònti·co -ca *adj* (**-ci -che**) mammoth

ma·stro -stra *adj* master || *m* ledger; master, e.g., **mastro meccanico** master mechanic

masturbare *tr & ref* to masturbate

matassa *f* skein; trouble

matemàti·co -ca (**-ci -che**) *adj* mathematical || *m* mathematician || *f* mathematics

materassino *m* (sports) mat; **materassino pneumatico** air mattress

materasso *m* mattress; (boxing) sparring partner

matèria *f* matter; substance; subject; (coll) pus; **dare materia a** to give ground for; **materia grigia** gray matter; **materie coloranti** dyestuffs; **materie prime** raw materials

materiale *adj* material; rough, bulky || *m* material; equipment, supplies; (fig) makings, stuff; **materiale ferroviario** (rr) rolling stock; **materiale stabile** (rr) permanent way

materni·tà *f* (**-tà**) maternity; maternity hospital; maternity ward
matèr·no -na *adj* maternal; mother (*tongue, country*)
matita *f* pencil; **matita per gli occhi** eye-shadow pencil; **matita per le labbra** lipstick; cosmetic pencil
matrice *f* matrix; stub
matrici·da *mf* (**-di -de**) matricide
matricì·dio *m* (**-di**) matricide
matrìcola *f* register, roll; registration (*number*); registry; beginner, novice; freshman (*in university*); **far la matricola a** to haze
matricola·to -ta *adj* notorious, arrant
matrigna *f* stepmother
matrimoniale *adj* matrimonial; double (*bed*); married (*life*)
matrimonialménte *adv* as husband and wife
matrimò·nio *m* (**-ni**) matrimony, marriage; wedding
matròna *f* matron
matronale *adj* matronly
matta *f* joker, wild card
mattacchió·ne -na *mf* jester, prankster
mattana *f* tantrum; fit of laughter
matta·tóio *m* (**-tói**) slaughterhouse
matterèllo *m* rolling pin
mattina *f* morning; **di prima mattina** early in the morning; **la mattina** in the morning
mattinale *adj* morning || *m* morning report
mattinata *f* morning; (theat) matinée
mattinié·ro -ra *adj* early-rising
mattino *m* morning; **di buon mattino** early in the morning
mat·to -ta *adj* crazy; whimsical; dull; false (*jewelry*); wild (*desire*); **andare matto per** to be crazy about; **da matti** unbelievable; **fare il matto** to cut a caper; **matto da legare** raving mad || *f* see **matta**
mattòide *adj* & *mf* madcap
mattonare (**mattóno**) *tr* to pave with bricks
mattonato *m* brick floor; **restare sul mattonato** to be utterly destitute
mattóne *m* brick; (fig) bore
mattonèlla *f* tile; cushion (*of billiard table*)
mattuti·no -na *adj* morning || *m* matins
maturan·do -da *mf* lycée student who has to take the baccalaureate examination
maturare *tr* to ripen; to ponder; to pass (*a lycée pupil*) || *intr* (ESSERE) to ripen, mature; to fall due
maturazióne *f* ripening
maturi·tà *f* (**-tà**) maturity; ripening; lycée final
matu·ro -ra *adj* ripe; mature; due
Matusalèmme *m* Methuselah
mausolèo *m* mausoleum
mazza *f* club; mallet; sledge hammer; cane; mace; golf club; (baseball) bat
mazzacavallo *m* well sweep
mazzapìc·chio *m* (**-chi**) mallet; sledge
mazzata *f* heavy blow, wallop (*with club*)
mazzeran·ga *f* (**-ghe**) (mach) tamper
mazzière *m* macer; (cards) dealer
mazzo *m* bunch; bouquet; deck (*of cards*); **fare il mazzo** to shuffle the cards
mazzuòla *f* sledge hammer
mazzuòlo *m* sledge; mallet; wedge (*of golf club*); drumstick (*for bass drum*)
me §5 *pron pers*
meandro *m* meander; labyrinth
MEC *m* (letterword) (**Mercato Europeo Comune**) European Economic Community, Common Market
Mècca, la Mecca; (fig) the Mecca
meccàni·co -ca (**-ci -che**) *adj* mechanical || *m* mechanic || *f* mechanics; process (*e.g., of digestion*); machinery
meccanismo *m* machinery; mechanism; movement (*of watch*)
meccanizzare [ddzz] *tr* to mechanize || *ref* to become mechanized
mecenate *m* patron (*of the arts*)
méco §5 *prep phrase* (lit) with me
medàglia *f* medal
medaglióne *m* medallion; locket; biographical sketch
medési·mo -ma *adj* & *pron* same; -self, e.g., **egli medesimo** he himself; very e.g., **la verità medesima** the very truth
mèdia *f* average; secondary school, middle school; (math) mean; **media oraria** average speed || **mèdia** *mpl* media (*of communication*)
mediana *f* median; (soccer) middle line
mediàni·co -ca *adj* (**-ci -che**) medium
media·no -na *adj* median || *m* (sports) halfback || *f* see **mediana**
mediante *prep* by means of
mediare §287 (**mèdio**) *tr* & *intr* (ESSERE) to mediate
media·to -ta *adj* indirect
media·tóre -trice *adj* mediating || *mf* mediator; broker; commission merchant
mediazióne *f* mediation; brokerage; broker's fee, commission
medicaménto *m* medicine
medicamentó·so -sa [s] *adj* medicinal
medicare §197 (**mèdico**) *tr* to medicate; to treat
medicastro *m* quack
medicazióne *f* medication; dressing
medichéssa *f* (pej) lady doctor
medicina *f* medicine
medicinale *adj* medicinal || *m* medicine
mèdi·co -ca (**-ci -che**) *adj* medical || *m* doctor, physician; healer; **fare il medico** to practice medicine; **medico chirurgo** surgeon; **medico condotto** board-of-health doctor; country doctor; **medico curante** family physician
medievale *adj* medieval
medievali·sta *mf* (**-sti -ste**) medievalist
mè·dio -dia (**-di -die**) *adj* average, median; middle; secondary (*school*) medium || *m* middle finger || *f* see **media**
mediòcre *adj* mediocre
mediocri·tà *f* (**-tà**) mediocrity
medioèvo *m* Middle Ages
medioleggèro *m* welterweight

mediomàssimo *m* light heavyweight
meditabón•do -da *adj* meditative
meditare (mèdito) *tr & intr* to meditate
medita•to -ta *adj* considered
meditazióne *f* meditation
mediterrà•neo -nea *adj* inland (*sea*) || **Mediterraneo** *adj & m* Mediterranean
mè•dium *mf* (**-dium**) medium
medusa *f* jellyfish
mefistofèli•co -ca *adj* (**-ci -che**) Mephistophelian
mefìti•co -ca *adj* (**-ci -che**) mephitic
megaciclo *m* megacycle
megàfono *m* megaphone
megalomanìa *f* megalomania
megalòpo•li *f* (**-li**) megalopolis
mega•òhm *m* (**-òhm**) megohm
megèra *f* hag, termagant, vixen
mèglio *adj invar* better; (coll) best || *m*—**il meglio** the best; **nel meglio di** (coll) in the middle of || *f*—**avere la meglio** to get the upper hand; **avere la meglio di** to get the better of || *adv* better; best; rather; **stare meglio** to feel better; to be becoming; to fit better; **stare meglio a** to be becoming to; to fit; **tanto meglio!** so much the better!
méla *f* apple; nozzle (*of sprinkling can*); **mela cotogna** quince (*fruit*); **mela renetta** pippin
melagrana *f* pomegranate
melanzana [dz] *f* eggplant
melassa *f* molasses, treacle
mela•to -ta *adj* honey, honeyed
melèn•so -sa *adj* dull, silly
melissa *f* (bot) balm
mellìflu•o -a *adj* mellifluous
mélma *f* mud, slime
melmó•so -sa [s] *adj* muddy, slimy
mélo *m* apple tree
melodìa *f* melody
melòdi•co -ca *adj* (**-ci -che**) melodic
melodió•so -sa [s] *adj* melodious
melodram•ma *m* (**-mi**) melodrama; lyric opera; (fig) melodrama
melodrammàti•co -ca *adj* (**-ci -che**) melodramatic
melograno *m* pomegranate tree
melóne *m* melon; cantaloupe; **melone d'acqua** watermelon
membrana *f* membrane; parchment; diaphragm (*of telephone*); (zool) web
membratura *f* frame
mèm•bro *m* (**-bri,** *considered individually*) limb; member; penis || *m* (**-bra** *fpl, considered collectively*) limb (*of human body*)
membru•to -ta *adj* burly, husky
memoràbile *adj* memorable
memoràn•dum *m* (**-dum**) memorandum; agenda, calendar; note; note paper
mèmore *adj* (lit) mindful, grateful
memòria *f* memory; souvenir; memoir; dissertation; (law) brief
memoriale *m* memoir; memorial
memorizzare [ddzz] *tr* to memorize
ména *f* intrigue
mena•bò *m* (**-bò**) (typ) layout, dummy
menadito *m*—**a menadito** at one's fingertips; perfectly
menare (méno) *tr* to lead; to bring (*luck*); to wag (*the tail*); to deliver (*a blow*); (coll) to hit; **menare a effetto** to carry out; **menare buono di** to approve of; **menare il can per l'aia** to beat around the bush; **menare per le lunghe** to delay; **menare vanto** to boast
mènda *f* (lit) fault, flaw
mendace *adj* lying, false, mendacious
mendà•cio *m* (**-ci**) (law) falsehood
mendicante *adj & m* mendicant
mendicare §197 (**méndico**) *tr & intr* to beg
mendici•tà *f* (**-tà**) indigence, poverty
mendi•co -ca *adj & mf* (**-chi -che**) mendicant
menefreghismo *m* I-don't-care attitude
menestrèllo *m* minstrel
méno *adj invar* less || *m* less; least; minus (*sign*); **i meno** the few; **per lo meno** at least || *adv* less; least; minus; **a meno che** unless; **da meno** inferior; **fare a meno di** to do without; to spare; **meno . . . di** less . . . than; **meno male** fortunately; **meno . . . meno** the less . . . the less; **non poter fare a meno di** + *inf* to not be able to help + *ger*, e.g., **la conferenza non poteva fare a meno di essere un successo** the conference could not help being a success; **quanto meno** at least; **senza meno** without fail; **venir meno** to swoon, pass out; to fail; to lose, e.g., **gli venne meno il cuore** he lost his courage; **venir meno di** to break (*one's word*) || *prep* except; less, minus; of, e.g., **le sette meno dieci** ten minutes of seven
menomare (mènomo) *tr* to lessen, diminish; (fig) to hurt, damage
mèno•mo -ma *adj* least
menopàusa *f* menopause
mènsa *f* (prepared) table; mess, mess hall; (eccl) altar; communion table; (poet) mass; (poet) altar; **mensa aziendale** company cafeteria
mensile *adj* monthly || *m* monthly salary or allowance
mensili•tà *f* (**-tà**) monthly installment
mènsola *f* bracket; corner shelf; neck (*of harp*); mantel (*of chimney*); console
ménta *f* mint
mentale *adj* mental; (anat) chin
mentali•tà *f* (**-tà**) mentality, mind
ménte *f* mind; **a mente di** according to; **avere in mente** to mean; to intend; **di mente** mental; **mente direttiva** mastermind; **scappare di mente a qlcu** to escape s.o.'s mind, e,g., **gli è scappato di mente** it escaped his mind; **uscire di mente** to go out of one's mind; **venire in mente a qlcu** to remember, e.g., **non gli è venuto in mente di spedire la lettera** he did not remember to mail the letter
mentecat•to -ta *adj & mf* lunatic
mentina *f* mint; **mentina digestiva** after-dinner mint
mentire §176 & (**mènto**) *intr* to lie;

mentire per la gola to lie through one's teeth
menti•to -ta *adj* false; disguised
menti•tóre -trice *adj* lying || *mf* liar
ménto *m* chin
mentòlo *m* menthol
méntre *m*—**in quel mentre** at that very moment; **nel mentre che** at the time when || *conj* while; whereas
me•nù *m* (-**nù**) menu
menzionare (**menzióno**) *tr* to mention
menzióne *f* mention
menzógna *f* lie
menzognè•ro -ra *adj* false, deceptive; lying, untruthful
meravìglia *f* marvel, wonder; **a meraviglia** wonderfully; **destare le meraviglie di** to amaze; **dire meraviglie di** to praise to the skies; **fare meraviglia** (with *dat*) to amaze; **far meraviglie** to work wonders
meravigliare §280 (**meravìglio**) *tr* to amaze; to astonish || *ref* to be astonished
meraviglió•so -sa [s] *adj* marvelous, wonderful || *m* (lit) supernatural
mercan•te -téssa *mf* merchant, dealer
mercanteggiare §290 (**mercantéggio**) *tr* to sell || *intr* to deal; to haggle
mercantile *adj* mercantile; merchant (*marine*) || *m* cargo boat, freighter
mercanzìa *f* merchandise; (coll) junk
mercato *m* market; trafficking; **a buon mercato** cheap; **far mercato di** to traffic in; **sopra mercato** besides; into the bargain
mèrce *f* merchandise, goods; commodity
mercé *f* favor, grace; mercy; **alla mercé di** at the mercy of; **mercé a** thanks to; **mercé sua** thanks to him (her, etc.)
mercéde *f* pay; (lit) reward
mercenà•rio -ria *adj* & *m* (**-ri -rie**) mercenary
mercerìa *f* notions store; **mercerie** notions
mercerizzare [ddzz] *tr* to mercerize
mèr•ci *adj invar* freight (*train, car, etc.*) || *m* (**-ci**) freight train
mer•ciàio -ciàia *mf* (**-ciài -ciàie**) notions store owner
merciaiòlo *m* small businessman; **merciaiolo ambulante** peddler
mercole•dì *m* (**-dì**) Wednesday
mercuriale *f* market report; price ceiling
mercùrio *m* mercury || **Mercurio** *m* Mercury
merènda *f* afternoon snack, bite
meretrice *f* harlot
meridia•no -na *adj* & *m* meridian || *f* sundial
meridionale *adj* meridional, southern || *mf* southerner
meridióne *m* south; South
merìg•gio *m* (**-gi**) noon
merin•ga *f* (**-ghe**) meringue
meritare (**mèrito**) *tr* to deserve; to win || *intr* (eccl) to merit; **bene meritare di** to deserve the gratitude of || *impers*—**merita** it is worth while to
meritévole *adj* deserving, worthy
mèrito *m* merit; **in merito a** concerning; **per merito di** thanks to; **render merito a** to reward
meritò•rio -ria *adj* (**-ri -rie**) meritorious
merlan•go *m* (**-ghi**) whiting
merlatura *f* battlement
merlétto *m* lace, needlepoint
mèrlo *m* blackbird; merlon; (fig) simpleton
merluzzo *m* cod
mè•ro -ra *adj* bare, mere; (poet) pure
merovìngi•co -ca (**-ci -che**) *adj* Merovingian || *f* Merovingian script
mesata [s] *f* month's wages
méscere (*pp* **mesciuto**) *tr* to pour (*e.g., wine*); (poet) to mix
meschini•tà *f* (**-tà**) pettiness; narrowmindedness; meanness, stinginess
meschi•no -na *adj* petty; narrowminded; wretched; puny || *mf* wretch
méscita *f* pouring; counter; bar
mescolanza *f* mixture, blend
mescolare (**méscolo**) *tr* to mix, blend; to shuffle (*cards*); to stir (*e.g.,* (*coffee*) || *ref* to mix, blend; to mingle; to consort; **mescolarsi in** to mind (*somebody else's business*)
mescolatrice *f* mixer, blender
mése [s] *m* month; month's pay
mesétto [s] *m* short month
mesóne *m* (phys) meson
méssa *f* (eccl & mus) Mass; **messa a fuoco** (phot) focusing; **messa a punto** adjustment; clear statement, outline of a problem; (aut) tune-up; **messa a terra** (elec) grounding; **messa cantata** high mass; **messa in marcia** or **in moto** (mach) starting; **messa in orbita** (rok) orbiting; **messa in piega** waving (*of hair*); **messa in scena** staging; **messa in vendita** putting up for sale
messaggerìe *fpl* delivery service
messaggè•ro -ra *mf* messenger; postal clerk
messàg•gio *m* (**-gi**) message
messale *m* missal
mèsse *f* harvest; crop
Messìa *m* Messiah
messiàni•co -ca *adj* (**-ci -che**) Messianic
messica•no -na *adj* & *mf* Mexican
Mèssico, il Mexico
messinscèna *f* staging; faking
mésso *m* clerk; (poet) messenger
mestare (**mésto**) *tr* to stir || *intr* to intrigue
mesta•tóre -trice *mf* ringleader; schemer
mèstica *f* (painting) filler
mesticare §197 (**mèstico**) *tr* to prime (*a canvas*); to mix (*colors*)
mestierante *mf* potboiler (*person*); tradesman, craftsman
mestière *m* trade, craft; (archaic) task; **di mestiere** by trade; habitual; **essere del mestiere** to be up in one's line
mestièri *m*—**essere di** or **far mestieri** to be necessary
mestìzia *f* sadness
mè•sto -sta *adj* sad
méstola *f* ladle; trowel
méstolo *m* kitchen spoon; **avere il mestolo in mano** to be the boss
mèstruo *m* menses, menstruation

mèta *f* goal, aim; (rugby) goal line
méta *f* heap, stack (*e.g., of hay*)
me•tà *f* (**-tà**) half; middle; halfway; better half; **a metà** halfway, in the middle; **aver qlco a metà con qlcu** to go half and half with s.o.
metabolismo *m* metabolism
metafìsi•co -ca (-ci -che) *adj* metaphysical || *m* metaphysician || *f* metaphysics
metafonèsi *f* umlaut, metaphony
metafonìa *f* umlaut, metaphony
metàfora *f* metaphor
metafòri•co -ca *adj* **(-ci -che)** metaphoric(al)
metàlli•co -ca *adj* **(-ci -che)** metallic
metallizzare [ddzz] *tr* to cover with metal
metallo *m* metal; timbre (*of voice*); (poet) metal object; **il vile metallo** filthy lucre
metallòide *m* nonmetal
metallurgìa *f* metallurgy
metallùrgi•co -ca (ci -che) *adj* metallurgic(al) || *m* metalworker
metalmeccàni•co -ca (-ci -che) *adj* metallurgic(al) and mechanical || *m* metalworker
metamòrfo•si *f* **(-si)** metamorphosis
metanizzare [ddzz] *tr* to provide with methane
metano *m* methane
metanodótto *m* natural gas pipeline
metàte•si *f* **(-si)** metathesis
metèora *f* meteor; atmospheric phenomenon
meteorite *m* & *f* meteorite
meteorologìa *f* meteorology
meteorològi•co -ca *adj* **(-ci -che)** meteorologic(al); weather (*forecast*)
meteoròlo•go -ga *mf* **(-gi -ghe)** meteorologist
metic•cio -cia *adj* & *mf* **(-ci -ce)** halfbreed
meticolό•so -sa [s] *adj* meticulous
metìli•co -ca *adj* **(-ci -che)** methyl
metòdi•co -ca (-ci -che) *adj* methodical; subject (*e.g., index*) || *mf* methodical person || *f* methodology
metodi•sta *adj* & *mf* **(-sti -ste)** Methodist
mètodo *m* method
metràg•gio *m* **(-gi)** length in meters; **corto metraggio** short; **lungo metraggio** full-length movie, feature film
metratura *f* length in meters
mètri•co -ca (-ci -che) *adj* metric(al) || *f* metrics, prosody
mètro *m* meter; (fig) yardstick; (lit) words
métro *m* (coll) subway
metrònomo *m* (mus) metronome
metronòt•te *m* **(-te)** night watchman
metròpo•li *f* **(-li)** metropolis
metropolita•no -na *adj* metropolitan || *m* policeman, traffic cop || *f* subway
metrovìa *f* subway
méttere §198 *tr* to put, place; to set (*e.g., foot*); to run (*e.g., a nail into a board*); to cause (*fear; fever*); to employ; to admit; to put forth; to give out; (coll) to charge; (coll) to install; (aut) to engage (*a gear*); **metterci** to take (*e.g., an hour*); **mettere a confronto** to compare; **mettere a freno** to check; **mettere a fuoco** (phot) to focus; **mettere al bando** to banish; **mettere all'asta** to auction off; **mettere al mondo** to give birth to; **mettere a nudo** to lay bare; **mettere fuori** to pull out; to give out (*news*); to throw (*s.o.*) out; **mettere giù** to lower; **mettere in onda** to broadcast; **mettere in pericolo** to endanger; **mettere la pulce nell'orecchio a** to put a bug in the ear of; **mettere qlcu alla porta** to show s.o. the door; **mettere su** to set up; (coll) to put (*e.g., a coat*) on; **mettere su qlcu contro qlcu** to excite s.o. against s.o. || *intr* to sprout; to lead (*said, e.g., of a road*) || *ref* to put on, to don; to place oneself, put oneself; to take shape; **mettersi a** to begin to; **mettersi al bello** to clear up (*said of weather*); **mettersi a letto** to go to bed; **mettersi a sedere** to sit down; **mettersi con** to start to work with; **mettersi in ferie** to take one's vacation; **mettersi in malattia** to fall ill; **mettersi in mare** to put to sea; **mettersi in maschera** to wear a masked costume; **mettersi in salvo** to get out of danger; to save oneself; **mettersi in viaggio** to set out on a journey; **mettersi in vista** to make oneself conspicuous || *impers*—**mette conto** it is worth while
mettima•le *mf* **(-le)** troublemaker
mezzadrìa [ddzz] *f* sharecropping
mezza•dro -dra [ddzz] *mf* sharecropper
mezzaluna [ddzz] *f* **(mezzelune)** halfmoon; crescent (*symbol of Turkey and Islam*); curved chopping knife; lunette (*of fortification*)
mezzana [ddzz] *f* procuress; (naut) mizzen
mezzanave [ddzz] *f*—**a mezzanave** amidships
mezzanino [ddzz] *m* mezzanine
mezza•no -na [ddzz] *adj* median; medium; middle || *m* procurer || *f* see **mezzana**
mezzanòtte [ddzz] *f* **(mezzenòtti)** midnight
mezzatinta [ddzz] *f* **(mezzetinte)** halftone
méz•zo -za *adj* overripe, rotten
mèz•zo -za [ddzz] *adj* half; middle || *m* half; middle; medium; means; vehicle; **a mezzo (di)** by (*e.g., messenger*); **andar di mezzo** to suffer the consequences; to be the loser; **entrare di mezzo** to interpose oneself; **esserci di mezzo** to be present; to be at stake; **giusto mezzo** happy medium; **in mezzo a** among; in the lap of, e.g., **in mezzo alle delicatezze** in the lap of luxury; **in quel mezzo** meanwhile; **levar di mezzo** to get rid of; **mezzi** means; facilities; **mezzi di comunicazione di massa** mass media; **per mezzo di** by means of
mezzobusto [ddzz] *m* **(mezzibusti)** (sculp) bust; **a mezzobusto** halflength (*e.g., portrait*)

mezzo·dì [ddzz] *m* (**-dì**) noon; south; South
mezzogiórno [ddzz] *m* noon; south; South
mezzùc·cio [ddzz] *m* (**-ci**) expedient
mi §5 *pron*
miagolare (**miàgolo**) *intr* to meow
miagolì·o *m* (**-i**) meow, mew
mi·ca *f* (**-che**) mica; (obs) crumb || *adv*—**mica male** (coll) not too bad!; **non . . . mica** not . . . ever; not at all
mìc·cia *f* (**-ce**) fuse
michelàc·cio *m* (**-ci**) (coll) lazy bum
micidiale *adj* deadly; (fig) unbearable
mì·cio -cia *mf* (**-ci -cie**) (coll) pussy cat
micrò·bio *m* (**-bi**) microbe
microbiologìa *f* microbiology
mìcrobo *m* microbe
microfà·rad *m* (**-rad**) microfarad
microferrovìa *f* model railroad
micro·film *m* (**-film**) microfilm
microfilmare *tr* to microfilm
micròfono *m* microphone
microlettóre *m* microfilm reader
micromotóre *m* small motor; motorcycle
microónda *f* microwave
microschèda *f* microcard
microscòpi·co -ca *adj* (**-ci -che**) microscopic(al)
microscò·pio *m* (**-pi**) microscope
microsól·co *adj invar* microgroove || *m* (**-chi**) microgroove; microgroove, long-playing record
microtelèfono *m* French telephone, handset
midólla *f* crumb; (coll) marrow
midól·lo *m* (**-là** *fpl*) marrow; (bot & fig) pith; **midollo spinale** (anat) spinal cord
mièle *m* honey
mietere (**mièto**) *tr* to reap; (lit) to kill
mietitrebbiatrice *f* combine
mieti·tóre -trice *mf* reaper, harvester
mietitura *f* harvesting
mi·gliàio *m* (**-gliàia** *fpl*) thousand
mì·glio *m* (**-glia** *fpl*) mile; milestone; **miglio marino** nautical mile; **miglio terrestre** mile || *m* (**-gli**) millet
miglioraménto *m* improvement
migliorare (**miglióro**) *tr, intr* (ESSERE & AVERE) & *ref* to improve
miglióre *adj* better; best
migliorìa *f* improvement (*e.g., of real estate*)
mignatta *f* leech
mìgnolo *adj masc* little (*finger or toe*) || *m* little finger; little toe
migrare *intr* to migrate
migra·tóre -trice *adj & m* migrant
migrazióne *f* migration
Milano *f* Milan
miliardà·rio -ria *adj & mf* (**-ri -rie**) billionaire
miliardo *m* billion
milionà·rio -ria *adj & mf* (**-ri -rie**) millionaire
milióne *m* million
milionèsi·mo -ma *adj & m* millionth
militante *adj & m* militant
militare *adj* military || *m* soldier || *v* (**mìlito**) *intr* to be a member; to militate; to be in the armed forces; **militare in** to be a member of (*e.g., a party*)
militaré·sco -sca *adj* (**-schi -sche**) military, soldierly
militarismo *m* militarism
militari·sta (**-sti -ste**) *adj* militaristic || *mf* militarist
militarizzare [ddzz] *tr* to militarize; to fortify
mìlite *m* militiaman; soldier; **milite del fuoco** fireman; **Milite Ignoto** Unknown Soldier
militesènte *adj* exempt from military service || *m* man exempt from military service
milìzia *f* militia; (mil) service; struggle; **milizie celesti** heavenly host
miliziano *m* militiaman
millantare *tr* to boast of || *ref* to brag, boast
millanta·tóre -trice *mf* braggart
millanterìa *f* bragging
mille *adj, m & pron* (**mila**) thousand, a thousand, one thousand || **il Mille** the eleventh century; the year one thousand
millecènto *m* eleven hundred || *f* car with a 1100 cc. motor
millefò·glie *m* (**-glie**) puff-paste cake
millenà·rio -ria (**-ri -rie**) *adj* millennial || *m* millennium
millèn·nio *m* (**-ni**) millennium
millepiè·di *m* (**-di**) millipede
millèsi·mo -ma *adj & m* thousandth
milliam·père *m* (**-père**) milliampere
milligrammo *m* milligram
millimetra·to -ta *adj* divided into squares of one millimeter square
millìmetro *m* millimeter
milli·vòlt *m* (**-vòlt**) millivolt
milza *f* spleen
mimare *tr & intr* to mime
mimetizzare [ddzz] *tr* (mil) to camouflage
mimetizzazióne [ddzz] *f* (mil) camouflage
mìmi·co -ca (**-ci -che**) *adj* mimic; sign (*language*) || *f* mimicry; (theat) gestures; (theat) miming
mi·mo -ma *mf* mime || *m* (orn) mockingbird
mina *f* lead (*of pencil*); (mil) mine; **mina anticarro** antitank mine; **mina antiuomo** antipersonnel mine
minaccévole *adj* (lit) threatening
minàc·cia *f* (**-ce**) threat, menace
minacciare §128 *tr* to threaten, menace
minacció·so -sa [s] *adj* threatening
minare *tr* to mine; to undermine
minaréto *m* minaret
minatóre *m* miner
minatò·rio -ria *adj* (**-ri -rie**) threatening
minchionare (**minchióno**) *tr* (slang) to make a sucker of
minchióne *m* (slang) sucker
minerale *adj* mineral || *m* mineral; ore
mineralogìa *f* mineralogy
minerà·rio -ria *adj* (**-ri -rie**) mining
minèr·va *m* (**-va**) safety match
minèstra *f* vegetable soup
minestróne *m* minestrone; hodgepodge

mìngere §199 *intr* to urinate
mingherli·no -na *adj* frail, thin
miniare §287 *tr* to paint in miniature; to illuminate
miniatura *f* miniature
miniaturizzare [ddzz] *tr* to miniaturize
miniaturizzazióne [ddzz] *f* miniaturization
minièra *f* mine
mini·gòlf *m* (**-gòlf**) miniature golf
minigònna *f* miniskirt
mìnima *f* lowest temperature; (mus) minim
minimizzare [ddzz] *tr* to minimize
mìni·mo -ma *adj* smallest, least; minimum || *m* minimum; **al minimo** at the least; **girare al minimo** or **tenere il minimo** (aut) to idle || *f* see **minima**
mìnio *m* red lead; rouge
ministeriale *adj* ministerial
ministèro *m* ministry; cabinet; department; **pubblico ministero** public prosecutor
ministra *f* (joc) wife of minister; (joc) female minister; (poet) minister
ministro *m* minister; secretary; administrator; **ministro degli Esteri** foreign minister; (U.S.A.) Secretary of State
minoranza *f* minority
minorare (**minóro**) *tr* to lessen; to disable
minora·to -ta *adj* disabled || *mf* disabled person
minorazióne *f* reduction; disability
minóre *adj* smaller, lesser; minor; smallest, least; younger; youngest || *m* minor
minorènne *adj* underage || *mf* minor
minorile *adj* juvenile (*e.g., court*)
minori·tà *f* (**-tà**) minority
minuétto *m* minuet
minù·gia *f* (**-gia & -gie**) (mus) catgut
minùsco·lo -la *adj* small (*letter*); diminutive || *m & f* small letter
minuta *f* first draft, rough copy
minutàglia *f* trifles; small fry
minutante *m* secretary; retailer
minuterìa *f* trinkets, notions
minu·to -ta *adj* minute; small (*change*); common (*people*) || *m* minute; **al minuto** retail; **di minuto in minuto** at any moment; **minuto secondo** second; **nel minuto** in detail; **per minuto** minutely || *f* see **minuta**
minùzia *f* trifle; **minuzie** minutiae
minuzió·so -sa [s] *adj* meticulous
minùzzolo *m* scrap, crumb; small boy
mìo mìa §6 *adj & pron poss* (**mièi mìe**)
mìope *adj* nearsighted || *mf* nearsighted person
miopìa *f* nearsightedness
mira *f* aim; sight; target, goal; **prendere di mira** to aim at; to torment
miràbile *adj* admirable || *m* wonder
mirabìlia *fpl* wonders; **far mirabilia** to perform wonders; **dir mirabilia di** to speak highly of
mirabolante *adj* amazing, astonishing
miracola·to -ta *adj* miraculously cured || *mf* miraculously cured person
miràcolo *m* miracle; wonder; **dir miracoli di** to praise to the skies; **per miracolo** by mere chance
miracoló·so -sa [s] *adj* miraculous; wonderful
miràg·gio *m* (**-gi**) mirage
mirare *tr* (lit) to look at; (lit) to aim at || *intr* to aim; **mirare a** to aim at; **mirare a** + *inf* to aim to + *inf;* to intend to + *inf*
mirìade *f* myriad
mirino *m* sight (*of gun*); (phot) finder
mirra *f* myrrh
mirtillo *m* blueberry; whortleberry, huckleberry
mirto *m* myrtle
misantropìa *f* misanthropy
misàntro·po -pa *adj* misanthropic || *mf* misanthrope
miscèla *f* mixture, blend
miscelare (**miscèlo**) *tr* to mix, blend
miscellàne·o -a *adj* miscellaneous || *f* miscellany
mìschia *f* fight; (sports) scrimmage
mischiare §287 *tr* to mix, blend; to shuffle (*cards*) || *ref* to mix
misconóscere §134 *tr* to not appreciate, undervalue
miscredènte *adj* misbelieving || *mf* misbeliever
miscù·glio *m* (**-gli**) mixture, blend
miseràbile *adj* pitiful, miserable; poor, wretched
miseran·do -da *adj* pitiable
miserère *m* Miserere; **essere al miserere** to be in one's last hours
miserévole *adj* pitiful; pitiable
misèria *f* destitution, misery; wretchedness; lack, want; trifle; **piangere miseria** to cry poverty
misericòrdia *f* mercy
misericordió·so -sa [s] *adj* merciful
mìse·ro -ra *adj* unhappy, wretched; poor; meager; mean; too small, too short
misfatto *m* misdeed, misdoing
misiriz·zi [s] *m* (**-zi**) tumbler (*toy*); (fig) chameleon
misògi·no -na *adj* misogynous || *m* misogynist
mìssile *adj & m* missile; **missile antimissile** antimissile missile; **missile intercontinentale** I.C.B.M.; **missile teleguidato** guided missile
missillìsti·co -ca *adj* (**-ci -che**) missile
missionà·rio -ria *adj & m* (**-ri -rie**) missionary
missióne *f* mission
missiva *f* missive
misterió·so -sa [s] *adj* mysterious
mistèro *m* mystery
mìstica *f* mysticism; mystical literature
misticismo *m* mysticism
mìsti·co -ca (**-ci -che**) *adj & mf* mystic || *f* see **mistica**
mistificare §197 (**mistìfico**) *tr* to hoax
mistificazióne *f* hoax
mi·sto -sta *adj* mixed || *m* mixture; mixed train
mistura *f* mixture
misura *f* measure; size; bounds; fitting; **a misura che** in proportion as; **di**

misura (sports) with a narrow margin; **su misura** made-to-order
misuràbile *adj* measurable
misurare *tr* to measure; to deliver (*e.g., a slap*); to budget (*expenses*); to try on (*clothes*); to weigh (*the outcome*) || *intr* to measure || *ref* to compete; to limit oneself; **misurarsi con** to try conclusions with
misura·to -ta *adj* moderate; scanty
misurino *m* measuring spoon or cup
mite *adj* mild; tame; low (*price*)
mìti·co -ca *adj* (**-ci -che**) mythical
mitigare §209 (**mìtigo**) *tr* to mitigate; to assuage, allay || *ref* to abate
mìtilo *m* mussel
mito *m* myth
mitologìa *f* mythology
mitològi·co -ca *adj* (**-ci -che**) mythologic(al)
mitòmane *mf* compulsive liar
mi·tra *m* (**-tra**) submachine gun || *f* miter
mitràglia *f* grapeshot; scrap iron; (coll) machine gun
mitragliare §280 (**mitràglio**) *tr* to machine-gun
mitragliatrice *f* machine gun
mitraglièra *f* heavy machine gun
mitraglière *m* machine gunner
mittènte *mf* sender; shipper
mo' *m*—apocopated form of **modo** by way of; **a mo' d'esempio** as an illustration
mòbile *adj* movable; personal (*property*); (fig) fickle; (rr) rolling (*stock*) || *m* piece of furniture; cabinet; (phys) body; **mobili** furniture
mobìlia *f* furniture
mobiliare *adj* (fin) security; (law) movable || §287 (**mobìlio**) *tr* to furnish
mobilière *m* furniture maker; furniture dealer
mobilità *f* mobility
mobilitare (**mobìlito**) *tr & intr* to mobilize
mobilitazióne *f* mobilization
mò·ca *m* (**-ca**) mocha; **caffè moca** Mocha coffee
mocassino *m* mocassin
moccicare §197 (**móccico**) *intr* (slang) to snivel; (slang) to run (*said of the nose*); (slang) to whimper
moccicó·so -sa [s] *adj* (slang) snotty
móc·cio *m* (**-ci**) snot, snivel
mocció·so -sa [s] *adj* snotty || *m* brat
mòccolo *m* end of candle, snuff; (joc) snot; (slang) curse word; **reggere il moccolo a qlcu** to be a third party to a couple's necking
mòda *f* fashion, vogue; **andar di moda** to be fashionable; to be all the rage; **fuori moda** outdated
modali·tà *f* (**-tà**) modality; method
modanatura *f* molding
mòdano *m* mold
modèlla *f* model
modellare (**modèllo**) *tr* to model; to mold || *ref* to pattern oneself
modella·tóre -trice *mf* pattern maker; molder
modellino *m* (archit) model, maquette
modèllo *adj invar* model || *m* model; fashion; style; pattern
moderare (**mòdero**) *tr* to moderate, control
moderatézza *f* moderation
modera·to -ta *adj* moderate; (mus) moderato || *m* middle-of-the-roader
modera·tóre -trice *adj* moderating || *m* moderator
modernizzare [ddzz] *tr & ref* to modernize
modèr·no -na *adj & m* modern
modèstia *f* modesty; scantiness, meagerness
modè·sto -sta *adj* modest; humble
mòdi·co -ca *adj* (**-ci -che**) reasonable
modìfi·ca *f* (**-che**) modification; alteration
modificare §197 (**modìfico**) *tr* to modify; to change; to alter
modiglióne *m* (archit) modillion
modista *f* milliner
modisterìa *f* millinery; millinery shop
mòdo *m* manner, mode, way; custom; idiom; (gram) mood; (mus) mode; **ad ogni modo** anyhow; nevertheless; **ad un modo** equally; **a modo** proper; properly; **a suo modo** in his own way; **bei modi** good manners; **di modo che** so that; **in malo modo** poorly; **in modo da** so as to; **in nessun modo** by no means; **in ogni modo** anyhow; **in qualche modo** somehow; **modo di dire** idiom; turn of phrase; **modo di fare** behavior; **modo di vedere** opinion; **per modo di dire** so to speak
modulare (**mòdulo**) *tr* to modulate
modulazióne *f* modulation; **modulazione d'ampiezza** amplitude modulation; **modulazione di frequenza** frequency modulation
mòdulo *m* module; blank, form
moffétta *f* skunk
mògano *m* mahogany
mòg·gio *m* (**-gi**) bushel
mò·gio -gia *adj* (**-gi -gie**) downcast, crestfallen
mó·glie *f* (**-gli**) wife
moìne *fpl* blandishments
mòla *f* grindstone; (coll) millstone
molare *adj* grinding; molar || *m* molar || *v* (**mòlo**) *tr* to grind
molassa *f* molasse, sandstone
molatóre *m* grinder (*person*); sander (*person*)
molatrice *f* grinder (*machine*); sander (*machine*); **molatrice di pavimenti** floor sander
mòle *f* size; pile; bulk, mass; huge structure
molècola *f* molecule
molestare (**molèsto**) *tr* to bother, annoy
molèstia *f* bother, trouble, annoyance
molè·sto -sta *adj* bothersome, troublesome
molibdèno *m* molybdenum
molinétto *m* (naut) winch
mòlla *f* spring; (fig) mainspring; **molla a balestra** leaf spring; **molle** tongs; **molle del letto** bedspring; **prendere**

qlco con le molle to keep at a reasonable distance from s.th
mollare (**mòllo**) *tr* to let go; to slacken; to drop (*anchor*); (coll) to soak || *intr* to give up; (coll) to soak; **molla!** (coll) cut it out!
mòlle *adj* wet, soaked; soft; mild; easy (*life*); weak (*character*); flexible || *m* softness; soft ground; **tenere a molle** to soak
mollécca *f* soft-shell crab
molleggiaménto *m* suspension; springiness
molleggiare §290 (**molléggio**) *tr* to provide with springs, to make elastic; (aut) to provide with suspension || *intr* to be springy, to have bounce || *ref* to bounce along
molléggio *m* (**-gi**) springs; (aut) suspension; springiness
mollétta *f* hairpin; clothespin; **mollette** sugar tongs
mollettièra *f* puttee
mollettóne *m* swansdown
mollézza *f* softness
molli·ca *f* (**-che**) crumb (*soft inner portion of bread*); **molliche** crumbs
mollificare §197 (**mollìfico**) *tr & ref* to mollify; to soften
mòl·lo -la *adj* soft || *m*—**mettere a mollo** to soak || *f* see **molla**
mollu·sco *m* (**-schi**) mollusk
mòlo *m* pier, wharf
moltéplice *adj* multiple, manifold
moltilaterale *adj* multilateral, many-sided
moltìpli·ca *f* (**-che**) front sprocket (*of bicycle*)
moltiplicare §197 (**moltìplico**) *tr & ref* to multiply
moltitùdine *f* multitude, crowd
mól·to -ta *adj* much, a lot of; very, e.g., **ho molta sete** I am very thirsty || *pron* much; a lot; **a dir molto** mostly; **ci corre molto** there is a great difference || **mol·ti -te** *adj & pron* many || **molto** *adv* very; quite; much; a lot; widely; long; **fra non molto** before long; **non . . . molto** (coll) not . . . at all
momentàne·o -a *adj* momentary
moménto *m* moment; opportune time; (slang) trifle; (phys) momentum; **dal momento che** since; **per il momento** for the time being; **sul momento** this very moment
mòna·ca *f* (**-che**) nun
monacale *adj* monachal, conventual
monacato *m* monkhood
monachésimo *m* monachism, monasticism
monachina *f* little nun; **monachine** sparks
mòna·co *m* (**-ci**) monk; (archit) king post || **Monaco** *m* Monaco || *f* Munich
monar·ca *m* (**-chi**) monarch
monarchìa *f* monarchy
monàrchi·co -ca *adj* (**-ci -che**) monarchical; monarchist(ic) (*advocating a monarch*) || *mf* monarchist
monastèro *m* monastery
monàsti·co -ca *adj* (**-ci -che**) monastic(al)
moncherino *m* stump (*without hand*)
món·co -ca (**-chi -che**) *adj* one-handed; one-armed; incomplete || *mf* cripple
moncóne *m* stump
mondana *f* prostitute
mondani·tà *f* (**-tà**) worldliness
monda·no -na *adj* mundane; worldly; society; fashionable || *m* playboy || *f* see **mondana**
mondare (**móndo**) *tr* to peel, pare; to thresh; to weed; to prune; (fig) to cleanse
mondari·so *mf* (**-so**) rice weeder
mondez·zàio *m* (**-zài**) dump
mondiale *adj* world, world-wide; (coll) stupendous
mondìglia *f* chaff; trash; refuse
mondina *f* rice weeder
món·do da *adj* clean-peeled; (lit) pure || *m* world; hopscotch; (coll) heap, bunch; **bel mondo** smart set; **cascasse il mondo!** (coll) come what may!; **da che mondo è mondo** since the world began; **essere nel mondo della luna** to be absent-minded; **mandare all'altro mondo** (coll) to send packing; **mettere al mondo** to give birth to; **mondo della luna** world of fancy; **un mondo** a lot; **venire al mondo** to be born || **Mondo** *m*—**Terzo Mondo** Third World
monega·sco -sca *adj & mf* (**-schi -sche**) Monacan
monellerìa *f* prank
monèl·lo -la *mf* urchin, brat || *f* romp
monéta *f* money; coin; piece of money; purse (*in horse races*); change; **batter moneta** to mint money; **moneta sonante** cash
monetà·rio -ria (**-ri -rie**) *adj* monetary || *m*—**falso monetario** counterfeiter
monetizzare [ddzz] *tr* to express in money; to transform into cash
mòngo·lo -la *adj & mf* Mongolian
monile *m* necklace; jewel
mònito *m* admonition, warning
monitóre *m* monitor
mònna *f* (obs) lady; (coll) monkey
monoàlbero *adj invar* (aut) single-camshaft, valve-in-head (*distribution*)
monoaurale *adj* monaural
monoblòc·co (**-co**) *adj* single-block || *m* (aut) cylinder block
monocilìndri·co -ca *adj* (**-ci -che**) (mach) single-cylinder
monòco·lo -la *adj* one-eyed || *m* monocle
monocolóre *adj invar* one-color; one-party
monofa·se *adj* (**-si & -se**) single-phase
monogamìa *f* monogamy
monòga·mo -ma *adj* monogamous || *m* monogamist
monografìa *f* monograph
monogram·ma *m* (**-mi**) monogram
monolìti·co -ca *adj* (**-ci -che**) monolithic
monolito *m* monolith
monòlo·go *m* (**-ghi**) monologue
monomanìa *f* monomania

monò·mio *m* (**-mi**) monomial
monopàttino *m* scooter
monopèt·to (**-to**) *adj* single-breasted || *m* single-breasted suit
monoplano *m* (aer) monoplane
monopò·lio *m* (**-li**) monopoly
monopolizzare [ddzz] *tr* to monopolize
monopósto *adj invar* one-man || *m* single-seater
monorotàia *adj invar* single-track || *f* monorail
monoscò·pio *m* (**-pi**) (telv) test pattern
monosìlla·bo -ba *adj* monosyllabic || *m* monosyllable
monòssido *m* monoxide
monoteìsti·co -ca *adj* (**-ci -che**) monotheistic
monotipìa *f* monotype
monotipo *m* monotype
monotonìa *f* monotony
monòto·no -na *adj* monotonous
monsignóre *m* monsignor
monsóne *m* monsoon
mónta *f* horseback riding; stud; jockey
montacàri·chi *m* (**-chi**) freight elevator
montàg·gio *m* (**-gi**) (mach) assembly; (mov) editing; (mov) montage
montagna *f* mountain; **montagna di ghiaccio** iceberg; **montagne russe** roller coaster
montagnó·so -sa [s] *adj* mountainous
montana·ro -ra *adj* mountain || *mf* mountaineer
monta·no -na *adj* mountain
montante *adj* rising || *m* riser, upright; (football) goal post; (aer) strut; (boxing) uppercut; (com) aggregate amount
montare (**mónto**) *tr* to mount; to go up (*the stairs*); to set (*jewels*); to frame (*a painting*); to whip (*e.g., eggs*); to excite; to exaggerate (*news*); to decorate (*a house*); to cover (*said of a male animal*); (mach) to assemble; (mov) to edit; **montare la testa a** to excite; to give a swell head to || *intr* (ESSERE) to jump; to climb; to go up; to rise; to swell; **montare alla testa a** to go to the head of; **montare in collera** to get angry || *impers*—**non monta** it doesn't matter, never mind
monta·tóre -trice *mf* (mach) assembler; (mov) editor
montatura *f* assembly; frame (*of glasses*); appliqué; setting (*of gem*); (journ) ballyhoo; (mov) editing; **montatura pubblicitaria** publicity stunt
montavivan·de *m* (**-de**) dumbwaiter
mónte *m* mountain; bank; mount (*in palmistry*); (cards) discard; **a monte** uphill; upstream; **andare a monte** to fail; **mandare a monte** to cause to fail; **monte di pietà** pawnbroker's; **monte di premi** pot (*in a lottery*)
montenegri·no -na *adj* & *mf* Montenegrin
montessoria·no -na *adj* Montessori
montóne *m* ram; mutton; rounded stone
montuó·so -sa [s] *adj* mountainous
montura *f* uniform
monumentale *adj* monumental
monuménto *m* monument
moquètte *f* (**moquètte**) wall-to-wall carpeting
mòra *f* mulberry; blackberry; brunette; Moorish woman; arrears; penalty (*for arrears*); (archaic) heap of stones
morale *adj* moral || *m* morale; **giù di morale** downcast; **su di morale** in high spirits || *f* morals, ethics; moral (*of a fable*)
moraleggiare §290 (**moraléggio**) *intr* to moralize
moralismo *m* moralism
morali·tà *f* (**-tà**) morality; morals
moralizzare [ddzz] *tr* & *intr* to moralize
moratòria *f* moratorium
morbidézza *f* softness
mòrbi·do -da *adj* soft; sleek; pliable || *m* soft ground
morbillo *m* measles
mòrbo *m* disease; plague
morbó·so -sa [s] *adj* morbid
mòrchia *f* sediment; dregs of oil
mordace *adj* biting, mordacious
mordènte *adj* biting; (chem) mordant; (mach) interlocking || *s* strength; (chem) mordant
mòrdere §200 *tr* to bite; to grab; to corrode; **mordere il freno** to champ the bit
mordicchiare §287 (**mordìcchio**) *tr* to nibble
morèl·lo -la *adj* blackish; black (*horse*) || *m* black horse
morènte *adj* dying || *mf* dying person
moré·sco -sca (**-schi -sche**) *adj* Moresque, Moorish || *f* Moorish dance
morét·to -ta *adj* brunet || *m* Negro boy; dark-skinned boy; chocolate-covered ice-cream bar || *f* Negro girl; dark-skinned girl; mask; (orn) scaup duck
morfè·ma *m* (**-mi**) morpheme
morfina *f* morphine
morfinòmane *mf* morphine addict
morfologìa *f* morphology
morìa *f* pestilence; high mortality
moribón·do -da *adj* moribund
morigera·to -ta *adj* temperate, moderate
morire §201 *intr* (ESSERE) to die; to die out; to end (*said of a street*); **morire di noia** to be bored to death
moritu·ro -ra *adj* about to die, doomed
mormóne *mf* Mormon
mormorare (**mórmoro**) *tr* to murmur; to whisper || *intr* to murmur; to whisper; to babble (*said of a brook*); to rustle; to gossip
mormorì·o *m* (**-i**) whisper; murmur
mò·ro -ra *adj* Moorish; dark-skinned; dark-brown || *mf* Moor || *m* mulberry tree || *f* see **mora**
morosi·tà [s] *f* (**-tà**) delinquency (*in paying one's bills*)
moró·so -sa [s] *adj* delinquent (*in paying one's bills*) || *m* (coll) boyfriend; **i morosi** (coll) the lovers || *f* (coll) girl friend
mòrsa *f* vise; (archit) toothing
morsétto *m* clamp; (elec) binding post

morsicare §197 (**mòrsico**) *tr* to bite
morsicatura *f* bite
morsicchiare §287 (**morsìcchio**) *tr* to nibble
mòrso *m* bite; bit
mor•tàio *m* (**-tài**) mortar
mortale *adj* mortal; deadly || *m* mortal
mortali•tà *f* (**-tà**) mortality
mortarétto *m* firecracker
mòrte *f* death; end; **averla a morte con** to harbor hatred for; **morte civile** (law) attainder, loss of civil rights
mortèlla *f* myrtle
mortificare §197 (**mortìfico**) *tr* to mortify || *ref* to feel ashamed
mòr•to -ta *adj* dead; still (*life*); **morto di fame** dying of hunger; **morto di paura** scared to death || *mf* dead person, deceased || *m* hidden treasure; (cards) dummy, widow; **fare il morto** to float on one's back; to play possum; **morto di fame** ne'er-do-well, good-for-nothing; **suonare a morto** to toll
mortò•rio *m* (**-ri**) funeral
mortuà•rio -ria *adj* (**-ri -rie**) mortuary
mosài•co -ca (**-ci -che**) *adj* Mosaic || *m* mosaic
mó•sca *f* (**-sche**) fly; imperial (*beard*); **mosca bianca** one in a million; **mosca cieca** blindman's buff; **fare venire la mosca al naso a** to make angry || **Mosca** *f* Moscow
moscaiòla *f* fly netting; flytrap
moscardino *m* dandy; (zool) dormouse
moscatèl•lo -la *adj* muscat || *m* muscatel
moscato *m* muscat grape; muscat wine
moscerino *m* gnat
moschèa *f* mosque
moschettière *m* musketeer; Italian National soccer player
moschétto *m* musket
moschettóne *m* snap hook
moschici•da *adj* (**-di -de**) fly-killing
mó•scio -scia *adj* (**-sci -sce**) flabby, soft
moscóne *m* big fly; pesky suitor
moscovi•ta *adj* & *mf* (**-ti -te**) Muscovite
Mosè *m* Moses
mòssa *f* gesture; movement; move; fake; post; **fare la mossa** to sprout (*said of plants*); **mossa di corpo** bowel movement; **prendere le mosse** to begin; **stare sulle mosse** to be about to begin; to be eager to take off (*said of a horse*)
mossière *m* starter (*in a race*)
mòs•so -sa *adj* moved; in motion; plowed; rough (*sea*); blurred (*picture*); wavy (*hair; ground*) || *f* see **mossa**
mostarda *f* mustard; candied fruit
mósto *m* must
móstra *f* show; pretense, simulation; exhibit; display window; lapel; face (*of watch*); sample; (mil) insignia; (obs) military parade; **far mostra di sé** to show off; **mettersi in mostra** to show off
mostrare (**móstro**) *tr* to show; to put on; **mostrare a dito** to point to; **mostrare la corda** to be threadbare || *ref* to show up; to show oneself
mostreggiatura *f* lapel; cuff
mostrina *f* (mil) insignia
móstro *m* monster
mostruó•so -sa [s] *adj* monstruous
mòta *f* mud, mire
mo•tèl *m* (**-tèl**) motel
motivare *tr* to cause; to justify
motivazióne *f* justification, reason
motivo *m* motive, reason; motif; theme; (coll) tune; **a motivo di** because of; **motivo per cui** wherefore
mò•to *m* (**-ti**) motion; movement; emotion; riot; **mettere in moto** to start || *f* (**-to**) (coll) motorcycle
motobar•ca *f* (**-che**) motorboat
motocannonièra *f* gunboat
motocarro *m* three-wheeler (*truck*)
motocarrozzétta *f* three-wheeler (*vehicle with sidecar*)
motociclétta *f* motorcycle
motocicli•sta *mf* (**-sti -ste**) motorcyclist
motocorazza•to -ta *adj* armored, panzer
motofalciatrice *f* power mower
motofurgóne *m* delivery truck
motolàn•cia *f* (**-ce**) motorboat, speedboat
motonàuti•co -ca (**-ci -che**) *adj* motorboat || *f* motorboating
motonave *f* motor ship
motopescheréc•cio *m* (**-ci**) motor fishing boat
mo•tóre -trice *adj* motive (*power*); (mach) drive || *m* motor; engine; car; **a motore** motorized, motor; **motore rotativo** (aut) rotary engine; **primo motore** prime mover || *f* see **motrice**
motorétta *f* motor scooter
motorino *m* small motor; motor bicycle; **motorino d'avviamento** (aut) starter
motori•sta *m* (**-sti**) mechanic
motorìsti•co -ca *adj* (**-ci -che**) motor
motorizzare [ddzz] *tr* to motorize
motoscafo *m* motorboat; **motoscafo da corsa** speedboat
motosé•ga *f* (**-ghe**) chain saw
motosilurante *f* torpedo boat
motoveìcolo *m* motor vehicle
motovelièro *m* motor sailer
motrice *f* (rr) engine, motor; (aut) tractor; **motrice a vapore** steam engine
motteggiare §290 (**mottéggio**) *tr* to mock, jeer at || *intr* to jest
mottég•gio *m* (**-gi**) mockery, jest
mòtto *m* witticism; motto; (lit) word
movènte *m* stimulus, motive
movènza *f* bearing, carriage; flow (*of a sentence*); cadence
movìbile *adj* movable
movimenta•to -ta *adj* lively; eventful
moviménto *m* motion, movement; traffic; **movimento di cassa** cash turnover
moviòla *f* (mov) viewer and splicer
mozióne *f* motion; (lit) movement
mozzare (**mózzo**) *tr* to lop off; to sever; **mozzare la testa a** to cut off the head of

mozzicóne *m* stump; butt (*e.g., of cigar*)
móz·zo -za *adj* cut off; truncated; cropped (*ears*); docked (*tail*); hard (*breathing*) || *m* cabin boy; **mozzo di stalla** stable boy
mòzzo [ddzz] *m* hub
muc·ca *f* (**-che**) milch cow
mùc·chio *m* (**-chi**) pile, heap; bunch
mucillàgine *f* mucilage
mu·co *m* (**-chi**) mucus, phlegm
mucó·so -sa [s] *adj* mucous || *f* mucous membrane
muda *f* molt
muffa *f* mold; mildew; **fare la muffa** to be musty
muffire §176 *intr* (ESSERE) to be musty
mùffola *f* mitten; muffle (*of furnace*)
muflóne *m* mouflon
mugghiare §287 (**mùgghio**) *intr* to bellow; to roar
mùggine *m* (ichth) mullet
muggire §176 & (**muggo**) *intr* to moo, low; to roar; to howl
muggito *m* bellow; moo, low; roar
mughétto *m* lily of the valley
mu·gnàio -gnàia *mf* (**-gnài -gnàie**) miller
mugolare (**mùgolo**) *intr* to yelp; to moan
mugolì·o *m* (**-i**) yelp; moan
mugò·lio *m* (**-li**) pine tar
mugugnare *intr* (coll) to mumble; (coll) to grumble
mugugno *m* (coll) grumble
mulattière *m* mule driver, muleteer
mulattiè·ro -ra *adj* mule || *f* mule track
mulat·to -ta *adj* & *mf* mulatto
mulìebre *adj* womanly, feminine
mulinare *tr* to twirl; to scheme || *intr* to whirl; to muse; to buzz (*in the mind*)
mulinèllo *m* twirl; whirlpool; whirlwind; fishing reel; whirligig; **fare mulinello con** to twirl
mulino *m* mill; **mulino ad acqua** water mill; **mulino a vento** windmill
mu·lo -la *mf* mule; (slang) bastard
multa *f* penalty, fine
multare *tr* to fine
multilaterale *adj* multilateral, many-sided
mùlti·plo -pla *adj* & *m* multiple
mùmmia *f* mummy
mummificare §197 (**mummìfico**) *tr* to mummify
mùngere §183 *tr* to milk
mungi·tóre -trice *mf* milker || *f* milking machine; milk maid
mungitura *f* milking
municipale *adj* municipal, city
municipalizzazióne [ddzz] *f* municipalization; city management
municì·pio *m* (**-pi**) municipality; city council; city hall
munificènza *f* munificence
munìfi·co -ca *adj* (**-ci -che**) munificent
munire §176 *tr* to fortify; to provide; **munire di** to equip with || *ref* to provide oneself
munizióne *f* (obs) fortification; **munizioni** ammunition; building supplies
muòvere §202 *tr* to move; to wag; to propel, run; to lift (*one's finger*); to take (*a step*); to pose (*a question*); to stir up (*laughter*); to institute (*a lawsuit*); **muovere accusa a** to reproach || *intr* (ESSERE) to begin; to move, start || *ref* to move; to travel; to stir; to set out; to be moved; **muoviti!** hurry up!
mura *fpl* see **muro**
muràglia *f* wall; (fig) obstacle; **muraglia cinese** Chinese Wall
muraglióne *m* high wall, rampart
murale *adj* & *m* mural
murare *tr* to wall; to wall in || *intr* to build a wall; **murare a secco** to build a dry wall || *ref* to close oneself in
murata *f* (naut) bulwark
muratóre *m* bricklayer, mason
muratura *f* bricklaying, stonework
murìati·co -ca *adj* (**-ci -che**) muriatic
mu·ro *m* (**-ri**) wall; **muro del pianto** Wailing Wall; **muro del suono** sound barrier || *m* (**-ra** *fpl*)—**mura** walls (*of a city*)
musa *f* muse
muschia·to -ta *adj* musk (*e.g., ox*)
mù·schio *m* (**-schi**) musk; (coll) moss
mu·sco *m* (**-schi**) moss
mùscolo *m* muscle; (fig) sinew; (coll) mussel
muscoló·so -sa [s] *adj* muscular
muscó·so -sa [s] *adj* (lit) mossy
musèo *m* museum
museruòla *f* muzzle
musétta *f* nose bag
mùsi·ca *f* (**-che**) music; band; **cambiare musica** to change one's tune
musicale *adj* musical
musicante *adj* music-playing (*angels*) || *mf* band player; second-rate musician
musicare §197 (**mùsico**) *tr* to set to music
musicassétta *f* cassette, tape cartridge
music-hall *m* (**-hall**) *m* vaudeville, burlesque
musici·sta *mf* (**-sti -ste**) musician
musicologìa *f* musicology
musicòlo·go *m* (**-gi**) musicologist
muso *m* muzzle, snout; (coll) mug; (fig) nose; **avere il muso lungo** to make a long face; **mettere il muso** to pout
musó·ne -na *mf* pouter, sulker
mussare *tr* to publish with great fanfare (*a piece of news*) || *intr* to foam (*said of wine*)
mùssola or **mussolina** *f* muslin
mussolinia·no -na *adj* of Mussolini
mùssolo *m* mussel
mustàc·chio *m* (**-chi**) shroud (*of bowsprit*); **mustacchi** moustache
musulma·no -na [s] *adj* & *mf* Moslem
muta *f* change; shift; molt; set (*of sails*); pack (*of hounds*); (mil) watch
mutàbile *adj* changeable
mutande *fpl* shorts, briefs, drawers
mutandine *fpl* panties; **mutandine da bagno** trunks
mutare *tr, intr* (ESSERE) & *ref* to change
mutazióne *f* mutation; (biol) mutation, sport
mutévole *adj* changeable; fickle

mutilare (mùtilo) *tr* to mutilate, maim
mutila•to -ta *adj* mutilated || *mf* cripple; amputee; **mutilato di guerra** disabled veteran
mutismo *m* silence, willful silence; (pathol) dumbness
mu•to -ta *adj* mute; dumb; silent (*movie*); unexpressed || *mf* mute || *f* see **muta**
mùtria *f* sulking attitude; proud demeanor
mùtua *f* mutual benefit society; medical insurance; **mettersi in mutua** to go on sick leave
mutuali•tà *f* **(-tà)** mutuality; mutual benefit institutions
mutuare (mùtuo) *tr* to borrow; to lend
mutua•to -ta *mf* person insured by mutual benefit society; person insured by medical insurance
mù•tuo -tua *adj* mutual; borrowing || *m* loan || *f* see **mutua**

N

N, n ['enne] *m* & *f* twelfth letter of the Italian alphabet
nababbo *m* nabob
Nabucodònosor *m* Nebuchadnezzar
nàcchera *f* castanet
nafta *f* crude oil; naphta; Diesel oil
naftalina *f* naphthalene
nàia *f* cobra; (slang) army discipline; (slang) military service
nàiade *f* naiad
nàilon *m* nylon
nanna *f* sleep (*of child*); **fare la nanna** to sleep (*said of child*)
na•no -na *adj* & *mf* dwarf
nàpalm *m* napalm
napoleòne *m* napoleon (*gold coin*) || **Napoleone** *m* Napoleon
napoleòni•co -ca *adj* **(-ci -che)** Napoleonic
napoleta•no -na *adj* & *mf* Neapolitan || *f* espresso coffee machine
Nàpoli *f* Naples
nappa tassel; tuft; kid (*leather*)
narciso *m* narcissus
narcòti•co -ca *adj* & *m* **(-ci -che)** narcotic
narcotizzare [ddzz] *tr* to drug, dope; to anesthetize
narghi•lè *m* **(-lè)** hookah
narice *f* nostril
narrare *tr* to narrate, tell, recount
narrati•vo -va *adj* narrative; fictional || *f* narrative; fiction
narra•tóre -trice *mf* narrator, storyteller
narrazióne *f* narration; tale, story; narrative
nasale [s] *adj* & *f* nasal
nascènte *adj* nascent; budding; rising (*sun*); dawning (*day*)
nàscere *m* beginning, origin || §203 *intr* (ESSERE) to be born; to bud; to shoot; to dawn; to rise; to spring up; **nascere con la camìcia** to be born with a silver spoon in one's mouth
nàscita *f* birth; birthday; origin
nascitu•ro -ra *adj* unborn, future || *mf* unborn child
nascóndere §204 *tr* to hide; **nascondere a** to hide from || *ref* to hide; to lurk
nascondì•glio *m* **(-gli)** hiding place; hideout; cache
nascondino *m* hide-and-seek; **giocare a nascondino** to play hide-and-seek
nascó•sto -sta *adj* hidden, concealed; secret; **di nascosto** secretly
nasèllo [s] *m* catch (*of latch*); (ichth) hake
nasièra [s] *f* nose ring
naso [s] *m* nose; (fig) face; **aver buon naso** to have a keen sense of smell; **ficcare il naso negli affari degli altri** to pry into the affairs of others; **menare per il naso** to lead by the nose; **naso adunco** hooknose; **restare con un palmo di naso** to be duped
nassa *f* pot (*for fishing*); **nassa per aragoste** lobster pot
nastrino *m* ribbon; badge
nastro *m* ribbon; band; tape; streamer; tape measure; **nastro del cappello** hatband; **nastro isolante** friction tape; **nastro per capelli** hair ribbon
nastùr•zio *m* **(-zi)** nasturtium
natale *adj* native, natal || **natali** *mpl* birth; birthday; **dare i natali a** to be the birthplace of || **Natale** *m* Christmas
natali•tà *f* **(-tà)** birth rate
natalì•zio -zia (-zi -zie) *adj* natal; Christmas || *m* birthday
natante *adj* swimming; floating || *m* craft
natatóia *f* fin
natató•rio -ria *adj* **(-ri -rie)** swimming
nàti•ca *f* **(-che)** buttock
natì•o -a *adj* (-i -e) (poet) native
nativi•tà *f* **(-tà)** birth, nativity || **Natività** *f* Nativity
nati•vo -va *adj* native; natural, inborn || *mf* native
N.A.T.O. *f* (acronym) **(North Atlantic Treaty Organization)—la N.A.T.O.** NATO
na•to -ta *adj* born; **nata** née; **nato e sputato** the spit and image of; **nato morto** stillborn || *mf* child
natura *f* nature; **natura morta** still life; **in natura** in kind
naturale *adj* natural || *m* nature, disposition; **al naturale** life-size
naturalézza *f* naturalness; spontaneity
naturalismo *m* naturalism
naturali•sta *mf* **(-sti -ste)** naturalist
naturali•tà *f* **(-tà)** naturalization
naturalizzare [ddzz] *tr* to naturalize || *ref* to become naturalized
naturalizzazióne [ddzz] *f* naturalization
naturalménte *adv* naturally; of course
naufragare §209 **(nàufrago)** *intr* (ESSERE

& AVERE) to be shipwrecked; to sink, to fail
naufrà·gio *m* (-gi) shipwreck; failure
nàufra·go -ga (-ghi -ghe) *adj* shipwrecked || *mf* shipwrecked person; (fig) outcast
nàusea *f* nausea; disgust; **avere la nausea** to be sick at one's stomach
nauseabón·do -da *adj* sickening, nauseating; (fig) unsavory
nauseante *adj* sickening, nauseous
nauseare (nàuseo) *tr* to nauseate, sicken
nausea·to -ta *adj* sickened, disgusted
nàuti·co -ca (-ci -che) *adj* nautical || *f* sailing, navigation
navale *adj* naval, navy, sea
navata *f* nave; **navata centrale** nave; **navata laterale** aisle
nave *f* ship, vessel, boat; craft; **nave ammiraglia** flagship; **nave a motore** motorboat; **nave appoggio** tender; **nave a vela** sailboat; **nave da carico** freighter; **nave da guerra** warship; **nave petroliera** tanker; **nave portaerei** aircraft carrier; **nave rompighiaccio** icebreaker; **nave traghetto** ferryboat
navétta *f* shuttle; **fare la navetta** to shuttle
navicèlla *f* nacelle, cabin (*of airship*); car (*of balloon*)
navigàbile *adj* navigable
navigabili·tà *f* (-tà) navigability; seaworthiness
navigante *adj* sailing || *m* sailor
navigare §209 **(nàvigo)** *tr & intr* to navigate, to sail
naviga·to -ta *adj* seawise; wordly-wise
naviga·tóre -trice *mf* navigator
navigazióne *f* navigation
navì·glio *m* (-gli) ship, craft, boat; fleet; navy; canal; **naviglio mercantile** merchant marine
nazionale *adj* national || *f* national team
nazionalismo *m* nationalism
nazionali·sta *mf* (-sti -ste) nationalist
nazionalìsti·co -ca *adj* (-ci -che) nationalistic
nazionali·tà *f* (-tà) nationality
nazionalizzare [ddzz] *tr* to nationalize
nazionalizzazióne [ddzz] *f* nationalization
nazióne *f* nation
nazi·sta *adj & mf* (-sti -ste) Nazi
nazzarè·no -na [ddzz] *adj & mf* Nazarene || **il Nazzareno** the Nazarene
ne §5 *pron & adv*
né *conj* neither, nor; **né . . . né** neither . . . nor
neanche *adv* not even; nor; not . . . either
nébbia *f* fog, haze, mist; **fa nebbia** it is foggy; **nebbia artificiale** smoke screen
nebbióne *m* thick fog, pea soup
nebbió·so -sa [s] *adj* foggy, hazy, misty
nebulare *adj* nebular
nebulizzare [ddzz] *tr* to atomize
nebulizzatóre [ddzz] *m* atomizer
nebulósa [s] *f* nebula
nebulosi·tà [s] *f* (-tà) fogginess, haziness, mistiness
nebuló·so -sa [s] *adj* foggy, hazy, misty || *f* see **nebulosa**
néces·saire *m* (-saire) vanity case; sewing kit
necessariaménte *adv* necessarily
necessà·rio -ria (-ri -rie) *adj* necessary, needed; essential || *m* necessity; necessities (*of life*)
necessi·tà *f* (-tà) necessity; need, want; **di necessità** necessarily
necessitare (necèssito) *tr* to require; to force || *intr* to be in want; to be necessary; **necessitare di** to need
necrologìa *f* necrology, obituary
necrològi·co -ca *adj* (-ci -che) obituary
necromanzìa *f* necromancy
necròsi *f* necrosis, gangrene
nefan·do -da *adj* heinous, nefarious
nefa·sto -sta *adj* ill-fated; ominous
nefrite *f* nephritis
negare §209 **(négo & nègo)** *tr* to deny, negate; to refuse
negati·vo -va *adj & f* negative
nega·to -ta *adj* unfit, unsuited
negazióne *f* negation, denial; (gram) negative
neghittó·so -sa [s] *adj* lazy, slothful
neglèt·to -ta *adj* neglected; untidy
négli §4
negligènte *adj* negligent, careless
negligènza *f* negligence, carelessness; dereliction (*of duty*)
neglìgere §205 *tr* to neglect
negoziàbile *adj* negotiable
negoziante *mf* merchant, shopkeeper; dealer; **negoziante all'ingrosso** wholesaler; **negoziante al minuto** retailer; shopkeeper, storekeeper
negoziare §287 **(negòzio)** *tr* to negotiate, transact || *intr* to negotiate, deal
negoziati *mpl* negotiations
negozia·tóre -trice *mf* negotiator
negò·zio *m* (-zi) business; transaction; store, shop; **negozio di cancelleria** stationery store
negrière *m* slave trader; slave driver
negriè·ro -ra *adj* slave || *m* slave trader; slave driver
né·gro -gra *adj & mf* Negro
negromante *m* sorcerer
néi §4
nél §4
nélla §4
nélle §4
néllo §4
némbo *m* rain cloud; cloud (*e.g., of dust*)
Nembròd *m* Nimrod
nèmesi *f invar* nemesis || **Nemesi** *f* Nemesis
nemi·co -ca (-ci -che) *adj* inimical, hostile, unfriendly; enemy; (fig) adverse || *mf* enemy, foe; **il Nemico** the Evil One
nemméno *adv* not even; nor; not . . . either
nènia *f* funeral dirge; lamentation
nenùfaro *m* water lily
nèo *m* mole (*on the skin*); flaw, blemish; neon; beauty spot
neoclassicheggiante *adj* in the direction of the neoclassical

neòfi•ta *mf* (**-ti -te**) neophite
neolati•no -na *adj* Neo-Latin, Romance
neologismo *m* neologism
neomicina *f* neomycin
nèon *m* neon
neona•to -ta *adj* newborn || *mf* infant, baby; newborn child
neozelandése [dz][s] *adj* New Zealand || *mf* New Zealander
nepènte *f* nepenthe
Nepóte *m* Nepos
neppure *adv* not even; nor; **not . . .** either
nequìzia *f* iniquity, wickedness
nera•stro -stra *adj* blackish
nerbata *f* heavy blow
nèrbo *m* whip; sinew; bulk; strength (*of an opposing force*)
nerboru•to -ta *adj* muscular, sinewy
nereggiare §290 (**neréggio**) *intr* to look black; to be blackish
nerétto *m* (*typ*) boldface
né•ro -ra *adj* black; dark; gloomy; dark-red (*wine*) || *mf* black; Negro || *m* black
nerofumo *m* lampblack
Neróne *m* Nero
nervatura *f* ribbing
nervi•no -na *adj* nerve (*gas*); nervine (*medicine*)
nèrvo *m* nerve; sinew; **avere i nervi** to be in a bad mood
nervosismo [s] *m* nervousness, irritability
nervó•so -sa [s] *adj* nervous, irritable; sinewy, vigorous (*style*) || *m* bad mood; **avere il nervoso** to be in a bad mood
nèsci *m*—**fare il nesci** to feign ignorance
nèspola *f* medlar; **nespole** (coll) blows
nèspolo *m* medlar tree
nèsso *m* connection, link; **avere nesso** to cohere
nessu•no -na *adj* no, not any || **nessuno** *pron* nobody, no one; none; not anybody; not anyone; **nessuno dei due** neither one
nettapén•ne *m* (**-ne**) penwiper
nettare (**nétto**) *tr* to clean, to cleanse
nèttare *m* nectar
nettézza *f* cleanness, cleanliness; neatness; **nettezza urbana** department of sanitation; garbage collection
nét•to -ta *adj* clean; clear; sharp; net || **netto** *adv* clearly, distinctly
nettùnio *m* neptunium
Nettuno *m* Neptune
netturbino *m* street cleaner
neurologìa *f* neurology
neurò•si *f* (**-si**) neurosis
neuròti•co -ca *adj* (**-ci -che**) neurotic
neutrale *adj & mf* neutral
neutrali•sta *adj & mf* (**-sti -ste**) neutralist
neutrali•tà *f* (**-tà**) neutrality
neutralizzare [ddzz] *tr* to neutralize
nèu•tro -tra *adj* neuter; neutral
neutróne *m* neutron
ne•vàio *m* (**-vài**) snowfield; snowdrift
néve *f* snow; **neve carbonica** dry ice
nevicare §197 (**névica**) *impers* (ESSERE) —**nevica** it is snowing
nevicata *f* snowfall
nevìschio *m* sleet
nevó•so -sa [s] *adj* snowy
nevralgìa *f* neuralgia
nevrastèni•co -ca *adj & mf* (**-ci -che**) neurasthenic
nevvéro (i.e., **n'è vero for non è vero**) see **non**
niacina *f* niacin
nìb•bio *m* (**-bi**) (orn) kite
nìcchia *f* niche; nook, recess
nicchiare §287 (**nìcchio**) *intr* to waver
nìc•chio *m* (**-chi**) shell; nook
nichel *m* nickel
nichelare (**nìchelo**) *tr* to nickel, to nickel-plate
nichelatura *f* nickel-plating
nichelino *m* nickel (*coin*)
nichèlio *m* var of **nichel**
Nicòla *m* Nicholas
nicotina *f* nicotine
nidiata *f* nestful; brood
nidificare §197 (**nidìfico**) *intr* to build a nest, to nest
nido *m* nest; home; nursery; den (*of thieves*)
niènte *m* nothing; nothingness; **dal niente** from scratch; **di niente** you're welcome || *pron* nothing; not . . . anything; **quasi niente** next to nothing
nientediméno *adv* no less, nothing less
Nilo *m* Nile
ninfa *f* nymph
ninfèa *f* white water lily
ninnananna *f* lullaby, cradlesong
nìnnolo *m* toy; trinket
nipóte *mf* grandchild || *m* grandson; nephew; **nipoti** descendants || *f* granddaughter; niece
nippòni•co -ca *adj* (**-ci -che**) Nipponese
nirvana, il nirvana
nìti•do -da *adj* clear, distinct
nitóre *m* brightness; elegance
nitrato *m* nitrate
nitrire §176 *intr* to neigh
nitrito *m* neigh; (chem) nitrite
nitro *m* niter; **nitro del Cile** Chile saltpeter
nitroglicerina *f* nitroglycerin
nitruro *m* nitride
niu•no -na *adj* (poet) var of **nessuno**
nìve•o -a *adj* snow-white
Nizza *f* Nice
no *adv* no; not; **come no?** why not; certainly; **dire di no** to say no; **no?** is it not so?; **non dir di no** to consent; **proprio no** certainly not
nòbile *adj* noble; second (*floor*) || *m* nobleman || *f* noblewoman
nobiliare *adj* noble, of nobility
nobilitare (**nobìlito**) *tr* to ennoble
nobil•tà *f* (**-tà**) nobility
nòc•ca *f* (**-che**) knuckle
nocchière *m* or **nocchièro** *m* petty officer; (poet) pilot, helmsman
nocchieru•to -ta *adj* knotty
nòc•chio *m* (**-chi**) knot (*in wood*)
nocciòla *adj invar* hazel (*in color*) || *f* hazelnut; filbert
nocciolina *f* little nut; **nocciolina americana** peanut; roasted peanut
nòcciolo *m* stone, pit, kernel; **il noc-**

ciolo della questione the crux of the matter
nocciòlo *m* hazel (*tree*); filbert (*tree*)
nóce *m* walnut tree || *f* walnut (*fruit*); **noce del collo** Adam's apple; **noce di cocco** coconut; **noce di vitello** filet of veal; **noce moscata** nutmeg
nocévole *adj* harmful
noci·vo -va *adj* harmful, detrimental
nòdo *m* knot; crux, gist (*of a question*); junction; lump (*in one's throat*); (naut) knot; (phys) node; **lì è il nodo** there's the rub; **nodo d'amore** true-love knot; **nodo ferroviario** rail center, junction; **nodo scorsoio** noose; **nodo stradale** highway center, crossroads
nodó·so -sa [s] *adj* knotty
Noè *m* Noah
noi §5 *pron pers* we; us; **noi altri** we, e.g., **noi altri italiani** we Italians
nòia *f* boredom; bother, trouble; bug (*in a motor*); **venire a noia** (with *dat*) to weary; **dar noia** (with *dat*) to bother
noial·tri -tre *pron* we; us; **noialtri italiani** we Italians
noió·so -sa [s] *adj* boring, annoying
noleggiare §290 (**noléggio**) *tr* to rent; to hire, to charter || *ref*—**si noleggia, si noleggiano** for rent
noleggiatóre *m* hirer; lessor (*e.g., of a car*)
nolég·gio *m* (**-gi**) rent, lease; car rental; chartering; freightage
nolènte *adj* unwilling
nòlo *m* rent, hire; **a nolo** for hire
nòmade *adj* nomad, nomadic || *mf* nomad
nóme *m* name; fame; reputation; (gram) noun; **a nome di** on behalf of; **in nome di** in the name of; **nome commerciale** firm name; **nome depositato** registered name; **nome di battesimo** Christian name; **nome e cognome** full name
nomèa *f* name, reputation; notoriety
nomìgnolo *m* nickname; **affibbiare un nomignolo a** to nickname
nòmina *f* appointment; **di prima nomina** newly appointed
nominale *adj* nominal; noun
nominare (**nòmino**) *tr* to name, call; to mention; to elect; to appoint
nominati·vo -va *adj* nominative; with names in alphabetical order; (fin) registered || *m* nominative; name; model number
non *adv* no, not; none, e.g., **non troppo presto** none too soon; **non appena** as soon as; **non c'è di che** you are welcome; **non . . . che** but, only; **non è vero?** is it not so?, isn't it so? La traduzione in inglese di questa domanda dipende generalmente dalla proposizione che la precede. Se la proposizione è affermativa, l'interrogazione sarà negativa, p.es. **Lei mi scriverà, non è vero?** You will write me. Won't you? Se la proposizione è negativa, l'interrogazione sarà positiva, p.es. **Lei non beve birra, non è vero?** You do not drink beer. Do you? Se il soggetto della proposizione è un nome sostantivo, sarà rappresentato nell'interrogazione da un pronome personale, p.es. **Giovanni ha finito, non è vero?** John has finished. Hasn't he?
nonagenà·rio -ria *adj & mf* (**-ri -rie**) nonagenarian
nonagèsi·mo -ma *adj, pron & m* ninetieth
nonconformi·sta *mf* (**-sti -ste**) nonconformist
noncurante *adj* careless, indifferent
noncuranza *f* carelessness, indifference
nondiméno *conj* yet, nevertheless
nòn·no -na *mf* grandparent || *m* grandfather || *f* grandmother
nonnulla *m invar* nothing, trifle
nò·no -na *adj, m & pron* ninth
nonostante *prep* in spite of, notwithstanding; **nonostante che** although, even though
nonpertanto *adv* nevertheless, still, yet
non plus ultra *m* ne plus ultra, acme
nonsènso *m* nonsense
non so ché *adj invar* indefinable || *m invar* something indefinable
nontiscordardi·mé *m* (**-mé**) forget-me-not
nòrd *m* north
nòrdi·co -ca (**-ci -che**) *adj* Nordic; northern, north || *mf* northerner
nòrma *f* rule, regulation; **a norma di legge** according to law; **per Sua norma** for your guidance
normale *adj* normal; normative; perpendicular || *f* perpendicular line
normali·tà *f* (**-tà**) normality, normalcy
normalizzare [ddzz] *tr* to normalize, to standardize
Normandìa, la Normandy
norman·no -na *adj & mf* Norman || *m* Norseman
normati·vo -va *adj* normative || *f* normativeness
normògrafo *m* stencil
norvegése [s] *adj & mf* Norwegian
Norvègia, la Norway
nosocò·mio *m* (**-mi**) hospital
nossignóra (*i.e.*, **no signora**) *adv* no, Madam
nossignóre (*i.e.*, **no signore**) *adv* no, Sir
nostalgìa *f* nostalgia, longing; homesickness
nostàlgi·co -ca (**-ci -che**) *adj* nostalgic; homesick || *m* worshiper of the good old days (*esp. of Fascism*)
nostra·no -na *adj* domestic, national; home-grown; regional
nò·stro -stra §6 *adj & pron poss*
nostròmo *m* boatswain
nòta *f* mark; score; memorandum; list; bill, invoice; report (*on a subordinate*); (mus) note; **note caratteristiche** personal folder, efficiency report (*of an employee*); **prender nota di** to take down
notàbile *adj* notable, noteworthy || *m* notable
no·tàio *m* (**-tài**) notary (public); lawyer

notare (nòto) *tr* to mark, check; to note, to jot down; to observe; to bring out; **farsi notare** to attract attention, make oneself conspicuous; **nota bene** note well, take notice
notariale or **notarile** *adj* notarial
notazióne *f* notation; annotation; observation
nò·tes *m* (**-tes**) notebook
notévole *adj* noteworthy, remarkable
notìfi·ca *f* (**-che**) notification, notice; service (*e.g., of a summons*)
notificare §197 (**notìfico**) *tr* to report; to serve (*a summons*); to declare (*e.g., one's income*)
notificazióne *f* notification, notice; service (*e.g., of a summons*)
notìzia *f* knowledge; report; piece of news; **aver notizie di** to hear from; **notizie** news; **una notizia** a news item
notizià·rio *m* (**-ri**) news; news report, news bulletin; (rad) newscast; **notiziario sportivo** sports page; (rad, telv) sports news
nò·to -ta *adj* known, well-known || *m* south wind; (coll) swimming || *f* see **nota**
notorie·tà *f* (**-tà**) general knowledge; affidavit; notoriety
notò·rio -ria *adj* (**-ri -rie**) well-known
nottàmbu·lo -la *adj* nighttime; night-wandering || *mf* nightwalker; night owl
nottata *f* night; **far nottata bianca** to spend a sleepless night
nòtte *f* night; **buona notte** good night; **di notte** at night, by night, in the nighttime; **la notte di lunedì** Sunday night; Monday night; **lunedì notte** Monday night; **notte bianca** sleepless night; **notte di San Silvestro** New Year's Eve; watch night
nottetèmpo *adv*—**di nottetempo** at night, in the nighttime
nòttola *f* wooden latch; (zool) bat
nottolino *m* small wooden latch; ratchet, catch
nottur·no -na *adj* nocturnal, night || *m* nocturne
novanta *adj, m & pron* ninety
novantènne *adj* ninety-year-old || *mf* ninety-year-old person
novantèsi·mo -ma *adj, m & pron* ninetieth
novantina *f* about ninety; **sulla novantina** about ninety years old
nòve *adj & pron* nine; **le nove** nine o'clock || *m* nine; ninth (*in dates*)
novecentismo *m* twentieth-century arts and letters
novecenti·sta (-sti -ste) *adj* twentieth-century || *mf* artist of the twentieth century
novecènto *adj, m & pron* nine hundred || **il Novecento** the twentieth century
novèlla *f* short story; (poet) news
novellìè·re -ra *mf* storyteller; short-story writer
novelli·no -na *adj* early, tender; inexperienced, green
novellìstica *f* storytelling; fiction
novèl·lo -la *adj* fresh, young, tender; new || *f* see **novella**
novèmbre *m* November
novenà·rio -ria *adj* (**-ri -rie**) nine-syllable
noverare (nòvero) *tr* to count; to enumerate; (poet) to remember
nòvero *m* number; class
novilù·nio *m* (**-ni**) new moon
novìssi·mo -ma *adj* (lit) last, newest
novi·tà *f* (**-tà**) newness, originality; novelty, innovation; latest idea; late news
noviziato *m* novitiate; apprenticeship
novì·zio -zia (-zi -zie) *mf* novice; apprentice || *f* novice (*in a convent*)
novocaina *f* novocaine
nozióne *f* notion, conception
nòzze *fpl* wedding, marriage; **nozze d'argento** silver wedding; **nozze d'oro** golden wedding
nube *f* cloud
nubifrà·gio *m* (**-gi**) cloudburst
nùbile *adj* unmarried, single (*woman*); marriageable || *f* unmarried girl
nu·ca *f* (**-che**) nape of the neck, scruff
nucleare *adj* nuclear
nùcleo *m* nucleus; group; (elec) core
nudismo *m* nudism
nudi·sta *adj & mf* (**-sti -ste**) nudist
nudi·tà *f* (**-tà**) nudity, nakedness
nu·do -da *adj* naked, bare; barren; simple; **mettere a nudo** to lay bare; **nudo e crudo** stark-naked; destitute || *m* nude
nùgolo *m* cloud; throng, swarm
nulla *pron* nothing || *m invar* nothing; nothingness
nulla òsta *m* permission; visa
nullatenènte *adj* poor || *mf* have-not
nullificare §197 (**nullìfico**) *tr* to nullify
nulli·tà *f* (**-tà**) nothingness; nonentity; invalidity (*of a document*)
nul·lo -la *adj* void, worthless || **nullo** *pron* (poet) none, no one || **nulla** *m & pron* see **nulla**
nume *m* divinity, deity
numerare (nùmero) *tr* to number
numeratóre *m* numerator; numbering machine
numèri·co -ca *adj* (**-ci -che**) numerical
nùmero *m* number; lottery ticket; size (*of shoes*); **numero dispari** odd number; **numero legale** quorum; **numero pari** even number
numeró·so -sa [s] *adj* numerous, large; harmonious
nùn·zio *m* (**-zi**) nuncio; (poet) news
nuòcere §206 *intr* to be harmful; (*with dat*) to harm
nuòra *f* daughter-in-law
nuotare (nuòto) *intr* to swim; to float; to wallow (*in wealth*)
nuotata *f* swim, dip, plunge
nuota·tóre -trice *mf* swimmer
nuòto *m* swimming; **gettarsi a nuoto** to jump into the water; **traversare a nuoto** to swim across
nuòva *f* news; late news

Nuòva York *f* New York
Nuova Zelanda, la [dz] New Zealand
nuòvo -va *adj* new; **di nuovo** again; **nuovo di zecca** brand-new; **nuovo fiammante** brand-new; **nuovo venuto** new arrival || *m*—**il nuovo** the new || *f* see **nuova**
nùtria *f* coypu
nutrice *f* wet nurse; (lit) provider
nutriènte *adj* nourishing
nutriménto *m* nourishment
nutrire §176 & **(nutro)** *tr* to nourish; to nurture; to harbor (*e.g., hatred*) || *ref*—**nutrirsi di** to feed on or upon
nutriti•vo -va *adj* nutritious, nutritive
nutri•to -ta *adj* well-fed; strong; rich (*food*); brisk, heavy (*gunfire*)
nutrizióne *f* nutrition; food
nùvo•lo -la *adj* cloudy || *m* cloudy weather; (lit) cloud; (fig) swarm || *f* cloud
nuvoló•so -sa [s] *adj* cloudy
nuziale *adj* wedding, nuptial
nuzialità *f* marriage rate

O

O, o [o] *m & f* thirteenth letter of the Italian alphabet
o *conj* or; now; **o . . . o** either . . . or; whether . . . or || *interj* oh!
òa•si *f* **(-si)** oasis
obbediènte *adj* var of **ubbidiente**
obbedièñza *f* obedience
obbedire §176 *tr & intr* var of **ubbidire**
obbiettare (obbiètto) *tr & intr* var of **obiettare**
obbligare §209 **(òbbligo)** *tr* to oblige; to compel, to force || *ref* to obligate oneself
obbligatìssi•mo -ma *adj* much obliged
obbligatò•rio -ria *adj* **(-ri -rie)** compulsory, obligatory
obbligazióne *f* obligation; burden; (com) debenture, bond
obbligazioni•sta *mf* **(-sti -ste)** bondholder
òbbli•go *m* **(-ghi)** obligation; duty; **d'obbligo** obligatory, mandatory; **fare d'obbligo a qlcu** + *inf* to be necessary for s.o. to + *inf, e.g.,* **gli fa d'obbligo lavorare** it is necessary for him to work
obbrò•brio *m* **(-bri)** opprobrium, disgrace; **obbrobri** insults
obbrobrió•so -sa [s] *adj* opprobrious, disgraceful
obeli•sco *m* **(-schi)** obelisk
obera•to -ta *adj* overburdened
obesità *f* obesity
obè•so -sa *adj* obese, stout
òbice *m* howitzer
obiettare (obiètto) *tr & intr* to argue; to object
obietti•vo -va *adj & m* objective
obiettóre *m* objector; **obiettore di coscienza** conscientious objector
obiezióne *f* objection
obitò•rio *m* **(-ri)** morgue
oblare (òblo) *tr* to willingly pay (*a fine*)
obla•tóre -trice *mf* donor
oblazióne *f* donation; (eccl) oblation; (law) payment of a fine
obliare §119 *tr* (lit) to forget
oblì•o *m* **(-i)** (lit) oblivion
oblì•quo -qua *adj* oblique
obliterare (oblìtero) *tr* to obliterate, cancel
o•blò *m* **(-blò)** (naut) porthole; **oblò di accesso** door (*of space capsule*)
oblun•go -ga *adj* **(-ghi -ghe)** oblong
òbo•e *m* **(-e)** oboe
oboi•sta *mf* **(-sti -ste)** oboist
òbolo *m* mite
ò•ca *f* **(-che)** goose; gander
ocarina *f* ocarina, sweet potato
occasionale *adj* chance; immediate (*cause*)
occasionare (occasióno) *tr* to occasion
occasióne *f* occasion; opportunity; ground, pretext; bargain; **all'occasione** on occasion; **d'occasione** second-hand; occasional (*verses*)
occhiàia *f* eye socket; **occhiaie** rings under the eyes
occhia•làio *m* **(-lài)** optician
occhiale *adj* eye, ocular || **occhiali** *mpl* glasses; goggles; **occhiali antisole** sunglasses; **occhiali a stringinaso** nose glasses
occhialétto *m* lorgnon; monocle
occhiata *f* glance
occhieggiare §290 **(occhiéggio)** *tr* to eye || *intr* to peep
occhièllo *m* buttonhole; boutonniere; eyelet; half title; subhead
occhièra *f* eyecup
òc•chio *m* **(-chi)** eye; speck of grease (*in soup*); handle (*of scissors*); ring (*of stirrup*); (typ) face; (fig) bit; **a occhio e croce** at a rough guess; **a quattr'occhi** in private; **battere gli occhi** to blink; **cavarsi gli occhi** to strain one's eyes; **dar nell'occhio** to attract attention; **di buon occhio** favorably; **fare l'occhio a** to get used to; **fare tanto d'occhi** to be amazed, to open one's eyes wide; **lasciare gli occhi su** to covet; **non chiudere un occhio** not to sleep a wink; **occhio!** watch out!; **occhio della testa** outrageous price; **occhio di bue** (naut) porthole; **occhio di cubia** (naut) hawsehole; **occhio di pavone** (zool) peacock butterfly; **occhio di triglia** sheep's eyes; **occhio pesto** black eye; **occhio pollino** corn (*on toes*); **tenere d'occhio** to keep an eye on
occhiolino *m* small eye; **far l'occhiolino** to wink
occidentale *adj* western, occidental
occidènte *adj* (poet) setting (*sun*) || *m* west, occident

occìpite *m* occipital bone
occlusióne *f* occlusion
occlusi·vo -va *adj & f* occlusive
occlu·so -sa *adj* occluded
occorrènte *adj* necessary || *m* necessary; (lit) occurrence
occorrènza *f* necessity; **all'occorrenza** if need be
occórrere §139 *intr* (ESSERE) to happen; (with *dat*) to need, e.g., **gli occorre dell'olio** he needs oil || *impers* (ESSERE)—**occorre** it is necessary
occultaménto *m* concealment
occultare *tr & ref* to hide
occul·to -ta *adj* occult; (lit) hidden
occupante *adj* occupying || *m* occupant
occupare (**òccupo**) *tr* to occupy; to employ || *ref* to take employment; **occuparsi di** to busy oneself with, to mind; to attend to
occupa·to -ta *adj* occupied; busy
occupazionale *adj* occupational
occupazióne *f* occupation
oceàni·co -ca *adj* (**-ci -che**) oceanic
ocèano *m* ocean
òcra *f* ocher
oculare *adj* ocular; see **testimone** || *m* eyepiece
oculatézza *f* circumspection, prudence
ocula·to -ta *adj* circumspect, prudent
oculi·sta *mf* (**-sti -ste**) oculist
od *conj* or
odali·sca *f* (**-sche**) odalisque
òde *f* ode
odepòri·co -ca (**-ci -che**) *adj* (lit) travel || *m* (lit) travelogue
odiare §287 (**òdio**) *tr* to hate
odièr·no -na *adj* today's, current
ò·dio *m* (**-di**) hatred; **avere in odio** to hate; **essere in odio a** to be hated by
odió·so -sa [s] *adj* hateful, odious
odissèa *f* odyssey || **Odissea** *f* Odyssey
Odissèo *m* Odysseus
odontoia·tra *mf* (**-tri -tre**) doctor of dental surgery, dentist
odontoiatrìa *f* odontology, dentistry
odorare (**odóro**) *tr & intr* to smell
odora·to -ta *adj* (poet) fragrant || *m* smell
odóre *m* smell, odor, scent; **cattivo odore** bad odor; **odori** herbs, spice
odoró·so -sa [s] *adj* odorous, fragrant
offèndere §148 *tr & intr* to offend || *ref* to take offense
offensi·vo -va *adj & f* offensive
offensóre *m* offender
offerènte *mf* bidder; **miglior offerente** highest bidder
offèrta *f* offer; offering, donation; (*at an auction*) bid; (com) supply
offésa [s] *f* offense; wrongdoing; ravage (*of time*); **da offesa** (mil) offensive; **recarsi a offesa qlco** to regard s.th as offensive
officina *f* shop, workshop; **officina meccanica** machine shop
officiò·so -sa [s] *adj* helpful, obliging
offrire §207 *tr* to offer; to sponsor (*a radio or TV program*); to dedicate (*a book*); to bid (*at an auction*); (com) to tender || *ref* to offer oneself, to volunteer
offuscare §197 *tr* to darken, obscure; to obfuscate; to dim (*mind; eyes*) || *ref* to grow dark; to grow dim
oftàlmi·co -ca *adj* (**-ci -che**) opthalmic
oftalmòlo·go -ga *mf* (**-gi -ghe**) ophthalmologist
oggettività *f* objectivity
oggetti·vo -va *adj & m* objective
oggètto *m* object; subject, argument; article; **oggetti preziosi** valuables
òggi *m* today; **dall'oggi al domani** suddenly; overnight || *adv* today; **d'oggi in poi** henceforth; **oggi a otto** a week hence; **oggi come oggi** at present; **oggi è un anno** one year ago
oggidì *m invar & adv* nowadays
oggigiórno *m invar & adv* nowadays
ogiva *f* ogive, pointed arch; nose cone
ógni *adj indef invar* each; every, e.g., **ogni due giorni** every two days; **ogni cosa** everything; **ogni tanto** every now and then; **per ogni dove** (lit) everywhere
ogniqualvòlta *conj* whenever
Ognissan·ti *m* (**-ti**) All Saints' Day
ognitèmpo *adj invar* all-weather
-ógno·lo -la *suf adj* -ish, e.g., **giallognolo** yellowish
ognóra *adv* (lit) always
ognù·no -na *adj* (obs) each || *pron* each one, everyone
oh *interj* oh!
òhi *interj* ouch!
ohibò *interj* fie!
ohimè *interj* alas!
ohm *m* (**ohm**) ohm
olanda *f* Dutch linen || **l'Olanda** *f* Holland
olandése [s] *adj* Dutch || *m* Dutch (*language*); Dutchman; Dutch cheese || *f* Dutch woman
oleandro *m* oleander
oleà·rio -ria *adj* (**-ri -rie**) oil
olea·to -ta *adj* oiled
oleifì·cio *m* (**-ci**) oil mill
oleodótto *m* pipeline
oleó·so -sa [s] *adj* oily
olezzare [ddzz] (**olézzo**) *intr* (lit) to smell sweet
olézzo [ddzz] *m* perfume, fragrance
olfatto *m* smell
oliare §287 (**òlio**) *tr* to oil
oliatóre *m* oiler, oil can
olìbano *m* frankincense
olièra *f* cruet
oligarchìa *f* oligarchy
olimpìade *f* Olympiad
olìmpi·co -ca *adj* (**-ci -che**) Olympic; Olympian
olimpiòni·co -ca *adj* (**-ci -che**) Olympic || *mf* Olympic athlete
ò·lio *m* (**-li**) oil; **ad olio** oil, e.g., **quadro ad olio** oil painting; **olio di fegato di merluzzo** cod-liver oil; **olio di lino** linseed oil; **olio di ricino** castor oil; **olio solare** sun-tan lotion
oliva *f* olive
oliva·stro -stra *adj* livid; swarthy || *m* wild olive (*tree*)
olivéto *m* olive grove
Olivièro *m* Oliver
olivo *m* olive tree

ólmo *m* elm tree
olocàu·sto -sta *adj* (lit) burnt; (lit) sacrificed || *m* holocaust; sacrifice
ològra·fo -fa *adj* holographic
olóna *f* sailcloth, canvas
oltracciò *adv* besides
oltraggiare §290 *tr* to outrage; to insult
oltràg·gio *m* (**-gi**) outrage; offense; ravages (*of time*); **oltraggio al pudore** offense to public morals; **oltraggio al tribunale** contempt of court
oltraggió·so -sa [s] *adj* outrageous
oltranza *f*—**a oltranza** to the bitter end
oltranzi·sta *mf* (**-sti -ste**) (pol) extremist
óltre *adv* beyond; ahead; further; **oltre a** apart from; in addition to; **troppo oltre** too far || *prep* beyond; past; more than
oltrecortina *adj invar* beyond-the-iron-curtain || *m* country beyond the iron curtain
oltremare *m invar* country overseas || *adv* overseas
oltremisura *adv* (lit) beyond measure
oltremòdo *adv* (lit) exceedingly
oltrepassare *tr* to overstep; to cross (*a river*); to be beyond (. . . *years old*); (sports) to overtake
oltretómba *m*—**l'oltretomba** the life beyond
omàg·gio *m* (**-gi**) homage; compliment; **in omaggio** complimentary; **rendere omaggio a** to pay tribute to
òmaro *m* Norway lobster
ombeli·co *m* (**-chi**) navel
ómbra *f* shade; shadow; umbrage; form, mass; **nemmeno per ombra** not in the least
ombreggiare §290 (**ombréggio**) *tr* to shade
ombrèlla *f* shade (*of trees*); (bot) umbel; (coll) umbrella
ombrel·làio *m* (**-lài**) umbrella maker
ombrellino *m* parasol
ombrèllo *m* umbrella
ombrellóne *m* beach umbrella
ombró·so -sa [s] *adj* shady; touchy; skittish (*horse*)
omelette *f* (**omelette**) omelet
omelìa *f* homily
omeopàti·co -ca (**-ci -che**) *adj* homeopathic || *m* homeopathist
omèri·co -ca *adj* (**-ci -che**) Homeric
òmero *m* (anat) humerus; (lit) shoulder
omertà *f* code of silence of underworld
ométtere §198 *tr* to omit
ométto *m* little man; (coll) clothes hanger; (billiards) pin; (archit) king post
omici·da (**-di -de**) *adj* homicidal, murderous || *mf* homicide, murderer
omicì·dio *m* (**-di**) homicide, murder; **omicidio colposo** (law) manslaughter; **omicidio doloso** (law) first-degree murder
ominó·so -sa [s] *adj* (lit) ominous
omissióne *f* omission
òmni·bus *m* (**-bus**) omnibus; way train
omnisciènte *adj* all-knowing, omniscient
omogène·o -a *adj* homogeneous
omologare §209 (**omòlogo**) *tr* to confirm, ratify; to probate (*a will*); (sports) to validate
omòni·mo -ma *adj* of the same name || *m* namesake; homonym
omosessuale [s] *adj & mf* homosexual
ón·cia *f* (**-ce**) ounce; **oncia a oncia** little by little
ónda *f* wave; **a onde** wavy; wavily; **essere in onda** (rad, telv) to be on the air; **farsi le onde** to have one's hair waved; **mettere in onda** (rad, telv) to put on the air; **onda crespa** whitecap; **onda portante** (rad, telv) carrier wave
ondata *f* wave, billow; gust (*e.g., of smoke*); rush (*of blood*); wave (*of cold weather*)
ondatra *f* muskrat
ónde *pron* from which; of which || *adv* whereof; hence; (poet) wherefrom || *prep* **onde** + *inf* in order to || *conj* **onde** + *subj* so that
ondeggiante *adj* waving, swaying
ondeggiare §290 (**ondéggio**) *intr* to wave, sway; to waver
ondina *f* mermaid; (mythol) undine; (mythol) mermaid
ondó·so -sa [s] *adj* wavy
ondulare (**óndulo & òndulo**) *tr* to wave; to corrugate (*e.g., metal*) || *intr* to sway
ondula·to -ta *adj* wavy (*hair*); corrugated (*e.g., metal*); bumpy (*road*)
ondulazióne *f* undulation; **ondulazione permanente** permanent wave
-óne -óna *suf mf* big, e.g., **librone** big book; **dormigliona** big sleeper || **-óne** *suf m* (applies to both sexes) big, e.g., **donnone** *m* big woman
ònere *m* (lit) onus, burden
oneró·so -sa [s] *adj* onerous, burdensome
onestà *f* honesty; (poet) modesty
onè·sto -sta *adj* honest; fair; (poet) modest || *m* moderate amount; honest gain; honest person
ònice *m* onyx
onnipossènte & onnipotènte *adj* almighty, omnipotent
onnisciènte *adj* omniscient
onniveggènte *adj* all-seeing
onnìvo·ro -ra *adj* omnivorous
onomàsti·co -ca (**-ci -che**) *adj* onomastic || *m* name day || *f* study of proper names
onomatopèi·co -ca *adj* (**-ci -che**) onomatopeic
onoràbile *adj* honorable
onoranza *f* honor; **onoranze** homage; **onoranze funebri** obsequies
onorare (**onóro**) *tr* to honor || *ref* to deem it an honor
onorà·rio -ria (**-ri -rie**) *adj* honorary || *m* fee, honorarium
onora·to -ta *adj* honored; honest; honorable
onóre *m* honor; **d'onore** honest, e.g., **uomo d'onore** honest man; **estremi onori** last rites; **fare gli onori di casa** to receive guests; **fare onore a** to honor; **onore al merito** credit where

credit is due; **onor del mento** (lit) beard
onorévole *adj* honorable || *m* honorable member (*of parliament*)
onorificènza *f* dignity; decoration
onorìfi·co -ca *adj* (**-ci -che**) honorific; honorary (*e.g., title*)
ónta *f* dishonor, shame; **a onta di** in spite of; **avere onta** to be ashamed; **fare onta a** to bring shame upon; **in onta a** against
ontano *m* alder
O.N.U. (acronym) *f* (**Organizzazione delle Nazioni Unite**) United Nations, U.N.
onu·sto -sta *adj* (poet) laden
opa·co -ca *adj* (**-chi -che**) opaque
opale *m* opal
opali·no -na *adj* opaline || *f* shiny cardboard; luster (*fabric*)
òpera *f* work; organization, foundation; day's work; (mus) opera; **mettere in opera** to install; to start work on; to make ready; to begin using; **opera di consultazione** reference work; **opera morta** (naut) upper works; **opera viva** (naut) quickwork; **per opera di** thanks to
ope·ràio -ràia (**-ràì -ràie**) *adj* workman's, worker's; working || *m* workman, worker; **operaio a cottimo** pieceworker; **operaio a giornata** day laborer; **operaio specializzato** craftsman, skilled workman || *f* workwoman
operante *adj* actively engaged; operative
operare (**òpero**) *tr* to operate; to work (*a miracle*); (surg) to operate on || *intr* to operate; to be actively engaged || *ref* to be operated on; to occur, take place
operati·vo -va *adj* operative; operations, e.g., **ricerca operativa** operations research
opera·to -ta *adj* operated; embossed || *m* behavior; patient operated on
opera·tóre -trice *mf* operator || *m* (mov) cameraman
operatò·rio -ria *adj* (**-ri -rie**) surgical (*operation*); operating (*room*); (math) operational
operazióne *f* operation; transaction
operétta *f* short work; (mus) operetta
operìsti·co -ca *adj* (**-ci -che**) operatic
operosi·tà [s] *f* (**-tà**) industry
operó·so -sa [s] *adj* industrious; active
opi·mo -ma *adj* (lit) fat; rich, fertile
opinare *intr* to opine, deem
opinióne *f* opinion
opòs·sum *m* (**-sum**) opossum
oppia·to -ta *adj* opiate (*mixed with opium*); dulled by drugs || *m* opiate (*medicine containing opium*)
òppio *m* opium
oppiòmane *adj* opium-eating; opium-smoking || *mf* opium addict
oppórre §218 *tr* to oppose; to offer, put up (*resistance*) || *ref* to be opposite; **opporsi a** to oppose, to be against
opportuni·sta *mf* (**-sti -ste**) opportunist
opportuni·tà *f* (**-tà**) opportunity; opportuneness
opportu·no -na *adj* opportune
opposi·tóre -trice *mf* opponent
opposizióne *f* opposition; (law) appeal; **fare opposizione a** to object to
oppó·sto -sta *adj* opposite; contrary || *m* opposite; **all'opposto** on the contrary
oppressióne *f* oppression
oppressi·vo -va *adj* oppressive
opprès·so -sa *adj* oppressed; overcome, overwhelmed || **oppressi** *mpl* oppressed people
oppressóre *m* oppressor
opprimènte *adj* oppressive
opprìmere §131 *tr* to oppress; to overcome, overwhelm; to weigh down
oppugnare *tr* to refute, contradict
oppure *adv* otherwise || *conj* or else; or rather
optare (**òpto**) *intr* to choose; (com) to exercise an option
optometri·sta *mf* (**-sti -ste**) optometrist
opulèn·to -ta *adj* opulent
opùscolo *m* booklet, brochure, pamphlet; **opuscolo d'informazioni** instruction manual
opzióne *f* option
ór *adv* now; **or ora** right now; **or sono** ago
óra *f* hour; time; period (*in school*); **alla buon'ora!** finally!; **a ore** by the hour; **a tarda ora** late; **che ora è?** or **che ore sono?** what time is it?; **da un'ora all'altra** from one moment to the next; **dell'ultima ora** up-to-date (*news*); **di buon'ora** early; early in the morning; **di ora in ora** at any moment; **d'ora in avanti** from this moment on; **d'ora in poi** from now on; **far l'ora** to kill time; **fin ora** until now; **non vedere l'ora di** + *inf* to be hardly able to wait until + *ind*; **ora di cena** suppertime; **ora di punta** rush hour, peak hour; **ora legale** daylight-saving time; **ore piccole** late hours; **un'ora di orologio** one full hour || *adv* now
oràcolo *m* oracle
òra·fo -fa *adj* goldsmith's || *m* goldsmith
orale *adj* & *m* oral
oralménte *adv* orally; by word of mouth
oramài *adv* now; already
oran·go *m* (**-ghi**) orangutan
orà·rio -ria (**-ri -rie**) *adj* hourly; per hour; clockwise || *m* timetable; schedule; roster; **essere in orario** to be on time; **orario di lavoro** working hours; **orario d'ufficio** office hours
ora·tóre -trice *mf* orator
oratò·rio -ria (**-ri -rie**) *adj* oratorical || *m* (eccl) oratory; (mus) oratorio || *f* oratory, public speaking
orazióne *f* oration; prayer; **orazione domenicale** Lord's Prayer
orbare (**òrbo**) *tr* (lit) to bereave; (lit) to deprive
òrbe *f* (lit) orb; (lit) world
orbène *adv* well

òrbita *f* orbit; (fig) sphere
orbitare (**òrbito**) *intr* to orbit
orbitaziòne *f* orbiting
òr•bo -ba *adj* bereaved; deprived; blind || *m* blind man
òrca *f* killer whale
Òrcadi *fpl* Orkney Islands
orchèstra *f* orchestra; band; orchestra pit
orchestrale *adj* orchestral || *mf* orchestra player, orchestra performer
orchestrare (**orchèstro**) *tr* to orchestrate; (fig) to organize
orchestrina *f* dance band; dance-band music
orchidèa *f* orchid
ór•cio *m* (**-ci**) jar, jug, crock
orciòlo *m*—**a orciolo** puckered up (*lips*)
òr•co *m* (**-chi**) ogre
òrda *f* horde
ordàlia *f* (hist) ordeal
ordigno *m* gadget, contrivance; tool; **ordigno esplosivo** infernal machine
ordinale *adj* & *m* ordinal
ordinaménto *m* disposition; regulation
ordinanza *f* ordinance; (mil) orderly; **d'ordinanza** regulation (*e.g., uniform*); **in ordinanza** (mil) in formation
ordinare (**órdino**) *tr* to order; to straighten up; to range; to regulate; to ordain; to trim
ordinà•rio -ria (**-ri -rie**) *adj* ordinary; plain; inferior; workday (*suit*) || *m* ordinary; full professor; **d'ordinario** ordinarily, usually
ordina•to -ta *adj* orderly, tidy; ordained || *f* ordinate; straightening up; (aer) frame; (naut) bulkhead
ordinaziòne *f* order; ordination
órdine *m* order; row; tier; series (*e.g., of years*); college (*e.g., of surgeons*); nature (*of things*); (law) warrant, writ; **in ordine a** concerning; **ordine del giorno** order of the day; **ordine d'idee** train of thought
ordire §176 *tr* to warp (*cloth*); to hatch (*a plot*)
ordi•to -ta *adj* plotted || *m* warp (*of fabric*)
orécchia *f* ear; dog-ear; **con le orecchie tese** all ears
orecchiale *m* earphone (*of sonar equipment*)
orecchiétta *f* (anat) auricle
orecchino *m* earring
oréc•chio *m* (**-chi**) ear; hearing; dog-ear; moldboard; **fare orecchio da mercante** to turn a deaf ear || *m* (**orécchia** *fpl*) (archaic) ear
orecchióne *m* long-eared bat; (mil) trunnion; **orecchioni** (pathol) mumps
oréfice *m* goldsmith; jeweler
oreficerìa *f* goldsmith shop; jewelry shop
orfanézza *f* orphanage (*condition*)
òrfa•no -na *adj* orphaned || *mf* orphan
orfanotrò•fio *m* (**-fi**) orphanage (*institution*)
Orfèo *m* Orpheus
organdi *m* organdy
organétto *m* hand organ; mouth organ; **organetto di Barberia** hand organ
orgàni•co -ca (**-ci -che**) *adj* organic || *m* personnel, staff || *f* (mil) organization
organigram•ma *m* (**-mi**) organization chart
organino *m* hand organ, barrel organ
organismo *m* organism
organi•sta *mf* (**-sti -ste**) organist
organizzare [ddzz] *tr* to organize
organizza•tóre -trice [ddzz] *mf* organizer
organizzazióne [ddzz] *f* organization; **Organizzazione delle Nazioni Unite** United Nations
òrgano *m* organ; part (*of a machine*); **organo di stampa** mouthpiece
orgasmo *m* orgasm; agitation, excitement
òr•gia *f* (**-ge**) orgy
orgó•glio *m* (**-gli**) pride
orgoglió•so -sa [s] *adj* proud
orientale *adj* & *mf* oriental; Oriental
orientaménto *m* orientation; bearing; trend; trim (*of sail*); **orientamento scolastico e professionale** aptitude test; vocational guidance
orientare (**oriènto**) *tr* to orient; to guide; to trim (*a sail*) || *ref* to find one's bearings
oriènte *m* orient; **grand'oriente** grand lodge || **Oriente** *m* Orient, East; **Estremo Oriente** Far East; **Medio Oriente** Middle East; **Vicino Oriente** Near East
orifì•zio *m* (**-zi**) orifice, opening
orìgano *m* wild marjoram
originale *adj* original; odd || *mf* queer character, odd person || *m* original; copy (*for printer*)
originare (**orìgino**) *tr* to originate || *intr* (ESSERE) & *ref* to originate
originà•rio -ria *adj* (**-ri -rie**) originating; native; original
orìgine *f* origin; source; extraction
origliare §280 *intr* to eavesdrop
orglière *m* (lit) pillow
orina *f* var of **urina**
orinale *m* chamber pot, urinal
orinare *tr* & *intr* to urinate
orina•tóio *m* (**-tói**) urinal, comfort station
oriòlo *m* (orn) oriole
oriun•do -da *adj* native || *m* (sports) native son
orizzontale [ddzz] *adj* horizontal || **orizzontali** *fpl* horizontal words (*in crossword puzzle*)
orizzontare [ddzz] (**orizzónto**) *tr* to orient || *ref* to get one's bearings
orizzónte [ddzz] *m* horizon
Orlando *m* Roland
orlare (**órlo**) *tr* to hem, border; **orlare a zigzag** to pink
órlo *m* edge; brim; hem, border; (fig) brink; **orlo a giorno** hemstitch
órma *f* footprint; **orme** remains, vestiges; **calcare le orme di** to follow the footsteps of
ormeggiare §290 (**orméggio**) *tr* & *ref* (naut) to moor
orméggio *m* (**-gi**) mooring; **mollare gli ormeggi** (naut) to cast off
ormóne *m* hormone

ornamentale *adj* ornamental
ornaménto *m* ornament
ornare (**órno**) *tr* to adorn
orna•to -ta *adj* adorned; ornate || *m* ornament; ornamental design
ornitòlo•go -ga *mf* (**-gi -ghe**) ornithologist
òro *m* gold; (fig) money; **d'oro** gold, golden; **ori** gold objects; jewels; suit of Neapolitan cards corresponding to diamonds; **oro zecchino** pure gold; **per tutto l'oro del mondo** for all the world
orologerìa *f* watchmaking; clockmaking; watchmaker's shop
orolo•giàio *m* (**-giài**) watchmaker; clockmaker
orolò•gio *m* (**-gi**) watch; clock; **orologio a pendolo** clock; **orologio a polvere** sandglass; **orologio a scatto** digital clock; **orologio da polso** wristwatch; **orologio della morte** deathwatch; **orologio solare** sundial
oròscopo *m* horoscope
orpèllo *m* Dutch gold; (fig) tinsel
orrèndo *m* horrible
orrìbile *adj* horrible
òrri•do -da *adj* horrid || *m* horridness; gorge, ravine
orripilante *adj* bloodcurdling, hair-raising
orróre *m* horror; awe; **aver in** or **per orrore** to loath; **fare orrore a** to horrify
órsa *f* she-bear || **Orsa** *f*—**Orsa maggiore** Great Bear; **Orsa minore** Little Bear
orsacchiòtto *m* bear cub; Teddy bear
ór•so -sa *mf* bear; **orso bianco** polar bear; **orso grigio** grizzly bear || *f* see **orsa**
orsù *interj* come on!
ortàg•gio *m* (**-gi**) vegetable
ortàglia *f* vegetable garden; vegetable
ortènsia *f* hydrangea
orti•ca *f* (**-che**) nettle; hives
orticària *f* hives, nettle rash
orticoltóre *m* truck gardener; horticulturist
òrto *m* garden, vegetable garden; (lit) sunrise; **orto botanico** botanical garden; **orto di guerra** Victory garden
ortodòs•so -sa *adj* orthodox || *m* Greek Catholic
ortografia *f* orthography; spelling
ortola•no -na *adj* garden || *m* truck farmer, gardener
ortopèdi•co -ca (**-ci -che**) *adj* orthopedic || *m* orthopedist
òrza *f* bowline; windward; **andare all'orza** to sail close to the wind
orzaiòlo [dz] *m* (pathol) sty
orzare (**òrzo**) *intr* to sail close to the wind; to luff
orzata [dz] *f* orgeat
orzata *f* (naut) luff
òrzo [dz] *m* barley
osannare *intr* to cry or sing hosanna; **osannare a** to acclaim, applaud
osare (**òso**) *intr* to dare
osceni•tà *f* (**-tà**) obscenity
oscè•no -na *adj* obscene; (coll) horrible
oscillante *adj* oscillating
oscillare *intr* to oscillate; to swing; to wobble; to waver, hesitate
oscillazióne *f* oscillation; fluctuation
oscuraménto *m* darkening, dimming; blackout
oscurare *tr* to darken; to blot out; to dim || *ref* to get dark; **oscurarsi in volto** to frown
oscuri•tà *f* (**-tà**) obscurity; darkness; ignorance
oscu•ro -ra *adj* obscure, dark; opaque (*style*) || *m* obscurity, darkness; **essere all'oscuro di** to be in the dark about
osmòsi *f* osmosis
ospedale *m* hospital
ospedalière *m* hospital worker
ospedaliè•ro -ra *adj* hospital || *m* hospitaler
ospedalizzare [ddzz] *tr* to hospitalize
ospitale *adj* hospitable || *m* hospital
ospitali•tà *f* (**-tà**) hospitality
ospitare (**òspito**) *tr* to lodge, shelter, accommodate; to entertain; (sports) to play (*an opposing team*) at home
òspite *mf* host; guest; **andarsene insalutato ospite** to take French leave; **ospiti** company (*guests at home*)
ospì•zio *m* (**-zi**) hospice; hostel; (lit) hospitality; **ospizio dei vecchi** nursing home; **ospizio di mendicità** poorhouse
ossatura *f* frame, framework; skeleton
òsse•o -a *adj* bony
ossequènte *adj* (lit) respectful; (lit) reverent
ossequiare §287 (**ossèquio**) *tr* to pay one's respects to; to honor
ossè•quio *m* (**-qui**) respect; reverence; **i miei ossequi** my best regards; **in ossequio a** in conformity with; **porgere i propri ossequi a** to pay one's respects to
ossequió•so -sa [s] *adj* obsequious; respectful
osservante *adj & m* observant
osservanza *f* observance; deference
osservare (**ossèrvo**) *tr* to observe
osserva•tóre -trice *adj* observing, observant || *mf* observer
osservatò•rio *m* (**-ri**) observatory
osservazióne *f* observation; rebuke
ossessionare (**ossessióno**) *tr* to obsess; to harass, bedevil
ossessióne *f* obsession
ossès•so -sa *adj* possessed || *mf* person possessed
ossìa *conj* or; to wit
ossidante *adj* oxidizing || *m* oxidizer
ossidare (**òssido**) *tr & ref* to oxidize
òssido *m* oxide; **ossido di carbone** carbon monoxide
ossìdulo *m* protoxide; **ossidulo di azoto** nitrous oxide
ossificare §197 (**ossìfico**) *tr & ref* to ossify
ossigenare (**ossìgeno**) *tr* to oxygenate; to bleach (*the hair*); to infuse strength into || *ref* to bleach (*the hair*)
ossìgeno *m* oxygen; (fig) transfusion, shot in the arm
ossìto•no -na *adj & m* oxytone

òs·so *m* (-si) bone (*of animal*); stone (*of fruit*); **osso di balena** whalebone; **osso di seppia** cuttlebone; **osso duro da rodere** hard nut to crack; **osso sacro** sacrum; **rimetterci l'osso del collo** to be thoroughly ruined; **rompersi l'osso del collo** to break one's neck || *m* (-sa *fpl*) bone (*of a person*); **avere le ossa rotte** to be dead-tired
ossu·to -ta *adj* bony; scrawny
ostacolare (ostàcolo) *tr* to hinder; to obstruct; **ostacolare l'azione** (sports) to interfere
ostàcolo *m* obstacle; obstruction; (golf) hazard; (sports) hurdle
ostàg·gio *m* (-gi) hostage
ostare (òsto) *intr* (lit) to be in the way; (with *dat*) to hinder; **nulla osta** no objection, permission granted
òste ostéssa *mf* innkeeper || **oste** *m* & *f* (lit) army in the field || *m* (poet) enemy
ostèllo *m* hostel; (poet) abode
ostentare (ostènto) *tr* to show, display; to affect, feign
ostenta·to -ta *adj* affected, ostentatious
ostentazióne *f* show, ostentation
osteopatìa *f* osteopathy
osterìa *f* tavern, inn, taproom
ostéssa *f* see **oste**
ostètri·ca *f* (-che) midwife
ostetrìcia *f* obstetrics
ostètri·co -ca (-ci -che) *adj* obstetrical || *m* obstetrician || *f* see **ostetrica**
òstia *f* wafer; Host; sacrificial victim
òsti·co -ca *adj* **(-ci -che)** hard; (lit) repugnant, distasteful
ostile *adj* hostile
ostili·tà *f* (-tà) hostility
ostinare *ref* to be stubborn; to persist
ostina·to -ta *adj* obstinate; persistent
ostinazióne *f* obstinacy
ostracismo *m* ostracism; **dare l'ostracismo a** to ostracize
ostracizzare [ddzz] *tr* (poet) to ostracize
òstri·ca *f* **(-che)** oyster; **ostrica perlifera** pearl oyster
ostri·càio *m* **(-cài)** oyster bed; oysterman
ostruire §176 *tr* to obstruct; to stop up
ostruzióne *f* obstruction
Otèllo *m* Othello
otorinolaringoia·tra *mf* **(-tri -tre)** ear, nose, and throat specialist, otorhinolaryngologist
ótre *f* wineskin; **otre di vento** windbag (*person*)
ottàni·co -ca *adj* **(-ci -che)** octane
ottano *m* octane
ottanta *adj, m* & *pron* eighty
ottantènne *adj* eighty-year-old || *mf* eighty-year-old person
ottantèsi·mo -ma *adj, m* & *pron* eightieth
ottantina *f* about eighty; **essere sull'ottantina** to be about eighty years old
ottava *f* octave
Ottaviano *m* Octavian
ottavino *m* (mus) piccolo; (com) commission of ⅛ of 1%
otta·vo -va *adj* & *pron* eighth || *m* eighth; octavo || *f* see **ottava**
ottemperare (ottèmpero) *intr* (with *dat*) to obey; **ottemperare a** to comply with
ottenebrare (ottènebro) *tr* to becloud
ottenére §271 *tr* to obtain, get
ottétto *m* octet
òtti·co -ca (-ci -che) *adj* optic(al) || *m* optician || *f* optics
ottimismo *m* optimism
ottimi·sta *mf* **(-sti -ste)** optimist
ottimìsti·co -ca *adj* **(-ci -che)** optimistic
òtti·mo -ma *adj* very good, excellent || *m* best; highest rating
òtto *adj* & *pron* eight; **le otto** eight o'clock || *m* eight; eighth (*in dates*); (sports) racing shell with eight oarsmen; **otto giorni a week; otto volante** roller coaster
ottóbre *m* October
ottocenté·sco -sca *adj* **(-schi -sche)** nineteenth-century
ottocènto *adj, m* & *pron* eight hundred || **l'Ottocento** the nineteenth century
ottoma·no -na *adj* & *m* Ottoman || *m* ottoman (*fabric*) || *f* ottoman (*sofa*)
ottomila *adj, m* & *pron* eight thousand
ottoname *m* brassware
ottonare (ottóno) *tr* to coat with brass
ottóne *m* brass; **ottoni** (mus) brasses || **Ottone** *m* Otto
ottuagenà·rio -ria *adj* & *mf* **(-ri -rie)** octogenerian
ottùndere §208 *tr* (fig) to deaden; (lit) to blunt
otturare *tr* to fill; to plug; to stop; to obstruct, stop up (*e.g., a channel*) || *ref* to clog up
otturatóre *m* breechblock; (phot, mov) shutter; (mach) cutoff (*of cylinder*)
otturazióne *f* filling (*of tooth*)
ottu·so -sa *adj* obtuse; blunt
ovàia *f* ovary
ovale *adj* oval || *m* oval; oval face
ovatta *f* wadding; absorbent cotton
ovattare *tr* to pad, wad; to muffle
ovazióne *f* ovation
óve *adv* (lit) where || *conj* (lit) if; (poet) while
òvest *m* west
Ovìdio *m* Ovid
ovile *m* sheepcote, fold
ovi·no -na *adj* ovine || **ovini** *mpl* sheep
òvo *m* var of **uovo**
ovoidale *adj* egg-shaped
òvulo *m* pill shaped like an egg; (biol) ovum; (bot) ovule
ovùnque *adv* (lit) wherever; (lit) everywhere
ovvéro *conj* or; to wit
ovvìa *interj* come on!
ovviare §119 *intr*—(with *dat*) to obviate
òv·vio -via *adj* **(-vi -vie)** obvious
oziare §287 **(òzio)** *intr* to idle, loiter
ò·zio *m* **(-zi)** idleness; leisure
oziosi·tà [s] *f* (-tà) idleness
ozió·so -sa [s] *adj* idle; useless, vain
ozòno [dz] *m* ozone

P

P, p [pi] *m & f* fourteenth letter of the Italian alphabet
pacare §197 *tr* (poet) to placate
pacatézza *f* tranquillity, serenity
paca•to -ta *adj* serene, tranquil
pac•ca *f* (**-che**) slap
pacchétto *m* parcel, package; book (*of matches*); pack (*of cigarettes*)
pàcchia *f* (coll) hearty meal; (coll) godsend, windfall
pacchia•no -na *adj* boorish, uncouth ‖ *mf* boor
pacciamantura *f* mulching
pacciame *m* mulch
pac•co *m* (**-chi**) package; **pacchi postali** parcel post (*service*); **pacco dono** gift package; **pacco postale** parcel by mail
paccottìglia *f* shoddy goods, junk; trinkets
pace *f* peace; **lasciare in pace** to leave alone; **mettersi il cuore in pace** to resign oneself
pachidèr•ma *m* (**-mi**) pachyderm
pachista•no -na *adj & mf* Pakistani
paciè•re -ra *mf* peacemaker
pacificare §197 (**pacìfico**) *tr* to pacify; to appease; to mediate ‖ *ref* to make one's peace
pacifica•tóre -trice *adj* pacifying ‖ *mf* peacemaker
pacificazióne *f* pacification; appeasement
pacìfi•co -ca (**-ci -che**) *adj* peaceful, pacific; **è pacifico che** it goes without saying that ‖ *m* peaceable person ‖ **Pacifico** *adj & m* Pacific
pacifismo *m* pacifism
pacifi•sta *mf* (**-sti -ste**) pacifist
pacioccó•ne -na *mf* chubby, easygoing person
padèlla *f* frying pan; bedpan; **cadere dalla padella nella brace** to jump from the frying pan into the fire
padiglióne *m* pavilion; hunting lodge; roof (*of car*); ward (*of a hospital*); (naut) rigging, tackle; **padiglione auricolare** (anat) auricle of the ear
Pàdova *f* Padua
padre *m* father; sire; **padre di famiglia** provider; (law) head of household; **Padre Eterno** Heavenly Father
padreggiare §290 (**padréggio**) *intr* to resemble one's father
padrino *m* godfather; second (*in duel*)
padrona *f* owner, boss, mistress; **padrona di casa** lady of the house
padronale *adj* proprietary; private (*e.g., car*)
padronanza *f* command; **padronanza di sé stesso** self-control
padróne *m* owner, boss, master; **essere padrone di** + *inf* to have the right to + *inf;* **padrone di casa** landlord; **padrone di sé** cool and collected
padroneggiare §290 (**padronéggio**) *tr* to master, control
paesàg•gio *m* (**-gi**) landscape
paesaggi•sta *mf* (**-sti -ste**) landscapist
paesa•no -na *adj* country ‖ *mf* villager ‖ *m* countryman ‖ *f* countrywoman; **alla paesana** according to local tradition
paése *m* country; village; **i Paesi Bassi** the Netherlands; (hist) the Low Countries; **mandare a quel paese** to send to blazes
paesi•sta *mf* (**-sti -ste**) landscapist
paffu•to -ta *adj* chubby, plump
pa•ga *f* (**-ghe**) salary; wages; repayment; **mala paga** poor pay (*person*)
pagàbile *adj* payable
pagàia *f* paddle
pagaménto *m* payment; **pagamento alla consegna** c.o.d.
paganésimo *m* paganism
paga•no -na *adj & mf* pagan, heathen
pagare §209 *tr* to pay; to pay for; **far pagare** to charge; **pagare di egual moneta** to repay in kind; **pagare il fio per** to pay (the penalty) for; **pagare in natura** to pay in kind; **pagare salato** to pay dearly; **pagare un occhio della testa** to pay through the nose ‖ *intr* to pay
paga•tóre -trice *mf* payer
pagèlla *f* report card
pàg•gio *m* (**-gi**) page (*boy attendant*)
paghe•rò *m* (**-rò**) promissory note, I.O.U.
pàgina *f* page (*e.g., of book*)
paginatura *f* pagination
pàglia *f* straw; thatch (*for roof*); **paglia di ferro** steel wool; **paglia di legno** excelsior
pagliaccé•sco -sca *adj* (**-schi -sche**) clownish
pagliaccétto *m* rompers
pagliacciata *f* buffoonery, antics
pagliàc•cio *m* (**-ci**) clown, buffoon; **fare il pagliaccio** to clown
pa•glià•io *m* (**-gliài**) heap of straw; haystack
paglieric•cio *m* (**-ci**) straw mattress
paglieri•no -na *adj* straw-colored
pagliétta *f* skimmer, boater; steel wool; (coll) pettifogger
pagnòtta *f* loaf of bread; (coll) bread
pa•go -ga *adj* (**-ghi -ghe**) satisfied ‖ *f* see **paga**
paguro *m* (zool) hermit crab
pà•io *m* (**-ia** *fpl*) pair, couple; **è un altro paio di maniche** this is a horse of another color; **fare il paio** to match perfectly
paiòlo *m* caldron, kettle; (mil) platform
Pakistan, il Pakistan
pala *f* shovel; blade (*e.g., of turbine*); paddle (*of waterwheel*); peel (*of baker*); **pala d'altare** altarpiece
paladi•no -na *mf* champion ‖ *m* paladin; **farsi paladino di** to champion
palafitta *f* pile dwelling; piles (*to support a structure*)
palafrenière *m* groom
palafréno *m* palfrey
palan•ca *f* (**-che**) beam, board; (naut)

gangplank; copper coin; **palanche** (coll) money
palanchino *m* palanquin; (naut) pulley
palandrana *f* (joc) long, full coat
palata *f* shovelful; stroke (*of oar*); **a palate** by the bucketful
palatale *adj & f* palatal
palati•no -na *adj* palatine; (anat) palatal
palato *m* palate
palazzina *f* villa
palazzo *m* palace; large office or government building; mansion; **palazzo dello sport** sports arena; **palazzo di città** city hall; **palazzo di giustizia** courthouse
palchetti•sta (-sti -ste) *mf* (theat) boxholder || *m* person who lays floors
palchétto *m* shelf; (theat) small box; (journ) box
pal•co *m* **(-chi)** flooring; scaffold; stand, platform; (theat) box; (theat) stage
palcoscèni•co *m* **(-ci)** (theat) stage
palesare (paléso) *tr* to reveal, manifest || *ref* to show oneself
palése *adj* plain, manifest; **fare palese** to manifest, reveal
palèstra *f* gymnasium; palestra
palétta *f* small shovel, scoop; blade (*of turbine*)
palettata *f* shovelful
palétto *m* stake; bolt (*of door*)
palificazióne *f* pile work (*in the ground for foundation*); line of telephone poles
pà•lio *m* **(-lii)** embroidered cloth (*given as prize*); **metter in palio** to offer as a prize; **palio di Siena** colorful horserace at Siena
palissandro *m* Brazilian rosewood
palizzata *f* palisade; picket fence
palla *f* ball; bullet; sphere; **dar palla nera a** to blackball; **palla da cannone** cannon ball; **palla di neve** snowball; **prendere la palla al balzo** to seize the opportunity
pallabase *f* baseball
pallacanè•stro *f* **(-stro)** basketball
pallamuro *m* handball
pallanuòto *f* water polo
pallavó•lo *f* **(-lo)** volleyball
palleggiare §290 (palléggio) *tr* to toss (*e.g., a javelin*); to shift from one hand to another || *intr* (tennis) to knock a few balls; (soccer) to dribble || *ref*—**palleggiarsi la responsabilità** to shift the responsibility
pallég•gio *m* **(-gi)** (tennis) knocking back and forth; (soccer) dribbling
palliati•vo -va *adj & m* palliative
pallidézza *f* paleness
pàlli•do -da *adj* pale; faint
pallina *f* marble; small ball; **pallina antitarmica** mothball
pallino *m* little ball; (bowling) jack; bullet; **a pallini** polka-dot; **avere il pallino di** to be crazy about; **pallini** buckshot; polka dots
palloncino *m* child's balloon; Chinese lantern
pallóne *m* (soccer) ball; (aer) balloon; **pallone di sbarramento** barrage balloon; **pallone gonfiato** (fig) stuffed shirt; **pallone sonda** trial balloon
pallonétto *m* (tennis) lob
pallóre *m* pallor, paleness
pallòttola *f* pellet; ball; bullet
pallottolière *m* abacus
pallovale *f* rugby
palma *f* palm; **tenere in palma di mano** to hold in the highest esteem
palmare *adj* evident, plain
palménto *m* millstone; **mangiare a quattro palmenti** (coll) to stuff oneself eating
palméto *m* palm grove
palmìpede *adj* palmate, web-footed
palmì•zio *m* **(-zi)** palm
palmo *m* span; palm (*of hand*); foot (*measure*); **a palmo a palmo** little by little; **restare con un palmo di naso** to be disappointed
palo *m* pole (*of wood or metal*); beam; pile; (soccer, football) goal post; **fare il palo** to be on the lookout (*said of thieves*); **palo indicatore** signpost; **saltare di palo in frasca** to digress
palombaro *m* diver
palómbo *m* dogfish
palpàbile *adj* palpable
palpare *tr* to touch; to palpate
pàlpebra *f* eyelid; **battere le palpebre** to blink
palpeggiare §290 (palpéggio) *tr* to finger, touch repeatedly
palpitante *adj* throbbing; burning (*question*); fluttering (*e.g., with love*)
palpitare (pàlpito) *intr* to palpitate, pulsate; (fig) to pine
palpitazióne *f* palpitation
pàlpito *m* heartbeat; (fig) throb
pal•tò *m* **(-tò)** overcoat
paltoncino *m* child's winter coat; lady's topcoat
paludaménto *m* (joc) array, attire
palude *f* marsh, bog
paludó•so -sa [s] *adj* marshy
palustre *adj* marshy
pàmpino *m* grape leaf
panacèa *f* panacea, cure-all
pàna•ma *m* **(-ma)** Panama hat
panamé•gno -gna *adj & mf* Panamenian
panamènse *adj & mf* Panamenian
panare *tr* (culin) to bread
pan•ca *f* **(-che)** bench; **scaldare le panche** (coll) to loaf around; (coll) to waste one's time at school
pancétta *f* potbelly; bacon
panchétto *m* footstool
panchina *f* bench
pàn•cia *f* **(-ce)** belly; **a pancia all'aria** on one's back; **mangiare a crepa pancia** to stuff oneself like a pig; **mettere su pancia** to grow a potbelly; **salvar la pancia per i fichi** to not take any chances; **tenersi la pancia dalle risate** to split one's side laughing
panciata *f* belly flop
pancièra *f* bellypiece; body girth
panciòlle *m*—**in panciolle** frittering one's time away

panciòtto *m* waistcoat; vest; **panciotto a maglia** cardigan
panciu•to -ta *adj* potbellied
pàncre•as *m* (**-as**) pancreas
pandemò•nio *m* (**-ni**) pandemonium
pane *m* bread; thread (*of screw*); cake (*e.g., of butter*); loaf (*of sugar*); (metallurgy) pig; **a pane di zucchero** conic(al); **dire pane al pane e vino al vino** to call a spade a spade; **essere come pane e cacio** to be hand and glove; **essere pane per i propri denti** to be a match for s.o.; **guadagnarsi il pane** to earn one's living; **pane a cassetta** sandwich bread; **pane azzimo** unleavened bread, matzoth; **pan di Spagna** angel food cake, sponge cake; **pane integrale** graham bread; **render pan per focaccia** to give tit for tat
panegìri•co *m* (**-ci**) panegyric
panetterìa *f* bakery
panettière *m* baker
panétto *m* pat (*e.g., of butter*)
pànfilo *m* yacht
panfrutto *m* plum cake
pangrattato *m* bread crumbs
pània *f* birdlime; **cadere nella pania** to fall into the trap
pàni•co -ca (-ci -che) *adj* panicky || *m* panic
pani•co *m* (**-chi**) (bot) Italian millet
panièra *f* basket; basketful
panière *m* basket; basketful
panificazióne *f* breadmaking
panifi•cio *m* (**-ci**) bakery
panino *m* roll, bun; **panino imbottito** sandwich
panna *f* cream, heavy cream; **essere in panna** (naut) to lie to; (aut) to have a breakdown; **mettere in panna** (naut) to heave to; **panna montata** whipped cream
panne *f* (aut) breakdown; **essere in panne** (aut) to have a breakdown
pannèllo *m* linen cloth; pane; panel (*of machine*); (archit; elec) panel
pannìcolo *m* (anat) membrane, tissue
panno *m* cloth; woolen cloth; film, membrane; **bianco come un panno** as white as a ghost; **mettersi nei panni di** to put oneself in the boots of; **non stare più nei propri panni** to be beside oneself with joy; **panni** clothes; **panno verde** baize
pannòcchia *f* ear (*of corn*)
pannolino *m* linen cloth; diaper; sanitary napkin
panòplia *f* panoply
panora•ma *m* (**-mi**) panorama
panoràmi•co -ca *adj* (**-ci -che**) panoramic || *f* panoramic view; (mov) panoramic scene
pantaloncini *mpl* trunks
pantalóni *mpl* trousers; **pantaloni da donna** slacks
pantano *m* bog, quagmire
panteismo *m* pantheism
pànteon *m* pantheon
pantèra *f* panther; (slang) police car
pantòfola *f* slipper
pantomima *f* pantomine, mimicry
panzana *f* (lit) fib, lie
Pàolo *m* Paul
paonaz•zo -za *adj* & *m* purple
pa•pa *m* (**-pi**) pope; **ad ogni morte di papa** once in a blue moon; **morto un papa se ne fa un altro** nobody is indispensable
pa•pà *m* (**-pà**) daddy, papa
papàbile *adj* likely to be elected || *mf* front runner || *m* cardinal likely to be elected to the papacy
papale *adj* papal (*e.g., benediction*); Papal (*States*)
papali•no -na *adj* papal || *m* advocate of papal temporal power || *f* skullcap
paparazzo *m* freelance photographer
papato *m* papacy
papàvero *m* poppy; **alto papavero** (fig) big shot
pàpera *f* young goose; slip of the tongue; spoonerism; **fare una papera** to make a boner
pàpero *m* gander
papiro *m* papyrus
pappa *f* bread soup, farina, pap; **pappa molla** (fig) jellyfish
pappafi•co *m* (**-chi**) (naut) topgallant; (slang) goatee
pappagallo *m* parrot; bedpan; (slang) masher
pappagòr•gia *f* (**-ge**) double chin, jowl
pappare *tr* (coll) to gulp; (fig) to gobble up fraudulently
pappata•ci *m* (**-ci**) gnat
pappina *f* light pap; poultice
pàpri•ca *f* (**-che**) paprika
para *f* crepe rubber
paràbola *f* parable; (geom) parabola
parabórdo *m* (naut) fender
parabréz•za [ddzz] *m* (**-za**) windshield
paracadutare *tr* to parachute, airdrop || *ref* to parachute
paracadu•te *m* (**-te**) parachute
paracadutismo *m* parachute jumping; (sports) sky diving
paracaduti•sta *mf* (**-sti -ste**) parachutist; skydiver || *m* paratrooper
paracarro *m* spur stone
paracól•pi *m* (**-pi**) doorstop
paràcqua *m* (**paràcqua**) umbrella
paradèn•ti *m* (**-ti**) (sports) mouthpiece
paradisìa•co -ca *adj* (**-ci -che**) heavenly
paradiso *m* paradise
paradossale *adj* paradoxical
paradòsso *m* paradox
parafa *f* initials
parafan•go *m* (**-ghi**) fender, mudguard
parafare *tr* to initial
paraffina *f* paraffin
parafiam•ma *m* (**-ma**) fire-proof partition
parafrasare (**paràfraso**) *tr* to paraphrase
paràfra•si *f* (**-si**) paraphrase
parafùlmine *m* lightning rod
parafuò•co *m* (**-co**) screen, fender (*in front of fireplace*)
paràg•gio *m* (**-gi**) lineage; **paraggi** neighborhood, vicinity
paragonàbile *adj* comparable
paragonare (**paragóno**) *tr* to compare
paragóne *m* comparison; **a paragone di**

in comparison with; **mettere a paragone** to compare; **senza paragone** beyond compare
paragrafare (paràgrafo) *tr* to paragraph
paràgrafo *m* paragraph
paraguaia·no -na *adj & mf* Paraguayan
paràli·si *f* **(-si)** paralysis
paraliti·co -ca *adj & mf* **(-ci -che)** paralytic
paralizzare [ddzz] *tr* to paralyze
parallè·lo -la *adj & m* parallel || *f* (geom) parallel line; **parallele** (sports) parallel bars
paralume *m* lamp shade
paramano *m* cuff, wristband; (archit) facing brick
paraménto *s* facing (*of a wall*); (eccl) vestment
parami·ne *m* **(-ne)** (nav) paravane
paramó·sche *m* **(-sche)** fly net
paran·co *m* **(-chi)** tackle
paranin·fo -fa *mf* matchmaker
paranòi·co -ca *adj & mf* **(-ci -che)** paranoiac
paraòc·chi *m* **(-chi)** blinker (*on horse*)
parapètto *m* parapet
parapì·glia *m* **(-glia)** hubbub
parapiòg·gia *m* **(-gia)** umbrella
parare *tr* to adorn; to hang; to protect; to parry (*a thrust*); to offer; to drive (*e.g., cattle*) || *intr*—**dove va a parare?** what are you driving at? || *ref* to protect oneself; (eccl) to don the vestments; **pararsi dinanzi a** to loom up in front of
parasóle *m* parasol; (aut) sun visor
paraspal·le *m* **(-le)** (sports) shoulder pad
parassi·ta (-ti -te) *adj* parasitic || *m* parasite
parassità·rio -ria *adj* **(-ri -rie)** parasitic(al)
parassìti·co -ca *adj* **(-ci -che)** parasitic(al)
parastatale *adj* government-controlled || *mf* employee of government-controlled agency
parastin·chi *m* **(-chi)** (sports) shin guard
parata *f* fence, bar; (fencing) parry; (soccer) catch; (mil) parade; **mala parata** dangerous situation
paratìa *f* bulkhead
parato *m* hangings; **parati** hangings; (naut) bilgeways
paratóia *f* sluice gate
paraur·ti *m* **(-ti)** (aut) bumper; (rr) buffer
paravènto *m* screen
Par·ca *f* **(-che)** Fate
parcare §197 *tr & intr* to park
parcèlla *f* bill, fee, honorarium; parcel, lot (*of land*)
parcheggiare §290 **(parchéggio)** *tr & intr* to park
parchég·gio *m* **(-gi)** parking; parking lot
parchìmetro *m* parking meter
par·co -ca (-chi -che) *adj* frugal; parsimonious || *m* park; parking; parking lot; **parco dei divertimenti** amusement park
paréc·chio -chia (-chi -chie) *adj indef* a good deal of, a lot of; **parecchi** several || *pron* a good deal, a lot; **parecchi** several || **parecchio** *adv* a lot; rather
pareggiare §290 **(paréggio)** *tr* to level; to equal; to match; to balance; to recognize || *intr* (sports) to tie
pareggia·to -ta *adj* accredited (*school*)
paré̀g·gio *m* **(-gi)** leveling; matching; (sports) tie; **pareggio del bilancio** balancing of the budget
parentado *m* kinsfolk, kindred; relationship; **concludere il parentado di** to arrange for the wedding of
parènte *mf* relative; (lit) parent; **parenti** kin
parentèla *f* relationship; relations
parènte·si *f* **(-si)** parenthesis; break, interval; **fra parentesi** parenthetically; in parentheses; **parentesi quadra** bracket
parére *m* opinion, mind; advice; **a mio parere** in my opinion || §210 *intr* (ESSERE) to seem; **che Le pare?** what is your opinion?; **ma Le pare!** not at all!; **mi pare che** + *subj* it seems to me that + *ind;* I guess that + *ind;* **non Le pare?** don't you think so?; **non mi pare vero** I can't believe it
paréte *f* wall; **tra le pareti domestiche** within the four walls of the home
pargolét·to -ta *adj* (poet) infantile || *mf* (poet) child
pàrgo·lo -la *adj* (poet) infantile || *mf* (poet) child
pari *adj invar* equal, even; **camminare di pari passo** to walk at the same rate; **essere pari** to be quits; **essere pari al proprio compito** to be equal to the task; **fare un salto a piè pari** to jump with feet together; **pari pari** verbatim; **rimanere pari con** (sports) to be tied with; **saltare a piè pari** to skip (*e.g., a page*); to dodge (*a difficulty*); **trattare da pari a pari** to treat as an equal || *m* peer; **al pari di** as, like; **del pari** also; **in pari** even, leveled; **senza pari** matchless, peerless || *f*—**stare alla pari con** to be an even match for
parìa *f* peerage
pà·ria *m* **(-ria)** pariah
parificare §197 **(parìfico)** *tr* to level; to match; to accredit (*a school*); to balance
Parigi *f* Paris
parigi·no -na *adj & mf* Parisian || *f* slow-burning stove; Parisian woman; (rr) switching spur
parìglia *f* pair, couple; team (*of horses*); (cards) two of a kind; **rendere la pariglia** to give tit for tat
pariménti *adv* likewise
pari·tà *f* **(-tà)** parity
paritèti·co -ca *adj* **(-ci -che)** joint (*e.g., committee*)
parlamentare *adj* parliamentary || *mf* member of parliament || *m* (mil) envoy || *v* **(parlaménto)** *intr* to parley
parlaménto *m* parliament
parlante *adj* talking; life-like || *mf* speaker
parlantina *f* glibness

arlare *m* talk, speech; dialect || *tr* to speak (*a language*) || *intr* to speak, talk; to discuss; **chi parla?** (telp) hello!; **far parlare di sé** to be talked about; **parlare chiaro** to speak bluntly; **parlare del più e del meno** to make small talk; **parlare tra sé e sé** to talk to oneself || *ref* to talk to one another

arla·to -ta *adj* spoken; current (*speech*); talking (*movie*) || *m* talkie; (mov) sound track; (theat) dialogue || *f* speech, talk; dialect

arla·tóre -trice *mf* speaker

arlatò·rio *m* (**-ri**) visting room (*e.g., in jail*)

arlottare (**parlòtto**) *intr* to whisper in secret

armigia·no -na *adj & mf* Parmesan || *m* Parmesan cheese

arnaso *m* Parnassus (*poetry, poets*) || **il Parnaso** Mount Parnassus

aro *m*—**in un par d'ore** in a couple of hours || *adv*—**andare a paro** to keep abreast; **mettere a paro** to compare

arodìa *f* parody; **fare la parodia di** to parody

arodiare §287 (**paròdio**) *tr* to parody

aròla *f* word; speech; **avere parole con** to have words with; **buttare la mezza parola** to make an allusion; **dare la parola a** to give the floor to; **di poche parole** of few words; **domandare la parola a** to ask for the floor; **essere di parola** to keep one's word; **essere in parola con** to have dealings with; **mangiarsi la parola** to break one's word; **mangiarsi le parole** to slur one's words; **non far parola** to not breathe a word; **parola crociata** crossword puzzle; **parola d'ordine** password; **parola macedonia** acronym **parola sdrucciola** proparoxytone; **parole** lyrics; **parole di circostanza** occasional words; **prendere la parola** to take the floor; **rivolgere la parola a** to address; **venire a parole** to begin to quarrel

arolàc·cia *f* (**-ce**) dirty word; swearword

aro·làio -làia (**-lài -làie**) *adj* wordy, verbose || *mf* windbag

arolière *m* lyricist

arossismo *m* paroxysm; climax

arossìto·no -na *adj* paroxytone

arotite *f* (pathol) parotitis; **parotite epidemica** (pathol) mumps

arrici·da *mf* (**-di -de**) patricide

arrocchétto *m* parakeet; (naut) foretopsail; (naut) fore-topmast

arròcchia *f* parish

arrocchia·no -na *mf* parishioner

àrro·co *m* (**-ci**) rector, parson

arruc·ca *f* (**-che**) wig; (fig) old fogey

arsimònia *f* parsimony

arsimonió·so -sa [s] *adj* parsimonious

artàc·cia *f*—**fare una partaccia** to break one's word; **fare una partaccia a** to make a scene in front of; to rebuke loudly

arte *f* part; share; section; side; party; partiality; (theat) role; **a parte** separately; (theat) aside; **d'altra parte** on the other hand; **da parte** aside; **da parte mia** as for me; **fare le parti** to divide in shares; **gran parte di** a great deal of; **in parte** partially; **la maggior parte di** most of; **parte civile** (law) plaintiff; **parte . . . parte** some . . . some; part . . . part; **prendere in mala parte** to take amiss

partecipante *adj* participating || *mf* participant; (sports) contestant

partecipare (**partécipo**) *tr* to announce; (lit) to share in || *intr*—**partecipare a** to share in; to participate in; **partecipare di** to partake of (*e.g., the nature of an animal*)

partecipazióne *f* announcement; card; announcement (*of a wedding*); share in a business); participation (*in some action*)

partécipe *adj* sharing, partaking

parteggiare §290 (**partéggio**) *intr* to side; **parteggiare per** to side with

Partenóne *m* Parthenon

partènte *adj* departing || *mf* person departing, traveler; (sports) starter

partènza *f* departure; sailing; (sports) start; **di partenza** or **in partenza** about to leave; **partenza lanciata** (sports) running start

particèlla *f* particle

particì·pio *m* (**-pi**) participle

particolare *adj* particular; private; **in particolare** especially || *m* detail

particolareggiare §290 (**particolaréggio**) *tr* to detail

particolarismo *m* regionalism, particularism

particolarìsti·co -ca *adj* (**-ci -che**) particularistic; individualistic

particolari·tà *f* (**-tà**) peculiarity; detail

partigianerìa *f* partisanship, factionalism

partigia·no -na *adj & mf* partisan

partire §176 *tr* (lit) to divide || *v* (**parto**) *intr* to depart; (fig) to arise; **a partire da** beginning with; **far partire** to start (*e.g., a car*) || *ref* to depart, leave

parti·to -ta *adj* parted || *m* match (*in marriage*); (pol) party; **ridotto a mal partito** in bad shape; **mettere la testa a partito** to reform; **partito preso** parti pris; **prendere partito** to take sides; to make up one's mind; **trarre il miglior partito da** to make the best of || *f* panel (*e.g., of door*); lot (*of goods*); game; match; party; round (*of golf*); (com) entry; **partita di caccia** hunting party; **partita doppia** (com) double entry; **partita semplice** (com) single entry

partitura *f* (mus) score

partizióne *f* partition, division

parto *m* birth, childbirth

partorire §176 *tr* to bear, bring forth

parvènza *f* (lit) appearance

parziale *adj* partial, one-sided

parziali·tà *f* (**-tà**) partiality

pàscere §211 *tr, intr & ref* to pasture, graze

pa·scià *m* (**-scià**) pasha

pasciu·to -ta *adj* well-fed

pascolare (pàscolo) *tr & intr* to pasture
pàscolo *m* pasture
Pàsqua *f* Easter; **contento come una Pasqua** as happy as a lark; **Pasqua fiorita** Palm Sunday
pasquale *adj* paschal (*e.g., lamb*)
passàbile *adj* passable, tolerable
passàg·gio *m* **(-gi)** passage; transfer; crossing; traffic; passageway; ride; promotion; (sports) pass; **aprirsi il passaggio** to make one's way; **di passaggio** in passing; transient (*visitor*); **essere di passaggio** to be passing by; **passaggio a livello** railroad crossing; **passaggio zebrato** zebra crossing; **vietato il passaggio** no thoroughfare
passamano *m* passing from hand to hand; ribbon; (coll) railing, handrail
passante *adj* passing (*shot*) || *mf* passer-by || *m* strap
passapòrto *m* passport
passare *tr* to cross; to pass; to undergo (*a medical examination*); to move; to hand; to pay; to send (*word*); to pierce; to spend (*time*); to strain; to go over; to let have (*e.g., a slap*); to overstep (*the bounds*); **passare in rassegna** to pass in review; **passare per le armi** to execute; **passare un brutto quarto d'ora** to have a bad ten minutes; **passare un guaio** to have a hard time; **passarla a qlcu** (coll) to forgive s.o.; **passarla liscia** (coll) to get off unscathed; **passarsela bene** (coll) to have a good time || *intr* (ESSERE) to pass; to go; to filter (*said of air, light*); to move; to spoil (*said of food*); to be overcooked; to be promoted; to become; to enter; (lit) to be over; **fare passare qlcu** to let s.o. come in; **passare a nozze** to get married; **passare a seconde nozze** to remarry; **passare avanti a** to overcome; **passare di mente a** to forget, e.g., **gli è passata di mente la riunione** he forgot the meeting; **passare di moda** to go out of style; **passare in giudicato** (law) to be no longer appealable; **passare per** to pass as; **passare per il rotto della cuffia** to barely make it; **passare sopra qlco** to overlook s.th; **passi!** come in!; **passo!** (rad) over!; **passo** (cards) pass
passata *f* purée; **dare una passata a** to glance at; **dare una passata di straccio a** to rub lightly with a rag; to give a lick and a promise to; **di passata** hurriedly
passatèmpo *m* pastime; hobby
passati·sta *mf* **(-sti -ste)** traditionalist
passa·to -ta *adj* past; last; overcooked; **essere passato** (coll) to be no longer in one's prime; **passato di moda** out of fashion || *m* past; purée; **passato prossimo** present perfect; **passato remoto** preterit || *f* see **passata**
passatóia *f* runner (*rug*)
passa·tóio *m* **(-tói)** stepping stone
passeggè·ro -ra *adj* passing || *mf* passenger; **passeggero clandestino** stowaway
passeggiare §290 (passéggio) *tr* to walk (*e.g., a horse*) || *intr* to walk, promenade
passeggiata *f* promenade; walk; drive, ride; drive, road; **fare una passeggiata** to take a walk; to take a ride
passeggiatrice *f* streetwalker
passég·gio *m* **(-gi)** walk; promenade; **andare a passeggio** to take a walk
passerèlla *f* gangway; catwalk; footbridge
pàsse·ro -ra *mf* sparrow || *f*—**passera di mare** (ichth) flounder
passìbile *adj*—**passibile di** subject to, liable to
passiflòra *f* passionflower
passino *m* colander, strainer
passióne *f* passion
passivi·tà *f* **(-tà)** passivity; (com) deficit
passi·vo -va *adj* passive || *m* (com) liabilities; (com) debit side; (gram) passive
pas·so -sa *adj*—see **uva** || *m* step; passage; pass (*in mountain*); pace; footstep; pitch (*of screw, helix, etc.*); (aut) wheelbase; (phot) tread; (phot) size (*of roll*); **a grandi passi** with great strides; **andare al passo** to march in step; to walk (*said of a horse*); **a passi di gigante** by leaps and bounds; **a passo di corsa** running; **a passo d'uomo** walking, at a walk; **aprire il passo** to open the way; **di buon passo** at a good clip; **di pari passo** at the same rate; **fare quattro passi** to take a stroll; **passo doppio** paso doble; **passo d'uomo** manhole; step; **passo falso** misstep; (fig) stumble; **sbarrare il passo** to block the way; **seguire i passi di** to walk in the footsteps of || *interj* (cards) pass!; over!
pasta *f* paste; dough; **di pasta grossa** uncouth, coarse; **pasta alimentare** pasta, macaroni products; **pasta all'uovo** egg noodles; **pasta asciutta** pasta with sauce and cheese; **pasta dentifricia** toothpaste; **una pasta d'uomo** a good-natured man
pastasciutta *f* pasta with sauce and cheese
pasteggiare §290 (pastéggio) *intr* to dine
pastèllo *adj invar & m* pastel || *m* crayon
pastétta *f* batter; (coll) trickery
pastic·ca *f* **(-che)** lozenge, tablet; **pasticche per la tosse** cough drops
pasticcerìa *f* pastrymaking; pastry; pastry shop
pasticciare §128 (pastìccio) *tr & intr* to bungle; to scribble
pasticciè·re -ra *mf* pastry cook; confectioner
pasticcino *m* cookie; patty
pastìc·cio *m* **(-ci)** pie (*of meat, macaroni, etc*); bungle; mess; **cacciarsi nei pasticci** to wind up in the soup
pasticció·ne -na *mf* bungler
pastifì·cio *m* **(-ci)** spaghetti and macaroni factory
pastìglia *f* lozenge, tablet; **pastiglia per la tosse** cough drop

pastina·ca *f* (**-che**) parsnip
pa·sto -sta *adj* (archaic) fed || *m* meal; **pasto a prezzo fisso** table d'hôte || *f* see **pasta**
pastóia *f* hobble; (fig) shackle
pastóne *m* mash
pastóra *f* shepherdess
pastorale *adj* pastoral
pastóre *m* shepherd; pastor
pastorì·zio -zia (**-zi -zie**) *adj* shepherd || *f* sheep raising
pastorizzare [ddzz] *tr* to pasteurize
pastó·so -sa [s] *adj* pasty; mellow
pastrano *m* overcoat
pastura *f* pasture; hay; fodder
patac·ca *f* (**-che**) large, worthless coin; fake; (coll) medal; (coll) spot
patata *f* potato
patatràc *m* (**patatràc**) crash
patèlla *f* kneecap; (zool) limpet
patè·ma *m* (**-mi**) affliction; **patema d'animo** anxiety
patenta·to -ta *adj* licensed; (coll) well-known
patènte *adj* patent || *f* license; driver's license; **patente sanitaria** (naut) bill of health
patentino *m* (aut) permit
paterèc·cio *m* (**-ci**) whitlow
paternale *adj* (obs) paternal || *f* reprimand
paterni·tà *f* (**-tà**) paternity; authorship
patèr·no -na *adj* paternal; fatherly
paternòstro *m* Lord's Prayer; **è vero come il paternostro** it is the gospel truth
patèti·co -ca (**-ci -che**) *adj* pathetic; mawkish || *m* pathos; mawkishness
pathos *m* pathos
patibile *adj* endurable
patibolare *adj* gallows
patìbolo *m* executioner's instrument; scaffold
patiménto *m* suffering
pàtina *f* patina; coating (*on paper*); varnish; fur (*on tongue*)
patinare (**pàtino**) *tr* to gloss, glaze (*e.g., paper*)
patire §176 *tr* to suffer; (gram) to be the recipient of (*an action*) || *intr* to suffer
pati·to -ta *adj* suffering, sickly || *mf* fan || *m* boyfriend || *f* girlfriend
patòge·no -na *adj* pathogenic
patologìa *f* pathology
patològi·co -ca *adj* (**-ci -che**) pathologic(al)
patos *m* var of **pathos**
patrasso *m*—**andare a patrasso** to die; to go to ruin; **mandare a patrasso** to kill; to ruin
pàtria *f* fatherland, native land
patriar·ca *m* (**-chi**) patriarch
patriarcale *adj* patriarchal
patrigno *m* stepfather
patrimoniale *adj* patrimonial; property (*tax*); capital (*e.g., transaction*)
patrimò·nio *m* (**-ni**) patrimony; estate; fortune; (fig) heritage
pà·trio -tria (**-tri -trie**) *adj* paternal; of one's country (*e.g., love*) || *f* see **patria**
patriò·ta *mf* (**-ti -te**) patriot; (coll) fellow citizen
patriòtti·co -ca *adj* (**-ci -che**) patriotic
patriottismo *m* patriotism
patrì·zio -zia (**-zi -zie**) *adj* & *m* patrician || **Patrizio** *m* Patrick
patrocinante *adj* pleading (*lawyer*)
patrocinare *tr* to favor, sponsor; to plead
patrocina·tóre -trice *mf* defender; pleader
patrocì·nio *m* (**-ni**) support; sponsorship; (law) defense; **patrocinio gratuito** public defense
patronato *m* patronage; charitable institution, foundation; **patronato scolastico** state aid fund
patronéssa *f* sponsor; trustee (*of charitable institution*)
patròno *m* patron saint; patron; sponsor; trustee (*of charitable institution*); (law) counsel
patta *f* flap (*of garment*); bill (*of anchor*); (coll) potholder; **essere** or **far patta** to be even, tie
patteggiaménto *m* negotiation
patteggiare §290 (**pattéggio**) *tr* & *intr* to negotiate
pattinàggio *m* skating
pattinare (**pàttino**) *intr* to skate; to skid (*said of a car*)
pattina·tóio *m* (**-tói**) skating rink
pattina·tóre -trice *mf* skater
pàttino *m* skate; guide block (*of an elevator*); (aer) skid, runner; **pattino a rotelle** roller skate
pattìno *m* racing shell with outrigger floats
patto *m* pact; **a nessun patto** by no means; **a patto che** provided (that); **patto sociale** social contract; **venire a patti** to come to terms
pattùglia *f* patrol
pattugliare §280 *tr* & *intr* to patrol
pattuire §176 *tr* & *intr* to negotiate
pattui·to -ta *adj* agreed || *m* agreement
pattume *m* litter, garbage
pattumièra *f* dustpan; trash bin
patùrnie *fpl*—**avere le paturnie** (coll) to be in the dumps
paura *f* fear; **aver paura di** to be afraid of; **da far paura** frightful; **dar** or **metter paura a** to frighten; **per paura che** for fear that, lest
pauró·so -sa [s] *adj* fearful
pàusa *f* pause
pausare (**pàuso**) *tr* (lit) to interrupt || *intr* (lit) to pause
paventare (**pavènto**) *tr* & *intr* to fear
pavesare (**pavéso**) *tr* to deck with flags; to dress (*a ship*)
pavése [s] *adj*—see **zuppa** || *m* pavis (*shield*); (naut) bunting
pàvi·do -da *adj* cowardly, timid
pavimentare (**paviménto**) *tr* to pave
pavimentazióne *f* paving, pavement
paviménto *m* floor; bottom (*of sea*); paving (*of street*)
pavoncèlla *f* lapwing
pavó·ne -na or **-néssa** *mf* peacock
pavoneggiare §290 (**pavonéggio**) *ref* to swagger, strut
pazientare (**paziènto**) *intr* to be patient

pazièn̂te *adj & mf* patient
pazièn̂za *f* patience; **fare scappare la pazienza a** to drive mad; **pazienza!** too bad!
pazzé·sco -sca *adj* (**-schi -sche**) crazy, wild
pazzìa *f* madness, insanity; folly; **fare pazzie** to act like a fool
paz·zo -za *adj* crazy, insane; **andar pazzo per** to be crazy about || *mf* crazy person
pèc·ca *f* (**-che**) imperfection
peccaminó·so -sa [s] *adj* sinful
peccare §197 (**pècco**) *intr* to sin; to be lacking; to be at fault
peccato *m* sin; **che peccato!** what a pity!; **è un peccato** it's a shame
pecca·tóre -trice *mf* sinner
pécchia *f* bee
pecchióne *m* drone
péce *f* pitch; **pece greca** rosin
pechinése [s] *adj & mf* Pekingese
Pechino *f* Peking
pècora *f* sheep
peco·ràio *m* (**-rài**) shepherd
pecorèlla *f* small sheep, lamb
pecori·no -na *adj* sheep; sheepish || *m* sheep-milk cheese || *f* sheep manure
peculato *m* embezzlement, peculation
peculiare *adj* peculiar
peculiari·tà *f* (**-tà**) peculiarity
pecù·lio *m* (**-lì**) nest egg, savings; (obs) cattle
pecùnia *m* (lit) money
pecunià·rio -ria *adj* (**-ri -rie**) pecuniary
pedàg·gio *m* (**-gi**) toll
pedagogìa *f* pedagogy, pedagogics
pedagògi·co -ca *adj* (**-ci -che**) pedagogic(al)
pedagò·go -ga *mf* (**-ghi -ghe**) pedagogue
pedalare *intr* to pedal
pedale *m* trunk (*of tree*); pedal; treadle (*e.g., of sewing machine*)
pedalièra *f* pedals, pedal keyboard; (aer) rudder bar
pedalino *m* (coll) sock, short stocking
pedana *f* footrest; platform; bedside rug; hem (*of skirt*); (aut) running board; (sports) springboard
pedante *adj* pedantic || *m* pedant
pedanterìa *f* pedantry
pedanté·sco -sca *adj* (**-schi -sche**) pedantic
pedata *f* kick; footprint; tread (*of step*)
pedèstre *adj* pedestrian
pedia·tra *mf* (**-tri -tre**) pediatrician
pediatrìa *f* pediatrics
pedicu·re *mf* (**-re**) pedicure
pedicu·ro -ra *mf* var of **pedicure**
pedilù·vio *m* (**-vi**) foot bath
pedina *f* (checkers) checker, man; (chess) pawn
pedinare *tr* to shadow, follow about
pedisse·quo -qua *adj* servile
pedivèlla *f* pedal crank
pedóne *m* pedestrian; (chess) pawn
pedule *m* stocking foot || *fpl* climbing shoes, sneakers
pedùncolo *m* (anat, bot, zool) peduncle
pegamòide *f* imitation leather
pèggio *adj invar* worse; **il peggio** the worst, e.g., **il peggio ragazzo** the worst boy; || *m* worst; **andare per il peggio** to be getting worse || *f* worst; **alla peggio** if worst comes to worst; **averne la peggio** to get the worst of it || *adv* worse; worst; at worst; **peggio** + *pp* less + *pp;* least + *pp;* **tanto peggio** so much the worse
peggioraménto *m* deterioration, worsening
peggiorare (**peggióro**) *tr & intr* to worsen
peggió·re (**-ri**) *adj* worse; worst || *m* worst
pégli §4
pégno *m* pledge, pawn
pégola *f* pitch; (coll) bad luck
péi §4
pél §4
pèla·go *m* (**-ghi**) (poet) open sea; (coll) mess; **pelago di guai** sea of trouble
pelame *m* hair, coat
pelandróne *m* (coll) shirker, do-nothing
pelapata·te *m* (**-te**) potato peeler
pelare (**pélo**) *tr* to fleece; to pluck; to pare, peel; to clear (*land*); (fig) to strip; to scald, burn || *ref* (coll) to shed; to become bald
pela·to -ta *adj* peeled; hairless, bald; barren || *m* (coll) baldy; **pelati** peeled tomatoes || *f* fleecing, plucking; (joc) baldness, bald spot
pélla §4
pellàc·cia *f* (**-ce**) tough hide
pellame *m* skins, hides
pèlle *f* skin, hide; **a fior di pelle** slightly, superficially; **essere nella pelle di** to be in the boots of; **fare la pelle a** to bump off; **non stare più nella pelle** to be beside oneself with joy; **pelle di dante** buckskin; **pelle d'oca** goose skin, goose flesh; **pelle d'uovo** mull; **pelle pelle** skin-deep, superficial
pélle §4
pellegrinàg·gio *m* (**-gi**) pilgrimage
pellegrinare *intr* (lit) to go on a pilgrimage
pellegri·no -na *adj* wandering; (lit) foreign; (lit) strange, quixotic || *mf* pilgrim, traveler
pelleróssa *mf* (**pellirosse**) redskin
pelletterìa *f* leather goods; leather goods store
pellicano *m* pelican
pellicceria *f* furrier's store; furrier's trade, fur industry
pellìc·cia *f* (**-ce**) fur
pellic·ciàio -ciàia *mf* (**-ciài -ciàie**) furrier
pelliccióne *m* fur jacket
pellìcola *f* film; **pellicola in rotolo** roll film; **pellicola piana** film pack; **pellicola sonora** sound film; **pellicola vergine** unexposed film
pelliró·sa *mf* (**-se**) var of **pellerossa**
pélo *m* hair (*of beard*); pile (*of carpet*); fur; **avere pelo sul cuore** not to be easily moved; **cercare il pelo nell'uovo** to split hairs; **di primo pelo** green, inexperienced; **non avere peli sulla lingua** to not mince one's words; **pelo dell'acqua** water surface; **per un pelo** by a hair's breadth

peloponnesìa•co -ca *adj* **(-ci -che)** Peloponnesian
peló•so -sa [s] *adj* hairy; self-serving (*e.g., charity*)
péltro *m* pewter
pelùria *f* down, soft hair
péna *f* penalty; concern; compassion; pain, suffering; grief; **a mala pena** barely; **essere in pena per** to worry about; **fare pena** to arouse compassion; **pena infamante** degrading punishment; loss of civil rights; **sotto pena di** under penalty of; **valere la pena** to be worthwhile
penale *adj* penal || *f* penalty
penali•sta *mf* **(-sti -ste)** criminal lawyer
penali•tà *f* **(-tà)** penalty
penalizzare [ddzz] *tr* (sports) to penalize
penare (péno) *intr* to suffer; to find it difficult
pencolare (pèncolo) *intr* to totter; to waver
pendà•glio *m* **(-gli)** pendant; **pendaglio da forca** gallows bird
pendènte *adj* leaning; hanging; pending || *m* pendant
pendènza *f* inclination, pitch; controversy; balance; **in pendenza** pending
pèndere §123 *intr* to hang; to lean; to slope; to pitch
pendice *f* slope, declivity
pen•dìo *m* **(-dìi)** slant; slope
pèndola *f* clock
pendolare *adj* pendulum-like; commuting; transient (*tourist*) || *mf* commuter || *v* **(pèndolo)** *intr* to sway back and forth; to waver; (nav) to cruise back and forth
pèndolo *m* pendulum; clock
pèndu•lo -la *adj* (lit) hanging
penetrante *adj* penetrating, piercing
penetrare (pènetro) *tr* to penetrate, pierce || *intr* to penetrate || *ref*—**penetrarsi di** to be convinced of; to become aware of
penicillina *f* penicillin
peninsulare *adj* peninsular
penìsola *f* peninsula
penitènte *adj* & *mf* penitent
penitènza *f* penitence; punishment
penitenzià•rio -ria *adj* & *mf* **(-ri -rie)** penitentiary
pénna *f* feather; pen; peen (*of hammer*); (mus) plectrum; **penna a sfera** ball-point pen; **penna d'oca** quill; **penna stilografica** fountain pen
pennàc•chio *m* **(-chi)** panache; plume, tuft; cloud (*of smoke*)
pennaiòlo *m* hack writer
pennarèllo *m* felt-tip pen
pennellare (pennèllo) *intr* to brush; (med) to pencil
pennellata *f* brush stroke
pennèllo *m* brush; (naut) signal flag; (naut) kedge; **pennello per la barba** shaving brush; **stare a pennello** to fit to a T
pennino *m* pen; penpoint, nib
pennóne *m* flagpole; (naut) yard; (mil) pennant
pennu•to -ta *adj* feathered || **pennuti** *mpl* birds
penómbra *f* penumbra; semidarkness; faint light; **vivere in penombra** to live in obscurity
penó•so -sa [s] *adj* painful
pensàbile *adj* thinkable
pensante *adj* thinking
pensare (pènso) *tr* to think; to think of || *intr* to think; to worry; **dar da pensare a** to cause worry to, e.g., **suo figlio gli dà da pensare** his son causes him worry; **pensa ai fatti tuoi** (coll) mind your own business; **pensa alla salute** (coll) don't worry!; **pensare a** to think of; **pensare di** to plan, intend to
pensata *f* bright idea, brainstorm
pensa•tóre -trice *mf* thinker
pensièro *m* thought; **dare pensiero a** to cause worry to; **darsi pensiero per** to worry about; **essere sopra pensiero** to be absorbed in thought
pensieró•so -sa [s] *adj* thoughtful, pensive
pènsile *adj* hanging, overhead
pensilina *f* marquee
pensionaménto *m* retirement
pensionante *mf* boarder, paying guest
pensionare (pensióno) *tr* to pension
pensiona•to -ta *adj* pensioned || *mf* pensioner || *m* boarding school
pensióne *f* pension; boarding house; **in pensione** retired; **tenere a pensione** to board (*a lodger*); **vivere a pensione** to board (*said of a lodger*)
pensó•so -sa [s] *adj* thoughtful, pensive
pentàgono *m* pentagon
pentagram•ma *m* **(-mi)** (mus) staff, stave
pentàmetro *m* pentameter
Pentecòste, la Pentecost, Whitsunday
pentiménto *m* repentance; correction (*e.g., in a manuscript*); change of heart
pentire (pènto) *ref* to repent; to change one's mind; **pentirsi di** to repent
penti•to -ta *adj* repentant, repenting; **pentito e contrito** in sackcloth and ashes
péntola *f* pot, kettle; potful; **pentola a pressione** pressure cooker
penùlti•mo -ma *adj* next to the last || *f* penult
penùria *f* shortage, scarcity
penzolare (pènzolo) [dz] *intr* to dangle, hang down
penzolóni [dz] *adv* dangling
peònia *f* peony
pepaiòla *f* pepper shaker; pepper mill
pepare (pépo) *tr* to pepper
pepa•to -ta *adj* peppered; peppery
pépe *m* pepper; **pepe della Giamaica** allspice; **pepe di Caienna** red pepper, cayenne pepper
peperóne *m* (bot) pepper
pepita *f* nugget
per *prep* by; through; throughout; for; because of; to, in order to; in favor of; considering; **essere per** to be about to; **per** + *adj* or *adv* + **che** + *subj* however + *adj* or *adv* + *ind*,

e.g., **per intelligente che sia** however intelligent he is; **per caso** perchance; **per che cosa?** what for?; **per l'appunto** exactly, just; **per lungo** lengthwise; **per me** as for me; **per ora** now; **per parte mia** as for me; **per poco** hardly, scarcely, **per quanto** + *adj* or *adv* + *subj* however + *adj* or *adv* + *pres ind*, e.g., **per quanto disperatamente provi** however desperately he attempts; **per tempo** early; **per traverso** diagonally; **per via che** (coll) because; **stare per** to be about to
péra *f* pear (*fruit*); bulb, light bulb; (joc) head
peraltro *adv* besides, moreover
peranco *adv* yet
perbacco *interj* by Jove!
perbène *adj invar* nice, well brought up
percalle *m* percale
percènto *m* percent; percentage
percentuale *adj* percentage || *f* percent; commission, bonus
percepìbile *adj* collectable
percepire §176 *tr* to perceive; to receive (*a salary*)
percettìbile *adj* perceptible
percetti·vo -va *adj* perceptive
percezióne *f* perception
perché *m* why, reason; **il perché e il percome** the why and the wherefore || *pron rel* for which || *adv* why || *conj* because; so that
perciò *conj* therefore, accordingly
percóme *m & conj* wherefore
percorrènza *f* stretch, distance
percórrere §139 *tr* to cross; to cover, go through
percórso *m* crossing, distance
percòssa *f* hit, blow; contusion
percuòtere §251 *tr* to hit, beat; (fig) to shake || *intr* to strike
percussióne *f* percussion
percussóre *m* firing pin
perdènte *adj* losing || *mf* loser
pèrdere §212 *tr* to lose; to waste; to miss (*e.g., a train*); to ruin; to leak || *intr* to lose; to leak; to be inferior || *ref* to get lost; to waste one's time; **perdersi d'animo** to lose heart; **perdersi in un bicchier d'acqua** to become discouraged for nothing
perdifiato *m*—**a perdifiato** at the top of one's lungs
perdigiór·no *mf* (**-no**) idler
perdinci *interj* good Heavens!
pèrdita *f* loss; leak; **a perdita d'occhio** as far as the eye can see; **perdite** (mil) casualties
perditèm·po *mf* (**-po**) idler || *m* waste of time
perdizióne *f* perdition
perdonàbile *adj* pardonable
perdonare (**perdóno**) *tr* to forgive; to spare; **perdonare a qlcu qlco** or **perdonare qlcu di qlco** to forgive s.o. for s.th || *intr* (with *dat*) to pardon
perdóno *m* forgiveness, pardon
perdurare *intr* (ESSERE & AVERE) to last; to persevere
perdu·to -ta *adj* lost; **andar perduto** to be desperately in love; to get lost
peregrinare *intr* to wander
peregrinazióne *f* wandering
peregri·no -na *adj* far-fetched, outlandish
perènne *adj* everlasting; perennial
perentò·rio -ria *adj* (**-ri -rie**) peremptory
perequare (**perèquo**) *tr* to equalize
perequazióne *f* equalization
perfèt·to -ta *adj & m* perfect
perfezionaménto *m* improvement; (educ) specialization
perfezionare (**perfezióno**) *tr* to improve, polish up; to perfect || *ref* to improve; (educ) to specialize
perfezióne *f* perfection; **a** or **alla perfezione** to perfection
perfìdia *f* perfidy
pèrfi·do -da *adj* perfidious, treacherous; (coll) foul, nasty
perfini·re *m* (**-re**) punch line
perfino *adv* even
perforante *adj* piercing, perforating
perforare (**perfóro**) *tr* to pierce; to perforate; to punch; to bore
perfora·tóre -trice *mf* key-punch operator || *m* drill || *f* punch; drill; pneumatic drill, rock drill
perforazióne *f* perforation
pergamèna *f* parchment, vellum
pèrgamo *m* (lit) pulpit
pèrgola *f* bower, pergola
pergolato *m* arbor, pergola; grape arbor
pericolante *adj* tottering, unsafe
perìcolo *m* danger; **non c'è pericolo** don't worry
pericoló·so -sa [s] *adj* dangerous
periferìa *f* periphery; suburbs
perifèri·co -ca *adj* (**-ci -che**) peripheral
perìfra·si *f* (**-si**) periphrasis
perìmetro *m* perimeter
periodare *m* writing style || *v* (**periodo**) *intr* to turn a phrase
periòdi·co -ca (**-ci -che**) *adj* periodic(al) || *m* periodical
perìodo *m* period; age; (gram) sentence; (phys) cycle; **il periodo delle feste** holiday time
peripezìa *f* vicissitude
pèriplo *m* circumnavigation
perire §176 *intr* (ESSERE) to perish
periscò·pio *m* (**-pi**) periscope
peritale *adj* expert
peritare (**pèrito**) *ref* (lit) to hesitate
peri·to -ta *adj* expert, skilled || *mf* expert; **perito agrario** land surveyor; **perito calligrafo** handwriting expert; **perito chimico** chemist; **perito industriale** industrial engineer
peritonèo *m* peritoneum
perìzia *f* skill; survey; appraisal
periziare §287 (**perìzio**) *tr* to estimate, appraise
pèrla *f* pearl; (med) capsule
perlàce·o -a *adj* pearly
perla·to -ta *adj* pearly, smooth
perlìfe·ro -ra *adj* pearl-producing
perlina *f* bead
perlomèno *adv* at least
perlopiù *adv* mostly, generally
perlustrare *tr* to patrol
perlustrazióne *f* patrol, patrolling

permaló•so -sa [s] *adj* touchy, grouchy
permanènte *adj* permanente || *f* permanent wave
permanènza *f* permanence; stay; continuance (*in office*); duration (*of a disease*); **in permanenza** permanent (*employee*); **buona permanenza!** may your stay be happy!
permanére §235 (*pp* **permaso**) *intr* (ESSERE) to remain, stay
permeàbile *adj* permeable
permeare (**pèrmeo**) *tr* to permeate
permés•so -sa *adj* permitted, allowed; **è permesso?** may I come in? || *m* permit; (mil) pass, leave
perméttere §198 *tr* to permit, allow, let; **permette?** do you mind? || *ref* to take the liberty; to afford
permissìbile *adj* permissible
pèrmuta *f* barter; exchange
permutàbile *adj* tradable, exchangeable
permutare (**pèrmuto**) *tr* to barter; (math) to permute
pernàcchia *f* (vulg) raspberry
pernice *f* partridge
pernició•so -sa [s] *adj* pernicious || *f* pernicious malaria
pèr•nio *m* (**-ni**) var of **perno**
pèrno *m* pivot; pin; kingbolt; swivel; heart (*of the matter*); kernel (*of the story*); support (*of the family*); (mach) journal; **fare perno** to pivot
pernottare (**pernòtto**) *intr* to spend the night, stay overnight
péro *m* pear tree
però *conj* but, yet; however, nevertheless; **e però** (lit) therefore
peróne *m* fibula
peronòspora *f* downy mildew
perorare (**pèroro**) *tr & intr* to perorate; (law) to plead
perorazióne *f* peroration; (law) pleading
peròssido *m* peroxide; **perossido d'idrogeno** hydrogen peroxide
perpendicolare *adj & f* perpendicular
perpendìcolo *m* plumb line; **a perpendìcolo** perpendicularly
perpetrare (**pèrpetro** & **perpètro**) *tr* (lit) to perpetrate
perpètua *f* priest's housekeeper
perpetuare (**perpètuo**) *tr* to perpetuate
perpè•tuo -tua *adj* perpetual, life || *f* see **perpetua**
perplessi•tà *f* (**-tà**) perplexity
perplès•so -sa *adj* perplexed; (lit) ambiguous
perquisire §176 *tr* to search
perquisizióne *f* search
persecu•tóre -trice *mf* persecutor, oppressor
persecuzióne *f* persecution
perseguire (**perséguo**) *tr* to pursue; to persecute; to pester
perseguitare (**perséguito**) *tr* to persecute; to pursue; to pester
perseveranza *f* perseverance
perseverare (**persèvero**) *intr* to persevere
persia•no -na *adj* Persian || *m* Persian; Persian lamb || *f* slatted shutter; **persiana avvolgibile** Venetian blind
pèrsi•co -ca (**-ci -che**) *adj* Persian || *m* (ichth) perch; (obs) peach || *f* (coll) peach
persino *adv* var of **perfino**
persistènte *adj* persistent
persistènza *f* persistence
persìstere §114 *intr* to persist
pèr•so -sa *adj* lost, wasted; (archaic) reddish-brown; **a tempo perso** in one's spare time
persóna *f* person; **per persona** apiece; per capita; **persona di servizio** servant; **persone** people
personàg•gio *m* (**-gi**) personage; character
personale *adj* personal || *m* figure, body; personnel, staff; crew || *f* one-man show
personali•tà *f* (**-tà**) personality; personage
personificare §197 (**personìfico**) *tr* to personify
perspicace *adj* perspicacious; far-sighted
perspicàcia *f* perspicacity
perspì•cuo -cua *adj* perspicuous
persuadére §213 *tr* to persuade || *ref* to become convinced
persuasióne *f* persuasion
persuasi•vo -va *adj* persuasive; pleasing || *f* persuasiveness
persua•so -sa *adj* convinced; resigned
pertanto *conj* therefore; **non pertanto** nevertheless
pèrti•ca *f* (**-che**) perch; pole
pertinace *adj* pertinacious, persistent
pertinà•cia *f* (**-cie**) pertinacity, obstinacy
pertinènte *adj* pertinent, relevant
pertinènza *f* pertinence; competence
pertósse *f* whooping cough
pertù•gio *m* (**-gi**) hole
perturbare *tr* to perturb || *ref* to be perturbed
perturbazióne *f* perturbation; disturbance
Perù, il Peru; **valere un Perù** to be worth a king's ransom
peruvia•no -na *adj & mf* Peruvian
pervàdere §172 *tr* (lit) to pervade
pervenire §282 *intr* (ESSERE) to arrive; to come; **pervenire a** to reach
perversióne *f* perversion
perversi•tà *f* (**-tà**) perversity
pervèr•so -sa *adj* perverse; wicked
pervertiménto *m* perversion
pervertire (**pervèrto**) *tr* to pervert || *ref* to become perverted
perverti•to -ta *adj* perverted || *mf* pervert
pervicace *adj* (lit) obstinate
pervin•ca *f* (**-che**) periwinkle
pésa [s] *f* weighing; scale
pesage *m* (**pesage**) weigh-in; place for weighing in jockeys
pesalètte•re [s] *m* (**-re**) postal scale
pesante [s] *adj* heavy
pesantézza [s] *f* heaviness; weight
pesare (**péso**) [s] *tr* to weigh || *intr* to weigh; **pesare a qlcu** to weigh upon s.o.
pesa•tóre -trice [s] *mf* scale or weigh-

bridge operator; **pesatore pubblico** inspector for the department of weights and measures
pesatura [s] *f* weighing
pé•sca *f* (**-sche**) fishing; catch (*of fish*) **pesca alla traina** trawling; **pesca d'altura** deep-sea fishing; **pesca di beneficenza** benefit lottery
pè•sca *f* (**-sche**) peach
pescàg•gio *m* (**-gi** (naut) draft
pescàia *f* dam, weir
pescare §197 (**pésco**) *tr* to fish; to draw (*a card*); to dig up (*a piece of news*); to dive for (*pearls*); **pescare con la lenza** to angle for (*fish*) || *intr* to fish; (naut) to displace; **pescare con la lenza** to angle; **pescare di frodo** to poach; **pescare nel torbido** to fish in troubled waters
pesca•tóre -trice *mf* fisher; **pescatore di canna** angler; **pescatore di frodo** poacher
pésce *m* fish; (typ) omission; (coll) biceps; **a pesce** headlong; **non sapere che pesci pigliare** to not know which way to turn; **pesce d'aprile** April fool; **pesce gatto** catfish; **pesce martello** hammerhead || **Pesci** *mpl* (astr) Pisces
pesceeane *m* (**pescecani & pescicani**) shark; (fig) war profiteer
pescheréc•cio -cia (**-ci -ce**) *adj* fishing || *m* fishing boat
pescherìa *f* fish market
peschièra *f* fishpond; fishpound (*net*)
pescivéndo•lo -la *mf* fishmonger, fish dealer || *f* fishwife, fishwoman
pè•sco *m* (**-schi**) peach tree
pesi•sta [s] *m* (**-sti**) (sports) weight lifter
péso -sa [s] *adj* (coll) heavy || *m* weight; burden; bob (*of clock*); (racing) weigh-in; (sports) shot; **di peso** bodily; **peso lordo** gross weight; **peso massimo** (sports) heavyweight; **peso specifico** specific gravity; **rubare sul peso** to give short weight; **usare due pesi e due misure** to have a double standard || *f* see **pesa**
pessimismo *m* pessimism
pessimi•sta *mf* (**-sti -ste**) pessimist
pessimìsti•co -ca *adj* (**-ci -che**) pessimistic
pèssi•mo -ma *adj* very bad, very poor
pésta *f* track, footprint; **lasciar nelle peste** to leave in the lurch; **seguir le peste di** to follow in the footsteps of
pestàggio *m* beating, clubbing
pestare (**pésto**) *tr* to pound; to trample; to step on; **pestare le orme di** to follow in the footsteps of; **pestare i piedi** to stamp the feet; **pestare sodo** to beat up
pèste *f* plague, pest
pestèllo *m* pestle
pestìfe•ro -ra *adj* pestiferous
pestilènza *f* pestilence; stench
pestilenziale *adj* pestilential; pernicious
pé•sto -sta *adj* crushed; thick (*darkness*) || *m* Genoese sauce || *f* see **pesta**
pètalo *m* petal
petardo *m* petard, firecracker
petènte *mf* petitioner
petizióne *f* petition; **petizione di principio** begging the question
péto *m* wind, gas
Petrarca *m* Petrarch
petrarché•sco -sca *adj* (**-schi -sche**) Petrarchan
petrolièra *f* (naut) tanker
petrolière *adj* incendiary || *m* petroleum-industry worker; incendiary; oilman (*producer*)
petrolìfe•ro -ra *adj* oil-yielding
petrò•lio *m* (**-li**) petroleum; coal oil, kerosene
petró•so -sa [s] *adj* (lit) stony
pettegolare (**pettégolo**) *intr* to gossip
pettegolézzo [ddzz] *m* gossip, rumor
pettégo•lo -la *adj* gossipy || *mf* gossip
pettinare (**pèttino**) *tr* to comb; to card; (coll) to scold
pettinatóre *m* carder
pettinatrice *f* hairdresser; carding machine
pettinatura *f* coiffure, hairstyling
pèttine *m* comb; (zool) scallop; **a pettine** perpendicular (*parking*)
pettino *m* dickey; bib (*of an apron*); plastron
pettirósso *m* robin redbreast
pètto *m* breast, chest; bust; bosom; **a un petto** single-breasted; **avere al petto** to feed at the breast; **a due petti** or **a doppio petto** double-breasted; **stare a petto** to be equal
pettorale *adj* pectoral || *m* pectoral; breast collar (*of horse*)
pettorina *f* var of **pettino**
pettoru•to -ta *adj* strutting, haughty
petulante *adj* importunate; impertinent
petulanza *f* importunity; impertinence
petùnia *f* petunia
pèzza *f* piece (*of cloth*); diaper; patch (*in suit or tire*); bolt (*of paper or cloth*); **pezza d'appoggio** supporting document, voucher; **trattare come una pezza da piedi** to wipe one's boots on
pezza•to -ta *adj* spotted, dappled
pezzatura *f* dapple (*on a horse*); size (*e.g., of a loaf of bread*)
pezzènte *mf* beggar
pezzétto *m* little bit; scrap, snip
pèzzo *m* piece; cut (*of meat*); coin; (journ) article; **andare** or **cadere a pezzi** to fall apart; **a pezzi e bocconi** by fits and starts; **fare a pezzi** to break to pieces; to blow to bits; **pezzo di ricambio** spare part; **pezzo d'uomo** hunk of a man; **pezzo duro** brick ice cream; **pezzo forte** forte; **pezzo fuso** cast, casting; **un bel pezzo** a good while; **un pezzo grosso** a big shot
pezzuòla *f* small piece of cloth; (coll) handkerchief
phy•lum *m* (**-lum**) phylum
piacènte *adj* attractive, pleasant
piacére *m* pleasure; **a piacere** at will; **a Suo piacere** as you please; **fare piacere a** to do a favor for; to please; **per piacere** please; **piacere!**

pleased to meet you! || §214 *intr* (ESSERE) to please; to be pleasing; (with *dat*) to please, e.g., **come piace a Dio** as it pleases God; to like, e.g., **gli piace il ballo** he likes dancing
piacévole *adj* pleasant, pleasing
piacevolézza *f* pleasantness; off-color joke
pia·ga *f* (**-ghe**) sore; ulcer; wound; plague; (joc) bore; **piaga di decubito** bedsore
piagare §209 *tr* to make sore, injure
piàg·gia *f* (**-ge**) (archaic) declivity; (lit) clime, country
piaggiare §290 *tr* (lit) to flatter, blandish || *intr* (archaic) to coast
piagnistèo *m* whining
piagnó·ne -na *mf* (coll) weeper, crybaby
piagnucolare (**piagnùcolo**) *intr* to whimper, whine
piagnucoló·ne -na *mf* whimperer, crybaby
piagnucoló·so -sa [s] *adj* whimpering, whining
pialla *f* (carp) plane
piallàc·cio *m* (**-ci**) veneer
piallare *tr* (carp) to plane
piallatrice *f* (carp) planer
piallatura *f* (carp) planing
piana *f* plain; wide table
pianale *m* plain; platform; (rr) flatcar, platform car
pianeggiante *adj* plane, level
pianèlla *f* mule (*slipper*); tile
pianeròttolo *m* landing (*of stairs*); ledge
piané·ta *m* (**-ti**) planet; horoscope || *f* (eccl) chasuble
piàngere §215 *tr* to shed (*tears*); to mourn, lament; **piangere miseria** to cry poverty || *intr* to cry, weep
piangimisè·ria *mf* (**-ria**) poverty-crying penny pincher
piangiucchiare §287 *intr* to whimper
pianificare §197 (**pianìfico**) *tr* to level; (econ) to plan
pianifica·tóre -trice *mf* planner
pianino *m* (coll) barrel organ
piani·sta *mf* (**-sti -ste**) pianist
pia·no -na *adj* plane; plain, flat || *m* plain; plane; floor; plateau; plan; map; (mus) piano; **di primo piano** first-class; **in piano** horizontal; **piano di coda** (aer) tail assembly; **piano di studio** curriculum; **piano regolatore** building plan; **piano terra** ground floor; **primo piano** (phot) close-up; (theat) foreground || *f* see **piana** || **piano** *adv* slowly; softly
pianofòrte *m* piano; **pianoforte a coda** grand piano
pianòla *f* player piano
pianòro *m* plateau
pianotèr·ra *m* (**-ra**) ground floor
pianta *f* plant; sole (*of foot*); plan, map; floor plan; **di sana pianta** wholly; **in pianta stabile** permanent (*employee*); **pianta rampicante** (bot) climber
piantagióne *f* plantation
piantana *f* scaffolding
piantare *tr* to plant; to set up (*e.g., a gun emplacement*); to pitch (*a tent*); **piantala!** (slang) cut it out!; **piantare baracca e burattini** (coll) to clear out; **piantar chiodi** (coll) to go into debt; **piantare gli occhi addosso a** to stare at; **piantare in asso** to leave in the lurch || *ref* to place oneself; to abandon one another
pianta·to -ta *adj* planted; stuck; driven; **bien piantato** well-built (*person*)
pianta·tóre -trice *mf* planter
pianterréno *m* ground floor
piantito *m* (coll) floor
pianto *m* weeping, tears; sadness; (bot) sap; (coll) sight, mess
piantonare (**piantóno**) *tr* to watch, guard
piantóne *m* watchman; (mil) orderly; (mil) sentry; (bot) cutting, shoot; **piantone di guida** (aut) steering wheel column
pianura *f* plain
piastra *f* plate; piaster (*coin*)
piastrèlla *f* tile; small flat stone; bounce (*of an airplane on landing*)
piastrellaménto *m* bump, bounce (*of motorboat or airplane*)
piastrelli·sta *m* (**-sti**) tiler, tile layer
piastrina *f* or **piastrino** *m* small plate; (mil) dog tag; (biol) platelet
piatire §176 *intr* (lit) to argue; (coll) to beg insistently
piattafórma *f* platform; roadbed (*of highway*); (rr) turntable; (pol) plank; **piattaforma di lancio** launching pad
piattèllo *m* small dish; bobêche; clay pigeon
piattina *f* electric cord; metal band; (min) wagon
piattino *m* saucer
piat·to -ta *adj* flat || *m* dish, plate; pan (*of scale*); pot (*in gambling*); course (*of meal*); cover (*of book*); flat (*e.g., of blade*); **piatti** (mus) cymbals; **piatto del grammofono** turntable; **piatto del giorno** plat du jour; **piatto di lenticchie** (*Bib & fig*) mess of pottage; **piatto fondo** soup dish; **piatto forte** pièce de résistance
piàttola *f* (zool) crab louse; (coll) cockroach; (vulg) bore
piazza *f* square; plaza; crowd; market; fortress; **andare in piazza** (coll) to become bald; **da piazza** common, ordinary; **di piazza** for hire (*e.g., cab*); **fare la piazza** (com) to canvass for customers; **far piazza pulita di** to get rid of; to clean out; **mettere in piazza** to noise abroad; **piazza d'armi** parade ground; **scendere in piazza** to take to the streets
piazzafòrte *f* (**piazzefòrti**) stronghold, fortress
piazzale *m* large square, esplanade, plaza
piazzaménto *m* placement; (sports) position (*of a team*)
piazzare *tr* to place; to sell || *ref* to place; to show (*said of a racing horse*)

piazza·to -ta *adj* placed; arrived (*at a high position*) || *f* row, brawl
piazzi·sta *m* (**-sti**) salesman; traveling salesman
piazzòla *f* court, place; rest area (*off a highway*); (mil) emplacement; **piazzola di partenza** (golf) tee
pi·ca *f* (**-che**) (orn) magpie
picaré·sco -sca *adj* (**-schi -sche**) picaresque
pic·ca *f* (**-che**) pike; pique; **per picca** out of spite; **picche** (cards) spades; **rispondere picche** (fig) to answer no
piccante *adj* piquant, racy
piccare §197 *tr* (obs) to prick || *ref* to become angry; **piccarsi di** to pride oneself on
pic·chè *f* (**-chè**) piqué
picchettaménto *m* picketing
picchettare (**picchétto**) *tr* to stake out; to picket
picchétto *m* stake; picket; (mil) detail
picchiare §287 *tr* to hit, strike || *intr* to knock; to strike; to tap (*said, e.g., of rain*); (aer) to nose-dive; **picchiare in testa** (aut) to knock || *ref* to hit one another
picchiata *f* hit, blow; (aer) nose dive
picchia·tóre -trice *mf* hitter || *m* (boxing) puncher
picchierellare (**picchierèllo**) *tr & intr* to tap
picchiettare (**picchiétto**) *tr* to tap; to scrape; to speckle || *intr* to tap
picchiet·tìo *m* (**-tìi**) patter (*e.g., of rain*)
pìc·chio *m* (**-chi**) knock; (orn) woodpecker; **di picchio** all of a sudden
picchiòtto *m* knocker (*on door*)
piccinerìa *f* pettiness
picci·no -na *adj* little, tiny; petty || *mf* child; baby
picciòlo *m* stem (*e.g., of cherry*); leafstalk, petiole
piccionàia *f* dovecote; loft; attic; (theat) upper gallery
piccióne -na *mf* pigeon; **pigliare due piccioni con una fava** to hit two birds with one stone
pic·co *m* (**-chi**) peak; (naut) gaff; **andare a picco** to sink; to go to ruin; **a picco** vertically; **picco di carico** (naut) derrick
piccolézza *f* smallness; trifle
pìcco·lo -la *adj* small; low (*speed*); short (*distance*); young; petty; **da piccolo** when young; **in piccolo** on a small scale; **nel mio piccolo** with my modest abilities || *mf* child
piccóne *m* pick
piccòzza *f* mattock (*for mountain climbing*)
pidocchierìa *f* stinginess; meanness
pidòc·chio *m* (**-chi**) louse; **pidocchio rifatto** (slang) parvenu
pidocchió·so -sa [s] *adj* lousy; stingy
piè *m* (**piè**) (lit) foot; **ad ogni piè sospinto** on every occasion; **saltare a piè pari** to skip with the feet together; (fig) to skip over
piède *m* foot; leg (*of table*); stalk (*of salad*); bottom (*of column*); trunk (*of tree*); footing; **alzarsi in piedi** to stand up; **a piede libero** free; **a piedi** on foot; **a piedi nudi** barefooted; **con i piedi di piombo** cautiously; **essere in piedi** to be up and around; **fare con i piedi** to botch; **mettere un piede in fallo** to stumble; **piede di porco** crowbar; **prendere piede** to take hold; **puntare i piedi** to balk; **su due piedi** offhand; **tenere il piede in due staffe** to carry water on both shoulders
piedestallo or **piedistallo** *m* pedestal
piedritto *m* buttress
piè·ga *f* (**-ghe**) bend; crease; pleat; crimp; wrinkle; (fig) turn; **prendere una cattiva piega** to take a turn for the worse
piegare §209 (**piègo**) *tr* to bend; to wave (*hair*); to fold; to pleat; to bow (*head*) || *intr* to turn || *ref* to bow; to bend; to buckle; to yield
piega·tóre -trice *mf* folder || *f* folding machine
piegatura *f* fold, crease
pieghettare (**pieghétto**) *tr* to pleat
pieghévole *adj* folding; pliant; (fig) versatile || *m* folder
pieghevolézza *f* flexibility
piè·go *m* (**-ghi**) folder; bundle of papers
pièna *f* flood; rise (*of river*); crowd; (fig) overflow; **in piena** overflowing
pienézza *f* plenitude, fullness
piè·no -na *adj* full; solid; broad (*daylight*); full (*honors*); **a pieno** or **in pieno** to the full; **colpire nel pieno** to hit the bull's eye; **pieno di** alive with; **pieno di sé** conceited; **pieno zeppo** replete, chock-full || *m* fullness; height (*e.g., of winter*); **fare il pieno** (aut) to fill up || *f* see **piena**
pie·tà *f* (**-tà**) mercy; pity; (lit) piety
pietanza *f* main course
pietó·so -sa [s] *adj* pitiful, piteous; merciful
piètra *f* stone; rock; **pietra angolare** cornerstone; **pietra da affilare** whetstone; **pietra da sarto** French chalk; **pietra dello scandalo** source of scandal; **pietra di paragone** touchstone; **pietra focaia** flint; **pietra miliare** milestone; **piètra tombale** tombstone; **posare la prima pietra** to lay the cornerstone
pietrificare §197 (**pietrìfico**) *tr & ref* to petrify
pietrina *f* flint (*for lighter*)
pietri·sco *m* (**-schi**) rubble; (rr) ballast
Piètro *m* Peter
pietró·so -sa [s] *adj* (lit) stony
pievano *m* parish priest
piffero *m* pipe, fife
pìgia *m*—**pigia pigia** crowd, throng
pigia·ma *m* (**-ma & -mi**) pajamas
pigiare §290 *tr* to squeeze, press || *intr* to insist || *ref* to squeeze
pigia·tóre -trice *mf* presser (*of grapes*) || *f* wine press
pigiatura *f* pressing, squeezing
pigionante *mf* tenant
pigióne *f* rent, rental; **dare a pigione** to rent; to grant the possession of; **prendere a pigione** to rent; to hold for payment

pigliamó·sche *m* (-sche) flypaper; flytrap; (orn) flycatcher
pigliare §280 *tr* to take, catch; to mistake; **che Le piglia?** what's the matter with you? ‖ *ref*—**pigliarsela (con)** to get angry (at)
pì·glio *m* (-gli) hold; countenance; **dar di piglio a** to grab
pigménto *m* pigment
pigmè·o -a *adj & mf* pygmy; Pygmy
pigna *f* strainer (*at the end of a suction pipe*); bunch (*of grapes*); (bot) pine cone
pignatta *f* pot
pignò·lo -la *adj* finicky, fussy ‖ *m* pine nut
pignóne *m* pinion; embankment
pignoraménto *m* (law) seizure
pignorare (pìgnoro) *tr* (law) to seize
pigolare (pìgolo) *intr* to peep (*said, e.g., of young birds*)
pigolì·o *m* (-i) peep (*e.g., of a young bird*)
pigrìzia *f* laziness
pi·gro -gra *adj* lazy; (lit) sluggish
pila *f* pier; buttress (*of bridge*); heap; sink; font; (elec) cell; (elec) battery; **pila atomica** atomic pile
pilastro *m* pier, pillar
pillàcchera *f* mud splash; (fig) fault
pìllola *f* pill; (slang) bullet; **addolcire la pillola** to sugar-coat the pill
pilóne *m* pier; pylon
pilò·ta (-ti -te) *adj* pilot ‖ *mf* pilot; (aut) driver
pilotàg·gio *m* (-gi) piloting; steering
pilotare (pilòto) *tr* to pilot; to drive
pilotina *f* (naut) pilot boat
piluccare §197 *tr* to pluck (*e.g., grapes one by one*); to nibble, pick at; to scrounge; (lit) to consume
piménto *m* allspice
pinacotè·ca *f* (-che) picture gallery
pinéta *f* pine grove
pìngue *adj* fat; rich
pinguèdine *f* fatness, corpulence
pinguino *m* penguin
pinna *f* fin (*of fish*); flipper; (zool) pen shell (*mussel*)
pinnàcolo *m* pinnacle
pino *m* pine tree; **pino marittimo** pinaster; **pino silvestre** Scotch fir
pinòlo *m* pine nut
pinta *f* pint
pinza *f* claw (*of lobster*); **pinza emostatica** hemostat; **pinza tagliafili** wire cutter; **pinze** clippers; pliers; pincers
pinzatrice *f* stapler
pinzétte *fpl* tweezers, pliers
pinzòche·ro -ra *mf* bigot
pì·o -a *adj* (-i -e) pious; charitable ‖ **Pio** *m* Pius
piòg·gia *f* (-ge) rain
piòlo *m* peg; rung (*of ladder*); picket, stake
piombàggine *f* graphite
piombare (piómbo) *tr* to lead; to seal; to knock down; to fill (*a tooth*) ‖ *intr* to fall; to swoop down
piombatura *f* leading; filling (*of tooth*)
piombino *m* weight; seal; plumb; plumb bob
piómbo *m* lead; **a piombo** perpendicularly; **di piombo** suddenly
pioneristi·co -ca *adj* (-ci -che) pioneering
pionière *m* pioneer
piòppo *m* poplar; **pioppo tremolo** aspen
piorrèa *f* pyorrhea
piotare (piòto) *tr* to sod
piova·no -na *adj* rain (*water*)
piova·sco *m* (-schi) rain squall
piovènte *m* pitch, slope
piòvere §216 *intr* (ESSERE) to rain; to pour; to flock (*said of people*); **piovere addosso a** to rain down on; **piovere su** to flow down over ‖ *impers* (ESSERE & AVERE)—**piove** it is raining; it is leaking (*from rain*); **piove a catinelle** or **a dirotto** it is raining cats and dogs
piovigginare (piovìggina) *impers* (ESSERE & AVERE)—**pioviggina** it is drizzling
piovigginó·so -sa [s] *adj* drizzling, drizzly
piovór·no -na *adj* (lit) var of **piovoso**
piovosi·tà [s] *f* (-tà) raininess; rainfall
piovó·so -sa [s] *adj* rainy
piòvra *f* octopus; (fig) leech
pipa *f* pipe; **non valere una pipa di tabacco** to not be worth a tinker's dam
pipare *intr* to smoke a pipe
pipata *f* pipe, pipeful
pipistrèllo *m* (zool) bat
pipita *f* hangnail; (vet) pip
pira *f* (lit) pyre
piràmide *f* pyramid
pira·ta *adj invar* pirate ‖ *m* (-ti) pirate; **pirata dell'aria** skyjacker; **pirata della strada** hit-and-run driver
pirateggiare §290 **(piratéggio)** *intr* to pirate
pirateria *f* piracy; **pirateria letteraria** piracy of literary works
Pirenèi *mpl* Pyrenees
pìri·co -ca *adj* (-ci -che) fireworks; **polvere pirica** gunpowder
pirite *f* pyrite
piroétta *f* pirouette
pirò·ga *f* (-ghe) pirogue
pirolisi *f* (chem) cracking
piróne *m* (mus) tuning pin
piròscafo *m* steamship; **piroscafo da carico** (naut) freighter; **piroscafo da passeggeri** passenger ship
piroscissióne *f* (chem) cracking
pirotècni·co -ca (-ci -che) *adj* pyrotecnic ‖ *m* pyrotecnist ‖ *f* fireworks, pyrotechnics
pisciare §128 *intr* (vulg) to urinate
piscia·tóio *m* (-tói) (vulg) street urinal
piscina *f* swimming pool
pisèllo [s] *m* pea; **pisello odoroso** sweet pea
pisolare (pìsolo) *intr* (coll) to doze
pìsolo *m* (coll) nap; **schiacciare un pisolo** (coll) to take a nap
pìsside *f* (eccl) pyx; (bot) pyxidium
pista *f* track; ring (*of circus*); race track, speedway (*for car races*); ski run; (aer) runway; **pista ciclabile** bicycle trail; **pista da ballo** dance

floor; **seguire una pista** to follow a clue
pistàc•chio *m* (**-chi**) pistachio
pistillo *m* (bot) pistil
pistòla *f* pistol
pistolettata *f* pistol shot
pistolòtto *m* lecture, talking-to; theatrical peroration
pistóne *m* piston; plunger
pitagòri•co -ca *adj & m* (**-ci -che**) Pythagorean
pitale *m* (coll) chamber pot
pitoccare §197 (**pitòcco**) *intr* to beg
pitòc•co *m* (**-chi**) beggar; miser
pitóne *m* python
pìttima *f* plaster; (fig) bore
pit•tóre -trice *mf* painter
pittoré•sco -sca *adj* (**-schi -sche**) picturesque
pittòri•co -ca *adj* (**-ci -che**) pictorial
pittura *f* painting; picture; (coll) paint
pitturare *tr* to paint; to varnish || *ref* to put on make-up
più *adj invar* more; several || *m* (**più**) plus; most; **credersi da più** to believe oneself superior; **dal più al meno** about, more or less; **i più** most, the majority; **parlare del più e del meno** (coll) to make small talk || *adv* more; again; **a più non posso** to the very utmost; **in più** besides; **mai più** never again; **non poterne più** to be exhausted; **per di più** besides; **per lo più** for the most part; **più o meno** more or less; **tanto più** moreover; **tutt'al più** mostly
piuma *f* feather, plume; **piume** (fig) bed
piumàc•cio *m* (**-ci**) feather pillow
piumàg•gio *m* (**-gi**) plumage
piumino *m* down; comforter; puff, powder puff; feather duster
piuttòsto *adv* rather; somewhat
piva *f* bagpipe; **tornare con le pive nel sacco** to return bitterly disappointed
pivèllo *m* greenhorn; whippersnapper
pivière *m* (orn) plover
pizza *f* pizza; (mov) canister; (coll) bore
pizzaiò•lo -la *mf* owner of pizzeria || *m* pizza baker || *f*—**alla pizzaiola** prepared with tomato and garlic sauce
pizzardóne *m* (coll) cop, officer
pizzicàgno•lo -la *mf* grocer; sausage dealer
pizzicare §197 (**pìzzico**) *tr* to pinch; to pluck; to bite, burn; (mus) to pick, twang
pizzicherìa *f* delicatessen, grocery
pizzi•co *m* (**-chi**) pinch
pizzicóre *m* itch
pizzicòtto *m* pinch; **dar pizzicotti a** to pinch
pizzo *m* peak (*of mountain*); goatee; lace
placare §197 *tr* to placate || *ref* to calm down
plac•ca *f* (**-che**) plate; plaque; tag, badge; (elec, rad) plate; (pathol) blotch, spot
placcare §197 *tr* to plate; (sports) to tackle
plàci•do -da *adj* placid
plafond *m* (**plafond**) ceiling; (aer) ceiling; (com) top credit
pla•ga *f* (**-ghe**) (lit) clime, region
plagiare §290 *tr* to plagiarize
plagià•rio -ria (**-ri -rie**) *adj* plagiaristic || *mf* plagiarist
plà•gio *m* (**-gi**) plagiarism
planare *intr* (aer) to glide
planata *f* (aer) gliding
plàn•cia *f* (**-ce**) (naut) gangplank; (naut) bridge
planetà•rio -ria (**-ri -rie**) *adj* planetary || *m* planetarium; (aut) planetary gear
plantare *m* arch support
pla•sma *m* (**-smi**) plasma
plasmare *tr* to mold, shape
plàsti•ca *f* (**-che**) plastic art; **plastics**; plastic surgery; plastic
plasticare §197 (**plàstico**) *tr* to mold, shape; to cover with plastic
plàsti•co -ca (**-ci -che**) *adj* plastic || *m* relief map; maquette; plastic bomb || *f* see **plastica**
plastilina *f* modeling clay
plastron *m* (**plastron**) ascot
plàtano *m* plane tree; **platano americano** buttonwood tree
platèa *f* audience; (theat) orchestra; (archit) foundation
plateale *adj* obvious; plebeian
plàtina *f* (typ) platen
platinare (**plàtino**) *tr* to platinize; **to** bleach (*hair*)
plàtino *m* platinum
Platóne *m* Plato
plaudènte *adj* enthusiastic
plàudere (**plàudo**) & **plaudire** (**plàudo**) *intr* to applaud; (with *dat*) to applaud, e.g., **plaudere alla generosità** to applaud the generosity
plausìbile *adj* plausible
plàuso *m* (lit) applause, praise
plebàglia *f* rabble
plèbe *f* populace; (lit) crowd
plebè•o -a *adj & mf* plebeian
plebiscito *m* plebiscite
plenà•rio -ria *adj* (**-ri -rie**) plenary
plenilù•nio *m* (**-ni**) full moon
plenipotenzià•rio -ria *adj & m* (**-ri -rie**) plenipotentiary
plètora *f* plethora
plèttro *m* (mus) pick, plectrum
pleurite *f* (pathol) pleurisy
pli•co *m* (**-chi**) sealed document; bundle of papers; **in plico a parte** or **in plico separato** under separate cover
plotóne *m* platoon; **plotone d'esecuzione** firing squad
plùmbe•o -a *adj* lead, leaden
plurale *adj & m* plural; **al plurale** in the plural
plurilìngue *adj* multilingual
plurimotóre *adj* multimotored || *m* multimotor
pluristàdio *adj invar* (rok) multistage
plusvalènza *f* unearned increment
plusvalóre *m;* surplus value (*in Marxist economics*)
Plutarco *m* Plutarch
plutocrazìa *f* plutocracy
Plutóne *m* Pluto

plutònio *m* plutonium
pluviale *adj* rain || *m* waterspout
pneumàti•co -ca (-ci -che) *adj* pneumatic, air || *m* tire; **pneumatico da neve** snow tire
po' *m* see **poco**
pochézza *f* lack, scarcity
pò•co -ca (-chi -che) *adj* little; short (*distance*); poor (*health*; *memory*); (*with collective nouns*) few, e.g., **poca gente** few people; (*with plural nouns*) a few, e.g., **fra pochi mesi** in a few months; (*with plural nouns having singular meaning in English*) little, e.g., **pochi quattrini** little money || *m invar* little; short distance; short time; **a ogni poco** often; **da poco** a little while ago; of no account; **da un bel po'** quite a while; quite a while ago; **fra poco** in a little while; **manca poco a** it won't be long till; **manca poco che** (*e.g., il ragazzo*) **non** + *subj* (e.g., the boy) almost + *ind;* **per poco non** almost; **poco di buono** good-for-nothing; **poco fa** a little while ago; **saper di poco** to taste flat; **un poco di** or **un po' di** a little || *f*—**poca di buono** hussy || **poco** *adv* little; **poco bene** poorly; **poco dopo** shortly after; **poco male** not too poorly
podagra *f* gout
podére *m* farm, country property
poderó•so -sa [s] *adj* powerful
pode•stà *m* **(-stà)** (hist) mayor; (hist) podesta
podia•tra *mf* **(-tri -tre)** chiropodist
pò•dio *m* **(-di)** podium; platform; (archit) base
podismo *m* foot racing
podi•sta *mf* **(-sti -ste)** foot racer
poè•ma *m* **(-mi)** long poem
poesìa *f* poetry; poem
poè•ta *m* **(-ti)** poet
poetéssa *f* poetess
poèti•co -ca (-ci -che) *adj* poetic(al) || *f* poetics
pòg•gia *f* **(-ge)** leeward
poggiare §290 **(pòggio)** *tr* to lean || *intr* to be based; (mil) to move; (naut) to sail before the wind; (archaic) to rise
poggiatè•sta *m* **(-sta)** headrest; (aut) head restrainer
pòg•gio *m* **(-gi)** hillock, knoll
poggiòlo *m* balcony
pòi *m* future || *adv* then; later; **a poi** until later; **poi dopo** later on
poiana *f* buzzard
poiché *conj* since, as; (lit) after
pòker *m* poker (*game*); four of a kind; **poker di re** four kings
polac•co -ca (-chi -che) *adj* Polish || *mf* Pole || *f* (mus) polonaise
polare *adj* pole, polar
polarizzare [ddzz] *tr* to polarize
pòl•ca *f* **(-che)** polka
polèmi•co -ca (-ci -che) *adj* polemical || *f* polemics
polemizzare [ddzz] *intr* to engage in polemics
polèna *f* (naut) figurehead
polènta *f* corn mush
polentina *f* poultice
poliambulanza *f* clinic, emergency ward
policlìni•co *m* **(-ci)** polyclinic
polifonìa *f* polyphony
polìga•mo -ma *adj* polygamous || *m* polygamist
poliglòt•ta *adj & mf* **(-ti -te)** polyglot
poliglòt•to -ta *adj & mf* polyglot
polìgono *m* polygon; **poligono di tiro** shooting range
polìgrafo *m* author skilled in many subjects; multigraph
polinesia•no -na *adj & mf* Polynesian
polinò•mio *m* **(-mi)** polynomial
pòlio *f* (coll) polio
poliomielite *f* poliomielitis, infantile paralysis
pòlipo *m* (pathol, zool) polyp
polisìlla•bo -ba *adj* polysyllabic || *m* polysyllable
poli•sta *m* **(-sti)** polo player
politea•ma *m* **(-mi)** theater
politècni•co -ca (-ci -che) *adj* polytechnic || *m* polytechnic institute
politei•sta (-sti -ste) *adj* polytheistic || *mf* polytheist
politeìsti•co -ca *adj* **(-ci -che)** polytheistic
politézza *f* smoothness
polìti•ca *f* **(-che)** politics; policy
politicante *mf* petty politician
polìti•co -ca (-ci -che) *adj* political || *m* politician || *f* see **politica**
polìtti•co *m* **(-ci)** polyptych
polizìa *f* police; **polizia sanitaria** health department; **polizia stradale** highway patrol; **polizia tributaria** income-tax investigation department
polizié•sco -sca *adj* **(-schi -sche)** police (*car*); detective (*story*)
poliziòtto *adj masc* police (*dog*) || *m* policeman; detective; **poliziotto in borghese** plain-clothes man
pòlizza *f* policy; ticket (*e.g., of pawnbroker*); **polizza di carico** bill of lading
pólla *f* spring (*of water*)
pol•làio *m* **(-lài)** chicken coop
pollaiò•lo -la *mf* chicken dealer
pollame *m* poultry
pollastra *f* pullet; (coll) chick
pollerìa *f* poultry shop
pòllice *m* thumb; big toe; inch
pollicoltura *f* poultry raising
pòlline *m* pollen
pollivéndo•lo -la *mf* poultry dealer
póllo *m* chicken; (fig) sucker; **conoscere i propri polli** (fig) to know one's onions; **pollo d'India** turkey
pollóne *m* (bot) shoot; (fig) offspring
polmóne *m* lung; **a pieni polmoni** at the top of one lungs; **polmone d'acciaio** iron lung
polmonite *f* pneumonia
pòlo *m* pole; polo shirt; (sports) polo
Polònia, la Poland
pólpa *f* meat; pulp; flesh (*of fruit*); (fig) gist; **in polpe** (hist) in knee breeches
polpàc•cio *m* **(-ci)** calf (*of leg*); cut of meat; ball of thumb

polpastrèllo *m* finger tip
polpétta *f* meat ball; meat patty, cutlet
polpettóne *m* meat loaf; (fig) hash
pólpo *m* (zool) octopus
polpó•so -sa [s] *adj* pulpy, fleshy
polpu•to -ta *adj* meaty
polsino *m* cuff
pólso *m* pulse; wrist; cuff, wristband; strong hand, energy; **di polso** energetic
poltiglia *f* mash; slush
poltrire §176 *intr* to idle; to loll in bed
poltróna *f* armchair; (theat) orchestra seat; **poltrona a orecchioni** wing chair; **poltrona a sdraio** chaise longue; **poltrona letto** day bed
poltroncina *f* parquet-circle seat
poltró•ne -na *mf* lazybones, sluggard || *f* see **poltrona**
poltroneria *f* laziness
poltronissima *f* (theat) first-row seat
pólvere *f* dust; powder; **in polvere** powdered; **polvere da sparo** gunpowder; **polvere di stelle** stardust; **polvere nera** or **pirica** gunpowder; **polveri** gunpowder
polverièra *f* powder magazine; (fig) tinderbox, trouble spot
polverifi•cio *m* (**-ci**) powder works
polverina *f* (pharm) powder
polverino *m* pounce, sand
polverizzare [ddzz] *tr* to crush, powder; to atomize; to pulverize
polverizza•to -ta [ddzz] *adj* powdered (*sugar*)
polverizzatóre [ddzz] *m* atomizer
polveróne *m* dust cloud
polveró•so -sa [s] *adj* dusty; powdery (*snow*)
pomata *f* ointment; pomade
pomella•to -ta *adj* dapple-grey
pomèllo *m* cheek; cheekbone; pommel, knob
pomeridia•no -na *adj* afternoon, P.M.
pomerig•gio *m* (**-gi**) afternoon
pomiciare §128 (**pómicio**) *tr* to pumice || *intr* (slang) to spoon
pomicióne *m* (slang) spooner
pomidòro *m* var of **pomodoro**
pómo *m* apple; knob; pommel (*of saddle*); **pomo della discordia** apple of discord; **pomo di Adamo** Adam's apple; **pomo di terra** potato
pomodòro *m* tomato; **pomodoro di mare** (zool) sea anemone
pómolo *m* (coll) knob, handle
pómpa *f* pump; pomp; state; **in pompa magna** all dressed up; **pompa aspirante** suction pump; **pompa premente** force pump; see **imprenditore** and **impresa**
pompare (**pómpo**) *tr* to pump; to pump up
pompèlmo *m* grapefruit
pompière *m* fireman
pompó•so -sa [s] *adj* pompous
pòn•ce *m* (**-ci**) punch
ponderare (**pòndero**) *tr* to weigh, ponder; to weight || *intr* to think it over
pondera•to -ta *adj* considerate, careful
ponderó•so -sa [s] *adj* ponderous
ponènte *m* west; west wind; West; West Wind
pónte *m* bridge; metal scaffolding; (aut) axle; (naut) deck; **fare il ponte** to take the day off between two holidays; **fare ponti d'oro a** to offer a good way out to; **ponte aereo** airlift; **ponte delle segnalazioni** (rr) gantry; **ponte di chiatte** pontoon bridge; **ponte di comando** (naut) bridge; **ponte di volo** flight deck; **ponte levatoio** drawbridge; **ponte radio** radio communication; **ponte sospeso** suspension bridge
pontéfice *m* pontiff; (hist) pontifex
pontéggio *m* scaffolding
ponticèllo *m* small bridge; nosepiece (*of eyeglasses*); (mus) bridge
pontière *m* (mil) engineer
pontificale *adj* pontifical || *m* pontifical mass
pontifi•cio -cia *adj* (**-ci -cie**) papal
pontile *m* pier
pontóne *m* pontoon, barge
ponzare (**pónzo**) *tr* (coll) to strain to accomplish || *intr* (coll) to rack one's brains
popeli•ne *f* (**-ne**) broadcloth
popola•no -na *adj* popular || *mf* commoner
popolare *adj* popular || *v* (**pòpolo**) *tr* to people, populate || *ref* to be inhabited
popolarità *f* popularity
popola•to -ta *adj* peopled; crowded
popolazióne *f* population
pòpolo *m* people; crowd; **popolo grasso** (hist) rich bourgeoisie; **popolo minuto** (hist) artisans, common people
popoló•so -sa [s] *adj* populous
popóne *m* (coll) melon
póppa *f* breast; (naut) stern; (lit) ship; **a poppa** astern, aft
poppante *adj* & *mf* suckling
poppare (**póppo**) *tr* to suckle
poppa•tóio *m* (**-tói**) nursing bottle
poppavia *f*—**a poppavia** astern, aft
pòr•ca *f* (**-che**) ridge (*between furrows*); sow
porcacció•ne -na *m* cad, rake || *f* slut
por•càio *m* (**-càì**) swineherd; pigsty
porcellana *f* porcelain, china; (bot) purslane
porcellino *m* piggy; **porcellino d'India** guinea pig
porcheria *f* dirt; (coll) dirty trick; (coll) botch
porchétta *f* roast suckling pig
porcile *m* pigsty
porci•no -na *adj* pig || *m* (bot) boletus
pòr•co -ca *mf* (**-ci -che**) pig, hog, swine; pork; **porco mondo!** (slang) heck! || *f* see **porca**
porcospino *m* porcupine
pòrfido *m* porphyry
pòrgere §217 *tr* to hand, offer; to relate; **porgere l'orecchio** to lend an ear || *intr* to declaim || *ref* to appear, show up
pornografia *f* pornography
pòro *m* pore
poró•so -sa [s] *adj* porous
pórpora *f* purple

porpora·to -ta *adj* purple || *m* purple; cardinal
porpori·no -na *adj* purple
pórre §218 *tr* to put; to repose (*trust*); to set (*a limit; one's foot*); to lay (*a stone*); to pose (*a question*); to pay (*attention*); to suppose; to advance (*the candidacy*); **porre gli occhi addosso a** to lay one's eyes on; **porre in dubbio** to cast doubt on; **porre mano a** to set to work at; **porre termine a** to put an end to; **posto che** since, provided || *ref* to place oneself; **porsi in cammino** to set out or forth; **porsi in salvo** to reach safety
pòrro *m* wart; (bot) leek
pòrta *f* door; gate; (cricket) wicket; (sports) goal; **di porta in porta** door-to-door; **fuori porta** outside the city limits; **mettere alla porta** to dismiss, fire; **porta di servizio** delivery entrance; **porta scorrevole** sliding door; **porta stagna** (naut; theat) safety door
portabagà·gli *m* (**-gli**) porter; baggage rack
portabandiè·ra *m* (**-ra**) standard-bearer
portàbile *adj* portable
portàbi·ti *m* (**-ti**) coat hanger
portabottì·glie *m* (**-glie**) bottle rack
portacar·te *adj invar & m* (**-te**) folder
portacati·no *adj invar* washstand-supporting || *m* (**-no**) washstand
portacéne·re *m* (**-re**) ashtray
portachia·vi *m* (**-vi**) key ring
portacì·pria *m* (**-pria**) compact
portadi·schi *m* (**-schi**) record cabinet, record rack; turntable
portadól·ci *m* (**-ci**) candy dish
portaère·i *f* (**-i**) aircraft carrier
portaferi·ti *m* (**-ti**) (mil) stretcher bearer
portafinèstra *f* (**portefinèstre**) French window
portafió·ri *m* (**-ri**) flower vase
portafò·gli *m* (**-gli**) or **portafò·glio** *m* (**-gli**) billfold, wallet; pocketbook; portfolio
portafortu·na *m* (**-na**) charm, amulet
portafrut·ta *m* (**-ta**) fruit dish
portafusìbi·li *m* (**-li**) fuse box
portagiò·ie *m* (**-ie**) jewel box
portaimmondì·zie *m* (**-zie**) trash can, garbage can
portainsé·gna *m* (**-gna**) standard-bearer
portalàmpa·da *m* (**-da**) (elec) socket
portale *m* portal
portalètte·re (**-re**) *mf* letter carrier || *m* postman, mailman
portamaz·ze *m* (**-ze**) caddie
portaménto *m* posture; gait; (fig) behavior
portami·na *m* (**-na**) mechanical pencil
portamìssi·li (**-li**) *adj invar* missile-carrying || *m* missile carrier
portamoné·te *m* (**-te**) purse
portamùsi·ca *m* (**-ca**) music stand
portante *adj* carrying; (archit) weight-bearing; (aer) lifting; (rad) carrier || *m* amble
portantina *f* sedan chair; stretcher
portantino *m* bearer (*of sedan chair*); stretcher bearer
portanza *f* (archit) capacity; (aer) lift
portaombrèl·li *m* (**-li**) umbrella stand
portaórdi·ni *m* (**-ni**) (mil) messenger
portapac·chi *m* (**-chi**) parcel delivery man; basket (*on bicycle*)
portapén·ne *m* (**-ne**) penholder
portapiat·ti *m* (**-ti**) dish rack
portaposa·te [s] *m* (**-te**) silverware chest
portapran·zi [dz] *m* (**-zi**) dinner pail
portaraz·zi (**-zi**) [ddzz] *adj invar* missile-carrying || *m* missile carrier
portare (**pòrto**) *tr* to carry; to bring; to take; to carry along; to lead; to herald; to praise; to wear; to drive (*car*); to run (*a candidate*); to adduce; to nurture (*hatred*); (aut) to hold (*e.g., five people*); **portare a conoscenza di** to let know; **portare avanti** to carry forward; **portare in alto** to lift; **portare via** to steal; to take away || *intr* to carry (*said of a gun*) || *ref* to move; to behave; to be (*a candidate*)
portaritrat·ti *m* (**-ti**) picture frame
portasapó·ne *m* (**-ne**) soap dish
portasigarét·te *m* (**-te**) cigarette case
portasìga·ri *m* (**-ri**) cigar case; humidor
portaspil·li *m* (**-li**) pincushion
portata *f* course (*of a meal*); capacity; flow (*of river*); compass (*of voice*); range (*of voice or gun*); importance; (naut) burden; (naut) tonnage; **a portata di mano** within reach; **a portata di voce** within call, within earshot
portatèsse·re *m* (**-re**) card case
portàtile *adj* portable
porta·to -ta *adj* worn; **portato a** leaning toward || *m* result, effect || *f* see **portata**
porta·tóre -trice *mf* bearer
portatovagliòlo *m* napkin ring
portauò·vo *m* (**-vo**) eggcup
portavó·ce *m* (**-ce**) megaphone; (fig) mouthpiece
porte-enfant *m* (**porte-enfant**) baby bunting
portèllo *m* wicket; leaf (*of cabinet door*); (naut) porthole
portènto *m* portent
portica·to -ta *adj* arcaded || *m* arcade
pòrti·co *m* (**-ci**) portico, arcade, colonnade; shed
portiè·re -ra *mf* concierge || *m* janitor, doorman; (sports) goalkeeper || *f* portiere (*in church door*); (aut) door
porti·nàio -nàia (**-nài -nàie**) *adj* door, door-keeping || *mf* doorkeeper, concierge
portinerìa *f* janitor's quarters
pòrto *m* port, harbor; transportation charge; port wine; goal; **condurre a buon porto** to carry to fruition; **franco di porto** prepaid, postpaid; **porto a carico del mittente** postage prepaid; **porto assegnato** charges to be paid by addressee; **porto d'armi** permit to carry arms; **porto franco** free port
Portogallo, il Portugal
portoghése [s] *adj & mf* Portuguese;

fare il portoghese (theat) to crash the gate
portóne *m* portal
portorica·no -na *adj & mf* Puerto Rican
Portorico *m* Puerto Rico
portuale *adj* port, harbor || *m* dock worker, longshoreman
porzióne *f* portion
pòsa [s] *f* laying (*e.g., of cornerstone*); posing (*for portrait*); posture, affectation, pose; dregs; (phot) exposure; (lit) rest; **senza posa** relentless; relentlessly
posami·ne (-ne) [s] *adj invar* minelaying || *f* minelayer
posare [s] **(pòso)** *tr* to lay, put down || *intr* to lie; to settle; to pose; **posare a** to pose as || *ref* to settle; to alight; (lit) to rest
posata [s] *f* cover, place (*at table*); table utensil (*knife, fork or spoon*); **posate** knife, fork and spoon
posaterìa [s] *f* service (*of knives, forks, and spoons*)
posa·to -ta [s] *adj* sedate, quiet; placed || *f* see **posata**
posa·tóre -trice [s] *mf* poseur || *m* layer, installer (*of cables or pipes*)
pòscia *adv* then, afterwards; **poscia che** after
poscritto *m* postscript
posdatare *tr* var of **postdatare**
posdomani *adv* (lit) day after tomorrow
positivaménte *adv* for sure
positi·vo -va *adj* positive || *f* (phot) positive, print
posizióne *f* position; status; (fig) stand
pospórre §218 *tr* to put off, postpone; to put last; **posporre qlco a qlco** to put or place s.th after s.th
pòssa *f* (lit) strength, vigor
possanza *f* (lit) power
possedére §252 *tr* to possess; to own; to master (*a language*); **essere posseduto da** to be enthralled with; to be possessed by
possediménto *m* possession, property
posseditrice *f* owner, possessor
possènte *adj* (lit) powerful
possessióne *f* possession
possessi·vo -va *adj* possessive
possèsso *m* possession
possessóre *m* owner, possessor
possìbile *adj* possible || *m*—**fare il possibile** to do one's best
possibili·sta (-sti -ste) *adj* pragmatically flexible || *mf* pragmatically flexible person, possibilist
possibili·tà *f* **(-tà)** possibility; opportunity; **possibilità** *fpl* means
possidènte *mf* proprietor, owner; **possidente terriero** landowner
pòsta *f* post; mail; post office; box (*in stable*); ambush; bet; **a giro di posta** by return mail; **a posta** on purpose; **darsi la posta** to set up an appointment; **fare la posta a** to have under surveillance; **fermo in posta** general delivery; **levare la posta** to pick up the mail; **posta aerea** air mail; **posta dei lettori** (journ) letters to the editor; **poste** postal department
pósta *f* (archaic) planting; (archaic) footprint
postagi·ro *m* **(-ro & -ri)** postal transfer of funds
postale *adj* postal, mail || *m* mail; mail train (boat, bus, or plane)
postare (pòsto) *tr* (mil) to post || *ref* (mil) to take a position
postazióne *f* (mil) emplacement
postbèlli·co -ca *adj* **(-ci -che)** postwar
postbruciatóre *m* (aer) afterburner
postdatare *tr* to postdate
posteggiare §290 **(postéggio)** *tr & intr* to park
posteggia·tóre -trice *mf* parking-lot attendant; customer (*in a parking lot*); (coll) outdoor merchant; **posteggiatore abusivo** parking violator
postég·gio *m* **(-gi)** parking lot; stand (*in outdoor market*); **posteggio di tassì** cabstand
posterióre *adj* back; subsequent, later
posteri·tà *f* **(-tà)** posterity
pòste·ro -ra *adj* later, subsequent || **posteri** *mpl* posterity, descendants
postìc·cio -cia (-ci -ce) *adj* artificial; false (*e.g., tooth*); temporary || *m* wiglet, ponytail || *f* row of trees
posticipare (postìcipo) *tr* to postpone
posticipa·to -ta *adj* deferred
postièrla *f* postern
postiglióne *m* postilion
postilla *f* marginal note
postillare *tr* to annotate
posti·no -na *mf* letter carrier || *m* mailman, postman
pósto *m* place; room; seat; job, position; spot; (mil) post; **a posto** in order; orderly; **al posto di** instead of; **essere a posto** to have a good job; **mettere a posto** to find a good job for; (coll) to keep quiet; **quel posto** (coll) seat of the pants; (coll) toilet; **posto a sedere** seat; **posto di blocco** road block; (rr) signal tower; **posto di guardia** (mil) guardhouse; **posto di medicazione** or **di pronto soccorso** first-aid station; **posto in piedi** standing room; **posto letto** bed (*e.g., in hospital*); **posto telefonico pubblico** public telephone, pay station; **rimettere a posto** to fix, repair; **saper stare al proprio posto** to know one's place; **sul posto** on the spot
postrè·mo -ma *adj* (lit) last
postrìbolo *m* (lit) brothel
postulante *adj* petitioning || *mf* petitioner, applicant; (eccl) postulant
postulare (pòstulo) *tr* to postulate
pòstu·mo -ma *adj* posthumous || **postumi** *mpl* sequel; (pathol) sequelae
potàbile *adj* drinkable
potare (póto) *tr* to trim, prune
potassa *f* potash
potàssio *m* potassium
potatura *f* pruning, polling
potentato *m* (lit) potentate
potènte *adj* powerful; influential || **i potenti** the powers that be
potènza *f* power, might; (math) power; **all'ennesima potenza** (math) to the nth power; (fig) to the nth degree; **in potenza** potential; potentially

potenziale *adj & m* potential
potére *m* ability; authority, power; **in potere di** in the hands of; **potere d'acquisto** purchasing power; **potere esecutivo** executive; **potere giudiziario** judiciary; **quarto potere** fourth estate || §219 *intr* to be powerful; **non ne posso più** I am at the end of my rope; **si può?** may I come in? || *aux* (ESSERE & AVERE) to be able; **non posso fare a meno di** + *inf* I can't help + *ger;* **non potere fare a meno di** to not be able to do without; **posso,** etc. I can; I may, etc.; **potrei,** etc. I could; I might, etc.
pote·stà *f* (-stà) power, authority
poveràc·cio -cia *mf* (-ci -ce) poor guy, poor soul
pòve·ro -ra *adj* poor; needy, wretched; lean (*gasoline mixture*); **povero in canna** as poor as a church mouse || *mf* pauper; beggar; poor devil || **i poveri** the poor
pover·tà *f* (-tà) poverty; paucity, scantiness
poveruòmo *m* (used only in *sg*) poor devil
pozióne *f* potion, brew
pózza *f* pool, puddle
pozzànghera *f* puddle
pozzétto *m* small well; manhole; forecastle (*in small boat*)
pózzo *m* well; shaft; **pozzo artesiano** artesian well; **pozzo delle catene** (naut) chain locker; **pozzo di scienza** fountain of knowledge; **pozzo di ventilazione** (min) air shaft; **pozzo nero** cesspool; **pozzo petrolifero** oil well; **pozzo trivellato** deep well; **un pozzo di** (fig) a barrel of
Praga *f* Prague
prammàti·co -ca (-ci -che) *adj* pragmatic || *f* social custom; **di prammatica** obligatory, de rigueur
pranzare [dz] *intr* to dine
pranzo [dz] *m* dinner; **dopo pranzo** afternoon
pras·si *f* (-si) practice, praxis
praterìa *f* prairie
pràti·ca *f* (-che) practice; knowledge; matter; file, dossier; business; experience; (naut) pratique; **aver pratica con** to be familiar with (*people*); **aver pratica di** to be familiar with (*things*); **far pratica** to be an apprentice; **fare le pratiche** to make an application; **in pratica** practically; **insabbiare una pratica** to pigeonhole a matter
praticàbile *adj* practicable; passable || *m* (theat) raised platform
praticante *adj* practicing || *mf* apprentice; novice; churchgoer
praticare §197 **(pràtico)** *tr* to practice; to frequent; to be familiar with; to make (*e.g., a hole*); to grant (*a discount*) || *intr* to practice; **praticare in** to frequent
pratici·tà *f* (-tà) utility; practicality
pràti·co -ca (-ci -che) *adj* practical; experienced || *f* see **pratica**
praticó·ne -na *mf* (pej) old hand
prato *m* meadow
pratolina *f* daisy
pra·vo -va *adj* (lit) wicked
preaccennare (preaccénno) *tr* to mention in advance
preaccenna·to -ta *adj* aforementioned
preallarme *m* early warning
Prealpi *fpl* foothills of the Alps
preàmbolo *m* preamble
preannunziare §287 **(preannùnzio)** *tr* to foretell, forebode
preannùn·zio *m* (-zi) advance information; foreboding
preautunnale *adj* pre-fall
preavvertire (preavvèrto) *tr* to forewarn
preavvisare *tr* to give advance notice to; to forewarn
preavviso *m* forewarning; notification of dismissal
prebèlli·co -ca *adj* (-ci -che) prewar
prebènda *f* prebend; (fig) easy money, sinecure
precà·rio -ria *adj* (-ri -rie) precarious
precauzióne *f* precaution
precedènte *adj* preceding || *m* precedent; **precedenti** background; **precedenti penali** previous offenses, record
precedènza *f* precedence; (aut) right of way; (fig) priority
precèdere §123 *tr & intr* to precede
precettare (precètto) *tr* (mil) to call back from furlough
precètto *m* precept; (eccl) obligation
precettóre *m* tutor
precipitare (precìpito) *tr* to precipitate; to hasten; (chem) to precipitate || *intr* (ESSERE) to fall; to fail; to rush (*said of events*); (chem) to precipitate || *ref* to rush
precipitó·so -sa [s] *adj* hasty, headlong
precipì·zio *m* (-zi) precipice, cliff; ruin; **a precipizio** headlong
precì·puo -pua *adj* chief, principal, primary
precisare *tr* to say exactly, specify, clarify; to fix (*a date*)
precisazióne *f* clarification
precisióne *f* precision
preci·so -sa *adj* precise, exact; punctilious; identical, same; sharp, e.g., **alle sette precise** at seven o'clock sharp
precla·ro -ra *adj* (lit) illustrious
preclùdere §105 *tr* to preclude
precòce *adj* precocious, premature
preconcèt·to -ta *adj* preconceived || *m* preconception; prejudice, bias
preconizzare [ddzz] *tr* to foretell, forecast; (eccl) to preconize
precórrere §139 *tr* (lit) to precede || *intr* (lit) to occur before
precursóre *m* precursor
prèda *f* booty, prize; prey
predace *adj* (lit) preying, predatory
predare (prèdo) *tr* to pillage; to prey upon
preda·tóre -trice *adj* predacious, rapacious || *mf* plunderer
predecessóre *m* predecessor
predèlla *f* dais; altar step; platform
predellino *m* footboard
predestinare (predestino & predèstino) *tr* to predestine

predét·to -ta *adj* aforementioned
prediale *adj* field, rural || *f* land tax
prèdi·ca *f* (**-che**) sermon
predicare §197 (**prèdico**) *tr & intr* to preach
predicato *m* predicate; **essere in predicato di** + *inf* to be rumored to + *inf;* **essere predicato per** to be considered for
predica·tóre -trice *mf* preacher
predicazióne *f* preaching; sermon
predicòzzo *m* (coll) lecture, scolding
predilèt·to -ta *adj & m* favorite
predilezióne *f* predilection
predilìgere §149 (*pres part* missing) *tr* to prefer; to like best
predire §151 *tr* to foretell
predispórre §218 *tr* to predispose, prearrange || *ref* to prepare oneself
predisposizióne *f* predisposition
predizióne *f* prediction
predominare (**predòmino**) *tr* to overcome || *intr* to predominate; to prevail
predomì·nio *m* (**-ni**) predominance
predóne *m* marauder; **predone del mare** pirate
preesìstere §114 *intr* (ESSERE) to preexist
prefabbricare §197 (**prefàbbrico**) *tr* to prefabricate
prefazióne *f* preface
preferènza *f* preference; **a preferenza** rather; **usar preferenze a** to favor
preferìbile *adj* preferable
preferire §176 *tr* to prefer
preferi·to -ta *adj* preferred, favored || *mf* favorite; pet
prefètto *m* prefect
prefettura *f* prefecture
prèfi·ca *f* (**-che**) professional mourner, paid mourner; (coll) crybaby
prefiggere §103 *tr* to set, fix; (gram) to prefix || *ref* to plan
prefis·so -sa *adj* appointed; prefixed || *m* (gram) prefix; (telp) area code
prefissòide *m* prefixed combining form
pregare §209 (**prègo**) *tr* to beg, pray; to ask, request; **farsi pregare** to take a lot of asking; **La prego** please; **prego!** please!; beg your pardon!; you are welcome!
pregévole *adj* valuable
preghièra *f* entreaty; prayer
pregiare §290 (**prègio**) *tr* (lit) to praise, esteem || *ref* to be honored, to have the pleasure
pregia·to -ta *adj* precious; esteemed; **la Sua pregiata (lettera)** your favor, your kind letter; **pregiatissimo Signore** (com) dear Sir; **pregiato Signore** (com) dear Sir
prè·gio *m* (**-gi**) value, worth; esteem; **avere in pregio** to value
pregiudicare §197 (**pregiùdico**) *tr* to damage, harm, jeopardize
pregiudica·to -ta *adj* prejudged; prejudiced; compromised; bound to fail || *m* previous offender
pregiudiziale *adj* (law) pretrial; (pol) essential || *f* (law) pretrial
pregiudiziévole *adj* prejudicial, detrimental
pregiudì·zio *m* (**-zi**) prejudice, bias; harm, damage
pregnante *adj* pregnant
pré·gno -gna *adj* pregnant; saturated
prè·go *m* (**-ghi**) (lit) prayer || *interj* please!; beg your pardon!; you are welcome!
pregustare *tr* to foretaste, anticipate with pleasure
preistòri·co -ca *adj* (**-ci -che**) prehistoric(al)
prelato *m* prelate
prelazióne *f* (law) preemption; (obs) privilege
prelevaménto *m* (com) withdrawal
prelevare (**prelèvo**) *tr* to withdraw (*money*); to capture
preliba·to -ta *adj* excellent, delicious
prelièvo *m* withdrawal; (med) specimen
preliminare *adj* preliminary || **preliminari** *mpl* preliminary negotiations
prelùdere §105 *intr* to make an introductory statement; (with *dat*) to precede, usher in
prelù·dio *m* (**-di**) prelude; (*of an opera*) overture
prematu·ro -ra *adj* premature
premeditare (**premèdito**) *tr* to premeditate
premeditazióne *f* premeditation; **con premeditazione** (law) with malice prepense
prèmere §123 *tr* to press; to push; to squeeze || *intr* (ESSERE & AVERE) to press; to be urgent; **premere a** to matter to, e.g., **gli preme** it matters to him; **premere su** to press, put pressure on
premèssa *f* premise; introduction (*to a book*)
preméttere §198 *tr* to state at the onset; to place at the beginning
premiare §287 (**prèmio**) *tr* to award a prize to, reward
premiazióne *f* awarding of prizes
preminènte *adj* prominent, preeminent
prè·mio *m* (**-mi**) prize; premium; bonus; award
prèmito *m* straining (*to defecate*)
premolare *adj & m* premolar
premonire §176 *tr* (lit) to foretell
premonizióne *f* premonition
premorire §201 *intr* (ESSERE) (with *dat*) to predecease
premunire §176 *tr* to fortify || *ref*—**premunirsi contro** to provide against; **premunirsi di** to provide oneself with
premura *f* haste; attention, care; **aver premura (di)** to be in a hurry (to); **di premura** hastily; **far premura** (with *dat*) to urge
premuró·so -sa [s] *adj* attentive, careful
prèndere §220 *tr* to take; to catch; to lift; to pick up; to fetch; to get; to receive; **prendere a calci** to kick; **prendere a pugni** to punch; **prendere a servizio** to employ, hire; **prendere commiato** to take leave; **prendere con le buone** to treat with kid gloves; **prendere in castagna** to catch in the act; **prendere il sole** to sun oneself; **prendere la fuga** to take flight;

prendere la mano to run away (*said of a horse*); **prendere le mosse** to begin (*said, e.g., of a story*); **prendere lucciole per lanterne** to commit a gross error; **prender paura** to get scared; **prendere per** to take for; **prendere per il naso** to lead by the nose; **prendere quota** (aer) to gain altitude; **prendere sonno** to fall asleep; **prendere un granchio** to make a blunder || *intr* to take root; to set (*said of cement*); to catch (*said of fire*); to turn (*left or right*); **prendere a** + *inf* to begin to + *inf* || *ref* to grab one another; to get along together; **prendersela con** to become angry with; to lay the blame on; **prendersi a** to take hold of
prendi·tóre -trice *mf* receiver; payee (*of a note*); margin buyer || *m* (baseball) catcher
prenóme *m* first name, given name
prenotare (prenòto) *tr* to reserve, book || *ref* to register
prenotazióne *f* reservation, booking
preoccupante *adj* worrisome
preoccupare (preòccupo) *tr* to preoccupy; **preoccupare la mente di** to win the favor of || *ref* to worry
preoccupazióne *f* preoccupation, worry
preordinare (preórdino) *tr* to foreordain; to prearrange
preparare *tr* to prepare; to prime; to steep, brew || *ref* to be prepared; to brew (*said, e.g., of a storm*)
peparati·vo -va *adj* preparatory || **preparativi** *mpl* preparations
prepara·to -ta *adj* prepared; well-equipped || *m* patent medicine; (med) preparation; **preparato anatomico** dissection, anatomical specimen
preparatò·rio -ria *adj* (**-ri -rie**) preparatory
preparazióne *f* preparation
preponderante *adj* preponderant, prevailing
preponderanza *f* preponderance
prepórre §218 *tr* to prefix; to place before; to prefer; **preporre (qlcu) a** to place (*s.o.*) at the head of
preposizióne *f* preposition
prepósto *m* chief; (eccl) provost
prepotènte *adj* arrogant, overbearing; urgent (*desire*) || *m* bully
prepotènza *f* arrogance; outrage; **di prepotenza** by force
prerogativa *f* prerogative
présa [s] *f* hold, grip; handle; potholder; capture; pinch (*e.g., of salt*); setting (*of cement*); intake; (cards) trick; (elec) jack; (mov) take; **a pronta presa** quick-setting (*cement*); **dar presa a** to give rise to; **essere alle prese** to come to grips; **far presa** to stick (*said of glue*); to set (*said of cement*); to take root; **far presa su** to impress; **mettere alle prese** to pit (*e.g., animals*); **presa d'acqua** spigot, faucet; **presa d'aria** outlet (*of air hose*); air shaft; **presa di corrente** (elec) wall socket, outlet, receptacle; **presa di terra** (elec) ground; **presa in giro** kidding, joke; **venire alle prese** to come to grips
presà·gio *m* (**-gi**) forecast; portent
presagire §176 *tr* to forecast; to portend
presalà·rio [s] *m* (**-ri**) (educ) stipend
prèsbite *adj* far-sighted || *mf* far-sighted person
presbiteria·no -na *adj* & *mf* Presbyterian
prescégliere §244 *tr* to choose, select
prescìndere §247 (*pret* **prescindéi** & **prescissi**) *intr*—**a prescindere da** except for; **prescindere da** to leave out
prescolàsti·co -ca *adj* (**-ci -che**) preschool
prescrit·to -ta *adj* prescribed
prescrìvere §250 *tr* to prescribe || *intr* (ESSERE) (law) to prescribe, to lapse
prescrizióne *f* prescription; (law) extinctive prescription
presegnale [s] *m* warning sign
presentàbile *adj* presentable
presentare (presènto) *tr* to present; to introduce; **presentare la candidatura di** to nominate; **presentat'arm!** present arms! || *ref* to show up, appear; to come, arise (*said, e.g., of an opportunity*)
presenta·tóre -trice *mf* presenter; (rad, telv) announcer || *m* master of ceremonies
presentazióne *f* presentation; introduction
presènte *adj* present; **avere presente** to have in mind; **fare presente qlco a qlcu** to bring s.th to s.o.'s attention; **tenere presente** to keep in mind || *m* present; bystander, onlooker; **al presente** at present; **di presente** immediately || *interj* here!
presentimènto [s] *m* presentiment, foreboding
presentire [s] (**presènto**) *tr* to have a presentiment of
presènza *f* presence; attendance; **di presenza** in person; **presenza di spirito** presence of mind
presenziare §287 (**presènzio**) *tr* to attend; to witness || *intr*—**presenziare a** to be present at; to witness
presè·pio *m* (**-pi**) Nativity, crèche
preservare [s] (**presèrvo**) *tr* to preserve, protect
preservati·vo -va [s] *adj* & *m* prophylactic
prèside [s] *m* principal (*of secondary school*); **preside di facoltà** dean
presidènte [s] *m* president; chairman; **presidente del Consiglio** premier
presidentéssa [s] *f* president; chairwoman
presidènza [s] *f* presidency; chairmanship
presi·dio [s] *m* (**-di**) garrison; (fig) defense, help; **presidi** medical aids
presièdere [s] §141 (**presièdo**) *tr* to preside over || *intr* to preside; **presiedere a** to preside over
prèssa *f* crowd; haste; (mach) press; **far pressa** (poet) to urge
pressacar·te *m* (**-te**) paperweight
pressaforàg·gio *m* (**-gio**) baler, hay baler

pressante *adj* pressing, urgent
pressappòco *adv* more or less
pressare (prèsso) *tr* to press; to urge
pressióne *f* pressure; **far pressione su** to put pressure on; **pressione sanguigna** blood pressure; **sotto pressione** under steam
prèsso *m*—**nei pressi di** in the neighborhood of || *adv* near, nearby; **a un di presso** approximately; **da presso** close; **press'a poco** more or less || *prep* near; about; at; according to; at the house of; at the office of; care of; with, e.g., **godere fama presso** to enjoy popularity with
pressoché *adv* almost, about, nearly
pressurizzare [ddzz] *tr* to pressurize
prestabilire §176 *tr* to preestablish
prestabili•to -ta *adj* appointed
prestanó•me *m* (**-me**) straw man, figurehead
prestante *adj* strong, vigorous; comely
prestanza *f* vigor; (lit) comeliness
prestare (prèsto) *tr* to lend; to loan; to give (*ear; help*); to pay (*attention*); to render (*obedience*); to take (*oath*); to keep (*faith*); **prestar man forte** to give aid; **prestar servizio** to work || *ref* to lend oneself; to be suitable; to be willing; to volunteer
presta•tóre -trice *mf* lender; **prestatore d'opera** worker; **prestatori d'opera** labor
prestazióne *f* service; performance
prestigia•tóre -trice *mf* magician, juggler
prestì•gio *m* (**-gi**) prestige; spell, influence; ledgerdemain
prestigió•so -sa [s] *adj* captivating, spellbinding; illusory
prèstito *m* loan; (philol) borrowing; **dare a prestito** to lend; **prendere a prestito** to borrow
prè•sto -sta *adj* (archaic) quick || *m* (mus) presto || **presto** *adv* soon; fast; quick, quickly; early; **al più presto** at the earliest possible time; **ben presto** soon; **far presto** to hurry; **più presto che può** as soon as you can; **presto detto** easy to say
presùmere §116 *tr & intr* to presume
presunti•vo -va *adj* presumptive; budgeted, estimated (*expenditure*)
presun•to -ta *adj* alleged, supposed; estimated (*expenditure*)
presuntuó•so -sa [s] *adj* presumptuous; bumptious
presunzióne *f* presumption; conceit
presuppórre [s] §218 *tr* to presuppose
presuppósto [s] *m* assumption
prète *m* priest; minister; wooden frame (*to hold bed warmer*)
pretendènte *m* suitor; pretender
pretèndere §270 *tr* to demand, claim; **pretenderla a** to pretend to be || *intr*—**pretendere a** to be a suitor for; to claim (*e.g., a throne*)
pretensióne *f* demand; pretention; pretense
pretensió•so -sa [s] or **pretenzió•so -sa** [s] *adj* pretentious
preterintenzionale *adj* (law) unintentional; (law) justifiable
pretèri•to -ta *adj & m* preterit
preté•so -sa [s] *adj* alleged, ostensible; assumed (*name*) || *f* pretense; pretension
pretèsto *m* pretext, excuse; **sotto il pretesto di** under pretense of
pretòni•co -ca *adj* (**-ci -che**) pretonic
pretóre *m* judge, magistrate (*of lower court*)
prèt•to -ta *adj* pure, genuine
pretura *f* lower court
prevalènte *adj* prevalent, prevailing
prevalènza *f* prevalence; **essere in prevalenza** to be in the majority; **in prevalenza** for the most part
prevalére §278 *intr* (ESSERE & AVERE) to prevail || *ref* to take advantage
prevaricare §197 (**prevàrico**) *intr* to transgress; to graft
prevarica•tóre -trice *mf* grafter
prevedére §279 *tr* to foresee; to provide for (*said of a statute*)
prevedìbile *adj* foreseeable
prevenire §282 *tr* to precede; to anticipate; to forewarn; to prejudice
preventivi•sta *mf* (**-sti -ste**) estimator
preventi•vo -va *adj* preventive; prior; estimated (*budget*) || *m* estimate
prevenu•to -ta *adj* forewarned; biased, prejudiced || *m* defendant
prevenzióne *f* prevention; prejudice, bias
previdènte *adj* provident, prudent
previdènza *f* providence; foresight; **previdenza sociale** social security
previdenziale *adj* social (*e.g., responsibility*); social-security (*e.g., contribution*)
prè•vio -via *adj* (**-vi -vie**) with previous, e.g., **previo accordo** with previous agreement
previsióne *f* foresightedness; **in previsione di** anticipating; **previsioni del tempo** weather forecast
previ•sto -sta *adj* foreseen, expected || *m* expected time; estimated amount
prezió•so -sa [s] *adj* precious, valuable; affected; **fare il prezioso** (coll) to play hard to get || **preziosi** *mpl* valuables, jewels
prezzare (prèzzo) *tr* to care about; to price
prezzémolo *m* parsley
prèzzo *m* price; cost; **mettere a prezzo** (fig) to sell; **prezzo di favore** special price; **prezzo d'ingresso** admission; **tenere in gran prezzo** to value highly, to esteem highly; **ultimo prezzo** rock-bottom price
prezzolare (prèzzolo) *tr* to hire (*e.g., a gunman*); to bribe
prigióne *f* prison, jail; (naut) brig
prigionìa *f* imprisonment; bondage
prigionè•ro -ra *adj* imprisoned || *mf* prisoner || *m* stud bolt
prillare *intr* to spin, whirl
prima *f* first grade (*in school*); (rr) first class; (theat) first night; (aut) first (gear); **alla prima** or **sulle prime** at the outset || *adv* before; first; prior; ahead; **di prima** previous; **prima che** before; **prima di** ahead of; before;

prima o poi sooner or later; **quanto prima** as soon as possible
primàrio -ria (-ri -rie) *adj* primary || *m* (elec) primary; (med) chief of staff
primati•sta *mf* **(-sti -ste)** (sports) record holder
primato *m* primacy; (sports) record
primavèra *f* spring; springtime; (bot) primrose
primaverile *adj* spring; spring-like
primeggiare §290 **(priméggio)** *intr* to excel
primiè•ro -ra *adj* (lit) prior; (lit) pristine || *f* (cards) meld
primiti•vo -va *adj & m* primitive
primìzia *f* first fruits; scoop, beat
pri•mo -ma *adj* first; early (*dawn*); prime (*cost*); raw (*material*); **sulle prime** at first || *m* first; minute; **primo arrivato** first comer || *f* see **prima**
primogèni•to -ta *adj* first-born; (fig) beloved || *mf* first-born child
primòrdi *mpl* beginning, origin
primordiale *adj* primordial, primeval
prìmula *f* primrose || **Primula** *f*—**la Primula Rossa** the Scarlet Pimpernel
principale *adj* principal, main || *m* (coll) boss, chief
principalménte *adv* chiefly, mainly
principato *m* principality
prìncipe *adj* princeps || *m* prince; **il principe di Galles** the Prince of Wales; **principe ereditario** crown prince
principé•sco -sca *adj* **(-schi -sche)** princely
principéssa *f* princess
principiante *adj* beginning || *mf* beginner
principiare §287 *tr & intr* (ESSERE & AVERE) to begin; **a principiare da** beginning with
princì•pio *m* **(-pi)** beginning; principle; **in principio** at the beginning, at first
princisbécco *m* pinchbeck; **restare** or **rimanere di princisbecco** to be dumfounded
prióre *m* prior
priori•tà *f* **(-tà)** priority
priorità•rio -ria *adj* **(-ri -rie)** priority, e.g., **progetto prioritario** priority project
pri•sma *m* **(-smi)** prism
privare *tr* to deprive; to remove
privativa *f* government monopoly; salt and tobacco store; patent
priva•to -ta *adj* private || *m* private individual
privazióne *f* privation, loss
privilegiare §290 **(privilègio)** *tr* to privilege; (fig) to endow
privilegia•to -ta *adj* privileged; preferred (*stock*) || *m* privileged person
privilè•gio *m* **(-gi)** privilege
pri•vo -va *adj* deprived; **privo di** lacking
prò *m* **(pro)** profit, advantage; **a che pro?** what's the use?; **buon pro!** good appetite!; **far pro** to be good for the health; **il pro e il contro** the pros and the cons || *prep* pro, in favor of
probàbile *adj* probable
probabili•tà *f* **(-tà)** probability; chance; odds
probante *adj* proving; evidential
probatò•rio -ria *adj* **(-ri -rie)** probative, evidential
problè•ma *m* **(-mi)** problem
prò•bo -ba *adj* (lit) honest
procàc•cia *mf* **(-cia)** messenger; mail carrier
procacciare §128 *tr* to get, procure || *ref* to eke out (*a living*); to get into (*trouble*)
procace *adj* buxom, sexy; saucy, petulant
procèdere §123 **(procèdo)** *intr* to proceed, take action || *intr* (ESSERE) to proceed, go ahead
procediménto *m* procedure; behavior
procedura *f* procedure
procèlla *f* (lit) storm, tempest
procellària *f* (orn) petrel
processare (procèsso) *tr* to try, prosecute
processióne *f* procession
procèsso *m* process; trial; **processo verbale** minutes
processuale *adj* trial
procinto *m*—**in procinto di** on the point of
procióne *m* raccoon
procla•ma *m* **(-mi)** proclamation
proclamare *tr* to proclaim
proclamazióne *f* proclamation
proclìti•co -ca *adj & f* **(-ci -che)** proclitic
proclive *adj* inclined, disposed
proclivi•tà *f* **(-tà)** proclivity
procrastinare (procràstino) *tr* to procrastinate, put off || *intr* to procrastinate
procreare (procrèo) *tr* to procreate
procura *f* agency; power of attorney; **Procura della Repubblica** attorney general's office; district attorney's office
procurare *tr* to procure, to get; to cause; **procurare che** to see to it that; **procurare di** to try to || *ref* to get, acquire
procura•tóre -trice *mf* proxy; agent; attorney-at-law; (sports) manager; **Procuratore della Repubblica** district attorney
pròda *f* shore, bank; (archaic) prow
pròde *adj* brave || *m* brave person, hero
prodézza *f* prowess; accomplishment
prodiè•ro -ra *adj* prow, e.g., **cannone prodiero** prow gun; preceding (*in a row of ships*)
prodigare §209 **(pròdigo)** *tr* to squander, lavish || *ref* to do one's best
prodì•gio *m* **(-gi)** prodigy; wonder
prodigió•so -sa [s] *adj* prodigious; wonderful
pròdi•go -ga *adj* **(-ghi -ghe)** lavish, prodigal; **prodigo di** profuse in
proditò•rio -ria *adj* **(-ri -rie)** traitorous
prodótto *m* product; result; **prodotti in scatola** canned goods; **prodotti (ortofrutticoli)** produce
produrre §102 *tr* to produce; to turn out; to yield; to breed; to cause; (lit)

to prolong; (law) to exhibit || *ref* (theat) to perform, appear
produtti•vo -va *adj* productive
produttivìsti•co -ca *adj* (**-ci -che**) productivity, e.g., **fine produttivistico** productivity policy
produt•tóre -trice *adj* producing || *mf* producer; agent; manufacturer's representative || *m* salesman || *f* saleswoman
produzióne *f* production; output; **produzione in massa** or **in serie** mass production
proè•mio *m* (**-mi**) preamble, proem
profanare *tr* to profane, desecrate
profanazióne *f* profanation, desecration
profa•no -na *adj* profane; lay, uninformed || *m* layman; **il profano** the profane
proferire §176 *tr* (lit) to utter; (lit) to proffer
professare (**profèsso**) *tr* to profess; to practice (*e.g., law*) || *intr* to practice || *ref* to profess oneself to be
professionale *adj* professional; occupational (*disease*); trade (*school*)
professióne *f* profession; **fare il ladro di professione** to be a confirmed thief; **fare qlco di professione** to pursue the trade of s.th, e.g., **fa il falegname di professione** he pursues the trade of carpenter
professioni•sta *mf* (**-sti -ste**) professional
professorale *adj* professorial; pedantic
profes•sóre -soréssa *mf* professor; teacher; **professore d'orchestra** orchestra member
profè•ta *m* (**-ti**) prophet
profetéssa *f* prophetess
profèti•co -ca *adj* (**-ci -che**) prophetic
profetizzare [ddzz] *tr* to prophesy
profezìa *f* prophecy
profferire §176 (*pp* **proffèrto;** *pret* **profferìi** & **proffèrsi**) *tr* to offer; (lit) to utter
profi•cuo -cua *adj* profitable
profilare *tr* to outline; to sketch; to hem; (mach) to shape || *ref* to be outlined; to loom
profilas•si *f* (**-si**) prophylaxis
profila•to -ta *adj* outlined; hemmed; (mach) shaped || *m* structural piece
profilàtti•co -ca *adj* (**-ci -che**) prophylactic
profilatura *f* hemming; (mach) shaping
profilo *m* profile; sketch; outline
profittare *intr* to profit, benefit
profitta•tóre -trice *mf* profiteer
profittévole *adj* (lit) profitable
profitto *m* profit; progress; **profitti e perdite** profit and loss
proflù•vio *m* (**-vi**) overflow; (pathol) discharge
profondare (**profóndo**) *tr* & *intr* to sink
profóndere §178 *tr* to squander, lavish || *ref* to be profuse
profondi•tà *f* (**-tà**) depth
profón•do -da *adj* deep; profound; searching (*e.g., investigation*) || *m* bottom; depth; subconscious
pro fórma *adj invar* pro forma; perfunctory || *m* (coll) formality
pròfu•go -ga (**-ghi -ghe**) *adj* fugitive || *mf* refugee
profumare *tr* to perfume || *intr* to smell
profumataménte *adv* lavishly
profuma•to -ta *adj* perfumed, fragrant
profumerìa *f* perfumery; perfume shop
profumo *m* perfume; bouquet (*of wine*)
profusióne *f* profusion; **a profusione** in profusion
profu•so -sa *adj* profuse
progè•nie *f* (**-nie**) progeny, offspring; (pej) breed
progeni•tóre -trice *mf* ancestor
progettare (**progètto**) *tr* to plan; to design
progetti•sta *mf* (**-sti -ste**) planner; designer; wild dreamer
progètto *m* project; plan; draft (*of law*); **far progetti** to plan; **progetto di scala reale** (cards) possible straight flush
pròngo•si *f* (**-si**) prognosis
program•ma *m* (**-mi**) program; plan; curriculum; cycle (*of washing machine*); (mov) feature; (theat) playbill; **programma politico** platform
programmare *tr* to program; to plan
programma•tóre -trice *mf* programmer
programmazióne *f* programming
progredire §176 *intr* (ESSERE & AVERE) to progress, advance
progredi•to -ta *adj* advanced
progressióne *f* progression
progressi•sta *adj* & *mf* (**-sti -ste**) progressive
progressi•vo -va *adj* progressive
progrèsso *m* progress; progression, advance; **fare progressi** to progress
proibire §176 *tr* to prohibit; to prevent
proibi•to -ta *adj* forbidden; **è proibito entrare** no admission; **è proibito fumare** no smoking
proibizióne *f* prohibition
proibizionismo *m* prohibition
proiettare (**proiètto**) *tr* to project; to cast (*a shadow*) || *intr* to project || *ref* to be projected, project
proièttile *m* projectile, missile
proiettóre *m* projector, projection machine; searchlight; (aut) headlight; **proiettore acustico** sonar projector
proiezióne *f* projection; **proiezione rallentata** slow motion
pròle *f invar* offspring, progeny
proletariato *m* proletariat
proletà•rio -ria *adj* & *mf* (**-ri -rie**) proletarian
proliferare (**prolìfero**) *intr* to proliferate
prolificare §197 (**prolìfico**) *intr* to proliferate
prolìfi•co -ca *adj* (**-ci -che**) prolific
prolis•so -sa *adj* prolix, long-winded; long (*e.g., beard*)
pròlo•go *m* (**-ghi**) prologue; preface
prolun•ga *f* (**-ghe**) extension
prolungaménto *m* prolongation, extension
prolungare §209 *tr* to prolong, extend || *ref* to extend; to speak at great length
prolunga•to -ta *adj* extended, protracted
prolusióne *f* inaugural lecture

promemò·ria or **pro memò·ria** *m* (**-ria**) reminder
promés·so -sa *adj* promised || *mf* betrothed || *f* promise; promising individual
promettènte *adj* promising
prométtere §198 *tr* to promise; to threaten (*e.g., a storm*) || *intr* to promise; **promettere bene** to be very promising || *ref*—**promettersi a Dio** to make a vow to God; **promettersi in matrimonio** to become engaged
prominènte *adj* prominent
promì·scuo -scua *adj* promiscuous; coeducational; mixed (*marriage; races*); (gram) epicene
promontò·rio *m* (**-ri**) promontory, cliff
promo·tóre -trice *adj* promoting || *mf* promoter
promozióne *f* promotion
promulgare §209 *tr* to promulgate
promuòvere §202 *tr* to promote; to pass (*a student*); to initiate (*legal suit*); to induce (*e.g., perspiration*)
pronipóte *mf* great-grandchild || *m* great-grandson; grandnephew; **pronipoti** descendants || *f* great-granddaughter; grandniece
prò·no -na *adj* (lit) prone
pronóme *m* pronoun
pronominale *adj* (gram) pronominal; (gram) reflexive (*verb*)
pronosticare §197 (**pronòstico**) *tr* to prognosticate, forecast
pronòsti·co *m* (**-ci**) prognostication, forecast; sign, omen
prontézza *f* readiness; quickness, promptness
prón·to -ta *adj* ready; first (*aid*); quick; prompt; ready (*cash*) || **pronto** *interj* (telp) hello!
prontuà·rio *m* (**-ri**) handbook
pronùn·cia *f* (**-cie**) or **pronunzia** *f* pronunciaton; (law) judgment
pronunziare §287 *tr* to pronounce; to utter; to pass (*sentence*); to make (*a speech*) || *ref* to pass judgment
pronunzia·to -ta *adj* pronounced, marked; prominent (*nose, chin, beard*) || *m* (law) sentence
propaganda *f* propaganda; advertisement; advertising
propagandi·sta *mf* (**-sti -ste**) propagandist; advertiser; agent; detail man
propagandìsti·co -ca *adj* (**-ci -che**) advertising
propagare §209 *tr* to propagate; to spread || *ref* to spread
propàggine *f* offspring; (geog) spur, counterfort; (hort) layer
propalare *tr* (lit) to spread, divulge
propellènte *adj* & *m* propellent
propèllere §168 *tr* to propel
propèndere §123 (*pp* **propènso**) *intr* to incline, tend
propensióne *f* propensity, inclination
propèn·so -sa *adj* inclined, bent
propinare *tr* to administer (*e.g., poison*); **propinare qlco a qlcu** to put s.th over on s.o.
propìn·quo -qua *adj* (lit) near; (lit) related
propiziare §287 *tr* to propitiate, appease
propì·zio -zia *adj* (**-zi -zie**) propitious, favorable
proponiménto *m* intention, plan
propórre §218 *tr* to propose, present; to propound; **proporre come candidato** to nominate || *ref*—**proporsi di** to propose to, resolve to
proporzionare (**proporzióno**) *tr* to proportion, prorate
proporzióne *f* proportion
propòsito *m* purpose; **a proposito** opportune; opportunely; proper; by the way; **a proposito di** on the subject of; **di proposito** deliberately; **fuor di proposito** out of place; **parlare a proposito** to speak to the point
proposizióne *f* proposition; (gram) clause; **proposizione subordinata** dependent clause
propósta *f* proposal; **proposta di legge** bill
propriaménte *adv* exactly; properly
proprie·tà *f* (**-tà**) propriety; ownership; property; **la proprietà** property owners; **proprietà immobiliare** real estate; **proprietà letteraria** copyright; **sulla proprietà** on the premises
proprietà·rio -ria *mf* (**-ri -rie**) owner, proprietor
prò·prio -pria (**-pri -prie**) *adj* peculiar, characteristic; proper (*e.g., name*); own, e.g., **il mio proprio libro** my own book || *m* one's own; **i propri** one's folks; **lavorare in proprio** to work for oneself || **proprio** *adv* just, really, exactly; **non . . . proprio** not . . . at all; **proprio adesso** just, just now
propugnare *tr* to advocate; (lit) to fight for
propugna·tóre -trice *mf* (lit) advocate
propulsare *tr* to propel; (lit) to repulse
propulsióne *f* propulsion
propulsóre *m* propeller, motor
pròra *f* prow, bow
proravìa *f*—**a proravia** (naut) fore
pròro·ga *f* (**-ghe**) delay, extension
prorogare §209 (**pròrogo**) *tr* to extend; to put off, delay
prorómpere §240 *intr* to overflow; to burst (*into tears*)
prosa *f* prose
prosàl·co -ca *adj* (**-ci -che**) prose; prosaic
prosàpia *f* (lit) ancestry
prosa·tóre -trice *mf* prose writer
proscè·nio *m* (**-ni**) forestage
prosciògliere §127 *tr* to free; to exonerate
prosciugare §209 *tr* to drain, reclaim || *ref* to dry up
prosciutto *m* ham; **prosciutto cotto** boiled ham; **prosciutto crudo** prosciutto
proscrìvere §250 *tr* to proscribe, outlaw
prosecuzióne [s] *f* prosecution, pursuit
proseguiménto [s] *m* prosecution, pursuit
proseguire [s] (**proséguo**) *tr* to follow, pursue || *intr* (ESSERE & AVERE) to continue

prosèlito *m* proselyte
prosodìa *f* prosody
prosopopèa *f* conceit
prosperare (**pròspero**) *intr* to prosper, thrive
prosperi·tà *f* (**-tà**) prosperity || *interj* gesundheit!
pròspe·ro -ra *adj* prosperous, thriving; flourishing; successful || *m* (coll) match
prosperó·so -sa [s] *adj* flourishing; healthy; buxom
prospettare (**prospètto**) *tr* to face, overlook; to outline || *intr*—**prospettare su** to face || *ref* to look; to appear; to loom up
prospetti·vo -va *adj* prospective || *f* perspective; prospect; view
prospètto *m* prospect, view; front (*of building*); diagram; outline; prospectus
prospettóre *m* prospector
prospiciènte *adj* facing
prossimaménte *adv* shortly
prossimi·tà *f* **-tà** proximity, nearness; **in prossimità di** near
pròssi·mo -ma *adj* near, close; next; immediate (*cause*) || *m* neighbor, fellow man
pròstata *f* prostate
prosternare (**prostèrno**) *ref* to prostrate oneself
prostituire §176 *tr* to prostitute
prostituta *f* prostitute
prostituzióne *f* prostitution
prostrare (**pròstro**) *ref* to prostrate oneself
prostrazióne *f* prostration
protagoni·sta *mf* (**-sti -ste**) protagonist
protèggere §193 *tr* to protect; to help, defend; to favor, promote
proteina *f* protein
protèndere §270 *tr & ref* to stretch
pròte·si *f* (**-si**) (philol) prothesis; (surg) prosthesis
protèsta *f* protest, protestation
protestante *adj & mf* protestant; Protestant
protestare (**protèsto**) *tr* to protest; to reject (*faulty merchandise*) || *intr & ref* to protest
protestatò·rio -ria (**-ri -rie**) *adj* protesting || *m* protester
protèsto *m* (com) protest
protèt·to -ta *adj* protected || *m* protegé || *f* protegée
protettorato *m* protectorate
protet·tóre -trice *adj* patron || *mf* protector, guardian || *m* patron || *f* patroness
protezióne *f* protection; patronage
pròto *m* (typ) foreman
protocòllo *adj invar* commercial (*size*) || *m* protocol; **mettere a protocollo** to register, record
protopla·sma *m* (**-smi**) protoplasm
protòtipo *m* prototype; (fig) epitome
protozòi [dz] *mpl* protozoa
protrarre §273 *tr* to protract, extend || *ref* to continue
protrùdere §190 *intr* to protrude (*said, e.g., of a broken bone*)
protuberante *adj* protruding, bulging
pròva *f* test, examination; proof; try, attempt; probationary period (*of employment*); trial; token (*e.g., of friendship*); (sports) competition, event; (theat) rehearsal; **a prova di bomba** bombproof; foolproof; **a tutta prova** thoroughly tested; **in prova** on approval; **mettere a dura prova** to test (*e.g., one's patience*); **mettere alla prova** to test (*e.g., one's ability*); **mettere in prova** to fit (*a suit*); **prova del fuoco** trial by fire; **prova dell'acido** acid test; **prova generale** dress rehearsal; **prova indiziaria** circumstantial evidence
provare (**pròvo**) *tr* to test; to try; to try on; to try out; to taste; to prove; to feel (*e.g., anger*); (theat) to rehearse || *intr* to try || *ref* to compete
proveniènza *f* origin
provenire §282 *intr* (ESSERE) to stem, originate
provènto *m* income, proceeds
provenzale *adj & mf* Provençal
provèr·bio *m* (**-bi**) proverb; byword
provétta *f* test tube
provèt·to -ta *adj* (lit) masterful
provìn·cia *f* (**-ce**) province; **in provincia** outside of the big cities
provinciale *adj* provincial || *mf* small-town person || *f* provincial highway, state highway
provino *m* gauge; (mov) screen test
provocare §197 (**pròvoco**) *tr* to provoke; to bring about, cause; to arouse; to entice
provoca·tóre -trice *adj* provoking || *mf* provoker
provocatò·rio -ria *adj* (**-ri -rie**) provoking, provocative
provocazióne *f* provocation; challenge
provvedére §221 *tr* to prepare; to supply; **provvedere che** to see to it that || *intr* to take the necessary steps; **provvedere a** to provide for; **provvedere a** + *inf* to provide for + *ger;* **provvedere nei confronti di** to take steps against
provvediménto *m* measure, step
provvedi·tóre -trice *mf* provider || *m* superintendent; **provveditore agli studi** superintendent of schools
provvedu·to -ta *adj* supplied; careful
provvidènza *f* providence; windfall; **provvidenze** provisions, help
provvidenziale *adj* providential
pròvvi·do -da *adj* (lit) provident
provvigióne *f* (com) commission
provvisò·rio -ria *adj* (**-ri -rie**) provisional, temporary
provvi·sto -sta *adj* supplied || *f* supply, provision; **fare le provviste** to shop
prozìa *f* grandaunt
prozì·o *m* (**-i**) granduncle
prua *f* bow, prow
prudènte *adj* prudent, cautious
prudènza *f* prudence, discretion
prùdere §222 *intr* to itch; **sentirsi prudere le mani** to feel like giving s.o. a beating
prugna *f* plum; **prugna secca** prune

prugno *m* plum tree
prùgnola *f* sloe
prùgnolo *m* sloe, blackthorn
pruno *m* thorn
prurito *m* itch
pseudònimo *m* pseudonym; alias; pen name
psicanàlisi *f* psychoanalysis
psicanali•sta *mf* **(-sti -ste)** psychoanalyst
psicanalizzare [ddzz] *tr* to psychoanalyze
psiche *f* psyche; cheval glass
psichia•tra *mf* **(-tri -tre)** psychiatrist
psichiatrìa *f* psychiatry
psìchi•co -ca *adj* **(-ci -che)** psychic
psicologìa *f* psychology
psicològi•co -ca *adj* **(-ci -che)** psychological
psicòlo•go -ga *mf* **(-gi -ghe)** psychologist
psicopàti•co -ca (-ci -che) *adj* psychopathic || *mf* psychopath
psicò•si *f* **(-si)** psychosis
psicosomàti•co -ca *adj* **(-ci -che)** psychosomatic
psicotècni•co -ca (-ci -che) *adj* psychotechnical || *m* industrial psychologist || *f* industrial psychology
psicòti•co -ca *adj* **(-ci -che)** psychotic
pubblicare §197 **(pùbblico)** *tr* to publish
pubblicazióne *f* publication; **pubblicazioni di matrimonio** marriage banns
pubblicismo *m* communications; advertising
pubblici•sta *mf* **(-sti -ste)** free-lance newspaper writer; publicist
pubblicìsti•co -ca (-ci -che) *adj* advertising; political-science || *f* newspaper business
pubblicità *f* publicity; advertising
pubblicità•rio -ria (-ri -rie) *adj* advertising || *mf* advertising agent
publicizzare [ddzz] *tr* to publicize
publicizzazióne [ddzz] *f* publicizing
pùbbli•co -ca *adj & m* **(-ci -che)** public; **mettere in pubblico** to publish
pubertà *f* puberty
pudibón•do -da *adj* (lit) modest, bashful; (lit) prudish
pudicìzia *f* modesty; prudery
pudi•co -ca *adj* **(-chi -che)** modest, chaste; bashful; (lit) reserved
pudóre *m* modesty; decency; shame
puericoltóre *m* pediatrician
puerile *adj* puerile, childish
puerili•tà *f* **(-tà)** puerility, childishness
puèrpera *f* lying-in patient
pugilato *m* boxing
pugilatóre *m* boxer, prize fighter
pùgile *m* boxer, prize fighter
pugili•sta *m* **(-sti)** boxer, prize fighter
pù•glia *f* **(-glie)** stake (*in gambling*)
pugnace *adj* (lit) pugnacious
pugnalare *tr* to stab
pugnalata *f* stab
pugnale *m* dagger
pugno *m* fist; fistful; punch; **avere in pugno** to have in one's grasp; **di proprio pugno** in one's own hand; **fare a pugni** to fight; to clash

pula *f* chaff
pulce *f* flea; **mettere una pulce nell'orecchio di** to put a bug in the ear of; **pulce tropicale** jigger, chigger
pulcèlla *f* maid, maiden
pulcinèlla *f*—**pulcinella di mare** (orn) Atlantic puffin || **Pulcinel•la** *m* **(-la)** buffoon; Punch, Punchinello
pulcino *m* chick
pulédra *f* filly
pulédro *m* colt, foal
pulég•gia *f* **(-ge)** pulley
pulire §176 *tr* to clean; to shine (*shoes*); to wipe; to polish
puliscipiè•di *m* **(-di)** doormat
puli•to -ta *adj* clean; polished; clear (*conscience*) || *f*—**dare una pulita a** to give a lick and a promise to
pulitura *f* cleaning; **pulitura a secco** dry cleaning
pulizìa *f* cleaning; cleanliness; **fare le pulizie** to clean house
pullulare (pùllulo) *intr* to swarm
pùlpito *m* pulpit
pulsante *m* knob; push button
pulsare *intr* to throb; to pulsate
pulvìscolo *m* fine dust; haze
pulzèlla *f* var of **pulcella**
pu•ma *m* **(-ma)** cougar
pungènte *adj* pungent; bitter (*cold*)
pùngere §183 *tr* to sting; (fig) to goad
pungiglióne *m* stinger (*of bee*); (fig) sting; (obs) goad
pungitòpo *m* (bot) butcher's broom
pungolare (pùngolo) *tr* to goad, prod
punire §176 *tr* to punish
punizióne *f* punishment; penalty
punta *f* point, tip; prong; brad; bit, trifle; needle (*of phonograph*); avant-garde; point (*of dog*); (lit) wound; (fig) peak; (mach) broach; **averne fino alla punta dei capelli** to be sick and tired; **fare la punta a** to sharpen; **in punta di penna** elegantly; **prendere di punta** to treat roughly; to face up to; **punta delle dita** fingertip; **punta di piedi** tiptoe
puntale *m* tip, ferrule
puntaménto *m* aiming
puntare *tr* to aim; to aim at; to point; to thrust; to dot; to bet; to stare at; to fix (*one's eyes*); **puntare i piedi** to stiffen up; (fig) to balk || *intr* to aim; to point; to pin; to bet; **puntare su** to count on; **puntare verso** to march on; to sail toward
puntaspil•li *m* **(-li)** pincushion
puntata *f* jab (*with weapon*); excursion; bet; issue, number (*of magazine*); installment (*of story*); (mil) incursion
punteggiare §290 **(puntéggio)** *tr* to dot; (gram) to punctuate
punteggiatura *f* dotting; punctuation
punté•gio *m* **(-gi)** score
puntellare (puntèllo) *tr* to prop, brace; to support
puntèllo *m* prop, brace; support
punterìa *f* aiming; aiming gear; (aut) tappet
punteruòlo *m* punch; awl
puntì•glio *m* **(-gli)** obstinacy, stubbornness; punctilio

puntiglió•so -sa [s] *adj* punctilious, scrupulous; obstinate, stubborn
puntina *f* brad; needle; thumbtack
puntino *m* small dot; G-string; **a puntino** to a T
punto *m* point; period; dot; place, spot; extent; stitch; **dare dei punti a** to be superior to; **di punto in bianco** all of a sudden; **di tutto punto** thoroughly; **due punti** colon; **essere a buon punto** to be well advanced; **essere sul punto di** + *inf* to be about to + *inf;* **fare il punto** (fig; naut) to take one's bearings; **in punto** on the dot; **in punto franco** in bond; **in un punto** together; **mettere a punto** to get in working order; (aut) to tune up; **mettere i punti sulle i** to dot one's i's; **punto assistenza** service agency; **punto di partenza** starting point; **punto di vista** viewpoint; **punto esclamativo** exclamation point; **punto e virgola** semicolon; **punto fermo** full stop; **punto interrogativo** question mark; **punto morto** (mach) dead center; **punto stimato** (naut) dead reckoning; **qui sta il punto!** here's the rub!; **vincere ai punti** (boxing) to win by points, win by decision || *adv*—**né punto né poco** not at all; **non . . . punto** not at all
puntóne *m* rafter
puntuale *adj* punctual, prompt
puntuali•tà *f* (-tà) punctuality, promptness
puntura *f* sting; stitch (*sharp pain*); (coll) injection; **puntura lombare** spinal anesthesia
punzecchiare §287 (**punzécchio**) *tr* to keep on stinging; to tease, torment
punzecchiatura *f* sting, bite
punzonare (**punzóno**) *tr* to mark or stamp with a punch
punzonatrice *f* punch press
punzóne *m* punch; nailset
pupa *f* doll; (zool) pupa
pupazzetti•sta *mf* (-sti -ste) cartoonist
pupazzétto *m* caricature; cartoon; **pupazzetto di carta** paper doll
pupazzo *m* puppet; **pupazzo di stoffa** rag doll
pupil•lo -la *mf* pupil; ward, protégé || *f* pupil (*of eye*); protégée
pupo *m* (coll) baby
purché *conj* provided, providing
pure *adv* too, also; indeed; (lit) only; **pur di** only in order to; **quando pure** even if; **se pure** even if || *conj* though, although; but, yet
pu•rè *m* (-rè) purée; **purè di patate** mashed potatoes
purézza *f* purity
pur•ga *f* (-ghe) laxative; purification; purge
purgante *adj* purging || *m* laxative
purgare §209 *tr* to purge; to purify; to expurgate || *ref* to take a laxative
purgati•vo -va *adj* laxative
purgatò•rio *m* (-ri) purgatory
purificare §197 (**purìfico**) *tr* to purify
purismo *m* purism
purità *f* purity
purita•no -na *adj & m* puritan; Puritan
pu•ro -ra *adj* pure; clear; simple, mere
purosàn•gue *adj invar & m* (-gue) thoroughbred
purpùre•o -a *adj* (lit) purple
purtròppo *adv* unfortunately
purulèn•to -ta *adj* purulent
pus *m* pus
pusillànime *adj* pusillanimous
pùstola *f* pustule; pimple
puta caso *adv* possibly, maybe
putifè•rio *m* (-ri) hubbub
putrefare §173 *intr* (ESSERE) *& ref* to putrefy, rot
putrefazióne *f* putrefaction
putrèlla *f* I beam
pùtri•do -da *adj* putrid || *m* corruption
putta *f* (coll) girl; (lit) prostitute
puttana *f* (vulg) whore
put•to -ta *adj* (archaic) meretricious || *m* figure of a child || *f* see **putta**
puzza *f* var of **puzzo**
puzzare *intr* to stink, smell
puzzo *m* stench, smell, bad odor
pùzzola *f* polecat, skunk
puzzolènte *adj* stinking, smelly
puzzonata *f* (coll) contemptible action; (coll) botch, bungle
puzzóne *m* (coll) skunk (*person*)

Q

Q, q [ku] *m & f* fifteenth letter of the Italian alphabet
qua *adv* here; **da un (giorno, mese, anno) in qua** for the past (day, month, year); **di qua da** on this side of; **in qua** on this side; here
quàcche•ro -ra or **quàcque•ro -ra** *adj & mf* Quaker; **alla quacquera** in a plain fashion
quadèrno *m* copybook; **quaderno di cassa** cash book
quadràngo•lo -la *adj* quadrangular || *m* quadrangle
quadrante *m* quadrant; dial; face (*of watch*); **quadrante solare** sundial
quadrare *tr* to square || *intr* (ESSERE & AVERE) to square; **quadrare a** to be satisfactory to; **quadrare con** to fit
quadra•to -ta *adj* square; sound (*mind*) || *m* square; diaper; (boxing) ring; (nav) wardroom
quadratura *f* squaring; concreteness; (astr) quadrature
quadrèl•lo *m* (-li) square ruler; square tile || *m* (-la *fpl*) (lit) bolt, arrow
quadrerìa *f* picture gallery; collection
quadretta•to -ta *adj* checkered
quadrétto *m* small painting; checker, small square; (fig) picture

quadriennale *adj* four-year || *f* quadrennial
quadrifò·glio *m* (**-gli**) four-leaf clover; **a quadrifoglio** cloverleaf
quadrì·glio *m* (**-gli**) (cards) quadrille
quadrimensionale *adj* four-dimensional
quadrimestrale *adj* four-month
quadrimèstre *m* four-month period; four-month payment
quadrimotóre *adj* four-motor || *m* four-motor plane
quadrireattóre *m* four-motor jet
qua·dro -dra *adj* square; (fig) solid || *m* picture; painting; sight; square; table, summary; panel, switchboard; (theat) scene; **quadri** bulletin board; (mil) cadres; (cards) diamonds
quadrùmane *adj* quadrumanous || *m* monkey; ape
quadruplicare §197 (**quadrùplico**) *tr & ref* to quadruple
quadrùplice *adj* quadruple; **in quadruplice copia** in four copies
quàdru·plo -pla *adj & m* quadruple
quaggiù *adv* down here
quàglia *f* quail
quagliare §280 *tr, intr* (ESSERE) *& ref* var of **cagliare**
qualche *adj invar* some, e.g., **qualche giorno** some day; some, e.g., **qualche elefante è bianco** some elephants are white; any, e.g., **ha qualche libro da vendere?** do you have any books to sell?; a few, e.g., **qualche giorno** a few days
qualchedu·no -na *pron indef* var of **qualcuno**
qualcòsa [s] *m* (fig) something; (fig) somebody || *pron indef* something; anything; **qualcosa di buono** something good
qualcu·no -na *pron indef* some; any; somebody; anybody || *m* somebody
quale *adj* which, what; what a, e.g., **quale onore!** what an honor!; as, e.g., **il pane, quale vedi, è fresco** the bread, as you can see, is fresh; **quale che sia** regardless of || *pron* which; what; (archaic) who; **il quale** who, whom; **per la quale** o.k.; well-bred; commendable; terrific; **quale . . . quale** some . . . some || *prep* as, e.g., **quale ministro** as a minister
qualifi·ca *f* (**-che**) rating; position; quality, qualification
qualificare §197 (**qualifico**) *tr* to qualify; to classify; to rate, give a rating to || *ref* to introduce oneself; to qualify
qualifica·to -ta *adj* aggravated (*assault*); qualified (*personnel*); specialized (*worker*)
quali·tà *f* (**-tà**) quality; capacity
qualóra *conj* if; (lit) whenever
qualsìasi [s] *adj invar* any; whatever; ordinary
qualunque *adj invar* any; whatever; common, ordinary; **in qualunque modo** anyway, anyhow; **qualunque altro** anybody else; **qualunque cosa** anything; no matter what
qualvòlta *conj* (lit) whenever
quando *m* when || *adv* when; **di quando in quando** from time to time; **quando . . . quando** sometimes . . . sometimes || *conj* when; whenever; while; **da quando** since
quantìsti·co -ca *adj* (**-ci -che**) quantum
quanti·tà *f* (**-tà**) quantity; number
quantitativo *m* quantity
quan·to -ta *adj* how much; as much; how great; how great a; what a; **quan·ti -te** how many; as many || *m* quantum || *pron* how much; as much; how great; how long; that which; what; whatever; **a quanto si dice** according to what is rumored; **da quanto** from what; for how long; **fra quanto** how soon; **per quanto io ne sappia** as far as I know; **quanto più** (or **meno**) . . . **tanto più** (or **meno**) the more (or the less) . . . the more (or the less); **quan·ti -te** how many; all those; as many as; **quanti ne abbiamo?** what's the date? || **quanto** *adv* how much; as much as; **in quanto** as; **in quanto che** inasmuch as; **per quanto** although; no matter; nevertheless; **quanto a** as to, as for; **quanto mai** as never before; **quanto meno** at least; **quanto prima** as soon as possible
quantunque *conj* although, though
quaranta *adj, m & pron* forty; **gli anni quaranta** the forties; **i quaranta** the forties (*in age*)
quarantèna *f* quarantine
quarantènne *adj* forty-year-old || *mf* forty-year-old person
quarantèsi·mo -ma *adj, m & pron* fortieth
quarantina *f* about forty; **essere sulla quarantina** to be about forty years old
quarantòtto *adj* forty-eight || *m* forty-eight; (coll) hubbub, uproar
quarésima *f* Lent
quartabuòno *m* triangle (*in drafting*); **tagliare a quartabuono** to miter
quartétto *m* quartet; **quartetto d'archi** string quartet
quartière *m* quarter, district; (mil) quarters; (coll) apartment; **quartier generale** headquarters; **senza quartiere** (*fight*) without quarter
quar·to -ta *adj & pron* fourth || *m* fourth; quarter; quarter of a kilo; quarter of a liter; (naut) watch; **l'una e un quarto** a quarter after one; **l'una meno un quarto** a quarter to one
quarzo *m* quartz
quasi *adv* almost, nearly; **quasi che** as if; **quasi mai** hardly ever; **senza quasi** without any ifs and buts
quassù *adv* up here
quat·to -ta *adj* crouching; squatting; **quatto quatto** stealthy, silent; **starsene quatto quatto** to not make a sound
quattordicènne *adj* fourteen-year-old || *mf* fourteen-year-old person
quattordicèsi·mo -ma *adj, m & pron* fourteenth
quattórdici *adj & pron* fourteen; **le**

quattordici two P.M. || *m* fourteen; fourteenth (*in dates*)
quattrino *m* penny; (fig) bit; **quattrini** money
quattro *adj* four; a few, e.g., **quattro gatti** a few people; **a quattro mani** (mus) for four hands || *pron* four; **dirne quattro a** to upbraid; **farsi in quattro** to go all out; **in quattro e quattr'otto** in a few minutes; **le quattro** four o'clock || *m* four; fourth (*in dates*); racing shell with four oarsmen
quattrocènto *adj, m & pron* four hundred || **il Quattrocento** the fifteenth century
quattromila *adj, m & pron* four thousand
quégli §7 *adj* || §8 *pron*
quéi §7 *adj*
quél §7 *adj* || §8 *pron*
quéll' §7 *adj*
quél·lo -la §7 *adj* || §8 *pron*—**per quello che so io** as far as I know
quèr·cia *f* (**-ce**) oak tree
querci·no -na *adj* oaken
querèla *f* complaint
querelante *adj* complaining || *mf* plaintiff
querelare (**querèlo**) *tr* to sue || *ref* (law) to sue; (lit) to complain
querela·to -ta *adj* accused || *mf* defendant
quèru·lo -la *adj* (lit) plaintive
quesito *m* question; problem; (lit) request
questi §7 *pron*
questionare (**questióno**) *intr* to quarrel
questionà·rio *m* (**-ri**) questionnaire
questióne *f* question; (coll) quarrel; **questione di gabinetto** call for a vote of confidence; **venire a questione** to quarrel
qué·sto -sta §7 *adj* || §8 *pron*—**e con questo?** so what?; **per questo** therefore; **questa** this matter; **questo . . . quello** the former . . . the latter
questóre *m* police commissioner; sergeant at arms (*of congress*)
questua *f* begging; collection of alms; **andare alla questua** to go begging; **vietata la questua** no begging
questura *f* police department; police headquarters
questurino *m* (coll) policeman
què·to -ta *adj* var of **quieto**
qui *adv* here; **di qui** hence, from here; this way; **di qui a un anno** one year hence; **di qui in avanti** from now on; **qui vicino** nearby
quiescènza *f* quiescence; retirement
quietanza *f* receipt
quietanzare *tr* to receipt
quietare (**quièto**) *tr* to quiet, calm; to satisfy (*e.g., thirst*) || *ref* to quiet down
quiète *f* quiet, calmness
quiè·to -ta *adj* quiet, calm; still; **stia quieto!** don't worry! || *m* quiet life
quindi *adv* then; therefore; (archaic) thence, from there
quindicènne *adj* fifteen-year-old || *mf* fifteen-year-old person
quindicèsi·mo -ma *adj, m & pron* fifteenth
quìndici *adj & pron* fifteen; **le quindici** three P.M. || *m* fifteen; fifteenth (*in dates*)
quindicina *f* about fifteen; two weeks, fortnight; semimonthly pay
quindicinale *adj* fortnightly
quinquennale *adj* five-year
quinta *f* (theat) wing; (mus) fifth; **dietro le quinte** behind the scenes
quintale *m* quintal (*100 kilos*)
quintèrno *m* signature of five sheets; (bb) quire
quintessènza *f* quintessence
quintétto *m* quintet
quin·to -ta *adj, m & pron* fifth || *f* see **quinta**
quisquìlia *f* trifle
quivi *adv* (lit) over there; (lit) then
quòrum *m* quorum
quòta *f* quota; share; altitude; elevation; level (*of stock market*); market average; odds (*in betting*); subscription (*to club*); **quota zero** (fig) point of departure
quotare (**quòto**) *tr* to quote (*a price*); to value, esteem || *ref* to sign up for, e.g., **si quotò duemila lire** he signed up for two thousand lire
quotazióne *f* quotation
quotidia·no -na *adj & m* daily
quoziènte *m* quotient; (sports) percentage; **quoziente d'intelligenza** I.Q.

R

R, r ['erre] *m & f* sixteenth letter of the Italian alphabet
rabàrbaro *m* rhubarb
rabberciare §128 (**rabbèrcio**) *tr* (coll) to patch up
ràbbia *f* rage, anger; rabies
rabbino *m* rabbi
rabbió·so -sa [s] *adj* furious; rabid
rabbonire §176 *tr* to pacify || *ref* to calm down
rabbrividire §176 *intr* (ESSERE) to shiver, shudder
rabbuffare *tr* to rebuke; to dishevel
rabbuffo *m* rebuke; **fare un rabbuffo a** to rebuke
rabbuiare §287 *ref* to darken, turn dark
rabdomante *m* dowser, diviner
rabé·sco *m* (**-schi**) arabesque; scrawl, scribble
ràbi·do -da *adj* rabid
raccapezzare (**raccapézzo**) *tr* to put together; to gather (*news*); to find (*one's way*); to make out (*what is*

meant) || *ref*—**non raccapezzarsi** to not be able to get one's bearings
raccapricciante *adj* bloodcurdling
raccapric•cio *m* (**-ci**) horror
raccartocciare §128 (**raccartòccio**) *tr* & *ref* to shrivel
raccattare *tr* to pick up; to gather
racchétta *f* racket; **racchetta da neve** snowshoe; **racchetta da sci** ski pole
ràc•chio -chia *adj* (**-chi -chie**) (coll) ugly, homely
racchiùdere §125 *tr* to contain, hold
raccògliere §127 *tr* to pick up; to gather; to collect (*e.g., stamps*); to take up (*the gauntlet*); to receive; to reap; to furl (*sail*); to draw in (*a net*); to fold (*the wings*); to shelter (*e.g., foundlings*); **raccogliere i passi** to stop walking || *ref* to gather; to concentrate
raccogliménto *m* concentration; meditation
raccogli•tóre -trice *mf* collector, compiler || *m* folder
raccòl•to -ta *adj* crouched; collected; engrossed; snug, intimate || *m* harvest || *f* harvest; collection; **chiamare a raccolta** to rally
raccomandàbile *adj* recommendable; **poco raccomandabile** unreliable
raccomandare *tr* to recommend; to secure (*e.g., a boat*); to register (*mail*); to exhort || *ref* to recommend oneself; to entreat; **mi raccomando** please; **raccomandarsi a** to beg, implore; **raccomandarsi alle gambe** to take to one's heels
raccomanda•to -ta *adj* recommended; registered || *m* protégé || *f* protégée; registered letter
raccomandazióne *f* recommendation; registration (*of mail*); exhortation
raccomodare (**raccòmodo**) *tr* to fix; to mend
racconciare §128 (**raccóncio**) *tr* to fix; to mend || *ref* to clear up (*said of the weather*); to tidy oneself up
raccontare (**raccónto**) *tr* to tell; **raccontarla bene** to be good at telling lies
raccónto *m* tale; story; narrative
raccorciaménto *m* shortening
raccorciare §128 (**raccòrcio**) *tr* to shorten
raccordare (**raccòrdo**) *tr* to link, connect
raccòrdo *m* link, connection; **raccordo a circolazione rotatoria** traffic circle; **raccordo anulare** (rr) belt line; **raccordo ferroviario** junction; spur; siding; **raccordo stradale** connecting road
raccostare (**raccòsto**) *tr* & *ref* to draw near
raccozzare (**raccòzzo**) *tr* to scrape together
ràchide *m* & *f* backbone; midrib (*of leaf*); shaft (*of feather*)
rachìti•co -ca *adj* (**-ci -che**) stunted; weak; (pathol) rickety
rachitismo *m* rickets
racimolare (**racìmolo**) *tr* to glean; to scrape together
rada *f* roadstead; cove
ràdar *m* radar
addobbare (**raddòbbo**) *tr* (naut) to refit
raddolcire §176 *tr* & *ref* to sweeten; to mellow
raddoppiare §287 (**raddóppio**) *tr*, *intr* (ESSERE) & *ref* to double, redouble
raddrizzare *tr* to straighten; (elec) to rectify || *ref* to straighten up
raddrizzatóre *m* (elec) rectifier
ràdere §223 *tr* to shave; to raze; to graze, skim || *ref* to shave
radézza *f* rarity, rareness; thinness; sparsity (*of vegetation*); space, distance (*e.g., between trees*)
radiante *adj* radiating
radiare §287 *tr* to strike off; to expel; to condemn (*a ship*); **radiare dall'albo degli avvocati** to disbar
radiatóre *m* radiator
radiazióne *f* radiation; explulsion
ràdi•ca *f* (**-che**) brier; (coll) root
radicale *adj* & *mf* radical || *m* & *f* (philol) radical, root || *m* (chem, math) radical
radicare §197 (**ràdico**) *tr* & *intr* to root
radice *f* root; base or foot (*e.g., of a mountain or tower*); **mettere radice** to take root; **svellere dalle radici** to pull up by the roots; to eradicate
rà•dio *adj invar* radio || *m* (**-di**) (anat) radius; (chem) radium || *f* (**-dio**) radio; **radio fante** (mil) grapevine
radioabbonato *m* (rad) subscriber (*to radio broadcasting*)
radioama•tóre -trice *mf* radio fan; radio ham
radioannunciatóre *m* radio announcer
radioascolta•tóre -trice *mf* radio listener
radioatti•vo -va *adj* radioactive
radiobùssola *f* radio compass
radiocanale *m* radio channel
radiocomanda•to -ta *adj* radio-controlled
radiocròna•ca *f* (**-che**) newscast
radiocroni•sta *mf* (**-sti -ste**) newscaster
radiodiffóndere §178 *tr* to broadcast
radiodiffusióne *f* broadcasting
radiofaro *m* radio beacon
radiofòni•co -ca *adj* (**-ci -che**) radio
radiofonògrafo *m* radiophonograph
radiofò•to *f* (**-to**) radiophoto
radiofrequènza *f* radiofrequency
radiologìa *f* radiology
radiomontatóre *m* radio assembler
radioónda *f* radio wave; **radioonde** airwaves
radioricevènte *adj* radio || *f* radio set; radio station
radioriparatóre *m* radio repairman
radiosegnale *m* radio signal
radiosentièro *m* range of a radio beacon
radió•so -sa [s] *adj* radiant
radiosorgènte *f* quasar
radiostazióne *f* radio station
radiostélla *f* quasar
radiotas•sì *m* (**-sì**) radio-dispatched taxi
radiotelescò•pio *m* (**-pi**) radiotelescope
radiotrasméttere §198 *tr* & *intr* to broadcast, radio
radiotrasmissióne *f* broadcast

radiotrasmittènte *adj* broadcasting || *f* broadcasting station
ra·do -da *adj* rare; thin; sheer; sparse, scattered; **di rado** seldom, rarely
radunare *tr & ref* to assemble, gather
radunata *f* gathering; (mil) assembly; **radunata sediziosa** unlawful assembly
raduno *m* assembly, gathering
radura *f* clearing, glade
ràfano *m* (bot) radish
raffazzonare (raffazzóno) *tr* to mend, patch up
raffazzonatura *f* patchwork, hodgepodge
rafférma *f* confirmation; stay (*in office*); return to office; (mil) reenlistment
raffermare (raffermo) *tr* to reaffirm; to secure; (coll) to reconfirm; to reappoint, reelect; to return (*e.g., a mayor*) to office || *intr* (ESSERE) & *ref* to reenlist; (coll) to harden
raffér·mo -ma *adj* stale (bread) || *f* see **rafferma**
ràffi·ca *f* (**-che**) gust; blast; burst (*e.g., of machine gun*); **a raffiche** gusty
raffigurare *tr* to represent; to symbolize
raffinare *tr* to refine; to polish || *intr* (ESSERE) to become refined
raffinatézza *f* refinement, polish
raffinatura *f* refinement (*of oil*)
raffinazióne *f* refining
raffinerìa *f* refinery
ràf·fio *m* (**-fi**) hook; grappling iron
rafforzare (raffòrzo) *tr* to strengthen
raffreddaménto *m* cooling
raffreddare (raffréddo) *tr* to make cold; to cool; **raffreddare gli spiriti di qlcu** to dampen s.o.'s enthusiasm || *intr* (ESSERE) & *ref* to get cold; to cool
raffreddóre *m* cold
raffrontare (raffrónto) *tr* to compare; (law) to bring face to face
raffrónto *m* comparison; confrontation
ràfia *f* raffia
raganèlla *f* rattle; (zool) tree frog
ragazza *f* girl; spinster; (coll) girl friend; **ragazza copertina** cover girl; **ragazza squillo** call girl
ragazzata *f* boyish prank
ragaz·zo -za *mf* youth, young person || *m* boy; (coll) boyfriend || *f* see **ragazza**
raggelare (raggèlo) *intr* (ESSERE) to freeze
raggiante *adj* radiant; beaming
raggiare §290 *tr & intr* to radiate
raggièra *f* rayed halo; **a raggiera** radially
ràg·gio *m* (**-gi**) ray; beam; spoke; (geom) radius; **raggio d'azione** radius, range of action; **raggio di sole** sunbeam
raggiornare (raggiórno) *tr* (coll) to bring up to date || *intr* (ESSERE) to dawn || *impers* (ESSERE)—**raggiorna** it is dawning
raggirare *tr* to trick, swindle || *ref* to roam, wander; **raggirarsi su** to turn on (*e.g., a certain subject*)
raggiro *m* trickery, swindle
raggiungere §183 *tr* to reach; to catch up with, rejoin
raggiungìbile *adj* attainable
raggomitolare (raggomìtolo) *tr* to roll up || *ref* to curl up; to cuddle
raggranellare (raggranèllo) *tr* to gather; to scrape together
raggrinzire §176 *tr & ref* to crease, wrinkle
raggrumare *tr & ref* to clot, coagulate
raggruppaménto *m* grouping; group
raggruppare *tr & ref* to group, assemble
ragguagliare §280 *tr* to compare; to balance; to inform in detail; to level
ragguà·glio *m* (**-gli**) comparison; detailed report
ragguardévole *adj* considerable, notable
ragionaménto *m* reasoning; discussion
ragionare (ragióno) *intr* to reason; to discuss || *impers ref*—**si ragiona** it is rumored
ragióne *f* reason; account; rate; justice; (math) ratio; **a maggior ragione** with all the more reason; **a ragione** within reason; **aver ragione** to be right; **aver ragione di** to get the best of; **dar ragione a qlcu** to admit that s.o. is right; **di santa ragione** hard, a great deal; **farsi ragione** to be resigned; **in ragione di** at the rate of; **ragion per cui** and therefore; **ragione sociale** (com) trade name; **rendere di pubblica ragione** to publicize
ragionerìa *f* accounting; bookkeeping
ragionévole *adj* reasonable
ragioniè·re -ra *mf* accountant; bookkeeper
ragliare §280 *intr* to bray
rà·glio *m* (**-gli**) bray
ragnatéla *f* spider web
ragno *m* spider
ra·gù *m* (**-gù**) meat gravy; stew
ràion *m* rayon
rallegraménto *m* congratulation, act of congratulating; **rallegramenti** congratulations
rallegrare (rallégro) *tr* to cheer up; to rejoice, gladden || *ref* to cheer up; to rejoice; **rallegrarsi con** to congratulate
rallentare (rallènto) *tr, intr & ref* to slow down; to lessen
rallentatóre *m* slow-motion projector; **al rallentatore** slow-motion
ra·màio *m* (**-mài**) tinker, coppersmith
ramaiòlo *m* ladle
ramanzina [dz] *f* reprimand
ramare *tr* to copperplate; (agr) to spray with copper sulfate
ramarro *m* green lizard
ramazza *f* broom; (mil) cleaning detail; (mil) soldier on cleaning detail
rame *m* copper; etching
ramerino *m* (coll) rosemary
ramificare §197 (**ramìfico**) *intr & ref* to branch; to branch off; to branch out, ramify
ramin·go -ga *adj* (**-ghi -ghe**) wandering
ramino *m* copper pot; rummy (*card game*)
rammagliare §280 *tr* to reknit; to mend a run in (*a stocking*)
rammaricare §197 (**rammàrico**) *tr* to afflict || *ref* to be sorry, regret; **rammaricarsi di** to be sorry for

rammàri·co *m* **(-chi)** regret
rammendare (rammèndo) *tr* to darn
rammèndo *m* darn
rammentare (ramménto) *tr* to remember; to remind || *ref*—**rammentarsi di** to remember
rammenta·tóre -trice *mf* prompter
rammollire §176 *tr & ref* to soften
rammolli·to -ta *adj* soft; soft-headed || *m* dodo, jellyfish
ramo *m* branch; bough; point (*of antler*); **ramo di pazzia** streak of madness
ramoscèllo *m* twig; **ramoscello d'olivo** olive branch
rampa *f* ramp; flight (*of stairs*); launching platform
rampicante *adj* climbing || *m* (ichth) perch; (orn) climber
rampino *m* hook; tine, prong; pretext
rampógna *f* (lit) reprimand
rampóllo *m* spring (*of water*); scion; shoot (*of a plant*); (joc) offspring
rampóne *m* harpoon; crampon
rana *f* frog
rànci·do -da *adj* rancid
ràn·cio -cia (-ci -ce) *adj* (poet) orange || *m* (mil) mess
rancóre *m* rancor; grudge; **serbar rancore** to bear malice
randa *f* (naut) spanker; (obs) edge
randà·gio -gia *adj* **(-gi -gie)** wandering; stray
randellare (randèllo) *tr* to cudgel; to bludgeon; to blackjack
randèllo *m* cudgel; bludgeon
ran·go *m* **(-ghi)** rank; station
rannicchiare §287 *tr* to cause to curl up || *ref* to crouch; to cower; to cuddle up
ranno *m* lye; **buttar via il ranno e il sapone** to waste one's time and effort
rannuvolare (rannùvolo) *tr & ref* to cloud; to darken
ranòcchia *f* frog
ranòc·chio *m* **(-chi)** frog
rantolare (ràntolo) *intr* to wheeze
ràntolo *m* wheezing; death rattle
ranùncolo *m* buttercup
rapa *f* turnip; **valere una rapa** to be not worth a fig
rapace *adj* rapacious || **rapaci** *mpl* birds of prey
rapare *tr* to shave (*s.o.'s head*) || *ref* to shave one's head; to have one's head shaved
rapidi·tà *f* **(-tà)** rapidity, swiftness
ràpi·do -da *adj* rapid, swift || *m* (rr) express || **rapide** *fpl* rapids
rapiménto *m* rape, abduction; rapture
rapina *f* pillage, plunder; misappropriation; prey; (lit) fury; **rapina a mano armata** armed robbery
rapinare *tr* to rob, plunder; to hold up; **rapinare qlco a qlcu** to rob s.o. of s.th
rapina·tóre -trice *mf* robber, plunderer
rapire §176 *tr* to rape, abduct; to kidnap; to enrapture
rapi·tóre -trice *mf* kidnaper
rappacificare §197 **(rappacìfico)** *tr* to reconcile || *ref* to become reconciled
rappezzare (rappèzzo) *tr* to patch; to piece; **rappezzarla** to get out of trouble
rappèzzo *m* patch; patchwork
rapportare (rappòrto) *tr* to report; to transfer (*a design*) || *ref* to refer
rapporta·tóre -trice *mf* reporter || *m* protractor
rappòrto *m* report; relation; relationship; (math) ratio; **chiamare a rapporto** to summon; **chiedere di mettersi a rapporto** to ask for a hearing; **fare rapporto** to report; **in rapporto a** concerning; **mettersi a rapporto** to report; **sotto ogni rapporto** in every respect
rapprèndere §220 *tr & ref* to coagulate
rappresàglia [s] *f* reprisal; retaliation
rappresentante *adj* representing; representative || *mf* representative; agent; **rappresentante di commercio** agent
rappresentanza *f* delegation; proxy; agency; representation
rappresentare (rappresènto) *tr* to represent; to play; to portray
rappresentati·vo -va *adj* representative
rappresentazióne *f* representation; description; (theat) performance; **rappresentazione teatrale diurna** matinée; **sacra rappresentazione** (theat) mystery, miracle play
rapsodìa *f* rhapsody
raraménte *adv* seldom, rarely
rarefare §173 *tr* to rarefy || *ref* to become rarefied
rari·tà *f* **(-tà)** rarity
ra·ro -ra *adj* rare; **di raro** seldom
rasare [s] *tr* to shave; to mow; to trim; to smooth || *ref* to shave
raschiare §287 **(ràschio)** *tr* to scrape; to scratch || *intr* to clear one's throat
raschiétto *m* scraper; erasing knife; footscraper
rà·schio *m* **(-schi)** clearing one's throat; hoarseness; frog in the throat
rasentare (rasènto) *tr* to graze; to scrape; to border on; to come close to
rasènte *adv* close; **rasente a** close to || *prep* close to
ra·so -sa [s] *adj* shaved; trimmed; brimful; disreputable (*clothes*); flush || *m* satin || *adv*—**raso terra** down-to-earth; **volare raso terra** to skim the ground; to hedgehop
ra·sóio [s] *m* **(-sói)** razor; **rasoio a mano libera** straight razor; **rasoio di sicurezza** safety razor
raspa *f* rasp
raspare *tr* to rasp; to irritate; to stamp, paw; (coll) to steal || *intr* to rasp; to scratch (*said of a chicken*); to scrawl
raspo *m* grape stalk; scraper; (vet) mange
rasségna *f* review; exposition
rassegnare (rasségno) *tr* to resign; **rassegnare le dimissioni** to resign || *ref* to resign oneself; to submit
rassegnazióne *f* resignation
rasserenare (rasseréno) *tr & ref* to brighten; to cheer up
rassettare (rassètto) *tr & ref* to tidy up

rassicurare *tr* to reassure || *ref* to be reassured
rassodare (**rassòdo**) *tr* to harden; to strengthen || *intr* (ESSERE) & *ref* to harden
rassomigliare §280 (**rassomìglio**) *tr* to compare || *intr* (ESSERE) (with *dat*) to resemble || *ref* to resemble each other
rastrellaménto *m* roundup; mop-up operation
rastrellare (**rastrèllo**) *tr* to rake; to round up; to mop up; to drag (*e.g., the bottom*)
rastrellièra *f* rack; crib
rastrèllo *m* rake
rastremare (**rastrèmo**) *tr* to taper
rata *f* installment; quota; **a rate** on time; by installments
rateale *adj* installment
rateizzare [ddzz] *tr* to prorate; to divide (*a payment*) into installments
ratìfi•ca *f* (**-che**) ratification
ratificare §197 (**ratìfico**) *tr* to ratify
rat•to -ta *adj* (lit) swift || *m* rat; (lit) rape || **ratto** *adv* (lit) swiftly
rattoppare (**rattòppo**) *tr* to patch, patch up
rattrappire §176 *tr* to cramp; to make numb, benumb || *ref* to become cramped; to become numb
rattristare *tr* & *ref* to sadden
raucèdine *f* hoarseness
ràu•co -ca *adj* (**-chi -che**) hoarse, raucous
ravanèllo *m* radish
ravizzóne *m* (bot) rape
ravvedére §279 (*fut* **ravvedrò** & **ravvederò**; *pp* **ravveduto**) *ref* to repent; to mend one's ways
ravvedu•to -ta *adj* repentant; reformed
ravviare §119 *tr* to arrange, adjust; to poke (*fire*) || *ref* to tidy up; (lit) to reform
ravvicinaménto *m* approach; reconciliation; rapprochement
ravvicinare *tr* to bring up; to reconcile || *ref* to approach; to become reconciled; **ravvicinarsi a** to approach
ravviluppare *tr* to wrap up; to wind up; to bamboozle || *ref* to become tangled
ravvisare *tr* to recognize
ravvivare *tr* to revive; to enliven; to brighten; to stir (*fire*) || *ref* to revive
ravvòlgere §289 *tr* to wrap up
raziocì•nio *m* (**-ni**) reasoning; reason; common sense
razionale *adj* rational
razionalizzare [ddzz] *tr* (com, math) to rationalize
razionaménto *m* rationing
razionare (**razióno**) *tr* to ration
razióne *f* ration; portion
razza *f* race; breed; kind; **di razza** purebred; **far razza** to reproduce; **passare a razza** to go to stud
razza [ddzz] *f* (ichth) ray; **razza cornuta** manta ray
razzìa *f* raid; foray; insect powder
razziale *adj* racial
razziare §119 *tr* & *intr* to foray
razzismo *m* racism
razzi•sta *mf* (**-sti -ste**) racist
razzo [ddzz] *m* rocket; (coll) spoke; (mil) flare
razzolare (**ràzzolo**) *intr* to scratch (*said of chickens*); (coll) to rummage
re [e] *m* (**re**) king
re [ɛ] *m* (**re**) (mus) re
reagènte *m* reagent
reagire §176 *intr* to react
reale *adj* real, actual; royal, regal
realismo *m* realism; royalism
reali•sta *mf* (**-sti -ste**) realist; royalist
realìsti•co -ca *adj* (**-ci -che**) realistic
realizzare [ddzz] *tr* to carry out; to realize; to build || *ref* to come true
realizzazióne [ddzz] *f* realization; **realizzazione scenica** production
realizzo [ddzz] *m* conversion into cash; profit taking; forced sale
realménte *adv* really, indeed
real•tà *f* (**-tà**) reality; actuality; **realtà romanzesca** truth stranger than fiction
reato *m* crime
reatti•vo -va *adj* reactive
reattóre *m* reactor; jet plane; jet engine
reazionà•rio -ria (**-ri -rie**) *adj* & *mf* reactionary
reazióne *f* reaction; (mach) backlash; **a reazione** jet-propelled
réb•bio *m* (**-bi**) prong
recalcitrante *adj* balky, restive; **essere recalcitrante a** to be opposed to, to resist
recalcitrare (**recàlcitro**) *intr* to be balky; to kick; (with *dat*) to buck, resist
recapitare (**recàpito**) *tr* to deliver
recàpito *m* address; delivery; **far recapito in** to be domiciled in; **recapiti** (com) notes
recare §197 (**rèco**) *tr* to bring; to cause; **recare ad effetto** to carry out; **recare qlco alla memoria di qlcu** to remind s.o. of s.th; **recare qlco a lode di qlcu** to praise s.o. for s.th || *ref* to go, betake oneself
recèdere §123 *intr* (ESSERE & AVERE) to recede
recensióne *f* book review; collation
recensire §176 *tr* to review; to collate
recensóre *m* reviewer
recènte *adj* recent; **di recente** recently
recessióne *f* recession
recèsso *m* recess; subsiding (*of fever*); ebb tide
recìdere §145 *tr* to cut off; to chop off
recidiva *f* relapse; second offense
recìngere §126 *tr* to enclose, pen in
recinto *m* enclosure; pen, yard; compound; playpen; paddock; **recinto delle grida** floor of the exchange
recipiènte *m* container
reciprocità *f* reciprocity
recìpro•co -ca *adj* (**-ci -che**) reciprocal
reci•so -sa *adj* cut off; abrupt
rècita *f* show, performance
recitare (**rècito**) *tr* to recite; to portray, play; **recitare la commedia** to put on an act || *intr* to perform, play; **recitare a soggetto** (theat) to improvise
recitazióne *f* recitation; diction; acting

reclamare *tr* to claim, demand ‖ *intr* to complain
récla•me *f* (**-me**) advertising; advertisement; **fare réclame a** to advertise; to boost
reclami•sta *mf* (**-sti -ste**) advertising agent; show-off ‖ *m* advertising man
reclamìsti•co -ca *adj* (**-ci -che**) advertising
reclamo *m* complaint; **fare reclamo** to complain
reclinare *tr* to bow ‖ *intr* to recline
reclusióne *f* seclusion; imprisonment
reclu•so -sa *adj* recluse ‖ *mf* recluse; prisoner
reclusò•rio *m* (**-ri**) penitentiary
rècluta *f* recruit; rookie
reclutaménto *m* recruitment
reclutare (**rècluto**) *tr* to recruit
recòndi•to -ta *adj* concealed; inmost; recondite
recriminare (**recrìmino**) *intr* to recriminate
recuperare (**recùpero**) *tr* see **ricuperare**
redarguire §176 *tr* to berate
redat•tóre -trice *mf* compiler; newspaper editor; **redattore capo** managing editor; **redattore pubblicitario** copywriter; **redattore responsabile** publisher; **redattore viaggiante** correspondent
redazionale *adj* editorial, editor's (*e.g., policy*)
redazióne *f* writing; draft; version; (journ) city room
redazza *f* mop; (naut) swab
redditi•zio -zia *adj* (**-zi -zie**) lucrative
rèddito *m* income, revenue; yield; **reddito nazionale** gross national product
redèn•to -ta *adj* redeemed, set free
reden•tóre -trice *mf* redeemer ‖ **Redentore** *m*—**il Redentore** the Redeemer
redenzióne *f* redemption
redìgere §224 *tr* to compile; to write up, compose
redìmere §225 *tr* to redeem; to ransom; to save
rèdine *f* rein
redivi•vo -va *adj* come back to life
rèduce *adj* back (*from war*) ‖ *mf* veteran
réfe *m* thread
referèn•dum *m* (**-dum**) referendum; **referendum postale** mail questionnaire
referènza *f* reference
referenziare (**referènzio**) *tr* to give references to; to write references for ‖ *intr* to have good references
referenzia•to -ta *adj* with good references, e.g., **impiegato referenziato** employee with good references
refèrto *m* report (*of a physician*)
refettò•rio *m* (**-ri**) refectory
refezióne *f* lunch, light meal; **refezione scolastica** school lunch
refrattà•rio -ria *adj* (**-ri -rie**) refractory
refrigerante *adj* cooling ‖ *m* refrigerator; (chem) condenser
refrigerare (**refrìgero**) *tr* to refrigerate; to cool ‖ *ref* to cool off
refrigè•rio *m* (**-ri**) relief, comfort
refurtiva *f* stolen goods
refuso *m* misprint
regalare *tr* to present; to deliver (*a slap*); to throw away (*money*); **è regalato** it's a steal
regale *adj* regal; royal; imposing
regalìa *f* gratuity; bonus
regalità *f* regality, royalty
regalo *m* present, gift
regata *f* regatta
reggènte *adj* & *m* regent
reggènza *f* regency
règgere §226 *tr* to hold, hold up; to stand, withstand; to guide; (gram) to govern; **reggere il sacco a** to connive with; **reggere l'animo di** + *inf* to bear or stand + *ger*, e.g., **non gli regge l'animo di vederla piangere** he cannot stand seeing her cry ‖ *intr* to hold; to be valid; to last, hold out (*said of weather*); **reggere** (with *dat*) to withstand (*e.g., the cold*); **reggere al paragone** to bear comparison ‖ *ref* to stand up; to hold; to be ruled; **reggersi a** to hold on to; to be governed as (*e.g., a republic*); **reggersi a galla** to float
règ•gia *f* (**-ge**) royal palace
reggical•ze *m* (**-ze**) girdle
reggilibro *m* book end
reggimentale *adj* regimental
reggiménto *m* regiment
reggipètto *m* brassiere
reggisé•no *m* (**-ni** & **-no**) brassiere
regìa *f* monopoly; (mov) direction; (theat) production
regici•da *mf* (**-di -de**) regicide
regicì•dio *m* (**-di**) regicide
regime *m* regime; diet; flow (*e.g., of river*); government; authoritarian government; (mach) rate; **regime secco** total abstinence
regina *f* queen; **regina claudia** greengage; **regina madre** queen mother
reginétta *f* young queen; queen (*of a beauty contest*)
rè•gio -gia *adj* (**-gi -gie**) royal ‖ **i regi** the king's soldiers
regióne *f* region
regi•sta *mf* (**-sti -ste**) coordinator; (theat) producer; (mov) director
registrare *tr* to register, record; to enter; to tally, log; to adjust; to tune up (*a musical instrument*) ‖ *ref* to register
registra•tóre -trice *mf* registrar ‖ *m* recorder; **registratore di cassa** cash register
registrazióne *f* registration; record, entry; adjustment; (aut) tune-up; (telv) videotaping; (telv) video-taping studio; (telv) video-taped program
registro *m* register; registration; classbook; regulator (*of watch*); stop (*of organ*); **cambiar registro** to change one's tune; **dar registro a** to regulate (*a watch*)
regnante *adj* reigning; prevailing ‖ **i regnanti** the rulers
regnare (**régno**) *intr* to reign, rule; to prevail; to take hold (*said of a root*)
régno *m* kingdom; reign

règola *f* rule; regulation; moderation; **a regola d'arte** to a T; **di regola** as a rule; **in regola** in good order; **mettere in regola** to put in order; **regole** menstruation; **secondo le regole** by the book
regolamentare *adj* regulation || *v* **(regolaménto)** *tr* to regulate
regolaménto *m* regulation; settlement; **regolamento edilizio** building code
regolare *adj* regular; steady (*employment*); stock (*material*) || *v* **(règolo)** *tr* to regulate; to adjust; to set (*a watch*); to focus (*a lens*); to settle (*an account*) || *ref* to behave; to control oneself
regolari·tà *f* **(-tà)** regularity
regolarizzare [ddzz] *tr* to regularize
regolatézza *f* regularity; moderation
regola·to -ta *adj* regular, orderly
regola·tóre -trice *adj* regulating; see **piano** || *m* ruler; regulator (*of watch*); (mach) governor; **regolatore dell'aria** register; **regolatore di volume** (rad, telv) volume control
regolazióne *f* regulation
regolìzia *f* (coll) licorice
règolo *m* ruler; slat; (orn, hist) kinglet; **regolo calcolatore** slide rule
regredire §176 (*pres participle* **regrediènte;** *pp* **regredito & regrèsso)** *intr* (ESSERE & AVERE) to retrogress
regrèsso *m* regression; abatement (*of fever*); (com) recourse
reièt·to -ta *adj* rejected || *mf* outcast
reimbarcare §197 *tr & ref* to reship; to transship
reimbar·co *m* **(-chi)** reshipment; transshipment
reincarnare *tr* to reincarnate || *ref* to become reincarnated
reincarnazióne *f* reincarnation
reinseriménto *m* integration
reintegrare (reìntegro) *tr* to restore; to reinstate; to indemnify
reità *f* guilt
reiterare (reìtero) *tr* to reiterate
relativi·tà *f* **(-tà)** relativity
relati·vo -va *adj* relative
rela·tóre -trice *adj* reporting || *mf* relator (*of proceedings*); presenter (*of a bill*); dissertation supervisor
relazióne *f* relation; relationship; report; **relazione amorosa** affair; **relazioni** relations; connections
re·lè *m* **(-lè)** (elec) relay
relegare §209 **(rèlego)** *tr* to banish; to store away
religióne *f* religion
religió·so -sa [s] *adj* religious || *m* clergyman || *f* nun
relìquia *f* relic
relit·to -ta *adj* residual || *m* shipwreck; air crash; derelict; shoal, bar
remare (rèmo & rémo) *intr* to row
rema·tóre -trice *mf* rower || *m* oarsman
reminiscènza *f* reminiscence
remissióne *f* submissiveness; remission
remissi·vo -va *adj* submissive
rèmo *m* oar; **remo alla battana** paddle
rèmora *f* hindrance; (lit) delay
remò·to -ta *adj* remote; **passato remoto** (gram) preterit

réna *f* sand
Renània, la the Rhineland
Renata *f* Renée
rèndere §227 *tr* to return, give back to give (*thanks*); to render (*justice*) to yield; to translate; to mak (*known*); **render conto di** to give a account of; **rendere di pubblica ra gione** to publicize; **rendere l'anima Dio** to give up the ghost; **rendere pa per focaccia** to give tit for tat *intr* to pay, yield || *ref* to make one self; to betake oneself; to become (lit) to surrender; **rendersi conto d** to realize
rendicónto *m* account; report; **rendi conti** proceedings
rendiménto *m* rendering; yield; output (mech) efficiency
rèndita *f* private income; yield; Italia Government bond
rène *m* kidney
renèlla *f* (pathol) gravel
renétta *f* pippin
réni *fpl* loins; **spezzare le reni a t** break the back of
renitènte *adj* opposed || *m*—**renitent alla leva** draft dodger
rènna *f* reindeer; reindeer skin
Rèno *m* Rhine
rè·o -a *adj* guilty; (lit) wicked || *n* guilty person; accused
reòstato *m* (elec) rheostat
reparto *m* department; (mil) unit; **re parto d'assalto** shock troops
repèllere §168 *tr* to repel
repentàglio *m* jeopardy; **mettere a re pentaglio** to jeopardize
repènte *adj*—**di repente** suddenly
repenti·no -na *adj* sudden
reperìbile *adj* available
reperiménto *m* finding
reperire §176 *tr* to find
repèrto *m* (archeol) find; (law) evi dence; (law) exhibit; (med) report
repertò·rio *m* **(-ri)** repertory; catalogu
rèpli·ca *f* **(-che)** repetition; replica (law) rebuttal; (theat) repeat per formance; **in replica** in reply
replicare §197 **(rèplico)** *tr* to repeat; t reply, answer; (theat) to repeat (*a performance*)
reportàg·gio *m* **(-gi)** news coverage reporting
repòr·ter *m* **(-ter)** reporter
repressióne *f* repression; constraint
repressi·vo -va *adj* repressive; control ling, checking (*e.g., a disease*)
reprìmere §131 *tr* to repress; to hol back (*tears*) || *ref* to restrain onesel
rèpro·bo -ba *adj & m* reprobate
repùbbli·ca *f* **(-che)** republic
repubblica·no -na *adj & mf* republica
repulisti *m*—**fare repulisti** (coll) t make a clean sweep
repulsióne *f* repulsion
repulsi·vo -va *adj* var of **ripulsivo**
reputare (rèputo) *tr* to think, esteem repute
reputazióne *f* reputation
rèquie *m & f* (eccl) requiem || *f* rest respite
Rèquiem *m & f* Requiem

requisire §176 *tr* to requisition, commandeer
requisito *m* requisite, requirement
requisitòria *f* scolding, reproach; (law) summation
requisizióne *f* requisition
résa [s] *f* surrender; rendering (*of an account*); delivery (*of merchandise*); return (*e.g., of newspapers*); yield; **resa a discrezione** unconditional surrender
rescìndere §247 *tr* to rescind
resezióne [s] *f* (surg) resection
residènte [s] *adj & mf* resident
residènza [s] *f* residence
residenziale [s] *adj* residential
residua·to -ta [s] *adj* residual
resì·duo -dua [s] *adj* residual ‖ *m* residue; remainder; balance
rèsina *f* resin
resipiscènza [s] *f* (lit) repentance
resistènte [s] *adj* resistant; strong; fast (*color*) ‖ *mf* member of the Resistance
resistènza [s] *f* resistance ‖ **Resistenza** *f* Resistance
resìstere [s] §114 *intr* to resist; (with *dat*) to withstand; (with *dat*) to endure; (with *dat*) to resist
rèso [s] *m* rhesus
resocónto [s] *m* report, relation
respingènte *m* (rr) bumper, buffer
respìngere §126 *tr* to drive back, beat off; to reject; to fail (*a student*); to vote down
respin·to -ta *adj* rejected ‖ *mf* failure (*pupil*)
respirare *tr & intr* to breathe, respire
respiratò·rio -ria *adj* (**-ri -rie**) respiratory
respirazióne *f* breathing
respiro *m* breath; breathing; respite
responsàbile *adj* responsible; **responsabile di** responsible for
responsabili·tà *f* (**-tà**) responsibility
respònso *m* decision (*of an oracle*); report (*of a physician*); return (*of an election*); (lit) response
rèssa *f* crowd; **far ressa** to crowd
rèsta *f* string (*of garlic or onions*); awn (*e.g., of wheat*); (coll) fishbone; (*for a lance*) (hist) rest
restante *adj* remaining ‖ *m* remainder
restare (rèsto) *intr* (ESSERE) to remain; to stay; to be located; (lit) to stop; **non restare a...che** to have no alternative but to, e.g., **non gli resta che andarsene** he has no alternative but to go; **non restare a qlcu qlco da** + *inf* to not have s.th + to + *inf*, e.g., **non gli resta molto da finire** he does not have much to finish; **resta a vedere** it remains to be seen; **restare qlco a qlcu** to have s.th left, e.g., **gli restano tre dollari** he has three dollars left; **restare sul colpo** to die on the spot; **resti comodo** please don't get up!
restaurare (restàuro) *tr* to restore, renovate
restaurazióne *f* restoration
restàuro *m* restoration (*of a building*)
restì·o -a (**-ì -e**) *adj* balky, restive ‖ *m* balkiness
restituire §176 *tr* to give back, return; (lit) to restore ‖ *ref* (lit) to return
restituzióne *f* restitution, return
rèsto *m* remainder; change; balance; **del resto** besides, after all; **resti** remains
restrìngere §265 (*pp* **ristrétto**) *tr* to narrow down; to shrink; to take in (*a suit*); to limit (*expenses*); to tighten (*a knot*); to bind (*the bowels*); to restrict ‖ *ref* to contract; to narrow
restrizióne *f* restriction
retàg·gio *m* (**-gi**) (lit) heritage
retata *f* haul; (fig) roundup
réte *f* net; network; (soccer) goal; **rete a strascico** trawl; **rete da pesca** fishing net; **rete del letto** bedspring; **rete metallica** wire mesh; window screen; **rete per i capelli** hair net; **rete viaria** highway network
reticèlla *f* small net; hair net; mantle (*of gas jet*)
reticènte *adj* secretive, dissembling; evasive, noncommittal
reticènza *f* secretiveness; evasiveness
reticolato *m* grid (*on map*); wire entanglement
retìcolo *m* grid
retina *f* small net
rètina *f* (anat) retina
retino *m* small net; (typ) screen
retòri·co -ca (**-ci -che**) *adj* rhetorical ‖ *m* rhetorician ‖ *f* rhetoric
retràttile *adj* retractile
retribuire §176 *tr* to remunerate
retributi·vo -va *adj* retributive; salary (*e.g., conditions*)
retri·vo -va *adj* backward
rètro *m* back; verso; back of store ‖ *adv* (lit) behind; **retro a** (lit) behind
retroatti·vo -va *adj* retroactive
retrobotté·ga *m & f* (**-ga** *mpl* **-ghe** *fpl*) back of store
retrocàmera *f* back room
retrocàrica *f*—**a retrocarica** breechloading
retrocèdere §228 *tr* to demote; (com) to return; (com) to give a discount to ‖ *intr* (ESSERE & AVERE) to retreat
retrocessióne *f* demotion; (sports) assignment to a lower division
retrodatare *tr* to antedate, predate
retrògra·do -da *adj* backward; retrograde
retroguàrdia *f* rearguard
retromàr·cia *f* (**-ce**) (aut) reverse
retrorazzo [ddzz] *m* retrorocket
retrosapóre *m* aftertaste
retroscè·na *m* (**-na**) intrigue, maneuver ‖ *f* backstage
retrospetti·vo -va *adj* retrospective
retrotèr·ra *m* (**-ra**) hinterland; (fig) background
retrotrèno *m* rear end (*of vehicle*); (aut) rear assembly
retroversióne *f* retroversion; retranslation
retrovìe *fpl* zone behind the front
retrovisi·vo -va *adj* rear-view, e.g., **specchietto retrovisivo** rear-view mirror

retrovisóre *m* rear-view mirror
rètta *f* board and lodging; straight line; **dar retta a** to pay attention to
rettangolare *adj* rectangular
rettàngolo *m* rectangle
rettìfi•ca *f* (**-che**) straightening; rectification; (mach) grinding; (mach) reboring
rettificare §197 (**rettìfico**) *tr* to straighten; to rectify; (mach) to grind; (mach) to rebore
rettifica•tóre -trice *adj* rectifying || *mf* rectifier (*person*) || *m* rectifier (*apparatus*)
rettifilo *m* straightaway
rèttile *m* reptile
rettilì•neo -nea *adj* rectilinear || *m* straightaway || *f* straight line
rettitùdine *f* straightness; uprightness, rectitude
rèt•to -ta *adj* straight; correct; upright; (geom) right || *m* right; recto; (anat) rectum || *f* see **retta**
rettóre *m* rector; president (*of university*)
reumàti•co -ca *adj* (**-ci -che**) rheumatic
reumatismo *m* rheumatism
reverèn•do -da *adj & m* reverend
reverènte *adj* var of **riverente**
reverènza *f* var of **riverenza**
revisióne *f* revision; (mach) overhaul
revisionismo *m* revisionism
revisóre *m* inspector; **revisore dei conti** auditor; **revisore di bozze** proofreader
reviviscènza *f* rebirth
rèvo•ca *f* (**-che**) revocation; recall; repeal
revocare §197 (**rèvoco**) *tr* to revoke; to recall; to repeal
revòl•ver *m* (**-ver**) revolver
revolverata *f* gun shot
revulsióne *f* (med) revulsion
ri- *pref* re-, e.g., **rivivere** to relive; again, e.g., **rifare** to do again; back, e.g., **riandare** to go back
riabbonare (**riabbòno**) *tr* to renew the subscription of || *ref* to renew one's subscription
riabbracciare §128 (**riabbràccio**) *tr* to embrace again; to greet again
riabilitare (**riabìlito**) *tr* to rehabilitate || *ref* to reestablish one's good name
riaccèndere §101 *tr* to rekindle || *ref* to become rekindled
riaccompagnare *tr* to take home
riaccostare (**riaccòsto**) *tr* to bring near; to bring together || *ref* to draw near
riacquistare *tr* to buy back; to recover
riaddormentare (**riaddorménto**) *tr* to put back to sleep || *ref* to go back to sleep
riaffacciare §128 (**riaffàccio**) *tr* to present again || *ref* to reappear
riaffermare (**riafférmo**) *tr* to reaffirm
riaggravare *tr* to make worse || *ref* to get worse again
rialesare (**rialèso**) *tr* to rebore
riallacciare §128 (**riallàccio**) *tr* to tie again || *ref* to be tied or connected
rialto *m* knoll, height; **fare rialto** (coll) to eat better than usual
rialzare *tr* to lift, raise; to increase || *ref* to rise
rialzi•sta *mf* (**-sti -ste**) bull (*in stock market*)
rialzo *m* rise; raise; knoll, height; **giocare al rialzo** to bull the market
riammobiliare §287 *tr* to refurnish
rianimare (**riànimo**) *tr* to revive; to encourage || *ref* to revive; to recover one's spirits, to rally
riapertura *f* reopening
riapparire §108 *intr* (ESSERE) to reappear
riapparizióne *f* reappearance
riaprire §110 *tr & ref* to reopen
riarmare *tr* to rearm; to reinforce; to refit || *intr & ref* to rearm
riarmo *m* rearmament
riar•so -sa *adj* dry, parched
riassaporare (**riassapóro**) *tr* to relish again
riassettare (**riassètto**) *tr* to tidy up
riassicurare *tr* to reinsure; to fasten again; to reassure
riassorbire §176 & (**riassòrbo**) *tr* to reabsorb
riassùmere §116 *tr* to hire again; to summarize, sum up
riassunto *m* précis, abstract; résumé
riassunzióne *f* rehiring; resumption
riattaccare §197 *tr* to attach again; (coll) to begin again; (telp) to hang up
riattare *tr* to repair, fix
riattivare *tr* to reactivate
riavére §229 *tr* to get again; to recover; to get back || *ref* to recover
riavvicinaménto *m* var of **ravvicinamento**
riavvicinare *tr & ref* var of **ravvicinare**
ribadire §176 *tr* to clinch (*a nail*); to rivet; to drive home (*an idea*); to back up (*a statement*)
ribaldo *m* scoundrel, rogue
ribalta *f* lid with hinge; trap door; (theat) footlights; (theat) forestage; (fig) limelight; **a ribalta** hinged
ribaltàbile *adj* collapsable (*e.g., seat*) || *m* dump-truck lift; dump truck
ribaltare *tr & ref* to upset, turn over
ribassare *tr & intr* (ESSERE) to lower
ribassi•sta *mf* (**-sti -ste**) bear (*in stock market*)
ribasso *m* fall, decline; discount, rebate; **giocare al ribasso** to be a bear
ribàttere *tr* to clinch (*a nail*); to return (*a ball*); to iron smooth; to belabor (*a point*) || *intr* to answer back
ribattezzare [ddzz] (**ribattézzo**) *tr* to rebaptize
ribattino *m* rivet
ribellare (**ribèllo**) *tr* to rouse to rebellion || *ref* to rebel; **ribellarsi a** to rebel against
ribèlle *adj* rebellious || *mf* rebel
ribellióne *f* rebellion
ri•bes *m* (**-bes**) currant; gooseberry
ribobinazióne *f* rewind (*of a tape*)
riboccare §197 (**ribócco**) *intr* (ESSERE & AVERE) to overflow
ribollire (**ribóllo**) *tr* to boil again ||

intr to boil over; to simmer; to ferment
ribrézzo [ddzz] *m* repugnance, disgust
ributtare *tr* to return (*a ball*); to throw up; to reject; to push back || *intr* to sprout; (with *dat*) to disgust, nauseate
ricacciare §128 *tr* to drive back || *intr* to sprout || *ref* to sneak away, disappear
ricadére §121 *intr* (ESSERE) to fall back; to fall down; to relapse; **ricadere su** to devolve upon
ricaduta *f* relapse
ricalcare §197 *tr* to transfer (*a design*); to imitate; **ricalcare le orme di** follow in the footsteps of
rical·co *m* (**-chi**) copy, copying; **a ricalco** multiple-copy
ricamare *tr* to embroider
ricambiare §287 *tr* to return; to repay || *ref* to change clothes
ricàm·bio *m* (**-bi**) exchange; spare part; refill; metabolism; **di ricambio** spare (*part*)
ricamo *m* embroidery; needlework; **ricami** (*fig*) embellishments
ricapitolare (**ricapìtolo**) *tr* to recapitulate
ricaricare §197 (**ricàrico**) *tr* to reload; to wind (*a watch*); to charge (*a battery*)
ricattare *tr* to blackmail
ricatta·tóre -trice *mf* blackmailer
ricatto *m* blackmail
ricavare *tr* to draw, extract; to obtain, derive
ricavato *m* proceeds; (fig) fruit, yield
ricavo *m* proceeds
ricchézza *f* wealth; **ricchezza mobile** income from personal property; **ricchezze** riches
ric·cio -cia (**-ci -ce**) *adj* curly || *m* curl; shaving; burr; scroll (*of violin*); crook (*of crozier*); (zool) hedgehog; **riccio di mare** (zool) sea urchin
ricciolo *m* curl
ricciolu·to -ta *adj* curly
ricciu·to -ta *adj* curly
ric·co -ca *adj* (**-chi -che**) rich || **i ricchi** the rich
ricér·ca *f* (**-che**) search; research; **ricerca operativa** operations research
ricercare §197 (**ricérco**) *tr* to search for again; to seek; to investigate; (poet) to pluck (*a musical instrument*)
ricercatézza *f* affectation; sophistication
ricerca·to -ta *adj* sought after, wanted; affected; sophisticated
ricetrasmettitóre *m* two-way radio
ricètta *f* prescription; recipe
ricettàcolo *m* receptacle; depository
ricettare (**ricètto**) *tr* to receive (*stolen goods*); to prescribe
ricettà·rio *m* (**-ri**) recipe book; prescription pad
ricetta·tóre -trice *mf* fence, receiver of stolen goods
ricetti·vo -va *adj* receptive
ricètto *m* (poet) refuge
ricévere §141 *tr* to receive; to get; to contain; to withstand
riceviménto *m* reception; receipt
ricevi·tóre -trice *mf* addressee || *m* receiver; collector; registrar of deeds; **ricevitore postale** postmaster
ricevitorìa *f* collection office; **ricevitoria postale** post office
ricevuta *f* receipt; **accusare ricevuta di** to acknowledge receipt of
ricezióne *f* (rad, telv) reception; **accusare ricezione** to acknowledge receipt
richiamare *tr* to call back; to recall; to call (*e.g., attention*); to quote; to chide || *ref* to refer
richiamato *m* soldier recalled to active duty
richiamo *m* call; recall; admonition; cross reference; advertisement
richièdere §124 *tr* to ask again; to demand; to require; to apply for || *ref* to be required
richiè·sto -sta *adj*—**essere richiesto** to be in demand || *f* request; demand; petition, application
richiùdere §125 *tr* & *ref* to shut again
riciclare *tr* to recycle (*e.g., in the chemical industry*)
ricino *m* castor-oil plant
ricognitóre *m* scout; reconnaissance plane; (law) recognition
ricognizióne *f* recognition; (mil) reconnaissance
ricollegare §209 (**ricollégo**) *tr* to connect || *ref* to be connected; to refer
ricolmare (**ricólmo**) *tr* to fill to the brim; to overwhelm
ricominciare §128 *tr* & *intr* (ESSERE) to begin again, resume
ricomparire §108 *intr* (ESSERE) to reappear
ricomparsa *f* reappearance
ricompènsa *f* compensation, recompense; reward; (mil) award
ricompensare (**ricompènso**) *tr* to compensate, recompense; to reward
ricomperare (**ricómpero**) *tr* var of **ricomprare**
ricompórre §218 *tr* to recompose; to plan again || *ref* to regain one's composure
ricomprare (**ricómpro**) *tr* to buy again; to buy back
riconcentrare (**riconcèntro**) *tr* to concentrate again; to gather (*one's thoughts*) || *ref* to be withdrawn
riconciliare §287 (**riconcìlio**) *tr* to reconcile || *ref* to become reconciled
ricondurre §102 *tr* to bring back; to take back || *ref* to go back
riconfermare (**riconférmo**) *tr* to reconfirm
riconfortare (**riconfòrto**) *tr* to comfort
ricongiùngere §183 *tr* & *ref* to reunite
riconoscènte *adj* grateful
riconoscènza *f* gratitude
riconóscere §134 *tr* to recognize; (mil) to reconnoiter
riconosciménto *m* recognition; **in riconoscimento di** in recognition of
riconquistare *tr* to reconquer
riconsegnare (**riconségno**) *tr* to give back, to return

riconsiderare (**riconsidero**) *tr* to reconsider
ricontare (**ricónto**) *tr* to recount, count again
riconversióne *f* reconversion
riconvertire §138 *tr* to reconvert; to recycle
ricopèr•to -ta *adj* covered; coated
ricopertura *f* covering; seat cover
ricopiare §287 (**ricòpio**) *tr* to make a fair copy of; to recopy; to copy
ricoprire §110 *tr* to cover; to coat; to hide || *ref* to become covered
ricordanza *f* (poet) memory
ricordare (**ricòrdo**) *tr* to remember; to remind; to mention || *ref* to remember; **ricordarsi di** to remember
ricòrdo *m* memory; souvenir; **ricordo marmoreo** marble statue
ricorrènte *adj* recurrent, recurring
ricorrènza *f* recurrence; anniversary
ricórrere §139 *intr* (ESSERE & AVERE) to run again; to run back; to resort; to recur; (law) to appeal; **ricorrere a** to have recourse to
ricórso *m* recurrence; recourse; appeal
ricostituènte *adj* invigorating || *m* tonic
ricostituire §176 *tr* to reconstitute, to reform; to reinvigorate
ricostruire §140 *tr* to rebuild; to reconstruct
ricostruzióne *f* rebuilding; reconstruction
ricòtta *f* Italian cottage cheese; **di ricotta** weak
ricoverare (**ricóvero**) *tr* to shelter || *ref* to take shelter
ricóvero *m* shelter; nursing home; (med) admission; **ricovero antiaereo** air-raid shelter
ricreare (**ricrèo**) *tr* to recreate; to refresh || *ref* to relax
ricreati•vo -va *adj* refreshing; recreational
ricreatò•rio -ria (**-ri -rie**) *adj* recreation, recreational || *m* recreation room; playground
ricreazióne *f* recreation; recess
ricrédere §141 *intr*—**far ricredere qlcu** to make s.o. change his mind || *ref* to change one's mind
ricréscere §142 *intr* (ESSERE) to grow again; to swell
ricucire §143 *tr* to sew up
ricuòcere §144a *tr* to cook again; to anneal
ricuperare (**ricùpero**) *tr* to recover; (naut) to salvage; (sports) to make up for (*rained-out game*)
ricùpero *m* recovery; salvage; rally; making up (*for lost time or postponed game*)
ricur•vo -va *adj* bent; bent over
ricusare *tr* to refuse
ridacchiare §287 *intr* to titter, giggle
ridancia•no -na *adj* prone to laughter; amusing
ridare §230 (*1st sg pres ind* **ridò**) *tr* to give back; to give again; **ridare fuori** to vomit || *intr* (coll) to reappear, e.g., **gli ha ridato il foruncolo** his boil has reappeared || *intr* (ESSERE)—**ridare giù** to have a relapse
ridda *f* round; confusion; throng
ridènte *adj* laughing; bright, pleasant
rìdere §231 *tr* (poet) to laugh at || *intr* to laugh; (poet) to shine; **far ridere i polli** to be utterly ridiculous; **ridere sotto i baffi** to laugh up one's sleeve || *ref*—**ridersi di** to laugh at
ridestare (**ridésto**) *tr* & *ref* to reawaken
ridicolizzare [ddzz] *tr* to ridicule; to twit
ridìco•lo -la *adj* ridiculous || *m* ridicule; ridiculousness
ridipìngere §126 *tr* to paint again
ridire §151 *tr* to tell again; to repeat; to tell (*to express*); **avere** or **trovare a** or **da ridire** (**su**) to find fault (with)
ridistribuzióne *f* redistribution
ridivenire §282 or **ridiventare** (**ridivènto**) *intr* (ESSERE) to become again
ridonare (**ridóno**) *tr* to give back
ridondante *adj* redundant
ridondare (**ridóndo**) *intr* (ESSERE & AVERE) (fig) to overflow; **ridondare a** or **in** to redound to
ridòsso *m* back; shelter; **a ridosso** sheltered; as a shelter; behind, close behind
ridót•to -ta *adj* reduced; **mal ridotto** down at the heel || *m* lounge; (theat) foyer || *f* (mil) redoubt
ridurre §102 *tr* to reduce; to adapt; to translate; to lead; to curtail; (mus) to arrange || *ref* to be reduced; to retire
riduttóre *m* (mach) reduction gear
riduzióne *f* reduction; (mus) arrangement
riecheggiare §290 (**riechéggio**) *tr* & *intr* to echo
riedificare §197 (**riedìfico**) *tr* to rebuild
rieducare §197 (**rièduco**) *tr* to reeducate
rielèggere §193 *tr* to reelect
rielezióne *f* reelection
riemèrgere §162 *intr* to resurface
riempiménto *m* fill
riempire §163 *tr* to fill; to stuff
riempiti•vo -va *adj* expletive || *m* expletive; fill-in
rientrante *adj* hollow (*cheeks*); (mil) reentrant
rientranza *f* recess
rientrare (**riéntro**) *intr* (ESSERE) to reenter; to come back; to recede; (coll) to shrink; **rientrare in** to recover (*one's expenses*); **rientrare in sé** to come to one's senses
riéntro *m* reentry
riepilogare §209 (**riepìlogo**) *tr* to sum up, recapitulate
riepìlo•go *m* (**-ghi**) recapitulation
riesame *m* reexamination
riesaminare (**riesàmino**) *tr* to reexamine
riesumare *tr* to exhume; (fig) to dig up; (fig) to bring back
rievocare §197 (**rièvoco**) *tr* to recall
rifaciménto *m* adaptation; recasting
rifare §173 (*3d sg* **rifà**) *tr* to do again, redo; to remake; to imitate; to indemnify; to prepare again; to repeat;

to make (*a bed*) || *ref* to recover; to become again; to recoup one's losses; to begin; **rifarsi con** to get even with; **rifarsi da** to begin with
rifasciare §128 *tr* to rebind
riferiménto *m* reference
riferire §176 *tr* to wound again; to refer; to relate || *ref*—**riferirsi a** to refer to; to concern
riffa *f* raffle; lottery; (coll) violence; **di riffa o di raffa** by hook or crook
rifilare *tr* to trim; (coll) to reel off (*a list of names*); (coll) to deal (*a blow*); (coll) to palm off
rifinire §176 *tr* to give the finishing touch to; to wear out || *intr* to stop || *ref* to wear oneself out
rifiorire §176 *tr* (lit) to revive || *intr* to bloom again || *intr* (ESSERE) to flourish; to grow better; to reappear
rifischiare §287 *tr* to whistle again; (coll) to report || *intr* to talk, gossip
rifiutare *tr* to refuse; (lit) to reject || *intr* (cards) to renege, renounce || *ref* to refuse, deny
rifiuto *m* refusal; refuse, rubbish; rejection; rebuff, spurn; (fig) wreck; (cards) renege; **di rifiuto** waste, e.g., **materiale di rifiuto** waste material
riflessióne *f* reflexion
riflessi·vo -va *adj* thoughtful; (gram) reflexive
riflès·so -sa *adj* reflex, e.g., **azione riflessa** reflex action || *m* reflection; (physiol) reflex; **di riflesso** vicarious
riflèttere §177 (*pp* **riflettuto** & **riflèsso**) *tr* & *intr* to reflect || *ref* to be reflected
riflettóre *m* searchlight; reflector
rifluire §176 *intr* (ESSERE & AVERE) to flow; to flow back
riflusso *m* flow; ebb, ebb tide
rifocillare *tr* to refresh (*with food*) || *ref* to take refreshment
rifóndere §178 *tr* to melt again; to recast; to refund; to reedit
rifórma *f* reform; (mil) rejection || **Riforma** *f*—**la Riforma** the Reformation
riformare (**rifórmo**) *tr* to reform; to amend; (mil) to reject
riformati·vo -va *adj* reformatory
riforma·tóre -trice *adj* reforming || *mf* reformer
riformatò·rio *m* (**-ri**) reform school, reformatory
rifornimiénto *m* supply; refueling; **fare rifornimento di** to fill up with; **rifornimenti** supplies
rifornire §176 *tr* to supply; to restock; **rifornire di benzina** to refuel
rifràngere §179 *tr* to crush || *ref* to break (*said of waves*) || §179 (*pp* **rifratto**) *tr* to refract || *ref* to be refracted
rifrat·tóre -trice *adj* refracting || *m* refractor
rifrazióne *f* refraction
rifriggere §180 *tr* to fry again; to rehash || *intr* to fry too long or in too much oil
rifrit·to -ta *adj* fried again; (fig) hackneyed || *m* taste of stale fat; (fig) rehash
rifuggire *tr* to avoid || *intr*—**rifuggire da** to abhor || *intr* (ESSERE) to take refuge
rifugiare §290 *ref* to take refuge, take shelter
rifugiato *m* refugee
rifù·gio *m* (**-gi**) refuge; **rifugio alpino** mountain hut; **rifugio antiaereo** air-raid shelter; **rifugio antiatomico** fall-out shelter
rifùlgere §233 *intr* (ESSERE & AVERE) to shine
rifusióne *f* recast; refund, reimbursement
ri·ga *f* (**-ghe**) line; row; rank; ruler; part (*in hair*); stripe; (fig) quality
rigàglie *fpl* giblets
rigàgnolo *m* rivulet; gutter (*at the side of a road*)
rigare §209 *tr* to rule, line; to stripe; to mark; to rifle (*gun*) || *intr*—**rigare diritto** to toe the line
rigatino *m* gingham
rigattière *m* second-hand dealer
rigatura *f* ruling; rifling (*of gun*)
rigenerare (**rigènero**) *tr* to regenerate; to reclaim; to recycle || *ref* to become regenerate
rigeneratóre *m*—**rigeneratore per i capelli** hair restorer
rigettare (**rigètto**) *tr* to throw back; to reject; to recast; (slang) to throw up || *intr* to sprout
rigètto *m* rejection
righèllo *m* ruler
rigidi·tà *f* (**-tà**) rigidity; rigor; stiffness; **rigidità cadaverica** rigor mortis
rigi·do -da *adj* rigid, stiff; severe
rigirare *tr* to keep turning; to dupe; to invest; to encircle || *intr* to ramble || *ref* to turn around; to tumble
ri·go *m* (**-ghi**) line; **rigo musicale** (mus) staff
rigò·glio *m* (**-gli**) luxuriance; bloom; gurgling
rigonfiare §287 (**rigónfio**) *tr* to inflate || *intr* (ESSERE) & *ref* to swell up
rigóre *m* rigor; severity; precision; **a rigor di termini** strictly speaking; **di rigore** de rigueur; (sports) penalty (*e.g., kick*)
rigorismo *m* rigorism, strictness, severity
rigori·sta *mf* (**-sti -ste**) rigorist || *m* (soccer) kicker of penalty goal
rigoró·so -sa [s] *adj* rigorous, strict
rigovernare (**rigovèrno**) *tr* to clean, wash (*dishes*); to groom, tend (*animals*)
riguadagnare *tr* to regain
riguardare *tr* to look again; to look back; to examine; to consider; to take care of; to concern || *intr*—**riguardare a** to look out for; to face (*said of a window*) || *ref* to take care of oneself; **riguardarsi da** to keep away from
riguardo *m* care; esteem; regard; **a questo riguardo** in this regard; **ri-**

guardo a as far as . . . is concerned; **senza riguardo a** irrespective of
riguardó·so -sa [s] *adj* considerate
rigurgitare (**rigùrgito**) *tr & intr* to regurgitate
rilanciare §128 *tr* to toss back; to reestablish (*e.g., fashions*); (poker) to raise
rilasciare §128 *tr* to free, let go; to relax; to grant || *ref* to relax
rilà·scio *m* (**-sci**) release; delivery; granting, issue (*of a document*)
rilassante *adj* relaxing
rilassare *tr & ref* to relax
rilassatézza *f* laxity
rilegare §209 (**rilégo**) *tr* to tie again; to bind, rebind (*a book*); to set (*a stone*)
rilega·tóre -trice *mf* binder
rilegatura *f* binding
rilèggere §193 *tr* to reread
rilènto *m*—**a rilento** slowly
rilevaménto *m* survey; (naut) bearing
rilevare (**rilèvo**) *tr* to lift again; to observe; to draw; to bring out; to survey; to take over; to pick up; (mil) to relieve || *intr* to be delineated; to be of import || *ref* to rise again; to recover
rilevatà·rio *m* (**-ri**) successor; (law) assignee
rilièvo *m* relief; survey; remark; assumption (*of debts*); taking over (*of business*); **mettere in rilievo** to bring out; to set off
rilò·ga *f* (**-ghe**) traverse rod
rilucènte *adj* shiny, shining
rilùcere §234 *intr* to shine
riluttante *adj* reluctant
riluttanza *f* reluctance
rima *f* rhyme; slit; crevice; **rispondere per le rime** to answer in kind, to retort
rimandare *tr* to send back; to refer; to dismiss; to put off, postpone; to refer; **rimandare a ottobre** to condition (*a student*)
rimando *m* delay; reference; footnote; repartee; postponement; (sports) return
rimaneggiare §290 (**rimanéggio**) *tr* to rearrange; to reshuffle; to shake up (*personnel*); to rewrite (*news*)
rimanènte *adj* remaining || *m* remainder; remnant; **i rimanenti** the rest
rimanènza *f* remainder
rimanére §235 *intr* (ESSERE) to remain, stay; to be in agreement; to have left, e.g., **mi sono rimasti solo tre dollari** I only have three dollars left; to be located; (poet) to stop; **rimanerci** (coll) to be killed; (coll) to be duped; **rimanere da** to depend on, e.g., **questo rimane da Lei** this depends on you
rimangiare §290 *tr* to eat again || *ref*—**rimangiarsi la parola** to go back on one's word
rimarcare §197 *tr* to mark again; to point out
rimar·co *m* (**-chi**) remark, notice
rimare *tr & intr* to rhyme
rimarginare (**rimàrgino**) *tr, intr & ref* to heal
rimaritare *tr & ref* to marry again
rimasù·glio *m* (**-gli**) leftover
rima·tóre -trice *mf* poet; rhymster
rimbalzare *intr* (ESSERE & AVERE) to bounce back, rebound
rimbalzo *m* rebound
rimbambire §176 *intr* (ESSERE) & *ref* to become feeble-minded (*from old age*)
rimbambi·to -ta *adj* feeble-minded || *mf* dotard
rimbeccare §197 (**rimbécco**) *tr* to peck; to retort
rimbecilli·to -ta *adj* feeble-minded
rimboccare §197 (**rimbócco**) *tr* to tuck up; to tuck in; to fill to the brim
rimbombare (**rimbómbo**) *intr* (ESSERE & AVERE) to thunder, boom
rimbómbo *m* thunder, boom
rimborsare (**rimbórso**) *tr* to reimburse, pay back
rimbórso *m* repayment
rimboscare §197 (**rimbòsco**) *tr* to reforest || *ref* to take to the woods
rimboschiménto *m* reforestation
rimboschire §176 *tr* to reforest || *intr* (ESSERE) to become wooded
rimbrottare (**rimbròtto**) *tr* to scold
rimbròtto *m* scolding
rimediare §287 (**rimèdio**) *tr* (coll) to scrape together; (coll) to patch up || *intr* (with *dat*) to remedy; to make up (*lost time*)
rimè·dio *m* (**-di**) remedy
rimembranza *f* remembrance
rimeritare (**rimèrito**) *tr* to reward
rimescolare (**riméscolo**) *tr* to stir; to shuffle (*cards*)
riméssa *f* remittance; shipment; harvest; store; loss; sprout; carriage house; garage; (sports) return; (sports) putting in play; **rimessa dei tram** carbarn
rimestare (**riméstо**) *tr* to stir
riméttere §198 *tr* to remit; to put back; to set back; to sprout; to postpone, defer; to ship; to vomit; to recover; to deliver; to straighten up; (sports) to return; **rimetterci** to lose; **rimettere a nuovo** to renovate; **rimettere in ordine** to tidy up; **rimettere in piedi** to rebuild, restore || *intr* (coll) to sprout; (coll) to grow; (lit) to abate || *ref* to recover; to quiet down; to defer; to be clearing (*said of weather*); **rimettersi a** to go back to (*e.g., bed*); **rimettersi a** + *inf* to start + *ger* + again; **rimettersi in cammino** to start off again
rimirare *tr* to stare at
rimmel *m* mascara
rimodellare (**rimodèllo**) *tr* to remodel
rimodernare (**rimodèrno**) *tr* to modernize; to remodel; to bring up to date || *ref* to become modern
rimónta *f* reassembly; return (*of migratory birds*); revamping (*of shoes*); (mil) remount
rimontare (**rimónto**) *tr* to rewind; to go up (*a stream*); to vamp (*shoes*); to

renovate; to regain; to reassemble (*a machine*); (mil) to remount || *intr* (ESSERE & AVERE) to climb again; to go back (*in time*)
rimorchiare §287 (**rimòrchio**) *tr* to tow; to drag along
rimorchiatóre *m* tugboat; tow car
rimòr·chio *m* (**-chi**) tow; trailer; **prendere a rimorchio** to take in tow
rimòrdere §200 *tr* to bite again; to prick (*said, e.g., of conscience*)
rimòrso *m* remorse
rimostranza *f* remonstrance
rimostrare (**rimóstro**) *tr* to show again || *intr* to remonstrate; **rimostrare a** to remonstrate with
rimozióne *f* removal; demotion
rimpannucciare §128 *tr* to outfit better || *ref* to be better dressed; to be better off
rimpastare *tr* to knead again; to reshuffle, remake
rimpasto *m* reshuffling, rearrangement
rimpatriare §287 *tr* to repatriate || *intr* to be repatriated
rimpà·trio *m* (**-tri**) repatriation
rimpètto *adv* opposite; **di rimpetto a** opposite to; in comparison with
rimpiàngere §215 *tr* to regret; to mourn
rimpianto *m* regret
rimpiattare *tr* & *ref* to hide; **giocare a rimpiattarsi** to play hide-and-seek
rimpiattino *m* hide-and-seek
rimpiazzare *tr* to replace
rimpiazzo *m* replacement, substitute
rimpiccolire §176 *tr* to make smaller || *intr* (ESSERE) to get smaller
rimpinzare *tr* to stuff, cram
rimproverare (**rimpròvero**) *tr* to chide, reproach; **rimproverare qlcu di qlco** or **rimproverare qlco a qlcu** to reproach s.o. for s.th
rimpròvero *m* reproach, rebuke
rimuginare (**rimùgino**) *tr* & *intr* to rummage; to stir; to ruminate
rimunerare (**rimùnero**) *tr* to reward || *intr* to pay
rimunerati·vo -va *adj* remunerative; rewarding
rimunerazióne *f* remuneration
rimuòvere §202 *tr* to remove; to demote; to move
rinàscere §203 *intr* (ESSERE) to be born again; to grow again; to revive; **far rinascere** to revive
rinasciménto *m* rebirth || **Rinascimento** *m* Renaissance
rinàscita *f* rebirth
rincagna·to -ta *adj* snub (*nose*)
rincalzare *tr* to hill (*plants*); to underpin; to tuck in
rincalzo *m* reinforcement; support
rincantucciare §128 *tr* & *ref* to hide in a corner
rincarare *tr* to raise the price of; to raise; **rincarare la dose** to add insult to injury || *intr* (ESSERE) to rise, go up (*said of prices*)
rincasare [s] *intr* (ESSERE) to return home
rinchiùdere §125 *tr* to enclose, shut in
rinchiu·so -sa [s] *adj* shut in; musty || *m*—**saper di rinchiuso** to smell musty
rincitrullire §176 *intr* (ESSERE) to grow stupid
rincóntro *m*—**a rincontro** opposite
rincorare §236 *tr* to encourage || *ref* to take heart
rincórrere §139 *tr* to pursue, chase
rincórsa *f*—**prendere la rincorsa** to take off (*for a jump*); to get a running start
rincréscere §142 *intr* (ESSERE) (with *dat*) to displease; to be sorry, e.g., **gli rincresce** he is sorry; to mind, **Le rincresce?** do you mind?
rincresciménto *m* regret
rincrudire §176 *tr* to sharpen; to embitter || *intr* (ESSERE) to become bitter; to get worse
rinculare *intr* (ESSERE & AVERE) to back up; to recoil
rinculo *m* recoil
rinfacciare §128 *tr* to throw in one's face
rinfarcire §176 *tr* to stuff
rinfiancare §197 *tr* to support
rinfocolare (**rinfòcolo**) *tr* to rekindle; to revive
rinfoderare (**rinfòdero**) *tr* sheathe
rinforzare (**rinfòrzo**) *tr* to reinforce; strengthen || *intr* (ESSERE) & *ref* to become stronger
rinfòrzo *m* reinforcement
rinfrancare §197 *tr* to reassure || *ref* to buck up
rinfrescante *adj* refreshing || *m* mild laxative
rinfrescare §197 (**rinfrésco**) *tr* to refresh; to restore; to renew || *intr* (ESSERE & AVERE) to cool off (*said of the weather*) || *ref* to have some refreshments; to cool off
rinfré·sco *m* (**-schi**) refreshment
rinfusa *f*—**alla rinfusa** at random; pell-mell; in bulk
ringalluzzire §176 *tr* & *ref* to perk up
ringhiare §287 *intr* to growl, to snarl
ringhièra *f* railing
rìn·ghio *m* (**-ghi**) growl, snarl
ringiovaniménto *m* rejuvenation
ringiovanire §176 *tr* to rejuvenate || *intr* (ESSERE) to grow or look younger
ringraziaménto *m* thanks
ringraziare §287 *tr* to thank; to dismiss
ringuainare (**ringuaino**) *tr* to sheathe
rinnegare §209 (**rinnègo** & **rinnégo**) *tr* to forswear; to repudiate
rinnega·to -ta *adj* & *m* renegade
rinnovaménto *m* renewal; reawakening
rinnovare (**rinnòvo**) *tr* to renew; to renovate; to restore; to replace || *ref* to occur again; to renew
rinnovellare (**rinnovèllo**) *tr* to repeat; (poet) to renew || *intr* (ESSERE) & *ref* to change; to renew
rinnòvo *m* renewal
rinocerónte *m* rhinoceros
rinomanza *f* renown
rinoma·to -ta *adj* renowned, famous
rinsaldare *tr* to starch; (fig) to strengthen || *ref* to become confirmed (*in one's opinion*)

rinsanguare (rinsànguo) *tr* to give new strength to || *ref* to regain strength; to recover
rinsavire §176 *intr* (ESSERE) to return to reason
rintanare *ref* to burrow; to hide
rintóc•co *m* **(-chi)** toll (*of bell*)
rintontire §176 *tr* to stun, to daze
rintracciare §128 *tr* to track down
rintronare (rintròno) *tr* to deafen; to make rumble || *intr* (ESSERE & AVERE) to thunder; to rumble
rintuzzare *tr* to dull, blunt; to repel; to repress
rinùn•cia *f* **(-ce)** or **rinùnzia** *f* renunciation
rinunziare §287 *tr* to renounce || *intr* (with *dat*) to give up, renounce, e.g., **rinunziò al trono** he renounced the throne
rinvangare §209 *tr & intr* var of **rivangare**
rinvenire §282 *tr* to find || *intr* (ESSERE) to come to; **far rinvenire** to bring to, revive
rinviare §119 *tr* to send back; to postpone; to refer; to adjourn; to remit (*to a lower court*)
rinvigorire §176 *tr* to strengthen || *intr* (ESSERE) & *ref* to regain strength
rinvì•o *m* **(-i)** return; postponement; adjournment; reference; (law) continuance
rì•o *m* **(-i)** (lit) sin; (lit) brook; (coll) canal
rioccupare (riòccupo) *tr* to reoccupy
rioccupazióne *f* reoccupation
rionale *adj* neighborhood
rióne *m* district; neighborhood
riordinare (riórdino) *tr* to rearrange; to reorganize; to order again
riorganizzare [ddzz] *tr* to reorganize
riottó•so -sa [s] *adj* (lit) quarrelsome; (lit) unruly, rebellious
ripa *f* (lit) bank (*of river*); (lit) escarpment
ripagare §209 *tr* to repay; to pay again
riparare *tr* to protect; to mend, fix, repair; to make up (*an exam*) || *intr* —**riparare a** to make up for || *intr* (ESSERE) & *ref* to take refuge; to betake oneself
riparazióne *f* repair; reparation; redress; (educ) make-up
riparlare *intr* to speak again; **ne riparleremo!** you will see!
riparo *m* repair; shelter
ripartire §176 *tr* to divide; to distribute; to share || **(riparto)** *intr* (ESSERE) to leave again; to start again || **§176** *ref* to split up
ripartizióne *f* division; distribution
riparto *m* division; distribution; allotment
ripassare *tr* to cross again; to brush up, review; to repass; to sift again; to check; to read over; (mach) to overhaul || *intr* (ESSERE) to go by; to come by
ripassata *f* checkup; review; (coll) rebuke
ripassa•tóre -trice *mf* checker
ripasso *m* return (*of birds*); (coll) review
ripensare (ripènso) *intr* to keep thinking; **ripensare a** to think of again; to think over again
ripentire (ripènto) *ref* to repent; **ripentirsi di** to repent
ripercórrere §139 *tr* to retrace
ripercuòtere §251 *tr* to reflect; to strike again || *ref* to reverberate
ripescare §197 (ripésco) *tr* to fish again; (fig) to dig up
ripètere *tr & intr* to repeat || *ref* to be repeated
ripeti•tóre -trice *mf* repeater; coach; tutor || *m* (rad, telv) rebroadcasting station; (rad) relay
ripetizióne *f* repetition; review; tutoring; **a ripetizione** repeating (*firearm*)
ripiano *m* terrace; ledge; shelf; landing; (com) balancing
ripic•co *m* **(-chi)** pique; spite
rìpi•do -da *adj* steep
ripiegaménto *m* bend; (mil) withdrawal, retreat
ripiegare §209 (ripiègo) *tr* to fold, fold over || *intr* to do better; (mil) to fall back || *ref* to bend over; to withdraw into oneself
ripiè•go *m* **(-ghi)** expedient
ripiè•no -na *adj* full; stuffed || *m* stuffing; (culin) filling
ripigliare §280 *tr* to reacquire; to catch again; to begin again || *intr* to recover || *ref* to renew a quarrel
ripiombare (ripiómbo) *tr* to make plumb; (fig) to plunge back || *intr* (ESSERE) (fig) to plunge back
ripopolare (ripòpolo) *tr* to repopulate; to restock (*e.g., a pond*)
ripórre §218 *tr* to put back; to place (*one's hope*); to repose (*one's trust*) || *ref* to back down; **riporsi a** + *inf* to start + *ger* again
riportare (ripòrto) *tr* to bring back; to report; to get; to transfer (*a design*); (com) to carry forward; (hunt) to retrieve; (math) to carry || *ref* to go back
ripòrto *m* filler; retrieving; (com) balance carried forward; (math) number carried
riposante [s] *adj* restful
riposare [s] **(ripòso)** *tr, intr & ref* to rest
ripòso [s] *m* rest; repose; Requiem; retirement; **buon riposo!** sleep well!; **mettere a riposo** to retire; **riposo!** (mil) at ease
riposti•glio *m* **(-gli)** closet
ripó•sto -sta *adj* innermost || *m* (coll) pantry
riprèndere §220 *tr* to take back; to take up again; to get back; to take in (*a garment*); to catch (*s.th thrown in the air*); to take up (*arms*); to get; to reconquer; to start again, resume; to reprehend; to recover; (mov, telv) to shoot; **riprendere moglie** to remarry || *intr* to start again; to recover, improve; to pick up (*said of a*

motor) || *ref* to recover; to catch oneself up
riprésa [s] *f* resumption; (aut) pickup; (theat) revival; (mov) shooting, take; (boxing) round; (soccer) second half; (mus, pros) refrain; **a più riprese** several times
ripresentare (ripresènto) *tr* to present again
ripristinare (riprìstino) *tr* to restore; to reestablish
riprìstino *m* revival, restoration
riprodurre §102 *tr* to reproduce; to express || *ref* to reproduce; to occur
riprodut·tóre -trice *adj* reproducing || *mf* reproducer || *m* reproducer (*e.g., of sound*)
riproduzióne *f* reproduction; playback (*e.g., of tape*)
ripromèttere §198 *tr* to promise again || *ref* to hope; to propose; to hope for
ripròva *f* new proof; confirmation
riprovare (ripròvo) *tr* to try again; to try on again; to feel, experience again; to flunk; to censure || *ref* to try again
riprovazióne *f* disapproval
ripudiare §287 *tr* to repudiate
ripugnante *adj* repugnant, repulsive
ripugnanza *f* repugnance; aversion
ripugnare *intr* (with *dat*) to disgust, revolt, be repugnant to
ripulire §176 *tr* to clean again; to tidy up; to clean up; to polish || *ref* to be dressed up; to become polished
ripulita *f*—**dare una ripulita a** to give a lick and a promise to; **fare una ripulita** (fig) to clean house
ripulsi·vo -va *adj* repulsive
riquadrare *tr* to square; to decorate (*a room*) || *intr* to measure; to square
riquadro *m* square
risac·ca [s] *f* (**-che**) undertow; backwash
risàia [s] *f* rice field
risalire [s] §242 *tr* to go up again; to stem (*the tide*); **risalire la corrente** to go upstream || *intr* (ESSERE) to climb again; to reascend; (com) to appreciate; to date back
risaltare [s] *tr* to jump again || *intr* (ESSERE & AVERE) to rebound || *intr* to stand out; **far risaltare** to emphasize
risalto [s] *m* emphasis; prominence; relief; foil
risanare [s] *tr* to heal; to reclaim (*land*); to redevelop (*urban areas*); to reorganize || *intr* (ESSERE) to heal; to improve
risapére [s] §243 *tr* to find out
risapu·to -ta [s] *adj* well-known
risarciménto [s] *m* indemnification, redress
risarcire [s] §176 *tr* to indemnify; to compensate
risata [s] *f* outburst of laughter
risatina [s] *f* chuckle
riscaldaménto *m* heating; inflammation
riscaldare *tr* to heat; to warm up; to inflame || *ref* to warm up; to go in heat; to perspire; to get excited
riscaldo *m* inflammation; prickly heat; padding (*for clothes*)
riscattare *tr* to ransom; to redeem || *intr* (ESSERE) to click again (*said, e.g., of a ratchet*)
riscatto *m* ransom; redemption
rischiarare *tr, intr* (ESSERE) & *ref* to clear, clear up
rischiare §287 *tr* to risk || *intr* to run a risk
ri·schio *m* (**-schi**) risk
rischió·so -sa [s] *adj* risky
risciacquare (risciàcquo) *tr* to rinse
risciacquatura *f* rinse; swill
risciàcquo *m* rinsing (*of mouth*); mouthwash
riscónto *m* (com) discount
riscontrare (riscóntro) *tr* to compare, collate; to check; to reply to || *intr* to reply; to tally || *ref* to tally
riscóntro *m* comparison; check, control; draft; correspondence; reply; **far riscontro** to correspond; **far riscontro con** to correspond to; **far riscontro di** to check; **mettere a riscontro** to compare; **riscontri** drafts (*of air*); parts (*that fit together*)
riscoprire §110 *tr* to rediscover
riscòssa *f* insurrection; recovery, reconquest; (mil) counterattack
riscossióne *f* collection
riscrìvere §250 *tr* to rewrite; to write back
riscuòtere §251 *tr* to shake; to wake up; to collect; to get; to redeem || *ref* to wake up; to come to one's senses
riseccare [s] §197 (**risécco**) *tr, intr* (ESSERE) & *ref* to dry up
risecchire [s] §176 *intr* (ESSERE) & *ref* to dry up
risentiménto [s] *m* resentment, pique
risentire [s] (**risènto**) *tr* to hear again; to feel || *intr*—**risentire di** to feel the effects of || *ref* to take offense; to wake up; to come to one's senses; (telp) to talk again; **a risentirci!** (telp) until we talk again!; **risentirsi con** to resent (*a person*); **risentirsi di** to feel the effects of; **risentirsi per** to resent (*an act*)
risenti·to -ta [s] *adj* heard again; resentful; strong; swift; incisive
riserbare [s] (**risèrbo**) *tr* var of **riservare**
risèrbo [s] *m* var of **risèrvo**
risèrva [s] *f* preservation; exclusive rights; preserve; reserve; supply; backlog; reservation; circumspection; vintage
riservare [s] (**risèrvo**) *tr* to reserve
riservatézza [s] *f* reservedness
riserva·to -ta [s] *adj* reserved; private; classified
riservista [s] *m* (**-sti**) reservist
risèrvo [s] *m* discretion
risguardo *m* end paper
risièdere [s] *intr* to reside
risma *f* ream; (fig) type
riso [s] *m* rice || *m* (**risa** *fpl*) laugh; laughter; jest; cheer; (lit) smile
risolare [s] §257 *tr* to resole
risolino [s] *m* smile; giggle

risollevare [s] (**risollèvo**) *tr* to raise again; to lift || *ref* to rise
risolutézza [s] *f* resoluteness
risolu·to -ta [s] *adj* resolved, determined
risoluzióne [s] *f* resolution; resolve; dissolution
risòlvere [s] §256 (*pret ind* **risolvéi** or **risolvètti** or **risòlsi**; *pp* **risòlto**) *tr* to resolve; to solve; to dissolve; to persuade || *ref* to dissolve; to resolve
risolvìbile [s] *adj* solvable
risonante [s] *adj* resounding
risonanza [s] *f* resonance; (fig) sensation
risonare [s] §257 *tr* to ring again; (lit) to repeat || *intr* (ESSERE & AVERE) to resonate; to resound; to ring again; to echo
risórgere [s] §258 *intr* (ESSERE) to rise again; to revive, to come back to life; to recover
risorgiménto [s] *m* renaissance; resurgence || **Risorgimento** *m* Risorgimento
risórsa [s] *f* resource
risór·to -ta [s] *adj* arisen; reborn
risòtto [s] *m* risotto, rice cooked with broth
risparmiare §287 *tr* to save; to spare
rispàr·mio *m* (**-mi**) saving; sparing; savings; **risparmi** savings; **senza risparmio** lavishly
rispecchiare §287 (**rispècchio**) *tr* to reflect
rispedire §176 *tr* to send back; to forward; to reship
rispedizióne *f* reshipment
rispettàbile *adj* respectable
rispettare (**rispètto**) *tr* to respect; **farsi rispettare** to command respect; **rispettare sé stesso** to have self-respect
rispetti·vo -va *adj* respective
rispètto *m* respect; observance; restriction (*e.g., in building*); comparison; regard; **con rispetto parlando** excuse the word; **di rispetto** (naut) spare (*e.g., parts*); **rispetti** regards; **rispetto di sé medesimo** self-respect; **rispetto umano** fear of what people will say
rispettó·so -sa [s] *adj* respectful; respectable (*distance*)
risplendènte *adj* resplendent
risplèndere §281 *intr* (ESSERE & AVERE) to shine
rispóndere §238 *tr* to answer; **risponder picche** (coll) to say no || *intr* to answer; **rispondere a** to answer (*e.g., a letter*); **rispondere con un cenno del capo** to nod assent; **rispondere di** to be responsible for; **rispondere in** to face, overlook
risposare (**rispòso**) *tr & ref* to marry again, remarry
rispósta *f* answer, reply, response
rissa *f* scuffle, brawl
rissó·so -sa [s] *adj* quarrelsome
ristabilire §176 *tr* to reestablish || *ref* to recover
ristagnare *tr* to tin; to solder || *intr* to stagnate
ristampa *f* reprint
ristampare *tr* to reprint
ristorante *m* restaurant
ristorare (**ristòro**) *tr & ref* to refresh
ristora·tóre -trice *adj* refreshing || *m* restaurant
ristòro *m* refreshment; compensation
ristrettézza *f* narrowness; scarcity; **ristrettezza d'idee** narrow-mindedness
ristrét·to -ta *adj* narrow; limited; in straitened circumstances; concentrated, condensed (*e.g., broth*)
ristrutturazióne *f* restructuring
risùc·chio [s] *m* (**-chi**) whirlpool
risultante [s] *adj* resulting || *m & f* resultant; (phys) resultant
risultare [s] *intr* (ESSERE) to result; to prove to be, turn out to be; to appear
risultato [s] *m* result
risurrezióne [s] *f* resurrection
risuscitare [s] (**risùscito**) *tr* to resurrect; to revive || *intr* to be resurrected; to be revived
risvegliare §280 (**risvéglio**) *tr & ref* to awaken; to reawaken
risvé·glio *m* (**-gli**) awakening, reawakening
risvòlto *m* cuff; lapel; inside flap (*of book*); minor aspect (*of a question*)
ritagliare §280 *tr* to cut again; to clip; to trim
rità·glio *m* (**-gli**) clipping (*of paper*); scrap (*of meat*); cutting (*of fabric*); bit (*of time*); **al ritaglio** retail
ritappezzare (**ritappézzo**) *tr* to repaper
ritardare *tr* to delay; to slow down, retard; || *intr* to tarry; to be late; to be slow (*said of a watch*)
ritardatà·rio -ria *mf* (**-ri -rie**) latecomer; (com) delinquent
ritardo *m* delay; retard; lateness; **essere in ritardo** to be late
ritégno *m* reservation; discretion; **senza ritegno** shamelessly
ritemprare (**ritèmpro**) *tr* to temper again; to invigorate || *ref* to harden
ritenére §271 *tr* to retain; to hold; to withhold; to believe, think || *ref* to restrain oneself; to consider oneself; to be considered
ritentare (**ritènto**) *tr* to try again; (law) to retry
ritirare *tr* to withdraw; to pay (*a note*); to throw back; to shoot again; to accept delivery of; to take back (*a promise*) || *intr* to shrink || *ref* to shrink; to withdraw; to fall back, retreat; to retire
ritirata *f* toilet; (mil) retreat
ritiro *m* withdrawal; retreat; retirement; shrinkage; (metallurgy) shrinking
ritma·to -ta *adj* measured (*step*)
ritmi·co -ca *adj* (**-ci -che**) rhythmic(al)
ritmo *m* rhythm; **a ritmo serrato** at a quick pace
rito *m* rite; (fig) ritual, ceremony; **di rito** customary
ritoccare §197 (**ritócco**) *tr* to retouch; to brush up
ritóc·co *m* (**-chi**) retouch; improvement; change

ritòrcere §272 *tr* to twist, twine; to wring; to retort
ritornare (ritórno) *tr* to return, give back || *intr* (ESSERE) to return, go back, come back; **ritornare in sé** to come back to one's senses
ritornèllo *m* refrain; chorus (*of song*)
ritórno *m* return; reoccurrence; **di ritorno** reoccurring; **essere di ritorno** to be back; **far ritorno** to return; **ritorno di fiamma** backfire
ritòr•to -ta *adj* twisted || *m* twist
ritrarre §273 *tr* to retract; to draw; to portray || *intr*—**ritrarre da** to look like || *ref* to retreat; to portray oneself
ritrasméttere §198 *tr* (rad, telv) to retransmit, rebroadcast
ritrattare *tr* to treat again; to retract; (coll) to portray || *ref* to recant
ritrattazióne *f* retraction
ritratti•sta *mf* (**-sti -ste**) portrait painter
ritratto *m* portrait, picture; photograph; **ritratto parlante** spit and image
ritri•to -ta *adj* (fig) stale, trite
ritrósa [s] *f* (coll) cowlick
ritrosìa [s] *f* coyness, shyness
ritró•so -sa [s] *adj* coy, shy; **a ritroso** backwards || *f* see **ritrosa**
ritrovare (ritròvo) *tr* to discover; to find; to regain; to meet again || *ref* to meet again; to find oneself; to find one's bearings; **non ritrovarcisi** to be out of sorts
ritrovato *m* discovery, find
ritròvo *m* meeting; nightspot; **ritrovo estivo** summer resort; **ritrovo notturno** night club
rit•to -ta *adj* upright; straight; right || *m* face (*of medal*); prop; (sports) post || *f* (lit) right hand
rituale *adj* & *m* ritual
riunióne *f* reunion; meeting; assembly; **riunione alla sommità** summit conference
riunire §176 *tr* to assemble; to reunite; to reconcile || *ref* to gather together; to meet; to be reunited; to rally
riuscire §277 *intr* (ESSERE) to go out again; to turn out, turn out to be; to lead (*said, e.g., of a door*); to succeed; **riuscire a** + *inf* to succeed in + *ger* || *impers*—**riesce** (with *dat*) **di** + *inf* to succeed in + *ger*, e.g., **non gli è riuscito di farsi ricevere** he did not succeed in being received
riuscita *f* success; result; outlet
riva *f* shore; bank; (naut) board
rivale *adj* & *mf* rival
rivaleggiare §290 **(rivaléggio)** *intr* to compete; **rivaleggiare con** to rival
rivalére §278 *ref*—**rivalersi di** to use; **rivalersi su qlcu** to resort to s.o. for compensation; to fall back on s.o., to have recourse to s.o.
rivali•tà *f* (**-tà**) rivalry
rivalsa *f* compensation; revenge; (com) recourse
rivalutare (rivàluto & rivaluto) *tr* to revalue
rivalutazióne *f* reassessment
rivangare §209 *tr* to rake up; to mull over || *intr* to reminisce
rivedére §279 *tr* to see again; to review; to check; to reread; to revise; to read (*proof*) || *ref* to see one another; **a rivederci!** good-bye!, au revoir!
rivedìbile *adj* deferred (*for draft*)
rivelare (rivélo) *tr* to reveal; to detect; (phot) to develop
rivela•tóre -trice *adj* revealing || *m* (phot) developer; (rad) detector; **rivelatore di mine** mine detector
rivelazióne *f* revelation
rivéndere §281 *tr* to resell; (fig) to surpass
rivendicare §197 **(rivéndico)** *tr* to demand; to claim
rivendicazióne *f* demand; claim
rivéndita *f* resale; shop; **rivendita sali e tabacchi** cigar store
rivendi•tóre -trice *mf* seller, dealer, retailer
rivendùgliolo *m* peddler; huckster
rivèrbero *m* reverberation; reflection; glare; echo
riverènte *adj* reverent
riverènza *f* reverence; curtsy, bow
riverire §176 *tr* to revere; to pay one's respects to
riversare (rivèrso) *tr* to pour again; to transfer || *ref* to overflow
rivèr•so -sa *adj* on one's back
rivestiménto *m* coating; covering; lining
rivestire (rivèsto) *tr* to dress again; to coat; to line; to cover; to wear; to have (*importance*); to hold (*a rank*) || *ref* to get dressed again; to wear; to be covered
rivièra *f* coast || **Riviera** *f* Riviera
riviera•sco -sca *adj* (**-schi -sche**) coastal; riverside
rivìncere §285 *tr* to win back
rivìncita *f* revenge; return match; **prendersi la rivincita** to get even
rivista *f* review; parade; magazine, journal; revue; proofreading
rivìvere §286 *tr* to relive || *intr* (ESSERE) to live again; to revive
rivo *m* (lit) rivulet, brook
rivolare (rivólo) *intr* (ESSERE & AVERE) to fly again
rivolére §288 *tr* to want back
rivòlgere §289 *tr* to turn again; to revolve; to overturn; to train (*a weapon*); to address; to deter || *ref* to turn; to turn around; **rivolgersi a** to apply to
rivolgiménto *m* turn; revolution; upheaval
rivòlta *f* revolt; cuff
rivoltante *adj* revolting
rivoltare (rivòlto) *tr* to overturn; to turn inside out; to toss (*salad*); to upset || *ref* to turn around; to revolt; to toss
rivoltèlla *f* revolver; spray gun
rivoltellata *f* revolver shot
rivoltó•so -sa [s] *adj* rebellious || *m* rioter; rebel
rivoluzionare (rivoluzióno) *tr* to revolutionize

rivoluzionà·rio -ria *adj & mf* **(-ri -rie)** revolutionary
rivoluzióne *f* revolution
rizza *f* (naut) rigging
rizzare *tr* to raise; to hoist; to pay (*attention*); to build; (naut) to lash || *ref* to rise; to bristle (*said of hair*); to rear up (*said of a horse*)
ròba *f* things, stuff; property
robìnia *f* locust tree
robivèc·chi *m* **(-chi)** junk dealer
robu·sto -sta *adj* robust; burly
róc·ca *f* **(-che)** distaff
ròc·ca *f* **(-che)** fortress
roccafòrte *f* **(rocchefòrti)** stronghold
rocchétto *m* spool; reel; coil; roll (*of film*); pinion, rear sprocket wheel; (eccl) rochet; **rocchetto d'accensione** ignition coil; **rocchetto d'induzione** induction coil
ròc·cia *f* **(-ce)** rock; crag; cliff
rocció·so -sa [s] *adj* rocky
rò·co -ca *adj* **(-chi -che)** hoarse; (poet) faint
rodàg·gio *m* **(-gi)** breaking in, running in; adjustment period (*to a new situation*); **in rodaggio** (aut) being run in
Ròdano *m* Rhone
rodare (ròdo) *tr* to break in; (aut) to run in
ródere §239 *tr* to gnaw; to bite; to corrode || *ref* to worry, to fret
Ròdi *f* Rhodes
rodì·o *m* **(-i)** gnawing
rodi·tóre -trice *adj* gnawing || *mf* rodent
rodomónte *m* braggart
rogare §209 **(rògo)** *tr* to draw up (*a contract*); (law) to request
rògito *m* (law) instrument, deed
rógna *f* mange; itch
rognóne *m* (culin) kidney
rognó·so -sa [s] *adj* scabby, mangy
rò·go *m* **(-ghi)** pyre; stake
rollì·o *m* **(-i)** roll (*of ship*)
Róma *f* Rome
romané·sco -sca *adj* **(-schi -sche)** Roman (*dialect*)
Romanìa, la Rumania
romàni·co -ca *adj & m* **(-ci -che)** Romanesque
roma·no -na *adj & mf* Roman; **pagare alla romana** to go Dutch
romanticismo *m* romanticism
romànti·co -ca (-ci -che) *adj* romantic || *mf* romanticist
romanza *f* romance; ballad
romanzare *tr* to fictionalize
romanzé·sco -sca *adj* **(-schi -sche)** romantic; of chivalry; novelistic
romanzière *m* novelist
roman·zo -za *adj* Romance (*language*) || *m* novel; story; romance; fiction; **romanzi** fiction; **romanzo a fumetti** comic strip; comic book; **romanzo d'appendice** serial story, feuilleton; **romanzo giallo** whodunit; **romanzo rosa** love story
rombare (rómbo) *intr* to thunder
rómbo *m* thunder, roar
romè·no -na *adj & mf* Rumanian
romi·to -ta *adj* (lit) lonely || *m* (coll) hermit
rómpere §240 *tr* to break; to bust; **rompere la testa a** to annoy, pester || *intr* to overflow; to be wrecked; to break; **rompere in pianto** to burst out crying || *ref* to fly to pieces; **rompersi la testa** to rack one's brains
rompicapo *m* annoyance; puzzle; jigsaw puzzle
rompicòllo *m* madcap; **a rompicollo** headlong, rashly; at breakneck speed
rompighiàc·cio *m* **(-cio)** icebreaker; ice pick
rompiscàto·le *m* **(-le)** bore, pest
roncì·glio *m* **(-gli)** (poet) hook
róncola *f* pruning hook
rónda *f* patrol; beat (*of policeman*)
rondèlla *f* (mach) washer
róndine *f* swallow
rondóne *m* European swift
ronfare (rónfo) *intr* (coll) to snore; (coll) to purr
ronzare [dz] **(rónzo)** *intr* to buzz; to hum
ronzino [dz] *m* jade, nag
ronzì·o [dz] *m* **(-i)** buzzing; humming
ròsa *adj invar & m* pink || *f* rose; group; rosette; **rosa dei venti** compass card; **rosa del Giappone** (bot) camelia; **rosa delle Alpi** (bot) rhododendron; **rosa di tiro** (mil) dispersion
ro·sàio *m* **(-sài)** rosebush
rosà·rio *m* **(-ri)** rosary; **recitare il rosario** to count one's beads
rosa·to -ta *adj* rosy
ròse·o -a *adj* rosy
roséto *m* rose garden
rosétta *f* rosette; hard roll; (mach) washer
rosicanti [s] *mpl* rodents
rosicchiare [s] §287 *tr* to gnaw; to pick (*a bone*); to bite (*one's fingernails*)
rosmarino *m* (bot) rosemary
rosolare (ròsolo) *tr* (culin) to brown
rosolìa *f* German measles
rosóne *m* (archit) rosette; (archit) rose window
ròspo *m* toad; ugly person; unsociable person; **ingoiare un rospo** to swallow a bitter pill
rossa·stro -stra *adj* reddish
rossétto *m* rouge; **rossetto per le labbra** lipstick
rós·so -sa *adj* red; red-headed; Red; **diventare rosso** to blush || *mf* redhead; Red (*Communist*) || *m* red
rossóre *m* redness; blush
rosticcerìa *f* grill; rotisserie
rotàbile *adj* open to vehicular traffic (*road*); (rr) rolling (*stock*) || *f* road open to vehicular traffic
rotàia *f* rail; rut; **uscire dalle rotaie** to jump the track; (fig) to go astray
rotare §257 *tr & intr* to rotate; to circle
rotativa *f* (typ) rotary press
rotazióne *f* rotation
roteare (ròteo) *tr* to roll (*the eyes*); to flourish (*a sword*) || *intr* to circle
rotèlla *f* small wheel; caster; roller; kneecap; disk (*of ski pole*); **gli**

manca una rotella he has a screw loose
rotocal•co *m* (**-chi**) rotogravure
rotolare (**ròtolo**) *tr* & *intr* (ESSERE) to roll || *ref* to turn over; to wallow
ròtolo *m* roll; bolt; coil; **a rotoli** to rack and ruin
rotolóne *m* tumble; **a rotoloni** falling down; to rack and ruin
rotón•do -da *adj* round; rotund || *f* rotunda; terrace
rótta *f* break; rout; (aer, naut) course; **a rotta di collo** at breakneck speed; **mettere in rotta** to rout
rottame *m* fragment; wreck; **rottami** scraps, debris; wreckage; **rottami di ferro** scrap iron
rót•to -ta *adj* broken; shattered; inured || *m* break, tear; **e rotti** odd, e.g., **duecento e rotti** two hundred odd; **per il rotto della cuffia** hardly; just about || *f* see **rotta**
rottura *f* break; breakage; rupture; breakdown (*of relations*); crack
ròtula *f* kneecap
rovèllo *m* (lit) anger
rovènte *adj* red-hot
róvere *m* & *f* oak tree || *m* oak (*lumber*)
rovè•scia *f* (**-sce**) cuff; **alla rovescia** inside out; upside down; the wrong way
rovesciaménto *m* upset; overturn
rovesciare §128 (**rovèscio**) *tr* to overturn; to upset; to throw back (*one's head*); to spill (*liquid*); to pour; to hurl (*insults*); to turn inside out || *intr* to throw up || *ref* to spill; to pour; to upset
rovè•scio -scia (**-sci -sce**) *adj* reverse; inverse; inside out; upside down; backwards || *m* reverse; wrong side; downpour; upset; (com) crash; (tennis) backhand; **a rovescio** upside down; backwards || *f* see **rovescia**
rovéto *m* bramble; brier patch
rovina *f* ruin; blight; **andare in rovina** to go to ruin; **mandare in rovina** to ruin; **rovine** ruins
rovinare *tr* to ruin || *intr* (ESSERE) to collapse || *ref* to go to ruin
rovinì•o *m* (**-i**) clatter; crash
rovinó•so -sa [s] *adj* ruinous
rovistare *tr* to rummage through
róvo *m* bramble
ròzza [ddzz] *f* nag
róz•zo -za [ddzz] *adj* rough; coarse
ruba *f*—**andare a ruba** to sell like hotcakes; **mettere a ruba** to plunder
rubacchiare §287 *tr* to pilfer
rubacuò•ri (**-ri**) *adj* ravishing || *m* lady-killer || *f* vamp
rubare *tr* to steal; **rubare a man salva** to pillage, loot || *intr* to steal; **rubare sul peso** to give short measure
ruberìa *f* thieving, stealing
rubicón•do -da *adj* rubicund
rubinétto *m* faucet; cock
rubino *m* ruby; jewel (*of watch*)
rubiz•zo -za *adj* well-preserved (*person*)
rubri•ca *f* (**-che**) title, heading; directory; (journ) section
rude *adj* (lit) rough; (lit) rude
rùdere *m* ruin
rudimentale *adj* rudimentary
rudiménto *m* rudiment
ruffia•no -na *mf* go-between || *m* pimp, panderer || *f* bawd, procuress
ru•ga *f* (**-ghe**) wrinkle; (bot) rocket
rùggine *f* rust; ill-will; (bot) blight
rugginó•so -sa [s] *adj* rusty
ruggire §176 *tr* & *intr* to roar
ruggito *m* roar
rugiada *f* dew
rugó•so -sa [s] *adj* wrinkled, wrinkly
rullàg•gio *m* (**-gi**) (aer) taxiing
rullare *tr* to roll || *intr* to roll; to taxi
rullì•o *m* (**-i**) roll; rub-a-dub
rullo *m* roll; platen (*of typewriter*); pin (*in tenpins*); **rullo compressore** road roller
rumè•no -na *adj* & *mf* var of **romeno**
ruminare (**rùmino**) *tr* & *intr* to ruminate
rumóre *m* noise; rumor; ado; **far molto rumore** to create a stir
rumoreggiare §290 (**rumoréggio**) *intr* to rumble
rumoró•so -sa [s] *adj* noisy; rumbling; controversial
ruolino *m* roster
ruòlo *m* roll; role; list; **di ruolo** regular, full-time; **fuori ruolo** temporary, part-time
ruòta *f* wheel; paddle wheel; revolving server (*in convent*); **a quattro ruote** four-wheel; **dar la ruota a** to sharpen; **esser l'ultima ruota del carro** to be the fifth wheel to a wagon; **fare la ruota** to spread its tail, strut (*said, e.g., of a peacock*); to turn cartwheels (*said, e.g., of an acrobat*); **ruota dentata** cog, cogwheel; **ruota idraulica** water wheel; **seguire a ruota** to follow closely
rupe *f* cliff
rurale *adj* rural, farm, farmer
ruscèllo *m* brook
ruspa *f* road grader
ruspante *m* barnyard chicken
russare *intr* to snore
Rùssia, la Russia
rus•so -sa *adj* & *mf* Russian
rustica•no -na *adj* rustic, boorish
rùsti•co -ca (**-ci -che**) *adj* rustic; coarse || *m* tool shed; cottage; (lit) peasant
rutilante *adj* (lit) shiny
ruttare *tr* (lit) to belch || *intr* (vulg) to belch
rutto *m* (vulg) belch
ruttóre *m* (elec) contact breaker
ruvidézza *f* or **ruvidi•tà** *f* (**-tà**) coarseness; roughness
rùvi•do -da *adj* coarse; rough
ruzzare [ddzz] *intr* to romp
ruzzolare (**rùzzolo**) *tr* to roll || *intr* (ESSERE) to tumble down; to roll
ruzzolóne *m* tumble; **a ruzzoloni** tumbling down

S

S, s ['esse] *m & f* seventeenth letter of the Italian alphabet
s- *pref* dis-, e.g., **sleale** disloyal; e.g., **sconto** discount; un-, e.g., **scatenare** to unchain, unleash
sàbato *m* Saturday; (*of Jews*) Sabbath; **sabato inglese** Saturday afternoon off
sabbàti·co -ca *adj* (**-ci -che**) sabbatical
sàbbia *f* sand; **sabbia mobile** quicksand
sabbiatura *f* sand bath; sandblast
sabbièra *f* (rr) sandbox
sabbió·so -sa [s] *adj* sandy
sabotàg·gio *m* (**-gi**) sabotage
sabotare (**sabòto**) *tr* to sabotage
sac·ca *f* (**-che**) bag; satchel; (mil) pocket; **sacca d'aria** (aer) air pocket; **sacca da viaggio** traveling bag; duffel bag
saccarina *f* saccharine
saccènte *mf* wiseacre, know-it-all
saccheggiare §290 (**sacchéggio**) *tr* to pillage, plunder
sacchég·gio *m* (**-gi**) pillage, plunder
sacchétto *m* little bag, pouch
sac·co *m* (**-chi**) bag; sack; sackcloth; pouch; (boxing) punching bag; (fig) heap, lot; **fare sacco** to sag; **mettere a sacco** to sack; **mettere nel sacco** to outwit; **sacco alpino** knapsack; **sacco a pelo** or **a piuma** sleeping bag; **sacco postale** mailbag
saccòc·cia *f* (**-ce**) (coll) pocket
sacerdòte *m* priest; (fig) devotee
sacerdotéssa *f* priestess
sacerdòzio *m* priesthood; ministry
sacramentale *adj* sacramental; (joc) habitual, ritual
sacraménto *m* sacrament
sacrà·rio *m* (**-ri**) memorial; sanctuary, shrine
sacrestìa *f* var of **sagrestìa**
sacrificare §197 (**sacrìfico**) *tr* to sacrifice; to waste; to force || *ref* to sacrifice oneself
sacrifi·cio *m* (**-ci**) sacrifice
sacrilè·gio *m* (**-gi**) sacrilege
sacrìle·go -ga *adj* (**-ghi -ghe**) sacrilegious
sacri·sta *m* (**-sti**) sexton
sacristìa *f* var of **sagrestìa**
sa·cro -cra *adj* sacred
sacrosan·to -ta *adj* sacrosanct; sacred (*truth*)
sàdi·co -ca (**-ci -che**) *adj* sadistic || *mf* sadist
sadismo *m* sadism
saétta *f* stroke of lightning; hand (*of watch*); (mach) bit; (lit) arrow
saettare (**saétto**) *tr* to shoot; **saettare sguardi a** to look daggers at
saettóne *m* (archit) strut
sagace *adj* sagacious, shrewd
sagà·cia *f* (**-cie**) sagacity
saggézza *f* wisdom
saggiare §290 *tr* to assay; to test; (dial) to taste
saggia·tóre -trice *mf* assayer || *m* assay balance
saggina *f* sorghum
sàg·gio -gia (**-gi -ge**) *adj* wise || *m* sage; assay; sample; proof; theme; test; rate (*of interest*); display; **di saggio** examination (*copy*)
saggi·sta *mf* (**-sti -ste**) essayist
sagittària *f* (bot) arrowhead
sagittà·rio *m* (**-ri**) (obs) archer || **Sagittario** *m* Sagittarius
sàgola *f* (naut) halyard
sàgoma *f* outline; target; model, pattern; (joc) character
sagomare (**sàgomo**) *tr* to outline; to mold; to shape
sagomato *m* billboard
sagra *f* anniversary consecration (*of church*); festival
sagrato *m* elevated square in front of a church; churchyard; (coll) curse
sagrestano *m* sexton, sacristan
sagrestìa *f* sacristy, vestry
sàia *f* serge
sàio *m* (**sài**) habit (*of monk or nun*); doublet; frock coat
sala *f* axletree; hall, room; (bot) cattail, reed mace; **sala da ballo** dance hall; **sala da pranzo** dining room; **sala d'aspetto** waiting room; anteroom; **sala operatoria** operating room
salac·ca *f* (**-che**) (coll) sardine; (coll) shad
salace *adj* salacious; pungent
salamandra *f* salamander
salame *m* salami
salamelèc·co *m* (**-chi**) salaam
salamòia *f* brine
salare *tr* to salt; (coll) to cut (*school*)
salaria·to -ta *adj* wage-earning || *m* wage earner
salà·rio *m* (**-ri**) pay, wages
salassare *tr* to bleed
salasso *m* bloodletting
sala·to -ta *adj* salted; salty; dear, expensive; (fig) sharp || *m* salt pork; cold cuts || *f* salting
salda *f* starch solution (*used in laundering*)
saldacón·ti *m* (**-ti**) bookkeeping department; credit department; ledger; bookkeeping machine
saldare *tr* to solder; to set (*a bone*); to weld; to pay, settle || *ref* to knit (*said of a bone*); (lit) to heal
saldatóre *m* solderer; welder; soldering iron
saldatura *f* soldering; setting (*of bones*); joint; continuity; **saldatura autogena** welding
saldézza *f* firmness
sal·do -da *adj* firm; valid (*reason*); flawless || *m* balance; clearance sale; job lot; payment; **saldi** remnants || *f* see **salda**
saldobrasatura *f* soldering
sale *m* salt; wit; (lit) sea; **restare di sale** to be dumbfounded; **sale inglese** Epsom salts; **sali aromatici** smelling salts; **sali da bagno** bath salts
salgèmma *f* rock salt

sàlice *m* willow tree; **salice piangente** weeping willow
salicilato *m* salicylate
saliènte *adj* projecting; (fig) salient || *m* projection
salièra *f* saltcellar, salt shaker
salini•tà *f* (**-tà**) salinity
sali•no -na *adj* saline; salty || *f* salt bed
salire §242 *tr* to climb || *intr* (ESSERE) to climb; to go up; to rise; **salire in** or **su** to get on (*e.g., a train*)
saliscén•di *m* (**-di**) latch; **saliscendi** *mpl* ups and downs
salita *f* climbing; ascent, rise; slope; **in salita** uphill
saliva *f* saliva
salma *f* corpse, body
salma•stro -stra *adj* briny; saltish || *m*—**sapere di salmastro** to smell or taste salty
salmerìe *fpl* wagon train; (mil) supplies
salmì *m*—**in salmì** (culin) in a stew
salmo *m* psalm
salmodiare §287 (**salmòdio**) *intr* to chant, sing hymns, intone
salmóne *m* salmon
salnitro *m* saltpeter
Salomóne *m* Solomon
salóne *m* hall; salon, drawing room; (naut) saloon; **salone da barbiere** barber shop; **salone dell'automobile** auto show
salòtto *m* drawing room; living room, parlor; reception room
salpare *tr* to weigh (*anchor*) || *intr* (ESSERE) to weigh anchor
salsa *f* sauce
salsapariglia *f* sarsaparilla
salsèdine *f* saltiness
salsìc•cia *f* (**-ce**) sausage
salsièra *f* gravy boat
sal•so -sa *adj* salty; saline || *m* saltiness || *f* see **salsa**
saltabeccare §197 (**saltabécco**) *intr* to hop
saltaleóne *m* coil spring
saltare *tr* to jump; to skip; to sauté; (sports) to vault, hurdle; **far saltare** to kick out; to blow up (*e.g., a mine*); **saltare la sbarra** (coll) to go A.W.O.L. || *intr* (ESSERE & AVERE) to jump; to pop off, e.g., **mi è saltato un bottone** one of my buttons has popped off; to blow out (*said of a fuse*); **saltare agli occhi** to be self-evident; **saltare a piè pari** to skip with both feet; **saltar fuori** to pop out (*said of the eyes*); to appear suddenly; **saltare in mente a** to come to the mind of; **saltare il ticchio a (qlcu) di** to feel like + *ger*, e.g., **gli è saltato il ticchio di cantare** he felt like singing; **saltare la mosca al naso a (qlcu)** to blow one's top, e.g., **le è saltata la mosca al naso** she blew her top; **saltare per aria** to blow up; **saltare su** to start (*to make a sudden jerk*); **saltare su a** + *inf* to begin suddenly to + *inf*
salta•tóre -trice *mf* jumper, hurdler
saltellare (**saltèllo**) *intr* to skip, hop
saltellóni *adv*—**a saltelloni** skipping, hopping
saltimban•co *m* (**-chi**) acrobat, tumbler; mountebank
salto *m* jump; leap; fall; skip; (*of animals*) mating; (fig) step; **a salti** skipping, jumping; **al salto** sauté; **fare quattro salti** to dance; **fare un salto** to hop, hurry; **salto a pesce** jackknife (*dive*); **salto coll'asta** pole vaulting; **salto in altezza** high jump; **salto in lunghezza** broad jump; **salto mortale** somersault; **salto nel vuoto** leap in the dark
saltuà•rio -ria *adj* (**-ri -rie**) desultory, occasional
salubre *adj* salubrious, healthy, healthful
salume *m* pork product
salumerìa *f* pork butcher shop
salumiè•re -ra *mf* pork butcher
salutare *adj* healthful || *tr* to greet; to salute; (lit) to proclaim
salute *f* health; salvation; safety || *interj* good luck; to your health!; gesundheit!
saluto *m* salute; greeting; salutation; **distinti saluti** sincerely yours
salva *f* salvo; outburst; **a salve** with blank cartridges, with blanks
salvacondótto *m* safe-conduct
salvada•nàio *m* (**-nài**) piggy bank
salvagèn•te *m* (**-te & -ti**) life preserver; fender (*of trolley car*) || *m* (**-te**) safety island
salvaguardare *tr* to safeguard
salvaguàrdia *f* safeguard
salvaménto *m* safety
salvamotóre *m* circuit breaker; fuse box
salvapun•te *m* (**-te**) pencil cap; tap (*on sole of shoe*)
salvare *tr* to save; to spare (*a life*); to rescue || *ref* to save oneself; to be rescued; **si salvi chi può!** every man for himself!
salvatàg•gio *m* (**-gi**) rescue
salvatóre *m* savior, rescuer || **il Salvatore** the Saviour
salvazióne *f* salvation
salve *interj* hello!, hail!
salvézza *f* salvation; safety
sàlvia *f* (bot) sage
salviétta *f* napkin; paper napkin; paper towel
sal•vo -va *adj* safe; saved; secure || *m* —**mettere in salvo** to put in a safe place; **mettersi in salvo** to reach safety || *f* see **salva** || **salvo** *prep* except; **salvo che** unless; **salvo il vero** unless I am mistaken
samarita•no -na *adj & mf* Samaritan
sambu•co *m* (**-chi**) elder tree
san *adj* apocopated and unstressed form of **santo**
sanàbile *adj* curable
sanare *tr* to heal; to remedy; to reclaim (*land*); to normalize
sanatò•rio *m* (**-ri**) sanatorium
sancire §176 *tr* to ratify, sanction; to establish
sàndalo *m* sandal; sandalwood; flat-bottom boat

sandolino *m* canoe, skiff, kayak
sangue *m* blood; **agitarsi il sangue** to fret; **all'ultimo sangue** (*duel*) to the death; **al sangue** rare (*meat*); **a sangue freddo** in cold blood; cold-blooded; **cavar sangue da una rapa** to draw blood from a stone; **farsi cattivo sangue** to get angry; **il sangue non è acqua** blood is thicker than water; **puro sangue** thoroughbred; **sangue dal naso** nosebleed; **sangue freddo** calmness, composure
sangui•gno -gna *adj* blood (*circulation*); bloody; sanguine, ruddy || *m* (lit) color of blood
sanguinante *adj* bloody, bleeding
sanguinare (**sànguino**) *intr* to bleed; to be rare (*said of meat*)
sanguinà•rio -ria *adj* (**-ri -rie**) sanguinary
sanguinó•so -sa [s] *adj* bloody; bleeding; (fig) stinging
sanguisu•ga [s] *f* (**-ghe**) leech
sani•tà *f* (**-tà**) health; healthfulness; soundness (*of body*); sanity; health department
sanità•rio -ria (**-ri -rie**) *adj* health; sanitary || *m* physician
sa•no -na *adj* healthy; sound; **sano e salvo** safe and sound
sant' *adj* apocopated form of **santo** and **santa**
santa *f* saint
santabàrbara *f* (**santebàrbare**) (nav) powder magazine
santarellina *f* goody-goody girl
santificare §197 (**santìfico**) *tr* to sanctify
santissi•mo -ma *adj* most holy || *m* Eucharist
santi•tà *f* (**-tà**) sanctity, holiness; sainthood, saintliness
san•to -ta *adj* saintly, holy; sacred; blessed, livelong, e.g., **tutto il santo giorno** all the livelong day || *m* saint; name day; (fig) someone || *f* see **santa**
santoré•gia *f* (**-ge**) (bot) savory
santuà•rio *m* (**-ri**) sanctuary
sanzionare (**sanzióno**) *tr* to sanction; to ratify
sanzióne *f* sanction
sapére *m* knowledge; **sapere fare** savoir-faire || §243 *tr* to know; to find out; to know how to; **far sapere** to let know; **saperla lunga** to know a thing or two; **un certo non so che** a certain something, something vague || *intr*—**sapere di** to know; to taste; to smell; to smack of; **mi sa che** I think that; **non voler più saperne di** to not want to have anything to do with; **sapere male** (with *dat*) to feel sorry, e.g., **gli sa male** he feels sorry || *ref*—**che io mi sappia** as far as I know
sàpido -da *adj* savory; witty
sapiènte *adj* wise; talented; trained (*dog*) || *m* wise man
sapientó•ne -na *mf* wiseacre, know-it-all
sapiènza *f* wisdom; knowledge
saponària *f* (bot) soapwort
saponata *f* soapsuds; lather; (fig) soft soap
sapóne *m* soap; **sapone da toletta** toilet soap; **sapone per la barba** shaving soap
saponétta *f* cake of soap
saponière *m* soap maker
saponifi•cio *m* (**-ci**) soap factory
saponó•so -sa [s] *adj* soapy
sapóre *m* taste; savor; flavor
saporire §176 *tr* to savor
saporitaménte *adv* heartily; soundly
sapori•to -ta *adj* tasty; flavorful; salty; expensive
saporó•so -sa [s] *adj* savory; witty
saputèl•lo -la *adj* cocksure || *m* smart aleck
sarac•co *m* (**-chi**) hand saw
saracè•no -na *adj* Saracen, Saracenic || *m* Saracen; quintain
saraciné•sca *f* (**-sche**) metal shutter (*of store*); sluice gate; (hist) portculis
sarcasmo *m* sarcasm
sarcàsti•co -ca *adj* (**-ci -che**) sarcastic
sarchiare §287 *tr* to weed
sarchia•tóre -trice *mf* weeder || *f* (agr) cultivator
sarchièllo *m* weeding hoe
sàr•chio *m* (**-chi**) hoe
sarcòfa•go *m* (**-gi & -ghi**) sarcophagus
sarcràuti *mpl* sauerkraut
Sardégna, la Sardinia
sardèlla *f* pilchard; sardine
sardina *f* pilchard; sardine
sar•do -da *adj & mf* Sardinian
sardòni•co -ca *adj* (**-ci -che**) sardonic
sarménto *m* vine shoot, running stem
sarta *f* dressmaker
sàrtie *fpl* (naut) shrouds
sarto *m* tailor
sartoria *f* dressmaker's shop; tailor shop; dressmaking; tailoring
sassaiòla *f* shower of stones
sassata *f* blow with a stone
sasso *m* stone, rock; pebble; (poet) tombstone; **di sasso** stony; **restare di sasso** to be taken aback; **tirare sassi in colombaia** to cut one's nose to spite one's face
sassòfono *m* saxophone
sàssone *adj & mf* Saxon
sassó•so -sa [s] *adj* stony
Sàtana *m* Satan
satanasso *m* Satan; devil
satèllite *m* satellite
sa•tin *m* (**-tin**) sateen
satinare *tr* to gloss
sàtira *f* satire
satireggiare §290 (**satiréggio**) *tr* to satirize, lampoon || *intr* to compose satires
satìri•co -ca *adj* (**-ci -che**) satiric(al) || *m* satirist
sàtiro *m* satyr
satól•lo -la *adj* sated, full
saturare *tr* (**sàturo**) *tr* to saturate; to steep; (fig) to fill; (com) to glut (*a market*)
saturni•no -na *adj* Saturnian; saturnine
Saturno *m* (astr) Saturn
sàtu•ro -ra *adj* saturated; (fig) full; (lit) sated

sàu·ro -ra *adj & m* sorrel (*horse*)
Savèrio *m* Xavier
sà·vio -via (-vi -vie) *adj* wise || *m* wise man, sage
savoiar·do -da *adj & mf* Savoyard || *m* ladyfinger
saxòfono *m* saxophone
saziare §287 *tr* to satisfy; to cloy, satiate
sazietà *f* satiety, surfeit; **mangiare a sazietà** to eat one's fill
sà·zio -zia *adj* (**-zi -zie**) sated; full; satisfied
sbaciucchiare §287 (**sbaciùcchio**) *tr* to kiss again and again || *ref* to neck
sbadatàggine *f* carelessness; oversight
sbada·to -ta *adj* careless; heedless
sbadigliare §280 *intr* to yawn
sbadì·glio *m* (**-gli**) yawn
sbafa·tóre -trice *mf* sponger
sbafo *m*—**a sbafo** sponging; **mangiare a sbafo** to sponge
sbagliare §280 *tr* to miss; to mistake; **sbagliarla** to be sadly mistaken || *intr & ref* to be mistaken; to make a mistake
sbaglia·to -ta *adj* wrong; mistaken
sbà·glio *m* (**-gli**) error, mistake
sbalestrare (**sbalèstro**) *tr* to fling with the crossbow; to send (*an employee*) far away || *intr* to speak amiss; to ramble; to blunder
sbalestra·to -ta *adj* unbalanced; ill-at-ease
sballare *tr* to unpack; **sballarle grosse** to tell tall tales || *intr* to overbid
sballa·to -ta *adj* unpacked; absurd, wild
sballottare (**sballòtto**) *tr* to toss
sbalordire §176 *tr* to stun; to amaze; to bewilder || *intr* to lose consciousness; to be dumfounded
sbalorditi·vo -va *adj* amazing
sbalzare *tr* to upset; to send far away; to overthrow; to emboss || *intr* (ESSERE) to bounce
sbalzo *m* leap, jump; climb; embossment, relief; **a sbalzi** by leaps and bounds; **di sbalzo** all of a sudden
sbancare §197 *tr* to clear (*ground*) of rocks; to ruin; (cards) to break (*the bank*)
sbandaménto *m* skid; swerve; disbandment; breaking up; (naut) list
sbandare *tr* to disband; (naut) to cause to list || *intr* to list; to skid; to swerve; to deviate || *ref* to disband; to break up
sbanda·to -ta *adj* disbanded; stray; alienated || *mf* alienated person || *m* straggler || *f* listing (*of ship*); skidding (*of vehicle*); **prendere una sbandata per** to get a crush on
sbandierare (**sbandièro**) *tr* to wave (*a flag*); to display
sbaragliare §280 *tr* to rout; to crush
sbaràglio *m*—**mettere allo sbaraglio** to endanger
sbarazzare *tr* to clear out; to free || *ref* —**sbarazzarsi di** to get rid of
sbarazzi·no -na *adj* mischievous || *mf* scamp; **alla sbarazzina** cocked, at an angle (*said of a hat*)
sbarbare *tr* to shave; to uproot || *ref* to shave
sbarbatèllo *m* greenhorn, fledgling
sbarcare §197 *tr* to unload; to discharge; to disembark; to pass; to strew (*fodder*); **sbarcare il lunario** to make ends meet || *intr* (ESSERE) to come ashore, land
sbarca·tóio *m* (**-tói**) landing pier
sbar·co *m* (**-chi**) unloading; landing
sbarra *f* bar; (typ) dash
sbarraménto *m* barrage; obstacle
sbarrare *tr* to bar; to block (*the way*); to open (*one's eyes*) wide, e.g., **sbarrò gli occhi** he opened his eyes wide
sbarrétta *f* bar; **sbarrette verticali** (typ) parallels
sbatacchiare §287 *tr* to slam; to flap || *intr* to slam
sbatàc·chio *m* (**-chi**) shore, prop
sbàttere *tr* to flap; to fling; to slam; to beat; to toss; to send away; to make pale; **sbatter fuori** to throw out || *intr* to flap; to slam
sbattighiàc·cio *m* (**-cio**) cocktail shaker
sbattitóre *m* electric mixer
sbattiuò·va *m* (**-va**) egg beater
sbattu·to -ta *adj* haggard, downcast
sbavare *tr* to slobber over; (mach) to trim || *intr* to drivel, slobber; to run (*said of colors*)
sbavatura *f* drivel; run (*of colors*); burr (*of metal*); deckle edge; verbosity
sbeccare §197 (**sbécco**) *tr & ref* to chip
sbeffeggiare §290 (**sbefféggio**) *tr* to make fun of
sbellicare §197 *ref*—**sbellicarsi dalle risa** to burst with laughter
sbèrla *f* (coll) slap
sberlèffo *m* scar; grimace; **fare gli sberleffi a** to make faces at
sbevazzare *intr* to guzzle
sbevucchiare §287 *intr* to tipple
sbiadire §176 *tr & intr* (ESSERE) to fade
sbiadi·to -ta *adj* faded; dull
sbiancare §197 *tr* to whiten || *ref* to become white; to pale
sbianchire §176 *tr* (culin) to blanch
sbiè·co -ca (-chi -che) *adj* oblique; **di sbieco** on the bias; **guardare di sbieco** to look askance at || *m* cloth cut diagonally
sbigottire §176 *tr* to terrify, dismay || *intr* (ESSERE) *& ref* to be dismayed
sbilanciare §128 *tr* to unbalance; to upset || *intr* to lose one's balance || *ref* to commit oneself
sbilàn·cio *m* (**-ci**) disequilibrium; (com) deficit
sbilèn·co -ca *adj* (**-chi -che**) twisted, crooked
sbirciare §128 *tr* to leer at, ogle; to eye closely
sbir·ro -ra *adj* (coll) smart || *m* (pej) cop
sbizzarrire [ddzz] §176 *tr* to cure the whims of || *ref* to indulge one's whims
sbloccare §197 (**sblòcco**) *tr* to unblock; to raise the blockade of; to free
sbòbba *f* slop, dishwater
sboccare §197 (**sbócco**) *tr* to break the

mouth of (*a bottle*); to remove a few drops from (*a bottle*) || *intr* (ESSERE) to flow; to open (*said of a street*); **sboccare in** to turn out to be
sbocca·to -ta *adj* foulmouthed; foul (*language*); chipped at the mouth (*said of a bottle*)
sbocciare §128 (**sbòccio**) *intr* (ESSERE) to bud, burgeon, bloom
sbóc·co *m* (**-chi**) outlet; **avere uno sbocco di sangue** to spit blood
sbocconcellare (**sbocconcèllo**) *tr* to nibble at; to chip, nick
sbollentare (**sbollènto**) *tr* to blanch
sbollire §176 *intr* to stop boiling; to calm down
sbolognare (**sbológno**) *tr* (coll) to palm off; (coll) to get rid of
sbòrnia *f* (coll) drunk, jag; **smaltire la sbornia** to sober up
sborsare (**sbórso**) *tr* to pay out, disburse
sbórso *m* disbursement, outlay
sbottare (**sbòtto**) *intr*—**sbottare a** + *inf* to burst out + *ger*
sbottonare (**sbottóno**) *tr* to unbutton || *ref* (fig) to unbosom oneself
sbozzare (**sbòzzo**) *tr* to rough-hew; to sketch, outline
sbraca·to -ta *adj* without pants; slovenly; vulgar
sbracciare §128 *intr* to gesticulate || *ref* to roll up one's sleeves; to wear sleeveless clothes; to gesticulate; to do one's best
sbraccia·to -ta *adj* bare-armed
sbraitare (**sbràito**) *intr* to scream
sbraitó·ne -na *mf* bigmouth
sbranare *tr* to tear to pieces
sbrano *m* tear, rent
sbrattare *tr* to clean; to clear
sbreccare §197 (**sbrécco**) *tr* to chip, nick
sbrecciare §128 (**sbréccio**) *tr* to open a gap in
sbréndolo *m* tatter, rag
sbriciolare (**sbrìciolo**) *tr* to crumb || *ref* to crumble
sbrigare §209 *tr* to transact; to take care of || *ref* to hasten, hurry; **sbrigarsela** to get out of trouble; **sbrigarsi di** to get rid of; **sbrigati!** make it snappy!, hurry up!
sbrigativ·o -va *adj* quick, brisk; businesslike
sbrigliare §280 *tr* to unbridle; to reduce (*a hernia*); to lance (*an infected wound*) || *ref* to cut loose
sbrinare *tr* to defrost
sbrindella·to -ta *adj* tattered
sbrodolare (**sbròdolo**) *tr* to soil; (fig) to drag out || *ref* to slobber
sbrogliare §280 (**sbròglio**) *tr* to untangle; to clean up || *ref* to extricate oneself; **sbrogliarsela** to get out of a tight spot
sbronzare (**sbrónzo**) *ref* (coll) to get drunk
sbruffare *tr* to squirt out of the mouth; to spatter; to bribe || *intr* to tell tall tales
sbruffo *m* sprinkle, squirt; bribe
sbruffó·ne -na *mf* braggart
sbucare §197 *intr* (ESSERE) to pop out, come out
sbucciare §128 *tr* to peel; to skin || *ref* to slough (*said of snakes*); **sbucciarsela** (coll) to goldbrick
sbucciatura *f* slight abrasion
sbudellare (**sbudèllo**) *tr* to disembowel || *ref*—**sbudellarsi dalle risa** to burst with laughter, split one's sides laughing
sbuffare *tr & intr* to puff
sbuffo *m* puff; gust (*of wind*); **a sbuffo** puffed (*sleeve*)
sbullonare (**sbullóno**) *tr* to unbolt
sc- *pref* dis-, e.g., **sconto** discount; es-, e.g., **scalare** to escalate; ex-, e.g., **scusare** to excuse
scàbbia *f* scabies
sca·bro -bra *adj* rough; stony; tight (*style*)
scabró·so -sa [s] *adj* scabrous
scacchièra *f* checkerboard; chessboard
scacchière *m* (mil) sector; (obs) checkerboard; exchequer
scacciaca·ni *m & f* (**-ni**) toy gun; gun shooting only blanks
scacciamó·sche *m* (**-sche**) fly swatter
scacciapensiè·ri *m* (**-ri**) jew's-harp
scacciare §128 *tr* to chase away, drive away; to expel
scaccino *m* sexton, sacristan
scac·co *m* (**-chi**) chessman; checker; check; square; **a scacchi** checkered; **dare scacco matto a** to checkmate; **in scacco** or **sotto scacco** in check; **scacchi** chess; **scacco matto** checkmate
scàccoli *mpl* cement piles
scaccomatto *m* checkmate
scadènte *adj* inferior, poor, shoddy
scadènza *f* term, maturity; obligation; **a breve scadenza** short-term; **a lunga scadenza** long-term
scadére §121 *intr* (ESSERE) to decay, to decline; to fall due; to expire; (naut) to drift
scafandro *m* diving suit; **scafandro astronautico** space suit
scaffale *m* bookcase; shelf
scafo *m* hull
scagionare (**scagióno**) *tr* to exonerate, exculpate
scàglia *f* scale (*of fish*); chip; plate (*of medieval armor*); flake (*of soap*); tile (*of slate roof*)
scagliare §280 *tr* to hurl, fling, throw; to scale (*fish*) || *ref* to dash, to rush; to flake
scaglionare (**scaglióno**) *tr* to echelon; to stagger (*e.g., payments*)
scaglióne *m* terrace (*of mountain*); echelon; scale; **a scaglioni** graded (*e.g., income tax*)
scala *f* stairs; ladder; scale; (cards) straight; (rad) dial; **a scale** scaled, graded; **fare le scale** to climb the stairs; **scala a chiocciola** spiral stairway; **scala a gradini** or **a libretto** stepladder; **scala mobile** escalator; (econ) sliding scale; **scala porta** aerial ladder; **scala reale** (poker)

straight flush; **su larga scala** large-scale; **su scala nazionale** on a national scale
scalandróne *m* (naut) gangway
scalare *adj* graded, scaled; gradual ‖ *m* (com) running balance ‖ *tr* to climb, ascend; to scale, grade; to reduce
scalata *f* climb, ascent; **dar la scalata a** to climb; to climb up to
scalcagna·to -ta *adj* down-at-the-heel
scalcare §197 *tr* to slice, carve
scalciare §128 *intr* to kick
scalcina·to -ta *adj* (*wall or plaster*) that is peeling off; worn-out; down-at-the-heels
scalda·acqua *m* (**-acqua**) hot-water heater
scaldaba·gno *m* (**-gno**) hot-water heater; **scaldabagno a gas** gas heater
scaldalèt·to *m* (**-ti** & **-to**) bedwarmer
scaldare *tr* to warm, warm up; to heat, heat up ‖ *intr* (mach) to become hot ‖ *ref* to warm up; to heat up; **scaldarsi la testa** to get excited
scaldavivan·de *m* (**-de**) hot plate
scaldino *m* hand warmer
scalèa *f* flight of stairs, stairway
scalèo *m* stepladder
scalétta *f* small ladder; small stairs; (mov) rough draft
scalfire §176 *tr* to graze, scratch; to cut (*e.g., glass*)
scalfittura *f* graze, scratch
scalinata *f* stairway, perron
scalino *m* step (*of a stair*); (fig) ladder
scalmana *f* chill; flush; **prendere una scalmana per** to take a fancy to
scalmanare *ref* to hustle, bustle; to fuss
scalmana·to -ta *adj* panting; hotheaded
scalmo *m* (naut) oarlock
scalo *m* pier, dock; (naut) ways; (naut) port of call; **fare scalo** (naut) to call, stop; (aer) to land; **scalo di alaggio** (naut) slip; **scalo merci** (rr) freight yard; **senza scalo** (aer, naut) nonstop
scalógna *f* (coll) bad luck
scalógno *m* (bot) scallion
scalòppa *f* veal chop
scaloppina *f* veal cutlet, scallop
scalpellare (**scalpèllo**) *tr* to chisel
scalpellino *m* stone cutter
scalpèllo *m* chisel; (surg) scalpel; **scalpello a taglio obliquo** skew chisel
scalpicciare §128 *tr* & *intr* to shuffle
scalpitare (**scàlpito**) *intr* to paw the ground
scalpóre *m* scene; **fare scalpore** to raise a fuss
scaltrézza *f* shrewdness, cunning
scaltrire §176 *tr* to polish, refine; to sharpen the wits of ‖ *ref* to catch on; to improve
scal·tro -tra *adj* shrewd, smart
scalzare *tr* to take the shoes or stockings off of; to undermine ‖ *ref* to take off one's shoes or stockings
scal·zo -za *adj* barefoot
scambiare §287 *tr* to exchange; to mistake ‖ *ref* to exchange (*presents*)
scambièvole *adj* mutual
scàm·bio *m* (**-bi**) exchange; (rr) switch; **libero scambio** free trade; **scambio di persona** mistaken identity
scamicia·to -ta *adj* in shirt sleeves; extremist ‖ *m* extremist; tunic, waist
scamoscia·to -ta *adj* chamois, suede
scampagnata *f* excursion, outing
scampanare *intr* to peal, chime; to flare (*said of a garment*)
scampanellare (**scampanèllo**) *intr* to ring loud and clear
scampanì·o *m* (**-i**) toll, peal
scampare *tr* to save, rescue; **scamparla bella** to have a narrow escape ‖ *intr* (ESSERE)—**scampare a** to escape from; to take refuge in
scampo *m* escape; safety; (zool) Norway lobster; **non c'è scampo** there is no way out
scàmpolo *m* remnant; **scampoli di tempo** free moments
scanalare *tr* to channel, groove, rabbet ‖ *intr* to overflow
scanalatura *f* channel, groove, rabbet
scandagliare §280 *tr* to sound
scandà·glio *m* (**-gli**) sounding lead; **fare uno scandaglio** to make a sounding or survey
scandalismo *m* scandalmongering, yellow journalism
scandalizzare [ddzz] *tr* to scandalize, shock ‖ *ref* to be scandalized
scàndalo *m* scandal
scandaló·so -sa [s] *adj* scandalous
scandina·vo -va *adj* & *mf* Scandinavian
scandire §176 *tr* to scan; to syllabize; (telv) to scan
scàndola *f* wood shingle
scannare *tr* to slaughter, butcher
scanna·tóio *m* (**-tói**) slaughterhouse; gyp joint
scanno *m* bench; seat; sand bar
scansafati·che *mf* (**-che**) loafer
scansare *tr* to move; to avoid ‖ *ref* to get out of the way
scansia *f* shelf; bookcase
scansióne *f* scansion; (telv) scanning
scanso *m*—**a scanso di** in order to avoid
scantinare *intr* to make a blunder; (mus) to be out of tune
scantinato *m* basement
scantonare (**scantóno**) *tr* to round (*a corner*) ‖ *intr* to duck around the corner
scanzona·to -ta *adj* flippant; unconventional
scapaccióne *m* clout; **dare uno scapaccione a** to clout, slap
scapa·to -ta *adj* scatterbrained ‖ *m* scatterbrain
scapestra·to -ta *adj* & *m* libertine
scapigliare §280 *tr* to dishevel ‖ *ref* to be disheveled
scapiglia·to -ta *adj* disheveled; libertine; unconventional; free and easy
scapitare (**scàpito**) *intr* to lose
scàpito *m* damage; loss; **a scapito di** to the detriment of
scàpola *f* shoulder blade
scapolare *m* scapular ‖ *v* (**scàpolo**) *tr* (coll) to escape, avoid ‖ *intr*—**scapolare da** to get out of (*danger*)

scàpo•lo -la *adj* unmarried || *m* bachelor || *f* see **scapola**
scappaménto *m* escapement (*of watch, of piano*); (aut) exhaust
scappare *tr*—**scapparla bella** to have a narrow escape || *intr* (ESSERE) to flee; to abscond; to run; to get away; to escape; to stick out; to burst out (*said, e.g., of sun*); **far scappare la pazienza a qlcu** to make s.o. lose his patience, to tax s.o.'s patience; **scappare a gambe levate** to run away, beat it; **scappare da** to burst out, e.g., **gli è scappato da ridere** he burst out laughing; **scappar detto di** to blurt out that, e.g., **gli scappò detto di non poterne più** he blurted out that he could not hold out; **scappare di mente** to escape one's mind; **scappar fuori con** to come out with
scappata *f* excursion; sally; escapade; bolt (*of horse*); **fare una scappata** to take a run; **scappata spiritosa** witticism
scappatóia *f* subterfuge; loophole
scappellare (scappèllo) *ref* to tip one's hat
scappellòtto *m* smack, slap (on the head); **entrare a scappellotto** (coll) to squeeze in; **passare a scappellotto** (coll) to squeeze through with influence
scapricciare §128 *tr* to satisfy the whims of
scarabèo *m* beetle; scarab (*stone*); **scarabeo sacro** scarab; **scarabeo stercorario** dung beetle
scarabocchiare §287 **(scarabòcchio)** *tr* to scribble; to blot (*with ink*)
scarabòc•chio *m* **(-chi)** ink blot; scribble; scrawl
scarafàg•gio *m* **(-gi)** cockroach
scaramanzia *f* exorcism; **per scaramanzia** to ward off the evil eye, for good luck
scaramazza *adj fem* irregular (*pearl*)
scaramùc•cia *f* **(-ce)** skirmish
scaraventare (scaravènto) *tr* to hurl, chuck; to transfer suddenly
scarcerare (scàrcero) *tr* to release from jail
scardinare (scàrdino) *tr* to unhinge
scàri•ca *f* **(-che)** discharge; volley; evacuation; (elec) discharge; (fig) shower
scaricabarili *m*—**giocare a scaricabarili** (fig) to pass the buck
scaricare §197 **(scàrico)** *tr* to unload; to discharge; to hurl (*insults*); to wreak (*anger*); to free (*from responsibility*) || *ref* to unburden oneself; to flow (*said of a river*); to discharge; to run down (*said of a battery or a watch*)
scaricatóre *m* longshoreman; (elec) lightning arrester
scàri•co -ca (-chi -che) *adj* empty, unloaded; discharged; clear (*sky*); free; run-down (*e.g., clock*) || *m* unloading; discharge; exhaust; waste, refuse; **a mio (tuo, etc.) scarico** in my (your, etc.) defense || *f* see **scarica**
scarlattina *f* scarlet fever
scarlat•to -ta *adj & m* scarlet
scarmigliare §280 *tr* to dishevel
scarnificare §197 **(scarnifico)** or **scarnire** §176 *tr* to bone, take the flesh off; to make thin; to wear down to the bone
scarni•to -ta or **scar•no -na** *adj* boned; meager; skinny
scaròla *f* escarole, endive
scarpa *f* shoe; wedge, skid; scarp; **fare le scarpe a** to undercut; **scarpe al sole** violent death; **scarpe da sci** ski boots
scarpata *f* escarp, escarpment; slope (*of embankment*); blow with a shoe; **scarpata continentale** continental slope
scarpétta *f* small shoe; low shoe; **scarpette chiodate** spikes; **scarpette da ginnastica** gym shoes
scarpinare *intr* to trudge
scarpóne *m* heavy boot; clodhopper
scarròc•cio *m* **(-ci)** (aer, naut) leeway
scarrozzare (scarròzzo) *tr* to take for a ride || *intr* to go for a ride; to go for a walk
scarrozzata *f* ride, drive
scarseggiare §290 **(scarséggio)** *intr* (ESSERE) to be scarce, be in short supply; **scarseggiare di** to be short of
scarsèlla *f* pocket; (obs) purse
scarsézza *f* or **scarsi•tà** *f* **(-tà)** scarcity, dearth, lack
scar•so -sa *adj* short; scarce; scanty, scant; weak (*wind*); **scarso a** short of
scartabellare (scartabèllo) *tr* to leaf through (*a book*)
scartafàc•cio *m* **(-ci)** note pad, notebook; poorly-bound copybook
scartaménto *m* (rr) gauge; **a scartamento ridotto** narrow-gauge; small-size; small-scale
scartare *tr* to unpack, unwrap; to discard (*cards*); to remove; to scrap (*e.g., a machine*); (mil) to reject || *intr* to swerve; to side-step
scartata *f* unwrapping; side step; swerving; (fig) scolding
scartina *f* discard
scarto *m* discard; reject; swerve; (mil) rejected soldier; (sports) difference; **di scarto** inferior
scartocciare §128 **(scartòccio)** *tr* to unwrap; to unfold; to husk (*corn*)
scartòffie *fpl* old papers, trash
scassare *tr* to uncrate; to plow up; (coll) to ruin, bust || *ref* (coll) to break down
scassinare *tr* to pick (*a lock*); to burglarize; to break open
scassina•tóre -trice *mf* burglar; **scassinatore di casseforti** safe-cracker
scasso *m* plowing, tilling; burglary
scatenare (scaténo) *tr* to unchain; to trigger; to excite, stir up || *ref* to break loose
scàtola *f* box; can; **a scatola chiusa** sight unseen; **in scatola** canned; **rompere le scatole a** (vulg) to bug, pester; **scatola armonica** music box; **scatola a sorpresa** jack-in-the-box;

scatola cranica cranium, skull; **scatola del cambio** (aut) transmission, gear box
scatolame *m* boxes; canned food
scatolifi•cio *m* (**-ci**) box factory
scattare *tr* to take (*a picture*) || *intr* (ESSERE & AVERE) to jump, spring; to go off (*said of a trap*); to go up (*said of the cost of living*); to go into action, begin
scatto *m* click (*of camera, gun*); outburst; sprint; automatic increase (*in salary*); shutter release; **a scatti** in jerks; **di scatto** suddenly
scaturire §176 *intr* (ESSERE) to spring; to pour, gush; to stem
scavalcare §197 *tr* to jump over; to pass over; to unsaddle; to skip (*a stitch*) || *intr* (ESSERE) to dismount || *ref* (coll) to rush
scavallare *intr* to caper, cavort
scavare *tr* to dig; to dig up, unearth
scava•tóre -trice *adj* excavating || *m* digger || *f* digger, excavator
scavezzacòllo *m* scamp; daredevil; **a scavezzacollo** headlong, at breakneck speed
scavezzare (**scavézzo**) *tr* to lop; to burst; to break; to take the halter off (*a horse*)
scavo *m* digging, excavation
scazzottare (**scazzòtto**) *tr* to beat up
scégliere §244 *tr* to choose; to pick out
sceic•co *m* (**-chi**) sheik
scelleratàggine *f* or **scelleratézza** *f* wickedness, villainy
scellera•to -ta *adj* wicked || *m* villain
scellino *m* shilling
scél•to -ta *adj* choice; selected; (mil) first-class || *f* choice; pick; selection; **di prima scelta** choice
scemare (**scémo**) *tr* to diminish, reduce; to lower the level of || *intr* (ESSERE) & *ref* to lessen, diminish
scemènza *f* foolishness, stupidity
scé•mo -ma *adj* silly, foolish || *mf* simpleton, fool
scempiàggine *f* silliness, foolishness
scém•pio -pia (**-pi -pie**) *adj* simple; single; (lit) wicked || *m* ruination; (lit) slaughter; **fare scempio di** to ruin; (lit) to slaughter
scèna *f* scene; stage; acting; scenery; **esser di scena** (theat) to be on; **mettere in scena** (theat) to stage; **scene di prossima programmazione** (mov) coming attractions
scenà•rio *m* (**-ri**) scenery; scenario, setting
scenari•sta *mf* (**-sti -ste**) scenarist; script writer
scenata *f* scene (*outbreak of anger*)
scéndere §245 *tr* to descend, go down; to bring down || *intr* (ESSERE) to descend, go down; to get off; to come (*to an agreement*); to step (*into the ring*); to put up (*at a hotel*); to check in (*at a hotel*)
scendilèt•to *m* (**-to**) scatter rug; bathrobe
sceneggiare §290 (**scenéggio**) *tr* to write a scenario for; to adapt for the stage
sceneggia•tóre -trice *mf* scenarist
sceneggiatura *f* (mov) screenplay; (rad, telv) continuity
scenètta *f* (theat) sketch
scenògrafo *m* scene designer
scenotècni•ca *f* (**-che**) stagecraft
sceriffo *m* sheriff
scèrnere §246 *tr* to discern; to distinguish; to select
scervellare (**scervèllo**) *ref* to rack one's brains
scervella•to -ta *adj* scatterbrained
scésa [s] *f* discent; slope
scespiria•no -na *adj* Shakesperean
scetticismo *m* skepticism
scètti•co -ca (**-ci -che**) *adj* skeptic(al) || *m* skeptic
scèttro *m* scepter
sceverare (**scévero**) *tr* (lit) to distinguish
scé•vro -vra *adj* (lit) free, exempt
schèda *f* card; slip, form; **scheda elettorale** ballot; **scheda perforata** punch card
schedare (**schèdo**) *tr* to file
schedà•rio *m* (**-ri**) card index, card catalogue; file cabinet
schég•gia *f* (**-ge**) splinter; chip
scheggiare §290 (**schéggio**) *tr* & *ref* to splinter
schelètri•co -ca *adj* (**-ci -che**) skeleton, skeletal; succint
schèletro *m* skeleton
schè•ma *m* (**-mi**) diagram; draft; model; scheme; **schema di montaggio** (electron) hookup
schérma *f* fencing
schermàglia *f* argument
schermare (**schérmo**) *tr* to screen; (elec) to shield
schermire §176 *tr* to protect; (obs) to fence with || *ref*—**schermirsi da** to ward off, parry; to protect oneself from
schermi•tóre -trice *mf* fencer
schérmo *m* screen; protection; (elec) shield; **farsi schermo di** to use as protection; **farsi schermo delle mani** to ward off a blow with one's hands
schernire §176 *tr* to deride
schérno *m* derision, ridicule, mockery
scherzare (**schérzo**) *tr* (coll) to mock || *intr* to play; to joke, trifle
schérzo *m* play; joke, jest; freak (*of nature*); child's play; trick; **neppure per scherzo** under no circumstances; **per scherzo** in jest; **stare allo scherzo** to take a joke
scherzó•so -sa [s] *adj* joking; playful
schiacciaménto *m* crushing; flattening
schiaccianó•ci *m* (**-ci**) nutcracker
schiacciante *adj* crushing
schiacciapata•te *m* (**-te**) ricer
schiacciare §128 *tr* to crush; to take (*a nap*); to squelch (*a rumor*); to subdue (*the details of a painting*); to mash (*potatoes*); to tread on, step on (*s.o.'s foot*); to flatten; to run (*s.o.*) over; to make (*s.o.'s figure*) look squatty; to crack (*nuts*); to flunk; (tennis) to smash
schiacciata *f* hot cake; (tennis) smash

schiaffare *tr* (coll) to fling, clap
schiaffeggiare §290 (**schiafféggio**) *tr* to slap; to buffet
schiaffo *m* slap, box
schiamazzare *intr* to squawk, cackle; to honk; to make a racket
schiamazzo *m* squawking, cackle; honk; hubbub
schiantare *tr* to crush, burst || *intr* (ESSERE) (coll) to burst; (coll) to croak || *ref* to break, crack, split
schianto *m* break, crack; crash; bang; knockout (*extraordinary, attractive person or thing*); **di schianto** all of a sudden; **schianto al cuore** heartache
schiappa *f* splinter; (coll) good-for-nothing
schiariménto *m* elucidation
schiarire §176 *tr* to make clearer; to make (*the hair*) light; to clear; to explain; to elucidate || *intr* (ESSERE) to become light || *ref* to clear up (*said of the weather*); to clear (*one's throat*); to fade || *impers* (ESSERE) —**schiarisce** it is getting light
schiarita *f* clearing (*of weather*); improvement (*in relations*)
schiatta *f* race, stock
schiattare *intr* (ESSERE) to burst
schiavi•sta (**-sti -ste**) *adj* slave (*e.g., state*) || *mf* antiabolitionist
schiavi•tù *f* (**-tù**) slavery; bondage
schia•vo -va *adj* enslaved || *mf* slave
schiccherare (**schìcchero**) *tr* to scribble; to soil; to sketch; to dash off; to blurt out; (coll) to clean out
schidionare (**schidióno**) *tr* to put on the spit
schidióne *m* spit
schièna *f* back; divide; crown (*of road*); **giocare di schiena** to buck
schienale *m* back (*of chair; cut of meat*)
schièra *f* crowd; flock; herd; (mil) rank
schieraménto *m* alignment
schierare (**schièro**) *tr* to line up || *ref* to line up; **schierarsi dalla parte di** to side with
schièt•to -ta *adj* pure; frank, honest
schifare *tr* to loathe; to disgust || *ref*—**schifarsi di** to feel disgusted with
schifa•to -ta *adj* disgusted
schifiltó•so -sa [s] *adj* fastidious; squeamish
schifo *m* disgust, loathing; skiff; shell; **fare schifo a** to disgust; to make sick
schifó•so -sa [s] *adj* disgusting; sickening; (slang) tremendous
schioccare §197 (**schiòcco**) *tr* to snap (*the fingers*); to click (*the tongue*); to smack (*the lips*); to crack (*a whip*) || *intr* to crack
schiòc•co *m* (**-chi**) crack, snap; click; smack
schiodare (**schiòdo**) *tr* to take the nails out of
schioppettata *f* gunshot; earshot
schiòppo *m* gun, shotgun; **a un tiro di schioppo** within earshot
schiùdere §125 *tr & ref* to open
schiuma *f* foam, froth; lather; head (*of beer*); dregs, scum; meerschaum; **avere la schiuma alla bocca** to froth at the mouth
schiumaiòla *f* skimmer
schiumare *tr* to scum; to skim || *intr* to foam, froth; to lather
schiumó•so -sa [s] *adj* foamy
schivare *tr* to avoid; to avert || *ref* to shy
schi•vo -va *adj* averse; bashful, shy
schizzare *tr* to spray; to sprinkle; to ooze (*venom*); to sketch; **schizzare fuoco dagli occhi** to have fire in one's eyes || *intr* (ESSERE) to gush; to squirt; to dart; **gli occhi gli schizzano dall'orbita** his eyes are popping out of his head
schizzétto *m* sprayer; syringe; water pistol
schizzinó•so -sa [s] *adj* finicky, fastidious
schizzo *m* spray; splash; sketch; survey (*e.g., of literature*)
sci *m* (**sci**) ski
scia *f* wake; track; trail; **scia di condensazione** contrail
sciàbola *f* saber
sciabordare (**sciabórdo**) *tr* to shake, agitate || *intr* to break (*said of waves*)
sciacallo *m* jackal
sciacquadi•ta *m* (**-ta**) finger bowl
sciacquare (**sciàcquo**) *tr* to rinse
sciacquatura *f* rinse
sciacquì•o *m* (**-i**) splash, dash
sciàcquo *m* rinsing (*of the mouth*); mouthwash
sciagura *f* calamity, misfortune
sciagura•to -ta *adj* unfortunate; wretched
scialacquare (**scialàcquo**) *tr* to squander
scialare *tr* to squander || *intr* to be well off; to live it up
scial•bo -ba *adj* pale, faded; wan
scialle *m* shawl; **scialle da viaggio** traveling blanket
scialo *m* squandering; opulence; **a scialo** lavishly
scialuppa *f* launch; lifeboat
sciamanna•to -ta *adj* slovenly
sciamannó•ne -na *mf* slovenly person || *f* slattern
sciamare *intr* (ESSERE & AVERE) to swarm
sciame *m* swarm; flock
sciampagna *f* champagne
scianca•to -ta *adj* cripple, lame; wobbly (*table*)
sciangai *m* pick-up-sticks || **Sciangai** *f* Shanghai
sciarada *f* charade
sciare §119 *intr* to ski; to back water
sciarpa *f* scarf; sash (*e.g., of an officer or of a mayor*)
scias•si *m* (**-si**) chassis
sciàtica *f* (pathol) sciatica
scia•tóre -trice *mf* skier
sciatterìa *f* or **sciattézza** *f* slovenliness
sciat•to -ta *adj* slovenly, sloppy
scibile *m* knowledge
sciènte *adj* conscious; knowing
scientìfi•co -ca *adj* (**-ci -che**) scientific
sciènza *f* science; knowledge

scienzia•to -ta *mf* scientist
scilinguàgnolo *m* frenum (*of tongue*); **avere lo scilinguagnolo sciolto** to have a loose tongue
Scilla *f* Scylla; **fra Scilla e Cariddi** between Scylla and Charibdis
scimitarra *f* scimitar
scìmmia *f* monkey; (coll) drunk; **fare la scimmia a** to ape; **scimmia antropomorfa** anthropoid ape
scimmié•sco -sca *adj* (**-schi -sche**) monkeyish; apish
scimmiottare (scimmiòtto) *tr* to ape
scimpan•zé *m* (**-zé**) chimpanzee
scimuni•to -ta *adj* idiotic || *mf* idiot
scìndere §247 *tr* (lit) to split; to separate
scintilla *f* spark; sparkle; (fig) scintilla; **scintilla elettrica** jump spark
scintillare *intr* to spark; to sparkle
scintillì•o *m* (**-ì**) sparkle, brilliance
scioccare §197 *tr* to shock
sciocchézza *f* silliness; trifle
sciòc•co -ca (**-chi -che**) *adj* silly, foolish || *mf* fool, blockhead
sciògliere §127 *tr* to loosen; to release; to unfasten, untie; to solve; to disperse; to dissolve; to limber; to fulfill (*a promise*); to unfurl (*sails*) || *ref* to loosen up; to get loose; to dissolve; to melt (*into tears*)
scioglilìn•gua *m*(**-gue**) tongue twister
scioglimento *m* melting; dissolution; fulfillment; denouement
sciolina *f* ski wax
scioltézza *f* nimbleness, agility; freedom (*of movement*); ease
sciòl•to -ta *adj* loose; glib; free; blank (*verse*)
scioperante *adj* striking || *mf* striker
scioperare (sciòpero) *intr* to strike
sciopera•to -ta *adj* loafing; lazy || *m* loafer
sciòpero *m* strike; walkout; **sciopero a singhiozzo** slowdown strike; **sciopero bianco** sit-down strike; **sciopero della fame** hunger strike; **sciopero di solidarietà** sympathy strike; **sciopero pignolo** slowdown
sciorinare *tr* to display; to tell (*lies*); to air (*laundry*)
sciovia *f* ski lift
sciovinismo *m* chauvinism, jingoism
scipi•to -ta *adj* insipid
scippo *m* snatching (*e.g., of a bag*)
sciròc•co *m* (**-chi**) sirocco; southeast
sciròppo *m* syrup
sci•sma *m* (**-smi**) schism
scismàti•co -ca *adj* (**-ci -che**) schismatic
scissióne *f* split; (biol, phys) fission
scis•so -sa *adj* split, rent
scisto *m* schist
sciupare *tr* to spoil; to wear out; to waste; to rumple || *ref* to wear; to run down (*said of health*); to get rumpled
sciupa•to -ta *adj* ruined; worn out; wasted; run down
sciupì•o *m* (**-ì**) waste
sciupó•ne -na *mf* waster, squanderer
sciu•scià *m* (**-scià**) bootblack; urchin
scìvola *f* chute
scivolare (scìvolo) *intr* (ESSERE & AVERE) to slide, glide; to steal; **scivolare d'ala** (aer) to sideslip
scivolata *f* slide, glide; **scivolata d'ala** (aer) sideslip
scìvolo *m* chute; (aer) slip (*for seaplanes*)
scivolóne *m* slip, slide
scivoló•so -sa [s] *adj* slippery
scoccare §197 (**scòcco**) *tr* to shoot (*an arrow*); to give (*a buss*); to strike (*the hour*) || *intr* (ESSERE) to dart; to spring; to strike (*said of a clock*); to shoot
scocciare §128 (**scòccio**) *tr* (coll) to break; (coll) to bother; (naut) to unhook || *ref* to be bored
scoccia•tóre -trice *mf* (coll) nuisance
scocciatura *f* (coll) bother, annoyance
scòc•co *m* (**-chi**) darting; stroke (*e.g., of three*); (naut) hook; **scocco di baci** bussing, kissing
scodèlla *f* bowl; soup plate
scodellare (scodèllo) *tr* to dish out
scodellino *m* small bowl; (mil) pan (*of musket lock*)
scodinzolare (scodìnzolo) *intr* to wag its tail; to waddle (*said of a woman*)
scoglièra *f* reef (*of rocks*); **scogliera corallina** coral reef
scò•glio *m* (**-gli**) rock; reef; cliff; stumbling block
scoiare §248 *tr* to skin
scoiàttolo *m* squirrel
scolabrò•do *m* (**-do**) colander, strainer
scolafrit•to *m* (**-to**) strainer
scolapa•sta *m* (**-sta**) (coll) colander
scolare (scólo) *tr* to drain; (fig) to polish off || *intr* (ESSERE) to drip || *ref* to melt
scolaré•sco -sca (-schi -sche) *adj* school || *f* schoolchildren; student body
scola•ro -ra *mf* pupil; student
scolàsti•co -ca (**-ci -che**) *adj* school; scholastic || *m* scholastic, schoolman || *f* scholasticism
scola•tóio *m* (**-tói**) drain; strainer
scolatura *f* drip, drippings; dregs
scollaccia•to -ta *adj* low-necked; wearing a low-cut dress; dirty, obscene
scollare (scòllo) *tr* to cut off at the neck; to unglue || *ref* to wear a low-necked dress; to come unglued
scollatura *f* neckline; ungluing; **scollatura a barchetta** low neck; **scollatura a punta** V neck
scòllo *m* neck, neckline
scólo *m* drain; drainage; (slang) clap
scolopèndra *f* centipede
scolorare (scolóro) *tr, intr* (ESSERE), & *ref* to fade, discolor; to pale
scolorire §176 *tr, intr* (ESSERE), & *ref* to fade, discolor
scolpare (scólpo) *tr* to excuse
scolpire §176 *tr* to sculpture; to engrave; to emphasize
scólta *f* (lit) sentry; **fare la scolta** to stand guard
scombaciare §128 *tr* to pull apart, separate
scombinare *tr* to disarrange; to upset
scómbro *m* mackerel

scombù·glio *m* (-gli) (coll) disorder
scombussolare (scombùssolo) *tr* to upset
scomméssa *f* bet, wager
scomméttere §198 *tr* to bet; to separate
scommetti·tóre -trice *mf* bettor
scomodare (scòmodo) *tr* to trouble, disturb || *ref* to take the trouble
scomodi·tà *f* (-tà) trouble, inconvenience
scòmo·do -da *adj* awkward, unwieldy; uncomfortable || *m* inconvenience
scompaginare (scompàgino) *tr* to upset; (typ) to pi
scompagna·to -ta *adj* odd
scomparire §108 *intr* (ESSERE) to disappear; to make a bad showing
scompar·so -sa *adj* disappeared; extinct || *mf* deceased || *f* disappearance; death
scompartiménto *m* compartment; partition
scompènso *m* lack of compensation; imbalance
scompigliare §280 *tr* to disarray; to trouble, upset
scompì·glio *m* (-gli) disarray; upset
scompisciare §128 *tr* (vulg) to piss on || *ref* (vulg) to wet oneself; **scompisciarsi dalle risa** (coll) to split one's sides laughing
scomplè·to -ta *adj* incomplete
scompórre §218 *tr* to decompose, disintegrate; to rumple; to dishevel; to upset; to dismantle, take apart; (typ) to pi || *ref* to lose one's composure
scompó·sto -sta *adj* unseemly
scomùni·ca *f* (-che) excommunication
scomunicare §197 **(scomùnico)** *tr* to excommunicate; (joc) to ostracize
sconcertare (sconcèrto) *tr* to upset; to disconcert || *ref* to become disconcerted
sconcézza *f* obscenity, indecency
scón·cio -cia (-ci -ce) *adj* dirty, filthy, obscene || *m* obscenity; shame
sconclusiona·to -ta *adj* inconsequential; incoherent; rambling
sconcordanza *f* disagreement; (gram) lack of agreement
scondi·to -ta *adj* unseasoned
sconfessare (sconfèsso) *tr* to disavow; to retract
sconfessióne *f* disavowal
sconfiggere §104 *tr* to defeat, rout; to pull (*a nail*); to unfasten
sconfinare *intr* to cross the border; **sconfinare da** to stray from
sconfina·to -ta *adj* boundless, unlimited
sconfitta *f* defeat, rout
sconfortante *adj* discouraging
sconfortare (sconfòrto) *tr* to discourage; to distress || *ref* to become discouraged
sconfòrto *m* depression; distress
scongelare (scongèlo) *tr* to thaw
scongiurare *tr* to conjure; to implore
scongiuro *m* conjuration; entreaty
sconnès·so -sa *adj* disconnected; incoherent
sconnèttere §107 *tr* to disconnect; to take apart || *intr* to be incoherent
sconoscènte *adj* unappreciative
sconosciu·to -ta *adj* unknown || *mf* stranger
sconquassare *tr* to smash, shatter
sconquassa·to -ta *adj* broken-down; upset
sconquasso *m* destruction; confusion; smash-up
sconsacrare *tr* to desecrate
sconsideratézza *f* thoughtlessness
sconsidera·to -ta *adj* inconsiderate
sconsigliare §280 *tr* to dissuade, discourage
sconsiglia·to -ta *adj* thoughtless
sconsola·to -ta *adj* disconsolate
scontare (scónto) *tr* to expiate; to discount; to serve (*time in jail*)
scontentare (scontènto) *tr* to dissatisfy
scontèn·to -ta *adj & m* discontent
scónto *m* discount; part payment; (fig) partial remission
scontrare (scóntro) *tr* to meet; (naut) to turn (*the wheel*) sharply || *ref* to clash; to collide; to come to blows
scontrino *m* check, ticket
scóntro *m* collision; battle, encounter; clash; ward (*of key*)
scontró·so -sa [s] *adj* peevish, cross
sconveniènte *adj* unfavorable; unseemly, unbecoming; indecent
sconvenire §282 *intr* (ESSERE) to be unseemly or unbecoming
sconvòlgere §289 *tr* to upset; to disconcert
sconvolgiménto *m* upsetting; **sconvolgimento di stomaco** stomach upset; **sconvolgimento tellurico** upheaval
sconvòl·to -ta *adj* upset; disconcerted; distracted
scópa *f* broom; **scopa per lavaggio** mop
scopare (scópo) *tr* to sweep
scopata *f* sweep
scoperchiare §287 **(scopèrchio)** *tr* to uncover; to take the lid off
scopèr·to -ta *adj* uncovered; open; bare; exposed; unpaid || *m* open ground; open air; overdraft; (econ) short sale; (com) balance; **allo scoperto** in the open; overdrawn (*check*); short (*sale*) || *f* discovery; **alla scoperta** openly
scòpo *m* purpose, goal, aim
scoppiare §287 **(scòppio)** *tr* to uncouple || *intr* (ESSERE) to burst; to blow; to explode; to break (*said, e.g., of news*); (fig) to die (*e.g., of overeating*); **scoppiare a** to burst out (*laughing or crying*)
scoppiettare (scoppiétto) *intr* to crackle
scoppietti·o *m* (-i) crackle
scòp·pio *m* (-pi) burst; explosion; outbreak; outburst; blowout (*of tire*); **a scoppio** internal-combustion (*engine*); **scoppio di tuono** clap of thunder
scòppola *f* drop (*of plane in air pocket*); (coll) rabbit punch
scopriménto *m* uncovering; unveiling
scoprire §110 *tr* to uncover; to unveil; to discover; to expose || *ref* to take off one's clothes; to take one's hat off; to reveal oneself

scopri•tóre -trice *mf* discoverer
scoraggiaménto *m* discouragement
scoraggiante *adj* discouraging
scoraggiare §290 *tr* to discourage, dishearten || *ref* to be or become discouraged
scoraménto *m* (lit) discouragement
scorbuto *m* scurvy
scorciare §128 (**scórcio**) *tr* to shorten; to foreshorten || *intr* (ESSERE) to shorten, grow shorter; to look foreshortened || *ref* to shorten, grow shorter
scorciatóia *f* shortcut, cutoff
scór•cio *m* (**-ci**) foreshortening; end, close (*of a period*); **di scorcio** foreshortened
scordare (**scòrdo**) *tr* to forget; to put out of tune || *ref* to forget; to get out of tune
scorég•gia *f* (**-ge**) (vulg) fart
scoreggiare §290 (**scoréggio**) *intr* (vulg) to fart
scòrgere §249 *tr* to perceive, to discern
scòria *f* slag, dross; (fig) scum, dregs; **scorie atomiche** atomic waste
scorna•to -ta *adj* humiliated, ridiculed; hornless
scòrno *m* humiliation, ridicule
scorpacciata *f* bellyful; **fare una scorpacciata di** to stuff oneself with
scorpióne *m* scorpion || **Scorpione** *m* (astrol) Scorpio
scorrazzare *tr* to wander over || *intr* to run around; to move about; (fig) to ramble; (mil) to raid
scórrere §139 *tr* to raid; to glance over || *intr* (ESSERE) to flow; to run; to glide
scorrerìa *f* raid, foray, incursion
scorrettézza *f* imprecision; impropriety
scorrèt•to -ta *adj* incorrect; improper
scorrévole *adj* sliding; flowing, fluent || *m* slide (*of slide rule*)
scorribanda *f* raid, foray, incursion
scór•so -sa *adj* past, last || *m* error, slip || *f* glance; short stay
scor•sóio -sóia *adj* (**-sói -sóie**) slip (*knot*)
scòrta *f* escort; provision, stock; **di scorta** spare (*tire*); **fare di scorta a** to escort; **scorta d'onore** (mil) honor guard; **scorte** (com) stockpile; (com) supplies; **scorte morte** agricultural supplies; **scorte vive** livestock
scortare (**scòrto**) *tr* to escort; to foreshorten
scortecciare §128 (**scortéccio**) *tr* to strip the bark from; to peel off; to scrape || *ref* to peel off
scortése *adj* discourteous, impolite
scortesìa *f* discourtesy, impoliteness
scorticare §197 (**scórtico**) *tr* to skin; to be overdemanding with (*students*); to fleece || *ref* to skin (*e.g., one's arm*)
scòrza *f* bark; skin, hide; (fig) appearance; **scorza di limone** lemon peel
scoscendiménto *m* landslide; cliff
scoscé•so -sa [s] *adj* sloping, steep
scòssa *f* shake; jerk; **scossa di pioggia** downpour; **scossa di terremoto** earth tremor; **scossa elettrica** electric shock; **scossa tellurica** earthquake
scossóne *m* jolt, jerk
scostaménto *m* removal; separation
scostare (**scòsto**) *tr* to move away; to try to avoid || *intr* (ESSERE) to stand away || *ref* to step aside; to stray
scostuma•to -ta *adj* dissolute, debauched
scotennare (**scoténno**) *tr* to scalp; to skin (*an animal*)
scòtta *f* whey; (naut) sheet
scottante *adj* burning (*question*); outrageous (*offense*)
scottare (**scòtto**) *tr* to burn; to scald; to sear; to boil (*eggs*); (fig) to sting || *intr* to burn; to be hot (*said of stolen goods*) || *ref* to get burnt
scottatura *f* burn; (fig) blow, jolt
scòt•to -ta *adj* overcooked, overdone || *m*—**pagare lo scotto** to foot the bill; **pagare lo scotto di** to expiate || *f* see **scotta**
scoutismo *m* scouting
scovare (**scóvo**) *tr* to rouse (*game*); to find, discover
scovolino *m* pipe cleaner; (mil) small swab
scóvolo *m* (mil) swab
scòzia *f* (archit) scotia || **la Scozia** Scotland
scozzése [s] *adj* Scotch, Scottish || *m* Scotch, Scottish (*language*); Scotchman || *f* Scotchwoman
scozzonare (**scozzóno**) *tr* to break in (*a horse*); to train
scranna *f* (hist) seat
screanza•to -ta *adj* ill-mannered, rude
screditare (**scrédito**) *tr* to discredit
scremare (**scrèmo**) *tr* to cream
scrematrice *f* cream separator
screpolare (**scrèpolo**) *tr, intr* (ESSERE), *& ref* to crack; to chap
screpolatura *f* crack; chap (*of skin*)
screziare §287 (**scrèzio**) *tr* to mottle, variegate
scrè•zio *m* (**-zi**) tiff
scri•ba *m* (**-bi**) scribe (*Jewish scholar*)
scribacchiare §287 *tr* to scribble, scrawl
scribacchino *m* scribbler; hack
scricchiolare (**scricchiolo**) *intr* to crack, creak
scricchiolì•o *m* (**-i**) crack, creak
scricciolo *m* wren
scrigno *m* jewel box
scriminatura *f* part (*in hair*)
scrit•to -ta *adj* written || *m* writing || *f* sign; inscription; contract; **scritta luminosa** electric sign
scrit•tóio *m* (**-tói**) writing desk
scrit•tóre -trice *mf* writer
scrittura *f* handwriting; penmanship; writing; contract; entry; (theat) booking; **Sacra Scrittura** Holy Scripture; **scrittura privata** contract; **scrittura pubblica** deed, indenture; **scrittura a macchina** typing
scritturale *adj* scriptural || *m* clerk; copyist; fundamentalist
scritturare *tr* (theat) to book, engage
scrivanìa *f* desk

scrivano *m* clerk, copyist, typist
scrìvere §250 *tr & intr* to write; **scrivere a macchina** to type
scroccare §197 (**scròcco**) *tr* to sponge (*a meal*); to manage to get (*a prize*) || *intr* to sponge
scrocca·tóre -trice *mf* sponger
scròc·co *m* (**-chi**) sponging; creaking; **a scrocco** sponging; spring (*lock*); switchblade (*knife*)
scroccó·ne -na *mf* sponger
scròfa *f* sow; slut
scrollare (**scròllo**) *tr* to shake; to shrug (*one's shoulders*) || *ref* to get into action; to pull oneself together
scrollata *f* shake; **scrollata di spalle** shrug
scrosciare §128 (**scròscio**) *intr* (ESSERE & AVERE) to pelt down; (fig) to thunder
scrò·scio *m* (**-sci**) thunder, roar; **scroscio di pioggia** downpour; **scroscio di tuono** thunderclap
scrostare (**scròsto**) *tr* to pick (*a scab*); to scrape; to peel off || *ref* to peel off
scrosta·to -ta *adj* peeling; scaly
scròto *m* scrotum
scrùpolo *m* scruple; scrupulousness
scrupoló·so -sa [s] *adj* scrupulous
scrutare *tr* to scan, scrutinize
scruta·tóre -trice *adj* inquisitive || *mf* teller (*of votes*)
scrutina·tóre -trice *mf* teller (*of votes*)
scrutì·nio *m* (**-ni**) poll, vote; evaluation (*of an examination*); count (*of votes*); **scrutinio segreto** secret ballot
scucire §143 *tr* to unstitch; (coll) to cough up || *ref* to come unstitched
scucitura *f* unstitching; rip
scuderìa *f* stable
scudétto *m* badge; escutcheon; (sports) badge of victory
scudièro *m* esquire
scudisciare §128 *tr* to whip
scudì·scio *m* (**-sci**) whip
scudo *m* shield; escutcheon; **far scudo a** to shield
scùffia *f* (coll) load (*intoxication*); **fare scuffia** to capsize; **prendersi una scuffia per** to fall for, to fall in love with
scugnizzo *m* Neapolitan urchin
sculacciare §128 *tr* to spank
sculacciata *f* spank, spanking
sculacció ne *m* spank, spanking
sculettare (**sculétto**) *intr* to waddle
scul·tóre -trice *mf* sculptor || *f* sculptress
scultura *f* sculpture
scuòla *f* school; **scuola allievi ufficiali** military academy; officers' candidate school; **scuola dell'obbligo** mandatory education; **scuola di danza** dancing school; **scuola di dressaggio** obedience school (*for dogs*); **scuola di guerra** war college; **scuola di guida** driving school; **scuola di perfezionamento per laureati** postgraduate school; **scuola di taglio** sewing school; **scuola materna** kindergarten; **scuola mista** coeducational school
scuòla·bus *m* (**-bus**) school bus
scuòtere §251 *tr* to shake; to shake up; **scuotere di dosso** to shake off
scure *f* ax; cleaver
scurire §176 *tr*, *intr* (ESSERE), & *ref* to darken
scu·ro -ra *adj* dark || *m* darkness; dark; shutter; **essere allo scuro** to be in the dark
scurrile *adj* scurrilous
scusa *f* excuse; apology; pretext; **chiedere scusa** to apologize
scusare *tr* to excuse; to pardon; to apologize for; **scusi!** pardon me! || *ref* to apologize; to beg off
sdaziare §287 *tr* to clear through customs
sdebitare (**sdébito**) *tr* to free from debt || *ref* to become free of debt; **sdebitarsi con** to repay a favor to
sdegnare (**sdégno**) *tr* to scorn; to arouse, enrage || *ref* to get mad
sdégno *m* indignation, anger; (lit) scorn
sdegnó·so -sa [s] *adj* indignant; haughty
sdenta·to -ta *adj* toothless
sdilinquire §176 *tr* to weaken || *intr* (ESSERE) & *ref* to swoon; to become mawkish
sdoganare *tr* to clear through customs
sdolcina·to -ta *adj* mawkish
sdolcinatura *f* mush, slobber
sdoppiare §287 (**sdóppio**) *tr & ref* to split
sdoppiaménto *m* splitting
sdottoreggiare §290 (**sdottoréggio**) *intr* to pontificate
sdràia *f* chaise longue; deck chair
sdraiare §287 *tr* to lay down || *ref* to stretch out (*e.g., on the ground*)
sdràio *m* (**sdrài**) stretching out; **mettersi a sdraio** to lie down
sdrucciolare (**sdrùcciolo**) *intr* (ESSERE & AVERE) to slip, slide
sdrucciolévole *adj* slippery
sdrùccio·lo -la *adj* proparoxytone || *m* slip; slope; proparoxytone
sdruccioloni *adv* slipping, sliding
sdrucire (**sdrùcio**) & §176 *tr* to tear, rend, rip
sdrucitura *f* tear, rend, rip
se *m* (**se**) if || §5 *pron* || *conj* if; whether; **se mai** in the event; **se no** otherwise; **se non tu (lui, lei, etc.)** nobody else but you (him, her, etc.), e.g., **non puoi essere stato se non tu** it could not have been anyone else but you; **se non altro** at least; **se non che** but; **se pure** even if
sé §5 *pron* himself; herself; itself; yourself; themselves; yourselves; oneself; **di per sé stesso** by itself; **fuori di sé** beside oneself; **rientrare in sé** to come back to one's senses; **uscire di sé** to be beside oneself
sebbène *conj* although, though
sèbo *m* sebum, tallow
séc·ca *f* (**-che**) sand bank, shoal; drought; **dare in secca** to run aground; **in secca** hard up
seccante *adj* drying; annoying
seccare §197 (**sécco**) *tr* to dry; to bore;

to bother, annoy || *intr* (ESSERE) to dry up || *ref* to dry up; to be annoyed
secca·tóio *m* (**-tói**) drying room; squeegee (*to remove water from wet decks*)
secca·tóre -trice *mf* bore, pest
seccatura *f* drying; trouble, nuisance
sécchia *f* bucket, pail; **piovere a secchie** to rain cats and dogs
secchièllo *m* little bucket
séc·chio *m* (**-chi**) bucket, pail; bucketful; **secchio dell'immondezza** trash can
séc·co -ca (**-chi -che**) *adj* dry; lanky; sharp || *m* dryness; dry land; drought; **a secco** dry (*cleaning*); **dare in secco** to run aground; **in secco** hard up; **lavare a secco** to dry-clean || *f* see **secca**
secenté·sco -sca *adj* (**-schi -sche**) seventeenth-century
secentèsi·mo -ma *adj, m & pron* six hundredth
secèrnere §153 (*pp* **secrèto**) *tr* to secrete
secessióne *f* secession
séco §5 *prep phrase* (lit) with oneself; along, e.g., **portare seco** to bring along
secolare *adj* secular; century-old; worldly || *m* layman
sècolo *m* century; age; world
secónda *f* second; second-year class; **a seconda** with the wind; **a seconda di** according to; **in seconda** (aut) in second; (mil) second in command
secondare (**secóndo**) *tr* to second
secondà·rio -ria *adj* (**-ri -rie**) secondary
secondino *m* prison guard, turnkey
secón·do -da *adj* second; (lit) favorable || *m* second; second course; (nav) executive officer || *f* see **seconda** || *pron* second || **secondo** *prep* according to; **secondo me (te, etc.)** in my (your, etc.) opinion
secondogèni·to -ta *adj* second-born
secrezióne *f* secretion
sèdano *m* celery
sedare (**sèdo**) *tr* to calm, placate
sedati·vo -va *adj & m* sedative
sède *f* seat; branch; residence; period; (gram) syllable; (rr) right of way; **in separata sede** in private; (law) with change of venue; **Santa Sede** Holy See; **sede centrale** main office, home office
sedentà·rio -ria (**-ri -rie**) *adj* sedentary || *m* sedentary person
sedére *m* sitting; rear, backside || *v* §252 *intr* (ESSERE) to sit, to be seated; to be in session; to be located || *ref* to sit down
sèdia *f* chair; seat; see; **sedia a braccioli** armchair; **sedia a dondolo** rocking chair; **sedia a pozzetto** bucket seat; **sedia a sdraio** deck chair; **sedia da posta** (hist) mail coach; **sedia di vimini** wicker chair; **sedia elettrica** electric chair; **sedia girevole** swivel chair
sedicènne *adj* sixteen-year-old || *mf* sixteen-year-old person
sedicènte *adj* so-called, self-styled
sedicèsi·mo -ma *adj, m & pron* sixteenth
sédici *adj & pron* sixteen; **le sedici** four P.M. || *m* sixteen; sixteenth (*in dates*)
sedile *m* seat; bench; bottom (*of chair*); (aut) bucket seat
sediménto *m* sediment
sediòlo *m* sulky
sedizióne *f* sedition
sedizió·so -sa [s] *adj* seditious
seducènte *adj* seductive; alluring
sedurre §102 *tr* to seduce; to allure; to lead astray; to charm, captivate
seduta *f* sitting; session, meeting; **seduta fiume** (pol) uninterrupted session; **seduta stante** on the spot
sedut·tóre -trice *adj* seductive; alluring; charming || *mf* seducer
seduzióne *f* seduction; allurement; charm
sefardi·ta (**-ti -te**) *adj* Sephardic || *mf* Sephardi
sé·ga *f* (**-ghe**) saw; **a sega** serrated; **sega a nastro** band saw; **sega circolare** buzz saw; **sega da carpentiere** lumberman's saw; **sega intelaiata a lama** bucksaw; **sega meccanica** power saw
ségala *f* rye
segali·gno -gna *adj* rye; lean, wiry
segare §209 (**ségo**) *tr* to saw; to cut
segatrice *f* power saw; **segatrice a disco** circular saw; **segatrice a nastro** band saw
segatura *f* cutting; sawdust
seggétta *f* commode
sèg·gio *m* (**-gi**) seat (*e.g., in congress*); **seggio elettorale** voting commission
sèggiola *f* chair; **seggiola a sdraio** deck chair
seggiolino *m* child's chair; stool; bucket seat; **seggiolino eiettabile** (aer) ejection seat
seggiolóne *m* highchair; easy chair
seggiovìa *f* chair lift
segherìa *f* sawmill
seghetta·to -ta *adj* serrated
seghétto *m* hacksaw; **seghetto da traforo** coping saw
segménto *m* segment; **segmento elastico** (aut) piston ring
segnaccènto *m* accent mark
segnàcolo *m* (lit) symbol, sign
segnalare *tr* to signal; to point out || *ref* to distinguish oneself
segnalazióne *f* signaling; sign, signal; nomination; recommendation; **dare la segnalazione a** to notify; **fare segnalazioni** to signal; **segnalazioni stradali** road signs
segnale *m* sign; signal; bookmark; **segnale di allarme** (mil) alarm; **segnale di occupato** (telp) busy signal; **segnale di via libera** (telp) dial tone; **segnale orario** (rad, telv) time signal; **segnali stradali** road signs
segnalèti·co -ca *adj* (**-ci -che**) identification (*mark*) || *f* road signs
segnalibro *m* bookmark
segnalìne·e *m* (**-e**) lineman
segnapósto *m* place card
segnapun·ti *m* (**-ti**) scorekeeper

segnare (**ségno**) *tr* to mark; to underscore, underline; to jot down; to say (*e.g., five o'clock, said of a watch*); to brand; (sports) to score; **segnare a dito** to point to || *ref* to cross oneself
segnatas·se *m* (-se) postage-due stamp
segnatura *f* signing; signature; library number; (eccl) chancery; (sports) final score; (typ) signature
segnavèn·to *m* (-to) weather vane
ségno *m* mark; bookmark; symbol; sign; signal; boundary; (mus) signature; **a segno che** so that; **a tal segno** to such a point; **essere fatto segno di** to be the target of; **in segno di** as a token of; **mettere a segno** to check, control; **segno della Croce** sign of the Cross; **segno di croce** cross (*mark*); **segno d'interpunzione,** or **di punteggiatura,** or **grafico** punctuation mark; **segno di riconoscimento** identification mark
ségo *m* tallow, suet
segregare §209 (**sègrego**) *tr* to segregate; to secrete || *ref* to withdraw
segregazióne *f* segregation; **segregazione cellulare** solitary confinement
segregazioni·sta *mf* (-**sti** -**ste**) segregationist
segretariato *m* secretariat
segretà·rio -ria *mf* secretary; clerk
segreterìa *f* secretary's office; secretaryship
segretézza *f* secrecy
segré·to -ta *adj* secret; secretive || *m* secret; secrecy; **segreto d'alcova** boudoir secret; **segreto di Pulcinella** open secret
seguace *mf* follower
seguènte *adj* following, next
segù·gio *m* (-**gi**) bloodhound; (fig) private eye
seguire (**séguo**) *tr* to follow; to attend || *intr* (ESSERE) to continue; to follow, ensue; (with *dat*) to follow
seguitare (**séguito**) *intr*—**seguitare a** + *inf* to keep on + *ger*, e.g., **seguitare a parlare** to keep on talking; **seguiti!** go ahead!
séguito *m* following; retinue; followers; sequence; sequel; pursuit; **di seguito** in succession; **far seguito a** to refer to; **in seguito** thereafter; **in seguito a** as a consequence of
sèi *adj & pron* six; **le sei** six o'clock || *m* six; sixth (*in dates*)
seicènto *adj, m & pron* six hundred || *f* car with a motor displacing 600 cubic centimeters || **il Seicento** the seventeenth century
seimila *adj, m, & pron* six thousand
sélce *f* silica; flint; (lit) stone; **selci** paving blocks
selciare §128 (**sélcio**) *tr* to pave
selcia·to -ta *adj* paved || *m* paving
seletti·vo -va *adj* selective
selezionare (**selezióno**) *tr* to select, sort out
selezióne *f* selection; choice
sèlla *f* saddle
sel·làio *m* (-**lài**) saddler
sellare (**sèllo**) *tr* to saddle
sellerìa *f* saddler's shop; saddlery; (**aut**) upholstery
sélva *f* woods, forest
selvaggina *f* game
selvàg·gio -gia (-**gi** -**ge**) *adj* savage; vicious (*horse*) || *m* savage; unsociable person
selvàti·co -ca *adj* (-**ci** -**che**) wild
selvicoltura *f* forestry
sèlz *m* (**sèlz**) seltzer, club soda
semàforo *m* traffic light; semaphore
semànti·co -ca (-**ci** -**che**) *adj* semantic || *f* semantics
sembiante *m* (lit) look; **fare sembianti di** to pretend
sembianza *f* look; (lit) similarity
sembrare (**sémbro**) *intr* (ESSERE) to seem, look, appear || *impers*—**sembra** it seems
séme *m* seed; stone (*of fruit*); (cards) suit
seménta *f* sowing season; (lit) seed
seménte *f* seed
semènza *f* seed; brads (*used in upholstery*)
semenzà·io *m* (-**zài**) hotbed, seedbed
semestrale *adj* semiannual, semiyearly
semèstre *m* semester; half year
sèmi- *pref adj* semi-, e.g., **semicircolare** semicircular; half-, e.g., **semichiuso** half-closed || *pref mf* semi-, e.g., **semicerchio** semicircle; half, e.g., **semitono** half tone; demi-, e.g., **semidio** demigod
semiapèr·to -ta *adj* half-open; ajar
semiasse *m* (mach) axle (*on each side of differential*)
semicér·chio *m* (-**chi**) semicircle
semichiu·so -sa [s] *adj* half-closed
semicingola·to -ta *adj & m* half-track
semicircolo *m* semicircle
semiconduttóre *m* semiconductor
semiconvit·tóre -trice *mf* day student
semicù·pio *m* (-**pi**) sitz bath
semi·dìo *m* (-**dèi**) demigod
semidòt·to -ta *adj* semilearned
semifinale *f* semifinal
sémina *f* sowing; sowing season
seminare (**sémino**) *tr* to sow, seed; to plant; (coll) to leave behind
seminà·rio *m* (-**ri**) seminary; seminar
seminari·sta *m* (-**sti**) seminarian
semina·to -ta *adj* sown, seeded || *m* sown land; **uscire dal seminato** to digress
semina·tóre -trice *mf* sower || *f* (mach) seeder, seeding machine
seminterrato *m* basement
seminu·do -da *adj* half-naked
semioscurità *f* partial darkness
semirìgi·do -da *adj* semirigid; inelastic
semirimòr·chio *m* (-**chi**) semitrailer
semisè·rio -ria [s] *adj* (-**ri** -**rie**) seriocomic
semisfèra *f* (geom) hemisphere
semì·ta (-**ti** -**te**) *adj* Semitic || *mf* Semite
semitòno *m* (mus) semitone, half tone
semmài *conj* if ever; in the event that
sémola *f* bran; (coll) freckles
semolino *m* semolina
semovènte *adj* self-propelled

sempitèr•no -na *adj* (lit) everlasting
sémplice *adj* simple; single; plain; mere; (mil) private; (nav) ordinary || *m* medicinal herb; **semplici** simple folk
semplició•ne -na *adj* simple || *mf* simpleton
semplici•tà *f* (-tà) simplicity
semplificare §197 (**semplìfico**) *tr* to simplify || *ref* to become easier or simpler
sèmpre *adv* always; ever; yet; **da sempre** from time immemorial; **di sempre** same, same old; **e poi sempre** ever and ever; **ma sempre** but only; **per sempre** forever; **sempre che** provided; **sempre meglio** better and better; **sempre meno** less and less; **sempre però** but only; **sempre vostro** very truly yours
sempreverde *adj, m & f* evergreen
sènape *f* mustard
senapismo *m* mustard plaster
senato *m* senate
sena•tóre -trice *mf* senator
senése [s] *adj & mf* Sienese
senile *adj* old; of old age
senilismo *m* (pathol) senility
senilità *f* old age
senióre *adj & m* elder, senior
Sènna *f* Seine
sénno *m* wisdom; **far senno** to come back to one's senses; **senno di poi** hindsight; **uscir di senno** to go out of one's mind
séno *m* chest; breast, bosom; cove; (anat) sinus; (math) sine; (fig) heart; **in seno a** within
senonché or **se non che** *conj* but
sensale *m* broker; commission merchant
sensa•to -ta *adj* sensible, reasonable; sane
sensazionale *adj* sensational
sensazióne *f* sensation
sensìbile *adj* sensible; perceptible; appreciable; sensitive; responsive (*e.g., to affection*) || *m* world of the senses
sensibili•tà *f* (-tà) sensitivity; sensibility
sensibilizzare [ddzz] *tr* to sensitize
sensiti•vo -va *adj* sensitive || *m* medium
sènso *m* sense; feeling; meaning; aspect; tone, fashion; direction; **ai sensi di legge** according to law; **a senso** free (*translation*); **doppio senso** double entendre; **in senso contrario** in the opposite direction; **perdere i sensi** to lose consciousness; **riprendere i sensi** to come to; **sensi** carnal appetite, flesh; **senso unico** one-way; **senso vietato** no entry, one-way
sensò•rio -ria *adj* (**-ri -rie**) sensory
sensuale *adj* sensual, carnal; sensuous
sensualità *f* sensuality
sentènza *f* sentence; maxim
sentenziare §287 (**sentènzio**) *tr* to pass sentence upon, sentence || *intr* to pontificate
sentenzió•so -sa [s] *adj* sententious
sentièro *m* path, pathway
sentimentale *adj* sentimental; mawkish
sentimentalismo *m* sentimentalism
sentiménto *m* feeling; sentiment; sense; **uscire di sentimento** (coll) to go out of one's mind
sentina *f* bilge; sink (*of vice*)
sentinèlla *f* sentry, sentinel
sentire *m* feeling || *v* (**sènto**) *tr* to feel; to hear; to listen to; to consult (*a doctor*); to smell; to taste **farsi sentire** to make oneself heard || *intr* to feel; to listen; to smell; to taste; **non sentirci di quell'orecchio** to turn a deaf ear; **sentirci bene** to have keen hearing || *ref* to feel; **non sentirsela di** to not have the courage to; **sentirsela** to feel up to it
senti•to -ta *adj* heartfelt
sentóre *m* inkling, feeling; sign; (lit) smell
sènza *prep* without; beyond (*e.g., comparison*); **senza** + *inf* without + *ger;* **senza che** + *subj* without + *ger;* **senza di** + *pron* without + *pron,* e.g., **senza di lui** without him; **senz'altro** without any doubt, of course
senza•dìo *m* (**-dìo**)—**i senzadio** the godless
senzapà•tria *m* (**-tria**) man without a country; renegade
senzatét•to *m* (**-to**) homeless person; **i senzatetto** the homeless
separare *tr & ref* to separate
separazióne *f* separation
sepolcrale *adj* sepulchral
sepolcréto *m* cemetery
sepólcro *m* sepulcher, grave
sepoltura *f* burial; grave
seppellire §253 *tr* to bury
séppia *adj invar* sepia || *f* cuttlefish
seppure *conj* even if
sè•psi *f* (**-psi**) sepsis
sequèla *f* series
sequènza *f* sequence
sequestrare (**sequèstro**) *tr* to seize, confiscate; to kidnap; to confine; to quarantine; (law) to attach, sequester
sequèstro *m* seizure; attachment; **sequestro di persona** unlawful detention
séra *f* evening; night; **da mezza sera** cocktail (*dress*); dark (*suit*); **da sera** evening (*gown*); formal (*attire*)
serac•co *m* (**-chi**) serac
serafino *m* seraph
serale *adj* evening; night
seralménte *adv* in the evening; every evening
serata *f* evening; soiree, evening party; **serata d'addio** (theat) farewell performance; **di beneficenza** benefit performance
serbare (**sèrbo**) *tr* to keep; to save (*e.g., a place*); to bear (*a grudge*) || *ref* to keep oneself; to stay
serba•tóio *m* (**-tói**) tank; reservoir; cartridge clip
sèr•bo -ba *adj & mf* Serbian || *m*—**in serbo** in store
serbocroa•to -ta *adj & mf* Serbo-Croatian
serenata *f* serenade
serenìssi•mo -ma *adj* Serene (*Highness*)
sereni•tà *f* (**-tà**) serenity

seré·no -na *adj* serene; clear, fair (*weather*)
sergènte *m* sergeant; carpenter's clamp; **sergente maggiore** first sergeant
sèri·co -ca *adj* (**-ci -che**) silk
sè·rie *f* (**-rie**) series; (sports) division; **fuori serie** (aut) custom-built; **in serie** (aut) standard; (elec) in series
serietà *f* seriousness; gravity
serigrafia *f* silkscreen process
sè·rio -ria (**-ri -rie**) *adj* serious; stern; **poco serio** unreliable (*man*); loose (*woman*) || *m* seriousness; **sul serio** in earnest; really, e.g., **bello sul serio** really beautiful
sermonare (**sermóno**) *tr* & *intr* (lit) to sermonize
sermóne *m* sermon
sermoneggiare §290 (**sermonéggio**) *intr* to preach; to lecture
seròti·no -na *adj* late; (lit) evening
sèrpa *f* coach box
sèrpe *f* snake, serpent; **a serpe** coiled, in a coil; **nutrirsi** or **scaldarsi la serpe in seno** to nourish a viper in one's bosom
serpeggiare §290 (**serpéggio**) *intr* to zigzag; to wind; to creep, spread
serpènte *m* snake, serpent; **serpente a sonagli** rattlesnake
serpenti·no -na *adj* serpentine || *m* serpentine; coil (*of pipe*) || *f* zigzag, turn (*of winding road*); coil (*of pipe*)
sérqua *f* dozen; lot, large number
sèrra *f* dike, levee; hothouse; sierra; **un serra serra** a milling crowd
serrafi·la *m* (**-le**) rear-guard soldier || *f* rear ship (*of convoy*)
serrafilo *m* electrician's pliers; (elec) binding post
serrà·glio *m* (**-gli**) menagerie; seraglio
serramànico *m*—**a serramanico** clasp (*knife*); switchblade (*knife*)
serrame *m* lock
serraménto *m* closing, bolting || **serramén·ti** & **-ta** *fpl* closing devices, doors, windows, and shutters
serranda *f* shutter (*of store*)
serrare (**sèrro**) *tr* to shut, close; to pursue (*the enemy*); to increase (*tempo*); to furl (*sails*); to lock; to clench (*one's teeth, one's fists*); to shake (*hands*) || *intr* to shut; to be tight || *ref* to be wrenched, e.g., **gli si serrò il cuore** his heart was wrenched; **serrarsi addosso a** to press (*the enemy*)
serrata *f* lockout
serrate *m*—**serrate finale** (sports) finish
serra·to -ta *adj* shut (*e.g., door*); concise (*style*); tight (*game*); rapid (*gallop*); closed (*ranks*); thick (*crowd*) || *f* see **serrata**
serratura *f* lock
sèrto *m* (poet) crown, wreath
sèrva *f* (pej) maidservant, maid
servènte *adj* (*gentleman*) in waiting || *m* gunner; (obs) servant
servìbile *adj* usable
serviènte *m* (eccl) server
servì·gio *m* (**-gi**) service; favor
servile *adj* servile; menial; modal (*auxiliary*)
servire (**sèrvo**) *tr* to serve; to wait on; **in che posso servirLa?** what can I do for you?; may I help you?; **per servirLa** at your service || *intr* to serve || *intr* (ESSERE & AVERE) to serve; to answer the purpose; to last; (with *dat*) (coll) to need, e.g., **gli serve il martello** he needs the hammer; **non servire a nulla** to be of no use; **servire da** to act as || *ref* to help oneself; **servirsi da** to patronize, deal with; **servirsi di** to avail oneself of, use
servitóre *m* servant; tea wagon; **servitor suo umilissimo** your humble servant
servi·tù *f* (**-tù**) servitude; captivity; servants, help; **servitù di passaggio** (law) easement
serviziévole *adj* obliging, accommodating
servì·zio *m* (**-zi**) service; favor; turn; **a mezzo servizio** part-time (*domestic help*); **di servizio** delivery (*entrance*); for hire (*car*); domestic (*help*); **fuori servizio** out of commission; **in servizio** in commission; **servizi** kitchen and bath; facilities; **servizi pubblici** public services; public works; **servizio attivo** active duty; **servizio permanente effettivo** service in the regular army
sèr·vo -va *adj* (lit) enslaved || *m* slave; servant; **servo della gleba** serf || *f* see **serva**
servoassisti·to -ta *adj* servocontrolled
servofréno *m* (aut) power brake
servomotóre *m* servomotor
servostèrzo *m* (aut) power steering
sèsamo *m* sesame; **apriti sesamo!** open sesame!
sessanta *adj*, *m* & *pron* sixty
sessantènne *adj* sixty-year-old || *mf* sixty-year-old person
sessantèsi·mo -ma *adj*, *m* & *pron* sixtieth
sessantina *f* about sixty
sessióne *f* session
sèsso *m* sex; **il sesso debole** the fair sex
sessuale *adj* sexual
sestante *m* sextant
sestétto *m* sextet
sestière *m* district, section
sè·sto -sta *adj* & *pron* sixth || *m* sixth; curve (*of an arch*); **fuori sesto** out of sorts; **mettere in sesto** to arrange; to set in order; **sesto acuto** (archit) ogive
sèt *m* (**sèt**) set; **set all'aperto** (mov) location
séta *f* silk; **seta artificiale** rayon
setacciare §128 *tr* to sift, sieve
setàc·cio *m* (**-ci**) sieve
setàce·o -a *adj* silky
séte *f* thirst; **aver sete** to be thirsty; to lust after; **sete di** thirst for
seteria *f* silk mill; **seterie** silk goods
setifi·cio *m* (**-ci**) silk mill
sétola *f* bristle; (joc) stubble
sètta *f* sect
settanta *adj*, *m* & *pron* seventy
settantènne *adj* seventy-year-old || *mf* seventy-year-old person
settantèsi·mo -ma *adj*, *m* & *pron* seventieth

settantina *f* about seventy
settà·rio -ria *adj & mf* (**-ri -rie**) sectarian
sètte *adj & pron* seven; **le sette** seven o'clock || *m* seven; seventh (*in dates*); V-shaped tear (*in clothing*)
settecentèsi·mo -ma *adj, m & pron* seven hundredth
settecènto *adj, m & pron* seven hundred || **il Settecento** the eighteenth century
settèmbre *m* September
settennale *adj* seven-year (*e.g., plan*)
settènne *adj* seven-year-old || *mf* seven-year-old child
settentrionale *adj* northern || *mf* northerner
settentrióne *m* north; (astr) Little Bear
setticemìa *f* septicemia
sètti·co -ca *adj* (**-ci -che**) septic
settimana *f* week; week's wages; **settimana corta** five-day week
settimanale *adj & m* weekly
settimi·no -na *adj* premature (*baby*) || *m* (mus) septet
sètti·mo -ma *adj, m & pron* seventh
sètto *m* septum
settóre *m* sector; section, branch; dissector, anatomist; coroner's pathologist
sevè·ro -ra *adj* severe, stern
seviziare §287 *tr* to torture
sevìzie *fpl* cruelty
sezionale *adj* sectional
sezionare (**sezióno**) *tr* to cut up; to divide up; to dissect
sezióne *f* section; dissection; chapter (*of club*); department (*of agency*); (geom) cross section
sfaccenda·to -ta *adj* loafing || *mf* loafer
sfaccettare (**sfaccétto**) *tr* to facet
sfacchinare *intr* (coll) to toil, drudge
sfacchinata *f* (coll) drudgery, grind
sfacciatàggine *f* brazenness, impudence
sfaccia·to -ta *adj* brazen, impudent; loud, gaudy; **fare lo sfacciato** to be fresh
sfacèlo *m* breakdown, collapse
sfà·glio *m* (**-gli**) swerve (*e.g., of horse*); (cards) discard
sfaldare *tr* to exfoliate; to cut into slices || *ref* to flake, scale; (fig) to collapse, crumble
sfamare *tr* to feed (*the hungry; the family*) || *ref* to get enough to eat
sfare §173 *tr* to undo || *ref* to spoil (*said, e.g., of meat*)
sfarzo *m* pomp, display; luxury
sfarzó·so -sa [s] *adj* sumptuous, luxurious
sfasare *tr* to throw out of phase; (coll) to depress || *intr* (ESSERE) (aut) to misfire; (elec) to be out of phase
sfasciare §128 *tr* to remove the bandage from; to unswathe; to smash, shatter || *ref* to go to pieces; to lose one's figure
sfatare *tr* to discredit; to unmask
sfatica·to -ta *adj* lazy || *mf* loafer
sfat·to -ta *adj* overdone; overripe; undone (*bed*); ravaged (*by age*)
sfavillare *intr* to spark, sparkle
sfavóre *m* disfavor
sfavorévole *adj* unfavorable
sfebbra·to -ta *adj* free of fever
sfegata·to -ta *adj* (coll) rabid, fanatical
sfèra *f* sphere; (coll) hand (*of clock*); **a sfera** ball-point (*pen*); **a sfere** ball (*bearing*); **sfera di cuoio** (sports) pigskin
sfèri·co -ca *adj* (**-ci -che**) spherical
sferrare (**sfèrro**) *tr* to unshoe (*a horse*); to unchain; to draw (*a weapon from a wound*); to deliver (*a blow*) || *ref* to hurl oneself
sfèrza *f* whip, scourge
sferzare (**sfèrzo**) *tr* to whip, scourge
sfiancare §197 *tr* to break open; to tire out; to fit (*clothes*) too tight || *ref* to burst open; to get worn out
sfiatare *intr* to leak (*said, e.g., of a tire*) || *intr* (ESSERE) to leak (*said of air or gas*) || *ref* to waste one's breath
sfiata·tóio *m* (**-tói**) vent
sfibbiare §287 *tr* to unbuckle, unfasten; to untie (*a knot*)
sfibrante *adj* exhausting
sfibrare *tr* to grind (*wood*) into fibers; to shred (*rags*) into fibers; to weaken, wear out
sfida *f* challenge
sfidare *tr* to challenge, dare; to brave, defy; to endure (*the challenge of time*); **sfidare che** to bet that
sfidù·cia *f* (**-cie**) mistrust; (pol) no confidence
sfiducia·to -ta *adj* downcast, depressed
sfigurare *tr* to disfigure || *intr* to make a bad impression; to lose face
sfilacciare §128 *tr & ref* to ravel, fray
sfilare *tr* to unstring; to take off (*one's shoes*); to count (*beads*); to unthread; to dull (*a blade*); to ravel || *intr* (ESSERE) to march, parade; to follow one another || *ref* to become unthreaded; to become frayed; to run (*said of knitted work*); to break one's back
sfilata *f* parade; row; **sfilata di moda** fashion show
sfilza *f* row, sequence
sfinge *f* sphinx
sfiniménto *m* exhaustion
sfinire §176 *tr* to exhaust, wear out || *ref* to be worn out
sfintère *m* sphincter
sfiorare (**sfióro**) *tr* to graze; to barely touch (*a subject*); to skim; (lit) to barely reach
sfioratóre *m* spillway
sfiorire §176 *intr* (ESSERE) to wither, fade
sfit·to -ta *adj* not rented
sfocare §197 (**sfòco**) *tr* to put out of focus; to blur
sfociare §128 (**sfócio**) *tr* to dredge (*the mouth of a river*) || *intr* (ESSERE) to flow; **sfociare in** (fig) to lead to
sfoderare (**sfòdero**) *tr* to unsheathe; to show off, sport, display; to take the cover or lining off || *intr* to be drawn out
sfogare §209 (**sfógo**) *tr* to vent, give vent to || *intr* (ESSERE) to flow; to pour out; **sfogare in** to turn into || *ref*—**sfogarsi a** + *inf* to have one's

fill of + *ger;* **sfogarsi con** to unburden oneself to; **sfogarsi su qlcu** to take it out on s.o.
sfoga•tóio *m* (-tói) vent
sfoggiare §290 (**sfòggio**) *tr* to display, sport; to show off
sfòg•gio *m* (-gi) display, ostentation
sfòglia *f* foil; skin (*of onion*); layer of puff paste; (ichth) sole
sfogliare §280 (**sfòglio**) *tr* to pluck (*a flower*); to defoliate (*a tree*); to leaf through (*a book*); to deal (*cards*); to husk (*corn*); to press (*dough*) into layers || *ref* to shed its leaves; to flake
sfogliata *f* defoliation; puff paste; **dare una sfogliata a** to glance through
sfó•go *m* (-ghi) exhaust; outlet; vent; (coll) eruption (*of skin*)
sfolgorare (**sfólgoro**) *intr* (ESSERE & AVERE) to shine, blaze
sfolgorì•o *m* (-i) glittering, blazing
sfollagèn•te *m* (-te) billy
sfollaménto *m* evacuation; layoff
sfollare (**sfòllo**) *tr* to clear; to cut the staff of || *intr* (ESSERE & AVERE) to disperse, evacuate; to cut down the staff
sfolla•to -ta *adj* driven from home || *mf* evacuee
sfoltire §176 *tr* to thin out
sfondare (**sfóndo**) *tr* to stave in; to break through; to be heavy on (*the stomach*) || *intr* to give || *ref* to break open
sfóndo *m* background
sfondóne *m* (coll) blunder, error
sforbiciare §128 (**sfòrbicio**) *tr* to clip, shear
sforbiciata *f* clipping; (sports) scissors; (sports) scissors kick
sformare (**sfórmo**) *tr* to pull out of shape; to take out of the mold || *intr* to get mad
sforma•to -ta *adj* out of shape || *m* pudding
sfornare (**sfórno**) *tr* to take out of the oven
sfornire §176 *tr* to deprive; to strip
sfortuna *f* bad luck, misfortune
sfortuna•to -ta *adj* unsuccessful; unlucky, unfortunate
sforzare (**sfòrzo**) *tr* to strain; to force || *ref* to strive, endeavor
sforza•to -ta *adj* forced, unnatural
sfòrzo *m* effort; strain; stretch (*of imagination*); **senza sforzo** effortlessly
sfóttere *tr* (vulg) to make fun of
sfracassare *tr* to smash, crash
sfracellare (**sfracèllo**) *tr & ref* to shatter, smash
sfrangiare §290 *tr* to ravel
sfrattare *tr* to evict; to deport || *intr* to be evicted
sfratto *m* eviction; notice of eviction
sfrecciare §128 (**sfréccio**) *intr* (ESSERE & AVERE) to speed by
sfregaménto *m* rubbing
sfregare §209 (**sfrégo**) *tr* to rub; to scrape; to strike (*a match*)
sfregiare §290 (**sfrégio & sfrègio**) *tr* to disfigure, slash
sfregia•to -ta *adj* disfigured, slashed || *m* scarface
sfré•gio or **sfrè•gio** *m* (-gi) slash, scar, gash; insult
sfrenare (**sfréno & sfrèno**) *tr* to take the brake off; to give free rein to || *ref* to kick over the traces
sfriggere §180 *intr* to sizzle
sfrigolì•o *m* (-i) sizzle
sfrondare (**sfróndo**) *tr* to defoliate; to lop off; to trim down || *ref* to lose leaves
sfrontatézza *f* effrontery, impudence
sfronta•to -ta *adj* brazen, impudent
sfrusciare §128 *intr* to rustle
sfruttare *tr* to exploit; to exhaust (*e.g., a mine*); to take advantage of
sfrutta•tóre -trice *mf* exploiter, developer (*e.g., of an invention*)
sfuggènte *adj* fleeting; receding (*forehead*); shifty (*glance*)
sfuggire *tr* to avoid, flee || *intr* (ESSERE) to flee, escape, get away; (with *dat*) to escape, e.g., **nulla gli sfugge** nothing escapes him; to break, e.g., **sfuggì a una promessa** he broke a promise; **lasciarsi sfuggire** to let slip
sfuggita *f*—**di sfuggita** hastily; incidentally; **dare una sfuggita** to run down (*e.g., to the post office*)
sfumare *tr* to shade down; to tone down; to trim (*hair*) || *intr* (ESSERE) to vanish; to shade
sfumatura *f* nuance, shade; razor clipping
sfumino *m* stump (*in drawing*)
sfuriare §287 *tr* to vent (*one's anger*) || *intr* to rave
sfuriata *f* outburst of anger; gust (*of wind*); **fare una sfuriata a** to give a scolding to
sgabèllo *m* stool, footstool
sgabuzzino *m* cubbyhole
sgambettare (**sgambétto**) *tr* to trip || *intr* to toddle; to kick (*said of a baby*); to scamper
sgambétto *m* trip, stumble; **dare lo sgambetto a** to trip
sganasciare §128 *tr* to dislocate the jaw of; to break the jaw of; to tear apart || *intr* to steal right and left || *ref* to break one's jaw; **sganasciarsi dalle risa** to split one's sides laughing
sganciare §128 *tr* to unhook; to lay out *money*); to drop (*bombs*) || *intr* to drop bombs; (coll) to go away || *ref* to get unhooked; (mil) to disengage oneself; **sganciarsi da** to get rid of
sgangherare (**sgànghero**) *tr* to unhinge; to burst || *ref*—**sgangherarsi dalle risa** to split one's sides laughing
spanghera•to -ta *adj* unhinged; broken down; rickety; coarse (*laughter*)
sgarbatéz•za *f* rudeness, incivility; clumsiness
sgarba•to -ta *adj* rude; clumsy
sgarberìa *f* var of **sgarbatezza**
sgarbo *m*—**fare uno sgarbo a** to be rude to
sgargiante *adj* loud, flashy, showy
sgarrare *intr* to go wrong
sgattaiolare (**sgattàiolo**) *intr* (ESSERE) to slip away; to wriggle out

sgelare (sgèlo) *tr & intr* to thaw, melt
sgèlo *m* thaw
sghém•bo -ba *adj* crooked; **a sghembo** askew || **sghembo** *adv* askew; sideways
sghèrro *m* hired assassin; gendarme
sghiacciare §128 *tr* to thaw
sghignazzare *intr* to guffaw
sghignazzata *f* guffaw
sghimbè•scio -scia *adj*—**a** or **di sghimbescio** askew, crooked
sghiribizzo [ddzz] *m* whim, fancy
sgobbare (sgòbbo) *intr* to drudge, plod, plug
sgobbó•ne -na *mf* plugger, plodder, drudge
sgocciolare (sgócciolo) *tr* to let drip || *intr* to drip (*said of container*) || *intr* (ESSERE) to drip (*said of liquid*)
sgocciola•tóio *m* **(-tói)** dish rack; drip pan
sgocciolatura *f* dripping; drippings
sgócciolo *m* last drop; **essere agli sgoccioli** to be coming to an end
sgolare (sgólo) *ref* to shout oneself hoarse
sgomberare (sgómbero) *tr & intr* var of **sgombrare**
sgómbero *m* moving
sgombrané•ve *m* **(-ve)** snowplow (*truck*)
sgombrare (sgómbro) *tr* to clear; to vacate || *intr* to move, vacate
sgóm•bro -bra *adj* clear || *m* moving; (ichth) mackerel
sgomentare (sgoménto) *tr* to frighten; to dismay
sgomén•to -ta *adj* dismayed || *m* dismay; **rimanere di sgomento** to be dismayed
sgominare (sgòmino) *tr* to rout
sgomma•to -ta *adj* unglued; without tires; with poor tires
sgonfiare §287 **(sgónfio)** *tr* to deflate; to damn with faint praise (*e.g., a play*); (coll) to bore || *intr* (ESSERE) to boast; to balloon || *ref* to go down (*said of swelling*); to go flat (*said of a tire*); (fig) to collapse
sgón•fio -fia *adj* deflated, flat
sgonfiòtto *m* jelly doughnut; puff (*in clothing*)
sgórbia *f* (carp) gouge
sgorbiare §287 **(sgòrbio)** *tr* to scribble; (carp) to gouge
sgòr•bio *m* **(-bi)** ink spot; scribble, scrawl
sgorgare §209 **(sgórgo)** *tr* to unclog || *intr* (ESSERE) to gush
sgottare (sgótto) *tr* to bail out (*a boat*)
sgozzare (sgózzo) *tr* to slaughter; to slit the throat of; (fig) to bleed, fleece
sgradévole *adj* disagreeable, unpleasant
sgradire §176 *tr* to refuse || *intr* to be displeasing
sgradi•to -ta *adj* unpleasant; unwelcome
sgraffignare *tr* to snitch, snatch
sgrammatica•to -ta *adj* ungrammatical
sgranare *tr* to shell (*e.g., peas*); to count (*one's beads*); to seed (*grapes*); to open (*one's eyes*) wide; (mach) to disengage || *ref* to crumble; to scratch oneself
sgranchire §176 *tr* to stretch (*e.g., one's legs*)
sgranocchiare §287 **(sgranòcchio)** *tr* to crunch, munch
sgrassare *tr* to remove the grease from; to skim (*broth*); to scour (*wool*)
sgravare *tr* to relieve, lighten || *ref* to be relieved; to give birth
sgrà•vio *m* **(-vi)** lightening, lessening; **a sgravio di coscienza** to ease one's conscience
sgrazia•to -ta *adj* gawky, clumsy
sgretolare (sgrétolo) *tr & ref* to crumble
sgretola•to -ta *adj* crumbling, falling down
sgridare *tr* to scold, chide
sgridata *f* scolding, reprimand
sgrondare (sgróndo) *tr* to cause to drip || *intr* to drip, trickle
sgroppare (sgròppo) *tr* to wear (*a horse*) out || *intr* to buck (*said of a horse*)
sgroppare (sgróppo) *tr* to untie
sgrossare (sgròsso) *tr* to rough-hew; (fig) to refine
sgrovigliare §280 *tr* to untangle
sguaiatàggine *f* uncouthness
sguaia•to -ta *adj* crude, vulgar; uncouth || *mf* vulgar person; uncouth person
sguainare *tr* to unsheathe; to show (*one's nails*)
sgualcire §176 *tr* to crumple || *ref* to become crumpled
sgualdrina *f* trollop, strumpet
sguardo *m* glance, look; eyes
sguarnire §176 *tr* to untrim; (mil) to strip, dismantle
sguàtte•ro -ra *mf* dishwasher, scullion || *f* kitchenmaid, scullery maid
sguazzare *tr* to waste, squander || *intr* to splash; to wallow; to be lost (*in shoes too big or clothes too loose*)
sguinzagliare §280 *tr* to unleash, let loose
sgusciare §128 *tr* to shell, hull || *intr* (ESSERE) to slip; **sgusciare di soppiatto** to slip away
shòp•ping *m* **(-ping)** shopping; shopping bag; **fare lo shopping** to go shopping
shràpnel *m* **(shràpnel)** shrapnel
si *m* **(-si)** (mus) si || §5 *pron*
sì *m* **(sì)** yes; yea; **stare tra il sì e il no** to not be able to make up one's mind; **un . . . sì e l'altro no** every other (*e.g., day*)
sìa *conj* see **essere**
siamése [s] *adj & mf* Siamese
siberia•no -na *adj & mf* Siberian
sibilante *adj & f* sibilant
sibilare (sìbilo) *intr* to hiss
sibilla *f* sibyl
sìbilo *m* hiss, hissing
sicà•rio *m* **(-ri)** hired assassin
sicché *conj* so that
siccità *f* drought
siccóme *adv* as || *conj* since; as; how
Sicìlia, la Sicily
sicilia•no -na *adj & mf* Sicilian
sicomòro *m* sycamore
sicumèra *f* cocksureness, overconfidence
sicura *f* safety lock (*on gun*)

sicurézza *f* security; assurance; safety; certainty; reliability; **di sicurezza** safety; **sicurezza sociale** social security
sicu•ro -ra *adj* sure; safe; steady; **di sicuro** certainly || *m* safety; **camminare sul sicuro** to take no chances || **sicuro** *adv* certainly || *f* see **sicura**
sicur•tà *f* (**-tà**) insurance
siderale *adj* sidereal
sidère•o -a *adj* sidereal
siderùrgi•co -ca (**-ci -che**) *adj* iron-and-steel || *m* iron-and-steel worker
sidro *m* cider, hard cider
sièpe *f* hedge; (fig) wall
sièro *m* serum
sièsta *f* siesta; **fare la siesta** to take a nap, take a siesta
siffat•to -ta *adj* such
sifilide *f* syphilis
sifóne *m* siphon; siphon bottle; trap
siga•ràio -ràia (**-rài -ràie**) *mf* cigar maker || *m* (ent) grape hopper; || *f* cigarette girl
sigarétta *f* cigarette
sìgaro *m* cigar
sigillare *tr* to seal
sigillo *m* seal; **avere il sigillo alle labbra** to have one's lips sealed; **sigillo sacramentale** seal of confession
sigla *f* acronym; initials; abbreviation; letterword; **sigla musicale** theme song
siglare *tr* to initial
significare §197 (**signìfico**) *tr* to mean; to signify; **significare qlco a qlcu** to inform s.o. of s.th
significati•vo -va *adj* significant; meaningful
significato *m* meaning; **senza significato** meaningless
signóra *f* Madam, Mrs.; lady; mistress, owner; wife || **Nostra Signora** Our Lady
signóre *m* sir, Mr.; gentleman; rich man; lord, master, owner; man; **il signore desidera?** what is your pleasure?; **per signori** stag || **Signore** *m* Lord
signoreggiare §290 (**signoréggio**) *tr* to rule over; to master; to tower over; to overshadow || *intr* to be the master
signorìa *f* seigniory; rule; **La Signoria Vostra** your Honor; **Sua Signoria** his Lordship; your Lordship
signorile *adj* seigniorial; gentlemanly; ladylike; elegant, refined
signorina *f* miss; Miss; young lady; spinster
signorino *m* master, young gentleman
signornò *adv* no, Sir
signoró•ne -na *mf* (coll) rich person
signoròtto *m* lordling
signorsì *adv* yes, Sir
silenziatóre *m* silencer (*of firearm*); (aut) muffler
silèn•zio *m* (**-zi**) silence; (mil) taps; **fare silenzio** to be silent; **ridurre al silenzio** (mil) to silence
silenzió•so -sa [s] *adj* silent; noiseless
silfide *f* sylphid
silfo *m* sylph
silhouèt•te *f* (**-te**) silhouette
sìlice *f* silica
silìcio *m* silicon
silicóne *m* silicone
siliquastro *m* redbud
sìllaba *f* syllable
sillabare (**sìllabo**) *tr* to syllabify; to spell
sillabà•rio *m* (**-ri**) reader, primer
sìllabo *m* syllabus
silo *m* silo
silòfono *m* xylophone
siluétta *f* silhouette
silurante *adj* torpedoing, torpedo || *f* destroyer; torpedo boat
silurare *tr* to torpedo; (fig) to fire, dismiss; (fig) to undermine
siluro *m* torpedo
silva•no -na *adj* sylvan
silvèstre *adj* (lit) sylvan; (lit) wild; (lit) hard, arduous
simboleggiare §290 (**simboléggio**) *tr* to symbolize
simbòli•co -ca *adj* (**-ci -che**) symbolic
simbolismo *m* symbolism
sìmbolo *m* symbol
similari•tà *f* (**-tà**) similarity
sìmile *adj* similar; such || *m* like; **i propri simili** fellow men
similòro *m* tombac
simmetrìa *f* symmetry
simmètri•co -ca *adj* (**-ci -che**) symmetrical
simonìa *f* simony
simpamina *f* benzedrine
simpatèti•co -ca *adj* (**-ci -che**) sympathetic
simpatìa *f* like, liking; **cattivarsi la simpatia di** to make oneself well liked by
simpàti•co -ca (**-ci -che**) *adj* nice, pleasant, congenial || *m* (anat) sympathetic system
simpatizzante [ddzz] *adj* sympathizing || *mf* sympathizer
simpatizzare [ddzz] *intr* to sympathize; to become friends
simpò•sio *m* (**-si**) symposium
simulare (**sìmulo**) *tr* to simulate
simula•tóre -trice *mf* faker, impostor || *m* simulator
simultàne•o -a *adj* simultaneous
sin- *pref adj* syn-, e.g., **sinonimo** synonymous || *pref m & f* syn-, e.g., **sinonimo** synonym
sin *adv*—**sin da** ever since
sinagò•ga *f* (**-ghe**) synagogue
sincerare (**sincèro**) *tr* (lit) to convince || *ref*—**sincerarsi di** to ascertain
sincè•ro -ra *adj* sincere; pure
sinché *conj* until
sìncope *f* fainting spell; (phonet) syncope; (mus) syncopation
sincronismo *m* syncronism; **sincronismo orrizzontale** (telv) horizontal hold; **sincronismo verticale** (telv) vertical hold
sincronizzare [ddzz] *tr* to syncronize
sìncro•no -na *adj* syncronous
sindacale *adj* mayoral; union
sindacalismo *m* trade unionism
sindacali•sta *mf* (**-sti -ste**) union member; union leader

sindacare §197 (**sìndaco**) *tr* to criticize; to scrutinize
sindaca·to -ta *adj* controlled, scrutinized || *m* control; labor union; syndicate; **sindacato giallo** company union
sìnda·co *m* (**-ci**) mayor; controller; auditor
sinecura *f* sinecure
sinfonìa *f* symphony; (*of an opera*) overture; (coll) racket (*noise*)
sinfòni·co -ca *adj* (**-ci -che**) symphonic
singhiozzare (**singhiózzo**) *intr* to sob; to hiccup; to jerk
singhiózzo *m* sob; hiccups; **a singhiozzo** in jerks; by fits and spurts
singolare *adj* singular || *m* singular; (tennis) singles
sìngo·lo -la *adj* single || *m* individual; shell for one oarsman; (rr) roomette; (telp) private line; (tennis) singles
singulto *m* hiccups; sob
sinistra *f* left hand; left
sinistrare *tr* to ruin; to damage
sinistra·to -ta *adj* injured, damaged, ruined || *mf* victim (*of bombing or flood*)
sinistrismo *m* leftism
sinistri·sta *adj* (**-sti -ste**) leftish, leftist
sini·stro -stra *adj* left; sinister || *m* accident; (boxing) left || *f* see **sinistra**
sinistròide *adj & mf* leftist
sino *adv* var of **fino**
sinologìa *f* Sinology
sinòni·mo -ma *adj* synonymous || *m* synonym
sinò·psi *f* (**-psi**) (mov) synopsis
sinóra *adv* var of **finora**
sinòs·si *f* (**-si**) synopsis
sinòtti·co -ca *adj* (**-ci -che**) synoptic(al)
sintas·si *f* (**-si**) syntax
sìnte·si *f* (**-si**) synthesis
sintèti·co -ca *adj* (**-ci -che**) synthetic(al); concise
sintetizzare [ddzz] *tr* to synthesize
sintogram·ma *m* (**-mi**) (rad) dial
sìntomo *m* symptom
sintonìa *f* harmony; (rad) tuning
sintonizzare [ddzz] *tr* (rad) to tune
sintonizzatóre [ddzz] *m* (rad) tuner
sinuó·so -sa [s] *adj* sinuous, winding
sionismo *m* Zionism
sipà·rio *m* (**-ri**) curtain; **sipario di ferro** iron curtain
sirèna *f* siren; mermaid; **sirena da nebbia** foghorn
Sìria, la Syria
siria·no -na *adj & mf* Syrian
sirin·ga *f* (**-ghe**) panpipe; syringe; catheter; grease gun; (orn) syrinx
siringare §209 *tr* to catheterize
siròcchia *f* (obs) sister
si·sma *m* (**-smi**) earthquake
sismògrafo *m* seismograph
sismologìa *f* seismology
sissignóre *adv* yes, Sir!
sistè·ma *m* (**-mi**) system
sistemare (**sistèmo**) *tr* to arrange; to put in order; to systematize; to settle; to find a job for; to find a husband for; (coll) to fix || *ref* to settle; to get married
sistemazióne *f* arrangement; settlement; job, position
sìstole *f* systole
sitibón·do -da *adj* (lit) thirsty
si·to -ta *adj* (lit) located || *m* (lit) site, spot, location; (mil) sight; (coll) musty odor
situare (**sìtuo**) *tr* to locate, place, situate
situazióne *f* situation; condition
slabbrare *tr* to chip; to open (*a wound*) || *intr* to overflow || *ref* to become chipped; to reopen (*said of a cut*)
slacciare §128 *tr* to untie; to unfasten; to unbutton || *ref* to get undone; to get unbuttoned
sladinare *tr* (sports) to train; (mach) to run in, break in
slanciare §128 *tr* to hurl, throw || *ref* to hurl oneself; to rise (*said, e.g., of a tower*)
slancia·to -ta *adj* slender; soaring
slàn·cio *m* (**-ci**) leap; outburst (*of feeling*); momentum; **di slancio** with a rush; **prendere lo slancio** to get a running start
slargare §209 *tr* to widen; to warm (*the heart*) || *ref* to widen, spread out
slattare *tr* to wean
slava·to -ta *adj* pale, washed out
sla·vo -va *adj* Slav, Slavic || *mf* Slav || *m* Slavic (*language*)
sleale *adj* disloyal; unfair (*competition*)
sleal·tà *f* (**-tà**) disloyalty
slegare §209 (**slégo**) *tr* to untie
slega·to -ta *adj* untied; disconnected
slip *m* (**slip**) briefs; tank suit, bathing suit (*for men*)
slitta *f* sled, sleigh; (mach) carriage
slittaménto *m* skid; slide
slittare *intr* to sled; to skid; to slide
slogare §209 (**slògo**) *tr* to dislocate || *ref* to become dislocated; to dislocate (*e.g., an arm*)
slogatura *f* dislocation
sloggiare §290 (**slòggio**) *tr* to dislodge; to evict || *intr* to vacate
slòg·gio *m* (**-gi**) moving; eviction
slovac·co -ca *adj & mf* (**-chi -che**) Slovak
smacchiare §287 *tr* to clean; to deforest
smacchia·tóre -trice *mf* cleaner || *m* cleaning fluid; spot remover
smac·co *m* (**-chi**) letdown; slap in the face
smagliante *adj* dazzling, shining
smagliare §280 *tr* to break the links of; to undo the meshes of; to remove (*a fish*) from the net || *intr* to shine, dazzle || *ref* to run (*said, e.g., of knitted fabric*); to free itself from the net
smagliatura *f* run (*in stockings*); (fig) break
smagrire §176 *tr* to impoverish || *intr* (ESSERE) & *ref* to become thin or lean
smaliziare §287 *tr* to make wiser || *ref* to get wiser
smaltare *tr* to enamel; to glaze
smaltire §176 *tr* to digest; to sleep off (*a drunk*); to swallow (*an offense*);

to sell off; to get rid of; to drain off (*water*)
smalti·tóio *m* **(-tói)** drain, sewer
smalto *m* enamel; **smalto per le unghie** nail polish
smancerìe *fpl* affectation; mawkishness
smanceró·so -sa [s] *adj* prissy
smangiare §290 *tr* to erode, eat away || *ref* to be consumed (*e.g., by hatred*)
smània *f* frenzy; craze, yearning; **dare in smanie** to be in a frenzy
smaniare §287 *intr* to be delirious; to yearn, crave
smanió·so -sa [s] *adj* eager; disturbing
smantellare (smantèllo) *tr* to dismantle; to demolish; to disable (*a ship*)
smargias·so -sa *mf* braggart, boaster
smarriménto *m* loss; bewilderment; discouragement
smarrire §176 *tr* to lose || *ref* to get lost; to get discouraged
smascellare (smascèllo) *ref*—**smascellarsi dalle risa** to split one's sides laughing
smascherare (smàschero) *tr* & *ref* to unmask
smazzata *f* (cards) deal; (cards) hand
smembraménto *m* dismemberment
smembrare (smèmbro) *tr* to dismember
smemorataggine *f* forgetfulness
smemora·to -ta *adj* absent-minded; forgetful || *mf* absent-minded or forgetful person
smentire §176 *tr* to belie; to refute; to retract; to be untrue to || *ref* to not be consistent, to contradict oneself
smentita *f* denial; retraction
smeraldo *m* emerald
smerciare §128 **(smèrcio)** *tr* to sell, sell out
smèr·cio *m* **(-ci)** sale
smèr·go *m* **(-ghi)** (zool) merganser
smerigliare §280 *tr* to grind, polish; to sand
smeriglia·to -ta *adj* polished; sand (*paper*); emery (*cloth*); frosted (*glass*)
smeri·glio *m* **(-gli)** emery; (orn) merlin; (ichth) porbeagle
smerlare (smèrlo) *tr* to scallop
smèrlo *m* scallop (*along the edge of a garment*)
smés·so -sa *adj* hand-me-down, castoff
sméttere §198 *tr* to stop; to stop wearing; to break up (*housekeeping*); **smetterla** to cut it out || *intr*—**smettere di** + *inf* to stop + *ger*
smezzare [ddzz] **(smèzzo)** *tr* to halve
smidollare (smidóllo) *tr* to remove the marrow from; (fig) to emasculate
smilitarizzare [ddzz] *tr* to demilitarize
smil·zo -za *adj* slender; poor, worthless
sminare *tr* to remove mines from
sminuire §176 *tr* to belittle
sminuzzare *tr* to crumble; to mince; to expatiate on || *ref* to crumble
smistaménto *m* sorting (*of mail*); (rr) shunting, shifting
smistare *tr* to sort; (rr) to shift; (soccer) to pass; (rad) to unscramble
smisura·to -ta *adj* immense, huge
smitizzante [ddzz] *adj* debunking, demythologizing
smitizzare [ddzz] *tr* to debunk; to demythologize
smobiliare §287 *tr* to remove the furniture from
smobilitare (smobìlito) *tr* to demobilize
smobilitazióne *f* demobilization
smoccolare (smòccolo & smóccolo) *tr* to snuff (*a candle*) || *intr* (slang) to swear, curse
smoda·to -ta *adj* excessive, immoderate
smòg *m* smog
smóking *m* **(smóking)** dinner jacket, tuxedo
smontàbile *adj* dismountable
smontàg·gio *m* **(-gi)** disassembling, dismantling
smontare (smónto) *tr* to take apart; to dismantle; to cause (*e.g., whipped cream*) to fall; to take (*a precious stone*) out of its setting; to dishearten; to dissuade; to drop (*s.o.*) off; **smontare la guardia** to come off guard duty || *intr* (ESSERE) to dismount; to get off or out (*of a conveyance*); to fade; to drop (*said, e.g., of beaten eggs*) || *ref* to become downcast
smòrfia *f* grimace; mawkishness; **fare le smorfie a** to make faces at
smorfió·so -sa [s] *adj* mawkish, prissy
smòr·to -ta *adj* pale, wan; faded
smorzare (smòrzo) *tr* to attenuate; to lessen; to tone down; to turn off (*light*); (phys) to dampen
smorzatóre *m* (mus) damper
smòs·so -sa *adj* moved; loose
smottaménto *m* mud slide
smozzicare §197 **(smózzico)** *tr* to crumble; to mince; to clip, mince (*one's words*)
smun·to -ta *adj* emaciated, pale, wan
smuòvere §202 *tr* to budge; to till; (fig) to move || *ref* to budge; to move away; **smuoviti!** get going!
smussare *tr* to blunt; to bevel; (fig) to soften
snaturalizzare [ddzz] *tr* to denaturalize; to denationalize
snaturare *tr* to change the nature of; to distort, misrepresent
snatura·to -ta *adj* distorted; monstrous, unnatural
snebbiare §287 **(snébbio)** *tr* to drive the fog from; to clear (*e.g., one's mind*)
snellézza *f* slenderness; nimbleness
snellire §176 *tr* & *ref* to slenderize
snèl·lo -la *adj* slender; nimble; lively
snervante *adj* enervating
snervare (snèrvo) *tr* to enervate, prostrate || *ref* to become enervated
snidare *tr* to drive out, flush
snòb *adj invar* snobbish || *mf* **(snòb)** snob
snobbare (snòbbo) *tr* to snub, slight
snobismo *m* snobbishness, snobbery
snobìsti·co -ca *adj* **(-ci -che)** snobbish
snocciolare (snòcciolo) *tr* to spill (*a secret*); to peel off (*sums of money*); to pit, stone (*fruit*)
snodare (snòdo) *tr* to untie; to limber up; to exercise; to loosen up (*e.g.,*

s.o.'s tongue) || *ref* to become loose; to wind (*said, e.g., of a road*)
snòdo *m* (mach) joint; **a snodo** flexible
soave *adj* sweet, gentle
sobbalzare *intr* to jerk, jolt
sobbalzo *m* jerk, jolt; **di sobbalzo** with a jolt
sobbarcare §197 *tr* to overburden || *ref* —**sobbarcarsi a** to take it upon oneself to
sobbór·go *m* (**-ghi**) suburb
sobillare *tr* to instigate, stir up
sobilla·tóre -trice *mf* instigator
sobrietà *f* sobriety, temperance
sò·brio -bria *adj* sober, temperate; plain
socchiùdere §125 *tr* to half-shut; to leave ajar
socchiu·so -sa [s] *adj* ajar
soccómbere §186 *intr* to succumb
soccórrere §139 *tr* to help || *intr* (lit) to occur
soccórso *m* help, succor; **mancato soccorso** failure to render assistance; hit-and-run driving
sociale *adj* social; company (*e.g., outing*)
socialismo *m* socialism
sociali·sta (**-sti -ste**) *adj* socialistic || *mf* socialist
sociali·tà *f* (**-tà**) gregariousness; social responsibility
socie·tà *f* (**-tà**) society; company; **in società** in partnership; **società anonima** corporation; **società a responsabilità limitata** limited company; **Società delle Nazioni** League of Nations; **società finanziaria** holding company; **società in accomandita** limited partnership; **società per azioni** corporation
sociévole *adj* sociable; gregarious
sò·cio *m* (**-ci**) member; cardholder; partner; shareholder; **socio fondatore** charter member; **socio sostenitore** patron, sustaining member
sociologìa *f* sociology
sociòlo·go -ga *mf* (**-gi -ghe**) sociologist
sòda *f* soda
sodalì·zio *m* (**-zi**) society; brotherhood, fraternity; friendship
soddisfacènte *adj* satisfying, satisfactory
soddisfare §173 (*2d sg pres ind* **soddisfài** or **soddisfi;** *3d pl pres* **soddisfanno** or **soddìsfano;** *1st, 2d & 3d sg pres subj* **soddisfaccia** or **soddisfi;** *3d pl pres subj* **soddisfàcciano** or **soddìsfino**) *tr* to satisfy || *intr* (with *dat*) to satisfy || *ref* to be satisfied
soddisfat·to -ta *adj* satisfied
soddisfazióne *f* satisfaction
sòdi·co -ca *adj* (**-ci -che**) sodium
sòdio *m* sodium
sò·do -da *adj* hard; hard-boiled; stubborn; solid; **prenderle sode** to get a good thrashing || *m* hard ground; untilled soil; solid foundation; **venire al sodo** to come to the point; **mettere in sodo** to ascertain || *f* see **soda** || **sodo** *adv* hard
sodomìa *f* sodomy
so·fà *m* (**-fà**) couch, sofa; **sofà a letto** sofa bed
sofferènte *adj* sickly, ailing; (lit) long-suffering
sofferènza *f* suffering, pain; bad debt; **in sofferenza** overdue
soffermare (**soffèrmo**) *tr*—**soffermare il passo** to come to a stop || *ref* to linger, pause
soffiare §287 (**sóffio**) *tr* to blow; to whisper; (checkers) to huff; (coll) to steal || *intr* to blow; to bellow; (slang) to squeal (*about somebody's offense*); **soffiare sul fuoco** to stir up trouble || *ref to* blow (*one's nose*)
soffia·to -ta *adj* blown || *m* soufflé || *f* (slang) squealing, **darsi una soffiata di naso** to blow one's nose
soffiatóre *m* glass blower
sòffice *adj* soft
soffierìa *f* glass factory; blower
soffiétto *m* bellows; hood (*of carriage*); (journ) puff, ballyhoo
sóf·fio *m* (**-fi**) blow; breath; **in un soffio** in a jiffy; **soffio al cuore** heart murmur
soffióne *m* blowpipe; fumarole; (bot) dandelion; (coll) spy
soffitta *f* attic, garret
soffitto *m* ceiling
soffocaménto *m* choking
soffocante *adj* stifling; oppressive
soffocare §197 (**sòffoco**) *tr* to choke; to stifle; to suffocate; to smother; to repress
sòffo·co *m* (**-chi**) sultriness
soffóndere §178 *tr* (lit) to suffuse
soffregare §209 (**soffrégo**) *tr* to rub lightly
soffrìggere §180 *tr* to fry lightly || *intr* to mutter
soffrire §207 *tr* to suffer; to endure; **non poter soffrire** to not be able to stand || *intr* to suffer; to ail; **soffrire di** to be troubled with
soffritto *m* fried onions and bacon
sofistica·to -ta *adj* adulterated; sophisticated, studied
sofisti·co -ca *adj* (**-ci -che**) sophistic; faultfinding || *f* sophistry
soggetti·sta *mf* (**-sti -ste**) scriptwriter
soggetti·vo -va *adj* subjective
soggèt·to -ta *adj* subject || *m* subject; (coll) character; (law) person; **cattivo soggetto** hoodlum; **recitare a soggetto** to improvise
soggezióne *f* subjection; awe, embarrassment; **mettere a soggezione** to awe
sogghignare *intr* to sneer
soggiacére §181 *intr* (ESSERE & AVERE) to be subject; to succumb
soggiogare §209 (**soggiógo**) *tr* to subjugate, subdue
soggiornare (**soggiórno**) *intr* to sojourn, stay
soggiórno *m* sojourn, stay; living room; sitting room (*in hotel*)
soggiùngere §183 *tr* to add
soggólo *m* wimple (*of nun*); throatlatch (*on horse*); (mil) chin strap
sòglia *f* doorsill; threshhold
sògliola *f* sole
sognare (**sógno**) *tr* to dream of || *intr*

to dream; **sognare ad occhi aperti** to daydream
sogna·tóre -trice *adj* dreaming ‖ *mf* dreamer
sógno *m* dream; **nemmeno per sogno** (coll) by no means
sòia *f* (bot) soy
sòl *m* (**sòl**) (mus) sol
so·làio *m* (**-lài**) attic, loft; (agr) crib
solare *adj* solar; bright; clear ‖ *v* §257 *tr* to sole
solàr·rio *m* (**-ri**) solarium
solatì·o -a (**-i -e**) *adj* sunny ‖ *m*—**a solatio** with a southern exposure
solcare §197 (**sólco**) *tr* to furrow; to plow (*the waves*)
sól·co *m* (**-chi**) furrow; rut; groove (*of phonograph record*); (fig) path; (naut) wake
solcòmetro *m* (naut) log
soldaté·sco -sca (**-schi -sche**) *adj* soldier ‖ *f* soldiery; soldiers; undisciplined troops
soldatino *m* toy soldier
soldato *m* soldier; **andare soldato** to enlist; **soldato di ventura** soldier of fortune; **soldato scelto** private first class; **soldato semplice** private
sòldo *m* soldo (*Italian coin*); coin; money; (mil) pay; (fig) penny; **a soldo a soldo** a penny at a time; **al soldo di** in the pay of; **tirare al soldo** to be a tightwad
sóle *m* sun; sunshine; (fig) day, daytime; **sole artificiale** sun lamp; **sole a scacchi** (joc) hoosegow, calaboose
soleggia·to -ta *adj* sunny
solènne *adj* solemn; (joc) first-class
solenni·tà *f* (**-tà**) solemnity
solennizzare [ddzz] *tr* to solemnize
solére §255 *intr* (ESSERE) + *inf* to be accustomed to + *inf*, *e.g.*, **suole arrivare alle sette** he is accustomed to arrive at seven ‖ *impers* (ESSERE) —**suole** + *inf* it generally + *3d sg ind*, e.g., **suole nevicare** it generally snows
solèrte *adj* (lit) diligent, industrious
solèrzia *f* (lit) diligence
solét·to -ta *adj* (lit) alone, lonely ‖ *f* sole; inner sole; (archit) slab, cement slab
sòlfa *f* (mus) solfeggio; **la solita solfa** the same old story
solfanèllo *m* var of **zofanello**
solfara *f* sulfur mine
solfato *m* sulfate
solfeggiare §290 (**solféggio**) *tr* to sol-fa
solfiè·ro -ra *adj* sulfur
solfito *m* sulfite
sólfo *m* var of **zolfo**
solfòri·co -ca *adj* (**-ci -che**) sulfuric
solforó·so -sa [s] *adj* sulfurous
solfuro *m* sulfide
solidale *adj* solidary; (law) joint; (law) jointly responsible; (mach) built-in; **solidale con** integral with
solidarie·tà *f* (**-tà**) solidarity; (law) joint liability
solidarizzare [ddzz] *intr* to make common cause, become united
solidificare §197 (**solidìfico**) *tr* to solidify; to settle
solidi·tà *f* (**-tà**) solidity; (fig) soundness
sòli·do -da *adj* solid; (law) joint ‖ *m* solid; **in solido** jointly
solilò·quio *m* (**-qui**) soliloquy
solin·go -ga *adj* (**-ghi -ghe**) (lit) lonely; (lit) solitary (*enjoying solitude*)
solino *m* detachable collar; **solino duro** stiff collar
soli·sta *mf* (**-sti -ste**) soloist
solità·rio -ria (**-ri -rie**) *adj* solitary, lonely ‖ *m* solitaire; solitary
sòli·to -ta *adj* usual, customary; **esser solito** to be accustomed to ‖ *m* habit, custom; **come il solito** as usual; **di solito** usually
solitùdine *f* solitude, loneliness
sollazzare *tr* to amuse ‖ *ref* to have a good time, amuse oneself
sollazzo *m* (lit) amusement; **essere il sollazzo di** to be the laughingstock of
sollecitare (**sollécito**) *tr* to solicit; to urge; to induce; (mach) to stress ‖ *intr* & *ref* to hasten
sollecitazióne *f* solicitation; urging; (mach) stress
solléci·to -ta *adj* quick, prompt; diligent; solicitous, anxious ‖ *m* (com) solicitation, urging
sollecitùdine *f* solicitude; promptness; diligence; **cortese sollecitudine** (com) prompt attention
solleóne *m* dog days
solleticare §197 (**sollético**) *tr* to tickle; (fig) to flatter
solléti·co *m* (**-chi**) tickling; stimulation; **fare il solletico a** to tickle
sollevaménto *m* lifting; **sollevamento di pesi** weight lifting
sollevare (**sollèvo**) *tr* to lift; to relieve; to pick up; to raise (*e.g., a question*); to excite; to elevate ‖ *ref* to rise; to lift oneself; to pick up (*said of courage or health*)
sollevazióne *f* uprising
sollièvo *m* relief
sollùchero *m*—**andare in solluchero** to become ecstatic; **mandare in solluchero** to thrill
só·lo -la *adj* lone, lonely, alone; only; single; **fare da solo** to operate all by oneself; **solo soletto** all by myself (yourself, himself, etc.); within oneself; **un solo** only one ‖ *m* (mus) solo ‖ **solo** *adv* only ‖ **solo** *conj* only; **solo che** provided that
solstì·zio *m* (**-zi**) solstice
soltanto *adv* only
solùbile *adj* soluble
soluzióne *f* solution; installment; **soluzione di comodo** compromise; **soluzione provvisoria** stopgap
solvènte *adj* & *m* solvent
solvènza *f* solvency
solvìbile *adj* collectable; solvent
sòma *f* burden, load
Somàlia, la Somaliland
sòma·lo -la *adj* & *mf* Somali
soma·ro -ra *mf* donkey, ass
someggia·to -ta *adj* carried by pack animal; carried on mule back
somigliante *adj* similar; **essere somigliante a** to look like ‖ *m* same thing
somiglianza *f* similarity, resemblance

somigliare §280 *tr* to resemble; (lit) to compare || *intr* (ESSERE & AVERE) (with *dat*) to resemble; to seem to be || *ref* to resemble each other
sómma *f* addition; sum; summary
sommare (**sómmo**) *tr* to add; to consider; **tutto sommato** all in all || *intr* to amount
sommà·rio -ria (**-ri -rie**) *adj* summary || *m* summary; abstract; (journ) subheading
sommèrgere §162 *tr* to submerge; (fig) to plunge; (fig) to flood (*with insults*) || *ref* to submerge
sommergibile *adj* & *m* submarine
sommés·so -sa *adj* submissive; subdued (*voice*)
somministrare *tr* to administer; to provide; to deliver (*a blow*); to adduce (*proof*)
somministrazióne *f* administration; provision
sommi·tà *f* (**-tà**) summit
sóm·mo -ma *adj* highest; supreme || *m* top; peak, summit || *f* see **somma**
sommòssa *f* insurrection, riot
sommoviménto *m* tremor (*of earth*); arousal (*of passions*); riot
sommozzatóre *m* skin diver; (nav) frogman
sommuòvere §202 *tr* (lit) to agitate; (lit) to stir up, excite
sonaglièra *f* collar with bells
sonà·glio *m* (**-gli**) bell; rattle; raindrop; pitter-patter (*of the rain*)
sonante *adj* ringing, sounding; ready (*cash*)
sonare §257 *tr* to sound; to play; to strike (*the hour*); to ring (*a bell*); (coll) to dupe, cheat; (coll) to give a sound thrashing to; **sonare le campane a distesa** to ring a full peal || *intr* (ESSERE & AVERE) to play; to ring (*said of a bell*); to sound; (lit) to spread (*said of reputation*)
sona·to -ta *adj* played; past, e.g., **le tre sonate** past three o'clock; **cinquant'anni sonati** past fifty years of age || *f* ring (*of bell*); (mus) sonata; (coll) thrashing; (coll) cheating
sona·tóre -trice *mf* (mus) player
sónda *f* sound; probe; drill
sondàg·gio *m* (**-gi**) sounding; probe; drilling; **sondaggio d'opinioni** opinion survey, public opinion poll
sondare (**sóndo**) *tr* to sound; to probe; to drill; to survey (*public opinion*)
soneria *f* alarm (*of clock*)
sonétto *m* sonnet
sonnacchió·so -sa [s] *adj* sleepy, drowsy
sonnàmbu·lo -la *mf* sleepwalker
sonnecchiare §287 (**sonnécchio**) *intr* to drowse, take a nap; to nap, nod
sonnellino *m* nap
sonnife·ro -ra *adj* soporific; narcotic || *m* sleeping medicine; narcotic
sónno *m* sleep; (lit) dream; **aver sonno** to be sleepy; **far venir sonno a** to bore; **prender sonno** to fall asleep
sonnolèn·to -ta *adj* sleepy; lazy
sonnolènza *f* drowsiness; laziness
sonori·tà *f* (**-tà**) sonority; acoustics
sonorizzare [ddzz] *tr* to voice; (mov) to dub || *ref* to voice
sonò·ro -ra *adj* sound (*wave*); sonorous; (phonet) sonant, voiced
sontuó·so -sa [s] *adj* sumptuous
sopèr·chio -chia *adj* & *m* (**-chi -chie**) var of **soverchio**
sopire §176 *tr* to appease, calm
sopóre *m* drowsiness
soporife·ro -ra *adj* soporific
soppanno *m* interlining; lining (*of shoes*)
sopperire §176 *intr*—**sopperire a** to provide for; to make up for
soppesare [s] (**soppéso**) *tr* to heft; (fig) to weigh
soppiantare *tr* to supplant by scheming; to kick out; to replace; to trick
soppiatto *m*—**di soppiatto** stealthily
sopportàbile *adj* bearable, tolerable
sopportare (**soppòrto**) *tr* to bear, support; to suffer, endure
sopportazióne *f* forbearance, endurance
soppressióne *f* suppression, abolition
sopprìmere §131 *tr* to suppress, do away with
sópra *adj invar* upper; above, preceding || *m* upper, upper part; **al di sopra** above; **al di sopra di** above, over; beyond; **di sopra** upper || *adv* above; up; on top || *prep* on; upon; on top of; over; beyond; above; versus; **sopra pensiero** absorbed in thought
sopràbito *m* overcoat, topcoat
sopraccàri·co -ca (**-chi -che**) *adj* overburdened || *m* overload; overweight; (naut) supercargo
sopraccenna·to -ta *adj* above-mentioned
sopraccì·glio *m* (**-gli** & **-glia** *fpl*) brow, eyebrow; window frame
sopraccita·to -ta *adj* above-mentioned
sopraccopèrta *f* bedspread; book jacket, dust jacket || *adv* (naut) on deck
sopraddét·to -ta *adj* above-mentioned
sopraffare §173 *tr* to overcome, overpower
sopraffazióne *f* overpowering; abuse
sopraffinèstra *f* transom window
sopraffi·no -na *adj* first-class; superfine
sopraggitto *m* (sew) overcasting
sopraggiùngere §183 *intr* (ESSERE) to arrive; to happen
sopraintèndere §270 *tr* var of **soprintendere**
sopralluò·go *m* (**-ghi**) inspection, investigation on the spot
sopralzo *m* var of **soprelevazione**
soprammercato *m*—**per soprammercato** in addition, to boot
soprammòbile *m* knicknack
soprannaturale *adj* & *m* supernatural
soprannóme *m* nickname
soprannominare (**soprannòmino**) *tr* to nickname
soprannùmero *adj invar* in excess; overtime || *m* —**in soprannumero** extra; in excess
sopra·no -na *adj* upper; (lit) supreme

|| **sopra•no** *mf* (**-ni -ne**) soprano (*person*) || *m* soprano (*voice*)
soprappensièro *adj invar & adv* immersed in thought
soprappéso [s] *m*—**per soprappeso** besides, into the bargain
soprap•più *m* (**-più**) plus, extra; **in soprappiù** besides, into the bargain
soprapprèzzo *m* extra charge, surcharge
soprascarpa *f* overshoe
soprascrit•to -ta *adj* written above || *f* address
soprassalto *m* start, jump; **di soprassalto** with a start
soprassedére §252 *intr* to wait; (with *dat*) to postpone
soprassòldo *m* extra pay; (mil) warzone indemnity
soprastare §263 *intr* (ESSERE) to be the boss
soprattac•co *m* (**-chi**) rubber heel
soprattassa *f* surtax; surcharge
soprattutto *adv* above all, especially
sopravanzare *tr* to overcome || *intr* (ESSERE) to be left over
sopravanzo *m* surplus
sopravvalutare *tr* to overrate
sopravvenire §282 *tr* (lit) to overrun || *intr* (ESSERE) to arrive; to happen, occur; (with *dat*) to befall
sopravvènto *m* windward; **avere il sopravvento** to have the upper hand || *adv* windward
sopravvissu•to -ta *adj* surviving || *mf* survivor
sopravvivènza *f* survival
sopravvìvere §286 *intr* (ESSERE) to survive; (with *dat*) to survive, to outlive
soprelevare (**soprelèvo**) *tr* to elevate (*e.g., a railroad*); to increase the height of (*building*)
soprelevazióne *f* elevation; addition of one or more floors
soprintendènte *m* superintendent
soprintendènza *f* superintendency
soprintèndere §270 *tr* to oversee
sopròsso *m* (coll) bony outgrowth
sopruso *m* abuse of power
soqquadro *m*—**a soqquadro** upside down, topsy-turvy
sòrba *f* sorb apple; (coll) hit, blow
sorbettièra *f* ice-cream freezer
sorbétto *m* ice cream; sherbet
sorbire §176 *tr* to sip; (fig) to swallow, endure
sòrbo *m* sorb; service tree
sór•cio *m* (**-ci**) mouse
sòrdi•do -da *adj* sordid; dirty
sordina *f* (mus) sordino, mute; (mus) soft pedal; **in sordina** quietly; stealthily; **mettere in sordina** (mus) to muffle
sór•do -da *adj* deaf; dull (*pain*); deep-seated (*hatred*); hollow (*sound*); (phonet) surd, voiceless; **sordo come una campana** stone-deaf || *mf* deaf person
sordomu•to -ta *adj* deaf and dumb || *mf* deafmute
sorèlla *f* sister
sorellastra *f* stepsister
sorgènte *adj* rising || *f* spring; well (*of oil*); (fig) source; **sorgente del fiume** riverhead
sórgere §258 *intr* (ESSERE) to rise; to arise; to spring forth; **sorgere su un'ancora** (naut) to lie at anchor
sorgi•vo -va *adj* spring (*water*)
sór•go *m* (**-ghi**) sorghum
sormontare (**sormónto**) *tr* to surmount; to overcome || *intr* to fit
sornió•ne -na *adj* cunning, sly || *m* sneak
sorpassare *tr* to get ahead of; to surpass; to overstep; to go above
sorpasso *m* (aut) passing
sorprendènte *adj* surprising, astonishing
sorprèndere §220 *tr* to surprise; to catch; **sorprendere la buona fede di** to take advantage of || *ref* to be surprised
sorprésa [s] *f* surprise; surprise investigation; **di sorpresa** suddenly; unprepared; by surprise
sorrèggere §226 *tr* to sustain, support; to bolster
sorrìdere §231 *tr* (lit) to say with a smile || *intr* to smile; **sorridere a** to appeal to, e.g., **le sorride l'idea di questa gita** the idea of this trip appeals to her; to smile upon, e.g., **gli sorrideva la vita** life was smiling upon him
sorriso [s] *m* smile
sorsata *f* gulp, draught
sorseggiare §290 (**sorséggio**) *tr* to sip
sórso *m* sip; **a sorso a sorso** sipping
sòrta *f* kind, sort
sòrte *f* luck, lot, fate; chance; kind; (com) principal; **per sorte** of each kind; by chance; **tirare a sorte** to cast lots
sorteggiare §290 (**sortéggio**) *tr* to choose by lot; to raffle; **sorteggiare un premio** to draw a prize
sortég•gio *m* (**-gi**) drawing
sortilè•gio *m* (**-gi**) sortilege; sorcery, magic
sortire §176 *tr* (lit) to get by lot; (lit) to have (*results*); (lit) to allot || (**sòrto**) *intr* (ESSERE) to come out (*said, e.g., of a newspaper*); (coll) to be drawn (*by lot*); (coll) to go out; (mil) to make a sally
sortita *f* witticism; (mil) sally, sortie; (theat) appearance
sorvegliante *adj* watchful || *mf* overseer, caretaker; guardian || *m* watchman; foreman
sorveglianza *f* surveillance; supervision
sorvegliare §280 (**sorvéglio**) *tr* to oversee, watch over; to check, control
sorvolare (**sorvólo**) *tr* to fly over; to overfly; (fig) to avoid, skip
sorvólo *m* overflight
sò•sia *m* (**-sia**) double, counterpart
sospèndere §259 *tr* to hang; to suspend; (chem) to prepare a suspension of; (law) to stay
sospensióne *f* suspension; suspense; (law) stay; **sospensione cardanica** gimbals

sospensò•rio *m* (**-ri**) jockstrap, supporter
sospé•so -sa [s] *adj* suspended; suspension (*bridge*); **in sospeso** in suspense; in abeyance || *m* employee who has been disciplined by suspension; (com) pending item
sospettare (sospètto) *tr* to suspect || *intr*—**sospettare di** to suspect; to fear
sospèt•to -ta *adj* suspected; suspicious || *m* dash; suspicion
sospettó•so -sa [s] *adj* suspicious
sospìngere §126 *tr* (fig) to drive; (lit) to push
sospirare *tr* to long for, crave; **fare sospirare** to keep waiting || *intr* to sigh
sospiro *m* sigh; longing; (lit) breath; **a sospiri** little by little
sossópra *adv* upside down
sòsta *f* stop; reprieve; (rr) demurrage
sostanti•vo -va *adj & m* substantive
sostanza *f* substance; **sostanza grigia** gray matter
sostanziale *adj* substantial
sostanzió•so -sa [s] *adj* substantial
sostare (sòsto) *intr* to stop, pause
sostégno *m* prop; (fig) support
sostenére §271 *tr* to support; to sustain; to take (*an examination*); to defend (*a thesis*); to prop up; to stand (*alcohol*); to play (*a role*) || *ref* to support oneself; to hold up (*said, e.g., of a theory*); to take nourishment
sosteni•tóre -trice *mf* backer, supporter
sostentaménto *m* sustenance, support
sostentare (sostènto) *tr* to support, keep || *ref* to feed, eat
sostenu•to -ta *adj* reserved, austere; rising (*prices*); bullish (*market*); starchy (*manner*)
sostituìbile *adj* replaceable
sostituire §176 *tr* to replace, substitute for, take the place of; **sostituire** (*qlco* or *qlcu*) **a** to substitute (*s.th* or *s.o.*) for
sostitu•to -ta *adj* acting; associate, assistant || *m* replacement, substitute
sostituzióne *f* replacement, substitution
sostrato *m* substratum
sottàbito *m* slip
sottacére §268 *tr* (lit) to withhold
sottacéto *adj invar* pickled || **sottaceti** *mpl* pickles
sott'àcqua *adv* underwater
sotta•no -na *adj* lower (*town*) || *f* skirt; petticoat; (eccl) cassock; **gettare la sottana alle ortiche** to doff the cassock
sottécchi *adv*—**di sottecchi** stealthily, secretly; **guardare di sottecchi** to peep, look furtively (at)
sottentrare (sotténtro) *intr* (ESSERE) (with *dat*) to replace
sotterfù•gio *m* (**-gi**) subterfuge
sottèrra *adv* underground
sotterràne•o -a *adj* subterranean, underground; secret, clandestine || *m* cave, vault; dungeon; underground passage || *f* (rr) subway, underground
sotterrare (sottèrro) *tr* to bury
sottigliézza *f* thinness; subtlety
sottile *adj* thin; subtle; (naut) lightweight || *m*—**guardare troppo per il sottile** to split hairs
sottilizzare [ddzz] *intr* to quibble
sottintèndere §270 *tr* to understand || *ref* to be understood, be implied
sottinté•so -sa [s] *adj* understood, implied || *m* innuendo
sótto *adj invar* lower || *m* lower part || *adv* under; underneath; **al di sotto** below; **al di sotto di** under, below; **di sotto** lower; underneath; downstairs; **di sotto a** under, below; **farsi sotto** to sneak up; **metter sotto** to run over (*with a vehicle*); **sotto a** under; **sotto di** under || *prep* under; beneath; below; just before; **prendere sotto gamba** to underestimate; **sotto braccio** arm in arm; **sotto carico** (naut) being loaded; **sotto i baffi** up one's sleeve; **sotto le armi** in the service; **sotto mano** within reach; **sotto voce** under one's breath, sottovoce
sottoascèl•la *m* (**-la**) underarm pad
sottobanco *adv* under the counter
sottobicchière *m* coaster
sottobò•sco *m* (**-schi**) underbrush, thicket
sottobràccio *adv* arm in arm
sottòcchio *adv* under one's eyes
sottoccupa•to -ta *adj* underemployed
sottochiave *adv* under lock and key
sottocó•da *m* (**-da**) crupper
sottocommissióne *f* subcommittee
sottocopèrta *adv* (naut) below decks
sottocòp•pa *m* (**-pa**) mat; coaster; (aut) oil pan
sottocòsto *adj invar & adv* below cost
sottocutàne•o -a *adj* subcutaneous
sottofà•scia *m* (**-scia**) wrapper; **spedire sottofascia** to mail (*a newspaper*) in a wrapper || *f* (**-sce**) wrapper (*for cigars*)
sottogamba *adv* lightly; **prendere sottogamba** to underestimate
sottogó•la *m & f* (**-la**) chin strap; throatlatch (*of harness*)
sottolineare (sottolìneo) *tr* to underline, underscore; to emphasize
sott'òlio *adv* in oil
sottomano *m* writing pad || *adv* underhand; within reach
sottomari•no -na *adj & m* submarine
sottomés•so -sa *adj* conquered; subdued; submissive
sottométtere §198 *tr* to subdue, crush; to defer, postpone; to present (*a bill*); to subject || *ref* to submit, yield
sottomissióne *f* submission
sottopan•cia *m* (**-cia**) bellyband, girth
sottopassàg•gio *m* (**-gi**) underpass; lower level (*of highway*)
sottopiatto *m* saucer
sottopórre §218 *tr* to subject; to submit || *ref* to submit; **sottoporsi a** to submit to; to undergo (*e.g., an operation*)
sottopó•sto -sta *adj* subject; exposed || *m* subordinate

sottoprèzzo *adj invar* cut-rate || *adv* at a cut rate
sottoprodótto *m* by-product
sottórdine *m* suborder; **in sottordine** secondary
sottosca•la *m* (**-la**) space under the stairs; closet under the stairs
sottoscrit•to -ta *adj* & *mf* undersigned
sottoscrit•tóre -trice *mf* subscriber
sottoscrìvere §250 *tr* to subscribe; to sign, undersign; to underwrite || *intr* to subscribe
sottoscrizióne *f* subscription
sottosegretà•rio *m* (**-ri**) undersecretary
sottosópra *adj invar* upset; **mettere sottosopra** to upset; to turn upside down || *m* confusion, disorder || *adv* upside down
sottostante *adj* lower; subordinate || *m* subordinate
sottostare §263 *intr* (ESSERE) to be located below; to be subject; to yield, submit; (with *dat*) to undergo (*e.g., an examination*)
sottosuòlo *m* subsoil; cellar
sottosviluppa•to -ta *adj* underdeveloped
sottotenènte *m* second lieutenant; **sottotenente di vascello** (nav) lieutenant j.g.
sottotèr•ra *m* (**-ra**) basement || *adv* underground
sottotétto *m* attic, garret
sottotìtolo *m* subtitle; (mov) caption
sottovalutare *tr* to underrate
sottovènto *m* & *adv* leeward
sottovèste *f* slip (*undergarment*)
sottovóce *adv* sotto voce, under one's breath
sottrarre §273 *tr* to subtract; **sottrarre a** to take away from, steal from || *ref*—**sottrarsi a** to avoid; to escape from
sottrazióne *f* subtraction
sottufficiale *m* noncommissioned officer
sovènte *adv* often
soverchiante *adj* overwhelming
soverchiare §287 (**sovèrchio**) *tr* to overwhelm; to excel; to bully; (lit) to overflow || *intr* to be in excess
soverchia•tóre -trice *adj* overbearing || *mf* overbearing person, oppressor
sovèr•chio -chia (**-chi -chie**) *adj* excessive; overbearing || *m* overbearing action
sovè•scio *m* (**-sci**) plowing under (*of green manure*)
sovièti•co -ca (**-ci -che**) *adj* Soviet || *mf* Soviet citizen
sovrabbondante *adj* superabundant
sovrabbondare (**sovrabbóndo**) *intr* (ESSERE & AVERE) to be superabundant; to go to excesses
sovraccaricare §197 (**sovraccàrico**) *tr* to overload
sovraccàri•co -ca (**-chi -che**) *adj* overburdened || *m* overload; overweight
sovraespó•sto -sta *adj* overexposed
sovraggiùngere §183 *intr* (ESSERE) var of **sopraggiungere**
sovralimentazióne *f* (aut) supercharging
sovrani•tà *f* (**-tà**) sovereignty
sovra•no -na *adj* & *mf* sovereign
sovrappopolare (**sovrappòpolo**) *tr* to overpopulate
sovrappórre §218 *tr* to overlay; to superimpose; **sovrapporre qlco a** to lay s.th on || *ref* to be superimposed; to be added; **sovrapporsi a** to put oneself above
sovrapproduzióne *f* overproduction
sovrastampa *f* overprint
sovrastante *adj* overlooking, overhanging; impending
sovrastare *tr* to tower over; to hang over; to surpass; to excel || *intr* (ESSERE & AVERE)—**sovrastare a** to tower over; to overlook; to hang over; to surpass; to excel
sovratensióne *f* (elec) surge
sovreccitare (**sovrèccito**) *tr* to overexcite
sovrespórre §218 *tr* to overexpose
sovrimpòsta *f* surtax
sovrimpressióne *f* double exposure
sovruma•no -na *adj* superhuman
sovvenire §282 *tr* (lit) to help || *intr* (with *dat*) (lit) to help || *impers* (ESSERE)—**sovviene** (with *dat*) **di** remember, e.g., **gli sovviene spesso dei suoi cari** he often remembers his dear ones || *ref*—**sovvenirsi di** to remember
sovvenzionare (**sovvenzióno**) *tr* to subsidize, grant a subvention to
sovvenzióne *f* subsidy, subvention
sovversi•vo -va *adj* & *m* subversive
sovvertire (**sovvèrto**) *tr* to subvert
sóz•zo -za *adj* dirty, filthy, foul
sozzura *f* dirt, filth
spaccalé•gna *m* (**-gna**) woodcutter
spaccamón•ti *m* (**-ti**) braggart
spaccaòs•sa *m* (**-sa**) butcher's cleaver
spaccare §197 *tr* to break, burst; to crack; to unpack; to chop; to split || *ref* to crack; to break; to split
spacca•to -ta *adj* broken; split; (coll) identical; (coll) true || *f* (sports, theat) splits
spaccatura *f* break; crack; cleavage; split
spacchétto *m* vent (*in jacket*)
spacciare §128 *tr* to sell out; to palm off; to spread (*reports*); to expedite; to abandon (*as hopeless*); (slang) to push (*e.g., dope*) || *ref*—**spacciarsi per** to pretend to be, pass oneself off as
spaccia•to -ta *adj* (coll) cooked, done for; (coll) hopeless
spaccia•tóre -trice *mf* passer (*of bad currency or stolen goods*); **spacciatore di notizie false** gossipmonger
spàc•cio *m* (**-ci**) sale; passing (*of counterfeit money*); spreading (*of false news*); post exchange; tobacco shop
spac•co *m* (**-chi**) break; split; tear; crack; vent (*in jacket*)
spacconata *f* brag, braggadocio
spaccó•ne -na *mf* braggart, braggadocio
spada *f* sword; **a spada tratta** dog-

gedly; **spade** suit of Neapolitan cards corresponding to spades
spadaccino *m* swordsman; swashbuckler
spadóne *m* two-handed sword
spadroneggiare §290 (**spadronéggio**) *intr* to be domineering or bossy
spaesa·to -ta *adj* out-of-place
spaghétto *m* (coll) fear, jitters; **avere lo spaghetto** (coll) to be scared stiff; **spaghetti** spaghetti
Spagna, la Spain
spagnòla *f* Spanish woman; Spanish influenza
spagnolétta *f* espagnolette; spool; (coll) cigarette; (coll) peanut
spagnò·lo -la *adj* Spanish || *m* Spaniard (*individual*); Spanish (*language*); **gli spagnoli** the Spanish || *f* see **spagnola**
spa·go *m* (**-ghi**) string, twine; (coll) fear, jitters
spaiare §287 *tr* to break a pair of
spaia·to -ta *adj* unmatched
spalancare §197 *tr* to open wide || *ref* to open up; to gape
spalare *tr* to shovel; to feather (*oar*)
spalla *f* shoulder; back; abutment (*of bridge*); (theat) stooge, straight man; **alle spalle di qlcu** behind s.o.'s back; **a spalla** on one's back; **fare spalla a** to help; **lavorare di spalle** to elbow one's way; (fig) to worm one's way up; **vivere alle spalle di** to sponge on
spallàrm *interj* (mil) shoulder arms!
spallata *f* push with the shoulder; shrug of the shoulders
spalleggiare §290 (**spalléggio**) *tr* to back, support; (mil) to carry on one's back
spallétta *f* parapet, retaining wall; jamb
spallièra *f* back (*of chair*); head (*of bed*); foot (*of bed*); espalier
spallina *f* epaulet; shoulder strap
spallùccia *f*—**fare spallucce** to shrug one's shoulders
spalmare *tr* to spread; to smear
spalto *m* glacis; **spalti** seats (*of a stadium*)
spanare *tr* to strip the thread of || *ref* to be stripped (*said, e.g., of the thread of a nut*)
spanciare §128 *tr* to disembowel, gut || *intr* to belly-flop; to bulge (*said of a wall*) || *ref*—**spanciarsi dalle risa** to split one's sides laughing
spanciata *f* belly flop; bellyful; **fare una spanciata** to stuff oneself
spàndere §260 *tr* to spread; to spill; to shed (*tears*); to squander || *ref* to spread
spanna *f* span
spannare *tr* to skim (*milk*)
spannocchiare §287 (**spannòcchio**) *tr* to husk (*corn*)
spappolare (**spàppolo**) *tr* to crush, squash || *ref* to become mushy
sparadrappo *m* adhesive tape; (obs) plaster, poultice
sparagnare *tr* (coll) to save
sparare *tr* to gut, disembowel; to shoot; to let go with (*a kick*); to remove the hangings from; **spararne delle grosse** to tell tall tales
sparato *m* shirt front, dickey
sparatòria *f* shooting
sparecchiare §287 (**sparécchio**) *tr* to clear (*the table*); to clear away (*one's tools*); to eat up
sparég·gio *m* (**-gi**) disparity; deficit; (sports) play-off
spàrgere §261 *tr* to spread; to shed; to spill || *ref* to spread
spargiménto *m* spreading; **spargimento di sangue** bloodshed
spargisa·le [s] *m* (**-le**) salt shaker
sparigliare §280 *tr* to break a pair of; to break (*a set*)
spariglia·to -ta *adj* unmatched
sparire §176 *intr* (ESSERE) to disappear
sparlare *intr* to backbite; **sparlare di** to backbite, slander
sparo *m* shot
sparpagliare §280 *tr & intr* to scatter
spar·so -sa *adj* scattered; dotted; speckled; hanging loosely (*e.g., hair*)
sparta·no -na *adj & mf* Spartan
spartiàc·que *m* (**-que**) watershed
spartiné·ve *m* (**-ve**) snowplow
spartire §176 *tr* to divide, share; to separate; **non aver nulla da spartire con** to have nothing to do with
spartito *m* (mus) score; (mus) arrangement
spartitràffi·co *m* (**-co**) median strip
spar·to -ta *adj* (lit) spread || *m* esparto grass
sparu·to -ta *adj* lean, wan; meager
sparvière *m* sparrow hawk; mortarboard
spasimante *m* (joc) lover, wooer
spasimare (**spàsimo**) *intr* to writhe; **spasimare per** to long for; to be madly in love with
spàsimo *m* pang; severe pain; longing
spasmo *m* spasm
spasmòdi·co -ca *adj* (**-ci -che**) spasmodic
spassare *tr* to amuse || *ref*—**spassarsela** to have a good time
spassiona·to -ta *adj* dispassionate, unbiased
spasso *m* fun, amusement; walk; (coll) funny guy; **andare a spasso** to go out for a walk; **essere a spasso** to be out of a job; **mandare a spasso** to fire, dismiss; to get rid of; **per spasso** for fun; **portare a spasso** to lead by the nose; **prendersi spasso di** to make fun of
spassó·so -sa [s] *adj* amusing, droll
spàsti·co -ca *adj & mf* spastic
spato *m* spar
spatofluòre *m* fluorspar
spàtola *f* spatula; putty knife; slapstick (*of harlequin*)
spauràc·chio *m* (**chi**) scarecrow; bugaboo, bugbear
spaurare *tr & ref* (lit) var of **spaurire**
spaurire §176 *tr* to frighten || *ref* to be scared
spaval·do -da *adj* bold, swaggering
spaventapàs·seri *m* (**-ri**) scarecrow

spaventare (**spavènto**) *tr* to scare, frighten || *ref* to be scared
spaventévole *adj* frightening, dreadful
spavènto *m* fright, fear
spaventó•so -sa [s] *adj* frightful, fearful
spaziale *adj* space
spaziare §287 *tr* (typ) to space || *intr* to soar; to range, rove (*said, e.g., of eye*)
spazia•tóre -trice *adj* spacing || *f* space bar (*of typewriter*)
spaziatura *f* spacing
spazientire §176 *tr* to make (*s.o.*) lose his patience || *intr* (ESSERE) & *ref* to lose patience
spà•zio *m* (**-zi**) space; (fig) room; **spazio aereo** air space; **spazio cosmico** outer space
spazió•so -sa [s] *adj* spacious, roomy; wide
spazzacamino *m* chimney sweep
spazzami•ne *m* (**-ne**) mine sweeper
spazzané•ve *m* (**-ve**) snowplow
spazzare *tr* to sweep; to plow (*snow*); to clean up
spazzata *f*—**dare una spazzata a** to give a lick and a promise to
spazzatrice *f* street sweeper
spazzatura *f* sweeping; sweepings; rubbish, trash
spazzatu•ràio *m* (**-rài**) or **spazzino** *m* street cleaner; trashman, garbage collector, trash collector
spàzzola *f* brush; **capelli a spazzola** crew cut
spazzolare (**spàzzolo**) *tr* to brush
spazzolino *m* little brush; (elec) brush; **spazzolino da denti** toothbrush; **spazzolino per le unghie** nailbrush
spazzolóne *m* push broom
specchiare §287 (**spècchio**) *tr* (lit) to reflect || *ref* to look at oneself (*in a mirror*); to be reflected; **specchiarsi in qlcu** to model oneself on s.o.
specchièra *f* mirror; dressing table; full-length mirror
specchiétto *m* mirror; synopsis; **specchietto retrovisivo** (aut) rear-view mirror
spèc•chio *m* (**-chi**) mirror; synopsis; shore (*of lake or river*); panel (*of door or window*); sheet (*of water*); (sports) goal line; (sports) board; **specchio di poppa** (naut) transom; **specchio ustorio** burning glass
speciale *adj* special
speciali•sta *mf* (**-sti -ste**) specialist
speciali•tà *f* (**-tà**) specialty; (mil) special services; **specialità farmaceutica** patent or proprietary medicine
specializzare [ddzz] *tr* & *ref* to specialize
spè•cie *f* (**-cie**) species; kind, sort; appearance, semblance; **fare specie** (with *dat*) (coll) to be surprised, e.g., **gli fa specie** he is surprised; **in specie** especially; **sotto specie di** under pretext of
specìfi•ca *f* (**-che**) itemized list; specification
specificare §197 (**specìfico**) *tr* to specify; to itemize
specìfi•co -ca (**-ci -che**) *adj* & *m* specific || *f* see **specifica**
specillo *m* (med) probe
speció•so -sa [s] *adj* specious
spè•co *m* (**-chi**) (lit) cave
spècola *f* observatory
spècolo *m* (med, surg) speculum
speculare (**spèculo**) *tr* to observe; to meditate on || *intr* to speculate
specula•tóre -trice *adj* speculating || *mf* speculator; **speculatore al rialzo** bull; **speculatore al ribasso** bear
speda•to -ta *adj* footworn
spedire §176 *tr* to expedite; to prepare; to ship, send, forward; (law) to deliver
spedi•to -ta *adj* rapid; free, easy
spedi•tóre -trice *mf* shipper, sender; shipping clerk
spedizióne *f* shipment, shipping; sending, forwarding; expedition; (naut) papers; **di spedizione** expeditionary
spedizionière *m* shipper, forwarder, forwarding agent
spègnere §262 *tr* to extinguish, put out; to turn off; to slake (*lime*); to kill; to mix (*flour*) with water or milk; to quench; to obliterate (*a memory*) || *ref* to burn out; to go out (*said of a light*); to fade, die away; to die
spegni•tóio *m* (**-tói**) snuffer
spegnitura *f* (theat) blackout
spelacchiare §287 *tr* to strip of hair || *ref* to shed hair or fur
spelacchia•to -ta *adj* mangy; (pej) baldy
spelare (**spélo**) *tr* to strip of hair; to pluck (*e.g., a chicken*); (fig) to fleece || *ref* to shed hair or fur; to get bald
spellare (**spèllo**) *tr* to skin; (fig) to skin, fleece
spelón•ca *f* (**-che**) cave; hovel, den
spème *f* (poet) hope
spendacció•ne -na *mf* spendthrift
spèndere §220 *tr* to spend
spenderéc•cio -cia *adj* (**-ci -ce**) spendthrift, prodigal
spennacchiare §287 *tr* to pluck; (fig) to fleece || *ref* to lose its feathers
spennare (**spénno**) *tr* & *ref* var of **spennacchiare**
spennellare (**spennèllo**) *tr* to dab
spensieratézza *f* thoughtlessness
spensiera•to -ta *adj* thoughtless, careless; carefree, happy-go-lucky
spèn•to -ta *adj* extinguished; turned off; slaked (*lime*); dull (*color*); low (*tone*)
spenzolare [dz] (**spènzolo**) *tr* & *intr* to hang || *ref*—**spenzolarsi da** to hang out of
speranza *f* hope; prospect, expectation
speranzó•so -sa [s] *adj* hopeful
sperare (**spèro**) *tr* to candle (*eggs*); to hope for; to expect || *intr* to hope; to trust
spèrdere §212 *tr* (lit) to scatter; (lit) to lose (*one's way*) || *ref* to lose one's way, get lost
sperdu•to -ta *adj* lost, astray; godforsaken (*place*)
sperequazióne *f* disproportion; inequality; unjust distribution

spergiurare *tr & intr* to swear falsely; **giurare e spergiurare** to swear over and over again
spergiu•ro -ra *adj* perjured || *mf* perjurer || *m* perjury
spericola•to -ta *adj* reckless, daring
sperimentale *adj* experimental
sperimentare (sperimento) *tr* to test, try out; to experience
sperimenta•to -ta *adj* experienced
spèr•ma *m* **(-mi)** sperm
speronare (speróno) *tr* (naut) to ram
speróne *m* spur; abutment; (nav) ram
sperperare (spèrpero) *tr* to squander
spèrpero *m* squandering
spèr•so -sa *adj* lost, stray
spertica•to -ta *adj* too long; too tall; exaggerated, excessive
spésa [s] *f* expense; shopping; buy, purchase; **fare la spesa** to shop; **fare le spese di** to be the butt of; **lavorare per le spese** to work for one's keep; **pagare le spese** to bear the charges; **spese** expenses; room and board; **spese di manutenzione** upkeep; **spese minute** petty expenses; **spese processuali** (law) costs
spesare [s] **(spéso)** *tr* to support
spesa•to -ta [s] *adj* with all expenses paid
spés•so -sa *adj* thick; many (*times*) || **spesso** *adv* often; **spesso spesso** again and again
spessóre *m* thickness
spettàbile *adj* esteemed; **Spettabile Ditta** (com) Gentlemen
spettàcolo *m* spectacle, show; sight; **dar spettacolo di sé** to make a show of oneself; **spettacolo all'aperto** outdoor performance
spettacolò•so -sa [s] *adj* spectacular; (coll) exceptional; (coll) sensational
spettanza *f* concern; pay
spettare (spètto) *intr* (ESSERE)—**spettare a** to belong to || *impers* (ESSERE) —**spetta a** it behooves, it is up to
spetta•tóre -trice *mf* spectator, bystander; **spettatori** public, audience
spettegolare (spettégolo) *intr* to gossip
spettinare (spèttino) *tr* to muss the hair of
spettrale *adj* ghost-like; spectral
spèttro *m* specter, ghost; spectrum
speziale *m* dealer in spices; (coll) pharmacist
spèzie *fpl* spices
spezierìa *f* grocery; (coll) drug store, pharmacy; **spezierie** spices
spezzare (spèzzo) *tr* to break; to smash; to interrupt || *ref* to break
spezzatino *m* stew; **spezzatini** change
spezza•to -ta *adj* broken; fragmentary; interrupted || *m* stew; (theat) set piece; **spezzati** change
spezzettare (spezzétto) *tr* to mince
spezzóne *m* small aerial bomb; fragmentation bomb; fragment
spìa *f* spy; indication; peephole; (aut) gauge; (aut) pilot light; **fare la spia** to be an informer
spiaccicare §197 **(spiàccico)** *tr* to squash, crush || *ref* to be squashed
spiacènte *adj* sorry; (lit) disliked
spiacére §214 *intr* (ESSERE) (with *dat*) to dislike, e.g., **queste parole gli spiacciono** he dislikes these words; to mind, e.g., **se non Le spiace** if you don't mind || *ref*—**spiacersi di** to be sorry for || *impers* (ESSERE) (with *dat*)—**gli spiace** he is sorry
spiacévole *adj* unpleasant
spiàg•gia *f* **(-ge)** beach, shore
spianare *tr* to grade (*land*); to roll (*dough*); to pave (*the way*); to iron (*pleats*); to raze, demolish; to level (*a gun*); **spianare la fronte** to smooth one's brow || *intr* (ESSERE) to be level
spianata *f* esplanade; **dare una spianata a** to level
spianatóia *f* board (*for rolling dough*)
spiana•tóio *m* **(-tói)** rolling pin
spianatrice *f* grader
spiano *m* leveling; esplanade; **a tutto spiano** at full blast; continuously
spiantare *tr* to uproot; to raze, level; to ruin (*financially*) || *ref* to ruin oneself
spianta•to -ta *adj* ruined || *m* pauper
spiare §119 *tr* to spy on; to keep an eye on
spiattellare (spiattèllo) *tr* to blurt out
spiazzo *m* square; plain; clearing
spiccare §197 *tr* to detach; to pick; to enunciate; to begin; to draw up (*a commercial paper*); to issue (*a warrant*); **spiccare il volo** (aer) to take off || *intr* to stand out || *ref* to separate (*said, e.g., of the stone of a peach*)
spicca•to -ta *adj* clear, distinct; typical; outstanding
spic•chio *m* **(-chi)** section (*of fruit*); clove (*of garlic*); slice (*e.g., of apple*); arm (*of cross*)
spicciare §128 *tr* to clear up; to wait on; to dispatch (*business*) || *intr* (ESSERE) to flow forth, gush out || *ref* to hurry up, make haste
spicciati•vo -va *adj* expeditious, quick; straightforward; gruff
spiccicare §197 **(spiccico)** *tr* to unglue; to enunciate; to utter || *ref* to come unglued; **spiccicarsi di** to get rid of
spic•cio -cia (-ci -ce) *adj* expeditious, quick; unhampered; small (*change*) || **spicci** *mpl* change
spicciolata *adj fem*—**alla spicciolata** little by little; a few at a time
spìccio•lo -la *adj* small (change); (coll) plain || **spiccioli** *mpl* small change
spic•co -ca (-chi -che) *adj* freestone (*e.g., peach*) || *m*—**fare spicco** to stand out
spidocchiare §287 **(spidòcchio)** *tr* to delouse
spièdo *m* spit; **allo spiedo** barbecued
spiegàbile *adj* explainable
spiegaménto *m* (mil) array; (mil) deployment
spiegare §209 **(spiègo)** *tr* to unfold; to let go (*with one's voice*); to unfurl; to spread (*wings*); to deploy (*troops*); to explain; to show, demonstrate; **spiegare il volo** (aer) to take off || *ref* to become unfurled or unfolded;

to make oneself understood; to come to an understanding; to realize
spiega·to -ta *adj* open; full (*voice*)
spiegazióne *f* explanation
spiegazzare *tr* to crumple, rumple
spieta·to -ta *adj* pitiless, ruthless
spifferare (spìffero) *tr* (coll) to blurt out || *intr* to blow in (*said of wind*)
spìffero *m* (coll) draft
spi·ga *f* **(ghe)** panicle (*of oats*); (bot) ear, spike; **a spiga** herringbone
spiga·to -ta *adj* herringbone
spighétta *f* braid; (bot) spikelet
spigionare (spigióno) *ref* to be or become vacant
spiglia·to -ta *adj* easy, free and easy
spi·go *m* **(-ghi)** lavender
spigolare (spìgolo) *tr* to glean
spigola·tóre -trice *mf* gleaner
spìgolo *m* corner; edge; (archit) arris
spilla *f* brooch, pin; **spilla da cravatta** tiepin; **spilla di sicurezza** safety pin
spillare *tr* to draw off, tap; to wheedle, worm (*money*) || *intr* to leak (*said of container*) || *intr* (ESSERE) to leak (*said of liquid*)
spillàti·co *m* **(-ci)** (law) pin money (*for one's wife*)
spillo *m* pin; gimlet; trifle; **a spillo** spikelike; **spillo da balia** or **di sicurezza** safety pin
spillóne *m* hatpin; bodkin
spilluzzicare §197 **(spillùzzico)** *tr* to pick at, nibble; to scrape together
spilorcerìa *f* stinginess
spilòr·cio -cia (-ci -ce) *adj* stingy || *mf* miser, tightwad
spilungó·ne -na *mf* lanky person
spina *f* thorn; quill, spine (*of porcupine*); bone (*of fish*); (fig) preoccupation, worry; **alla spina** (*beer*) on tap; **a spina di pesce** herringbone (*fabric*); **con una spina nel cuore** sick at heart; **essere sulle spine** to be on pins and needles; **spina della botte** tap; bunghole; **spina dorsale** spinal column; (fig) backbone; **spina elettrica** plug
spinà·cio *m* **(-ci)** spinach (*plant*); **spinaci** spinach (*as food*)
spinapésce *m*—**a spinapesce** herringbone
spina·to -ta *adj* barbed (*wire*); herringbone (*fabric*)
spìngere §126 *tr* to push, press; to prod, goad || *ref* to push; to reach
spi·no -na *adj* thorny || *m* thorn || *f* see **spina**
spinóne *m* griffon
spinó·so -sa [s] *adj* thorny
spinòtto *m* wrist pin
spinta *f* push; pressure; poke, prod; stress
spinterògeno *m* (aut) distributor unit, ignition system
spin·to -ta *adj* pushed; bent, inclined; (coll) risqué; (coll) far-out, offbeat || *f* see **spinta**
spintóne *m* (coll) push, shove
spionàg·gio *m* **(-gi)** espionage, spying
spioncino *m* peephole
spió·ne -na *mf* spy, stool pigeon
spiovènte *adj* drooping; sloping; falling || *m* slope; drainage area (*of a mountain*)
spiòvere §216 *intr* to fall, to hang down (*said, e.g., of hair*); to flow down || *impers* (ESSERE)—**è spiovuto** it stopped raining
spira *f* turn (*of a coil*); coil (*of serpent*); **a spire** spiral
spirà·glio *m* **(-gli)** small opening; gleam (*of light or hope*)
spirale *adj* spiral || *f* spiral; hairspring; wreath (*of smoke*); **spirale di fumo** smoke ring
spirare *tr* to send forth; (lit) to inspire, infuse; (lit) to show (*kindness*) || *intr* to blow; to emanate; to die; to expire
spirita·to -ta *adj* possessed; wild, mad
spirìti·co -ca *adj* **(-ci -che)** spiritual; spiritualistic
spiritismo *m* spiritualism
spìrito *m* spirit; wit; mind; spirits, alcohol; sprite; **bello spirito** wit (*person*); **fare dello spirito** to be witty; to crack jokes; **l'ultimo spirito** (lit) one's last breath; **spirito di corpo** esprit de corps; **spirito di parte** partisanship; **spirito sportivo** sportsmanship
spiritosàggine [s] *f* witticism
spiritó·so -sa [s] *adj* witty; alcoholic
spirituale *adj* spiritual
spìzzi·co *m* **(-chi)**—**a spizzico** or **a spizzichi** little by little; a little at a time
splendènte *adj* resplendent, shining
splèndere §281 *intr* (ESSERE & AVERE) to shine
splèndi·do -da *adj* splendid; gorgeous; bright || *m*—**fare lo splendido** to be a big spender
splendóre *m* splendor; brightness; beauty
splène *m* (anat) spleen
spòcchia *f* haughtiness
spodestare (spodèsto) *tr* to dispossess; to dethrone; to oust
spoetizzare [ddzz] *tr* to disillusion
spòglia *f* slough (*of snake*); skin (*of onion*); husk (*of corn*); (lit) body; (lit) outer garment; **sotto mentite spoglie** under false pretense; **spoglie** spoils
spogliare §280 **(spòglio)** *tr* to undress, strip; to strip of armor; to defraud, deprive; to free; to check, examine; to husk (*corn*); to go through (*e.g., correspondence*) || *ref* to undress; to slough (*said, e.g., of a snake*); **spogliarsi di** to get rid of; to divest oneself of; to shake (*a habit*)
spogliarelli·sta *f* **(-ste)** stripteaser
spogliarèllo *m* striptease
spoglia·tóio *m* **(-tói)** dressing room; locker room
spò·glio -glia (-gli -glie) *adj* stripped, bare; free || *m* cast-off clothing; sorting; scrutiny; counting (*of votes*); **di spoglio** second-hand (*material*) || *f* see **spoglia**
spòla *f* bobbin; shuttle; **fare la spola** to shuttle

spolétta *f* bobbin, spool; (mil) fuse
spolmonare (**spolmóno**) *ref* (coll) to talk, sing, or shout oneself hoarse
spolpare (**spólpo**) *tr* to gnaw (*a bone*); to eat up (*fruit*); (fig) to fleece
spolverare (**spólvero**) *tr* to dust off, whisk; to powder, dust; to pounce
spolveratura *f* dusting; powdering; sprinkling, smattering (*of knowledge*); **dare una spolveratura a** to brush up on
spolverina *f* (coll) duster
spolverino *m* duster, smock; powder-sugar duster; pounce; (coll) whisk broom
spolverizzaménto [ddzz] *m* sprinkling (*with powder*)
spolverizzare [ddzz] *tr* to dust, powder, pounce
spólvero *m* dusting; powdering; pounce; smattering, sprinkling (*of knowledge*); display
spónda *f* bank (*of river*); side; cushion (*of billiard table*)
sponsale *adj* (lit) wedding || **sponsali** *mpl* (lit) wedding
spontàne•o -a *adj* spontaneous; artless
spopolare (**spòpolo**) *tr* to depopulate || *intr* to be a hit; to become depopulated or deserted
spoppare (**spóppo**) *tr* to wean
sporàdi•co -ca *adj* (**-ci -che**) sporadic
sporcacció•ne -na *adj* filthy || *mf* filthy person; (fig) dirty mouth
sporcare §197 (**spòrco**) *tr* to dirty; to soil || *ref* to get dirty; to soil oneself; **sporcarsi la fedina** (coll) to get a black mark on one's record
sporcìzia *f* dirt, filth
spòr•co -ca (-chi -che) *adj* dirty, filthy; foul; **farla sporca** to pull a dirty trick || *m* dirt, filth
sporgènte *adj* leaning; protruding; beetle (*brow*)
sporgènza *f* prominence, projection
spòrgere §217 *tr* to stick out; to stretch out; to lodge (*a complaint*) || *intr* (ESSERE) to project, jut out || *ref* to lean out
spòrt *m* (**spòrt**) sport; game; **per sport** for fun, for pleasure
spòrta *f* shopping bag; bagful; basket; basketful; shopping; **a sporta** wide-brimmed (*hat*)
sportèllo *m* door; panel; window (*in bank, station, etc.*); wicket; branch (*of a bank*); (theat) box office
sportivi•tà *f* (**-tà**) sportsmanship
sporti•vo -va *adj* sporting; sportsmanlike; athletic || *m* sportsman
spòr•to -ta *adj* projecting; jutting out || *m* projection; removable shutter (*on store door or window*) || *f* see **sporta**
spòsa *f* bride; wife; **andare in sposa a** to get married to; **sposa promessa** fiancée
sposalì•zio -zia (-zi -zie) *adj* (lit) nuptial || *m* wedding
sposare (**spòso**) *tr* to marry; to unite; to embrace (*a cause*); to fit perfectly; to give in marriage || *ref* to get married, marry
spòso *m* bridegroom; **sposi** newlyweds
spossare (**spòsso**) *tr* to exhaust || *ref* to become worn out
spossatézza *f* exhaustion
spostaménto *m* shift; movement; displacement; change
spostare (**spòsto**) *tr* to move; to change, shift; to upset || *ref* to move; to shift; to get out of place; to be upset
sposta•to -ta *adj* ill-adjusted, out of place || *mf* misfit
spran•ga *f* (**-ghe**) bar, crossbar
sprangare §209 *tr* to bar, bolt
sprazzo *m* spray; flash; burst
sprecare §197 (**sprèco**) *tr* to waste; to miss (*an opportunity*) || *ref* to waste one's efforts
sprè•co *m* (**-chi**) waste; squandering
sprecó•ne -na *adj & mf* spendthrift
spregévole *adj* contemptible, despicable
spregiare §290 (**sprègio**) *tr* to despise
sprè•gio *m* (**-gi**) contempt, scorn
spregiudica•to -ta *adj* open-minded, unbiased || *m* open-minded person
sprèmere §123 *tr* to squeeze, press; **spremere le lacrime a** to move to tears || *ref*—**spremersi il cervello** to rack one's brain
spremifrut•ta *m* (**-ta**) squeezer
spremilimó•ni *m* (**-ni**) lemon squeezer
spremuta *f* squeezing; **spremuta d'arancia** orange juice
spretare (**sprèto**) *ref* to doff the cassock
sprezzante *adj* contemptuous, haughty
sprezzare (**sprèzzo**) *tr* (lit) to despise
sprèzzo *m* disdain, contempt
sprigionare (**sprigióno**) *tr* to exhale, emit; to free from prison || *ref* to free oneself; to escape, come forth, issue (*said, e.g., of steam*)
sprimacciare §128 *tr* to beat, fluff (*e.g., a pillow*)
sprizzare *tr* to spout; to sparkle with (*joy, health*) || *intr* (ESSERE) to spurt; to fly (*said of sparks*); to sparkle
sprizzo *m* sprinkle; spurt; spark
sprofondare (**sprofóndo**) *tr* to send to the bottom; to destroy, ruin; to sink || *intr* (ESSERE) to sink; to founder; to cave in; to be sunk (*e.g., in meditation*)
sprolò•quio *m* (**-qui**) long rigmarole
spronare (**spróno**) *tr* to spur, goad
spróne *m* spur; prodding; example; guimpe; buttress; abutment (*of bridge*); **a sprone battuto** at full speed; at once; **dar di sprone a** to spur on; **sprone di cavaliere** (bot) rocket larkspur
sproporziona•to -ta *adj* out of proportion, disproportionate
sproporzióne *f* disproportion
sproposita•to -ta *adj* out of proportion; excessive; gross (*error*)
spropòsito *m* blunder, gross error; excessive amount; **a sproposito** out of place; inopportunely
sprovvedu•to -ta *adj* deprived; brainless, witless
sprovvi•sto -sta *adj* deprived; devoid, lacking; **alla sprovvista** suddenly; unawares, off guard

spruzzabianche•rìa *m* **(-rìa)** sprinkler (*to sprinkle clothes*)
spruzzare *tr* to sprinkle, spray; to powder (*sugar*)
spruzzatóre *m* sprayer; (aut) nozzle (*of carburetor*)
spruzzo *m* spray; splash (*of mud*)
spudora•to -ta *adj* shameless; impudent
spugna *f* sponge; **dare un colpo di spugna** to wipe the slate clean; **gettare la spugna** to throw in the towel
spugnare *tr* to sponge; to swab
spugnatura *f* sponge bath
spugnó•so -sa [s] *adj* spongy
spulciare §128 *tr* to pick the fleas off; to scrutinize, examine minutely
spuma *f* foam, froth
spumante *adj* sparkling ‖ *m* sparkling wine; champagne
spumare *intr* to froth
spumeggiante *adj* sparkling; vaporous; foamy
spumeggiare §290 **(spuméggio)** *intr* to foam
spumóne *m* spumoni
spumó•so -sa [s] *adj* foamy, frothy
spunta *f* check; check list; check mark
spuntare *tr* to blunt; to unpin; to overcome; to clip, trim; to check off; **spuntarla** to come out on top; to overcome ‖ *intr* (ESSERE) to appear; to sprout; to rise; to well up (*said of tears*); to pop out; to break through ‖ *ref* to become blunt; to die down
spuntino *m* bite, snack; **fare uno spuntino** to have a bite
spunto *m* sourness (*of wine*); (theat) cue; (sports) sprint; (fig) starting point, origin
spuntóne *m* spike; pike; crag
spurgare §209 *tr* to purge, clear; to clean up ‖ *ref* to expectorate
spur•go *m* **(-ghi)** discharge; reject (*e.g., book*)
spù•rio -ria *adj* **(-ri -rie)** spurious
sputacchiare §287 *tr* to spit upon ‖ *intr* to sputter
sputacchièra *f* spittoon, cuspidor
sputare *tr* to spit; to cough up; (fig) to spew (*venom*); **sputare sangue** to spit blood; (fig) to sweat blood ‖ *intr* to spit
sputasentènze *mf* **(-ze)** wiseacre
sputo *m* spit, sputum; spitting
squadernare (squadèrno) *tr* to leaf through; **squadernare qlco a qlcu** to put s.th under the nose of s.o. ‖ *ref* to come apart (*said of a book*)
squadra *f* square (*for measuring right angles*); squad, group; (mil) squadron; (sports) team; **a squadra** at right angles; **fuori squadra** out of kilter; **squadra di pompieri** fire company; **squadra mobile** flying squad
squadrare *tr* to square; (fig) to examine, study
squadrìglia *f* (aer, nav) squadron
squadróne *m* squadron (*of cavalry*)
squagliare §280 *tr* to melt ‖ *ref* to melt; **squagliarsela** to take French leave
squalìfi•ca *f* **(-che)** disqualification
squalificare §197 **(squalìfico)** *tr* to disqualify ‖ *ref* to disqualify oneself; to prove to be unqualified
squàlli•do -da *adj* wretched, dreary, gloomy; faint (*smile*); (lit) emaciated
squallóre *m* wretchedness, dreariness, gloominess
squalo *m* shark
squama *f* scurf (*shed by the skin*); (bot, pathol, zool) scale
squamare *tr & ref* to scale
squamó•so -sa [s] *adj* scaly
squarciagóla *adv*—**a squarciagola** at the top of one's voice
squarciare §128 *tr* to rend, tear apart; to dispel (*a doubt*) ‖ *ref* to become torn; to open
squàr•cio *m* **(-ci)** tear, rip; passage (*of book*)
squartare *tr* to quarter
squartatura *f* quartering
squassare *tr* to shake violently; to wreck
squattrina•to -ta *adj* penniless ‖ *m* pauper
squilibra•to -ta *adj* unbalanced, deranged ‖ *mf* mad or insane person
squilì•brio *m* **(-bri)** lack of balance; **squilibrio mentale** insanity; unbalanced mental condition
squillante *adj* ringing, shrill; sharp
squillare *intr* to ring; to ring out; to blare
squillo *m* ring; peal; blare, blast (*of horn*); ‖ *f* call girl
squinternare (squintèrno) *tr* to tear (*a book*) to pieces; (fig) to upset
squisi•to -ta *adj* exquisite
squittire §176 *intr* to squeak; to squeal
sradicare §197 **(sràdico)** *tr* to uproot; to eradicate; to pull (*a tooth*)
sragionare (sragióno) *intr* to talk nonsense
sregola•to -ta *adj* intemperate; dissolute
srotolare (sròtolo) *tr* to unroll
stàb•bio *m* **(-bi)** pen; manure, dung
stabbiòlo *m* pigpen
stàbile *adj* stable; real (*estate*); permanent; stock (*company*) ‖ *m* building
stabiliménto *m* plant, factory; establishment; settlement, colony; conclusion (*of a deal*)
stabilire §176 *tr* to establish; to decide ‖ *ref* to settle
stabili•tà *f* **(-tà)** stability, steadiness
stabilito *m* (law) agreement of sale (*drawn up by a broker*)
stabilizzare [ddzz] *tr & ref* to stabilize
stabilizza•tóre -trice [ddzz] *mf* stabilizing person ‖ *m* (aer) stabilizer; (elec) voltage stabilizer
staccare §197 *tr* to detach; to unhitch; to outdistance; to draw (*a check*); to tear off; to take (*one's eyes*) away; to begin; to enunciate (*words*) ‖ *intr* to stand out; (coll) to stop working ‖ *ref* to come off; **staccarsi da** to come off (*e.g., the wall*); to leave (*one's home; the shore*); (aer) to take off from
stacciare §128 *tr* to sift, sieve

stàc·cio *m* (**-ci**) sieve
staccionata *f* fence; hurdle; stockade
stac·co *m* (**-chi**) tearing off; cut of cloth (*for a suit*); interval; **fare stacco** to stand out
stadèra *f* steelyard; **stadera a ponte** weighbridge
stàdia *f* leveling rod
stà·dio *m* (**-di**) stadium; stage
staffa *f* stirrup; heel (*of sock*); gaiter strap; clamp; (mach) bracket; **perdere le staffe** to lose one's nerve
staffétta *f* courier, messenger; pilot (*car*); **a staffetta** relay
staffière *m* groom, footman; servant
staffilare *tr* to whip, belt, lash
staffilata *f* lash
staffile *m* stirrup strap; whip
stàg·gio *m* (**-gi**) stay, upright
stagionale *adj* seasonal || *mf* seasonal worker
stagionare (**stagióno**) *tr* to season, cure
stagiona·to -ta *adj* seasoned, ripe
stagióne *f* season; **da mezza stagione** spring-and-fall (*coat*); **di fine stagione** year-end (*sale*)
stagliare §280 *tr* to hack || *ref* to stand out
staglia·to -ta *adj* sheer (*cliff*)
sta·gnàio *m* (**-gnài**) tinsmith; plumber
stagnante *adj* stagnant
stagnare *tr* to tin; to solder; to stanch || *intr* to stagnate
stagnaro *m* var of **stagnaio**
stagnina *f* tin can
stagnino *m* (coll) var of **stagnaio**
sta·gno -gna *adj* watertight; airtight || *m* tin; pond, pool
stagnòla *f* tin foil; tin can
stàio *m* (**stài**) bushel (*container*); **a staio** (coll) top (*hat*) || *m* (**stàia** *fpl*) bushel (*measure*); **a staia** in abundance
stalla *f* stable
stallìa *f* (com) lay day
stallière *m* stableman, stableboy
stallo *m* seat; stall; (chess) stalemate
stallóne *m* stallion
stamane, stamani or **stamattina** *adv* this morning
stambéc·co *m* (**-chi**) ibex
stambèr·ga *f* (**-ghe**) hovel
stambù·gio *m* (**-gi**) hole, hovel
stamburare *tr* to puff up, to boast about || *intr* to drum
stame *m* (bot) stamen; thread, yarn
stamigna *f* cheesecloth
stampa *f* printing; print; (fig) print; (fig) mold; **stampe** printed matter
stampàg·gio *m* (**-gi**) (mach) stamping
stampare *tr* to stamp; to print; to impress; to publish || *ref* (fig) to be ingraved
stampatèllo *m*—**in stampatello** in block letters; **scrivere in stampatello** to print (*with pen or pencil*)
stampa·to -ta *adj* printed; impressed || *m* printed form; **stampati** printed matter
stampa·tóre -trice *mf* printer
stampèlla *f* crutch
stamperìa *f* print shop
stampìglia *f* rubber stamp; billboard; overprint
stampigliare §280 *tr* to stamp; to overprint
stampinare *tr* to stencil
stampino *m* stencil
stampo *m* mold; stencil; stamp, kind; decoy
stanare *tr* to flush (*game*); (fig) to dig up
stancare §197 *tr* to tire, fatigue; to bore || *ref* to tire, weary
stanchézza *f* tiredness, weariness
stan·co -ca *adj* (**-chi -che**) tired; tired out; (lit) left (*hand*)
standardizzare [ddzz] *tr* to standardize
stan·ga *f* (**-ghe**) bar; shaft (*of cart*); beam (*of plow*)
stangata *f* blow
stanghétta *f* small bar; bolt (*of lock*); temple (*of spectacles*); (mus) bar
stanòtte *adv* tonight; last night
stante *adj* being; standing; **a sé stante** by itself, independent || *prep* because of; **stante che** since
stan·tìo -tìa *adj* (**-tìi; -tìe**) stale; musty
stantuffo *m* piston; plunger
stanza *f* room; stanza; **essere di stanza** (mil) to be stationed; **stanza da bagno** bath room; **stanza di compensazione** clearing house; **stanza di soggiorno** living room
stanziare §287 *tr* to allocate; to appropriate; to budget || *ref* to settle
stanzino *m* small room; closet
stappare *tr* to uncork
stare §263 *intr* (ESSERE) to stay; to stand; to live; to be; to be located; to linger; to last; to stick (*e.g., to a rule*); (poker) to stand pat; **come sta?** how are you?; **lasciar stare** to leave alone; **lasciar stare che** to leave aside that; **non stare in sé dalla gioia** to be beside oneself with joy; **sta bene!** O.K.!; **starci** to fit, e.g., **ci stanno trecento persone** three hundred people fit there; **starci di** to be in favor of, e.g., **io ci starei d'andare al cine** I would be in favor of going to the movies; **stare** + *ger* to be + *ger*, e.g., **stava leggendo** he was reading; **stare a** to be up to; to stand on (*ceremony*); to base oneself on; to take (*a joke*); to cost, e.g., **a quanto sta il prosciutto?** how much does the ham cost?; **stare a** + *inf* to keep + *ger*, e.g., **stai sempre a sognare** you always keep dreaming; to take + *inf*, e.g., **stette poco a decidere** he took little time to decide; **stare a cuore** (with *dat*) to deem important, e.g., **gli sta a cuore il lavoro** he deems his work important; **stare a pancia all'aria** to not do a stroke of work; **stare al proprio posto** to keep one's place; **stare a segno** to behave properly; **stare a vedere** to be possible, e.g., **sta a vedere che non viene?** could it be possible that he won't come?; **stare bene** to be well; to be well-off; (with *dat*) to fit, to become, e.g., **questo vestito gli sta**

bene this suit fits him well, this suit becomes him; to serve right, e.g., **gli sta bene!** it serves him right!; **stare comodo** to be at ease; to remain seated; **stare con** (fig) to be on the side of; **starsene** to stay apart, e.g., **se ne sta solo soletto** he stays apart or all alone; **stare fermo** to be quiet; to not move; **stare in forse** to doubt; to be doubtful; **stare sulle proprie** to stand aloof; **stare su** to stand erect; **stare su tardi** to stay up late; **stia comodo!** remain seated!

starna *f* gray partridge

starnazzare *intr* to flap its wings; to flutter; to cackle

starnutare *intr* to sneeze

starnuto *m* sneeze

stasare [s] *tr* to unplug, unblock

staséra [s] *adv* tonight, this evening

sta•si *f* (**-si**) (com) stagnation; (pathol) stasis

statale *adj* government; state ‖ *mf* government employee

stàti•co -ca (**-ci -che**) static ‖ *f* statics

stati•no -na *adj* (coll) migratory ‖ *m* itemized list; (educ) registration form

stati•sta *m* (**-sti**) statesman

statìsti•co -ca (**-ci -che**) *adj* statistical ‖ *m* statistician ‖ *f* statistics; **fare una statistica (di)** to survey; **statistiche** statistics (*data*)

stati•vo -va *adj* nonmigratory; permanent ‖ *m* stand (*of microscope*)

stato *m* state; condition; plight; frame (*of mind*); status; estate (*social class*); **di stato** public (*e.g., school*); **essere in stato di arresto** to be under arrest; **stati** extracts from vital statistics; **Stati Pontifici** Papal States; **Stati Uniti** United States; **stato civile** marital status; vital statistics; **stato confessionale** state under ecclesiastical rule; **stato cuscinetto** buffer state; **stato di preallarme** state of emergency; **stato di previsione** preliminary budget; **stato interessante** pregnancy; **stato maggiore** (mil) general staff

statoreattóre *m* ramjet engine

stàtua *f* statue

statuà•rio -ria (**-ri -rie**) *adj* statuary; statuesque ‖ *m* sculptor

statunitènse *adj* & *mf* American (*U.S.A.*)

statura *f* stature; height

statuto *m* statute

stavòlta *adv* (coll) this time

stazionaménto *m* parking; **stazionamento vietato** no parking

stazionare (**staziόno**) *intr* to park

stazionà•rio -ria *adj* (**-ri -rie**) stationary

staziόne *f* station; bearing, posture; **stazione balneare** shore resort; **stazione climatica** health resort, spa; **stazione di rifornimento** service station; **stazione di tassametri** cab stand; **stazione estiva** summer resort; **stazione generatrice** power plant; **stazione orbitale** orbiting station; **stazione sanitaria** clinic

stazza *f* tonnage; (naut) displacement

stazzare *tr* (naut) to gauge; (naut) to displace

stazzonare (**stazzόno**) *tr* to crumple

steatite *f* French chalk

stéc•ca *f* (**-che**) small stick; slat (*of shutter*); rib (*of umbrella*); bone (*of whale*); carton (*of cigarettes*); rail (*of fence*); letter opener; chisel (*of sculptor*); (billiards) cue; (billiards) miscue; (surg) splint; **fare una stecca** (billiards) to miscue; (mus) to sing or play a sour note

steccadèn•ti *m* (**-ti**) (coll) toothpick

steccare §197 (**stécco**) *tr* to fence; to put in a splint ‖ *intr* to play or sing a sour note; (billiards) to miscue

steccato *m* fence; (racing) inside track

stecchétto *m* small stick; **tenere a stecchetto** to keep on a strict diet; to keep short of money

stecchino *m* toothpick

stecchi•to -ta *adj* stiff; lean, lank; dry (*twig*); dumfounded

stéc•co *m* (**-chi**) stick, twig

stecconata *f* stockade; fence

stélla *f* star; rowel (*of spur*); speck of fat (*in soup*); (fig) sky; **a stella** star-shaped; stellar; **montare alle stelle** to be sky-high (*said, e.g., of prices*); **portare alle stelle** to praise to the skies; **stella alpina** edelweiss; **stella cadente** shooting star; **stella di mare** starfish; **stella filante** shooting star; confetti; **stella polare** polestar, lodestar

stellare *adj* stellar; (mach) radial ‖ *v* (**stéllo**) *tr* to spangle with stars; to stud

stella•to -ta *adj* starry; star-spangled; star-shaped; studded

stellétta *f* (mil) star; (typ) asterisk; **guadagnarsi le stellette** (mil) to earn a promotion; **portare le stellette** (mil) to be in the service

stellina *f* starlet

stelloncino *m* (journ) short paragraph

stèlo *m* stem, stalk

stèm•ma *m* (**-mi**) coat of arms; genealogy (*of a manuscript*)

stemperare (**stèmpero**) *tr* to dilute; to blunt; to untemper; (lit) to waste ‖ *ref* to melt; to become dull or blunt

stendardo *m* banner, standard

stèndere §270 *tr* to stretch; to hang up (*laundry*); to spread; to draw up (*a document*); (mil) to deploy; **stendere a terra** to knock down ‖ *ref* to stretch out

stendibianche•rìa *m* (**-rìa**) clothes rack, clotheshorse

stenodattilògra•fo -fa *mf* shorthand typist

stenografare (**stenògrafo**) *tr* to take down in shorthand

stenografìa *f* shorthand, stenography

stenogràfi•co -ca *adj* (**-ci -che**) stenographic, shorthand

stenògra•fo -fa *mf* stenographer

stenòsi *f* (pathol) stricture

stenotipìa *f* stenotypy

stentare (**stènto**) *tr* to eke out (*a living*)

|| *intr* to barely make ends meet; **stentare a** to hardly be able to; to find it hard to
stenta·to -ta *adj* hard; stunted; strained (*smile*)
stènto *m* privation; hardship; **a stento** hardly; with difficulty; **senza stento** without any trouble
stèr·co *m* (**-chi**) dung
stereofòni·co -ca *adj* (**-ci -che**) stereo, stereophonic
stereoscòpi·co -ca *adj* (**-ci -che**) stereoscopic
stereoscò·pio *m* (**-pi**) stereoscope
stereotipa·to -ta *adj* stereotyped
sterilizzare [ddzz] *tr* to sterilize
sterlina *f* pound sterling
sterminare (**stèrmino**) *tr* to exterminate
sterminа·to -ta *adj* immense, boundless
stermì·nio *m* (**-ni**) extermination; (coll) large amount, lots
stèrno *m* breastbone
sterpàglia *f* brushwood; undergrowth
stèrpo *m* dry twig; bramble
sterrare (**stèrro**) *tr* to excavate
sterratóre *m* digger
sterzare (**stèrzo**) *tr* to diminish by one third; to thin out (*woodland*); (aut) to steer || *intr* to swerve
sterzata *f* swerve
stèrzo *m* handle bar; (aut) steering gear; (aut) steering wheel
stésa [s] *f* coat (*of paint*); string (*of clothes on line*)
stés·so -sa *adj* same, e.g., **lo stesso mese** the same month; very, e.g., **tuo fratello stesso** your very brother; **essere alle stesse** to be just the same; **io stesso** I myself; **lui stesso** he himself, etc.; **per sé stesso** by himself; by itself || *pron* same; same thing; **fa lo stesso** it's all the same, it makes no difference
stesura [s] *f* drawing up (*of a contract*); **prima stesura** first draft
stetoscò·pio *m* (**-pi**) stethoscope
stìa *f* chicken coop
Stige *m* Styx
stì·gio -gia *adj* (**-gi -gie**) Stygian
stìgmate *fpl* stigmata
stilare *tr* to draft properly
stile *m* style
stilè *adj invar* stylish
stilétto *m* dagger, stiletto
stilizzare [ddzz] *tr* to stylize
stilla *f* (lit) drop, droplet
stillare *tr* to exude; to distill || *intr* (ESSERE) to ooze, drip, exude || *ref*—**stillarsi il cervello** to rack one's brains
stillicì·dio *m* (**-di**) dripping; repetition
stilo *m* stylus; arm (*of steelyard*); dagger; gnomon (*of sundial*); (poet) style || *f* (coll) fountain pen
stilogràfi·ca *f* (**-che**) fountain pen
stima *f* appraisal; esteem; (naut) dead reckoning; **a stima d'occhio** more or less
stimare *tr* to estimate; to deem; to esteem || *ref* (coll) to think a lot of oneself
stima·tóre -trice *mf* appraiser; admirer
stìmmate *fpl* var of **stigmate**
stimolante *adj* & *m* stimulant
stimolare (**stìmolo**) *tr* to stimulate
stìmolo *m* influence; stimulus
stin·co *m* (**-chi**) shinbone; shin; **stinco di santo** saintly person, saint; **rompere gli stinchi a** to annoy
stìngere §126 *tr, intr* (ESSERE) & *ref* to fade
stipa *f* kindling wood, brushwood
stipare *tr* & *ref* to crowd, jam
stipendiare §287 (**stipèndio**) *tr* to employ, hire; to pay a salary to
stipendia·to -ta *adj* salaried || *mf* salaried person
stipèn·dio *m* (**-di**) pay, salary
stipétto *m* (naut) closet, cabinet
stìpite *m* jamb; stock, family; (bot) trunk (*of palm tree*)
stipo *m* cabinet
stipulare (**stìpulo**) *tr* to draw up (*a contract*); to stipulate
stiracchiare §287 *tr* to stretch; to eke out (*a living*); to twist (*a meaning*); to haggle over || *intr* to haggle; to economize || *ref* to stretch out
stirare *tr* to stretch; to iron, press || *intr* to iron || *ref* to stretch out
stira·tóre -trice *mf* ironer, presser
stiratura *f* ironing; stretching
stirerìa *f* ironing shop
stiro *m*—**ferro da stiro** see **ferro**
stirpe *f* family; birth, origin
stitichézza *f* constipation
stìti·co -ca *adj* (**-ci -che**) constipated; (fig) tight
stiva *f* (naut) hold; (lit) beam (*of plow*)
stivàg·gio *m* **-gi**) stowage
stivale *m* boot; **dei miei stivali** good-for-nothing; **lustrare gli stivali a qlcu** to lick s.o.'s boots
stivalétto *m* high shoe
stivalóne *m* boot; **stivaloni da equitazione** riding boots; **stivaloni da palude** hip boots
stivare *tr* to stow
stivatóre *m* stevedore
stizza *f* anger; irritation
stizzire §176 *tr* to anger, vex || *ref* to get angry
stizzó·so -sa [s] *adj* peevish, irritable
stoccafisso *m* stockfish
stoccata *f* thrust (*with dagger or rapier*); dig, sarcastic remark; touch (*for money*)
stòc·co *m* (**-chi**) dagger; rapier; stalk (*of corn*)
Stoccólma *f* Stockholm
stòffa *f* cloth, material; (fig) stuff, makings
stoicismo *m* stoicism
stòi·co -ca (**-ci -che**) *adj* stoic, stoical || *m* stoic; Stoic
stoino *m* doormat
stòla *f* stole
stòli·do -da *adj* foolish, silly
stoltézza *f* foolishness, silliness
stól·to -ta *adj* silly || *mf* fool
stomacare §197 (**stòmaco**) *tr* to disgust; to nauseate
stomachévole *adj* disgusting, sickening

stòma·co *m* (**-ci** or **-chi**) stomach; maw (*of animal*); **dare di stomaco** to vomit
stonare (**stòno**) *tr* to sing or play out of tune; to upset || *intr* to sing or play out of tune; to be out of place; to not harmonize
stona·to -ta *adj* out-of-tune; upset; clashing (*color*)
stonatura *f* jarring sound; clash (*of colors*); lack of harmony
stóppa *f* tow; oakum; **di stoppa** flaxen; weak, trembling; **stoppa incatramata** oakum
stoppàc·cio *m* (**-ci**) wad
stóppie *fpl* stubble
stoppino *m* wick
stoppó·so -sa [s] *adj* stubby; stringy
stórcere §272 *tr* to twist; to twitch; to wrench (*one's ankle*); to roll (*one's eyes*) || *ref* to twist; to writhe; to bend
stordiménto *m* bewilderment; dizziness
stordire §176 *tr* to bewilder; to daze || *intr* to be bewildered || *ref* to dull one's senses
storditàggine *f* carelessness; mistake, blunder
stordi·to -ta *adj* careless; bewildered; amazed; dizzy || *mf* scatterbrain
stòria *f* history; story, tale; fact; **fare storie** to stand on ceremony; **un'altra storia** a horse of another color
stòri·co -ca (**-ci -che**) *adj* historical || *m* historian
storièlla *f* tale, short story; joke
storiografia *f* historiography
storióne *m* sturgeon
stormire §176 *intr* to rustle
stórmo *m* swarm, flock; (aer) group
stornare (**stórno**) *tr* to ward off; to dissuade; to divert (*funds*); to write off (*as noncollectable*)
stornèllo *m* Italian folksong; (orn) starling
stór·no -na *adj* dapple-gray || *m* (com) transfer; (orn) starling
storpiare §287 (**stòrpio**) *tr* to cripple; to clip (*one's words*)
stòr·pio -pia (**-pi -pie**) *adj* crippled || *m* cripple
stòr·to -ta *adj* twisted; crooked; crippled || *f* twist; dislocation; retort
stovìglie *fpl* dishes; **lavare le stoviglie** to wash the dishes
stra- *pref adj* extra-, e.g., **straordinario** extraordinary; over-, e.g., **stracarico** overloaded
stràbi·co -ca *adj* (**-ci -che**) crosseyed
strabiliante *adj* astonishing, amazing
strabiliare §287 *tr* to amaze || *intr* & *ref* to be amazed
strabismo *m* strabismus, squint
straboccare §197 (**strabócco**) *intr* to overflow
strabocchévole *adj* overflowing
strabuzzare [ddzz] *tr* (coll) to roll (*one's eyes*)
stracàri·co -ca *adj* (**-chi -che**) overloaded, overburdened
stracca *f*—**pigliare una stracca** to be dead tired
straccale *m* breeching (*of harness*); **straccali** (coll) suspenders
straccare §197 *tr* (coll) to tire
stracciaiò·lo -la *mf* ragpicker
stracciare §128 *tr* to tear, rend; to comb (*natural silk*)
stràc·cio -cia (**-ci -ce**) *adj* torn, in rags; waste (*paper*) || *m* rag, tatter; tear, rend; combed silk
stracció·ne -na *mf* tatterdemalion
straccivéndo·lo -la *mf* ragpicker; rag dealer
strac·co -ca *adj* (**-chi -che**) tired; worn-out; **alla stracca** lazily || *f* see **stracca**
stracòt·to -ta *adj* overcooked, overdone || *m* stew
stracuòcere §144a *tr* to overcook, overdo
strada *f* roadway; street; **da strada** vulgar, common; **divorare la strada** to burn up the road; **essere in mezzo a una strada** to be in a bad way; **fare strada a** to pave the way for; **farsi strada** to make one's way; **prender la strada** to set forth; **strada carrozzabile** carriage road; **strada dell'orto** easy way out; **strada ferrata** railroad; **strada maestra** main road; **tagliare la strada a** to stand in the way of; (aut) to cut in front of
stradale *adj* road; street; traffic (*e.g., accident*); highway (*police*) || *m* avenue || *f* highway patrol
stradà·rio *m* (**-ri**) street directory
strafalcióne *m* blunder, gross error
strafare §173 *tr* to overdo; to overcook
strafóro *m* drilled hole; **di straforo** stealthily
strafottènte *adj* unconcerned, nonchalant; arrogant, impudent
strafottènza *f* nonchalance, unconcern; arrogance, impudence
strage *f* butchery, massacre, carnage; (coll) multitude, lot
stragrande *adj* enormous, huge
stralciare §128 *tr* to prune, trim (*grapevines*); to eliminate, remove; (com) to liquidate
stràl·cio *adj invar* interim; emergency (*e.g., law*); liquidating || *m* (**-ci**) excerpt; clearance sale; **a stralcio** at a bargain
strale *m* (lit) arrow
strallo *m* (naut) stay
stralunare *tr* to roll (*one's eyes*)
straluna·to -ta *adj* upset; wild-eyed
stramazzare *tr* to fell || *intr* (ESSERE) to fall down
stramazzo *m* sluice; (coll) straw mattress
stramberìa *f* eccentricity
stram·bo -ba *adj* odd, queer, eccentric; crooked (*legs*); squint (*eyes*)
strame *m* litter; fodder
strampala·to -ta *adj* strange; preposterous, absurd
stranézza *f* strangeness; oddity
strangolare (**stràngolo**) *tr* to strangle; (naut) to furl
strangola·tóre -trice *mf* strangler
straniare §287 *tr* (lit) to draw away || *ref* to become estranged

straniè·ro -ra *adj* foreign, alien; (lit) strange || *mf* foreigner, alien
stra·no -na *adj* strange, odd; (lit) estranged
straordinà·rio -ria (-ri -rie) *adj* extraordinary; extra || *mf* temporary employee || *m* overtime
strapagare §209 *tr* to overpay; to pay too much for
strapazzare *tr* to rebuke, upbraid; to mishandle; to bungle || *ref* to overwork oneself
strapazza·to -ta *adj* crumpled; bungled; scrambled (*eggs*); overworked || *f* upbraiding, rebuke; fatigue
strapazzo *m* misuse; fatigue; excess; **da strapazzo** working (*clothes*); hackneyed, second-rate
straperdere §212 *tr & intr* to lose hopelessly || *intr* to be wiped out
strapiè·no -na *adj* chock-full
strapiombare (strapiómbo) *intr* to overhang, jut out
strapiómbo *m* overhang; **a strapiombo** sheer (*cliff*)
strapotènte *adj* overpowerful
strappare *tr* to pull; to tear, rend; to wring (*s.o.'s heart*); **strappare le lacrime a qlcu** to move s.o. to tears; **strappare qlco a qlcu** to pry s.th out of s.o.; to snatch s.th from s.o. || *ref* to tear (*e.g., one's hair*)
strappata *f* pull, tug, snatch
strappo *m* pull; tear, rip; infraction, breach; pulling away (*on a bicycle*); patch (*of sky*); **a strappi** in jerks; **strappo muscolare** pulled muscle; sprain
strapuntino *m* folding seat, jump seat; bucket seat; (naut) mattress
straric·co -ca *adj* (**-chi -che**) (coll) immensely rich
straripare *intr* (ESSERE & AVERE) to overflow
strascicare §197 (stràscico) *tr* to drag; to shuffle; **strascicare le parole** to drawl
strascichì·o *m* (**-i**) shuffle (*of feet*)
stràsci·co *m* (**-chi**) train (*of skirt*); trail; sequel, aftermath; **a strascico** dragging
strascinare (stràscino) *tr* to drag || *ref* to drag oneself, drag
strascinì·o *m* (**-i**) shuffle
stràscino *m* dragnet, trawl
stratagèm·ma *m* (**-mi**) stratagem
strategìa *f* strategy
stratègi·co -ca *adj* (**-ci -che**) strategic
stratè·go *m* (**-ghi**) strategist; general, commander
stratificare §197 (stratìfico) *tr* to stratify
strato *m* layer; coat, coating; stratum; (meteor) stratus
stratosfèra *f* stratosphere
strattóne *m* jerk, tug
stravagante *adj* extravagant; whimsical, capricious || *mf* eccentric
stravèc·chio -chia *adj* (**-chi -chie**) aged (*cheese, wine, etc.*); very old
stravìncere §285 *tr* to overpower
straviziare §287 *intr* to be intemperate
stravì·zio *m* (**-zi**) intemperance, excess
stravòlgere §289 *tr* to roll (*the eyes*); to distort; to derange
straziante *adj* heartbreaking; excruciating (*pain*); horrible
straziare §287 *tr* to torture; to dismay; to mangle; to murder (*a language*)
strazia·to -ta *adj* torn, stricken
strà·zio *m* (**-zi**) suffering, pain; torture; shame; boredom; **fare strazio di** to squander
stré·ga *f* (**-ghe**) witch; sorceress
stregare §209 (strégo) *tr* to bewitch
stregóne *m* sorcerer; witch doctor
stregonerìa *f* witchcraft; sorcery
strègua *f* standard, criterion; **alla stregua di** on the basis of
strema·to -ta *adj* exhausted
strènna *f* Christmas gift, New Year's gift; special New Year's issue
strè·nuo -nua *adj* strenuous
strepitare (strèpito) *intr* to make a noise; to shout, make a racket
strèpito *m* noise, racket; **fare strepito** to make a hit
strepitó·so -sa [s] *adj* loud, noisy; resounding (*success*)
streptomicina *f* streptomycin
stressa·to -ta *adj* under stress
strétta *f* grasp, clench; tightening (*of brakes*); hold; press, crush; pang; mountain pass; **mettere alle strette** to drive into a corner; **stretta dei conti** rendering of accounts; **stretta di mano** handshake; **stretta finale** climax
strettézza *f* narrowness; **strettezze** straits, hardship
strét·to -ta *adj* narrow; tight; bare (*necessities*); pure (*e.g., dialect*); strict; clenched (*fist*); heavy (*heart*); minimum (*price*); (phonet) close || *m* straits, narrows || *f* see **stretta** || **stretto** *adv* tightly
strettóia *f* narrow stretch; hardship; bandage
strìa *f* stripe, streak
striare §119 *tr* to stripe, streak
stricnina *f* strychnine
stridènte *adj* jarring; clashing (*colors*); strident (*sound*)
strìdere §264 *tr* to grit (*one's teeth*) || *intr* to shriek; to squeak; to creak; to clash (*said of colors*); to croak (*said of raven*); to hoot (*said of owl*); to howl (*said of wind*) || *ref* (coll) to be resigned
strido *m* (**-di & -da** *fpl*) shriek; squeak
stridóre *m* shriek; creak, squeak; gnashing (*of teeth*)
strìdu·lo -la *adj* shrill
strigare §209 *tr* to disentangle || *ref* to extricate oneself
strìglia *f* currycomb
strigliare §280 *tr* to curry; to upbraid || *ref* to groom oneself
strillare *tr* to shout; (coll) to scold; (coll) to hawk (*newspapers*) || *intr* to scream
strillo *m* shriek; shout, scream
strilló·ne -na *mf* loud-mouthed person || *m* newsdealer; newsboy, paperboy

striminzi·to -ta *adj* shrunken; tight; stunted; skinny
strimpellare (strimpèllo) *tr* to thrum; to thrum on
strinare *tr* to singe; to burn (*with a flatiron*)
strin·ga *f* (-**ghe**) lace; shoelace
stringa·to -ta *adj* terse, concise
stringere §265 *tr* to tighten; to grip; to shake, clasp (*a hand*); to drive into a corner; to squeeze; to embrace; to close (*an alliance, a deal*); to wring (*one's heart*); to clench (*the fist*); (lit) to gird (*a sword*); (mus) to accelerate; **stringere d'assedio** to besiege; **stringere i freni** to put the brakes on || *intr* to be tight; **il tempo stringe** time is running short; **stringi, stringi** at the very end, in conclusion || *ref* to squeeze close together; to shrink; to coagulate; to draw close; **stringersi a** to snuggle up to; **stringersi addosso a** to attack; **stringersi nelle spalle** to shrug one's shoulders
stringina·so [s] *m* (-**so**) pince-nez
strì·scia *f* (-**sce**) strip, band; trail; stripe; line; **a strisce** striped; **striscia d'atterramento** airstrip; **striscia di cuoio** strop
strisciante *adj* crawling; (fig) fawning
strisciare §128 *tr* to shuffle (*feet*); to graze; **strisciare una riverenza** to curtsy || *intr* to creep, crawl; to graze by || *ref* to fawn; **strisciarsi a** to rub one's back against
strisciata or **strisciatura** *f* sliding; trail
strì·scio *m* (-**sci**) rubbing; shuffling; **ballare di striscio** to shuffle; **da** or **di striscio** superficial (*wound*)
striscióne *m* festoon; festooned sign; flatterer; **striscione d'arrivo** landing (*in gymnastics*); **striscione del traguardo** (sports) tape
striscióni *adv* crawling
stritolare (strìtolo) *tr* to crush, smash
strizzalimó·ni *m*(-**ni**) lemon squeezer
strizzare *tr* to squeeze, press; to wink (*the eye*); **strizzare l'occhio** to wink
strizza·tóio *m* (-**tói**) wringer
strò·fa or **strò·fe** *f* (-**fe**) strophe
strofinàc·cio *m* (-**ci**) dust cloth
strofinare *tr* to rub; to polish || *ref* to rub oneself; to fawn
strofinata *f*—**dare una strofinata a** to give a lick and a promise to
strofinì·o *m* (-**i**) rubbing; wiping
stròla·ga *f* (-**ghe**) (orn) loon
strombatura *f* embrasure
strombazzare *tr* to glorify; **strombazzare i propri meriti** to toot one's own horn || *intr* to blast away on the trumpet
strombazza·tóre -trice *mf* show-off
strombettare (strombétto) *tr* to trumpet, toot
stroncare §197 **(strónco)** *tr* to break off; to break down; to eliminate; (fig) to criticize severely
stroncatura *f* devastating criticism
stronzio *m* strontium
strónzo *m* (vulg) turd
stropicciare §128 *tr* to rub (*hands*); to drag, shuffle (*feet*); (coll) to crumple || *ref*—**stropicciarsene** (coll) to not give a hoot
stropiccì·o *m* (-**i**) rubbing; shuffling
stròzza *f* (coll) gullet, throat
strozzare (stròzzo) *tr* to strangle; to stop up; to fleece, swindle || *ref* to choke; to narrow
strozza·to -ta *adj* choked; choking; strangulated (*hernia*)
strozzatura *f* narrowing
strozzinàg·gio *m* (-**gi**) usury
strozzino *m* usurer, loan shark
strùggere §266 *tr* to melt; to consume || *ref* to melt; to pine away; to be upset; **struggersi di** to be consumed by
struggiménto *m* melting; longing; torment
strumentale *adj* instrument (*flying*); capital (*goods*); instructional (*language, in multi-lingual regions*); (gram, mus) instrumental
strumentali·sta *mf* (-**sti -ste**) instrumentalist
strumentalizzare [ddzz] *tr* to use, take advantage of
strumentare (struménto) *tr* to orchestrate
struménto *m* instrument; tool, implement; **strumento a corda** stringed instrument; **strumento a fiato** wind instrument; **strumento di bordo** (aer) flight recorder
strusciare §128 *tr* to rub; to shuffle (*feet*); to crumple; to wear out || *ref*—**strusciarsi a** to fawn on
strutto *m* lard, shortening
struttura *f* structure
strutturare *tr* to organize, structure
struzzo *m* ostrich
stuccare §197 *tr* to putty; to stucco; to surfeit || *ref* to grow weary
stucchévole *adj* sickening
stuc·co -ca (-chi -che) *adj* bored; **stucco e ristucco** sick and tired || *m* putty; stucco; plaster of Paris; **rimanere di stucco** to be taken aback
studèn·te -téssa *mf* student
studenté·sco -sca (-schi -sche) *adj* student; student-like || *f* student body
studiare §287 *tr* to study; **studiarle tutte** to consider every angle || *intr* to study; to try || *ref* to try; to gaze at oneself
studia·to -ta *adj* affected, studied
stù·dio *m* (-**di**) study; school district; office (*of professional man*); studio; (hist) university; (lit) wish; (mus) étude; **a studio** on purpose; **essere allo studio** to be under consideration
studió·so -sa [s] *adj* studious || *m* scholar
stufa *f* stove, heater; hothouse
stufare *tr* to warm up, heat up; to stew; (coll) to bore
stufato *m* stew
stu·fo -fa *adj* (coll) bored, sick and tired || *f* see **stufa**
stuòia *f* mat; matting
stuòlo *m* throng, crowd; flock; (lit) army

stupefacènte *adj* amazing; habit-forming || *m* dope
stupefare §173 *tr* to amaze, astonish
stupefazióne *f* amazement, astonishment; stupefaction
stupèn·do -da *adj* stupendous
stupidàggine *f* stupidity; silliness; child's play, cinch
stùpi·do -da *adj* stupid; silly; (lit) amazed
stupire §176 *tr* to amaze || *ref* to be amazed
stupóre *m* amazement
stuprare *tr* to rape
stura *f* tapping; uncorking; **dar la stura a** to begin (*a speech*)
sturabottì·glie *m* (**-glie**) bottle opener
sturalavandi·ni *m* (**-ni**) plunger (*to open up clogged sink*)
sturare *tr* to uncork; to take the wax out of (*ears*); to open up (*clogged line*)
stuzzicadèn·ti *m* (**-ti**) toothpick
stuzzicare §197 (**stùzzico**) *tr* to pick (*e.g., one's teeth*); to bother; to excite, arouse; to tease; to sharpen (*appetite*)
su *adv* up; on top; upstairs; **da . . . in su** from . . . on, e.g., **dal mese scorso in su** from last month on; **di su** from upstairs; **in su** up; **metter su** to put on the fire; to instigate; **metter su bottega** to set up shop; **metter su casa** to set up housekeeping; **più su** higher; further up; **su!** come on!; let's go!; **su di** on; **su e giù** back and forth; up and down; **su per giù** more or less; **tirarsi su** to lift oneself up; to sit up; to get better, recover; **tirar su** to pick up; to grow, raise; **venir su** to grow; to come up || §4 *prep* on, upon; up; towards; over, above; onto; against; at, e.g., **sul far del giorno** at daybreak; on top of; out of, e.g., **due volte su tre** two times out of three; **mettere su superbia** to become proud; **stare sulle sue** to be reserved; **sul serio** in earnest; **su misura** made to order
suaccenna·to -ta *adj* above-mentioned
sub *m* (**sub**) (coll) skindiver
subàcque·o -a *adj* submarine
subaffittare *tr* to sublet
subaffitto *m* subletting, sublet; **prendere in subaffitto** to sublet
subaltèr·no -na *adj* & *m* subaltern; subordinate
subastare *tr* to auction off
sùbbia *f* stonecutter's chisel
subbù·glio *m* (**-gli**) turmoil, hubbub
subcosciènte *adj* & *m* subconscious
sùbdo·lo -la *adj* treacherous, deceitful
subentrare (**subéntro**) *intr* (ESSERE) (with *dat*) to succeed, follow
subire §176 *tr* to suffer; to undergo
subissare *tr* to ruin; to sink; to overwhelm || *intr* (ESSERE) to sink; to go to rack and ruin
subisso *m* ruin; (coll) lots, plenty
subitàne·o -a *adj* sudden
sùbi·to -ta *adj* (lit) sudden || *m*—**d'un subito** all of a sudden || **subito** *adv* rapidly; immediately; right away; **subito al principio** at the very beginning; **subito dopo** right after; **subito prima** right before || *interj* right away!
sublima·to -ta *adj* sublimated || *m* **sublimato corrosivo** corrosive sublimate
sublime *adj* & *m* sublime
subodorare (**subodóro**) *tr* to suspect; to get wind of
subordinare (**subórdino**) *tr* to subordinate
subordina·to -ta *adj* & *m* subordinate || *f* subordinate clause
subornare (**subórno**) *tr* to bribe
substrato *m* substratum
suburba·no -na *adj* suburban
subùr·bio *m* (**-bi**) suburb
succedàne·o -a *adj* & *m* substitute
succèdere §132 (*pp* **succeduto** or **succèsso**) *intr* (ESSERE) (with *dat*) to succede, to follow || *ref* to follow one another, follow one after the other || (*pret* **successi;** *pp* **succèsso**) *intr* (ESSERE) to happen, to come to pass; (with *dat*) to happen to, to come over, e.g., **che gli è successo?** what happened to him?
successióne *f* succession; **in successione** in succession; in a row
successi·vo -va *adj* successive; next
succèsso *m* success; outcome
successóre *m* successor
successò·rio -ria *adj* (**-ri -rie**) inheritance (*tax*)
succhiare §287 *tr* to suck
succhièllo *m* gimlet
succhiétto *m* pacifier
sùc·chio *m* (**-chi**) suck, sucking; (bot) sap; (coll) gimlet
succiaca·pre *m* (**-pre**) goatsucker, whippoorwill
succin·to -ta *adj* scanty (*clothing*); succinct, concise
suc·co *m* (**-chi**) juice; (fig) gist
succó·so -sa [s] *adj* juicy; pithy
succursale *f* branch, branch office
sud *m* south
sudafrica·no -na *adj* & *mf* South African
sudamerica·no -na *adj* & *mf* South American
sudàmina *f* prickly heat
sudare *tr* to sweat; to ooze; **sudare il pane** to earn one's living by the sweat of one's brow; **sudare sette camicie** to toil very hard || *intr* to perspire, sweat; to reek
sudà·rio *m* (**-ri**) shroud
suda·to -ta *adj* wet with perspiration; hard-earned || *f* sweat, sweating
suddét·to -ta *adj* aforesaid, above
sùddi·to -ta *adj* & *mf* subject
suddivìdere §158 *tr* to subdivide
sud-èst *m* southeast
sudicerìa *f* filth, filthiness; smut
sùdi·cio -cia (**-ci -cie**) *adj* dirty, filthy || *m* dirt, filth
sudiciume *m* dirt, filth
sudi·sta *mf* (**-sti -ste**) Southerner
sudóre *m* sweat, perspiration

sud-òvest *m* southwest
sufficiènte *adj* sufficient, adequate; self-sufficient ‖ *m* sufficient
sufficiènza *f* sufficiency; self-sufficiency; (educ) minimum passing grade
suffisso *m* suffix
suffragare §209 *tr* to support; to pray for
suffragétta *f* suffragette
suffrà·gio *m* (**-gi**) suffrage
suffumicare §197 (**suffùmico**) *tr* to fumigate
suffumi·gio *m* (**-gi**) treatment by inhalation; fumigation
suggellare (**suggèllo**) *tr* to seal
suggèllo *m* seal
suggeriménto *m* suggestion
suggerire §176 *tr* to suggest; to prompt
suggeri·tóre -trice *mf* prompter ‖ *m* (baseball) coach
suggestionàbile *adj* suggestible
suggestionare (**suggestióno**) *tr* to influence by suggestion ‖ *ref*—**suggestionarsi a** + *inf* to talk oneself into + *ger*
suggestióne *f* suggestion; fascination
suggesti·vo -va *adj* suggestive; fascinating; (law) leading (*question*)
sùghero *m* cork
sugli §4
sugna *f* fat; lard
su·go *m* (**-ghi**) juice; gravy; gist, pith; **non c'è sugo** it's no fun; there's nothing to it; **senza sugo** pointless, dull
sugó·so -sa [s] *adj* juicy
sui §4
suici·da (**-di -de**) *adj* suicidal ‖ *mf* suicide (*person*)
suicidare *ref* to commit suicide
suici·dio *m* (**-di**) suicide (*act*)
sui·no -na *adj* swinish; see **carne** ‖ *m* swine
sul §4
sulfamìdi·co -ca (**-ci -che**) *adj* sulfa ‖ *m* sulfa drug
sulla §4
sulle §4
sulli §4
sullo §4
sulloda·to -ta *adj* above-mentioned
sultano *m* sultan
summentova·to -ta, summenziona·to -ta, sunnomina·to -ta *adj* above-mentioned
sunteggiare §290 (**suntéggio**) *tr* to summarize
sunto *m* résumé, summary
suo sua §6 *adj & pron poss* (**suòi sue**)
suòcera *f* mother-in-law
suòcero *m* father-in-law; **i suoceri** the in-laws
suòla *f* sole (*of shoe*); share (*of plow*); (naut) sliding ways; (rr) flange (*of rail*)
suòlo *m* ground; soil; floor ‖ *m* (**suola** *fpl*) (coll) layer; (coll) sole (*of shoe*)
suonare (**suòno**) *tr & intr* var of **sonare**
suòno *m* sound; (fig) ring; **a suon di bastonate** with a sound thrashing; **a suon di fischi** with loud boos; **suono armonico** (mus) overtone
suòno·stère·o *m* (**-o**) stereo tape player
suòra *f* nun, sister
super- *pref adj & mf* super-, e.g., **supersonico** supersonic; over-, e.g., **superallenamento** overtraining
superaffollaménto *m* overcrowding
superare (**sùpero**) *tr* to surpass; to cross; to overcome; to pass; to exceed; (cards) to trump
supera·to -ta *adj* out-of-date, passé
supèrbia *f* pride, haughtiness; **montare in superbia** to get a swelled head
superbió·so -sa [s] *adj* proud, haughty
supèr·bo -ba *adj* proud, haughty; superb; spirited ‖ **i superbi** the haughty ones
supercarburante *m* high-octane gas
supercolòsso *m* supercolossal film
superdònna *f*—**si da arie di superdonna** she thinks she's hot stuff
supereterodina *f* superheterodyne
superficiale *adj* superficial; surface; cursory, perfunctory ‖ *m* superficial fellow
superfi·cie *f* (**-ci & cie**) surface; area; **superficie portante** airfoil
supèr·fluo -flua *adj* superfluous ‖ *m* surplus
super-ìo *m* (**-ìo**) superego
superióra *f* (eccl) mother superior
superióre *adj* superior; upper; higher; above; **superiore a** higher than; more than; larger than ‖ *m* superior
superlati·vo -va *adj & m* superlative
superlavóro *m* overwork
supermercato *m* supermarket
supersòni·co -ca *adj* (**-ci -che**) supersonic
supèrstite *adj* surviving; remaining ‖ *mf* survivor
superstizióne *f* superstition
superstizió·so -sa [s] *adj* superstitious
superstrada *f* superhighway
superuòmo *m* superman
supervisióne *f* supervision
supervisóre *m* supervisor; (mov) director
supi·no -na *adj* supine; on one's back
suppellèttile *f* furnishings; equipment; fixtures; fund (*of knowledge*)
supplementare *adj* supplementary
suppleménto *m* supplement; (mil) reinforcement
supplènte *adj & mf* substitute
supplènza *f* substitute assignment
suppleti·vo -va *adj* additional; (gram) suppletive
sùppli·ca *f* (**-che**) supplication; plea; petition
supplicante *mf* supplicant
supplicare §197 (**sùpplico**) *tr* to beseech; to plead with; to appeal to
supplichévole *adj* beseeching, imploring
supplire §176 *tr* to replace ‖ *intr* (with *dat*) to supplement, make up for
suppliziare §287 *tr* to torture; to execute
supplì·zio *m* (**-zi**) torture, torment; **estremo supplizio** capital punishment
suppórre §218 *tr* to suppose
suppòrto *m* support, prop
suppositò·rio *m* (**-ri**) suppository

supposizióne *f* supposition; presumption
suppó·sto -sta *adj* alleged || *m* supposition || *f* suppository
suppurare *intr* (ESSERE & AVERE) to suppurate
supremazìa *f* supremacy
suprè·mo -ma *adj* supreme
surclassare *tr* to outclass
surgelare (surgèlo) *tr* to quick-freeze
surreali·sta *mf* (**-sti -ste**) surrealist
surrenale *adj* adrenal (*gland*)
surrène *m* (anat) adrenal gland
surriscaldare *tr* to overheat
surrogare §209 (**surrògo**) *tr* to replace
surroga·to -ta *adj* replaceable || *m* makeshift, substitute, ersatz
suscettìbile *adj* susceptible; touchy
suscitare (sùscito) *tr* to rouse; to give rise to; to provoke
susina *f* plum
susino *m* plum tree
susseguènte *adj* subsequent, following
susseguire (susséguo) *intr* (ESSERE) (with *dat*) to follow || *ref* to follow one after the other
sussidiare §287 *tr* to subsidize
sussidià·rio -ria (-ri -rie) *adj* subsidiary; (nav) auxiliary || *m* supplementary text book; subsidiary
sussì·dio *m* (**-di**) subsidy; assistance, relief; **sussidi audiovisivi** audio-visual aids; **sussidi didattici** teaching aids; **sussidio di disoccupazione** unemployment compensation
sussiè·go *m* (**-ghi**) stiffness, haughtiness
sussistènza *f* substance; subsistence; (mil) quartermaster corps
sussìstere §114 *intr* (ESSERE & AVERE) to subsist; to be, exist
sussultare *intr* to start, jump; to quake
sussulto *m* start, jump; **sussulto di terremoto** earth tremor
sussurrare *tr* to whisper; to murmur, mutter || *intr* to whisper; to rustle || *ref*—**si sussurra** it is rumored
sussurra·-tóre -trice *mf* whisperer; grumbler
sussurrì·o *m* (**-i**) whispering; murmur; rustle
sussurro *m* whisper; murmur
susta *f* temple (*of spectacles*); (coll) spring
suvvìa *interj* come!, come on!
svagare §209 *tr* to entertain; to distract || *ref* to have a good time; to relax
svaga·to -ta *adj* absent-minded; inattentive
sva·go *m* (**-ghi**) entertainment, diversion; avocation, hobby
svaligiare §290 *tr* to ransack; to rob; to pirate
svaligia·tóre -trice *mf* thief, robber
svalutare (svàluto & svaluto) *tr* to devaluate; to depreciate; to belittle || *ref* to depreciate
svalutazióne *f* depreciation
svanire §176 *intr* (ESSERE) to evaporate; to vanish
svani·to -ta *adj* faded, evaporated; vanished; enfeebled
svantàg·gio *m* (**-gi**) disadvantage
svantaggió·so -sa [s] *adj* disadvantageous
svaporare (svapóro) *intr* (ESSERE) to evaporate; to vanish
svaria·to -ta *adj* varied; **svaria·ti -te** several
svarióne *m* blunder, gross error
svasare *tr* to transplant from a pot; to make (*e.g., a gown*) flare
svasa·to -ta *adj* bell-mouthed, flaring
svecchiare §287 (**svècchio**) *tr* to renew; to rejuvenate; to modernize
svedése [s] *adj* Swedish; safety (*match*) || *mf* Swede || *m* Swedish
svéglia *f* awakening; reveille; alarm clock; **dare la sveglia a** to wake up
svegliare §280 *tr & ref* to wake up
svegliarino *m* alarm clock; (coll) rebuke
své·glio -glia *adj* (**-gli -glie**) awake; alert || *f* see **sveglia**
svelare (svélo) *tr* to reveal; to unveil || *ref* to reveal oneself; **svelarsi per** to reveal oneself to be
svèllere §267 *tr* (lit) to eradicate
sveltézza *f* quickness; slenderness
sveltire §176 *tr* to make shrewd; to quicken, accelerate || *ref* to become smart
svèl·to -ta *adj* quick; slender; brisk; quick-witted; **alla svelta** quickly; **svelto di lingua** loose-tongued; **svelto di mano** light-fingered || **svelto** *interj* quick!
svenare (svéno) *tr* to bleed to death; (fig) to bleed || *ref* to bleed to death; (fig) to bleed oneself white
svéndere §281 *tr* to sell below cost; to undersell
svéndita *f* clearance sale
svenévole *adj* maudlin, mawkish
svenevolézza *f* maudlinness, mawkishness
sveniménto *m* faint, swoon
svenire §282 *intr* (ESSERE) to faint
sventagliare §280 *tr* to fan; to flash, display
sventagliata *f* blow with a fan; volley
sventare (svènto) *tr* to foil, thwart; (naut) to spill (*a sail*)
sventa·to -ta *adj* careless, thoughtless
svèntola *f* fan (*to kindle fire*); (coll) box, slap; **a sventola** (*ears*) that stick out
sventolare (svèntolo) *tr* to wave; to fan; to winnow || *intr* to flutter || *ref* to fan oneself
sventolì·o *m* (**-i**) fluttering, flutter
sventraménto *m* demolition; disembowelment; hernia
sventrare (svèntro) *tr* to demolish; to disembowel; to draw (*a fowl*)
sventura *f* misfortune, mishap; bad luck
sventura·to -ta *adj* unfortunate, unlucky
sverginare (svérgino) *tr* to deflower
svergognare (svergógno) *tr* to put to shame; to unmask
svergogna·to -ta *adj* shameless

svergolare (svérgolo) *tr & ref* to warp; (mach) to twist
svernare (svèrno) *intr* to winter
svérza [dz] *f* big splinter
sverzino [dz] *m* lash, whipcord
svestire (svèsto) *tr* to undress; to hull (*rice*); (fig) to strip || *ref* to undress; **svestirsi di** to shed (*e.g., leaves*)
svettare (svétto) *tr* to pollard, top || *intr* to stand out; to sway (*said of a tree*)
Svè•vo -va *adj & m* Swabian
Svèzia, la Sweden
svezzaménto *m* weaning
svezzare (svézzo) *tr* to wean; **svezzare da** to break (*s.o.*) of (*e.g., a habit*)
sviare §119 *tr* to turn aside; to lead astray || *intr & ref* to go astray; to straggle; (rr) to run off the track
svignare *intr* (ESSERE) to slip away || *ref*—**svignarsela** to sneak away
svilire §176 *tr* to devaluate
svillaneggiare §290 **(svillanéggio)** *tr* to insult, abuse
sviluppare *tr* to develop; to cause; (lit) to uncoil || *intr* (ESSERE & AVERE) & *ref* to develop; to break out (*said of fire*)
sviluppo *m* development; puberty
svincolare (svìncolo) *tr* to free; to clear (*at customs*)
svìncolo *m*—**svincolo autostradale** interchange; **svincolo doganale** customs clearance
svirilizzare [ddzz] *tr* (fig) to emasculate
svisare *tr* to alter, distort
sviscerare (svìscero) *tr* to eviscerate; to examine thoroughly || *ref*—**sviscerarsi per** to be crazy about; to bow and scrape to
sviscera•to -ta *adj* ardent, passionate; obsequious
svista *f* slip, error, oversight
svitare *tr* to unscrew
svìzze•ro -ra *adj & mf* Swiss || **la Svizzera** Switzerland
svocia•to -ta *adj* hoarse
svogliatézza *f* laziness; listlessness
svoglia•to -ta *adj* lazy; listless
svolazzare *intr* to flutter, flit
svolazzo *m* flutter; short flight; curlicue, flourish
svòlgere §289 *tr* to unwrap; to unfold; to unwind; to develop; to pursue (*an activity*); to dissuade || *ref* to unwind; to free oneself; to develop; to take place; to unfold
svolgiménto *m* development; composition
svòlta *f* turn; curve; turning point
svoltare (svòlto) *tr* to unwrap || *intr* to turn
svotare §257 or **svuotare (svuòto)** *tr* to empty

T

T, t [ti] *m & f* eighteenth letter of the Italian alphabet
tabac•càio -càia *mf* **(-cài -càie)** tobacconist
tabaccare §197 *intr* to take snuff
tabaccherìa *f* cigar store
tabacchièra *f* snuffbox
tabac•co *m* **(-chi)** tobacco; **tabacco da fiuto** snuff
tabarro *m* winter coat; cloak
tabèlla *f* tablet; list; schedule; (coll) clapper, noisemaker; **tabella di marcia** timetable
tabellare *adj* (typ) on wooden blocks; scheduled
tabellóne *m* board; bulletin board; (basketball) backboard
tabernàcolo *m* tabernacle
ta•bù *adj invar & m* **(-bù)** taboo
tàbula *f*—**far tabula rasa di** to make a clean sweep of
tabulare (tàbulo) *tr* to tabulate
tabulatóre *m* tabulator
tabulatrice *f* printer (*of computer*)
tac•ca *f* **(-che)** notch; size; kind; tally; blemish; (typ) nick; **di mezza tacca** middle-sized; mediocre; **tacca di mira** rear sight (*of firearm*)
tacca•gno -gna *adj* stingy, closefisted || *mf* miser
taccheggia•tóre -trice *mf* shoplifter || *f* prostitute, streetwalker
taccheggiatura *f* or **tacchég•gio** *m* **(-gi)** shoplifting
tacchétto *m* high heel; cleat (*on soccer or football shoe*)
tacchina *f* turkey hen
tacchino *m* turkey
tàc•cia *f* **(-ce)** notoriety
tacciare §128 *tr*—**tacciare di** to accuse of, charge with
tac•co *m* **(-chi)** heel; block; (typ) underlay; **battere i tacchi** to take to one's heels
taccóne *m* (coll) patch; (coll) hobnail; **battere il taccone** to take to one's heels
taccuino *m* pocketbook; notebook
tacére *m* silence; **mettere a tacere** to silence || §268 *tr* to conceal, withhold; to imply, understand || *intr* to keep quiet; to stop playing; to quiet down; to be silent; **far tacere** to silence; **taci!** (coll) shut up!
tachìmetro *m* tachometer; (aut) speedometer
tacitare (tàcito) *tr* to silence, satisfy (*a creditor*); to pay off
tàci•to -ta *adj* silent; tacit
tacitur•no -na *adj* taciturn
tafano *m* horsefly, gadfly
tafferù•glio *m* **(-gli)** scuffle
taffe•tà *m* **(-tà)** taffeta; **taffetà adesivo**

or **inglese** adhesive plaster, court plaster
tàglia *f* ransom, reward; size; build; tally; (mach) tackle
tagliabór•se *m* (**-se**) pickpocket
tagliabò•schi *m* (**-schi**) woodcutter, woodsman
tagliacar•te *m* (**-te**) letter opener, paper knife
tagli•àcque *m* (**-àcque**) cutwater (*of bridge*)
tagliaèrba *adj invar* grass-cutting
tagliafèr•ro *m* (**-ro**) cold chisel
taglialé•gna *m* (**-gna**) woodcutter
tagliama•re *m* (**-re**) cutwater (*of ship*)
tagliando *m* coupon
tagliapiè•tre *m* (**-tre**) stonecutter
tagliare **§280** *tr* to cut; to cut down; to cut off; to pick (*a pocket*); to cross (*finish line*); to tailor (*a suit*); to blend (*wine*); to turn off (*e.g., water*); **tagliare a fette** to slice; **tagliare in due** to split; **tagliare i panni addosso a qlcu** to slander s.o.; **tagliare i ponti con** to sever relations with; **tagliare i viveri a** to cut off supplies from; **tagliare la corda** to run away; **tagliare la strada a** to stand in the way of; (aut) to cut in front of; **tagliare le gambe a** to make wobbly (*said of wine*) || *intr* to cut; to bite (*said of cold*); **tagliare per una scorciatoia** to take a shortcut || *ref* to cut oneself; to tear (*said of material*)
tagliasìga•ri *m* (**-ri**) cigar cutter
tagliata *f* cut; clearing; (mil) abatis; **tagliata ai capelli** haircut
tagliatèlle *fpl* noodles
taglia•to -ta *adj* cut; fashioned; **essere tagliato per** to be cut out for; **tagliato all'antica** old-fashioned; **tagliato con l'accetta** rough-hewn || *f* see **tagliata**
taglia•tóre -trice *mf* cutter
tagliènte *adj* cutting || *m* edge
taglière *m* carving board
taglierina *f* paper cutter
tà•glio *m* (**-gli**) cut; cutting; dressmaking; cutting edge; sharpness; blending (*of wines*); size; denomination (*of paper money*); crossing (*of t*); (bb) fore edge; **a due tagli** double-edged; **a tagli** by the slice; **dare un taglio a** to chop; **di taglio** edgewise; **rifare il taglio a** to sharpen; **taglio cesareo** Caesarean section; **taglio d'abito** suiting; **taglio dei capelli** haircut; **venire in taglio** to come in handy
tagliòla *f* trap
tagliuzzare *tr* to shred, cut into shreds
tailandése [s] *adj & mf* Thai
Tailàndia, la Thailand
tailleur *m* (**tailleur**) woman's tailored costume
talal•tro -tra *pron indef* another, some other
tàlamo *m* (lit) nuptial bed
talare *adj* ankle-length || *f* soutane, cassock
talché *conj* so that
talco *m* talcum; talcum powder
tale *adj* such; such a; that; **il tale** such and such a; **un tale** such a; a certain; **un tal quale** such a; a certain || *pron* so-and-so; **il tal dei tali** so-and-so; Mr. so-and-so; **il tale** that fellow; that guy; **quel tale** that fellow, that guy; **tale e quale** like; **tali e quali** exactly, word for word; **un tale** someone, a certain person
talèa *f* (hort) cutting
talènto *m* talent; inclination; **a proprio talento** gladly, willingly; **di mal talento** grudgingly; **andare a talento a** to suit, e.g., **non gli va a talento nulla** nothing suits him
talismano *m* talisman
tallire **§176** *intr* (ESSERE & AVERE) to sprout
tallonare (**tallóno**) *tr* (sports) to be at the heels of
talloncino *m* coupon, stub
tallóne *m* heel; coupon, stub; tang (*of knife*); **tallone d'Achille** Achilles heel
talménte *adv* so, so much
talóra *adv* sometimes
talpa *f* mole
talu•no -na *pron indef* some; someone, somebody || **talu•ni -ne** *adj & pron indef* some
talvòlta *adv* sometimes
tamarindo *m* tamarind
tambureggiare **§290** (**tamburéggio**) *intr* to drum; to beat down (*said, e.g., of hail*)
tamburèllo *m* tambour (*for embroidering*); (mus) tambourine
tamburino *m* drummer
tamburo *m* drum; barrel (*of watch; of windlass*); **a tamburo battente** on the spot
tamerice *f* tamarisk
Tamigi *m* Thames
tampòco *adv*—**né tampoco** (archaic) nor . . . either
tamponaménto *m* stopping, plugging; rear-end collision
tamponare (**tampóno**) *tr* to tampon, plug; to collide with; to hit from the rear; (surg) to tampon
tampóne *m* plug, tampon; pad; (mus) drumstick; (rr) buffer; (surg) tampon; **tampone di vapore** vapor lock
tana *f* burrow; den; hole; hovel; base (*in children games*)
tanàglie *fpl* var of **tenaglie**
tan•ca *f* (**-che**) can, jerry can; tank
tanfo *m* musty or stuffy smell
tangènte *adj* tangent || *f* tangent; (com) commission
tàngere **§269** *tr* (lit) to touch
Tàngeri *f* Tangier
tànghero *m* boor, lout
tangìbile *adj* tangible
tàni•ca *f* (**-che**) var of **tanca**
tantino *m*—**un tantino** a little, e.g., **è un tantino arrabbiato** he is a little angry; a little bit, e.g., **un tantino di dolce** a little bit of cake
tan•to -ta *adj & pron indef* such, such a; so much; as much; **a dir tanto** or **a far tanto** at the most; **ai tanti**

(*del mese*) on such and such a day (*of the month*); **a tanto** to such a point; to such a level; **e tanto** odd, e.g., **mille dollari e tanto** a thousand odd dollars; **è tanto** it has been a long time, e.g., **è tanto che lo conosco** it has been a long time since I made his acquaintance; **fra tanto** meanwhile; **senza tanto chiasso** without any noise; **tan·ti -te** many; so many; as many; **a** lot, e.g., **grazie tante!** thanks a lot! **tanti . . . che** so many . . . that; **tanti . . . quanti** as many . . . as; **tanto di guadagnato** so much the better || **tanto** *adv* so much; so; only, e.g., **tanto per passare il tempo** only to pass the time; anyhow; anyway; **nè tanto nè quanto** at all; **tant'è** it's the same; **tanto che** so much that, e.g., **mi ha annoiato tanto che l'ho mandato via** he bothered me so much that I dismissed him; **tanto . . . che** both . . . and, e.g., **tanto Maria che Roberto** both Mary and Robert; so much . . . that; **tanto fa** or **vale** it's all the same; **tanto meglio** so much the better; **tanto meno** so much the less; **tanto per cambiare** as usual; **tanto più . . . quanto più** the more . . . the more; **tanto . . . quanto** as . . . as || *s*— **ascoltare con tanto d'orecchie** to be all ears; **di tanto in tanto** from time to time

tapi·no -na *adj* (lit) wretched || *mf* (lit) wretch

tappa *f* stopping place; stop; stage, leg; (sports) lap; **bruciare le tappe** to press on, keep going; **fare tappa** to stop

tappabu·chi *mf* (**-chi**) makeshift, pinch hitter, substitute

tappare *tr* to cork, plug; to shut up tight || *ref* to shut oneself in; to plug (*e.g., one's ears*)

tapparèlla *f* (coll) inside rolling shutter

tappéto *m* rug, carpet; (sports) canvas, mat; **mettere al tappeto** (boxing) to knock out; **tappeto erboso** lawn, green; **tappeto verde** gambling table

tappezzare (**tappèzzo**) *tr* to paper (*a wall*); to upholster

tappezzerìa *f* wallpaper; upholstery; upholsterer's shop; tapestry; wallflower

tappezzière *m* paperhanger; upholsterer

tappo *m* cork, stopper; cap; plug; **tappo a corona** bottle cap; **tappo a vite** screw cap

tara *f* tare

taràntola *f* tarantula

tarare *tr* to tare; to set, adjust

tara·to -ta *adj* net (*weight*); calibrated (*instrument*); sickly, weak

tarchia·to -ta *adj* stocky, sturdy

tardare *tr* to delay || *intr* to delay; to be late

tardi *adv* late; **al più tardi** at the latest; **a più tardi!** so long!; **fare tardi** to be late; **più tardi** later; later on; **sul tardi** in the late afternoon

tardi·vo -va *adj* late; retarded, slow; belated

tar·do -da *adj* slow; late; **di età tarda** of advanced years; **tardo d'ingegno** slow-witted

tardó·ne -na *adj* slow-moving || *mf* slowpoke || *f* old dame, middle-aged vamp

tar·ga *f* (**-ghe**) plate; nameplate; shield; (aut) license plate; (sports) trophy

targare §209 *tr* (aut) to register

targatura *f* (aut) registration

targhétta *f* nameplate

tariffa *f* tariff; rate; rates

tariffà·rio -ria (**-ri -rie**) *adj* tariff; rate || *m* price list; rate book

tarlare *tr* to eat (*said of woodworms or moths*) || *intr* (ESSERE) & *ref* to become worm-eaten; to become moth-eaten

tarlo *m* woodworm; moth; bookworm; (fig) gnawing

tarma *f* moth; clothes moth

tarmare *tr* to eat (*said of moths*) || *intr* (ESSERE) & *ref* to become moth-eaten

tarmici·da (**-di -de**) *adj* moth-repelling || *m* moth repellent

taròc·co *m* (**-chi**) tarot; tarok

tarpare *tr* to clip; **tarpare le ali a** to clip the wings of

tartagliare §280 *tr* & *intr* to stutter, stammer

tàrta·ro -ra *adj* Tartar || *m* tartar; Tartar || **Tartaro** *m* Tartarus

tartaru·ga *f* (**-ghe**) turtle, tortoise; tortoise shell

tartassare *tr* to ill-treat; to harass

tartina *f* slice of bread and butter; canapé

tartufo *m* truffle; (fig) tartuffe, hypocrite

ta·sca *f* (**-sche**) pocket; briefcase; **aver le tasche piene di** to be sick and tired of; **da tasca** pocket; **rompere le tasche a** (vulg) to bother, annoy; **tasca in petto** inside pocket

tascàbile *adj* pocket; vest-pocket

tascapane *m* knapsack, rucksack

tascata *f* pocketful

taschino *m* vest pocket, small pocket

tassa *f* tax; (coll) duty, fee; **tassa complementare** surtax; **tassa di circolazione** road-use tax; **tassa di registro** registration fee; **tassa scolastica** tuition

tassàbile *adj* taxable

tassàmetro *m* taximeter; **tassametro di parcheggio** parking meter

tassare *tr* to tax; to assess || *ref* to pledge money

tassati·vo -va *adj* positive; specific; peremptory

tassazióne *f* taxation; tax

tassèllo *m* dowel; inlay; plug; patch; reinforcement

tas·sì *m* (**-sì**) taxi, taxicab

tassi·sta *m* (**-sti**) taxi driver

tasso *m* stake (*anvil*); yew tree; (com) rate (*e.g., of interest*); (zool) badger; **tasso valutario fluttuante** (econ) fluctuation of currency rate

tastare *tr* to touch; to feel; to probe; **tastare il terreno** (fig) to see how the land lies

tastièra *f* keyboard; manual (*of organ*)

tasto *m* touch, feeling, feel; plug (*e.g., in watermellon*); key (*of piano or typewriter*); sample (*in drilling*); **tasto bianco** white key, natural; **toccare un tasto falso** to strike a sour note
tastóni *adv*—**a tastoni** gropingly
tàtti·co -ca (-ci -che) *adj* tactical; tactful || *m* tactician || *f* tactics; prudence; tactfulness
tatto *m* touch; tact
tatuàg·gio *m* (**-gi**) tattoo
tatuare (tàtuo) *tr* to tattoo
taumatur·go *m* (**-gi** & **-ghi**) wonder-worker
tauri·no -na *adj* taurine, bull-like; bull
tavèrna *f* tavern, inn
tavernière *m* tavernkeeper
tàvola *f* board, plank; slab; table; tablet; bookplate; list; **tavola a ribalta** drop-leaf table; **tavola armonica** (mus) sound board; **tavola calda** cafeteria, snack bar; **tavola da stirare** ironing board; **tavola di salvezza** (fig) last recourse, lifesaver; **tavola imbandita** open house; **tavola nera** blackboard; **tavola operatoria** operating table; **tavola pitagorica** multiplication table; **tavola reale** backgammon; **tavole di fondazione** charter (*of a charitable institution*)
tavolàc·cio *m* (**-ci**) wooden board (*on which soldiers on guard and prisoners used to sleep*)
tavolare (tàvolo) *tr* to board up
tavolata *f* tableful
tavolato *m* planking; plateau
tavolétta *f* small table; tablet; bar (*e.g., of chocolate*)
tavolière *m* chessboard table; card table; plateau, tableland
tavolino *m* small table; desk
tàvolo *m* table; desk; **tavolo di gioco** gambling table; **tavolo d'ufficio** office desk
tavolòzza *f* palette
tazza *f* cup; bowl
tazzina *f* demitasse
tazzóna *f* mug
te §5 *pron pers*
tè *m* (**tè**) tea; **tè danzante** tea dance, thé dansant
tèa *adj fem*—**rosa tea** tea rose
teatrale *adj* theatrical
teatro *m* theater; performance; drama; stage; (fig) scene; **che teatro!** what fun!; **teatro dell'opera** or **teatro lirico** opera house; **teatro di posa** (mov) studio; **teatro di prosa** legitimate theater
teatróne *m* large theater; (coll) excellent box office
Tèbe *f* Thebes
tè·ca *f* (**-che**) case; (eccl) reliquary
tecnicismo *m* technicality
tècni·co -ca (-ci -che) *adj* technical || *m* technician; engineer || *f* technique; technics
téco §5 *prep phrase* (lit) with you
tedé·sco -sca *adj* & *mf* (**-schi -sche**) German
tediare §287 **(tèdio)** *tr* to bore || *ref* to get bored
tè·dio *m* (**-di**) dullness, tedium, boredom; **recare tedio a** to annoy, bother
tedió·so -sa [s] *adj* dull, tedious
tegame *m* pan; **al tegame** fried (*e.g., eggs*)
tegamino *m* small pan; **uova al tegamino** fried eggs
téglia *f* pan; baking pan
tégola *f* tile; (fig) blow
tégolo *m* tile
teièra *f* teapot, teakettle
tèk *m* teak
téla *f* linen; cloth; material; canvas, oil painting; (fig) plot, trap; (lit) weft; (theat) curtain; **far tela** (coll) to beat it; **tela batista** batiste; **tela cerata** oilcloth; **tela da imballaggio** burlap; **tela di ragno** cobweb; **tela di sacco** sackcloth; **tela greggia** gunny, burlap; **tela smeriglio** emery cloth
te·làio *m* (**-lài**) loom; frame; embroidery frame; sash; stretcher (*for oil painting*); (aut) chassis; **telaio di finestra** window sash
teleama·tóre -trice *mf* TV viewer
telear·ma *f* (**-mi**) guided missile
telecabina *f* cable car
telecàmera *f* TV camera
telecomanda·to -ta *adj* remote-control
telecomando *m* remote control
telecommentatóre *m* TV newscaster
telecròna·ca *f* (**-che**) TV broadcast; **telecronaca diretta** live broadcast
telecroni·sta *mf* (**-sti -ste**) TV news announcer, TV newscaster
telediffusióne *f* TV broadcasting
teledram·ma *m* (**-mi**) teleplay
telefèri·ca *f* (**-che**) cableway, telpherage
telefonare (telèfono) *tr* & *intr* to telephone || *ref* to call one another
telefonata *f* telephone call
telefòni·co -ca *adj* (**-ci -che**) telephone
telefoni·sta *mf* (**-sti -ste**) telephone operator, central; telephone installer
telèfono *m* telephone; **telefono a gettone** pay telephone (*operated by tokens*); **telefono a moneta** pay telephone; **telefono interno** intercommunication system, intercom
telegèni·co -ca *adj* (**-ci -che**) telegenic, videogenic
telegiornale *m* TV newscast
telegrafare (telègrafo) *tr* & *intr* to telegraph
telegràfi·co -ca *adj* (**-ci -che**) telegraphic
telegrafi·sta *mf* (**-sti -ste**) telegrapher; telegraph installer
telègrafo *m* telegraph; **telegrafo di macchina** (naut) engine-room telegraph; **telegrafo ottico** heliograph; wigwag; **telegrafo senza fili** wireless
telegram·ma *m* (**-mi**) telegram
teleguida *f* remote control
teleguidare *tr* to control from a distance, to operate by remote control
Telèmaco *m* Telemachus
telèmetro *m* telemeter; range finder
teleobbiettivo *m* (phot) telephoto lens
telepatìa *f* telepathy
teleproiètto *m* guided missile
telericévere §141 *tr* to receive by TV; to teleview
teleschérmo *m* television screen

telescò•pio *m* (**-pi**) telescope
telescrivènte *f* teletypewriter; ticker
telescriventi•sta *mf* (**-sti -ste**) teletype operator
teleselezióne *f* (telp) direct distance dialing
telespetta•tóre -trice *mf* televiewer
teletrasméttere §198 *tr* to televise, telecast
teletrasmissióne *f* telecast
televisióne *f* television, TV
televisi•vo -va *adj* television, TV
televisóre *m* television set
tellina *f* sunset shell or clam
télo *m* piece of cloth; yardage, length of material; (mil) side (*of tent*)
tèlo *m* (lit) dart, arrow
telóne *m* canvas; (theat) curtain
tè•ma *m* (**-mi**) theme; (gram) stem
téma *f* (lit) fear; **per tema di** (lit) for fear of
temerarie•tà *f* (**-tà**) recklessness, rashness
temerà•rio -ria *adj* (**-ri -rie**) reckless, rash; ill-founded
temére (**témo** & **tèmo**) *tr* to fear; to respect || *intr* to fear; **temere di** to be afraid to
temeri•tà *f* (**-tà**) temerity
temìbile *adj* frightening
tèmpera *f* tempera, distemper
temperala•pis *m* (**-pis**) or **temperamati•te** *m* (**-te**) pencil sharpener
temperaménto *m* middle course, compromise; temper, temperament
temperante *adj* temperate, moderate
temperanza *f* temperance
temperare (**tèmpero**) *tr* to mitigate; to temper; to sharpen (*a pencil*)
tempera•to -ta *adj* temperate; tempered (*metal*); watered (*wine*)
temperatura *f* temperature; **temperatura ambiente** room temperature
temperino *m* penknife, pocketknife
tempèsta *f* tempest, storm; **tempesta in un bicchier d'acqua** tempest in a teapot
tempestare (**tempèsto**) *tr* to pound; to pepper, pelt; to pester || *intr* to storm
tempesta•to -ta *adj* studded, spangled
tempesti•vo -va *adj* timely
tempestó•so -sa [s] *adj* stormy, tempestuous
tèmpia *f* temple (*side of forehead*); **tempie** (lit) head
tempiale *m* temple (*in loom; of spectacles*)
tempière *m* Templar
tèm•pio *m* (**-pi** & **-pli**) temple (*edifice*)
tempi•sta *mf* (**-sti -ste**) person or athlete showing good timing; (mus) rhythmist
tèmpo *m* time; weather; age; period, stage; cycle (*of internal-combustion engine*); (gram) tense; (mus) tempo, (mus) movement; (sports) period; (theat, mov) part; **ad un tempo** at the same time; **al tempo che Berta filava** long ago; **a suo tempo** in due time; long ago; **a tempo debito** in due time; **a tempo e luogo** at the opportune time; **a tempo perso** in one's spare time; **aver fatto il proprio tempo** to be outdated; **c'è sempre tempo** we are still in time; **col tempo** in time; **dare tempo al tempo** to allow time to heal things; **darsi del bel tempo** to have a good time; **da tempo** for a long time; **del tempo di** from the time of; **è scaduto il tempo utile** the time is up; **è tanto tempo** it's been a long time; **fa bel tempo** the weather is fine; **il Tempo** Father Time; **lasciare il tempo che trova** to have no effect; **molto tempo dopo** long afterward; **nel tempo che** while; **per tempo** early; **prima del tempo** formerly; **quanto tempo** how long; **sentire il tempo** to feel the weather in one's bones; **senza por tempo in mezzo** without any delay; **tempi che corrono** present times; **tempo fa** some time ago; **tempo legale** legal time limit; **tempo libero** leisure time; **tempo supplementare** (sports) overtime; **tempo un . . .** within (*e.g., one month*); **un tempo** long ago
temporale *adj* temporal || *m* storm
temporàne•o -a *adj* temporary, provisional
temporeggiare §290 (**temporéggio**) *intr* to temporize
tèmpra *f* (metallurgy) tempering, temper; (mus) timbre; (fig) fiber, timber
temprare (**tèmpro**) *tr* to temper (*metal*); to harden, inure || *ref* to become hardened or inured
tenace *adj* tenacious; tough
tenàcia *f* tenacity
tenaci•tà *f* (**-tà**) strength, resistance; tenacity
tenàglie *fpl* nippers, pincers, pliers; tongs; **a tenaglie** (mil) pincers (*e.g., action*)
tènda *f* curtain; awning; tent
tendènza *f* tendency; trend
tendenzió•so -sa [s] *adj* tendentious
tèn•der *m* (**-der**) (rr) tender
tèndere §270 *tr* to stretch; to tighten; to draw (*a bow*); to cast (*nets*); to lay (*snares*); to reach out (*one's hand*); to prick up (*one's ears*); to draw (*s.o.'s attention*); to set (*sail*) || *intr* to aim; to lean; to tend; to tend to be
tendina *f* curtain, blind
tèndine *m* (anat) tendon
tendiscar•pe *m* (**-pe**) shoetree
tenditóre *m* turnbuckle; **tenditore della racchetta** (tennis) press
tendóne *m* big curtain; canvas; tent (*of circus*); (theat) curtain
tendòpo•li *f* (**-li**) tent city
tènebre *fpl* darkness
tenebró•so -sa [s] *adj* dark, gloomy
tenènte *m* lieutenant; (mil) first lieutenant; (nav) lieutenant junior grade; **tenente colonnello** (mil) lieutenant colonel; **tenente di vascello** (nav) lieutenant senior grade
tenére §271 *tr* to hold; to have; to keep; to stand (*e.g., rough sea*); to wear; to make (*a speech*); to follow

(*a course*); **tenere a battesimo** to stand for, sponsor; **tenere al corrente** to keep informed; **tenere a memoria** to remember; **tenere da conto** to hold in high esteem; to take good care of (*s.th*); **tenere d'occhio** to keep an eye on; **tenere la destra** to keep to the right; **tenere la strada** (aut) to hug the road; **tenere la testa a partito** to mend one's ways; **tenere le distanze** to keep aloof; **tenere mano a** to connive with; **tenere presente** to bear in mind; **tenere qlco a conto** to take good care of s.th || *intr* to hold; to take root; **tenerci che** to be anxious for, e.g., **ci tengo che vinca le elezioni** I am anxious for him to win the elections; **tenere a destra** to keep to the right; **tenere alle apparenze** to stand on ceremony; to keep up appearances; **tenere da** to hail from; to take after; **tenere dietro a** to follow; to keep abreast of; **tenere duro** to hold fast; **tenere per** (sports) to be a fan of || *ref* to hold; to hold on; to keep; to keep (*e.g., ready*); to regard oneself; **tenersi a** to adhere to (*e.g., a treaty*); to hold on to; to stick to; to follow; **tenersi a galla** to stay afloat; **tenersi al largo** (naut) to keep to the open sea; **tenersi al vento** (naut) to sail to leeward; (fig) to follow a safe course; **tenersi in piedi** to stand up; **tenersi per mano** to hold hands; **tenersi sulle proprie** to keep aloof

tenerézza *f* tenderness; fondness, endearment

tène•ro -ra *adj* tender || *m* tender portion

tènia *f* tapeworm

teni•tóre -trice *mf* keeper

tènnis *m* tennis; **tennis da tavolo** table tennis, ping-pong

tenni•sta *mf* (**-sti -ste**) tennis player

tennìsti•co -ca *adj* (**-ci -che**) tennis

tenóne *m* tenon

tenóre *m* character, tone; tenor; alcoholic content; manner (*of living*); **tenore di vita** way of life; standard of living

tensióne *f* tension; **alta tensione** high tension; **tensione sanguigna** blood pressure

tentàcolo *m* tentacle

tentare (**tènto**) *tr* to try, attempt; to assay; to tempt; (lit) to touch

tentativo *m* attempt; **tentativo di furto** attempted robbery

tenta•tóre -trice *adj* tempting || *m* tempter || *f* temptress

tentazióne *f* temptation

tentennare (**tenténno**) *tr* to shake; to rock || *intr* to shake; to wobble; to hesitate; to stagger

tentóne or **tentóni** *adv* blindly; gropingly; at random

tènue *adj* small (*intestine*); (lit) tenuous, thin

tenu•to -ta *adj* bound, obliged || *f* capacity, volume; estate, farm; uniform; outfit; (sports) endurance, resistance; **a tenuta d'acqua** watertight; **a tenuta d'aria** airtight; **tenuta dei libri** bookkeeping; **tenuta di gala** (mil, nav) full-dress uniform; **tenuta di servizio** (mil) fatigues; **tenuta di strada** (aut) roadability

tenzóne *f* combat; poetic contest

teologìa *f* theology

teòlo•go *m* (**-gi**) theologian

teorè•ma *m* (**-mi**) theorem

teorèti•co -ca *adj* (**-ci -che**) theoretic(al)

teorìa *f* theory; (lit) series, row

teòri•co -ca (**-ci -che**) *adj* theoretical || *m* theoretician

tèpi•do -da *adj* var of **tiepido**

tepóre *m* warmth

téppa *f* underworld, rabble

teppi•sta *m* (**-sti**) hoodlum, hooligan

terapèuti•co -ca (**-ci -che**) *adj* therapeutic || *f* therapeutics

terapìa *f* therapy; **terapia convulsivante** or **terapia d'urto** shock therapy

Terèsa *f* Theresa

tèrgere §162 *tr* (lit) to wipe

tergicristallo *m* windshield wiper

tergiversare (**tergivèrso**) *intr* to stall; to beat around the bush

tèr•go *m* (**-ghi**) back (*of a coin*); **a tergo** on the reverse side || *m* (**-ga** *fpl*) (lit) back; **volgere le terga** (lit) to turn one's back

termale *adj* thermal (*e.g., waters*)

tèrme *fpl* spa, hot spring

tèrmi•co -ca *adj* (**-ci -che**) thermal; heat, heating

terminale *adj* & *m* terminal

terminare (**tèrmino**) *tr* to border; to end, terminate || *intr* (ESSERE) to end, terminate

terminazióne *f* termination; completion; (gram) ending

tèrmine *m* border; marker; term; deadline; end; goal; boundary, bounds; (fig) point; **a termini di legge** according to law; **avere termine** to end; **in altri termini** in other words; **mezzo termine** half measure; **porre termine a** to put an end to; **portare a termine** to put through

terminologìa *f* terminology

termistóre *m* (elec) thermistor

tèrmite *f* termite

termoconvettóre *m* baseboard radiator

termocòppia *f* thermocouple

termodinàmi•co -ca (**-ci -che**) *adj* thermodynamic || *f* thermodynamics

termòforo *m* heating pad

termòmetro *m* thermometer

termonucleare *adj* thermonuclear

tèr•mos *m* (**-mos**) thermos bottle

termosifóne *m* radiator; hot-water heating system; steam heating system

termòstato *m* thermostat

termovisièra *f* electric defroster

tèrno *m* tern (*in lotto*); **vincere un terno al lotto** to hit the jackpot

tèrra *f* earth; land; ground; world; city, town; dirt, soil; clay; **essere a terra** to be downcast; to be broke; to be flat (*said of a tire*); **rimanere a terra** to miss the boat; **sotto terra** underground; **terra bruciata** scorched

earth; **terra di nessuno** no man's land; **terra di Siena** sienna; **terra ferma** terra firma; mainland; **terra terra** skimming the ground; (naut) close to the shore; (fig) mediocre, second-rate
terracòtta *f* (**terrecòtte**) terra cotta; earthenware
terrafèrma *f* mainland (*as distinguished from adjacent islands*); terra firma (*dry land, not air or water*)
terràglia *f* crockery; **terraglie** earthenware
terranò•va *m* (**-va**) Newfoundland (*dog*) || **Terranova** *f* Newfoundland
terrapièno *m* embankment
terrazza *f* terrace; **a terrazza** terraced
terrazza•no -na *mf* villager
terrazzo *m* balcony; terrace; ledge, shelf; terrazzo
terremota•to -ta *adj* hit by an earthquake || *mf* earthquake victim
terremòto *m* earthquake
terré•no -na *adj* terrestrial, earthly; ground-floor; first-floor || *m* ground floor; first floor; ground; soil; land, plot of ground; combat zone, terrain; **preparare il terreno** to work the soil; (fig) to pave the way; **scendere sul terreno** to fight a duel; **tastare il terreno** to feel one's way; **terreno di gioco** (sports) field
tèrre•o -a *adj* wan, sallow
terrèstre *adj* terrestrial; ground; land || *m* earthling
terrìbile *adj* terrible; awesome, awful
terrìc•cio *m* (**-ci**) soil; top soil
terriè•ro -ra *adj* land; landed
terrificare §197 (**terrìfico**) *tr* to terrify
terrina *f* tureen
territò•rio *m* (**-ri**) territory
terróre *m* terror
terrorismo *m* terrorism
terrori•sta *mf* (**-sti -ste**) terrorist
terrorizzare [ddzz] *tr* to terrorize
terró•so -sa [s] *adj* dirty (*e.g., spinach*); dirty-earth (*color*); (chem) rare-earth (*metal*)
tèr•so -sa *adj* clear
tèrza *f* third grade; (aut) third; (eccl) tierce; (rr) third class
terzaforzì•sta (**-sti -ste**) *adj* of the third force || *m* partisan of the third force
terzaròlo *m* (naut) reef
terzétto *m* trio
terzià•rio -ria *adj* (**-ri -rie**) tertiary
terzina *f* tercet
terzino *m* (soccer) back
tèr•zo -za *adj & pron* third || *m* third; third party || *f* see **terza**
terzùlti•mo -ma *adj* third from the end
tésa [s] *f* brim (*of hat*); snare, net
tesare [s] (**téso**) *tr* to pull taut
tè•schio *m* (**-schi**) skull
tè•si *f* (**-si**) thesis; dissertation
té•so -sa [s] *adj* taut, tight; strained; outstretched (*hand*); **con le orecchie tese** all ears || *f* see **tesa**
tesorerìa *f* treasury; liquid assets
tesorière *m* treasurer
tesòro *m* treasure; treasury; thesaurus; bank vault; **far tesoro di** to treasure, prize; **tesoro mio!** my darling!
Tèspi *m* Thespis
tèssera *f* card; domino (*piece*); tessera (*of mosaic*)
tessera•to -ta *adj* card-carrying; rationed || *mf* card-carrying member; holder of ration card
tèssere *tr* to weave; to spin
tèssile *adj* textile || *m* textile; **tessili** textile workers
tessilsac•co *m* (**-chi**) garment bag
tessi•tóre -trice *mf* weaver
tessitura *f* weaving; spinning mill; (mus) range; (fig) plot
tessuto *m* cloth, fabric; tissue
tèsta *f* head; mind; bulb (*of garlic*); spindle (*of wheel*); warhead (*of torpedo*); row (*of bricks*); **a testa** apiece; per capita; **a testa a testa** neck and neck; **fare di testa propria** to act on one's own; **fare la testa grossa a** to stun; to annoy; **levarsi di testa** to forget about; **mettersi in testa di** to get it into one's head to; **non avere testa di** + *inf* to not feel like + *ger;* **non sapere dove battere la testa** to not know which way to turn; **per una corta testa** by a neck; **rompersi la testa** to rack one's brains; **tenere testa a** to face up to; **testa coda** (aut) spin; **testa di ponte** (mil) bridgehead; **testa di sbarco** beachhead; **testa e croce** head or tails
testaménto *m* will, testament || **Antico** or **Vecchio Testamento** Old Testament; **Nuovo Testamento** New Testament
testardàggine *f* stubborness
testar•do -da *adj* stubborn
testata *f* headboard (*of bed*); top; end (*e.g., of beam*); heading (*of newspaper*); butt with the head; nose (*of rocket*)
tèste *m* witness
testé *adv* (lit) a short time ago; (lit) presently, in a little while
testìcolo *m* testicle
testièra *f* headboard; crown (*of harness*); battering ram
testimòne *m* witness; **testimone di nozze** best man; **testimone di veduta** or **testimone oculare** eyewitness
testimonianza *f* testimony
testimoniare §287 (**testimònio**) *tr* to attest; to depose, testify; **testimoniare il falso** to bear false witness || *intr* to bear witness
testimò•nio *m* (**-ni**) (coll) witness
testina *f* small head; whimsical person; boiled head of veal; head (*e.g., of tape recorder*)
tèsto *m* text; pie dish; (coll) flower vase; **fare testo** to serve as a model
testó•ne -na *mf* dolt; stubborn person
testuale *adj* textual; word-for-word
testùggine *f* turtle; tortoise
tètano *m* tetanus
tè•tro -tra *adj* (lit) gloomy, dark
tétta *f* (coll) teat
tettarèlla *f* nipple
tétto *m* roof; ceiling price; home; **senza tetto** homeless; **tetto a capanna** gable roof; **tetto a padiglione** hip

roof; **tetto a una falda** lean-to roof; **tetto di paglia** thatched roof
tettóia *f* shed; pillared roof
tettóia-garage *f* (**tettóie-garage**) carport
tettùc•cio *m* (**-ci**) (aut) roof; (aut) top; **tettuccio a bulbo** dome; **tettuccio rigido** (aut) convertible top
ti §5 *pron*
tìbia *f* tibia, shinbone
tic *m* (**tic**) twitch; habit
ticchettì•o *m* (**-i**) click (*of typewriter*); patter (*of rain*); tick (*of clock*)
tìc•chio *m* (**-chi**) whim; tic; viciousness (*of animal*); blemish
tièpi•do -da *adj* tepid, lukewarm
tifo *m* typhus; **fare il tifo per** to root for; to be a fan of
tifoidèa *f* typhoid fever
tifóne *m* typhoon
tifó•so -sa [s] *adj* rooting || *mf* fan, rooter
tì•glio *m* (**-gli**) linden, lime; bast; fiber
tigliò•so -sa [s] *adj* tough, fibrous
tigna *f* ringworm; (coll) tightwad
tignòla *f* clothes moth
tigra•to -ta *adj* striped; tabby
tigre *f* tiger
timballo *m* pie, meat pie; timbale; (lit) drum
timbrare *tr* to stamp; to cancel (*stamps*)
timbro *m* stamp; character (*of a writer*); (mus) timbre; **timbro di gomma** rubber stamp; **timbro postale** postmark
timidézza *f* shyness, bashfulness; timidity
tìmi•do -da *adj* shy, bashful; timid || *mf* shy person
timo *m* (anat) thymus; (bot) thyme
timóne *m* rudder, helm; shaft, pole (*of cart*); **timone di direzione** (aer) rudder; **timone di profondità** (aer) elevator; (nav) diving plane (*of submarine*)
timonièra *f* (naut) pilot house
timonière *m* helmsman, steersman; coxswain
timonié•ro -ra *adj* rudder; tail (*feather*) || *f* see **timoniera**
timora•to -ta *adj* conscientious; **timorato di Dio** God-fearing
timóre *m* fear; awe; **avere timore di** to fear
timoró•so -sa [s] *adj* timorous
tìmpano *m* (archit) tympanum; (anat) eardrum; (mus) kettledrum; **rompere i timpani a** to deafen
tin•ca *f* (**-che**) (ichth) tench
tinèllo *m* pantry; breakfast room
tìngere §126 *tr* to dye; to dirty, soil; to color || *ref* to dye (*e.g., one's hair*); to put on make-up; to become colored
tino *m* tub, vat
tinòzza *f* tub, washtub
tinta *f* paint; color; dye; shade; stain; **calcare le tinte** to exaggerate; **mezza tinta** halftone, shade; **vedere qlco a fosche tinte** to take a dim view of s.th; **vedere qlco a tinte rosee** to see s.th through rose-colored glasses
tintarèlla *f* (coll) suntan
tinteggiare §290 (**tintéggio**) *tr* to calcimine; to whitewash; to tint; to paint (*e.g., a house*)
tintinnare *intr* (ESSERE & AVERE) to jingle; to clink
tintinnì•o *m* (**-i**) jingling; clink
tin•to -ta *adj* dyed; tinged; soiled; (lit) dark || *f* see **tinta**
tintó•re -ra *mf* dyer; dry cleaner
tintorìa *f* dyeworks; dry cleaning establishment; dyeing
tintura *f* dyeing; dyestuff; tincture; smattering; **tintura di iodio** iodine
tìpi•co -ca *adj* (**-ci -che**) typical
tipificare §197 (**tipìfico**) *tr* to standardize
tipizzare [ddzz] *tr* to standardize
tipo *adj invar* typical, e.g., **famiglia tipo** typical family || *m* type; standard, model; fellow, guy; phylum (*in taxonomy*); **bel tipo** (coll) character, card; **coi tipi di** printed in the shop of; **sul tipo di** similar to; **vero tipo** prototype, epitome
tipografìa *f* typography; print shop
tipogràfi•co -ca *adj* (**-ci -che**) typographical
tipògrafo *m* typographer; owner of print shop, printer
tipòmetro *m* (typ) line gauge
tiptologìa *f* table rapping (*during séance*); tapping in code (*among jailbirds*)
tiraba•ci *m* (**-ci**) (coll) spitcurl
tiràg•gio *m* (**-gi**) draft; **a tiraggio forzato** forced-draft
tiralìne•e *m* (**-e**) ruling pen
tirannìa *f* tyranny
tirànni•co -ca *adj* (**-ci -che**) tyrannical
tiran•no -na *adj* tyrannical || *mf* tyrant
tirante *m* brace; rod; strap; trace (*of harness*); **tirante degli stivali** bootstrap
tirapiè•di *m* (**-di**) hangman's assistant; underling
tirapu•gni *m* (**-gni**) brass knuckles
tirare *tr* to pull; to draw; to tug; to suck; to haul in (*nets*); to deserve (*a slap*); to pluck; to throw; to give (*blows*); to utter (*oaths*); to shoot (*arrows, bullets*); to stretch; to tighten (*one's belt*); to print; to make (*an addition*); (sports) to force (*the pace*); **tirare a lucido** to polish; **tirare a sé** to attract; **tirare a sorte** to draw lots for; **tirare fuori** to draw out; to pull out; to get out; **tirare giù** to lower; to jot down; (coll) to gulp down; **tirare gli orecchi a** to punish by yanking the ears of; **tirare il collo a** to wring the neck of; **tirare in ballo** to bring up (*a subject*); **tirare l'acqua al proprio mulino** to look out for number one; **tirare l'anima coi denti** to be at the end of one's rope; **tirare l'aria** to draw (*said of a chimney*); **tirare le cuoia** (slang) to kick the bucket; **tirare per i capelli** to drag by the hair; to drag in; to push, coerce; **tirare per le lunghe** to stretch out; **tirare su** to lift; to raise (*children*); to pull up || *intr* to be too tight (*said of clothes*); to shoot; to blow (*said of wind*); to

draw (*said, e.g., of chimney*); **tirare a** to tend toward, lean toward; **tirare a** + *inf* to try to + *inf;* **tirare a campare** (coll) to goldbrick; **tirare avanti** to go ahead; to manage to get along; **tirare di boxe** to box; **tirare diritto** to go straight ahead; **tirare di scherma** to fence; **tirare in lungo** to delay, linger; to dillydally; **tirare innanzi** to keep on going; to go ahead; **tirare sul prezzo** to haggle; **tirare via** to hurry along || *ref*—**tirarsi addosso** (coll) to bring upon oneself; **tirarsi dietro** to drag along; **tirarsi fuori da** to get out of (*e.g., trouble*); **tirarsi gente in casa** to keep open house; **tirarsi indietro** to move back; **tirarsi in là** to move aside; **tirarsi su** to get up; to recover; to roll up (*one's sleeves*); **tirarsi un colpo di rivoltella** to shoot oneself

tirastiva·li *m* (**-li**) bootjack

tirata *f* pull; stretch; tirade

tirati·ra *m* (**-ra**) (coll) yen; **fare a tiratira per** (coll) to scramble for

tira·to -ta *adj* taut; forced (*smile*); drawn (*face*); tight, closefisted; **tirato con** short of || *f* see **tirata**

tira·tóre -trice *mf* shot; **tiratore scelto** sharpshooter; **franco tiratore** sniper

tiratura *f* printing

tirchierìa *f* stinginess

tìr·chio -chia (-chi -chie) *adj* stingy, closefisted || *mf* miser

tirèlla *f* trace (*of harness*)

tirétto *m* (coll) drawer

tiritèra *f* rigmarole

tiro *m* pull; pair, brace (*e.g., of oxen*); throw; fire, shot; trick; **a tiro** within reach; **a un tiro di schioppo** within gunshot; **da tiro** draft; **fuori del tiro dell'orecchio** out of earshot; **tiro alla fune** tug of war; **tiro al piattello** trapshooting; **tiro a quattro** four-in-hand; **tiro a segno** rifle range; shooting gallery

tirocì·nio *m* (**-ni**) apprenticeship; internship; **tirocinio didattico** practice teaching

tiròide *f* thyroid

tirolése [s] *adj & mf* Tyrolean

tirrèni·co -ca *adj* (**-ci -che**) Tyrrhenian

Tirrèno *m* Tyrrhenian Sea

tisana *f* tea, infusion

tisi *f* consumption, tuberculosis

tìsi·co -ca (-ci -che) *adj* consumptive; stunted || *mf* consumptive

titàni·co -ca *adj* (**-ci -che**) titanic

titànio *m* titanium

titillare *tr* to tickle

titolare *adj* titular; regular, full-time || *m* owner, boss; incumbent || *v* (**tìtolo**) *tr* to name, call

tìtolo *m* title; heading; name; caption; entry (*in dictionary*); grade; fineness (*of gold*); (chem) titer; (educ) credit; **avere titolo a** to have a right to; **a titolo di** as, by way of; **titoli di testa** (mov) credits; **titolo al portatore** security payable to bearer; **titolo azionario** share; **titolo corrente** subtitle; **titolo di credito** instrument of credit; certificate; deed; conveyance; **titolo di studio** degree, diploma; credits; **titolo di trasporto** travel document

titubare (**tìtubo**) *intr* to hesitate; to waver

tiziané·sco -sca *adj* (**-schi -sche**) titian; Titian

tì·zio *m* (**-zi**) fellow, guy

tizzo or **tizzóne** *m* brand, firebrand

to' *interj* here!; well!

tobò·ga *m* (**-ga**) toboggan

toccafèrro *m* tag (*game*)

toccamano *m* handshake (*to close a deal*); bribe, under-the-table tip

toccante *adj* touching, moving

toccare §197 (**tócco**) *tr* to touch; to reach; to concern; to push (*a button*); to play (*an instrument*); to feel; to hit (*the target*); to border on (*e.g., the age of forty*); **toccare con mano** to make sure of; **toccare il cielo col dito** to be in seventh heaven; **toccare nel vivo** to touch to the quick; **toccare terra** to land; **toccarne molte** to get a good thrashing; **toccato!** touché! || *intr* (ESSERE) to be touching; **toccare a** to be up to, e.g., **tocca a lui** it's up to him; to have to, e.g., **le tocca partire domani** she has to leave tomorrow; to deserve, e.g., **gli è toccato il premio** he deserved the prize || *ref* to meet, e.g., **gli estremi si toccano** extremes meet

toccasa·na [s] *m* (**-na**) cure-all, panacea

tocca·to -ta *adj* touché; touched in the head, nutty; **già toccato** abovementioned || *f* (mus) toccata

tóc·co -ca (-chi -che) *adj* touched, nutty; spoiled (*fruit*) || *m* touch; knock; one o'clock (*P.M.*); (coll) stroke

tòc·co *m* (**-chi**) chunk, piece; mortarboard; toque; **un bel tocco di ragazza** a buxom lass

tò·ga *f* (**-ghe**) gown, academic gown; (hist) toga

tògliere §127 *tr* to remove, take away; to take; to cut (*telephone connection*); to deduct; to take off; to preclude, prevent; **togliere a** to take away from; **togliere al cielo** (lit) to praise to the skies; **togliere di mezzo** to remove; to do away with; **togliere la parola a** to take the floor from; **togliere l'onore a** to dishonor; **togliere una spina dal cuore a** to relieve the heart and mind of || *intr*—**tolga Dio!** God forbid! || *ref* to take off (*e.g., one's coat*); to have (*e.g., a tooth*) pulled; to satisfy (*a whim*); **togliersi di mezzo** to get out of the way; **togliersi la vita** to take one's life; **togliersi qlcu dai piedi** to get rid of s.o.

tòlda *f* (naut) deck

tolemài·co -ca *adj* (**-ci -che**) Ptolemaic

tolétta *f* dressing table; dressing room; toilet, washroom; dress, gown; **fare toletta** or **farsi la toletta** to make one's toilet

tolleràbile *adj* tolerable

tollerante *adj* tolerant; liberal
tolleranza *f* tolerance; leeway
tollerare **(tòllero)** *tr* to tolerate; to bear, stand
tòl·to -ta *adj* taken; except, leaving out, e.g., **tolta sua figlia** leaving his daughter out || *m*—**il mal tolto** ill-gotten goods
to·màio *m* (**-mài** & **-màia** *fpl*) or **to·màia** *f* (**-màie**) upper (*of shoe*)
tómba *f* tomb, grave
tombale *adj* grave (*e.g., stone*)
tombino *m* sewer inlet
tómbola *f* bingo; (coll) tumble
tombolare **(tómbolo)** *tr* (coll) to tumble down (*the steps*) || *intr* (ESSERE) to fall headlong; (coll) to go to rack and ruin; (aer) to tumble
tómbolo *m* fall, tumble; bolster; lace pillow; (coll) fatso; **fare un tombolo** to go to rack and ruin; to lose one's position
Tommaso *m* Thomas
tòmo *m* volume; (coll) character
tòna·ca *f* (**-che**) (eccl) frock; (eccl) soutane; **gettare la tonaca alle ortiche** to doff the cassock
tonare **§257** *intr* to peal; to thunder || *impers* (ESSERE & AVERE)—**tuona** it is thundering
tondeggiante *adj* round; rounded; chubby; curvaceous
tondino *m* coaster; iron rod (*for reinforced concrete*); (archit) molding (*at top or bottom of column*); (archit) astragal
tón·do -da *adj* round; (typ) roman || *m* round; circle; plate, dish; (typ) roman; **in tondo** around
tónfo *m* splash; thump
tòni·co -ca **(-ci -che)** *adj* tonic || *m* tonic (*medicine*) || *f* (mus) tonic
tonificare **§197** **(tonìfico)** *tr* to invigorate
tonnara *f* tuna nets
tonnellàg·gio *m* (**-gi**) tonnage
tonnellata *f* ton; **tonnellata di stazza** displacement ton
tónno *m* tuna
tòno *m* tone; tune; hue; style; (mus) pitch; (mus) key; **darsi tono** to put on airs; **di tono** stylish; **fuori di tono** out of tune
tonsilla *f* tonsil
tonsura *f* tonsure
tón·to -ta *adj* (coll) dumb, stupid
topàia *f* rat's nest; hovel
topà·zio *m* (**-zi**) topaz
tòpi·co -ca **(-ci -che)** *adj* topical || *f* topic; (coll) blunder
tòpo *m* mouse; rat; **topo campagnolo** field mouse; **topo d'acqua** water rat; **topo d'albergo** hotel thief; **topo d'auto** car thief; **topo di biblioteca** bookworm
topografìa *f* topography
topolino *m* little mouse || **Topolino** *m* Mickey Mouse
toporagno *m* shrew
tòppa *f* patch; keyhole
tòppo *m* stump; headstock (*of lathe*)
torace *m* thorax
tórba *f* peat
tórbi·do -da *adj* cloudy; murky || *m* trouble; **pescare nel torbido** to fish in troubled waters; **torbidi** disorder
torbièra *f* peatbog
tòrcere **§272** *tr* to twist; to wring; to bend, curve; to curl (*the lips*); to lead astray || *intr* (ESSERE) to bend, curve || *ref* to writhe; to bend over; **torcersi dalle risa** to split with laughter
torchiare **§287** **(tòrchio)** *tr* to press
tòr·chio *m* (**-chi**) press; printing press
tòr·cia *f* (**-ce**) torch
torcicòllo *m* stiff neck; (orn) wryneck
torcinaso [s] *m* (vet) twitch
tórdo *m* thrush; simpleton
torèllo *m* young bull; (naut) garboard
torèro *m* bullfighter
tórlo *m* yolk
tórma *f* crowd, throng; herd
torménta *f* blizzard
tormentare **(torménto)** *tr* to torture, torment; to pester, nag || *ref* to worry
torménto *m* torture, torment; pang; bore, pest, annoyance
tornacónto *m* interest, advantage
tornante *m* curve
tornare **(tórno)** *tr* (lit) to restore; (obs) to turn || *intr* (ESSERE) to return; to go back; (coll) to jibe, agree, square; **tornare a** to be profitable to; **tornare a** + *inf* verb + again, e.g., **tornare a essere** to become again; **tornare a fare** to do again; **tornare a bomba** to return to the point; **tornare a galla** to come back to the surface; **tornare a gola** to repeat (*said of food*); **tornare a onore a qlcu** to do credit to s.o.; **tornare a pennello** to fit to a T; **tornare in sé** to come to; **tornare opportuno** or **utile a** to suit, e.g., **non gli tornó opportuno vendere la casa** it did not suit him to sell the house; **tornare utile** to come in handy; **tornare sulle proprie decisioni** to change one's mind
tornasóle *m* litmus
tornèllo *m* turnstile
tornèo *m* tournament, tourney
tór·nio *m* (**-ni**) lathe
tornire **§176** *tr* to turn, turn up (*on a lathe*); to polish
tornitóre *m* lathe operator
tórno *m* turn; period (*of time*); **levarsi di torno** to get rid of; **torno torno** all around
tòro *m* bull; (archit, geom) torus; (lit) marital bed || **Toro** *m* (astrol) Taurus
torpèdine *f* torpedo
torpedinièra *f* destroyer escort; torpedo-boat destroyer
torpè·do *f* (**-do**) (aut) touring car
torpedóne *m* bus, motor coach
tòrpi·do -da *adj* torpid, sluggish; numb
torpóre *m* torpor, sluggishness; numbness
tórre *f* tower; (chess) castle; (nav) turret; **torre campanaria** bell tower; **torre d'avorio** ivory tower; **torre di**

lancio (rok) gantry; **torre pendente** leaning tower
torrefare §173 *tr* to roast (*coffee*)
torreggiante *adj* towering
torreggiare §290 (**torréggio**) *intr* to tower
torrènte *m* torrent
torrenziale *adj* torrential
torrétta *f* turret; (nav) conning tower (*of submarine*); (archit) bartizan
tòrri·do -da *adj* torrid
torrióne *m* donjon; (nav) conning tower (*of battleship*)
torróne *m* nougat
torsióne *f* torsion
tórso *m* stalk; core (*of fruit*); torso, trunk; **a torso nudo** bare-chested
tórsolo *m* core; stalk; stem; **non vale un torsolo** it's not worth a fig
tórta *f* pie; cake, tart; **torta di mele** apple pie
tòrta *f* twist
tortièra *f* baking pan
tòr·to -ta *adj* twisted; crooked; gloomy (*face*) || *m* wrong; **a torto** unjustly; **avere torto** to be wrong; **avere torto marcio** to be dead wrong; **dar torto a** to lay the blame on; **fare torto a** to wrong, e.g., **fece torto al proprio fratello** he wronged his own brother; to bring discredit upon || *f* see **tòrta** || **torto** *adv* askance
tórtora *f* turtledove
tortuó·so -sa [s] *adj* winding; ambiguous; (fig) devious
tortura *f* torture
torturare *tr* to torture; to pester || *ref* to torment oneself; **torturarsi il cervello** to rack one's brain
tosare (**tóso**) *tr* to clip, crop; to shear; (fig) to fleece
tosa·tóre -trice *mf* clipper, shearer || *f* clippers; lawn mower
tosatura *f* sheepshearing; clip (*of wool*)
tosca·no -na *adj* & *mf* Tuscan || *m* stogy || **Toscana, la** Tuscany
tósse *f* cough; **tosse asinina** or **canina** whooping cough
tòssi·co -ca (**-ci -che**) toxic || *m* (archaic) poison
tossicòmane *mf* drug addict
tossicomanìa *f* drug addiction
tossina *f* toxin
tossire (**tósso**) & §176 *intr* to cough
tostapa·ne *m* (**-ne**) toaster
tostare (**tòsto**) *tr* to toast; to roast (*e.g., coffee*)
tò·sto -sta *adj* (lit) prompt; (lit) impudent; (lit) brazen (*face*) || **tosto** *adv* (lit) soon; **ben tosto** (lit) very soon; **tosto che** (lit) as soon as
tòt *adj pl invar* so many, that many || *pron invar* so much, that much
totale *adj* & *m* total
totalità·rio -ria *adj* (**-ri -rie**) total, complete; totalitarian
totalizzare [ddzz] *tr* to add up; to make (*so many points*)
totalizzatóre [ddzz] *m* pari-mutuel; betting window; (mach) totalizator
tòtano *m* squid; (orn) tattler
totocàlcio *m* soccer pool
tovàglia *f* tablecloth
tovagliòlo *m* napkin
tòz·zo -za *adj* stubby, stocky || *m* piece (*of fresh bread*); crust (*of bread*)
tra *prep* among; between
trabàccolo *m* small fishing boat
traballare *intr* to shake; to totter; to wobble; to stagger; to toddle
trabìccolo *m* frame for bedwarmer; jalopy; hulk
traboccante *adj* overflowing
traboccare §197 (**trabócco**) *tr* to knock down || *intr* to overflow (*said of container*) || *intr* (ESSERE) to overflow (*said of liquid*) || *intr* (ESSERE & AVERE) to tip (*said of scales*); **far traboccare** to make (*the scales*) tip
trabocchétto *m* pitfall; trapdoor
trabóc·co *m* (**-chi**)—**trabocco di sangue** internal hemorrhage
tracagnòt·to -ta *adj* stubby, stocky || *mf* stocky person
tracannare *tr* to gulp down
tracchég·gio *m* (**-gi**) delay; (fencing) feint
tràc·cia *f* (**-ce**) track; trace, clue; trail; outline, plan; (lit) line, row; **buona traccia** right track; **fare la traccia a** to open the way for; **in** or **sotto traccia** concealed (*e.g., wiring*); **tracce** tinge; (chem) traces
tracciante *adj* tracer (*bullet*)
tracciare §128 *tr* to trace; to pave (*the way*); to outline; (lit) to track
tracciato *m* tracing, drawing; outline; map; layout
trachèa *f* trachea, windpipe
tracòlla *f* baldric; shoulder strap; **a tracolla** slung across the shoulders
tracòllo *m* collapse, debacle
tracotanza *f* arrogance
tradiménto *m* treason; treachery; **a tradimento** unawares, unexpectedly; treacherously
tradire §176 *tr* to betray; to fail (*a person; said of memory*) || *ref* to give oneself away
tradi·tóre -trice *adj* charming, seductive; treacherous; deceitful, faithless || *mf* traitor; betrayer || *f* traitress
tradizionale *adj* traditional
tradizióne *f* tradition
tradótta *f* military train
tradurre §102 *tr* to translate
tradut·tóre -trice *mf* translator
traduzióne *f* translation
traènte *mf* (com) drawer
trafela·to -ta *adj* breathless, out of breath
trafèrro *m* (elec) air gap; (elec) spark gap
trafficante *m* dealer, trader; trafficker
trafficare §197 (**tràffico**) *tr* to sell; to traffic in || *intr* to trade, deal; to hustle
tràffi·co *m* (**-ci**) traffic
trafficó·ne -na *mf* hustler
trafiggere §104 *tr* to pierce, stab, transfix; to wound
trafila *f* routine; red tape; (mach) drawplate
trafilare *tr* to wiredraw

trafilétto *m* (journ) short feature, special item; (journ) notice
trafitta *f* stab wound; shooting pain
trafittura *f* stab; shooting pain
traforare (**trafòro** & **trafóro**) *tr* to bore; to pierce; to carve (*wood*); to pink (*leather*); to embroider with open work
trafóro *m* boring; tunnel; open work
trafugare §209 *tr* to purloin; to sneak off with
tragèdia *f* tragedy; **far tragedie** (coll) to make a fuss
traghettare (**traghétto**) *tr* to ferry
traghétto *m* ferry; **traghetto spaziale** space shuttle
tràgi•co -ca (**-ci -che**) *adj* tragic ‖ *m* tragedian; **il tragico** (fig) the tragic
tragitto *m* journey; (obs) ferry
traguardo *m* sight; aim; goal; finish line; (phot) viewfinder; (sports) tape
traiettòria *f* trajectory; path
tràina *f* towline; **pescare alla traina** to troll
trainare (**tràino**) *tr* to drag, tug, pull
tràino *m* drag; load; trailer
tralasciare §128 *tr* to interrupt; to omit; **non tralasciare di** to not fail to
tràl•cio *m* (**-ci**) stem (*of vine*)
tralìc•cio *m* (**-ci**) ticking, bedtick; trellis; tower (*of high-tension line*)
tralice *m*—**in tralice** askance
tralignare *intr* (ESSERE & AVERE) to degenerate
tram *m* (**tram**) streetcar
trama *f* woof, weft; plot (*of play*); texture (*of cloth*)
tramà•glio *m* (**-gli**) trammel net
tramandare *tr* to hand down
tramare *tr* & *intr* to weave; to plot
trambusto *m* bustle
tramestì•o *m* (**-i**) bustle, confusion
tramèzza [ddzz] *f* partition
tramezzare (**tramèzzo**) [ddzz] *tr* to interpose; to partition
tramezzino [ddzz] *m* small partition; sandwich; sandwich man
tramèzzo [ddzz] *m* partition; side dish; (sew) insertion ‖ *adv* in between; **tramezzo a** among
tràmite *m* intermediary; (lit) pass; **per tramite di** through ‖ *prep* (coll) by; by means of
tramòg•gia *f* (**-ge**) hopper
tramontana *f* north wind; **perdere la tramontana** to lose one's bearings
tramontare (**tramónto**) *intr* (ESSERE) to set (*said, e.g., of sun*); to end
tramónto *m* setting; sunset; decline
tramortire §176 *tr* to stun ‖ *intr* (ESSERE) to faint, swoon
trampolière *m* wading bird; (orn) stilt
tràmpoli *mpl* stilts
trampolino *m* diving board; springboard; ski jump; (fig) springboard
tramutare *tr* to transfer; to transform
tràn•cia *f* (**-ce**) slice; (mach) shears
tranèllo *m* trap, snare
trangugiare §290 *tr* to swallow; to gulp down
tranne *prep* except, save; **tranne che** unless
tranquillante *m* tranquilizer
tranquillare *tr* & *ref* (lit) to tranquilize; to calm down
tranquilli•tà *f* (**-tà**) tranquillity
tranquillizzare [ddzz] *tr* to tranquilize; to reassure ‖ *ref* to become reassured
tranquil•lo -la *adj* tranquil, calm; clear (*conscience*)
transatlànti•co -ca *adj* & *m* (**-ci -che**) transatlantic
transazióne *f* compromise
transènna *f* bar, barrier
transètto *m* (archit) transept
trànsfu•ga *m* (**-ghi**) (lit) deserter
transìgere §165 *tr* to settle ‖ *intr* to compromise
transistóre *m* transistor
transitàbile *adj* passable
transitare (**trànsito**) *intr* to move; to walk
transiti•vo -va *adj* transitive
trànsito *m* passage; traffic; (lit) passing; **di transito** transient
transitò•rio -ria *adj* (**-ri -rie**) temporary; transitory; transitional
transizióne *f* transition
transoceàni•co -ca *adj* (**-ci -che**) transoceanic
transòni•co -ca *adj* (**-ci -che**) transonic
transunto *m* abstract, summary (*of a document*)
trantràn *m* routine
tran•vài *m* (**-vài**) (coll) streetcar
tranvìa *f* streetcar line
tranvià•rio -ria *adj* (**-ri -rie**) streetcar
tranvière *m* streetcar conductor; motorman
trapanare (**tràpano**) *tr* to drill; (surg) to trephine
tràpano *m* drill; (surg) trephine; **trapano a vite** automatic drill
trapassare *tr* to pierce; (fig) to grieve; (poet) to cross; (lit) to pass, spend ‖ *intr* (ESSERE) to go through; to pass (*said of an inheritance*); (lit) to pass away; **trapassare da, per** or **al di là di** to come through (*said, e.g., of a nail, light*)
trapassato *m* (lit) deceased; **trapassato prossimo** past perfect
trapasso *m* crossing; transfer; transition; (lit) passing, death
trapelare (**trapélo**) *intr* (ESSERE) to ooze; to trickle out; to leak through; (fig) to leak out
trapè•zio *m* (**-zi**) trapeze; (geom) trapezoid
trapezòide *adj* trapezoidal ‖ *m* trapezoid
trapiantare *tr* to transplant ‖ *ref* to transfer
trapianto *m* transplantation; transplant; **trapianto cardiaco** heart transplant
tràppola *f* trap; (coll) gadget; (fig) lie; **trappola esplosiva** booby trap
trapunta *f* quilt
trapuntare *tr* to quilt; to embroider
trapun•to -ta *adj* quilted; embroidered; studded ‖ *m* embroidery ‖ *f* see **trapunta**
trarre §273 *tr* to pull; to drag; to draw; to bring; to deduct; to lead; to un-

sheathe (*a sword*); to heave (*a sigh*); to spin (*silk, wool,* etc.); **il dado è tratto** the die is cast; **trarre dalla prigione** to free from prison; **trarre d'impaccio** to get (*s.o.*) out of trouble; **trarre fuori** to extract; **trarre in inganno** to deceive; **trarre in rovina** to ruin; **trarre per mano** to lead by the hand || *intr* to kick (*said of a mule*); (lit) to run; (lit) to blow (*said of the wind*) || *ref* to take off (*e.g., one's hat*); **trarsi d'impaccio** to get out of trouble; **trarsi indietro** to pull back; **trarsi in disparte** to move aside

trasalire [s] §176 *intr* (ESSERE & AVERE) to start, jump

trasanda·to -ta *adj* untidy, slovenly

trasbordare (trasbórdo) *tr* to transfer, transship

trasbórdo *m* transfer, transshipment

trascéndere §245 *tr* to transcend || *intr* (ESSERE) to go to excesses

trascinare *tr* to drag; to stir; to enthrall; to lead astray; **trascinare la vita** to barely make ends meet || *ref* to drag oneself; to drag on

trascolorare (trascolóro) *tr* to discolor; to change the color of || *intr* (ESSERE) & *ref* to discolor; to change color

trascórrere §139 *tr* to pass (*time*); to skim through (*e.g., a book*); (lit) to go through || *intr* to go to excesses || *intr* (ESSERE) to elapse, pass

trascórso *m* slip (*e.g., of pen*); peccadillo

trascrìvere §250 *tr* to transcribe

trascrizióne *f* transcription; registration (*e.g., of a deed*)

trascuràbile *adj* negligible

trascurare *tr* to neglect; to fail; to disregard || *ref* to not take care of oneself

trascuratézza *f* negligence, neglect; carelessness; slovenliness

trascura·to -ta *adj* neglected; careless; slovenly

trasecolare (trasècolo) [s] *intr* (ESSERE & AVERE) to marvel, be astonished

trasferìbile *adj* transferable

trasferiménto *m* transfer; conveyance

trasferire §176 *tr* to transfer; to assign, convey || *ref* to move

trasfèrta *f* business trip; traveling expenses, per diem

trasfigurare *tr* to transfigure; to distort (*the truth*) || *ref* to be transfigured; to change countenance

trasfocatóre *m* (phot) zoom lens

trasfóndere §178 *tr* to transfuse; (fig) to instill

trasformàbile *adj* transformable; (aut) convertible

trasformare (trasfórmo) *tr* to transform; to alter || *ref* to transform oneself; to be converted

trasformati·vo -va *adj* (gram) transformational

trasformatóre *m* transformer

trasformazióne *f* transformation

trasformi·sta *mf* (-sti -ste) quick-change artist

trasfusióne *f* transfusion

trasgredire §176 *tr* & *intr* to transgress

trasgressióne *f* transgression

trasgressóre *m* transgressor

trasla·to -ta *adj* figurative; metaphorical; (lit) transferred || *m* figure of speech; metaphor

traslitterare (traslìttero) *tr* to transliterate

traslocare §197 **(traslòco)** *tr* to transfer; to move || *intr* & *ref* to move

traslò·co *m* (-chi) moving

traslùci·do -da *adj* translucent

trasméttere §198 *tr* to transmit; (rad) to broadcast

trasmetti·tóre -trice *mf* transmitter || *m* (naut) engine-room telegraph; (telg) sender

trasmigrare *intr* (ESSERE & AVERE) to transmigrate || *intr* (ESSERE) to pass, pass on

trasmissióne *f* transmission; conveyance; broadcast; telecast; **trasmissione del pensiero** thought transference

trasmittènte *adj* transmitting; broadcasting || *f* broadcasting station

trasmutare *tr* to transmute; to change

trasogna·to -ta [s] *adj* dreamy; daydreaming; dazed

trasparènte *adj* transparent || *m* transparency

trasparènza *f* transparence; **in trasparenza** against the light

trasparire §108 *intr* (ESSERE) to appear; to shine; to show through; to show, be revealed (*said of feelings*); **far trasparire** to reveal

traspirare *intr* to perspire || *intr* (ESSERE) to show, be revealed

traspirazióne *f* perspiration

traspórre §218 *tr* to transpose

trasportare (traspòrto) *tr* to transport; to carry away; to transfer; to translate; to postpone; (mus) to transpose; **lasciarsi trasportare** to be carried away || *ref* to move; (fig) to go back

trasporta·tóre -trice *mf* carrier || *m* (mach) conveyor belt; (phot) sprocket

traspòrto *m* transportation; transport; transfer; eagerness; moving; (mus) transposition; **trasporto funebre** funeral procession

trasposi·tóre -trice *mf* (mus) transposer

trassa·to -ta *adj* paying || *m* drawee

trastullare *tr* to amuse; to entice || *ref* to have a good time; to loiter

trastullo *m* play, game; fun; plaything

trasudare [s] *tr* to ooze; (fig) to exude || *intr* to ooze (*said of a wall*) || *intr* (ESSERE) to drip (*said of perspiration*)

trasversale *adj* transverse, cross || *f* crossroad

trasvèr·so -sa *adj* transverse || *m* transverse beam

trasvolare (trasvólo) *tr* to fly over, cross by air || *intr*—**trasvolare su** to skip over

trasvolata *f* non-stop flight

tratta *f* tug, pull; (rr) stretch; (com)

draft; (lit) crowd; **tratta dei neri** slave trade; **tratta delle bianche** white slavery

trattàbile *adj* negotiable; friendly, sociable

trattaménto *m* treatment; working conditions; food, spread; reception, welcome; **trattamento di favore** special treatment; **trattamento di quiescenza** retirement benefits

trattare *tr* to treat; to deal with; to transact; to wield; to play (*an instrument*); to work (*e.g., iron*); to deal in; **trattare qlcu da bugiardo** to call s.o. a liar; **trattare da cane** to treat like a dog || *intr* to bargain; **trattare di** to deal with; to take care of; to treat, handle || *ref* to take good care of oneself || *impers* (ESSERE) **si tratta di** it's question of

trattà•rio -ria *mf* (-ri -rie) drawee

trattativa *f* negotiation

trattato *m* treatise; treaty

trattazióne *f* treatment

tratteggiare §290 (**trattéggio**) *tr* to sketch; to outline; to hatch

trattég•gio *m* (-gi) hatching

trattenére §271 *tr* to keep; to entertain; to withhold; to hold back; to detain || *ref* to stop; to refrain; to remain

tratteniménto *m* entertainment, party; delay

trattenuta *f* withholding; checkoff

trattino *m* dash; hyphen

trat•to -ta *adj* drawn, extracted || *m* stretch; span; passage; tract; gesture; throw (*of dice*); stroke (*of pen*); bearing; section; (chess) move; **a larghi tratti** in broad outline; **a tratti** from time to time; **a un tratto** all of a sudden; at the same time; **dare un tratto alla bilancia** to tip the scales; **tratti** features; **tratti del volto** features; **tratto di corda** strappado; **tratto di unione** hyphen; **tutto d'un tratto** all of a sudden; **un bel tratto** quite a while

trat•tóre -trice *mf* innkeeper; restaurateur || *m* tractor; **trattore a cingoli** caterpillar tractor || *f* tractor (*vehicle*)

trattorìa *f* inn, restaurant

tratturo *m* cow path

traumatizzare [ddzz] *tr* to traumatize

travagliare §280 *tr* to torment; to molest || *intr & ref* to toil, labor

travà•glio *m* (-gli) suffering; toil; trave (*to inhibit horse being shod*); **travaglio di parto** labor pains; **travaglio di stomaco** upset stomach

travasare *tr* to pour off; to decant; to transfer || *ref* to spill

travaso *m* pouring off; transfer; **travaso di bile** gall bladder attack; **travaso di sangue** hemorrhage

travatura *f* roof timbers; **travatura maestra** ridgepole

trave *f* beam; joist; **fare una trave d'un fuscello** to make a mountain out of a molehill

travedére §279 *tr* to glimpse || *intr* to be mistaken

travéggole *fpl*—**avere le traveggole** to see things; to see one thing for another

travèrsa *f* crossbar; crossroad; crosspiece; rung; bar (*of goalpost*); dam; rail (*of fence*); transom; slat (*to hold bedspring*); rubber pad; (rr) tie

traversare (**travèrso**) *tr* to cross

traversata *f* passage, crossing

traversìa *f* strong wind; **traversie** misfortunes

traversina *f* (rr) tie

travèr•so -sa *adj* cross; devious || *m* width; crossbar; (naut) beam; (naut) side; **a traverso** (naut) on the beam; **capire a traverso** to misunderstand; **di traverso** askance; crosswise; the wrong way || *f* see **traversa**

traversóne *m* large crossbar; westerly gale; side blow with saber

travestiménto *m* disguise; travesty

travestire (**travèsto**) *tr* to disguise; to travesty, parody || *ref* to disguise oneself

traviare §119 *tr* to lead astray || *intr & ref* to go astray

travicèllo *m* joist

travisare *tr* to distort

travolgènte *adj* impetuous; fascinating; sweeping

travòlgere §289 *tr* to overwhelm; to overturn; to sweep away

trazióne *f* traction

tre [e] *adj & pron* three; **le tre** three o'clock || *m* three; third (*in dates*)

trébbia *f* thresher; threshing

trebbiare §287 (**trébbio**) *tr & intr* to thresh

trebbiatrice *f* thresher, threshing machine

trebbiatura *f* threshing

tréc•cia *f* (-ce) plait; braid; **treccia a ciambella** bun, knot

trecentèsi•mo -ma *adj, m & pron* three hundredth

trecènto *adj, m & pron* three hundred || **il Trecento** the fourteenth century

tredicèsi•mo -ma *adj, m & pron* thirteenth || *f* Xmas bonus

trédici *adj & pron* thirteen; **le tredici** one P.M. || *m* thirteen; thirteenth (*in dates*)

trégua *f* truce; respite; **tregua atomica** nuclear test ban; **senza tregua** without letup

tremare (**trèmo**) *intr* to shake, tremble; to quiver; **far tremare** to shake

tremarèlla *f*—**avere la tremarella** (coll) to shake in one's boots

tremebón•do -da *adj* (lit) shaky

tremèn•do -da *adj* tremendous

trementina *f* turpentine

tremila *adj, m & pron* three thousand

trèmito *m* trembling; quivering

tremolare (**trèmolo**) *intr* to shake; to quiver; to flicker

trèmo•lo -la *adj* tremulous || *m* (bot) aspen; (mus) tremolo

trèno *m* train; quarter (*of animal*); **set** (*of tires*); threnody, lamentation; **treno accelerato** local; **treno di lusso** Pullman train; **treno direttissimo** ex-

press; **treno di vita** mode of life; mode of living; **treno merci** freight train; **treno stradale** tractor-trailer
trenodìa *f* threnody
trénta *adj & pron* thirty ‖ *m* thirty; thirtieth (*in dates*)
trentèsi·mo -ma *adj, m & pron* thirtieth
trentina *f* about thirty
Trènto *f* Trent
trepidare (**trèpido**) *intr* to fear; to worry
trepidazióne *f* fear, trepidation
treppiède *m* tripod; trivet
tré·sca *f* (**-sche**) intrigue; liaison
tréspolo *m* stool; pedestal; stand, perch; (coll) jalopy
triàngolo *m* triangle; **triangolo rettangolo** right triangle
tribolare (**trìbolo**) *tr* to torment, afflict ‖ *intr* to suffer
tribolazióne *f* tribulation, ordeal
tribórdo *m* (naut) starboard
tri·bù *f* (**-bù**) tribe
tribuna *f* rostrum, platform; (sports) grandstand; **tribuna stampa** press box
tribunale *m* court, tribunal; courthouse; **tribunale dei minorenni** juvenile court; **tribunale di prima istanza** court of first instance
tributare *tr* to bestow
tributà·rio -ria (**-ri -rie**) *adj* tributary; tax ‖ *m* tributary
tributo *m* tribute; tax
trichè·co *m* (**-chi**) walrus
triciclo *m* tricycle
tricolóre *adj & m* tricolor
tricòrno *m* cocked hat, tricorn
tricromìa *f* three-color printing; three-color print
tridènte *m* trident
trifase *adj* three-phase
trifocale *adj* trifocal
trifò·glio *m* (**-gli**) clover; three-leaf clover
trìfola *f* (coll) truffle
trìglia *f* red mullet
trigonometrìa *f* trigonometry
trilióne *m* trillion
trillare *intr* to trill; to vibrate
trillo *m* trill; ringing
trilogìa *f* trilogy
trimestrale *adj* quarterly
trimèstre *m* quarter; quarterly dues; quarterly payment; (educ) quarter, trimester
trimotóre *m* three-engine plane
trina *f* lace
trin·ca *f* (**-che**) (naut) gammoning; **di trinca** clearly, cleanly; **nuovo di trinca** brand-new
trincare §197 *tr* (coll) to gulp down, swill
trincèa *f* trench
trincerare (**trincèro**) *tr* to dig trenches in ‖ *ref* to entrench oneself
trincétto *m* shoemaker's blade
trinchétto *m* (naut) foremast; (naut) foresail
trinciante *adj* cutting ‖ *m* carving knife
trinciapóllo *m* meat shears
trinciare §128 *tr* to carve; to shred; to advance (*rash opinions*); to cut up
trinciato *m* smoking tobacco
trinciatrice *f* shredder; slicer
Trinità *f* Trinity
trionfale *adj* triumphal
trionfante *adj* triumphant
trionfare (**trionfo**) *intr* to triumph
trionfo *m* triumph; center piece; tidbit dish with three or four tiers; trump (*in game of tarot*)
triparti·to -ta *adj* tripartite
triplicare §197 (**trìplico**) *tr & ref* to triple
trìplice *adj* threefold
tri·plo -pla *adj & m* triple
trìpode *m* tripod
trippa *f* tripe; (coll) belly
tripudiare §287 *intr* to exult
tripù·dio *m* (**-di**) exultation
tris *m* (**tris**) (poker) three of a kind
trisàvola *f* great-great-grandmother
trisàvolo *m* great-great-grandfather; **trisavoli** great-great-grandparents
trisma *m* lockjaw
triste *adj* sad; gloomy, bleak
tristézza *f* sadness
tri·sto -sta *adj* wicked; wretched; poor (*figure*); (lit) sad
tritacar·ne *m* (**-ne**) meat grinder
tritaghiàc·cio *m* (**-cio**) ice crusher
tritare *tr* to chop; to grind; to mince, hash; to pound
tri·to -ta *adj* minced, hashed; worn, trite
tritòlo *m* T.N.T.
tritóne *m* (zool) newt; (fig) merman ‖ **Tritone** *m* Triton
trìtti·co *m* (**-ci**) triptych; export document in triplicate; trilogy
trittòn·go *m* (**-ghi**) triphthong
triturare *tr* to mince, hash
trivèlla *f* auger, drill; post-hole digger
trivellare (**trivèllo**) *tr* to drill, bore
triviale *adj* vulgar
triviali·tà *f* (**-tà**) vulgarity
trì·vio *m* (**-vi**) crossroads; trivium; **da trivio** vulgar
trofèo *m* trophy; (mil) insignia (*on headpiece*)
trògolo *m* trough
tròia *f* sow; slut ‖ **Troia** *f* Troy
troia·no -na *adj & m* Trojan
trómba *f* trumpet; bugle, clarion; trunk (*of elephant*); leg (*of boot*); (anat) tube; (aut, rad) horn; **con le trombe nel sacco** crestfallen, dejected; **tromba d'aria** whirlwind; tornado; **tromba marina** waterspout; **tromba delle scale** stairwell
trombétta *f* trumpet
trombettière *m* (mil) trumpeter
trombetti·sta *m* (**-sti**) trumpet player
trombóne *m* trombone; blunderbuss
trombò·si *f* (**-si**) thrombosis
troncare §197 (**trónco**) *tr* to chop; to cut off; to clip (*words*); to break, sever; to block (*s.o.'s progress*); to apocopate
tronchése [s] *m* wire cutter
trón·co -ca (**-chi -che**) *adj* truncate; oxytone; apocopated; exhausted, dead-tired; incomplete; **in tronco** in the middle; (*dismissal*) on the spot ‖ *m* trunk; stub (*of receipt book*);

section (*of highway*); log; strain (*of a family*); (rr) branch; **tronco di cono** truncated cone; **tronco maggiore** (naut) lower mast
troncóne *m* stump
troneggiare §290 (**tronéggio**) *intr* to tower; to hold forth; **troneggiare su** to lord it over
trón•fio -fia *adj* (**-fi -fie**) haughty; bombastic
tròno *m* throne
tropicale *adj* tropical
tròpi•co *m* (**-ci**) tropic
troposfèra *f* troposphere
tròp•po -pa *adj & pron* too much; **trop•pi -pe** too many || *m* too much; **questo è troppo!** enough is enough! || **troppo** *adv* too; too much; **essere di troppo** to be in the way
tròta *f* trout
trottare (**tròtto**) *intr* to trot
trotterellare (**trotterèllo**) *intr* to trot along; to toddle
tròtto *m* trot; **piccolo trotto** jog trot
tròttola *f* top
trovare (**tròvo**) *tr* to find; to visit; **trovare a or da ridire (su)** to find fault (with); **trovi?** don't you think so? || *ref* to find oneself; to meet; to be; to be located; to happen, e.g., **mi trovai a passare di fronte a casa sua** I happened to pass in front of his house
trovarò•be *m* (**-be**) (theat) property man || *f* (theat) dresser
trovata *f* find; trick, gimmick
trovatèl•lo -la *mf* foundling, waif
trovatóre *m* troubadour
trovièro *m* trouvère
truccare §197 *tr* to make up; to falsify; (aut) to soup up || *ref* to put on make-up
truccatura *f* make-up; trick, gimmick
truc•co *m* (**-chi**) make-up; trick, gimmick
truce *adj* fierce, cruel; menacing
trucidare (**trùcido**) *tr* to massacre
trùciolo *m* chip, shaving
truculènto *adj* truculent
truffa *f* cheat, fraud, swindle; **truffa all'americana** confidence game
truffare *tr* to cheat, swindle
truffa•tóre -trice *mf* cheat, swindler
truismo *m* truism
truògolo *m* var of **trogolo**
truppa *f* troop; soldiers; **di truppa** (mil) enlisted (*man or woman*); **in truppa** in a flock
tu §5 *pron pers;* **a tu per tu** face to face; **dare del tu a** to address in the familiar form
tuba *f* tuba; (hist) horn, trumpet; (joc) top hat, stovepipe; (anat) tube
tubare *intr* to coo
tubatura *f* piping, tubing; pipe, tube; pipeline
tubazióne *f* tubes, pipes
tubèrcolo *m* tubercle
tubercolosà•rio [s] *m* (**-ri**) tuberculosis sanitarium
tubercolò•si *f* (**-si**) tuberculosis
tubercoló•so -sa [s] *adj* tuberculous || *mf* T.B. patient
tùbero *m* tuber
tubétto *m* tube (*for pills or toothpaste*); spool
tubino *m* small tube; derby (hat)
tubo *m* tube; pipe; (anat) canal, duct; **a tubo** tubular; **tubo di scarico** exhaust pipe; **tubo di troppopieno** overflow; **tubo di ventilazione** air shaft
tubolare *adj* tubular || *m* tire (*for racing bicycle*)
tuffare *tr* to dip; to plunge || *ref* to plunge; to dive
tuffa•tóre -trice *mf* diver || *m* dive bomber
tuffétto *m* (orn) dabchick, grebe
tuffo *m* dive; plunge; throb; **a tuffo** (aer) diving; **scendere a tuffo** (aer) to dive; **tuffo ad angelo** (sports) swan dive; **tuffo d'acqua** downpour
tufo *m* tufa
tu•ga *f* (**-ghe**) (naut) deckhouse
tugù•rio *m* (**-ri**) hovel
tulipano *m* tulip
tumefare §173 *tr & ref* to swell
tumefazióne *f* swelling
tùmi•do -da *adj* tumid
tumóre *m* tumor
tùmulo *m* tomb; tumulus
tumulto *m* tumult, riot; commotion
tumultuó•so -sa [s] *adj* tumultuous
tungstèno *m* tungsten
tùni•ca *f* (**-che**) tunic
Tùnisi *f* Tunis
Tunisìa, la Tunisia
tunisi•no -na *adj & mf* Tunisian
tuo tua §6 *adj & pron poss* (**tuòi tue**)
tuòno *m* thunder
tuòrlo *m* yolk
turàcciolo *m* cork, stopper
turare *tr* to plug, stop; to cork
turba *f* crowd; mob; (pathol) upset
turbaménto *m* commotion, perturbation; disturbance, breach (*of law and order*)
turbante *m* turban
turbare *tr* to muddy; to disturb; to upset || *ref* to become cloudy; to become upset
turba•to -ta *adj* upset; disturbed; distracted
tùrbi•do -da *adj* turbid
turbina *f* turbine
turbinare (**tùrbino**) *tr* to separate in a centrifuge || *intr* to whirl
tùrbine *m* whirlwind; swarm; tumult
turbinó•so -sa [s] *adj* whirling; tumultuous
turboèli•ca *m* (**-ca**) turboprop
turbogètto *m* turbojet
turbolèn•to -ta *adj* turbulent
turbolènza *f* turbulence
turbomotrice *f* (rr) turbine engine
turboreattóre *m* turbojet
turcasso *m* quiver
turchése [s] *m* turquoise
Turchìa, la Turkey
turchinétto *m* bluing
turchi•no -na *adj* dark-blue || *m* dark blue
tur•co -ca (**-chi -che**) *adj* Turkish; **sedere alla turca** to sit cross-legged || *mf* Turk || *m* Turkish (*language*); **bestemmiare come un turco** to swear

like a trooper; **fumare come un turco** to smoke like a steam engine
tùrgi•do -da *adj* turgid
turìbolo *m* thurible, censer
turismo *m* tourism
turi•sta *mf* (**-sti -ste**) tourist
turìsti•co -ca *adj* (**-ci -che**) tourist; travel (*e.g., bureau*); traveler's (*check*)
turlupinare *tr* to hoodwink, swindle
turlupinatura *f* swindle, confidence game
turno *m* turn; shift; **a turno** in turn; **di turno** on duty; **fare a turno** to take turns
turpe *adj* base, abject; (lit) ugly
turpilò•quio *m* (**-qui**) foul language
turpitùdine *f* turpitude
tuta *f* overalls; **tuta antigravità** anti-G suit; **tuta da bambini** jumpers; **tuta spaziale** spacesuit
tutèla *f* guardianship; defense, protection
tutelare *adj* tutelary || *v* (**tutèlo**) *tr* to protect, defend
tùtolo *m* corncob
tu•tóre -trice *mf* guardian; protector
tuttavìa *adv* yet, nevertheless; (lit) always, continuously
tut•to -ta *adj* whole; all; full; **con tutto** in spite of, e.g., **con tutto quello che ho fatto per lui** in spite of all I have done for him; **del tutto** fully, completely; **è tutt'uno** it's all the same; **tutt'altro** completely different; on the contrary; **tutt'altro che** anything but; **tutti** every, e.g., **tutti gli scolari** every pupil; **tutti e due** both || *m* everything; whole; **con tutto che** although; **fare di tutto** to do everything possible; **in tutto** altogether || *pron* **tut•ti -te** all, everybody (*of a group*); **tutti** everybody || **tutto** *adv* quite; **tutt'a un tratto** all of a sudden; **tutto al contrario** quite the opposite
tuttofa•re *adj invar* of all trades; of all work || *m* (**-re**) factotum, jack-of-all-trades || *f* (**-re**) maid of all work
tuttóra *adv* yet, still
tziga•no -na *adj & mf* var of **zigano**

U

U, u [u] *m & f* nineteenth letter of the Italian alphabet
ubbìa *f* prejudice, bias; complex; whim
ubbidiènte *adj* obedient
ubbidire §176 *tr* to obey || *intr* to obey; to respond (*said of a car*); (with *dat*) to obey, e.g., **gli ubbedì** he obeyed him
ubertó•so -sa [s] *adj* fruitful; fertile
ubicazióne *f* location
ubiquità *f* ubiquity; **non ho il dono dell'ubiquità** I can't be everywhere at the same time
ubì•quo -qua *adj* ubiquitous
ubriacare §197 *tr* to make drunk, intoxicate || *ref* to get drunk
ubriacatura or **ubriachézza** *f* drunkenness, intoxication
ubria•co -ca (**-chi -che**) *adj* drunk; **ubriaco fradicio** dead drunk || *mf* drunkard
ubriacó•ne -na *mf* drunkard
uccellare (**uccèllo**) *tr* to take in, cajole || *intr* to snare; to fowl; to hunt birds
uccèllo *m* bird; **uccello di bosco** fugitive; **uccello di galera** gallows bird; **uccello di passo** bird of passage
uccella•tóre -trice *mf* live-bird catcher
uccellièra *f* aviary; large birdcage
uccìdere §274 *tr* to kill || *ref* to kill oneself; to get killed; to kill one another
-ùccio -ùccia (**-ucci -ucce**) *suf adj* not very, e.g., **calduccio** not very hot; rather, e.g., **magruccio** rather thin; poor little, e.g., **caruccio** poor little darling || *suf m & f* small e.g., **cappelluccio** small hat
uccisióne *f* killing; murder
ucci•so -sa *adj* killed || *mf* victim
ucci•sóre -ditrice *mf* killer
ucrai•no -na *adj & mf* Ukrainian || **l'Ucraina** *f* the Ukraine
udìbile *adj* audible
udiènza *f* audience; hearing; **l'udienza è aperta!** the court is now in session!
udire §275 *tr* to hear; to listen to
udito *m* hearing
uditòfono *m* hearing aid
udi•tóre -trice *adj* hearing || *mf* (educ) auditor || *m* magistrate
uditò•rio -ria (**-ri -rie**) *adj* auditory || *m* audience
ufficiale *adj* official || *m* official; officer; **primo ufficiale** (naut) first officer, mate; **ufficiale di giornata** (mil) officer of the day; **ufficiale di rotta** (aer, naut) navigator; **ufficiale giudiziario** clerk of the court; process server, bailiff; **ufficiale medico** (mil) medical officer
ufficiare §128 *tr* to officiate
uffì•cio *m* (**-ci**) duty; office; bureau; department (*of agency*); **d'ufficio** ex-officio; public, e.g., **avvocato d'ufficio** public defender; **ufficio di collocamento** placement bureau; **ufficio di compensazione** clearing house; **ufficio d'igiene** board of health
uffició•so -sa [s] *adj* unofficial; kindly; white (*lie*)
uffì•zio *m* (**-zi**) (eccl) office
ufo *m*—**a ufo** gratis, without paying
ugèllo *m* nozzle
ùg•gia *f* (**-ge**) darkness; gloom; dislike; **avere in uggia** to dislike
uggiolare (**ùggiolo**) *intr* to whine (*said of a dog*)
uggió•so -sa [s] *adj* gloomy; boring
ugnare *tr* to bevel; to miter

ugnatura *f* bevel; miter
ùgola *f* uvula; **bagnarsi l'ugola** (coll) to wet one's whistle
ugonòtto *m* Huguenot
uguaglianza *f* equality
uguagliare §280 *tr* to equal; to make equal; to equalize; to level; to compare || *ref* to compare oneself; to be equal; to be compared
uguale *adj* equal; same; even; level; **per me è uguale** it's the same to me || *m* equal; (math) equal sign
ùlcera *f* ulcer; sore
ulcerare (ùlcero) *tr & ref* to ulcerate
uliva *f* var of **oliva**
ulterióre *adj* further, subsequent, ulterior
ùltima *f* latest news; last straw
ultimare (ùltimo) *tr* to complete, finish
ultimato *m* ultimatum
ultimìssima *f* latest edition (*of newspaper*); **ultimissime** late news
ùlti·mo- ma *adj* last; final; latest; latter; farthest; ultimate; least; top (*floor*); **all'ultimo, dall'ultimo, nell'ultimo** or **sull'ultimo** lately; finally, at the end || *f* see **ultima**
ultimogèni·to -ta *adj* last-born || *mf* last-born child
ultra- *pref adj* and *m & f* ultra-, e.g., **ultraelevato** ultrahigh; super-, e.g., **ultrasonico** supersonic (*speed*)
ultracór·to -ta *adj* ultrashort
ultraróss·so -sa *adj & m* infrared
ultraterré·no -na *adj* ultramundane; unearthly
ultraviolét·to -ta *adj & m* ultraviolet
ululare (ùlulo) *intr* to howl
ululato *m* howl
umanésimo *m* humanism
umani·sta *mf* (**-sti -ste**) humanist
umani·tà *f* (**-tà**) humanity; **umanità** *fpl* humanities
umanità·rio -ria *adj & mf* (**-ri -rie**) humanitarian
uma·no -na *adj* human; humane || *m* human nature; **umani** human beings
um·bro -bra *adj & m* Umbrian
umettare (umétto) *tr* to moisten, dampen
umidìc·cio -cia *adj* (**-ci -ce**) dampish
umidi·tà *f* (**-tà**) humidity, dampness
ùmi·do -da *adj* humid, damp || *m* humidity, dampness; **in umido** stewed (*e.g., meat*)
ùmile *adj* humble || **gli umili** *mpl* the meek
umiliare §287 *tr* to humiliate, humble || *ref* to humble oneself
umiliazióne *f* humiliation
umiltà *f* humility
umóre *m* humor, mood, temper; whim; (bot) sap; **un bell'umore** (coll) quite a character
umorismo *m* humor
umori·sta *mf* (**-sti -ste**) humorist
umorìsti·co -ca *adj* (**-ci -che**) humorous; amusing, comic, funny
un (apocopated form of **uno**) §9 *indef art* a, an || §9 *numeral adj* one || §12 *reciprocal indef pron*—**l'un l'altro** each other, one another
unànime *adj* unanimous
unanimità *f* unanimity
unàni·mo -ma *adj* unanimous
uncinare *tr* to hook, grapple
uncinétto *m* small hook; crochet hook
uncino *m* hook; grapnel; clasp; pothook; (fig) pretext; **a uncino** hooked
undicèsi·mo -ma *adj, m & pron* eleventh
ùndici *adj & pron* eleven; **le undici** eleven o'clock || *m* eleven; eleventh (*in dates*); (soccer) squad
ùngere §183 *tr* to grease; to oil; to smear; to anoint; to flatter || *ref* to smear oneself
Ungherìa, l' *f* Hungary
ungherése [s] *adj & mf* Hungarian
ùnghia *f* nail; fingernail; claw; hoof; fluke (*of anchor*); (fig) hairbreadth; **avere le unghie lunghe** to be light-fingered; **unghia del piede** toenail; **unghie** (fig) clutches
unghiata *f* nail scratch
unguènto *m* unguent, ointment
ùni·co -ca *adj* (**-ci -che**) only, sole; unique; single (*copy*); complete (*text*) || *f*—**l'unica** the only solution
unicòrno *m* unicorn
unificare §197 (**unìfico**) *tr* to unify; to standardize
unificazióne *f* unification; standardization
uniformare (unifórmo) *tr* to make uniform, standardize || *ref*—**uniformarsi a** to conform to; to comply with
unifórme *adj* uniform; standard || *f* uniform; **alta uniforme** (mil) full dress
unilaterale *adj* unilateral
unióne *f* union; agreement; **unione libera** free love
unire §176 *tr & ref* to unite
unìsono [s] *m* unison; **all'unisono** in unison
uni·tà *f* (**-tà**) unity; unit; **unità di misura** unit of measurement
unità·rio -ria (-ri -rie) *adj* unit (*e.g., price*); united || *m* Unitarian
uni·to -ta *adj* united; joined; compact; plain (*color*); consolidated
universale *adj* universal; last (*judgment*)
universi·tà *f* (**-tà**) university
università·rio -ria (-ri -rie) *adj* university; college || *mf* university or college student; university or college professor
univer·so -sa *adj* universal || *m* universe
unno *m* Hun
u·no -na §9 *indef art* a, an || §9 *numeral adj* one || *m* one || §10 *pron indef* one; **le una, la una,** or **l'una** one o'clock; **l'uno e l'altro** both; **l'uno o l'altro** either, either one; **per uno** in single file; **uno per uno** one by one; each other || §11 *correlative pron* one
un·to -ta *adj* greasy || *m* grease, fat; flattery; anointed one
untuosità [s] *f* greasiness; unction, unctuousness
untuó·so -sa [s] *adj* greasy; unctuous

unzióne *f* unction
uò•mo *m* (**-mini**) man; **come un sol uomo** to a man; **uomo d'affari** businessman; **uomo del giorno** man of the hour; **uomo della strada** man of the street; **uomo di chiesa** churchman; **uomo di fatica** laborer; **uomo di fiducia** trusted man; **uomo di mare** seaman; **uomo di paglia** straw man; **uomo di parola** man of his word; **uomo in mare!** man overboard!; **uomo meccanico** automaton; **uomo morto** (rr) deadman brake; **uomo nuovo** nouveau riche; **uomo rana** frogman
uòpo *m*—**all'uopo** if need be; **essere d'uopo** (lit) to be necessary
uòse [s] *fpl* leggings
uò•vo *m* (**-va** *fpl*) egg; **meglio un uovo oggi che una gallina domani** a bird in a hand is worth two in the bush; **rompere le uova nel paniere a qlcu** to spoil s.o.'s plans; **uovo affogato** poached egg; **uovo alla coque** soft-boiled egg; **uovo all'occhio di bue** fried egg; **uovo da tè** tea ball; **uovo strapazzato** scrambled egg
uragano *m* hurricane; storm (*of applause*); **uragano di neve** blizzard
Urali *mpl* Ural Mountains
uranìfe•ro -ra *adj* uranium-bearing
urànio *m* uranium
urbanésimo *m* urbanization, migration toward the cities
urbanìsti•co -ca (**-ci -che**) *adj* city-planning || *f* city planning
urbani•tà *f* (**-tà**) urbanity, civility; city population
urbanizzare [ddzz] *tr* to urbanize
urba•no -na *adj* urban; urbane
urètra *f* urethra
urgènte *adj* urgent, pressing
urgènza *f* urgency; **d'urgenza** urgent; emergency (*e.g., operation*); **fare urgenza a** to urge
ùrgere §276 *tr* to urge, press || *intr* to be urgent
urina *f* urine
urinà•rio -ria *adj* (**-ri -rie**) urinary
urlare *tr* to shout; to shout down || *intr* to howl; to shout, yell
urla•tóre -trice *adj* screaming || *mf* screamer; loud singer
ur•lo *m* howl || *m* (**-la** *fpl*) yell, scream
urna *f* urn; ballot box; (poet) grave; **urne** polls
-uro *suf m* (chem) -ide, e.g., **cloruro** chloride
urologìa *f* urology
urrà *interj* hurrah!
ursóne *m* Canada porcupine
urtare *tr* to hit; to bump; to annoy || *intr*—**urtare contro** to hit, strike against; **urtare in** to hit; to stumble into || *ref* to get annoyed; to clash; to bump into one another
urto *m* hit; bump; collision; onslaught; clash, disagreement; **urto di nervi** huff
Uruguai, l' *m* Uruguay
uruguaia•no -na *adj & mf* Uruguayan
usanza *f* usage, custom; habit, practice
usare *tr* to use, employ; to wear out; (lit) to frequent; **usare** + *inf* to be accustomed to + *ger* || *intr* to be fashionable; **usare di** to use, employ || *ref* to become accustomed; **si usa** + *inf* it is customary to + *inf*
usa•to -ta *adj* used, second-hand; worn; worn-out; (lit) usual || *m* usage, custom; norm; second-hand goods
usbèr•go *m* (**-ghi**) hauberk; (fig) shield, protection
uscènte *adj* ending, terminating; retiring
uscière *m* receptionist; office boy, errand boy; (coll) court clerk; (coll) bailiff; (coll) tipstaff
ù•scio *m* (**-sci**) door; **infilar l'uscio** to take French leave; **metter tra l'uscio e il muro** (fig) to corner
uscire §277 *intr* (ESSERE) to go out, leave; to come out; to flow out; to escape; to turn out, ensue; **essere uscito** to be out; **uscire da** to leave; to run off (*the track*); **uscire dai gangheri** to get mad; **uscire dal comune** to be out of the ordinary; **uscire dal segno** to go too far; **uscire dal seminato** to go astray; **uscire di mente a** to escape one's mind, e.g., **gli è uscito di mente** it escaped his mind; **uscire di sentimento** to pass out; **uscire di vita** to die; **uscire in** to lead into; **uscire per il rotto della cuffia** to barely make it
uscita *f* exit; outlay; quip, sally; gate (*e.g., in an airport*); (gram) ending; **all'uscita** on the way out; **buona uscita** severance pay; bonus; **libera uscita** day off (*of servant*); (mil) pass; **uscita di sicurezza** emergency exit
usignòlo *m* nightingale
u•so -sa *adj* (lit) accustomed || *m* practice; usage; use; wear; faculty; power (*e.g., of hearing*); (lit) intimate relations; **all'uso di** in the fashion of; **avere per uso di** to be wont to; **come d'uso** as usual; **farci l'uso** to get used to it!; **fuori d'uso** worn-out, out of commission; **uso esterno!** (pharm) not to be taken internally!
ustionare (**ustióno**) *tr* to burn, scorch
ustióne *f* burn
usuale *adj* usual; ordinary, common
usufruire §176 *intr*—**usufruire di** to have the use of; to enjoy
usura *f* usury; (mach) wear and tear; **ad usura** abundantly
usu•ràio -ràia (**-rài -ràie**) *adj* usurious || *mf* usurer, loanshark
usurpare *tr* to usurp
utensile *adj* tool, e.g., **macchina utensile** machine tool || *m* utensil; tool
utènte *m* user; customer, consumer
ùtero *m* uterus, womb
ùtile *adj* useful; usable; workable; legal, prescribed (*e.g., time*); **essere utile a** to help; **venire utile** to come in handy || *m* usefulness; profit, gain
utili•tà *f* (**-tà**) utility, usefulness; profit, gain
utilitària *f* economy car, compact
utilizzare [ddzz] *tr* to utilize

utopìa *f* utopia
utopi·sta *mf* (**-sti -ste**) utopian
utopìsti·co -ca *adj* (**-ci -che**) utopian
uva *f* grapes; **un grano di uva passa** a raisin; **uva passa** raisins
uxorici·da *m* (**-di**) uxoricide || *f* (**-de**) murderer of one's husband
uxoricì·dio *m* (**-di**) uxoricide; murder of one's husband
ùzzolo [ddzz] *m* whim, fancy, caprice

V

V, v [vu] *m & f* twentieth letter of the Italian alphabet
V. *abbr* (**vostro**) your
vacante *adj* vacant
vacanza *f* vacancy; vacation; **fare vacanza** to be on vacation; **vacanze** vacation
vacanzière *m* vacationer
vac·ca *f* (**-che**) cow
vac·càio *m* (**-cài**) cowboy; stable boy
vaccherìa *f* dairy farm
vacchétta *f* cowhide
vaccina *f* cow manure; cow
vaccinare *tr* to vaccinate
vaccinazióne *f* vaccination
vacci·no -na *adj* cow; bovine || *m* vaccine || *f* see **vaccina**
vacillante *adj* vacillating
vacillare *intr* to totter; to vacillate; to shake; to flicker; to fail, e.g., **la memoria gli vacilla** his memory is failing; **far vacillare** to rock
vacui·tà *f* (**-tà**) vacuity
và·cuo -cua *adj* empty || *m* vacuum
vademè·cum *m* (**-cum**) almanac, ready-reference handbook
vagabondàg·gio *m* (**-gi**) vagrancy; wandering; rambling
vagabondare (**vagabóndo**) *intr* to wander, rove
vagabón·do -da *adj* wandering; vagabond || *mf* vagrant, bum, tramp; rover
vagare §209 *intr* to wander, ramble, rove
vagheggiare §290 (**vaghéggio**) *tr* to gaze fondly at; to cherish
vagire §176 *intr* to cry, whimper
vagito *m* cry, whimper
và·glia *m* (**-glia**) money order || *f*—**di vaglia** worthy, capable
vagliare §280 *tr* to sift, bolt
và·glio *m* (**-gli**) sieve; **mettere al vaglio** to scrutinize
va·go -ga (**-ghi -ghe**) *adj* vague; vacant (*stare*); (lit) beautiful; (lit) roving; (poet) desirous || *m* vagueness; (lit) rover; (anat) vagus
vagonata *f* carload
vagóne *m* (rr) car; **vagone frigorifero** (rr) refrigerator car; **vagone letto** (rr) sleeping car, sleeper; **vagone ristorante** (rr) dining car; **vagone volante** (aer) flying boxcar
vàio vàia (**vài vàie**) *adj* dark-grey || *m* dark grey; (heral) vair; (zool) Siberian squirrel
vaiòlo *m* smallpox
valan·ga *f* (**-ghe**) avalanche
valènte *adj* capable, skillful; clever
valentìa *f* skill; cleverness
valentino *m* Valentine (*sweetheart*)
valènza *f* (chem) valence
valére §278 *tr* to win, get (*e.g., an honor for s.o.*); **che vale?** what's the use?; **valere la pena** to be worthwhile; **valere un Perù** to be worth a king's ransom || *intr* (ESSERE & AVERE) to be worth: to be of avail; to be valid; to mean; to be the equivalent; **far valere** to enforce; **farsi valere** to assert oneself; **tanto vale** it's all the same; **vale a dire** that is to say; **valere meglio** to be better || *ref*—**valersi di** to avail oneself of; to play on; to employ
valévole *adj* valid, good
valicare §197 (**vàlico**) *tr* to cross, pass
vàli·co *m* (**-chi**) mountain pass; passage; opening (*in a hedge*)
validi·tà *f* (**-tà**) validity
vàli·do -da *adj* valid; able, able-bodied; strong
valigerìa *f* luggage; luggage store
valigétta *f* valise; **valigetta diplomatica** attaché case
valì·gia *f* (**-ge**) suitcase; traveling bag; **fare le valige** to pack one's bags; **valigia diplomatica** diplomatic pouch; attaché case; **valigia per abiti** suit carrier
vallata *f* valley
valle *f* valley; **a valle** downhill; downstream
vallétta *f* (telv) assistant
vallétto *m* valet; page; (telv) assistant
valló·ne -na *adj & mf* Walloon || *m* narrow valley
valóre *m* value; valor, bravery; force; (fig) jewel; (math) variable; **mettere in valore** to raise the value of; **valore di mercato** market value; **valore facciale** face value; **valore locativo** rental value; **valori** valuables; securities; **valori mobiliari** securities
valorizzare [ddzz] *tr* to enhance the value of
valoró·so -sa [s] *adj* brave, valiant
valuta *f* currency; (com) effective date; (com) value (*of promissory note*)
valutare *tr* to estimate, appraise; to value, prize; to count, reckon; to take into consideration
valutazióne *f* estimation, appraisal; evaluation
valva *f* (bot, zool) valve
vàlvola *f* (anat, mach) valve; (elec) fuse; (rad, telv) tube, valve; **valvola a galleggiante** ball cock; **valvola di sicurezza** safety valve; **valvola in testa** overhead valve
vàl·zer *m* (**-zer**) waltz

vamp *f* (**vamp**) vamp
vampa *f* flame; blaze; flash; flush
vampata *f* burst (*of heat*); blast (*of hot air*); flash, flush
vampiro *m* vampire
vanàdio *m* vanadium
vanaglòria *f* vainglory, boastfulness
vanaglorió·so -sa [s] *adj* vainglorious
vandalismo *m* vandalism
vànda·lo -la *adj* & *m* vandal ‖ **Vandalo** *m* Vandal
vaneggiare §290 (**vanéggio**) *intr* to rave; to be delirious; (lit) to open, yawn
vanè·sio -sia *adj* (**-si -sie**) vain
van·ga *f* (**-ghe**) spade
vangare §209 *tr* to spade up; to dig with a spade
vangèlo *m* gospel ‖ **Vangelo** *m* Gospel
vanghétto *m* spud
vaniglia *f* vanilla
vanilò·quio *m* (**-qui**) empty talk
vani·tà *f* (**-tà**) vanity
vanitó·so -sa [s] *adj* vain, conceited
va·no -na *adj* vain; (lit) empty, hollow; **in vano** in vain ‖ *m* empty space; room
vantàg·gio *m* (**-gi**) advantage; profit; odds, handicap; discount; (coll) extra; (typ) galley; **a vantaggio di** on behalf of
vantaggió·so -sa [s] *adj* advantageous
vantare *tr* to boast of; to set up (*a claim*) ‖ *ref* to boast; **vantarsi di** to brag about, vaunt
vanterìa *f* brag, boast, vaunt
vanto *m* brag, boast; **aver vanto su** (lit) to overcome
vànvera *f*—**a vanvera** at random
vapóre *m* vapor; steam; locomotive; steamship; **a tutto vapore** at full speed
vaporétto *m* small river boat; vaporetto (*in Venice*)
vaporizzare [ddzz] *tr* to vaporize; to spray ‖ *intr* (ESSERE) & *ref* to evaporate
vaporizzatóre [ddzz] *m* vaporizer; sprayer
vaporó·so -sa [s] *adj* vaporous
varaménto *m* assemblage (*of prefab pieces*)
varano *m* monitor lizard
varare *tr* to launch; to pass (*a law*); (coll) to back, promote (*a candidate*)
varcare §197 *tr* to cross ‖ *intr* (poet) to pass (*said of time*)
var·co *m* (**-chi**) opening; mountain pass; breach; **attendere al varco** to lie in wait for; **cogliere al varco** to catch unawares; **fare varco in** to breach
varechina *f* (laundry) bleach
variàbile *adj* & *f* variable
variante *f* variant; detour; (aut) model
variare §287 *tr* & *intr* (ESSERE & AVERE) to vary
variazióne *f* variation
varicèlla *f* chicken pox
varicó·so -sa [s] *adj* varicose
variega·to -ta *adj* variegated
varie·tà *m* (**-tà**) (theat) vaudeville ‖ *f* variety
và·rio -ria (**-ri -rie**) *adj* varied; various; variable; different; **va·ri -rie** several ‖ *m* variety ‖ **varie** *fpl* miscellanies ‖ **va·ri -rie** *pron indef* several
variopin·to -ta *adj* multicolored
varo *m* (naut) launch
vas *m* (**vas**) subchaser
va·sàio *m* (**-sài**) potter
va·sca *f* (**-sche**) tub; basin; pool; **vasca da bagno** bathtub; **vasca dei pesci** aquarium; **vasca navale** (naut) basin
vascèllo *m* vessel, ship
vaselina or **vasellina** *f* vaseline
vasellame *m* dishes; set of dishes; **vasellame da cucina** kitchen ware; **vasellame d'argento** silverware; **vasellame di porcellana** chinaware
vasèllo *m* (lit) vessel
vasi·stas [s] *m* (**-stas**) transom
vaso *m* vase; vessel; jar, pot; nave (*of church*); hall (*of building*); (naut) shipway; (poet) cup; **vasi vinari** wine containers; **vaso da fiori** flowerpot; **vaso da notte** chamber pot; **vaso d'elezione** (eccl) chosen vessel (*viz., Saint Paul*)
vassallo *m* vassal; (obs) helper
vas·sóio *m* (**-sói**) tray; mortarboard
vasti·tà *f* (**-tà**) vastness
va·sto -sta *adj* spacious; vast; (fig) deep
vate *m* (lit) prophet, poet
vatica·no -na *adj* Vatican ‖ **Vaticano** *m* Vatican
vaticinare (**vatìcino** & **vaticino**) *tr* to prophesy
vaticì·nio *m* (**-ni**) prophecy
ve §5 *pron*
V.E. *abbr* (**Vostra Eccellenza**) Your Excellency
vècchia *f* old woman
vecchiàia *f* old age
vecchiézza *f* old age
vèc·chio -chia (**-chi -chie**) *adj* old; elder; **vecchio come il cucco** as old as the hills ‖ *m* old man; **vecchi** old people; **vecchio del mestiere** old hand ‖ *f* see **vecchia**
véc·cia *f* (**-ce**) vetch
véce *f* stead, e.g., **in vece mia** in my stead; (lit) vicissitude; **fare le veci di** to act for or as
vedére *m* seeing; looks; view, opinion ‖ §279 *tr* to see; to review; to look over; **chi s'è visto s'è visto!** good-by and good luck!; **dare a vedere** to make believe; **stare a vedere** to watch; observe; **non poter vedere** to not be able to stand; **non vedere l'ora di** to be hardly able to wait for; **vedere male qlcu** to be ill-disposed toward s.o. ‖ *intr*—**stare a vedere** to wait and see; **vederci bene** to see (*e.g., in the dark*); **vederci chiaro** to look into it; **vedere di** to try to ‖ *ref* to see oneself; to see each other; **vedersela brutta** to anticipate trouble
vedétta *f* lookout; (nav) vedette
védova *f* widow
vedovanza *f* widowhood
vedovile *adj* widow's; widower's ‖ *m* dower

védo•vo -va *adj* widowed || *m* widower || *f* see **vedova**
veduta *f* view; (lit) eyesight; **di corte vedute** narrowminded; **di larghe vedute** broadminded
veemènte *adj* vehement; violent; impassioned
veemènza *f* vehemence; violence
vegetale *adj* vegetable || *m* plant, vegetable
vegetare (vègeto) *intr* to vegetate
vegetaria•no -na *adj & mf* vegetarian
vegetazióne *f* vegetation
vège•to -ta *adj* vigorous, spry
veggènte *adj* (obs) seeing || *mf* fortuneteller || *m* seer, prophet; **i veggenti** people having eyesight || *f* seeress, prophetess
véglia *f* vigil, watch; wakefulness; evening party, soirée; party, crowd; **a veglia** unbelievable (*tale*); **veglia danzante** dance; **veglia funebre** wake
vegliardo *m* old man
vegliare §280 **(véglio)** *tr* to keep watch over || *intr* to stay awake; to keep watch; to stay up
veglióne *m* masked ball
veicolo *m* vehicle; carrier (*of disease*)
véla *f* sail; sailing; **alzare le vele** to set sail; **ammainare le vele** to take in sail; **a vela** under sail; **far vela** to set sail; **vela aurica** lugsail; **vela bermudiana** or **Marconi** jib; **vela maestra** mainsail
ve•làio *m* (**-lài**) sailmaker
velare *adj & f* (phonet) velar || *v* **(vélo)** *tr* to veil; to cover; to muffle (*sound*); to attenuate, reduce (*a shock*); to dim, cloud; to conceal; (phot) to fog || *ref* to cover oneself with a veil; to take the veil; to get dim, e.g., **gli si è velata la vista** his eyesight got dim
velà•rio *m* (**-ri**) (hist) velarium; (theat) curtain
vela•to -ta *adj* veiled; sheer (*hosiery*)
velatura *f* coating; (aer) airfoil; (naut) sails
veleggiare §290 **(veléggio)** *tr* (lit) to sail over (*the sea*) || *intr* to sail; (aer) to glide
veleggiatóre *m* sailboat; (aer) glider
veléno *m* poison; (fig) venom
velenó•so -sa [s] *adj* poisonous; (fig) venomous
velétta *f* veil; (naut) topgallant
vèli•co -ca *adj* (**-ci -che**) sail, sailing
velièro *m* sailing ship
veli•no -na *adj* thin (*paper*) || *f* carbon copy; onionskin; slant (*given to a news item*)
velivo•lo -la *adj* (lit) gliding; (lit) sailing || *m* (lit) airplane, aircraft
vellei•tà *f* (**-tà**) wild ambition, dream
vellicare §197 **(vèllico)** *tr* to tickle
vèllo *m* (lit) fleece; **vello d'oro** Golden Fleece
velló•so -sa [s] *adj* hairy
velluta•to -ta *adj* velvety
vellutino *m* thin velvet; velvet ribbon; **vellutino di cotone** velveteen
vellu•to -ta *adj* (lit) hairy || *m* velvet; **velluto a coste** corduroy
vélo *m* veil; coating; film; skin (*e.g., of onion*); (anat, bot) velum; (fig) body; **fare velo a** to becloud; to fog
velóce *adj* speedy, quick, fast; fleeting
velocipedastro *m* poor or reckless bicycle rider
veloci•sta *mf* (**-sti -ste**) (sports) sprinter
veloci•tà *f* (**-tà**) velocity; speed; (aut) speed; **a grande velocità** by express; **a piccola velocità** by freight; **velocità di crociera** cruising speed; **velocità di fuga** (rok) escape velocity
velòdromo *m* bicycle ring or track
véna *f* vein; grain (*in wood or stone*); mood; streak (*of madness*); **di vena** willingly; **essere in vena di** to be in the mood to
venale *adj* venal
venare (véno) *tr* to vein
vena•to -ta *adj* veined; streaked; suffused; **venato di sangue** bloodshot
venatura *f* veining; (fig) streak
vendémmia *f* vintage
vendemmiare §287 **(vendémmio)** *tr* to harvest (*grapes*) || *intr* to gather grapes; (fig) to make a killing
vendemmia•tóre -trice *mf* vintager
véndere §281 *tr* to sell; **da vendere** plenty, more than enough; **vendere allo scoperto** (fin) to sell short; **vendere fumo** to peddle influence || *intr* to sell; **vendere allo scoperto** (fin) to sell short || *ref* to sell; **si vende** for sale
vendétta *f* vengeance; revenge; **gridare vendetta** to cry out for retribution
vendicare §197 **(véndico)** *tr* to avenge || *ref* to get revenge
vendicati•vo -va *adj* vengeful, vindictive
vendica•tóre -trice *adj* avenging || *mf* avenger
vendifu•mo *mf* (**-mo**) influence peddler
véndita *f* sale; shop; **in vendita** for sale; **vendita allo scoperto** (fin) short sale; **vendita per corrispondenza** catalogue sale
vendi•tóre -trice *mf* seller; clerk (*in store*) || *m* salesman; **venditore ambulante** peddler; **venditore di fumo** influence peddler || *f* saleslady
venefì•cio *m* (**-ci**) poisoning
venèfi•co -ca (**-ci -che**) *adj* poisonous; unhealthy || *m* (lit) poisonmaker
veneràbile or **venerando** *adj* venerable
venerare (vènero) *tr* to venerate, revere; to worship
venerazióne *f* veneration; worship
vener•dì *m* (**-dì**) Friday || **Venerdì Santo** Good Friday
Vènere *m* (astr) Venus || *f* (mythol & fig) Venus
venè•reo -rea *adj* (**-rei -ree**) venereal
Venèzia *f* Venice; Venetia (*province*)
venezia•no -na *adj & mf* Venetian || *f* Venetian blind
venezola•no -na *adj & mf* Venezuelan
vènia *f* (lit) forgiveness, pardon
venire §282 *intr* (ESSERE) to come; to turn out (*well or badly*); to turn out to be; **che viene** next, e.g., **il mese che viene** next month; **come viene** as it is; **far venire** to send for; to

give, cause; **un va e vieni** a backward-and-forward motion; **venire** + *ger* to keep + *ger;* **venire** + *pp* to be + *pp, e.g.*, **il portone viene aperto alle tre** the gate is opened at three; **venire a capo di** to solve; **venire ai ferri corti** to come into open conflict; **venire al dunque** or **al fatto** to come to the point; **venire alle corte** to get down to brass tacks; **venire alle mani** or **alle prese** to come to blows; **venire a parole** to have words; **venire a patti con** to come to terms with; **venire a proposito** to come in handy; **venire incontro a** to go to meet; **venire in possesso di** to come into possession of (*s.th*); to come into the hands of (*s.o.*); **venire meno** to faint; **venir meno a** to fail to keep (*one's word*); **venir su** to grow, come up; **venire via** to give way || *ref*—**venirsene** to stroll along || *impers* (with *dat*)—**viene da** feel the urge to, e.g., **gli venne da starnutire** he felt the urge to sneeze; **gli è venuto da ridere** he felt the urge to laugh; **viene detto** blurt out, e.g., **gli è venuto detto che non gli piaceva quel tipo** he blurted out that he did not like that fellow; **viene fatto di**+*inf* succeed in+*ger*, e.g., **le venne fatto di convincerli** she succeeded in convincing them; happen to + *inf*, e.g., **gli venne fatto di incontrarmi per istrada** he happened to meet me on the way

ventà·glio *m* (**-gli**) fan; (fig) spread; **a ventaglio** fanlike; **diramarsi a ventaglio** to fan out

ventaròla *f* weather vane

ventata *f* gust of wind; (fig) wave

ventènne *adj* twenty-year-old || *mf* twenty-year-old person

ventèsi·mo -ma *adj, m & pron* twentieth

vénti *adj & pron* twenty; **le venti** eight P.M. || *m* twenty; twentieth (*in dates*)

ventidue *adj & pron* twenty-two **le ventidue** ten P.M. || *m* twenty-two; twenty-second (*in dates*)

ventilare (**vèntilo**) *tr* to air, ventilate; to winnow (*grain*); to discuss minutely; to air (*a subject*); to broach (*a subject*); to unfurl (*a flag*) || *ref* to fan oneself

ventilatóre *m* fan, ventilator; vent; (min) ventilation shaft; (naut) funnel

ventilazióne *f* ventilation; winnowing

ventina *f* score; **una ventina (di)** twenty, about twenty

ventino *m* twenty-cent coin

ventiquattro *adj & pron* twenty-four; **le ventiquattro** twelve P.M. || *m* twenty-four; twenty-fourth (*in dates*)

ventiquattró·re *f* (**-re**) overnight bag; twenty-four-hour race; **ventiquattrore** *fpl* period of twenty-four hours

ventitré *adj & pron* twenty-three; **le ventitré** eleven P.M.; **portare il cappello alle ventitré** to wear one's hat cocked || *m* twenty-three; twenty-third (*in dates*)

vènto *m* wind; air; guy wire; **presentarsi al vento** to sail into the wind; **farsi vento** to fan oneself; **a vento** windproof; wind-propelled; **col vento in prora** downwind; **col vento in poppa** upwind; favorably, famously

vèntola *f* fireside fan; lampshade; candle sconce; blade (*of fan*)

ventó·so -sa [s] *adj* windy || *f* cupping glass; suction cup; (zool) sucker

vèntre *m* belly; **a ventre a terra** on one's belly; on one's face; at full speed (*said of a horse*)

ventrìcolo *m* ventricle

ventrièra *f* abdominal band or belt

ventrilòquia *f* ventriloquism

ventrìlo·quo -qua *mf* ventriloquist

ventuno *adj & pron* twenty-one; **le ventuno** nine P.M. || *m* twenty-one; twenty-first (*in dates*); (cards) blackjack

ventu·ro -ra *adj* next || *f* (lit) luck, fortune; (lit) good fortune; **alla ventura** at random, at a venture; **di ventura** of fortune, e.g., **soldato di ventura** soldier of fortune

venustà *f* (lit) pulchritude

venu·to -ta *mf*—**nuovo venuto** newcomer; **primo venuto** firstcomer || *f* coming, arrival

véra *f* curbstone (*of well*); (coll) wedding ring

verace *adj* true; truthful, veracious

veraci·tà *f* (**-tà**) veracity, truthfulness

veranda *f* veranda; porch

verbale *adj* verbal || *m* minutes; ticket (*given by a policeman*); **mettere a verbale** to enter into the record

verbèna *f* verbena

vèrbo *m* verb; (lit) word || **Verbo** *m* (theol) Word

verbosità [s] *f* verbiage, verbosity

verbó·so -sa [s] *adj* windy, long-winded, verbose

verda·stro -stra *adj* greenish

vérde *adj* green; young, youthful || *m* green; **al verde** (coll) broke, penniless; **nel verde degli anni** in the prime of life

verdeggiante *adj* verdant

verderame *m* blue vitriol; verdigris

verdét·to -ta *adj* greenish || *m* verdict

verdógno·lo -la *adj* greenish; sallow (*face*)

verdura *f* vegetables

verecóndia *f* modesty, bashfulness

verecón·do -da *adj* modest, bashful

vér·ga *f* (**-ghe**) switch; rod; ingot, bar; pole; penis; (eccl) staff, crosier; (naut) yard; **tremare a verga a verga** to shake like a leaf

vergare §209 (**vérgo**) *tr* to switch; to rule (*paper*); to stripe; to write

vergati·no -na *adj* thin (*paper*) || *m* striped cloth

verga·to -ta *adj* striped; watermarked with stripes || *m* (obs) serge

verginale *adj* maidenly, virginal

vérgine *adj & f* virgin || **Vergine** *f* (eccl) Virgin; (astr) Virgo

verginità *f* virginity, maidenhood

vergógna *f* shame; **aver vergogna to be**

ashamed; **vergogne** privates || *interj* for shame!
vergognare (**vergógno**) *ref* to be ashamed; to feel cheap; **vergognati!** shame on you!
vergognó·so -sa [s] *adj* ashamed; bashful; shameful
veridici·tà *f* (**-tà**) veracity
verìdi·co -ca *adj* (**-ci -che**) veracious
verìfi·ca *f* (**-che**) verification; control; **verifica fiscale** auditing (*of tax return*)
verificare §197 (**verìfico**) *tr* to verify; to control, check; to audit || *ref* to come true; to happen
verifica·tóre -trice *mf* checker, inspector
verismo *m* verism (*as developed in Italy*)
veri·sta *adj* & *mf* (**-sti -ste**) verist
veri·tà *f* (**-tà**) truth; **in verità** truthfully, verily
veritiè·ro -ra *adj* truthful
vèrme *m* worm; (mach) thread; **verme solitario** tapeworm
vermì·glio -glia (**-gli -glie**) *adj* vermilion; ruby (*lips*) || *m* vermilion
vèr·mut *m* (**-mut**) vermouth
vernàcolo *m* vernacular
vernice *f* varnish; paint; polish; patina; (painting) private viewing; (fig) veneer; **scarpe di vernice** patent-leather shoes; **vernice a olio** oil paint; **vernice a spruzzo** spray paint; **vernice da scarpe** shoe polish
verniciare §128 *tr* to varnish; to paint
vé·ro -ra *adj* true; real; right; pure; **non è vero?** isn't that so? La traduzione precedente è generalmente rimpiazzata da molte altre frasi. Se la prima espressione è negativa, la domanda equivalente a **non è vero?** sarà affermativa, per esempio, **Lei non lavora, non è vero?** You are not working, are you? Se la prima espressione è affermativa, la domanda sarà negativa, per esempio, **Lei lavora, non è vero?** You are working, are you not? or aren't you? Se la prima espressione contiene un ausiliare, la domanda conterrà l'ausiliare stesso senza infinito o senza participio passato, per esempio, **Arriveranno domani, non è vero?** They will arrive tomorrow, won't they? **Ha finito il compito, non è vero?** He has finished his homework, hasn't he? Se la prima espressione non contiene né un ausiliare, né una delle forme del verbo "to be" in funzione di copula, la domanda conterrà l'ausiliare "do" o "did" senza l'infinito del verbo, per esempio, **Lei è vissuto a Milano, non è vero?** You lived in Milano, did you not? **Lei non va mai al parco, non è vero?** You never go to the park, do you?; **non mi par vero** it seems unbelievable || *m* truth; actuality; **a dire il vero** to tell the truth, as a matter of fact; **dal vero** from nature; **salvo il vero** if I am not mistaken || *f* see **vera**
veróne *m* (lit) balcony
verosimiglianza *f* verisimilitude; probability, likelihood
verosìmile *adj* verisimilar; probable, likely
verricèllo *m* winch, windlass
vèrro *m* boar
verru·ca *f* (**-che**) wart
versaménto *m* spilling; payment; deposit
versante *m* depositor; slope, side
versare (**vèrso**) *tr* to pour; to spill; to shed; to pay; to deposit || *intr* to overflow; **versare in gravi condizioni** to be in a bad way || *ref* to spill; to pour (*said of people*); to empty (*said of a river*)
versàtile *adj* versatile; fickle
versa·to -ta *adj* versed; gifted; fully subscribed to (*e.g., stock of a corporation*)
verseggia·tóre -trice *mf* verse writer
versétto *m* verse (*of Bible*)
versificare §197 (**versìfico**) *tr* & *intr* to versify
versificazióne *f* versification
versióne *f* version; translation
vèrso *adj invar*—**pollice verso** (hist) thumbs down || *m* verse; local accent; voice, cry; reverse (*of coin*); verso (*of page*); line (*of poetry*); singsong; gesture; direction, way, manner; respect; **andare a verso** (with *dat*) to suit, e.g., **le sue maniere non gli vanno a verso** her manners do not suit him; **a verso** properly; **contro verso** against the grain; **fare un verso** to make faces; **per un verso** on one hand; **rifare il verso** (with *dat*) to mimick; **senza verso** without rhyme or reason; **verso sciolto** blank verse || *prep* toward; near, around; about; for, toward; upon, in return for; as compared with; **verso di** toward
vèrtebra *f* vertebra
vertebrale *adj* vertebral; spinal
vertebra·to -ta *adj* & *m* vertebrate
vertènza *f* quarrel, dispute; **vertenza sindacale** labor dispute
vèrtere §283 *intr*—**vertere su** to deal with, to turn on
verticale *adj* & *f* vertical
vèrtice *m* top, summit; vertex; **summit conference**
vertigine *f* vertigo, dizziness; **avere le vertigini** to feel dizzy
vertiginó·so -sa [s] *adj* dizzy; breathtaking
vérza [dz] *f* cabbage
verzière [dz] *m* (lit) fruit, vegetable, and flower garden; (coll) produce market
verzura [dz] *f* verdure
vesci·ca *f* (**-che**) bladder; blister; **vescica di vento** (fig) windbag; **vescica gonfiata** swellhead; **vescica natatoria** air bladder
vescichétta *f* blister; vescicle; **vescichetta biliare** gall bladder
vescìcola *f* blister
vescovado *m* bishopric
véscovo *m* bishop

vè·spa *f* wasp, yellowjacket || *f* (**-spe** & **-spa**) motor scooter
ve·spàio *m* (**-spài**) wasp's nest; (fig) hornet's nest
vespasiano *m* public urinal
Vèspero *m* Vesper
vesperti·no -na *adj* (lit) evening
vèspro *m* (eccl) vespers; (lit) vespertide
vessare (**vèsso**) *tr* (lit) to oppress
vessatò·rio -ria *adj* (**-ri -rie**) vexatious
vessazióne *f* oppression
vessillo *m* flag
vestàglia *f* negligee, dressing gown; **vestaglia da bagno** bathrobe
vèste *f* dress; cover; (lit) body; **in veste di** in the quality of; as; in the guise of; **veste da camera** negligee, dressing gown; bathrobe; **veste talare** (eccl) long vestment; **vesti** clothes
vestià·rio *m* (**-ri**) wardrobe
vestìbolo *m* vestibule, lobby
vestì·gio *m* (**-gi** & **-gia** *fpl*) vestige, trace; (lit) footprint
vestire (**vèsto**) *tr* to dress; to don; to wear; to clothe; to cover, bedeck || *intr* to dress; to fit || *ref* to get dressed; to dress; to dress oneself; to buy one's own clothes
vesti·to -ta *adj* dressed; covered || *m* dress; suit; clothing; **vestiti** clothes; **vestito da donna** dress; **vestito da festa** Sunday best; **vestito da sera** evening clothes, formal suit; evening gown; **vestito da uomo** suit
Vesùvio, il Vesuvius
vetera·no -na *adj & mf* veteran
veterinà·rio -ria (**-ri -rie**) *adj* veterinary || *m* veterinarian || *f* veterinary medicine
vèto *m* veto; **porre il veto a** to veto
ve·tràio *m* (**-trài**) glass manufacturer; glass dealer; glass blower
vetra·to -ta *adj* glass, glass-enclosed; sand (*paper*) || *m* glare ice, glaze || *f* glass door; glass window; glass enclosure; **vetrata a colori** or **vetrata istoriata** stained-glass window
vetrerìa *f* glassworks; **vetrerie** glassware
vetria·to -ta *adj* glassy; glass-covered
vetrificare §197 (**vetrifico**) *tr* to vitrify || *ref* to become vitrified
vetrina *f* show window; showcase, glass cabinet; **mettersi in vetrina** to show off; **vetrine** (coll) eyeglasses
vetrini·sta *mf* (**-sti -ste**) window dresser
vetri·no -na *adj* glass-like; brittle, fragile || *m* slide (*of microscope*) || *f* see **vetrina**
vetriòlo *m* vitriol
vétro *m* glass; glassware; window pane; piece of glass; **vetro aderente** contact lens; **vetro infrangibile** (aut) safety glass; **vetro smerigliato** ground glass, frosted glass
vetrorèsina *f* fiberglass
vetró·so -sa [s] *adj* vitreous, glassy
vétta *f* peak; top, tip; limb (*of tree*); (naut) end (*of hawser*); **tremare come una vetta** to shake like a leaf
vet·tóre -trice *adj* leading, guiding; spreading, carrying || *m* carrier; (math, phys) vector
vettovagliare §280 *tr* to supply with food
vettovàglie *fpl* victuals, food; supplies
vettura *f* forwarding; coach; car; freight; **in vettura!** (rr) all aboard!; **prendere in vettura** to hire (*a conveyance*); **vettura belvedere** (rr) observation car; **vettura da turismo** (aut) pleasure car; **vettura di piazza** hack, hackney; **vettura letto** (rr) sleeping car; **vettura ristorante** (rr) diner
vetturétta *f* economy car, compact
vetturino *m* hackman, cab driver
vetu·sto -sta *adj* old, ancient
vezzeggiare §290 (**vezzéggio**) *tr* to coddle || *intr* (lit) to strut
vezzeggiati·vo -va *adj* endearing || *m* endearing expression; diminutive
vézzo *m* habit; caress; necklace; bad habit; **vezzi** fondling, petting; mawkish behavior; charms
vezzó·so -sa [s] *adj* graceful, charming; affected, mincing
vi §5
via *m* (**vìa**) starting signal; **dare il via a** to give the go-ahead to || *f* street; road, way; route; career; **dare la via a** to open the way to; **in via confidenziale** in confidence; **in via eccezionale** as an exception; **per via di** via, through; (coll) because of; **per via gerarchica** through administrative channels; **per via orale** orally; **per via rettale** rectally; **prendere la via** to be on one's way; **venire a vie di fatto** to come to blows; **Via Crucis** Way of the Cross; **via d'acqua** waterway; **via di scampo** (fig) way out; **via d'uscita** way out; **Via Lattea** Milky Way; **vie di fatto** assault and battery; **vie legali** legal steps || *adv* away; (math) times, by; **e così via** and so on; **e via dicendo** and so on; **tirar via** to hurry along; **via via che** as || *prep* via, by way of
viadótto *m* viaduct
viaggiare §290 *intr* to travel; (com) to deal
viaggia·tóre -trice *adj* traveling; homing (*pigeon*) || *mf* traveler || *m* traveling salesman
viàg·gio *m* (**-gi**) travel; journey, trip; **buon viaggio!** bon voyage!; **viaggio d'andata e ritorno** round trip; **viaggio di prova** (naut) trial run, shakedown cruise
viale *m* boulevard
viandante *mf* (lit) wayfarer
vià·rio -ria *adj* (**-ri -rie**) road, highway
viàti·co *m* (**-ci**) viaticum
viavài *m* coming and going; hustle and bustle
vibrante *adj* vibrant; wiry; (phonet) vibrant || *f* (phonet) trill, vibrant
vibrare *tr* to jar; to deliver (*a blow*); to vibrate; (lit) to hurl || *intr* to vibrate
vibra·to -ta *adj* vibrant; resolute, vigorous || *m* vibrating sound
vibrazióne *f* vibration
vicariato *m* vicarage
vicà·rio *m* (**-ri**) vicar

vice- *pref adj* vice-, e.g., **vicereale** viceroyal || *pref m & f* vice-, e.g., **viceammiraglio** vice-admiral; assistant, e.g., **vicegovernatore** assistant governor; deputy, e.g., **vicesindaco** deputy mayor
vicediret•tóre -trice *mf* assistant manager
vicènda *f* vicissitude; rotation (*of crops*); **a vicenda** in turn
vicendévole *adj* mutual, reciprocal
vicepresidènte [s] *mf* vice president
vice•ré *m* (**-ré**) viceroy
vicevèrsa *adv* vice versa; (coll) instead, on the contrary
vichin•go -ga *adj & mf* (**-ghi -ghe**) Viking
vicinanza *f* nearness; **in vicinanza di** in the neighborhood of; **vicinanze** vicinity, neighborhood
vicinato *m* neighborhood
vici•no -na *adj* near; neighboring; next; close (*relative*) || *mf* neighbor || **vicino** *adv* nearby, near; **da vicino** closely; at close quarters; **vicino a** near; next to, close to
vicissitùdine *f* vicissitude
vi•co *m* (**-chi**) alley, lane; village; (lit) region
vìcolo *m* alley, court, place; **vicolo cieco** blind alley, dead end
videocassétta *f* video cassette
vidimare (**vìdimo**) *tr* to validate, visa; to sign
vidimazióne *f* validation, visa; signature
viennése [s] *adj & mf* Viennese
viepiù *adv* (lit) more and more
vietare (**vièto**) *tr* to forbid, prohibit
vieta•to -ta *adj* forbidden; **senso vietato** one way; **sosta vietata** no parking; no stopping; **vietato fumare** no smoking
Vietnam, il Vietnam
vietnami•ta *adj & mf* (**-ti -te**) Vietnamese
viè•to -ta *adj* (lit) old-fashioned; (coll) musty-smelling, rancid
vigènte *adj* current, in force
vìgere §284 *intr* to be in force
vigèsi•mo -ma *adj* twentieth
vigilante *adj* watchful, vigilant || *m* watchman
vigilanza *f* vigilance; surveillance
vigilare (**vìgilo**) *tr* to watch; to watch over; to police || *intr* to watch; **vigilare che** to see to it that
vigila•tóre -trice *mf* inspector || *f* camp counselor; **vigilatrice sanitaria** child health inspector
vìgile *adj* (lit) watchful || *m* watch; **vigile del fuoco** fireman; **vigile urbano** policeman
vigìlia *f* fast; vigil; **la vigilia di** on the eve of, the night before
vigliaccherìa *f* cowardice
vigliac•co -ca (**-chi -che**) *adj* cowardly || *m* coward
vigna *f* vineyard
vignaiòlo *m* vine dresser
vignéto *m* vineyard
vignétta *f* vignette; **vignetta umoristica** cartoon
vignetti•sta *mf* (**-sti -ste**) cartoonist
vigógna *f* vicuña
vigóre *m* vigor; **in vigore** in force
vigorìa *f* vigor
vigoró•so -sa [s] *adj* vigorous
vile *adj* cowardly; vile, low, cheap; base (*metal*)
vilificare §197 (**vilìfico**) *tr* to vilify
vilipèndere §148 *tr* to despise; to show scorn for
villa *f* villa; country house; one-family detached house; (lit) country
villàg•gio *m* (**-gi**) village; **villaggio del fanciullo** boys' town
villanata *f* boorishness
villanìa *f* boorishness, rudeness; insult
villa•no -na *adj* rude, churlish || *mf* boor, churl; (lit) peasant
villanzó•ne -na *mf* boor, uncouth person
villeggiante *mf* vacationist
villeggiare §290 (**villéggio**) *intr* to vacation
villeggiatura *f* vacation, summer vacation
villétta *f* or **villino** *m* bungalow
villó•so -sa [s] *adj* hairy
vil•tà *f* (**-tà**) baseness; cowardice
viluppo *m* tangle, twist
vìmine *m* withe, wicker, osier
vinàcce *fpl* pressed grapes
vi•nàio *m* (**-nài**) wine merchant
vincènte *adj* winning || *mf* winner
vìncere §285 *tr* to overcome; to win; to convince; to check; to defeat; **vincere per un pelo** to nose out; **vincerla** to come out on top || *ref* to control oneself
vincetòssi•co *m* (**-ci**) swallowwort, tame poison
vincipèr•di *m* (**-di**) giveaway
vìncita *f* gain; winnings
vinci•tóre -trice *adj* conquering, victorious || *mf* winner; conqueror; victor
vincolare *adj* binding; bound || *v* (**vìncolo**) *tr* to tie; to bind, obligate; to restrict the use of (*real-estate property*)
vìncolo *m* tie, bond; (law) entail; (law) restriction (*in a real-estate deed*)
vinìco•lo -la *adj* wine, wine-producing
vinile *m* vinyl
vino *m* wine; **vin caldo** mulled wine; **vino da pasto** table wine; **vino di marca** vintage wine; **vino di mele** cider
vin•to -ta *adj* vanquished, overcome, defeated; victorious (*battle*); **averla vinta su** to overcome; **darla vinta a qlcu** to let s.o. get away with murder; **darsi per vinto** to give in, yield || *m* vanquished person; **i vinti** the vanquished
viò•la *adj invar* violet || *m* (**-la**) violet (*color*) || *f* violet; (mus) viola; **viola del pensiero** pansy; **viola mammola** sweet violet
violacciòc•ca *f* (**-che**) (bot) wallflower
violà•ceo -cea *adj* violet
violare (**vìolo**) *tr* to violate; to run (*a blockade*)
violazióne *f* violation; **violazione di**

domicilio housebreaking, burglary; **violazione di proprietà** trespass
violentare (**violènto**) *tr* to violate, force; to do violence to; to rape
violèn•to -ta *adj* violent || *m* violent person
violènza *f* violence; **violenza carnale** rape
violét•to -ta *adj & m* violet || *f* (bot) violet
violini•sta *mf* (**-sti -ste**) violinist
violino *m* violin; **primo violino** concertmaster
violoncelli•sta *mf* (**-sti -ste**) violoncellist
violoncèllo *m* violoncello, cello
viòttolo *m* path
vìpera *f* viper, adder
viràg•gio *m* (**-gi**) turn; (aer) banking; (naut) tacking; (phot) toning
virare *tr* to veer; to turn (*a winch*); (aer) to bank; (phot) to tone || *intr* to veer, steer; **virare di bordo** (naut) to put about; (naut) to tack
virata *f* turn, veer; (aer) banking; (naut) tacking
virginale *adj* var of **verginale**
virgì•nia *m* (**-nia**) Virginia tobacco || *f* (**-nia**) Virginia cigarette
vìrgola *f* comma; (*used in Italian to set off the decimal fraction from the integer*) decimal point; **doppia virgola** quotation mark
virgolétta *f* quotation mark
virgulto *m* (lit) shoot; (lit) shrub
virile *adj* virile
virilità *f* virility
viròla *f* (mach) male piece
virologìa *f* virology
vir•tù *f* (**-tù**) virtue; (lit) valor
virtuale *adj* virtual
virtualménte *adv* virtually, to all intents and purposes
virtuosismo [s] *m* virtuosity; showing off
virtuosità [s] *f* virtuosity
virtuó•so -sa [s] *adj* virtuous || *mf* virtuoso
virulèn•to -ta *adj* virulent
virulènza *f* virulence
vi•rus *m* (**-rus**) virus
vìsce•re *m* (**-ri**) internal organ; **visceri** entrails, viscera || **viscere** *fpl* entrails, viscera; (fig) heart, feeling; (fig) bowels (*of the earth*)
vì•schio *m* (**-schi**) mistletoe; birdlime; (fig) trap
vischió•so -sa [s] *adj* sticky, viscous; (com) steady
vìsci•do -da *adj* viscid; clammy; (fig) unctuous
vìsciola *f* sour cherry
vìsciolo *m* sour cherry tree
viscónte *m* viscount
viscontéssa *f* viscountess
viscó•so -sa [s] *adj* viscous, sticky || *f* viscose
visétto *m* small face; baby face
visìbile *adj* visible; obvious
visibì•lio *m* (**-li**) (coll) crowd; (coll) bunch; **andare in visibilio** to become ecstatic; **mandare in visibilio** to throw into ecstasy, enrapture
visibilità *f* visibility
visièra *f* visor; fencing mask; eyeshade; **visiera termica** (aut) electric defroster
visigò•to -ta *adj* Visigothic || *mf* Visigoth
visionà•rio -ria *adj & mf* (**-ri -rie**) visionary
visióne *f* vision; sight; (mov, telv) showing; **in visione gratuita** for free examination; **mandare qlco a qlcu in visione** to send s.th to s.o. for his (or her) opinion; **prendere visione di** to examine; to peruse
vi•sìr *m* (**-sìr**) vizier
vìsita *f* visit; visitation; **fare una visita** to pay a visit; **marcare visita** (mil) to report sick; **visita doganale** customs inspection
visitare (**vìsito**) *tr* to visit; to inspect
visita•tóre -trice *mf* visitor || *f* social worker
visitazióne *f* visitation
visi•vo -va *adj* visual
viso *m* face; **far buon viso a cattivo gioco** to grin and bear it
visóne *m* mink
visóre *m* (phot) viewer; (phot) viewfinder
vi•spo -spa *adj* brisk, lively
vissu•to -ta *adj* wordly-wise
vista *f* sight, eyesight; view; vista; glance; (poet) window; **a vista** exposed, visible; **a vista d'occhio** as far as the eye can see; **essere in vista** to be expected; to be imminent; to be in the limelight; **far vista di** to pretend to; **in vista di** in view of; **mettere in vista** to show off; **vista a volo d'uccello** bird's-eye view; **vista corta** poor eyesight
vistare *tr* to validate, visa
vi•sto -sta *adj*—**visto che** seeing that, inasmuch as || *m* visa; approval || *f* see **vista**
vistó•so -sa [s] *adj* showy, flashy; (fig) considerable
visuale *adj* visual || *f* view; line of sight
visualizzare [ddzz] *tr* to visualize
vita *f* life; livelihood; living; waist; **avere breve vita** to be short-lived; **fare la vita** to be a prostitute; **vita natural durante** for life; during one's lifetime
vitaiòlo *m* man about town; playboy, bon vivant
vitale *adj* vital
vitalità *f* vitality
vitalì•zio -zia (**-zi -zie**) *adj* life, lifetime || *m* life annuity
vitamina *f* vitamin
vite *f* (bot) grapevine; (mach) screw; **a vite** threaded; (aer) in a tailspin; **vite autofilettante** self-tapping screw; **vite del Canadà** woodbine, Virginia creeper; **vite per legno** wood screw; **vite per metallo** machine screw; **vite perpetua** (mach) endless screw, worm gear; **vite prigioniera** stud bolt
vitèllo *m* calf; veal
vitìc•cio *m* (**-ci**) tendril
vìtre•o -a *adj* vitreous; glassy (*eyes*)

vìttima *f* victim
vitto *m* food; diet; **vitto e alloggio** room and board
vittòria *f* victory; **cantar vittoria** to crow; to crow too soon
vittorió·so -sa [s] *adj* victorious
vituperare (**vitùpero**) *tr* to vituperate
vituperévole *adj* contemptible, shameful
vitupè·rio *m* (**-ri**) shame, infamy; insult; (lit) blame
viuzza *f* narrow street, lane
viva *interj* long live!
vivacchiare §287 *intr* (coll) to get along || *ref*—**si vivacchia** (coll) so, so
vivace *adj* lively, brisk; brilliant; vivacious
vivacità *f* liveliness, briskness; brilliancy, brightness; vivacity
vivaddìo *interj* yes, of course!; by Jove!
vivagno *m* selvage; edge
vi·vàio *m* (**-vài**) fishpond; fish tank; tree nursery; (fig) seedbed
vivanda *f* food
vivandiè·re -ra *mf* (mil) sutler
vìvere *m* life; living; cost of living; **viveri** food, provisions; allowance || §286 *tr* to live; **vivere un brutto momento** to spend an uncomfortable moment || *intr* (ESSERE) to live; **vive** (typ) **stet**; **vivere alla giornata** to live from hand to mouth
vivézza *f* liveliness
vìvi·do -da *adj* vivid, lively
vivificare §197 (**vivìfico**) *tr* to vivify
vivisezionare (**vivisezióno**) *tr* to vivisect; to scrutinize
vivisezióne *f* vivisection
vi·vo -va *adj* alive; living; live, vivacious; lively; vivid; high (*flame*); bright (*light*); raw (*flesh*); sharp, acute (*pain*); hearty (*thanks*); outright (*expense*); gross (*weight*); brute (*strength*); modern (*language*); kinetic (*energy*); running (*water*) || *m* living being; heart (*of a question*); **al vivo** lively; lifelike; **i vivi e i morti** the quick and the dead; **toccare nel vivo** to sting to the quick || **viva** *interj* see **viva**
viziare §287 *tr* to spoil; to ruin; (law) to vitiate || *ref* to become spoiled
vizia·to -ta *adj* spoiled; ruined; stale (*air*)
vì·zio *m* (**-zi**) vice; defect; flaw; (law) vitiation
vizió·so -sa [s] *adj* vicious; defective || *mf* profligate
viz·zo -za *adj* withered
vocabolà·rio *m* (**-ri**) dictionary; vocabulary
vocàbolo *m* word
vocale *adj* vocal; (lit) sonorous || *f* vowel
vocalizzare [ddzz] *tr & ref* to vocalize
vocativo *m* vocative
vocazióne *f* vocation
vóce *f* voice; noise, roar; word; rumor; entry; tone; **ad alta voce** aloud; **a bassa voce** in a low voice; **a viva voce** by word of mouth; **a voce** orally; **dare una voce a** (coll) to call; **dare sulla voce a** to rebuke; to contradict; **fare la voce grossa** to raise one's voice; **non avere voce in capitolo** to have no say; **schiarirsi la voce** to clear one's throat; **senza voce** hoarse; **sotto voce** in a low tone; **voce bianca** child's voice (*in singing*)
vociare *m* bawl || §128 (**vócio**) *intr* to bawl
vociferare (**vocìfero**) *intr* to vociferate, shout || *ref*—**si vocifera** it is rumored
vó·ga *f* (**-ghe**) fashion, vogue; energy, enthusiasm; rowing
vogare §209 (**vógo**) *tr & intr* to row
voga·tóre -trice *mf* rower || *m* oarsman; rowing machine
vòglia *f* wish; whim, fancy; willingness; birthmark; **aver voglia di** to feel like, have a notion to; **di buona voglia** willingly; **di mala voglia** unwillingly
voglió·so -sa [s] *adj* fanciful; (lit) desirous
vói §5 *pron pers* you; **voi altri** you, e.g., **voi altri americani** you Americans
voial·tri -tre *pron pl* you, e.g., **voialtri americani** you Americans
volano *m* shuttlecock; (mach) flywheel
volante *adj* flying; loose (*sheet*); free (*agent*) || *m* steering wheel; (mach) hand wheel; shuttlecock
volantino *m* leaflet; fringe; (mach) hand wheel
volare (**vólo**) *tr* (soccer) to overthrow || *intr* (ESSERE & AVERE) to fly
volata *f* flight; sprint; run; mouth (*of gun*); (tennis) volley; **di volata** in a hurry
volàtile *adj* volatile; flying (*animal*) || **volatili** *mpl* birds
volatilizzare [ddzz] *tr & intr* (ESSERE) to volatilize
volènte *adj*—**Dio volente** God willing; **volente o nolente** willy-nilly
volentièri *adv* gladly, willingly
volére *m* will, wish; **al volere di** at the bidding of || §288 *tr* to will; to want, desire; (lit) to believe, affirm; **l'hai voluto tu** it's your fault; **non vuol dire!** never mind!; **qui ti voglio** here's the rub, that's the trouble; **senza volere** without meaning to; **voglia Dio!** may God grant!; **voler bene** (with *dat*) to like; **volerci** to take, e.g., **ci vorranno due anni per finire questo palazzo** it will take two years to complete this building; **ce ne vogliono ancora tre** it takes three more of them; **voler dire** to mean; to try, e.g., **vuole piovere** it is trying to rain; **volere che** + *subj* to want + *inf*, e.g., **vuole che vengano** he wants them to come; **volere piuttosto** to prefer; **volere è potere** where there is a will there is a way; **voler male** (with *dat*) to dislike; **volerne a** to bear a grudge against; **vorrei** I should like, I'd like; **vuoi . . . vuoi** either . . . or
volgare *adj* vernacular, popular, common; vulgar || *m* vernacular
volgari·tà *f* (**-tà**) vulgarity

volgarizzare [ddzz] *tr* to popularize
vòlgere §289 *tr* to turn; (lit) to translate || *intr* to turn; (lit) to go by; **volgere a** to turn toward; to draw near, to approach; **volgere in fuga** to take to flight || *ref* to turn; to devote oneself
vól•go *m* (**-ghi**) (lit) crowd, mob
volièra *f* aviary
voliti•vo -va *adj* volitional; strong-minded, strong-willed
vólo *m* flight; fall; **al volo** on the spot; on the wing; **a volo d'uccello** as the crow flies; bird's-eye (*e.g., view*); **di volo** at top speed, immediately; **in volo** aloft, in the air; **prendere il volo** to take flight; **volo a vela** or **volo planato** gliding; **volo strumentale** instrument flying; **volo veleggiato** gliding
volon•tà *f* (**-tà**) will; **di spontanea volontà** of one's own volition; **pieno di buona volontà** eager to please; **ultime volontà** last will and testament
volontariato *m* volunteer work; apprenticeship without pay; (mil) volunteer service
volontà•rio -ria (-ri -rie) *adj* voluntary || *m* volunteer
volonteró•so -sa [s] *adj* willing, well-disposed
volpacchiòtto *m* fox cub; (fig) sly fox
vólpe *f* fox; (agr) smut; **volpe argentata** silver fox
volpi•no -na *adj* fox; fox-colored; foxy || *m* Pomeranian
volpó•ne -na *mf* sly fox
vòlt *m* (**vòlt**) (elec) volt
vòl•ta *m* (**-ta**) (elec) volt || *f* turn; time; vault; roof (*of mouth*); **alla volta di** toward; **a volta di corriere** by return mail; **a volte** sometimes; **c'era una volta** once upon a time there was; **certe volte** sometimes; **dare di volta il cervello a** to go crazy, e.g., **gli ha dato di volta il cervello** he went crazy; **dar la volta** to turn sour (*said of wine*); **due volte** twice; **molte volte** often; **per una volta tanto** only once; **poche volte** seldom; **tante volte** often; **tutto in una volta** at one swoop, at one stroke; in one gulp, in one swallow; **una volta** once; **una volta che** (coll) inasmuch as; **una volta per sempre** once and for all; **una volta tanto** for once; **volta a crociera** cross vault; **volta per volta** little by little; **volte** (math) times, e.g., **cinque volte cinque** five times five
voltafàc•cia *m* (**-cia**) volte-face; **fare voltafaccia** to wheel around (*said of a horse*)
voltagabba•na *mf* (**-na**) turncoat
voltàg•gio *m* (**-gi**) voltage
voltài•co -ca *adj* (**-ci -che**) voltaic
voltare (**vòlto**) *tr, intr & ref* to turn
voltastòma•co *m* (**-chi**) (coll) nausea; **fare venire il voltastomaco a qlcu** (coll) to turn s.o.'s stomach
voltata *f* turn; curve
volteggiare §290 (**voltéggio**) *tr* to put (*a horse*) through its paces || *intr* to hover; to flit, flutter; (sports) to vault (*e.g., on horseback or trapeze*)
voltég•gio *m* (**-gi**) (sports) vaulting
vòltmetro *m* voltmeter
vólto *m* (lit) face
voltura *f* (com, law) transfer
volùbile *adj* fickle
volubilità *f* fickleness
volume *m* volume; bulk; mass
voluminó•so -sa [s] *adj* voluminous, bulky
volu•to -ta *adj* desired; intentional || *f* (archit) volute, scroll
volut•tà *f* (**-tà**) pleasure, enjoyment; voluptuousness
voluttuà•rio -ria *adj* (**-ri -rie**) luxury (*goods*)
voluttuó•so -sa [s] *adj* voluptuous, sensuous
vòmere *m* plowshare; trail spade (*of gun*)
vòmi•co -ca *adj* (**-ci -che**) emetic
vomitare (**vòmito**) *tr & intr* to vomit
vomitati•vo -va *adj & m* emetic
vòmito *m* vomit
vóngola *f* clam
vorace *adj* voracious
voraci•tà *f* (**-tà**) voracity
voràgine *f* chasm, gulf, abyss
vòrtice *m* vortex, whirlpool; whirlwind
vorticó•so -sa [s] *adj* whirling, swirling
vò•stro -stra §6 *adj & pron poss*
votare (**vóto**) *tr* to devote; to vote || *intr* to vote || *ref* to devote oneself
votazióne *f* vote, voting, poll; (educ) grades
voti•vo -va *adj* votive
vóto *m* vow; wish; votive offering; vote, ballot; grade, mark; **a pieni voti** with highest honors; **fare un voto** to make a vow; **pronunciare i voti** to take vows; **voto di fiducia** vote of confidence; **voto preferenziale** write-in vote; preferential ballot
vudù *m* voodoo
vudui•sta *mf* (**-sti -ste**) voodoo (*person*)
vulcàni•co -ca *adj* (**-ci -che**) volcanic
vulcanizzare [ddzz] *tr* to vulcanize
vulcano *m* volcano
vulga•to -ta *adj* disseminated || **Vulgata** *f* Vulgate
vulneràbile *adj* vulnerable
vuotare (**vuòto**) *tr* to empty; **vuotare il sacco** to speak one's mind, unburden oneself || *ref* to empty
vuò•to -ta *adj* empty; devoid || *m* vacuum; emptiness; empty space; empty seat; empty feeling; empty (*e.g., container*); **a vuoto** in vain; wide of the mark; (*check*) without sufficient funds; **andare a vuoto** to fail; (mach) to idle; **cadere nel vuoto** to fall on deaf ears; **mandare a vuoto** to thwart; **sotto vuoto** in a vacuum; **vuoto d'aria** (aer) air pocket; **vuoto di cassa** deficit; **vuoto di potere** power vacuum

W

W, w ['doppjo 'vu] *m & f*
wà•fer *m* **(-fer)** wafer
water-clòset *m* **(-clòset)** flush toilet
watt *m* **(watt)** watt
watt•óra *m* **(-óra)** watt-hour
wèstera *m* **(wèstern)** (mov) western
whisky *m* **(whisky)** whiskey
wìgwam *m* **(wìgwam)** wigwam

X

X, x [ɪks] *m & f*
xèno *m* xenon
xenòfo•bo -ba *mf* xenophobe
xè•res *m* **(-res)** sherry
xerografìa *f* xerography
xerófito *m* xerophyte

Y

Y, y ['ɪpsɪlon] *m & f*
yacht *m* **(yachts)** yacht
yak *m* **(yak)** yak
yànkee *m* **(yànkees)** Yankee
yìddish *adj invar & m* Yiddish

Z

Z, z ['dzɛta] *m & f* twenty-first letter of the Italian alphabet
zabaióne [dz] *m* eggnog
zàcchera *f* splash of mud
zaffare *tr* to plug; to bung
zaffata *f* unpleasant whiff, stench; gust
zafferano [dz] *m* saffron
zaffiro [dz] *m* sapphire
zaffo *m* plug; bung; tampon
zàgara [dz] *f* orange blossom
zàino [dz] *m* knapsack; (mil) pack
zampa *f* paw; (culin) leg; **a quattro zampe** on all fours; **zampa di gallina** crow's-foot; illegible scrawl; **zampa di porco** crowbar
zampare *intr* to paw; to stamp
zampettare (zampétto) *intr* to toddle; to scamper
zampillare *intr* (ESSERE & AVERE) to spurt, gush, spring
zampillo *m* spurt, gush, spring
zampino *m* little paw; **metterci lo zampino** to put one's finger in the pie
zampiróne *m* slow-burning mosquito repellent; foul-smelling cigarette
zampógna *f* bagpipe
zampognare (zampógno) *intr* to pipe, play the bagpipe
zampóne *m* Modena salami (*stuffed forepaw of a hog*)
zanèlla *f* gully
zàngola *f* butter churn
zanna *f* tusk; fang; **mostrare le zanne** to show one's teeth
zanzara [dz] [dz] *f* mosquito
zanzarièra [dz] [dz] *f* mosquito net; window screen
zappa *f* hoe; **darsi la zappa sui piedi** to cut one's nose off to spite one's face
zappare *tr* to hoe
zappatóre *m* hoer, digger; (mil) sapper
zar *m* **(zar)** czar
zàttera *f* raft; **zattera di salvataggio** life raft
zatterière *m* log driver
zavòrra [dz] *f* ballast; (fig) deadwood
zavorrare [dz] **(zavòrro)** *tr* to ballast
zàzzera *f* mop (*of hair*)
zèbra [dz] *f* zebra; **zebre** zebra crossing
zebra•to -ta [dz] *adj* zebra-striped
ze•bù [dz] *m* **(-bù)** zebu
zéc•ca *f* **(-che)** mint; (ent) tick; **nuovo di zecca** brand-new
zecchino *m* sequin, gold coin
zèfiro [dz] *m* zephyr
zelante [dz] *adj* zealous; studious || *mf* zealot; eager beaver
zèlo [dz] *m* zeal; **zelo pubblico** public spirit
zènit [dz] *m* zenith
zénzero [dz] [dz] *m* ginger
zép•po -pa *adj* crammed, jammed || *f* wedge; (fig) padding
zerbino [dz] *m* doormat; dandy
zerbinòtto [dz] *m* dandy, sporty fellow
zèro [dz] *m* zero
zìa *f* aunt
zibaldóne [dz] *m* notebook; collection of thoughts; (pej) hodgepodge
zibellino [dz] *m* sable
zibétto [dz] *m* civet cat; civet (*substance used in perfumery*)
zibibbo [dz] *m* raisin
ziga•no -na *adj & mf* gypsy
zìgomo [dz] *m* cheekbone

zigrinare [dz] *tr* to grain (*leather*); to mill, knurl (*metal*)
zigrina•to -ta [dz] *adj* shagreened, grained (*leather*); knurled
zigzàg [dz] [dz] *m* (**zigzàg**) zigzag; **andare a zigzag** to zigzag
zigzagare §209 [dz] [dz] *intr* to zigzag
zimarra [dz] *f* cassock; (obs) overcoat
zimbèllo *m* decoy (*bird*); laughingstock
zincare §197 *tr* to zinc
zinco *m* zinc
zingaré•sco -sca (**-schi -sche**) *adj & mf* gypsy
zìnga•ro -ra *mf* gypsy
zìnnia [dz] *f* zinnia
zìo *m* uncle; **zio d'America** rich uncle
zìpolo *m* peg, bung
zircóne [dz] *m* zircon
zircònio [dz] *m* zirconium
zirlare *intr* to warble; to squeak (*said of mouse*)
zitèlla *f* old maid
zittire §176 *tr & intr* to hoot, hiss
zit•to -ta *adj* silent; **far stare zitto** to hush up; **stare zitto** to keep quiet || *m* whisper || **zitto** *interj* quiet!; hush!; shut up!
zizzània [dz] [ddzz] *f* (bot) darnel; **seminar zizzania** to sow discord
zòccolo *m* clog, sabot; clump, clod; clodhopper; base (*of column*); pedestal; wide baseboard; (zool) hoof
zodìaco [dz] *m* zodiac
zolfanèllo *m* sulfur match
zolfara *f* var of **solfara**
zólfo *m* sulfur
zòlla *f* clod, clump; turf; lump, cube (*of sugar*)
zollétta *f* lump, cube (*of sugar*)
zòna [dz] *f* zone; area; girdle; band, stripe; ticker tape; (pathol) shingles; (telg) tape; **zona glaciale** frigid zone; **zona tropicale** tropics, tropical zone
zónzo [dz] [dz] *m*—**andare a zonzo** to stroll, loiter along
zoòfito [dz] *m* zoophite
zoologìa [dz] *f* zoology
zoològi•co -ca [dz] *adj* (**-ci -che**) zoological
zoòlo•go -ga [dz] *mf* (**-gi -ghe**) zoologist
zootecnìa [dz] *f* animal husbandry
zootècni•co -ca [dz] (**-ci -che**) *adj* livestock || *m* livestock specialist
zoppicante *adj* limping; halting; shaky
zoppicare §197 (**zòppico**) *intr* to limp; to be shaky (*in one's studies*); to wobble
zoppicatura *f* limp; wobble
zòp•po -pa *adj* crippled; lame; wobbly || *mf* cripple; lame person
zòti•co -ca [dz] (**-ci -che**) *adj* uncouth, boorish || *m* churl, boor
zuc•ca *f* (**-che**) pumpkin; (joc) pate; (coll) empty head
zuccata *f* bump with the head
zuccherare (**zùcchero**) *tr* to sweeten, sugar
zuccherièra *f* sugar bowl
zuccherifì•cio *m* (**-ci**) sugar refinery
zuccheri•no -na *adj* sugary || *m* candy; sugar plum; sugar-coated pill
zùcchero *m* sugar; **zucchero filato** cotton candy; **zucchero in polvere** powdered sugar
zuccheró•so -sa [s] *adj* sugary
zucchétto *m* scull cap; zucchetto
zucchi•no -na *m & f* zucchini
zuccó•ne -na *mf* dunce, dumbbell
zuffa *f* brawl, fight
zufolare (**zùfolo**) *tr & intr* to whistle
zùfolo *m* (mus) whistle, pipe
zu•lù (**-lù**) [dz] *adj & mf* Zulu
zumare [dz] *tr & intr* (mov, telv) to zoom
zumata [dz] *f* (mov, telv) zoom
zuppa *f* soup; (fig) mess; **zuppa inglese** cake with brandy and whipped cream; **zuppa pavese** consommé with toast and eggs
zuppièra *f* tureen
zup•po -pa *adj* drenched, soaked || *f* see **zuppa**
Zurigo *f* Zurich
zuzzurulló•ne -na [dz] [ddzz] *mf* overgrown child, just a big kid

PART TWO

Inglese-Italiano

La pronunzia dell'inglese

I simboli seguenti rappresentano approssimativamente tutti i suoni della lingua inglese.

VOCALI

SIMBOLO	SUONO	ESEMPIO
[æ]	Più chiuso della **a** in **caso.**	**hat** [hæt]
[ɑ]	Come la **a** in **basso.**	**father** ['fɑðər] **proper** ['prɑpər]
[ɛ]	Come la **e** in **sella.**	**met** [mɛt]
[e]	Più chiuso della **e** in **ché.** Specialmente in posizione finale, si pronunzia come se fosse seguita da [ɪ].	**fate** [fet] **they** [ðe]
[ə]	Come la seconda **e** nella parola francese **gouvernement.**	**heaven** ['hɛvən] **pardon** ['pɑrdən]
[i]	Come la **i** in **nido.**	**she** [ʃi] **machine** [mə'ʃin]
[ɪ]	Come la **i** in **ritto.**	**fit** [fɪt] **beer** [bɪr]
[o]	Più chiuso della **o** in **sole.** Specialmente in posizione finale, si pronunzia come se fosse seguito da [ʊ].	**nose** [noz] **road** [rod] **row** [ro]
[ɔ]	Meno chiuso della **o** in **torre.**	**bought** [bɔt] **law** [lɔ]
[ʌ]	Piuttosto simile alla **eu** nella parola francese **peur**	**cup** [kʌp] **come** [kʌm] **mother** ['mʌðər]
[ʊ]	Meno chiuso della **u** in **insulto.**	**pull** [pʊl] **book** [bʊk] **wolf** [wʊlf]
[u]	Come la **u** in **acuto.**	**rude** [rud] **move** [muv] **tomb** [tum]

DITTONGHI

SIMBOLO	SUONO	ESEMPIO
[aɪ]	Come **ai** in **laico.**	**night** [naɪt] **eye** [aɪ]
[aʊ]	Come **au** in **causa.**	**found** [faʊnd] **cow** [kaʊ]
[ɔɪ]	Come **oi** in **poi.**	**voice** [vɔis] **oil** [ɔɪl]

SIMBOLO	SUONO	ESEMPIO
[b]	Come la **b** in **bambino.** Suono bilabiale occlusivo sonoro.	**bed** [bɛd] **robber** [ˈrɑbər]
[d]	Come la **d** in **caldo.** Suono dentale occlusivo sonoro.	**dead** [dɛd] **add** [æd]
[dʒ]	Come la **g** in **gente.** Suono palatale affricato sonoro.	**gem** [dʒɛm] **jail** [dʒel]
[ð]	Come la **d** nella pronuncia castigliana di **nada.** Suono interdentale fricativo sonoro.	**this** [ðɪs] **father** [ˈfɑðər]
[f]	Come la **f** in **fare.** Suono labiodentale fricativo sordo.	**face** [fes] **phone** [fon]
[g]	Come la **g** in **gatto.** Suono velare occlusivo sonoro.	**go** [go] **get** [gɛt]
[h]	Come la **c** aspirata nella pronuncia toscana di **casa.**	**hot** [hɔt] **alcohol** [ˈælkə ˌhɔl]
[j]	Come la **i** in **ieri** o la **y** in **yo-yo.** Semiconsonante di suono palatale sonoro.	**yes** [jɛs] **unit** [ˈjunɪt]
[k]	Come la **c** in **casa** ma accompagnato da un'aspirazione. Suono velare occlusivo sordo.	**cat** [kæt] **chord** [kɔrd] **kill** [kɪl]
[l]	Come la **l** in **latino.** Suono alveolare fricativo laterale sonoro.	**late** [let] **allow** [əˈlaʊ]
[m]	Come la **m** in **madre.** Suono bilabiale nasale sonoro.	**more** [mor] **command** [kəˈmænd]
[n]	Come la **n** in **notte.** Suono alveolare nasale sonoro.	**nest** [nɛst] **manner** [ˈmænər]
[ŋ]	Come la **n** in **manca.** Suono velare nasale sonoro.	**king** [kɪŋ] **conquer** [ˈkɑŋkər]
[p]	Come la **p** in **patto** ma accompagnato da un'aspirazione. Suono bilabiale occlusivo sordo.	**pen** [pɛn] **cap** [kæp]
[r]	La **r** più comune in molte parti dell'Inghilterra e nella maggior parte degli Stati Uniti e del Canadà è un suono semivocalico articolato con la punta della lingua elevata verso la volta del palato. Questa consonante è debolissima in posizione intervocalica o alla fine di una sillaba, e può appena percepirsi. L'articolazione di questa consonante ha la tendenza di influenzare il suono delle vocali contigue. La **r,** preceduta dai suoni [ʌ] o [ə], dà il proprio colorito a questi suoni e sparisce completamente come suono consonantico.	**run** [rʌn] **far** [fɑr] **art** [ɑrt] **carry** [ˈkæri] **burn** [bʌrn] **learn** [lʌrn] **weather** [ˈwɛðər]
[s]	Come la **s** in **sette.** Suono alveolare fricativo sordo.	**send** [sɛnd] **cellar** [ˈsɛlər]
[ʃ]	Come **sc** in **lasciare.** Suono palatale fricativo sordo.	**shall** [ʃæl] **machine** [məˈʃin]
[t]	Come la **t** in **tavolo** ma accompagnato da un'aspirazione. Suono dentale occlusivo sordo.	**ten** [tɛn] **dropped** [drɑpt]
[tʃ]	Come **c** in **cibo.** Suono palatale affricato sordo.	**child** [tʃaɪld] **much** [mʌtʃ] **nature** [ˈnetʃər]
[θ]	Come la **z** castigliana in **zapato.** Suono interdentale fricativo sordo.	**think** [θɪŋk] **truth** [truθ]
[v]	Come la **v** in **vento.** Suono labiodentale fricativo sonoro.	**vest** [vɛst] **over** [ˈovər] **of** [ɑv]

SIMBOLO	SUONO	ESEMPIO
[w]	Come la **u** in **quadro.** Suono labiovelare fricativo sonoro.	**work** [wʌrk] **tweed** [twid] **queen** [kwin]
[z]	Come la **s** in **asilo.** Suono alveolare fricativo sonoro.	**zeal** [zil] **busy** ['bɪzi] **his** [hɪz]
[ʒ]	Come la seconda **g** nella parola francese **garage.** Suono palatale fricativo sonoro.	**azure** ['eʒər] **measure** ['mɛʒər]

ACCENTO

L'accento tonico principale, indicato col segno grafico ', e l'accento secondario, indicato col segno grafico ,, precedono la sillaba sulla quale cadono, per es., **fascinate** ['fæsɪ ,net].

La pronunzia delle parole composte

Nella parte inglese-italiano di questo Dizionario la pronunzia figurata di tutte le parole inglesi semplici è indicata in parentesi quadre che seguono immediatamente l'esponente, secondo un nuovo adattamento dell'alfabeto fonetico internazionale.

Vi sono tre generi di parole composte in inglese: (1) le parole in cui gli elementi componenti si sono uniti per formare una parola solida, come per es., **steamboat** vapore; (2) la parole in cui gli elementi componenti sono uniti da un trattino, come per es., **high'-grade'** di qualità superiore; (3) le parole in cui gli elementi componenti rimangono graficamente indipendenti gli uni da gli altri, per es., **post card** cartolina postale. La pronunzia delle parole inglesi composte non è indicata in questo Dizionario qualora gli elementi componenti appaiono come esponenti indipendenti nella loro normale posizione alfabetica e mostrano quindi la loro pronunzia figurata. Solo gli accenti principali e secondari di tali parole sono indicati, come per es., **steam'boat'**, **high'-grade'**, **post' card'**. Se i due membri di una parola composta inglese solida non sono separati da un accento grafico, si usa un punto leggermente elevato sopra il rigo per indicarne la divisione, come per es., **la'dy•like'**.

Nei nomi in cui l'accento secondario cade sul membro **-man** o **-men,** le vocali di tali membri si pronunziano come nelle parole semplici **man** e **men,** come per es., **mailman** ['mel ,mæn] e **mailmen** ['mel ,men]. Nei nomi in cui tali membri componenti non sono accentati, le loro vocali si pronunziano come se fossero un'**e** muta francese, come per es., **policeman** [pə'lismən] e **policemen** [pə'lismən]. In questo Dizionario la trascrizione fonetica di tali nomi non è stata indicata qualora il primo membro componente appaia come esponente con la sua pronunzia in alfabeto fonetico internazionale. Gli accenti sono ciò nondimeno indicati:

mail'man' *s* (**-men'**)
police'man *s* (**-men**)

La pronunzia dei participi passati

La pronunzia di una parola la cui desinenza è **-ed** (o **-d** dopo una **e** muta) non è indicata nel presente Dizionario, purché la pronunzia della parola stessa senza tale suffisso appaia con il suo esponente nella sua posizione alfabetica. In tale caso la pronunzia segue le regole indicate qui sotto. Si osservi che il raddoppiamento della vocale finale dopo una semplice vocale tonica non muta la pronunzia del suffisso **-ed,** per es.: **batted** ['bætɪd], **dropped** [drɑpt], **robbed** [rɑbd].

La desinenza **-ed** (o **-d** dopo una **e** muta) del preterito, del participio passato e di certi aggettivi ha tre pronunzie differenti, che dipendono dal suono in cui il tema termina:

1) Se il tema termina in suono consonantico sonoro (che non sia [d]), cioè [b], [g], [l], [m], [n], [ŋ], [r], [v], [z], [ð], [ʒ] o [dʒ] o in un suono vocalico, l'**-ed** è pronunziato [d]:

SUONO IN CUI TERMINA IL TEMA	INFINITO	PRETERITO E PARTICIPIO PASSATO
[b]	**ebb** [ɛb] **rob** [rɑb] **robe** [rob]	**ebbed** [ɛbd] **robbed** [rɑbd] **robed** [robd]

SUONO IN CUI TERMINA IL TEMA	INFINITO	PRETERITO E PARTICIPIO PASSATO
[g]	**egg** [ɛg] **sag** [sæg]	**egged** [ɛgd] **sagged** [sægd]
[l]	**mail** [mel] **scale** [skel]	**mailed** [meld] **scaled** [skeld]
[m]	**storm** [stɔrm] **bomb** [bɑm] **name** [nem]	**stormed** [stɔrmd] **bombed** [bɑmd] **named** [nemd]
[n]	**tan** [tæn] **sign** [saɪn] **mine** [maɪn]	**tanned** [tænd] **signed** [saɪnd] **mined** [maɪnd]
[ŋ]	**hang** [hæŋ]	**hanged** [hæŋd]
[r]	**fear** [fɪr] **care** [kɛr]	**feared** [fɪrd] **cared** [kɛrd]
[v]	**rev** [rɛv] **save** [sev]	**revved** [rɛvd] **saved** [sevd]
[z]	**buzz** [bʌz] **fuze** [fjuz]	**buzzed** [bʌzd] **fuzed** [fjuzd]
[ð]	**smooth** [smuð] **bathe** [beð]	**smoothed** [smuðd] **bathed** [beðd]
[ʒ]	**massage** [mə'sɑʒ]	**massaged** [mə'sɑʒd]
[dʒ]	**page** [pedʒ]	**paged** [pedʒd]
suono vocalico	**key** [ki] **sigh** [saɪ] **paw** [pɔ]	**keyed** [kid] **sighed** [saɪd] **pawed** [pɔd]

2) Se il tema termina in un suono consonantico sordo (che non sia [t]), cioè [f], [k], [p], [s], [θ], [ʃ] o [tʃ], l'**-ed** si pronunzia [t]:

SUONO IN CUI TERMINA IL TEMA	INFINITO	PRETERITO E PARTICIPIO PASSATO
[f]	**loaf** [lof] **knife** [naɪf]	**loafed** [loft] **knifed** [naɪft]
[k]	**back** [bæk] **bake** [bek]	**backed** [bækt] **baked** [bekt]
[p]	**cap** [kæp] **wipe** [waɪp]	**capped** [kæpt] **wiped** [waɪpt]
[s]	**hiss** [hɪs] **mix** [mɪks]	**hissed** [hɪst] **mixed** [mɪkst]
[θ]	**lath** [læθ]	**lathed** [læθt]
[ʃ]	**mash** [mæʃ]	**mashed** [mæʃt]
[tʃ]	**match** [mætʃ]	**matched** [mætʃt]

3) Se il tema termina in un suono dentale, cioè [t] o [d], l'**-ed** si pronunzia [ɪd] o [əd]:

SUONO IN CUI TERMINA IL TEMA	INFINITO	PRETERITO E PARTICIPIO PASSATO
[t]	**wait** [wet] **mate** [met]	**waited** ['wetɪd] **mated** ['metɪd]
[d]	**mend** [mɛnd] **wade** [wed]	**mended** ['mɛndɪd] **waded** ['wedɪd]

L'-ed di alcuni aggettivi aggiunto ad un tema che termina in suono consonantico (oltre a quelli che terminano in [d] o [t]), è ciò nonostante talvolta pronunziato [ɪd] e tale fenomeno è idicato con la piena pronunzia della parola in simboli dell'alfabeto fonetico internazionale, per es., **blessed** ['blesɪd], **crabbed** ['kræbɪd].

A, a [e] *s* prima lettera dell'alfabeto inglese
a [e] *art indef* un, uno, una, un'
aback [ə'bæk] *adv* all'indietro; **taken aback** colto alla sprovvista, sconcertato
aba·cus ['æbəkəs] *s* (**-cuses** or **-ci** [ˌsaɪ]) pallottoliere *m;* (archit) abaco
abaft [ə'bæft] or [ə'bɑft] *adv* a poppa || *prep* dietro a
abandon [ə'bændən] *s* disinvoltura || *tr* abbandonare
abase [ə'bes] *tr* umiliare, degradare
abash [ə'bæʃ] *tr* imbarazzare; sconcertare
abate [ə'bet] *tr* ridurre; omettere; (law) terminare || *intr* diminuire, calmarsi
aba·tis ['æbətɪs] or [ə'bætɪs] *s* (**-tis** or **-tises**) (mil) tagliata
abattoir ['æbəˌtwɑr] *s* macello
abba·cy ['æbəsi] *s* (**-cies**) abbazia
abbess ['æbɪs] *s* badessa
abbey ['æbi] *s* badia, abbazia
abbot ['æbət] *s* abate *m*
abbreviate [ə'brivɪˌet] *tr* abbreviare, raccorciare
abbreviation [əˌbrivɪ'eʃən] *s* (*abbreviated form*) abbreviazione; (*shortening*) abbreviamento
A B C [ˌeˌbi'si] *s* (letterword) abbiccì *m;* **A B C's** abbecedario
abdicate ['æbdɪˌket] *tr* abdicare a || *intr* abdicare
abdomen ['æbdəmən] or [æb'domən] *s* addome *m*
abduct [æb'dʌkt] *tr* rapire
abed [ə'bɛd] *adv* a letto
abet [ə'bɛt] *v* (*pret & pp* **abetted;** *ger* **abetting**) *tr* favoreggiare
abeyance [ə'be·əns] *s* sospensione; **in abeyance** in sospeso
ab·hor [æb'hɔr] *v* (*pret & pp* **-horred;** *ger* **-horring**) *tr* aborrire
abhorrent [æb'hɑrənt] or [æb'hɔrənt] *adj* detestabile
abide [ə'baɪd] *v* (*pret & pp* **abode** or **abided**) *tr* aspettare; tollerare || *intr* **—to abide by** attenersi a; rimanere fedele a
abili·ty [ə'bɪlɪti] *s* (**-ties**) abilità *f,* bravura
abject ['æbdʒɛkt] or [æb'dʒɛkt] *adj* abietto, turpe
abjure [æb'dʒʊr] *tr* abiurare
ablative ['æblətɪv] *adj & s* ablativo
ablaut ['æblaʊt] *s* apofonia
ablaze [ə'blez] *adj* in fiamme; risplendente
able ['ebəl] *adj* abile, esperto; **to be able to** + *inf* potere + *inf*
able-bodied ['ebəl'bɑdid] *adj* sano; forte
abloom [ə'blum] *adj & adv* in fiore
abnormal [æb'nɔrməl] *adj* anormale
aboard [ə'bord] *adv* a bordo; **all aboard!** (rr) signori, in vettura!; **to go aboard** imbarcarsi; **to take aboard** imbarcare || *prep* a bordo di; (*a bus, train, etc.*) in, su
abode [ə'bod] *s* abitazione, dimora
abolish [ə'bɑlɪʃ] *tr* abolire
A-bomb ['eˌbɑm] *s* bomba atomica
abominable [ə'bɑmənəbəl] *adj* abominevole
abomination [əˌbɑmɪ'neʃən] *s* abominazione
aborigenes [ˌæbə'rɪdʒɪˌniz] *spl* aborigeni *mpl*
abort [ə'bɔrt] *tr* terminare prematuramente; provocare un aborto in || *intr* abortire
abortion [ə'bɔrʃən] *s* aborto
abound [ə'baʊnd] *intr* abbondare; **to abound in** or **with** abbondare di
about [ə'baʊt] *adv* circa, press'a poco; qua intorno; qua e là; in direzione opposta; (coll) quasi; **to be about to** star sul punto di || *prep* intorno a; circa a; addosso a; tutt'intorno a; riguardo a
about'-face' *interj* (mil) dietro front!
about'-face' or **about'-face'** *s* voltafaccia; (mil) dietro front *m* || **about'-face'** *intr* fare dietro front
above [ə'bʌv] *adj* soprammenzionato; superiore || *s*—**from above** dal cielo; dall'alto || *adv* in alto; su; più sopra || *prep* sopra, sopra a; più di; al di là di, oltre; **above all** soprattutto
above-mentioned [ə'bʌv'mɛnʃənd] *adj* summenzionato, sunnominato
abrasive [ə'bresɪv] or [ə'brezɪv] *adj & s* abrasivo
abreast [ə'brɛst] *adj & adv* in fila, in linea; **to keep abreast of** tenersi alla pari con; essere al corrente di
abridge [ə'brɪdʒ] *tr* compendiare; ridurre
abroad [ə'brɔd] *adv* all'estero; all'aria aperta; **to be abroad** (*said of news*) circolare
abrupt [ə'brʌpt] *adj* brusco, improvviso; (*very steep*) scosceso
abscess ['æbsɛs] *s* ascesso
abscond [æb'skɑnd] *intr* scappare; **to abscond with** svignarsela con
absence ['æbsəns] *s* assenza; **in the absence of** in mancanza di
absent ['æbsənt] *adj* assente || [æb-ˌsɛnt] *tr*—**to absent oneself** assentarsi
absentee [ˌæbsən'ti] *s* assente *mf*
absent-minded ['æbsənt'maɪndɪd] *adj* distratto, assente
absinth ['æbsɪnθ] *s* assenzio
absolute ['æbsəˌlut] *adj & s* assoluto
absolutely ['æbsəˌlutli] *adv* assolutamente, certamente || [ˌæbsə'lutli] *interj* certamente!
absolve [æb'sɑlv] *tr* assolvere
absorb [æb'sɔrb] *tr* assorbire; **to be or become absorbed** essere assorto
absorbent [æb'sɔrbənt] *adj* assorbente; (*cotton*) idrofilo || *s* sostanza assorbente
absorbing [æb'sɔrbɪŋ] *adj* interessantissimo
abstain [æb'sten] *intr* astenersi
abstemious [æb'stimɪ·əs] *adj* astemio
abstention [æb'stɛnʃən] *s* astensione; astenuto (*vote withheld*)

abstinent [ˈæbstɪnənt] *adj* astinente
abstract [ˈæbstrækt] *adj* astratto || *s* compendio, sommario || *tr* compendiare || (æbˈstrækt] *tr* astrarre; (*to steal*) sottrarre
abstruse [æbˈstrus] *adj* astruso
absurd [æbˈsʌrd] or [æbˈzʌrd] *adj* assurdo
absurdi•ty [æbˈsʌrdɪti] or [æbˈzʌrdɪti] *s* (**-ties**) assurdità *f*
abundant [əˈbʌndənt] *adj* abbondante
abuse [əˈbjus] *s* (*misuse*) abuso; maltrattamento; insulto || [əˈbjuz] *tr* (*to misuse, take unfair advantage of*) abusare di; maltrattare; insultare
abusive [əˈbjusɪv] *adj* abusivo; insultante
abut [əˈbʌt] *v* (*pret & pp* **abutted;** *ger* **abutting**) *intr*—**to abut on** confinare con
abutment [əˈbʌtmənt] *s* rinfianco; (*at either end of bridge*) spalla; (*of buttresses of bridge*) sprone *m*
abysmal (əˈbɪzməl] *adj* abissale; (*e.g., ignorance*) spropositato
abyss [əˈbɪs] *s* abisso
academic [ˌækəˈdɛmɪk] *adj* accademico
ac'ademic cos'tume *s* toga accademica
academician [əˌkædəˈmɪʃən] *s* accademico
ac'adem'ic year' *s* anno scolastico
acade•my [əˈkædəmi] *s* (**-mies**) accademia
accede [ækˈsid] *intr* accedere; **to accede to** salire a; accedere a
accelerate [ækˈsɛləˌret] *tr & intr* accelerare
accelerator [ækˈsɛləˌretər] *s* acceleratore *m*
accent [ˈæksɛnt] *s* accento || [ˈæksɛnt] or [ækˈsɛnt] *tr* accentare; (*to accentuate*) accentuare
ac'cent mark' *s* segnaccento, accento grafico
accentuate [ækˈsɛntʃʊˌet] *tr* accentuare
accept [ækˈsɛpt] *tr* accettare
acceptable [ækˈsɛptəbəl] *adj* accettabile
acceptance [ækˈsɛptəns] *s* accettazione
access [ˈæksɛs] *s* accesso
accessible [ækˈsɛsɪbəl] *adj* accessibile; (*person*) abbordabile
accession [ækˈsɛʃən] *s* accessione, acquisto; (*e.g., to the throne*) adito
accesso•ry [ækˈsɛsəri] *adj* accessorio || *s* (**-ries**) accessorio; (*to a crime*) complice *m*
accident [ˈæksɪdənt] *s* accidente *m;* **by accident** accidentalmente, per caso
accidental [ˌæksɪˈdɛntəl] *adj* accidentale || *s* (mus) accidente *m*
acclaim [əˈklem] *s* acclamazione, applauso || *tr & intr* acclamare, applaudire
acclimate [ˈæklɪˌmet] *tr* acclimatare || *intr* acclimatarsi
accolade [ˌækəˈled] *s* accollata; (fig) elogio
accommodate [əˈkɑməˌdet] *tr* (*to adjust, make fit*) accomodare; (*to provide with a loan*) venire incontro a; (*to supply with lodging*) alloggiare; (*to oblige*) favorire; (*to have room for*) aver posto per
accommodating [əˈkɑməˌdetɪŋ] *adj* servizievole, compiacente
accommodation [əˌkɑməˈdeʃən] *s* (*favor*) favore *m;* (*loan*) prestito; (*adaptation*) adattamento; (*reconciliation*) conciliazione; (*compromise*) accomodamento; **accommodations** (*traveling space*) posto; (*in a hotel*) alloggio
accommoda'tion train' *s* treno accelerato
accompaniment [əˈkʌmpənɪmənt] *s* accompagnamento
accompanist [əˈkʌmpənɪst] *s* accompagnatore *m*
accompa•ny [əˈkʌmpəni] *v* (*pret & pp* **-nied**) *tr* accompagnare
accomplice [əˈkɑmplɪs] *s* complice *mf*
accomplish [əˈkɑmplɪʃ] *tr* compiere
accomplished [əˈkɑmplɪʃt] *adj* (*completed*) compiuto, terminato; (*skilled*) finito, compiuto
accomplishment [əˈkɑmplɪʃmənt] *s* (*completion*) esecuzione, realizzazione; (*something accomplished*) opera; (*acquired ability*) talento; (*military achievement*) prodezza; (*social skill*) compitezza
accord [əˈkɔrd] *s* accordo; **in accord with** in conformità con; **of one's own accord** spontaneamente; **with one accord** di comune accordo || *tr* concedere || *intr* accordarsi
accordance [əˈkɔrdəns] *s* accordo; **in accordance with** in conformità con
according [əˈkɔrdɪŋ] *adv*—**according as** a seconda che; **according to** secondo, a seconda di
accordingly [əˈkɔrdɪŋli] *adv* per conseguenza, perciò; in conformità
accordion [əˈkɔrdɪ·ən] *s* fisarmonica
accost [əˈkɔst] or [əˈkɑst] *tr* accostare, abbordare
accouchement [əˈkuʃmənt] *s* parto
account [əˈkaunt] *s* (*explanation*) versione; (*report*) resoconto; conto; (*statement*) estratto conto; **by all accounts** secondo la voce comune; **of account** d'importanza; **of no account** senza importanza; **on account** in acconto; **on account of** a causa di; per l'amor di; **on all accounts** in ogni modo; **on no account** in nessuna maniera; **to call to account** chiedere conto di; **to give a good account of oneself** comportarsi bene; **to take account of** prendere in considerazione; **to turn to account** trarre profitto da || *intr*—**to account for** render conto di; essere responsabile per
accountable [əˈkauntəbəl] *adj* responsabile; (*explainable*) spiegabile
accountant [əˈkauntənt] *s* contabile *mf,* ragioniere *m*
accounting [əˈkauntɪŋ] *s* contabilità *f,* ragioneria
accouterments [əˈkutərmənts] *spl* (mil)

buffetterie *fpl;* (*trappings*) ornamenti *mpl*
accredit [ə'kredɪt] *tr* accreditare; **to accredit s.o. with s.th** ascrivere qlco a credito di qlcu
accrue [ə'kru] *intr* accumularsi; (*said of interest*) maturare
acculturation [ə,kʌltʃə'reʃən] *s* acculturazione
accumulate [ə'kjumjə,let] *tr* accumulare || *intr* accumularsi
accuracy ['ækjərəsi] *s* esattezza, precisione; fedeltà *f*
accurate ['ækjərɪt] *adj* esatto, preciso; fedele
accursed [ə'kʌrsɪd] or [ə'kʌrst] *adj* maledetto
accusation [,ækjə'zeʃən] *s* accusa
accusative [ə'kjuzətɪv] *adj & s* accusativo
accuse [ə'kjuz] *tr* accusare
accustom [ə'kʌstəm] *tr* abituare
ace [es] *s* asso; **to be within an ace of** essere quasi sul punto di
ace' in the hole' *s* asso nella manica
acetate ['æsɪ,tet] *s* acetato
ace'tic ac'id [ə'sitɪk] *s* acido acetico
aceti·fy [ə'setɪ,faɪ] *v* (*pret & pp* **-fied**) *tr* acetificare || *intr* acetificarsi
acetone ['æsɪ,ton] *s* acetone *m*
acetylene [ə'setɪ,lin] *s* acetilene *m*
acet'ylene torch' *s* cannello ossiacetilenico
ache [ek] *s* dolore *m* || *intr* dolere, e.g., **my tooth aches** mi duole il dente
Acheron ['ækə,rɑn] *s* Acheronte *m*
achieve [ə'tʃiv] *tr* compiere, conseguire
achievement [ə'tʃivmənt] *s* compimento; successo; (*exploit*) impresa, prodezza
Achil'les heel' [ə'kɪliz] *s* tallone *m* d'Achille
acid ['æsɪd] *adj & s* acido
acidi·fy [ə'sɪdɪ,faɪ] *v* (*pret & pp* **-fied**) *tr & intr* acidificare
acidity [ə'sɪdɪti] *s* acidità *f*
acid' test' *s* prova del fuoco
ack-ack ['æk'æk] *s* (slang) cannone antiaereo
acknowledge [æk'nɑlɪdʒ] *tr* riconoscere; (*receipt of a letter*) accusare; (*a claim*) ammettere; mostrare la gratitudine per; (law) certificare
acknowledgment [æk'nɑlɪdʒmənt] *s* riconoscimento; (*of receipt of a letter*) accusa, cenno
acme ['ækmi] *s* acme *f*
acolyte ['ækə,laɪt] *s* accolito
acorn ['ekɔrn] or ['ekərn] *s* ghianda
acoustic [ə'kustɪk] *adj* acustico || **acoustics** *s* acustica
acquaint [ə'kwent] *tr* mettere al corrente; **to be acquainted with** conoscere; essere al corrente di; **to become acquainted** (*with each other*) conoscersi
acquaintance [ə'kwentəns] *s* conoscenza; (*person*) conoscente *mf,* conoscenza
acquiesce [,ækwɪ'es] *intr* acconsentire, accondiscendere
acquiescence [,ækwɪ'esəns] *s* accondiscendenza
acquire [ə'kwaɪr] *tr* acquistare
acquisition [,ækwɪ'zɪʃən] *s* acquisto
acquit [ə'kwɪt] *v* (*pret & pp* **acquitted;** *ger* **acquitting**) *tr* (*to pay*) ripagare; (*to declare not guilty*) assolvere; **to acquit oneself** condursi
acquittal [ə'kwɪtəl] *s* assoluzione
acre ['ekər] *s* acro
acrid ['ækrɪd] *adj* acrido, pungente
acrobat ['ækrə,bæt] *s* acrobata *mf*
acrobatic [,ækrə'bætɪk] *adj* acrobatico || **acrobatics** *ssg* (*e.g., of a stunt pilot*) acrobazie *fpl;* **acrobatics** *spl* (*gymnastics*) acrobatica
acronym ['ækrənɪm] *s* acronimo, parola macedonia
acropolis [ə'krɑpəlɪs] *s* acropoli *f*
across [ə'krɔs] or [ə'krɑs] *adv* dall'altra parte; **to get an idea across to** farsi capire da || *prep* attraverso; (*on the other side of*) al di là di, dall'altra parte di; **to come across** (*a person*) imbattersi in; **to go across** attraversare
across'-the-board' *adj* generale
act [ækt] *s* atto; legge *f;* rappresentazione; **in the act** in flagrante || *tr* (*a drama*) rappresentare; (*a role*) recitare || *intr* (*on the stage*) recitare; (*to behave*) comportarsi; (*to perform special duties; to reach a decision*) agire; (*to have an effect*) reagire; **to act as** fungere da; **to act for** rimpiazzare; **to act on** eseguire; **to act up** (coll) fare il matto; non funzionare bene (*said, e.g., of a motor*); **to act up to** (coll) fare festa a
acting ['æktɪŋ] *adj* facente funzione, interino || *s* recita
action ['ækʃən] *s* azione; (*moving parts*) meccanismo; **to take action** iniziare azione; (law) intentare causa
activate ['æktɪ,vet] *tr* attivare
active ['æktɪv] *adj & s* attivo
activi·ty [æk'tɪvɪti] *s* (**-ties**) attività *f*
act' of God' *s* forza maggiore
actor ['æktər] *s* attore *m*
actress ['æktrɪs] *s* attrice *f*
actual ['æktʃʊ·əl] *adj* reale
actually ['æktʃʊ·əli] *adv* realmente, in realtà
actuar·y ['æktʃʊ,eri] *s* (**-ies**) attuario
actuate ['æktʃʊ,et] *tr* attuare, mettere in azione; (*to motivate*) stimulare
acuity [ə'kju·ɪti] *s* acuità *f*
acumen [ə'kjumən] *s* acume *m*
acupuncture ['ækjʊ,pʌŋktʃər] *s* agopuntura
acute [ə'kjut] *adj* acuto
ad [æd] *s* (coll) inserzione pubblicitaria
Adam ['ædəm] *s* Adamo; **not to know from Adam** non conoscere affatto
adamant ['ædəmənt] *adj* saldo, inflessibile
Ad'am's ap'ple *s* pomo d'Adamo
adapt [ə'dæpt] *tr* adattare
adaptation [,ædæp'teʃən] *s* adattamento; (*e.g., of a play*) rifacimento
add [æd] *tr* aggiungere; (*numbers*)

sommare || *intr* aggiungere; far di conto; **to add up to** ammontare a; (coll) voler dire
adder ['ædər] *s* vipera
addict ['ædɪkt] *s* (*to drugs*) tossicomane *mf;* (*to a sport*) tifoso || [ə'dɪkt] *tr* abituare; rendere propenso alla tossicomania; **to addict oneself to** darsi a, abbandonarsi a
addiction [ə'dɪkʃən] *s* dedizione; (*to drugs*) tossicomania; (*to sports*) tifo
add'ing machine' *s* calcolatrice *f*
addition [ə'dɪʃən] *s* addizione; (*building*) annessi *mpl;* **in addition** inoltre, per di più; **in addition to** oltre a
additive ['ædɪtɪv] *adj & s* additivo
address [ə'drɛs] or ['ædrɛs] *s* (*speech*) discorso; (*place and destination of mail*) indirizzo; (*skill*) destrezza; (*formal request*) petizione; **to deliver an address** pronunciare un discorso || [ə'drɛs] *tr* indirizzare; (*to speak to*) rivolgere la parola a
addressee [,ædrɛ'si] *s* destinatario
address'ing machine' *s* macchina per indirizzi
adduce [ə'djus] or [ə'dus] *tr* addurre
adenoids ['ædə,nɔɪds] *spl* vegetazioni *fpl* adenoidi, adenoidi *fpl*
adept [ə'dɛpt] *adj & s* esperto
adequate ['ædɪkwɪt] *adj* sufficiente; (*suitable*) conveniente
adhere [æd'hɪr] *intr* aderire
adherence [æd'hɪrəns] *s* aderenza
adherent [æd'hɪrənt] *adj & s* aderente *m*
adhesion [æd'hiʒən] *s* adesione; (pathol) aderenza
adhesive [æd'hisɪv] or [æd'hizɪv] *adj & s* adesivo
adhe'sive tape' *s* tela adesiva, cerotto
adieu [ə'dju] or [ə'du] *s* (**adieus** or **adieux**) addio || *interj* addio!
adjacent [ə'dʒesənt] *adj* adiacente
adjective ['ædʒɪktɪv] *adj* aggettivale; accessorio, secondario || *s* aggettivo
adjoin [ə'dʒɔɪn] *tr* confinare con || *intr* essere confinanti
adjoining [ə'dʒɔɪnɪŋ] *adj* confinante; vicino, attiguo
adjourn [ə'dʒʌrn] *tr* aggiornare, rinviare || *intr* rinviarsi
adjournment [ə'dʒʌrnmənt] s aggiornamento, rinvio
adjust [ə'dʒʌst] *tr* accomodare; regolare; (ins) liquidare || *intr* abituarsi
adjustable [ə'dʒʌstəbəl] *adj* regolabile
adjustment [ə'dʒʌstmənt] *s* aggiustamento; accomodamento; (ins) liquidazione del danno
adjutant ['ædʒətənt] *s* aiutante *mf*
ad·lib [,æd'lɪb] *v* (*pret & pp* **-libbed;** *ger* **-libbing**) *tr & intr* improvvisare
administer [æd'mɪnɪstər] *tr* amministrare; (*medicine*) somministrare; (*an oath*) dare || *intr*—**to administer to** ministrare, prestare aiuto a
administrator [æd'mɪnɪs,tretər] *s* amministratore *m*
admirable ['ædmɪrəbəl] *adj* ammirabile, ammirevole
admiral ['ædmɪrəl] *s* ammiraglio
admiral·ty ['ædmɪrəlti] *s* (**-ties**) ammiragliato
admire [æd'maɪr] *tr* ammirare
admirer [æd'maɪrər] *s* ammiratore *m*
admissible [æd'mɪsɪbəl] *adj* ammissibile
admission [æd'mɪʃən] *s* ammissione; confessione; (*entrance fee*) prezzo d'ingresso; **to gain admission** arrivare a entrare
ad·mit [æd'mɪt] *v* (*pret & pp* **-mitted;** *ger* **-mitting**) *tr* ammettere; confessare || *intr* dare l'ingresso; **to admit of** permettere, ammettere; consentire
admittance [æd'mɪtəns] *s* ammissione; permesso di entrare; **no admittance** divieto d'ingresso
admonish [æd'mɑnɪʃ] *tr* ammonire
ado [ə'du] *s* confusione, trambusto; **much ado about nothing** molto rumore per nulla; **to make a big ado** fare cerimonie
adobe [ə'dobi] *s* mattone crudo
adolescence [,ædə'lɛsəns] *s* adolescenza
adolescent [,ædə'lɛsənt] *adj & s* adolescente *mf*
adopt [ə'dɑpt] *tr* adottare
adoption [ə'dɑpʃən] *s* adozione
adorable [ə'dorəbəl] *adj* adorabile
adore [ə'dor] *tr* adorare
adorn [ə'dɔrn] *tr* adornare
adornment [ə'dɔrnmənt] *s* ornamento
adre'nal gland' [æd'rinəl] *s* glandola surrenale
Adriatic [,edrɪ'ætɪk] or [,ædrɪ'ætɪk] *adj* adriatico || *adj & s* Adriatico
adrift [ə'drɪft] *adj & adv* alla deriva
adroit [ə'drɔɪt] *adj* destro
adult [ə'dʌlt] or ['ædʌlt] *adj & s* adulto
adulterate [ə'dʌltə,ret] *tr* adulterare
adulterer [ə'dʌltərər] *s* adultero
adulteress [ə'dʌltərɪs] *s* adultera
adulter·y [ə'dʌltəri] *s* (**-ies**) adulterio
advance [æd'væns] or [æd'vɑns] *adj* avanzato || *s* avanzata; (*increase in price*) aumento; (*of money*) anticipo; **advances** approcci *mpl;* **in advance** in anticipo || *tr* avanzare; aumentare; (*to make earlier*) anticipare; (*money*) anticipare; (*a clock*) mettere avanti || *intr* avanzare; (*said, e.g., of prices*) aumentare
advanced [æd'vænst] or [æd'vɑnst] *adj* avanzato, progredito
advanced' stand'ing *s* trasferimento di voti scolastici
advancement [æd'vænsmənt] or [æd'vɑnsmənt] *s* progresso; promozione; (mil) avanzata
advance' public'ity *s* pubblicità *f* di lancio
advantage [æd'væntɪdʒ] or [æd'vɑntɪdʒ] *s* vantaggio; **to advantage** in maniera favorevole; **to take advantage of** approfittarsi di; abusare di || *tr* avantaggiare
advantageous [,ædvən'tedʒəs] *adj* vantaggioso
advent ['ædvɛnt] *s* avvento

adventure [æd'ventʃər] *s* avventura || *tr* avventurare || *intr* avventurarsi
adventurer [æd'ventʃərər] *s* avventuriero
adventuresome [æd'vəntʃərsəm] *adj* avventuroso
adventuress [æd'ventʃərɪs] *s* avventuriera
adventurous [æd'ventʃərəs] *adj* avventuroso
adverb ['ædvʌrb] *s* avverbio
adversar•y ['ædvər,seri] *s* (**-ies**) avversario
adverse [æd'vʌrs] or ['ædvʌrs] *adj* avverso, contrario
adversi•ty [æd'vʌrsɪti] *s* (**-ties**) avversità *f*
advertise ['ædvər,taɪz] or [,ædvər'taɪz] *tr* propagandare; reclamizzare || *intr* fare la pubblicità; inserire un annunzio; inserzionare
advertisement [,ædvər'taɪzmənt] or [æd'vʌrtɪsmənt] *s* annuncio pubblicitario, inserzione
advertiser ['ædvər,taɪzer] or [,ædvər'taɪzər] *s* inserzionista *mf*
advertising ['ædvər,taɪzɪŋ] *s* pubblicità *f*, pubblicismo
ad'vertising a'gent *s* pubblicista *mf*
ad'vertising campaign' *s* campagna pubblicitaria
ad'vertising man' *s* agente *m* di pubblicità, reclamista *m*
advice [æd'vaɪs] *s* consiglio; **a piece of advice** un consiglio
advisable [æd'vaɪzəbəl] *adj* consigliabile
advise [æd'vaɪz] *tr* consigliare; informare || *intr*—**to advise with** chiedere il consiglio di; avere una conferenza con
advisement [æd'vaɪzmənt] *s* considerazione; **to take under advisement** prendere in considerazione
adviser [æd'vaɪzər] *s* consigliere *m*
advisory [æd'vaɪzəri] *adj* consultivo
advocate ['ædvə,ket] *s* difensore *m*; (*lawyer*) avvocato || *tr* sostenere, propugnare
adze [ædz] *s* ascia
Aege'an Sea' [ɪ'dʒi·ən] *s* mare Egeo
aegis ['idʒɪs] *s* egida
Aeneid [i'ni·ɪd] *s* Eneide *f*
aerate ['eret] or ['e·ə,ret] *tr* aerare
aerial ['ɛrɪ·əl] or [e'ɪrɪ·əl] *adj* aereo || ['ɛri·əl] *s* (rad & telv) antenna
aer'ial pho'tograph *s* aerofotogramma *m*
aerodrome ['ɛrə,drom] *s* aerodromo
aerodynamic [,ɛrodaɪ'næmɪk] *adj* aerodinamico || **aerodynamics** *ssg* aerodinamica
aeronaut ['ɛrə,nɔt] *s* aeronauta *m*
aeronautic [,ɛrə'nɔtɪk] *adj* aeronautico || **aeronautics** *ssg* aeronautica
aerosol ['ɛrə,sol] *s* aerosol *m*
aerospace ['ɛro,spes] *adj* aerospaziale || *s* aerospazio
Aesop ['isɑp] *s* Esopo
aesthete ['esθit] *s* esteta *mf*
aesthetic [ɛs'θetɪk] *adj* estetico || **aesthetics** *ssg* estetica
afar [ə'fɑr] *adv* lontano; **from afar** da lontano
affable ['æfəbəl] *adj* affabile
affair [ə'fɛr] *s* affare *m*; (*romance*) relazione amorosa
affect [ə'fekt] *tr* influenzare; (*to touch the heart of*) commuovere; (*to pretend to have*) affettare
affectation [,æfɛk'teʃən] *s* affettazione
affected [ə'fɛktɪd] *adj* affettato
affection [ə'fɛkʃən] *s* affezione
affectionate [ə'fɛkʃənɪt] *adj* affettuoso, affezionato
affidavit [,æfɪ'devɪt] *s* affidavit *m*, dichiarazione sotto giuramento
affiliate [ə'fɪlɪ,et] *adj* & *s* affiliato || *tr* affiliare || *intr* affiliarsi
affini•ty [ə'fɪnɪti] *s* (**-ties**) affinità *f*
affirm [ə'fʌrm] *tr* affermare; confermare
affirmative [ə'fʌrmətɪv] *adj* affermativo || *s* affermativa
affix ['æfɪks] *s* affisso || [ə'fɪks] *tr* affiggere; (*a signature*) apporre; (*e.g.*, *blame*) attribuire
afflict [ə'flɪkt] *tr* affliggere
affliction [ə'flɪkʃən] *s* afflizione
affluence ['æflʊ·əns] *s* opulenza, abbondanza
affluent ['æflʊ·ənt] *adj* opulento, abbondante; ricco || *s* affluente *m*
afford [ə'fɔrd] *tr* permettersi il lusso di; (*to furnish*) provvedere; (*to give*) dare
affray [ə'fre] *s* rissa
affront [ə'frʌnt] *s* affronto || *tr* fare un affronto a
afghan ['æfgən] or ['æfgæn] *s* coperta di lana all'uncinetto || **Afghan** *adj* & *s* afgano
afield [ə'fild] *adv* sul campo; **far afield** lontano
afire [ə'faɪr] *adj* ardente; in fuoco, in fiamme
aflame [ə'flem] *adj* in fiamme
afloat [ə'flot] *adj* & *adv* a galla; a bordo; (*drifting*) alla deriva; (*said of a rumor*) in circolazione
afoot [ə'fʊt] *adj* & *adv* a piedi; in movimento, in moto
aforementioned [ə'for,menʃənd] or **aforesaid** [ə'for,sed] *adj* suddetto
afoul [ə'faʊl] *adj* & *adv* in collisione; **to run afoul of** finire nelle mani di, impigliarsi con
afraid [ə'fred] *adj* impaurito, spaventato; **to be afraid (of)** aver paura (di)
African ['æfrɪkən] *adj* & *s* africano
aft [æft] or [ɑft] *adv* a poppa; indietro
after ['æftər] or ['ɑftər] *adj* seguente; di poppa || *adv* dopo; (*behind*) dietro || *prep* dopo; dopo di; (*in the manner of*) secondo; **to run after** correre dietro a || *conj* dopo che
afterburner ['æftər,bʌrnər] or ['ɑftər,bʌrnər] *s* (aer) postbruciatore *m*
af'ter-din'ner *adj* dopo la cena
aftereffect ['æftərɪ,fɛkt] or ['ɑftəri,fɛkt] *s* conseguenza
af'ter-hours' *adj* dopo le ore di ufficio
af'ter•life' *s* aldilà *m*; vita susseguente

aftermath ['æftər,mæθ] or ['ɑftər,mæθ] *s* conseguenze *fpl;* gravi conseguenze *fpl*
af'ter·noon' *adj* pomeridiano || *s* pomeriggio
after-shaving ['æftər,ʃevɪŋ] or ['ɑftər,ʃevɪŋ] *adj* dopobarba
af'ter·taste' *s* retrosapore *m*
af'ter·thought' *s* pensiero tardivo
afterward ['æftərwərd] or ['ɑftərwərd] *adv* dopo; **long afterward** molto tempo dopo
af'ter·while' *adv* fra un po'
again [ə'gɛn] *adv* di nuovo; ancora; un'altra volta; **again and again** ripetutamente; **as much again** due volte tanto, altrettanto; **to** + *inf* + **again** tornare a + *inf,* e.g., **to cook again** tornare a cuocere
against [ə'gɛnst] *prep* contro; (*opposite*) in faccia a; **to be against** opporsi a; **to go against the grain** ripugnare
agape [ə'gep] *adj & adv* a bocca aperta
age [edʒ] *s* età *f;* (*old age*) vecchiaia; (*full term of life*) vita; (*historical or geological period*) evo; generazione; **of age** maggiorenne; **to come of age** diventare maggiorenne; **under age** minorenne || *tr & intr* invecchiare
aged [edʒd] *adj* dell'età di || ['edʒɪd] *adj* vecchio, invecchiato
ageless ['edʒlɪs] *adj* eternamente giovane, che non invecchia mai
agen·cy ['edʒənsi] *s* **(-cies)** azione; agenzia; mediazione; (*of government*) ente *m*
agenda [ə'dʒɛndə] *s* agenda, ordine *m* del giorno
agent ['edʒənt] *s* agente *m;* (coll) commesso viaggiatore, agente *m* di commercio; (rr) gestore *m*
Age' of Enlight'enment *s* illuminismo
agglomeration [ə,glɑmə'reʃən] *s* agglomerazione
aggrandizement [ə'grændɪzmənt] *s* aumento, innalzamento
aggravate ['ægrə,vet] *tr* aggravare; (coll) irritare, esasperare
aggregate ['ægrɪ,get] *adj & s* aggregato, totale *m;* **in the aggregate** nel complesso || *tr* aggregare; ammontare a
aggression [ə'grɛʃən] *s* aggressione
aggressive [ə'grɛsɪv] *adj* aggressivo, attivo
aggressor [ə'grɛsər] *s* aggressore *m*
aggrieve [ə'griv] *tr* affliggere
aghast [ə'gæst] or [ə'gɑst] *adj* atterrito
agile ['ædʒɪl] *adj* agile
agitate ['ædʒɪ,tet] *tr* agitare || *intr* agitarsi
agitator ['ædʒɪ,tetər] *s* agitatore *m*
aglow [ə'glo] *adj* splendente
agnostic [æg'nɑstɪk] *adj & s* agnostico
ago [ə'go] *adv* fa, e.g., **a year ago** un anno fa; **long ago** molto tempo fa
agog [ə'gɑg] *adj & adv* ansioso; **to set agog** riempire di ansietà
agonize ['ægə,naɪz] *intr* soffrire straziantemente; (*to struggle*) dibattersi
ago·ny ['ægəni] *s* **(-nies)** agonia
agrarian [ə'grɛrɪ·ən] *adj* agrario || *s* membro del partito agrario
agree [ə'gri] *intr* aderire, andar d'accordo; (*to consent*) acconsentire; (gram) concordare; **to agree with** confarsi a, e.g., **eggs do not agree with him** le uova non gli si confanno
agreeable [ə'gri·əbəl] *adj* gentile; gradevole; (*willing to agree*) consenziente
agreement [ə'grimənt] *s* accordo; **in agreement** d'accordo
agriculture ['ægrɪ,kʌltʃər] *s* agricoltura
agriculturist [,ægrɪ'kʌltʃərɪst] *s* (*farmer*) agricoltore *m;* perito in agricoltura, agronomo
agronomy [ə'grɑnəmi] *s* agronomia
aground [ə'graʊnd] *adv* alla riva; **to run aground** andare or dare in secca
ague ['egju] *s* (*chill*) brivido; febbre *f*
ahead [ə'hɛd] *adv* davanti, avanti; **to get ahead** (coll) andare avanti, aver successo; **to get ahead of** sorpassare; **to go ahead** avanzare; continuare
ahoy [ə'hɔɪ] *interj*—**ship ahoy!** ehi della barca!
aid [ed] *s* aiuto; assistente *m;* (mil) aiutante *m* di campo || *tr* aiutare; **to aid and abet** essere complice di
aide [ed] *s* assistente *m*
aide-de-camp ['eddə'kæmp] *s* **(aides-de-camp)** aiutante *m* di campo
ail [el] *tr* affliggere; **what ails you?** che ha? || *intr* soffrire, essere malato
aileron ['elə,rɑn] *s* alerone *m*
ailing ['elɪŋ] *adj* ammalato
ailment ['elmənt] *s* malattia, indisposizione; (*chronic*) acciacco
aim [em] *s* mira; intento || *tr* (*a gun*) puntare; (*words*) dirigere || *intr* mirare; **to aim to** cercare di, aver l'intenzione di
air [ɛr] *adj* (*e.g., pocket*) d'aria; (*e.g., show*) aeronautico || *s* aria; **by air** per via aerea; **in the open air** all'aria aperta; **to be in the air** circolare; **to be on the air** (rad, telv) essere in onda; **to go on the air** (rad, telv) andare in onda; **to put on airs** darsi delle arie; **to take the air** andar fuori; **up in the air** incerto; (slang) arrabbiato || *tr* aerare, ventilare
airborne ['ɛr,bɔrn] or ['ɛr,born] *adj* aerosostentato; aerotrasportato
air' brake' *s* freno ad aria compressa
air' cas'tle *s* castello in aria
air'-condi'tion *tr* climatizzare
air' condi'tioner *s* condizionatore *m*
air' condi'tioning *s* aria condizionata, climatizzazione
air-'cool' *tr* raffreddare con aria
air' corps' *s* aviazione, arma aeronautica
air'craft' *s* **(-craft)** aeromobile *m*
air'craft car'rier *s* portaerei *f*
airdrome ['ɛr,drom] *s* aerodromo
air'drop' *tr* paracadutare
air'field' *s* campo d'aviazione
air'foil' *s* superficie *f* portante, velatura
air' force' *s* forza aerea
air' gap' *s* (elec) intraferro

airing ['erɪŋ] *s* aerazione; passeggiata all'aria aperta; pubblica discussione
air' jack'et *s* (aer, naut) giubbotto salvagente
air' lane' *s* aerovia
air'lift' *s* ponte aereo, aerotrasporto || *tr* aerotrasportare
air'line' *s* linea aerea; tubo dell'aria
air' mail' *s* posta aerea
air'-mail' *adj* per via aerea || *s* lettera per posta aerea || *adv* per posta aerea || *tr* spedire per posta aerea
air'-mail let'ter *s* lettera per posta aerea
air'-mail stamp' *s* francobollo posta aerea
air'man *s* (**-men**) aviatore *m*, aviere *m*
air' mat'tress *s* materassino pneumatico
air'plane' *s* aeroplano, aereo
air'plane car'rier *s* portaerei *f*
air' pock'et *s* vuoto d'aria
air' pollu'tion *s* contaminazione atmosferica, inquinamento atmosferico
air' port' *s* aeroporto
air' pump' *s* pompa pneumatica
air' raid' *s* incursione aerea
air'-raid shel'ter *s* rifugio antiaereo
air'-raid warn'ing *s* allerta
air' ri'fle *s* fucile *m* ad aria compressa
air' serv'ice *s* aeroservizio
air' shaft' *s* tubo di ventilazione
air'ship' s aeronave *f*
airsickness ['er ,sɪknɪs] *s* male *m* d'aria
air' sleeve' *s* manica a vento
airspace ['er ,spes] *s* aerospazio
air'strip' *s* aviopista
air' ter'minal *s* aerostazione
air'tight' *adj* impermeabile all'aria, ermetico
air'waves' *spl* onde *fpl*, radioonde *fpl*
air'way' *s* aerovia; **airways** (rad) onda, onde *fpl*
air•y ['eri] *adj* (**-ier; -iest**) arioso; leggero; aereo
aisle [aɪl] *s* (*between rows of seats*) corsia; (*of a church*) navata laterale; (theat) canale *m*
ajar [ə'dʒɑr] *adj* socchiuso; in disaccordo
akimbo [ə'kɪmbo] *adj* & *adv*—**with arms akimbo** con le mani sui fianchi
akin [ə'kɪn] *adj* affine; congiunto
alabaster ['ælə ,bæstər] or ['ælə-,bɑstər] *s* alabastro
à la carte [,ɑlə'kɑrt] *adv* alla carta
à la mode [,ɑlə'mod] or [,ælə'mod] *adv* alla moda; servito con gelato
alarm [ə'lɑrm] *s* allarme *m* || *tr* allarmare
alarm' clock' *s* sveglia
alas [ə'læs] or [ə'lɑs] *interj* ahimé!; povero me!
Albanian [æl'benɪ•ən] *adj* & *s* albanese *mf*
albatross ['ælbə ,trɔs] or ['ælbə ,trɑs] *s* albatro, diomedea
album ['ælbəm] *s* album *m*
albumen [æl'bjumən] *s* albume *m*
alchemy ['ælkəmi] *s* alchimia
alcohol ['ælkə ,hɔl] or ['ælkə ,hɑl] *s* alcole *m*
alcoholic [,ælkə'hɔlɪk] or [,ælkə'hɑlɪk] *adj* alcolico || *s* alcolizzato

alcove ['ælkov] *s* (*recess*) alcova; (*in a garden*) chiosco, padiglione *m*; cameretta attigua
alder ['ɔldər] *s* ontano, alno
al'der•man *s* (**-men**) assessore *m* municipale, consigliere *m* municipale
ale [el] *s* birra amara
alembic [ə'lɛmbɪk] *s* alambicco
alert [ə'lʌrt] *adj* attento; vispo || *s* allerta; **to be on the alert** stare allerta || *tr* dare l'allerta a
Aleu'tian Is'lands [ə'luʃən] *spl* Isole Aleutine
Alexander [,ælɪg'zændər] or [,ælɪg-'zɑndər] *s* Alessandro
Alexan'der the Great' *s* Alessandro Magno
Alexandrine [,ælɪg'zændrɪn] *adj* & *s* alessandrino
alfalfa [æl'fælfə] *s* (bot) erba medica
algae ['ældʒi] *spl* alghe *fpl*
algebra ['ældʒɪbrə] *s* algebra
algebraic [,ældʒɪ'bre•ɪk] *adj* algebrico
Algeria [æl'dʒɪrɪ•ə] *s* l'Algeria
Algerian [æl'dʒɪrɪ•ən] *adj* & *s* algerino
Algiers [æl'dʒɪrz] *s* Algeri *f*
alias ['elɪ•əs] *s* pseudonimo || *adv* alias
ali•bi ['ælɪ ,baɪ] *s* (**-bis**) alibi *m*
alien ['eljən] or ['elɪ•ən] *adj* straniero; (*strange*) strano || *s* straniero; (*outsider*) estraneo
alienate ['eljə ,net] or ['elɪ•ə ,net] *tr* alienare
alight [ə'laɪt] *v* (*pret & pp* **alighted** or **alit** [ə'lɪt]) *intr* scendere; **to alight on** or **upon** posarsi su
align [ə'laɪn] *tr* allineare || *intr* allinearsi
alike [ə'laɪk] *adj* uguali; **to look alike** assomigliarsi || *adv* nello stesso modo
alimen'tary canal' [,ælɪ'mɛntəri] *s* tubo digestivo
alimony ['ælɪ ,moni] *s* alimonia
alive [ə'laɪv] *adj* vivo, in vita; (*lively*) vivace; **alive to** conscio di; **alive with** brulicante di, pieno zeppo di; **look alive!** fa presto!
alka•li ['ælkə ,laɪ] *s* (**-lis** or **-lies**) alcali *m*
alkaline ['ælkə ,laɪn] or ['ælkəlɪn] *adj* alcalino
all [ɔl] *adj indef* tutto, tutto il, ogni || *s* tutto || *pron* tutto; tutti; **all of** tutti || *adv* completamente; **all but** quasi; **all in** (slang) stanco morto; **all in all** tutto considerato; **all the better** tanto meglio; **all the worse** tanto peggio; **far all that** per quello che, e.g., **for all that I know** per quello che io ne sappia; **in all** tutto contato; **it's all right!** va bene!; **not at all** niente affatto; prego
allay [ə'le] *tr* calmare, mitigare
all' clear' *s* fine *f* dell'allarme, cessato allarme
allegation [,ælɪ'geʃən] *s* asserzione, affermazione
allege [ə'lɛdʒ] *tr* asserire, affermare; addurre
allegiance [ə'lidʒəns] *s* fedeltà *f*, lealtà *f*

allegoric(al) [ˌælɪˈgɑrɪk(əl)] or [ˌælɪˈgɔrɪk(əl)] *adj* allegorico
allego·ry [ˈælɪˌgori] *s* **(-ries)** allegoria
aller·gy [ˈælərdʒi] *s* **(-gies)** allergia
alleviate [əˈlivɪˌet] *tr* alleviare
alley [ˈæli] *s* vicolo, calle *f*; (*for bowling*) pista; (*tennis*) corridoio
All' Fools' Day' *s* primo d'aprile
all' fours' *spl*—**on all fours** a quattro gambe
alliance [əˈlaɪ·əns] *s* alleanza
alligator [ˈælɪˌgetər] *s* alligatore *m*
alliteration [əˌlɪtəˈreʃən] *s* allitterazione
all-knowing [ˈɔlˈno·ɪŋ] *adj* onnisciente
allocate [ˈæləˌket] *tr* assegnare; (*funds*) stanziare; (*to fix the place of*) allogare
allot [əˈlɑt] *v* (*pret & pp* **allotted**; *ger* **allotting**) *tr* distribuire, assegnare
all'-out' *adj* completo; (*ruthless*) acerrimo
allow [əˈlaʊ] *tr* permettere; ammettere; concedere ‖ *intr* **to allow for** prendere in considerazione
allowance [əˈlaʊ·əns] *s* (*limited share*) assegno; concessione; (*reduction in price*) sconto; tolleranza; **to make allowance for** prendere in considerazione
alloy [ˈælɔɪ] or [əˈlɔɪ] *s* lega; impurezza ‖ [əˈlɔɪ] *tr* far lega di, legare; adulterare
all-powerful [ˈɔlˈpaʊ·ərfəl] *adj* onnipotente
all' right' *adj* esatto; bene; in buona salute; (slang) dabbene
All' Saints'' Day' *s* Ognissanti *m*
All' Souls'' Day' *s* giorno dei morti
all'spice' *s* pimento, pepe *m* della Giamaica
all'-star game' *s* partita sportiva in cui tutti i giocatori sono scelti fra i migliori
allude [əˈlud] *intr* alludere
allure [əˈlʊr] *s* fascino, incanto ‖ *tr* affascinare, incantare
alluring [əˈlʊrɪŋ] *adj* affascinante, seducente
allusion [əˈluʃən] *s* allusione
al·ly [ˈælaɪ] or [əˈlaɪ] *s* **(-lies)** alleato ‖ [əˈlaɪ] *v* (*pret & pp* **-lied**) *tr* alleare; associare; **to become allied** allearsi; imparentarsi ‖ *intr* allearsi
almanac [ˈɔlməˌnæk] *s* almanacco
almighty [ɔlˈmaɪti] *adj* onnipotente
almond [ˈɑmənd] or [ˈæmənd] *s* (*nut*) mandorla; (*tree*) mandorlo
al'mond brittle' *s* croccante *m*
almost [ˈɔlmost] or [ɔlˈmost] *adv* quasi
alms [ɑmz] *s* elemosina
aloe [ˈælo] *s* aloe *m*
aloft [əˈlɔft] or [əˈlɑft] *adv* in alto, sopra; (aer) in volo; (naut) nell'alberatura
alone [əˈlon] *adj* solo; **let alone** senza menzionare; **to leave alone** non disturbare ‖ *adv* solo, solamente
along [əˈlɔŋ] or [əˈlɑŋ] *adv* (*lengthwise*) per il lungo; (*onward*) avanti; **all along** tutto il tempo; **along with** con; **to get along** andar d'accordo; andarsene; avanzare; aver successo; **to take along** prendere con sè ‖ *prep* lungo
along'side' *adv* a lato; **alongside of** a lato di ‖ *prep* a lato di, vicino a
aloof [əˈluf] *adj* riservato, freddo; **to keep** or **stand aloof from** tenersi a distanza da ‖ *adv* lontano; da solo
aloud [əˈlaʊd] *adv* ad alta voce
alphabet [ˈælfəˌbɛt] *s* alfabeto
alpine [ˈælpaɪn] *adj* alpino
Alps [ælps] *spl* Alpi *fpl*
already [ɔlˈrɛdi] *adv* già
Alsace [ælˈses] or [ˈælsæs] *s* l'Alsazia
Alsatian [ælˈseʃən] *adj & s* alsaziano
also [ˈɔlso] *adv* anche
altar [ˈɔltər] *s* altare *m*
al'tar boy' *s* accolito, chierico
al'tar·piece' *s* pala d'altare
alter [ˈɔltər] *tr* alterare; (*a male animal*) castrare ‖ *intr* diventare differente, cambiare
alteration [ˌɔltəˈreʃən] *s* alterazione, modifica
alternate [ˈɔltərnɪt] or [ˈæltərnɪt] *s* sostituto, supplente *mf* ‖ [ˈɔltərˌnet] or [ˈæltərˌnet] *tr* alternare ‖ *intr* alternarsi, avvicendarsi
al'ternating cur'rent *s* corrente alternata
alternator [ˈɔltərˌnetər] or [ˈæltərˌnetər] *s* alternatore *m*
although [ɔlˈðo] *conj* benchè, per quanto, malgrado
altimeter [ælˈtɪmɪtər] or [ˈæltəˌmitər] *s* altimetro
altitude [ˈæltɪˌtjud] or [ˈæltɪˌtud] *s* altitudine *f*
al·to [ˈælto] *s* **(-tos)** contralto
altogether [ˌɔltəˈgɛðər] *adv* completamente, affatto, tutt'insieme
altruist [ˈæltrʊ·ɪst] *s* altruista *mf*
altruistic [ˌæltrʊˈɪstɪk] *adj* altruistico
alum [ˈæləm] *s* allume *m*
aluminum [əˈlumɪnəm] *s* alluminio
alum·na [əˈlʌmnə] *s* **(-nae** [ni]**)** diplomata, laureata
alum·nus [əˈlʌmnəs] *s* **(-ni** [naɪ]**)** diplomato, laureato
alveo·lus [ælˈvi·ələs] *s* **(-li** [ˌlaɪ]**)** alveolo
always [ˈɔlwɪz] or [ˈɔlwez] *adv* sempre
amalgam [əˈmælgəm] *s* amalgama *m*
amalgamate [əˈmælgəˌmet] *tr* amalgamare ‖ *intr* amalgamarsi
amass [əˈmæs] *tr* ammassare
amateur [ˈæmətʃər] *adj* da dilettante ‖ *s* amatore *m*, dilettante *mf*
amaze [əˈmez] *tr* stupire, meravigliare
amazing [əˈmezɪŋ] *adj* straordinario
Amazon [ˈæməˌzɑn] or [ˈæməzən] *s* rio delle Amazzoni; (myth) Amazzone *f*
ambassador [æmˈbæsədər] *s* ambasciatore *m*
ambassadress [æmˈbæsədrɪs] *s* ambasciatrice *f*
amber [ˈæmbər] *s* ambra
ambigui·ty [ˌæmbɪˈgju·ɪti] *s* **(-ties)** ambiguità *f*
ambiguous [æmˈbɪgju·əs] *adj* ambiguo

ambition [æm'bɪʃən] *s* ambizione
ambitious [æm'bɪʃəs] *adj* ambizioso
amble ['æmbəl] *s* ambio || *intr* ambiare
ambulance ['æmbjələns] *s* ambulanza
ambush ['æmbʊʃ] *s* imboscata; **to lie in ambush** tendere un'imboscata || *tr* appostare || *intr* appostarsi
amelioration [ə,miljə'reʃən] *s* miglioramento
amen ['e'men] or ['ɑ'men] *s* amen *m* || *interj* amen!
amenable [ə'minəbəl] or [ə'mɛnəbəl] *adj* docile, aperto; (*accountable*) responsabile
amend [ə'mɛnd] *tr* emendare || **amends** *spl* ammenda, contravvenzione; **to make amends for** fare ammenda per
amendment [ə'mɛndmənt] *s* emendamento
ameni·ty [ə'minɪti] or [ə'mɛnɪti] *s* (**-ties**) amenità *f*
American [ə'mɛrɪkən] *adj* & *s* americano
Americanize [ə'mɛrɪkə,naɪz] *tr* americanizzare
amethyst ['æmɪθɪst] *s* ametista
amiable ['emɪ·əbəl] *adj* amabile
amicable ['æmɪkəbəl] *adj* amichevole
amid [ə'mɪd] *prep* in mezzo a, fra, tra
amidship [ə'mɪdʃɪp] *adv* a mezzanave
amiss [ə'mɪs] *adj* erroneo, sbagliato || *adv* erroneamente; **to take amiss** offendersi, prendere in mala parte
ami·ty ['æmɪti] *s* (**-ties**) amicizia
ammeter ['æm,mitər] *s* amperometro
ammonia [ə'monɪ·ə] *s* ammoniaca; acqua ammoniacale
ammunition [,æmjə'nɪʃən] *s* munizione, munizioni *fpl*
amnes·ty ['æmnɪsti] *s* (**-ties**) amnistia || *v* (*pret* & *pp* **-tied**) *tr* amnistiare
amoeba [ə'mibə] *s* ameba
among [ə'mʌŋ] *prep* fra, tra, in mezzo a
amorous ['æmərəs] *adj* amoroso; erotico
amortize ['æmər,taɪz] *tr* ammortare
amount [ə'maunt] *s* ammontare *m* || *intr*—**to amount to** ammontare a
ampere ['æmpɪr] *s* ampere *m*
am'pere-hour' *s* amperora *m*
amphibious [æm'fɪbɪ·əs] *adj* anfibio
amphitheater ['æmfɪ,θi·ətər] *s* anfiteatro
ample ['æmpəl] *adj* ampio
amplifier ['æmplɪ,faɪ·ər] *s* amplificatore *m*
ampli·fy ['æmplɪ,faɪ] *v* (*pret* & *pp* **-fied**) *tr* amplificare
amplitude ['æmplɪ,tjud] or ['æmplɪ,tud] *s* ampiezza
am'plitude modula'tion *s* modulazione d'ampiezza
amputate ['æmpjə,tet] *tr* amputare
amputee [,æmpjə'ti] *s* chi ha subito l'amputazione di un arto
amuck [ə'mʌk] *adv* freneticamente; **to run amuck** dare in un accesso di pazzia; attaccare alla cieca
amulet ['æmjəlɪt] *s* amuleto
amuse [ə'mjuz] *tr* divertire
amusement [ə'mjuzmənt] *s* divertimento
amuse'ment park' *s* parco dei divertimenti, luna park *m*
amusing [ə'mjuzɪŋ] *adj* divertente
an [æn] or [ən] *art indef* var of **a,** used before words beginning with vowel or mute *h*
anachronism [ə'nækrə,nɪzəm] *s* anacronismo
anaemia [ə'nimɪ·ə] *s* var of **anemia**
anaesthesia [,ænɪs'θiʒə] *s* anestesia
anaesthetic [,ænɪs'θɛtɪk] *adj* & *s* anestetico
anaesthetize [æ'nɛsθɪ,taɪz] *tr* anestetizzare
analogous [ə'næləgəs] *adj* analogo
analo·gy [ə'nælədʒi] *s* (**-gies**) analogia
analy·sis [ə'nælɪsɪs] *s* (**-ses** [,siz]) analisi *f*
analyst ['ænəlɪst] *s* analista *mf*
analytic(al) [,ænə'lɪtɪk(əl)] *adj* analitico
analyze ['ænə,laɪz] *tr* analizzare
anarchist ['ænərkɪst] *s* anarchico
anarchy ['ænərki] *s* anarchia
anathema [ə'næθɪmə] *s* anatema *m*
anatomic(al) [,ænə'tɑmɪk(əl)] *adj* anatomico
anato·my [ə'nætəmi] *s* (**-mies**) anatomia
ancestor ['ænsɛstər] *s* antenato
ances·try ['ænsɛstri] *s* (**-tries**) lignaggio, prosapia
anchor ['æŋkər] *s* ancora; **to cast anchor** gettare l'ancora; **to ride at anchor** stare all'ancora; **to weigh anchor** salpare l'ancora, salpare || *tr* ancorare || *intr* ancorarsi, stare all'ancora
ancho·vy ['æntʃovi] *s* (**-vies**) acciuga
ancient ['enʃənt] *adj* antico || *s* vecchio, anziano; **the ancients** gli antichi
ancillary ['ænsɪ,lɛri] *adj* dipendente; ausiliario, ausiliare
and [ænd] or [ənd] *conj* e, ed; **and so on, and so forth** e così via
Andean [æn'di·ən] or ['ændɪ·ən] *adj* andino || *s* abitante *mf* della regione andina
Andes ['ændiz] *spl* Ande *fpl*
andiron ['ænd,aɪ·ərn] *s* alare *m*
anecdote ['ænɪk,dot] *s* aneddoto
anemia [ə'nimɪ·ə] *s* anemia
anemic [ə'nimɪk] *adj* anemico
an'eroid barom'eter ['ænə,rɔɪd] *s* barometro aneroide
anesthesia [,ænɪs'θiʒə] *s* anestesia
anesthetic [,ænɪs'θɛtɪk] *adj* & *s* anestetico
anesthetize [æ'nɛsθɪ,taɪz] *tr* anestetizzare
aneurysm ['ænjə,rɪzəm] *s* aneurisma *m*
anew [ə'nju] or [ə'nu] *adv* di nuovo, nuovamente
angel ['endʒəl] *s* angelo; (*financial backer*) (coll) finanziatore *m*
angelic(al) [æn'dʒɛlɪk(əl)] *adj* angelico
anger ['æŋgər] *s* ira, collera || *tr* adirare || *intr* adirarsi, incollerirsi
angle ['æŋgəl] *s* angolo; punto di vista

|| *intr* intrigare; **to angle for** darsi da fare per
an'gle i'ron *s* cantonale *m*, angolare *m*
angler ['æŋglər] *s* pescatore *m* alla lenza; (fig) intrigante *m*
Anglo-Saxon ['æŋglo'sæksən] *adj & s* anglosassone *mf*
an·gry ['æŋgri] *adj* (**-grier; -griest**) arrabbiato; (pathol) infiammato; **to become angry at** incollerirsi per; **to become angry with** adirarsi con
anguish ['æŋgwɪʃ] *s* angoscia, pena
angular ['æŋgjələr] *adj* angolare
anhydrous [æn'haɪdrəs] *adj* anidro
aniline ['ænɪlɪn] or ['ænɪ,laɪn] *s* anilina
animal ['ænɪməl] *adj & s* animale *m*
an'imated cartoon' ['ænɪ,metɪd] *s* cartone animato
animation [,ænɪ'meʃən] *s* animazione
animosi·ty [,ænɪ'mɑsɪti] *s* (**-ties**) animosità *f*
animus ['ænɪməs] *s* odio, malanimo
anion ['æn,aɪ·ən] *s* anione *m*
anise ['ænɪs] *s* anice *f*
anisette [,ænɪ'zɛt] *s* anisetta
ankle ['æŋkəl] *s* caviglia
an'kle·bone' *s* malleolo
an'kle support' *s* cavigliera
anklet ['æŋklɪt] *s* calzino corto; bracciale *m* da caviglia
annals ['ænəlz] *spl* annali *mpl*
annex ['ænɛks] *s* annesso, dipendenza || [ə'nɛks] *tr* annettere, appropriarsi di
annihilate [ə'naɪ·ɪ,let] *tr* annientare
anniversa·ry [,ænɪ'vʌrsəri] *adj* anniversario || *s* (**-ries**) anniversario
annotate ['ænə,tet] *tr* annotare
announce [ə'naʊns] *tr* annunciare
announcement [ə'naʊnsmənt] *s* annuncio, partecipazione
announcer [ə'naʊnsər] *s* annunziatore *m*
annoy [ə'nɔɪ] *tr* annoiare, seccare
annoyance [ə'nɔɪ·əns] *s* fastidio, seccatura
annoying [ə'nɔɪ·ɪŋ] *adj* noioso
annual ['ænjʊ·əl] *adj* annuale || *s* annuario; pianta annuale
annui·ty [ə'nju·ɪti] or [ə'nu·ɪti] *s* (**-ties**) annualità *f*; (*for life*) vitalizio
an·nul [ə'nʌl] *v* (*pret & pp* **-nulled**; *ger* **-nulling**) *tr* annullare, cassare
annunciation [ə,nʌnsɪ'eʃən] *s* annunzio || **Annunciation** *s* Annunciazione
anode ['ænod] *s* anodo
anoint [ə'nɔɪnt] *tr* ungere
anomalous [ə'nɑmələs] *adj* anomalo
anoma·ly [ə'nɑməli] *s* (**-lies**) anomalia
anonymi·ty [,ænə'nɪmɪti] *s* (**-ties**) anonimia; **to preserve one's anonymity** serbare l'anonimo
anonymous [ə'nɑnɪməs] *adj* anonimo
another [ə'nʌðər] *adj & pron indef* un altro
answer ['ænsər] or ['ɑnsər] *s* risposta; (*to a problem*) soluzione || *tr* rispondere a; **this will answer your purpose** questo fa per Lei; **to answer back** (slang) dare una rispostaccia a; **to answer the door** andare a rispondere || *intr* rispondere; corrispondere; essere responsabile; **to answer back** (slang) dare una rispostaccia
ant [ænt] *s* formica
antagonism [æn'tægə,nɪzəm] *s* antagonismo
antagonize [æn'tægə,naɪz] *tr* opporsi a; creare antagonismo in
antarctic [ænt'ɑrktɪk] *adj* antartico || **the Antarctic** la regione antartica
anteater ['ænt,itər] *s* formichiere *m*
antecedent [,æntɪ'sidənt] *adj & s* antecedente *m*; **antecedents** antenati *mpl*
antechamber ['æntɪ,tʃembər] *s* anticamera
antedate ['æntɪ,det] *tr* antidatare; (*to happen before*) antecedere
antelope ['æntɪ,lop] *s* antilope *f*
anten·na [æn'tɛnə] *s* (**-nae** [ni]) (*of insect*) antenna || *s* (**-nas**) (rad, telv) antenna
antepenult [,æntɪ'pinʌlt] *s* terzultima sillaba
anteroom ['æntɪ,rum] or ['æntɪ,rʊm] *s* anticamera, sala d'aspetto
anthem ['ænθəm] *s* inno
ant'hill' *s* formicaio
antholo·gy [æn'θɑlədʒi] *s* (**-gies**) antologia
anthracite ['ænθrə,saɪt] *s* antracite *f*
anthrax ['ænθræks] *s* antrace *m*
anthropoid ['ænθrə,pɔɪd] *adj* antropoide, antropomorfo
anthropology [,ænθrə'pɑlədʒi] *s* antropologia
antiaircraft [,æntɪ'ɛr,kræft] or [,æntɪ'ɛr,krɑft] *adj* antiaereo
antibiotic [,æntɪbaɪ'ɑtɪk] *adj & s* antibiotico
antibod·y ['æntɪ,bɑdi] *s* (**-ies**) anticorpo
anticipate [æn'tɪsɪ,pet] *tr* anticipare, prevedere; ripromettersi
anticipation [æn,tɪsɪ'peʃən] *s* anticipazione, previsione
antics ['æntɪks] *spl* pagliacciate *fpl*, buffonate *fpl*
antidote ['æntɪ,dot] *s* antidoto
antifreeze ['æntɪ,friz] *s* anticongelante *m*
antiglare [,æntɪ'glɛr] *adj* antiabbagliante
anti-G' suit' *s* tuta antigravità
antiknock [,æntɪ'nɑk] *adj* antidetonante
antimissile [,æntɪ'mɪsɪl] *adj* antimissile
antimony ['æntɪ,moni] *s* antimonio
antinoise [,æntɪ'nɔɪz] *adj* antirumore
antipa·thy [æn'tɪpəθi] *s* (**-thies**) antipatia
antipersonnel [,æntɪ,pʌrsə'nɛl] *adj* (*e.g., mine*) antiuomo
antiquarian [,æntɪ'kwɛrɪ·ən] *adj & s* antiquario
antiquar·y ['æntɪ,kwɛri] *s* (**-ies**) antiquario
antiquated ['æntɪ,kwetɪd] *adj* antiquato
antique [æn'tik] *adj* antico, vecchio; antiquato || *s* oggetto d'epoca, antichità *f*

antique' deal'er *s* antiquario
antique' store' *s* negozio d'antiquariato
antiqui•ty [æn'tɪkwɪti] *s* (**-ties**) antichità *f*
anti-Semitic [ˌæntɪsɪ'mɪtɪk] *adj* antisemita
antiseptic [ˌæntɪ'septɪk] *adj* & *s* antisettico
antislavery [ˌæntɪ'slevəri] *adj* antischiavista
antitank [ˌæntɪ'tæŋk] *adj* anticarro
antitheft [ˌæntɪ'θɛft] *adj* antifurto
antithe•sis [æn'tɪθɪsɪs] *s* (**-ses** [ˌsiz]) antitesi *f*
antitoxin [ˌæntɪ'tɑksɪn] *s* antitossina
antitrust [ˌæntɪ'trʌst] *adj* antitrust
antler ['æntlər] *s* corno di cervo
antonym ['æntənɪm] *s* antonimo
Antwerp ['æntwərp] *s* Anversa
anvil ['ænvɪl] *s* incudine *m*
anxie•ty [æŋ'zaɪ•əti] *s* (**-ties**) ansietà *f;* (*psychol*) angoscia
anxious ['æŋkʃəs] *adj* ansioso; **anxious about** sollecito di; **anxious for** desideroso di
any ['ɛni] *adj indef* ogni, qualunque, qualsiasi; qualche, e.g., **do you know any boy who could help me?** conosce qualche ragazzo che possa aiutarmi?; di + *art,* e.g., **do you want any cheese?** vuole del formaggio?; **not . . . any** non . . . nessuno, e.g., **he does not read any newspaper** non legge nessun giornale ‖ *adv* un po', e.g., **do you want any?** ne vuole un po'?; **not . . . any longer** non . . . più; **not . . . any more** non . . . più ‖ *pron* ne, e.g., **do you want any?** ne vuole?
an'y•bod'y *pron indef* chiunque; (*in interrogative sentences*) qualcuno; **not . . . anybody** non . . . nessuno
an'y•how' *adv* in qualunque modo, comunque; in ogni caso; (*haphazardly*) alla rinfusa
an'y•one' *pron indef* chiunque; (*in interrogative sentences*) qualcuno; **not . . . anyone** non . . . nessuno
an'y•thing' *s* qualunque cosa ‖ *pron indef* qualcosa; qualunque cosa; tutto quanto; checchessia; **anything at all** qualunque cosa; **not . . . anything** non . . . niente; **not . . . anything at all** non . . . niente affatto, non . . . nulla; **not . . . anything else** non . . . nient'altro
an'y•way' *adv* in qualunque modo, comunque; in ogni caso; (*haphazardly*) alla rinfusa
an'y•where' *adv* dovunque, in qualsiasi luogo; **not . . . anywhere** non . . . in nessun luogo
apace [ə'pes] *adv* presto, rapidamente
apart [ə'pɑrt] *adv* a parte, a pezzi; separatamente; **apart from** a parte da; oltre a; **to come apart** andare a pezzi, cadere a pezzi; **to set apart** mettere in disparte; **to take apart** smontare; **to tear apart** fare a pezzi; **to tell apart** distinguere
apartment [ə'pɑrtmənt] *s* appartamento; (*single room*) stanza
apart'ment house' *s* casa d'appartamenti
apathetic [ˌæpə'θɛtɪk] *adj* apatico
apathy ['æpəθi] *s* apatia
ape [ep] *s* scimmia antropomorfa; scimmia ‖ *tr* imitare, scimmiottare
Apennines ['æpəˌnaɪnz] *spl* Appennini *mpl*
aperture ['æpərtʃər] *s* apertura
apex ['epɛks] *s* (**apexes** or **apices** ['æpɪˌsiz]) apice *m*
apheresis [ə'fɛrɪsɪs] *s* aferesi *f*
aphorism ['æfəˌrɪzəm] *s* aforisma *m*
aphrodisiac [ˌæfrə'dɪzɪˌæk] *adj* & *s* afrodisiaco
apiar•y ['epɪˌɛri] *s* (**-ies**) apiario
apiece [ə'pis] *adv* a testa, per persona; ciascuno
apish ['epɪʃ] *adj* scimmiesco; da scimmia
aplomb [ə'plɑm] *s* disinvoltura, baldanza
apocalypse [ə'pɑkəˌlɪps] *s* apocalisse *f*
apogee ['æpəˌdʒi] *s* apogeo
apologetic [əˌpɑlə'dʒɛtɪk] *adj* pieno di scuse
apologize [ə'pɑləˌdʒaɪz] *intr* chiedere scusa, scusarsi
apolo•gy [ə'pɑlədzi] *s* (**-gies**) scusa; (*makeshift*) surrogato
apoplectic [ˌæpə'plɛktɪk] *adj* & *s* apoplettico
apoplexy ['æpəˌplɛksi] *s* apoplessia
apostle [ə'pɑsəl] *s* apostolo
apostrophe [ə'pɑstrəfi] *s* (*mark*) apostrofo; (rhet) apostrofe *f*
apothecar•y [ə'pɑθɪˌkɛri] *s* (**-ies**) farmacista *mf*
appall [ə'pɔl] *tr* sgomentare, sbigottire
appalling [ə'pɔlɪŋ] *adj* sconcertante
appara•tus [ˌæpə'retəs] or [ˌæpə'rætəs] *s* (**-tus** or **-tuses**) apparato
apparel [ə'pærəl] *s* confezioni *fpl,* vestiario
apparent [ə'pærənt] or [ə'pɛrənt] *adj* apparente; chiaramente visibile
apparition [ˌæpə'rɪʃən] *s* apparizione
appeal [ə'pil] *s* appello; (*attraction*) attrattiva, fascino ‖ *tr* (*a sentence*) appellare contro ‖ *intr* dare nell'occhio; **to appeal from** (law) appellarsi contro; **to appeal to** supplicare, pregare; piacere a, e.g., **his idea appeals to me** la sua idea mi piace
appear [ə'pɪr] *intr* apparire; (*to seem*) sembrare; (*said of a book*) uscire; (*before the public*) presentarsi; (law) comparire
appearance [ə'pɪrəns] *s* apparizione; (*of a book*) pubblicazione; (*outward look*) apparenza; (law) comparizione; **to keep up appearances** salvare le apparenze
appease [ə'piz] *tr* pacificare, placare; (*a desire*) soddisfare
appeasement [ə'pizmənt] *s* pacificazione, tranquillizzazione
appel'late court' [ə'pɛlɪt] *s* corte *f* d'appello
appellation [ˌæpə'leʃən] *s* denominazione, nome *m*
append [ə'pɛnd] *tr* allegare, aggiungere

appendage [ə'pɛndɪdʒ] *s* appendice *f*
appendicitis [ə,pɛndɪ'saɪtɪs] *s* appendicite *f*
appen·dix [ə'pɛndɪks] *s* (**-dixes** or **-dices** [dɪ,siz]) appendice *f*
appertain [,æpər'ten] *intr* spettare, riferirsi
appetite ['æpɪ,taɪt] *s* appetito
appetizer ['æpɪ,taɪzər] *s* (*drink*) aperitivo; (*food*) stimulante *m* dell'appetito
appetizing ['æpɪ,taɪzɪŋ] *adj* appetitoso
applaud *tr* applaudire, applaudire (with *dat*) || *intr* applaudire
applause [ə'plɔz] *s* applauso, applausi *mpl*
apple ['æpəl] *s* mela, pomo; (*tree*) melo, pomo
ap'plejack' *s* acquavite *f* di mele
ap'ple of dis'cord *s* pomo della discordia
ap'ple of one's eye' *s* pupilla degli occhi di qlcu, beniamino di qlcu
ap'ple pie' *s* torta di mele
ap'ple pol'isher *s* leccapiedi *mf*
ap'ple·sauce' *s* marmellata di mele; (slang) scemenza
appliance [ə'plaɪ·əns] *s* apparecchio, apparato; (*complicated instrument*) congegno; (*for domestic chores*) utensile *m*; (*act of applying*) applicazione
applicant ['æplɪkənt] *s* postulante *mf*, aspirante *m*, candidato
application [,æplɪ'keʃən] *s* applicazione; uso; richiesta, domanda
ap·ply [ə'plaɪ] *v* (*pret & pp* **-plied**) *tr* applicare; (*the brakes*) mettere; (*e.g., a nickname*) affibbiare || *intr* (*said of a rule*) essere applicabile; fare richiesta; **to apply for** sollecitare
appoint [ə'pɔɪnt] *tr* nominare; assegnare; (*to furnish*) ammobiliare
appointee [,æpɔɪn'ti] *s* persona nominata a una carica
appointive [ə'pɔɪntɪv] *adj* a nomina
appointment [ə'pɔɪntmənt] *s* nomina; (*position*) ufficio; (*agreement to meet*) appuntamento; **appointments** mobilia, arredamento; **by appointment** previo appuntamento
apportion [ə'porʃən] *tr* spartire, dividere proporzionatamente
appraisal [ə'prezəl] *s* stima, valutazione; (*of real estate*) estimo
appraise [ə'prez] *tr* stimare, valutare
appreciable [ə'priʃɪ·əbəl] *adj* apprezzabile, notevole
appreciate [ə'priʃɪ,et] *tr* apprezzare, valutare; (*to be grateful for*) gradire; (*to be aware of*) rendersi conto di; (*to raise in value*) valorizzare || *intr* aumentare di valore
appreciation [ə,priʃɪ'eʃən] *s* apprezzamento, valutazione; (*grateful recognition*) gradimento, riconoscenza; valorizzazione
appreciative [ə'prɪʃɪ,etɪv] *adj* grato, riconoscente
apprehend [,æprɪ'hend] *tr* (*to fear*) temere; (*to understand*) comprendere; (*to arrest*) arrestare
apprehension [,æprɪ'henʃən] *s* timore *m*, apprensione; comprensione; arresto
apprehensive [,æprɪ'hensɪv] *adj* apprensivo
apprentice [ə'prentɪs] *s* apprendista *mf*, novizio || *tr* mettere in apprendistato; accettare in apprendistato
apprenticeship [ə'prentɪs,ʃɪp] *s* apprendistato, carovana
apprise or **apprize** [ə'praɪz] *tr* avvertire, avvisare; stimare, valutare
approach [ə'protʃ] *s* (*a coming near*) avvicinamento; (*of night*) avvicinarsi *m*, far *m*; approssimazione; (*access*) via d'accesso; (*to a problem*) impostazione; **approaches** approcci *mpl* || *tr* avvicinarsi a, avvicinare; fare approcci con || *intr* avvicinarsi, approssimarsi
approbation [,æprə'beʃən] *s* approvazione
appropriate [ə'proprɪ·ɪt] *adj* appropriato, acconcio || [ə'proprɪ,et] *tr* (*to take*) appropriarsi di; (*to set aside for some specific use*) stanziare
approval [ə'pruvəl] *s* approvazione; consenso; **on approval** in prova
approve [ə'pruv] *tr & intr* approvare
approximate [ə'prɑksɪmɪt] *adj* approssimato, approssimativo || [ə'prɑksɪ,met] *tr* approssimarsi a || *intr* approssimarsi
apricot ['eprɪ,kɑt] or ['æprɪ,kɑt] *adj* color albicocca || *s* (*fruit*) albicocca; (*tree*) albicocco
April ['eprɪl] *s* aprile *m*
A'pril fool' *s* pesce *m* d'aprile
A'pril Fools'' Day' *s* primo d'aprile
apron ['eprən] *s* grembiale *m*, grembiule *m*; **tied to the apron strings of** attaccato alle sottane di
apropos [,æprə'po] *adj* opportuno || *adv*—**apropos of** a proposito di
apse [æps] *s* abside *f*
apt [æpt] *adj* atto, appropriato; (*quick*) pronto; **to be apt to** essere propenso a, portato a
aptitude ['æptɪ,tjud] or ['æptɪ,tud] *s* attitudine *f*
ap'titude test' *s* esame *m* attitudinale
Apulia [ə'pjulɪ·ə] *s* la Puglia
aqualung ['ækwə,lʌŋ] *s* autorespiratore *m*
aquamarine [,ækwəmə'rin] *s* acquamarina
aquaplane ['ækwə,plen] *s* acquaplano || *intr* andare in acquaplano
aquari·um [ə'kwerɪ·əm] *s* (**-ums** or **-a** [ə]) acquario, vasca dei pesci
Aquarius [ə'kwerɪ·əs] *s* (astr) Acquario
aquatic [ə'kwætɪk] or [ə'kwɑtɪk] *adj* acquatico || *s* animale acquatico; pianta acquatica; **aquatics** sport acquatici
aqueduct ['ækwə,dʌkt] *s* acquedotto
aqueous ['ekwɪ·əs] or ['ækwɪ·əs] *adj* acquoso
aq'uiline nose' ['ækwɪ,laɪn] *s* naso aquilino
Arab ['ærəb] *adj & s* arabo
Arabic ['ærəbɪk] *adj & s* arabo

arbiter [ˈɑrbɪtər] *s* arbitro
arbitrary [ˈɑrbɪ ˌtreri] *adj* arbitrario
arbitrate [ˈɑrbɪ ˌtret] *tr* arbitrare || *intr* fare l'arbitro
arbitration [ˌɑrbɪˈtreʃən] *s* arbitrato
arbitrator [ˈɑrbɪ ˌtretər] *s* arbitro
arbor [ˈɑrbər] *s* pergola, pergolato; (mach) albero, asse *m*
arbore·tum [ˌɑrbəˈritəm] *s* (**-tums** or **-ta** [tə]) arboreto
arbutus [ɑrˈbjutəs] *s* (*Arbutus unedo*) corbezzolo
arc [ɑrk] *s* arco; (elec) arco voltaico || *intr* (elec) formare un arco
arcade [ɑrˈked] *s* arcata, portico
arch [ɑrtʃ] *adj* malizioso || *s* arco; (anat) arco del piede || *tr* attraversare; arcuare || *intr* inarcarsi
archaeology [ˌɑrkɪˈɑlədʒi] *s* archeologia
archaic [ɑrˈke·ɪk] *adj* arcaico
archaism [ˈɑrke ˌɪzəm] or [ˈɑrki ˌɪzəm] *s* arcaismo
archangel [ˈɑrk ˌendʒəl] *s* arcangelo
archbishop [ˈɑrtʃˈbɪʃəp] *s* arcivescovo
archduke [ˈɑrtʃˈdjuk] or [ˈɑrtʃˈduk] *s* arciduca *m*
archene·my [ˈɑrtʃˈenɪmi] *s* (**-mies**) nemico giurato
archer [ˈɑrtʃər] *s* arciere *m*
archery [ˈɑrtʃəri] *s* tiro con l'arco
archetype [ˈɑrkɪ ˌtaɪp] *s* archetipo, prototipo
archipela·go [ˌɑrkɪˈpeləgo] *s* (**-gos** or **-goes**) arcipelago
architect [ˈɑrkɪ ˌtekt] *s* architetto
architectural [ˌɑrkɪˈtektʃərəl] *adj* architetturale, architettonico
architecture [ˈɑrkɪ ˌtektʃər] *s* architettura
archives [ˈɑrkaɪvz] *spl* archivio
arch'way' *s* arcata
arc' lamp' *s* lampada ad arco
arctic [ˈɑrktɪk] *adj* artico || **the Arctic** la regione artica
arc' weld'ing *s* saldatura ad arco
ardent [ˈɑrdənt] *adj* ardente
ardor [ˈɑrdər] *s* ardore *m*
arduous [ˈɑrdʒʊ·əs] or [ˈɑrdjʊ·əs] *adj* arduo
area [ˈerɪ·ə] *s* area
ar'ea code' *s* prefisso
Argentina [ˌɑrdʒənˈtinə] *s* l'Argentina
Argentine [ˈɑrdʒən ˌtin] or [ˈɑrdʒən ˌtaɪn] *adj & s* argentino || **the Argentine** l'Argentina
Argonaut [ˈɑrgə ˌnɔt] *s* argonauta *m*
argue [ˈɑrgju] *tr* dibattere; (*to indicate*) indicare, provare; **to argue out of** dissuadere da; **to argue s.o. into s.th** persuadere qlcu di qlco || *intr* argomentare, discutere
argument [ˈɑrgjəmənt] *s* discussione, argomentazione; (*theme*) argomento
argumentative [ˌɑrgjəˈmentətɪv] *adj* litigioso
aria [ˈɑrɪ·ə] or [ˈerɪ·ə] *s* aria
arid [ˈærɪd] *adj* arido
aridity [əˈrɪdɪti] *s* aridità *f*
Aries [ˈeriz] or [ˈeri ˌiz] *s* (astr) Ariete *m*
aright [əˈraɪt] *adv* correttamente; **to set aright** rettificare
arise [əˈraɪz] *v* (*pret* **arose** [əˈroz]; *pp* **arisen** [əˈrɪzən]) *intr* alzarsi; (*to originate*) provenire, trarre origine; (*to occur*) succedere, avvenire; (*to be raised, as objections*) avanzarsi
aristocra·cy [ˌærɪsˈtɑkrəsi] *s* (**-cies**) aristocrazia
aristocrat [əˈrɪstə ˌkræt] *s* aristocratico
aristocratic [ə ˌrɪstəˈkrætɪk] *adj* aristocratico
Aristotelian [ˌærɪstəˈtilɪ·ən] *adj & s* aristotelico
Aristotle [ˈærɪ ˌstɑtəl] *s* Aristotele *m*
arithmetic [əˈrɪθmətɪk] *s* aritmetica
arithmetical [ˌærɪθˈmetɪkəl] *adj* aritmetico
arithmetician [ˌærɪθməˈtɪʃən] or [ə ˌrɪθməˈtɪʃən] *s* aritmetico
ark [ɑrk] *s* arca
ark' of the cov'enant *s* arca dell'alleanza
arm [ɑrm] *s* braccio; (*e.g., of a bear*) zampa; (*of a chair*) bracciolo; (*weapon*) arma; **arm in arm** a braccetto; **to be up in arms** essere in armi; essere indignato; **to lay down one's arms** deporre le armi; **to rise up in arms** levarsi in armi; **with open arms** a braccia aperte || *tr* armare || *intr* armarsi
armament [ˈɑrməmənt] *s* armamento
armature [ˈɑrmə ˌtʃər] *s* (*of an animal*) corazza; (*of motor or dynamo*) indotto; (*of a buzzer or electric bell*) ancora
arm'chair' *s* poltrona
Armenian [ɑrˈminɪ·ən] *adj & s* armeno
armful [ˈɑrm ˌful] *s* bracciata
arm'hole' *s* giro manica
armistice [ˈɑrmɪstɪs] *s* armistizio
armlet [ˈɑrmlɪt] *s* bracciale *m*
armor [ˈɑrmər] *s* armatura, corazza || *tr* corazzare, blindare
ar'mored car' *s* carro armato
ar'mor plate' *s* lamiera di corazza
armor·y [ˈɑrməri] *s* (**-ies**) armeria; arsenale *m*
arm'pit' *s* ascella
arm'rest' *s* bracciolo
ar·my [ˈɑrmi] *adj* dell'esercito, militare || *s* (**-mies**) esercito; (*two or more army corps*) armata
ar'my corps' *s* corpo d'armata
aromatic [ˌærəˈmætɪk] *adj* aromatico
around [əˈraʊnd] *adv* intorno; all'intorno; dappertutto; **to turn around** voltarsi || *prep* intorno a; (coll) vicino a; (*approximately*) (coll) circa
arouse [əˈraʊz] *tr* eccitare, incitare; svegliare
arpeg·gio [ɑrˈpedʒo] *s* (**-gios**) arpeggio
arraign [əˈren] *tr* citare, portare in giudizio; accusare
arrange [əˈrendʒ] *tr* disporre, sistemare; (*a dispute*) comporre, accomodare; (mus) ridurre, arrangiare
arrangement [əˈrendʒmənt] *s* disposizione, sistemazione; composizione, accomodamento; (mus) riduzione,

arrangiamento; **arrangements** preparazione, preparativi *mpl*
array [ə're] *s* ordine *m;* (*clothes*) abbigliamento; (mil) spiegamento, schiera || *tr* disporre; abbigliare, adornare; (mil) spiegare, schierare
arrears [ə'rɪrz] *spl* arretrati *mpl;* **in arrears** in arretrato
arrest [ə'rest] *s* arresto; **under arrest** in arresto || *tr* arrestare; (*the attention*) attrarre
arresting [ə'restɪŋ] *adj* interessante, che fa colpo
arrival [ə'raɪvəl] *s* arrivo; persona arrivata
arrive [ə'raɪv] *intr* arrivare
arrogance ['ærəgəns] *s* arroganza
arrogant ['ærəgənt] *adj* arrogante
arrogate ['ærə,get] *tr* (*to take without right*) arrogare per sé, arrogarsi; (*to claim for another*) attribuire ingiustamente
arrow ['æro] *s* freccia, saetta
ar'row·head' *s* punta di freccia; (bot) sagittaria
arsenal ['ɑrsənəl] *s* arsenale *m*
arsenic ['ɑrsɪnɪk] *s* arsenico
arson ['ɑrsən] *s* incendio doloso
art [ɑrt] *s* arte *f*
arter·y ['ɑrtəri] *s* (**-ies**) arteria
artful ['ɑrtfəl] *adj* artificioso; (*clever*) destro; (*crafty*) astuto
arthritic [ɑr'θrɪtɪk] *adj & s* artritico
arthritis [ɑr'θraɪtɪs] *s* artrite *f*
artichoke ['ɑrtɪ,tʃok] *s* carciofo
article ['ɑrtɪkəl] *s* articolo
articulate [ɑr'tɪkjəlɪt] *adj* articolato; facile di parola || ['ɑrtɪkjə,let] *tr* articolare || *intr* pronunziare in modo articolato
articulation [ɑr,tɪkjə'leʃən] *s* articolazione
artifact ['ɑrtɪ,fækt] *s* manufatto
artifice ['ɑrtɪfɪs] *s* artificio
artificial [,ɑrtɪ'fɪʃəl] *adj* artificiale
artillery [ɑr'tɪləri] *s* artiglieria
artil'lery·man *s* (**-men**) artigliere *m,* cannoniere *m*
artisan ['ɑrtɪzən] *s* artigiano
artist ['ɑrtɪst] *s* artista *mf*
artistic [ɑr'tɪstɪk] *adj* artistico
artistry ['ɑrtɪstri] *s* abilità artistica
artless ['ɑrtlɪs] *adj* ingenuo, naturale; ignorante; (*clumsy*) grossolano
arts' and crafts' *spl* arti *fpl* e mestieri *mpl*
art·y ['ɑrti] *adj* (**-ier; -iest**) (coll) interessato nell'arte con ostentazione
Aryan ['ɛrɪ·ən] or ['ɑrjən] *adj & s* ariano
as [æz] or [əz] *pron rel* che; **the same as** lo stesso che || *adv* come; per esempio; **as . . . as** così . . . come; **as far as** fino a; **as far as I know** per quanto mi consta; **as for** in quanto a, per quanto concerne; **as is** (slang) com'è, nelle condizioni in cui si trova; **as long as** tanto che, mentre che; **as per** secondo; **as soon as** appena, non appena, non appena che; **as to** per quanto concerne; **as well** pure, anche; **as yet** ancora || *prep* come; da; **as a rule** come regola || *conj* come; mentre; dato che; per quanto; **as if** come se; **as it were** per così dire; **as though** come se
asbestos [æs'bestəs] *s* asbesto, amianto
ascend [ə'send] *tr* ascendere, scalare || *intr* ascendere, salire
ascension [ə'senʃən] *s* ascensione, scalata || **Ascension** *s* Ascensione
ascent [ə'sent] *s* scalata; salita; (*slope*) erta
ascertain [,æsər'ten] *tr* sincerarsi di, verificare
ascertainable [,æsər'tenəbəl] *adj* verificabile
ascetic [ə'setɪk] *adj* ascetico || *s* asceta *m*
ascor'bic ac'id [ə'skɔrbɪk] *s* acido ascorbico
ascribe [ə'skraɪb] *tr* attribuire, imputare
aseptic [ə'septɪk] or [e'septɪk] *adj* asettico
ash [æʃ] *s* cenere *f;* (bot) frassino
ashamed [ə'ʃemd] *adj* vergognoso; **to be or feel ashamed** vergognarsi
ash'can' *s* pattumiera; (coll) bomba antisommergibile
ashen ['æʃən] *adj* cinereo
ashlar ['æʃlər] *s* bugna, bugnato
ashore [ə'ʃor] *adv* a terra; **to come ashore** andare a terra, sbarcare; **to run ashore** arenarsi
ash'tray' *s* portacenere *m*
Ash' Wednes'day *s* le Ceneri
Asia ['eʒə] or ['eʃə] *s* l'Asia *f*
A'sia Mi'nor *s* l'Asia *f* Minore
Asian ['eʒən] or ['eʃən] or **Asiatic** [,eʒɪ'ætɪk] or [,eʃɪ'ætɪk] *adj & s* asiatico
aside [ə'saɪd] *s* parola detta a parte; (theat) a parte *m* || *adv* da parte; a parte; **aside from** (coll) eccetto; separato da; **to step aside** farsi da un lato
asinine ['æsɪnaɪn] *adj* (*like an ass*) asinino; (*stupid*) asinesco
ask [æsk] or [ɑsk] *tr* chiedere (with *dat*), domandare (with *dat*); invitare; (*a question*) fare; **to ask s.o. for s.th** chiedere or domandare qlco a qlcu; **to ask s.o. to** + *inf* chiedere a qlcu di + *inf* || *intr* chiedere; **to ask about** chiedere informazioni di; **to ask for** chiedere, domandare; **to ask for it** (coll) andare in cerca di disgrazie; (coll) volerlo, e.g., **he asked for it** l'ha voluto
askance [ə'skæns] *adv* di traverso, di sbieco; (fig) con sospetto
asleep [ə'slip] *adj* addormentato; **to fall asleep** addormentarsi
asp [æsp] *s* aspide *m*
asparagus [ə'spærəgəs] *s* asparago; (*as food*) asparagi *mpl*
aspect ['æspekt] *s* aspetto; (*direction anything faces*) esposizione
aspen ['æspən] *s* pioppo tremolo, tremolo
aspersion [ə'spʌrʒən] or [ə'spʌrʃən] *s* diffamazione, calunnia; (eccl) aspersione
asphalt ['æsfɔlt] or ['æsfælt] *s* asfalto || *tr* asfaltare

asphyxiate [æs'fɪksɪ ˌet] *tr* asfissiare
aspirant [ə'spaɪrənt] or ['æspɪrənt] *s* aspirante *mf*
aspire [ə'spaɪr] *intr* aspirare
aspirin ['æspɪrɪn] *s* aspirina
ass [æs] *s* asino
assail [ə'sel] *tr* assalire, assaltare
assassin [ə'sæsɪn] *s* assassino
assassinate [ə'sæsɪ ˌnet] *tr* assassinare
assassination [ə ˌsæsɪ'neʃən] *s* assassinio
assault [ə'sɔlt] *s* assalto || *tr* assaltare
assault' and bat'tery *s* vie *fpl* di fatto
assay [ə'se] or ['æse] *s* saggio, esame *m* || [ə'se] *tr* saggiare
assemblage [ə'semblɪdʒ] *s* assemblea; (mach) montaggio
assemble [ə'sembəl] *tr* riunire; (mach) montare, mettere insieme || *intr* assembrarsi, riunirsi
assembler [ə'semblər] *s* montatore *m*
assem•bly [ə'sembli] *s* (**-blies**) assemblea, riunione; (mach) montaggio
assem'bly hall' *s* sala di riunioni
assem'bly line' *s* catena di montaggio
assem'bly•man *s* (**-men**) membro dell'assemblea legislativa
assent [ə'sent] *s* assenso || *intr* assentire
assert [ə'sʌrt] *tr* asserire; **to assert oneself** far valere i propri diritti
assertion [ə'sʌrʃən] *s* asserzione
assess [ə'ses] *tr* stimare, valutare; (*for taxation or fine*) tassare
assessment [ə'sesmənt] *s* valutazione; tassazione
assessor [ə'sesər] *s* agente *m* delle tasse
asset ['æsət] *s* vantaggio; persona di valore; **assets** (com) attivo; (law) beni *mpl*
assiduous [ə'sɪdʒu·əs] or [ə'sɪdju·əs] *adj* assiduo
assign [ə'saɪn] *s* cessionario || *tr* assegnare; (*e.g., a date*) fissare; (*a right*) trasferire
assignation [ˌæsɪg'neʃən] *s* assegnazione; trasferimento; (*date*) appuntamento amoroso
assignment [ə'saɪnmənt] *s* assegnamento; (*of rights*) trasferimento; (*schoolwork*) compito
assimilate [ə'sɪmɪ ˌlet] *tr* assimilare || *intr* essere assimilato; assimilarsi
assist [ə'sɪst] *s* aiuto || *tr* aiutare, assistere
assistance [ə'sɪstəns] *s* assistenza, aiuto
assistant [ə'sɪstənt] *adj & s* assistente *m*
associate [ə'soʃɪ·ɪt] or [ə'soʃɪ ˌet] *adj* associato || *s* associato; membro limitato || [ə'soʃɪ ˌet] *tr* associare || *intr* associarsi
association [ə ˌsoʃɪ'eʃən] *s* associazione
assort [ə'sɔrt] *tr* assortire || *intr* associarsi
assortment [ə'sɔrtmənt] *s* assortimento
assuage [ə'swedʒ] *tr* alleviare
assume [ə'sum] or [ə'sjum] *tr* assumere; (*to appropriate*) usurpare; (*to pretend*) fingere; (*to suppose*) supporre
assumed [ə'sumd] or [ə'sjumd] *adj* supposto, immaginario
assumption [ə'sʌmpʃən] *s* (*arrogance*) aria, arroganza; (*thing taken for granted*) supposizione; (*of an undertaking*) assunzione
assurance [ə'ʃurəns] *s* assicurazione, certezza; baldanza, fiducia in sè; (*too much boldness*) sicumera
assure [ə'ʃur] *tr* assicurare
assuredly [ə'ʃurɪdli] *adv* sicuramente
astatine ['æstə ˌtin] *s* astato
asterisk ['æstə ˌrɪsk] *s* asterisco, stelloncino
astern [ə'stʌrn] *adv* a poppa, a poppavia
asthma ['æzmə] or ['æsmə] *s* asma
astonish [ə'stɑnɪʃ] *tr* meravigliare, stupefare
astonishing [ə'stɑnɪʃɪŋ] *adj* stupefacente, sorprendente
astound [ə'staund] *tr* stupefare, sbalordire
astounding [ə'staundɪŋ] *adj* stupefacente
astraddle [ə'strædəl] *adv* a cavaliere, a cavalcioni
astray [ə'stre] *adv* sulla cattiva via; **to go astray** traviarsi; **to lead astray** traviare
astride [ə'straɪd] *adj & adv* a cavaliere; (*said of a person*) a cavalcioni || *prep* a cavaliere di; a cavalcioni di
astrology [ə'strɑlədʒi] *s* astrologia
astronaut ['æstrə ˌnɔt] *s* astronauta *mf*
astronautic [ˌæstrə'nɔtɪk] *adj* astronautico || **astronautics** *ssg* astronautica
astronomer [ə'strɑnəmər] *s* astronomo
astronomic(al) [ˌæstrə'nɑmɪk(əl)] *adj* astronomico
astronomy [ə'strɑnəmi] *s* astronomia
astute [ə'stjut] or [ə'stut] *adj* astuto
asunder [ə'sʌndər] *adv* a pezzi; **to tear asunder** separare, fare a pezzi
asylum [ə'saɪləm] *s* asilo
asymmetry [ə'sɪmɪtri] *s* asimmetria
at [æt] or [ət] *prep* a; in; a casa di, e.g., **at John's** a casa di Giovanni; da, **e.g., at Mary's** da Maria; di, **e.g., to be surprised at** essere sorpreso di; **to laugh at** ridersi di
atheist ['eθi·ɪst] *s* ateista *mf*
Athenian [ə'θinɪ·ən] *adj & s* ateniese *mf*
Athens ['æθɪnz] *s* Atene *f*
athirst [ə'θʌrst] *adj* assetato
athlete ['æθlit] *s* atleta *mf*
athletic [æθ'letɪk] *adj* atletico || **athletics** *ssg & spl* atletica
Atlantic [æt'læntɪk] *adj* atlantico || *adj & s* Atlantico
atlas ['ætləs] *s* atlante *m* || **Atlas** *s* Atlante *m*
atmosphere ['ætməs ˌfɪr] *s* atmosfera
atmospheric [ˌætməs'ferɪk] *adj* atmosferico || **atmospherics** *spl* disturbi atmosferici
atom ['ætəm] *s* atomo
at'om bomb' *s* bomba atomica
atomic [ə'tɑmɪk] *adj* atomico
atom'ic age' *s* era atomica
atom'ic sub'marine *s* sommergibile *m* nucleare
atomize ['ætə ˌmaɪz] *tr* atomizzare

atomizer ['ætə ˌmaɪzər] *s* nebulizzatore *m*
at'om smash'er *s* acceleratore *m* di particelle
atone [ə'ton] *intr*—**to atone for** espiare
atonement [ə'tonmənt] *s* riparazione; espiazione
atop [ə'tɑp] *adv* in cima || *prep* in cima a
atrocious [ə'troʃəs] *adj* atroce
atroci·ty [ə'trɑsɪti] *s* (**-ties**) atrocità *f*
atro·phy ['ætrəfi] *s* atrofia || *v* (*pret & pp* **-phied**) *tr* atrofizzare || *intr* atrofizzarsi
attach [ə'tætʃ] *tr* attaccare; (*to affix*) apporre; (*to attribute*) attribuire; (law) sequestrare; **to be attached to** essere legato a; fare parte di || *intr*—**to attach to** essere pertinente a
attaché [ˌætə'ʃe] or [ə'tæʃe] *s* attaché *m*., addetto
attaché' case' *s* valigetta diplomatica
attachment [ə'tætʃmənt] *s* attacco, unione; affezione; (mach) accessorio; (law) sequestro
attack [ə'tæk] *s* attacco || *tr & intr* attaccare
attain [ə'ten] *tr* raggiungere || *intr*—**to attain to** raggiungere, conseguire
attainder [ə'tendər] *s* morte *f* civile
attainment [ə'tenmənt] *s* raggiungimento, realizzazione; (*accomplishment*) dote *f*
attempt [ə'tɛmpt] *s* tentativo; (*attack*) attentato || *tr* tentare; (*s.o.'s life*) attentare a
attend [ə'tɛnd] *tr* (*to be present at*) presenziare, presenziare a, assistere a; (*to accompany*) accompagnare; (*to take care of; to pay attention to*) assistere || *intr*—**to attend to** occuparsi di, attendere a
attendance [ə'tɛndəns] *s* (*attending*) presenza; (*company present*) concorso; **to dance attendance** essere al servizio completo
attendant [ə'tɛndənt] *adj* assistente; (*accompanying*) concomitante || *s* (*servant*) inserviente *mf;* presente *m*
attention [ə'tɛnʃən] *s* attenzione; (mil) attenti *m;* **attentions** attenzioni *fpl;* **to call s.o.'s attention to s.th** fare presente qlco a qlcu; **to stand at attention** stare sull'attenti || *interj* attenti!
attentive [ə'tɛntɪv] *adj* attento, premuroso
attenuate [ə'tɛnjʊˌet] *tr* attenuare
attest [ə'tɛst] *tr* attestare || *intr*—**to attest to** attestare, testimoniare
attic ['ætɪk] *s* attico, solaio || **Attic** *adj & s* attico
attire [ə'taɪr] *s* vestiti *mpl,* vestiario || *tr* vestire
attitude ['ætɪˌtjud] or ['ætɪˌtud] *s* atteggiamento, attitudine *f;* **to strike an attitude** atteggiarsi
attorney [ə'tʌrni] *s* avvocato; (*proxy*) procuratore *m*
attor'ney gen'eral *s* (**attor'neys gen'eral** or **attor'ney gen'erals**) procuratore *m* generale || **Attorney General** *s* (U.S.A.) ministro di grazia e giustizia
attract [ə'trækt] *tr* attrarre; (*attention*) chiamare
attraction [ə'trækʃən] *s* attrazione
attractive [ə'træktɪv] *adj* attrattivo
attribute ['ætrɪˌbjut] *s* attributo || [ə'trɪbjut] *tr* attribuire
attrition [ə'trɪʃən] *s* attrito; diminuzione di numero
auburn ['ɔbərn] *adj & s* biondo fulvo, rosso tizianesco
auction ['ɔkʃən] *s* asta, incanto || *tr* vendere all'asta
auctioneer [ˌɔkʃə'nɪr] *s* banditore *m* || *tr & intr* vendere all'asta
audacious [ɔ'deʃəs] *adj* audace
audaci·ty [ɔ'dæsɪti] *s* (**-ties**) audacia
audience ['ɔdɪ·əns] *s* (*hearing*) udienza; uditorio, pubblico
au'dio fre'quency ['ɔdɪˌo] *s* audiofrequenza
au'dio-vis'ual aids' *spl* sussidi audiovisivi
audit ['ɔdɪt] *s* verifica or esame *m* dei conti || *tr* esaminare i conti di; (*a class*) assistere a, come uditore || *intr* assistere a una classe come uditore
audition [ɔ'dɪʃən] *s* audizione || *tr* dare un'audizione a
auditor ['ɔdɪtər] *s* revisore *m* dei conti; (educ) uditore *m*
auditorium [ˌɔdɪ'torɪ·əm] *s* auditorio
auger ['ɔgər] *s* succhiello, trivella
aught [ɔt] *s* zero; **for aught I know** per quanto ne so || *adv* affatto
augment [ɔg'mɛnt] *tr & intr* aumentare
augur ['ɔgər] *s* augure *m* || *tr & intr* vaticinare
augu·ry ['ɔgəri] *s* (**-ries**) augurio
august [ɔ'gʌst] *adj* augusto || **August** ['ɔgəst] *s* agosto
aunt [ænt] or [ɑnt] *s* zia
aurora [ə'rorə] *s* aurora
auspice ['ɔspɪs] *s* auspicio; **under the auspices of** sotto gli auspici di
austere [ɔs'tɪr] *adj* austero
Australia [ɔ'streljə] *s* l'Australia *f*
Australian [ɔ'streljən] *adj & s* australiano
Austria ['ɔstrɪ·ə] *s* l'Austria *f*
Austrian ['ɔstrɪ·ən] *adj & s* austriaco
authentic [ɔ'θɛntɪk] *adj* autentico
authenticate [ɔ'θɛntɪˌket] *tr* autenticare
author ['ɔθər] *s* autore *m*
authoress ['ɔθərɪs] *s* autrice *f*
authoritarian [ɔˌθɑrɪ'tɛrɪ·ən] or [ɔˌθɔrɪ'tɛrɪ·ən] *adj* autoritario || *s* persona autoritaria
authoritative [ɔ'θɑrɪˌtetɪv] or [ɔ'θɔrɪˌtetɪv] *adj* autorevole; autoritario
authori·ty [ɔ'θɑrɪti] or [ɔ'θɔrɪti] *s* (**-ties**) autorità *f;* **on good authority** da buona fonte, da fonte autorevole
authorize ['ɔθəˌraɪz] *tr* autorizzare
authorship ['ɔθərˌʃɪp] *s* paternità letteraria
au·to ['ɔto] *s* (**-tos**) (coll) auto *f*
autobiogra·phy [ˌɔtobaɪ'ɑgrəfi] or [ˌɔtobɪ'ɑgrəfi] *s* (**-phies**) autobiografia

autobus ['ɔto ˌbʌs] *s* autobus *m*
autocratic(al) [ˌɔtə'krætɪk(əl)] *adj* autocratico
autograph ['ɔtə ˌgræf] or ['ɔtə ˌgrɑf] *adj & s* autografo || *tr* porre l'autografo su, firmare con firma autografa
automat ['ɔtə ˌmæt] *s* ristorante *m* self-service a distribuzione automatica
automate ['ɔtə ˌmet] *tr* automatizzare
automatic [ˌɔtə'mætɪk] *adj* automatico || *s* pistola automatica
automat'ic transmis'sion *s* trasmissione automatica
automation [ˌɔtə'meʃən] *s* automazione
automa•ton [ɔ'tɑmə ˌtɑn] *s* (**-tons** or **-ta** [tə]) automa *m*
automobile [ˌɔtəmo'bil] or [ˌɔtə'mobil] *adj & s* automobile *f*
automobile' show' *s* salone *m* dell'automobile
automotive [ˌɔtə'motɪv] *adj* (*self-propelled*) automotore; automobilistico
autonomous [ɔ'tɑnəməs] *adj* autonomo
autonomy [ɔ'tɑnəmi] *s* autonomia
autop•sy ['ɔtɑpsi] *s* (**-sies**) autopsia
au'to trans'port rig' *s* autotreno per trasporto di automobili
autumn ['ɔtəm] *s* autunno
autumnal [ɔ'tʌmnəl] *adj* autunnale
auxilia•ry [ɔg'zɪljəri] *adj & s* (**-ries**) ausiliare *m*
avail [ə'vel] *s* utilità *f*; **of no avail** che non serve a nulla || *tr* servire (with *dat*); **to avail oneself of** servirsi di; approfittare di || *intr* servire
available [ə'veləbəl] *adj* disponibile; **to make available to** mettere alla disposizione di
avalanche ['ævə ˌlæntʃ] or ['ævə ˌlɑntʃ] *s* valanga
avant-garde [əvɑ̃'gard] *adj* d'avanguardia
avant-gardism [ə'vɑ̃'gardɪzəm] *s* avanguardismo
avarice ['ævərɪs] *s* avarizia
avaricious [ˌævə'rɪʃəs] *adj* avaro
avenge [ə'vendʒ] *tr* vendicare; **to avenge oneself on** vendicarsi di
avenue ['ævə ˌnju] or ['ævənu] *s* viale *m*, corso
aver [ə'vʌr] *v* (*pret & pp* **averred**; *ger* **averring**) *tr* asserire, affermare
average ['ævərɪdʒ] *adj* medio || *s* media; (naut) avaria; (*e.g., of goals*) (sports) quoziente *m*; **on the average** di media || *tr* fare la media di; fare . . . di media, e.g., **he averages one hundred dollars a week** fa cento dollari di media alla settimana
averse [ə'vʌrs] *adj* avverso
aversion [ə'vʌrʒən] *s* avversione
avert [ə'vʌrt] *tr* (*to ward off*) evitare; (*to turn away*) distogliere
aviar•y ['evɪ ˌeri] *s* (**-ies**) aviario, voliera
aviation [ˌevɪ'eʃən] *s* aviazione
aviator ['evɪ ˌetər] *s* aviatore *m*
avid ['ævɪd] *adj* avido
avidity [ə'vɪdɪti] *s* avidità *f*
avocation [ˌævə'keʃən] *s* svago, passatempo
avoid [ə'vɔɪd] *tr* evitare
avoidable [ə'vɔɪdəbəl] *adj* evitabile
avow [ə'vaʊ] *tr* confessare, ammettere
avowal [ə'vaʊ•əl] *s* confessione, ammissione
await [ə'wet] *tr* aspettare, attendere
awake [ə'wek] *adj* sveglio || *v* (*pret & pp* **awoke** [ə'wok] or **awaked**) *tr* svegliare || *intr* svegliarsi
awaken [ə'wekən] *tr* svegliare || *intr* svegliarsi
awakening [ə'wekənɪŋ] *s* risveglio
award [ə'wɔrd] *s* (*prize*) premio; (*decision by judge*) sentenza || *tr* aggiudicare
aware [ə'wer] *adj* conscio, consapevole; **to become aware of** rendersi conto di
awareness [ə'wernɪs] *s* coscienza
awash [ə'wɑʃ] or [ə'wɔʃ] *adj & adv* a fior d'acqua
away [ə'we] *adj* distante, assente || *adv* lontano; via; continuamente; **away back** (coll) molto tempo fa; **away from** lontano da; **to do away with** disfarsi di, sopprimere; **to get away** scappare, sfuggire; **to go away** andarsene; **to run away** fuggire; **to send away** mandar via; **to take away** portar via
awe [ɔ] *s* estremo rispetto; sacro timore || *tr* infondere rispetto a; infondere un sacro timore a
aweigh [ə'we] *adj* (*anchor*) levato
awesome ['ɔsəm] *adj* grandioso, imponente
awestruck ['ɔ ˌstrʌk] *adj* pieno di sacro timore
awful ['ɔfəl] *adj* terribile; imponente || *adv* (coll) terribilmente
awfully ['ɔfəli] *adv* tremendamente, terribilmente; (coll) molto
awhile [ə'hwaɪl] *adv* un po', un po' di tempo
awkward ['ɔkwərd] *adj* (*clumsy*) goffo, maldestro; (*unwieldly*) scomodo; (*embarrassing*) imbarazzante
awl [ɔl] *s* punteruolo
awning ['ɔnɪŋ] *s* tenda; (*in front of a store*) tendone *m*
A.W.O.L. ['ewɔl] (acronym) or ['e'dʌbəl ˌju'o'el] (letterword) *adj* (mil) assente al contrappello
awry [ə'raɪ] *adv*—**to go awry** andare a capovescio; **to look awry** guardare di sbieco
ax or **axe** [æks] *s* scure *f*; **to have an axe to grind** (coll) avere un interesse speciale
axiom ['æksɪ•əm] *s* assioma *m*
axiomatic [ˌæksɪ•ə'mætɪk] *adj* assiomatico
axis ['æksɪs] *s* (**axes** ['æksiz]) asse *m*
axle ['æksəl] *s* assale *m*, asse *m*
ax'le•tree' *s* assale *m*
ay [aɪ] *s & adv* sì *m*
Azores [ə'zorz] or ['ezorz] *spl* Azzorre *fpl*
azure ['æʒər] or ['eʒər] *adj & s* azzurro, blu *m*

B

B, b [bi] *s* seconda lettera dell'alfabeto inglese
baa [bɑ] *s* belato || *intr* belare
babble [ˈbæbəl] *s* (*murmuring sound*) mormorio; (*senseless prattle*) balbettio || *tr* (*e.g., a secret*) divulgare || *intr* mormorare; balbettare; (*to talk idly*) parlare a vanvera
babe [beb] *s* bebè *m*, bambino; persona inesperta; (slang) ragazza
baboon [bæˈbun] *s* babbuino
ba·by [ˈbebi] *s* (**-bies**) bebè *m*, neonato; bambino; (*the youngest child*) piccolo || *v* (*pret & pp* **-bied**) *tr* coccolare, ninnare
ba'by car'riage *s* carrozzella
ba'by grand' *s* piano a mezza coda
babyhood [ˈbebi ˌhʊd] *s* infanzia
babyish [ˈbebi·ɪʃ] *adj* infantile
Babylon [ˈbæbɪlən] or [ˈbæbɪ ˌlɑn] *s* Babilonia
ba'by sit'ter *s* bambinaia ad ore
ba'by teeth' *spl* denti *mpl* di latte
baccalaureate [ˌbækəˈlɔrɪ·ɪt] *s* baccalaureato; servizio religioso prima del baccalaureato
bacchanal [ˈbækənəl] *adj* bacchico || *s* baccanale *m*; (*person*) ubriacone *m*, bisboccione *m*
bachelor [ˈbætʃələr] *s* (*unmarried man*) scapolo, celibe *m*; (*holder of bachelor's degree*) diplomato; (*apprentice knight*) baccelliere *m*
bachelorhood [ˈbætʃələr ˌhʊd] *s* celibato
bacil·lus [bəˈsɪləs] *s* (**-li** [laɪ]) bacillo
back [bæk] *adj* di dietro, posteriore; arretrato; contrario || *s* dorso, schiena; parte *f* posteriore, didietro; (*of a sheet or coin*) tergo; (*of a knife*) costola; (*of a room*) fondo; (*of a book*) fine *f*; (*of a chair*) schienale *m*; **behind one's back** dietro le spalle di uno; **to turn one's back on** volgere la schiena a || *adv* dietro; indietro; **a few weeks back** alcune settimane fa; **as far back as** sino da; **back of** dietro, dietro a; **to go back on one's word** mancare di parola; **to go back to** ritornare a; **to pay back** ripagare; **to send back** restituire || *tr* appoggiare; far indietreggiare || *intr* indietreggiare; rinculare; **to back down** rinunciarci; **to back off** or **out** ritirarsi; **to back up** (*said of a car*) fare marcia indietro
back'ache' *s* mal *m* di schiena
back'bite' *v* (*pret* **-bit**; *pp* **-bitten** or **-bit**) *tr* sparlare di || *intr* sparlare
back'bit'er *s* maldicente *mf*
back'board' *s* (basketball) tabellone *m*
back'bone' *s* spina dorsale; (*of a book*) costola, dorso; (fig) fermezza
back'break'ing *adj* sfiancante
back'door' *adj* segreto, clandestino
back' door' *s* porta di dietro; (fig) mezzo clandestino
back'drop' *s* (theat) fondale *m*
backer [ˈbækər] *s* sostenitore *m*, difensore *m*; (com) finanziatore *m*
back'fire' *s* (*for firefighting*) controfuoco; (aut) ritorno di fiamma || *intr* (aut) avere un ritorno di fiamma; (fig) raggiungere l'effetto opposto
back'ground' *s* fondo, sfondo; precedenti *mpl*; origine *f*
back'ground mu'sic *s* musica di fondo
backhand [ˈbæk ˌhænd] *adj* obliquo || *s* scrittura inclinata a sinistra; (tennis) rovescio
back'hand'ed *adj* obliquo; sarcastico; insincero
backing [ˈbækɪŋ] *s* appoggio; sostegno; (bb) dorso
back'ing light' *s* (aut) faro retromarcia; (theat) luce *f* per il fondale
back'lash' *s* reazione; contraccolpo; (mach) gioco
back'log' *s* ceppo; (fig) riserva
back' num'ber *s* numero arretrato; (coll) persona all'antica
back' pay' *s* paga arretrata, arretrati *mpl*
back' scratch'er *s* manina per grattare la schiena; (coll) leccapiedi *m*
back' seat' *s* (aut) sedile *m* posteriore; (fig) posizione secondaria
back'side' *s* dorso; didietro
back'slide' *v* (*pret & pp* **-slid** [ˌslɪd]) *intr* ricadere
back'spac'er *s* tasto ritorno
back'spin' *s* effetto
back'stage' *adj* dietro alle quinte || *s* retroscena *m* || *adv* a retroscena, dietro alle quinte
back'stairs' *adj* indiretto, segreto
back' stairs' *spl* scala di servizio
back'stitch' *s* impuntura || *tr & intr* impunturare
back'stroke' *s* (swimming) bracciata sul dorso
back'swept wing' *s* ala a freccia
back' talk' *s* risposta impertinente
back'track' *intr* ritornare sulle proprie tracce; (fig) fare macchina indietro
back'up light' *s* (aut) faro retromarcia
backward [ˈbækwərd] *adj* ritroso; poco progredito, retrogrado || *adv* a ritroso, all'indietro; verso il passato; alla rovescia; **backward and forward** (coll) completamente, perfettamente; **to go backward and forward** andare avanti e indietro
back'wash' *s* risacca
back'wa'ter *s* gora, ristagno; (fig) eremo
back'woods' *spl* zona boscosa lontana dai centri popolati
back'yard' *s* cortile *m* posteriore
bacon [ˈbekən] *s* pancetta
bacteria [bækˈtɪrɪ·ə] *spl* batteri *mpl*
bacterial [bækˈtɪrɪ·əl] *adj* batterico
bacteriologist [bæk ˌtɪrɪˈɑlədʒɪst] *s* batteriologo
bacteriology [bæk ˌtɪrɪˈɑlədʒi] *s* batteriologia
bad [bæd] *adj* (**worse** [wʌrs]; **worst** [wʌrst]) cattivo; (*coin*) falso; (*weather*) brutto; (*debt*) insolvibile; severo || *s* male *m*; **from bad to**

worse da male in peggio || *adv* male; **to be too bad** essere peccato; **to feel bad** esser spiacente; sentirsi male; **to look bad** aver brutta cera
bad' breath' *s* fiato cattivo
bad' egg' *s* (slang) cattivo soggetto
badge [bædʒ] *s* divisa; decorazione; simbolo, placca
badger ['bædʒər] *s* tasso || *tr* molestare
badly ['bædli] *adv* male; gravemente; molto
bad'ly off' *adj* in cattive condizioni
badminton ['bædmɪntən] *s* badminton *m*
baffle ['bæfəl] *s* (mach) deflettore *m;* (rad) schermo acustico || *tr* frustrare, confondere
baffling ['bæflɪŋ] *adj* sconcertante
bag [bæg] *s* sacco; borsetta; (*of a marsupial*) borsa; (hunt) presa; **bag and baggage** con armi e bagagli; **to be in the bag** (slang) averlo nel sacco; **to be left holding the bag** (coll) essere piantato in asso || *v* (*pret & pp* **bagged;** *ger* **bagging**) *tr* insaccare; (hunt) pigliare || *intr* (*to hang loosely*) far pieghe
baggage ['bægɪdʒ] *s* bagaglio
bag'gage car' *s* bagagliaio
bag'gage check' *s* scontrino del bagaglio
bag'gage room' *s* deposito bagagli
bag·gy ['bægi] *adj* (**-gier; -giest**) come un sacco
bag'pipe' *s* cornamusa, zampogna
bag'pip'er *s* zampognaro
bail [bel] *s* cauzione; libertà provvisoria sotto cauzione; (*bucket*) sassola || *tr* liberare sotto cauzione; **to bail out** (*a boat*) sgottare || *intr*—**to bail out** (aer) gettarsi col paracadute
bailiwick ['belɪwɪk] *s* (fig) sfera di competenza
bait [bet] *s* esca; (fig) allettamento || *tr* adescare; (fig) allettare
baize [bez] *s* panno verde
bake [bek] *tr* cuocere al forno || *intr* cuocersi al forno; abbrustolirsi
bakelite ['bekə,laɪt] *s* bachelite *f*
baker ['bekər] *s* fornaio, panettiere *m*
bak'er's doz'en *s* tredici per ogni dozzina
baker·y ['bekəri] *s* (**-ies**) panetteria
bak'ing pan' ['bekɪŋ] *s* tortiera
bak'ing pow'der *s* lievito in polvere
bak'ing so'da *s* bicarbonato di soda
balance ['bæləns] *s* (*scales*) bilancia; equilibrio; armonia; (*of watch*) bilanciere *m;* (*remainder; amount due*) resto; (*of budget*) pareggio; **in the balance** in bilico; **to lose one's balance** perdere l'equilibrio; **to strike a balance** fare il bilancio || *tr* bilanciare, pesare; (com) bilanciare, pareggiare || *intr* bilanciarsi
bal'ance of pay'ments *s* bilancia dei pagamenti
bal'ance of pow'er *s* equilibrio politico
bal'ance of trade' *s* bilancia commerciale
bal'ance sheet' *s* bilancio
balco·ny ['bælkəni] *s* (**-nies**) balcone *m;* (theat) galleria
bald [bɔld] *adj* calvo; (*bare*) nudo; (*unadorned*) semplice
bald' ea'gle *s* aquila col capo bianco dell'America del Nord
baldness ['bɔldnɪs] *s* calvizie *f*
baldric ['bɔldrɪk] *s* tracolla
bale [bel] *s* balla; collo || *tr* imballare
baleful ['belfəl] *adj* minaccioso, funesto
balk [bɔk] *tr* ostacolare || *intr* intestarsi, impuntarsi
Balkan ['bɔlkən] *adj* balcanico || **the Balkans** i Balcani
balk·y ['bɔki] *adj* (**-ier; -iest**) caparbio, ostinato
ball [bɔl] *s* palla; pallone *m;* sfera; (*of the thumb*) polpastrello; (*of wool*) gomitolo; (*projectile*) palla, pallottola; (*dance*) ballo; **on the ball** (slang) capace, efficiente; (slang) in gamba; **to play ball** giocare alla palla; **to play ball with** essere in cooperazione con || *tr*—**to ball up** (slang) confondere
ballad ['bæləd] *s* ballata
ball' and chain' *s* palla di piombo; (fig) impedimento; (slang) moglie *f*
ball'-and-sock'et joint' ['bɔlən'sɑkɪt] *s* giunto a sfere
ballast ['bæləst] *s* zavorra; (rr) pietrisco || *tr* zavorrare
ball' bear'ing *s* cuscinetto a sfere
ballet ['bæle] *s* balletto
ballistic [bə'lɪstɪk] *adj* balistico || **ballistics** *ssg* balistica
balloon [bə'lun] *s* pallone *m;* (*for children*) palloncino; (*in comic strip*) fumetto
ballot ['bælət] *s* scheda elettorale; voto || *intr* votare, ballottare
bal'lot box' *s* bussola, urna
ball'play'er *s* giocatore *m* di palla, giocatore *m* di baseball
ball'-point pen' *s* penna a sfera
ball'room' *s* salone *m* da ballo
ballyhoo ['bælɪ,hu] *s* chiasso; montatura || *tr* far chiasso a favore di
balm [bɑm] *s* balsamo
balm·y ['bɑmi] *adj* (**-ier; -iest**) balsamico; salubre; (slang) pazzo
balsam ['bɔlsəm] *s* balsamo; (*plant*) balsamina
Baltic ['bɔltɪk] *adj* baltico
baluster ['bæləstər] *s* balaustro
balustrade [,bæləs'tred] *s* balaustrata
bamboo [bæm'bu] *s* bambù *m*
bamboozle [bæm'buzəl] *tr* ingannare, raggirare
bamboozler [bæm'buzlər] *s* raggiratore *m*
ban [bæn] *s* bando; (*of marriage*) pubblicazione matrimoniale; (eccl) interdetto, scomunica || *v* (*pret & pp* **banned;** *ger* **banning**) *tr* proibire
banal ['benəl] or [bə'næl] *adj* banale
banana [bə'nænə] *s* banana, (*tree*) banano
band [bænd] *s* banda, striscia; (*of thin cloth*) benda; (*of metal, rubber*) fascia, nastro; (*of hat*) nastro; (mus) banda, fanfara; **to beat the band** fortemente; abbondantemente || *tr* unire || *intr*—**to band together** unirsi

bandage ['bændɪdʒ] *s* benda, bendaggio || *tr* fasciare
bandanna [bæn'dænə] *s* fazzolettone colorato
band'box' *s* cappelliera
bandit ['bændɪt] *s* bandito
band'mas'ter *s* capomusica *m*
bandoleer [,bændə'lɪr] *s* bandoliera
band' saw' *s* sega a nastro
band'stand' *s* chiosco della banda
band'wag'on *s* carrozzone *m* da circo; **to jump on the bandwagon** prendere le parti del vincitore
baneful ['benfəl] *adj* nocivo; funesto
bang [bæŋ] *s* rumore *m*, scoppio; (coll) energia; (*pleasure*) (slang) piacere *m*, eccitazione; **bangs** frangetta || *adv* tutto d'un colpo || *tr* sbattere || *intr* rimbombare || *interj* bum!
bang'-up' *adj* (slang) eccellente, di prim'ordine
banish ['bænɪʃ] *tr* sbandire, mettere al bando
banishment ['bænɪʃmənt] *s* bando, esilio
banister ['bænɪstər] *s* balaustra; **banisters** balaustrata
bank [bæŋk] *s* (*of fish; of fog*) banco; (*of a river*) sponda; (*for coins*) salvadanaio; (*financial institution*) banca, banco; (*of earth, snow*) mucchio, banco; (*of clouds*) cumulo; (aer) inclinazione laterale; (billiards) sponda || *tr* (*a fire*) coprire di cenere; (*to pile up*) ammonticchiare; (*a curve*) sopraelevare; (*money*) depositare || *intr* depositare denaro; (aer) inclinarsi lateralmente; **to bank on** (coll) contare su (di)
bank'book' *s* libretto bancario, libretto di deposito
banker ['bæŋkər] *s* banchiere *m*
banking ['bæŋkɪŋ] *adj* bancario || *s* attività bancaria; professione di banchiere
bank' note' *s* biglietto di banca
bank'roll' *s* rotolo di carta moneta; soldi *mpl* || *tr* (slang) finanziare
bankrupt ['bæŋkrʌpt] *adj & s* fallito; **to go bankrupt** andare in fallimento || *tr* dichiarare in fallimento; far fallire
bankrupt·cy ['bæŋkrʌptsi] *s* (**-cies**) fallimento
banner ['bænər] *adj* importante || *s* bandiera, stendardo; (journ) titolo in grassetto
banns [bænz] *spl* bandi *mpl* matrimoniali
banquet ['bæŋqwɪt] *s* banchetto || *tr* dar un banchetto a || *intr* banchettare
bantam ['bæntəm] *adj* piccolo || *s* pollo nano
ban'tam·weight' *s* peso gallo, bantam *m*
banter ['bæntər] *s* scherzo, facezia || *intr* scherzare, celiare
baptism ['bæptɪzəm] *s* battesimo
baptismal [bæp'tɪzməl] *adj* battesimale; (*certificate*) di battesimo
Baptist ['bæptɪst] *adj & s* battista *mf*
baptister·y ['bæptɪstəri] *s* (**-ies**) battistero
baptize [bæp'taɪz] or ['bæptaɪz] *tr* battezzare
bar [bɑr] *s* barra; sbarra; (*of soap*) saponetta; (*of chocolate*) tavoletta; (*of sand*) banco; (*obstacle*) barriera; bar *m;* (*of public opinion*) tribunale *m;* (*legal profession*) avvocatura; (*of door or window*) spranga; (*of lead*) (typ) lingotto; (mus) battuta; **behind bars** in guardina; **to be admitted to the bar** diventare avvocato; **to tend bar** fare il barista || *prep* eccetto, salvo; **bar none** senza eccezione || *v* (*pret & pp* **barred;** *ger* **barring**) *tr* sbarrare; sprangare; bloccare; escludere
bar' associa'tion *s* associazione dell'ordine degli avvocati
barb [bɑrb] *s* (*of arrow*) barbiglio
barbarian [bɑr'berɪ·ən] *s* barbaro
barbaric [bɑr'bærɪk] *adj* barbaro
barbarism ['bɑrbə,rɪzəm] *s* barbarismo
barbari·ty [bɑr'bærɪti] *s* (**-ties**) barbarie *f*
barbarous ['bɑrbərəs] *adj* barbaro, crudele
Bar'bary ape' ['bɑrbəri] *s* bertuccia
barbecue ['bɑrbɪ,kju] *s* arrosto allo spiedo || *tr* arrostire allo spiedo
barbed [bɑrbd] *adj* irto di punte; mordace, pungente
barbed' wire' *s* filo spinato
barber ['bɑrbər] *s* barbiere *m;* (*who cuts and styles hair*) parrucchiere *m*
bar'ber·shop' *s* barbieria, negozio di barbiere; negozio di parrucchiere
barbiturate [bɑr'bɪtʃə,ret] *s* barbiturato, barbiturico
bard [bɑrd] *s* bardo, poeta *m*
bare [ber] *adj* nudo; (*head*) a capo scoperto; (*unconcealed*) palese; (*empty*) vuoto; (*wire*) senza isolante; (*unadorned*) semplice; **to lay bare** mettere a nudo || *tr* denudare, scoprire
bare'back' *adj & adv* senza sella
barefaced ['ber,fest] *adj* impudente, sfacciato, spudorato
bare'foot' *adj* scalzo
barehanded ['ber,hændɪd] *adj & adv* a mani nude
bareheaded ['ber,hedɪd] *adj* a capo scoperto
barelegged ['ber,legɪd] *adj* a gambe nude
barely ['berli] *adv* appena, soltanto
bargain ['bɑrgɪn] *s* affare *m*, buon affare *m;* contrattazione; **at a bargain** a buon prezzo; **into the bargain** in soprappiù || *tr*—**to bargain away** vendere a buonissimo prezzo || *intr* contrattare, mercanteggiare; **to bargain for** aspettarsi
bar'gain sale' *s* vendita sottoprezzo
barge [bɑrdʒ] *s* barcone *m*, chiatta || *intr*—**to barge in** entrare senza chiedere permesso
baritone ['bærɪ,ton] *adj* di baritono || *s* baritono *m*
barium ['berɪ·əm] *s* bario
bark [bɑrk] *s* corteccia, scorza; (*of dog*) abbaiamento, latrato || *tr* (*e.g.,*

insults) lanciare || *intr* abbaiare, latrare
bar'keep'er *s* barista *mf*
barker ['barkər] *s* banditore *m*, imbonitore *m*
barley ['barli] *s* orzo
bar' mag'net *s* calamita a forma di barra allungata
bar'maid' *s* barista *f*
bar'man *s* (**-men**) barista *m*
barn [barn] *s* granaio; (*for hay*) fienile *m*; (*for livestock*) stalla
barnacle ['barnəkəl] *s* cirripede *m*
barn' owl' *s* civetta
barn'yard' *s* bassacorte *f*, aia
barn'yard fowl' *s* animale *m* da cortile || *spl* animali *mpl* da cortile
barometer [bə'ramɪtər] *s* barometro
baron ['bærən] *s* barone *m*; (*industrialist*) cavaliere *m* d'industria
baroness ['bærənɪs] *s* baronessa
baroque [bə'rok] *adj* & *s* barocco
bar'rack-room' *adj* da caserma || *s* camerata
barracks ['bærəks] *spl* caserma; camerata
barrage [bə'raʒ] *s* (mil) fuoco di sbarramento
barrel ['bærəl] *s* barile *m*, botte *f*; (*of gun*) canna; (mach) cilindro
bar'rel or'gan *s* organetto di Barberia
barren ['bærən] *adj* sterile; (*without vegetation*) brullo
barricade [,bærɪ'ked] *s* barricata || *tr* barricare
barrier ['bærɪ·ər] *s* barriera
bar'rier reef' *s* barriera corallina
barring ['barɪŋ] *prep* eccetto, salvo
barrister ['bærɪstər] *s* (Brit) avvocato
bar'room' *s* bar *m*, cantina, mescita
bar'tend'er *s* barista *mf*, barman *m*
barter ['bartər] *s* baratto || *tr* & *intr* barattare, permutare
basalt [bə'sɔlt] *s* basalto
base [bes] *adj* basale; basso; servile; (*morally low*) turpe; (*metal*) vile, non prezioso || *s* base *f*; (*in children's games*) tana; (*of a word*) radice *f* basale || *tr* basare
base'ball' *s* baseball *m*, pallabase *f*
base'board' *s* basamento; (*of wall*) zoccolo
Basel ['bazəl] *s* Basilea
baseless ['beslɪs] *adj* infondato
basement ['besmənt] *s* scantinato, piano interrato
bashful ['bæʃfəl] *adj* timido
basic ['besɪk] *adj* fondamentale; (chem) basico
ba'sic commod'ities *spl* articoli *mpl* di prima necessità
basilica [bə'sɪlɪkə] *s* basilica
basin ['besɪn] *s* catino; vasca; (*of balance*) piatto; (*of river*) bacino; (*of harbor*) darsena
ba•sis ['besɪs] *s* (**-ses** [siz]) base *f*
bask [bæsk] or [bask] *intr* crogiolarsi
basket ['bæskɪt] or ['baskɪt] *s* cesta; (sports) cesto
bas'ket•ball' *s* pallacanestro *f*
Basque [bæsk] *adj* & *s* basco
bas-relief [,barɪ'lif] or [,bærɪ'lif] *s* bassorilievo
bass [bes] *adj* & *s* (mus) basso || [bæs] *s* (ichth) pesce persico
bass' drum' *s* grancassa
bass' horn' *s* bassotuba *m*
bassinet ['bæsə,nɛt] or [,bæsə'nɛt] *s* culla a forma di cesto; carrozzina a forma di cesto
bas•so ['bæso] or ['baso] *s* (**-sos** or **-si** [si]) basso
bassoon [bə'sun] *s* fagotto
bass' vi'ol ['vaɪ·əl] *s* contrabbasso
bastard ['bæstərd] *adj* & *s* bastardo
baste [best] *tr* (*to sew*) imbastire; (*meat*) inumidire con acqua o grasso
bastion ['bæstʃən] or ['bæstɪ·ən] *s* bastione *m*
bat [bæt] *s* mazza; (*in cricket*) maglio; (coll) colpo; (zool) pipistrello || *v* (*pret* & *pp* **batted**; *ger* **batting**) *tr* colpire con la mazza; **without batting an eye** (coll) senza batter ciglio
batch [bætʃ] *s* (*of bread*) infornata; gruppo, numero
bath [bæθ] or [baθ] *s* bagno; **to take a bath** fare il bagno
bathe [beð] *tr* bagnare, lavare || *intr* bagnarsi, fare il bagno
bather ['beðər] *s* bagnante *mf*
bath'house' *s* (*individual*) cabina; spogliatoio
bath'ing beau'ty *s* bellezza in costume da bagno
bath'ing cap' *s* cuffia da bagno
bath'ing resort' *s* stazione balneare
bath'ing suit' *s* costume *m* da bagno
bath'ing trunks' *spl* mutandine *fpl* da bagno
bath'robe' *s* accappatoio
bath'room' *s* stanza da bagno
bath' salts' *spl* sali *mpl* da bagno
bath'tub' *s* bagno, vasca da bagno
baton [bæ'tan] or ['bætən] *s* bastone *m*; (mus) bacchetta
battalion [bə'tæljən] *s* battaglione *m*
batten ['bætən] *tr* assicella; piccola traversa; (naut) bietta || *tr*—**to batten down the hatches** chiudere ermeticamente i boccaporti
batter ['bætər] *s* pasta, farina pastosa; (baseball) battitore *m* || *tr* battere, tempestare di colpi; (*to wear out*) logorare
bat'tering ram' *s* ariete *m*
batter•y ['bætəri] *s* (**-ies**) (*primary cell*) pila; (*secondary cell*) accumulatore *m*; (*group of batteries*) batteria; (law) assalto; (mil & mus) batteria
battle ['bætəl] *s* battaglia; **to do battle** dar battaglia || *tr* combattere contro || *intr* combattere
bat'tle cry' *s* grido di guerra
battledore ['bætəl,dor] *s* racchetta; **battledore and shuttlecock** gioco del volano
bat'tle•field' *s* campo di battaglia
bat'tle•front' *s* fronte *m* di combattimento
battlement ['bætəlmənt] *s* merlatura
bat'tle roy'al *s* baruffa generale, zuffa generale
bat'tle•ship' *s* corazzata
battue [bæ'tu] or [bæ'tju] *s* (hunt) battuta

bat·ty ['bæti] *adj* **(-tier; -tiest)** (slang) pazzo, eccentrico
bauble ['bɔbəl] *s* bazzecola, gingillo
Bavaria [bə'verɪ·ə] *s* la Baviera
Bavarian [bə'verɪ·ən] *adj & s* bavarese *mf*
bawd [bɔd] *s* ruffiano; ruffiana
bawd·y ['bɔdi] *adj* **(-ier; -iest)** indecente, osceno
bawd'y·house' *s* casa di malaffare
bawl [bɔl] *s* grido; (coll) pianto || *tr*— **to bawl out** (slang) fare una ramanzina a || *intr* strillare; (coll) piangere
bay [be] *adj* baio || *s* baia; vano, alcova; (*recess in wall*) apertura nel muro; finestra sporgente; (*of dog*) latrato; cavallo baio; (bot) lauro; **at bay** in una posizione disperata || *intr* latrare
bayonet ['be·ənɪt] *s* baionetta || *tr* dare baionettate a || *intr* dare baionettate
bay' win'dow *s* finestra sporgente; (slang) pancia
bazooka [bə'zukə] *s* bazooka *m*
be [bi] *v* (*pres* **am** [æm], **is** [ɪz], **are** [ɑr]; *pret* **was** [wɑz] or [wʌz], **were** [wʌr]; *pp* **been** [bɪn]) *intr* essere; fare, e.g., **to be a mason** fare il muratore; fare, e.g., **3 times 3 is 9** tre volte tre fa nove; **be as it may be** comunque sia; **here is** or **here are** ecco; **there are** ci sono; **there is** c'è; **to be** futuro, e.g., **my wife to be** la mia futura sposa; **to be ashamed** aver vergogna; **to be cold** aver freddo; **to be hot** aver caldo; **to be hungry** aver fame; **to be in** stare a casa; **to be in a hurry** aver fretta; **to be in with** (coll) essere amico intimo di; **to be off** andarsene; **to be out** essere fuori; **to be out of** (coll) non aver più; **to be right** aver ragione; **to be sleepy** aver sonno; **to be thirsty** avere sete; **to be up** essere alzato; **to be up to** essere all'altezza di; toccare, e.g., **it's up to you** tocca a Lei; **to be warm** avere caldo; **to be wrong** avere torto; sbagliarsi; **to be . . . years old** avere . . . anni || *aux* stare, e.g., **to be waiting** stare aspettando; essere, e.g., **the murder has been committed** l'omicidio è stato commesso; dovere, e.g., **he is to clean the stables tomorrow** domani deve pulire la stalla || *impers* essere, e.g., **it is necessary** è necessario; fare, e.g., **it is cold** fa freddo; **it is hot** fa caldo
beach [bitʃ] *s* spiaggia || *tr* (*a boat*) arenare || *intr* arenarsi
beach'comb' *intr* raccogliere relitti sulla spiaggia
beach'comb'er *s* girellone *m* di spiaggia
beach'head' *s* testa di sbarco
beach' robe' *s* accappatoio
beach' shoe' *s* sandalo da spiaggia
beach' umbrel'la *s* ombrellone *m* da spiaggia
beacon ['bikən] *s* faro || *tr* rischiarare; fare da guida a || *intr* brillare
bead [bid] *s* perlina; grano, chicco; (*drop*) goccia; **beads** (*in a necklace or rosary*) conterie *fpl;* **to count one's beads** recitare il rosario
beagle ['bigəl] *s* segugio, bracco
beak [bik] *s* becco; promontorio
beam [bim] *s* trave *f;* (*of balance*) braccio; (*of light*) raggio; (*ship's breadth*) larghezza; (*smile*) sorriso; (*radio signal*) fascio direttore; (*course indicated by radio beam*) aerovia; (naut) traverso || *tr* (*a radio signal*) dirigere; (*e.g., light*) irraggiare || *intr* raggiare
bean [bin] *s* fagiolo; (*of coffee*) chicco; (slang) testa
beaner·y ['binəri] *s* **(-ies)** (slang) gargotta, taverna di secondo ordine
bean'pole' *s* puntello per i fagioli; (coll) palo del telegrafo
bear [ber] *s* orso; (astr) orsa; (com) ribassista *m,* giocatore *m* al ribasso || *v* (*pret* **bore** [bor]; *pp* **borne** [born]) *tr* (*to carry*) portare; (*to give birth to*) partorire; (*to sustain*) sostenere; (*to withstand*) sopportare; (*a grudge*) serbare; (*in mind*) tenere; (*interest*) produrre; (*to pay*) pagare; **to bear the date** aver la data; **to bear out** confermare; **to bear witness** testimoniare || *intr* (*to be productive*) fruttificare; (*to move*) dirigersi; (*to be oppressive*) fare pressione; **to bear down on** fare pressione su; avvicinarsi a; **to bear up** resistere; **to bear with** tollerare
bearable ['berəbəl] *adj* tollerabile
beard [bɪrd] *s* barba; (*e.g., in wheat*) arista
bearded *adj* barbuto
beardless ['bɪrdlɪs] *adj* imberbe
bearer ['berər] *s* portatore *m*
bearing ['berɪŋ] *s* portamento; relazione; importanza; (mach) bronzina, cuscinetto; **bearings** orientamento; **to lose one's bearings** perdere la bussola; perdere l'orientamento
bearish ['berɪʃ] *adj* (*like a bear*) orsino; (*e.g., prices*) in ribasso; (*market*) al ribasso; (*speculator*) ribassista
bear'skin' *s* pelle *f* dell'orso; (mil) colbacco
beast [bist] *s* bestia
beast·ly ['bistli] *adj* **(-lier; -liest)** bestiale || *adv* (coll) malissimo
beast' of bur'den *s* bestia da soma
beast' of prey' *s* animale *m* da rapina
beat [bit] *s* (*of heart*) battito; (*of policeman*) ronda; (*stroke*) colpo; (*habitual route*) cammino battuto; (mus) tempo; (phys) battimento || *v* (*pret* **beat;** *pp* **beat** or **beaten**) *tr* battere; percuotere; (*eggs*) frullare; (*to whip*) frustare; (coll) confondere; **beat it!** (slang) vattene!; **to beat a retreat** battere in ritirata; **to beat back** respingere; **to beat down** sopprimere; **to beat off** respingere; **to beat up** (*eggs*) frullare; (*people*) dargliene a || *intr* battere; pulsare; **to beat around the bush** (coll) menare il can per l'aia
beat'en path' ['bitən] *s* cammino battuto
beater ['bitər] *s* frullino
beati·fy [bɪ'ætɪ ,faɪ] *v* (*pret & pp* **-fied**) *tr* beatificare

beating ['bitɪŋ] *s* battitura; (*whipping*) frustatura; (*throbbing*) pulsazione, battito; (*defeat*) sconfitta
beau [bo] *s* (**beaus** or **beaux** [boz]) (*dandy*) bellimbusto; (*girl's sweetheart*) spasimante *m*
beautician [bju'tɪʃən] *s* estetista *mf*
beautiful ['bjutɪfəl] *adj* bello
beauti•fy ['bjutɪ,faɪ] *v* (*pret & pp* **-fied**) *tr* abbellire
beau•ty ['bjuti] *s* (**-ties**) bellezza
beau'ty con'test *s* concorso di bellezza
beau'ty par'lor *s* istituto di bellezza
beau'ty sleep' *s* primo sonno
beau'ty spot' *s* neo; posto pittoresco
beaver ['bivər] *s* castoro; pelle *f* di castoro; cappello a cilindro
because [bɪ'kɔz] *conj* perchè; **because of** a causa di
beck [bɛk] *s* gesto; **at the beck and call of** agli ordini di
beckon ['bɛkən] *s* gesto || *tr* fare gesto a || *intr* fare gesto
becloud [bɪ'klaʊd] *tr* annebbiare; oscurare
be•come [bɪ'kʌm] *v* (*pret* **-came;** *pp* **-come**) *tr* convenire a; stare bene a, e.g., **this hat becomes you** questo cappello Le sta bene || *intr* diventare; farsi; convertirsi, e.g., **water became wine** l'acqua si convertì in vino; succedere, e.g., **what became of my coat?** che è successo del mio pastrano?; essere, e.g., **what will become of me?** che sarà di me?; **to become accustomed** abituarsi; **to become angry** entrare in collera; **to become crazy** impazzire; **to become ill** ammalarsi
becoming [bɪ'kʌmɪŋ] *adj* conveniente; appropriato; acconcio; **this is very becoming to you** questo Le sta molto bene
bed [bɛd] *s* letto; (*layer*) strato; giacimento; **to go to bed** andare a letto; **to take to one's bed** mettersi a letto
bed' and board' *s* vitto e alloggio; pensione completa
bed'bug' *s* cimice *f*
bed'clothes' *spl* lenzuola *fpl* e coperte *fpl*, biancheria da letto
bed'cov'er *s* coperta da letto
bedding ['bɛdɪŋ] *s* lenzuola *fpl* e coperte *fpl;* (*litter*) lettiera; (*foundation*) fondamenta *fpl*
bedeck [bɪ'dɛk] *tr* ornare, adornare
bedev•il [bɪ'devɪl] *v* (*pret & pp* **-iled** or **-illed;** *ger* **-iling** or **-illing**) *tr* tormentare diabolicamente; confondere
bed'fast' *adj* confinato a letto
bed'fel'low *s* compagno di letto; compagno di stanza; compagno
bedlam ['bɛdləm] *s* manicomio; pandemonio
bed' lin'en *s* biancheria da letto
bed'pan' *s* padella
bedridden ['bed,rɪdən] *adj* degente a letto
bed'room' *s* stanza da letto, camera da letto
bed'room slip'per *s* babbuccia, pantofola
bed'side' *s* capezzale *m*
bed'side man'ner *s* maniera di fare coi pazienti
bed'sore' *s* piaga da decubito
bed'spread' *s* coperta da letto
bed'spring' *s* rete *f* del letto; molla del letto
bed'stead' *s* fusto del letto
bed'tick' *s* traliccio
bed'time' *s* ora di coricarsi
bed'warm'er *s* scaldaletto
bee [bi] *s* ape *f*
beech [bitʃ] *s* faggio
beech'nut' *s* faggiola
beef [bif] *s* bue *m*, manzo; carne *f* di manzo; (coll) forza; (slang) lamentela || *tr*—**to beef up** (coll) rinforzare || *intr* (slang) lamentarsi
beef' cat'tle *s* manzi *mpl* da carne
beef'steak' *s* bistecca
beef' stew' *s* stufato di manzo
bee'hive' *s* alveare *m*
bee'keep'er *s* apicoltore *m*
bee'line' *s*—**to make a beeline for** (coll) andare direttamente verso
beer [bɪr] *s* birra
beer' saloon' *s* birreria
beeswax ['biz,wæks] *s* cera d'api
beet [bit] *s* barbabietola
beetle ['bitəl] *adj* sporgente, folto || *s* scarafaggio
bee'tle-browed' *adj* dalle sopracciglia folte
beet' su'gar *s* zucchero di barbabietola
be•fall [bɪ'fɔl] *v* (*pret* **-fell** ['fel]; *pp* **-fallen** ['fɔlən]) *tr* succedere a || *intr* succedere
befitting [bɪ'fɪtɪŋ] *adj* appropriato
before [bɪ'for] *adv* prima, prima d'ora || *prep* (*in time*) prima di; (*in place*) dinnanzi a, davanti a; **before Christ** avanti Cristo || *conj* prima che
before'hand' *adv* in anticipo; precedentemente
befriend [bɪ'frend] *tr* diventare amico di, proteggere, favorire; aiutare
befuddle [bɪ'fʌdəl] *tr* confondere
beg [bɛg] *v* (*pret & pp* **begged;** *ger* **begging**) *tr* chiedere; implorare; (*alms*) mendicare; **I beg your pardon** Le chiedo scusa; **to beg s.o. for s.th** chiedere qlco a qlcu || *intr* chiedere la carità; **to beg for** sollecitare; **to beg off** scusarsi; **to go begging** rimanere invenduto
be•get [bɪ'get] *v* (*pret* **-got** ['gɑt]; *pp* **-gotten** or **-got;** *ger* **-getting**) *tr* generare
beggar ['bɛgər] *s* accattone *m*, mendicante *m*
be•gin [bɪ'gɪn] *v* (*pret* **-gan** ['gæn]; *pp* **-gun** ['gʌn]; *ger* **-ginning**) *tr & intr* cominciare, iniziare; **beginning with** a partire da; **to begin with** per cominciare
beginner [bɪ'gɪnər] *s* principiante *mf*
beginning [bɪ'gɪnɪŋ] *s* inizio, origine *f*, principio, esordio
begrudge [bɪ'grʌdʒ] *tr* invidiare; concedere con riluttanza
beguile [bɪ'gaɪl] *tr* ingannare; sedurre; (*to delight*) divertire
behalf [bɪ'hæf] or [bɪ'hɑf] *s*—**on behalf of** nell'interesse di; a nome di

behave [bɪˈhev] *intr* comportarsi; comportarsi bene
behavior [bɪˈhevjər] *s* comportamento, condotta; funzionamento
behead [bɪˈhed] *tr* decapitare
behest [bɪˈhest] *s* ordine *m*, comando
behind [bɪˈhaɪnd] *s* didietro; (slang) sedere *m* || *adv* dietro; (*in arrears*) in arretrato; **from behind** dal didietro || *prep* dietro a, dietro di; **behind time** in ritardo
be•hold [bɪˈhold] *v* (*pret & pp* **-held** [ˈhɛld]) *tr* contemplare; ammirare || *interj* guarda!
behoove [bɪˈhuv] *impers*—**it behooves him to** gli conviene di
being [ˈbi•ɪŋ] *adj* esistente; **for the time being** per ora || *s* essere *m*, ente *m*
belabor [bɪˈlebər] *tr* attaccare; (fig) ribattere, confutare; (fig) insistere su
belated [bɪˈletɪd] *adj* tardivo
belch [bɛltʃ] *s* rutto || *tr* eruttare, vomitare || *intr* ruttare
beleaguer [bɪˈligər] *tr* assediare
bel•fry [ˈbɛlfri] *s* (**-fries**) (*tower*) campanile *m;* (*site of bell*) cella campanaria; (slang) testa
Belgian [ˈbɛldʒən] *adj & s* belga *mf*
Belgium [ˈbɛldʒəm] *s* il Belgio
be•lie [bɪˈlaɪ] *v* (*pret & pp* **-lied** [ˈlaɪd]; *ger* **-lying** [ˈlaɪ•ɪŋ]) *tr* (*to misrepresent*) tradire; (*to prove false*) smentire
belief [bɪˈlif] *s* fede *f*, credenza
believable [bɪˈlivəbəl] *adj* credibile
believe [bɪˈliv] *tr* credere || *intr* credere, aver fede; **to believe in** credere in
believer [bɪˈlivər] *s* credente *mf*
belittle [bɪˈlɪtəl] *tr* menomare
bell [bɛl] *s* campana; (*for a door*) campanello; (*sound*) rintocco; (*on cattle*) campanaccio; (*of deer*) bramito || *intr* bramire
belladonna [ˌbɛləˈdɑnə] *s* belladonna
bell'-bot'tom *adj* a campana
bell'boy' *s* cameriere *m*, ragazzo
belle [bɛl] *s* bella
belles-lettres [ˌbɛlˈlɛtrə] *spl* belle lettere
bell' glass' *s* campana di vetro
bell'hop' *s* cameriere *m*, ragazzo
bellicose [ˈbɛlɪˌkos] *adj* bellicoso
belligerent [bəˈlɪdʒərənt] *adj & s* belligerante *m*
bellow [ˈbɛlo] *s* muggito; **bellows** mantice *m;* (*of camera*) soffietto || *tr* gridare || *intr* muggire
bell' ring'er [ˈrɪŋər] *s* campanaro
bellwether [ˈbɛlˌwɛðər] *s* pecora guida
bel•ly [ˈbɛli] *s* (**-lies**) ventre *m*, pancia || *v* (*pret & pp* **-lied**) *intr* far pancia
bel'ly•ache' *s* (coll) mal *m* di pancia || *intr* (slang) lamentarsi
bel'ly•but'ton *s* (coll) ombelico
bel'ly dance' *s* (coll) danza del ventre
bel'ly flop' *s* panciata
bellyful [ˈbɛlɪˌfʊl] *s*—**to have a bellyful** (slang) averne fino agli occhi
bel'ly•land' *intr* (aer) atterrare sul ventre
belong [bɪˈlɔŋ] or [bɪˈlɑŋ] *intr* appartenere; stare bene, e.g., **this chair belongs in this room** questa sedia sta bene in questa stanza
belongings [bɪˈlɔŋɪŋz] or [bɪˈlɑŋɪŋz] *spl* effetti *mpl* personali
beloved [bɪˈlʌvɪd] or [bɪˈlʌvd] *adj & s* diletto, amato
below [bɪˈlo] *adv* sotto; più sotto; sotto zero, e.g., **ten below** dieci gradi sotto zero || *prep* sotto, sotto di
belt [bɛlt] *s* cintura, cinghia; (mach) nastro; (mil) cinturone *m;* (geog) fascia, zona; **to tighten one's belt** far cintura || *tr* cingere; (slang) staffilare
belt'ed tire' *s* copertone cinturato
belt' line' *s* linea di circonvallazione
beltway [ˈbɛltˌwe] *s* raccordo anulare
bemoan [bɪˈmon] *tr* lamentare; compiangere
bench [bɛntʃ] *s* banco, panca; tribunale *m;* (mach) banco di prova; **to be on the bench** (law) essere giudice
bend [bɛnd] *s* curva; (*e.g., of pipe*) gomito, angolo || *v* (*pret & pp* **bent** [bɛnt]) *tr* curvare; piegare; far piegare || *intr* deviare; piegare, piegarsi; **to bend over** inchinarsi
beneath [bɪˈniθ] *adv* sotto; più sotto || *prep* sotto, sotto di
benediction [ˌbɛnɪˈdɪkʃən] *s* benedizione
benefactor [ˈbɛnɪˌfæktər] or [ˌbɛnɪˈfæktər] *s* benefattore *m*
benefactress [ˈbɛnɪˌfæktrɪs] or [ˌbɛnɪˈfæktrɪs] *s* benefattrice *f*
beneficence [bɪˈnɛfɪsəns] *s* beneficenza
beneficent [bɪˈnɛfɪsənt] *adj* caritatevole; benefico
beneficial [ˌbɛnɪˈfɪʃəl] *adj* benefico
beneficiar•y [ˌbɛnɪˈfɪʃɪˌɛri] *s* (**-ies**) beneficiario
benefit [ˈbɛnɪfɪt] *s* beneficio; festa di beneficenza; **for the benefit of** a beneficio di || *tr & intr* beneficiare
ben'efit perfor'mance *s* beneficiata
benevolence [bɪˈnɛvələns] *s* benevolenza; carità *f*
benevolent [bɪˈnɛvələnt] *adj* benevolo; (*institution*) benefico
benign [bɪˈnaɪn] *adj* benigno
bent [bɛnt] *adj* curvo; **bent on** deciso a || *s* curva; tendenza, propensità *f*
Benzedrine [ˈbɛnzɪˌdrin] (trademark) *s* benzedrina
benzene [ˈbɛnzin] *s* benzolo
benzine [bɛnˈzin] *s* benzina
bequeath [bɪˈkwiθ] or [bɪˈkwið] *tr* legare, lasciare in eredità
bequest [bɪˈkwɛst] *s* legato, lascito
berate [bɪˈret] *tr* redarguire
be•reave [bɪˈriv] *v* (*pret & pp* **-reaved** or **-reft** [ˈrɛft]) *tr* spogliare
bereavement [bɪˈrivmənt] *s* lutto, perdita
beret [bəˈre] or [ˈbere] *s* berretto
Berlin [bərˈlɪn] *adj* berlinese || *s* Berlino
Berliner [bərˈlɪnər] *s* berlinese *mf*
Bermuda [bərˈmjudə] *s* le Bermude
ber•ry [ˈbɛri] *s* (**-ries**) (*dry seed*) chicco; (*fruit*) bacca

berserk [bʌr'sʌrk] *adj* infuriato || *adv* —**to go berserk** impazzire
berth [bʌrθ] *s* (*for a ship*) posto di ormeggio; (*bed*) cuccetta; (coll) posto
beryllium [bə'rɪlɪ·əm] *s* berillio
be·seech [bɪ'sitʃ] *v* (*pret & pp* **-sought** ['sɔt] or **-seeched**) *tr* supplicare
be·set [bɪ'sɛt] *v* (*pret & pp* **-set;** *ger* **-setting**) *tr* assediare, circondare; (*e.g., with problems*) assillare
beside [bɪ'saɪd] *adv* oltre, inoltre || *prep* vicino a; in confronto di; oltre a; **beside oneself** fuori di sé; **beside the point** fuori del seminato
besides [bɪ'saɪdz] *adv* inoltre; d'altronde || *prep* oltre a
besiege [bɪ'sidʒ] *tr* assediare; (*with questions*) bombardare
besmear [bɪ'smɪr] *tr* imbrattare, sgorbiare; sporcare
besmirch [bɪ'smʌrtʃ] *tr* insudiciare
bespatter [bɪ'spætər] *tr* inzaccherare
be·speak [bɪ'spik] *v* (**-spoke** ['spok]; **-spoken**) *tr* chiedere anticipatamente a; (*to show*) dimostrare
best [best] *adj super* (il) migliore; ottimo || *s* meglio; **at best** nella miglior delle ipotesi; **to do one's best** fare del proprio meglio; **to get the best of** avere la meglio di; **to make the best of** adattarsi a || *adv super* meglio; **had best,** e.g., **I had best** dovrei || *tr* battere; riuscire superiore a
bestial ['bestjəl] or ['bestʃəl] *adj* bestiale
be·stir [bɪ'stʌr] *v* (*pret & pp* **-stirred;** *ger* **-stirring**) *tr* eccitare; **to bestir oneself** darsi da fare
best' man' *s* testimone *m* di nozze
bestow [bɪ'sto] *tr* accordare; conferire
best' sell'er *s* best-seller *m*
bet [bɛt] *s* scommessa || *v* (*pret & pp* **bet** or **betted;** *ger* **betting**) *tr & intr* scommettere; **I bet** ci scommetto; **you bet** (coll) evidentemente
be·take [bɪ'tek] *v* (*pret* **-took** ['tʊk]; *pp* **-taken**) *tr*—**to betake oneself** andare, dirigersi
be·think [bɪ'θɪŋk] *v* (*pret & pp* **-thought** ['θɔt]) *tr* **to bethink oneself** pensare; ricordarsi
Bethlehem ['bɛθlɪ·əm] or ['bɛθlɪ,hɛm] *s* Betlemme *f*
betide [bɪ'taɪd] *tr* accadere a || *intr* accadere
betoken [bɪ'tokən] *tr* indicare, presagire
betray [bɪ'tre] *tr* tradire, ingannare; (*to reveal*) rivelare
betroth [bɪ'troð] or [bɪ'trɔθ] *tr* promettere in matrimonio a
betrothal [bɪ'troðəl] or [bɪ'trɔθəl] *s* fidanzamento
betrothed [bɪ'troðd] or [bɪ'trɔθt] *adj* fidanzato || *s* promesso sposo, fidanzato
better ['bɛtər] *adj comp* migliore; **to grow better** migliorare || *s*—**betters** superiori *mpl;* ottimati *mpl;* **to get the better of** avere la meglio di || *adv* meglio; **had better** dovere, e.g., **I had better** dovrei; **to be better off** stare meglio; **to think better of** riconsiderare; **you ought to know better** dovrebbe vergognarsi || *tr* sorpassare; migliorare; **to better oneself** migliorare la propria situazione
bet'ter half' *s* metà *f*
betterment ['bɛtərmənt] *s* miglioramento
bettor ['bɛtər] *s* scommettitore *m*
between [bɪ'twin] *adv* in mezzo; **in between** in mezzo, fra i piedi || *prep* fra, tra
between'-decks' *s* interponte *m*
bev·el ['bɛvəl] *s* (*instrument*) falsa squadra; (*sloping part*) augnatura || *v* (*pret & pp* **-eled** or **-elled;** *ger* **-eling** or **-elling**) *tr* augnare
beverage ['bɛvərɪdʒ] *s* bevanda
bev·y ['bɛvi] *s* (**-ies**) (*of women*) gruppo; (*of birds*) stormo
bewail [bɪ'wel] *tr* lamentare
beware [bɪ'wɛr] *tr* fare attenzione **a,** guardarsi da || *intr* fare attenzione, guardarsi
bewilder [bɪ'wɪldər] *tr* lasciar perplesso, confondere, disorientare
bewilderment [bɪ'wɪldərmənt] *s* perplessità *f,* disorientamento
bewitch [bɪ'wɪtʃ] *tr* stregare
beyond [bɪ'jɑnd] *s*—**the beyond** l'aldilà *m* || *adv* più lontano || *prep* al di là di; oltre a; più tardi di; **beyond a doubt** fuori dubbio; **beyond repair** irreparabile
bias ['baɪ·əs] *s* linea diagonale; pregiudizio; **on the bias** diagonalmente || *tr* prevenire
bib [bɪb] *s* bavaglino
Bible ['baɪbəl] *s* Bibbia
Biblical ['bɪblɪkəl] *adj* biblico
bibliogra·phy [,bɪblɪ'ɑgrəfi] *s* (**-phies**) bibliografia
bibliophile ['bɪblɪ·ə,faɪl] *s* bibliofilo
bicarbonate [baɪ'kɑrbə,net] *s* bicarbonato
biceps ['baɪsɛps] *s* bicipite *m*
bicker ['bɪkər] *s* bisticcio, disputa || *intr* bisticciare, disputare
bicycle ['baɪsɪkəl] *s* bicicletta
bid [bɪd] *s* offerta; (cards) dichiarazione; (coll) invito || *v* (*pret* **bade** [bæd] or **bid;** *pp* **bidden** ['bɪdən] or **bid;** *ger* **bidding**) *tr & intr* offrire; comandare; (cards) dichiarare
bidder ['bɪdər] *s* offerente *mf;* (cards) dichiarante *mf;* **the highest bidder** il miglior offerente
bidding ['bɪdɪŋ] *s* ordine *m;* offerte *fpl;* (cards) dichiarazione
bide [baɪd] *tr*—**to bide one's time** attendere l'ora propizia
biennial [baɪ'ɛnɪ·əl] *adj* biennale
bier [bɪr] *s* catafalco
bifocal [baɪ'fokəl] *adj* bifocale || **bifocals** *spl* occhiali *mpl* bifocali
big [bɪg] *adj* (**bigger; biggest**) grande; (coll) importante; (coll) stravagante; **big with child** incinta || *adv*—**to talk big** (coll) parlare con iattanza
bigamist ['bɪgəmɪst] *s* bigamo
bigamous ['bɪgəməs] *adj* bigamo

big-bellied ['bɪg ,belid] *adj* panciuto
Big' Dip'per *s* Gran Carro
big' game' *s* caccia grossa
big-hearted ['bɪg ,hartɪd] *adj* magnanimo, generoso
big' mouth' *s* (slang) sbraitone *m*
bigot ['bɪgət] *s* bigotto, bacchettone *m*
bigoted ['bɪgətɪd] *adj* (*in religion*) bigotto; intransigente
bigot·ry ['bɪgətri] *s* (**-ries**) bigottismo; intransigenza
big' shot' *s* (slang) pezzo grosso, (un) qualcuno
big' slam' *s* (bridge) grande slam *m*
big'-time op'erator *s* (slang) grosso trafficante
big' toe' *s* alluce *m*
big' wheel' *s* (slang) pezzo grosso
bike [baɪk] *s* (coll) bicicletta
bile [baɪl] *s* bile *f*
bilge [bɪldʒ] *s* sentina; (*of barrel*) ventre *m*
bilge'ways' *spl* parati *mpl*
bilingual [baɪ'lɪŋgwəl] *adj* bilingue
bilious ['bɪljəs] *adj* bilioso
bilk [bɪlk] *tr* defraudare
bill [bɪl] *s* (*of bird*) becco; (*statement of charges*) conto; (*e.g., for electricity*) bolletta; (*menu*) lista; (*money*) biglietto; (*proposed law*) disegno di legge; (*handbill*) annunzio; (law) atto; (theat) cartellone *m;* **to fill the bill** (coll) riempire i requisiti; **to foot the bill** (coll) pagare lo scotto || *tr* fare una lista di; mettere in conto a || *intr* (*said of doves*) beccuzzarsi; (*said of lovers*) baciucchiarsi
bill'board' *s* cartellone *m;* (rad, telv) titolo di testa
billet ['bɪlɪt] *s* (mil) alloggiamento; (mil) ordine *m* d'alloggiamento || *tr* (mil) alloggiare, accasermare
bill'fold' *s* portafoglio
bill'head' *s* intestazione di fattura
billiards ['bɪljərdz] *s* bigliardo
bil'ling clerk' *s* fatturista *mf*
billion ['bɪljən] *s* (U.S.A.) miliardo; (Brit) bilione *m*
bill' of exchange' *s* tratta
bill' of fare' *s* menu *m,* lista delle vivande
bill' of lad'ing ['ledɪŋ] *s* polizza di carico
bill' of rights' *s* dichiarazione dei diritti
bill' of sale' *s* atto di vendita
billow ['bɪlo] *s* ondata, cavallone *m*
bill'post'er *s* attacchino
bil·ly ['bɪli] *s* (**-lies**) manganello
bil'ly goat' *s* capro, caprone *m*
bimonthly [baɪ'mʌnθli] *adj* (*occurring every two months*) bimestrale; (*occurring twice a month*) bimensile
bin [bɪn] *s* cassone *m;* (*for bread*) madia; (*e.g., for coal*) deposito
binaural [baɪ'nɔrəl] *adj* biauricolare
bind [baɪnd] *v* (*pret & pp* **bound** [baʊnd]) *tr* legare; allacciare; (*to bandage*) fasciare; (*to constipate*) costipare; (*a book*) rilegare; (*to oblige*) obbligare; (mach) grippare
binder ['baɪndər] *s* rilegatore *m;* (*cover*) cartella
binder·y ['baɪndəri] *s* (**-ies**) rilegatoria
binding ['baɪndɪŋ] *adj* obbligatorio || *s* (*of book*) rilegatura; legatura; fasciatura
bind'ing post' *s* (elec) capocorda; (*e.g., of battery*) (elec) serrafilo
binge [bɪndʒ] *s*—**to go on a binge** (coll) far baldoria
bingo ['bɪngo] *s* tombola
binnacle ['bɪnəkəl] *s* abitacolo
binoculars [bɪ'nakjələrz] or [baɪ'nakjələrz] *spl* binocolo
biochemical [,baɪ·ə'kemɪkəl] *adj* biochimico
biochemist [,baɪ·ə'kemɪst] *s* biochimico
biochemistry [,baɪ·ə'kemɪstri] *s* biochimica
biodegradable [,baɪ·odɪ'gredəbəl] *adj* biodegradabile
biographer [baɪ'agrəfər] *s* biografo
biographic(al) [,baɪ·ə'græfɪk(əl)] *adj* biografico
biogra·phy [baɪ'agrəfi] *s* (**-phies**) biografia
biologist [baɪ'alədʒɪst] *s* biologo
biology [baɪ'alədʒi] *s* biologia
biophysics [,baɪ·ə'fɪzɪks] *s* biofisica
biop·sy ['baɪ ,apsi] *s* (**-sies**) biopsia
bipartisan [baɪ'partɪzən] *adj* (*system*) bipartitico; (*government*) bipartito
biped ['baɪped] *adj & s* bipede *m*
birch [bʌrtʃ] *s* betulla || *tr* scudisciare
bird [bʌrd] *s* uccello; **a bird in the hand is worth two in the bush** un uovo oggi vale meglio di una gallina domani; **birds of a feather** gente *f* della stessa risma; **to kill two birds with one stone** pigliare due piccioni con una fava
bird' cage' *s* gabbia
bird' call' *s* richiamo
birdie ['bʌrdi] *s* uccellino; (golf) giocata di un colpo sotto la media
bird'lime' *s* pania
bird' of pas'sage *s* uccello di passo
bird' of prey' *s* uccello da preda
bird'seed' *s* becchime *m*
bird's'-eye view' *s* vista a volo d'uccello
bird' shot' *s* pallini *mpl* da caccia
birth [bʌrθ] *s* nascita; **to give birth to** dare i natali a; mettere alla luce
birth' certif'icate *s* certificato di nascita
birth' control' *s* limitazione delle nascite
birth'day' *s* natalizio, compleanno; (*of an event*) anniversario
birth'mark' *s* voglia
birth'place' *s* patria; (*e.g., city*) luogo di nascita; **to be the birthplace of** dare i natali a
birth' rate' *s* natalità *f*
birth'right' *s* diritto acquisito sin dalla nascita
biscuit ['bɪskɪt] *s* panino soffice; (Brit) biscotto
bisect [baɪ'sekt] *tr* bisecare || *intr* (*said of roads*) incrociarsi
bisection [baɪ'sekʃən] *s* bisezione
bishop ['bɪʃəp] *s* vescovo; (chess) alfiere *m*
bishopric ['bɪʃəprɪk] *s* vescovado

bismuth ['bɪzməθ] *s* bismuto
bison ['baɪsən] or ['baɪzən] *s* bisonte *m*
bisulfate [baɪ'sʌlfet] *s* bisolfato
bisulfite [baɪ'sʌlfaɪt] *s* bisolfito
bit [bɪt] *s* (*of bridle*) morso; (*of key*) mappa; (*tool*) punta, trivella; (*small piece*) briciolo; **a bit** un po'; (coll) un momento; **a good bit** una buona quantità; **bit by bit** poco a poco; **to blow to bits** fare a pezzi; **to champ the bit** mordere il freno; **two bits** (slang) quarto di dollaro, cinque soldi
bitch [bɪtʃ] *s* cagna; (vulg) donnaccia || *intr* (slang) lamentarsi
bite [baɪt] *s* morso; (*mouthful*) boccone *m*; **to take a bite** fare uno spuntino; mangiare un boccone || *v* (*pret* **bit** [bɪt]; *pp* **bit** or **bitten** ['bɪtən]) *tr* mordere, addentare; pungere; (*the dust*) baciare || *intr* mordere; (*said of insects*) pungere; (*said of fish*) abboccare
biting ['baɪtɪŋ] *adj* mordace; pungente
bitter ['bɪtər] *adj* amaro; (*e.g., fight*) accanito; (*cold*) pungente || *s* amaro; **bitters** amaro
bit'ter end' *s*—**to the bitter end** fino alla fine; fino alla morte
bit'ter•en'der *s* (coll) intransigente *mf*
bitterness ['bɪtərnɪs] *s* amarezza
bit'ter•sweet' *adj* dolceamaro; (fig) agrodolce || *s* dulcamara
bitumen [bɪ'tjumən] or [bɪ'tumən] *s* bitume *m*
bivou•ac ['bɪvʊ,æk] or ['bɪvwæk] *s* bivacco || *v* (*pret & pp* **-acked**; *ger* **-acking**) *intr* bivaccare
biweekly [baɪ'wikli] *adj* bisettimanale; quindicinale || *adv* ogni due settimane
biyearly [baɪ'jɪrli] *adj* semestrale || *adv* semestralmente
bizarre [bɪ'zɑr] *adj* bizzarro
blab [blæb] *s* chiacchierone *m* || *v* (*pret & pp* **blabbed**; *ger* **blabbing**) *tr* rivelare || *intr* chiacchierare
black [blæk] *adj* nero; (*without light*) buio || *s* nero; **to wear black** vestire a lutto, vestire di nero || *intr*—**to black out** perdere i sensi
black'-and-blue' *adj* livido e pesto
black'-and-white' *adj* in bianco e nero
black'ball' *s* palla nera, voto contrario || *tr* dare la palla nera a
black'ber'ry *s* (**-ries**) mora
black'bird' *s* merlo
black'board' *s* lavagna, **tavola nera**
black'cap' *s* capinera
black'damp' *s* putizza
Black' Death' *s* peste bubbonica
blacken ['blækən] *tr* annerire; (*shoes*) lucidare; (*reputation*) sporcare
black' eye' *s* occhio pesto; (fig) cattiva reputazione
blackguard ['blægɑrd] *s* canaglia
black'head' *s* comedone *m*
blackish ['blækɪʃ] *adj* nerastro
black'jack' *s* randello; (cards) ventuno || *tr* randellare
black' mag'ic *s* magia nera
black'mail' *s* ricatto || *tr* ricattare
blackmailer ['blæk,melər] *s* ricattatore *m*
Black' Mari'a [mə'raɪ•ə] *s* (coll) furgone *m* cellulare
black' mar'ket *s* borsa nera
black' marketeer' [,mɑrkɪ'tɪr] *s* borsanerista *mf*
blackness ['blæknɪs] *s* nerezza
black'out' *s* oscuramento; (theat) spegnitura; (pathol) svenimento passeggero
black' sheep' *s* (fig) pecora nera
black'smith' *s* fabbro
black' tie' *s* cravatta da smoking; smoking *m*
bladder ['blædər] *s* vescica
blade [bled] *s* (*of a leaf*) pagina; (*of grass*) stelo, filo; (*of oar*) pala; (*of turbine*) paletta; (*of fan*) ventola; (*of knife*) lama; (coll) caposcarico
blame [blem] *s* colpa; **to be to blame for** aver la colpa di; **to put the blame on s.o. for s.th** attribuire a qlcu la colpa di qlco; **you are to blame** è colpa Sua || *tr* biasimare, incolpare
blameless ['blemlɪs] *adj* innocente, senza colpa
blanch [blæntʃ] or [blɑntʃ] *tr* bianchire || *intr* impallidire
bland [blænd] *adj* blando; (*weather*) mite
blandish ['blændɪʃ] *tr* blandire
blank [blæŋk] *adj* (*not written on*) in bianco; (*e.g., stare*) vuoto; (*utter*) completo || *s* (*printed form*) modulo; (*cartridge*) cartuccia a salve; (*of the mind*) lacuna; **to draw a blank** (coll) non avere alcun successo || *tr*—**to blank out** cancellare
blank' check' *s* assegno in bianco; (fig) carta bianca
blanket ['blæŋkɪt] *adj* generale, combinato || *s* coperta; (*of snow*) cappa || *tr* coprire con una coperta; oscurare
blank' verse' *s* verso sciolto
blare [bler] *s* squillo || *tr* proclamare; fare echeggiare || *intr* squillare; echeggiare
blaspheme [blæs'fim] *tr & intr* bestemmiare
blasphemous ['blæsfɪməs] *adj* bestemmiatore
blasphe•my ['blæsfɪmi] *s* (**-mies**) bestemmia
blast [blæst] or [blɑst] *s* (*of air*) raffica; (*of a horn*) squillo; (*blight*) rovina; scoppio, esplosione; **at full blast** a piena velocità || *tr* rovinare; fare scoppiare, far saltare || *intr* —**to blast off** (rok) lanciarsi
blast' fur'nace *s* altoforno
blast'off' *s* lancio di missile or di nave spaziale
blatant ['bletənt] *adj* (*noisy*) rumoroso; (*obtrusive*) palmare; (*flashy*) chiassoso
blaze [blez] *s* fiammata; splendore *m*; (*on a horse's head*) stella; **in a blaze** in fiamme || *tr* proclamare; **to blaze a**

trail marcare il cammino || *intr* divampare
bleach [blitʃ] *s* candeggio, candeggina || *tr* imbiancare, candeggiare
bleachers ['blitʃərz] *spl* posti *mpl* allo scoperto or di gradinata
bleak [blik] *adj* nudo, deserto; (*cold*) freddo; (*gloomy*) triste
blear•y ['blɪri] *adj* (**-ier; iest**) (*sight*) cisposo; confuso; offuscato
bleat [blit] *s* belato || *intr* belare
bleed [blid] *v* (*pret & pp* **bled** [blɛd]) *tr* (*to draw blood from*) salassare; (*a tree*) estrare linfa da; (coll) sfruttare || *intr* sanguinare; (*said of a tree*) dar linfa; **to bleed to death** morire dissanguato
blemish ['blɛmɪʃ] *s* difetto; macchia || *tr* danneggiare; macchiare
blend [blɛnd] *s* mescolanza, miscuglio; (*of gasoline*) miscela || *v* (*pret & pp* **blended** or **blent** [blɛnt]) *tr* mescolare, miscelare || *intr* mescolarsi, miscelarsi; armonizzare; fondersi
bless [blɛs] *tr* benedire; (*to endow*) dotare; (*to make happy*) allietare
blessed ['blɛsɪd] *adj* benedetto; beato; fortunato; dotato
bless'ed event' *s* lieto evento
blessing ['blɛsɪŋ] *s* benedizione
blight [blaɪt] *s* (*insect; disease*) piaga; rovina; (*fungus*) ruggine *f* || *tr* rovinare, guastare
blimp [blɪmp] *s* piccolo dirigibile
blind [blaɪnd] *adj* cieco; (slang) ubriaco || *s* persiana; tendina; (*decoy*) mascheratura; pretesto || *adv* alla cieca || *tr* accecare
blind' al'ley *s* vicolo cieco
blinder ['blaɪndər] *s* paraocchi *m*
blind' fly'ing *s* (aer) volo senza visibilità
blind'fold' *adj* bendato, cogli occhi bendati || *s* benda || *tr* bendare gli occhi a
blindly ['blaɪndli] *adv* alla cieca
blind' man' *s* cieco
blind'man's buff' *s* mosca cieca
blindness ['blaɪndnɪs] *s* cecità *f*
blind' spot' *s* (anat) punto cieco; (rad) zona di silenzio; (fig) debole *m*
blink [blɪŋk] *s* batter *m* di ciglio; (*glimpse*) occhiata; (*glimmer*) barlume *m;* **on the blink** (slang) fuori servizio || *tr*—**to blink one's eyes** batter il ciglio || *intr* occhieggiare; (*to wink*) ammiccare; (*to flash on and off*) lampeggiare; **to blink at** ignorare; far finta di non vedere
blinker ['blɪŋkər] *s* (*at a crossing*) luce *f* intermittente; (*on a horse*) paraocchi *m*
blip [blɪp] *s* guizzo sullo schermo radar
bliss [blɪs] *s* beatitudine *f,* felicità *f*
blissful ['blɪsfəl] *adj* beato, felice
blister ['blɪstər] *s* vescica, bolla || *tr* coprire di vesciche; (fig) bollare || *intr* coprirsi di vesciche
blithe [blaɪð] *adj* gaio, giocondo
blitzkrieg ['blɪts,krig] *s* guerra lampo
blizzard ['blɪzərd] *s* tormenta, ventoneve *m*
bloat [blot] *tr* gonfiare || *intr* gonfiarsi
blob [blɑb] *s* (*lump*) zolla; (*of liquid*) macchia
block [blɑk] *s* (*e.g., of wood*) blocco; (*for chopping*) ceppo; (*pulley*) puleggia; ostacolo; (*of houses*) isolato; (typ) cliché *m* || *tr* bloccare; (*a hat*) mettere in forma; **to block up** tappare
blockade [blɑ'ked] *s* blocco; **to run a blockade** forzare il blocco || *tr* bloccare
block' and tack'le *s* bozzello
block'bust'er *s* (coll) superbomba
block'head' *s* imbecille *mf*
block' let'ter *s* carattere *m* stampatello
block' sig'nal *s* (rr) segnale di blocco
blond [blɑnd] *adj & s* biondo
blonde [blɑnd] *s* bionda
blood [blʌd] *s* sangue *m;* **in cold blood** a sangue freddo; **to draw blood** ferire, fare sanguinare
blood' bank' *s* emoteca
bloodcurdling ['blʌd,kʌrdlɪŋ] *adj* orripilante
blood' do'nor *s* donatore *m* di sangue
blood'hound' *s* segugio
bloodless ['blʌdlɪs] *adj* esangue; (*e.g., revolution*) senza effusione di sangue
blood'mobile' [mo,bil] *s* autoemoteca
blood' poi'soning *s* avvelenamento del sangue
blood' pres'sure *s* pressione sanguigna
blood' rela'tion *s* consanguineo
blood'shed' *s* spargimento di sangue, carneficina
blood'shot' *adj* iniettato di sangue
blood'stained' *adj* macchiato di sangue
blood'stream' *s* circolazione sanguigna
blood'suck'er *s* sanguisuga
blood' test' *s* esame *m* del sangue
blood'thirst'y *adj* assetato di sangue
blood' transfu'sion *s* trasfusione di sangue
blood' type' *s* gruppo sanguigno
blood' ves'sel *s* vaso sanguigno
blood•y ['blʌdi] *adj* (**-ier; -iest**) sanguinoso; (*bloodthirsty*) avido di sangue || *v* (*pret & pp* **-ied**) *tr* macchiare di sangue
bloom [blum] *s* fiore *m;* (*state of having open buds*) sboccio; (*youthful glow*) incarnato || *intr* fiorire; sbocciare
bloomers ['blumərz] *spl* pantaloni *mpl* femminili larghi fermati sotto il ginocchio
blossom ['blɑsəm] *s* fiore *m;* sboccio || *intr* sbocciare
blot [blɑt] *s* macchia || *v* (*pret & pp* **blotted;** *ger* **blotting**) *tr* macchiare; (*with blotting paper*) asciugare; **to blot out** cancellare; oscurare || *intr* macchiarsi; (*to be absorbent*) essere assorbente; (*said of a pen*) fare macchie
blotch [blɑtʃ] *s* chiazza, macchia || *tr* chiazzare
blotter ['blɑtər] *s* carta asciugante, carta assorbente; (*book*) registro
blouse [blaʊs] *s* blusa
blow [blo] *s* colpo; (*blast*) folata; (*of*

horn) squillo; (*sudden reverse*) batosta; **at one blow** d'un sol colpo; **to come to blows** venire alle mani; **without striking a blow** senza colpo ferire || *v* (*pret* **blew** [blu]; *pp* **blown**) *tr* soffiare, soffiare su; (*an instrument*) suonare; (*one's nose*) soffiarsi; **to blow in** sfondare; **to blow one's brains out** bruciarsi le cervella; **to blow open** aprire completamente; **to blow out** (*e.g., a candle*) spegnere; (*a fuse*) fondere; **to blow up** (*e.g., a mine*) far brillare; (phot) ingrandire || *intr* soffiare; (*to pant*) ansimare; (*with an instrument*) suonare; (*to puff*) sbuffare; (slang) andarsene; **to blow hot and cold** cambiare d'opinione ogni cinque minuti; **to blow in** (coll) arrivare inaspettatamente; **to blow out** (*said, e.g., of a candle*) spegnersi; (*said of a fuse*) saltare, fondersi; (*said of a tire*) scoppiare; **to blow over** passare; **to blow up** saltar per aria; (*said of a storm*) scoppiare; (coll) perdere la pazienza, scoppiare d'ira

blow'out' *s* scoppio di un pneumatico

blow'pipe' *s* (*tube*) soffione *m;* (*peashooter*) cerbottana

blow'torch' *s* saldatrice *f* a benzina

blubber ['blʌbər] *s* grasso di balena || *intr* piangere, lamentarsi

bludgeon ['blʌdʒən] *s* randello || *tr* randellare

blue [blu] *adj* blu, azzurro; (*gloomy*) triste; (*e.g., laws*) puritanico || *s* blu *m,* azzurro; **out of the blue** inaspettatamente; **the blues** la malinconia; (mus) blues *m;* **to have the blues** essere giù di morale || *tr* tingere di azzurro; (*a metal*) brunire

blue'ber'ry *s* (**-ries**) mirtillo

blue'bird' *s* uccello azzurro

blue' blood' *s* sangue *m* blu

blue' cheese' *s* gorgonzola americano

blue' chip' *s* (fin) azione di prim'ordine

blue' jay' *s* ghiandaia azzurra

blue' moon' *s*—**once in a blue moon** ad ogni morte di papa

blue'-pen'cil *v* (*pret & pp* **-ciled** or **-cilled;** *ger* **-ciling** or **-cilling**) *tr* correggere col lapis blu

blue'print' *s* riproduzione cianografica; (*plan*) piano || *tr* riprodurre in cianografia; preparare dettagliatamente

blue'stock'ing *s* saccente *f,* sapientona

blue' streak' *s*—**like a blue streak** (coll) come un razzo

bluff [blʌf] *adj* scosceso; brusco, burbero || *s* promontorio scosceso; bluff *m;* bluffatore *m* || *intr* bluffare

bluing ['bluɪŋ] *s* turchinetto

bluish ['blu·ɪʃ] *adj* bluastro

blunder ['blʌndər] *s* errore *m* madornale || *intr* pigliare un granchio

blunt [blʌnt] *adj* ottuso; (*plain-spoken*) franco || *tr* rendere ottuso

bluntness ['blʌntnɪs] *s* ottusità *f;* franchezza

blur [blʌr] *s* macchia; offuscamento; confusione || *v* (*pret & pp* **blurred;** *ger* **blurring**) *tr* macchiare; (*the view*) offuscare

blurb [blʌrb] *s* annuncio pubblicitario

blurt [blʌrt] *tr*—**to blurt out** prorompere a dire, lasciarsi sfuggire

blush [blʌʃ] *s* rossore *m;* (*pinkish natural tinge*) incarnato || *intr* arrossire; **to blush at** vergognarsi di

bluster ['blʌstər] *s* frastuono; (fig) boria || *intr* (*said of the wind*) infuriare; fare il bravaccio

blustery ['blʌstəri] *adj* tempestuoso; violento; (*swaggering*) borioso

boar [bor] *s* verro; (*wild hog*) porco selvatico, cinghiale *m*

board [bord] *s* asse *m;* (*notice*) cartello; (*pasteboard*) cartone *m;* (*table*) tavola; (*meals*) vitto; (*group of administrators*) consiglio; (naut) bordo; **above board** franco; **in boards** rilegato; **on board** a bordo; (rr) in vettura; **to go by the board** andare in rovina; **to tread the boards** fare l'attore || *tr* chiudere con assi; (*to provide with meals*) dare pensione a, tenere a dozzina; (*a ship*) salire a bordo di; (*a train*) salire su; (naut) abbordare || *intr* essere a pensione

board' and lodg'ing *s* pensione completa

boarder ['bordər] *s* pensionante *mf*

board'ing house' *s* pensione di famiglia

board'ing school' *s* collegio di pensionanti

board' of direc'tors *s* consiglio d'amministrazione

board' of health' *s* ufficio d'igiene

board' of trade' *s* camera di commercio

board'walk' *s* passeggiata a mare

boast [bost] *s* millanteria, vanteria || *intr* vantarsi

boastful ['bostfəl] *adj* millantatore

boat [bot] *s* nave *f,* battello; (*small ship*) barca, imbarcazione; (*dish*) salsiera; **in the same boat** nella stessa situazione

boat' hook' *s* alighiero

boat'house' *s* capannone *m* per i canotti

boating ['botɪŋ] *s* escursione in barca

boat'man *s* (**-men**) barcaiolo

boat' race' *s* regata

boatswain ['bosən] or ['bot,swen] *s* nostromo

bob [bɑb] *s* (*plumb*) piombino; (*short haircut*) taglio alla bebè; coda mozza (di cavallo); (*jerky motion*) strattone *m;* (*on pendulum of clock*) lente *f;* (*on fishing line*) sughero || *v* (*pret & pp* **bobbed;** *ger* **bobbing**) *tr* tagliare alla bebè; far muovere a scatti || *intr* muoversi a scatti; fare mossa; **to bob up** apparire

bobbin ['bɑbɪn] *s* bobina

bob'by pin' ['bɑbi] *s* forcina

bob'by·socks' *spl* (coll) calzini *mpl* da ragazza

bobbysoxer ['bɑbɪ,sɑksər] *s* (coll) ragazzina

bobolink ['bɑbə,lɪŋk] *s* doliconice *m*

bob'sled' *s* guidoslitta

bode [bod] *tr & intr* presagire

bodice ['bɑdɪs] *s* giubbetto, copribusto

bodily ['badɪli] *adj* fisico, corporeo || *adv* fisicamente, corporeamente; di persona; in massa
bodkin ['badkɪn] *s* punteruolo; (*for lady's hair*) spillone *m*
bod•y ['badi] *s* (**-ies**) corpo; (*corpse*) cadavere *m;* (*of water*) massa; (*of people*) gruppo; (*of a liquid*) sostanza; (*of truck*) cassone *m;* (*of car*) carrozzeria; (*of tree*) tronco; (coll) persona; **in a body** in massa
bod'y•guard' *s* (*of a high official*) guardia del corpo; (*e.g., of a movie star*) guardaspalle *m*
bod'y suit' *s* calzamaglia
bog [bag] *s* pantano, palude *m* || (*pret & pp* **bogged;** *ger* **bogging**) *intr*—**to bog down** impelagarsi
bogey•man ['bogi ˌmæn] *s* (**-men** [mɛn]) babau *m*
bogus ['bogəs] *adj* (coll) falso, finto
Bohemian [bo'himɪ•ən] *adj* boemo; da bohémien || *s* boemo; (fig) bohémien *m*
boil [bɔɪl] *s* bollore *m,* ebollizione; (pathol) foruncolo; **to come to a boil** cominciare a bollire || *tr* bollire; **to boil down** condensare || *intr* bollire; **to boil away** evaporare completamente; **to boil down** condensarsi; **to boil over** andare per il fuoco
boiled' ham' *s* prosciutto cotto
boiler ['bɔɪlər] *s* caldaia; (*for cooking*) caldaio
boil'er•mak'er *s* calderaio
boiling ['bɔɪlɪŋ] *adj* bollente || *s* bollore *m,* ebollizione
boisterous ['bɔɪstərəs] *adj* (*storm*) violento; (*loud*) rumoroso
bold [bold] *adj* (*daring*) coraggioso; (*impudent*) sfacciato; (*steep*) scosceso; (*clear, sharp*) netto
bold'face' *s* (typ) neretto, grassetto
boldness ['boldnɪs] *s* coraggio, audacia; sfacciataggine *f,* impudenza
boll' wee'vil [bol] *s* antonomo del cotone
bologna [bə'lonə] or [bə'lonjə] *s* mortadella
Bolshevik ['balʃəvɪk] or ['bolʃəvɪk] *adj & mf* bolscevico
bolster ['bolstər] *s* cuscino; cuscinetto; (*support*) sostegno || *tr* sorreggere; **to bolster up** sostenere
bolt [bolt] *s* (*arrow*) freccia; (*of lightning*) fulmine *m;* (*sliding bar*) chiavistello; (*threaded rod*) bullone *m;* (*of paper or cloth*) pezza, rotolo || *adv*—**bolt upright** dritto come un fuso || *tr* (*to swallow hurriedly*) ingollare; (*to fasten, e.g., a door*) sprangare; (*to fasten, e.g., two metal parts*) bullonare; (*e.g., a political party*) abbandonare || *intr* (*said of people*) spiccare un salto; (*said of a horse*) prendere la mano; precipitarsi
bolt' from the blue' *s* fulmine *m* a ciel sereno
bomb [bam] *s* bomba; (*e.g., for spraying*) bombola || *tr* bombardare
bombard [bam'bard] *tr* bombardare; (*with questions*) bersagliare
bombardment [bam'bardmənt] *s* bombardamento
bombast ['bambæst] *s* ampollosità *f*
bombastic [bam'bæstɪk] *adj* ampolloso
bomb' cra'ter *s* cratere *m*
bomber ['bamər] *s* bombardiere *m*
bomb'proof' *adj* a prova di bomba
bomb'shell' *s* bomba; (fig) colpo di bomba, colpo di sorpresa
bomb' shel'ter *s* rifugio antiaereo
bomb'sight' *s* traguardo aereo
bona fide ['bonə ˌfaɪdə] *adj* sincero || *adv* in buona fede
bonanza [bə'nænzə] *s* (min) ricca vena; (coll) fortuna
bond [band] *s* legame *m,* vincolo; (*contractual obligation*) obbligazione; (*interest-bearing certificate*) buono, obbligazione; (*surety*) cauzione; **bonds** catene *fpl;* **in bond** sotto cauzione; (*said of goods*) in punto franco || *tr* unire, connettere
bondage ['bandɪdʒ] *s* schiavitù *f*
bond'ed ware'house *s* deposito in punto franco
bond'hold'er *s* obbligazionista *mf*
bonds'man *s* (**-men**) garante *m*
bone [bon] *s* osso; (*of fish*) spina; (*of whale*) stecca; **bones** ossa *fpl;* **to have a bone to pick with** avere un conto da regolare con; **to make no bones about** (coll) ammettere; (coll) parlare esplicitamente || *tr* disossare; cavare le spine a || *intr*—**to bone up on** (coll) ripassare
bone'head' *s* (coll) testa dura
boneless ['bonlɪs] *adj* senz'osso; (*fish*) senza spine
boner ['bonər] *s* (slang) errore *m* madornale
bonfire ['ban ˌfaɪr] *s* falò *m*
bonnet ['banɪt] *s* cappello da donna; (*of child*) berrettino
bonus ['bonəs] *s* gratifica; indennità *f;* (*to an outgoing employee*) buonuscita
bon•y ['boni] *adj* (**-ier; -iest**) (*having bones*) osseo; (*emaciated*) scarno; (*fish*) spinoso
boo [bu] *s* fischio, urlaccio || *tr & intr* fischiare, disapprovare
boo•by ['bubi] *s* (**-bies**) stupido
boo'by hatch' *s* (naut) portello; (slang) manicomio; (slang) prigione *f*
boo'by prize' *s* premio dato al peggior giocatore
boo'by trap' *s* (mil) trappola esplosiva; (fig) tranello
boogie-woogie ['bugi'wugi] *s* bughi-bughi *m*
book [buk] *s* libro; (*e.g., of matches*) pacchetto; (mus) libretto; (fig) regole *fpl;* **the Book** la Bibbia; **to be in one's book** essere nelle grazie di; **to bring s.o. to book** fare una ramanzina a || *tr* registrare; (*e.g., on a horse*) allibrare; (*e.g., a room*) prenotare; (*an actor*) scritturare
book'bind'er *s* rilegatore *m*
book'bind'er•y *s* (**-ies**) rilegatoria
book'bind'ing *s* rilegatura
book'case' *s* scaffale *m*
book' end' *s* reggilibri *m*

bookie ['buki] *s* (coll) allibratore *m*
booking ['bukɪŋ] *s* (*of a trip*) prenotazione; (*of an actor*) scrittura
book'ing clerk' *s* impiegato alla biglietteria
bookish ['bukɪʃ] *adj* studioso; libresco
book'keep'er *s* contabile *mf*
booklet ['buklɪt] *s* libretto; (*pamphlet*) opuscolo
book'keep'ing *s* contabilità *f*
book'mak'er *s* (*one who accepts bets*) allibratore *m*
book'mark' *s* segnalibro
bookmobile ['bukmo ,bil] *s* bibliobus *m*
book'plate' *s* ex libris *m*
book' review' *s* rassegna, recensione
book'sell'er *s* libraio
book'shelf' *s* (**-shelves**) scaffale *m*
book'stand' *s* (*rack*) scansia; (*stall*) edicola
book'store' *s* libreria
book'worm' *s* (zool) tarlo dei libri; (fig) topo da biblioteca
boom [bum] *s* (*of crane*) braccio; (*barrier*) barriera galleggiante; (*noise*) bum *m;* (fin) boom *m;* (naut) boma; (mov, telv) giraffa || *intr* rimbombare; essere in condizioni floride
boomerang ['bumə,ræŋ] *s* bumerang *m*
boom' town' *s* città *f* fungo
boon [bun] *s* fortuna, benedizione
boon' compan'ion *s* compagnone *m*
boor [bur] *s* bifolco, zotico
boorish ['burɪʃ] *adj* grossolano
boost [bust] *s* aumento; (coll) spinta || *tr* spingere in su; sostenere; (*prices*) alzare; parlare a favore di
booster ['bustər] *s* (*backer*) sostenitore *m;* propulsore *m* a razzo; (rok) propulsore *m* del primo stadio; (med) seconda iniezione
boot [but] *s* stivale *m;* (*kick*) calcio; (*patch*) (aut) pezza; **the boot is on the other foot** la situazione è rovesciata; **to be in the boots of** essere nella pelle di; **to boot** per di più; **to get the boot** (coll) essere messo sulla strada; **to lick the boots of** leccare i piedi a; **to wipe one's boots on** trattare come una pezza da piedi || *tr* dare un calcio a; **to boot out** (slang) buttar fuori
boot'black' *s* lustrascarpe *m*
booth [buθ] *s* (*stall*) banco da mercato; (*for telephoning, voting*) cabina
boot'jack' *s* tirastivali *m*
boot'leg' *adj* di contrabbando || *s* liquore *m* di contrabbando || *v* (*pret & pp* **-legged**; *ger* **-legging**) *tr* vendere di contrabbando || *intr* vendere alcol di contrabbando
bootlegger ['but ,legər] *s* contrabbandiere *m* di liquori
boot'lick'er [,lɪkər] *s* (coll) leccapiedi *mf*
boot'strap' *s* tirante *m* degli stivali
boo•ty ['buti] *s* (**-ties**) bottino
booze [buz] *s* (coll) bevanda alcolica || *intr* (coll) ubriacarsi
borax ['boræks] *s* borace *m*
border ['bɔrdər] *adj* confinario, confinante || *s* bordo, margine *m;* (*between two countries*) confine *m* || *tr* bordare; confinare con || *intr* confinare
bor'der clash' *s* incidente *m* ai confini
bor'der•line' *adj* incerto || *s* frontiera
bore [bor] *s* (*drill hole*) buco, foro; (*hollow part of gun*) anima; (*caliber*) calibro; (*dull person*) seccatore *m;* (*annoyance*) seccatura; (mach) alesaggio || *tr* bucare, forare; seccare; (mach) alesare
boredom ['bordəm] *s* noia, tedio
boring ['borɪŋ] *adj* noioso || *s* trivellazione
born [bɔrn] *adj* nato, partorito; **to be born** nascere; **to be born again** rinascere; **to be born with a silver spoon in one's mouth** nascere con la camicia
borough ['bʌro] *s* borgata, comune *m*
borrow ['bɑro] or ['bɔro] *tr* chiedere a or in prestito; prendere a or in prestito; ricevere a or in prestito; (*to adopt*) adottare; **to borrow trouble** preoccuparsi per nulla
borrower ['bɑro•ər] or ['bɔro•ər] *s* chi riceve a prestito; (law) comodatario, prestatario
borrowing ['bɑro•ɪŋ] or ['bɔro•ɪŋ] *s* prestito; prestito linguistico, forestierismo
bosom ['buzəm] *s* petto, seno; (*e.g., of the family*) grembo, seno; (*of shirt*) pettorina
bos'om friend' *s* amico del cuore
Bosporus ['bɑspərəs] *s* Bosforo
boss [bɔs] or [bɑs] *s* (coll) padrone *m;* (coll) direttore *m;* (coll) capintesta *m;* (coll) principale *m;* (archit) bugna, bozza || *tr* fare da padrone a || *intr* fare da padrone
boss•y ['bɔsi] or ['bɑsi] *adj* (**-ier; -iest**) autoritario
botanical [bə'tænɪkəl] *adj* botanico
botanist ['bɑtənɪst] *s* botanico
botany ['bɑtəni] *s* botanica
botch [bɑtʃ] *s* abborracciatura || *tr* abborracciare
both [boθ] *adj* entrambi i, tutti e due i || *pron* entrambi, tutti e due || *conj* del pari, al medesimo tempo; **both . . . and** tanto . . . quanto
bother ['bɑðər] *s* (*worry*) noia, seccatura; (*person*) seccatore *m* || *tr* dar noia a, seccare || *intr* preoccuparsi; **to bother about** or **with** occuparsi di; **to bother to** + *inf* molestarsi di + *inf*
bothersome ['bɑðərsəm] *adj* incomodo
bottle ['bɑtəl] *s* bottiglia, fiasco || *tr* imbottigliare; **to bottle up** imbottigliare
bot'tle cap' *s* tappo a corona
bot'tle•neck' *s* collo di bottiglia; (*of traffic*) congestione, imbottigliamento
bot'tle o'pener ['opənər] *s* apribottiglie *m*
bottom ['bɑtəm] *adj* basso; (*price, dollar*) ultimo; infimo || *s* fondo; (*of chair*) sedile *m;* base *f;* (*of bottle*) culo; (*of ship*) scafo; **at bottom** in realtà; **to begin at the bottom** comin-

ciare dalla gavetta; **to get at the bottom of** andare a fondo di; **to go to the bottom** andare a picco
bottomless ['bɑtəmlɪs] *adj* senza fondo
boudoir [bu'dwɑr] *s* gabinetto di toletta (da signora)
bough [baʊ] *s* ramo
bouillon ['bʊjɑn] *s* brodo schietto
boulder ['boldər] *s* masso, roccia
boulevard ['bʊlə,vɑrd] *s* corso
bounce [baʊns] *s* balzo; salto; elasticità *f;* (*of boat or plane*) piastrellamento; (fig) spirito; **to get the bounce** (slang) essere licenziato || *tr* far balzare; (slang) buttar fuori || *intr* rimbalzare; saltare; (aer, naut) piastrellare
bouncer ['baʊnsər] *s* (*in night club*) (slang) buttafuori *m*
bouncing ['baʊnsɪŋ] *adj* forte, vigoroso; grande, rumoroso
bound [baʊnd] *adj* legato; collegato; obbligato; (bb) rilegato; (coll) risoluto; **bound for** destinato a, diretto per; **bound up in** or **with** in strette relazioni con; assorto in || *s* salto; rimbalzo; limite *m;* **bounds** zona limitrofa; **out of bounds** fuori limiti; al di là delle convenienze || *tr* delimitare
bounda·ry ['baʊndəri] *s* (**-ries**) confine *m*, limite *m*
bound'ary stone' *s* pietra di confine
boundless ['baʊndlɪs] *adj* illimitato, sconfinato
bountiful ['baʊntɪfəl] *adj* generoso; abbondante
boun·ty ['baʊnti] *s* (**-ties**) dono generoso; generosità *f*, abbondanza; (*reward*) premio
bouquet [bu'ke] or [bo'ke] *s* mazzo, mazzolino; profumo, aroma *m*
bourgeois ['burʒwɑ] *adj & s* borghese *mf*
bourgeoisie [,burʒwɑ'zi] *s* borghesia
bout [baʊt] *s* lotta, contesa; (*of illness*) attacco
bow [baʊ] *s* inchino, riverenza; (naut) prua; **to take a bow** ricevere gli applausi || *tr* chinare, piegare || *intr* inchinarsi; sottomettersi; **to bow and scrape** fare riverenze || [bo] *s* (*weapon*) arco; (*knot*) nodo; (mus) archetto; (*stroke of bow*) (mus) arcata || *tr & intr* (mus) suonare con l'archetto
bowdlerize ['baʊdlə,raɪz] *tr* espurgare
bowel ['baʊ·əl] *s* budello; **bowels** viscere *fpl*
bow'el move'ment *s* evacuazione; **to have a bowel movement** andar di corpo
bower ['baʊ·ər] *s* pergolato
bowery ['baʊ·əri] *adj* frondoso
bowknot ['bo,nɑt] *s* nodo scorsoio
bowl [bol] *s* (*dish*) ciotola; (*cup*) tazza; (*of pipe*) fornello; (*basin*) catino; (*amphitheater*) arena; (*ball*) boccia; (*delivery of ball*) bocciata; **bowls** bocce *fpl* || *tr* bocciare; **to bowl down** or **over** abbattere || *intr* giocare alle bocce
bowlegged ['bo,lɛgd] or ['bo,lɛgɪd] *adj* con le gambe storte
bowler ['bolər] *s* giocatore *m* di bocce
bowling ['bolɪŋ] *s* bocce *fpl;* bowling *m*, birilli *mpl*
bowl'ing al'ley *s* pista per il bowling; bowling *m*
bowl'ing green' *s* campo di bocce erboso
bowshot ['bo,ʃɑt] *s* tiro d'arco
bowsprit ['baʊsprit] or ['bosprɪt] *s* (naut) bompresso
bow' tie' [bo] *s* cravatta a farfalla
bowwow ['baʊ,waʊ] *interj* bau bau!
box [bɑks] *s* scatola; cassa; (*for jury*) banco; (*for sentry*) garitta; (*on coach*) cassetta; (*in stable*) posta; (*slap*) ceffone *m;* (*with fist*) pugno; (bot) bosso; (theat) palco, barcaccia; (baseball) posto del battitore; (typ) riquadratura || *tr* mettere in scatola; (*to slap*) schiaffeggiare; (*to hit with fist*) fare a pugilato con; **to box in** or **up** rinchiudere || *intr* fare a pugni; combattere
box'car' *s* vagone *m* merci coperto
boxer ['bɑksər] *s* pugile *m*
box'hold'er *s* palchettista *mf*
boxing ['bɑksɪŋ] *s* pugilato
box'ing gloves' *spl* guantoni *mpl* da pugilato
box' of'fice *s* sportello, biglietteria; (theat) incasso; (theat) successo
box'-of'fice hit' *s* grande successo
box' pleat' *s* (*of skirt*) cannone *m*
box' seat' *s* posto in palco
box'wood' *s* bosso
boy [bɔɪ] *s* ragazzo, giovane *m* || *interj* accidempoli!
boycott ['bɔɪkɑt] *s* boicottaggio || *tr* boicottare
boy'friend' *s* innamorato, amico
boyhood ['bɔɪhʊd] *s* fanciullezza
boyish ['bɔɪ·ɪʃ] *adj* giovanile
boy' scout' *s* giovane esploratore *m*
bra [brɑ] *s* (coll) reggiseno
brace [bres] *s* (*couple*) paio; (*device for maintaining tension*) tirante *m;* (*prop*) sostegno; (*tool*) trapano; (typ) graffa; **braces** (Brit) bretelle *fpl* || *tr* legare; serrare; puntellare; sostenere; invigorare; **to brace oneself** pigliare animo || *intr*—**to brace up** (coll) pigliare animo
brace' and bit' *s* menarola, trapano
bracelet ['breslɪt] *s* braccialetto
bracer ['bresər] *s* (coll) bicchierino
bracket ['brækɪt] *s* mensola; (*for lamp*) braccio; angolo; classifica; (typ) parentesi quadra || *tr* sostenere con mensola; mettere tra parentesi quadra; classificare
brackish ['brækɪʃ] *adj* salmastro
brad [bræd] *s* chiodino, punta
brag [bræg] *s* vanto || *v* (*pret & pp* **bragged;** *ger* **bragging**) *intr* vantare
braggart ['brægərt] *s* millantatore *m*
Brah·man ['brɑmən] *s* (**-mans**) bramino
braid [bred] *s* treccia; (*strip of cloth*) spighetta; (mil) cordellina || *tr* intrecciare; decorare con spighette

brain [bren] *s* cervello; **brains** cervello, intelligenza; **to rack one's brains** rompersi la testa || *tr* far saltare le cervella di
brain'child' *s* (coll) parto dell'ingegno, idea geniale
brain' drain' *s* (coll) fuga di cervelli
brainless ['brenlɪs] *adj* senza testa
brain' pow'er *s* intelligenza
brain'storm' *s* (coll) ispirazione
brain' trust' *s* consiglio d'esperti
brain'wash'ing *s* lavaggio del cervello
brain' wave' *s* onda encefalica; (coll) idea geniale
brain'work' *s* lavoro intellettuale
brain·y ['breni] *adj* **(-ier; -iest)** intelligente
braise [brez] *tr* (culin) brasare
brake [brek] *s* freno; (*thicket*) macchia || *tr & intr* frenare
brake' drum' *s* tamburo del freno
brake' lin'ing *s* ferodo
brake'man *s* **(-men)** frenatore *m*
brake' shoe' *s* ganascia
bramble ['bræmbəl] *s* rovo
bran [bræn] *s* crusca
branch [bræntʃ] *s* (*of tree*) **branca,** ramo; (*of river*) braccio; (*of a family*) ramo; (*of business*) filiale *f;* (rr) diramazione || *intr* biforcarsi; **to branch off** or **out** ramificarsi, diramarsi
branch' line' *s* ferrovia di diramazione
branch' of'fice *s* succursale *f*
brand [brænd] *s* (*burning stick*) tizzone *m;* (*mark; stigma*) marchio; (*label; make*) marca || *tr* (*to mark with a brand*) marchiare; (*to put a stigma on*) bollare; **to brand as** tacciare di
brandied ['brændid] *adj* conservato in acquavite
brand'ing i'ron *s* ferro da marchio
brandish ['brændɪʃ] *tr* brandire
brand'-new' *adj* nuovo fiammante
bran·dy ['brændi] *s* **(-dies)** cognac *m,* acquavite *f*
brash [bræʃ] *adj* (*too hasty*) avventato; (*insolent*) impudente || *s* frammenti *mpl;* attacco (di malattia), indigestione
brass [bræs] or [brɑs] *s* ottone *m;* (coll) faccia tosta; (slang) alti ufficiali; **brasses** (mus) ottoni *mpl*
brass' band' *s* fanfara
brassiere [brə'zir] *s* reggiseno
brass' knuck'les *spl* tirapugni *m*
brass' tack' *s* chiodino or borchia d'ottone; **to get down to brass tacks** (coll) venire al sodo
brass·y ['bræsi] or ['brɑsi] *adj* **(-ier; -iest)** fatto d'ottone; sfacciato, impudente
brat [bræt] *s* marmocchio, monello
brava·do [brə'vɑdo] *s* **(-does** or **-dos)** bravata
brave [brev] *adj* coraggioso || *s* persona coraggiosa; guerriero indiano || *tr* (*to defy*) sfidare; (*to meet with courage*) affrontare
bravery ['brevəri] *s* coraggio
bra·vo ['brɑvo] *s* **(-vos)** **bravo;** applauso || *interj* bravo!

brawl [brɔl] *s* zuffa, rissa || *intr* azzuffarsi, rissare
brawn [brɔn] *s* forza muscolare
brawn·y ['brɔni] *adj* **(-ier; -iest)** muscoloso
bray [bre] *s* raglio || *intr* ragliare
braze [brez] *s* brasatura || *tr* brasare
brazen ['brezən] *adj* d'ottone; (*shameless*) sfrontato; (*sound*) penetrante || *tr*—**to brazen out** or **through** affrontare sfacciatamente
brazier ['breʃər] *s* caldano, braciere *m;* (*workman*) ottonaio
Brazil [brə'zɪl] *s* il Brasile
Brazilian [brə'zɪljən] *adj & s* brasiliano
Brazil' nut' *s* noce *f* del Brasile
breach [britʃ] *s* (*gap*) breccia; (*failure to observe a law*) infrazione || *tr* fare breccia su, fare varco in
breach' of faith' *s* abuso di confidenza
breach' of prom'ise *s* rottura di promessa di matrimonio
breach' of the peace' *s* violazione dell'ordine pubblico
bread [bred] *s* pane *m;* **to break bread with** sedersi a tavola con || *tr* impannare
bread' and but'ter *s* pane *m* e **burro;** (coll) pane quotidiano
bread' crumbs' *spl* pangrattato
breaded ['brɛdɪd] *adj* impannato
bread' knife' *s* coltello da pane
bread' line' *s* coda del pane
bread' stick' *s* grissino
breadth [bredθ] *s* (*width*) **larghezza;** (*scope*) ampiezza
bread'win'ner *s* sostegno della famiglia
break [brek] *s* interruzione; intervallo; omissione; (*breaking*) rottura; (*of bones*) frattura; (*of day*) fare *m,* spuntare *m;* (*sudden change*) mutamento; (*from jail*) evasione; (*luck*) (coll) fortuna; **to give s.o. a break** dare a qlcu l'opportunità || *v* (*pret* **broke** [brok]; *pp* **broken**) *tr* (*to smash*) rompere, spezzare; (*to tame*) domare; (*to demote*) destituire; (*a record*) superare; (*to violate*) violare; (*to make bankrupt*) mandare al fallimento; (*to interrupt*) interrompere; (*to reduce the effects of*) attutire; (*to disclose*) rivelare; (*to bring to an end by force*) battere; (*a banknote*) cambiare; (*one's word*) mancare (with *dat*); (*a law*) rompere; **to break asunder** separare; **to break down** analizzare; **to break in** forzare; **to break open** forzare, scassinare; **to break up** dissolvere || *intr* (*to divide*) rompersi; (*to burst*) scoppiare; (*said of voice of youngster*) cambiare; (*said of voice*) indebolirsi; (*said of a crowd*) disperdersi; (*said of weather*) rischiararsi; (*said of prices*) ribassare; (*to come into being*) scoppiare; (boxing) separarsi; **to break asunder** separarsi; **to break away** scappare; **to break down** abbattersi; (aut) essere or rimanere in panna; **to break even** fare patta; **to break in** irrompere; interrompere; **to break into** forzare; **to break into a run** inco-

minciare a correre; **to break loose** liberarsi; (*said of a storm*) scatenarsi; **to break off** interrompere; **to break out** (*said of the skin*) avere un'eruzione; (*said, e.g., of war*) scoppiare; **to break through** aprirsi il varco; **to break up** disperdersi; **to break with** rompere le relazioni con
breakable ['brekəbəl] *adj* fragile
breakage ['brekɪdʒ] *s* rottura
break'down' *s* (*in negotiations*) rottura; (aut) panna; (chem) analisi *f;* (pathol) colasso
breaker ['brekər] *s* (*wave*) frangente *m*
breakfast ['brɛkfəst] *s* prima colazione || *intr* fare prima colazione
break'neck' *adj* pericoloso; **at breakneck speed** a rotta di collo, a rompicollo
break' of day' *s* alba
break'through' *s* (mil) penetrazione; (fig) scoperta sensazionale
break'up' *s* dispersione; dissoluzione; (*of a friendship*) rottura
break'wa'ter *s* diga, frangiflutti *m*
breast [brest] *s* petto; (*of female*) seno; (*source of emotions*) animo; **to make a clean breast of** fare una piena confessione di
breast'bone' *s* sterno
breast' drill' *s* trapano da petto
breast'feed' *v* (*pret & pp* **-fed** [fɛd]) *tr* allattare
breast'pin' *s* spilla
breast'stroke' *s* bracciata a rana
breath [brɛθ] *s* respiro, respirazione; (*odor*) alito; (*breeze*) soffio; (*whisper*) sussurro; (fig) vita; **out of breath** ansimante; **short of breath** corto di respiro; **to gasp for breath** respirare affannosamente; **under one's breath** sottovoce
breathe [brið] *tr* respirare; (*to whisper*) sussurrare; **to breathe one's last** esalare l'ultimo sospiro; **to not breathe a word** non dire una parola || *intr* respirare; **to breathe in** inspirare; **to breathe out** espirare
breath'ing spell' *s* attimo di respiro
breathless ['brɛθlɪs] *adj* senza fiato, ansimante; soffocante
breath'tak'ing *s* emozionante, commovente
breech [britʃ] *s* (*buttocks*) natiche *fpl;* (*rear part*) parte *f* posteriore; (*of gun*) culatta; **breeches** ['brɪtʃɪz] pantaloni *mpl* al ginocchio; pantaloni *mpl* da cavallo; **to wear the breeches** (coll) portare le brache
breed [brid] *s* razza; tipo; (*stock*) origine *f* || *v* (*pret & pp* **bred** [brɛd]) *tr* produrre; (*to raise*) allevare
breeder ['bridər] *s* allevatore *m;* riproduttore *m*
breeding ['bridɪŋ] *s* (*e.g., of livestock*) allevamento; educazione
breeze [briz] *s* brezza
breez·y ['brizi] *adj* (**-ier; -iest**) ventilato; (*brisk*) vivace, brioso
brethren ['brɛðrɪn] *spl* fratelli *mpl*
brevi·ty ['brɛvɪti] *s* (**-ties**) brevità *f*
brew [bru] *s* pozione; bevanda || *tr* (*beer*) fabbricare; (*to steep*) preparare; (*to plot*) complottare || *intr* (*said of beer*) fermentare; (*said of a storm*) prepararsi
brewer ['bru·ər] *s* birraio
brew'er's yeast' *s* lievito di birra
brewer·y ['bru·əri] *s* (**-ies**) birreria, fabbrica di birra
bribe [braɪb] *s* subornazione, bustarella || *tr* subornare, dare la bustarella a
briber·y ['braɪbəri] *s* (**-ies**) subornazione, corruzione
bric-a-brac ['brɪkə,bræk] *s* bric-a-brac *m,* cianfrusaglia, cianfrusaglie *fpl*
brick [brɪk] *s* mattone *m* || *tr* mattonare
brick'bat' *s* pezzo di mattone; (coll) insulto
brick'kiln' *s* fornace *f* per mattoni
bricklayer ['brɪk,le·ər] *s* muratore *m*
brick'yard' *s* deposito di mattoni
bridal ['braɪdəl] *adj* nuziale, da sposa
brid'al wreath' *s* serto nuziale
bride [braɪd] *s* sposa
bride'groom' *s* sposo
bridesmaid ['braɪdz,med] *s* damigella d'onore
bridge [brɪdʒ] *s* ponte *m;* (*of violin*) ponticello; (*on a ship*) ponte *m* di comando || *tr* gettare un ponte su; congiungere; **to bridge a gap** colmare una lacuna
bridge'head' *s* testa di ponte
bridle ['braɪdəl] *s* briglia || *tr* mettere la briglia a; (fig) frenare || *intr* drizzare il capo, insuperbirsi
bri'dle path' *s* strada cavalcabile
brief [brif] *adj* breve || *s* sommario; (law) esposto; (eccl) breve *m;* **briefs** slip *m* || *tr* dare istruzioni a, mettere al corrente
brief' case' *s* cartella, borsa d'avvocato
brier ['braɪ·ər] *s* radica; pipa di radica
brig [brɪg] *s* (naut) brigantino; (naut) prigione
brigade [brɪ'ged] *s* brigata
brigadier [,brɪgə'dir] *s* (coll) brigadier generale *m,* generale *m* di brigata
brigand ['brɪgənd] *s* brigante *m*
brigantine ['brɪgən,tin] or ['brɪgən,taɪn] *s* (naut) brigantino goletta
bright [braɪt] *adj* (*shining*) lucido; (*light*) brillante; (*lively*) vivo; intelligente; famoso; (*idea*) luminoso
brighten ['braɪtən] *tr* illuminare; ravvivare || *intr* illuminarsi; ravvivarsi; rischiararsi
bright' lights' *spl* luci *fpl* abbaglianti; (aut) fari *mpl* abbaglianti
brilliance ['brɪljəns] or **brilliancy** ['brɪljənsi] *s* splendore *m,* scintillio
brilliant ['brɪljənt] *adj* brillante
brim [brɪm] *s* (*e.g., of cup*) orlo, bordo; (*of hat*) ala, tesa || *v* (*pret & pp* **brimmed;** *ger* **brimming**) *intr* essere pieno sino all'orlo
brim'stone' *s* zolfo
brine [braɪn] *s* salamoia; acqua di mare
bring [brɪŋ] *v* (*pret & pp* **brought**

[brɔt]) *tr* far venire; provocare; (*to carry along*) portare con sè; **to bring about** causare; **to bring around** persuadere; **to bring back** restituire; **to bring down** far abbassare; (fig) umiliare; **to bring forth** dare alla luce; **to bring forward** (*an excuse*) addurre; (math) riportare; **to bring in** introdurre; far entrare; **to bring off** compiere; **to bring on** causare; **to bring oneself to** rassegnarsi a; **to bring out** (*to expose*) rivelare; (*to offer to the public*) presentare al pubblico; (*a book*) far uscire; **to bring to** far rinvenire; (*a ship*) fermare; **to bring together** riunire; **to bring up** (*children*) allevare, tirar su; (*to introduce*) allegare; (*to cough up*) rigettare
bringing-up [ˈbrɪŋɪŋˈʌp] *s* educazione
brink [brɪŋk] *s* orlo
briquet [brɪˈkɛt] *s* bricchetta
brisk [brɪsk] *adj* (*quick*) svelto; (*sharp*) acuto; (*invigorating*) frizzante; (*gunfire*) nutrito
bristle [ˈbrɪsəl] *s* setola ‖ *intr* (*to be stiff*) irrigidirsi; (*said of hair*) rizzarsi; (*with anger*) adirarsi
bris•tly [brɪsli] *adj* (**-tlier; -tliest**) irto di setole
British [ˈbrɪtɪʃ] *adj* britannico ‖ **the British** i britannici, gl'inglesi
Britisher [ˈbrɪtɪʃər] *s* britannico
Briton [ˈbrɪtən] *s* britannico
Brittany [ˈbrɪtəni] *s* la Bretagna
brittle [ˈbrɪtəl] *adj* fragile, friabile; (*crisp*) croccante
broach [brotʃ] *s* (*pin*) spilla; (*spit*) spiedo; (mach) alesatore *m* ‖ *tr* perforare; (*a subject*) intavolare
broad [brɔd] *adj* largo; tollerante, liberale; (*daylight*) pieno; (*story*) grossolano; (*extensive*) lato; (*accent*) pronunciato
broad'cast' *s* disseminazione; (rad) radiodiffusione ‖ *v* (*pret & pp* **-cast**) *tr* disseminare, diffondere ‖ (*pret & pp* **-cast** or **-casted**) *tr* radiodiffondere
broad'casting sta'tion *s* stazione radiotrasmittente
broad'cloth' *s* (*wool*) panno di lana; (*cotton*) popeline *f*
broaden [ˈbrɔdən] *tr* allargare, estendere ‖ *intr* allargarsi, estendersi
broad' jump' *s* salto in lunghezza
broadloom [ˈbrɔd,lum] *adj* tessuto su telaio largo
broad-minded [ˈbrɔdˈmaɪndɪd] *adj* di ampie vedute, liberale
broad-shouldered [ˈbrɔdˈʃoldəred] *adj* largo di spalle
broad'side' *s* (nav) bordo; (nav) bordata; (*verbal criticism*) (coll) sfuriata; (*written criticism*) (coll) attacco violento
broad'sword' *s* spada da taglio
brocade [broˈked] *s* broccato
broccoli [ˈbrɑkəli] *s* broccolo; (*as food*) broccoli *mpl*
brochure [broˈʃur] *s* opuscolo, libriccino
brogue [brog] *s* accento irlandese; scarpa forte e comoda
broil [brɔɪl] *s* cottura alla graticola; carne *f* cotta alla graticola; (*quarrel*) rissa, zuffa ‖ *tr* cucinare alla graticola; bruciare ‖ *intr* cucinare alla graticola; (*to quarrel*) rissare, azzuffarsi
broiler [ˈbrɔɪlər] *s* graticola, gratella; (*chicken*) pollo da cucinare alla gratella or allo spiedo
broke [brok] *adj* (coll) al verde
broken [ˈbrokən] *adj* rotto; fratturato; (*e.g., English*) parlato male; (*tamed*) domato
bro'ken-down' *adj* avvilito; rovinato
broken-hearted [ˈbrokənˈhɑrtɪd] *adj* affranto
broker [ˈbrokər] *s* sensale *m;* (*on the stock exchange*) agente *m* di cambio
brokerage [ˈbrokərɪdʒ] *s* mediazione
bromide [ˈbromaɪd] *s* bromuro; (coll) banalità *f*
bromine [ˈbromin] *s* bromo
bronchitis [brɑŋˈkaɪtɪs] *s* bronchite *f*
bron•co [ˈbrɑŋko] *s* (**-cos**) puledro brado
broncobuster [ˈbrɑŋko,bʌstər] *s* domatore *m* di puledri bradi
bronze [brɑnz] *adj* bronzeo ‖ *s* bronzo ‖ *tr* bronzare ‖ *intr* abbronzarsi
brooch [brotʃ] or [brutʃ] *s* spilla
brood [brud] *s* covata, nidiata ‖ *tr* covare ‖ *intr* chiocciare; meditare; **to brood on** or **over** meditare con tristezza (su)
brook [brʊk] *s* ruscello ‖ *tr*—**to brook no** non sopportare
broom [brum] or [brʊm] *s* scopa; (*shrub*) saggina
broom'corn' *s* sorgo
broom'stick' *s* manico di scopa
broth [brɔθ] or [brɑθ] *s* brodo
brothel [ˈbrɑθəl] or [ˈbrɑðəl] *s* postribolo, bordello
brother [ˈbrʌðər] *s* fratello
brotherhood [ˈbrʌðər,hʊd] *s* fratellanza; (*association*) confraternita
broth'er-in-law' *s* (**brothers-in-law**) cognato
brotherly [ˈbrʌðərli] *adj* fraterno ‖ *adv* fraternamente
brow [braʊ] *s* ciglio; (*forehead*) fronte *f;* **to knit one's brow** aggrottare la fronte
brow'beat' *v* (*pret* **-beat;** *pp* **-beaten**) *tr* intimidire, intimorire
brown [braʊn] *adj* bruno; (*tanned*) abbronzato ‖ *s* color bruno ‖ *tr* colorare di bruno; abbronzare; (*metal*) brunire; (culin) dorare ‖ *intr* colorarsi di bruno; abbronzarsi; brunirsi; (culin) dorarsi
brownish [ˈbraʊnɪʃ] *adj* brunastro
brown' stud'y *s*—**in a brown study** assorto in fantasticherie
brown' sug'ar *s* zucchero greggio
browse [braʊz] *intr* (*said of cattle*) brucare; sfogliare; **to browse around** curiosare
bruise [bruz] *s* ammaccatura, contu-

sione || *tr* ammaccare || *intr* ammaccarsi
brunet [bru'net] *adj* bruno
brunette [bru'net] *adj & s* bruna
brunt [brʌnt] *s* forza; scontro; peso
brush [brʌʃ] *s* pennello; spazzola; (*stroke*) pennellata; (*light touch*) tocco; (*brushwood*) macchia; (*brief encounter*) scaramuccia; (elec) spazzola || *tr* spazzolare; pennellare; **to brush aside** rigettare; **to brush up** ritoccare || *intr*—**to brush by** passar vicino; **to brush up on** ripassare
brush'-off' *s* (slang) scortesia; **to give the brush-off to** (slang) snobbare
brush'wood' *s* macchia, fratta
brusque [brʌsk] *adj* brusco
brusqueness ['brʌsknɪs] *s* bruschezza
Brussels ['brʌsəlz] *s* Bruxelles *f*
Brus'sels sprouts' *spl* cavolini *mpl*
brutal ['brutəl] *adj* brutale
brutali·ty [bru'tælɪti] *s* (**-ties**) brutalità *f*
brute [brut] *adj & s* bruto
brutish ['brutɪʃ] *adj* bruto
bubble ['bʌbəl] *s* bolla; (fig) chimera || *intr* bollire; (*to make a bubbling sound*) barbugliare; **to bubble over** traboccare
bub'ble bath' *s* bagno di schiuma
buccaneer [,bʌkə'nɪr] *s* bucaniere *m*
buck [bʌk] *s* (*deer*) cervo; (*goat*) caprone *m;* (*sawhorse*) cavalletto; (*rabbit*) coniglio maschio; (*bucking*) groppata; (*dandy*) damerino; (slang) dollaro; **to pass the buck** (coll) giocare a scaricabarile || *tr* resistere accanitamente || *intr* (*said of a horse*) fare salti da caprone; **to buck for** (slang) cercare di ottenere; **to buck up** (coll) rianimarsi, prender animo
bucket ['bʌkɪt] *s* secchio; bigoncia; (*e.g., of dredge*) benna; **to kick the bucket** (slang) tirare le cuoia
buck'et seat' *s* sedile *m,* strapuntino
buckle ['bʌkəl] *s* (*clasp*) fibbia, boccola; piega || *tr* affibbiare || *intr* piegarsi, curvarsi; **to buckle down to** (coll) mettersi di buzzo buono a
buck' pri'vate *s* (slang) soldato semplice
buckram ['bʌkrəm] *s* tela da fusto
buck'saw' *s* cavalletto
buck'shot' *s* pallini *mpl* da caccia
buck'tooth' *s* (**-teeth**) dente *m* in fuori, dente *m* sporgente
buck'wheat' *s* grano saraceno
bud [bʌd] *s* bocciolo, gemma; **to nip in the bud** troncare sul nascere || *v* (*pret & pp* **budded;** *ger* **budding**) *intr* sbocciare; nascere
Buddhism ['bʊdɪzəm] *s* buddismo
bud·dy ['bʌdi] *s* (**-dies**) (coll) amico, compare *m*
budge [bʌdʒ] *tr* smuovere || *intr* muoversi
budget ['bʌdʒɪt] *s* bilancio || *tr* stanziare, preventivare; (*to schedule*) anticipare; (*time*) calcolare in anticipo
budgetary ['bʌdʒɪ,teri] *adj* preventivo, di bilancio
buff [bʌf] *adj* bruno giallastro; di pelle || *s* (*leather*) pelle gialla; dilettante *m;* (mil) giacca di pelle gialla; (coll) pelle nuda || *tr* lucidare; (*to reduce the force of*) ammortizzare
buffa·lo ['bʌfə,lo] *s* (**-loes** or **-los**) bufalo || *tr* (coll) intimidire
buffer ['bʌfər] *s* ammortizzatore *m;* cuscinetto; (*worker*) lucidatore *m;* (mach) lucidatrice *f;* (rr) respingente *m*
buff'er state' *s* stato cuscinetto
buffet [bʊ'fe] *s* (*piece of furniture*) credenza; (*counter*) buffet *m* || ['bʌfɪt] *s* pugno; schiaffo || *tr* dar pugni a; schiaffeggiare; lottare con; (*to push about*) sballottare
buffet' car' [bʊ'fe] *s* vagone *m* ristorante
buffoon [bə'fun] *s* buffone *m*
buffoner·y [bə'funəri] *s* (**-ies**) buffoneria
bug [bʌg] *s* insetto; (coll) germe *m;* (*in motor*) (slang) noia; (slang) pazzo; **to put a bug in the ear of** mettere una pulce nell'orecchio di || *v* (*pret & pp* **bugged;** *ger* **bugging**) *tr* (slang) installare un sistema d'ascolto nel telefono di; (*to annoy*) (slang) seccare || *intr*—**to bug out** (slang) andarsene
bug'bear' *s* spauracchio
bug·gy ['bʌgi] *adj* (**-gier; -giest**) pieno di cimici; (slang) pazzo || *s* (**-gies**) carrozzino
bug'house' *adj* (slang) pazzo || *s* (slang) manicomio
bugle ['bjugəl] *s* tromba, cornetta
bugler ['bjuglər] *s* trombettiere *m*
build [bɪld] *s* corporatura, taglia || *v* (*pret & pp* **built** [bɪlt]) *tr* costruire, edificare; fondare, basare; **to build up** sviluppare
builder ['bɪldər] *s* costruttore *m;* costruttore *m* edile
building ['bɪldɪŋ] *s* edificio, stabile *m;* costruzione; edilizia
build'ing and loan' associa'tion *s* società *f* di credito fondiario
build'ing lot' *s* (coll) terreno da costruzioni
build'ing trades' *spl* edilizia
build'-up' *s* concentrazione; sviluppo; processo di preparazione; propaganda favorevole
built'-in' *adj* (*in a wall*) murato; (*in a cabinet*) incassato, incorporato
built'-in clos'et *s* armadio a muro
built'-up' *adj* armato; popolato
bulb [bʌlb] *s* bulbo; (*lamp*) lampadina; (*of a lamp*) globo, cipolla
Bulgarian [bʌl'gerɪ·ən] *adj & s* bulgaro
bulge [bʌldʒ] *s* protuberanza, sporgenza || *intr* sporgere, gonfiarsi
bulk [bʌlk] *s* volume *m,* massa; **in bulk** in blocco; sciolto || *intr* avere importanza; aumentare d'importanza
bulk'head' *s* diga; (naut) paratia
bulk·y ['bʌlki] *adj* (**-ier; -iest**) voluminoso
bull [bʊl] *s* toro; (*in the stockmarket*) rialzista *mf;* (slang) scemenza; (eccl) bulla || *tr*—**to bull the market** giocare al rialzo
bull'dog' *s* molosso

bulldoze ['bʊl,doz] *tr* intimidire; (*land*) livellare
bulldozer ['bʊl,dozər] *s* livellatrice *f*, apripista *m*
bullet ['bʊlɪt] *s* palla, pallottola
bulletin ['bʊlətɪn] *s* bollettino; (*of a school*) albo; (journ) comunicato
bul'letin board' s tabellone *m*
bul'let•proof' *adj* blindato
bull'fight' *s* corrida
bull'fight'er *s* torero
bull'finch' *s* (orn) ciuffolotto
bull'frog' *s* rana americana
bull•headed ['bʊl,hedɪd] *adj* testardo
bullion ['bʊljən] *s* lingotti *mpl* d'oro or d'argento; frangia d'oro; (*on an Italian general's hat*) greca
bullish ['bʊlɪʃ] *adj* ostinato; (*market*) al rialzo; (*speculator*) rialzista
bullock ['bʊlək] *s* manzo
bull'ring' *s* arena
bull's-eye ['bʊlz,aɪ] *s* centro, tiro in pieno sul bersaglio; **to hit the bull's-eye** fare centro
bul•ly ['bʊli] *adj* (coll) eccellente || *s* (**-lies**) bravaccio || *v* (*pret & pp* **-lied**) *tr* intimidire
bulrush ['bʊl,rʌʃ] *s* giunco; (Bibl) papiro
bulwark ['bʊlwərk] *s* baluardo; protezione || *tr* proteggere
bum [bʌm] *adj* (slang) pessimo || *s* (slang) vagabondo; **on the bum** (slang) rotto, fuori servizio || *v* (*pret & pp* **bummed**; *ger* **bumming**) *tr* (slang) scroccare || *intr* (slang) oziare; (slang) vivere d'elemosina; (slang) fare lo scroccatore
bumble ['bʌmbəl] *tr* abborracciare || *intr* abborracciare; (*to stagger*) barcollare; (*to stumble*) balbettare; (*said of a bee*) ronzare
bum'blebee' *s* calabrone *m*
bump [bʌmp] *s* botta, botto; (*collision*) colpo, urto; (*swelling*) bernoccolo || *tr* urtare; **to bump off** (slang) uccidere || *intr* urtare, cozzare; **to bump into** incontrarsi con; cozzare contro
bumper ['bʌmpər] *adj* (coll) abbondante || *s* bicchiere pieno fino all'orlo; (aut) paraurti *m*; (rr) respingente *m*
bumpkin ['bʌmpkɪn] *s* beota *m*
bumptious ['bʌmpʃəs] *adj* vanitoso, presuntuoso
bump•y ['bʌmpi] *adj* (**-ier**; **-iest**) (*road*) irregolare, ondulato; (*air*) agitato
bun [bʌn] *s* panino; (*of hair*) crocchia, treccia a ciambella
bunch [bʌntʃ] *s* (*of grapes*) grappolo; (*of keys*) mazzo; (*of grass*) ciuffo; (*of people*) gruppo; (*of twigs*) fastello; (*of animals*) branco || *tr* (*things*) ammonticchiare; (*people*) raggruppare || *intr* raggrupparsi
bundle ['bʌndəl] *s* fascio, fastello; (*package*) pacco; (*large package*) collo; (*bunch*) mucchio || *tr* affastellare; impacchettare; ammucchiare; **to bundle off** or **out** cacciare precipitosamente; **to bundle up** infagottare || *intr*—**to bundle up** infagottarsi
bung [bʌŋ] *s* spina, cannella
bungalow ['bʌngə,lo] *s* casetta, villino, bungalow *m*
bung'hole' *s* spina, foro della botte
bungle ['bʌŋgəl] *s* abborracciatura || *tr* abborracciare || *intr* lavorare alla carlona
bungler ['bʌŋglər] *s* abborraccione *m*
bungling ['bʌŋglɪŋ] *adj* goffo; mal fatto || *s* abborracciatura
bunion ['bʌnjən] *s* gonfiore *m* dell'alluce
bunk [bʌŋk] *s* letto a castello; (nav) cuccetta; (slang) sciocchezza || *intr* dormire in cuccetta
bunk' bed' *s* letto a castello
bunker ['bʌŋkər] *s* (*bin*) carbonile *m*; (mil) casamatta; (golf) ostacolo
bun•ny ['bʌni] *s* (**-nies**) coniglietto
bunting ['bʌntɪŋ] *s* ornamento di bandiere; (nav) gala; (orn) zigolo
buoy [bɔɪ] or ['bu•i] *s* boa; (*life preserver*) salvagente *m* || *tr*—**to buoy up** tenere a galla; (fig) rincuorare
buoyancy ['bɔɪ•ənsi] or ['bujənsi] *s* galleggiabilità *f*; (*cheerfulness*) allegria, esuberanza
buoyant ['bɔɪ•ənt] or ['bujənt] *adj* galleggiante; allegro, esuberante
bur [bʌr] *s* riccio, aculeo
burble ['bʌrbəl] *s* gorgoglio || *intr* gorgogliare
burden ['bʌrdən] *s* carico, peso, fardello; (*of a speech*) tema *m*; (*chorus*) ritornello; (naut) portata || *tr* caricare
bur'den of proof' *s* onere *m* della prova
burdensome ['bʌrdənsəm] *adj* oneroso
burdock ['bʌrdɑk] *s* lappa, lappola
bureau ['bjʊro] *s* comò *m*; (*agency*) ufficio, servizio
bureaucra•cy [bjʊ'rɑkrəsi] *s* (**-cies**) burocrazia
bureaucrat ['bjʊrə,kræt] *s* burocrate *m*
burglar ['bʌrglər] *s* scassinatore *m*
bur'glar alarm' *s* campanello antifurto
burglarize ['bʌrglə,raɪz] *tr* scassinare
bur'glar•proof' *adj* a prova di furto
burgla•ry ['bʌrgləri] *s* (**-ries**) furto con scasso, scassinatura
Burgundy ['bʌrgəndi] *s* la Borgogna; (*wine*) borgogna *m*
burial ['berɪ•əl] *s* sepoltura
bur'ial ground' *s* cimitero
burin ['bjʊrɪn] *s* burino, cesello
burlap ['bʌrlæp] *s* tela di iuta
burlesque [bʌr'lesk] *adj* burlesco || *s* farsa, burlesque *m* || *tr* parodiare
burlesque' show' *s* spettacolo di varietà, music-hall *m*
bur•ly ['bʌrli] *adj* (**-lier**; **-liest**) membruto, robusto
Burma ['bʌrmə] *s* la Birmania
burn [bʌrn] *s* bruciatura, scottatura || *v* (*pret & pp* **burned** or **burnt** [bʌrnt]) *tr* bruciare; (*to set on fire*) dar fuoco a; (*bricks*) cuocere; **to burn down** radere al suolo; **to burn up** consumare; (*the road*) divorare; (coll) fare arrabbiare || *intr* bruciare, bruciarsi; (*said of lights*) essere acceso, e.g., **the lights were burning** la luce era accesa; **to burn out** (*said of an electric bulb or a fuse*) bruciarsi;

to burn to (fig) agognare di; **to burn up** (coll) essere arrabiato; **to burn with** (*e.g., envy*) ardere di

burner ['bʌrnər] *s* (*of gas fixture or lamp*) becco; (*of furnace*) bruciatore *m*

burning ['bʌrnɪŋ] *adj* bruciante, scottante || *s* incendio; (*ceramic*) cottura finale

burn'ing ques'tion *s* questione di attualità palpitante

burnish ['bʌrnɪʃ] *s* lucidatura || *tr* brunire

burnt' al'mond [bʌrnt] *s* mandorla tostata

burp [bʌrp] *s* (coll) rutto || *intr* (coll) ruttare

burr [bʌr] *s* riccio, aculeo; (*rough edge*) bava; (*dentist's drill*) fresa

burrow ['bʌro] *s* tana, buca || *intr* imbucarsi, rintanarsi

bursar ['bʌrsər] *s* tesoriere universitario

burst [bʌrst] *s* esplosione; (*e.g., of machine gun*) raffica; (*break*) crepa; (*of passion*) accesso; (*of speed*) slancio || *tr* far scoppiare || *intr* scoppiare, esplodere; **to burst into** (*e.g., a room*) irrompere in; (*e.g., angry words*) esplodere in; **to burst out crying** scoppiare in lacrime; **to burst with laughter** scoppiare dalle risa

bur•y ['beri] *v* (*pret & pp* **-ied**) *tr* sotterrare; **to be buried in thought** essere immerso nel pensiero; **to bury the hatchet** fare la pace

bus [bʌs] *s* (**buses** or **busses**) bus *m*, autobus *m* || *v* (*pret & pp* **bused** or **bussed**; *ger* **busing** or **bussing**) *tr* trasportare con autobus

bus'boy' *s* secondo cameriere

bus•by ['bʌzbi] *s* (**-bies**) colbacco

bus' driv'er *s* conducente *mf* di autobus

bush [bʊʃ] *s* cespuglio, arbusto; **to beat around the bush** menare il can per l'aia

bushed [bʊʃt] *adj* (coll) stanco morto

bushel ['bʊʃəl] *s* staio

bushing ['bʊʃɪŋ] *s* (mach) bronzina

bush•y ['bʊʃi] *adj* (**-ier; -iest**) ricco di arbusti; (*face*) barbuto

business ['bɪznɪs] *adj* commerciale || *s* occupazione; commercio; affare *m*, negozio; faccenda; impiego; **it is not your business** non è affare Suo; **to know one's business** sapere il fatto proprio; **to make it one's business to** proporsi di; **to mean business** (coll) farla sul serio; **to mind one's own business** impicciarsi degli affari propri

businesslike ['bɪznɪs,laɪk] *adj* metodico; serio; efficace

busi'ness•man' *s* (**-men'**) commerciante *m*, uomo d'affari

busi'ness suit' *s* abito da passeggio

busi'ness•wom'an *s* (**wom'en**) commerciante *f*

bus'man *s* (**-men**) guidatore *m* d'autobus

buss [bʌs] *s* (coll) bacione sonoro || *tr* (coll) baciare sonoramente

bus' stop' *s* fermata degli autobus

bust [bʌst] *s* busto; petto; (slang) fallimento; (slang) pugno || *tr* (slang) rompere; (slang) far fallire; (slang) colpire, dare pugni a; (mil) degradare

buster ['bʌstər] *s* (coll) ragazzo; (coll) rompitore *m*

bustle ['bʌsəl] *s* (*on a dress*) guardinfante *m*; attività *f* || *intr* affrettarsi

bus•y ['bɪzi] *adj* (**-ier; -iest**) occupato || *v* (*pret & pp* **-ied**) *tr* occupare, tenere occupato; **to busy oneself with** occuparsi di

bus'y•bod'y *s* (**-ies**) ficcanaso

bus'y sig'nal *s* (telp) segnale *m* d'occupato

but [bʌt] *s* ma *m* || *adv* solo, solamente; **but for** se non . . . per || *prep* eccetto, ad eccezione di, meno, se non; **all but** quasi || *conj* ma; che non, e.g., **I never go out in the rain but I catch a cold** non esco mai con la pioggia che non mi pigli un raffreddore

butcher ['bʊtʃər] *s* macellaio || *tr* macellare; massacrare

butch'er knife' *s* coltello da cucina, coltella

butch'er shop' *s* macelleria

butcher•y ['bʊtʃəri] *s* (**-ies**) macello; carneficina

butler ['bʌtlər] *s* cantiniere *m*, credenziere *m*

butt [bʌt] *s* (*butting*) cornata; (*of rifle or gun*) calcio; (*of cigar*) mozzicone *m*; (*target*) bersaglio; (*end*) estremità *f*; (*of ridicule*) zimbello; (*cask*) botte *f* || *tr* dare cornate a; cozzare contro || *intr*—**to butt into** (slang) intromettersi in

butter ['bʌtər] *s* burro || *tr* imburrare; **to butter up** (coll) adulare

but'ter•cup' *s* (bot) bottone *m* d'oro, ranuncolo

but'ter dish' *s* piattino per il burro, burriera

but'ter•fat' *s* grasso nel latte

but'ter•fly' *s* (**-flies**) farfalla

but'ter knife' *s* coltello per il burro

but'ter•milk' *s* latticello

but'ter sauce' *s* burro fuso

but'ter•scotch' *s* caramella al burro

buttocks ['bʌtəks] *spl* chiappe *fpl*, natiche *fpl*

button ['bʌtən] *s* bottone *m* || *tr* abbottonare

but'ton•hole' *s* occhiello, asola || *tr* attaccare un bottone a

but'ton•hook' *s* allacciabottoni *m*

buttress ['bʌtrɪs] *s* contrafforte *m*; piedritto || *tr* rinforzare

buxom ['bʌksəm] *adj* avvenente, procace

buy [baɪ] *s* compra || *v* (*pret & pp* **bought** [bɔt]) *tr* comprare; **to buy off** corrompere; **to buy out** comprare la parte di

buyer ['baɪ•ər] *s* compratore *m*

buzz [bʌz] *s* brusio, ronzio || *tr* volare a bassa quota sopra; (coll) fare una telefonata a || *intr* ronzare

buzzard ['bʌzərd] *s* (*hawk*) poiana; avvoltoio americano

buzzer ['bʌzər] *s* suoneria ronzante

buzz' saw' *s* sega circolare, segatrice *f* a disco
by [baɪ] *adv* oltre, e.g., **to speed by** correre velocemente oltre; **by and by** fra poco; **by and large** generalmente || *prep* vicino a; di, durante, e.g., **by night** di notte, durante la notte; a, e.g., **they work by the hour** lavorano all'ora; (*not later than, through*) per; (*past*) in fronte a; (*through the agency of*) da; (*according to*) secondo; (math) per, volte; **by far** di molto; **by the way** a proposito
bygone ['baɪ,gɔn] or ['baɪ,gɑn] *adj & s* passato; **to let bygones be bygones** dimenticare il passato
bylaw ['baɪ,lɔ] *s* legge *f* locale, regolamento di una società
by'-line' *s* (journ) firma
by'pass' *s* linea secondaria; (*detour*) deviazione || *tr* fare una deviazione oltre a; (*a difficulty*) evitare
by'path' *s* sentiero secondario; sentiero privato
by'prod'uct *s* sottoprodotto
bystander ['baɪ,stændər] *s* astante *m*, spettatore *m*
byway ['baɪ,we] *s* via traversa
byword ['baɪ,wʌrd] *s* proverbio; oggetto di obbrobrio
Byzantium [bɪ'zænʃɪ·əm] or [bɪ'zæntɪ·əm] *s* Bisanzio

C

C, c [si] *s* terza lettera dell'alfabeto inglese
cab [kæb] *s* vettura di piazza; tassì *m*; (*of truck or locomotive*) cabina
cabbage ['kæbɪdʒ] *s* cavolo, verza
cab' driv'er *s* autista *m* di piazza; (*of horse-drawn cab*) vetturino
cabin ['kæbɪn] *s* (*shed*) capanna; (*hut*) baracca; (aer, naut) cabina
cab'in boy' *s* mozzo
cabinet ['kæbɪnɪt] *s* (*piece of furniture*) vetrina; (*for a radio*) armadietto; (*small room; ministry of a government*) gabinetto
cab'inet·mak'er *s* ebanista *m*
cab'inet·mak'ing *s* ebanisteria
cable ['kebəl] *s* cavo; cablogramma; (elec) cablaggio || *tr* cablare, mandare un cablogramma a
ca'ble address' *s* indirizzo telegrafico
ca'ble car' *s* funicolare *f*, teleferica
cablegram ['kebel,græm] *s* cablogramma *m*
caboose [kə'bus] *s* (rr) vagone *m* di coda
cab'stand' *s* stazione di tassametri
cache [kæʃ] *s* nascondiglio || *tr* mettere in un nascondiglio
cachet [kæ'ʃe] *s* sigillo; (*distinguishing feature*) impronta
cackle ['kækəl] *s* (*of chickens*) coccodè *m*; (*of people*) chiaccherio || *intr* fare coccodè; ciarlare
cac·tus ['kæktəs] *s* (**-tuses** or **-ti** [taɪ]) cactus *m*
cad [kæd] *s* mascalzone *m*
cadaver [kə'dævər] *s* cadavere *m*
cadaverous [kə'dævərəs] *adj* cadaverico
caddie ['kædi] *s* portamazze *m*
cadence ['kedəns] *s* cadenza
cadet [kə'dɛt] *s* cadetto
cadmium ['kædmɪ·əm] *s* cadmio
cadres ['kædriz] *spl* (mil) quadri *mpl*
Caesar'ean sec'tion [sɪ'zɛrɪ·ən] *s* taglio cesareo
café [kæ'fe] *s* caffè *m*, bar *m*, ristorante *m*
ca'fé soci'ety *s* bel mondo
cafeteria [,kæfə'tɪrɪ·ə] *s* mensa, tavola calda, caffetteria
caffeine [kæ'fin] or ['kæfi·ɪn] *s* caffeina
cage [kedʒ] *s* gabbia; (*of elevator*) cabina || *tr* ingabbiare
ca·gey ['kedʒi] *adj* (**-gier**; **-giest**) (coll) astuto, cauto
cahoots [kə'huts] *s*—**to be in cahoots** (slang) far lega, essere in combutta; **to go cahoots** (slang) dividere in parti eguali
Cain [ken] *s* Caino; **to raise Cain** (slang) arrabbiarsi; (slang) fare una sfuriata
Cairo ['kaɪro] *s* il Cairo
caisson ['kesən] *s* cassone *m*; (archit) cassettone *m*
cajole [kə'dʒol] *tr* lusingare; persuadere con lusinghe
cajoler·y [kə'dʒoləri] *s* (**-ies**) lusinga
cake [kek] *s* dolce *m*; torta, pasta; (*with bread-like dough*) focaccia; (*of soap*) saponetta; (*of earth*) zolla; **to take the cake** (coll) essere il colmo || *tr* incrostare || *intr* indurirsi; incrostarsi
calabash ['kælə,bæʃ] *s* zucca a fiasca
calaboose ['kælə,bus] *s* (coll) gattabuia
calamitous [kə'læmɪtəs] *adj* calamitoso
calami·ty [kə'læmɪti] *s* (**-ties**) calamità *f*
calci·fy ['kælsɪ,faɪ] *v* (*pret & pp* **-fied**) *tr* calcificare || *intr* calcificarsi
calcium ['kælsɪ·əm] *s* calcio
calculate ['kælkjə,let] *tr* calcolare || *intr* calcolare; **to calculate on** contare su
cal'culating machine' *s* (macchina) calcolatrice
calcu·lus ['kælkjələs] *s* (**-luses** or **-li** [,laɪ]) (math, pathol) calcolo
calendar ['kæləndər] *s* calendario; (*agenda*) ordine *m* del giorno
calf [kæf] or [kɑf] *s* (**calves** [kævz] or [kɑvz]) vitello; (*of shoes or binding*) pelle *f* di vitello; (*of the leg*) polpaccio
calf'skin' *s* pelle *f* di vitello

caliber ['kælɪbər] *s* calibro
calibrate ['kælɪ,bret] *tr* calibrare
cali•co ['kælɪ,ko] *s* (**-coes** or **-cos**) cotone stampato, calico
California [,kælɪ'fɔrnɪ•ə] *s* la California
calipers ['kælɪpərz] *spl* compasso a grossezze, calibro
caliph ['kelɪf] or ['kælɪf] *s* califfo
calisthenic [,kælɪs'θenɪk] *adj* ginnastico || **calisthenics** *spl* ginnastica a corpo libero
calk [kɔk] *tr* var of **caulk**
call [kɔl] *s* chiamata; visita; (*shout*) grido, richiamo; (*of bugle*) squillo; (*of telephone*) colpo; (*of ship*) scalo; obbligo; vocazione; (com) richiesta; **on call** disponibile; **within call** a portata di voce || *tr* chiamare; convocare; (*to awaken*) svegliare; **to call back** richiamare; **to call in** (*e.g., an expert*) fare venire; (*e.g., currency*) domandare, esigere; **to call off** annullare; **to call out** chiamare; **to call together** convocare; **to call up** chiamare per telefono || *intr* chiamare; visitare; **to call at** passare per la casa di; (naut) fare scalo a; **to call for** venire a prendere; **to call out** gridare; **to go calling** andare a fare visite
cal'la lil'y ['kælə] *s* (*Zantedeschia aethiopica*) calla dei fioristi
call'boy' *s* (*in a hotel*) fattorino; (theat) buttafuori *m*
caller ['kɔlər] *s* visitatore *m*
call' girl' *s* ragazza squillo
calling ['kɔlɪŋ] *s* appello; professione
call'ing card' *s* biglietto da visita
call' num'ber *s* numero telefonico; numero di biblioteca
callous ['kæləs] *adj* calloso; insensibile
callow ['kælo] *adj* inesperto, immaturo
call' to arms' *s* chiamata alle armi
call' to the col'ors *s* chiamata sotto la bandiera
callus ['kæləs] *s* callo
calm [kɑm] *adj* calmo, tranquillo || *s* calma || *tr* calmare, tranquillizzare || *intr*—**to calm down** calmarsi; (*said of weather*) abbonacciarsi
calmness ['kɑmnɪs] *s* calma, placidità *f*, tranquillità *f*
calomel ['kælə,mel] *s* calomelano
calorie ['kæləri] *s* caloria
calum•ny ['kæləmni] *s* (**-nies**) calunnia
Calvary ['kælvəri] *s* (Bib) Calvario
cam [kæm] *s* camma
camber ['kæmbər] *s* curvatura; convessità *f* || *tr* arcuare || *intr* curvarsi
cambric ['kembrɪk] *s* cambrì *m*
camel ['kæməl] *s* cammello
came•o ['kæmi,o] *s* (**-os**) cammeo
camera ['kæmərə] *s* macchina fotografica; (mov) cinepresa
cam'era•man' *s* (**-men'**) operatore *m*
camomile ['kæmə,maɪl] *s* camomilla
camouflage ['kæmə,flɑʒ] *s* mascheramento || *tr* mascherare, camuffare
camp [kæmp] *s* accampamento, campo || *intr* accamparsi
campaign [kæm'pen] *s* campagna || *intr* fare una campagna
campaigner [kæm'penər] *s* veterano; (pol) propagandista *mf*
camp' bed' *s* letto da campo, branda
camper ['kæmpər] *s* campeggiatore *m*, campeggista *mf*
camp'fire' *s* fuoco di accampamento
camp'ground' *s* terreno per campeggio
camphor ['kæmfər] *s* canfora
camp'stool' *s* seggiolino pieghevole
campus ['kæmpəs] *s* campo, terreno dell'università
cam'shaft' *s* albero di distribuzione, albero a camme
can [kæn] *s* lattina, barattolo; (*of gasoline or oil*) bidone *m* || *v* (*pret & pp* **canned**; *ger* **canning**) *tr* inscatolare; (slang) licenziare || *v* (*pret & cond* **could**) *aux* **I can speak English** so parlare inglese; **can he go now?** se ne può andare ora?
Canada ['kænədə] *s* il Canadà
Canadian [kə'nedɪ•ən] *adj* & *s* canadese *mf*
canal [kə'næl] *s* canale *m*
canar•y [kə'neri] *s* (**-ies**) canarino || **Canaries** *spl* Canarie *fpl*
can•cel ['kænsəl] *v* (*pret & pp* **-celed** or **-celled**; *ger* **-celing** or **-celling**) *tr* cancellare; annullare; revocare; (*stamps*) timbrare, annullare
cancellation [,kænsə'leʃən] *s* cancellazione, annullamento; cassazione; (*of a stamp*) bollo
cancer ['kænsər] *s* cancro || **Cancer** *s* Cancro
cancerous ['kænsərəs] *adj* canceroso
candela•brum [,kændə'lɑbrəm] *s* (**-bra** [brə] or **-brums**) candelabro
candid ['kændɪd] *adj* candido; sincero, franco
candida•cy ['kændɪdəsi] *s* (**-cies**) candidatura
candidate ['kændɪ,det] *s* candidato; (*for a degree*) laureando
can'did cam'era *s* camera fotografica indiscreta
candied ['kændid] *adj* candito
candle ['kændəl] *s* candela || *tr* (*eggs*) sperare
can'dle•hold'er *s* var of **candlestick**
can'dle•light' *s* luce *f* or lume *m* di candela
can'dle•pow'er *s* (phys) candela
can'dle•stick' *s* (*ornate*) candeliere *m*; (*plain*) bugia
candor ['kændər] *s* candore *m*; ingenuità *f*
can•dy ['kændi] *s* (**-dies**) dolciumi *mpl*; **a piece of candy** un bombon || *v* (*pret & pp* **-died**) *tr* candire
can'dy box' *s* bomboniere
can'dy dish' *s* bomboniera; (*three-tier-high*) alzata
can'dy store' *s* confetteria
cane [ken] *s* canna, giunco; (*for walking*) bastone *m* || *tr* bastonare; (*chairs*) impagliare
cane' seat' *s* sedia impagliata
cane' sug'ar *s* zucchero di canna
canine ['kenaɪn] *adj* canino || *s* (*tooth*) canino; (*dog*) cane *m*
canister ['kænɪstər] *s* barattolo

canned' goods' *spl* conserve *fpl* alimentari; prodotti *mpl* in scatola
canned' mu'sic *s* (slang) musica su dischi
canner·y ['kænəri] *s* (**-ies**) fabbrica di conserve alimentari
cannibal ['kænɪbəl] *adj & s* cannibale *mf*, antropofago
canning ['kænɪŋ] *s* conservazione
cannon ['kænən] *s* cannone *m*
cannonade [,kænə'ned] *s* cannonata || *tr* cannoneggiare
can'non·ball' *s* palla da cannone
can'non fod'der *s* carne *f* da cannone
can·ny ['kæni] *adj* (**-nier; -niest**) astuto, fino; malizioso
canoe [kə'nu] *s* canoa, piroga
canon ['kænən] *s* canone *m*; (*priest*) canonico
canonical [kə'nɑnɪkəl] *adj* canonico || **canonicals** *spl* paramenti liturgici
canonize ['kænə,naɪz] *tr* canonizzare
can'on law' *s* diritto canonico
canon·ry ['kænənri] *s* (**-ries**) canonicato
can' o'pener ['opənər] *s* apriscatole *m*
cano·py ['kænəpi] *s* (**-pies**) tenda; baldacchino; (*of sky*) (fig) volta
cant [kænt] *adj* ipocrita || *s* linguaggio ipocrita; gergo; (*slope*) inclinazione
cantaloupe ['kæntə,lop] *s* melone *m*
cantankerous [kæn'tæŋkərəs] *adj* bisbetico, attaccabrighe
canteen [kæn'tin] *s* cantina, spaccio; (*metal bottle*) borraccia
canter ['kæntər] *s* piccolo galoppo || *intr* andare al piccolo galoppo
cantiliver ['kæntɪ,livər] *adj* a cantiliver || *s* trave *f* a sbalzo; (archit) trave *f* a mensola
cantle ['kæntəl] *s* arcione *m* posteriore
canton [kæn'tɑn] *s* cantone *m*; regione || *tr* accantonare
cantonment [kæn'tɑnmənt] *s* accantonamento
cantor ['kæntər] or ['kæntɔr] *s* cantore *m*
canvas ['kænvəs] *s* (*cloth*) olona; (*e.g. on open truck*) copertone *m*; (*painting*) tela; (naut) vela; **under canvas** (naut) a vele spiegate
canvass ['kænvəs] *s* discussione; dibattito; (pol) sollecitazione di voti || *tr* discutere; (*votes*) sollecitare; (*to investigate*) indagare; (com) fare la piazza a || *intr* discutere; sollecitare voti; indagare; (com) fare la piazza
canyon ['kænjən] *s* cañon *m*
cap [kæp] *s* berretto; cuffia; (*of academic costume*) berrettone *m*; (*of bottle*) tappo, capsula; (*e.g., of fountain pen*) cappuccio || *v* (*pret & pp* **capped**; *ger* **capping**) *tr* (*a person*) coprire il capo di; (*s.o.'s head*) coprire con il berretto; (*a bottle*) mettere il tappo a; terminare; **to cap the climax** essere il colmo
capabili·ty [,kepə'bɪlɪti] *s* (**-ties**) capacità *f*, abilità *f*
capable ['kepəbəl] *adj* capace, abile
capacious [kə'peʃəs] *adj* ampio, capace
capaci·ty [kə'pæsɪti] *s* (**-ties**) capacità *f*; **filled to capacity** pieno zeppo; **in the capacity of** in veste di
cap' and bells' *spl* berretto a sonagli; scettro di buffone
cap' and gown' *s* costume accademico, toga e tocco
caparison [kə'pærɪsən] *s* bardatura || *tr* bardare
cape [kep] *s* cappa, mantello; (mil) mantella; (geog) capo
Cape' of Good' Hope' *s* Capo di Buona Speranza
caper ['kepər] *s* capriola; (bot) cappero; **to cut capers** far capriole; (fig) fare monellerie || *intr* fare capriole; saltellare
Cape' Town' *s* Città *f* del Capo
capital ['kæpɪtəl] *adj* capitale || *s* (*money*) capitale *m*; (*city*) capitale *f*; (*of column*) capitello
cap'ital expen'ditures *spl* spese *fpl* d'impianto
cap'ital goods' *spl* beni *mpl* strumentali
capitalism ['kæpɪtə,lɪzəm] *s* capitalismo
capitalize ['kæpɪtə,laɪz] *tr* capitalizzare; scrivere con la maiuscola || *intr*—**to capitalize on** approfittare di
cap'ital let'ter *s* lettera maiuscola
cap'ital pun'ishment *s* pena capitale
cap'ital stock' *s* capitale *m* sociale
capitol ['kæpɪtəl] *s* campidoglio
capitulate [kə'pɪtʃə,let] *intr* capitolare
capon ['kepɑn] *s* cappone *m*
caprice [kə'pris] *s* capriccio, ghiribizzo
capricious [kə'prɪʃəs] *adj* capriccioso, estroso
Capricorn ['kæprɪ,kɔrn] *s* Capricorno
capsize ['kæpsaɪz] *tr* capovolgere || *intr* capovolgersi
capstan ['kæpstən] *s* argano
cap'stone' *s* (archit) coronamento
capsule ['kæpsəl] *adj* in miniatura; riassuntivo || *s* capsula
captain ['kæptən] *s* capitano; (naut) comandante *m*; || *tr* capitanare
caption ['kæpʃən] *s* titolo; (mov) didascalia; (journ) leggenda
captivate ['kæptɪ,vet] *tr* cattivare, affascinare
captive ['kæptɪv] *adj & s* prigioniero
captivi·ty [kæp'tɪvɪti] *s* (**-ties**) cattività *f*, prigionia
captor ['kæptər] *s* persona che cattura
capture ['kæptʃər] *s* cattura, presa; (*person*) prigioniero; (*thing*) bottino || *tr* catturare; prendere
car [kɑr] *s* (*of train*) vagone *m*, vettura; (*automobile*) automobile *m & f*, macchina, vettura; (*of elevator*) cabina; (*of balloon*) navicella; (*for narrow-gauge track*) carrello
carafe [kə'ræf] *s* caraffa
caramel ['kærəməl] or ['kɑrməl] *s* (*burnt sugar*) caramello; (*candy*) caramella appiccicaticcia
carat ['kærət] *s* carato
caravan ['kærə,væn] *s* carovana; (*covered vehicle*) furgone *m*
caravansa·ry [,kærə'vænsəri] *s* (**-ries**) caravanserraglio
caraway ['kærə,we] *s* cumino
car'barn' *s* rimessa del tram

carbide ['kɑrbaɪd] *s* carburo
carbine ['kɑrbaɪn] *s* carabina
carbol'ic ac'id [kɑr'bɑlɪk] *s* acido fenico
carbon ['kɑrbən] *s* (*in arc light, battery, auto cylinder*) carbone *m;* carta carbone; (chem) carbonio
car'bon cop'y *s* copia a carbone, velina
car'bon diox'ide *s* anidride carbonica
car'bon monox'ide *s* ossido di carbonio, monossido di carbonio
car'bon pa'per *s* carta carbone
carbuncle ['kɑrbʌŋkəl] *s* (*stone; boil*) carbonchio; (*boil*) foruncolo
carburetor ['kɑrbə,retər] or ['kɑrbjə,retər] *s* carburatore *m*
carcass ['kɑrkəs] *s* carcassa; (*in state of decay*) carogna
card [kɑrd] *s* (*file*) scheda; (*post card*) cartolina; (*personal card*) biglietto; (*announcement*) partecipazione; (*playing card*) carta da gioco; (coll) tipo divertente, bel tipo
card'board' *s* cartone *m*
card'-car'rying mem'ber *s* tesserato
card' case' *s* portatessere *m*
card' cat'alogue *s* schedario
card'hold'er *s* socio, tesserato
cardiac ['kɑrdɪ,æk] *adj & s* cardiaco
cardigan ['kɑrdɪgən] *s* panciotto a maglia
cardinal ['kɑrdɪnəl] *adj* cardinale, fondamentale || *s* cardinale *m*
card' in'dex *s* schedario
cardiogram ['kɑrdɪ·o,græm] *s* cardiogramma *m*
card' par'ty *s* riunione per giocare a carte
card'sharp' *s* baro
card' ta'ble *s* tavoliere *m,* tavolino da gioco
card' trick' *s* gioco di prestigio colle carte
care [ker] *s* cura, custodia; inquietudine *f,* preoccupazione; cautela; **care of** presso, e.g., **R. Smith care of Jones** R. Smith presso Jones; **to take care** fare attenzione; **to take care of** prendersi cura di, badare a; **to take care of oneself** badare alla salute || *intr* curarsi, badare; **I don't care** non m'importa; **to care about** preoccuparsi di; **to care for** voler bene a; curarsi di; **to care to** volere
careen [kə'rin] *s* carenaggio || *intr* sbandare
career [kə'rir] *adj* di carriera || *s* carriera
care'free' *adj* spensierato
careful ['kerfəl] *adj* attento; diligente; premuroso; **careful!** faccia attenzione!
careless ['kerlɪs] *adj* trascurato; imprudente; indifferente
carelessness ['kerlɪsnɪs] *s* trascuratezza; imprudenza; indifferenza
caress [kə'res] *s* carezza || *tr* carezzare, accarezzare
caretaker ['ker,tekər] *adj* interinale, provvisorio || *s* custode *m;* guardiano; (*of school*) bidello
care'taker gov'ernment *s* governo interinale
care'worn' *adj* accasciato dalle preoccupazioni
car'fare' *s* passaggio, denaro per il tram; (*small sum of money*) spiccioli *mpl*
car·go ['kɑrgo] *s* (**-goes** or **-gos**) carico mercantile
car'go boat' *s* battello da carico
Caribbean [,kærɪ'bi·ən] or [kə'rɪbɪ·ən] *s* Mare *m* dei Caraibi
caricature ['kærɪkətʃər] *s* caricatura || *tr* mettere in caricatura
carillon ['kærɪ,lɑn] or [kə'rɪljən] *s* carillon *m* || *intr* suonare il carillon
car'load' *s* vagone completo, vagonata
carnage ['kɑrnɪdʒ] *s* carnaio, carneficina
carnal ['kɑrnəl] *adj* carnale
carnation [kɑr'neʃən] *adj* incarnato || *s* garofano; (*color*) incarnato
carnival ['kɑrnɪvəl] *adj* carnevalesco || *s* carnevale *m;* festa, spettacolo all'aperto
carob ['kærəb] *s* (*fruit*) carruba; (*tree*) carrubo
car·ol ['kærəl] *s* canzone *f* popolare; pastorella di Natale || *v* (*pret & pp* **-oled** or **-olled;** *ger* **-oling** or **-olling**) *tr* cantare
carom ['kærəm] *s* carambola || *intr* carambolare
carousal [kə'rauzəl] *s* baldoria, gozzoviglia
carouse [kə'rauz] *intr* fare baldoria, gozzovigliare
carousel [,kærə'zel] or [,kæru'zel] *s* giostra, carosello
carp ['kɑrp] *s* carpa || *intr* lagnarsi, criticare
carpenter ['kɑrpəntər] *s* falegname *m*
carpentry ['kɑrpəntri] *s* falegnameria
carpet ['kɑrpɪt] *s* tappeto || *tr* coprire con un tappeto, tappetare
carpetbagger ['kɑrpɪt,bægər] *s* avventuriero; (hist) politicante *m*
car'pet sweep'er *s* spazzolone elettrico per tappeti
car'port' *s* tettoia-garage *f*
car'-ren'tal serv'ice *s* servizio di autonoleggi
carriage ['kærɪdʒ] *s* carrozza; (*of gun*) affusto; (*of typewriter*) carrello; (*bearing*) portamento; (mach) slitta
carrier ['kærɪ·ər] *s* portatore *m;* (*person or organization in business of carrying goods*) spedizioniere *m;* (*of mail*) postino; (*e.g., on top of station wagon*) portabagagli *m;* (*of a disease*) veicolo
car'rier pig'eon *s* piccione *m* viaggiatore
car'rier wave' *s* (rad) onda portante
carrion ['kærɪ·ən] *s* carogne *fpl*
carrot ['kærət] *s* carota
car·ry ['kæri] *v* (*pret & pp* **-ried**) *tr* portare; trasportare; (*a burden*) sopportare; (*an election*) guadagnare; (*to keep in stock*) avere in assortimento; **to carry along** portare con sé; **to carry away** trasportare; entusiasmare; **to carry forward** riportare; **to carry out** eseguire; **to carry**

through completare; **to carry weight** aver importanza || *intr* avere la portata (di), e.g., **this gun carries two miles** questo cannone ha la portata di due miglia; **to carry on** continuare; (coll) fare baccano
cart [kɑrt] *s* carro, carretto; (*for shopping*) carrello; **to put the cart before the horse** mettere il carro davanti ai buoi || *tr* trasportare col carro
carte blanche ['kɑrt'blɑnʃ] *s* carta bianca
cartel [kɑr'tel] *s* cartello
Carthage ['kɑrθɪdʒ] *s* Cartagine *f*
cart' horse' *s* cavallo da tiro
cartilage ['kɑrtɪlɪdʒ] *s* cartilagine *f*
carton ['kɑrtən] *s* cartone *m;* scatola di cartone; (*of cigarettes*) stecca
cartoon [kɑr'tun] *s* disegno; caricatura; (*comic strip*) fumetto; (mov) disegno animato || *tr* fare caricature di
cartoonist [kɑr'tunɪst] *s* disegnatore *m;* caricaturista *mf*
cartridge ['kɑrtrɪdʒ] *s* cartuccia; (*e.g., of camera*) caricatore *m*
car'tridge belt' *s* cartucciera; (mil) giberna
car'tridge clip' *s* serbatoio
cart'wheel' *s* ruota di carro; **to turn cartwheels** fare la ruota
carve [kɑrv] *tr* (*meats*) trinciare; scolpire, intagliare
carv'ing knife' *s* trinciante *m*
car' wash'er *s* lavamacchine *m*
cascade [kæs'ked] *s* cascata || *intr* cadere a mo' di cascata
case [kes] *s* (*box*) cassetta; (*of watch*) calotta; (*outer covering*) astuccio; (*instance*) caso; (gram) caso; (law) causa; (typ) cassa; **in case** in caso, nel caso; **in no case** in nessun modo || *tr* rinchiudere; (*to package*) impaccare; (slang) ispezionare
casement ['kesmənt] *s* telaio di finestra; finestra a gangheri
case' stud'y *s* casistica
cash [kæʃ] *s* contante *m;* **cash on delivery** spedizione contro assegno; **for cash** in contanti; a pronta cassa || *tr* (*a check*) cambiare, incassare || *intr* —**to cash in on** (coll) trarre profitto da
cash' box' *s* cassa
cashew ['kæʃu] *s* (*tree*) anacardio; (*nut*) mandorla indiana
cashier [kæ'ʃɪr] *s* cassiere *m* || *tr* (*to dismiss*) silurare
cashier's' check' *s* assegno circolare
cash' reg'ister *s* registratore *m* cassa
casing ['kesɪŋ] *s* rivestimento; tubo di rivestimento; (*for salami*) budello; (*of tire*) copertone *m*
cask [kæsk] or [kɑsk] *s* barile *m,* botte *f*
casket ['kæskɪt] or ['kɑskɪt] *s* scrigno, cofanetto; (*coffin*) bara, cassa da morto
casserole ['kæsə,rol] *s* tegame *m* di terracotta or vetro; (*food*) pasticcio, timballo
cassette [kə'set] *s* (mus) musicassetta; (mus & phot) caricatore *m*
cassock ['kæsək] *s* sottana, tonaca; **to doff the cassock** gettar la tonaca alle ortiche
cast [kæst] or [kɑst] *s* getto; lancio; forma; (mach) pezzo fuso; (surg) gesso; (theat) complesso artistico, cast *m* || *v* (*pret & pp* **cast**) *tr* gettare; fondere; (*a ballot*) dare; (*the roles*) distribuire; (*actors*) scegliere; **to cast aside** abbandonare; **to cast down** deprimere; **to cast lots** tirare a sorte; **to cast off** abbandonare; **to cast out** buttar fuori || *intr* tirare i dadi; **to cast off** (naut) mollare gli ormeggi
castanets [,kæstə'nets] *spl* nacchere *fpl*
cast'a•way' *adj & s* naufrago; (fig) reprobo
caste [kæst] or [kɑst] *s* casta; **to lose caste** perdere prestigio
caster ['kæstər] or ['kɑstər] *s* ampollina, saliera, pepaiola; (*roller*) rotella per i mobili
castigate ['kæstɪ,get] *tr* castigare, punire; correggere
Castile [kæs'til] *s* (la) Castiglia
Castilian [kæs'tɪljən] *adj & s* castigliano
casting ['kæstɪŋ] or ['kɑstɪŋ] *s* getto, getto fuso; (*in fishing*) pesca a getto
cast' i'ron *s* ghisa
cast'-i'ron *adj* fatto di ghisa; (*e.g., stomach*) fatto d'acciaio, di struzzo
castle ['kæsəl] or ['kɑsəl] *s* castello; (chess) torre *f* || *tr & intr* (chess) arroccare
cas'tle in Spain' or **cas'tle in the air'** *s* castello in aria
cast'off' *adj* abbandonato || *s* rigetto; persona abbandonata; (typ) stima
cas'tor oil' ['kæstər] or ['kɑstər] *s* olio di ricino
castrate ['kæstret] *tr* castrare
casual ['kæʒʊ•əl] *adj* casuale, fortuito; (*clothing*) semplice, sportivo
casually ['kæʒʊ•əli] *adv* con disinvoltura; (*by chance*) fortuitamente
casual•ty ['kæʒʊ•əlti] *s* (**-ties**) accidente *m,* disastro; vittima; **casualties** (*in war*) perdite *fpl*
casuist•ry ['kæʃʊ•ɪstri] *s* (**-ries**) (*specious reasoning*) speciosità *f;* (philos) casistica
cat [kæt] *s* gatto; donna perfida; **to let the cat out of the bag** lasciarsi scappare il segreto
cataclysm ['kætə,klɪzəm] *s* cataclisma *m*
catacomb ['kætə,kom] *s* catacomba
catalogue ['kætə,lɔg] or ['kætə,lɑg] *s* catalogo || *tr* catalogare
cat'alogue sale' *s* vendita per corrispondenza
catalyst ['kætəlɪst] *s* catalizzatore *m*
catapult ['kætə,pʌlt] *s* catapulta || *tr* catapultare
cataract ['kætə,rækt] *s* cataratta
catarrh [kə'tɑr] *s* catarro
catastrophe [kə'tæstrəfi] *s* catastrofe *f,* disastro

cat'call' *s* urlo di disapprovazione
catch [kætʃ] *s* presa; cattura; (*of door*) paletto; (*in marriage*) partito; (*trick*) inganno; (*of fish*) pesca; (mach) nottolino || *v* (*pret & pp* **caught** [kɔt]) *tr* prendere, acchiappare; (*a cold*) pigliare, buscarsi; **to catch hold of** afferrare; **to catch it** (coll) prendersele; **to catch oneself** contenersi; **to catch up** sorprendere sul fatto || *intr* agganciarsi; (*said of a disease*) trasmettersi; **to catch on** capire l'antifona; **to catch up** mettersi al corrente; **to catch up with** raggiungere
catch'-as-catch'-can' *s* lotta libera americana
catch' ba'sin *s* ricettacolo di fogna
catcher ['kætʃər] *s* ricevitore *m*, catcher *m*
catching ['kætʃɪŋ] *adj* (*alluring*) seducente; (*infectious*) contagioso
catch'word' *s* slogan *m;* (typ) chiamata; (typ) esponente *m* in testa di pagina
catch•y ['kætʃi] *adj* (**-ier; -iest**) attraente, vivo; (*tricky*) insidioso
catechism ['kætɪ,kɪzəm] *s* catechismo
catego•ry ['kætɪ,gori] *s* (**-ries**) categoria
cater ['ketər] *intr* provvedere cibo; **to cater to** servire
cater-cornered ['kætər,kɔrnərd] *adj* diagonale || *adv* diagonalmente
caterer ['ketərər] *s* provveditore *m*
caterpillar ['kætər,pɪlər] *s* bruco
cat'erpillar trac'tor *s* trattore *m* a cingoli
cat'fish' *s* pesce *m* gatto
cat'gut' *s* (mus) corda di minugia; (surg) catgut *m*, cattegù *m*
cathartic [kə'θɑrtɪk] *adj & s* catartico
cathedral [kə'θidrəl] *s* cattedrale *f*
catheter ['kæθɪtər] *s* catetere *m*
catheterize ['kæθɪtə,raɪz] *tr* cateterizzare
cathode ['kæθod] *s* catodo
catholic ['kæθəlɪk] *adj* cattolico; (*e.g., mind*) liberale || **Catholic** *adj & s* cattolico
catkin ['kætkɪn] *s* (bot) amento, gattino
cat'nap' *s* corta siesta, sonnellino
cat-o'-nine-tails [,kætə'naɪn,telz] *s* gatto a nove code
cat's'-paw' *s* gonzo; (*breeze*) brezzolina
catsup ['kætsəp] or ['ketʃəp] *s* salsa piccante di pomodoro, ketchup *m*
cat'tail' *s* stiancia
cattle ['kætəl] *s* bestiame grosso
cat'tle•man *s* (**-men**) allevatore *m* di bestiame
cat•ty ['kæti] *adj* (**-tier; -tiest**) malizioso, maligno; felino, gattesco
cat'walk' *s* passerella, ballatoio
Caucasian [kɔ'keʒən] or [kɔ'keʃən] *adj & s* caucasico
caucus ['kɔkəs] *s* comitato elettorale; conciliabolo politico
cauldron ['kɔldrən] *s* calderone *m*
cauliflower ['kɔlɪ,flaʊ•ər] *s* cavolfiore *m*
caulk [kɔk] *tr* calafatare, stoppare
cause [kɔz] *s* causa, cagione || *tr* causare, cagionare; **to cause to** + *inf* fare + *inf*, e.g., **she caused him to fall** l'ha fatto cadere
cause'way' *s* strada rialzata, scarpata
caustic ['kɔstɪk] *adj* caustico
cauterize ['kɔtə,raɪz] *tr* cauterizzare
caution ['kɔʃən] *s* cautela, prudenza; ammonizione || *tr* ammonire
cautious ['kɔʃəs] *adj* prudente
cavalcade ['kævəl,ked] or [,kævəl'ked] *s* cavalcata
cavalier [,kævə'lir] or ['kævə,lir] *adj* altero, sdegnoso; disinvolto || *s* cavaliere *m*
caval•ry ['kævəlri] *s* (**-ries**) cavalleria
cav'alry•man' or **cav'alry•man** *s* (**-men'** or **-men**) cavalleggero, soldato di cavalleria
cave [kev] *s* caverna, grotta || *intr*—**to cave in** sprofondarsi; (*to give in*) (coll) cedere; (*to become exhausted*) (coll) diventare spossato
cave'-in' *s* sprofondamento
cave' man' *s* troglodita *m*
cavern ['kævərn] *s* caverna
caviar ['kævɪ,ɑr] or [,kævɪ'ɑr] *s* caviale *m*
cav•il ['kævɪl] *v* (*pret & pp* **-iled** or **-illed**; *ger* **-iling** or **-illing**) *intr* cavillare
cavi•ty ['kævɪti] *s* (**-ties**) cavità *f;* (*in tooth*) carie *f*
cavort [kə'vɔrt] *intr* far capriole
caw [kɔ] *s* gracchiamento || *intr* gracchiare
cease [sis] *tr* cessare, interrompere || *intr* cessare, interrompersi; **to cease** + *ger* cessare di + *inf*
cease'-fire' *s* sospensione delle ostilità
ceaseless ['sislɪs] *adj* incessante
cedar ['sidər] *s* cedro; legno di cedro
cede [sid] *tr* cedere, trasferire
ceiling ['silɪŋ] *s* soffitto; (aer) altezza massima; **to hit the ceiling** (slang) uscire dai gangheri
ceil'ing price' *s* calmiere *m*, tetto
celebrate ['sɛlɪ,bret] *tr* celebrare || *intr* celebrare; far festa
celebrated ['sɛlɪ,bretɪd] *adj* celebre, famoso
celebration [,sɛlɪ'breʃən] *s* celebrazione
celebri•ty [sɪ'lɛbrɪti] *s* (**-ties**) celebrità *f*
celery ['sɛləri] *s* sedano
celestial [sɪ'lɛstʃəl] *adj* celestiale, celeste
celibacy ['sɛləbəsi] *s* celibato
celibate ['sɛlə,bet] or ['sɛləbɪt] *adj & s* celibe *m;* nubile *f*
cell [sɛl] *s* (*e.g., of jail*) cella; (*of electric battery*) elemento; (biol, phys, pol) cellula
cellar ['sɛlər] *s* cantina; (*partly above ground*) seminterrato
cellist or **'cellist** ['tʃɛlɪst] *s* violoncellista *mf*
cel•lo or **'cel•lo** ['tʃɛlo] *s* (**-los**) violoncello
cellophane ['sɛlə,fen] *s* cellofan *m*
celluloid ['sɛljə,lɔɪd] *s* celluloide *f*
Celtic ['sɛltɪk] or ['kɛltɪk] *adj* celtico || *s* lingua celtica

cement [sɪ'ment] *s* cemento ‖ *tr* cementare
cemete•ry ['semɪ,teri] *s* **(-ries)** cimitero
censer ['sensər] *s* turibolo
censor ['sensər] *s* censore *m* ‖ *tr* censurare
censure ['senʃər] *s* censura, critica ‖ *tr* censurare, criticare
census ['sensəs] *s* censo, censimento
cent [sent] *s* centesimo di dollaro, cent *m;* **not to have a red cent to one's name** non avere il becco di un quattrino
centaur ['sentɔr] *s* centauro
centennial [sen'tenɪ•əl] *adj* & *s* centenario
center ['sentər] *s* centro ‖ *tr* centrare, concentrare ‖ *intr*—**to center on** concentrarsi su
cen'ter•board' *s* chiglia mobile
cen'ter•piece' *s* centro tavola
cen'ter punch' *s* punzone *m,* punteruolo
centigrade ['sentɪ,gred] *adj* centigrado
centimeter ['sentɪ,mitər] *s* centimetro
centipede ['sentɪ,pid] *s* centopiedi *m*
cento ['sento] *s* centone *m*
central ['sentrəl] *adj* centrale ‖ *s* centrale *f,* centrale telefonica; (*operator*) telefonista *mf*
Cen'tral Amer'ica *s* l'America Centrale
centralize ['sentrə,laɪz] *tr* centralizzare ‖ *intr* centralizzarsi
centu•ry ['sentʃəri] *s* **(-ries)** secolo
ceramic [sɪ'ræmɪk] *adj* ceramico ‖ **ceramics** *ssg* ceramica; *spl* oggetti *mpl* di ceramica
cereal ['sɪrɪ•əl] *adj* cerealicolo ‖ *s* (*grain*) cereale *m;* (*uncooked breakfast food, e.g., cornflakes*) fiocchi *mpl;* (*breakfast food to be cooked*) farina
cerebral ['serɪbrəl] *adj* cerebrale
ceremonious [,serɪ'monɪ•əs] *adj* cerimonioso
ceremo•ny ['serɪ,moni] *s* **(-nies)** cerimonia; **to stand on ceremony** fare cerimonie
certain ['sʌrtən] *adj* certo; **for certain** di or per certo; **to be certain to** + *inf* non mancare di + *inf*
certainly ['sʌrtənli] *adv* certamente; (*gladly*) con piacere
certain•ty ['sʌrtənti] *s* **(-ties)** certezza
certificate [sər'tɪfɪkɪt] *s* certificato; (com) titolo ‖ [sər'tɪfɪ,ket] *tr* certificare
cer'tified check' *s* assegno a copertura garantita
cer'tified cop'y *s* estratto; (*as a formula on a document*) per copia conforme
cer'tified pub'lic account'ant *s* esperto contabile
certi•fy ['sʌrtɪ,faɪ] *v* (*pret & pp* **-fied**) *tr* certificare, garantire
cervix ['sʌrvɪks] *s* **(cervices** [sər'vaɪsiz] cervice *f*
cessation [se'seʃən] *s* cessazione
cesspool ['ses,pul] *s* pozzo nero
Ceylo•nese [,silə'niz] *adj* & *s* **(-nese)** singalese *mf*
chafe [tʃef] *s* irritazione ‖ *tr* (*the hands*) strofinare; irritare; (*to wear away*) logorare ‖ *intr* irritarsi; logorarsi
chaff [tʃæf] or [tʃɑf] *s* lolla; pula; (*joke*) burla; (fig) loppa
chaf'ing dish' *s* fornello a spirito
cha•grin [ʃə'grɪn] *s* cruccio, dispiacere *m* ‖ *v* (*pret* **-grined** or **-grinned;** *ger* **-grining** or **-grinning**) *tr* crucciare, affliggere
chain [tʃen] *s* catena; (*e.g., for necklace*) catenella ‖ *tr* incatenare
chain' gang' *s* catena di forzati
chain' reac'tion *s* reazione a catena
chain' saw' *s* motosega
chain'-smoke' *intr* fumare come un turco
chain' store' *s* negozio a catena
chair [tʃer] *s* sedia, seggiola; (*of important person*) seggio; (*at a university*) cattedra; (*chairman*) presidente *m,* presidenza; **to take the chair** cominciare una riunione ‖ *tr* (*a meeting*) presiedere
chair' lift' *s* seggiovia
chair'man *s* **(-men)** presidente *m*
chair'man•ship' *s* presidenza
chair'wom'an *s* **(-wom'en)** *s* presidentessa
chalice ['tʃælɪs] *s* calice *m*
chalk [tʃɔk] *s* gesso ‖ *tr* marcare or scrivere col gesso; **to chalk up** prendere appunti di; attribuire
chalk' talk' *s* conferenza illustrata
chalk•y ['tʃɔki] *adj* **(-ier; -iest)** gessoso
challenge ['tʃælɪndʒ] *s* sfida; (law) ricusazione; (mil) chi va là *m* ‖ *tr* sfidare; (*a juror*) (law) ricusare; (mil) dare il chi va là a
chamber ['tʃembər] *s* camera, stanza; (*of a palace*) aula; (*of a judge*) gabinetto
chamberlain ['tʃembərlɪn] *s* ciambellano
cham'ber•maid' *s* cameriera
cham'ber of com'merce *s* camera di commercio
cham'ber pot' *s* orinale *m*
chameleon [kə'milɪ•ən] *s* camaleonte *m*
cham•ois ['ʃæmi] *s* **(-ois)** camoscio
champ [tʃæmp] *s* (slang) campione *m* ‖ *tr* masticare rumorosamente; (*the bit*) mordere ‖ *intr* masticare rumorosamente
champagne [ʃæm'pen] *s* champagne *m,* spumante *m*
champion ['tʃæmpɪ•ən] *s* campione *m* ‖ *tr* difendere; farsi paladino di
championship ['tʃæmpɪ•ən,ʃɪp] *s* campionato
chance [tʃæns] or [tʃɑns] *adj* casuale, fortuito ‖ *s* occasione; caso; probabilità *f;* rischio; biglietto di lotteria; **by chance** per caso; **not to stand a chance** non avere la probabilità di riuscita; **to take one's chances** arrischiarsi; **to wait for a chance** attendere l'opportunità ‖ *intr* succedere; **to chance upon** imbattersi in
chancel ['tʃænsəl] or ['tʃɑnsəl] *s* presbiterio, coro
chanceller•y ['tʃænsələri] or ['tʃɑnsələri] *s* **(-ies)** cancelleria

chancellor ['tʃænsələr] or ['tʃɑnsələr] *s* cancelliere *m*
chandelier [,ʃændə'lir] *s* lampadario
change [tʃendʒ] *s* cambiamento; (*of clothes*) muta; (*of currency*) cambio; (*coins*) spiccioli *mpl;* **for a change** tanto per cambiare; **to keep the change** tenere il resto || *tr* cambiare, rimpiazzare; (*clothes*) cambiare, cambiarsi di || *intr* cambiare, mutare
changeable ['tʃendʒəbəl] *adj* mutevole, variabile, incostante
change' of heart' *s* pentimento, conversione
change' of life' *s* menopausa
chan•nel ['tʃænəl] *s* canale *m;* tubo, passaggio; stretto; (*of river*) alveo; (*groove*) solco; (rad, telv) canale *m;* **through channels** per via gerarchica || *v* (*pret & pp* **-neled** or **-nelled;** *ger* **-neling** or **-nelling**) *tr* incanalare; (*a river*) incassare || **the Channel** il Canale della Manica
chant [tʃænt] or [tʃɑnt] *s* canto; salmodia; canzone *f* || *tr & intr* cantare
chanticleer ['tʃæntɪ,klɪr] *s* il gallo
chaos ['ke•ɑs] *s* caos *m*
chaotic [ke'ɑtɪk] *adj* caotico
chap [tʃæp] *s* (*fellow*) individuo, tipo; (*of skin*) screpolatura; **chaps** pantaloni *mpl* di cuoio || *v* (*pret & pp* **chapped;** *ger* **chapping**) *tr* screpolare || *intr* screpolarsi
chapel ['tʃæpəl] *s* cappella
chaperon or **chaperone** ['ʃæpə,ron] *s* accompagnatrice *f* (di signorina) || *tr* accompagnare
chaplain ['tʃæplɪn] *s* cappellano
chaplet ['tʃæplɪt] *s* (*wreath*) corona, ghirlanda; rosario
chapter ['tʃæptər] *s* capitolo; (*of a club*) sezione
chap'ter and verse' *s*—**to give chapter and verse** citare le autorità
char [tʃɑr] *v* (*pret & pp* **charred;** *ger* **charring**) *tr* carbonizzare; bruciare
character ['kærɪktər] *s* carattere *m;* lettera, scrittura; indole *f;* (theat) personaggio; (coll) tipo; **in character** caratteristico di lui (lei, loro, etc.)
char'acter ac'tor *s* caratterista *m*
char'acter ac'tress *s* caratterista *f*
char'acter assassina'tion *s* linciaggio morale
characteristic [,kærɪktə'rɪstɪk] *adj* caratteristico || *s* caratteristica
characterize ['kærɪktə,raɪz] *tr* caratterizzare
char'coal' *s* carbone *m* di legna, carbone *m* dolce; (*for sketching*) carboncino; (*sketch*) disegno al carboncino
charge [tʃɑrdʒ] s carica; incarico; responsibilità *f;* (*indictment*) accusa; costo; prezzo; debito; **in charge** in comando; **in charge of** a cura di; **to take charge of** prendersi cura di || *tr* caricare; comandare; accusare; (*a price*) fare pagare; mettere in conto; **to charge s.o. with s.th** addebitare qlco a qlcu; accusare qlcu di qlco || *intr* fare una carica
charge' account' *s* conto corrente
chargé d'affaires [ʃɑr'ʒe də'fer] *s* (**chargés d'affaires**) incaricato d'affari
charger ['tʃɑrdʒər] *s* cavallo di battaglia; (*of a battery*) caricatore *m*
chariot ['tʃærɪ•ət] *s* cocchio
charioteer [,tʃærɪ•ə'tɪr] *s* auriga *m*
charis•ma [kə'rɪzmə] *s* (**-mata** [mətə]) fascino personale; (theol) carisma *m*
charitable ['tʃærɪtəbəl] *adj* (*person*) caritatevole; (*institution*) caritativo
chari•ty ['tʃærɪti] *s* (**-ties**) carità *f;* associazione di beneficenza
charlatan ['ʃɑrlətən] *s* ciarlatano
charlatanism ['ʃɑrlətən,ɪzəm] *s* ciarlataneria
Charlemagne ['ʃɑrlə,men] *s* Carlomagno
Charles [tʃɑrlz] *s* Carlo
char'ley horse' ['tʃɑrli] *s* (coll) crampo
charlotte ['ʃɑrlət] *s* charlotte *f* || **Charlotte** *s* Carlotta
charm [tʃɑrm] *s* fascino; amuleto; portafortuna *m* || *tr* incantare, stregare
charming ['tʃɑrmɪŋ] *adj* affascinante
charnel ['tʃɑrnəl] *adj* orribile || *s* ossario
chart [tʃɑrt] *s* carta geografica; lista; diagramma *m* || *tr* tracciare
charter ['tʃɑrtər] *s* statuto; privilegio || *tr* (*a company*) fondare; (*a conveyance*) noleggiare
char'ter mem'ber *s* socio fondatore
char'wom'an *s* (**-wom'en**) domestica per la pulizia
chase [tʃes] *s* inseguimento; caccia; (typ) telaio || *tr* inseguire; cacciare; (*to chisel*) cesellare; **to chase away** scacciare || *intr*—**to chase after** inseguire
chaser ['tʃesər] *s* cacciatore *m;* (coll) bibita da bersi dopo un liquore
chasm ['kæzəm] *s* abisso, baratro
chas•sis ['tʃæsi] *s* (**-sis** [siz]) **telaio**
chaste [tʃest] *adj* casto
chasten ['tʃesən] *tr* castigare
chastise [tʃæs'taɪz] *tr* castigare
chastity ['tʃæstɪti] *s* castità *f*
chat [tʃæt] *s* chiacchierata || *v* (*pret & pp* **chatted;** *ger* **chatting**) *intr* chiacchierare
chatelaine ['ʃætə,len] *s* castellana
chattels ['tʃætəlz] *spl* beni *mpl* mobili
chatter ['tʃætər] *s* cicaleccio; balbettio; (*of teeth*) battito || *intr* cicalare; balbettare; (*said of teeth*) battere
chat'ter•box' *s* chiacchierone *m*
chauffeur ['ʃofər] or [ʃo'fʌr] *s* autista *mf* || *intr* fare l'autista
cheap [tʃip] *adj* a buon mercato, economico; (*of poor quality*) scadente; **to feel cheap** vergognarsi || *adv* a buon mercato
cheapen ['tʃipən] *tr* deprezzare; avvilire; rendere di cattivo gusto
cheapness ['tʃipnəs] *s* buon mercato, prezzo basso
cheat [tʃit] *s* truffa; truffatore *m* || *tr* imbrogliare, truffare || *intr* truffare; (*at cards*) barare
check [tʃek] *s* arresto, pausa; ostacolo;

esame *m;* verifica, controllo; (*of bank*) assegno; (*for baggage*) tagliando, scontrino; (*square pattern*) quadretto; (*fabric in squares*) tessuto a scacchi; (*in a restaurant*) conto; **in check** controllato, sotto controllo; (chess) sotto scacco || *tr* fermare; confrontare; ispezionare; marcare; (*e.g., a coat*) depositare; disegnare a quadretti; (chess) dare scacco a; **to check off** controllare marcando; **to check on** controllare, verificare || *intr* fermarsi; corrispondere perfettamente; **to check in** scendere (a un albergo); **to check out** andar via; pagare il conto; **to check up on** controllare

check'book' s libretto d'assegni

checker ['tʃɛkər] *s* ispettore *m;* quadretto; (*in game of checkers*) pedina; **checkers** dama || *tr* variegare; marcare a quadretti

check'er•board' *s* scacchiera

check'ered *adj* (*e.g., career*) pieno di vicissitudini; (*marked with squares*) a scacchi; (*in color*) variegato

check'ing account' *s* conto corrente

check'mate' *s* scacco matto || *tr* dare scacco matto a || *interj* scacco matto!

check'off' dues' *spl* trattenute *fpl* sindacali

check'-out' *s* (*from hotel room*) partenza; (*time*) ora della partenza; (*examination*) esame *m* di controllo; (*in a supermarket*) cassa

check'point' *s* punto di ispezione

check'room' *s* guardaroba *m*

check'up' *s* (*of car*) ispezione; (*of patient*) esame *m* (fisico)

cheek [tʃik] *s* guancia, gota; (coll) faccia tosta

cheek'bone' *s* zigomo

cheek•y ['tʃiki] *adj* (**-ier; -iest**) (coll) impudente, sfacciato

cheer [tʃɪr] *s* gioia, allegria; applauso; **of good cheer** di buon umore || *tr* riempire di gioia, rallegrare; applaudire; ricevere con applausi || *intr* rallegrarsi; **cheer up!** animo!, coraggio!

cheerful ['tʃɪrfəl] *adj* allegro, di buon umore; (*willing*) volonteroso

cheerless ['tʃɪrlɪs] *adj* tetro, triste

cheese [tʃiz] *s* formaggio || *intr*—**cheese it!** (slang) scappa via!

cheese' cake' *s* torta di formaggio; (slang) pin-up girl *f*

cheese'cloth' *s* etamine *f*, stamigna

chees•y [tʃisi] *adj* (**-ier; -iest**) di formaggio; come il formaggio; (slang) meschino, di cattiva qualità

chef [ʃɛf] *s* chef *m*, capocuoco

chemical ['kɛmɪkəl] *adj* chimico || *s* prodotto chimico

chemise [ʃə'miz] *s* sottoveste *f*

chemist ['kɛmɪst] *s* chimico

chemistry ['kɛmɪstri] *s* chimica

cherish ['tʃɛrɪʃ] *tr* accarezzare; (*a memory*) custodire; (*a hope*) nutrire

cher•ry ['tʃɛri] *s* (**-ries**) (*tree*) ciliegio; (*fruit*) ciliegia

cher•ub ['tʃɛrəb] *s* (**-ubim** [əbɪm] & **-ubs**) cherubino

chess [tʃɛs] *s* scacchi *mpl*

chess'board' *s* scacchiera

chess'man' or **chess'man** *s* (**-men'** or **-men**) scacco

chest [tʃɛst] *s* petto; (*box*) cassapanca; (*furniture with drawers*) cassettone *m;* (*for money*) forziere *m*

chestnut ['tʃɛsnət] *s* (*tree, wood, color*) castagno; (*nut*) castagna

chest' of drawers' *s* cassettone *m*

cheval' glass' [ʃə'væl] *s* psiche *f*

chevalier [,ʃɛvə'lɪr] *s* cavaliere *m*

chevron ['ʃɛvrən] *s* gallone *m*

chew [tʃu] *tr* masticare; **to chew the cud** ruminare; **to chew the rag** (slang) chiacchierare || *intr* masticare

chew'ing gum' *s* gomma da masticare

chic [ʃik] *adj* & *s* chic

chicaner•y [ʃɪ'kenəri] *s* (**-ies**) trucco, rigiro

chick [tʃɪk] *s* pulcino; (slang) ragazza

chicken ['tʃɪkən] *s* pollo, pollastro; (coll) giovane *mf;* **to be chicken** (slang) avere la fifa || *intr*—**to chicken out** (coll) indietreggiare

chick'en coop' *s* pollaio

chick'en feed' *s* (slang) spiccioli *mpl*

chicken-hearted ['tʃɪkən,hartɪd] *adj* timido, fifone

chick'en pox' *s* varicella

chick'en store' *s* polleria

chick'en wire' *s* rete metallica esagonale

chick'pea' *s* cece *m*

chico•ry ['tʃɪkəri] *s* (**-ries**) cicoria

chide [tʃaɪd] *v* (*pret* **chided** or **chid** [tʃɪd]; *pp* **chided, chid,** or **chidden** ['tʃɪdən]) *tr* & *intr* rimproverare, correggere

chief [tʃif] *adj* principale, sommo, supremo || *s* capo, comandante supremo; (slang) padrone *m*

chief' exec'utive *s* capo del governo

chief' jus'tice *s* presidente *m* di una corte; presidente *m* della corte suprema

chiefly ['tʃifli] *adv* principalmente

chief' of staff' *s* capo di stato maggiore

chief' of state' *s* capo dello stato

chieftain ['tʃiftən] *s* capo

chiffon [ʃɪ'fan] *s* velo trasparente, chiffon *m;* **chiffons** trine *fpl*

chiffonier [,ʃɪfə'nɪr] *s* mobile *m* a cassettini, chiffonier *m*

chilblain ['tʃɪl,blen] *s* gelone *m*

child [tʃaɪld] *s* (**children** ['tʃɪldrən]) bebè *mf*, bambino; figlio; discendente *mf;* **with child** incinta

child'birth' *s* parto

childhood ['tʃaɪldhʊd] *s* infanzia

childish ['tʃaɪldɪʃ] *adj* infantile

childishness ['tʃaɪldɪʃnɪs] *s* puerilità *f*, infanzia

child' la'bor *s* lavoro dei minorenni

childless ['tʃaɪldlɪs] *adj* senza figli

child'like' *adj* infantile, innocente

child's' play' *s* un gioco

child' wel'fare *s* protezione dell'infanzia

Chile ['tʃɪli] *s* il Cile

Chilean ['tʃɪlɪ•ən] *adj* cileno

chil'i sauce' ['tʃɪli] *s* salsa di pomodoro con peperoni
chill [tʃɪl] *adj* freddo || s freddo; brivido di freddo; freddezza; (*depression*) abbattimento || *tr* raffreddare; (*a metal*) temprare; (fig) scoraggiare || *intr* raffreddarsi
chill·y ['tʃɪli] *adj* (**-ier; -iest**) fresco, freddiccio; (*reception*) freddo
chime [tʃaɪm] *s* scampanio; **chimes** campanello || *intr* scampanare; **to chime in** cominciare a cantare all'unisono; (coll) intromettersi
chime' clock' *s* orologio con carillon
chimney ['tʃɪmni] *s* camino; (*of factory*) ciminiera; **to smoke like a chimney** fumare come un turco
chim'ney flue' *s* tubo di stufa, canna del camino
chim'ney pot' *s* testa della canna fumaria, comignolo
chim'ney sweep' *s* spazzacamino
chimpanzee [tʃɪm'pænzi] or [ˌtʃɪmpæn'zi] *s* scimpanzé *m*
chin [tʃɪn] *s* mento; **to keep one's chin up** (coll) non perdersi di coraggio; **to take it on the chin** (slang) subire una sconfitta || *v* (*pret & pp* **chinned;** *ger* **chinning**) *tr*—**to chin oneself** sollevarsi fino al mento (ai manubri) || *intr* (slang) chiacchierare
china ['tʃaɪnə] *s* porcellana || **China** *s* la Cina
chi'na clos'et *s* armadio per le stoviglie
chi'na·ware' *s* porcellana, stoviglie *fpl*
Chi·nese [tʃaɪ'niz] *adj* cinese || *s* (**-nese**) cinese *mf*
Chi'nese lan'tern *s* lampioncino alla veneziana
Chi'nese puz'zle *s* rebus *m*
chink [tʃɪŋk] *s* fessura
chin' strap' *s* sottogola
chintz [tʃɪnts] *s* chintz *m*
chip [tʃɪp] *s* scheggia; frammento; (*in card games*) gettone *m;* (*of wood*) truciolo; **chip off the old block** vero figlio di suo padre (di sua madre); **chip on one's shoulder** propensità *f* a attaccar brighe || *v* (*pret & pp* **chipped;** *ger* **chipping**) *tr* scheggiare; **to chip in** contribuire || *intr* scheggiarsi
chipmunk ['tʃɪpˌmʌŋk] *s* tamia
chipper ['tʃɪpər] *adj* (coll) allegro, vivo
chiropodist [kaɪ'rɑpədɪst] or [kɪ'rɑpədɪst] *s* callista *mf*, pedicure *mf*
chiropractice ['kaɪrəˌpræktɪs] *s* chiropratica
chirp [tʃʌrp] *s* (*of birds*) cinguettio; (*of crickets*) cri cri *m* || *intr* cinguettare; fare cri cri
chis·el ['tʃɪzəl] *s* (*for wood and metal*) scalpello; (*for metal*) cesello || *v* (*pret & pp* **-eled** or **-elled;** *ger* **-eling** or **-elling**) *tr* scalpellare; cesellare; (slang) imbrogliare || *intr* (slang) imbrogliare, fare l'imbroglione
chiseler ['tʃɪzələr] *s* scalpellino; cesellatore *m;* (slang) imbroglione *m*
chit-chat ['tʃɪtˌtʃæt] *s* chiacchierata
chivalrous ['ʃɪvəlrəs] *adj* cavalleresco
chivalry ['ʃɪvəlri] *s* cavalleria
chive [tʃaɪv] *s* cipolla porraia
chloride ['klorаɪd] *s* cloruro
chlorine ['klorin] *s* cloro
chloroform ['kloreˌfɔrm] *s* cloroformio || *tr* cloroformizzare
chlorophyll ['klorəfɪl] *s* clorofilla
chock [tʃɑk] *s* (*wedge*) bietta, cuneo
chock-full ['tʃɑk'ful] *adj* colmo, pieno zeppo
chocolate ['tʃɔkəlɪt] or ['tʃɑkəlɪt] *s* (*candy*) cioccolato; (*drink*) cioccolata
choc'olate bar' *s* barretta di cioccolato
choice [tʃɔɪs] *adj* di prima scelta, superiore || *s* scelta; (*variety*) assortimento
choir [kwaɪr] *s* coro
choir'boy' *s* ragazzo cantore
choir' loft' *s* coro
choir'mas'ter *s* maestro di cappella
choke [tʃok] *s* strozzatura; (aut) farfalla del carburatore || *tr* strozzare; ostruire; (*an internal-combustion engine*) arricchire la miscela di; **to choke back** trattenere; **to choke up** tappare, ostruire || *intr* soffocarsi; **to choke up** tapparsi; (coll) soffocarsi
choker ['tʃokər] *s* (*necklace*) (coll) collana; (*scarf*) (coll) foulard *m*
cholera ['kɑlərə] *s* colera *m*
choleric ['kɑlərɪk] *adj* collerico
cholesterol [kə'lɛstəˌrol] or [kə'lɛstəˌrɑl] *s* colesterina
choose [tʃuz] *v* (*pret* **chose** [tʃoz]; *pp* **chosen** ['tʃozən]) *tr* scegliere || *intr* —**to choose to** decidere di
choos·y ['tʃuzi] *adj* (**-ier; -iest**) (coll) di difficile contentatura
chop [tʃɑp] *s* colpo; (*of meat*) cotoletta; **chops** labbra *fpl*, bocca || *v* (*pret & pp* **chopped;** *ger* **chopping**) *tr* tagliare; (*meat*) tritare; **to chop off** troncare; **to chop up** sminuzzare
chopper ['tʃɑpər] *s* (*man*) tagliatore *m;* interruttore automatico; coltello da macellaio; (slang) elicottero; **choppers** (slang) i denti
chop'ping block' *s* tagliere *m*
chop·py ['tʃɑpi] *adj* (**-pier; -piest**) (*wind*) variabile; (*sea*) agitato; (*style*) instabile
choral ['korəl] *adj & s* corale *m*
chorale [ko'rɑl] *s* corale *m*
chord [kɔrd] *s* corda; (mus) accordo
chore [tʃor] *s* lavoro; lavoro spiacevole; **chores** faccende domestiche
choreography [ˌkorɪ'ɑgrəfi] *s* coreografia
chorine [ko'rin] *s* (slang) ballerina
chorus ['korəs] *s* coro; (*group of dancers*) corpo di ballo; (*of a song*) ritornello
cho'rus girl' *s* ballerina
cho'rus man' *s* (**men'**) corista *m*
chow [tʃaʊ] *s* (*dog*) chow chow *m;* (slang) cibo, pappa
chowder ['tʃaʊdər] *s* zuppa di vongole; zuppa di pesce
Christ [kraɪst] *s* Cristo
christen ['krɪsən] *tr* battezzare
Christendom ['krɪsəndəm] *s* cristianità *f*

christening ['krɪsənɪŋ] *s* battesimo
Christian ['krɪstʃən] *adj* & *s* cristiano
Christianity [,krɪstʃɪ'ænɪti] *s* (*Christendom*) cristianità *f*; (*religion*) cristianesimo
Chris'tian name' *s* nome *m* di battesimo
Christmas ['krɪsməs] *adj* natalizio ‖ *s* Natale *m*; **Merry Christmas!** Buon Natale!
Christ'mas card' *s* cartoncino natalizio
Christ'mas car'ol *s* pastorella di Natale
Christ'mas Eve' *s* vigilia di Natale
Christ'mas gift' *s* strenna natalizia
Christ'mas tree' *s* albero di Natale
chrome [krom] *adj* cromato ‖ *s* cromo ‖ *tr* cromare
chromium ['kromɪ·əm] *s* cromo
chromosome ['kromə,som] *s* cromosoma *m*
chronic ['krɑnɪk] *adj* cronico
chronicle ['krɑnɪkəl] *s* cronaca ‖ *tr* fare la storia di
chronicler ['krɑnɪklər] *s* cronista *mf*
chronolo·gy [krə'nɑlədʒi] *s* (**-gies**) cronologia
chronometer [krə'nɑmɪtər] *s* cronometro
chrysanthemum [krɪ'sænθɪməm] *s* crisantemo
chub·by ['tʃʌbi] *adj* (**-bier; -biest**) paffuto
chuck [tʃʌk] *s* buffetto sotto il mento; (*cut of meat*) reale *m*; (*of lathe*) coppaia ‖ *tr* accarezzare sotto il mento; (*to throw*) (coll) gettare
chuckle ['tʃʌkəl] *s* risatina ‖ *intr* ridacchiare
chum [tʃʌm] *s* (coll) amico intimo; (coll) compagno di stanza ‖ *v* (*pret & pp* **chummed**; *ger* **chumming**) *intr* (coll) essere amico intimo; essere compagno di stanza
chum·my ['tʃʌmi] *adj* (**-mier; -miest**) (coll) intimo, amicone
chump [tʃʌmp] *s* ciocco, ceppo; (coll) sciocco
chunk [tʃʌŋk] *s* grosso pezzo
church [tʃʌrtʃ] *s* chiesa
churchgoer ['tʃʌrtʃ,go·ər] *s* praticante *mf*
church'man *s* (**-men**) parrocchiano; (*clergyman*) sacerdote *m*
Church' of Eng'land *s* chiesa anglicana
church'yard' *s* camposanto
churl [tʃʌrl] *s* zotico, villano
churlish ['tʃʌrlɪʃ] *adj* villano
churn [tʃʌrn] *s* zangola ‖ *tr* agitare violentemente, sbattere ‖ *intr* (*said of water*) ribollire
chute [ʃut] *s* piano inclinato, canna; (*in a river*) cascata, rapida; paracadute *m*; (*into a swimming pool*) toboga *m*
Cicero ['sɪsə,ro] *s* Cicerone *m*
cider ['saɪdər] *s* sidro
cigar [sɪ'gɑr] *s* sigaro
cigar' case' *s* portasigari *m*
cigar' cut'ter *s* tagliasigari *m*
cigarette [,sɪgə'rɛt] *s* sigaretta
cigarette' butt' *s* cicca
cigarette' case' *s* portasigarette *m*
cigarette' hold'er *s* bocchino
cigarette' light'er *s* accendisigaro, accendino
cigarette' pa'per *s* cartina da sigarette
cigar' store' *s* tabaccheria, rivendita di sali e tabacchi
cinch [sɪntʃ] *s* (*on a horse*) sottopancia *m*; (*hold*) (coll) presa; (slang) giochetto ‖ *tr* legare con una cinghia; (slang) agguantare
cinder ['sɪndər] *s* tizzone *m*; (*slag*) scoria; **cinders** cenere *f*
cin'der block' *s* concio di scoria
Cinderella [,sɪndə'rɛlə] *s* (la) Cenerentola
cinema ['sɪnəmə] *s* cine *m*, cinema *m*
cinnabar ['sɪnə,bɑr] *s* cinabro
cinnamon ['sɪnəmən] *s* cannella
cipher ['saɪfər] *s* zero; cifra; codice *m*; monogramma *m* ‖ *tr* calcolare; (*to write in code*) cifrare
circle ['sʌrkəl] *s* cerchio; (*of theater*) prima galleria; (*of friends*) cerchia ‖ *tr* cerchiare, compiere una rotazione intorno a
circuit ['sʌrkɪt] *s* circuito; (*district*) circoscrizione
cir'cuit break'er *s* salvamotore *m*, interruttore automatico
circuitous [sər'kju·ɪtəs] *adj* tortuoso
circuitry ['sʌrkɪtri] *s* (*plan*) schema *m* di montaggio; (*components*) elementi *mpl* di un circuito
circular ['sʌrkjələr] *adj* & *s* circolare *f*
circulate ['sʌrkjə,let] *tr* mettere in circolazione, diffondere ‖ *intr* circolare
cir'culating li'brary *s* biblioteca circolante
circulation [,sʌrkjə'leʃən] *s* circolazione; (*of newspaper*) diffusione
circumcise ['sʌrkəm,saɪz] *tr* circoncidere
circumference [sər'kʌmfərəns] *s* circonferenza
circumflex ['sʌrkəm,flɛks] *adj* circonflesso ‖ *s* accento circonflesso
circumscribe [,sʌrkəm'skraɪb] *tr* circoscrivere
circumspect ['sʌrkəm,spɛkt] *adj* circospetto
circumstance ['sʌrkəm,stæns] *s* circostanza; (*fact*) dettaglio; solennità *f*; **circumstances** condizioni *fpl*; dettagli *mpl*; condizioni economiche; **under no circumstances** a nessuna condizione; **under the circumstances** le cose essendo come sono
circumstantial [,sʌrkəm'stænʃəl] *adj* circostanziale, indiziario; (*incidental*) secondario; (*complete*) circostanziato
cir'cumstan'tial ev'idence *s* prova indiziaria
circumstantiate [,sʌrkəm'stænʃɪ,et] *tr* (*to support with particulars*) comprovare; (*to describe in detail*) circonstanziare
circumvent [,sʌrkəm'vent] *tr* (*to surround*) accerchiare; (*to outwit*) circuire; (*a difficulty*) eludere, scansare
circus ['sʌrkəs] *s* circo equestre
cistern ['sɪstərn] *s* cisterna, serbatoio
citadel ['sɪtədəl] *s* cittadella
citation [saɪ'teʃən] *s* citazione

cite [saɪt] *tr* citare
cither ['sɪðər] *s* cetra
citizen ['sɪtɪzən] *s* cittadino; (*civilian*) civile *mf*
citizenship ['sɪtɪzən ,ʃɪp] *s* cittadinanza
citric ['sɪtrɪk] *adj* citrico
citron ['sɪtrən] *s* cedro; cedro candito
cit'rus fruit' ['sɪtrəs] *s* agrumi *mpl*
cit•y ['sɪti] *s* (**-ies**) città *f*
cit'y counc'il *s* consiglio municipale
cit'y ed'itor *s* capocronista *m*
cit'y fa'thers *spl* maggiorenti *mpl;* consiglieri *mpl* municipali
cit'y hall' *s* municipio
cit'y plan'ning *s* urbanistica
cit'y room' *s* (journ) redazione
civic ['sɪvɪk] *adj* civico ‖ **civics** *s* educazione civica
civil ['sɪvɪl] *adj* civile
civ'il engineer'ing *s* genio civile
civilian [sɪ'vɪljən] *adj* & *s* civile *mf,* borghese *mf*
civili•ty [sɪ'vɪlɪti] *s* (**-ties**) cortesia; **civilities** ossequi *mpl*
civilization [,sɪvɪlɪ'zeʃən] *s* civilizzazione, civiltà *f*
civilize ['sɪvɪ ,laɪz] *tr* civilizzare
civ'il law' *s* diritto civile
civ'il serv'ant *s* impiegato statale
civ'il war' *s* guerra civile ‖ **Civil War** *s* (*of the U.S.A.*) guerra di secessione
claim [klem] *s* pretesa; richiesta; (min) concessione ‖ *tr* (*one's rights*) rivendicare; (*one's property*) richiedere; dichiarare; **to claim to be** pretendere d'essere
claim' check' *s* tagliando
clairvoyance [kler'vɔɪ•əns] *s* chiaroveggenza
clairvoyant [kler'vɔɪ•ənt] *adj* chiaroveggente ‖ *s* veggente *mf,* chiaroveggente *mf*
clam [klæm] *s* vongola ‖ *intr*—**to clam up** (coll) essere muto come un pesce
clamber ['klæmər] *intr* arrampicarsi
clam•my ['klæmi] *adj* (**-mier; -miest**) coperto di sudore freddo; morbido
clamor ['klæmər] *s* clamore *m* ‖ *intr* fare clamore
clamorous ['klæmərəs] *adj* clamoroso
clamp [klæmp] *s* graffa, morsetto; (*e.g., to hold a hose*) fascetta ‖ *tr* assicurare con graffa, aggrappare; (*a tool*) montare ‖ *intr*—**to clamp down on** (coll) fare pressione su, mettere i freni a
clan [klæn] *s* clan *m*
clandestine [klæn'destɪn] *adj* clandestino
clang [klæŋ] *s* clangore *m* ‖ *intr* risonare con clangore
clannish ['klænɪʃ] *adj* esclusivista, partigiano
clap [klæp] *s* applauso; (*of thunder*) scoppio ‖ *v* (*pret & pp* **clapped;** *ger* **clapping**) *tr* (*the hands*) battere; (*e.g., in jail*) schiaffare; **to clap shut** sbattere ‖ *intr* applaudire
clapper ['klæpər] *s* applauditore *m;* (*of bell*) batacchio
clap'trap' *s* imbonimento
claret ['klærɪt] *adj* & *s* chiaretto
clari•fy ['klærɪ ,faɪ] *v* (*pret & pp* **-fied**) *tr* chiarificare, chiarire
clarinet [,klærɪ'net] *s* clarinetto
clarion ['klærɪ•ən] *adj* chiaro e metallico ‖ *s* tromba, clarino
clash [klæʃ] *s* cozzo, urto; conflitto di opinioni ‖ *intr* cozzare, urtarsi; essere in conflitto
clasp [klæsp] or [klɑsp] *s* gancio, fermaglio; (*hold*) presa; (*grip*) stretta ‖ *tr* agganciare; (*to hold in the arms*) abbracciare; (*to grip*) stringere
class [klæs] or [klɑs] *s* classe *f* ‖ *tr* classificare
class'book' *s* registro
classic ['klæsɪk] *adj* & *s* classico
classical ['klæsɪkəl] *adj* classico
classicism ['klæsɪ ,sɪzəm] *s* classicismo
classicist ['klæsɪsɪst] *s* classicista *mf*
classified ['klæsɪ ,faɪd] *adj* segreto
clas'sified ad' *s* annunzio economico
classi•fy ['klæsɪ ,faɪ] *v* (*pret & pp* **-fied**) *tr* classificare
class'mate' *s* compagno di scuola
class'room' *s* aula scolastica
class' strug'gle *s* lotta di classe
class•y [klæsi] *adj* (**-ier; -iest**) (slang) di lusso, di prim'ordine
clatter ['klætər] *s* (*of dishes*) acciottolio; vocio, schiamazzo ‖ *tr* acciottolare ‖ *intr* fare schiamazzo
clause [klɔz] *s* clausola; (gram) proposizione
clavicle ['klævɪkəl] *s* clavicola
claw [klɔ] *s* artiglio; (*of lobster*) pinza; (*tool*) raffio; (*of hammer*) granchio; (coll) dita *fpl* ‖ *tr* aggraffiare; artigliare
claw' ham'mer *s* levachiodi *m*
clay [kle] *s* argilla, creta
clay' pipe' *s* pipa di terracotta
clean [klin] *adj* pulito; (*precise*) netto; (*e.g., break*) completo ‖ *adv* completamente ‖ *tr* pulire; **to clean out** pulire, fare repulisti di; (slang) ripulire; **to clean up** pulire completamente; mettere in ordine ‖ *intr* pulirsi, fare pulizia
clean' bill' of health' *s* patente sanitaria; (fig) esonero completo
clean'-cut' *adj* ben delineato, deciso
cleaner ['klinər] *s* pulitore *m,* smacchiatore *m;* (*machine*) pulitrice *f,* smacchiatrice *f;* **to send to the cleaners** (slang) spolpare
clean'ing fluid' *s* smacchiatore *m*
clean'ing wom'an *s* donna di servizio per fare la pulizia
clean•ly ['klenli] *adj* (**-lier; -liest**) pulito, netto
cleanse [klenz] *tr* pulire; detergere; purificare
cleanser ['klenzər] *s* detergente *m*
clean'-sha'ven *adj* sbarbato di fresco
clean'up' *s* pulizia; (slang) guadagno enorme
clear [klɪr] *adj* chiaro; evidente; completo; innocente; (*profit*) netto; **clear of** libero da ‖ *s* posto libero; **in the clear** libero; esonerato; non in codice ‖ *adv* chiaramente; completamente ‖ *tr* (*e.g., trees*) rischiarare; (*e.g., peo-*

ple) sgombrare; (*the table*) sparecchiare; (*an obstacle*) superare; (*from guilt*) discolpare; (*a profit*) guadagnare; (*goods at customs*) svincolare; (*a ship through customs*) dichiarare il carico di; (*checks*) compensare; **to clear away** or **off** liberare; **to clear out** sgomberare, sbarazzare; **to clear up** spiegare; (*a doubt*) dissipare || *intr* rasserenarsi; (*said of a ship*) partire; **to clear away** or **off** sparire; **to clear out** (coll) andarsene; **to clear up** rasserenarsi
clearance ['klɪrəns] *s* liberazione; (*of a ship*) partenza; (*of goods through customs*) sdoganamento; (*of checks*) compensazione; (*of goods*) liquidazione; (mach) gioco
clear'ance sale' *s* liquidazione
clear'-cut' *adj* chiaro, distinto
clearing ['klɪrɪŋ] *s* (*open space*) radura; (*of checks*) compensazione
clear'ing house' *s* stanza di compensazione
cleat [klit] *s* bietta, cuneo; (*on the sole of shoe*) tacchetto; (naut) galloccia
cleavage ['klivɪdʒ] *s* divisione; fessura
cleave [kliv] *v* (*pret & pp* **cleft** [kleft] or **cleaved**) *tr* dividere, fendere || *intr* aderire, essere fedele
cleaver ['klivər] *s* scure *f*, accetta; (*of butcher*) spaccaossa *m*, fenditoio
clef [klɛf] *s* (mus) chiave *f*
cleft [klɛft] *adj* diviso, fesso || *s* fessura, crepaccio
cleft' pal'ate *s* palato spaccato, gola lupina
clematis ['klɛmətɪs] *s* clematide *f*
clemen•cy ['klɛmənsi] *s* (**-cies**) clemenza
clement ['klɛmənt] *adj* clemente
clench [klɛntʃ] *s* stretta || *tr* stringere; afferrare
clergy ['klʌrdʒi] *s* clero
cler'gy•man *s* (**-men**) ecclesiastico
cleric ['klɛrɪk] *s* ecclesiastico, sacerdote *m*
clerical ['klɛrɪkəl] *adj* da impiegato; (*error*) burocratico; (*of clergy*) clericale || *s* ecclesiastico; **clericals** abiti ecclesiastici
cler'ical work' *s* lavoro d'ufficio
clerk [klʌrk] *s* impiegato, commesso; (*accountant*) contabile *mf*; (*e.g., in a record office*) ufficiale *m*; cancelliere *m*; (*copyist, typist*) scrivano
clever ['klɛvər] *adj* intelligente; bravo, abile; destro
cleverness ['klɛvərnɪs] *s* intelligenza; bravura, abilità *f*
clew [klu] *s* indizio, traccia; (*of yarn*) gomitolo; (naut) bugna
cliché [kli'ʃe] *s* cliché *m*, luogo comune
click [klɪk] *s* (*of camera or gun*) scatto; (*of typewriter*) battito, ticchettio || *tr* (*the tongue*) schioccare; (*the heels*) battere || *intr* ticchettare; (slang) andare d'accordo; (slang) avere fortuna
client ['klaɪ·ənt] *s* cliente *mf*
clientele [,klaɪ·ən'tɛl] *s* clientela
cliff [klɪf] *s* rupe *f*, precipizio
climate ['klaɪmɪt] *s* clima *m*
climax ['klaɪmæks] *s* apice *m*; (*acute phase*) parossismo
climb [klaɪm] *s* salita; (*of a mountain*) scalata, ascensione || *tr* (*the stairs*) salire; (*a mountain*) scalare, ascendere || *intr* salire, arrampicarsi; **to climb down** discendere a carponi; (coll) ritirarsi
climber ['klaɪmər] *s* scalatore *m*; pianta rampicante; (*ambitious person*) (coll) arrampicatore *m*
clinch [klɪntʃ] *s* stretta, presa; (*boxing*) corpo a corpo *m* || *tr* (*nails*) ribattere, ribadire
clincher ['klɪntʃər] *s* chiodo per ribaditura; argomento decisivo
cling [klɪŋ] *v* (*pret & pp* **clung** [klʌŋ]) *intr* avviticchiare, attaccarsi; aderire, rimanere attaccato
cling'stone' peach' *s* pesca duracino
clinic ['klɪnɪk] *s* clinica
clinical ['klɪnɪkəl] *adj* clinico
clinician [klɪ'nɪʃən] *s* clinico
clink [klɪŋk] *s* tintinnio; (slang) gattabuia || *tr* (*glasses*) toccare || *intr* tintinnare
clinker ['klɪŋkər] *s* clinker *m*; mattone vetrificato; (slang) sbaglio
clip [klɪp] *s* (*of hair*) taglio; (*of wool*) tosatura; (*speed*) passo rapido; clip *f*, fermaglio; (*large clip*) fermacarte *m*; (*for cartridges*) caricatore *m*; (coll) colpo || *v* (*pret & pp* **clipped**; *ger* **clipping**) *tr* tagliare, tosare; (*words*) mangiare, storpiare; (*paper*) ritagliare; ritenere; (coll) battere || *intr* andare di buon passo
clipper ['klɪpər] *s* tagliatore *m*; (aer, naut) clipper *m*; **clippers** (*for hair*) tosatrice *f*; (*for nails*) pinze *fpl* per le unghie
clipping ['klɪpɪŋ] *s* taglio; (*from newspaper*) ritaglio
clique [klik] *s* cricca, chiesuola
cloak [klok] *s* mantello, manto; (fig) velo, maschera || *tr* ammantare, velare
cloak'-and-dag'ger *adj* d'avventura
cloak'-and-sword' *adj* di cappa e spada
cloak'room' *s* guardaroba *m*
clock [klɑk] *s* orologio; (*with pendulum*) pendolo, pendola; (*on stocking*) freccia || *tr* registrare, cronometrare
clock'mak'er *s* orologiaio
clock' tow'er *s* torre *f* dell'orologio
clock'wise' *adj & adv* nella direzione delle lancette dell'orologio
clock'work' *s* movimento d'orologeria; **like clockwork** come un orologio
clod [klɑd] *s* zolla; (fig) tonto
clod'hop'per *s* (*shoe*) scarpone *m*; (fig) villano, bifolco
clog [klɑg] *s* intoppo; (*to impede movement*) pastoia; scarpone *m*, zoccolo || *v* (*pret & pp* **clogged**; *ger* **clogging**) *tr* intoppare; (*to hold back*) impastoiare || *intr* otturarsi, ostruirsi
cloister ['klɔɪstər] *s* chiostro || *tr* rinchiudere in un chiostro
close [klos] *adj* vicino; (*translation*)

fedele; (*air in room*) male arieggiato; (*weather*) soffocante; (*stingy*) avaro; limitato, senza gioco; (*haircut*) corto; (*friend*) intimo; (*hit*) preciso; (*enclosed*) chiuso; (*narrow*) stretto || *adv* da vicino; **close to** vicino a || [kloz] *s* fine *f*, conclusione; **to bring to a close** concludere || *tr* chiudere; otturare; concludere; **to close down** chiudere completamente; **to close out** vendere in liquidazione; **to close up** bloccare || *intr* chiudersi; serrarsi; **to close down** chiudersi completamente; **to close in on** venire alle prese con; **to close up** bloccarsi; (*said of a wound*) rimarginarsi

close' call' [klos] *s* rischio scampato per miracolo

closed' chap'ter *s* affare chiuso

closed' cir'cuit *s* circuito chiuso

closed' sea'son *s* periodo di caccia o pesca vietata

closefisted ['klos'fɪstɪd] *adj* taccagno

close'-fit'ing [klos] *adj* attillato

close-lipped ['klos'lɪpt] *adj* riservato

closely ['klosli] *adv* da vicino; strettamente; fedelmente; attentamente

close' quar'ters [klos] *spl* (*cramped space*) pigia pigia *m;* **at close quarters** a corpo a corpo

close' quote' [kloz] *s* fine *f* della citazione

close' shave' [klos] *s*—**to have a close shave** farsi fare la barba a contropelo; (coll) scamparla per un pelo

closet ['klɑzɪt] *s* armadio a muro; (*small private room*) gabinetto; (*for keeping clothing*) ripostiglio || *tr*—**to be closeted with** essere in conciliabolo con

close'-up' [klos] *s* (mov) primo piano

closing ['klozɪŋ] *s* fine *f*, conclusione

clos'ing price' *s* ultimo corso

clot [klɑt] *s* grumo, coagulo || *v* (*pret & pp* **clotted;** *ger* **clotting**) *intr* raggrumarsi, coagularsi

cloth [klɔθ] or [klɑθ] *s* panno, tessuto, stoffa; abito; (*for binding books*) tela; **the cloth** il clero

clothe [kloð] *v* (*pret & pp* **clothed** or **clad** [klæd]) *tr* vestire, rivestire, coprire

clothes [kloz] or [kloðz] *spl* vestiti *mpl*, abiti *mpl;* (*for a bed*) coltre *f;* **to change clothes** cambiarsi

clothes'bas'ket *s* cesto della biancheria

clothes'brush' *s* spazzola per vestiti

clothes' dry'er *s* asciugatrice *f*

clothes' hang'er *s* attaccapanni *m*

clothes'horse' s cavalletto per stendere il bucato; elegantone *m*

clothes'line' *s* corda per stendere il bucato

clothes' moth' *s* tarma, tignola

clothes'pin' *s* molletta

clothes' tree' *s* attaccapanni *m*

clothier ['kloðjər] *s* negoziante *m* di confezioni; mercante *m* di panno

clothing ['kloðɪŋ] *s* vestiti *mpl*, vestiario

cloud [klaʊd] *s* nuvola, nube *f;* (*great number*) nuvolo; macchia; sospetto || *tr* annuvolare; offuscare || *intr* annuvolarsi; offuscarsi

cloud' bank' *s* banco di nubi

cloud'burst' *s* acquazzone *m*, nubifragio

cloud'-capped' *adj* coperto di nubi

cloudless ['klaʊdlɪs] *adj* senza nubi

cloud•y ['klaʊdi] *adj* (**-ier; -iest**) nuvoloso, annuvolato; confuso; tenebroso

clout [klaʊt] *s* (coll) schiaffo || *tr* (coll) schiaffeggiare

clove [klov] *s* chiodo di garofano; (*of garlic*) spicchio

cloven-hoofed ['klovən'huft] *adj* dal piede biforcuto; demoniaco

clover ['klovər] *s* trifoglio; **in clover** come un papa

clo'ver•leaf' *s* (**-leaves** [,livz]) foglia di trifoglio; incrocio stradale a quadrifoglio

clown [klaʊn] *s* pagliaccio, buffone *m* || *intr* fare il pagliaccio

clownish ['klaʊnɪʃ] *adj* buffonesco, clownesco, claunesco

cloy [klɔɪ] *tr* saziare fino alla nausea

club [klʌb] *s* bastone *m;* circolo, società *f;* (*playing card*) fiore *m* || *v* (*pret & pp* **clubbed;** *ger* **clubbing**) *tr* bastonare || *intr*—**to club together** unirsi

club' car' *s* vagone *m* con servizio di buffet

club'house' *s* sede *f* di un circolo

club'man' *s* (**-men'**) frequentatore *m* di circoli

club'room' *s* sala delle riunioni

club' sand'wich *s* sandwich *m* a tre fette di pane con insalata

club'wom'an *s* (**-wom'en**) frequentatrice *f* di circoli

cluck [klʌk] *s* (il) chiocciare || *intr* chiocciare

clue [klu] *s* traccia, indizio

clump [klʌmp] *s* gruppo, massa; (*of earth*) zolla || *intr* camminare con passo pesante

clum•sy ['klʌmzi] *adj* (**-sier; -siest**) goffo, malaccorto, sgraziato

cluster ['klʌstər] *s* gruppo; (*of grapes*) grappolo; (*of bees*) sciame *m;* (*of stars*) ammasso; (*of people*) folla || *tr* raggruppare || *intr* raggrupparsi

clutch [klʌtʃ] *s* presa; (*claw*) grinfia; (*of chickens*) covata; (mach) innesto; (aut) frizione; **clutches** grinfie *fpl;* **to throw the clutch in** innestare la marcia; **to throw the clutch out** disinnestare la marcia || *tr* afferrare, aggrappare || *intr*—**to clutch at** aggrapparsi a

clutter ['klʌtər] *tr*—**to clutter up** ingombrare alla rinfusa

coach [kotʃ] *s* carrozza, vettura; vagone *m;* (*automobile*) berlina; autobus *m;* (*trainer*) allenatore *m;* (*teacher*) ripetitore *m* || *tr* allenare; preparare

coach' house' *s* rimessa

coaching ['kotʃɪŋ] *s* suggerimento; (*in school*) ripetizione; (sports) allenamento

coach'man *s* (**-men**) cocchiere *m*

coagulate [ko'ægjə,let] *tr* coagulare || *intr* coagularsi
coal [kol] *s* carbone *m;* (*piece of burning wood*) tizzone *m;* **to call** or **haul over the coals** rimproverare || *tr* rifornire di carbone || *intr* rifornirsi di carbone; (naut) fare carbone
coal'bin' *s* carbonaia
coal' deal'er *s* (*wholesale*) negoziante *m* di carbone; (*retail*) carbonaio
coal' field' *s* bacino carbonifero
coal' gas' *s* gas *m* illuminante
coalition [,ko·ə'lɪʃən] *s* coalizione
coal' mine' *s* miniera di carbone
coal' oil' *s* cherosene *m*
coal' scut'tle *s* secchio del carbone
coal' tar' *s* catrame *m*
coal' yard' *s* carbonaia, carboniera
coarse [kors] *adj* (*manners*) volgare, ordinario; (*unrefined*) greggio; (*lacking refinement in manners*) rozzo, grossolano
coast [kost] *s* costa; discesa a ruota libera; **the coast is clear** la via è libera || *tr* costeggiare || *intr* costeggiare; scendere a ruota libera
coastal ['kostəl] *adj* costiero
coaster ['kostər] *s* nave *f* di cabotaggio; (*amusement*) otto volante, montagna russa; (*small tray*) sottobicchiere *m*
coast'er brake' *s* freno a contropedale
coast' guard' *s* guardacoste *m*
coast'-guard cut'ter *s* guardacoste *m*
coast'ing trade' *s* cabotaggio
coast'land' *s* costa
coast'line' *s* linea costiera, litorale *m*
coast'wise' *adv* lungo la costa
coat [kot] *s* soprabito; cappotto; (*jacket*) giacca; (*hide of man and animals*) mantello; (*of paint*) mano *f;* (*layer*) strato || *tr* vestire, proteggere; ricoprire, coprire
coat'ed ['kotɪd] *adj* rivestito; (*tongue*) patinato
coat' hang'er *s* attaccapanni *m*
coating ['kotɪŋ] *s* rivestimento; (*of paint*) mano *f;* (*of cement*) strato; (*cloth*) tessuto per abiti
coat' of arms' *s* scudo, stemma *m*
coat'room' *s* guardaroba *m*
coat'tail' *s* falda
coax [koks] *tr* blandire; ottenere con lusinghe
cob [kɑb] *s* spiga di granturco; (*horse*) cavallo da tiro; (*swan*) cigno maschio
cobalt ['kobɔlt] *s* cobalto
cobble ['kɑbəl] *s* ciottolo || *tr* acciottolare; (*to mend*) raccomodare, riparare
cobbler ['kɑblər] *s* calzolaio, ciabattino; (*pie*) torta di frutta
cob'ble·stone' *s* ciottolo
cob'web' *s* tela di ragno, ragnatela
cocaine [ko'ken] *s* cocaina
cock [kɑk] *s* gallo; (*faucet*) rubinetto; (*of gun*) cane *m;* (*of the eye*) ammicco; (*of nose*) angolo (del naso) rivolto all'insù; (*of hay*) covone *m* || *tr* (*a gun*) armare; (*the head*) drizzare
cockade [kɑ'ked] *s* coccarda
cock-a-doodle-doo ['kɑkə,dudəl'du] *s* chicchirichì *m*
cock'-and-bull' sto'ry *s* racconto incredibile
cocked' hat' *s* tricorno, cappello tricorno; **to knock into a cocked hat** (slang) distruggere completamente
cockeyed ['kɑk,aɪd] *adj* strabico; (slang) sbilenco; (slang) sciocco, scemo
cockle ['kɑkəl] *s* (*mollusk*) cardio; (*weed*) loglio; (*boat*) barchetta; (*wrinkle*) grinza; **to warm the cockles of one's heart** far bene al cuore || *intr* raggrinzirsi
cock' of the walk' *s* gallo del pollaio
cock'pit' *s* (*of boat*) cabina; (aer) carlinga; (naut) cassero di poppa
cock'roach' *s* scarafaggio, blatta
cocks'comb' *s* cresta di gallo; berretto da buffone
cock'sure' *adj* ostinato; troppo sicuro di sé stesso
cock'tail' *s* cocktail *m*
cock'tail par'ty *s* cocktail *m*
cock·y ['kɑki] *adj* (**-ier; -iest**) impudente, presuntuoso
cocoa ['koko] *s* (*bean*) cacao; (*drink*) cioccolata; (*tree*) cocco
coconut ['kokə,nʌt] *s* noce *f* di cocco
co'conut palm' or **tree'** *s* cocco
cocoon [kə'kun] *s* bozzolo
cod [kɑd] *s* merluzzo
C.O.D. ['si'o'di] *s* (letterword) (**Collect on Delivery**) contro assegno
coddle ['kɑdəl] *tr* vezzeggiare
code [kod] *s* codice *m,* cifra; **in code** in codice, in cifra || *tr* mettere in codice or in cifra; cifrare
codex ['kodɛks] *s* (**codices** ['kodɪ,siz] or ['kɑdɪ,siz]) codice *m*
cod'fish' *s* merluzzo
codger ['kɑdʒər] *s*—**old codger** (coll) vecchietto
codicil ['kɑdɪsɪl] *s* codicillo
codi·fy ['kɑdɪ,faɪ] or ['kodɪ,faɪ] *v* (*pret & pp* **-fied**) *tr* codificare
cod'-liver oil' *s* olio di fegato di merluzzo
coed ['co,ɛd] *s* studentessa di scuola mista
coeducation [,ko,ɛdʒə'keʃən] *s* coeducazione
co'educa'tional school' [,ko·ɛdʒə'keʃənəl] *s* scuola mista
coefficient [,ko·ɪ'fɪʃənt] *s* coefficiente *m*
coerce [ko'ʌrs] *tr* forzare, costringere
coercion [ko'ʌrʃən] *s* coercizione
coexist [,ko·ɪg'zɪst] *intr* coesistere
coffee ['kɔfi] or ['kɑfi] *s* caffè *m;* **ground coffee** caffè macinato; **roasted coffee** caffè torrefatto
cof'fee bean' *s* chicco di caffè
cof'fee·cake' *s* pasticcino (da mangiarsi con il caffè)
cof'fee grind'er *s* macinino da caffè, macinacaffè *m*
cof'fee grounds' *spl* fondi *mpl* di caffè
cof'fee house' *s* caffè *m*
cof'fee mak'er *s* macchinetta del caffè

cof'fee mill' *s* macinino del caffè, macinacaffè *m*
cof'fee·pot' *s* caffettiera
cof'fee shop' *s* caffè *m*
coffer ['kɔfər] or ['kɑfər] *s* forziere *m;* (*ceiling*) soffitto a cassettoni; (archit) cassettone *m;* **coffers** tesoro
coffin ['kɔfɪn] or ['kɑfɪn] *s* bara
cog [kɑg] *s* dente *m* d'ingranaggio; ruota dentata; **to slip a cog** fare un errore
cogent ['kodʒənt] *adj* convincente, persuasivo
cogitate ['kɑdʒɪ,tet] *tr & intr* cogitare, ponzare
cognac ['konjæk] or ['kɑnjæk] *s* cognac *m*
cognate ['kɑgnet] *adj* consanguineo, parente, affine || *s* parola dello stesso ceppo linguistico; consanguineo, parente *mf*
cognizance ['kɑgnɪzəns] or ['kɑnɪzəns] *s* conoscenza; **to take cognizance of** prendere conoscenza di
cognizant ['kɑgnɪzənt] or ['kɑnɪzənt] *adj* informato, al corrente
cog'wheel' *s* ruota dentata
cohabit [ko'hæbɪt] *intr* convivere; (archaic) coabitare
coheir [ko'er] *s* coerede *mf*
cohere [ko'hɪr] *intr* aderire; (fig) avere nesso
coherent [ko'hɪrənt] *adj* coerente
coiffeur [kwɑ'fʌr] *s* parrucchiere *m* per signora; (Brit) parrucchiere *m*
coiffure [kwɑ'fjʊr] *s* pettinatura || *tr* pettinare
coil [kɔɪl] *s* (*of rope*) rotolo; (*of pipe*) serpentino; (*of wire*) bobina, avvolgimento || *tr* arrotolare || *intr* arrotolarsi
coil' spring' *s* molla a spirale, molla elicoidale
coin [kɔɪn] *s* moneta; **to pay back in one's own coin** pagare della stessa moneta; **to toss a coin** giocare a testa o croce || *tr* (*money*) coniare, battere; (*words*) inventare, creare; **to coin money** battere moneta; (coll) fare soldoni
coincide [,ko·ɪn'saɪd] *intr* coincidere
coincidence [ko'ɪnsɪdəns] *s* coincidenza
coke [kok] *s* coke *m*, carbone *m* coke
colander ['kʌləndər] or ['kɑləndər] *s* colabrodo, colapasta *m*
cold [kold] *adj* freddo; **it is cold** (*said of weather*) fa freddo; **to be cold** (*said of a person*) avere freddo || *s* freddo; (*ailment*) raffreddore *m;* **out in the cold** solo soletto; **to catch cold** pigliare freddo, pigliarsi un raffreddore
cold' blood' *s*—**in cold blood** a sangue freddo
cold'-blood'ed *adj* insensibile; (*sensitive to cold*) freddoloso; (*animal*) a sangue freddo
cold' chis'el *s* tagliaferro
cold' com'fort *s* magra consolazione
cold' cream' *s* crema emolliente
cold' cuts' *spl* salumi *mpl*, affettato
cold' feet' *spl*—**to get cold feet** (coll) perdersi d'animo
cold'-heart'ed *adj*—**to be coldhearted** avere il cuore duro
coldness ['koldnɪs] *s* freddezza
cold' shoul'der *s*—**to get the cold shoulder** (coll) essere trattato con freddezza; **to turn a cold shoulder on** (coll) trattare con freddezza
cold' snap' *s* freddo breve e improvviso
cold' stor'age *s* conservazione a freddo
cold' war' *s* guerra fredda
cold' wave' *s* ondata di freddo
coleslaw ['kol,slɔ] *s* insalata di cavolo cappuccio
colic ['kɑlɪk] *adj* colico || *s* colica
coliseum [,kɑlɪ'si·əm] *s* stadio, arena || **Coliseum** *s* Colosseo
collaborate [kə'læbə,ret] *intr* collaborare
collaborationist [kə,læbə'reʃənɪst] *s* collaborazionista *mf*
collaborator [kə'læbə,retər] *s* collaboratore *m*
collapse [kə'læps] *s* (*of business*) fallimento; (*e.g., of a roof*) caduta; (*of a person*) collasso || *tr* piegare || *intr* (*to shrink*) restringersi, sgonfiarsi; (*said of a business*) fallire; (*said of health*) venir meno; (*said, e.g., of a roof*) cadere, crollare
collapsible [kə'læpsɪbəl] *adj* pieghevole, smontabile
collar ['kɑlər] *s* (*of shirt*) colletto; (*for dog or horse*) collare *m;* (*ring*) anello; (*short piece of pipe*) manicotto || *tr* afferrare per il collo, catturare
col'lar·band' *s* cinturino della camicia
col'lar·bone' *s* clavicola
collate [kə'let] or ['kɑlet] *tr* collazionare, confrontare
collateral [kə'lætərəl] *adj* collaterale; accessorio, addizionale || *s* collaterale *m*
colleague ['kɑlig] *s* collega *mf*
collect ['kɑlɛkt] *s* (eccl) colletta || [kə'lɛkt] *adv* contro assegno; (telp) pagamento all'abbonato chiamato || *tr* raccogliere, riunire; (*e.g., stamps*) collezionare; (*mail*) levare; (*bills*) incassare; (*ideas*) coordinare; (*thoughts*) riordinare; (*e.g., classroom papers*) raccogliere; (*taxes*) riscuotere; **to collect oneself** riprendersi, riprendere il controllo di sé stesso || *intr* (*for the poor*) fare la colletta; riunirsi, raccogliersi
collected [kə'lɛktɪd] *adj* raccolto; equilibrato, padrone di sè
collection [kə'lɛkʃən] *s* collezione; (*for the poor*) colletta; (*of mail*) levata; (*heap*) deposito; (*of taxes*) esazione; (*of bills*) riscossione
collec'tion a'gency *s* agenzia di riscossione
collective [kə'lɛktɪv] *adj* collettivo
collector [kə'lɛktər] *s* (*of stamps*) collezionista *mf;* (*of taxes*) esattore *m;* (*of tickets*) controllore *m*
college ['kɑlɪdʒ] *s* scuola superiore,

università *f;* (*e.g., of medicine*) facoltà *f;* (*electoral*) collegio
collide [kə'laɪd] *intr* collidere, scontrarsi
collie ['kɑli] *s* collie *m*
collier ['kɑljər] *s* (*ship*) carboniera; (min) minatore *m* di carbone
collier·y ['kɑljəri] *s* (**-ies**) miniera di carbone
collision [kə'lɪʒən] *s* collisione
colloid ['kɑlɔɪd] *adj* colloidale ‖ *s* colloide *m*
colloquial [kə'lokwɪ·əl] *adj* familiare, colloquiale
colloquialism [kə'lokwɪ·ə,lɪzəm] *s* espressione familiare
collo·quy ['kɑləkwi] *s* (**-quies**) colloquio
collusion [kə'luʒən] *s* collusione; **to be in collusion with** essere d'intelligenza con
cologne [kə'lon] *s* acqua di colonia, colonia ‖ **Cologne** *s* Colonia
colon ['kolən] *s* (anat) colon *m;* (gram) due punti *mpl*
colonel ['kʌrnəl] *s* colonnello
colonist ['kɑlənɪst] *s* colono, coloniale *m*
colonize ['kɑlə,naɪz] *tr & intr* colonizzare
colonnade [,kɑlə'ned] *s* colonnato
colo·ny ['kɑləni] *s* (**-nies**) colonia
color ['kʌlər] *s* colore *m;* **off color** sbiadito, scolorito; (slang) sporco, volgare; **the colors** i colori, la bandiera; **to call to the colors** chiamare in servizio militare; **to change color** cambiar colore; arrossire; impallidire; **to give** or **lend color to** far parere probabile; **to lose color** impallidire; **to show one's colors** mostrarsi come si è; **under color of** sotto il pretesto di ‖ *tr* colorare; (fig) colorire ‖ *intr* arrossire
col'or-blind' *adj* daltonico
colored ['kʌlərd] *adj* colorato; (*person*) di colore; esagerato
colorful ['kʌlərfəl] *adj* colorito, espressivo
col'or guard' *s* guardia d'onore alla bandiera
coloring ['kʌlərɪŋ] *s* colorazione; colore *m;* pigmento; (fig) specie *f*
colorless ['kʌlərlɪs] *adj* incolore, incoloro
col'or photog'raphy *s* fotografia a colori
col'or ser'geant *s* sergente *m* portabandiera
col'or tel'evision *s* televisione a colori
colossal [kə'lɑsəl] *adj* colossale
colossus [kə'lɑsəs] *s* colosso
colt [kolt] *s* puledro
Columbus [kə'lʌmbəs] *s* Colombo
column ['kɑləm] *s* colonna
columnist ['kɑləmɪst] *s* giornalista incaricato di una colonna speciale; articolista *mf*
coma ['komə] *s* coma *m*
comb [kom] *s* pettine *m;* (*for horse*) striglia; (*of hen or wave*) cresta; (*honeycomb*) favo ‖ *tr* pettinare; (fig) esaminare minuziosamente ‖ *intr* (*said of waves*) frangersi
com·bat ['kɑmbæt] *s* combattimento ‖ ['kɑmbæt] or [kəm'bæt] *v* (*pret & pp* **-bated** or **-batted;** *ger* **-bating** or **-batting**) *tr & intr* combattere
combatant ['kɑmbətənt] *s* combattente *mf*
com'bat du'ty *s* servizio in zona di guerra
combination [,kɑmbɪ'neʃən] *s* combinazione
combine ['kɑmbaɪn] *s* consorzio; (pol) coalizione; mieto-trebbiatrice *f* ‖ [kəm'baɪn] *tr* combinare ‖ *intr* combinarsi
combin'ing form' *s* membro di parola composta
combo ['kɑmbo] *s* orchestrina
combustible [kəm'bʌstɪbəl] *adj & s* combustibile *m*
combustion [kəm'bʌstʃən] *s* combustione
come [kʌm] *v* (*pret* **came** [kem]; *pp* **come**) *intr* venire; arrivare; (*to become*) diventare; (*to amount*) ammontare; **come!** macchè!; **come along!** andiamo!; **come in!** avanti!, entri!; **come on!** andiamo!; avanti!, coraggio!; **to come about** accadere, succedere; **to come across** incontrarsi con; (slang) pagare; **to come around** cedere; mettersi d'accordo; (*said of health*) rimettersi; **to come at** raggiungere; (*to attack*) attaccare; **to come back** ritornare; **to come between** mettersi fra; **to come by** ottenere; **to come down** scendere; decadere; essere trasmesso; **to come down with** ammalarsi di; **to come forward** farsi avanti; **to come in** entrare, passare; **to come in for** ricevere; **to come into** ricevere; ereditare; **to come off** succedere; riuscire; **to come on** mostrarsi; migliorare; incontrarsi; **to come out** uscire; debuttare in società; andare a finire; **to come out with** uscire con; mostrare; **to come over** succedere a, e.g., **what came over him?** che gli è successo?; **to come through** riuscire; **to come to** riprendere i sensi; **to come under** essere di competenza di; appartenere a; **to come up** salire; **to come up to** salire fino a; avvicinarsi a; **to come up with** raggiungere; produrre, fornire; proporre
come'back' *s* (coll) ritorno; (slang) pronta risposta; **to stage a comeback** (coll) ritornare in auge
comedian [kə'midɪ·ən] *s* attore comico; (*author*) commediografo; (*amusing person*) commediante *mf*
comedienne [kə,midɪ'ɛn] *s* attrice comica
come'down' *s* (coll) rovescio di fortuna
come·dy ['kɑmədi] *s* (**-dies**) commedia
come·ly ['kʌmli] *adj* (**-lier; -liest**) bello, grazioso
comet ['kɑmɪt] *s* cometa
comfort ['kʌmfərt] *s* conforto, sollievo;

(*ease*) benessere *m* || *tr* confortare, alleviare
comfortable ['kʌmfərtəbəl] *adj* comodo, agiato; (*e.g.*, *income*) (coll) bastante || *s* coltre *f*
comforter ['kʌmfərtər] *s* consolatore *m;* (*bedcover*) coltre *f;* sciarpa di lana || **the Comforter** lo Spirito Santo, lo Spirito Consolatore
comforting ['kʌmfərtɪŋ] *adj* confortante
com'fort sta'tion *s* latrina pubblica
comic ['kamɪk] *adj* comico || *s* (*actor*) comico; comicità *f;* **comics** fumetti *mpl*
comical ['kamɪkəl] *adj* comico
com'ic book' *s* libretto a fumetti
com'ic op'era *s* opera buffa
com'ic strip' *s* racconto umoristico a fumetti
coming ['kʌmɪŋ] *adj* venturo, prossimo; promettente || *s* venuta
com'ing out' *s* debutto in società; (*e.g.*, *of stock*) emissione
comma ['kamə] *s* virgola
command [kə'mænd] or [kə'mand] *s* comando; (*e.g.*, *of a language*) padronanza || *tr* comandare, ordinare; (*to overlook*) dominare; (*to be able to have*) disporre di || *intr* avere il comando
commandant [,kamən'dænt] or [,kamən'dant] *s* comandante *m*
commandeer [,kamən'dɪr] *tr* requisire
commander [kə'mændər] or [kə'mandər] *s* (*of knighthood*) commendatore *m;* (mil) comandante *m;* (nav) capitano di vascello
command'er in chief' *s* comandante *m* in capo
command'ing of'ficer *s* comandante *m*
commandment [kə'mændmənt] or [kə'mandmənt] *s* comandamento
command' mod'ule *s* (rok) modulo di comando
commando [kə'mændo] *s* guastatore *m*
commemorate [kə'memə,ret] *tr* commemorare, celebrare
commence [kə'mens] *tr & intr* cominciare
commencement [kə'mensmənt] *s* inizio, esordio; (*in a school*) cerimonia per la distribuzione dei diplomi
commend [kə'mend] *tr* lodare; (*to entrust*) raccomandare, affidare
commendable [kə'mendəbəl] *adj* (*person*) lodevole; (*act*) commendevole
commendation [,kamən'deʃən] *s* lode *f;* raccomandazione; (mil) citazione
comment ['kament] *s* commento || *tr* commentare || *intr* fare commenti; **to comment on** fare commenti su
commentar·y ['kamən,teri] *s* (**-ies**) commentario
commentator ['kamən,tetər] *s* commentatore *m*
commerce ['kamərs] *s* commercio
commercial [kə'merʃəl] *adj* commerciale || *s* (rad, telv) programma *m* di pubblicità; (rad, telv) annunzio pubblicitario
commiserate [kə'mɪzə,ret] *intr*—**to commiserate with** commiserare, compiangere
commissar ['kamɪ,sar] or [,kamɪ'sar] *s* commissario del popolo
commissar·y ['kamɪ,seri] *s* (**-ies**) (*store*) economato; (*deputy*) commissario; (*in army*) intendente *m*
commission [kə'mɪʃən] *s* commissione; (*e.g.*, *in army*) nomina, brevetto; autorità *f;* (*of a crime*) perpetrazione; (il) fare; **in commission** in servizio, in uso; **out of commission** fuori servizio || *tr* nominare, dare un brevetto a; autorizzare; (*a ship*) armare
commis'sioned of'ficer *s* (mil, nav) ufficiale *m*
commissioner [kə'mɪʃənər] *s* commissario; membro di una commissione
commis'sion mer'chant *s* sensale *m*
com·mit [kə'mɪt] *v* (*pret & pp* **-mitted;** *ger* **-mitting**) *tr* commettere, perpetrare; (*to deliver*) affidare, consegnare; (*to imprison*) mandare in prigione; (*an insane person*) internare; (*to refer*) rinviare; (*to involve*) compromettere; **to commit oneself** compromettersi; **to commit to memory** imparare a memoria; **to commit to writing** mettere in iscritto
commitment [kə'mɪtmənt] *s* (*act of committing*) commissione; (*to an asylum*) internamento; promessa; (law) mandato
committal [kə'mɪtəl] *s* consegna; promessa
committee [kə'mɪti] *s* comitato, commissione
commode [kə'mod] *s* (*chest of drawers*) cassettone *m;* (*washstand*) lavabo; seggetta, comoda
commodious [kə'modɪ·əs] *adj* spazioso; conveniente
commodi·ty [kə'madɪti] *s* (**-ties**) merce *f;* articolo di prima necessità
commod'ity exchange' *s* borsa merci
common ['kamən] *adj* comune || *s* fondo comunale; pascolo comune; **commons** gente *f* non nobile; refettorio; **in common** in comune || **the Commons** la Camera dei Comuni
com'mon car'rier *s* impresa di trasporti pubblici
commoner ['kamənər] *s* plebeo, borghese *m;* membro della Camera dei Comuni
com'mon law' *s* consuetudine *f,* diritto consuetudinario
com'mon-law mar'riage *s* matrimonio basato sulla mera convivenza
commonly ['kamənli] *adv* generalmente
com'mon·place' *adj* banale, ordinario || *s* banalità *f,* cosa ordinaria
com'mon sense' *s* senso comune
com'mon-sense' *adj* giudizioso
com'mon stock' *s* azione ordinaria; azioni ordinarie
commonweal ['kamən,wil] *s* bene pubblico
com'mon·wealth' *s* (*citizens of a state*) cittadinanza; repubblica; (*one of the*

50 states of the U.S.A.) stato; comunità *f*, federazione
commotion [kə'moʃən] *s* agitazione
commune [kə'mjun] *s* comune *m* || *intr* confabulare; (eccl) comunicarsi
communicate [kə'mjunɪ,ket] *tr & intr* comunicare
communicating [kə'mjunɪ,ketɪŋ] *adj* comunicante
communication [kə,mjunɪ'keʃən] *s* comunicazione; **communications** sistema *m* di comunicazione; mezzi *mpl* di comunicazione
communicative [kə'mjunɪ,ketɪv] *adj* comunicativo
Communion [kə'mjunjən] *s* Comunione; **to take Communion** comunicarsi
communiqué [kə,mjunɪ'ke] or [kə'mjunɪ,ke] *s* comunicato
communism ['kɑmjə,nɪzəm] *s* comunismo
communist ['kɑmjənɪst] *s* comunista *mf*
communi·ty [kə'mjunɪti] *s* (**-ties**) (*people living together*) comunità *f*; (*sharing together*) comunanza; (*neighborhood*) circondario
commu'nity cen'ter *s* centro sociale
commu'nity chest' *s* fondo di beneficenza
commuta'tion tick'et [,kɑmjə'teʃən] *s* biglietto d'abbonamento
commutator ['kɑmjə,tetər] *s* (*switch*) commutatore *m;* (*of dynamo or motor*) collettore *m*
commute [kə'mjut] *tr* commutare || *intr* commutare; fare il pendolare
commuter [kə'mjutər] *s* pendolare *mf*
compact [kəm'pækt] *adj* compatto || ['kɑmpækt] *s* (*small case for face powder*) portacipria *m;* (*agreement*) accordo; (*small car*) utilitaria
companion [kəm'pænjən] *s* compagno; (*one of two items*) pendant *m;* (*lady*) dama di compagnia
compan'ion·ship' *s* cameratismo
compan'ion·way' *s* (naut) scaletta per andare sottocoperta
compa·ny ['kʌmpəni] *s* (**-nies**) compagnia; (coll) ospite *m* or ospiti *mpl;* (naut) equipaggio; **to bear company** accompagnare; **to be good company** essere simpatico; **to keep company** (*said of a couple*) andare insieme; **to keep company with** accompagnare; (coll) fare la corte a; **to part company** separarsi
comparable ['kɑmpərəbəl] *adj* comparabile, paragonabile
comparative [kəm'pærətɪv] *adj* comparativo; (*e.g., anatomy*) comparato || *s* (gram) comparativo
compare [kəm'per] *s*—**beyond compare** incomparabile || *tr* confrontare; **compared to** a confronto di, in confronto a
comparison [kəm'pærɪsən] *s* confronto; (gram) comparazione; **in comparison with** in confronto a, a confronto di
compartment [kəm'pɑrtmənt] *s* compartimento; (naut) compartimento stagno; (rr) compartimento
compass ['kʌmpəs] *s* (*instrument for showing direction*) bussola; (*boundary*) limite *m;* (*range*) ambito; (*range of voice*) portata; (*of a wall*) cerchia; (*circuit*) circuito; (*drawing instrument*) compasso; **compasses** (*drawing instrument*) compasso || *tr* girare intorno a; comprendere; **to compass about** accerchiare
com'pass card' *s* rosa dei venti
compassion [kəm'pæʃən] *s* compassione
compassionate [kəm'pæʃənɪt] *adj* compassionevole
com'pass saw' *s* gattuccio
com·pel [kəm'pɛl] *v* (*pret & pp* **-pelled;** *ger* **-pelling**) *tr* forzare, obbligare
compelling [kəm'pelɪŋ] *adj* imperioso, coercitivo
compendious [kəm'pɛndɪ·əs] *adj* compendioso, conciso
compensate ['kɑmpən,set] *tr & intr* compensare
compensation [,kɑmpən'seʃən] *s* compensazione; (*pay*) pagamento; (*something given to offset a loss*) risarcimento, indennità *f*
compete [kəm'pit] *intr* competere
competence ['kɑmpɪtəns] or **competency** ['kɑmpɪtənsi] *s* (*fitness*) abilità *f;* (*money*) agiatezza; (*authority*) competenza
competent ['kɑmpɪtənt] *adj* abile; competente
competition [,kɑmpɪ'tɪʃən] *s* competizione, gara; (*in business*) concorrenza
competitive [kəm'pɛtɪtɪv] *adj* competitivo; (*based on competition*) di concorso
compet'itive pric'es *spl* prezzi *mpl* di concorrenza
competitor [kəm'pɛtɪtər] *s* competitore *m*, concorrente *mf;* rivale *mf*
compilation [,kɑmpɪ'leʃən] *s* compilazione
compile [kəm'paɪl] *tr* compilare
complacence [kəm'plesəns] or **complacency** [kəm'plesənsi] *s* compiacenza; compiacenza di sé stesso
complacent [kəm'plesənt] *adj* compiaciuto or soddisfatto con sé stesso
complain [kəm'plen] *intr* lagnarsi
complainant [kəm'plenənt] *s* (law) querelante *mf*
complaint [kəm'plent] *s* lagnanza, reclamo; (*sickness*) malattia; (law) querela
complaisance [kəm'plezəns] or ['kɑmplɪ,zæns] *s* compiacenza
complaisant [kəm'plezənt] or ['kɑmplɪ,zænt] *adj* compiacente, cortese
complement ['kɑmplɪmənt] *s* complemento; (naut) equipaggio || ['kɑmplɪ,mɛnt] *tr* completare
complete [kəm'plit] *adj* completo; (*done*) finito || *tr* completare, finire
completion [kəm'pliʃən] *s* completamento, compimento
complex [kəm'plɛks] or ['kɑmplɛks]

adj complesso, complicato || ['kampleks] *s* complesso
complexion [kəm'plekʃən] *s* (*of skin*) carnagione; (*appearance*) aspetto; (*viewpoint*) punto di vista
compliance [kəm'plaɪ·əns] *s* condiscendenza, arrendevolezza; **in compliance with** in conformità di
complicate ['kamplɪ,ket] *tr* complicare
complicated ['kamplɪ,ketɪd] *adj* complicato
complici·ty [kəm'plɪsɪti] *s* (**-ties**) complicità *f*
compliment ['kamplɪmənt] *s* complimento, omaggio || ['kamplɪ,ment] *tr*—**to compliment s.o. on s.th** felicitarsi con qlcu per qlco; **to compliment s.o. with s.th** regalare qlco a qlcu
complimentary [,kamplɪ'mentəri] *adj* complimentoso, lusinghiero; (*free*) in omaggio, gratis; (*ticket*) di favore
com·ply [kəm'plaɪ] *v* (*pret & pp* **-plied**) *intr* acconsentire, accondiscendere; **to comply with** accedere a
component [kəm'ponənt] *adj* componente, costituente || *s* (*component part*) componente *m;* (*force*) componente *f*
compose [kəm'poz] *tr* comporre; **to be composed of** essere composto di; **to compose oneself** calmarsi
composed [kəm'pozd] *adj* calmo, tranquillo
composer [kəm'pozər] *s* (*peacemaker*) conciliatore *m;* (mus) compositore *m*
compos'ing stick' *s* (typ) compositoio
composite [kəm'pazɪt] *adj & s* composto, composito
composition [,kampə'zɪʃən] *s* composizione; (*agreement*) compromesso
compositor [kəm'pazɪtər] *s* compositore *m*
compost ['kampost] *s* concime *m* naturale
composure [kəm'poʒər] *s* calma
compote ['kampot] *s* (*stewed fruit*) composta; (*dish*) compostiera
compound ['kampaʊnd] *adj* composto; (*fracture*) complesso; (archit, bot) composito || *s* composto; parola composta; (*yard*) recinto || [kam'paʊnd] *tr* (*to mix*) combinare; (*to settle*) comporre; (*interest*) capitalizzare
comprehend [,kamprɪ'hend] *tr* comprendere
comprehensible [,kamprɪ'hensɪbəl] *adj* comprensibile
comprehension [,kamprɪ'henʃən] *s* comprensione
comprehensive [,kamprɪ'hensɪv] *adj* comprensivo
compress ['kampres] *s* compressa || [kəm'pres] *tr* comprimere
compressed' air' *s* aria compressa
compression [kəm'preʃən] *s* compressione
comprise [kəm'praɪz] *tr* comprendere, includere; **to be comprised of** consistere di
compromise ['kamprə,maɪz] *s* compromesso || *tr* (*a dispute*) transigere, comporre; (*to put in danger*) compromettere || *intr* transigere, fare un compromesso
comptroller [kən'trolər] *s* economo, amministratore *m*, controllore *m*
compulsive [kəm'pʌlsɪv] *adj* obbligatorio, coercitivo; (psychol) compulsivo
compulsory [kəm'pʌlsəri] *adj* obbligatorio
compute [kəm'pjut] *tr & intr* computare, calcolare
computer [kəm'pjutər] *s* calcolatore *m;* elaboratore *m*
comrade ['kamræd] or ['kamrɪd] *s* camerata *m*, compagno
com'rade in arms' *s* compagno d'armi
con [kan] *s* contro || *v* (*pret & pp* **conned;** *ger* **conning**) *tr* imparare a memoria; (slang) imbrogliare
concave ['kankev] or [kan'kev] *adj* concavo
conceal [kən'sil] *tr* nascondere; (*to keep secret*) celare
concealment [kən'silmənt] *s* occultamento; (*place*) nascondiglio
concede [kən'sid] *tr* concedere
conceit [kən'sit] *s* (*high opinion of oneself*) presunzione; (*fanciful notion*) concetto sottile
conceited [kən'sitɪd] *adj* vanitoso
conceivable [kən'sivəbəl] *adj* concepibile
conceive [kən'siv] *tr & intr* concepire
concentrate ['kansən,tret] *s* concentrato || *tr* concentrare || *intr* concentrarsi; **to concentrate on** concentrarsi in
concentra'tion camp' [,kansən'treʃən] *s* campo di concentrazione
concept ['kansept] *s* concetto
conception [kən'sepʃən] *s* concezione
concern [kən'sʌrn] *s* interesse *m;* (*worry*) ansietà *f;* (*firm*) ditta, compagnia; **of concern** d'interesse || *tr* concernere; **as concerns** circa; **to concern oneself** interessarsi; **to whom it may concern** a chiunque possa averne interesse
concerning [kən'sʌrnɪŋ] *prep* riguardo a
concert ['kansərt] *s* concerto || [kən'sʌrt] *tr & intr* concertare
con'cert·mas'ter *s* primo violino
concer·to [kən'tʃerto] *s* (**-tos** or **-ti** [ti]) concerto
concession [kən'seʃən] *s* concessione
conciliate [kən'sɪlɪ,et] *tr* conciliare, conciliarsi con
concise [kən'saɪs] *adj* conciso
conclude [kən'klud] *tr* concludere || *intr* concludersi, terminare
conclusion [kən'kluʒən] *s* conclusione; **in conclusion** per finire; **to try conclusions with** misurarsi con
conclusive [kən'klusɪv] *adj* decisivo, convincente
concoct [kən'kakt] *tr* preparare, confezionare; (*a story*) inventare
concoction [kan'kakʃən] *s* prepara-

zione, mescolanza; (*unpleasant in taste*) intruglio
concomitant [kən'kamɪtənt] *adj* concomitante || *s* fatto or sintomo concomitante
concord ['kaŋkɔrd] *s* concordia, armonia; (*treaty*) accordo; (gram) concordanza
concourse ['kaŋkors] *s* confluenza; (*crowd*) affluenza, concorso; (*boulevard*) viale *m;* (rr) salone *m* principale
concrete ['kankrit] or [kan'krit] *adj* concreto; fatto di cemento; solido || *s* cemento, calcestruzzo || *tr* (*e.g., a sidewalk*) cementare
con'crete mix'er *s* betoniera
con·cur [kən'kʌr] *v* (*pret & pp* **-curred;** *ger* **-curring**) *intr* (*to work together*) concorrere; (*to agree*) essere d'accordo, aderire
concurrence [kən'kʌrəns] *s* concorso; (*agreement*) accordo
concurrent [kən'kʌrənt] *adj* concomitante, simultaneo; cooperante; armonioso
concussion [kən'kʌʃən] *s* scossa, urto; (*of brain*) commozione cerebrale
condemn [kən'dɛm] *tr* condannare; (*to take for public use*) espropriare
condemnation [,kandɛm'neʃən] *s* condanna
condense [kən'dɛns] *tr* condensare || *intr* condensarsi
condescend [,kandɪ'sɛnd] *intr* condiscendere, degnarsi
condescending [,kandɪ'sɛndɪŋ] *adj* condiscendente
condescension [,kandɪ'sɛnʃən] *s* condiscendenza, degnazione
condiment ['kandɪmənt] *s* condimento
condition [kən'dɪʃən] *s* condizione; clausola; **on condition that** a condizione che || *tr* condizionare; mettere in buone condizioni fisiche
conditional [kən'dɪʃənəl] *adj & s* condizionale *m*
condole [kən'dol] *intr* condolersi
condolence [kən'doləns] *s* condoglianza
condone [kən'don] *tr* condonare
conduce [kən'djus] or [kən'dus] *intr* contribuire, indurre
conducive [kən'djusiv] or [kən'dusɪv] *adj* contribuente
conduct ['kandʌkt] *s* condotta; direzione || [kən'dʌkt] *tr* condurre; (*an orchestra*) dirigere; **to conduct oneself** condursi, comportarsi || *intr* dirigere
conductor [kən'dʌktər] *s* direttore *m;* (*of a streetcar*) fattorino, conduttore *m;* (phys) conduttore *m;* (rr) capotreno
conduit ['kandɪt] or ['kandu·ɪt] *s* condotto
cone [kon] *s* cono; (bot) pigna
Con'estoga wag'on ['kanɪ'stogə] *s* carriaggio coperto
confectioner [kən'fɛkʃənər] *s* confettiere *m,* pasticcere *m*
confec'tioners' sug'ar *s* zucchero in polvere finissimo
confectioner·y [kən'fɛkʃə,nɛri] *s* (**-ies**) confetteria, pasticceria; (*candies*) confetture *fpl*
confedera·cy [kən'fɛdərəsi] *s* (**-cies**) confederazione; lega
confederate [kən'fɛdərɪt] *s* alleato; (*in crime*) complice *mf* || [kən'fɛdə,ret] *tr* confederare || *intr* confederarsi
con·fer [kən'fʌr] *v* (*pret & pp* **-ferred;** *ger* **-ferring**) *tr* conferire || *intr* conferire, abboccarsi
conference ['kanfərəns] *s* conferenza
confess [kən'fɛs] *tr* confessare, ammettere || *intr* confessare, confessarsi
confession [kən'fɛʃən] *s* confessione
confessional [kən'fɛʃənəl] *s* confessionale *m*
confes'sion of faith' *s* professione di fede
confessor [kən'fɛsər] *s* confessore *m*
confetti [kən'fɛti] *s* coriandoli *mpl*
confide [kən'faɪd] *tr* confidare; (*to entrust*) affidare || *intr* confidarsi
confidence ['kanfɪdəns] *s* fiducia; sicurezza di sé; (*boldness*) baldanza; (*secrecy*) confidenza
confident ['kanfɪdənt] *adj* fiducioso; baldanzoso || *s* confidente *mf*
confidential [,kanfɪ'dɛnʃəl] *adj* confidenziale
confine ['kanfaɪn] *s* confine *m* || [kən'faɪn] *tr* limitare; confinare; **to be confined** essere in altro stato; **to be confined to bed** dover stare a letto
confinement [kən'faɪnmənt] *s* confino; (*childbirth*) parto; (*imprisonment*) prigionia
confirm [kən'fʌrm] *tr* confermare; (eccl) cresimare
confirmed [kən'fʌrmd] *adj* (*e.g., piece of news*) confermato; (*bachelor; drunkard*) impenitente; inveterato; (*e.g., invalid*) cronico
confiscate ['kanfɪs,ket] *tr* confiscare
conflagration [,kanflə'greʃən] *s* conflagrazione
conflict ['kanflɪkt] *s* conflitto || [kən'flɪkt] *intr* lottare; essere in conflitto
conflicting [kən'flɪktɪŋ] *adj* contrastante; contraddittorio
confluence ['kanflu·əns] *s* confluenza
conform [kən'fɔrm] *tr* conformare || *intr* conformarsi
conformi·ty [kən'fɔrmɪti] *s* (**-ties**) conformità *f;* **in conformity with** in conformità di
confound [kan'faʊnd] *tr* confondere || ['kan'faʊnd] *tr* maledire; **confound it!** accidenti!
confounded [kan'faʊndɪd] or ['kan'faʊndɪd] *adj* maledetto; (*hateful*) odioso
confront [kən'frʌnt] *tr* affrontare, opporsi a; (*to bring face to face*) raffrontare; (*to compare*) confrontare
confrontation [,kanfrən'teʃən] *s* contestazione
confuse [kən'fjuz] *tr* confondere; **to get confused** confondersi
confusion [kən'fjuʒən] *s* confusione

congeal [kən'dʒil] *tr* congelare; coagulare || *intr* congelarsi; (*said, e.g., of blood*) coagularsi
congenial [kən'dʒinjəl] *adj* (*agreeable*) simpatico; (*having similar tastes*) affine; (*suited to one's needs or tastes*) congeniale
congenital [kən'dʒenɪtəl] *adj* congenito
con'ger eel' ['kɑŋgər] *s* grongo
congest [kən'dʒest] *tr* congestionare || *intr* essere congestionato
congestion [kən'dʒestʃən] *s* congestione
conglomerate [kən'glɑmərɪt] *adj & s* conglomerato || [kən'glɑmə,ret] *tr* conglomerare || *intr* conglomerarsi
congratulate [kən'grætʃə,let] *tr* congratularsi con
congratulation [kən,grætʃə'leʃən] *s* congratulazione, felicitazione
congregate ['kɑŋgrɪ,get] *intr* congregarsi
congregation [,kɑŋgrɪ'geʃən] *s* congregazione; fedeli *mpl* di una chiesa
congress ['kɑŋgrɪs] *s* parlamento; congresso
con'gress•man *s* (**-men**) deputato al congresso degli S.U.
con'gress•wom'an *s* (**-wom'en**) deputatessa al congresso degli S.U.
conical ['kɑnɪkəl] *adj* conico
conjecture [kən'dʒektʃər] *s* congettura || *tr & intr* congetturare
conjugate ['kɑndʒə,get] *tr* coniugare
conjugation [,kɑndʒə'geʃən] *s* coniugazione
conjunction [kən'dʒʌŋkʃən] *s* congiunzione
conjure [kən'dʒur] *tr* (*to entreat*) scongiurare || ['kɑndʒər] or ['kʌndʒər] *tr* evocare, stregare; **to conjure up** evocare || *intr* fare delle stregonerie
conk [kɑŋk] *intr*—**to conk out** (slang) essere in panna; (slang) svenire
connect [kə'nekt] *tr* connettere, unire || *intr* connettersi, essere associato; (*said of public conveyances*) operare in coincidenza
connect'ing rod' [kə'nektɪŋ] *s* (mach) biella
connection [kə'nekʃən] *s* connessione; unione, associazione; (*of trains*) coincidenza; (*relative*) parente *mf;* (*e.g., of a water pipe*) allacciamento; **in connection with** rispetto a
con'ning tow'er ['kɑnɪŋ] *s* (nav) torretta
conniption [kə'nɪpʃən] *s* (slang) attacco di rabbia
connive [kə'naɪv] *intr* essere connivente; **to connive at** chiudere un occhio su
connote [kə'not] *tr* indicare, suggerire
conquer ['kɑŋkər] *tr & intr* conquistare
conqueror ['kɑŋkərər] *s* conquistatore *m*
conquest ['kɑŋkwest] *s* conquista
conscience ['kɑnʃəns] *s* coscienza; **in all conscience** a prezzo onesto; certamente
conscientious [,kɑnʃɪ'enʃəs] *adj* coscienzioso
conscien'tious objec'tor [ɑb'dʒektər] *s* obiettore *m* di coscienza
conscious ['kɑnʃəs] *adj* (*aware of one's existence*) cosciente; (*aware*) conscio, consapevole; (*lie*) consapevole; **to become conscious** riprendere i sensi
consciousness ['kɑnʃəsnɪs] *s* coscienza, conoscenza; **to lose consciousness** perdere la conoscenza
conscript ['kɑnskrɪpt] *s* coscritto || [kən'skrɪpt] *tr* coscrivere, arruolare
conscription [kən'skrɪpʃən] *s* coscrizione
consecrate ['kɑnsɪ,kret] *tr* consacrare
consecutive [kən'sekjətɪv] *adj* consecutivo; di seguito
consensus [kən'sensəs] *s* consenso
consent [kən'sent] *s* consenso; **by common consent** per comune consenso || *intr* consentire
consequence ['kɑnsɪ,kwens] *s* conseguenza
consequential [,kɑnsɪ'kwenʃəl] *adj* conseguente; importante, d'importanza; pomposo, pieno di sé
consequently ['kɑnsɪ,kwentli] *adv* conseguentemente, per conseguenza
conservation [,kɑnsər'veʃən] *s* conservazione; preservazione delle foreste
conservatism [kən'sʌrvə,tɪzəm] *s* conservatorismo
conservative [kən'sʌrvətɪv] *adj* conservatore; (*cautious*) cauto; (*preserving*) conservativo; (*free from fads*) tradizionale || *s* conservatore *m*
conservato•ry [kən'sʌrvə,tori] *s* (**-ries**) (*greenhouse*) serra; (mus) conservatorio
conserve [kən'sʌrv] *tr* conservare
consider [kən'sɪdər] *tr* considerare
considerable [kən'sɪdərəbəl] *adj* (*fairly large*) considerevole; (*worth thinking about*) considerabile
considerate [kən'sɪdərɪt] *adj* riguardoso, premuroso
consideration [kən,sɪdə'reʃən] *s* considerazione; (*reason*) motivo; (*money*) pagamento; **in consideration of** a cagione di; in cambio di; **on no consideration** in nessuna maniera, mai; **under consideration** in considerazione, sotto esame; **without due consideration** senza riflessione, alla leggera
considering [kən'sɪdərɪŋ] *adv* tutto considerato || *prep* per, visto || *conj* considerando che, visto che
consign [kən'saɪn] *tr* consegnare; (*to send*) inviare; (*to set apart*) assegnare
consignee [,kɑnsaɪ'ni] *s* consegnatario
consignment [kən'saɪnmənt] *s* consegna; **on consignment** in consegna
consist [kən'sɪst] *intr*—**to consist in** consistere in; **to consist of** consistere in, constare di
consisten•cy [kən'sɪstənsi] *s* (**-cies**) (*firmness, amount of firmness*) consistenza; (*logical connection*) coerenza
consistent [kən'sɪstənt] *adj* (*holding firmly together*) consistente; (*agree-*

ing with itself or oneself) conseguente, coerente; compatibile
consolation [ˌkɑnsəˈleʃən] *s* consolazione
console [ˈkɑnsol] *s* (*table*) console *f;* (rad, telv) mobile *m;* (mus) console *f* || [kənˈsol] *tr* consolare
consonant [ˈkɑnsənənt] *adj* consonante, armonioso; (gram) consonantico || *s* consonante *f*
consort [ˈkɑnsɔrt] *s* consorte *mf* || [kənˈsɔrt] *intr* associarsi; (*to agree*) concordarsi
conspicuous [kənˈspɪkju·əs] *adj* visibile, manifesto; notevole; (*too noticeable*) appariscente; **to make oneself conspicuous** farsi notare
conspira•cy [kənˈspɪrəsi] *s* (**-cies**) cospirazione, congiura
conspire [kənˈspaɪr] *intr* cospirare, congiurare; (*to act together*) cooperare
constable [ˈkɑnstəbəl] or [ˈkʌnstəbəl] *s* poliziotto; (*keeper of a castle*) conestabile *m*
constancy [ˈkɑnstənsi] *s* costanza
constant [ˈkɑnstənt] *adj & s* costante *f*
constellation [ˌkɑnstəˈleʃən] *s* costellazione
constipate [ˈkɑnstɪˌpet] *tr* costipare
constipation [ˌkɑnstɪˈpeʃən] *s* costipazione
constituen•cy [kənˈstɪtʃʊ·ənsi] *s* (**-cies**) (*voters*) elettorato; (*district*) circoscrizione elettorale
constituent [kənˈstɪtʃʊ·ənt] *adj* costituente || *s* (*component*) parte *f* costituente; (*voter*) elettore *m;* (*of a chemical substance*) costituente *m*
constitute [ˈkɑnstɪˌtjut] or [ˈkɑnstɪˌtut] *tr* costituire
constitution [ˌkɑnstɪˈtjuʃən] or [ˌkɑnstɪˈtuʃən] *s* costituzione
constrain [kənˈstren] *tr* (*to force*) costringere; (*to restrain*) restringere, comprimere
constrict [kənˈstrɪkt] *tr* stringere, comprimere
construct [kənˈstrʌkt] *tr* costruire
construction [kənˈstrʌkʃən] *s* costruzione; (*meaning*) interpretazione
construe [kənˈstru] *tr* (*to interpret*) interpretare; (*to translate*) tradurre; (gram) analizzare
consul [ˈkɑnsəl] *s* console *m*
consular [ˈkɑnsələr] or [ˈkɑnsjələr] *adj* consolare
consulate [ˈkɑnsəlɪt] or [ˈkɑnsjəlɪt] *s* consolato
consult [kənˈsʌlt] *tr* consultare || *intr* consultarsi
consultation [ˌkɑnsəlˈteʃən] *s* consultazione, conferenza
consume [kənˈsum] or [kənˈsjum] *tr* consumare; distruggere; **consumed with** (*passion*) arso di; (*curiosity*) assorbito da
consumer [kənˈsumər] or [kənˈsjumər] *s* consumatore *m*
consum'er goods' *spl* beni *mpl* di consumo
consumerism [kənˈsumərˌɪzem] *s* consumismo
consummate [kənˈsʌmɪt] *adj* consumato || [ˈkɑnsəˌmet] *tr* consumare
consumption [kənˈsʌmpʃən] *s* (*decay*) consunzione; (*using up*) consumo; (pathol) consunzione
consumptive [kənˈsʌmptɪv] *adj* tubercolotico, tisico; (*wasteful*) logorante || *s* tisico, etico
contact [ˈkɑntækt] *s* contatto; (elec) contatto; (elec) presa di corrente || *tr* (coll) mettersi in contatto con || *intr* (coll) mettersi in contatto
con'tact break'er *s* ruttore *m*
con'tact lens' *s* lente *f* a contatto
contagion [kənˈtedʒən] *s* contagio
contagious [kənˈtedʒəs] *adj* contagioso
contain [kənˈten] *tr* contenere; **to contain oneself** frenarsi
container [kənˈtenər] *s* recipiente *m,* contenitore *m*
contaminate [kənˈtæmɪˌnet] *tr* contaminare
contamination [kənˌtæmɪˈneʃən] *s* contaminazione
contemplate [ˈkɑntəmˌplet] *tr* contemplare; (*to think about*) meditare; (*to have in mind*) progettare, avere in mente || *intr* meditare
contemplation [ˌkɑntəmˈpleʃən] *s* contemplazione; (*intention*) intenzione
contemporaneous [kənˌtɛmpəˈrenɪ·əs] *adj* contemporaneo, coevo
contemporar•y [kənˈtɛmpəˌrɛri] *adj* contemporaneo, coevo || *s* (**-ies**) contemporaneo
contempt [kənˈtɛmpt] *s* (*despising*) disprezzo; (*condition of being despised*) dispregio; (*of the law*) disprezzo
contemptible [kənˈtɛmptɪbəl] *adj* disprezzabile, spregevole
contempt' of court' *s* (law) offesa alla magistratura, oltraggio al tribunale
contemptuous [kənˈtɛmptʃʊ·əs] *adj* sprezzante, sdegnoso
contend [kənˈtɛnd] *tr* dichiarare || *intr* (*to argue*) disputare, contendere; (*to fight*) lottare
contender [kənˈtɛndər] *s* competitore *m,* concorrente *m*
content [kənˈtɛnt] *adj* contento; (*willing*) pronto || *s* contentezza || [ˈkɑntɛnt] *s* contenuto; **contents** contenuto || [kənˈtɛnt] *tr* contentare
contented [kənˈtɛntɪd] *adj* soddisfatto
contention [kənˈtɛnʃən] *s* disputa, litigio; contenzione
contentious [kənˈtɛnʃəs] *adj* litigioso
contentment [kənˈtɛntmənt] *s* contentezza
contest [ˈkɑntɛst] *s* contesa, controversia; (*game*) gara || [kənˈtɛst] *tr* disputare, contestare || *intr* combattere, fare resistenza
contestant [kənˈtɛstənt] *s* concorrente *m;* (law) contendente *m*
context [ˈkɑntɛkst] *s* contesto
contiguous [kənˈtɪgjʊ·əs] *adj* contiguo
continence [ˈkɑntɪnəns] *s* continenza
continent [ˈkɑntɪnənt] *adj & s* conti-

nente *m;* **on the Continent** nel continente europeo
continental [ˌkɑntɪˈnɛntəl] *adj & s* continentale *mf*
contingen·cy [kənˈtɪndʒənsi] *s* **(-cies)** contingenza, congiuntura; (*chance*) eventualità *f*
contingent [kənˈtɪndʒənt] *adj* eventuale; imprevisto; (philos) contingente; **to be contingent upon** dipendere da
continual [kənˈtɪnju·əl] *adj* continuo
continuance [kənˈtɪnjuəns] *s* continuazione; (*in office*) permanenza; (law) rinvio
continue [kənˈtɪnju] *tr* continuare; (*to cause to remain*) mantenere; (law) rinviare ‖ *intr* continuare; rimanere
continui·ty [ˌkɑntɪˈnju·ɪti] or [ˌkɑntɪˈnu·ɪti] *s* **(-ties)** continuità *f;* (mov & telv) sceneggiatura; (rad) copione *m*
continuous [kənˈtɪnju·əs] *adj* continuo
contin'uous show'ing *s* (mov) spettacolo permanente
contortion [kənˈtɔrʃən] *s* contorsione; (*of facts*) distorsione
contour [ˈkɑntʊr] *s* contorno
con'tour line' *s* curva di livello, isoipsa
contraband [ˈkɑntrəˌbænd] *adj* di contrabbando ‖ *s* contrabbando
contrabass [ˈkɑntrəˌbes] *s* contrabasso
contraceptive [ˌkɑntrəˈsɛptɪv] *adj & s* antifecondativo
contract [ˈkɑntrækt] *s* contratto ‖ [ˈkɑntrækt] or [kənˈtrækt] *tr* (*a business deal*) contrattare; (*marriage*) contrarre ‖ *intr* (*to shrink*) contrarsi; **to contract for** contrattare, appaltare
contraction [kənˈtrækʃən] *s* contrazione
contractor [kənˈtræktər] *s* (*person who makes a contract*) contraente *m;* (*person who contracts to supply material*) appaltatore *m,* imprenditore *m;* (*in building*) capomastro
contradict [ˌkɑntrəˈdɪkt] *tr* contraddire
contradiction [ˌkɑntrəˈdɪkʃən] *s* contraddizione
contradictory [ˌkɑntrəˈdɪktəri] *adj* contraddittorio
contrail [ˈkɑnˌtrel] *s* (aer) scia di condensazione
contral·to [kənˈtrælto] *s* **(-tos)** (*person*) contralto *mf;* (*voice*) contralto *m*
contraption [kənˈtræpʃən] *s* (coll) aggeggio
contra·ry [ˈkɑntreri] *adj* contrario ‖ [kənˈtreri] *adj* ostinato, caparbio ‖ [ˈkɑntreri] *s* **(-ries)** contrario; **on the contrary** al contrario ‖ *adv* contrariamente
contrast [ˈkɑntræst] *s* contrasto ‖ [kənˈtræst] *tr* confrontare ‖ *intr* contrastare
contravene [ˌkɑntrəˈvin] *tr* contraddire; (*a law*) contravvenire (with *dat*)
contribute [kənˈtrɪbjut] *tr* contribuire ‖ *intr* contribuire; (*to a newspaper*) collaborare
contribution [ˌkɑntrɪˈbjuʃən] *s* contribuzione; (*to a newspaper*) collaborazione
contributor [kənˈtrɪbjutər] *s* contributore *m;* (*to a newspaper*) collaboratore *m*
contrite [kənˈtraɪt] *adj* contrito
contrition [kənˈtrɪʃən] *s* contrizione
contrivance [kənˈtraɪvəns] *s* dispositivo, congegno; (*faculty*) invenzione; (*scheme*) artificio, piano
contrive [kənˈtraɪv] *tr* inventare; (*to scheme up*) macchinare; (*to bring about*) effettuare; **to contrive to** trovare il modo di
con·trol [kənˈtrol] *s* controllo; (*check*) freno; **controls** comandi *mpl;* **to get under control** riuscire a controllare ‖ *v* (*pret & pp* **-trolled;** *ger* **-trolling**) *tr* controllare
controller [kənˈtrolər] *s* controllore *m;* analista *mf* di gestione; economo; (mach) regolatore *m;* (elec) interruttore *m* di linea
control'ling in'terest *s* maggioranza delle azioni
control' stick' *s* leva di comando
controversial [ˌkɑntrəˈvʌrʃəl] *adj* controverso, polemico, discusso
controver·sy [ˈkɑntrəˌvʌrsi] *s* **(-sies)** controversia
controvert [ˈkɑntrəˌvʌrt] or [ˌkɑntrəˈvʌrt] *tr* contraddire
contumacious [ˌkɑntjʊˈmeʃəs] or [ˌkɑntʊˈmeʃəs] *adj* ribelle, contumace
contuma·cy [ˈkɑntjuməsi] or [ˈkɑntuməsi] *s* **(-cies)** contumacia
contusion [kənˈtjuʒən] or [kənˈtuʒən] *s* contusione
conundrum [kəˈnʌndrəm] *s* indovinello
convalesce [ˌkɑnvəˈlɛs] *intr* essere convalescente
convalescence [ˌkɑnvəˈlɛsəns] *s* convalescenza
convalescent [ˌkɑnvəˈlɛsənt] *adj & s* convalescente *mf*
con'vales'cent home' *s* convalescenziario
convene [kənˈvin] *tr* convocare ‖ *intr* convenire
convenience [kənˈvinjəns] *s* convenienza; (*comfort*) agio; (*anything that saves work*) conforto; **at your earliest convenience** quanto prima
convenient [kənˈvinjənt] *adj* conveniente, adatto; comodo; **convenient to** (*near*) (coll) vicino a
convent [ˈkɑnvɛnt] *s* convento di religiose
convention [kənˈvenʃən] *s* convenzione, assemblea; **conventions** (*customs*) convenzioni *fpl*
conventional [kənˈvenʃənəl] *adj* convenzionale
converge [kənˈvʌrdʒ] *intr* convergere
conversant [kənˈvʌrsənt] *adj* versato, esperto, dotto
conversation [ˌkɑnvərˈseʃən] *s* conversazione
converse [ˈkɑnvʌrs] *adj & s* contrario ‖ [kənˈvʌrs] *intr* conversare

conversion [kən'vʌrʒən] *s* conversione; (*unlawful appropriation*) malversazione
convert ['kɑnvʌrt] *s* convertito || [kən'vʌrt] *tr* convertire; misappropriare || *intr* convertirsi
convertible [kən'vʌrtɪbəl] *adj & s* convertibile *f;* (aut) trasformabile *f,* decappottabile *f*
convex ['kɑnvɛks] or [kɑn'vɛks] *adj* convesso
convey [kən've] *tr* (*to carry*) trasportare; (*liquids*) convogliare; (*sounds*) trasmettere; (*to express*) esprimere; (*e.g., property*) trasferire
conveyance [kən've·əns] *s* trasporto; veicolo; comunicazione; (*of property*) trasferimento; (*deed*) titolo di proprietà
convey'or belt' [kən've·ər] *s* trasportatore *m*
convict ['kɑnvɪkt] *s* condannato || [kən'vɪkt] *tr* convincere, condannare
conviction [kən'vɪkʃən] *s* condanna; (*belief*) convinzione, convincimento
convince [kən'vɪns] *tr* convincere
convincing [kən'vɪnsɪŋ] *adj* convincente
convivial [kən'vɪvɪ·əl] *adj* (*festive*) conviviale; gioviale, bonaccione
convocation [,kɑnvə'keʃən] *s* convocazione, assemblea
convoke [kən'vok] *tr* convocare
convoy ['kɑnvɔɪ] *s* (*of ships*) convoglio; (*of vehicles*) carovana || *tr* convogliare
convulse [kən'vʌls] *tr* (*to shake*) scuotere; (*to throw into convulsions*) mettere in convulsioni; (*to cause to shake with laughter*) far torcere dalle risa
coo [ku] *intr* tubare, gemere
cook [kʊk] *s* cuoco || *tr* cuocere; **to cook up** (coll) preparare, macchinare || *intr* (*said of food*) cuocere; (*said of a person*) fare il cuoco
cook'book' *s* libro di cucina
cookie ['kʊki] *s* var of **cooky**
cooking ['kʊkɪŋ] *s* culinaria
cook'out' *s* picnic *m,* spuntino all'aperto
cook'stove' *s* cucina economica
cook·y ['kʊki] *s* (**-ies**) pasticcino, biscotto
cool [kul] *adj* fresco; calmo; (*not cordial*) freddo; (*bold*) sfacciato || *s* fresco || *tr* rinfrescare; **to cool one's heels** fare anticamera || *intr* rinfrescarsi; **to cool off** rinfrescarsi; calmarsi
coolant ['kulənt] *s* miscela refrigerante
cooler ['kulər] s ghiacciaia; (slang) prigione
cool'-head'ed *adj* calmo, imperturbabile
coolish ['kulɪʃ] *adj* freschetto
coon [kun] *s* procione *m*
coop [kʊp] *s* pollaio; conigliera; **to fly the coop** (slang) scapparsene || *tr*—**to coop up** rinchiudere tra quattro mura
cooper ['kupər] *s* bottaio
cooperate [ko'ɑpə,ret] *intr* cooperare
cooperation [ko,ɑpə'reʃən] *s* cooperazione
cooperative [ko'ɑpə,retɪv] *adj* cooperativo || *s* cooperativa
coordinate [ko'ɔrdɪnɪt] *adj* coordinato; (gram) coordinativo || *s* (math) coordinata || [ko'ɔrdɪ,net] *tr & intr* coordinare
coot [kut] *s* (zool) folaga; (slang) vecchio pazzo
cootie ['kuti] *s* (slang) pidocchio
cop [kɑp] *s* (slang) poliziotto || *v* (*pret & pp* **copped; ger copping**) *tr* (slang) rubare
copartner [ko'pɑrtnər] *s* consocio, socio
cope [kop] *intr*—**to cope with** **tener testa a**
cope'stone' *s* pietra da cimasa
copier ['kɑpɪ·ər] *s* (*person*) copista *mf;* imitatore *m;* (*machine*) duplicatore *m*
copilot ['ko,paɪlət] *s* copilota *mf*
coping ['kopɪŋ] *s* coronamento, cimasa
cop'ing saw' *s* seghetto da traforo
copious ['kopɪ·əs] *adj* copioso
copper [kɑp'ər] *s* rame *m;* (*coin*) soldo; (*boiler*) calderone *m;* (slang) poliziotto
cop'per·head' *s* vipera (*Ancistrodon contortrix*)
cop'per·smith' *s* battirame *m,* calderaio
coppice ['kɑpɪs] or **copse** [kɑps] *s* boschetto
copulate ['kɑpjə,let] *intr* copularsi, congiungersi carnalmente
cop·y ['kɑpi] *s* (**-ies**) copia; modello; manoscritto || *v* (*pret & pp* **-ied**) *tr* copiare, imitare || *intr* copiare; **to copy after** imitare
cop'y·book' *s* quaderno
copyist ['kɑpɪ·ɪst] *s* copista *mf;* imitatore *m*
cop'y·right' *s* copyright *m,* diritto di proprietà letteraria || *tr* registrare; proteggere con copyright
cop'y·writ'er *s* copy-writer *m,* redattore *m* pubblicitario
coquet·ry ['kokətri] or [ko'ketri] *s* (**-ries**) civetteria
coquette [ko'kɛt] *s* civetta
coquettish [ko'kɛtɪʃ] *adj* civettuolo
coral ['kɑrəl] or ['kɔrəl] *adj* corallino || *s* corallo
cor'al reef' *s* banco di coralli
cord [kɔrd] *s* corda, fune *f;* (*corduroy*) tessuto cordonato; (elec) cordone *m* || *tr* legare con corda
cordial ['kɔrdʒəl] *adj & s* cordiale *m*
corduroy ['kɔrdə,rɔɪ] *s* velluto a coste; **corduroys** pantaloni *mpl* alla cacciatora
core [kor] *s* (*of fruit*) torsolo; (*central part*) centro; (*of problem*) nocciolo; (*of earth*) barisfera, nucleo centrale; (phys) nucleo; **rotten to the core** guasto nelle ossa
corespondent [,korɪs'pɑndənt] *s* coimputato in un processo di divorzio
cork [kɔrk] *s* (*bark*) sughero; (*stopper*) tappo, tappo di sughero || *tr* tappare
cork' oak' *s* sughero

cork'screw' *s* cavatappi *m*
cormorant ['kɔrmərənt] *s* cormorano
corn [kɔrn] *s* granturco, mais *m;* (*kernel*) chicco; (*thickening of skin*) callo; (*whiskey*) whisky *m* di granturco; (Brit) grano; (Scot) avena; (slang) banalità *f*
corn' bread' *s* pane *m* di farina gialla
corn' cake' *s* omelette *f* di granturco
corn'cob' *s* tutolo
corn'cob pipe' *s* pipa fatta di un tutolo di pannocchia
corn'crib' *s* granaio per le pannocchie
corn' cure' *s* callifugo
cornea ['kɔrnɪ·ə] *s* cornea
corner ['kɔrnər] *s* angolo; (*of street*) cantonata; situazione difficile; (*of the eye*) coda dell'occhio; (com) accaparramento, incetta, bagarinaggio; **to cut corners** tagliare le spese; **to turn the corner** passare il punto più pericoloso ‖ *tr* mettere in una situazione difficile; (*the market*) incettare, accaparrare
cor'ner cup'board *s* cantoniera, armadio d'angolo
cor'ner stone' *s* pietra angolare; (*of new building*) prima pietra
cornet [kɔr'nɛt] *s* cornetta
corn' exchange' *s* borsa dei cereali
corn'field' *s* (*in U.S.A.*) campo di granturco; (*in England*) campo di grano; (*in Scotland*) campo di avena
corn'flakes' *spl* fiocchi *mpl* di granturco
corn' flour' *s* farina di granturco
corn'flow'er *s* fiordaliso
corn'husk' *s* brattea, cartoccio
cornice ['kɔrnɪs] *s* (*of house*) cornicione *m;* (*of room*) cornice *f*
corn' liq'uor *s* whisky *m* di granturco
corn' meal' *s* farina di granturco
corn' on the cob' *s* granturco servito in pannocchia
corn' plas'ter *s* cerotto per i calli
corn' silk' *s* barba del granturco
corn'stalk' *s* fusto di granturco
corn'starch' *s* amido di granturco
corn·y ['kɔrni] *adj* (**-ier; -iest**) (slang) banale, trito, triviale
coronation [,kɑrə'neʃən] or [,kɔrə'neʃən] *s* incoronazione
coroner ['kɑrənər] or ['kɔrənər] *s* magistrato inquirente
cor'oner's in'quest *s* inchiesta giudiziaria dinanzi a giuria
coronet ['kɑrə,nɛt] or ['kɔrə,nɛt] *s* corona (non reale); diadema *m*
corporal ['kɔrpərəl] *adj* caporalesco ‖ *s* caporale *m*
corporation [,kɔrpə'reʃən] *s* società anonima
corps [kor] *s* (**corps** [korz]) corpo
corps' de bal'let *s* corpo di ballo
corpse [kɔrps] *s* cadavere *m*
corpulent ['kɔrpjələnt] *adj* corpulento
corpuscle ['kɔrpəsəl] *s* (anat) globulo; (phys) corpuscolo
cor·ral [kə'ræl] *s* recinto per bestiame ‖ *v* (*pret & pp* **-ralled;** *ger* **-ralling**) *tr* mettere in un recinto; catturrare
correct [kə'rɛkt] *adj* corretto ‖ *tr* correggere
correction [kə'rɛkʃən] *s* correzione
corrective [kə'rɛktɪv] *adj & s* correttivo
correctness [kə'rɛktnɪs] *s* correttezza
correlate ['kɑrə,let] or ['kɔrə,let] *tr* correlare ‖ *intr* essere in correlazione
correlation [,kɑrə'leʃən] or [,kɔrə'leʃən] *s* correlazione
correspond [,kɑrɪ'spɑnd] or [,kɔrɪ'spɑnd] *intr* corrispondere
correspondence [,kɑrɪ'spɑndəns] or [,kɔrɪ'spɑndəns] *s* corrispondenza
correspond'ence school' *s* scuola per corrispondenza
correspondent [,kɑrɪ'spɑndənt] or [,kɔrɪ'spɑndənt] *adj & s* corrispondente *mf*
corridor ['kɑrɪdər] or ['kɔrɪdər] *s* corridoio
corroborate [kə'rɑbə,ret] *tr* corroborare
corrode [kə'rod] *tr* corrodere ‖ *intr* corrodersi
corrosion [kə'roʒən] *s* corrosione
corrosive [kə'rosɪv] *adj & s* corrosivo
corrugated ['kɑrə,getɪd] or ['kɔrə,getɪd] *adj* ondulato
corrupt [kə'rʌpt] *adj* corrotto ‖ *tr* corrompere; (*a language*) imbarbarire ‖ *intr* corrompersi
corruption [kə'rʌpʃən] *s* corruzione
corsage [kɔr'sɑʒ] *s* (*bodice*) corpetto; (*bouquet*) mazzolino di fiori da appuntarsi al vestito
corsair ['kɔr,sɛr] *s* corsaro
corset ['kɔrsɪt] *s* corsetto
Corsican ['kɔrsɪkən] *adj & s* corso
cortege [kɔr'tɛʒ] *s* corteggio
cor·tex ['kɔr,tɛks] *s* (**-tices** [tɪ,siz]) cortice *f*
cortisone ['kɔrtɪ,son] *s* cortisone *m*
corvette [kɔr'vɛt] *s* corvetta
cosmetic [kɑz'mɛtɪk] *adj & s* cosmetico
cosmic ['kɑzmɪk] *adj* cosmico
cosmonaut ['kɑzmə,nɔt] *s* cosmonauta *mf*
cosmopolitan [,kɑzmə'pɑlɪtən] *adj & s* cosmopolita *mf*
cosmos ['kɑzməs] *s* cosmo
cost [kɔst] or [kɑst] *s* costo, prezzo; **at all costs** or **at any cost** ad ogni costo; **costs** (law) spese *fpl* processuali ‖ *v* (*pret & pp* **cost**) *intr* costare
cost·ly ['kɔstli] or ['kɑstli] *adj* (**-lier; -liest**) costoso; (*sumptuous*) lussuoso
cost' of liv'ing *s* costo della vita
costume ['kɑstjum] or ['kɑstum] *s* costume *m*
cos'tume ball' *s* ballo in costume
cos'tume jew'elry *s* gioielli falsi
cot [kɑt] *s* (*narrow bed*) branda; (*cottage*) capanna, cabina
coterie ['kotəri] *s* gruppo; (*clique*) chiesuola
cottage ['kɑtɪdʒ] *s* casetta, villino
cot'tage cheese' *s* ricotta americana
cot'ter pin' ['kɑtər] *s* copiglia, coppiglia
cotton ['kɑtən] *s* cotone *m* ‖ *intr*—**to cotton up to** (coll) cominciare a provare della simpatia per; (coll) andare d'accordo con
cot'ton can'dy *s* zucchero filato

cot'ton gin' *s* sgranatrice *f*
cot'ton pick'er ['pɪkər] *s* chi raccoglie il cotone; macchina che raccoglie il cotone
cot'tonseed oil' *s* olio di semi di cotone
cot'ton waste' *s* cascame *m* di cotone
cot'ton•wood' *s* pioppo deltoide
couch [kautʃ] *s* canapè *m*, sofà *m*, divano || *tr* esprimere
couch' grass' *s* gramigna
cougar ['kugər] *s* puma *m*
cough [kɔf] or [kɑf] *s* tosse *f* || *tr*—**to cough up** sputare, sputare tossendo; (slang) dare, pagare || *intr* tossire
cough' drop' *s* pastiglia per la tosse
cough' syr'up *s* sciroppo per la tosse
could [kud] *v aux*—**I could not come yesterday** non ho potuto venire ieri; **I could not see you tomorrow** non potrei vederLa domani; **it could not be so** non potrebbe essere così
council ['kaunsəl] *s* consiglio; (eccl) concilio
coun'cil•man *s* (**-men**) consigliere *m* or assessore *m* municipale
coun•sel ['kaunsəl] *s* consiglio; (*lawyer*) avvocato; **to keep one's counsel** essere riservato; **to take counsel with** consultarsi con || *v* (*pret & pp* **-seled** or **-selled**; *ger* **-seling** or **-selling**) *tr* consigliare || *intr* consigliare; consigliarsi
counselor ['kaunsələr] *s* consigliere *m*; avvocato
count [kaunt] *s* conto; (*nobleman*) conte *m*; (law) capo d'accusa || *tr* contare; **to count off by** (*twos, threes*) contare per (*due, tre*); **to count out** escludere; (boxing) contare || *intr* contare; (*to be worth*) valere; **to count on** contare su
count'down' *s* conteggio alla rovescia
countenance ['kauntɪnəns] *s* espressione; (*face*) faccia; (*approval*) approvazione || *tr* approvare, incoraggiare
counter ['kauntər] *adj* contrario || *s* contatore *m*; (*token*) gettone *m*; (*table in store*) banco; (*opposite*) contrario || *adv* contro, contrariamente || *tr* contrariare, opporre || *intr* (boxing) rispondere
coun'ter•act' *tr* contrariare, neutralizzare
coun'ter•attack' *s* contrattacco || **coun'ter•attack'** *tr & intr* contrattaccare
coun'ter•bal'ance *s* contrappeso || **coun'ter•bal'ance** *tr* controbilanciare
coun'ter•clock'wise' *adj* antiorario || *adv* in senso antiorario
coun'ter•es'pionage' *s* controspionaggio
counterfeit ['kauntərfɪt] *adj* contraffatto || *s* contraffazione; moneta falsa || *tr & intr* contraffare
counterfeiter ['kauntər,fɪtər] *s* contraffattore *m*
coun'ter•feit mon'ey *s* moneta falsa
countermand ['kauntər,mænd] or ['kauntər,mɑnd] *tr* (*troops*) dare un contrordine a; (*an order; a payment*) cancellare
coun'ter•march' *s* contromarcia || *intr* fare contromarcia
coun'ter•offen'sive *s* controffensiva
coun'ter•pane' *s* sopraccoperta
coun'ter•part' *s* copia; (*person*) sosia
coun'ter•point' *s* (mus) contrappunto; (mus) controcanto
Coun'ter Reforma'tion *s* controriforma
coun'ter•rev'olu'tion *s* controrivoluzione
coun'ter•sign' *s* (*password*) parola d'ordine; (*signature*) controfirma || *tr* controfirmare
coun'ter•sink' *v* (*pret & pp* **-sunk**) *tr* incassare, accecare
coun'ter•spy' *s* (**-spies**) membro del controspionaggio
coun'ter•stroke' *s* contraccolpo
coun'ter•weight' *s* contrappeso
countess ['kauntɪs] *s* contessa
countless ['kauntlɪs] *adj* innumerevole
countrified ['kʌntrɪ,faɪd] *adj* rustico, rurale
coun•try ['kʌntri] *s* (**-tries**) (*land*) terreno; (*nation*) paese *m*; (*land of one's birth*) patria; (*rural region*) campagna
coun'try club' *s* circolo privato sportivo situato nei sobborghi
coun'try cous'in *s* campagnolo
coun'try estate' *s* tenuta
coun'try•folk' *s* campagnoli *mpl*
coun'try gen'tleman *s* proprietario terriero, signorotto di campagna
coun'try house' *s* casa di campagna
coun'try jake' *s* (coll) zoticone *m*
coun'try life' *s* vita rustica
coun'try•man *s* (**-men**) paesano, compaesano
coun'try•peo'ple *s* gente *f* di campagna
coun'try•side' *s* campagna
coun'try-wide' *adj* nazionale
coun'try•wom'an *s* (**-wom'en**) *s* paesana, compaesana
coun•ty ['kaunti] *s* (**-ties**) contea, distretto
coun'ty seat' *s* capoluogo di contea
coup [ku] *s* colpo; colpo di stato
coup de grâce [ku də 'grɑs] *s* colpo di grazia
coup d'état [ku de'tɑ] *s* colpo di stato
coupe [kup] or **coupé** [ku'pe] *s* coupé *m*
couple ['kʌpəl] *s* (*of people or animals*) paio, coppia; (*of things*) paio; (*link*) unione || *tr* accoppiare; (*to link*) unire, agganciare || *intr* accoppiarsi
couplet ['kʌplɪt] *s* coppia di versi; (mus) couplet *m*
coupling ['kʌplɪŋ] *s* unione; (mach) giunto
coupon ['kupɑn] or ['kjupɑn] *s* coupon *m*, tagliando
courage ['kʌrɪdʒ] *s* coraggio; **to have the courage of one's convictions** avere il coraggio delle proprie opinioni
courageous [kə'redʒəs] *adj* coraggioso
courier ['kʌrɪ•ər] or ['kurɪ•ər] *s* corriere *m*
course [kors] *s* corso; (*part of meal*) portata; (*place for games*) campo;

(*row*) fila; **in due course** a tempo debito; **in the course of** durante, nel corso di; **of course** certamente, senza dubbio
court [kort] *s* (*uncovered place surrounded by walls*) corte *f*, cortile *m;* (*royal residence; courtship*) corte *f;* (*short street*) vicolo; (*playing area*) campo; (law) corte *f* || *tr* corteggiare; (*e.g., disaster*) andare in cerca di
courteous ['kʌrtɪ·əs] *adj* cortese
courtesan ['kʌrtɪzən] or ['kortɪzən] *s* cortigiana, meretrice *f*
courte·sy ['kʌrtɪsi] *s* (**-sies**) cortesia, gentilezza; **through the courtesy of** con il gentile permesso di
court'house' *s* palazzo di giustizia
courtier ['kortɪ·ər] *s* cortigiano
court' jest'er *s* buffone *m* di corte
court·ly ['kortli] *adj* (**-lier; -liest**) cortese, cortigiano; ossequioso
court'-mar'tial *s* (**courts-martial**) corte *f* marziale || *v* (*pret & pp* **-tialed** or **-tialled;** *ger* **-tialing** or **-tialling**) *tr* sottomettere a corte marziale
court' plas'ter *s* taffettà *m*
court'room' *s* aula di giustizia
courtship ['kortʃɪp] *s* corte *f*, corteggiamento
court'yard' *s* corte *f*, cortile *m*
cousin ['kʌzɪn] *s* cugino
cove [kov] *s* piccola baia, cala
covenant ['kʌvənənt] *s* convenzione, patto || *tr* promettere solennemente
cover ['kʌvər] *s* (*lid*) coperchio; (*tablecloth; shelter*) coperto; (*of book*) copertina; **to take cover** nascondersi; **under cover** in segreto, segretamente; **under cover of** sotto la protezione di; **under separate cover** in busta a parte, in plico a parte || *tr* coprire; puntare un'arma verso; (journ) riferire, riportare; **to cover up** coprire completamente || *intr* (*said of paint*) spandersi
coverage ['kʌvərɪdʒ] *s* copertura; (journ) servizio giornalistico; (rad, telv) raggio di udibilità
coveralls ['kʌvər ,ɔlz] *spl* tuta
cov'er charge' *s* coperto
cov'ered wag'on *s* carro coperto da tendone
cov'er girl' *s* ragazza-copertina
covering ['kʌvərɪŋ] *s* copertura; involucro
covert ['kʌvərt] *adj* nascosto, segreto
cov'er-up' *s* dissimulazione; sotterfugio
covet ['kʌvɪt] *tr* desiderare, agognare
covetous ['kʌvɪtəs] *adj* cupido
covey ['kʌvi] *s* covata
cow [kaʊ] *s* vacca; (*of seal, elephant, etc.*) femmina || *tr* spaventare, intimidire
coward ['kaʊ·ərd] *s* codardo, vile *m*
cowardice ['kaʊ·ərdɪs] *s* codardia, viltà *f*
cowardly ['kaʊ·ərdli] *adj* codardo, vile || *adv* vilmente
cow'bell' *s* campano, campanaccio
cow'boy' *s* cowboy *m*
cow'catch'er *s* (rr) cacciapietre *m*
cower ['kaʊ·ər] *intr* rannicchiarsi
cow'herd' *s* guardiano d'armenti
cow'hide' *s* pelle *f* di vacca
cowl [kaʊl] *s* (*hood*) cappuccio; (*monk's cloak*) cappa; (*of car*) sostegno del cofano; (*of chimney*) cappello; (aer) cappottatura
cow'lick' *s* ritrosa
cow'pox' *s* (vet) vaiolo bovino
coxcomb ['kɑks ,kom] *s* zerbinotto
coxwain ['kɑksən] or ['kɑk ,swen] *s* timoniere *m*
coy [kɔɪ] *adj* timido, ritroso
co·zy ['kozi] *adj* (**-zier; -ziest**) comodo || *s* (**-zies**) copriteiera *m*
C.P.A. ['si'pi'e] *s* (letterword) (**certified public accountant**) esperto contabile
crab [kræb] *s* granchio; (aer) scarroccio; (*complaining person*) (coll) scontroso || *v* (*pret & pp* **crabbed;** *ger* **crabbing**) *intr* (coll) lamentarsi
crab' apple' *s* mela selvatica; (*tree*) melo selvatico
crabbed ['kræbɪd] *adj* sgarbato; (*handwriting*) da gallina; (*style*) oscuro, ermetico
crab' louse' *s* piattola
crab·by ['kræbi] *adj* (**-bier; -biest**) scontroso, sgarbato
crack [kræk] *adj* (slang) di prim'ordine, eccellente || *s* (*noise*) schiocco; (*break*) rottura, screpolatura, crepa; (*opening*) fessura; (slang) tentativo; (slang) barzelletta || *tr* (*e.g., a whip*) schioccare; (*to break*) rompere, screpolare; (*oil*) ridurre con distillazione; (coll) risolvere; (*a safe*) (slang) forzare; (*a joke*) (slang) dire; **cracked up to be** (slang) avendo fama di || *intr* (*to make a noise*) scricchiolare; (*to break*) rompersi, screpolarsi; (*said of voice*) diventare fesso; (slang) avere un esaurimento nervoso; **to crack down** (slang) essere severo; **to crack up** (slang) andare a pezzi
cracked [krækt] *adj* rotto, spezzato; (*voice*) fesso; (coll) pazzo
cracker ['krækər] *s* cracker *m*, galletta
crack'er·bar'rel *adj* in piccolo, alla buona
crack'er·jack' *adj* (slang) di prim'ordine || *s* (slang) persona di prim'ordine
cracking ['krækɪŋ] *s* piroscissione
crackle ['krækəl] *s* crepitio, crepito || *intr* crepitare
crack'pot' *adj & s* (coll) mattoide *mf*
crack'-up' *s* accidente *m;* collisione; (*breakdown in health or in relations*) (coll) colasso; (aer) accidente *m* d'atterraggio
cradle ['kredəl] *s* culla; (*of handset*) forcella || *tr* cullare
crad'le·song' *s* ninnananna
craft [kræft] or [krɑft] *s* (*skill*) abilità *f;* (*trade*) mestiere *m;* (*guile*) astuzia, furberia; (*ship*) nave *f;* aeronave
craftiness ['kræftfɪnɪs] or ['krɑftɪnɪs] *s* astuzia, furberia
crafts'man *s* (**-men**) operaio specializzato, artigiano

craft' un'ion *s* artigianato, sindacato artigiano
craft·y ['kræfti] or ['krɑfti] *adj* (**-ier; -iest**) astuto, furbo
crag [kræg] *s* roccia scoscesa, rupe *f*
cram [kræm] *v* (*pret & pp* **crammed;** *ger* **cramming**) *tr* (*to pack full*) riempire fino all'orlo; (*to stuff with food*) rimpinzare || *intr* rimpinzarsi; (coll) preparare un esame alla svelta
cramp [kræmp] *s* (*painful contraction*) crampo; (*bar with hooks*) grappa; (fig) ostacolo || *tr* ostacolare, restringere
cranber·ry ['kræn,bɛri] *s* (**-ries**) mirtillo
crane [kren] *s* (orn, mach) gru *f;* (*boom*) (telv, mov) giraffa || *tr* (*one's neck*) allungare || *intr* allungare il collo
crani·um ['krenɪ·əm] *s* (**-a** [ə]) cranio
crank [kræŋk] *s* manovella; (aut) alzacristalli *m;* (coll) eccentrico || *tr* girare con la manovella; mettere in moto con la manovella
crank'case' *s* coppa dell'olio, carter *m*
crank'shaft' *s* albero a gomito
crank·y ['kræŋki] *adj* (**-ier; -iest**) irritabile; eccentrico
cran·ny ['kræni] *s* (**-nies**) (*crevice*) crepaccio; (*crack*) fessura
crape [krep] *s* crespo
crape'hang'er *s* (slang) pessimista uggioso, guastafeste *mf*
craps [kræps] *s* gioco dei dadi; **to shoot craps** giocare ai dadi
crash [kræʃ] *adj* (coll) d'emergenza || *s* (*noise*) scoppio, schianto; accidente *m;* (*collapse of business*) crac *m,* rovescio; (*bad landing*) atterraggio senza carrello || *tr* fracassare; **to crash the gate** (coll) entrare senza invito || *intr* fracassarsi; (com) fallire; **to cash into** investire, cozzare contro; **to cash through** sfondare
crash' dive' *s* immersione rapida di un sottomarino
crash' hel'met *s* casco
crass [kræs] *adj* crasso
crate [kret] *s* gabbia d'imballaggio || *tr* imballare in una gabbia
crater ['kretər] *s* cratere *m*
cravat [krə'væt] *s* cravatta
crave [krev] *tr* anelare; (*to beg*) implorare || *intr*—**to crave for** desiderare ardentemente
craven ['krevən] *adj & s* codardo
craving ['krevɪŋ] *s* anelito, desiderio
craw [krɔ] *s* gozzo
crawl [krɔl] *s* strisciamento, avanzata striscioni; (sports) crawl *m* || *intr* strisciare, avanzare striscioni; (*said of worms*) brulicare; (*said of insects*) formicolare; (*to feel creepy*) sentirsi il formicolio
crayfish ['krefɪʃ] *s* (*Palinurus vulgaris*) aragosta; (*Astacus; Cambarus*) gambero
crayon ['kre·ən] *s* pastello; disegno a pastello || *tr* disegnare a pastello
craze [krez] *s* mania, moda || *tr* fare impazzire
cra·zy ['krezi] *adj* (**-zier; -ziest**) pazzo, matto; **to be crazy about** (coll) esser matto per; **to drive crazy** fare impazzire
cra'zy bone' *s* osso rabbioso (del gomito)
creak [krik] *s* scricchiolio, cigolio || *intr* scricchiolare, cigolare
creak·y ['kriki] *adj* (**-ier; -iest**) stridente, cigolante
cream [krim] *s* crema, panna; (*finest part*) fior fiore *m* || *tr* rendere di consistenza cremosa; (*to remove cream from*) scremare; prendere il meglio di
creamer·y ['krimәri] *s* (**-ies**) (*factory*) caseificio; (*store*) cremeria
cream' puff' *s* bignè *m*
cream·y ['krimi] *adj* (**-ier; -iest**) cremoso; butirroso
crease [kris] *s* piega, grinza || *tr* piegare, raggrinzire || *intr* piegarsi, raggrinzirsi, far pieghe
crease'-resis'tant *adj* antipiega
create [kri'et] *tr* creare
creation [kri'eʃən] *s* creazione; **the Creation** il creato
creative [kri'etɪv] *adj* creativo
creator [kri'etər] *s* creatore *m*
creature ['kritʃər] *s* creatura
credence ['kridəns] *s* credenza
credentials [krɪ'dɛnʃəlz] *spl* lettere *fpl* credenziali; documento d'autorizzazione
credible ['krɛdɪbəl] *adj* credibile
credit ['krɛdɪt] *s* credito; (*in a school*) unità *f* di promozione; (com) avere *m;* **credits** (mov, telv) titoli *mpl* di testa || *tr* accreditare; **to credit s.o. with s.th** attribuire qlco a qlcu
creditable ['krɛdɪtəbəl] *adj* lodevole
cred'it card' *s* carta di credito
creditor ['krɛdɪtər] *s* creditore *m*
cre·do ['krido] or ['kredo] *s* (**-dos**) credo
credulous ['krɛdʒələs] *adj* credulo
creed [krid] *s* credo
creek [krik] *s* fiumicello
creep [krip] *v* (*pret & pp* **crept** [krɛpt]) *intr* strisciare, avanzare striscioni; (*to grow along a wall*) arrampicarsi; (*to feel creepy*) sentirsi il formicolio
creeper ['kripər] *s* strisciante *m;* (*plant*) rampicante *f*
creeping ['kripɪŋ] *adj* lento; (*plant*) rampicante
cremate ['krimet] *tr* cremare
cremato·ry ['krimə,tori] *adj* crematorio || *s* (**-ries**) forno crematorio
Creole ['kri·ol] *adj & s* creolo
crescent ['krɛsənt] *s* (*of Islam*) mezzaluna; (*of moon*) crescente *m;* (*roll*) cornetto
cress [krɛs] *s* crescione *m*
crest [krɛst] *s* cresta; (heral) stemma *m,* insegna
crestfallen ['krɛst,fɔlən] *adj* depresso
Cretan ['kritən] *adj & s* cretese *mf*
cretin ['kritən] *s* cretino
crevice ['krɛvɪs] *s* fessura, fenditura
crew [kru] *s* (*group working together*) personale *m;* (*group of workmen;*

mob) ciurma; (*of a ship or racing boat*) equipaggio; (sports) canottaggio
crew' cut' *s* capelli *mpl* a spazzola
crib [krɪb] *s* (*bed*) lettino; (*rack*) rastrelliera; (*building*) capanna, granaio; (coll) bigino || *v* (*pret & pp* **cribbed;** *ger* **cribbing**) *tr* (coll) usare un bigino in || *intr* (coll) usare un bigino; (coll) commettere un plagio
cricket ['krɪkɪt] *s* grillo; (sports) cricket *m*, palla a spatola
crier ['kraɪ·ər] *s* banditore *m*
crime [kraɪm] *s* delitto, crimine *m*
criminal ['krɪmɪnəl] *adj* criminale; (*code*) penale || *s* delinquente *mf*
crimp [krɪmp] *s* piega, pieghettatura; **to put a crimp in** (slang) mettere i bastoni fra le ruote a || *tr* pieghettare; (*the hair*) arricciare
crimson ['krɪmzən] *adj & s* cremisi *m* || *intr* imporporarsi
cringe [krɪndʒ] *intr* rannicchiarsi; (*to fawn*) umiliarsi
crinkle ['krɪŋkəl] *tr* arricciare || *intr* (*to rustle*) sfrusciare
cripple ['krɪpəl] *s* zoppo, sciancato || *tr* storpiare; (*e.g., business*) paralizzare
cri·sis ['kraɪsɪs] *s* (**-ses** [siz]) crisi *f*
crisp [krɪsp] *adj* (*brittle*) croccante, friabile; (*air*) frizzante; (*sharp and clear*) acuto
criteri·on [kraɪ'tɪrɪ·ən] *s* (**-a** [ə] or **-ons**) criterio
critic ['krɪtɪk] *s* critico
critical ['krɪtɪkəl] *adj* critico
criticism ['krɪtɪ,sɪzəm] *s* critica
criticize ['krɪtɪ,saɪz] *tr & intr* criticare
critique [krɪ'tik] *s* critica
croak [krok] *s* (*of frogs*) gracidio; (*of crows*) gracchiamento || *intr* gracidare; gracchiare; (slang) crepare
Croat ['kro·æt] *s* croato
Croatian [kro'eʃən] *adj & s* croato
cro·chet [kro'ʃe] *s* lavoro all'uncinetto || *v* (*pret & pp* **-cheted** ['ʃed]; *ger* **-cheting** ['ʃe·ɪŋ]) *tr & intr* lavorare all'uncinetto
crock [krɑk] *s* vaso di terracotta, giara, orcio
crockery ['krɑkəri] *s* vasellame *m* di terracotta, terracotta
crocodile ['krɑkə,daɪl] *s* coccodrillo
croc'odile tears' *spl* lacrime *fpl* di coccodrillo
crocus ['krokəs] *s* croco
crone [kron] *s* vecchia incartapecorita
cro·ny ['kroni] *s* (**-nies**) amicone *m*, compare *m*
crook [krʊk] *s* (*hook*) uncino; (*staff*) pastorale *m;* (*bend*) curva; (*bend of pipe*) gomito; (coll) imbroglione *m* || *tr* piegare || *intr* piegarsi
crooked ['krʊkɪd] *adj* uncinato; curvo, piegato; (coll) disonesto
croon [krun] *intr* canterellare; cantare in modo sentimentale
crop [krɑp] *s* (*of bird*) gozzo; (*agricultural product, growing or harvested*) messe *f;* (*agricultural product harvested*) raccolto; (*riding whip*) frustino; (*hair cut close*) capelli corti; gruppo || *v* (*pret & pp* **cropped;** *ger* **cropping**) *tr* (*to cut the ends off of*) spuntare; (*to reap*) raccogliere; (*to cut short*) tosare || *intr*—**to crop out or up** apparire inaspettatamente
crop'-dust'ing *s* fumigazione aerea
cropper ['krɑpər] *s* mietitore *m;* (*sharecropper*) mezzadro; **to come a cropper** (coll) fare una cascataccia; (coll) andare in rovina
croquet [kro'ke] *s* croquet *m*, pallamaglio *m & f*
croquette [kro'ket] *s* crocchetta
crosier ['kroʒər] *s* pastorale *m*
cross [krɔs] or [krɑs] *adj* trasversale, contrario, obliquo; (*irritable*) bisbetico, di cattivo umore; (*of mixed breed*) incrociato || *s* croce *f;* (*crossing of breeds*) incrocio; **to take the cross** farsi crociato || *tr* crociare, segnare con una croce; (*the street*) attraversare; (*e.g., the legs*) incrociare; (*to draw a line across*) barrare; (*to thwart*) ostacolare; **to cross oneself** farsi il segno della croce; **to cross one's mind** venire in mente a uno; **to cross out** cancellare || *intr* incrociarsi
cross'bones' *spl* teschio e tibie incrociate (*simbolo della morte*)
cross'bow' *s* balestra
cross'breed' *v* (*pret & pp* **-bred** [,brɛd]) *tr* incrociare, ibridare
cross'-coun'try *adj* campestre; attraverso il paese
cross'-examina'tion *s* (law) confronto, interrogatorio in contraddittorio
cross-eyed ['krɔs,aɪd] or ['krɑs,aɪd] *adj* guercio, strabico
crossing ['krɔsɪŋ] or ['krɑsɪŋ] *s* incrocio; ostacolo; (*of the sea*) traversata; (*of a river*) guado; (rr) passaggio a livello
cross'patch' *s* (coll) bisbetico
cross'piece' *s* traversa
cross' ref'erence *s* richiamo, rimando
cross'road' *s* strada trasversale; **at the crossroads** al bivio; **crossroads** crocicchio
cross' sec'tion *s* sezione trasversale
cross' street' *s* traversa
cross' talk' *s* conversazione; (telp) diafonia
cross'word puz'zle *s* cruciverba *m*, parole incrociate
crotch [krɑtʃ] *s* inforcatura; (*of pants*) cavallo
crotchety ['krɑtʃɪti] *adj* bisbetico
crouch [krautʃ] *intr* accoccolarsi
croup [krup] *s* (pathol) crup *m*
crouton ['krutɑn] *s* crostino
crow [kro] *s* corvo, cornacchia; (*cry of rooster*) chicchirichì *m;* **as the crow flies** in linea retta, a volo d'uccello; **to eat crow** (coll) rimangiarsi le parole || *intr* fare chicchirichì; **to crow over** vantarsi di, esultare per
crow'bar' *s* bastone *m* a leva
crowd [kraud] *s* folla; (*common people*) masse *fpl;* (coll) gruppo || *tr*

affollare; (*to push*) spingere || *intr* affollarsi; (*to press forward*) spingersi
crowded ['kraudɪd] *adj* affollato
crown [kraun] *s* corona; (*of hat*) cupola; (*highest point*) sommo || *tr* coronare; (*checkers*) damare; **to crown s.o.** (coll) battere qlcu sulla testa
crown' prince' *s* principe ereditario
crown' prin'cess *s* principessa ereditaria
crow's'-foot' *s* (**-feet**) zampa di gallina
crow's'-nest' *s* coffa, gabbia
crucial ['kruʃəl] *adj* cruciale, critico
crucible ['krusɪbəl] *s* crogiolo
crucifix ['krusɪfɪks] *s* crocefisso
crucifixion [ˌkrusɪ'fɪkʃən] *s* crocifissione
cruci•fy ['krusɪˌfaɪ] *v* (*pret & pp* **-fied**) *tr* crocifiggere
crude [krud] *adj* (*raw*) grezzo; (*unripe*) acerbo; (*roughly made; uncultured*) rozzo
crudi•ty ['krudɪti] *s* (**-ties**) rozzezza
cruel ['kru·əl] *adj* crudele
cruel•ty ['kru·əlti] *s* (**-ties**) crudeltà *f*
cruet ['kru·ɪt] *s* oliera
cruise [kruz] *s* crociera || *tr* navigare || *intr* andare in crociera; andare avanti e indietro
cruiser ['kruzər] *s* (nav) incrociatore *m*
cruising ['kruzɪŋ] *adj* di crociera
cruis'ing ra'dius *s* autonomia di crociera
cruller ['krʌlər] *s* frittella
crumb [krʌm] *s* briciola || *tr* sbriciolare; (*e.g., a cutlet*) impannare || *intr* sbriciolarsi
crumble ['krʌmbəl] *tr* sbriciolare, polverizzare || *intr* andare a pezzi, polverizzarsi, sbriciolarsi
crum•my ['krʌmi] *adj* (**-mier; -miest**) (slang) sporco; (*miserable*) (slang) schifoso; (*e.g., joke*) (slang) povero
crumple ['krʌmpəl] *tr* sgualcire, spiegazzare; **to crumple into a ball** appallottolare || *intr* spiegazzarsi
crunch [krʌntʃ] *s* crocchio; (coll) stretta, morsa || *tr* sgranocchiare || *intr* crocchiare
crusade [kru'sed] *s* crociata || *intr* crociarsi; (*to take up a cause*) farsi paladino
crusader [kru'sedər] *s* crociato; (*of a cause*) paladino
crush [krʌʃ] *s* pigiatura, schiacciatura; (*crowd*) calca; (coll) infatuazione || *tr* schiacciare; (*to grind*) frantumare; (*to subdue*) sottomettere; (*to extract by squeezing*) pigiare
crust [krʌst] *s* crosta; (slang) faccia tosta || *tr* incrostare || *intr* incrostare, incrostarsi
crustacean [krʌs'teʃən] *s* crostaceo
crust•y ['krʌsti] *adj* (**-ier; -iest**) crostoso; duro; rude
crutch [krʌtʃ] *s* gruccia, stampella; (fig) sostegno
crux [krʌks] *s* difficoltà *f*, busillis *m*; (*crucial point*) punto cruciale
cry [kraɪ] *s* (**cries**) (*shout*) grido; (*fit of weeping*) pianto; (*entreaty*) richiamo; (*of animal*) urlo; **a far cry** ben lontano, ben distinto; **to have a good cry** sfogarsi, piangere a calde lacrime || *tr* gridare; (*to proclaim*) bandire; **to cry down** disprezzare; **to cry one's heart out** piangere a calde lacrime; **to cry out** proclamare; **to cry up** elogiare || *intr* gridare, urlare; piangere; **to cry for** implorare
cry'ba'by *s* (**-bies**) piagnucolone *m*
crypt [krɪpt] *s* cripta
cryptic(al) ['krɪptɪk(əl)] *adj* segreto, occulto, misterioso
crystal ['krɪstəl] *s* cristallo
crys'tal ball' *s* globo di cristallo
crystalline ['krɪstəlɪn] or ['krɪstəˌlaɪn] *adj* cristallino
crystallize ['krɪstəˌlaɪz] *tr* cristallizzare || *intr* cristallizzarsi
cub [kʌb] *s* cucciolo; (*of lion*) leoncino; (*of fox*) volpicino, volpacchiotto
cubbyhole ['kʌbɪˌhol] *s* sgabuzzino, bugigattolo
cube [kjub] *adj* cubico || *s* cubo; (*of sugar*) zolla || *tr* elevare al cubo; (*to shape*) tagliare in quadretti
cubic ['kjubɪk] *adj* cubico
cub' report'er *s* giornalista novello
cuckold ['kʌkəld] *adj & s* cornuto, becco || *tr* cornificare
cuckoo ['kuku] *adj* (slang) pazzo || *s* cuculo
cuck'oo clock' *s* orologio a cucù
cucumber ['kjukʌmbər] *s* cetriolo
cud [kʌd] *s* mangime masticato; **to chew the cud** ruminare
cuddle ['kʌdəl] *tr* abbracciare affettuosamente || *intr* (*to lie close*) giacere vicino; (*to curl up*) rannicchiarsi, raggomitolarsi
cudg•el ['kʌdʒəl] *s* manganello, randello; **to take up the cudgels for** farsi paladino di || *v* (*pret & pp* **-eled** or **-elled**; *ger* **-eling** or **-elling**) *tr* bastonare, randellare; **to cudgel one's brains** rompersi la testa
cue [kju] *s* suggerimento, imbeccata; (billiards) stecca; **to miss a cue** (theat) mancare la battuta; (coll) non capire l'antifona || *tr*—**to cue s.o. (in) on** (coll) dare a qlcu informazioni su
cuff [kʌf] *s* (*of shirt*) polsino; (*of trousers*) risvolto; (*slap*) schiaffo || *tr* schiaffeggiare
cuff' links' *spl* bottoni doppi, gemelli *mpl*
cuirass [kwɪ'ræs] *s* corazza
cuisine [kwɪ'zin] *s* cucina
culinary ['kjulɪˌneri] *adj* culinario
cull [kʌl] *s* scarto || *tr* (*to gather, pluck*) cogliere; selezionare, scegliere
culminate ['kʌlmɪˌnet] *intr* culminare
culottes [ku'lɑts] *spl* gonna pantaloni
culpable ['kʌlpəbəl] *adj* colpevole
culprit ['kʌlprɪt] *s* colpevole *m*, imputato
cult [kʌlt] *s* culto
cultivate ['kʌltɪˌvet] *tr* coltivare

cultivated ['kʌltɪ,vetɪd] *adj* colto, coltivato
cultivation [,kʌltɪ'veʃən] *s* coltivazione, cultura
culture ['kʌltʃər] *s* cultura
cultured ['kʌltʃərd] *adj* colto
cul'tured pearl' *s* perla coltivata
culvert ['kʌlvərt] *s* chiavica
cumbersome ['kʌmbərsəm] *adj* ingombrante, incomodo; (*clumsy*) goffo
cumulative ['kjumjə,letɪv] *adj* cumulativo
cunning ['kʌnɪŋ] *adj* (*sly*) astuto; (*skillful*) abile; (*pretty*) bello; (*created with skill*) ben fatto, fine || *s* astuzia; abilità *f*, destrezza
cup [kʌp] *s* tazza; (mach, sports) coppa; (eccl) calice *m*; **in one's cups** ubriaco || *v* (*pret & pp* **cupped**; *ger* **cupping**) *tr* mettere ventose a; **to cup one's hands** foggiare le mani a mo' di conca
cupboard ['kʌbərd] *s* armadio a muro, dispensa; (*buffet*) credenza
Cupid ['kjupɪd] *s* Cupido
cupidity [kju'pɪdɪti] *s* cupidigia
cup' of tea' *s* tazza di tè; (coll) forte *m*, e.g., **physics is not my cup of tea** la fisica non è il mio forte
cupola ['kjupələ] *s* cupola
cur [kʌr] *s* cane bastardo; (*despicable fellow*) canaglia, gaglioffo
curate ['kjurɪt] *s* curato
curative ['kjurətɪv] *adj* curativo
curator [kju'retər] *s* conservatore *m*
curb [kʌrb] *s* (*of bit*) barbazzale *m*; (*of pavement*) orlo del marciapiede; (*check*) freno || *tr* frenare
curb'stone' *s* cordone *m*; (*of well*) sponda del pozzo
curd [kʌrd] *s* cagliata || *tr* cagliare || *intr* cagliarsi
curdle ['kʌrdəl] *tr* cagliare; (*the blood*) far gelare || *intr* cagliarsi; (*said of custard*) impazzare
cure [kjur] *s* cura || *tr* curare; (*e.g., meat*) conservare; (*wood*) stagionare
cure'-all' *s* panacea
curfew ['kʌrfju] *s* coprifuoco
curi·o ['kjurɪ,o] *s* (**-os**) curiosità *f*
curiosi·ty [,kjurɪ'ɑsɪti] *s* (**-ties**) curiosità *f*
curious ['kjurɪ·əs] *adj* curioso
curl [kʌrl] *s* (*of hair*) ricciolo; (*anything curled*) rotolo, spirale *f* || *tr* arricciare; arrotolare; (*the lips*) torcere || *intr* arricciarsi; arrotolarsi; **to curl up** raggomitolarsi
curlicue ['kʌrlɪ,kju] *s* ghirigoro
curl'ing i'ron *s* ferro da arricciare
curl'pa'per *s* bigodino
curl·y ['kʌrli] *adj* (**-ier; -iest**) ricciuto
curmudgeon [kər'mʌdʒən] *s* bisbetico
currant ['kʌrənt] *s* (*seedless raisin*) uva passa di Corinto, uva sultanina; (*shrub and berry of genus Ribes*) ribes *m*
curren·cy ['kʌrənsi] *s* (**-cies**) (*circulation*) circolazione; (*money*) denaro circolante; (*general use*) corso
current ['kʌrənt] *adj & s* corrente *f*
cur'rent account' *s* conto corrente
cur'rent events' *spl* attualità *fpl*, eventi *mpl* correnti
curricu·lum [kə'rɪkjələm] *s* (**-lums** or **-la** [lə]) programma *m*; piano educativo
cur·ry ['kʌri] *s* (**-ries**) (*spice*) curry *m* || *v* (*pret & pp* **-ried**) *tr* (*a horse*) strigliare; (*leather*) conciare; **to curry favor** cercare di compiacere
cur'ry·comb' *s* striglia || *tr* strigliare
curse [kʌrs] *s* maledizione; bestemmia || *tr* maledire || *intr* imprecare, bestemmiare
cursed ['kʌrsɪd] or [kʌrst] *adj* maledetto; (*hateful*) odiato
cursive ['kʌrsɪv] *adj & s* corsivo
cursory ['kʌrsəri] *adj* rapido, superficiale
curt [kʌrt] *adj* (*rude*) brusco, sgarbato; (*short*) breve, conciso
curtail [kər'tel] *tr* ridurre, restringere
curtain ['kʌrtən] *s* (*in front of stage*) sipario; (*for window*) tendina; (fig) cortina || *tr* coprire con tenda; separare con tenda; coprire, nascondere
cur'tain call' *s* (theat) chiamata
cur'tain rais'er ['rezər] *s* (theat) avanspettacolo; (sports) incontro preliminare
cur'tain ring' *s* campanella
cur'tain rod' *s* bastone *m* su cui si fissano le tende
curt·sy ['kʌrtsi] *s* (**-sies**) riverenza, inchino || *v* (*pret & pp* **-sied**) *intr* fare la riverenza, inchinarsi
curve [kʌrv] *s* curva || *tr* curvare || *intr* curvarsi
curved [kʌrvd] *adj* curvo, curvato
cushion ['kuʃən] *s* cuscino; (*of billiard table*) mattonella || *tr* proteggere, ammortizzare, attutire
cuspidor ['kʌspɪ,dɔr] *s* sputacchiera
cuss [kʌs] *s* (coll) bestemmia; (coll) tipo perverso || *tr* maledire || *intr* bestemmiare
custard ['kʌstərd] *s* crema
custodian [kəs'todɪ·ən] *s* (*caretaker*) custode *m*, guardiano *m*; (*person who is entrusted with s.th*) conservatore *m*; (*janitor of school*) bidello
custo·dy ['kʌstədi] *s* (**-dies**) custodia; (*imprisonment*) arresto; **in custody** in prigione; **to take into custody** arrestare
custom ['kʌstəm] *s* costume *m*; (*customers*) clientela; **customs** dogana; diritti *mpl* doganali
customary ['kʌstə,meri] *adj* consueto, abituale
custom-built ['kʌstəm'bɪlt] *adj* fatto su misura; (*car*) fuori serie
customer ['kʌstəmər] *s* cliente *mf*
cus'tom·house' *adj* doganale || *s* dogana
custom-made ['kʌstəm'med] *adj* fatto su misura
cus'toms inspec'tion *s* visita doganale
cus'toms of'ficer *s* doganiere *m*
cus'tom work' *s* lavoro fatto su misura
cut [kʌt] *adj* (*prices*) ridotto; **to be cut out for** essere tagliato per || *s* taglio; (*reduction*) ribasso; (typ) cliché *m*;

(*snub*) (coll) affronto; (coll) assenza non autorizzata; (coll) parte *f;* **a cut above** (coll) un po' meglio di || *tr* tagliare; (*cards*) alzare; (*prices*) ridurre; (coll) far finta di non riconoscere; (coll) marinare; **cut it out!** basta!; **to cut back** ridurre; **to cut off** tagliare; diseredare; (surg) amputare; **to cut short** interrompere; **to cut teeth** fare i denti; **to cut up** sminuzzare; criticare || *intr* tagliare, tagliarsi; **to cut across** attraversare; **to cut in** interrompere; **to cut under** vendere sottoprezzo; **to cut up** (slang) fare il pagliaccio
cut-and-dried ['kʌtən'draɪd] *adj* monotono, stantio; bell'e fatto, fatto in anticipo
cutaneous [kju'tenɪ·əs] *adj* cutaneo
cut'away' coat' ['kʌtə,we] *s* marsina da giorno
cut'back' *s* riduzione; eliminazione; (mov) ritorno dell'azione a un'epoca anteriore
cute [kjut] *adj* (coll) carino, grazioso; (*shrewd*) (coll) furbo
cut' glass' *s* cristallo intagliato
cuticle ['kjutɪkəl] *s* cuticola
cutlass ['kʌtləs] *s* sciabola
cutler ['kʌtlər] *s* coltellinaio
cutlery ['kʌtləri] *s* coltelleria
cutlet ['kʌtlɪt] *s* cotoletta; (*flat croquette*) polpetta
cut'off' *s* taglio; (*road*) scorciatoia; (*of cylinder*) otturatore *m*, chiusura dell'ammissione; (*of river*) braccio diretto
cut'out' *s* ritaglio; (aut) valvola di scappamento libero
cut'-rate' *adj* a prezzo ridotto
cutter ['kʌtər] *s* tagliatore *m;* (naut) cutter *m*
cut'throat' *adj* spietato; (*relentless*) senza posa || *s* assassino
cutting ['kʌtɪŋ] *adj* tagliente || *s* taglio; (*from a newspaper*) ritaglio; (*e.g., of prices*) riduzione; (hort) talea
cut'ting board' *s* tagliere *m;* (*of dishwasher*) piano d'appoggio
cut'ting edge' *s* taglio
cuttlefish ['kʌtəl,fɪʃ] *s* seppia
cut'wat'er *s* (*of bridge*) tagliacque *m;* (*of boat*) tagliamare *m*
cyanamide [saɪ'ænə,maɪd] *s* cianamide *f;* cianamide *f* di calcio
cyanide ['saɪ·ə,naɪd] *s* cianuro
cycle ['saɪkəl] *s* ciclo; bicicletta; (*of internal combustion engine*) tempo; (phys) periodo || *intr* andare in bicicletta
cyclic(al) ['saɪklɪk(əl)] or ['sɪklɪk(əl)] *adj* ciclico
cyclone ['saɪklon] *s* ciclone *m*
cyclops ['saɪklɑps] *s* ciclope *m*
cyclotron ['saɪklo,trɑn] or ['sɪklo,trɑn] *s* ciclotrone *m*
cylinder ['sɪlɪndər] *s* cilindro; (*container*) bombola
cyl'inder block' *s* monoblocco
cyl'inder bore' *s* alesaggio
cyl'inder head' *s* testa
cylindric(al) [sɪ'lɪndrɪk(əl)] *adj* cilindrico
cymbals ['sɪmbəls] *spl* piatti *mpl*
cynic ['sɪnɪk] *adj & s* cinico
cynical ['sɪnɪkəl] *adj* cinico
cynicism ['sɪnɪ,sɪzəm] *s* cinismo
cynosure ['saɪnə,ʃʊr] or ['sɪnə,ʃʊr] *s* centro dell'attenzione
cypress ['saɪprəs] *s* cipresso
Cyprus ['saɪprəs] *s* Cipro
Cyrus ['saɪrəs] *s* Ciro
cyst [sɪst] *s* ciste *f*, cisti *f*
czar [zɑr] *s* zar *m*
czarina [zɑ'rɪnə] *s* zarina
Czech [tʃɛk] *adj & s* ceco
Czecho-Slovak ['tʃɛko'slovæk] *adj & s* cecoslovacco
Czecho-Slovakia [,tʃɛkoslo'vækɪ·ə] *s* la Cecoslovacchia

D

D, d [di] *s* quarta lettera dell'alfabeto inglese
dab [dæb] *s* tocco; (*of mud*) schizzo; (*e.g., of butter*) spalmata || *v* (*pret & pp* **dabbed;** *ger* **dabbing**) *tr* toccare leggermente; (*to apply a substance to*) spennellare
dabble ['dæbəl] *tr* spruzzare || *intr* diguazzare; **to dabble in** occuparsi di; (*stocks*) speculare in
dad [dæd] *s* (coll) papà *m*
dad·dy ['dædi] *s* (**-dies**) (coll) papà *m*
daffodil ['dæfədɪl] *s* trombone *m*
daff·y ['dæfi] *adj* (**-ier; -iest**) (coll) pazzo
dagger ['dægər] *s* daga, pugnale *m;* (typ) croce *f;* **to look daggers at** fulminare con lo sguardo
dahlia ['dæljə] *s* dalia
dai·ly ['deli] *adj* quotidiano, diurno || *s* (**-lies**) quotidiano || *adv* giornalmente
dai'ly dou'ble *s* duplice *f*, accoppiata
dain·ty ['denti] *adj* (**-tier; -tiest**) delicato || *s* (**-ties**) manicaretto
dair·y ['dɛri] *s* (**-ies**) (*store*) latteria; (*factory*) caseificio
dair'y farm' *s* vaccheria
dair'y·man *s* (**-men**) lattaio
dais ['de·ɪs] *s* predella
dai·sy ['dezi] *s* (**-sies**) margherita
dal·ly ['dæli] *v* (*pret & pp* **-lied**) *intr* (*to loiter*) bighellonare; (*to trifle*) scherzare
dam [dæm] *s* diga; (*for fishing*) pescaia; (zool) fattrice *f* || *v* (*pret & pp* **dammed;** *ger* **damming**) *tr* arginare; ostruire; tappare

damage ['dæmɪdʒ] *s* danno, scapito; (fig) menomazione; (com) avaria; **damages** danni *mpl* || *tr* danneggiare, ledere; sinistrare
damascene ['dæmə,sin] or [,dæmə'sin] *adj* damasceno || *s* damaschinatura || *tr* damaschinare
dame [dem] *s* dama, signora; (slang) donna
damn [dæm] *s*—**I don't give a damn** (slang) me ne impipo; **that's not worth a damn** (slang) non vale un fico || *tr* dannare, condannare || *intr* maledire || *interj* maledizione!
damnation [dæm'neʃən] *s* dannazione; (theol) condanna
damned [dæmd] *adj* dannato, maledetto || **the damned** i dannati || *adv* maledettamente
damp [dæmp] *adj* umido || *s* umidità *f;* (*firedamp*) grisou *m* || *tr* inumidire; umettare; (*to muffle*) smorzare; (*waves*) (elec) smorzare; **to damp s.o.'s enthusiasm** raffreddare gli spiriti di qlcu; scoraggiare qlcu
dampen ['dæmpən] *tr* inumidire; umettare; smorzare; (*s.o.'s enthusiasm*) raffreddare
damper ['dæmpər] *s* (*of chimney*) valvola di tiraggio; (fig) doccia fredda; (mus) smorzatore *m;* (mus) sordina
damsel ['dæmzəl] *s* damigella
dance [dæns] or [dɑns] *s* ballo, danza || *tr & intr* ballare, danzare
dance' band' *s* orchestrina
dance' floor' *s* pista da ballo
dance' hall' *s* sala da ballo
dancer ['dænsər] or ['dɑnsər] *s* danzatore *m;* (*expert or professional*) ballerino
danc'ing part'ner *s* cavaliere *m;* dama
danc'ing par'ty *s* festa da ballo
dandelion ['dændɪ,laɪ·ən] *s* dente *m* di leone, soffione *m*
dandruff ['dændrəf] *s* forfora
dan•dy ['dændi] *adj* (**-dier; -diest**) (coll) eccellente, magnifico || *s* (**-dies**) damerino, elegantone *m*
Dane [den] *s* danese *mf*
danger ['dendʒər] *s* pericolo
dangerous ['dendʒərəs] *adj* pericoloso
dangle ['dæŋgəl] *tr* dondolare || *intr* penzolare, ciondolare
Danish ['denɪʃ] *adj & s* danese *m*
dank [dæŋk] *adj* umido
Danube ['dænjub] *s* Danubio
dapper ['dæpər] *adj* azzimato
dapple ['dæpəl] *adj* pezzato || *tr* chiazzare
dap'ple-gray' *adj* storno
dare [dɛr] *s* sfida || *tr* sfidare || *intr* osare; **I dare say** oserei dire; forse, e.g., **I dare say we will be done at seven** forse avremo finito alle sette; **to dare to** (*to have the courage to*) osare di, fidarsi a
dare'dev'il *s* scavezzacollo
daring ['dɛrɪŋ] *adj* temerario, spericolato || *s* audacia, temerarietà *f*
dark [dɑrk] *adj* scuro; (*complexion*) bruno; oscuro, segreto; (*gloomy*) tetro, fosco || *s* oscurità *f,* scuro; tenebre *fpl;* **in the dark** al buio
Dark' Ag'es *spl* alto medio evo
dark-complexioned ['dɑrkkəm'plɛkʃənd] *adj* bruno
darken ['dɑrkən] *tr* scurire, oscurare || *intr* scurirsi, oscurarsi
dark' horse' *s* vincitore imprevisto, outsider *m*
darkly ['dɑrkli] *adv* oscuramente; segretamente
dark' meat' *s* gamba o anca (di pollo o tacchino)
darkness ['dɑrknɪs] *s* oscurità *f*
dark'room' *s* camera oscura
darling ['dɑrlɪŋ] *adj & s* caro, amato
darn [dɑrn] *s* rammendo || *tr* rammendare || *interj* (coll) accidenti!
darned [dɑrnd] *adj* (coll) maledetto || *adv* maledettamente; (coll) tremendamente
darnel ['dɑrnəl] *s* zizzania
darning ['dɑrnɪŋ] *s* rammendo
darn'ing nee'dle *s* ago da rammendo
dart [dɑrt] *s* freccia, dardo; (*game*) frecciolo || *intr* dardeggiare; lanciarsi, precipitarsi
dash [dæʃ] *s* sciacquio; piccola quantità, sospetto; (*spirit*) brio; (typ, telg) trattino, lineetta || *tr* lanciare; mescolare; (*s.o.'s hopes*) frustrare; deprimere; **to dash off** gettar giù; **to dash to pieces** fare a pezzi || *intr* precipitarsi; **to dash against** gettarsi contro; **to dash by** passare a gran velocità; **to dash in** entrare come un razzo; **to dash off** or **out** andarsene in fretta; lanciarsi fuori
dash'board' *s* cruscotto; (*in an open carriage*) parafango
dashing ['dæʃɪŋ] *adj* impetuoso; vistoso || *s* (*of waves*) sciacquio
dastard ['dæstərd] *adj & s* vile *mf,* codardo
da'ta proc'essing *s* elaborazione
date [det] *s* (*time*) data; (*palm*) palma da datteri; (*fruit*) dattero; (*appointment*) (coll) appuntamento; **out of date** fuori moda; **to date** sinora; **up to date** a giorno || *tr* datare; (coll) avere un appuntamento con || *intr*—**to date from** partire da
date' line' *s* linea del cambiamento di data
dative ['detɪv] *adj & s* dativo
datum ['detəm] or ['dætəm] *s* (**data** ['detə] or ['dætə]) dato
daub [dɔb] *s* imbratto || *tr* imbrattare
daughter ['dɔtər] *s* figlia, figliola
daughter-in-law ['dɔtərɪn,lɔ] *s* (**daughters-in-law**) nuora
daunt [dɔnt] *tr* spaventare; intimidire
dauntless ['dɔntlɪs] *adj* intrepido
dauphin ['dɔfɪn] *s* delfino
davenport ['dævən,port] *s* sofà *m,* sofà *m* letto
davit ['dævɪt] *s* gru *f* per lancia
daw [dɔ] *s* cornacchia
dawdle ['dɔdəl] *intr* bighellonare
dawn [dɔn] *s* alba || *intr* (*said of the day*) farsi, nascere, spuntare; **to dawn on** cominciare a apparire nella mente di
day [de] *adj* diurno; (*student*) esterno || *s* giorno; (*of travel, work, etc.*)

giornata; **a few days ago** giorni fa; **any day now** da un giorno all'altro; **by day** di giorno; **the day after** il giorno dopo; **the day after tomorrow** dopodomani; **the day before yesterday** ieri l'altro; **to call it a day** (coll) finire di lavorare
day' bed' *s* sofà *m* letto
day'book' *s* brogliaccio
day'break' *s* far *m* del giorno
day'dream' *s* fantasticheria || *intr* fantasticare
day' la'borer *s* giornaliero
day'light' *s* luce *f* del giorno; alba; **in broad daylight** alla luce del sole; **to see daylight** comprendere; vedere la fine
day'light-sav'ing time' *s* ora legale, ora estiva
day' nurs'ery *s* asilo infantile
day' off' *s* giorno di vacanza; (*of servant*) libera uscita
day' of reck'oning *s* giorno di rendiconto; (*last judgment*) giorno del giudizio
day' shift' *s* turno diurno
day'time' *adj* diurno || *s* giornata
daze [dez] *s* stordimento; **in a daze** stordito || *tr* stordire
dazzle ['dæzəl] *s* abbagliamento || *tr* abbagliare
dazzling ['dæzlɪŋ] *adj* abbagliante
deacon ['dikən] *s* diacono
dead [ded] *adj* morto || *s*—**in the dead of** (*e.g., night*) nel pieno di; **the dead** i morti || *adv* (coll) completamente; (*abruptly*) (coll) di colpo
dead' beat' *adj* (coll) stanco morto
dead'beat' *s* (coll) scroccone *m*
dead' cen'ter *s* punto morto
dead'drunk' *adj* ubriaco fradicio
deaden ['dedən] *tr* attutire; (*e.g., s.o.'s senses*) ottundere
dead' end' *s* vicolo cieco
dead' let'ter *s* lettera morta; lettera non reclamata
dead'line' *s* termine *m*
dead'lock' *s* punto morto || *tr* portare al punto morto || *intr* giungere al punto morto
dead·ly ['dedli] *adj* (**-lier; -liest**) mortale; insopportabile
dead' pan' *s* (slang) faccia senza espressione
dead'pan' *adj* senza espressione
dead' reck'oning *s* (naut) stima
dead'wood' *s* legna secca; (fig) zavorra
deaf [def] *adj* sordo; **to turn a deaf ear** fare orecchio di mercante
deaf'-and-dumb' *adj* sordomuto
deafen ['defən] *tr* assordare, intronare
deafening ['defənɪŋ] *adj* assordante
deaf'-mute' *s* sordomuto
deafness ['defnɪs] *s* sordità *f*
deal [dil] *s* accordo; quantità *f;* (cards) mano, girata; (coll) affare *m;* (coll) trattamento; **a good deal (of)** or **a great deal (of)** moltissimo || *v* (*pret & pp* **dealt** [delt]) *tr* (*a blow*) menare; (cards) fare, sfogliare; **to deal s.o. in** (coll) includere || *intr* mercanteggiare, commerciare; fare le carte; **to deal with** trattare con; trattare di
dealer ['dilər] *s* commerciante *mf,* esercente *mf;* (cards) mazziere *m*
dean [din] *s* decano
dear [dir] *adj* (*beloved; expensive*) caro; **dear me!** povero me!; **Dear Sir** egregio Signore || *s* caro
dearie ['dɪri] *s* (coll) caro
dearth [dʌrθ] *s* scarsezza; insufficienza
death [deθ] *s* morte *f;* **to bleed to death** morire dissanguato; **to burn to death** morire bruciato; **to choke to death** morire di soffocazione; **to freeze to death** morire di gelo; **to put to death** dare la morte a; **to shoot to death** uccidere a fucilate; **to stab to death** scannare; **to starve to death** far morire di fame; morire di fame
death'bed' *s* letto di morte
death'blow' *s* colpo mortale
deathless ['deθlɪs] *adj* immortale, eterno
deathly ['deθli] *adj* mortale || *adv* mortalmente; assolutamente
death' pen'alty *s* pena di morte
death' rate' *s* mortalità *f*
death' rat'tle *s* rantolo della morte
death' ray' *s* raggio della morte
death' sen'tence *s* pena di morte
death' war'rant *s* pena di morte; fine *f* di ogni speranza
death'watch' *s* veglia mortuaria; (zool) orologio della morte
debacle [de'bɑkəl] *s* disastro; (*downfall*) tracollo; (*in a river*) sgelo repentino
de·bar [dɪ'bɑr] *v* (*pret & pp* **-barred;** *ger* **-barring**) *tr* escludere; proibire (with *dat*)
debark [dɪ'bɑrk] *tr & intr* sbarcare
debarkation [,dibɑr'keʃən] *s* sbarco
debase [dɪ'bes] *tr* degradare; adulterare
debatable [dɪ'betəbəl] *adj* discutibile
debate [dɪ'bet] *s* discussione || *tr & intr* discutere
debauch [dɪ'bɔtʃ] *s* dissolutezza, corruzione || *tr* corrompere
debauchee [,debɔ'ʃi] or [,debɔ'tʃi] *s* degenerato, vizioso
debaucher·y [di'bɔtʃəri] *s* (**-ies**) dissolutezza, corruzione
debenture [dɪ'bentʃər] *s* (*bond*) obbligazione; (*voucher*) buono
debilitate [dɪ'bɪlɪ,tet] *tr* debilitare
debili·ty [dɪ'bɪlɪti] *s* (**-ties**) debolezza
debit ['debɪt] *s* debito; (*debit side*) (com) dare *m* || *tr* addebitare
debonair [,debə'ner] *adj* gioviale; cortese
debris [de'bri] *s* detrito, rottami *mpl*
debt [det] *s* debito; **to run into debt** indebitarsi
debtor ['detər] *s* debitore *m*
debut [de'bju] or ['debju] *s* debutto; **to make one's debut** debuttare || *intr* debuttare
debutante [,debjʊ'tɑnt] or ['debjə,tænt] *s* debuttante *f,* esordiente *f*
decade ['deked] *s* decennio
decadence [dɪ'kedəns] *s* decadenza

decadent [dɪ'kedənt] *adj & s* decadente *mf*
decanter [dɪ'kæntər] *s* boccia
decapitate [dɪ'kæpɪ,tet] *tr* decapitare
decay [dɪ'ke] *s* (*decline*) decadimento; (*rotting*) marciume *m*, putredine *f*; (*of teeth*) carie *f* || *tr* imputridire || *intr* imputridire, marcire; (*said of teeth*) cariarsi
decease [dɪ'sis] *s* decesso || *intr* decedere
deceased [dɪ'sist] *adj & s* defunto
deceit [dɪ'sit] *s* inganno, frode *f*
deceitful [dɪ'sitfəl] *adj* ingannatore, menzognero, subdolo
deceive [dɪ'siv] *tr & intr* ingannare
decelerate [dɪ'sɛlə,ret] *tr & intr* decelerare
December [dɪ'sɛmbər] *s* dicembre *m*
decen·cy ['disənsi] *s* (**-cies**) decenza, pudore *m*; **decencies** convenienze *fpl*
decent ['disənt] *adj* decente; (*proper*) conveniente
decentralize [dɪ'sɛntrə,laɪz] *tr* decentrare
deception [dɪ'sɛpʃən] *s* inganno
deceptive [dɪ'sɛptɪv] *adj* ingannevole
decide [dɪ'saɪd] *tr* decidere || *intr* decidere, decidersi
decimal ['dɛsɪməl] *adj & s* decimale *m*
dec'imal point' *s* (*in Italian the comma is used to separate the decimal fraction from the integer*) virgola
decimate ['dɛsɪ,met] *tr* decimare
decipher [dɪ'saɪfər] *tr* decifrare
decision [dɪ'sɪʒən] *s* decisione
decisive [dɪ'saɪsɪv] *adj* decisivo; (*resolute*) fermo
deck [dɛk] *s* (*of cards*) mazzo; (naut) coperta, tolda, ponte *m*; **on deck** (coll) pronto; (coll) prossimo || *tr*—**to deck out** adornare; (*with flags*) imbandierare
deck' chair' *s* sedia a sdraio
deck' hand' *s* marinaio di coperta
deck'house' *s* (naut) tuga
deck'le edge' ['dɛkəl] *s* sbavatura
declaim [dɪ'klem] *tr & intr* declamare
declaration [,dɛklə'reʃən] *s* dichiarazione
declarative [dɪ'klærətɪv] *adj* declaratorio; (gram) enunciativo
declare [dɪ'kler] *tr* dichiarare || *intr* dichiararsi
declension [dɪ'klenʃən] *s* declinazione
declination [,dɛklɪ'neʃən] *s* declinazione
decline [dɪ'klaɪn] *s* decadenza; (*in prices*) ribasso; (*in health*) deperimento; (*of sun*) tramonto || *tr* declinare || *intr* declinare; decadere, scadere
declivi·ty [dɪ'klɪvɪti] *s* (**-ties**) declivio, pendice *f*
decode [di'kod] *tr* decifrare
décolleté [,dekɑl'te] *adj* scollato
decompose [,dɪkəm'poz] *tr* decomporre || *intr* decomporsi
decomposition [,dikɑmpə'zɪʃən] *s* decomposizione
décor [de'kɔr] *s* decorazione; (*of a room*) stile *m*; (theat) scenario
decorate ['dɛkə,ret] *tr* decorare
decoration [,dɛkə'reʃən] *s* decorazione
decorator ['dɛkə,retər] *s* decoratore *m*
decorous ['dɛkərəs] or [dɪ'korəs] *adj* corretto, decoroso
decorum [dɪ'korəm] *s* decoro, correttezza
decoy [dɪ'kɔɪ] or ['dikɔɪ] *s* richiamo; (*for birds*) zimbello; (*person*) adescatore *m* || *tr* (*to lure*) adescare; (*to deceive*) abbindolare
decrease ['dikris] or [dɪ'kris] *s* diminuzione; (*of salary*) decurtazione || [dɪ'kris] *tr* decurtare || *intr* diminuire
decree [dɪ'kri] *s* decreto || *tr* decretare
de·cry [dɪ'kraɪ] *v* (*pret & pp* **-cried**) *tr* denigrare, screditare
dedicate ['dɛdɪ,ket] *tr* dedicare
dedication [,dɛdɪ'keʃən] s dedizione; (*inscription in a book*) dedica
deduce [dɪ'djus] or [dɪ'dus] *tr* dedurre
deduct [dɪ'dʌkt] *tr* dedurre, defalcare
deductible [dɪ'dʌktɪbəl] *adj* defalcabile || *s* (ins) franchigia
deduction [dɪ'dʌkʃən] *s* deduzione
deed [did] *s* fatto; (*exploit*) prodezza; (law) titolo || *tr* trasferire legalmente
deem [dim] *tr & intr* credere, giudicare
deep [dip] *adj* profondo; basso; (*woods*) folto; (*friendship*) intimo; **deep in debt** carico di debiti; **deep in thought** assorto in pensieri || *adv* profondamente; **deep into the night** a notte fatta; **to go deep into** approfondirsi in
deepen ['dipən] *tr* approfondire || *intr* approfondirsi
deep'-freeze' *tr* (*pret* **-froze** [froz]; *pp* **-frozen** [frozən]) *tr* surgelare
deep-laid ['dip,led] *adj* preparato astutamente
deep' mourn'ing *s* lutto stretto
deep-rooted ['dip,rutɪd] *adj* profondo
deep'-sea' fish'ing *s* pesca d'alto mare or d'altura
deep-seated ['dip,sitɪd] *adj* profondo, connaturato
Deep' South' *s* Profondo Sud
deer [dɪr] *s* cervo
deer'skin' *s* pelle *f* di daino
deface [dɪ'fes] *tr* sfigurare
defamation [,dɛfə'meʃən] or [,difə'meʃən] *s* diffamazione
defame [dɪ'fem] *tr* diffamare
default [dɪ'fɔlt] *s* mancanza; (*failure to act*) inadempienza; **in default of** per mancanza di; **to lose by default** dichiarare forfeit || *tr* essere inadempiente a || *intr* essere inadempiente; (sports) dichiarare forfeit
defeat [dɪ'fit] *s* sconfitta, disfatta || *tr* sconfiggere, vincere
defeatism [dɪ'fitɪzəm] *s* disfattismo
defeatist [dɪ'fitɪst] *adj & s* disfattista *mf*
defecate ['dɛfɪ,ket] *intr* defecare
defect [dɪ'fɛkt] or ['difɛkt] *s* vizio, difetto || [dɪ'fɛkt] *intr* defezionare
defection [dɪ'fɛkʃən] *s* defezione
defective [dɪ'fɛktɪv] *adj* difettivo, difettoso

defend [dɪˈfɛnd] *tr* difendere, proteggere
defendant [dɪˈfɛndənt] *s* (law) imputato, querelato
defender [dɪˈfɛndər] *s* difensore *m*
defense [dɪˈfɛns] *s* difesa
defenseless [dɪˈfɛnslɪs] *adj* indifeso
defensive [dɪˈfɛnsɪv] *adj* difensivo || *s* difensiva
de·fer [dɪˈfʌr] *v* (*pret & pp* **-ferred;** *ger* **-ferring**) *tr* differire, rinviare || *intr* rimettersi
deference [ˈdɛfərəns] *s* deferenza
deferential [ˌdɛfəˈrɛnʃəl] *adj* deferente
deferment [dɪˈfʌrmənt] *s* differimento
defiance [dɪˈfaɪ·əns] *s* opposizione; sfida; **in defiance of** a dispetto di
defiant [dɪˈfaɪ·ənt] *adj* provocante, ostile
deficien·cy [dɪˈfɪʃənsi] *s* (**-cies**) deficienza; (com) ammanco
deficient [dɪˈfɪʃənt] *adj* deficiente
deficit [ˈdefɪsɪt] *adj* deficitario || *s* deficit *m*, disavanzo
defile [dɪˈfaɪl] or [ˈdifaɪl] *s* gola, passo || [dɪˈfaɪl] *tr* profanare || *intr* marciare in fila
define [dɪˈfaɪn] *tr* definire
definite [ˈdɛfɪnɪt] *adj* definito; (gram) determinativo, determinato
definition [ˌdɛfɪˈnɪʃən] *s* definizione
definitive [dɪˈfɪnɪtɪv] *adj* definitivo
deflate [dɪˈflet] *tr* sgonfiare; (*s.o.'s hopes*) deprimere; (*e.g., currency*) deflazionare
deflation [dɪˈfleʃən] *s* sgonfiamento; (*of prices*) deflazione
deflect [dɪˈflɛkt] *tr* far deflettere || *intr* deflettere
deflower [diˈflaʊ·ər] *tr* privare dei fiori; (*a woman*) deflorare
deforest [diˈfɑrest] or [diˈfɔrest] *tr* disboscare, smacchiare
deform [dɪˈfɔrm] *tr* deformare
deformed [dɪˈfɔrmd] *adj* deforme
deformi·ty [dɪˈfɔrmɪti] *s* (**-ties**) deformità *f*
defraud [dɪˈfrɔd] *tr* defraudare
defray [dɪˈfre] *tr* pagare
defrost [diˈfrɔst] or [diˈfrɑst] *tr* sgelare, sbrinare
defroster [diˈfrɔstər] or [diˈfrɑstər] *s* (aut) visiera termica
deft [deft] *adj* destro, lesto
defunct [dɪˈfʌŋkt] *adj* defunto
de·fy [dɪˈfaɪ] *v* (*pret & pp* **-fied**) *tr* sfidare, provocare
degeneracy [dɪˈdʒɛnərəsi] *s* degenerazione
degenerate [dɪˈdʒɛnərɪt] *adj & s* degenerato || [dɪˈdʒɛnəˌret] *intr* degenerare, tralignare
degrade [dɪˈgred] *tr* degradare
degrading [dɪˈgredɪŋ] *adj* degradante
degree [dɪˈgri] *s* grado; titolo accademico; **by degrees** a grado a grado; **to a degree** fino a un certo punto; troppo; **to take a degree** ricevere un titolo di studio
dehydrate [diˈhaɪdret] *tr* disidratare
deice [diˈaɪs] *tr* sgelare
dei·fy [ˈdi·ɪˌfaɪ] *v* (*pret & pp* **-fied**) *tr* deificare
deign [den] *intr* degnarsi
dei·ty [ˈdi·ɪti] *s* (**-ties**) deità *f;* **the Deity** Dio
dejected [dɪˈdʒɛktɪd] *adj* demoralizzato
dejection [dɪˈdʒɛkʃən] *s* (*in spirits*) demoralizzazione; (*evacuation*) deiezione
delay [dɪˈle] *s* ritardo, proroga; dilazione; **without further delay** senza ulteriore indugio || *tr* tardare; (*to put off*) differire || *intr* tardare, ritardare
delayed'-ac'tion *adj* a azione differita
delectable [dɪˈlɛktəbəl] *adj* dilettevole
delegate [ˈdɛlɪˌget] or [ˈdɛlɪgɪt] *s* delegato, incaricato; (*to a convention*) congressista *mf* || [ˈdɛlɪˌget] *tr* delegare, incaricare
delegation [ˌdɛlɪˈgeʃən] *s* delegazione
delete [dɪˈlit] *tr* cancellare, sopprimere
deletion [dɪˈliʃən] *s* cancellazione
deliberate [dɪˈlɪbərɪt] *adj* meditato; (*slow in deciding*) cauto; (*slow in moving*) lento || [dɪˈlɪbəˌret] *tr & intr* deliberare
deliberately [dɪˈlɪbərɪtli] *adv* (*on purpose*) deliberatamente; (*without hurrying*) con ponderatezza
delica·cy [ˈdɛlɪkəsi] *s* (**-cies**) delicatezza; (*choice food*) leccornia
delicatessen [ˌdɛlɪkəˈtɛsən] *s* negozio di salumerie || *spl* salumerie *fpl*, articoli alimentari scelti
delicious [dɪˈlɪʃəs] *adj* delizioso
delight [dɪˈlaɪt] *s* gioia, delizia || *tr* dilettare || *intr* dilettarsi
delightful [dɪˈlaɪtfəl] *adj* delizioso
delinquen·cy [dɪˈlɪŋkwənsi] *s* (**-cies**) colpa; (*offense*) delinquenza; (*in payment of a debt*) morosità *f*
delinquent [dɪˈlɪŋkwənt] *adj* colpevole; (*in payment*) moroso; non pagato || *s* delinquente *m;* debitore moroso
delirious [dɪˈlɪrɪ·əs] *adj* in delirio
deliri·um [dɪˈlɪrɪ·əm] *s* (**-ums** or **-a** [ə]) delirio
deliver [dɪˈlɪvər] *tr* consegnare; (*a blow*) affibbiare; (*a speech*) fare; (*a letter*) recapitare; (*electricity or gas*) erogare; (*said of a pregnant woman*) partorire; (*said of a doctor*) assistere durante il parto
deliver·y [dɪˈlɪvəri] *s* (**-ies**) consegna; (*of mail*) distribuzione; (*of merchandise*) fornitura; (*of a speech*) dizione; (*childbirth*) parto; (sports) lancio
deliv'ery·man' *s* (**-men'**) fattorino
deliv'ery room' *s* sala parto
deliv'ery truck' *s* furgoncino
dell [dɛl] *s* valletta
delouse [diˈlaʊs] or [diˈlaʊz] *tr* spidocchiare
delude [dɪˈlud] *tr* illudere, ingannare
deluge [ˈdeljudʒ] *s* diluvio, inondazione || **the Deluge** il diluvio universale || *tr* inondare
delusion [dɪˈluʒən] *s* illusione, inganno; (psychopath) allucinazione;

(psychopath) idea fissa; **delusions of grandeur** mania di grandezza
de luxe [dɪ'luks] or [dɪ'lʌks] *adj* di lusso || *adv* in gran lusso
delve [delv] *intr* frugare; **to delve into** approfondirsi in
demagnetize [di'mægnɪ,taɪz] *tr* smagnetizzare
demagogue ['demə,gɑg] *s* demagogo
demand [dɪ'mænd] or [dɪ'mɑnd] *s* esigenza; (com) richiesta, domanda; **to be in demand** essere in richiesta || *tr* esigere
demanding [dɪ'mændɪŋ] or [dɪ'mɑndɪŋ] *adj* esigente, impegnativo
demarcate [dɪ'mɑrket] or ['dimɑr,ket] *tr* demarcare
démarche [de'mɑrʃ] *s* progetto, piano
demean [dɪ'min] *tr* degradare; **to demean oneself** comportarsi; degradarsi
demeanor [dɪ'minər] *s* condotta, contegno
demented [dɪ'mentɪd] *adj* demente
demigod ['demɪ,gɑd] *s* semidio
demijohn ['demɪ,dʒɑn] *s* damigiana
demilitarize [di'mɪlɪtə,raɪz] *tr* smilitarizzare
demimonde ['demɪ,mɑnd] *s* donne *fpl* della società equivoca
demise [dɪ'maɪz] *s* decesso
demitasse ['demɪ,tæs] or ['demi,tɑs] *s* tazzina da caffè; (*contents*) caffè nero
demobilize [di'mobɪ,laɪz] *tr* smobilitare
democra•cy [dɪ'mɑkrəsi] *s* (**-cies**) democrazia
democrat ['demə,kræt] *s* democratico
democratic [,demə'krætɪk] *adj* democratico
demolish [dɪ'mɑlɪʃ] *tr* demolire
demolition [,demə'lɪʃən] or [,dimə'lɪʃən] *s* demolizione
demon ['dimən] *s* demonio
demoniacal [,dɪmə'naɪ·əkəl] *adj* demoniaco
demonstrate ['demən,stret] *tr & intr* dimostrare
demonstration [,demən'streʃən] *s* dimostrazione
demonstrative [dɪ'mɑnstrətɪv] *adj* dimostrativo; (*giving open exhibition of emotion*) espansivo
demonstrator ['demən,stretər] *s* (*of a product*) dimostratore *m;* (*in a public gathering*) dimostrante *m;* (*product*) prodotto usato da dimostratori
demoralize [dɪ'mɑrə,laɪz] or [dɪ'mɔrə,laɪz] *tr* demoralizzare
demote [dɪ'mot] *tr* retrocedere
demotion [dɪ'moʃən] *s* retrocessione
de•mur [dɪ'mʌr] *v* (*pret & pp* **-murred;** *ger* **-murring**) *intr* sollevare obiezioni
demure [dɪ'mjur] *adj* modesto; sobrio
demurrage [dɪ'mʌrɪdʒ] *s* (com) controstallie *fpl;* (rr) sosta
den [den] *s* (*of animals, thieves*) tana; (*little room*) bugigattolo; (*little room for studying or writing*) studiolo; (*of lions*) (Bib) fossa
denaturalize [di'nætjərə,laɪz] *tr* snaturare; privare della nazionalità
dena'tured al'cohol [di'netʃərd] *s* alcole denaturato
denial [dɪ'naɪ·əl] *s* diniego; (*disavowal*) smentita
denim ['denɪm] *s* tessuto di cotone per tuta; **denims** tuta; (*trousers*) jeans *mpl*
denizen ['denɪzən] *s* abitante *mf*
Denmark ['denmɑrk] *s* la Danimarca
denomination [dɪ,nɑmɪ'neʃən] *s* denominazione; categoria; (com) taglio; (eccl) confessione
denote [dɪ'not] *tr* denotare, significare
denouement [denu'mɑ̃] *s* scioglimento
denounce [dɪ'nauns] *tr* denunziare
dense [dens] *adj* denso; stupido
densi•ty ['densɪti] *s* (**-ties**) densità *f*
dent [dent] *s* ammaccatura; (*in a gearwheel*) tacca, dente *m;* **to make a dent** fare progresso; fare impressione || *tr* ammaccare; (fig) ferire
dental ['dentəl] *adj* dentale, dentario || *s* dentale *f*
den'tal floss' *s* filo cerato dentario
dentifrice ['dentɪfrɪs] *s* dentifricio
dentist ['dentɪst] *s* dentista *mf*
dentistry ['dentɪstri] *s* odontoiatria
denture ['dentʃər] *s* dentiera
denunciation [dɪ,nʌnsɪ'eʃən] or [dɪ,nʌnʃɪ'eʃən] *s* denunzia
de•ny [dɪ'nai] *v* (*pret & pp* **-nied**) *tr* (*to declare not to be true*) negare; (*to refuse*) rifiutare; **to deny oneself to callers** sottrarsi alle visite || *intr* negare; rifiutare
deodorant [di'odərənt] *adj & s* deodorante *m*
deo'dorant spray' *s* deodorante *m* spray
deodorize [di'odə,raɪz] *tr* deodorare
depart [dɪ'pɑrt] *intr* partire, andarsene; (*to diverge*) dipartire
departed [dɪ'pɑrtɪd] *adj* morto, defunto || **the departed** i defunti
department [dɪ'pɑrtmənt] *s* dipartimento; (*of government*) ministero; (*e.g., of a hospital*) reparto; (*of agency*) sezione, ufficio
depart'ment store' *s* grandi magazzini *mpl*
departure [dɪ'pɑrtʃər] *s* partenza; divergenza, deviazione
depend [dɪ'pend] *intr* dipendere; **to depend on** (*to rely on*) contare su; dipendere da
dependable [dɪ'pendəbəl] *adj* sicuro, fidato
dependence [dɪ'pendəns] *s* dipendenza; (*trust*) fiducia
dependen•cy [dɪ'pendənsi] *s* (**-cies**) dipendenza; (*territory*) possessione
dependent [dɪ'pendənt] *adj* dipendente; a carico; **to be dependent on** dipendere da || *s* persona a carico
depend'ent clause' *s* proposizione subordinata
depict [dɪ'pɪkt] *tr* descrivere, dipingere
deplete [dɪ'plit] *tr* esaurire
depletion [dɪ'pliʃən] *s* esaurimento
deplorable [dɪ'plorəbəl] *adj* deplorevole
deplore [dɪ'plor] *tr* deplorare
deploy [dɪ'plɔɪ] *tr* (mil) spiegare, stendere

deployment [dɪ'plɔɪmənt] *s* (mil) dispositivo, spiegamento
depolarize [di'polə,raɪz] *tr* depolarizzare
depopulate [di'pɑpjə,let] *tr* spopolare
deport [dɪ'port] *tr* deportare; **to deport oneself** comportarsi
deportation [,dipor'teʃən] *s* deportazione
deportee [,dipor'ti] *s* deportato
deportment [dɪ'portmənt] *s* condotta, comportamento
depose [dɪ'poz] *tr & intr* deporre
deposit [dɪ'pɑzɪt] *s* deposito; (*down payment*) caparra || *tr* depositare || *intr* depositarsi
depos'it account' *s* conto corrente
depositor [dɪ'pɑzɪtər] *s* versante *mf;* (*to the credit of an established account*) correntista *mf*
deposito·ry [dɪ'pɑzɪ,tori] *s* **(-ries)** deposito; (*person*) depositario
depos'it slip' *s* distinta di versamento
depot ['dipo] or ['dɛpo] *s* magazzino; (mil) deposito; (rr) stazione
depraved [dɪ'prevd] *adj* depravato
depravi·ty [dɪ'prævɪti] *s* **(-ties)** depravazione
deprecate ['dɛprɪ,ket] *tr* deprecare
depreciate [dɪ'priʃɪ,et] *tr* svalutare, deprezzare || *intr* deprezzarsi
depreciation [dɪ,priʃɪ'eʃən] *s* (*drop in value*) deprezzamento; (*disparagement*) disprezzo
depredation [,dɛprɪ'deʃən] *s* depredazione
depress [dɪ'prɛs] *tr* deprimere; avvilire; (*prices*) far abbassare
depression [dɪ'prɛʃən] *s* depressione; (*gloom*) sconforto; (*slump*) crisi *f*
deprive [dɪ'praɪv] *tr* privare; **to deprive oneself** espropriarsi
depth [dɛpθ] *s* profondità *f;* (*of a house or room*) lunghezza; (*of sea*) fondale *m;* (fig) vastità *f;* **in the depth of** nel cuor di; **to go beyond one's depth** non toccare più; (fig) andare oltre le proprie possibilità
depth' bomb' *s* (aer) bomba antisommergibile
depth' charge' *s* (nav) granata antisommergibile
depth' of hold' *s* (naut) puntale *m*
deputation [,dɛpjə'teʃən] *s* deputazione
deputize ['dɛpjə,taɪz] *tr* deputare
depu·ty ['dɛpjəti] *s* **(-ties)** deputato
derail [dɪ'rel] *tr* far deragliare || *intr* deragliare, deviare
derailment [dɪ'relmənt] *s* deragliamento, deviamento
derange [dɪ'rendʒ] *tr* (*to disarrange*) dissestare; (*to make insane*) squilibrare, render pazzo
derangement [dɪ'rendʒmənt] *s* (*disorder*) disordine *m;* (*insanity*) squilibrio mentale, pazzia
der·by ['dʌrbi] *s* **(-bies)** bombetta; (*race*) derby *m*
derelict ['dɛrɪlɪkt] *adj* derelitto; negligente || *s* derelitto; (naut) relitto
dereliction [,dɛrɪ'lɪkʃən] *s* (*in one's duty*) negligenza; (law) derelizione
deride [dɪ'raɪd] *tr* deridere, schernire, farsi beffe di
derision [dɪ'rɪʒən] *s* derisione, scherno
derisive [dɪ'raɪsɪv] *adj* derisorio
derivation [,dɛrɪ'veʃən] *s* derivazione
derivative [dɪ'rɪvətɪv] *adj & s* derivato
derive [dɪ'raɪv] *tr & intr* derivare
dermatology [,dʌrmə'tɑlədʒi] *s* dermatologia
derogatory [dɪ'rɑgə,tori] *adj* dispregiativo
derrick ['dɛrɪk] *s* gru *f;* (naut) picco di carico
dervish ['dʌrvɪʃ] *s* dervis *m*
desalinization [di,selɪnɪ'zeʃən] *s* desalazione
desalt [di'sɔlt] *tr* desalificare
descend [dɪ'sɛnd] *tr* discendere || *intr* discendere; **to descend on** calare su, gettarsi su
descendant [dɪ'sɛndənt] *adj & s* discendente *mf*
descendent [dɪ'sɛndənt] *adj* discendente
descent [dɪ'sɛnt] *s* (*slope*) china; (*decline*) declino; discesa; (*lineage*) stirpe *f,* discendenza; (*sudden raid*) calata
Descent' from the Cross' *s* Deposizione dalla Croce
describe [dɪ'skraɪb] *tr* descrivere
description [dɪ'skrɪpʃən] *s* descrizione
descriptive [dɪ'skrɪptɪv] *adj* descrittivo
de·scry [dɪ'skraɪ] *v* (*pret & pp* **-scried**) *tr* avvistare
desecrate ['dɛsɪ,kret] *tr* profanare, dissacrare
desecration [,dɛsɪ'kreʃən] *s* profanazione, dissacrazione
desegregate [di'sɛgrɪ,get] *intr* sopprimere la segregazione razziale
desegregation [di,sɛgrɪ'geʃən] *s* desegregazione
desensitize [di'sɛnsɪ,taɪz] *tr* desensibilizzare
desert ['dɛzərt] *adj & s* deserto || [dɪ'zʌrt] *s* merito; **he received his just deserts** ricevette quanto meritava || *tr & intr* disertare
deserter [dɪ'zʌrtər] *s* disertore *m*
deserted [dɪ'zɛrtɪd] *adj* (*person*) abbandonato; (*place*) deserto
desertion [dɪ'zʌrʃən] *s* diserzione; abbandono del coniuge
deserve [dɪ'zʌrv] *tr & intr* meritare
deservedly [dɪ'zʌrvɪdli] *adv* meritatamente, meritevolmente
design [dɪ'zaɪn] *s* disegno; (*of a play*) congegno; **to have designs on** aver mire su || *tr* disegnare; progettare || *intr* disegnare; **designed for** destinato a
designate ['dɛzɪg,net] *tr* designare
designer [dɪ'saɪnər] *s* disegnatore *m*
designing [dɪ'zaɪnɪŋ] *adj* intrigante, macchinatore || *s* disegnazione
desirable [dɪ'zaɪrəbəl] *adj* desiderabile
desire [dɪ'zaɪr] *s* desiderio || *tr* desiderare
desirous [dɪ'zaɪrəs] *adj* desideroso
desist [di'zɪst] *intr* desistere
desk [dɛsk] *s* scrittoio; tavolo d'ufficio;

(*lectern*) leggio; (*of professor*) cattedra; (*of pupil*) banco; (com) cassa
desk'bound' *adj* sedentario; legato al tavolino
desk' pad' *s* blocco da tavolo; blocco per appunti
desolate ['desəlɪt] *adj* desolato, deserto; (*hopeless*) disperato; (*dismal*) lugubre || ['desə,let] *tr* desolare; devastare
desolation [,desə'leʃən] *s* desolazione; devastazione
despair [dɪ'sper] *s* disperazione; **to be in despair** disperarsi || *intr* disperare, disperarsi
despairing [dɪ'sperɪŋ] *adj* disperato
despera•do [,despə'redo] or [,despə'rɑdo] *s* (**-does** or **-dos**) fuorilegge disposto a tutto
desperate ['despərɪt] *adj* disposto a tutto; (*hopeless*) disperato; (*very bad*) atroce, terribile; (*bitter, excessive*) accanito; (*remedy*) estremo
desperation [,despə'reʃən] *s* disperazione
despicable ['despɪkəbəl] *adj* spregevole, incanaglito
despise [dɪ'spaɪz] *tr* sprezzare, disprezzare, vilipendere
despite [dɪ'spaɪt] *prep* malgrado
despoil [dɪ'spɔɪl] *tr* spogliare
desponden•cy [dɪ'spɑndənsi] *s* (**-cies**) scoraggiamento, abbattimento
despondent [dɪ'spɑndənt] *adj* scoraggiato, abbattuto
despot ['despɑt] *s* despota *m*
despotic [des'pɑtɪk] *adj* dispotico
despotism ['despə,tɪzəm] *s* dispotismo
dessert [dɪ'zʌrt] *s* dessert *m*
dessert' spoon' *s* cucchiaio or cucchiaino da dessert
destination [,destɪ'neʃən] *s* destinazione
destine ['destɪn] *tr* destinare
desti•ny ['destɪni] *s* (**-nies**) destino
destitute ['destɪ,tjut] or ['destɪ,tut] *adj* (*poverty-stricken*) indigente; (*lacking*) privo
destitution [,destɪ'tjuʃən] or [,destɪ'tuʃən] *s* indigenza, miseria
destroy [dɪ'strɔɪ] *tr* distruggere
destroyer [dɪ'strɔɪ•ər] *s* (nav) cacciatorpediniere *m*
destruction [dɪ'strʌkʃən] *s* distruzione
destructive [dɪ'strʌktɪv] *adj* distruttivo
desultory ['desəl,tori] *adj* saltuario, sconnesso
detach [dɪ'tætʃ] *tr* staccare, distaccare; (mil) distaccare
detachable [dɪ'tætʃəbəl] *adj* staccabile; separabile
detached [dɪ'tætʃt] *adj* (*e.g., stub*) staccato; (*e.g., house*) discosto; (*aloof*) riservato, freddo; imparziale
detachment [dɪ'tætʃmənt] *s* distacco; imparzialità *f;* (mil) distaccamento
detail [dɪ'tel] or ['ditel] *s* dettaglio, ragguaglio; (mil) distaccamento || [dɪ'tel] *tr* dettagliare; (mil) distaccare
detain [dɪ'ten] *tr* detenere, trattenere
detect [dɪ'tekt] *tr* scoprire, discernere; (rad) rivelare
detection [dɪ'tekʃən] *s* scoperta; (rad) rivelazione
detective [dɪ'tektɪv] *s* detective *m*
detec'tive sto'ry *s* romanzo poliziesco, romanzo giallo
detector [dɪ'tektər] *s* (rad) detector *m*, rivelatore *m*
detention [dɪ'tenʃən] *s* detenzione
de•ter [dɪ'tʌr] *v* (*pret & pp* **-terred;** *ger* **-terring**) *tr* distogliere, impedire
detergent [dɪ'tʌrdʒənt] *adj & s* detergente *m*
deteriorate [dɪ'tɪrɪ•ə,ret] *tr* deteriorare || *intr* deteriorarsi, andar giù
determination [dɪ,tʌrmɪ'neʃən] *s* determinazione
determine [dɪ'tʌrmɪn] *tr* determinare
determined [dɪ'tʌrmɪnd] *adj* determinato, risoluto
deterrent [dɪ'tʌrənt] *s* deterrente *m*
detest [dɪ'test] *tr* detestare, odiare
dethrone [dɪ'θron] *tr* detronizzare
detonate ['detə,net] or ['ditə,net] *tr* far scoppiare || *intr* detonare
detonator ['detə,netər] *s* innesco
detour ['ditʊr] or [dɪ'tʊr] *s* deviazione || *tr* far deviare || *intr* deviare
detract [dɪ'trækt] *tr* detrarre || *intr*—**to detract from** diminuire
detractor [dɪ'træktər] *s* detrattore *m*
detriment ['detrɪmənt] *s* detrimento; **to the detriment of** a danno di
detrimental [,detrɪ'mentəl] *adj* pregiudizievole
deuce [djus] or [dus] *s* (cards) due *m;* **the deuce!** diavolo!
devaluate [di'vælju,et] *tr* svalutare
devaluation [di,vælju'eʃən] *s* devalutazione, svalutazione
devastate ['devəs,tet] *tr* devastare
devastating ['devəs,tetɪŋ] *adj* devastatore, devastante; (*e.g., reply*) schiacciante, annichilante
devastation [,devəs'teʃən] *s* devastazione
develop [dɪ'veləp] *tr* sviluppare; (phot) sviluppare, rivelare || *intr* svilupparsi; manifestarsi
developer [dɪ'veləpər] *s* (*e.g., of a new engine*) sfruttatore *m;* (*in real estate*) specialista *mf* in lottizzazione; (phot) sviluppatore *m*, rivelatore *m*
development [dɪ'veləpmənt] *s* sviluppo; valorizzazione; sfruttamento; (phot) rivelazione
deviate ['divɪ,et] *tr* sviare || *intr* deviare, sviarsi
deviation [,divɪ'eʃən] *s* deviazione
deviationism [,divɪ'eʃə,nɪzəm] *s* deviazionismo
deviationist [,divɪ'eʃənɪst] *s* deviazionista *mf*
device [dɪ'vaɪs] *s* dispositivo, congegno; (*trick*) stratagemma *m;* (*motto*) divisa, emblema *m;* **to leave s.o. to his own devices** lasciare che qlcu faccia come gli pare e piace
dev•il ['devəl] *s* diavolo; **between the devil and the deep blue sea** fra l'incudine e il martello; **to raise the devil** (slang) fare diavolo a quattro || *v* (*pret & pp* **-iled** or **-illed;** *ger*

-iling or **-illing**) *tr* condire con spezie or con pepe; (coll) infastidire
devilish ['dɛvəlɪʃ] *adj* diabolico
devilment ['dɛvəlmənt] *s* (*mischief*) diavoleria; (*evil*) cattiveria
devil·try ['dɛvəltri] *s* (**-tries**) malvagità *f*, crudeltà *f*; (*mischief*) diavoleria
devious ['divɪ·əs] *adj* (*tricky*) traverso; (*roundabout*) tortuoso
devise [dɪ'vaɪz] *tr* ideare, inventare; (law) legare, disporre per testamento
devoid [dɪ'vɔɪd] *adj* sprovvisto
devolve [dɪ'vɑlv] *intr*—**to devolve on** ricadere su
devote [dɪ'vot] *tr* dedicare
devoted [dɪ'votɪd] *adj* devoto; dedito, dedicato
devotee [ˌdɛvə'ti] *s* devoto; (*fan*) fanatico, tifoso, entusiasta *mf*
devotion [dɪ'voʃən] *s* devozione; (*e.g., to work*) dedizione; **devotions** orazioni *mpl*, preghiere *fpl*
devour [dɪ'vaʊr] *tr* divorare
devout [dɪ'vaʊt] *adj* devoto; sincero
dew [dju] or [du] *s* rugiada
dew'drop' *s* goccia di rugiada
dew'lap' *s* giogaia
dew·y ['dju·i] or ['du·i] *adj* (**-ier; -iest**) rugiadoso
dexterity [dɛks'terɪti] *s* destrezza
diabetes [ˌdaɪ·ə'bitɪs] or [ˌdaɪ·ə'bitiz] *s* diabete *m*
diabetic [ˌdaɪ·ə'bɛtɪk] or [ˌdaɪ·ə'bitɪk] *adj & s* diabetico
diabolic(al) [ˌdaɪ·ə'bɑlɪk(əl)] *adj* diabolico
diadem ['daɪ·əˌdɛm] *s* diadema *m*
diaere·sis [daɪ'ɛrɪsɪs] *s* (**-ses** [ˌsiz]) dieresi *f*
diagnose [ˌdaɪ·əg'nos] or [ˌdaɪ·əg'noz] *tr* diagnosticare
diagno·sis [ˌdaɪ·əg'nosɪs] *s* (**-ses** [siz]) diagnosi *f*
diagonal [daɪ'ægənəl] *adj & s* diagonale *f*
dia·gram ['daɪ·əˌgræm] *s* diagramma *m*; (*drawing*) schema *m*; (*plan*) prospetto ‖ *v* (*pret & pp* **-gramed** or **-grammed**; *ger* **-graming** or **-gramming**) *tr* diagrammare
dial ['daɪ·əl] *s* (*of watch*) quadrante *m*; (rad) tabella graduata, sintogramma *m*; (telp) disco combinatore ‖ *tr* (rad) sintonizzare; (*a person*) (telp) chiamare; (*a number*) (telp) comporre; (*the phone*) (telp) comporre il numero di ‖ *intr* (telp) comporre il numero
dialect ['daɪ·əˌlɛkt] *s* dialetto
dialing ['daɪ·əlɪŋ] *s* composizione del numero
dialogue ['daɪ·əˌlɔg] or ['daɪ·əˌlɑg] *s* dialogo
di'al tel'ephone *s* telefono automatico
di'al tone' *s* (telp) segnale *m* di via libera
diameter [daɪ'æmɪtər] *s* diametro
diametric(al) [ˌdaɪ·ə'metrɪk(əl)] *adj* diametrico, diametrale
diamond ['daɪmənd] *s* diamante *m*; (*figure of a rhombus*) losanga; (baseball) diamante *m*; **diamonds** (cards) quadri *mpl*
diaper ['daɪ·pər] *s* pannolino
diaphanous [daɪ'æfənəs] *adj* diafano
diaphragm ['daɪ·əˌfræm] *s* diaframma *m*; (telp) membrana
diarrhea [ˌdaɪ·ə'ri·ə] *s* diarrea
dia·ry ['daɪ·əri] *s* (**-ries**) diario
diastole [daɪ'æstəli] *s* diastole *f*
diathermy ['daɪ·əˌθʌrmi] *s* diatermia
dice [daɪs] *spl* dadi *mpl*; (*small cubes*) cubetti *mpl*; **no dice** (slang) niente da fare; (slang) risposta a picche
dice' cup' *s* bussolotto
dichloride [daɪ'kloraɪd] *s* bicloruro
dichoto·my [daɪ'kɑtəmi] *s* (**-mies**) dicotomia
dickey ['dɪki] *s* camiciola; (*starched insert*) sparato; (*bib*) bavaglino
dictaphone ['dɪktəˌfon] *s* dittafono
dictate ['dɪktet] *s* dettato ‖ ['dɪktet] or [dɪk'tet] *tr* dettare
dictation [dɪk'teʃən] *s* dettato; (*act of ordering*) ordine *m*; **to take dictation** scrivere sotto dettatura
dictator ['dɪktetər] or [dɪk'tetər] *s* dittatore *m*
dictatorship ['dɪktetərˌʃɪp] or [dɪk'tetərʃɪp] *s* dittatura
diction ['dɪkʃən] *s* dizione
dictionar·y ['dɪkʃənˌɛri] *s* (**-ies**) dizionario, vocabolario
dic·tum ['dɪktəm] *s* (**-ta** [tə]) detto, sentenza
didactic(al) [daɪ'dæktɪk(əl)] or [dɪ'dæktɪk(əl)] *adj* didattico
die [daɪ] *s* (**dice** [daɪs]) dado; **the die is cast** il dado è tratto ‖ *s* (**dies**) (*for stamping coins, medals,* etc.) stampo; (*for cutting threads*) filiera ‖ *v* (*pret & pp* **died**; *ger* **dying**) *intr* morire; **to die hard** morire lentamente; morire lottando; **to die laughing** morire dalle risa; **to die off** morire uno per uno
die'-hard' *adj & s* intransigente *m*
die'sel oil' ['dizəl] *s* nafta, gasolio
die'stock' *s* girafiliera
diet ['daɪ·ət] *s* dieta, regime *m* ‖ *intr* stare a dieta
dietetic [ˌdaɪ·ə'tɛtɪk] *adj* dietetico ‖ **dietetics** *ssg* dietetica
dietitian [ˌdaɪ·ə'tɪʃən] *s* dietista *mf*
differ ['dɪfər] *intr* (*to be different*) differire, differenziarsi; **to differ with** dissentire da
difference ['dɪfərəns] *s* differenza; **to make no difference** fare lo stesso; **to split the difference** dividere la differenza; (fig) venire a un compromesso
different ['dɪfərənt] *adj* differente
differential [ˌdɪfə'renʃəl] *adj & s* differenziale *m*
differentiate [ˌdɪfə'renʃɪˌet] *tr* differenziare ‖ *intr* differenziarsi
difficult ['dɪfɪˌkʌlt] *adj* difficile
difficul·ty ['dɪfɪˌkʌlti] *s* (**-ties**) difficoltà *f*
diffident ['dɪfɪdənt] *adj* timido, imbarazzato
diffuse [dɪ'fjus] *adj* diffuso ‖ [dɪ'fjuz] *tr* diffondere ‖ *intr* diffondersi
dig [dɪg] *s* (*poke*) botta, spintone *m*; (*jibe*) stoccata, fiancata ‖ *v* (*pret & pp* **dug** [dʌg]; *ger* **digging**) *tr* sca-

vare, sterrare; **to dig up** dissodare; (*to uncover*) dissotterrare || *intr* scavare; **to dig in** (mil) fortificarsi; **to dig into** (coll) sprofondarsi in
digest ['daɪdʒest] *s* compendio; (law) digesto || [dɪ'dʒest] or [daɪ'dʒest] *tr & intr* digerire
digestible [dɪ'dʒestɪbəl] or [daɪ'dʒestɪbəl] *adj* digeribile, digestibile
digestion [dɪ'dʒestʃən] or [daɪ'dʒestʃən] *s* digestione
digestive [dɪ'dʒestɪv] or [daɪ'dʒestɪv] *adj* (*tube*) digerente || *s* digestivo
digit ['dɪdʒɪt] *s* cifra, unità *f;* (*finger*) dito; (*toe*) dito del piede
dig'ital clock' *s* orologio a scatto
digitalis [,dɪdʒɪ'tælɪs] or [,dɪdʒɪ'telɪs] *s* (bot) digitale *f;* (pharm) digitalina
dignified ['dɪgnɪ,faɪd] *adj* dignitoso, fiero, contegnoso
digni•fy ['dɪgnɪ,faɪ] *v* (*pret & pp* **-fied**) *tr* (*to ennoble*) nobilitare; onorare, esaltare; dare la dignità a
dignitar•y ['dɪgnɪ,teri] *s* (**-ies**) dignitario; **dignitaries** dignità *fpl*
digni•ty ['dɪgnɪti] *s* (**-ties**) dignità *f,* decoro; **to stand on one's dignity** mantenere la propria dignità
digress [dɪ'gres] or [daɪ'gres] *intr* digredire, divagare
digression [dɪ'greʃən] or [daɪ'greʃən] *s* digressione, divagazione
dike [daɪk] *s* diga; (*in a river*) argine *m;* (*ditch*) fosso; scarpata
dilapidated [dɪ'læpɪ,detɪd] *adj* dilapidato, decrepito
dilate [daɪ'let] *tr* dilatare || *intr* dilatarsi
dilatory ['dɪlə,tori] *adj* lento, tardivo; (*e.g., strategy*) dilatorio
dilemma [dɪ'lemə] *s* dilemma *m*
dilettan•te [,dɪlə'tænti] *adj* dilettantesco || *s* (**-tes** or **-ti** [ti]) dilettante *mf*
diligence ['dɪlɪdʒəns] *s* diligenza
diligent ['dɪlɪdʒənt] *adj* diligente
dill [dɪl] *s* (bot) aneto
dillydal•ly ['dɪlɪ,dæli] *v* (*pret & pp* **-lied**) *intr* farla lunga
dilute [dɪ'lut] or [daɪ'lut] *adj* diluito || [dɪ'lut] *tr* diluire || *intr* diluirsi
dilution [dɪ'luʃən] *s* diluizione
dim [dɪm] *adj* (**dimmer; dimmest**) (*light*) fioco; (*sight*) debole; (*memory*) vago; (*color*) smorzato; (*sound*) sordo; **to take a dim view of** avere una visione pessimistica di || *v* (*pret & pp* **dimmed; ger dimming**) *tr* (*lights*) smorzare; **to dim the headlights** abbassare i fari
dime [daɪm] *s* moneta di dieci centesimi di dollaro
dimension [dɪ'menʃən] *s* dimensione
diminish [dɪ'mɪnɪʃ] *tr & intr* diminuire, scemare
diminutive [dɪ'mɪnjətɪv] *adj* (*tiny*) minuscolo; (gram) diminutivo || *s* diminutivo
dimly ['dɪmli] *adv* indistintamente
dimmer ['dɪmər] *s* smorzatore *m;* (aut) luce *f* di incrocio; **dimmers** fari *mpl* antiabbaglianti
dimple ['dɪmpəl] *s* fossetta
dimwit ['dɪm,wɪt] *s* (slang) stupido, cretino
din [dɪn] *s* fragore *m,* frastuono || *v* (*pret & pp* **dinned;** *ger* **dinning**) *tr* assordare; **to din s.th into s.o.'s ears** rintronare qlco nelle orecchie di qlcu
dine [daɪn] *tr* offrire un pranzo a; offire una cena a || *intr* pasteggiare; cenare; **to dine out** mangiare fuori di casa
diner ['daɪnər] *s* commensale *m;* (rr) vettura ristorante; (U.S.A.) ristorante *m* a forma di vagone
ding-dong ['dɪŋ,dəŋ] or ['dɪŋ,dɑŋ] *s* dindon *m*
din•gy ['dɪndʒi] *adj* (**-gier; -giest**) sporco, sbiadito
din'ing car' *s* vagone *m* ristorante
din'ing room' *s* sala da pranzo
dinner ['dɪnər] *s* cena; pranzo; (*formal meal*) banchetto
din'ner coat' or **jack'et** *s* smoking *m*
din'ner knife' *s* coltello da tavola
din'ner set' *s* servizio da tavola
din'ner ta'ble *s* desco
din'ner time' *s* ora di pranzo or di cena
dinosaur ['daɪnə,sɔr] *s* dinosauro
dint [dɪnt] *s* tacca, ammaccatura; **by dint of** a forza di || *tr* ammaccare
diocese ['daɪ•ə,sis] or ['daɪ•əsɪs] *s* diocesi *f*
diode ['daɪ•od] *s* diodo
dioxide [daɪ'ɑksaɪd] *s* biossido
dip [dɪp] *s* immersione; (*brief swim*) tuffo, nuotata; (*in a road*) depressione; inclinazione magnetica || *v* (*pret & pp* **dipped;** *ger* **dipping**) *tr* immergere, tuffare; (*the flag*) abbassare; (*bread*) inzuppare || *intr* immergersi, tuffarsi; inclinarsi; (*to drop down*) sparire subitamente; **to dip into** (*a book*) sfogliare; (*business*) mettersi in; (*a container of liquids*) intingere; **to dip into one's purse** spendere soldi
diphtheria [dɪf'θɪrɪ•ə] *s* difterite *f*
diphthong ['dɪfθəŋ] or ['dɪfθɑŋ] *s* dittongo
diphthongize ['dɪfθəŋ,gaɪz] or ['dɪfθɑŋ,gaɪz] *tr & intr* dittongare
diploma [dɪ'plomə] *s* diploma *m*
diploma•cy [dɪ'ploməsi] *s* (**-cies**) diplomazia
diplomat ['dɪplə,mæt] *s* diplomatico
diplomatic [,dɪplə'mætɪk] *adj* diplomatico
dip'lomat'ic pouch' *s* valigia diplomatica
dipper ['dɪpər] *s* mestolo
dip'stick' *s* asta di livello
dire [daɪr] *adj* terribile, orrendo
direct [dɪ'rekt] or [daɪ'rekt] *adj* diretto; sincero || *tr* dirigere; ordinare
direct' cur'rent *s* corrente continua
direct' dis'course *s* discorso diretto
direct' dis'tance di'aling *s* (telp) teleselezione *f*
direct' hit' *s* colpo centrato
direction [dɪ'rekʃən] or [daɪ'rekʃən] *s* direzione; **directions** istruzioni *fpl;* (*for use*) indicazioni *fpl* per l'uso

directional [dɪ'rɛkʃənəl] or [daɪ'rɛkʃənəl] *adj* direzionale
directive [dɪ'rɛktɪv] or [daɪ'rɛktɪv] *s* direttiva
direct' ob'ject *s* (gram) complemento diretto, complemento oggetto
director [dɪ'rɛktər] or [daɪ'rɛktər] *s* direttore *m*, gerente *m*; (*member of a governing body*) consigliere *m*
directorship [dɪ'rɛktər,ʃɪp] or [daɪ'rɛktər,ʃɪp] *s* direzione; amministrazione
directo•ry [dɪ'rɛktəri] or [daɪ'rɛktəri] *s* **(-ries)** (*board of directors*) direzione, direttorio; (*list of names and addresses*) rubrica, elenco; (telp) elenco dei telefoni, guida telefonica
dirge [dʌrdʒ] *s* canto funebre
dirigible ['dɪrɪdʒɪbəl] *adj & s* dirigibile *m*
dirt [dʌrt] *s* (*soil*) terra, suolo; (*dust*) polvere *m*; (*mud*) fango; (*accumulation of dirt*) sudiciume *m*, lerciume *m*; (*moral filth*) porcheria, sozzura; (*gossip*) pettegolezzi *mpl*; **to do s.o. dirt** (slang) calunniare qlcu
dirt'-cheap' *adj* a prezzo bassissimo
dirt' road' *s* strada di terra battuta
dirt•y ['dʌrti] *adj* **(-ier; -iest)** sporco, sudicio; fangoso; polveroso; (*e.g., spinach*) terroso; (*obscene*) sconcio, lurido; immondo || *v* (*pret & pp* **(-ied)** *tr* sporcare, insudiciare, imbrattare
dir'ty lin'en *s* roba sporca; **to air one's dirty linen in public** mettere i panni al sole
dir'ty trick' *s* brutto tiro
disabili•ty [,dɪsə'bɪlɪti] *s* **(-ties)** incapacità *f*, invalidità *f*
disabil'ity insur'ance *s* assicurazione invalidità
disable [dɪs'ebəl] *tr* mutilare, storpiare; (*a ship*) smantellare; (law) invalidare
disabuse [,dɪsə'bjuz] *tr* disingannare
disadvantage [,dɪsəd'væntɪdʒ] or [,dɪsəd'vɑntɪdʒ] *s* svantaggio
disadvantageous [dɪs,ædvən'tedʒəs] *adj* svantaggioso
disagree [,dɪsə'gri] *intr* discordare, disconvenire; (*to quarrel*) litigare, altercare; **to disagree with** non essere del parere di
disagreeable [,dɪsə'gri•əbəl] *adj* sgradevole
disagreement [,dɪsə'grimənt] *s* sconcordanza, dissidio, dissenso
disallow [,dɪsə'laʊ] *tr* non permettere, rifiutare
disappear [,dɪsə'pɪr] *intr* sparire, scomparire
disappearance [,dɪsə'pɪrəns] *s* scomparsa
disappoint [,dɪsə'pɔɪnt] *tr* deludere, disilludere; **to be disappointed** rimanere deluso
disappointment [,dɪsə'pɔɪntmənt] *s* delusione, disinganno, disappunto
disapproval [,dɪsə'pruvəl] *s* disapprovazione, riprova
disapprove [,dɪsə'pruv] *tr & intr* disapprovare

disarm [dɪs'ɑrm] *tr* disarmare || *intr* disarmare, disarmarsi
disarmament [dɪs'ɑrməmənt] *s* disarmo
disarming [dɪs'ɑrmɪŋ] *adj* ingraziante, simpatico
disarray [,dɪsə're] *s* disordine *m*, scompiglio; (*of apparel*) sciatteria || *tr* scomporre, scompigliare
disassemble [,dɪsə'sɛmbəl] *tr* smontare, sconnettere
disassociate [,dɪsə'soʃɪ,et] *tr* dissociare, disassociare
disaster [dɪ'zæstər] or [dɪ'zɑstər] *s* disastro, sinistro
disastrous [dɪ'zæstrəs] or [dɪ'zɑstrəs] *adj* disastroso
disavow [,dɪsə'vaʊ] *tr* sconfessare
disavowal [,dɪsə'vaʊ•əl] *s* sconfessione
disband [dɪs'bænd] *tr* (*an assembly*) sciogliere; (*troops*) congedare; (*any group*) sbandare || *intr* sbandarsi
dis•bar [dɪs'bɑr] *v* (*pret & pp* **-barred; ger -barring**) *tr* (law) radiare dall'albo degli avvocati
disbelief [,dɪsbɪ'lif] *s* incredulità *f*
disbelieve [,dɪsbɪ'liv] *tr* rifiutarsi di credere a || *intr* rifiutarsi di credere
disburse [dɪs'bʌrs] *tr* sborsare
disbursement [dɪs'bʌrsmənt] *s* sborso, disborso
discard [dɪs'kɑrd] *s* scarto, scartina; **to put into the discard** scartare || *tr* scartare
discern [dɪ'zʌrn] or [dɪ'sʌrn] *tr* scernere, discernere, sceverare
discernible [dɪ'zʌrnɪbəl] or [dɪ'sʌrnɪbəl] *adj* discernibile
discerning [dɪ'zʌrnɪŋ] or [dɪ'sʌrnɪŋ] *adj* perspicace, oculato
discernment [dɪ'zʌrnmənt] or [dɪ'sʌrnmənt] *s* discernimento
discharge [dɪs'tʃɑrdʒ] *s* (*of a load*) scarico; (*of a gun; of electricity*) scarica; (*of a prisoner*) liberazione; (*of a duty*) adempimento; (*of a debt*) pagamento; (*from a job*) licenziamento; (mil) foglio di congedo; (pathol) spurgo || *tr* scaricare; (*a duty*) adempiere; (*a prisoner*) liberare; (*a debt*) pagare; (*an employee*) licenziare; (*a patient*) lasciar uscire; (*a passenger from a ship*) sbarcare; (*a battery*) scaricare; (mil) congedare || *intr* (*said, e.g., of a liquid*) sboccare; (*said of a gun or a battery*) scaricarsi
disciple [dɪ'saɪpəl] *s* discepolo
disciplinarian [,dɪsɪplɪ'nɛrɪ•ən] *s* disciplinatore *m*; partigiano di una forte disciplina
disciplinary ['dɪsɪplɪ,nɛri] *adj* disciplinare
discipline ['dɪsɪplɪn] *s* disciplina; castigo || *tr* disciplinare; castigare
disclaim [dɪs'klem] *tr* non riconoscere, negare
disclose [dɪs'kloz] *tr* rivelare, scoprire
disclosure [dɪs'kloʒər] *s* rivelazione, scoperta; divulgazione
discolor [dɪs'kʌlər] *tr* scolorare, scolorire || *intr* scolorirsi
discoloration [dɪs,kʌlə'reʃən] *s* discolorazione

discomfit [dɪsˈkʌmfɪt] *tr* sconcertare, turbare; frustrare, battere, mettere in fuga
discomfiture [dɪsˈkʌmfɪtʃər] *s* sconcerto, turbamento; frustrazione; disfatta
discomfort [dɪsˈkʌmfərt] *s* disagio ‖ *tr* incomodare
disconcert [ˌdɪskənˈsʌrt] *tr* sconcertare
disconnect [ˌdɪskəˈnekt] *tr* sconnettere; (elec) disinserire
disconsolate [dɪsˈkɑnsəlɪt] *adj* sconsolato, desolato
discontent [ˌdɪskənˈtent] *adj & s* scontento ‖ *tr* scontentare
discontented [ˌdɪskənˈtentɪd] *adj* scontento
discontinue [ˌdɪskənˈtɪnju] *tr* cessare, interrompere
discord [ˈdɪskɔrd] *s* discordia, dissidio
discordance [dɪsˈkɔrdəns] *s* discordanza
discotheque [ˌdɪskoˈtek] *s* discoteca
discount [ˈdɪskaʊnt] *s* sconto ‖ [ˈdɪskaʊnt] or [dɪsˈkaʊnt] *tr* scontare; (*news*) fare la tara a
dis′count rate′ *s* tasso di sconto
discourage [dɪsˈkʌrɪdʒ] *tr* scoraggiare, sconfortare; (*to dissuade*) sconsigliare
discouragement [dɪsˈkʌrɪdʒmənt] *s* scoraggiamento; disapprovazione
discourse [ˈdɪskors] or [dɪsˈkors] *s* discorso ‖ [dɪsˈkors] *intr* discorrere
discourteous [dɪsˈkʌrtɪ·əs] *adj* scortese
discourte·sy [dɪsˈkʌrtəsi] *s* (**-sies**) scortesia
discover [dɪsˈkʌvər] *tr* scoprire
discoverer [dɪsˈkʌvərər] *s* scopritore *m*
discover·y [dɪsˈkʌvəri] *s* (**-ies**) scoperta
discredit [dɪsˈkredɪt] *s* discredito ‖ *tr* screditare
discreditable [dɪsˈkredɪtəbəl] *adj* indegno, disonorevole
discreet [dɪsˈkrit] *adj* discreto
discrepan·cy [dɪsˈkrepənsi] *s* (**-cies**) discrepanza, divario
discretion [dɪsˈkreʃən] *s* discrezione
discriminate [dɪsˈkrɪmɪˌnet] *tr* discriminare ‖ *intr*—**to discriminate against** fare delle discriminazioni contro
discrimination [dɪsˌkrɪmɪˈneʃən] *s* discriminazione
discriminatory [dɪsˈkrɪmɪnəˌtori] *adj* discriminante
discuss [dɪsˈkʌs] *tr & intr* discutere
discussion [dɪsˈkʌʃən] *s* discussione
discus thrower [ˈdɪskəs ˈθro·ər] *s* discobolo
disdain [dɪsˈden] *s* disdegno ‖ *tr* disdegnare, sdegnare
disdainful [dɪsˈdenfəl] *adj* sdegnoso
disease [dɪˈziz] *s* malattia
diseased [dɪˈzizd] *adj* malato
disembark [ˌdɪsemˈbɑrk] *tr & intr* sbarcare
disembarkation [dɪsˌembɑrˈkeʃən] *s* sbarco
disembowel [ˌdɪsemˈbaʊ·əl] *tr* sbudellare, sventrare
disenchant [ˌdɪsenˈtʃænt] or [ˌdɪsenˈtʃɑnt] *tr* disincantare
disenchantment [ˌdɪsenˈtʃæntmənt] or [ˌdɪsenˈtʃɑntmənt] *s* disinganno
disengage [ˌdɪsenˈgedʒ] *tr* (*from a pledge*) svincolare; (*to disconnect*) sgranare, disinnestare; (mil) sganciare
disengagement [ˌdɪsenˈgedʒmənt] *s* liberazione; disinnesto; svincolamento
disentangle [ˌdɪsenˈtæŋgəl] *tr* disincagliare, districare
disentanglement [ˌdɪsenˈtæŋgəlmənt] *s* districamento
disestablish [ˌdɪsesˈtæblɪʃ] *tr* (*the Church*) separare dallo Stato
disfavor [dɪsˈfevər] *s* disfavore *m*
disfigure [dɪsˈfɪgjər] *tr* sfigurare, deturpare
disfigurement [dɪsˈfɪgjərmənt] *s* deturpazione
disfranchise [dɪsˈfræntʃaɪz] *tr* privare dei diritti civili
disgorge [dɪsˈgɔrdʒ] *tr* vomitare; (*something illicitly obtained*) restituire; (*said of a river*) scaricare ‖ *intr* vomitare; scaricarsi
disgrace [dɪsˈgres] *s* vergogna; disgrazia ‖ *tr* disonorare; privare del favore
disgraceful [dɪsˈgresfəl] *adj* infamante, disonorante
disgruntle [dɪsˈgrʌntəl] *tr* scontentare, irritare
disgruntled [dɪsˈgrʌntəld] *adj* irritato, di cattivo umore
disguise [dɪsˈgaɪz] *s* travestimento ‖ *tr* travestire, dissimulare
disgust [dɪsˈgʌst] *s* disgusto, schifo ‖ *tr* disgustare, fare schifo a
disgusting [dɪsˈgʌstɪŋ] *adj* disgustoso, schifoso
dish [dɪʃ] *s* piatto, **dishes** vasellame *m;* **to wash the dishes** fare i piatti ‖ *tr* scodellare; (*to defeat*) (slang) sconfiggere; **to dish out** (slang) distribuire
dish′cloth′ *s* canovaccio, strofinaccio
dishearten [dɪsˈhɑrtən] *tr* scoraggiare, disanimare, desolare
dishev·el [dɪˈʃevəl] *v* (*pret & pp* **-eled** or **-elled;** *ger* **-eling** or **-elling**) *tr* scomporre, scarmigliare, scapigliare
dishonest [dɪsˈɑnɪst] *adj* disonesto
dishones·ty [dɪsˈɑnɪsti] *s* (**-ties**) disonestà *f*
dishonor [dɪsˈɑnər] *s* disonore *m* ‖ *tr* disonorare; (com) rifiutare di pagare
dishonorable [dɪsˈɑnərəbəl] *adj* disonorevole, disonorante
dish′pan′ *s* bacinella per lavare i piatti
dish′rack′ *s* portapiatti *m,* sgocciolatoio
dish′rag′ *s* canovaccio, strofinaccio
dish′towel′ *s* canovaccio per le stoviglie
dish′wash′er *s* (*person*) sguattero, lavapiatti *m;* (*machine*) lavastoviglie *m & f*
dish′wa′ter *s* lavatura di piatti
disillusion [ˌdɪsɪˈluʒən] *s* disillusione ‖ *tr* disilludere
disillusionment [ˌdɪsɪˈluʒənmənt] *s* disillusione
disinclination [dɪsˌɪnklɪˈneʃən] *s* riluttanza, avversione
disinclined [ˌdɪsɪnˈklaɪnd] *adj* riluttante, avverso

disinfect [ˌdɪsɪn'fɛkt] *tr* disinfettare
disinfectant [ˌdɪsɪn'fɛktənt] *adj & s* disinfettante *m*
disingenuous [ˌdɪsɪn'dʒɛnjʊ·əs] *adj* poco schietto, insincero
disinherit [ˌdɪsɪn'hɛrɪt] *tr* diseredare
disintegrate [dɪs'ɪntɪˌgret] *tr* disintegrare, disgregare || *intr* disintegrarsi, disgregarsi
disintegration [dɪsˌɪntɪ'greʃən] *s* disintegrazione, disgregamento
disin·ter [ˌdɪsɪn'tʌr] *v* (*pret & pp* **-terred;** *ger* **-terring**) *tr* dissotterrare
disinterested [dɪs'ɪntəˌrestɪd] or [dɪs'ɪntrɪstɪd] *adj* disinteressato
disjunctive [dɪs'dʒʌŋktɪv] *adj* disgiuntivo
disk [dɪsk] *s* disco; (*of ski pole*) rotella
disk' jock'ey *s* presentatore *m* di un programma radiodiffuso di dischi
dislike [dɪs'laɪk] *s* antipatia, avversione; **to take a dislike for** prendere in uggia || *tr* non piacere (with *dat*), e.g., **he dislikes wine** non gli piace il vino
dislocate ['dɪsloˌket] *tr* spostare, mettere fuori posto; (*a bone*) slogare
dislodge [dɪs'lɑdʒ] *tr* sloggiare
disloyal [dɪs'lɔɪ·əl] *adj* sleale
disloyal·ty [dɪs'lɔɪ·əlti] *s* (**-ties**) slealtà *f*
dismal ['dɪzməl] *adj* tetro, triste; cattivo, orribile
dismantle [dɪs'mæntəl] *tr* smontare, smantellare; (*a fortress*) sguarnire
dismay [dɪs'me] *s* costernazione || *tr* costernare
dismember [dɪs'mɛmbər] *tr* smembrare
dismiss [dɪs'mɪs] *tr* congedare; (*to fire*) licenziare; (*a subject*) scartare; (*from the mind*) scacciare
dismissal [dɪs'mɪsəl] *s* congedo; licenziamento
dismount [dɪs'maʊnt] *tr* disarcionare || *intr* scendere, smontare
disobedience [ˌdɪsə'bidɪ·əns] *s* disubbidienza
disobedient [ˌdɪsə'bidɪ·ənt] *adj* disubbidiente
disobey [ˌdɪsə'be] *tr* disubbidire (with *dat*) || *intr* disubbidire
disorder [dɪs'ɔrdər] *s* disordine *m* || *tr* disordinare, confondere
disorderly [dɪs'ɔrdərli] *adj* disordinato, confuso; (*unruly*) turbolento
disor'derly con'duct *s* contegno contrario all'ordine pubblico
disor'derly house' *s* bordello, lupanare *m*
disorganize [dɪs'ɔrgəˌnaɪz] *tr* disorganizzare
disoriented [dɪs'orɪˌɛntɪd] *adj* disorientato
disown [dɪs'on] *tr* disconoscere
disparage [dɪs'pærɪdʒ] *tr* svilire, deprezzare
disparagement [dɪs'pærɪdʒmənt] *s* discredito, deprezzamento
disparate ['dɪspərɪt] *adj* disparato
dispari·ty [dɪs'pærɪti] *s* (**-ties**) disparità *f*, spareggio
dispassionate [dɪs'pæʃənɪt] *adj* spassionato

dispatch [dɪs'pætʃ] *s* dispaccio || *tr* spedire; (*to dismiss*) congedare; uccidere; (*a meal*) (coll) liquidare
dis·pel [dɪs'pɛl] *v* (*pret & pp* **-pelled;** *ger* **-pelling**) *tr* dissipare
dispensa·ry [dɪs'pensəri] *s* (**-ries**) dispensario
dispensation [ˌdɪspen'seʃən] *s* (*dispensing*) distribuzione, dispensa; (*exemption*) dispensa
dispense [dɪs'pɛns] *tr* (*medicines*) distribuire; (*justice*) amministrare; (*to distribute*) dispensare; (*to exempt*) esimere || *intr*—**to dispense with** fare a meno di; esimersi da
dispenser [dɪ'spɛnsər] *s* dispensatore *m;* (*automatic*) distributore *m*
disperse [dɪs'pʌrs] *tr* disperdere || *intr* disperdersi
dispersion [dɪ'spʌrʒən] or [di'sperʃən] *s* dispersione
dispersive [dɪ'spʌrsɪv] *adj* dispersivo
dispirit [dɪ'spɪrɪt] *tr* scoraggiare
displace [dɪs'ples] *tr* muovere; costringere a lasciare il proprio paese; (*to supplant*) rimpiazzare; (naut) dislocare
displaced' per'son *s* rifugiato politico
displacement [dɪs'plesmənt] *s* spostamento; sostituzione; (*of a piston*) cilindrata; (naut) dislocamento
display [dɪs'ple] *s* sfoggio, mostra || *tr* mostrare; (*e.g., in a store window*) mettere in mostra; (*to unfold*) spiegare; (*to show ostentatiously*) sfoggiare, ostentare; (*ignorance*) rivelare
display' cab'inet *s* bacheca
display' win'dow *s* mostra, vetrina
displease [dɪs'pliz] *tr* dispiacere (with *dat*)
displeasing [dɪs'plizɪŋ] *adj* spiacevole
displeasure [dɪs'plɛʒər] *s* dispiacere *m;* sfavore *m*
disposable [dɪs'pozəbəl] *adj* (*available*) disponibile; (*made to be thrown away after use*) scartabile, da gettarsi via, usa e getta
disposal [dɪs'pozəl] *s* disposizione; eliminazione; **to have at one's disposal** disporre di
dispose [dɪs'poz] *tr* disporre; **to dispose of** disporre di; (*to get rid of*) sbarazzarsi di; vendere
disposed [dɪ'spozd] *adj*—**to be disposed to** essere disposto a
disposition [ˌdɪspə'zɪʃən] *s* disposizione; (*mental outlook*) indole *f;* tendenza; (mil) ordinamento
dispossess [ˌdɪspə'zɛs] *tr* spodestare, bandire; (*to evict*) sfrattare
disproof [dɪs'pruf] *s* confutazione
disproportionate [ˌdɪsprə'porʃənɪt] *adj* sproporzionato
disprove [dɪs'pruv] *tr* confutare
dispute [dɪs'pjut] *s* disputa; **beyond dispute** incontestabile; **in dispute** in discussione || *tr & intr* disputare
disquali·fy [dɪs'kwɑlɪˌfaɪ] *v* (*pret & pp* **-fied**) *tr* squalificare
disquiet [dɪs'kwaɪ·ət] *s* inquietudine *f* || *tr* inquietare, turbare
disquisition [ˌdɪskwɪ'zɪʃən] *s* disquisizione

disregard [ˌdɪsrɪˈgɑrd] *s* (*of a rule*) inosservanza; (*of danger*) disprezzo, noncuranza || *tr* non fare attenzione a
disrepair [ˌdɪsrɪˈpɛr] *s* cattivo stato, rovina
disreputable [dɪsˈrɛpjətəbəl] *adj* malfamato; disonorevole; (*in bad condition*) raso, logoro
disrepute [ˌdɪsrɪˈpjut] *s* cattiva fama; **to bring into disrepute** rovinare la reputazione di
disrespect [ˌdɪsrɪˈspɛkt] *s* mancanza di rispetto || *tr* mancare di rispetto a
disrespectful [ˌdɪsrɪˈspɛktfəl] *adj* non rispettoso, irriverente
disrobe [dɪsˈrob] *tr* svestire || *intr* svestirsi, spogliarsi
disrupt [dɪsˈrʌpt] *tr* disorganizzare; interrompere
disruption [dɪsˈrʌpʃən] *s* rottura; disorganizzazione
dissatisfaction [ˌdɪssætɪsˈfækʃən] *s* scontento, malcontento
dissatisfied [dɪsˈsætɪsˌfaɪd] *adj* scontento, malcontento; insoddisfatto
dissatis·fy [dɪsˈsætɪs,faɪ] *v* (*pret & pp* **-fied**) *tr* scontentare
dissect [dɪˈsɛkt] *tr* sezionare
dissemble [dɪˈsɛmbəl] *tr & intr* dissimulare
disseminate [dɪˈsɛmɪˌnet] *tr* disseminare, divulgare
dissension [dɪˈsɛnʃən] *s* dissensione
dissent [dɪˈsɛnt] *s* dissenso; (*nonconformity*) dissidio || *intr* dissentire
dissenter [dɪˈsɛntər] *s* dissenziente *m*
dissertation [ˌdɪsərˈteʃən] *s* dissertazione
disservice [dɪˈsʌrvɪs] *s* danno; cattivo servizio
dissidence [ˈdɪsɪdəns] *s* dissidenza
dissident [ˈdɪsɪdənt] *adj & s* dissidente *m*
dissimilar [dɪˈsɪmɪlər] *adj* dissimile
dissimilate [dɪˈsɪmɪˌlet] *tr* dissimilare || *intr* dissimilarsi
dissimulate [dɪˈsɪmjəˌlet] *tr & intr* dissimulare
dissipate [ˈdɪsɪˌpet] *tr* dissipare || *intr* dissiparsi; (*to indulge oneself*) darsi alla dissipatezza
dissipated [ˈdɪsɪˌpetɪd] *adj* dissipato
dissipation [ˌdɪsɪˈpeʃən] *s* dissipazione
dissociate [dɪˈsoʃɪˌet] *tr* dissociare || *intr* dissociarsi
dissolute [ˈdɪsəˌlut] *adj* dissoluto
dissolution [ˌdɪsəˈluʃən] *s* dissoluzione
dissolve [dɪˈzɑlv] *tr* sciogliere, disciogliere || *intr* sciogliersi, disciogliersi
dissonance [ˈdɪsənəns] *s* dissonanza
dissuade [dɪˈswed] *tr* dissuadere
dissyllabic [ˌdɪsɪˈlæbɪk] *adj* disillabo
dissyllable [dɪˈsɪləbəl] *s* disillabo
distaff [ˈdɪstæf] or [ˈdɪstɑf] *s* rocca
dis′taff side′ *s* ramo femminile di una famiglia
distance [ˈdɪstəns] *s* distanza; **a long distance** (fig) moltissimo; **in the distance** in lontananza; **to keep at a distance** or **to keep one's distance** mantenere le distanze || *tr* distanziare
distant [ˈdɪstənt] *adj* distante; (*relative*) lontano; (*aloof*) freddo, riservato
distaste [dɪsˈtest] *s* ripugnanza
distasteful [dɪsˈtestfəl] *adj* ripugnante, sgradevole
distemper [dɪsˈtɛmpər] *s* cimurro; (*painting*) tempera || *tr* dipingere a tempera
distend [dɪsˈtɛnd] *tr* stendere, distendere; gonfiare || *intr* stendersi, distendersi; gonfiarsi
distension [dɪsˈtɛnʃən] *s* distensione; gonfiamento
distill [dɪsˈtɪl] *tr* distillare
distillation [ˌdɪstɪˈleʃən] *s* distillazione
distiller·y [dɪsˈtɪləri] *s* (**-ies**) distilleria
distinct [dɪsˈtɪŋkt] *adj* distinto, chiaro; (*not blurred*) nitido
distinction [dɪsˈtɪŋkʃən] *s* distinzione
distinctive [dɪsˈtɪŋktɪv] *adj* distintivo
distinguish [dɪsˈtɪŋgwɪʃ] *tr* distinguere
distinguished [dɪsˈtɪŋgwɪʃt] *adj* distinto
distort [dɪsˈtɔrt] *tr* distorcere; (*the truth*) svisare, snaturare
distortion [dɪsˈtɔrʃən] *s* deformazione; (*of the truth*) alterazione, svisamento; (rad) distorsione
distract [dɪsˈtrækt] *tr* distrarre
distracted [dɪsˈtræktɪd] *adj* distratto; (*irrational*) turbato, sconvolto
distraction [dɪsˈtrækʃən] *s* distrazione
distraught [dɪsˈtrɔt] *adj* turbato, stordito
distress [dɪsˈtrɛs] *s* pena, dispiacere *m;* pericolo; (naut) difficoltà *f* || *tr* sconfortare, affliggere
distressing [dɪsˈtrɛsɪŋ] *adj* penoso
distress′ mer′chandise *s* merce *f* sotto costo
distress′ sig′nal *s* segnale *m* di soccorso
distribute [dɪsˈtrɪbjut] *tr* distribuire
distribution [ˌdɪstrɪˈbjuʃən] *s* distribuzione, erogazione
distributor [dɪsˈtrɪbjətər] *s* distributore *m;* (aut) distributore *m* d'accensione
district [ˈdɪstrɪkt] *s* regione; (*of a city*) rione *m*, quartiere *m;* (*administrative division*) distretto || *tr* dividere in distretti
dis′trict attor′ney *s* procuratore *m* generale
distrust [dɪsˈtrʌst] *s* diffidenza || *tr* diffidare di
distrustful [dɪsˈtrʌstfəl] *adj* diffidente
disturb [dɪsˈtʌrb] *tr* disturbare, turbare; disordinare
disturbance [dɪsˈtʌrbəns] *s* disturbo, turbamento, perturbazione; disordine *m*
disuse [dɪsˈjus] *s* disuso
ditch [dɪtʃ] *s* fossa, fossato || *tr* scavare un fosso in; (rr) far deragliare; (slang) piantare in asso || *intr* fare un ammaraggio forzato
dither [ˈdɪðər] *s* agitazione; **to be in a dither** (coll) essere agitato
dit·to [ˈdɪto] *s* (**-tos**) lo stesso; (*ditto symbol*) virgolette *fpl* || *adv* ugualmente, idem || *tr* copiare, duplicare
dit′to marks′ *spl* virgolette *fpl*

dit·ty ['dɪti] *s* (**-ties**) canzonetta
diva ['divɑ) *s* (mus) diva
divan ['daɪvæn] or [dɪ'væn] *s* divano
dive [daɪv] *s* tuffo; (*of a submarine*) immersione; (aer) picchiata; (coll) taverna; (com) discesa ‖ *v* (*pret & pp* **dived** or **dove** [dov]) *intr* tuffarsi; (*said of submarine*) immergersi; (*to plunge*) lanciarsi; (aer) scendere in picchiata; **to dive for** (*e.g., pearls*) pescare
dive'-bomb' *tr* bombardare in picchiata ‖ *intr* scendere a tuffo
dive' bomb'ing *s* bombardamento in picchiata
diver ['daɪvər] *s* tuffatore *m;* (*person who works under water*) palombaro; (orn) tuffetto
diverge [dɪ'vʌrdʒ] or [daɪ'vʌrdʒ] *intr* divergere
divers ['daɪvərz] *adj* diversi, vari
diverse [dɪ'vʌrs], [daɪ'vʌrs] or ['daɪvʌrs] *adj* (*different*) diverso; (*of various kinds*) multiforme
diversification [dɪ ,vʌrsɪfɪ'keʃən] or [daɪ ,vʌrsɪfɪ'keʃən] *s* diversificazione
diversi·fy [dɪ'vʌrsɪ ,faɪ] or [daɪ'vʌrsɪ ,faɪ] *v* (*pret & pp* **-fied**) *tr* diversificare ‖ *intr* diversificarsi
diversion [dɪ'vʌrʒən] or [daɪ'vʌrʒən] *s* diversione; (*pastime*) svago
diversi·ty [dɪ'vʌrsɪti] or [daɪ'vʌrsɪti] *s* (**-ties**) diversità *f*
divert [dɪ'vʌrt] or [daɪ'vʌrt] *tr* deviare; (*to entertain*) divertire; (*money*) stornare, distrarre
diverting [dɪ'vʌrtɪŋ] or [daɪ'vʌrtɪŋ] *adj* divertente
divest [dɪ'vest] or [daɪ'vest] *tr* spogliare; spossessare; **to divest oneself of** spogliarsi di, espropriarsi di
divide [dɪ'vaɪd] *s* spartiacque *m* ‖ *tr* dividere ‖ *intr* dividersi
dividend ['dɪvɪ ,dend] *s* dividendo
dividers [dɪ'vaɪdərz] *spl* compasso a punte fisse
divination [,dɪvɪ'neʃən] *s* divinazione
divine [dɪ'vaɪn] *adj* divino ‖ *s* sacerdote *m*, prete *m* ‖ *tr* divinare
diviner [dɪ'vaɪnər] *s* divinatore *m*
diving ['daɪvɪŋ] *s* tuffo, immersione
div'ing bell' *s* campana da palombaro
div'ing board' *s* trampolino
div'ing suit' *s* scafandro
divin'ing rod' [dɪ'vaɪnɪŋ] *s* bacchetta rabdomantica
divini·ty [dɪ'vɪnɪti] *s* (**-ties**) divinità *f;* teologia; **the Divinity** Dio
divisible [dɪ'vɪsɪbəl] *adj* divisibile
division [dɪ'vɪʒən] *s* divisione
divisor [dɪ'vaɪzər] *s* divisore *m*
divorce [dɪ'vors] *s* divorzio; **to get a divorce** divorziare ‖ *tr* (*a married couple*) divorziare; (*one's spouse*) divorziare da ‖ *intr* divorziare
divorcé [dɪvor'se] *s* divorziato
divorcee [dɪvor'si] *s* divorziata
divulge [dɪ'vʌldʒ] *tr* divulgare
dizziness ['dɪzɪnɪs] *s* vertigine *f*, stordimento; confusione
diz·zy ['dɪzi] *adj* (**-zier; -ziest**) (*causing dizziness*) vertiginoso; (*suffering dizziness*) preso da vertigine, stordito; (coll) stupido
do [du] *v* (*3rd pers* **does** [dʌz]; *pret* **did** [dɪd]; *pp* **done** [dʌn]; *ger* **doing** ['du·ɪŋ]) *tr* fare; (*a problem*) risolvere; (*a distance*) percorrere; (*to study*) studiare; (*to explore*) attraversare; (*to tire*) stancare; **to do one's best** fare del proprio meglio; **to do over** tornare a fare; ripetere; **to do right by** trattare bene; **to do s.o. out of s.th** (coll) portare via qlco a qlcu; **to do to death** mettere a morte; **to do up** (coll) impacchettare; stancare; (*one's hair*) farsi; vestire; (*a shirt*) lavare e stirare; **to have done** far fare ‖ *intr* fare; agire; comportarsi; servire; bastare; stare; succedere; **how do you do?** come sta?; **that will do** basta; è sufficiente; **to have done with** non aver più nulla a che fare con; **to have nothing to do with** non aver nulla a che vedere con; **to have to do with** aver a che fare con, trattarsi di; **to do away with** togliere di mezzo; **to do for** servire da; **to do well** crescere bene; **to do without** fare a meno di ‖ *v aux* used 1) in interrogative sentences: **Do you speak Italian?** Parla italiano?; 2) in negative sentences: **I do not speak Italian** Non parlo italiano; 3) to avoid repetition of a verb or full verbal expression: **Did you go to church this morning? Yes, I did.** È stato in chiesa questa mattina? Sì, ci sono stato; 4) to lend emphasis to a principal verb: **I do believe what you told me** Ci credo a quello che mi ha detto; 5) in inverted constructions after certain adverbs: **Seldom does he come to see me** Mi viene a vedere di raro; 6) in a supplicating tone with imperatives: **Do come in** entri per favore
docile ['dɑsɪl] *adj* docile
dock [dɑk] *s* (*wharf*) molo; (*waterway between two piers*) darsena; (*area including piers and waterways*) scalo portuario; (law) gabbia degli imputati ‖ *tr* (*to deduct from the wages of*) fare una deduzione a; (*to deduct s.o.'s salary*) dedurre da; (*an animal*) scodare; (naut) attraccare ‖ *intr* (aer) agganciarsi; (naut) attraccare
dockage ['dɑkɪdʒ] *s* attracco; (*charges*) diritti *mpl* di porto
docket ['dɑkɪt] *s* ordine *m* del giorno; (law) ruolo delle sentenze; **on the docket** (coll) pendente, in sospeso
dock' hand' *s* portuale *m*
docking ['dɑkɪŋ] *s* (aer) aggancio; (naut) attracco
dock'yard' *s* cantiere *m* navale
doctor ['dɑktər] *s* dottore *m;* (*physician*) medico ‖ *tr* curare; aggiustare; falsificare; adulterare ‖ *intr* esercitare la medicina; (coll) curarsi, prendere medicine
doctorate ['dɑktərɪt] *s* dottorato
doctrine ['dɑktrɪn] *s* dottrina
document ['dɑkjəmənt] *s* documento ‖ ['dɑkjə ,ment] *tr* documentare

documenta·ry [ˌdɑkjəˈmɛntəri] *adj & s* (**-ries**) documentario
documentation [ˌdɑkəmɛnˈteʃən] *s* documentazione
doddering [ˈdɑdərɪŋ] *adj* tremante, rimbambito
dodge [dɑdʒ] *s* scarto, schivata; (fig) stratagemma *m* || *tr* schivare, evitare || *intr* schivarsi; (fig) rispondere evasivamente; **to dodge around the corner** scantonare
do·do [ˈdodo] *s* (**-dos** or **-does**) (coll) rimbecillito
doe [do] *s* (*of deer*) cerva; (*of goat*) capretta; (*of rabbit*) coniglia
doeskin [ˈdoˌskɪn] *s* pelle *f* di daino, pelle *f* di dante; lana finissima
doff [dɑf] or [dɔf] *tr* (*one's hat*) togliersi; (*clothing*) deporre
dog [dɔg] or [dɑg] *s* cane *m;* **to go to the dogs** (coll) andare in malora; **to put on the dog** (coll) darsi delle arie || *v* (*pret & pp* **dogged;** *ger* **dogging**) *tr* seguire; perseguitare
dog′catch′er *s* accalappiacani *m*
dog′ days′ *s* solleone *m,* canicola
doge [dodʒ] *s* doge *m*
dog′-ear′ *s* orecchia, orecchio
dog′fight′ *s* duello aereo
dogged [ˈdɔgɪd] or [ˈdɑgɪd] *adj* accanito
doggerel [ˈdɔgərəl] or [ˈdɑgərəl] *s* versi *mpl* da colascione
dog·gy [ˈdɔgi] or [ˈdɑgi] *adj* (**-gier; -giest**) vistoso; canino || *s* (**-gies**) cagnolino
dog′house′ *s* canile *m;* **to be in the doghouse** (slang) essere in disgrazia
dog′ Lat′in *s* latino maccheronico
dogma [ˈdɔgmə] or [ˈdɑgmə] *s* dogma *m*
dogmatic [dɔgˈmætɪk] or [dɑgˈmætɪk] *adj* dogmatico
dog′ rac′ing *s* corse *fpl* dei cani
dog′ show′ *s* mostra canina
dog's′ life′ *s* vita da cani
Dog′ Star′ *s* canicola
dog′ tag′ *s* (mil) piastrina, piastrino
dog′-tired′ *adj* (coll) stanco morto
dog′tooth′ *s* (**-teeth** [ˌtiθ]) canino
dog′ track′ *s* cinodromo
dog′watch′ *s* (naut) quarto di solo due ore, gaettone *m*
dog′wood′ *s* corniolo
doi·ly [ˈdɔɪli] *s* (**-lies**) centrino
doings [ˈdu·ɪŋz] *spl* azioni *fpl,* fatti *mpl*
do′-it-your·self′ *s* il fare tutto da sé
doldrums [ˈdɑldrəmz] *spl* calma equatoriale; inattività *f;* depressione
dole [dol] *s* elemosina; (*to the jobless*) sussidio di disoccupazione || *tr*—**to dole out** distribuire parsimoniosamente
doleful [ˈdolfəl] *adj* lugubre, triste
doll [dɑl] *s* bambola || *intr*—**to doll up** (slang) agghindarsi
dollar [ˈdɑlər] *s* dollaro
dol′lar·wise′ *adv* in termini finanziari
dol·ly [ˈdɑli] *s* (**-lies**) pupattola; (*low, wheeled frame for moving heavy loads*) carrello; (mov, telv) carrello || *v* (*pret & pp* **-lied**) *intr* (mov, telv) carrellare
dol′ly shot′ *s* (mov, telv) carrellata
dolphin [ˈdɑlfɪn] *s* delfino
dolt [dolt] *s* gonzo, balordo
doltish [ˈdoltɪʃ] *adj* gonzo, balordo
domain [doˈmen] *s* dominio; (law) proprietà *f;* (fig) campo, orbita
dome [dom] *s* cupola
dome′ light′ *s* lampadario
domestic [dəˈmɛstɪk] *adj & s* domestico
domesticate [dəˈmɛstɪˌket] *tr* domesticare
domicile [ˈdɑmɪsɪl] or [ˈdɑmɪˌsaɪl] *s* domicilio || *tr* domiciliare
dominance [ˈdɑmɪnəns] *s* dominio
dominant [ˈdɑmɪnənt] *adj & s* dominante *f*
dominate [ˈdɑmɪˌnet] *tr & intr* dominare
domination [ˌdɑmɪˈneʃən] *s* dominazione
domineer [ˌdɑmɪˈnɪr] *intr* spadroneggiare
domineering [ˌdɑmɪˈnɪrɪŋ] *adj* dispotico, tirannico
Dominican [dəˈmɪnɪkən] *adj & s* dominicano; (*eccl*) domenicano
dominion [dəˈmɪnjən] *s* dominio
domi·no [ˈdɑmɪˌno] *s* (**-noes** or **-nos**) (*costume and person*) domino; (*piece*) tessera di domino; **dominoes** (*game*) domino
don [dɑn] *s* signore *m;* don *m;* membro di un collegio universitario inglese || *v* (*pret & pp* **donned; ger donning**) *tr* (*clothes*) mettersi, vestire
donate [ˈdonet] *tr* donare, dare
donation [doˈneʃən] *s* donazione
done [dʌn] *adj* fatto; finito; stanco; (culin) ben cotto, ben rosolato
done′ for′ *adj* (coll) stanco morto; (coll) rovinato; (coll) fuori combattimento; (coll) morto
donjon [ˈdʌndʒən] or [ˈdɑndʒən] *s* torrione *m,* maschio
Don Juan [dɑn ˈwɑn] or [dɔn ˈhwɑn] *s* Don Giovanni
donkey [ˈdɑŋki] or [ˈdʌŋki] *s* asino, somaro
donnish [ˈdɑnɪʃ] *adj* pedante
donor [ˈdonər] *s* donatore *m*
doodle [ˈdudəl] *tr & intr* scarabocchiare, riempire di ghirigori
doom [dum] *s* destino; morte *f,* rovina; sentenza di morte; giudizio finale || *tr* destinare; condannare; condannare a morte
doomsday [ˈdumzˌde] *s* giorno del giudizio
door [dor] *s* porta; (*of a carriage or automobile*) portiera, sportello; (*one part of a double door*) battente *m;* **behind closed doors** a porte chiuse; **to see to the door** accompagnare alla porta; **to show s.o. the door** mettere qlcu alla porta
door′bell′ *s* campanello della porta
door′ check′ *s* chiusura automatica di porta, scontro
door′frame′ *s* cornice *f*

door'head' *s* architrave *m*
door'jamb' *s* stipite *m*
door'keep'er *s* portinaio
door'knob' s maniglia della porta
door' knock'er *s* battente *m*
door' latch' *s* paletto
door'man' *s* (**-men'**) portiere *m*, portinaio; (*of large apartment house*) guardaportone *m*
door'mat' *s* stoino, zerbino
door'nail' *s* borchione *m*; **dead as a doornail** morto e ben morto
door'post' *s* stipite *m*
door' scrap'er *s* raschietto
door'sill' *s* soglia
door'step' *s* gradino davanti la porta
door'stop' *s* paracolpi *m*
door'-to-door' *adj* (*shipment*) diretto; (*selling*) di porta in porta
door'way' *s* vano della porta; porta
dope [dop] *s* lubrificante *m*; (aer) vernice *f*; (slang) stupido, scemo; (slang) informazioni *fpl*; (slang) narcotico ‖ *tr* (slang) narcotizzare; **to dope out** (slang) indovinare, decifrare, immaginare
dope' fiend' *s* (slang) tossicomane *mf*
dope'sheet' *s* giornaletto con le previsioni della corse ippiche
dormant ['dɔrmənt] *adj* dormente; latente
dor'mer win'dow ['dɔrmər] *s* abbaino
dormito·ry ['dɔrmɪ,tori] *s* (**-ries**) dormitorio
dor·mouse ['dɔr,maʊs] *s* (**-mice** [,maɪs]) ghiro
dosage ['dosɪdʒ] *s* dosatura
dose [dos] *s* dose *f*; (coll) boccone amaro ‖ *tr* dosare; somministrare
dossier ['dɑsɪ,e] *s* incartamento
dot [dɑt] *s* punto; **on the dot** (coll) in punto ‖ *v* (*pret & pp* **dotted**; *ger* **dotting**) *tr* punteggiare; **to dot one's i's** mettere i punti sulle i
dotage ['dotɪdʒ] *s* rimbecillimento; **to be in one's dotage** essere rimbambito
dotard ['dotərd] *s* vecchio rimbambito
dote [dot] *intr* rimbambirsi; **to dote on** essere pazzo per
doting ['dotɪŋ] *adj* che ama alla follia; (*from old age*) rimbambito, rimbecillito
dots' and dash'es *spl* (telg) punti *mpl* e tratti *mpl*
dot'ted line' *s* linea punteggiata; **to sign on the dotted line** firmare inconsideratamente
double ['dʌbəl] *adj* doppio ‖ *s* doppio; (bridge) contre *m*; **doubles** (tennis) doppio ‖ *tr* raddoppiare; (bridge) contrare ‖ *intr* raddoppiarsi; (bridge) contrare; (mov, theat) sostenere due ruoli; (mov) doppiare; **to double up** (*said of two people*) dividere la stessa camera, dividere lo stesso letto; piegarsi in due
double-barreled ['dʌbəl'bærəld] *adj* a due canne; (fig) a doppio fine
dou'ble bass' *s* contrabbasso
dou'ble bed' *s* letto matrimoniale
dou'ble boil'er *s* bagnomaria *m*
double-breasted ['dʌbəl'brɛstɪd] *adj* a doppio petto, doppiopetto
dou'ble chin' *s* pappagorgia
dou'ble-cross' *tr* (coll) tradire
dou'ble date' *s* (coll) appuntamento amoroso di due coppie
dou'ble-deal'ing *adj* doppio
dou'ble-deck'er *s* (*bed*) letto a castello; (*sandwich*) tramezzino doppio; autobus *m* a due piani; (naut) nave *f* due ponti; (aer) aereo due ponti
double-edged ['dʌbəl'ɛdʒd] *adj* a due tagli, a doppio taglio
dou'ble en'try *s* (com) partita doppia
dou'ble fea'ture *s* (mov) programma *m* di due lungometraggio
double-header ['dʌbəl'hɛdər] *s* treno con due locomotive; due partite di baseball giocate successivamente
double-jointed ['dʌbəl'dʒɔɪntɪd] *adj* snodato
dou'ble-park' *tr & intr* parcheggiare in doppia fila
dou'ble-quick' *adj & adv* a passo di carica
dou'ble stand'ard *s*—**to have a double standard** usare due pesi e due misure
doublet ['dʌblɪt] *s* (*close-fitting jacket*) farsetto; (philol) doppione *m*
dou'ble-talk' *s* discorso incomprensibile; **to give s.o. double-talk** parlare evasivamente a qlcu ‖ *intr* parlare evasivamente
dou'ble time' *s* paga doppia; (mil) passo di carica
doubleton ['dʌbəltən] *s* doppio
doubly ['dʌbli] *adv* doppiamente
doubt [daʊt] *s* dubbio; **beyond doubt** senza dubbio; **if in doubt** in caso di dubbio; **no doubt** senza dubbio ‖ *tr* dubitare di ‖ *intr* dubitare
doubter ['daʊtər] *s* incredulo
doubtful ['daʊtfəl] *adj* incerto; dubbioso
doubtless ['daʊtlɪs] *adj* indubitabile ‖ *adv* senza dubbio; probabilmente
douche [duʃ] *s* irrigazione *f*; (*instrument*) irrigatore *m* ‖ *tr* irrigare ‖ *intr* fare irrigazioni
dough [do] *s* pasta di pane; (*money*) (slang) soldi *mpl*, quattrini *mpl*
dough'boy' *s* fantaccino americano
dough'nut' *s* ciambella; (*with filling*) sgonfiotto
dough·ty ['daʊti] *adj* (**-tier; -tiest**) forte, coraggioso
dough·y ['do·i] *adj* (**-ier; -iest**) pastoso, molle
dour [daʊr] or [dʊr] *adj* triste, severo
douse [daʊs] *tr* immergere; bagnare; (*the light*) (coll) spegnere
dove [dʌv] *s* colomba, tortora
dovecote ['dʌv,kot] *s* piccionaia
dove'tail' *s* coda di rondine ‖ *tr* calettare a coda di rondine; (*to make fit*) adattare, far combaciare ‖ *intr* (*to fit*) combaciare; corrispondere
dowager ['daʊ·ədʒər] *s* vedova titolata; vecchia signora austera; **queen dowager** regina madre
dow·dy ['daʊdi] *adj* (**-dier; -diest**) trasandato

dow•el ['dau·əl] *s* caviglia, tassello || *v* (*pret & pp* **-eled** or **-elled;** *ger* **-eling** or **-elling**) *tr* tassellare

dower ['dau·ər] *s* (*widow's portion*) legittima, vedovile *m;* (*marriage portion; natural gift*) dote *f* || *tr* dotare; assegnare un vedovile a

down [daun] *adj* che discende; basso; (*train*) che va al centro; depresso; finito; (*money, payment*) anticipato; (*storage battery*) esaurito || *s* (*of fruit and human body*) lanugine *f;* (*of birds*) piumino; (*upset*) rovescio; discesa; (*sandhill*) duna || *adv* giù; all'ingiù, in giù; dabbasso; a terra; al sud; (*in cash*) a contanti; **down and out** rovinato; senza una soldo; **down from** da; **down on one's knees** in ginocchio; **down to** fino a; **down under** agli antipodi; **down with . . . !** abasso . . . !; **to get down to work** mettersi seriamente al lavoro; **to go down** scendere; **to lie down** sdraiarsi; andare a letto; **to sit down** sedersi || *prep* giù per; **down the river** a valle; **down the street** giù per la strada || *tr* abbattere; (coll) buttar giù, tracannare

down'cast' *adj* mogio, sfiduciato

down'fall' *s* rovina, rovescio

down'grade' *adj & adv* in declivio, a valle || *s* discesa; **to be on the downgrade** essere in declino || *tr* attribuire minor importanza a; degradare

downhearted ['daun,hartıd] *adj* scoraggiato, abbattuto

down'hill' *adj & adv* in declivio; **to go downhill** declinare

down' pay'ment *s* acconto

down'pour' *s* acquazzone *m,* rovescio

down'right' *adj* assoluto; completo; franco, diretto || *adv* completamente

down'stairs' *adj* del piano di sotto || *s* il piano di sotto; i piani di sotto || *adv* dabbasso, di sotto, giù

down'stream' *adv* a valle

down'stroke' *s* corsa discendente

down'town' *adj* centrale || *s* centro della città || *adv* al centro della città

down' train' *s* treno discendente, treno che va al centro

down'trend' *s* tendenza al ribasso

downtrodden ['daun,tradən] *adj* calpestato, oppresso

downward ['daunwərd] *adj & adv* all'ingiù

down•y ['dauni] *adj* (**-ier; -iest**) piumoso, lanuginoso; (*soft*) molle, morbido

dow•ry ['dauri] *s* (**-ries**) dote *f*

doze [doz] *s* pisolo || *intr* dormicchiare; **to doze off** appisolarsi

dozen ['dʌzən] *s* dozzina

dozy ['dozi] *adj* sonnolento

drab [dræb] *adj* (**drabber; drabbest**) grigiastro; (*dull*) scialbo || *s* colore grigiastro; (*fabric*) tela naturale; donna di malaffare

drach•ma ['drækmə] *s* (**-mas** or **-mae** [mi]) dramma

draft [dræft] or [draft] *s* corrente *f* d'aria; (*pulling*) tiro; (*in a chimney*) tiraggio; (*sketch, outline*) schizzo; (*first form of a writing*) prima stesura; (*drink*) sorso, bicchiere *m;* (com) tratta, lettera di credito; (law) progetto, disegno; (naut) pesca; (mil) coscrizione *f,* leva; **on draft** alla spina || *tr* disegnare; fare uno schizzo di; (*a document*) stendere; (mil) coscrivere; **to be drafted** essere di leva, andar coscritto

draft' age' *s* età *f* di leva

draft' beer' *s* birra alla spina

draft' board' *s* consiglio di leva

draft' dodg'er ['dadʒər] *s* renitente *m* alla leva, imboscato

draftee [,dræf'ti] or [,draf'ti] *s* coscritto

draft' horse' *s* cavallo da tiro

drafts'man *s* (**-men**) disegnatore *m;* (*man who draws up documents*) redattore *m*

draft' trea'ty *s* progetto di trattato

draft•y ['dræfti] or ['drafti] *adj* (**-ier; -iest**) pieno di correnti d'aria

drag [dræg] *s* (*sledge for conveying heavy bodies*) traino, treggia; (*on a cigarette*) boccata; (aer) resistenza aerodinamica; (naut) pressione idrostatica; (naut) draga; (fig) noia; (*influence*) (slang) aderenze *fpl;* (*a bore*) (slang) rompiscatole *m* || *v* (*pret & pp* **dragged;** *ger* **dragging**) *tr* strascinare, strascicare; (naut) rastrellare || *intr* strascicare, strascicarsi; dilungarsi; **to drag on** andare per le lunghe

drag'net' *s* paranza; (fig) retata

dragon ['drægən] *s* drago, dragone *m*

drag'on•fly' *s* (**-flies**) libellula

dragoon [drə'gun] *s* (mil) dragone *m* || *tr* forzare, costringere

drain [dren] *s* scolo; prosciugamento; (geog) spiovente *m;* (surg) drenaggio; (fig) salasso || *tr* (*a liquid*) scolare; prosciugare; (*humid land; a wound*) drenare || *intr* scolare; prosciugarsi; (geog) defluire

drainage ['drenıdʒ] *s* drenaggio; (geog) displuvio, spartiacque *m*

drain'board' *s* scolatoio per le stoviglie

drain' cock' *s* rubinetto di scarico

drain'pipe' *s* tubo di scarico

drake [drek] *s* anatra maschio

dram [dræm] *s* dramma; bicchierino di liquore

drama ['dramə] or ['dræmə] *s* dramma *m;* (*art and genre*) drammatica

dramatic [drə'mætık] *adj* drammatico || **dramatics** *ssg* drammatica; *spl* rappresentazione dilettantesca; comportamento drammatico

dramatist ['dræmətıst] *s* drammaturgo

dramatize ['dræmə,taız] *tr* drammatizzare

drape [drep] *s* tenda, cortina; (*of a curtain*) drappeggio; (*of a skirt*) taglio || *tr* drappeggiare

draper•y ['drepəri] *s* (**-ies**) drapperia; negozio di tessuti; **draperies** tendaggi *mpl*

drastic ['dræstık] *adj* drastico

draught [dræft] or [drɑft] *s & tr* var of **draft**
draught' beer' *s* birra alla spina
draw [drɔ] *s* (*in a game*) patta; (*in a lottery*) sorteggio; (*act of drawing*) tiro; (*of chimney*) tiraggio; (*attraction*) attrazione; (*of a drawbridge*) ala || *v* (*pret* **drew** [dru]; *pp* **drawn** [drɔn]) *tr* (*a line*) tirare; (*to attract*) richiamare; (*butter*) fondere; (*a sword*) sguainare; (*a nail*) estrarre; (*people*) attrarre; (*a sigh*) emettere; (*a curtain*) far scorrere; (*a salary*) pigliare; (*a prize*) ricevere; (*a game*) impattare; (*in card games*) pescare; (*a drawbridge*) sollevare; (*said of a ship*) pescare; (*a comparison*) fare; (*a profit*) ricavare; (*a chicken*) sventrare; (*e.g., a picture*) disegnare, ritrarre; (*to sketch in words*) descrivere; (*a contract*) stipulare; (*interest*) ricevere; (com) spiccare, staccare; **to draw forth** far uscire; **to draw off** estrarre; (*a liquid*) spillare; **to draw** (*shoes*) **on** mettersi; **to draw** (*money*) **on** ritirare da; **to draw** (*a draft*) **on** domiciliare presso; **to draw oneself up** raddrizzarsi; **to draw out** (*to persuade to talk*) far parlare, tirar fuori le parole a; **to draw up** (*a document*) estendere; (mil) schierare || *intr* (*said of chimney*) tirare; impattare; sorteggiare un premio; aver attrazione; disegnare; **to draw aside** scostarsi; **to draw back** retrocedere, ritirarsi; **to draw near** avvicinarsi; volgere a; **to draw to a close** essere quasi finito; **to draw together** unirsi
draw'back' *s* inconveniente *m*
draw'bridge' *s* ponte levatoio
drawee [ˌdrɔ'i] *s* trattario, trassato
drawer ['drɔ·ər] *s* disegnatore *m;* (com) traente *m* || [drɔr] *s* cassetto; **drawers** mutande *fpl*
drawing ['drɔ·ɪŋ] *s* disegno; (*in a lottery*) sorteggio
draw'ing board' *s* tavolo da disegno
draw'ing card' *s* attrazione
draw'ing room' *s* salotto, salottino
draw'knife' *s* (**-knives** [ˌnaɪvz]) coltello a petto
drawl [drɔl] *s* accento strascicato || *tr* dire con accento strascicato || *intr* strascicare le parole
drawn' but'ter *s* burro fuso
drawn' work' *s* lavoro a giorno
dray [dre] *s* carro pesante; slitta, treggia; autocarro
drayage ['dre·ɪdʒ] *s* carreggio
dray'man *s* (**-men**) carrettiere *m*
dread [drɛd] *adj* spaventoso, terribile || *s* spavento, terrore *m* || *tr & intr* temere
dreadful ['drɛdfəl] *adj* spaventevole, terribile; (coll) orribile
dread'nought' *s* corazzata
dream [drim] *s* sogno; illusione, fantasticheria; **dream come true** sogno fatto realtà || *v* (*pret & pp* **dreamed** or **dreamt** [drɛmt]) *tr* sognare; **to dream up** (coll) immaginare, fantasticare || *intr* sognare
dreamer ['drimər] *s* sognatore *m*
dream'land' *s* paese *m* dei sogni
dream·y ['drimi] *adj* (**-ier; -iest**) sognante; (*visionary*) trasognato; vago
drear·y ['drɪri] *adj* (**-ier; -iest**) squallido; triste; (*boring*) noioso
dredge [drɛdʒ] *s* draga || *tr* dragare; (culin) infarinare
dredger ['drɛdʒər] *s* (*boat*) draga; (*container*) spolverino
dredging ['drɛdʒɪŋ] *s* dragaggio
dregs [drɛgz] *spl* feccia
drench [drɛntʃ] *tr* infradiciare, inzuppare
dress [drɛs] *s* vestito; vestiti *mpl;* vestito da donna; abito; abito da cerimonia; (*of a bird*) piumaggio || *tr* vestire; adornare, decorare; (*hair*) pettinare; (*a wound*) medicare; (*leather*) conciare; (*food*) condire; (*a boat*) pavesare; **to dress down** (coll) rimproverare; **to get dressed** vestirsi || *intr* vestire; vestirsi; (mil) schierarsi; **to dress up** vestirsi da sera; farsi bello, mettersi in gala
dress' ball' *s* ballo di gala
dress' coat' *s* frac *m*
dresser ['drɛsər] *s* toletta; (*sideboard*) credenza; **to be a good dresser** vestire con eleganza
dress' goods' *spl* stoffa per abiti
dressing ['drɛsɪŋ] *s* ornamento; (*for food*) condimento, salsa; (*stuffing for fowl*) ripieno; (*fertilizer*) concime *m;* (*for a wound*) medicazione
dress'ing down' *s* ramanzina
dress'ing gown' *s* vestaglia
dress'ing room' *s* spogliatoio, toletta; (theat) camerino
dress'ing sta'tion *s* posto di pronto soccorso
dress'ing ta'ble *s* toletta, specchiera
dress'mak'er *s* sarta, sarto per donna
dress'mak'ing *s* taglio, sartoria
dress' rehears'al *s* prova generale
dress' shirt' *s* camicia inamidata
dress' suit' *s* marsina
dress' u'niform *s* (mil) alta uniforme
dress·y ['drɛsi] *adj* (**-ier; iest**) (coll) elegante, ricercato
dribble ['drɪbəl] *s* goccia || *tr* (sports) palleggiare, dribblare || *intr* gocciolare; (*at the mouth*) sbavare; (sports) dribblare
driblet ['drɪblɪt] *s* piccola quantità; **in driblets** col contagocce
dried' beef' [draɪd] *s* carne seccata
dried' fruit' *s* frutta secca
drier ['draɪ·ər] *s* (*for hair*) asciugacapelli *m;* (*for clothes*) asciugatrice *f*
drift [drɪft] *s* movimento; (*of sand, snow, etc.*) cumulo; (*snowdrift*) neve accumulata dal vento; tendenza, corrente *f;* intenzione; (aer, naut) deriva; (rad, telv) deviazione || *intr* andare alla deriva; (*said of snow*) accumularsi; (aer, naut) derivare, scadere
drift' ice' *s* ghiaccio alla deriva
drift'pin' *s* (mach) mandrino
drift'wood' *s* legname andato alla deriva

drill [drɪl] *s* esercizio; (*fabric*) tela cruda; (agr) seminatrice *f;* (mach) trapano, trivella; (mil) esercitazioni *fpl* militari || *tr* trivellare; istruire; (mil) insegnare gli esercizi militari a || *intr* addestrarsi; (mil) fare gli esercizi militari
drill'mas'ter *s* istruttore *m*
drill' press' *s* trapano a colonna
drink [drɪŋk] *s* bevanda; **the drinks are on the house!** paga il proprietario! || *v* (*pret* **drank** [dræŋk]; *pp* **drunk** [drʌŋk]) *tr* bere; assorbire; **to drink down** tracannare; **to drink in** bere, assorbire; (*air*) aspirare || *intr* bere; **to drink out of** bere da; **to drink to the health of** bere alla salute di
drinkable ['drɪŋkəbəl] *adj* bevibile, potabile
drinker ['drɪŋkər] *s* bevitore *m*
drinking ['drɪnkɪŋ] *s* (il) bere
drink'ing foun'tain *s* fontanella pubblica
drink'ing song' *s* canzone bacchica
drink'ing straw' *s* cannuccia
drink'ing trough' *s* abbeveratoio
drink'ing wa'ter *s* acqua potabile
drip [drɪp] *s* sgocciolo, sgocciolatura || *v* (*pret & pp* **dripped;** *ger* **dripping**) *intr* sgocciolare, stillare; (*said of perspiration*) trasudare
drip' cof'fee *s* caffè fatto con la macchinetta
drip'-dry' *adj* non-stiro
drip' pan' *s* (culin) ghiotta; (mach) coppa
dripping ['drɪpɪŋ] *s* gocciolio; **drippings** grasso che cola dall'arrosto
drive [draɪv] *s* scarrozzata; strada; passeggiata; impulso; forza, iniziativa; urgenza; spinta; campagna; (aut) trazione; (mach) trasmissione || *v* (*pret* **drove** [drov]; *ger* **driven** ['drɪvən]) *tr* (*a nail*) ficcare, piantare; (*e.g., cattle*) condurre, parare; (*s.o. in a carriage or auto*) condurre, portare; spingere; stimulare; forzare; spingere a lavorare; (sports) colpire molto forte; **to drive away** scacciare; **to drive back** respingere; **to drive mad** far impazzire; **to drive out** scacciare || *intr* fare una scarrozzata; **to drive at** parare a; voler dire; **to drive hard** lavorare sodo; **to drive in** entrare in automobile; (*a place*) entrare in automobile in; **to drive on the right** guidare a destra; **to drive out** uscire in macchina; **to drive up** arrivare in macchina
drive'-in' mov'ie the'ater *s* cineparco
drive'-in' res'taurant *s* ristorante *m* con servizio alla portiera
driv•el ['drɪvəl] *s* (*slobber*) bava; (*nonsense*) scemenza || *v* (*pret* **-eled** or **-elled;** *ger* **-eling** or **-elling**) *intr* sbavare; dire scemenze
driver ['draɪvər] *s* guidatore *m;* (*of a carriage*) cocchiere *m;* (*of a locomotive*) macchinista *m;* (*of pack animals*) carrettiere *m,* mulattiere *m*
driv'er's li'cense *s* patente automobilistica
driv'er's seat' *s* posto di guida
drive' shaft' *s* albero motore
drive'way' *s* strada privata d'accesso; carrozzabile *f*
drive' wheel' *s* ruota motrice
driv'ing school' ['draɪvɪŋ] *s* autoscuola, scuola guida
drizzle ['drɪzəl] *s* pioviggine *f* || *intr* piovigginare
droll [drol] *adj* buffo, spassoso
dromedar•y ['drɑmə ˌdɛri] *s* (**-ies**) dromedario
drone [dron] *s* fuco, pecchione *m;* (*hum*) ronzio; (*of bagpipe*) bordone *m;* areoplano teleguidato || *tr* dire in tono monotono || *intr* (*to live in idleness*) fare il fannullone; (*to buzz, hum*) ronzare
drool [drul] *s* (*slobber*) bava; (slang) scemenza || *intr* sbavare; (slang) dire scemenze
droop [drup] *s* accasciamento || *intr* (*to sag*) pendere; (*to lose spirit*) accasciarsi; (*said, e.g., of wheat*) avvizzire
drooping ['drupɪŋ] *adj* (*eyelid*) abbassato; (*shoulder*) spiovente; (fig) accasciato
drop [drɑp] *s* goccia; (*slope*) pendenza; (*earring*) pendente *m;* (*in temperature*) discesa; (*from an airplane*) lancio; (*trap door*) botola; (*gallows*) trabocchetto della forca; (*lozenge*) pastiglia; (*slit for letters*) buca; (*curtain*) tela; (*in prices*) calo; **a drop in the bucket** una goccia nell'oceano || *v* (*pret & pp* **dropped;** *ger* **dropping**) *tr* lasciar cadere; (*a letter*) imbucare; (*a curtain*) abbassare; (*a remark*) lasciar scappare; (*a note*) scrivere; omettere; abbandonare; (*anchor*) gettare; (*from an airplane*) lanciare; (*from an automobile*) lasciare; (*from a list*) cancellare || *intr* cadere; lasciarsi cadere; terminare; **to drop dead** cader morto; **to drop in** entrare un momento; **to drop off** sparire; addormentarsi; morire improvvisamente; **to drop out** scomparire; ritirarsi; dare le dimissioni
drop' cur'tain *s* telone *m*
drop' ham'mer *s* maglio
drop'-leaf' ta'ble *s* tavola a ribalta
drop'light' *s* lampada sospesa
drop'out' *s* studente *m* che abbandona permanentemente la scuola media
dropper ['drɑpər] *s* contagocce *m*
dropsical ['drɑpsɪkəl] *adj* idropico
dropsy ['drɑpsi] *s* idropisia
dross [drɔs] or [drɑs] *s* scoria; (fig) feccia
drought [draʊt] *s* siccità *f;* (*shortage*) mancanza
drove [drov] *s* branco; folla; **in droves** in massa
drover ['drovər] *s* mandriano
drown [draʊn] *tr & intr* affogare, annegare
drowse [draʊz] *intr* sonnecchiare
drow•sy ['draʊzi] *adj* (**-sier; -siest**) sonnolento, insonnolito
drub [drʌb] *v* (*pret & pp* **drubbed;** *ger* **drubbing**) *tr* bastonare; battere

drudge [drʌdʒ] *s* sgobbone *m* || *intr* sgobbare, sfacchinare
drudger·y ['drʌdʒəri] *s* (**-ies**) lavoro ingrato, sfacchinata
drug [drʌg] *s* droga, medicina; narcotico; **drug on the market** merce *f* invendibile || *v* (*pret & pp* **drugged**; *ger* **drugging**) *tr* drogare, narcotizzare
drug' ad'dict *s* tossicomane *mf*
drug' addic'tion *s* tossicomania
druggist ['drʌgɪst] *s* farmacista *mf*
drug' hab'it *s* tossicomania
drug'store' *s* farmacia
drug' traf'fic *s* traffico in stupefacenti
druid ['dru·ɪd] *s* druida *m*
drum [drʌm] *s* (*cylinder; instrument*) tamburo; (*container*) fusto || *v* (*pret & pp* **drummed**; *ger* **drumming**) *tr* stamburare; **to drum up** (*customers*) farsi; (*enthusiasm*) creare || *intr* tambureggiare; (*with the fingers*) tamburellare
drum'beat' *s* rullo di tamburi
drum' corps' *s* banda di tamburi
drum'fire' *s* fuoco nutrito
drum'head' *s* membrana del tamburo
drum' ma'jor *s* tamburo maggiore
drummer ['drʌmər] *s* (*salesman*) agente *m* viaggiatore; (mus) tamburo; (mil) tamburino
drum'stick' *s* bacchetta del tamburo; (*of cooked fowl*) coscia
drunk [drʌŋk] *adj* ubriaco; **to get drunk** ubriacarsi || *s* ubriaco; (*spree*) sbornia; **to go on a drunk** (coll) ubriacarsi
drunkard ['drʌŋkərd] *s* ubriacone *m*
drunken ['drʌŋkən] *adj* ubriaco
drunk'en driv'ing *s*—**to be arrested for drunken driving** esser arrestato per aver guidato in stato di ubriachezza
drunkenness ['drʌŋkənnɪs] *s* ubriachezza, ebbrezza
dry [draɪ] *adj* (**drier**; **driest**) secco; (*boring*) arido; **to be dry** aver sete || *s* (**drys**) abolizionista *mf* || *v* (*pret & pp* **dried**) *tr* seccare; (*to wipe dry*) asciugare || *intr* seccarsi; **to dry up** prosciugarsi, essiccarsi; (slang) star zitto
dry' bat'tery *s* pila a secco; (*group of dry cells*) batteria a secco
dry' cell' *s* pila a secco
dry'-clean' *tr* lavare a secco, pulire a secco
dry' clean'er *s* tintore *m*
dry' clean'ing *s* lavaggio a secco, pulitura a secco
dry'-clean'ing estab'lishment *s* tintoria
dry' dock' *s* bacino di carenaggio
dryer ['draɪ·ər] *s* var of **drier**
dry'-eyed' *adj* a occhi asciutti
dry' farm'ing *s* coltivazione di terreno arido
dry' goods' *spl* tessuti *mpl*; aridi *mpl*
dry'-goods store' *s* drapperia, negozio di tessuti
dry' ice' *s* neve carbonica, ghiaccio secco
dry' law' *s* legge *f* proibizionista
dry' meas'ure *s* misura per solidi
dryness ['draɪnɪs] *s* siccità *f*; (*e.g., of a speaker*) aridità *f*
dry' nurse' *s* balia asciutta
dry' run' *s* esercizio di prova; (mil) esercitazione senza munizioni
dry' sea'son *s* stagione arida
dry' wash' *s* roba lavata e asciugata ma non stirata
dual ['dju·əl] or ['du·əl] *adj & s* duale *m*
duali·ty [dju'ælɪti] or [du'ælɪti] *s* (**-ties**) dualità *f*
dub [dʌb] *s* (slang) giocatore inesperto || *v* (*pret & pp* **dubbed**; *ger* **dubbing**) *tr* chiamare, affibbiare il nome di; (*a knight*) armare; (mov) doppiare
dubbing ['dʌbɪŋ] *s* doppiaggio
dubious ['djubɪ·əs] or ['dubɪ·əs] *adj* dubbioso; incerto
ducat ['dʌkət] *s* ducato
duchess ['dʌtʃɪs] *s* duchessa
duch·y ['dʌtʃi] *s* (**-ies**) ducato
duck [dʌk] *s* anatra; mossa rapida; (*in the water*) tuffo; (*dodge*) schivata; **ducks** pantaloni *mpl* di tela cruda || *tr* (*one's head*) abbassare rapidamente; (*in water*) tuffare; (*a blow*) schivare || *intr* tuffarsi; **to duck out** (coll) svignarsela
duckling ['dʌklɪŋ] *s* anatroccolo
ducks' and drakes' *s*—**to play ducks and drakes with** buttar via, sperperare
duck' soup' *s* (slang) cosa facilissima
duct [dʌkt] *s* tubo, condotto
ductile ['dʌktɪl] *adj* duttile
duct'less gland' ['dʌktlɪs] *s* ghiandola a secrezione interna
duct'work' *s* condotto, canalizzazione
dud [dʌd] *s* (slang) bomba inesplosa; (*person*) (slang) fallito; (*enterprise*) (slang) fallimento; **duds** (coll) vestito; roba
dude [djud] or [dud] *s* elegantone *m*
due [dju] or [du] *adj* dovuto; atteso, debito; pagabile; **due to** dovuto a; **to fall due** scadere; **when is the train due?** a che ora arriva il treno? || *s* spettanza; debito; **dues** (*of a member*) quota sociale; **to get one's due** ricevere quanto uno merita; **to give the devil his due** trattare ognuno con giustizia || *adv* in direzione, e.g., **due north** in direzione nord
duel ['dju·əl] or ['du·əl] *s* duello; **to fight a duel** battersi a duello || *v* (*pret & pp* **dueled** or **duelled**; *ger* **dueling** or **duelling**) *intr* duellare
duelist or **duellist** ['dju·əlɪst] or ['du·əlɪst] *s* duellante *mf*
dues-paying ['djuz,pe·ɪŋ] or ['duz,pe·ɪŋ] *adj* regolare, effettivo
duet [dju'et] or [du'et] *s* duetto
duf'fel bag' ['dʌfəl] *s* sacca da viaggio
duke [djuk] or [duk] *s* duca *m*
dukedom ['djukdəm] or ['dukdəm] *s* ducato
dull [dʌl] *adj* (*not sharp*) spuntato, senza filo; (*color*) spento, sbiadito; (*sound, pain*) sordo; (*stupid*) ebete, tonto; (*business*) inattivo; (*boring*) noioso, melenso; (*flat*) opaco, appannato || *tr* spuntare; sbiadire; inebetire; ottundere; (*enthusiasm*) raffreddare; (*pain*) alleviare || *intr*

spuntarsi; sbiadirsi; inebetirsi; raffreddarsi
dullard ['dʌlərd] *s* stupido
duly ['djuli] or ['duli] *adv* debitamente
dumb [dʌm] *adj* (*lacking the power to speak*) muto; (coll) tonto, stupido
dumb'bell' *s* manubrio; (slang) zuccone *m*, stupido
dumb' crea'ture *s* animale *m*, bruto
dumb' show' *s* pantomima
dumb'wai'ter *s* montavivande *m*
dumfound [,dʌm'faʊnd] *tr* interdire, lasciare esterrefatto
dum•my ['dʌmi] *adj* copiato; falso || *s* (**-mies**) (*dress form*) manichino; (*in card games*) morto; (*figurehead*) uomo di paglia, prestanome *m;* (*skeleton copy of a book*) menabò *m;* copia; (slang) stupido, tonto
dump [dʌmp] *s* immondezzaio; mucchio di spazzature; (mil) deposito munizioni; (min) montagnetta di scarico; **to be down in the dumps** (coll) avere le paturnie || *tr* scaricare; (*to tip over*) rovesciare; (com) scaricare sul mercato; (com) vendere sottocosto
dumping ['dʌmpɪŋ] *s* scarico; (com) dumping *m*
dumpling ['dʌmplɪŋ] *s* gnocco
dump' truck' *s* ribaltabile *m*
dump•y ['dʌmpi] *adj* (**-ier; -iest**) grassoccio, tarchiato
dun [dʌn] *adj* bruno grigiastro || *s* creditore importuno; (*demand for payment*) sollecitazione di pagamento || *v* (*pret & pp* **dunned;** *ger* **dunning**) *tr* sollecitare
dunce [dʌns] *s* ignorante *mf*, zuccone *m*
dunce' cap' *s* berretto d'asino
dune [djun] or [dun] *s* duna
dung [dʌŋ] *s* sterco, letame *m* || *tr* concimare con il letame
dungarees [,dʌŋgə'riz] *spl* tuta di cotone blu
dungeon ['dʌndʒən] *s* carcere sotterraneo; (*fortified tower*) torrione *m*, maschio
dung'hill' *s* letamaio
dunk [dʌŋk] *tr* inzuppare
du•o ['dju•o] or ['du•o] *s* (**-os**) duo
duode•num [,dju•ə'dinəm] or [,du•ə'dinəm] *s* (**-na** [nə]) duodeno
dupe [djup] or [dup] *s* gonzo || *tr* gabbare, ingannare
du'plex house' ['djuplɛks] or ['duplɛks] *s* casa di due appartamenti
duplicate ['djuplɪkɪt] or ['duplɪkɪt] *adj & s* duplicato || ['djuplɪ,ket] or ['duplɪ,ket] *tr* duplicare
du'plicating machine' *s* duplicatore *m*
duplici•ty [dju'plɪsɪti] or [du'plɪsɪti] *s* (**-ties**) duplicità *f*, doppiezza
durable ['djurəbəl] or ['durəbəl] *adj* durabile, duraturo
du'rable goods' *spl* beni *mpl* durevoli
duration [djʊ'reʃən] or [dʊ'reʃən] *s* durata
during ['djurɪŋ] or ['durɪŋ] *prep* durante
du'rum wheat' ['durəm] or ['djurəm] *s* grano duro
dusk [dʌsk] *s* crepuscolo
dust [dʌst] *s* polvere *f* || *tr* (*to free of dust*) spolverare; (*to sprinkle with dust*) spolverizzare; **to dust off** (slang) rimettere in uso; (slang) spolverare le spalle a
dust' bowl' *s* regione polverosissima
dust'cloth' *s* strofinaccio
dust' cloud' *s* polverone *m*
duster ['dʌstər] *s* (*cloth*) cencio; (*light overgarment*) spolverino
dust' jack'et *s* sopraccoperta
dust'pan' *s* pattumiera
dust' rag' *s* strofinaccio
dust•y ['dʌsti] *adj* (**-ier; -iest**) polveroso; grigiastro
Dutch [dʌtʃ] *adj* olandese; (slang) tedesco || *s* (*language*) olandese *m;* (*language*) (slang) tedesco; **in Dutch** (slang) in disgrazia; (slang) nei pasticci; **the Dutch** gli olandesi; (slang) i tedeschi; **to go Dutch** (coll) pagare alla romana
Dutch'man *s* (**-men**) olandese *m;* (slang) tedesco
Dutch' treat' *s* invito alla romana
dutiable ['djutɪ•əbəl] or ['dutɪ•əbəl] *adj* soggetto a dogana
dutiful ['djutɪfəl] or ['dutɪfəl] *adj* obbediente, doveroso
du•ty ['djuti] or ['duti] *s* (**-ties**) dovere *m;* (*task*) funzione; dazio, dogana; **off duty** libero; in libera uscita; **on duty** in servizio; di guardia; **to do one's duty** fare il proprio dovere; **to take up one's duties** entrare in servizio
du'ty-free' *adj* esente da dogana
dwarf [dwɔrf] *adj & s* nano || *tr* rimpiccolire || *intr* rimpiccolire; apparire più piccolo
dwarfish ['dwɔrfɪʃ] *adj* nano, da nano
dwell [dwɛl] *v* (*pret & pp* **dwelled** or **dwelt** [dwɛlt]) *intr* dimorare, abitare; **to dwell on** or **upon** intrattenersi su
dwelling ['dwɛlɪŋ] *s* abitazione, residenza
dwell'ing house' *s* casa d'abitazione
dwindle ['dwɪndəl] *intr* diminuire; restringersi, consumarsi
dye [daɪ] *s* tinta, colore *m* || *v* (*pret & pp* **dyed;** *ger* **dyeing**) *tr* tingere
dyed-in-the-wool ['daɪdɪnðə,wʊl] *adj* tinto prima della tessitura; completo, intransigente
dyeing ['daɪ•ɪŋ] *s* tintura
dyer ['daɪ•ər] *s* tintore *m*
dye'stuff' *s* tintura, materia colorante
dying ['daɪ•ɪŋ] *adj* morente
dynamic [daɪ'næmɪk] or [dɪ'næmɪk] *adj* dinamico
dynamite ['daɪnə,maɪt] *s* dinamite *f* || *tr* far saltare con la dinamite
dyna•mo ['daɪnə,mo] *s* (**-mos**) dinamo *f*
dynast ['daɪnæst] *s* dinasta *m*
dynas•ty ['daɪnəsti] *s* (**-ties**) dinastia
dysentery ['dɪsən,tɛri] *s* dissenteria
dyspepsia [dɪs'pɛpsɪ•ə] or [dɪs'pɛpʃə] *s* dispepsia

E

E, e [i] *s* quinta lettera dell'alfabeto inglese
each [itʃ] *adj indef* ogni || *pron indef* ognuno, ciascuno; **each other** ci; vi; si; l'un l'altro || *adv* l'uno; a testa
eager ['igər] *adj* (*enthusiastic*) ardente; **eager for** avido di; **eager to** + *inf* desideroso di + *inf*
ea'ger bea'ver *s* zelante *mf*
eagerness ['igərnɪs] *s* ardore *m;* brama
eagle ['igəl] *s* aquila
ea'gle owl' *s* gufo reale
eaglet ['iglɪt] *s* aquilotto
ear [ir] *s* orecchio; (*of corn*) pannocchia; (*of wheat*) spiga; **to be all ears** essere tutt'orecchi; **to prick up one's ears** tendere l'orecchio; **to turn a deaf ear** far l'orecchio di mercante
ear'ache' *s* mal *m* d'orecchi
ear'drop' *s* pendente *m*
ear'drum' *s* timpano
ear'flap' *s* paraorecchi *m*
earl [ʌrl] *s* conte *m*
earldom ['ʌrldəm] *s* contea
ear·ly ['ʌrli] (**-lier; -liest**) *adj* (*occurring before customary time*) di buon'ora; (*first in a series*) primo; (*far back in time*) remoto, antico; (*occurring in near future*) prossimo || *adv* presto; per tempo, di buon'ora; **as early as** (*a certain time of day*) già a; (*a certain time or date*) fin da, già in; **as early as possible** quanto prima possibile; **early in** (*e.g., the month*) all'inizio di; **early in the morning** di mattina presto, di buon mattino; **early in the year** all'inizio dell'anno
ear'ly bird' *s* persona mattiniera
ear'ly mass' *s* prima messa
ear'ly ris'er *s* persona mattiniera
ear'mark' *s* contrassegno || *tr* contrassegnare; assegnare a scopo speciale
ear'muff' *s* paraorecchi *m*
earn [ʌrn] *tr* guadagnare, guadagnarsi; (*to get one's due*) meritarsi; (*interest*) (com) produrre || *intr* trarre profitto, rendere
earnest ['ʌrnɪst] *adj* serio; fervente; **in earnest** sul serio || *s* caparra
ear'nest mon'ey *s* caparra
earnings ['ʌrnɪŋz] *s* guadagno; salario
ear'phone' *s* (*of sonar*) orecchiale *m;* (rad, telp) cuffia
ear'piece' *s* (*of eyeglasses*) susta; (telp) ricevitore *m*
ear'ring' *s* orecchino
ear'shot' *s* tiro dell'orecchio; **within earshot** a portata di voce
ear'split'ting *adj* assordante
earth [ʌrθ] *s* terra; **to come back to** or **down to earth** scendere dalle nuvole
earthen ['ʌrθən] *adj* di terra; di terracotta
ear'then·ware' *s* coccio, terraglie *fpl,* terracotta
earthling ['ʌrθlɪŋ] *s* terrestre *mf*
earthly ['ʌrθli] *adj* terreno, terrestre; **to be of no earthly use** non servire assolutamente a niente
earthmover ['ʌrθ ˌmuvər] *s* ruspa
earth'quake' *s* terremoto
earth'work' *s* terrapieno
earth'worm' *s* lombrico
earth·y ['ʌrθi] *adj* (**-ier; -iest**) terroso; (*coarse*) rozzo; pratico; sincero, diretto
ear' trum'pet *s* corno acustico
ear'wax' *s* cerume *m*
ease [iz] *s* facilità *f;* (*naturalness*) spigliatezza, disinvoltura; (*comfort*) benestare *m;* tranquillità *f;* **at ease!** (mil) riposo!; **with ease** con facilità || *tr* facilitare; (*a burden*) alleggerire; (*to let up on*) rallentare; mitigare; **to ease out** licenziare con le buone maniere || *intr* alleviarsi, mitigarsi, diminuire; rallentare
easel ['izəl] *s* cavalletto
easement ['izmənt] *s* attenuamento; (law) servitù *f*
easily ['izɪli] *adv* facilmente; senza dubbio; probabilmente
easiness ['izɪnɪs] *s* facilità *f;* disinvoltura; grazia, agilità *f;* indifferenza
east [ist] *adj* orientale, dell'est || *s* est *m* || *adv* verso l'est
Easter ['istər] *s* Pasqua
East'er egg' *s* uovo di Pasqua
East'er Mon'day *s* lunedì *m* di Pasqua
eastern ['istərn] *adj* orientale
East'er·tide' *s* tempo pasquale
eastward ['istwərd] *adv* verso l'est
eas·y ['izi] *adj* (**-ier; -iest**) facile; (*conducive to ease*) comodo, agiato; (*free from worry*) tranquillo; (*easygoing*) disinvolto, spigliato; (*not tight*) ampio; (*not hurried*) lento, moderato || *adv* (coll) facilmente; (coll) tranquillamente; **to take it easy** (coll) riposarsi; (coll) non prendersela; (coll) andar piano
eas'y chair' *s* poltrona
eas'y·go'ing *adj* (*person*) comodone; (*horse*) sciolto nell'andatura
eas'y mark' *s* (coll) gonzo
eas'y mon'ey *s* denaro fatto senza fatica; soldi rubati
eas'y terms' *spl* facilitazioni *fpl* di pagamento
eat [it] *v* (*pret* **ate** [et]; *pp* **eaten** ['itən]) *tr* mangiare; **to eat away** smangiare; **to eat up** mangiarsi || *intr* mangiare
eatable ['itəbəl] *adj* mangiabile || **eatables** *spl* commestibili *mpl*
eaves [ivz] *spl* gronda
eaves'drop' *v* (*pret & pp* **-dropped;** *ger* **-dropping**) *intr* origliare
ebb [ɛb] *s* riflusso; decadenza || *intr* (*said of the tide*) ritirarsi; decadere
ebb' and flow' *s* flusso e riflusso
ebb' tide' *s* riflusso, deflusso
ebon·y ['ɛbəni] *s* (**-ies**) ebano
ebullient [ɪ'bʌljənt] *adj* bollente
eccentric [ɛk'sɛntrɪk] *adj & s* eccentrico

eccentrici•ty [ˌɛksɛnˈtrɪsɪti] *s* **(-ties)** eccentricità *f*, originalità *f*
ecclesiastic [ɪˌklizɪˈæstɪk] *adj & s* ecclesiastico
echelon [ˈɛʃəˌlɑn] *s* scaglione *m;* (mil) scaglione *m* || *tr* scaglionare
ech•o [ˈɛko] *s* **(-oes)** eco || *tr* far eco a || *intr* echeggiare, riecheggiare
éclair [eˈkler] *s* dolce ripieno di crema
eclectic [ɛkˈlɛktɪk] *adj & s* eclettico
eclipse [ɪˈklɪps] *s* eclisse *f*, eclissi *f* || *tr* eclissare
eclogue [ˈɛklɔg] or [ˈɛklɑg] *s* egloga
ecology [ɪˈkɑlədʒi] *s* ecologia
economic(al) [ˌikəˈnɑmɪk(əl)] or [ˌɛkəˈnɑmɪk(əl)] *adj* economico
economics [ˌikəˈnɑmɪks] or [ˌɛkəˈnɑmɪks] *s* economia (politica)
economist [ɪˈkɑnəmɪst] *s* economista *mf*
economize [ɪˈkɑnəˌmaɪz] *tr & intr* economizzare
econo•my [ɪˈkɑnəmi] *s* **(-mies)** economia
ecosystem [ˈɛkoˌsɪstəm] *s* ecosistema *m*
ecsta•sy [ˈɛkstəsi] *s* **(-sies)** estasi *f*
ecstatic [ɛkˈstætɪk] *adj* estatico
ecumenic(al) [ˌɛkjəˈmɛnɪk(əl)] *adj* ecumenico
eczema [ˈɛksɪmə] or [ɛgˈzimə] *s* eczema *m*
ed•dy [ˈɛdi] *s* **(-dies)** turbine *m* || *v* (*pret & pp* **-died**) *tr & intr* turbinare
edelweiss [ˈedəlˌvaɪs] *s* stella alpina
edge [ɛdʒ] *s* (*of knife, sword, etc*) filo, tagliente *m;* (*border at which a surface terminates*) orlo, bordo; (*of a wound*) labbro, margine *m;* (*of a book*) taglio; (*of a tumbler*) giro; (*of clothing*) vivagno; (*of a table*) spigolo; (slang) vantaggio; **on edge** nervoso; **to have the edge on** (coll) avere il vantaggio su; **to set the teeth on edge** far allegare i denti || *tr* affilare, aguzzare; orlare, bordare; **to edge out** riuscire ad eliminare || *intr* avanzare lentamente
edgeways [ˈɛdʒˌwez] *adv* di taglio; **to not let s.o. get a word in edgeways** non lasciar dire una parola a qlcu
edging [ˈɛdʒɪŋ] *s* orlo, bordo
edg•y [ˈɛdʒi] *adj* **(-ier; -iest)** acuto, angolare; nervoso, ansioso
edible [ˈɛdɪbəl] *adj* mangereccio, mangiabile || **edibles** *spl* commestibili *mpl*
edict [ˈidɪkt] *s* editto
edification [ˌɛdɪfɪˈkeʃən] *s* edificazione
edifice [ˈɛdɪfɪs] *s* edificio
edi•fy [ˈɛdɪˌfaɪ] *v* (*pret & pp* **-fied**) *tr* edificare
edifying [ˈɛdɪˌfaɪ•ɪŋ] *adj* edificante
edit [ˈɛdɪt] *tr* redigere; (*e.g., a manuscript*) correggere; (*an edition*) curare; (*a newspaper*) dirigere; (mov) montare
edition [ɪˈdɪʃən] *s* edizione
editor [ˈɛdɪtər] *s* (*of a newspaper or magazine*) direttore *m*, gerente *mf;* (*of an editorial*) redattore *m*, cronista *mf;* (*of a critical edition*) editore *m;* (*of a manuscript*) revisore *m*
editorial [ˌɛdɪˈtorɪ•əl] *adj* editoriale || *s* capocronaca *m*, articolo di fondo
ed'ito'rial staff' *s* redazione
ed'itor in chief' *s* gerente *mf* responsabile
educate [ˈɛdʒʊˌket] *tr* educare, erudire
education [ˌɛdʒʊˈkeʃən] *s* educazione; istruzione, insegnamento
educational [ˌɛdʒʊˈkeʃənəl] *adj* educativo
educa'tional institu'tion *s* istituto di magistero
educator [ˈɛdʒʊˌketər] *s* educatore *m*
eel [il] *s* anguilla; **to be as slippery as an eel** guizzare di mano come un'anguilla
ee•rie or **ee•ry** [ˈɪri] *adj* **(-rier; -riest)** spettrale, pauroso
efface [ɪˈfes] *tr* cancellare; **to efface oneself** eclissarsi, mettersi in disparte
effect [ɪˈfɛkt] *s* effetto; (*main idea*) tenore *m;* **in effect** in vigore; in realtà; **to go into effect** or **to take effect** andare in vigore; **to put into effect** mandare ad effetto || *tr* effettuare
effective [ɪˈfɛktɪv] *adj* efficace; (*actually in effect*) effettivo; (*striking*) che colpisce; **to become effective** entrare in vigore
effectual [ɪˈfɛktʃʊ•əl] *adj* efficace
effectuate [ɪˈfɛktʃʊˌet] *tr* effettuare
effeminacy [ɪˈfɛmɪnəsi] *s* effemminatezza
effeminate [ɪˈfɛmɪnɪt] *adj* effemminato
effervesce [ˌɛfərˈvɛs] *intr* essere in effervescenza
effervescence [ˌɛfərˈvɛsəns] *s* effervescenza
effervescent [ˌɛfərˈvɛsənt] *adj* effervescente
effete [ɪˈfit] *adj* esausto, sterile
efficacious [ˌɛfɪˈkeʃəs] *adj* efficace
effica•cy [ɛfɪkəsi] *s* **(-cies)** efficacia
efficien•cy [ɪˈfɪʃənsi] *s* **(-cies)** efficienza; (mech) rendimento, efficienza
effi'ciency engineer' *s* analista *mf* tempi e metodi
efficient [ɪˈfɪʃənt] *adj* efficiente; (*person*) abile; (mech) efficiente
effi•gy [ˈɛfɪdʒi] *s* **(-gies)** effigie *f*
effort [ˈɛfərt] *s* sforzo
effronter•y [ɪˈfrʌntəri] *s* **(-ies)** sfrontatezza, sfacciataggine *f*
effusion [ɪˈfjuʒən] *s* effusione
effusive [ɪˈfjusɪv] *adj* espansivo
egg [ɛg] *s* uovo; (slang) bravo ragazzo || *tr*—**to egg on** incitare
egg'beat'er *s* frullino, sbattiuova *m*
egg'cup' *s* portauovo
egg'head' *s* (coll) intellettuale *mf*
eggnog [ˈɛgˌnɑg] *s* zabaione *m*
egg'plant' *s* melanzana, petonciano
egg'shell' *s* guscio d'uovo
egoism [ˈɛgoˌɪzəm] or [ˈigoˌɪzəm] *s* egoismo
egoist [ˈɛgo•ɪst] or [ˈigo•ɪst] *s* egoista *mf*
egotism [ˈɛgoˌtɪzəm] or [ˈigoˌtɪzəm] *s* egotismo
egotist [ˈɛgotɪst] or [ˈigotɪst] *s* egotista *mf*

egregious [ɪˈgridʒəs] *adj* gigantesco, tremendo, marchiano
egress [ˈigres] *s* uscita
Egypt [ˈidʒɪpt] *s* l'Egitto
Egyptian [ɪˈdʒɪpʃən] *adj & s* egiziano
ei'der down' [ˈaɪdər] *s* piumino
ei'der duck' *s* edredone *m*
eight [et] *adj & pron* otto || *s* otto; **eight o'clock** le otto
eighteen [ˈetˈtin] *adj, s & pron* diciotto
eighteenth [ˈetˈtinθ] *adj, s & pron* diciottesimo || *s* (*in dates*) diciotto
eighth [etθ] *adj & s* ottavo || *s* (*in dates*) otto
eight' hun'dred *adj, s & pron* ottocento
eightieth [ˈetɪ·ɪθ] *adj, s & pron* ottantesimo
eight·y [ˈeti] *adj & pron* ottanta || *s* (**-ies**) ottanta *m;* **the eighties** gli anni ottanta
either [ˈiðər] or [ˈaɪðər] *adj* l'uno o l'altro; l'uno e l'altro; ciascuno; entrambi i, tutti e due i || *pron* l'uno o l'altro; l'uno e l'altro; entrambi || *adv*—**not either** nemmeno || *conj*—**either . . . or** o . . . o
ejaculate [ɪˈdʒækjəˌlet] *tr* esclamare; (physiol) emettere || *intr* esclamare; (physiol) avere un'eiaculazione
eject [ɪˈdʒekt] *tr* espellere, gettar fuori; (*to evict*) sfrattare
ejection [ɪˈdʒekʃən] *s* espulsione; (*of a tenant*) sfratto
ejec'tion seat' *s* sedile *m* eiettabile
eke [ik] *tr*—**to eke out a living** sbarcare il lunario
elaborate [ɪˈlæbərɪt] *adj* (*done with great care*) elaborato; (*detailed*) minuzioso; (*ornate*) ornato || [ɪˈlæbəˌret] *tr* elaborare || *intr*—**to elaborate on** or **upon** circonstanziare, particolareggiare
elapse [ɪˈlæps] *intr* passare, trascorrere
elastic [ɪˈlæstɪk] *adj & s* elastico
elasticity [ɪˌlæsˈtɪsɪti] or [ˌilæsˈtɪsɪti] *s* elasticità *f*
elated [ɪˈletɪd] *adj* esultante, gongolante
elation [ɪˈleʃən] *s* esultanza, gaudio
elbow [ˈɛlbo] *s* gomito; (*in a river*) ansa; (*of a chair*) braccio; **at one's elbow** sotto mano; **out at the elbows** coi gomiti logori; **to crook the elbow** alzare il gomito; **to rub elbows** stare gomito a gomito; **up to the elbows** fino al collo || *tr*—**to elbow one's way** aprirsi il passo a gomitate || *intr* dar gomitate
el'bow grease' *s* (coll) olio di gomiti
el'bow patch' *s* toppa al gomito
el'bow rest' *s* bracciolo
el'bow·room' *s* spazio sufficiente; libertà *f* d'azione
elder [ˈɛldər] *adj* seniore, maggiore || *s* (bot) sambuco; (eccl) maggiore *m*
el'der·ber'ry *s* (**-ries**) sambuco; (*fruit*) bacca del sambuco
elderly [ˈɛldərli] *adj* attempato, anziano
eld'er states'man *s* uomo di stato esperto
eldest [ˈɛldɪst] *adj* (il) maggiore; (il) più vecchio
elect [ɪˈlɛkt] *adj & s* eletto; **the elect** gli eletti || *tr* eleggere
election [ɪˈlɛkʃən] *s* elezione
electioneer [ɪˌlɛkʃəˈnɪr] *intr* fare una campagna elettorale
elective [ɪˈlɛktɪv] *adj* elettivo || *s* corso facoltativo
electorate [ɪˈlɛktərɪt] *s* elettorato
electric(al) [ɪˈlɛktrɪk(əl)] *adj* elettrico
elec'tric blend'er *s* frullatore *m*
elec'tric chair' *s* sedia elettrica
elec'tric cord' *s* piattina, filo elettrico
elec'tric eel' *s* gimnoto
elec'tric eye' *s* occhio elettrico
electrician [ɪˌlɛkˈtrɪʃən] or [ˌɛlɛkˈtrɪʃən] *s* elettricista *m*
electricity [ɪˌlɛkˈtrɪsɪti] or [ˌɛlɛkˈtrɪsɪti] *s* elettricità *f*
elec'tric me'ter *s* contatore *m* della luce
elec'tric per'cola'tor *s* caffettiera elettrica
elec'tric shav'er *s* rasoio elettrico
elec'tric shock' *s* scossa elettrica, elettrosquasso
elec'tric tape' *s* nastro isolante
elec'tric train' *s* elettrotreno
electri·fy [ɪˈlɛktrɪˌfaɪ] *v* (*pret & pp* **-fied**) *tr* (*to provide with electric power*) elettrificare; (*to communicate electricity to; to thrill*) elettrizzare
electrocute [ɪˈlɛktrəˌkjut] *tr* fulminare con la corrente; far morire sulla sedia elettrica
electrode [ɪˈlɛktrod] *s* elettrodo
electrolysis [ɪˌlɛkˈtrɑlɪsɪs] or [ˌɛlɛkˈtrɑlɪsɪs] *s* elettrolisi *f*
electrolyte [ɪˈlɛktrəˌlaɪt] *s* elettrolito
electromagnet [ɪˌlɛktrəˈmægnɪt] *s* elettrocalamita
electromagnetic [ɪˌlɛktrəmægˈnɛtɪk] *adj* elettromagnetico
electromotive [ɪˌlɛktrəˈmotɪv] *adj* elettromotore
electron [ɪˈlɛktrɑn] *s* elettrone *m*
electronic [ɪˌlɛkˈtrɑnɪk] or [ˌɛlɛkˈtrɑnɪk] *adj* elettronico || **electronics** *s* elettronica
electroplating [ɪˈlɛktrəˌpletɪŋ] *s* galvanostegia
electrostatic [ɪˌlɛktrəˈstætɪk] *adj* elettrostatico
electrotype [ɪˈlɛktrəˌtaɪp] *s* stereotipia || *tr* stereotipare
eleemosynary [ˌɛlɪˈmɑsɪˌnɛri] *adj* caritatevole, di beneficenza
elegance [ˈɛlɪgəns] *s* eleganza
elegant [ˈɛlɪgənt] *adj* elegante
elegiac [ˌɛlɪˈdʒaɪ·æk] *adj* elegiaco
ele·gy [ˈɛlɪdʒi] *s* (**-gies**) elegia
element [ˈɛlɪmənt] *s* elemento; **to be out of one's element** essere fuori del proprio ambiente
elementary [ˌɛlɪˈmɛntəri] *adj* elementare
elephant [ˈɛlɪfənt] *s* elefante *m*
elevate [ˈɛlɪˌvet] *tr* elevare, innalzare
elevated [ˈɛlɪˌvetɪd] *adj* elevato || *s* ferrovia soprelevata, metropolitana soprelevata
elevation [ˌɛlɪˈveʃən] *s* elevazione; (surv) quota
elevator [ˈɛlɪˌvetər] *s* ascensore *m;*

(*for freight*) montacarichi *m;* (*for hoisting grain*) elevatore *m* di grano; (*warehouse for storing grain*) deposito granaglie; (aer) timone *m* di profondità
eleven [ɪ'levən] *adj & pron* undici || *s* undici *m;* **eleven o'clock** le undici
eleventh [ɪ'levənθ] *adj, s & pron* undicesimo || *s* (*in dates*) undici *m*
elev'enth hour' *s* ultimo momento
elf [ɛlf] *s* (**elves** [ɛlvz]) elfo
elicit [ɪ'lɪsɪt] *tr* cavare, sottrarre
elide [ɪ'laɪd] *tr* elidere
eligible ['ɛlɪdʒɪbəl] *adj* eleggibile; accettabile
eliminate [ɪ'lɪmɪ,net] *tr* eliminare
elision [ɪ'lɪʒən] *s* elisione
elite [e'lit] *adj* eletto, scelto || *s*—**the elite** l'élite *f*
elk [ɛlk] *s* alce *m*
ellipse [ɪ'lɪps] *s* (geom) ellisse *f*
ellip·sis [ɪ'lɪpsɪs] *s* (**-ses** [siz]) (gram) ellissi *f*
elliptic(al) [ɪ'lɪptɪk(əl)] *adj* ellittico
elm [ɛlm] *s* olmo
elongate [ɪ'lɔŋget] or [ɪ'lɑŋget] *tr* allungare, prolungare
elope [ɪ'lop] *intr* fuggire con un amante
elopement [ɪ'lopmənt] *s* fuga con un amante
eloquence ['ɛləkwəns] *s* eloquenza
eloquent ['ɛləkwənt] *adj* eloquente
else [ɛls] *adj*—**nobody else** nessun altro; **nothing else** nient'altro; **somebody else** qualcun altro; **something else** qualcosa d'altro; **what else** che altro; **who else** chi altro; **whose else** di che altra persona || *adv*—**how else** in che altra maniera; **or else** se no; altrimenti; **when else** in che altro momento; in che altro periodo; **where else** dove mai, da che parte
else'where' *adv* altrove
elucidate [ɪ'lusɪ,det] *tr* dilucidare
elude [ɪ'lud] *tr* eludere
elusive [ɪ'lusɪv] *adj* elusivo; (*evasive*) fugace, sfuggente
emaciated [ɪ'meʃɪ,etɪd] *adj* smunto, emaciato, macilento
emanate ['ɛmə,net] *tr & intr* emanare
emancipate [ɪ'mænsɪ,pet] *tr* emancipare
embalm [ɛm'bɑm] *tr* imbalsamare
embankment [ɛm'bæŋkmənt] *s* terrapieno
embar·go [ɛm'bɑrgo] *s* (**-goes**) embargo || *tr* mettere l'embargo a
embark [ɛm'bɑrk] *intr* imbarcarsi
embarkation [,ɛmbɑr'keʃən] *s* imbarco
embarrass [ɛm'bærəs] *tr* imbarazzare, mettere a disagio; (*to impede*) imbarazzare, impacciare; mettere in difficoltà economiche
embarrassing [ɛm'bærəsɪŋ] *adj* sconcertante; imbarazzante
embarrassment [ɛm'bærəsmənt] *s* imbarazzo, disagio, confusione; impaccio; difficoltà finanziaria, dissesto
embas·sy ['ɛmbəsi] *s* (**-sies**) ambasciata
em·bed [ɛm'bɛd] *s* (*pret & pp* **-bedded;** *ger* **-bedding**) *tr* incastrare, incassare

embellish [ɛm'bɛlɪʃ] *tr* imbellire
embellishment [ɛm'bɛlɪʃmənt] *s* abbellimento; (fig) fioretto
ember ['ɛmbər] *s* brace *f;* **embers** braci *fpl*
Em'ber days' *spl* tempora *fpl*
embezzle [ɛm'bɛzəl] *tr* appropriare, malversare || *intr* appropriarsi
embezzlement [ɛm'bɛzəlmənt] *s* appropriazione indebita, malversazione; (*of public funds*) peculato
embezzler [ɛm'bɛzlər] *s* malversatore *m*
embitter [ɛm'bɪtər] *tr* amareggiare
emblazon [ɛm'blezən] *tr* blasonare; celebrare
emblem ['ɛmbləm] *s* emblema *m*
emblematic(al) [,ɛmblə'mætɪk(əl)] *adj* emblematico
embodiment [ɛm'bɑdɪmənt] *s* incarnazione, personificazione
embod·y [ɛm'bɑdi] *v* (*pret & pp* **-ied**) *tr* incarnare, personificare; incorporare
embolden [ɛm'boldən] *tr* imbaldanzire
embolism ['ɛmbə,lɪzəm] *s* embolia
emboss [ɛm'bɔs] or [ɛm'bɑs] *tr* (*metal*) sbalzare; (*paper*) goffrare
embrace [ɛm'bres] *s* abbraccio || *tr* abbracciare || *intr* abbracciarsi
embrasure [ɛm'breʒər] *s* (archit) strombatura; (mil) feritoia
embroider [ɛm'brɔɪdər] *tr* ricamare, trapuntare
embroider·y [ɛm'brɔɪdəri] *s* (**-ies**) ricamo, trapunto
embroil [ɛm'brɔɪl] *tr* ingarbugliare; (*to involve in contention*) coinvolgere
embroilment [ɛm'brɔɪlmənt] *s* imbroglio; (*in contention*) disaccordo
embry·o ['ɛmbrɪ,o] *s* (**-os**) embrione *m*
embryology [,ɛmbrɪ'ɑlədʒi] *s* embriologia
embryonic [,ɛmbrɪ'ɑnɪk] *adj* embrionale
emcee ['ɛm'si] *s* presentatore *m* || *tr* presentare
emend [ɪ'mɛnd] *tr* emendare
emendation [,imɛn'deʃən] *s* emendamento
emerald ['ɛmərəld] *s* smeraldo
emerge [ɪ'mʌrdʒ] *intr* emergere
emergence [ɪ'mʌrdʒəns] *s* emergenza
emergen·cy [ɪ'mʌrdʒənsi] *s* (**-cies**) emergenza
emer'gency brake' *s* freno a mano
emer'gency ex'it *s* uscita di sicurezza
emer'gency land'ing *s* atterragio di fortuna
emer'gency ward' *s* sala d'urgenza
emeritus [ɪ'mɛrɪtəs] *adj* emerito
emersion [ɪ'mʌrʒən] or [ɪ'mʌrʃən] *s* emersione
emery ['ɛməri] *s* smeriglio
em'ery cloth' *s* tela smeriglio
em'ery wheel' *s* mola a smeriglio
emetic [ɪ'mɛtɪk] *adj & s* emetico
emigrant ['ɛmɪgrənt] *adj & s* emigrante *mf*
emigrate ['ɛmɪ,gret] *intr* emigrare
émigré [emi'gre] or ['ɛmɪ,gre] *s* emigrato

eminence ['ɛmɪnəns] *s* eminenza; (eccl) Eminenza
eminent ['ɛmɪnənt] *adj* eminente
emissar·y ['ɛmɪ,seri] *s* (**-ies**) emissario
emission [ɪ'mɪʃən] *s* emissione
emit [ɪ'mɪt] *v* (*pret & pp* **emitted;** *ger* **emitting**) *tr* emettere
emolument [ɪ'mɑljəmənt] *s* emolumento
emotion [ɪ'moʃən] *s* emozione
emotional [ɪ'moʃənəl] *adj* emotivo
emperor ['ɛmpərər] *s* imperatore *m*
empha·sis ['ɛmfəsɪs] *s* (**-ses** [,siz]) enfasi *f*. risalto
emphasize ['ɛmfə,saɪz] *tr* dar rilievo a, sottolineare
emphatic [ɛm'fætɪk] *adj* enfatico
emphysema [,ɛmfɪ'simə] *s* enfisema *m*
empire ['ɛmpaɪr] *s* impero
empiric(al) [ɛm'pɪrɪk(əl)] *adj* empirico
empiricist [ɛm'pɪrɪsɪst] *s* empirista *mf*
emplacement [ɛm'plesmənt] *s* piazzola, postazione
employ [ɛm'plɔɪ] *s* impiego || *tr* impiegare, usare; valersi di
employee [ɛm'plɔɪ·i] or [,ɛmplɔɪ'i] *s* impiegato, dipendente *mf*
employer [ɛm'plɔɪ·ər] *s* dirigente *mf*, datore *m* di lavoro
employment [ɛm'plɔɪmənt] *s* impiego, occupazione
employ'ment a'gency *s* agenzia di collocamento
empower [ɛm'pau·ər] *tr* autorizzare; permettere
empress ['ɛmprɪs] *s* imperatrice *f*
emptiness ['ɛmptɪnɪs] *s* vuoto
emp·ty ['ɛmpti] *adj* (**-tier; -tiest**) vuoto; (*gun*) scarico; (*hungry*) (coll) digiuno; (fig) esausto || *v* (*pret & pp* **-tied**) *tr* vuotare || *intr* vuotarsi
empty-handed ['ɛmpti'hændɪd] *adj* a mani vuote
empty-headed ['ɛmpti'hɛdɪd] *adj* dalla testa vuota, balordo
empyrean [,ɛmpɪ'ri·ən] *adj & s* empireo
emulate ['ɛmjə,let] *tr* emulare
emulator ['ɛmjə,letər] *s* emulo
emulous ['ɛmjələs] *adj* emulo
emulsi·fy [ɪ'mʌlsɪ,faɪ] *v* (*pret & pp* **-fied**) *tr* emulsionare
emulsion [ɪ'mʌlʃən] *s* emulsione
enable [ɛn'ebəl] *tr* abilitare; permettere (with *dat*)
enact [ɛn'ækt] *tr* decretare; (*a role*) rappresentare
enactment [ɛn'æktmənt] *s* legge *f*; (*of a law*) promulgazione; (*of a play*) rappresentazione
enam·el [ɪn'æməl] *s* smalto || *v* (*pret & pp* **-eled** or **-elled;** *ger* **-eling** or **-elling**) *tr* smaltare
enam'el·ware' *s* utensili *mpl* di cucina di ferro smaltato
enamor [ɛn'æmər] *tr* innamorare; **to become enamored of** innamorarsi di
encamp [ɛn'kæmp] *tr* accampare || *intr* accamparsi
encampment [ɛn'kæmpmənt] *s* campeggio; (mil) accampamento
encase [ɛn'kes] *tr* incassare
encephalitis [ɛn,sɛfə'laɪtɪs] *s* encefalite *f*
enchain [ɛn'tʃen] *tr* incatenare
enchant [ɛn'tʃænt] or [ɛn'tʃɑnt] *tr* incantare
enchantment [ɛn'tʃæntmənt] or [ɛn'tʃɑntmənt] *s* incanto, malia
enchanting [ɛn'tʃæntɪŋ] or [ɛn'tʃɑntɪŋ] *adj* incantatore, incantevole
enchantress [ɛn'tʃæntrɪs] or [ɛn'tʃɑntrɪs] *s* incantatrice *f*, maliarda
enchase [ɛn'tʃes] *tr* incastonare
encircle [ɛn'sʌrkəl] *tr* rigirare, girare intorno a; (mil) circondare
enclave ['ɛnklev] *s* enclave *f*
enclitic [ɛn'klɪtɪk] *adj* enclitico || *s* enclitica
enclose [ɛn'kloz] *tr* rinchiudere; (*in a letter*) accludere, includere; **to enclose herewith** accludere alla presente
enclosure [ɛn'kloʒər] *s* (*land surrounded by fence*) recinto, chiuso; (*e.g., letter*) allegato
encomi·um [ɛn'komɪ·əm] *s* (**-ums** or **-a** [ə]) encomio, elogio
encompass [ɛn'kʌmpəs] *tr* circondare; racchiudere, contenere
encore ['ɑŋkor] *s* bis *m* || *tr* (*a performance*) chiedere il bis di; (*a performer*) chiedere il bis a || *interj* bis!
encounter [ɛn'kauntər] *s* (*casual meeting*) incontro; (*combat*) scontro || *tr* incontrare || *intr* scontrarsi
encourage [ɛn'kʌrɪdʒ] *tr* incoraggiare; (*to foster*) favorire
encouragement [ɛn'kʌrɪdʒmənt] *s* incoraggiamento; favoreggiamento
encroach [ɛn'krotʃ] *intr*—**to encroach on** or **upon** invadere; usurpare; occupare il territorio di
encumber [ɛn'kʌmbər] *tr* imbarazzare; ingombrare; (*to load with debts, etc*) gravare
encumbrance [ɛn'kʌmbrəns] *s* imbarazzo; ingombro; gravame *m*
encyclical [ɛn'siklɪkəl] or [ɛn'saɪklɪkəl] *s* enciclica
encyclopedia [ɛn,saɪklə'pidɪ·ə] *s* enciclopedia
encyclopedic [ɛn,saɪklə'pidɪk] *adj* enciclopedico
end [ɛnd] *s* (*extremity; concluding part*) fine *f*; (*e.g., of the week*) fine *f*; (*purpose*) fine *m*; (*part adjacent to an extremity*) lembo; (*small piece*) pezza, avanzo; (*of a beam*) testata; (sports) estrema; **at the end of** in capo a; in fondo a; **in the end** alla fine, all'ultimo; **no end** (coll) moltissimo; **no end of** (coll) un mucchio di; **to make both ends meet** sbarcare il lunario; **to no end** senza effetto; **to stand on end** mettere in piedi, drizzare; mettersi diritto; (*said of hair*) drizzarsi; **to the end that** affinché || *tr* finire, terminare; **to end up** andare a finire || *intr* finire, terminare; **to end up** finire
endanger [ɛn'dendʒər] *tr* mettere in pericolo

endear [ɛn'dɪr] *tr* affezionare; **to endear oneself to** rendersi caro a
endeavor [ɛn'dɛvər] *s* tentativo, sforzo || *intr* tentare, sforzarsi
endemic [ɛn'dɛmɪk] *adj* endemico || *s* endemia
ending ['ɛndɪŋ] *s* fine *f*, conclusione; (gram) terminazione, desinenza
endive ['ɛndaɪv] *s* indivia
endless ['ɛndlɪs] *adj* interminabile; sterminato; (mach) senza fine
end'most' *adj* estremo, ultimo
endorse [ɛn'dɔrs] *tr* girare; (fig) approvare, confermare
endorsee [,ɛndɔr'si] *s* giratario
endorsement [ɛn'dɔrsmənt] *s* girata; approvazione, conferma
endorser [ɛn'dɔrsər] *s* girante *mf*
endow [ɛn'daʊ] *tr* dotare
endowment [ɛn'daʊmənt] *adj* dotale || *s* (*of an institution*) dotazione; (*gift, talent*) dote *f*
end' pap'er *s* risguardo
endurance [ɛn'djʊrəns] or [ɛn'dʊrəns] *s* sopportazione, tolleranza; (*ability to hold out*) resistenza, forza; (*lasting time*) durata
endure [ɛn'djʊr] or [ɛn'dʊr] *tr* sopportare, tollerare; resistere (with *dat*) || *intr* durare, resistere
enduring [ɛn'djʊrɪŋ] or [ɛn'dʊrɪŋ] *adj* duraturo, durevole; paziente
enema ['ɛnəmə] *s* clistere *m*
ene·my ['ɛnəmi] *adj* nemico || *s* **(-mies)** nemico
en'emy al'ien *s* straniero nemico
energetic [,ɛnər'dʒɛtɪk] *adj* energetico, vigoroso
ener·gy ['ɛnərdʒi] *s* **(-gies)** energia
enervate ['ɛnər,vet] *tr* snervare
enfeeble [ɛn'fibəl] *tr* indebolire
enfold [ɛn'fold] *tr* avvolgere; abbracciare
enforce [ɛn'fors] *tr* far osservare; ottenere per forza; (*e.g., obedience*) imporre; (*an argument*) far valere
enforcement [ɛn'forsmənt] *s* imposizione; (*of a law*) esecuzione
enfranchise [ɛn'fræntʃaɪz] *tr* liberare; concedere il diritto di voto a
engage [ɛn'gedʒ] *tr* occupare; riservare; (*s.o.'s attention*) attrarre; (*a gear*) ingranare; (*the enemy*) ingaggiare; (*to hire*) assumere; (theat) scritturare; **to be engaged, to be engaged to be married** essere fidanzato; **to engage s.o. in conversation** intavolare una conversazione con qlcu || *intr* essere occupato; essere impiegato; assumere un'obbligazione; (mil) impegnarsi; (mach) ingranare, incastrarsi
engaged [ɛn'gedʒd] *adj* fidanzato; occupato, impegnato; (*column*) murato
engagement [ɛn'gedʒmənt] *s* accordo; fidanzamento; impegno, contratto; (*appointment*) appuntamento; (mil) azione; (mach) innesto
engage'ment ring' *s* anello di fidanzamento
engaging [ɛn'gedʒɪŋ] *adj* attrattivo
engender [ɛn'dʒɛndər] *tr* ingenerare
engine ['ɛndʒɪn] *s* macchina; (aut) motore *m;* (rr) locomotiva, motrice *f*
engineer [,ɛndʒə'nɪr] *s* ingegnere *m;* (rr) macchinista *m;* (mil) zappatore *m*, geniere *m* || *tr* costruire; progettare
engineering [,ɛndʒə'nɪrɪŋ] *s* ingegneria
en'gine house' *s* stazione dei pompieri
en'gine·man' *s* **(-men)** (rr) macchinista *m*
en'gine room' *s* sala macchine
en'gine-room' tel'egraph *s* (naut) telegrafo di macchina, trasmettitore *m*
England ['ɪŋglənd] *s* l'Inghilterra
Englander ['ɪŋglənder] *s* nativo dell'Inghilterra
English ['ɪŋglɪʃ] *adj* inglese || *s* inglese *m;* (billiards) effetto; **the English** gli inglesi
Eng'lish Chan'nel *s* Canale *m* della Manica
Eng'lish dai'sy *s* margherita
Eng'lish horn' *s* (mus) corno inglese
Eng'lish·man *s* **(-men)** inglese *m*
Eng'lish-speak'ing *adj* di lingua inglese, anglofono
Eng'lish·wom'an *s* **(-wom'en)** inglese *f*
engraft [ɛn'græft] or [ɛn'grɑft] *tr* (hort) innestare; (fig) inculcare
engrave [ɛn'grev] *tr* incidere
engraver [ɛn'grevər] *s* incisore *m*
engraving [ɛn'grevɪŋ] *s* incisione
engross [ɛn'gros] *tr* preoccupare, assorbire; redigere ufficialmente, scrivere a grandi caratteri; monopolizzare
engrossing [ɛn'grosɪŋ] *adj* assorbente
engulf [ɛn'gʌlf] *tr* sommergere, inondare
enhance [ɛn'hæns] or [ɛn'hɑns] *tr* valorizzare; far risaltare
enigma [ɪ'nɪgmə] *s* enigma *m*
enigmatic(al) [,ɪnɪg'mætɪk(əl)] *adj* enigmatico
enjambment [ɛn'dʒæmmənt] or [ɛn'dʒæmbmənt] *s* inarcatura
enjoin [ɛn'dʒɔɪn] *tr* ingiungere, intimare
enjoy [ɛn'dʒɔɪ] *tr* godere; **to enjoy** + *ger* provar piacere in + *inf;* **to enjoy oneself** divertirsi
enjoyable [ɛn'dʒɔɪ·əbəl] *adj* gradevole
enjoyment [ɛn'dʒɔɪmənt] *s* (*pleasure*) piacere *m;* (*pleasurable use*) godimento
enkindle [ɛn'kɪndəl] *tr* infiammare
enlarge [ɛn'lɑrdʒ] *tr* aumentare; ingrossare; (phot) ingrandire || *intr* aumentare; **to enlarge on** or **upon** dilungarsi su
enlargement [ɛn'lɑrdʒmənt] *s* aumento; ingrossamento; (phot) ingrandimento
enlighten [ɛn'laɪtən] *tr* illustrare, illuminare
enlightenment [ɛn'laɪtənmənt] *s* spiegazione, schiarimento || **Enlightenment** *s* illuminismo
enlist [ɛn'lɪst] *tr* (*e.g., s.o.'s favor*) guadagnarsi; (*the help of a person*) ottenere; (mil) ingaggiare || *intr* (mil) ingaggiarsi, arruolarsi; **to enlist**

in (*a cause*) dare il proprio appoggio a
enlistment [ɛn'lɪstmənt] *s* arruolamento, ingaggio
enliven [ɛn'laɪvən] *tr* ravvivare
enmesh [ɛn'mɛʃ] *tr* irretire
enmi·ty ['ɛnmɪti] *s* (**-ties**) inimicizia
ennoble [ɛn'nobəl] *tr* nobilitare
ennui ['ɑnwi] *s* noia, tedio
enormous [ɪ'nɔrməs] *adj* enorme
enormously [ɪ'nɔrməsli] *adv* enormemente
enough [ɪ'nʌf] *adj* abbastanza || *s* il sufficiente || *adv* abbastanza || *interj* basta!
enounce [ɪ'nauns] *tr* enunciare; (*to declare*) affermare
enrage [ɛn'redʒ] *tr* infuriare, irritare
enrapture [ɛn'ræptʃər] *tr* mandare in visibilio, estasiare
enrich [ɛn'rɪtʃ] *tr* arricchire
enroll [ɛn'rol] *tr* arruolare, ingaggiare; (*a student*) iscrivere || *intr* arruolarsi, ingaggiarsi; (*said of a student*) iscriversi
enrollment [ɛn'rolmənt] *s* arruolamento, ingaggio; (*of a student*) iscrizione
en route [ɑn 'rut] *adv* in cammino; **en route to** in via per
ensconce [ɛn'skɑns] *tr* nascondere; **to esconce oneself** rannicchiarsi, istallarsi comodamente
ensemble [ɑn'sɑmbəl] *s* insieme *m;* (mus) concertato
ensign ['ɛnsaɪn] *s* (*standard*) bandiera, insegna; (*badge*) distintivo || ['ɛnsən] or ['ɛnsaɪn] *s* guardamarina *m*
ensilage ['ɛnsəlɪdʒ] *s* (*preservation of fodder*) insilamento; (*preserved fodder*) insilato
ensile ['ɛnsaɪl] or [ɛn'saɪl] *tr* insilare
enslave [ɛn'slev] *tr* fare schiavo, asservire
enslavement [ɛn'slevmənt] *s* asservimento
ensnare [ɛn'snɛr] *tr* irretire
ensue [ɛn'su] or [ɛn'sju] *intr* risultare; seguire, conseguire
ensuing [ɛn'su·ɪŋ] or [ɛn'sju·ɪŋ] *adj* risultante, conseguente; seguente
ensure [ɛn'ʃʊr] *tr* assicurare, garantire
entail [ɛn'tel] *s* (law) obbligo || *tr* provocare, comportare; (law) obbligare
entangle [ɛn'tæŋgəl] *tr* intricare, imbrogliare, impigliare
entanglement [ɛn'tæŋgəlmənt] *s* groviglio, garbuglio
enter ['ɛntər] *tr* (*a house*) entrare in; (*in the customhouse*) dichiarare; (*to make a record of*) registrare; (*a student*) iscrivere; iscriversi a; fare membro; (*to undertake*) intraprendere; **to enter s.o.'s head** passare per la testa a qlcu || *intr* entrare; (theat) entrare in scena; **to enter into** entrare in; (*a contract*) impegnarsi in; **to enter on** or **upon** intraprendere
enterprise ['ɛntər ˌpraɪz] *s* (*undertaking*) impresa; (*spirit, push*) intraprendenza
enterprising ['ɛntər ˌpraɪzɪŋ] *adj* intraprendente
entertain [ˌɛntər'ten] *tr* divertire, intrattenere; (*guests*) ospitare; (*a hope*) accarezzare; (*a proposal*) considerare || *intr* ricevere
entertainer [ˌɛntər'tenər] *s* (*host*) ospite *mf;* (*in public*) attore *m,* cantante *mf,* fine dicitore *m*
entertaining [ˌɛntər'tenɪŋ] *adj* divertente
entertainment [ˌɛntər'tenmənt] *s* trattenimento, svago; spettacolo, attrazione; buon trattamento
enthrall [ɛn'θrɔl] *tr* affascinare, incantare; (*to subjugate*) asservire, soggiogare
enthrone [ɛn'θron] *tr* mettere sul trono, intronizzare; esaltare, innalzare
enthuse [ɛn'θuz] or [ɛn'θjuz] *tr* (coll) entusiasmare || *intr* (coll) entusiasmarsi
enthusiasm [ɛn'θuzɪ ˌæzəm] or [ɛn'θjuzɪ ˌæzəm] *s* entusiasmo
enthusiast [ɛn'θuzɪ ˌæst] or [ɛn'θjuzɪ ˌæst] *s* entusiasta *mf,* maniaco
enthusiastic [ɛn ˌθuzɪ'æstɪk] or [ɛn ˌθjuzɪ'æstɪk] *adj* entusiastico
entice [ɛn'taɪs] *tr* attrarre, provocare; tentare
enticement [ɛn'taɪsmənt] *s* attrazione, provocazione; tentazione
entire [ɛn'taɪr] *adj* intero
entirely [ɛn'taɪrli] *adv* interamente; (*solely*) solamente
entire·ty [ɛn'taɪrti] *s* (**-ties**) interezza; totalità *f*
entitle [ɛn'taɪtəl] *tr* dar diritto a; (*to give a name to*) intitolare
enti·ty ['ɛntɪti] *s* (**-ties**) (*something real; organization, institution*) ente *m;* (*existence*) entità *f*
entomb [ɛn'tum] *tr* seppellire
entombment [ɛn'tummənt] *s* sepoltura
entomology [ˌɛntə'mɑlədʒi] *s* entomologia
entourage [ˌɑntu'rɑʒ] *s* seguito
entrails ['ɛntrelz] or ['ɛntrəlz] *spl* visceri *mpl*
entrain [ɛn'tren] *tr* far salire sul treno || *intr* imbarcarsi sul treno
entrance ['ɛntrəns] *s* entrata, ingresso || [ɛn'træns] or [ɛn'trɑns] *tr* ipnotizzare, incantare
en'trance exam'ina'tion *s* esame *m* d'ammissione
entrancing [ɛn'trænsɪŋ] or [ɛn'trɑnsɪŋ] *adj* incantatore
entrant ['ɛntrənt] *s* nuovo membro; (sports) concorrente *mf*
en·trap [ɛn'træp] *v* (*pret & pp* **-trapped; ger -trapping**) *tr* intrappolare, irretire
entreat [ɛn'trit] *tr* implorare
entreat·y [ɛn'triti] *s* (**-ies**) implorazione, supplica
entree ['ɑntre] *s* entrata, ingresso; (culin) prima portata
entrench [ɛn'trɛntʃ] *tr* trincerare || *intr* —**to entrench on** or **upon** violare

entrust [ɛn'trʌst] *tr* affidare, confidare
en·try ['ɛntri] *s* (**-tries**) entrata; (*item*) partita, registrazione; (*in a dictionary*) lemma, esponente *m;* (sports) concorrente *mf*
entwine [ɛn'twaɪn] *tr* intrecciare || *intr* intrecciarsi
enumerate [ɪ'njumə,ret] or [ɪ'numə,ret] *tr* enumerare
enunciate [ɪ'nʌnsɪ,et] or [ɪ'nʌnʃɪ,et] *tr* enunciare, staccare
envelop [ɛn'vɛləp] *tr* involgere
envelope ['ɛnvə,lop] or ['ɑnvə,lop] *s* (*for a letter*) busta; (*wrapper*) involucro
envenom [ɛn'venəm] *tr* avvelenare
enviable ['ɛnvɪ·əbəl] *adj* invidiabile
envious ['ɛnvɪ·əs] *adj* invidioso
environment [ɛn'vaɪrənmənt] *s* ambiente *m;* condizioni *fpl* ambientali
environs [ɛn'vaɪrənz] *spl* dintorni *mpl,* sobborghi *mpl*
envisage [ɛn'vɪzɪdʒ] *tr* considerare, immaginare
envoi ['ɛnvɔɪ] *s* (pros) congedo
envoy ['ɛnvɔɪ] *s* inviato; (mil) parlamentare *m;* (pros) congedo
en·vy ['ɛnvi] *s* (**-vies**) invidia || *v* (*pret & pp* **-vied**) *tr* invidiare
enzyme ['ɛnzaɪm] or ['ɛnzɪm] *s* enzima *m*
epaulet or **epaulette** ['ɛpə,lɛt] *s* spallina
epenthe·sis [ɛ'pɛnθɪsɪs] *s* (**-ses** [,siz]) epentesi *f*
ephemeral [ɪ'fɛmərəl] *adj* effimero
epic ['ɛpɪk] *adj* epico || *s* epica
epicure ['ɛpɪ,kjʊr] *s* epicureo
epicurean [,ɛpɪkjʊ'ri·ən] *adj & s* epicureo
epidemic [,ɛpɪ'dɛmɪk] *adj* epidemico || *s* epidemia
epidermis [,ɛpɪ'dʌrmɪs] *s* epidermide *f*
epiglottis [,ɛpɪ'glɑtɪs] *s* epiglottide *f*
epigram ['ɛpɪ,græm] *s* epigramma *m*
epilepsy ['ɛpɪ,lɛpsi] *s* epilessia
epileptic [,ɛpɪ'lɛptɪk] *adj & s* epilettico
epilogue ['ɛpɪ,lɔg] or ['ɛpɪ,lɑg] *s* epilogo
Epiphany [ɪ'pɪfəni] *s* Epifania
Episcopalian [ɪ,pɪskə'pelɪ·ən] *adj & s* episcopaliano
episode ['ɛpɪ,sod] *s* episodio
epistle [ɪ'pɪsəl] *s* epistola
epitaph ['ɛpɪ,tæf] *s* epitaffio
epithet ['ɛpɪ,θɛt] *s* epiteto
epitome [ɪ'pɪtəmi] *s* epitome *f;* (fig) prototipo, personificazione
epitomize [ɪ'pɪtə,maɪz] *tr* epitomare; (fig) incarnare, personificare
epoch ['ɛpək] or ['ipɑk] *s* epoca
epochal ['ɛpəkəl] *adj* memorabile
ep'och-mak'ing *adj*—**to be epoch-making** fare epoca
Ep'som salt' ['ɛpsəm] *s* sale *m* inglese
equable ['ɛkwəbəl] or ['ikwəbəl] *adj* uniforme; tranquillo
equal ['ikwəl] *adj* uguale; **equal to** pari a, all'altezza di || *s* uguale *m* || *v* (*pret & pp* **equaled** or **equalled**; *ger* **equaling** or **equalling**) *tr* uguagliare
equali·ty [ɪ'kwɑlɪti] *s* (**-ties**) uguaglianza
equalize ['ikwə,laɪz] *tr* uguagliare; (*to make uniform*) perequare, pareggiare
equally ['ikwəli] *adv* ugualmente
equanimity [,ikwə'nɪmɪti] *s* equanimità *f*
equate [i'kwet] *tr* mettere in forma di equazione; considerare uguale or uguali
equation [i'kweʒən] or [i'kweʃən] *s* equazione
equator [i'kwetər] *s* equatore *m*
equatorial [,ikwə'torɪ·əl] *adj* equatoriale
equer·ry ['ɛkwəri] or [ɪ'kwɛri] *s* (**-ries**) scudiero
equestrian [ɪ'kwɛstrɪ·ən] *adj* equestre || *s* cavallerizzo
equilateral [,ikwɪ'lætərəl] *adj* equilatero
equilibrium [,ikwɪ'lɪbrɪ·əm] *s* equilibrio
equinoctial [,ikwɪ'nɑkʃəl] *adj* equinoziale
equinox ['ikwɪ,nɑks] *s* equinozio
equip [ɪ'kwɪp] *v* (*pret & pp* **equipped**; *ger* **equipping**) *tr* equipaggiare; **to equip** (*e.g., a ship*) **with** munire di
equipment [ɪ'kwɪpmənt] *s* equipaggiamento; (*skill*) attitudine *f*, capacità *f*
equipoise ['ikwɪ,pɔɪz] or ['ɛkwɪ,pɔɪz] *s* equilibrio || *tr* equilibrare
equitable ['ɛkwɪtəbəl] *adj* equo
equi·ty ['ɛkwɪti] *s* (**-ties**) (*fairness*) equità *f;* valore *m* al netto; (*in a corporation*) interessenza azionaria
equivalent [ɪ'kwɪvələnt] *adj* equivalente || *s* equivalente *m;* (com) controvalore *m*
equivocal [ɪ'kwɪvəkəl] *adj* equivoco
equivocate [ɪ'kwɪvə,ket] *intr* giocare sulle parole, parlare in maniera equivoca
equivocation [ɪ,kwɪvə'keʃən] *s* equivocità *f;* equivoco
era ['ɪrə] or ['irə] *s* era, evo
eradicate [ɪ'rædɪ,ket] *tr* sradicare
erase [ɪ'res] *tr* cancellare
eraser [ɪ'resər] *s* gomma da cancellare; (*for blackboard*) spugna
erasure [ɪ'reʃər] or [ɪ'reʒər] *s* cancellatura; (*of a tape*) cancellazione
ere [ɛr] *prep* (lit) prima di || *conj* (lit) prima che
erect [ɪ'rɛkt] *adj* dritto, eretto; (*hair*) irto || *tr* (*to set in upright position*) drizzare; (*a building*) erigere, costruire; (*a machine*) montare
erection [ɪ'rɛkʃən] *s* erezione
ermine ['ʌrmɪn] *s* ermellino; (fig) carica di giudice, toga, magistratura
erode [ɪ'rod] *tr* erodere || *intr* corrodersi, consumarsi
erosion [ɪ'roʒən] *s* erosione
erotic [ɪ'rɑtɪk] *adj* erotico
err [ʌr] *intr* errare; (*to be incorrect*) sbagliarsi
errand ['ɛrənd] *s* corsa, commissione; **to run an errand** fare una commissione
er'rand boy' *s* fattorino, galoppino

erratic [ɪ'rætɪk] *adj* erratico; strano, eccentrico
erra·tum [ɪ'retəm] or [ɪ'rɑtəm] *s* (**-ta** [tə]) errore *m* di stampa
erroneous [ɪ'ronɪ·əs] *adj* erroneo
error ['ɛrər] *s* errore *m*, sbaglio
erudite ['ɛrʊ,daɪt] or ['ɛrjʊ,daɪt] *adj* erudito, dotto
erudition [,ɛrʊ'dɪʃən] or [,ɛrjʊ'dɪʃən] *s* erudizione
erupt [ɪ'rʌpt] *intr* (*said of a volcano*) eruttare; (*said of a skin rash*) fiorire; (*said of a tooth*) spuntare; (fig) erompere
eruption [ɪ'rʌpʃən] *s* eruzione
escalate ['ɛskə,let] *tr & intr* aumentare
escalation [,ɛskə'leʃən] *s* aumento
escalator ['ɛskə,letər] *s* scala mobile
escallop [ɛs'kæləp] *s* (*on edge of cloth*) dentellatura, festone *m*; (*mollusk*) pettine *m* || *tr* cuocere in conchiglia; cuocere al forno con salsa e pane grattugiato
escapade [,ɛskə'ped] *s* scappatella
escape [ɛs'kep] *s* (*getaway*) fuga; (*from responsibility, duties, etc.*) scampo || *tr* sottrarsi a, eludere; **to escape s.o.** scappare da qlcu; scappar di mente a qlcu || *intr* scappare; sprigionarsi; **to escape from** (*a person*) sfuggire a; (*jail*) evadere da
escapee [,ɛskə'pi] *s* evaso
escape' lit'erature' *s* letteratura di evasione
escapement [ɛs'kepmənt] *s* scappamento
escape' veloc'ity *s* (rok) velocità *f* di fuga
escarpment [ɛs'kɑrpmənt] *s* scarpata
eschew [ɛs'tʃu] *tr* evitare, rifuggire da
escort ['ɛskɔrt] *s* scorta; (*of a woman or girl*) compagno, cavaliere *m* || [ɛs'kɔrt] *tr* scortare
escutcheon [ɛs'kʌtʃən] *s* scudo; (*plate in front of lock on door*) bocchetta
Esk·imo ['ɛskɪ,mo] *adj* eschimese || *s* (**-mos** or **-mo**) eschimese *mf*
esopha·gus [ɪ'sɑfəgəs] *s* (**-gi** [,dʒaɪ]) esofago
espalier [ɛs'pæljər] *s* spalliera
especial [ɛs'pɛʃəl] *adj* speciale
espionage ['ɛspɪ·ənɪdʒ] or [,ɛspɪ·ə'nɑʒ] *s* spionaggio
esplanade [,ɛsplə'ned] or [,ɛsplə'nɑd] *s* spianata, piazzale *m*
espousal [ɛs'pauzəl] *s* sposalizio; (*of a cause*) adozione
espouse [ɛs'pauz] *tr* sposare; (*to advocate*) abbracciare, adottare
esquire [ɛs'kwaɪr] or ['ɛskwaɪr] *s* scudiero || **Esquire** *s* titolo di cortesia usato generalmente con persone di riguardo
essay ['ɛse] *s* saggio
essayist ['ɛse·ɪst] *s* saggista *mf*
essence ['ɛsəns] *s* essenza
essential [ɛ'senʃəl] *adj & s* essenziale *m*
establish [ɛs'tæblɪʃ] *tr* stabilire
establishment [ɛs'tæblɪʃmənt] *s* stabilimento; fondazione; **the Establishment** l'autorità costituita
estate [ɛs'tet] *s* stato; condizione sociale; (*landed property*) tenuta; (*a person's possessions*) patrimonio; (*left by a decedent*) massa ereditaria
esteem [ɛs'tim] *s* stima || *tr* stimare
esthete ['ɛsθit] *s* esteta *mf*
esthetic [ɛs'θɛtɪk] *adj* estetico || **esthetics** *ssg* estetica
estimable ['ɛstɪməbəl] *adj* stimabile
estimate ['ɛstɪ,met] or ['ɛstɪmɪt] *s* stima, valutazione; (*statement of cost of work to be done*) preventivo || ['ɛstɪ,met] *tr* stimare, valutare; preventivare
estimation [,ɛstɪ'meʃən] *s* stima; **in my estimation** a mio parere
estimator ['ɛstɪ,metər] *s* preventivista *mf*
estrangement [ɛs'trendʒmənt] *s* alienazione, disaffezione
estuar·y ['ɛstʃʊ,ɛri] *s* (**-ies**) estuario
etch [ɛtʃ] *tr & intr* incidere all'acquaforte
etcher ['ɛtʃər] *s* acquafortista *mf*
etching ['ɛtʃɪŋ] *s* acquaforte *f*
eternal [ɪ'tʌrnəl] *adj* eterno
eterni·ty [ɪ'tʌrnɪti] *s* (**-ties**) eternità *f*
ether ['iθər] *s* etere *m*
ethereal [ɪ'θɪrɪ·əl] *adj* etereo
ethical ['ɛθɪkəl] *adj* etico
ethics ['ɛθɪks] *ssg* etica
Ethiopian [,iθɪ'opɪ·ən] *adj & s* etiope *mf*
ethnic(al) ['ɛθnɪk(əl)] *adj* etnico
ethnography [ɛθ'nɑgrəfi] *s* etnografia
ethnology [ɛθ'nɑlədʒi] *s* etnologia
ethyl ['ɛθɪl] *s* etile *m*
ethylene ['ɛθɪ,lin] *s* etilene *m*
etiquette ['ɛtɪ,kɛt] *s* etichetta
étude [e'tjud] *s* (mus) studio
etymology [,ɛtɪ'mɑlədʒi] *s* etimologia
ety·mon ['ɛtɪ,mɑn] *s* (**-mons** or **-ma** [mə]) etimo
eucalyp·tus [,jukə'lɪptəs] *s* (**-tuses** or **-ti** [taɪ]) eucalipto
Eucharist ['jukərɪst] *s* Eucaristia
eugenics [jʊ'dʒɛnɪks] *ssg* eugenetica
eulogistic [,julə'dʒɪstɪk] *adj* elogiativo
eulogize ['julə,dʒaɪz] *tr* elogiare
eulo·gy ['julədʒi] *s* (**-gies**) elogio; elogio funebre
eunuch ['junək] *s* eunuco
euphemism ['jufɪ,mɪzəm] *s* eufemismo
euphemistic [,jufɪ'mɪstɪk] *adj* eufemistico
euphonic [jʊ'fɑnɪk] *adj* eufonico
eupho·ny ['jufəni] *s* (**-nies**) eufonia
euphoria [jʊ'forɪ·ə] *s* euforia
euphuism ['jufjʊ,ɪzəm] *s* eufuismo
Europe ['jʊrəp] *s* l'Europa
European [,jʊrə'pi·ən] *adj & s* europeo
euthanasia [,juθə'neʒə] *s* eutanasia
evacuate [ɪ'vækjʊ,et] *tr & intr* evacuare
evacuation [ɪ,vækjʊ'eʃən] *s* evacuazione
evacuee [ɪ'vækjʊ,i] or [ɪ,vækjʊ'i] *s* sfollato
evade [ɪ'ved] *tr* eludere || *intr* evadere
evaluate [ɪ'væljʊ,et] *tr* valutare
evaluation [ɪ,væljʊ'eʃən] *s* valutazione
Evangel [ɪ'vændʒəl] *s* Vangelo
evangelic(al) [,ivæn'dʒɛlɪk(əl)] or [,ɛvən'dʒɛlɪk(əl)] *adj* evangelico

Evangelist [ɪ'vændʒəlɪst] *s* evangelista *m*
evaporate [ɪ'væpə,ret] *tr & intr* evaporare
evasion [ɪ'veʒən] *s* evasione; (*subterfuge*) scappatoia
evasive [ɪ'vesɪv] *adj* evasivo
eve [iv] *s* vigilia; **on the eve of** la vigilia di
even ['ivən] *adj* (*smooth*) piano, regolare; (*number*) pari; uguale, uniforme; (*temperament*) calmo, placido; **even with** a livello di; **to be even** mettersi in pari; **to get even** prendersi la rivincita || *adv* anche; fino, perfino; pure; esattamente; magari; **even as** proprio mentre; **even if** anche se, quando pure; **even so** anche se così; **even though** quantunque; **even when** anche quando; **not even** neppure, nemmeno; **to break even** impattare || *tr* spianare; **to even up** bilanciare
evening ['ivnɪŋ] *adj* serale || *s* sera, serata; **all evening** tutta la sera; **every evening** tutte le sere; **in the evening** la sera
eve'ning clothes' *spl* vestito da sera
eve'ning gown' *s* vestito da sera da signora
eve'ning star' *s* espero
e'ven·song' *s* (eccl) vespro
event [ɪ'vent] *s* avvenimento; (*outcome*) evenienza; (*public function*) manifestazione; (sports) prova; **at all events** or **in any event** in ogni caso; **in the event that** in caso che, se mai
eventful [ɪ'ventfəl] *adj* ricco di avvenimenti; movimentato
eventual [ɪ'ventʃʊ·əl] *adj* finale
eventuali·ty [ɪ,ventʃʊ'ælɪti] *s* (**-ties**) eventualità *f*, evenienza
eventually [ɪ'ventʃʊ·əli] *adv* finalmente, alla fine
eventuate [ɪ'ventʃʊ,et] *intr* risultare; accadere
ever ['evər] *adv* (*at all times*) sempre; (*at any time*) mai; **as ever** come sempre; **as much as ever** tanto come prima; **ever since** (*since that time*) sin da; da allora in poi; **ever so** molto; **ever so much** moltissimo; **hardly ever** or **scarcely ever** quasi mai; **not . . . ever** non . . . mai
ev'er·glade' *s* terreno paludoso coperto di erbe
ev'er·green' *adj & s* sempreverde *m & f*; **evergreens** decorazione di sempreverdi
ev'er·last'ing *adj* eterno; incessante; (*lasting indefinitely*) duraturo; (*wearisome*) noioso || *s* eternità *f*; (bot) semprevivo
ev'er·more' *adv* eternamente; **for evermore** per sempre
every ['evri] *adj* tutti i; (*each*) ogni, ciascuno; (*being each in a series*) ogni, e.g., **every three days** ogni tre giorni; **every bit** (coll) in tutto e per tutto, e.g., **every bit a man** un uomo in tutto e per tutto; **every now and then** di quando in quando; **every once in a while** una volta ogni tanto; **every other day** ogni secondo giorno; **every which way** (coll) da tutte le parti; (coll) in disordine
ev'ery·bod'y *pron indef* ognuno, tutti
ev'ery·day' *adj* di ogni giorno; quotidiano; ordinario
ev'ery·man' *s* l'uomo qualunque || *pron* chiunque
ev'ery·one' or **ev'ery one'** *pron indef* ciascuno, tutti
ev'ery·thing' *pron indef* tutto, ogni cosa, tutto quanto
ev'ery·where' *adv* dappertutto, dovunque
evict [ɪ'vɪkt] *tr* sfrattare, sloggiare
eviction [ɪ'vɪkʃən] *s* sfratto, sloggio
evidence ['evɪdəns] *s* evidenza; (law) prova
evident ['evɪdənt] *adj* evidente
evil ['ivəl] *adj* cattivo, malvagio || *s* male *m*; disgrazia
evildoer ['ivəl,du·ər] *s* malfattore *m*, malvagio
e'vil·do'ing *s* malafatta, malvagità *f*
e'vil eye' *s* iettatura, malocchio
evil-minded ['ivəl'maɪndɪd] *adj* malintenzionato
e'vil one', **the** il nemico
evince [ɪ'vɪns] *tr* mostrare, manifestare
evoke [ɪ'vok] *tr* evocare
evolution [,evə'luʃən] *s* evoluzione
evolve [ɪ'vɑlv] *tr* sviluppare || *intr* evolversi
ewe [ju] *s* pecora
ewer ['ju·ər] *s* brocca
ex [eks] *prep* senza includere
exacerbation [ɪg,zæsər'beʃən] *s* esulcerazione, esacerbazione
exacerbate [ɪg'zæsər,bet] *tr* esacerbare, esulcerare
exact [eg'zækt] *adj* esatto || *tr* esigere
exacting [eg'zæktɪŋ] *adj* esigente
exaction [eg'zækʃən] *s* esazione
exactly [eg'zæktli] *adv* esattamente; (*sharp, on the dot*) in punto
exactness [eg'zæktnɪs] *s* esattezza
exaggerate [eg'zædʒə,ret] *tr* esagerare
exalt [eg'zɔlt] *tr* elevare, esaltare
exam [eg'zæm] *s* (coll) esame *m*
examination [eg,zæmɪ'neʃən] *s* esame *m*; **to take an examination** sostenere un esame
examine [eg'zæmɪn] *tr* esaminare
examiner [eg'zæmɪnər] *s* esaminatore *m*
example [eg'zæmpəl] or [eg'zɑmpəl] *s* esempio; (*precedent*) precedente *m*; (*of mathematics*) problema *m*; **for example** per esempio
exasperate [eg'zæspə,ret] *tr* esasperare
excavate ['ekskə,vet] *tr* scavare
exceed [ek'sid] *tr* eccedere
exceedingly [ek'sidɪŋli] *adv* estremamente, sommamente
ex·cel [ek'sel] *v* (*pret & pp* **-celled**; *ger* **-celling**) *tr* sorpassare || *intr* eccellere
excellence ['eksələns] *s* eccellenza
excellen·cy ['eksələnsi] *s* (**-cies**) eccellenza; **Your Excellency** Sua Eccellenza
excelsior [ek'selsɪ·ər] *s* trucioli *mpl* per imballaggio
except [ek'sept] *prep* eccetto; **except**

for tranne, ad eccezione di; **except that** eccetto che || *tr* eccettuare
exception [ɛk'sɛpʃən] *s* eccezione; **to take exception** obiettare; scandalizzarsi; **with the exception of** a esclusione di, eccetto
exceptional [ɛk'sɛpʃənəl] *adj* eccezionale
excerpt ['ɛksʌrpt] or [ɛk'sʌrpt] *s* brano, selezione || [ɛk'sʌrpt] *tr* scegliere, selezionare
excess ['ɛksɛs] or [ɛk'sɛs] *adj* eccedente || [ɛk'sɛs] *s* (*amount or degree by which one thing exceeds another*) eccedente *m*, eccedenza; (*excessive amount; immoderate indulgence; unlawful conduct*) eccesso; **in excess of** più di
ex'cess bag'gage *s* bagaglio eccedente
ex'cess fare' *s* (rr) supplemento
excessive [ɛk'sɛsɪv] *adj* eccessivo
ex'cess-prof'its tax' *s* tassa sui soprapprofitti
exchange [ɛks'tʃendʒ] *s* scambio; (*place for buying and selling*) borsa; (*transactions in the currencies of two different countries*) cambio; (telp) centrale *f*, centralino; **in exchange for** in cambio di || *tr* scambiare, scambiarsi; **to exchange blows** venire alle mani; **to exchange greetings** salutarsi
exchequer [ɛks'tʃɛkər] or ['ɛkstʃɛkər] *s* erario, tesoro
ex'cise tax' [ɛk'saɪz] or ['ɛksaɪz] *s* imposta sul consumo
excitable [ɛk'saɪtəbəl] *adj* eccitabile
excite [ɛk'saɪt] *tr* eccitare
excitement [ɛk'saɪtmənt] *s* eccitazione
exciting [ɛk'saɪtɪŋ] *adj* emozionante; (*stimulating*) eccitante
exclaim [ɛks'klem] *tr & intr* esclamare
exclamation [,ɛksklə'meʃən] *s* esclamazione
exclama'tion mark' or **point'** *s* punto esclamativo
exclude [ɛks'klud] *tr* escludere
excluding [ɛks'kludɪŋ] *prep* a esclusione di, senza contare
exclusion [ɛks'kluʒən] *s* esclusione; **to the exclusion of** tranne, salvo
exclusive [ɛks'klusɪv] *adj* esclusivo; **exclusive of** escluso, senza contare || *s* (journ) esclusiva
excommunicate [,ɛkskə'mjunɪ,ket] *tr* scomunicare
excommunication [,ɛkskə,mjunɪ'keʃən] *s* scomunica
excoriate [ɛks'korɪ,et] *tr* criticare aspramente, vituperare
excrement ['ɛkskrəmənt] *s* escremento
excruciating [ɛks'kruʃɪ,etɪŋ] *adj* (*e.g., pleasure*) estremo; (*e.g., pain*) atroce, lancinante, straziante
exculpate ['ɛkskʌl,pet] or [ɛks'kʌlpet] *tr* scolpare, scagionare
excursion [ɛks'kʌrʒən] or [ɛks'kʌrʃən] *s* escursione, gita
excursionist [ɛks'kʌrʒənɪst] or [ɛks'kʌrʃənɪst] *s* escursionista *mf*
excusable [ɛks'kjuzəbəl] *adj* scusabile
excuse [ɛks'kjus] *s* scusa || [ɛks'kjuz] *tr* scusare; esentare; (*a debt*) rimettere
execute ['ɛksɪ,kjut] *tr* (*to carry out; to produce*) eseguire; (*to put to death*) giustiziare; (law) rendere esecutorio
execution [,ɛksɪ'kjuʃən] *s* esecuzione; (*e.g., of a criminal*) esecuzione capitale
executioner [,ɛksɪ'kjuʃənər] *s* giustiziere *m*, boia *m*, carnefice *m*
executive [ɛg'zɛkjətɪv] *adj* esecutivo || *s* esecutivo; (*of a school, business, etc.*) dirigente *mf*
Exec'utive Man'sion *s* palazzo del governatore; residenza del capo del governo statunitense
executor [ɛg'zɛkjətər] *s* (law) esecutore testamentario
executrix [ɛg'zɛkjətrɪks] *s* (law) esecutrice testamentaria
exemplary [ɛg'zɛmpləri] or ['ɛgzəm,plɛri] *adj* esemplare
exempli·fy [ɛg'zɛmplɪ,faɪ] *v* (*pret & pp* **-fied**) *tr* esemplificare
exempt [ɛg'zɛmpt] *adj* esente || *tr* esimere, esentare
exemption [ɛg'zɛmpʃən] *s* esenzione
exercise ['ɛksər,saɪz] *s* esercizio; cerimonia; **to take exercise** fare del moto || *tr* esercitare; (*care*) usare; (*to worry*) preoccupare || *intr* esercitarsi
exert [ɛg'zʌrt] *tr* (*e.g., power*) esercitare; **to exert oneself** sforzarsi
exertion [ɛg'zʌrʃən] *s* sforzo, tentativo; (*active use*) uso, esercizio
exhalation [,ɛks·hə'leʃən] *s* (*of gas, vapors*) esalazione; (*of air from lungs*) espirazione
exhale [ɛks'hel] or [ɛg'zel] *tr* (*gases, vapors, etc.*) esalare; (*air from lungs*) espirare || *intr* esalare; espirare
exhaust [ɛg'zɔst] *s* scarico, scappamento; tubo di scarico or scappamento || *tr* (*to wear out*) spossare, finire; (*to use up*) esaurire, dar fondo a; vuotare
exhaust' fan' *s* aspiratore *m*
exhaustion [ɛg'zɔstʃən] *s* esaurimento; estenuazione; (sports) cotta
exhaustive [ɛg'zɔstɪv] *adj* esauriente
exhaust' man'ifold *s* collettore *m* di scarico
exhaust' pipe' *s* tubo di scarico
exhaust' valve' *s* valvola di scappamento
exhibit [ɛg'zɪbɪt] *s* esposizione; (law) documento in giudizio || *tr* esibire
exhibition [,ɛksɪ'bɪʃən] *s* esibizione
exhibitor [ɛg'zɪbɪtər] *s* espositore *m*
exhilarating [ɛg'zɪlə,retɪŋ] *adj* esilarante
exhort [ɛg'zɔrt] *tr* esortare
exhume [ɛks'hjum] or [ɛg'zjum] *tr* esumare, dissotterrare
exigen·cy ['ɛksɪdʒənsi] *s* (**-cies**) esigenza
exigent ['ɛksɪdʒənt] *adj* esigente
exile ['ɛgzaɪl] or ['ɛksaɪl] *s* esilio; (*person*) esule *mf* || *tr* esiliare
exist [ɛg'zɪst] *intr* esistere
existence [ɛg'zɪstəns] *s* esistenza
existing [ɛg'zɪstɪŋ] *adj* esistente
exit ['ɛgzɪt] or ['ɛksɪt] *s* uscita || *intr* uscire

exodus ['ɛksədəs] *s* esodo
exonerate [ɛg'zɑnə,ret] *tr* (*from an obligation*) esonerare; (*from blame*) scagionare
exorbitant [ɛg'zɔrbɪtənt] *adj* esorbitante
exorcise ['ɛksɔr,saɪz] *tr* esorcizzare
exotic [ɛg'zɑtɪk] *adj* esotico
expand [ɛks'pænd] *tr* (*a metal*) dilatare; (*gas*) espandere; (*to enlarge*) allargare, ampliare; (*to unfold*) spiegare; (math) svolgere, sviluppare ‖ *intr* dilatarsi; espandersi; allargarsi, ampliarsi; spiegarsi, estendersi
expanse [ɛks'pæns] *s* vastità *f*
expansion [ɛks'pænʃən] *s* espansione
expansive [ɛks'pænsɪv] *adj* espansivo
expatiate [ɛks'peʃɪ,et] *intr* dilungarsi
expatriate [ɛks'petrɪ·ɪt] *adj* esiliato ‖ *s* esule *mf* ‖ [ɛks'petri,et] *tr* esiliare; **to expatriate oneself** espatriare
expect [ɛks'pɛkt] *tr* aspettare, attendere; (coll) credere, supporre; **to expect it** aspettarselo, aspettarsela
expectan•cy [ɛks'pɛktənsi] *s* (**-cies**) aspettativa, aspettazione
expect'ant moth'er [ɛks'pɛktənt] *s* futura madre
expectation [,ɛkspɛk'teʃən] *s* aspettativa
expectorate [ɛks'pɛktə,ret] *tr & intr* espettorare
expedien•cy [ɛks'pidɪ·ənsi] *s* (**-cies**) industria, ingegno; opportunismo, vantaggio personale
expedient [ɛks'pidɪ·ənt] *adj* conveniente; vantaggioso; (*acting with self-interest*) opportunista ‖ *s* espediente *m*
expedite ['ɛkspɪ,daɪt] *tr* sbrigare, accelerare; (*a document*) dar corso a
expedition [,ɛkspɪ'dɪʃən] *s* spedizione; (*speed*) celerità *f*
expeditionary [,ɛkspɪ'dɪʃən,ɛri] *adj* (*e.g., corps*) di spedizione
expeditious [,ɛkspɪ'dɪʃəs] *adj* spicciativo, spiccio
ex•pel [ɛks'pɛl] *v* (*pret & pp* **-pelled;** *ger* **-pelling**) *tr* espellere, scacciare
expend [ɛks'pɛnd] *tr* spendere, consumare
expendable [ɛks'pɛndəbəl] *adj* spendibile; da buttarsi via; (mil) da sacrificare
expenditure [ɛks'pɛndɪtʃər] *s* spesa
expense [ɛks'pɛns] *s* spesa; **at the expense of** al costo di; **expenses** spese *fpl;* **to meet expenses** far fronte alle spese
expense' account' *s* conto delle spese risarcibili
expensive [ɛks'pɛnsɪv] *adj* caro, costoso
experience [ɛks'pɪrɪ·əns] *s* esperienza ‖ *tr* sperimentare, provare
experienced [ɛks'pɪrɪ·ənst] *adj* esperto, sperimentato
experiment [ɛks'pɛrɪmənt] *s* esperimento ‖ [ɛks'pɛrɪ,mɛnt] *intr* sperimentare
expert ['ɛkspərt] *adj & s* esperto
expertise [,ɛkspər'tiz] *s* maestria
expiate ['ɛkspɪ,et] *tr* espiare
expiation [,ɛkspɪ'eʃən] *s* espiazione
expire [ɛks'paɪr] *tr* espirare ‖ *intr* (*to breathe out*) espirare; (*said of a contract*) scadere; (*to die*) morire
explain [ɛks'plen] *tr* spiegare; **to explain away** giustificare; dar ragione di ‖ *intr* spiegare, spiegarsi
explainable [ɛks'plenəbəl] *adj* spiegabile
explanation [,ɛksplə'neʃən] *s* spiegazione, delucidazione
explanatory [ɛks'plænə,tori] *adj* esplicativo
explicit [ɛks'plɪsɪt] *adj* esplicito
explode [ɛks'plod] *tr* far scoppiare; (*a theory*) smontare ‖ *intr* scoppiare
exploit [ɛks'plɔɪt] or ['ɛksplɔɪt] *s* impresa, prodezza ‖ [ɛks'plɔɪt] *tr* utilizzare, sfruttare
exploitation [,ɛksplɔɪ'teʃən] *s* utilizzazione, sfruttamento
exploration [,ɛksplə'reʃən] *s* esplorazione
explore [ɛks'plor] *tr* esplorare
explorer [ɛks'plorər] *s* esploratore *m*
explosion [ɛks'ploʒən] *s* esplosione, scoppio; (*of a theory*) confutazione
explosive [ɛks'plosɪv] *adj & s* esplosivo
exponent [ɛks'ponənt] *s* esponente *m*
export ['ɛksport] *adj* di esportazione ‖ *s* esportazione, articolo di esportazione ‖ [ɛks'port] or ['ɛksport] *tr & intr* esportare
exportation [,ɛkspor'teʃən] *s* esportazione
exporter ['ɛksportər] or [ɛks'portər] *s* esportatore *m*
expose [ɛks'poz] *tr* esporre; (*to unmask*) smascherare
exposé [,ɛkspo'ze] *s* rivelazione scandalosa, smascheramento
exposition [,ɛkspə'zɪʃən] *s* esposizione; interpretazione, commento
expostulate [ɛks'pɑstʃə,let] *intr* protestare; **to expostulate with** lagnarsi con
exposure [ɛks'poʒər] *s* (*disclosure*) rivelazione; (*situation with regard to sunlight*) esposizione; (phot) esposizione
expo'sure me'ter *s* (phot) fotometro, esposimetro
expound [ɛks'paʊnd] *tr* esporre
express [ɛks'prɛs] *adj* espresso ‖ *s* (rr) celere *m*, rapido, direttissimo; **by express** per espresso, a grande velocità ‖ *adv* per espresso, a grande velocità ‖ *tr* esprimere; mandare per espresso; (*to squeeze out*) spremere; **to express oneself** esprimersi
ex'press com'pany *s* servizio corriere
expression [ɛks'prɛʃən] *s* espressione
expressive [ɛks'prɛsɪv] *adj* espressivo
expressly [ɛks'prɛsli] *adv* espressamente
express'man *s* (**-men**) fattorino di servizio corriere
express'way' *s* autostrada
expropriate [ɛks'proprɪ,et] *tr* espropriare
expulsion [ɛks'pʌlʃən] *s* espulsione

expunge [ɛks'pʌndʒ] *tr* espungere
expurgate ['ɛkspər,get] *tr* espurgare
exquisite ['ɛkskwɪzɪt] or [ɛks'kwɪzɪt] *adj* squisito; intenso
ex'serv'ice-man' *s* (**-men'**) ex combattente *m*
extant ['ɛkstənt] or [ɛks'tænt] *adj* ancora esistente
extemporaneous [ɛks,tɛmpə'renɪ·əs] *adj* estemporaneo; (*made for the occasion*) improvvisato
extempore [ɛks'tɛmpəri] *adj* improvvisato || *adv* senza preparazione
extemporize [ɛks'tɛmpə,raɪz] *tr* & *intr* improvvisare
extend [ɛks'tɛnd] *tr* allungare; estendere; (*e.g., aid*) offrire; (*payment of a debt*) dilazionare || *intr* estendersi
extended [ɛks'tɛndɪd] *adj* esteso; prolungato
extension [ɛks'tɛnʃən] *s* estensione; prolungamento; (com) proroga; (telp) derivazione
exten'sion lad'der *s* scala porta, scala a prolunga
exten'sion ta'ble *s* tavola allungabile
exten'sion tel'ephone' *s* telefono interno
extensive [ɛks'tɛnsɪv] *adj* (*wide*) vasto; (*lengthy*) lungo; (*characterized by extention*) estensivo
extent [ɛks'tɛnt] *s* estensione; **to a certain extent** fino a un certo punto; **to a great extent** in larga misura; **to the full extent** all'estremo limite
extenuate [ɛks'tɛnju,et] *tr* (*to make seem less serious*) attenuare; (*to underrate*) sottovalutare
exterior [ɛks'tɪrɪ·ər] *adj* & *s* esteriore *m*
exterminate [ɛks'tʌrmɪ,net] *tr* sterminare
external [ɛks'tʌrnəl] *adj* esterno || **externals** *spl* esteriorità *f*, di fuori *m*
extinct [ɛks'tɪŋkt] *adj* estinto
extinction [ɛks'tɪŋkʃən] *s* estinzione
extinguish [ɛks'tɪŋgwɪʃ] *tr* estinguere
extinguisher [ɛks'tɪŋgwɪʃər] *s* estintore *m*
extirpate ['ɛkstər,pet] or [ɛks'tʌrpet] *tr* estirpare
ex·tol [ɛks'tol] or [ɛks'tɑl] *v* (*pret* & *pp* **-tolled**; *ger* **-tolling**) *tr* inneggiare
extort [ɛks'tɔrt] *tr* estorcere
extortion [ɛks'tɔrʃən] *s* estorsione
extra ['ɛkstrə] *adj* extra; (*spare*) di scorta || *s* (*of a newspaper*) edizione straordinaria; (*something additional*) soprappiù *m*; (theat) figurante *mf* || *adv* straordinariamente
ex'tra charge' *s* supplemento
extract ['ɛkstrækt] *s* estratto || [ɛks'trækt] *tr* (*to pull out*) estrarre; (*to take from a book*) scegliere, selezionare
extraction [ɛks'trækʃən] *s* estrazione
extracurricular [,ɛkstrəkə'rɪkjələr] *adj* fuori del programma normale
extradition [,ɛkstrə'dɪʃən] *s* estradizione
ex'tra·dry' *adj* molto secco, brut
ex'tra fare' *s* supplemento al biglietto
ex'tra·mar'ital *adj* extraconiugale
extramural [,ɛkstrə'mjurəl] *adj* fuori della scuola, interscolastico; fuori delle mura
extraneous [ɛks'trenɪ·əs] *adj* estraneo
extraordinary [,ɛkstrə'ɔrdɪ,nɛri] or [ɛks'trɔrdɪ,nɛri] *adj* straordinario
extrapolate [ɛks'træpə,let] *tr* & *intr* estrapolare
extrasensory [,ɛkstrə'sɛnsəri] *adj* extrasensoriale
extravagance [ɛks'trævəgəns] *s* prodigalità *f*; (*wildness, folly*) stravaganza
extravagant [ɛks'trævəgənt] *adj* prodigo; (*wild, foolish*) stravagante
extreme [ɛks'trim] *adj* & *s* estremo; **in the extreme** in massimo grado; **to go to extremes** andare agli estremi
extremely [ɛks'trimli] *adv* estremamente, in sommo grado
extreme' unc'tion *s* Estrema Unzione
extremist [ɛks'trimɪst] *adj* & *s* estremista *mf*
extremi·ty [ɛks'trɛmɪti] *s* (**-ties**) estremità *f*; (*great want*) estrema necessità; **extremities** estremi *mpl*; (*hands and feet*) estremità *fpl*
extricate ['ɛkstrɪ,ket] *tr* districare
extrinsic [ɛks'trɪnsɪk] *adj* estrinseco
extrovert ['ɛkstrə,vʌrt] *s* estroverso
extrude [ɛks'trud] *tr* estrudere || *intr* protrudere
exuberant [ɛg'zubərənt] or [ɛg'zjubərənt] *adj* esuberante
exude [ɛg'zud] or [ɛk'sud] *tr* & *intr* trasudare, stillare
exult [ɛg'zʌlt] *intr* esultare, tripudiare
exultant [ɛg'zʌltənt] *adj* esultante
eye [aɪ] *s* occhio; (*of hook and eye*) occhiello; **to catch one's eye** attirare l'attenzione di qlcu; **to feast one's eyes on** deliziarsi la vista con; **to lay eyes on** riuscire a vedere; **to make eyes at** fare gli occhi dolci a; **to roll one's eyes** stralunare gli occhi; **to see eye to eye** andare perfettamente d'accordo; **to shut one's eyes to** chiudere un occhio a; far finta di non vedere; **without batting an eye** senza batter ciglio || *v* (*pret* & *pp* **eyed**; *ger* **eying** or **eyeing**) *tr* occhieggiare; **to eye up and down** guardare da capo a piedi
eye'ball' *s* globo oculare
eye'bolt' *s* bullone *m* ad anello
eye'brow' *s* sopracciglio; **to raise one's eyebrows** inarcare le sopracciglia
eye'cup' *s* occhiera
eye'drop'per *s* contagocce *m*
eyeful ['aɪ,ful] *s* vista, colpo d'occhio; (coll) bellezza
eye'glass' *s* (*of optical instrument*) lente *f*, oculare *m*; (*eyecup*) occhiera; **eyeglasses** occhiali *mpl*
eye'lash' *s* ciglio
eyelet ['aɪlɪt] *s* occhiello, maglietta, asola; (*hole to look through*) feritoia
eye'lid' *s* palpebra
eye' o'pener ['opənər] *s* affare *m* che apre gli occhi; (coll) bicchierino bevuto di mattina presto

eye'piece' *s* oculare *m*
eye'shade' *s* visiera
eye' shad'ow *s* rimmel *m*
eye'shot' *s*—**within eyeshot** a portata di vista
eye'sight' *s* vista; (*range*) capacità visiva
eye' sock'et *s* occhiaia, orbita
eye'sore' *s* pugno in un occhio
eye'strain' *s* vista affaticata
eye'-test chart' *s* tabella optometrica
eye'tooth' *s* (**-teeth**) dente canino; **to cut one's eyeteeth** (coll) fare esperienza; **to give one's eyeteeth for** (coll) dare un occhio della testa per
eye'wash' *s* (*flattery*) burro, lusinga; (pharm) collirio; (slang) balla
eye' wit'ness *s* testimone *m* oculare

F

F, f [ef] *s* sesta lettera dell'alfabeto inglese
fable ['febəl] *s* favola
fabric ['fæbrɪk] *s* stoffa, tessuto; fabbrica, struttura
fabricate ['fæbrɪ,ket] *tr* fabbricare
fabrication [,fæbrɪ'keʃən] *s* fabbricazione; falsificazione, invenzione
fabulous ['fæbjələs] *adj* favoloso
façade [fə'sɑd] *s* facciata
face [fes] *s* volto, viso, faccia; (*surface*) superficie *f;* (*of coin*) diritto; (*of precious stone*) faccetta; (*of watch*) mostra; (*grimace*) smorfia; (*of building*) facciata; (typ) occhio; **in the face of** di fronte a; **to have a long face** fare il muso lungo; **to keep a straight face** contenere le risa; **to show one's face** farsi vedere || *tr* far fronte a, fronteggiare; (*a wall*) ricoprire; (*a suit*) foderare; **facing** di fronte a || *intr*—**to face about** voltarsi, fare dietro front; **to face on** dare a; **to face up to** guardare in faccia
face' card' *s* figura
face' lift'ing *s* plastica facciale
face' pow'der *s* cipria
facet ['fæsɪt] *s* faccetta; (fig) faccia
facetious [fə'siʃəs] *adj* faceto
face' val'ue *s* valore *m* facciale
facial ['feʃəl] *adj* facciale || *s* massaggio facciale
fa'cial tis'sue *s* velina detergente
facilitate [fə'sɪlɪ,tet] *tr* facilitare
facili•ty [fə'sɪlɪti] *s* (**-ties**) facilità *f;* **facilities** (*installations*) attrezzature *fpl;* (*for transportation*) mezzi *mpl;* (*services*) servizi *mpl*
facing ['fesɪŋ] *s* rivestimento
facsimile [fæk'sɪmɪli] *s* facsimile *m*
fact [fækt] *s* fatto; **in fact** in realtà; **the fact is that** il fatto si è che
faction ['fækʃən] *s* fazione; discordia
factional ['fækʃənəl] *adj* fazioso; (*partisan*) partigiano
factionalism ['fækʃənə,lɪzəm] *s* partigianeria; parzialità *f*
factor ['fæktər] *s* fattore *m* || *tr* scomporre in fattori
facto•ry ['fæktəri] *s* (**-ries**) fabbrica
factual ['fæktʃʊ·əl] *adj* effettivo, reale
facul•ty ['fækəlti] *s* (**-ties**) facoltà *f*
fad [fæd] *s* moda passeggera
fade [fed] *tr* stingere || *intr* (*said of colors*) stingersi, sbiadire; (*said of sounds, sight, radio signals, memory, etc.*) svanire, affievolirsi; (*said of beauty*) sfiorire
fade'-out' *s* affievolimento, affievolirsi *m;* (mov) chiusura in dissolvenza; (rad, telv) evanescenza
fading ['fedɪŋ] *s* affievolimento; (mov) dissolvenza; (rad, telv) evanescenza
fag [fæg] *s* schiavo del lavoro; (coll) sigaretta || *tr*—**to fag out** stancare
fagot ['fægət] *s* fascina, fastello
fail [fel] *s*—**without fail** senza meno || *tr* mancare (with *dat*); (*a student*) riprovare; (*an examination*) farsi bocciare in || *intr* fallire, venire a meno; (*said of a student*) farsi riprovare; (*said of a motor*) rompersi, fermarsi; (com) cadere in fallimento; **to fail to** mancare di
failure ['feljər] *s* insuccesso; insufficienza; (*student*) bocciato; (com) fallimento
faint [fent] *adj* debole; **to feel faint** sentirsi mancare || *s* svenimento || *intr* svenire
faint-hearted ['fent'hɑrtɪd] *adj* codardo, timido
fair [fer] *adj* giusto, onesto; (*moderately large*) discreto; (*even*) liscio; (*civil*) gentile; (*hair*) biondo; (*complexion*) chiaro; (*sky, weather*) sereno || *s* (*exhibition*) fiera; (*carnival*) sagra || *adv* direttamente; **to play fair** agire onestamente
fair'ground' *s* terreno dell'esposizione, campo della fiera
fairly ['ferli] *adv* giustamente, imparzialmente; discretamente, abbastanza; completamente
fair-minded ['fer'maɪndɪd] *adj* equanime, equo, giusto
fairness ['fernɪs] *s* giustizia, imparzialità *f;* bellezza; (*of complexion*) bianchezza
fair' play' *s* comportamento leale
fair' sex' *s* bel sesso
fair'-weath'er *adj*—**a fair-weather friend** un amico del tempo felice
fair•y ['feri] *adj* fatato || *s* (**-ies**) fata; (slang) finocchio
fair'y god'mother *s* buona fata
fair'y•land' *s* terra delle fate
fair'y tale' *s* fiaba, racconto delle fate
faith [feθ] *s* fede *f;* **to break faith with** venir meno alla parola data a; **to keep faith with** tener fede alla parola

data a; **to pin one's faith on** porre tutte le proprie speranze su; **upon my faith!** in fede mia!

faithful ['feθfəl] *adj* fedele || **the faithful** i fedeli

faithless ['feθlɪs] *adj* infedele, sleale

fake [fek] *adj* falso, finto || *s* contraffazione; (*person*) imbroglione *m* || *tr & intr* contraffare, falsificare

faker ['fekər] *s* (coll) imbroglione *m*

falcon ['fɔkən] or ['fɔlkən] *s* falcone *m*

falconer ['fɔkənər] or ['fɔlkənər] *s* falconiere *m*

falconry ['fɔkənri] or ['fɔlkənri] *s* falconeria

fall [fɔl] *adj* autunnale || *s* caduta; (*of water*) cataratta, cascata; (*of prices*) ribasso; (*autumn*) autunno; **falls** cataratta, cascate *fpl* || *v* (*pret* **fell** [fɛl]; *pp* **fallen** ['fɔlən]) *intr* cadere; discendere; **to fall apart** farsi a pezzi; **to fall back** (mil) ripiegare; **to fall behind** rimanere indietro; **to fall down** cadere; stramazzare; **to fall due** scadere; **to fall flat** stramazzare; essere un insuccesso; **to fall for** (slang) lasciarsi abbindolare da; (slang) innamorarsi di; **to fall in** (*said of a building*) crollare; (mil) allinearsi; **to fall in with** imbattersi in; mettersi d'accordo con; **to fall off** ritirarsi; diminuire; **to fall out** accadere; essere in disaccordo; (mil) rompere i ranghi; **to fall out of** cadere da; **to fall out with** inimicarsi con; **to fall over** cadere; (coll) adulare; **to fall through** fallire; **to fall to** cominciare; (coll) cominciare a mangiare; (*said, e.g., of an inheritance*) ricadere su; **to fall under** rientrare in

fallacious [fə'leʃəs] *adj* fallace

falla•cy ['fæləsi] *s* **(-cies)** fallacia

fall' guy' *s* (slang) testa di turco

fallible ['fælɪbəl] *adj* fallibile

fall'ing star' *s* stella cadente

fall'out' *s* pulviscolo radioattivo

fall'out shel'ter *s* rifugio antiatomico

fallow ['fælo] *adj* incolto; **to lie fallow** rimanere incolto || *s* maggese *m* || *tr* maggesare

false [fɔls] *adj* falso; (*hair, teeth, etc.*) posticcio, finto || *adv* falsamente; **to play false** tradire

false' bot'tom *s* doppio fondo

false' col'ors *spl* apparenze mentite

false' face' *s* maschera; (*ugly false face*) mascherone *m*

false'-heart'ed ['fɑls'hɑrtɪd] *adj* perfido

falsehood ['fɔls•hʊd] *s* falsità *f*, falso

false' pretens'es *spl* falso, impostura; **under false pretenses** allegando ragioni false

falset•to [fɔl'sɛto] *s* **(-tos)** (*voice*) falsetto; (*person*) cantante *m* in falsetto

falsi•fy ['fɔlsɪ,faɪ] *v* (*pret & pp* **-fied**) *tr* falsificare; (*to disprove*) smentire || *intr* mentire

falsi•ty ['fɔlsɪti] *s* **(-ties)** falsità *f*

falter ['fɔltər] *s* vacillamento; (*in speech*) balbettio || *intr* vacillare; balbettare

fame [fem] *s* fama

famed [femd] *adj* famoso

familiar [fə'mɪljər] *adj* familiare; intimo; **to be familiar with** (*people*) aver pratica con; (*things*) aver pratica di

familiari•ty [fə,mɪlɪ'ærɪti] *s* **(-ties)** familiarità *f*, dimestichezza

familiarize [fə'mɪljə,raɪz] *tr* far conoscere

fami•ly ['fæmɪli] *adj* familiare; **in the family way** (coll) in altro stato || *s* **(-lies)** famiglia

fam'ily man' *s* **(men')** padre *m* di famiglia

fam'ily name' *s* cognome *m*

fam'ily tree' *s* albero genealogico

famine ['fæmɪn] *s* carestia

famished ['fæmɪʃt] *adj* famelico; **to be famished** avere una fame da lupo

famous ['feməs] *adj* famoso; (coll) eccellente

fan [fæn] *s* ventaglio; (elec) ventilatore *m;* (coll) tifoso, patito || *v* (*pret & pp* **fanned;** *ger* **fanning**) *tr* sventagliare; (*to winnow*) vagliare; (*fire, passions*) attizzare || *intr* sventagliarsi; **to fan out** (*said of a road*) diramarsi a ventaglio

fanatic [fə'nætɪk] *adj & s* fanatico

fanatical [fə'nætɪkəl] *adj* fanatico

fanaticism [fə'nætɪ,sɪzəm] *s* fanatismo

fan' belt' *s* (aut) cinghia del ventilatore

fancied ['fænsid] *adj* immaginario

fancier ['fænsɪ•ər] *s* maniaco, tifoso; (*of animals*) conoscitore *m*, allevatore *m*

fanciful ['fænsɪfəl] *adj* fantasioso, estroso; immaginario

fan•cy ['fænsi] *adj* **(-cier; -ciest)** immaginario; immaginativo; ornamentale; di lusso; fantasioso, estroso || *s* fantasia; (*whim*) grillo, estro; **to take a fancy to** prendere una passione per || *v* (*pret & pp* **-cied**) *tr* immaginare

fan'cy ball' *s* ballo in costume

fan'cy dress' *s* costume *m*

fan'cy foods' *spl* cibi *mpl* di lusso

fan'cy-free' *adj* libero dai lacci dell'amore

fan'cy skat'ing *s* pattinaggio artistico

fan'cy•work' *s* (sew) ricamo ornamentale

fanfare ['fænfer] *s* fanfara

fang [fæŋ] *s* zanna; (*of reptile*) dente velenoso

fan'light' *s* lunetta

fantastic(al) [fæn'tæstɪk(əl)] *adj* fantastico

fanta•sy ['fæntəzi] or ['fæntəsi] *s* **(-sies)** fantasia

far [fɑr] *adj* distante; **on the far side of** dall'altra parte di || *adv* lontano; **as far as** fino a; **as far as I am concerned** per quanto mi riguardi; **as far as I know** per quanto io sappia; **by far** di gran lunga; **far and near** in lungo e in largo; **far away** molto lontano; **far be it from me** Dio me ne scampi e liberi; **far better** molto meglio; molto migliore; **far different** molto differente; **far from** lontano da; **far from it** tutto al contrario; **far into** fino al fondo di; **far into the night** fino a tarda ora; **far more** molto più; **far off** lontanissimo; **how far** quanto lontano; **how far is it?** a che distanza è da qui?; **in so far as** in quanto; **thus far** sinora; **to go far towards** contribuire molto a

faraway ['fɑrə,we] *adj* distante, lontano; distratto

farce [fɑrs] *s* farsa

farcical ['fɑrsɪkəl] *adj* farsesco

fare [fɛr] *s* prezzo della corsa; passeggero; (*food*) vitto || *intr* andare, e.g., **how did you fare?** come Le è andata?

Far' East' *s* Estremo Oriente

fare'well' *s* congedo, commiato; **to bid farewell to** or **to take farewell of** prender commiato da || *interj* addio!

far-fetched ['fɑr'fetʃt] *adj* peregrino, campato in aria

far-flung ['fɑr'flʌŋ] *adj* ampio; d'ampia distribuzione

farm [fɑrm] *adj* agricolo || *s* fattoria, tenuta || *tr* (*land*) coltivare || *intr* fare l'agricoltore or l'allevatore

farmer ['fɑrmər] *s* agricoltore *m*, contadino

farm' hand' *s* bracciante *m*

farm'house' *s* casa colonica, masseria

farming ['fɑrmɪŋ] *s* agricoltura, coltivazione

farm'yard' *s* aia

far'-off' *adj* lontano

far-reaching ['fɑr'ritʃɪŋ] *adj* di grande portata

far-sighted ['fɑr'saɪtɪd] *adj* lungimirante; perspicace; presbite

farther ['fɑrðər] *adj* più lontano; addizionale || *adv* più lontano, più in là; inoltre; **farther on** più oltre

farthest ['fɑrðɪst] *adj* (il) più lontano; ultimo || *adv* al massimo

farthing ['fɑrðɪŋ] *s* (Brit) quarto di centesimo

Far' West' *s* (U.S.A.) lontano Occidente

fascinate ['fæsɪ,net] *tr* affascinare

fascinating ['fæsɪ,netɪŋ] *adj* incantatore, affascinante

fascism ['fæsɪzəm] *s* fascismo

fascist ['fæsɪst] *adj & s* fascista *mf*

fashion ['fæʃən] *s* voga, moda; foggia, maniera; alta società; **after a fashion** in certo modo; **in fashion** di moda; **out of fashion** fuori moda; **to go out of fashion** passare di moda || *tr* fare, foggiare

fashionable ['fæʃənəbəl] *adj* elegante, alla moda

fash'ion design'ing *s* alta moda

fash'ion plate' *s* figurino

fash'ion show' *s* sfilata di moda

fast [fæst] or [fɑst] *adj* veloce; (*clock*) che corre, in anticipo; dissoluto; ben legato; (*color*) solido; (*friend*) fedele || *s* digiuno; **to break fast** rompere il digiuno || *adv* rapidamente; fortemente; (*asleep*) profondamente; **to hold fast** tenersi saldo; **to live fast** condurre una vita dissoluta || *intr* digiunare, fare vigilia

fast' day' *s* giorno di magro

fasten ['fæsən] or ['fɑsən] *tr* fissare; attaccare; (*a door*) sbarrare; (*a nickname; blows*) affibbiare; (*a dress*) allacciarsi || *intr* attaccarsi

fastener ['fæsənər] or ['fɑsənər] *s* legaccio, laccio; (*snap, clasp*) fermaglio; (*for papers*) fermacarte *m*

fastidious [fæs'tɪdɪ·əs] *adj* schizzinoso; meticoloso

fasting ['fæstɪŋ] or ['fɑstɪŋ] *s* digiuno

fat [fæt] *adj* (**fatter; fattest**) grasso; (*productive*) forte, ricco, pingue; **to get fat** ingrassare || *s* grasso, unto; (*of pork*) sugna

fatal ['fetəl] *adj* fatale

fatalism ['fetə,lɪzəm] *s* fatalismo

fatalist ['fetəlɪst] *s* fatalista *mf*

fatali·ty [fə'tælɪti] *s* (**-ties**) (*in an accident*) morte *f;* accidente *m* mortale; fatalità *f*

fate [fet] *s* fato; **the Fates** le Parche || *tr* predestinare

fated ['fetɪd] *adj* destinato

fateful ['fetfəl] *adj* fatidico, fatale

fat'head' *s* (coll) zuccone *m*

father ['fɑðər] *s* padre *m;* (*male ancestor*) antenato || *tr* procreare; creare; assumere la paternità di

fatherhood ['fɑðər,hʊd] *s* paternità *f*

fa'ther-in-law' *s* (**fathers-in-law**) suocero

fa'ther·land' *s* patria

fatherless ['fɑðərlɪs] *adj* orfano di padre; senza padre

fatherly ['fɑðərli] *adj* paterno

Fa'ther's Day' *s* festa del papà

Fa'ther Time' *s* il Tempo

fathom ['fæðəm] *s* braccio || *tr* sondare

fathomless ['fæðəmlɪs] *adj* senza fondo; imponderabile

fatigue [fə'tig] *s* fatica, strapazzo; (mil) comandata || *tr* stancare, affaticare

fatigue' clothes' *spl* (mil) tenuta di servizio, tenuta di fatica

fatten ['fætən] *tr & intr* ingrassare

fat·ty ['fæti] *adj* (**-tier; -tiest**) grasso; (pathol) adiposo || *s* (**-ties**) (coll) tombolo

fatuous ['fætʃʊ·əs] *adj* fatuo

faucet ['fɔsɪt] *s* rubinetto

fault [fɔlt] *s* (*misdeed, blame*) colpa; (*defect*) difetto, magagna; (geol) faglia; (sports) fallo; **it's your fault** è colpa Sua; **to a fault** all'eccesso; **to find fault with** trovare a ridire sul conto di

fault'find'er *s* ipercritico, criticone *m*

fault'find'ing *adj* criticone || *s* ipercritica

faultless ['fɔltlɪs] *adj* perfetto, inappuntabile

fault·y ['fɔlti] *adj* (**-ier; -iest**) manchevole, difettuoso

faun [fɔn] *s* fauno

fauna ['fɔnə] *s* fauna

favor ['fevər] *s* favore *m;* (*letter*) pregiata; **do me the favor to** mi faccia il

piacere di; **by your favor** col Suo permesso; **favors** regali *mpl* di festa; **to be in favor with** essere nelle grazie di; **to be out of favor** cadere in disgrazia || *tr* favorire; (coll) assomigliare (with *dat*)
favorable ['fevərəbəl] *adj* favorevole
favorite ['fevərɪt] *adj & s* favorito
favoritism ['fevərɪ,tɪzəm] *s* favoritismo
fawn [fɔn] *s* cerbiatto || *intr*—**to fawn on** adulare, strusciarsi a
faze [fez] *tr* (coll) perturbare
fear [fɪr] *s* paura; **for fear of** per paura di; **for fear that** per paura che; **no fear** non c'è pericolo; **to be in fear of** aver timore di || *tr & intr* temere
fearful ['fɪrfəl] *adj* pauroso, timorato; (coll) spaventoso
fearless ['fɪrlɪs] *adj* impavido
feasible ['fizɪbəl] *adj* fattibile, possibile
feast [fist] *s* festa; (*sumptuous meal*) festino, banchetto || *tr* intrattenere || *intr* banchettare; **to feast on** rallegrarsi alla vista di
feat [fit] *s* fatto, prodezza
feather ['fɛðər] *s* penna; (*soft and fluffy structure covering bird*) piuma; (*type*) qualità *f*, conio; (*tuft*) pennacchio; **in fine feather** di buon umore; in buona salute || *tr* impennare; coprire di piume; (naut) spalare; (aer) bandierare; **to feather one's nest** arricchirsi
feath'er bed' *s* letto di piume
feath'er•bed'ding *s* impiego di mano d'opera non necessaria richiesto da un sindacato operaio
feath'er•brain' *s* cervello di gallina
feath'er•edge' *s* (*of board*) augnatura; (*of sharpened tool*) filo morto
feath'er•weight' *s* peso piuma
feathery ['fɛðəri] *adj* piumato; leggero
feature ['fitʃər] *s* fattezza; caratteristica; (journ) articolo principale; (mov) attrazione; **features** fattezze *fpl* || *tr* caratterizzare; mettere in evidenza; (coll) immaginare
fea'ture film' *s* lungometraggio
fea'ture sto'ry *s* articolo di spalla
February ['fɛbrʊ,ɛri] *s* febbraio
feces ['fisiz] *spl* feci *fpl*
feckless ['fɛklɪs] *adj* debole; inetto
federal ['fɛdərəl] *adj* federale || *s* federalista *mf*
federate ['fɛdə,ret] *adj* federato || *tr* federare || *intr* federarsi
federation [,fɛdə'reʃən] *s* federazione
federative ['fɛdə,retɪv] or ['fɛdərətɪv] *adj* federativo
fedora [fɪ'dorə] *s* cappello floscio di feltro
fed' up' [fɛd] *adj* stanco e stufo; **to be fed up with** averne fin sopra gli occhi di
fee [fi] *s* onorario; (*charge allowed by law*) diritto; (*tip*) mancia; (*for tuition*) tassa; (*for admission*) ingresso || *tr* pagare
feeble ['fibəl] *adj* debole, fievole
feeble-minded ['fibəl'maɪndɪd] *adj* rimbecillito; debole, vacillante
feed [fid] *s* mangime *m;* (coll) mangiata; (mach) dispositivo d'alimentazione || *v* (*pret & pp* **fed** [fɛd]) *tr* nutrire; (*a machine*) alimentare; (*cattle*) pascere; (theat) imbeccare || *intr* mangiare; **to feed upon** nutrirsi di
feed'back' *s* (*of a computer*) ritorno d'informazioni; (electron) reazione
feed' bag' *s* musetta
feed' pump' *s* pompa di alimentazione
feed' trough' *s* (*for cattle*) vasca; (*for hogs*) trogolo
feed' wire' *s* cavo di alimentazione
feel [fil] *s* sensazione; (*touch*) tocco; (*vague mental impression*) senso || *v* (*pret & pp* **felt** [fɛlt]) *tr* sentire; (*e.g., with the hands*) palpare, toccare; (*s.o.'s pulse*) tastare || *intr* (*sick, tired, etc.*) sentirsi; **to feel bad** sentirsi male; (*to be unhappy*) essere spiacente; **to feel cheap** vergognarsi; **to feel comfortable** sentirsi a proprio agio; **to feel for** cercare di toccare; avere compassione per; **to feel like** aver voglia di; **to feel safe** sentirsi al sicuro; **to feel sorry** essere spiacente; pentirsi; **to feel sorry for** aver compassione di; pentirsi di
feeler ['filər] *s* (*hint*) sondaggio; **feelers** (*of insect*) antenne *fpl;* (*of mollusk*) tentacoli *mpl;* **to put out feelers** (fig) tastare il terreno
feeling ['filɪŋ] *s* (*with senses*) senso; (*impression, emotion*) sentimento, sensazione; opinione
feign [fen] *tr* fingere; inventare; imitare || *intr* far finta; **to feign to be** fingersi
feint [fent] *s* finta || *intr* fare una finta
feldspar ['fɛld,spɑr] *s* feldspato
felicitate [fə'lɪsɪ,tet] *tr* felicitarsi con
felicitous [fə'lɪsɪtəs] *adj* felice, indovinato; eloquente
fell [fɛl] *adj* crudele, mortale || *tr* (*trees*) abbattere
felloe ['fɛlo] *s* cerchione *m;* (*part of the rim*) gavello
fellow ['fɛlo] *s* compagno; collega *m;* (*of a society*) membro, socio; (*holder of fellowship*) borsista *mf;* (coll) tipo, tizio; (coll) innamorato; **good fellow** buon diavolo; galantuomo
fel'low cit'izen *s* concittadino
fel'low coun'try•man *s* (**-men**) concittadino
fel'low crea'ture *s* prossimo
fel'low-man' *s* (**-men'**) prossimo
fel'low mem'ber *s* consocio
fellowship ['fɛlo,ʃɪp] *s* compagnia; (*for study*) borsa di studio
fel'low trav'eler *s* simpatizzante *mf;* criptocomunista *mf;* compagno di viaggio
felon ['fɛlən] *s* criminale *mf;* (pathol) patereccio, giradito
felo•ny ['fɛləni] *s* (**-nies**) delitto doloso
felt [fɛlt] *s* feltro
felt' board' *s* lavagna di panno
felt'-tip pen' *s* pennarello
female ['fimel] *adj* (*sex*) femminile;

(*animal, plant, piece of a device*) femmina || *s* femmina
feminine [ˈfɛmɪnɪn] *adj & s* femminile *m*
feminism [ˈfɛmɪˌnɪzəm] *s* femminismo
fence [fɛns] *s* steccato, staccionata; (*for stolen goods*) ricettatore *m;* (carp) squadra di guida; (sports) scherma; **on the fence** (coll) indeciso || *tr* recingere || *intr* tirare di scherma
fencing [ˈfɛnsɪŋ] *s* scherma; (fig) schermaglia
fenc'ing mask' *s* visiera
fend [fɛnd] *tr*—**to fend off** parare || *intr*—**to fend for oneself** (coll) badare a sé stesso
fender [ˈfɛndər] *s* (*of trolley car*) salvagente *m;* (*of fireplace*) parafuoco; (aut) parafango; (naut) parabordo
fennel [ˈfɛnəl] *s* finocchio
ferment [ˈfʌrmɛnt] *s* fermento || [fərˈmɛnt] *tr & intr* fermentare
fern [fʌrn] *s* felce *f*
ferocious [fəˈroʃəs] *adj* feroce
ferocity [fəˈrɑsɪti] *s* ferocia
ferret [ˈfɛrɪt] *s* furetto || *tr*—**to ferret out** scovare || *intr* indagare
Fer'ris wheel' [ˈfɛrɪs] *s* ruota (del parco dei divertimenti)
fer•ry [ˈfɛri] *s* (**-ries**) traghetto; nave *f* traghetto || *v* (*pret & pp* **-ried**) *tr* traghettare || *intr* attraversare
fer'ry•boat' *s* nave *f* traghetto, ferryboat *m*
fertile [ˈfʌrtɪl] *adj* fertile
fertilize [ˈfʌrtɪˌlaɪz] *tr* fertilizzare; (*to impregnate*) fecondare
fertilizer [ˈfʌrtɪˌlaɪzər] *s* fertilizzante *m;* (*e.g., of flowers*) fecondatore *m*
fervent [ˈfʌrvənt] *adj* fervente, fervido
fervid [ˈfʌrvɪd] *adj* fervido
fervor [ˈfʌrvər] *s* fervore *m*
fester [ˈfɛstər] *s* ulcera, piaga || *tr* corrompere || *intr* suppurare; (fig) corrompersi
festival [ˈfɛstɪvəl] *adj* festivo || *s* festa; (*of music*) festival *m*
festive [ˈfɛstɪv] *adj* festivo
festivi•ty [fɛsˈtɪvɪti] *s* (**-ties**) festività *f*
festoon [fɛsˈtun] *s* festone *m* || *tr* ornare di festoni
fetch [fɛtʃ] *tr* andare a prendere; (*a price*) fruttare, vendersi per
fetching [ˈfɛtʃɪŋ] *adj* (coll) cattivante, attraente
fete [fet] *s* festa || *tr* festeggiare
fetid [ˈfɛtɪd] or [ˈfitɪd] *adj* fetido
fetish [ˈfitɪʃ] or [ˈfɛtɪʃ] *s* feticcio
fetlock [ˈfɛtlɑk] *s* nocca; (*tuft of hair*) barbetta
fetter [ˈfɛtər] *s* ceppo, catena || *tr* mettere ai ceppi, incatenare
fettle [ˈfɛtəl] *s* stato, condizione; **in fine fettle** in buone condizioni
fetus [ˈfitəs] *s* feto
feud [fjud] *s* antagonismo; odio ereditario || *intr* essere in lotta
feudal [ˈfjudəl] *adj* feudale
feudalism [ˈfjudəˌlɪzəm] *s* feudalismo
fever [ˈfivər] *s* febbre *f*
feverish [fivərɪʃ] *adj* febbrile
few [fju] *adj & pron* pochi; **a few** alcuni; **quite a few** molti

fiancé [ˌfi·ɑnˈse] *s* fidanzato
fiancée [ˌfi·ɑnˈse] *s* fidanzata
fias•co [fɪˈæsko] *s* (**-cos** or **-coes**) fiasco
fib [fɪb] *s* menzogna, frottola || *v* (*pret & pp* **fibbed;** *ger* **fibbing**) *intr* raccontar frottole
fiber [ˈfaɪbər] *s* fibra; (fig) tempra
fi'ber•glass' *s* vetroresina
fibrous [ˈfaɪbrəs] *adj* fibroso
fickle [ˈfɪkəl] *adj* volubile, incostante, mobile
fiction [ˈfɪkʃən] *s* (*invention*) finzione; (*branch of literature*) novellistica
fictional [ˈfɪkʃənəl] *adj* immaginario
fictionalize [ˈfɪkʃənəˌlaɪz] *tr* romanzare
fictitious [fɪkˈtɪʃəs] *adj* fittizio
fiddle [ˈfɪdəl] *s* violino; **fit as a fiddle** in perfetta salute || *tr* (coll) suonare sul violino; **to fiddle away** (coll) sprecare || *intr* (coll) suonare il violino; **to fiddle with** (coll) giocherellare con
fiddler [ˈfɪdlər] *s* (coll) violinista *mf*
fiddling [ˈfɪdlɪŋ] *adj* triviale, futile, insignificante
fideli•ty [faɪˈdɛlɪti] or [fɪˈdɛlɪti] *s* (**-ties**) fedeltà *f*
fidget [ˈfɪdʒɪt] *intr* agitarsi; **to fidget with** giocherellare con
fidgety [ˈfɪdʒɪti] *adj* irrequieto
fiduciar•y [fɪˈdjuʃɪˌɛri] or [fɪˈduʃɪˌɛri] *adj* fiduciario || *s* (**-ies**) fiduciario
fie [faɪ] *interj* vergogna!
fief [fif] *s* feudo
field [fild] *adj* (mil) da campagna || *s* campo; (sports) terreno; (min) giacimento; (*of motor or dynamo*) (elec) induttore *m;* (phys) campo
fielder [ˈfildər] *s* (*outfielder*) giocatore *m* del campo esterno
field' glass'es *spl* binocolo
field' hock'ey *s* hockey *m* su prato
field' mag'net *s* induttore *m,* calamita induttrice
field' mar'shal *s* (mil) maresciallo di campo
field' mouse' *s* topo di campagna
field'piece' *s* pezzo da campagna
fiend [find] *s* diavolo; (coll) addetto, tifoso
fiendish [ˈfindɪʃ] *adj* diabolico
fierce [fɪrs] *adj* fiero, feroce; (*wind*) furioso; (coll) maledetto
fierceness [ˈfɪrsnɪs] *s* ferocia
fier•y [ˈfaɪri] or [ˈfaɪ·əri] *adj* (**-ier; -iest**) ardente, focoso
fife [faɪf] *s* piffero
fifteen [ˈfɪfˈtin] *adj, s & pron* quindici *m*
fifteenth [ˈfɪfˈtinθ] *adj, s & pron* quindicesimo || *s* (*in dates*) quindici *m*
fifth [fɪfθ] *adj, s & pron* quinto || *s* (*in dates*) cinque *m*
fifth' col'umn *s* quinta colonna
fiftieth [ˈfɪftɪ·ɪθ] *adj, s & pron* cinquantesimo
fif•ty [ˈfɪfti] *adj & pron* cinquanta || *s* (**-ties**) cinquanta *m;* **the fifties** gli anni cinquanta

fif'ty-fif'ty *adv*—**to go fifty-fifty** fare a metà
fig [fɪg] *s* fico
fight [faɪt] *s* lotta; baruffa; combattimento; spirito combattivo; (sports) incontro; **to pick a fight with** attaccar briga con ‖ *v* (*pret & pp* **fought** [fɔt]) *tr* lottare con; combattere contro; opporsi a ‖ *intr* lottare; combattere; **to fight shy of** cercar di evitare
fighter ['faɪtər] *s* lottatore *m;* (*warrior*) combattente *m;* (aer) caccia *m*
fig' leaf' *s* foglia di fico
figment ['fɪgmənt] *s* finzione
figurative ['fɪgjərətɪv] *adj* (fa) figurativo; (rhet) figurato
figure ['fɪgjər] *s* figura; numero; prezzo; **to be good at figures** far bene di conto; **to cut a figure** fare una buona figura; **to keep one's figure** conservare la linea ‖ *tr* figurare; immaginare; raffigurare; supporre, calcolare; **to figure out** calcolare; decifrare ‖ *intr* apparire; **to figure on** (coll) contare su
fig'ure·head' *s* uomo di paglia, prestanome *m;* (naut) polena
fig'ure of speech' *s* figura retorica
fig'ure skat'ing *s* pattinaggio artistico
figurine [ˌfɪgjə'rin] *s* figurina
filament ['fɪləmənt] *s* filamento
filbert ['fɪlbərt] *s* (*tree*) nocciolo, avellano; (*nut*) nocciola, avellana
filch [fɪltʃ] *tr* rubacchiare
file [faɪl] *s* (*row*) fila; (*tool*) lima; (*folder*) filza; (*room*) archivio; (*of cards*) schedario ‖ *tr* mettere in fila; limare; archiviare, schedare; (journ) trasmettere ‖ *intr* sfilare; **to file for** fare domanda di
file' clerk' *s* schedarista *mf*
filet [fɪ'le] or ['fɪle] *s* filetto ‖ *tr* tagliare in filetti
filial ['fɪlɪ·əl] or ['fɪljəl] *adj* filiale
filiation [ˌfɪlɪ'eʃən] *s* filiazione
filibuster ['fɪlɪˌbʌstər] *s* (*tactics*) ostruzionismo; (*speech*) discorso ostruzionista; (*person making such a speech*) ostruzionista *mf;* (*buccaneer*) filibustiere *m* ‖ *tr* fare ostruzionismo contro ‖ *intr* fare dell'ostruzionismo
filigree ['fɪlɪˌgri] *adj* filigranato ‖ *s* filigrana ‖ *tr* lavorare in filigrana
filing ['faɪlɪŋ] *s* (*of documents*) schedatura; limatura; **filings** limatura
fil'ing cab'inet *s* schedario
fil'ing card' *s* cartellino, scheda
fill [fɪl] *s* sazietà *f;* (*place filled with earth*) terrapieno; **to have** or **get one's fill** mangiare a sazietà ‖ *tr* riempire; (*an order*) eseguire; (*a hole*) otturare; (*a tooth*) piombare; (*a tire*) gonfiare; (*a place*) occupare; (*with sand*) interrare; **to fill out** (*a form*) riempire; **to fill up** (aut) fare il pieno di ‖ *intr* riempirsi; **to fill in** prendere il posto; **to fill up** riempirsi
filler ['fɪlər] *s* ripieno; (*person*) riempitore *m;* (painting) mestica; (journ) articolo riempitivo
fillet ['fɪlɪt] *s* nastro, fascia; (*for hair*) nastro; (archit) listello ‖ *tr* filettare ‖ ['fɪle] or ['fɪlɪt] *s* (*of meat or fish*) filetto ‖ *tr* tagliare a filetti
filling ['fɪlɪŋ] *s* (*of a tooth*) impiombatura; (*of turkey*) ripieno
fill'ing sta'tion *s* stazione di rifornimento
fillip ['fɪlɪp] *s* stimolo; colpetto col dito ‖ *tr* dare un colpetto col dito a; (fig) stimulare
fil·ly ['fɪli] *s* (**-lies**) puledra
film [fɪlm] *s* pellicola; (mov, phot) pellicola, film *m* ‖ *tr* filmare
film' li'brary *s* cineteca, filmoteca
film'strip' *s* filmina
film·y ['fɪlmi] *adj* (**-ier; -iest**) sottile, delicato; (*look*) annebbiato
filter ['fɪltər] *s* filtro ‖ *tr & intr* filtrare
filtering ['fɪltərɪŋ] *s* filtrazione
fil'ter pa'per *s* carta da filtro
fil'ter tip' *s* filtro, bocchino filtro
filth [fɪlθ] *s* sporco, sporcizia
filth·y ['fɪlθi] *adj* (**-ier; -iest**) sporco, sudicio
filth'y lu'cre ['lukər] *s* il vile metallo
filtrate ['fɪltret] *s* liquido filtrato ‖ *tr & intr* filtrare
fin [fɪn] *s* pinna; (slang) biglietto da cinque dollari
final ['faɪnəl] *adj* finale; (*last in a series*) ultimo; definitivo, insindacabile ‖ *s* esame *m* finale; **finals** (sports) finale *f*
finale [fɪ'nɑli] *s* (mus) finale *m*
finalist ['faɪnəlɪst] *s* finalista *mf*
finally ['faɪnəli] *adv* finalmente
finance [fɪ'næns] or ['faɪnæns] *s* finanza; **finances** finanze *fpl* ‖ *tr* finanziare
financial [fɪ'nænʃəl] or [faɪ'nænʃəl] *adj* finanziario
financier [ˌfɪnən'sɪr] or [ˌfaɪnən'sɪr] *s* finanziere *m*
financing [fɪ'nænsɪŋ] or ['faɪnænsɪŋ] *s* finanziamento
finch [fɪntʃ] *s* fringuello
find [faɪnd] *s* trovata ‖ *v* (*pret & pp* **found** [faʊnd]) *tr* trovare; rinvenire; (*s.o. innocent or guilty*) dichiarare; **to find out** venire a sapere ‖ *intr* (law) sentenziare; **to find out about** informarsi su
finder ['faɪndər] *s* (phot) mirino; (astr) cannochiale cercatore
finding ['faɪndɪŋ] *s* scoperta; (law) sentenza
fine [faɪn] *adj* buono; bello; fino, fine ‖ *s* multa ‖ *adv* (coll) benissimo; **to feel fine** (coll) sentirsi benissimo ‖ *tr* multare
fine' arts' *spl* belle arti
fineness ['faɪnnɪs] *s* finezza; (*of metal*) titolo
fine' print' *s* testo in caratteri minuti
finer·y ['faɪnəri] *s* (**-ies**) ornamenti *mpl,* fronzoli *mpl;* abito vistoso
fine-spun ['faɪnˌspʌn] *adj* sottile
finesse [fɪ'nes] *s* finezza; (bridge) impasse *f* ‖ *tr* fare l'impasse a ‖ *intr* fare l'impasse
fine'-tooth comb' *s* pettine fitto; **to go over with a fine-tooth comb** esaminare minuziosamente

finger ['fɪŋgər] *s* dito; **to have a finger in the pie** avere le mani in pasta; **to put one's finger on the spot** mettere il dito nella piaga; **to slip between the fingers** sfuggire di tra le dita; **to snap one's fingers at** infischiarsi di; **to twist around one's little finger** fare ciò che si vuole di || *tr* toccare con le dita; (*to pilfer*) rubacchiare; (slang) mostrare a dito
fin'ger board' *s* (mus) tastiera
fin'ger bowl' *s* sciacquadita *m*
fingering ['fɪŋgərɪŋ] *s* palpeggiamento; (mus) diteggiatura
fin'ger mark' *s* ditata
fin'ger•nail' *s* unghia
fin'ger•print' *s* impronta digitale || *tr* prendere le impronte digitali di
fin'ger•tip' *s* polpastrello; **to have at one's fingertips** avere sulla punta delle dita, sapere a menadito
finical ['fɪnɪkəl] or **finicky** ['fɪnɪki] *adj* pignolo, schizzinoso
finish ['fɪnɪʃ] *s* fine *f;* finitura; (sports) finale *m* || *tr* finire; **to finish off** distruggere || *intr* finire; **to finish** + *ger* finire di + *inf;* **to finish by** + *ger* finire per + *inf*
fin'ishing school' *s* scuola di perfezionamento per signorine
fin'ishing touch' *s* ultimo tocco
finite ['faɪnaɪt] *adj* finito
Finland ['fɪnlənd] *s* la Finlandia
Finlander ['fɪnləndər] *s* finlandese *mf*
Finn [fɪn] *s* (*member of a Finnish-speaking group of people*) finnico; (*native or inhabitant of Finland*) finlandese *mf*
Finnic ['fɪnɪk] *adj & s* finnico
Finnish ['fɪnɪʃ] *adj* finlandese || *s* (*language*) finlandese *m*
fir [fʌr] *s* abete *m*
fire [faɪr] *s* fuoco; (*destructive burning*) incendio; **to be on fire** ardere; **to be under enemy fire** essere sotto tiro nemico; **to catch fire** infiammarsi; **to hang fire** essere in sospeso; **to open fire** aprire il fuoco; **to set on fire, to set fire to** dar fuoco a; **under fire** sotto fuoco nemico; accusato || *tr* accendere; (*an oven*) scaldare; (*bricks*) cuocere; (*a weapon*) sparare; (*the imagination*) riscaldare; (*an employee*) (coll) licenziare || *intr* accendersi; **to fire on** far fuoco su; **to fire up** attivare una caldaia
fire' alarm' *s* avvisatore *m* d'incendio
fire'arm' *s* arma da fuoco
fire'ball' *s* palla da cannone esplosiva; (*lightning*) lampo a forma di globo infocato; meteorite *m* a forma di globo infocato; globo infocato
fire'boat' *s* lancia dei pompieri
fire'box' *s* (*of a boiler*) fornello; (*to give alarm*) stazione d'allarme
fire'brand' *s* tizzone *m;* (fig) fiaccola della discordia
fire'brick' *s* mattone refrattario
fire' brigade' *s* corpo di pompieri volontari
fire'bug' *s* (coll) incendiario
fire' com'pany *s* corpo dei pompieri; compagnia d'assicurazioni contro gli incendi
fire'crack'er *s* mortaretto
fire'damp' *s* grisou *m*
fire' depart'ment *s* corpo dei pompieri
fire'dog' *s* alare *m*
fire' drill' *s* esercitazione in caso d'incendio
fire' en'gine *s* autopompa
fire' escape' *s* scala di sicurezza
fire' extin'guisher *s* estintore *m*
fire'fly' *s* (**-flies**) lucciola
fire'guard' *s* parafuoco
fire' hose' *s* manichetta
fire'house' *s* caserma dei pompieri
fire' hy'drant *s* bocca d'incendi
fire' insur'ance *s* assicurazione contro gli incendi
fire' i'rons *spl* arnesi *mpl* del camino
fire'man *s* (**-men**) (*man who extinguishes fires*) pompiere *m,* vigile *m* del fuoco; (*stoker*) fochista *m*
fire'place' *s* camino
fire'plug' *s* bocca da incendio, idrante *m*
fire'proof' *adj* incombustibile || *tr* rendere incombustibile
fire' sale' *s* vendita di merce avariata dal fuoco
fire' screen' *s* parafuoco
fire' ship' *s* brulotto
fire'side' *s* focolare *m*
fire'trap' *s* edificio senza mezzi adeguati per combattere incendi
fire' wall' *s* paratia antincendio
fire'wa'ter *s* (coll) acquavite *f*
fire'wood' *s* legna
fire'works' *spl* fuochi *mpl* artificiali
firing ['faɪrɪŋ] *s* (*of furnace*) alimentazione; (*of bricks*) cottura; (*of a gun*) sparo; (*of soldiers*) tiro; (*of an internal-combustion engine*) accensione; (*of an employee*) (coll) licenziamento
fir'ing line' *s* linea del fuoco
fir'ing or'der *s* (aut) ordine *m* d'accensione
fir'ing pin' *s* percussore *m*
fir'ing squad' *s* (*for saluting at a burial*) plotone *m* d'onore; (*for executing*) plotone *m* d'esecuzione
firm [fʌrm] *adj* forte, fermo || *s* ditta, compagnia
firmament ['fʌrməmənt] *s* firmamento
firm' name' *s* ragione *f* sociale
firmness ['fʌrmnɪs] *s* fermezza
first [fʌrst] *adj* primo || *s* primo; (aut) prima; (mus) voce *f* principale; **at first** sulle prime; **from the first** da bel principio || *adv* prima; **first of all** per prima cosa
first' aid' *s* pronto soccorso
first'-aid' kit' *s* cassetta farmaceutica d'urgenza
first'-aid' sta'tion *s* posto di pronto soccorso
first'-born' *adj & s* primogenito
first'-class' *adj* di prim'ordine, sopraffino || *adv* in prima classe
first' cous'in *s* cugino primo
first'-day cov'er *s* busta primo giorno
first' draft' *s* brutta copia

first' fin'ger *s* dito indice
first' floor' *s* pianoterra *m*
first' fruits' *spl* primizie *fpl*
first' lieuten'ant *s* tenente *m*
firstly ['fʌrstli] *adv* in primo luogo
first' mate' *s* (naut) primo ufficiale, comandante *m* in seconda, secondo
first' name' *s* nome *m* di battesimo
first' night' *s* (theat) prima
first' of'ficer *s* (naut) primo ufficiale, comandante *m* in seconda, secondo
first'-rate' *adj* di prima forza; eccellente || *adv* (coll) benissimo
first'-run' *adj* di prima visione
fiscal ['fɪskəl] *adj* (*pertaining to public treasury*) fiscale; finanziario || *s* avvocato fiscale
fis'cal year' *s* esercizio finanziario
fish [fɪʃ] *s* pesce *m;* **to be like a fish out of water** essere come un pesce fuor d'acqua; **to be neither fish nor fowl** non essere né carne né pesce; **to drink like a fish** bere come una spugna || *tr* pescare || *intr* pescare; **to fish for compliments** cercare di farsi fare dei complimenti; **to go fishing** andare alla pesca; **to take fishing** portare con sé alla pesca
fish'bone' *s* lisca, spina di pesce
fish'bowl' *s* vaschetta per i pesci rossi
fisher ['fɪʃər] *s* pescatore *m;* (zool) martora canadese
fish'er•man *s* **(-men)** pescatore *m;* (*boat*) peschereccio
fisher•y ['fɪʃəri] *s* **(-ies)** (*activity*) pesca; (*business*) pescheria; (*grounds*) riserva di pesca, luogo dove si pesca
fish' glue' *s* colla di pesce
fish'hook' *s* amo
fishing ['fɪʃɪŋ] *adj* da pesca || *s* pesca
fish'ing reel' *s* mulinello
fish'ing rod' *s* canna da pesca
fish'ing tack'le *s* attrezzatura da pesca
fish'line' *s* lenza
fish' mar'ket *s* pescheria
fish'pool' *s* peschiera
fish' spear' *s* fiocina
fish' sto'ry *s* (coll) fandonia; **to tell fish stories** spararle grosse
fish'tail' *s* (aut) imbardata (aer) spedalata || *intr* (aut) imbardare; (aer) compiere una spedalata
fish'wife' *s* **(-wives')** pescivendola; (*foul-mouthed woman*) ciana
fish'worm' *s* lombrico
fish•y ['fɪʃi] *adj* **(-ier; -iest)** che sa di pesce; (coll) dubbioso, inverosimile
fission ['fɪʃən] *s* (biol) scissione; (phys) fissione
fissionable ['fɪʃənəbəl] *adj* fissionabile
fissure ['fɪʃər] *s* fenditura; (*in rock*) crepaccio
fist [fɪst] *s* pugno; (typ) indice *m;* **to shake one's fist at** mostrare i pugni a
fist'fight' *s* scontro a pugni
fist'ful' *s* pugno, manciata
fisticuff ['fɪstɪ,kʌf] *s* pugno; **fisticuffs** scontro a pugni
fit [fɪt] *adj* **(fitter; fittest)** indicato; idoneo, adatto; in buona salute; **fit to be tied** (coll) infuriato, arrabbiatissimo; **fit to eat** mangiabile; **to feel fit** sentirsi in buona salute; **to see fit** giudicare conveniente || *s* equipaggiamento; (*of a suit*) taglio; (*of one piece with another*) incastro; (*of coughing*) accesso; (*of anger*) attacco; **by fits and starts** a pezzi e a bocconi || *v* (*pret & pp* **fitted;** *ger* **fitting**) *tr* adattare; quadrare a; andar bene a; equipaggiare; preparare; servire a; esser d'accordo con; **to fit out** or **up** attrezzare, equipaggiare || *intr* stare; incastrare; (*said of clothes*) cascare; entrare; **to fit in** entrarci
fitful ['fɪtfəl] *adj* capriccioso; incostante, irregolare
fitness ['fɪtnɪs] *s* convenienza; idoneità *f;* buona salute
fitter ['fɪtər] *s* aggiustatore *m;* (*of machinery*) montatore *m;* (*of clothing*) sarto che mette in prova
fitting ['fɪtɪŋ] *adj* appropriato, adatto, conveniente || *s* adattamento; (*of a garment*) prova; tubo adattabile; (carp) incastro; **fittings** accessori *mpl;* utensili *mpl;* (*iron trimmings*) ferramenta *fpl*
five [faɪv] *adj & pron* cinque || *s* cinque *m;* **five o' clock** le cinque
five' hun'dred *adj, s & pron* cinquecento
five'-year plan' *s* piano quinquennale
fix [fɪks] *s*—**in a tight fix** (coll) nei pasticci; **to be in a fix** (coll) star fresco, essere nei guai || *tr* riparare; fissare; (*a meal*) preparare; (*a bayonet*) inastare; (*attention*) attrarre, fermare; (*hair*) mettere a posto; (coll) arrangiare || *intr* fissarsi, stabilirsi; **to fix on** scegliere
fixed [fɪkst] *adj* fisso; (*time*) improrogabile; (coll) arrangiato
fixing ['fɪksɪŋ] *adj* fissativo || *s* (*fastening*) attacco; (phot) fissaggio; **with all the fixings** (coll) con tutti i contorni
fix'ing bath' *s* bagno di fissaggio
fixture ['fɪkstʃər] *s* infisso; accessorio; (*of a lamp*) guarnizione; **fixtures** (*e.g., of a store*) suppellettili *fpl*
fizz [fɪz] *s* effervescenza; gazosa; (Brit) spumante *m* || *intr* frizzare
fizzle ['fɪzəl] *s* (coll) fiasco || *intr* crepitare; (coll) fare fiasco
flabbergast ['flæbər,gæst] *tr* (coll) sbalordire, lasciare stupefatto
flab•by ['flæbi] *adj* **(-bier; -biest)** floscio, flaccido, cascante
flag [flæg] *s* bandiera || *v* (*pret & pp* **flagged;** *ger* **flagging**) *tr* imbandierare; segnalare; (rr) far fermare || *intr* ammosciarsi, afflosciarsi
flageolet [,flædʒə'lɛt] *s* flautino
flag'man *s* **(-men)** (rr) manovratore *m*
flag' of truce' *s* bandiera parlamentaria
flag'pole' *s* pennone *m*
flagrant ['flegrənt] *adj* flagrante; scandaloso
flag'ship' *s* nave ammiraglia
flag'staff' *s* pennone *m*
flag' sta'tion *s* (rr) stazione facoltativa
flag'stone' *s* lastra di pietra

flag' stop' *s* (rr) fermata facoltativa
flail [flel] *s* correggiato ‖ *tr* battere col correggiato; battere
flair [flɛr] *s* fiuto, istinto
flak [flæk] *s* fuoco antiaereo
flake [flek] *s* falda; (*of snow*) fiocco, falda; (*of cereal*) fiocco; ‖ *tr* sfaldare; (*fish*) scagliare ‖ *intr* sfaldarsi
flak•y ['fleki] *adj* (**-ier; -iest**) a falde, faldoso
flamboyant [flæm'bɔɪ·ənt] *adj* sgargiante; (archit) fiammeggiante
flame [flem] *s* fiamma ‖ *tr & intr* fiammeggiare
flamethrower ['flem,θro·ər] *s* lanciafiamme *m*
flaming ['flemɪŋ] *adj* fiammeggiante; appassionato; (culin) alla fiamma
flamin•go [flə'mɪŋgo] *s* (**-gos** or **-goes**) fenícottero, fiammingo
flammable ['flæməbəl] *adj* infiammabile
Flanders ['flændərz] *s* le Fiandre
flange [flændʒ] *s* (*e.g., on a pipe*) flangia; (*on I beam*) bordo; (*of a wheel*) cerchione *m*
flank [flæŋk] *s* fianco ‖ *tr* fiancheggiare
flannel ['flænəl] *s* flanella
flap [flæp] *s* (*in clothing*) falda; (*of hat*) tesa; (*of book*) risvolto; (*of pocket*) patta; (*of shoe*) linguetta; (*blow*) colpo; (*of a table*) pannello; (*of the counter in a store*) ribalta; (*of wings*) alata ‖ *v* (*pret & pp* **flapped;** *ger* **flapping**) *tr* battere, sbattere; (*to move violently*) sbatacchiare ‖ *intr* penzolare
flare [flɛr] *s* vampa; scintillio; (*of a dress*) svasatura; (mil) fuoco di segnalazione; **flares** (*trousers*) calzoni *mpl* a zampe d'elefante ‖ *tr* svasare ‖ *intr* scintillare; (*said of a garment*) scampanare; **to flare up** divampare; (*said of an illness*) aggravarsi, infiammarsi
flare'-up' *s* vampa, fiammata; (*of an illness*) recrudescenza; scoppio d'ira, accesso di collera
flash [flæʃ] *s* (*of light*) sprazzo; (*of lightning*) lampo, baleno; (*of hope*) raggio; (*of joy*) accesso; (journ, phot) flash *m;* (fig) lampo; **flash in the pan** fuoco di paglia ‖ *tr* (*powder*) accendere; (*a sword*) brandire; (journ) diffondere; (*e.g., money*) (coll) ostentare ‖ *intr* lampeggiare, balenare, folgorare; **to flash by** passare come un lampo
flash'back' *s* flashback *m*
flash' bulb' *s* lampada lampo
flash' cube' *s* cuboflash *m*
flash' flood' *s* inondazione torrenziale
flashing ['flæʃɪŋ] *s* metallo per coprire la conversa; commessura metallica fra tetto e comignolo
flash'light' *s* lampadina tascabile; (*of a lighthouse*) luce *f* intermittente; (phot) fotolampo, lampeggiatore *m*
flash'light bulb' *s* lampada per fotolampo
flash•y ['flæʃi] *adj* (**-ier; -iest**) sgargiante, chiassoso, vistoso
flask [flæsk] or [flɑsk] *s* fiasco, fiasca; (*for laboratory use*) beuta
flat [flæt] *adj* (**flatter; flattest**) piano; (*nose*) camuso; (*boat*) a fondo piatto; (*surface*) liscio; (*beer*) svanito; (*tire*) sgonfio; (*denial*) deciso; (mus) bemolle; (coll) al verde ‖ *s* (*flat surface*) piatto; (*flat area*) piano; (*apartment*) appartamento; (mus) bemolle *m;* (coll) gomma a terra ‖ *adv*—**to fall flat** fallire
flat'boat' *s* chiatta
flat'car' *s* (rr) pianale *m*
flat-footed ['flæt,fʊtɪd] *adj* dai piedi piatti; (coll) inflessibile
flat'head' *s* (*of a bolt*) testa piatta; (coll) testa di legno
flat'i'ron *s* ferro da stiro
flat' race' *s* corsa piana
flatten ['flætən] *tr* schiacciare; distendere ‖ *intr* appiattirsi; indebolirsi; **to flatten out** appiattirsi; (aer) porsi in linea orizzontale di volo
flatter ['flætər] *tr* adulare, lusingare; (*to make seem more attractive*) favorire ‖ *intr* adulare
flatterer ['flætərər] *s* adulatore *m,* lusingatore *m*
flattering ['flætərɪŋ] *adj* lusinghiero
flatter•y ['flætəri] *s* (**-ies**) lusinga
flat' tire' *s* gomma a terra
flat'top' *s* portaerei *f*
flatulence ['flætʃələns] *s* flatulenza
flat'ware' *s* argenteria, vasellame *m*
flaunt [flɔnt] or [flɑnt] *tr* sfoggiare, ostentare
flautist ['flɔtɪst] *s* flautista *mf*
flavor ['flevər] *s* sapore *m,* gusto; condimento ‖ *tr* insaporire; condire; aromatizzare, profumare
flavoring ['flevərɪŋ] *s* condimento, sapore *m*
flaw [flɔ] *s* difetto, menda, fallo; (*crack*) incrinatura
flawless ['flɔlɪs] *adj* senza difetti
flax [flæks] *s* lino
flaxen ['flæksən] *adj* di lino; biondo
flax'seed' *s* linosa
flay [fle] *tr* scorticare, scoiare
flea [fli] *s* pulce *f*
flea'bite' *s* morso di pulce; (fig) inezia, seccatura secondaria
fleck [flɛk] *s* macchia; efelide *f* ‖ *tr* chiazzare, macchiare
fledgling ['flɛdʒlɪŋ] *s* uccellino appena nato; (fig) pivello
flee [fli] *v* (*pret & pp* **fled** [flɛd]) *tr & intr* fuggire, sfuggire
fleece [flis] *s* vello; (*e.g., of clouds*) bioccolo ‖ *tr* tosare; (fig) pelare
fleec•y ['flisi] *adj* (**-ier; -iest**) lanoso; (*sky*) a pecorelle
fleet [flit] *adj* rapido ‖ *s* flotta
fleeting ['flitɪŋ] *adj* fugace, passeggero
Fleming ['flemɪŋ] *s* fiammingo
Flemish ['flemɪʃ] *adj & s* fiammingo
flesh [fleʃ] *s* carne *f;* (*of fruit*) polpa; **in the flesh** in carne ed ossa; **to lose flesh** dimagrire; **to put on flesh** ingrassare
flesh' and blood' *s* (*relatives*) carne *f* della carne, i miei, i suoi, etc.; il corpo umano

flesh-colored ['fleʃ ,kʌlərd] *adj* color carne
fleshiness ['fleʃɪnɪs] *s* carnosità *f*
fleshless ['fleʃlɪs] *adj* scarno
flesh'pot' *s* piatto di carne; locale *m* di dissoluzione; **fleshpots** vita dissoluta
flesh' wound' *s* ferita superficiale
flesh·y ['fleʃi] *adj* (**-ier; -iest**) carnoso; polposo
flex [fleks] *tr* piegare || *intr* piegarsi
flexible ['fleksɪbəl] *adj* flessibile; (*joint*) a snodo
flick [flɪk] *s* schiocco; (slang) pellicola cinematografica || *tr* schioccare
flicker ['flɪkər] *s* fiamma tremolante; (*of eyelids*) battito; (*of hope*) bagliore *m* || *intr* tremolare; vacillare
flier ['flaɪ·ər] *s* aviatore *m;* (*venture*) (coll) impresa rischiosa; (coll) foglio volante
flight [flaɪt] *s* fuga; (*of an airplane*) volo; (*of birds*) stormo; (*of stairs*) rampa; (*of fancy*) slancio; **to put to flight** mettere in fuga; **to take flight** prendere la fuga
flight' deck' *s* ponte *m* di volo
flight·y ['flaɪti] *adj* (**-ier; -iest**) frivolo; volubile
flim-flam ['flɪm ,flæm] *s* (coll) imbroglio, truffa || *v* (*pret & pp* **-flammed;** *ger* **-flamming**) *tr* (coll) imbrogliare, truffare
flim·sy ['flɪmzi] *adj* (**-sier; -siest**) leggero; (*material*) di scarsa consistenza; (*excuse*) inconsistente
flinch [flɪntʃ] *intr* indietreggiare; **without flinching** senza scomporsi
fling [flɪŋ] *s* tiro; ballo scozzese; **to go on a fling** darsi alla pazza gioia; **to have a fling at** tentare di fare; **to have one's fling** correre la cavallina || *v* (*pret & pp* **flung** [flʌŋ]) *tr* sbattere, scagliare; (*e.g., in jail*) schiaffare; **to fling open** spalancare; **to fling shut** chiudere improvvisamente
flint [flɪnt] *s* selce *f*, pietra focaia
flint'lock' *s* fucile *m* a pietra focaia
flint·y ['flɪnti] *adj* (**-ier; -iest**) pietroso; (*unmerciful*) spietato; duro come un macigno
flip [flɪp] *adj* (**flipper; flippest**) impertinente || *s* buffetto; salto mortale || *v* (*pret & pp* **flipped;** *ger* **flipping**) *tr* sbattere in aria; muovere d'un tratto **to flip a coin** giocare a testa e croce; **to flip shut** (*e.g., a fan*) chiudere improvvisamente
flippancy ['flɪpənsi] *s* leggerezza
flippant ['flɪpənt] *adj* scanzonato, leggero
flirt [flʌrt] *s* (*woman*) civetta; (*man*) vagheggino || *intr* (*said of a woman*) civettare; (*said of a man*) fare il damerino; **to flirt with** flirtare con; (*an idea*) accarezzare; (*death*) giocare con
flit [flɪt] *v* (*pret & pp* **flitted;** *ger* **flitting**) *intr* svolazzare, volteggiare; passare rapidamente, volare
flitch [flɪtʃ] *s* fetta di pancetta
float [flot] *s* (*raft*) galleggiante *m;* (*of mason*) cazzuola; carro allegorico || *tr* far galleggiare; (*a business*) lanciare; (*stocks, bonds*) emettere || *intr* galleggiare, tenersi a galla
floating ['flotɪŋ] *adj* galleggiante
flock [flɑk] *s* (*of birds*) stormo; (*of sheep*) gregge *m;* (*of people*) stuolo; (*of wool*) fiocco; (fig) mucchio || *intr* affollarsi, riunirsi, radunarsi
floe [flo] *s* tavola di ghiaccio
flog [flɑg] *v* (*pret & pp* **flogged;** *ger* **flogging**) *tr* battere, fustigare
flood [flʌd] *s* (*caused by rain*) diluvio; (*sudden rise of river*) piena, fiumana; (*of tide*) flusso || *tr* inondare; (aut) ingolfare || *intr* straripare; (aut) ingolfarsi || **the Flood** il diluvio universale
flood'gate' *s* (*of a canal*) chiusa; (*of a dam*) saracinesca
flood'light' *s* riflettore *m*
flood' tide' *s* flusso
floor [flor] *s* (*inside bottom surface of room*) pavimento; (*story of building*) piano; (*of the sea, a swimming pool, etc.*) fondo; (*of the exchange*) recinto delle grida; (*of an assembly hall*) emiciclo; (naut) madiere *m;* **to ask for the floor** chiedere la parola; **to have the floor** avere la parola; **to take the floor** prendere la parola || *tr* pavimentare; abbattere, gettare al suolo; (coll) confondere; (coll) vincere
flooring ['florɪŋ] *s* palco, impiantito
floor' mop' *s* redazza
floor' plan' *s* pianta
floor' show' *s* spettacolo di caffè concerto
floor'walk'er *s* direttore *m* di sezione
floor' wax' *s* cera da pavimenti
flop [flɑp] *s* (coll) fiasco || *v* (*pret & pp* **flopped;** *ger* **flopping**) *tr* lasciar cadere; sbattere || *intr* lasciarsi cadere; (coll) fare fiasco; **to flop over** (*to change sides*) cambiare casacca
flora ['florə] *s* flora
floral ['florəl] *adj* floreale
Florence ['flɔrəns] or ['flɑrəns] *s* Firenze *f*
Florentine ['flɑrən ,tin] or ['flɔrən ,tin] *adj & s* fiorentino
florescence [flo'resəns] *s* infiorescenza
florid ['flɑrɪd] or ['flɔrɪd] *adj* florido
florist ['florɪst] *s* fiorista *mf*, fioraio
floss [flɔs] or [flɑs] *s* lanugine *f;* (*of corn*) barba
floss·y ['flɔsi] or ['flɑsi] *adj* (**-ier; -iest**) serico; (*downy*) lanuginoso; (coll) vistoso
flotsam ['flɑtsəm] *s* relitti gettati a mare
flot'sam and jet'sam *s* relitti *mpl* di naufragio; (*trifles*) cianfrusaglie *fpl;* gentaglia, vagabondi *mpl*
flounce [flɑuns] *s* balza, falda, falpalà *m* || *tr* ornare di falpalà || *intr*—**to flounce out** andarsene irosamente
flounder ['flaundər] *s* (ichth) passera || *intr* dibattersi
flour [flaur] *adj* farinoso || *s* farina || *tr* infarinare
flourish ['flʌrɪʃ] *s* (*with the sword*) mulinello; (*with the pen*) ghirigoro; (*as part of signature*) svolazzo; (mus)

fioritura || *tr* (*one's sword*) roteare || *intr* rifiorire, prosperare
flourishing [ˈflʌrɪʃɪŋ] *adj* prosperoso
flour' mill' *s* mulino per grano
floury [ˈflaʊri] *adj* farinoso; infarinato
flout [flaʊt] *tr* burlarsi di || *intr* burlare, motteggiare
flow [flo] *s* flusso; (*of a river*) regime *m* || *intr* fluire; (*said of tide*) montare; (*said of hair in the air*) ondeggiare; **to flow into** gettarsi in, sfociare in; **to flow over** traboccare; **to flow with** abbondare di
flower [ˈflaʊ·ər] *s* fiore *m* || *tr* infiorare || *intr* fiorire
flow'er bed' *s* aiola fiorita
flow'er gar'den *s* giardino
flow'er girl' *s* fioraia; (*at a wedding*) damigella d'onore
flow'er·pot' *s* vaso da fiori
flow'er shop' *s* negozio di fiori
flow'er show' *s* esposizione di fiori
flow'er·stand' *s* portafiori *m*
flowery [ˈflaʊ·əri] *adj* fiorito
flowing [ˈflo·ɪŋ] *adj* (*water*) corrente; (*language*) scorrevole; (*e.g., hair*) fluente; (*e.g., lines of a dress*) filante
flu [flu] *s* influenza
fluctuate [ˈflʌktʃʊ,et] *intr* fluttuare, ondeggiare; (*said of prices*) oscillare
flue [flu] *s* gola, fumaiolo
fluency [ˈflu·ənsi] *s* facilità *f* di parola
fluent [ˈflu·ənt] *adj* (*speaker*) facondo; (*style*) fluido
fluently [ˈflu·əntli] *adv* correntemente
fluff [flʌf] *s* lanugine *f;* vaporosità *f;* (*of an actor*) papera || *tr* sprimacciare || *intr* sprimacciarsi; (coll) impaperarsi
fluff·y [ˈflʌfi] *adj* (**-ier; -iest**) lanuginoso; vaporoso
fluid [ˈflu·ɪd] *adj* & *s* fluido
flu'id drive' *s* trasmissione idraulica
fluidity [fluˈɪdɪti] *s* fluidità *f*
fluke [fluk] *s* (*of anchor*) marra, dente *m;* (*in billiards*) colpo fortunato; (ichth) passera
flume [flum] *s* gora; condotta forzata
flunk [flʌŋk] *s* (coll) bocciatura || *tr* (coll) bocciare; (*a course*) (coll) farsi bocciare in || *intr* (coll) fare fiasco; **to flunk out** (coll) farsi bocciare
flunk·y [ˈflʌŋki] *s* (**-ies**) valletto; parassita *m*
fluor [ˈflu·ɔr] *s* fluorite *f*
fluorescence [,flu·əˈrɛsəns] *s* fluorescenza
fluorescent [,flu·əˈrɛsənt] *adj* fluorescente
fluoridation [,flu·ərɪˈdeʃən] *s* fluorizzazione
fluoride [ˈflu·ə,raɪd] *s* fluoruro
fluorine [ˈflu·ə,rin] *s* fluoro
fluoroscope [ˈflu·ərə,skop] *s* schermo fluorescente
fluorspar [ˈflu·er,spɑr] *s* spatofluore *m*
flur·ry [ˈflʌri] *s* (**-ries**) agitazione; (*of wind*) raffica; (*of rain*) acquazzone *m;* (*of snow*) turbine *m* || *v* (*pret* & *pp* **-ried**) *tr* agitare
flush [flʌʃ] *adj* livellato; contiguo; prospero, ben provvisto; abbondante; vigoroso; (*full to overflowing*) rigurgitante; arrossito; **flush with** allo stesso livello che || *s* (*of water*) flusso improvviso; (*in the cheeks*) caldana, scalmana; (*of spring*) germogliare *m;* (*of joy*) ebbrezza; (*of youth*) rigoglio; (*in poker*) colore *m* || *adv* rasente, raso || *tr* (*to cause to blush*) far arrossire; lavare con un getto d'acqua; (*e.g., a rabbit*) snidare || *intr* essere accaldato; (*to blush*) arrossire; (*to gush*) zampillare
flush' tank' *s* sciacquone *m*
flush' toi'let *s* gabinetto a sciacquone
fluster [ˈflʌstər] *s* nervosismo, eccitazione || *tr* innervosire, eccitare
flute [flut] *s* (*of a column*) scanalatura; (mus) flauto || *tr* scanalare
flutist [ˈflutɪst] *s* flautista *mf*
flutter [ˈflʌtər] *s* svolazzo; agitazione; sensazione || *intr* frullare; svolazzare; agitarsi; (*said of the heart*) palpitare; (*said of the heartbeat*) essere irregolare
flux [flʌks] *s* (*flow*) flusso; (*for fusing metals*) fondente *m*
fly [flaɪ] *s* (*flies*) mosca; (*of trousers*) finta; (*for fishing*) mosca artificiale || *v* (*pret* **flew** [flu]; *pp* **flown** [flon]) *tr* (*an airplane*) pilotare, far volare; trasportare a volo; (*e.g., an ocean*) trasvolare; (*a flag*) battere || *intr* volare; fuggire, scappare; (*said of a flag*) ondeggiare; **to fly away** involarsi; **to fly into a rage** andare in eccessi; **to fly off** volare via; scappare; **to fly over** trasvolare; **to fly shut** chiudersi improvvisamente
fly'blow' *s* uovo di mosca
fly'-by-night' *adj* poco raccomandabile; di breve durata
fly'catch'er *s* (orn) pigliamosche *m*
flyer [ˈflaɪ·ər] *s* var of **flier**
fly'-fish' *intr* pescare con le mosche artificiali
flying [ˈflaɪ·ɪŋ] *adj* volante; rapido; in fuga; (*start*) lanciato || *s* volo
fly'ing boat' *s* idrovolante *m* a scafo centrale
fly'ing but'tress *s* contrafforte *m*
fly'ing col'ors *spl* successo; **with flying colors** a bandiere spiegate
fly'ing field' *s* campo d'aviazione
fly'ing sau'cer *s* disco volante
fly'ing sick'ness *s* male *m* d'aria
fly'ing squad' *s* squadra mobile
fly'ing time' *s* ore *fpl* di volo
fly'leaf' *s* (**-leaves'**) (bb) guardia
fly' net' *s* (*for a bed*) moschettiera; (*for a horse*) scacciamosche *m*
fly'pa'per *s* carta moschicida
fly'speck' *s* macchia di mosca; macchiolina
fly' swat'ter [ˈswɑtər] *s* scacciamosche *m*
fly'trap' *s* pigliamosche *m*
fly'wheel' *s* volano
foal [fol] *s* puledro || *intr* (*said of a mare*) figliare
foam [fom] *s* schiuma || *intr* schiumare
foam' rub'ber *s* gommapiuma

foam·y ['fomi] *adj* **(-ier; -iest)** spumoso, schiumeggiante
fob [fɑb] *s* taschino per l'orologio; (*chain*) catenina per l'orologio || *v* (*pret & pp* **fobbed**; *ger* **fobbing**) *tr*—**to fob off s.th on s.o.** rifilare qlco a qlcu
f.o.b. or **F.O.B.** [ˌefˌo'bi] *adv* (letterword) **(free on board)** franco
focal ['fokəl] *adj* focale
fo·cus ['fokəs] *s* **(-cuses** or **-ci** [saɪ]) fuoco; (*of a disease*) focolaio || *v* (*pret & pp* **-cused** or **-cussed**; *ger* **-cusing** or **-cussing**) *tr* mettere a fuoco; (*attention*) concentrare || *intr* convergere
fodder ['fɑdər] *s* foraggio
foe [fo] *s* nemico
fog [fɑg] or [fɔg] *s* nebbia; (phot) velo || *v* (*pret & pp* **fogged**; *ger* **fogging**) *tr* annebbiare; (phot) velare || *intr* annebbiarsi; (phot) velarsi
fog' bank' *s* banco di nebbia
fog'bound' *adj* avvolto nella nebbia
fog·gy ['fɑgi] or ['fɔgi] *adj* **(-gier; -giest)** annebbiato; nebbioso; (*idea*) vago; (phot) velato; **it is foggy** fa nebbia
fog'horn' *s* sirena da nebbia
foible ['fɔɪbəl] *s* debolezza, debole *m*
foil [fɔɪl] *s* (*thin sheet of metal*) foglia; (*of mirror*) argentatura; contrasto, risalto; (*sword*) fioretto || *tr* sventare; (*a mirror*) argentare
foist [fɔɪst] *tr*—**to foist s.th on s.o.** rifilare qlco a qlcu
fold [fold] *s* piega; drappeggio; (*for sheep*) ovile *m;* (*of sheep; of the faithful*) gregge *m;* (geol) corrugamento || *tr* piegare; (*the arms*) incrociare; **to fold up** ripiegare || *intr* piegarsi; **to fold up** (coll) fare fallimento
folder ['foldər] *s* (*pamphlet*) pieghevole *m;* (*cover*) portacarte *m*
folding ['foldɪŋ] *adj* pieghevole
fold'ing cam'era *s* macchina fotografica a soffietto
fold'ing chair' *s* sedia pieghevole
fold'ing cot' *s* branda
fold'ing door' *s* porta a libro
fold'ing seat' *s* strapuntino
foliage ['folɪ·ɪdʒ] *s* fogliame *m*
foli·o ['folɪˌo] *adj* in-folio || *s* **(-os)** foglio; (*book*) in-folio || *tr* numerare
folk [fok] *adj* popolare || *s* **(folk** or **folks)** gente *f;* **your folks** i Suoi
folk'lore' *s* folclore *m*
folk' mu'sic *s* musica folcloristica
folk' song' *s* canzone *f* tradizionale
folk·sy ['foksi] *adj* **(-sier; -siest)** socievole; alla buona, alla mano
folk'ways' *spl* costumi *mpl* tradizionali
follicle ['fɑlɪkəl] *s* follicolo
follow ['fɑlo] *tr* seguire; (*to keep up with*) interessarsi di; **to follow suit** seguire l'esempio; (cards) rispondere al colore || *intr* seguire; derivare; **as follows** come segue; **it follows** ne risulta
follower ['fɑlo·ər] *s* seguace *m;* discepolo; partigiano
following ['fɑlo·ɪŋ] *adj* susseguente || *s* seguito; aderenti *mpl*
fol'low-up' *adj* susseguente; ricordativo; da continuarsi || *s* prosecuzione; lettera ricordativa
fol·ly ['fɑli] *s* **(-lies)** follia; **follies** rivista di varietà
foment [fo'ment] *tr* fomentare
fond [fɑnd] *adj* appassionato; (*of food*) ghiotto; **to become fond of** appassionarsi di
fondle ['fɑndəl] *tr* accarezzare, vezzeggiare
fondness ['fɑndnɪs] *s* tenerezza; passione
font [fɑnt] *s* acquasantiera, pila; fonte *f* battesimale; (typ) fondita
food [fud] *adj* alimentare || *s* cibo, vitto; (*for animals*) mangiare *m;* **food for thought** materia di che pensare
food' store' *s* negozio di commestibili
food'stuffs' *spl* commestibili *mpl*
fool [ful] *s* scemo, sciocco; (*jester*) buffone *m;* (*person imposed on*) vittima, zimbello; **to make a fool of** beffarsi di; **to play the fool** fare lo stupido || *tr* infinocchiare, ingannare; **to fool away** sprecare || *intr* giocare, fare per gioco; **to fool around** perdere il proprio tempo; **to fool with** giocherellare con
fooler·y ['fuləri] *s* **(-ies)** pazzia, buffonata
fool'har'dy *adj* **(-dier; -diest)** temerario
fooling ['fulɪŋ] *s* scherzo; **no fooling** senza scherzi, parlando sul serio
foolish ['fulɪʃ] *adj* sciocco; matto
fool'proof' *adj* a tutta prova; infallibile
fools'cap' *s* berretto a sonagli; carta formato protocollo
fool's' er'rand *s* impresa inutile
fool's' par'adise *s* felicità immaginaria
foot [fut] *s* **(feet** [fit]) piede *m;* (*of an animal*) zampa; (*of horse*) zoccolo; **to drag one's feet** procedere a passo di lumaca; **to put one's best foot forward** fare del proprio meglio; **to put one's foot down** farsi valere, imporsi; **to put one's foot in it** (coll) fare una topica; **to stand on one's own two feet** agire indipendentemente; **to tread under foot** calcare || *tr* (*the bill*) pagare; **to foot it** andare a piedi; ballare
footage ['futɪdʒ] *s* distanza or lunghezza in piedi; (*of film measured in meters*) metraggio
foot'-and-mouth' disease' *s* (vet) afta epizootica
foot'ball' *s* (*ball*) pallone *m;* (*game*) pallovale *f;* (*soccer*) calcio, football *m*
foot'board' *s* (*support for foot*) predellino; (*of bed*) spalliera
foot' brake' *s* freno a pedale
foot'bridge' *s* passerella, ponte riservato ai pedoni
foot'fall' *s* passo
foot'hill' *s* collina ai piedi di una montagna

foot'hold' *s* stabilità *f;* **to gain a foothold** prender piede
footing ['futɪŋ] *s* piede *m,* e.g., **he lost his footing** perse piede; **on a friendly footing** in relazioni amichevoli; **on an equal footing** su un piede di parità; **on a war footing** su un piede di guerra
foot'lights' *spl* luci *fpl* della ribalta; (fig) ribalta, scena
foot'loose' *adj* completamente libero
foot'man *s* (**-men**) staffiere *m*
foot'mark' *s* orma
foot'note' *s* rimando, rinvio
foot'path' *s* sentiero
foot'print' *s* orma, pesta
foot' race' *s* corsa podistica
foot'rest' *s* pedana
foot' rule' *s* regolo di un piede
foot' soldier' *s* fante *m,* fantaccino
foot'sore' *adj* coi piedi stanchi
foot'step' *s* passo; **to follow in the footsteps of** seguire le orme di
foot'stone' *s* pietra tombale a piè di un sepolcro; (archit) pietra di sostegno
foot'stool' *s* sgabello
foot' warm'er *s* scaldino
foot'wear' *s* calzature *fpl*
foot'work' *s* allenamento delle gambe; (fig) manovra delicata
foot'worn' *adj* (*road*) battuto; (*person*) spedato
foozle ['fuzəl] *s* schiappinata ‖ *tr & intr* mancare completamente
fop [fɑp] *s* bellimbusto, gagà *m*
for [fɔr] *prep* per; malgrado, e.g., **for all his wealth** malgrado tutta la sua ricchezza; come, e.g., **he uses his house for an office** adopera la casa come ufficio; di, e.g., **time for bed** ora di andare a letto; da, e.g., **he has been here for three days** è qui da tre giorni; per amor di; **to go for a walk** andare a fare una passeggiata ‖ *conj* perchè, poichè
forage ['fɑrɪdʒ] or ['fɔrɪdʒ] *adj* foraggero ‖ *s* foraggio ‖ *tr* foraggiare ‖ *intr* andare in cerca di foraggio
foray ['fɑre] or ['fɔre] *s* razzia, scorreria ‖ *intr* razziare
for•bear [fɔr'ber] *v* (*pret* **-bore** ['bor]; *pp* **-borne** ['born]) *tr* astenersi da ‖ *intr* essere longanime
forbearance [fɔr'berəns] *s* longanimità *f,* tolleranza; astensione
for•bid [fɔr'bɪd] *v* (*pret* **-bade** ['bæd] or **-bad** ['bæd]; *pp* **-bidden** ['bɪdən]; *ger* **-bidding**) *tr* proibire, vietare ‖ *intr*—**God forbid!** Dio ci scampi!
forbidding [fɔr'bɪdɪŋ] *adj* severo, sinistro
force [fors] *s* forza; (*staff of workers*) forza, personale *m;* (phys) forza; **by force of** a forza di; **by main force** con tutte le sue forze; **in force** vigente; in gran numero; **to join forces** allearsi ‖ *tr* forzare; obbligare; **to force back** respingere; **to force open** forzare; **to force s.th on s.o.** obbligare qlcu a accettare qlco
forced [forst] *adj* forzato; studiato
forced' air' *s* aria sotto pressione
forced' draft' *s* tiraggio forzato
forced' land'ing *s* atterraggio forzato
forced' march' *s* marcia forzata
forceful ['forsfəl] *adj* vigoroso, energico
for•ceps ['fɔrsəps] *s* (**-ceps** or **-cipes** [sɪ,piz]) (dent, surg) pinze *fpl;* (obstet) forcipe *m*
force' pump' *s* pompa premente
forcible ['forsɪbəl] *adj* impetuoso, energico; efficace
ford [ford] *s* guado ‖ *tr* guadare
fore [for] *adj* davanti; (naut) prodiero ‖ *s* davanti *m;* (naut) prua; **to the fore** alla ribalta; d'attualità ‖ *adv* prima; (naut) a proravia ‖ *interj* attenzione!
fore' and aft' *adv* a poppa e a prua
fore'arm' *s* avambraccio ‖ **fore•arm'** *tr* premunire; prevenire
fore'bears' *spl* antenati *mpl*
forebode [for'bod] *tr* (*to portend*) preannunziare; (*to have a presentiment of*) presentire
foreboding [for'bodɪŋ] *s* preannunzio; presentimento
fore'cast' *s* pronostico ‖ *v* (*pret & pp* **-cast** or **-casted**) *tr* pronosticare
forecastle ['foksəl], ['for,kæsəl] or ['for,kɑsəl] *s* castello, pozzetto
fore•close' *tr* escludere, precludere; (*a mortgage*) (law) precludere il riscatto di
fore•doom' *tr* condannare all'insuccesso
fore' edge' *s* (bb) taglio
fore'fa'ther *s* antenato
fore'fin'ger *s* dito indice
fore'front' *s*—**in the forefront** all'avanguardia
fore•go' *v* (*pret* **-went'**; *pp* **-gone'**) *tr & intr* precedere
fore•go'ing *adj* precedente, anteriore
fore'gone' conclu'sion *s* conclusione inevitabile; decisione già scontata
fore'ground' *s* primo piano
forehanded ['for,hændɪd] *adj* previdente; (*thrifty*) risparmiatore
forehead ['fɑrɪd] or ['fɔrɪd] *s* fronte *f*
foreign ['fɑrɪn] or ['fɔrɪn] *adj* straniero; (*product; affairs*) estero; **foreign to** estraneo a
for'eign affairs' *spl* affari esteri
for'eign-born' *adj* nato all'estero
foreigner ['fɑrɪnər] or ['fɔrɪnər] *s* straniero, forestiero
for'eign exchange' *s* divise *fpl;* (*money*) valuta
for'eign min'ister *s* ministro degli affari esteri
for'eign of'fice *s* ministero degli affari esteri
for'eign serv'ice *s* servizio diplomatico e consolare; (Brit) servizio militare in paesi d'oltremare
fore'leg' *s* zampa anteriore
fore'lock' *s* ciuffo sulla fronte; **to take time by the forelock** acchiappare l'occasione
fore'man *s* (**-men**) sorvegliante *m,* capomastro; presidente *m* dei giurati
foremast ['formәst], ['for,mæst] or ['for,mɑst] *s* trinchetto
foremost ['for,most] *adj* primo, principale, più importante

fore'noon' *adj* mattinale || *s* mattina
fore'part' *s* parte *f* anteriore; prima parte
fore'paw' *s* zampa anteriore
fore'quar'ter *s* quarto anteriore
fore'run'ner *s* precursore *m*, predecessore *m*, foriero
fore•sail ['forsəl] or ['for,sel] *s* trinchetto
fore•see' *v* (*pret* **-saw'**; *pp* **-seen'**) *tr* prevedere
foreseeable [for'si•əbəl] *adj* prevedibile
fore•shad'ow *tr* presagire
fore•short'en *tr* scorciare
fore'sight' *s* (*prudence*) previdenza; (*foreknowledge*) previsione
fore'sight'ed *adj* previdente
fore'skin' *s* prepuzio
forest ['fɑrɪst] or ['fɔrɪst] *adj* forestale || *s* foresta, bosco
fore•stall' *tr* prevenire; anticipare; (*to buy up*) accapparrare
for'est rang'er ['rendʒər] *s* guardaboschi *m*, guardia forestale
forestry ['fɑrɪstri] or ['fɔrɪstri] *s* selvicoltura
fore'taste' *s* pregustazione || *tr* pregustare
fore•tell' *v* (*pret & pp* **-told'**) *tr* predire, presagire, preannunziare
fore'thought' *s* premeditazione; previdenza
forever [fɔr'ɛvər] *adv* per sempre; continuamente
fore•warn' *tr* prevenire, preavvertire
fore'word' *s* avvertenza, prefazione
forfeit ['fɔrfɪt] *adj* perduto || *s* perdita, confisca; multa; (*article deposited*) pegno; **forfeits** (*game*) pegni *mpl* || *tr* decadere da
forfeiture ['fɔrfɪtʃər] *s* perdita di un pegno
forgather [fɔr'gæðər] *intr* riunirsi; incontrarsi
forge [fordʒ] *s* fucina, forgia || *tr* forgiare; (*a lie*) inventare; (*e.g., handwriting*) falsificare || *intr* forgiare; commettere un falso; **to forge ahead** farsi strada
forger•y ['fordʒəri] *s* (**-ies**) falsificazione, falso, contraffazione
for•get [fɔr'get] *v* (*pret* **-got** ['gɑt]; *pp* **-got** or **-gotten** ['gɑtən]) *tr* dimenticare; **forget it!** non si preoccupi!; **to forget oneself** venir meno alla propria dignità; **to forget to** passare di mente a (qlcu) di, e.g., **he forgot to turn off the lights** gli è passato di mente di spegnere la luce
forgetful [fɔr'getfəl] *adj* (*apt to forget*) smemorato; (*neglectful*) dimentico, immemore
forgetfulness [fɔr'getfəlnɪs] *s* (*inability to recall*) smemorataggine *f*; (*neglectfulness*) dimenticanza
for•get'-me-not' *s* nontiscordardimé *m*
forgivable [fɔr'gɪvəbəl] *adj* perdonabile
for•give [fɔr'gɪv] *v* (*pret* **-gave'**; *pp* **-giv'en**) *tr* perdonare
forgiveness [fɔr'gɪvnɪs] *s* perdono
forgiving [fɔr'gɪvɪŋ] *adj* clemente
for•go [fɔr'go] *v* (*pret* **-went**; *pp* **-gone**) *tr* rinunciare (with *dat*)

fork [fɔrk] *s* (*pitchfork*) forca, forcone *m*; (*of a bicycle*) forcella; (*for eating*) forchetta; (*of a tree or road*) biforcazione, diramazione || *tr* muovere col forcone; inforcare; **to fork out** (slang) cacciar fuori || *intr* biforcarsi, diramarsi
forked [fɔrkt] *adj* biforcuto
fork'-lift truck' *s* carrello elevatore a forca
forlorn [fɔr'lɔrn] *adj* abbandonato; disperato; miserabile
forlorn' hope' *s* impresa disperata
form [fɔrm] *s* forma; (*paper to be filled out*) formulario; (*construction to give shape to cement*) cassaforma || *tr* formare || *intr* formarsi
formal ['fɔrməl] *adj* formale; di gala, da sera, da etichetta
for'mal attire' *s* vestito da cerimonia
for'mal call' *s* visita di prammatica
formali•ty [fɔr'mælɪti] *s* (**-ties**) formalità *f*; (*excessive adherence to rules*) formalismo
for'mal par'ty *s* ricevimento di gala
for'mal speech' *s* discorso ufficiale
format ['fɔrmæt] *s* formato
formation [fɔr'meʃən] *s* formazione
former ['fɔrmər] *adj* (*preceding*) anteriore; (*long past*) passato, antico; (*having once been*) già, ex; (*of two*) primo; **the former** quello
formerly ['fɔrmərli] *adv* già, prima, in tempi passati
form'fit'ting *adj* aderente al corpo
formidable ['fɔrmɪdəbəl] *adj* formidabile
formless ['fɔrmlɪs] *adj* informe
form' let'ter *s* lettera a formulario, stampato
formu•la ['fɔrmjələ] *s* (**-las** or **-lae** [,li]) formula
formulate ['fɔrmjə,let] *tr* formulare
for•sake [fɔr'sek] *v* (*pret* **-sook** ['sʊk]; *pp* **-saken** ['sekən]) *tr* abbandonare
fort [fort] *s* forte *m*, fortezza
forte [fort] *s* forte *m*
forth [forθ] *adv* avanti; **and so forth** e così via; **from this day forth** da oggi in poi; **to go forth** uscire
forth'com'ing *adj* prossimo; immediatamente disponibile
forth'right' *adj* diretto || *adv* direttamente; senza ambagi; immediatamente
forth'with' *adv* immediatamente
fortieth ['fɔrtɪ•ɪθ] *adj, s & pron* quarantesimo
fortification [,fɔrtɪfɪ'keʃən] *s* fortificazione
forti•fy ['fɔrtɪ,faɪ] *v* (*pret & pp* **-fied**) *tr* fortificare; aumentare il livello alcolico di
fortitude ['fɔrtɪ,tjud] or ['fɔrtɪ,tud] *s* fortezza, fermezza
fortnight ['fɔrtnaɪt] or ['fɔrtnɪt] *s* quindicina, due settimane
fortress ['fɔrtrɪs] *s* fortezza, forte *m*
fortuitous [fɔr'tju•ɪtəs] or [fɔr'tu•ɪtəs] *adj* fortuito, occasionale
fortunate ['fɔrtʃənɪt] *adj* fortunato
fortune ['fɔrtjən] *s* fortuna; **to make a fortune** farsi un patrimonio; **to tell**

s.o. **his fortune** leggere il futuro a qlcu
for'tune hunt'er *s* cacciatore *m* di dote
for'tune•tel'ler *s* indovino, cartomante *mf*
for•ty ['fɔrti] *adj & pron* quaranta || *s* (**-ties**) quaranta *m;* **the forties** gli anni quaranta
fo•rum ['forəm] *s* (**-rums** or **-ra** [rə]) foro
forward ['fɔrwərd] *adj* avanzato; precoce; impertinente || *s* (soccer) avanti *m* || *adv* avanti; **to bring forward** mettere in luce; riportare; **to come forward** avanzare; **to look forward to** anticipare il piacere di || *tr* inoltrare, trasmettere; promuovere
fossil ['fɑsɪl] *adj & s* fossile *m*
foster ['fɑstər] or ['fɔstər] *adj* adottivo; di latte || *tr* allevare; promuovere
fos'ter home' *s* famiglia adottiva
foul [faʊl] *adj* sporco; (*air*) viziato; (*wind*) contrario; (*weather; breath*) cattivo; (baseball) fuori linea di gioco || *s* (*of boats*) urto, collisione; (baseball) palla colpita fuori linea di gioco; (boxing) colpo basso; (sports) fallo || *adv* slealmente; (baseball) fuori linea di gioco; **to fall foul of** entrare in collisione con; urtarsi con; **to run foul of** avere una controversia con || *tr* sporcare; otturare; (baseball) colpire fuori linea di gioco || *intr* (*said of two boats*) entrare in collisione; (*said, e.g., of a rope*) imbrogliarsi
foul-mouthed ['faʊl'maʊðd] or ['faʊl'maʊθt] *adj* sboccato, osceno
foul' play' *s* reato; (sports) gioco sleale
found [faʊnd] *tr* fondare; (*to melt, to cast*) fondere
foundation [faʊn'deʃən] *s* fondazione; (*endowment*) dotazione; (*charitable*) patronato; (*masonry support*) platea, fondamenta *fpl;* (*make-up*) fondo tinta; (fig) fondatezza
founder ['faʊndər] *s* fondatore *m;* (*of family*) capostipite *m;* (*of metals*) fonditore *m* || *intr* (*said of a ship*) affondare; (*said of a horse*) azzopparsi; (*to fail*) fare fiasco
foundling ['faʊndlɪŋ] *s* trovatello
found'ling hos'pital *s* brefotrofio
found•ry ['faʊndri] *s* (**-ries**) fonderia
found'ry•man *s* (**-men**) fonditore *m*
fount [faʊnt] *s* fonte *f*
fountain ['faʊntən] *s* fonte *f*, fontana; (*of knowledge*) pozzo
foun'tain•head' *s* sorgente *f*
foun'tain pen' *s* penna stilografica
foun'tain syringe' *s* clistere *m* a pera
four [for] *adj & pron* quattro || *s* quattro; **four o'clock** le quattro; **on all fours** gattoni, carponi
four'-cy'cle *adj* a quattro tempi
four'-cyl'inder *adj* a quattro cilindri
four'-flush' *intr* (coll) millantarsi
fourflusher ['for ,flʌʃər] *s* (coll) millantatore *m*
four-footed ['for'futɪd] *adj* quadrupede
four' hun'dred *adj, s & pron* quattrocento || **the Four Hundred** l'alta società
four'-in-hand' *s* cravatta a cappio; tiro a quattro
four'-lane' *adj* a quattro corsie
four'-leaf clo'ver *s* quadrifoglio
four-legged ['for'lɛgɪd] or ['for'lɛgd] *adj* a quattro zampe; (*schooner*) (coll) a quattro alberi
four'-letter word' *s* parolaccia di quattro lettere
four'-mo'tor plane' *s* quadrimotore *m*
four'-o'clock' *s* (bot) bella di notte
four' of a kind' *s* (cards) poker *m*
four'post'er *s* letto a baldacchino
four'score' *adj* ottanta
foursome ['forsəm] *s* gruppo di quattro giocatori
fourteen ['for'tin] *adj, s & pron* quattordici *m*
fourteenth ['for'tinθ] *adj, s & pron* quattordicesimo || *s* (*in dates*) quattordici *m*
fourth [forθ] *adj, s & pron* quarto || *s* (*in dates*) quattro
fourth' estate' *s* quarto potere
four'-way' *adj* a quattro orifizi; fra quattro persone; quadruplice
fowl [faʊl] *s* pollo || *intr* uccellare
fowl'ing piece' *s* fucile *m* da caccia
fox [fɑks] *s* volpe *f* || *tr* (coll) ingannare
fox'glove' *s* digitale *f*
fox'hole' *s* buca ricovero
fox'hound' *s* segugio
fox' hunt' *s* caccia alla volpe
fox' ter'rier *s* fox-terrier *m*
fox'-trot' *s* (*of a horse*) piccolo trotto; (*dance*) fox-trot *m*
fox•y ['fɑksi] *adj* (**-ier; -iest**) volpino, astuto
foyer ['fɔɪ•ər] *s* (*of a private house*) ingresso, vestibolo; (theat) ridotto
fracas ['frekəs] *s* lite *f*, tumulto
fraction ['frækʃən] *s* frazione; frammento
fractional ['frækʃənəl] *adj* frazionario; insignificante
fractious ['frækʃəs] *adj* litigioso, permaloso; indisciplinato
fracture ['fræktʃər] *s* frattura || *tr* fratturare; (*e.g., an arm*) fratturarsi, rompersi || *intr* fratturarsi
fragile ['frædʒɪl] *adj* fragile
fragment ['frægmənt] *s* frammento; (*e.g., of a movie*) spezzone *m* || *tr* frammentare, spezzare
fragmenta'tion bomb' [,frægmən'teʃən] *s* bomba dirompente
fragrant ['fregrənt] *adj* fragrante
frail [frel] *adj* (*not robust*) gracile; (*easily broken*) fragile; (*morally weak*) debole || *s* canestro di giunco
frail•ty ['frelti] *s* (**-ties**) fragilità *f;* (*of a person*) debolezza
frame [frem] *s* (*of picture*) cornice *f;* (*of glasses*) montatura; (*structure*) ossatura; (*of a building*) ingabbiatura, impalcatura; (*for embroidering*) telaio; (*of a window*) intelaiatura; (*of mind*) stato; (*of government*) sistema *m;* (mov) inquadratura; (phot) fotogramma *m;* (aer) ordinata;

(naut) costa || *tr* (*to put in a frame*) incorniciare; montare; costruire; inventare; esprimere; (slang) architettare un' accusa contro
frame' house' *s* casa con l'ossatura di legno
frame'-up' *s* (slang) complotto per incriminare un innocente
frame'work' *s* intelaiatura, impalcatura; palificazione
franc [fræŋk] *s* franco
France [fræns] or [frɑns] *s* la Francia
Frances ['frænsɪs] or ['frɑnsɪs] *s* Francesca
franchise ['fræntʃaɪz] *s* diritto di voto; concessione; (*privilege*) franchigia
Francis ['frænsɪs] or ['frɑnsɪs] *s* Francesco
Franciscan [fræn'sɪskən] *adj & s* francescano
frank [fræŋk] *adj* sincero, schietto || *s* affrancatura postale; lettera affrancata; (*franking privilege*) franchigia postale || *tr* affrancare || **Frank** *s* (*member of Frankish tribe*) franco; (*masculine name*) Franco
frankfurter ['fræŋkfərtər] *s* salsiccia di Francoforte, Frankfurter *m*
frankincense ['fræŋkɪn,sens] *s* olibano
Frankish ['fræŋkɪʃ] *adj & s* franco
frankness ['fræŋknɪs] *s* franchezza
frantic ['fræntɪk] *adj* frenetico
frappé [fræ'pe] *adj & s* frappé *m*
frat [fræt] *s* (slang) associazione di studenti
fraternal [frə'tʌrnəl] *adj* fraterno
fraterni·ty ['frə'tʌrnɪti] *s* (**-ties**) (*brotherliness*) fraternità *f;* sodalizio; (eccl) confraternita; (U.S.A.) associazione di studenti
fraternize ['frætər,naɪz] *intr* fraternizzare
fraud [frɔd] *s* truffa, frode *f;* (*person*) (coll) truffatore *m*
fraudulent ['frɔdjələnt] *adj* fraudolento; (*conversion*) indebito
fraught [frɔt] *adj*—**fraught with** carico di, gravido di
fray [fre] *s* zuffa, rissa, lotta || *intr* sfilacciarsi, logorarsi
freak [frik] *s* (*sudden fancy*) capriccio, ticchio; (*person, animal*) fenomeno
freakish ['frikɪʃ] *adj* capriccioso; strano, grottesco
freckle ['frɛkəl] *s* lentiggine *f*, efelide *f*
freckle-faced ['frɛkəl,fest] *adj* lentigginoso
freckly ['frɛkli] *adj* lentigginoso
Frederick ['frɛdərɪk] *s* Federico
free [fri] *adj* (**freer** ['fri·ər]; **freest** ['fri·ɪst]) libero; gratis; franco; sciolto; esente; generoso; **to be free with** essere prodigo di; **to set free** liberare || *adv* liberamente; in libertà; gratis || *v* (*pret & pp* **freed** [frid]; *ger* **freeing** ['fri·ɪŋ]) *tr* liberare; (*from customs*) svincolare; esimere
freebooter ['fri,butər] *s* pirata *m*
free'born' *adj* nato in libertà; proprio di un popolo libero
freedom ['fridəm] *s* libertà *f*
free'dom of speech' *s* libertà *f* di parola
free'dom of the press' *s* libertà *f* di stampa
free'dom of the seas' *s* libertà *f* di navigazione
free'dom of wor'ship *s* libertà religiosa
free' en'terprise *s* economia libera
free'-for-all' *s* rissa, tafferuglio
free' hand' *s* libertà assoluta
free'-hand' *adj* a mano libera
freehanded ['fri'hændɪd] *adj* liberale, generoso
free' lance' *s* giornalista *mf* pubblicista; scrittore *m* che lavora senza contratto; soldato di ventura
free'load'er ['lodər] *s* (coll) mangiatore *m* a sbafo
free'man *s* (**-men**) uomo libero; cittadino
Free'ma'son *s* frammassone *m*
Free'ma'sonry *s* frammassoneria
free' of charge' *adj* gratis, senza spese
free' port' *s* porto franco
free' serv'ice *s* manutenzione gratuita
free'-spo'ken *adj* franco, aperto
free'stone' *adj* spiccagnolo || *s* pesca spicca
free'think'er *s* libero pensatore
free' thought' *s* libero pensiero
free' trade' *s* libero scambio
free'trad'er *s* liberoscambista *mf*
free'way' *s* autostrada
free' will' *s* libero arbitrio
freeze [friz] *s* gelo, gelata; (*e.g., of prices*) blocco || *v* (*pret* **froze** [froz]; *pp* **frozen**) *tr* gelare; (*credits, rentals, etc.*) bloccare || *intr* gelarsi; (*said of brakes*) inchiodarsi; morire assiderato; (*to become immobilized*) irrigidirsi
freeze'-dry' *v* (*pret & pp* **-dried'**) *tr* liofilizzare
freezer ['frizər] *s* congelatore *m;* (*for making ice cream*) sorbettiera
freight [fret] *s* carico; (*charge*) porto; (naut) nolo; **by freight** come carico mercantile; (rr) a piccola velocità || *tr* spedire come carico
freight' car' *s* vagone *m* or carro merci
freighter ['fretər] *s* speditore *m;* nave *f* da carico
freight' plat'form *s* (rr) banchina adibita al traffico merci
freight' sta'tion *s* (rr) stazione merci
freight' train' *s* treno merci, merci *m*
freight' yard' *s* (rr) scalo merci
French [frentʃ] *adj & s* francese *m;* **the French** i francesi
French' bread' *s* pane *m* a bastone
French' chalk' *s* pietra da sarto
French' door' *s* porta a vetri
French' dress'ing *s* salsa verde con aceto
French' fried' pota'toes *spl* patate fritte affettate
French' horn' *s* (mus) corno
French' leave' *s*—**to take French leave** andarsene all'inglese, filare all'inglese
French'man *s* (**-men**) francese *m*
French' tel'ephone *s* microtelefono
French' toast' *s* pane dorato al salto
French' win'dow *s* portafinestra
French'wom'an *s* (**-wom'en**) francese *f*

frenzied ['frenzid] *adj* frenetico
fren•zy ['frenzi] *s* (**-zies**) frenesia
frequen•cy ['frikwənsi] *s* (**-cies**) frequenza
fre'quency modula'tion *s* modulazione di frequenza
frequent ['frikwənt] *adj* frequente || [frɪ'kwent] or ['frikwənt] *tr* frequentare, praticare
frequently ['frikwəntli] *adv* frequentemente
fres•co ['fresko] *s* (**-coes** or **-cos**) affresco || *tr* affrescare
fresh [freʃ] *adj* fresco; (*water*) dolce; (*new*) nuovo; (*wind*) moderato; (*inexperienced*) novizio; (*cheeky*) (slang) sfacciato || *adv* recentemente, di recente; **fresh in** (coll) appena arrivato; **fresh out** (coll) appena esaurito
freshen ['freʃən] *tr* rinfrescare || *intr* rinfrescarsi
freshet ['freʃɪt] *s* piena, crescita
fresh'man *s* (**-men**) (*newcomer*) novizio; (educ) matricola
freshness ['freʃnɪs] *s* freschezza; (*of air*) frescura; (*cheek*) (slang) sfacciataggine *f*
fresh'-wa'ter *adj* d'acqua dolce; poco conosciuto; piccolo
fret [fret] *s* (*interlaced design*) fregio, greca; irritazione; (mus) tasto || *v* (*pret & pp* **fretted**; *ger* **fretting**) *tr* fregiare || *intr* fremere, trepidare, agitarsi
fretful ['fretfəl] *adj* irritabile, permaloso
fret'work' *s* greca
Freudianism ['frɔɪdɪ•ə,nɪzəm] *s* freudismo
friar ['fraɪ•ər] *s* frate *m*
friar•y ['fraɪ•əri] *s* (**-ies**) convento di frati
fricassee [,frɪkə'si] *s* fricassea
friction ['frɪkʃən] *s* frizione; disaccordo, dissenso
fric'tion tape' *s* nastro isolante
Friday ['fraɪdi] *s* venerdì *m*
fried [fraɪd] *adj* fritto
fried' egg' *s* uovo al tegame, uovo occhio di manzo
friend [frend] *s* amico; **to be friends with** essere amico di; **to make friends** allacciare amicizie; **to make friends with** fare l'amicizia di
friend•ly ['frendli] *adj* (**-lier**; **-liest**) amico, amichevole
friendship ['frendʃɪp] *s* amicizia
frieze [friz] *s* (archit) fregio
frigate ['frɪgɪt] *s* fregata
fright [fraɪt] *s* spavento; **to take fright at** spaventarsi di
frighten ['fraɪtən] *tr* intimorire, spaventare; **to frighten away** mettere in fuga, sgomentare || *intr* spaventarsi
frightful ['fraɪtfəl] *adj* spaventevole, orribile; (coll) enorme
frightfulness ['fraɪtfəlnɪs] *s* spavento; terrorismo
frigid ['frɪdʒɪd] *adj* freddo; (*zone*) glaciale
frigidity [frɪ'dʒɪdɪti] *s* (fig) frigidezza; (pathol) frigidità *f*
frill [frɪl] *s* pieghettatura; (*of birds and other animals*) collarino; (*in dress, speech, etc.*) affettazione
fringe [frɪndʒ] *s* frangia; (*in dressmaking*) volantino; (*on curtains*) balza; **on the fringe of** all'orlo di || *tr* orlare
fringe' ben'efits *spl* assegni *mpl*, benefici *mpl* marginali
fripper•y ['frɪpəri] *s* (**-ies**) (*finery*) fronzoli *mpl*; ostentazione; (*trifles*) cianfrusaglie *fpl*
frisk [frɪsk] *tr* perquisire; (slang) derubare || *intr* fare capriole
frisk•y ['frɪski] *adj* (**-ier**; **-iest**) gaio, vivace
fritter ['frɪtər] *s* frittella; frammento || *tr*—**to fritter away** sprecare
frivolous ['frɪvələs] *adj* frivolo
friz [frɪz] *s* (**frizzes**) ricciolo || *v* (*pret & pp* **frizzed**; *ger* **frizzing**) *tr* arricciare
frizzle ['frɪzəl] *s* ricciolo || *tr* arricciare || *intr* arricciarsi
friz•zly ['frɪzli] *adj* (**-zlier**; **-zliest**) crespo, riccio
fro [fro] *adv*—**to and fro** avanti e indietro; **to go to and fro** andare e venire
frock [frɑk] *s* gabbano; (*smock*) grembiule *m*; blusa; (*of priest*) tonaca
frock' coat' *s* finanziera
frog [frɑg] or [frɔg] *s* rana; (*button and loop on a garment*) alamaro; (*in throat*) raschio
frog'man' *s* (**-men'**) sommozzatore *m*, uomo rana
frol•ic ['frɑlɪk] *s* scherzo, monelleria || *v* (*pret & pp* **-icked**; *ger* **-icking**) *intr* scherzare, folleggiare
frolicsome ['frɑlɪksəm] *adj* scherzoso
from [frʌm], [frɑm] or [frəm] *prep* da; di, e.g., **I am from New York** sono di New York; da parte di; a, e.g., **to take s.th away from s.o.** portar via qlco a qlcu
front [frʌnt] *adj* frontale, anteriore; di fronte || *s* fronte *m & f*; (*of a building*) prospetto; (*of a book*) principio; (*of a shirt*) sparato; (*e.g., of wealth*) apparenza; (theat) boccascena *m*; (mil) fronte *m*; **in front of** dinanzi a; **to put on a front** (coll) fare ostentazione; **to put up a bold front** (coll) farsi coraggio || *tr* (*to face*) fronteggiare; (*to confront*) affrontare; (*to supply with a front*) coprire; servire da facciata a || *intr*—**to front on** dare su
frontage ['frʌntɪdʒ] *s* facciata, veduta; terreno di fronte alla casa
front' door' *s* porta d'entrata
front' drive' *s* (aut) trazione anteriore
frontier [frʌn'tɪr] *adj* limitrofo || *s* frontiera
fron'tiers'man *s* (**-men**) pioniere *m*
frontispiece ['frʌntɪs,pis] *s* (*of book*) pagina illustrata di fronte al frontispizio; (*of building*) facciata
front' mat'ter *s* (*of book*) parte *f* preliminare
front'-page' *tr* stampare in prima pagina
front' porch' *s* porticato

front′ room′ *s* stanza con vista sulla strada
front′ row′ *s* prima fila
front′ seat′ *s* posto in una delle file davanti; (aut) sedile *m* anteriore
front′ steps′ *spl* scalinata d'ingresso
front′ view′ *s* vista sulla strada
frost [frɔst] or [frɑst] *s* gelo, brina, gelata; (fig) freddezza; (slang) fiasco || *tr* agghiacciare; (*with sugar*) glassare; (*glass*) smerigliare
frost′bite′ *s* congelamento
frost′ed glass′ *s* vetro smerigliato
frosting [ˈfrɔstɪŋ] or [ˈfrɑstɪŋ] *s* glassatura; (*of glass*) smerigliatura
frost·y [ˈfrɔsti] or [ˈfrɑsti] *adj* (**-ier; -iest**) brinato; (*hair*) canuto; (fig) gelido
froth [frɔθ] or [frɑθ] *s* schiuma; (fig) frivolezza || *intr* schiumare; (*at the mouth*) avere la schiuma
froth·y [ˈfrɔθi] or [ˈfrɑθi] *adj* (**-ier; -iest**) spumoso; frivolo
froward [ˈfroʷərd] *adj* indocile
frown [fraʊn] *s* aggrottare *m* delle ciglia; (*of disapproval*) cipiglio || *intr* aggrottare le ciglia; **to frown at** or **on** disapprovare
frows·y or **frowz·y** [ˈfraʊzi] *adj* (**-ier; -iest**) sporco; puzzolente
fro′zen foods′ [ˈfrozən] *spl* cibi congelati; cibi surgelati
frugal [ˈfrugəl] *adj* parsimonioso; (*in food and drink*) frugale
fruit [frut] *adj* (*tree*) fruttifero; (*dish*) da frutta || *s* (*such as apple*) frutto; (*collectively*) frutta, e.g., **I like fruit** mi piace la frutta; (fig) frutto
fruit′ cake′ *s* torta con noci e canditi
fruit′ cup′ *s* macedonia di frutta
fruit′ dish′ *s* fruttiera, portafrutta *m*
fruit′ fly′ *s* moscerino del vino
fruitful [ˈfrutfəl] *adj* fruttuoso
fruition [fruˈɪʃən] *s* realizzazione; **to come to fruition** giungere a buon fine
fruit′ jar′ *s* vaso da frutta
fruit′ juice′ *s* sugo or spremuta di frutta
fruitless [ˈfrutlɪs] *adj* infruttuoso
fruit′ sal′ad *s* macedonia di frutta
fruit′ stand′ *s* bancarella da fruttivendolo
fruit′ store′ *s* negozio di frutta
frumpish [ˈfrʌmpɪʃ] *adj* trasandato
frustrate [ˈfrʌstret] *tr* frustrare
fry [fraɪ] *s* (**fries**) fritto || *v* (*pret & pp* **fried**) *tr & intr* friggere
fry′ing pan′ *s* padella; **out of the frying pan into the fire** dalla padella nella brace
fudge [fʌdʒ] *s* dolce *m* di cioccolato
fuel [ˈfju·əl] *s* combustibile *m;* (fig) cibo || *v* (*pret & pp* **fueled** or **fuelled;** *ger* **fueling** or **fuelling**) *tr* rifornire di carburante || *intr* rifornirsi di carburante
fuel′ cell′ *s* cellula elettrogena
fu′el oil′ *s* nafta, olio pesante
fu′el tank′ *s* serbatoio del carburante
fugitive [ˈfjudʒɪtɪv] *adj & s* fuggiasco, fuggitivo
fugue [fjug] *s* (mus) fuga
ful·crum [ˈfʌlkrəm] *s* (**-crums** or **-cra** [krə]) fulcro
fulfill [fʊlˈfɪl] *tr* (*to carry out*) eseguire; (*an obligation*) mantenere; (*to bring to an end*) completare
fulfillment [fʊlˈfɪlmənt] *s* adempimento; realizzazione
full [fʊl] *adj* pieno; (*speed*) tutto; (*garment*) ampio; (*voice*) spiegato; (*of food*) sazio; (*member*) effettivo; **full of aches and pains** pieno d'acciacchi; **full of fun** divertentissimo; **full of play** pieno di vita || *s* pieno; colmo; **in full** per estenso, in pieno; **to the full** completamente || *adv* completamente; **full many** (a) moltissimi; **full well** perfettamente || *tr* follare
full-blooded [ˈfʊlˈblʌdɪd] *adj* vigoroso; purosangue
full-blown [ˈfʊlˈblon] *adj* completamente sbocciato; maturo
full-bodied [ˈfʊlˈbɑdid] *adj* forte, ricco
full′ dress′ *s* vestito da sera; (mil) tenuta di gala, alta uniforme
full-faced [ˈfʊlˈfest] *adj* paffuto; (*view*) intero; (typ) grassetto
full-fledged [ˈfʊlˈflɛdʒd] *adj* completamente sviluppato; vero, autentico
full-grown [ˈfʊlˈgron] *adj* completamente sviluppato, adulto
full′ house′ *s* (theat) piena; (poker) full *m*
full′-length′ mir′ror *s* specchiera
full′-length mo′vie *s* lungometraggio
full′ moon′ *s* luna piena
full′ name′ *s* nome *m* e cognome *m*
full′-page′ *adj* di tutta una pagina
full′ pow′ers *spl* pieni poteri
full′ sail′ *adv* a vele spiegate
full′-scale′ *adj* in grandezza naturale; completo
full-sized [ˈfʊlˈsaɪzd] *adj* in grandezza naturale
full′ speed′ *adv* a tutta velocità
full′ stop′ *s* fermata; (gram) punto
full′ swing′ *s* piena attività
full′ tilt′ *adv* a tutta forza
full′-time′ *adj* a orario completo
fully [ˈfʊli] or [ˈfʊlli] *adv* completamente, del tutto
fulsome [ˈfʊlsəm] or [ˈfʌlsəm] *adj* basso, volgare; nauseante
fumble [ˈfʌmbəl] *tr* (*a ball*) lasciar cadere || *intr* titubare; andare a tentoni; (*in one's pocket*) cercare alla cieca
fume [fjum] *s* fumo, vapore *m,* esalazione || *tr* affumicare || *intr* fumare, esalare fumo; (*to show anger*) irritarsi
fumigate [ˈfjumɪ ˌget] *tr* fumigare
fumigation [ˌfjumɪˈgeʃən] *s* fumigazione
fun [fʌn] *s* divertimento, spasso; **to be fun** essere divertente; **to have fun** divertirsi; **to make fun of** prendersi gioco di
function [ˈfʌŋkʃən] *s* funzione || *intr* funzionare, marciare, camminare
functional [ˈfʌŋkʃənəl] *adj* funzionale
functionalism [ˈfʌŋkʃənəl ˌɪzəm] *s* funzionalismo
functionar·y [ˈfʌŋkʃə ˌnɛri] *s* (**-ies**) funzionario

fund [fʌnd] *s* fondo; (*of knowledge*) suppellettile *f* || *tr* (*debts*) consolidare
fundamental [ˌfʌndəˈmentəl] *adj* fondamentale || *s* fondamento
fundamentalist [ˌfʌndəˈmentəlɪst] *adj* & *s* scritturale *m*
funeral [ˈfjunərəl] *adj* funebre, funerario || *s* funerale *m*, trasporto funebre; **it's not my funeral** (slang) non sono affari miei
fu'neral direc'tor *s* imprenditore *m* di pompe funebri
fu'neral home' or **par'lor** *s* impresa di pompe funebri
fu'neral serv'ice *s* ufficio dei defunti
funereal [fjuˈnɪrɪ·əl] *adj* funebre
fungous [ˈfʌŋgəs] *adj* fungoso
fungus [ˈfʌŋgəs] *s* (**funguses** or **fungi** [ˈfʌndʒaɪ]) fungo
funicular [fjuˈnɪkjələr] *adj* & *s* funicolare *f*
funk [fʌŋk] *s* (coll) paura; (coll) codardo; **in a funk** (coll) con una paura matta
fun·nel [ˈfʌnəl] *s* imbuto; (*smokestack*) fumaiolo; (*for ventilation*) manica a vento || *v* (*pret & pp* **-neled** or **-nelled**; *ger* **-neling** or **-nelling**) *tr* incanalare
funnies [ˈfʌniz] *spl* pagine *fpl* fumetti
fun·ny [ˈfʌni] *adj* (**-nier**; **-niest**) comico, buffo; (coll) strano; **to strike as funny** parere strano or buffo a
fun'ny bone' *s* osso rabbioso (del gomito); **to strike s.o.'s funny bone** far ridere qlcu
fur [fʌr] *s* pelo; (*garment*) pelliccia; (*on the tongue*) patina
furbelow [ˈfʌrbəˌlo] *s* falpalà *m*
furbish [ˈfʌrbɪʃ] *tr* lustrare; mettere a nuovo; **to furbish up** rinfrescare
furious [ˈfjurɪ·əs] *adj* furioso
furl [fʌrl] *tr* (*a flag*) incazzottare; (naut) raccogliere, strangolare
fur-lined [ˈfʌrˌlaɪnd] *adj* foderato di pelliccia
furlong [ˈfʌrlɔŋ] or [ˈfʌrlɑŋ] *s* un ottavo di miglio terrestre
furlough [ˈfʌrlo] *s* licenza || *tr* licenziare
furnace [ˈfʌrnɪs] *s* fornace *f*; (*to heat a house*) caldaia del calorifero
furnish [ˈfʌrnɪʃ] *tr* fornire; ammobiliare
furnishings [ˈfʌrnɪʃɪŋz] *spl* mobilia; (*things to wear*) accessori *mpl* da uomo
furniture [ˈfʌrnɪtʃər] *s* mobili *mpl*, mobilia; (naut) attrezzatura; **a piece of furniture** un mobile
fur'ni·ture deal'er *s* mobiliere *m*
furor [ˈfjurər] *s* furore *m*
furrier [ˈfʌrɪ·ər] *s* pellicciaio
furrier·y [ˈfʌrɪ·əri] *s* (**-ies**) pellicceria
furrow [ˈfʌro] *s* solco || *tr* solcare
further [ˈfʌrðər] *adj* più lontano; ulteriore || *adv* oltre; più; inoltre || *tr* favorire, incoraggiare
furtherance [ˈfʌrðərəns] *s* avanzamento, incoraggiamento
furthermore [ˈfʌrðərˌmor] *adv* inoltre
furthest [ˈfʌrðɪst] *adj* (il) più lontano || *adv* al massimo
furtive [ˈfʌrtɪv] *adj* furtivo
fu·ry [ˈfjuri] *s* (**-ries**) furia
furze [fʌrz] *s* ginestra spinosa
fuse [fjuz] *s* (*for igniting an explosive*) miccia; (*for detonating an explosive*) spoletta; (elec) fusibile *m*; **to burn out a fuse** bruciare un fusibile || *tr* fondere || *intr* fondersi; (elec) saltare
fuse' box' *s* valvoliera
fuselage [ˈfjuzəlɪdʒ] or [ˌfjuzəˈlɑʒ] *s* fusoliera
fusible [ˈfjuzɪbəl] *adj* fusibile
fusillade [ˌfjuzɪˈled] *s* fucileria; (fig) gragnola || *tr* attaccare con fuoco di fucileria
fusion [ˈfjuʒən] *s* fusione
fuss [fʌs] *s* agitazione inutile; (coll) alterco per nulla; **to make a fuss** accogliere festosamente; fare molte storie; **to make a fuss over** aver un alterco su || *tr* disturbare || *intr* agitarsi per un nonnulla
fuss·y [ˈfʌsi] *adj* (**-ier**; **-iest**) (*person*) pignolo, meticoloso; (*object*) carico di fronzoli; (*writing*) complicato
fustian [ˈfʌstʃən] *s* fustagno; (fig) verbosità *f*, magniloquenza
fust·y [ˈfʌsti] *adj* (**-ier**; **-iest**) ammuffito, che sa di muffa; antico, sorpassato
futile [ˈfjutɪl] *adj* (*unproductive*) sterile; (*unimportant*) futile
futili·ty [fjuˈtɪlɪti] *s* (**-ties**) sterilità *f*; futilità *f*
future [ˈfjutʃər] *adj* futuro || *s* futuro; **futures** contratto con consegna a termine; **in the near future** nel prossimo avvenire
fuze [fjuz] *s* (*for igniting an explosive*) miccia; (*for detonating an explosive*) spoletta; (elec) fusibile *m* || *tr* innestare la spoletta a
fuzz [fʌz] *s* lanugine *f*, peluria; (*in corners*) polvere *f*; (slang) poliziotto; (slang) polizia
fuzz·y [ˈfʌzi] *adj* (**-ier**; **-iest**) lanuginoso; coperto di polvere; (*indistinct*) confuso

G

G, g [dʒi] *s* settima lettera dell'alfabeto inglese
gab [gæb] *s* (coll) parlantina || *v* (*pret & pp* **gabbed**; *ger* **gabbing**) *intr* (coll) chiacchierare
gabardine [ˈgæbərˌdin] *s* gabardine *f*
gabble [ˈgæbəl] *s* barbugliamento || *intr* barbugliare
gable [ˈgebəl] *s* (archit) timpano
ga'ble roof' *s* tetto a due falde, tetto a capanna
gad [gæd] *v* (*pret & pp* **gadded**; *ger* **gadding**) *intr* bighellonare
gad'about' *adj* ozioso || *s* vagabondo, bighellone *m*; fannullone *m*
gad'fly' *s* (**-flies**) tafano, moscone *m*

gadget ['gædʒɪt] *s* congegno, dispositivo, macchinetta
Gaelic ['gelɪk] *adj & s* gaelico
gaff [gæf] *s* arpione *m;* (naut) picco; **to stand the gaff** (slang) aver pazienza
gag [gæg] *s* bavaglio; (*joke*) barzelletta; (theat) battuta improvvisata || *v* (*pret & pp* **gagged;** *ger* **gagging**) *tr* imbavagliare; soffocare || *intr* sentirsi venire la nausea
gage [gedʒ] *s* (*pledge*) pegno; (*challenge*) sfida
gaie·ty ['ge·ɪti] *s* (**-ties**) gaiezza
gaily ['geli] *adv* allegramente
gain [gen] *s* profitto; (*increase*) aumento || *tr* guadagnare; (*to reach*) raggiungere; (*altitude*) prendere || *intr* (*said of a patient*) migliorare; (*said of a watch*) correre; **to gain on** guadagnare terreno su; sorpassare
gainful ['genfəl] *adj* rimunerativo
gain'say' *v* (*pret & pp* **-said** [,sed] or [,sɛd]) *tr* disdire, misconoscere; negare
gait [get] *s* portamento, andatura
gaiter ['getər] *s* ghetta
gala ['gælə] or ['gelə] *adj* di gala || *s* gala *m & f,* festa
galax·y ['gæləksi] *s* (**-ies**) galassia
gale [gel] *s* (*of wind*) bufera; (*of laughter*) scoppio; **to weather the gale** resistere alla tempesta
gall [gɔl] *s* fiele *m;* bile *f;* cistifellea; scorticatura; (*gallnut*) galla; (*audacity*) (coll) faccia tosta || *tr* irritare || *intr* irritarsi; (naut) logorarsi
gallant ['gælənt] or [gə'lænt] *adj* galante || ['gælənt] *adj* (*brave*) valoroso; (*grand*) magnifico; (*showy*) festivo || *s* prode *m;* (*man attentive to women*) galante *m*
gallant·ry ['gæləntri] *s* (**-ries**) galanteria; valore *m*
gall' blad'der *s* vescichetta biliare
gall'-blad'der attack' *s* travaso di bile
galleon ['gælɪ·ən] *s* galeone *m*
galler·y ['gæləri] *s* (**-ies**) galleria; tribuna; (*cheapest seats in theater*) loggione *m*
galley ['gæli] *s* (*vessel*) galera; (*kitchen*) (aer) cucina; (*kitchen*) (naut) cambusa; (*galley proof*) (typ) bozza in colonna; (*tray*) (typ) vantaggio
gal'ley proof' *s* bozza in colonna
gal'ley slave' *s* galeotto
Gallic ['gælɪk] *adj* gallo, gallico
galling ['gɔlɪŋ] *adj* irritante
gallivant ['gælɪ,vænt] *intr* andare a spasso; fare il galante
gall'nut' *s* galla
gallon ['gælən] *s* gallone *m*
galloon [gə'lun] *s* gallone *m,* nastro
gallop ['gæləp] *s* galoppo; **at a gallop** al galoppo || *tr* far galoppare || *intr* galoppare
gal·lows ['gæloz] *s* (**-lows** or **-lowses**) forca; (min) castelletto
gal'lows bird' *s* (coll) remo di galera, pendaglio da forca
gall'stone' *s* calcolo biliare
galore [gə'lor] *adv* in abbondanza
galosh [gə'lɑʃ] *s* stivaletto di gomma
galvanize ['gælvə,naɪz] *tr* galvanizzare
gal'vanized i'ron *s* ferro zincato
gambit ['gæmbɪt] *s* gambetto
gamble ['gæmbəl] *s* azzardo; (*game*) gioco d'azzardo || *tr* giocare; **to gamble away** giocarsi || *intr* giocare d'azzardo; (com) speculare
gambler ['gæmblər] *s* giocatore *m;* speculatore *m*
gambling ['gæmblɪŋ] *s* gioco (d'azzardo)
gam'bling den' *s* bisca
gam'bling house' *s* casa da gioco
gam·bol ['gæmbəl] *s* salto, capriola || *v* (*pret & pp* **-boled** or **-bolled;** *ger* **-boling** or **-bolling**) *intr* saltare, far capriole
gambrel ['gæmbrəl] *s* garretto
gam'brel roof' *s* tetto a mansarda
game [gem] *adj* da caccia; coraggioso; (*leg*) (coll) zoppo; (coll) pronto || *s* (*amusement*) gioco; (*contest*) partita; (*any sport*) sport *m;* (*wild animals hunted*) selvaggina; (*any pursuit*) attività *f;* (*object of pursuit*) bersaglio; (bridge) manche *f;* **the game is up** il gioco è fallito; **to make game of** farsi gioco di; **to play the game** giocare onestamente
game' bag' *s* carniere *m*
game'cock' *s* gallo da combattimento
game'keep'er *s* guardacaccia *m*
game' of chance' *s* gioco d'azzardo
game' preserve' *s* bandita di caccia
game' war'den *s* guardacaccia *m*
gamut ['gæmət] *s* (mus, fig) gamma
gam·y ['gemi] *adj* (**-ier; -iest**) coraggioso; (culin) che sa di selvatico
gander ['gændər] *s* papero, oca
gang [gæŋ] *adj* multiplo || *s* (*of workers*) ganga; (*of thugs*) cricca || *intr*—**to gang up** riunirsi; **to gang up against** or **on** (coll) gettarsi insieme contro
gangling ['gæŋglɪŋ] *adj* dinoccolato
gangli·on ['gæŋglɪ·ən] *s* (**-ons** or **-a** [ə]) ganglio
gang'plank' *s* palanca, plancia
gangrene ['gæŋgrin] *s* cancrena || *tr* far andare in cancrena || *intr* andare in cancrena
gangster ['gæŋstər] *s* gangster *m*
gang'way' *s* (*passageway*) corridoio; (*gangplank*) passerella, scalandrone *m;* (*in ship's side*) barcarizzo || *interj* lasciar passare!
gan·try ['gæntri] *s* (**-tries**) (*of crane*) cavalletto; (rr) ponte *m* delle segnalazioni; (rok) piattaforma verticale, torre *f* di lancio
gap [gæp] *s* (*pass*) passo; (*in a wall*) breccia; (*interval*) lacuna; (*between two points of view*) abisso; (mach) gioco
gape [gep] or [gæp] *s* apertura; (*yawn*) sbadiglio; sguardo di meraviglia || *intr* stare a bocca aperta; **to gape at** guardare a bocca aperta
garage [gə'rɑʒ] *s* rimessa
garb [gɑrb] *s* veste *f* || *tr* vestire
garbage ['gɑrbɪdʒ] *s* pattume *m,* immondizia, immondizie *fpl*
gar'bage can' *s* portaimmondizie *m*

gar'bage collec'tor *s* spazzaturaio, spazzino, netturbino
garble ['gɑrbəl] *tr* falsare, mutilare
garden ['gɑrdən] *s* (*of vegetables*) orto; (*of flowers*) giardino
gardener ['gɑrdnər] *s* (*of vegetables*) ortolano; (*of flowers*) giardiniere *m*
gardenia [gɑr'dinɪ·ə] *s* gardenia
gardening ['gɑrdnɪŋ] *s* orticoltura; giardinaggio
gar'den par'ty *s* trattenimento in giardino
gargle ['gɑrgəl] *s* gargarismo ‖ *intr* gargarizzare
gargoyle ['gɑrgɔɪl] *s* doccione *m*, gargolla
garish ['gerɪʃ] or ['gærɪʃ] *adj* appariscente; abbagliante
garland ['gɑrlənd] *s* ghirlanda ‖ *tr* inghirlandare
garlic ['gɑrlɪk] *s* aglio
garment ['gɑrmənt] *s* capo di vestiario
gar'ment bag' *s* tessilsacco
garner ['gɑrnər] *tr* mettere in granaio; (*to get*) acquistarsi; (*to hoard*) incettare
garnet ['gɑrnɪt] *adj & s* granata
garnish ['gɑrnɪʃ] *s* guarnizione; ‖ *tr* guarnire; (law) sequestrare
garret ['gærɪt] *s* sottotetto, soffitta
garrison ['gærɪsən] *s* guarnigione, presidio ‖ *tr* presidiare
garrote [gə'rɑt] or [gə'rot] *s* strangolamento; garrotta ‖ *tr* strangolare; giustiziare con la garrotta
garrulous ['gærələs] or ['gærjələs] *adj* garrulo, loquace
garter ['gɑrtər] *s* giarrettiera
gas [gæs] *s* gas *m;* (coll) benzina; (slang) successo; (slang) chiacchiere *fpl* ‖ *v* (*pret & pp* **gassed; ger gassing**) *tr* fornire di gas; (mil) gassare; (slang) divertire ‖ *intr* emettere gas; (slang) chiacchierare; **to gas up** fare il pieno
gas'bag' *s* involucro per il gas; (coll) chiacchierone *m*
gas' burn'er *s* becco a gas; (*on a stove*) fornello a gas
Gascony ['gæskəni] *s* la Guascogna
gaseous ['gæsɪ·əs] *adj* gassoso
gas' fit'ter *s* gassista *m*
gash [gæʃ] *s* sfregio ‖ *tr* sfregiare
gas' heat' *s* calefazione a gas
gas'hold'er *s* gassometro
gasi·fy ['gæsɪ,faɪ] *v* (*pret & pp* **-fied**) *tr* gassificare ‖ *intr* gassificarsi
gas' jet' *s* fornello a gas; fiamma
gasket ['gæskɪt] *s* guarnizione
gas'light' *s* luce *f* del gas
gas' main' *s* tubatura principale del gas
gas' mask' *s* maschera antigas
gas' me'ter *s* contatore *m* del gas
gasoline ['gæsə,lin] or [,gæsə'lin] *s* benzina
gas'oline' deal'er *s* benzinaio
gas'oline' pump' *s* colonnetta, distributore *m* di benzina
gasp [gæsp] or [gɑsp] *s* respirazione affannosa; (*of death*) rantolo ‖ *tr* dire affannosamente ‖ *intr* boccheggiare
gas' range' *s* cucina a gas, fornello a gas
gas'-sta'tion attend'ant *s* benzinaio
gas' stove' *s* cucina a gas
gas' tank' *s* gassometro; (aut) serbatoio di benzina
gastric ['gæstrɪk] *adj* gastrico
gastronomy [gæs'trɑnəmi] *s* gastronomia
gas' works' *s* officina del gas
gate [get] *s* porta; (*in fence or wall*) cancello; (*of sluice*) saracinesca; (*in an airport or station*) uscita; (rr) barriera; (sports, theat) incasso totale; **to crash the gate** (coll) fare il portoghese
gate'keep'er *s* portiere *m;* (rr) guardiabarriere *m*
gate'way' *s* passaggio, entrata
gather ['gæðər] *tr* raccogliere, cogliere; (*news*) raccapezzare; (*dust*) coprirsi di; (*e.g., a shawl*) avvolgere; (*speed*) aumentare (di); concludere, dedurre; (*signatures*) (bb) riunire; (sew) increspare ‖ *intr* riunirsi; raccogliersi; accumularsi
gathering ['gæðərɪŋ] *s* riunione; (bb) raccolta e piegatura; (pathol) ascesso; (sew) pieghettatura
gaud·y ['gɔdi] *adj* (**-ier; -iest**) chiassoso, vistoso
gauge [gedʒ] *s* misura; calibro; (*for liquids*) indicatore *m* di livello; (*of carpenter*) graffietto; indice *m;* diametro; (aut) spia; (rr) scartamento ‖ *tr* misurare; calibrare; (naut) stazzare
Gaul [gɔl] *s* gallo
gaunt [gɔnt] or [gɑnt] *adj* magro, emaciato; (*e.g., landscape*) desolato
gauntlet ['gɔntlɪt] or ['gɑntlɪt] *s* guanto; guanto di ferro; guantone *m*, manopola; **to run the gauntlet** (fig) esporsi alla critica; **to take up the gauntlet** raccogliere il guanto; **to throw down the gauntlet** gettare il guanto
gauze [gɔz] *s* garza
gavel ['gævəl] *s* martello, martelletto
gavotte [gə'vɑt] *s* gavotta
gawk [gɔk] *s* sciocco ‖ *intr* guardare a bocca aperta
gawk·y ['gɔki] *adj* (**-ier; -iest**) sgraziato, goffo
gay [ge] *adj* gaio; brillante; dissipato; (slang) omosessuale
gaye·ty ['ge·ɪti] *s* (**-ties**) gaiezza
gaze [gez] *s* sguardo fisso ‖ *intr* fissare lo sguardo
gazelle [gə'zel] *s* gazzella
gazette [gə'zet] *s* gazzetta
gazetteer [,gæzə'tɪr] *s* dizionario geografico
gear [gɪr] *s* utensili *mpl*, attrezzi *mpl;* (*mechanism*) meccanismo, dispositivo; (aut) marcia; (mach) ingranaggio **out of gear** disingranato; (fig) disturbato; **to throw into gear** ingranare; **to throw out of gear** disingranare; (fig) disturbare ‖ *tr* adattare ‖ *intr* adattarsi
gear' box' *s* scatola del cambio
gear'shift' *s* cambio di velocità

gear'shift lev'er *s* leva del cambio
gear'wheel' *s* ruota dentata
gee [dʒi] *interj* oh!; che bellezza!; **gee up!** (*command to a draft animal*) arri!
Gei'ger count'er ['gaɪgər] *s* contatore *m* Geiger
gel [dʒel] *s* gel *m* || *v* (*pret & pp* **gelled**; *ger* **gelling**) *intr* gelatinizzarsi
gelatine ['dʒelətɪn] *s* gelatina
geld [geld] *v* (*pret & pp* **gelded** or **gelt** [gelt]) *tr* castrare
gem [dʒem] *s* gemma, gioia
Gemini ['dʒemɪ,naɪ] *spl* i Gemelli
gender ['dʒendər] *s* (gram) genere *m;* (coll) sesso
gene [dʒin] *s* (biol) gene *m*
genealo•gy [,dʒenɪ'ælədʒi] or [,dʒinɪ'ælədʒi] *s* (**-gies**) genealogia
general ['dʒenərəl] *adj & s* generale *m*
gen'eral deliv'ery *s* fermo in posta, fermo posta *m*
generalissi•mo [,dʒenərə'lɪsɪmo] *s* (**-mos**) generalissimo
generali•ty [,dʒenə'rælɪti] *s* (**-ties**) generalità *f*
generalize ['dʒenərə,laɪz] *tr & intr* generalizzare
generally ['dʒenərəli] *adv* in genere, generalmente
gen'eral part'ner *s* accomandatario
gen'eral practi'tioner *s* medico generico
generalship ['dʒenərəl,ʃɪp] *s* generalato; strategia, abilità *f* militare; abilità amministrativa
gen'eral staff' *s* stato maggiore
generate ['dʒenə,ret] *tr* (*offspring; electricity*) generare; (math) originare
gen'erat'ing sta'tion *s* centrale elettrica
generation [,dʒenə'reʃən] *s* generazione
generative ['dʒenə,retɪv] *adj* generativo
gen'erative gram'mar *s* grammatica generativa
generator ['dʒenə,retər] *s* generatore *m;* (elec) generatrice *f*
generic [dʒɪ'nerɪk] *adj* generico
generous ['dʒenərəs] *adj* generoso; abbondante, copioso
gene•sis ['dʒenɪsɪs] *s* (**-ses** [,siz]) genesi *f* || **Genesis** *s* (Bib) Genesi *m*
genetic [dʒɪ'netɪk] *adj* genetico || **genetics** *ssg* genetica
Geneva [dʒɪ'nivə] *s* Ginevra
Genevan [dʒɪ'nivən] *adj & s* ginevrino
genial ['dʒinɪ·əl] *adj* affabile, geniale
genie ['dʒini] *s* genio
genital ['dʒenɪtəl] *adj* genitale || **genitals** *spl* genitali *mpl*
genitive ['dʒenɪtɪv] *adj & s* genitivo
genius ['dʒinjəs] or ['dʒinɪ·əs] *s* (**geniuses**) genio || *s* (**genii**) ['dʒinɪ,aɪ] (*spirit; deity*) genio
Genoa ['dʒeno·ə] *s* Genova
genocide ['dʒenə,saɪd] *s* (*act*) genocidio; (*person*) genocida *mf*
Geno•ese [,dʒeno'iz] *adj* genovese || *s* (**-ese**) genovese *mf*
genre ['ʒɑnrə] *adj* (*e.g., painting*) di genere || *s* genere *m*
genteel [dʒen'til] *adj* (*well-bred*) beneducato; (*affectedly polite*) manieroso, manierato
gentian ['dʒenʃən] *s* genziana
gentile ['dʒentɪl] or ['dʒentaɪl] *adj* gentilizio || ['dʒentaɪl] *adj & s* non circonciso; non ebreo; cristiano; (*pagan*) gentile
gentili•ty [dʒen'tɪlɪti] *s* (**-ties**) distinzione, raffinatezza
gentle ['dʒentəl] *adj* (*e.g., manner*) gentile; (*e.g., wind*) dolce, soave; (*wellborn*) bennato; (*tap*) leggero
gen'tle•folk' *s* gente *f* per bene
gen'tle•man *s* (**-men**) signore *m;* (*attendant to a person of high rank*) gentiluomo; (*well-mannered man*) gentleman *m*
gen'tleman in wait'ing *s* gentiluomo di camera
gentlemanly ['dʒentəlmənli] *adj* signorile
gen'tleman of the road' *s* brigante *m;* vagabondo
gen'tlemen's agree'ment *s* accordo fondato sulla buona fede
gen'tle sex' *s* gentil sesso
gentry ['dʒentri] *s* gente *f* per bene
genuine ['dʒenju·ɪn] *adj* genuino
genus ['dʒinəs] *s* (**genera** ['dʒenərə] or **genuses**) genere *m*
geographer [dʒɪ'ɑgrəfər] *s* geografo
geographic(al) [,dʒɪ·ə'græfɪk(əl)] *adj* geografico
geogra•phy [dʒɪ'ɑgrəfi] *s* (**-phies**) geografia
geologic(al) [,dʒi·ə'lɑdʒɪk(əl)] *adj* geologico
geologist [dʒɪ'ɑlədʒɪst] *s* geologo
geolo•gy [dʒɪ'ɑlədʒi] *s* (**-gies**) geologia
geometric(al) [,dʒi·ə'metrɪk(əl)] *adj* geometrico
geometrician [dʒɪ,ɑmɪ'trɪʃən] *s* geometra *mf*
geome•try [dʒɪ'ɑmɪtri] *s* (**-tries**) geometria
George [dʒɔrdʒ] *s* Giorgio
geranium [dʒɪ'renɪ·əm] *s* geranio
geriatrics [,dʒerɪ'ætrɪks] *ssg* geriatria
germ [dʒʌrm] *s* germe *m*
German ['dʒʌrmən] *adj & s* tedesco
germane [dʒər'men] *adj* pertinente
Germanize ['dʒʌrmə,naɪz] *tr* germanizzare
Ger'man mea'sles *s* rosolia, rubeola
Ger'man sil'ver *s* alpacca
Germany ['dʒʌrməni] *s* la Germania
germ' car'rier *s* portatore *m* di germi
germ' cell' *s* cellula germinale
germicidal [,dʒʌrmɪ'saɪdəl] *adj* germicida
germicide ['dʒʌrmɪ,saɪd] *s* germicida *m*
germinate ['dʒʌrmɪ,net] *intr* germinare
germ' war'fare *s* guerra batteriologica
gerontology [,dʒerɑn'tɑlədʒi] *s* gerontologia
gerund ['dʒerənd] *s* gerundio
gestation [dʒes'teʃən] *s* gestazione
gesticulate [dʒes'tɪkjə,let] *intr* gesticolare

gesticulation [dʒes ˌtɪkjəˈleʃən] *s* gesticolazione
gesture [ˈdʒestʃər] *s* gesto || *intr* gestire, gesticolare
get [get] *v* (*pret* **got** [gɑt]; *pp* **got** or **gotten** [ˈgɑtən]; *ger* **getting**) *tr* ottenere; ricevere; prendere; andare a comprare; procacciare; riportare; procurarsi; riscuotere; guadagnare; **to get across** far capire; **to get back** riacquistare; **to get down** staccare; (*to swallow*) trangugiare; **to get off** togliere, cavare; **to get s.o. to** + *inf* indurre che qlcu + *subj;* **to get done** far fare; **to have got** (coll) avere; **to have got to** + *inf* (coll) dovere + *inf* || *intr* (*to become*) diventare, farsi; (*to arrive*) arrivare, venire; **to get out** (*said of a convalescent*) alzarsi; **to get along** andarsene; andare avanti; tirare avanti, giostrare; aver successo; **to get along in years** essere avanti con gli anni; **to get along with** andare d'accordo con; **to get angry** arrabbiarsi; **to get around** uscire; divulgarsi; rigirare; **to get away** scappare, darsela a gambe; **to get away with s.th** scappare con qlco; (coll) farla franca; **to get back** ritornare; ricuperare; **to get back at** (coll) vendicarsi di; **to get behind** rimanere indietro; (*to support*) appoggiare, patrocinare; **to get better** migliorare; **to get by** passare oltre; (*to succeed*) arrivare a farcela; passare inosservato; **to get even with** rifarsi con, prendersi la rivincita con; **to get going** mettersi in moto; **to get in** entrare; rientrare; arrivare; **to get in deeper and deeper** cacciarsi nei pasticci; **to get in with** diventare amico di; **to get married** sposarsi **to get off** andarsene; smontare da; **to get old** invecchiare; **to get on** andare avanti; andare d'accordo; **to get out** uscire; propagarsi; **to get out of** (*a car*) uscire da; (*trouble*) trarsi di; **to get out of the way** togliersi di mezzo; **to get run over** essere investito; **to get through** finire; arrivare; farsi capire; **to get to be** finire per essere; **to get under way** mettersi in cammino; **to get up** alzarsi; **to not get over it** (coll) non arrivare a rassegnarsi
get'a•way' *s* fuga; (sports) partenza
get'-to•geth'er *s* riunione, crocchio
get'up' *s* (coll) stile *m*, presentazione; (coll) costume *m*, abbigliamento
gewgaw [ˈgjugɔ] *s* cianfrusaglia
geyser [ˈgaɪzər] *s* geyser *m*
ghast•ly [ˈgæstli] or [ˈgɑstli] *adj* (**-lier; -liest**) orribile, orrendo; spettrale
gherkin [ˈgʌrkɪn] *s* cetriolino
ghet•to [ˈgeto] *s* (**-tos** or **-toes**) ghetto
ghost [gost] *s* spettro, fantasma *m;* **not a ghost of** nemmeno l'ombra di; **to give up the ghost** rendere l'anima
ghost•ly [ˈgostli] *adj* (**-lier; -liest**) spettrale, fantomatico
ghost' sto'ry *s* storia di fantasmi
ghost' town' *s* città morta
ghost' writ'er *s* collaboratore anonimo
ghoul [gul] *s* spirito necrofago; ladro di tombe
ghoulish [ˈgulɪʃ] *adj* demoniaco, macabro
GI [ˈdʒiˈaɪ] (letterword) (**General Issue**) *s* (**GI's**) soldato degli Stati Uniti
giant [ˈdʒaɪ•ənt] *adj & s* gigante *m*
giantess [ˈdʒaɪ•əntɪs] *s* gigantessa
gibberish [ˈdʒɪbərɪʃ] or [ˈgɪbərɪʃ] *s* linguaggio inintelligibile
gibbet [ˈdʒɪbɪt] *s* forca || *tr* impiccare sulla forca; (*to hold up to scorn*) mettere alla berlina
gibe [dʒaɪb] *s* scherno, frecciata || *intr* schernire; **to gibe at** beffarsi di
giblets [ˈdʒɪblɪts] *spl* rigaglie *fpl*
giddiness [ˈgɪdɪnɪs] *s* vertigine *f;* frivolezza
gid•dy [ˈgɪdi] *adj* (**-dier; -diest**) vertiginoso; preso dalle vertigini; frivolo
gift [gɪft] *s* regalo; (*natural ability*) dono, dote *f;* (*for Christmas*) strenna
gifted [ˈgɪftɪd] *adj* dotato
gift' horse' *s*—**never look a gift horse in the mouth** a caval donato non si guarda in bocca
gift' of gab' *s* (coll) facondia; **to have the gift of gab** (coll) avere la lingua sciolta
gift' pack'age *s* pacco-dono
gift' shop' *s* negozio di regali
gift'-wrap' *v* (*pret & pp* **-wrapped;** *ger* **-wrapping**) *tr* incartare in carta speciale per regali
gigantic [dʒaɪˈgæntɪk] *adj* gigantesco
giggle [ˈgɪgəl] *s* risolino || *intr* ridere scioccamente, ridacchiare
gigo•lo [ˈdʒɪgəˌlo] *s* (**-los**) gigolo
gild [gɪld] *v* (*pret & pp* **gilded** or **gilt** [gɪlt]) *tr* dorare, indorare
gilding [ˈgɪldɪŋ] *s* doratura
gill [gɪl] *s* (*of fish*) branchia || [dʒɪl] *s* quarto di pinta
gilt [gɪlt] *adj & s* dorato
gilt-edged [ˈgɪlt ˌedʒd] *adj* a bordo dorato; di primissima qualità
gimcrack [ˈdʒɪm ˌkræk] *adj* di nessun valore || *s* cianfrusaglia
gimlet [ˈgɪmlɪt] *s* succhiello
gimmick [ˈgɪmɪk] *s* (slang) trucco
gin [dʒɪn] *s* (*liquor*) gin *m;* (*trap*) trappola; (mach) arganello; (tex) sgranatrice *f* di cotone || *v* (*pret & pp* **ginned;** *ger* **ginning**) *tr* ginnare, sgranare
ginger [ˈdʒɪndʒər] *s* zenzero; (coll) energia, vivacità *f*
gin'ger ale' *s* gazosa allo zenzero
gin'ger•bread' *s* pan di zenzero; ornamento di cattivo gusto
gingerly [ˈdʒɪndʒərli] *adj* cauto || *adv* con cautela
gin'ger•snap' *s* biscotto allo zenzero
gingham [ˈgɪŋəm] *s* rigatino
giraffe [dʒɪˈræf] or [dʒɪˈrɑf] *s* giraffa
girandole [ˈdʒɪrən ˌdol] *s* girandola
gird [gʌrd] *v* (*pret & pp* **girt** [gʌrt] or **girded**) *tr* cingere; (*to equip*) dotare; (*to prepare*) preparare; (*to surround*) circondare
girder [ˈgʌrdər] *s* longherina

girdle ['gʌrdəl] *s* reggicalze *m*, zona, fascetta || *tr* fasciare; circondare
girl [gʌrl] *s* fanciulla; ragazza
girl' friend' *s* amica, innamorata
girlhood ['gʌrlhʊd] *s* adolescenza, giovinezza
girlish ['gʌrlɪʃ] *adj* fanciullesco; da ragazza
girl' scout' *s* giovane esploratrice *f*
girth [gʌrθ] *s* circonferenza; fascia; (*to hold a saddle*) sottopancia *m*
gist [dʒɪst] *s* sugo, nocciolo, essenza
give [gɪv] *s* elasticità *f* || *v* (*pret* **gave** [gev]; *pp* **given** ['gɪvən]) *tr* dare; (*trouble*) causare; (*a play*) rappresentare; (*a speech; fruit; a sigh*) fare; **to give away** distribuire gratuitamente; (*to reveal*) lasciarsi sfuggire; (*a bride*) accompagnare all'altare; (coll) tradire; **to give back** restituire; **to give forth** (*odors*) emettere; **to give oneself up** darsi; **to give up** cedere; (*a position*) abbandonare || *intr* dare; cedere; (*said, e.g., of a rope*) rompersi; **to give in** cedere; darsi per vinto; **to give out** esaurirsi; venir meno; **to give up** darsi per vinto
give'-and-take' *s* compromesso; conversazione briosa
give'a·way' *s* premio gratuito; rivelazione involontaria; (*game*) vinciperdi *m;* (rad, telv) programma *m* a premi
given ['gɪvən] *adj* dato; **given that** dato che, concesso che
giv'en name' *s* nome *m* di battesimo
giver ['gɪvər] *s* donatore *m;* dispensatore *m*
gizzard ['gɪzərd] *s* magone *m*
glacial ['gleʃəl] *adj* glaciale
glacier ['gleʃər] *s* ghiacciaio
glad [glæd] *adj* (**gladder; gladdest**) felice, lieto, contento; **to be glad (to)** essere felice (di)
gladden ['glædən] *tr* rallegrare
glade [gled] *s* radura
glad' hand' *s* (coll) accoglienza calorosa
gladiator ['glædɪ,etər] *s* gladiatore *m*
gladiola [,glædɪ'olə] or [glə'daɪ·ələ] *s* gladiolo
gladly ['glædli] *adv* volentieri, di buon grado
gladness ['glædnɪs] *s* contentezza
glad' rags' *s* (coll) panni *mpl* da festa; (coll) vestito da sera
glamorous ['glæmərəs] *adj* affascinante, attraente
glamour ['glæmər] *s* fascino, malia
glam'our girl' *s* ragazza sci-sci
glance [glæns] or [glɑns] *s* occhiata, guardata; **at first glance** a prima vista || *intr* lanciare uno sguardo; **to glance at** dare un'occhiata a; **to glance off** sorvolare su; deviare da; **to glance over** dare una scorsa a
gland [glænd] *s* ghiandola
glanders ['glændərz] *spl* morva
glare [gler] *s* splendore *m*, luce *f* abbagliante; sguardo minaccioso || *intr* risplendere; lanciare occhiatacce; **to glare at** fare la faccia feroce a
glare' ice' *s* vetrato
glaring ['glerɪŋ] *adj* risplendente, abbagliante; (*look*) torvo; evidente
glass [glæs] or [glɑs] *s* vetro; (*tumbler*) bicchiere *m;* (*mirror*) specchio; (*glassware*) cristalleria; **glasses** occhiali *mpl*
glass' blow'er ['blo·ər] *s* vetraio
glass' case' *s* vetrinetta
glass' cut'ter *s* tagliatore *m* di cristallo; (*tool*) diamante *m* tagliavetro
glass' door' *s* porta a vetri
glassful ['glæsfʊl] or ['glɑsfʊl] *s* bicchiere *m*
glass'house' *s* vetreria; (fig) casa di vetro
glass'ware' *s* vetreria, cristalleria
glass' wool' *s* vetro filato
glass'work'er *s* vetraio
glass'works' *s* vetreria, cristalleria
glass·y ['glæsi] or ['glɑsi] *adj* (**-ier; -iest**) vetriato, vetroso
glaze [glez] *s* vernice vitrea; smalto; (*of ice*) superficie invetriata; (culin) glassa || *tr* smaltare; invetriare; (culin) glassare
glazier ['gleʒər] *s* vetraio
gleam [glim] *s* barlume *m*, raggio || *intr* baluginare
glean [glin] *tr* spigolare, racimolare; (*to gather facts*) raccogliere
glee [gli] *s* gioia, esultanza
glee' club' *s* società *f* corale
glib [glɪb] *adj* (**glibber; glibbest**) loquace; (*tongue*) facile, sciolto
glide [glaɪd] *s* scivolata; (aer) volo a vela, volo planato; (mus) legamento || *intr* scivolare; (aer) librarsi, planare; **to glide away** scorrere
glider ['glaɪdər] *s* (aer) libratore *m*, veleggiatore *m*
glimmer ['glɪmər] *s* barlume *m* || *intr* brillare, luccicare; tralucere
glimmering ['glɪmərɪŋ] *adj* tenue, tremulo || *s* luce fioca; barlume *m*
glimpse [glɪmps] *s* occhiata; **to catch a glimpse of** intravedere || *tr* travedere
glint [glɪnt] *s* scintillio || *intr* scintillare
glisten ['glɪsən] *s* scintillio, luccichio || *intr* scintillare, luccicare
glitter ['glɪtər] *s* luccichio || *intr* rilucere, sfolgorare
gloaming ['glomɪŋ] *s* crepuscolo (vespertino)
gloat [glot] *intr* guardare con maligna soddisfazione; **to gloat over** godere di
global ['globəl] *adj* globale; universale; globulare
globe [glob] *s* globo; (*with map of earth*) mappamondo
globe-trotter ['glob ,trɑtər] *s* giramondo
globule ['glɑbjʊl] *s* globulo
glockenspiel ['glɑkən ,spil] *s* vibrafono
gloom [glum] *s* oscurità *f;* malinconia, uggia
gloom·y ['glumi] *adj* (**-ier; -iest**) lugubre, triste, tetro
glori·fy ['glorɪ ,faɪ] *v* (*pret & pp* **-fied**) *tr* glorificare; (*to enhance*) esaltare

glorious ['glorɪ·əs] *adj* glorioso; magnifico, splendido
glo·ry ['glori] *s* (**-ries**) gloria; **to go to glory** morire || *v* (*pret & pp* **-ried**) *intr* gloriarsi
gloss [glɔs] or [glɑs] *s* lucentezza, patina; (*commentary*) glossa || *tr* satinare, patinare; (*to annotate*) glossare; **to gloss over** nascondere, discolpare
glossa·ry ['glɑsəri] *s* (**-ries**) glossario
gloss·y ['glɔsi] or ['glɑsi] *adj* (**-ier; -iest**) lucido; (*paper*) satinato
glottal ['glɑtəl] *adj* articolato alla glottide
glottis ['glɑtɪs] *s* glottide *f*
glove [glʌv] *s* guanto
glove' compart'ment *s* cassetto portaoggetti
glow [glo] *s* fuoco, incandescenza; splendore *m*, scintillio; calore *m;* colorito acceso || *intr* essere incandescente; (*said of cheeks*) avvampare; (*said of cat's eyes*) fosforeggiare
glower ['glaʊ·ər] *s* sguardo torvo || *intr* guardare col viso torvo
glowing ['glo·ɪŋ] *adj* incandescente; acceso; entusiasta, entusiastico
glow'worm' *s* lucciola; lampiride *m*
glucose ['glukos] *s* glucosio
glue [glu] *s* colla, mastice *m* || *tr* incollare, ingommare
glue'pot' *s* pentolino per la colla
gluey ['glu·i] *adj* (**gluier; gluiest**) attaccaticcio; (*smeared with glue*) incollato
glum [glʌm] *adj* (**glummer; glummest**) tetro, accigliato
glut [glʌt] *s* abbondanza; eccesso; **there is a glut on the market** il mercato è saturo || *v* (*pret & pp* **glutted;** *ger* **glutting**) *tr* saziare; (*the market*) saturare; (*a channel*) otturare
glutton ['glʌtən] *adj & s* ghiottone *m*
gluttonous ['glʌtənəs] *adj* ghiotto
glutton·y ['glʌtəni] *s* (**-ies**) ghiottoneria, golosità *f*
glycerine ['glɪsərɪn] *s* glicerina
G'-man' *s* (**-men'**) agente *m* federale
gnarl [nɑrl] *s* nodo || *tr* torcere || *intr* ringhiare
gnarled [nɑrld] *adj* nodoso; (*wrinkled*) grinzoso
gnash [næʃ] *tr* digrignare || *intr* digrignare i denti
gnat [næt] *s* moscerino, pappataci *m*
gnaw [nɔ] *tr* rosicchiare, rodere || *intr* —**to gnaw at** (fig) rimordere
gnome [nom] *s* gnomo
go [go] *s* (**goes**) andata; energia; (*for traffic*) via libera; **it's a go** è un affare fatto; **it's all the go** (coll) è all'ultimo grido; **it's no go** (coll) è impossibile; **on the go** in continuo andare e venire; **to make a go of** (coll) aver successo con || *v* (*pret* **went** [wɛnt]; *pp* **gone** [gɔn] or [gɑn]) *tr* (coll) sopportare; (coll) scommettere; (coll) pagare; **to go it alone** fare da sé || *intr* andare; (*to operate*) camminare, funzionare; (*e.g., mad*) diventare; (*said of numbers*) entrare; **gone!** venduto!; **so it goes** così va il mondo; **to be going to** + *inf* andare a + *inf*, e.g., **I am going to New York to see him** vado a New York a vederlo; (*to express futurity*) use *fut ind*, e.g., **I am going to stay home today** starò a casa oggi; **to be gone** essere andato; esser morto; **to go against** opporsi a; **to go ahead** andar avanti; tirare avanti; **to go around** andare in giro; **to go away** andarsene; **to go back** tornare; **to go by** passare per; regolarsi su; (*said of time*) passare; **to go down** discendere; (*said of a boat*) affondare; **to go fishing** andare a pescare; **to go for** vendersi per; andare a pigliare; attaccare; favorire; **to go get** andare a pigliare; **to go house hunting** andare in cerca di una casa; **to go hunting** andare a caccia; **to go in** entrare in; (*to fit in*) starci in; **to go in for** dedicarsi a; **to go into** investigare; darsi a, dedicarsi a; (*gear*) (aut) ingranare; **to go in with** associarsi con; **to go off** andarsene; aver luogo; (*said of a bomb*) esplodere; (*said of a rifle*) sparare; (*said of a trap*) scattare; **to go on** continuare, protrarsi; **to go on** + *ger* continuare a + *inf;* **to go out** uscire; passare di moda; (*said, e.g., of fire*) spegnersi; (*to strike*) mettersi in sciopero; **to go over** aver successo; leggere; esaminare; **to go over to** passare ai ranghi di; **to go skiing** andare a sciare; **to go swimming** andare a nuotare, andare al bagno; **to go through** esperimentare; (*to examine carefully*) rovistare; (*said, e.g., of a plan or a project*) aver successo; (*a fortune*) dissipare; **to go through a red light** passare la strada col semaforo rosso; **to go with** andare con, accompagnare; (*a girl*) essere l'amico di; **to go without** fare a meno di
goad [god] *s* pungolo || *tr* pungolare; (fig) spronare
go'-ahead' *adj* intraprendente || *s* via *m*
goal [gol] *s* meta; (football) gol *m*
goalie ['goli] *s* portiere *m*
goal'keep'er *s* portiere *m*
goal' line' *s* linea di porta
goal' post' *s* montante *m*
goat [got] *s* capra; (*male*) becco; (coll) capro espiatorio; **to get the goat of** (coll) irritare
goatee [go'ti] *s* barbetta, pizzo
goat'herd' *s* capraio
goat'skin' *s* pelle *f* di capra
goat'suck'er *s* caprimulgo
gob [gɑb] *s* massa informe; **gobs** (coll) mucchio, quantità *f* enorme
gobble ['gɑbəl] *s* gloglottio || *tr* ingozzare; **to gobble up** (coll) trangugiare; (coll) impadronirsi di || *intr* trangugiare; (*said of a turkey*) gloglottare
gobbledegook ['gɑbəldɪ,gʊk] *s* linguaggio oscuro
go'-between' *s* intermediario; (*pander*) mezzano; (poet) pronubo
goblet ['gɑblɪt] *s* coppa
goblin ['gɑblɪn] *s* folletto
go'-by' *s*—**to give s.o. the go-by** (coll) schivare qlcu
go'-cart' *s* carrettino; (*walker*) girello

god [gɑd] *s* dio; **God forbid** Dio ci scampi; **God grant** voglia Dio; **God willing** se Dio vuole
god'child' *s* (**-chil'dren**) figlioccio
god'daugh'ter *s* figlioccia
goddess ['gɑdɪs] *s* dea, diva
god'fa'ther *s* padrino
God'-fear'ing *adj* timorato di Dio
God'for•sak'en *adj* miserabile; (*place*) sperduto, fuori di mano
god'head' *s* deità *f* || **Godhead** *s* Ente Supremo, Dio
godless ['gɑdlɪs] *adj* ateo; malvagio || **the godless** i senza Dio
god•ly ['gɑdli] *adj* (**-lier; -liest**) devoto, pio
god'moth'er *s* madrina
God's' a'cre *s* camposanto
god'send' *s* manna, provvidenza
god'son' *s* figlioccio
God'speed' *s* successo, buona fortuna
go-getter ['go ˌgetər] *s* (coll) persona intraprendente
goggle ['gɑgəl] *intr* stralunare gli occhi
goggle-eyed ['gɑgəl ˌaɪd] *adj* dagli occhi sporgenti
goggles ['gɑgəlz] *spl* occhiali *mpl* da protezione
going ['go•ɪŋ] *adj* in moto, in funzione; **going on** quasi, e.g., **it is going on seven o'clock** sono quasi le sette || *s* andata; progresso
go'ings on' *s* (coll) comportamento, contegno; (coll) avvenimenti *mpl*
goiter ['gɔɪtər] *s* gozzo
gold [gold] *adj* aureo, d'oro || *s* oro
gold'beat'er *s* battiloro
gold'brick' *s* imitazione, frode *f;* (slang) fannullone *m*
gold' dig'ger ['dɪgər] *s* cercatore *m* d'oro; (coll) donna unicamente interessata nel denaro
golden ['goldən] *adj* aureo, d'oro; (*gilt*) dorato; (fig) splendido
gold'en age' *s* età *f* dell'oro
gold'en calf' *s* vitello d'oro
Gold'en Fleece' *s* vello d'oro
gold'en mean' *s* aurea mediocrità
gold'en•rod' *s* (bot) verga d'oro
gold'en rule' *s* regola della carità cristiana
gold'en wed'ding *s* nozze *fpl* d'oro
gold-filled ['gold ˌfɪld] *adj* otturato in oro
gold'finch' *s* cardellino
gold'fish' *s* pesce rosso
goldilocks ['goldɪ ˌlɑks] *s* bionda; (bot) ranuncolo
gold' leaf' *s* oro in foglia
gold' mine' *s* miniera d'oro
gold' plate' *s* vasellame *m* d'oro
gold'-plate' *tr* dorare
gold' rush' *s* febbre *f* dell'oro
gold'smith' *s* orefice *m*
gold' stand'ard *s* regime aureo
golf [gɑlf] *s* golf *m* || *intr* giocare a golf
golf' cart' *s* mini-auto *f* per campi da golf
golf' club' *s* mazza; associazione di giocatori di golf
golfer ['gɑlfər] *s* giocatore *m* di golf
golf' links' *spl* campo di golf
Golgotha ['gɑlgəθə] *s* il Golgota
gondola ['gɑndələ] *s* gondola
gondolier [ˌgɑndə'lɪr] *s* gondoliere *m*
gone [gɔn] or [gɑn] *adj* partito; rovinato; andato; morto; **gone on** (coll) innamorato di
gong [gɔŋ] or [gɑŋ] *s* gong *m*
goo [gu] *s* (coll) sostanza appiccicaticcia
good [gʊd] *adj* (**better; best**) buono; **good and . . .** (coll) molto, e.g., **good and cheap** molto a buon mercato; **good for** buono per; responsabile per; (*equivalent*) valido per; **to be good at** esser bravo a; **to be no good** (coll) non servire a nulla; (coll) essere un perdigiorno; **to make good** avere successo; (*one's promise*) mantenere; (*a debt*) pagare; (*damages*) indennizzare || *s* bene *m;* utile *m,* profitto; **for good** per sempre; **for good and all** una volta per sempre; **goods** merce *f,* mercanzia; **the good** il bene; i buoni; **to catch with the goods** (coll) cogliere in flagrante; **to deliver the goods** (slang) mantenere le promesse; **to do good** fare del bene; **to the good** come profitto; come attivo; **what is the good of . . . ?** a che serve . . . ?
good' afternoon' *s* buon pomeriggio
good'-by' [ˌgʊd'baɪ] *s* addio || *interj* addio!; arrivederci!
good' day' *s* buon giorno
good' deed' *s* buona azione
good' egg' *s* (slang) bonaccione *m,* gran brava persona
good' eve'ning *s* buona sera; buona notte
good' fel'low *s* buon ragazzo
good'-fel'low•ship' *s* cameratismo
good'-for-noth'ing *adj* inutile, senza valore || *s* pelandrone *m,* inetto
Good' Fri'day *s* Venerdì Santo
good' grac'es *spl* buone grazie
good-hearted ['gʊd'hɑrtɪd] *adj* di buon cuore
good'-hum'ored *adj* di buon umore
good'-look'ing *adj* bello
good' looks' *s* bellezza
good•ly ['gʊdli] *adj* (**-lier; -liest**) bello; di buona qualità; ampio, considerevole
good' morn'ing *s* buon giorno
good-natured ['gʊd'netʃərd] *adj* bonaccione, affabile
goodness ['gʊdnɪs] *s* bontà *f;* **for goodness sake!** per amor di Dio!; **goodness knows!** chi sa mai! || *interj* Dio mio!
good' night' *s* buona notte
good'-sized' *adj* piuttosto grande
good' speed' *s* buona fortuna
good'-tem'pered *adj* di carattere mite, gioviale
good' time' *s* periodo gradevole; **to have a good time** divertirsi; **to make good time** andare di buon passo
good' turn' *s* favore *m,* servizio
good' will' *s* buona volontà; (com) reputazione; (com) clientela
good•y ['gʊdi] *adj* (coll) troppo buono || *s* (**-ies**) (coll) santerello; **goodies**

(coll) ghiottonerie *fpl* || *interj* (coll) bene!, benissimo!
gooey ['gu·i] *adj* **(gooier; gooiest)** (slang) attaccaticcio
goof [guf] *s* (slang) sciocco || *tr* (slang) rovinare; **to goof up** (*an opportunity*) (slang) mancare || *intr* (slang) pigliare un granchio; **to goof off** (slang) battere la fiacca; **to goof up** (slang) farla grossa
goof·y ['gufi] *adj* **(-ier; -iest)** (slang) sciocco
goon [gun] *s* (slang) scemo; (coll) crumiro, gaglioffo, terrorista *m*
goose [gus] *s* **(geese** [gis]) oca; **the goose hangs high** tutto va per il meglio; **to cook one's goose** rompere le uova nel paniere di qlcu; **to kill the goose that lays the golden eggs** uccidere la gallina delle uova d'oro || *s* **(gooses)** ferro da stiro per sarto
goose'ber'ry *s* **(-ries)** uva spina; (*berry*) bacca d'uva spina
goose' egg' *s* (slang) zero; (*lump on the head*) (coll) bernoccolo
goose' flesh' *s* pelle *f* d'oca
goose'neck' *s* collo d'oca
goose' pim'ples *spl* pelle *f* d'oca
goose' step' *s* passo dell'oca
gopher ['gofər] *s* scoiattolo di terra, citillo
gore [gor] *s* sangue coagulato; (*in a garment*) gherone *m* || *tr* (*with a horn*) incornare; inserire gheroni in
gorge [gɔrdʒ] *s* gola, burrone *m;* (*meal*) mangiata || *tr* rimpinzare || *intr* rimpinzarsi
gorgeous ['gɔrdʒəs] *adj* splendido, magnifico
gorilla [gə'rɪlə] *s* gorilla *m*
gorse [gɔrs] *s* gineprone *m*
gor·y ['gori] *adj* **(-ier; -iest)** sanguinolento
gosh [gɑʃ] *interj* perbacco!
goshawk ['gɑs,hɔk] *s* sparviere *m,* astore *m*
gospel ['gɑspəl] *s* vangelo || **Gospel** *s* Vangelo
gos'pel truth' *s* santissima verità
gossamer ['gɑsəmər] *s* ragnatela; (*variety of gauze*) garza finissima; tessuto impermeabile finissimo
gossip ['gɑsɪp] *s* maldicenza; (*person*) pettegolo; **piece of gossip** maldicenza || *intr* spettegolare
gossipy ['gɑsɪpi] *adj* pettegolo
Goth [gɑθ] *s* Goto
Gothic ['gɑθɪk] *adj & s* gotico
gouge [gaʊdʒ] *s* (*cut made with a gouge*) scanalatura; (*tool*) sgorbia; (coll) truffa || *tr* sgorbiare; (coll) truffare
goulash ['gulɑʃ] *s* gulasch *m*
gourd [gord] or [gʊrd] *s* zucca
gourmand ['gʊrmənd] *s* ghiottone *m*
gourmet ['gʊrme] *s* buongustaio
gout [gaʊt] *s* gotta, podagra
gout·y ['gaʊti] *adj* **(-ier; -iest)** gottoso
govern ['gʌvərn] *tr* governare; (gram) reggere
governess ['gʌvərnɪs] *s* governante *f,* istitutrice *f*
government ['gʌvərnmənt] *s* governo; (gram) reggenza
governmental [,gʌvərn'mentəl] *adj* governativo
governor ['gʌvərnər] *s* governatore *m;* (mach) regolatore *m*
governorship ['gʌvərnər,ʃɪp] *s* governatorato
gown [gaʊn] *s* (*of a woman*) vestito; (*academic*) toga; (*of a physician or patient*) gabbanella; (*of a priest*) veste *f* talare
grab [græb] *s* presa; **up for grabs** (coll) pronto a esser pigliato || *v* (*pret & pp* **grabbed;** *ger* **grabbing**) *tr* pigliare, afferrare
grace [gres] *s* (*charm; favor*) grazia; (*pardon*) mercé *f;* (*prayer*) benedicite *m;* (com) dilazione; **to say grace** recitare il benedicite; **with good grace** di buona voglia || *tr* adornare
graceful ['gresfəl] *adj* grazioso, vezzoso, leggiadro
grace' note' *s* (mus) appoggiatura
gracious ['greʃəs] *adj* grazioso; misericordioso || *interj* Dio buono!
gradation [gre'deʃən] *s* gradazione; (*step in a series*) passo
grade [gred] *s* grado; (*slope*) pendenza; (*mark in school*) voto; **to make the grade** raggiungere la meta || *tr* selezionare; (*a student*) dare un voto a; (*land*) spianare
grade' cros'sing *s* (rr) passaggio a livello
grade' school' *s* scuola elementare
gradient ['gredɪ·ənt] *adj* in pendenza || *s* pendenza; (phys) gradiente *m*
gradual ['grædʒʊ·əl] *adj* graduale
graduate ['grædʒʊ·ɪt] *adj* graduato; superiore; (*student*) laureato; (*candidate for degree*) laureando || ['grædʒʊ,et] *tr* graduare; laureare, diplomare || *intr* laurearsi, diplomarsi
grad'uate school' *s* facoltà *f* di studi avanzati
graduation [,grædʒʊ'eʃən] *s* graduazione; laurea; cerimonia della consegna delle lauree
graft [græft] or [grɑft] *s* (hort) innesto; (surg) trapianto; (coll) prevaricazione || *tr* (hort) innestare; (surg) trapiantare || *intr* (coll) prevaricare
gra'ham bread' ['gre·əm] *s* pane *m* integrale
grain [gren] *s* chicco; (*of sand*) granello; (*cereal seeds*) granaglie *fpl;* (*in wood*) venatura; (*in stone*) grana; **against the grain** di cattivo verso || *tr* granulare; (*leather*) zigrinare; (*metal*) granire
grain' el'evator *s* elevatore *m* di grano; (*building*) deposito di cereali
graining ['grenɪŋ] *s* venatura
gram [græm] *s* grammo
grammar ['græmər] *s* grammatica
grammarian [grə'merɪ·ən] *s* grammatico
gram'mar school' *s* scuola elementare
grammatical [grə'mætɪkəl] *adj* grammatico

gramophone ['græmə,fon] *s* (trademark) grammofono
grana·ry ['grænəri] *s* (**-ries**) granaio
grand [grænd] *adj* grandioso; grande, famoso
grand'aunt' *s* prozia
grand'child' *s* (**-chil'dren**) nipote *mf*
grand'daugh'ter *s* nipote *f*
grand' duch'ess *s* granduchessa
grand' duke' *s* granduca *m*
grandee [græn'di] *s* grande *m*
grandeur ['grændʒər] or ['grændʒur] *s* grande *m*, grandiosità *f*
grand'fa'ther *s* nonno; (*forefather*) antenato
grand'father's clock' *s* grande orologio a pendolo
grandiose ['grændɪ,os] *adj* grandioso
grand' ju'ry *s* giuria investigativa
grand' lar'ceny *s* furto importante
grand' lodge' *s* grande oriente *m*
grandma ['grænd,mɑ], ['græm,mɑ] or ['græmə] *s* (coll) nonna
grand'moth'er *s* nonna
grand'neph'ew *s* pronipote *m*
grand'niece' *s* pronipote *f*
grand' op'era *s* opera, opera lirica
grandpa ['grænd,pɑ], ['græn,pɑ] or ['græmpə] *s* (coll) nonno
grand'par'ent *s* nonno, nonna
grand' pian'o *s* pianoforte *m* a coda
grand'son' *s* nipote *m*
grand'stand' *s* tribuna
grand' to'tal *s* somma totale; importo globale
grand'un'cle *s* prozio
grand' vizier' *s* gran visir *m*
grange [grendʒ] *s* (*farm*) fattoria; (*organization of farmers*) sindacato di agricoltori
granite ['grænɪt] *s* granito
grant [grænt] or [grɑnt] *s* concessione; (*sum of money*) sovvenzione; trapasso di proprietà || *tr* concedere; (*a wish*) esaudire; (*a permit*) rilasciare; (law) trasferire; **to take for granted** ammettere come vero; trattare con indifferenza
grantee [græn'ti] or [grɑn'ti] *s* concessionario; beneficiario
grant'-in-aid' *s* (**grants'-in-aid'**) sussidio governativo a un ente pubblico; borsa di studio
grantor [græn'tər] or [grɑn'tər] *s* concedente *m*, concessore *m*
granular ['grænjələr] *adj* granulare
granulate ['grænjə,let] *tr* granulare || *intr* diventare granulato
gran'ulated sug'ar *s* zucchero cristallizzato
granule ['grænjul] *s* granulo
grape [grep] *s* chicco d'uva; (*vine*) vite *f*; **grapes** uva
grape' ar'bor *s* pergolato
grape'fruit' *s* pompelmo
grape' juice' *s* succo d'uva
grape'shot' *s* mitraglia
grape'vine' *s* vite *f*; **by the grapevine** di bocca in bocca; (mil) attraverso la radio fante
graph [græf] or [grɑf] *s* (*diagram*) grafico; (gram) segno grafico
graphic(al) ['græfɪk(əl)] *adj* grafico
graphite ['græfaɪt] *s* grafite *f*
graph' pa'per *s* carta millimetrata
grapnel ['græpnəl] *s* uncino; (*anchor*) grappino
grapple ['græpəl] *s* uncino; lotta corpo a corpo || *tr* uncinare || *intr* combattere; **to grapple with** lottare con
grap'pling i'ron *s* raffio, grappino
grasp [græsp] or [grɑsp] *s* impugnatura; (*power*) possesso; **to have a good grasp of** sapere a fondo; **within the grasp of** nei limiti della comprensione di || *tr* (*with hand*) impugnare; (*to get control of*) impadronirsi di; (fig) capire || *intr*—**to grasp at** cercare di afferrare
grasping ['græspɪŋ] or ['grɑspɪŋ] *adj* tenace; avido, cupido
grass [græs] or [grɑs] *s* erba; (*pasture land*) pastura; (*lawn*) tappeto erboso; **to go to grass** (*said of cattle*) andare al pascolo; andare in vacanza; ritirarsi; andare in rovina; morire; **to not let the grass grow under one's feet** non dormire in piuma
grass' court' *s* campo da tennis d'erba
grass'hop'per *s* cavalletta
grass'-roots' *adj* popolare
grass' seed' *s* semente *f* d'erba
grass' wid'ow *s* donna separata dal marito
grass·y ['græsi] or ['grɑsi] *adj* (**-ier; -iest**) erboso
grate [gret] *s* (*for cooking*) griglia; (*at a window*) grata || *tr* mettere una grata a; (*one's teeth*) digrignare; (*e.g., cheese*) grattugiare || *intr* stridere, cigolare; **to grate on one's nerves** dare sui nervi di qlcu
grateful ['gretfəl] *adj* riconoscente; (*pleasing*) piacevole, gradito
grater ['gretər] *s* grattugia
grati·fy ['grætɪ,faɪ] *v* (*pret & pp* **-fied**) *tr* gratificare, soddisfare
gratifying ['grætɪ,faɪ·ɪŋ] *adj* soddisfacente, piacevole
grating ['gretɪŋ] *adj* irritante; (*sound*) stridente || *s* inferriata
gratis ['gretɪs] or ['grætɪs] *adj* gratuito || *adv* gratis
gratitude ['grætɪ,tjud] or ['grætɪ,tud] *s* gratitudine *f*, riconoscenza
gratuitous [grə'tju·ɪtəs] or [grə'tu·ɪtəs] *adj* gratuito
gratui·ty [grə'tju·ɪti] or [grə'tu·ɪti] *s* (**-ties**) mancia, regalia
grave [grev] *adj* grave || *s* tomba, sepolcro, fossa
gravedigger ['grev,dɪgər] *s* becchino
gravel ['grævəl] *s* ghiaia; (pathol) renella
grav'en im'age ['grevən] *s* idolo
grave'stone' *s* pietra tombale
grave'yard' *s* cimitero, camposanto
gravitate ['grævɪ,tet] *intr* gravitare
gravitation [,grævɪ'teʃən] *s* gravitazione
gravi·ty ['grævɪti] *s* (**-ties**) gravità *f*
gravure [grə'vjur] or ['grevjur] *s* fotoincisione
gra·vy ['grevi] *s* (**-vies**) (*juice from*

cooking meat) sugo; (*sauce made with it*) salsa, intingolo; (slang) guadagni *mpl* facili
gra'vy boat' *s* salsiera
gra'vy train' *s* (slang) greppia, mangiatoia
gray [gre] *adj* grigio; (*gray-haired*) canuto || *s* grigio; cavallo grigio || *intr* incanutire
gray'beard' *s* vecchio
gray-haired ['gre ,herd] *adj* canuto
gray'hound' *s* levriere *m*
grayish ['gre·ɪʃ] *adj* grigiastro
gray' mat'ter *s* materia grigia
graze [grez] *tr* (*to touch lightly*) sfiorare; (*to scratch lightly*) scalfire; (*grass*) brucare; (*cattle*) pascere, pascolare || *intr* pascere, brucare
grease [gris] *s* grasso, unto || [gris] or [griz] *tr* ingrassare, ungere
grease' cup' [gris] *s* coppa dell'olio
grease' gun' [gris] *s* ingrassatore *m*
grease' lift' [gris] *s* piattaforma di lubrificazione
grease' paint' [gris] *s* cerone *m*
grease' pit' [gris] *s* fossa di riparazione
greas·y ['grisi] or ['grizi] *adj* (**-ier; -iest**) grasso, unto, untuoso
great [gret] *adj* grande; (coll) eccellente || **the great** i grandi
great'-aunt' *s* prozia
Great' Bear' *s* Orsa Maggiore
Great' Brit'ain ['brɪtən] *s* la Gran Bretagna
Great' Dane' *s* danese *m*, alano
Great'er New York' *s* Nuova York e i suoi sobborghi
great'-grand'child' *s* (**-chil'dren**) pronipote *mf*
great'-grand'daught'er *s* pronipote *f*
great'-grand'fa'ther *s* bisnonno
great'-grand'moth'er *s* bisnonna
great'-grand'par'ent *s* bisnonno, bisnonna
great'-grand'son' *s* pronipote *m*
greatly ['gretli] *adj* molto
great'-neph'ew *s* pronipote *m*
greatness ['gretnɪs] *s* grandezza
great'-niece' *s* pronipote *f*
great'-un'cle *s* prozio
Grecian ['griʃən] *adj* & *s* greco
Greece [gris] *s* la Grecia
greed [grid] *s* avarizia, avidità *f*
greediness ['gridɪnɪs] *s* bramosia
greed·y ['gridi] *adj* (**-ier; -iest**) avaro; ingordo, bramoso
Greek [grik] *adj* & *s* greco
green [grin] *adj* verde; (fig) verde, inesperto || *s* verde *m;* (*lawn*) tappeto erboso; **greens** verdura, insalata
green'back' *s* (U.S.A.) biglietto di banca
green' earth' *s* verdaccio
greener·y ['grinəri] *s* (**-ies**) (*foliage*) vegetazione; (*hothouse*) serra
green'-eyed' *adj* dagli occhi verdi; (coll) geloso
green'gage' *s* regina claudia
green'horn' *s* (slang) pivello, sempliciotto
green'house' *s* serra
greenish ['grinɪʃ] *adj* verdastro
Greenland ['grinlənd] *s* la Groenlandia
green' light' *s* semaforo verde; (coll) via *m*
greenness ['grinnɪs] *s* verdore *m*, verdezza; inesperienza
green' pep'per *s* peperone *m* verde
greensward ['grin ,swɔrd] *s* tappeto erboso
green' thumb' *s* abilità *f* speciale per il giardinaggio
green' veg'etables *spl* verdura
green'wood' *s* bosco verde
greet [grit] *tr* salutare; ricevere; (*e.g., one's ears*) offrirsi a
greeting ['gritɪŋ] *s* saluto; accoglienza || **greetings** *interj* saluti!
greet'ing card' *s* cartolina d'auguri
gregarious [grɪ'gerɪ·əs] *adj* (*living in the midst of others*) gregario; (*sociable*) sociale
Gregorian [grɪ'gorɪ·ən] *adj* gregoriano
grenade [grɪ'ned] *s* granata
grenadier [,grenə'dɪr] *s* granatiere *m*
grenadine [,grenə'din] *s* granatina
grey [gre] *adj*, *s* & *intr* var of **gray**
grid [grɪd] *s* (*network*) rete *f;* (*on map*) reticolato; (electron) griglia
griddle ['grɪdəl] *s* tegame *m*
grid'dle·cake' *s* frittella cotta in teglia, crêpe *m*
grid'i'ron *s* griglia; campo di football; (theat) graticcia
grief [grif] *s* affanno, dolore *m;* disgrazia; **to come to grief** andare in rovina
grievance ['grivəns] *s* lagnanza; motivo di lagnanza
grieve [griv] *tr* affliggere || *intr* affliggersi, dolersi; **to grieve over** soffrire per
grievous ['grivəs] *adj* doloroso, penoso; (*error*) grave; (*deplorable*) deplorevole
griffin ['grɪfɪn] *s* grifo, grifone *m*
grill [grɪl] *s* griglia || *tr* mettere alla griglia; (coll) interrogare insistentemente
grille [grɪl] *s* inferriata; (aut) mascherina, calandra
grill'room' *s* grill-room *m*, rosticceria
grim [grɪm] *adj* (**grimmer; grimmest**) (*stern*) accigliato; (*fierce*) feroce; (*sinister*) sinistro; (*unyielding*) implacabile
grimace ['grɪməs] or [grɪ'mes] *s* smorfia, sberleffo || *intr* fare le boccacce
grime [graɪm] *s* sporco; (*soot*) fuliggine *f*
grim·y ['graɪmi] *adj* (**-ier; -iest**) sporco; fuligginoso
grin [grɪn] *s* sorriso; (*malicious in intent*) ghigno || *v* (*pret* & *pp* **grinned;** *ger* **grinning**) *intr* sorridere; ghignare
grind [graɪnd] *s* macinata; (*laborious work*) (coll) macina; (slang) sgobbone *m* || *v* (*pret* & *pp* **ground** [graund]) *tr* macinare; (*to sharpen*) molare; (*lenses*) smerigliare; (*meat*) tritare; opprimere; (*a crank*) girare; (mach) rettificare || *intr* macinare; frantumarsi; cigolare; (coll) sgobbare
grinder ['graɪndər] *s* (*to sharpen tools*) mola; (*to grind coffee*) macinino;

(*back tooth*) molare *m;* (*person*) molatore *m*

grind'stone' *s* mola; **to keep one's nose to the grindstone** lavorare senza posa

grin·go ['grɪŋgo] *s* (**-gos**) (disparaging) gringo

grip [grɪp] *s* (*grasp*) presa; (*with hand*) stretta; (*handle*) impugnatura; **to come to grips** venire alle prese || *v* (*pret & pp* **gripped;** *ger* **gripping**) *tr* stringere; impugnare; attirare l'attenzione di

gripe [graɪp] *s* (coll) lamentela; (naut) rizza; **gripes** colica || *intr* (coll) lamentarsi, brontolare

grippe [grɪp] *s* influenza

gripping ['grɪpɪŋ] *adj* interessantissimo, affascinante

gris·ly ['grɪzli] *adj* (**-lier; -liest**) orribile, spaventoso

grist [grɪst] *s* (*grain to be ground*) macinata; (*ground grain*) farina; (coll) mucchio; **to be grist to the mill of** (coll) fare comodo a

gristle ['grɪsəl] *s* cartilagine *f*

gris·tly ['grɪsli] *adj* (**-tlier; -tliest**) cartilaginoso

grist'mill' *s* mulino

grit [grɪt] *s* sabbia, arenaria; (fig) forza d'animo || *v* (*pret & pp* **gritted;** *ger* **gritting**) *tr* (*one's teeth*) far stridere, digrignare

grit·ty ['grɪti] *adj* (**-tier; -tiest**) sabbioso, granuloso; (fig) forte, coraggioso

griz·zly ['grɪzli] *adj* (**-zlier; -zliest**) brizzolato, canuto || *s* (**-zlies**) orso grigio

groan [gron] *s* gemito || *intr* gemere; (*to be overburdened*) essere sovraccarico

grocer ['grosər] *s* droghiere *m;* pizzicagnolo; proprietario di negozio di generi alimentari

grocer·y ['grosəri] *s* (**-ies**) (*store selling spices, soap, etc.*) drogheria; (*store selling cheese, cold cuts, etc.*) negozio di pizzicagnolo; negozio di generi alimentari; **groceries** generi *mpl* alimentari, commestibili *mpl*

grog [grɑg] *s* grog *m*

grog·gy ['grɑgi] *adj* (**-gier; -giest**) (coll) groggy, intontito

groin [grɔɪn] *s* (anat) inguine *m;* (archit) costolone *m*

groom [grum] *s* mozzo di stalla; (*bridegroom*) sposo || *tr* rassettare; (*horses*) rigovernare; (pol) preparare per le elezioni

grooms'man *s* (**-men**) compare *m* di nozze

groove [gruv] *s* scanalatura; (*of a pulley*) gola; (*of a phonograph record*) solco; (fig) routine *f* || *tr* scanalare, incavare

grope [grop] *intr* brancicare; (*for words*) cercare; **to grope for** cercare a tastoni

gropingly ['gropɪŋli] *adv* a tastoni

gross [gros] *adj* (*thick*) spesso; (*coarse*) volgare; (*fat*) grosso; (*error*) marchiano; (*without deductions*) lordo || *s* grossa || *tr* fare un incasso lordo di

grossly ['grosli] *adv* approssimativamente; totalmente

gross' na'tional prod'uct *s* reddito nazionale

grotesque [gro'tesk] *adj & s* grottesco

grot·to ['grɑto] *s* (**-toes** or **-tos**) grotta

grouch [graʊtʃ] *s* (coll) malumore *m;* (coll) persona stizzosa || *intr* (coll) brontolare

grouch·y ['graʊtʃi] *adj* (**-ier; -iest**) (coll) stizzoso, brontolone

ground [graʊnd] *s* (*earth, soil, land*) terra; (*piece of land*) terreno; (*basis*) causa, fondatezza; (elec) terra, massa; (fig) occasione, motivo; **grounds** giardini *mpl,* terreno; (*of coffee*) fondi *mpl;* **on the ground of** per motivo di; **to break ground** dare la prima palata; (fig) mettere la prima pietra; **to fall to the ground** cadere al suolo; (fig) fallire; **to gain ground** guadagnar terreno; **to give ground** ceder terreno; **to lose ground** perder terreno; **to stand one's ground** non indietreggiare || *tr* fondare; (elec) mettere a massa; **to be grounded** (*said of an airplane*) essere forzato di rimanere a terra; **to be well grounded** essere bene al corrente || *intr* incagliarsi

ground' connec'tion *s* messa a terra

ground' crew' *s* (aer) personale *m* di servizio

ground' floor' *s* pianterreno

ground' glass' *s* vetro smerigliato

ground' hog' *s* marmotta americana

ground' lead' [lid] *s* (elec) collegamento a massa

groundless ['graʊndlɪs] *adj* infondato

ground' meat' *s* carne tritata

ground' plan' *s* progetto, pianta

ground' swell' *s* mareggiata

ground' wire' *s* filo di terra, filo di massa

ground'work' *s* fondamento, base *f*

group [grup] *adj* collettivo || *s* gruppo; (aer) stormo || *tr* raggruppare || *intr* raggrupparsi

grouse [graʊs] *s* gallo cedrone; (slang) brontolio || *intr* (slang) brontolare

grout [graʊt] *s* stucco || *tr* stuccare

grove [grov] *s* boschetto

grov·el ['grʌvəl] or ['grɑvəl] *v* (*pret & pp* **-eled** or **-elled;** *ger* **-eling** or **-elling**) *intr* umiliarsi

grow [gro] *v* (*pret* **grew** [gru]; *pp* **grown** [gron]) *tr* (*plants*) coltivare; (*animals*) allevare; (*a beard*) farsi crescere || *intr* crescere; svilupparsi; nascere; venir su; (*to become*) diventare; farsi; **to grow angry** arrabbiarsi; **to grow old** invecchiare; **to grow out of** (*fashion*) passare di; originare da; **to grow up** svilupparsi

growing ['gro·ɪŋ] *adj* crescente; (*pains*) di crescenza; (*child*) in crescita

growl [graʊl] *s* ringhio; brontolio || *intr* (*said of animals*) ringhiare; brontolare

grown'-up' *adj* adulto, grande || *s* (**grown-ups**) adulto
growth [groθ] *s* crescita, sviluppo; aumento; (pathol) escrescenza
growth' stock' *s* azione *f* che promette di aumentare di valore
grub [grʌb] *s* (*drudge*) sgobbone *m;* larva di coleottero; (coll) mangiare *m* || *v* (*pret & pp* **grubbed;** *ger* **grubbing**) *tr* scavare, zappare, dissodare || *intr* cercare assiduamente; scavare; sgobbare
grub·by ['grʌbi] *adj* (**-bier; -biest**) sporco; bacato; infestato di larve
grudge [grʌdʒ] *s* rancore *m;* **to have a grudge against** nutrire rancore contro || *tr* (*to spend unwillingly*) lesinare; invidiare
grudgingly ['grʌdʒɪŋli] *adv* di cattiva voglia
gru·el ['gru·əl] *s* farinata d'avena || *v* (*pret & pp* **-eled** or **-elled;** *ger* **-eling** or **-elling**) *tr* estenuare
gruesome ['grusəm] *adj* raccapricciante
gruff [grʌf] *adj* brusco, burbero; (*voice*) rauco, roco
grumble ['grʌmbəl] *s* brontolio || *intr* brontolare, borbottare
grump·y ['grʌmpi] *adj* (**-ier; -iest**) di cattivo umore, scontroso
grunt [grʌnt] *s* grugnito || *intr* grugnire
G-string ['dʒi ,strɪŋ] *s* (*loincloth*) perizoma *m;* (*worn by a female entertainer*) triangolino di stoffa; (mus) corda di sol
guarantee [,gærən'ti] *s* garanzia; (*guarantor*) garante *mf* || *tr* garantire
guarantor ['gærən ,tɔr] *s* garante *mf*
guaran·ty ['gærənti] *s* (**-ties**) garanzia || *v* (*pret & pp* **-tied**) *tr* garantire
guard [gɑrd] *s* guardia; (*safeguard*) protezione; (*in a prison*) guardia carceraria; (*of a sword*) guardamano; (football) mediano; **off guard** alla sprovvista; **on guard** in guardia; di fazione; **to mount a guard** montare la guardia; **under guard** ben custodito || *tr* guardare || *intr* fare la sentinella; **to guard against** guardarsi da
guarded ['gɑrdɪd] *adj* (*remark*) prudente
guard'house' *s* locale *m* di detenzione; (mil) corpo di guardia
guardian ['gɑrdɪ·ən] *adj* tutelare || *s* guardiano; (law) tutore *m*
guard'ian an'gel *s* angelo custode
guardianship ['gɑrdɪ·ən ,ʃɪp] *s* protezione; (law) tutela
guard'rail' *s* guardavia *m;* (naut) parapetto
guard'room' *s* (mil) corpo di guardia
guards'man *s* (**-men**) guardia
guerrilla [gə'rɪlə] *s* guerrigliero
guerril'la war'fare *s* guerriglia
guess [gɛs] *s* congettura, supposizione || *tr & intr* congetturare, supporre; (*to estimate correctly*) indovinare; (coll) credere; **I guess so** credo di sì
guess'work' *s* congettura
guest [gɛst] *s* invitato, ospite *m;* (*of a hotel*) cliente *mf;* (*of a boarding house*) pensionante *mf*
guest' book' *s* albo d'onore; (*in a hotel*) registro
guffaw [gə'fɔ] *s* sghignazzata || *intr* sghignazzare
Guiana [gɪ'ɑnə] or [gɪ'ænə] *s* la Guayana
guidance ['gaɪdəns] *s* guida, governo; **for your guidance** per Sua norma
guide [gaɪd] *s* guida || *tr* guidare
guide'board' *s* indicatore *m* stradale
guide'book' *s* guida
guid'ed mis'sile ['gaɪdɪd] *s* telearma, teleproietto, missile teleguidato
guide' dog' *s* cane *m* conduttore di un cieco
guide'line' *s* falsariga; corda fissa; linea di condotta, direttiva
guide'post' *s* indicatore *m* stradale
guide' word' *s* esponente *m* in testa di pagina
guidon ['gaɪdən] *s* guidone *m*
guild [gɪld] *s* associazione mutua; (hist) gilda
guild'hall' *s* palazzo delle corporazioni
guile [gaɪl] *s* astuzia, frode *f*
guileful ['gaɪlfəl] *adj* astuto, insidioso
guileless ['gaɪllɪs] *adj* sincero, innocente
guillotine ['gɪlə ,tin] *s* ghigliottina || [,gɪlə'tin] *tr* ghigliottinare
guilt [gɪlt] *s* colpa, reità *f*
guiltless ['gɪltlɪs] *adj* innocente
guilt·y ['gɪlti] *adj* (**-ier; -iest**) colpevole, reo
guimpe [gɪmp] or [gæmp] *s* sprone *m*
guinea ['gɪni] *s* ghinea; gallina faraona || **Guinea** *s* la Guinea
guin'ea fowl' *s* gallina faraona
guin'ea pig' *s* porcellino d'India, cavia; (fig) cavia
guise [gaɪz] *s* aspetto; veste *f;* **under the guise of** in guisa di
guitar [gɪ'tɑr] *s* chitarra
guitarist [gɪ'tɑrɪst] *s* chitarrista *mf*
gulch [gʌltʃ] *s* burrone *m*
gulf [gʌlf] *s* golfo; abisso
Gulf' Stream' *s* corrente *f* del Golfo
gull [gʌl] *s* gabbiano; (coll) credulone *m* || *tr* darla da bere a
gullet ['gʌlɪt] *s* gargarozzo; esofago
gullible ['gʌlɪbəl] *adj* credulone
gul·ly ['gʌli] *s* (**-lies**) borro, zanella
gulp [gʌlp] *s* sorsata || *tr*—**to gulp down** (*food*) ingoiare; (*drink*) tracannare; (fig) ingoiare, trangugiare
gum [gʌm] *s* gomma; (*mucus on eyelids*) cispa; **gums** (anat) gengive *fpl* || *v* (*pret & pp* **gummed;** *ger* **gumming**) *tr* ingommare; **to gum up** (slang) guastare || *intr* secernere gomma
gum' ar'abic *s* gomma arabica
gum'boil' *s* flemmone *m* gengivale
gum' boot' *s* stivale *m* da palude
gum'drop' *s* caramella alla gelatina di frutta, pasticca di gomma, drop *m*
gum·my ['gʌmi] *adj* (**-mier; -miest**) gommoso, vischioso; (*eyelid*) cisposo
gumption ['gʌmpʃən] *s* (coll) iniziativa; (coll) coraggio, fegato
gum'shoe' *s* caloscia; (slang) poliziotto || *v* (*pret & pp* **-shoed;** *ger* **-shoeing**)

intr (slang) camminare silenziosamente
gun [gʌn] *s* (*rifle*) fucile *m;* (*revolver*) revolver *m;* (*pistol*) rivoltella; (*e.g., for spraying*) rivoltella; **to stick to one's guns** tener duro || *v* (*pret & pp* **gunned;** *ger* **gunning**) *tr* far fuoco su, freddare; (*a motor*) (slang) accelerare rapidamente || *intr* andare a caccia; sparare; **to gun for** andare a caccia di
gun'boat' *s* cannoniera, esploratore *m*
gun' car'riage *s* affusto
gun'cot'ton *s* fulmicotone *m*
gun'fire' *s* fuoco, tiro
gun'man *s* (**-men**) bandito, sicario
gun' met'al *s* bronzo da cannoni; acciaio brunito
gunnel ['gʌnəl] *s* (naut) frisata
gunner ['gʌnər] *s* artigliere *m,* servente *m*
gunnery ['gʌnəri] *s* artiglieria, tiro
gunnysack ['gʌni ˌsæk] *s* sacco di tela greggia
gunpoint ['gʌn ˌpɔɪnt] *s* mirino; **at gunpoint** a mano armata, e.g., **he was held up at gunpoint** subì una rapina a mano armata
gun'pow'der *s* polvere nera or pirica
gun'run'ner *s* contrabbandiere *m* di armi da fuoco
gun'shot' *s* schioppettata; revolverata; **within gunshot** a tiro di schioppo
gun'shot' wound' *s* schioppettata
gun'smith' *s* armaiolo
gun'stock' *s* cassa del fucile
gunwale ['gʌnəl] *s* frisata
gup•py ['gʌpi] *s* (**-pies**) lebiste *m*
gurgle ['gʌrgəl] *s* gorgoglio, borboglio || *intr* gorgogliare, borbogliare; (*said of a human being*) barbugliare
gush [gʌʃ] *s* getto, fiotto || *intr* zampillare, sgorgare; (coll) dare in effusioni
gusher ['gʌʃər] *s* pozzo di petrolio; (coll) persona espansiva
gushing ['gʌʃɪŋ] *adj* zampillante, sgorgante; (coll) espansivo || *s* zampillo; (coll) espansione, effusione
gush•y ['gʌʃi] *adj* (**-ier; -iest**) (coll) espansivo, effusivo
gusset ['gʌsɪt] *s* gherone *m*
gust [gʌst] *s* (*of wind*) raffica; (*of smoke*) ondata, zaffata; (*of noise*) esplosione; (*of anger*) sfuriata
gusto ['gʌsto] *s* gusto; entusiasmo
gust•y ['gʌsti] *adj* (**-ier; -iest**) a raffiche, burrascoso
gut [gʌt] *s* budello; **guts** budello; (slang) fegato, coraggio || *v* (*pret & pp* **gutted;** *ger* **gutting**) *tr* sparare, spanciare; distruggere l'interno di
gutta-percha ['gʌtə'pʌrtʃə] *s* guttaperca
gutter ['gʌtər] *s* (*on side of road*) cunetta; (*in street*) rigagnolo; (*of roof*) doccia, grondaia; (fig) bassifondi *mpl*
gut'ter•snipe' *s* monello
guttural ['gʌtərəl] *adj & s* gutturale *f*
guy [gaɪ] *s* cavo di sicurezza; (coll) tipo, tizio || *tr* burlarsi di
guzzle ['gʌzəl] *tr & intr* trincare, bere a garganella
guzzler ['gʌzlər] *s* ubriacone *m*
gym [dʒɪm] *s* (coll) palestra
gymnasi•um [dʒɪm'nezɪ•əm] *s* (**-ums** or **-a** [ə]) palestra
gymnast ['dʒɪmnæst] *s* ginnasta *mf*
gymnastic [dʒɪm'næstɪk] *adj* ginnastico || **gymnastics** *spl* ginnastica
gynecologist [ˌgaɪnə'kɑlədʒɪst], [ˌdʒaɪnə'kɑlədʒɪst] or [ˌdʒɪnə'kɑlədʒɪst] *s* ginecologo
gyp [dʒɪp] *s* (coll) imbroglio; (*person*) (coll) imbroglione *m* || *v* (*pret & pp* **gypped;** *ger* **gypping**) *tr* imbrogliare
gypsum ['dʒɪpsəm] *s* gesso
gyp•sy ['dʒɪpsi] *adj* zingaresco, zingaro || *s* (**-sies**) zingaro || **Gypsy** *s* (*language*) zingaresco
gypsyish ['dʒɪpsɪ•ɪʃ] *adj* zingaresco
gyrate ['dʒaɪret] *intr* turbinare
gyrocompass ['dʒaɪro ˌkʌmpəs] *s* girobussola
gyroscope ['dʒaɪrə ˌskop] *s* giroscopio

H

H, h [etʃ] *s* ottava lettera dell'alfabeto inglese
haberdasher ['hæbər ˌdæʃər] *s* camiciaio; (*dealer in notions*) merciaio
haberdasher•y ['hæbər ˌdæʃəri] *s* (**-ies**) camiceria; merceria
habit ['hæbɪt] *s* abitudine *f;* (*addiction*) vizio; (*garb*) saio; **to be in the habit of** aver l'usanza di
habitat ['hæbɪ ˌtæt] *s* habitat *m*
habitation [ˌhæbɪ'teʃən] *s* abitazione
habit-forming ['hæbɪt ˌfɔrmɪŋ] *adj* (*e.g., drugs*) stupefacente; (*e.g., T.V.*) assuefacente, che fa venire il vizio
habitual [hə'bɪtʃʊ•əl] *adj* abituale
habitué [hə ˌbɪtʃʊ'e] *s* habitué *m*
hack [hæk] *s* (*cut*) taglio; (*notch*) tacca; (*cough*) tosse secca; cavallo da nolo; vettura di piazza; (*nag*) ronzino; (*poor writer*) scribacchino || *tr* tagliare; stagliare
hack'man *s* (**-men**) vetturino
hackney ['hækni] *s* cavallo da sella; vettura di piazza
hackneyed ['hæknid] *adj* banale, trito
hack'saw' *s* seghetto per metalli
haddock ['hædək] *s* eglefino
haft [hæft] or [hɑft] *s* impugnatura
hag [hæg] *s* (*ugly old woman*) megera; (*witch*) strega
haggard ['hægərd] *adj* sparuto, macilento; (*wild-looking*) stralunato

haggle [ˈhægəl] *intr* mercanteggiare
hagiographer [ˌhægiˈɑgrəfer] or [ˌhedʒiˈɑgrəfər] *s* agiografo
hagiography [ˌhægiˈɑgrəfi] or [ˌhedʒiˈɑgrəfi] *s* agiografia
Hague, The [heg] *s* L'Aia *f*
hail [hel] *s* (*precipitation*) grandine *f;* (*greeting*) saluto; **within hail** a portata di voce || *tr* salutare; accogliere; chiamare; (*e.g., blows*) far cadere || *intr* grandinare; **to hail from** venire da || *interj* salute!; salve!
hail'-fel'low *adj* gioviale
Hail' Mar'y *s* Ave Maria, avemaria
hail'stone' *s* chicco di grandine
hail'storm' *s* grandinata
hair [her] *s* capelli *mpl;* (*of animals*) pelame *m* or pelo; **a hair** (*a single filament*) un capello or un pelo; **to a hair** a perfezione; **to get in one's hair** (slang) dare sui nervi a qlcu; **to let one's hair down** (slang) parlare francamente; (slang) comportarsi alla buona; **to make one's hair stand on end** far rizzare i capelli a qlcu; **to not turn a hair** non scomporsi; **to split hairs** cercare il pelo nell'uovo
hair'breadth' *s* spessore *m* di un capello; **to escape by a hairbreadth** scamparla per un pelo
hair'brush' *s* spazzola per i capelli
hair'cloth' s cilicio
hair'cut' *s* taglio dei capelli; **to get a haircut** farsi tagliare i capelli
hair'do' *s* (**-dos**) acconciatura
hair'dress'er *s* parrucchiere *m* per signora; pettinatrice *f*
hair' dri'er *s* asciugacapelli *m*
hair' dye' *s* tintura per i capelli
hairless [ˈherlɪs] *adj* pelato, calvo
hair' net' *s* rete *f* per i capelli
hair'pin' *s* forcella, forcina, molletta
hair-raising [ˈher ˌrezɪŋ] *adj* orripilante
hair' re•mov'er *s* depilatorio
hair' restor'er [rɪˈstorər] *s* rigeneratore *m* per i capelli
hair' rib'bon *s* nastro per i capelli
hairsplitting [ˈher ˌsplɪtɪŋ] *adj* meticoloso, pignolo
hair'spring' *s* spirale *f*
hair' styl'ing *s* pettinatura per signora
hair•y [ˈheri] *adj* (**-ier; -iest**) peloso, villoso, irsuto
hake [hek] *s* merluzzo, nasello
halberd [ˈhælbərd] *s* alabarda
halberdier [ˌhælbərˈdɪr] *s* alabardiere *m*
halcyon [ˈhælsɪ•ən] *adj* calmo, pacifico
hale [hel] *adj* sano, robusto || *tr* trascinare a viva forza
half [hæf] or [hɑf] *adj* mezzo; **a half** or **half a** mezzo; **half the** la metà di || *s* (**halves** [hævz] or [hɑvz]) metà *f;* (arith) mezzo; **in half** a metà; **to go halves** fare a metà || *adv* mezzo, e.g., **half asleep** mezzo addormentato; a metà, e.g., **half finished** a metà finito; **half past** e mezzo or e mezza, e.g., **half past three** le tre e mezzo or le tre e mezza; **half . . . half** metà . . . metà
half'-and-half' *adj* mezzo e mezzo || *s* mezza crema e mezzo latte; mezza birra chiara e mezza scura || *adv* a metà, in parti uguali
half'back' *s* (football) mediano; (soccer) laterale *m*
half-baked [ˈhæf ˌbekt] or [ˈhɑf ˌbekt] *adj* mezzo cotto; (*ideas*) infondato, inesperto
half' bind'ing *s* rilegatura in mezza pelle
half'-blood' *s* meticcio; fratellastro; sorellastra
half'-breed' *s* meticcio
half' broth'er *s* fratellastro
half-cocked [ˈhæf ˌkɑkt] or [ˈhɑf ˌkɑkt] *adj* immaturo, precipitato || *adv* (coll) precipitatamente
half' fare' *s* mezza corsa
half'-full' *adj* mezzo pieno
half-hearted [ˈhæf ˌhɑrtɪd] or [ˈhɑf ˌhɑrtɪd] *adj* indifferente, freddo
half'-hol'iday *s* mezza festa
half' hose' *s* calzini *mpl* corti
half'-hour' *s* mezz'ora; **on the half-hour** ogni trenta minuti allo scoccare dell'ora e della mezz'ora
half'-length' *adj* a mezzo busto || *s* ritratto a mezzo busto
half'life' *s* (phys) vita media
half'-mast' *s*—**at half-mast** a mezz'asta
half'moon' *s* mezzaluna
half' mourn'ing *s* mezzo lutto
half' note' *s* (mus) minima
half' pay' *s* mezza paga
halfpen•ny [ˈhepəni] or [ˈhepni] *s* (**-nies**) mezzo penny
half' pint' *s* mezza pinta; (slang) mezza cartuccia, mezza calzetta
half'-seas o'ver *adj*—**to be half-seas over** (slang) essere sbronzato
half' shell' *s*—**on the half shell** in conchiglia
half' sis'ter *s* sorellastra
half' sole' *s* mezza suola
half'-sole' *tr* mettere la mezza suola a
half'-staff' *s*—**at half-staff** a mezz'asta
half-timbered [ˈhæf ˌtɪmbərd] or [ˈhɑf ˌtɪmbərd] *adj* in legno e muratura
half' ti'tle *s* occhiello, occhietto
half'tone' *s* mezzatinta
half'-track' *s* semicingolato
half'truth' *s* mezza verità, mezza bugia
half'way' *adj* a metà strada; parziale, mezzo || *adv* a metà strada; **halfway through** nel mezzo di; **to meet halfway** fare concessioni mutue
half-witted [ˈhæf ˌwɪtɪd] or [ˈhɑf ˌwɪtɪd] *adj* mezzo scemo
halibut [ˈhælɪbət] *s* ippoglosso
halide [ˈhælaɪd] or [ˈhelaɪd] *s* alogenuro
halitosis [ˌhælɪˈtosɪs] *s* alito cattivo, fiato puzzolente
hall [hɔl] *s* (*passageway*) corridoio; (*entranceway*) vestibolo; (*large meeting room*) salone *m;* (*assembly room of a university*) aula magna; (*building of a university*) edificio
halleluiah or **hallelujah** [ˌhælɪˈlujə] *s* alleluia *m* || *interj* alleluia!
hall'mark' *s* punzone *m* di garanzia; (fig) contrassegno, caratteristica
hal•lo [həˈlo] *s* (**-los**) grido || *interj* ehi!
hallow [ˈhælo] *tr* santificare

hallowed ['hælod] *adj* consacrato
Halloween or **Hallowe'en** [,hælo'in] *s* vigilia di Ognissanti
hallucination [hə,lusɪ'neʃən] *s* allucinazione
hall'way' *s* corridoio; entrata
ha·lo ['helo] *s* (**-los** or **-loes**) alone *m*
halogen ['hælədʒən] *s* alogeno
halt [hɔlt] *adj* zoppicante || *s* fermata; **to call a halt** dare ordine di fermarsi; **to come to a halt** fermarsi || *tr* fermare || *intr* fermarsi, esitare || *interj* altolà!
halter ['hɔltər] *s* (*for leading horse*) cavezza; (*noose*) capestro; (*hanging*) impiccagione; corpino bagno di sole
halting ['hɔltɪŋ] *adj* zoppicante; esitante
halve [hæv] or [hɑv] *tr* dimezzare
halyard ['hæljərd] *s* (naut) drizza
ham [hæm] *s* (*part of leg behind knee*) polpaccio; (*thigh and buttock*) coscia; (*cured meat from hog's hind leg*) prosciutto; (slang) istrione *m;* (slang) radioamatore *m;* **hams** natiche *fpl*
ham' and eggs' *spl* uova *fpl* col prosciutto
hamburger ['hæm,bʌrgər] *s* hamburger *m*
hamlet ['hæmlɪt] *s* frazione, paese *m* || **Hamlet** *s* Amleto
hammer ['hæmər] *s* martello; (*of gun*) cane *m;* (*of piano*) martelletto; **under the hammer** all'asta pubblica || *tr* martellare; **to hammer out** battere; portare a fine faticosamente || *intr* martellare; **to hammer away** lavorare accanitamente
hammock ['hæmək] *s* amaca
hamper ['hæmpər] *s* cesta || *tr* imbarazzare, intralciare
hamster ['hæmstər] *s* criceto
ham·string ['hæm,strɪŋ] *v* (*pret & pp* **-strung**) *tr* azzoppare; tagliare i garretti a; (fig) impastoiare
hand [hænd] *adj* manuale; fatto a mano || *s* mano *f;* (*workman*) garzone *m,* operaio; (*way of writing*) scrittura; (*signature*) firma; (*clapping of hands*) applauso; (*of clock or watch*) lancetta; (*all the cards in one's hand*) gioco; (*a round of play*) smazzata, mano *f;* (*player*) giocatore *m;* (*skill*) destrezza; (*side*) lato; **all hands** (naut) tutto l'equipaggio; (coll) tutti *mpl;* **at first hand** direttamente; **at hand** a portata di mano; **hand in glove** in perfetta unione; **hand in hand** tenendosi per mano; **hands up!** le mani in alto!; **hand to hand** corpo a corpo; **in hand** tra le mani; **in his own hand** di proprio pugno; **on hand** disponibile; **on hands and knees** (*crawling*) a gattoni; (*beseeching*) in ginocchio; **on the one hand** da un canto; **on the other hand** per contro; **to change hands** cambiare di mano; **to clap hands** battere le mani; **to eat out of one's hand** essere sottomesso a qlcu; **to get out of hand** diventare incontrollabile; **to have a hand in** prender parte a; **to have one's hands full** essere occupatissimo; **to hold hands** tenersi per mano; **to hold up one's hands** (*as a sign of surrender*) alzare le mani; **to join hands** darsi la mano; **to keep one's hands off** non mettere il naso in; **to lend a hand** dare una mano; **to live from hand to mouth** vivere alla giornata; **to not lift a hand** non alzare un dito; **to play into the hands of** fare il gioco di; **to shake hands** darsi la mano; **to show one's hand** scoprire il proprio gioco; **to take in hand** prendere in mano; (*a matter*) prendere in esame; **to throw up one's hands** darsi per vinto; **to try one's hand** mettere la propria abilità alla prova; **to turn one's hand to** dedicarsi a; **to wash one's hands of** lavarsi le mani di; **under my hand** di mia firma autografa; **under the hand and seal of** firmato di pugno da || *tr* dare, porgere; **to hand down** tramandare; **to hand in** consegnare; **to hand on** trasmettere; **to hand out** distribuire
hand'bag' *s* borsetta
hand' bag'gage *s* valigie *fpl* a mano
hand'ball' *s* palla a mano
hand'bill' *s* manifestino, foglio volante
hand'book' *s* manuale *m;* guida; (*of a particular field*) prontuario
hand'breadth' *s* palmo
hand'car' *s* (rr) carrello a mano
hand'cart' *s* carretto a mano
hand'cuffs' *spl* manette *fpl* || *tr* mettere le manette a
handful ['hænd,fʊl] *s* manata, manciata
hand' glass' *s* lente *f* di ingrandimento; specchietto
hand' grenade' *s* bomba a mano
handi·cap ['hændɪ,kæp] *s* svantaggio; (sports) handicap *m* || *v* (*pret & pp* **-capped;** *ger* **-capping**) *tr* andicappare
handicraft ['hændɪ,kræft] or ['hændɪ,krɑft] *s* destrezza manuale; artigianato
handiwork ['hændɪ,wʌrk] *s* lavoro fatto a mano; opera, lavoro
handkerchief ['hæŋkərtʃɪf] or ['hæŋkər,tʃif] *s* fazzoletto
handle ['hændəl] *s* manico; (*of a sword*) impugnatura; (*of a door*) maniglia; (*of a drawer*) pomolo; (*of a hand organ*) manovella; espediente *m;* **to fly off the handle** (slang) uscire dai gangheri || *tr* maneggiare; manovrare, dirigere; commerciare in || *intr* comportarsi
handle'bar' *s* manubrio
handler ['hændlər] *s* (sports) allenatore *m*
hand'made' *adj* fatto a mano
hand'maid' or **hand'maid'en** *s* domestica, serva; (fig) ancella
hand'-me-down' *adj* smesso || *s* vestito smesso or di seconda mano
hand' or'gan *s* organetto, organino, organetto di Barberia
hand'out' *s* elemosina di cibo; articolo distribuito gratis; comunicato stampa
hand-picked ['hænd,pɪkt] *adj* colto a mano; scelto specialmente

hand'rail' *s* guardamano, passamano
hand'saw' *s* sega a mano
hand'set' *s* microtelefono
hand'shake' *s* stretta di mano
handsome ['hænsəm] *adj* bello; considerevole; generoso
hand'spring' *s* capriola, salto mortale fatto toccando il terreno con le mani
hand'-to-hand' *adj* corpo a corpo
hand'-to-mouth' *adj* precario, da un giorno all'altro
hand'work' *s* lavoro fatto a mano
hand'writ'ing *s* scrittura
hand'wrought' *adj* lavorato a mano
hand•y ['hændi] *adj* **(-ier; -iest)** (*easy to handle*) maneggevole; (*within easy reach*) vicino; (*skillful*) destro, abile; **to come in handy** tornare utile
hand'y•man' *s* **(-men')** factotum *m*
hang [hæŋ] *s* maniera di cadere; **to get the hang of** (coll) imparare a adoperare; **to not give a hang** (coll) non importare un fico a || *v* (*pret & pp* **hung** [hʌŋ]) *tr* sospendere; (*laundry*) stendere; (*to attach*) attaccare; (*a door or window*) mettere sui cardini; (*one's head*) abbassare; **hang it!** (coll) al diavolo!; **to hang up** appendere; sospendere il progesso di || *intr* pendere, penzolare; esitare; essere sospeso; essere attaccato; **to hang around** ciondolare, oziare, gironzolare; **to hang on** essere sospeso a; dipendere da; persistere; (*s.o.'s words*) pendere; **to hang out** sporgersi; (slang) raccogliersi; (slang) vivere; **to hang over** esser sospeso; (*to threaten*) minacciare; **to hang together** mantenersi uniti; **to hang up** (telp) riattaccare || *v* (*pret* **hanged** or **hung**) *tr* (*to execute*) impiccare || *intr* impiccarsi
hangar ['hæŋər] or ['hæŋgɑr] *s* rimessa; (aer) aviorimessa, hangar *m*
hanger ['hæŋər] *s* gancio, uncino; (*for clothes*) attaccapanni *m*
hang'er-on' *s* **(hangers-on)** seguace *mf;* seccatore *m;* (*sponger*) parassita *m*
hanging ['hæŋɪŋ] *adj* pendente, pensile || *s* impiccagione; **hangings** parati *mpl*
hang'man *s* **(-men)** boia *m*
hang'nail' *s* pipita delle unghie
hang'out' *s* (coll) ritrovo abituale
hang'o'ver *s* mal *m* di testa dopo una sbornia
hank [hæŋk] *s* matassa
hanker ['hæŋkər] *intr* agognare
Hannibal ['hænɪbəl] *s* Annibale *m*
haphazard [,hæp'hæzərd] *adj* fortuito, a caso || *adv* a caso; alla carlona
hapless ['hæplɪs] *adj* sfortunato
happen ['hæpən] *intr* succedere; **to happen along** sopravvenire; **to happen on** incontrarsi per caso con; **to happen to** + *inf* per caso + *ind*, e.g., **I happened to see her at the theater** l'ho incontrata per caso a teatro
happening ['hæpənɪŋ] *s* avvenimento, fatto
happily ['hæpɪli] *adv* felicemente; fortunatamente
happiness ['hæpɪnɪs] *s* felicità *f;* gioia, piacere *m*
hap•py ['hæpi] *adj* **(-pier; -piest)** lieto, felice, contento; **to be happy to** avere il piacere di
hap'py-go-luck'y *adj* spensierato
hap'py me'dium *s* giusto mezzo
Hap'py New Year' *interj* buon anno!, felice anno nuovo!
harangue [hə'ræŋ] *s* arringa, concione || *tr & intr* arringare
harass ['hærəs] or [hə'ræs] *tr* bersagliare; tartassare, tormentare
harbinger ['hɑrbɪndʒər] *s* foriero; annunzio || *tr* annunziare
harbor ['hɑrbər] *adj* di porto, portuario || *s* porto || *tr* albergare; (*love or hatred*) nutrire; (*e.g., a criminal*) dare ricetto a
har'bor mas'ter *s* capitano di porto
hard [hɑrd] *adj* duro; (*difficult*) difficile; (*work*) improbo; (*solder*) forte; (*hearing or breathing*) grosso; (*drinker*) impenitente; (*liquor*) fortemente alcolico; **to be hard on** essere severo con; (*to wear out fast*) logorare rapidamente || *adv* duro; forte; molto; **hard upon** subito dopo
hard'-and-fast' *adj* inflessibile
hard-bitten ['hɑrd'bɪtən] *adj* duro, incallito
hard-boiled ['hɑrd'bɔɪld] *adj* (*egg*) sodo; (coll) duro
hard' can'dy *s* caramelle *fpl;* **piece of hard candy** caramella
hard' cash' *s* denaro contante
hard' ci'der *s* sidro fermentato
hard' coal' *s* antracite *f*
hard'-earned' *adj* guadagnato a stento
harden ['hɑrdən] *tr* indurire || *intr* indurirsi
hardening ['hɑrdənɪŋ] *s* indurimento; (metallurgy) tempra
hard' facts' *spl* realtà *f*
hard-fought ['hɑrd'fɔt] *adj* accanito
hard-headed ['hɑrd'hɛdɪd] *adj* astuto; ostinato, caparbio
hard-hearted ['hɑrd'hɑrtɪd] *adj* dal cuore duro
hardihood ['hɑrdɪ,hʊd] *s* forza, coraggio; insolenza
hardiness ['hɑrdɪnɪs] *s* ardire *m;* vigore *m*, robustezza fisica
hard' la'bor *s* lavori forzati
hard' luck' *s* mala sorte
hard'-luck' sto'ry *s* storia delle proprie disgrazie
hardly ['hɑrdli] *adv* appena, quasi no; (*with great difficulty*) a malapena, a fatica; **hardly ever** quasi mai
hardness ['hɑrdnɪs] *s* durezza
hard'-of-hear'ing *adj* duro d'orecchio
hard-pressed ['hɑrd'prɛst] *adj* oppresso; **to be hard-pressed for** essere a corto di
hard' rub'ber *s* ebanite *f*
hard' sauce' *s* miscela di burro e zucchero
hard'-shell crab' *s* granchio con la corazza
hardship ['hɑrdʃɪp] *s* pena, privazione; **hardships** privazioni *fpl*, strettezze *fpl*

hard'tack' *s* galletta
hard' times' *spl* strettezze *fpl*
hard' to please' *adj* di difficile contentatura
hard' up' *adj* (coll) in urgente bisogno; **to be hard up for** (coll) essere a corto di
hard'ware' *s* ferramenta *fpl;* macchinario
hard'ware store' *s* negozio di ferramenta
hard-won ['hard,wʌn] *adj* (*victory, battle*) conquistato con molti sforzi; (*money*) acquistato con molti sforzi
hard'wood' *s* legno forte
hard'wood floor' *s* pavimento di legno, parquet *m*
har•dy ['hardi] *adj* (**-dier; -diest**) forte, resistente; (*rash*) temerario; (hort) resistente al freddo
hare [her] *s* lepre *f*
harebrained ['her,brend] *adj* scervellato, sventato
hare'lip' *s* labbro leporino
harem ['herəm] *s* arem *m*
hark [hark] *intr* ascoltare; **to hark back** (*said of hounds*) ritornare sulla pista; riandare col pensiero || *interj* ascolta!
harken ['harkən] *intr* ascoltare
harlequin ['harləkwɪn] *s* arlecchino
harlot ['harlət] *s* meretrice *f*, baldracca
harm [harm] *s* danno || *tr* rovinare; nuocere (with *dat*), fare del male (with *dat*)
harmful ['harmfəl] *adj* nocivo
harmless ['harmlɪs] *adj* innocuo
harmonic [har'manɪk] *adj* armonico || *s* (phys) armonica || **harmonics** *ssg* armonica; *spl* suoni armonici
harmonica [har'manɪkə] *s* armonica a bocca
harmonious [har'monɪ•əs] *adj* armonioso
harmonize ['harmə,naɪz] *tr* intonare; (mus) armonizzare || *intr* intonarsi; (mus) cantare all'unisono
harmo•ny ['harməni] *s* (**-nies**) armonia
harness ['harnɪs] *s* bardatura, finimenti *mpl;* (fig) routine *f;* **to die in the harness** morire sulla breccia || *tr* bardare, imbrigliare; (*a waterfall*) captare
har'ness mak'er *s* sellaio
har'ness race' *s* corsa al trotto, corsa di cavalli col sulky
harp [harp] *s* arpa || *intr*—**to harp on** ripetere ostinatamente
harpist ['harpɪst] *s* arpista *mf*
harpoon [har'pun] *s* rampone *m* || *tr* & *intr* arpionare
harpsichord ['harpsɪ,kərd] *s* arpicordo, clavicembalo
har•py ['harpi] *s* (**-pies**) arpia
harrow ['hæro] *s* erpice *m* || *tr* (agr) erpicare; (fig) tormentare
harrowing ['hæro•ɪŋ] *adj* straziante
har•ry ['hæri] *v* (*pret* & *pp* **-ried**) *tr* saccheggiare; tormentare
harsh [harʃ] *adj* (*to touch*) ruvido; (*to taste or hearing*) aspro; inclemente
harshness ['harʃnɪs] *s* ruvidezza; asprezza; inclemenza
hart [hart] *s* cervo
harum-scarum ['herəm'skerəm] *adj* & *s* scervellato
harvest ['harvɪst] *s* raccolta, mietitura || *tr* raccogliere, mietere
harvester ['harvɪstər] *s* (*person*) mietitore *m;* (*machine*) mietitrice *f*
har'vest home' *s* fine *f* della mietitura; festa dei mietitori; canzone *f* dei mietitori
har'vest moon' *s* luna di settembre
has-been ['hæz,bɪn] *s* (*person*) fallito; (*thing*) anticaglia
hash [hæʃ] *s* polpettone *m* || *tr* tritare
hash' house' *s* osteria di terz'ordine
hashish ['hæʃiʃ] *s* ascisc *m*
hasp [hæsp] or [hasp] *s* boncinello
hassle ['hæsəl] *s* (coll) rissa, disputa
hassock ['hæsək] *s* cuscino poggiapiedi
haste [hest] *s* premura; **in haste** di premura; **to make haste** fare presto
hasten ['hesən] *tr* affrettare || *intr* affrettarsi
hast•y ['hesti] *adj* (**-ier; -iest**) frettoloso; precipitato
hat [hæt] *s* cappello; **to keep under one's hat** (coll) mantenere il segreto su; **to throw one's hat in the ring** (coll) dichiarare la propria candidatura
hat'band' *s* nastro del cappello
hat' block' *s* forma da cappelli
hat'box' *s* cappelliera
hatch [hætʃ] *s* (*brood*) nidiata; (*shading line*) tratteggio; (*trap door*) porta a ribalta; (*lower half of door*) mezza porta; (naut) boccaporto || *tr* (*eggs*) covare; (*a drawing*) tratteggiare; complottare, tramare || *intr* schiudersi
hat'check' girl' *s* guardarobiera
hatchet ['hætʃɪt] *s* accetta; **to bury the hatchet** fare la pace
hatch'way' *s* (*trap door*) porta a ribalta; (naut) boccaporto
hate [het] *s* odio || *tr* & *intr* odiare
hateful ['hetfəl] *adj* odioso
hat'pin' *s* spillone *m*
hat'rack' *s* attaccapanni *m*
hatred ['hetrɪd] *s* odio, livore *m*
hatter ['hætər] *s* cappellaio
haughtiness ['hɔtɪnɪs] *s* superbia
haugh•ty ['hɔti] *adj* (**-tier; -tiest**) superbo, sprezzante
haul [hɔl] *s* (*tug*) tiro; (*amount caught*) retata; (*distance transported*) percorso, pezzo || *tr* trasportare; tirare; (naut) alare
haunch [hɔntʃ] or [hantʃ] *s* fianco; anca; (*hind quarter of an animal*) coscia; (*same used for food*) cosciotto
haunt [hɔnt] or [hant] *s* ritrovo, nido || *tr* frequentare assiduamente; perseguitare
haunt'ed house' *s* casa frequentata dai fantasmi
haute couture [ot ku'tyr] *s* alta moda
have [hæv] *s*—**the haves and the have-nots** gli abbienti e i nullatenenti || *v*

(*pret & pp* **had** [hæd]) *tr* avere; (*a dream*) fare; (*to get, take*) prendere, ottenere, ricevere; **to have got** (coll) avere; **to have got to** + *inf* (coll) dovere + *inf;* **to have it in for** (coll) serbar rancore per; **to have it out with** avere a che dire con; **to have on** portare; **to have (s.th) to do with** avere (qlco) a che fare con, e.g., **I don't want to have anything to do with him** non voglio aver nulla a che fare con lui; **to have** + *inf* fare + *inf,* e.g., **I had him pay the bill** gli ho fatto pagare il conto; **to have** + *pp* fare + *inf,* e.g., **I had my watch repaired** ho fatto aggiustare l'orologio || *intr*—**to have at** attaccare, mettersi di buzzo buono con; **to have to** + *inf* dovere + *inf;* **to have to do with** avere a che fare con; trattare di, e.g., **this book has to do with superstition** questo libro tratta di superstizione || *v aux* avere, e.g., **he has studied his lesson** ha studiato la sua lezione

havelock ['hævlɑk] *s* coprinuca *m*

haven ['hevən] *s* porto; asilo

haversack ['hævər,sæk] *s* bisaccia; (mil) zaino

havoc ['hævək] *s* rovina; **to play havoc with** rovinare; scompigliare

haw [hɔ] *s* (*of hawthorn*) bacca; (*in speech*) esitazione || *intr* voltare a sinistra || *interj* voltare a sinistra!

hawk [hɔk] *s* falco; (*mortarboard*) sparviere *m;* (coll) persona rapace || *tr* imbonire; (*newspapers*) strillare; **to hawk up** sputare raschiandosi la gola || *intr* fare il merciaiolo ambulante; schiarirsi la gola

hawker ['hɔkər] *s* merciaiolo ambulante

hawse [hɔz] *s* (naut) cubia; (*hole*) (naut) occhio di cubia; (naut) altezza di cubia

hawse'hole' *s* occhio di cubia

hawser ['hɔzər] *s* cavo, gomena

haw'thorn' *s* biancospino

hay [he] *s* fieno; **to hit the hay** (slang) andare a letto; **to make hay while the sun shines** battere il ferro fin ch'è caldo

hay' fe'ver *s* febbre *f* da fieno, raffreddore *m* da fieno

hay'field' *s* prato seminato a fieno

hay'fork' *s* forcone *m;* (mach) rastrello

hay'loft' *s* fienile *m*

haymow ['he,maʊ] *s* fienile *m*

hay'rack' *s* rastrelliera

hay'ride' *s* gita notturna in carro da fieno

hay'seed' *s* semente *f* d'erba; (coll) semplicione *m,* campagnolo

hay'stack' *s* meta, pagliaio

hay'wire' *adj* (coll) disordinato, in confusione; (coll) impazzito || *s* filo per legare il fieno

hazard ['hæzərd] *s* pericolo; (*chance*) rischio; (golf) ostacolo || *tr* rischiare; (*an opinion*) arrischiare

hazardous ['hæzərdəs] *adj* pericoloso

haze [hez] *s* foschia; (fig) confusione || *tr* far la matricola a

hazel ['hezəl] *adj* nocciola || *s* (*tree*) nocciolo; (*fruit*) nocciola

ha'zel•nut' *s* nocciola

hazing ['hezɪŋ] *s* vessazione, angheria; (*at university*) matricola

ha•zy ['hezi] *adj* (**-zier; -ziest**) nebbioso; confuso

H-bomb ['etʃ,bɑm] *s* bomba H

he [hi] *s* (**hes**) maschio || *pron pers* (**they**) lui, egli, esso

head [hɛd] *s* testa, capo; (*of bed*) testiera; (*caption*) testata; (*of a nail*) cappello; (*on a glass of beer*) schiuma; (*of a boil*) punta purulenta; (*e.g., of cattle*) capo; **at the head of** a capo di; **from head to foot** da capo a piedi; **head over heels** a gambe levate; completamente; **heads or tails** testa o croce; **over one's head** al di sopra della capacità intellettuale di qlcu; (*going to a higher authority*) al di sopra di qlcu; **to be out of one's head** (coll) esser matto; **to bring to a head** far giungere alla crisi; **to come into one's head** passar per la mente a qlcu; **to go to one's head** dare al cervello a qlcu; **to keep one's head** non perdere la testa; **to keep one's head above water** arrivare a sbarcare il lunario; **to not make head or tail of** non riuscire a raccappezzarsi su || *tr* dirigere, comandare; essere alla testa di || *intr*—**to head towards** dirigersi verso

head'ache' *s* mal di capo, emicrania

head'band' *s* fascia sul capo; (bb) capitello; (typ) filetto

head'board' *s* testiera del letto

head' cheese' *s* salame *m* di testa

head'dress' *s* acconciatura

header ['hɛdər] *s*—**to take a header** (coll) gettarsi a capofitto

head'first' *adv* a capofitto

head'gear' *s* copricapo; (*for protection*) casco

head'hunt'er *s* cacciatore *m* di teste

heading ['hɛdɪŋ] *s* intestazione; (*of a chapter of a book*) titolo; (journ) testata, capopagina *m*

headland ['hɛdlənd] *s* promontorio

headless ['hɛdlɪs] *adj* senza testa

head'light' *s* (naut, rr) fanale *m;* (aut) faro

head'line' *s* (*of a page of a book*) titolo; (journ) testata || *tr* intestare; fare pubblicità a

head'lin'er *s* (slang) attrazione principale

head'long' *adj* precipitoso || *adv* a precipizio; a capofitto

head'man *s* (**-men**) capo; giustizere *m*

head'mas'ter *s* direttore *m* di un collegio per ragazzi

head'most' *adj* primo, più avanzato

head' of'fice *s* sede *f* centrale

head' of hair' *s* capigliatura

head'-on' *adj* frontale || *adv* di fronte, frontalmente

head'phones' *spl* cuffia

head'piece' *s* (*any covering for the head*) copricapo; (*helmet*) elmo; (*brains, judgment*) testa; (*of bed*)

spalliera; (*headset*) cuffia; (typ) testata
head'quar'ters *s* sede *f* centrale, direzione; (mil) quartier *m* generale
head'rest' *s* poggiatesta *m*, testiera
head'set' *s* cuffia
head'ship' *s* direzione
head'stone' *s* pietra angolare; (*on a grave*) pietra tombale
head'stream' *s* affluente *m* principale
head'strong' *adj* testardo, ostinato
head'wait'er *s* capocameriere *m*
head'wa'ters *spl* fonti *fpl* or sorgenti *fpl* d'un fiume
head'way' *s* progresso; **to make headway** progredire
head'wear' *s* copricapo
head'wind' *s* vento di prua
head'work' *s* lavoro intellettuale
head•y ['hɛdi] *adj* (**-ier; -iest**) eccitante; impetuoso; violento; (*clever*) astuto; intossicante
heal [hil] *tr* sanare, guarire; purificare ‖ *intr* risanarsi, guarire; (*said of a wound*) rimarginare
healer ['hilər] *s* guaritore *m*
health [hɛlθ] *s* salute *f*; **to radiate health** sprizzare salute da tutti i pori; **to your health!** alla Sua salute!
health' depart'ment *s* sanità *f*
healthful ['hɛlθfəl] *adj* salutare
health' insur'ance *s* assicurazione malattia
health•y ['hɛlθi] *adj* (**-ier; -iest**) sano; salubre
heap [hip] *s* mucchio; (coll) insalata, mare *m* ‖ *tr* ammucchiare; **to heap s.th upon s.o.** colmare qlcu di qlco; **to heap with** colmare di
hear [hɪr] *v* (*pret & pp* **heard** [hʌrd]) *tr* udire; **to hear it said** sentirlo dire ‖ *intr* udire; **hear!, hear!** bravo!; **to hear about** sentir parlare di; **to hear from** aver notizie di; **to hear of** sentir parlare di; **to hear that** sentir dire che
hearer ['hɪrər] *s* ascoltatore *m*
hearing ['hɪrɪŋ] *s* (*sense*) udito, orecchio; (*act*) udienza; **in the hearing of** in presenza di; **within hearing** a portata d'orecchio
hear'ing aid' *s* uditofono
hear'say' *s* diceria; **by hearsay** per sentito dire
hearse [hʌrs] *s* carro, carrozzone *m*, or furgone *m* funebre
heart [hɑrt] *s* cuore *m*; (*e.g., of lettuce*) grumolo; **after one's heart** di gusto di qlcu; **by heart** a memoria; **heart and soul** di tutto cuore; **to break the heart of** spezzare il cuore di; **to die of a broken heart** morire di crepacuore; **to eat one's heart out** piangere silenziosamente; **to get to the heart of** sviscerare il nocciolo di; **to have one's heart in one's work** lavorare di buzzo buono; **to have one's heart in the right place** avere buone intenzioni; **to lose heart** scoraggiarsi; **to open one's heart to** aprire il cuore a; **to take heart** prender coraggio; **to take to heart** prendersi a cuore; **to wear one's heart on one's sleeve** parlare a cuore aperto; **with one's heart in one's mouth** col cuore in bocca
heart'ache' *s* angustia, angoscia
heart' attack' *s* attacco cardiaco
heart'beat' *s* battito del cuore
heart'break' *s* angoscia straziante
heart'break'er *s* rubacuori *m*
heartbroken ['hɑrt ,brokən] *adj* col cuore spezzato
heart'burn' *s* bruciore *m* di stomaco
heart' disease' *s* mal *m* di cuore
hearten ['hɑrtən] *tr* rincuorare
heart' fail'ure *s* (*death*) arresto cardiaco; collasso cardiaco
heartfelt ['hɑrt ,fɛlt] *adj* sentito
hearth [hɑrθ] *s* focolare *m*
hearth'stone' *s* pietra del focolare
heartily ['hɑrtɪli] *adv* di cuore, cordialmente; saporitamente
heartless ['hɑrtlɪs] *adj* senza cuore, insensibile
heart' mur'mur *s* soffio al cuore
heart-rending ['hɑrt ,rɛndɪŋ] *adj* da far male al cuore
heart'sick' *adj* afflitto, sconsolato
heart'strings' *spl* precordi *mpl*
heart'-to-heart' *adj* cuore a cuore
heart' trans'plant *s* trapianto cardiaco
heart'wood' *s* cuore *m* del legno
heart•y ['hɑrti] *adj* (**-ier; -iest**) cordiale, di cuore; abbondante; (*eater*) grande
heat [hit] *adj* termico ‖ *s* calore *m*; (*of room, house, etc.*) riscaldamento; (zool) fregola; (sports) batteria; (fig) fervore *m*; **in heat** (zool) in amore ‖ *tr* scaldare, riscaldare; (fig) eccitare ‖ *intr* riscaldarsi; (fig) accalorarsi
heated ['hitɪd] *adj* accalorato
heater ['hitər] *s* riscaldatore *m*; (*for central heating*) calorifero; (*to heat hands or bed*) scaldino; (*to heat water in tub*) scaldabagno
heath [hiθ] *s* (*shrub*) brugo, erica; (*tract of land*) brughiera
hea•then ['hiðən] *adj* pagano; irreligioso ‖ *s* (**-then** or **-thens**) pagano
heathendom ['hiðəndəm] *s* (*worship*) paganesimo; (*land*) pagania
heather ['hɛðər] *s* erica, brugo
heating ['hitɪŋ] *adj* di riscaldamento ‖ *s* riscaldamento
heat'ing pad' *s* termoforo
heat' light'ning *s* lampo di caldo
heat' shield' *s* (rok) scudo termico
heat'stroke' *s* colpo di calore
heat' wave' *s* ondata di caldo
heave [hiv] *s* sollevamento, sforzo; **heaves** (vet) bolsaggine *f* ‖ *v* (*pret & pp* **heaved** or **hove** [hov]) *tr* sollevare, alzare; rigettare; (*a sigh*) emettere ‖ *intr* alzarsi e abbassarsi; (*said of one's chest*) palpitare; avere conati di vomito
heaven ['hɛvən] *s* cielo; **for heaven's sake!** or **good heavens!** per amor del cielo!; **heavens** (*firmament*) cielo ‖ **Heaven** *s* cielo
heavenly ['hɛvənli] *adj* celeste
heav'enly bod'y *s* corpo celeste
heav•y ['hɛvi] *adj* (**-ier; -iest**) (*of great

weight) pesante; (*liquid*) denso; (*cloth, sea*) grosso; (*traffic*) forte; (*serious*) grave; (*crop*) abbondante; (*rain*) dirotto; (*features*) grossolano; (*heart*) stretto; (*ponderous*) macchinoso; (*industry*) grande; (*stock market*) abbattuto || *adv* (coll) pesantemente; **to hang heavy** (*said of time*) passar lentamente
heav'y-du'ty *adj* extraforte
heavy-hearted ['hɛvɪ'hartɪd] *adj* afflitto, triste
heav'y·set' *adj* forte, corpulento
heav'y·weight' *s* peso massimo
Hebrew ['hibru] *adj & s* ebreo; (*language*) ebraico
hecatomb ['hɛkə,tom] or ['hɛkə,tum] *s* ecatombe *f*
heckle ['hɛkəl] *tr* interrompere con domande imbarazzanti
hectic ['hɛktɪk] *adj* febbrile
hedge [hɛdʒ] *s* barriera; (*of bushes*) siepe *f;* (*in stock market*) operazione controbilanciante || *tr* circondare con siepe; **to hedge in** circondare || *intr* evitare di compromettersi; (com) coprirsi
hedge'hog' *s* (zool) riccio; (*porcupine*) (zool) porcospino
hedge'hop' *v* (*pret & pp* **-hopped;** *ger* **hopping**) *intr* volare a volo radente
hedgehopping ['hɛdʒ,hapɪŋ] *s* volo radente
hedge'row' [ro] *s* siepe *f*
heed [hid] *s* attenzione; **to take heed** fare attenzione || *tr* badare a || *intr* fare attenzione, badare
heedless [hidlɪs] *adj* sbadato
heehaw ['hi,hɔ] *s* (*of donkey*) raglio d'asino; risata || *intr* ragliare; ridere fragorosamente
heel [hil] *s* (*of shoe, of foot*) calcagno, tallone *m;* (*of stocking or shoe*) tallone *m;* (*raised part of shoe below heel*) tacco; (coll) farabutto; **down at the heel** mal ridotto; **to cool one's heels** aspettare a lungo; **to kick up one's heels** darsi alla pazza gioia; **to show a clean pair of heels** or **to take to one's heels** battere i tacchi
heeler ['hilər] *s* politicante *mf*
heft·y ['hɛfti] *adj* (**-ier; -iest**) (*heavy*) pesante; (*strong*) forte
hegemon·y [hɪ'dʒɛməni] or ['hɛdʒɪ,moni] *s* (**-ies**) egemonia
hegira [hɪ'dʒaɪrə] or ['hɛdʒɪrə] *s* fuga
heifer ['hɛfər] *s* manza, giovenca
height [haɪt] *s* altezza; (*of a person*) altezza, statura; (*e.g., of folly*) colmo
heighten ['haɪtən] *tr* innalzare; (*to increase the amount of*) accrescere, aumentare || *intr* aumentare
heinous ['henəs] *adj* nefando, odioso
heir [ɛr] *s* erede *m*
heir' appar'ent *s* (**heirs' appar'ent**) erede necessario
heirdom ['ɛrdəm] *s* eredità *f*
heiress ['ɛrɪs] *s* ereditiera, erede *f*
heirloom ['ɛr,lum] *s* cimelio di famiglia
Helen ['hɛlən] *s* Elena
helicopter ['hɛlɪ,kaptər] *s* elicottero
heliport ['hɛlɪ,port] *s* eliporto
helium ['hilɪ·əm] *s* elio
helix ['hɪlɪks] *s* (**helixes** or **helices** ['hɛlɪ,siz]) spirale *f;* (geom) elica
hell [hɛl] *s* inferno
hell-bent ['hɛl'bɛnt] *adj* (coll) risoluto; **to be hell-bent on** (coll) avere un chiodo in testa di
hell'cat' *s* arpia, megera
hellebore ['hɛlɪ,bor] *s* elleboro
Hellene ['hɛlin] *s* greco
Hellenic [hɛ'lɛnɪk] or [hɛ'linɪk] *adj* ellenico
hell'fire' *s* fuoco dell'inferno
hellish ['hɛlɪʃ] *adj* infernale
hel·lo [hɛ'lo] *s* saluto || *interj* **ciao!;** (*on telephone*) pronto!
helm [hɛlm] *s* barra del timone; ruota del timone; timone *m* || *tr* dirigere
helmet ['hɛlmɪt] *s* (mil) elmetto; (sports) casco; (hist) elmo
helms'man *s* (**-men**) timoniere *m*
help [hɛlp] *s* aiuto; (*relief*) rimedio, e.g., **there's no help for it** non c'è rimedio; servitù *f;* impiegati *mpl;* operai *mpl;* **to come to the help of** venire in aiuto di || *tr* aiutare; soccorrere, mitigare; (*to wait on*) servire; **it can't be helped** non c'è rimedio; **so help me God!** Dio mi sia testimonio!; **to help down** aiutare a scendere; **to help s.o. with his coat** aiutare qlcu a mettersi il cappotto; **to help oneself** servirsi da solo; **to help up** aiutare a salire; aiutare ad alzarsi; **to not be able to help** + *ger* non poter fare a meno di + *inf*, e.g., **he can't help laughing** non può fare a meno di ridere || *intr* aiutare || *interj* aiuto!
helper ['hɛlpər] *s* aiutante *m;* (*in a shop*) garzone *m*, lavorante *m*
helpful ['hɛlpfəl] *adj* utile, servizievole
helping ['hɛlpɪŋ] *s* (*of food*) razione
helpless ['hɛlplɪs] *adj* (*weak*) debole; (*powerless*) impotente; senza risorse; (*confused*) perplesso; (*situation*) irrimediabile
help'mate' *s* compagno; (*wife*) compagna
helter-skelter ['hɛltər'skɛltər] *adj & adv* in fretta e furia; alla rinfusa
hem [hɛm] *s* (*any edge*) orlo; (*of skirt*) basta, pedana; (*of suit*) falda || *v* (*pret & pp* **hemmed;** *ger* **hemming**) *tr* orlare, bordare; **to hem in** insaccare || *intr* esitare; **to hem and haw** esitare; essere evasivo
hemisphere ['hɛmɪ,sfɪr] *s* emisfero
hemistich ['hɛmɪ,stɪk] *s* emistichio
hem'line' *s* orlo della gonna
hem'lock' *s* (*herb and poison*) cicuta; (*Tsuga canadensis*) abete *m* del Canada
hemoglobin [,hɛmə'globɪn] or [,himə'globɪn] *s* emoglobina
hemophilia [,hɛmə'fɪlɪ·ə] or [,himə'fɪlɪ·ə] *s* emofilia
hemorrhage ['hɛmərɪdʒ] *s* emorragia
hemorrhoids ['hɛmə,rɔɪdz] *spl* emorroidi *fpl*
hemostat ['hɛmə,stæt] or ['himə,stæt] *s* pinza emostatica
hemp [hɛmp] *s* canapa

hemstitch ['hem ˌstɪtʃ] *s* orlo a giorno || *tr & intr* orlare a giorno
hen [hen] *s* gallina
hence [hens] *adv* di qui; da ora; quindi; di qui a, e.g., **three weeks hence** di qui a tre settimane
hence'forth' *adv* d'ora innanzi
hench·man ['hɛntʃmən] *s* (**-men** [mən]) accolito; politicante *m*
hen'house' *s* pollaio
henna ['hɛnə] *s* henna || *tr* tingere con la henna
hen'peck' *tr* (*a husband*) trovare a ridire con
hen'pecked' hus'band *s* marito dominato dalla moglie
her [hʌr] *adj poss* suo, il suo || *pron pers* la, lei; **to her** le, a lei
herald ['herəld] *s* araldo; annunziatore *m* || *tr* annunziare
heraldic [he'rældɪk] *adj* araldico
herald·ry ['herəldri] *s* (**-ries**) (*office*) consulta araldica; (*science*) araldica; (*coat of arms*) blasone *m*
herb [ʌrb] or [hʌrb] *s* erba; erba medicinale
herbaceous [hʌr'beʃəs] *adj* erbaceo
herbage ['ʌrbɪdʒ] or ['hʌrbɪdʒ] *s* erba; (law) erbatico
herbalist ['hʌrbəlɪst] or ['ʌrbəlɪst] *s* erborista *mf*
herbari·um [hʌr'berɪ·əm] *s* (**-ums** or **-a** [ə]) erbario
herb' doc'tor *s* erborista *mf*
herculean [hʌr'kjulɪ·ən] or [ˌhʌrkju'li·ən] *adj* erculeo
herd [hʌrd] *s* (*of sheep*) gregge *m;* (*of cattle*) mandria; (*of men*) torma || *tr & intr* imbrancare
herds'man *s* (**-men**) (*of cattle*) mandriano, vaccaio; (*of sheep*) pastore *m*
here [hɪr] *adj* presente || *s*—**the here and the hereafter** la vita presente e l'aldilà || *adv* qui, qua; **here and there** qua e là; **here is** or **here are** ecco; **that's neither here not there** ciò non ha nulla a che vedere || *interj* presente!
hereabouts ['hɪrə ˌbauts] *adv* qua vicino
here·af'ter *s* aldilà *m* || *adv* d'ora innanzi; nel futuro
here·by' *adv* con la presente
hereditary [hɪ'redɪ ˌteri] *adj* ereditario
heredi·ty [hɪ'redɪti] *s* (**-ties**) eredità *f*
here·in' *adv* qui; in questo posto
here·of' *adv* di questo
here·on' *adv* in questo; su questo
here·sy ['herəsi] *s* (**-sies**) eresia
heretic ['herətɪk] *adj & s* eretico
heretical [hɪ'retɪkəl] *adj* eretico
heretofore [ˌhɪrtu'for] *adv* sinora
here'u·pon' *adv* su questo; in questo; immediatamente dopo
here·with' *adv* accluso; con la presente
heritage ['herɪtɪdʒ] *s* eredità *f*
hermetic(al) [hʌr'metɪk(əl)] *adj* ermetico
hermit ['hʌrmɪt] *s* eremita *m*
hermitage ['hʌrmɪtɪdʒ] *s* eremitaggio
herni·a ['hʌrnɪ·ə] *s* (**-as** or **-ae** [ˌi]) ernia
he·ro ['hɪro] *s* (**-roes**) eroe *m*
heroic [hɪ'ro·ɪk] *adj* eroico || **heroics** *spl* linguaggio altisonante
heroin ['hero·ɪn] *s* (pharm) eroina
heroine ['hero·ɪn] *s* eroina
heroism ['hero ˌɪzəm] *s* eroismo
heron ['herən] *s* airone *m*
herring ['herɪŋ] *s* aringa
her'ring·bone' *s* (*in fabrics*) spina di pesce; (*in hardwood floors*) spiga
hers [hʌrz] *pron poss* il suo; **of hers** suo
herself [hʌr'self] *pron pers* lei stessa; sé stessa; si, e.g., **she enjoyed herself** si divertì; **with herself** con sé
hertz [hʌrts] *s* hertz *m*
hesitan·cy ['hezɪtənsi] *s* (**-cies**) titubanza, esitanza
hesitant ['hezɪtənt] *adj* esitante
hesitate ['hezɪ ˌtet] *intr* esitare, titubare; (*to stutter*) balbettare
hesitation [ˌhezɪ'teʃən] *s* esitazione
heterodox ['hetərə ˌdɑks] *adj* eterodosso
heterodyne ['hetərə ˌdaɪn] *s* eterodina
heterogeneous [ˌhetərə'dʒinɪ·əs] *adj* eterogenco
hew [hju] *v* (*pret* **hewed;** *pp* **hewed** or **hewn**) *tr* tagliare; (*a passage*) aprirsi; (*a statue*) abbozzare; **to hew down** abbattere || *intr*—**to hew close to the line** (coll) filare diritto
hex [heks] *s* strega; incantesimo || *tr* stregare, incantare
hexameter [heks'æmɪtər] *s* esametro
hey [he] *interj* ehi!
hey'day' *s* apogeo
hia·tus [haɪ'etəs] *s* (**-tuses** or **-tus**) (*gap*) lacuna; (gram) iato
hibernate ['haɪbər ˌnet] *intr* ibernare; (*said of people*) svernare
hibiscus [hɪ'bɪskəs] or [haɪ'bɪskəs] *s* ibisco
hic·cup ['hɪkəp] *s* singhiozzo || *v* (*pret & pp* **-cuped** or **-cupped;** *ger* **-cuping** or **-cupping**) *intr* singhiozzare
hick [hɪk] *adj & s* (coll) rustico
hicko·ry ['hɪkəri] *s* (**-ries**) hickory *m*
hidden ['hɪdən] *adj* nascosto
hide [haɪd] *s* cuoio, pelle *f;* **hides** cuoio; **neither hide nor hair** nemmeno una traccia; **to tan s.o.'s hide** (coll) dargliele sode a qlcu || *v* (*pret* **hid** [hɪd]; *pp* **hid** or **hidden** ['hɪdən]) *tr* nascondere || *intr* nascondersi; **to hide out** (coll) rintanarsi
hide'-and-seek' *s* rimpiattino; **to play hide-and-seek** giocare a rimpiattino or a nascondino
hide'bound' *adj* retrogrado, conservatore
hideous ['hɪdɪ·əs] *adj* orribile, brutto
hide'out' *s* nascondiglio
hiding ['haɪdɪŋ] *s* nascondere *m;* (*place*) nascondiglio; **in hiding** nascosto
hid'ing place' *s* nascondiglio
hie [haɪ] *v* (*pret & pp* **hied;** *ger* **hieing** or **hying**) *tr*—**hie thee home** affrettati a tornare a casa || *intr* affrettarsi
hierar·chy ['haɪ·ə ˌrɑrki] *s* (**-chies**) gerarchia
hieroglyphic [ˌhaɪ·ərə'glɪfɪk] *adj & s* geroglifico

hi-fi ['haɪ'faɪ] *adj* di alta fedeltà || *s* alta fedeltà
higgledy-piggledy ['hɪgəldi'pɪgəldi] *adj* confuso || *adv* alla rinfusa
high [haɪ] *adj* alto; (*color*) forte; (*merry*) allegro; (*luxurious*) lussuoso; (coll) ubriaco; (culin) frollo; **high and dry** abbandonato; **high and mighty** (coll) arrogante || *adv* molto; riccamente; **to aim high** mirare in alto; **to come high** essere caro || *s* (aut) quarta, diretta; **on high** in cielo
high' al'tar *s* altare *m* maggiore
high'ball' *s* whiskey con ghiaccio e gazosa || *intr* (slang) andare di carriera
high' blood' pres'sure *s* ipertensione
high'born' *adj* di nobile lignaggio
high'boy' *s* cassettone alto
high'brow' *s* intellettuale *mf;* (coll) intellettualoide *mf*
high'chair' *s* seggiolino per bambini
high' command' *s* comando supremo
high' cost' of liv'ing *s* carovita *m*, caroviveri *m*
high'er educa'tion *s* insegnamento universitario, istruzione superiore
higher-up [,haɪ·ər'ʌp] *s* (coll) superiore *m*
high' explo'sive *s* esplosivo ad alta potenza
highfalutin [,haɪfə'lutən] *adj* (coll) pomposo, pretenzioso
high' fidel'ity *s* high fidelity, alta fedeltà
high'-fre'quency *adj* ad alta frequenza
high' gear' *s* (aut) presa diretta
high'-grade' *adj* di qualità superiore
high-handed ['haɪ'hændɪd] *adj* arbitrario
high' hat' *s* cappello a cilindro
high'-hat' *adj* (coll) snob *m* || *v* (*pret & pp* **-hatted;** *ger* **-hatting**) *tr* (coll) snobbare
high'-heeled' shoe' ['haɪ ,hild] *s* scarpa coi tacchi alti
high' horse' *s* comportamento arrogante; **to get up on one's high horse** darsi delle grandi arie
high' jinks' [dʒɪŋks] *s* (slang) pagliacciata, gazzarra
high' jump' *s* salto in altezza
highland ['haɪlənd] *adj* montagnoso || **highlands** *spl* regione montagnosa
high' life' *s* high-life *f*, alta società
high'light' *s* punto culminante || *tr* mettere in risalto
highly ['haɪli] *adv* altamente, molto; (*paid*) profumatamente; **to speak highly of** parlar molto bene di
High' Mass' *s* messa cantata
high-minded ['haɪ'maɪndɪd] *adj* magnanimo
highness ['haɪnɪs] *s* altezza || **Highness** *s* Altezza
high' noon' *s* mezzogiorno in punto; (fig) sommo
high-pitched ['haɪ'pɪtʃt] *adj* acuto; intenso, emozionante
high-powered ['haɪ'pau·ərd] *adj* ad alta potenza; (*binoculars*) ad alto ingrandimento
high'pres'sure *adj* ad alta pressione || *tr* sollecitare con insistenza
high-priced ['haɪ'praɪst] *adj* caro, di alto prezzo
high' priest' *s* sommo sacerdote
high' rise' *s* edificio di molti piani
high'road' *s* strada principale
high'school' *s* scuola media; (*in Italy*) liceo
high' sea' *s* alto mare; **high seas** alto mare
high' soci'ety *s* l'alta società
high'-sound'ing *adj* altisonante
high'-speed' *adj* ad alta velocità
high-spirited ['haɪ'spɪrɪtɪd] *adj* fiero, vivace, focoso
high' spir'its *spl* allegria, vivacità *f*
high-strung ['haɪ'strʌŋ] *adj* teso, nervoso
high'-test' fuel' *s* supercarburante *m*
high' tide' *s* alta marea; punto culminante
high' time' *s* ora, e.g., **it is high time for you to go** è proprio ora che Lei se ne vada; (coll) baldoria
high' trea'son *s* (*against the sovereign*) lesa maestà; (*against the state*) alto tradimento
high' wa'ter *s* alta marea; (*in a river*) straripamento
high'way' *adj* autostradale || *s* autostrada
high'way'man *s* (**-men**) grassatore *m*
hijack ['haɪ ,dʒæk] *tr* rubare; (*e.g., an airplane*) dirottare || *intr* effettuare un dirottamento
hijacker ['haɪ ,dʒækər] *s* ladro a mano armata; (*e.g., of an airplane*) dirottatore *m*
hijacking ['haɪ ,dʒækɪŋ] *s* furto a mano armata; dirottamento
hike [haɪk] *s* (*for pleasure*) gita, camminata; (*increase*) aumento; (mil) marcia || *tr* tirar su; aumentare || *intr* fare una gita; (mil) fare una marcia
hiker ['haɪkər] *s* camminatore *m*
hilarious [hɪ'lɛrɪ·əs] or [haɪ'lɛrɪ·əs] *adj* ilare; (*e.g., joke*) allegro, divertente
hill [hɪl] *s* collina || *tr* rincalzare
hillbil·ly ['hɪl ,bɪli] *s* (**-lies**) (coll) montanaro rustico
hillock ['hɪlək] *s* poggio, collinetta
hill'side' *s* pendio
hill'top' *s* cima
hill·y ['hɪli] *adj* (**-ier; -iest**) collinoso; ripido
hilt [hɪlt] *s* impugnatura, elsa; **up to the hilt** completamente
him [hɪm] *pron pers* lo; lui; **to him gli,** a lui
himself [hɪm'sɛlf] *pron pers* lui stesso; sé stesso; si, e.g., **he enjoyed himself** si è divertito; **with himself** con sé
hind [haɪnd] *adj* posteriore, di dietro || *s* cerva
hinder ['hɪndər] *tr* ostacolare, impedire
hindmost ['haɪnd ,most] *adj* ultimo
hind'quar'ter *s* quarto posteriore
hindrance ['hɪndrəns] *s* ostacolo, impedimento

hind'sight' *s* senno di poi
Hindu ['hɪndu] *adj & s* indù *mf*
hinge [hɪndʒ] *s* cardine *m;* (bb) cerniera; (philately) listello gommato; punto principale || *tr* munire di cardini || *intr*—**to hinge on** dipendere da
hin•ny ['hɪni] *s* (**-nies**) bardotto
hint [hɪnt] *s* insinuazione; **to take the hint** capire l'antifona || *tr & intr* insinuare; **to hint at** alludere a
hinterland ['hɪntər,lænd] *s* retroterra *m,* entroterra *m*
hip [hɪp] *adj*—**to be hip to** (slang) essere al corrente di || *s* anca, fianco; (*of a roof*) spigolo
hip'bone' *s* ileo, osso iliaco
hipped [hɪpt] *adj* (*livestock*) zoppicante; (*roof*) a padiglione; **hipped on** (coll) ossessionato per
hippie ['hɪpi] *s* capellone *m*
hip•po ['hɪpo] *s* (**-pos**) (coll) ippopotamo
hippodrome ['hɪpə,drom] *s* ippodromo
hippopota•mus [,hɪpə'patəməs] *s* (**-muses** or **-mi** [,maɪ]) ippopotamo
hip' roof' *s* tetto a padiglione
hire [haɪr] *s* paga, salario; nolo; **for hire** a nolo || *tr* (*help*) impiegare; (*a conveyance*) noleggiare || *intr*—**to hire out** mettersi a servizio
hired' girl' *s* lavorante *f* di campagna
hired' hand' *s* lavorante *mf*
hired' man' *s* (**men'**) lavorante *m* di campagna
hireling ['haɪrlɪŋ] *adj* venale || *s* persona prezzolata
his [hɪz] *adj poss* suo, il suo || *pron poss* il suo
Hispanic [hɪs'pænɪk] *adj* ispano
Hispanist ['hɪspənɪst] *s* ispanista *mf*
hiss [hɪs] *s* (*of fire, wind, serpent, etc.*) sibilo; (*of disapproval*) fischio, zittio || *tr* zittire || *intr* zittire; sibilare; (*said of a kettle*) fischiare
histology [hɪs'talədʒi] *s* istologia
historian [hɪs'torɪ•ən] *s* storico
historic(al) [hɪs'tarɪk(əl)] or [hɪs'tɔrɪk(əl)] *adj* storico
histo•ry ['hɪstəri] *s* (**-ries**) storia
histrionic [,hɪstrɪ'anɪk] *adj* teatrale; (*artificial, affected*) istrionico, teatrale || **histrionics** *s* istrionismo, teatralità *f*
hit [hɪt] *s* colpo; successo; (*sarcastic remark*) frecciata; **to be a hit** far furore; **to make a hit with** fare ottima impressione con || *v* (*pret & pp* **hit;** *ger* **hitting**) *tr* colpire; (*to bump*) cozzare; (*the target*) toccare, imbroccare, infilare; (*with a car*) metter sotto; (*a certain speed*) andare a || *intr* battere; **to hit on** (*s.th new*) imbroccare; **to hit out at** attaccare
hit'-and-run' *adj* (*driver*) colpevole di mancato soccorso
hit'-and-run' driv'er *s* pirata *m* della strada
hitch [hɪtʃ] *s* (*jerk*) strattone *m;* (*knot*) nodo; difficoltà *f,* ostacolo; || *tr* (*to tie*) attaccare; (*oxen*) aggiogare; (slang) sposare
hitch'hike' *intr* fare l'autostop
hitch'hik'er *s* autostoppista *mf*
hitch'ing post' *s* palo per attaccare un cavallo
hither ['hɪðər] *adv* qua, qui; **hither and thither** qua e là
hith'er•to' *adv* sinora
hit'-or-miss' *adj* fatto alla carlona
hit' rec'ord *s* disco di grande successo
hive [haɪv] *s* (*box for bees*) alveare *m;* (*swarm*) sciame *m;* **hives** orticaria || *tr* (*bees*) raccogliere
hoard [hord] *s* cumulo; (*of money*) gruzzolo || *tr & intr* custodire gelosamente; tesaurizzare
hoarding ['hordɪŋ] *s* ammassamento, tesaurizzazione
hoarfrost ['hor,frɔst] *s* brina
hoarse [hors] *adj* rauco, svociato
hoarseness ['horsnɪs] *s* raucedine *f*
hoar•y ['hori] *adj* (**-ier; -iest**) canuto, incanutito
hoax [hoks] *s* mistificazione || *tr* mistificare
hob [hab] *s* mensola del focolare; **to play hob with** (coll) mettere a soqquadro
hobble ['habəl] *s* zoppicamento; (*to tie legs of animal*) pastoia || *tr* far zoppicare; imbarazzare; mettere le pastoie a || *intr* zoppicare
hob•by ['habi] *s* (**-bies**) svago, passatempo; **to ride a hobby** dedicarsi troppo alla propria occupazione favorita
hob'by-horse' *s* cavallo a dondolo
hob'gob'lin *s* folletto
hob'nail' *s* brocca, bulletta
hob•nob ['hab,nab] *v* (*pret & pp* **-nobbed;** *ger* **-nobbing**) *intr* essere amiconi; **to hobnob with** essere intimo di
ho•bo ['hobo] *s* (**-bos** or **-boes**) girovago, vagabondo
Hob'son's choice' ['habsənz] *s* scelta fra quanto viene offerto o niente
hock [hak] *s* garretto; (coll) pegno; **in hock** (coll) impegnato, al monte di pietà || *tr* tagliare i garretti a; (coll) impegnare
hockey ['haki] *s* hockey *m*
hock'ey play'er *s* hockeista *m,* discatore *m*
hock'shop' *s* (coll) negozio di prestiti su pegno
hocus-pocus ['hokəs'pokəs] *s* (*meaningless formula*) abracadabra *m;* gherminella
hod [had] *s* vassoio; secchio per il carbone
hod' car'rier *s* manovale *m*
hodgepodge ['hadʒ,padʒ] *s* farragine *f*
hoe [ho] *s* marra, zappa || *tr & intr* zappare
hog [hag] or [hɔg] *s* suino, porco, maiale *m* || *v* (*pret & pp* **hogged;** *ger* **hogging**) *tr* (slang) mangiarsi il meglio di
hoggish ['hagɪʃ] or ['hɔgɪʃ] *adj* maialesco; egoista
hogs'head' *s* barilozzo di sessantatrè galloni
hog'wash' *s* broda da maiali

hoist [hɔɪst] *s* montacarichi *m;* (*lift*) spinta || *tr* alzare, rizzare; (*a flag*) inastare; (naut) issare
hoity-toity ['hɔɪti'tɔɪti] *adj* arrogante, altezzoso
hokum ['hokəm] *s* (coll) fandonie *fpl;* (coll) sentimentalismo volgare
hold [hold] *s* presa, piglio; (*handle*) impugnatura; autorità *f,* ascendente *m;* (wrestling) presa; (aer) cabina bagagli; (mus) corona; (naut) cala, stiva; **to take hold of** afferare; impossessarsi di || *v* (*pret & pp* **held** [hɛld]) *tr* tenere; (*to hold up*) sostenere; (*e.g., with a pin*) assicurare; (*a rank*) rivestire; contenere; (*a meeting*) avere; (*a note*) (mus) filare; **to hold back** trattenere; **to hold in** trattenere; **to hold one's own** non perdere terreno; **to hold over** differire; **to hold up** reggere, sostenere; (*to rob*) (coll) derubare, rapinare || *intr* stare; (*to cling*) reggere; restare valido; **hold on!** un momento!; **to hold back** frenarsi; **to hold forth** fare un discorso; **to hold off** astenersi; mantenersi a distanza; **to hold on** continuare; **to hold on to** attaccarsi a; **to hold out** tener duro, resistere; **to hold out for** mantenersi fermo per
holder ['holdər] *s* possessore *m,* detentore *m;* (*e.g., for a cigar*) bocchino; (*e.g., for a pot*) manico, impugnatura
holding ['holdɪŋ] *s* possesso; **holdings** valori *mpl,* patrimonio
hold'ing com'pany *s* società finanziaria
hold'up' *s* (*delay*) interruzione; (coll) rapina a mano armata; (fig) furto
hold'up man' *s* grassatore *m*
hole [hol] *s* buco; (*in cheese*) occhio; (*in a road*) buca; (*den*) tana; (*burrow*) fossa; **in a hole** in grane, in difficoltà; **to burn a hole in one's pocket** (*said of money*) scorrere attraverso le mani bucate di qlcu; **to pick holes in** trovare a ridire su || *intr*—**to hole up** (coll) imbucarsi
holiday ['hɑlɪ,de] *s* giorno festivo, festa; vacanza
holiness ['holɪnɪs] *s* santità *f;* **his Holiness** sua Santità
Holland ['hɑlənd] *s* l'Olanda *f*
Hollander ['hɑləndər] *s* olandese *mf*
hollow ['hɑlo] *adj* vuoto; (*sound*) sordo; (*eyes, cheeks*) infossato; vano, futile || *s* buca, cavità *f;* (*small valley*) valletta || *adv*—**to beat all hollow** (coll) battere completamente || *tr* scavare
hol·ly ['hɑli] *s* (**-lies**) agrifoglio
holly'hock' *s* altea, malvone *m*
holm' oak' [hom] *s* leccio
holocaust ['hɑlə,kɔst] *s* olocausto
holster ['holstər] *s* fondina
ho·ly ['holi] *adj* (**-lier; -liest**) santo; (*writing*) sacro; (*water*) benedetto
Ho'ly Ghost' *s* Spirito Santo
ho'ly or'ders *spl* ordini sacri; **to take holy orders** entrare in un ordine religioso
Ho'ly Rood' [rud] *s* Santa Croce
Ho'ly Scrip'ture *s* Sacra Scrittura
Ho'ly See' *s* Santa Sede
Ho'ly Sep'ulcher *s* Santo Sepolcro
Ho'ly Thurs'day *s* l'Ascensione; il giovedì santo
ho'ly wa'ter *s* acqua benedetta, acquasanta
Ho'ly Writ' *s* Sacra Scrittura
homage ['hɑmɪdʒ] or ['ɑmɪdʒ] *s* omaggio
homburg ['hɑmbʌrg] *s* lobbia *m & f*
home [hom] *adj* casalingo, domestico; nazionale || *s* casa, dimora; (*fatherland*) patria; (*for the sick, aged, etc.*) ricovero; (sports) meta, traguardo; **at home** a casa; (*at ease*) a proprio agio; (sports) nel proprio campo; **away from home** fuori di casa; **make yourself at home** stia comodo; **to be at home** (*to receive callers*) ricevere || *adv* a casa; **to see home** accompagnare a casa; **to strike home** toccare nel vivo
home'bod'y *s* (**-ies**) persona casalinga
homebred ['hom,brɛd] *adj* domestico; rozzo; semplice
home'brew' *s* bevanda fatta in casa
home-coming ['hom,kʌmɪŋ] *s* ritorno a casa
home' coun'try *s* paese *m* natale
home' deliv'ery *s* trasporto a domicilio
home' front' *s* fronte domestico
home'land' *s* paese natio
homeless ['homlɪs] *adj* senza tetto
home' life' *s* vita familiare
home-loving ['hom,lʌvɪŋ] *adj* casalingo
home·ly ['homli] *adj* (**-lier; -liest**) (*not goodlooking*) brutto; (*not elegant*) semplice, scialbo
homemade ['hom'med] *adj* fatto in casa
homemaker ['hom,mekər] *s* casalinga
home' of'fice *s* sede *f* centrale || **Home Office** *s* (Brit) ministero degli interni
homeopath ['homɪ·ə,pæθ] or ['hɑmɪ·ə,pæθ] *s* omeopatico
home' plate' *s* casa base
home' port' *s* porto d'iscrizione (nel registro marittimo)
home' rule' *s* autogoverno
home' run' *s* colpo che permette al battitore di percorrere tutte le basi del diamante fino alla casa base
home'sick' *adj* nostalgico; **to be homesick for** sentire la nostalgia per
home'sick'ness *s* nostalgia
homespun ['hom,spʌn] *adj* filato a casa; semplice
home'stead *s* casa e terreno
home'stretch' *s* (sports) dirittura d'arrivo; (fig) fase *f* finale
home'town' *s* città *f* natale
homeward ['homwərd] *adj* di ritorno || *adv* verso casa; verso la patria
home'work' *s* lavoro a domicilio; (*of a student*) dovere *m,* esercizio
homey ['homi] *adj* (**homier; homiest**) intimo, comodo
homicidal [,hɑmɪ'saɪdəl] *adj* omicida
homicide ['hɑmɪ,saɪd] *s* (*act*) omicidio; (*person*) omicida *mf*
homi·ly ['hɑmɪli] *s* (**-lies**) omelia

homing ['homɪŋ] *adj* (*pigeon*) viaggiatore; (*weapon*) cercatore del bersaglio
hominy ['hɑmɪni] *s* granturco macinato
homogenei•ty [ˌhoməd͡ʒɪ'ni·ɪti] or [ˌhɑməd͡ʒɪ'ni·ɪti] *s* (**-ties**) omogeneità *f*
homogeneous [ˌhomə'd͡ʒinɪ·əs] or [ˌhɑmə'd͡ʒinɪ·əs] *adj* omogeneo
homogenize [hə'mɑd͡ʒəˌnaɪz] *tr* omogeneizzare
homonym ['hɑmənɪm] *s* omonimo
homonymous [hə'mɑnɪməs] *adj* omonimo
homosexual [ˌhomə'sekʃu·əl] *adj & s* omosessuale *mf*
hone [hon] *s* cote *f* || *tr* affilare
honest ['ɑnɪst] *adj* onesto; guadagnato onestamente; integro, schietto
honesty ['ɑnɪsti] *s* onestà *f*; (bot) lunaria
hon•ey ['hʌni] *adj* melato, dolce || *s* miele *m*; nettare *m*; (coll) caro || *v* (*pret & pp* **-eyed** or **-ied**) *tr* dire parole melate a
hon'ey•bee' *s* ape domestica
hon'ey•comb' *s* favo || *tr* crivellare
honeyed ['hʌnid] *adj* melato
hon'eydew mel'on *s* melone *m* dolce dalla scorza liscia
hon'ey lo'cust *s* acacia a tre spine
hon'ey•moon' *s* luna di miele || *intr* andare in viaggio di nozze
honeysuckle ['hʌniˌsʌkəl] *s* caprifoglio
honk [hɑŋk] or [hɔŋk] *s* (*of wild goose*) schiamazzo; (*of automobile horn*) suono del clacson || *tr* (aut) suonare || *intr* schiamazzare; (aut) suonare
honkytonk ['hɑŋkiˌtɑŋk] or ['hɔŋkiˌtɔŋk] *s* (coll) locale notturno rumoroso
honor ['ɑnər] *s* onore *m* || *tr* onorare; (com) accettare e pagare
honorable ['ɑnərəbəl] *adj* (*upright*) onorato; (*bringing honor; worthy of honor*) onorevole
honorari•um [ˌɑnə'rɛrɪ·əm] *s* (**-ums** or **-a** [ə]) onorario
honorary ['ɑnəˌrɛri] *adj* onorario
honorific [ˌɑnə'rɪfɪk] *adj* onorifico || *s* titolo onorifico; formula di gentilezza
hon'or sys'tem *s* sistema scolastico basato sulla parola d'onore
hood [hud] *s* cappuccio; cappuccio di toga universitaria; (*of carriage*) soffietto; (aut) cofano; (slang) gangster *m* || *tr* incappucciare
hoodlum ['hudləm] *s* (slang) facinoroso, gangster *m*, teppista *m*
hoodoo ['hudu] *s* (*body of primitive rites*) vuduismo; (*bad luck*) iettatura; (*person who brings bad luck*) iettatore *m* || *tr* iettare
hood'wink' *tr* turlupinare, imbrogliare
hooey ['hu·i] *s* (coll) sciocchezze *fpl*
hoof [huf] or [huf] *s* zoccolo, unghia; **on the hoof** (*cattle*) vivo || *tr*—**to hoof it** (slang) camminare; ballare
hoof'beat' *s* rumore *m* degli zoccoli
hook [huk] *s* gancio; (*for fishing*) amo; (*to join two things*) agganciamento; (*for pulling*) raffio, rampino; (*curve*) curva; (*of hook and eye*) uncinello; (boxing) hook *m*, gancio; **by hook or by crook** di riffa o di raffa; **to swallow the hook** abboccare all'amo || *tr* agganciare; (*to bend*) curvare; (*fish*) pigliare; (*to wound with the horns*) incornare; **to hook up** agganciare; (*e.g., a loudspeaking system*) montare || *intr* agganciarsi; curvarsi
hookah ['hukə] *s* narghilè *m*
hook' and eye' *s* uncinello e occhiello
hook' and lad'der *s* autoscala
hooked' rug' *s* tappeto fatto all'uncinetto
hook'nose' *s* naso gobbo
hook'up' *s* (electron) diagramma *m*, schema *m* di montaggio; (rad, telv) rete *f*
hook'worm' *s* anchilostoma *m*
hooky ['huki] *s*—**to play hooky** marinare la scuola
hooligan ['hulɪgən] *s* teppista *m*
hooliganism ['hulɪgənˌɪzəm] *s* teppismo
hoop [hup] or [hup] *s* cerchio || *tr* cerchiare
hoop' skirt' *s* crinolina
hoot [hut] *s* grido della civetta; grido di derisione || *tr* zittire || *intr* stridere; **to hoot at** fischiare
hoot' owl' *s* allocco
hop [hɑp] *s* salto, saltello; (aer) breve volo; (bot) luppolo; (coll) corsa; **hops** (*dried flowers of hop vine*) luppolo || *v* (*pret & pp* **hopped**; *ger* **hopping**) *tr* saltare su; (aer) trasvolare || *intr* saltellare; saltellare su un piede; **to hop over** saltare su; fare una corsa a
hope [hop] *s* speranza || *tr & intr* sperare; **to hope for** sperare
hope' chest' *s* corredo da sposa
hopeful ['hopfəl] *adj* (*feeling hope*) fiducioso; (*giving hope*) promettente
hopeless ['hoplɪs] *adj* disperato
hopper ['hɑpər] *s* tramoggia
hop'scotch' *s* gioco del mondo
horde [hord] *s* orda
horehound ['horˌhaund] *s* marrubio; pastiglie *fpl* per la tosse al marrubio
horizon [hə'raɪzən] *s* orizzonte *m*
horizontal [ˌhɑrɪ'zɑntəl] or [ˌhɔrɪ'zɑntəl] *adj & s* orizzontale *f*
hormone ['hɔrmon] *s* ormone *m*
horn [hɔrn] *s* corno; (aut) clacson *m*, avvisatore acustico; (mus) corno; (*trumpet*) (slang) tromba; **to blow one's horn** cantare le proprie lodi; **to lock horns** lottare, disputare; **to pull in one's horns** battere in ritirata || *intr*—**to horn in** (slang) intromettersi (in)
horned' owl' [hɔrned] *s* allocco
hornet ['hɔrnɪt] *s* calabrone *m*
hor'net's nest' *s* vespaio; **to stir up a hornet's nest** suscitare un vespaio
horn' of plen'ty *s* corno dell'abbondanza
horn'pipe' *s* clarinetto contadinesco inglese fatto di corno di bue

horn'-rimmed glass'es ['hɔrn'rɪmd] *spl* occhiali cerchiati di corno or con la montatura di corno
horn•y ['hɔrni] *adj* **(-ier; -iest)** corneo; (*callous*) calloso; (*having hornlike projections*) cornuto; (slang) preso da desiderio lussurioso
horoscope ['harə,skop] or ['hɔrə,skop] *s* oroscopo
horrible ['harɪbəl] or ['hɔrɪbəl] *adj* orrendo, orribile
horrid ['harɪd] or ['hɔrɪd] *adj* orrido, orribile
horri•fy ['harɪ,faɪ] or ['hɔrɪ,faɪ] *v* (*pret & pp* **-fied**) *tr* inorridire
horror ['harər] or ['hɔrər] *s* orrore *m;* **to have a horror of** provare orrore per
hors d'oeuvre [ɔr 'dʌrv] *s* **(hors d'oeuvres** [ɔr 'dʌrvz]) *s* antipasto
horse [hɔrs] *s* cavallo; (*of carpenter*) cavalletto; **hold your horses!** (coll) aspetti un momento!; **to back the wrong horse** (coll) puntare sul perdente; **to be a horse of another color** (coll) essere un altro paio di maniche || *intr*—**to horse around** (slang) giocherellare; (slang) fare tiri burloni
horse'back' *s*—**on horseback** a cavallo || *adv*—**to ride horseback** montare a cavallo
horse' block' *s* montatoio
horse'break'er *s* domatore *m* di cavalli
horse'car' *s* tram *m* a cavalli
horse' chest'nut *s* (*tree*) ippocastano; (*nut*) castagna d'India
horse' deal'er *s* mercante *m* di cavalli
horse' doc'tor *s* veterinario
horse'fly' *s* **(-flies)** tafano
horse'hair' *s* crine *m* di cavallo; (*fabric*) cilicio
horse'hide' *s* cuoio di cavallo
horse'laugh' *s* risataccia
horse'man *s* **(-men)** cavallerizzo
horsemanship ['hɔrsmən,ʃɪp] *s* equitazione, maneggio
horse' meat' *s* carne equina
horse' op'era *s* western *m*
horse' pis'tol *s* pistola da sella
horse'play' *s* gioco violento, tiro burlone
horse'pow'er *s* cavallo vapore inglese
horse' race' *s* corsa ippica
horse'rad'ish *s* cren *m,* barbaforte *m*
horse' sense' *s* (coll) senso comune
horse'shoe' *s* ferro di cavallo
horse'shoe mag'net *s* calamita a ferro di cavallo
horse'shoe nail' *s* chiodo da cavallo
horse' show' *s* concorso ippico
horse' thief' *s* ladro di cavalli
horse'-trade' *intr* trafficare
horse'whip' *s* staffile *m* || *v* (*pret & pp* **-whipped;** *ger* **-whipping)** *tr* staffilare
horse'wom'an *s* **(-wom'en)** amazzone *f*
hors•y ['hɔrsi] *adj* **(-ier; -iest)** equestre; (*interested in horses*) appassionato ai cavalli; (coll) goffo
horticulture ['hɔrtɪ,kʌltʃər] *s* orticoltura
horticulturist [,hɔrtɪ'kʌltʃərɪst] *s* orticoltore *m*
hose [hoz] *s* (*stocking*) calza; (*sock*) calzino corto; (*flexible tube*) manica || **hose** *spl* calze *fpl*
hosier ['hoʒər] *s* calzettaio
hosiery ['hoʒəri] *s* calze *fpl;* calzificio
hospice ['haspɪs] *s* ospizio
hospitable ['haspɪtəbəl] or [has'pɪtəbəl] *adj* ospitale
hospital ['haspɪtəl] *s* ospedale *m*
hospitali•ty [,haspɪ'tælɪti] *s* **(-ties)** ospitalità *f*
hospitalize ['haspɪtə,laɪz] *tr* ospedalizzare
host [host] s ospite *m;* (*at an inn*) oste *m;* (*army*) milizia; (*crowd*) folla || **Host** *s* (eccl) ostia
hostage ['hastɪdʒ] *s* ostaggio
hostel ['hastəl] *s* ostello della gioventù
hostel•ry ['hastəlri] *s* **(-ries)** albergo
hostess ['hostɪs] *s* ospite *f,* padrona di casa; (*e.g., on a bus*) accompagnatrice *f,* guida *f;* (aer) assistente *f* di volo
hostile ['hastɪl] *adj* ostile
hostili•ty [has'tɪlɪti] *s* **(-ties)** ostilità *f*
hostler ['haslər] or ['aslər] *s* stalliere *m*
hot [hat] *adj* **(hotter; hottest)** caldo; (*reception*) caloroso; (*e.g., pepper*) piccante; (*fresh*) fresco; (*pursuit*) impetuoso; (*in rut*) in calore; (coll) radioattivo; **to be hot** (*said of a person*) aver caldo; (*said of the weather*) fare caldo; **to make it hot for** (coll) dare del filo da torcere a
hot' air' *s* aria calda; (slang) fumo
hot'-air fur'nace *s* impianto di riscaldamento ad aria calda
hot' baths' *spl* terme *fpl*
hot'bed' *s* (*e.g., of revolt*) focolaio; (hort) semenzaio, letto caldo
hot'-blood'ed *adj* ardente; impetuoso
hot' cake' *s* frittella; **to sell like hot cakes** vendersi come se fosse regalato
hot' dog' *s* Frankfurter *m,* Würstel *m*
hotel [ho'tel] *adj* alberghiero || *s* albergo
ho•tel'keep'er *s* albergatore *m*
hot'head' *s* testa calda
hotheaded ['hat,hedɪd] *adj* esaltato, scalmanato
hot'house' *s* serra
hot' plate' *s* fornello elettrico, scaldavivande *m*
hot' springs' *spl* terme *fpl*
hot-tempered ['hat'tempərd] *adj* impulsivo, irascibile
hot' wa'ter *s*—**to be in hot water** (coll) essere nei guai
hot'-wa'ter boil'er *s* caldaia del termosifone
hot'-wa'ter bot'tle *s* borsa dell'acqua calda
hot'-wa'ter heat'er *s* scaldabagno
hot'-wa'ter heat'ing *s* riscaldamento a circolazione di acqua calda
hound [haund] *s* bracco; **to follow the hounds** or **to ride to hounds** andare a caccia alla volpe || *tr* perseguitare
hour [aur] *s* ora; **by the hour** a ore; **in an evil hour** in un brutto momento; **on the hour** ogni ora al suonar del-

l'ora; **to keep late hours** andare a letto tardi
hour'glass' *s* clessidra
hour' hand' *s* lancetta delle ore
hourly ['aurli] *adj* orario || *adv* ogni ora; spesso
house [haus] *s* (**houses** ['hauzɪz]) casa; (*legislative body*) camera; (*size of audience*) concorso di pubblico; teatro; **to keep house** fare le faccende domestiche; **to put one's house in order** migliorare il proprio comportamento; accomodare le proprie faccende || [hauz] *tr* allogare
house' arrest' *s* arresto a domicilio
house'boat' *s* casa galleggiante
house'break'er *s* scassinatore *m*
housebreaking ['haus ˌbrekɪŋ] *s* violazione di domicilio, scasso
housebroken ['haus ˌbrokən] *adj* (*e.g., cat*) che è stato addestrato a tenersi pulito
house'clean'ing *s* pulizia della casa; (fig) pulizia, repulisti *m*
house'coat' *s* vestaglia da casa
house' cur'rent *s* corrente *f* di rete
house'fly' *s* (**-flies**) mosca domestica
houseful ['haus ˌful] *s* casa piena
house' fur'nishings *spl* arredi domestici
house'hold' *adj* domestico || *s* famiglia
house'hold'er *s* capo della famiglia
house'-hunt' *intr*—**to go house-hunting** andare in cerca di casa
house'keep'er *s* governante *f*
house'keep'ing *s* faccende domestiche; **to set up housekeeping** metter su casa
house'keeping apart'ment *s* appartamentino
house'maid' *s* domestica
house' me'ter *s* contatore domestico
house'moth'er *s* maestra in pensionato per studenti
house' of cards' *s* castello di carte
house' of ill' repute' *s* casa di malaffare
house' paint'er *s* imbianchino
house' physi'cian *s* medico residente
house'top' *s* tetto; **to shout from the housetops** proclamare ai quattro venti
housewarming ['haus ˌwɔrmɪŋ] *s* festa per l'inaugurazione di una casa
house'wife' *s* (**-wives'**) donna di casa
house'work' *s* faccende domestiche
housing ['hauzɪŋ] *s* (*of a horse*) gualdrappa; (*dwelling*) abitazioni *fpl;* (carp) alloggiamento; (mach) gabbia, custodia; (aut) coppa; (*of transmission*) (aut) scatola
hous'ing short'age *s* crisi *f* degli alloggi
hovel ['hʌvəl] or ['hɑvəl] *s* catapecchia, stamberga; (*shed*) baracca
hover ['hʌvər] or ['hɑvər] *intr* librarsi; (*on the lips*) trapelare; (fig) ondeggiare, esitare
how [hau] *adv* come; (*at what price*) a quanto; **how early** quando, a che ora; **how else** in che altro modo; **how far** fino a dove; quanto, e.g., **how far is it to the station?** quanto c'è da qui alla stazione?; **how long** quanto tempo; **how many** quanti; **how much** quanto; **how often** quante volte; **how old are you?** quanti anni ha?; **how soon** quando, a che ora; **how** + *adj* quanto + *adj,* e.g., **how beautiful she is!** quanto è bella!
how•ev'er *adv* comunque; in qualunque modo; per quanto . . . , e.g., **however wrong he may be** per quanto torto possa avere || *conj* come, e.g., **do it however you want** lo faccia come vuole
howitzer ['hau·ɪtsər] *s* obice *m*
howl [haul] *s* ululato, urlo; scoppio di risa || *tr* gridare; **to howl down** sopraffare a grida; || *intr* ululare, urlare
howler ['haulər] *s* urlatore *m;* (coll) strafalcione *m,* topica
hoyden ['hɔɪdən] *s* ragazzaccia
hub [hʌb] *s* mozzo; (fig) centro
hubbub ['hʌbəb] *s* putiferio, fracasso
hub'cap' *s* (aut) calotta della ruota
huckleber•ry ['hʌkəl ˌberi] *s* (**-ries**) mirtillo
huckster ['hʌkstər] *s* venditore *m* ambulante; trafficante *m*
huddle ['hʌdəl] *s* conferenza segreta || *intr* affollarsi, accalcarsi
hue [hju] *s* tono, tinta; **hue and cry** grido d'indignazione
huff [hʌf] *s* stizza; **in a huff** di cattivo umore || *tr* (checkers) buffare
hug [hʌg] *s* abbraccio || *v* (*pret & pp* **hugged;** *ger* **hugging**) *tr* abbracciare; (*e.g., a wall*) costeggiare || *intr* abbracciarsi
huge [hjudʒ] *adj* smisurato, immane
huh [hʌ] *interj* eh!
hulk [hʌlk] *s* scafo, carcassa; (*unwieldy object*) trabiccolo
hulking ['hʌlkɪŋ] *adj* grosso e goffo
hull [hʌl] *s* (*of ship or hydroplane*) scafo; (*of dirigible*) intelaiatura; (*of airplane*) fusoliera; (*e.g., of a nut*) guscio || *tr* sgusciare; (*rice*) brillare
hullabaloo ['hʌləbə ˌlu] or [ˌhʌləbə'lu] *s* fracasso, baccano
hum [hʌm] *s* canterellio; (*of bee, machine, etc.*) ronzio || *v* (*pret & pp* **hummed;** *ger* **humming**) *tr* canterellare || *intr* canterellare; (*to buzz*) ronzare; (coll) vibrare, essere attivo
human ['hjumən] *adj* umano
hu'man be'ing *s* essere umano
humane [hju'men] *adj* umano; compassionevole
humanist ['hjumənɪst] *adj* umanistico || *s* umanista *mf*
humanitarian [hju ˌmænɪ'terɪ·ən] *adj & s* umanitario
humani•ty [hju'mænɪti] *s* (**-ties**) umanità *f;* **humanities** (*of Greece and Rome*) studi umanistici; (*literature, art, philosophy*) scienze umanistiche
hu'man•kind' *s* genere umano
humble ['hʌmbəl] or ['ʌmbəl] *adj* umile || *tr* umiliare
hum'ble pie' *s*—**to eat humble pie** accettare un'umiliazione
hum'bug' *s* frottola; (*person*) impostore *m* || *v* (*pret & pp* **-bugged;** *ger*

-bugging) *tr* imbrogliare || *intr* fare l'imbroglione
hum'drum' *adj* noioso, monotono
humer·us ['hjumərəs] *s* (**-i** [,aɪ]) omero
humid ['hjumɪd] *adj* umido
humidifier [hju'mɪdɪ,faɪ·ər] *s* evaporatore *m*
humidi·fy [hju'mɪdɪ,faɪ] *v* (*pret & pp* **-fied)** *tr* inumidire
humidity [hju'mɪdɪti] *s* umidità *f*
humiliate [hju'mɪlɪ,et] *tr* umiliare
humiliating [hju'mɪlɪ,etɪŋ] *adj* umiliante
humility [hju'mɪlɪti] *s* umiltà *f*
hummingbird ['hʌmɪŋ,bʌrd] *s* colibrì *m*
humor ['hjumər] or ['jumər] *s* umore *m;* umorismo; **out of humor** di cattivo umore || *tr* adattarsi alle fisime di, assecondare
humorist ['hjumərɪst] or ['jumərɪst] *s* umorista *mf*
humorous ['hjumərəs] or ['jumərəs] *adj* umoristico
hump [hʌmp] *s* gobba; (*in the ground*) monticello
hump'back' *s* gobba; (*person*) gobbo
humus ['hjuməs] *s* humus *m*
hunch [hʌntʃ] *s* gobba; (*premonition*) (coll) sospetto || *tr* piegare || *intr* accovacciarsi
hunch'back' *s* gobba; (*person*) gobbo
hundred ['hʌndrəd] *adj, s & pron* cento; **a hundred** or **one hundred** cento; **by the hundreds** a centinaia
hundredth ['hʌndrədθ] *adj, s & pron* centesimo
hun'dred·weight' *s* cento libbre
Hungarian [hʌŋ'gerɪ·ən] *adj & s* ungherese *mf*
Hungary ['hʌŋgəri] *s* l'Ungheria *f*
hunger ['hʌŋgər] *s* fame *f* || *intr* aver fame; **to hunger for** aver un desiderio ardente di, agognare
hun'ger strike' *s* sciopero della fame
hun·gry ['hʌŋgri] *adj* (**-grier; -griest)** affamato; **to be hungry** aver fame; **to go hungry** andare digiuno
hunk [hʌŋk] *s* (coll) bel pezzo
hunt [hʌnt] *s* caccia; **on the hunt for** a caccia di || *tr* cacciare; (*to look for*) cercare || *intr* andare a caccia; cercare; **to go hunting** andare a caccia; **to hunt for** cercare
hunter ['hʌntər] *s* cacciatore *m;* (*dog*) cane *m* da caccia
hunting ['hʌntɪŋ] *adj* da caccia || *s* caccia
hunt'ing box' *s* capanno
hunt'ing dog' *s* cane *m* da caccia
hunt'ing ground' *s* terreno di caccia
hunt'ing horn' *s* corno da caccia
hunt'ing jack'et *s* cacciatora
hunt'ing lodge' *s* (*hut*) capanno; villino da caccia
hunt'ing sea'son *s* stagione della caccia
huntress ['hʌntrɪs] *s* cacciatrice *f*
hunts'man *s* (**-men)** cacciatore *m*
hurdle ['hʌrdəl] *s* (*hedge*) siepe *f;* (*wooden frame*) barriera; (sports, fig) ostacolo; **hurdles** corsa ad ostacoli || *tr* saltare, superare
hur'dle race' *s* corsa agli ostacoli
hurl [hʌrl] *s* lancio || *tr* lanciare; **to hurl back** respingere
hurrah [hʊ'rɑ] or **hurray** [hʊ're] *s* viva *m* || *tr* applaudire || *intr* gridare urrà || *interj* evviva!, urrà!; **hurrah for . . . !** viva . . . !
hurricane ['hʌrɪ,ken] *s* uragano
hurried ['hʌrid] *adj* frettoloso
hur·ry ['hʌri] *s* (**-ries)** fretta; **to be in a hurry** avere fretta || *v* (*pret & pp* **-ried)** *tr* affrettare, sollecitare || *intr* affrettarsi; **to hurry after** correr dietro a; **to hurry away** andarsene di furia; **to hurry back** ritornare presto; **to hurry up** spicciarsi
hurt [hʌrt] *adj* (*injured*) ferito; (*offended*) risentito || *s* (*harm*) danno; (*injury*) ferita; (*pain*) dolore *m* || *v* (*pret & pp* **hurt)** *tr* (*to harm*) fare male a; (*to injure*) ferire; (*to offend*) offendere; (*to pain*) dolere (with *dat*) || *intr* fare male, dolere; aver male, e.g., **my head hurts** ho male alla testa
hurtle ['hʌrtəl] *intr* sferrarsi, scagliarsi, precipitarsi
husband ['hʌzbənd] *s* marito || *tr* amministrare con economia
hus'band·man *s* (**-men)** agricoltore *m*
husbandry ['hʌzbəndri] *s* agricoltura; (*management of domestic affairs*) governo, economia domestica
hush [hʌʃ] *s* silenzio || *tr* far tacere; **to hush up** (*a scandal*) soffocare || *intr* tacere || *interj* zitto!
hushaby ['hʌʃə,baɪ] *interj* fa' la nanna!
hush'-hush' *adj* segretissimo
hush' mon'ey *s* prezzo del silenzio
husk [hʌsk] *s* guscio; (*of corn*) spoglia || *tr* sgusciare; (*rice*) brillare; (*corn*) scartocciare, spogliare
husk·y ['hʌski] *adj* (**-ier; -iest)** forte; (*voice*) rauco
hus·sy ['hʌzi] or ['hʌsi] *s* (**-sies)** poca di buono; ragazza impudente
hustle ['hʌsəl] *s* vigore *m;* (slang) traffico || *tr* forzare, spingere || *intr* affrettarsi, scalmanarsi; (slang) trafficare; (*said of a prostitute*) (slang) accostare un cliente
hustler ['hʌslər] *s* (*go-getter*) persona intraprendente; (slang) trafficone *m,* imbroglione *m;* (slang) passeggiatrice *f*
hut [hʌt] *s* casolare *m,* casupola
hyacinth ['haɪ·əsɪnθ] *s* giacinto
hybrid ['haɪbrɪd] *adj & s* ibrido
hybridize ['haɪbrɪ,daɪz] *tr & intr* ibridare
hy·dra ['haɪdrə] *s* (**-dras** or **-drae** [dri]) idra
hydrant ['haɪdrənt] *s* idrante *m;* (*water faucet*) rubinetto
hydrate ['haɪdret] *s* idrato || *tr* idratare || *intr* idratarsi
hydraulic [haɪ'drɔlɪk] *adj* idraulico || **hydraulics** *s* idraulica
hydrau'lic ram' *s* pompa idraulica
hydriodic [,haɪdrɪ'ɑdɪk] *adj* iodidrico
hydrobromic [,haɪdrə'bromɪk] *adj* bromidrico

hydrocarbon [,haɪdrə'kɑrbən] *s* idrocarburo
hydrochloric [,haɪdrə'klorɪk] *adj* cloridrico
hydroelectric [,haɪdro·ɪ'lɛktrɪk] *adj* idroelettrico
hydrofluoric [,haɪdrəflu'ɑrɪk] or [,haɪdrəflu'ɔrɪk] *adj* fluoridrico
hydrofoil ['haɪdrə,fɔɪl] *s* superificie idrodinamica; (*winglike member*) aletta idrodinamica; (*vessel*) aliscafo, idroplano
hydrogen ['haɪdrədʒən] *s* idrogeno
hy'drogen bomb' *s* bomba all'idrogeno
hy'drogen perox'ide *s* perossido d'idrogeno, acqua ossigenata
hy'drogen sul'fide *s* solfuro d'idrogeno
hydrometer [haɪ'drɑmɪtər] *s* areometro
hydrophobia [,haɪdrə'fobɪ·ə] *s* idrofobia
hydroplane ['haɪdrə,plen] *s* (aer) idrovolante *m;* (naut) idroscivolante *m,* idroplano
hydroxide [haɪ'drɑksaɪd] *s* idrossido
hyena [haɪ'inə] *s* iena
hygiene ['haɪdʒin] or ['haɪdʒɪ,in] *s* igiene *f*
hygienic [,haɪdʒɪ'ɛnɪk] or [haɪ'dʒinɪk] *adj* igienico
hymn [hɪm] *s* inno
hymnal ['hɪmnəl] *s* innario
hyperacidity [,haɪpərə'sɪdɪti] *s* iperacidità *f*
hyperbola [haɪ'pʌrbələ] *s* (geom) iperbole *f*
hyperbole [haɪ'pʌrbəli] *s* (rhet) iperbole *f*
hyperbolic [,haɪpər'bɑlɪk] *adj* iperbolico
hypersensitive [,haɪpər'sɛnsɪtɪv] *adj* ipersensibile
hypertension [,haɪpər'tɛnʃən] *s* ipertensione
hyphen ['haɪfən] *s* trattino
hyphenate ['haɪfə,net] *tr* unire con trattino; scrivere con trattino
hypno·sis [hɪp'nosɪs] *s* (**-ses** [siz]) ipnosi *f*
hypnotic [hɪp'nɑtɪk] *adj & s* ipnotico
hypnotism ['hɪpnə,tɪzəm] *s* ipnotismo
hypnotize ['hɪpnə,taɪz] *tr* ipnotizzare
hypochondriac [,haɪpə'kɑndrɪ,æk] or [,hɪpə'kɑndrɪ,æk] *s* ipocondriaco
hypocri·sy [hɪ'pɑkrəsi] *s* (**-sies**) ipocrisia
hypocrite ['hɪpəkrɪt] *s* ipocrita *mf*
hypocritical [,hɪpə'krɪtɪkəl] *adj* ipocrita
hypodermic [,haɪpə'dʌrmɪk] *adj* ipodermico
hyposulfite [,haɪpə'sʌlfaɪt] *s* iposolfito
hypotenuse [haɪ'pɑtɪ,nus] or [haɪ'pɑtɪ,njus] *s* ipotenusa
hypothesis [haɪ'pɑθɪsɪs] *s* (**-ses** [,siz]) ipotesi *f*
hypothesize [haɪ'poθɪ,saɪz] *tr* ipotizzare
hypothetic(al) [,haɪpə'θɛtɪk(əl)] *adj* ipotetico
hyssop ['hɪsəp] *s* issopo
hysteria [hɪs'tɪrɪ·ə] *s* isterismo
hysteric [hɪs'tɛrɪk] *adj* isterico || **hysterics** *s* isterismo
hysterical [hɪs'tɛrɪkəl] *adj* isterico

I

I, i [aɪ] *s* nona lettera dell'alfabeto inglese
I [aɪ] *pron pers* (**we** [wi]) io; **it is I** sono io
iambic [aɪ'æmbɪk] *adj* giambico
iam·bus [aɪ'æmbəs] *s* (**-bi** [baɪ]) giambo
I'-beam' *s* putrella
Iberian [aɪ'bɪrɪ·ən] *adj* iberico || *s* abitante *mf* dell'Iberia; lingua iberica
ibex ['aɪbɛks] *s* (**ibexes** or **ibices** ['ɪbɪ,siz]) stambecco
ice [aɪs] *s* ghiaccio; **to break the ice** rompere il ghiaccio; **to cut no ice** (coll) non avere importanza; **to skate on thin ice** cacciarsi in una situazione delicata || *tr* gelare; (*to cover with icing*) glassare || *intr* gelarsi
ice' age' *s* epoca glaciale
ice' bag' *s* borsa di ghiaccio
iceberg ['aɪs,bʌrg] *s* borgognone *m,* montagna di ghiaccio
ice'boat' *s* slitta a vela; (*icebreaker*) rompighiaccio
icebound ['aɪs,baʊnd] *adj* chiuso dal ghiaccio
ice'box' *s* ghiacciaia
ice'break'er *s* rompighiaccio
ice' buck'et *s* secchiello da ghiaccio
ice'cap' *s* calotta glaciale
ice'-cold' *adj* gelido, ghiacciato
ice' cream' *s* gelato, sorbetto
ice'-cream cone' *s* cono gelato
ice'-cream freez'er *s* gelatiera
ice'-cream par'lor *s* gelateria
ice' cube' *s* cubetto di ghiaccio
ice' hock'ey *s* hockey *m* su ghiaccio
Iceland ['aɪslənd] *s* l'Islanda *f*
Icelander ['aɪs,lændər] or ['aɪsləndər] *s* islandese *mf*
Icelandic [aɪs'lændɪk] *adj* islandese || *s* (*language*) islandese *m*
ice'man' *s* (**-men'**) venditore *m* di ghiaccio
ice' pack' *s* banco di ghiaccio; (*ice bag*) borsa di ghiaccio
ice' pick' *s* rompighiaccio
ice' shelf' *s* tavolato di ghiaccio
ice' skate' *s* pattino da ghiaccio
ice' wa'ter *s* acqua gelata
ichthyology [,ɪkθɪ'ɑlədʒi] *s* ittiologia
icicle ['aɪsɪkəl] *s* ghiacciolo
icing ['aɪsɪŋ] *s* glassa; (meteor) gelo
iconoclast [aɪ'kɑnə,klæst] *s* iconoclasta *mf*

iconoscope [aɪˈkɑnəˌskop] *s* (trademark) iconoscopio
icy [ˈaɪsi] *adj* (**icier; iciest**) ghiacciato; (*e.g., wind, hands*) gelido; (fig) glaciale
idea [aɪˈdi·ə] *s* idea
ideal [aɪˈdi·əl] *adj & s* ideale *m*
idealist [aɪˈdi·əlɪst] *adj & s* idealista *mf*
idealistic [aɪˌdɪ·əlˈɪstɪk] *adj* idealistico
idealize [aɪˈdi·əˌlaɪz] *tr* idealizzare
identic(al) [aɪˈdɛntɪk(əl)] *adj* identico
identification [aɪˌdɛntɪfɪˈkeʃən] *s* identificazione, riconoscimento
identifica'tion card' *s* carta d'identità
identifica'tion tag' *s* piastrina
identi·fy [aɪˈdɛntɪˌfaɪ] *v* (*pret & pp* **-fied**) *tr* identificare
identi·ty [aɪˈdɛntɪti] *s* (**-ties**) identità *f*
ideolo·gy [ˌaɪdɪˈɑlədʒi] or [ˌɪdɪˈɑlədʒi] *s* (**-gies**) ideologia
ides [aɪdz] *spl* idi *mpl & fpl*
idio·cy [ˈɪdɪ·əsi] *s* (**-cies**) idiozia
idiom [ˈɪdɪ·əm] *s* (*expression that is contrary to the usual patterns of the language*) locuzione idiomatica, idiotismo; (*style of language*) lingua, idioma *m;* (*style of an author*) stile *m;* (*character of a language*) indole *f*
idiomatic [ˌɪdɪ·əˈmætɪk] *adj* idiomatico
idiosyncra·sy [ˌɪdɪ·əˈsɪnkrəsi] *s* (**-sies**) eccentricità *f,* originalità *f;* (med) idiosincrasia
idiot [ˈɪdɪ·ət] *s* idiota *mf*
idiotic [ˌɪdɪˈɑtɪk] *adj* idiota
idle [ˈaɪdəl] *adj* (*unemployed*) disoccupato; (*machine*) fermo; (*capital*) giacente; (*time*) perso; (*talk*) vano; (*lazy*) fannullone, ozioso; **to run idle** girare a vuoto || *tr*—**to idle away** (*time*) sprecare || *intr* poltrire, fare il fannullone; (aut) girare al minimo
idleness [ˈaɪdəlnɪs] *s* ozio
idler [ˈaɪdlər] *s* fannullone *m*
idling [ˈaɪdlɪŋ] *s* (*of motor*) minimo
idol [ˈaɪdəl] *s* idolo
idola·try [aɪˈdɑlətri] *s* (**-tries**) idolatria
idolize [ˈaɪdəˌlaɪz] *tr* idolatrare
idyll [ˈaɪdəl] *s* idillio
idyllic [aɪˈdɪlɪk] *adj* idilliaco
if [ɪf] *conj* se; **as if** come se; **even if** anche se; **if so** se è così; **if true** se è vero
ignis fatuus [ˈɪgnɪsˈfætʃʊ·əs] *s* (**ignes fatui** [ˈɪgnizˈfætʃʊˌaɪ]) fuoco fatuo
ignite [ɪgˈnaɪt] *tr* infiammare || *intr* infiammarsi
ignition [ɪgˈnɪʃən] *s* ignizione; (aut) accensione
igni'tion switch' *s* (aut) chiavetta dell'accensione
igni'tion sys'tem *s* (aut) apparecchiatura d'accensione
ignoble [ɪgˈnobəl] *adj* ignobile
ignominious [ˌɪgnəˈmɪnɪ·əs] *adj* ignominioso
ignoramus [ˌɪgnəˈreməs] *s* ignorante *mf*
ignorance [ˈɪgnərəns] *s* ignoranza
ignorant [ˈɪgnərənt] *adj* ignorante; **to be ignorant of** ignorare
ignore [ɪgˈnor] *tr* (*a person; a person's kindness*) ignorare
ill [ɪl] *adj* (**worse** [wʌrs]; **worst** [wʌrst]) malato; **to take ill** cadere malato || *adv* male; **to take ill** prendere in mala parte
ill-advised [ˈɪlədˈvaɪzd] *adj* inconsulto, sconsiderato
ill'-at-ease' *adj* imbarazzato, spaesato
ill-bred [ˈɪlˈbrɛd] *adj* maleducato
ill-considered [ˈɪlkənˈsɪdərd] *adj* sconsiderato
ill-disposed [ˈɪldɪsˈpozd] *adj* maldisposto, malintenzionato
illegal [ɪˈligəl] *adj* illegale
illegible [ɪˈlɛdʒɪbəl] *adj* illeggibile
illegitimate [ˌɪlɪˈdʒɪtɪmɪt] *adj* illegittimo
ill' fame' *s* pessima fama
ill-fated [ˈɪlˈfetɪd] *adj* infausto
ill-gotten [ˈɪlˈgɑtən] *adj* male acquistato
ill-humored [ˈɪlˈhjumərd] *adj* di cattivo umore
illicit [ɪˈlɪsɪt] *adj* illecito
illitera·cy [ɪˈlɪtərəsi] *s* (**-cies**) analfabetismo; (*mistake*) solecismo; ignoranza
illiterate [ɪˈlɪtərɪt] *adj* (*uneducated*) illetterato; (*unable to read or write*) analfabeta || *s* analfabeta *mf*
ill-mannered [ˈɪlˈmænərd] *adj* screanzato, ineducato
illness [ˈɪlnɪs] *s* malattia
illogical [ɪˈlɑdʒɪkəl] *adj* illogico
ill-spent [ˈɪlˈspɛnt] *adj* sprecato
ill-starred [ˈɪlˈstɑrd] *adj* nato sotto una cattiva stella; sfortunato, funesto
ill-tempered [ˈɪlˈtɛmpərd] *adj* di cattivo umore
ill-timed [ˈɪlˈtaɪmd] *adj* inopportuno
ill'-treat' *tr* maltrattare, tartassare
illuminate [ɪˈlumɪˌnet] *tr* illuminare; (*a manuscript*) miniare
illumination [ɪˌlumɪˈneʃən] *s* illuminazione; (*in manuscript*) miniatura
illusion [ɪˈluʒən] *s* illusione
illusive [ɪˈlusɪv] *adj* illusorio
illusory [ɪˈlusəri] *adj* illusorio
illustrate [ˈɪləsˌtret] or [ɪˈlʌstret] *tr* illustrare
illustration [ˌɪləsˈtreʃən] *s* illustrazione
illustrator [ˈɪləsˌtretər] *s* illustratore *m*
illustrious [ɪˈlʌstrɪ·əs] *adj* illustre
ill' will' *s* astio, ruggine *f,* malevolenza
image [ˈɪmɪdʒ] *s* immagine *f;* **the very image of** il ritratto parlante di
image·ry [ˈɪmɪdʒri] or [ˈɪmɪdʒəri] *s* (**-ries**) (*mental images*) fantasia; (*images collectively*) immagini *fpl;* (rhet) linguaggio figurato
imaginary [ɪˈmædʒɪˌnɛri] *adj* immaginario
imagination [ɪˌmædʒɪˈneʃən] *s* immaginazione
imagine [ɪˈmædʒɪn] *tr & intr* immaginare; (*to conjecture*) immaginarsi; **imagine!** si figuri!
imbalance [ɪmˈbæləns] *s* scompenso
imbecile [ˈɪmbɪsɪl] *adj & s* imbecille *mf*

imbecili·ty [ˌɪmbɪˈsɪlɪti] *s* (**-ties**) imbecillità *f*, imbecillaggine *f*
imbibe [ɪmˈbaɪb] *tr* (*to drink*) bere; assorbire || *intr* bere
imbue [ɪmˈbju] *tr* imbevere
imitate [ˈɪmɪ ˌtet] *tr* imitare
imitation [ˌɪmɪˈteʃən] *adj* (*e.g., jewelry*) falso || *s* imitazione
imitator [ˈɪmɪ ˌtetər] *s* imitatore *m*
immaculate [ɪˈmækjəlɪt] *adj* immacolato
immaterial [ˌɪməˈtɪrɪ·əl] *adj* immateriale; poco importante; **it's immaterial to me** a me fa lo stesso
immature [ˌɪməˈtjur] or [ˌɪməˈtur] *adj* immaturo
immeasurable [ɪˈmɛʒərəbəl] *adj* incommensurabile, smisurato
immediacy [ɪˈmidɪ·əsi] *s* immediatezza
immediate [ɪˈmidɪ·ɪt] *adj* immediato
immediately [ɪˈmidɪ·ɪtli] *adv* immediatamente
immemorial [ˌɪmɪˈmorɪ·əl] *adj* immemorabile
immense [ɪˈmɛns] *adj* immenso
immerge [ɪˈmʌrdʒ] *intr* sommergersi
immerse [ɪˈmʌrs] *tr* immergere
immersion [ɪˈmʌrʃən] or [ɪˈmʌrʒən] *s* immersione
immigrant [ˈɪmɪgrənt] *adj & s* immigrante *mf*
immigrate [ˈɪmɪ ˌgret] *intr* immigrare
immigration [ˌɪmɪˈgreʃən] *s* immigrazione
imminent [ˈɪmɪnənt] *adj* imminente
immobile [ɪˈmobɪl] or [ɪˈmobil] *adj* immobile
immobilize [ɪˈmobɪ ˌlaɪz] *tr* immobilizzare
immoderate [ɪˈmɑdərɪt] *adj* smodato, sregolato
immodest [ɪˈmɑdɪst] *adj* immodesto
immoral [ɪˈmɑrəl] or [ɪˈmɔrəl] *adj* immorale
immortal [ɪˈmɔrtəl] *adj & s* immortale *mf*
immortalize [ɪˈmɔrtə ˌlaɪz] *tr* eternare, immortalare
immune [ɪˈmjun] *adj* immune
immunize [ˈɪmjə ˌnaɪz] or [ɪˈmjunaɪz] *tr* immunizzare
imp [ɪmp] *s* diavoletto; (*child*) frugolo
impact [ˈɪmpækt] *s* impatto
impair [ɪmˈper] *tr* danneggiare; (*to weaken*) indebolire
impan·el [ɪmˈpænəl] *v* (*pret & pp* **-eled** or **-elled;** *ger* **-eling** or **-elling**) *tr* iscrivere nella lista dei giurati; (*a jury*) selezionare
impart [ɪmˈpɑrt] *tr* (*a secret*) far conoscere; (*knowledge*) impartire; (*motion*) imprimere
impartial [ɪmˈpɑrʃəl] *adj* imparziale
impassable [ɪmˈpæsəbəl] or [ɪmˈpɑsəbəl] *adj* impraticabile, intransitabile
impasse [ɪmˈpæs] or [ˈɪmpæs] *s* vicolo cieco, impasse *f*
impassible [ɪmˈpæsɪbəl] *adj* impassibile
impassioned [ɪmˈpæʃənd] *adj* caloroso, veemente
impassive [ɪmˈpæsɪv] *adj* impassibile
impatience [ɪmˈpeʃəns] *s* impazienza
impatient [ɪmˈpeʃənt] *adj* impaziente
impeach [ɪmˈpitʃ] *tr* accusare; (*a public official*) sottoporre a un'inchiesta; (*a statement*) mettere in dubbio
impeachment [ɪmˈpitʃmənt] *s* accusa; inchiesta
impeccable [ɪmˈpɛkəbəl] *adj* impeccabile
impecunious [ˌɪmpɪˈkjunɪ·əs] *adj* indigente
impedance [ɪmˈpidəns] *s* impedenza
impede [ɪmˈpid] *tr* impedire, intralciare
impediment [ɪmˈpɛdɪmənt] *s* impedimento; ostacolo
im·pel [ɪmˈpɛl] *v* (*pret & pp* **-peled** or **-pelled;** *ger* **-peling** or **-pelling**) *tr* spingere, forzare
impending [ɪmˈpɛndɪŋ] *adj* imminente, incombente
impenetrable [ɪmˈpɛnətrəbəl] *adj* impenetrabile
impenitent [ɪmˈpɛnɪtənt] *adj* impenitente || *s* persona impenitente
imperative [ɪmˈpɛrɪtɪv] *adj* (*commanding*) imperativo; (*urgent*) imperioso || *s* imperativo
imperceptible [ˌɪmpərˈsɛptɪbəl] *adj* impercettibile
imperfect [ɪmˈpʌrfɪkt] *adj & s* imperfetto
imperfection [ˌɪmpərˈfɛkʃən] *s* imperfezione
imperial [ɪmˈpɪrɪ·əl] *adj* imperiale || *s* (*goatee*) barbetta, mosca; (*top of coach*) imperiale *m*
imperialist [ɪmˈpɪrɪ·əlɪst] *adj & s* imperialista *mf*
imper·il [ɪmˈpɛrɪl] *v* (*pret & pp* **-iled** or **-illed;** *ger* **-iling** or **-illing**) *tr* mettere in pericolo
imperious [ɪmˈpɪrɪ·əs] *adj* imperioso
imperishable [ɪmˈpɛrɪʃəbəl] *adj* imperituro, duraturo
impersonate [ɪmˈpʌrsə ˌnet] *tr* (*to pretend to be*) spacciarsi per; (*on the stage*) impersonare
impertinence [ɪmˈpʌrtɪnəns] *s* impertinenza
impertinent [ɪmˈpʌrtɪnənt] *adj* impertinente
impetuous [ɪmˈpɛtʃʊ·əs] *adj* impetuoso
impetus [ˈɪmpɪtəs] *s* impeto, foga
impie·ty [ɪmˈpaɪ·əti] *s* (**-ties**) empietà *f*
impinge [ɪmˈpɪndʒ] *intr*—**to impinge on** or **upon** violare; (*said, e.g., of the sun*) ferire; (*the imagination*) colpire
impious [ˈɪmpɪ·əs] *adj* empio
impish [ˈɪmpɪʃ] *adj* indiavolato
implant [ɪmˈplænt] *tr* innestare; instillare, istillare
implement [ˈɪmplɪmənt] *s* utensile *m*, strumento || [ˈɪmplɪ ˌmɛnt] *tr* completare, mettere in opera; (*to provide with implements*) attrezzare
implicate [ˈɪmplɪ ˌket] *tr* implicare
implicit [ɪmˈplɪsɪt] *adj* implicito; (*unquestioning*) assoluto, cieco
implied [ɪmˈplaɪd] *adj* implicito
implore [ɪmˈplor] *tr* (*a person; pardon*)

implorare; (*to entreat*) raccomandarsi a
im·ply [ɪm'plaɪ] *v* (*pret & pp* **-plied**) *tr* voler dire, significare; implicare, sottintendere
impolite [,ɪmpə'laɪt] *adj* scortese
import ['ɪmport] *s* importazione; articolo d'importazione; importanza || [ɪm'port] or ['ɪmport] *tr* importare; significare || *intr* importare
importance [ɪm'pɔrtəns] *s* importanza
important [ɪm'pɔrtənt] *adj* importante
importation [,ɪmpor'teʃən] *s* importazione
importer [ɪm'portər] *s* importatore *m*
importunate [ɪm'pɔrtʃənɪt] *adj* importuno
importune [,ɪmpər'tjun] or [,ɪmpər'tun] *tr* importunare
impose [ɪm'poz] *tr* imporre || *intr*—**to impose on** or **upon** abusare di; abusare della gentilezza di
imposing [ɪm'pozɪŋ] *adj* imponente
imposition [,ɪmpə'zɪʃən] *s* imposizione; abuso; abuso della gentilezza; inganno
impossible [ɪm'pɑsɪbəl] *adj* impossibile
impostor [ɪm'pɑstər] *s* impostore *m*
imposture [ɪm'pɑstjər] *s* impostura
impotence ['ɪmpətəns] *s* impotenza
impotent ['ɪmpətənt] *adj* impotente
impound [ɪm'paʊnd] *tr* rinchiudere, recintare; (*water*) raccogliere; (law) sequestrare, confiscare
impoverish [ɪm'pɑvərɪʃ] *tr* impoverire
impracticable [ɪm'præktɪkəbəl] *adj* impraticabile; (*intractable*) intrattabile
impractical [ɪm'præktɪkəl] *adj* poco pratico
impregnable [ɪm'pregnəbəl] *adj* inespugnabile, imprendibile
impregnate [ɪm'pregnet] *tr* impregnare
impresari·o [,ɪmprɪ'sɑrɪ,o] *s* (**-os**) impresario
impress [ɪm'pres] *tr* (*to affect in mind or feelings*) impressionare; (*to produce by pressure; to fix on s.o.'s mind*) imprimere; (mil) arruolare
impression [ɪm'preʃən] *s* impressione
impressionable [ɪm'preʃənəbəl] *adj* impressionabile
impressive [ɪm'presɪv] *adj* impressionante, imponente
imprint ['ɪmprɪnt] *s* impronta; (typ) indicazione dell'editore || [ɪm'prɪnt] *tr* imprimere
imprison [ɪm'prɪzən] *tr* imprigionare
imprisonment [ɪm'prɪzənmənt] *s* prigione, prigionia
improbable [ɪm'prɑbəbəl] *adj* improbabile
impromptu [ɪm'prɑmptju] or [ɪm'prɑmptu] *adj* improvvisato || *s* improvvisazione; (mus) impromptu *m* || *adv* all'improvviso
improper [ɪm'prɑpər] *adj* (*erroneous*) improprio; (*inappropriate; unseemly*) scorretto; (math) improprio
improve [ɪm'pruv] *tr* migliorare; (*an opportunity*) approfittare di || *intr* migliorare; **to improve on** or **upon** perfezionare
improvement [ɪm'pruvmənt] *s* miglioramento, perfezionamento; (*in real estate*) miglioria; (*e.g., of time*) buon uso
improvident [ɪm'prɑvɪdənt] *adj* improvvido, imprevidente
improvise ['ɪmprə,vaɪz] *tr & intr* improvvisare
imprudence [ɪm'prudəns] *s* imprudenza
imprudent [ɪm'prudənt] *adj* imprudente
impudence ['ɪmpjədəns] *s* impudenza, sfrontatezza, sfacciataggine *f*
impudent ['ɪmpjədənt] *adj* sfrontato, sfacciato, spudorato
impugn [ɪm'pjun] *tr* impugnare
impulse ['ɪmpʌls] *s* impulso
impulsive [ɪm'pʌlsɪv] *adj* impulsivo
impunity [ɪm'pjunɪti] *s* impunità *f*
impure [ɪm'pjʊr] *adj* impuro
impuri·ty [ɪm'pjʊrɪti] *s* (**-ties**) impurità *f*
impute [ɪm'pjut] *tr* imputare
in [ɪn] *adj* interno; (coll) moderno, alla moda || *s* relazione; **the ins and outs** tutti i dettagli || *adv* dentro; a casa; in ufficio; **in here** qui dentro; **in there** lì dentro; **to be in** essere a casa; **to be in for** essere destinato a; **to be in with** essere in intimità con || *prep* in; (*within*) dentro a; (*over, through*) per; di, e.g., **the best in the class** il migliore della classe; **dressed in** vestito di; **in so far as** per quanto; **in that** per quanto, dato che
inability [,ɪnə'bɪlɪti] *s* inabilità *f*
inaccessible [,ɪnæk'sesɪbəl] *adj* inaccessibile
inaccura·cy [ɪn'ækjərəsi] *s* (**-cies**) inesattezza, imprecisione
inaccurate [ɪn'ækjərɪt] *adj* inesatto
inaction [ɪn'ækʃən] *s* inazione
inactive [ɪn'æktɪv] *adj* inattivo
inadequate [ɪn'ædɪkwɪt] *adj* inadeguato, inadatto
inadvertent [,ɪnəd'vʌrtənt] *adj* disattento; inavvertito
inadvisable [,ɪnəd'vaɪzəbəl] *adj* poco consigliabile
inane [ɪn'en] *adj* insensato, assurdo
inanimate [ɪn'ænɪmɪt] *adj* inanimato
inappreciable [,ɪnə'priʃɪ·əbəl] *adj* inapprezzabile
inappropriate [,ɪnə'proprɪ·ɪt] *adj* non appropriato, improprio
inarticulate [,ɪnɑr'tɪkjəlɪt] *adj* (*sounds, words*) inarticolato; (*person*) incapace di esprimersi
inasmuch as [,ɪnəs'mʌtʃ,æz] *conj* dato che, visto che, in quanto che
inattentive [,ɪnə'tentɪv] *adj* disattento
inaugural [ɪn'ɔgjərəl] *adj* inaugurale || *s* discorso inaugurale
inaugurate [ɪn'ɔgjə,ret] *tr* inaugurare
inauguration [ɪn,ɔgjə'reʃən] *s* inaugurazione; (*investiture of a head of government*) assunzione dei poteri
inborn ['ɪn,bɔrn] *adj* innato, ingenito
inbreeding ['ɪn,bridɪŋ] *s* incrocio fra animali o piante affini
incandescent [,ɪnkən'desənt] *adj* incandescente

incapable [ɪn'kepəbəl] *adj* incapace
incapacitate [,ɪnkə'pæsɪ,tet] *tr* inabilitare; (law) interdire
incapaci·ty [,ɪnkə'pæsɪti] *s* **(-ties)** incapacità *f*
incarcerate [ɪn'kɑrsə,ret] *tr* incarcerare
incarnate [ɪn'kɑrnɪt] or [ɪn'kɑrnet] *adj* incarnato || [ɪn'kɑrnet] *tr* incarnare
incarnation [,ɪnkɑr'neʃən] *s* incarnazione
incendiarism [ɪn'sɛndɪ·ə,rɪzəm] *s* incendio doloso; (*agitation*) sobillazione
incendiar·y [ɪn'sɛndɪ,ɛri] *adj* incendiario || *s* **(-ies)** incendiario; (fig) sobillatore *m*
incense ['ɪnsɛns] *s* incenso || *tr* (*to burn incense for*) incensare || [ɪn'sɛns] *tr* irritare, esasperare
in'cense burn'er *s* (*person*) incensatore *m;* (*vessel*) incensiere *m*
incentive [ɪn'sɛntɪv] *adj & s* incentivo
inception [ɪn'sɛpʃən] *s* principio
incertitude [ɪn'sʌrtɪ,tjud] or [ɪn'sʌrtɪ,tud] *s* incertezza
incest ['ɪnsɛst] *s* incesto
incestuous [ɪn'sɛstʃʊ·əs] *adj* incestuoso
inch [ɪntʃ] *s* pollice *m;* **to be within an inch of** essere a due dita da || *intr*—**to inch ahead** spingersi avanti poco a poco
incidence ['ɪnsɪdəns] *s* incidenza
incident ['ɪnsɪdənt] *adj* incidente, incidentale || *s* incidente *m*
incidental [,ɪnsɪ'dɛntəl] *adj* incidentale || *s* elemento incidentale; **incidentals** piccole spese
incidentally [,ɪnsɪ'dɛntəli] *adv* incidentalmente, per inciso; a proposito
incinerator [ɪn'sɪnə,retər] *s* inceneritore *m*
incision [ɪn'sɪʒən] *s* incisione
incisive [ɪn'saɪsɪv] *adj* incisivo
incite [ɪn'saɪt] *tr* incitare, stimulare
inclemen·cy [ɪn'klɛmənsi] *s* **(-cies)** inclemenza
inclination [,ɪnklɪ'neʃən] *s* inclinazione
incline ['ɪnklaɪn] or [ɪn'klaɪn] *s* declivio || [ɪn'klaɪn] *tr* inclinare || *intr* inclinarsi
inclose [ɪn'kloz] *tr* includere, accludere; **to inclose herewith** accludere alla presente
inclosure [ɪn'kloʒər] *s* (*land surrounded by fence*) recinto; (*e.g., letter*) allegato
include [ɪn'klud] *tr* includere; **including** incluso, e.g., **three books including the grammar** tre libri inclusa la grammatica
inclusive [ɪn'klusɪv] *adj* incluso, e.g., **until next Friday inclusive** fino a venerdì prossimo incluso; **inclusive of** inclusivo di, e.g., **price inclusive of freight** prezzo inclusivo delle spese di trasporto
incogni·to [ɪn'kɑgnɪ,to] *adj* incognito || *s* **(-tos)** incognito || *adv* in incognito
incoherent [,ɪnko'hɪrənt] *adj* incoerente
incombustible [,ɪnkəm'bʌstɪbəl] *adj* incombustibile
income ['ɪnkʌm] *s* reddito, provento
in'come tax' *s* imposta sul reddito
incoming ['ɪn,kʌmɪŋ] *adj* entrante; futuro; (*tide*) ascendente || *s* entrata
incomparable [ɪn'kɑmpərəbəl] *adj* incomparabile, impareggiabile
incompatible [,ɪnkəm'pætɪbəl] *adj* incompatibile
incomplete [,ɪnkəm'plit] *adj* incompleto, tronco, scompleto
incomprehensible [,ɪnkɑmprɪ'hɛnsɪbəl] *adj* incomprensibile
inconceivable [,ɪnkən'sivəbəl] *adj* inconcepibile
inconclusive [,ɪnkən'klusɪv] *adj* inconcludente
incongruous [ɪn'kɑŋgrʊ·əs] *adj* incongruo
inconsequential [ɪn,kɑnsɪ'kwɛnʃəl] *adj* (*lacking proper sequence of thought or speech*) inconseguente; (*trivial*) di poca importanza
inconsiderate [,ɪnkən'sɪdərɪt] *adj* inconsiderato, sconsiderato
inconsisten·cy [,ɪnkən'sɪstənsi] *s* **(-cies)** inconsistenza
inconsistent [,ɪnkən'sɪstənt] *adj* inconsistente, inconseguente
inconsolable [,ɪnkən'soləbəl] *adj* inconsolabile, sconsolato
inconspicuous [,ɪnkən'spɪkjʊ·əs] *adj* poco appariscente, poco apparente
inconstant [ɪn'kɑnstənt] *adj* incostante
incontinence [ɪn'kɑntɪnəns] *s* incontinenza
incontrovertible [,ɪnkɑntrə'vʌrtɪbəl] *adj* incontrovertibile
inconvenience [,ɪnkən'vinɪ·əns] *s* scomodo, incomodo || *tr* scomodare
inconvenient [,ɪnkən'vinɪ·ənt] *adj* incomodo, inconveniente
incorporate [ɪn'kɔrpə,ret] *tr* incorporare; costituire in società anonima || *intr* incorporarsi; costituirsi in società anonima
incorrect [,ɪnkə'rɛkt] *adj* scorretto
increase ['ɪnkris] *s* aumento; crescita; **to be on the increase** essere in aumento || [ɪn'kris] *tr* aumentare; (*by propagation*) moltiplicare || *intr* aumentare; moltiplicarsi
increasingly [ɪn'krisɪŋli] *adv* sempre più
incredible [ɪn'krɛdɪbəl] *adj* incredibile
incredulous [ɪn'krɛdʒələs] *adj* incredulo
increment ['ɪnkrɪmənt] *s* aumento, incremento
incriminate [ɪn'krɪmɪ,net] *tr* incriminare
incrust [ɪn'krʌst] *tr* incrostare
incubate ['ɪnkjə,bet] *tr* incubare || *intr* essere in incubazione; (*said, e.g., of a hen*) covare; (fig) covare
incubator ['ɪnkjə,betər] *s* incubatrice *f*
inculcate [ɪn'kʌlket] or ['ɪnkʌl,ket] *tr* inculcare

incumben·cy [ɪn'kʌmbənsi] *s* **(-cies)** incombenza
incumbent [ɪn'kʌmbənt] *adj*—**to be incumbent on** incombere a, spettare a || *s* titolare *mf*
incunabula [,ɪnkjʊ'næbjələ] *spl* (*beginnings*) origini *fpl;* (*early printed books*) incunaboli *mpl*
in·cur [ɪn'kʌr] *v* (*pret & pp* **-curred;** *ger* **-curring**) *tr* incorrere in; (*a debt*) assumere, contrarre
incurable [ɪn'kjʊrəbəl] *adj & s* incurabile *mf*
incursion [ɪn'kʌrʒən] or [ɪn'kʌrʃən] *s* incursione, scorreria
indebted [ɪn'dɛtɪd] *adj* indebitato; obbligato
indecen·cy [ɪn'disənsi] *s* **(-cies)** indecenza, sconcezza
indecent [ɪn'disənt] *adj* indecente, sconveniente
indecisive [,ɪndɪ'saɪsɪv] *adj* indeciso; (*e.g., event*) non decisivo
indeed [ɪn'did] *adv* difatti, infatti || *interj* davvero!
indefatigable [,ɪndɪ'fætɪgəbəl] *adj* indefesso, infaticabile
indefensible [,ɪndɪ'fensɪbəl] *adj* indifendibile, insostenibile
indefinable [ɪndɪ'fainəbəl] *adj* indefinibile
indefinite [ɪn'defɪinɪt] *adj* indefinito
indelible [ɪn'dɛlɪbəl] *adj* indelebile
indemnification [ɪn,dɛmnɪfɪ'keʃən] *s* indennità *f*, indennizzo
indemni·fy [ɪn'dɛmnɪ,faɪ] *v* (*pret & pp* **-fied**) *tr* indennizzare
indemni·ty [ɪn'dɛmnɪti] *s* **(-ties)** indennità *f*, indennizzo
indent [ɪn'dent] *tr* frastagliare, dentellare; (typ) far rientrare
indentation [,ɪnden'teʃən] *s* frastaglio, dentellatura; (typ) accapo
indenture [ɪn'dentʃər] *s* scrittura pubblica; contratto di apprendista || *tr* obbligare per contratto
independence [,ɪndɪ'pendəns] *s* indipendenza
independent [,ɪndɪ'pendənt] *adj & s* indipendente *mf*
indescribable [,ɪndɪ'skraɪbəbəl] *adj* indescrivibile
indestructible [,ɪndɪ'strʌktɪbəl] *adj* indistruttibile
indeterminate [,ɪndɪ'tʌrmɪnɪt] *adj* indeterminato
index ['ɪndɛks] *s* **(indexes** or **indices** ['ɪndɪ,siz]) indice *m;* (typ) indice *m* indicatore || *tr* mettere un indice a; mettere all'indice || **Index** *s* Indice *m*
in'dex card' *s* scheda di catalogo
in'dex fin'ger *s* dito indice
India ['ɪndɪ·ə] *s* l'India *f*
In'dia ink' *s* inchiostro di china
Indian ['ɪndɪ·ən] *adj & s* indiano
In'dian club' *s* clava di ginnastica
In'dian corn' *s* granoturco
In'dian file' *s* fila indiana || *adv* in fila indiana
In'dian O'cean *s* Oceano Indiano
In'dian sum'mer *s* estate *f* di San Martino
In'dian wres'tling *s* braccio di ferro
In'dia pa'per *s* carta bibbia, carta d'India
In'dia rub'ber *s* caucciù *m*
indicate ['ɪndɪ,ket] *tr* indicare
indication [,ɪndɪ'keʃən] *s* indicazione
indicative [ɪn'dɪkətɪv] *adj & s* indicativo
indicator ['ɪndɪ,ketər] *s* indicatore *m*, indice *m*
indict [ɪn'daɪt] *tr* accusare
indictment [ɪn'daɪtmənt] *s* accusa, atto d'accusa
indifferent [ɪn'dɪfərənt] *adj* indifferente; (*not particularly good*) passabile
indigenous [ɪn'dɪdʒɪnəs] *adj* indigeno
indigent ['ɪndɪdʒənt] *adj* indigente || **the indigent** gli indigenti
indigestion [,ɪndɪ'dʒɛstʃən] *s* indigestione
indignant [ɪn'dɪgnənt] *adj* indignato
indignation [,ɪndɪg'neʃən] *s* indignazione
indigni·ty [ɪn'dɪgnɪti] *s* **(-ties)** indignità *f*
indi·go ['ɪndɪ,go] *adj* indaco || *s* **(-gos** or **-goes)** indaco
indirect [,ɪndɪ'rɛkt] or [,ɪndaɪ'rɛkt] *adj* indiretto
in'direct dis'course *s* discorso indiretto
indiscernible [,ɪndɪ'zʌrnɪbəl] or [,ɪndɪ'sʌrnɪbəl] *adj* indiscernibile
indiscreet [,ɪndɪs'krit] *adj* indiscreto
indispensable [,ɪndɪs'pensəbəl] *adj* indispensabile, imprescindibile
indispose [,ɪndɪs'poz] *tr* indisporre
indisposed [,ɪndɪs'pozd] *adj* (*disinclined*) mal disposto; (*slightly ill*) indisposto
indissoluble [,ɪndɪ'sɑljəbəl] *adj* indissolubile
indistinct [,ɪndɪ'stɪŋkt] *adj* indistinto
indite [ɪn'daɪt] *tr* redigere
individual [,ɪndɪ'vɪdʒʊ·əl] *adj* individuale || *s* individuo
individuali·ty [,ɪndɪ,vɪdʒʊ'ælɪti] *s* **(-ties)** individualità *f;* (*person of distinctive character*) individuo
Indochina ['ɪndo'tʃaɪnə] *s* l'Indocina *f*
Indo-Chi·nese ['ɪndotʃaɪ'niz] *adj* indocinese || *s* **(-nese)** indocinese *mf*
Indo-European ['ɪndo,jʊrə'pi·ən] *adj & s* indoeuropeo
indolent ['ɪndələnt] *adj* indolente
Indonesia [,ɪndo'niʃə] or [,ɪndo'niʒə] *s* l'Indonesia *f*
Indonesian [,ɪndo'niʃən] or [,ɪndo'niʒən] *adj & s* indonesiano
indoor ['ɪn,dor] *adj* situato in casa; da farsi in casa
indoors ['ɪn'dorz] *adv* dentro, a casa, al coperto
indorse [ɪn'dɔrs] *tr* (com) girare; (fig) appoggiare, approvare
indorsee [,ɪndɔr'si] *s* giratario
indorsement [ɪn'dɔrsmənt] *s* (com) girata; (fig) appoggio, approvazione
indorser [ɪn'dɔrsər] *s* girante *mf*
induce [ɪn'djus] or [ɪn'dus] *tr* indurre
inducement [ɪn'djusmənt] or [ɪn'dusmənt] *s* stimolo, incentivo

induct [ɪn'dʌkt] *tr* installare; iniziare; (mil) arruolare
induction [ɪn'dʌkʃən] *s* iniziazione; (elec & log) induzione; (mil) arruolamento
indulge [ɪn'dʌldʒ] *tr* indulgere (with *dat*) || *intr* cedere, lasciarsi andare; **to indulge in** abbandonarsi a; permettersi il lusso di
indulgence [ɪn'dʌldʒəns] *s* compiacenza; intemperanza, abbandono; (*leniency*) indulgenza
indulgent [ɪn'dʌldʒənt] *adj* indulgente
industrial [ɪn'dʌstrɪ·əl] *adj* industriale
industrialist [ɪn'dʌstrɪ·əlɪst] *s* industriale *m*
industrialize [ɪn'dʌstrɪ·ə,laɪz] *tr* industrializzare
industrious [ɪn'dʌstrɪ·əs] *adj* industrioso, laborioso
indus·try ['ɪndʌstri] *s* **(-tries)** industria
inebriation [ɪn,ibrɪ'eʃən] *s* ubriachezza
inedible [ɪn'edɪbəl] *adj* immangiabile
ineffable [ɪn'efəbəl] *adj* ineffabile
ineffective [,ɪnɪ'fektɪv] *adj* inefficace; (*person*) incapace
ineffectual [,ɪnɪ'fektʃʊ·əl] *adj* inefficace
inefficient [,ɪnɪ'fɪʃənt] *adj* inefficiente
ineligible [ɪn'elɪdʒɪbəl] *adj* ineleggibile
inequali·ty [,ɪnɪ'kwɑlɪti] *s* **(-ties)** disuguaglianza
inequi·ty [ɪn'ekwɪti] *s* **(-ties)** ingiustizia
ineradicable [,ɪnɪ'rædɪkəbəl] *adj* inestirpabile
inertia [ɪn'ʌrʃe] *s* inerzia
inescapable [,ɪnes'kepəbəl] *adj* ineluttabile, inderogabile
inevitable [ɪn'evɪtəbəl] *adj* inevitabile
inexact [,ɪneg'zækt] *adj* inesatto
inexcusable [,ɪneks'kjuzəbəl] *adj* inescusabile
inexhaustible [,ɪneg'zɔstɪbəl] *adj* inesauribile
inexorable [ɪn'eksərəbəl] *adj* inesorabile
inexpedient [,ɪnek'spidɪ·ənt] *adj* inopportuno
inexpensive [,ɪnek'spensɪv] *adj* poco costoso, a buon mercato
inexperience [,ɪnek'spɪrɪ·əns] *s* inesperienza
inexplicable [ɪn'eksplɪkəbəl] *adj* inesplicabile
inexpressible [,ɪnek'spresɪbəl] *adj* indicibile, inesprimibile
infallible [ɪn'fælɪbəl] *adj* infallibile
infamous ['ɪnfəməs] *adj* infame
infa·my ['ɪnfəmi] *s* **(-mies)** infamia
infan·cy ['ɪnfənsi] *s* **(-cies)** infanzia
infant ['ɪnfənt] *adj* infantile; (*in the earliest stage*) (fig) nascente || *s* neonato, bebè *m*
infantile ['ɪnfən,taɪl] or ['ɪnfəntɪl] *adj* infantile
infan·try ['ɪnfəntri] *s* **(-tries)** fanteria
in'fantry·man *s* **(-men)** fante *m*
infatuated [ɪn'fætʃʊ,etɪd] *adj* infatuato
infect [ɪn'fekt] *tr* infettare
infection [ɪn'fekʃən] *s* infezione
infectious [ɪn'fekʃəs] *adj* infettivo
in·fer [ɪn'fʌr] *v* (*pret & pp* **-ferred;** *ger* **-ferring**) *tr* inferire; (coll) dedurre, supporre
inferior [ɪn'fɪrɪ·ər] *adj & s* inferiore *m*
inferiority [ɪn,fɪrɪ'ɑrɪti] *s* inferiorità *f*
inferior'ity com'plex *s* complesso di inferiorità
infernal [ɪn'fʌrnəl] *adj* infernale
infest [ɪn'fest] *tr* infestare
infidel ['ɪnfɪdəl] *adj & s* infedele *mf*
infideli·ty [,ɪnfɪ'delɪti] *s* **(-ties)** infedeltà *f*
in'field' *s* campo interno, diamante *m*
infiltrate [ɪn'fɪltret] or ['ɪnfɪl,tret] *tr* infiltrarsi in || *intr* infiltrarsi
infinite ['ɪnfɪnɪt] *adj & s* infinito
infinitive [ɪn'fɪnɪtɪv] *adj* infinitivo || *s* infinito
infini·ty [ɪn'fɪnɪti] *s* **(-ties)** infinità *f;* (math) infinito
infirm [ɪn'fʌrm] *adj* infermo; (*not firm*) debole
infirma·ry [ɪn'fʌrməri] *s* **(-ries)** infermeria
infirmi·ty [ɪn'fʌrmɪti] *s* **(-ties)** infermità *f*
inflame [ɪn'flem] *tr* infiammare || *intr* infiammarsi
inflammable [ɪn'flæməbəl] *adj* infiammabile
inflammation [,ɪnflə'meʃən] *s* infiammazione
inflate [ɪn'flet] *tr* gonfiare; (*currency, prices*) inflazionare || *intr* gonfiarsi
inflation [ɪn'fleʃən] *s* inflazione; (*of a tire*) gonfiatura
inflect [ɪn'flekt] *tr* curvare; (*voice*) modulare; (gram) flettere
inflection [ɪn'flekʃən] *s* inflessione; (gram) flessione
inflexible [ɪn'fleksɪbəl] *adj* inflessibile
inflict [ɪn'flɪkt] *tr* infliggere, inferire
influence ['ɪnflu·əns] *s* influenza || *tr* influire su, influenzare
influential [,ɪnflu'enʃəl] *adj* influente
influenza [,ɪnflu'enzə] *s* influenza
inform [ɪn'fɔrm] *tr* informare || *intr* dare informazioni; **to inform on** denunziare, fare la spia contro
informal [ɪn'fɔrməl] *adj* non ufficiale, ufficioso; (*unceremonious*) alla buona, familiare
informant [ɪn'fɔrmənt] *s* informatore *m;* (*informer*) delatore *m;* (ling) fonte *f* orale, informatore *m*
information [,ɪnfər'meʃən] *s* informazioni *fpl;* conoscenze *fpl*
informational [,ɪnfər'meʃənəl] *adj* informativo
informed' sour'ces *spl* fonti *fpl* attendibili
informer [ɪn'fɔrmər] *s* (*informant*) informatore *m;* (*spy*) delatore *m*
infraction [ɪn'frækʃən] *s* infrazione
infrared [,ɪnfrə'red] *adj & s* infrarosso
infrequent [ɪn'frikwənt] *adj* infrequente
infringe [ɪn'frɪndʒ] *tr* violare || *intr*—**to infringe on** or **upon** violare, contravvenire a
infringement [ɪn'frɪndʒmənt] *s* infrazione

infuriate [ɪn'fjʊrɪ,et] *tr* infuriare
infuse [ɪn'fjuz] *tr* infondere
infusion [ɪn'fjuʒən] *s* infusione
ingenious [ɪn'dʒinjəs] *adj* ingegnoso
ingenui·ty [,ɪndʒɪ'nu·ɪti] or [,ɪndʒɪ'nju·ɪti] *s* **(-ties)** ingegnosità *f*
ingenuous [ɪn'dʒɛnjʊ·əs] *adj* ingenuo
ingenuousness [ɪn'dʒɛnjʊ·əsnɪs] *s* ingenuità *f*
ingest [ɪn'dʒɛst] *tr* ingerire
ingoing ['ɪn,goɪŋ] *adj* entrante
ingot ['ɪŋgət] *s* lingotto, massello
ingraft [ɪn'græft] or [ɪn'grɑft] *tr* (hort & surg) innestare; (fig) inculcare
ingrate ['ɪngret] *s* ingrato
ingratiate [ɪn'greʃɪ,et] *tr*—**to ingratiate oneself with** ingraziarsi
ingratiating [ɪn'greʃɪ,etɪŋ] *adj* attraente, affascinante, insinuante
ingratitude [ɪn'grætɪ,tjud] or [ɪn'grætɪ,tud] *s* ingratitudine *f*
ingredient [ɪn'gridɪ·ənt] *s* ingrediente *m*
in'grown nail' ['ɪngron] *s* unghia incarnita
ingulf [ɪn'gʌlf] *tr* sommergere, inondare
inhabit [ɪn'hæbɪt] *tr* abitare, popolare
inhabitant [ɪn'hæbɪtənt] *s* abitante *mf*
inhale [ɪn'hel] *tr & intr* inspirare
inherent [ɪn'hɪrənt] *adj* inerente
inherit [ɪn'hɛrɪt] *tr & intr* ereditare
inheritance [ɪn'hɛrɪtəns] *s* eredità *f*
inheritor [ɪn'hɛrɪtər] *s* erede *mf*
inhibit [ɪn'hɪbɪt] *tr* inibire
inhospitable [ɪn'hɑspɪtəbəl] or [,ɪnhɑs'pɪtəbəl] *adj* inospitale
inhuman [ɪn'hjumən] *adj* inumano
inhumane [,ɪnhju'men] *adj* inumano
inimical [ɪ'nɪmɪkəl] *adj* nemico
iniqui·ty [ɪ'nɪkwɪti] *s* **(-ties)** iniquità *f*
ini·tial [ɪ'nɪʃəl] *adj & s* iniziale *f* || *v* (*pret* **-tialed** or **-tialled**; *ger* **-tialing** or **-tialling**) *tr* siglare
initiate [ɪ'nɪʃɪ,et] *tr* iniziare
initiation [ɪ,nɪʃɪ'eʃən] *s* iniziazione
initiative [ɪ'nɪʃɪ·ətɪv] or [ɪ'nɪʃətɪv] *s* iniziativa
inject [ɪn'dʒɛkt] *tr* iniettare; introdurre
injection [ɪn'dʒɛkʃən] *s* iniezione
injudicious [,ɪndʒu'dɪʃəs] *adj* avventato, sconsiderato
injunction [ɪn'dʒʌŋkʃən] *s* ingiunzione
injure ['ɪndʒər] *tr* (*to harm*) danneggiare; (*to wound*) ferire; (*to offend*) offendere, ingiuriare
injurious [ɪn'dʒʊrɪ·əs] *adj* dannoso; offensivo, ingiurioso
inju·ry ['ɪndʒəri] *s* **(-ries)** (*harm*) danno; (*wound*) ferita, lesione; offesa, ingiuria
injustice [ɪn'dʒʌstɪs] *s* ingiustizia
ink [ɪŋk] *s* inchiostro || *tr* inchiostrare
inkling ['ɪŋklɪŋ] *s* sentore *m*, indizio
ink'stand' *s* (*container*) calamaio; (*stand*) calamaiera
ink'well' *s* calamaio
ink·y ['ɪŋki] *adj* **(-ier; -iest)** nero come l'inchiostro; nero d'inchiostro
inlaid ['ɪn,led] or [,ɪn'led] *adj* intarsiato, incrostato
inland ['ɪnlənd] *adj & s* interno || *adv* verso l'interno
in'-law' *s* affine *mf*
in·lay ['ɪn,le] *s* intarsio, tassello || [ɪn'le] or ['ɪn,le] *v* (*pret & pp* **-laid**) *tr* intarsiare
in'let *s* (*of the shore*) insenatura; (*entrance*) ammissione
in'mate' *s* (*patient, e.g., in an insane asylum*) internato; (*in a jail*) prigioniero
inn [ɪn] *s* taverna, osteria
innate [ɪ'net] or ['ɪnet] *adj* innato
inner ['ɪnər] *adj* interno, interiore; intimo, profondo
in'ner·spring' mat'tress *s* materasso a molle
in'ner tube' *s* camera d'aria
inning ['ɪnɪŋ] *s* (baseball) turno
inn'keep'er *s* locandiere *m*, oste *m*
innocence ['ɪnəsəns] *s* innocenza
innocent ['ɪnəsənt] *adj & s* innocente *mf*
innovate ['ɪnə,vet] *tr* innovare
innovation [,ɪnə'veʃən] *s* innovazione
innuen·do [,ɪnjʊ'ɛndo] *s* **(-does)** sottinteso, insinuazione
innumerable [ɪ'njumərəbəl] or [ɪ'numərəbəl] *adj* innumerevole
inoculate [ɪn'ɑkjə,let] *tr* inoculare; (*e.g., with hatred*) inoculare; permeare
inoculation [ɪn,ɑkjə'leʃən] *s* inoculazione
inoffensive [,ɪnə'fɛnsɪv] *adj* inoffensivo
inopportune [ɪn,ɑpər'tjun] or [ɪn,ɑpər'tun] *adj* inopportuno
inordinate [ɪn'ɔrdɪnɪt] *adj* smoderato
inorganic [,ɪnɔr'gænɪk] *adj* inorganico
in'pa'tient *s* degente *mf*
in'put' *s* entrata; (elec, mach) energia immessa
inquest ['ɪnkwɛst] *s* inchiesta
inquire [ɪn'kwaɪr] *tr* domandare, chiedere || *intr*—**to inquire about, after, or for** chiedere di; **to inquire into** investigare
inquir·y [ɪn'kwaɪri] or ['ɪnkwɪri] *s* **(-ies)** indagine *f*, inchiesta
inquisition [,ɪnkwɪ'zɪʃən] *s* inquisizione
inquisitive [ɪn'kwɪzɪtɪv] *adj* indagatore, curioso
in'road' *s* incursione, invasione
insane [ɪn'sen] *adj* pazzo, matto
insane' asy'lum *s* manicomio
insani·ty [ɪn'sænɪti] *s* **(-ties)** pazzia, follia, demenza
insatiable [ɪn'seʃəbəl] *adj* insaziabile
inscribe [ɪn'skraɪb] *tr* iscrivere; (*a book*) dedicare; (geom) inscrivere
inscription [ɪn'skrɪpʃən] *s* scritta, iscrizione; (*of a book*) dedica
inscrutable [ɪn'skrutəbəl] *adj* imperscrutabile
insect ['ɪnsɛkt] *s* insetto
insecticide [ɪn'sɛktɪ,saɪd] *adj & s* insetticida *m*
insecure [,ɪnsɪ'kjʊr] *adj* malsicuro
inseparable [ɪn'sɛpərəbəl] *adj* inseparabile

insert [ˈɪnsʌrt] *s* inserzione; (*circular*) inserto || [ɪnˈsʌrt] *tr* inserire
insertion [ɪnˈsʌrʃən] *s* inserzione; (*in lunar orbit*) immissione; (*of lace*) tramezzo
in·set [ˈɪn,sɛt] *s* intercalazione || [ɪnˈsɛt] or [ˈɪn,sɛt] *v* (*pret & pp* **-set**; *ger* **-setting**) *tr* intercalare
in'shore' *adj & adv* vicino alla spiaggia
in'side' *adj* interno; privato, confidenziale || *s* interno; **insides** (coll) interiora *fpl;* **to be on the inside** avere informazioni confidenziali || *adv* dentro; all'interno; **inside of** dentro, dentro a, dentro di; **to turn inside out** rovesciare, voltare il diritto al rovescio || *prep* dentro, dentro a
in'side flap' *s* (bb) risvolto
insider [,ɪnˈsaɪdər] *s* persona informata
in'side track' *s* (racing) steccato; **to have the inside track** (coll) trovarsi in una situazione vantaggiosa
insidious [ɪnˈsɪdɪ·əs] *adj* insidioso
in'sight' *s* intuito, penetrazione
insigni·a [ɪnˈsɪgnɪ·ə] *s* (**-a** or **-as**) distintivo; (*distinguishing sign*) segno
insignificant [,ɪnsɪgˈnɪfɪkənt] *adj* insignificante
insincere [,ɪnsɪnˈsɪr] *adj* insincero
insinuate [ɪnˈsɪnjʊ,et] *tr* insinuare
insist [ɪnˈsɪst] *intr* insistere
insofar as [,ɪnsoˈfɑr,æz] *conj* per quanto
insolence [ˈɪnsələns] *s* insolenza
insolent [ˈɪnsələnt] *adj* insolente
insoluble [ɪnˈsɑljəbəl] *adj* insolubile
insolven·cy [ɪnˈsɑlvənsi] *s* (**-cies**) insolvenza
insomnia [ɪnˈsɑmnɪ·ə] *s* insonnia
insomuch [,ɪnsoˈmʌtʃ] *adv* fino al punto; **insomuch as** giacché, visto che; **insomuch that** fino al punto che
inspect [ɪnˈspɛkt] *tr* ispezionare
inspection [ɪnˈspɛkʃən] *s* ispezione
inspector [ɪnˈspɛktər] *s* ispettore *m*
inspiration [,ɪnspɪˈreʃən] *s* ispirazione
inspire [ɪnˈspaɪr] *tr & intr* ispirare
install [ɪnˈstɔl] *tr* istallare
installment [ɪnˈstɔlmənt] *s* rata; (*of a book*) dispensa; **in installments** a rate
install'ment plan' *s* pagamento rateale; **on the installment plan** con facilitazioni di pagamento
instance [ˈɪnstəns] *s* esempio; (law) istanza; **for instance** per esempio
instant [ˈɪnstənt] *adj* istantaneo || *s* istante *m;* mese *m* corrente
instantaneous [,ɪnstənˈtenɪ·əs] *adj* istantaneo
instantly [ˈɪnstəntli] *adv* immediatamente, istantaneamente
instead [ɪnˈstɛd] *adv* invece; **instead of** invece di
in'step' *s* collo del piede
instigate [ˈɪnstɪ,get] *tr* istigare
instigation [,ɪnstɪˈgeʃən] *s* istigazione
in·still' *tr* instillare, istillare
instinct [ˈɪnstɪŋkt] *s* istinto
instinctive [ɪnˈstɪŋktɪv] *adj* istintivo
institute [ˈɪnstɪ,tjut] or [ˈɪnstɪ,tut] *s* istituto || *tr* istituire
institution [,ɪnstɪˈtjuʃən] or [,ɪnstɪˈtuʃən] *s* istituzione
institutionalize [,ɪnstɪˈtjuʃənə,laɪz] or [,ɪnstɪˈtuʃənə,laɪz] *tr* istituzionalizzare
instruct [ɪnˈstrʌkt] *tr* istruire
instruction [ɪnˈstrʌkʃən] *s* istruzione
instructive [ɪnˈstrʌktɪv] *adj* istruttivo
instructor [ɪnˈstrʌktər] *s* istruttore *m*
instrument [ˈɪnstrəmənt] *s* strumento; (law) istrumento || [ˈɪnstrə,mɛnt] *tr* strumentare
instrumental [,ɪnstrəˈmɛntəl] *adj* strumentale; **to be instrumental in** contribuire a
instrumentalist [,ɪnstrəˈmɛntəlɪst] *s* strumentista *mf*
instrumentali·ty [,ɪnstrəmənˈtælɪti] *s* (**-ties**) mediazione, aiuto
in'strument fly'ing *s* volo strumentale
in'strument pan'el *s* (aut) cruscotto
insubordinate [,ɪnsəˈbɔrdɪnɪt] *adj* insubordinato
insufferable [ɪnˈsʌfərəbəl] *adj* insoffribile
insufficient [,ɪnsəˈfɪʃənt] *adj* insufficiente
insular [ˈɪnsələr] or [ˈɪnsjʊlər] *adj* insulare; (*e.g., attitude*) gretto
insulate [ˈɪnsə,let] *tr* isolare
in'sulating tape' [ˈɪnsəletɪŋ] *s* nastro isolante
insulation [,ɪnsəˈleʃən] *s* isolamento
insulator [ˈɪnsə,letər] *s* isolatore *m*
insulin [ˈɪnsəlɪn] *s* insulina
insult [ˈɪnsʌlt] *s* insulto || [ɪnˈsʌlt] *tr* insultare, insolentire
insulting [ɪnˈsʌltɪŋ] *adj* insultante
insurance [ɪnˈʃʊrəns] *s* assicurazione
insure [ɪnˈʃʊr] *tr* assicurare
insurer [ɪnˈʃʊrər] *s* assicuratore *m*
insurgent [ɪnˈsʌrdʒənt] *adj & s* insorgente *mf*
insurmountable [,ɪnsərˈmaʊntəbəl] *adj* insormontabile
insurrection [,ɪnsəˈrɛkʃən] *s* insurrezione
insusceptible [,ɪnsəˈsɛptɪbəl] *adj* non suscettibile
intact [ɪnˈtækt] *adj* intatto, integro
in'take' *s* (*place of taking in*) entrata; (*act of taking in*) ammissione; (mach) presa, immissione, aspirazione
in'take man'ifold' *s* collettore *m* d'ammissione
intangible [ɪnˈtændʒɪbəl] *adj* intangibile; (fig) vago, inafferrabile
integer [ˈɪntɪdʒər] *s* numero intero
integral [ˈɪntɪgrəl] *adj* integrale; (*part of a whole*) integrante || *s* (math) integrale *m*
integration [,ɪntɪˈgreʃən] *s* integrazione
integrity [ɪnˈtɛgrɪti] *s* integrità *f*
intellect [ˈɪntə,lɛkt] *s* intelletto
intellectual [,ɪntəˈlɛktʃʊ·əl] *adj & s* intellettuale *mf*
intelligence [ɪnˈtɛlɪdʒəns] *s* intelligenza; informazione, conoscenza

intel'ligence bu'reau *s* ufficio spionaggi
intel'ligence quo'tient *s* quoziente *m* d'intelligenza
intelligent [ɪn'telɪdʒənt] *adj* intelligente
intelligentsia [ɪn,telɪ'dʒentsɪ·ə] or [ɪn,telɪ'gentsɪ·ə] *s* intellighenzia, intellettualità *f*
intelligible [ɪn'telɪdʒɪbəl] *adj* intelligibile, comprensibile
intemperance [ɪn'tempərəns] *s* intemperanza, sregolatezza
intemperate [ɪn'tempərɪt] *adj* intemperante; (*climate*) rigoroso
intend [ɪn'tend] *tr* intendere, prefiggersi; (*to mean for a particular purpose*) destinare; (*to signify*) voler dire
intendance [ɪn'tendəns] *s* intendenza
intendant [ɪn'tendənt] *s* intendente *m*
intended [ɪn'tendɪd] *adj & s* (coll) promesso, promessa
intense [ɪn'tens] *adj* intenso
intensi·fy [ɪn'tensɪ·faɪ] *v* (*pret & pp* **-fied**) *tr* intensificare, rinforzare; (phot) rinforzare || *intr* intensificarsi, rinforzarsi
intensi·ty [ɪn'tensɪti] *s* (**-ties**) intensità *f*
intensive [ɪn'tensɪv] *adj* intensivo
intent [ɪn'tent] *adj* intento, attento; **intent on** deciso a || *s* (*purpose*) intento, scopo; (*meaning*) significato; **to all intents and purposes** virtualmente, in realtà
intention [ɪn'tenʃən] *s* intenzione
intentional [ɪn'tenʃənəl] *adj* intenzionale, deliberato
intentionally [ɪn'tenʃənəli] *adv* apposta, deliberatamente
in·ter [ɪn'tʌr] *v* (*pret & pp* **-terred;** *ger* **-terring**) *tr* interrare, inumare
interact [,ɪntər'ækt] *intr* esercitare un'azione reciproca
interaction [,ɪntər'ækʃən] *s* azione reciproca
inter·breed [,ɪntər'brid] *s* (*pret & pp* **-bred** ['bred]) *tr* incrociare || *intr* incrociarsi
intercalate [ɪn'tʌrkə,let] *tr* intercalare
intercede [,ɪntər'sid] *intr* intercedere
intercept [,ɪntər'sept] *tr* intercettare
interceptor [,ɪntər'septər] *s* (*person*) intercettatore *m;* (aer) intercettore *m*
interchange ['ɪntər,tʃendʒ] *s* interscambio; (*on a highway*) svincolo autostradale || [,ɪntər'tʃendʒ] *tr* scambiare || *intr* scambiarsi
intercollegiate [,ɪntərkə'lidʒɪ·ɪt] *adj* interscolastico, fra università
intercom ['ɪntər,kɑm] *s* citofono
intercourse ['ɪntər,kors] *s* comunicazione; (*of products, ideas, etc.*) scambio; (*copulation*) copula, coito; **to have intercourse** accoppiarsi sessualmente
intercross [,ɪntər'krɔs] or [,ɪntər'krɑs] *tr* incrociare || *intr* incrociarsi
interdict ['ɪntər,dɪkt] *s* interdetto || [,ɪntər'dɪkt] *tr* interdire; **to interdict s.o. from** + *ger* interdire a qlcu di + *inf*
interest ['ɪntərɪst] or ['ɪntrɪst] *s* interesse *m;* **the interests** i potenti || ['ɪntərɪst], ['ɪntrɪst] or ['ɪntə,rest] *tr* interessare
interested ['ɪntrɪstɪd] or ['ɪntə,restɪd] *adj* interessato
interesting ['ɪntrɪstɪŋ] or ['ɪntə,restɪŋ] *adj* interessante
interfere [,ɪntər'fɪr] *intr* interferire; (sports) ostacolare l'azione; **to interfere with** interferire in
interference [,ɪntər'fɪrəns] *s* interferenza
interim ['ɪntərɪm] *adj* interino || *s* interim *m;* **in the interim** frattanto
interior [ɪn'tɪrɪ·ər] *adj & s* interno
interject [,ɪntər'dʒekt] *tr* interporre || *intr* interporsi
interjection [,ɪntər'dʒekʃən] *s* interposizione; esclamazione; (gram) interiezione
interlard [,ɪntər'lɑrd] *tr* infiorare, lardellare
interline [,ɪntər'laɪn] *tr* scrivere nell'interlinea di; (*a garment*) foderare con ovattina
interlining ['ɪntər,laɪnɪŋ] *s* soppanno
interlink [,ɪntər'lɪŋk] *tr* concatenare
interlock [,ɪntər'lɑk] *tr* connettere || *intr* connettersi
interlope [,ɪntər'lop] *intr* intromettersi; trafficare senza permesso
interloper [,ɪntər'lopər] *s* intruso
interlude ['ɪntər,lud] *s* interludio; (theat) intermezzo
intermarriage [,ɪntər,mærɪdʒ] *s* matrimonio tra consanguinei; matrimonio fra membri di razze diverse
intermediar·y [,ɪntər'midɪ,eri] *adj* intermediario || (**-ies**) *s* intermediario
intermediate [,ɪntər'midɪ·ɪt] *adj* intermedio
interment [ɪn'tʌrmənt] *s* inumazione
intermingle [,ɪntər'mɪŋgəl] *tr* mescolare || *intr* mescolarsi
intermission [,ɪntər'mɪʃən] *s* interruzione; (theat) intervallo
intermittent [,ɪntər'mɪtənt] *adj* intermittente
intermix [,ɪntər'mɪks] *tr* mescolare || *intr* mescolarsi
intern ['ɪntʌrn] *s* interno || [ɪn'tʌrn] *tr* internare
internal [ɪn'tʌrnəl] *adj* interno
inter'nal-combus'tion en'gine *s* motore *m* a combustione interna, motore *m* a scoppio
inter'nal rev'enue *s* fisco
international [,ɪntər'næʃənəl] *adj* internazionale
in'terna'tional date' line' *s* linea del cambiamento di data
internationalize [,ɪntər'næʃənə,laɪz] *tr* internazionalizzare
internecine [,ɪntər'nisɪn] *adj* micidiale, sanguinario
internee [,ɪntʌr'ni] *s* internato
internist [ɪn'tʌrnɪst] *s* internista *mf*
internment [ɪn'tʌrnmənt] *s* internamento
internship ['ɪntʌrn,ʃɪp] *s* tirocinio in un ospedale, internato

interpellate [ˌɪntərˈpelet] or [ɪnˈtʌrpɪˌlet] *tr* interpellare
interplanetary [ˌɪntərˈplænəˌteri] *adj* interplanetario
interplay [ˈɪntərˌple] *s* azione reciproca
interpolate [ɪnˈtʌrpəˌlet] *tr* interpolare
interpose [ˌɪntərˈpoz] *tr* frapporre
interpret [ɪnˈtʌrprɪt] *tr* interpretare
interpreter [ɪnˈtʌrprətər] *s* interprete *mf*
interrogate [ɪnˈterəˌget] *tr & intr* interrogare
interrogation [ɪnˌterəˈgeʃən] *s* interrogazione
interroga'tion mark' or **point'** *s* punto interrogativo
interrupt [ˌɪntəˈrʌpt] *tr* interrompere
interruption [ˌɪntəˈrʌpʃən] *s* interruzione
interscholastic [ˌɪntərskəˈlæstɪk] *adj* interscolastico
intersect [ˌɪntərˈsekt] *tr* intersecare || *intr* intersecarsi
intersection [ˌɪntərˈsekʃən] *s* (*of streets, roads, etc.*) crocevia *m;* (geom) intersezione
intersperse [ˌɪntərˈspʌrs] *tr* cospargere, inframezzare
interstellar [ˌɪntərˈstelər] *adj* interstellare
interstice [ɪnˈtʌrstɪs] *s* interstizio
intertwine [ˌɪntərˈtwaɪn] *tr* intrecciare || *intr* intrecciarsi
interval [ˈɪntərvəl] *s* intervallo; **at intervals** a intervalli; di tanto in tanto
intervene [ˌɪntərˈvin] *intr* intervenire; (*to happen*) succedere
intervening [ˌɪntərˈvinɪŋ] *adj*—**in the intervening time** nel frattempo
intervention [ˌɪntərˈvenʃən] *s* intervenzione
interview [ˈɪntərˌvju] *s* intervista || *tr* intervistare
inter·weave [ˌɪntərˈwiv] *v* (*pret* **-wove** [ˈwov] or **-weaved;** *pp* **-wove, -woven** or **-weaved**) *tr* intessere
intestate [ɪnˈtestet] or [ɪnˈtestɪt] *adj* intestato
intestine [ɪnˈtestɪn] *s* intestino
inthrall [ɪnˈθrɔl] *tr* affascinare, incantare; (*to subjugate*) asservire, soggiogare
inthrone [ɪnˈθron] *tr* mettere sul trono, intronizzare; esaltare, innalzare
intima·cy [ˈɪntɪməsi] *s* (**-cies**) intimità *f*
intimate [ˈɪntɪmɪt] *adj & s* intimo || [ˈɪntɪˌmet] *tr* insinuare
intimation [ˌɪntɪˈmeʃən] *s* insinuazione
intimidate [ɪnˈtɪmɪˌdet] *tr* intimidire
into [ˈɪntu] or [ˈɪntʊ] *prep* in; verso; contro
intolerant [ɪnˈtɑlərənt] *adj & s* intollerante *mf,* insofferente *mf*
intomb [ɪnˈtum] *tr* inumare, seppellire
intombment [ɪnˈtummənt] *s* sepoltura
intonation [ˌɪntoˈneʃən] *s* intonazione
intone [ɪnˈton] *tr* intonare || *intr* salmodiare
intoxicant [ɪnˈtɑksɪkənt] *s* bevanda alcoolica
intoxicate [ɪnˈtɑksɪˌket] *tr* ubriacare; esilarare; (*to poison*) avvelenare, intossicare
intoxication [ɪnˌtɑksɪˈkeʃən] *s* ubriachezza; ebbrezza, allegria; (*poisoning*) avvelenamento, intossicazione
intractable [ɪnˈtræktəbəl] *adj* intrattabile
intransigent [ɪnˈtrænsɪdʒənt] *adj & s* intransigente *mf*
intransitive [ɪnˈtrænsɪtɪv] *adj* intransitivo
intravenous [ˌɪntrəˈvinəs] *adj* intravenoso, endovenoso
intrench [ɪnˈtrentʃ] *tr & intr* var of **entrench**
intrepid [ɪnˈtrepɪd] *adj* intrepido
intrepidity [ˌɪntrɪˈpɪdɪti] *s* intrepidezza
intricate [ˈɪntrɪkɪt] *adj* intricato
intrigue [ɪnˈtrig] or [ˈɪntrig] *s* intrigo; tresca, intrigo amoroso; (theat) intreccio || [ɪnˈtrig] *tr* incuriosire || *intr* intrigare; trescare
intrinsic(al) [ɪnˈtrɪnsɪk(əl)] *adj* intrinseco
introduce [ˌɪntrəˈdjus] or [ˌɪntrəˈdus] *tr* introdurre; (*a product*) lanciare; (*a person*) presentare
introduction [ˌɪntrəˈdʌkʃən] *s* introduzione; presentazione
introductory [ˌɪntrəˈdʌktəri] *adj* introduttivo
introit [ˈɪntro·ɪt] *s* (eccl) introito
introspective [ˌɪntrəˈspektɪv] *adj* introspettivo
introvert [ˈɪntrəˌvʌrt] *adj & s* introverso
intrude [ɪnˈtrud] *intr* intrudersi, intrufolarsi
intruder [ɪnˈtrudər] *s* intruso; importuno
intrusion [ɪnˈtruʒən] *s* intrusione
intrusive [ɪnˈtrusɪv] *adj* invadente
intrust [ɪnˈtrʌst] *tr* affidare, confidare
intuition [ˌɪntʊˈɪʃən] or [ˌɪntjʊˈɪʃən] *s* intuizione, intuito
inundate [ˈɪnənˌdet] *tr* inondare
inundation [ˌɪnənˈdeʃən] *s* inondazione
inure [ɪnˈjʊr] *tr* indurire, assuefare || *intr* entrare in vigore; **to inure to** ridondare in favore di
invade [ɪnˈved] *tr* invadere
invader [ɪnˈvedər] *s* invasore *m*
invalid [ɪnˈvælɪd] *adj* (*non valid*) invalido || [ˈɪnvəlɪd] *adj* (*person*) invalido; (*thing*) povero; (*diet*) per malati || [ˈɪnvəlɪd] *s* invalido
invalidate [ɪnˈvælɪˌdet] *tr* invalidare
invalidity [ˌɪnvəˈlɪdɪtɪ] *s* invalidità *f*
invaluable [ɪnˈvæljʊ·əbəl] *adj* inestimabile, inapprezzabile
invariable [ɪnˈverɪ·əbəl] *adj* invariabile
invasion [ɪnˈveʒən] *s* invasione
invective [ɪnˈvektɪv] *s* invettiva
inveigh [ɪnˈve] *intr*—**to inveigh against** inveire contro
inveigle [ɪnˈvegəl] or [ɪnˈvigəl] *tr* sedurre, abbindolare
invent [ɪnˈvent] *tr* inventare
invention [ɪnˈvenʃən] *s* invenzione

inventiveness [ɪn'vɛntɪvnɪs] *s* inventiva
inventor [ɪn'ventər] *s* inventore *m*
invento·ry ['ɪnvən ,tori] *s* (**-ries**) inventario || *v* (*pret & pp* **-ried**) *tr* inventariare
inverse [ɪn'vʌrs] *adj & s* inverso
inversion [ɪn'vʌrʒən] or [ɪn'vʌrʃən] *s* inversione
invert ['ɪnvʌrt] *s* invertito || [ɪn'vʌrt] *tr* invertire
invertebrate [ɪn'vʌrtɪ ,bret] or [ɪn'vʌrtɪbrɪt] *adj & s* invertebrato
invest [ɪn'vɛst] *tr* investire || *intr* fare un investimento; fare investimenti
investigate [ɪn'vestɪ ,get] *tr* investigare
investigation [ɪn ,vɛstɪ'geʃən] *s* investigazione
investigator [ɪn'vestɪ ,getər] *s* investigatore *m*
investment [ɪn'vestmənt] *s* (*of money*) investimento; (*e.g., with an office*) investitura; (*siege*) assedio
investor [ɪn'vɛstər] *s* investitore *m*
inveterate [ɪn'vɛtərɪt] *adj* inveterato
invidious [ɪn'vɪdɪ·əs] *adj* irritante, odioso
invigorate [ɪn'vɪgə ,ret] *tr* invigorire
invigorating [ɪn'vɪgə ,retɪŋ] *adj* ritemprante, ricostituente, rinforzante
invincible [ɪn'vɪnsɪbəl] *adj* invincibile
invisible [ɪn'vizɪbəl] *adj* invisibile
invis'ible ink' *s* inchiostro simpatico
invitation [,ɪnvɪ'teʃən] *s* invito
invite [ɪn'vaɪt] *tr* invitare
inviting [ɪn'vaɪtɪŋ] *adj* invitante, attrattivo; (*food*) appetitoso; accogliente
invoice ['ɪnvɔɪs] *s* fattura; **as per invoice** secondo fattura || *tr* fatturare
invoke [ɪn'vok] *tr* invocare; (*a spirit*) evocare
involuntary [ɪn'vɑlən ,tɛri] *adj* involontario
involve [ɪn'vɑlv] *tr* involvere, includere; occupare; (*to bring unpleasantness upon*) implicare, coinvolgere; complicare
invulnerable [ɪn'vʌlnərəbəl] *adj* invulnerabile
inward ['ɪnwərd] *adj* interno || *adv* al di dentro, verso l'interno
iodide ['aɪ·ə ,daɪd] *s* ioduro
iodine ['aɪ·ə ,din] *s* iodio || ['aɪ·ə ,daɪn] *s* tintura di iodio
ion ['aɪ·ən] or ['aɪ·ɑn] *s* ione *m*
ionize ['aɪ·ə ,naɪz] *tr* ionizzare
IOU ['aɪ ,o'ju] *s* (letterword) (**I owe you**) cambiale *f*, pagherò *m*
I.Q. ['aɪ'kju] *s* (letterword) (**intelligence quotient**) quoziente *m* d'intelligenza
Iranian [aɪ'renɪ·ən] *adj & s* iraniano
Ira·qi [ɪ'rɑki] *adj* iracheno || *s* (**-qis**) iracheno
irate ['aɪret] or [aɪ'ret] *adj* irato
ire [aɪr] *s* ira, collera
Ireland ['aɪrlənd] *s* l'Irlanda *f*
iris ['aɪrɪs] *s* iride *f*
I'rish·man *s* (**-men**) irlandese *m*
I'rish stew' *s* stufato all'irlandese
I'rish·wom'an *s* (**-wom'en**) irlandese *f*
irk [ʌrk] *tr* infastidire, annoiare
irksome ['ʌrksəm] *adj* fastidioso
iron ['aɪ·ərn] *adj* ferreo || *s* ferro; (*to press clothes*) ferro da stiro; **irons** ferri *mpl;* **strike while the iron is hot** batti il ferro fin ch'è caldo || *tr* (*clothes*) stirare; **to iron out** (*a difficulty*) (coll) appianare
i'ron·bound' *adj* ferrato; (*unyielding*) ferreo, inflessibile; (*rock-bound*) roccioso, scabroso
ironclad ['aɪ·ərn ,klæd] *adj* corazzato, blindato; inflessibile, ferreo
i'ron constitu'tion *s* salute *f* di ferro
i'ron cur'tain *s* cortina di ferro
i'ron horse' *s* locomotiva a vapore
ironic(al) [aɪ'rɑnɪk(əl)] *adj* ironico
ironing ['aɪ·ərnɪŋ] *s* stiratura; roba stirata; roba da stirare
i'roning board' *s* tavolo or asse *m* da stiro
i'ron lung' *s* polmone *m* d'acciaio
i'ron·ware' *s* ferrame *m*
i'ron will' *s* volontà *f* di ferro
i'ron·work' *s* lavoro in ferro; **ironworks** *ssg* ferriera
i'ron-work'er *s* ferraio; metalmeccanico, siderurgico
iro·ny ['aɪrəni] *s* (**-nies**) ironia
irradiate [ɪ'redɪ ,et] *tr* irradiare || *intr* irradiare, irradiarsi
irrational [ɪ'ræʃənəl] *adj* irrazionale
irrecoverable [,ɪrɪ'kʌvərəbəl] *adj* irrecuperabile
irredeemable [,ɪrɪ'diməbəl] *adj* irredimibile
irrefutable [,ɪrɪ'fjutəbəl] *adj* irrefutabile
irregular [ɪ'rɛgjələr] *adj* irregolare || *s* (mil) irregolare *m*
irrelevance [ɪ'rɛləvəns] *s* irrilevanza
irrelevant [ɪ'rɛləvənt] *adj* irrilevante
irreligious [,ɪrɪ'lɪdʒəs] *adj* irreligioso
irremediable [,ɪrɪ'midɪ·əbəl] *adj* irrimediabile
irremovable [,ɪrɪ'muvəbəl] *adj* irremovibile, inamovibile
irreplaceable [,ɪrɪ'plesəbəl] *adj* insostituibile
irrepressible [,ɪrɪ'prɛsɪbəl] *adj* irreprimibile, incontenibile
irreproachable [,ɪrɪ'protʃəbəl] *adj* irreprensibile
irresistible [,ɪrɪ'zɪstɪbəl] *adj* irresistibile
irrespective [,ɪrɪ'spɛktɪv] *adj*—**irrespective of** senza riguardo a
irresponsible [,ɪrɪ'spɑnsɪbəl] *adj* irresponsabile
irretrievable [,ɪrɪ'trivəbəl] *adj* irrecuperabile
irreverent [ɪ'rɛvərənt] *adj* irriverente
irrevocable [ɪ'rɛvəkəbəl] *adj* irrevocabile
irrigate ['ɪrɪ ,get] *tr* irrigare
irrigation [,ɪrɪ'geʃən] *s* irrigazione
irritant ['ɪrɪtənt] *adj & s* irritante *m*
irritate ['ɪrɪ ,tet] *tr* irritare
irritation [,ɪrɪ'teʃən] *s* irritazione
irruption [ɪ'rʌpʃən] *s* irruzione
isinglass ['aɪzɪŋ ,glæs] or ['aɪzɪŋ ,glɑs] *s* (*gelatine*) colla di pesce; mica
Islam ['ɪsləm] or [ɪs'lɑm] *s* l'Islam *m*

island ['aɪlənd] *adj* isolano || *s* isola; (*for safety of pedestrians*) salvagente *m*
islander ['aɪləndər] *s* isolano
isle [aɪl] *s* isoletta
isolate ['aɪsə,let] or ['ɪsə,let] *tr* isolare
isolation [,aɪsə'leʃən] or [,ɪsə'leʃən] *s* isolamento
isolationist [,aɪsə'leʃənɪst] or [,ɪsə'leʃənɪst] *s* isolazionista *mf*
isosceles [aɪ'sɑsə,liz] *adj* isoscele
isotope ['aɪsə,top] *s* isotopo
Israel ['ɪzrɪ·əl] *s* l'Israele *m*
Israe•li [ɪz'reli] *adj* israeliano || *s* (**-lis** [liz]) israeliano
Israelite ['ɪzrɪ·ə,laɪt] *adj & s* israelita *mf*
issuance ['ɪʃʊ·əns] *s* (*of stamps, stocks, bonds, etc.*) emissione; (*e.g., of clothes*) distribuzione; (*of a law*) emanazione
issue ['ɪʃʊ] *s* (*outlet*) uscita; distribuzione; (*result*) conseguenza; (*offspring*) prole *f;* (*of a magazine*) puntata, fascicolo; (*of a bond*) emissione; (*yield*) prodotto; (*of a law*) promulgazione; (pathol) flusso; **at issue** in discussione; **to face the issue** affrontare la situazione; **to force the issue** forzare la soluzione; **to take issue with** non essere d'accordo con, dissentire da || *tr* (*e.g., a book*) pubblicare; (*bonds, orders*) emettere; (*a communiqué*) diramare; (*e.g., food*) distribuire || *intr* uscire; **to issue from** provenire da
isthmus ['ɪsməs] *s* istmo
it [ɪt] *pron pers* esso, essa; lo, la; **it is I** sono io; **it is raining** piove; **it is four o'clock** sono le quattro
Italian [ɪ'tæljən] *adj & s* italiano
Ital'ian-speak'ing *adj* italofono
italic [ɪ'tælɪc] *adj* (typ) corsivo || **italics** *s* (typ) corsivo || **Italic** *adj* italico
italicize [ɪ'tælɪ,saɪz] *tr* stampare in carattere corsivo; sottolineare
Italy ['ɪtəli] *s* l'Italia *f*
itch [ɪtʃ] *s* prurito; (pathol) rogna; (*eagerness*) (fig) pizzicore *m* || *tr* prudere, e.g., **his foot itches him** gli prude il piede || *intr* (*said of a part of body*) prudere; (*said of a person*) avere il prurito; **to itch to** avere il pizzicore di
itch•y ['ɪtʃi] *adj* (**-ier; -iest**) che prude; (pathol) rognoso
item ['aɪtəm] *s* articolo; notizia; (*on the agenda*) questione; (slang) notizia scottante
itemize ['aɪtə,maɪz] *tr* dettagliare, specificare
itinerant [aɪ'tɪnərənt] or [ɪ'tɪnərənt] *adj* itinerante, ambulante || *s* viaggiatore *m,* viandante *m*
itinerar•y [aɪ'tɪnə,reri] or [ɪ'tɪnə,reri] *adj* itinerario || *s* (**-ies**) itinerario
its [ɪts] *adj & pron poss* il suo
itself [ɪt'self] *pron pers* sé stesso; si, e.g., **it opened itself** si è aperto
ivied ['aɪvid] *adj* coperto di edera
ivo•ry ['aɪvəri] *adj* d'avorio || *s* (**-ries**) avorio; **ivories** (slang) tasti *mpl* del piano; (slang) palle *fpl* da bigliardo; (*dice*) (slang) dadi *mpl;* (slang) denti *mpl*
i'vory tow'er *s* torre *f* d'avorio
ivy ['aɪvi] *s* (**ivies**) edera

J

J, j [dʒe] *s* decima lettera dell'alfabeto inglese
jab [dʒæb] *s* puntata; (*prick*) puntura; (*with elbow*) gomitata || *v* (*pret & pp* **jabbed;** *ger* **jabbing**) *tr* pugnalare; pungere; dare una gomitata a || *intr* dare colpi
jabber ['dʒæbər] *s* borbottamento, ciarla || *tr & intr* borbottare, ciarlare
jack [dʒæk] *s* (*for lifting heavy objects*) cricco, martinetto; (*jackass*) asino; (*device for turning a spit*) girarrosto; (*to remove a boot*) cavastivali *m;* (cards) fante *m;* (bowling) pallino; (rad & telv) jack *m;* (elec) presa; (slang) soldi *mpl;* **every man jack** ognuno, tutti *mpl* || **Jack** *s* marinaio; (coll) buonuomo || *tr*—**to jack up** alzare col cricco; (*prices*) (coll) alzare
jackal ['dʒækəl] *s* sciacallo
jack'ass' *s* asino
jack'daw' *s* cornacchia
jacket ['dʒækɪt] *s* giacca; (*of boiled potatoes*) buccia; (*of book*) sopraccoperta; (*metal casing*) camicia
jack'ham'mer *s* martello perforatore
jack'-in-the-box' *s* scatola a sorpresa
jack'knife' *s* (**-knives**) coltello a serramanico; (sports) salto a pesce
jack'-of-all'-trades' *s* factotum *m*
jack-o'-lantern ['dʒækə,læntərn] *s* lanterna a forma di testa umana fatta con una zucca; fuoco fatuo
jack'pot' *s* monte *m* premi; **to hit the jackpot** (slang) vincere un terno al lotto
jack' rab'bit *s* lepre nordamericana di taglia grande
jack'screw' *s* cricco a verme
jack'-tar' *s* (coll) marinaio
jade [dʒed] *adj* di giada, come la giada || *s* (*ornamental stone*) giada; (*worn-out horse*) ronzino; (*disreputable woman*) donnaccia || *tr* logorare
jad'ed ['dʒedɪd] *adj* logoro, stanco; (*appetite*) stucco
jag [dʒæg] *s* slabbratura; **to have a jag on** (slang) avere la sborniа

jagged ['dʒægɪd] *adj* dentato, slabbrato
jaguar ['dʒægwɑr] *s* giaguaro
jail [dʒel] *s* prigione *f;* **to break jail** evadere dal carcere || *tr* carcerare
jail'bird' *s* galeotto, remo di galera
jail'break' *s* evasione *f* dal carcere
jailer ['dʒelər] *s* carceriere *m*
jalop•y [dʒə'lɑpi] *s* **(-ies)** carcassa, trespolo, trabiccolo
jam [dʒæm] *s* stretta, compressione; (*in traffic*) imbottigliamento; (*preserve*) marmellata, confettura; (*difficult situation*) (coll) pasticcio || *v* (*pret & pp* **jammed;** *ger* **jamming**) *tr* stipare; (*e.g., one's finger*) schiacciare, schiacciarsi; (rad) disturbare; **to jam on the brakes** bloccare i freni || *intr* schiacciarsi; (*said of firearms*) incepparsi; (mach) grippare
jamb [dʒæm] *s* stipite *m*
jamboree [,dʒæmbə'ri] *s* riunione nazionale di giovani esploratori; (coll) riunione
James [dʒəmz] *s* Giacomo
jamming ['dʒæmɪŋ] *s* radiodisturbo
jam-packed ['dʒæm'pækt] *adj* gremito, pieno fino all'orlo
jangle ['dʒæŋgəl] *s* suono stridente; (*quarrel*) baruffa || *tr* fare suoni stridenti con || *intr* stridere; litigare
janitor ['dʒænɪtər] *s* portiere *m*
janitress ['dʒænɪtrɪs] *s* portinaia
January ['dʒænjʊ,eri] *s* gennaio
ja•pan [dʒə'pæn] *s* lacca giapponese; oggetto di lacca || *v* (*pret & pp* **-panned;** *ger* **-panning**) *tr* laccare || **Japan** *s* il Giappone
Japa•nese [,dʒæpə'niz] *adj* giapponese || *s* **(-nese)** giapponese *mf*
Jap'anese bee'tle *s* scarabeo giapponese
Jap'anese lan'tern *s* lampioncino alla veneziana
Jap'anese persim'mon *s* cachi *m*
jar [dʒɑr] *s* barattolo; (*earthenware container*) orcio, giara; discordanza; (*jolt*) scossa; (fig) brutta sorpresa; **on the jar** (*said of a door*) socchiuso || *v* (*pret & pp* **jarred;** *ger* **jarring**) *tr* scuotere; far stridere || *intr* vibrare; stridere; essere in conflitto; **to jar on** irritare
jardiniere [,dʒɑrdɪ'nɪr] *s* (*pot*) vaso da fiori; giardiniera
jargon ['dʒɑrgən] *s* gergo
jasmine ['dʒæsmɪn] or ['dʒæzmɪn] *s* gelsomino
jasper ['dʒæspər] *s* diaspro
jaundice ['dʒɔndɪs] or ['dʒɑndɪs] *s* itterizia; (fig) invidia
jaundiced ['dʒɔndɪst] or ['dʒɑndɪst] *adj* itterico; (fig) invidioso
jaunt [dʒɔnt] or [dʒɑnt] *s* passeggiata, gita
jaun•ty ['dʒɔnti] or ['dʒɑnti] *adj* **(-tier; -tiest)** disinvolto; elegante
Java•nese [,dʒævə'niz] *adj* giavanese || *s* **(-nese)** giavanese *m*
javelin ['dʒævlɪn] or ['dʒævəlɪn] *s* giavellotto
jaw [dʒɔ] *s* mascella, mandibola; (mach) ganascia; **jaws** fauci *fpl;* gola, stretta || *tr* (slang) rimproverare || *intr* (slang) chiacchierare; (slang) fare la predica
jaw'bone' *s* mascella, mandibola
jaw'break'er *s* (coll) parola difficile da pronunciare; (coll) caramella durissima; (mach) frantoio a mascelle
jay [dʒe] *s* (orn) ghiandaia; (coll) sempliciotto
jay'walk' *intr* attraversare la strada contro la luce rossa del semaforo
jay'walk'er *s* (coll) pedone distratto che attraversa la strada contro la luce rossa del semaforo
jazz [dʒæz] *s* jazz *m;* (slang) spirito || *tr*—**to jazz up** (slang) dar vita a
jazz' band' *s* orchestra jazz
jealous ['dʒɛləs] *adj* geloso; (*envious*) invidioso; vigilante
jealous•y ['dʒɛləsi] *s* **(-ies)** gelosia; invidia; vigilanza
jean [dʒin] *s* tela cruda; **jeans** pantaloni *mpl* di tela cruda
jeep [dʒip] *s* gip *f,* jeep *f*
jeer [dʒɪr] *s* beffa || *tr* beffare || *intr* beffarsi; **to jeer at** motteggiare
Jeho'vah's Wit'nesses [dʒɪ'hovəs] *spl* Testimoni *mpl* di Geova
jell [dʒel] *s* gelatina || *intr* (*to congeal*) gelatinizzarsi; (*to become substantial*) cristallizzarsi
jel•ly ['dʒeli] *s* **(-lies)** gelatina || *v* (*pret & pp* **-lied**) *tr* gelatinizzare || *intr* gelatinizzarsi
jel'ly•fish' *s* medusa; (*weak person*) (coll) fiaccone *m*
jeopardize ['dʒɛpər,daɪz] *tr* compromettere, mettere a repentaglio
jeopardy ['dʒɛpərdi] *s* pericolo, repentaglio
jeremiad [,dʒerɪ'maɪ·æd] *s* geremiade *f*
Jericho ['dʒerɪ,ko] *s* Gerico *f*
jerk [dʒʌrk] *s* strattone *m,* scatto; tic *m;* (*stupid person*) scempio, sciocco; **by jerks** a scatti || *tr* tirare a strattoni; (*meat*) essiccare || *intr* sobbalzare
jerked' beef' *s* fetta di carne di bue essicata
jerkin ['dʒʌrkɪn] *s* giubbetto
jerk'wa'ter *adj* di scarsa importanza
jerk•y ['dʒʌrki] *adj* **(-ier; -iest)** sussultante; (*style*) disuguale
Jerome [dʒə'rom] *s* Gerolamo
jersey ['dʒʌrzi] *s* jersey *m,* maglione *m*
Jerusalem [dʒɪ'rusələm] *s* Gerusalemme *f*
jest [dʒest] *s* scherzo, burla; **in jest** per celia || *intr* scherzare
jester ['dʒestər] *s* motteggiatore *m,* burlone *m;* (hist) buffone *m*
Jesuit ['dʒeʒʊ·ɪt] or ['dʒezjʊ·ɪt] *adj & s* gesuita *m*
Jesuitic(al) [,dʒeʒʊ'ɪtɪk(əl)] or [,dʒezjʊ'ɪtɪk(əl)] *adj* gesuitico
Jesus ['dʒizəs] *s* Gesù *m*
Je'sus Christ' *s* Gesù *m* Cristo
jet [dʒet] *adj* di giaietto || *s* (*of a fountain*) zampillo; (*stream shooting forth from nozzle*) getto; (*mineral; lustrous black*) giaietto; (aer) aereo a getto || *v* (*pret & pp* **jetted;** *ger* **jetting**) *tr*

spruzzare || *intr* zampillare; volare in aereo a getto
jet' age' *s* era dell'aviogetto
jet'-black' *adj* nero come il carbone
jet' bomb'er *s* bombardiere *m* a reazione
jet' coal' *s* carbone *m* a lunga fiamma
jet' en'gine *s* motore *m* a reazione
jet' fight'er *s* caccia *m* a reazione
jet'lin'er *s* aviogetto da trasporto passeggeri
jet' plane' *s* aviogetto
jet' propul'sion *s* gettopropulsione
jetsam ['dʒetsəm] *s* relitto
jet' stream' *s* corrente *f* a getto; scappamento di motore a razzo
jettison ['dʒetɪsən] *s* (naut) alleggerimento || *tr* (naut) alleggerirsi di; (fig) disfarsi di
jet·ty ['dʒeti] *s* **(-ties)** gettata; (*wharf*) molo, imbarcadero
Jew [dʒu] *s* giudeo
jewel ['dʒu·əl] *s* pietra preziosa; (*valuable personal ornament*) gioia, gioiello; (*of a watch*) rubino; (*costume jewelry*) gioia finta; (fig) valore *m*, gioiello
jew'el case' *s* scrigno, portagioie *m*
jeweler or **jeweller** ['dʒu·ələr] *s* gioielliere *m*, orefice *m*
jewelry ['dʒu·əlri] *s* gioielli *mpl*
jew'elry shop' *s* gioielleria
Jewess ['dʒu·ɪs] *s* giudea
Jewish ['dʒu·ɪʃ] *adj* giudeo
jews'-harp or **jew's-harp** ['djuz ,hɑrp] *s* scacciapensieri *m*
jib [dʒɪb] *s* (*of a crane*) (mach) braccio (di gru); (naut) fiocco, vela Marconi
jib' boom' *s* asta di fiocco
jibe [dʒaɪb] *s* burla, beffa || *intr* beffarsi; accordarsi; **to jibe at** beffarsi di
jif·fy ['dʒɪfi] *s*—**in a jiffy** (coll) in men che non si dica
jig [dʒɪg] *s* (*dance*) giga; **the jig is up** (slang) tutto è perduto
jigger ['dʒɪgər] *s* bicchierino di liquore d'un'oncia e mezza; (*flea*) pulce *f* tropicale; (*gadget*) (coll) aggeggio; (naut) bozzello; (min) crivello
jiggle ['dʒɪgəl] *s* scossa || *tr* scuotere, agitare || *intr* scuotersi
jig' saw' *s* sega da traforo
jig'saw puz'zle *s* gioco di pazienza, rompicapo
jilt [dʒɪlt] *tr* piantare
jim·my ['dʒɪmi] *s* **(-mies)** piccolo piede di porco || *v* (*pret & pp* **-mied**) *tr* scassinare; **to jimmy open** scassinare
jingle ['dʒɪŋgəl] *s* sonaglio, bubbolo; (*sound*) rumore *m* di sonagliera; cantilena, rima infantile || *tr* far suonare || *intr* tintinnare
jin·go ['dʒɪŋgo] *adj* sciovinista || *s* **(-goes)** sciovinista *mf*; **by jingo!** perbacco!
jingoism ['dʒɪŋgo ,ɪzəm] *s* sciovinismo
jinx [dʒɪŋks] *s* iettatura; (*person*) iettatore *m* || *tr* portare la iettatura a
jitters ['dʒɪtərz] *spl* (coll) nervosismo; **to have the jitters** (coll) essere nervoso
jittery ['dʒɪtəri] *adj* nervoso
job [dʒɑb] *s* (*piece of work*) lavoro; (*task*) mansione; (*employment*) posto, impiego; (slang) furto; **by the job** a cottimo; **on the job** (slang) attento, sollecito; **to be out of a job** essere disoccupato; **to lie down on the job** (slang) dormire sul lavoro
job' anal'ysis *s* valutazione delle mansioni
jobber ['dʒɑbər] *s* grossista *mf*; (*pieceworker*) lavoratore *m* a cottimo; funzionario disonesto
job'hold'er *s* impiegato; (*in the government*) burocrate *m*
jobless ['jɑblɪs] *adj* disoccupato
job' lot' *s* (com) saldo
job' print'er *s* piccolo tipografo non specializzato
job' print'ing *s* piccolo lavoro tipografico
jockey ['dʒɑki] *s* fantino || *tr* (*a horse*) montare; manovrare; (*to trick*) abbindolare
jockstrap ['dʒɑk ,stræp] *s* sospensorio
jocose [dʒo'kos] *adj* giocoso
jocular ['dʒɑkjələr] *adj* scherzoso
jog [dʒɑg] *s* spinta; piccolo trotto || *v* (*pret & pp* **jogged**; *ger* **jogging**) *tr* spingere leggermente; (*the memory*) rinfrescare || *intr* barcarellare; **to jog along** continuare col solito tran tran
jog' trot' *s* piccolo trotto; (fig) tran tran *m*
John [dʒɑn] *s* Giovanni *m*
John' Bull' *s* il tipico inglese; gli inglesi, il popolo inglese
John' Han'cock ['hænkɑk] *s* (coll) la firma
johnnycake ['dʒɑni ,kek] *s* pane *m* di granturco
John'ny-come'-late'ly *s* (coll) ultimo arrivato
John'ny-jump'-up' *s* violetta, viola del pensiero
John'ny-on-the-spot' *s* (coll) persona sempre pronta
John' the Bap'tist *s* San Giovanni Battista
join [dʒɔɪn] *tr* giungere, congiungere; associarsi a; unire; (*e.g., a party*) farsi membro di; (*the army*) arruolarsi in; (*battle*) ingaggiare; (*to empty into*) sfociare in || *intr* congiungersi, unirsi; (*said, e.g., of two rivers*) confluire
joiner ['dʒɔɪnər] *s* falegname *m*; membro di molte società
joint [dʒɔɪnt] *adj* congiunto || *s* (*in a pipe*) giuntura; (*of bones*) giuntura, articolazione; (*hinge of book*) brachetta; (*in woodwork*) incastro, commettitura; (*of meat*) taglio; (mach) snodo; (*gambling den*) (slang) bisca; (elec) innesto; (slang) bettola; **out of joint** slogato; (fig) fuori luogo; **to throw** (*e.g., one's arm*) **out of joint** slogarsi
joint' account' *s* conto in comune
joint' commit'tee *s* commissione mista
jointly ['dʒɔɪntli] *adv* unitamente
joint' own'er *s* condomino
joint'-stock' com'pany *s* società *f* per azioni a responsabilità illimitata
joist [dʒɔɪst] *s* trave *f*

joke [dʒok] *s* burla, barzelletta; (*trifling matter*) cosa da nulla; (*person laughed at*) zimbello; **to tell a joke** raccontare una barzelletta; **to play a joke on** fare uno scherzo a || *tr*—**to joke one's way into** ottenere dicendo barzellette || *intr* burlare, dire storielle; **joking aside** senza scherzi
joker ['dʒokər] *s* burlone *m*; fumista *m;* (*wise guy*) saputello; (*hidden provision*) clausola ingannatrice; (cards) matta
jol·ly ['dʒɑli] *adj* (**-lier; -liest**) allegro, gaio || *adv* (coll) molto || *v* (*pret & pp* **-lied**) *tr* (coll) prendersi gioco di
jolt [dʒolt] *s* scossa || *tr* scuotere || *intr* sobbalzare
Jonah ['dʒonə] *s* Giona; (fig) uccello di mal augurio
jongleur ['dʒɑŋglər] *s* giullare *m*
jonquil ['dʒɑŋkwɪl] *s* giunchiglia
Jordan ['dʒɔrdən] *s* (*country*) la Giordania; (*river*) Giordano
Jordanian [dʒɔr'denɪ·ən] *adj & s* giordano
josh [dʒɑʃ] *tr & intr* (coll) canzonare
jostle ['dʒɑsəl] *s* spintone *m* || *tr* spingere || *intr* scontrarsi; farsi strada a gomitate
jot [dʒɑt] *s*—**I don't care a jot for** non mi importa un fico di || *v* (*pret & pp* **jotted;** *ger* **jotting**) *tr*—**to jot down** notare, gettar giù
jounce [dʒauns] *s* scossa || *tr* scuotere || *intr* sobbalzare
journal ['dʒʌrnəl] *s* (*newspaper*) giornale *m;* (*magazine*) rivista; (*daily record*) diario; (com) giornale *m;* (mach) perno; (naut) giornale *m* di bordo
journalese [,dʒʌrnə'liz] *s* linguaggio giornalistico
journalism ['dʒʌrnə,lɪzəm] *s* giornalismo
journalist ['dʒʌrnəlɪst] *s* giornalista *mf*
journey ['dʒʌrni] *s* viaggio || *intr* viaggiare
jour'ney·man *s* (**-men**) operaio specializzato
joust [dʒʌst] or [dʒust] or [dʒaust] *s* giostra || *intr* giostrare
jovial ['dʒovɪ·əl] *adj* gioviale
jowl [dʒaul] *s* (*cheek*) guancia; (*jawbone*) mascella; (*of cattle*) giogaia; (*of fowl*) bargiglio; (*of fat person*) pappagorgia
joy [dʒɔɪ] *s* gioia, allegria; **to leap with joy** ballare dalla gioia
joyful ['dʒɔɪfəl] *adj* gioioso, festoso; **joyful over** lieto di
joyless ['dʒɔɪlɪs] *adj* senza gioia
joyous ['dʒɔɪ·əs] *adj* gioioso
joy' ride' *s* (coll) gita in auto; (coll) gita all'impazzata in auto
jubilant ['dʒubɪlənt] *adj* esultante
jubilation [,dʒubɪ'leʃən] *s* giubilo
jubilee ['dʒubɪ,li] *s* (*jubilation*) giubilo; (eccl) giubileo
Judaism ['dʒude,ɪzəm] *s* giudaismo
judge [dʒʌdʒ] *s* giudice *m* || *tr & intr* giudicare; **judging by** a giudicare da
judge' ad'vocate *s* avvocato militare; avvocato della marina da guerra
judgeship ['dʒʌdʒʃɪp] *s* carica di giudice
judgment ['dʒʌdʒmənt] *s* giudizio; (*legal decision*) sentenza
judg'ment day' *s* giorno del giudizio
judg'ment seat' *s* banco dei giudici; tribunale *m*
judicature ['dʒudɪkətʃər] *s* carica di giudice
judicial [dʒu'dɪʃəl] *adj* giudiziario; (*becoming a judge*) giudizioso
judiciar·y [dʒu'dɪʃɪ,ɛri] *adj* giudiziario || *s* (**-ies**) (*judges collectively*) magistratura; (*judicial branch*) potere giudiziario
judicious [dʒu'dɪʃəs] *adj* giudizioso
jug [dʒʌg] *s* brocca, boccale *m;* (*narrow-necked vessel*) orcio; (*jail*) (slang) prigione
juggle ['dʒʌgəl] *s* gioco di prestigio || *tr* fare il giocoliere con; (*documents, facts*) alterare frodolentamente; **to juggle away** ghermire, trafugare || *intr* fare il giocoliere; fare l'imbroglione
juggler ['dʒʌglər] *s* giocoliere *m,* prestigiatore *m;* impostore *m*
juggling ['dʒʌglɪŋ] *s* giochi *mpl* di prestigio
Jugoslav ['jugo'slɑv] *adj & s* iugoslavo, jugoslavo
Jugoslavia ['jugo'slɑvɪ·ə] *s* la Iugoslavia, la Jugoslavia
jugular ['dʒʌgjələr] or ['dʒugjələr] *adj & s* giugulare *f*
juice [dʒus] *s* sugo; (*natural fluid of an animal body*) succo; (slang) elettricità *f;* (slang) benzina; **to stew in one's own juice** (coll) annegarsi nel proprio sugo
juic·y ['dʒusi] *adj* (**-ier; -iest**) sugoso, succoso; (*spicy*) piccante
jukebox ['dʒuk,bɑks] *s* grammofono a gettone, juke-box *m*
julep ['dʒulɪp] *s* bibita di menta col ghiaccio; (pharm) giulebbe *m*
julienne [,dʒulɪ'en] *s* giuliana
July [dʒu'laɪ] *s* luglio
jumble ['dʒʌmbəl] *s* intrico, garbuglio || *tr* ingarbugliare
jum·bo ['dʒʌmbo] *adj* (coll) enorme || *s* (**-bos**) (*person*) (coll) elefante *m;* (*thing*) (coll) oggetto enorme
jump [dʒʌmp] *s* salto; (*in a parachute*) lancio; (*of prices*) sbalzo; (*start*) soprassalto; **on the jump** in moto; **to get or to have the jump on** (coll) avere il vantaggio su || *tr* saltare; (*a horse*) far saltare; (*prices*) alzare; uscire da, e.g., **the train jumped the track** il treno uscì dalle rotaie; (*to attack*) (coll) balzare su; (checkers) suffiare || *intr* saltare; (*from surprise*) trasalire; (*said of prices*) salire; (*in a parachute*) lanciarsi; **to jump at** (*e.g., an offer*) afferrare; **to jump on** saltare su; (coll) sgridare, arrabbiarsi con; **to jump over** oltrepassare; (*a page*) saltare; **to jump to a conclusion** arrivare precipitosamente a una conclusione
jumper ['dʒʌmpər] *s* saltatore *m;* camiciotto; **jumpers** tuta da bambini

jump'ing jack' ['dʒʌmpɪŋ] *s* marionetta
jump'ing-off' place' *s* fine *f* del mondo; (fig) trampolino, punto di partenza
jump' seat' *s* strapuntino
jump' spark' *s* scintilla elettrica; (*of induction coil*) (elec) scintilla d'intraferro
jump' wire' *s* filo elettrico di contatto
jump•y ['dʒʌmpi] *adj* (**-ier; -iest**) nervoso, eccitato
junction ['dʒʌŋktʃən] *s* congiunzione; (*of two rivers*) confluenza; (carp) commettitura; (rr) raccordo ferroviario
juncture ['dʒʌŋktʃər] *s* giuntura; (*occasion*) congiuntura; (*moment*) momento
June [dʒun] *s* giugno
jungle ['dʒʌŋgəl] *s* giungla
junglegym ['dʒʌŋgəl,dʒɪm] *s* (trademark) castello
junior ['dʒunjər] *adj* minore, di minore età; giovane; (*in American university*) del penultimo anno; figlio, e.g., **John H. Smith, Junior** Giovanni H. Smith, figlio || *s* minore *m;* socio secondario; studente *m* del penultimo anno
jun'ior col'lege *s* scuola universitaria unicamente di primo biennio
jun'ior high' school' *s* scuola media; ginnasio
juniper ['dʒunɪpər] *s* ginepro
ju'niper ber'ry *s* coccola di ginepro
junk [dʒʌŋk] *s* roba vecchia, ferro vecchio; (*Chinese ship*) giunca; (naut) carne salata || *tr* (slang) gettar via
junk' deal'er *s* robivecchi *m*
junket ['dʒʌŋkɪt] *s* budino di giuncata; (*outing*) viaggio di piacere; viaggio pagato a spese del tesoro || *intr* far un viaggio di piacere; far un viaggio a spese del tesoro
junk'man' *s* (**-men'**) ferravecchio; rigattiere *m*
junk' room' *s* ripostiglio
junk' shop' *s* negozio di robivecchi
junk'yard' *s* cantiere *m* di ferravecchio
juridical [dʒʊ'rɪdɪkəl] *adj* giuridico
jurisdiction [,dʒʊrɪs'dɪkʃən] *s* giurisdizione
jurisprudence [,dʒʊrɪs'prudəns] *s* giurisprudenza
jurist ['dʒʊrɪst] *s* giurista *mf*
juror ['dʒʊrər] *s* giurato
ju•ry ['dʒʊri] *s* (**-ries**) giuria
ju'ry box' *s* banco della giuria
ju'ry•man *s* (**-men**) giurato
just [dʒʌst] *adj* giusto || *adv* giustamente, giusto; appena; proprio; **just as** come, proprio come; **just beyond** un po' più in là (di); **just now** poco fa, or ora; **just out** appena uscito, appena pubblicato
justice ['dʒʌstɪs] *s* giustizia; (*judge*) giudice *m;* **to bring to justice** arrestare e condannare; **to do justice to** render giustizia a; apprezzare bastantemente
jus'tice of the peace' *s* giudice *m* conciliatore
justifiable ['dʒʌstɪ,faɪ•əbəl] *adj* giustificabile
justi•fy ['dʒʌstɪ,faɪ] *v* (*pret & pp* **-fied**) *tr* giustificare; (typ) giustificare
justly ['dʒʌstli] *adj* giustamente
jut [dʒʌt] *v* (*pret & pp* **jutted;** *ger* **jutting**) *intr*—**to jut out** strapiombare, sporgere
jute [dʒut] *s* iuta || **Jute** *s* Juto
juvenile ['dʒuvənɪl] or ['dʒuvə,naɪl] *adj* giovanile; minorile || *s* giovane *mf;* libro per la gioventù; (theat) amoroso
ju'venile court' *s* tribunale *m* per i minorenni
ju'venile delin'quency *s* delinquenza minorile
juvenilia [,dʒuvə'nɪlɪ•ə] *spl* opere *fpl* giovanili; libri *mpl* per ragazzi
juxtapose [,dʒʌkstə'poz] *tr* giustapporre

K

K, k [ke] *s* undicesima lettera dell'alfabeto inglese
kale [kel] *s* verza; (slang) cocuzza, soldi *mpl*
kaleidoscope [kə'laɪdə,skop] *s* caleidoscopio
kangaroo [,kæŋgə'ru] *s* canguro
katydid ['ketidɪd] *s* grossa cavalletta verde nordamericana
kedge [kedʒ] *s* (naut) ancorotto
keel [kil] *s* chiglia || *intr*—**to keel over** (naut) abbattersi in carena, capovolgersi; (fig) svenire
keelson ['kelsən] or ['kilsən] *s* (naut) controchiglia
keen [kin] *adj* (*sharpened*) affilato; (*wind; wit*) tagliente, mordente; (*eyes*) penetrante; (*ears; mind*) acuto, fine; (*eager*) entusiasta; intenso, vivo; (slang) meraviglioso; **to be keen on** essere appassionato per
keep [kip] *s* mantenimento; (*of medieval castle*) torrione *m,* maschio; **for keeps** (coll) seriamente; (coll) per sempre; **to earn one's keep** guadagnarsi la vita || *v* (*pret & pp* **kept** [kept]) *tr* mantenere; (*watch*) fare; (*one's word*) mantenere; (*to withhold*) trattenere; (*accounts*) tenere; (*servants, guests*) avere; (*a garden*) coltivare; (*a business*) esercitare; (*a holiday*) festeggiare; (*to support*) sostentare; (*a secret; one's seat*) serbare; (*to decide to purchase*) prendere **to keep away** tener lontano; **to keep back** trattenere; (*a secret*) man-

tenere; **to keep down** reprimere; (*expenses*) ridurre al minimo; **to keep s.o. from** + *ger* impedire a qlcu di + *inf;* **to keep in** tener chiuso; **to keep off** tenere a distanza; (*e.g., moisture*) non lasciar penetrare; **to keep s.o. informed about s.th** tenere qlcu al corrente di qlco; **to keep s.o. waiting** fare aspettare qlcu; **to keep up** mantenere, sostenere || *intr* **to keep** + *ger* continuare a + *inf;* **to keep away** tenersi lontano; **to keep from** + *ger* evitare di + *inf;* **to keep informed (about)** tenersi al corrente (di); **to keep in with** (coll) stare nelle buone grazie di; **to keep off** stare lontano (da); (*the grass*) non calpestare; **to keep on** + *ger* seguitare a + *inf;* **to keep out** star fuori, non entrare; **to keep out of** non entrare in; (*danger*) stare lontano da; non immischiarsi in; **to keep quiet** stare tranquillo; **to keep to** (*left or right*) tenere; **to keep to oneself** stare in disparte; **to keep up** continuare; **to keep up with** stare alla pari con; (*e.g., the news*) tenersi al corrente di

keeper ['kipər] *s* (*of a shop*) tenitore *m;* guardiano; (*of a game preserve*) guardacaccia *m;* (*of a magnet*) ancora

keeping ['kipɪŋ] *s* custodia; (*of a holiday*) celebrazione; **in keeping with** in armonia con; **in safe keeping** in luogo sicuro; **out of keeping with** in cattivo accordo con

keep'sake' *s* ricordo

keg [kɛg] *s* barilotto, botticella

ken [kɛn] *s* portata; **beyond the ken of** al di là dell'ambito di

kennel ['kɛnəl] *s* canile *m*

kep·i ['kepi] or ['kɛpi] *s* (**-is**) chepì *m*

kept' wo'man [kɛpt] *s* (**wom'en**) mantenuta

kerchief ['kʌrtʃɪf] *s* fisciù *m*

kernel ['kʌrnəl] *s* (*of a nut*) gheriglio; (*of wheat*) chicco; (fig) nucleo

kerosene ['kɛrə,sin] or [,kɛrə'sin] *s* cherosene *m,* petrolio da illuminazione

kerplunk [kər'plʌŋk] *interj* patapum!

ketchup ['kɛtʃəp] *s* salsa piccante di pomodoro, ketchup *m*

kettle ['kɛtəl] *s* marmitta, paiolo; (*teakettle*) bricco, teiera

ket'tle·drum' *s* timpano

key [ki] *adj* a chiave; chiave || *s* chiave *f;* (*of piano, typewriter, etc.*) tasto; (*cotter pin*) chiavetta, coppiglia; (*reef*) isolotto; (*tone of voice*) tono; (fig, mus) chiave *f;* (bot) samara; (telg) tasto trasmettitore, manipolatore *m;* **off key** stonato || *tr* aggiustare; inchiavardare; **to key up** eccitare, portare al parossismo

key'board' *s* tastiera

key'hole' *s* toppa, buco della serratura; (*of a clock*) buco della chiave

key'note' *s* (mus) tono; (fig) principio informatore

key'note address' *s* discorso d'apertura

key'punch op'era'tor *s* perforatore *m*

key' ring' *s* portachiavi *m*

key'stone' *s* chiave *f* di volta

key' word' *s* parola chiave

kha·ki ['kɑki] or ['kæki] *adj* cachi || *s* (**-kis**) cachi *m*

khedive [kə'div] *s* kedivè *m*

kibitz ['kɪbɪts] *intr* (coll) dare consigli non richiesti

kibitzer ['kɪbɪtsər] *s* (*at a card game*) (coll) consigliere *m* importuno; (coll) ficcanaso *mf*

kibosh ['kaɪbɑʃ] or [kɪ'bɑʃ] *s* (coll) sciocchezza; **to put the kibosh on** (coll) impossibilitare

kick [kɪk] *s* calcio, pedata; (*of a gun*) rinculo; (*complaint*) (slang) protesta; (*of liquor*) (slang) forza; **to get a kick out of** (slang) pigliar piacere da || *tr* prendere a calci; (*a ball*) calciare; (*one's feet*) battere; **to kick out** (coll) sbatter fuori a pedate; **to kick up a row** scatenare un putiferio || *intr* calciare; (*said of an animal*) scalciare, trarre; (*said of a firearm*) rinculare; (coll) lamentarsi; **to kick against the pricks** dar calci al vento; **to kick off** (football) dare il calcio d'inizio

kick'back' *s* (coll) contraccolpo; (coll) intrallazzo, bustarella

kick'off' *s* calcio d'inizio

kid [kɪd] *s* capretto; (coll) piccolo; **kids** guanti *mpl* or scarpe *fpl* di capretto || *v* (*pret & pp* **kidded;** *ger* **kidding**) *tr* (coll) prendere in giro; **to kid oneself** (coll) farsi illusioni || *intr* (coll) dirlo per scherzo

kidder ['kɪdər] *s* (coll) burlone *m*

kid' gloves' *spl* guanti *mpl* di capretto; **to handle with kid gloves** trattare con la massima cautela

kid'nap' *v* (*pret & pp* **-naped** or **-napped;** *ger* **-naping** or **-napping**) *tr* rapire, sequestrare

kidnaper or **kidnapper** ['kɪd,næpər] *s* rapitore *m* a scopo d'estorsione

kidnaping or **kidnapping** ['kɪd,næpɪŋ] *s* rapimento a scopo di estorsione

kidney ['kɪdni] *s* rene *m;* (culin) rognone *m;* (*temperament*) carattere *m;* (*kind*) tipo

kid'ney bean' *s* fagiolo

kid'ney stone' *s* calcolo renale

kill [kɪl] *s* uccisione; (*game killed*) cacciagione; (coll) fiumicello; **for the kill** per il colpo finale || *tr* uccidere; eliminare; (*a bill*) bocciare; (fig) opprimere

killer ['kɪlər] *s* uccisore *m*

kill'er whale' *s* orca

killing ['kɪlɪŋ] *adj* mortale; (*exhausting*) opprimente; (coll) molto divertente || *s* uccisione; (*game killed*) cacciagione; (coll) fortuna; **to make a killing** (coll) fare una fortuna da un giorno all'altro

kill'-joy' *s* guastafeste *mf*

kiln [kɪl] or [kɪln] *s* forno, fornace *f*

kil·o ['kɪlo] or ['kilo] *s* (**-os**) chilogrammo; chilometro

kilocycle ['kɪlə,saɪkəl] *s* chilociclo

kilogram ['kɪlə,græm] *s* chilogrammo

kilo·hertz ['kɪlə,hʌrts] *s* (**-hertz**) chilohertz

kilometer ['kɪlə ˌmitər] or [kɪ'lamɪtər] *s* chilometro
kilowatt ['kɪlə ˌwat] *s* kilowatt *m*, chilowatt *m*
kilowatt-hour ['kɪlə ˌwat'aur] *s* (**kilowatt-hours**) chilowattora *m*
kilt [kɪlt] *s* gonnellino
kilter ['kɪltər] *s*—**to be out of kilter** (coll) essere fuori squadra
kimo•no [kɪ'monə] or [kɪ'mono] *s* (**-nos**) chimono
kin [kɪn] *s* (*family relationship*) parentela; (*relatives*) parenti *mpl;* **of kin** parente, affine; **the next of kin** il parente più prossimo, i parenti più prossimi
kind [kaɪnd] *adj* gentile; **kind to** buono con || *s* genere *m*, specie *f;* **a kind of** una specie di; **all kinds of** (coll) ogni sorta di; **in kind** in natura; **kind of** (coll) quasi, piuttosto; **of a kind** dello stesso stampo; (*mediocre*) di poco valore
kindergarten ['kɪndər ˌgartən] *s* scuola materna, giardino d'infanzia
kindergartner ['kɪndər ˌgartnər] *s* allievo della scuola d'infanzia; (*teacher*) maestra giardiniera
kind-hearted ['kaɪnd'hartɪd] *adj* gentile, di buon cuore
kindle ['kɪndəl] *tr* accendere || *intr* accendersi
kindling ['kɪndlɪŋ] *s* accensione; legna minuta
kin'dling wood' *s* legna minuta per accendere il fuoco
kind•ly ['kaɪndli] *adj* (**-lier; -liest**) gentile; (*climate*) benigno; favorevole || *adv* gentilmente; cordialmente; per gentilezza; **to not take kindly to** non accettare di buon grado
kindness ['kaɪndnɪs] *s* gentilezza; **have the kindness to** abbia la bontà di
kindred ['kɪndrɪd] *adj* imparentato; affine || *s* parentela; affinità *f*
kinescope ['kɪnɪ ˌskop] *s* (trademark) cinescopio
kinetic [kɪ'netɪk] or [kaɪ'netɪk] *adj* cinetico || **kinetics** *s* cinetica
kinet'ic en'ergy *s* forza viva, energia cinetica
king [kɪŋ] *s* re *m;* (checkers) dama; (cards, chess) re *m*
king'bolt' *s* perno
kingdom ['kɪŋdəm] *s* regno
king'fish'er *s* martin pescatore *m*
king•ly ['kɪŋli] *adj* (**-lier; -liest**) reale; (*stately*) maestoso || *adv* regalmente
king'pin' *s* birillo centrale; (aut) perno dello sterzo; (fig) figura principale
king' post' *s* (archit) ometto, monaco
king's' e'vil *s* scrofola
kingship ['kɪŋʃɪp] *s* regalità *f*
king'-size' *adj* extra-grande
king's' ran'som *s* ricchezza di Creso
kink [kɪŋk] *s* (*in a rope*) arricciatura; (*in hair*) crespatura; (*soreness in neck*) torcicollo; (*flaw*) ostacolo; (*mental twist*) ghiribizzo || *tr* attorcigliare || *intr* attorcigliarsi
kink•y ['kɪŋki] *adj* (**-ier; -iest**) attorcigliato; (*hair*) crespo
kinsfolk ['kɪnz ˌfok] *s* parentado
kinship ['kɪnʃɪp] *s* parentela; affinità *f*
kins'man *s* (**-men**) parente *m*
kins'wom'an *s* (**-wom'en**) parente *f*
kipper ['kɪpər] *s* aringa affumicata || *tr* (*herring or salmon*) affumicare
kiss [kɪs] *s* bacio; (*billiards*) rimpallo leggerissimo; (*confection*) meringa || *tr* baciare; **to kiss away** (*tears*) asciugare con baci || *intr* baciare, baciarsi; (billiards) rimpallare leggermente
kit [kɪt] *s* (*case*) cassetta dei ferri; (*tools*) ferri *mpl* del mestiere; (*set of supplies*) corredo; (*of small tools*) astuccio; (*of a traveler*) borsa da viaggio; (*pail*) secchio; **the whole kit and caboodle** (coll) tutti quanti
kitchen ['kɪtʃən] *s* cucina
kitchenette [ˌkɪtʃə'net] *s* cucinetta
kitch'en gar'den *s* orto
kitch'en•maid' *s* sguattera
kitch'en police' *s* (mil) corvè *f* di cucina
kitch'en range' *s* cucina economica
kitch'en sink' *s* acquaio
kitch'en•ware' *s* utensili *mpl* di cucina
kite [kaɪt] *s* cervo volante, aquilone *m;* (orn) nibbio
kith' and kin' [kɪθ] *spl* amici *mpl* e parenti *mpl*
kitten ['kɪtən] *s* gattino
kittenish ['kɪtənɪʃ] *adj* giocattolone; civettuolo
kit•ty ['kɪti] *s* (**-ties**) gattino; (cards) piatto || *interj* micio!
kleptomaniac [ˌkleptə'menɪ ˌæk] *s* cleptomane *mf*
knack [næk] *s* abilità *f*, destrezza
knapsack ['næp ˌsæk] *s* zaino
knave [nev] *s* furfante *m;* (cards) fante *m*
knaver•y ['nevəri] *s* (**-ies**) furfanteria
knead [nid] *tr* maneggiare, intridere; (*a muscle*) massaggiare
knee [ni] *s* ginocchio; (*of trousers*) ginocchiera; (mach) gomito; **to bring s.o. to his knees** ridurre qlcu all'obbedienza; **to go down on one's knees (to)** gettarsi in ginocchio (davanti a)
knee' breech'es [ˌbrɪtʃɪz] *spl* calzoni *mpl* al ginocchio
knee'cap' *s* rotula, patella; (*protective covering*) ginocchiera
knee'-deep' *adj* fino al ginocchio
knee'-high' *adj* fino al ginocchio
knee' jerk' *s* riflesso patellare
kneel [nil] *v* (*pret & pp* **knelt** [nelt] or **kneeled**) *intr* inginocchiarsi
knee'pad' *s* ginocchiera
knee'pan' *s* rotula, patella
knell [nel] *s* rintocco funebre, campana a morto; **to toll the knell of** annunciare la morte di || *intr* suonare a morte
knickers ['nɪkərz] *spl* knickerbockers *mpl*, calzoni *mpl* alla zuava
knickknack ['nɪk ˌnæk] *s* soprammobile *m;* gingillo, ninnolo
knife [naɪf] *s* (**knives** [naɪvz]) coltello; (*of a paper cutter*) mannaia; (*of a milling machine*) fresa; **to go under the knife** essere sulla tavola operatoria || *tr* accoltellare; mettere il coltello nella schiena di
knife' sharp'ener *s* affilatoio

knife' switch' *s* (elec) coltella
knight [naɪt] *s* cavaliere *m;* (chess) cavallo || *tr* armare cavaliere
knight-errant ['naɪt'ɛrənt] *s* (**knights-errant**) cavaliere *m* errante
knighthood ['naɪt·hud] *s* cavalleria
knightly ['naɪtli] *adj* cavalleresco
knit [nɪt] *v* (*pret & pp* **knitted** or **knit;** *ger* **knitting**) *tr* lavorare a maglia; (*to join*) unire; (*e.g., the brow*) corrugare || *intr* lavorare a maglia; fare la calza; unirsi; (*said of a bone*) saldarsi
knitting ['nɪtɪŋ] *s* maglia, lavoro a maglia
knit'ting machine' *s* macchina per maglieria
knit'ting mill' *s* maglieria
knit'ting nee'dle *s* ferro da calza
knit'wear' *s* maglieria
knit'wear store' *s* maglieria
knob [nɑb] *s* (*lump*) bozza, protuberanza; (*of a door*) maniglia; (*on furniture*) pomolo; (*hill*) collinetta rotondeggiante; (rad, telv) manopola, pulsante *m*
knock [nɑk] *s* colpo; (*on a door*) tocco; (slang) attacco, critica || *tr* battere; (*repeatedly*) sbatacchiare; (slang) attaccare, criticare; **to knock down** (*with a punch*) stendere a terra; (*a wall*) diroccare; (*to the highest bidder*) aggiudicare; (*e.g., a machine*) smontare; **to knock off** (*work*) (slang) sospendere; (slang) terminare; (slang) uccidere; **to knock out** mettere fuori combattimento || *intr* battere; (aut) battere in testa; (slang) criticare; **to knock about** (slang) gironzolare; **to knock against** urtare contro; **to knock at** (*e.g., a door*) battere a, bussare a; **to knock off** (slang) cessare di lavorare
knock'down' *adj* (*blow*) knock down, che atterra; (*dismountable*) smontabile || *s* (*blow*) colpo che atterra; (*discount*) sconto
knocker ['nɑkər] *s* (*on a door*) battaglio, bussatoio; (coll) criticone *m*
knock-kneed ['nɑk,nid] *adj* con le gambe a X [iks]
knock'out' *s* pugno che mette fuori combattimento; fuori combattimento; (coll) pezzo di giovane
knock'out drops' *spl* (slang) narcotico
knoll [nol] *s* poggio, rialzo
knot [nɑt] *s* nodo; (*worn as an ornament*) fiocco; (*in wood*) nocchio; gruppo; protuberanza; (*tie*) nodo; (naut) nodo; **to tie the knot** (coll) sposarsi || *v* (*pret & pp* **knotted;** *ger* **knotting**) *tr* annodare; (*the brow*) corrugare || *intr* annodarsi
knot'hole' *s* buco lasciato da un nodo (nel legno)
knot·ty ['nɑti] *adj* (**-tier; -tiest**) nodoso; (fig) spinoso
know [no] *s*—**to be in the know** (coll) essere al corrente || *v* (*pret* **knew** [nju] or [nu]; *pp* **known**) *tr & intr* (*by reasoning or learning*) sapere; (*by the senses or by perception; through acquaintance or recognition*) conoscere; **as far as I know** per quanto io ne sappia; **to know about** essere al corrente di; **to know best** essere il miglior giudice; **to know how to** + *inf* sapere + *inf;* **to know it all** (coll) sapere tutto; **to know what's what** (coll) saperla lunga; **you ought to know better** dovresti vergognarti
knowable ['no·əbəl] *adj* conoscibile
know'-how' *s* sapere *m,* abilità *f*
knowingly ['no·ɪŋli] *adv* con conoscenza di causa; (*on purpose*) apposta
know'-it-all' *adj & s* (coll) saputello
knowledge ['nɑlɪdʒ] *s* (*faculty*) scibile *m,* sapere *m,* sapienza; (*awareness, acquaintance, familiarity*) conoscenza; **to have a thorough knowledge of** conoscere a fondo; **to my knowledge** per quanto io ne sappia; **with full knowledge** con conoscenza di causa; **without my knowledge** a mia insaputa
knowledgeable ['nɑlɪdʒəbəl] *adj* intelligente, bene informato
knuckle ['nʌkəl] *s* nocca; foro del cardine, cardine *m;* **knuckles** pugno di ferro || *intr*—**to knuckle down** (coll) lavorare di impegno; **to knuckle under** (coll) darsi per vinto
knurl [nʌrl] *s* granitura || *tr* godranare, zigrinare
Koran [ko'rɑn] or [ko'ræn] *s* Corano
Korea [ko'ri·ə] *s* la Corea
Korean [ko'ri·ən] *adj & s* coreanò
kosher ['koʃər] *adj* kasher, casher, puro secondo la legge giudaica; (coll) autentico
kowtow ['kau'tau] or ['ko'tau] *intr* inchinarsi servilmente
Kremlin ['krɛmlɪn] *s* Cremlino
Kremlinology [,krɛmlɪ'nɑlədʒi] *s* Cremlinologia
kudos ['kjudɑs] or ['kudɑs] *s* (coll) gloria, fama, approvazione

L

L, l [ɛl] *s* dodicesima lettera dell'alfabeto inglese
la·bel ['lebəl] *s* marca, etichetta; (*descriptive word*) qualifica || *v* (*pret & pp* **-beled** or **-belled;** *ger* **-beling** or **-belling**) *tr* etichettare; qualificare
labial ['lebɪ·əl] *adj & s* labiale *f*
labor ['lebər] *adj* operaio || *s* lavoro; (*toil*) fatica; (*childbirth*) parto; (*body of wage earners*) manodopera; (*class as contrasted with management*) prestatori *mpl* d'opera, lavoro; **labors** fatiche *fpl;* **to be in labor** avere le doglie || *intr* lavorare; (*to exert one-*

self) travagliare; (*said of a ship*) rollare e beccheggiare; **to labor for** lottare per; **to labor under** soffrire di
laborato•ry ['læbərə,tori] *s* (**-ries**) laboratorio
la'bor dispute' *s* vertenza sindacale
labored ['lebərd] *adj* elaborato, artificiale; penoso, difficile
laborer ['lebərər] *s* lavoratore *m;* (*unskilled worker*) bracciante *m*, manovale *m*, uomo di fatica
laborious [lə'borɪ•əs] *adj* laborioso
la'bor un'ion *s* sindacato
Labourite ['lebə,raɪt] *s* laburista *mf*
labyrinth ['læbɪrɪnθ] *s* labirinto
lace [les] *s* (*cord or string*) stringa; (*netlike ornament*) trina, merletto; (*braid*) gallone *m* || *tr* stringare; merlettare; (coll) fustigare
lace'work' *s* trina, merletto, pizzo
lachrymose ['lækrɪ,mos] *adj* lacrimoso
lacing ['lesɪŋ] *s* stringa, cordone *m;* gallone *m;* (coll) battuta, frustata
lack [læk] *s* mancanza, scarsezza, difetto || *tr* mancare di, scarseggiare di || *intr* mancare, scarseggiare, difettare
lackadaisical [,lækə'dezɪkəl] *adj* letargico, indifferente
lackey ['læki] *s* lacchè *m*
lacking ['lækɪŋ] *prep* privo di
lack'lus'ter *adj* smorto, spento
laconic [lə'kɑnɪk] *adj* laconico
lacquer ['lækər] *s* lacca || *tr* laccare
lac'quer spray' *s* lacca spray
lac'quer ware' *s* oggetti *mpl* laccati
lacu•na [le'kjunə] *s* (**-nas** or **-nae** [ni]) lacuna
lac•y ['lesi] *adj* (**-ier; -iest**) simile al merletto
lad [læd] *s* ragazzo, fanciullo
ladder ['lædər] *s* scala; (*stepladder hinged on top*) scaleo; (*stepping stone*) (fig) scalino
lad'der truck' *s* autocarro di pompieri munito di scale
la'dies' man' *s* beato fra le donne
la'dies' room' *s* gabinetto per signore
ladle ['ledəl] *s* ramaiolo, mestolo; (*of tinsmith*) cucchiaio || *tr* scodellare
la•dy ['ledi] *s* (**-dies**) signora, dama
la'dy•bug' *s* coccinella
la'dy•fin'ger *s* savoiardo, lingua di gatto
la'dy-in-wait'ing *s* (**ladies-in-waiting**) dama di corte
la'dy-kil'ler *s* rubacuori *m*
la'dy•like' *adj* signorile; **to be ladylike** comportarsi come una signora
la'dy•love' *s* amata
la'dy of the house' *s* padrona di casa
ladyship ['ledi,ʃɪp] *s* signoria
la'dy's maid' *s* cameriera personale della signora
lag [læg] *s* ritardo || *v* (*pret & pp* **lagged;** *ger* **lagging**) *intr* ritardare; **to lag behind** rimanere indietro
la'ger beer' ['lɑgər] *s* birra invecchiata
laggard ['lægərd] *s* tardo, pigro
lagoon [lə'gun] *s* laguna
laid' pa'per [led] *s* carta vergata
laid' up' *adj* messo da parte; (naut) disarmato; (coll) costretto a letto
lair [lɛr] *s* tana, covo
laity ['le•ɪti] *s* laicato
lake [lek] *adj* lacustre || *s* lago
lamb [læm] *s* agnello
lambaste [læm'best] *tr* (*to thrash*) sferzare; (*to reprimand*) riprovare
lamb' chop' *s* cotoletta d'agnello
lambkin ['læmkɪn] *s* agnellino; (fig) innocente *mf*
lamb'skin' *s* (*leather*) pelle *f* d'agnello; (*skin with its wool*) agnello
lame [lem] *adj* zoppo; difettoso; (*disabled*) invalido; (*excuse*) debole || *tr* azzoppare
lament [lə'ment] *s* lamento; lamento funebre || *tr* lamentare || *intr* lamentarsi
lamentable ['læməntəbəl] or [lə'mentəbəl] *adj* lamentevole
lamentation [,læmən'teʃən] *s* lamentazione
laminate ['læmɪ,net] *tr* laminare
lamp [læmp] *s* lampada
lamp'black' *s* nerofumo
lamp' chim'ney *s* tubo di vetro di lampada a petrolio
lamp'light' *s* luce *f* di lampada
lamp'light'er *s* lampionaio
lampoon [læm'pun] *s* satira || *tr* satireggiare
lamp'post' *s* colonna del lampione
lamp'shade' *s* paralume *m*, ventola
lamp'wick' *s* lucignolo
lance [læns] or [lɑns] *s* lancia; (surg) lancetta || *tr* (*with an oxygen lance*) tagliare col cannello ossidrico; (surg) sbrigliare, incidere col bisturi
lance' rest' *s* resta
lancet ['lænsɪt] or ['lɑnsɪt] *s* (surg) lancetta
land [lænd] *adj* terrestre; (*wind*) di terra || *s* terra; **on land, on sea, and in the air** per mare, per terra e nel cielo; **to make land** toccare terra; **to see how the land lies** tastare terreno || *tr* sbarcare; (aer) fare atterrare; (coll) pigliare || *intr* sbarcare; (*to come to rest*) andare a finire; (naut) toccar terra; (aer) atterrare; **to land on one's feet** cadere in piedi; **to land on one's head** andare a gambe all'aria; **to land on the moon** allunare; **to land on the water** ammarare
land' breeze' *s* vento di terra
landed ['lændɪd] *adj* (*owning land*) terriero; (*real estate*) immobile
land'fall' *s* (*sighting land*) avvistamento; terra avvistata; (*landslide*) frana
land' grant' *s* terreno ricevuto in dono dallo stato
land'hold'er *s* proprietario terriero
landing ['lændɪŋ] *s* (*of passengers*) sbarco; (*place where passengers and goods are landed*) imbarcadero; (*of stairway*) pianerottolo; (aer, naut) atterraggio
land'ing bea'con *s* radiofaro d'atterraggio
land'ing card' *s* cartoncino di sbarco
land'ing craft' *s* imbarcazione da sbarco
land'ing field' *s* campo d'atterraggio

land'ing flap' *s* (aer) iposostentatore *m*
land'ing gear' *s* (aer) carrello d'atterraggio
land'ing strip' *s* (aer) pista d'atterraggio
land'la'dy *s* (**-dies**) (*of an apartment*) padrona di casa; (*of a lodging house*) affittacamere *f*; (*of an inn*) ostessa
landlocked ['lænd,lakt] *adj* circondato da terra
land'lord' *s* (*of an apartment*) padrone *m* di casa; (*of a lodging house*) affittacamere *m*; (*of an inn*) oste *m*
land•lubber ['lænd,lʌbər] *s* marinaio d'acqua dolce
land'mark' *s* (*boundary stone*) pietra di confine; (*distinguishing landscape feature*) punto di riferimento; (fig) pietra miliare
land' of'fice *s* ufficio del catasto
land'-office busi'ness *s* (coll) sacco d'affari
land'own'er *s* proprietario terriero
landscape ['lænd,skep] *s* paesaggio ‖ *tr* abbellire
land'scape gar'dener *s* giardiniere *m* ornamentale
land'scape paint'er *s* paesista *mf*
landscapist ['lænd,skepɪst] *s* paesista *mf*
land'slide' *s* frana; (fig) vittoria strepitosa
landward ['lændwərd] *adv* verso terra, verso la costa
land' wind' *s* vento di terra
lane [len] *s* (*narrow street*) vicolo, viuzza; (*of a highway*) corsia; (naut) rotta; (aer) corridoio
langsyne [,læŋ'saɪn] *s* (Scotch) tempo passato ‖ *adv* (Scotch) molto tempo fa
language ['læŋgwɪdʒ] *s* lingua; (*style of language*) linguaggio; (*of a special group of people*) gergo
lan'guage lab'oratory *s* laboratorio linguistico
languid ['læŋgwɪd] *adj* languido
languish ['læŋgwɪʃ] *intr* languire; affettare languore
languor ['læŋgər] *s* languore *m*
languorous ['læŋgərəs] *adj* languido; (*causing languor*) snervante
lank [læŋk] *adj* scarnito, sparuto
lank•y ['læŋki] *adj* (**-ier; -iest**) scarnito, sparuto
lantern ['læntərn] *s* lanterna
lan'tern slide' *s* diapositiva
lanyard ['lænjərd] *s* (naut) drizza; (mil) aghetto, cordellina
lap [læp] *s* (*of human body or clothing*) grembo; (*with the tongue*) leccata; (*of the waves*) sciacquio; (sports) giro, tappa; **in the lap of** in mezzo a, e.g., **in the lap of luxury** in mezzo alle delicatezze ‖ *v* (*pret & pp* **lapped**; *ger* **lapping**) *tr* lappare; (*said, e.g., of waves*) lambire; (*to fold*) piegare; (*to overlap*); sovrapporre; **to lap up** lappare; (coll) accettare con entusiasmo ‖ *intr* sovrapporsi; **to lap against** (*said of the waves*) lambire; **to lap over** traboccare
lap'board' *s* tavolino da lavoro da tenersi sulle ginocchia
lap' dissolve' *s* (mov) dissolvenza incrociata
lap' dog' *s* cagnolino da salotto
lapel [lə'pel] *s* risvolto
Lap'land' *s* la Lapponia
Laplander ['læp,lændər] *s* lappone *mf*
Lapp [læp] *s* lappone *mf*; (*language*) lappone *m*
lap' robe' *s* coperta da viaggio
lapse [læps] *s* (*interval*) spazio di tempo; (*fall, decline*) caduta; (*of memory*) perdita; errore *m*; (ins) risoluzione; (law) decadenza ‖ *intr* cadere, ricadere; cadere in disuso; (*said of time*) passare; (ins) risolversi; (law) decadere
lap'wing' *s* pavoncella
larce•ny ['larsəni] *s* (**-nies**) furto
larch [lartʃ] *s* larice *m*
lard [lard] *s* strutto ‖ *tr* lardellare
larder ['lardər] *s* dispensa
large [lardʒ] *adj* grande, grosso ‖ *s*—**at large** in libertà
large' intes'tine *s* intestino crasso
largely ['lardʒli] *adv* in gran parte
large'-scale' *adj* su larga scala
lariat ['lærɪ•ət] *s* lazo, laccio
lark [lark] *s* allodola; (coll) burla; **to go on a lark** (coll) far festa
lark'spur' *s* (*rocket larkspur*) sprone *m* di cavaliere; (*field larkspur*) consolida reale
lar•va ['larvə] *s* (**-vae** [vi]) larva
laryngitis [,lærɪn'dʒaɪtɪs] *s* laringite *f*
laryngoscope [lə'rɪŋgə,skop] *s* laringoscopio
larynx ['lærɪŋks] *s* (**larynxes** or **larynges** [lə'rɪndʒiz]) laringe *f*
lascivious [lə'sɪvɪ•əs] *adj* lascivo
lasciviousness [lə'sɪvɪ•əsnɪs] *s* lascivia
laser ['lesər] *s* (acronym) (**light amplification by stimulated emission of radiation**) laser *m*
lash [læʃ] *s* (*cord on end of whip*) sverzino; (*blow with whip; scolding*) staffilata; (*of animal's tail*) colpo; (*eyelash*) ciglio; (fig) assalto ‖ *tr* (*to whip*) frustare; (*to bind*) legare; (*to shake*) agitare; (*to attack with words*) staffilare ‖ *intr* lanciarsi; **to lash out at** attaccare violentemente
lashing ['læʃɪŋ] *s* legatura; (*severe scolding*) staffilata; (*fastening with a rope*) (naut) rizza
lass [læs] *s* ragazza, giovane *f*; innamorata
las•so ['læso] or [læ'su] *s* (**-sos** or **-soes**) lasso, lazo ‖ *tr* pigliare col lasso
last [læst] or [last] *adj* ultimo, passato; (*most recent*) scorso; **before last** ierlaltro, e.g., **the night before last** ierlaltro notte; **every last one** tutti senza eccezione; **last but one** penultimo ‖ *s* ultima persona; ultima cosa; fine *f*; (*for holding shoes*) forma; **at last** alla fine; **at long last!** finalmente!; **stick to your last!** fa' il mestiere tuo!; **the last of the month** alla fine del mese; **to breathe one's last** dare l'ultimo sospiro; **to see the last of s.o.** vedere qlcu per l'ultima

volta; **to the last** fino alla fine || *adv* ultimo, per ultimo, alla fine || *intr* durare, continuare
lasting ['læstɪŋ] or ['lɑstɪŋ] *adj* duraturo, durevole
lastly ['læstli] or ['lɑstli] *adv* finalmente, in conclusione
last'-min'ute news' *s* notizie *fpl* dell'ultima ora
last' name' *s* cognome *m*
last' night' *adv* ieri sera; la notte scorsa
last' quar'ter *s* ultimo quarto
last' sleep' *s* ultimo sonno
last' straw' *s* ultima, colmo
Last' Sup'per *s* Ultima Cena
last will' and tes'tament *s* ultime volontà *fpl*
last' word' *s* ultima parola; (*latest style*) ultima novità, ultimo grido
latch [lætʃ] *s* saliscendi *m;* (*wooden*) nottola || *tr* chiudere col saliscendi
latch'key' *s* chiave *f* per saliscendi
latch'string' *s*—**the latchstring is out** faccia come fosse a casa Sua
late [let] *adj* (*happening after the usual time*) tardo; (*person*) in ritardo; (*hour of the night*) avanzato; (*news*) dell'ultima ora, recente; (*incumbent of an office*) predecessore, ex, passato; (*coming toward the end of a period*) tardivo; (*deceased*) defunto, fu; **in the late 30's, 40's, etc.** verso la fine del decennio che va dal 1930, 1940, etc. al 1940, 1950, etc.; **of late** recentemente; **to be late in** + *ger* essere in ritardo a + *inf;* **to grow late** farsi tardi; **to keep late hours** fare le ore piccole || *adv* tardi; in ritardo; **late in** (*the week, the month, etc.*) alla fine di; **late in life** a un'età avanzata
latecomer ['let ˌkʌmər] *s* ritardatario
lateen' sail' [læ'tin] *s* vela latina
lately ['letli] *adv* recentemente
latent ['letənt] *adj* latente
later ['letər] *adj comp* più tardi; (*event*) susseguente; **later than** posteriore a || *adv comp* più tardi; **later on** più tardi; **see you later** (coll) arrivederci, a ben presto
lateral ['lætərəl] *adj* laterale
lath [læθ] or [lɑθ] *s* listello, striscia di legno || *tr* mettere listelli su
lathe [leð] *s* tornio
lather ['læðər] *s* schiuma di sapone; schiuma || *tr* insaponare; (coll) bastonare || *intr* schiumare
lathery ['læðəri] *adj* schiumoso
lathing ['læθɪŋ] or ['lɑθɪŋ] *s* costruzione con listelli
Latin ['lætɪn] or ['lætən] *adj* & *s* latino
Lat'in Amer'ica *s* l'America latina
Lat'in-Amer'ican *adj* dell'America latina
Lat'in Amer'ican *s* abitante *mf* dell'America latina
latitude ['lætɪ ˌtjud] or ['lætɪ ˌtud] *s* latitudine *f*
latrine [lə'trin] *s* latrina militare
latter ['lætər] *adj* (*more recent*) posteriore; (*of two*) secondo; **the latter** questo; **the latter part of** la fine di
lattice ['lætɪs] *s* graticcio || *tr* munire di graticcio, graticciare
lat'tice gird'er *s* trave *f* a traliccio
lat'tice·work' *s* graticcio, traliccio
Latvia ['lætvɪ·ə] *s* la Lettonia
laud [lɔd] *tr* lodare
laudable ['lɔdəbəl] *adj* lodevole
laudanum ['lɔdənəm] or ['lɔdnəm] *s* laudano
laudatory ['lɔdə ˌtori] *adj* lodativo
laugh [læf] or [lɑf] *s* riso || *tr*—**to laugh away** dissipare ridendo; **to laugh off** prendere sotto gamba, non dare importanza a || *intr* ridere, ridersi; **to laugh at** ridersi di; **to laugh up one's sleeve** ridere sotto i baffi
laughable ['læfəbəl] or ['lɑfəbəl] *adj* risibile
laughing ['læfɪŋ] or ['lɑfɪŋ] *adj* che ride; **to be no laughing matter** non esserci niente da ridere || *s* riso
laugh'ing gas' *s* gas *m* esilarante
laugh'ing·stock' *s* ludibrio, zimbello
laughter ['læftər] or ['lɑftər] *s* riso
launch [lɔntʃ] or [lɑntʃ] *s* (*of a ship*) varo; (*of a rocket*) lancio; (naut) lancia, scialuppa || *tr* (*to throw; to send forth*) lanciare; (naut) varare || *intr* lanciarsi
launching ['lɔntʃɪŋ] or ['lɑntʃɪŋ] *s* lancio; (*of a ship*) varo
launch'ing pad' *s* piattaforma di lancio
launder ['lɔndər] or ['lɑndər] *tr* lavare e stirare || *intr* riuscire dopo il lavaggio
launderer ['lɔndərər] or ['lɑndərər] *s* lavandaio stiratore *m*
laundress ['lɔndrɪs] or ['lɑndrɪs] *s* lavandaia stiratrice *f*
laundromat ['lɔndrə ˌmæt] or ['lɑndrə ˌmæt] *s* (trademark) lavanderia a gettone
laun·dry ['lɔndri] or ['lɑndri] *s* (**-dries**) lavanderia; (*clothing*) bucato
laun'dry·man' *s* (**-men'**) lavandaio
laun'dry·wom'an *s* (**-wom'en**) lavandaia
laureate ['lɔrɪ·ɪt] *adj* laureato || *s* laureato; poeta laureato
lau·rel ['lɔrəl] or ['lɑrəl] *s* lauro, alloro; **laurels** (fig) alloro; **to rest or sleep on one's laurels** dormire sugli allori || *v* (*pret & pp* **-reled** or **-relled;** *ger* **-reling** or **-relling**) *tr* laureare
lava ['lɑvə] or ['lævə] *s* lava
lavato·ry ['lævə ˌtori] *s* (**-ries**) (*room*) gabinetto da bagno; (*bowl*) lavabo; (*toilet*) gabinetto di decenza, cesso
lavender ['lævəndər] *s* lavanda
lavish ['lævɪʃ] *adj* prodigo || *tr* prodigare, profondere
law [lɔ] *s* (*of man, of nature, of science*) legge *f;* (*study, profession of law*) diritto; **to enter the law** farsi avvocato; **to go to law** ricorrere alla legge; **to lay down the law** dettar legge; **to maintain law and order** mantenere la pace interna; **to practice law** fare l'avvocato
law-abiding ['lɔ·ə ˌbaɪdɪŋ] *adj* osservante della legge
law'break'er *s* violatore *m* della legge

law' court' *s* tribunale *m* di giustizia
lawful ['lɔfəl] *adj* legale, legittimo
lawless ['lɔlɪs] *adj* illegale; (*unbridled*) sfrenato
law'mak'er *s* legislatore *m*
lawn [lɔn] *s* tappeto erboso; (*fabric*) batista
lawn' mow'er *s* tosatrice *f*
law' of'fice *s* ufficio d'avvocato
law' of na'tions *s* diritto delle genti
law' of the jun'gle *s* legge *f* della giungla
law' stu'dent *s* studente *m* di legge
law'suit' *s* causa, lite *f*, processo
lawyer ['lɔjər] *s* avvocato, legale *m*
lax [læks] *adj* (*in morals*) lasso, rilassato; (*rope*) lento; (*negligent*) trascurato; vago, indeterminato
laxative ['læksətɪv] *adj* purgativo ‖ *s* purga, purgante *m*
lay [le] *adj* (*not belonging to the clergy*) laico; (*not having special training*) non dotto, profano ‖ *s* configurazione, disposizione ‖ *v* (*pret & pp* **laid** [led]) *tr* mettere, collocare; (*snares*) tendere; (*one's eyes; a stone*) porre; (*blame*) dare, gettare; (*a bet*) fare; (*for consideration*) presentare; (*the table*) imbandire; (*said of a hen*) deporre; (*plans*) impostare; (*to locate*) disporre; **to be laid in** (*said of a scene*) aver luogo in; **to lay aside** mettere da parte; **to lay down** dichiarare; (*one's life*) dare; (*one's arms*) deporre; **to lay low** abbattere; uccidere; **to lay off** (*workers*) licenziare; (*to measure*) marcare; (slang) lasciare in pace; **to lay open** rivelare; (*to a danger*) esporre; **to lay out** estendere; preparare, disporre; (*a corpse*) comporre; (*money*) (coll) sborsare; **to lay over** posporre; **to lay up** mettere da parte; obbligare a letto; (naut) disarmare ‖ *intr* (*said of a hen*) fare le uova; **to lay about** dar botte da orbi; **to lay for** (slang) attendere al varco; **to lay off** (coll) cessare di lavorare; **to lay over** trattenersi, fermarsi; **to lay to** (naut) navigare alla cappa
lay' broth'er *s* frate *m* secolare; converso
lay' day' *s* (com) stallia
layer ['le·ər] *s* (*of paint*) mano *f*; (*of bricks*) testa; (*e.g., of rocks*) strato, falda; (anat) pannicolo; (hort) propaggine *f* ‖ *tr* (hort) propagginare
lay'er cake' *s* dolce *m* a strati
layette [le'et] *s* corredino
lay' fig'ure *s* manichino
laying ['le·ɪŋ] *s* posa; (*of eggs*) deporre *m*; (*of a wire*) tendere *m*
lay'man *s* (**-men**) (*member of the laity*) laico, secolare *m*; (*not a member of a special profession*) laico, profano
lay'off' *s* (*dismissal of workers*) licenziamento; (*period of unemployment*) disoccupazione
lay' of the land' *s* andamento generale
lay'out' *s* piano; (*sketch*) tracciato; (*of tools*) armamentario; (coll) residenza; (typ) menabò *m*; (coll) banchetto, festino
lay'o'ver *s* fermata in un viaggio
lay' sis'ter *s* suora al secolo; conversa
laziness ['lezɪnɪs] *s* pigrizia
la•zy ['lezi] *adj* (**-zier; -ziest**) pigro
la'zy•bones' *s* (coll) poltrone *m*
lea [li] *s* (*fallow land*) maggese *m*; (*meadow*) prato
lead [led] *adj* plumbeo ‖ *s* piombo; (*of lead pencil*) mina; (*for sounding depth*) (naut) scandaglio; (typ) interlinea ‖ [led] *v* (*pret & pp* **leaded; ger leading**) *tr* impiombare; (typ) interlineare ‖ [lid] *s* (*foremost place*) primato; (*guidance*) guida, direzione; (*leash*) guinzaglio; (journ) testata; (cards) mano *f*, prima mano; (elec) conduttore *m*; (mach) passo; (min) filone *m*; (rad, telv) filo d'entrata; (theat) ruolo principale; (theat) primo attore; (theat) prima attrice; **to take the lead** prendere il comando ‖ [lid] *v* (*pret & pp* **led** [led]) *tr* condurre, portare; (*to command*) comandare, essere alla testa di; (*an orchestra*) dirigere; (*a good or bad life*) fare; (*s.o. into vice*) trascinare; (cards) cominciare a giocare; (elec, mach) anticipare; **to lead astray** forviare ‖ *intr* essere in testa, guidare; prendere l'offensiva; (*said of a road*) condurre; (cards) cominciare a giocare; **to lead to** risultare in; **to lead up to** andare a condurre a
leaden ['ledən] *adj* (*of lead; like lead*) plumbeo; (*sluggish*) tardo; (*with sleep*) carico; triste
leader ['lidər] *s* capo, comandante *m*; (*ringleader*) capobanda *m*; (*of an orchestra*) direttore *m*; (*among animals*) guidaiolo; (*in a dance*) ballerino guidaiolo; (sports) capintesta *m*; (journ) articolo di fondo
lead'er dog' *s* cane *m* guida di ciechi
leadership ['lidər,ʃɪp] *s* comando, direzione; doti *fpl* di comando
leading ['lidɪŋ] *adj* principale; primo; dirigente, preeminente
lead'ing ar'ticle *s* articolo di fondo
lead'ing edge' *s* (aer) bordo d'attacco
lead'ing la'dy *s* prima attrice
lead'ing man' *s* (**men'**) primo attore
lead'ing ques'tion *s* domanda suggestiva, domanda orientatrice
lead'ing strings' *spl* dande *fpl*
lead'-in wire' ['lid ,ɪn] *s* filo d'antenna
lead' pen'cil [led] *s* lapis *m*, matita
leaf [lif] *s* (**leaves** [livz]) (*of plant*) foglia; (*of vine*) pampino; (*of paper*) foglio; (*of double door*) battente *m*; (*of table*) asse *m* a ribalta; **to turn over a new leaf** ricominciare una nuova vita ‖ *intr* fogliare; **to leaf through** sfogliare
leafless ['liflɪs] *adj* senza foglie
leaflet ['liflɪt] *s* manifestino, volantino; (*of plant*) foglietta
leaf' spring' *s* molla a balestra
leaf'stalk' *s* picciolo
leaf•y ['lifi] *adj* (**-ier; -iest**) foglioso, frondoso
league [lig] *s* lega ‖ *tr* associare ‖ *intr* associarsi

League' of Na'tions *s* Società *f* delle Nazioni
leak [lik] *s* (*in a roof*) stillicidio; (*in a ship*) falla; (*of water, gas, steam*) fuga; (*of electricity*) dispersione; buco, fessura; (*of news*) filtrazione; **to spring a leak** avere una perdita; (naut) cominciare a far acqua || *tr* (*gas, liquids*) perdere, lasciar scappare; (*news*) lasciar trapelare || *intr* (*said of water, gas etc.,*) perdere, scappare; (*said of a barrel*) spillare; (naut) fare acqua; **to leak away** (*said of money*) andarsene; **to leak out** (*said of news*) trapelare
leakage ['likɪdʒ] *s* perdita, fuoruscita, fuga; (elec) dispersione; (com) colaggio
leak•y ['liki] *adj* (**-ier; -iest**) che perde; (naut) che fa acqua; (coll) indiscreto
lean [lin] *adj* magro, secco; (*gasoline mixture*) povero || *v* (*pret & pp* **leaned** or **leant** [lɛnt]) *tr* inclinare; appoggiare || *intr* pendere, inclinarsi; (fig) inclinare, tendere; **to lean against** appoggiarsi a, addossarsi a; **to lean back** sdraiarsi; **to lean on** appoggiarsi su; **to lean out (of)** sporgersi (da); **to lean over backwards** fare di tutto; **to lean toward** (fig) tendere a, avere un'inclinazione per
leaning ['linɪŋ] *adj* inclinato, pendente || *s* inclinazione
lean'ing tow'er *s* torre *f* pendente
lean'-to' *s* (**-tos**) tetto a una falda
leap [lip] *s* salto, balzo; **by leaps and bounds** a passi da gigante; **leap in the dark** salto nel vuoto || *v* (*pret & pp* **leaped** or **leapt** [lept]) *tr* saltare || *intr* saltare; (*said of one's heart*) balzare
leap'frog' *s* cavallina; **to play leapfrog** giocare alla cavallina
leap' year' *s* anno bisestile
learn [lʌrn] *s* (*pret & pp* **learned** or **learnt** [lʌrnt]) *tr* imparare; imparare a memoria; (*news*) apprendere || *intr* istruirsi, apprendere
learned ['lʌrnɪd] *adj* dotto; (*word*) colto
learn'ed jour'nal *s* rivista scientifica
learn'ed soci'ety *s* associazione di eruditi
learn'ed word' *s* parola dotta
learn'ed world' *s* mondo di dotti
learner ['lʌrnər] *s* apprendista *mf;* studente *m;* (*beginner*) principiante *mf*
learning ['lʌrnɪŋ] *s* istruzione; (*scholarship*) erudizione
lease [lis] *s* locazione, contratto d'affitto; **a new lease on life** nuove prospettive di felicità; vita nuova (dopo una malattia) || *tr* locare; prendere in affitto || *intr* affittare
lease'hold' *adj* affittato || *s* beni *mpl* sotto locazione
leash [liʃ] *s* guinzaglio; **to strain at the leash** mordere il freno || *tr* frenare, controllare
least [list] *adj* minore, menomo, minimo || *s* (il) meno; **at least** or **at the least** per lo meno, quanto meno; **not in the least** nient'affatto || *adv* meno
leather ['lɛðər] *s* cuoio
leath'er•back tur'tle *s* tartaruga di mare
leath'er goods' store' *s* pelletteria
leathery ['lɛðəri] *adj* coriaceo
leave [liv] *s* (*permission*) permesso; (*permission to be absent*) licenza; (*farewell*) commiato; **on leave** in licenza; **to take French leave** andarsene all'inglese; **to take leave (of)** prender congedo (da) || *v* (*pret & pp* **left** [lɛft]) *tr* (*to go away from*) lasciare, uscire da; (*to let stay*) lasciare; (*to bequeath*) lasciare in testamento; **leave it to me!** lasciami fare!; **to be left** restare, e.g., **the door was left open** la porta restò aperta; esserci, e.g., **there is no bread left** non c'è più pane; **to leave alone** lasciare in pace; **to leave no stone unturned** cercare ogni possibilità; **to leave off** abbandonare, lasciare; **to leave out** omettere; **to leave things as they are** lasciar stare le cose || *intr* andarsene; (*said of a conveyance*) partire
leaven ['lɛvən] *s* lievito || *tr* lievitare; (fig) impregnare, permeare
leavening ['lɛvənɪŋ] *s* lievito
leave' of ab'sence *s* licenza; (*without pay*) aspettativa
leave'-tak'ing *s* commiato
leavings ['livɪŋz] *spl* rifiuti *mpl*
Leba•nese [,lɛbə'niz] *adj* libanese || *s* (**-nese**) libanese *mf*
Lebanon ['lɛbənən] *s* il Libano
lecher ['lɛtʃər] *s* libertino
lecherous ['lɛtʃərəs] *adj* libidinoso
lechery ['lɛtʃəri] *s* lussuria
lectern ['lɛktərn] *s* leggio
lecture ['lɛktʃər] *s* conferenza; (*tedious reprimand*) pistolotto || *tr* dare una conferenza a; sermoneggiare || *intr* fare una conferenza; sermoneggiare
lecturer ['lɛktʃərər] *s* conferenziere *m*
ledge [lɛdʒ] *s* cornice *f*, cornicione *m*
ledger ['lɛdʒər] *s* (com) libro mastro
ledg'er line' *s* (mus) rigo supplementare
lee [li] *s* (*shelter*) rifugio; (naut) parte *f* sottovento; **lees** feccia
leech [litʃ] *s* mignatta, sanguisuga; **to stick like a leech** attaccarsi come una sanguisuga
leek [lik] *s* porro
leer [lɪr] *s* occhiata lussuriosa or maligna || *intr*—**to leer at** guardare di sbieco, sbirciare
leer•y ['lɪri] *adj* (**-ier; -iest**) sospettoso
leeward ['liwərd] or ['lu•ərd] *adj* di sottovento || *s* sottovento, poggia || *adv* sottovento
lee'way' *s* (aer, naut) deriva, scarroccio; (*in time*) (coll) tolleranza; (coll) libertà *f* d'azione
left [lɛft] *adj* sinistro; (pol) di sinistra || *s* sinistra; (boxing) sinistro || *adv* alla sinistra
left' field' *s* fuoricampo di sinistra
left'-hand' drive' *s* guida a sinistra
left-handed ['lɛft'hændɪd] *adj* (*individual*) mancino; (*awkward*) goffo;

(*compliment*) ambiguo; (mach) sinistrorso
leftish ['lɛftɪʃ] *adj* sinistrista
leftist ['lɛftɪst] *adj* di sinistra || *s* membro della sinistra
left'o'ver *adj & s* rimanente *m;* **leftovers** resti *mpl*
left'-wing' *adj* di sinistra
left-winger ['lɛft'wɪŋər] *s* (coll) membro dell'estrema sinistra; (coll) membro della sinistra
leg [lɛg] *s* (*of man, animal, table, chair; of trousers*) gamba; (*of fowl; of lamb*) coscia; (*of boot*) gambale *m;* (*of a journey*) tappa; **to be on one's last legs** essere agli estremi, essere ridotto alla disperazione; **to not have a leg to stand on** (coll) non avere la minima giustificazione; **to pull the leg of** (coll) prendere in giro, burlarsi di; **to shake a leg** (coll) affrettarsi; (*to dance*) (coll) ballare; **to stretch one's legs** sgranchirsi le gambe
lega·cy ['lɛgəsi] *s* (**-cies**) legato
legal ['ligəl] *adj* legale
legali·ty [lɪ'gælɪti] *s* (**-ties**) legalità *f*
legalize ['ligə,laɪz] *tr* legalizzare
le'gal ten'der *s* denaro a corso legale
legate ['lɛgɪt] *s* legato
legatee [,lɛgə'ti] *s* legatario
legation [lɪ'geʃən] *s* legazione
legend ['lɛdʒənd] *s* leggenda
legendary ['lɛdʒən,dɛri] *adj* leggendario
legerdemain [,lɛdʒərdɪ'men] *s* gioco di prestigio; (*trickery*) imbroglio
legging ['lɛgɪŋ] *s* gambale *m*
leg·gy ['lɛgi] *adj* (**-gier; -giest**) dalle gambe lunghe
leg'horn' *s* cappello di paglia di Firenze; gallina bianca livornese || **Leghorn** *s* Livorno
legible ['lɛdʒɪbəl] *adj* leggibile
legion ['lidʒən] *s* legione *f*
legislate ['lɛdʒɪs,let] *tr* ordinare per mezzo di legge || *intr* legiferare
legislation [,lɛdʒɪs'leʃən] *s* legislazione
legislative ['lɛdʒɪs,letɪv] *adj* legislativo
legislator ['lɛdʒɪs,letər] *s* legislatore *m*
legislature ['lɛdʒɪs,letʃər] *s* legislatura; corpo legislativo
legitimacy [lɪ'dʒɪtɪməsi] *s* legittimità *f*
legitimate [lɪ'dʒɪtɪmɪt] *adj* legittimo || [lɪ'dʒɪtɪ,met] *tr* legittimare
legit'imate dra'ma *s* teatro serio
legitimize [lɪ'dʒɪtɪ,maɪz] *tr* legittimare
leg' of lamb' *s* cosciotto d'agnello
legume ['lɛgjum] or [lɪ'gjum] *s* (*pod*) legume *m;* (*table vegetables*) legumi *mpl;* (bot) leguminose *fpl*
leg'work' *s* lavoro che involve molto cammino
leisure ['liʒər] or ['lɛʒər] *s* ozio; **at leisure** senza fretta; disoccupato; **at one's leisure** quando si abbia un po' di tempo libero
lei'sure class' *s* gente agiata
lei'sure hours' *spl* ore *fpl* d'ozio
leisurely ['liʒərli] or ['lɛʒərli] *adj* lento || *adv* lentamente, a tempo perso
lei'sure time' *s* tempo libero
lemon ['lɛmən] *s* limone *m;* (*car*) (coll) catorcio
lemonade [,lɛmə'ned] *s* limonata
lem'on squeez'er *s* spremilimoni *m*
lend [lɛnd] *s* (*pret & pp* **lent** [lɛnt]) *tr* prestare; (*a hand*) dare
lender ['lɛndər] *s* prestatore *m*
lend'ing li'brary *s* biblioteca circolante
length [lɛŋθ] *s* lunghezza; (*of time*) durata; **at length** finalmente; **to go to any lengths** fare quanto è possibile; essere disposto a tutto; **to keep at arm's length** (*someone else*) tenere a distanza (qlcu); (*said of oneself*) tenere la distanza
lengthen ['lɛŋθən] *tr* allungare || *intr* allungarsi
length'wise' *adj* longitudinale || *adv* per il lungo
length·y ['lɛŋθi] *adj* (**-ier; -iest**) lungo, prolungato
lenien·cy ['linɪ·ənsi] *s* (**-cies**) indulgenza
lenient ['linɪ·ənt] *adj* indulgente, clemente
lens [lɛnz] *s* lente *f;* (*of the eye*) cristallino
Lent [lɛnt] *s* quaresima
Lenten ['lɛntən] *adj* quaresimale
lentil ['lɛntəl] *s* lenticchia
Leo ['li·o] *s* (astr) il Leone
leopard ['lɛpərd] *s* leopardo
leotard ['li·ə,tɑrd] *s* calzamaglia
leper ['lɛpər] *s* lebbroso
leprosy ['lɛprəsi] *s* lebbra
leprous ['lɛprəs] *adj* lebbroso; (*of an animal or plant*) squamoso
Lesbian ['lɛzbɪ·ən] *adj* lesbico || *s* lesbico; (*female homosexual*) lesbica
lesbianism ['lɛzbɪ·ə,nɪzəm] *s* lesbismo
lese majesty ['liz'mædʒɪsti] *s* delitto di lesa maestà
lesion ['liʒən] *s* lesione
less [lɛs] *adj* minore || *adv* meno; **less and less** sempre meno; **less than** meno che; (*followed by numeral or personal pron*) meno di; (*followed by verb*) meno di quanto || *s* meno
lessee [lɛs'i] *s* locatario; (*of business establishment*) concessionario
lessen ['lɛsən] *tr* diminuire, ridurre || *intr* diminuire, ridursi
lesser ['lɛsər] *adj comp* minore
lesson ['lɛsən] *s* lezione
lessor ['lɛsər] *s* locatore *m*
lest [lɛst] *conj* per paura che
let [lɛt] *v* (*pret & pp* **let;** *ger* **letting**) *tr* permettere; (*to rent*) affittare; **let** + *inf* che + *subj,* e.g., **let him go** che vada; **let alone** tanto meno; senza menzionare; **let good enough alone** essere contento dell'onesto; **let us** + *inf* = *1st pl impv,* e.g., **let us sing** cantiamo; **to let** da affittare; **to let alone** lasciare in pace; **to let be** lasciar stare; **to let by** lasciar passare; **to let down** far scendere; deludere; tradire; abbandonare; **to let fly** (*insults*) lanciare; **to let go** lasciar libero; vendere; **to let in** fare entrare; **to let it go at that** non parlarne più; **to let know** far sapere; **to**

let loose sciogliere; **to let out** lasciar uscire; (*a secret*) divulgare; (*a scream*) lasciarsi scappare; (*to enlarge*) allargare; affittare; **to let through** lasciar passare; **to let up** lasciar salire; lasciar alzare || *intr* affittare; **to let down** diminuire gli sforzi; **to let go of** disfarsi di; **to let on** (coll) fare finta; **to not let on** (coll) non lasciar trapelare; **to let out** (*said, e.g., of school*) terminare; **to let up** (coll) cessare; (coll) diminuire
let'down' *s* diminuzione; smacco, umiliazione; delusione
lethal ['liθəl] *adj* letale
lethargic [lɪ'θɑrdʒɪk] *adj* letargico
lethar·gy ['lɛθərdʒi] *s* (**-gies**) letargo
Lett [lɛt] *s* lettone *mf*; (*language*) lettone *m*
letter ['lɛtər] *s* lettera; **letters** (*literature*) lettere *fpl*, letteratura; **to the letter** alla lettera || *tr* marcare con lettere
let'ter box' *s* cassetta delle lettere
let'ter car'rier *s* postino
let'ter drop' *s* buca delle lettere
let'ter·head' *s* capolettera *m*; (*paper with printed heading*) carta da lettera intestata
lettering ['lɛtərɪŋ] *s* iscrizione; lettere *fpl*
let'ter of cred'it *s* lettera di credito
let'ter o'pener ['opənər] *s* tagliacarte *m*
let'ter pa'per *s* carta da lettere
let'ter-per'fect *adj* alla lettera; che sa alla perfezione
let'ter·press' *s* stampato in tipografia || *adv* a stampa tipografica
let'ter scales' *spl* pesalettere *m*
let'ter·word' *s* sigla
Lettish ['lɛtɪʃ] *adj* & *s* lettone *m*
lettuce ['lɛtɪs] *s* lattuga
let'up' *s* (coll) pausa, sosta; (coll) tregua; **without letup** (coll) senza posa
leucorrhea [,lukə'ri·ə] *s* leucorrea
leukemia [lu'kimɪ·ə] *s* leucemia
Levant [lɪ'vænt] *s* levante *m*
levee ['lɛvi] *s* (*embankment*) argine *m*; (*reception*) ricevimento
lev·el ['lɛvəl] *adj* piano; livellato; equilibrato; **level with** a livello di; **one's level best** (coll) il proprio meglio || *s* (*instrument*) livella; (*degree of elevation*) livello; (*flat surface*) spianata, pianura; **on the level** (slang) onesto; onestamente; **to find one's level** trovare il proprio ambiente || *v* (*pret & pp* **-eled** or **-elled**; *ger* **-eling** or **-elling**) *tr* livellare; (*to flatten out*) spianare; (*e.g., prices*) pareggiare, ragguagliare; (*a gun*) puntare; (coll) gettare a terra; (fig) dirigere || *intr*—**to level off** (aer) volare orizzontalmente
level-headed ['lɛvəl'hedɪd] *adj* equilibrato
lev'eling rod' *s* stadia
lever ['livər] or ['lɛvər] *s* leva || *tr* far leva su || *intr* far leva
leverage ['livərɪdʒ] or ['lɛvərɪdʒ] *s* azione di una leva; (fig) potere *m*
leviathan [lɪ'vaɪ·əθən] *s* leviatano
levitation [,lɛvɪ'teʃən] *s* levitazione
levi·ty ['lɛvɪti] *s* (**-ties**) leggerezza
lev·y ['lɛvi] *s* (**-ies**) (*of taxes*) esazione; (*of money*) tributo; (*of troops*) leva || *v* (*pret & pp* **-ied**) *tr* (*a tax*) imporre; (*soldiers*) reclutare; (*war*) fare
lewd [lud] *adj* (*lustful*) lascivo; osceno
lexical ['lɛksɪkəl] *adj* lessicale
lexicographer [,lɛksɪ'kɑgrəfər] *s* lessicografo
lexicographic(al) [,lɛksɪko'græfɪk(əl)] *adj* lessicografico
lexicography [,lɛksɪ'kɑgrəfi] *s* lessicografia
lexicology [,lɛksɪ'kɑlədʒi] *s* lessicologia
lexicon ['lɛksɪkən] *s* lessico
liabili·ty [,laɪ·ə'bɪlɪti] *s* (**-ties**) svantaggio; responsabilità *f*; (*e.g., to disease*) tendenza; (com) passivo; **liabilities** debiti *mpl*; (com) passivo
liabil'ity insur'ance *s* assicurazione sulla responsabilità civile
liable ['laɪ·əbəl] *adj* (*e.g., to disease; e.g., to make mistakes*) soggetto; responsabile; probabile; (*e.g., to a fine*) passibile
liaison ['li·ə,zɑn] or [li'ezən] *s* legame *m*; relazione illecita; (mil, nav) collegamento; (phonet) legamento
li'aison of'ficer *s* ufficiale *m* di collegamento
liar ['laɪ·ər] *s* bugiardo, mentitore *m*
libation [laɪ'beʃən] *s* (joc) libazione, bevuta
li·bel ['laɪbəl] *s* diffamazione; (*defamatory writing*) libello || *v* (*pret & pp* **-beled** or **-belled**; *ger* **-beling** or **-belling**) *tr* diffamare
libelous ['laɪbələs] *adj* diffamatorio
liberal ['lɪbərəl] *adj* liberale; (*translation*) libero || *s* liberale *mf*
liberali·ty [,lɪbə'rælɪti] *s* (**-ties**) liberalità *f*; (*breadth of mind*) ampiezza di vedute
liberal-minded ['lɪbərəl'maɪndɪd] *adj* liberale, tollerante
liberate ['lɪbə,ret] *tr* liberare
liberation [,lɪbə'reʃən] *s* liberazione
liberator ['lɪbə,retər] *s* liberatore *m*
libertine ['lɪbər,tin] *adj* & *s* libertino
liber·ty ['lɪbərti] *s* (**-ties**) libertà *f*; **to take the liberty to** permettersi di
liberty-loving ['lɪbərti'lʌvɪŋ] *adj* amante della libertà
libidinous [lɪ'bɪdɪnəs] *adj* libidinoso
libido [lɪ'bido] or [lɪ'baɪdo] *s* libidine *f*; (psychoanal) libido *f*
Libra ['librə] or ['laɪbrə] *s* (astr) Bilancia
librarian [laɪ'brɛrɪ·ən] *s* bibliotecario
librar·y ['laɪ,breri] or ['laɪbrəri] *s* (**-ies**) biblioteca; (*room in a house; collection of books*) libreria
li'brary num'ber *s* segnatura
li'brary sci'ence *s* biblioteconomia
libret·to [lɪ'brɛto] *s* (**-tos**) (mus) libretto
Libya ['lɪbɪ·ə] *s* la Libia
license ['laɪsəns] *s* licenza; (aut) patente *f* || *tr* dare la licenza a

li'cense num'ber *s* numero di targa di circolazione
li'cense plate' or **tag'** *s* targa di circolazione
licentious [laɪ'senʃəs] *adj* licenzioso
lichen ['laɪkən] *s* lichene *m*
lick [lɪk] *s* leccata, leccatura; (coll) esplosione di energia; (coll) velocità *f;* (coll) battitura; (coll) ripulita; **to give a lick and a promise to** (coll) fare rapidamente e con poca attenzione || *tr* leccare; (*said of waves, flames, etc.*) lambire; (*to defeat*) (*coll*) battere, vincere; (*e.g., with a stick*) (coll) bastonare
licorice ['lɪkərɪs] *s* liquirizia
lid [lɪd] *s* coperchio; (*eyelid*) palpebra; (*curb*) (coll) restrizione, freno; (*hat*) (slang) cappello
lie [laɪ] *s* menzogna; **to catch in a lie** pigliare in castagna; **to give the lie to** smentire || *v* (*pret & pp* **lied;** *ger* **lying**) *tr*—**to lie oneself out of** or **to lie one's way out of** trarsi fuori da (*un impaccio*) con una menzogna || *intr* mentire || *v* (*pret* **lay** [le]; *pp* **lain** [len]; *ger* **lying**) *intr* essere sdraiato; trovarsi; (*in the grave*) giacere; **to lie down** sdraiarsi
lie' detec'tor *s* macchina della verità
lien [lin] or ['li·ən] *s* diritto di pegno, diritto di garanzia
lieu [lu] *s*—**in lieu of** in luogo di
lieutenant [lu'tenənt] *s* luogotenente *m;* (mil) tenente *m;* (nav) tenente *m* di vascello
lieuten'ant colo'nel *s* (mil) tenente *m* colonnello
lieuten'ant command'er *s* (nav) capitano di corvetta
lieuten'ant gen'eral *s* (mil) generale *m* di corpo d'armata
lieuten'ant gov'ernor *s* (USA) vicegovernatore *m*
lieuten'ant jun'ior grade' *s* (nav) sottotenente *m* di vascello
life [laɪf] *adj* (*animate*) vitale; (*lifelong*) perpetuo; (*annuity*) vitalizio; (*working from nature*) dal vero || *s* (**lives** [laɪvz]) vita; (*of an insurance policy*) forza; **for life** a vita; **for the life of me** per quanto io provi; **the life and soul of** (*e.g., the party*) l'anima di; **to come to life** tornare a sé; riprender vita; **to depart this life** passar a miglior vita; **to run for one's life** scappare a tutta corsa
life' annu'ity *s* rendita vitalizia
life' belt' *s* cintura di salvataggio
life'boat' *s* imbarcazione di salvataggio, lancia di salvataggio
life' buoy' *s* salvagente *m*
life' float' *s* zattera di salvataggio
life'guard' *s* bagnino
life' impris'onment *s* ergastolo
life' insur'ance *s* assicurazione sulla vita
life' jack'et *s* cintura or giubbotto di salvataggio
lifeless ['laɪflɪs] *adj* inanimato; (*in a faint*) esanime; senza vita
life'like' *adj* (*e.g., portrait*) parlante; naturale
life' line' *s* sagola di salvataggio; (fig) linea di comunicazioni vitale
life'long' *adj* perpetuo, a vita
life' of Ri'ley ['raɪli] *s* vita del michelaccio
life' of the par'ty *s* anima della festa
life' preserv'er [prɪ'zʌrvər] *s* salvagente *m*
lifer ['laɪfər] *s* (slang) ergastolano
life' raft' *s* zattera di salvataggio
life'sav'er *s* salvatore *m* della vita; (*something that saves from a predicament*) ancora di salvezza
life' sen'tence *s* condanna all'ergastolo
life'-size' *adj* in grandezza naturale
life'time' *adj* vitalizio || *s* corso della vita
life' vest' *s* (air, naut) giubbotto salvagente or di salvataggio
life'work' *s* lavoro di tutta una vita
lift [lɪft] *s* sollevamento; (*act of helping*) aiuto; (*ride*) passaggio; (*apparatus*) elevatore *m;* (aer) portanza || *tr* sollevare, alzare; (*one's hat*) levarsi; rimuovere; (coll) plagiare; (coll) rubare; (*fire*) (mil) sospendere || *intr* sollevare, sollevarsi; (*said, e.g., of fog*) dissiparsi
lift'-off' *s* (aer) decollo verticale
lift' truck' *s* carrello elevatore
ligament ['lɪgəmənt] *s* legamento
ligature ['lɪgətʃər] *s* legatura
light [laɪt] *adj* (*in weight*) leggero; (*hair*) biondo; (*complexion*) chiaro; (*oil*) fluido; (naut) con poco carico; (*room*) chiaro, illuminato; (*beer*) chiaro; **light in the head** (*dizzy*) allegro; (*silly*) scimunito; **to make light of** prendere sotto gamba || *s* luce *f;* (*to light a cigarette*) fuoco; (*to control traffic*) segnale *m;* (*shining example*) luminare *m;* (*lighthouse*) faro; (*window*) luce *f;* **according to one's lights** secondo l'intelligenza che il buon Dio gli (le) ha dato; **against the light** controluce; **in this light** sotto questo punto di vista; **lights** esempio; (*of sheep*) polmone *m;* **to come to light** venire alla luce; **to shed** or **throw light on** mettere in luce; **to strike a light** accendere un fiammifero || *v* (*pret & pp* **lighted** or **lit** [lɪt] *tr* (*to furnish with illumination*) illuminare; (*to ignite*) accendere; **to light up** illuminare || *intr* illuminarsi; accendersi; (*said, e.g., of a bird*) posarsi; (*from a car*) scendere; **to light into** (coll) gettarsi contro; **to light out** (slang) darsela a gambe; **to light upon** imbattersi in || *adv* senza bagagli; senza carico
light' bulb' *s* lampadina
light-complexioned ['laɪtkəm'plekʃənd] *adj* dal colorito chiaro
lighten ['laɪtən] *tr* alleggerire, sgravare; illuminare; (*to cheer up*) rallegrare || *intr* alleggerirsi; (*to become less dark*) illuminarsi; (*to give off flashes of lightning*) lampeggiare
lighter ['laɪtər] *s* accenditore *m;* (naut) burchio
light-fingered ['laɪt'fɪŋgərd] *adj* svelto di mano, con le mani lunghe

light-footed ['laɪt'fʊtɪd] *adj* agile
light-headed ['laɪt'hɛdɪd] *adj* (*dizzy*) allegro; (*simple*) scemo
light-hearted ['laɪt'hɑrtɪd] *adj* allegro
light'house' *s* faro
lighting ['laɪtɪŋ] *s* illuminazione
lightly ['laɪtli] *adv* alla leggera
light' me'ter *s* esposimetro
lightness ['laɪtnɪs] *s* (*in weight*) leggerezza; (*in illumination*) chiarezza
light•ning ['laɪtnɪŋ] *s* lampo, fulmine *m* || *v* (*ger* **-ning**) *intr* lampeggiare
light'ning arrest'er [ə'rɛstər] *s* scaricatore *m*
light'ning bug' *s* lucciola
light'ning rod' *s* parafulmine *m*
light' op'era *s* operetta
light'ship' *s* battello faro
light-struck ['laɪt,strʌk] *adj* che ha preso luce
light'weight' *adj* leggero; da mezza stagione, e.g., **lightweight coat** cappotto da mezza stagione
light'-year' *s* anno luce
likable ['laɪkəbəl] *adj* simpatico
like [laɪk] *adj* uguale, simile; uguale a, simile a, e.g., **this hat is like mine** questo cappello è simile al mio; (elec) di segno uguale; **like father like son** tale il padre quale il figlio; **to feel like** + *ger* aver voglia di + *inf;* **to look like** assomigliare a; sembrare, e.g., **it looks like rain** sembra che pioverà || *s* (*liking*) preferenza; (*fellow man*) simile *m;* **and the like** e cose dello stesso genere; **to give like for like** rendere pane per focaccia || *adv* come; **like enough** (coll) probabilmente || *prep* come || *conj* (coll) come; come se; (coll) che, e.g., **it seems like he is afraid** sembra che abbia paura || *tr* voler bene (with *dat*), e.g., **I like her very much** le voglio molto bene; trovar piacere in, e.g., **I like music** trovo piacere nella musica; piacere (with *dat*), e.g., **John likes apples** le mele piacciono a Giovanni; **to like best** or **better** preferire; **to like it in** trovarsi a proprio agio in; **to like to** + *inf* piacere (with *dat*) + *inf,* e.g., **she likes to dance** le piace ballare; gradire che + *subj,* e.g., **I should like him to pay a visit to my parents** gradirei che facesse una visita ai miei genitori || *intr* volere, desiderare, e.g., **as you like** come desidera; **if you like** se vuole
likelihood ['laɪklɪ,hʊd] *s* probabilità *f*
like•ly ['laɪkli] *adj* (**-lier; -liest**) probabile; verosimile; a proposito; promettente; **to be likely to** + *inf* essere probabile che + *fut,* e.g., **Mary is likely to get married in the spring** è probabile che Maria si sposerà in primavera || *adv* probabilmente
like-minded ['laɪk'maɪndɪd] *adj* dello stesso parere, della stessa opinione
liken ['laɪkən] *tr* paragonare
likeness ['laɪknɪs] *s* (*picture*) ritratto; (*similarity*) rassomiglianza; apparenza
like'wise' *adv* ugualmente; inoltre; **to do likewise** fare lo stesso
liking ['laɪkɪŋ] *s* simpatia; **to be to the liking of** essere di gusto di; **to have a liking for** (*things*) prendere gusto per; (*people*) affezionarsi a
lilac ['laɪlək] *adj* & *s* lilla *m*
Lilliputian [,lɪlɪ'pju∫ən] *adj* & *s* lillipuziano
lilt [lɪlt] *s* canzone *f* a cadenza; movimento a cadenza; (*in verse*) cadenza
lil•y ['lɪli] *s* (**-ies**) giglio; **to gild the lily** cercare di migliorare quanto è già perfetto
lil'y of the val'ley *s* mughetto
li'ma bean' ['laɪmə] *s* fagiolo bianco
limb [lɪm] *s* (*of body*) membro, arto; (*of tree*) ramo; (*of cross*) braccio; **to be out on a limb** (coll) essere nei guai
limber ['lɪmbər] *adj* agile || *intr*—**to limber up** sciogliersi i muscoli, sgranchirsi le gambe
lim•bo ['lɪmbo] *s* (**-bos**) esilio; dimenticatoio; (theol) limbo
lime [laɪm] *s* (*calcium oxide*) calce *f;* (*Citrus aurantifolia*) limetta agra; (*linden tree*) tiglio || *tr* gessare
lime'kiln' *s* fornace *f* da calce
lime'light' *s*—**to be in the limelight** essere in vista
limerick ['lɪmərɪk] *s* canzoncina umoristica di cinque versi
lime'stone' *s* calcare *m*
limit ['lɪmɪt] *s* limite *m;* (coll) colmo; **to go to the limit** andare agli estremi || *tr* limitare
limitation [,lɪmɪ'te∫ən] *s* limitazione
lim'ited-ac'cess high'way ['lɪmɪtɪd] *s* autostrada, strada con corsia d'accesso
lim'ited com'pany *s* società *f* a responsabilità limitata
lim'ited mon'archy *s* monarchia costituzionale
limitless ['lɪmɪtlɪs] *adj* illimitato
limousine ['lɪmə,zin] or [,lɪmə'zin] *s* berlina
limp [lɪmp] *adj* floscio; debole || *s* zoppicatura || *intr* zoppicare
limpid ['lɪmpɪd] *adj* limpido
linage ['laɪnɪdʒ] *s* (typ) numero di linee
linchpin ['lɪnt∫,pɪn] *s* acciarino
linden ['lɪndən] *s* tiglio
line [laɪn] *s* linea; (*e.g., of people*) fila; (*of trees*) filare *m;* (*for fishing*) lenza; (*written or printed*) rigo, riga; (*wrinkle*) ruga; (*of goods*) ramo; (naut) gherlino; **all along the line** su tutta la linea; **in line** allineato; sotto controllo; **in line with** secondo; **out of line** fuori d'allineamento; (slang) in disaccordo; **to bring into line** far filare; **to draw the line at** fermarsi a; stabilire il limite a; **to fall in line** conformarsi; allinearsi; **to have a line on** (coll) aver informazioni su; **to read between the lines** leggere fra le righe; **to stand in line** fare la coda; **to toe the line** filare diritto; **to wait in line** fare la fila || *tr* rigare; (*e.g., the street*) schierare lungo; (*a suit*) foderare; (*a brake*) rivestire; **to line up** allineare; trovare, scovare || *intr*

—to line up mettersi in fila; fare la coda
lineage ['lɪnɪ·ɪdʒ] *s* lignaggio
lineaments ['lɪnɪ·əmənts] *spl* lineamenti *mpl*
linear ['lɪnɪ·ər] *adj* lineare
line'man *s* (**-men**) (elec) guardafili *m;* (sports) guardalinee *m;* (surv) assistente geometra *m*
linen ['lɪnən] *adj* di tela di lino ‖ *s* (*fabric*) tela di lino, lino; (*yarn*) filo di lino; biancheria
lin'en clos'et *s* guardaroba *m* per la biancheria
line' of fire' *s* (mil) linea di tiro
line' of least' resist'ance *s* principio del minimo sforzo; **to follow the line of least resistance** prendere la via più facile
line' of sight' *s* visuale *f;* (mil) linea di mira
liner ['laɪnər] *s* transatlantico
line'-up' *s* disposizione; (*of prisoners*) allineamento; (sports) formazione
linger ['lɪŋgər] *intr* indugiare, soffermarsi; (*to be tardy*) tardare; rimanere in vita; **to linger over** contemplare
lingerie [ˌlænʒə'ri] *s* biancheria intima
lingering ['lɪŋgərɪŋ] *adj* prolungato
lingual ['lɪŋgwəl] *adj* linguale ‖ *s* suono linguale
linguist ['lɪŋgwɪst] *s* poliglotto; (*specialist in linguistics*) glottologo
linguistic [lɪŋ'gwɪstɪk] *adj* linguistico ‖ **linguistics** *s* linguistica, glottologia
lining ['laɪnɪŋ] *s* (*of a coat*) fodera; (*of auto brake*) guarnizione; (*of a furnace*) rivestimento interno; (*of wall*) rivestimento
link [lɪŋk] *s* anello, maglia; unione; (*of sausage*) nocco; **links** campo di golf ‖ *tr* connettere ‖ *intr* connettersi
linnet ['lɪnɪt] *s* fanello
linotype ['laɪnə ˌtaɪp] *s* linotype *f* ‖ *tr* comporre in linotipia
lin'otype op'erator *s* linotipista *mf*
linseed ['lɪn ˌsid] *s* linosa
lin'seed oil' *s* olio di lino
lint [lɪnt] *s* peluria, sfilacciatura; (*for dressing wounds*) filaccia
lintel ['lɪntəl] *s* architrave *m*
lion ['laɪ·ən] *s* leone *m;* celebrità *f;* **to beard the lion in his den** affrontare l'avversario a casa sua; **to put one's head in the lion's mouth** cacciarsi nei pericoli
lioness ['laɪ·ənɪs] *s* leonessa
lion-hearted ['laɪ·ən ˌhɑrtɪd] *adj* cuor di leone, coraggioso
lionize ['laɪ·ə ˌnaɪz] *tr* festeggiare come una celebrità
li'ons' den' *s* fossa dei leoni
li'on's share' *s* parte *f* del leone
lip [lɪp] *s* labbro; (*of a jar*) beccuccio; (slang) linguaggio insolente; **to smack one's lips** leccarsi le labbra
lip'read' *v* (*pret & pp* **-read** [ˌred]) *tr* leggere le labbra di ‖ *intr* leggere le labbra
lip' read'ing *s* labiolettura
lip' serv'ice *s* omaggio non sentito
lip'stick' *s* rossetto per le labbra, matita per le labbra
lique·fy ['lɪkwɪ ˌfaɪ] *v* (*pret & pp* **-fied**) *tr & intr* liquefare
liqueur [lɪ'kʌr] *s* liquore *m*
liquid ['lɪkwɪd] *adj* liquido ‖ *s* liquido; (phonet) liquida
liquidate ['lɪkwɪ ˌdet] *tr & intr* liquidare
liquidity [lɪ'kwɪdɪti] *s* liquidità *f*
liq'uid meas'ure *s* misura di capacità per liquidi
liquor ['lɪkər] *s* distillato alcolico, bevanda alcolica; (*broth*) brodo
Lisbon ['lɪzbən] *s* Lisbona
lisp [lɪsp] *s* pronuncia blesa ‖ *intr* parlare bleso
lissome ['lɪsəm] *adj* flessibile, agile
list [lɪst] *s* lista, elenco; (*border*) orlo; (*selvage*) cimossa, vivagno; (naut) sbandamento; **lists** lizza; **to enter the lists** entrare in lizza ‖ *tr* elencare, listare ‖ *intr* (naut) sbandare, andare alla banda
listen ['lɪsən] *intr* ascoltare; obbedire; **to listen in** ascoltare una conversazione; (rad) captare una comunicazione; **to listen to** ascoltare; obbedire a, prestare attenzione a; **to listen to reason** intendere ragione
listener ['lɪsənər] *s* ascoltatore *m;* radioascoltatore *m*
lis'tening post' *s* (mil) posto di ascolto
listless ['lɪstlɪs] *adj* svogliato
list' price' *s* prezzo di catalogo
lita·ny ['lɪtəni] *s* (**-nies**) litania
liter ['litər] *s* litro
literacy ['lɪtərəsi] *s* abilità *f* di leggere e scrivere; istruzione
literal ['lɪtərəl] *adj* letterale
literary ['lɪtə ˌreri] *adj* letterario; (*individual*) letterato
literate ['lɪtərɪt] *adj* che sa leggere e scrivere; (*educated*) istruito; (*well-read*) letterato ‖ *s* persona che sa leggere e scrivere; letterato
literature ['lɪtərətʃər] *s* letteratura; (*printed matter*) opuscoli pubblicitari
lithe [laɪθ] *adj* flessibile, agile
lithium ['lɪθɪ·əm] *s* litio
lithograph ['lɪθə ˌgræf] or ['lɪθə ˌgrɑf] *s* litografia ‖ *tr* litografare
lithographer [lɪ'θɑgrəfər] *s* litografo
lithography [lɪ'θɑgrəfi] *s* litografia
Lithuania [ˌlɪθu'enɪ·ə] *s* la Lituania
Lithuanian [ˌlɪθu'enɪ·ən] *adj & s* lituano
litigant ['lɪtɪgənt] *adj & s* litigante *mf*
litigate ['lɪtɪ ˌget] *tr & intr* litigare
litigation [ˌlɪtɪ'geʃən] *s* litigio; (*lawsuit*) lite *f*, causa
litmus ['lɪtməs] *s* tornasole *m*
lit'mus pa'per *s* cartina al tornasole
litter ['lɪtər] *s* disordine *m;* (*scattered rubbish*) pattume *m;* (*young brought forth at one birth*) figliata; (*of puppies*) cucciolata; (*bedding for animals*) strame *m;* (*stretcher; bed carried by men or animals*) lettiga, portantina ‖ *tr* mettere in disordine; spargere rifiuti per; coprire di strame ‖ *intr* partorire

lit'ter·bug' *s* sparpagliatore *m* di rifiuti
littering ['lɪtərɪŋ] *s*—**no littering** vietato gettare rifiuti
little ['lɪtəl] *adj* (*in size*) piccolo; (*in amount*) poco, e.g., **little salt** poco sale; **a little** un po' di, e.g., **a little salt** un po' di sale; **the little ones** i piccini || *s* poco; **a little** un po'; **to make little of** farsi gioco di; non pigliar sul serio; **to think little of** non tener di conto || *adv* poco; **little by little** poco a poco, mano a mano
Lit'tle Bear' *s* Orsa minore
Lit'tle Dip'per *s* Piccolo Carro
lit'tle fin'ger *s* mignolo; **to twist around one's little finger** maneggiare come un fantoccio
lit'tle·neck' *s* piccola vongola (*Venus mercenaria*)
lit'tle owl' *s* civetta
lit'tle peo'ple *spl* fate *fpl;* folletti *mpl*
Lit'tle Red Rid'inghood' ['raɪdɪŋ ,hʊd] *s* Cappuccetto Rosso
lit'tle slam' *s* (bridge) piccolo slam
liturgic(al) [lɪ'tʌrdʒɪk(əl)] *adj* liturgico
litur·gy ['lɪtərdʒi] *s* (**-gies**) liturgia
livable ['lɪvəbəl] *adj* abitabile; socievole; tollerabile
live [laɪv] *adj* vivo; (*flame*) ardente; di attualità; (elec) sotto tensione; (telv) in diretta || [lɪv] *tr* vivere; **to live down** (*one's past*) far dimenticare; **to live it up** (coll) darsi alla bella vita, scialare; **to live out** (*e.g., a war*) sopravvivere (with *dat*) || *intr* vivere; **to live from hand to mouth** vivere alla giornata; **to live high** darsi alla bella vita; **to live on** continuare a vivere; (*e.g., vegetables*) vivere di; vivere alle spalle di; **to live up to** (*one's promises*) compiere; (*one's earnings*) spendere
live' coal' [laɪv] *s* brace *f*
livelihood ['laɪvlɪ ,hʊd] *s* vita; **to earn one's livelihood** guadagnarsi la vita
livelong ['lɪv ,lɔŋ] or ['lɪv ,lɑŋ] *adj*—**all the livelong day** tutto il santo giorno
live·ly ['laɪvli] *adj* (**-lier; -liest**) vivo, vivace; (*color*) vivido; (*resilient*) elastico; (*tune*) brioso
liven ['laɪvən] *tr* animare || *intr* animarsi, rianimarsi
liver ['lɪvər] *s* abitante *mf;* (anat) fegato
liver·y ['lɪvəri] *s* (**-ies**) livrea
liv'ery·man *s* (**-men**) stalliere *m*
liv'ery sta'ble *s* stallaggio
livestock ['laɪv ,stɑk] *adj* zootecnico || *s* bestiame *m*
live' wire' [laɪv] *s* (elec) filo carico di corrente; (slang) persona energica
livid ['lɪvɪd] *adj* livido; (*with anger*) incollerito
living ['lɪvɪŋ] *adj* vivo; (*conditions*) abitativo || *s* vivere *m;* **to earn a living** guadagnarsi la vita
liv'ing quar'ters *spl* abitazione, alloggio
liv'ing room' *s* stanza di soggiorno
liv'ing wage' *s* salario sufficiente per vivere
lizard ['lɪzərd] *s* lucertola

load [lod] *s* peso, carico; **loads of** (coll) un mucchio di; **to get a load of** (slang) stare a vedere; (slang) stare a sentire; **to have a load on** (slang) essere ubriaco || *tr* caricare || *intr* caricarsi
loaded ['lodɪd] *adj* caricato; (slang) ubriaco fradicio; (slang) ricchissimo
load'ed dice' *spl* dadi truccati
load'stone' *s* magnetite *f;* (fig) calamita
loaf [lof] *s* (**loaves** [lovz]) pane *m;* (*molded mass*) forma; (*of sugar*) pane *m;* (*long and thin loaf*) filone *m* || *intr* batter fiacca, oziare
loafer ['lofər] *s* fannullone *m*
loam [lom] *s* ricca argilla sabbiosa; terra da fonderia
loan [lon] *s* prestito; **to hit for a loan** (coll) dare una stoccata a || *tr* prestare
loan' shark' *s* (coll) strozzino
loan' word' *s* (ling) prestito
loath [loθ] *adj* poco disposto; **nothing loath** molto volentieri
loathe [loð] *tr* detestare, aborrire
loathsome ['loðsəm] *adj* abominevole, disgustoso
lob [lɑb] *s* (tennis) pallonetto || *v* (*pret & pp* **lobbed;** *ger* **lobbing**) *tr* (tennis) dare un pallonetto a
lob·by ['lɑbi] *s* (**-bies**) anticamera, vestibolo; sollecitazione di voti || *v* (*pret & pp* **-bied**) *intr* sollecitare voti, influenzare il voto dietro le quinte
lobbyist ['lɑbɪ·ɪst] *s* politicante *m* che cerca di influenzare il voto dietro le quinte
lobe [lob] *s* lobo
lobster ['lɑbstər] *s* (*Palinurus vulgaris*) aragosta; (*Hommarus vulgaris*) astice *m*
lob'ster pot' *s* nassa per aragoste
local ['lokəl] *adj* locale || *s* treno accelerato; notizia di interesse locale; (*of a union*) sezione
locale [lo'kæl] *s* località *f*
locali·ty [lo'kælɪti] *s* (**-ties**) località *f*
localize ['lokə ,laɪz] *tr* localizzare
lo'cal op'tion *s* referendum *m* locale sulla vendita di alcolici
locate [lo'ket] or ['loket] *tr* (*to discover the location of*) localizzare; (*to place, settle*) situare, stabilire; (*to ascribe a location to*) individuare || *intr* stabilirsi
location [lo'keʃən] *s* localizzazione; posizione; sito; **on location** (mov) in esterno
lock [lɑk] *s* serratura; (*of a canal*) chiusa; (*of hair*) ciocca; (*of a firearm*) percussore *m;* (mach) freno; **lock, stock, and barrel** (coll) completamente; **under lock and key** sotto chiave || *tr* chiudere a chiave; serrare; (*a boat*) far passare per una chiusa; unire; abbracciare; **to lock in** chiudere sotto chiave; **to lock out** chiudere fuori; (*workers*) sbarrare dal lavoro; **to lock up** chiudere a chiave; incarcerare
locker ['lɑkər] *s* armadietto a chiave; (*in the form of a chest*) bauletto

lock'er room' *s* spogliatoio
locket ['lakɪt] *s* medaglione *m*
lock'jaw' *s* tetano, trisma *m*
lock' nut' *s* controdado
lock'out' s serrata
lock'smith' *s* magnano, fabbro
lock' step' *s*—**to march in lock step** marciare a passo serrato
lock' stitch' *s* punto a filo doppio
lock' ten'der *s* guardiano di chiusa
lock'up' *s* prigione; (typ) messa in forma
lock' wash'er *s* rondella di sicurezza
locomotive [,lokə'motɪv] *s* locomotiva
lo•cus ['lokəs] *s* (**-ci** [saɪ]) luogo
locust ['lokəst] *s* (ent) locusta; (*cicada*) (ent) cicala; (bot) robinia
lode [lod] *s* filone *m*, vena
lode'star' *s* stella polare; guida
lodge [ladʒ] *s* casetta; padiglione *m* da caccia; albergo; (*e.g., of Masons*) loggia || *tr* alloggiare, ospitare; depositare; contenere; (*a complaint*) sporgere || *intr* alloggiare; essere contenuto, trovarsi; andar a finire
lodger ['ladʒər] *s* inquilino
lodging ['ladʒɪŋ] *s* alloggio
loft [lɔft] or [laft] *s* (*attic*) solaio; (*hayloft*) fienile *m*; (*in theater or church*) galleria
loft•y ['lɔfti] or ['lafti] *adj* (**-ier; -iest**) alto, elevato; (*haughty*) orgoglioso
log [lɔg] or [lag] *s* ceppo, ciocco; (naut) solcometro; (aer, naut) giornale *m* di bordo; **to sleep like a log** dormire della grossa || *v* (*pret & pp* **logged; ger logging**) *tr* registrare; (*a speed*) fare; (*a distance*) percorrere
logarithm ['lɔgə,rɪðəm] or ['lagə,rɪðəm] *s* logaritmo
log'book' *s* (aer, naut) libro di bordo
log' cab'in *s* capanna di tronchi
log' chip' *s* (naut) barchetta
log' driv'er *s* zatteriere *m*
log' driv'ing ['draɪvɪŋ] *s* fluitazione
logger ['lɔgər] or ['lagər] *s* taglialegna *m*; trattore *m* per trasporto tronchi
log'ger•head' *s* testone *m*; **at loggerheads** in lite
loggia ['lodʒə] *s* loggia
logic ['ladʒɪk] *s* logica
logical ['ladʒɪkəl] *adj* logico
logician [lo'dʒɪʃən] *s* logico
logistic(al) [lo'dʒɪstɪk(əl)] *adj* logistico
logistics [lo'dʒɪstɪks] *s* logistica
log'jam' *s* ingorgo fluviale dovuto a ammasso di tronchi; (fig) ristagno
log' line' *s* (naut) sagola
log'roll' *intr* barattare favori politici
log'wood' *s* campeggio
loin [lɔɪn] *s* lombo; **to gird up one's loins** prepararsi per l'azione
loin'cloth' *s* perizoma *m*, copripudende *m*
loiter ['lɔɪtər] *tr*—**to loiter away** (*time*) sprecare in ozio || *intr* bighellonare, trastullarsi
loiterer ['lɔɪtərər] *s* perdigiorno
loll [lal] *intr* sdraiarsi pigramente, adagiarsi pigramente; pendere
lollipop ['lali,pap] *s* caramella sullo stecchetto, lecca-lecca *m*

Lombard ['lambard] or ['lambərd] *adj & s* lombardo; (hist) longobardo
Lom'bardy pop'lar *s* pioppo italico
London ['lʌndən] *adj* londinese || *s* Londra
Londoner ['lʌndənər] *s* londinese *mf*
lone [lon] *adj* solo; solitario
loneliness ['lonlinɪs] *s* solitudine *f*
lone•ly ['lonli] *adj* (**-lier; -liest**) solingo, solo, solitario
lonesome ['lonsəm] *adj* solitario
lone' wolf' *s* (coll) orso, solitario
long [lɔŋ] or [laŋ] (**longer** ['lɔŋgər] or ['laŋgər]; **longest** ['lɔŋgɪst] or ['laŋgɪst]) *adj* lungo; **three meters long** lungo tre metri || *adv* molto, molto tempo; **as long as** mentre; (*provided*) fin tanto che; (*inasmuch as*) dato che; **before long** fra poco; **how long?** quanto?; **long ago** molto tempo fa; **long before** molto prima; **long since** molto tempo fa; **no longer** non più; **so long!** (coll) ciao!, arrivederci!; **so long as** fino a che, finché || *intr* anelare; **to long for** sviscerarsi per, sospirare per
long'boat' *s* (naut) lancia
long'-dis'tance *adj* (telp) interurbano, intercomunale; (sports) di fondo; (aer) a distanza
long'-drawn'-out' *adj* prolungato
longeron ['landʒərən] *s* longherone *m*
longevity [lan'dʒɛvɪti] *s* longevità *f*
long' face' *s* (coll) faccia triste, muso lungo
long'hair' *adj & s* (coll) intellettuale *mf*; (coll) musicomane *mf*
long'hand' *adj* (scritto) a mano || *s* scrittura a mano; **in longhand** scritto a mano
longing ['lɔŋɪŋ] or ['laŋɪŋ] *adj* bramoso, anelante || *s* brama, anelito
longitude ['landʒɪ,tjud] or ['landʒɪ,tud] *s* longitudine *f*
long•lived ['lɔŋ'laɪvd], ['lɔŋ'lɪvd], ['laŋ'laɪvd] or ['laŋ'lɪvd] *adj* (*person*) longevo, di lunga vita; (*e.g., rumor*) di lunga durata
long'-play'ing rec'ord *s* disco di grande durata
long'-range' *adj* a lunga portata
long'shore'man *s* (**-men**) portuale *m*, scaricatore *m*
long'stand'ing *adj* vecchio, che esiste da lungo tempo
long'-suf'fering *adj* paziente, longanime
long' suit' *s* (cards) serie lunga; (fig) forte *m*
long'-term' *adj* a lunga scadenza
long'-wind'ed *adj* verboso; (*speech*) chilometrico
look [lʊk] *s* (*appearance*) aspetto; (*glance*) sguardo; (*search*) ricerca; **looks** aspetto, apparenza; **to take a look at** dare un'occhiata a || *tr* guardare; (*one's age*) mostrare; **to look daggers at** fulminare con lo sguardo; **to look up** (*e.g., in a dictionary*) cercare; andare a visitare; venire a visitare || *intr* guardare; cercare; parere; **look out!** attenzione!; **to look after** badare a; occuparsi di; **to look at** guardare; **to look back** riguardare;

(fig) guardare al passato; **to look down on s.o.** guardare qlcu dall'alto in basso; **to look for** cercare; aspettarsi; **to look forward to** antecipare il piacere di; **to look ill** avere una brutta cera; **to look in on** passare per la casa di; **to look into** esaminare a fondo; **to look like** sembrare, parere; **to look out** fare attenzione; **to look out for** aver cura di; **to look out of** guardare da; **to look out on** dare su; **to look through** guardare per; (*a book*) sfogliare; **to look toward** dare su; **to look up to** ammirare, guardare con ammirazione; **to look well** avere una buona cera; fare figura

looker-on [ˌlʊkərˈɑn] or [ˌlʊkərˈɔn] *s* (**lookers-on**) astante *m*

look'ing glass' [ˈlʊkɪŋ] *s* specchio

look'out' *s* guardia; (*person; watch kept; place from which a watch is kept*) vedetta; (*concern*) (coll) affare *m;* **to be on the lookout** stare in guardia; **to be on the lookout for** essere in cerca di

loom [lum] *s* telaio ‖ *intr* apparire indistintamente; pararsi dinanzi; apparire

loon [lun] *s* scemo; fannullone *m;* (orn) (*Gavia*) strolaga

loon·y [ˈluni] *adj* (**-ier; -iest**) (slang) pazzo ‖ *s* (**-ies**) (slang) pazzo

loop [lup] *s* cappio; (*e.g., of a road*) tortuosità *f;* (*for fastening a button*) occhiello; (aer) cerchio or giro della morte; (phys) ventre *m;* ‖ *tr* fare cappi in; annodare; **to loop the loop** (aer) fare il giro della morte ‖ *intr* avanzare tortuosamente, girare

loop'hole' *s* (*narrow opening*) feritoia; (*means of evasion*) scappatoia

loose [lus] *adj* libero, sciolto; (*available*) disponibile; (*not firm*) rilasciato; (*tooth*) che balla; (*unchaste*) facile; (*garment*) ampio; (*soil*) smosso; (*translation*) libero; (*rein*) lento; **to become loose** sciogliersi; **to break loose** mettersi in libertà; **to have loose bowels** avere la diarrea; **to turn loose** liberare ‖ *s*—**to be on the loose** (coll) essere in libertà; (coll) correre la cavallina ‖ *tr* sciogliere; slegare; lanciare

loose' change' *s* spiccioli *mpl*

loose' end' *s* capo sciolto; **at loose ends** indeciso; disoccupato, senza nulla da fare

loose'-leaf' *adj* a fogli mobili

loosen [ˈlusən] *tr* snodare; rilasciare; smuovere; allentare; (*the bowels*) liberare dalla stitichezza ‖ *intr* snodarsi; rilasciarsi; smuoversi; allentarsi

looseness [ˈlusnɪs] *s* scioltezza; (*in morals*) rilassamento

loose-tongued [ˈlusˈtʌŋd] *adj* sciolto di lingua; linguacciuto, maldicente

loot [lut] *s* bottino ‖ *tr* saccheggiare

lop [lɑp] *v* (*pret & pp* **lopped; ger lopping**) *tr* lasciar cadere, lasciar penzolare; **to lop off** mozzare; (*a tree*) potare; (*a vine*) stralciare ‖ *intr* penzolare

lopsided [ˈlɑpˈsaɪdɪd] *adj* che pende da una parte; asimmetrico, sproporzionato

loquacious [loˈkweʃəs] *adj* loquace

lord [lɔrd] *s* signore *m;* (Brit) lord *m* ‖ *tr*—**to lord it over** signoreggiare su

lord·ly [ˈlɔrdli] *adj* (**-lier; -liest**) signorile, magnifico; altero, disdegnoso, arrogante

Lord's' Day', the la domenica, il giorno del Signore

lordship [ˈlɔrdʃɪp] *s* signoria

Lord's' Prayer' *s* paternostro

Lord's' Sup'per *s* Eucarestia; Ultima Cena

lore [lor] *s* tradizioni *fpl* popolari; cognizioni *fpl*

lorgnette [lɔrnˈjet] *s* occhialetto, lorgnette *f;* binocolo da teatro col manico

lor·ry [ˈlɑri] or [ˈlɔri] *s* (**-ries**) (rr) vagoncino; (Brit) camion *m*

lose [luz] *v* (*pret & pp* **lost** [lɔst] or [lɑst]) *tr* perdere; (*said of a physician*) non riuscire a salvare; **to lose heart** perdersi d'animo; **to lose oneself** perdersi, smarrirsi ‖ *intr* perdere; (*said of a watch*) ritardare; **to lose out** rimetterci

loser [ˈluzər] *s* perdente *mf*

losing [ˈluzɪŋ] *adj* perdente ‖ **losings** *spl* perdite *fpl*

loss [lɔs] or [lɑs] *s* perdita; **to be at a loss** essere perplesso; **to be at a loss to** + *inf* non saper come + *inf;* **to sell at a loss** vendere in perdita

loss' of face' *s* perdita di faccia

lost [lɔst] or [lɑst] *adj* perduto; **lost in thought** assorto in sè stesso; **lost to** perso per; insensibile a

lost'-and-found' depart'ment *s* ufficio degli oggetti smarriti

lost' sheep' *s* percorella smarrita

lot [lɑt] *s* (*for building*) lotto; (*fate*) sorte *f;* (*parcel, portion*) partita; (*of people*) gruppo; (coll) grande quantità *f;* (coll) tipo, soggetto; **a lot (of)** or **lots of** (coll) molto, molti; **to cast** or **to throw in one's lot with** condividere la sorte di; **to draw** or **to cast lots** tirare a sorte

lotion [ˈloʃən] *s* lozione

lotter·y [ˈlɑtəri] *s* (**-ies**) lotteria, riffa

lotto [ˈlɑto] *s* tombola, lotto

lotus [ˈlotəs] *s* loto

loud [laʊd] *adj* forte; (*noisy*) rumoroso; (*voice*) alto; (*garish*) sgargiante, chiassoso, appariscente; (*foul-smelling*) puzzolente ‖ *adv* a voce alta; rumorosamente

loud-mouthed [ˈlaʊd ˌmaʊθt] or [ˈlaʊd ˌmaʊðd] *adj* chiassone

loud'speak'er *s* altoparlante *m*

lounge [laʊndʒ] *s* divano, sofà *m;* sala soggiorno; ridotto ‖ *intr* oziare, star senza far niente; bighellonare; **to lounge around** bighellonare

lounge' liz'ard *s* (slang) damerino, bellimbusto, gagà *m*

louse [laʊs] *s* (**lice** [laɪs]) pidocchio ‖ *tr*—**to louse up** (slang) rovinare

lous·y [ˈlaʊzi] *adj* (**-ier; -iest**) pidocchioso; (*mean; bungling*) (coll) schi-

foso; (*filthy*) (coll) sporco; **lousy with** (*e.g., money*) (slang) pieno di
lout [laut] *s* gaglioffo, tanghero
louver ['luvər] *s* sportello girevole di persiana; (aut) feritoia per ventilazione
lovable ['lʌvəbəl] *adj* amabile
love [lʌv] *s* amore *m;* (tennis) zero; **not for love nor money** a nessun prezzo; **to be in love (with)** essere innamorato (di); **to make love to** fare l'amore con || *tr* amare; voler bene a; piacere (with *dat*), e.g., **she loves short skirts** le piacciono le sottane corte
love' affair' *s* passione, amori *mpl*
love'bird' *s* (orn) inseparabile *m;* **lovebirds** (slang) amanti appassionati
love' child' *s* figlio naturale
love' feast' *s* agape *f*
loveless ['lʌvlɪs] *adj* senza amore
lovelorn ['lʌv,lɔrn] *adj* abbandonato dalla persona amata
love·ly ['lʌvli] *adj* (**-lier; -liest**) bello; (coll) delizioso
love' match' *s* matrimonio d'amore
love' po'tion *s* filtro d'amore
lover ['lʌvər] *s* amante *m;* (*e.g., of music*) amico, appassionato
love' seat' *s* amorino
love'sick' *adj* malato d'amore
love'sick'ness *s* mal *m* d'amore
love' song' *s* canzone *f* d'amore
loving ['lʌvɪŋ] *adj* affezionato, amoroso; **your loving son** il vostro affezionato figlio
lov'ing-kind'ness *s* tenera sollecitudine
low [lo] *adj* basso; (*deep*) profondo; (*diet*) magro; (*visibility*) cattivo; (*dress*) scollato; (*dejected*) abbattuto; (*fire*) lento; (*flame; speed*) piccolo; **to lay low** ammazzare; abbattere; **to lie low** rimanere nascosto; attendere || *s* punto basso; prezzo minimo; (*of cow*) muggito; (aut) prima velocità; (meteor) depressione || *adv* basso, a basso, in basso || *intr* (*said of a cow*) muggire
low'born' *adj* di umili origini
low'boy' *s* cassettone basso con le gambe corte
low'brow' *adj* & *s* (coll) ignorante *mf*
low'-cost hous'ing *s* case *fpl* popolari
Low' Coun'tries, the i Paesi Bassi
low'-down' *adj* (coll) basso, vile || **low'-down'** *s* (coll) semplice verità *f*, notizie *fpl* confidenziali
lower ['lo·ər] *adj* inferiore, disotto || *tr* abbassare; (*prices*) ribassare || *intr* diminuire; discendere || ['lau·ər] *intr* aggrottare le ciglia; (*said of the weather*) imbronciarsi
low'er berth' ['lo·ər] *s* cuccetta inferiore
low'er case' ['lo·ər] *s* (typ) cassa inferiore
lower-case ['lo·ər,kes] *adj* (typ) minuscolo
low'er mid'dle class' ['lo·ər] *s* piccola borghesia
lowermost ['lo·ər,most] *adj* (il) più basso, (l') infimo
low'-fre'quency *adj* a bassa frequenza
low' gear' *s* prima velocità, prima
lowland ['lolənd] *s* pianura || **Lowlands** *spl* Scozia meridionale, bassa Scozia
low·ly ['loli] *adj* (**-lier; -liest**) umile
Low' Mass' *s* messa bassa
low-minded ['lo'maɪndɪd] *adj* vile, basso
low-necked ['lo'nɛkt] *adj* scollato
low-pitched ['lo'pɪtʃt] *adj* (*sound*) basso, grave; (*roof*) poco inclinato
low'-pres'sure *adj* a bassa pressione
low-priced ['lo'praɪst] *adj* a buon mercato, a basso prezzo
low' shoe' *s* scarpa bassa
low'-speed' *adj* di piccola velocità
low-spirited ['lo'spɪrɪtɪd] *adj* depresso
low' tide' *s* bassa marea; (fig) punto più basso
low' visibil'ity *s* scarsa visibilità
low' wa'ter *s* (*low tide*) bassa marea; (*of a river*) magra
loyal ['lɔɪ·əl] *adj* leale
loyalist ['lɔɪ·əlɪst] *s* lealista *mf*
loyal·ty ['lɔɪ·əlti] *s* (**-ties**) lealtà *f*
lozenge ['lɑzɪndʒ] *s* losanga; (*candy cough drop*) pasticca, pastiglia
LP ['ɛl'pi] *s* (letterword) (trademark) disco di grande durata
lubricant ['lubrɪkənt] *adj* & *s* lubrificante *m*
lubricate ['lubrɪ,ket] *tr* lubrificare; (*e.g., one's hands*) ungersi
lubrication [,lubrɪ'keʃən] *s* lubrificazione
lubricous ['lubrɪkəs] *adj* lubrico; incerto, incostante
lucerne [lu'sʌrn] *s* erba medica
lucid ['lusɪd] *adj* lucido
Lucifer ['lusɪfər] *s* Lucifero
luck [lʌk] *s* (*good or bad*) sorte *f;* (*good*) sorte *f*, fortuna; **down on one's luck** in cattive condizioni; **in luck** fortunato; **out of luck** sfortunato; **to bring luck** portare (buona) fortuna; **to try one's luck** tentare la sorte; **worse luck** disgraziatamente
luckily ['lʌkɪli] *adv* fortunatamente
luckless ['lʌklɪs] *adj* sfortunato
luck·y ['lʌki] *adj* (**-ier; -iest**) fortunato; (*supposed to bring luck*) portafortuna; (*foretelling good luck*) di buon augurio; **to be lucky** aver fortuna
luck'y hit' *s* (coll) colpo di fortuna
lucrative ['lukrətɪv] *adj* lucrativo
ludicrous ['ludɪkrəs] *adj* ridicolo
lug [lʌg] *s* manico; (*pull*) tiro; **to put the lug on s.o.** (slang) batter cassa a qlcu || *v* (*pret & pp* **lugged;** *ger* **lugging**) *tr* tirarsi dietro; (coll) introdurre a sproposito
luggage ['lʌgɪdʒ] *s* (*used in traveling*) bagaglio; (*found in a store*) valigeria
lug'gage store' *s* valigeria
lugubrious [lu'gubrɪ·əs] or [lu'gjubrɪ·əs] *adj* lugubre
lukewarm ['luk,wɔrm] *adj* tiepido
lull [lʌl] *s* momento di calma, calma || *tr* calmare, pacificare; addormentare
lulla·by ['lʌlə,baɪ] *s* (**-bies**) ninnananna
lumbago [lʌm'bego] *s* lombaggine *f*

lumber ['lʌmbər] *s* legname *m*, legno da costruzione; cianfrusaglie *fpl* || *intr* muoversi pesantemente
lum'ber·jack' *s* boscaiolo
lum'ber jack'et *s* giaccone *m*
lum'ber·man *s* (**-men**) (*dealer*) commerciante *m* in legname; (*man who cuts down lumber*) boscaiolo
lum'ber room' *s* ripostiglio
lum'ber·yard' *s* deposito legnami
luminar·y ['lumɪ,neri] *s* (**-ies**) luminare *m*
luminous ['lumɪnəs] *adj* luminoso
lummox ['lʌməks] *s* (coll) scimunito
lump [lʌmp] *s* grumo; mucchio; cumulo; (*swelling*) bernoccolo; (*of sugar*) zolletta; (*in one's throat*) groppo; (coll) stupidone *m*; **in the lump** in blocco; nell'insieme || *tr* mescolare; (*to make into lumps*) raggrumare; **to lump it** (coll) mandarla giù
lumpish ['lʌmpɪʃ] *adj* grumoso; goffo; balordo
lump' sum' *s* ammontare unico, somma globale
lump·y ['lʌmpi] *adj* (**-ier; -iest**) grumoso; (*person*) pesante, ottuso; (*sea*) agitato
luna·cy ['lunəsi] *s* (**-cies**) pazzia
lunar ['lunər] *adj* lunare
lu'nar land'ing *s* allunaggio
lu'nar mod'ule *s* modulo lunare
lu'nar rov'er *s* auto *f* lunare
lunatic ['lunətɪk] *adj* & *s* demente *mf*
lu'natic asy'lum *s* manicomio
lu'natic fringe' *s* estremisti *mpl* fanatici
lunch [lʌntʃ] *s* (*regular midday meal*) seconda colazione; (*light meal*) spuntino, merenda || *intr* fare colazione; fare uno spuntino
lunch' bas'ket *s* portavivande *m*
luncheon ['lʌntʃən] *s* seconda colazione; pranzo ufficiale
luncheonette [,lʌntʃə'nɛt] *s* tavola calda
lunch'eon meat' *s* insaccati *mpl*
lunch'room' *s* tavola calda
lung [lʌŋ] *s* polmone *m*
lunge [lʌndʒ] *s* slancio; (*fencing*) affondo || *intr* slanciarsi
lurch [lʌrtʃ] *s* barcollamento; (*at close of a game*) cappotto; (naut) sbandata; **to leave in the lurch** piantare in asso || *intr* barcollare; (naut) sbandare
lure [lur] *s* esca; (fig) insidie *fpl* || *tr* adescare; **to lure away** distogliere, sviare
lurid ['lurɪd] *adj* (*fiery*) ardente, acceso; sensazionale; (*gruesome*) orripilante
lurk [lʌrk] *intr* stare in agguato, nascondersi; (fig) essere latente
luscious ['lʌʃəs] *adj* delizioso; lussuoso, lussureggiante; voluttuoso
lush [lʌʃ] *adj* lussureggiante, lussuoso
lust [lʌst] *s* desiderio sfrenato; libidine *f*, lussuria || *intr*—**to lust after** or **for** aver sete di
luster ['lʌstər] *s* (*gloss*) lustro, lucentezza; (*glory*) lustro, onore *m*
lus'ter·ware' *s* ceramiche smaltate
lustful ['lʌstfəl] *adj* lussurioso
lustrous ['lʌstrəs] *adj* lucido
lust·y ['lʌsti] *adj* (**-ier; -iest**) vigoroso, gagliardo
lute [lut] *s* (mus) liuto; (chem) luto
Lutheran ['luθərən] *adj* & *s* luterano
luxuriance [lʌg'ʒurɪ·əns] *s* rigoglio
luxuriant [lʌg'ʒurɪ·ənt] *adj* lussureggiante; (*imagery*) ridondante
luxuriate [lʌg'ʒurɪ,et] or [lʌk'ʃurɪ,et] *intr* lussureggiare; trovare piacere
luxurious [lʌg'ʒurɪ·əs] or [lʌk'ʃurɪ·əs] *adj* lussuoso, fastoso
luxu·ry ['lʌkʃəri] or ['lʌgʒəri] *s* (**-ries**) lusso, sfarzo
lye [laɪ] *s* ranno, liscivia
lying ['laɪ·ɪŋ] *adj* menzognero || *s* il mentire
ly'ing-in' hos'pital *s* clinica ostetrica, maternità *f*
lymph [lɪmf] *s* linfa
lymphatic [lɪm'fætɪk] *adj* linfatico
lynch [lɪntʃ] *tr* linciare
lynching ['lɪntʃɪŋ] *s* linciaggio
lynx [lɪŋks] *s* lince *f*
lynx-eyed ['lɪŋks,aɪd] *adj* dagli occhi di lince
lyonnaise [,laɪ·ə'nez] *adj* (culin) alla maniera di Lione
lyre [laɪr] *s* lira
lyric ['lɪrɪk] *adj* lirico || *s* lirica; (*words of a song*) parole *fpl*
lyrical ['lɪrɪkəl] *adj* lirico
lyricism ['lɪrɪ,sɪzəm] *s* lirismo
lyricist ['lɪrɪsɪst] *s* (*writer of words for songs*) paroliere *m*; (*poet*) lirico

M

M, m [ɛm] *s* tredicesima lettera dell'alfabeto inglese
ma'am [mæm] or [mɑm] *s* (coll) signora
macadam [mə'kædəm] *s* macadàm *m*
macadamize [mə'kædə,maɪz] *tr* macadamizzare
macaroni [,mækə'roni] *s* maccheroni *mpl*
macaroon [,mækə'run] *s* amaretto
macaw [mə'kɔ] *s* ara
mace [mes] *s* mazza; (*spice*) macis *m* & *f*
mace' bear'er *s* mazziere *m*
machination [,mækɪ'neʃən] *s* macchinazione, macchina
machine [mə'ʃin] *s* macchina || *tr* fare a macchina
machine' gun' *s* mitragliatrice *f*
machine'-gun' *v* (*pret* & *pp* **-gunned**; *ger* **-gunning**) *tr* mitragliare
machine'-made' *adj* fatto a macchina

machiner•y [mə'ʃinəri] *s* **(-ies)** macchinario, meccanismo
machine' screw' *s* vite *f* per metallo
machine' shop' *s* officina meccanica
machine' tool' *s* macchina utensile
machinist [mə'ʃinɪst] *s* meccanico; (nav) secondo macchinista
mackerel ['mækərəl] *s* maccarello
mack'erel sky' *s* cielo a pecorelle
mackintosh ['mækɪn,tɑʃ] *s* impermeabile *m*
mad [mæd] *adj* **(madder; maddest)** (*angry; rabid*) arrabbiato; (*insane; foolish*) pazzo, folle; furioso; **to be mad about** (coll) andar pazzo per; **to drive mad** far impazzire; **to go mad** impazzire; (*said of a dog*) diventare idrofobo
madam ['mædəm] *s* signora
mad'cap' *s* mattoide *m*, rompicollo
madden ['mædən] *tr* (*to make angry*) inferocire; (*to make insane*) fare impazzire
made-to-order ['medtə'ɔrdər] *adj* fatto apposta; (*clothing*) fatto su misura
made'-up' *adj* inventato; (*using cosmetics*) truccato
mad'house' *s* manicomio
mad'man' *s* **(-men')** pazzo
madness ['mædnɪs] *s* rabbia; pazzia
Madonna lily [mə'dɑnə] *s* giglio
maelstrom ['melstrəm] *s* vortice *m*
magazine ['mægə,zin] or [,mægə'zin] *s* (*periodical*) rivista, giornale *m;* (*warehouse*) magazzino; (*for cartridges*) caricatore *m;* (*for powder*) polveriera; (naut) santabarbara; (phot) magazzino
maggot ['mægət] *s* larva di dittero
Magi ['medʒaɪ] *spl* Re Magi
magic ['mædʒɪk] *adj* magico || *s* magia; illusionismo; **as if by magic** come per incanto
magician [mə'dʒɪʃən] *s* (*entertainer*) illusionista *mf;* (*sorcerer*) mago
magistrate ['mædʒɪs,tret] *s* magistrato
magnanimous [mæg'nænɪməs] *adj* magnanimo
magnesium [mæg'niʃɪ·əm] or [mæg'niʒɪ·əm] *s* magnesio
magnet ['mægnɪt] *s* calamita, magnete *m*
magnetic [mæg'netɪk] *adj* magnetico
magnetism ['mægnɪ,tɪzəm] *s* magnetismo
magnetize ['mægnɪ,taɪz] *tr* calamitare, magnetizzare
magne•to [mæg'nito] *s* **(-tos)** magnete *m*
magnificent [mæg'nɪfɪsənt] *adj* magnifico
magni•fy ['mægnɪ,faɪ] *v* (*pret & pp* **-fied**) *tr* ingrandire; (*to exaggerate*) magnificare
mag'nifying glass' *s* lente *f* d'ingrandimento
magnitude ['mægnɪ,tjud] or ['mægnɪ,tud] *s* grandezza
magpie ['mæg,paɪ] *s* gazza
mahlstick ['mɑl,stɪk] or ['mɔl,stɪk] *s* appoggiamano
mahoga•ny [mə'hɑgəni] *s* **(-nies)** mogano
Mahomet [mə'hɑmɪt] *s* Maometto
maid [med] *s* (*girl*) ragazza; (*servant*) cameriera, domestica
maiden ['medən] *s* pulzella
maid'en•hair' *s* (bot) capelvenere *m*
maid'en•head' *s* imene *m*
maidenhood ['medən,hud] *s* verginità *f*
maid'en la'dy *s* zitella
maid'en name' *s* nome *m* da signorina
maid'en voy'age *s* viaggio inaugurale
maid'-in-wait'ing *s* **(maids-in-waiting)** (*of a princess*) damigella d'onore; (*of a queen*) dama d'onore
maid' of hon'or *s* (*attendant at a wedding; attendant of a princess*) damigella d'onore; (*attendant of a queen*) dama d'onore
maid'serv'ant *s* domestica, ancella
mail [mel] *s* posta; (*of armor*) maglia; **by return mail** a volta di corriere || *tr* impostare
mail'bag' *s* sacco postale
mail'boat' *s* battello postale
mail'box' *s* cassetta or buca delle lettere
mail' car' *s* vagone *m* postale
mail' car'rier *s* postino, portalettere *m*
mail'ing list' *s* indirizzario
mail'ing per'mit *s* abbonamento postale
mail'man' *s* **(-men')** portalettere *m*
mail' or'der *s* ordinazione per corrispondenza
mail'-order house' *s* ditta che fa affari unicamente per corrispondenza
mail'plane' *s* areoplano postale
mail' train' *s* treno postale
maim [mem] *tr* mutilare
main [men] *adj* principale, maggiore || *s* condotta principale; **in the main** principalmente, per lo più
main' clause' *s* proposizione principale
main' course' *s* piatto forte
main' deck' *s* ponte *m* principale
mainland ['men,lænd] or ['menlənd] *s* terra ferma, continente *m*
main' line' *s* (rr) linea principale
mainly ['menli] *adv* principalmente
mainmast ['menməst], ['men,mæst] or ['men,mɑst] *s* albero maestro
mainsail ['mensəl] or ['men,sel] *s* vela maestra
main'spring' *s* molla motrice; (fig) molla
main'stay' *s* (naut) strallo di maestra; (fig) cardine *m*
main' street' *s* strada principale
maintain [men'ten] *tr* mantenere
maintenance ['mentɪnəns] *s* mantenimento; (*upkeep*) manutenzione
maître d'hôtel [,metər do'tel] *s* (*butler*) maggiordomo; (*headwaiter*) capocameriere *m*
maize [mez] *s* mais *m*
majestic [mə'dʒestɪk] *adj* maestoso
majes•ty ['mædʒɪsti] *s* **(-ties)** maestà *f*
major ['medʒər] *adj* maggiore || *s* (educ) specializzazione; (mil) maggiore *m* || *intr* (educ) specializzarsi
major•do•mo [,medʒər'domo] *s* **(-mos)** maggiordomo
ma'jor gen'eral *s* generale *m* di divisione

majori·ty [mə'dʒɑrɪti] or [mə'dʒɔrɪti] *adj* maggioritario || *s* (**-ties**) (*being of full age*) maggiore età *f;* (*larger number or part*) maggioranza; (mil) grado di maggiore
make [mek] *s* (*brand*) marca; (*form*) stile *m;* produzione; **on the make** (slang) tirando l'acqua al proprio mulino || *v* (*pret & pp* **made** [med]) *tr* fare; (*a train*) pigliare; (*a circuit*) chiudere; essere, e.g., **she will make a good typist** sarà una buona dattilografa; **to make** + *inf* fare + *inf,* e.g., **she made him study** lo fece studiare; **to make into** trasformare in; **to make known** far sapere; **to make of** pensare di; **to make oneself known** darsi a conoscere; **to make out** decifrare; (*a prescription*) scrivere, preparare; (*a check*) riempire; **to make over** convertire; (com) trasferire; **to make up** preparare, comporre; (*a story*) inventare; (*lost time*) riguadagnare; (typ) impaginare; (theat) truccare || *intr* essere fatto; **to make away with** rubare; disfarsi di; **to make believe that** + *ind* far finta di + *inf,* e.g., **he made believe (that) he was sleeping** fece finta di dormire; **to make for** avvicinarsi a; attaccare; (*better relations*) contribuire a cementare; **to make much of** (coll) fare le feste a; **to make off** andarsene; **to make off with** svignarsela con; **to make out** (coll) farcela; **to make toward** incamminarsi verso; **to make up** truccarsi; fare la pace; **to make up for** compensare per, supplire a; **to make up to** (coll) ingraziarsi; (coll) fare la corte a
make'-be·lieve' *adj* immaginario || *s* finzione, sembianza
maker ['mekər] *s* fabbricante *mf,* costruttore *m* || **Maker** *s* Fattore *m*
make'shift' *adj* improvvisato, di fortuna || *s* espediente *m,* ripiego; (*person*) tappabuchi *mf*
make'-up' *s* composizione, costituzione; truccatura, cosmetico; (typ) impaginazione; (journ) caratteristica
make'-up man' *s* truccatore *m*
make'-up test' *s* esame *m* di riparazione
make'weight' *s* giunta, contentino; (fig) supplemento, di più *m*
making ['mekɪŋ] *s* fabbricazione; costituzione; causa del successo; **makings** materiale *m;* (*potential*) stoffa
maladjusted [,mælə'dʒʌstɪd] *adj* spostato
mala·dy ['mælədi] *s* (**-dies**) malattia
malaise [mæ'lez] *s* malessere *m*
malapropos [,mælæprə'po] *adj* inopportuno || *adv* a sproposito
malaria [mə'lerɪ·ə] *s* malaria
Malay ['mele] or [mə'le] *adj & s* malese *mf*
malcontent ['mælkən,tent] *adj & s* malcontento
male [mel] *adj & s* maschio
malediction [,mælɪ'dɪkʃən] *s* maledizione
malefactor ['mælɪ,fæktər] *s* malfattore *m*
male' nurse' *s* infermiere *m*
malevolent [mə'lɛvələnt] *adj* malevolo
malfeasance [mæl'fizəns] *s* reato di pubblico funzionario
malice ['mælɪs] *s* malizia; (law) dolo; **to bear malice** serbar rancore; **with malice prepense** (law) con premeditazione
malicious [mə'lɪʃəs] *adj* malizioso, maligno
malign [mə'laɪn] *adj* maligno || *tr* calunniare
malignan·cy [mə'lɪgnənsi] *s* (**-cies**) malignità *f;* (pathol) malignità *f*
malignant [mə'lɪgnənt] *adj* maligno
maligni·ty [mə'lɪgnɪti] *s* (**-ties**) malignità *f*
malinger [mə'lɪŋgər] *intr* fingersi ammalato, darsi malato (per sottrarsi al proprio dovere)
mall [mɔl] or [mæl] *s* viale *m;* (*strip of land in a boulevard*) aiola
mallet ['mælɪt] *s* maglio; (*of a stone cutter*) mazzuolo
mallow ['mælo] *s* malva
malnutrition [,mælnju'trɪʃən] or [,mælnu'trɪʃən] *s* malnutrizione
malodorous [mæl'odərəs] *adj* puzzolente
malpractice [mæl'præktɪs] *s* incuria, negligenza; (*of physician or lawyer*) negligenza colposa
malt [mɔlt] *s* malto
maltreat [mæl'trit] *tr* maltrattare
mamma ['mɑmə] or [mə'mɑ] *s* (coll) mamma
mammal ['mæməl] *s* mammifero
mammalian [mæ'melɪ·ən] *adj & s* mammifero
mammoth ['mæməθ] *adj* mastodontico || *s* mammut *m*
man [mæn] *s* (**men** [men]) uomo; (*in chess*) pedina; (*in checkers*) pezzo; **a man** uno, e.g., **a man can get lost in this town** uno può perdersi in questa città; **as one man** come un sol uomo; **man alive!** accidenti!; **man and wife** marito e moglie; **to be one's own man** essere completamente indipendente || *v* (*pret & pp* **manned;** *ger* **manning**) *tr* (*a boat*) equipaggiare; (*a fortress*) guarnire; (*a cannon*) maneggiare
man' about town' *s* vitaiolo
manacle ['mænəkəl] *s*—**manacles** manette *fpl* || *tr* ammanettare
manage ['mænɪdʒ] *tr* (*a business*) gestire; (*e.g., a tool*) maneggiare || *intr* sbrogliarsela; **to manage to** fare in modo di; ingegnarsi a; **to manage to get along** barcamenarsi
manageable ['mænɪdʒəbəl] *adj* maneggevole
management ['mænɪdʒmənt] *s* direzione, gestione; (*executives collectively*) classe *f* dirigente; direzione; (*college course*) economia aziendale
manager ['mænədʒər] *s* direttore *m,* gerente *mf;* (theat) impresario; (sports) procuratore *m,* manager *m*
managerial [,mænə'dʒɪrɪ·əl] *adj* direttoriale, imprenditoriale

man'aging ed'itor *s* gerente *m* responsabile, redattore *m* in capo
mandate ['mændet] *s* mandato || *tr* dare in mandato a
mandatory ['mændə,tori] *adj* obbligatorio
mandolin ['mændəlɪn] *s* mandolino
mandrake ['mændrek] *s* mandragola
mandrel ['mændrəl] *s* (mach) mandrino
mane [men] *s* criniera
maneuver [mə'nuvər] *s* manovra || *tr* manovrare || *intr* manovrare; (aer, nav) evoluire; (fig) intrigare
manful ['mænfəl] *adj* maschile, risoluto
manganese ['mæŋgə,nis] or ['mæŋgə,niz] *s* manganese *m*
mange [mendʒ] *s* rogna
manger ['mendʒər] *s* presepio
mangle ['mæŋgəl] *tr* straziare, lacerare
man•gy ['mendʒi] *adj* (**-gier; -giest**) rognoso; (*squalid*) misero
man'han'dle *tr* malmenare, maltrattare
man'hole' *s* passo d'uomo, pozzetto
manhood ['mænhud] *s* virilità *f;* uomini *mpl,* umanità *f*
man'hunt' *s* caccia all'uomo
mania ['menɪ·ə] *s* mania
maniac ['menɪ,æk] *adj & s* maniaco
manicure ['mænɪ,kjur] *s* (*treatment*) manicure *f;* (*manicurist*) manicure *mf* || *tr* (*a person*) curare le mani di; (*the hands*) curare
manicurist ['mænɪ,kjurɪst] *s* manicurista *mf,* manicure *mf*
manifest ['mænɪ,fɛst] *adj* manifesto || *s* (naut) manifesto di carico || *tr* manifestare
manifes•to [,mænɪ'fɛsto] *s* (**-toes**) manifesto
manifold ['mænɪ,fold] *adj* molteplice || *s* copia; carta velina; (aut, mach) collettore *m*
manikin ['mænɪkɪn] *s* manichino; (*dwarf*) nano
man' in the moon' *s* faccia di uomo che appare nella luna piena
man' in the street' *s* uomo qualunque, uomo della strada
manipulate [mə'nɪpjə,let] *tr* manipolare
man'kind' *s* genere umano || **man'kind'** *s* il sesso maschile
manliness ['mænlɪnɪs] *s* virilità *f*
man•ly ['mænli] *adj* (**-lier; -liest**) maschio, virile
manned' space'ship *s* astronave pilotata
mannequin ['mænɪkɪn] *s* (*figure*) manichino; (*person*) indossatrice *f*
manner ['mænər] *s* maniera; **by all manner of means** in tutti i modi; **in a manner of speaking** in una certa maniera; **in the manner of** alla moda di; **manners** maniere, *fpl,* educazione; **to the manner born** avvezzo sin dalla nascita
mannish ['mænɪʃ] *adj* maschile; (*woman*) mascolino
man' of God' *s* santo; profeta *m;* (*priest*) uomo al servizio di Dio
man' of let'ters *s* letterato
man' of means' *s* uomo danaroso
man' of parts' *s* uomo di talento
man' of straw' *s* uomo di paglia
man' of the world' *s* uomo di mondo
man-of-war [,mænəv'wɔr] *s* (**men-of-war** [,menəv'wɔr] nave *f* da guerra
manor ['mænər] *s* maniero; feudo
man'or house' *s* maniero, palazzo
man' o'verboard *interj* uomo in mare!
man'pow'er *s* manodopera; (mil) effettivo
mansard ['mænsɑrd] *s* mansarda
man'serv'ant *s* (**men'serv'ants**) servo, servitore *m*
mansion ['mænʃən] *s* palazzo, palazzina; (*manor house*) maniero
man'slaugh'ter *s* omicidio colposo
mantel ['mæntəl] *s* parte *f* anteriore dei pilastri del camino; (*shelf above it*) mensola
man'tel•piece' *s* mensola del camino
man'tis shrimp' ['mæntɪs] *s* canocchia
mantle ['mæntəl] *s* mantello, cappa || *tr* ammantare; (*to conceal*) nascondere || *intr* (*to blush*) arrossire
manual ['mænju·əl] *adj* manuale || *s* (*book*) manuale *m;* (mil) esercizio; (mus) tastiera d'organo
man'ual train'ing *s* istruzione nelle arti e mestieri
manufacture [,mænjə'fæktjər] *s* fabbricazione; (*thing manufactured*) manufatto || *tr* fabbricare
manufacturer [,mænjə'fæktjərər] *s* fabbricante *mf,* industriale *m*
manure [mə'njur] or [mə'nur] *s* letame *m* || *tr* concimare
manuscript ['mænjə,skrɪpt] *adj & s* manoscritto
many ['meni] *adj & pron* molti; **a good many** or **a great many** un buon numero; **as many . . . as** tanti . . . quanti; **as many as** fino a, e.g., **they sell as many as five thousand dozen** vendono fino a cinquemila dozzine; **how many** quanti; **many a** molti, e.g., **many a day** molti giorni; **many another** molti altri; **many more** molti di più; **so many** tanti; **too many** troppi; **twice as many** altrettanti, il doppio
many-sided ['meni,saɪdɪd] *adj* multilaterale; versatile
map [mæp] *s* mappa; (*of a city*) piano || *v* (*pret & pp* **mapped;** *ger* **mapping**) *tr* tracciare la mappa di; mostrare sulla mappa; **to map out** fare il piano di
maple ['mepəl] *s* acero
maquette [mɑ'ket] *s* plastico
mar [mɑr] *v* (*pret & pp* **marred;** *ger* **marring**) *tr* deturpare, sfigurare
maraud [mə'rɔd] *tr & intr* predare
marauder [mə'rɔdər] *s* predone *m*
marble ['mɑrbəl] *adj* marmoreo || *s* marmo; (*little ball of glass*) bilia; **marbles** bilie *fpl;* **to lose one's marbles** (slang) mancare una rotella a qlcu || *tr* marmorizzare
march [mɑrtʃ] *s* marcia; (hist) marca; **to steal a march on** guadagnare il

vantaggio su || *tr* far marciare || *intr* marciare || **March** *s* marzo
marchioness ['mɑrʃənɪs] *s* marchesa
mare [mer] *s* (*female horse*) cavalla; (*female donkey*) asina
margarine ['mɑrdʒərɪn] *s* margarina
margin ['mɑrdʒɪn] *s* margine *m;* (econ) scoperto
mar'gin stop' *s* marginatore *m*
marigold ['mærɪ,gold] *s* fiorrancio
marihuana or **marijuana** [,mɑrɪ'hwɑnə] *s* marijuana
marina [mə'rinə] *s* porto turistico di imbarcazioni, porticciolo turistico
marinate ['mærɪ,net] *tr* marinare
marine [mə'rin] *adj* marino, marittimo || *s* marina; soldato di fanteria da sbarco; **marines** fanteria da sbarco; **tell that to the marines!** (coll) va a raccontarlo ai frati!
mariner ['mærɪnər] *s* marinaio
marionette [,mærɪ-ə'net] *s* marionetta
mar'ital sta'tus ['mærɪtəl] *s* stato civile
maritime ['mærɪ,taɪm] *adj* marittimo
marjoram ['mɑrdʒərəm] *s* origano; (*sweet marjoram*) maggiorana
mark [mɑrk] *s* segno; (*brand*) marca; (*of punctuation*) punto; (*in an examination*) voto; (*sign made by illiterate person*) croce *f;* (*landmark*) segnale *m;* (*target*) bersaglio; (*spot*) macchia; (*starting point in a race*) linea di partenza; (*of confidence*) voto; (*coin*) marco; impronta; **to be beside the mark** essere fuori del seminato; **to hit the mark** colpire il bersaglio; **to leave one's mark** lasciare la propria impronta; **to make one's mark** raggiungere il successo; **to miss the mark** fallire il colpo; **to toe the mark** mettersi in fila; filare diritto || *tr* marcare, segnare, contrassegnare; (*a student*) dar il voto a; (*a test*) esaminare; improntare; notare, avvertire; **to mark down** mettere in iscritto; ribassare il prezzo di
mark'down' *s* riduzione di prezzo
market ['mɑrkɪt] *s* mercato; **to bear the market** giocare al ribasso; **to bull the market** giocare al rialzo; **to play the market** giocare in borsa; **to put on the market** lanciare sul mercato || *tr* mettere sul mercato
marketable ['mɑrkɪtəbəl] *adj* commerciabile, vendibile
marketing ['mɑrkɪtɪŋ] *s* compravendita; marketing *m*
mar'ket-place' *s* piazza del mercato
mar'ket price' *s* prezzo corrente
mark'ing gauge' ['mɑrkɪŋ] *s* graffietto
marks'man *s* (**-men**) tiratore *m;* **a good marksman** un tiratore scelto
marksmanship ['mɑrksmən,ʃɪp] *s* qualità *f* di tiratore scelto
mark'up' *s* margine *m* di rivendita
marl [mɑrl] *s* marna || *tr* marnare
marmalade ['mɑrmə,led] *s* marmellata d'arance
marmot ['mɑrmət] *s* marmotta
maroon [mə'run] *adj* & *s* marrone *m* || *tr* abbandonare (*in un luogo deserto*)
marquee [mɑr'ki] *s* pensilina
marquess ['mɑrkwɪs] *s* marchese *m*
marque-try ['mɑrkətri] *s* (**-tries**) intarsio
marquis ['mɑrkwɪs] *s* marchese *m*
marquise [mɑr'kiz] *s* marchesa; (**Brit**) pensilina
marriage ['mærɪdʒ] *s* matrimonio
marriageable ['mærɪdʒəbəl] *adj* adatto al matrimonio; (*woman*) nubile
mar'riage por'tion *s* dote *f*
mar'riage rate' *s* nuzialità *f*
mar'ried life' *s* vita coniugale
marrow ['mæro] *s* midollo
mar-ry ['mæri] *v* (*pret* & *pp* **-ried**) *tr* sposare; **to get married** to sposarsi con || *intr* sposarsi; **to marry into** (*e.g., a noble family*) imparentarsi con; **to marry the second time** risposarsi
Mars [mɑrz] *s* Marte *m*
Marseilles [mɑr'selz] *s* Marsiglia
marsh [mɑrʃ] *s* palude *f*, lama
mar-shal ['mɑrʃəl] *s* direttore *m* di una sfilata; maestro di cerimonie; (mil) maresciallo; (U.S.A.) ufficiale *m* di giustizia || *v* (*pret* & *pp* **-shaled** or **-shalled;** *ger* **-shaling** or **-shalling**) *tr* introdurre cerimoniosamente; mettere in buon ordine
marsh' mal'low *s* (bot) altea
marsh'mal'low *s* dolce *m* di gelatina e zucchero
marsh-y ['mɑrʃi] *adj* (**-ier; -iest**) paludoso, palustre
marten ['mɑrtən] *s* (*Martes martes*) martora; (*Martes zibellina*) zibellino
martial ['mɑrʃəl] *adj* marziale
mar'tial law' *s* legge *f* marziale
Martian ['mɑrʃən] *adj* & *s* marziano
martin ['mɑrtɪn] *s* rondicchio
martinet [,mɑrtɪ'net] or ['mɑrtɪ,net] *s* pignolo
martyr ['mɑrtər] *s* martire *mf*
martyrdom ['mɑrtərdəm] *s* martirio
mar-vel ['mɑrvəl] *s* meraviglia || *v* (*pret* & *pp* **-veled** or **-velled;** *ger* **-veling** or **-velling**) *intr* meravigliarsi; **to marvel at** stupirsi di, meravigliarsi di
marvelous ['mɑrvələs] *adj* meraviglioso
Marxist ['mɑrksɪst] *adj* & *s* marxista *mf*
mascara [mæs'kærə] *s* bistro, rimmel *m*
mascot ['mæskɑt] *s* mascotte *f*
masculine ['mæskjəlɪn] *adj* & *s* maschile *m*
mash [mæʃ] *s* (*crushed mass*) poltiglia; (*to form wort*) decotto d'orzo germinato; (*e.g., for poultry*) intriso || *tr* schiacciare; impastare
mashed' pota'toes *spl* purè *m* di patate
masher ['mæʃər] *s* utensile *m* per schiacciare; (slang) pappagallo
mask [mæsk] or [mɑsk] *s* maschera; (phot) mascherina || *tr* mascherare; (phot) mettere una mascherina a || *intr* mascherarsi
masked' ball' *s* ballo in maschera
mason ['mesən] *s* muratore *m* || **Mason** *s* massone *m*
mason-ry ['mesənri] *s* (**-ries**) arte *f* del

muratore; muratura || **Masonry** *s* massoneria
masquerade [ˌmæskəˈred] or [ˌmɑskəˈred] *s* mascherata; (*disguise*) maschera; (*pretense*) finzione || *intr* mascherarsi; **to masquerade as** mascherarsi da; farsi passare per
mass [mæs] *s* massa; (*celebration of the Eucharist*) messa; **in the mass** nell'insieme; **the masses** le masse || *tr* ammassare || *intr* ammassarsi, accumularsi
massacre [ˈmæsəkər] *s* massacro, strage *f* || *tr* massacrare, trucidare
massage [məˈsɑʒ] *s* massaggio || *tr* massaggiare
masseur [mæˈsœr] *s* massaggiatore *m*
masseuse [mæˈsœz] *s* massaggiatrice *f*
massive [ˈmæsɪv] *adj* massiccio; (*e.g., dose*) massivo; solido
mass' me'dia [ˈmidɪ·ə] *s* mezzi *mpl* di comunicazione di massa
mass' meet'ing *s* assemblea popolare; adunanza in massa
mass' produc'tion *s* produzione in serie
mast [mæst] or [mɑst] *s* (*post*) palo; (agr) ghiande *fpl*, faggiole *fpl;* (naut) albero; **before the mast** come marinaio semplice
master [ˈmæstər] or [ˈmɑstər] *s* (*employer*) padrone *m;* (*male head of household*) capo di casa; (*man who possesses some special skill*) maestro; (*title of respect for a boy*) signorino; (naut) capitano || *tr* dominare; (*a language*) possedere
mas'ter bed'room *s* camera da letto padronale
mas'ter blade' *s* foglia maestra (di una balestra)
mas'ter build'er *s* capomastro
masterful [ˈmæstərfəl] or [ˈmɑstərfəl] *adj* autoritario; provetto, magistrale
mas'ter key' *s* chiave maestra
masterly [ˈmæstərli] or [ˈmɑstərli] *adj* magistrale || *adv* magistralmente
mas'ter mechan'ic *s* mastro meccanico
mas'ter·mind' *s* mente direttiva || *tr* organizzare, dirigere
mas'ter of cer'emonies *s* maestro di cerimonia; (*in a night club, radio, etc.*) presentatore *m*
mas'ter·piece' *s* capolavoro
mas'ter ser'geant *s* (mil) sergente *m* maggiore
mas'ter stroke' *s* colpo da maestro
mas'ter·work' *s* capolavoro
master·y [ˈmæstəri] or [ˈmɑstəri] *s* (**-ies**) (*command of a subject*) dominio; (*skill*) maestria
mast'head' *s* (journ) titolo; (naut) testa d'albero
masticate [ˈmæstɪˌket] *tr* masticare
mastiff [ˈmæstɪf] or [ˈmɑstɪf] *s* mastino
masturbate [ˈmæstərˌbet] *tr* masturbare || *intr* masturbarsi
mat [mæt] *s* (*for floor*) tappeto, stuoia; (*under a dish*) tondo, sottocoppa, centrino; (*before a door*) stoino, zerbino; (*around a picture*) bordo di cartone; (sports) materassino; (typ) flan *m;* flano || *v* (*pret & pp* **matted;** *ger* **matting**) *tr* coprire di stuoie; arruffare || *intr* **arruffarsi**
match [mætʃ] *s* (*counterpart*) uguale *m;* (*suitably associated pair*) paio; (*light*) fiammifero; (*wick*) miccia; (*prospective mate*) partito; (sports) partita, gara; **to be a match for** essere pari a, fare fronte a; **to meet one's match** trovare un degno rivale || *tr* uguagliare, pareggiare; (*colors*) combinare; (*in pairs*) appaiare; giocarsi, e.g., **to match s.o. for the drinks** giocarsi le bevande con qlcu || *intr* corrispondersi, fare il paio
match'box' *s* scatola di fiammiferi; (*of wax matches*) scatola di cerini
matchless [ˈmætʃlɪs] *adj* incomparabile, senza pari
match'mak'er *s* paraninfo
mate [met] *s* compagno; (*husband or wife*) consorte *mf;* (*to a female*) maschio; (*to a male*) femmina; (chess) scacco matto; (naut) primo ufficiale || *tr* appaiare; (chess) dar scacco matto a; **to be well mated** esser ben appaiato || *intr* accoppiarsi
material [məˈtɪrɪ·əl] *adj* materiale; importante || *s* materiale *m*, materia; (*cloth, fabric*) tela, stoffa; **materials** occorrente *m*
materialist [məˈtɪrɪ·əlɪst] *s* materialista *mf*
materialize [məˈtɪrɪ·əˌlaɪz] *intr* materializzarsi
matériel [məˌtɪrɪˈel] *s* materiale *m;* materiale bellico
maternal [məˈtʌrnəl] *adj* materno
maternity [məˈtʌrnɪti] *s* maternità *f*
mater'nity ward' *s* maternità *f*
mathematical [ˌmæθɪˈmætɪkəl] *adj* matematico
mathematician [ˌmæθɪməˈtɪʃən] *s* matematico
mathematics [ˌmæθɪˈmætɪks] *s* matematica
matinée [ˌmætɪˈne] *s* mattinata, diurna
mat'ing sea'son *s* calore *m*
matins [ˈmætɪnz] *spl* mattutino
matriarch [ˈmetrɪˌɑrk] *s* matrona dignitosa; donna che possiede l'autorità matriarcale
matricidal [ˌmetrɪˈsaɪdəl] or [ˌmætrɪˈsaɪdəl] *adj* matricida
matricide [ˈmetrɪˌsaɪd] or [ˈmætrɪˌsaɪd] *s* (*act*) matricidio; (*person*) matricida *mf*
matriculate [məˈtrɪkjəˌlet] *tr* immatricolare || *intr* immatricolarsi
matriculation [məˌtrɪkjəˈleʃən] *s* immatricolazione, iscrizione
matrimonial [ˌmætrɪˈmonɪ·əl] *adj* matrimoniale
matrimo·ny [ˈmætrɪˌmoni] *s* (**-nies**) matrimonio
ma·trix [ˈmetrɪks] or [ˈmætrɪks] *s* (**-trices**[trɪˌsiz] or **-trixes**) matrice *f*
matron [ˈmetrən] *s* matrona; direttrice *f;* guardiana
matronly [ˈmetrənli] *adj* matronale
matter [ˈmætər] *s* (*physical substance*) materia; (*pus*) materia; (*affair, busi-*

ness) faccenda; (*material of a book*) contenuto; (*reason*) motivo; (*copy for printer*) manoscritto; (*printed material*) stampati *mpl;* **a matter of** un caso di; **for that matter** per quanto riguarda ciò; **in the matter** al soggetto; **no matter** non importa; **no matter how** non importa come; **no matter when** non importa quando; **no matter where** non importa dove; **what is the matter?** cosa succede?; **what is the matter with you?** cosa ha? || *intr* importare

mat'ter of course' *s*—**as a matter of course** come se nulla fosse, come se fosse una cosa naturale

mat'ter of fact' *s*—**as a matter of fact** in realtà, a onor del vero

matter-of-fact ['mætərəv,fækt] *adj* prosaico, pratico

mattock ['mætək] *s* piccone *m*

mattress ['mætrɪs] *s* materasso

mature [mə'tʃur] or [mə'tur] *adj* maturo; (*due*) scaduto || *tr* maturare || *intr* maturare; (com) scadere

maturity [mə'tʃurɪti] or [mə'turɪti] *s* maturità *f;* (com) scadenza

maudlin ['mɔdlɪn] *adj* sentimentale, lagrimoso; piagnucoloso e ubriaco

maul [mɔl] *tr* maltrattare, bistrattare

maulstick ['mɔl,stɪk] *s* appoggiamano

maundy ['mɔndi] *s* lavanda

Maun'dy Thurs'day *s* giovedì santo

mausole·um [,mɔsə'li·əm] *s* (**-ums** or **-a** [ə]) mausoleo

maw [mɔ] *s* (*e.g., of a hog*) stomaco; (*of carnivorous mammal*) fauci *fpl;* (*of fowl*) gozzo; (fig) bocca, fauci *fpl*

mawkish ['mɔkɪʃ] *adj* (*sickening*) nauseante; (*sentimental*) svenevole

maxim ['mæksɪm] *s* massima

maximum ['mæksɪməm] *adj* & *s* massimo

may [me] *v aux*—**it may be** può essere; **may I come in?** si può?; **may you be happy!** possa tu essere felice! || **May** *s* maggio

maybe ['mebi] *adv* forse

May' Day' *s* primo maggio; festa della primavera; (hist) calendimaggio (*in Florence*)

mayhem ['mehem] or ['me·əm] *s* mutilazione dolosa

mayonnaise [,me·ə'nez] *s* maionese *f*

mayor ['me·ər] or [mer] *s* sindaco

mayoress ['me·ərɪs] or ['merɪs] *s* donna sindaco

May'pole' *s* maio, maggio, palo per le danze di calendimaggio

May'pole dance' *s* ballo figurato con nastri per la festa di primavera

May' queen' *s* reginetta di maggio

maze [mez] *s* dedalo, labirinto

me [mi] *pron* me; mi; **to me** mi; a me

meadow ['medo] *s* prato

mead'ow·land' *s* prateria

meager ['migər] *adj* magro

meal [mil] *s* (*food*) pasto; (*unbolted grain*) farina

meal'time' *s* ora del pasto

mean [min] *adj* (*intermediate*) medio; (*low in rank*) basso, umile; (*shabby*) misero; (*of poor quality*) inferiore; (*stingy*) taccagno; (*nasty*) villano; (*vicious, as a horse*) intrattabile; (coll) indisposto; (coll) vergognoso; (slang) splendido; **no mean** eccellente || *s* media, termine medio; **by all means** certamente, senza dubbio; **by means of** per mezzo di; **by no means** in nessuna maniera; **means** beni *mpl;* (*agency*) mezzo, maniera; **to live on one's means** vivere di rendita || *v* (*pret & pp* **meant** [ment]) *tr* significare, voler dire; **to mean to** pensare || *intr*—**to mean well** aver buone intenzioni

meander [mɪ'ændər] *s* meandro || *intr* serpeggiare, vagare

meaning ['minɪŋ] *s* senso, significato

meaningful ['minɪŋfəl] *adj* significativo

meaningless ['minɪŋlɪs] *adj* senza senso, senza significato

meanness ['minnɪs] *s* viltà *f*, bassezza; (*stinginess*) meschinità *f;* (*lowliness*) umiltà *f*, povertà *f*

mean'time' *s*—**in the meantime** nel frattempo || *adv* frattanto, intanto

mean'while' *s & adv* var of **meantime**

measles ['mizəlz] *s* morbillo; (*German measles*) rosolia

mea·sly ['mizli] *adj* (**-slier; -sliest**) col morbillo; (coll) miserabile

measurable ['meʒərəbəl] *adj* misurabile

measure ['meʒər] *s* misura; (*legislative bill*) progetto di legge; (mus) battuta; **in a measure** in un certo senso; **to take the measure of** prendere le misure di; giudicare accuratamente || *tr* misurare; (*a distance*) percorrere; **to measure out** somministrare || *intr* misurare; **to measure up to** essere all'altezza di

measurement ['meʒərmənt] *s* misura; **to take s.o.'s measurements** prendere le misure di qlcu

meas'uring cup' *s* vetro graduato

meat [mit] *s* carne *f;* (*food in general*) cibo; (*of nut*) gheriglio; (fig) sostanza, midollo

meat'ball' *s* polpetta

meat' grind'er *s* tritacarne *m*

meat' loaf' *s* polpettone *m*

meat' mar'ket *s* macelleria

meat·y ['miti] *adj* (**-ier; -iest**) carnoso, polputo; (fig) sostanzioso

Mecca ['mekə] *s* la Mecca; **the Mecca** (fig) la Mecca

mechanic [mɪ'kænɪk] *s* meccanico; (aut) motorista *m*

mechanical [mɪ'kænɪkəl] *adj* meccanico; (*machinelike*) (fig) macchinale

mechan'ical engineer'ing *s* ingegneria meccanica

mechan'ical pen'cil *s* matita automatica

mechanics [mɪ'kænɪks] *s* meccanica

mechanism ['mekə,nɪzəm] *s* meccanismo, congegno

mechanize ['mekə,naɪz] *tr* meccanizzare

medal ['medəl] *s* medaglia

medallion [mɪ'dæljən] *s* medaglione *m*

meddle ['mɛdəl] *intr* intromettersi
meddler ['mɛdlər] *s* ficcanaso
meddlesome ['mɛdəlsəm] *adj* invadente, indiscreto
median ['midɪ·ən] *adj* medio, mediano || *s* punto medio, numero medio
me'dian strip' *s* spartitraffico
mediate ['midɪ,et] *tr* (*a dispute*) comporre; (*parties*) pacificare || *intr* (*to be in the middle*) mediare; fare da paciere
mediation [,midɪ'eʃən] *s* mediazione
mediator ['midɪ,etər] *s* mediatore *m*
medical ['mɛdɪkəl] *adj* medico; (*student*) di medicina
medicinal [mə'dɪsɪnəl] *adj* medicinale
medicine ['mɛdɪsɪn] *s* medicina
med'icine cab'inet *s* armadietto farmaceutico
med'icine kit' *s* cassetta farmaceutica
med'icine man' *s* (**men'**) stregone indiano
medieval [,midɪ'ivəl] or [,mɛdɪ'ivəl] *adj* medievale
medievalist [,midɪ'ivəlɪst] or [,mɛdɪ'ivəlɪst] *s* medievalista *mf*
mediocre ['midɪ,okər] or [,midɪ'okər] *adj* mediocre
mediocri·ty [,midɪ'ɑkrɪti] *s* (**-ties**) mediocrità *f*
meditate ['mɛdɪ,tet] *tr* & *intr* meditare
meditation [,mɛdɪ'teʃən] *s* meditazione
Mediterranean [,mɛdɪtə'renɪ·ən] *adj* & *s* Mediterraneo
medi·um ['midɪ·əm] *adj* medio; (*heat*) moderato; (*meat*) cotto moderatamente || *s* (**-ums** or **-a** [ə]) (*middle state; mean*) media; mezzo; (*in spiritualism*) medium *m;* **media** (*of communication*) media *mpl;* **through the medium of** per mezzo di
medlar ['mɛdlər] *s* (*tree*) nespolo; (*fruit*) nespola
medley ['mɛdli] *s* farragine *f*, mescolanza; (mus) pot-pourri *m*
medul·la [mɪ'dʌlə] *s* (**-lae** [li]) midollo
meek [mik] *adj* mansueto, umile
meekness ['miknɪs] *s* mansuetudine *f*
meerschaum ['mɪrʃəm] or ['mɪrʃɔm] *s* schiuma; pipa di schiuma
meet [mit] *adj* conveniente || *s* incontro || *v* (*pret* & *pp* **met** [met]) *tr* incontrare, incontrarsi con; (*to become acquainted with*) fare la conoscenza di; riunirsi con; (*to cope with*) sopperire a; (*said of a public carrier*) fare coincidenza con; andar incontro a; (*one's obligations*) far fronte a; (*bad luck*) avere; **to meet the eyes of** presentarsi agli occhi di || *intr* incontrarsi; riunirsi; conoscersi; **till we meet again** arrivederci; **to meet with** incontrare, incontrarsi con; (*an accident*) avere; (*said of a public carrier*) fare coincidenza con
meeting ['mitɪŋ] *s* riunione, ritrovo; seduta, convegno; (*political*) comizio; (*e.g., of two rivers*) confluenza; duello
meet'ing of the minds' *s* accordo, consonanza di voleri
meet'ing place' *s* luogo di riunione
megacycle ['mɛgə,saɪkəl] *s* megaciclo
megaphone ['mɛgə,fon] *s* megafono, portavoce *m*
megohm ['mɛg,om] *s* megaohm *m*
melancholia [,mɛlən'kolɪ·ə] *s* melanconia, malinconia
melanchol·y ['mɛlən,kɑli] *adj* malinconico || *s* (**-ies**) malinconia
melee ['mele] or ['mɛle] *s* (*fight*) mischia; confusione
mellow ['mɛlo] *adj* (*fruit*) maturo; (*wine*) pastoso; (*voice*) soave, melodioso || *tr* raddolcire || *intr* raddolcirsi
melodic [mɪ'lɑdɪk] *adj* melodico
melodious [mɪ'lodɪ·əs] *adj* melodioso
melodramatic [,mɛlədrə'mætɪk] *adj* melodrammatico
melo·dy ['mɛlədi] *s* (**-dies**) melodia
melon ['mɛlən] *s* melone *m*, popone *m*
melt [mɛlt] *tr* sciogliere; (*metals*) fondere; (fig) intenerire || *intr* sciogliersi; fondersi; (fig) intenerirsi; **to melt away** svanire; **to melt into** convertirsi in, diventare; (*tears*) struggersi in
melt'ing pot' *s* crogiolo
member ['mɛmbər] *s* membro
membership ['mɛmbər,ʃɪp] *s* associazione; numero di membri
membrane ['mɛmbren] *s* membrana
memen·to [mɪ'mɛnto] *s* (**-tos** or **-toes**) oggetto ricordo
mem·o ['mɛmo] *s* (**-os**) (coll) memorandum *m*
memoir ['mɛmwɑr] *s* memoria, memoriale *m;* biografia; **memoirs** memorie *fpl*
memoran·dum [,mɛmə'rændəm] *s* (**-dums** or **-da** [də]) memorandum *m*
memorial [mɪ'morɪ·əl] *adj* commemorativo || *s* sacrario; (*petition*) memoriale *m*
Memo'rial Day' *s* giorno dei caduti
memorialize [mɪ'morɪ·ə,laɪz] *tr* commemorare
memorize ['mɛmə,raɪz] *tr* imparare a memoria
memo·ry ['mɛməri] *s* (**-ries**) memoria; **to commit to memory** imparare a memoria
menace ['mɛnɪs] *s* minaccia || *tr* & *intr* minacciare
ménage [me'nɑʒ] *s* casa; (*housekeeping*) economia domestica
menagerie [mə'næʒəri] or [mə'nædʒəri] *s* serraglio
mend [mɛnd] *s* riparo; **to be on the mend** migliorare || *tr* (*to repair*) raccomodare, riparare; (*to patch*) rammendare; (fig) correggere || *intr* correggersi
mendacious [mɛn'deʃəs] *adj* mendace
mendicant ['mɛndɪkənt] *adj* & *s* mendicante *mf*
menfolk ['mɛn,fok] *spl* uomini *mpl*
menial ['minɪ·əl] *adj* basso, servile || *s* servitore *m*, servo
menses ['mɛnsiz] *spl* mestruazione, mestrui *mpl*
men's' fur'nishings *spl* articoli *mpl* d'abbigliamento maschile
men's' room' *s* gabinetto per signori

menstruate ['menstrʊ,et] *intr* avere le mestruazioni
men'tal arith'metic ['mentəl] *s* calcolo mentale
men'tal hos'pital *s* manicomio
men'tal ill'ness *s* malattia mentale
men'tal reserva'tion *s* riserva mentale
men'tal test' *s* test *m* mentale
mention ['menʃən] *s* menzione || *tr* menzionare; **don't mention it** non c'è di che
menu ['menju] or ['menju] *s* menu *m,* lista
meow [mɪ'aʊ] *s* miagolio || *intr* miagolare
Mephistophelian [,mefɪstə'filɪ·ən] *adj* mefistofelico
mercantile ['mʌrkən,til] or ['mʌrkən,taɪl] *adj* mercantile
mercenar·y ['mʌrsə,neri] *adj* mercenario || *s* **(-ies)** mercenario
merchandise ['mʌrtʃən,daɪz] *s* mercanzia, merce *f*
merchant ['mʌrtʃənt] *adj* mercantile || *s* mercante *m,* commerciante *mf*
mer'chant·man *s* **(-men)** mercantile *m*
mer'chant marine' *s* marina mercantile
merciful ['mʌrsɪfəl] *adj* misericordioso
merciless ['mʌrsɪlɪs] *adj* spietato
mercu·ry ['mʌrkjəri] *s* **(-ries)** mercurio || **Mercury** *s* Mercurio
mer·cy ['mʌrsi] *s* **(-cies)** misericordia; **at the mercy of** alla mercé di
mere [mɪr] *adj* mero, puro
meretricious [,merɪ'trɪʃəs] *adj* vistoso, chiassoso, sgargiante; artificiale, falso, finto
merge [mʌrdʒ] *tr* fondere || *intr* fondersi; (*said of two roads*) convergere; **to merge into** convertirsi lentamente in
merger ['mʌrdʒər] *s* fusione
meridian [mə'rɪdɪ·ən] *adj* meridiano; culminante || *s* meridiano; apogeo
meringue [mə'ræŋ] *s* meringa
merit ['merɪt] *s* merito || *tr* meritare
meritorious [,merɪ'torɪ·əs] *adj* meritorio
merlon ['mʌrlən] *s* merlo
mermaid ['mʌr,med] *s* sirena
mer'man' *s* **(-men')** tritone *m*
merriment ['merɪmənt] *s* allegria
mer·ry ['meri] *adj* **(-rier; -riest)** allegro, giocondo; **to make merry** divertirsi
Mer'ry Christ'mas *interj* Buon Natale!
mer'ry-go-round' *s* giostra, carosello; (*of parties*) serie ininterrotta
mer'ry·mak'er *s* festaiolo
mesh [meʃ] *s* (*network*) rete *f;* (*each open space of net*) maglia; (mach) ingranaggio; **meshes** rete *f* || *tr* irretire; (mach) ingranare || *intr* irretirsi; (mach) ingranarsi
mess [mes] *s* (*dirty condition*) disordine *m;* (*meal for a group of people*) mensa, rancio; porzione; **to get into a mess** mettersi nei pasticci; **to make a mess of** rovinare || *tr* sporcare; disordinare; rovinare || *intr* mangiare in comune; **to mess around** (coll) perdersi in cose inutili
message ['mesɪdʒ] *s* messaggio
messenger ['mesəndʒər] *s* messaggero; (*person who goes on an errand*) fattorino; (mil) portaordini *m*
mess' hall' *s* mensa
Messiah [mə'saɪ·ə] *s* Messia *m*
mess' kit' *s* gavetta, gamella
mess'mate' *s* compagno di rancio
mess' of pot'tage ['pɑtɪdʒ] *s* (Bib & fig) piatto di lenticchie
Messrs. ['mesərz] *pl* of **Mr.**
mess·y ['mesi] *adj* **(-ier; -iest)** disordinato; sporco
metal ['metəl] *adj* metallico || *s* metallo
metallic [mɪ'tælɪk] *adj* metallico
metallurgy ['metə,lʌrdʒi] *s* metallurgia
met'al pol'ish *s* lucido per metalli
met'al·work' *s* lavoro di metallo
metamorpho·sis [,metə'mɔrfəsɪs] *s* **(-ses** [,siz]**)** metamorfosi *f*
metaphony [mə'tæfəni] *s* metafonia, metafonesi *f*
metaphor ['metəfər] or ['metə,fɔr] *s* metafora
metaphorical [,metə'fɑrɪkəl] or [,metə'fɔrɪkəl] *adj* metaforico
metathe·sis [mɪ'tæθɪsɪs] *s* **(-ses** [,siz]**)** metatesi *f*
mete [mit] *tr*—**to mete out** distribuire
meteor ['mitɪ·ər] *s* meteora
meteoric [,mitɪ'ɑrɪk] or [,mitɪ'ɔrɪk] *adj* meteorico; (fig) rapidissimo, folgorante
meteorite ['mitɪ·ə,raɪt] *s* meteorite *m* & *f*
meteorology [,mitɪ·ə'rɑlədʒi] *s* meteorologia
meter ['mitər] *s* (*unit of length; verse*) metro; (*instrument for measuring gas, water, etc.*) contatore *m;* (mus) tempo || *tr* misurare col contatore
me'ter read'er *s* lettore *m,* letturista *m*
methane ['meθen] *s* metano
method ['meθəd] *s* metodo
methodic(al) [mɪ'θɑdɪk(əl)] *adj* metodico
Methodist ['meθədɪst] *adj* & *s* metodista *mf*
Methuselah [mɪ'θuzələ] *s* Matusalemme *m*
meticulous [mɪ'tɪkjələs] *adj* meticoloso
metric(al) ['metrɪk(əl)] *adj* metrico
metronome ['metrə,nom] *s* metronomo
metropolis [mɪ'trɑpəlɪs] *s* metropoli *f*
metropolitan [,metrə'pɑlɪtən] *adj* & *s* metropolitano
mettle ['metəl] *s* disposizione, temperamento; brio, animo; **to be on one's mettle** impegnarsi a fondo
mettlesome ['metəlsəm] *adj* brioso
mew [mju] *s* miagolio; (orn) gabbiano; **mews** scuderie *fpl*
Mexican ['meksɪkən] *adj* & *s* messicano
Mexico ['meksɪ,ko] *s* il Messico
mezzanine ['mezə,nin] *s* mezzanino
mica ['maɪkə] *s* mica
microbe ['maɪkrob] *s* microbio
microbiology [,maɪkrəbaɪ'ɑlədʒi] *s* microbiologia
microcard ['maɪkrə,kɑrd] *s* microscheda

microfarad [ˌmaɪkrəˈfæræd] *s* microfarad *m*
microfilm [ˈmaɪkrəˌfɪlm] *s* microfilm *m* || *tr* microfilmare
microgroove [ˈmaɪkrəˌgruv] *adj* microsolco || *s* microsolco; disco microsolco
microphone [ˈmaɪkrəˌfon] *s* microfono
microscope [ˈmaɪkrəˌskop] *s* microscopio
microscopic [ˌmaɪkrəˈskɑpɪk] *adj* microscopico
microwave [ˈmaɪkrəˌwev] *s* microonda
mid [mɪd] *adj* mezzo, la metà di, e.g., **mid October** la metà di ottobre
mid'day' *adj* di mezzogiorno || *s* mezzogiorno
middle [ˈmɪdəl] *adj* medio, mezzo || *s* mezzo, metà *f;* (*of human body*) cintura; **about the middle of** verso la metà di; **in the middle of** nel mezzo di
mid'dle age' *s* mezza età || **Middle Ages** *spl* Medio Evo
mid'dle class' *s* ceto medio, borghesia
Mid'dle East' *s* Medio Oriente
Mid'dle Eng'lish *s* inglese *m* medievale parlato fra il 1150 e il 1500
mid'dle fin'ger *s* dito medio
mid'dle•man' *s* (**-men'**) intermediario
middling [ˈmɪdlɪŋ] *adj* mediocre, passabile || *s* (*coarsely ground wheat*) farina grossa integrale; **middlings** articoli *mpl* di qualità mediocre || *adv* moderatamente
mid•dy [ˈmɪdi] *s* (**-dies**) aspirante *m* di marina
mid'dy blouse' *s* marinara
midget [ˈmɪdʒɪt] *s* nano
midland [ˈmɪdlənd] *adj* centrale, interno || *s* regione centrale
mid'night' *adj* di mezzanotte; **to burn the midnight oil** studiare a lume di candela || *s* mezzanotte *f*
midriff [ˈmɪdrɪf] *s* diaframma *m;* (*middle part of body*) cintura, vita
mid'ship'man *s* (**-men**) aspirante *m* di marina
midst [mɪdst] *s* mezzo, centro; **in the midst of** in mezzo a
mid'stream' *s*—**in midstream** in mezzo al fiume
mid'sum'mer *s* cuore *m* dell'estate
mid'way' *adj* situato a metà strada || *s* metà strada; viale *m* principale di un' esposizione || *adv* a metà strada
mid'week' *s* mezzo della settimana
mid'wife' *s* (**-wives'**) levatrice *f*
mid'win'ter *s* cuore *m* dell'inverno
mid'year' *adj* nel mezzo dell'anno || *s* mezzo dell'anno; **midyears** (coll) esami *mpl* nel mezzo dell'anno scolastico
mien [min] *s* aspetto, portamento
miff [mɪf] *s* (coll) battibecco || *tr* (coll) offendere
might [maɪt] *s* forza, potenza; **with might and main** a tutta forza || *v aux* used to form the potential, e.g., **he might change his mind** è possibile che cambi opinione
might•y [ˈmaɪti] *adj* (**-ier; -iest**) potente; (*huge*) grandissimo || *adv* (coll) moltissimo, grandemente
migraine [ˈmaɪgren] *s* emicrania
migrate [ˈmaɪgret] *intr* migrare
migratory [ˈmaɪgrəˌtori] *adj* migratore
milch [mɪltʃ] *adj* lattifero
mild [maɪld] *adj* dolce, mite, gentile; (*disease*) leggero
mildew [ˈmɪlˌdju] or [ˈmɪlˌdu] *s* (*mold*) muffa; (*plant disease*) peronospora
mile [maɪl] *s* miglio terrestre; miglio marino
mileage [ˈmaɪlɪdʒ] *s* distanza in miglia
mile'age tick'et *s* biglietto calcolato in miglia simile al biglietto chilometraggio
mile'post' *s* colonnina miliare
mile'stone' *s* pietra miliare
milieu [mɪlˈjʊ] *s* ambiente *m*
militancy [ˈmɪlɪtənsi] *s* bellicismo; spirito militante
militant [ˈmɪlɪtənt] *adj* & *s* militante *mf*
militarism [ˈmɪlɪtəˌrɪzəm] *s* militarismo
militarist [ˈmɪlɪtərɪst] *adj* & *s* militarista *mf*
militarize [ˈmɪlɪtəˌraɪz] *tr* militarizzare
military [ˈmɪlɪˌteri] *adj* militare || *s*—**the military** le forze armate
mil'itary acad'emy *s* scuola allievi ufficiali, accademia militare
mil'itary police' *s* polizia militare
militate [ˈmɪlɪˌtet] *intr* militare
militia [mɪˈlɪʃə] *s* milizia
mili'tia•man *s* (**-men**) miliziano
milk [mɪlk] *adj* lattifero; di latte; **al latte** || *s* latte *m* || *tr* mungere; (fig) spillare || *intr* dare latte
milk' can' *s* bidone *m* per il latte
milk' choc'olate *s* cioccolato al latte
milk' diet' *s* regime latteo
milking [ˈmɪlkɪŋ] *s* mungitura
milk'maid' *s* lattaia
milk'man' *s* (**-men'**) lattaio
milk' of hu'man kind'ness *s* grande compassione
milk' pail' *s* secchio da latte
milk' shake' *s* frappé *m* or frullato di latte
milk'sop' *s* effeminato
milk'weed' *s* vincetossico
milk•y [ˈmɪlki] *adj* (**-ier; -iest**) latteo; (*whitish*) lattiginoso
Milk'y Way' *s* Via Lattea
mill [mɪl] *s* (*for grinding grain*) mulino; (*for making fabrics*) filanda; (*for cutting wood*) segheria; (*for refining sugar*) zuccherificio; (*for producing steel*) acciaieria; (*to grind coffee*) macinino; (*part of a dollar*) millesimo; **to put through the mill** mettere a dura prova || *tr* (*grains*) macinare; (*coins*) zigrinare; (*steel*) laminare; (*ore*) frantumare; (*with a milling machine*) fresare; (*chocolate*) frullare || *intr*—**to mill about** or **around** girare intorno
millennial [mɪˈlenɪ•əl] *adj* millenario

millenni•um [mɪˈlenɪ·əm] *s* (**-ums** or **-a** [ə]) millennio
miller [ˈmɪlər] *s* mugnaio; (ent) tignola notturna
millet [ˈmɪlɪt] *s* panico, miglio
milliampere [ˌmɪlɪˈæmpɪr] *s* milliampere *m*
milliard [ˈmɪljərd] or [ˈmɪljɑrd] *s* (Brit) miliardo, bilione *m*
milligram [ˈmɪlɪ ˌgræm] *s* milligrammo
millimeter [ˈmɪlɪ ˌmitər] *s* millimetro
milliner [ˈmɪlɪnər] *s* modista
milliner•y [ˈmɪlɪ ˌneri] or [ˈmɪlɪnəri] *s* (**-ies**) cappelli *mpl* per signora; modisteria; articoli *mpl* di modisteria
mil'linery shop' *s* modisteria
milling [ˈmɪlɪŋ] *s* (*of grain*) macinatura; (*of coins*) granitura; (mach) fresatura
mill'ing machine' *s* fresatrice *f*
million [ˈmɪljən] *adj* milione di, milioni di || *s* milione *m*
millionaire [ˌmɪljənˈɛr] *s* milionario
millionth [ˈmɪljənθ] *adj, s & pron* milionesimo
millivolt [ˈmɪlɪ ˌvolt] *s* millivolt *m*
mill'pond' *s* gora
mill'race' *s* corrente *f* che aziona il mulino; canale *m* di presa
mill'stone' *s* mola, macina, palmento; (fig) peso, gravame *m*
mill' wheel' *s* ruota del mulino
mill'work' *s* lavoro di falegnameria; lavoro di falegnameria fatto a macchina
mime [maɪm] *s* mimo || *tr* mimare
mimeograph [ˈmɪmɪ·ə ˌgræf] or [ˈmɪmɪə ˌgrɑf] *s* (trademark) ciclostile *m* || *tr* ciclostilare
mim•ic [ˈmɪmɪk] *s* mimo, imitatore *m* || *v* (*pret & pp* **-icked**; *ger* **-icking**) *tr* imitare, scimmiottare
mimic•ry [ˈmɪmɪkri] *s* (**-ries**) mimica; (biol) mimetismo
minaret [ˌmɪnəˈret] or [ˈmɪnə ˌret] *s* minareto
mince [mɪns] *tr* tagliuzzare, triturare; (*words*) pronunziare con affettazione; **to not mince one's words** non aver peli sulla lingua
mince'meat' *s* carne tritata; **to make mincemeat of** annientare completamente
mince' pie' *s* torta di frutta secca e carne tritata
mind [maɪnd] *s* mente *f;* opinione; **to bear in mind** tener presente; **to be not in one's right mind** essere fuori di senno; **to be of one mind** essere d'accordo; **to be out of one's mind** essere impazzito; **to change one's mind** cambiare d'opinione; **to go out of one's mind** impazzire; **to have a mind to** aver voglia di; **to have in mind to** pensare a; **to have on one's mind** avere in mente; **to lose one's mind** uscire di mente; **to make up one's mind** decidersi; **to my mind** a mio modo di vedere; **to say whatever comes to one's mind** dire quanto salta in testa, e.g., **John always says whatever comes to his mind** Giovanni dice sempre quanto gli salta in testa; **to set one's mind on** risolversi a; **to slip one's mind** scappare di mente (with *dat*), e.g., **it slipped his mind** gli è scappato di mente; **to speak one's mind** dire la propria opinione; **with one mind** unanimamente || *tr* (*to take care of*) occuparsi di; obbedire (with *dat*); **do you mind the smoke?** Le disturba il fumo?; **mind your own business** si occupi degli affari Suoi || *intr* osservare, fare attenzione; rincrescere, e.g., **do you mind if I go?** Le rincresce se vado?; **never mind** non si preoccupi
mindful [ˈmaɪndfəl] *adj* memore
mind' read'er *s* lettore *m* del pensiero
mind' read'ing *s* lettura del pensiero
mine [maɪn] *s* (*e.g., of coal*) miniera; (mil & nav) mina || *pron poss* il mio; mio || *tr* minare; (*earth*) scavare; (*ore*) estrarre || *intr* lavorare una miniera; (mil & nav) minare
mine' detec'tor *s* rivelatore *m* di mine
mine'field' *s* campo minato
mine'lay'er *s* posamine *m*
miner [ˈmaɪnər] *s* minatore *m*
mineral [ˈmɪnərəl] *adj & s* minerale *m*
mineralogy [ˌmɪnəˈrælədʒi] *s* mineralogia
min'eral wool' *s* cotone *m* or lana minerale
mine' sweep'er *s* dragamine *m*
mingle [ˈmɪŋgəl] *tr* mescolare; unire || *intr* mescolarsi, associarsi
miniature [ˈmɪnɪ·ətʃər] or [ˈmɪnɪtʃər] *s* miniatura; **to paint in miniature** miniare, dipingere in miniatura
min'iature golf' *s* minigolf *m*
miniaturization [ˌmɪnɪ·ətʃərɪˈzeʃən] or [ˌmɪnɪtʃərɪˈzeʃən] *s* miniaturizzazione
minimal [ˈmɪnɪməl] *adj* minimo
minimize [ˈmɪnɪ ˌmaɪz] *tr* minimizzare
minimum [ˈmɪnɪməm] *adj & s* minimo
min'imum wage' *s* salario minimo
mining [ˈmaɪnɪŋ] *adj* minerario || *s* estrazione di minerali; (nav) posa di mine
minion [ˈmɪnjən] *s* servo; favorito, beniamino
min'ion of the law' *s* poliziotto
miniskirt [ˈmɪnə ˌskʌrt] *s* minigonna
minister [ˈmɪnɪstər] *s* ministro; pastore *m* protestante || *tr & intr* ministrare
ministerial [ˌmɪnɪsˈtɪrɪ·əl] *adj* ministeriale
minis•try [ˈmɪnɪstri] *s* (**-tries**) ministero; sacerdozio
mink [mɪŋk] *s* visone *m*
minnow [ˈmɪno] *s* pesciolino; (ichth) ciprino
minor [ˈmaɪnər] *adj* minore || *s* minore *m*, minorenne *mf;* (educ) corso secondario
minori•ty [mɪˈnɑrɪti] or [mɪˈnɔrɪti] *adj* minoritario || *s* (**-ties**) (*smaller number or part; group differing in race, etc., from majority*) minoranza; (*under legal age*) minorità *f*
minstrel [ˈmɪnstrəl] *s* (hist) mene-

strello; (U.S.A.) comico vestito da nero
minstrel·sy ['mɪnstrəlsi] *s* (**-sies**) giulleria; poesia giullaresca
mint [mɪnt] *s* zecca; (*plant*) menta; (*losenge*) mentina; (fig) miniera d'oro || *tr* coniare
minuet [,mɪnjʊ'et] *s* minuetto
minus ['maɪnəs] *adj* meno || *s* meno, perdita || *prep* meno, senza
minute [maɪ'njut] or [maɪ'nut] *adj* minuto || ['mɪnɪt] *adj* fatto in un minuto || *s* minuto; momento; **minutes** processo verbale; **to write up the minutes** tenere i verbali; **up to the minute** al corrente; dell'ultima ora
min'ute hand' ['mɪnɪt] *s* sfera or lancetta dei minuti
minutiae [mɪ'njuʃɪ,i] or [mɪ'nuʃɪ,i] *spl* minuzie *fpl*
minx [mɪŋks] *s* sfacciata, civetta
miracle ['mɪrəkəl] *s* miracolo
mir'acle play' *s* sacra rappresentazione
miraculous [mɪ'rækjələs] *adj* miracoloso
mirage [mɪ'rɑʒ] *s* miraggio
mire [maɪr] *s* limo, mota
mirror ['mɪrər] *s* specchio || *tr* specchiare, riflettere
mirth [mʌrθ] *s* allegria, gioia
mir·y ['maɪri] *adj* (**-ier; -iest**) fangoso, limaccioso
misadventure [,mɪsəd'ventʃər] *s* disavventura, contrattempo
misanthrope ['mɪsən,θrop] *s* misantropo
misanthropy [mɪs'ænθrəpi] *s* misantropia
misapprehension [,mɪsæprɪ'henʃən] *s* malinteso
misappropriation [,mɪsə,proprɪ'eʃən] *s* malversazione
misbehave [,mɪsbɪ'hev] *intr* comportarsi male
misbehavior [,mɪsbɪ'hevɪ·ər] *s* cattiva condotta
miscalculation [,mɪskælkjə'leʃən] *s* calcolo errato
miscarriage [mɪs'kærɪdʒ] *s* (*of justice*) errore *m;* (*of a letter*) disguido; (pathol) aborto
miscar·ry [mɪs'kæri] *v* (*pret & pp* **-ried**) *intr* (*said of a project*) fallire; (*said of a letter*) smarrirsi; (pathol) abortire
miscellaneous [,mɪsə'lenɪ·əs] *adj* miscellaneo
miscella·ny ['mɪsə,leni] *s* (**-nies**) miscellanea
mischief ['mɪstʃɪf] *s* (*harm*) danno; (*disposition to annoy*) malizia; (*prankishness*) birichinata
mis'chief·mak'er *s* mettimale *mf*
mischievous ['mɪstʃɪvəs] *adj* dannoso; malizioso; birichino
misconception [,mɪskən'sepʃən] *s* concetto erroneo, fraintendimento
misconduct [mɪs'kɑndəkt] *s* cattiva condotta; (*of a public official*) malgoverno || [,mɪskən'dʌkt] *tr* male amministrare; **to misconduct oneself** comportarsi male
misconstrue [,mɪskən'stru] or [mɪs'kɑnstru] *tr* fraintendere
miscount [mɪs'kaʊnt] *s* conteggio erroneo || *tr & intr* contare male
miscue [mɪs'kju] *s* sbaglio; (*in billiards*) stecca || *intr* steccare; (theat) sbagliarsi di battuta
mis·deal ['mɪs,dil] *s* distribuzione sbagliata || [mɪs'dil] *v* (*pret & pp* **-dealt** [dɛlt]) *tr & intr* distribuire erroneamente
misdeed [mɪs'did] or ['mɪs,did] *s* misfatto, malfatto
misdemeanor [,mɪsdɪ'minər] *s* cattiva condotta; (law) delitto colposo
misdirect [,mɪsdɪ'rɛkt] or [,mɪsdaɪ'rɛkt] *tr* dare un indirizzo sbagliato a; (*a letter*) mettere un indirizzo sbagliato su
misdoing [mɪs'du·ɪŋ] *s* misfatto
miser ['maɪzər] *s* avaro, spilorcio
miserable ['mɪzərəbəl] *adj* miserabile, miserevole; (coll) malissimo; (coll) schifoso
miserly ['maɪzərli] *adj* spilorcio
miser·y ['mɪzəri] *s* (**-ies**) miseria
misfeasance [mɪs'fizəns] *s* infrazione della legge; abuso di autorità commesso da pubblico funzionario
misfire [mɪs'faɪr] *s* difetto di esplosione; (aut) difetto d'accensione || *intr* (*said of a gun*) fare cilecca; (aut) dare accensione irregolare; (fig) fallire
mis·fit ['mɪs,fɪt] *s* vestito che non va bene; (*person*) spostato, pesce *m* fuor d'acqua || [mɪs'fɪt] *v* (*pret & pp* **-fitted;** *ger* **-fitting**) *intr* andar male
misfortune [mɪs'fɔrtʃən] *s* disgrazia
misgiving [mɪs'gɪvɪŋ] *s* dubbio, timore *m,* cattivo presentimento
misgovern [mɪs'gʌvərn] *tr* amministrare male
misguided [mɪs'gaɪdɪd] *adj* fuorviato; (*e.g., kindness*) sconsigliato
mishap ['mɪshæp] or [mɪs'hæp] *s* accidente *m,* infortunio
misinform [,mɪsɪn'fɔrm] *tr* dare informazioni errate a
misinterpret [,mɪsɪn'terprɪt] *tr* interpretare male, trasfigurare
misjudge [mɪs'dʒʌdʒ] *tr & intr* giudicare male
mis·lay [mɪs'le] *v* (*pret & pp* **-laid** [,led]) *tr* (*e.g., tile*) applicare in maniera sbagliata; (*e.g., papers*) smarrire, mettere al posto sbagliato
mis·lead [mɪs'lid] *v* (*pret & pp* **-led** [,lɛd]) *tr* sviare, traviare
misleading [mɪs'lidɪŋ] *adj* ingannatore
mismanagement [mɪs'mænɪdʒmənt] *s* malgoverno
misnomer [mɪs'nomər] *s* termine improprio
misplace [mɪs'ples] *tr* mettere fuori di posto; (*trust*) riporre erroneamente
misprint ['mɪs,prɪnt] *s* errore *m* di stampa, refuso || [mɪs'prɪnt] *tr* stampare erroneamente
mispronounce [,mɪsprə'naʊns] *tr* pronunciare in modo erroneo
mispronunciation [,mɪsprə,nʌnsɪ-

'eʃən] or [ˌmɪsprəˌnʌnʃɪ'eʃən] *s* errore *m* di pronuncia
misquote [mɪs'kwot] *tr* citare incorrettamente
misrepresent [ˌmɪsreprɪ'zent] *tr* travisare, snaturare; (pol) rappresentare slealmente
miss [mɪs] *s* sbaglio, omissione; tiro fuori bersaglio; signorina || *tr* (*a train, an opportunity*) perdere; (*the target*) fallire; (*an appointment*) mancare; (*the point*) non vedere, non capire; per poco, e.g., **the car missed hitting him** l'automobile non l'ha investito per poco || *intr* sbagliare, fallire; mancare il bersaglio || **Miss** *s* signorina, la signorina
missal ['mɪsəl] *s* messale *m*
misshapen [mɪs'ʃepən] *adj* deforme, malfatto
missile ['mɪsɪl] *adj* missilistico || *s* missile *m*
mis'sile launch'er *s* lanciamissili *m*
missing ['mɪsɪŋ] *adj* mancante; assente; (*in action*) disperso
mis'sing link' *s* anello di congiunzione
miss'ing per'son *s* disperso
mission ['mɪʃən] *s* missione
missionar•y ['mɪʃənˌeri] *adj* missionario || *s* (**-ies**) (eccl) missionario; (dipl) incaricato in missione
missive ['mɪsɪv] *s* missiva
mis•spell [mɪs'spel] *v* (*pret & pp* **-spelled** or **-spelt** ['spelt]) *tr & intr* scrivere male
misspelling [mɪs'spelɪŋ] *s* errore *m* di ortografia
misspent [mɪs'spent] *adj* sprecato
misstatement [mɪs'stetmənt] *s* dichiarazione inesatta
misstep [mɪs'step] *s* passo falso
miss•y ['mɪsi] *s* (**-ies**) (coll) signorina
mist [mɪst] *s* caligine *f*, foschia; (*of tears*) velo; (*of smoke, vapors, etc.*) nuvola
mis•take [mɪs'tek] *s* errore *m*, sbaglio; **and no mistake** (coll) di sicuro; **by mistake** per sbaglio; **to make a mistake** sbagliarsi || *v* (*pret* **-took** ['tʊk]; *pp* **-taken**) *tr* fraintendere; **to be mistaken for** essere preso per; **to mistake for** pigliare per
mistaken [mɪs'tekən] *adj* errato, sbagliato; **to be mistaken** essere in errore, sbagliarsi
mister ['mɪstər] *s* (mil, nav) signore *m*; (coll) marito || *interj* (coll) signore!; (coll) Lei!; (coll) buonuomo! || **Mister** *s* Signore *m*
mistletoe ['mɪsəlˌto] *s* vischio
mistreat [mɪs'trit] *tr* maltrattare
mistreatment [mɪs'tritmənt] *s* maltrattamento
mistress ['mɪstrɪs] *s* (*of a household*) signora, padrona; (*paramour*) amante *f*, ganza; (Brit) maestra di scuola
mistrial [mɪs'traɪ•əl] *s* processo viziato da errore giudiziario
mistrust [mɪs'trʌst] *s* diffidenza || *tr* diffidare di || *intr* diffidarsi
mistrustful [mɪs'trʌstfəl] *adj* diffidente
mist•y ['mɪsti] *adj* (**-ier; -iest**) fosco, brumoso; (fig) vago, confuso

misunder•stand [ˌmɪsʌndər'stænd] *v* (*pret & pp* **-stood** ['stʊd] *tr* fraintendere, equivocare
misunderstanding [ˌmɪsʌndər'stændɪŋ] *s* malinteso
misuse [mɪs'jus] *s* abuso; (*of funds*) malversazione || [mɪs'juz] *tr* abusare di; (*funds*) malversare
misword [mɪs'wʌrd] *tr* comporre male
mite [maɪt] obolo; (ent) acaro
miter ['maɪtər] *s* (carp) ugnatura; (carp) giunto a quartabuono; (eccl) mitra || *tr* tagliare a quartabuono, ugnare; giungere a quartabuono
mi'ter box' *s* cassetta per ugnature
mi'ter joint' *s* giunto a quartabuono
mitigate ['mɪtɪˌget] *tr* mitigare
mitten ['mɪtən] *s* manopola, muffola
mix [mɪks] *tr* mescolare; (*colors*) mesticare; (*dough*) impastare; (*salad*) condire; **to mix up** confondere || *intr* confondersi, mescolarsi
mixed [mɪkst] *adj* misto; (*candy*) assortito; (coll) confuso
mixed' com'pany *s* riunione *f* di ambo i sessi
mixed' drink' *s* miscela di liquori diversi
mixed' feel'ing *s* sentimento ambivalente
mixed' met'aphor *s* metafora incongruente
mixer ['mɪksər] *s* (mach) mescolatrice *f*; **to be a good mixer** essere socievole
mixture ['mɪkstʃər] *s* mistura, mescolanza; (aut) miscela, carburazione
mix'-up' *s* confusione; (coll) baruffa
mizzen ['mɪzən] *s* mezzana
moan [mon] *s* gemito || *intr* gemere
moat [mot] *s* fosso, fossato
mob [mɑb] *s* turba || *v* (*pret & pp* **mobbed**; *ger* **mobbing**) *tr* assaltare; affollarsi intorno a; (*a place*) affollare
mobile ['mobɪl] or ['mobil] *adj* mobile
mo'bile home' *s* caravan *m*, roulotte *f*
mobility [mo'bɪlɪti] *s* mobilità *f*
mobilization [ˌmobɪlɪ'zeʃən] *s* mobilitazione
mobilize ['mobɪˌlaɪz] *tr & intr* mobilitare
mob' rule' *s* legge *f* della teppa
mobster ['mɑbstər] *s* gangster *m*
moccasin ['mɑkəsɪn] *s* mocassino
Mo'cha cof'fee ['mokə] *s* caffè *m* moca
mock [mɑk] *adj* finto, imitato || *s* dileggio, burla || *tr* deridere, canzonare; ingannare || *intr* motteggiare; **to mock at** farsi gioco di
mocker•y ['mɑkəri] *s* (**-ies**) dileggio, scherno; (*subject of derision*) zimbello; (*poor imitation*) contraffazione
mock'-hero'ic *adj* eroicomico
mockingbird ['mɑkɪŋˌbʌrd] *s* mimo
mock' or'ange *s* gelsomino selvatico
mock' tur'tle soup' *s* finto brodo di tartaruga
mock'-up' *s* modello dimostrativo
mode [mod] *s* modo, maniera; (*fashion*) moda; (gram) modo
mod•el ['mɑdəl] *adj* modello, e.g., **model student** studente modello || *s*

modello; (*woman serving as subject for artists*) modello *f*; (*woman wearing clothes at fashion show*) indossatrice *f* || *v* (*pret & pp* **-eled** or **-elled**; *ger* **-eling** or **-elling**) *tr* modellare || *intr* modellarsi; fare il manichino
mod'el air'plane *s* aeromodello
mo'del-air'plane build'er *s* aeromodellista *mf*
mod'eling clay' *s* plastilina
moderate ['madərɪt] *adj* moderato || ['madə ,ret] *tr* moderare; (*a meeting*) presiedere a || *intr* moderarsi
moderator ['madə ,retər] *s* moderatore *m*; (*mediator*) arbitro; (phys) moderatore *m*
modern ['madərn] *adj* moderno
modernize ['madər ,naɪz] *tr* modernizzare, rimodernare
modest ['madɪst] *adj* modesto
modes·ty ['madɪsti] *s* (**-ties**) modestia
modicum ['madɪkəm] *s* piccola quantità
modi·fy ['madɪ ,faɪ] *v* (*pret & pp* **-fied**) *tr* modificare; (gram) determinare
modish ['modɪʃ] *adj* alla moda
modulate ['madʒə ,let] *tr & intr* modulare
modulation [,madʒə'leʃən] *s* modulazione
mohair ['mo ,her] *s* mohair *m*
Mohammedan [mo'hæmɪdən] *adj & s* maomettano
Mohammedanism [mo'hæmɪdə ,nɪzəm] *s* maomettismo
moist [mɔɪst] *adj* umido; lacrimoso
moisten ['mɔɪsən] *tr* inumidire || *intr* inumidirsi
moisture ['mɔɪstʃər] *s* umidità *f*
molar ['molər] *s* molare *m*
molasses [mə'læsɪz] *s* melassa
mold [mold] *s* stampo, forma; (*fungus*) muffa; humus *m*; (fig) indole *f* || *tr* plasmare, conformare; (*to make moldy*) fare ammuffire || *intr* ammuffire
molder ['moldər] *s* modellatore *m* || *intr* sgretolarsi; polverizzarsi
molding ['moldɪŋ] *s* modellato; (archit, carp) modanatura
mold·y ['moldi] *adj* (**-ier**; **-iest**) ammuffito
mole [mol] *s* (*pier*) molo; (*harbor*) darsena; (*spot on skin*) neo; (*small mammal*) talpa
molecule ['malɪ ,kjul] *s* molecola
mole'hill' *s* mucchio di terra sopra la tana di talpe
mole'skin' *s* pelle *f* di talpa; (*fabric*) fustagno di prima qualità
molest [mə'lest] *tr* molestare; fare proposte disoneste a
moll [mal] *s* (slang) ragazza della malavita; (slang) puttana
molli·fy ['malɪ ,faɪ] *v* (*pret & pp* **-fied**) *tr* pacificare, placare
mollusk ['maləsk] *s* mollusco
mollycoddle ['malɪ ,kadəl] *s* effeminato || *tr* viziare, coccolare
Mo'lotov cock'tail ['malə ,tɔf] *s* bottiglia Molotov
molt [molt] *s* muda || *intr* andare in muda
molten ['moltən] *adj* fuso
molybdenum [mə'lɪbdɪnəm] or [,malɪb'dinəm] *s* molibdeno
moment ['momənt] *s* momento; **at any moment** da un momento all'altro
momentary ['momən ,teri] *adj* momentaneo
momentous [mo'mentəs] *adj* grave, importante
momen·tum [mo'mentəm] *s* (**-tums** or **-ta** [tə]) slancio; (mech) momento
monarch ['manərk] *s* monarca *m*
monarchic(al) [mə'narkɪk(əl)] *adj* monarchico
monarchist ['manərkɪst] *adj & s* monarchico
monar·chy ['manərki] *s* (**-chies**) monarchia
monaster·y ['manəs ,teri] *s* (**-ies**) monastero
monastic [mə'næstɪk] *adj* monastico, monacale
monasticism [mə'næstɪ ,sɪzəm] *s* monachesimo
Monday ['mʌndi] *s* lunedì *m*
monetary ['manɪ ,teri] *adj* monetario; pecuniario
money ['mʌni] *s* denaro; **to be in the money** esser carico di soldi; **to make money** far quattrini
mon'ey·bag' *s* borsa per denaro; **moneybags** (coll) riccone sfondato
moneychanger ['mʌnɪ ,tʃendʒər] *s* cambiavalute *m*
moneyed ['mʌnid] *adj* danaroso
moneylender ['mʌni ,lendər] *s* prestatore *m* di denaro
mon'ey·mak'er *s* capitalista *mf*; affare vantaggioso
mon'ey or'der *s* vaglia *m*
Mongolian [maŋ'golɪ·ən] *adj & s* mongolo
mon·goose ['maŋgus] *s* (**-gooses**) mangusta
mongrel ['mʌŋgrəl] or ['maŋgrəl] *adj* ibrido || *s* ibrido; cane bastardo
monitor ['manɪtər] *s* (educ) capoclasse *mf*; (rad, telv) monitore *m* || *tr* osservare; (*a signal*) controllare; (*a broadcast*) ascoltare
monk [mʌŋk] *s* monaco
monkey ['mʌŋki] *s* scimmia; **to make a monkey of** farsi gioco di || *intr*—**to monkey around** (coll) oziare; **to monkey around with** (coll) giocherellare con
mon'key·shines' *spl* (slang) monellerie *fpl*, pagliacciate *fpl*
mon'key wrench' *s* chiave *f* inglese
monkhood ['mʌŋkhud] *s* monacato
monkshood [mʌŋks ,hud] *s* (bot) aconito
monocle ['manəkəl] *s* monocolo
monogamy [mə'nagəmi] *s* monogamia
monogram ['manə ,græm] *s* monogramma *m*
monograph ['manə ,græf] or ['manə ,graf] *s* monografia
monolithic [,manə'lɪθɪk] *adj* monolitico

monologue ['mɑnə,lɔg] or ['mɑnə,lɑg] *s* monologo
monomania [,mɑnə'menɪ·ə] *s* monomania
monomial [mə'nomɪ·əl] *s* monomio
monopolize [mə'nɑpə,laɪz] *tr* monopolizzare, accaparrare
monopo·ly [mə'nɑpəli] *s* (**-lies**) monopolio, privativa
monorail ['mɑnə,rel] *s* monorotaia
monosyllable ['mɑnə,sɪləbəl] *s* monosillabo
monotheist ['mɑnə,θi·ɪst] *adj & s* monoteista *mf*
monotonous [mə'nɑtənəs] *adj* monotono
monotype ['mɑnə,taɪp] *s* (*method*) monotipia; (typ) monotipo
monoxide [mə'nɑksaɪd] *s* monossido
monseigneur [,mɑnsen'jœr] *s* monsignore *m*
monsignor [mɑn'sinjər] *s* (**-monsignors** or **monsignori** [,mɔnsi'njori]) (eccl) monsignore *m*
monsoon [mɑn'sun] *s* monsone *m*
monster ['mɑnstər] *adj* mostruoso || *s* mostro
monstrance ['mɑnstrəns] *s* ostensorio
monstrosi·ty [mɑn'strɑsɪti] *s* (**-ties**) mostruosità *f*
monstrous ['mɑnstrəs] *adj* mostruoso
month [mʌnθ] *s* mese *m*
month·ly ['mʌnθli] *adj* mensile || *s* (**-lies**) rivista mensile; **monthlies** (coll) mestruazione || *adv* mensilmente
monument ['mɑnjəmənt] *s* monumento
moo [mu] *s* muggito || *intr* muggire
mood [mud] *s* umore *m*, vena; (gram) modo; **moods** luna, malumore *m*
mood·y ['mudi] *adj* (**-ier; -iest**) triste, malinconico; lunatico, capriccioso
moon [mun] *s* luna; **once in a blue moon** ad ogni morte di papa || *tr*—**to moon away** (*time*) (coll) sprecare || *intr*—**to moon about** (coll) gingillarsi, baloccarsi; (*to daydream about*) (coll) sognarsi di
moon'beam' *s* raggio di luna
moon'light' *s* chiaro *m* di luna
moon'light'ing *s* secondo lavoro notturno
moon'shine' *s* chiaro di luna; (coll) chiacchiere *fpl*, balle *fpl;* (coll) whisky *m* distillato illegalmente
moon'shot' *s* lancio alla luna
moon'stone' *s* lunaria
moor [mur] *s* brughiera, landa || *tr* ormeggiare || *intr* ormeggiarsi || **Moor** *s* moro
Moorish ['murɪʃ] *adj* moresco
moor'land' *s* brughiera, landa
moose [mus] *s* (**moose**) alce americano
moot [mut] *adj* controverso, discutibile
mop [mɑp] *s* scopa di filacce; (naut) redazza; (*of hair*) zazzera || *v* (*pret & pp* **mopped;** *ger* **mopping**) *tr* (*a floor*) pulire, asciugare; (*one's brow*) asciugarsi; **to mop up** rastrellare
mope [mop] *intr* andare rattristato
mopish ['mopɪʃ] *adj* triste, avvilito
moral ['mɑrəl] or ['mɔrəl] *adj* morale || *s* (*of a fable*) morale *f;* **morals** (*ethics*) morale *f;* (*modes of conduct*) costumi *mpl*
morale [mə'ræl] or [mə'rɑl] *s* morale *m*
morali·ty [mə'rælɪti] *s* (**-ties**) moralità *f*
mor'als charge' *s* accusa di oltraggio al pudore
morass [mə'ræs] *s* palude *f*
moratori·um [,mɔrə'torɪ·əm] or [,mɑrə'torɪ·əm] *s* (**-ums** or **-a** [ə]) moratoria
morbid ['mɔrbɪd] *adj* (*gruesome*) orribile; (*feelings; curiosity; pertaining to disease; pathologic*) morboso
mordacious [mɔr'deʃəs] *adj* mordace
mordant ['mɔrdənt] *adj & s* mordente *m*
more [mor] *adj & s* più *m* || *adv* più; **more and more** sempre più; **more than** più di; (*followed by verb*] più di quanto; **the more . . . the less** tanto più . . . quanto meno
more·o'er *adv* per di più, inoltre
Moresque [mo'rɛsk] *adj* moresco
morgue [mɔrg] *s* deposito, obitorio; (journ) archivio di un giornale, frigorifero
moribund ['mɔrɪ,bʌnd] or ['mɑrɪ,bʌnd] *adj* moribondo
morning ['mɔrnɪŋ] *adj* mattiniero || *s* mattina, mattino; **good morning** buon giorno; **in the morning** di mattina
morn'ing coat' *s* giacca nera a code
morn'ing-glo'ry *s* (**-ries**) convolvolo; (*Ipomea*) campanella; (*Convolvulus tricolor*) bella di giorno
morn'ing sick'ness *s* vomito di gravidanza
morn'ing star' *s* Lucifero, stella del mattino
Moroccan [mə'rɑkən] *adj & s* marocchino
morocco [mə'rɑko] *s* (*leather*) marocchino || **Morocco** *s* il Marocco
moron ['morɑn] *s* deficiente *mf*
morose [mə'ros] *adj* tetro, imbronciato
morphine ['mɔrfin] *s* morfina
morphology [mɔr'fɑlədʒi] *s* morfologia
morrow ['mɑro] or ['mɔro] *s*—**on the morrow** l'indomani, il giorno seguente; domani
morsel ['mɔrsəl] *s* boccone *m*, bocconcino; pezzetto
mortal ['mɔrtəl] *adj & s* mortale *m*
mortality [mɔr'tælɪti] *s* mortalità *f;* (*death or destruction on a large scale*) moria
mortar ['mɔrtər] *s* (*mixture of lime or cement*) malta, calcina; (*bowl*) mortaio; (mil) mortaio, lanciabombe *m*
mor'tar·board' *s* sparviere *m;* (*cap*) tocco accademico
mortgage ['mɔrgɪdʒ] *s* ipoteca || *tr* ipotecare
mortgagee [,mɔrgɪ'dʒi] *s* creditore *m* ipotecario
mortgagor ['mɔrgɪdʒər] *s* debitore *m* ipotecario

mortician [mɔrˈtɪʃən] *s* impresario di pompe funebri
morti•fy [ˈmɔrtɪ,faɪ] *v* (*pret & pp* **-fied**) *tr* mortificare; **to be mortified** vergognarsi
mortise [ˈmɔrtɪs] *s* intaccatura, incastro ‖ *tr* incassare, incastrare
mor'tise lock' *s* serratura incastrata
mortuar•y [ˈmɔrtʃʊ,eri] *adj* mortuario ‖ *s* (**-ies**) camera mortuaria
mosaic [moˈze·ɪk] *s* mosaico
Moscow [ˈmɑskaʊ] or [ˈmɑsko] *s* Mosca
Moses [ˈmozɪz] or [ˈmozɪs] *s* Mosè *m*
Mos•lem [ˈmɑzləm] or [ˈmɑsləm] *adj* musulmano ‖ *s* (**-lems** or **-lem**) musulmano
mosque [mɑsk] *s* moschea
mosqui•to [məsˈkito] *s* (**-toes** or **-tos**) zanzara
mosqui'to net' *s* zanzariera
moss [mɔs] or [mɑs] *s* musco
moss'back' *s* (coll) ultraconservatore *m*, fossile *m*
moss•y [ˈmɔsi] or [ˈmɑsi] *adj* (**-ier; -iest**) muscoso
most [most] *adj* il più di, la maggior parte di ‖ *s* la maggioranza, i più; **most of** la maggior parte di; **to make the most of** trarre il massimo da ‖ *adv* più, maggiormente, al massimo
mostly [ˈmostli] *adv* per lo più, maggiormente, al massimo
motel [moˈtɛl] *s* motel *m*, autostello
moth [mɔθ] or [mɑθ] *s* falena; (*clothes moth*) tarma
moth'ball' *s* pallina antitarmica
moth-eaten [ˈmɔθ,itən] or [ˈmɑθ,itən] *adj* tarmato; antiquato
mother [ˈmʌðər] *adj* (*love, tongue*) materno; (*country*) natio; (*church, company*) madre ‖ *s* madre *f;* (*elderly woman*) (coll) zia ‖ *tr* fare da madre a; creare; procreare; assumere la maternità di
moth'er coun'try *s* madrepatria
Moth'er Goose' *s* supposta autrice di una raccolta di favole infantili
motherhood [ˈmʌðər,hʊd] *s* maternità *f*
moth'er-in-law' *s* (**moth'ers-in-law'**) suocera
moth'er•land' *s* madrepatria
motherless [ˈmʌðərlɪs] *adj* orfano di madre, senza madre
mother-of-pearl [ˈmʌðərəvˈpʌrl] *adj* madreperlaceo ‖ *s* madreperla
motherly [ˈmʌθərli] *adj* materno
Moth'er's Day' *s* giorno della madre, festa della mamma
moth'er supe'rior *s* madre superiora
moth'er tongue' *s* madrelingua; (*language from which another language is derived*) lingua madre
moth'er wit' *s* intelligenza nativa
moth' hole' *s* tarlatura
moth•y [ˈmɔθi] or [ˈmɑθi] *adj* (**-ier; -iest**) tarmato
motif [moˈtif] *s* motivo
motion [ˈmoʃən] *s* movimento; (*e.g., of a dancer*) movenza, mossa; (*in parliamentary procedure*) mozione; **in motion** in moto ‖ *intr* fare cenno
motionless [ˈmoʃənlɪs] *adj* immobile
mo'tion pic'ture *s* pellicola cinematografica; **motion pictures** cinematografia
mo'tion-picture' *adj* cinematografico
motivate [ˈmotɪ,vet] *tr* animare, incitare
motive [ˈmotɪv] *adj* motivo; (*producing motion*) motore ‖ *s* motivo; (*incentive*) movente *m*
mo'tive pow'er *s* forza motrice; impianto motore; (rr) insieme *m* di locomotive
motley [ˈmɑtli] *adj* eterogeneo; variato, variopinto
motor [ˈmotər] *adj* motore; (*operated by motor*) motorizzato; (*pertaining to motor vehicles*) motoristico ‖ *s* motore *m;* (aut) macchina ‖ *intr* viaggiare in macchina
mo'tor•boat' *s* motobarca, motoscafo
mo'tor•bus' *s* torpedone *m;* autobus *m*
motorcade [ˈmotər,ked] *s* carovana di automobili
mo'tor•car' *s* automobile *f*
mo'tor•cy'le *s* motocicletta
motorist [ˈmotərɪst] *s* automobilista *mf*
motorize [ˈmotə,raɪz] *tr* motorizzare
mo'torman *s* (**-men**) guidatore *m* di tram; guidatore *m* di locomotore
mo'tor sail'er *s* motoveliero
mo'tor scoot'er *s* motoretta
mot'or ship' *s* motonave *f*
mo'tor truck' *s* autocarro, camion *m*
mo'tor ve'hicle *s* motoveicolo
mottle [ˈmɑtəl] *tr* chiazzare, screziare
mot•to [ˈmɑto] *s* (**-toes** or **-tos**) motto, divisa
mould [mold] *s, tr, & intr* var of **mold**
mound [maʊnd] *s* monticello, collinetta
mount [maʊnt] *s* monte *m*, montagna; (*horse for riding*) cavalcatura, monta; (*setting for a jewel*) montatura; supporto; (*for a picture*) incorniciatura ‖ *tr* montare; (*a wall*) scalare; (theat) allestire ‖ *intr* montare; (*to climb*) salire
mountain [ˈmaʊntən] *s* montagna; **to make a mountain out of a molehill** fare di un bruscolo una trave, fare d'una mosca un elefante
moun'tain climb'ing *s* alpinismo
mountaineer [,maʊntəˈnɪr] *s* montanaro
mountainous [ˈmaʊntənəs] *adj* montagnoso
moun'tain rail'road *s* ferrovia a dentiera
moun'tain range' *s* catena di montagne
moun'tain sick'ness *s* mal *m* di montagna
mountebank [ˈmaʊntɪ,bæŋk] *s* ciarlatano
mounting [ˈmaʊntɪŋ] *s* (*act*) il montare, montaggio; (*setting*) montatura; (mach) supporto
mourn [morn] *tr* (*the loss of s.o.*) piangere; (*a misfortune*) lamentare ‖ *intr* piangere; vestire a lutto
mourner [ˈmornər] *s* persona in lutto; (*penitent sinner*) penitente *mf;*

(*woman hired to attend a funeral or funerals*) prefica
mourn'er's bench' *s* banco dei penitenti
mournful ['mornfəl] *adj* luttuoso, funesto; (*gloomy*) lugubre
mourning ['mornɪŋ] *s* lutto; **to be in mourning** portare il lutto
mourn'ing band' *s* bracciale *m* a lutto
mouse [maʊs] *s* (**mice** [maɪs]) topo, sorcio
mouse'hole' *s* topaia; piccolo buco
mouser ['maʊzər] *s* cacciatore *m* di topi
mouse'trap' *s* trappola per topi
moustache [məs'tæʃ] or [məs'tɑʃ] *s* baffi *mpl*, mustacchi *mpl*
mouth [maʊθ] s (**mouths** [maʊðz]) bocca; **by mouth** per via orale; **to be born with a silver spoon in one's mouth** essere nato con la camicia; **to make one's mouth water** fare venire a qlcu l'acquolina in bocca
mouthful ['maʊθ,fʊl] *s* boccata
mouth' or'gan *s* armonica a bocca
mouth'piece' *s* (*of wind instrument*) bocchetta; (*of bridle*) imboccatura; (*of megaphone*) boccaglio; (*of cigarette*) bocchino; (*of telephone*) imboccatura; (*spokesman*) portavoce *m*
mouth'wash' *s* sciacquo, risciacquo
movable ['muvəbəl] *adj* mobile, movibile; (law) mobiliare
move [muv] *s* movimento; (*change of residence*) trasloco; (*step*) passo; (*e.g., in chess*) mossa; **on the move** in moto, in movimento; **to get a move on** (coll) affrettarsi || *tr* muovere; (*the bowels*) provocare l'evacuazione di; (*to prompt*) spingere; (*to stir the feelings of*) emozionare, commuovere; (law) proporre; (com) svendere; **to move up** (*a date*) anticipare || *intr* muoversi; passare; (*to another house*) traslocare; (*to another city*) trasferirsi; (*said of goods*) avere una vendita; (*said of the bowels*) evacuare; procedere; (law) presentare una mozione; (coll) andarsene; **to move away** andarsene; trasferirsi; **to move back** tirarsi indietro; **to move in** avanzare; (*society*) frequentare; **to move off** allontanarsi
movement ['muvmənt] *s* movimento; (*of a watch*) meccanismo; (*of the bowels*) evacuazione; (mus) movimento, tempo
movie ['muvi] *s* (coll) film *m*, pellicola
movie·goer ['movi,go·ər] *s* frequentatore *m* del cinema
mov'ie house' *s* (coll) cinematografo
mov'ie·land' *s* (coll) cinelandia
moving ['muvɪŋ] *adj* commovente, emozionante || *s* trasporto; (*from one house to another*) trasloco
mov'ing pic'ture *s* film *m*, pellicola
mov'ing stair'case' *s* scala mobile
mow [mo] *v* (*pret* **mowed**; *pp* **mowed** or **mown**) *tr* & *intr* falciare
mower ['mo·ər] *s* falciatore *m;* (mach) falciatrice *f*
Mr. ['mɪstər] *s* (**Messrs.** ['mesərz]) Signore *m*
Mrs. ['mɪsɪz] *s* Signora

much [mʌtʃ] *adj* & *pron* molto; **as much . . . as** tanto . . . quanto; **too much** troppo || *adv* molto; **however much** per quanto; **how much** quanto; **too much** troppo; **very much** moltissimo
mucilage ['mjusɪlɪdʒ] *s* colla; (*gummy secretion in plants*) mucillagine *f*
muck [mʌk] *s* letame *m;* (*dirt*) sudiciume *m;* (min) materiale *m* di scoria
muck'rake' *intr* (coll) sollevare scandali
mucous ['mjukəs] *adj* mucoso
mucus ['mjukəs] *s* muco
mud [mʌd] *s* fango, melma, limo; **to sling mud at** calunniare
muddle ['mʌdəl] *s* confusione, guazzabuglio || *tr* confondere, intorbidire || *intr*—**to muddle through** arrangiarsi; cavarsela alla meno peggio in
mud'dle·head' *s* (coll) semplicione *m*
mud·dy ['mʌdi] *adj* (**-dier; -diest**) fangoso, melmoso; (*obscure*) torbido || *v* (*pret* & *pp* **-died**) *tr* turbare, intorbidare; (*to soil with mud*) infangare
mud'guard' *s* parafango
mud'hole' *s* pozzanghera, fangaia
mud' slide' *s* smottamento
mudslinger ['mʌd,slɪŋgər] *s* calunniatore *m*
muff [mʌf] *s* manicotto || *tr* (coll) mancare; (*to handle badly*) (coll) abborracciare; (sports) mancare di pigliare
muffin ['mʌfɪn] *s* panino soffice
muffle ['mʌfəl] *tr* infagottare, imbacuccare; (*a sound*) velare, smorzare
muffler ['mʌflər] *s* sciarpa; (aut) silenziatore *m*, marmitta
mufti ['mʌfti] *s*—**in mufti** in borghese
mug [mʌg] *s* tazzona; (slang) muso, grugno || *v* (*pret* & *pp* **mugged**; *ger* **mugging**) *tr* (slang) fotografare; (slang) attaccare proditoriamente || *intr* fare le smorfie
mug·gy ['mʌgi] *adj* (**-gier; -giest**) afoso, opprimente
mulat·to [mjʊ'læto] or [mə'læto] *s* (**-toes**) mulatto
mulber·ry ['mʌl,beri] *s* (**-ries**) (*tree*) gelso; (*fruit*) mora di gelso
mulct [mʌlkt] *tr* defraudare
mule [mjul] *s* mulo; (*slipper*) pianella
muleteer [,mjulə'tɪr] *s* mulattiere *m*
mulish ['mjulɪʃ] *adj* testardo
mull [mʌl] *tr* (*wine*) scaldare aggiungendo spezie || *intr*—**to mull over** pensarci sopra, rinvangare
mulled' wine' *s* vino caldo
mullion ['mʌljən] *s* colonnina che divide una bifora
multigraph ['mʌltɪ,græf] or ['mʌltɪ,grɑf] *s* (trademark) poligrafo || *tr* poligrafare
multilateral [,mʌltɪ'lætərəl] *adj* multilaterale
multimotor [,mʌltɪ'motər] *s* plurimotore *m*
multiple ['mʌltɪpəl] *adj* & *s* multiplo
multiplici·ty [,mʌltɪ'plɪsɪti] *s* (**-ties**) molteplicità *f*
multi·ply ['mʌltɪ,plaɪ] *v* (*pret* & *pp* **-plied**) *tr* moltiplicare || *intr* moltiplicarsi

multistage ['mʌltɪ,stedʒ] *adj* (rok) pluristadio
multitude ['mʌltɪ,tjud] or ['mʌltɪ,tud] s moltitudine *f*
mum [mʌm] *adj* zitto; **mum's the word!** acqua in bocca!; **to keep mum** stare zitto || *interj* zitto!
mumble ['mʌmbəl] *tr* biascicare || *intr* farfugliare
mummer·y ['mʌməri] *s* **(-ies)** buffonata, mascherata
mum·my ['mʌmi] *s* **(-mies)** mummia
mumps [mʌmps] *s* orecchioni *mpl*
munch [mʌntʃ] *tr* sgranocchiare
mundane ['mʌnden] *adj* mondano
municipal [mju'nɪsɪpəl] *adj* municipale
municipali·ty [mju,nɪsɪ'pælɪti] *s* **(-ties)** municipio
munificent [mju'nɪfɪsənt] *adj* munifico
munition [mju'nɪʃən] *s* munizione || *tr* fornire di munizioni
muni'tion dump' *s* deposito munizioni
mural ['mjurəl] *adj* murale || *s* pittura murale
murder ['mʌrdər] *s* omicidio || *tr* assassinare
murderer ['mʌrdərər] *s* omicida *m*
murderess ['mʌrdərɪs] *s* omicida *f*
murderous ['mʌrdərəs] *adj* omicida, crudele, sanguinario
murk·y ['mʌrki] *adj* **(-ier; -iest)** fosco, tenebroso; brumoso, nebbioso
murmur ['mʌrmər] *s* mormorio || *tr & intr* mormorare
Mur'phy bed' ['mʌrfi] *s* letto a scomparsa
muscle ['mʌsəl] *s* muscolo
muscular ['mʌskjələr] *adj* muscolare; (*having well-developed muscles*) muscoloso
muse [mjuz] *s* musa; **the Muses** le Muse || *intr* meditare, rimuginare
museum [mju'zi·əm] *s* museo
mush [mʌʃ] *s* pappa, polentina; (fig) leziosaggine *f*, sdolcinatura
mush'room *s* fungo || *intr* venir su come i funghi; **to mushroom into** diventare rapidamente
mush'room cloud' *s* fungo atomico
mush·y ['mʌʃi] *adj* **(-ier; -iest)** polposo, spappolato; (fig) sdolcinato, sentimentale
music ['mjuzɪk] *s* musica; **to face the music** (coll) affrontare le conseguenze; **to set to music** mettere in musica
musical ['mjuzɪkəl] *adj* musicale
mu'sical com'edy *s* operetta, commedia musicale
musicale [,mjuzɪ'kæl] *s* serata musicale
mu'sic box' *s* scatola armonica
mu'sic cab'inet *s* scaffaletto per la musica
mu'sic hall' *s* salone *m* da concerti; (Brit) teatro di varietà, music-hall *m*
musician [mju'zɪʃən] *s* musicista *mf*
musicianship [mju'zɪʃən,ʃɪp] *s* abilità *f* musicale, virtuosismo
musicologist [,mjuzɪ'kɑlədʒɪst] *s* musicologo
musicology [,mjuzɪ'kɑlədʒi] *s* musicologia
mu'sic stand' *s* portamusica *m*
musk [mʌsk] *s* muschio
musk' deer' *s* mosco
musket ['mʌskɪt] *s* moschetto
musketeer [,mʌskɪ'tɪr] *s* moschettiere *m*
musk'mel'on *s* melone *m*
musk' ox' *s* bue muschiato
musk'rat' *s* ondatra, topo muschiato
muslin ['mʌzlɪn] *s* mussolina
muss [mʌs] *tr* (*the hair*) scompigliare, arruffare; (*clothing*) (coll) sciupare
mussel ['mʌsəl] *s* mussolo
Mussulman ['mʌsəlmən] *adj & s* musulmano
muss·y ['mʌsi] *adj* **(-ier; -iest)** (coll) arruffato, scompigliato
must [mʌst] *s* (*new wine*) mosto; (*mold*) muffa; (coll) cosa assolutamente indispensabile || *v aux*—**I must go now** devo andarmene ora; **it must be Ann** deve assere Anna; **she must be ill** dev'essere malata; **they must have known it** devono averlo saputo
mustache [məs'tæʃ], [məs'tɑʃ] or ['mʌstæʃ] *s* baffi *mpl*, mustacchi *mpl*
mustard ['mʌstərd] *s* mostarda
mus'tard plas'ter *s* senapismo
muster ['mʌstər] *s* adunata, rivista; **to pass muster** passar ispezione || *tr* chiamare a raccolta; riunire; **to muster in** arruolare; **to muster out** congedare; **to muster up courage** prendere coraggio a quattro mani
mus'ter roll' *s* ruolo; (naut) appello
mus·ty ['mʌsti] *adj* **(-tier; -tiest)** (*moldy*) ammuffito; (*stale*) stantio; (fig) ammuffito, stantio
mutation [mju'teʃən] *s* mutazione
mute [mjut] *adj & s* muto || *tr* mettere la sordina a
mutilate ['mjutɪ,let] *tr* mutilare
mutineer [,mjutɪ'nɪr] *s* ammutinato
mutinous ['mjutɪnəs] *adj* ammutinato
muti·ny ['mjutɪni] *s* **(-nies)** ammutinamento || *v* (*pret & pp* **-nied**) *intr* ammutinarsi
mutt [mʌt] *s* (slang) cane bastardo; (slang) scemo
mutter ['mʌtər] *tr & intr* borbottare
mutton ['mʌtən] *s* montone *m*
mut'ton chop' *s* cotoletta di montone
mutual ['mutʃu·əl] *adj* mutuo, vicendevole
mu'tual aid' *s* mutualità *f*
mu'tual fund' *s* fondo comune di investimento
muzzle ['mʌzəl] *s* (*of animal*) muso; (*device to keep animal from biting*) museruola; (*of firearm*) bocca || *tr* mettere la museruola a; (fig) imbavagliare
my [maɪ] *adj poss* mio, il mio || *interj* (coll) corbezzoli!
myriad ['mɪrɪ·əd] *s* miriade *f*
myrrh [mʌr] *s* mirra
myrtle ['mʌrtəl] *s* mirto, mortella
myself [maɪ'self] *pron pers* io stesso; me, me stesso; mi, e.g., **I hurt myself** mi sono fatto male

mysterious [mɪs'tɪrɪ·əs] *adj* misterioso
myster·y ['mɪstəri] *s* (**-ies**) mistero
mystic ['mɪstɪk] *adj & s* mistico
mystical ['mɪstɪkəl] *adj* mistico
mysticism ['mɪstɪ,sɪzəm] *s* misticismo
mystification [,mɪstɪfɪ'keʃən] *s* mistificazione
mysti·fy ['mɪstɪ,faɪ] *v* (*pret & pp* **-fied**) *tr* avvolgere nel mistero; (*to hoax*) mistificare
myth [mɪθ] *s* mito
mythical ['mɪθɪkəl] *adj* mitico
mythological [,mɪθə'lɑdʒɪkəl] *adj* mitologico
mytholo·gy [mɪ'θɑlədʒi] *s* (**-gies**) mitologia

N

N, n [en] *s* quattordicesima lettera dell'alfabeto inglese
nab [næb] *v* (*pret & pp* **nabbed**; *ger* **nabbing**) *tr* (slang) afferrare, agguantare
nag [næg] *s* ronzino || *v* (*pret & pp* **nagged**; *ger* **nagging**) *tr & intr* tormentare, infastidire
naiad ['ne·æd] or ['naɪ·æd] *s* naiade *f*
nail [nel] *s* (*of finger or toe*) unghia; (*of metal*) chiodo; **to hit the nail on the head** cogliere nel giusto || *tr* inchiodare
nail'brush' spazzolino per le unghie
nail' file' *s* lima per le unghie
nail' pol'ish *s* smalto per le unghie
nail' set' *s* punzone *m*
naïve [nɑ'iv] *adj* candido, ingenuo
naked ['nekɪd] *adj* nudo, ignudo; **to strip naked** denudare; denudarsi; **with the naked eye** a occhio nudo
name [nem] *s* nome *m;* (*first name*) nome *m;* (*last name*) cognome *m;* fama, reputazione; titolo; lignaggio; **in the name of** nel nome di; **to call s.o. names** coprire qlco di ingiurie; **to go by the name of** essere conosciuto sotto il nome di; **to make a name for oneself** farsi un nome; **what is your name?** come si chiama Lei? || *tr* nominare; menzionare; battezzare; (*a price*) fissare
name' day' *s* onomastico
nameless ['nemlɪs] *adj* senza nome, anonimo
namely ['nemli] *adv* cioè, vale a dire
name'plate' *s* targa, targhetta
namesake ['nem,sek] *s* omonimo; persona chiamata in onore di qualcun altro
nan'ny goat' ['næni] *s* capra
nap [næp] *s* lanugine *f;* (*pile*) pelo; pisolino, sonnellino; **to take a nap** schiacciare un sonnellino || *v* (*pret & pp* **napped**; *ger* **napping**) *intr* sonnecchiare; **to catch napping** cogliere alla sprovvista
napalm ['nepɑm] *s* napalm *m*
nape [nep] *s* nuca
naphtha ['næfθə] *s* nafta
napkin ['næpkɪn] *s* tovagliolo
nap'kin ring' *s* portatovagliolo
Naples ['neplәz] *s* Napoli *f*
Napoleonic [nə,polɪ'ɑnɪk] *adj* napoleonico
narcissus [nɑr'sɪsəs] *s* narciso
narcotic [nɑr'kɑtɪk] *adj & s* narcotico
narrate [næ'ret] *tr* narrare
narration [næ'reʃən] *s* narrazione
narrative ['nærətɪv] *adj* narrativo || *s* narrazione; (*genre*) narrativa
narrator [næ'retər] *s* narratore *m*
narrow ['næro] *adj* stretto; limitato; (*illiberal*) meschino, ristretto || **narrows** *spl* stretti *mpl* || *tr* limitare, restringere || *intr* limitarsi, restringersi
nar'row escape' *s*—**to have a narrow escape** scamparla bella
nar'row-gauge' *adj* a scartamento ridotto
narrow-minded ['næro'maɪndɪd] *adj* gretto, ristretto d'idee
nasal ['nezəl] *adj & s* nasale *f*
nasturtium [nə'stʌrʃəm] *s* nasturzio
nas·ty ['næsti] or ['nɑsti] *adj* (**-tier; -tiest**) brutto, cattivo; sgradevole, orribile; sudicio; (*foul*) perfido
natatorium [,netə'torɪ·əm] *s* piscina
nation ['neʃən] *s* nazione
national ['næʃənəl] *adj & s* nazionale *mf*
na'tional an'them *s* inno nazionale
na'tional debt' *s* debito pubblico
na'tional hol'iday *s* festa nazionale
nationalism ['næʃənə,lɪzəm] *s* nazionalismo
nationali·ty [,næʃən'ælɪti] *s* (**-ties**) nazionalità *f*
nationalize ['næʃənə,laɪz] *tr* nazionalizzare
na'tion·wide' *adj* su scala nazionale
native ['netɪv] *adj* nativo, indigeno, oriundo; (*language*) materno || *s* indigeno, nativo
na'tive land' *s* patria, paese natio
nativi·ty [nə'tɪvɪti] *s* (**-ties**) nascita, natività *f* || **Nativity** *s* Natività *f*
Nato ['neto] *s* (acronym) (**North Atlantic Treaty Organization**) la N.A.T.O.
nat·ty ['næti] *adj* (**-tier; -tiest**) accurato, elegante
natural ['nætʃərəl] *adj* naturale || *s* imbecille *mf;* (mus) bequadro; (mus) tono naturale; (mus) tasto bianco; **a natural** (coll) proprio quello che ci vuole
naturalism ['nætʃərə,lɪzəm] *s* naturalismo
naturalist ['nætʃərəlɪst] *s* naturalista *mf*
naturalization [,nætʃərəlɪ'zeʃən] *s* naturalizzazione
nat'uraliza'tion pa'pers *spl* documenti *mpl* di naturalizzazione

naturalize ['nætʃərə,laɪz] *tr* naturalizzare
naturally ['nætʃərəli] *adv* naturalmente
nature ['netʃər] *s* natura; **from nature** dal vero
naught [nɔt] *s* niente *m;* zero; **to come to naught** ridursi al nulla; **to set at naught** disprezzare
naugh•ty ['nɔti] *adj* (**-tier; -tiest**) cattivo, disubbidiente; (*joke*) di cattivo genere
nausea ['nɔʃɪ•ə] or ['nɔsɪ•ə] *s* nausea
nauseate ['nɔʃɪ,et] or ['nɔsɪ,et] *tr* nauseare ‖ *intr* essere nauseato
nauseating ['nɔʃɪ,etɪŋ] or ['nɔsɪ,etɪŋ] *adj* nauseabondo, stomachevole
nauseous ['nɔʃɪ•əs] or ['nɔsɪ•əs] *adj* nauseabondo
nautical ['nɔtɪkəl] *adj* nautico, marittimo, marino
naval ['nevəl] *adj* navale
na'val acad'emy *s* accademia navale
na'val of'ficer *s* ufficiale *m* di marina
na'val sta'tion *s* base *f* navale
nave [nev] *s* navata centrale; (*of a wheel*) mozzo
navel ['nevəl] *s* ombelico
na'vel or'ange *s* arancia (con depressione alla sommità)
navigability [,nævɪgə'bɪlɪti] *s* navigabilità *f;* (*of a ship*) manovrabilità *f*
navigable ['nævɪgəbəl] *adj* (*river*) navigabile; (*ship*) manovrabile
navigate ['nævɪ,get] *tr & intr* navigare
navigation [,nævɪ'geʃən] *s* navigazione
navigator ['nævɪ,getər] *s* navigatore *m;* (*in charge of navigating ship or plane*) ufficiale *m* di rotta
na•vy ['nevi] *adj* blu marino ‖ *s* (**-vies**) marina (da guerra)
na'vy bean' *s* fagiolo secco
na'vy blue' *s* blu marino
na'vy yard' *s* arsenale *m*
nay [ne] *s* no; voto negativo ‖ *adv* no; anzi
Nazarene [,næzə'rin] *adj & s* nazzareno; **the Nazarene** il Nazzareno
Nazi ['nɑtsi] or ['nætsi] *adj & s* nazista *mf*
N-bomb ['en,bɑm] *s* bomba al neutrone
Neapolitan [,ni•ə'pɑlɪtən] *adj & s* napoletano
neap' tide' [nip] *s* marea di quadratura
near [nɪr] *adj* vicino, prossimo; intimo; esatto ‖ *adv* vicino, da vicino ‖ *prep* vicino a, accanto a; **to come near** avvicinarsi a ‖ *tr* avvicinarsi a ‖ *intr* avvicinarsi
nearby ['nɪr,baɪ] *adj* vicino ‖ *adv* vicino, qui vicino
Near' East' *s* Medio Oriente
nearly ['nɪrli] *adv* quasi; (*a little more or less*) press'a poco; per poco non, e.g., **he nearly died** per poco non morì
near-sighted ['nɪr'saɪtɪd] *adj* miope
near'-sight'ed•ness *s* miopia
neat [nit] *adj* netto, pulito; elegante, accurato; puro
neat's'-foot oil' *s* olio di piede di bue
Nebuchadnezzar [,nebjəkəd'nezər] *s* Nabucodonosor *m*
nebu•la ['nebjələ] *s* (**-lae** [,li] or **-las**) nebulosa
nebular ['nebjələr] *adj* nebulare
nebulous ['nebjələs] *adj* nebuloso
necessary ['nesɪ,seri] *adj* necessario
necessitate [nɪ'sesɪ,tet] *tr* necessitare, esigere
necessitous [nɪ'sesɪtəs] *adj* bisognoso
necessi•ty [nɪ'sesɪti] *s* (**-ties**) necessità *f*
neck [nek] *s* collo; (*of a horse*) incollatura; (*of violin*) manico; (*of mountain*) gola, passo; **neck and neck** testa a testa; **to stick one's neck out** (coll) esporsi al pericolo; **to win by a neck** vincere per una corta testa ‖ *intr* (slang) abbracciarsi, sbaciucchiarsi
neck'band' *s* colletto
neckerchief ['nekər,tʃɪf] *s* fazzoletto da collo
necklace ['neklɪs] *s* collana
neck'line' *s* giro collo, scollatura
necktie ['nek,taɪ] *s* cravatta
neck'tie pin' *s* spilla da cravatta
necrolo•gy [ne'krɑlədʒi] *s* (**-gies**) necrologia
necromancy ['nekrə,mænsi] *s* necromanzia
nectar ['nektər] *s* nettare *m*
née or **nee** [ne] *adj* nata
need [nid] *s* necessità *f,* bisogno; povertà *f;* **if need be** se ci fosse bisogno; **in need** in strettezze ‖ *tr* aver bisogno di ‖ *intr* necessitare, essere in necessità ‖ *v aux*—**to need (to)** + *inf* dovere + *inf*
needful ['nidfəl] *adj* necessario
needle ['nidəl] *s* ago; (*of phonograph*) puntina; **to look for a needle in a haystack** cercare l'ago nel pagliaio ‖ *tr* cucire; (fig) aguzzare, eccitare
nee'dle bath' *s* bagno a doccia filiforme
nee'dle•case' *s* agoraio
nee'dle•point' *s* merletto; ricamo su canovaccio
needless ['nidlɪs] *adj* inutile
nee'dle•work' *s* lavoro di cucito; (*embroidery*) ricamo; (*needlepoint*) merletto
needs [nidz] *adv* necessariamente; **it must needs be** dev'essere proprio così
need•y [nidi] *adj* (**-ier; -iest**) bisognoso, indigente ‖ **the needy** i bisognosi
ne'er-do-well ['nerdu,wel] *adj & s* buono a nulla
negate ['neget] or [nɪ'get] *tr* invalidare; negare
negation [nɪ'geʃən] *s* negazione
negative ['negətɪv] *adj* negativo ‖ *s* negativa; (elec) polo negativo; (gram) negazione ‖ *tr* respingere, votare contro; neutralizzare
neglect [nɪ'glekt] *s* negligenza, trascuratezza ‖ *tr* trascurare; **to neglect to** trascurare di; dimenticarsi di
neglectful [nɪ'glektfəl] *adj* negligente, trascurato
négligée or **negligee** [,neglɪ'ʒe] *s* veste *f* da camera or vestaglia per signora
negligence ['neglɪdʒəns] *s* negligenza, trascuratezza

negligent ['neglɪdʒənt] *adj* negligente, trascurato
negligible ['neglɪdʒɪbəl] *adj* trascurabile, insignificante
negotiable [nɪ'goʃɪ·əbəl] *adj* negoziabile; (*security*) al portatore; (*road*) transitabile
negotiate [nɪ'goʃɪ,et] *tr* negoziare; (*to overcome*) superare || *intr* negoziare
negotiation [nɪ,goʃɪ'eʃən] *s* negoziazione, negoziato
Ne·gro ['nigro] *adj* negro || *s* **(-groes)** negro, nero
neigh [ne] *s* nitrito || *intr* nitrire
neighbor ['nebər] *adj* vicino, adiacente || *s* vicino; (*fellow man*) prossimo || *tr* essere vicino a || *intr* essere vicino
neighborhood ['nebər,hud] *s* vicinanza, vicinato; **in the neighborhood of** nei pressi di; (coll) a un dipresso, all'incirca
neighboring ['nebərɪŋ] *adj* vicino, attiguo; (*country*) limitrofo
neighborly ['nebərli] *adj* da buon vicino, socievole
neither ['niðər] or ['naɪðər] *adj indef* nessuno dei due, e.g., **neither boy** nessuno dei due ragazzi || *pron indef* nessuno dei due, nè l'uno nè l'altro || *conj* neppure, nemmeno, e.g., **neither do I** nemmeno io; **neither . . . nor** nè . . . nè
neme·sis ['nemɪsɪs] *s* **(-ses** [,siz]**)** nemesi *f* || **Nemesis** *s* Nemesi *f*
neologism [ni'ɑlə,dʒɪzəm] *s* neologismo
neomycin [,ni·ə'maɪsɪn] *s* neomicina
ne'on lamp' ['ni·ɑn] *s* lampada al neon
neophyte ['nɪ·ə,faɪt] *s* neofita *mf*
nepenthe [nɪ'penθi] *s* nepente *f*
nephew ['nefju] or ['nevju] *s* nipote *m*
Nepos ['nipɑs] or ['nepɑs] *s* Nipote *m*
Neptune ['neptʃun] or ['neptjun] *s* Nettuno
neptunium [nep'tʃunɪ·əm] or [nep'tjunɪ·əm] *s* (chem) nettunio
Nero ['nɪro] *s* Nerone *m*
nerve [nʌrv] *adj* nervoso || *s* nervo; (*courage*) coraggio; (*boldness*) (coll) faccia tosta; **to get on one's nerves** dare ai nervi di qlcu; **to lose one's nerve** perdere le staffe
nerve-racking ['nʌrv,rækɪŋ] *adj* irritante, esasperante
nervous ['nʌrvəs] *adj* nervoso
nerv'ous break'down *s* esaurimento nervoso
nervousness ['nʌrvəsnɪs] *s* nervosismo
nerv·y ['nʌrvi] *adj* **(-ier; -iest)** (*strong*) forte, vigoroso; audace; (coll) insolente, sfacciato
nest [nest] *s* nido; (*of hen*) cova; (*retreat*) rifugio; (*hangout*) tana; (*brood*) nidiata; **to feather one's nest** farsi il gruzzolo || *tr* (*e.g., tables*) mettere l'uno nell'altro || *intr* nidificare
nest' egg' *s* endice *m;* (fig) gruzzolo
nestle ['nesəl] *tr* annidare || *intr* annidarsi, nidificare; (*to cuddle up*) rannicchiarsi
net [net] *adj* netto || *s* rete *f;* (*snare*) laccio, trappola; guadagno netto || *tr* prendere con la rete; (*a sum of money*) fare un guadagno netto di
nether ['neðər] *adj* inferiore, infero
Netherlander ['neðər,lændər] or ['neðərləndər] *s* olandese *mf*
Netherlands, The ['neðərləndz] *spl* i Paesi Bassi
netting ['netɪŋ] *s* rete *f*
nettle ['netəl] *s* ortica || *tr* irritare, provocare
net'work' *s* rete *f*
neuralgia [nju'rældʒə] or [nu'rældʒə] *s* nevralgia
neurology [nju'rɑlədʒi] or [nu'rɑlədʒi] *s* neurologia
neuro·sis [nju'rosɪs] or [nu'rosɪs] **(-ses** [siz]**)** *s* neurosi *f*
neurotic [nju'rɑtɪk] or [nu'rɑtɪk] *adj & s* neurotico
neuter ['njutər] or ['nutər] *adj* neutro || *s* genere neutro
neutral ['njutrəl] or ['nutrəl] *adj* neutro; (*not aligned*) neutrale || *s* neutrale *m;* (mach) folle *m*
neutralist ['njutrəlɪst] or ['nutrəlɪst] *adj & s* neutralista *mf*
neutrality [nju'trælɪti] or [nu'trælɪti] *s* neutralità *f*
neutralize ['njutrə,laɪz] or ['nutrə,laɪz] *tr* neutralizzare
neutron ['njutrɑn] or ['nutrɑn] *s* neutrone *m*
neu'tron bomb' *s* bomba al neutrone
never ['nevər] *adv* mai, giammai; **non . . . mai; never mind** non importa
nev'er·more' *adv* mai più
nevertheless [,nevərðə'les] *adv* ciò nonostante, ciò nondimeno, tuttavia
new [nju] or [nu] *adj* nuovo; **what's new?** che c'è di nuovo?
new' arri'val *s* nuovo venuto; (*baby*) neonato
new'born' *adj* neonato; (*e.g., faith*) rinato
New'cas'tle *s*—**to carry coals to Newcastle** portare l'acqua al mare, portare vasi a Samo
newcomer ['nju,kʌmər] or ['nu,kʌmər] *s* nuovo venuto
New' Eng'land *s* la Nuova Inghilterra
newfangled ['nju,fæŋgəld] or ['nu,fæŋgəld] *adj* all'ultima moda; di nuovo conio, di nuova invenzione
Newfoundland ['njufənd,lænd] or ['nufənd,lænd] *s* la Terranova || [nju'faundlənd] or [nu'faundlənd] *s* (*dog*) terranova *m*
newly ['njuli] or ['nuli] *adv* di recente, di fresco
new'ly·wed' *s* sposino or sposina; **the newlyweds** gli sposi
new' moon' *s* luna nuova, novilunio
news [njuz] or [nuz] *s* notizie *fpl;* **a news item** una notizia; **a piece of news** una notizia
news' a'gency *s* agenzia d'informazioni
news'beat' *s* colpo giornalistico
news'boy' *s* strillone *m*
news'cast' *s* notiziario
news'cast'er *s* annunziatore *m,* radiocommentatore *m,* telecommentatore *m*
news' con'ference *s* conferenza stampa

news' cov'erage *s* reportaggio
news'deal'er *s* venditore *m* di giornali
news'man' *s* (**-men'**) (*reporter*) giornalista *m;* giornalaio
newsmonger ['njuz ˌmʌŋgər] or ['nuz ˌmʌŋgər] *s* persona pettegola, gazzettino
news'pa'per *adj* giornalistico || *s* giornale *m*
news'pa'per•man' *s* (**-men'**) giornalista *m*
news'print' *s* carta da giornale
news'reel' *s* cinegiornale *m*
news'stand' *s* chiosco, edicola
news'week'ly *s* (**-lies**) settimanale *m* d'informazione
news'wor'thy *adj* degno d'essere pubblicato, di viva attualità
news•y ['njuzi] or ['nuzi] *adj* (**-ier; -iest**) (coll) informativo
New' Tes'tament *s* Nuovo Testamento
New' Year's' card' *s* cartolina d'auguri di capodanno
New' Year's' Day' *s* il capo d'anno, il capodanno
New' Year's' Eve' *s* la vigilia di capodanno, la sera di San Silvestro
New' York' [jɔrk] *adj* nuovayorchese || *s* New York *f,* Nuova York
New' York'er ['jɔrkər] *s* nuovayorchese *mf*
New' Zea'land ['zilənd] *adj* neozelandese || *s* la Nuova Zelanda
New' Zea'lander ['ziləndər] *s* neozelandese *mf*
next [nekst] *adj* prossimo, seguente; (*month*) prossimo, entrante || *adv* la prossima volta; dopo, in seguito; **next to** vicino a; **next to nothing** quasi nulla; **to come next** essere il prossimo
next'-door' *adj* della casa vicina || **next'-door'** *adv* nella casa vicina
next' of kin' *s* (**next' of kin'**) parente più prossimo
niacin ['naɪ·əsɪn] *s* niacina
Niag'ara Falls' [naɪ'ægərə] *spl* le Cascate del Niagara
nib [nɪb] *s* becco; punta; **his nibs** (slang & pej) sua eccellenza
nibble ['nɪbəl] *s* piccolo morso || *tr & intr* mordicchiare, sbocconcellare; (*said of a fish*) abboccare
nice [naɪs] *adj* (*pleasant*) simpatico, gentile; (*requiring skill*) buono, bello; (*fine*) sottile; (*refined*) raffinato, per bene; (*fussy*) esigente, difficile; rispettabile; (*weather*) bello; (*attractive*) bello; **nice . . . and** (coll) bello, e.g., **it is nice and warm** fa un bel caldo
nice-looking ['naɪs'lʊkɪŋ] *adj* bello, attraente
nicely ['naɪsli] *adv* precisamente, esattamente; (coll) benissimo
nice•ty ['naɪsəti] *s* (**-ties**) esattezza, precisione; **to a nicety** con la massima precisione
niche [nɪtʃ] *s* nicchia
Nicholas ['nɪkələs] *s* Nicola *m*
nick [nɪk] *s* intaccatura; (*of a dish*) slabbratura; **in the nick of time** al momento giusto || *tr* intaccare; (*to cut*) tagliare; (*a dish*) slabbrare
nickel ['nɪkəl] *s* nichel *m;* moneta americana di cinque cents || *tr* nichelare
nick'el plate' *s* nichelatura
nick'el-plate' *tr* nichelare
nicknack ['nɪk ˌnæk] *s* soprammobile *m;* gingillo, ninnolo
nick'name' *s* nomignolo, soprannome *m* || *tr* soprannominare
nicotine ['nɪkə ˌtin] *s* nicotina
niece [nis] *s* nipote *f*
nif•ty ['nɪfti] *adj* (**-tier; -tiest**) (coll) elegante; (coll) eccellente
niggard ['nɪgərd] *adj & s* spilorcio
night [naɪt] *adj* notturno || *s* notte *f;* **at** or **by night** di notte; **the night before last** l'altra notte; **to make a night of it** (coll) fare le ore piccole
night'cap' *s* berretto da notte; bicchierino di liquore che si beve prima di coricarsi
night' club' *s* night-club *m*
night' driv'ing *s* il guidare di notte
night'fall' *s* crepuscolo; **at nightfall** sul cader della notte, all'imbrunire
night'gown' *s* camicia da notte
nightingale ['naɪtən ˌgel] *s* usignolo
night' latch' *s* serratura a molla
night' let'ter *s* telegramma notturno
night'long' *adj* di tutta la notte || *adv* tutta la notte
nightly ['naɪtli] *adj* di notte; di ogni notte || *adv* di notte; ogni notte
night'mare' *s* incubo
nightmarish ['naɪt ˌmerɪʃ] *adj* raccapricciante
night' owl' *s* (coll) nottambulo
night' school' *s* scuola serale
night'shirt' *s* camicia da notte
night'time' *s* notte *f*
night'walk'er *s* nottambulo; vagabondo notturno; (*prostitute*) passeggiatrice *f*
night' watch' *s* guardia notturna
night' watch'man *s* (**-men**) guardiano notturno
nihilist ['naɪ·ɪlɪst] *s* nichilista *mf*
nil [nɪl] *s* nulla *m,* niente *m*
Nile [naɪl] *s* Nilo
nimble ['nɪmbəl] *adj* agile, svelto
Nimrod ['nɪmrɑd] *s* Nembrod *m*
nincompoop ['nɪnkəm ˌpup] *s* babbeo, tonto, semplicione *m*
nine [naɪn] *adj & pron* nove || *s* nove *m;* **nine o' clock** le nove
nine' hun'dred *adj, s & pron* novecento
nineteen ['naɪn'tin] *adj, s & pron* diciannove *m*
nineteenth ['naɪn'tinθ] *adj & s* diciannovesimo; (*century*) decimonono || *s* (*in dates*) diciannove *m* || *pron* diciannovesimo
ninetieth ['naɪntɪ·ɪθ] *adj, s & pron* novantesimo
nine•ty ['naɪnti] *adj & pron* novanta || *s* (**-ties**) novanta *m;* **the gay nineties** il decennio scapestrato dal 1890 al 1900
ninth [naɪnθ] *adj, s & pron* nono || *s* (*in dates*) nove *m*
nip [nɪp] *s* morso, pizzicotto; freddo pungente; (*of liquor*) bicchierino,

sorso; **nip and tuck** testa a testa || *v* (*pret & pp* **nipped;** *ger* **nipping**) *tr* pizzicare, mordere; (*to squeeze*) spremere; (*to freeze*) gelare; (*liquor*) sorseggiare; **to nip in the bud** arrestare di bel principio || *intr* bere a sorsi
nipple ['nɪpəl] *s* capezzolo; (*of rubber*) tettarella; (mach) corto tubo filettato a entrambe le estremità, manicotto, cappuccio
Nippon [nɪ'pɑn] or ['nɪpɑn] *s* il Giappone
Nippon·ese [,nɪpə'niz] *adj* nipponico || *s* (**-ese**) Giapponese *mf*
nip·py ['nɪpi] *adj* (**-pier; -piest**) mordente, pizzicante; gelato
nirvana [nɪr'vɑnə] *s* il nirvana
nit [nɪt] *s* lendine *m;* pidocchio
niter ['naɪtər] *s* nitro
nit'-pick' *intr* (coll) cercare il pelo nell'uovo
nitrate ['naɪtret] *s* nitrato; (agr) nitrato di soda; (agr) nitrato di potassio
ni'tric ac'id ['naɪtrɪk] *s* acido nitrico
nitride ['naɪtraɪd] *s* azoturo, nitruro
nitrogen ['naɪtrədʒən] *s* azoto
nitroglycerin [,naɪtrə'glɪsərɪn] *s* nitroglicerina
ni'trous ox'ide ['naɪtrəs] *s* ossidulo di azoto
nitwit ['nɪt,wɪt] *s* (slang) baggiano
no [no] *adj* nessuno; **no admittance** vietato l'ingresso; **no doubt** senza dubbio; **no matter** non importa; **no parking** divieto di sosta; **no smoking** vietato fumare; **no thoroughfare** divieto di transito; **no use** inutilmente; **with no** senza || *s* no; voto negativo || *adv* no; non; **no longer** non . . . più; **no sooner** non appena
Noah ['no·ə] *s* Noè *m*
nob·by ['nɑbi] *adj* (**-bier; -biest**) (slang) elegante; (slang) eccellente
nobili·ty [no'bɪlɪti] *s* (**-ties**) nobiltà *f*
noble ['nobəl] *adj & s* nobile *m*
no'ble·man *s* (**-men**) nobile *m,* nobiluomo
no'ble·wom'an *s* (**-wom'en**) nobile *f,* nobildonna
nobod·y ['no,bɑdi] or ['nobədi] *s* (**-ies**) nessuno, illustre sconosciuto || *pron indef* nessuno; **nobody but** nessun altro che; **nobody else** nessun altro
nocturnal [nɑk'tʌrnəl] *adj* notturno
nod [nɑd] *s* cenno d'assenso, cenno del capo; (*of person going to sleep*) crollo del capo || *v* (*pret & pp* **nodded;** *ger* **nodding**) *tr* (*one's head*) inclinare; **to nod assent** fare cenno di sì || *intr* inclinare il capo; (*to drowse*) assopirsi
node [nod] *s* nodo; protuberanza; (phys) nodo
no'-good' *adj & s* (coll) buono a nulla
nohow ['no,haʊ] *adv* (coll) in nessuna maniera
noise [nɔɪz] *s* rumore *m* || *tr* divulgare
noiseless ['nɔɪzlɪs] *adj* silenzioso
nois·y ['nɔɪzi] *adj* (**-ier; -iest**) rumoroso, chiassoso
nomad ['nomæd] *adj & s* nomade *m*
no' man's' land' *s* terra di nessuno
nominal ['nɑmɪnəl] *adj* nominale; simbolico
nominate ['nɑmɪ,net] *tr* presentare la candidatura di; (*to appoint*) nominare, designare
nomination [,nɑmɪ'neʃən] *s* candidatura; nomina
nominative ['nɑmɪnətɪv] *adj & s* nominativo
nominee [,nɑmɪ'ni] *s* candidato designato
nonbelligerent [,nɑnbə'lɪdʒərənt] *adj & s* non belligerante *m*
nonbreakable [nɑn'brekəbəl] *adj* infrangibile
nonce [nɑns] *s*—**for the nonce** per l'occasione
nonchalance ['nɑnʃələns] or [,nɑnʃə'lɑns] *s* disinvoltura, indifferenza
nonchalant ['nɑnʃələnt] or [,nɑnʃə'lɑnt] *adj* disinvolto, indifferente
noncom ['nɑn,kɑm] *s* (coll) sottufficiale *m*
noncombatant [nɑn'kɑmbətənt] *adj* non combattente || *s* persona non combattente
non'commis'sioned of'ficer [,nɑnkə'mɪʃənd] *s* sottufficiale *m*
noncommittal [,nɑnkə'mɪtəl] *adj* ambiguo, evasivo
non compos mentis ['nɑn'kɑmpəs'mentɪs] *adj* pazzo; (law) incapace
nonconformist [,nɑnkən'fɔrmɪst] *s* anticonformista *mf,* nonconformista *mf*
nondelivery [,nɑndɪ'lɪvəri] *s* mancata consegna
nondescript ['nɑndɪ,skrɪpt] *adj* indefinibile, inclassificabile
none [nʌn] *pron indef* nessuno; **none of** nessuno di; **none other** nessun altro || *adv* non; affatto, niente affatto; **none the less** ciò nonostante, nondimeno
nonenti·ty [nɑn'entɪti] *s* (**-ties**) inesistenza; (*person*) nullità *f*
nonfiction [nɑn'fɪkʃən] *s* letteratura non romanzesca
nonfulfillment [,nɑnfʊl'fɪlmənt] *s* mancanza di esecuzione
nonintervention [,nɑnɪntər'venʃən] *s* non intervento
nonmetal ['nɑn,metəl] *s* metalloide *m*
nonpayment [nɑn'pemənt] *s* mancato pagamento
non·plus ['nɑnplʌs] or [nɑn'plʌs] *s* perplessità *f* || *v* (*pret & pp* **-plussed** or **plused;** *ger* **-plussing** or **-plusing**) *tr* lasciare perplesso
nonprofit [nɑn'prɑfɪt] *adj* senza scopo lucrativo
nonrefillable [,nɑnrɪ'fɪləbəl] *adj* (*prescription*) non ripetibile; (*e.g., bottle*) non ricaricabile
nonresident [nɑn'rezɪdənt] *s* persona di passaggio, non residente *mf*
nonresidential [nɑn,rezɪ'denʃəl] *adj* commerciale, non residenziale
nonscientific [nɑn,saɪ·ən'tɪfɪk] *adj* non scientifico

nonsectarian [ˌnɑnsek'terɪ·ən] *adj* che non segue nessuna confessione religiosa
nonsense ['nɑnsens] *s* sciocchezza, assurdità *f*, nonsenso
nonsensical [nɑn'sensɪkəl] *adj* sciocco, assurdo, illogico
nonskid ['nɑn'skɪd] *adj* antiderapante
nonstop ['nɑn'stɑp] *adj & adv* senza scalo
nonsupport [ˌnɑnsə'port] *s* mancato pagamento degli alimenti
noodle ['nudəl] *s* (slang) scemo; (slang) testa; **noodles** tagliatelle *fpl*
noo'dle soup' *s* tagliatelle *fpl* in brodo
nook [nʊk] *s* angolo, cantuccio
noon [nun] *s* mezzogiorno; **at high noon** a mezzogiorno in punto
no one or **no-one** ['no ˌwʌn] *pron indef* nessuno; **no one else** nessun altro
noontime ['nun ˌtaɪm] *s* mezzogiorno
noose [nus] *s* laccio, nodo scorsoio
nor [nɔr] *conj* nè
Nordic ['nɔrdɪk] *adj* nordico
norm [nɔrm] *s* norma, media, tipo
normal ['nɔrməl] *adj* normale || *s* condizione normale; norma; (geom) normale *f*
Norman ['nɔrmən] *adj & s* normanno
Normandy ['nɔrməndi] *s* la Normandia
Norse [nɔrs] *adj* norvegese; scandinavo || *s* (*ancient Scandinavian language*) scandinavo; (*language of Norway*) norvegese *m;* **the Norse** gli scandinavi; i norvegesi
Norse'man *s* (**-men**) normanno
north [nɔrθ] *adj* del nord, settentrionale || *s* nord *m* || *adv* al nord, verso il nord
North' Amer'ica *s* l'America del Nord
North' Amer'ican *adj & s* nordamericano
north'east' *adj* di nord-est || *s* nord-est *m* || *adv* al nord-est
north'east'er *s* vento di nord-est
northern ['nɔrðərn] *adj* settentrionale; (*Hemisphere*) boreale
North' Kore'a *s* la Corea del Nord
North' Pole' *s* polo nord
northward ['nɔrθwərd] *adv* verso il nord
north'west' *adj* di nord-ovest || *s* nord-ovest *m* || *adv* al nord-ovest
north' wind' *s* vento del nord, aquilone *m*
Norway ['nɔrwe] *s* la Norvegia
Norwegian [nɔr'widʒən] *adj & s* norvegese *mf* || *s* (*language*) norvegese *m*
nose [noz] *s* naso; (*of missile*) testata; **to blow one's nose** soffiarsi il naso; **to count noses** contare il numero dei presenti; **to follow one's nose** andare a lume di naso; **to lead by the nose** menare per il naso; **to look down one's nose at** (coll) guardare dall'alto in basso; **to pay through the nose** pagare un occhio della testa; **to pick one's nose** mettersi le dita nel naso; **to speak through the nose** parlare nel naso; **to thumb one's nose at** fare marameo a; **to turn up one's nose at** guardare dall'alto in basso, guardare con disprezzo || *tr* fiutare; **to nose out** vincere per un pelo || *intr* fiutare; **to nose about** curiosare
nose' bag' *s* musetta
nose'band' *s* museruola di cavallo
nose'bleed' *s* sangue *m* dal naso
nose' cone' *s* ogiva
nose' dive' *s* (*of prices*) subita discesa; (aer) discesa in picchiata
nose'-dive' *intr* discendere in picchiata
nosegay ['noz ˌge] *s* mazzolino di fiori
nose' glass'es *spl* occhiali *mpl* a stringinaso
nose' ring' *s* nasiera
nose'wheel' *s* (aer) ruota del carrello anteriore
no'-show' *s* (coll) passeggero che si è prenotato e non parte
nostalgia [nɑ'stældʒə] *s* nostalgia
nostalgic [nɑ'stældʒɪk] *adj* nostalgico
nostril ['nɑstrɪl] *s* narice *f*
nos·y ['nozi] *adj* (**-ier; -iest**) (coll) curioso
not [nɑt] *adv* no; non; **not at all** niente affatto; **not yet** non ancora; **to think not** credere di no; **why not?** come no?
notable ['notəbəl] *adj* notevole, notabile || *s* notabile *m*
notarize ['notə ˌraɪz] *tr* munire di fede notarile
nota·ry ['notəri] *s* (**-ries**) notaio
notch [nɑtʃ] *s* tacca; (*in mountain*) passo; (coll) tantino; **notches** (coll) di gran lunga, e.g., **notches above** di gran lunga migliore || *tr* intaccare
note [not] *s* nota, annotazione; (*currency*) banconota; (*communication*) memorandum *m;* (*of bird*) canto; (*tone of voice*) tono; (*reputation*) riguardo; (*short letter*) biglietto, letterina; (mus) nota; (com) cambiale *f* || *tr* notare, annotare; osservare
note'book' *s* (*for school*) quaderno; taccuino, notes *m*
noted ['notɪd] *adj* ben noto, eminente
note' pa'per *s* carta da lettera
note'wor'thy *adj* notevole
nothing ['nʌθɪŋ] *s* niente *m*, nulla; **for nothing** gratis; inutilmente; **next to nothing** quasi niente || *pron indef* niente, nulla, non . . . niente, non . . . nulla; **nothing else** nient'altro; **to make nothing of it** non farne caso || *adv* per nulla; **nothing less** non meno
notice ['notɪs] *s* attenzione; notizia, notifica; annunzio, preavviso; (*in newspaper*) trafiletto; (law) disdetta; **on short notice** senza preavviso; (com) a breve scadenza; **to escape the notice of** passare inavvertito a; **to serve notice to** far sapere a, far constatare a || *tr* osservare, notare, prendere nota di
noticeable ['notɪsəbəl] *adj* notevole; (*e.g., difference*) percettibile
noti·fy ['notɪ ˌfaɪ] *v* (*pret & pp* **-fied**) *tr* informare, far sapere
notion ['noʃən] *s* nozione; (*whim*) capriccio; **notions** mercerie *fpl;* **to have a notion to** aver voglia di
notorie·ty [ˌnotə'raɪ·ɪti] *s* (**-ties**) (*state*

of being well known) notorietà *f;* cattiva fama
notorious [no'torɪ·əs] *adj* (*generally known*) notorio; (*unfavorably known*) famigerato
no'-trump' *adj & s* senza atout *m*
notwithstanding [,nɑtwɪð'stændɪŋ] or [,nɑtwɪθ'stændɪŋ] *adv* ciò nonostante || *prep* malgrado || *conj* sebbene
nougat ['nugət] *s* torrone *m*
noun [naʊn] *s* nome *m,* sostantivo
nourish ['nʌrɪʃ] *tr* nutrire
nourishing ['nʌrɪʃɪŋ] *adj* nutriente
nourishment ['nʌrɪʃmənt] *s* nutrimento
novel ['nɑvəl] *adj* nuovo, novello, insolito, originale || *s* romanzo
novelist ['nɑvəlɪst] *s* romanziere *m*
novel·ty ['nɑvəlti] *s* (**-ties**) novità *f;* **novelties** chincaglierie *fpl*
November [no'vembər] *s* novembre *m*
novice ['nɑvɪs] *s* novizio
novitiate [no'vɪʃɪ·ɪt] *s* noviziato
novocaine ['novə,ken] *s* novocaina
now [naʊ] *s* presente *m* || *adv* adesso; **from now on** d'ora in poi; **just now** un momento fa; **now and then** di tempo in tempo; **now that** visto che || *conj* visto che, dato che
nowadays ['naʊ·ə,dez] *adv* al giorno d'oggi, oggidì
no'way' *adv* in nessun modo; nient'affatto
no'where' *adv* da nessuna parte; **nowhere else** da nessun'altra parte, in nessun altro luogo
noxious ['nɑkʃəs] *adj* nocivo
nozzle ['nɑzəl] *s* (*of hose or pipe*) boccaglio; (*of tea pot, gas burner*) becco; (*of gun*) bocca; (*of sprinkling can*) bocchetta; (aut, mach) becco; (slang) naso
nth [enθ] *adj* ennesimo; **to the nth degree** all'ennesima potenza
nuance [nju'ɑns] or ['nju·ɑns] *s* sfumatura
nub [nʌb] *s* protuberanza; (*of coal*) pezzo; (coll) nocciolo, cuore *m*
nuclear ['njuklɪ·ər] or ['nuklɪ·ər] *adj* nucleare
nu'clear fis'sion *s* fissione nucleare
nu'clear fu'sion *s* fusione nucleare
nu'clear test' ban' *s* accordo per la tregua atomica
nucle·us ['njuklɪ·əs] or ['nuklɪ·əs] *s* (**-i** [,aɪ] or **-uses**) nucleo
nude [njud] or [nud] *adj* nudo || *s*—**in the nude** nudo
nudge [nʌdʒ] *s* gomitatina || *tr* dare di gomito a
nudist ['njudɪst] or ['nudɪst] *adj & s* nudista *mf*
nudi·ty ['njudɪti] or ['nudɪti] *s* (**-ties**) nudità *f*
nugget ['nʌgɪt] *s* pepita
nuisance ['njusəns] or ['nusəns] *s* noia, seccatura; (*person*) seccatore *m,* pittima *mf*
null [nʌl] *adj* nullo; **null and void** invalido
nulli·fy ['nʌlɪ,faɪ] *v* (*pret & pp* **-fied**) *tr* annullare, invalidare
nulli·ty ['nʌlɪti] *s* (**-ties**) nullità *f*
numb [nʌm] *adj* intorpidito; (*from cold*) intirizzito; **to become numb** intorpidirsi || *tr* intorpidire
number ['nʌmbər] *s* numero; (*for sale*) articolo di vendita; (*publication*) fascicolo; (*of a serial*) dispensa, puntata; **a number of** parecchi; **beyond** or **without number** senza numero, infiniti || *tr* numerare, contare; **his days are numbered** i suoi giorni sono contati || *intr*—**to number among** essere tra
numberless ['nʌmbərlɪs] *adj* innumerevole
numeral ['njumərəl] or ['numərəl] *adj* numerale || *s* numero
numerical [nju'merɪkəl] or [nu'merɪkəl] *adj* numerico
numerous ['njumərəs] or ['numərəs] *adj* numeroso
numskull ['nʌm,skʌl] *s* (coll) stupido
nun [nʌn] *s* monaca, religiosa
nuptial ['nʌpʃəl] *adj* nuziale || **nuptials** *spl* nozze *fpl*
nurse [nʌrs] *s* infermiera; (*to suckle a child*) nutrice *f;* (*to take care of a child*) bambinaia || *tr* (*to minister to*) curare; allattare; allevare; (*e.g., hatred*) covare || *intr* fare l'infermiera
nurser·y ['nʌrsəri] *s* (**-ies**) stanza dei bambini; (*shelter for children*) asilo infantile; (hort) vivaio
nurs'ery·man *s* (**-men**) orticoltore *m*
nurs'ery rhyme' *s* canzoncina per i più piccini
nurs'ery school' *s* scuola materna
nursing ['nʌrsɪŋ] *adj* infermieristico || *s* allattamento; professione d'infermiera
nurs'ing bot'tle *s* biberon *m,* poppatoio
nurs'ing home' *s* convalescenziario; ospizio dei vecchi, gerontocomio
nurture ['nʌrtʃər] *s* allevamento; nutrimento || *tr* allevare; alimentare; (*e.g., hope*) accarezzare
nut [nʌt] *s* noce *f;* (*eccentric*) (slang) esaltato, pazzoide *m;* (mus) capotasto; (mach) madrevite *f,* dado; **a hard nut to crack** un osso duro da rodere; **to be nuts for** (coll) essere pazzo per
nut'crack'er *s* schiaccianoci *m*
nutmeg ['nʌt,meg] *s* noce moscata
nutrition [nju'trɪʃən] or [nu'trɪʃən] *s* (*process*) nutrizione; (*food*) nutrimento
nutritious [nju'trɪʃəs] or [nu'trɪʃəs] *adj* nutriente
nut'shell' *s* guscio di noce; **in a nutshell** in breve, in poche parole
nut·ty ['nʌti] *adj* (**-tier; -tiest**) che sa di noci; (slang) pazzo; **nutty about** (slang) pazzo per
nuzzle ['nʌzəl] *tr* toccare col muso, ammusare || *intr* (*said of swine*) grufolare; (*said of other animals*) stare muso a muso, ammusare; (*to snuggle*) rannicchiarsi
nylon ['naɪlɑn] *s* nailon *m*
nymph [nɪmf] *s* ninfa

O

O, o [o] *s* quindicesima lettera dell'alfabeto inglese
O *interj* o!, oh!
oaf [of] *s* balordo, scemo, imbecille *mf*
oak [ok] *s* quercia
oaken ['okən] *adj* di quercia, quercino
oakum ['okəm] *s* stoppa incatramata
oar [or] *s* remo; **to lie** or **rest on one's oars** dormire sugli allori; non lavorare più || *tr* spingere coi remi || *intr* remare
oar'lock' *s* scalmo
oars'man *s* (**-men**) rematore *m*
oa•sis [o'esɪs] *s* (**-ses** [siz]) oasi *f*
oat [ot] *s* avena; **oats** (*seeds*) avena; **to feel one's oats** (coll) essere pieno di vita; (coll) sentirsi importante; **to sow one's wild oats** correre la cavallina
oath [oθ] *s* giuramento; **on oath** sotto giuramento; **to take an oath** giurare, prestar giuramento
oat'meal' *s* (*breakfast food*) fiocchi *mpl* d'avena; farina d'avena
obdurate ['ɑbdjərɪt] *adj* indurito, inesorabile; impenitente, incallito
obedience [o'bidɪ•əns] *s* obbedienza, ubbidienza
obedient [o'bidɪ•ənt] *adj* ubbidiente
obeisance [o'besəns] or [o'bisəns] *s* saluto rispettoso; omaggio
obelisk ['ɑbəlɪsk] *s* obelisco
obese [o'bis] *adj* obeso
obesity [o'bisɪti] *s* obesità *f*
obey ['obe] *tr* ubbidire (with *dat*), ubbidire || *intr* ubbidire
obfuscate [ɑb'fʌsket] or ['ɑbfəs,ket] *tr* offuscare
obituar•y [o'bɪtʃʊ,eri] *adj* necrologico || *s* (**-ies**) necrologia
object ['ɑbdʒɪkt] *s* oggetto || [əb'dʒekt] *tr* obiettare || *intr* fare obiezioni, obiettare
objection [ɑb'dʒɛkʃən] *s* obiezione
objectionable [ɑb'dʒɛkʃənəbəl] *adj* reprensibile; (*e.g., odor*) sgradevole; offensivo
objective [ɑb'dʒɛktɪv] *adj* & *s* obiettivo
obligate ['ɑblɪ,get] *tr* obbligare
obligation [,ɑblɪ'geʃən] *s* obbligo, obbligazione
oblige [ə'blaɪdʒ] *tr* obbligare; favorire; **much obliged** obbligatissimo
obliging [ə'blaɪdʒɪŋ] *adj* compiacente, accomodante, servizievole
oblique [ə'blik] *adj* obliquo; indiretto
obliterate [ə'blɪtə,ret] *tr* obliterare; spegnere, distruggere
oblivion [ə'blɪvɪ•ən] *s* oblio
oblivious [ə'blɪvɪ•əs] *adj* (*forgetful*) dimentico; (*unaware*) ignaro
oblong ['ɑblɔŋ] or ['ɑblɑŋ] *adj* oblungo
obnoxious [əb'nɑkʃəs] *adj* detestabile
oboe ['obo] *s* oboe *m*
oboist ['obo•ɪst] *s* oboista *mf*
obscene [ɑb'sin] *adj* osceno
obsceni•ty [ɑb'sɛnɪti] or [ɑb'sinɪti] *s* (**-ties**) oscenità *f*, sconcezza
obscure [əb'skjʊr] *adj* oscuro || *tr* oscurare
obscuri•ty [əb'skjʊrɪti] *s* (**-ties**) oscurità *f*
obsequies ['ɑbsɪkwiz] *spl* esequie *fpl*
obsequious [əb'sikwɪ•əs] *adj* ossequioso, servile
observance [əb'zʌrvəns] *s* osservanza; **observances** pratiche *fpl;* cerimonie *fpl*
observation [,ɑbzər'veʃən] *s* osservazione; osservanza
observa'tion car' *s* (rr) vettura belvedere
observato•ry [əb'zʌrvə,tori] *s* (**-ries**) osservatorio
observe [əb'zʌrv] *tr* osservare
observer [əb'zʌrvər] *s* osservatore *m*
obsess [əb'sɛs] *tr* ossessionare
obsession [əb'sɛʃən] *s* ossessione
obsolescent [,ɑbsə'lɛsənt] *adj* che sta cadendo in disuso
obsolete ['ɑbsə,lit] *adj* disusato
obstacle ['ɑbstəkəl] *s* ostacolo
obstetrical [ɑb'stɛtrɪkəl] *adj* ostetrico
obstetrics [ɑb'stetrɪks] *s* ostetricia
obstina•cy ['ɑbstɪnəsi] *s* (**-cies**) ostinazione
obstinate ['ɑbstɪnɪt] *adj* ostinato
obstreperous [ɑb'strɛpərəs] *adj* turbolento; rumoroso
obstruct [əb'strʌkt] *tr* ostruire
obstruction [əb'strʌkʃən] *s* ostruzione
obtain [əb'ten] *tr* ottenere || *intr* prevalere, essere in voga
obtrusive [əb'trusɪv] *adj* intruso, importuno; sporgente
obtuse [əb'tjus] or [əb'tus] *adj* ottuso
obviate ['ɑbvɪ,et] *tr* ovviare (with *dat*)
obvious ['ɑbvɪ•əs] *adj* ovvio, palmare
occasion [ə'keʒən] *s* occasione; **on occasion** di quando in quando || *tr* occasionare
occasional [ə'keʒənəl] *adj* saltuario; (*e.g., verses*) d'occasione
occasionally [ə'keʒənəli] *adv* occasionalmente, di tanto in quanto
occident ['ɑksɪdənt] *s* occidente *m*
occidental [,ɑksɪ'dentəl] *adj* & *s* occidentale *mf*
occlud'ed front' [ə'kludɪd] *s* fronte occluso
occlusion [ə'kluʒən] *s* occlusione
occlusive [ə'klusɪv] *adj* occlusivo || *s* occlusiva
occult [ə'kʌlt] or ['ɑkʌlt] *adj* occulto
occupancy ['ɑkjəpənsi] *s* occupazione, presa di possesso; (*tenancy*) locazione
occupant ['ɑkjəpənt] *s* occupante *m;* (*tenant*) inquilino
occupation [,ɑkjə'peʃən] *s* occupazione
occupational [,ɑkjə'peʃənəl] *adj* occupazionale; (*e.g., disease*) professionale, del lavoro
occu•py ['ɑkjə,paɪ] *v* (*pret* & *pp* **-pied**) *tr* occupare; (*to dwell in*) abitare
oc•cur [ə'kʌr] *v* (*pret* & *pp* **-curred;**

ger **-curring)** *intr* accadere, succedere; incontrarsi; (*to come to mind*) venir in mente, e.g., **it occurs to me** mi viene in mente
occurrence [ə'kʌrəns] *s* evento, avvenimento; apparizione
ocean ['oʃən] *s* oceano
o'cean lin'er *s* transatlantico
o'clock [ə'klɑk] *adv* secondo l'orologio; **it is one o'clock** è la una; **it is two o'clock** sono le due
octane ['ɑkten] *adj* ottanico || *s* ottano
octave ['ɑktɪv] or ['ɑktev] *s* ottava
Octavian [ɑk'tevɪ·ən] *s* Ottaviano
October [ɑk'tobər] *s* ottobre *m*
octo·pus ['ɑktəpəs] *s* **(-puses** or **-pi** [,paɪ]) (*small*) polpo; (*large*) piovra; (fig) piovra
ocular ['ɑkjələr] *adj* & *s* ocùlare *m*
oculist ['ɑkjəlɪst] *s* oculista *mf*
odd [ɑd] *adj* (*number*) dispari; strambo, bizzarro; (*not matching*) scompagnato, spaiato; strano; e rotti, e.g., **three hundred odd** tre cento e rotti || **odds** *ssg* or *spl* probabilità *f;* (*advantage*) vantaggio, superiorità *f;* **at odds** in disaccordo; **by all odds** senza dubbio; **it makes no odds** fa lo stesso; **the odds are** la quota è; **to set at odds** seminare zizzania fra
oddi·ty ['ɑdɪti] *s* **(-ties)** stranezza
odd' jobs' *spl* lavori saltuari
odd' lot' *s* (fin) compravendita di meno di cento unità
odds' and ends' *spl* un po' di tutto
odious ['odɪ·əs] *adj* odioso
odor ['odər] *s* odore *m;* **to be in bad odor** aver cattiva fama
odorless ['odərlɪs] *adj* inodoro
odorous ['odərəs] *adj* odoroso
Odysseus [o'dɪsjus] or [o'dɪsɪ·əs] *s* Odisseo
Odyssey ['ɑdɪsi] *s* Odissea
Oedipus ['ɛdɪpəs] or ['idɪpəs] *s* Edipo
of [ɑv] or [əv] *prep* di, e.g., **the lead of the pencil** la mina della matita; a, e.g., **to think of** pensare a; meno, e.g., **a quarter of ten** le dieci meno un quarto
off [ɔf] or [ɑf] *adj* (*wrong*) sbagliato; (*slightly abnormal*) matto, pazzo; inferiore; (*electricity*) tagliato; (*agreement*) sospeso; libero, in libertà; distante; destro; (*season*) morto || *adv* via; fuori, lontano, distante; **to be off** mettersi in marcia || *prep* da; fuori da; al disotto di; lontano da; distolto da, e.g., **his eyes were off the target** i suoi occhi erano distolti dal bersaglio; (naut) al largo di
offal ['ɑfəl] or ['ɔfəl] *s* (*of butchered animal*) frattaglie *fpl;* rifiuti *mpl*
off' and on' *adv* di tempo in tempo
off'beat' *adj* insolito, originale
off' chance' *s* possibilità remota
off'-col'or *adj* scolorito; indisposto; (*joke*) di dubbio gusto
offend [ə'fɛnd] *tr* & *intr* offendere
offender [ə'fɛndər] *s* offensore *m*
offense [ə'fɛns] *s* offesa; **to take offense (at)** offendersi (di)
offensive [ə'fɛnsɪv] *adj* offensivo || *s* offensiva
offer ['ɔfər] or ['ɑfər] *s* offerta || *tr* offrire; (*thanks*) porgere; (*resistance*) opporre || *intr* offrirsi
offering ['ɔfərɪŋ] or ['ɑfərɪŋ] *s* offerta
off'hand' *adj* fatto all'improvviso; sbrigativo, alla buona || *adv* all'improvviso; bruscamente
office ['ɔfɪs] or ['ɑfɪs] *s* ufficio; funzione, incombenza; (*of a doctor*) gabinetto; (*of a lawyer*) studio; (eccl) uffizio; **through the good offices of** per tramite di
of'fice boy' *s* fattorino
of'fice·hold'er *s* pubblico funzionario
of'fice hours' *spl* orario d'ufficio
officer ['ɔfɪsər] or ['ɑfɪsər] *s* (*in a corporation*) funzionario; (*policeman*) agente *m;* (mil, nav, naut) ufficiale *m;* **officer of the day** (mil) ufficiale *m* di giornata
of'fice seek'er ['sikər] *s* aspirante *m* a un ufficio pubblico
of'fice supplies' *spl* articoli *mpl* di cancelleria
official [ə'fɪʃəl] *adj* ufficiale || *s* funzionario, ufficiale *m*
officiate [ə'fɪʃɪ,et] *intr* ufficiare
officious [ə'fɪʃəs] *adj* invadente, inframettente; **to be officious** essere un impiccione
offing ['ɔfɪŋ] or ['ɑfɪŋ] *s*—**in the offing** al largo; (fig) in preparazione, probabile
off'-lim'its *adj* proibito; **off-limits to** ingresso proibito a
off'-peak' heat'er *s* (elec) scaldabagno azionato unicamente in periodi di consumo minimo
off'-peak' load' *s* (elec) carico di consumo minimo
off'print' *s* estratto
off'set' *s* compensazione; (typ) offset *m* || **off'set'** *v* (*pret* & *pp* **-set;** *ger* **-setting)** *tr* compensare; stampare in offset
off'shoot' *s* (*of plant*) germoglio; (*of family or race*) discendente *mf;* (*branch*) ramo; (fig) conseguenza
off'shore' *adj* (*wind*) di terra; (*fishing*) vicino alla costa; (*island*) costiero || *adv* al largo
off'side' *adv* (sports) fuori gioco
off'spring' *s* discendente *m;* prole *f;* figlio; figli *mpl*
off'stage' *adv* tra le quinte
off'-the-rec'ord *adj* confidenziale || *adv* confidenzialmente
often ['ɔfən] or ['ɑfən] *adv* sovente, spesso; **how often?** quante volte?; **once too often** una volta di troppo
ogive ['odʒaɪv] or [o'dʒaɪv] *s* ogiva
ogle ['ogəl] *tr* adocchiare, occhieggiare
ogre ['ogər] *s* orco
ohm [om] *s* ohm *m*
oil [ɔɪl] *adj* (*pertaining to edible oil*) oleario; (*e.g., well*) di petrolio; (*e.g., lamp*) a olio; (*tanker*) petroliero; (*field*) petrolifero || *s* olio; petrolio; **to burn the midnight oil** studiare a lume di candela; **to pour oil on troubled waters** pacificare; **to strike oil** trovare petrolio || *tr* oliare; lubrifi-

care; ungere || *intr* (*said of a motorship*) fare petrolio
oil' burn'er *s* bruciatore *m* a gasolio
oil'can' *s* oliatore *m*
oil'cloth' *s* incerata, tela cerata
oil' field' *s* giacimento petrolifero
oil' lamp' *s* lampada a petrolio
oil'man *s* (**-men**) (*retailer*) mercante *m* di petrolio; (*operator*) petroliere *m*
oil' paint'ing *s* quadro a olio
oil' slick' *s* macchia d'olio
oil' tank'er *s* petroliera
oil' well' *s* pozzo di petrolio
oil•y ['ɔɪli] *adj* (**-ier; -iest**) oleoso; untuoso
ointment ['ɔɪntmənt] *s* unguento
O.K. ['o'ke] *adj* (coll) corretto || *s* (coll) approvazione || *adv* (coll) benissimo, d'accordo || *v* (*pret & pp* **O.K.'d**; *ger* **O.K.'ing**) *tr* (coll) dare l'approvazione a || *interj* benissimo!
okra ['okrə] *s* (bot) ibisco esculento; (bot) baccello dell'ibisco esculento
old [old] *adj* vecchio; antico, vetusto; **how old is . . . ?** quanti anni ha . . . ?; **of old** anticamente; **to be . . . years old** avere . . . anni
old' age' *s* vecchiaia
old' boy' *s* vecchietto arzillo; (Brit) vecchio mio
old'-clothes'man' *s* (**-men'**) rigattiere *m*
old' coun'try *s* madre patria
old-fashioned ['old'fæʃənd] *adj* all'antica; fuori moda
old' fo'gey or **old' fo'gy** ['fogi] *s* (**-gies**) uomo di idee antiquate, reazionario
Old' Glo'ry *s* la bandiera degli Stati Uniti
Old' Guard' *s* (U.S.A.) parte *f* più conservatrice di un partito
old' hand' *s* vecchio del mestiere
old' maid' *s* zitella
old' mas'ter *s* grande maestro; quadro di un gran maestro
old' moon' *s* luna calante
old' salt' *s* lupo di mare
old' school' *s* gente *f* all'antica
old' school' tie' *s* (Brit) cravatta coi colori della propria scuola; (fig) tradizionalismo
Old' Tes'tament *s* Antico Testamento
old'-time' *adj* all'antica; del tempo antico
old-timer ['old'taɪmər] *s* (coll) veterano; (coll) vecchio
old' wives'' tale' *s* superstizione da donnicciole; racconto di vecchie comari
Old' World' *s* mondo antico
oleander [ˌolɪ'ændər] *s* oleandro
oligar•chy ['alɪˌgarki] *s* (**-chies**) oligarchia
olive ['alɪv] *adj* oleario; (*color*) olivastro || *s* (*tree*) olivo; (*fruit*) oliva
ol'ive branch' *s* ramoscello d'olivo
ol'ive grove' *s* oliveto
ol'ive oil' *s* olio d'oliva
Oliver ['alɪvər] *s* Oliviero
ol'ive tree' *s* olivo
Olympiad [o'lɪmpɪˌæd] *s* olimpiade *f*
Olympian [o'lɪmpɪ·ən] *adj* olimpico || *s* deità olimpica; giocatore olimpico
Olympic [o'lɪmpɪk] *adj* olimpico, olimpionico
omelet or **omelette** ['amələt] or ['amlɪt] *s* frittata, omelette *f*
omen ['omən] *s* augurio
ominous ['amɪnəs] *adj* infausto, ominoso
omission [o'mɪʃən] *s* omissione
omit [o'mɪt] *v* (*pret & pp* **omitted**; *ger* **omitting**) *tr* omettere
omnibus ['amnɪˌbʌs] or ['amnɪbəs] *adj* di interesse generale || *s* bus *m*; volume collettivo
omnipotent [am'nɪpətənt] *adj* onnipotente
omniscient [am'nɪʃənt] *adj* onnisciente
omnivorous [am'nɪvərəs] *adj* onnivoro
on [an] or [ɔn] *adj* addosso, e.g., **with his hat on** col cappello addosso; in uso, in funzione; (*light*) acceso; (*deal*) fatto, concluso; (*e.g., game*) già cominciato; **what is on at the theater?** che cosa si dà al teatro? || *adv* su; avanti; dietro, e.g., **to drag on** tirarsi dietro; **and so on** e così via; **come on!** va via!; **farther on** più in là; **later on** più tardi; **to be on to s.o.** (coll) scoprire il gioco di qlcu; **to have on** avere addosso; **to . . . on** continuare a, e.g., **the band played on** la banda continuò a suonare; **to put on** mettersi || *prep* su, sopra; a, e.g., **on foot** a piedi; **on his arrival** al suo arrivo; sotto, e.g., **on my responsibility** sotto la mia responsabilità; contro, e.g., **an attack on the government** un attacco contro il governo; da, e.g., **on good authority** da buona fonte; **on all sides** da tutte le parti; verso, e.g., **to march on the capital** marciare verso la capitale; dopo, e.g., **victory on victory** vittoria dopo vittoria
on' and on' *adv* senza cessa
once [wʌns] *s* una volta; volta, e.g., **this once** questa volta || *adv* una volta; mai, e.g., **if this once becomes known** se questo si risapesse mai; **all at once** repentinamente; **at once** subito; allo stesso tempo; **for once** almeno una volta; **once and again** ripetutamente; **once in a blue moon** ad ogni morte di papa; **once in a while** di tanto in tanto; **once upon a time there was** c'era una volta || *conj* se appena; una volta che
once'-o'ver *s* (coll) occhiata rapida; **to give s.th the once-over** (coll) esaminare qlco rapidamente; (coll) pulire qlco superficialmente
one [wʌn] *adj* uno; un certo, e.g., **one Smith** un certo Smith; unico e.g., **one price** prezzo unico || *s* uno || *pron* uno, e.g., **how can one live here?** come è possibile che uno viva qui?; si, e.g., **how does one go to the museum?** come si va al museo?; **I for one** per lo meno io; **it's all one and the same to me** per me fa lo stesso; **my little one** piccolo mio; **one and all** tutti; **one another** si, e.g., **they wrote one another** si scrissero;

l'un(o) l'altro, e.g., **they looked at one another** si guardarono l'un l'altro; **one o'clock** la una; **one's** il suo, il proprio; **the blue hat and the red one** il cappello blu e quello rosso; **the one and only** l'unico; **the one that** chi, quello che; **this one** questo; **that one** quello; **to make one** unire

one'-eyed' *adj* monocolo

one'-horse' *adj* a un solo cavallo; (coll) da nulla, poco importante

one'-man' show' *s* personale *f*

onerous ['ɑnərəs] *adj* oneroso

one•self' *pron* sé stesso; se; si; **to be oneself** essere normale; comportarsi normalmente

one-sided ['wʌn'saɪdɪd] *adj* unilaterale; ingiusto, parziale

one'-track' *adj* a un solo binario; (coll) unilaterale, limitato

one'-way' *adj* a senso unico; (*ticket*) semplice, d'andata

onion ['ʌnjən] *s* cipolla; **to know one's onions** (coll) conoscere i propri polli

on'ion•skin' *s* carta pelle aglio, carta velina

on'look'er *s* presente *m*, spettatore *m*

only ['onlɪ] *adj* solo, unico || *adv* solo, soltanto, non . . . più di; **not only . . . but also** non solo . . . ma anche || *conj* ma; se non che

on'set' *s* attacco; (*beginning*) inizio; **at the onset** dapprincipio

onslaught ['ɑn,slɔt] or ['ɔn,slɔt] *s* attacco

on'to *prep* su, sopra a; **to be onto** (coll) rendersi conto del gioco di

onward ['ɑnwərd] or **onwards** ['ɑnwərdz] *adv* avanti, più avanti

onyx ['ɑnɪks] *s* onice *m*

ooze [uz] *s* trasudazione; liquido per concia || *tr* sudare || *intr* trasudare; (*said, e.g., of blood*) stillare; (*said, e.g., of air*) filtrare; (fig) trapelare

opal ['opəl] *s* opale *m*

opaque [o'pek] *adj* opaco; (*writer's style*) oscuro; stupido

open ['opən] *adj* aperto, scoperto; (*job*) vacante; (*time*) libero; (*hunting season*) legale; indeciso; manifesto; (*hand*) liberale; (*needlework*) a giorno; **to break** or **to crack open** forzare; **to throw open** aprire completamente || *s* apertura; (*in the woods*) radura; **in the open** all'aperto; all'aria aperta; in alto mare; apertamente || *tr* aprire; (*an account*) impostare; **to open up** spalancare; (*one's eyes*) sbarrare || *intr* aprire, aprirsi; (theat) esordire; **to open into** sboccare in; **to open on** dare su; **to open up** sbottonarsi

o'pen-air' *adj* all'aria aperta

open-eyed ['opən,aɪd] *adj* con gli occhi aperti; meravigliato; fatto con piena conoscenza

open-handed ['opən'hændɪd] *adj* generoso, liberale

open-hearted ['opən'hɑrtɪd] *adj* franco, sincero; gentile

o'pen house' *s* tavola imbandita; **to keep open house** aver sempre ospiti

opening ['opənɪŋ] *s* apertura; (*of dress*) giro collo; (*e.g., of sewer*) imbocco; (*in the woods*) radura; (*vacancy*) posto vacante; (*beginning*) inizio; (*chance to say something*) occasione

o'pening night' *s* debutto, prima

o'pening num'ber *s* primo numero

o'pening price' *s* prezzo d'apertura

open-minded ['opən'maɪndɪd] *adj* di larghe vedute; imparziale

o'pen se'cret *s* segreto di Pulcinella

o'pen shop' *s* officina che impiega chi non è membro del sindacato

o'pen•work' *s* traforo

opera ['ɑpərə] *s* opera

op'era glass'es *spl* binocolo da teatro

op'era hat' *s* gibus m

op'era house' *s* teatro dell'opera

operate ['ɑpə,ret] *tr* (*a machine*) far funzionare; (*a shop*) gestire; operare || *intr* funzionare; operare; **to operate on** (surg) operare

operatic [,ɑpə'rætɪk] *adj* operistico

op'erating expens'es *spl* spese *fpl* di ordinaria amministrazione

op'erating room' *s* sala operatoria

op'erating ta'ble *s* tavola operatoria

operation [,ɑpə'reʃən] *s* operazione; funzionamento, marcia

opera'tions research' *s* ricerca operativa

operator ['ɑpə,retər] *s* operatore *m;* (*of a conveyance*) conduttore *m*, conducente *mf;* (com) gestore *m;* (telp) telefonista *mf;* (surg) chirurgo operatore; (slang) faccendiere *m*

opiate ['opɪ•ɪt] or ['opɪ,et] *adj & s* oppiato

opinion [ə'pɪnjən] *s* opinione; **in my opinion** a mio modo di vedere; **to have a high opinion of** avere una grande stima di

opinionated [ə'pɪnjə,netɪd] *adj* ostinato, testardo, dogmatico

opium ['opɪ•əm] *s* oppio

o'pium den' *s* fumeria d'oppio

opossum [ə'pɑsəm] *s* opossum *m*

opponent [ə'ponənt] *s* avversario

opportune [,ɑpər'tjun] or [,ɑpər'tun] *adj* opportuno

opportunist [,ɑpər'tjunɪst] or [,ɑpər'tunɪst] *s* opportunista *mf*

opportuni•ty [,ɑpər'tjunɪti] or [,ɑpər'tunɪti] *s* (**-ties**) opportunità *f*, occasione

oppose [ə'poz] *tr* opporsi a

opposite ['ɑpəsɪt] *adj* opposto; di rimpetto, e.g., **the house opposite** la casa di rimpetto || *s* contrario || *prep* di faccia a, di rimpetto a

op'posite num'ber *s* persona di grado corrispondente

opposition [,ɑpə'zɪʃən] *s* opposizione

oppress [ə'pres] *tr* opprimere

oppressive [ə'presɪv] *adj* oppressivo; opprimente, soffocante

oppressor [ə'presər] *s* oppressore *m*

opprobrious [ə'probrɪ•əs] *adj* obbrobrioso

opprobrium [ə'probrɪ·əm] *s* obbrobrio
optic ['aptɪk] *adj* ottico || **optics** *ssg* ottica
optical ['aptɪkəl] *adj* ottico
optician [ap'tɪʃən] *s* ottico, occhialaio
optimism ['aptɪ,mɪzəm] *s* ottimismo
optimist ['aptɪmɪst] *s* ottimista *mf*
optimistic [,aptɪ'mɪstɪk] *adj* ottimistico
option ['apʃən] *s* opzione
optional ['apʃənəl] *adj* facoltativo
optometrist [ap'tamɪtrɪst] *s* optometrista *mf*
opulent ['apjələnt] *adj* opulento
or [ɔr] *conj* o; (*or else*) oppure
oracle ['arəkəl] or ['ɔrəkəl] *s* oracolo
oracular [o'rækjələr] *adj* profetico; ambiguo; misterioso; sentenzioso
oral ['orəl] *adj* orale
orange ['arɪndʒ] or ['ɔrɪndʒ] *adj* di arance; arancio || *s* arancia
orangeade [,arɪndʒ'ed] or [,ɔrɪndʒ'ed] *s* aranciata
or'ange blos'som *s* zagara
or'ange grove' *s* aranceto
or'ange juice' *s* sugo d'arancia
or'ange squeez'er *s* spremiagrumi *m*
or'ange tree' *s* arancio
orang-outang [o'ræŋʊ,tæŋ] *s* orango
oration [o'reʃən] *s* orazione, discorso
orator ['arətər] or ['ɔrətər] *s* oratore *m*
oratorical [,arə'tarɪkəl] or [,ɔrə'tɔrɪkəl] *adj* oratorio
oratori·o [,arə'torɪ,o] or [,ɔrə'torɪ,o] *s* (**-os**) (mus) oratorio
orato·ry ['arə,tori] or ['ɔrə,tori] *s* (**-ries**) oratoria; (eccl) oratorio
orb [ɔrb] *s* orbe *m*
orbit ['ɔrbɪt] *s* orbita; **to go into orbit** entrare in orbita || *tr* mettere in orbita; orbitare intorno a || *intr* orbitare
or'biting sta'tion *s* stazione orbitale
orchard ['ɔrtʃərd] *s* frutteto
orchestra ['ɔrkɪstrə] *s* orchestra; (*parquet*) platea
orchestral [ɔr'kɛstrəl] *adj* orchestrale
or'chestra pit' *s* golfo mistico
or'chestra seat' *s* poltrona di platea
orchestrate ['ɔrkɪs,tret] *tr* orchestrare
orchid ['ɔrkɪd] *s* orchidea
ordain [ɔr'den] *tr* predestinare; decretare; (eccl) ordinare
ordeal [ɔr'dil] or [ɔr'di·əl] *s* sfacchinata; (hist) ordalia
order ['ɔrdər] *s* ordine *m;* compito, e.g., **a big order** un compito difficile; (com) commessa, ordinazione; (mil) consegna; **in order that** affinché; **in order to** + *inf* per + *inf;* **made to order** fatto su misura; **to get out of order** guastarsi; **to give an order** dare un ordine; (com) fare una commessa || *tr* (*e.g., a drink*) ordinare; (*a person*) ordinare (with *dat*); (*e.g., a suit of clothes*) far fare; **to order around** mandare attorno; **to order s.o. away** mandar via qlcu
or'der blank' *s* cedola d'ordinazione
order·ly ['ɔrdərli] *adj* ordinato; disciplinato || *s* (**-lies**) (*in a hospital*) inserviente *mf;* (mil) ordinanza, attendente *m*
ordinal ['ɔrdɪnəl] *adj* & *s* ordinale *m*
ordinance ['ɔrdɪnəns] *s* ordinanza
ordinary ['ɔrdɪ,nɛri] *adj* ordinario
ordnance ['ɔrdnəns] *s* artiglieria; bocche *fpl* da fuoco; munizionamento
ore [or] *s* minerale *m* (metallifero)
organ ['ɔrgən] *s* organo
organ·dy ['ɔrgəndi] *s* (**-dies**) organdi *m*
or'gan grind'er *s* suonatore *m* d'organetto
organic [ɔr'gænɪk] *adj* organico
organism ['ɔrgə,nɪzəm] *s* organismo
organist ['ɔrgənɪst] *s* organista *mf*
organization [,ɔrgənɪ'zeʃən] *s* organizzazione
organize ['ɔrgə,naɪz] *tr* organizzare
organizer ['ɔrgə,naɪzər] *s* organizzatore *m*
or'gan loft' *s* palco, galleria per l'organo
orgasm ['ɔrgæzəm] *s* orgasmo
or·gy ['ɔrdʒi] *s* (**-gies**) orgia
orient ['orɪ·ənt] *s* oriente *m* || **Orient** *s* Oriente *m* || **orient** ['orɪ,ɛnt] *tr* orientare, orizzontare
oriental [,orɪ'ɛntəl] *adj* orientale || **Oriental** *s* orientale *mf*
orifice ['arɪfɪs] or ['ɔrɪfɪs] *s* orifizio
origin ['arɪdʒɪn] or ['ɔrɪdʒɪn] *s* origine *f*, provenienza
original [ə'rɪdʒɪnəl] *adj* & *s* originale *mf*
originate [ə'rɪdʒɪ,net] *tr* originare || *intr* originare, originarsi
oriole ['orɪ,ol] *s* oriolo, rigogolo
Ork'ney Is'lands ['ɔrkni] *spl* Orcadi *fpl*
ormolu ['ɔrmə'lu] *s* (*alloy*) similoro; (*gold powder*) polvere *f* d'oro; (*gilded metal*) bronzo dorato
ornament ['ɔrnəmənt] *s* ornamento || ['ərnə,mɛnt] *tr* ornamentare
ornamental [,ɔrnə'mɛntəl] *adj* ornamentale
ornate [ɔr'net] or ['ɔrnet] *adj* ornato; (*style*) elaborato
ornithologist [,ɔrnɪ'θalədʒɪst] *s* ornitologo
orphan ['ɔrfən] *adj* & *s* orfano || *tr* rendere orfano
orphanage ['ɔrfənɪdʒ] *s* (*institution*) orfanotrofio; (*condition*) orfanezza
Orpheus ['ɔrfjus] or ['ɔrfɪ·əs] *s* Orfeo
orthodox ['ɔrθə,daks] *adj* ortodosso
orthogra·phy [ɔr'θagrəfi] *s* (**-phies**) ortografia
oscillate ['asɪ,let] *intr* oscillare
osier ['oʒər] *s* vimine *m;* (bot) vinco
osmosis [az'mosɪs] or [as'mosɪs] *s* osmosi *f*
osprey ['aspri] *s* falco pescatore
ossi·fy ['asɪ,faɪ] *v* (*pret* & *pp* **-fied**) *tr* ossificare || *intr* ossificarsi
ostensible [as'tɛnsɪbəl] *adj* apparente, preteso
ostentatious [,astɛn'teʃəs] *adj* ostentato
osteopathy [,astɪ'apəθi] *s* osteopatia
ostracism ['astrə,sɪzəm] *s* ostracismo

ostracize [ˈɑstrəˌsaɪz] *tr* dare l'ostracismo a, ostracizzare
ostrich [ˈɑstrɪtʃ] *s* struzzo
Othello [oˈθɛlo] or [əˈθɛlo] *s* Otello
other [ˈʌðər] *adj & pron indef* altro || *adv*—**other than** diversamente che
otherwise [ˈʌðərˌwaɪz] *adv* altrimenti; differentemente
otter [ˈɑtər] *s* lontra
ottoman [ˈɑtəmən] *s* (*fabric*) ottomano; (*sofa*) ottomana; cuscino per i piedi || **Ottoman** *adj & s* ottomano
ouch [aʊtʃ] *interj* ahi!
ought [ɔt] *s* qualcosa; zero; **for ought I know** per quanto io sappia || *v aux* is rendered in Italian by the conditional of *dovere*, e.g., **you ought to be ashamed** dovresti vergognarti
ounce [aʊns] *s* oncia
our [aʊr] *adj poss* nostro, il nostro
ours [aʊrz] *pron poss* il nostro
ourselves [aʊrˈsɛlvz] *pron pers* noi stessi; ci, e.g., **we enjoyed ourselves** ci siamo divertiti
oust [aʊst] *tr* espellere; (*a tenant*) sfrattare
out [aʊt] *adj* erroneo; esterno; fuori pratica; svenuto; ubriaco; finito; (*book*) pubblicato; (*lights*) spento; fuori moda; introvabile; palmare; di permesso, e.g., **my night out** la mia serata di permesso; (*e.g., at the knees*) frusto; (sports) fuori gioco || *s* via d'uscita; **to be on the outs** or **at outs with** (coll) essere in disaccordo con || *adv* fuori, all'infuori; all'aria libera; **out for** in cerca di; **out of** fuori, fuori di; di; da; (*e.g., money*) a corto di, senza; su, e.g., **two students out of three** due studenti su tre || *prep* fuori di; per, lungo || *interj* fuori!
out' and away' *adv* di gran lunga
out'-and-out' *adj* perfetto, completo || *adv* perfettamente, completamente
out'bid' *v* (*pret* **-bid**; *pp* **-bid** or **-bidden**; *ger* **-bidding**) *tr* fare un'offerta migliore di; (bridge) fare una dichiarazione più alta di
out'board mo'tor *s* fuoribordo, motore *m* fuoribordo
out'break' *s* insurrezione; (*of hives*) eruzione; (*of anger; of war*) scoppio
out'build'ing *s* dipendenza
out'burst' *s* (*of tears; of laughter*) scoppio; (*of energy*) impeto, slancio
out'cast' *s* vagabondo reietto
out'come' *s* risultato
out'cry' *s* (**-cries**) grido, chiasso
out'dat'ed *adj* fuori moda
out'dis'tance *tr* distanziare
out'do' *v* (*pret* **-did**; *pp* **-done**) *tr* sorpassare; **to outdo oneself** sorpassare sé stesso
out'door' *adj* all'aria aperta
out'doors' *s* aria libera, aperta campagna || *adv* all'aria aperta, fuori di casa
out'er space' [ˈaʊtər] *s* spazio cosmico
out'field' *s* (baseball) campo esterno
out'field'er *s* (baseball) esterno
out'fit' *s* equipaggiamento; (*female costume*) insieme *m;* (*of bride*) corredo; (*group*) (coll) corpo; (com) compagnia || *v* (*pret & pp* **-fitted**; *ger* **-fitting**) *tr* equipaggiare
out'flow' *s* efflusso
out'go'ing *adj* in partenza; (*tide*) decrescente; (*character*) espansivo || *s* efflusso
out'grow' *v* (*pret* **-grew**; *pp* **-grown**) *tr* essere troppo grande per; sorpassare in statura; perdere l'interesse per || *intr* protrudere
out'growth' *s* risultato, conseguenza; crescita
outing [ˈaʊtɪŋ] *s* gita, scampagnata
outlandish [aʊtˈlændɪʃ] *adj* strano, bizzarro; dall'aspetto straniero; (*remote, far away*) in capo al mondo
out'last' *tr* sopravvivere (with *dat*)
out'law' *s* fuorilegge *mf* || *tr* proscrivere; dichiarare illegale
out'lay' *s* disborso || **out·lay'** *v* (*pret & pp* **-laid**) *tr* sborsare
out'let *s* uscita; (*e.g., of river*) sbocco; (com) mercato; (elec) presa di corrente; (fig) sfogo
out'line' *s* contorno; traccia, tracciato; sagoma, profilo; prospetto || *tr* delineare; tracciare, tratteggiare; sagomare, profilare; prospettare
out'live' *tr* sopravvivere (with *dat*)
out'look' *s* prospettiva; (*watch*) guardia; (*mental view*) modo di vedere, opinione
out'ly'ing *adj* lontano, fuori di mano; periferico
outmoded [ˌaʊtˈmodɪd] *adj* fuori moda, antiquato
out'num'ber *tr* superare in numero
out'-of-date' *adj* fuori moda
out'-of-door' *adj* all'aria aperta
out'-of-doors' *adj* all'aria aperta || *s* aria aperta || *adv* all'aria aperta; fuori di casa
out'-of-print' *adj* esaurito
out'-of-the-way' *adj* appartato, fuori mano; inusitato, strano
out' of tune' *adj* stonato || *adv* fuori di tono
out' of work' *adj* disoccupato
out'pa'tient *s* paziente *mf* esterno
out'post' *s* (mil) posto avanzato
out'put' *s* produzione; (elec) uscita; (mach) rendimento, potenza utile
out'rage *s* oltraggio, indecenza || *tr* oltraggiare; (*a woman*) violare
outrageous [aʊtˈredʒəs] *adj* oltraggioso; (*excessive*) eccessivo; atroce, feroce
out'rank' *tr* superare in grado
out'rid'er *s* battistrada *m*
out'right' *adj* completo, intero || *adv* completamente; apertamente; sul colpo, sull'istante
out'set' *s* inizio, principio
out'side' *adj* esterno; (*unlikely*) improbabile; (*price*) massimo || *s* esterno, di fuori *m;* aspetto esteriore; vita fuori del carcere || *adv* fuori, di fuori; **outside of** fuori di || *prep* fuori di; (coll) all'infuori di

outsider [ˌautˈsaɪdər] *s* estraneo, intruso; (sports) outsider *m*
out'skirts' *spl* sobborghi *mpl*, periferia
out'spo'ken *adj* franco, esplicito
out'stand'ing *adj* saliente, eminente; (*debt*) arretrato, non pagato
outward [ˈautwərd] *adj* esterno, superficiale || *adv* al di fuori
out'weigh' *tr* pesare più di; eccedere in importanza
out'wit' *v* (*pret & pp* **-witted**; *ger* **-witting**) *tr* farla in barba di; (*a pursuer*) far perdere la traccia or la pista a
oval [ˈovəl] *adj & s* ovale *m*
ova·ry [ˈovəri] *s* (**-ries**) ovaia
ovation [oˈveʃən] *s* ovazione
oven [ˈʌvən] *s* forno
over [ˈovər] *adj* superiore; esterno; finito, concluso || *adv* su, sopra; dall'altra parte; dall'altra sponda; al rovescio; di nuovo; (*at the bottom of a page*) continua; qui, e.g., **hand over the money** dammi qui il denaro; **over again** di nuovo; **over against** contro; **over and over** ripetutamente; **over here** qui; **over there** là || *prep* su, sopra; dall'altra parte di; attraverso, per; (*a certain number*) più di; a causa di; **over and above** in eccesso di
o'ver·all' *adj* completo, totale || **overalls** *spl* tuta
o'ver·bear'ing *adj* arrogante, prepotente
o'ver·board' *adv* in acqua; **man overboard!** uomo in mare!; **to go overboard** andare agli estremi
o'ver·cast' *adj* annuvolato || *s* cielo annuvolato || *v* (*pret & pp* **-cast**) *tr* coprire, annuvolare
o'ver·charge' *s* prezzo eccessivo; sovraccarico; (elec) carica eccessiva || **o'ver·charge'** *tr* far pagare eccessivamente; sovraccaricare
o'ver·coat' *s* soprabito, pastrano
o'ver·come' *v* (*pret* **-came**; *pp* **-come**) *tr* vincere, sopraffare; (*e.g., passions*) frenare; opprimere
o'vercon'fidence *s* sicumera
o'ver·crowd' *tr* gremire
o'ver·do' *v* (*pret* **-did**; *pp* **-done**) *tr* esagerare; strafare; esaurire; (*meat*) stracuocere || *intr* esaurirsi
o'ver·dose' *s* dose eccessiva
o'ver·draft' *s* assegno allo scoperto
o'ver·draw' *v* (*pret* **-drew**; *pp* **-drawn**) *tr* (*a check*) emettere allo scoperto; (*a character*) esagerare la descrizione di
o'ver·due' *adj* in ritardo; (com) in sofferenza, scaduto
o'ver·eat' *v* (*pret* **-ate**; *pp* **-eaten**) *tr & intr* mangiare troppo
o'ver·exer'tion *s* sforzo eccessivo
o'ver·expose' *tr* sovresporre
o'ver·expo'sure *s* sovresposizione
o'ver·flow' *s* (*of a river*) piena, straripamento; (*excess*) sovrabbondanza; (*e.g., of a fountain*) trabocco; (*outlet*) tubo di troppopieno || **o'ver·flow'** *intr* (*said of a river*) straripare; (*said of a container*) traboccare
o'ver·fly' *v* (*pret* **-flew**; *pp* **-flown**) *tr* sorvolare; (*a target*) oltrepassare
o'ver·grown' *adj* cresciuto troppo; coperto, denso
o'ver·hang' *s* strapiombo || **o'ver·hang'** *v* (*pret & pp* **-hung**) *tr* sovrastare (with *dat*); sovrastare; (*to threaten*) minacciare; pervadere, permeare || *intr* sovrastare, strapiombare
o'ver·haul' *s* riparazione; esame *m*, revisione || *tr* riparare; esaminare, ripassare, rivedere; raggiungere, mettersi alla pari con
o'ver·head' *adj* in alto, sopra la testa; aereo; elevato, pensile; generale || **o'ver·head'** *adv* in alto, di sopra || **o'ver·head'** *s* spese *fpl* generali
o'ver·head projec'tor *s* lavagna luminosa
o'ver·head valve' *s* valvola in testa
o'ver·hear' *v* (*pret & pp* **-heard**) *tr* sentire per caso, udire per caso
o'ver·heat' *tr* surriscaldare || *intr* surriscaldarsi; eccitarsi
overjoyed [ˌovərˈdʒɔɪd] *adj* felicissimo; **to be overjoyed** non stare in sé dalla contentezza
overland [ˈovərˌlænd] or [ˈovərlənd] *adj & adv* per via di terra
o'ver·lap' *v* (*pret & pp* **-lapped**; *ger* **-lapping**) *tr* sovrapporre, estendersi sopra || *intr* sovrapporsi, estendersi; coincidere parzialmente
o'ver·load' *s* sovraccarico || **o'ver·load'** *tr* sovraccaricare, stracaricare
o'ver·look' *tr* sovrastare su, dominare; ispezionare, sorvegliare; passare sopra, trascurare; dare su, e.g., **the window overlooks the street** la finestra dà sulla strada
o'ver·lord' *s* dominatore *m* || *tr* dominare despoticamente
overly [ˈovərli] *adv* eccessivamente
o'ver·night' *adj* per la notte, per solo una notte || **o'ver·night'** *adv* durante la notte; la notte prima
o'vernight bag' *s* astuccio di toletta per la notte
o'ver·pass' *s* cavalcavia, viadotto
o'ver·pop'ulate' *tr* sovrappopolare
o'ver·pow'er *tr* sopraffare
o'ver·pow'ering *adj* schiacciante
o'ver·produc'tion *s* sovrapproduzione
o'ver·rate' *tr* sopravvalutare
o'ver·run' *v* (*pret* **-ran**; *pp* **-run**; *ger* **-running**) *tr* invadere, infestare; inondare; (*one's time*) oltrepassare, eccedere
o'ver·sea' or **o'ver·seas'** *adj* di oltremare || **o'ver·sea'** or **o'ver·seas'** *adv* oltremare, al di là dei mari
o'ver·see' *v* (*pret* **-saw**; *pp* **-seen**) *tr* sorvegliare
o'ver·seer' *s* sorvegliante *mf*
o'ver·shad'ow *tr* oscurare, eclissare
o'ver·shoe' *s* soprascarpa
o'ver·shoot' *v* (*pret & pp* **-shot**) *tr* (*the target*) oltrepassare; (*said of water*) scorrere sopra; **to overshoot oneself** andare troppo in là || *intr* (aer) atterrare lungo e richiamare
o'ver·sight' *s* sbadataggine *f*, svista; sorveglianza, supervisione

o'ver·sleep' *v* (*pret & pp* **-slept**) *tr* (*a certain hour*) dormire oltre || *intr* dormire troppo a lungo
o'ver·step' *v* (*pret & pp* **-stepped; ger -stepping**) *tr* eccedere, oltrepassare
o'ver·stock' *tr* riempire eccessivamente
o'ver·sup·ply' *s* (**-plies**) fornitura superiore alla richiesta || **o'ver·sup·ply'** *v* (*pret & pp* **-plied**) *tr* fornire in quantità superiore alla richiesta
overt ['ovərt] or [o'vʌrt] *adj* palmare, chiaro, manifesto
o'ver·take' *v* (*pret* **-took;** *pp* **-taken**) *tr* raggiungere, sorpassare; sorprendere
o'ver-the-count'er *adj* (*securities*) venduto direttamente al compratore
o'ver·throw' *s* rovesciamento; disfatta || **o'ver·throw'** *s* (*pret* **-threw;** *pp* **-thrown**) *tr* rovesciare, sconfiggere
o'ver·time' *adj* supplementare, fuori orario || *s* straordinario; (sports) tempo supplementare || *adv* fuori orario
o'ver·tone' *s* (mus) suono armonico; (fig) sottinteso
o'ver·trump' *s* taglio con atout più alto || **o'ver·trump'** *tr & intr* tagliare con atout più alto
overture ['ovərtʃər] *s* apertura; (mus) preludio, sinfonia
o'ver·turn' *s* rovesciamento || **o'ver·turn'** *tr* rovesciare, travolgere || *intr* rovesciarsi, ribaltarsi
overweening [,ovər'winɪŋ] *adj* presuntuoso, vanitoso; esagerato, eccessivo
o'ver·weight' *adj* troppo grasso; oltrepassante i limiti di peso || **o'ver·weight'** *s* sovraccarico; preponderanza; eccesso di peso
overwhelm [,ovər'hwelm] *tr* schiacciare, debellare; coprire; (*e.g., with kindness*) colmare, ricolmare
o'ver·work' *s* lavoro straordinario; superlavoro || **o'ver·work'** *tr* far lavorare eccessivamente || *intr* lavorare eccessivamente
Ovid ['ɑvɪd] *s* Ovidio
ow [aʊ] *interj* ahi!
owe [o] *tr* dovere || *intr* essere in debito
owing ['o·ɪŋ] *adj* dovuto; **owing to** a causa di
owl [aʊl] *s* gufo, barbagianni *m*
own [on] *adj* proprio, e.g., **my own brother** il mio proprio fratello || *s* il proprio; **on one's own** (coll) per proprio conto; (*without anybody's advice*) di testa propria; **to come into one's own** entrare in possesso del proprio; essere riconosciuto per quanto si vale; **to hold one's own** non perdere terreno; essere pari || *tr* possedere; riconoscere || *intr*—**to own up to** confessare
owner ['onər] *s* padrone *m*, proprietario, titolare *m*
ownership ['onər,ʃɪp] *s* proprietà *f*
own'er's li'cence *s* permesso di circolazione
ox [ɑks] *s* (**oxen** ['ɑksən]) bue *m*
ox'cart' *s* carro tirato da buoi
oxide ['ɑksaɪd] *s* ossido
oxidize ['ɑksɪ,daɪz] *tr* ossidare || *intr* ossidarsi
oxygen ['ɑksɪdʒən] *s* ossigeno
ox'ygen mask' *s* maschera respiratoria
ox'ygen tent' *s* tenda ad ossigeno
oxytone ['ɑksɪ,ton] *adj* tronco, ossitono || *s* ossitono
oyster ['ɔɪstər] *adj* di ostriche || *s* ostrica
oys'ter bed' *s* ostricaio, banco di ostriche
oys'ter cock'tail *s* ostriche *fpl* servite in valva
oys'ter fork' *s* forchettina da ostriche
oys'ter·house' *s* ristorante *m* per la vendita delle ostriche
oys'ter·knife' *s* coltello per aprire le ostriche
oys'ter·man *s* (**-men**) ostricaio
oys'ter shell' *s* conchiglia d'ostrica
oys'ter stew' *s* brodetto d'ostriche
ozone ['ozon] *s* ozono

P

P, p [pi] *s* sedicesima lettera dell'alfabeto inglese
pace [pes] *s* passo, andatura; (*of a horse*) ambio; **to keep pace with** andare di pari passo con; **to put s.o. through his paces** mettere qlcu a dura prova; **to set the pace for** fare l'andatura per; dare l'esempio a || *tr* misurare a passi, percorrere; **to pace the floor** andare avanti e indietro per la stanza || *intr* camminare lentamente; andare al passo; (*said of a horse*) ambiare
pace'mak'er *s* battistrada *m;* (*in races*) chi stabilisce il passo; (med) pacemaker *m*
pacific [pə'sɪfɪk] *adj* pacifico || **Pacific** *adj & s* Pacifico
pacifier ['pæsɪ,faɪ·ər] *s* paciere *m;* (*teething ring*) succhietto, tettarella
pacifism ['pæsɪ,fɪzəm] *s* pacifismo
pacifist ['pæsɪfɪst] *adj & s* pacifista *mf*
paci·fy ['pæsɪ,faɪ] *v* (*pret & pp* **-fied**) *tr* pacificare
pack [pæk] *s* fardello, pacco; (*of merchandise*) balla; (*of lies*) mucchio; (*of cards*) mazzo; (*of thieves*) banda; (*of dogs*) muta; (*of animals*) branco; (*of birds*) stormo; (*of cigarettes*) pacchetto; (*of ice*) banchiglia; (*of people*) turba || *tr* affardellare, impaccare; (*to wrap*) imballare; ammucchiare; (*in cans*) mettere in conserva; (*people*) stipare; (*a trunk*) fare; **to pack in** stipare; **to pack off** mandare via || *intr* ammucchiarsi,

pigiarsi, accalcarsi; **to pack up** fare il baule
package ['pækɪdʒ] *s* pacco, collo; (*small*) pacchetto || *tr* impacchettare
pack' an'imal *s* bestia da soma
packer ['pækər] *s* imballatore *m;* (*of canned goods*) proprietario (di fabbrica di conserve alimentari)
packet ['pækɪt] *s* pacchetto; (*boat*) vapore *m* postale
packing ['pækɪŋ] *s* imballaggio; (*on shoulders of suit*) spallina; (mach) stoppa; (*ring*) (mach) guarnizione
pack'ing box' or **case'** *s* cassa d'imballaggio
pack'ing house' *s* fabbrica di conserve alimentari; fabbrica di carne in conserva
pack'ing slip' *s* foglio d'imballaggio
pack'sad'dle *s* basto
pack'thread' *s* spago d'imballaggio
pack'train' *s* fila di animali da soma
pact [pækt] *s* patto
pad [pæd] *s* cuscinetto, tampone *m;* imbottitura; (*of writing paper*) blocco da annotazioni; (*of an animal*) superficie *f* plantare, zampa; (*of a water lily*) foglia; (rok) piattaforma || *v* (*pret & pp* **padded;** *ger* **padding**) *tr* imbottire, ovattare; (*e.g., a speech*) infarcire || *intr* camminare pesantemente
pad'ding *s* imbottitura
paddle ['pædəl] *s* pagaia; (*of waterwheel*) pala || *tr* remare; (*to spank*) bastonare || *intr* remare; (*to splash*) diguazzare
pad'dle wheel' *s* ruota a pale
paddock ['pædək] *s* prato d'allenamento, paddock *m*
pad'lock' *s* lucchetto || *tr* chiudere col lucchetto
pagan ['pegən] *adj & s* pagano
paganism ['pegə,nɪzəm] *s* paganesimo
page [pedʒ] *s* (*of a book*) pagina; (*at court*) paggio; (*in hotels*) fattorino, valletto || *tr* impaginare; (*in hotels*) chiamare, far chiamare
pageant ['pædʒənt] *s* parata, corteo, spettacolo
pageant•ry ['pædʒəntri] *s* (**-ries**) pompa, fasto
paginate ['pædʒɪ,net] *tr* impaginare
pail [pel] *s* secchio
pain [pen] *s* dolore *m;* **on pain of** sotto pena di; **to take pains to** prendersi cura di; **to take pains not to** guardarsi da || *tr & intr* dolere
painful ['penfəl] *adj* doloroso, penoso
pain'kill'er *s* (coll) analgesico
painless ['penlɪs] *adj* indolore
painstaking ['penz,tekɪŋ] *adj* meticoloso
paint [pent] *s* (*for pictures*) colore *m;* (*for a house*) vernice *f;* (*make-up*) trucco || *tr* dipingere; (*a house*) verniciare, tinteggiare || *intr* (*with make-up*) dipingersi; essere pittore
paint'box' *s* scatola da colori
paint'brush' *s* pennello
painter ['pentər] *s* (*of pictures*) pittore *m;* (*of a house*) verniciatore *m;* (naut) barbetta
painting ['pentɪŋ] *s* pittura, dipinto
paint' remov'er [rɪ'muvər] *s* solvente *m* per levar la vernice
paint' thin'ner *s* diluente *m*
pair [per] *s* paio; (*of people*) coppia || *tr* appaiare, accoppiare || *intr* appaiarsi, accoppiarsi
pair' of scis'sors *s* forbici *fpl*
pair' of trou'sers *s* calzoni *mpl*
pajamas [pə'dʒɑməz] or [pə'dʒæməz] *spl* pigiama *m*
Pakistan [,pɑkɪ'stɑn] *s* il Pakistan
Pakistani [,pɑkɪ'stɑni] *adj & s* pachistano
pal [pæl] *s* (coll) compagno || *v* (*pret & pp* **palled;** *ger* **palling**) *intr* (coll) essere compagni
palace ['pælɪs] *s* palazzo
palatable ['pælətəbəl] *adj* gustoso, appetitoso; accettabile
palatal ['pælətəl] *adj & s* palatale *f*
palate ['pælɪt] *s* palato
pale [pel] *adj* pallido || *s* palo; (*enclosure*) recinto; (fig) ambito || *intr* impallidire
pale'face' *s* faccia pallida
palette ['pælɪt] *s* tavolozza
palfrey ['pɔlfri] *s* palafreno
palisade [,pælɪ'sed] *s* palizzata; (*line of cliffs*) dirupo
pall [pɔl] *s* panno mortuario; (*of smoke*) cappa || *tr* saziare, infastidire || *intr* saziarsi, perdere l'appetito
pall'bear'er *s* chi accompagna il feretro; chi porta il feretro
palliate ['pælɪ,et] *tr* attenuare, alleviare
pallid ['pælɪd] *adj* pallido
pallor ['pælər] *s* pallore *m*
palm [pɑm] *s* (*tree and leaf*) palma; (*of hand; measure*) palmo; **to carry off the palm** riportare la palma; **to grease the palm of** ungere le ruote a || *tr* far sparire nella mano; nascondere; **to palm off s.th on s.o.** rifilare qlco a qlcu
palmet•to [pæl'meto] *s* (**-tos** or **-toes**) palmeto
palmist ['pɑmɪst] *s* chiromante *mf*
palmistry ['pɑmɪstri] *s* chiromanzia
palm' leaf' *s* palma, foglia di palma
palm' oil' *s* olio di palma
Palm' Sun'day *s* Domenica delle Palme
palpable ['pælpəbəl] *adj* palpabile
palpitate ['pælpɪ,tet] *intr* palpitare
pal•sy ['pɔlzi] *s* (**-sies**) paralisi *f* || *v* (*pret & pp* **-sied**) *tr* paralizzare
pal•try ['pɔltri] *adj* (**-trier; -triest**) vile, meschino, irrisorio
pamper ['pæmpər] *tr* viziare; (*the appetite*) saziare
pamphlet ['pæmflɪt] *s* opuscolo, libello
pan [pæn] *s* padella, casseruola; (*of a balance*) coppa, piatto; (phot) bacinella || *v* (*pret & pp* **panned;** *ger* **panning**) *tr* friggere; (*gold*) vagliare in padella; (*salt*) estrarre in salina; (coll) criticare || *intr* essere estratto; **to pan out** (coll) riuscire || **Pan** *s* Pan *m*
panacea [,pænə'si·ə] *s* panacea
Pan'ama Canal' ['pænə,mɑ] *s* Canale *m* di Panama

Pan'ama hat' *s* panama *m*
Panamanian [ˌpænəˈmenɪ·ən] or [ˌpænəˈmɑnɪ·ən] *adj & s* panamegno
pan'cake' *s* frittella ‖ *intr* (aer) atterrare a piatto
pan'cake land'ing *s* atterraggio a piatto
pancreas [ˈpænkrɪ·əs] *s* pancreas *m*
pander [ˈpændər] *s* mezzano ‖ *intr* ruffianeggiare; **to pander to** favorire, assecondare i desideri di
pane [pen] *s* pannello, vetro di finestra
pan·el [ˈpænəl] *s* pannello; gruppo che discute in faccia al pubblico, telequiz *m;* discussione pubblica; (*of door or window*) specchio; (law) lista di giurati ‖ *v* (*pret & pp* **-eled** or **-elled;** *ger* **-eling** or **-elling**) *tr* coprire di pannelli
pan'el discus'sion *s* colloquio di esperti in faccia al pubblico
panelist [ˈpænəlɪst] *s* partecipante *mf* a una discussione in faccia al pubblico
pan'el lights' *spl* luci *fpl* del cruscotto
pan'el truck' *s* camioncino
pang [pæŋ] *s* (*sharp pain*) spasimo; (*of remorse*) tormento
pan'han'dle *s* manico della padella ‖ *intr* accattare, mendicare
pan·ic [ˈpænɪk] *adj & s* panico ‖ *v* (*pret & pp* **-icked;** *ger* **-icking**) *tr* riempire di panico ‖ *intr* essere colto dal panico
pan'ic·strick'en *adj* morto di paura, in preda al panico
pano·ply [ˈpænəpli] *s* (**-plies**) panoplia; abbigliamento in pompa magna
panorama [ˌpænəˈræmə] or [ˌpænəˈrɑmə] *s* panorama *m*
pan·sy [ˈpænzi] *s* (**-sies**) viola del pensiero
pant [pænt] *s* anelito, affanno; **pants** pantaloni *mpl*, calzoni *mpl;* **to wear the pants** portare i calzoni ‖ *intr* ansare; (*said of heart*) palpitare
pantheism [ˈpænθɪ ˌɪzəm] *s* panteismo
pantheon [ˈpænθɪ ˌɑn] or [ˈpænθɪ·ən] *s* panteon *m*, pantheon *m*
panther [ˈpænθər] *s* pantera
panties [ˈpæntiz] *spl* mutandine *fpl*
pantomime [ˈpæntə ˌmaɪm] *s* pantomima
pan·try [ˈpæntri] *s* (**-tries**) dispensa
pap [pæp] *s* pappa
papa·cy [ˈpepəsi] *s* (**-cies**) papato
Pa'pal States' [ˈpəpəl] *spl* Stati *mpl* pontifici
paper [ˈpepər] *adj* di carta, cartaceo ‖ *s* carta; (*newspaper*) giornale *m;* (*of a student*) tema *m*, saggio; (*of a scholar*) dissertazione; **on paper** per iscritto ‖ *tr* (*a wall*) tappezzare
pa'per·back' *s* libro in brossura
pa'per·boy' *s* giornalaio, strillone *m*
pa'per clip' *s* fermaglio per le carte, clip *m*
pa'per cone' *s* cartoccio
pa'per cut'ter *s* rifilatrice *f*
pa'per doll' *s* pupazzetto di carta
pa'per·hang'er *s* tappezziere *m*
pa'per knife' *s* tagliacarte *m*
pa'per mill' *s* cartiera
pa'per mon'ey *s* carta moneta
pa'per prof'its *spl* guadagni *mpl* non realizzati su valori non venduti
pa'per tape' *s* (*of teletype*) nastro di carta; (*of computer*) nastro perforato
pa'per·weight' *s* fermacarte *m*
pa'per work' *s* lavoro a tavolino
papier-mâché [ˌpepərməˈʃe] *s* cartapesta
paprika [pæˈprikə] or [ˈpæprɪkə] *s* paprica
papy·rus [pəˈpaɪrəs] *s* (**-ri** [raɪ]) papiro
par [pɑr] *adj* alla pari, nominale; normale ‖ *s* parità *f*, valore *m* nominale; **at par** alla pari
parable [ˈpærəbəl] *s* parabola
parabola [pəˈræbələ] *s* parabola
parachute [ˈpærə ˌʃut] *s* paracadute *m* ‖ *intr* lanciarsi col paracadute
par'a·chute jump' *s* lancio col paracadute
parachutist [ˈpærə ˌʃutɪst] *s* paracadutista *mf*
parade [pəˈred] *s* parata, sfilata; ostentazione, sfoggio ‖ *tr* ostentare, sfoggiare; disporre in parata ‖ *intr* fare mostra di sé; (mil) sfilare
paradise [ˈpærə ˌdaɪs] *s* paradiso
paradox [ˈpærə ˌdɑks] *s* paradosso
paradoxical [ˌpærəˈdɑksɪkəl] *adj* paradossale
paraffin [ˈpærəfɪn] *s* paraffina
paragon [ˈpærə ˌgɑn] *s* paragone *m*
paragraph [ˈpærə ˌgræf] or [ˈpærə ˌgrɑf] *s* paragrafo, capoverso; (*in a newspaper*) trafiletto; (*of law*) comma *m*
parakeet [ˈpærə ˌkit] *s* parrocchetto
paral·lel [ˈpærə ˌlel] *adj* parallelo ‖ *s* (geog, fig) parallelo; (geom) parallela; **parallels** (typ) sbarrette *fpl* verticali ‖ *v* (*pret & pp* **-leled** or **-lelled;** *ger* **-leling** or **-lelling**) *tr* collocare parallelamente; correre parallelo a; confrontare
par'allel bars' *spl* parallele *fpl*
paraly·sis [pəˈrælɪsɪs] *s* (**-ses** [ˌsiz]) paralisi *f*
paralytic [ˌpærəˈlɪtɪk] *adj & s* paralitico
paralyze [ˈpærə ˌlaɪz] *tr* paralizzare
paramount [ˈpærə ˌmaunt] *adj* capitale, supremo
paramour [ˈpærə ˌmur] *s* amante *mf*
paranoiac [ˌpærəˈnɔɪ·æk] *adj & s* paranoico
parapet [ˈpærə ˌpet] *s* parapetto
paraphernalia [ˌpærəfərˈnelɪ·ə] *spl* roba, cose *fpl;* attrezzi *mpl*, aggeggi *mpl*
parasite [ˈpærə ˌsaɪt] *s* parassita *m*
parasitic(al) [ˌpærəˈsɪtɪk(əl)] *adj* parassitico, parassitario
parasol [ˈpærə ˌsɔl] or [ˈpærə ˌsɑl] *s* parasole *m*, ombrellino da sole
par'a·troop'er *s* paracadutista *m*
par'a·troops' *spl* truppe *fpl* paracadutiste
parboil [ˈpɑr ˌbɔɪl] *tr* bollire parzialmente; (fig) far bollire
parcel [ˈpɑrsəl] *s* pacchetto; (*of land*) appezzamento ‖ *v* (*pret & pp* **-celed** or **-celled;** *ger* **-celing** or **-celling**) *tr*

impacchettare; **to parcel out** dividere, distribuire
par'cel post' *s* servizio pacchi postali
parch [partʃ] *tr* bruciare; (*land*) inaridire; (*e.g., beans*) essiccare; **to be parched** bruciare dalla sete || *intr* arrostirsi; inaridire
parchment ['partʃmənt] *s* pergamena
pardon ['pardən] *s* perdono, grazia; **I beg your pardon** scusi || *tr* perdonare; (*an offense*) graziare
pardonable ['pardənəbəl] *adj* perdonabile, veniale
par'don board' *s* ufficio per la decisione delle grazie
pare [per] *tr* (*fruit, potatoes*) sbucciare, pelare; (*nails*) tagliare; (*expenses*) ridurre
parent ['perənt] *adj* madre, principale || *s* genitore *m* or genitrice *f;* (fig) origine *f;* **parents** genitori *mpl*
parentage ['perəntɪdʒ] *s* discendenza, lignaggio
parenthesis [pə'renθɪsɪs] *s* (**-ses** [,siz]) parentesi *f;* **in parenthesis** tra parentesi
parenthetically [,pærən'θetɪkəli] *adv* tra parentesi
parenthood ['perənt,hud] *s* paternità *f* or maternità *f*
pariah [pə'raɪ·ə] or ['parɪ·ə] *s* paria *m*
pari-mutuel ['pærɪ'mjutʃu·əl] *s* totalizzatore *m*
par'ing knife' ['perɪŋ] *s* coltello per sbucciare
Paris ['pærɪs] *s* Parigi *f*
parish ['pærɪʃ] *s* parrocchia
parishioner [pə'rɪʃənər] *s* parrocchiano
Parisian [pə'rɪʒən] *adj* & *s* parigino
parity ['pærɪti] *s* parità *f*
park [park] *s* parco || *tr* parcare, parcheggiare || *intr* parcare, parcheggiare, stazionare
parking ['parkɪŋ] *s* posteggio, parcheggio; **no parking** divieto di parcheggio
park'ing lights' *spl* luci *fpl* di posizione
park'ing lot' *s* posteggio, parcheggio
park'ing me'ter *s* parchimetro
park'ing tick'et *s* contravvenzione per parcheggio abusivo
park'way' *s* boulevard *m*
parlay ['parli] or [par'le] *tr* rigiocare
parley ['parli] *s* trattativa, conferenza || *tr* parlamentare
parliament ['parlɪmənt] *s* parlamento
parlor ['parlər] *s* salotto; (*of beautician or undertaker*) salone *m;* (*of convent*) parlatorio
par'lor car' *s* vettura salone
par'lor game' *s* gioco di società
par'lor pol'itics *s* politica da caffè
Parmesan [,parmɪ'zæn] *adj* & *s* parmigiano
Parnassus [par'næsəs] *s* (*poetry; poets*) parnaso; il Parnaso
parochial [pə'rokɪ·əl] *adj* parrocchiale; ristretto, limitato; (*school*) confessionale
paro·dy ['pærədi] *s* (**-dies**) parodia || *v* (*pret* & *pp* **-died**) *tr* parodiare
parole [pə'rol] *s* parola d'onore; libertà *f* condizionale, condizionale *f* || *tr* mettere in libertà condizionale
paroxytone [pær'aksɪ,ton] *adj* parossitono || *s* parola parossitona
par·quet [par'ke] *s* pavimento di legno tassellato, tassellato; (theat) platea || *v* (*pret* & *pp* **-queted** ['ked]; *ger* **-queting** ['ke·ɪŋ]) *tr* pavimentare in legno tassellato
par'quet cir'cle *s* poltroncine *fpl*
parricide ['pærɪ,saɪd] *s* (*act*) patricidio, parricidio; (*person*) patricida *mf,* parricida *mf*
parrot ['pærət] *s* pappagallo || *tr* scimmiottare, fare il pappagallo a
par·ry ['pæri] *s* (**-ries**) parata || *v* (*pret* & *pp* **-ried**) *tr* parare; (fig) evitare
parse [pars] *tr* (gram) analizzare grammaticalmente
parsimonious [,parsɪ'monɪ·əs] *adj* parsimonioso
parsley ['parsli] *s* prezzemolo
parsnip ['parsnɪp] *s* pastinaca
parson ['parsən] *s* parroco; pastore *m* protestante
part [part] *s* parte *f;* (*of a machine*) pezzo, organo; (*of hair*) riga; **for my part** per parte mia; **on the part of** da parte di; **part and parcel** parte *f* integrante; **parts** abilità *f,* dote *f;* regione *f,* paesi *mpl;* **to do one's part** fare il proprio dovere || *adv* parzialmente, in part || *tr* dividere, separare; **to part company** separasi; **to part one's hair** farsi la riga || *intr* separarsi; **to part from** separarsi da, dividersi da; **to part with** rinunciare a
par·take [par'tek] *v* (*pret* **-took** ['tuk]; *pp* **-taken**) *tr* condividere || *intr*—**to partake in** partecipare a; **to partake of** condividere
parterre [par'ter] *s* aiola; (theat) platea
Parthenon ['parθɪ,nan] *s* Partenone *m*
partial ['parʃəl] *adj* parziale
participate [par'tɪsɪ,pet] *intr* partecipare; **to participate in** partecipare a
participation [par,tɪsɪ'peʃən] *s* partecipazione
participle ['partɪ,sɪpəl] *s* participio
particle ['partɪkəl] *s* particella
particular [pər'tɪkjələr] *adj* (*belonging to a single person*) particolare; (*exacting*) esigente, fastidioso || *s* particolare *m;* **in particular** specialmente, particolarmente
part'ing *adj* (*words*) di commiato; (*last*) ultimo || *s* commiato; separazione
partisan ['partɪzən] *adj* & *s* partigiano
partition [par'tɪʃən] *s* partizione, divisione; (*or house*) tramezzo || *tr* dividere; tramezzare
partner ['partnər] *s* (*in sports*) compagno; (*in dancing*) cavaliere *m,* dama; (*husband or wife*) consorte *mf;* (com) socio
partnership ['partnər,ʃɪp] *s* associazione; (com) società *f*
part' of speech' *s* parte *f* del discorso
partridge ['partrɪdʒ] *s* pernice *f*
part' time' *adj* a orario ridotto, a ore
par·ty ['parti] *adj* comune; di gala || *s* (**-ties**) festa, ricevimento, trattenimento; (*of people*) gruppo; (*indi-*

vidual) persona; (pol) partito; (law) contraente *mf;* (mil) distaccamento; **to be a party to** prendere parte a; essere complice di
par'ty girl' *s* ragazza che fa la vita
par'ty-go'er *s* frequentatore *m* di trattenimenti
part'y line' *s* (*boundary*) linea di confine; (*of Communist party*) politica del partito; (telp) linea in coutenza
pass [pæs] or [pɑs] *s* passaggio; (*state*) stato, situazione; (*free ticket*) ingresso gratuito; (*leave of absence given to a soldier*) congedo, permesso; (*of a hypnotist*) gesto; (*between mountains*) passo; (slang) tentativo d'abbraccio; **a pretty pass** (coll) un bell'affare || *tr* (*a course in school*) passare; (*to promote*) promuovere; (*a law*) approvare; (*a sentence*) pronunciare; (*an opinion*) esprimere, avanzare; (*to excrete*) evacuare; far muovere; **to pass by** non fare attenzione a; **to pass off** (*e.g., bogus money*) azzeccare; **to pass on** trasmettere; **to pass out** distribuire; **to pass over** omettere || *intr* (*to go*) passare; (*said of a law*) essere approvato; (*said of a student*) essere promosso; (*to be accepted*) farsi passare; (*said, e.g., of two trains*) incrociarsi; **to come to pass** accadere, succedere; **to pass as** passare per; **to pass away** morire; **to pass out** (slang) svenire; **to pass over** or **through** attraversare, passare per
passable ['pæsəbəl] or ['pɑsəbəl] *adj* praticabile; (*by boat*) navigabile; (*adequate*) passabile; (*law*) promulgabile
passage ['pæsɪdʒ] *s* passaggio; (*of a law*) approvazione; (*ticket*) biglietto di passaggio; (*of the bowels*) evacuazione
pass'book' *s* libretto di banca; libretto della cassa di risparmio
passenger ['pæsəndʒər] *s* passeggero
passer-by ['pæsər'baɪ] or ['pɑsər'baɪ] *s* (**passers-by**) passante *mf*
passing ['pæsɪŋ] or ['pɑsɪŋ] *adj* (*fleeting*) fuggente; (*casual*) incidentale; (*grade*) che concede la promozione || *s* passaggio; (*death*) morte *f;* promozione
passion ['pæʃən] *s* passione
passionate ['pæʃənɪt] *adj* appassionato; (*hot-tempered*) collerico; veemente, ardente
passive ['pæsɪv] *adj & s* passivo
pass'key' *s* chiave maestra; (*for use of hotel help*) comunella
Pass'o'ver *s* Pasqua ebraica
pass'port' *s* passaporto
pass'word' *s* parola d'ordine
past [pæst] or [pɑst] *adj* passato, scorso; ex, e.g., **past president** ex presidente || *s* passato || *adv* oltre; al di fuori; al di là || *prep* oltre; al di là di; dopo (di); **past belief** incredibile; **past cure** incurabile; **past hope** senza speranza; **past recovery** incurabile; **past three o'clock** le tre passate
paste [pest] *s* (*dough*) pasta; (*adhesive*) colla; diamante *m* artificiale || *tr* incollare; (slang) dare pugni a
paste'board' *s* cartone *m*
pastel [pæs'tɛl] *adj & s* pastello
pasteurize ['pæstə ,raɪz] *tr* pastorizzare
pastime ['pæs ,taɪm] or ['pɑs ,taɪm] *s* diversione, passatempo
pastor ['pæstər] or ['pɑstər] *s* pastore *m*, sacerdote *m*
pastoral ['pæstərəl] or ['pɑstərəl] *adj* pastorale || *s* (*poem, letter*) pastorale *f;* (*crosier*) pastorale *m*
pas·try ['pestri] *s* (**-tries**) pasticceria
pas'try cook' *s* pasticciere *m*
pas'try shop' *s* pasticceria
pasture ['pæstʃər] or ['pɑstʃər] *s* pastura, pascolo || *tr* condurre al pascolo || *intr* brucare
past·y ['pesti] *adj* (**-ier; -iest**) pastoso; flaccido
pat [pæt] *s* colpetto; (*of butter*) panetto || *v* (*pret & pp* **patted;** *ger* **patting**) *tr* accarezzare leggermente; battere leggermente; **to pat on the back** elogiare, incoraggiare battendo sulla spalla
patch [pætʃ] *s* (*on a suit or shoes*) toppa; (*in a tire*) pezza; (*on wound*) benda; (*of ground*) appezzamento; (*small area*) lembo || *tr* rammendare; **to patch up** (*an argument*) comporre; (*to produce crudely*) raffazzonare
patent ['petənt] *adj* patente, palmare || ['pætənt] *adj* brevettato || *s* (*of invention*) brevetto; (*sole right*) privativa || *tr* brevettare
pat'ent leath'er ['pætent] *s* copale *m & f*, pelle *f* di vernice
pat'ent med'icine ['pætent] *s* specialità *f* medicinale
pat'ent right' ['pætent] *s* proprietà brevettata
paternal [pə'tʌrnəl] *adj* paterno
paternity [pə'tʌrnɪti] *s* paternità *f*
path [pæθ] or [pɑθ] *s* via battuta, sentiero; (fig) via
pathetic [pə'θɛtɪk] *adj* patetico
path'find'er *s* esploratore *m*
pathology [pə'θɑlədʒi] *s* patologia
pathos ['peθɑs] *s* patos *m*, pathos *m*
path'way' *s* sentiero, cammino
patience ['peʃəns] *s* pazienza
patient ['peʃənt] *adj & s* paziente *mf*
patriarch ['petrɪ ,ɑrk] *s* patriarca *m*
patrician [pə'trɪʃən] *adj & s* patrizio
patricide ['pætrɪ ,saɪd] *s* (*act*) parricidio; (*person*) parricida *mf*
Patrick ['pætrɪk] *s* Patrizio
patrimo·ny ['pætrɪ ,moni] *s* (**-nies**) patrimonio
patriot ['petrɪ·ət] or ['pætrɪ·ət] *s* patriota *mf*
patriotic [,petrɪ'ɑtɪk] or [,pætrɪ'ɑtɪk] *adj* patriottico
patriotism ['petrɪ·ə ,tɪzəm] or ['pætrɪ·ə ,tɪzəm] *s* patriottismo
pa·trol [pə'trol] *s* (*group*) pattuglia; (*individual*) soldato or agente *m* di pattuglia || *v* (*pret & pp* **-trolled;** *ger* **-trolling**) *tr & intr* pattugliare
patrol'man *s* (**-men**) agente *m*, poliziotto

patrol' wag'on *s* carrozzone *m* cellulare, cellulare *m*
patron ['petrən] or ['pætrən] *s* patrono, sostenitore *m;* (*customer*) cliente *mf*
patronize ['petrə,naɪz] or ['pætrə,naɪz] *tr* (*to support*) sostenere; trattare con condiscendenza; essere cliente abituale di
pa'tron saint' *s* patrono
patter ['pætər] *s* (*e.g., of rain*) battito; (*of feet*) scalpiccio; (*speech*) chiacchierio || *intr* battere, picchiettare; chiacchierare
pattern ['pætərn] *s* modello; disegno; (*of flight*) procedura || *tr* modellare
pat•ty ['pæti] *s* (**-ties**) pasticcino; (*meat cake*) polpetta
paucity ['pɔsɪti] *s* pochezza, scarsità *f,* insufficienza
Paul [pɔl] *s* Paolo
paunch [pɔntʃ] *s* pancia
paunch•y ['pɔntʃi] *adj* (**-ier; -iest**) panciuto
pauper ['pɔpər] *s* povero, indigente *mf*
pause [pɔz] *s* pausa; (*of a tape recorder*) arresto momentaneo; **to give pause (to)** dar di che pensare (a) || *intr* far pausa, fermarsi; (*to hesitate*) esitare, vacillare
pave [pev] *tr* pavimentare, lastricare; **to pave the way (for)** aprire il cammino (a)
pavement ['pevmənt] *s* pavimentazione, lastricato; (*sidewalk*) marciapiede *m*
pavilion [pə'vɪljən] *s* padiglione *m;* (*of circus*) tendone *m*
paw [pɔ] *s* zampa || *tr* (*to touch with paws*) dar zampate a; (*to handle clumsily*) maneggiare goffamente; (coll) palpeggiare || *intr* zampare
pawn [pɔn] *s* (*security*) pegno; (*tool of another person*) pedina; (chess) pedina, pedone *m;* (fig) ostaggio || *tr* dare in pegno, impegnare
pawn'bro'ker *s* prestatore *m* su pegno
pawn'shop' *s* agenzia di prestiti su pegno, monte *m* di pietà
pawn' tick'et *s* ricevuta di pegno, polizza del monte di pietà
pay [pe] *s* pagamento; (*wages*) paga, salario; (mil) soldo || *v* (*pret & pp* **paid** [ped]) *tr* pagare; (*wages*) conguagliare; (*one's respects*) presentare; (*a visit*) fare; (*a bill*) saldare; (*attention*) fare, presentare; **to pay back** ripagare; (fig) pagare pan per focaccia a; **to pay for** pagare; **to pay off** liquidare; (*in order to discharge*) pagare e licenziare; **to pay up** saldare || *intr* pagare; valere la pena; **pay as you enter** pagare all'ingresso; **pay as you go** pagare le tasse per trattenuta; **pay as you leave** pagare all'uscita
payable ['pe•əbəl] *adj* pagabile
pay' boost' *s* aumento di salario
pay'check' *s* assegno in pagamento del salario; salario, paga
pay'day' *s* giorno di paga
payee [pe'i] *s* beneficiario
pay' en'velope *s* bustapaga
payer ['pe•ər] *s* pagatore *m*
pay'load' *s* peso utile
pay'mas'ter *s* ufficiale *m* pagatore
payment ['pemənt] *s* pagamento
pay'off' *s* pagamento, regolamento; (coll) conclusione
pay' phone' *s* telefono a moneta
pay'roll' *s* lista degli impiegati; libro paga
pay' sta'tion *s* telefono pubblico
pea [pi] *s* pisello
peace [pis] *s* pace *f;* **to hold one's peace** tacere, stare zitto
peaceable ['pisəbəl] *adj* pacifico
peaceful ['pisfəl] *adj* pacifico
peace'mak'er *s* paciere *m*
peace' of mind' *s* serenità *f* d'animo
peace' pipe' *s* calumet *m* della pace
peach [pitʃ] *s* pesca; (coll) persona or cosa stupenda
peach' tree' *s* pesco
peach•y ['pitʃi] *adj* (**-ier; -iest**) (coll) stupendo
pea'cock' *s* pavone *m*
peak [pik] *s* picco; (*of traffic*) punta; (*of one's career*) sommo
peak' hour' *s* ora di punta
peak' load' *s* carico delle ore di punta, carico massimo
peal [pil] *s* (*of bells*) squillo; (*of gun*) rombo; (*of laughter*) scoppio; (*of thunder*) scroscio || *intr* scampanare, squillare
pea'nut' *s* nocciolina americana; (*plant*) arachide *f*
pea'nut but'ter *s* pasta d'arachidi
pear [per] *s* (*fruit*) pera; (*tree*) pero
pearl [pʌrl] *s* perla; (*mother-of-pearl*) madreperla; colore perlaceo
pearl' oys'ter *s* ostrica perlifera
pear' tree' *s* pero
peasant ['pezənt] *adj & s* contadino
pea'shoot'er *s* cerbottana
pea' soup' *s* minestra di piselli; (coll) nebbione *m*
peat [pit] *s* torba
pebble ['pebəl] *s* ciottolo
peck [pek] *s* beccata; misura di due galloni; **a peck of trouble** un mare di guai || *tr* beccare || *intr* beccare; **to peck at** beccucciare
peculation [,pekjə'leʃən] *s* malversazione, peculato
peculiar [pɪ'kjuljər] *adj* peculiare; (*odd*) strano
pedagogue ['pedə,gɑg] *s* pedagogo
pedagogy ['pedə,godʒi] or ['pedə,gɑdʒi] *s* pedagogia
ped•al ['pedəl] *s* pedale *m* || *v* (*pret & pp* **-aled** or **-alled;** *ger* **-aling** or **-alling**) *tr* spingere coi pedali || *intr* pedalare
pedant ['pedənt] *s* pedante *mf*
pedantic [pɪ'dæntɪk] *adj* pedantesco
pedant•ry ['pedəntri] *s* (**-ries**) pedanteria
peddle ['pedəl] *tr* vendere di porta in porta || *intr* fare il venditore ambulante
peddler ['pedlər] *s* venditore *m* or merciaiolo ambulante

pedestal ['pɛdɪstəl] *s* piedistallo
pedestrian [pɪ'destrɪ·ən] *adj* pedestre || *s* pedone *m*
pediatrics [ˌpidɪ'ætrɪks] or [ˌpɛdɪ'ætrɪks] *s* pediatria
pedigree ['pɛdɪˌgri] *s* albero genealogico; discendenza, lignaggio
pediment ['pɛdɪmənt] *s* frontone *m*
peek [pik] *s* sbirciata || *intr* sbirciare
peel [pil] *s* scorza, buccia; (*of baker*) pala || *tr* sbucciare; **to keep one's eyes peeled** (slang) tenere gli occhi aperti || *intr* pelarsi
peep [pip] *s* sbirciata; (*sound*) pigolio || *intr* guardare attraverso una fessura; (*said of birds*) pigolare; (*to begin to appear*) fare capolino
peep'hole' *s* spioncino
Peep'ing Tom' *s* guardone *m*
peep' show' *s* cosmorama *m*
peer [pɪr] *s* pari *m*, uguale *m;* (Brit) pari *m* || *intr* guardare da vicino
peerless ['pɪrlɪs] *adj* senza pari
peeve [piv] *s* (coll) seccatura, irritazione || *tr* (coll) seccare, irritare
peevish ['pivɪʃ] *adj* irritabile
peg [pɛg] *s* (*to plug holes*) zipolo; (*pin*) cavicchio; (mus) bischero; (coll) grado; **to take down a peg** (coll) fare abbassare la testa a || *v* (*pret & pp* **pegged;** *ger* **pegging**) *tr* fissare con cavicchi; (*prices*) stabilizzare || *intr*—**to peg away** lavorare di lena
peg' leg' *s* gamba di legno
Peking ['pi'kɪŋ] *s* Pechino *f*
Peking·ese [ˌpikɪ'niz] *adj* pechinese || *s* (**-ese**) pechinese *mf*
pelf [pɛlf] *s* (pej) denaro rubacchiato, maltolto
pelican ['pɛlɪkən] *s* pellicano
pellet ['pɛlɪt] *s* pallottola; (*for shotgun*) pallino; (*pill*) pillola
pell-mell ['pɛl'mɛl] *adj* confuso, disordinato || *adv* alla rinfusa
Peloponnesian [ˌpɛləpə'niʃən] *adj* & *s* peloponnesiaco
pelt [pɛlt] *s* pelle grezza; (*blow*) colpo || *tr* scagliare contro; (*to beat*) battere violentemente || *intr* battere, scrosciare
pen [pɛn] *s* (*enclosure*) recinto; (*for writing*) penna; (*pen point*) pennino || *v* (*pret & pp* **penned;** *ger* **penning**) *tr* scrivere a penna; (*to compose*) redigere || *v* (*pret & pp* **penned** or **pent;** *ger* **penning**) *tr* recintare
penalize ['pinəˌlaɪz] *tr* punire; (sports) penalizzare
penal·ty ['pɛnəlti] *s* (**-ties**) punizione; (*fine*) multa; (*for late payment*) penale *f;* **under penalty of** sotto pena di
pen'alty goal' *s* calcio di rigore
penance ['pɛnəns] *s* penitenza
penchant ['pɛnʃənt] *s* propensione
pen·cil ['pɛnsəl] *s* matita; (*of rays*) fascio || *v* (*pret & pp* **-ciled** or **-cilled;** *ger* **-ciling** or **-cilling**) *tr* scrivere a matita; (med) pennellare
pen'cil sharp'ener *s* temperalapis *m*
pendent ['pɛndənt] *adj* pendente, sospeso || *s* pendente *m*, ciondolo
pending ['pɛndɪŋ] *adj* imminente; in sospeso || *prep* durante; fino a
pendulum ['pɛndʒələm] *s* pendolo
pen'dulum bob' *s* lente *f*
penetrate ['pɛnɪˌtret] *tr* & *intr* penetrare
penguin ['pɛŋgwɪn] *s* pinguino
pen'hold'er *s* portapenne *m*
penicillin [ˌpɛnɪ'sɪlɪŋ] *s* penicillina
peninsula [pe'nɪnsələ] *s* penisola
peninsular [pə'nɪnsələr] *adj* & *s* peninsulare
penitence ['pɛnɪtəns] *s* penitenza
penitent ['pɛnɪtənt] *adj* & *s* penitente *mf*
pen'knife' *s* (**-knives**) temperino
penmanship ['pɛnmənˌʃɪp] *s* calligrafia
pen' name' *s* nome *m* di penna, pseudonimo
pennant ['pɛnənt] *s* pennone *m*
penniless ['pɛnɪlɪs] *adj* povero in canna, senza un soldo
pennon ['pɛnən] *s* pennone *m*
pen·ny ['pɛni] *s* (**-nies**) (U.S.A.) centesimo || *s* (**penee** [pens]) (Brit) penny *m*
pen'ny pinch'er ['pɪntʃər] *s* spilorcio
pen' pal' *s* amico corrispondente
pen'point' *s* pennino; (*of ball-point pen*) punta
pension ['pɛnʃən] *s* pensione || *tr* pensionare, mettere in pensione
pensioner ['pɛnʃənər] *s* pensionato
pensive ['pɛnsɪv] *adj* pensieroso
Pentecost ['pɛntɪˌkɔst] or ['pɛntɪˌkɑst] *s* la Pentecoste
penthouse ['pɛntˌhaus] *s* appartamento di lusso sul tetto; tettoia
pent-up ['pɛntˌʌp] *adj* represso
penult ['pinʌlt] *s* penultima
penum·bra [pɪ'nʌmbrə] *s* (**-brae** [bri] or **-bras**) penombra
penurious [pɪ'nurɪ·əs] *adj* taccagno, meschino; indigente
penury ['pɛnjəri] *s* taccagneria; estrema povertà, miseria
pen'wip'er *s* nettapenne *m*
people ['pipəl] *spl* popolo, gente *f;* (*relatives*) famiglia; gente *f* del popolo; si, e.g., **people say** si dice || *ssg* (**peoples**) nazione, popolazione || *tr* popolare
pep [pɛp] *s* (coll) animo, brio || *v* (*pret & pp* **pepped;** *ger* **pepping**) *tr*—**to pep up** (coll) dar animo a
pepper ['pɛpər] *s* pepe *m* || *tr* pepare; (*to pelt*) tempestare
pep'per·box' *s* pepaiola
pep'per·mint' *s* menta piperita
per [pʌr] *prep* per; (*for each*) il, e.g., **three dollars per meter** tre dollari il metro; **as per** secondo
perambulator [pər'æmbjəˌletər] *s* carrozzella, carrozzino
per capita [pər 'kæpɪtə] per persona, a testa
perceive [pər'siv] *tr* percepire
percent [pər'sɛnt] *s* percento, per cento
percentage [pər'sɛntɪdʒ] *s* percento, percentuale *f;* (coll) vantaggio
perception [pər'sepʃən] *s* percezione

perch [pʌrtʃ] *s* (*roost*) posatoio; (*horizontal rod*) ballatoio; (ichth) pesce persico || *intr* appollaiarsi
percolator ['pʌrkə ,letər] *s* caffettiera filtro a circolazione
percus'sion cap' [pər'kʌʃən] *s* capsula di percussione
per diem [pər 'daɪ·əm] *s* assegno giornaliero
perdition [pər'dɪʃən] *s* perdizione
perennial [pə'renɪ·əl] *adj* perenne || *s* pianta perenne
perfect ['pʌrfɪkt] *adj & s* perfetto || [pər'fɛkt] *tr* perfezionare
perfidious [pər'fɪdɪ·əs] *adj* perfido
perfi·dy ['pʌrfɪdi] *s* (**-dies**) perfidia
perforate ['pʌrfə ,ret] *tr* perforare
perforation [,pʌrfə'reʃən] *s* perforazione; (*of postage stamp*) dentellatura
perforce [pər'fors] *adv* per forza, necessariamente
perform [pər'fɔrm] *tr* (*a task*) eseguire; (*a promise*) adempiere; (*to enact*) rappresentare || *intr* recitare; (*said, e.g., of a machine*) funzionare
performance [pər'fɔrməns] *s* esecuzione; (*of a machine*) funzionamento; (*deed*) atto di prodezza; (theat) rappresentazione
performer [pər'fɔrmər] *s* esecutore *m;* attore *m;* acrobata *mf*
perform'ing arts' *spl* arti *fpl* dello spettacolo
perfume ['pʌrfjum] *s* profumo || [pər'fjum] *tr* profumare
perfumer·y [pər'fjuməri] *s* (**-ies**) profumeria
perfunctory [pər'fʌŋktəri] *adj* superficiale, pro forma; indifferente
perhaps [pər'hæps] *adv* forse
per·il ['perəl] *s* pericolo || *v* (*pret & pp* **-iled** or **-illed;** *ger* **-iling** or **-illing**) *tr* mettere in pericolo
perilous ['perɪləs] *adj* pericoloso
period ['pɪrɪ·əd] *s* periodo; mestruazione; (*in school*) ora; (sports) tempo; (gram) punto
pe'riod cos'tume *s* costume *m* dell'epoca
periodic [,pɪrɪ'ɑdɪk] *adj* periodico
periodical [,pɪrɪ'ɑdɪkəl] *adj & s* periodico
peripher·y [pə'rɪfəri] *s* (**-ies**) periferia
periscope ['perɪ ,skop] *s* periscopio
perish ['perɪʃ] *intr* perire
perishable ['perɪʃəbəl] *adj* deteriorabile
periwig ['perɪ ,wɪg] *s* parrucca
perjure ['pʌrdʒər] *tr*—**to perjure oneself** spergiurare, giurare il falso
perju·ry ['pʌrdʒəri] *s* (**-ries**) spergiuro
perk [pʌrk] *tr* (*the head, the ears*) alzare; **to perk oneself up** agghindarsi || *intr*—**to perk up** ringalluzzirsi
permanence ['pʌrmənəns] *s* permanenza
permanen·cy ['pʌrmənənsi] *s* (**-cies**) permanenza
permanent ['pʌrmənənt] *adj* permanente || *s* permanente *f,* ondulazione permanente
per'manent fix'ture *s* cosa or persona permanente
per'manent ten'ure *s* inamovibilità *f*
per'manent way' *s* (rr) sede *f* stradale ed armamento
permeate ['pʌrmɪ ,et] *tr* permeare || *intr* permearsi
permissible [pər'mɪsɪbəl] *adj* permissibile
permission [pər'mɪʃən] *s* permesso
per·mit ['pʌrmɪt] *s* permesso; patente *f,* licenza || [pər'mɪt] *v* (*pret & pp* **-mitted;** *ger* **-mitting**) *tr* permettere
permute [pər'mjut] *tr* permutare
pernicious [pər'nɪʃəs] *adj* pernicioso
pernickety [pər'nɪkɪti] *adj* (coll) incontentabile, meticoloso
perorate ['perə ,ret] *intr* perorare
peroxide [pər'ɑksaɪd] *s* perossido; perossido d'idrogeno
perox'ide blonde' *s* bionda ossigenata
perpendicular [,pʌrpən'dɪkjələr] *adj & s* perpendicolare *f*
perpetrate ['pʌrpɪ ,tret] *tr* (*a crime*) perpetrare; (*a blunder*) commettere
perpetual [pər'pɛtʃʊ·əl] *adj* perpetuo
perpetuate [pər'pɛtʃʊ ,et] *tr* perpetuare
perplex [pər'plɛks] *tr* lasciare perplesso
perplexed [pər'plɛkst] *adj* perplesso
perplexi·ty [pər'plɛksɪti] *s* (**-ties**) perplessità *f*
per se [pər 'si] di per se
persecute ['pʌrsɪ ,kjut] *tr* perseguitare
persevere [,pərsɪ'vɪr] *intr* perseverare
Persian ['pʌrʒən] *adj & s* persiano
Per'sian Gulf' *s* Golfo Persico
persimmon [pər'sɪmən] *s* diospiro virginiano; cachi *m*
persist [pər'sɪst] or [pər'zɪst] *intr* persistere
persistent [pər'sɪstənt] or [pər'zɪstənt] *adj* persistente
person ['pʌrsən] *s* persona; **no person** nessuno
personage ['pʌrsənɪdʒ] *s* personaggio; persona
personal ['pʌrsənəl] *adj* personale; (*goods*) mobile || *s* inserzione personale; trafiletto di società
personali·ty [,pʌrsə'nælɪti] *s* (**-ties**) personalità *f;* offesa personale
personal'ity cult' *s* culto della personalità
per'sonal prop'erty *s* beni *mpl* mobili
personi·fy [pər'sɑnɪ ,faɪ] *v* (*pret & pp* **-fied**) *tr* personificare
personnel [,pʌrsə'nɛl] *s* personale *m*
per'son-to-per'son call' *s* (telp) chiamata con preavviso
perspective [pər'spɛktɪv] *s* prospettiva
perspicacious [,pʌrspɪ'keʃəs] *adj* perspicace
perspire [pər'spaɪr] *intr* sudare
persuade [pər'swed] *tr* persuadere
persuasion [pər'sweʒən] *s* persuasione; fede religiosa
pert [pʌrt] *adj* impertinente, sfacciato; vivace
pertain [pər'ten] *intr* appartenere; (*to have reference*) riferirsi
pertinacious [,pʌrtɪ'neʃəs] *adj* pertinace

pertinent ['pʌrtɪnənt] *adj* pertinente
perturb [pər'tʌrb] *tr* perturbare
Peru [pə'ru] *s* il Perù
perusal [pə'ruzəl] *s* attenta lettura
peruse [pə'ruz] *tr* leggere attentamente
pervade [pər'ved] *tr* pervadere
perverse [pər'vʌrs] *adj* perverso; (*obstinate*) ostinato
perversion [pər'vʌrʒən] *s* perversione
perversi·ty [pər'vʌrsɪti] *s* (**-ties**) perversità *f;* contrarietà *f*
pervert ['pʌrvərt] *s* pervertito, degenerato || [pər'vʌrt] *tr* pervertire, degenerare
pes·ky ['peski] *adj* (**-kier; -kiest**) (coll) noioso, molesto
pessimism ['pesɪ,mɪzəm] *s* pessimismo
pessimist ['pesɪmɪst] *s* pessimista *mf*
pessimistic [,pesɪ'mɪstɪk] *adj* pessimistico
pest [pest] *s* peste *f,* pestilenza; insetto; animale nocivo; (*person*) peste *f,* seccatore *m*
pester ['pestər] *tr* seccare, annoiare
pest'house' *s* lazzaretto
pesticide ['pestɪ,saɪd] *s* insetticida *m*
pestiferous [pest'tɪfərəs] *adj* pestifero
pestilence ['pestɪləns] *s* pestilenza
pestle ['pesəl] *s* pestello
pet [pet] *s* animale favorito; beniamino || *v* (*pret & pp* **petted;** *ger* **petting**) *tr* accarezzare || *intr* (coll) pomiciare
petal ['petəl] *s* petalo
petard [pɪ'tɑrd] *s* petardo
pet'cock' *s* chiavetta
Peter ['pitər] *s* Pietro; **to rob Peter to pay Paul** fare un buco per tapparne un altro || *intr*—**to peter out** (coll) affievolirsi
petition [pɪ'tɪʃən] *s* petizione || *tr* rivolgere un'istanza a
pet' name' *s* nomignolo vezzeggiativo
Petrarch ['pitrɑrk] *s* Petrarca *m*
petri·fy ['petrɪ,faɪ] *v* (*pret & pp* **-fied**) *tr* pietrificare || *intr* pietrificarsi
petrol ['petrəl] *s* (Brit) benzina
petroleum [pɪ'trolɪ·əm] *s* petrolio
pet' shop' *s* negozio di animali domestici
petticoat ['petɪ,kot] *s* sottoveste *f;* (coll) sottana, gonnella
pet·ty ['peti] *adj* (**-tier; -tiest**) insignificante, minore; meschino
pet'ty cash' *s* cassa delle piccole spese
pet'ty lar'ceny *s* furterello
pet'ty of'ficer *s* (nav) sottufficiale *m* di marina
petulant ['petjələnt] *adj* stizzoso, irritabile
pew [pju] *s* banco di chiesa
pewter ['pjutər] *s* peltro; oggetti *mpl* di peltro
phalanx ['felæŋks] or ['fælæŋks] *s* falange *f*
phantasm ['fæntæzəm] *s* fantasma *m*
phantom ['fæntəm] *s* fantasma *m*
Pharaoh ['fero] *s* Faraone *m*
pharisee ['færɪ,si] *s* fariseo || **Pharisee** *s* fariseo
pharmaceutical [,fɑrmə'sutɪkəl] *adj* farmaceutico
pharmacist ['fɑrməsɪst] *s* farmacista *mf*
pharma·cy ['fɑrməsi] *s* (**-cies**) farmacia
pharynx ['færɪŋks] *s* faringe *f*
phase [fez] *s* fase *f* || *tr* mettere in fase; sincronizzare; **to phase in** mettere in operazione gradualmente; **to phase out** eliminare gradualmente
pheasant ['fezənt] *s* fagiano
phenobarbital [,fino'bɑrbɪ,tæl] *s* acido fenil-etilbarbiturico, barbiturato
phenomenal [fɪ'nɑmɪnəl] *adj* fenomenale
phenome·non [fɪ'nɑmɪ,nɑn] *s* (**-na** [nə]) fenomeno
phial ['faɪ·əl] *s* fiala
philanderer [fɪ'lændərər] *s* donnaiolo
philanthropist [fɪ'lænθrəpɪist] *s* filantropo
philanthro·py [fɪ'lænθrəpi] *s* (**-pies**) filantropia
philatelist [fɪ'lætəlɪst] *s* filatelico
philately [fi'lætəli] *s* filatelia
Philip ['fɪlɪp] *s* Filippo
Philippine ['fɪlɪ,pin] *adj* filippino || **Philippines** *spl* isole *fpl* Filippine
Philistine [fɪ'lɪstin], ['fɪlɪ,stin] or ['fɪlɪ,staɪn] *adj & s* filisteo
philologist [fɪ'lɑlədʒɪst] *s* filologo
philology [fɪ'lɑlədʒi] *s* filologia
philosopher [fɪ'lɑsəfər] *s* filosofo
philosophic(al) [,fɪlə'sɑfɪk(əl)] *adj* filosofico
philoso·phy [fɪ'lɑsəfi] *s* (**-phies**) filosofia
philter ['fɪltər] *s* filtro
phlebitis [flɪ'baɪtɪs] *s* flebite *f*
phlegm [flem] *s* (*secretion*) muco, catarro; (*self-possession*) flemma; apatia
phlegmatic(al) [fleg'mætɪk(əl)] *adj* flemmatico
Phoebus ['fibəs] *s* Febo
Phoenician [fɪ'nɪʃən] or [fɪ'niʃən] *adj & s* fenicio
phoenix ['finɪks] *s* fenice *f*
phone [fon] *s* (coll) telefono || *tr & intr* (coll) telefonare
phone' call' *s* chiamata telefonica
phonetic [fo'netɪk] *adj* fonetico || **phonetics** *s* fonetica
phonograph ['fonə,græf] or ['fonə,grɑf] *s* fonografo
phonology [fə'nɑlədʒi] *s* fonologia
pho·ny ['foni] *adj* (**-nier; -niest**) (coll) falso || *s* (**-nies**) (coll) frode *f;* (*person*) (coll) impostore *m*
phosphate ['fɑsfet] *s* fosfato
phosphorescent [,fɑsfə'resənt] *adj* fosforescente
phospho·rus ['fɑsfərəs] *s* (**-ri** [,raɪ]) fosforo
pho·to ['foto] *s* (**-tos**) (coll) foto *f*
photo·cop·y ['fotə,kɑpi] *s* (**-ies**) fotocopia || *tr* fotocopiare
pho'toelec'tric cell' [,foto·ɪ'lektrɪk] *s* cellula fotoelettrica
photoengraving [,foto·en'grevɪŋ] *s* fotoincisione
pho'to fin'ish *s* photofinish *m,* arrivo con fotografia

photogenic [ˌfotoˈdʒɛnɪk] *adj* fotogenico
photograph [ˈfotəˌgræf] or [ˈfotəˌgrɑf] *s* fotografia ‖ *tr* fotografare ‖ *intr*—**to photograph well** riuscire in fotografia
photographer [fəˈtɑgrəfər] *s* fotografo
photography [fəˈtɑgrəfi] *s* fotografia
photojournalism [ˌfotəˈdʒʌrnəˌlɪzəm] *s* giornalismo fotografico
pho'to•play' *s* dramma adattato per il cinematografo
photostat [ˈfotəˌstæt] *s* (trademark) copia fotostatica ‖ *tr* riprodurre fotostaticamente
phototube [ˈfotəˌtjub] or [ˈfotəˌtub] *s* fototubo
phrase [frez] *s* (gram) locuzione; (mus) frase *f* ‖ *tr* esprimere, formulare ‖ *intr* (mus) fraseggiare
phrenology [frɪˈnɑlədʒi] *s* frenologia
Phyllis [ˈfɪlɪs] *s* Fillide *f*
phy•lum [ˈfaɪləm] *s* (**-la** [lə]) phylum *m*, tipo
phys•ic [ˈfɪzɪk] *s* purgante *m* ‖ *v* (*pret & pp* **-icked**; *ger* **-icking**) *tr* dare il purgante a, purgare
physical [ˈfɪzɪkəl] *adj* fisico
physician [fɪˈzɪʃən *s* medico
physicist [ˈfɪzɪsɪst] *s* fisico
physics [ˈfɪzɪks] *s* fisica
physiognomy [ˌfɪzɪˈɑgnəmi] or [ˌfɪzɪˈɑnəmi] *s* fisionomia
physiological [ˌfɪzɪ·əˈlɑdʒɪkəl] *adj* fisiologico
physiology [ˌfɪzɪˈɑlədʒi] *s* fisiologia
physique [fɪˈzɪk] *s* fisico
pi [paɪ] *s* (math) pi greco; (typ) tipi scartati ‖ *v* (*pret & pp* **pied**; *ger* **piing**) *tr* (typ) scompaginare, scomporre
pian•o [pɪˈæno] *s* (**-os**) piano
picaresque [ˌpɪkəˈrɛsk] *adj* picaresco
picayune [ˌpɪkəˈjun] *adj* meschino, minore, di poca importanza
picco•lo [ˈpɪkəˌlo] *s* (**-los**) ottavino
pick [pɪk] *s* (*tool*) piccone *m*; (*choice*) scelta; (*the best*) fiore *m*; (mus) plettro ‖ *tr* scavare; (*to scratch at*) grattare; (*to gather*) cogliere; (*to pluck*) spennare; (*to pull apart*) separare; (*one's teeth*) stuzzicarsi; (*a bone*) rosicchiare; (*to choose*) scegliere; (*a lock*) scassinare; (*a pocket*) tagliare, rubare; (mus) pizzicare; **to pick a fight** attaccare briga; **to pick faults** trovare a ridire; **to pick out** scegliere; distinguere; discriminare; **to pick s.o. to pieces** (coll) tagliare i panni addosso a qlcu; **to pick up** sollevare; (*to find*) trovare; (*to learn*) arrivare a sapere; (*a radio signal*) captare; (*speed*) acquistare ‖ *intr* usare il piccone; **to pick at** (*food*) spilluzzicare; (coll) criticare; **to pick on** (coll) scegliere; (coll) criticare; **to pick up** (coll) migliorarsi
pick'ax' *s* piccone *m*
picket [ˈpɪkɪt] *s* picchetto ‖ *tr* rinchiudere con palizzata; (*to hitch*) legare; (*to post*) (mil) mettere di picchetto; (*e.g., a factory*) picchettare
pick'et fence' *s* steccato
pick'et line' *s* corteo di scioperanti; corteo di dimostranti
pickle [ˈpɪkəl] *s* salamoia, sottaceto; (*cucumber*) cetriolo sottaceto; **to get into a pickle** (coll) cacciarsi in un imbroglio ‖ *tr* mettere sottaceto; (metallurgy) decapare
pick-me-up [ˈpɪkmiˌʌp] *s* (coll) spuntino; (coll) bevanda stimulante
pick'pock'et *s* borseggiatore *m*, borsaiolo
pick'up' *s* sollevamento; (*in speed*) accelerazione; (*of phonograph*) pick-up *m*, fonorivelatore *m*; (aut) camioncino; (coll) persona conosciuta per caso; (coll) miglioramento
pick'-up-sticks' *spl* sciangai *m*
pic•nic [ˈpɪknɪk] *s* picnic *m* ‖ *v* (*pret & pp* **-nicked**; *ger* **-nicking**) *intr* fare merenda all'aperto
pictorial [pɪkˈtorɪ·əl] *adj* pittorico; illustrato; vivido ‖ *s* rivista illustrata
picture [ˈpɪktʃər] *s* illustrazione, disegno; (*painting*) quadro, dipinto; (*of a person*) ritratto; fotografia; film *m*, pellicola ‖ *tr* fare il ritratto di; disegnare; dipingere; fotografare; descrivere; immaginare, immaginarsi
pic'ture frame' *s* cornice *f*
pic'ture gal'lery *s* pinacoteca, galleria di quadri, quadreria
pic'ture post' card' *s* cartolina illustrata
pic'ture show' *s* cinematografo; mostra di quadri
picturesque [ˌpɪktʃəˈrɛsk] *adj* pittoresco
pic'ture tube' *s* tubo televisivo
pic'ture win'dow *s* finestra panoramica
piddling [ˈpɪdlɪŋ] *adj* insignificante
pie [paɪ] *s* (*with fruit*) torta; (*with meat*) timballo; (orn) pica ‖ *v* (*pret & pp* **pied**; *ger* **pieing**) *tr* (typ) scompaginare, scomporre
piece [pis] *s* pezzo; (*e.g., of cloth*) pezza; **a piece of advice** un consiglio; **a piece of baggage** un collo; **a piece of furniture** un mobile *m*; **a piece of news** una notizia; **by the piece** a cottimo; **to break to pieces** frantumare; frantumarsi; **to cut to pieces** fare a pezzi; **to fall to pieces** cadere a pezzi; **to fly to pieces** rompersi in mille pezzi; **to give s.o. a piece of one's mind** dirne a qlcu di tutti i colori; **to go to pieces** perdere il controllo di sé stesso; **to take to pieces** confutare punto per punto ‖ *tr* rappezzare, mettere insieme ‖ *intr* (coll) mangiucchiare
piece'meal' *adv* poco a poco
piece'work' *s* lavoro a cottimo
piece'work'er *s* cottimista *mf*
pier [pɪr] *s* (*of a bridge*) pila; (*over water*) molo; (archit) pilastro, pilone *m*
pierce [pɪrs] *tr* forare, bucare; penetrare; (*to stab*) trapassare ‖ *intr* penetrare
piercing [ˈpɪrsɪŋ] *adj* acuto; (*eyes*) penetrante; (*pain*) lancinante

pier' glass' *s* specchiera
pie•ty ['paɪ-əti] *s* (**-ties**) pietà *f*
piffle ['pɪfəl] *s* (coll) fesserie *fpl*
pig [pɪg] *s* maiale *m*, porco; (metallurgy) lingotto, massello; **to buy a pig in the poke** comprare il gatto nel sacco
pigeon ['pɪdʒən] *s* piccione *m*
pi'geon•hole' *s* nicchia nella piccionaia; (*for filing*) casella ‖ *tr* (*to lay aside for later time*) archiviare; (*to shelve, e.g., an application*) insabbiare
pi'geon house' *s* colombaia, piccionaia
piggish ['pɪgɪʃ] *adj* porcino, maialesco
pig'gy•back' ['pɪgi ˌbæk] *adv* sulle spalle, sulla schiena; (rr) su carrello stradale per trasporto carri
pig'head'ed *adj* ostinato, cocciuto
pig' i'ron *s* ghisa, ferro grezzo
pigment ['pɪgmənt] *s* pigmento ‖ *tr* pigmentare ‖ *intr* pigmentarsi
pig'pen' *s* porcile *m*
pig'skin' *s* pelle *f* di maiale; (coll) pallone *m* da football, sfera di cuoio
pig'sty' *s* (**-sties**) porcile *m*
pig'tail' *s* codino; (*of girl*) treccia; treccia di tabacco
pike [paɪk] *s* (*weapon*) picca; (*road*) autostrada; (ichth) luccio
piker ['paɪkər] *s* (coll) uomo piccino
pile [paɪl] *s* (*heap*) pila; (*for burning a corpse*) pira; (*large building*) mole *f;* (*beam*) palo; (*of carpet*) pelo; (*of money*) (slang) gruzzolo; (coll) mucchio; **piles** emorroidi *fpl* ‖ *tr* ammucchiare, accumulare; **to pile up** ammonticchiare ‖ *intr* accumularsi; **to pile into** pigiarsi in; **to pile up** accumularsi
pile' driv'er *s* battipalo, berta
pilfer ['pɪlfər] *tr & intr* rubacchiare
pilgrim ['pɪlgrɪm] *s* pellegrino
pilgrimage ['pɪlgrɪmɪdʒ] *s* pellegrinaggio
pill [pɪl] *s* pillola; amara pillola; (coll) rompiscatole *mf;* **to sugar-coat the pill** addolcire la pillola
pillage ['pɪlɪdʒ] *s* saccheggio, rapina ‖ *tr & intr* saccheggiare, rapinare
pillar ['pɪlər] *s* pilastro, colonna; **from pillar to post** da Erode a Pilato
pill'box' *s* scatoletta per le pillole; (mil) casamatta
pillo•ry ['pɪləri] *s* (**-ries**) gogna, berlina ‖ *v* (*pret & pp* **-ried**) *tr* mettere alla berlina
pillow ['pɪlo] *s* cuscino, guanciale *m*
pil'low•case' *s* federa
pilot ['paɪlət] *adj* pilota ‖ *s* pilota *m;* (*of locomotive*) respingente *m* ‖ *tr* pilotare
pi'lot light' *s* fiammella automatica
pimp [pɪmp] *s* ruffiano, lenone *m*
pimple ['pɪmpəl] *s* bitorzolo
pim•ply ['pɪmpli] *adj* (**-plier; -pliest**) bitorzoluto
pin [pɪn] *s* (*of metal*) spillo; (*peg*) caviglia; (*adornment*) spilla; (*linchpin*) acciarino; (*of key*) mappa; (*clothespin*) molletta; (*bowling pin*) birillo; **to be on pins and needles** stare sulle spine ‖ *tr* appuntare; (*to hold*) immobilizzare; **to pin s.o. down** forzare qlcu a rivelare i propri piani **to pin s.th on s.o.** (coll) dare la colpa a qlcu per qlco
pinafore ['pɪnə ˌfor] *s* grembiulino
pinaster [paɪ'næstər] *s* pino marittimo
pin'ball machine' *s* biliardino
pince-nez ['pæns ˌne] *s* occhiali *mpl* a stringinaso
pincers ['pɪnsərz] *ssg* or *spl* tenaglie *fpl;* (zool) pinze *fpl*
pinch [pɪntʃ] *s* (*squeeze*) pizzicotto; (*of tobacco*) presa; (*of salt*) pizzico; (*hardship*) strettoia; **in a pinch** in caso di necessità ‖ *tr* stringere, pizzicare; (*to press*) comprimere; ridurre alle strettezze; (slang) rubare; (slang) arrestare ‖ *intr* stringere; (*to be stingy*) fare l'avaro
pin'cush'ion *s* puntaspilli *m*
pine [paɪn] *s* pino ‖ *intr*—**to pine away** struggersi; **to pine for** spasimare per
pine'ap'ple *s* ananas *m*
pine' cone' *s* pigna
pine' nee'dle *s* ago del pino
ping [pɪŋ] *s* rumore secco; rumore metallico ‖ *intr* fare un rumore secco or metallico
pin'head' *s* capocchia di spillo; (slang) testa quadra
pin'hole' *s* forellino
pink [pɪŋk] *adj* rosa ‖ *s* color *m* rosa; condizione perfetta; (bot) garofano ‖ *tr* orlare a zig-zag; (*to stab*) perforare
pin' mon'ey *s* denaro per le piccole spese
pinnacle ['pɪnəkəl] *s* pinnacolo
pin'point' *adj* di precisione ‖ *s* punta di spillo ‖ *tr* mettere in rilievo
pin'prick' *s* puntura di spillo
pint [paɪnt] *s* pinta
pintle ['pɪntəl] *s* maschietto
pin'up' *s* pin-up-girl *f*
pin'wheel' *s* girandola
pioneer [ˌpaɪ-ə'nɪr] *s* pioniere *m* ‖ *tr* aprire la via a ‖ *intr* fare il pioniere
pioneering [ˌpaɪ-ə'nɪrɪŋ] *adj* pioneristico
pious ['paɪ-əs] *adj* pio, devoto
pip [pɪp] *s* (*seed*) seme *m;* (vet) pipita
pipe [paɪp] *s* tubo, canna; (*of stove*) cannone *m;* (*for smoking*) pipa; (mus) legno; (mus) cornamusa ‖ *tr* suonare; cantare ad alta voce; fischiare; condurre in una tubatura; munire di tubatura ‖ *intr* suonare la zampogna; **to pipe down** (slang) stare zitto
pipe' clean'er *s* scovolino
pipe' dream' *s* castello in aria
pipe' line' *s* oleodotto; (fig) fonte *f* (d'informazioni)
pipe' or'gan *s* organo a canne
piper ['paɪpər] *s* zampognaro; **to pay the piper** pagare lo scotto
pipe' wrench' *s* chiave *f* per tubi
piping ['paɪpɪŋ] *adj* (*voice*) acuto; (*sound*) di cornamusa ‖ *s* tubatura; suono di cornamuse; suono acuto; (*on cakes*) fregio; (*on garments*) cor-

doncino ornamentale || *adv*—**piping hot** scottante, bollente
pippin ['pɪpɪn] *s* mela renetta; (*seed*) seme *m;* (fig) gran brava persona
piquant ['pikənt] *adj* piccante
pique [pik] *s* picca, ripicco || *tr* offendere, eccitare
pira•cy ['paɪrəsi] *s* (**-cies**) pirateria
pirate ['paɪrɪt] *s* pirata *mf* || *tr* derubare; (*a book*) svaligiare, pubblicare illegalmente || *intr* pirateggiare
pirouette [,pɪru'ɛt] *s* piroetta || *intr* piroettare
Pisces ['paɪsiz] or ['pɪsiz] *s* (astr) Pesci *mpl*
pistol ['pɪstəl] *s* pistola
piston ['pɪstən] *s* pistone *m*
pis'ton displace'ment *s* cilindrata
pis'ton ring' *s* segmento elastico
pis'ton rod' *s* (*of a steam engine*) biella d'accoppiamento; (*of a motor*) asta del pistone, biella
pis'ton stroke' *s* corsa dello stantuffo
pit [pɪt] *s* (*in the ground*) buca; (*trap*) trappola; (*of fruit*) nocciolo; (*of stomach*) bocca; (*scar*) buttero; (*in exchange*) recinto delle grida; (*for fights*) arena; (theat) platea; (min) miniera; (aut) fossa di riparazione || *v* (*pret & pp* **pitted;** *ger* **pitting**) *tr* infossare; butterare; opporre; (*to remove pits from*) snocciolare
pitch [pɪtʃ] *s* (*black sticky substance*) pece *f;* (*throw*) lancio; (*of a roof*) pendenza, inclinazione; (*of a boat*) beccheggio; (*of a screw*) passo; (*of sound*) altezza || *tr* lanciare; (*a tent*) rizzare || *intr* beccheggiare; **to pitch in** (coll) mettersi al lavoro; (coll) cominciare a mangiare
pitch' ac'cent *s* accento di altezza
pitch' at'titude *s* assetto longitudinale
pitch'-dark' *adj* nero come la pece
pitched' bat'tle *s* battaglia campale
pitcher ['pɪtʃər] *s* brocca; (baseball) lanciatore *m*
pitch'fork' *s* forca, tridente *m;* **to rain pitchforks** (coll) piovere a dirotto
pitch' pipe' *s* (mus) corista *m*
pit'fall' *s* trappola, trabocchetto
pith [pɪθ] *s* midollo; (*strength*) (fig) forza; (fig) succo, essenza
pith•y ['piθi] *adj* (**-ier; -iest**) midolloso; succoso, essenziale
pitiful ['pɪtɪfəl] *adj* pietoso
pitiless ['pɪtɪlɪs] *adj* spietato
pit•y ['pɪti] *s* (**-ies**) pietà *f;* **it is a pity that** è un peccato che; **what a pity!** che peccato! || *v* (*pret & pp* **-ied**) *tr* aver pietà di
Pius ['paɪ-əs] *s* Pio
pivot ['pɪvət] *s* asse *m,* perno; (fig) asse *m* || *tr* imperniare || *intr* imperniarsi; **to pivot on** fare perno su; dipendere da
placard ['plækɑrd] *s* manifesto, affisso || *tr* affiggere
place [ples] *s* luogo; locale *m;* (*court*) piazzetta; (*short street*) vicolo; residenza; sito, luogo, località *f;* (*point*) punto; (*space occupied*) posto; (*office*) posto, impiego; **in no place** da nessuna parte; **in place** a posto; **in place of** al posto di, invece di; **in the first place** in primo luogo; **in the next place** in secondo luogo; **to know one's place** saper stare al proprio posto; **to take place** aver luogo || *tr* piazzare, mettere; (*to find employment for*) collocare; (*to identify*) ravvisare || *intr* (sports) piazzarsi
place•bo [plə'sibo] *s* (**-bos** or **-boes**) rimedio fittizio
place' card' *s* segnaposto
placement ['plesmənt] *s* (*e.g., of furniture*) collocazione; (*employment*) collocamento
place' name' *s* toponimo
place' of busi'ness *s* ufficio, negozio
placid ['plæsɪd] *adj* placido
plagiarism ['pledʒə,rɪzəm] *s* plagio
plagiarize ['pledʒə,raɪz] *tr* plagiare
plague [pleg] *s* peste bubbonica; (*widespread affliction*) piaga, flagello || *tr* infestare, appestare; tormentare
plaid [plæd] *s* tessuto scozzese
plain [plen] *adj* piano; aperto; evidente, esplicito; semplice; (*undyed*) naturale; comune, ordinario; **in plain English** senz'ambagi; **in plain view** di fronte a tutti || *s* pianura
plain'-clothes' man' *s* (**-men'**) agente *m* in borghese
plains'man *s* (**-men**) abitante *m* della pianura
plaintiff ['plentɪf] *s* querelante *mf*
plaintive ['plentɪv] *adj* lamentevole
plan [plæn] *s* piano, progetto || *v* (*pret & pp* **planned;** *ger* **planning**) *tr & intr* progettare
plane [plen] *adj* piano || *m* piano; (*tool*) pialla; (aer) aeroplano; (aer) ala d'aeroplano; (bot) platano || *tr* piallare || *intr* andare in areoplano
plane' sick'ness *s* male *m* d'aria
planet ['plænɪt] *s* pianeta *m*
plane' tree' *s* platano
plan'ing mill' *s* officina di piallatura
plank [plæŋk] *s* tavola, asse *m;* (*of political party*) piattaforma || *tr* coprire d'assi; cucinare sulla graticola e servire sul tagliere; **to plank down** (*e.g., money*) (coll) snocciolare
plant [plænt] or [plɑnt] *s* (*factory*) impianto, stabilimento; (*e.g;, of a college*) complesso di edifici; (bot) pianta; (mach) apparato motore; (slang) trappola || *tr* (*e.g., a tree*) piantare; (*seeds*) seminare; (*to stock*) fornire
plantation [plæn'teʃən] *s* piantagione
planter ['plæntər] *s* piantatore *m;* (mach) piantatrice *f*
plaster ['plæstər] or ['plɑstər] *s* (*gypsum*) gesso; (*mixture to cover walls*) intonaco, malta; (*poultice*) impiastro || *tr* ingessare; intonacare; impiastrare; (*with posters*) affiggere, ricoprire
plas'ter•board' *s* cartone *m* di gesso
plas'ter cast' *s* (sculp) gesso; (surg) ingessatura
plas'ter of Par'is *s* gesso, stucco
plastic ['plæstɪk] *adj & s* plastico

plate [plet] *s* (*dish*) piatto; (*sheet of metal*) placca, piastra; (*thin sheet of metal*) lamina; (*of vacuum tube*) placca; (*of auto license*) targa; (*of condenser*) armatura; (*tableware*) vasellame *m* d'argento, vasellame *m* d'oro; dentiera; (baseball) casa base; (phot) lastra; (typ) cliché *m* || *tr* (*with gold or silver*) placcare; (*with armor*) blindare, corazzare
plateau [plæ'to] *s* altipiano
plate' glass' *s* lastrone *m*
platen ['plætən] *s* rullo
platform ['plæt,fɔrm] *s* piattaforma; (*for speaker*) tribuna, palco; (*for passengers*) (rr) marciapiede *m;* (*at end of car*) (rr) piattaforma
plat'form car' *s* (rr) pianale *m*
platinum ['plætɪnəm] *s* platino
plat'inum blonde' *s* bionda platinata
platitude ['plætɪ,tjud] or ['plætɪ,tud] *s* trivialità *f*, banalità *f*
Plato ['pleto] *s* Platone *m*
platoon [plə'tun] *s* plotone *m*
platter ['plætər] *s* piatto di portata; (slang) disco di grammofono
plausible ['plɔzɪbəl] *adj* plausibile; (*person*) credibile, attendibile
play [ple] *s* gioco; libertà *f* d'azione; recreazione; turno, volta; (theat) dramma *m;* (mach) gioco || *tr* giocare; giocare contro; causare, produrre; (*a drama*) rappresentare; (*a character*) fare la parte di; (*to wield*) esercitare; (mus) suonare; **to play back** (*e.g., a tape*) riprodurre; **to play down** diminuire l'importanza di; **to play one off against another** mettere uno contro l'altro; **to play up** dare importanza a || *intr* giocare; (*to act*) giocare, comportarsi; (theat) recitare; (mus) suonare; (mach) aver gioco; **to play on** continuare a giocare; continuare a suonare; valersi di; **to play safe** non prendere rischi; **to play sick** fare il malato; **to play up to** fare la corte a
play'back' *s* riproduzione; apparechiatura di riproduzione
play'bill' *s* (theat) programma *m*
play'boy' *s* playboy *m*, gaudente *m*
player ['ple·ər] *s* giocatore *m;* (theat) attore *m;* (mus) suonatore *m*
play'er pian'o *s* pianola
playful ['plefəl] *adj* giocoso
playgoer ['ple,go·ər] *s* frequentatore *m* del teatro
play'ground' *s* parco di ricreazione; (*resort*) posto di villeggiatura
play'house' *s* teatro; casa di bambole
play'ing card' ['ple·ɪŋ] *s* carta da gioco
play'ing field' *s* campo da gioco
play'mate' *s* compagno di gioco
play'-off' *s* (sports) spareggio
play'pen' *s* recinto, box *m*
play'thing' *s* giocattolo
play'time' *s* ricreazione
playwright ['ple,raɪt] *s* drammaturgo, commediografo
play'writ'ing *s* drammaturgia
plaza ['plæzə] or ['plɑzə] *s* piazzale *m*
plea [pli] *s* scusa; richiesta, domanda; (law) dichiarazione
plead [plid] *v* (*pret & pp* **pleaded** or **pled** [plɛd]) *tr* (*ignorance*) dichiarare; (*a case*) perorare || *intr* supplicare; argomentare; **to plead guilty** dichiararsi colpevole
pleasant ['plɛzənt] *adj* piacevole; (*person*) simpatico
pleasant·ry ['plɛzəntri] *s* (**-ries**) facezia, motto
please [pliz] *tr* piacere (with *dat*) || *intr* piacere; **as you please** come vuole; **if you please** per favore; **please** per cortesia; **to be pleased to** avere il piacere di; **to be pleased with** essere soddisfatto con; **to do as one pleases** fare come par e piace
pleasing ['plizɪŋ] *adj* piacevole
pleasure ['plɛʒər] *s* piacere *m;* desiderio; **what is your pleasure?** cosa desidera?
pleas'ure car' *s* vettura da turismo
pleat [plit] *s* piega || *tr* piegare, pieghettare
plebeian [plɪ'bi·ən] *adj & s* plebeo
plebiscite ['plɛbɪ,saɪt] *s* plebiscito
pledge [plɛdʒ] *s* pegno; promessa; voto; (*person*) ostaggio; (*toast*) brindisi *m;* **as a pledge** in pegno; **to take the pledge** giurare d'astenersi dal bere || *tr* dare in pegno; (*to bind*) far promettere a
plentiful ['plɛntɪfəl] *adj* abbondante
plenty ['plɛnti] *s* abbondanza || *adv* (coll) abbastanza
pleurisy ['plʊrɪsi] *s* pleurite *f*
pliable ['plaɪ·əbəl] *adj* flessibile, pieghevole; docile
pliers ['plaɪ·ərz] *ssg* or *spl* pinze *fpl*
plight [plaɪt] *s* condizione or situazione precaria || *tr*—**to plight one's troth** fidanzarsi
plod [plɑd] *v* (*pret & pp* **plodded;** *ger* **plodding**) *tr* percorrere pesantemente || *intr* camminare pesantemente; (*to drudge*) sgobbare
plot [plɑt] *s* (*of ground*) appezzamento; (*of a play*) trama, intreccio; (*evil scheme*) cospirazione, trama || *v* (*pret & pp* **plotted;** *ger* **plotting**) *tr* fare il piano di; macchinare; preparare la trama di; (aer, naut) fare il punto di || *intr* tramare, cospirare
plover ['plʌvər] or ['plovər] *s* piviere *m*
plow [plaʊ] *s* aratro; (*for snow*) spazzaneve *m* || *tr* arare; (*e.g., water*) solcare; (*snow*) spazzare; **to plow back** reinvestire || *intr* arare; aprirsi la via; camminare pesantemente
plow'man *s* (**-men**) aratore *m;* contadino
plow'share' *s* vomere *m*
pluck [plʌk] *s* strattone *m;* coraggio; (*giblets*) frattaglie *fpl* || *tr* (*to snatch*) tirare; (*e.g., fruit*) svellere; (*a fowl*) spennare; (mus) pizzicare || *intr* tirare; **to pluck up** farsi coraggio
pluck·y ['plʌki] *adj* (**-ier; -iest**) coraggioso
plug [plʌg] *s* tappo, zaffo; tavoletta di

tabacco; bocca da incendi; (elec) spina; (*horse*) (slang) ronzino; (slang) raccomandazione || *v* (*pret & pp* **plugged;** *ger* **plugging**) *tr* tappare, otturare; colpire; inserire; (slang) fare la pubblicità di; **to plug in** (elec) innestare, connettere || *intr* (coll) sgobbare
plum [plʌm] *s* (*fruit*) susina; (*tree*) susino; (slang) cosa bellissima; (slang) colpo di fortuna
plumage ['plumɪdʒ] *s* piumaggio
plumb [plʌm] *adj* appiombo || *s* piombino || *adv* appiombo; (coll) completamente || *tr* determinare la verticale col piombino; assodare
plumb' bob' *s* piombino
plumber ['plʌmər] *s* installatore *m*, idraulico
plumbing ['plʌmɪŋ] *s* impianto idraulico; mestiere *m* d'idraulico; sondaggio
plumb'ing fix'tures *spl* rubinetteria; impianti *mpl* sanitari
plumb' line' *s* filo a piombo
plum' cake' *s* panfrutto
plume [plum] *s* piuma; (*tuft of feathers*) pennacchio || *tr* coprire di piume; **to plume oneself on** piccarsi di; **to plume one's feathers** pulirsi le penne
plummet ['plʌmɪt] *s* piombino || *intr* cadere a piombo
plump [plʌmp] *adj* grassoccio, paffuto; franco || *s* caduta || *adv* francamente || *intr* cadere a piombo
plum' pud'ding *s* budino con uva passa
plum' tree' *s* susino
plunder ['plʌndər] *s* (*act*) saccheggio; (*loot*) bottino || *tr & intr* saccheggiare
plunge [plʌndʒ] *s* (*fall*) caduta; (*dive*) nuotata, tuffo || *tr* gettare; tuffare; (*e.g., a knife*) configgere || *intr* (*to rush*) precipitarsi; (*to gamble*) (coll) darsi al gioco; (fig) ripiombare
plunger ['plʌndʒər] *s* tuffatore *m;* (*for clearing clogged drains*) sturalavandini *m;* (mach) stantuffo; (coll) giocatore temerario
plunk [plʌŋk] *adv* (coll) proprio; (coll) con un colpo secco || *tr* (coll) gettare; lasciar cadere; (mus) pizzicare || *intr* (coll) lasciarsi cadere
plural ['plurəl] *adj & s* plurale *m*
plus [plʌs] *adj* superiore; (elec) positivo; (coll) con lode || *s* più *m;* soprappiù *m* || *prep* più
plush [plʌʃ] *adj* di lusso || *s* peluche *f*, felpa
Plutarch ['plutɑrk] *s* Plutarco
Pluto ['pluto] *s* Plutone *m*
plutonium [plu'tonɪ·əm] *s* plutonio
ply [plaɪ] *s* (**plies**) spessore *m;* (*layer*) strato; (*of rope*) legnolo || *v* (*pret & pp* **plied**) *tr* (*a trade*) esercitare; (*a tool*) maneggiare; (*to assail*) premere, incalzare || *intr* lavorare assiduamente; **to ply between** fare la spola tra
ply'wood' *s* legno compensato
pneumatic [nju'mætɪk] or [nu'mætɪk] *adj* pneumatico
pneumat'ic drill' *s* martello perforatore or pneumatico
pneumonia [nju'monɪ·ə] or [nu'monɪ·ə] *s* polmonite *f*
poach [potʃ] *tr* (*eggs*) affogare || *intr* cacciare or pescare di frodo
poacher ['potʃər] *s* bracconiere *m;* pescatore *m* di frodo
pock [pɑk] *s* buttero
pocket ['pɑkɪt] *adj* tascabile || *s* tasca; (billiards) buca; (aer) vuoto; (min) deposito || *tr* intascare; (*e.g., one's pride*) ingoiare
pock'et·book' *s* portafoglio; (*woman's purse*) borsetta
pock'et book' *s* libro tascabile
pock'et-hand'kerchief *s* fazzoletto
pock'et·knife' *s* (**-knives**) temperino
pock'et mon'ey *s* spiccioli *mpl*
pock'mark' *s* buttero
pod [pɑd] *s* baccello; (aer) contenitore *m*
poem ['po·ɪm] *s* poesia; (*of some length*) poema *m*
poet ['po·ɪt] *s* poeta *m*
poetess ['po·ɪtɪs] *s* poetessa
poetic [po'etɪk] *adj* poetico || **poetics** *ssg* poetica
poetry ['po·ɪtri] *s* poesia
pogrom ['pogrəm] *s* pogrom *m*
poignancy ['pɔɪnjənsi] or ['pɔɪnənsi] *s* strazio; intensità *f*
poignant ['pɔɪnjənt] or ['pɔɪnənt] *adj* straziante; intenso
point [pɔɪnt] *s* (*sharp end*) punta; (*something essential*) essenziale *m;* (*hint*) suggerimento; (*dot, decimal point, spot, degree, instant, position of compass*) punto; (coll) costrutto; **beside the point** fuori del seminato; **in point of** per quanto concerne; **to come to the point** venire al sodo; **to get the point** capire l'antifona; **to make a point of** dar importanza a; insistere di; **to stretch a point** fare un'eccezione, fare uno strappo alla regola; **to the point** a proposito || *tr* (*e.g., a weapon*) puntare; (*to sharpen*) aguzzare; (*to dot*) punteggiare; (*to give force to*) dare enfasi a; (*with mortar*) rinzaffare || *intr* puntare; **to point at** puntare il dito a; **to point to** mostrare a dito
point'blank' *adj & adv* a bruciapelo
pointed ['pɔɪntɪd] *adj* appuntito; personale, diretto, acuto
pointer ['pɔɪntər] *s* (*rod*) bacchetta; indice *m*, indicatore *m;* cane *m* da punta, pointer *m;* (coll) direttiva
poise [pɔɪz] *s* equilibrio, stabilità *f;* dignità *f* || *tr* equilibrare || *intr* equilibrarsi, stare in equilibrio
poison ['pɔɪzən] *s* veleno || *tr* avvelenare
poi'son i'vy *s* edera del Canada, tossicodendro
poisonous ['pɔɪzənəs] *adj* velenoso
poke [pok] *s* spinta, urto; (*with elbow*) gomitata; (slang) polentone *m* || *tr* (*to prod*) spingere, urtare; (*the head*) sporgere; (*the fire*) attizzare; **to poke fun at** burlarsi di; **to poke one's nose into** ficcare il naso in || *intr* (*to jab*)

urtare; (*to thrust oneself*) ficcarsi; (*to pry*) ficcare il naso; **to poke around** gironzolare; **to poke out** spuntare, protrudere
poker ['pokər] *s* (*game*) poker *m;* (*bar*) attizzatoio
pok'er face' *s* faccia impassibile
pok•y ['poki] *adj* **(-ier; -iest)** (coll) lento; (coll) meschino, modesto || **(-ies)** *s* (slang) gattabuia
Poland ['polənd] *s* la Polonia
po'lar bear' ['polər] *s* orso bianco
polarize ['polə,raɪz] *tr* polarizzare
pole [pol] *s* palo; (*long rod*) pertica; (*of wagon*) timone *m;* (*for jumping*) asta; (astr, biol, elec, geog, math) polo || *tr* (*a boat*) spingere con un palo || *intr* spingere una barca con un palo || **Pole** *s* polacco
pole'cat' *s* puzzola
pole' lamp' *s* lampada a stelo
pole'star' *s* stella polare
pole' vault' *s* salto coll'asta
police [pə'lis] *s* polizia || *tr* vigilare, proteggere; (mil) pulire
police'man *s* **(-men)** agente *m* di polizia, vigile urbano
police' state' *s* governo poliziesco
police' sta'tion *s* commissariato di polizia
poli•cy ['palɪsi] *s* **(-cies)** politica; (ins) polizza
polio ['polɪ,o] *s* (coll) polio *f*
polish ['palɪʃ] *s* lustro, lucentezza; (*for shoes or furniture*) cera; (fig) raffinatezza, eleganza || *tr* pulire; (*e.g., a stone*) levigare; **to polish off** (slang) finire; **to polish up** (slang) migliorare || *intr* pulirsi; diventar lucido || **Polish** ['polɪʃ] *adj & s* polacco
polisher ['palɪʃər] *s* lucidatore *m;* (mach) lucidatrice *f*
polite [pə'laɪt] *adj* raffinato, cortese
politeness [pə'laɪtnɪs] *s* cortesia
politic ['palɪtɪk] *adj* prudente; (*expedient*) diplomatico
political [pə'lɪtɪkəl] *adj* politico
politician [,palɪ'tɪʃən] *s* politico; (pej) politicante *m,* politicastro
politics ['palɪtɪks] *ssg* or *spl* politica
poll [pol] *s* votazione; (*registering of votes*) scrutinio; lista elettorale; (*analysis of public opinion*) referendum *m,* sondaggio; (*head*) testa; **to go to the polls** andare alle urne; **to take a poll** fare un'inchiesta || *tr* ricevere i voti di; contare i voti di; (*a tree*) potare; fare un'inchiesta di
pollen ['palən] *s* polline *m*
pollinate ['palɪ,net] *tr* fecondare col polline
poll'ing booth' ['polɪŋ] *s* cabina elettorale
polliwog ['palɪ,wag] *s* girino
poll' tax' *s* capitazione
pollute [pə'lut] *tr* insudiciare; (*to defile*) desecrare, profanare; (*e.g., the environment*) inquinare, contaminare
pollution [pə'luʃən] *s* inquinamento, contaminazione
poll' watch'er *s* rappresentante *m* di lista
polo ['polo] *s* polo
po'lo play'er *s* giocatore *m* di polo, polista *m*
po'lo shirt' *s* maglietta, polo
polygamist [pə'lɪgəmɪst] *s* poligamo
polygamous [pə'lɪgəməs] *adj* poligamo
polyglot ['palɪ,glat] *adj & s* poliglotto
polygon ['palɪ,gan] *s* poligono
polynomial [,palɪ'nomɪ•əl] *adj* polinomiale || *s* polinomio
polyp ['palɪp] *s* (pathol, zool) polipo
polytheist ['palɪ,θi•ɪst] *s* politeista *mf*
polytheistic [,palɪθi'ɪstɪk] *adj* politeistico
pomade [pə'med] or [pə'mad] *s* pomata
pomegranate ['pam,grænɪt] *s* (*shrub*) melograno; (*fruit*) melagrana
pom•mel ['pʌməl] or ['paməl] *s* (*of sword*) pomello; (*of saddle*) arcione *m* || *v* (*pret & pp* **-meled** or **-melled;** *ger* **-meling** or **-melling**) *tr* prendere a pugni
pomp [pamp] *s* pompa
pompadour ['pampə,dor] or ['pampə,dur] *s* acconciatura a ciuffo
pompous ['pampəs] *adj* pomposo
pon•cho ['pantʃo] *s* **(-chos)** poncho
pond [pand] *s* stagno
ponder ['pandər] *tr & intr* ponderare; **to ponder over** pensare sopra
ponderous ['pandərəs] *adj* ponderoso
poniard ['panjərd] *s* pugnale *m*
pontiff ['pantɪf] *s* pontefice *m*
pontifical [pan'tɪfɪkəl] *adj* pontificale
pontoon [pan'tun] *s* (*boat*) chiatta, pontone *m;* (aer) galleggiante *m*
po•ny ['poni] *s* **(-nies)** pony *m;* (*glass and drink*) bicchierino; (*for cheating*) (slang) bigino
poodle ['pudəl] *s* barbone *m,* cane *m* barbone
pool [pul] *s* (*pond*) stagno; (*puddle*) pozza; (*for swimming*) piscina; (*game*) biliardo; (com) cartello, consorzio; (com) fondo comune || *tr* mettere in un fondo comune || *intr* formare un cartello or un consorzio
pool'room' *s* sala da biliardo
pool' ta'ble *s* tavolo da biliardo
poop [pup] *s* poppa; (*deck*) casseretto
poor [pur] *adj* povero; (*inferior*) scadente || **the poor** *spl* i poveri
poor' box' *s* cassetta per l'elemosina
poor'house' *s* asilo dei poveri
poorly ['purli] *adv* male
pop [pap] *s* scoppio; (*soda*) gazzosa || *v* (*pret & pp* **popped;** *ger* **popping**) *tr* far scoppiare; **to pop the question** (coll) fare la domanda di matrimonio || *intr* esplodere con fragore; **to pop in** fare una capatina; entrare all'improvviso
pop'corn' *s* pop-corn *m*
pope [pop] *s* papa *m*
popeyed ['pap,aɪd] *adj* con gli occhi sporgenti; con gli occhi fuori dalle orbite
pop'gun' *s* fucile *m* ad aria compressa
poplar ['paplər] *s* pioppo
pop•py ['papi] *s* **(-pies)** papavero
pop'py•cock' *s* (coll) scemenza

popsicle ['pɑpsɪkəl] *s* (trademark) gelato da passeggio
populace ['pɑpjəlɪs] *s* gente *f*, popolino
popular ['pɑpjələr] *adj* popolare
popularize ['pɑpjələ,raɪz] *tr* divulgare, volgarizzare
populate ['pɑpjə,let] *tr* popolare
population [,pɑpjə'leʃən] *s* popolazione
populous ['pɑpjələs] *adj* popoloso
porcelain ['pɔrsəlɪn] or ['pɔrslɪn] *s* porcellana
porch [portʃ] *s* portico
porcupine ['pɔrkjə'paɪn] *s* (*Hystrix cristata*) istrice *m & f*, porcospino; (*Erethizon dorsatum*) ursone *m*, porcospino americano
pore [por] *s* poro || *intr*—**to pore over** studiare minutamente
pork [pork] *s* carne *f* di maiale
pork' butch'er shop' *s* salumeria
pork'chop' *s* cotoletta di maiale
porous ['porəs] *adj* poroso
po'rous plas'ter *s* cataplasma *m*
porphy•ry ['pɔrfɪri] *s* (**-ries**) porfido
porpoise ['pɔrpəs] *s* focena; (*dolphin*) delfino
porridge ['pɑrɪdʒ] or ['pɔrɪdʒ] *s* pappa, farinata
port [port] *adj* portuario || *s* (*harbor; wine*) porto; (naut) babordo, sinistra; (*opening in side of ship*) portello; (*round opening*) (naut) oblò *m*
portable ['portəbəl] *adj* portabile
portal ['portəl] *s* portale *m*
portend [por'tend] *tr* presagire
portent ['portent] *s* presagio
portentous [por'tentəs] *adj* sinistro, funesto, premonitore; (*amazing*) portentoso
porter ['portər] *s* (*doorman*) portiere *m;* (*man who carries luggage*) facchino; (*of a sleeper*) conduttore *m;* (*in a store*) inserviente *mf;* (*beverage*) birra scura e amara
portfoli•o [port'folɪ,o] *s* (**-os**) cartella; (*office; holdings*) portafoglio
port'hole' *s* (*opening in side of ship*) portello; (*round opening*) (naut) oblò *m*
porti•co ['portɪ,ko] *s* (**-cos** or **-coes**) portico
portion ['porʃən] *s* porzione; (*dowry*) dote *f* || *tr*—**to portion out** dividere, ripartire
port•ly ['portli] *adj* (**-lier; -liest**) obeso, corpulento
port' of call' *s* scalo
portrait ['portret] or ['portrɪt] *s* ritratto
portray [por'tre] *tr* ritrarre
portrayal [por'tre•əl] *s* delineazione; ritratto
Portugal ['portʃəgəl] *s* il Portogallo
Portu•guese ['portʃə,giz] *adj* portoghese || *s* (**-guese**) portoghese *mf*
pose [poz] *s* posa || *tr* (*a question*) avanzare; (*a model*) mettere in posa || *intr* posare; **to pose as** posare a, atteggiarsi a
posh [pɑʃ] *adj* (coll) di lusso
position [pə'zɪʃən] *s* posizione; rango; impiego, posto; **to be in a position to** essere in grado di
positive ['pɑzɪtɪv] *adj* positivo || *s* positivo; (phot) positiva
possess [pə'zes] *tr* possedere
possession [pə'zeʃən] *s* possedimento; (*of mental faculties*) possesso; **possessions** (*wealth*) beni *mpl*
possessive [pə'zesɪv] *adj* possessivo; (*e.g., mother*) opprimente, soffocante
possible ['pɑsɪbəl] *adj* possibile
possum ['pɑsəm] *s* opossum *m;* **to play possum** (coll) fare il morto
post [post] *s* (*mail*) posta; (*pole*) palo; (*in horse racing*) linea di partenza; posizione, rango; (*job*) posto; (mil) presidio || *tr* mettere in una lista; impostare; tenere al corrente; **post no bills** divieto d'affissione
postage ['postɪdʒ] *s* affrancatura
post'age me'ter *s* affrancatrice *f*
post'age stamp' *s* francobollo
postal ['postəl] *adj* postale
post'al card' *s* cartolina postale
pos'tal per'mit *s* abbonamento postale
post'al sav'ings bank' *s* cassa di risparmio postale
post'al scale' *s* pesalettere *m*
post' card' *s* cartolina illustrata; cartolina postale
post'date' *tr* postdatare
poster ['postər] *s* cartellone *m*, manifesto pubblicitario
posterity [pɑs'terɪti] *s* posterità *f*
postern ['postərn] *adj* posteriore || *s* postierla
post' exchange' *s* spaccio militare
post'haste' *adv* al più presto possibile
posthumous ['pɑstʃuməs] *adj* postumo
post'man *s* (**-men**) portalettere *m*
post'mark' *s* bollo, timbro postale || *tr* bollare, timbrare
post'mas'ter *s* ricevitore *m* postale
post'master gen'eral *s* (**postmasters general**) ministro delle poste
post-mortem ['post'mɔrtəm] *adj* postumo || *s* autopsia
post' of'fice *s* ufficio postale
post'-office box' *s* casella postale
postpaid ['post,ped] *adj* franco di porto
postpone [post'pon] *tr* differire, posporre
postscript ['post,scrɪpt] *s* poscritto
postulant ['pɑstʃələnt] *s* postulatore *m*, postulante *mf*
posture ['pɑstʃər] *s* portamento; posa || *intr* posare
post'war' *adj* del dopoguerra
po•sy ['pozi] *s* (**-sies**) fiore *m;* (*nosegay*) mazzolino di fiori
pot [pɑt] *s* pentola, pignatta; pitale *m*, orinale *m;* (*in gambling*) (coll) piatto; **to go to pot** andare a gambe all'aria
potash ['pɑt,æʃ] *s* potassa
potassium [pə'tæsɪ•əm] *s* potassio
pota•to [pə'teto] *s* (**-toes**) patata
pota'to om'elet *s* omelette *f* con patate
potbellied ['pɑt,belid] *adj* panciuto
poten•cy ['potənsi] *s* (**-cies**) potenza
potent ['potənt] *adj* potente

potentate ['potən ,tet] *s* potentato
potential [pə'tɛnʃəl] *adj & s* potenziale *m*
pot'hold'er *s* patta, presa
pot'hook' *s* uncino
potion ['poʃən] *s* pozione
pot'luck' *s*—**to take potluck** mangiare quello che passa il convento
pot' shot' *s* colpo sparato a casaccio
potter ['pɑtər] *s* vasaio
pot'ter's clay' *s* argilla per stoviglie
pot'ter's field' *s* cimitero dei poveri
potter•y ['pɑtəri] *s* (**-ies**) vasellame *m;* fabbrica di vasellame; ceramica
pouch [paʊtʃ] *s* sacchetto, borsa; (*of kangaroo*) borsa
poultice ['poltɪs] *s* cataplasma *m*
poultry ['poltri] *s* pollame *m*
poul'try•man *s* (**-men**) pollivendolo
pounce [paʊns] *intr*—**to pounce on** balzare su
pound ['paʊnd] *s* libbra; lira sterlina; (*for stray animals*) recinto || *tr* battere, picchiare; tempestare di colpi; (*to crush*) polverizzare || *intr* battere
pound' cake' *s* dolce *m* fatto con una libbra di burro, una di zucchero ed una di farina
pound' ster'ling *s* lira sterlina
pour [por] *tr* versare; (*e.g., tea*) servire; (*wine*) mescere; (*stones upon an enemy*) far piovere || *intr* fluire; (*to rain*) diluviare; **to pour in** affluire; **to pour out** uscire in massa
pout [paʊt] *s* broncio || *intr* tenere il broncio
poverty ['pɑvərti] *s* povertà *f*
POW ['pi'o'dʌbl ,ju] *s* (letterword) (**prisoner of war**) prigioniero di guerra
powder ['paʊdər] *s* polvere *f;* (*for the face*) cipria; (med) polverina || *tr* incipriare; (*to sprinkle with powder*) spolverizzare
pow'dered sug'ar *s* zucchero in polvere
pow'der puff' *s* piumino
pow'der room' *s* toletta
powdery ['paʊdəri] *adj* polveroso; fragile; (*snow*) farinoso
power ['paʊ·ər] *s* (*ability, authority*) potere *m;* forza, energia; (*nation*) potenza; (math, phys) potenza; **in power** al potere; **the powers that be** i potenti || *tr* azionare
pow'er•boat' *s* barca a motore
pow'er brake' *s* (aut) servofreno
pow'er com'pany *s* compagnia di elettricità
pow'er drive' *s* picchiata
powerful ['paʊ·ərfəl] *adj* poderoso
pow'er•house' *s* centrale elettrica
powerless ['paʊ·ərlɪs] *adj* impotente
pow'er line' *s* elettrodotto
pow'er mow'er *s* motofalciatrice *f*
pow'er of attor'ney *s* procura legale
pow'er plant' *s* stazione *f* generatrice; (aut) gruppo motore
pow'er steer'ing *s* servosterzo
pow'er tool' *s* apparecchiatura a motore
pow'er vac'uum *s* vuoto di potere
practical ['præktɪkəl] *adj* pratico
prac'tical joke' *s* scherzo da prete
practically ['præktɪkəli] *adv* (*in a practical manner; virtually, really*) praticamente; più o meno, quasi
practice ['præktɪs] *s* pratica; (*of a profession*) esercizio; (*e.g., of a doctor*) clientela; (*process of doing something*) prassi *f;* (*habitual performance*) abitudine *f* || *tr* praticare, esercitare || *intr* esercitarsi, praticare; (*to be active in a profession*) esercitare; **to practice as** esercitare la professione di
practitioner [præk'tɪʃənər] *s* professionista *mf*
Prague [prɑg] or [preg] *s* Praga
prairie ['prɛri] *s* prateria
prai'rie dog' *s* cinomio
prai'rie wolf' *s* coyote *m*
praise [prez] *s* lode *f,* elogio || *tr* lodare, elogiare; **to praise to the skies** levare alle stelle
praise'wor'thy *adj* lodevole
pram [præm] *s* (coll) carrozzella
prance [præns] or [prɑns] *s* caracollo || *intr* caracollare; (*to caper*) ballonzolare
prank [præŋk] *s* burla, tiro
prate [pret] *intr* cianciare
prattle ['prætəl] *s* ciancia, chiacchierio || *intr* cianciare, parlare a vanvera
pray [pre] *tr & intr* pregare
prayer [prɛr] *s* preghiera
prayer' book' *s* libro di preghiere
preach [pritʃ] *tr & intr* predicare
preacher ['pritʃər] *s* predicatore *m*
preamble ['pri ,æmbəl] *s* preambolo
precarious [prɪ'kɛrɪ·əs] *adj* precario
precaution [prɪ'kɔʃən] *s* precauzione
precede [prɪ'sid] *tr & intr* precedere
precedent ['prɛsɪdənt] *s* precedente *m*
precept ['prisɛpt] *s* precetto
precinct ['prisɪŋkt] *s* distretto; circoscrizione elettorale; **precincts** dintorni *mpl*
precious ['prɛʃəs] *adj* prezioso || *adv*—**precious little** (coll) molto poco
precipice ['prɛsɪpɪs] *s* precipizio
precipitate [prɪ'sɪpɪ ,tet] *adj* precipitoso || *s* precipitato || *tr & intr* precipitare
precipitous [prɪ'sɪpɪtəs] *adj* precipitoso, a precipizio
precise [prɪ'saɪs] *adj* preciso
precision [prɪ'sɪʒən] *s* precisione
preclude [prɪ'klud] *tr* precludere; escludere
precocious [prɪ'koʃəs] *adj* precoce
predatory ['predə ,tori] *adj* da preda, predatore
predicament [prɪ'dɪkəmənt] *s* situazione critica or imbarazzante
predict [prɪ'dɪkt] *tr* predire
prediction [prɪ'dɪkʃən] *s* predizione
predispose [,pridɪs'poz] *tr* predisporre
predominant [prɪ'dɑmɪnənt] *adj* predominante
preeminent [prɪ'ɛmɪnənt] *adj* preminente
preempt [prɪ'ɛmpt] *tr* occupare or acquistare in precedenza
preen [prin] *tr* (*feathers, fur*) lisciarsi;

to **preen oneself** agghindarsi, attillarsi
prefabricate [pri'fæbrɪ,ket] *tr* prefabbricare
preface ['prɛfɪs] *s* prefazione || *tr* prefazionare; essere la prefazione di
pre•fer [prɪ'fʌr] *v* (*pret & pp* **-ferred;** *ger* **-ferring**) *tr* preferire; (*to advance*) promuovere; (law) presentare, avanzare
preferable ['prɛfərəbəl] *adj* preferibile
preference ['prɛfərəns] *s* preferenza
preferred' stock' *s* azioni *fpl* privilegiate
prefix ['prifɪks] *s* prefisso || *tr* prefiggere
pregnan•cy ['prɛgnənsi] *s* (**-cies**) gravidanza
pregnant ['prɛgnənt] *adj* incinta, gravida; (fig) gravido
prehistoric [,prihɪs'tɑrɪk] or [,prihɪs'tɔrɪk] *adj* preistorico
prejudice ['prɛdʒədɪs] *s* pregiudizio; preconcetto; **without prejudice** senza detrimento || *tr* (*to harm*) pregiudicare; predisporre; **to prejudice against** prevenire contro
prejudicial ['prɛdʒə'dɪʃəl] *adj* pregiudizievole
prelate ['prɛlɪt] *s* prelato
preliminar•y [prɪ'lɪmɪ,nɛri] *adj* preliminare || *s* (**-ies**) preliminare *m*
prelude ['preljud] or ['prilud] *s* preludio || *tr* preludere a || *intr* preludere
premeditate [pri'mɛdɪ,tet] *tr* premeditare
premier [prɪ'mɪr] or ['primɪ·ər] *s* primo ministro, presidente *m* del consiglio
premiere [prə'mjɛr or [prɪ'mɪr] *s* prima; prima attrice
premise ['prɛmɪs] *s* premessa; **on the premises** nella proprietà, sul luogo; **premises** proprietà *f*
premium ['primɪ·əm] *s* premio; **at a premium** in gran richiesta; a prezzo altissimo
premonition [,primə'nɪʃən] *s* presentimento; indizio
preoccupation [pri,ɑkjə'peʃən] *s* preoccupazione
preoccu•py [pri'ɑkjə,paɪ] *v* (*pret & pp* **-pied**) *tr* preoccupare; (*to occupy beforehand*) occupare prima
prepaid [pri'ped] *adj* pagato in anticipo; franco di porto
preparation [,prɛpə'reʃən] *s* preparazione; (*for a trip*) preparativo; (pharm) preparato
preparatory [prɪ'pærə,tori] *adj* preparatorio
prepare [prɪ'pɛr] *tr* preparare || *intr* prepararsi
preparedness [prɪ'pɛrɪdnəs] or [prɪ'pɛrdnɪs] *s* preparazione; preparazione militare
pre•pay [pri'pe] *v* (*pret & pp* **-paid**) *tr* pagare anticipatamente
preponderant [prɪ'pɑndərənt] *adj* preponderante
preposition [,prɛpə'zɪʃən] *s* preposizione
prepossessing [,pripə'zɛsɪŋ] *adj* simpatico, attraente, piacevole
preposterous [prɪ'pɑstərəs] *adj* assurdo, ridicolo
prep' school' [prɛp] *s* (coll) scuola preparatoria
prerecorded [,prirɪ'kɔrdɪd] *adj* (rad & telv) a registrazione differita
prerequisite [pri'rɛkwɪzɪt] *s* requisito
prerogative [prɪ'rɑgətɪv] *s* prerogativa
presage ['prɛsɪdʒ] *s* presagio || [prɪ'sedʒ] *tr* presagire
Presbyterian [,prɛzbɪ'tɪrɪ·ən] *adj & s* presbiteriano; Presbiteriano
prescribe [prɪ'skraɪb] *tr & intr* prescrivere
prescription [prɪ'skrɪpʃən] *s* prescrizione; (pharm) ricetta
presence ['prɛzəns] *s* presenza; **in the presence of** alla presenza di
present ['prɛzənt] *adj* presente || *s* presente *m*, regalo || [prɪ'zɛnt] *tr* presentare; **present arms!** presentat'arm!; **to present s.o. with s.th** regalare qlco a qlcu
presentable [prɪ'zɛntəbəl] *adj* presentabile
presentation [,prɛzən'teʃən] or [,prizən'teʃən] *s* presentazione; (theat) rappresentazione
presenta'tion cop'y *s* copia d'omaggio
presentiment [prɪ'zɛntɪmənt] *s* presentimento
presently ['prɛzəntli] *adv* fra poco; attualmente
preserve [prɪ'zʌrv] *s* (*for hunting*) riserva; **preserves** conserva, marmellata || *tr* preservare; conservare
preserved' fruit' *s* frutta in conserva
preside [prɪ'zaɪd] *intr* presiedere; **to preside over** presiedere, presiedere **a**
presiden•cy ['prɛzɪdənsi] *s* (**-cies**) presidenza
president ['prɛzɪdənt] *s* presidente *m;* (*of a university*) rettore *m*
press [prɛs] *s* pressione; (*crowd*) folla; (*closet*) armadio; (mach) pressa; (typ) stampa; **to go to press** andare in macchina || *tr* (*to push*) spingere, premere; (*to squeeze*) spremere; (*to embrace*) abbracciare; forzare; costringere; urgere, sollecitare; (*to iron*) stirare || *intr* premere; avanzare
press' a'gent *s* agente pubblicitario
press' con'ference *s* conferenza stampa
pressing ['prɛsɪŋ] *adj* pressante, urgente || *s* (*of records*) incisione
press' release' *s* comunicato stampa
pressure ['prɛʃər] *s* pressione; tensione, urgenza || *tr* pressare, incalzare con insistenza
pres'sure cook'er ['kʊkər] *s* pentola a pressione
pressurize ['prɛʃə,raɪz] *tr* pressurizzare
prestige [prɛs'tiʒ] or ['prɛstɪdʒ] *s* prestigio
prestigious [prɛ'stɪdʒɪ·əs] or [prɛ'stɪdʒəs] *adj* onorato, stimato
presumably [prɪ'zuməbli] or [prɪ'zjuməbli] *adv* presumibilmente
presume [prɪ'zum] or [prɪ'zjum] *tr* presumere; **to presume to** prendersi

la libertà di || *intr* assumere; **to presume on** or **upon** abusare di
presumption [prɪ'zʌmpʃən] *s* presunzione; supposizione
presumptuous [prɪ'zʌmptʃʊ·əs] *adj* presuntuoso
presuppose [,prisə'poz] *tr* presupporre
pretend [prɪ'tɛnd] *tr* fingere, fare finta di || *intr* fingere; **to pretend to** (*e.g., the throne*) pretendere a
pretender [prɪ'tɛndər] *s* pretendente *mf;* impostore *m*
pretense [prɪ'tɛns] or ['pritɛns] *s* pretesa; finzione; **under false pretenses** allegando ragioni false; **under pretense of** sotto l'apparenza di
pretentious [prɪ'tɛnʃəs] *adj* pretenzioso
preterit ['prɛtərɪt] *adj* passato, preterito || *s* passato remoto, preterito
pretext ['pritɛkst] *s* pretesto
pretonic [prɪ'tɑnɪk] *adj* pretonico
pret·ty ['prɪti] *adj* (**-tier; -tiest**) grazioso, carino; (*e.g., sum of money*) (coll) bello || *adv* abbastanza; molto; **sitting pretty** (slang) ben messo
prevail [prɪ'vel] *intr* prevalere; **to prevail on** or **upon** persuadere
prevailing [prɪ'velɪŋ] *adj* prevalente
prevalent ['prɛvələnt] *adj* comune
prevaricate [prɪ'værɪ,ket] *intr* mentire
prevent [prɪ'vɛnt] *tr* impedire; **to prevent from** + *ger* impedire (with *dat*) di + *inf* or che + *subj*
prevention [prɪ'vɛnʃən] *s* prevenzione
preventive [prɪ'vɛntɪv] *adj* preventivo || *s* rimedio preventivo
preview ['pri,vju] *s* indizio; (*private showing*) (mov) anteprima; (*showing of brief scenes for advertising*) (mov) scene *fpl* di prossima programmazione
previous ['privɪ·əs] *adj* previo, precedente || *adv* precedentemente; **previous to** prima di
prewar ['pri,wɔr] *adj* anteguerra
prey [pre] *s* preda; **to be prey to** essere preda di || *intr* predare; **to prey on** or **upon** predare, sfruttare; preoccupare
price [praɪs] *s* prezzo; **at any price** a qualunque costo || *tr* chiedere il prezzo di; fissare il prezzo di
price' control' *s* calmiere *m*
price' cut'ting *s* riduzione di prezzo
price' fix'ing *s* regolamento dei prezzi
price' freez'ing *s* congelamento dei prezzi
priceless ['praɪslɪs] *adj* inestimabile; (coll) molto divertente
price' list' *s* listino prezzi
price' tag' *s* cartellino del prezzo
price' war' *s* guerra dei prezzi
prick [prɪk] *s* punta; puntura; **to kick against the pricks** tirare calci al vento || *tr* bucare, forare; pungere; (*to goad*) spronare; (*the ears*) ergere; (*said, e.g., of the conscience*) rimordere (with *dat*)
prick·ly ['prɪkli] *adj* (**-lier; -liest**) spinoso, pungente
prick'ly heat' *s* sudamina
prick'ly pear' *s* ficodindia *m*
pride [praɪd] *s* orgoglio; arroganza; **the pride of** il fiore di || *tr*—**to pride oneself on** or **upon** inorgoglirsi di
priest [prist] *s* prete *m*, sacerdote *m*
priesthood ['prist·hʊd] *s* sacerdozio
priest·ly ['pristli] *adj* (**-lier; -liest**) sacerdotale
prig [prɪg] *s* pedante *mf*, moralista *mf*
prim [prɪm] *adj* (**primmer; primmest**) formale, corretto, compito
prima·ry ['praɪ,mɛri] or ['praɪməri] *adj* primario || *s* (**-ries**) elezione preferenziale; (elec) bobina primaria; (elec) primario
prime [praɪm] *adj* primo; originale; di prima qualità || *s* (*earliest part*) inizio; (*best period*) fiore *m;* (*choicest part*) fior fiore *m;* (math) numero primo; (*mark*) (math) primo || *tr* preparare; (*a pump*) adescare; (*a firearm*) innescare; (*a canvas*) mesticare; (*a wall*) dare la prima mano a; (*to supply with information*) istruire
prime' min'ister *s* primo ministro
primer ['prɪmər] *s* sillabario, abbecedario || ['praɪmər] *s* innesco, detonatore *m*
primeval [praɪ'mivəl] *adj* primordiale
primitive ['prɪmɪtɪv] *adj* primitivo
primp [prɪmp] *tr* agghindare || *intr* agghindarsi
prim'rose' *s* primula
prim'rose path' *s* sentiero dei piaceri
prince [prɪns] *s* principe *m;* **to live like a prince** vivere da principe
prince' roy'al *s* principe ereditario
princess ['prɪnsɪs] *s* principessa
principal ['prɪnsɪpəl] *adj* principale || *s* (*chief*) padrone *m*, principale *m;* (*of school*) direttore *m*, preside *m;* (*actor*) primo attore; (com) capitale *m;* (law) mandante *mf*
principle ['prɪnsɪpəl] *s* principio; **on principle** per principio
print [prɪnt] *s* stampa; (*cloth*) tessuto stampato; (*printed matter*) stampato; (*newsprint*) giornale *m;* (*mark made by one's thumb*) impronta; (phot) positiva; **in print** stampato; disponibile; **out of print** esaurito || *tr* stampare, tirare; (*to write in print*) scrivere in stampatello; (*in the memory*) imprimere
print'ed cir'cuit *s* circuito stampato
print'ed mat'ter *s* stampati *mpl*
printer ['prɪntər] *s* stampatore *m;* (*of computer*) tabulatrice *f*
print'er's dev'il *s* apprendista *m* tipografo
print'er's ink' *s* inchiostro da stampa
printing ['prɪntɪŋ] *s* stampa; stampato; tiratura, edizione; (*writing in printed letters*) stampatello
prior ['praɪ·ər] *adj* anteriore, precedente || *s* priore *m* || *adv* prima; **prior to** prima di
priori·ty [praɪ'ɑrɪti] or [praɪ'ɔrɪti] *s* (**-ties**) priorità *f*
prism ['prɪzəm] *s* prisma *m*
prison ['prɪzən] *s* prigione, carcere *m*
prisoner ['prɪzənər] or ['prɪznər] *s* prigioniero
pris'on van' *s* furgone *m* cellulare

pris•sy ['prɪsi] *adj* (**-sier; -siest**) smanceroso, smorfioso
priva•cy ['praɪvəsi] *s* (**-cies**) ritiro; segreto; **to have no privacy** non esser mai lasciato in pace
private ['praɪvɪt] *adj* privato, personale ‖ *s* soldato semplice; **in private** privatamente; **privates** pudende *fpl*
pri'vate eye' *s* poliziotto privato
pri'vate first' class' *s* soldato scelto
pri'vate hos'pital *s* clinica
priv'ate view'ing *s* (mov) anteprima; (painting) vernice *f*
privet ['prɪvɪt] *s* ligustro
privilege ['prɪvɪlɪdʒ] *s* privilegio
priv•y ['prɪvi] *adj* privato; **privy to** segretamente a conoscenza di ‖ *s* (**-ies**) latrina
prize [praɪz] *s* premio; (nav) preda ‖ *tr* valutare, stimare
prize' fight' *s* incontro di pugilato
prize' fight'er *s* pugile *m*, pugilista *m*
prize' ring' *s* ring *m*, quadrato
pro [pro] *s* (**pros**) pro; voto favorevole; argomento favorevole; (coll) professionista *m;* **the pros and the cons** il pro e il contro
probabili•ty [,prɑbə'bɪlɪti] *s* (**-ties**) probabilità *f*
probable ['prɑbəbəl] *adj* probabile
probate ['probet] *s* omologazione di un testamento; copia autentica di un testamento ‖ *tr* (*a will*) omologare
probation [pro'beʃən] *s* prova; periodo di prova; (law) condizionale *f*, libertà vigilata; (educ) provvedimento disciplinare
probe [prob] *s* inchiesta; (surg) sonda ‖ *tr* indagare; sondare
problem ['prɑbləm] *s* problema *m*
procedure [pro'sidʒər] *s* procedura
proceed ['prosid] *s*—**proceeds** provento ‖ [pro'sid] *intr* procedere
proceeding [pro'sidɪŋ] *s* procedimento; **proceedings** atti *mpl;* (law) procedimenti *mpl*
process ['proses] *s* processo; **in the process of time** in processo di tempo ‖ *tr* trattare
procession [pro'sɛʃən] *s* processione
proc'ess serv'er *s* ufficiale giudiziario
proclaim [pro'klem] *tr* proclamare
proclitic [pro'klɪtɪk] *adj* proclitico ‖ *s* parola proclitica
procrastinate [pro'kræstɪ,net] *tr & intr* procrastinare
procure [pro'kjʊr] *tr* ottenere ‖ *intr* ruffianeggiare
prod [prɑd] *s* pungolo, stimolo ‖ *v* (*pret & pp* **prodded;** *ger* **prodding**) *tr* stimulare, pungolare, incitare
prodigal ['prɑdɪgəl] *adj & s* prodigo
prodigious [pro'dɪdʒəs] *adj* prodigioso
prodi•gy ['prɑdɪdʒi] *s* (**-gies**) prodigio
produce ['prodjus] or ['produs] *s* produzione; prodotti *mpl* agricoli ‖ [pro'djus] or [pro'dus] *tr* produrre; (theat) presentare
producer [pro'djusər] or [pro'dusər] *s* produttore *m;* (*of a play*) impresario; (mov) produttore *m*
product ['prɑdəkt] *s* prodotto
production [pro'dʌkʃən] *s* produzione
profane [pro'fen] *adj* profano; blasfemo ‖ *tr* profanare
profani•ty [pro'fænɪti] *s* (**-ties**) bestemmia
profess [pro'fɛs] *tr & intr* professare
profession [pro'fɛʃən] *s* professione
professor [pro'fɛsər] *s* professore *m*
proffer ['prɑfər] *s* offerta ‖ *tr* offrire
proficient [pro'fɪʃənt] *adj* abile, competente
profile ['profaɪl] *s* profilo ‖ *tr* profilare
profit ['prɑfɪt] *s* profitto; vantaggio; **at a profit** con guadagno ‖ *tr* avvantaggiare; giovare (with *dat*) ‖ *intr* avvantaggiarsi; **to profit by** approfittare di
profitable ['prɑfɪtəbəl] *adj* vantaggioso
prof'it and loss' *s* profitti *mpl* e perdite *fpl*
profiteer [,prɑfɪ'tɪr] *s* profittatore *m* ‖ *intr* fare il profittatore
prof'it shar'ing *s* cointeressenza, partecipazione agli utili
prof'it tak'ing *s* realizzo
profligate ['prɑflɪgɪt] *adj & s* dissoluto; prodigo
pro for'ma in'voice ['fɔrmə] *s* fattura fittizia
profound [pro'faʊnd] *adj* profondo
profuse [prə'fjus] *adj* profuso, abbondante; **profuse in** prodigo di
proge•ny ['prɑdʒəni] *s* (**-nies**) prole *f*
progno•sis [prɑg'nosɪs] *s* (**-ses** [siz]) prognosi *f*
prognostic [prɑg'nɑstɪk] *s* pronostico
prognosticate [prɑg'nɑstɪ,ket] *tr* pronosticare
pro•gram ['progræm] *s* programma *m* ‖ *v* (*pret & pp* **-gramed** or **-grammed;** *ger* **-graming** or **-gramming**) *tr* programmare
programmer ['progræmər] *s* pannellista *mf*, programmatore *m*
progress ['prɑgrɛs] *s* progresso; **in progress** in corso; **to make progress** fare dei progressi ‖ [prə'grɛs] *intr* progredire; migliorare
progressive [prə'grɛsɪv] *adj* (*proceeding step by step*) progressivo; progressista ‖ *s* progressista *mf*
prohibit [pro'hɪbɪt] *tr* proibire
prohibition [,pro•ə'bɪʃən] *s* proibizione; (hist) proibizionismo
project ['prɑdʒɛkt] *s* progetto ‖ [prə'dʒɛkt] *tr* (*to propose, plan*) progettare; (*light, a shadow, etc.*) proiettare ‖ *intr* sporgere, protrudere
projectile [prə'dʒɛktɪl] *s* proiettile *m*
projection [prə'dʒɛkʃən] *s* proiezione, sporgenza
projector [prə'dʒɛktər] *s* (*apparatus*) proiettore *m;* (*person*) progettista *mf*
proletarian [,prolɪ'tɛrɪ•ən] *adj & s* proletario
proliferate [prə'lɪfə,ret] *intr* proliferare
prolific [prə'lɪfɪk] *adj* prolifico
prolix ['prolɪks] or [pro'lɪks] *adj* prolisso
prologue ['prolɔg] or ['prolɑg] *s* prologo

prolong [pro'lɔŋ] or pro'lɑŋ] *tr* prolungare
promenade [,prɑmɪ'ned] or [,prɑmɪ'nɑd] *s* passeggiata; ballo di gala ‖ *tr & intr* passeggiare
promenade' deck' *s* ponte *m* passeggiata
prominent ['prɑmɪnənt] *adj* prominente
promise ['prɑmɪs] *s* promessa ‖ *tr & intr* promettere
prom'ising young' man' *s* giovane *m* di belle speranze
prom'issory note' ['prɑmɪ,sori] *s* cambiale *f*, pagherò *m*
promonto·ry ['prɑmən,tori] *s* **(-ries)** promontorio
promote [prə'mot] *tr* promuovere
promotion [prə'moʃən] *s* promozione
prompt [prɑmpt] *adj* pronto ‖ *tr* incitare, istigare; (theat) suggerire
prompter ['prɑmptər] *s* suggeritore *m*, rammentatore *m*
prompt'er's box' *s* buca del suggeritore
promptness ['prɑmptnɪs] *s* prontezza
promulgate ['prɑməl,get] or [pro'mʌlget] *tr* promulgare
prone [pron] *adj* prono
prong [prɔŋ] or [prɑŋ] *s* punta; (*of fork*) dente *m;* (*of pitchfork*) rebbio
pronoun ['pronaʊn] *s* pronome *m*
pronounce [prə'naʊns] *tr* pronunziare
pronounced [prə'naʊnst] *adj* pronunziato, marcato
pronouncement [prə'naʊnsmənt] *s* dichiarazione ufficiale
pronunciamen·to [prə,nʌnsɪ·ə'mento] *s* **(-tos)** pronunciamento
pronunciation [prə,nʌnsɪ'eʃən] or [prə,nʌnʃɪ'eʃən] *s* pronunzia
proof [pruf] *adj*—**proof against** a prova di ‖ *s* prova; (*of alcoholic beverages*) gradazione; (typ) bozza
proof'read'er *s* correttore *m* di bozze
prop [prɑp] *s* sostegno, puntello; (*pole*) palo; **props** attrezzi *mpl* teatrali ‖ *v* (*pret & pp* **propped;** *ger* **propping**) *tr* sostenere, puntellare
propaganda [,prɑpə'gændə] *s* propaganda
propagate ['prɑpə,get] *tr* propagare ‖ *intr* propagarsi
pro·pel [prə'pel] *v* (*pret & pp* **-pelled;** *ger* **-pelling**) *tr* propulsare, spingere, azionare; (*a rocket*) propellere
propeller [prə'pelər] *s* elica
propensi·ty [prə'pensɪti] *s* **(-ties)** propensione
proper ['prɑpər] *adj* appropriato, corretto; decente, convenevole; (gram) proprio; **proper to** proprio di
proper·ty ['prɑpərti] *s* **(-ties)** proprietà *f;* **properties** attrezzi *mpl* teatrali
prop'erty man' *s* trovarobe *m*, attrezzista *m*
prop'erty own'er *s* proprietario fondiario
prophe·cy ['prɑfɪsi] *s* **(-cies)** profezia
prophe·sy ['prɑfɪ,saɪ] *v* (*pret & pp* **-sied**) *tr* profetizzare
prophet ['prɑfɪt] *s* profeta *m*
prophetess ['prɑfɪtɪs] *s* profetessa
prophylactic [,profɪ'læktɪk] *adj* profilattico ‖ *s* rimedio profilattico; preservativo
propitiate [prə'pɪʃɪ,et] *tr* propiziare
propitious [prə'pɪʃəs] *adj* propizio
prop'jet' *s* turboelica *m*
proportion [prə'porʃən] *s* proporzione; **in proportion as** a misura che; **in proportion to** in proporzione a; **out of proportion** sproporzionato ‖ *tr* proporzionare, commensurare
proportionate [prə'porʃənɪt] *adj* proporzionato
proposal [prə'pozəl] *s* proposta; proposta di matrimonio
propose [prə'poz] *tr* proporre ‖ *intr* fare una proposta di matrimonio; **to propose to** chiedere la mano di; proporsi di + *inf*
proposition [,prɑpə'zɪʃən] *s* proposizione, proposta; (coll) progetto ‖ *tr* fare delle proposte indecenti a
propound [prə'paʊnd] *tr* proporre
proprietary [prə'praɪ·ə,teri] *adj* padronale; esclusivo, patentato
proprietor [prə'praɪ·ətər] *s* proprietario
proprietress [prə'praɪ·ətrɪs] *s* proprietaria
proprie·ty [prə'praɪ·əti] *s* **(-ties)** correttezza, decoro; **proprieties** convenzioni *fpl* sociali
propulsion [prə'pʌlʃən] *s* propulsione
prorate [pro'ret] *tr* rateizzare
prosaic [pro'ze·ɪk] *adj* prosaico
proscribe [pro'skraɪb] *tr* proscrivere
prose [proz] *adj* prosaico ‖ *s* prosa
prosecute ['prɑsɪ,kjut] *tr* eseguire; (law) processare
prosecutor ['prɑsɪ,kjutər] *s* esecutore *m;* (law) querelante *m;* (law) avvocato d'accusa
proselyte ['prɑsɪ,laɪt] *s* proselito
prose' writ'er *s* prosatore *m*
prosody ['prɑsədi] *s* prosodia, metrica
prospect ['prɑspekt] *s* vista; prospettiva; candidato; probabile cliente *m;* **prospects** speranze *fpl* ‖ *intr* fare il cercatore; **to prospect for** fare il cercatore di
prospectus [prə'spektəs] *s* prospetto
prosper ['prɑspər] *tr & intr* prosperare
prosperi·ty [prɑs'perɪti] *s* **(-ties)** prosperità *f*, benessere *m*
prosperous ['prɑspərəs] *adj* prospero
prostitute ['prɑstɪ,tjut] or ['prɑstɪ,tut] *s* prostituta ‖ *tr* prostituire
prostrate ['prɑstret] *adj* prostrato ‖ *tr* prostrare
prostration [prɑs'treʃən] *s* prostrazione
protagonist [pro'tægənɪst] *s* protagonista *mf*
protect [prə'tekt] *tr* proteggere
protection [prə'tekʃən] *s* protezione
protégé ['protə,ʒe] *s* protetto, favorito
protégée ['protə,ʒe] *s* protetta, favorita
protein ['proti·ɪn] or ['protin] *s* proteina
pro tempore [pro'tempə,ri] *adj* provvisorio, interinale
protest ['protest] *s* protesta; (com)

protesto || [pro'test] *tr & intr* protestare
Protestant ['prɑtɪstənt] *adj & s* protestante *mf*
protester [prə'tɛstər] *s* protestatario
prothonotar·y [pro'θɑnə,teri] *s* **(-ies)** (law) cancelliere *m* capo
protocol ['protə,kɑl] *s* protocollo
protoplasm ['protə,plæzəm] *s* protoplasma *m*
prototype ['protə,taɪp] *s* prototipo
proto·zoon [,protə'zo·ɑn] *s* **(-zoa** ['zo·ə]) protozoo
protract [pro'trækt] *tr* prolungare
protractor [pro'træktər] *s* rapportatore *m*
protrude [pro'trud] *intr* sporgere
proud [praʊd] *adj* fiero; arrogante; maestoso, magnifico
proud' flesh' *s* tessuto di granulazione
prove [pruv] *v* (*pret* **proved;** *pp* **proved** or **proven**) *tr* provare; (*ore*) analizzare; (law) omologare; (math) fare la prova di || *intr* risultare
proverb ['prɑvərb] *s* proverbio
provide [prə'vaɪd] *tr* provvedere || *intr*—**to provide for** provvedere a; (*to be ready for*) prepararsi a
provided [prə'vaɪdɪd] *conj* a condizione che, purché; **provided that** a condizione che, purché
providence ['prɑvɪdəns] *s* provvidenza
providential [,prɑvɪ'dɛnʃəl] *adj* provvidenziale
providing [prə'vaɪdɪŋ] *conj* var of **provided**
province ['prɑvɪns] *s* provincia; (fig) pertinenza, competenza
provision [prə'vɪʃən] *s* provvedimento; clausola; **provisions** viveri *mpl*
provi·so [prə'vaɪzo] *s* **(-sos** or **-soes)** stipulazione, clausola
provoke [prə'vok] *tr* provocare; contrariare, irritare
prow [praʊ] *s* prora, prua
prowess ['praʊ·ɪs] *s* prodezza; maestria
prowl [praʊl] *intr* andare in cerca di preda; vagabondare
prowler ['praʊlər] *s* vagabondo; ladro
proximity [prɑk'sɪmɪti] *s* prossimità *f*
prox·y ['prɑksi] *s* **(-ies)** procura; (*person*) procuratore *m*
prude [prud] *s* pudibondo
prudence ['prudəns] *s* prudenza
prudent ['prudənt] *adj* prudente
pruder·y ['prudəri] *s* **(-ies)** attitudine pudibonda
prudish ['prudɪʃ] *adj* pudibondo
prune [prun] *s* prugna secca || *tr* potare
pry [praɪ] *v* (*pret & pp* **pried**) *tr*—**to pry open** forzare con una leva; **to pry s.th out of s.o.** strappare qlco a qlcu || *intr* intromettersi, cacciarsi
psalm [sɑm] *s* salmo
pseudo ['sudo] or ['sjudo] *adj* falso, finto, sedicente
pseudonym ['sudənɪm] or ['sjudənɪm] *s* pseudonimo
psychiatrist [saɪ'kaɪ·ətrɪst] *s* psichiatra *mf*
psychiatry [saɪ'kaɪ·ətri] *s* psichiatria
psychic ['saɪkɪk] *adj* psichico || *s* medium *mf*
psychoanalysis [,saɪko·ə'nælɪsɪs] *s* psicanalisi *f*
psychoanalyze [,saɪko'ænə,laɪz] *tr* psicanalizzare
psychologic(al) [,saɪko'lɑdʒɪk(əl)] *adj* psicologico
psychologist [saɪ'kɑlədʒɪst] *s* psicologo
psycholo·gy [saɪ'kɑlədʒi] *s* **(-gies)** psicologia
psychopath ['saɪkə,pæθ] *s* psicopatico
psycho·sis [saɪ'kosɪs] *s* **(-ses** [siz]) psicosi *f*
psychotic [saɪ'kɑtɪk] *adj* psicotico
pub [pʌb] *s* (Brit) taverna, bar *m*
puberty ['pjubərti] *s* pubertà *f*
public ['pʌblɪk] *adj & s* pubblico
pub'lic-address' sys'tem *s* sistema *m* d'amplificazione per discorsi in pubblico
publication [,pʌblɪ'keʃən] *s* pubblicazione
pub'lic convey'ance *s* veicolo di servizi pubblici
publicity [pʌb'lɪsɪti] *s* pubblicità *f*
publicize ['pʌblɪ,saɪz] *tr* pubblicare, divulgare
pub'lic li'brary *s* biblioteca comunale
pub'lic-opin'ion poll' *s* sondaggio d'opinioni
pub'lic pros'ecutor *s* pubblico ministero
pub'lic school' *s* (U.S.A.) scuola dell'obbligo; (Brit) scuola privata, collegio
pub'lic serv'ant *s* funzionario pubblico
pub'lic speak'ing *s* oratoria
pub'lic spir'it *s* civismo
pub'lic toi'let *s* gabinetto pubblico
pub'lic util'ity *s* impresa di servizio pubblico; **public utilities** azioni emesse da imprese di servizi pubblici
publish ['pʌblɪʃ] *tr* pubblicare
publisher ['pʌblɪʃər] *s* editore *m;* (journ) direttore *m* responsabile
pub'lishing house' *s* casa editrice
pucker ['pʌkər] *s* grinza || *tr* raggrinzire || *intr* raggrinzirsi
pudding ['pʊdɪŋ] *s* budino, torta
puddle ['pʌdəl] *s* pozza, pozzanghera || *intr* diguazzare
pudg·y ['pʌdʒi] *adj* **(-ier; -iest)** grassoccio
puerile ['pju·ərɪl] *adj* puerile
Puerto Rican ['pwɛrto'rikən] *adj & s* portoricano
puff [pʌf] *s* soffio, sbuffo; (*e.g., of cigar*) boccata; (*pad*) piumino; (*exaggerated praise*) pistolotto; (culin) bigné *m* || *tr* sbuffare; gonfiare; adulare || *intr* soffiare, sbuffare; (*to breathe heavily*) ansimare, ansare; gonfiarsi; tirare boccate
puff' paste' *s* pasta sfoglia
pugilist ['pjudʒɪlɪst] *s* pugile *m*
pug-nosed ['pʌg,nozd] *adj* camuso
puke [pjuk] *tr & intr* (slang) vomitare
pull [pʊl] *s* tiro; (*act of drawing in*) tirata; (*handle*) tirante *m;* (slang) influenza, appoggi *mpl* || *tr* tirare; (*a tooth*) cavare; (*a muscle*) strappare;

(*a punch*) (coll) limitare la forza di; **to pull apart** fare a pezzi; **to pull down** abbattere; degradare; **to pull on** (*e.g., one's pants*) infilarsi; **to pull oneself together** ricomporsi; **to pull s.o.'s leg** beffarsi di qlcu || *intr* tirare; **to pull apart** andare a pezzi; **to pull at** tirare; **to pull away** andarsene; **to pull for** (coll) fare il tifo per; **to pull in** (*said of a train*) arrivare, entrare in stazione; **to pull out** (*said of a train*) partire; **to pull through** guarire, riuscire a cavarsela; **to pull up to** avanzare fino a
pullet ['pulɪt] *s* pollastra
pulley ['puli] *s* puleggia, carrucola
pulp [pʌlp] *s* polpa; (*for making paper*) pasta
pulpit ['pulpɪt] *s* pulpito
pulsate ['pʌlset] *intr* pulsare
pulsation [pʌl'seʃən] *s* pulsazione
pulse [pʌls] *s* polso; **to feel or take the pulse of** tastare il polso a
pulverize ['pʌlvə,raɪz] *tr* polverizzare
pum'ice stone' *s* ['pʌmɪs] *s* pomice *f*, pietra pomice
pum·mel ['pʌməl] *v* (*pret & pp* **-meled** or **-melled**; *ger* **-meling** or **-melling**) *tr* prendere a pugni
pump [pʌmp] *s* pompa; (*slipper*) scarpina || *tr* pompare; (coll) cavare un segreto a; **to pump up** pompare
pumpkin ['pʌmpkɪn] or ['puŋkɪn] *s* zucca
pump-priming ['pʌmp ,praɪmɪŋ] *s* stimolo governativo per sostentare l'economia
pun [pʌn] *s* gioco di parole || *v* (*pret & pp* **punned**; *ger* **punning**) *intr* fare giochi di parole
punch [pʌntʃ] *s* pugno; (*tool*) punteruolo, punzone *m;* (*drink*) ponce *m;* (coll) forza || *tr* dare un pugno a; (*metal*) punzonare; (*a ticket*) perforare || **Punch** *s* Pulcinella *m;* **pleased as Punch** soddisfattissimo
punch' bowl' *s* vaso per il ponce
punch' card' *s* scheda perforata
punch' clock' *s* orologio di controllo
punch'-drunk' *adj* stordito
punched' tape' *s* nastro perforato
punch'ing bag' *s* sacco
punch' line' *s* perfinire *m*, motto finale
punctilious [pʌŋk'tɪlɪ·əs] *adj* cerimonioso, pignolo
punctual ['pʌŋktʃu·əl] *adj* puntuale
punctuate ['pʌŋktʃu ,et] *tr* punteggiare
punctuation [,pʌŋktʃu'eʃən] *s* punteggiatura
punctua'tion mark' *s* segno d'interpunzione
puncture ['pʌŋktʃər] *s* puntura; (*hole*) bucatura; **to have a puncture** avere una gomma a terra || *tr* bucare, perforare || *intr* essere bucato
punct'ure-proof' *adj* antiperforante
pundit ['pʌndɪt] *s* esperto, autorità *f*
pungent ['pʌndʒənt] *adj* pungente
punish ['pʌnɪʃ] *tr* punire
punishment ['pʌnɪʃmənt] *s* punizione, castigo
punk [pʌŋk] *adj* (slang) di pessima qualità || *s* esca; (*decayed wood*) legno marcio; (slang) malandrino
punster ['pʌnstər] *s* freddurista *mf*
punt [pʌnt] *s* (football) calcio dato al pallone prima che tocchi il terreno
pu·ny ['pjuni] *adj* (**-nier; -niest**) insignificante, meschino; (*weak*) debole
pup [pʌp] *s* cucciolo
pupil ['pjupəl] *s* allievo, scolaro; (anat) pupilla
puppet ['pʌpɪt] *s* marionetta, burattino; (fig) fantoccio
puppeteer [,pʌpɪ'tɪr] *s* burattinaio
pup'pet gov'ernment *s* governo fantoccio or pupazzo
pup'pet show' *s* spettacolo di marionette
pup·py ['pʌpi] *s* (**-pies**) cucciolo
pup'py love' *s* amore *m* giovanile
purchase ['pʌrtʃəs] *s* compra, acquisto; (*grip*) presa, leva || *tr* comprare, acquistare
pur'chasing pow'er *s* potere *m* d'acquisto
pure [pjur] *adj* puro
purgative ['pʌrgətɪv] *adj* purgativo || *s* purga
purge [pʌrdʒ] *s* purga || *tr* purgare
puri·fy ['pjurɪ,faɪ] *v* (*pret & pp* **-fied**) *tr* purificare || *intr* purificarsi
puritan ['pjurɪtən] *adj & s* puritano || **Puritan** *adj & s* puritano
purity ['pjurɪti] *s* purezza
purloin [pər'lɔɪn] *tr & intr* rubare
purple ['pʌrpəl] *adj* purpureo || *s* porpora
purport ['pʌrport] *s* senso, significato || [pər'port] *tr* significare; **to purport to** + *inf* pretendere di + *inf*
purpose ['pʌrpəs] *s* scopo, fine *m;* **on purpose** apposta; **to good purpose** con buoni risultati; **to no purpose** inutilmente; **to serve one's purpose** fare al caso proprio
purposely ['pʌrpəsli] *adv* a bella posta, apposta
purr [pʌr] *s* ronfare *m* || *intr* fare le fusa
purse [pʌrs] *s* borsa; (*woman's handbag*) borsetta; (*for men*) borsetto || *tr* (*one's lips*) arricciare
purser ['pʌrsər] *s* commissario di bordo
purse' snatch'er ['snætʃər] *s* borsaiolo
purse' strings' *spl* cordini *mpl* della borsa; **to hold the purse strings** controllare le spese
purslane ['pʌrslen] or ['pʌrslɪn] *s* (bot) porcellana
pursue [pər'su] or [pər'sju] *tr* perseguire; (*to harass*) perseguitare; (*a career*) proseguire
pursuit [pər'sut] or [pər'sjut] *s* inseguimento, caccia; occupazione, esercizio
pursuit' plane' *s* caccia *m*
purvey [pər've] *tr* provvedere, fornire
pus [pʌs] *s* pus *m*
push [puʃ] *s* spinta; (*advance*) avanzata; (coll) impulso, energia || *tr* premere, spingere; (*a product*) promuovere la vendita di; dare impulso a; (*narcotics*) (slang) spacciare; **to**

push around (coll) dare spintoni a; (fig) fare pressione su; **to push back** ricacciare || *intr* spingere; **to push ahead** avanzarsi a spintoni, avanzarsi; **to push on** avanzare
push' but'ton *s* pulsante *m*, bottone *m*
push'-button con'trol *s* controllo a pulsanti
push'cart' *s* carretto a mano
pusher ['pʊʃər] *adj* spingente; (aer) propulsivo || *s* spingitore *m;* (aer) aeroplano a elica propulsiva; (slang) spacciatore *m* di stupefacenti
pushing ['pʊʃɪŋ] *adj* aggressivo, intraprendente
puss [pʊs] *s* micio
puss' in the cor'ner *s* gioco dei quattro cantoni
puss·y ['pʊsi] *s* (**-ies**) micio
puss'y wil'low *s* salice americano a gattini
pustule ['pʌstʃʊl] *s* pustola
put [pʊt] *v* (*pret & pp* **put;** *ger* **putting**) *tr* mettere; (*to estimate*) stimare; (*a question*) rivolgere; (*to throw*) lanciare; imporre; **to put across** (slang) far accettare; **to put aside, away** or **by** mettere da parte; **to put down** annotare; (*to suppress*) reprimere; **to put off** differire; evadere; **to put on** (*clothes*) mettersi; (*a brake*) azionare; (*to assume*) fingere; (*airs*) darsi; **to put out** spegnere; imbarazzare; incomodare; deludere; annoiare, irritare; (*of a game*) espellere; **to put it over on s.o.** fargliela a qlcu; **to put off** rinviare; **to put over** mandare ad effetto; **to put to flight** mettere in fuga; **to put to shame** svergognare; **to put through** portare a termine; **to put up** offrire; mettere in conserva; alloggiare; costruire; (*money*) contribuire; (coll) incitare || *intr* dirigersi; **to put to sea** mettersi in mare; **to put up** prendere alloggio; **to put up with** tollerare
put'-out' *adj* sconcertato, seccato
putrid ['pjutrɪd] *adj* putrido
Putsch [pʊtʃ] *s* tentativo di sollevazione, sollevazione
putter ['pʌtər] *intr* occuparsi di inezie; **to putter about** andare avanti e indietro
put·ty ['pʌti] *s* (**-ties**) stucco, mastice *m* || *v* (*pret & pp* **-tied**) *tr* stuccare
put'ty knife' *s* spatola
put'-up' *adj* (coll) complottato
puzzle ['pʌzəl] *s* enigma *m;* (*toy*) indovinello || *tr* rendere perplesso, confondere; **to puzzle out** decifrare || *intr* essere perplesso
puzzler ['pʌzlər] *s* enigma *m*
puzzling ['pʌzlɪŋ] *adj* enigmatico
pyg·my ['pɪgmi] *s* (**-mies**) pigmeo
pylon *s* pilone *m*
pyramid ['pɪrəmɪd] *s* piramide *f* || *tr* (*e.g., costs*) aumentare gradualmente; (*one's money*) aumentare giocando in margine
pyre [paɪr] *s* pira
Pyrenees ['pɪrɪ ,niz] *spl* Pirenei *mpl*
pyrites [paɪ'raɪtiz] or ['paɪraɪts] *s* pirite *f*
pyrotechnics [,paɪrə'tɛknɪks] *spl* pirotecnica
python ['paɪθɑn] or ['paɪθən] *s* pitone *m*
pythoness ['paɪθənɪs] *s* pitonessa
pyx [pɪks] *s* (eccl) pisside *f*

Q

Q, q [kju] *s* diciassettesima lettera dell'alfabeto inglese
quack [kwæk] *adj* falso || *s* medicastro; ciarlatano; qua qua *m* || *intr* (*said of a duck*) fare qua qua
quacker·y ['kwækəri] *s* (**-ies**) ciarlataneria
quadrangle ['kwɑd ,ræŋgəl] *s* quadrangolo
quadrant ['kwɑdrənt] *s* quadrante *m*
quadruped ['kwɑdrʊ ,pɛd] *adj & s* quadrupede *m*
quadruple ['kwɑdrʊpəl] or [kwɑ'drupəl] *adj* quadruplo; (*alliance*) quadruplice || *s* quadruplo || *tr* quadruplicare || *intr* quadruplicarsi
quaff [kwɑf] or [kwæf] *s* lungo sorso || *tr & intr* bere a lunghi sorsi
quail [kwel] *s* quaglia || *intr* sgomentarsi
quaint [kwent] *adj* strano, strambo, originale; all'antica ma bello
quake [kwek] *s* terremoto || *intr* tremare, sussultare
Quaker ['kwekər] *adj & s* quacchero, quacquero
Quak'er meet'ing *s* riunione di quaccheri; (coll) riunione in cui si parla poco
quali·fy ['kwɑlɪ ,faɪ] *v* (*pret & pp* **-fied**) *tr* qualificare; (*for a profession*) abilitare || *intr* qualificarsi; abilitarsi
quali·ty ['kwɑlɪti] *s* (**-ties**) qualità *f;* (*of a sound*) timbro
qualm [kwɑm] *s* scrupolo di coscienza; preoccupazione; nausea
quanda·ry ['kwɑndəri] *s* (**-ries**) incertezza, perplessità *f*
quanti·ty ['kwɑntɪti] *s* (**-ties**) quantità *f*
quan·tum ['kwɑntəm] *adj* quantistico || *s* (**-ta** [tə]) quanto
quarantine ['kwɑrən ,tin] or ['kwɔrən ,tin] *s* quarantena || *tr* mettere in quarantena
quar·rel ['kwɑrəl] or ['kwɔrəl] *s* litigio, diverbio; **to have no quarrel with** non essere in disaccordo con; **to pick a quarrel with** venire a diverbio con || *v* (*pret & pp* **-reled** or **-relled;** *ger* **-reling** or **-relling**) *intr* litigare

quarrelsome ['kwɑrəlsəm] or ['kwɔrəlsəm] *adj* litigioso, rissoso
quar•ry ['kwɑri] or ['kwɔri] *s* **(-ries)** cava; (*game*) selvaggina, cacciagione || *v* (*pret & pp* **-ried**) *tr* cavare
quart [kwɔrt] *s* quarto di gallone
quarter ['kwɔrtər] *adj* quarto || *s* quarto; moneta di un quarto di dollaro; (*three months*) trimestre *m;* (*of town*) quartiere *m;* **a quarter after one** l'una e un quarto; **a quarter of an hour** un quarto d'ora; **a quarter to one** l'una meno un quarto; **at close quarters** corpo a corpo; **quarters** quartiere *m* || *tr* squartare; (*soldiers*) accasermare
quar'ter-deck' *s* cassero
quar'ter-hour' *s* quarto d'ora; **on the quarter-hour** ogni quindici minuti allo scoccare del quarto d'ora
quarter•ly ['kwɔrtərli] *adj* trimestrale || *s* **(-lies)** pubblicazione trimestrale || *adv* trimestralmente
quar'ter•mas'ter *s* (mil) intendente *m* militare; (nav) secondo capo
quartet [kwɔr'tet] *s* quartetto
quartz [kwɔrts] *s* quarzo
quasar ['kwesɑr] *s* (astr) radiostella
quash [kwɑʃ] *tr* sopprimere; annullare
quaver ['kwevər] *s* tremito; (mus) tremolo; (mus) croma || *intr* tremare
quay [ki] *s* molo
queen [kwin] *s* regina; (*in cards*) donna; (chess) regina
queen' bee' *s* ape regina; (fig) basilessa
queen' dow'ager *s* regina vedova
queen•ly ['kwinli] *adj* **(-lier; -liest)** da regina; regio
queen' moth'er *s* regina madre
queen' post' *s* monaco
queen's' Eng'lish *s* inglese corretto
queer [kwɪr] *adj* strano, curioso; poco bene, indisposto; falso; (slang) omosessuale || *s* (slang) finocchio || *tr* rovinare, mettere in pericolo
quell [kwɛl] *tr* soffocare, domare; (*pain*) calmare
quench [kwɛntʃ] *tr* (*fire, thirst*) spegnere, estinguere; (*rebellion*) soffocare; (elec) ammortizzare
que•ry ['kwɪri] *s* **(-ries)** domanda; punto interrogativo; dubbio || *v* (*pret & pp* **-ried**) *tr* interrogare; (typ) apporre punto interrogativo a
quest [kwɛst] *s* ricerca; **in quest of** in cerca di
question ['kwɛstʃən] *s* domanda; problema *m,* quesito; (*matter*) questione; **beyond question** senza dubbio; **out of the question** impossibile; **this is beside the question** questo non c'entra; **to ask a question** fare una domanda; **to be a question of** trattarsi di; **to call in** or **into question** mettere in dubbio; **without question** senza dubbio || *tr* interrogare; mettere in dubbio; (pol) interpellare
questionable ['kwɛstʃənəbəl] *adj* discutibile
ques'tion mark' *s* punto interrogativo
questionnaire [,kwɛstʃən'ɛr] *s* questionario
queue [kju] *s* (*of hair*) codino; (*of people*) coda || *intr* fare la coda
quibble ['kwɪbəl] *intr* sottilizzare
quick [kwɪk] *adj* pronto, sollecito; sbrigativo; veloce, rapido; vivo || *s*—**the quick and the dead** i vivi e i morti; **to cut to the quick** toccare nel vivo
quicken ['kwɪkən] *tr* sveltire; animare; ravvivare
quick'lime' *s* calce viva
quick' lunch' *s* tavola calda
quickly ['kwɪkli] *adv* svelto, alla svelta; presto
quick'sand' *s* sabbia mobile
quick'-set'ting *adj* a presa rapida
quick'sil'ver *s* argento vivo
quick'work' *s* (naut) opera viva
quiet ['kwaɪ•ət] *adj* quieto; silenzioso; (com) calmo; **to keep quiet** stare zitto || *s* quiete *f,* tranquillità *f;* pace *f,* calma || *tr* quietare; calmare || *intr*—**to quiet down** quietarsi, calmarsi
quill [kwɪl] *s* penna d'oca; (*basal part of feather*) calamo; (*e.g., of porcupine*) aculeo
quilt [kwɪlt] *s* trapunta, imbottita || *tr* trapuntare
quince [kwɪns] *s* cotogna; (*tree*) cotogno
quinine ['kwaɪnaɪn] *s* (*alkaloid*) chinina; (*salt of the alkaloid*) chinino
quinsy ['kwɪnzi] *s* angina
quintessence [kwɪn'tesəns] *s* quintessenza
quintet [kwɪn'tet] *s* quintetto
quintuplet [kwɪn'tjuplet] or [kwɪn'tuplet] *s* gemello nato da un parto quintuplice
quip [kwɪp] *s* frizzo, uscita || *v* (*pret & pp* **quipped;** *ger* **quipping**) *tr & intr* uscire a dire, dire come battuta
quire [kwaɪr] *s* ventiquattro fogli; (bb) quinterno
quirk [kwʌrk] *s* stranezza, manierismo; (*quibble*) cavillo; (*sudden turn*) mutamento improvviso
quit [kwɪt] *adj* libero; **to be quits** esser pari; **to call it quits** finirla, farla finita || *v* (*pret & pp* **quit** or **quitted;** *ger* **quitting**) *tr* abbandonare || *intr* andarsene; abbandonare l'impiego; smettere (di + *inf*)
quite [kwaɪt] *adv* completamente; molto, del tutto
quitter ['kwɪtər] *s* persona che abbandona facilmente
quiver ['kwɪvər] *s* fremito; (*to hold arrows*) faretra, turcasso || *intr* fremere, tremare
quixotic [kwɪks'ɑtɪk] *adj* donchisciottesco
quiz [kwɪz] *s* **(quizzes)** esame *m;* interrogatorio || *v* (*pret & pp* **quizzed;** *ger* **quizzing**) *tr* esaminare; interrogare
quiz' game' *s* quiz *m*
quiz' pro'gram *s* programma *m* di quiz
quiz' sec'tion *s* (educ) classe *f* a base di esercizi (e non di conferenze)
quizzical ['kwɪzɪkəl] *adj* strano, curioso; (*derisive*) canzonatore
quoin [kɔɪn] or [kwɔɪn] *s* cantone *m,*

pietra angolare; (*piece of wood*) zeppa; (typ) serraforme *m* || *tr* fissare con serraforme
quoit [kwɔɪt] or [kɔɪt] *s* anello di corda o di metallo da lanciarsi come gioco; **quoits** *ssg* gioco consistente nel lancio di anelli su di un piolo
quondam ['kwɑndæm] *adj* quondam
quorum ['kworəm] *s* quorum *m*
quota ['kwotə] *s* (*share*) quota; (*of imports*) contingentamento; (*of persons*) contingente *m*
quotation [kwo'teʃən] *s* (*from a book*) citazione; (*of prices*) quotazione
quota'tion mark' *s* doppia virgola, virgoletta
quote [kwot] *s* citazione, richiamo || *tr & intr* citare, richiamare; (com) quotare; **quote** cito
quotient ['kwoʃənt] *s* quoziente *m*

R

R, r [ɑr] *s* diciottesima lettera dell'alfabeto inglese
rabbet ['ræbɪt] *s* scanalatura, incastro || *tr* scanalare, incastrare
rab·bi ['ræbaɪ] *s* (**-bis**) rabbino
rabbit ['ræbɪt] *s* coniglio
rab'bit ears' *spl* (telv) doppia antenna a stilo
rabble ['ræbəl] *s* gentaglia, marmaglia
rab'ble-rous'er ['rauzər] *s* arruffapopoli *m*
rabies ['rebiz] or ['rebɪ,iz] *s* rabbia
raccoon [ræ'kun] *s* procione *m*
race [res] *s* (*branch of human stock*) razza; (*contest in speed*) corsa; (*contest of any kind*) gara; (*channel*) canale *m* di adduzione || *tr* far correre; gareggiare (in velocità) con; (*a motor*) imballare || *intr* correre; fare le corse; (*said of a motor*) imballarsi; (naut) fare le regate
race' horse' *s* cavallo da corsa
race' ri'ot *s* contestazione di razza
race' track' *s* pista
racial ['reʃəl] *adj* razziale
rac'ing car' *s* automobile *f* da corsa
rack [ræk] *s* (*to hang clothes*) attaccapanni *m;* (*framework to hold fodder, baggage, guns, etc.*) rastrelliera; (mach) cremagliera; **to go to rack and ruin** andare a rotoli || *tr* tormentare, torturare; **to rack off** (*wine*) travasare; **to rack one's brains** rompersi il capo, lambiccarsi il cervello
racket ['rækɪt] *s* racchetta; (*noise*) chiasso, gazzarra; (coll) racket *m;* **to raise a racket** fare gazzarra
racketeer [,rækɪ'tɪr] *s* chi è nel racket; (*engaged in extortion*) ricattatore *m* || *intr* essere nel racket; fare il ricattatore
rack' rail'way *s* ferrovia a cremagliera
rac·y ['resi] *adj* (**-ier; -iest**) pungente, vigoroso; piccante
radar ['redɑr] *s* radar *m*
radiant ['redɪ·ənt] *adj* raggiante, radioso
radiate ['redɪ,et] *tr* irradiare || *intr* irradiarsi
radiation [,redɪ'eʃən] *s* radiazione
radia'tion sick'ness *s* malattia causata da radiazione atomica
radiator ['redɪ,etər] *s* radiatore *m*
ra'diator cap' *s* tappo del radiatore
radical ['rædɪkəl] *adj* radicale || *s* radicale *mf;* (chem, math) radicale *m*
radi·o ['redɪ,o] *s* (**-os**) radio *f;* radiogramma *m* || *tr* radiotrasmettere
radioactive [,redɪ·o'æktɪv] *adj* radioattivo
ra'dio am'ateur *s* radioamatore *m*
ra'dio announc'er *s* radioannunciatore *m*
ra'dio bea'con *s* radiofaro
ra'dio·broad'cast *s* radiodiffusione || *tr* radiodiffondere
ra'dio com'pass *s* radiobussola
ra'dio·fre'quency *s* radiofrequenza
ra'dio lis'tener *s* radioascoltatore *m*
radiology [,redɪ'ɑlədʒi] *s* radiologia
ra'dio net'work *s* rete *f*
ra'dio news'caster *s* radiocronista *mf*
ra'dio·pho'to *s* (**-tos**) (coll) radiofoto *f*
ra'dio set' *s* radioricevente *f*
ra'dio sta'tion *s* stazione radio
radish ['rædɪʃ] *s* ravanello
radium ['redɪ·əm] *s* radio
radi·us ['redɪ·əs] *s* (**-i** [,aɪ] or **-uses**) (anat) radio; (fig, geom) raggio; **within a radius of** entro un raggio di
raffle ['ræfəl] *s* riffa || *tr* sorteggiare
raft [ræft] or [rɑft] *s* zattera; (coll) mucchio
rafter ['ræftər] or ['rɑftər] *s* puntone *m*
rag [ræg] *s* straccio; **to chew the rag** (slang) chiacchierare
ragamuffin ['rægə,mʌfɪn] *s* straccione *m*
rag' doll' *s* bambola di pezza
rage [redʒ] *s* rabbia; **to be all the rage** furoreggiare; **to fly into a rage** montare in bestia || *intr* infuriare
ragged ['rægɪd] *adj* cencioso; (*torn*) stracciato; (*edge*) rozzo, scabroso
ragpicker ['ræg,pɪkər] *s* cenciaiolo, straccivendolo
rag'weed' *s* (bot) ambrosia
raid [red] *s* irruzione, razzia || *tr* scorrere || *intr* scorrazzare
rail [rel] *s* (*of fence*) stecca, traversa; (*fence*) stecconata; (*railing*) ringhiera; (rr) rotaia; **by rail** per ferrovia; **rails** titoli *mpl* ferroviari || *intr* inveire; **to rail at** inveire contro
rail'car' *s* automotrice *f*
rail' fence' *s* stecconata fatta di traverse piallate alla buona

rail'head' *s* fine *f* della linea ferroviaria
railing ['relɪŋ] *s* ringhiera
rail'road' *adj* ferroviario || *s* ferrovia || *tr* trasportare in ferrovia; (*a bill*) far passare precipitosamente; (coll) imprigionare falsamente
rail'road cros'sing *s* passaggio a livello
rail'road'er *s* ferroviere *m*
rail'way' *s* ferrovia, strada ferrata
raiment ['remənt] *s* (lit) abbigliamento
rain [ren] *s* pioggia; **rain or shine** con qualunque tempo || *tr* fare piovere; (lit) piovere; **to rain cats and dogs** piovere a catinelle; **to rain out** far sospendere per via della pioggia || *intr* piovere
rainbow ['ren,bo] *s* arcobaleno
rain'coat' *s* impermeabile *m*
rain'fall' *s* acquazzone *m;* piovosità *f*
rain•y ['reni] *adj* (**-ier; -iest**) piovoso, piovano
rain'y day' *s* giorno piovoso; (fig) tempi *mpl* difficili
raise [rez] *s* aumento || *tr* levare, rialzare; (*children, animals*) allevare; (*to build*) tirare su; (*a question*) sollevare; (*the dead*) risollevare; (*to increase*) aumentare; (*money*) raccogliere; (*a siege*) togliere; (*at cards*) rilanciare; (*anchor*) salpare; (math) elevare
raisin ['rezən] *s* grano d'uva passa, grano d'uva secca; **raisins** uva passa, uva secca
rake [rek] *s* rastrello; (*person*) porcaccione *m,* libertino || *tr* rastrellare; **to rake in money** far soldoni
rake'-off' *s* (coll) compenso illecito, bustarella; (coll) sconto
rakish ['rekɪʃ] *adj* libertino; brioso, vivace; **to wear one's hat at a rakish angle** portare il cappello sulle ventitré
ral•ly ['ræli] *s* (**-lies**) riunione, comizio; adunata; ricupero || *v* (*pret & pp* **-lied**) *tr* riunire, chiamare a raccolta; rianimare || *intr* riunirsi; rianimarsi; (*said of stock prices*) rialzarsi; rimettersi in forze; **to rally to the side of** correre all'aiuto di
ram [ræm] *s* (*male sheep*) montone *m;* (mil) ariete *m;* (nav) sperone *m;* (mach) maglio del battipalo || *v* (*pret & pp* **rammed;** *ger* **ramming**) *tr* battere, sbattere contro; cacciare, conficcare; forzare; (nav) speronare || *intr*—**to ram into** sbattere contro
ramble ['ræmbəl] *s* girata || *intr* (*to wander around*) gironzolare; vagare; (*said of a vine*) crescere disordinatamente; (*said, e.g., of a river*) serpeggiare; (fig) scorrazzare, divagare
rami•fy ['ræmɪ,faɪ] *v* (*pret & pp* **-fied**) *tr* ramificare || *intr* ramificarsi
ram'jet en'gine *s* statoreattore *m*
ramp [ræmp] *s* rampa
rampage ['ræmpedʒ] *s* stato d'eccitazione; **to go on a rampage** infierire, comportarsi furiosamente
rampart ['ræmpɑrt] *s* baluardo, muraglione *m*
ram'rod' *s* (*for ramming*) (mil) bacchetta; (*for cleaning*) (mil) scovolo
ram'shack'le *adj* cadente, in rovina
ranch [ræntʃ] *s* fattoria agricola
rancid ['rænsɪd] *adj* rancido
rancor ['ræŋkər] *s* rancore *m*
random ['rændəm] *adj* fortuito; **at random** alla rinfusa, a casaccio
range [rendʒ] *s* (*row*) fila; (*rank*) classe *f;* (*distance*) portata; campo di tiro a segno; raggio d'azione; (*scope*) gamma; (*for grazing*) pascolo; (*stove*) fornello, cucina economica; **within range of** alla portata di || *tr* allineare; ordinare; passare attraverso; mandare al pascolo || *intr* variare, fluttuare; estendersi; trovarsi; (mil) portare; **to range over** percorrere; (fig) trattare
range' find'er *s* telemetro
rank [ræŋk] *adj* esuberante; grossolano; denso, spesso; puzzolente; eccessivo; completo, assoluto || *s* rango, grado; (*row*) fila, schiera; **ranks** truppe *fpl,* ranghi *mpl* || *tr* arrangiare, allineare; classificare; avere rango superiore a || *intr* avere il massimo rango; **to rank high** avere un'alta posizione; **to rank low** avere una posizione bassa; **to rank with** essere allo stesso livello di
rank' and file' *s* truppa; massa
rankle ['ræŋkəl] *tr* irritare || *intr* inasprirsi
ransack ['rænsæk] *tr* (*to search thoroughly*) frugare, rovistare; (*to pillage*) svaligiare, saccheggiare
ransom ['rænsəm] *s* taglia, riscatto || *tr* riscattare
rant [rænt] *intr* farneticare, parlare a vanvera
rap [ræp] *s* colpo, colpetto; **I don't care a rap** non m'importa un fico; **to take the rap** (slang) prendersi la colpa || *v* (*pret & pp* **rapped;** *ger* **rapping**) *tr* dare colpi a; battere; **to rap out** (*e.g., a command*) lanciare || *intr* dare colpi, bussare
rapacious [rə'peʃəs] *adj* rapace
rape [rep] *s* rapimento; (*of a woman*) stupro; (bot) ravizzone *m* || *tr* rapire; forzare, violentare
rapid ['ræpɪd] *adj* rapido || **rapids** *spl* rapide *fpl*
rap'id-fire' *adj* a tiro rapido
rapidity [rə'pɪdəti] *s* rapidità *f*
rapier ['repɪ•ər] *s* spada, stocco
rapt [ræpt] *adj* assorto; estatico
rapture ['ræptʃər] *s* rapimento, estasi *f*
rare [rɛr] *adj* raro; (*thinly distributed*) rado; (*gas*) rarefatto; (*meat*) al sangue; (*gem*) prezioso
rare'-earth' met'al *s* metallo delle terre rare
rare•fy ['rɛrɪ,faɪ] *v* (*pret & pp* **-fied**) *tr* rarefare || *intr* rarefarsi
rarely ['rɛrli] *adv* di rado, raramente
rascal ['ræskəl] *s* briccone *m,* birbante *m*
rash [ræʃ] *adj* temerario, precipitato || *s* eruzione; (fig) mucchio
rasp [ræsp] or [rɑsp] *s* raspa; rumore

m di raspa || *tr* raspare; irritare; dire con voce roca || *intr* fare rumore raspante
raspber·ry ['ræz,beri] or ['rɑz,beri] *s* (**-ries**) lampone *m;* (slang) pernacchia
rat [ræt] *s* ratto; (*to give fullness to hair*) posticcio; (slang) traditore *m;* **to smell a rat** (coll) subodorare un inganno
ratchet ['rætʃɪt] *s* nottolino
rate [ret] *s* (*of interest*) saggio, tasso; prezzo; costo; velocità *f;* (*degree of action*) ragione; tariffa; **at any rate** ad ogni modo; **at the rate of** in ragione di || *tr* valutare, classificare || *intr* essere considerato; essere classificato
rate' of exchange' *s* corso del cambio
rather ['ræðər] or ['rɑðər] *adv* piuttosto; a preferenza; per meglio dire; bensì; discretamente; **rather than** piuttosto di || *interj* e come!
rati·fy ['rætɪ,faɪ] *v* (*pret & pp* **-fied**) *tr* ratificare, sancire
rating ['retɪŋ] *s* classifica; (nav) grado; (com) valutazione
ra·tio ['reʃo] or ['reʃɪ,o] *s* (**-tios**) ragione, rapporto; proporzione
ration ['reʃən] or ['ræʃən] *s* razione || *tr* razionare
rational ['ræʃənəl] *adj* razionale
ra'tion book' *s* tessera di razionamento
rat' poi'son *s* veleno per i topi
rat' race' *s* (coll) corsa dei barberi
rattle ['rætəl] *s* (*sharp sounds*) fracasso; (*child's toy*) sonaglio; (*noisemaking device*) raganella; (*in throat*) rantolo || *tr* scuotere; (*to confuse*) sconcertare; **to rattle off** dire rapidamente, snocciolare || *intr* risuonare; scuotersi; cianciare
rat'tle·snake' *s* serpente *m* a sonagli
rat'trap' *s* trappola per topi; (*hovel*) topaia; (*jam*) (fig) frangente *m*
raucous ['rɔkəs] *adj* rauco
ravage ['rævɪdʒ] *s* distruzione; **ravages** (*of time*) oltraggio || *tr* distruggere, disfare
rave [rev] *intr* farneticare, delirare; infuriare; andare in estasi; **to rave about** levare alle stelle
raven ['revən] *s* corvo
ravenous ['rævənəs] *adj* famelico
ravine [rə'vin] *s* canalone *m*, burrone *m*
ravish ['rævɪʃ] *tr* incantare, entusiasmare; rapire; (*a woman*) stuprare
raw [rɔ] *adj* crudo; (*e.g., silk*) grezzo; (*flesh*) vivo; inesperto
raw' deal' *s* trattamento brutale e ingiusto
raw'hide' *s* pelle greggia
raw' mate'rial *s* materia prima
ray [re] *s* raggio; (*fish*) razza
rayon ['re·ɑn] *s* raion *m*
raze [rez] *tr* radere al suolo
razor ['rezər] *s* rasoio
ra'zor blade' *s* lametta
ra'zor strop' *s* coramella
razz [ræz] *s* (slang) pernacchia || *tr* (slang) prendere in giro
reach [ritʃ] *s* portata; estensione; **out of reach (of)** fuori della portata (di); oltre alle possibilità (di); fuori tiro (di); **within reach of** alla portata di || *tr* raggiungere; toccare; (*customers*) guadagnare || *intr* estendere la mano; **to reach for** cercare di raggiungere
react [rɪ'ækt] *intr* reagire
reaction [rɪ'ækʃən] *s* reazione
reactionar·y [rɪ'ækʃə,neri] *adj* reazionario || *s* (**-ies**) reazionario
reactor [rɪ'æktər] *s* reattore *m*
read [rid] *v* (*pret & pp* **read** [red]) *tr* leggere; (*s.o.'s thoughts*) leggere in; **to read over** ripassare || *intr* leggere; saper leggere; essere concepito, e.g., **your cable reads thus** il vostro telegramma è concepito così; leggersi, e.g., **this books reads easily** questo libro si legge facilmente; **to read on** continuare a leggere
reader ['ridər] *s* lettore *m;* libro di lettura, sillabo
readily ['redɪli] *adv* velocemente; facilmente; di buona voglia
reading ['ridɪŋ] *s* lettura; dizione
read'ing desk' *s* leggio
read'ing glass' *s* lente *f* d'ingrandimento; **reading glasses** occhiali *mpl* per la lettura
read'ing lamp' *s* lampada da scrittoio
read'ing room' *s* sala di lettura
read·y ['redi] *adj* (**-ier; -iest**) pronto; disponibile; **to make ready** preparare; prepararsi || *v* (*pret & pp* **-ied**) *tr* preparare || *intr* prepararsi
read'y cash' *s* denaro contante
read'y-made cloth'ing *s* confezioni *fpl*
read'y-made suit' *s* vestito già fatto
reaffirm [,ri·ə'fʌrm] *tr* riaffermare
reagent [rɪ'edʒənt] *s* reagente *m*
real ['ri·əl] *adj* effettivo, reale
re'al estate' *s* beni *mpl* immobili, proprietà *f* immobiliare
re'al-estate' *adj* immobiliare, fondiario
realism ['ri·ə,lɪzəm] *s* realismo
realist ['ri·əlɪst] *s* realista *mf*
realistic [,ri·ə'lɪstɪk] *adj* realistico
reali·ty [rɪ'ælɪti] *s* (**-ties**) realtà *f*
realize ['ri·ə,laɪz] *tr* rendersi conto di; concretare; realizzare || *intr* convertire proprietà in contanti
realm [relm] *s* regno
realtor ['ri·əl,tɔr] or ['ri·əltər] *s* (trademark) agente *m* d'immobili membro dell'associazione nazionale
realty ['ri·əlti] *s* proprietà *f* immobiliare
ream [rim] *s* risma; **reams** pagine *fpl* e pagine || *tr* alesare
reamer ['rimər] *s* (mach) alesatore *m;* (dentistry) fresa
reap [rip] *tr & intr* (*to cut*) mietere; (*to gather*) raccogliere
reaper ['ripər] *s* (*person*) mietitore *m;* (mach) mietitrice *f*
reappear [,ri·ə'pɪr] *intr* ricomparire, riapparire
reappearance [,ri·ə'pɪrəns] *s* riapparizione, ricomparsa
reapportionment [,ri·ə'porʃənmənt] *s* ridistribuzione
rear [rɪr] *adj* posteriore, di dietro || *s*

retro, di dietro; posteriore *m;* (mil) retroguardia || *tr* alzare, elevare; allevare, educare || *intr* (*said of a horse*) impennarsi
rear' ad'miral *s* contrammiraglio
rear' drive' *s* trazione posteriore
rear' end' *s* retro, di dietro; (coll) posteriore *m;* (aut) retrotreno
rearmament [ri'ɑrməmənt] *s* riarmo
rear'-view mir'ror *s* specchietto retrovisivo
rear' win'dow *s* (aut) lunetta posteriore
reason ['rizən] *s* ragione; **by reason of** per causa di; **to bring s.o. to reason** indurre qlcu alla ragione; **to stand to reason** esser logico || *tr & intr* ragionare
reasonable ['rizənəbəl] *adj* ragionevole
reassessment [,ri·ə'sesmənt] *s* rivalutazione
reassure [,ri·ə'ʃur] *tr* rassicurare, riassicurare
reawaken [,ri·ə'wekən] *tr* risvegliare || *intr* risvegliarsi
rebate ['ribet] or [rɪ'bet] *s* ribasso || *tr* ribassare
rebel ['rɛbəl] *adj & s* ribelle *mf* || **re•bel** [rɪ'bɛl] *v* (*pret & pp* **-belled;** *ger* **-belling**) *intr* ribellarsi
rebellion [rɪ'bɛljən] *s* ribellione
rebellious [rɪ'bɛljəs] *adj* ribelle
re•bind [ri'baɪnd] *v* (*pret & pp* **-bound** ['baʊnd]) *tr* rifasciare; (bb) rilegare
rebirth ['ribʌrθ] or [ri'bʌrθ] *s* rinascita
rebore [ri'bor] *tr* rialesare, rettificare
rebound ['rɪ,baʊnd] or [ri'baʊnd] *s* rimbalzo || [ri'baʊnd] *intr* rimbalzare
rebroad'casting sta'tion *s* stazione ripetitrice
rebuff [rɪ'bʌf] *s* rifiuto || *tr* respingere, rifiutare
rebuild [ri'bɪld] *v* (*pret & pp* **-built** ['bɪlt]) *tr* ricostruire, riedificare
rebuke [rɪ'bjuk] *s* rabbuffo || *tr* rabbuffare
re•but [rɪ'bʌt] *v* (*pret & pp* **-butted;** *ger* **-butting**) *tr* confutare
rebuttal [rɪ'bʌtəl] *s* confutazione
recall [rɪ'kɔl] or ['rikɔl] *s* richiamo; revoca || [rɪ'kɔl] *tr* richiamare; ricordare, ricordarsi di; richiamare alla memoria
recant [rɪ'kænt] *tr* ritrattare || *intr* ritrattarsi
re•cap ['ri,kæp] or [ri'kæp] *v* (*pret & pp* **-capped;** *ger* **-capping**) *tr* ricapitolare, riepilogare; (*a tire*) rifare il battistrada a
recapitulation [,rikə,pɪtʃə'leʃən] *s* ricapitolazione, riepilogo
re•cast ['ri,kæst] or ['ri,kɑst] *s* rifusione || [ri'kæst] or [ri'kɑst] *v* (*pret & pp* **-cast**) *tr* rifondere
recede [rɪ'sid] *intr* ritirarsi, allontanarsi; recedere, retrocedere; (*said, e.g., of chin*) sfuggire
receipt [rɪ'sit] *s* ricevimento; (*acknowledgment of payment*) ricevuta; (*recipe*) ricetta; **receipts** incasso, introito || *tr* quietanzare
receive [rɪ'siv] *tr* ricevere; (*stolen goods*) ricettare; (*to have inflicted upon one*) subire || *intr* ricevere
receiver [rɪ'sivər] *s* ricevitore *m;* ricettatore *m;* (law) curatore *m* fallimentare; (telp) auricolare *m*
receiv'ing set' *s* apparecchio radioricevente
receiv'ing tell'er *s* cassiere *m* incaricato delle riscossioni
recent ['risənt] *adj* recente
recently ['risəntli] *adv* recentemente, di recente
receptacle [rɪ'sɛptəkəl] *s* recipiente *m;* (elec) presa
reception [rɪ'sɛpʃən] *s* accoglienza; (*function*) ricevimento
recep'tion desk' *s* ufficio informazioni, bureau *m*
receptionist [rɪ'sɛpʃənɪst] *s* accoglitrice *f;* (*male*) usciere *m*
receptive [rɪ'sɛptɪv] *adj* ricettivo
recess [rɪ'sɛs] or ['risɛs] *s* intermezzo, interludio; ora di ricreazione; (*in a line*) rientranza; (*in a wall*) nicchia, alcova; (fig) recesso || [rɪ'sɛs] *tr* aggiornare, dare vacanza a; incassare, mettere in una nicchia || *intr* aggiornarsi, prendersi vacanza
recession [rɪ'sɛʃən] *s* ritirata; processione finale; (com) recessione
recipe ['rɛsɪ,pi] *s* ricetta
reciprocal [rɪ'sɪprəkəl] *adj* reciproco
reciprocity [,rɛsɪ'prɑsɪti] *s* reciprocità *f*
recital [rɪ'saɪtəl] *s* narrazione; (*of music or poetry*) recital *m*
recite [rɪ'saɪt] *tr* raccontare; (*music or poetry*) recitare
reckless ['rɛklɪs] *adj* temerario, spericolato
reckon ['rɛkən] *tr* calcolare; considerare; (coll) supporre || *intr* contare; **to reckon with** prevedere, tener conto di
reclaim [rɪ'klem] *tr* (*land*) sanare, prosciugare; (*substances*) rigenerare; (fig) rigenerare
recline [rɪ'klaɪn] *tr* reclinare || *intr* reclinarsi, adagiarsi
recluse [rɪ'klus] or ['rɛklus] *adj & s* recluso
recognition [,rɛkəg'nɪʃən] *s* riconoscimento
recognize ['rɛkəg,naɪz] *tr* riconoscere
recoil [rɪ'kɔɪl] *s* indietreggiamento; (*of a firearm*) rinculo || *intr* indietreggiare; rinculare
recollect [,rɛkə'lɛkt] *tr & intr* ricordare
recollection [,rɛkə'lɛkʃən] *s* ricordo
recommend [,rɛkə'mɛnd] *tr* raccomandare
recompense ['rɛkəm,pɛns] *s* ricompensa || *tr* ricompensare
reconcile ['rɛkən,saɪl] *tr* riconciliare; **to reconcile oneself** rassegnarsi
reconnaissance [rɪ'kɑnɪsəns] *s* ricognizione
reconnoiter [,rɛkə'nɔɪtər] or [,rikə'nɔɪtər] *tr & intr* perlustrare
reconsider [,rikən'sɪdər] *tr* riconsiderare

reconstruct [ˌrikənˈstrʌkt] *tr* ricostruire
reconversion [ˌrikənˈvʌrʒən] *s* riconversione
record [ˈrɛkərd] *s* registrazione; annotazione; (*official report*) verbale *m*, protocollo; (*criminal*) fedina sporca; (*of a phonograph*) disco; (educ) documenti *mpl* scolastici; (sports) record *m*, primato; **off the record** confidenziale; confidenzialmente; **records** annali *mpl*, documenti *mpl*; **to break a record** battere un record ‖ [rɪˈkɔrd] *tr* registrare; mettere a verbale; (*e.g., a song*) incidere
rec'ord break'er *s* (sports) primatista *mf*
rec'ord chang'er [ˈtʃendʒər] *s* cambiadischi *m*
recorder [rɪˈkɔrdər] *s* (*apparatus*) registratore *m*; (law) cancelliere *m*; (mus) flauto a imboccatura a tubo
rec'ord hold'er *s* (sports) primatista *mf*
recording [rɪˈkɔrdɪŋ] *s* registrazione; (*of a record*) incisione; (*record*) disco
record'ing sec'retary *s* cancelliere *m*
rec'ord play'er *s* giradischi *m*
recount [ˈri ˌkaunt] *s* nuovo conteggio ‖ [riˈkaunt] *tr* (*to count again*) ricontare ‖ [rɪˈkaunt] *tr* (*to narrate*) raccontare
recourse [rɪˈkors] or [ˈrikors] *s* ricorso; (com) rivalsa; **to have recourse to** ricorrere a
recover [rɪˈkʌvər] *tr* ricuperare, riacquistare; (*a substance*) rigenerare; **to recover consciousness** riaversi, riprendere conoscenza ‖ *intr* rimettersi; guadagnare una causa
recover•y [rɪˈkʌvəri] *s* (**-ies**) ricupero; guarigione; **past recovery** incurabile
recreant [ˈrɛkrɪ·ənt] *adj* & *s* codardo; traditore *m*
recreation [ˌrɛkrɪˈeʃən] *s* ricreazione
recruit [rɪˈkrut] *s* recluta ‖ *tr* & *intr* reclutare
rectangle [ˈrɛk ˌtæŋgəl] *s* rettangolo
rectifier [ˈrɛktə ˌfaɪ·ər] *s* rettificatore *m*; (elec) raddrizzatore *m*
recti•fy [ˈrɛktɪ ˌfaɪ] *v* (*pret* & *pp* **-fied**) *tr* rettificare; (elec) raddrizzare
rectitude [ˈrɛktɪ ˌtud] or [ˈrɛktɪ ˌtjud] *s* rettitudine *f*
rec•tum [ˈrɛktəm] *s* (**-tums** or **-ta** [tə]) retto
recumbent [rɪˈkʌmbənt] *adj* sdraiato
recuperate [rɪˈkjupə ˌret] *tr* ricuperare ‖ *intr* ristabilirsi, rimettersi
re•cur [rɪˈkʌr] *v* (*pret* & *pp* **-curred**; *ger* **-curring**) *intr* ricorrere; ritornare; tornare a mente
recurrent [rɪˈkʌrənt] *adj* ricorrente
recycle [riˈsaɪkəl] *tr* riconvertire; (*e.g., in chemical industry*) riciclare
red [rɛd] *adj* (**redder; reddest**) rosso ‖ *s* rosso; **in the red** in debito , in rosso ‖ **Red** *adj* & *s* (*Communist*) rosso
red'bait' *tr* dare del comunista a
red'bird' *s* cardinale *m*
red-blooded [ˈrɛd ˌblʌdɪd] *adj* sanguigno; vigoroso
red'breast' *s* pettirosso
red'bud' *s* siliquastro
red'cap' *s* (Brit) poliziotto militare; (U.S.A.) facchino
red' cell' *s* globulo rosso
red' cent' *s*—**to not have a red cent** (coll) non avere il becco di un quattrino
Red' Cross' *s* Croce Rossa
redden [ˈrɛdən] *tr* arrossare ‖ *intr* arrossire
redeem [rɪˈdim] *tr* redimere; (*a promise*) disimpegnare
redeemer [rɪˈdimər] *s* redentore *m*
redemption [rɪˈdɛmpʃən] *s* redenzione; disimpegno
red-handed [ˈrɛdˈhændɪd] *adj*—**to be caught red-handed** esser colto sul fatto or con le mani nel sacco
red'head' *s* persona dai capelli rossi
red' her'ring *s* argomento usato per sviare l'attenzione; aringa affumicata
red'-hot' *adj* rovente, incandescente; fresco fresco, appena uscito
rediscover [ˌridɪsˈkʌvər] *tr* riscoprire
red'-let'ter *adj* memorabile
red'-light' dis'trict *s* quartiere *m* delle case di tolleranza
red' man' *s* pellerossa *m*
re•do [ˈriˈdu] *v* (*pret* **-did** [ˈdɪd]; *pp* **-done** [ˈdʌn]) *tr* rifare
redolent [ˈrɛdələnt] *adj* fragrante, profumato; **redolent of** che sa di
redoubt [rɪˈdaut] *s* (mil) ridotta
redound [rɪˈdaund] *intr* ridondare
red' pep'per *s* pepe *m* di Caienna
redress [rɪˈdrɛs] or [ˈridrɛs] *s* riparazione, risarcimento ‖ [rɪˈdrɛs] *tr* riparare, risarcire
red'skin' *s* pellerossa *mf*
red' tape' *s* trafila, burocrazia
reduce [rɪˈdjus] or [rɪˈdus] *tr* ridurre; diluire; (mil) retrocedere; (*a hernia*) (surg) sbrigliare ‖ *intr* ridursi; (*to lose weight*) dimagrire
reducing [rɪˈdjusɪŋ] or [rɪˈdusɪŋ] *adj* dimagrante; (chem) riducente
reduction [rɪˈdʌkʃən] *s* riduzione
redundant [rɪˈdʌndənt] *adj* ridondante
red'wood' *s* sequoia
reed [rid] *s* (*stalk*) calamo; (*plant*) canna; (mus) linguetta; (mus) strumento a linguetta
reedit [riˈɛdit] *tr* rifondere
reef [rif] *s* scoglio, barriera; (naut) terzarolo; (min) vena, filone *m* ‖ *tr* (*sail*) imbrogliare
reefer [ˈrifər] *s* giacchetta a doppio petto; (slang) sigaretta di marijuana
reek [rik] *intr* puzzare; sudare, evaporare, fumare
reel [ril] *s* (*spool*) bobina; (*sway*) vacillamento; (*for fishing*) mulinello; **off the reel** senza esitazione ‖ *tr* bobinare; **to reel off** rifilare ‖ *intr* barcollare
reelection [ˌri·ɪˈlɛkʃən] *s* rielezione
reenlist [ˌri·ɛnˈlɪst] *tr* arruolare di nuovo ‖ *intr* arruolarsi di nuovo
reen•try [rɪˈɛntri] *s* (**-tries**) rientro
reexamination [ˌri·ɛg ˌzæmɪˈneʃən] *s* riesame *m*

re•fer [rɪˈfʌr] *v* (*pret & pp* **-ferred;** *ger* **-ferring**) *tr* riferire ‖ *intr* riferirsi
referee [ˌrɛfəˈri] *s* arbitro ‖ *tr & intr* arbitrare
reference [ˈrɛfərəns] *s* riferimento; (*testimonial*) referenza; (*e.g., in a book*) rinvio, rimando
ref'erence book' *s* libro di consultazione
referen•dum [ˌrɛfəˈrɛndəm] *s* (**-dums** or **-da** [də]) referendum *m*
refill [ˈrifɪl] *s* ricambio ‖ [rɪˈfɪl] *tr* riempire di nuovo
refine [rɪˈfaɪn] *tr* raffinare
refinement [rɪˈfaɪnmənt] *s* raffinatezza; (*of oil*) raffinatura
refiner•y [rɪˈfaɪnəri] *s* (**-ies**) raffineria
reflect [rɪˈflɛkt] *tr* riflettere ‖ *intr* riflettere, riflettersi
reflection [rɪˈflɛkʃən] *s* riflessione
reflex [ˈriflɛks] *adj* riflesso ‖ *s* riflesso; (*camera*) reflex *m*
reflexive [rɪˈflɛksɪv] *adj* riflessivo
reforestation [ˌrifɑrɪsˈteʃən] or [ˌrifɔrɪsˈteʃən] *s* rimboschimento
reform [rɪˈfɔrm] *s* riforma ‖ *tr* riformare ‖ *intr* correggersi
reformation [ˌrɛfərˈmeʃən] *s* riforma ‖ **Reformation** *s*—**the Reformation** la Riforma
reformato•ry [rɪˈfɔrməˌtori] *adj* riformativo ‖ *s* (**-ries**) riformatorio
reformer [rɪˈfɔrmər] *s* riformatore *m*
reform' school' *s* riformatorio
refraction [rɪˈfrækʃən] *s* rifrazione
refrain [rɪˈfren] *s* ritornello, intercalare *m* ‖ *intr* astenersi
refresh [rɪˈfrɛʃ] *tr* rinfrescare; ristorare ‖ *intr* ristorarsi
refreshing [rɪˈfrɛʃɪŋ] *adj* rinfrescante; ristoratore; ricreativo
refreshment [rɪˈfrɛʃmənt] *s* rinfresco
refrigerate [rɪˈfrɪdʒəˌret] *tr* refrigerare
refrigerator [rɪˈfrɪdʒəˌretər] *s* refrigerante *m*, frigorifero
refrig'erator car' *s* vagone frigorifero
re•fuel [riˈfjul] *v* (*pret & pp* **-fueled** or **-fuelled;** *ger* **-fueling** or **-fuelling**) *tr* rifornire di carburante ‖ *intr* rifornirsi di carburante
refuge [ˈrɛfjudʒ] *s* rifugio; scampo; **to take refuge (in)** rifugiarsi (in)
refugee [ˌrɛfjuˈdʒi] *s* rifugiato
refund [ˈrifʌnd] *s* rifusione ‖ [rɪˈfʌnd] *tr* (*to repay*) rifondere ‖ [riˈfʌnd] *tr* (*bonds*) consolidare; (*to fund anew*) rifondere
refurnish [riˈfʌrnɪʃ] *tr* riammobiliare
refusal [rɪˈfjuzəl] *s* rifiuto
refuse [ˈrɛfjus] *s* rifiuto, spazzatura ‖ [rɪˈfjuz] *tr* rifiutare; **to refuse to** rifiutarsi di
refute [rɪˈfjut] *tr* smentire, confutare
regain [rɪˈgen] *tr* riguadagnare; **to regain consciousness** tornare in sé
regal [ˈrigəl] *adj* reale, regale
regale [rɪˈgel] *tr* intrattenere, rallegrare
regalia [rɪˈgelɪ·ə] *spl* (*of royalty*) prerogative *fpl* reali; alta uniforme
regard [rɪˈgɑrd] *s* riguardo; (*look*) sguardo; (*esteem*) rispetto; **in regard to** rispetto a; **regards** rispetti *mpl;* **warm regards** cordiali saluti *mpl;* **without regard to** senza considerare ‖ *tr* considerare; osservare; concernere; **as regards** per quanto concerne
regarding [rɪˈgɑrdɪŋ] *prep* per quanto concerne
regardless [rɪˈgɑrdlɪs] *adj* incurante ‖ *adv* ciò nonostante; costi quello che costi; **regardless of** malgrado
regatta [rɪˈgætə] *s* regata
regen•cy [ˈridʒənsi] *s* (**-cies**) reggenza
regenerate [rɪˈdʒenəˌret] *tr* rigenerare ‖ *intr* rigenerarsi
regent [ˈridʒənt] *s* reggente *mf*
regicide [ˈrɛdʒɪˌsaɪd] *s* (*act*) regicidio; (*person*) regicida *mf*
regiment [ˈrɛdʒɪmənt] *s* reggimento ‖ [ˈrɛdʒɪˌmɛnt] *tr* irregimentare
regimental [ˌrɛdʒɪˈmɛntəl] *adj* reggimentale ‖ **regimentals** *spl* uniforme *f* reggimentale
region [ˈridʒən] *s* regione
register [ˈrɛdʒɪstər] *s* registro; (*for controlling the flow of air*) regolatore *m* dell'aria ‖ *tr* registrare; (*e.g., a student*) iscrivere; (*e.g., anger*) dimostrare; (*a letter*) raccomandare ‖ *intr* registrarsi; iscriversi; fare impressione
reg'istered let'ter *s* raccomandata
reg'istered nurse' *s* infermiera diplomata
registrar [ˈrɛdʒɪsˌtrɑr] *s* registratore *m*, archivista *mf;* (*of deeds*) ricevitore *m*
registration [ˌrɛdʒɪsˈtreʃən] *s* registrazione; (*e.g., of a student*) iscrizione; (*of mail*) raccomandazione
registra'tion fee' *s* diritto di segreteria
re•gret [rɪˈgret] *s* pentimento, rammarico; **regrets** scuse *fpl* ‖ *v* (*pret & pp* **-gretted;** *ger* **-gretting**) *tr* rimpiangere; **to regret to** essere spiacente di
regrettable [rɪˈgretəbəl] *adj* deplorevole
regular [ˈrɛgjələr] *adj* regolare; (*life*) regolato; (coll) vero ‖ *s* cliente *m* abituale; (mil) effettivo
regularity [ˌrɛgjuˈlærɪti] *s* regolarità *f*
regularize [ˈrɛgjələˌraɪz] *tr* regoralizzare
regulate [ˈrɛgjəˌlet] *tr* regolare
regulation [ˌrɛgjəˈleʃən] *s* regolazione; (*rule*) regolamento
rehabilitate [ˌrihəˈbɪlɪˌtet] *tr* riabilitare
rehearsal [rɪˈhʌrsəl] *s* prova
rehearse [rɪˈhʌrs] *tr* provare ‖ *intr* fare le prove
rehiring [riˈhaɪrɪŋ] *s* riassunzione
reign [ren] *s* regno ‖ *intr* regnare
reimburse [ˌri·ɪmˈbʌrs] *tr* rimborsare
rein [ren] *s* redine *f;* **to give full rein to** dare briglia sciolta a ‖ *tr* guidare con le redini; frenare
reincarnation [ˌri·ɪnkɑrˈneʃən] *s* reincarnazione
reindeer [ˈrenˌdɪr] *s* renna
reinforce [ˌri·ɪnˈfors] *tr* rinforzare; (*a wall*) armare
re'inforced con'crete *s* cemento armato

reinforcement [ˌri·ɪnˈforsmənt] *s* rinforzo
reinstate [ˌri·ɪnˈstet] *tr* reintegrare
reiterate [riˈɪtəˌret] *tr* reiterare
reject [ˈridʒɛkt] *s* rigetto, rifiuto; **rejects** scarti *mpl* || [rɪˈdʒɛkt] *tr* rigettare; (*to refuse*) rifiutare
rejection [rɪˈdʒɛkʃən] *s* rigetto; rifiuto
rejoice [rɪˈdʒɔɪs] *intr* rallegrarsi
rejoin [riˈdʒɔɪn] *tr* raggiungere; (*to reunite*) riunire; (*to reply*) rispondere
rejoinder [rɪˈdʒɔɪndər] *s* risposta; (law) controreplica
rejuvenation [rɪˌdʒuvɪˈneʃən] *s* ringiovanimento
rekindle [riˈkɪndəl] *tr* riaccendere
relapse [rɪˈlæps] *s* ricaduta || *intr* ricadere
relate [rɪˈlet] *tr* mettere in relazione; (*to tell*) narrare
relation [rɪˈleʃən] *s* relazione; (*account*) resoconto; (*relative*) parente *mf;* (*kinship*) parentela; **in relation to** or **with** in relazione a
relationship [rɪˈleʃənˌʃɪp] *s* rapporto, relazione; (*kinship*) parentela
relative [ˈrɛlətɪv] *adj* relativo || *s* congiunto, parente *mf*
relativity [ˌrɛləˈtɪvɪti] *s* relatività *f*
relax [rɪˈlæks] *tr* rilasciare, rilassare || *intr* rilasciarsi, rilassarsi
relaxation [ˌrilæksˈeʃən] *s* distensione; (*entertainment*) ricreazione
relaxa'tion of ten'sion *s* distensione
relaxing [rɪˈlæksɪŋ] *adj* rilassante; divertente
relay [ˈrile] or [rɪˈle] *s* (elec) relè *m;* (rad) ripetitore *m;* (mil, sports) staffetta; (sports) corsa a staffetta || *v* (*pret & pp* **-layed**) *tr* trasmettere, ritrasmettere || [rɪˈle] *v* (*pret & pp* **-laid**) *tr* rimettere, porre di nuovo
re'lay race' *s* corsa a staffetta
release [rɪˈlis] *s* (*e.g., from jail*) liberazione; (*from obligation*) disimpegno; (*for publication*) autorizzazione; (mov) distribuzione; (journ) comunicato; (aer) lancio; (mach) scappamento || *tr* liberare; disimpegnare; autorizzare la pubblicazione di; (mov) distribuire; (*a bomb*) (aer) lanciare; **to release s.o. from a debt** rimettere un debito a qlcu
relent [rɪˈlɛnt] *intr* placarsi
relentless [riˈlɛntlɪs] *adj* implacabile
relevant [ˈrɛlɪvənt] *adj* pertinente
reliable [rɪˈlaɪ·əbəl] *adj* (*person*) fidato; (*source*) attendibile
reliance [rɪˈlaɪ·əns] *s* fiducia, fede *f*
relic [ˈrɛlɪk] *s* reliquia
relief [rɪˈlif] *s* sollievo; sussidio; (*prominence; projection*) rilievo; (mil) cambio; **in relief** in rilievo; **on relief** sotto sussidio
relieve [rɪˈliv] *tr* (*e.g., pain*) alleviare; (*e.g., a load*) sgravare; (mil) rilevare
religion [rɪˈlɪdʒən] *s* religione
religious [rɪˈlɪdʒəs] *adj* religioso
relinquish [rɪˈlɪŋkwɪʃ] *tr* abbandonare
relish [ˈrɛlɪʃ] *s* piacere *m,* gusto; sapore *m,* aroma *m;* (culin) condimento || *tr* gustare, apprezzare; dare gusto a
reluctance [rɪˈlʌktəns] *s* riluttanza
reluctant [rɪˈlʌktənt] *adj* riluttante
re·ly [rɪˈlaɪ] *v* (*pret & pp* **-lied**) *intr* fare assegnamento; **to rely on** fidarsi di, fondarsi su
remain [rɪˈmen] *s*—**remains** resti *mpl;* resti *mpl* mortali || *intr* restare, rimanere
remainder [rɪˈmendər] *s* resto, restante *m;* (*unsold books*) fondi *mpl* di libreria || *tr* vendere come rimanenza
re·make [riˈmek] *v* (*pret & pp* **-made** [ˈmed]) *tr* rifare
remark [rɪˈmɑrk] *s* osservazione, rimarco || *tr & intr* osservare; **to remark on** fare osservazioni su
remarkable [rɪˈmɑrkəbəl] *adj* notevole
remar·ry [riˈmæri] *v* (*pret & pp* **-ried**) *intr* riprendere moglie, risposarsi
reme·dy [ˈrɛmɪdi] *s* (**-dies**) rimedio || *v* (*pret & pp* **-died**) *tr* rimediare (with *dat*)
remember [rɪˈmɛmbər] *tr* ricordarsi di; (*to send greetings to*) ricordare || *intr* ricordare, ricordarsi
remembrance [rɪˈmɛmbrəns] *s* rimembranza, ricordo
remind [rɪˈmaɪnd] *tr* rammentare
reminder [rɪˈmaɪndər] *s* promemoria
reminisce [ˌrɛmɪˈnɪs] *intr* ricordare il passato
reminiscence [ˌrɛmɪˈnɪsəns] *s* reminiscenza
remiss [rɪˈmɪs] *adj* negligente
re·mit [rɪˈmɪt] *v* (*pret & pp* **-mitted;** *ger* **-mitting**) *tr* rimettere; (*to a lower court*) (law) rinviare
remittance [rɪˈmɪtəns] *s* rimessa
remnant [ˈrɛmnənt] *s* (*remaining quantity*) rimanente *m;* (*of cloth*) scampolo; vestigio; **remnants** (*of merchandise*) rimanenze *fpl,* fondi *mpl* di magazzino
remod·el [riˈmɑdəl] *v* (*pret & pp* **-eled** or **-elled;** *ger* **-eling** or **-elling**) *tr* rimodellare; ricostruire
remonstrance [rɪˈmɑnstrəns] *s* rimostranza
remonstrate [rɪˈmɑnstret] *intr* protestare, rimostrare; **to remonstrate with** rimostrare a
remorse [rɪˈmɔrs] *s* rimorso
remorseful [rɪˈmɔrsfəl] *adj* tormentato dal rimorso, pentito
remote [rɪˈmot] *adj* remoto
remote' control' *s* telecomando
removable [rɪˈmuvəbəl] *adj* amovibile
removal [rɪˈmuvəl] *s* rimozione; trasferimento; (*dismissal*) destituzione
remove [rɪˈmuv] *tr* rimuovere; (*one's jacket*) togliersi, cavarsi; (*from office*) destituire; eliminare || *intr* trasferirsi; andarsene
remuneration [rɪˌmjunəˈreʃən] *s* rimunerazione
renaissance [ˌrɛnəˈsɑns] or [rɪˈnesəns] *s* rinascimento, rinascita || **Renaissance** *s* Rinascimento
rend [rɛnd] *v* (*pret & pp* **rent** [rɛnt]) *tr* (*to tear*) stracciare; (*to split*) fendere, squarciare
render [ˈrɛndər] *tr* (*justice*) rendere;

(*a service*) fare; (*aid*) prestare; (*a bill*) presentare; (*to translate*) tradurre; (*a piece of music*) interpretare; (*e.g., fat*) struggere
rendez•vous ['rɑndə,vu] *s* (**-vous** [,vuz]) appuntamento; (*in space*) incontro || *v* (*pret & pp* **-voused** [,vud]; *ger* **-vousing** [,vu·ɪŋ]) *intr* incontrarsi
rendition [rɛn'dɪʃən] *s* restituzione, resa; traduzione; interpretazione
renege [rɪ'nɪg] *s* rifiuto || *intr* rifiutare; (coll) venire meno
renew [rɪ'nju] or [rɪ'nu] *tr* rinnovare || *intr* rinnovarsi
renewal [rɪ'nju·əl] or [rɪ'nu·əl] *s* rinnovo, rinnovamento
renounce [rɪ'naʊns] *tr* rinunziare (with *dat*); ripudiare
renovate ['rɛnə,vet] *tr* rinnovare; (*a building*) restaurare; (*a room*) rimettere a nuovo
renown [rɪ'naʊn] *s* rinomanza
renowned [rɪ'naʊnd] *adj* rinomato
rent [rɛnt] *adj* scisso || *s* fitto, pigione; (*tear*) squarcio || *tr* locare, dare a pigione || *intr* prendere a pigione
rental ['rɛntəl] *s* affitto
renter ['rɛntər] *s* affittuario, locatario
renunciation [rɪ,nʌnsɪ'eʃən] or [rɪ,nʌnʃɪ'eʃən] *s* rinunzia
reopen [ri'opən] *tr* riaprire || *intr* riaprirsi
reopening [ri'opənɪŋ] *s* riapertura
reorganize [ri'ɔrgə,naɪz] *tr* riorganizzare || *intr* riorganizzarsi
repair [rɪ'pɛr] *s* riparazione; **in good repair** in buono stato || *tr* riparare || *intr* riparare, dirigersi
repair'man' *s* (**-men'**) aggiustatore *m*
repaper [ri'pepər] *tr* ritappezzare
reparation [,rɛpə'reʃən] *s* riparazione
repartee [,rɛpɑr'ti] *s* replica arguta, rimando
repast [rɪ'pæst] or [rɪ'pɑst] *s* pasto
repatriate [ri'petrɪ,et] *tr* rimpatriare
re•pay [rɪ'pe] *v* (*pret & pp* **-paid** ['ped]) *tr* ripagare
repayment [rɪ'pemənt] *s* rimborso; risarcimento, compensazione
repeal [rɪ'pil] *s* revoca, abrogazione || *tr* revocare, abrogare
repeat [rɪ'pit] *s* ripetizione || *tr* ripetere || *intr* ripetere; (*said of food*) tornare a gola
re•pel [rɪ'pɛl] *v* (*pret & pp* **-pelled;** *ger* **-pelling**) *tr* respingere, ricacciare; ripugnare (with *dat*)
repent [rɪ'pɛnt] *tr* pentirsi di || *intr* pentirsi, ravvedersi
repentance [rɪ'pɛntəns] *s* pentimento
repentant [rɪ'pɛntənt] *adj* pentito
repercussion [,ripər'kʌʃən] *s* ripercussione
reperto•ry ['rɛpər,tori] *s* (**-ries**) (com) magazzino; (theat) repertorio
repetition [,rɛpɪ'tɪʃən] *s* ripetizione
repine [rɪ'paɪn] *intr* lamentarsi
replace [rɪ'ples] *tr* (*to put back*) rimettere; (*to take the place of*) rimpiazzare
replaceable [rɪ'plesəbəl] *adj* sostituibile
replacement [rɪ'plesmənt] *s* rimpiazzo, sostituzione; **as a replacement for** al posto di
replenish [rɪ'plɛnɪʃ] *tr* rifornire
replete [rɪ'plit] *adj* pieno zeppo
replica ['rɛplɪkə] *s* replica
re•ply [rɪ'plaɪ] *s* (**-plies**) risposta || *v* (*pret & pp* **-plied**) *tr & intr* rispondere
report [rɪ'port] *s* rapporto, informazione; voce *f*, rumore *m;* (*of a physician*) responso; (*of a firearm*) detonazione || *tr* riportare, rapportare; denunziare || *intr* fare un rapporto; fare il cronista; presentarsi; **to report sick** (mil) marcare visita
report' card' *s* pagella
reportedly [rɪ'portɪdli] *adv* secondo la voce comune
reporter [rɪ'portər] *s* cronista *mf*, reporter *m*
reporting [rɪ'portɪŋ] *s* reportage *m*
repose [rɪ'poz] *s* riposo || *tr* posare, riporre || *intr* riposare
reprehend [,rɛprɪ'hɛnd] *tr* riprovare, rimproverare
represent [,rɛprɪ'zɛnt] *tr* rappresentare
representation [,rɛprɪsɛn'teʃən] *s* rappresentazione; protesta; **representations** dichiarazioni *fpl*
representative [,rɛprɪ'zɛntətɪv] *adj* rappresentativo || *s* rappresentante *mf;* (pol) deputato
repress [rɪ'prɛs] *tr* reprimere
repression [rɪ'prɛʃən] *s* repressione
reprieve [rɪ'priv] *s* tregua temporanea; sospensione della pena capitale || *tr* accordare una tregua a; sospendere l'esecuzione di
reprimand ['rɛprɪ,mænd] or ['rɛprɪ,mɑnd] *s* sgridata, ramanzina || *tr* sgridare, rimproverare
reprint ['ri,prɪnt] *s* ristampa; (*offprint*) estratto || [ri'prɪnt] *tr* ristampare
reprisal [rɪ'praɪzəl] *s* rappresaglia
reproach [rɪ'protʃ] *s* rimprovero; vituperio || *tr* rimproverare; **to reproach s.o. for s.th** rimproverare qlcu di qlco, rimproverare qlco a qlcu
reproduce [,riprə'djus] or [,riprə'dus] *tr* riprodurre || *intr* riprodursi
reproduction [,riprə'dʌkʃən] *s* riproduzione
reproof [rɪ'pruf] *s* rimprovero
reprove [rɪ'pruv] *tr* rimproverare; disapprovare
reptile ['rɛptɪl] *s* rettile *m*
republic [rɪ'pʌblɪk] *s* repubblica
republican [rɪ'pʌblɪkən] *adj & s* repubblicano
repudiate [rɪ'pjudɪ,et] *tr* ripudiare; rinnegare
repugnant [rɪ'pʌgnənt] *adj* ripugnante
repulse [rɪ'pʌls] *s* rifiuto; sconfitta || *tr* rifiutare; (*e.g., an enemy*) sconfiggere
repulsive [rɪ'pʌlsɪv] *adj* ripulsivo
reputation [,rɛpjə'teʃən] *s* reputazione

repute [rɪˈpjut] *s* reputazione, fama || *tr* reputare
reputedly [rɪˈpjutɪdli] *adv* secondo l'opinione corrente
request [rɪˈkwɛst] *s* domanda, richiesta; **at the request of** su domanda di || *tr* richiedere
Requiem [ˈrikwɪ ˌɛm] or [ˈrɛkwɪ ˌɛm] *adj* di Requiem || *s* Requiem *m & f;* Messa di Requiem
require [rɪˈkwaɪr] *tr* richiedere
requirement [rɪˈkwaɪrmənt] *s* requisito; richiesta, fabbisogno
requisite [ˈrekwɪzɪt] *adj* requisito, richiesto || *s* requisito
requisition [ˌrɛkwɪˈzɪʃən] *s* requisizione
requital [rɪˈkwaɪtəl] *s* contraccambio
requite [rɪˈkwaɪt] *tr* (*e.g., an injury*) contraccambiare; (*a person*) contraccambiare (with *dat*)
re·read [riˈrid] *v* (*pret & pp* **-read** [ˈrɛd]) *tr* rileggere
resale [ˈri ˌsel] or [riˈsel] *s* rivendita
rescind [rɪˈsɪnd] *tr* annullare, cancellare; (law) rescindere
rescue [ˈrɛskju] *s* salvataggio, liberazione; **to go to the rescue of** andare al soccorso di || *tr* salvare, liberare, soccorrere
research [rɪˈsʌrtʃ] or [ˈrisʌrtʃ] *s* ricerca, indagine *f* || *intr* investigare
re·sell [riˈsel] *v* (*pret & pp* **-sold** [ˈsold]) *tr* rivendere
resemblance [rɪˈzɛmbləns] *s* somiglianza
resemble [rɪˈzɛmbəl] *tr* somigliare (with *dat*), rassomigliare (with *dat*); **to resemble one another** rassomigliarsi
resent [rɪˈzɛnt] *tr* (*a remark*) risentirsi per; (*a person*) risentirsi con
resentful [rɪˈzɛntfəl] *adj* risentito
resentment [rɪˈzɛntmənt] *s* risentimento
reservation [ˌrɛzərˈveʃən] *s* riserva; (*e.g., for a room*) prenotazione
reserve [rɪˈzʌrv] *s* riserva; (*self-restraint*) riserbo, contegno || *tr* riservare; prenotare
reservist [rɪˈzʌrvɪst] *s* riservista *m*
reservoir [ˈrɛzər ˌvwɑr] *s* serbatoio, cisterna; (*large storage place for supplying community with water*) bacino di riserva; (fig) pozzo
re·set [riˈsɛt] *v* (*pret & pp* **-set;** *ger* **-setting**) *tr* rimettere a posto; (*a watch*) regolare; (*a gem*) incastonare di nuovo; (*a machine*) rimontare
re·ship [riˈʃɪp] *v* (*pret & pp* **-shipped;** *ger* **-shipping**) *tr* rispedire; (*on a ship*) reimbarcare || *intr* reimbarcarsi
reshipment [riˈʃɪpmənt] *s* rispedizione; (*on a ship*) reimbarco
reside [rɪˈzaɪd] *intr* risiedere
residence [ˈrɛzɪdəns] *s* residenza
resident [ˈrɛzɪdənt] *adj & s* residente *mf*
residential [ˌrɛzɪˈdɛnʃəl] *adj* residenziale
residue [ˈrɛzɪ ˌdju] or [ˈrɛsɪ ˌdu] *s* residuo

resign [rɪˈzaɪn] *tr* rassegnare, abbandonare; **to be resigned to** rassegnarsi a || *intr* dimettersi, rassegnare le dimissioni
resignation [ˌrɛzɪgˈneʃən] *s* (*from a job*) dimissione; (*submission*) rassegnazione
resin [ˈrɛzɪn] *s* resina
resist [rɪˈzɪst] *tr* resistere (with *dat*) || *intr* resistere
resistance [rɪˈzɪstəns] *s* resistenza
resole [riˈsol] *tr* risolare
resolute [ˈrɛzə ˌlut] *adj* risoluto
resolution [ˌrɛzəˈluʃən] *s* risoluzione; **good resolutions** buoni propositi
resolve [rɪˈzɑlv] *s* risoluzione || *tr* risolvere || *intr* risolversi
resonance [ˈrɛzənəns] *s* risonanza
resort [rɪˈzɔrt] *s* (*appeal*) ricorso; (*for vacation*) centro di villeggiatura || *intr* ricorrere
resound [rɪˈzaund] *intr* risonare
resounding [rɪˈzaundɪŋ] *adj* risonante; (*success*) strepitoso
resource [rɪˈsors] or [ˈrisors] *s* risorsa
resourceful [rɪˈsorsfəl] *adj* ingegnoso
respect [rɪˈspɛkt] *s* rispetto; **respects** rispetti *mpl,* ossequi *mpl;* **with respect to** rispetto a || *tr* rispettare
respectable [rɪˈspɛktəbəl] *adj* rispettabile; onesto, per bene
respectful [rɪˈspɛktfəl] *adj* rispettoso
respecting [rɪˈspɛktɪŋ] *prep* rispetto a
respective [rɪˈspɛktɪv] *adj* rispettivo
respiratory [ˈrɛspɪrə ˌtori] or [rɪˈspaɪrə ˌtori] *adj* respiratorio
respire [rɪˈspaɪr] *tr & intr* respirare
respite [ˈrɛspɪt] *s* tregua, requie *f;* (*reprieve*) proroga, dilazione
resplendent [rɪˈsplɛndənt] *adj* risplendente
respond [rɪˈspɑnd] *intr* rispondere
response [rɪˈspɑns] *s* risposta
responsibili·ty [rɪ ˌspɑnsɪˈbɪlɪti] *s* (**-ties**) responsibilità *f*
responsible [rɪˈspɑnsɪbəl] *adj* responsabile; (*job*) di fiducia; **responsible for** responsabile di
responsive [rɪˈspɑnsɪv] *adj* rispondente; (*e.g., to affection*) sensibile; (*e.g., motor*) che risponde
rest [rɛst] *s* riposo; (*what remains*) resto; (mus) pausa; **at rest** in riposo; tranquillo, in pace; (*dead*) morto; **the rest** il resto, gli altri; **to come to rest** andare a finire; **to lay to rest** sotterrare || *tr* riposare; (*to direct one's eyes*) dirigere; (*faith*) porre || *intr* riposarsi, riposare; appoggiarsi; **to rest assured (that)** esser sicuro (che); **to rest on** aver fiducia in; basarsi su; (*one's laurels*) dormire su
restaurant [ˈrɛstərənt] or [ˈrɛstə ˌrɑnt] *s* ristorante *m*
restful [ˈrɛstfəl] *adj* riposante, tranquillo
rest' home' *s* casa di riposo
rest'ing place' *s* luogo di riposo; (*of a staircase*) pianerottolo; (*of the dead*) ultima dimora
restitution [ˌrɛstɪˈtjuʃən] or [ˌrɛstɪˈtuʃən] *s* restituzione

restive [ˈrɛstɪv] *adj* irrequieto; (*e.g., horse*) recalcitrante
restless [ˈrɛstlɪs] *adj* irrequieto; (*night*) insonne, in bianco
restock [riˈstɑk] *tr* rifornire; (*e.g., with fish*) ripopolare
restoration [ˌrɛstəˈreʃən] *s* restaurazione
restore [rɪˈstor] *tr* restaurare, ripristinare
restrain [rɪˈstren] *tr* ritenere, frenare; limitare
restraint [rɪˈstrent] *s* restrizione; controllo, ritegno; detenzione
restrict [rɪˈstrɪkt] *tr* restingere, limitare
restriction [rɪˈstrɪkʃən] *s* restrizione
rest′ room′ *s* toletta; gabinetto di decenza
restructuring [rɪˈstrʌktʃərɪŋ] *s* ristrutturazione
result [rɪˈzʌlt] *s* risultato || *intr* risultare; **to result in** risolversi in, concludersi con
resume [rɪˈzum] or [rɪˈzjum] *tr* riprendere || *intr* ricominciare
résumé [ˌrɛzʊˈme] or [ˌrɛzjʊˈme] *s* sunto, riassunto
resumption [rɪˈzʌmpʃən] *s* ripresa
resurface [riˈsʌrfɪs] *tr* mettere copertura nuova a || *intr* riemergere
resurrect [ˌrɛzəˌrɛkt] *tr & intr* risuscitare
resurrection [ˌrɛzəˈrɛkʃən] *s* risurrezione
resuscitate [rɪˈsʌsɪˌtet] *tr* rendere alla vita
retail [ˈritel] *adj & adv* al dettaglio, al minuto || *s* dettaglio || *tr* dettagliare, vendere al minuto || *intr* vendere or vendersi al minuto
retailer [ˈritelər] *s* dettagliante *mf*
retain [rɪˈten] *tr* ritenere; (*a lawyer*) assicurarsi i servizi di
retaliate [rɪˈtælɪˌet] *intr* fare rappresaglie; **to retaliate for** ricambiare
retaliation [rɪˌtælɪˈeʃən] *s* rappresaglia
retard [rɪˈtɑrd] *s* ritardo || *tr* ritardare
retch [retʃ] *intr* avere sforzi di vomito
reticence [ˈrɛtɪsəns] *s* riservatezza
reticent [ˈrɛtɪsənt] *adj* riservato, taciturno
retina [ˈrɛtɪnə] *s* retina
retinue [ˈrɛtɪˌnju] or [ˈrɛtɪˌnu] *s* seguito, corteggio
retire [rɪˈtaɪr] *tr* ritirare; (*an employee*) giubilare, mettere a riposo || *intr* ritirarsi; andare a riposo; (*to go to bed*) andare a letto
retired [rɪˈtaɪrd] *adj* (*employee*) in pensione; (*officer*) a riposo
retirement [rɪˈtaɪrmənt] *s* ritiro; (*of an employee*) pensionamento, quiescenza
retort [rɪˈtɔrt] *s* risposta per le rime; controreplica; (chem) storta || *tr* rispondere per le rime a || *intr* rispondere per le rime
retouch [riˈtʌtʃ] *tr* ritoccare
retrace [rɪˈtres] *tr* ripercorrere; **to retrace one's steps** ritornare sui propri passi
retract [rɪˈtrækt] *tr* ritrattare, disdire || *intr* disdirsi
re•tread [ˈriˌtrɛd] *s* pneumatico col copertone ricostruito || [riˈtrɛd] *v* (*pret & pp* **-treaded**) *tr* ricostruire il copertone di || *v* (*pret* **-trod** [ˈtrɑd]; *pp* **-trod** or **-trodden**) *tr* ripercorrere || *intr* rimettere il piede
retreat [rɪˈtrit] *s* (*seclusion*) ritiro; (mil) ritirata; (eccl) esercizio spirituale; **to beat a retreat** battere in ritirata || *intr* ritirarsi
retrench [rɪˈtrentʃ] *tr* ridurre, tagliare; (mil) trincerare || *intr* ridurre le spese; (mil) trincerarsi
retribution [ˌrɛtrɪˈbjuʃən] *s* ricompensa; (theol) giudizio finale
retributive [rɪˈtrɪbjətɪv] *adj* retributivo
retrieve [rɪˈtriv] *tr* riguadagnare, riconquistare; (*to repair*) risarcire; (hunt) riportare || *intr* riportare la presa
retriever [rɪˈtrivər] *s* cane *m* da presa
retroactive [ˌrɛtroˈæktɪv] *adj* retroattivo
retrofiring [ˌrɛtroˈfaɪrɪŋ] *s* accensione dei retrorazzi
retrogress [ˈrɛtrəˌgrɛs] *intr* regredire; retrocedere
retrorocket [ˌrɛtroˈrɑkɪt] *s* retrorazzo
retrospect [ˈrɛtrəˌspɛkt] *s* esame retrospettivo; **in retrospect** retrospettivamente
retrospective [ˌrɛtrəˈspɛktɪv] *adj* retrospettivo
re•try [riˈtraɪ] *v* (*pret & pp* **-tried**) *tr* (*a person*) riprocessare; (*a case*) ritentare
return [rɪˈtʌrn] *adj* di ritorno; ripetuto || *s* restituzione; ritorno; profitto; (*of income tax*) dichiarazione; risposta; rapporto ufficiale; (*of an election*) responso; (sports) rimando, rimessa; **in return (for)** in cambio (di); **many happy returns of the day!** cento di questi giorni!; **returns** (*of an election*) responso, risultato || *tr* tornare, ritornare restituire; (*a favor*) contraccambiare; (*a profit*) dare; (*thanks; a decision*) rendere; (sports) ribattere || *intr* tornare; rispondere
return′ ad′dress *s* indirizzo del mittente
return′ bout′ *s* (boxing) rivincita
return′ mail′ *s*—**by return mail** a volta di corriere, a giro di posta
return′ tick′et *s* biglietto di ritorno; (Brit) biglietto di andata e ritorno
reunification [riˌjunɪfɪˈkeʃən] *s* riunione, unificazione
reunion [riˈjunjən] *s* riunione
reunite [ˌrijʊˈnaɪt] *tr* riunire || *intr* riunirsi
rev [rev] *s* (coll) giro || *v* (*pret & pp* **revved**; *ger* **revving**) *tr*—**to rev up** (coll) imballare || *intr* (coll) accelerare, imballarsi
revamp [riˈvæmp] *tr* rinnovare, rappezzare
reveal [rɪˈvil] *tr* rivelare, svelare
reveille [ˈrɛvəli] *s* sveglia, levata
rev•el [ˈrɛvəl] *s* baldoria || *v* (*pret &*

pp **-eled** or **-elled;** *ger* **-eling** or **-elling)** *intr* gozzovigliare; bearsi
revelation [ˌrɛvə'leʃən] *s* rivelazione ‖ **Revelation** *s* (Bib) Apocalisse *f*
revel·ry ['rɛvəlri] *s* **(-ries)** baldoria
revenge [rɪ'vendʒ] *s* vendetta ‖ *tr* vendicare
revengeful [rɪ'vendʒfəl] *adj* vendicativo
revenue ['rɛvəˌnju] or ['rɛvəˌnu] *s* entrata, profitto; (*government income*) entrate *fpl* erariali
rev'enue cut'ter *s* motobarca della guardia di finanza
rev'enue stamp' *s* marca da bollo
reverberate [rɪ'vʌrbəˌret] *intr* riverberarsi; (*said, e.g., of sound*) ripercuotersi, risonare; (*said of an echo*) rimbalzare
revere [rɪ'vɪr] *tr* venerare, riverire
reverence ['rɛvərəns] *s* riverenza ‖ *tr* ossequiare
reverend ['rɛvərənd] *adj & s* reverendo
reverent ['rɛvərənt] *adj* reverente
reverie ['rɛvəri] *s* sogno, fantasticheria
reversal [rɪ'vʌrsəl] *s* inversione, cambio; (law) annullamento
reverse [rɪ'vʌrs] *adj* rovescio, contrario; (mach) di retromarcia ‖ *s* contrario; (*rear*) dietro; (*misfortune; side of a coin not bearing principal design*) rovescio; (mach) retromarcia ‖ *tr* invertire; rovesciare; mettere in marcia indietro; **to reverse oneself** cambiare d'opinione; **to reverse the charges** far pagare al destinatario; (telp) far pagare al numero chiamato ‖ *intr* invertirsi
revert [rɪ'vʌrt] *intr* ritornare
review [rɪ'vju] *s* (*critical article*) recensione; (*magazine*) rivista; (educ) ripasso, ripetizione; (mil) rivista ‖ *tr* recensire; rivedere; (*a lesson*) ripassare; (mil) passare in rassegna
revile [rɪ'vaɪl] *tr* insultare, offendere
revise [rɪ'vaɪz] *s* revisione; (typ) seconda bozza ‖ *tr* rivedere; correggere
revision [rɪ'vɪʒən] *s* revisione
revisionism [rɪ'vɪʒəˌnɪzəm] *s* revisionismo
revival [rɪ'vaɪvəl] *s* ripresa delle forze; (*restoration*) ripristino; (*of learning*) rinascimento; risveglio religioso; (theat, mov) ripresa
revive [rɪ'vaɪv] *tr* ravvivare; (*a custom*) ripristinare; (theat) dare la ripresa di ‖ *intr* ravvivarsi; risorgere
revoke [rɪ'vok] *tr* revocare
revolt [rɪ'volt] *s* rivolta ‖ *tr* rivoltare ‖ *intr* rivoltarsi
revolting [rɪ'voltɪŋ] *adj* rivoltante
revolution [ˌrɛvə'luʃən] *s* rivoluzione
revolutionar·y [ˌrɛvə'luʃəˌnɛri] *adj* rivoluzionario ‖ *s* **(-ies)** rivoluzionario
revolve [rɪ'vɑlv] *tr* far rotare; (*in one's mind*) rivolgere ‖ *intr* girare, rotare
revolver [rɪ'vɑlvər] *s* rivoltella
revolv'ing book'case *s* scaffale *m* girevole
revolv'ing cred'it *s* credito rotativo
revolv'ing door' *s* porta girevole
revolv'ing fund' *s* fondo rotativo
revue [rɪ'vju] *s* rivista
revulsion [rɪ'vʌlʃən] *s* ripugnanza, avversione; (med) revulsione
reward [rɪ'wɔrd] *s* premio, ricompensa; (*money offered for capture*) taglia; (*for return of articles lost*) mancia competente ‖ *tr* premiare, ricompensare
rewarding [rɪ'wɔrdɪŋ] *adj* rimunerativo; gradevole
re·wind [rɪ'waɪnd] *s* (*of a tape*) ribobinazione ‖ *v* (*pret & pp* **-wound** [waʊnd]) *tr* ribobinare
re·write [ri'raɪt] *v* (*pret* **-wrote** ['rot]; *pp* **-written** ['rɪtən]) *tr* riscrivere; (*news*) rimaneggiare, correggere
rhapso·dy ['ræpsədi] *s* **(-dies)** rapsodia
rheostat ['ri·əˌstæt] *s* reostato
rhesus ['risəs] *s* reso
rhetoric ['rɛtərɪk] *s* retorica
rhetorical [rɪ'tɑrɪkəl] or [rɪ'tɔrɪkəl] *adj* retorico
rheumatic [ru'mætɪk] *adj & s* reumatico
rheumatism ['rumə,tɪzəm] *s* reumatismo
Rhine [raɪn] *s* Reno
Rhineland ['rain ˌlænd] *s* la Renania
rhine'stone' *s* gemma artificiale
rhinoceros [raɪ'nɑsərəs] *s* rinoceronte *m*
Rhodes [rodz] *s* Rodi *f*
Rhone [ron] *s* Rodano
rhubarb ['rubɑrb] *s* rabarbaro; (slang) baruffa
rhyme [raɪm] *s* rima; **without rhyme or reason** senza capo né coda ‖ *tr & intr* rimare
rhythm ['rɪðəm] *s* ritmo
rhythmic(al) ['rɪðmɪk(əl)] *adj* ritmico
rial·to [rɪ'ælto] *s* **(-tos)** mercato ‖ **the Rialto** il ponte di Rialto; il centro teatrale di New York
rib [rɪb] *s* costola; (*cut of meat*) costata; (*of umbrella*) stecca; (*of leaf*) nervatura; (aer, archit) centina; (naut) costa ‖ (*pret & pp* **ribbed;** *ger* **ribbing)** *tr* (slang) prendersi gioco di
ribald ['rɪbəld] *adj* volgare, indecente
ribbon ['rɪbən] *s* nastro; (*decoration*) nastrino; **ribbons** (*shreds*) brandelli *mpl*
rice [raɪs] *s* riso
rich [rɪtʃ] *adj* ricco; (*food*) nutrito, grasso; (*wine*) generoso; (*voice*) caldo; (*color*) vivo; (*odor*) forte; (coll) divertente; (coll) assurdo; **to strike it rich** trovare la miniera d'oro ‖ **riches** *spl* ricchezze *fpl;* **the rich** i ricchi
rickets ['rɪkɪts] *s* rachitismo
rickety ['rɪkɪti] *adj* (*object*) sgangherato; (*person*) vacillante; (*suffering from rickets*) rachitico
rid [rɪd] *v* (*pret & pp* **rid;** *ger* **ridding)** *tr* liberare, sbarazzare; **to get rid of** liberarsi di, sbarazzarsi di
riddance ['rɪdəns] *s* liberazione; **good riddance!** che sollievo!
riddle ['rɪdəl] *s* enigma *m,* indovi-

nello; (*sieve*) crivello || *tr* crivellare; (*to sift*) vagliare; (*s.o.'s reputation*) rovinare; **to riddle with** crivellare di

ride [raɪd] *s* scarrozzata; cavalcata; gita || *v* (*pret* **rode** [rod]; *pp* **ridden** ['rɪdən]) *tr* cavalcare, montare, montare su; (*e.g., a bus*) andare in; (*the waves*) galleggiare su; attraversare; tiranneggiare; farsi gioco di; **to ride down** travolgere; sorpassare; **to ride out** uscire felicemente da || *intr* cavalcare; fare una passeggiata, fare una gita; (*to float*) galleggiare; **to let ride** lasciar correre; **to ride on** dipendere da

rider ['raɪdər] *s* cavallerizzo; ciclista *mf;* viaggiatore *m,* passeggero

ridge [rɪdʒ] *s* (*of mountains*) crinale *m,* dorsale *f;* (*of roof*) displuvio; (agr) porca

ridge'pole' *s* trave maestra, colmo

ridicule ['rɪdɪ ˌkjul] *s* ridicolo; **to expose to ridicule** porre in ridicolo || *tr* ridicolizzare

ridiculous [rɪ'dɪkjələs] *adj* ridicolo

rid'ing boot' *s* stivalone *m* d'equitazione

rid'ing school' *s* maneggio

rife [raɪf] *adj* comune, prevalente; **rife with** pieno di

riffraff ['rɪf ˌræf] *s* gentaglia

rifle ['raɪfəl] *s* fucile *m;* cannone rigato || *tr* (*a place*) svaligiare; (*a person*) derubare; (*a gun*) rigare

rifle' range' *s* tiro a segno

rift [rɪft] *s* crepa, fessura; disaccordo

rig [rɪg] *s* attrezzatura, equipaggio; impianto di sondaggio (per il petrolio); (*outfit*) tenuta || *v* (*pret & pp* **rigged;** *ger* **rigging**) *tr* attrezzare, equipaggiare; guarnire; abbigliare in maniera strana

rigging ['rɪgɪŋ] *s* (naut) padiglione *m;* (*tackle*) (naut) rizza; (coll) vestiti *mpl*

right [raɪt] *adj* giusto; corretto; (*mind*) sano; destro, diritto; (geom) retto; (geom) perpendicolare; **right or wrong** a torto o a ragione; **to be all right** star bene di salute; **to be right** avér ragione || *s* diritto; quanto è giusto, (il) giusto; (*in a company*) interessenza; (*right hand*) destra; (*turn*) giro a destra; (boxing) diritto; (tex) dritto; (pol) destra; **by right** in giustizia; **on the right** alla destra; **to be in the right** aver ragione || *adv* direttamente; completamente; immediatamente; proprio, precisamente; correttamente, giustamente; bene; alla destra; (coll) molto; **all right** benissimo || *tr* drizzare; correggere; rimettere a posto || *intr* drizzarsi

righteous ['raɪtʃəs] *adj* retto; virtuoso

right' field' *s* (baseball) campo destro

rightful ['raɪtfəl] *adj* giusto; legittimo

right'-hand drive' *s* guida a destra

right-handed ['raɪt'hændɪd] *adj* che usa la destra; destrorso

right'-hand man' *s* braccio destro

rightist ['raɪtɪst] *adj* conservatore || *s* conservatore *m,* membro della destra

rightly ['raɪtli] *adv* correttamente; giustamente; **rightly or wrongly** a torto o a ragione

right' mind' *s*—**in one's right mind** nel pieno possesso delle proprie facoltà, con la testa a posto

right' of way' *s* precedenza; (law) servitù *f* di passaggio; (rr) sede *f*

rights' of man' *s* diritti *mpl* dell'uomo

right'-wing' *adj* della destra

right-winger ['raɪt'wɪŋər] *s* membro della destra, conservatore *m*

rigid ['rɪdʒɪd] *adj* rigido

rigmarole ['rɪgmə ˌrol] *s* sproloquio

rigorous ['rɪgərəs] *adj* rigoroso

rile [raɪl] *tr* irritare, esasperare

rill [rɪl] *s* rigagnolo

rim [rɪm] *s* orlo, bordo; (*of a wheel*) cerchione *m*

rime [raɪm] *s* brina; (*in verse*) rima || *tr* brinare; rimare || *intr* rimare

rind [raɪnd] *s* (*of animals*) cotenna; (*of fruit or cheese*) scorza

ring [rɪŋ] *s* (*for finger*) anello; (*anything round*) cerchio; (*circular course*) pista; (*of people*) crocchio; (*of evildoers*) combriccola; (*of anchor*) anello; (*sound of bell*) squillo; (*loud sound of bell*) scampanellata; (*of small bell; of glassware*) tintinnio; (*act of ringing*) sonata; (telp) chiamata; (fig) suono; (boxing) quadrato; (mach) ghiera; (fig, taur) arena; **to run rings around** essere molto migliore di || *v* (*pret & pp* **ringed**) *tr* accerchiare; mettere un anello a || *intr* formare cerchi || *v* (*pret* **rang** [ræŋ]; *pp* **rung** [rʌŋ]) *tr* sonare; squillare; tintinnare; chiamare al telefono; **to ring up** chiamare al telefono; (*a sale*) battere sul registratore di cassa || *intr* sonare; squillare; tintinnare; chiamare; (*said of one's ears*) fischiare; **to ring for** chiamare col campanello; **to ring off** terminare una conversazione telefonica; **to ring up** chiamare al telefono

ring-around-a-rosy ['rɪŋə ˌraʊndə'rozi] *s* girotondo

ringing ['rɪŋɪŋ] *adj* alto, sonoro || *s* accerchiamento; squillo; tintinnio; (*in the ears*) fischio

ring'lead'er *s* capobanda *m*

ringlet ['rɪŋlɪt] *s* anellino

ring'mas'ter *s* direttore *m* di circo equestre

ring'side' *s* posto vicino al quadrato

ring'worm' *s* tigna

rink [rɪŋk] *s* pattinatoio

rinse [rɪns] *s* risciacquatura || *tr* risciacquare

riot ['raɪ·ət] *s* sommossa, tumulto; profusione; **to be a riot** (coll) essere divertentissimo; **to run riot** sfrenarsi; (*said of plants*) crescere disordinatamente || *intr* tumultuare; darsi alle gozzoviglie

rioter ['raɪ·ətər] *s* rivoltoso

rip [rɪp] *s* sdrucitura; (*open seam*) scucitura || *v* (*pret & pp* **ripped;** *ger* **ripping**) *tr* sdrucire; (*to open the*

seam of) scucire || *intr* sdrucirsi; scucirsi; **to rip out with insults** (coll) prorompere in improperi
ripe [raɪp] *adj* maturo; (*lips*) turgido; (*cheese*) stagionato; pronto
ripen [ˈraɪpən] *tr & intr* maturare
ripple [ˈrɪpəl] *s* increspatura; (*sound*) mormorio || *tr* increspare || *intr* incresparsi; mormorare
rise [raɪz] *s* (*of prices, temperature*) aumento; (*of a road*) salita; (*of ground*) elevazione; (*of a heavenly body*) levata; (*in rank*) ascesa; (*of a step*) alzata; (*of a stream*) sorgente *f;* (*of water*) crescita; **to get a rise out of** (coll) farsi rispondere per le rime da; **to give rise to** dar origine a || *v* (*pret* **rose** [roz]; *pp* **risen** [ˈrɪzən]) *intr* (*said of the sun*) sorgere; rialzarsi; (*said of plants*) crescere; (*said of the wind*) alzarsi; (*said of a building*) ergersi; (*to return from the dead*) risorgere; (*to increase*) aumentare; **to rise above** alzarsi al di sopra di; essere al di sopra di; **to rise to** sorgere all'altezza di
riser [ˈraɪzər] *s* (*of step*) alzata; (*upright*) montante *m;* **early riser** persona mattiniera; **late riser** dormiglione *m*
risk [rɪsk] *s* rischio; **to run** or **take a risk** correre un rischio || *tr* rischiare
risk•y [ˈrɪski] *adj* (**-ier; -iest**) rischioso
risqué [rɪsˈke] *adj* audace, spinto
rite [raɪt] *s* rito; **last rites** riti *mpl* funebri
ritual [ˈrɪtʃʊ•əl] *adj & s* rituale *m*
ri•val [ˈraɪvəl] *s* rivale *mf* || *v* (*pret & pp* **-valed** or **-valled;** *ger* **-valing** or **-valling**) *tr* rivaleggiare con
rival•ry [ˈraɪvəlri] *s* (**-ries**) rivalità *f*
river [ˈrɪvər] *s* fiume *m;* **down the river** a valle; **up the river** a monte
riv'er ba'sin *s* bacino fluviale
riv'er•bed' *s* letto di fiume
riv'er front' *s* riva di fiume
riv'er•head' *s* sorgente *f* di fiume
riv'er•side' *adj* rivierasco || *s* riva del fiume
rivet [ˈrɪvɪt] *s* ribattino; (*of scissors*) perno || *tr* ribadire; (*s.o.'s attention*) concentrare
roach [rotʃ] *s* scarafaggio
road [rod] *adj* stradale || *s* strada; via; (naut) rada; **to be in the road of** ostacolare il cammino a; **to burn up the road** divorare la strada; **to get out of the road** togliersi di mezzo
roadability [ˌrodəˈbɪlɪti] *s* tenuta di strada
road'bed' *s* (*of highway*) piattaforma; (rr) massicciata, infrastruttura
road'block' *s* (mil) barricata; (fig) impedimento
road'house' *s* taverna su autostrada
road' la'borer *s* cantoniere *m*
road' map' *s* carta stradale
road' roll'er *s* compressore *m* stradale, rullo compressore
road' serv'ice *s* servizio di assistenza stradale
road'side' *s* bordo della strada
road'side inn' *s* taverna posta su autostrada
road' sign' *s* indicatore *m* stradale
road'stead' *s* rada
road'way' *s* carreggiata; strada
roam [rom] *s* vagabondaggio || *tr* girovagare per || *intr* girovagare
roar [ror] *s* ruggito, muggito; boato, fragore *m* || *intr* muggire; **to roar with laughter** fare una risata
roast [rost] *s* arrosto; torrefazione || *tr* arrostire; (*coffee*) tostare, torrefare; (coll) farsi beffe di || *intr* arrostirsi
roast' beef' *s* rosbif *m*
roast'ed pea'nut *s* nocciolina americana abbrustolita
roast' pork' *s* arrosto di maiale
rob [rɑb] *v* (*pret & pp* **robbed;** *ger* **robbing**) *tr & intr* derubare
robber [ˈrɑbər] *s* ladro, malandrino
robber•y [ˈrɑbəri] *s* (**-ies**) furto
robe [rob] *s* (*of a woman*) vestito; (*of a professor*) toga; (*of a priest*) abito talare; (*dressing gown*) vestaglia; (*for lap*) coperta da viaggio; **robes** vestiti *mpl* || *tr* vestire || *intr* vestirsi
robin [ˈrɑbɪn] *s* pettirosso
robot [ˈrobɑt] *s* robot *m*
robust [roˈbʌst] *adj* robusto
rock [rɑk] *s* roccia; (*any stone*) pietra; (*sticking out of water*) scoglio; (*one that is thrown*) sasso; (*hill*) rocca; (slang) pietra preziosa; **on the rocks** (coll) in rovina; (coll) al verde; (*said, e.g., of whiskey*) sul ghiaccio || *tr* far vacillare; dondolare || *intr* vacillare; dondolare
rock'-bot'tom *adj* (l') ultimo; (il) minimo
rock' can'dy *s* zucchero candito
rock' crys'tal *s* cristallo di rocca
rocker [ˈrɑkər] *s* (*curved piece at bottom of rocking chair*) dondolo; sedia a dondolo; (mach) bilanciere *m;* **off one's rocker** (slang) matto
rocket [ˈrɑkɪt] *s* razzo || *intr* partire come un razzo
rock'et launch'er [ˈlɔntʃər] or [ˈlɑntʃər] *s* lanciarazzo
rock' gar'den *s* giardino piantato fra le rocce
rock'ing chair' *s* sedia a dondolo
rock'ing horse' *s* cavallo a dondolo
rock' salt' *s* salgemma *m*
rock' wool' *s* cotone *m* or lana minerale
rock•y [ˈrɑki] *adj* (**-ier; -iest**) roccioso; traballante; (coll) debole
rod [rɑd] *s* verga, bacchetta; scettro; punizione; (*bar*) asta; (*for fishing*) canna da pesca; (anat, biol) bastoncino; (mach) biella; (surv) biffa; (Bib) razza, tribù *f;* (slang) pistola; **spare the rod and spoil the child** la madre pietosa fa la piaga cancrenosa
rodent [ˈrodənt] *adj & s* roditore *m*
rod'man *s* (**-men**) *s* aiutante *m* geometra
roe [ro] *s* capriolo; (*of fish*) uova *fpl*
rogue [rog] *s* furfante *m;* (*scamp*) picaro

rogues'' gal'lery *s* collezione di fotografie di malviventi
rôle or **role** [rol] *s* ruolo, parte *f;* **to play a role** fare la parte
roll [rol] *s* (*of film, paper, etc.*) rotolo, bobina; (*of fat*) strato; (*roller*) rotella; (*of bread*) panino; ondulazione; (*noise*) rullio, rullo; (*of a boat*) rollio; (*of thunder*) rombo; (*list*) ruolo; (*of money*) (slang) fascio; **to call the roll** fare la chiama || *tr* far rotolare; (*one's r's*) arrotare; (*one's eyes*) stralunare; (*e.g., dough*) spianare; (*steel*) laminare; (*to wrap*) arrotolare; (*a drum*) rullare; **to roll back** (*prices*) ridurre; **to roll out** spianare; srotolare; **to roll up** (*one's sleeves*) arrotolarsi; accumulare; aumentare || *intr* rotolare; rullare; arrotolarsi; raggomitolarsi; **to roll on** passare; **to roll out** srotolarsi; (*to get out of bed*) (slang) alzarsi
roll' call' *s* chiama, appello
roller ['rolər] *s* rotella; (*for hair*) bigodino; rotolo; (*wave*) ondata lunga
roll'er bear'ing *s* cuscinetto a rotolamento
roll'er coast'er *s* montagne russe
roll'er skate' *s* pattino a rotelle
roll'er-skate' *intr* pattinare coi pattini a rotelle
roll'er tow'el *s* bandinella
roll'ing mill' ['rolɪŋ] *s* laminatoio
roll'ing pin' *s* matterello
roll'ing stock' *s* (rr) materiale *m* rotabile
roll'-top desk' *s* scrivania a piano scorrevole
roly-poly ['roli'poli] *adj* grassoccio
roman ['romən] *adj* (typ) romano, tondo || *s* (typ) carattere romano, tondo || **Roman** *adj & s* romano
Ro'man can'dle *s* candela romana
Ro'man Cath'olic Church' *s* Chiesa Cattolica Apostolica Romana
romance [ro'mæns] or ['romæns] *s* romanzo; sentimentalità *f;* idillio, intrigo amoroso; (mus) romanza || [ro'mæns] *intr* scrivere romanzi; raccontare romanzi; fare il romantico || **Romance** ['romæns] or [ro'mæns] *adj* romanzo, neolatino
Ro'man Em'pire *s* Impero Romano
romanesque [,romən'ɛsk] *adj* romantico || **Romanesque** *adj & s* romanico
Ro'man nose' *s* naso aquilino
romantic [ro'mæntɪk] *adj* romantico
romanticism [ro'mæntɪ,sɪzəm] *s* romanticismo
romanticist [ro'mæntɪsɪst] *s* romantico
romp [rɑmp] *intr* ruzzare
rompers ['rɑmpərz] *spl* pagliaccetto
roof [ruf] or [rʊf] *s* (*of house*) tetto; (*of heaven*) volta; (*of car*) tetto, padiglione *m;* **to hit the roof** (slang) andare fuori dai gangheri; **to raise the roof** (slang) fare molto chiasso; (slang) protestare violentemente || *tr* ricoprire con tetto
roofer ['rufər] or ['rʊfər] *s* conciatetti *m*
roof' gar'den *s* giardino pensile
rook [rʊk] *s* (*bird*) cornacchia; (*in chess*) torre *f* || *tr* truffare
rookie ['rʊki] *s* novizio; (mil) recluta
room [rum] or [rʊm] *s* stanza, camera; vano, locale *m;* posto, spazio; opportunità *f;* **to make room** far luogo || *intr* alloggiare
room' and board' *s* vitto e alloggio
room' clerk' *s* impiegato d'albergo assegnato alle prenotazioni
roomer ['rumər] or ['rʊmər] *s* inquilino
room'ing house' *s* casa con camere d'affittare
room'mate' *s* compagno di stanza
room·y ['rumi] or ['rʊmi] *adj* (**-ier; -iest**) ampio, spazioso
roost [rust] *s* (*perch*) ballatoio; (*house for chickens*) pollaio; (*place for resting*) posto di riposo; **to rule the roost** essere il gallo del pollaio || *intr* appollaiarsi; andare a dormire
rooster ['rustər] *s* gallo
root [rut] or [rʊt] *s* radice *f;* **to get to the root of** andare al fondo di; **to take root** metter radici || *tr* inchiodare, piantare || *intr* radicare; (*said of swine*) grufolare; **to root for** fare il tifo per
rooter ['rutər] or ['rʊtər] *s* tifoso
rope [rop] *s* fune *f,* corda; (*of a hangman*) capestro; laccio, lasso; **to know the ropes** (coll) conoscere la faccenda a fondo, saperla lunga || *tr* legare con fune; prendere al laccio; **to rope in** (slang) imbrogliare
rope'danc'er or **rope'walk'er** *s* funambolo
rosa·ry ['rozəri] *s* (**-ries**) rosario
rose [roz] *adj & s* rosa
rose'bud' *s* bottoncino di rosa
rose'bush' *s* rosaio
rose'-col'ored *adj* color di rosa
rose'-colored glass'es *spl* occhiali *mpl* rosa
rose' gar'den *s* roseto
rosemar·y ['roz,meri] *s* (**-ies**) rosmarino
rose' of Shar'on ['ʃerən] *s* altea
rosette [ro'zet] *s* rosetta; (archit) rosone *m*
rose' win'dow *s* rosone *m*
rose'wood' *s* palissandro
rosin ['rɑzɪn] *s* colofonia
roster ['rɑstər] *s* ruolino; orario scolastico
rostrum ['rɑstrəm] *s* tribuna
ros·y ['rozi] *adj* (**-ier; -iest**) rosa, roseo
rot [rɑt] *s* marcio; (coll) stupidaggine *f* || *v* (*pret & pp* **rotted;** *ger* **rotting**) *tr & intr* imputridire
ro'tary en'gine ['rotəri] *s* motore rotativo
ro'tary press' *s* rotativa
rotate ['rotet] or [ro'tet] *tr & intr* rotare
rotation [ro'teʃən] *s* rotazione; **in rotation** in successione, a turno
rote [rot] *s* ripetizione macchinale; **by rote** a memoria
rot'gut' *s* (slang) acquavite *f* di infima qualità

rotisserie [ro'tɪsəri] *s* girarrosto a motore
rotten ['rɑtən] *adj* marcio, fradicio; corrotto
rotund [ro'tʌnd] *adj* (*plump*) rotondetto; (*voice*) profondo; (*speech*) enfatico
rouge [ruʒ] *s* belletto, rossetto || *tr* dare il belletto a || *intr* darsi il belletto
rough [rʌf] *adj* scabroso; (*sea*) agitato; (*crude*) rozzo, rude; (*road*) accidentato; approssimativo || *tr*—**to rough it** vivere primitivamente; **to rough up** malmenare
rough'cast' *s* intonaco; modello disgrossato || *v* (*pret & pp* **-cast**) *tr* (*a wall*) intonacare; disgrossare, dirozzare
rough' cop'y *s* brutta copia
rough-hew ['rʌf'hju] *tr* digrossare, dirozzare
roughly ['rʌfli] *adv* aspramente; rozzamente; approssimativamente
round [raʊnd] *adj* rotondo || *s* tondo; (*of applause; of guns*) salva; (*of a single gun*) colpo, tiro; (*of a chair*) piolo; (*of a doctor*) giro; (*of a policeman*) ronda; serie *f;* (*of golf*) partita; (*e.g., of bridge*) mano *f;* cerchio; (boxing) ripresa || *adv* intorno; dal principio alla fine || *prep* intorno a; attraverso || *tr* (*to make round*) arrotondare; circondare; (*a corner*) scantonare; **to round off** arrotondare; completare, perfezionare; **to round up** raccogliere; (*cattle*) condurre
roundabout ['raʊndə,baʊt] *adj* indiretto || *s* giacca attillata; via traversa; giro di parole; (Brit) giostra; (Brit) anello stradale
round'house' *s* rimessa per locomotive
round-shouldered ['raʊnd'ʃoldərd] *adj* dalle spalle spioventi
round'-trip tick'et *s* biglietto d'andata e ritorno
round'up' *s* (*of cattle*) riunione; (*of criminals*) retata; (*of facts*) riassunto
rouse [raʊz] *tr* svegliare; suscitare; (*game*) scovare || *intr* svegliarsi
rout [raʊt] *s* sconfitta, rotta || *tr* sconfiggere, mettere in rotta || *intr* grufolare
route [rut] or [raʊt] *s* via, rotta; itinerario || *tr* istradare
routine [ru'tin] *adj* ordinario || *s* trafila, routine *f*
rove [rov] *intr* vagabondare, vagare
rover ['rovər] *s* vagabondo
row [raʊ] *s* piazzata, scenata; (*clamor*) (coll) baccano; **to raise a row** (coll) fare baccano || [ro] *s* fila; (*of figures*) finca; (*e.g., of trees*) filare *m;* **in a row** in continuazione, di seguito || *tr* vogare || *intr* remare, vogare
rowboat ['ro,bot] *s* barca a remi
row•dy ['raʊdi] *adj* (**-dier; -diest**) turbolento || *s* (**-dies**) attaccabrighe *mf*
rower ['ro•ər] *s* rematore *m*
rowing ['ro•ɪŋ] *s* (*action*) voga; (*sport*) canottaggio
royal ['rɔɪ•əl] *adj* reale, regio
royalist ['rɔɪ•əlɪst] *adj* sostenitore del re || *s* realista *mf*
royal•ty ['rɔɪ•əlti] *s* (**-ties**) regalità *f;* membro della famiglia reale; nobiltà *f;* diritto d'autore; diritto d'inventore; percentuale *f* sugli utili
rub [rʌb] *s* frizione; difficile *m;* **here's the rub** qui sta il busillis || *v* (*pret & pp* **rubbed;** *ger* **rubbing**) *tr* fregare; **to rub elbows with** stare giunto a gomiti con; **to rub out** cancellare con la gomma; (slang) togliere di mezzo || *intr* sfregare; **to rub off** venir via sfregando; cancellarsi
rubber ['rʌbər] *s* gomma, caucciù *m;* gomma da cancellare; (*overshoe*) caloscia; (*in cards*) rubber *m;* (sports) bella
rub'ber band' *s* elastico
rub'ber•neck' *s* (coll) ficcanaso; (coll) turista curioso || *intr* (coll) allungare il collo
rub'ber plant' *s* albero del caucciù
rub'ber stamp' *s* timbro di gomma; (coll) persona che approva inconsultamente
rub'ber-stamp' *tr* timbrare; (coll) approvare inconsultamente
rubbish ['rʌbɪʃ] *s* spazzatura; immondizia; (fig) detrito; (coll) sciocchezza
rubble ['rʌbəl] *s* (*broken stone*) pietrisco; (*masonry*) mistura di malta e pietrame; (*broken bits*) calcinacci *mpl*
rub'down' *s* fregagione
rube [rub] *s* (slang) contadino gonzo
ru•by ['rubi] *adj* vermiglio || (**-bies**) *s* rubino
rudder ['rʌdər] *s* timone *m;* (aer) timone *m* di direzione
rud•dy ['rʌdi] *adj* (**-dier; -diest**) rubicondo
rude [rud] *adj* rude, sgarbato
rudiment ['rudɪmənt] *s* rudimento
rue [ru] *tr* lamentare, rimpiangere
rueful ['rufəl] *adj* lamentevole; triste
ruffian ['rʌfɪ•ən] *s* ribaldo
ruffle ['rʌfəl] *s* increspatura; (*of drum*) rullo; (sew) gala, crespa || *tr* increspare; arruffare; irritare; (*a drum*) far rullare; (sew) guarnire di gala or crespa
rug [rʌg] *s* tappeto
rugged ['rʌgɪd] *adj* aspro, irregolare; rugoso; rozzo; forte; tempestuoso
ruin ['ru•ɪn] *s* rovina || *tr* rovinare, mandare in rovina
rule [rul] *s* regola; dominazione; (*reign*) regno; (law) ordinanza; (typ) filetto; **as a rule** in generale || *tr* governare; dominare; (*with lines*) rigare; (law) deliberare; **to rule out** escludere || *intr* governare; regnare; **to rule over** governare
rule' of thumb' *s* regola basata sull'esperienza; **by rule of thumb** secondo la propria esperienza
ruler ['rulər] *s* governante *m,* dominatore *m;* (*for ruling lines*) riga, regolo
ruling ['rulɪŋ] *adj* dirigente || *s* (*ruled lines*) rigatura; (law) decisione
rum [rʌm] *s* rum *m;* (*any alcoholic drink*) acquavite *f*

Rumanian [ru'menɪ·ən] *adj & s* rumeno
rumble ['rʌmbəl] *s* rimbombo; (*of the intestines*) gorgoglio; (*slang*) rissa fra ganghe rivali || *intr* rimbombare; gorgogliare
ruminate ['rumɪ,net] *tr & intr* ruminare
rummage ['rʌmɪdʒ] *tr & intr* rovistare, frugare
rum'mage sale' *s* vendita di cianfrusaglie
rumor ['rumər] *s* voce *f*, diceria || *tr* vociferare; **it is rumored that** corre voce che
rump [rʌmp] *s* anca; posteriore *m;* (*of beef*) quarto posteriore
rumple ['rʌmpəl] *s* piega || *tr* spiegazzare, sgualcire || *intr* sgualcirsi
rumpus ['rʌmpəs] *s* tumulto; rissa; **to raise a rumpus** fare baccano
run [rʌn] *s* corsa; percorso; produzione; (*e.g., in a stocking*) smagliatura; direzione; (*spell*) serie *f;* (*in cards*) scala; (*of goods*) richiesta; (*on a bank*) afflusso; **in the long run** a lungo andare; **on the run** (coll) di corsa; in fuga; **the common run of men** la media della gente; **to give s.o. a run for his money** dare a qlcu del filo da torcere; essere denaro ben speso per qlcu, e.g., **that sweater gave me a run for my money** quello sweater è stato denaro ben speso per me; **to have a long run** tenere il cartellone per lungo tempo; **to have the run of** avere la libertà di andare e venire per || *v* (*pret* **ran** [ræn]; *pp* **run;** *ger* **running**) *tr* muovere; (*a horse*) far correre; (*the street*) vivere liberamente in; (*game*) inseguire; trasportare; (*a machine*) far camminare; (*a store*) esercire; (*a candidate*) portare; (*a risk*) correre; (*a blockade*) violare; mettere, ficcare; (*a line*) tirare; **to run down** cacciare; esaminare; trovare; (*a pedestrian*) investire; denigrare, criticare; **to run in** (*a machine*) rodare; (slang) schiaffare in prigione; **to run off** creare di getto; cacciare; (typ) tirare; **to run up** ammassare || *intr* correre; scappare; (*in a race*) arrivare; (*said of a candidate*) portarsi; passare; (*said of knitted material*) smagliarsi; (*said of a liquid*) scorrere; (*said of a color*) sbavare; (*said of fish*) migrare; funzionare; (*to become*) diventare; (*to be worded*) essere del tenore; (com) decorrere; (theat, mov) durare in cartellone; **to run across** imbattersi in; **to run aground** incagliarsi; **to run away** fuggire; (*said of a horse*) prendere la mano; **to run down** (*said of a liquid*) scorrere; (*said of a battery, a watch*) scaricarsi; (*in health*) sciuparsi; **to run for** presentarsi candidato per; **to run in the family** essere una caratteristica familiare; **to run into** imbattersi in; ammontare a; (*to follow*) succedersi a; **to run off the track** (rr) uscire dalle rotaie; **to run out** aver termine; scadere; esaurirsi; **to run out of** rimanere senza; **to run over** oltrepassare; (*e.g., with a car*) investire; **to run through** trapassare; (*a fortune*) dilapidare; esaminare rapidamente
run'a·way' *adj* fuggiasco; (*horse*) che ha preso la mano || *s* fuggiasco; cavallo che ha preso la mano; fuga
run'-down' *adj* esausto; negletto, cadente; (*watch, battery*) scarico
rung [rʌŋ] *s* (*of chair or ladder*) piolo
runner ['rʌnər] *s* corridore *m;* messaggero; fattorino, messo; (*of sleigh*) pattino; (*of ice skate*) lama; (*rug*) guida; (*on a table*) striscia di pizzo; (*in stocking*) smagliatura
run'ner-up' *s* (**runners-up**) finalista *mf* secondo
running ['rʌnɪŋ] *adj* in corsa; da corsa; (*water*) corrente; (*vine*) rampicante; (*knot*) scorsoio; (*sore*) purulento; (*writing*) corsivo; consecutivo; (*start*) (sports) lanciato || *s* corsa; (*of a business*) esercizio; direzione; funzionamento; **to be in the running** avere possibilità di vittoria
run'ning board' *s* (aut) pedana
run'ning head' *s* titolo corrente
run·ny ['rʌni] *adj* (**-nier; -niest**) (*liquid*) scorrevole; (*color*) sbavante; **to have a runny nose** avere la goccia al naso
run'off' *s* ballottagio
run-of-the-mill ['rʌnəvðə'mɪl] *adj* ordinario, corrente
run'proof' *adj* indemagliabile
runt [rʌnt] *s* nanerottolo; animale deperito
run'way' *s* pista; (*of a stream*) letto; (*for animals*) chiusa; (aut) corsia
rupture ['rʌptʃər] *s* rottura; (pathol) ernia || *tr* rompere; causare un'ernia a || *intr* rompersi; soffrire di ernia
ru'ral free' deliv'ery ['rurəl] *s* distribuzione postale campestre
ruse [ruz] *s* astuzia, stratagemma *m*
rush [rʌʃ] *adj* urgente || *s* fretta; slancio, corsa; (*of blood*) ondata; (*rushing of persons to a new mine*) febbre *f;* (bot) giunco; **in a rush** in fretta e furia || *tr* affrettare; portare di fretta; spingere; (coll) fare la corte a; **to rush through** fare di fretta; (*e.g., a bill through Congress*) far approvare di fretta || *intr* lanciarsi; affrettarsi; passare velocemente; **to rush through** (*a book*) leggere velocemente; (*one's work*) fare in fretta; (*a town*) attraversare velocemente
rush'-bot'tomed chair' *s* sedia di giunchi
rush' can'dle *s* lumicino con lo stoppino fatto di midollo di giunco
rush' hour' *s* ora di punta
russet ['rʌsɪt] *adj* color cannella
Russia ['rʌʃə] *s* la Russia
Russian ['rʌʃən] *adj & s* russo
rust [rʌst] *s* ruggine *f;* (fig) torpore *m* || *tr* arrugginire || *intr* arrugginirsi
rustic ['rʌstɪk] *adj & s* rustico
rustle ['rʌsəl] *s* fruscio; (*of leaves*) stormire *m* || *tr* far frusciare; far

stormire; (*cattle*) (coll) rubare || *intr* frusciare; stormire; (coll) lavorare di buzzo buono
rust·y [ˈrʌsti] *adj* (**-ier; -iest**) rugginoso; color ruggine; fuori pratica
rut [rʌt] *s* (*track*) solco, carrareccia; (*of animals*) fregola; (il) solito tran tran
ruthless [ˈruθlɪs] *adj* spietato
rye [raɪ] *s* segala; whiskey *m* di segala

S

S, s [ɛs] *s* diciannovesima lettera dell'alfabeto inglese
Sabbath [ˈsæbəθ] *s* (*of Jews*) sabato; (*of Christians*) domenica; **to keep the Sabbath** osservare il riposo domenicale
sabbat'ical year' [səˈbætɪkəl] *s* anno di congedo; (Bib) anno sabbatico
saber [ˈsebər] *s* sciabola
sa'ber rat'tling *s* minacce *fpl* di guerra
sable [ˈsebəl] *adj* nero || *s* zibellino; **sables** vestiti di lutto
sabotage [ˈsæbəˌtɑʒ] *s* sabotaggio || *tr & intr* sabotare
saccharin [ˈsækərɪn] *s* saccarina
sachet [ˈsæʃe] or [sæˈʃe] *s* sacchetto profumato (per la biancheria)
sack [sæk] *s* sacco; (*of an employee*) (slang) licenziamento; (slang) letto || *tr* insaccare; (*to lay waste*) saccheggiare, mettere a sacco; (slang) licenziare
sack'cloth' *s* tela di sacco; (*for penitence*) sacco, cilicio; **in sackcloth and ashes** pentito e contrito
sacrament [ˈsækrəmənt] *s* sacramento
sacramental [ˌsækrəˈmentəl] *adj* sacramentale
sacred [ˈsekrəd] *adj* sacro
sacrifice [ˈsækrɪˌfaɪs] *s* sacrificio; **at a sacrifice** in perdita || *tr* sacrificare; (com) svendere
sacrilege [ˈsækrɪlɪdʒ] *s* sacrilegio
sacrilegious [ˌsækrɪˈlɪdʒəs] or [ˌsækrɪˈlidʒəs] *adj* sacrilego
sacristan [ˈsækrɪstən] *s* sagrestano
sacris·ty [ˈsækrɪsti] *s* (**-ties**) sagrestia
sad [sæd] *adj* (**sadder; saddest**) triste; (*bad*) cattivo; (*color*) tetro
sadden [ˈsædən] *tr* rattristare || *intr* rattristarsi
saddle [ˈsædəl] *s* sella || *tr* insellare; **to saddle with** gravare di
saddle'bag' *s* fonda
saddlebow [ˈsædəlˌbo] *s* arcione *m* anteriore
sad'dle·cloth' *s* gualdrappa
saddler [ˈsædlər] *s* sellaio
sad'dle·tree' *s* arcione *m*
sadist [ˈsædɪst] or [ˈsedɪst] *s* sadico
sadistic [sæˈdɪstɪk] or [seˈdɪstɪk] *adj* sadico
sadness [ˈsædnɪs] *s* tristezza
sad' sack' *s* (coll) marmittone *m*
safe [sef] *adj* sicuro; cauto; (*distance*) rispettoso; **safe and sound** sano e salvo || *s* cassaforte *f*
safe'-con'duct *s* salvacondotto
safe'-depos'it box' *s* cassetta di sicurezza
safe'guard' *s* salvaguardia || *tr* salvaguardare
safe·ty [ˈsefti] *adj* di sicurezza || *s* (**-ties**) sicurezza; (*of a gun*) sicura; **to reach safety** mettersi in salvo
safe'ty belt' *s* (*of a worker*) imbraca; (aer, aut) cintura di sicurezza; (naut) cintura di salvataggio
safe'ty glass' *s* vetro infrangibile
safe'ty is'land *s* salvagente *m*
safe'ty match' *s* fiammifero svedese
safe'ty pin' *s* spillo di sicurezza
safe'ty ra'zor *s* rasoio di sicurezza
safe'ty valve' *s* valvola di sicurezza
saffron [ˈsæfrən] *s* zafferano
sag [sæg] *s* cedimento; depressione; (*of a rope*) allentamento || *v* (*pret & pp* **sagged**; *ger* **sagging**) *intr* curvarsi; cedere, afflosciarsi; allentarsi; (*said of prices*) calare
sagacious [səˈgeʃəs] *adj* sagace
sage [sedʒ] *adj* saggio, savio || *s* saggio, savio; (bot) salvia
sage'brush' *s* artemisia
Sagittarius [ˌsædʒɪˈteri·əs] *s* Sagittario
sail [sel] *s* vela; (*of windmill*) ala; gita a vela; **to set sail** far vela; **under full sail** a piena velatura || *tr* veleggiare, navigare; (*a boat*) far navigare || *intr* veleggiare, navigare; far vela; volare; (*said of a vessel*) partire; **to sail into** (coll) attaccare
sail'boat' *s* nave *f* a vela, veliero
sail'cloth' *s* tela di olona
sailing [ˈselɪŋ] *adj* in partenza || *s* partenza; navigazione; navigazione a vela
sail'ing ship' *s* veliero
sail'mak'er *s* velaio
sailor [ˈselər] *s* marinaio
saint [sent] *adj & s* santo || *tr* santificare, canonizzare
saint'hood *s* santità *f*
saintliness [ˈsentlɪnɪs] *s* santità *f*
Saint' Vi'tus's dance' [ˈvaɪtəsəz] *s* (pathol) ballo di San Vito
sake [sek] *s* causa, interesse *m*; **for the sake of** per il bene di, per l'amor di
salaam [səˈlɑm] *s* salamelecco || *tr* fare salamelecchi a
salable [ˈseləbəl] *adj* vendibile
salacious [səˈleʃəs] *adj* salace
salad [ˈsæləd] *s* insalata
sal'ad bowl' *s* insalatiera
sal'ad oil' *s* olio da tavola
sala·ry [ˈsæləri] *s* (**-ries**) stipendio
sale [sel] *s* vendita; (*at reduced prices*) svendita, saldo; **for sale** in vendita; si vende, si vendono
sales'clerk' *s* commesso, impiegato

sales'la'dy *s* (**-dies**) commessa, impiegata
sales'man *s* (**-men**) venditore *m;* commesso; (*traveling*) piazzista *m*
sales'man·ship' *s* arte *f* di vendere
sales' promo'tion *s* promozione delle vendite, promotion *f*
sales'room' *s* sala di esposizione; sala vendite
sales' talk' *s* discorso da venditore; (*e.g., of a barker*) imbonimento
sales' tax' *s* imposta sulle vendite
saliva [sə'laɪvə] *s* saliva
sallow ['sælo] *adj* giallastro, olivastro
sal·ly ['sæli] *s* (**-lies**) escursione, gita; (*outburst*) esplosione; (*witty remark*) uscita; (mil) sortita || *v* (*pret & pp* **-lied**) *intr* fare una sortita; **to sally forth** balzar fuori
salmon ['sæmən] *s* salmone *m*
salon [sæ'lɑn] *s* salone *m*
saloon [sə'lun] *s* taverna; (*on a passenger vessel*) salone *m*
saloon' keep'er *s* taverniere *m*
salt [sɔlt] *s* sale *m;* **to be worth one's salt** valere il pane che si mangia || *tr* salare; (*cattle*) dare sale a; **to salt away** (coll) metter via, conservare
salt' bed' *s* salina
salt'cel'lar *s* saliera
saltine [sɔl'tin] *s* galletta salata
saltish ['sɔltɪʃ] *adj* salmastro
salt'pe'ter *s* (*potassium nitrate*) salnitro; (*sodium nitrate*) nitro del Cile
salt' shak'er *s* saliera
salt·y ['sɔlti] *adj* (**-ier; -iest**) salato
salubrious [sə'lubrɪ·əs] *adj* salubre
salutation [,sæljə'teʃən] *s* saluto
salute [sə'lut] *s* saluto || *tr* salutare
salvage ['sælvɪdʒ] *s* ricupero || *tr* ricuperare
salvation [sæl'veʃən] *s* salvezza
Salva'tion Ar'my *s* Esercito della Salvezza
salve [sæv] or [sɑv] *s* unguento || *tr* lenire, alleviare
sal·vo ['sælvo] *s* (**-vos** or **-voes**) salva
Samaritan [sə'mærɪtən] *adj & s* samaritano
same [sem] *adj & pron indef* medesimo, stesso; **it's all the same to me** a me fa lo stesso; **just the same** lo stesso, ugualmente; ciò nonostante; **same . . . as** lo stesso . . . che
sameness ['semnɪs] *s* uniformità *f;* monotonia
sample ['sæmpəl] *s* campione *m,* saggio || *tr* (*to take a sample of*) campionare; (*to taste*) assaggiare; provare
sam'ple cop'y *s* esemplare *m* di campione
sancti·fy ['sæŋktɪ,faɪ] *v* (*pret & pp* **-fied**) *tr* santificare
sanctimonious [,sæŋktɪ'monɪ·əs] *adj* che affetta devozione ipocrita
sanction ['sæŋkʃən] *s* sanzione || *tr* sanzionare
sanctuar·y ['sæŋktʃʊ,ɛri] *s* (**-ies**) santuario; **to take sanctuary** prendere asilo, rifugiarsi
sand [sænd] *s* sabbia || *tr* insabbiare; (*to polish*) smerigliare; cospergere di sabbia
sandal ['sændəl] *s* sandalo
san'dal·wood' *s* sandalo
sand'bag' *s* sacchetto a terra
sand'bank' *s* banco di sabbia
sand' bar' *s* cordone *m* litorale, banco di sabbia
sand'blast' *s* sabbiatura || *tr* pulire con sabbiatura, sabbiare
sand'box' *s* cassone *m* pieno di sabbia; (rr) sabbiera
sand'glass' *s* orologio a polvere or a sabbia
sand'pa'per *s* carta vetrata || *tr* pulire con carta vetrata
sand'stone' *s* arenaria
sandwich ['sændwɪtʃ] *s* panino imbottito, tramezzino || *tr* inserire
sand'wich man' *s* tramezzino, uomo sandwich
sand·y ['sændi] *adj* (**-ier; -iest**) sabbioso; (*hair*) biondo rossiccio
sane [sen] *adj* sensato
sanguinary ['sæŋgwɪn,ɛri] *adj* sanguinario
sanguine ['sæŋgwɪn] *adj* fiducioso; (*complexion*) sanguigno
sanitary ['sænɪ,tɛri] *adj* sanitario
san'itary nap'kin *s* pannolino igienico
sanitation [,sænɪ'teʃən] *s* sanità *f*
sanity ['sænɪti] *s* sanità *f* di mente
Santa Claus ['sæntə,klɔz] *s* Babbo Natale
sap [sæp] *s* linfa, succhio; (mil) trincea; (coll) scemo || *v* (*pret & pp* **sapped;** *ger* **sapping**) *tr* scavare; insidiare, minare; (*to weaken*) indebolire
sapling ['sæplɪŋ] *s* alberello; (*youth*) giovanetto
sapphire ['sæfaɪr] *s* zaffiro
Saracen ['særesən] *adj & s* saraceno
sarcasm ['sɑrkæzəm] *s* sarcasmo
sarcastic [sɑr'kæstɪk] *adj* sarcastico
sardine [sɑr'din] *s* sardina; **packed in like sardines** pigiati come le acciughe
Sardinia [sɑr'dɪnɪ·ə] *s* la Sardegna
Sardinian [sɑr'dɪnɪ·ən] *adj & s* sardo
sarsaparilla [,sɑrsəpə'rɪlə] *s* salsapariglia
sash [sæʃ] *s* sciarpa; (*around one's waist*) fusciacca; (*of window*) telaio
sash' win'dow *s* finestra a ghigliottina
sas·sy ['sæsi] *adj* (**-sier; -siest**) (coll) impertinente; (*pert*) (coll) vivace
satchel ['sætʃəl] *s* sacca; (*of schoolboy*) cartella
sateen [sæ'tin] *s* satin *m*
satellite ['sætə,laɪt] *s* satellite *m*
satiate ['seʃɪ,et] *tr* saziare
satin ['sætən] *s* raso
satire ['sætaɪr] *s* satira
satiric(al) [sə'tɪrɪk(əl)] *adj* satirico
satirist ['sætɪrɪst] *s* satirico
satirize ['sætɪ,raɪz] *tr* satireggiare
satisfaction [,sætɪs'fækʃən] *s* soddisfazione
satisfactory [,sætɪs'fæktəri] *adj* soddisfacente
satis·fy ['sætɪs,faɪ] *v* (*pret & pp* **-fied**) *tr & intr* soddisfare
saturate ['sætʃə,ret] *tr* saturare

Saturday ['sætərdi] *s* sabato
Saturn ['sætərn] *s* (astr) Saturno
sauce [sɔs] *s* salsa; (*of fruit*) conserva; (*of chocolate*) crema; (coll) insolenza, impertinenza ‖ *tr* condire; rendere piccante ‖ [sɔs] or [sæs] *tr* (coll) rispondere con impertinenza a
sauce'pan' *s* casseruola
saucer ['sɔsər] *s* piattino
sau·cy ['sɔsi] *adj* (**-cier; -ciest**) impertinente; (*pert*) vivace
sauerkraut ['saur ,kraut] *s* sarcrauti *mpl*, crauti *mpl*
saunter ['sɔntər] *s* giro, bighellonata ‖ *intr* girandolare, bighellonare
sausage ['sɔsɪdʒ] *s* salsiccia
savage ['sævɪdʒ] *adj* & *s* selvaggio
savant ['sævənt] *s* erudito
save [sev] *prep* tranne, salvo ‖ *tr* salvare; (*money*) risparmiare; (*to set apart*) serbare; **to save face** salvare le apparenze ‖ *intr* fare economia
saving ['sevɪŋ] *adj* economico; che redime ‖ **savings** *spl* risparmi *mpl*, economie *fpl* ‖ **saving** *prep* eccetto, salvo
sav'ings account' *s* conto di risparmio
sav'ings and loan' associa'tion *s* cassa di risparmio che concede mutui
sav'ings bank' *s* cassa di risparmio
savior ['sevjər] *s* salvatore *m*
Saviour ['sevjər] *s* Salvatore *m*
savor ['sevər] *s* sapore *m* ‖ *tr* assaporare; (*to flavor*) saporire ‖ *intr* odorare; **to savor of** sapere di; odorare di
savor·y ['sevəri] *adj* (**-ier; -iest**) saporoso; piccante; delizioso ‖ *s* (**-ies**) (bot) santoreggia
saw [sɔ] *s* (*tool*) sega; detto, proverbio ‖ *tr* segare
saw'buck' *s* cavalletto
saw'dust' *s* segatura
saw'horse' *s* cavalletto
saw'mill' *s* segheria
Saxon ['sæksən] *adj* & *s* sassone *m*
saxophone ['sæksə ,fon] *s* sassofono
say [se] *s* dire *m;* **to have no say** non aver voce in capitolo; **to have one's say** esprimere la propria opinione; **to have the say** avere l'ultima parola ‖ *v* (*pret* & *pp* **said** [sed]) *tr* dire; **I should say so!** certamente!; **it is said** si dice; **no sooner said than done** detto fatto; **that is to say** vale a dire; **to go without saying** essere ovvio
saying ['se·ɪŋ] *s* detto, proverbio
scab [skæb] *s* crosta; (*strikebreaker*) crumiro
scabbard ['skæbərd] *s* guaina, fodero
scab·by ['skæbi] *adj* (**-bier; -biest**) crostoso; (*animal*) rognoso; (slang) vile
scabrous ['skæbrəs] *adj* scabroso
scads [skædz] *spl* (slang) un mucchio
scaffold ['skæfəld] *s* impalcatura; (*to execute a criminal*) patibolo
scaffolding ['skæfəldɪŋ] *s* incastellatura, ponteggio
scald [skɔld] *tr* scottare; (*e.g., milk*) cuocere al disotto del punto d'ebollizione
scale [skel] *s* (*e.g., of map*) scala; piatto della bilancia; (*of fish*) squama; **on a large scale** in grande scala; **scales** bilancia; **to tip the scales** far inclinare la bilancia ‖ *tr* squamare; (*to incrust*) incrostare; (*to weigh*) pesare; scalare; graduare; ridurre a scala ‖ *intr* squamarsi; scrostarsi
scallion ['skæljən] *s* scalogno
scallop ['skɑləp] or ['skæləp] *s* (*for cooking*) conchiglia; (*mollusk*) pettine *m;* (*slice of meat*) scaloppina; (*on edge of cloth*) dentello, smerlo ‖ *tr* (*fish*) cuocere in conchiglia; dentellare, smerlare
scalp [skælp] *s* cuoio capelluto ‖ *tr* scotennare; (*tickets*) fare il bagarinaggio di
scalpel ['skælpəl] *s* scalpello
scalper ['skælpər] *s* bagarino
scal·y ['skeli] *adj* (**-ier; -iest**) squamoso; scrostato
scamp [skæmp] *s* cattivo soggetto, briccone *m*
scamper ['skæmpər] *intr* sgambettare; **to scamper away** darsela a gambe
scan [skæn] *v* (*pret* & *pp* **scanned;** *ger* **scanning**) *tr* scrutare; dare un'occhiata a; (*verse*) scandire; (telv) analizzare, scandire, esplorare
scandal ['skændəl] *s* scandalo
scandalize ['skændə ,laɪz] *tr* scandalizzare
scandalous ['skændələs] *adj* scandaloso
Scandinavian [,skændɪ'nevɪ·ən] *adj* & *s* scandinavo
scanning ['skænɪŋ] *s* (telv) esplorazione
scan'ning line' *s* (telv) riga di analisi
scant [skænt] *adj* scarso; corto ‖ *tr* diminuire; lesinare
scant·y ['skænti] *adj* (**-ier; -iest**) appena sufficiente; povero, magro; (*clothing*) succinto
scapegoat ['skep ,got] *s* capro espiatorio
scar [skɑr] *s* cicatrice *f;* (fig) sfregio ‖ *v* (*pret* & *pp* **scarred;** *ger* **scarring**) *tr* segnare, marcare; sfregiare ‖ *intr* cicatrizzarsi
scarce [skers] *adj* scarso, raro; **to make oneself scarce** (coll) non farsi vedere
scarcely ['skersli] *adv* appena; a mala pena; non . . . affatto; **scarcely ever** raramente; non . . . affatto
scarci·ty ['skersɪti] *s* (**-ties**) scarsità *f*, scarsezza; carestia
scare [sker] *s* spavento ‖ *tr* spaventare, impaurire; **to scare away** fare scappare per lo spavento; **to scare up** (*money*) (coll) metter insieme
scare'crow' *s* spaventapasseri *m*
scarf [skɑrf] *s* (**scarfs** or **scarves** [skɑrvz]) sciarpa; cravattone *m;* (*cover for table*) centro, striscia
scarf'pin' *s* spilla da cravatta
scarlet ['skɑrlɪt] *adj* scarlatto
scar'let fe'ver *s* scarlattina
scar·y ['skeri] *adj* (**-ier; -iest**) (*timid*) (coll) fifone; (*causing fright*) (coll) spaventevole

scathing ['skeðɪŋ] *adj* severo, bruciante
scatter [skætər] *tr* disperdere, sparpagliare || *intr* disperdersi, sparpagliarsi
scatterbrained ['skætər,brend] *adj* scervellato, stordito
scenari•o [sɪ'nɛrɪ,o] or [sɪ'nɑrɪ,o] *s* (**-os**) scenario
scenarist [sɪ'nɛrɪst] or [sɪ'nɑrɪst] *s* scenarista *mf*, sceneggiatore *m*
scene [sin] *s* (*view*) paesaggio; (*place*) scena; (theat) scena, quadro; **behind the scenes** dietro le quinte; **to make a scene** fare una scenata
scener•y ['sinəri] *s* (**-ies**) paesaggio; (theat) scenario
scenic ['sinɪk] or ['sɛnɪk] *adj* pittoresco; (*pertaining to the stage*) scenico
scent [sɛnt] *s* odore *m;* profumo; (*sense of smell*) fiuto, odorato; (*trail*) traccia, pista || *tr* profumare; (*to detect*) fiutare, annusare
scepter ['sɛptər] *s* scettro
sceptic ['skɛptɪk] *adj* & *s* scettico
sceptical ['skɛptɪkəl] *adj* scettico
scepticism ['skɛptɪ,sɪzəm] *s* scetticismo
schedule ['skedjʊl] *s* lista; programma *m;* (*of trains, planes, etc.*) orario || *tr* programmare; mettere in orario
scheme [skim] *s* schema *m;* piano, progetto; (*plot*) trama || *tr* progettare; tramare
schemer ['skimər] *s* progettista *mf;* (*underhanded*) manipolatore *m*, concertatore *m*
scheming ['skimɪŋ] *adj* intrigante, scaltro
schism ['sɪzəm] *s* scisma *m*
schist [ʃɪst] *s* scisto
scholar ['skɑlər] *s* (*pupil*) alunno; detentore *m* di una borsa di studio; (*learned person*) dotto, studioso
scholarly ['skɑlərli] *adj* erudito, studioso
scholarship ['skɑlər,ʃɪp] *s* erudizione; (*money*) borsa di studio
scholasticism [skə'læstɪ,sɪzəm] *s* scolastica
school [skul] *s* scuola; (*of a university*) facoltà *f;* (*of fish*) banco || *tr* istruire, insegnare
school' age' *s* età scolastica
school'bag' *s* cartella
school' board' *s* comitato scolastico
school'boy' *s* alunno, scolaro
school' bus' *s* scuolabus *m*
school' day' *s* giorno di scuola; durata della giornata scolastica
school'girl' *s* alunna, scolara
school'house' *s* scuola, edificio scolastico
schooling ['skulɪŋ] *s* istruzione
school'mas'ter *s* maestro di scuola; direttore scolastico
school'mate' *s* compagno di scuola, condiscepolo
school'room' *s* aula scolastica
school'teach'er *s* maestro
school' year' *s* anno scolastico
schooner ['skunər] *s* goletta
sciatica [saɪ'ætɪkə] *s* (pathol) sciatica
science ['saɪ•əns] *s* scienza
sci'ence fic'tion *s* fantascienza
sci'ence-fic'tion *adj* fantascientifico
scientific [,saɪ•ən'tɪfɪk] *adj* scientifico
scientist ['saɪ•əntɪst] *s* scienziato
scimitar ['sɪmɪtər] *s* scimitarra
scintillate ['sɪntɪ,let] *intr* scintillare
scion ['saɪ•ən] *s* rampollo, discendente *m*
scissors ['sɪzərz] *ssg* or *spl* forbici *fpl*
scoff [skɔf] or [skɑf] *s* dileggio, beffa || *intr* burlarsi; **to scoff at** burlarsi di, dileggiare
scold [skold] *s* megera || *tr* & *intr* sgridare, rimproverare
scoop [skup] *s* (*ladlelike utensil*) paletta; (*kitchen utensil*) cucchiaio, cucchiaione *m;* cucchiaiata; palettata; (*of dredge*) benna; (*hollow*) buco; (naut) gottazza; (journ) primizia, esclusiva; (coll) colpo || *tr* vuotare a cucchiaiate; (journ) battere; (naut) gottare; **to scoop out** (*e.g., sand*) scavare; (*soup*) scodellare
scoot [skut] *s* (coll) corsa || *intr* (coll) correre precipitosamente
scooter ['skutər] *s* monopattino
scope [skop] *s* ampiezza; lunghezza; **to give full scope to** dare piena libertà d'azione a
scorch [skɔrtʃ] *s* scottatura || *tr* bruciacchiare; bruciare, inaridire; (fig) ferire || *intr* bruciarsi
scorching ['skɔrtʃɪŋ] *adj* bruciante
score [skor] *s* (*in a game*) punteggio; (*in an examination*) nota; linea, segno, marca; (*twenty*) ventina; (mus) partitura; **scores** un mucchio; **to keep score** segnare il punteggio; **to settle a score** (fig) saldare un conto || *tr* raggiungere il punteggio di, fare; marcare; guadagnare; (*to censure*) sgridare, rimproverare; (mus) orchestrare
score'board' *s* quadro del punteggio
score'keep'er *s* segnapunti *m*
scorn [skɔrn] *s* disdegno, disprezzo || *tr* & *intr* disdegnare, disprezzare
scornful ['skɔrnfəl] *adj* disdegnoso
Scorpio ['skɔrpi,o] *s* Scorpione *m*
scorpion ['skɔrpɪ•ən] *s* scorpione *m*
Scot [skɑt] *s* scozzese *mf*
Scotch [skɑtʃ] *adj* scozzese || *s* scozzese *m;* whisky *m* scozzese; **the Scotch** gli scozzesi
Scotch'man *s* (**-men**) scozzese *m*
Scotch' pine' *s* pino silvestre
Scotch' tape' *s* (trademark) nastro autoadesivo Scotch
scot'-free' *adj* impune; **to get off scot-free** farla franca
Scotland ['skɑtlənd] *s* la Scozia
Scottish ['skɑtɪʃ] *adj* scozzese || *s* scozzese *mf;* **the Scottish** gli scozzesi
scoundrel ['skaʊndrəl] *s* birbante *m*, farabutto, manigoldo
scour [skaʊr] *tr* sgrassare fregando, pulire fregando; (*the countryside*) battere
scourge [skʌrdʒ] *s* sferza; (fig) flagello || *tr* sferzare

scout [skaʊt] *s* esplorazione; giovane esploratore *m;* giovane esploratrice *f;* (mil) ricognitore *m;* (nav) esploratore *m;* (slang) tipo || *tr* esplorare, riconoscere; cercar di trovare; disdegnare
scouting ['skaʊtɪŋ] *s* scoutismo
scowl [skaʊl] *s* cipiglio || *intr* aggrottare le ciglia; guardare torvamente
scram [skræm] *v* (*pret & pp* **scrammed;** *ger* **scramming**) *intr* (coll) tagliare la corda; **scram!** (coll) vattene!, (coll) escimi di tra i piedi!
scramble ['skræmbəl] *s* ruffa, gara || *tr* (*to grab up*) arraffare; confondere, mescolare; (*eggs*) strapazzare || *intr* arrampicarsi; (*to struggle*) azzuffarsi
scram'bled eggs' *spl* uova strapazzate
scrap [skræp] *s* pezzetto, frammento; ritaglio, rottame *m;* (coll) baruffa; **scraps** avanzi *mpl;* || *v* (*pret & pp* **scrapped;** *ger* **scrapping**) *tr* scartare || *intr* (coll) fare baruffa
scrap'book' *s* album *m* di ritagli (di giornale o fotografie)
scrape [skrep] *s* impiccio, imbroglio; baruffa || *tr* raschiare, graffiare; **to scrape together** racimolare || *intr* raschiare; **to scrape along** vivacchiare; **to scrape through** passare per il rotto della cuffia
scraper ['skrepər] *s* raschietto
scrap' i'ron *s* rottami *mpl* di ferro
scrap' pa'per *s* carta straccia; carta da appunti
scratch [skrætʃ] *s* graffio, scalfittura; scarabocchio; (billiards) punto perduto; (sports) linea di partenza; **from scratch** da bel principio; dal niente; **up to scratch** soddisfacente || *tr* graffiare, grattare; (*e.g., a horse*) cancellare || *intr* graffiare; (*said of a chicken*) raspare; (*said of a pen*) grattare
scratch' pad' *s* quaderno per appunti
scratch' pa'per *s* carta da appunti
scrawl [skrɔl] *s* scarabocchio || *tr & intr* scarabocchiare
scraw·ny ['skrɔni] *adj* (**-nier; -niest**) ossuto, scarno
scream [skrim] *s* grido, strillo; cosa divertentissima; persona divertentissima || *intr* gridare, strillare
screech [skritʃ] *s* stridio || *intr* stridere
screech' owl' *s* gufo; (*barn owl*) barbagianni *m*
screen [skrin] *s* (*movable partition*) paravento; (*in front of fire*) parafuoco; rete metallica; (*sieve*) vaglio; (mov; phys) schermo; (telv) teleschermo || *tr* schermare; riparare, proteggere; (*to sieve*) vagliare; (*a film*) proiettare; (*to adapt*) (mov) sceneggiare
screen' grid' *s* (rad, telv) griglia schermo
screen' test' *s* provino
screw [skru] *s* vite *f;* giro di vite; (*of a boat*) elica; **to have a screw loose** (slang) avere una rotella fuori di posto; **to put the screws on** far pressione su || *tr* avvitare; (*to twist*) torcere; **to screw up** (slang) rovinare; **to screw up one's courage** prendere il coraggio a quattro mani || *intr* avvitarsi
screw'ball' *s* (slang) pazzoide *m*, svitato
screw'driv'er *s* cacciavite *m*
screw' eye' *s* occhiello a vite
screw' jack' *s* martinetto a vite
screw' propel'ler *s* elica
screw·y ['skru·i] *adj* (**-ier; -iest**) (slang) pazzo; (slang) fuori di posto, strano
scribble ['skrɪbəl] *s* scarabocchio || *tr & intr* scarabocchiare
scribe [skraɪb] *s* (*Jewish scholar*) scriba *m;* copista *mf* || *tr* tracciare, incidere
scrimmage ['skrɪmɪdʒ] *s* ruffa; (*football*) azione
scrimp [skrɪmp] *tr & intr* lesinare
script [skrɪpt] *s* scrittura, scrittura a mano; manoscritto; testo; (*e.g., of a play*) copione *m;* (typ) carattere *m* inglese
scriptural ['skrɪptʃərəl] *adj* scritturale, biblico
scripture ['skrɪptʃər] *s* scrittura || **Scripture** *s* Scrittura
script'writ'er *s* soggettista *mf*
scrofula ['skrɑfjələ] *s* scrofola
scroll [skrol] *s* rotolo di carta, rotolo di pergamena; (*of violin*) riccio; (archit) voluta, cartoccio
scroll'work' *s* ornamentazione a voluta
scro·tum ['skrotəm] *s* (**-ta** [tə] or **-tums**) scroto
scrub [skrʌb] *s* boscaglia; alberelli *mpl;* animale bastardo; persona di poco conto; (*act of scrubbing*) fregata; (sports) giocatore *m* di riserva || *v* (*pret & pp* **scrubbed;** *ger* **scrubbing**) *tr* pulire, fregare
scrub' oak' *s* rovere basso
scrub'wom'an *s* (**-wom'en**) lavatrice *f*, donna a giornata
scruff [skrʌf] *s* nuca, collottola
scruple ['skrupəl] *s* scrupolo
scrupulous ['skrupjələs] *adj* scrupoloso
scrutinize ['skrutɪ,naɪz] *tr* scrutare, disaminare
scruti·ny ['skrutɪni] *s* (**-nies**) attento esame, disamina
scuff [skʌf] *s* graffio, logorio || *tr* logorare, graffiare
scuffle ['skʌfəl] *s* zuffa, rissa || *intr* azzuffarsi, colluttare
scull [skʌl] *s* (*oar*) remo a bratto; (*boat*) canotto || *tr* spingere a bratto || *intr* vogare a bratto
sculler·y ['skʌləri] *s* (**-ies**) retrocucina
scul'lery maid' *s* sguattera
scullion ['skʌljən] *s* sguattero
sculptor ['skʌlptər] *s* scultore *m*
sculptress ['skʌlptrɪs] *s* scultrice *f*
sculpture ['skʌlptʃər] *s* scultura || *tr & intr* scolpire
scum [skʌm] *s* schiuma; (*slag*) scoria; (*rabble*) feccia, gentaglia || *v* (*pret & pp* **scummed;** *ger* **scumming**) *tr & intr* schiumare

scum·my ['skʌmi] *adj* (**-mier; -miest**) spumoso; (coll) vile, schifoso
scurf [skʌrf] *s* (*shed by the skin*) squama; incrostazione
scurrilous ['skʌrɪləs] *adj* scurrile
scur·ry ['skʌri] *v* (*pret & pp* **-ried**) *intr* affrettarsi; **to scurry around** dimenarsi
scur·vy ['skʌrvi] *adj* (**-vier; -viest**) spregevole, meschino || *s* scorbuto
scuttle ['skʌtəl] *s* (*for coal*) secchio; (*trap door*) botola; corsa, fuga; (naut) boccaporto || *tr* aprire una falla in, affondare || *intr* affrettarsi, darsi alla corsa
scut'tle·butt' *s* (naut) barilozzo dell'acqua; (coll) rumore *m*, diceria
scuttling ['skʌtlɪŋ] *s* autoaffondamento
Scylla ['sɪlə] *s* Scilla; **between Scylla and Charybdis** fra Scilla e Cariddi
scythe [saɪð] *s* falce *f*
sea [si] *s* mare *m;* (*wave*) maroso; **at sea** in alto mare; **by the sea** a mare, sulla costa; **to follow the sea** farsi marinaio; **to put to sea** prendere il largo
sea'board' *adj* costiero || *s* litorale *m*
sea' breeze' *s* brezza marina
sea'coast' *s* costa, litorale *m*
sea' dog' *s* (*seal*) foca; (*sailor*) lupo di mare
seafarer ['si ˌferər] *s* marinaio; viaggiatore marittimo
sea'food' *s* pesce *m;* (*shellfish*) frutti *mpl* di mare
seagoing ['si ˌgo·ɪŋ] *adj* di alto mare
sea' gull' *s* gabbiano
seal [sil] *s* sigillo; (*sea animal*) foca; (fig) suggello || *tr* sigillare, apporre i sigilli a; (fig) suggellare
sea' legs' *spl*—**to have good sea legs** avere piede marino
sea' lev'el *s* livello del mare
seal'ing wax' *s* ceralacca
seal'skin' *s* pelle *f* di foca
seam [sim] *s* (*abutting of edges*) giuntura; (*stitches*) costura, cucitura; (*scar*) cicatrice *f;* (*wrinkle*) ruga; (*in metal*) commettitura; (min) filone *m*, vena
sea'man *s* (**-men**) marinaio
sea' mile' *s* miglio marino
seamless ['simlɪs] *adj* senza giuntura; (*stockings*) senza cucitura
seamstress ['simstrɪs] *s* cucitrice *f*
seam·y ['simi] *adj* (**-ier; -iest**) pieno di cuciture; basso, sordido; (*unpleasant*) spiacevole
séance ['se·ɑns] *s* seduta spiritica
sea'plane' *s* idrovolante *m*
sea'port' *s* porto di mare
sea' pow'er *s* potenza navale
sear [sɪr] *adj* secco || *s* scottatura || *tr* scottare, bruciare; (*to brand*) marcare a fuoco; inaridire; (fig) indurire
search [sʌrtʃ] *s* ricerca, investigazione; (*frisking a person*) perquisizione; **in search of** in cerca di || *tr* cercare, investigare; perquisire, frugare || *intr* investigare; **to search for** cercare; **to search into** investigare
searching ['sʌrtʃɪŋ] *adj* (*e.g., inspection*) profondo; (*e.g., glance*) indagatore, penetrante
search'light' *s* proiettore *m*, riflettore *m;* (mil) fotoelettrica
search' war'rant *s* mandato di perquisizione
sea'scape' *s* vista del mare; (*painting*) marina
sea' shell' *s* conchiglia
sea'shore' *s* costa, marina, mare *m*
sea'sick' *adj*—**to be seasick** aver mal di mare
sea'sick'ness *s* mal *m* di mare
sea'side' *s* costa, riviera, marina
season ['sizən] *s* stagione; **in season di stagione**; **in season and out of season** sempre, continuamente; **out of season** fuori stagione || *tr* (*food*) condire; (*to mature*) stagionare; (*e.g., wood*) stagionare
seasonal ['sizənəl] *adj* stagionale
seasoning ['sizənɪŋ] *s* condimento; (*of wood*) stagionamento
sea'son's greet'ings *spl* migliori auguri *mpl* per le feste natalizie
sea'son tick'et *s* biglietto d'abbonamento
seat [sit] *s* sedia; (*part of chair*) sedile *m;* (*of human body*) sedere *m;* (*of pants*) fondo; sito, posto; (*e.g., of government*) sede *f;* (*in parliament*) seggio; (*e.g., of learning*) centro; (rr, theat) posto || *tr* far sedere; aver posti per; (*a chair*) mettere il sedile a; (*pants*) mettere il fondo a; (*an official*) insediare; (mach) installare; **to be seated** essere seduto; **to seat oneself** sedersi
seat' belt' *s* cintura di sicurezza
seat' cov'er *s* guaina, foderina
seat'ing room' *s* posti *mpl* a sedere
sea' wall' *s* diga
sea'way' *s* via marittima; alto mare; mare grosso; rotta percorsa; via di fiume accessibile a navi da trasporto
sea'weed' *s* alga marina; pianta marina
sea'wor'thy *adj* atto a tenere il mare
secede [sɪ'sid] *intr* separarsi, distaccarsi
secession [sɪ'seʃən] *s* secessione
seclude [sɪ'klud] *tr* appartare; isolare
seclusion [sɪ'kluʒən] *s* reclusione; solitudine *f*, intimità *f*
second ['sekənd] *adj & pron* secondo; **to be second to none** non cederla a nessuno || *s* secondo; (*in a duel*) padrino; (*in dates*) due *m;* (aut, mus) seconda; **seconds** (com) articoli *mpl* di seconda qualità; **to have seconds on** servirsi una seconda volta di || *tr* assecondare; (*a motion*) appoggiare || *adv* in secondo luogo
secondar·y ['sekən ˌderi] *adj* secondario || *s* (**-ies**) (elec) secondario
sec'ond-best' *adj* (il) migliore dopo il primo; **to come off second-best** arrivare secondo
sec'-ond-class' *adj* di seconda qualità; (aer, naut, rr) di seconda classe
sec'ond hand' *s* lancetta dei secondi
sec'ond·hand' *adj* di seconda mano, d'occasione

sec'ond lieuten'ant *s* sottotenente *m*
sec'ond-rate' *adj* di seconda categoria; (*inferior*) da strapazzo
sec'ond sight' *s* chiaroveggenza
sec'ond wind' [wɪnd] *s*—**to get one's second wind** riprendere fiato
secre·cy ['sikrəsi] *s* (**-cies**) segretezza; **in secrecy** in segreto
secret ['sikrɪt] *adj* & *s* segreto; **in secret** in segreto
secretar·y ['sɛkrɪ,teri] *s* (**-ies**) segretario; (*desk*) scrittoio
se'cret bal'lot *s* scrutinio segreto
secrete [sɪ'krit] *tr* nascondere; (physiol) secernere
secretive ['sikrɪtɪv] or [sɪ'kritɪv] *adj* riservato, poco comunicativo
sect [sɛkt] *s* setta
sectarian [sɛk'terɪ·ən] *adj* & *s* settario
section ['sɛkʃən] *s* sezione; (*of city*) rione *m;* (*of fruit*) spicchio; (*of highway*) tronco; (rr) tratta || *tr* sezionare
sectional ['sɛkʃənəl] *adj* (*e.g., bookcase*) componibile; sezionale; locale, regionale
secular ['sɛkjələr] *adj* & *s* secolare *m*
secularism ['sɛkjələ,rɪzəm] *s* laicismo
secure [sɪ'kjʊr] *adj* salvo, sicuro || *tr* ottenere; assicurare; fissare; (law) garantire
securi·ty [sɪ'kjʊrɪti] *s* (**-ties**) sicurezza; protezione; garanzia; (*person*) garante *m;* **securities** valori *mpl,* titoli *mpl*
sedan [sɪ'dæn] *s* (aut) berlina
sedan' chair' *s* bussola, portantina
sedate [sɪ'det] *adj* calmo, posato
sedation [sɪ'deʃən] *s* ritorno alla calma; stato di calma mentale
sedative ['sɛdətɪv] *adj* & *s* sedativo
sedentary ['sɛdən,teri] *adj* sedentario
sedge [sɛdʒ] *s* carice *m*
sediment ['sɛdɪmənt] *s* sedimento
sedition [sɪ'dɪʃən] *s* sedizione
seditious [sɪ'dɪʃəs] *adj* sedizioso
seduce [sɪ'djus] or [sɪ'dus] *tr* sedurre
seducer [sɪ'djusər] or [sɪ'dusər] *s* seduttore *m,* corruttore *m*
seduction [sɪ'dʌkʃən] *s* seduzione
seductive [sɪ'dʌktɪv] *adj* seduttore
sedulous ['sɛdjələs] *adj* diligente
see [si] *s* (eccl) sede *f* || *v* (*pret* **saw** [sɔ]; *pp* **seen** [sin]) *tr* vedere; **to see off** andare ad accompagnare; **to see through** portare a termine || *intr* vedere; **see here!** faccia attenzione!; **to see after** prender cura di; **to see through** conoscere il gioco di
seed [sid] *s* seme *m,* semenza; **to go to seed** andare in semenza; deteriorarsi || *tr* seminare; (*fruit*) togliere i semi da || *intr* seminare; produrre semi
seed'bed' *s* semenzaio; (fig) vivaio
seeder ['sidər] *s* (*person*) seminatore *m;* (*machine*) seminatrice *f*
seedling ['sidlɪŋ] *s* piantina da trapianto
seed·y ['sidi] *adj* (**-ier; -iest**) pieno di semi; (*unkempt*) malmesso, malvestito
seeing ['si·ɪŋ] *conj* visto che, dato che
See'ing Eye' dog' *s* cane *m* guida per ciechi
seek [sik] *v* (*pret* & *pp* **sought** [sɔt]) *tr* cercare, ricercare; **to be sought after** essere ricercato; **to seek to** cercare di
seem [sim] *intr* parere, sembrare
seemingly ['simɪŋli] *adv* apparentemente
seem·ly ['simli] *adj* (**-lier; -liest**) decoroso; appropriato
seep [sip] *intr* colare, filtrare
seer [sɪr] *s* profeta *m,* veggente *m*
see'saw' *s* altalena; (*motion*) viavai *m* || *intr* altalenare
seethe [sið] *intr* bollire
segment ['sɛgmənt] *s* segmento
segregate ['sɛgrɪ,get] *tr* segregare
segregation [,sɛgrɪ'geʃən] *s* segregazione
segregationist [,sɛgrɪ'geʃənɪst] *s* segregazionista *mf*
Seine [sen] *s* Senna
seismograph ['saɪzmə,græf] or ['saɪzmə,grɑf] *s* sismografo
seismology [saɪz'mɑlədʒi] *s* sismologia
seize [siz] *tr* afferrare; impossessarsi di; (*with one's clenched fist*) impugnare; comprendere; (law) sequestrare, confiscare
seizure ['siʒər] *s* conquista, cattura; (*of an illness*) attacco; (law) sequestro, pignoramento
seldom ['sɛldəm] *adj* di raro, raramente
select [sɪ'lɛkt] *adj* scelto, selezionato || *tr* prescegliere, selezionare
selectee [sɪ,lɛk'ti] *s* (mil) recluta
selection [sɪ'lɛkʃən] *s* selezione, scelta
selective [sɪ'lɛktɪv] *adj* selettivo
self [sɛlf] *adj* stesso || *s* (**selves** [sɛlvz]) sé stesso; io, personalità *f;* **all by one's self** senza aiuto altrui || *pron* sé stesso
self'-abuse' *s* abuso delle proprie forze; masturbazione
self'-addressed' *adj* col nome e l'indirizzo del mittente
self'-cen'tered *adj* egocentrico
self'-con'scious *adj* imbarazzato, vergognoso, timido
self'-control' *s* padronanza di sé stesso, autocontrollo
self'-defense' *s* autodifesa; **in self-defense** in legittima difesa
self'-deni'al *s* abnegazione
self'-deter'mina'tion *s* autodeterminazione
self'-dis'cipline *s* autodisciplina
self'-ed'ucat'ed *adj* autodidatta
self'-employed' *adj* che lavora in proprio
self'-ev'i·dent *adj* evidente, lampante
self'-ex·plan'a·tor'y *adj* ovvio, che si spiega da sé
self'-gov'ernment *s* autogoverno; controllo sopra sé stesso
self'-im·por'tant *adj* presuntuoso
self'-in·dul'gence *s* intemperanza
self'-in'terest *s* egoismo, interesse *m*
selfish ['sɛlfɪʃ] *adj* egoista
selfishness ['sɛlfɪʃnɪs] *s* egoismo

selfless ['sɛlflɪs] *adj* disinteressato; altruista
self'-liq'ui•dat'ing *adj* autoammortizzabile
self'-love' *s* amor proprio
self'-made' *adj* che si è fatto da sé
self'-por'trait *s* autoritratto
self'-pos•sessed' *adj* calmo, padrone di sé
self'-pres'er•va'tion *s* conservazione
self'-pro•pelled' *adj* semovente
self'-re•li'ant *adj* pieno di fiducia in sé stesso
self'-re•spect' *s* rispetto di sé stesso
self'-right'eous *adj* che si considera più morale degli altri, ipocrita
self'-sac'ri•fice' *s* sacrificio di sé, spirito di sacrifico
self'-same' *adj* stesso e medesimo
self'-sat'is•fied' *adj* contento di sé
self'-seek'ing *adj* egoista || *s* egoismo
self'-serv'ice *s* autoservizio
self'-start'er *s* motorino d'avviamento
self'-styled' *adj* sedicente
self'-support' *s* indipendenza economica
self'-tap'ping screw' *s* vite *f* autofilettante
self'-taught' *adj* autodidatta
self-threading ['sɛlf'θredɪŋ] *adj* autofilettante
self'-willed' *adj* ostinato, caparbio
self'-wind'ing *adj* a carica automatica
sell [sɛl] *v* (*pret & pp* **sold** [sold]) *tr* vendere; (*an idea*) fare accettare; **to sell off** svendere, liquidare; **to sell out** smerciare; vendere a stralcio; (coll) tradire || *intr* vendere, vendersi; fare il venditore; **to sell off** (*said of the stock market*) essere in ribasso; **to sell out** vendere a stralcio; vendersi
seller ['sɛlər] *s* venditore *m*
Selt'zer wa'ter ['sɛltsər] *s* selz *m*
selvage ['sɛlvɪdʒ] *s* cimosa, vivagno
semantic [sɪ'mæntɪk] *adj* semantico || **semantics** *s* semantica
semaphore ['sɛmə,for] *s* semaforo
semblance ['sɛmbləns] *s* apparenza, specie *f;* apparizione
semen ['simen] *s* sperma *m*
semester [sɪ'mɛstər] *adj* semestrale || *s* semestre *m*
semicircle ['sɛmɪ,sʌrkəl] *s* semicircolo
semicolon ['sɛmɪ,kolən] *s* punto e virgola
semiconductor [,sɛmikən'dʌktər] *s* semiconduttore *m*
semiconscious [,sɛmi'kɑnʃəs] *adj* mezzo cosciente
semifinal [,sɛmi'faɪnəl] *s* semifinale *f*
semilearned [,sɛmi'lʌrnɪd] *adj* semidotto
semimonth•ly [,sɛmi'mʌnθli] or [,sɛmaɪ'mʌnθli] *adj* quindicinale || *s* **(-lies)** rivista quindicinale
seminar ['sɛmɪ,nɑr] or [,sɛmɪ'nɑr] *s* seminario
seminar•y ['sɛmɪ,neri] *s* **(-ies)** seminario
Semite ['sɛmaɪt] or ['simaɪt] *s* semita *mf*
Semitic [sɪ'mɪtɪk] *adj* semitico || *s* lingua semitica; (*family of languages*) semitico
semitrailer ['sɛmɪ,trelər] *s* semirimorchio
semiweek•ly [,sɛmi'wikli] or [,sɛmaɪ'wikli] *adj* bisettimanale || *s* **(-lies)** periodico bisettimanale
semiyearly [,sɛmi'jɪrli] or [,sɛmaɪ'jɪrli] *adj* semestrale || *adv* due volte all'anno
senate ['sɛnɪt] *s* senato
senator ['sɛnətər] *s* senatore *m*
send [sɛnd] *v* (*pret & pp* **sent** [sɛnt]) *tr* inviare, mandare; spedire; (*e.g., a punch*) lanciare; **to send back** rimandare; **to send forth** emettere; **to send packing** licenziare su due piedi || *intr* (rad) trasmettere; **to send for** mandare a chiamare, far venire
sender ['sɛndər] *s* speditore *m,* mittente *m;* (telg) trasmettitore *m*
send'-off' *s* (coll) addio affettuoso; (coll) lancio
senility [sɪ'nɪlɪti] *s* (pathol) senilismo
senior ['sinjər] *adj* maggiore, più anziano; seniore, di grado più elevato; dell'ultimo anno, laureando; senior, il vecchio || *s* maggiore *m;* seniore *m,* persona di grado più elevato; studente *m* dell'ultimo anno, laureando
sen'ior cit'izen *s* vecchio, pensionato
seniority [sin'jɑrɪti] or [sin'jɔrɪti] *s* anzianità *f*
sensation [sɛn'seʃən] *s* sensazione
sensational [sɛn'seʃənəl] *adj* sensazionale
sense [sɛns] *s* senso; **in a sense** in un certo senso; **to come to one's senses** riprendere il giudizio; **to make sense out of** arrivare a capire; **to take leave of one's senses** perdere il ben dell'intelletto || *tr* intuire; comprendere
senseless ['sɛnslɪs] *adj* (*unconscious*) privo di sensi; (*meaningless*) insensato, privo di senso
sense' or'gan *s* organo di senso
sensibili•ty [,sɛnsɪ'bɪlɪti] *s* **(-ties)** sensibilità *f;* **sensibilities** suscettibilità *f*
sensible ['sɛnsɪbəl] *adj* sensato; (*keenly aware*) sensibile; cosciente
sensitive ['sɛnsɪtɪv] *adj* sensitivo, sensibile; delicato
sensitize ['sɛnsɪ,taɪz] *tr* sensibilizzare
sensory ['sɛnsəri] *adj* sensorio
sensual ['sɛnʃʊ·əl] *adj* sensuale
sensuous ['sɛnʃʊ·əs] *adj* sensuale
sentence ['sɛntəns] *s* (gram) frase; (law) sentenza, condanna || *tr* sentenziare, condannare
sentiment ['sɛntɪmənt] *s* sentimento
sentimental [,sɛntɪ'mɛntəl] *adj* sentimentale
sentimentalism [,sɛntɪ'mɛntəl,ɪzəm] *s* sentimentalismo
sentinel ['sɛntɪnəl] *s* sentinella; **to stand sentinel** montare di sentinella
sen•try ['sɛntri] *s* **(-tries)** sentinella
sen'try box' *s* garitta, casotto
separate ['sɛpərɪt] *adj* separato ||

['sɛpə,ret] *tr* separare || *intr* separarsi
separation [,sɛpə'reʃən] *s* separazione
Sephardic [sɪ'fɑrdɪk] *adj* sefardita
September [sep'tembər] *s* settembre *m*
septic ['sɛptɪk] *adj* settico
sep'tic tank' *s* fossa settica
sepulcher ['sɛpəlkər] *s* sepolcro
sequel ['sikwəl] *s* seguito
sequence ['sikwəns] *s* serie *f*, sequenza, successione; conseguenza; (cards, eccl, mov) sequenza; (gram) correlazione
sequester [sɪ'kwɛstər] *tr* isolare, appartare; (law) sequestrare
sequin ['sikwɪn] *s* lustrino
ser•aph ['sɛrəf] *s* (**-aphs** or **-aphim** [əfɪm]) serafino
Serbian ['sʌrbɪ·ən] *adj & s* serbo
Serbo-Croatian [,sʌrbokro'eʃən] *adj & s* serbocroato
sere [sɪr] *adj* secco, appassito
serenade [,sɛrə'ned] *s* serenata || *tr* fare la serenata a || *intr* fare la serenata
serene [sɪ'rin] *adj* sereno
serenity [sɪ'rɛnɪti] *s* serenità *f*
serf [sʌrf] *s* servo della gleba
serfdom ['sʌrfdəm] *s* servitù *f* della gleba
serge [sʌrdʒ] *s* saia
sergeant ['sɑrdʒənt] *s* sergente *m*
ser'geant at arms' *s* (**ser'geants at arms'**) ufficiale *m* delegato a mantenere l'ordine
ser'geant ma'jor *s* (**sergeants major** or **sergeant majors**) (*in U.S. Army*) sergente *m* maggiore; (*in Italian Army*) maresciallo
serial ['sɪrɪ·əl] *adj* a puntate, a dispense || *s* periodico; romanzo a puntate; programma *m* a serie
se'rial num'ber *s* matricola; (*of a book*) segnatura; (aut) matricola di telaio
se•ries ['sɪriz] *s* (**-ries**) serie *f*; (*works dealing with the same topic*) collana; **in series** (elec) in serie
serious ['sɪrɪ·əs] *adj* serio
seriousness ['sɪrɪ·əsnɪs] *s* serietà *f*; **in all seriousness** molto sul serio
sermon ['sʌrmən] *s* sermone *m*
sermonize ['sʌrmə,naɪz] *tr & intr* sermonare
serpent ['sʌrpənt] *s* serpente *m*
se•rum ['sɪrəm] *s* (**-rums** or **-ra** [rə]) siero
servant ['sʌrvənt] *s* servo, domestico; (*civil servant*) funzionario; (fig) servitore *m*
serv'ant girl' *s* serva, domestica
serv'ant prob'lem *s* crisi *f* ancillare
serve [sʌrv] *s* (*in tennis*) servizio || *tr* servire; (*a sentence*) espiare; (*to suffice*) bastare (with *dat*); (*a writ*) notificare; **to serve s.o. right** stare bene (with *dat*), e.g., **it serves him right** gli sta bene || *intr* servire; **to serve as** fare da
service ['sʌrvɪs] *s* servizio; (*of a writ*) notifica; (*branch of the armed forces*) arma; **at your service** per servirLa || *tr* rifornire, riparare
serviceable ['sʌrvɪsəbəl] *adj* utile; durevole; pratico; riparabile
serv'ice club' *s* casa del soldato
serv'ice•man' *s* (**-men'**) militare *m*; riparatore *m*, aggiustatore *m*
serv'ice mod'ule *s* modulo di servizio
serv'ice rec'ord *s* stato di servizio
serv'ice sta'tion *s* stazione di servizio or di rifornimento
serv'ice-sta'tion attend'ant *s* benzinaio
serv'ice stripe' *s* gallone *m*
servile ['sʌrvɪl] *adj* servile
servitude ['sʌrvɪ,tjud] or ['sʌrvɪ,tud] *s* servitù *f*; lavori forzati
sesame ['sɛsəmi] *s* sesamo; **open sesame** apriti sesamo
session ['sɛʃən] *s* sessione *f*, seduta
set [sɛt] *adj* determinato, preordinato; abituale; fisso, rigido; (*ready*) pronto; meditato, studiato || *s* (*e.g., of books*) collezione, serie *f*; (*e.g., of chess*) gioco; set *m*, insieme *m*, completo; (*of tires*) treno; (*of horses*) pariglia; (*of tennis*) partita; (*of dishes*) servizio; (*of kitchen utensils*) batteria; posizione, atteggiamento; (*of a garment*) linea; (*e.g., of cement*) presa; (*of people*) gruppo; (*of thieves*) genia; (*of sails*) muta; (*of lines*) (geom) fascio; (rad, telv) apparato; (theat, mov) set *m* || *v* (*pret & pp* **set**; *ger* **setting**) *tr* porre, deporre; mettere; (*fire*) dare; (*the table*) imbandire; (*a watch*) regolare; (*s.o. a certain number of tricks*) far cadere di; (*a price*) fissare; (*a gem*) incastonare; (*a fracture*) mettere a posto; (*a saw*) allicciare; (*a trap*) tendere; (*hair*) acconciare; stabilire; insediare; (*to plant*) piantare; (*a sail*) tendere; (*e.g., milk*) rapprendere; calibrare, tarare; (*cement*) solidificare; (typ) comporre; **to set back** ritardare; (*a clock*) mettere indietro; **to set forth** descrivere; **to set one's heart on** desiderare ardentemente; **to set store by** tenere in gran conto; **to set up** metter su; impiantare; (*drinks*) (slang) pagare || *intr* (*said, e.g., of the sun*) tramontare; (*said of a liquid*) solidificarsi; (*said of cement*) fare presa; (*said of milk*) rapprendersi; (*said of a hen*) covare; (*said of a garment*) cascare; (*said of hair*) prendere la piega; **to set about** mettersi a; **to set out** porsi in cammino; **to set out to** mettersi a; **to set to work** mettersi a lavorare; **to set upon** attaccare
set'back' *s* rovescio, contrarietà *f*
set'screw' *s* vite *f* di pressione
setting ['sɛtɪŋ] *s* (*environment*) ambiente *m*; (*of a gem*) montatura; (*of cement*) presa; (*e.g., of the sun*) tramonto; (theat) scenario; (mus) arrangiamento
set'ting-up' ex'ercises *spl* ginnastica da camera
settle ['sɛtəl] *tr* determinare, risolvere; sistemare, regolare; (*a bill*) liquidare; installarsi in, colonizzare; calmare; (*a liquid*) far depositare; (law)

conciliare || *intr* mettersi d'accordo; saldare un conto; stanziarsi, domiciliarsi; fermarsi, posare; (*said of a liquid*) depositare, calmarsi; solidificarsi; **to settle down to work** mettersi a lavorare di buzzo buono; **to settle on** scegliere, fissare

settlement ['sɛtəlmənt] *s* stabilimento; sistemazione, regolamento; colonia, comunità *f;* (*of a building*) infossamento; agenzia di beneficenza

settler ['sɛtlər] *s* fondatore *m;* colono; conciliatore *m*

set'up' *s* portamento; (*e.g., of tools*) disposizione; quanto è necessario per mescolare una bibita alcolica; (coll) incontro truccato

seven ['sɛvən] *adj & pron* sette || *s* sette *m;* **seven o'clock** le sette

sev'en hun'dred *adj, s & pron* settecento

seventeen ['sɛvən'tin] *adj, s & pron* diciassette *m*

seventeenth ['sɛvən'tinθ] *adj, s & pron* diciassettesimo || *s* (*in dates*) diciassette *m*

seventh ['sɛvənθ] *adj, s & pron* settimo || *s* (*in dates*) sette *m*

seventieth ['sɛvəntɪ·ɪθ] *adj, s & pron* settantesimo

seven·ty ['sɛvənti] *adj & pron* settanta || *s* (**-ties**) settanta *m;* **the seventies** gli anni settanta

sever ['sɛvər] *tr* tagliare, mozzare; (*relations*) troncare || *intr* separarsi

several ['sɛvərəl] *adj* parecchi, vari; rispettivi || *spl* parecchi *mpl*

sev'erance pay' ['sɛvərəns] *s* buonuscita, indennità *f* di licenziamento

severe [sɪ'vɪr] *adj* severo; (*weather*) rigido; (*pain*) acuto; (*illness*) grave

sew [so] *v* (*pret* **sewed;** *pp* **sewed** or **sewn**) *tr & intr* cucire

sewage ['su·ɪdʒ] or ['sju·ɪdʒ] *s* acque *fpl* di scolo or di rifiuto

sewer ['su·ər] or ['sju·ər] *s* fogna, chiavica

sewerage ['su·ərɪdʒ] or ['sju·ərɪdʒ] *s* fognatura; drenaggio, rimozione delle acque di rifiuto

sew'ing machine' ['so·ɪŋ] *s* macchina da cucire

sex [sɛks] *s* sesso

sex' appeal' *s* attrattiva fisica, sex appeal *m*

sextant ['sɛkstənt] *s* sestante *m*

sextet [sɛks'tɛt] *s* sestetto

sexton ['sɛkstən] *s* sagrestano

sexual ['sɛkʃʊ·əl] *adj* sessuale

sex·y ['sɛksi] *adj* (**-ier; -iest**) (coll) erotico; (coll) procace

shab·by ['ʃæbi] *adj* (**-bier; -biest**) (*clothes*) frusto; (*house*) malandato; (*person*) malvestito; (*deal*) cattivo

shack [ʃæk] *s* baracca

shackle ['ʃækəl] *s* ceppo; (*to tie an animal*) pastoia; (fig) ostacolo; **shackles** ceppi *mpl,* manette *fpl* || *tr* mettere in ceppi; (fig) inceppare

shad [ʃæd] *s* alosa

shade [ʃed] *s* ombra; (*of lamp*) paralume *m;* (*of window*) tendina; (*for the eyes*) visiera; (*hue*) tinta, sfumatura; **a shade of** un po' di; **shades** tenebre *fpl;* ombre *fpl* || *tr* ombreggiare; sfumare, digradare; (*a price*) ribassare leggermente

shadow ['ʃædo] *s* ombra || *tr* ombreggiare; (*to follow*) pedinare; **to shadow forth** adombrare, preannunciare

shadowy ['ʃædo·i] *adj* ombroso, ombreggiato; illusorio, chimerico

shad·y ['ʃedi] *adj* (**-ier; -iest**) ombroso; spettrale; (coll) losco; **to keep shady** (slang) starsene lontano

shaft [ʃæft] or [ʃɑft] *s* (*of arrow*) asta; (*of feather*) rachide *f;* (*of light*) raggio; (*handle*) manico; (*of wagon*) stanga, timone *m;* (*of motor*) albero; (*of column*) fusto; (*of elevator*) pozzo; (*in a mountain*) camino; (min) fornello; (fig) frecciata

shag·gy ['ʃægi] *adj* (**-gier; -giest**) peloso, irsuto; (*unkempt*) trasandato; (*cloth*) ruvido

shag'gy dog' sto'ry *s* storiella senza capo né coda

shake [ʃek] *s* scossa; stretta di mano; momento, istante *m;* **the shakes** la tremarella || *v* (*pret* **shook** [ʃʊk]; *pp* **shaken**) *tr* scuotere; scrollare; (*s.o.'s hands*) serrare; (*e.g., with a mixer*) sbattere; agitare, perturbare; eludere, disfarsi di || *intr* tremare; (*to totter*) traballare, tentennare; scuotere; darsi la mano

shake'down' *s* estorzione, concussione; (*bed*) lettuccio di fortuna

shake'down' cruise' *s* (naut) viaggio di prova

shaker ['ʃekər] *s* (*e.g., for sugar*) spolverino; (*for cocktails*) sbattighiaccio, shaker *m*

shake'-up' *s* cambiamento completo, riorganizzazione, rimaneggiamento

shak·y ['ʃeki] *adj* (**-ier; -iest**) tremebondo; traballante, zoppicante

shall [ʃæl] *v* (*cond* **should** [ʃʊd]) *v aux* si usa per formare (1) il futuro dell'indicativo, per es., **I shall do it** lo farò; (2) il futuro perfetto dell'indicativo, per es., **I shall have done it** l'avrò fatto; (3) espressioni di obbligo o necessità, per es., **what shall I do?** che devo fare?, che vuole che faccia?

shallow ['ʃælo] *adj* basso, poco profondo; leggero, superficiale

sham [ʃæm] *adj* falso, finto || *s* frode *f,* contraffazione || *v* (*pret & pp* **shammed;** *ger* **shamming**) *tr & intr* fingere

sham' bat'tle *s* finta battaglia

shambles ['ʃæmbəlz] *s* macello; confusione, disordine

shame [ʃem] *s* vergogna; **shame on you!** vergogna!; **what a shame!** che peccato! || *tr* svergognare, disonorare

shame'faced' *adj* timido, vergognoso

shameful ['ʃemfəl] *adj* vergognoso

shameless ['ʃemlɪs] *adj* sfrontato, impudente, svergognato

shampoo [ʃæm'pu] *s* shampoo *m* || *tr* fare lo shampoo a
shamrock ['ʃæmrɑk] *s* trifoglio irlandese
shanghai ['ʃæŋhaɪ] or [ʃæŋ'haɪ] *tr* imbarcare a viva forza || **Shanghai** *s* Sciangai *f*
shank [ʃæŋk] *s* fusto; (*of tool*) codolo; (*stem*) gambo; (*of bird*) zampa; (*of anchor*) fuso; (coll) principio; (coll) fine *f*; **to ride shank's mare** andare col cavallo di San Francesco
shan•ty ['ʃænti] *s* (**-ties**) bicocca
shan'ty•town' *s* bidonville *f*
shape [ʃep] *s* forma; **in bad shape** in cattive condizioni; **out of shape** sformato || *tr* formare, foggiare; plasmare, conformare || *intr* formarsi; **to take shape** prender forma
shapeless ['ʃeplɪs] *adj* informe
shape•ly ['ʃepli] *adj* (**-lier; -liest**) ben fatto, formoso
share [ʃɛr] *s* parte *f*; interesse *m*; (*of stock*) azione *f*; (*of plow*) suola; **to go shares** dividere in parti eguali || *tr* (*to enjoy jointly*) condividere; (*to apportion*) ripartire || *intr* partecipare, prender parte
sharecropper ['ʃɛr ˌkrɑpər] *s* mezzadro
share'hold'er *s* azionista *mf*
shark [ʃɑrk] *s* pescecane *m*; (*schemer*) piovra; (slang) esperto
sharp [ʃɑrp] *adj* affilato, acuto; angoloso; (*e.g., curve*) forte; distinto, ben delineato; (*taste*) pungente, salato; (*pain*) vivo; (*words*) mordace; (slang) elegante || *s* (mus) diesis *m* || *adv* acutamente; in punto, e.g., **at seven o'clock sharp** alle sette in punto
sharpen ['ʃɑrpən] *tr* affilare; (*a pencil*) fare la punta a || *intr* affilarsi
sharpener ['ʃɑrpənər] *s* (*person*) affilatore *m*; (*machine*) affilatrice *f*
sharper ['ʃɑrpər] *s* gabbamondo
sharp'shoot'er *s* tiratore scèlto
shatter ['ʃætər] *tr* frantumare; sfracellare; (*health*) rovinare; (*nerves*) sconvolgere; distruggere || *intr* frantumarsi, andare in pezzi
shat'ter•proof' *adj* infrangibile
shave [ʃev] *s* rasatura; **to have a close shave** scapparla or scamparla bella || *tr* (*the face*) radere, sbarbare; (*wood*) piallare; (*to scrape*) sfiorare; (*prices*) ridurre; (*a lawn*) tosare || *intr* rasarsi
shaving ['ʃevɪŋ] *adj* da barba, per barba, e.g., **shaving cream** crema da or per barba || *s* rasatura; **shavings** trucioli *mpl*
shav'ing brush' *s* pennello da barba
shav'ing soap' *s* sapone *m* per la barba
shawl [ʃɔl] *s* scialle *m*
she [ʃi] *s* (**shes**) femmina || *pron pers* (**they**) essa, lei
sheaf [ʃif] *s* (**sheaves** [ʃivz]) covone *m*; (*of paper*) fascio
shear [ʃɪr] *s* lama di cesoia; tagliatura; **shears** cesoie *fpl* || *v* (*pret* **sheared**; *pp* **sheared** or **shorn** [ʃorn]) *tr* (*sheep*) tosare; (*cloth*) tagliare; **to shear s.o. of** privare qlcu di
sheath [ʃiθ] *s* (**sheaths** [ʃiðz]) guaina, coperta; (*of a sword*) fodero
sheathe [ʃið] *tr* rinfoderare, inguainare
shed [ʃɛd] *s* portico, tettoia; (geog) spartiacque *m*, versante *m* || *v* (*pret & pp* **shed**; *ger* **shedding**) *tr* (*e.g., blood*) spargere, versare; (*light*) dare, fare; (*feathers*) spogliarsi di, lasciar cadere
sheen [ʃin] *s* lucentezza
sheep [ʃip] *s* (**sheep**) pecora; **sheep's eyes** occhio di triglia; **to separate the sheep from the goats** separare i buoni dai cattivi
sheep'dog' *s* cane *m* da pastore
sheepish ['ʃipɪʃ] *adj* timido, goffo; pecoresco, pedissequo
sheep'skin' *s* pelle *f* di pecora; (*parchment*) cartapecora; (bb) bazzana; (coll) diploma *m*
sheer [ʃɪr] *adj* trasparente, fino, velato; puro; (*cliff*) stagliato || *adv* completamente || *intr* deviare
sheet [ʃit] *s* (*for bed*) lenzuolo; (*of paper*) foglio; (*of metal*) lamina; (*of water*) specchio; (naut) scotta
sheet' light'ning *s* lampeggio all'orizzonte
sheet' met'al *s* lamiera
sheet' mu'sic *s* spartito non rilegato
sheik [ʃik] *s* sceicco; (*great lover*) (slang) rubacuori *m*
shelf [ʃɛlf] *s* (**shelves** [ʃɛlvz]) scaffale *m*, scansia; (*ledge*) terrazzo, ripiano; banco di sabbia; **on the shelf** in disparte, dimenticato
shell [ʃɛl] *s* (*of egg or crustacean*) guscio; (*of mollusk*) conchiglia; (*of vegetable*) baccello; proietto, proiettile *m*; (*cartridge*) cartuccia; (*of a cartridge*) bossolo; (*framework*) armatura; (*of boiler*) involucro; imbarcazione da regata, schifo, iole *f* || *tr* (*vegetables*) sgranare; bombardare, cannoneggiare; **to shell out** (slang) tirar fuori
shel•lac [ʃə'læk] *s* gomma lacca || *v* (*pret & pp* **-lacked**; *ger* **-lacking**) *tr* verniciare con gomma lacca; (slang) dare una batosta a
shell'fish' *ssg* (**-fish**) frutto di mare; crostaceo; *spl* frutti *mpl* di mare; crostacei *mpl*
shell' hole' *s* cratere *m*
shell' shock' *s* psicosi traumatica bellica
shelter ['ʃɛltər] *s* rifugio, ricovero; **to take shelter** rifugiarsi || *tr* raccogliere, ospitare, dare rifugio a
shelve [ʃɛlv] *tr* mettere sullo scaffale; (*a bill*) insabbiare; mettere a riposo
shepherd ['ʃɛpərd] *s* pastore *m* || *tr* guardare, curarsi di
shep'herd dog' *s* cane *m* da pastore
shepherdess ['ʃɛpərdɪs] *s* pastora
sherbet ['ʃʌrbət] *s* sorbetto
sheriff ['ʃɛrɪf] *s* sceriffo
sher•ry ['ʃɛri] *s* (**-ries**) xeres *m*
shield [ʃild] *s* scudo; (*for armpit*) sottoascella *m*; (*badge*) scudetto; (elec) schermo || *tr* proteggere; (elec) schermare
shift [ʃɪft] *s* cambio, cambiamento;

(*period of work*) turno; (*group of workmen*) operai *mpl* di turno, squadra di lavoro; espediente *m*, sotterfugio || *tr* cambiare; spostare; (*blame*) riversare; || *intr* cambiare; spostarsi; fare da sé; vivere di espedienti; (rr) manovrare; (aut) cambiare marcia
shift' key' *s* tasto maiuscole
shiftless ['ʃɪftlɪs] *adj* pigro, ozioso
shift·y ['ʃɪfti] *adj* (**-ier; -iest**) astuto; evasivo; pieno d'espedienti; (*glance*) sfuggente
shilling ['ʃɪlɪŋ] *s* scellino
shimmer ['ʃɪmər] *s* luccichio || *intr* luccicare, mandare bagliori
shim·my ['ʃɪmi] *s* (**-mies**) (*dance*) shimmy *m;* (aut) farfallamento delle ruote, shimmy *m* || *intr* ballare lo shimmy; vibrare
shin [ʃɪn] *s* stinco; (*of cattle*) cannone *m* || *v* (*pret & pp* **shinned;** *ger* **shinning**) *tr* arrampicarsi su || *intr* arrampicarsi
shin'bone' *s* stinco, tibia
shine [ʃaɪn] *s* splendore *m;* luce *f;* bel tempo; lucidatura, lucido; **to take a shine to** (coll) prender simpatia per || *v* (*pret & pp* **shined**) *tr* pulire, lucidare || *v* (*pret & pp* **shone** [ʃon]) *tr* (*e.g., a flashlight*) dirigere i raggi di || *intr* brillare, luccicare, risplendere; (*to excel*) essere brillante, eccellere
shiner ['ʃaɪnər] *s* (slang) occhio pesto
shingle ['ʃɪŋgəl] *s* assicella di copertura; (*to cover a wall*) mattoncino di rivestimento; (Brit) greto ciottoloso; (coll) capelli *mpl* alla bebé; **shingles** (pathol) erpete *m*, zona; **to hang out one's shingle** (coll) aprire un ufficio professionale || *tr* coprire di assicelle or mattoncini; (*hair*) tagliare alla bebé
shining ['ʃaɪnɪŋ] *adj* brillante, lucente
shin·y ['ʃaɪni] *adj* (**-ier; -iest**) lucente, lucido; (*paper*) patinato
ship [ʃɪp] *s* nave *f*, bastimento; aeronave *f;* aeroplano; (*crew*) equipaggio || *v* (*pret & pp* **shipped;** *ger* **shipping**) *tr* imbarcare; mandare, spedire; (*oars*) disarmare; (*water*) imbarcare || *intr* imbarcarsi
ship'board' *s*—**on shipboard** a bordo
ship'build'er *s* costruttore *m* navale
ship'build'ing *s* architettura navale
ship'mate' *s* compagno di bordo
shipment ['ʃɪpmənt] *s* invio, spedizione
ship'own'er *s* armatore *m*
shipper ['ʃɪpər] *s* speditore *m*, spedizioniere *m*, mittente *m*
shipping ['ʃɪpɪŋ] *s* imbarco; spedizione; (naut) trasporto marittimo
ship'ping clerk' *s* speditore *m*
ship'ping room' *s* ufficio impaccatura
ship'shape' *adj & adv* in perfette condizioni
ship'side' *s* molo
ship's' pa'pers *spl* documenti *mpl* di bordo
ship'wreck' *s* naufragio; (*remains*) relitto || *tr* far naufragare || *intr* naufragare
ship'yard' *s* cantiere *m* navale
shirk [ʃʌrk] *tr* (*work*) evitare; (*responsibility*) sottrarsi a || *intr* imboscarsi
shirt [ʃʌrt] *s* camicia; **to keep one's shirt on** (slang) non perdere la calma; **to lose one's shirt** (slang) perdere la camicia
shirt' front' *s* sparato
shirt' sleeve' *s* manica di camicia
shirt'tail' *s* falda della camicia
shirt'waist' *s* blusa da donna
shiver ['ʃɪvər] *s* brivido || *intr* rabbrividire, battere i denti
shoal [ʃol] *s* secca, banco di sabbia
shock [ʃɑk] *s* urto, collisione; scossa; scossa elettrica; (pathol) shock *m* || *tr* scuotere; (*to strike against*) urtare; scandalizzare, indignare; dare la scossa elettrica a; (fig) scioccare
shock' absorb'er [æb'sɔrbər] *s* ammortizzatore *m* di colpi
shocking ['ʃɑkɪŋ] *adj* disgustoso, scandalizzante
shock' ther'apy *s* terapia d'urto
shock' troops' *spl* truppe *fpl* d'assalto
shod·dy ['ʃɑdi] *adj* (**-dier; -diest**) scadente, falso
shoe [ʃu] *s* scarpa; (*horseshoe*) ferro da cavallo; (*of a tire*) copertone *m;* (*of brake*) ganascia, ceppo || *v* (*pret & pp* **shod** [ʃɑd]) *tr* calzare; (*a horse*) ferrare
shoe'black' *s* lustrascarpe *m*
shoe'horn' *s* corno da scarpe, calzatoio
shoe'lace' *s* laccio delle scarpe
shoe'mak'er *s* calzolaio
shoe' pol'ish *s* crema or cera da scarpe
shoe'shine' *s* lucidatura, lustramento di scarpe
shoe' store' *s* calzoleria
shoe'string' *s* laccio delle scarpe; **on a shoestring** con quattro soldi
shoe'tree' *s* tendiscarpe *m*
shoo [ʃu] *tr* fare sció a || *intr* fare sció
shoot [ʃut] *s* (*e.g., with a firearm*) tiro; gara di tiro; (*chute*) scivolo; (rok) lancio; (bot) getto, virgulto || *v* (*pret & pp* **shot** [ʃɑt]) *tr* (*any missile*) tirare; (*a bullet*) sparare; (*to execute with a bullet*) fucilare; (*to fling*) lanciare; (*the sun*) prendere l'altezza di; (*dice*) gettare; (mov, telv) girare, riprendere; **to shoot down** (*a plane*) abbattere; **to shoot up** (coll) terrorizzare sparando a casaccio || *intr* tirare, sparare; passare rapidamente; nascere; (*said of pain*) dare fitte; (mov) cinematografare; **to shoot at** tirare a; (coll) cercare di ottenere
shoot'ing gal'lery *s* tiro a segno
shoot'ing match' *s* gara di tiro a segno; (slang) tutto, ogni cosa
shoot'ing star' *s* stella cadente
shop [ʃɑp] *s* (*store*) negozio, rivendita; (*workshop*) officina; **to talk shop** parlare del proprio lavoro || *v* (*pret & pp* **shopped;** *ger* **shopping**) *intr* fare la spesa; **to go shopping** andare a fare la spesa; **to shop around** cercare un'occasione di negozio in negozio
shop'girl' *s* venditrice *f*

shop'keep'er *s* negoziante *mf*
shoplifter ['ʃɑp ˌlɪftər] *s* taccheggiatore *m*
shopper ['ʃɑpər] *s* compratore *m*
shopping ['ʃɑpɪŋ] *s* compra; (*purchases*) compre *fpl,* shopping *m*
shop'ping bag' *s* sporta, shopping *m*
shop'ping cen'ter *s* centro d'acquisto, ipermercato
shop'ping dis'trict *s* zona commerciale
shop'win'dow *s* vetrina
shop'worn' *adj* sciupato, usato
shore [ʃor] *s* costa, riva; spiaggia, lido; (fig) regione; (*support*) sostegno, puntello || *tr* puntellare
shore' din'ner *s* pranzo di pesce
shore' leave' *s* (naut) franchigia
shore'line' *s* frangia costiera
shore' patrol' *s* polizia della marina
short [ʃɔrt] *adj* (*in stature*) piccolo, basso; (*in space, time*) breve; (*scanty*) scarso; succinto; (*in quantity*) poco, piccolo; (*rude*) brusco; **in a short time** in breve; **in short** per farla breve; **on short notice** senza preavviso; **short of breath** corto di fiato; **to be short of** scarseggiare di || *s* (elec) cortocircuito; (mov) cortometraggio; **shorts** (*underwear*) mutande *fpl;* (*sports attire*) calzoncini *mpl,* shorts *mpl* || *adv* brevemente; bruscamente; (com) allo scoperto, e.g., **to sell short** vendere allo scoperto; **to run short of** essere a corto di; **to stop short** fermarsi di colpo || *tr* (elec) causare un cortocircuito in || *intr* (elec) andare in cortocircuito
shortage ['ʃɔrtɪdʒ] *s* mancanza; (*of food*) carestia; (*from pilfering*) ammanco
short'cake' *s* torta di pasta frolla; torta ricoperta di frutta fresca
short'-change' *tr* non dare il cambio giusto a; (coll) imbrogliare
short' cir'cuit *s* (elec) cortocircuito
short'-cir'cuit *tr* mandare in cortocircuito; (coll) rovinare || *intr* andare in cortocircuito
short'com'ing *s* difetto, manchevolezza
short'cut' *s* scorciatoia
shorten ['ʃɔrtən] *tr* raccorciare, abbreviare || *intr* raccorciarsi, abbreviarsi
shortening ['ʃɔrtənɪŋ] *s* raccorciamento; (culin) grasso, strutto
short'hand' *adj* stenografico || *s* stenografia; **to take shorthand** stenografare
short'hand' typ'ist *s* stenodattilografo
short-lived ['ʃɔrt'laɪvd] or ['ʃɔrt'lɪvd] *adj* effimero, di breve vita
shortly ['ʃɔrtli] *adv* in breve, brevemente; fra poco; bruscamente; **shortly after** poco dopo
short'-range' *adj* di corta portata
short' sale' *s* vendita allo scoperto
short-sighted ['ʃɔrt'saɪtɪd] *adj* miope; (fig) miope
short'stop' *s* (baseball) interbase *m*
short' sto'ry *s* novella
short-tempered ['ʃɔrt'tɛmpərd] *adj* irascibile
short'-term' *adj* a breve scadenza
short'wave' *adj* alle onde corte || *s* onda corta
short' weight' *s*—**to give short weight** rubare sul peso
shot [ʃɑt] *s* tiro, sparo; (*cartridge*) cartuccia; (*for cannon*) palla; (*pellets of lead*) pallini *mpl;* (*person*) tiratore *m;* (*hypodermic injection*) iniezione; (*of liquor*) bicchierino; (phot) istantanea; (sports) peso; (mov) inquadratura; **not by a long shot** nemmeno a pensarci; **to start like a shot** partire come una palla da cannone; **to take a shot at** tirare un colpo a; (*to attempt to*) provarsi a
shot'gun' *s* schioppo, fucile *m* da caccia
shot' put' *s* lancio del peso
should [ʃʊd] *v aux* si usa nelle seguenti situazioni: 1) per formare il condizionale presente, per es., **if I should wait for him, I should miss the train** se lo aspettassi, perderei il treno; 2) per formare il perfetto del condizionale, per es., **if I had waited for him, I should have missed the train** se lo avessi aspettato, avrei perso il treno; 3) per indicare la necessità di un'azione, per es., **he should go at once** dovrebbe andare immediatamente; **he should have gone immediately** sarebbe dovuto andare immediatamente
shoulder ['ʃoldər] *s* spalla; (*of highway*) banchina; **across the shoulder** a bandoliera; **to put one's shoulders to the wheel** mettersi a lavorare di buzzo buono; **to turn a cold shoulder to** volgere le spalle a || *tr* portare sulle spalle; (*a responsibility*) addossarsi; spingere con le spalle
shoul'der blade' *s* scapola
shoul'der strap' s spallina; (mil) tracolla
shout [ʃaʊt] *s* urlo, grido || *tr* urlare, gridare; **to shout down** far tacere a forza di strilli || *intr* gridare
shove [ʃʌv] *s* spintone *m* || *tr* spingere || *intr* spingere, dare spintoni; **to shove off** allontanarsi dalla riva; (slang) andarsene
shov·el ['ʃʌvəl] *s* pala || *v* (*pret & pp* **-eled** or **-elled;** *ger* **-eling** or **-elling**) *tr* spalare || *intr* lavorare di pala
show [ʃo] *s* mostra; apparenza; traccia; ostentazione; (mov, telv, theat) spettacolo; **to make a show of** dar spettacolo di; **to steal the show from** ricevere tutti gli applausi invece di || *tr* mostrare, esporre; (*a movie*) presentare; dimostrare, insegnare; provare; (*to register*) segnare; (*one's feelings*) manifestare; (*to the door*) accompagnare; **to show in** fare entrare; **to show off** mettere in mostra || *intr* mostrarsi; presentarsi, apparire; (*said of a horse*) (sports) arrivare terzo, piazzarsi; **to show off** mettersi in mostra; **to show up** (coll) mostrarsi; (coll) farsi vedere
show' bill' *s* cartellone *m*
show'boat' *s* battello per spettacoli teatrali

show' busi'ness *s* industria dello spettacolo
show'case' *s* bacheca, vetrina
show'down' *s* carte scoperte; chiarificazione
shower ['ʃaʊ·ər] *s* (*of rain*) acquazzone *m;* (*shower bath*) doccia; (*e.g., for a bride*) ricevimento cui i partecipanti devono portare un regalo; (fig) pioggia || *tr* inaffiare; **to shower with** colmare di || *intr* diluviare; fare la doccia
show'er bath' *s* doccia
show' girl' *s* ballerina, girl *f*
show'man *s* (**-men**) impresario teatrale; persona che ha molta scena
show'-off' *s* reclamista *m,* strombazzatore *m*
show'piece' *s* capolavoro, oggetto d'arte
show'place' *s* luogo celebre; **to be a showplace** (*said, e.g., of a house*) essere arredato perfettamente
show'room' *s* sala di mostra
show' win'dow *s* vetrina
show·y ['ʃo·i] *adj* (**-ier; -iest**) vistoso, sgargiante
shrapnel ['ʃræpnəl] *s* shrapnel *m*
shred [ʃrɛd] *s* brano, brandello; ritaglio; (fig) granello; **to cut to shreds** fare a brandelli || *v* (*pret & pp* **shredded** or **shred; *ger* shredding**) *tr* fare a brandelli; (*paper*) tagliuzzare
shrew [ʃru] *s* (*woman*) bisbetica; (*animal*) toporagno
shrewd [ʃrud] *adj* astuto, scaltro
shriek [ʃrik] *s* strido; strillo; risata stridula || *intr* stridere; strillare
shrill [ʃrɪl] *adj* stridulo, squillante
shrimp [ʃrɪmp] *s* gamberetto; (*person*) omiciattolo, nanerottolo
shrine [ʃraɪn] *s* santuario, sacrario
shrink [ʃrɪŋk] *v* (*pret* **shrank** [ʃræŋk] or **shrunk** [ʃrʌŋk]; *pp* **shrunk** or **shrunken**) *tr* contrarre, restringere || *intr* contrarsi, restringersi; ritirarsi
shrinkage ['ʃrɪŋkɪdʒ] *s* restringimento; (*in weight*) calo
shriv·el ['ʃrɪvəl] *v* (*pret & pp* **-eled** or **-elled;** *ger* **-eling** or **-elling**) *tr* raggrinzire; (*from heat*) raccartocciare; (*to wither*) avvizzire || *intr* raggrinzirsi; accartocciarsi; avvizzire; **to shrivel up** incartapecorire
shroud [ʃraʊd] *s* sudario, lenzuolo funebre; (fig) cappa || *tr* avvolgere
Shrove' Tues'day [ʃrov] *s* martedì grasso
shrub [ʃrʌb] *s* arbusto
shrubber·y ['ʃrʌbəri] *s* (**-ies**) arbusti *mpl,* cespugli *mpl*
shrug [ʃrʌg] *s* scrollata di spalle || *v* (*pret & pp* **shrugged;** *ger* **shrugging**) *tr* scrollare; **to shrug one's shoulders** scrollare le spalle || *intr* fare spallucce
shudder ['ʃʌdər] *s* brivido, fremito || *intr* rabbrividire, fremere
shuffle ['ʃʌfəl] *s* (*of cards*) mescolata; turno di fare il mazzo; (*of feet*) strascichio; evasione || *tr* mescolare; strisciare, strascicare || *intr* fare il mazzo; scalpicciare; ballare di striscio; **to shuffle off** strascicarsi, scalpicciare; **to shuffle out of** evadere da
shun [ʃʌn] *v* (*pret & pp* **shunned;** *ger* **shunning**) *tr* evitare, schivare
shunt [ʃʌnt] *tr* sviare; (elec) shuntare; (rr) deviare
shut [ʃʌt] *adj* chiuso || *v* (*pret & pp* **shut;** *ger* **shutting**) *tr* chiudere, serrare; **to shut in** rinchiudere; **to shut off** (*e.g., gas*) tagliare; **to shut up** tappare; imprigionare; (coll) fare star zitto || *intr* chiudersi; **to shut up** (coll) stare zitto, tacere
shut'down' *s* chiusura
shutter ['ʃʌtər] *s* (*outside a window*) persiana, gelosia; (*outside a store window*) serranda, saracinesca; (phot) otturatore *m*
shuttle ['ʃʌtəl] *s* spola, navetta || *intr* fare la spola
shut'tle·cock' *s* volano, volante *m*
shut'tle train' *s* treno che fa la spola fra due stazioni
shy [ʃaɪ] *adj* (**shyer** or **shier; shyest** or **shiest**) timido; (*fearful*) schivo, ritroso; corto, a corto, e.g., **he is shy of funds** è a corto di denaro || *v* (*pret & pp* **shied**) *intr* ritirarsi; schivarsi; (*said of a horse*) adombrarsi; **to shy away** tenersi discosto
shyster ['ʃaɪstər] *s* (coll) azzeccagarbugli *m*
Sia·mese [ˌsaɪ·ə'miz] *adj* siamese || *s* (**-mese**) siamese *mf*
Si'amese twins' *spl* fratelli *mpl* siamesi
Siberian [saɪ'bɪrɪ·ən] *adj & s* siberiano
sibilant ['sɪbɪlənt] *adj & s* sibilante *f*
sibyl ['sɪbɪl] *s* sibilla
sic [sik] *adv* sic || [sɪk] *v* (*pret & pp* **sicked;** *ger* **sicking**) *tr* aizzare; **sick 'em!** va!; **to sick on** aizzare contro
Sicilian [sɪ'sɪljən] *adj & s* siciliano
Sicily ['sɪsɪli] *s* la Sicilia
sick [sɪk] *adj* ammalato; nauseato; (*bored*) stucco; **sick at heart** con una spina nel cuore; **to be sick and tired** averne sin sopra i capelli; **to be sick at one's stomach** avere la nausea; **to take sick** cader malato || *tr* (*a dog*) aizzare
sick'bed' *s* letto d'ammalato
sicken ['sɪkən] *tr* ammalare; disgustare || *intr* ammalarsi
sickening ['sɪkənɪŋ] *adj* stomachevole
sick' head'ache *s* emicrania accompagnata da nausea
sickle ['sɪkəl] *s* falce messoria, falcetto
sick' leave' *s* congedo per motivi di salute
sick·ly ['sɪkli] *adj* (**-lier; -liest**) cagionevole, malaticcio
sickness ['sɪknɪs] *s* malattia; nausea
side [saɪd] *adj* laterale || *s* parte *f,* lato; (*e.g., of a coin*) faccia; (*slope*) versante *m;* (*of human body, of a ship*) fianco; **to take sides** parteggiare || *intr* parteggiare; **to side with** schierarsi dalla parte di
side'board' *s* credenza
side'burns' *spl* basette *fpl,* favoriti *mpl*

side'car' *s* motocarrozzetta; carrozzino laterale (di motocarrozzetta)
side' dish' *s* portata extra
side' door' *s* porta laterale
side' effect' *s* effetto secondario
side'-glance' *s* occhiata di sbieco
side' is'sue *s* questione secondaria
side'line' *s* linea laterale; impiego secondario; attività secondaria
sidereal [saɪ'dɪrɪ·əl] *adj* siderale
side'sad'dle *adv* all'amazzone
side' show' *s* spettacolo secondario di baraccone; affare secondario
side'slip' *intr* (aer) scivolare d'ala
side'split'ting *adj* che fa sbellicare dalle risa
side' step' *s* passo laterale; scartata
side'-step' *v* (*pret & pp* **-stepped;** *ger* **-stepping**) *tr* evitare || *intr* farsi da parte; fare una scartata
side'track' *s* binario morto di smistamento || *tr* sviare; (rr) smistare
side' view' *s* vista di profilo
side'walk' *s* marciapiede *m*
side'walk café' *s* caffè *m* con tavolini all'aperto
sideward ['saɪdwərd] *adj* obliquo, a sghembo || *adv* verso un lato; di sghembo
side'ways' *adj* sghembo || *adv* di sghembo; di fianco
side' whisk'ers *spl* favoriti *mpl*
siding ['saɪdɪŋ] *s* (rr) diramazione, binario morto, raccordo ferroviario
sidle ['saɪdəl] *intr* andare al lato; muoversi furtivamente
siege [sidʒ] *s* assedio; (*of illness*) ricorrenza d'attacchi; **to lay siege to** cingere d'assedio, assediare
siesta [si'ɛstə] *s* siesta; **to take a siesta** fare la siesta
sieve [sɪv] *s* vaglio, setaccio || *tr* vagliare, setacciare
sift [sɪft] *tr* (*flour*) abburattare; setacciare; (*to scatter with a sieve*) spolverare; (fig) vagliare
sigh [saɪ] *s* sospiro || *tr* mormorare sospirando || *intr* sospirare; **to sigh for** sospirare
sight [saɪt] *s* vista, visione; spettacolo, veduta; (opt) mira, traguardo; (mil) mirino, tacca di mira; (coll) mucchio; **a sight of** (coll) molto; **at first sight** a prima vista; **at sight** ad apertura di libro; (com) a vista; **out of sight** fuori di vista; lontano dagli occhi; (*prices*) astronomico; **sights** luoghi *mpl* interessanti; **sight unseen** senza averlo visto prima, a occhi chiusi; **to be a sight** (coll) essere un orrore; **to catch sight of** arrivare a intravedere; **to know by sight** conoscere di vista; **to not be able to stand the sight of s.o.** not poter vedere qlcu nemmeno dipinto || *tr* avvistare; (*a weapon*) mirare || *intr* mirare, prendere di mira; osservare attentamente
sight' draft' *s* (com) tratta a vista
sight'-read' *v* (*pret & pp* **-read** [,rɛd]) *tr & intr* leggere a libro aperto
sight'see'ing *adj* turistico || *s* turismo, visite *fpl* turistiche
sightseer ['saɪt,si·ər] *s* turista *mf*

sign [saɪn] *s* segno; segnale *m;* (*e.g., on a store*) insegna, cartello; **signs** tracce *fpl* || *tr* firmare; ingaggiare; indicare, segnalare || *intr* firmare; fare segno; **to sign off** (rad, telv) terminare la trasmissione; **to sign up** iscriversi
sig·nal ['sɪgnəl] *adj* insigne, segnalato || *s* segnale *m* || *v* (*pret & pp* **-naled** or **-nalled;** *ger* **-naling** or **-nalling**) *tr* segnalare || *intr* fare segnalazioni
sig'nal corps' *s* (mil) armi *fpl* di trasmissione
sig'nal tow'er *s* (rr) posto di blocco
signato·ry ['sɪgnɪ,tori] *s* (**-ries**) firmatario
signature ['sɪgnətʃər] *s* firma; segno musicale; (typ) segnatura
sign'board' *s* cartellone *m*
signer ['saɪnər] *s* firmatario
sig'net ring' ['sɪgnɪt] *s* anello col sigillo
significance [sɪg'nɪfɪkəns] *s* importanza; (*meaning*) significato
significant [sɪg'nɪfɪkənt] *adj* importante
signi·fy ['sɪgnɪ,faɪ] *v* (*pret & pp* **-fied**) *tr* significare
sign'post' *s* palo indicatore
silence ['saɪləns] *s* silenzio || *tr* far tacere; (mil) ridurre al silenzio
silent ['saɪlənt] *adj* silenzioso, tacito
si'lent mov'ie *s* cinema muto
silhouette [,sɪlu'ɛt] *s* silhouette *f*, siluetta
silicon ['sɪlɪkən] *s* silicio
silicone ['sɪlɪ,kon] *s* silicone *m*
silk [sɪlk] *adj* di seta || *s* seta; **to hit the silk** (slang) gettarsi col paracadute
silken ['sɪlkən] *adj* serico, di seta
silk' hat' *s* cappello a cilindro
silk'screen proc'ess *s* serigrafia
silk'-stock'ing *adj & s* aristocratico
silk'worm' *s* baco da seta, filugello
silk·y ['sɪlki] *adj* (**-ier; -iest**) di seta; come la seta
sill [sɪl] *s* basamento; (*of a door*) soglia; (*of a window*) davanzale *m*
sil·ly ['sɪli] *adj* (**-lier; -liest**) sciocco, scemo
si·lo ['saɪlo] *s* (**-los**) silo || *tr* insilare
silt [sɪlt] *s* sedimento
silver ['sɪlvər] *adj* d'argento; (*voice*) argentino; (*plated with silver*) argentato || *s* argento || *tr* inargentare
sil'ver·fish' *s* (ent) lepisma
sil'ver foil' *s* foglia d'argento
sil'ver fox' *s* volpe argentata
sil'ver lin'ing *s* spiraglio di speranza
sil'ver plate' *s* vasellame *m* d'argento; argentatura
sil'ver screen' *s* (mov) schermo
sil'ver·smith' *s* argentiere *m*
sil'ver spoon' *s* ricchezza ereditata; **to be born with a silver spoon in one's mouth** esser nato con la camicia
sil'ver·ware' *s* argenteria
sil'ver·ware' chest' *s* portaposate *m*
similar ['sɪmɪlər] *adj* simile
similari·ty [,sɪmɪ'lærɪti] *s* (**-ties**) similarità *f*, somiglianza
simile ['sɪmɪli] *s* similitudine *f*

simmer ['sɪmər] *tr* cuocere a fuoco lento || *intr* cuocere a fuoco lento; (fig) ribollire; **to simmer down** (slang) calmarsi
simper ['sɪmpər] *s* sorriso scemo || *intr* fare un sorriso scemo
simple ['sɪmpəl] *adj* semplice
simple-minded ['sɪmpəl'maɪndɪd] *adj* semplicione, scemo
simpleton ['sɪmpəltən] *s* semplicione *m*
simulate ['sɪmjə,let] *tr* simulare
simultaneous [,saɪməl'tenɪ·əs] or [,sɪməl'tenɪ·əs] *adj* simultaneo
sin [sɪn] *s* peccato || *v* (*pret & pp* **sinned; ***ger* **sinning**) *intr* peccare
since [sɪns] *adv* da allora, da allora in poi; da tempo fa || *prep* da || *conj* dacché; poiché, dato che
sincere [sɪn'sɪr] *adj* sincero
sincerity [sɪn'serɪti] *s* sincerità *f*
sine [saɪn] *s* (math) seno
sinecure ['saɪnɪ,kjur] or ['sɪnɪ,kjur] *s* sinecura
sinew ['sɪnju] *s* tendine *m;* (fig) nerbo
sinful ['sɪnfəl] *adj* (*person*) peccatore; (*act, intention, etc.*) peccaminoso
sing [sɪŋ] *v* (*pret* **sang** [sæŋ] or **sung** [sʌŋ]; *pp* **sung**) *tr* cantare; **to sing to sleep** ninnare || *intr* cantare; (*said, e.g., of the ears*) fischiare
singe [sɪndʒ] *v* (*ger* **singeing**) *tr* strinare, bruciacchiare
singer ['sɪŋər] *s* cantante *mf;* (*in night club*) canzonettista *mf*
single [sɪŋgəl] *adj* unico, solo; (*room*) a un letto; (*bed*) a una piazza; (*man*) celibe; (*woman*) nubile; (*combat*) corpo a corpo; semplice, sincero || **singles** *ssg* singolare *m* || *tr* scegliere; **to single out** individuare
single-breasted ['sɪŋgəl'brestɪd] *adj* a un petto, monopetto
sin'gle entry' *s* partita semplice
sin'gle file' *s* fila indiana
single-handed ['sɪŋgəl'hændɪd] *adj* da solo, senza aiuto altrui
sin'gle-phase' *adj* (elec) monofase
sin'gle room' *s* camera a un letto
sin'gle-track' *adj* (rr) a binario semplice; (fig) di corte vedute
sing'song' *adj* monotono || *s* cantilena
singular ['sɪŋgjələr] *adj & s* singolare *m*
sinister ['sɪnɪstər] *adj* sinistro
sink [sɪŋk] *s* acquaio; (*sewer*) scolo, fogna; (fig) sentina || *v* (*pret* **sank** [sæŋk] or **sunk** [sʌŋk]; *pp* **sunk**) *tr* sprofondare; infiggere; (*a well*) scavare; (*in tone*) abbassare; (*a boat*) mandare a picco; rovinare; investire; pérdere || *intr* sprofondarsi; abbassarsi; (*said, of the sun, prices, etc.*) calare; andare a picco; lasciarsi cadere; (*in vice*) impantanarsi; (*said of one's cheeks*) infossarsi; (*in thought*) perdersi; **to sink down** sedersi; **to sink in** penetrare
sink'ing fund' *s* fondo d'ammortamento
sinner ['sɪnər] *s* peccatore *m*
Sinology [si'nɑlədʒi] *s* sinologia
sinuous ['sɪnjʊ·əs] *adj* sinuoso
sinus ['saɪnəs] *s* seno
sip [sɪp] *s* sorso || *v* (*pret & pp* **sipped;** *ger* **sipping**) *tr* sorbire, sorseggiare
siphon ['saɪfən] *s* sifone *m* || *tr* travasare con un sifone
si'phon bot'tle *s* sifone *m*
sir [sʌr] *s* signore *m;* (Brit) sir *m;* **Dear Sir** Illustrissimo signore; (com) Egregio signore
sire [saɪr] *s* (*king*) sire *m;* padre *m,* stallone *m* || *tr* generare
siren ['saɪrən] *s* sirena
sirloin ['sʌrlɔɪn] *s* lombata, lombo
sirup ['sɪrəp] or ['sʌrəp] *tr* sciroppo
sis·sy ['sɪsi] *s* (**-sies**) effemminato
sister ['sɪstər] *adj* (*ship*) gemello; (*language*) sorella; (*corporation*) consorella || *s* sorella; (*nun*) suora, monaca
sis'ter-in-law' *s* (**sis'ters-in-law'**) cognata
Sis'tine Chap'el ['sɪstin] *s* Cappella Sistina
sit [sɪt] *v* (*pret & pp* **sat** [sæt]; *ger* **sitting**) *intr* sedere; posare; (*said of a hen*) covare; (*said of a jacket*) stare; essere in sessione; **to sit down** sedersi; **to sit in on** partecipare a; assistere a; **to sit still** stare tranquillo; **to sit up** alzarsi; (coll) essere sorpreso
sit'-down strike' *s* sciopero bianco
site [saɪt] *s* sito, luogo, posizione
sitting ['sɪtɪŋ] *s* seduta; (*of a court*) sessione; (*of a hen*) covata; (*serving of a meal*) turno
sit'ting duck' *s* (slang) facile bersaglio
sit'ting room' *s* soggiorno
situate ['sɪtʃʊ,et] *tr* situare
situation [,sɪtʃʊ'eʃən] *s* situazione, posizione; posto
sitz' bath' [sɪts] *s* semicupio
six [sɪks] *adj & pron* sei || *s* sei *m;* **at sixes and sevens** in disordine; **six o'clock** le sei
six' hun'dred *adj, s & pron* seicento
sixteen ['sɪks'tin] *adj, s & pron* sedici *m*
sixteenth ['sɪks'tinθ] *adj, s & pron* sedicesimo || *s* (*in dates*) sedici *m*
sixth [sɪksθ] *adj, s & pron* sesto || *s* (*in dates*) sei *m*
sixtieth ['sɪkstɪ·ɪθ] *adj, s & pron* sessantesimo
six·ty ['sɪksti] *adj & pron* sessanta || *s* (**-ies**) sessanta *m;* **the sixties** gli anni sessanta
sizable ['saɪzəbəl] *adj* considerevole
size [saɪz] *s* grandezza; quantità *f;* (*of person or garment*) taglia; (*of shoes*) numero; (*of hat*) giro; (*of a pipe*) diametro; (*for gilding*) colla; (fig) situazione || *tr* misurare, classificare secondo grandezza; incollare; **to size up** (coll) stimare, giudicare
sizzle ['sɪzəl] *s* sfrigolio || *intr* sfriggere
skate [sket] *s* pattino; (slang) tipo || *intr* pattinare; **to skate on thin ice** andare in cerca di disgrazie
skat'ing rink' *s* pattinatoio
skein [sken] *s* gomitolo, matassa
skeleton ['skelɪtən] *adj* scheletrico || *s* scheletro
skel'eton key' *s* chiave maestra
skeptic ['skeptɪk] *adj & s* scettico

skeptical ['skeptɪkəl] *adj* scettico
sketch [sketʃ] *s* schizzo, disegno; abbozzo, bozzetto; (theat) scenetta || *tr* schizzare, disegnare; abbozzare
sketch'book' *s* album *m* di schizzi; quaderno per abbozzi
skew [skju] *adj* obliquo || *s* movimento obliquo; (*chisel*) scalpello a taglio obliquo || *tr* tagliare di sghembo || *intr* (*to swerve*) deviare; (*to look obliquely*) guardare di sghembo
skew' chis'el *s* scalpello a taglio obliquo
skewer ['skju·ər] *s* spiedino || *tr* mettere allo spiedo
ski [ski] *s* (**skis** or **ski**) sci *m* || *intr* sciare
ski' boot' *s* scarpa da sci
skid [skɪd] *s* (*device to check a wheel*) scarpa; (*skidding forward*) slittamento; (*skidding sideway*) sbandamento; (aer, mach) pattino || *v* (*pret & pp* **skidded**; *ger* **skidding**) *tr* frenare || *intr* (*forward*) slittare; (*sideways*) sbandare
skid' row' [ro] *s* quartiere malfamato
skier ['ski·ər] *s* sciatore *m*
skiff [skɪf] *s* skiff *m*, singolo
skiing ['ski·ɪŋ] *s* sci *m*
ski' jump' *s* salto con gli sci; trampolino di salto
ski' lift' *s* sciovia
skill [skɪl] *s* destrezza, perizia
skilled [skɪld] *adj* abile, esperto
skilled' la'bor *s* manodopera qualificata
skillet ['skɪlɪt] *s* padella
skillful ['skɪlfəl] *adj* destro, abile
skim [skɪm] *v* (*pret & pp* **skimmed**; *ger* **skimming**) *tr* (*milk*) scremare; (*e.g., broth*) sgrassare; (*to graze*) sfiorare; (*the ground*) radere; (*a page*) trascorrere || *intr* sfiorare; **to skim over** scorrere
ski' mask' *s* passamontagna *m*
skimmer ['skɪmər] *s* schiumaiola; (*hat*) canottiera
skim' milk' *s* latte scremato or magro
skimp [skɪmp] *tr* lesinare || *intr* economizzare, risparmiare
skimp·y ['skɪmpi] *adj* (**-ier**; **-iest**) corto, scarso; taccagno
skin [skɪn] *s* pelle *f*; (*rind*) scorza; (*of onion*) spoglia; **by the skin of one's teeth** (coll) per il rotto della cuffia; **soaked to the skin** bagnato fino alle ossa; **to have a thin skin** offendersi facilmente || *v* (*pret & pp* **skinned**; *ger* **skinning**) *tr* pelare, spellare; (*e.g., one's knee*) spellarsi; (slang) tosare; **to skin alive** (slang) scotennare; (slang) battere in pieno
skin'-deep' *adj* a fior di pelle
skin'-div'er *s* nuotatore subacqueo, sub *m*; (mil) sommozzatore *m*
skin'flint' *s* avaro
skin' game' *s* truffa
skin·ny ['skɪni] *adj* (**-nier**; **-niest**) magro, scarno
skin' test' *s* cutireazione
skip [skɪp] *s* salto || *v* (*pret & pp* **skipped**; *ger* **skipping**) *tr* (*a fence; a meal*) saltare; (*a subject*) sorvolare; (*school*) (coll) marinare || *intr* saltare, salterellare; (*said of typewriter*) saltare uno spazio; (coll) svignarsela
ski' pole' *s* racchetta da sci
skipper ['skɪpər] *s* capitano, comandante *m*
skirmish ['skʌrmɪʃ] *s* scaramuccia || *intr* battersi in una scaramuccia
skirt [skʌrt] *s* sottana, gonna; (*edge*) orlo; (*woman*) (slang) gonnella || *tr* orlare; costeggiare; (*a subject*) evitare
ski' run' *s* pista da sci
skit [skɪt] *s* (theat) quadretto comico
skittish ['skɪtɪʃ] *adj* bizzarro, balzano; timido; (*horse*) ombroso
skulduggery [skʌl'dʌgəri] *s* trucco disonesto
skull [skʌl] *s* cranio, teschio
skull' and cross'bones *s* due tibie incrociate ed un teschio
skull'cap' *s* papalina
skunk [skʌŋk] *s* puzzola, moffetta; (coll) puzzone *m*
sky [skaɪ] *s* (**skies**) cielo; firmamento; **to praise to the skies** portare al cielo
sky'div'er *s* paracadutista *mf*
sky'jack'er *s* pirata *m* dell'aria
sky'lark' *s* allodola || *intr* (coll) darsi alla pazza gioia
sky'light' *s* lucernario
sky'line' *s* linea dell'orizzonte; (*of city*) profilo
sky'rock'et *s* razzo || *intr* salire come un razzo
sky'scrap'er *s* grattacielo
sky'writ'ing *s* scrittura pubblicitaria aerea
slab [slæb] *s* (*of stone*) lastra, lastrone *m*; (*of wood*) tavola; (*slice*) fetta
slack [slæk] *adj* lento, allentato; negligente, indolente; (fig) fiacco, morto || *s* lentezza; negligenza; stagione morta, inattività *f*; **slacks** pantaloni *mpl* da donna; pantaloni sciolti || *tr* allentare; trascurare; (*lime*) spegnere || *intr* rilasciarsi; essere negligente; **to slack up** rallentare
slacker ['slækər] *s* fannullone *m*; (mil) imboscato
slag [slæg] *s* scoria
slake [slek] *tr* spegnere
slalom ['slɑləm] *s* slalom *m*
slam [slæm] *s* colpo; (*of door*) sbatacchiamento; (*in cards*) cappotto; (coll) strapazzata || *v* (*pret & pp* **slammed**; *ger* **slamming**) *tr* sbattere, sbatacchiare; (coll) strapazzare || *intr* sbattere, sbatacchiare
slam'bang' *adv* (coll) con gran rumore, precipitosamente
slander ['slændər] *s* calunnia, maldicenza || *tr* calunniare, diffamare
slanderous ['slændərəs] *adj* calunnioso, diffamatorio
slang [slæŋ] *s* gergo
slant [slænt] *s* inclinazione; punto di vista || *tr* inclinare; (*news*) snaturare || *intr* inclinarsi; deviare

slap [slæp] *s* manata; (*in the face*) schiaffo, ceffone *m;* (*noise*) rumore *m;* insulto || *v* (*pret & pp* **slapped;** *ger* **slapping**) *tr* dare una manata a; schiaffeggiare
slap′dash′ *adj* raffazzonato, fatto a casaccio || *adv* a casaccio
slap′hap′py *adj* (*punch-drunk*) stordito; (*giddy*) allegro, brillo
slap′stick′ *adj* buffonesco || *s* bastone *m* d'Arlecchino; buffonata
slash [slæʃ] *s* sfregio; (*of prices*) riduzione || *tr* sfregiare; (*cloth*) tagliare; (*prices*) ridurre
slat [slæt] s travicello, regolo; (*for bed*) traversa; (*of shutter*) stecca
slate [slet] *s* ardesia, lavagna; lista elettorale; **clean slate** buon certificato || *tr* coprire con tegole d'ardesia; proporre la nomina di; (*to schedule*) mettere in cantiere
slate′ roof′ *s* tetto d'ardesia
slattern ['slætərn] *s* (*slovenly woman*) sciamannona; (*harlot*) puttana
slaughter ['slɔtər] *s* eccidio, carneficina || *tr* sgozzare, scannare
slaugh′ter·house′ *s* macello, scannatoio
Slav [slɑv] or [slæv] *adj & s* slavo
slave [slev] *adj & s* schiavo || *intr* lavorare come uno schiavo
slave′ driv′er *s* negriere *m*
slavery ['slevəri] *s* schiavitù *f*
slave′ trade′ *s* tratta degli schiavi
Slavic ['slɑvɪk] or ['slævɪk] *adj & s* slavo
slay [sle] *v* (*pret* **slew** [slu]; *pp* **slain** [slen]) *tr* scannare, uccidere
slayer ['sle·ər] *s* uccisore *m*
sled [slɛd] *s* slittino, slitta || *v* (*pret & pp* **sledded;** *ger* **sledding**) *intr* slittare
sledge′ ham′mer *s* [slɛdʒ] *s* mazza
sleek [slik] *adj* liscio, lustro; elegante || *tr* lisciare, ammorbidire
sleep [slip] *s* sonno; **to go to sleep** addormentarsi; **to put to sleep** addormentare; uccidere con un anestetico || *v* (*pret & pp* **slept** [slɛpt]) *tr* dormire; aver posto a dormire per; **to sleep it over** dormirci sopra; **to sleep off a hangover** smaltire una sbornia dormendo || *intr* dormire; **to sleep in** dormire fino a tardi; passare la notte a casa; **to sleep out** passare la notte fuori di casa
sleeper ['slipər] *s* (*person*) dormiente *mf;* (*beam, timber*) trave *f*
sleep′ing bag′ *s* sacco a pelo
sleep′ing car′ *s* vettura letto
sleep′ing pill′ *s* sonnifero
sleepless ['sliplɪs] *adj* insonne; (*night*) bianco
sleep′walk′er *s* sonnambulo
sleep·y ['slipi] *adj* (**-ier; -iest**) insonnolito, sonnolento; **to be sleepy** aver sonno
sleep′y-head′ *s* dormiglione *m*
sleet [slit] *s* nevischio || *impers* **it is sleeting** cade il nevischio
sleeve [sliv] *s* manica; (*of phonograph record*) busta; (mach) manicotto; **to laugh in** or **up one's sleeve** ridere sotto i baffi
sleigh [sle] *s* slitta || *intr* andare in slitta
sleigh′ bells′ *spl* bubboli *mpl* da slitta, sonagliera da slitta
sleigh′ ride′ *s* passeggiata in slitta
sleight′ of hand′ [slaɪt] *s* gioco di prestigio
slender ['slɛndər] *adj* smilzo, snello; esiguo, esile
sleuth [sluθ] *s* segugio
slew [slu] *s* (coll) mucchio
slice [slaɪs] *s* fetta; (*of an orange*) spicchio || *tr* tagliare a fette; (fig) fendere
slick [slɪk] *adj* liscio, lustro; scivoloso; astuto; (slang) ottimo || *s* posto scivoloso; (coll) rivista stampata su carta patinata || *tr* lisciare, lustrare; **to slick up** (coll) acconciare
slicker ['slɪkər] *s* impermeabile *m* di tela cerata; (coll) furbo di tre cotte
slide [slaɪd] *s* scivolata, scivolone *m;* (*chute*) scivolo; (*landslide*) frana; (*for projection*) diapositiva; (*of a microscope*) vetrino; (mach) guida; (*of a slide rule*) (mach) cursore *m* || *v* (*pret & pp* **slid** [slɪd]) *tr* far scivolare || *intr* sdrucciolare, scivolare; (*said of a car*) pattinare, slittare; **to let slide** lasciar correre
slide′ fas′tener *s* chiusura lampo
slide′ projec′tor *s* diascopio
slide′ rule′ *s* regolo calcolatore
slide′ valve′ *s* (mach) cassetto di distribuzione
slid′ing door′ *s* porta scorrevole
slid′ing scale′ *s* scala mobile
slight [slaɪt] *adj* leggero, lieve; delicato || *s* noncuranza, disattenzione; affronto || *tr* fare con negligenza; (*to snub*) trattare con noncuranza, snobbare
slim [slɪm] *adj* (**slimmer; slimmest**) sottile; magro
slime [slaɪm] *s* melma; (*e.g., of a snail*) bava
slim·y ['slaɪmi] *adj* (**-ier; -iest**) melmoso; bavoso; sudicio
sling [slɪŋ] *s* (*to shoot stones*) fionda; (naut) braca; **in a sling** (*arm*) al collo || *v* (*pret & pp* **slung** [slʌŋ]) *tr* gettare; lanciare; (*freight*) imbracare; sospendere; mettere a bandoliera
sling′shot′ *s* fionda
slink [slɪŋk] *v* (*pret & pp* **slunk** [slʌŋk]) *intr* andare furtivamente; **to slink away** eclissarsi
slip [slɪp] *s* scivolone *m;* svista, errore *m;* (*in prices*) discesa; (*underdress*) sottoveste *f;* (*pillowcase*) federa; (*of paper*) pezzo; (*space between two wharves*) darsena, imbarcatoio; (*form*) modulo; personcina; (*inclined plane*) (naut) scalo d'alaggio; (bot) innesto; **to give the slip to** eludere || *v* (*pret & pp* **slipped;** *ger* **slipping**) *tr* infilare; liberare; liberarsi da; omettere; **to slip off** togliersi; **to slip on** mettersi; **to slip one's mind** dimenticarsi di, e.g., **it slipped my mind** me ne sono dimenticato || *intr* scivolare,

scorrere; sdrucciolare; sbagliare; peggiorare; **to let slip** lasciarsi sfuggire; **to slip away** svignarsela; **to slip by** (*said of time*) passare, fuggire; **to slip out of s.o.'s hands** sgusciare dalle mani di qlcu; **to slip up** sbagliarsi

slip'cov'er *s* fodera

slip'knot' *s* nodo scorsoio

slip' of the tongue' *s* errore *m* nel parlare

slipper ['slɪpər] *s* pantofola

slippery ['slɪpəri] *adj* sdrucciolevole, scivoloso; evasivo; incerto

slip'shod' *adj* trasandato, mal fatto

slip'-up' *s* (coll) sbaglio

slit [slɪt] *s* taglio, fenditura || *v* (*pret & pp* **slit**; *ger* **slitting**) *tr* tagliare, fendere; **to slit the throat of** sgozzare

slob [slɑb] *s* (slang) rozzo, villanzone *m*

slobber ['slɑbər] *s* bava; sdolcinatura || *intr* sbavare; parlare sdolcinatamente

sloe [slo] *s* (*shrub*) prugnolo; (*fruit*) prugnola

slogan ['slogən] *s* slogan *m*

sloop [slup] *s* cutter *m*

slop [slɑp] *s* pastone *m;* (slang) sbobba || *v* (*pret & pp* **slopped**; *ger* **slopping**) *tr* versare, imbrodare || *intr* rovesciarsi, scorrere; (slang) perdersi in smancerie

slope [slop] *s* costa, pendice *f;* (*of mountain or roof*) spiovente *m* || *tr* inclinare || *intr* digradare, scendere

slop•py ['slɑpi] *adj* (**-pier; -piest**) fangoso; bagnato; (*slovenly*) sciatto; (*done badly*) abborracciato

slot [slɑt] *s* scanalatura; (*for letters*) buca; (*e.g., on a broadcasting schedule*) posizione

sloth [sloθ] or [slɔθ] *s* pigrizia; (zool) bradipo, poltrone *m*

slot' machine' *s* macchina a gettone

slouch [slaʊtʃ] *s* postura goffa; persona goffa; (coll) poltrone *m* || *intr* muoversi goffamente; **to slouch in a chair** sdraiarsi

slouch' hat' *s* cappello floscio

slough [slaʊ] *s* pantano; (fig) abisso || [slʌf] *s* (*of snake*) spoglia; (pathol) crosta || *tr*—**to slough off** spogliarsi di || *intr* sbucciarsi, cadere

Slovak ['slovæk] or [slo'væk] *adj & s* slovacco

sloven•ly ['slʌvənli] *adj* (**-lier; -liest**) sciatto, trasandato

slow [slo] *adj* lento; (*sluggish*) tardo; (*clock*) indietro, in ritardo; (*in understanding*) tardivo || *adv* piano || *tr* rallentare || *intr* rallentarsi; (*said of a watch*) ritardare

slow'down' *s* sciopero pignolo

slow' mo'tion *s*—**in slow motion** al rallentatore

slow'-motion projec'tor *s* rallentatore *m*

slow'poke' *s* (coll) poltrone *m*

slug [slʌg] *s* (*heavy piece of metal*) lingotto; (*metal disk*) gettone *m;* (fig) poltrone *m;* (zool) lumaca; (coll) colpo, mazzata || *v* (*pret & pp* **slugged**; *ger* **slugging**) *tr* picchiare sodo

sluggard ['slʌgərd] *s* poltrone *m*

sluggish ['slʌgɪʃ] *adj* pigro, indolente; lento, fiacco

sluice [slus] *s* canale *m;* stramazzo

sluice' gate' *s* paratoia

slum [slʌm] *s* bassifondi *mpl* || *v* (*pret & pp* **slummed**; *ger* **slumming**) *intr* visitare i bassifondi

slumber ['slʌmbər] *s* dormiveglia *m,* sonnellino || *intr* dormire, dormicchiare

slump [slʌmp] *s* depressione, crisi *f;* (*in prices*) ribasso, calo || *intr* impantanarsi; peggiorare; (*said of prices*) ribassare, calare

slur [slʌr] *s* insulto, macchia; critica; (mus) legatura || *v* (*pret & pp* **slurred**; *ger* **slurring**) *tr* pronunziare indistintamente; (*a subject*) sorvolare; insultare, calunniare; (mus) legare

slush [slʌʃ] *s* poltiglia di neve; fanghiglia; (fig) sdolcinatezza

slut [slʌt] *s* cagna; (*slovenly woman*) sciamannona; troia, puttana

sly [slaɪ] *adj* (**slyer** or **slier; slyest** or **sliest**) furbo; insidioso; (*hiding one's true feelings*) sornione; **on the sly** furtivamente

smack [smæk] *s* schiaffo; (*of whip or lips*) schiocco; (*taste*) traccia, sapore *m;* (coll) bacio collo schiocco || *adv* di colpo, direttamente || *tr* dare uno schiaffo a; colpire; (*the whip or one's lips*) schioccare; schioccare un bacio a || *intr*—**to smack of** sapere di

small [smɔl] *adj* piccolo; povero; basso, umile; (*change*) spicciolo; (typ) minuscolo

small' arms' *spl* armi *fpl* portatili

small' busi'ness *s* piccolo commercio

small' cap'ital *s* (typ) maiuscoletto

small' change' *s* spiccioli *mpl*

small' fry' *s* minutaglia; bambini *mpl;* gente *f* di poca importanza

small' hours' *spl* ore *fpl* piccole

small' intes'tine *s* intestino tenue

small-minded ['smɔl'maɪndɪd] *adj* di corte vedute, gretto

small' of the back' *s* fine *f* della schiena, reni *fpl*

smallpox ['smɔl ˌpɑks] *s* vaiolo

small' talk' *s* conversazione futile

small'-time' *adj* di poca importanza

small'-town' *adj* di provincia

smart [smɑrt] *adj* intelligente; scaltro, furbo; (*pain*) acuto; (*in appearance*) elegante; (*pert*) impertinente; (coll) grande, abbondante || *s* dolore acuto, sofferenza || *intr* bruciare; dolere; soffrire

smart' al'eck ['ælɪk] *s* saputello

smart' set' *s* bel mondo

smash [smæʃ] *s* sconquasso; colpo; collisione; rovina, fallimento; (tennis) smash *m,* schiacciata || *tr* sconquassare; sfracellare; rovinare; (tennis) schiacciare || *intr* sconquassarsi; sfracellarsi; andare in rovina; **to smash into** scontrarsi con

smash' hit' *s* successone *m*

smash'-up' *s* sconquasso
smattering ['smætərɪŋ] *s* infarinatura, spolvero
smear [smɪr] *s* macchia, imbrattatura; calunnia; (bact) striscio || *tr* imbrattare; spalmare; calunniare
smear' campaign' *s* campagna di vilipendio
smell [smɛl] *s* odore *m;* (*sense*) olfatto, odorato; profumo || *v* (*pret & pp* **smelled** or **smelt**) *tr* fiutare, odorare || *intr* odorare; (*to stink*) puzzare; profumare; **to smell of** odorare di; puzzare di
smell'ing salts' *spl* sali aromatici
smell•y ['smɛli] *adj* (**-ier; -iest**) puzzolente
smelt [smelt] *s* (ichth) eperlano || *tr & intr* fondere
smile [smaɪl] *s* sorriso || *intr* sorridere
smiling ['smaɪlɪŋ] *adj* sorridente
smirk [smʌrk] *s* ghigno || *intr* ghignare
smite [smaɪt] *v* (*pret* **smote** [smot]; *pp* **smitten** ['smɪtən] or **smit** [smɪt]) *tr* colpire; percuotere; affliggere, castigare
smith [smɪθ] *s* fabbro
smith•y ['smɪθi] *s* (**-ies**) fucina
smit'ten *adj* afflitto; innamorato
smock [smɑk] *s* camice *m;* (*of mechanic*) camiciotto
smock' frock' *s* blusa da lavoro
smog [smɑg] *s* foschia, smog *m*
smoke [smok] *s* fumo; **to go up in smoke** andare in cenere || *tr* affumicare; (*tobacco*) fumare; **to smoke out** cacciare col fumo; scoprire || *intr* fumare; (*said, e.g., of the earth*) fumigare
smoke'-filled room' *s* stanza da riunioni piena di fumo
smoke'less pow'der ['smoklɪs] *s* polvere *f* senza fumo
smoker ['smokər] *s* fumatore *m;* salone *m* fumatori; (rr) vagone *m* fumatori
smoke' rings' *spl* anelli *mpl* di fumo
smoke' screen' *s* cortina di fumo
smoke'stack' *s* fumaiolo
smoking ['smokɪŋ] *s* (il) fumare; **no smoking** vietato fumare
smok'ing car' *s* vagone *m* fumatori
smok'ing jack'et *s* giacca da casa
smok'ing room' *s* stanza per fumatori
smok•y ['smoki] *adj* (**-ier; -iest**) fumoso
smolder ['smoldər] *s* fumo derivante da fuoco che cova || *intr* (*said of fire or passion*) covare; (*said of s.o.'s eyes*) ardere
smooch [smutʃ] *intr* (coll) baciarsi, baciucchiarsi
smooth [smuð] *adj* liscio, levigato; (*face*) glabro; di consistenza uniforme; (*flat*) piano; senza interruzioni; tranquillo; elegante; (*sound*) armonioso; (*taste*) gradevole; (*wine*) abboccato; (*sea*) calmo; (*style*) fluido || *tr* lisciare, levigare; appianare, facilitare; calmare; **to smooth away** appianare
smooth-faced ['smuð,fest] *adj* (*beardless*) glabro; liscio
smooth-spoken ['smuð,spokən] *adj* mellifluo
smooth•y ['smuði] *s* (**-ies**) galante *m*
smother ['smʌðər] *tr* affoggare, soffocare
smudge [smʌdʒ] *s* macchia, imbrattatura || *tr* macchiare, imbrattare; (*a garden*) affumicare
smudge' pot' *s* apparecchiatura per affumicare
smug [smʌg] *adj* (**smugger; smuggest**) pieno di sé stesso; liscio, lisciato
smuggle ['smʌgəl] *tr* contrabbandare || *intr* praticare il contrabbando
smuggler ['smʌglər] *s* contrabbandiere *m*
smuggling ['smʌglɪŋ] *s* contrabbando
smut [smʌt] *s* sudiciume *m;* oscenità *f;* (agr) volpe *f*, golpe *f*
smut•ty ['smʌti] *adj* (**-tier; -tiest**) sudicio; osceno; (agr) malato di volpe
snack [snæk] *s* spuntino, merenda; porzione
snack' bar' *s* tavola calda
snag [snæg] *s* tronco sommerso; protuberanza, sporgenza; (*tooth*) dente rotto; (fig) intoppo, ostacolo; **to hit a snag** incontrare un ostacolo || *v* (*pret & pp* **snagged;** *ger* **snagging**) *tr* fare uno straccio a; (fig) ostacolare
snail [snel] *s* chiocciola, lumaca; **at a snail's pace** come una lumaca
snake [snek] *s* serpente *m;* (*nonvenomous*) biscia
snake' in the grass' *s* pericolo nascosto; (*person*) serpe *f* in seno
snap [snæp] *s* (*sharp sound*) schiocco; (*bite*) morso; (*fastener*) bottone automatico; (*of cold weather*) breve periodo; (*manner of speaking*) tono tagliente; (phot) istantanea; (coll) vigore *m;* (coll) cosa da nulla || *v* (*pret & pp* **snapped;** *ger* **snapping**) *tr* schioccare; chiudere di colpo; spezzare di colpo; (*a picture*) scattare; **to snap one's fingers at** infischiarsi di; **to snap up** afferrare; (*a person*) tagliare la parola a || *intr* schioccare; (*to crack*) rompersi di colpo; **to snap at** cercare di mordere; (*a bargain*) cercare di afferrare; **to snap out of it** (coll) riprendersi; **to snap shut** chiudersi di colpo
snap'drag'on *s* (bot) bocca di leone
snap' fas'tener *s* bottone automatico
snap' judg'ment *s* decisione presa senza riflessione
snap•py ['snæpi] *adj* (**-pier; -piest**) mordente, mordace; (coll) vivo, vivace; (coll) elegante; **to make it snappy** (slang) sbrigarsi
snap'shot' *s* istantanea
snare [snɛr] *s* laccio, lacciolo; (*of a drum*) corda
snare' drum' *s* cassa rullante
snarl [snɑrl] *s* (*of a dog*) ringhio; groviglio; (*of traffic*) ingorgo; (fig) confusione || *tr* urlare con un ringhio; (*to tangle*) aggrovigliare; complicare || *intr* ringhiare; aggrovigliarsi; complicarsi
snatch [snætʃ] *s* strappo, strappone *m;* presa; pezzetto; momentino || *tr &*

intr strappare; **to snatch at** cercare di afferrare; **to snatch from** strappare a
sneak [snik] *s* furfante *m* || *tr* mettere di nascosto; pigliare di nascosto || *intr*—**to sneak in** entrare di nascosto; **to sneak out** svignarsela
sneaker ['snikər] *s* furfante *m;* scarpetta da ginnastica
sneak' thief' *s* ladro, topo
sneak·y ['sniki] *adj* (**-ier; -iest**) furtivo
sneer [snɪr] *s* ghigno || *intr* sogghignare; **to sneer at** beffarsi si
sneeze [sniz] *s* starnuto || *intr* starnutare; **not to be sneezed at** (coll) non essere disprezzabile
snicker ['snɪkər] *s* risatina || *intr* fare una risatina
snide [snaɪd] *adj* malizioso
sniff [snɪf] *s* fiuto, fiutata; (*scent*) odore *m* || *tr* fiutare || *intr* aspirare rumorosamente; (*with emotion*) moccicare; **to sniff at** annusare; mostrare disprezzo per
sniffle ['snɪfəl] *s* moccio; **to have the sniffles** moccicare || *intr* moccicare
snip [snɪp] *s* taglio; pezzetto; (*person*) (coll) mezza cartuccia || *v* (*pret & pp* **snipped;** *ger* **snipping**) *tr* tagliuzzare
snipe [snaɪp] *s* tiro di nascosto; (orn) beccaccino || *intr* sparare in appostamento; attaccare da lontano
sniper ['snaɪpər] *s* franco tiratore, cecchino
snippet ['snɪpɪt] *s* ritaglio, frammento; (fig) mezza cartuccia
snip·py ['snɪpi] *adj* (**-pier; -piest**) frammentario; (coll) corto, brusco; (coll) arrogante
snitch [snɪtʃ] *tr & intr* (coll) graffignare, sgraffignare
sniv·el ['snɪvəl] *s* moccio; singhiozzo, piagnisteo; falsa commozione || *v* (*pret & pp* **-eled** or **-elled;** *ger* **-eling** or **-elling**) *intr* singhiozzare, piagnucolare; (*to have a runny nose*) moccicare, avere il moccio
snob [snɑb] *s* snob *mf*
snobbery ['snɑbəri] *s* snobismo
snobbish ['snɑbɪʃ] *adj* snobistico
snoop [snup] *s* (coll) ficcanaso || *intr* (coll) ficcare il naso
snoop·y ['snupi] *adj* (**-ier; -iest**) (coll) curioso, invadente
snoot [snut] *s* (slang) naso
snoot·y ['snuti] *adj* (**-ier; -iest**) (coll) snobistico
snooze [snuz] *s* (coll) sonnellino || *intr* (coll) fare un sonnellino
snore [snor] *s* russamento || *intr* russare
snort [snɔrt] *s* sbuffo || *intr* sbuffare
snot [snɑt] *s* (slang) moccio
snot·ty ['snɑti] *adj* (**-tier; -tiest**) (coll) snobistico; (coll) arrogante; (slang) moccioso
snout [snaʊt] *s* muso; (*of pig*) grugno; (*of person*) muso, grugno
snow [sno] *s* neve *f* || *intr* nevicare
snow'ball' *s* palla di neve || *tr* gettare palle di neve a || *intr* aumentare come una palla di neve
snow'blind' *adj* accecato dalla neve
snow'bound' *adj* prigioniero della neve
snow-capped ['sno ,kæpt] *adj* coperto di neve
snow'drift' *s* banco di neve
snow'fall' *s* nevicata
snow' fence' *s* barriera contro la neve
snow'flake' *s* fiocco di neve
snow' flur'ry *s* neve portata da raffiche
snow' line' *s* limite *m* delle nevi perenni
snow'man' *s* (**-men'**) uomo di neve
snow'plow' *s* spazzaneve *m*
snow'shoe' *s* racchetta da neve
snow'slide' *s* valanga
snow'storm' *s* bufera di neve
snow' tire' *s* gomma da neve, pneumatico da neve
snow'-white' *adj* bianco come la neve
snow·y ['sno·i] *adj* (**-ier; -iest**) nevoso
snub [snʌb] *s* affronto || *v* (*pret & pp* **snubbed;** *ger* **snubbing**) *tr* snobbare
snub·by ['snʌbi] *adj* (**-bier; -biest**) camuso, rincagnato
snuff [snʌf] *s* fiutata; tabacco da fiuto; (*of a candlewick*) moccolo; **up to snuff** (coll) soddisfacente; (coll) bene || *tr* fiutare; tabaccare; (*a candle*) smoccolare; **to snuff out** spegnere; (fig) soffocare
snuff'box' *s* tabacchiera
snuffers ['snʌfərz] *spl* smoccolatoio
snug [snʌg] *adj* (**snugger; snuggest**) comodo; (*dress*) attillato; compatto; (*well-off*) agiato; (*sum*) discreto; (*sheltered*) ben protetto; (*well-hidden*) nascosto
snuggle ['snʌgəl] *intr* rannicchiarsi; **to snuggle up to** stringersi a
so [so] *adv* così; così or tanto + *adj* or *adv;* per quanto; **and so** certamente; pure; **and so on** e così via; **or so** più o meno; **to think so** credere di sì; **so as to** + *inf* per + *inf;* **so far** sinora, finora; **so long!** arrivederci!; **so many** tanti; **so much** tanto; **so so** così così; **so that** in maniera che, di modo che; **so to speak** per così dire || *conj* cosicché || *interj* bene!; basta!; così!
soak [sok] *s* bagnata; (*toper*) (slang) ubriacone *m* || *tr* bagnare, inzuppare; imbevere; (coll) ubriacare; (slang) far pagare un prezzo esorbitante a; **to soak up** assorbire; **soaked to the skin** bagnato fino alle ossa || *intr* stare a molle, macerare; inzupparsi
so'-and-so' *s* (**-sos**) tal *m* dei tali; tal cosa
soap [sop] *s* sapone *m* || *tr* insaponare
soap'box' *s* cassa di sapone; tribuna improvvisata
soap'box or'ator *s* oratore *m* che parla da una tribuna improvvisata
soap' bub'ble *s* bolla di sapone
soap' dish' *s* portasapone *m*
soap' flakes' *spl* sapone *m* a scaglie
soap' op'era *s* (coll) trasmissione radiofonica o televisiva lacrimogena
soap' pow'der *s* sapone *m* in polvere
soap'stone' *s* pietra da sarto
soap'suds' *spl* saponata
soap·y ['sopi] *adj* (**-ier; -iest**) saponoso

soar [sor] *intr* spaziare, slanciarsi; (aer) librarsi
sob [sɑb] *s* singhiozzo || *v* (*pret & pp* **sobbed;** *ger* **sobbing**) *tr* dire a singhiozzi || *intr* singhiozzare
sober ['sobər] *adj* sobrio; non ubriaco || *intr* smaltire la sbornia; **to sober down** calmarsi; **to sober up** smaltire la sbornia
sobriety [so'braɪ·əti] *s* sobrietà *f*
sobriquet ['sobrɪ ,ke] *s* nomignolo
sob' sis'ter *s* giornalista lacrimogeno
sob' sto'ry *s* storia lacrimogena
so'-called' *adj* cosiddetto
soccer ['sɑkər] *s* calcio, football *m*
sociable ['soʃəbəl] *adj* sociale, socievole
social ['soʃəl] *adj* sociale || *s* riunione sociale
so'cial climb'er ['klaɪmər] *s* arrampicatore *m* sociale
so'cial con'tract *s* patto sociale
socialism ['soʃə ,lɪzəm] *s* socialismo
socialist ['soʃəlɪst] *s* socialista *mf*
socialite ['soʃə ,laɪt] *s* persona che appartiene all'alta società
So'cial Reg'ister *s* (trademark) annuario dell'alta società
so'cial secu'rity *s* sicurezza sociale
so'cial work'er *s* visitatrice *f*, assistente *mf* sociale
socie·ty [sə'saɪ·əti] *s* (**-ties**) società *f;* (*companionship or company*) compagnia
soci'ety ed'itor *s* cronista mondano
sociology [,sosɪ'ɑlədʒi] or [,soʃɪ'ɑlədʒi] *s* sociologia
sock [sɑk] *s* calzino; (slang) colpo forte; (slang) attore *m* di prim'ordine; (slang) spettacolo eccezionale || *tr* (slang) dare un forte colpo a
socket ['sɑkɪt] *s* (*of eye*) occhiaia; (*of tooth*) alveolo; (*of candlestick*) bocciolo; (*wall socket*) (elec) presa di corrente; (elec) portalampada *m*
sock'et wrench' *s* chiave *f* a tubo
sod [sɑd] *s* zolla; terreno erboso || *v* (*pret & pp* **sodded;** *ger* **sodding**) *tr* piotare
soda ['sodə] *s* soda
so'da crack'er *s* galletta fatta al bicarbonato
so'da wa'ter *s* soda, gazosa
sodium ['sodɪ·əm] *adj* sodico || *s* sodio
sofa ['sofə] *s* sofà *m*, divano
so'fa bed' *s* sofà *m* letto
soft [sɔft] or [sɑft] *adj* molle; (*smooth*) morbido; (*iron*) dolce; (*hat*) floscio; (*person*) rammollito; (coll) facile
soft'-boiled' egg' ['sɔft'bɔɪld] or ['sɑft'bɔɪld] *s* uovo alla coque
soft' coal' *s* carbone bituminoso
soft' drink' *s* bibita
soften ['sɔfən] or ['sɑfən] *tr* mollificare, rammollire; (fig) intenerire || *intr* intenerirsi
softener ['sɔfənər] or ['sɑfənər] *s* ammorbidente *m*
soft' land'ing *s* allunaggio morbido
soft'-ped'al *v* (*pret & pp* **-aled** or **-alled;** *ger* **-aling** or **-alling**) *tr* mettere in sordina; (coll) moderare
soft'-shell crab' *s* mollecca
soft' soap' *s* sapone *m* molle; (coll) adulazione
soft'-soap' *tr* (coll) insaponare
sog·gy ['sɑgi] *adj* (**-gier; -giest**) rammollito, inzuppato
soil [sɔɪl] *s* suolo, terreno; territorio; (*spot*) macchia; (*filth*) porcheria, lordura || *tr* sporcare, macchiare || *intr* sporcarsi, macchiarsi
soil' pipe' *s* tubo di scarico
soiree or **soirée** [swɑ're] *s* serata
sojourn ['sodʒʌrn] *s* soggiorno || ['sodʒʌrn] or [so'dʒʌrn] *intr* soggiornare
solace ['sɑlɪs] *s* conforto || *tr* confortare, consolare
solar ['solər] *adj* solare
so'lar bat'tery *s* batteria solare
solder ['sɑdər] *s* saldatura; lega per saldatura || *tr* saldare
sol'dering i'ron *s* saldatoio
soldier ['soldʒər] *s* (*man of rank and file*) soldato; (*man in military service*) militare *m* || *intr* fare il soldato
sol'dier of for'tune *s* soldato di ventura
soldier·y ['soldʒəri] *s* (**-ies**) soldatesca
sold-out ['sold ,aʊt] *adj* esaurito; (*e.g., theater*) completo
sole [sol] *adj* solo, unico; esclusivo || *s* (*of foot*) pianta; (*of stocking*) soletta; (*of shoe*) suola; (*fish*) sfoglia || *tr* solare
solely ['solli] *adv* solamente
solemn ['sɑləm] *adj* solenne
solicit [sə'lɪsɪt] *tr* sollecitare; adescare, accostare
solicitor [sə'lɪsɪtər] *s* sollecitatore *m;* agente *m;* (law) procuratore *m*
solicitous [sə'lɪsɪtəs] *adj* sollecito
solicitude [sə'lɪsɪ ,tjud] or [sə'lɪsɪ ,tud] *s* sollecitudine *f*
solid ['sɑlɪd] *adj* solido; (*not hollow*) sodo; (*e.g., clouds*) denso; (*wall*) pieno, massiccio; (*word*) con grafia unita; intero; unanime, solidale; (*good*) buono; (*e.g., gold*) puro, massiccio
solidity [sə'lɪdɪti] *s* solidità *f*
sol'id-state' *adj* transistorizzato, senza valvole
solilo·quy [sə'lɪləkwi] *s* (**-quies**) soliloquio
solitaire ['sɑlɪ ,tɛr] *s* solitario
solitar·y ['sɑlɪ ,tɛri] *adj* solitario; unico || *s* (**-ies**) persona solitaria
sol'itary confine'ment *s* segregazione cellulare
solitude ['sɑlɪ ,tjud] or ['sɑlɪ ,tud] *s* solitudine *f*
so·lo ['solo] *adj* solo, solitario; (mus) solista || *s* (**-los**) (mus) solo
soloist ['solo·ɪst] *s* solista *mf*
so' long' *interj* (coll) ciao!; (coll) addio!; (coll) arrivederci!
solstice ['sɑlstɪs] *s* solstizio
soluble ['sɑljəbəl] *adj* solubile
solution [sə'luʃən] *s* soluzione
solvable ['sɑlvəbəl] *adj* risolvibile
solve [sɑlv] *tr* risolvere, sciogliere

solvency ['sɑlvənsi] *s* solvenza
solvent ['sɑlvənt] *adj & s* solvente *m*
somber ['sɑmbər] *adj* tetro
some [sʌm] *adj indef* qualche; di + *art*, e.g., **some apples** delle mele; (coll) forte, grande || *pron indef* alcuni, taluni; ne, e.g., **I have some** ne ho
some'bod'y *pron indef* taluno, qualcuno; **somebody else** qualcun altro || *s* (**-ies**) (coll) qualcuno
some'day' *adv* qualche giorno
some'how' *adv* in qualche modo; **somehow or other** in un modo o nell'altro
some'one' *pron indef* qualcuno, taluno; **someone else** qualcun altro
somersault ['sʌmər ˌsɔlt] *s* salto mortale || *intr* fare un salto mortale
something ['sʌmθɪŋ] *pron indef* qualcosa; **something else** qualcos'altro || *adv* un po'; (coll) molto, moltissimo
some'time' *adj* antico, di un tempo || *adv* un giorno o l'altro, uno di questi giorni
some'times' *adv* talora, talvolta
some'way' *adv* in qualche modo
some'what' *s* qualcosa || *adv* piuttosto, un po'
some'where' *adv* in qualche luogo, da qualche parte; a qualche momento; **somewhere else** altrove
somnambulist [sɑm'næmbjəlɪst] *s* sonnambulo
somnolent ['sɑmnələnt] *adj* sonnolento
son [sʌn] *s* figlio
sonar ['sonɑr] *s* ecogoniometro, sonar *m*
song [sɔŋ] or [sɑŋ] *s* canto, canzone *f*; **for a song** per un soldo
song'bird' *s* uccello canoro
Song' of Songs' *s* Cantico dei Cantici
songster ['sɑŋgstər] *s* cantante *m*, canzonettista *m*
songstress ['sɑŋgstrɪs] *s* cantante *f*, canzonettista *f*
song'writ'er *s* canzoniere *m*
son'ic boom' ['sɑnɪk] *s* boato sonico
son'-in-law' *s* (**sons'-in-law'**) genero
sonnet ['sɑnɪt] *s* sonetto
son•ny ['sʌni] *s* (**-nies**) figliolo
sonori•ty [sə'nɑrɪti] or [sə'nɔrɪti] *s* (**-ties**) sonorità *f*
soon [sun] *adv* in breve, ben presto; subito, presto; **as soon as** non appena, quanto prima; **as soon as possible** quanto prima; **I had sooner** preferirei; **how soon?** quando?; **soon after** poco dopo; **sooner or later** prima o poi, tosto o tardi
soot [sʊt] or [sut] *s* fuliggine *f*
soothe [suð] *tr* calmare, lenire
soothsayer ['suθ ˌse·ər] *s* indovino
soot•y ['sʊti] or ['suti] *adj* (**-ier; -iest**) fuligginoso
sop [sɑp] *s* (*soaked food*) zuppa; (*bribe*) dono, offa || *v* (*pret & pp* **sopped**; *ger* **sopping**) *tr* intingere, inzuppare; **to sop up** assorbire
sophisticated [sə'fɪstɪ ˌketɪd] *adj* sofisticato, smaliziato
sophistication [sə ˌfɪstɪ'keʃən] *s* eccessiva ricercatezza; gusti *mpl* raffinati
sophomore ['sɑfə ˌmor] *s* studente *m* del secondo anno, fagiolo
sophomoric [ˌsɑfə'mɔrɪk] *adj* saputello, presuntuoso; ingenuo, imberbe
sopping ['sɑpɪŋ] *adv*—**sopping wet** inzuppato
sopran•o [sə'præno] or [sə'prɑno] *adj* per soprano, da soprano || *s* (**-os**) soprano *mf*
sorcerer ['sɔrsərər] *s* mago, stregone *m*
sorceress ['sɔrsərɪs] *s* maga, strega
sorcer•y ['sɔrsəri] *s* (**-ies**) stregoneria
sordid ['sɔrdɪd] *adj* sordido
sore [sor] *adj* irritato; indolenzito; estremo, grave; **to be sore at** (coll) aversela con || *s* piaga, ulcera; dolore *m*, afflizione; **to open an old sore** riaprire una ferita
sorely ['sorli] *adv* penosamente; gravemente, urgentemente
soreness ['sornɪs] *s* dolore *m*, afflizione
sore' spot' *s* (fig) piaga
sore' throat' *s* mal *m* di gola
sorori•ty [sə'rɑrɪti] or [sə'rɔrɪti] *s* (**-ties**) associazione femminile universitaria
sorrel ['sɑrəl] or ['sɔrəl] *adj* sauro
sorrow ['sɑro] or ['sɔro] *s* dolore *m*, cordoglio || *intr* affliggersi, provar cordoglio; **to sorrow for** rimpiangere
sorrowful ['sɑrəfəl] or ['sɔrəfəl] *adj* doloroso
sor•ry ['sɑri] or ['sɔri] *adj* (**-rier; -riest**) spiacente, desolato, dolente; povero, cattivo; **to be sorry** dolersi; dispiacere a, e.g., **he is sorry** gli dispiace || *interj* mi dispiace!, scusi!
sort [sɔrt] *s* tipo, specie *f*; maniera; **a sort of** una specie di; **out of sorts** depresso; ammalato; di mal umore; **sort of** (coll) piuttosto; (coll) un certo, e.g., **sort of a headache** un certo mal di testa || *tr* assortire; (*mail*) smistare
so'-so' *adj* passabile || *adv* così così
sot [sɑt] *s* ubriacone *m*
soubrette [su'brɛt] *s* (theat) soubrette *f*
soul [sol] *s* anima; **upon my soul!** sulla mia parola!
sound [saʊnd] *adj* sano; solido, forte; valido, buono; (*sleep*) profondo; valido, legale; onesto || *s* suono; rumore *m*; (*of an animal*) verso; (*passage of water*) stretto; (surg) sonda; (ichth) vescica natatoria; **within sound of** alla portata di || *adv* profondamente || *tr* (*an instrument*) sonare; pronunciare; (*e.g., s.o.'s chest*) auscultare; (*praises*) cantare; (*to measure*) sondare || *intr* sonare; parere, sembrare; fare uno scandaglio; **to sound like** avere il suono di; dare l'impressione di, parere
sound' bar'rier *s* muro del suono
sound' film' *s* pellicola sonora
soundly ['saʊndli] *adv* solidamente; profondamente; completamente
sound'proof' *adj* a prova di suono || *tr* insonorizzare

sound' track' *s* (mov) sonoro, colonna sonora
sound' truck' *s* autoveicolo con impianto sonoro
sound' wave' *s* onda sonora
soup [sup] *s* zuppa, minestra
soup' dish' *s* piatto fondo
soup' kitch'en *s* asilo dei poveri che serve zuppa gratuitamente
soup'spoon' *s* cucchiaio (da minestra)
sour [saʊr] *adj* acido; (*fruit*) acerbo ‖ *tr* inacidire ‖ *intr* inacidirsi
source [sors] *s* fonte *f*, sorgente *f*
source' lan'guage *s* lingua di partenza
source' mate'rial *s* fonti *fpl* originali
sour' cher'ry *s* (*fruit*) amarena; (*tree*) amareno
sour' grapes' *interj* l'uva è verde!
south [saʊθ] *adj* meridionale, del sud ‖ *s* sud *m*, meridione *m* ‖ *adv* verso il sud
South' Amer'ica *s* l'America *f* del Sud
South' Amer'ican *adj* & *s* sudamericano
southeast [,saʊθ'ist] *adj* di sud-est ‖ *s* sud-est ‖ *adv* al sud-est
southern ['sʌðərn] *adj* meridionale
South'ern Cross' *s* Croce *f* del Sud
southerner ['sʌðərnər] *s* meridionale *mf*
South' Kore'a *s* la Corea del Sud
south'paw' *adj* & *s* (coll) mancino
South' Pole' *s* Polo sud
South' Vietnam·ese' [vɪ,etnə'miz] *adj* vietnamita del sud ‖ *s* (**-ese**) vietnamita *mf* del sud
southward ['saʊθwərd] *adv* verso il sud
south'west' *adj* di sud-ovest ‖ *s* sud-ovest *m* ‖ *adv* al sud-ovest
souvenir [,suvə'nɪr] or ['suvə,nɪr] *s* ricordo, memoria
sovereign ['sɑvrɪn] or ['sʌvrɪn] *adj* sovrano ‖ *s* (*king*) sovrano; (*queen; coin*) sovrana
sovereign·ty ['sɑvrɪnti] or ['sʌvrɪnti] *s* (**-ties**) sovranità *f*
soviet ['sovɪ,et] or [,sovɪ'et] *adj* sovietico ‖ *s* soviet *m*
So'viet Rus'sia *s* la Russia Sovietica
sow [saʊ] *s* porca, troia ‖ [so] *v* (*pret* **sowed**; *pp* **sown** or **sowed**) *tr* seminare
soybean ['sɔɪ,bin] *s* soia; seme *m* di soia
spa [spɑ] *s* terme *fpl*
space [spes] *adj* spaziale ‖ *s* spazio; periodo; **after a space** dopo un po' ‖ *tr* spaziare; **to space out** diradare
space' bar' *s* barra spaziatrice, spaziatrice *f*
space' cen'ter *s* cosmodromo
space'craft' *s* astronave *f*
space' flight' *s* volo spaziale
space'man' *s* (**-men'**) navigatore *m* spaziale
spacer ['spesər] *s* spaziatrice *f*, barra spaziatrice
space'ship' *s* astronave *f*
space'suit' *s* scafandro astronautico, tuta spaziale
spacious ['speʃəs] *adj* spazioso
spade [sped] *s* vanga; (cards) picca; **to call a spade a spade** dire pane al pane, vino al vino ‖ *tr* vangare
spade'work' *s* lavoro preliminare
spaghetti [spə'gɛti] *s* spaghetti *mpl*
Spain [spen] *s* la Spagna
span [spæn] *s* (*of the hand*) spanna; (*of time*) tratto; (*of a bridge*) campata, luce *f*; (*of horses*) paio; (aer) apertura ‖ *v* (*pret* & *pp* **spanned**; *ger* **spanning**) *tr* misurare a spanne; attraversare, oltrepassare; (*said of time*) abbracciare
spangle ['spæŋgəl] *s* lustrino ‖ *tr* tempestare di lustrini; (*with bright objects*) stellare ‖ *intr* brillare
Spaniard ['spænjərd] *s* spagnolo
Spanish ['spænɪʃ] *adj* & *s* spagnolo; **the Spanish** gli spagnoli
Span'ish-Amer'ican *adj* & *s* ispanoamericano
Span'ish broom' *s* ginestra
Span'ish fly' mosca cantaride
Span'ish om'elet *s* frittata di pomodori, cipolle e peperoni
Span'ish-speak'ing *adj* di lingua spagnola
spank [spæŋk] *tr* sculacciare
spanking ['spæŋkɪŋ] *adj* rapido; forte; (coll) eccellente, straordinario ‖ *s* sculacciata
spar [spɑr] *s* (*mineral*) spato; (naut) asta, pennone *m*; (aer) longherone *m* ‖ *v* (*pret* & *pp* **sparred**; *ger* **sparring**) *intr* fare la box
spare [spɛr] *adj* di riserva; libero, in eccesso; (*e.g., diet*) frugale; (*lean*) magro ‖ *tr* salvare, risparmiare; perdonare; (*to do without*) fare a meno di, privarsi di; **to have . . . to spare** aver . . . d'avanzo; **to spare oneself** risparmiarsi
spare' parts' *s* pezzi *mpl* di ricambio
spare' room' *s* camera per gli ospiti
spare' tire' *s* ruota di scorta, pneumatico di scorta
spare' wheel' *s* ruota di scorta
sparing ['spɛrɪŋ] *adj* economico; (*scanty*) scarso
spark [spɑrk] *s* scintilla; traccia ‖ *tr* (coll) rianimare; (coll) corteggiare ‖ *intr* scintillare
spark' coil' *s* bobina d'accensione
spark' gap' *s* (elec) traferro, intraferro
sparkle ['spɑrkəl] *s* scintilla; (*luster*) scintillio; allegria, vivacità *f* ‖ *intr* scintillare; (*said, e.g., of eyes*) brillare, luccicare; (*said of wine*) frizzare, spumeggiare
sparkling ['spɑrklɪŋ] *adj* scintillante; (*wine*) frizzante, spumeggiante; (*water*) gassoso
spark' plug' *s* candela
sparrow ['spæro] *s* passero
sparse [spɑrs] *adj* rado
Spartan ['spɑrtən] *adj* & *s* spartano
spasm ['spæzəm] *s* spasmo; sprazzo d'energia
spasmodic [spæz'mɑdɪk] *adj* spasmodico; intermittente, a sprazzi
spastic ['spæstɪk] *adj* & *s* spastico
spat [spæt] *s* litigio, battibecco; **spats**

ghette *fpl* || *v* (*pret & pp* **spatted; ger spatting**) *intr* avere un battibecco
spatial ['speʃəl] *adj* spaziale
spatter ['spætər] *tr* schizzare, spruzzare || *intr* gocciolare
spatula ['spætʃələ] *s* spatola
spawn [spɔn] *s* prole *f*, progenie *f*; risultato || *tr* produrre, generare || *intr* (ichth) deporre le uova
spay [spe] *tr* asportare le ovaie a
speak [spik] *v* (*pret* **spoke** [spok]; *pp* **spoken**) *tr* (*a language*) parlare; (*the truth*) dire || *intr* parlare; **so to speak** per così dire; **speaking!** al telefono!; **to speak of** importante, che valga parlarne; **to speak out** dire la propria opinione
speak'-eas'y *s* (**-ies**) bar clandestino
speaker ['spikər] *s* conferenziere *m*, oratore *m*; (*of a language*) parlante *mf*; (pol) presidente *m*; (rad) altoparlante *m*
speaking ['spikɪŋ] *adj* parlante; **to be on speaking terms** parlarsi || *s* parlare *m*, discorso
speak'ing tube' *s* tubo acustico
spear [spɪr] *s* lancia; (*for fishing*) arpione *m*; (*of grass*) stelo || *tr* trafiggere con la lancia
spear' gun' *s* fucile subacqueo
spear'head' *s* punta di lancia || *tr* condurre, dirigere
spear'mint' *s* menta romana spicata
special ['speʃəl] *adj* speciale || *s* prezzo speciale; treno speciale
spe'cial deliv'ery *s* espresso
spe'cial draw'ing rights' *spl* (econ) diritti *mpl* speciali di prelievo
specialist ['speʃəlɪst] *s* specialista *mf*
specialize ['speʃə,laɪz] *tr* specializzare || *intr* specializzarsi
spe'cial part'ner *s* accomandante *mf*
special·ty ['speʃəlti] *s* (**-ties**) specialità *f*
spe·cies ['spisiz] *s* (**-cies**) specie *f*
specific [spɪ'sɪfɪk] *adj & s* specifico
specification [,spesɪfɪ'keʃən] *s* specifica; (com) capitolato
specif'ic grav'ity *s* peso specifico
speci·fy ['spesɪ,faɪ] *v* (*pret & pp* **-fied**) *tr* specificare
specimen ['spesɪmən] *s* esemplare *m*; (coll) tipo
specious ['spiʃəs] *adj* specioso
speck [spek] *s* macchiolina; (*of dust*) granello; (*of hope*) filo || *tr* macchiettare
speckle ['spekəl] *s* macchiolina || *tr* macchiettare, picchiettare
spectacle ['spektəkəl] *s* spettacolo; **spectacles** occhiali *mpl*
spectator ['spektetər] or [spek'tetər] *s* spettatore *m*
specter ['spektər] *s* spettro
spec·trum ['spektrəm] *s* (**-tra** [trə] or **-trums**) spettro; (fig) gamma
speculate ['spekjə,let] *intr* speculare
speech [spitʃ] *s* parola, parlata; (*before an audience*) discorso; (*of an actor*) elocuzione; **in speech** oralmente
speech' clin'ic *s* clinica per la correzione dei difetti del linguaggio
speechless ['spitʃlɪs] *adj* senza parole, muto
speed [spid] *s* velocità *f*; (aut) marcia || *tr* accelerare, affrettare || *intr* accelerare, affrettarsi; guidare oltre la velocità massima
speed'boat' *s* motoscafo da corsa
speeding ['spidɪŋ] *s* eccesso di velocità
speed' king' *s* asso del volante
speed' lim'it *s* limite *m* di velocità
speedometer [spi'dɑmɪtər] *s* tachimetro; (*to record the distance covered*) contachilometri *m*
speed'-up' *s* accelerazione
speed'way' *s* (*highway*) autostrada; (*for races*) pista
speed·y ['spidi] *adj* (**-ier; -iest**) veloce, rapido
spell [spel] *s* malia, incantesimo; fascino; turno; attacco; periodo di tempo; **to cast a spell on** incantare || *v* (*pret & pp* **spelled** or **spelt** [spelt]) *tr* compitare; scrivere in tutte lettere; voler dire; **to spell out** (coll) spiegare dettagliatamente || *intr* scrivere, sillabare || *v* (*pret & pp* **spelled**) *tr* rimpiazzare
spell'bind' *v* (*pret & pp* **-bound**) *tr* affascinare
spell'bind'er *s* oratore *m* abbagliante
spelling ['spelɪŋ] *adj* ortografico || *s* (*act*) compitazione; (*way a word is spelled*) grafia; (*subject of study*) ortografia
spell'ing bee' *s* gara di ortografia
spelunker [spɪ'lʌŋkər] *s* esploratore *m* di caverne
spend [spend] *v* (*pret & pp* **spent** [spent]) *tr* spendere; (*time*) passare
spender ['spendər] *s* spenditore *m*
spend'ing mon'ey *s* denaro per le piccole spese personali
spend'thrift' *s* sprecone *m*, spendaccione *m*
sperm [spʌrm] *s* sperma *m*
sperm' whale' *s* capodoglio
spew [spju] *tr & intr* vomitare
sphere [sfɪr] *s* sfera
spherical ['sferɪkəl] *adj* sferico
sphinx [sfɪŋks] *s* (**sphinxes** or **sphinges** ['sfɪndʒiz]) sfinge *f*
spice [spaɪs] *s* droga; spezie *fpl*; (fig) gusto, sapore *m* || *tr* drogare; dare gusto a, rendere piccante
spick-and-span ['spɪkənd'spæn] *adj* ordinato e pulito
spic·y ['spaɪsi] *adj* (**-ier; -iest**) drogato; piccante
spider ['spaɪdər] *s* ragno
spi'der·web' *s* ragnatela
spiff·y ['spɪfi] *adj* (**-ier; -iest**) (slang) elegante, bello
spigot ['spɪgət] *s* (*peg*) zipolo; (*faucet*) rubinetto
spike [spaɪk] *s* chiodo, chiodone *m*; (*sharp-pointed piece*) spuntone *m*; (rr) arpione *m*; (bot) spiga || *tr* inchiodare; mettere chiodi a; (*a rumor*) porre fine a; (coll) alcolizzare
spill [spɪl] *s* rovesciamento; liquido rovesciato; (coll) caduta || *v* (*pret & pp* **spilled** or **spilt** [spɪlt]) *tr* rove-

sciare, spandere; versare; (naut) sventare; (coll) far cadere; (slang) snocciolare || *intr* rovesciarsi; versarsi
spill'way' *s* sfioratore *m*, stramazzo
spin [spɪn] *s* giro; (*twirl*) mulinello; corsa; **to go into a spin** (aer) cadere a vite || *v* (*pret & pp* **spun** [spʌn]; *ger* **spinning**) *tr* far girare; (*e.g., thread*) filare; **to spin out** prolungare; **to spin a yarn** raccontare una storia || *intr* girare; (*said of a top*) prillare; filare
spinach ['spɪnɪtʃ] or ['spɪnɪdʒ] *s* spinacio; (*leaves used as food*) spinaci *mpl*
spi'nal col'umn ['spaɪnəl] *s* spina dorsale, colonna vertebrale
spi'nal cord' *s* midollo spinale
spindle ['spɪndəl] *s* (*rounded rod*) fuso; (*shaft, axle*) asse *m;* balaustro
spine [spaɪn] *s* spina; spina dorsale; (bb) costola; (fig) forza, carattere *m*
spineless ['spaɪnlɪs] *adj* senza spine; senza carattere
spinet ['spɪnɪt] *s* spinetta
spinner ['spɪnər] *s* filatore *m;* (*machine*) filatrice *f*
spinning ['spɪnɪŋ] *adj* filante || *s* filatura; rotazione
spin'ning mill' *s* filanda
spin'ning wheel' *s* filatoio
spinster ['spɪnstər] *s* zitella
spi•ral ['spaɪrəl] *adj & s* spirale *f* || *v* (*pret & pp* **-raled** or **-ralled;** *ger* **-raling** or **-ralling**) *intr* muoversi lungo una spirale
spi'ral stair'case *s* scala a chiocciola
spire [spaɪr] *s* (*of a steeple*) guglia, freccia; (*of grass*) foglia; (*spiral*) spirale *f*
spirit ['spɪrɪt] *s* spirito; valore *m*, vigore *m;* bevanda spiritosa; **out of spirits** giù di morale || *tr*—**to spirit away** portar via misteriosamente
spirited ['spɪrɪtɪd] *adj* brioso; (*horse*) superbo, vivace
spir'it lamp' *s* lampada a spirito
spiritless ['spɪrɪtlɪs] *adj* senza anima, senza vita
spir'it lev'el *s* livella a bolla d'aria
spiritual ['spɪrɪtʃʊ·əl] *adj* spirituale; (*séance*) spiritico
spiritualism ['spɪrɪtʃʊə,lɪzəm] *s* spiritismo; (philos) spiritualismo
spiritualist ['spɪrɪtʃʊ·əlɪst] *s* spiritista *mf;* (philos) spiritualista *mf*
spirituous ['spɪrɪtʃʊ·əs] *adj* alcolico
spit [spɪt] *s* sputo; (*for roasting*) spiedo, schidione *m;* punta; **the spit and image of** (coll) il ritratto parlante di || *v* (*pret & pp* **spat** [spæt] or **spit;** *ger* **spitting**) *tr & intr* sputare
spite [spaɪt] *s* dispetto, ripicco; **in spite of** a dispetto di, a onta di; **out of spite** per picca || *tr* far dispetto a; offendere; contrariare
spiteful ['spaɪtfəl] *adj* dispettoso
spit'fire' *s* persona collerica; (*woman*) bisbetica
spit'ting im'age *s* (coll) ritratto parlante
spittoon [spɪ'tun] *s* sputacchiera
splash [splæʃ] *s* schizzo, spruzzo; (*of mud*) zacchera; (*sound*) tonfo; **to make a splash** fare molto sci-sci || *tr & intr* sguazzare
splash'down' *s* (rok) ammaraggio, urto con l'acqua
spleen [splin] *s* cattivo umore, bile *f;* (anat) milza, splene *m*
splendid ['splendɪd] *adj* splendido; ottimo, magnifico
splendor ['splendər] *s* splendore *m*
splice [splaɪs] *s* giuntura || *tr* giuntare
splint [splɪnt] *s* stecca || *tr* steccare
splinter ['splɪntər] *s* scheggia || *tr* scheggiare || *intr* scheggiarsi
splin'ter group' *s* gruppo dissidente
split [splɪt] *adj* spaccato; diviso || *s* spaccatura; fessura; rottura, divisione; **splits** (sports) spaccato || *v* (*pret & pp* **split;** *ger* **splitting**) *tr* spaccare; dividere; **to split one's sides with laughter** scoppiare dalle risa || *intr* scindersi, dividersi; **to split up** separarsi
split' personal'ity *s* sdoppiamento della personalità
splitting ['splɪtɪŋ] *adj* che fende; che si fende; violento, fortissimo || *s*—**splittings** frammenti *mpl*
splotch [splɑtʃ] *s* macchia, chiazza || *tr* macchiare, chiazzare
splurge [splʌrdʒ] *s* ostentazione || *intr* fare ostentazione; fare una spesa matta
splutter ['splʌtər] *s* crepitio; (*utterance*) barbugliamento || *tr* barbugliare || *intr* crepitare; barbugliare
spoil [spɔɪl] *s* spoglia, bottino; **spoils** (mil) spoglie *fpl;* (pol) profitto, vantaggio || *v* (*pret & pp* **spoiled** or **spoilt** [spɔɪlt]) *tr* rovinare, sciupare; (*a child*) viziare; (*food*) deteriorare || *intr* guastarsi, andare a male
spoilage ['spɔɪlɪdʒ] *s* deterioramento
spoiled [spɔɪld] *adj* (*child*) viziato; (*food*) andato a male, passato
spoils' sys'tem *s* sistema politico secondo il quale le cariche vanno al partito vincitore
spoke [spok] *s* (*of a wheel*) raggio; (*of a ladder*) piolo
spokes'man *s* (**-men**) portavoce *m*
sponge [spʌndʒ] *s* spugna; **to throw in the sponge** (slang) gettare la spugna || *tr* pulire con spugna; assorbire; (coll) scroccare || *intr* assorbire; **to sponge off** (coll) vivere alle spalle di
sponge' bath' *s* spugnatura
sponge' cake' *s* pan *m* di Spagna
sponger ['spʌndʒər] *s* scroccatore *m*
sponge' rub'ber *s* gommapiuma
spon•gy ['spʌndʒi] *adj* (**-gier; -giest**) spugnoso
sponsor ['spɑnsər] *s* patrocinatore *m;* (*of a charitable institution*) patrono; (*godfather*) padrino; (*godmother*) madrina || *tr* patrocinare; (rad, telv) offrire
sponsorship ['spɑnsər,ʃɪp] *s* patrocinio
spontaneous [spɑn'tenɪ·əs] *adj* spontaneo

spoof [spuf] *s* mistificazione; parodia || *tr* mistificare; parodiare || *intr* mistificare; fare una parodia
spook [spuk] *s* (coll) spettro
spook·y ['spuki] *adj* (**-ier; -iest**) (coll) spettrale; (*horse*) (coll) nervoso
spool [spul] *s* spola, rocchetto
spoon [spun] *s* cucchiaio; (*lure*) cucchiaino; **born with a silver spoon in one's mouth** nato con la camicia || *tr* servire col cucchiaio || *intr* (coll) limonare
spoonerism ['spunə,rɪzəm] *s* papera
spoon'-feed' *v* (*pret & pp* **-fed**) *tr* nutrire col cucchiaino; (fig) coccolare
spoonful ['spun,fʊl] *s* cucchiaiata
spoon·y ['spuni] *adj* (**-ier; -iest**) (coll) svenevole
sporadic(al) [spə'rædɪk(əl)] *adj* sporadico
spore [spor] *s* spora
sport [sport] *adj* sportivo || *s* sport *m;* gioco; (*laughingstock*) zimbello; (*gambler*) (coll) giocatore *m;* (*person who behaves in a sportsmanlike manner*) (coll) spirito sportivo; (*flashy fellow*) (coll) tipo fino; (biol) mutazione; **to make sport of** farsi gioco di || *tr* (coll) sfoggiare; **to sport away** dissipare || *intr* divertirsi; giocare; farsi beffe
sport' clothes' *spl* vestiti *mpl* sport
sport'ing chance' *s* pari opportunità *f* di vincere
sport'ing goods' *spl* articoli *mpl* sportivi
sport'ing house' *s* (coll) bordello
sports'cast'er *s* annunziatore sportivo
sports' fan' *s* appassionato agli spettacoli sportivi, tifoso
sports'man *s* (**-men**) sportivo
sports'man·ship' *s* sportività *f,* spirito sportivo
sports' news' *s* notiziario sportivo
sports'wear' *s* articoli *mpl* d'abbigliamento sportivo
sports'writ'er *s* cronista sportivo
sport·y ['sporti] *adj* (**-ier; -iest**) (coll) elegante; (coll) sportivo; (coll) appariscente
spot [spɑt] *s* macchia; luogo, punto, posto; (*e.g., of tea*) goccia; **spots** locali *mpl;* **on the spot** sul posto; (*right now*) seduta stante; (slang) in difficoltà; **to hit the spot** (slang) soddisfare completamente || *v* (*pret & pp* **spotted;** *ger* **spotting**) *tr* macchiare; spargere; (coll) riconoscere || *intr* macchiare; macchiarsi
spot' cash' *s* pronta cassa
spot'-check' *tr* fare un breve sondaggio di; controllare rapidamente
spot' check' *s* breve sondaggio; rapido controllo
spotless ['spɑtlɪs] *adj* immacolato, senza macchia
spot'light' *s* riflettore *m;* (aut) proiettore *m;* **to be in the spotlight** (fig) essere il centro d'attenzione
spot' remov'er [rɪ'muvər] *s* smacchiatore *m*
spot' weld'ing *s* saldatura per punti
spouse [spaʊz] or [spaʊs] *s* consorte *mf*
spout [spaʊt] *s* (*to carry water from roof*) doccia; (*of jar, pitcher, etc.*) becco, beccuccio; (*jet*) zampillo, getto || *tr & intr* sprizzare, zampillare; (coll) declamare
sprain [spren] *s* distorsione || *tr* distorcere, distorcersi
sprawl [sprɔl] *intr* sdraiarsi
spray [spre] *s* spruzzo; (*of the sea*) schiuma; (*device*) spruzzatore *m;* (*twig*) ramoscello || *tr & intr* spruzzare
sprayer ['spre·ər] *s* spruzzatore *m,* schizzetto, vaporizzatore *m;* (hort) irroratrice *f*
spray' gun' *s* pistola a spruzzo; (hort) irroratrice *f*
spray' paint' *s* vernice *f* a spruzzo
spread [sprɛd] *s* espansione; diffusione; differenza; tappeto, coperta; elasticità *f;* (*of the wings of bird or airplane*) apertura; cibo da spalmare; (coll) festino; (journ) articolo di fondo or pubblicitario su varie colonne || *v* (*pret & pp* **spread**) *tr* tendere, estendere; (*one's legs*) divaricare; (*wings*) spiegare; spargere, cospargere; (*the table*) preparare; (*butter*) spalmare; diffondere || *intr* estendersi; spiegarsi; spargersi; spalmarsi; diffondersi
spree [spri] *s* baldoria, bisboccia; **to go on a spree** darsi alla pazza gioia
sprig [sprɪg] *s* ramoscello
spright·ly ['spraɪtli] *adj* (**-lier; -liest**) brioso, vivace
spring [sprɪŋ] *adj* primaverile; sorgivo; a molla || *s* (*season*) primavera; (*issue of water from earth*) fonte *f,* polla; (*elastic device*) molla; elasticità *f;* (*leap*) salto; (*crack*) fenditura; (aut) balestra || *v* (*pret* **sprang** [spræŋ] or **sprung** [sprʌŋ]; *pp* **sprung**) *tr* (*e.g., a lock*) far scattare; (*a leak*) aprire; (*a mine*) far brillare || *intr* saltare; (*said of a metal spring*) scattare; scaturire, zampillare; nascere, derivare; esplodere; **to spring forth** or **up** sorgere
spring'board' *s* pedana, trampolino
spring' chick'en *s* pollo giovanissimo; (slang) ragazzina
spring' fe'ver *s* indolenza primaverile
spring' mat'tress *s* materasso a molle
spring' tide' *s* marea di sizigia
spring'time' *s* primavera
sprinkle ['sprɪŋkəl] *s* spruzzo, spruzzatina; (*small amount*) pizzico || *tr* spruzzare; (*e.g., sugar*) spolverizzare || *intr* sprizzare; piovigginare
sprinkler ['sprɪŋklər] *s* annaffiatoio; (*person*) annaffiattore *m*
sprinkling ['sprɪŋklɪŋ] *s* sprizzo, spruzzo; (*with holy water*) aspersione; (*with powder*) spolverizzamento; (*e.g., of knowledge*) spolvero, spolveratura; (*of people*) piccolo numero
sprin'kling can' *s* annaffiatoio

sprint [sprɪnt] *s* (sports) scatto, volata || *intr* (sports) scattare
sprite [spraɪt] *s* spirito folletto
sprocket ['sprɑkɪt] *s* moltiplica; (phot) trasportatore *m*
sprout [spraʊt] *s* germoglio || *intr* germogliare; crescere rapidamente
spruce [sprus] *adj* elegante, attillato || *s* abete rosso || *tr* attillare, azzimare || *intr* attillarsi, azzimarsi
spry [spraɪ] *adj* (**spryer** or **sprier; spryest** or **spriest**) vegeto
spud [spʌd] *s* vanghetto, tagliaradici *m;* (coll) patata
spun' glass' *s* lana di vetro
spunk [spʌŋk] *s* (coll) coraggio, fegato
spur [spʌr] *s* sperone *m;* (rr) raccordo ferroviario; (fig) pungolo; **on the spur of the moment** lì per lì || *v* (*pret & pp* **spurred;** *ger* **spurring**) *tr* spronare; **to spur on** spronare, incitare
spurious ['spjʊrɪ·əs] *adj* spurio
spurn [spʌrn] *s* disprezzo, sdegno; rifiuto || *tr* disprezzare, sdegnare; rifiutare
spurt [spʌrt] *s* spruzzo, zampillo; (*sudden burst*) scatto repentino || *intr* sprizzare, zampillare; scattare
sputter ['spʌtər] *s* barbugliamento; (*sizzling*) crepitio || *tr* barbugliare || *intr* barbugliare; crepitare
spu·tum ['spjutəm] *s* (**-ta** [tə]) sputo
spy [spaɪ] *s* (**spies**) spia || *v* (*pret & pp* **spied**) *tr* spiare; osservare || *intr* fare la spia; **to spy on** spiare
spy'glass' *s* cannocchiale *m*
spying ['spaɪ·ɪŋ] *s* spionaggio
squabble ['skwɑbəl] *s* battibecco || *intr* litigare
squad [skwɑd] *s* squadra
squadron ['skwɑdrən] *s* (*of cavalry*) squadrone *m;* (aer, nav) squadriglia; (mil) squadra
squalid ['skwɑlɪd] *adj* sordido; squallido, misero
squall [skwɔl] *s* groppo, turbine *m;* urlo || *intr* gridare, urlare
squalor ['skwɑlər] *s* sordidezza; squallore *m,* miseria
squander ['skwɑndər] *tr* scialacquare, dilapidare, sperperare
square [skwer] *adj* quadrato, e.g., **two square miles** due miglia quadrate; di . . . di lato, e.g., **two miles square** di due miglia di lato; ad angolo retto; solido; saldato; (coll) onesto; (coll) diretto; (coll) sostanzioso; (slang) all'antica; **to get square with** (coll) fargliela pagare a || *s* quadrato; (*small square, e.g., of checkerboard*) quadretto; (*city block*) isolato; (*open area in city*) piazza, piazzale *m;* (*of carpenter*) squadra; **on the square** ad angolo retto; (coll) onesto || *adv* ad angolo retto; (coll) onestamente || *tr* squadrare; dividere in quadretti; elevare al quadrato; quadrare; (*a debt*) saldare; **to square with** adattare a || *intr* quadrare; **to square off** prepararsi, mettersi in posizione difensiva
square' dance' *s* danza figurata americana
square' meal' *s* (coll) pasto abbondante
square' root' *s* radice quadrata
square' shoot'er ['ʃutər] *s* (coll) persona onesta
squash [skwɑʃ] *s* spappolamento; (bot) zucca; (sports) squash *m* || *tr* spappolare; spiaciccare; (*e.g., a rumor*) sopprimere; (*a person*) (coll) ridurre al silenzio || *intr* spiaciccarsi
squash·y ['skwɑʃi] *adj* (**-ier; -iest**) tenero; (*ground*) fangoso, pantanoso; (*fruit*) maturo
squat [skwɑt] *adj* tozzo || *v* (*pret & pp* **squatted;** *ger* **squatting**) *intr* accoccolarsi; stabilirsi illegalmente su territorio altrui; stabilirsi su terreno pubblico per ottenerne titolo
squatter ['skwɑtər] *s* intruso
squaw [skwɔ] *s* squaw *f;* (coll) donna
squawk [skwɔk] *s* schiamazzo; (slang) lamento stridulo || *intr* schiamazzare; (slang) lamentarsi strillando
squaw' man' *s* bianco sposato con una pellerossa
squeak [skwik] *s* strido; cigolio || *intr* stridere; cigolare; (*said of a mouse*) squittire; **to squeak through** farcela per il rotto della cuffia
squeal [skwil] *s* strido || *intr* stridere; (slang) cantare, fare il delatore
squealer ['skwilər] *s* (slang) delatore *m*
squeamish ['skwɪmɪʃ] *adj* pudibondo; scrupoloso; (*easily nauseated*) schifiltoso, schizzinoso
squeeze [skwiz] *s* spremuta; stretta, abbraccio; **to put the squeeze on** (coll) far pressione su || *tr* premere; spremere, pigiare; stringere || *intr* stringere; **to squeeze through** aprirsi il passo attraverso; (fig) farcela a pena
squeezer ['skwizər] *s* spremifrutta *m*
squelch [skweltʃ] *s* osservazione schiacciante || *tr* schiacciare
squid [skwɪd] *s* calamaro, totano
squint [skwɪnt] *s* tendenza losca; (coll) occhiata; (pathol) strabismo || *tr* (*one's eyes*) socchiudere || *intr* socchiudere gli occhi; guardare furtivamente
squint-eyed ['skwɪnt,aɪd] *adj* guercio, losco; malevolo
squire [skwaɪr] *s* (*of a lady*) cavalier *m* servente; (Brit) proprietario terriero; (U.S.A.) giudice *m* conciliatore || *tr* (*a woman*) accompagnare
squirm [skwʌrm] *s* contorsione || *intr* contorcersi; mostrare imbarazzo; **to squirm out of** cavarsela da
squirrel ['skwʌrəl] *s* scoiattolo
squirt [skwʌrt] *s* schizzo; (*instrument*) schizzetto; (coll) saputello || *tr & intr* schizzare
stab [stæb] *s* pugnalata; (*of pain*) fitta; **to make a stab at** (coll) provare || *v* (*pret & pp* **stabbed;** *ger* **stabbing**) *tr* pugnalare, trafiggere || *intr* pugnalare
stabilize ['stebəl,aɪz] *tr* stabilizzare
stab' in the back' *s* pugnalata nella schiena or alle spalle

stable [ˈstebəl] *adj* stabile || *s* stalla; (*of race horses*) scuderia
sta′ble•boy′ *s* stalliere *m*
stack [stæk] *s* pila; (*of hay or straw*) pagliaio; (*of firewood*) catasta; (*of books*) scaffale *m;* camino; (coll) mucchio, sacco || *tr* ammonticchiare, accatastare
stadi•um [ˈstedɪ·əm] *s* (**-ums** or **-a** [ə]) stadio
staff [stæf] or [stɑf] *s* bastone *m;* asta, albero; personale *m,* corpo; (mil) stato maggiore; (mus) rigo, pentagramma *m* || *tr* dotare di personale
staff′ of′ficer *s* ufficiale *m* di stato maggiore
stag [stæg] *adj* per signori soli || *s* (*deer*) cervo; maschio; (coll) signore *m* || *adv* senza compagna
stage [stedʒ] *s* fase *f,* stadio; tappa, giornata; (*coach*) diligenza; teatro; piattaforma; (*of microscope*) piatto portaoggetti; (theat) scena, palcoscenico; **by easy stages** poco a poco; **to go on the stage** diventare attore || *tr* mettere in scena; organizzare
stage′coach′ *s* diligenza
stage′craft′ *s* scenotecnica
stage′ door′ *s* (theat) ingresso degli artisti
stage′ fright′ *s* tremarella
stage′hand′ *s* macchinista *m*
stage′ left′ *s* (theat) la sinistra della scena guardando il pubblico
stage′ man′ager *s* direttore *m* di scena
stage′ right′ *s* (theat) la destra della scena guardando il pubblico
stage′-struck′ *adj* innamorato del teatro
stage′ whis′per *s* a parte *m*
stagger [ˈstægər] *tr* far traballare; impressionare; (*troops; hours*) scaglionare || *intr* traballare
stag′gering *adj* traballante; impressionante, stupefacente
staging [ˈstedʒɪŋ] *s* impalcatura; (theat) messa in scena
stagnant [ˈstægnənt] *adj* stagnante
staid [sted] *adj* serio, grave
stain [sten] *s* macchia; tinta; colorante *m* || *tr* macchiare; tingere; colorare || *intr* macchiarsi
stained′ glass′ *s* vetro colorato
stained′-glass window′ *s* vetrata a colori
stainless [ˈstenlɪs] *adj* immacolato; (*steel*) inossidabile
stair [ster] *s* scala
stair′case′ *s* scala
stair′way′ *s* scala
stair′well′ *s* tromba delle scale
stake [stek] *s* picchetto; (*e.g., of cart*) staggio; (*to support a plant*) puntello; (*in gambling*) puglia, giocata; **at stake** in gioco; **to die at the stake** morire sul rogo; **to pull up stakes** (coll) andarsene, traslocare || *tr* picchettare; puntellare; attaccare a un palo; arrischiare; (coll) aiutare; **to stake out** picchettare; (slang) tenere sotto sorveglianza; **to stake out a claim** avanzare una pretesa
stale [stel] *adj* stantio; (*air*) viziato; (fig) ritrito
stale′mate′ *s* (chess) stallo; **to reach a stalemate** essere in una posizione di stallo || *tr* mettere in una posizione di stallo
stalk [stɔk] *s* stelo; (*of corn*) stocco; (*of salad*) piede *m* || *tr* braccare || *intr* avanzare furtivamente; camminare con andatura maestosa
stall [stɔl] *s* (*in a stable*) posta; (*booth in a market*) bancarella; (*seat*) stallo; (*space in a parking lot*) spazio per il parcheggio || *tr* (*an animal*) stallare; (*a car*) parcheggiare; (*a motor*) far fermare; **to stall off** eludere, tenere a bada || *intr* impantanarsi; stare nella posta; (*said of a motor*) fermarsi; (*to temporize*) menare il can per l'aia
stallion [ˈstæljən] *s* stallone *m*
stalwart [ˈstɔlwərt] *adj* forte, gagliardo || *s* sostenitore *m*
stamen [ˈstemən] *s* stame *m*
stamina [ˈstæmɪnə] *s* forza, vigore *m*
stammer [ˈstæmər] *s* balbuzie *f* || *tr & intr* balbettare
stammerer [ˈstæmərər] *s* balbuziente *mf*
stamp [stæmp] *s* (*postage stamp*) francobollo; (*device to show that a fee has been paid*) timbro, bollo; impressione; carattere *m;* sigillo; (*tool for stamping coins*) conio; (*tool for crushing ore*) maglio || *tr* timbrare, stampigliare, bollare; sigillare; coniare; (*one's foot*) battere, pestare; imprimere; caratterizzare; (mach) stampare; **to stamp out** spegnere; sopprimere || *intr* battere il piede; (*said of a horse*) zampare
stampede [stæmˈpid] *s* fuga precipitosa || *tr* precipitarsi verso; far fuggire precipitosamente || *intr* precipitarsi
stamp′ing ground′ *s* (coll) luogo di ritrovo abituale
stamp′ pad′ *s* tampone *m*
stamp′-vend′ing machine′ *s* distributore automatico di francobolli
stance [stæns] *s* posizione
stanch [stɑntʃ] *adj* leale; forte; a tenuta d'acqua || *s* chiusa || *tr* arrestare il flusso da; (*blood*) stagnare
stand [stænd] *s* posizione; resistenza, difesa; tribuna, palco; sostegno, supporto; (*booth in market*) posteggio; posto di sosta || *v* (*pret & pp* **stood** [stʊd]) *tr* mettere in piedi; reggere, sostenere; sopportare, tollerare; (*one's ground*) mantenere; (*a chance*) avere; (*watch*) fare; (coll) pagare; **to stand off** tenere a distanza || *intr* stare; essere alto; fermarsi; stare in piedi; trovarsi; aver forza; essere; (*e.g., apart*) tenersi; **to stand back of** spalleggiare; **to stand by** appoggiare; **to stand for** rappresentare, voler dire; appoggiare, favorire; tenere a battesimo; (coll) tollerare; **to stand in line** fare la fila or la coda; **to stand in with** (coll) essere nelle buone grazie di; **to stand out** stagliarsi, distaccarsi, risaltare; **to stand up** tenersi in piedi; resistere, durare; **to stand up to** affrontare
standard [ˈstændərd] *adj* (*usual*) nor-

male; uniforme, standard; (*language*) corretto, preferito || *s* standard *m;* (*model*) modello, campione *m;* (*flag*) stendardo
stand'ard·bear'er *s* portabandiera *m*
standardize ['stændər ˌdaɪz] *tr* standardizzare
stand'ard of liv'ing *s* tenore *m* di vita
stand'ard time' *s* ora ufficiale, ora legale
standee [stæn'di] *s* passeggero in piedi; spettatore *m* in piedi
stand'-in' *s* (mov) controfigura; **to have a stand-in with** (coll) essere nelle buone grazie di
standing ['stændɪŋ] *adj* (*jump*) da fermo; in piedi; fermo; (*water*) stagnante; vigente, permanente; (*idle*) fuori uso || *s* posizione, rango, situazione; classifica; **in good standing** riconosciuto da tutti; **of long standing** vecchio, da lungo tempo
stand'ing ar'my *s* esercito permanente
stand'ing room' *s* posto in piedi
standpatter ['stænd'pætər] *s* (coll) seguace *mf* dell'immobilismo
stand'point' *s* punto di vista
stand'still' *s* fermata; riposo; **to come to a standstill** fermarsi
stanza ['stænzə] *s* stanza
staple ['stepəl] *adj* principale || *s* articolo di prima necessità; elemento indispensabile; (*e.g., to hold wire*) cavallottino, cambretta; (*to fasten papers*) grappetta; fibra tessile || *tr* aggraffare
stapler ['steplər] *s* cucitrice *f* a grappe
star [stɑr] *s* (*any heavenly body, except the moon, appearing in the sky*) astro; (*heavenly body radiating self-produced energy*) stella; (*actor*) divo; (*actress*) diva, stella (*athlete*) asso; (fig, mov) stella; (typ) stelletta; **to thank one's lucky stars** ringraziare la propria stella || *v* (*pret & pp* **starred;** *ger* **starring**) *tr* costellare, stellare; presentare come stella; (typ) marcare con stelletta || *intr* primeggiare
starboard ['stɑrbərd] or ['stɑr ˌbord] *adj* di dritta, di tribordo || *s* dritta, tribordo || *adv* a dritta, a tribordo
starch [stɑrtʃ] *s* amido, fecola; (*in laundering*) salda; (coll) forza || *tr* inamidare
starch·y ['stɑrtʃi] *adj* (**-ier; -iest**) amidaceo; (*e.g., collar*) inamidato; (*manner*) sostenuto, contegnoso
star' dust' *s* polveri *fpl* meteoriche; (fig) polvere *f* di stelle
stare [stɛr] *s* sguardo fisso || *intr* rimirare; **to stare at** fissare gli occhi addosso a
star'fish' *s* stella di mare
star'gaze' *intr* guardare le stelle; sognare ad occhi aperti
stark [stɑrk] *adj* completo; desolato; severo, serio; duro, rigido || *adv* completamente
stark'-na'ked *adj* nudo e crudo
starlet ['stɑrlɪt] *s* stellina, divetta
star'light' *s* lume *f* delle stelle
starling ['stɑrlɪŋ] *s* storno, stornello
Stars' and Stripes' *s* bandiera stellata
Star'-Spangled Ban'ner *s* bandiera stellata
star' sys'tem *s* (mov) divismo
start [stɑrt] *s* inizio, principio; partenza; linea di partenza; (*sudden jerk*) sussulto, soprassalto; (*advantage*) vantaggio; (*spurt*) scatto || *tr* iniziare, principiare; mettere in moto; dare il via a; (*a conversation*) intavolare; (*game*) stanare || *intr* iniziare, principiare; mettersi in moto; incamminarsi; (*to be startled*) trasalire, sussultare; **to start** + *ger* mettersi a + *inf;* **to start** + *ger* + **again** rimettersi a + *inf;* **to start after** andare in cerca di
starter ['stɑrtər] *s* (*of a venture*) iniziatore *m;* partente *m;* (aut) motorino d'avviamento; (sports) mossiere *m*
starting ['stɑrtɪŋ] *adj* di partenza || *s* messa in marcia
start'ing crank' *s* manovella d'avviamento
start'ing point' *s* punto di partenza
startle ['stɑrtəl] *tr* far trasalire || *intr* trasalire, sussultare
startling ['stɑrtlɪŋ] *adj* allarmante, sorprendente
starvation [stɑr'veʃən] *s* fame *f*, inedia, inanizione
starva'tion wag'es *spl* paga da fame
starve [stɑrv] *tr* affamare; far morire di fame; **to starve out** prendere per fame || *intr* essere affamato; morire di fame
starving ['stɑrvɪŋ] *adj* famelico
state [stet] *adj* statale; ufficiale; di gala, di lusso || *s* condizione; stato; gala, pompa; **to lie in state** essere esposto in camera ardente; **to live in state** vivere sfarzosamente || *tr* dichiarare, affermare; (*a problem*) impostare
stateless ['stetlɪs] *adj* apolide
state·ly ['stetli] *adj* (**-lier; -liest**) maestoso, imponente
statement ['stetmənt] *s* dichiarazione, affermazione; comunicazione; (com) estratto conto
state' of mind' *s* stato d'animo
state'room' *s* cabina; (rr) compartimento privato
states'man *s* (**-men**) statista *m*, uomo di stato
static ['stætɪk] *adj* statico; (rad) atmosferico || *s* disturbi *mpl* atmosferici
station ['steʃən] *s* stazione; rango, condizione || *tr* stazionare
sta'tion a'gent *s* capostazione *m*
stationary ['steʃən ˌɛri] *adj* stazionario
sta'tion break' *s* (rad, telv) intervallo
stationer ['steʃənər] *s* cartolaio
stationery ['steʃən ˌɛri] *s* (*writing paper*) carta da lettere; (*writing materials*) cancelleria
sta'tionery store' *s* cartoleria
sta'tion house' *s* posto di polizia
sta'tion·mas'ter *s* capostazione *m*
sta'tion wag'on *s* giardinetta
statistical [stə'tɪstɪkəl] *adj* statistico
statistician [ˌstætɪs'tɪʃən] *s* statistico

statistics [stəˈtɪstɪks] *ssg* (*science*) statistica; *spl* (*data*) statistiche *fpl*
statue [ˈstætʃu] *s* statua
statuesque [ˌstætʃuˈɛsk] *adj* statuario
stature [ˈstætʃər] *s* statura
status [ˈstetəs] *s* stato, condizione; condizione sociale
sta'tus sym'bol *s* simbolo della posizione sociale
statute [ˈstætʃut] *s* legge *f;* regolamento
stat'ute of limita'tions *s* legge *f* che governa la prescrizione
statutory [ˈstætʃuˌtori] *adj* legale
staunch [stɔntʃ] or [stantʃ] *adj, s & tr* var of **stanch**
stave [stev] *s* (*of barrel*) doga; (*of ladder*) piolo; (mus) rigo, pentagramma *m* || *v* (*pret & pp* **staved** or **stove** [stov]) *tr* bucare; (*to smash*) sfondare; **to stave off** tenere a bada
stay [ste] *s* permanenza, soggiorno; (*brace*) staggio; (*of corset*) stecca di balena; sostegno; (law) sospensione; (naut) strallo || *tr* fermare; sospendere; poner freno a || *intr* stare; mantenersi; restare, rimanere; (*at a hotel*) sostare; **to stay up** stare alzato
stay'-at-home' *adj* casalingo || *s* persona casalinga
stead [stɛd] *s* posto; **in his stead** in suo luogo; **to stand in good stead** esser utile
stead'fast' *adj* fermo, risoluto
stead•y [ˈstedi] *adj* (**-ier; -iest**) stabile, fermo; regolare, costante; abituale; calmo, sicuro || *v* (*pret & pp* **-ied**) *tr* rinforzare; calmare || *intr* rinforzarsi; calmarsi
steak [stek] *s* bistecca
steal [stil] *s* (coll) furto || *v* (*pret* **stole** [stol]; *pp* **stolen**) *tr* rubare; involare; (*the attention*) cattivare || *intr* rubare; **to steal away** svignarsela; **to steal out** uscire di soppiatto; **to steal upon** approssimarsi silenziosamente a
stealth [stɛlθ] *s* clandestinità *f;* **by stealth** di straforo, di soppiatto
steam [stim] *adj* a vapore || *s* vapore *m;* fumo; **to get up steam** aumentare la pressione; **to let off steam** scaricare la pressione; (slang) sfogarsi || *tr* (*a steamship*) guidare; esalare; esporre al vapore; (*e.g., glasses*) appannare || *intr* dar vapore, fumigare; bollire; (*to become clouded*) appannarsi; andare a vapore; **to steam ahead** avanzare a tutto vapore
steam'boat' *s* vapore *m*
steam' en'gine *s* macchina a vapore
steamer [ˈstimər] *s* vapore *m*
steam'er rug' *s* coperta da viaggio
steam'er trunk' *s* bauletto da cabina
steam' heat' *s* riscaldamento a vapore
steam' roll'er *s* rullo compressore; (fig) rullo compressore
steam'ship' *s* piroscafo, vapore *m*
steam' shov'el *s* escavatore *m* a vapore
steam' ta'ble *s* tavola riscaldata a vapore per mantenere calde le vivande
steed [stid] *s* destriere *m*
steel [stil] *adj* d'acciaio; (*industry*) siderurgico || *s* acciaio; (*bar*) stecca d'acciaio; (*for sharpening knives*) affilacoltelli *m;* (fig) spada, brando || *tr* acciaiare; **to steel oneself** corazzarsi, indurirsi; armarsi di coraggio
steel' wool' *s* paglia di ferro
steel'works' *spl* acciaieria
steelyard [ˈstilˌjard] or [ˈstiljərd] *s* stadera
steep [stip] *adj* erto, scosceso, ripido; (*price*) alto || *tr* immergere, saturare, imbevere
steeple [ˈstipəl] *s* campanile *m;* (*spire*) cuspide *f,* guglia
stee'ple•chase' *s* corsa ad ostacoli
stee'ple•jack' *s* aggiustatore *m* di campanili
steer [stɪr] *s* bue *m,* manzo || *tr* governare, guidare; (aer) pilotare || *intr* governare; **to steer clear of** evitare
steerage [ˈstɪrɪdʒ] *s* (naut) alloggio passeggeri di terza classe
steer'ing wheel' *s* (aut) volante *m,* sterzo; (naut) ruota del timone
stellar [ˈstelər] *adj* stellare; (*role*) da stella
stem [stem] *s* (*of pipe, of key*) cannello; (*of goblet*) gambo; (*of column*) fusto; (*of spoon*) manico; (*of watch*) corona; (*of a word*) tema *m;* (*of note*) (mus) gamba; (bot) peduncolo, stelo; (bot) gambo; **from stem to stern** da poppa a prua || *v* (*pret & pp* **stemmed;** *ger* **stemming**) *tr* togliere il gambo a; (*to check*) arrestare; (*to dam up*) arginare; (*to plug*) otturare; (*the tide*) risalire, andare contro || *intr* originare, derivare
stem'-win'der *s* orologio a corona
stench [stentʃ] *s* tanfo, fetore *m*
sten•cil [ˈstensəl] *s* stampo, stampino; parole *fpl* a stampo || *v* (*pret & pp* **-ciled** or **-cilled;** *ger* **-ciling** or **-cilling**) *tr* stampinare
stenographer [stəˈnagrəfər] *s* stenografo
stenography [stəˈnagrəfi] *s* stenografia
step [stɛp] *s* passo; (*footprint*) orma, impronta; (*of ladder*) piolo; (*of staircase*) gradino; (*of carriage*) montatoio; **step by step** passo passo; **to watch one's step** fare molta attenzione || *v* (*pret & pp* **stepped;** *ger* **stepping**) *tr* scaglionare; **to step off** misurare a passi || *intr* camminare, andare a passi; mettere il piede; **to step aside** scostarsi; **to step back** indietreggiare; **to step on it** (slang) fare presto; **to step on the gas** (coll) accelerare; **to step on the starter** avviare il motore
step'broth'er *s* fratellastro, fratello consanguineo
step'child' *s* (**-children** [ˌtʃɪldrən]) figliastro
step'daugh'ter *s* figliastra
step'fa'ther *s* patrigno
step'lad'der *s* scala a gradini or a libretto
step'moth'er *s* matrigna
steppe [step] *s* steppa

step'ping stone' *s* passatoio, pietra per guadare; (fig) gradino
step'sis'ter *s* sorellastra
step'son' *s* figliastro
stere•o ['sterɪ ,o] or ['stɪrɪ ,o] *adj* stereofonico; stereoscopico || *s* (-**os**) musica stereofonica; sistema stereofonico; fotografia stereoscopica
stereotyped ['sterɪ-ə,taɪpt] or ['stɪrɪ-ə-,taɪpt] *adj* stereotipato
sterile ['sterɪl] *adj* sterile
sterilize ['sterɪ ,laɪz] *tr* sterilizzare
sterling ['stʌrlɪŋ] *adj* di lira sterlina; d'argento; puro; eccellente || *s* argento .925; vasellame *m* d'argento puro
stern [stʌrn] *adj* severo || *s* poppa
stet [stet] *v* (*pret & pp* **stetted**; *ger* **stetting**) *tr* marcare con la parola "vive"
stethoscope ['steθə ,skop] *s* stetoscopio
stevedore ['stivə ,dor] *s* stivatore *m*
stew [stju] or [stu] *s* stufato, guazzetto || *tr* stufare || *intr* cuocere a fuoco lento; (coll) preoccuparsi
steward ['stju•ərd] or ['stu•ərd] *s* amministratore *m*, agente *m;* maggiordomo; (aer, naut) cambusiere *m*, cameriere *m*
stewardess ['stju•ərdɪs] or ['stu•ərdɪs] *s* (naut) cameriera; (aer) hostess *f*, assistente *f* di volo
stewed' fruit' *s* composta di frutta
stewed' toma'toes *spl* pomodori *mpl* in umido
stick [stɪk] *s* stecco; legno; bacchetta; bastone *m;* (*e.g., of candy*) cannello; (naut) albero; (typ) compositoio; **in the sticks** (coll) in casa del diavolo || *v* (*pret & pp* **stuck** [stʌk]) *tr* pungere; ficcare, infiggere; attaccare; confondere; **to be stuck** essere insabbiato; essere attaccato; (fig) essere confuso; **to stick out** (*the head*) sporgere; (*the tongue*) cacciare; **to stick up** (slang) assaltare a mano armata, rapinare || *intr* rimanere attaccato; persistere; (*said of glue*) appiccicarsi; (*to one opinion*) tenersi; stare; **to stick out** sporgere; **to stick together** rimanere uniti; **to stick up** risaltare; (*said, e.g., of quills*) rizzarsi; **to stick up for** (coll) stare dalla parte di
sticker ['stɪkər] *s* etichetta gommata; spina; persona zelante; (coll) busillis *m*
stick'ing plas'ter *s* cerotto
stick'pin' *s* spilla da cravatta
stick'up' *s* (slang) grassazione
stick•y ['stɪki] *adj* (-**ier**; -**iest**) attaccaticcio; vischioso; (*weather*) afoso, soffocante; (fig) difficile
stiff [stɪf] *adj* rigido, duro; forte; (*price*) alto; denso || *s* (slang) cadavere *m;* **poor stiff** (slang) povero diavolo
stiff' col'lar *s* colletto duro
stiffen ['stɪfən] *tr* irrigidire || *intr* irrigidirsi
stiff' neck' *s* torcicollo; ostinazione
stiff'-necked' *adj* testardo
stiff' shirt' *s* camicia inamidata
stifle ['staɪfəl] *tr* soffocare
stigma ['stɪgmə] *s* (-**mas** or -**mata** [mətə]) stigma *m*
stigmatize ['stɪgmə ,taɪz] *tr* stigmatizzare
still [stɪl] *adj* fermo, tranquillo; silenzioso; (*wine*) non spumante || *s* calma; distillatore *m;* distilleria; (phot) fotografia singola || *adv* ancora; tuttora || *conj* tuttavia || *tr* calmare || *intr* calmarsi
still'birth' *s* parto di infante nato morto
still'born' *adj* nato morto
still' life' *s* (**lifes'**) natura morta
stilt [stɪlt] *s* trampolo; (*in water*) palafitta; (orn) trampoliere *m*
stilted ['stɪltɪd] *adj* elevato; pomposo
stimulant ['stɪmjələnt] *adj & s* stimulante *m*, eccitante *m*
stimulate ['stɪmjə ,let] *tr* stimulare
stimu•lus ['stɪmjələs] *s* (-**li** [,laɪ]) stimolo
sting [stɪŋ] *s* puntura; (*of insect*) pungiglione; (fig) scottatura || *v* (*pret & pp* **stung** [stʌŋ]) *tr & intr* pungere
stin•gy ['stɪndʒi] *adj* (-**gier**; -**giest**) tirchio, taccagno
stink [stɪŋk] *s* puzza || *v* (*pret* **stank** [stæŋk] or **stunk** [stʌŋk]; *pp* **stunk**) *tr* far puzzare || *intr* puzzare; **to stink of money** (slang) aver soldi a palate
stinker ['stɪŋkər] *s* (slang) puzzone *m*
stint [stɪnt] *s* limite *m;* lavoro assegnato, compito || *intr* lesinarsi
stipend ['staɪpənd] *s* stipendio; assegno di studio, presalario
stipulate ['stɪpjə ,let] *tr* stipulare
stir [stʌr] *s* agitazione, movimento; (*poke*) spinta; **to create a stir** creare una sensazione || *v* (*pret & pp* **stirred**; *ger* **stirring**) *tr* mescolare; muovere; (*fire*) ravvivare; (*pity*) fare; **to stir up** eccitare, svegliare; (*to rebellion*) sommuovere || *intr* muoversi, agitarsi
stirring ['stʌrɪŋ] *adj* commovente
stirrup ['stʌrəp] or ['stɪrəp] *s* staffa
stitch [stɪtʃ] *s* punto; maglia; (*pain*) fitta; (*bit*) poco, po' *m;* **to be in stitches** (coll) sbellicarsi dalle risa || *tr* cucire; aggraffare || *intr* cucire
stock [stɑk] *adj* regolare, comune; banale, ordinario; di bestiame; borsistico; azionario; (aut) di serie; (theat) stabile || *s* provvista, scorta; capitale *m* sociale; azione *f;* azioni *fpl*, titoli *mpl;* (*of tree*) tronco; (*of family; of anchor; of anvil*) ceppo; razza, famiglia; materia prima; (*of rifle*) cassa; (*broth*) brodo; (*handle*) manico; (*livestock*) bestiame *m;* (theat) compagnia stabile; **in stock** in magazzino, disponibile; **out of stock** esaurito; **stocks** gogna, berlina; **to take stock** fare l'inventario; **to take stock in** (coll) aver fede in || *tr* fornire; fornire di bestiame; fornire di pesci || *intr*—**to stock up** fare rifornimenti
stockade [stɑ'ked] *s* staccionata
stock'breed'er *s* allevatore *m* di bestiame

stock'bro'ker *s* agente *m* di cambio
stock' car' *s* automobile *f* di serie; (rr) carro bestiame
stock' com'pany *s* (theat) compagnia stabile; (com) società anonima
stock' div'idend *s* dividendo pagato in azioni
stock' exchange' *s* borsa valori
stock'fish' *s* stoccafisso
stock'hold'er *s* azionista *mf*
stock'holder of rec'ord *s* azionista *mf* registrato nei libri della compagnia
Stockholm ['stɑkhom] *s* Stoccolma
stocking ['stɑkɪŋ] *s* calza
stock' in trade' *s* stock *m;* ferri *mpl* del mestiere
stock' mar'ket *s* borsa valori
stock'pile' *s* riserva, scorta || *tr* mettere in riserva || *intr* mettere in riserva materie prime
stock' rais'ing *s* allevamento bestiame
stock'room' *s* magazzino, deposito
stock•y ['stɑki] *adj* **(-ier; -iest)** tozzo, tarchiato
stock'yard' *s* chiuso per il bestiame
stoic ['sto•ɪk] *adj & s* stoico
stoicism ['sto•ɪ ,sɪzəm] *s* stoicismo
stoke [stok] *tr* (*fire*) attizzare; (*a furnace*) caricare
stoker ['stokər] *s* fochista *m*
stolid ['stɑlɪd] *adj* impassibile
stomach ['stʌmək] *s* stomaco || *tr* (fig) digerire
stone [ston] *s* sasso, pietra; (*of fruit*) osso; (pathol) calcolo || *tr* lapidare; affilare con la pietra; (*fruit*) snocciolare
stone'-broke' *adj* (coll) senza un soldo, senza il becco di un quattrino
stone'-deaf' *adj* sordo come una campana
stone'ma'son *s* tagliapietra *m*
stone' quar'ry *s* cava di pietra
stone's' throw' *s* tiro di sasso; **within a stone's throw** a un tiro di schioppo
ston•y ['stoni] *adj* **(-ier; -iest)** di sasso, sassoso, pietroso
stooge [studʒ] *s* (theat) spalla; (slang) complice *mf*
stool [stul] *s* sgabello, seggiolino; gabinetto; (*mass evacuated*) feci *fpl*
stool' pi'geon *s* piccione *m* di richiamo; (slang) spia
stoop [stup] *s* curvatura, inclinazione; scalini *mpl* d'ingresso || *intr* inclinarsi, piegarsi; degnarsi, umiliarsi
stoop-shouldered ['stup'ʃoldərd] *adj* con le spalle cadenti
stop [stɑp] *s* fermata, sosta; arresto; otturazione, blocco; cessazione; ostacolo; (*of a check*) fermo; (*restraint*) freno; (*of organ*) registro; **to come to a stop** fermarsi; cessare; **to put a stop to** metter fine a || *v* (*pret & pp* **stopped;** *ger* **stopping**) *tr* fermare, cessare; arrestare, sospendere; tappare, otturare; (*a check*) mettere il fermo a; **to stop up** tappare, otturare || *intr* fermarsi; arrestarsi; (*said of a ship*) fare scalo; (*at an hotel*) scendere; **to stop** + *ger* smettere di or cessare di + *inf*
stop'cock' *s* rubinetto di arresto
stop'gap' *adj* provvisorio || *s* soluzione provvisoria; (*person*) tappabuchi *m*
stop'light' *s* (*traffic light*) semaforo; (aut) luce *f* di stop
stop'o'ver *s* fermata intermedia
stoppage ['stɑpɪdʒ] *s* fermata, arresto; (*of work, wages, etc.*) sospensione
stopper ['stɑpər] *s* tappo, turacciolo
stop' sign' *s* segnale *m* di fermata
stop'watch' *s* cronometro a scatto
storage ['storɪdʒ] *s* magazzinaggio; (*place for storing*) magazzino; (*of a computer*) memoria
stor'age bat'tery *s* (elec) accumulatore *m*
store [stor] *s* negozio; magazzino; (*supply*) scorta; **in store** in serbo; **to set store by** dare molta importanza a || *tr* immagazzinare; **to store away** accumulare
store'house' *s* magazzino, deposito; (*of knowledge*) miniera
store'keep'er *s* negoziante *m*
store'room' *s* magazzino; (naut) dispensa
stork [stɔrk] *s* cicogna
storm [stɔrm] *s* tempesta, temporale *m;* (*on the Beaufort scale*) burrasca; (mil) assalto; (fig) scoppio || *tr* assaltare || *intr* tempestare; imperversare; (mil) andare all'attacco
storm' cloud' *s* nuvolone *m*
storm' door' *s* controporta
storm' sash' *s* controfinestra
storm' troops' *spl* truppe *fpl* d'assalto
storm' win'dow *s* controfinestra
storm•y ['stɔrmi] *adj* **(-ier; -iest)** tempestoso, burrascoso; (fig) inquieto, violento
sto•ry ['stori] *s* **(-ries)** storia, racconto, romanzo; (*plot*) trama; (*level*) piano; (coll) storia, menzogna || *v* (*pret & pp* **-ried**) *tr* istoriare
sto'ry•tell'er *s* narratore *m,* novelliere *m;* (coll) mentitore *m*
stoup [stup] *s* (eccl) acquasantiera
stout [staʊt] *adj* grasso, obeso; forte, robusto; leale; coraggioso || *s* birra nera forte
stout-hearted ['staʊt,hɑrtɪd] *adj* coraggioso
stove [stov] *s* (*for warmth*) stufa; (*for cooking*) fornello, cucina economica
stove'pipe' *s* tubo della stufa, cannone *m;* (*hat*) (coll) tuba
stow [sto] *tr* mettere in riserva; riempire; (naut) stivare || *intr*—**to stow away** imbarcarsi clandestinamente
stowage ['sto•ɪdʒ] *s* stivaggio; (*place*) stiva
stow'a•way' *s* passeggero clandestino
straddle ['strædəl] *s* divaricamento || *tr* (*a horse*) cavalcare; (*the legs*) divaricare; favorire entrambe le parti in || *intr* cavalcare; stare a gambe divaricate; (coll) tenere il piede tra due staffe
strafe [strɑf] or [stref] *s* attacco violento || *tr* attaccare violentemente con fuoco aereo; bombardare violentemente; (slang) punire

straggle ['strægəl] *intr* sbandarsi, sviarsi; sparpagliarsi, essere sparpagliato
straggler ['stræglər] *s* ritardatario
straight [stret] *adj* diritto, ritto; (*e.g., shoulders*) quadro; candido, franco; (*honest, upright*) retto; inalterato; (*hair; whiskey*) liscio; **to set s.o. straight** mettere qlcu sulla retta via; mostrare la verità a qlcu || *s* rettilinea; (cards) scala || *adv* dritto; sinceramente; rettamente; **straight ahead** sempre diritto; **straight away** immediatamente; **to go straight** vivere onestamente
straighten ['stretən] *tr* ordinare; raddrizzare || *intr* raddrizzarsi
straight' face' *s* faccia seria
straight' flush' *s* (cards) scala reale
straight'for'ward *adj* diretto; onesto
straight' man' *s* (theat) spalla
straight' ra'zor *s* rasoio a mano libera
straight'way' *adv* immediatamente
strain [stren] *s* sforzo; fatica eccessiva; tensione, pressione; strappo muscolare; tono, stile *m;* (*family*) famiglia; tendenza, vena; (coll) lavoro severo; (mus) aria, melodia || *tr* passare, colare; (*e.g., a rope*) tirare al massimo; (*one's ear*) tendere; (*a muscle*) strappare; (*the ankle*) slogare; (*e.g., words*) storcere, forzare || *intr* colare, filtrare; tendersi, tirare; sforzarsi; fare resistenza; **to strain at** tirare; resistere a
strained [strend] *adj* (*smile*) stentato; (*relations*) teso
strainer ['strenər] *s* scolatoio
strait [stret] *s* stretto; **straits** stretto; (fig) strettezze *fpl;* **to be in dire straits** essere nei frangenti
strait' jack'et *s* camicia di forza
strait'-laced' *adj* puritano, pudibondo
strand [strænd] *s* sponda, lido; (*of metal cable*) trefolo; (*of rope*) legnolo; (*of pearls*) filo || *tr* sfilare; (*e.g., a rope*) ritorcere, intrecciare; (*e.g., a boat*) lasciare incagliato; **to be stranded** trovarsi incagliato
stranded ['strændɪd] *adj* (*ship*) incagliato, arenato; (*e.g., rope*) ritorto, intrecciato
strange [strendʒ] *adj* strano; straniero; non abituato; inusitato
stranger ['strendʒər] *s* forestiero; nuovo venuto, intruso
strangle ['stræŋgəl] *tr* strangolare; soffocare || *intr* strangolarsi; soffocarsi
strap [stræp] *s* (*of leather*) correggia; (*for holding things together*) tirante *m;* (*shoulder strap*) bretella; (*for passengers to hold on to*) manopola; (*to hold a sandal*) guiggia; (*to hold a baby*) falda; (*strop*) coramella || *v* (*pret & pp* **strapped;** *ger* **strapping**) *tr* legare con correggia or tirante; (*a razor*) affilare
strap'hang'er *s* (coll) passeggero senza posto a sedere
strapping ['stræpɪŋ] *adj* robusto; (coll) grande, enorme
stratagem ['strætədʒəm] *s* stratagemma *m*
strategic(al) [strə'tidʒɪk(əl)] *adj* strategico
strategist ['strætɪdʒɪst] *s* stratego
strate·gy ['strætɪdʒi] *s* (**-gies**) strategia
strati·fy ['strætɪ,faɪ] *v* (*pret & pp* **-fied**) *tr* stratificare || *intr* stratificarsi
stratosphere ['strætə,sfɪr] or ['stretə,sfɪr] *s* stratosfera
stra·tum ['stretəm] or ['strætəm] *s* (**-ta** [tə] or **-tums**) strato
straw [strɔ] *adj* di paglia; di nessun valore; falso, fittizio || *s* paglia; (*for drinking*) cannuccia; **I don't care a straw** non mi importa un fico; **to be the last straw** essere il colmo
straw'ber·ry *s* (**-ries**) fragola
straw'hat' *s* cappello di paglia; (*with hard crown*) paglietta
straw' man' *s* (*figurehead*) uomo di paglia; (*scarecrow*) spaventapasseri *m*
straw' mat'tress *s* paglericcio
straw' vote' *s* votazione esplorativa
stray [stre] *adj* sbandato, randagio; casuale, fortuito || *s* animale randagio || *intr* sviarsi; (fig) sbandarsi
streak [strik] *s* stria; (*of light*) raggio; (*of madness*) ramo, vena; (*of luck*) (coll) periodo; **like a streak** (coll) come un lampo || *tr* striare, venare || *intr* striarsi, venarsi; andare come un lampo
stream [strim] *s* corrente *f;* (*of light*) raggio; (*of people*) fiumana, torrente *m;* (*of cars*) fila || *intr* colare; filtrare, penetrare; (*said of a flag*) fluttuare
streamer ['strimər] *s* pennone *m;* nastro; raggio di luce
streamlined ['strim,laɪnd] *adj* aerodinamico; (aer) carenato
stream'lin'er *s* treno dal profilo aerodinamico
street [strit] *adj* stradale || *s* via, strada
street'car' *s* tram *m*
street' clean'er *s* spazzino; (mach) spazzatrice *f*
street' clothes' *spl* vestiti *mpl* da passeggio; vestito da passeggio
street' floor' *s* pianterreno
street'light' *s* lampione *m*
street' map' *s* pianta della città; stradario
street' sign' *s* segnale *m* stradale
street' sprin'kler *s* carro annaffiatoio
street' walk'er *s* passeggiatrice *f*
strength [streŋθ] *s* forza; resistenza; (*of spirituous liquors*) gradazione; (com) tendenza al rialzo; (mil) numero; **on the strength of** basandosi su
strengthen ['streŋθən] *tr* rinforzare; (fig) convalidare, rinsaldare || *intr* rinforzarsi, ingagliardirsi
strenuous ['strenju·əs] *adj* vigoroso; strenuo
stress [stres] *s* enfasi *f,* importanza; spinta; tensione, preoccupazione; accento; (mech) sollecitazione; **to lay**

stress on mettere in rilievo || *tr* (*a word*) accentare, accentuare; (*to emphasize*) accentuare; (mech) sollecitare
stress' ac'cent *s* accento di intensità
stretch [stretʃ] *s* tiro, tirata; (*in time or space*) periodo; (*of road*) tratto, percorrenza; (*of imagination*) sforzo; (rr) tratta; (slang) periodo di detenzione; **at a stretch** di un tiro || *tr* tirare; tendere, distendere; (*the imagination*) forzare; (*facts*) esagerare; (*money*) stiracchiare; (*one's legs*) sgranchirsi; (*the truth*) esagerare; **to stretch oneself** sdraiarsi || *intr* estendersi; stiracchiarsi; distendersi; **to stretch out** sdraiarsi
stretcher ['stretʃər] *s* (*for a painting*) telaio; (*tool*) tenditore *m*, tenditoio; (*to carry wounded*) barella, lettiga
stretch'er-bear'er *s* portantino
strew [stru] *v* (*pret* **strewed;** *pp* **strewed** or **strewn**) *tr* spargere, cospargere; disseminare
stricken ['strɪkən] *adj* afflitto; ferito; danneggiato
strict [strɪkt] *adj* stretto, severo
stricture ['strɪktʃər] *s* aspra critica; (pathol) stenosi *f*
stride [straɪd] *s* passo; andatura; **rapid strides** grandi passi *mpl;* **to hit one's stride** avanzare a andatura regolare; **to take s.th in one's stride** fare qlco senza sforzi || *v* (*pret* **strode** [strod]; *pp* **stridden** ['strɪdən]) *tr* attraversare a grandi passi; attraversare di un salto || *intr* camminare a grandi passi; (*majestically*) incedere
strident ['straɪdənt] *adj* stridente
strife [straɪf] *s* discordia; concorrenza
strike [straɪk] *s* (*blow*) colpo; (*stopping of work*) sciopero; (*discovery of oil, ore, etc.*) scoperta; (*of fish*) abboccatura; colpo di fortuna || *v* (*pret & pp* **struck** [strʌk]) *tr* colpire, percuotere; infiggere; (*a match*) strofinare; (*fire*) accendere; fare impressione su; incontrare improvvisamente; (*e.g., ore*) scoprire; (*roots*) mettere; (*a coin*) coniare; andare in sciopero contro; arrivare a; (*a posture*) prendere; (*the hour*) scoccare; cancellare, eliminare; (*sails*) calare; (*attention*) richiamare; **to strike it rich** scoprire una miniera; avere un colpo di fortuna || *intr* dare un colpo; cadere; (*said of a bell*) suonare; accendersi; scioperare; (mil) attaccare; **to strike out** mettersi in marcia; (*to fail*) (fig) fallire, venir meno
strike'break'er *s* crumiro
striker ['straɪkər] *s* battitore *m;* (*clapper in clock*) martelletto; (*worker*) scioperante *m*
striking ['straɪkɪŋ] *adj* impressionante, sorprendente; notevole; scioperante
strik'ing pow'er *s* potere *m* d'assalto
string [strɪŋ] *s* spago, cordicella; (*e.g., of apron*) laccio; (*of pearls*) filo; (*of onions; of lies*) filza; (*row*) fila, infilata; (mus) corda; **no strings attached** (coll) senza condizioni; **strings** strumenti *mpl* a corda; (coll) condizioni *fpl;* **to pull strings** usare influenza || *v* (*pret & pp* **strung** [strʌŋ]) *tr* legare; allacciare; infilare; infilzare; (*a racket*) munire di corde; (*to stretch*) tendere; (*a musical instrument*) mettere le corde a; (slang) ingannare; **to string along** (slang) menare per il naso; **to string up** impiccare || *intr*—**to string along with** (slang) andare d'accordo con
string' bean' *s* fagiolino
stringed' in'strument *s* strumento a corda
stringent ['strɪndʒənt] *adj* stringente; urgente; severo
string' quartet' *s* quartetto d'archi
strip [strɪp] *s* striscia; (*of metal*) lamina; (*of land*) lingua || *v* (*pret & pp* **stripped;** *ger* **stripping**) *tr* spogliare; denudare; (*a fruit*) pelare; (*a ship*) sguarnire; (*tobacco*) togliere le nervature da; scortecciare; (*thread*) spanare; **to strip of** spogliare di || *intr* spogliarsi; denudarsi; fare lo spogliarello
stripe [straɪp] *s* stria, striscia, riga, lista; tipo, qualità *f;* (mil) gallone *m* || *tr* striare, filettare, rigare
strip' min'ing *s* sfruttamento minerario a cielo aperto
strip'tease' *s* spogliarello
stripteaser ['strɪp ˌtizər] *s* spogliarellista
strive [straɪv] *v* (*pret* **strove** [strov]; *pp* **striven** ['strɪvən]) *intr* sforzarsi; lottare; **to strive to** sforzarsi di
stroke [strok] *s* colpo; (*of bell or clock*) rintocco; (*of pen*) tratto, frego; (*of brush*) pennellata; (*of arms in swimming*) bracciata; colpo apoplettico; (*caress*) carezza; (*with oar*) vogata; (*of oar or paddle*) palata; (*of a master*) tocco; (*of a piston*) corsa; (*keystroke*) battuta; (*of genius*) lampo; (*of the hour*) scocco; **to not do a stroke of work** non muovere un dito || *tr* accarezzare
stroll [strol] *s* passeggiata; **to take a stroll** fare una passeggiata || *intr* fare una passeggiata, andare a zonzo; errare
stroller ['strolər] *s* girovago; carrozzella; (*itinerant performer*) (theat) guitto
strong [strɔŋ] or [strɑŋ] *adj* forte, vigoroso; valido; acceso, zelante; (*butter*) rancido; (*cheese*) piccante; (com) sostenuto
strong'box' *s* cassaforte *f*
strong' drink' *s* bevanda alcolica
strong'hold' *s* piazzaforte *f*
strong' man' *s* (*in a circus*) maciste *m;* (*leader*) anima; dittatore *m*
strong-minded ['strɔŋ ˌmaɪndɪd] or ['strɑŋ ˌmaɪndɪd] *adj* volitivo
strong'point' *s* luogo fortificato
strontium ['strɑnʃɪ·əm] *s* stronzio
strop [strɑp] *s* coramella, affilarasoio || *v* (*pret & pp* **stropped;** *ger* **stropping**) *tr* affilare
strophe ['strofi] *s* strofa, strofe *f*

struc'tural steel' ['strʌktʃərəl] *s* profilato di acciaio
structure ['strʌktʃər] *s* struttura; edificio || *tr* strutturare
struggle ['strʌgəl] *s* lotta; sforzo || *intr* lottare; sforzare, dibattersi
strum [strʌm] *v* (*pret & pp* **strummed;** *ger* **strumming**) *tr & intr* strimpellare
strumpet ['strʌmpɪt] *s* sgualdrina, puttana
strut [strʌt] *s* controvento, puntello, saettone *m;* incedere impettito; (aer) montante || *v* (*pret & pp* **strutted;** *ger* **strutting**) *intr* pavoneggiarsi, fare la ruota
strychnine ['strɪknaɪn] or ['strɪknin] *s* stricnina
stub [stʌb] *s* (*of tree*) coppo; (*e.g., of cigar*) mozzicone *m;* (*of a check*) matrice *f,* madre *f* || *v* (*pret & pp* **stubbed;** *ger* **stubbing**) *tr* sradicare; **to stub one's toe** inciampare
stubble ['stʌbəl] *s* (*of beard*) pelo ispido; **stubbles** stoppie *fpl*
stubborn ['stʌbərn] *adj* (*headstrong*) testardo; (*resolute*) accanito; (*e.g., resistance*) ostinato; (*e.g., illness*) ribelle; (*soil*) ingrato
stuc•co ['stʌko] *s* (**-coes** or **-cos**) stucco || *tr* stuccare
stuck [stʌk] *adj* infisso; attaccato; (*glued*) incollato; (*unable to continue*) in panna; **stuck on** (slang) invaghito di
stuck'-up' *adj* (coll) presuntuoso, arrogante
stud [stʌd] *s* (*in upholstery*) borchia; bottone *m* da sparato; (*of walls*) montante *m;* (*stallion*) stallone *m;* (*for mares*) monta; (archit) bugna, bugnato || *v* (*pret & pp* **studded;** *ger* **studding**) *tr* cospergere; (*with stars*) costellare; (*with jewels*) incastonare, ingioiellare
stud' bolt' *s* prigioniero
stud'book' *s* registro della genealogia
student ['stjudənt] or ['studənt] *adj* studentesco || *s* studente *m;* scolaro; (*investigator*) studioso
stu'dent bod'y *s* scolaresca
stud'horse' *s* stallone *m*
studied ['stʌdid] *adj* premeditato; (*affected*) studiato
studi•o ['studɪ,o] or ['stjudɪ,o] *s* (**-os**) studio
studious ['stjudɪ•əs] or ['studɪ•əs] *adj* studioso; assiduo, zelante
stud•y ['stʌdi] *s* (**-ies**) studio || *v* (*pret & pp* **-ied**) *tr & intr* studiare
stuff [stʌf] *s* roba, cosa; stoffa; materiale *m;* (*nonsense*) scemenze *fpl;* medicina; (coll) mestiere *m* || *tr* riempire, inzeppare; (*one's stomach*) rimpinzare; (*e.g., poultry*) farcire; (*e.g., salami*) insaccare; (*a dead animal*) impagliare; **to stuff up** intasare || *intr* rimpinzarsi
stuffed' shirt' *s* persona altezzosa
stuffing ['stʌfɪŋ] *s* ripieno
stuff•y ['stʌfi] *adj* (**-ier; -iest**) soffocante, opprimente; (*nose*) chiuso; pedante
stumble ['stʌmbəl] *intr* incespicare, inciampare; sbagliare, impaperarsi; **to stumble on** or **upon** intopparsi in
stum'bling block' *s* inciampo, scoglio
stump [stʌmp] *s* (*of tree*) toppo, ceppo; (*e.g., of arm*) moncherino, moncone *m;* (*of cigar, candle*) mozzicone *m;* dente rotto; tribuna popolare; (*for drawing*) sfumino; **up a stump** (coll) completamente perplesso || *tr* mozzare; lasciare perplesso; (coll) fare discorsi politici in
stump' speech' *s* discorso politico
stun [stʌn] *v* (*pret & pp* **stunned;** *ger* **stunning**) *tr* tramortire; (fig) sbalordire
stunning ['stʌnɪŋ] *adj* (*blow*) che stordisce; sbalorditivo, magnifico
stunt [stʌnt] *s* atrofia; creatura striminzita; bravata, prodezza; (*for publicity*) montatura || *tr* striminzire; arrestare la crescita di || *intr* fare delle acrobazie
stunt'ed *adj* striminzito
stunt' fly'ing *s* acrobazia aerea
stunt' man' *s* (mov) controfigura
stupe•fy ['stjupɪ,faɪ] or ['stupɪ,faɪ] *v* (*pret & pp* **-fied**) *tr* istupidire, intontire
stupendous [stju'pendəs] or [stu'pendəs] *adj* stupendo
stupid ['stjupɪd] or ['stupɪd] *adj* stupido, ebete, scemo
stupor ['stjupər] or ['stupər] *s* torpore *m,* stupore *m*
stur•dy ['stʌrdi] *adj* (**-dier; -diest**) forte; (*robust*) tarchiato; risoluto
sturgeon ['stʌrdʒən] *s* storione *m*
stutter ['stʌtər] *s* tartagliamento || *tr & intr* tartagliare
sty [staɪ] *s* (**sties**) porcile *m;* (pathol) orzaiolo
style [staɪl] *s* stile *m;* tono; (*mode of living*) treno || *tr* chiamare col nome di
stylish ['staɪlɪʃ] *adj* alla moda, di tono
sty•mie ['staɪmi] *v* (*pret & pp* **-mied;** *ger* **-mieing**) *tr* ostacolare, contrastare
styp'tic pen'cil ['stɪptɪk] *s* matita emostatica
Styx [stɪks] *s* Stige *m*
suave [swɑv] or [swev] *adj* soave
subaltern [səb'ɔltərn] *adj & s* subalterno
subcommittee ['sʌbkə,mɪti] *s* sottocommissione
subconscious [səb'kɑnʃəs] *adj & s* subcosciente *m*
subconsciousness [səb'kɑnʃəsnɪs] *s* subcosciente *m,* subcoscienza
sub'deb' *s* (coll) signorina più giovane di una debuttante
subdivide ['sʌbdɪ,vaɪd] or [,sʌbdɪ'vaɪd] *tr* suddividere || *intr* suddividersi
subdue [səb'dju] or [səb'du] *tr* soggiogare, sottomettere; (*color, voice*) attenuare
subdued [səb'djud] or [səb'dud] *adj* (*voice*) sommesso; (*light*) tenue

subheading ['sʌb ˌhɛdɪŋ] *s* sottotitolo; (journ) sommario
subject ['sʌbdʒɪkt] *adj* soggetto; **subject to** (*e.g., a cold*) soggetto a; (*e.g., a fine*) passibile di || *s* soggetto, materia, proposito; (*of a ruler*) suddito; (gram, med, philos) soggetto || [səb'dʒɛkt] *tr* sottomettere
sub'ject cat'alogue *s* catalogo per materie
sub'ject in'dex *s* indice *m* per materie
subjection [səb'dʒɛkʃən] *s* soggezione
subjective [səb'dʒɛktɪv] *adj* soggettivo
sub'ject mat'ter *s* soggetto
subjugate ['sʌbdʒəˌget] *tr* soggiogare
subjunctive [səb'dʒʌŋktɪv] *adj & s* congiuntivo
sublease ['sʌb ˌlis] *s* subaffitto || [ˌsʌb'lis] *tr* subaffittare
sub•let [sʌb'let] or ['sʌb ˌlɛt] *v* (*pret & pp* **-let; ger -letting**) *tr* subaffittare
sub•machine' gun' [ˌsʌbmə'ʃin] *s* mitra *m*
submarine ['sʌbməˌrin] *adj & s* sottomarino
sub'marine chas'er ['tʃesər] *s* cacciasommergibili *m*
submerge [səb'mʌrdʒ] *tr* sommergere || *intr* sommergersi
submersion [səb'mʌrʒən] or [səb'mʌrʃən] *s* sommersione
submission [səb'mɪʃən] *s* sottomissione
submissive [səb'mɪsɪv] *adj* sottomesso
sub•mit [səb'mɪt] *v* (*pret & pp* **-mitted; ger -mitting**) *tr* sottomettere; presentare, deferire; osservare rispettosamente || *intr* sottomettersi
subordinate [səb'ɔrdɪnɪt] *adj & s* subordinato || [səb'ɔrdɪˌnet] *tr* subordinare
suborna'tion of per'jury [ˌsʌbər'neʃən] *s* subornazione
subplot ['sʌb ˌplɑt] *s* intreccio secondario
subpoena or **subpena** [sʌb'pinə] or [sə'pinə] *s* mandato di comparizione || *tr* citare
sub rosa [sʌb'rozə] *adv* in segreto
subscribe [səb'skraɪb] *tr* sottoscrivere || *intr* sottoscrivere; **to subscribe to** sottoscrivere a; (*a magazine*) abbonarsi a; (*an opinion*) approvare
subscriber [səb'skraɪbər] *s* sottoscrittore *m;* abbonato
subscription [sʌb'skrɪpʃən] *s* sottoscrizione; (*e.g., to a newspaper*) abbonamento; (*e.g., to club*) quota
subsequent ['sʌbsɪkwənt] *adj* susseguente, posteriore
subservient [səb'sʌrvɪ•ənt] *adj* subordinato; ossequioso, servile
subside [səb'saɪd] *intr* calmarsi; (*said of water*) decrescere
subsidiar•y [səb'sɪdɪˌɛri] *adj* sussidiario || *s* (**-ies**) sussidiario
subsidize ['sʌbsɪˌdaɪz] *tr* sussidiare, sovvenzionare; (*by bribery*) subornare
subsi•dy ['sʌbsɪdi] *s* (**-dies**) sussidio, sovvenzione
subsist [səb'sɪst] *intr* sussistere
subsistence [səb'sɪstəns] *s* sussistenza
subsoil ['sʌb ˌsɔɪl] *s* sottosuolo
substance ['sʌbstəns] *s* sostanza
substandard [sʌb'stændərd] *adj* inferiore al livello normale
substantial [səb'stænʃəl] *adj* considerevole; ricco, influente; (*food*) sostanzioso; (*e.g., reason*) sostanziale
substantiate [səb'stænʃɪˌet] *tr* provare, verificare; dare prova di, sostanziare
substantive ['sʌbstəntɪv] *adj & s* sostantivo
substation ['sʌb ˌsteʃən] *s* ufficio postale secondario; (elec) sottostazione
substitute ['sʌbstɪˌtjut] or ['sʌbstɪˌtut] *adj* provvisorio, interino || *s* (*thing*) sostituto, surrogato; (*person*) sostituto, supplente *mf;* **beware of substitutes** guardarsi dalle contraffazioni || *tr*—**to substitute for** sostituire (*qlco* or *qlcu*) a || *intr*—**to substitute for** sostituire, rimpiazzare, e.g., **he substituted for the teacher** sostituì il maestro
substitution [ˌsʌbstɪ'tjuʃən] or [ˌsʌbstɪ'tuʃən] *s* sostituzione; (*by fraud*) contraffazione
substra•tum [sʌb'strætəm] *s* (**-ta** [tə]) sostrato, substrato
subterfuge ['sʌbtərˌfjudʒ] *s* sotterfugio
subterranean [ˌsʌbtə'renɪ•ən] *adj & s* sotterraneo
subtitle ['sʌb ˌtaɪtəl] *s* sottotitolo; (journ) titolo corrente; (mov) didascalia || *tr* dare una didascalia a
subtle ['sʌtəl] *adj* sottile
subtle•ty ['sʌtəlti] *s* (**-ties**) sottigliezza
subtract [səb'trækt] *tr* sottrarre
subtraction [sʌb'trækʃən] *s* sottrazione
suburb ['sʌbʌrb] *s* suburbio, sobborgo; **the suburbs** la periferia
suburban [sə'bʌrbən] *adj* suburbano
suburbanite [sə'bʌrbəˌnaɪt] *s* abitante *mf* dei suburbi
subvention [səb'venʃən] *s* sovvenzione || *tr* sovvenzionare
subversive [səb'vʌrsɪv] *adj & s* sovversivo
subvert [səb'vʌrt] *tr* sovvertire
subway ['sʌb ˌwe] *s* sotterranea, metropolitana, metrovia; sottopassaggio
sub'way sta'tion *s* stazione della metropolitana
succeed [sək'sid] *tr* succedere (with *dat*), subentrare (with *dat*) || *intr* riuscire; **to succeed to** (*the throne*) succedere a
success [sək'ses] *s* successo, riuscita
successful [sək'sesfəl] *adj* felice, fortunato; che ha avuto successo
succession [sək'sɛʃən] *s* successione; **in succession** in seguito, uno dopo l'altro
successive [sək'sesɪv] *adj* successivo
succor ['sʌkər] *s* soccorso || *tr* soccorrere
succotash ['sʌkəˌtæʃ] *s* verdura di fagioli e granturco
succumb [sə'kʌm] *intr* soccombere
such [sʌtʃ] *adj & pron indef* tale, simile; **such a** un simile, un tale; **such**

a + *adj* tanto + *adj*, e.g., **such a beautiful story** una storia tanto bella; **such as** tale quale, come
suck [sʌk] *s* succhio || *tr* succhiare; (*air*) aspirare; **to suck in** (slang) ingannare
sucker ['sʌkər] *s* lattante *mf;* (bot) succhione *m;* (mach) pistone *m;* (coll) fesso, pollo, minchione *m*
suckle ['sʌkəl] *tr* allattare; nutrire || *intr* poppare
suck'ling pig' ['sʌklɪŋ] *s* maiale *m* di latte
suction ['sʌkʃən] *s* aspirazione
suc'tion cup' *s* ventosa
suc'tion pump' *s* pompa aspirante
sudden ['sʌdən] *adj* subito, improvviso; **all of a sudden** all'improvviso
suddenly ['sʌdənli] *adv* all'improvviso
suds [sʌdz] *spl* saponata; schiuma; (coll) birra
sue [su] or [sju] *tr* querelare || *intr* querelarsi; **to sue for damages** chiedere i danni; **to sue for peace** chiedere la pace
suede [swed] *s* pelle scamosciata
suet ['su·ɪt] or ['sju·ɪt] *s* grasso, sego
suffer ['sʌfər] *tr* soffrire; (*e.g., heavy losses*) subire || *intr* soffrire, patire
sufferance ['sʌfərəns] *s* tolleranza
suffering ['sʌfərɪŋ] *adj* sofferente || *s* sofferenza, strazio, patimento
suffice [sə'faɪs] *intr* bastare
sufficient [sə'fɪʃənt] *adj* sufficiente
suffix ['sʌfɪks] *s* suffisso
suffocate ['sʌfə,ket] *tr & intr* soffocare
suffrage ['sʌfrɪdʒ] *s* suffragio
suffragette [,sʌfrə'dʒet] *s* suffragetta
suffuse [sə'fjuz] *tr* soffondere
sugar ['ʃʊgər] *adj* (*water*) zuccherato; (*industry*) zuccheriero || *s* zucchero || *tr* zuccherare
sug'ar beet' *s* barbabietola da zucchero
sug'ar bowl' *s* zuccheriera
sug'ar cane' *s* canna da zucchero
sug'ar-coat' *tr* inzuccherare; (*e.g., the pill*) addolcire
sug'ar ma'ple *s* acero
sug'ar·plum' *s* zuccherino
sug'ar spoon' *s* cucchiaino per lo zucchero
sug'ar tongs' *spl* mollette *fpl* per lo zucchero
sugary ['ʃʊgəri] *adj* zuccherino, zuccheroso
suggest [səg'dʒest] *tr* suggerire
suggestion [səg'dʒestʃən] *s* suggerimento; (psychol) suggestione; ombra, traccia
suggestive [səg'dʒestɪv] *adj* suggestivo; (*risqué*) scabroso
suicidal [,su·ɪ'saɪdəl] or [,sju·ɪ'saɪdəl] *adj* suicida
suicide ['su·ɪ,saɪd] or ['sju·ɪ,saɪd] *s* (*person*) suicida *mf;* (*act*) suicidio; **to commit suicide** suicidarsi
suit [sut] or [sjut] *s* vestito da uomo; (*of a lady*) tailleur *m;* (*of cards*) seme *m*, colore *m;* (*for bathing*) costume *m;* corte *f*, corteggiamento; domanda, supplica; (law) causa; **to follow suit** seguire l'esempio; (cards) rispondere a colore || *tr* adattarsi (with *dat*); convenire (with *dat*); **suit yourself** faccia come vuole || *intr* convenire, andare a proposito
suitable ['sutəbəl] or ['sjutəbəl] *adj* indicato, conveniente
suit'case' *s* valigia
suite [swit] *s* gruppo, serie *f;* serie *f* di stanze; (*of furniture*) mobilia; (*retinue*) seguito; (mus) suite *f*
suiting ['sutɪŋ] or ['sjutɪŋ] *s* taglio d'abito
suit' of clothes' *s* completo maschile
suitor ['sutər] or ['sjutər] *s* pretendente *m;* (law) querelante *mf*
sul'fa drugs' ['sʌlfə] *spl* sulfamidici *mpl*
sulfate ['sʌlfet] *s* solfato
sulfide ['sʌlfaɪd] *s* solfuro
sulfite ['sʌlfaɪt] *s* solfito
sulfur ['sʌlfər] *adj* solfiero || *s* **zolfo;** color *m* zolfo
sulfuric [sʌl'fjʊrɪk] *adj* solforico
sul'fur mine' *s* solfara
sulfurous ['sʌlfərəs] *adj* solforoso
sulk [sʌlk] *s* broncio || *intr* imbronciarsi
sulk·y ['sʌlki] *adj* (**-ier; -iest**) imbronciato ||*s* (**-ies**) (*in horse racing*) sediolo, sulky *m*
sullen ['sʌlən] *adj* bieco, triste, tetro
sul·ly ['sʌli] *v* (*pret & pp* **-lied**) *tr* insudiciare, insozzare
sulphur ['sʌlfər] *adj & s* var of **sulfur**
sultan ['sʌltən] *s* sultano
sul·try ['sʌltri] *adj* (**-trier; -triest**) soffocante; infocato, appassionato
sum [sʌm] *s* somma; sommario; problema *m* di aritmetica || *v* (*pret & pp* **summed;** *ger* **summing**) *tr* sommare; **to sum up** riepilogare
sumac or **sumach** ['ʃumæk] or ['sumæk] *s* (bot) sommacco
summarize ['sʌmə,raɪz] *tr* riassumere
summa·ry ['sʌməri] *adj* sommario || *s* (**-ries**) sommario, sunto
summer ['sʌmər] *adj* estivo || *s* estate *f* || *intr* passare l'estate
sum'mer resort' *s* stazione estiva
summersault ['sʌmər,sɔlt] *s & intr* var of **somersault**
sum'mer school' *s* scuola estiva
summery ['sʌməri] *adj* estivo
summit ['sʌmɪt] *s* sommità *f*
sum'mit con'ference *s* riunione al vertice
summon ['sʌmən] *tr* convocare, invitare; evocare; (law) compulsare
summons ['sʌmənz] *s* ordine *m*, comando; (law) citazione || *tr* (law) citare
sumptuous ['sʌmptʃʊ·əs] *adj* sontuoso
sun [sʌn] *s* sole *m;* **place in the sun** posto al sole || *v* (*pret & pp* **sunned;** *ger* **sunning**) *tr* esporre al sole || *intr* prendere il sole
sun' bath' *s* bagno di sole
sun'beam' *s* raggio di sole
sun'burn' *s* abbronzatura || *v* (*pret & pp* **-burned** or **-burnt**) *tr* abbronzare || *intr* abbronzarsi

sundae ['sʌndi] *s* gelato con sciroppo, frutta o noci
Sunday ['sʌndi] *adj* domenicale ‖ *s* domenica
Sun'day best' *s* (coll) vestito da festa
Sun'day's child' *s* bambino nato con la camicia
Sun'day school' *s* scuola domenicale della dottrina
sunder ['sʌndər] *tr* separare
sun'di'al *s* meridiana
sun'down' *s* tramonto
sundries ['sʌndriz] *spl* generi *mpl* diversi
sundry ['sʌndri] *adj* vari, diversi
sun'fish' *s* pesce *m* mola, pesce *m* luna
sun'flow'er *s* girasole *m*
sun'glass'es *spl* occhiali *mpl* da sole
sunken ['sʌŋkən] *adj* affondato, sommerso; (*hollow*) incavato
sun' lamp' *s* sole *m* artificiale
sun'light' *s* luce *f* del sole
sun'lit' *adj* illuminato dal sole
sun•ny ['sʌni] *adj* (**-nier; -niest**) solatio, soleggiato; allegro, ridente; **it is sunny** fa sole
sun'ny side' *s* parte soleggiata; lato buono; **on the sunny side of** (*e.g., thirty*) al disotto dei . . . anni
sun' porch' *s* veranda a solatio
sun'rise' *s* sorgere *m* del sole; **from sunrise to sunset** dall'alba al tramonto
sun'set' *s* tramonto
sun'shade' *s* tenda; parasole *m*
sun'shine' *s* sole *m*, luce *f* del sole; **in the sunshine** al sole
sun'spot' *s* macchia solare
sun'stroke' *s* insolazione
sun' tan' *s* tintarella
sun'tan lo'tion *s* pomata antisole, abbronzante *m*
sun'up' *s* sorgere *m*, levare *m* del sole
sun' vi'sor *s* (aut) aletta parasole, parasole *m*
sup [sʌp] *v* (*pret & pp* **supped;** *ger* **supping**) *intr* cenare
super ['supər] *adj* (coll) superficiale; (coll) di prim'ordine, super ‖ *s* (coll) sovrintendente *m;* (coll) articolo di prim'ordine, super *m*
superabundant [,supərə'bʌndənt] *adj* sovrabbondante
superannuated [,super'ænjʊ,etɪd] *adj* giubilato, pensionato; messo a riposo per limiti di età; antiquato
superb [sʊ'pʌrb] or [sə'pʌrb] *adj* superbo
supercar•go ['supər,kɑrgo] *s* (**-goes**) (naut) sopraccarico
supercharge [,supər'tʃɑrdʒ] *tr* sovralimentare
supercilious [,supər'sɪlɪ•əs] *adj* altero, arrogante
superficial [,supər'fɪʃəl] *adj* superficiale
superfluous [sʊ'pʌrflʊ•əs] *adj* superfluo
su'per•high'way *s* autostrada
superhuman [,supər'hjumən] *adj* sovrumano
superimpose [,supərɪm'poz] *tr* sovrapporre
superintendent [,supərɪn'tendənt] *s* soprintendente *m;* (*of schools*) provveditore *m*
superior [sə'pɪrɪ•ər] or [sʊ'pɪrɪ•ər] *adj* superiore; di superiorità; (typ) esponente ‖ *s* superiore *m*
superiority [sə'pɪrɪ'ɑrɪti] or [sʊ,pɪrɪ'ɑrɪti] *s* superiorità *f*
superlative [sə'pʌrlətɪv] or [sʊ'pʌrlətɪv] *adj & s* superlativo
su'per•man' *s* (**-men'**) superuomo
supermarket ['supər,mɑrkɪt] *s* supermercato
supernatural [,supər'nætʃərəl] *adj* soprannaturale
superpose [,supər'poz] *tr* sovrapporre
supersede [,supər'sid] *tr* rimpiazzare, sostituire
supersensitive [,supər'sensɪtɪv] *adj* ipersensibile
supersonic [,supər'sɑnɪk] *adj* supersonico
superstition [,supər'stɪʃən] *s* superstizione
superstitious [,supər'stɪʃəs] *adj* superstizioso
supervene [,supər'vin] *intr* sopravvenire
supervise ['supər,vaɪz] *tr* sorvegliare, dirigere
supervision [,supər'vɪʃən] *s* supervisione, sorveglianza, direzione
supervisor ['supər,vaɪzər] *s* supervisore *m*, sorvegliante *mf;* ispettore *m*
supper ['sʌpər] *s* cena
sup'per•time' *s* ora di cena
supplant [sə'plænt] *tr* rimpiazzare
supple ['sʌpəl] *adj* flessibile; docile
supplement ['sʌplɪmənt] *s* supplemento ‖ ['sʌplɪ,ment] *tr* completare, supplire (with *dat*)
suppliant ['sʌplɪ•ənt] *adj & s* supplicante *mf*
supplicant ['sʌplɪkənt] *s* supplicante *mf*
supplication [,sʌplɪ'keʃən] *s* supplica
supplier [sʌ'plaɪ•ər] *s* fornitore *m*
sup•ply [sə'plaɪ] *s* (**-plies**) rifornimento, fornitura; provvista, scorta; (com) offerta; **supplies** rifornimenti *mpl*, vettovaglie *fpl* ‖ *v* (*pret & pp* **-plied**) *tr* fornire, provvedere; (*food*) vettovagliare
supply' and demand' *s* domanda ed offerta
support [sə'port] *s* sostegno, appoggio; puntello, rincalzo; mantenimento ‖ *tr* sostenere, appoggiare; puntellare; (*a cause*) caldeggiare; mantenere
supporter [sə'portər] *s* fautore *m*, sostenitore *m;* (*jockstrap*) sospensorio; giarrettiera; fascia elastica
suppose [sə'poz] *tr* supporre; ammettere; **suppose we take a walk?** che ne dice se facessimo una passeggiata?; **to be supposed to be** aver fama di essere; **to suppose so** credere di sì
supposed [sə'pozd] *adj* presunto
supposition [,sʌpə'zɪʃən] *s* supposizione
supposito•ry [sə'pɑzɪ,tori] *s* (**-ries**) suppositorio, supposta
suppress [sə'pres] *tr* sopprimere

suppression [sə'prɛʃən] *s* soppressione
suppurate ['sʌpjə,ret] *intr* suppurare
supreme [sə'prim] or [sʊ'prim] *adj* supremo, sommo
Supreme' Court' *s* (*in Italy*) Corte *f* di Cassazione; (*in U.S.A.*) tribunale *m* di ultima istanza
surcharge ['sʌr,tʃɑrdʒ] *s* soprapprezzo; soprattassa; sovraccarico; (philately) sovrastampa ‖ [,sʌr'tʃɑrdʒ] or ['sʌr,tʃɑrdʒ] *tr* sovraccaricare
sure [ʃʊr] *adj* sicuro; **to be sure!** certamente!, senza dubbio! ‖ *interj* (coll) certamente!; **sure enough!** (coll) difatti
sure-footed ['ʃʊr'fʊtɪd] *adj* dal piede sicuro
sure' thing' *s* (coll) successo garantito ‖ *adv* (coll) certamente ‖ *interj* (coll) di sicuro!
sure•ty ['ʃʊrti] or ['ʃʊrɪti] *s* (**-ties**) malleveria
surf [sʌrf] *s* frangente *m*
surface ['sʌrfɪs] *adj* superficiale ‖ *s* superficie *f* ‖ *tr* rifinire; spianare; ricoprire ‖ *intr* emergere
sur'face mail' *s* posta ordinaria
surf'board' *s* tavola per il surfing
surfeit ['sʌrfɪt] *s* eccesso; sazietà *f* ‖ *tr* saziare, rimpinzare ‖ *intr* saziarsi, rimpinzarsi
surf'ing *s* surfing *m*
surge [sʌrdʒ] *s* ondata; fiotto; (elec) sovratensione ‖ *intr* ondeggiare, fluttuare; (*said, e.g., of a crowd*) affluire
surgeon ['sʌrdʒən] *s* (medico) chirurgo
surger•y ['sʌrdʒəri] *s* (**-ies**) chirurgia; sala operatoria
surgical ['sʌrdʒɪkəl] *adj* chirurgico
sur•ly ['sʌrli] *adj* (**-lier; -liest**) arcigno, imbronciato
surmise [sər'maɪz] or ['sʌrmaɪz] *s* congettura, supposizione ‖ [sər'maɪz] *tr & intr* congetturare, supporre
surmount [sər'maʊnt] *tr* sormontare; coronare
surname ['sʌr,nem] *s* cognome *m;* (*added name*) soprannome *m* ‖ *tr* dare il cognome a; soprannominare
surpass [sər'pæs] or [sər'pɑs] *tr* sorpassare, superare
surplice ['sʌrplɪs] *s* cotta
surplus ['sʌrplʌs] *adj* eccedente ‖ *s* sopravanzo, eccedenza
surprise [sər'praɪz] *adj* insperato, improvviso ‖ *s* sorpresa ‖ *tr* sorprendere
surprise' par'ty *s* improvvisata
surprising [sər'praɪzɪŋ] *adj* sorprendente
surrender [sə'rɛndər] *s* resa ‖ *tr* arrendere ‖ *intr* arrendersi
surren'der val'ue *s* (ins) valore *m* di riscatto
surreptitious [,sʌrɛp'tɪʃəs] *adj* clandestino, nascosto, furtivo
surround [sə'raʊnd] *tr* circondare, contornare; (mil) aggirare
surrounding [sə'raʊndɪŋ] *adj* circostante, circonvicino ‖ **surroundings** *spl* dintorni *mpl;* ambiente *m*
surtax ['sʌr,tæks] *s* sovrimposta, soprattassa; imposta complementare
surveillance [sər'veləns] or [sər'veljəns] *s* sorveglianza, vigilanza
survey ['sʌrve] *s* quadro generale, schizzo; indagine *f;* (*of opinion*) sondaggio; rapporto; rilievo topografico; perizia ‖ [sʌr've] or ['sʌrve] *tr* fare un'indagine di; sondare; rilevare; misurare ‖ *intr* fare un rilievo
sur'vey course' *s* corso di rassegna generale
surveyor [sər've•ər] *s* livellatore *m*, geometra *m*
survival [sər'vaɪvəl] *s* sopravvivenza
survive [sər'vaɪv] *tr* sopravvivere (with *dat*) ‖ *intr* sopravvivere
surviving [sər'vaɪvɪŋ] *adj* superstite
survivor [sər'vaɪvər] *s* sopravvissuto, superstite *mf*
survivorship [sər'vaɪvər,ʃɪp] *s* (law) sopravvivenza
susceptible [sə'sɛptɪbəl] *adj* suscettibile, ricettivo; impressionabile; **susceptible to** (*e.g., colds*) soggetto a
suspect ['sʌspɛkt] or [səs'pɛkt] *adj* sospetto ‖ ['sʌspɛkt] *s* sospetto ‖ [səs'pɛkt] *tr* sospettare
suspend [səs'pɛnd] *tr* sospendere ‖ *intr* essere sospeso; fermarsi; fermare i pagamenti
suspenders [səs'pɛndərz] *spl* bretelle *fpl*
suspense [səs'pɛns] *s* sospensione; sospeso; **in suspense** in sospeso
suspen'sion bridge' [səs'pɛnʃən] *s* ponte sospeso
suspicion [səs'pɪʃən] *s* sospetto
suspicious [səs'pɪʃəs] *adj* (*subject to suspicion*) sospetto; (*inclined to suspect*) sospettoso
sustain [səs'ten] *tr* sostenere, sorreggere; (*with food*) sostentare; (*a conversation*) mantenere; (*a loss*) soffrire; (law) confermare
sustenance ['sʌstɪnəns] *s* sostentamento
sutler ['sʌtlər] *s* (mil) vivandiere *m*
swab [swɑb] *s* (mil) scovolo; (naut) redazza; (surg) batufolo di cotone ‖ *v* (*pret & pp* **swabbed;** *ger* **swabbing**) *tr* pulire con la redazza; spugnare; assorbire col cotone
swaddle ['swɑdəl] *tr* fasciare
swad'dling clothes' *spl* fasce *fpl* del neonato
swagger ['swægər] *s* spavalderia ‖ *intr* fare lo spavaldo
swain [swen] *s* innamorato; (*lad*) contadinotto
swallow ['swɑlo] *s* (*of liquid*) sorso; (*of food*) boccone *m;* (orn) rondine *f* ‖ *tr & intr* trangugiare, inghiottire
swal'low-tailed coat' ['swɑlo,teld] *s* frac *m*, marsina, abito a coda di rondine
swal'low•wort' *s* vincetossico
swamp [swɑmp] *s* pantano, palude *f* ‖ *tr* inondare, sommergere
swamp•y ['swɑmpi] *adj* (**-ier; -iest**) paludoso, pantanoso
swan [swɑn] *s* cigno
swan' dive' *s* volo dell'angelo

swank [swæŋk] *adj* (coll) elegante, vistoso || *s* (coll) eleganza vistosa
swan's-down ['swɑnz,daʊn] *s* piuma di cigno, piumino; mollettone *m*
swan' song' *s* canto del cigno
swap [swɑp] *s* scambio, baratto || *v* (*pret & pp* **swapped;** *ger* **swapping**) *tr & intr* scambiare, barattare
swarm [swɔrm] *s* sciame *m* || *intr* sciamare; (fig) formicolare
swarth·y ['swɔrði] or ['swɔrθi] *adj* (**-ier; -iest**) olivastro, abbronzato
swashbuckler ['swɑʃ,bʌklər] *s* spadaccino, rodomonte *m*
swat [swɑt] *s* colpo || *v* (*pret & pp* **swatted;** *ger* **swatting**) *tr* colpire; (*a fly*) schiacciare
sway [swe] *s* dondolio, ondeggiamento; dominio || *tr* dondolare, fare oscillare; influenzare; dominare || *intr* dondolarsi, ondulare; oscillare
swear [swer] *v* (*pret* **swore** [swor]; *pp* **sworn** [sworn]) *tr* giurare; (*to secrecy*) fare giurare; **to swear in** fare prestar giuramento a; **to swear off** giurare di rinunziare a; **to swear out a warrant** ottenere un atto di accusa sotto giuramento || *intr* giurare; (*to blaspheme*) bestemmiare; **to swear at** maledire; **to swear by** giurare su, avere certezza di; **to swear to** dichiarare sotto giuramento; giurare di + *inf*
swear'word' *s* bestemmia, parolaccia
sweat [swet] *s* sudata; sudore *m* || *v* (*pret & pp* **sweat** or **sweated**) *tr* sudare; far sudare; **to sweat it out** (slang) farcela fino alla fine; **to sweat off** (*weight*) perdere sudando || *intr* sudare
sweater ['swetər] *s* maglione *m*, golf *m*, sweater *m*
sweat' shirt' *s* maglione *m* da ginnastica
sweat·y ['sweti] *adj* (**-ier; -iest**) sudato; che fa sudare
Swede [swid] *s* svedese *mf*
Sweden ['swidən] *s* la Svezia
Swedish ['swidɪʃ] *adj & s* svedese *m*
sweep [swip] *s* scopata; movimento circolare; estensione; curva; (*of wind*) soffio; (*of well*) mazzacavallo; **to make a clean sweep of** far piazza pulita di || *v* (*pret & pp* **swept** [swept]) *tr* spazzare, scopare; percorrere con lo sguardo; (*eyes*) dirigere; travolgere || *intr* scopare; passare; estendersi; dragare
sweeper ['swipər] *s* spazzino; (*machine*) spazzatrice *f;* (nav) dragamine *m*
sweeping ['swipɪŋ] *adj* esteso; travolgente, decisivo || **sweepings** *spl* spazzatura
sweep'-sec'ond *s* lancetta dei secondi a perno centrale
sweep'stakes' *ssg* or *spl* lotteria abbinata alle corse dei cavalli
sweet [swit] *adj* dolce; (*butter*) senza sale; (*cider*) analcolico; **to be sweet on** (coll) essere innamorato di || **sweets** *spl* dolci *mpl;* (coll) patate *fpl* dolci || *adv* dolcemente; **to smell sweet** saper di buono
sweet'bread' *s* animella
sweet'bri'er *s* eglantina
sweeten ['switən] *tr* inzuccherare; raddolcire; purificare || *intr* raddolcirsi; purificarsi
sweet'heart' *s* innamorato; innamorata; caro, amore *m*
sweet' mar'joram *s* maggiorana
sweet'meats' *spl* dolci *mpl,* confetti *mpl*
sweet' pea' *s* pisello odoroso
sweet' pota'to *s* batata, patata americana; (mus) ocarina
sweet-scented ['swit,sentɪd] *adj* odoroso, profumato
sweet' tooth' *s* debole *m* per i dolci
sweet-toothed ['swit,tuθt] *adj* goloso
sweet' wil'liam *s* garofano barbuto
swell [swel] *adj* (slang) elegante; (slang) eccellente, di prim'ordine || *s* gonfiore *m;* onda, ondata; aumento; (mus) crescendo; (slang) elegantone *m* || *v* (*pret* **swelled;** *pp* **swelled** or **swollen** ['swolən]) *tr* gonfiare, ingrossare; aumentare || *intr* gonfiare, ingrossarsi; aumentare; (*said of the sea*) alzarsi; (*with pride*) montarsi
swelled' head' *s* borioso; **to have a swelled head** montarsi, essere pieno di sé
swelter ['sweltər] *intr* soffocare dal caldo
swept'back wing' *s* ala a freccia
swerve [swʌrv] *s* scarto, sbandamento || *tr* sviare || *intr* scartare, sbandare
swift [swɪft] *adj* rapido || *s* rondone *m* || *adv* rapidamente
swig [swɪg] *s* (coll) sorso || *v* (*pret & pp* **swigged;** *ger* **swigging**) *tr & intr* (coll) bere a grandi sorsi
swill [swɪl] *s* imbratto; risciacquatura || *tr* tracannare, trincare || *intr* bere a lunghi sorsi
swim [swɪm] *s* nuoto; **the swim** (*in social activities*) la corrente || *v* (*pret* **swam** [swæm]; *pp* **swum** [swʌm]; *ger* **swimming**) *tr* traversare a nuoto || *intr* nuotare; essere inondato; (*said of one's head*) girare, e.g., **her head is swimming** le gira la testa
swimmer ['swɪmər] *s* nuotatore *m*
swimming ['swɪmɪŋ] *s* nuoto
swim'ming pool' *s* piscina
swim'ming trunks' *spl* mutandine *fpl* da bagno
swim'suit' *s* costume *m* da bagno
swindle ['swɪndəl] *s* truffa, imbroglio || *tr* truffare, imbrogliare
swine [swaɪn] *s* suino, maiale *m,* porco; **swine** *spl* suini *mpl*
swing [swɪŋ] *s* oscillazione; dondolio; curva; (*suspended seat*) altalena; alternarsi *m;* piena attività; (boxing) sventola; (mus) swing *m;* **free swing** libertà *f* d'azione; **in full swing** (coll) in piena attività || *v* (*pret & pp* **swung** [swʌŋ]) *tr* (*e.g., one's arms*) dondo-

lare, oscillare; (*a weapon*) brandire; (*e.g., a club*) rotare; far girare; appendere; (*a deal*) (coll) riuscire ad ottenere || *intr* dondolare, dondolarsi, oscillare; girare; essere sospeso; cambiare; (boxing) dare una sventola; **to swing open** aprirsi di colpo
swing'ing door' ['swɪŋɪŋ] *s* porta oscillante
swinish ['swaɪnɪʃ] *adj* porcino
swipe [swaɪp] *s* (coll) colpo forte || *tr* (coll) dare un forte colpo a; (slang) portare via, rubare
swirl [swʌrl] *s* turbine *m*, vortice *m* || *tr* far girare || *intr* turbinare
swirling ['swʌrlɪŋ] *adj* vorticoso
swish [swɪʃ] *s* (*of whip*) schiocco; (*of silk*) fruscio || *tr* (*a whip*) schioccare; || *intr* schioccare; frusciare
Swiss [swɪs] *adj* svizzero || *s* svizzero; **the Swiss** gli svizzeri
Swiss' chard' [tʃard] *s* bietola
Swiss' cheese' *s* groviera
Swiss' Guards' *spl* guardie *fpl* svizzere
switch [swɪtʃ] *s* verga; vergata; (*false hair*) posticcio; cambio, trapasso; (elec) interruttore *m;* (rr) scambio || *tr* battere, frustare; (elec) commutare; (rr) deviare; (fig) girare; **to switch off** (*light, radio, etc.*) spegnere; **to switch on** (*light, radio, etc.*) accendere || *intr* fustigare; cambiare; (rr) deviare
switch'back' *s* strada a zigzag; (rr) tracciato a zigzag
switch'blade knife' *s* coltello a serramanico
switch'board' *s* quadro
switch'board op'erator *s* centralinista *mf*
switch'ing en'gine *s* locomotiva da manovra
switch'man *s* (**-men**) deviatore *m*
switch'yard' *s* stazione smistamento
Switzerland ['swɪtsərlənd] *s* la Svizzera
swiv•el ['swɪvəl] *s* perno, gancio girevole || *v* (*pret & pp* **-eled** or **-elled;** *ger* **-eling** or **-elling**) *intr* girare
swiv'el chair' *s* sedia girevole
swoon [swun] *s* deliquio, svenimento || *intr* svenire
swoop [swup] *s* calata a piombo || *intr* calare a piombo, piombare
sword [sord] *s* spada; **at swords' points** pronti a incrociare le spade; **to put to the sword** passare a fil di spada
sword' belt' *s* cinturone *m*
sword' cane' *s* bastone animato
sword'fish' *s* pesce *m* spada
swords'man *s* (**-men**) spadaccino
sword' swal'lower ['swalo•ər] *s* giocoliere *m* che ingoia spade
sword' thrust' *s* stoccata
sworn [sworn] *adj* giurato
sycophant ['sɪkəfənt] *s* adulatore *m;* parassita *mf*
syllable ['sɪləbəl] *s* sillaba
sylla•bus ['sɪləbəs] *s* (**-bi** [,baɪ]) sillabo, sommario scolastico
syllogism ['sɪlə,dʒɪzəm] *s* sillogismo
sylph [sɪlf] *s* silfo; silfide *f;* (fig) silfide *f*
sylvan ['sɪlvən] *adj* silvano
symbol ['sɪmbəl] *s* simbolo
symbolic(al) [sɪm'balɪk(əl)] *adj* simbolico
symbolism ['sɪmbə,lɪzəm] *s* simbolismo
symbolize ['sɪmbə,laɪz] *tr* simboleggiare
symmetric(al) [sɪ'metrɪk(əl)] *adj* simmetrico
symme•try ['sɪmɪtri] *s* (**-tries**) simmetria
sympathetic [,sɪmpə'θetɪk] *adj* simpatetico; ben disposto
sympathize ['sɪmpə,θaɪz] *intr*—**to sympathize with** aver compassione di; mostrar comprensione per; (*to be in accord with*) simpatizzare con
sympa•thy ['sɪmpəθi] *s* (**-thies**) compassione, commiserazione; **to be in sympathy with** essere d'accordo con; **to extend one's sympathy to** fare le condoglianze a
sym'pathy strike' *s* sciopero di solidarietà
symphonic [sɪm'fanɪk] *adj* sinfonico
sympho•ny ['sɪmfəni] *s* (**-nies**) sinfonia
symposi•um [sɪm'pozɪ•əm] *s* (**-a** [ə]) simposio, colloquio
symptom ['sɪmptəm] *s* sintomo
synagogue ['sɪnə,gɔg] or ['sɪnə,gag] *s* sinagoga
synchronize ['sɪŋkrə,naɪz] *tr & intr* sincronizzare
synchronous ['sɪŋkrənəs] *adj* sincrono
sincopation [,sɪŋkə'peʃən] *s* sincope *f*
syncope ['sɪŋkə,pi] *s* (phonet) sincope *f*
syndicate ['sɪndɪkɪt] *s* sindacato || ['sɪndɪ,ket] *tr* organizzare in un sindacato
synonym ['sɪnənɪm] *s* sinonimo
synonymous [sɪ'nanɪməs] *adj* sinonimo
synop•sis [sɪ'napsɪs] *s* (**-ses** [siz]) sinossi *f;* (mov) sinopsi *f*
synoptic(al) [sɪ'naptɪk(əl)] *adj* sinottico
syntax ['sɪntæks] *s* sintassi *f*
synthe•sis ['sɪnθɪsɪs] *s* (**-ses** [,siz]) sintesi *f*
synthesize ['sɪnθɪ,saɪz] *tr* sintetizzare
synthetic(al) [sɪn'θetɪk(əl)] *adj* sintetico
syphilis ['sɪfɪlɪs] *s* sifilide *f*
Syria ['sɪrɪ•ə] *s* la Siria
Syrian ['sɪrɪ•ən] *adj & s* siriano
syringe [sɪ'rɪndʒ] or ['sɪrɪndʒ] *s* (*fountain syringe*) schizzetto; (*for hypodermic injections*) siringa || *tr* schizzettare; iniettare
syrup ['sɪrəp] or ['sʌrəp] *s* sciroppo
system ['sɪstəm] *s* sistema *m*
systematic(al) [,sɪstə'mætɪk(əl)] *adj* sistematico
systematize ['sɪstəmə,taɪz] *tr* ridurre a sistema
systole ['sɪstəli] *s* sistole *f*

T

T, t [ti] *s* ventesima lettera dell'alfabeto inglese; **to fit to a T** calzare come un guanto
tab [tæb] *s* (*strap*) linguetta; (*of a pocket*) patta; targa; (*label*) etichetta; **to keep tabs on** (coll) sorvegliare; **to pick up the tab** (coll) pagare il conto
tab•by ['tæbi] *s* (**-bies**) gatto tigrato; gatta; (*spinster*) zitella; vecchia pettegola
tabernacle ['tæbər ,nækəl] *s* tabernacolo
table ['tebəl] *s* tavola; (*food*) mensa; (*people at a table*) tavolata; (*synopsis*) quadro, prospetto; (*list or catalogue*) indice *m;* **to turn the tables** rovesciare la posizione; **under the table** ubriaco fradicio || *tr* aggiornare, rinviare
tab•leau ['tæblo] *s* (**-leaus** or **-leaux** [loz]) quadro vivente
ta'ble•cloth' *s* tovaglia
table d'hôte ['tɑbəl'dot] *s* pasto a prezzo fisso
tableful ['tebəl ,fʊl] *s* (*persons*) tavolata; (*food*) tavola apparecchiata
ta'ble•land' *s* tavoliere *m*
ta'ble lin'en *s* biancheria da tavola
ta'ble man'ners *spl* maniere *fpl* a tavola
ta'ble of con'tents *s* indice *m* delle materie
ta'ble•spoon' *s* cucchiaio
tablespoonful ['tebəl ,spun ,fʊl] *s* cucchiaiata
tablet ['tæblɪt] *s* (*writing pad*) blocco; (*slab*) lapide *f;* (*flat rigid sheet*) tabella, tavoletta; (pharm) disco, pastiglia
ta'ble talk' *s* conversazione familiare a tavola
ta'ble ten'nis *s* ping-pong *m,* tennis *m* da tavolo
ta'ble•ware' *s* servizio da tavola
ta'ble wine' *s* vino da pasto
tabloid ['tæblɔɪd] *s* giornale *m* a carattere sensazionale
taboo [tə'bu] *adj & s* tabù *m* || *tr* proibire assolutamente
tabulate ['tæbjə ,let] *tr* tabulare
tabulator ['tæbjə ,letər] *s* tabulatore *m,* incolonnatore *m*
tachometer [tə'kɑmɪtər] *s* tachimetro
tacit ['tæsɪt] *adj* tacito
taciturn ['tæsɪ ,tʌrn] *adj* taciturno
tack [tæk] *s* bulletta; cambio di direzione; (naut) virata; (sew) imbastitura || *tr* imbullettare; attaccare; (naut) bordeggiare; (sew) imbastire || *intr* virare; mutare di direzione
tackle ['tækəl] *s* attrezzatura; (mach) taglia, paranco; (*gear*) (naut) padiglione *m* || *tr* attaccare, affrontare; (sports) placcare, bloccare
tack•y ['tæki] *adj* (**-ier; -iest**) appiccicaticcio; (coll) trasandato
tact [tækt] *s* tatto
tactful ['tæktfəl] *adj* pieno di tatto
tactical ['tæktɪkəl] *adj* tattico
tactician [tæk'tɪʃən] *s* tattico
tactics ['tæktɪks] *ssg* (mil) tattica || *spl* tattica
tactless ['tæktlɪs] *adj* che non ha tatto, indiscreto
tadpole ['tæd ,pol] *s* girino
taffeta ['tæfɪtə] *s* taffettà *m*
taffy ['tæfi] *s* caramella, zucchero d'orzo; (coll) lisciata
tag [tæg] *s* etichetta; (*on a shoelace*) punta dell'aghetto; conclusione; (*last words of speech*) pistolotto finale; epiteto; frase fatta; (*of hair*) ciocca; (*in writing*) ghirigoro; (*game*) toccaferro || *v* (*pret & pp* **tagged;** *ger* **tagging**) *tr* etichettare; (*to fine*) multare; aggiungere; soprannominare; accusare; stabilire il prezzo di; (coll) pedinare || *intr* seguire da presso
tag' end' *s* (*e.g., of day*) fine *f;* estremità logorata; avanzo
tail [tel] *adj* di coda || *s* coda; fine *f;* (*of coin*) croce *f;* **tails** falde *fpl,* frac *m;* **to turn tails** darsela a gambe || *tr* attaccare; finire; (coll) pedinare
tail' assem'bly *s* (aer) impennaggio
tail' end' *s* coda, fine *f*
tail'light' *s* fanale *m* di coda
tailor ['telər] *s* sarto || *tr* (*a suit*) tagliare, confezionare; (*one's conduct*) adattare || *intr* fare il sarto
tailoring ['telərɪŋ] *s* sartoria
tai'lor-made' *adj* fatto su misura
tai'lor shop' *s* sartoria
tail'piece' *s* coda, estremità *f;* (mus) cordiera; (typ) fusello finale
tail'race' *s* canale *m* di scarico
tail'spin' *s* avvitamento
tail'wind' *s* (aer) vento di coda; (naut) vento in poppa
taint [tent] *s* macchia; infezione || *tr* macchiare, infettare, corrompere
take [tek] *s* presa; (*of fish*) retata; (mov) presa; ripresa; (slang) incasso || *v* (*pret* **took** [tʊk]; *pp* **taken**) *tr* prendere, pigliare; ricevere, accettare; portare; (*to get by force*) portar via; (*a nap*) schiacciare; (*a bath*) fare; (*a joke*) stare a; (*an examination*) sostenere; (*one's own life*) togliersi; (*to deduct*) cavare; (*a purchase*) comprare; (*to convey*) portare; (*time*) impiegare; (*a step, a walk*) fare; (*a subject*) studiare; (*a responsibility, role, etc.*) assumere; (*an oath*) prestare; (*root*) mettere; (*exception*) sollevare; credere; (*e.g., a photograph*) fare, scattare; (slang) fregare; **it takes** ci vuole, ci vogliono; **to take amiss** prendere a male; **to take apart** scomporre; smontare; **to take back** riprendere; **to take down** abbassare; smontare; prender nota di; **to take for** prendere per; **to take from** portar via a; **to take in** (*to admit*) ammettere, ricevere; (*to encompass*) includere; (*a dress*) restringere; (*to cheat*) ingannare; (*water*) fare; (*a point of inter-*

est) visitare; **to take it** accettare, ammettere; (slang) resistere; **to take off** (*e.g., one's coat*) togliersi; portar via; scontare, defalcare; (slang) imitare; **to take on** ingaggiare; assumere; intraprendere; accettare la sfida di; **to take out** cavare, togliere; (*e.g., a girl*) portar fuori; (*e.g., a patent*) ottenere; **to take over** rilevare; (slang) imbrogliare; **to take place** aver luogo; **to take s.o.'s eye** attrarre l'attenzione di qlcu; **to take the place of** sottentrare a; **to take up** cominciare a studiare; sollevare, tirar su; (*a duty*) assumere; (*time, space*) occupare || *intr* prendere; scattare; darsi; diventare; **to take after** rassomigliare a; **to take off** (coll) partire, andarsene; (aer) decollare, involare; **to take up with** (coll) fare amicizia con; (coll) vivere con; **to take well** riuscire bene in fotografia

take'off' *s* parodia; (aer) decollaggio; (mach) presa di forza

tal'cum pow'der ['tælkəm] *s* talco

tale [tel] *s* storia, racconto; favola, fiaba; (*lie*) bugia, frottola; (*piece of gossip*) maldicenza

tale'bear'er *s* pettegolo

talent ['tælənt] *s* talento; persona di talento; gente *f* di talento

talented ['tæləntɪd] *adj* dotato di talento, dotato d'ingegno

tal'ent scout' *s* scopritore *m* di talenti

talk [tɔk] *s* chiacchierata; discorso, conferenza; (*language*) parlata; (*gossip*) pettegolezzo; **to cause talk** originare pettegolezzi || *tr* parlare; convincere parlando; **to talk up** elogiare || *intr* parlare; discutere; **to talk on** discutere; continuare a parlare; **to talk up** parlare apertamente

talkative ['tɔkətɪv] *adj* loquace

talker ['tɔkər] *s* parlatore *m*

talkie ['tɔki] *s* (coll) parlato

talk'ing machine' *s* grammofono

talk'ing pic'ture *s* film parlato

tall [tɔl] *adj* alto; (coll) stravagante, esagerato

tallow ['tælo] *s* sego

tal·ly ['tæli] *s* (**-lies**) tacca, taglia || *v* (*pret & pp* **-lied**) *tr* contare, registrare || *intr* riscontrare

tal'ly sheet' *s* foglio di spunta

talon ['tælən] *s* artiglio

tambourine [,tæmbə'rin] *s* tamburello

tame [tem] *adj* addomesticato; docile, mansueto; mite || *tr* addomesticare; domare; (*water power*) captare

tamp [tæmp] *tr* pigiare, comprimere; (*e.g., ground*) costipare

tamper ['tæmpər] *s* (*person*) pigiatore *m;* (*tool*) mazzeranga || *intr* intrigare; **to tamper with** (*a lock*) forzare; (*a document*) manomettere; (*a witness*) corrompere

tampon ['tæmpɑn] *s* (surg) tampone *m* || *tr* (surg) tamponare

tan [tæn] *adj* marrone; (*by sun*) abbronzato || *v* (*pret & pp* **tanned;** *ger* **tanning**) *tr* (*leather*) conciare; abbronzare; (coll) picchiare, sculacciare

tandem ['tændəm] *adj & adv* in tandem || *s* tandem *m*

tang [tæŋ] *s* sapore *m* piccante; odore *m* forte; traccia; (*of knife*) tallone *m;* (*sound*) tintinnio

tangent ['tændʒənt] *adj* tangente || *s* tangente *f;* **to fly off at a tangent** cambiare improvvisamente d'idea

tangerine [,tændʒə'rin] *s* mandarino

tangible ['tændʒɪbəl] *adj* tangibile

Tangier [tæn'dʒɪr] *s* Tangeri *f*

tangle ['tæŋgəl] *s* intrico; (coll) litigio || *tr* intricare || *intr* intricarsi; (coll) litigare

tank [tæŋk] *s* conserva, serbatoio; (mil) carro armato

tankard ['tæŋkərd] *s* boccale *m*

tank' car' *s* (rr) carro botte

tanker ['tæŋkər] *s* petroliera; (aer) aerocisterna

tank' farm'ing *s* idroponica

tank' truck' *s* autocisterna

tanner ['tænər] *s* conciapelli *m*

tanner·y ['tænəri] *s* (**-ies**) conceria

tantalize ['tæntə,laɪz] *tr* stuzzicare con vane promesse

tantamount ['tæntə,maunt] *adj* equivalente

tantrum ['tæntrəm] *s* bizze *fpl*

tap [tæp] *s* colpetto, buffetto; (*in a keg*) spina, cannella; (*faucet*) rubinetto; (elec) presa; (mach) maschio; **on tap** alla spina; (coll) disponibile; **taps** (mil) silenzio || *v* (*pret & pp* **tapped;** *ger* **tapping**) *tr* battere; picchiare, picchiettare; (*from a barrel*) spillare; mettere il cannello a; (*resources*) usare; (*a telephone*) intercettare; (*water, electricity*) derivare; (mach) maschiare || *intr* picchiare

tap' dance' *s* tip tap *m*

tap'-dance' *intr* ballare il tip tap

tape [tep] *s* nastro; (sports) striscione *m* del traguardo || *tr* legare con nastro; misurare col metro a nastro; registrare su nastro magnetico

tape' meas'ure *s* metro a nastro; nastro per misurare

tape' play'er *s* riproduttore *m* a nastro magnetico

taper ['tepər] *s* cerino || *tr* affusolare || *intr* affusolarsi; **to taper off** rastremarsi; diminuire in intensità; diminuire a poco a poco

tape'-re·cord' *tr* registrare su nastro magnetico

tape' record'er *s* magnetofono, registratore *m* a nastro

tapes·try ['tæpɪstri] *s* (**-tries**) tappezzeria || *v* (*pret & pp* **-tried**) *tr* tappezzare

tape'worm' *s* verme solitario, tenia

tappet ['tæpɪt] *s* (aut) punteria

tap'room' *s* taverna, osteria

tap'root' *s* radice *f* a fittone

tap' wa'ter *s* acqua corrente

tap' wrench' *s* giramaschio

tar [tɑr] *s* catrame *m* || *v* (*pret & pp* **tarred;** *ger* **tarring**) *tr* incatramare

tar•dy ['tɑrdi] *adj* (**-dier; -diest**) in ritardo; lento
tare [tɛr] *s* tara || *tr* tarare
target ['tɑrgɪt] *s* segno, bersaglio
tar'get date' *s* data progettata
tar'get lan'guage *s* lingua obbiettivo, lingua di arrivo
tar'get prac'tice *s* esercizio di tiro a segno
tariff ['tærif] *s* (*duties*) tariffa doganale; (*charge or fare*) tariffa
tarnish ['tɑrnɪʃ] *s* ossidazione; (fig) macchia || *tr* appannare || *intr* appannarsi, perdere il lustro
tar' pa'per *s* carta catramata
tarpaulin [tɑr'pɔlɪn] *s* telone *m* impermeabile incatramato
tarragon ['tærəgən] *s* dragoncello
tar•ry ['tɑri] *adj* incatramato || ['tæri] *v* (*pret & pp* **-ried**) *intr* rimanere; ritardare
tart [tɑrt] *adj* acido, pungente || *s* torta; (slang) puttana
tartar ['tɑrtər] *s* tartaro; cremore *m* di tartaro; (*shrew*) megera; **to catch a tartar** imbattersi in un muso duro
Tartarus ['tɑrtərəs] *s* Tartaro
task [tæsk] or [tɑsk] *s* compito, incarico; **to take to task** rimproverare
task' force' *s* gruppo formato per una missione speciale
task'mas'ter *s* sorvegliante *m;* sorvegliante severo
tassel ['tæsəl] *s* nappa; (bot) ciuffo
taste [test] *s* gusto, sapore *m;* buon gusto; (*sampling, e.g., of wine*) assaggio; esperienza; **to one's taste** a genio di qlcu || *tr* gustare, assaggiare || *intr* sentire, sapere; **to taste of** degustare; sapere di
tasteless ['testlɪs] *adj* insipido; di cattivo gusto
tast•y ['testi] *adj* (**-ier; -iest**) saporito; (coll) di buon gusto
tatter ['tætər] *s* brandello, sbrendolo || *tr* sbrindellare
tattered ['tætərd] *adj* sbrindellato
tattle ['tætəl] *s* chiacchiera; (*gossip*) pettegolezzo || *intr* chiacchierare; spettegolare
tat'tle•tale' *adj* rivelatore || *s* gazzetta, chiacchierone *m*
tattoo [tæ'tu] *s* tatuaggio; (mil) ritirata || *tr* tatuare
taunt [tɔnt] or [tɑnt] *s* rimprovero sarcastico, insulto || *tr* rimproverare sarcasticamente, insultare
Taurus ['tɔrəs] *s* (astr) Toro
taut [tɔt] *adj* teso, tirato
tavern ['tævərn] *s* osteria
taw•dry ['tɔdri] *adj* (**-drier; -driest**) vistoso, sgargiante, pacchiano
taw•ny ['tɔni] *adj* (**-nier; -niest**) falbo, fulvo
tax [tæks] *s* tassa, imposta || *tr* tassare; (*s.o.'s patience*) mettere a dura prova
taxable ['tæksəbəl] *adj* tassabile
tax'able in'come *s* imponibile *m*
taxation [tæk'seʃən] *s* imposizione, tassazione, contribuzione
tax' collec'tor *s* esattore *m* delle imposte
tax' deduc'tion *s* detrazione
tax'-ex•empt' *adj* esente da tasse
tax' evad'er [ɪ'vedər] *s* evasore *m*
tax•i ['tæksi] *s* (**-is**) tassì *m* || *v* (*pret & pp* **-ied;** *ger* **-iing** or **-ying**) *tr* far rullare || *intr* andare in tassì; (aer) rullare
tax'i•cab' *s* tassì *m*
tax'i driv'er *s* tassista *m*
tax'i•plane' *s* aeroplano da noleggio, aerotassì *m*
taxi' stand' *s* posteggio di tassì
tax'pay'er *s* contribuente *mf*
tax' rate' *s* imponibilità *f*
tea [ti] *s* tè *m;* (*medicinal infusion*) tisana; (*beef broth*) brodo di carne
tea' bag' *s* sacchetto di tè
tea' ball' *s* uovo da tè
tea'cart' *s* servitore *m*
teach [titʃ] *v* (*pret & pp* **taught** [tɔt]) *tr & intr* insegnare
teacher ['titʃər] *s* maestro, insegnante *mf*
teach'ers col'lege *s* scuola magistrale
teach'er's pet' *s* beniamino del maestro
teaching ['titʃɪŋ] *adj* insegnante || *s* insegnamento, dottrina
teach'ing aids' *spl* sussidi *mpl* didattici
teach'ing staff' *s* corpo insegnante
tea'cup' *s* tazza da tè
tea' dance' *s* tè *m* danzante
teak [tik] *s* tek *m*
tea'ket'tle *s* bricco del tè
team [tim] *s* (*e.g., of horses*) pariglia; (sports) squadra, equipaggio || *tr* apparigliare; tirare or trasportare con pariglia || *intr*—**to team up** unirsi, associarsi
team'mate' *s* compagno di squadra
teamster ['timstər] *s* (*of horses*) carrettiere *m;* (*of truck*) camionista *m,* autotrenista *m*
team'work' *s* affiatamento, collaborazione
tea'pot' *s* teiera
tear [tɪr] *s* lacrima; **to hold back one's tears** ingoiare le lacrime; **to laugh away one's tears** cambiare dal pianto al riso || [tɛr] *s* strappo || [tɛr] *v* (*pret* **tore** [tor]; *pp* **torn** [torn]) *tr* strappare; stracciare; (*one's heart*) squarciare; (*to wound*) sbranare; (*one's hair*) strapparsi; **to tear apart** rompere in due; separare; **to tear down** demolire; (*a piece of equipment*) smontare; **to tear off** staccare; **to tear to pieces** dilaniare; fare a pezzi; **to tear up** (*a piece of paper*) stracciare; (*a street*) scavare || *intr* strapparsi, stracciarsi; **to tear along** precipitarsi; correre all'impazzata
tear' bomb' [tɪr] *s* bomba lacrimogena
tearful ['tɪrfəl] *adj* lacrimoso
tear' gas' [tɪr] *s* gas lacrimogeno
tear-jerker ['tɪr ,dʒʌrkər] *s* (coll) storia lacrimogena
tear-off ['tɛr ,ɔf] *adj* da staccarsi, perforato
tea'room' *s* sala da tè
tear' sheet' [tɛr] *s* copia di annuncio pubblicitario
tease [tiz] *tr* stuzzicare, molestare;

(*hair*) accotonare; (*e.g., wool*) cardare
tea'spoon' *s* cucchiaino
teaspoonful ['ti ,spun ,fʊl] *s* cucchiaino
teat [tit] *s* capezzolo
tea'time' *s* l'ora del tè
tea' wag'on *s* servitore *m*
technical ['tɛknɪkəl] *adj* tecnico
technicali·ty [,tɛknɪ'kælɪti] *s* (**-ties**) tecnicismo; dettaglio tecnico
technician [tɛk'nɪʃən] *s* tecnico
technics ['tɛknɪks] *ssg* or *spl* tecnica
technique [tɛk'nik] *s* tecnica
ted'dy bear' ['tɛdi] *s* orsacchiotto
tedious ['tidɪ·əs] or ['tidʒəs] *adj* tedioso, noioso
tee [ti] *adj* fatto a T || *s* giunto a tre vie; (golf) piazzola di partenza || *tr*—**to tee off** (slang) cominciare || *intr*—**to be teed off** (slang) essere arrabbiato; **to tee off** (golf) colpire la palla dalla piazzola di partenza; **to tee off on** (slang) rimproverare severamente
teem [tim] *intr* brulicare; piovere a dirotto; **to teem with** abbondare di
teeming ['timɪŋ] *adj* brulicante; (*rain*) torrenziale
teen-ager ['tin ,edʒər] *s* giovane *mf* dai 13 ai 19 anni
teens [tinz] *spl* numeri inglesi che finiscono in **-teen** (dal 13 al 19); **to be in one's teens** avere dai 13 ai 19 anni
tee·ny ['tini] *adj* (**-nier; -niest**) (coll) piccolo, piccolissimo
teeter ['titər] *s* altalena, dondolio || *intr* dondolarsi, oscillare
teethe [tið] *intr* mettere i denti
teething ['tiðɪŋ] *s* dentizione
teeth'ing ring' *s* dentaruolo
teetotaler [ti'totələr] *s* astemio
tele·cast ['tɛlɪ ,kæst] or ['tɛlɪ ,kɑst] *s* teletrasmissione || *v* (*pret & pp* **-cast** or **-casted**) *tr & intr* teletrasmettere
telegram ['tɛlɪ ,græm] *s* telegramma *m*
telegraph ['tɛlɪ ,græf] or ['tɛlɪ ,grɑf] *s* telegrafo || *tr & intr* telegrafare
tel'egraph pole' *s* palo del telegrafo
Telemachus [tɪ'lɛməkəs] *s* Telemaco
telemeter [tɪ'lɛmɪtər] *s* telemetro || *tr* misurare col telemetro
telepathy [tɪ'lɛpəθi] *s* telepatia
telephone ['tɛlɪ ,fon] *s* telefono || *tr & intr* telefonare
tel'ephone book' *s* elenco or guida dei telefoni
tel'ephone booth' *s* cabina telefonica
tel'ephone call' *s* chiamata telefonica, colpo di telefono
tel'ephone direc'tory *s* elenco or guida dei telefoni
tel'ephone exchange' *s* centrale telefonica
tel'ephone op'erator *s* centralinista *mf*, telefonista *mf*
tel'ephone receiv'er *s* ricevitore *m*
tel'ephoto lens' ['tɛlɪ ,foto] *s* teleobbiettivo
teleplay ['tɛlɪ ,ple] *s* teledramma *m*
teleprinter ['tɛlɪ ,prɪntər] *s* telescrivente *f*
telescope ['tɛlɪ ,skop] *s* telescopio || *tr* snodare; condensare || *intr* essere snodabile; (*in a collision*) incastrarsi
teletype ['tɛlɪ ,taɪp] *s* telescrivente *f* || *tr & intr* trasmettere per telescrivente
teleview ['tɛlɪ ,vju] *tr* telericevere
televiewer ['tɛlɪ ,vju·ər] *s* telespettatore *m*
televise ['tɛlɪ ,vaɪz] *tr* teletrasmettere
television ['tɛlɪ ,vɪʃən] *adj* televisivo || *s* televisione
tel'evision screen' *s* teleschermo
tel'evision set' *s* televisore *m*
tell [tɛl] *v* (*pret & pp* **told** [told]) *tr* dire; (*to narrate*) raccontare; (*to count*) contare; distinguere; **I told you so!** te l'avevo detto!; **to tell off** (coll) dire il fatto suo a || *intr* dire; prevedere; avere effetto; **to tell on** (*s.o.'s health*) pesare a, e.g., **age was telling on his health** l'età pesava alla sua salute; (coll) denunciare
teller ['tɛlər] *s* narratore *m;* (*of bank*) cassiere *m;* (*of votes*) scrutatore *m*
temper ['tɛmpər] *s* indole *f*, temperamento; umore *m;* calma; (metallurgy) tempra; **to keep one's temper** mantenersi calmo; **to lose one's temper** perdere la pazienza || *tr* temprare || *intr* temprarsi
temperament ['tɛmpərəmənt] *s* indole *f*, temperamento, carattere *m*
temperamental [,tɛmpərə'mɛntəl] *adj* emotivo, capriccioso
temperance ['tɛmpərəns] *s* (*self-restraint in action*) temperanza; (*abstinence from alcoholic beverages*) sobrietà *f*
temperate ['tɛmpərɪt] *adj* temperato
temperature ['tɛmpərətʃər] *s* temperatura
tempest ['tɛmpɪst] *s* tempesta; **tempest in a teapot** tempesta in un bicchier d'acqua
tempestuous [tɛm'pɛstʃʊ·əs] *adj* tempestoso
temple ['tɛmpəl] *s* (*place of worship*) tempio; (*of spectacles*) susta, stanghetta; (anat) tempia
tem·po ['tɛmpo] *s* (**-pos** or **-pi** [pi]) (mus) tempo; (fig) ritmo
temporal ['tɛmpərəl] *adj* temporale
temporary ['tɛmpə ,rɛri] *adj* temporaneo, provvisorio, transitorio, interino
temporize ['tɛmpə ,raɪz] *intr* temporeggiare
tempt [tɛmpt] *tr* tentare
temptation [tɛmp'teʃən] *s* tentazione
tempter ['tɛmptər] *s* tentatore *m*
tempting ['tɛmptɪŋ] *adj* tentatore
ten [tɛn] *adj & pron* dieci || *s* dieci *m;* **ten o'clock** le dieci
tenable ['tɛnəbəl] *adj* difendibile
tenacious [tɪ'neʃəs] *adj* tenace
tenant ['tɛnənt] *s* inquilino, pigionante *mf;* (*of land*) fittavolo
tend [tɛnd] *tr* riguardare, governare; accudire (with *dat*), e.g., **he tends the fire** accudisce al fuoco || *intr* tendere; **to tend to** propendere verso; (*e.g., one's own business*) attendere a; **to tend to** + *inf* tendere a + *inf*
tenden·cy ['tɛndənsi] *s* (**-cies**) tendenza, propensione

tender ['tɛndər] *adj* tenero; sensibile, dolorante || *s* offerta; (naut) nave *f* rifornimento; (naut) lancia; (rr) carboniera || *tr* offrire
tender-hearted ['tɛndər ,hartɪd] *adj* dal cuore tenero
ten'der·loin' *s* filetto || **Tenderloin** *s* rione *m* della mala vita
tenderness ['tɛndərnɪs] *s* tenerezza
tendon ['tɛndən] *s* tendine *m*
tendril ['tɛndrɪl] *s* viticcio
tenement ['tɛnɪmənt] *s* appartamento; casa; casamento
ten'ement house' *s* casamento
tenet ['tɛnɪt] *s* dogma *m*, dottrina
tennis ['tɛnɪs] *s* tennis *m*
ten'nis court' *s* campo da tennis
ten'nis play'er *s* tennista *mf*
tenor ['tɛnər] *s* tenore *m*
tense [tɛns] *adj* teso || *s* (gram) tempo
tension ['tɛnʃən] *s* tensione
tent [tɛnt] *s* tenda; (*of circus*) tendone *m*
tentacle ['tɛntəkəl] *s* tentacolo
tentative ['tɛntətɪv] *adj* a titolo di prova; (*smile*) esile
tenth [tɛnθ] *adj, s & pron* decimo || *s* (*in dates*) dieci *m*
tenuous ['tɛnjʊ·əs] *adj* tenue
tenure ['tɛnjər] *s* (*in office*) rafferma; (*permanency of employment*) inamovibilità *f;* (law) possesso
tepid ['tɛpɪd] *adj* tiepido
tercet ['tʌrsɪt] *s* terzina
term [tʌrm] *s* vocabolo, voce *f;* periodo, durata; termine *m;* (com) scadenza; **terms** condizioni *fpl;* **to be on good terms** essere in buone relazioni; **to come to terms** venire a patti || *tr* chiamare, definire
termagant ['tʌrməgənt] *s* megera
terminal ['tʌrmɪnəl] *adj* terminale || *s* (*end or extremity*) terminale *m;* (elec) morsetto; (rr) capolinea *m*
terminate ['tʌrmɪ ,net] *tr & intr* terminare
terminus ['tʌrmɪnəs] *s* termine *m*, fine *m;* (rr) capolinea *m*
termite ['tʌrmaɪt] *s* termite *f*
terrace ['tɛrəs] *s* terrazza, terrazzo; (agr) gradino, scaglione *m*
terra firma ['tɛrə 'fʌrmə] *s* terra ferma
terrain [tɛ'ren] *s* terreno
terrestrial [tə'rɛstrɪ·əl] *adj* terrestre
terrific [tə'rɪfɪk] *adj* terrificante; (coll) tremendo
terri·fy ['tɛrɪ ,faɪ] *v* (*pret & pp* **-fied**) *tr* terrificare, inorridire
territo·ry ['tɛrɪ ,tori] *s* (**-ries**) territorio
terror ['tɛrər] *s* terrore *m*
terrorize ['tɛrə ,raɪz] *tr* terrorizzare; dominare col terrore
ter'ry cloth' ['tɛri] *s* tessuto a spugna
terse [tʌrs] *adj* conciso, terso
tertiary ['tʌrʃɪ ,ɛri] or ['tʌrʃəri] *adj* terziario
test [tɛst] *s* prova, saggio; esame *m* || *tr* provare, saggiare; esaminare; (*e.g., a machine*) collaudare
testament ['tɛstəmənt] *s* testamento || **Testament** *s* Testamento Nuovo
test' ban' *s* interdizione degli esperimenti nucleari
test' flight' *s* volo di prova
testicle ['tɛstɪkəl] *s* testicolo
testi·fy ['tɛstɪ ,faɪ] *v* (*pret & pp* **-fied**) *tr & intr* testimoniare
testimonial [,tɛstɪ'monɪ·əl] *s* (*certificate*) benservito, referenza; (*expression of esteem*) segno di gratitudine
testimo·ny ['tɛstɪ ,moni] *s* (**-nies**) testimonianza
test' pat'tern *s* (telv) monoscopio
test' pi'lot *s* pilota *m* collaudatore
test' tube' *s* provetta
tetanus ['tɛtənəs] *s* tetano
tether ['tɛðər] *s* cavezza, pastoia; **at the end of one's tether** al limite delle proprie risorse || *tr* legare; incavezzare, impastoiare
tetter ['tɛtər] *s* eczema *m*, impetigine *f*
text [tɛkst] *s* testo; tema *m*
text'book' *s* libro di testo
textile ['tɛkstɪl] or ['tɛkstaɪl] *adj & s* tessile *m*
textual ['tɛkstʃʊ·əl] *adj* testuale
texture ['tɛkstʃər] *s* (*of cloth*) trama; caratteristica, proprietà *f*
Thai ['tɑ·i] or ['taɪ] *adj & s* tailandese *mf*
Thailand ['taɪlənd] *s* la Tailandia
Thames [tɛmz] *s* Tamigi *m*
than [ðæn] *conj* di, e.g., **he is faster than you** è più veloce di te; (*before a verb*) di quanto, e.g., **he is smarter than I thought** è più intelligente di quanto pensavo; che, e.g., **he had barely begun to eat than it was time to leave** non aveva appena cominciato a mangiare che era ora di andarsene
thank [θæŋk] *s*—**thanks** ringraziamenti *mpl;* **thanks to** grazie a, in grazie di || *tr* ringraziare || **thanks** *interj* grazie!
thankful ['θæŋkfəl] *adj* grato
thankless ['θæŋklɪs] *adj* ingrato
Thanksgiv'ing Day' [,θæŋks'gɪvɪŋ] *s* giorno del Ringraziamento
that [ðæt] *adj dem* (**those**) quel; codesto; **that one** quello, quello là || *pron dem* (**those**) quello; codesto || *pron rel* che, quello che, il quale; **that is** cioè; **that's that** (coll) ecco fatto, ecco tutto || *adv* (coll) tanto, così; **that far** così lontano; **that many** tanti; **that much** tanto || *conj* che
thatch [θætʃ] *s* paglia, copertura di paglia; (*hair*) capigliatura || *tr* coprire di paglia
thaw [θɔ] *s* sgelo || *tr* sgelare || *intr* sgelarsi
the [ðə], [ðɪ], or [ði] *art def* il; al, e.g., **one dollar the dozen** un dollaro alla dozzina || *adv*—**so much the worse for him** tanto peggio per lui; **the more . . . the more** quanto più . . . tanto più
theater ['θi·ətər] *s* teatro
the'ater·go'er *s* frequentatore *m* abituale del teatro
the'ater news' *s* cronaca teatrale
theatrical [θɪ'ætrɪkəl] *adj* teatrale
Thebes [θibz] *s* Tebe *f*
thee [ði] *pron pers* (Bib; poet) ti; te
theft [θɛft] *s* furto, ruberia

their [ðɛr] *adj poss* il loro, loro
theirs [ðɛrz] *pron poss* il loro
them [ðɛm] *pron pers* li; loro; **to them** loro
theme [θim] *s* tema *m*, soggetto; saggio; (mus) tema *m*
theme' song' *s* (mus) tema *m* centrale; (rad) sigla musicale
them·selves' *pron pers* essi stessi, loro stessi; si, e.g., **they enjoyed themselves** si divertirono
then [ðɛn] *adj* allora, di allora ‖ *s* quel tempo; **by then** a quell'epoca; **from then on** da quel giorno in poi ‖ *adv* allora; indi, poi; **then and there** a quel momento
thence [ðɛns] *adv* indi, quindi; da lì; da allora in poi
thence'forth' *adv* da allora in poi
theolo·gy [θi'ɑlədʒi] *s* (**-gies**) telogia
theorem ['θi·ərəm] *s* teorema *m*
theoretical [,θi·ə'rɛtɪkəl] *adj* teoretico
theo·ry ['θi·əri] *s* (**-ries**) teoria
therapeutic [,θɛrə'pjutɪk] *adj* terapeutico ‖ **therapeutics** *ssg* terapeutica
thera·py ['θɛrəpi] *s* (**-pies**) terapia
there [ðɛr] *adv* lì, là; **there are** ci sono; **there is** c'è; ecco, e.g., **there it is** eccolo
there'abouts' *adv* circa, approssimativamente, giù di lì
there'af'ter *adv* in seguito, dipoi
there'by' *adv* quindi, perciò, così
therefore ['ðɛrfor] *adv* per questo, quindi, dunque
there'in' *adv* lì; in quel rispetto
there'of' *adv* di ciò, da ciò
Theresa [tə'risə] or [tə'rɛsə] *s* Teresa
there'upon' *adv* su questo; a quel momento; come conseguenza
thermal ['θʌrməl] *adj* (*water*) termale; (*capacity*) termico
thermistor [θər'mɪstər] *s* (elec) termistore *m*
thermocouple ['θʌrmo ,kʌpəl] *s* termocoppia
thermodynamic [,θʌrmodaɪ'næmɪk] *adj* termodinamico ‖ **thermodynamics** *ssg* termodinamica
thermometer [θər'mɑmɪtər] *s* termometro
thermonuclear [,θʌrmo'njuklɪ·ər] or [,θʌrmo'nuklɪ·ər] *adj* termonucleare
ther'mos bot'tle ['θʌrməs] *s* termos *m*
thermostat ['θʌrmə ,stæt] *s* termostato
thesau·rus [θɪ'sɔrəs] *s* (**-ri** [raɪ] or **-ruses**) tesoro, lessico, compendio
these [ðiz] *pl of* **this**
the·sis ['θisɪs] *s* (**-ses** [siz]) tesi *f*
Thespis ['θɛspɪs] *s* Tespi *m*
they [ðe] *pron pers* essi, loro
thick [θɪk] *adj* spesso, grosso; folto, denso; pieno, coperto; viscoso; stupido; (coll) intimo ‖ *s* spessore *m*; **in the thick of** nel folto di; **through thick and thin** nei tempi buoni e cattivi
thicken ['θɪkən] *tr* ispessire; ingrossare; infoltire ‖ *intr* ispessirsi; ingrossarsi; (*said of a plot*) complicarsi
thicket ['θɪkɪt] *s* boscaglia, macchia
thick-headed ['θɪk ,hɛdɪd] *adj* indietro, stupido
thick'set' *adj* tarchiato; (*hedge*) fitto, denso
thief [θif] *s* (**thieves** [θivz]) ladro
thieve [θiv] *intr* rubare
thiever·y ['θivəri] *s* (**-ies**) furto
thigh [θaɪ] *s* coscia
thigh'bone' *s* femore *m*
thimble ['θɪmbəl] *s* ditale *m*
thin [θɪn] *adj* (**thinner**; **thinnest**) (*paper, ice*) sottile; (*lean*) magro, smilzo; (*e.g., hair*) rado; (*air*) fine; (*excuse*) tenue; (*voice*) esile; (*wine*) leggero, annacquato ‖ *v* (*pret & pp* **thinned**; *ger* **thinning**) *tr* assottigliare; (*paint*) diluire ‖ *intr* assottigliarsi; **to thin out** (*said of a crowd; one's hair*) diradarsi
thine [ðaɪn] *adj & pron poss* (Bib & poet) tuo, il tuo
thing [θɪŋ] *s* cosa; **not to get a thing out of** non riuscire a capire; non cavare un briciolo d'informazione da; **of all things!** che cosa!; che sorpresa!; **the thing** l'ultima moda; **things** roba; **to see things** avere allucinazioni
think [θɪŋk] *v* (*pret & pp* **thought** [θɔt]) *tr* pensare; credere; **to think it over** ripensarci; **to think nothing of it** non darci la minima importanza; **to think of** (*to have as an opinion of*) pensare di, e.g., **what do you think of that doctor?** cosa ne pensa di quel medico?; **to think out** decifrare; **to think up** immaginare ‖ *intr* pensare; **to think not** credere di no; **to think of** (*to turn one's thoughts to*) pensare a, e.g., **he is thinking of the future** pensa al futuro; (*to imagine*) immaginare; **to think so** credere di sì; **to think well of** avere una buona opinione di
thinkable ['θɪŋkəbəl] *adj* pensabile
thinker ['θɪŋkər] *s* pensatore *m*
third [θʌrd] *adj, s & pron* terzo ‖ *s* terzo; (*in dates*) tre *m*; (aut) terza
third' degree' *s* interrogatorio di terzo grado
third' rail' *s* (rr) rotaia elettrificata di contatto
third'-rate' *adj* di terz'ordine
Third' World' *s* Terzo Mondo
thirst [θʌrst] *s* sete *f* ‖ *intr* aver sete; **to thirst for** aver sete di
thirst·y ['θʌrsti] *adj* (**-ier**; **-iest**) assetato, sitibondo; **to be thirsty** avere sete
thirteen ['θʌr'tin] *adj, s & pron* tredici *m*
thirteenth ['θʌr'tinθ] *adj, s & pron* tredicesimo ‖ *s* (*in dates*) tredici *m*
thirtieth ['θʌrtɪ·ɪθ] *adj, s & pron* trentesimo ‖ *s* (*in dates*) trenta *m*
thir·ty ['θʌrti] *adj & pron* trenta ‖ *s* (**-ties**) trenta *m*; **the thirties** gli anni trenta
this [ðɪs] *adj dem* (**these**) questo; **this one** questo, questo qui ‖ *pron dem* (**these**) questo, questo qui ‖ *adv* (coll) tanto, così
thistle ['θɪsəl] *s* cardo
thither ['θɪðər] or ['ðɪðər] *adv* là, da quella parte

Thomas ['tɑməs] *s* Tommaso
thong [θɔŋ] or [θɑŋ] *s* coreggia
thorax ['θoræks] *s* (**-raxes** or **-races** [rə ˌsiz]) torace *m*
thorn [θɔrn] *s* spina
thorn•y ['θɔrni] *adj* (**-ier; -iest**) spinoso
thorough ['θʌro] *adj* completo, esauriente
thor'ough•bred' *adj* di razza; (*horse*) purosangue ‖ *s* individuo di razza; (*horse*) purosangue *mf*
thor'ough•fare' *s* passaggio; **no thoroughfare** divieto di passaggio
thor'ough•go'ing *adj* completo, esauriente
thoroughly ['θʌroli] *adv* a fondo
those [ðoz] *pl* of **that**
thou [ðaʊ] *pron pers* (Bib; poet) tu ‖ *tr* dare del tu a
though [ðo] *adv* tuttavia ‖ *conj* malgrado, sebbene; **as though** come se
thought [θɔt] *s* pensiero; **perish the thought!** (coll) nemmeno a pensarci!
thoughtful ['θɔtfəl] *adj* pensieroso, riflessivo; (*considerate*) sollecito
thoughtless ['θɔtlɪs] *adj* irriflessivo; sconsiderato; (*reckless*) incurante
thought' transfer'ence *s* trasmissione del pensiero
thousand ['θaʊzənd] *adj, s & pron* mille *m;* **a thousand** or **one thousand** mille *m*
thousandth ['θaʊzəndθ] *adj, s & pron* millesimo
thralldom ['θrɔldəm] *s* schiavitù *f*
thrash [θræʃ] *tr* battere; (agr) trebbiare; **to thrash out** discutere a fondo ‖ *intr* agitarsi, dibattersi
thread [θrɛd] *s* filo; (mach) filetto, verme *m;* **to lose the thread of** perdere il filo di ‖ *tr* infilare; (fig) pervadere; (mach) filettare, impanare; **to thread one's way through** aprirsi il passaggio attraverso
thread'bare' *adj* frusto, logoro
threat [θrɛt] *s* minaccia
threaten ['θrɛtən] *tr & intr* minacciare
threatening ['θrɛtənɪŋ] *adj* minaccioso; (*e.g., letter*) minatorio
three [θri] *adj & pron* tre ‖ *s* tre *m;* **three o'clock** le tre
three'-cor'nered *adj* triangolare; (*hat*) a tre punte
three' hun'dred *adj, s & pron* trecento
threepenny ['θrɛpəni] or ['θrɪpəni] *adj* del valore di tre penny; di nessun valore
three'-phase' *adj* trifase
three'-ply' *adj* a tre spessori
three' R's' [ɑrz] *spl* lettura, scrittura e aritmetica
three'score' *adj* sessanta
three' thou'sand *adj, s & pron* tre mila *mpl*
threno•dy ['θrɛnədi] *s* (**-dies**) trenodia
thresh [θrɛʃ] *tr* (agr) trebbiare; **to thresh out** discutere a fondo ‖ *intr* trebbiare; battere
thresh'ing machine' *s* trebbiatrice *f*
threshold ['θrɛʃold] *s* soglia
thrice [θraɪs] *adv* tre volte; molto
thrift [θrɪft] *s* economia
thrift•y ['θrɪfti] *adj* (**-ier; -iest**) economo, economico; vigoroso; prospero
thrill [θrɪl] *s* fremito d'emozione; esperienza emozionante ‖ *tr* emozionare ‖ *intr* emozionarsi; vibrare
thriller ['θrɪlər] *s* (coll) thrilling *m*
thrilling ['θrɪlɪŋ] *adj* emozionante, thrilling
thrive [θraɪv] *v* (*pret* **thrived** or **throve** [θrov]; *pp* **thrived** or **thriven** ['θrɪvən]) *intr* prosperare, fiorire
throat [θrot] *s* gola; **to clear one's throat** schiarirsi la voce
throb [θrɑb] *s* battito, palpito, tuffo ‖ *v* (*pret & pp* **throbbed;** *ger* **throbbing**) *intr* palpitare, pulsare
throe [θro] *s* agonia, travaglio, spasimo; **in the throes of** nel travaglio di; (*e.g., battle*) nel momento più penoso di
throne [θron] *s* trono
throng [θrɔŋ] or [θrɑŋ] *s* folla, stuolo ‖ *intr* affollarsi
throttle ['θrɑtəl] *s* (*of locomotive*) leva di comando; (*of motorcycle*) manetta; (*of car*) acceleratore *m;* (mach) valvola di controllo ‖ *tr* soffocare; (mach) regolare
through [θru] *adj* diretto, senza fermate; **to be through** aver finito; **to be through with** farla finita con ‖ *adv* attraverso; da una parte all'altra; completamente; ‖ *prep* attraverso, per; durante; fino alla fine di; per mezzo di
through•out' *adv* completamente, da un capo all'altro; dappertutto ‖ *prep* durante tutto, e.g., **throughout the afternoon** durante tutto il pomeriggio; per tutto, e.g., **throughout the house** per tutta la casa
throw [θro] *s* getto, tiro, lancio; gettata; coperta leggera ‖ *v* (*pret* **threw** [θru]; *pp* **thrown**) *tr* gettare, tirare, lanciare; (*a shadow*) proiettare; (*the current*) connettere; (*said of a horse*) disarcionare; (wrestling) gettare a terra; (*a game*) (coll) perdere intenzionalmente; (coll) stupire; **to throw away** gettar via; perdere; **to throw back** rigettare; ritardare; **to throw in** (*the clutch*) innestare; (coll) aggiungere; **to throw oneself into** darsi a; **to throw out** sbatter fuori; (*the clutch*) disinnestare; **to throw over** abbandonare ‖ *intr* gettare, tirare, lanciare; **to throw up** vomitare
thrum [θrʌm] *v* (*pret & pp* **thrummed;** *ger* **thrumming**) *intr* tambureggiare; (mus) far scorrere la mano sulle corde di uno strumento
thrush [θrʌʃ] *s* tordo
thrust [θrʌst] *s* (*push*) spinta; botta; (*with dagger*) pugnalata; (*with sword*) stoccata ‖ *v* (*pret & pp* **thrust**) *tr* spingere; conficcare, configgere; **to thrust oneself** (*e.g., into a conversation*) ficcarsi
thru'way' *s* autostrada
thud [θʌd] *s* tonfo ‖ *v* (*pret & pp* **thudded;** *ger* **thudding**) *intr* fare un rumore sordo
thug [θʌg] *s* fascinoroso

thumb [θʌm] *s* pollice *m;* **all thumbs** maldestro, goffo; **thumbs down** pollice verso; **to twiddle one's thumbs** girare i pollici, essere ozioso; **under the thumb of** sotto l'influenza di || *tr* sporcare con le dita; (*a book*) sfogliare; **to thumb a ride** chiedere l'autostop; **to thumb one's nose (at)** fare marameo (a)
thumb' in'dex *s* margine *m* a scaletta
thumb'nail' *adj* breve, conciso || *s* unghia del pollice
thumb'screw' *s* vite *f* ad aletta
thumb'tack' *s* puntina
thump [θʌmp] *s* tonfo || *tr* battere, percuotere || *intr* battere; cadere con un tonfo; camminare a passi pesanti; (*said of the heart*) palpitare violentemente
thumping ['θʌmpɪŋ] *adj* (coll) straordinario, eccezionale; (coll) grande
thunder ['θʌndər] *s* tuono; (*of applause*) scroscio; (*of a cannon*) rombo || *tr* lanciare || *intr* tonare, rombare; (fig) scrosciare
thun'der•bolt' *s* folgore *f*, fulmine *m*
thun'der•clap' *s* scroscio di tuono
thunderous ['θʌndərəs] *adj* fragoroso
thun'der•show'er *s* acquazzone *m* accompagnato da tuoni
thun'der•storm' *s* temporale *m*
thun'der•struck' *adj* attonito
Thursday ['θʌrsdi] *s* giovedì *m*
thus [ðʌs] *adv* così; **thus far** sino qui
thwack [θwæk] *s* colpo || *tr* colpire
thwart [θwɔrt] *adj* obliquo || *adv* di traverso || *tr* contrariare, sventare
thy [θaɪ] *adj poss* (Bib; poet) tuo, il tuo
thyme [taɪm] *s* timo
thy'roid gland' ['θaɪrɔɪd] *s* tiroide *f*
thyself [ðaɪ'self] *pron* (Bib; poet) te stesso; te, ti
tiara [taɪ'ɑrə] or [taɪ'ɛrə] *s* (*female adornment*) diadema *m;* (eccl) tiara
tick [tɪk] *s* (*of pillow*) fodera; (*of mattress*) guscio; (*of clock*) ticchettio; (*dot*) punto; (ent) zecca; **on tick** (coll) a credito || *intr* fare ticchettio; **to make s.o. tick** mandare avanti qlcu
ticker ['tɪkər] *s* telescrivente *f;* (slang) orologio; (slang) cuore *m*
tick'er tape' *s* nastro della telescrivente
ticket ['tɪkɪt] *s* biglietto; (*e.g., of pawnbroker*) polizza; (*slip of paper or identifying tag*) bolletta, bollettino; (*summons*) verbale *m;* (*e.g., to indicate price*) etichetta; lista dei candidati; **that's the ticket** (coll) questo è quello che fa
tick'et a'gent *s* bigliettaio
tick'et of'fice *s* biglietteria
tick'et scalp'er ['skælpər] *s* bagarino
tick'et win'dow *s* sportello
ticking ['tɪkɪŋ] *s* traliccio
tickle ['tɪkəl] *s* solletico || *tr* solleticare; divertire || *intr* avere il solletico
ticklish ['tɪklɪʃ] *adj* sensibile al solletico; delicato; permaloso; **to be ticklish** soffrire il solletico
tick-tock ['tɪk ,tɑk] *s* tic tac *m*
tid'al wave' ['taɪdəl] *s* onda di marea; (fig) ondata
tidbit ['tɪd ,bɪt] *s* bocconcino
tiddlywinks ['tɪdli ,wɪŋks] *s* gioco della pulce
tide [taɪd] *s* marea; **to go against the tide** andare contro la corrente; **to stem the tide** fermare la corrente || *tr* portare sulla cresta delle onde; **to tide over** aiutare; (*a difficulty*) sormontare
tide'wa'ter *s* marea; costa marina
tidings ['taɪdɪŋz] *spl* notizie *fpl*
ti•dy ['taɪdi] *adj* (**-dier; -diest**) pulito, ordinato || *s* (**-dies**) cofanetto, astuccio; appoggiacapo || *v* (*pret & pp* **-died**) *tr* rassettare, mettere in ordine || *intr* rassettarsi
tie [taɪ] *s* laccio, nodo, vincolo; (*in games*) patta; (*necktie*) cravatta; (archit) traversa; (rr) traversina; (mus) legatura || *v* (*pret & pp* **tied;** *ger* **tying**) *tr* allacciare, annodare; legare; confinare; (*a game*) impattare; (*a person*) impattarla con; **to be tied up** essere occupato; **to tie down** confinare, limitare; **to tie up** legare; impedire; (*e.g., traffic*) intasare || *intr* allacciare; (*in games*) impattare
tie' beam' *s* catena
tie'pin' *s* spilla da cravatta
tier [tɪr] *s* gradinata; ordine *m*, livello
tiff [tɪf] *s* screzio, litigio
tiger ['taɪgər] *s* tigre *f*
ti'ger lil'y *s* giglio cinese
tight [taɪt] *adj* teso; stretto; compatto; impermeabile, ermetico; pieno; (*game*) (coll) serrato; (coll) tirato; (slang) ubriaco || **tights** *spl* calzamaglia || *adv* strettamente; **to hold tight** tenere stretto
tighten ['taɪtən] *tr* (*e.g., one's belt*) tirare; (*e.g., a screw*) stringere || *intr* tirarsi; stringersi
tight-fisted ['taɪt'fɪstɪd] *adj* taccagno
tight'-fit'ting *adj* attillato
tight'rope' *s* corda tesa
tight' squeeze' *s*—**to be in a tight squeeze** (coll) essere alle strette
tight'wad' *s* (coll) spilorcio
tigress ['taɪgrɪs] *s* tigre femmina
tile [taɪl] *s* mattonella; (*for floor*) piastrella; (*for roof*) tegola, coppo || *tr* coprire di mattonelle; coprire di piastrelle; coprire di coppi
tile' roof' *s* tetto di tegole
till [tɪl] *s* cassetto dei soldi || *prep* fino a || *conj* fino a che . . . non, fino a che, sinché . . . non, sinché || *tr* lavorare, coltivare
tilt [tɪlt] *s* inclinazione; giostra, torneo; **full tilt** di gran carriera; a tutta forza || *tr* inclinare; (*a lance*) mettere in resta; attaccare || *intr* inclinarsi; giostrare; **to tilt at** combattere con
timber ['tɪmbər] *s* legno, legname *m* da costruzione; alberi *mpl;* (fig) tempra
tim'ber•land' *s* bosco destinato a produrre legname
tim'ber line' *s* linea della vegetazione

timbre ['tɪmbər] *s* (phonet & phys) timbro
time [taɪm] *s* tempo; ora, e.g., **what time is it?** che ora è?; volta, e.g., **three times** tre volte; giorni *mpl*, e.g., **in our time** ai giorni nostri; momento; ultima ora; ore *fpl* lavorative; periodo, e.g., **Xmas time** periodo natalizio; **for a long time** da lungo; **for the time being** per ora, per il momento; **in time** presto; col tempo; **on time** a tempo; a rate; (*said, e.g., of a bus*) in orario; **times** volte, e.g., **seven times seven** sette volte sette; **to bide one's time** aspettare l'ora propizia; **to do time** (coll) essere in prigione; **to have a good time** divertirsi; **to have no time for** non poter sopportare; **to lose time** (*said of a watch*) ritardare; **to make time** avanzare rapidamente; guadagnare terreno; **to pass the time of day** fare una chiacchierata; salutarsi; **to take one's time** fare le cose senza fretta; **to tell time** leggere l'orologio || *tr* fissare il momento di; calcolare il tempo di; (sports) cronometrare
time' bomb' *s* bomba a orologeria
time'card' *s* cartellino di presenza
time' clock' *s* orologio di controllo (delle presenze)
time' expo'sure *s* (phot) posa
time' fuse' *s* spoletta a tempo
time'keep'er *s* marcatempo; orologio; (sports) cronometrista *mf*
timeless ['taɪmlɪs] *adj* senza fine, eterno
time·ly ['taɪmli] *adj* (**-lier; -liest**) opportuno, tempestivo
time'piece' *s* orologio; cronometro
time' sig'nal *s* segnale orario
time'ta'ble *s* orario; tabella di marcia
time'work' *s* lavoro a ore
time'worn' *adj* logorato dal tempo
time' zone' *s* fuso orario
timid ['tɪmɪd] *adj* timido, pavido
tim'ing gears' ['taɪmɪŋ] *spl* ingranaggi *mpl* di distribuzione
timorous ['tɪmərəs] *adj* timoroso
tin [tɪn] *s* (*element*) stagno; (*tin plate; can*) latta || *v* (*pret & pp* **tinned**; *ger* **tinning**) *tr* stagnare
tin' can' *s* latta
tincture ['tɪŋktʃər] *s* tintura
tin' cup' *s* tazzina metallica
tinder ['tɪndər] *s* esca
tin'der·box' *s* cassetta con l'esca e l'acciarino; persona eccitabile; (fig) polveriera
tin' foil' *s* stagnola
ting-a-ling ['tɪŋə,lɪŋ] *s* dindìn *m*
tinge [tɪndʒ] *s* sfumatura; pizzico, punta || *v* (*ger* **tingeing** or **tinging**) *tr* sfumare; dare una traccia di sapore a
tingle ['tɪŋgəl] *s* formicolio, pizzicore *m* || *intr* informicolirsi, pizzicare; (*said of the ears*) ronzare; (*with enthusiasm*) fremere
tin' hat' *s* (slang) elmetto
tinker ['tɪŋkər] *s* calderaio, ramaio || *intr* armeggiare
tinkle ['tɪŋkəl] *s* tintinnio || *tr* far tintinnare || *intr* tintinnare
tin' plate' *s* latta
tin' roof' *s* tetto di lamiera di latta
tinsel ['tɪnsəl] *s* orpello, lustrino
tin'smith' *s* lattoniere *m*, stagnino
tin' sol'dier *s* soldatino di piombo
tint [tɪnt] *s* tinta, sfumatura || *tr* tinteggiare
tin'ware' *s* articoli *mpl* di latta
ti·ny ['taɪni] *adj* (**-nier; -niest**) piccino
tip [tɪp] *s* punta; (*of mountain*) vetta; (*of umbrella*) gorbia; (*of shoe*) mascherina; (*of cigarette*) bocchino; (*of shoestring*) aghetto; colpetto; (*fee*) mancia; informazione confidenziale; inclinazione || *v* (*pret & pp* **tipped**; *ger* **tipping**) *tr* mettere la punta a; inclinare, rovesciare; (*one's hat*) levarsi; dare la mancia a; toccare, battere; (*the scales*) far traboccare; **to tip in** (bb) inserire fuori testo; **to tip off** (coll) dare informazioni confidenziali a || *intr* inclinarsi; dare la mancia
tip'cart' *s* carro ribaltabile
tip'-off' *s* (coll) avvertimento confidenziale
tipped'-in' *adj* (bb) fuori testo
tipple ['tɪpəl] *intr* sbevucchiare
tip'staff' *s* usciere *m*
tip·sy ['tɪpsi] *adj* (**-sier; -siest**) brillo
tip'toe' *s* punta di piedi || *v* (*pret & pp* **-toed**; *ger* **-toeing**) *intr* camminare in punta di piedi
tirade ['taɪred] *s* tirata
tire [taɪr] *s* gomma, pneumatico; (*of metal*) cerchione *m* || *tr* stancare || *intr* stancarsi; infastidirsi
tire' chain' *s* catena antineve
tired [taɪrd] *adj* stanco, stracco
tire' gauge' *s* manometro della pressione delle gomme
tireless ['taɪrlɪs] *adj* infaticabile
tire' pres'sure *s* pressione (delle gomme)
tire' pump' *s* pompa (per i pneumatici)
tiresome ['taɪrsəm] *adj* faticoso; (*boring*) noioso
tissue ['tɪsjʊ] *s* tessuto; tessuto finissimo, velina
tis'sue pa'per *s* carta velina
titanium [tai'tenɪ·əm] or [tɪ'tenɪ·əm] *s* titanio
tithe [taɪð] *s* decima || *tr* imporre la decima su; pagare la decima di
Titian ['tɪʃən] *adj* tizianesco || *s* Tiziano
title ['taɪtəl] *s* titolo; (sports) campionato || *tr* intitolare
ti'tle deed' *s* titolo di proprietà
ti'tle·hold'er *s* campione *m*, primatista *mf*
ti'tle page' *s* frontespizio
ti'tle role' *s* (theat) ruolo principale
tit'mouse' *s* (**-mice**) (orn) cincia
titter ['tɪtər] *s* risatina || *intr* ridacchiare
titular ['tɪtʃələr] *adj* titolare
TNT ['ti,en'ti] *s* (letterword) tritolo
to [tu], [tʊ] or [tə] *adv*—**to and fro** da una parte all'altra, avanti e indietro; **to come to** tornare in sè || *prep* a, e.g., **he is going to Rome** va a Roma; **he gave a kiss to his mother**

diede un bacio a sua madre; **she is learning to sew** impara a cucire; per, e.g., **he has been a true friend to me** è stato un vero amico per me; da, e.g., **there is still a lot of work to do** c'è ancora molto lavoro da fare; con, e.g., **she was very kind to me** è stata molto gentile con me; in, e.g., **we went to church** siamo andati in chiesa; fino a, e.g., **to see s.o. to the station** accompagnare qlcu fino alla stazione; in confronto di, e.g., **the accounts are nothing to what really happened** le storie non sono nulla, in confronto di quanto è realmente successo; meno, e.g., **ten minutes to seven** le sette meno dieci

toad [tod] *s* rospo

toad'stool' *s* agarico, fungo velenoso

to-and-fro [tu-ənd'fro] *adj* avanti e indietro

toast [tost] *s* pane tostato; (*drink to s.o.'s health*) brindisi *m;* **a piece of toast** una fetta di pane tostato || *tr* tostare; brindare alla salute di || *intr* tostarsi; brindare

toaster ['tostər] *s* (*of bread*) tostapane *m;* persona che fa un brindisi

toast'mas'ter *s* persona che annuncia i brindisi, maestro di cerimonie

tobac•co [tə'bæko] *s* (**-cos**) tabacco

tobacconist [tə'bækənɪst] *s* tabaccaio

tobac'co pouch' *s* borsa da tabacco

toboggan [tə'bɑgən] *s* toboga *m*

tocsin ['tɑksɪn] *s* campana a martello; scampanata d'allarme

today [tʊ'de] *s & adv* oggi *m*

toddle ['tɑdəl] *s* passo vacillante || *intr* traballare, trotterellare

tod•dy ['tɑdi] *s* (**-dies**) ponce *m*

to-do [tə'du] *s* (**-dos**) (coll) daffare *m*, rumore *m*

toe [to] *s* dito del piede; (*of shoe*) punta || *v* (*pret & pp* **toed;** *ger* **toeing**) *tr*—**to toe the line** filare diritto

toe'nail' *s* unghia del piede

together [tʊ'geðər] *adv* insieme; **to bring together** riunire; riconciliare; **to call together** chiamare a raccolta; **to stick together** (coll) rimanere uniti, stare insieme

togs [tɑgz] *spl* vestiti *mpl*

toil [tɔɪl] *s* travaglio, sfacchinata; **toils** reti *fpl*, lacci *mpl* || *intr* travagliare, sfacchinare

toilet ['tɔɪlɪt] *s* toletta; gabinetto, ritirata; **to make one's toilet** farsi la toletta

toi'let pa'per *s* carta igienica

toi'let pow'der *s* polvere *f* di talco

toi'let soap' *s* sapone *m* da toletta

toi'let wa'ter *s* acqua da toletta

token ['tokən] *s* segno, marca; ricordo; (*used as money*) gettone *m;* **by the same token** per di più; **in token of** in segno di, come prova di

tolerance ['tɑlərəns] *s* tolleranza

tolerate ['tɑlə,ret] *tr* tollerare

toll [tol] *s* (*of bell*) rintocco; (*e.g., for passage over bridge*) pedaggio; (*tax*) dazio; (*compensation for grinding grains*) molenda; (*number of victims*) perdite *fpl;* (telp) tariffa interurbana || *tr* (*a bell*) sonare a morto; (*the faithful*) chiamare a raccolta || *intr* sonare a morto

toll' bridge' *s* ponte *m* a pedaggio

toll' call' *s* (telp) chiamata interurbana

toll'gate' *s* barriera di pedaggio; (*in a turnpike*) casello

toma•to [tə'meto] or [tə'mɑto] *s* (**-toes**) pomodoro

toma'to juice' *s* sugo di pomodoro

tomb [tum] *s* tomba

tomboy ['tɑm,bɔɪ] *s* maschietta

tomb'stone' *s* pietra tombale, lapide *f*

tomcat ['tɑm,kæt] *s* gatto maschio

tome [tom] *s* tomo

tomorrow [tʊ'mɑro] or [tʊ'mɔro] *s* domani *m;* **the day after tomorrow** dopodomani *m* || *adv* domani

tom-tom ['tɑm,tɑm] *s* tam-tam *m*

ton [tʌn] *s* tonnellata; **tons** (coll) montagne *fpl*

tone [ton] *s* tono; (fig) tenore *m* || *tr* intonare; **to tone down** (*colors*) smorzare; (*sounds*) sfumare || *intr* intonarsi; **to tone down** moderarsi; **to tone up** rinforzarsi

tone' po'em *s* poema sinfonico

tongs [tɔŋz] or [tɑŋz] *spl* tenaglie *fpl;* (*e.g., for sugar*) molle *fpl*

tongue [tʌŋ] *s* (*language*) lingua; (*of bell*) battaglio; (*of shoe*) linguetta; (*of wagon*) timone *m;* (anat) lingua; (carp) maschio; **tongue in cheek** poco sinceramente; **to hold one's tongue** mordersi la lingua; **to speak with forked tongue** essere di due lingue

tongue' depres'sor *s* abbassalingua *m*

tongue'-lash'ing *s* sgridata

tongue' twist'er *s* scioglilingua *m*

tonic ['tɑnɪk] *adj & s* tonico

tonight [tʊ'naɪt] *s* questa sera, questa notte || *adv* stasera; stanotte

tonnage ['tʌnɪdʒ] *s* tonnellaggio, stazza

tonsil ['tɑnsəl] *s* tonsilla

ton•y ['toni] *adj* (**-ier; -iest**) (slang) elegante, di lusso

too [tu] *adv* (*also*) anche, pure; (*more than enough*) troppo; **too bad!** peccato!; **too many** troppi; **too much** troppo

tool [tul] *s* utensile *m*, attrezzo; (*person*) strumento; (*of lathe*) punta || *tr* lavorare; (bb) decorare

tool' bag' *s* borsa degli attrezzi

tool'box' *s* cassetta attrezzi

tool'mak'er *s* attrezzista *m*

tool'shed' *s* barchessa

toot [tut] *s* (*of horn*) suono; (*of locomotive*) fischio; (*of car's horn*) colpo; (coll) gazzarra || *tr* strombettare; **to toot one's own horn** strombazzare i propri meriti || *intr* strombettare

tooth [tuθ] *s* (**teeth** [tiθ]) dente *m*

tooth'ache' *s* mal *m* di denti

tooth'brush' *s* spazzolino da denti

toothless ['tuθlɪs] *adj* sdentato

tooth'paste' *s* pasta dentifricia

tooth'pick' *s* stuzzicadenti *m*

tooth' pow'der *s* polvere dentifricia

top [tɑp] *s* cima, sommo, vertice *m;* (*upper part of anything*) disopra *m;*

(*of mountain, tree*) vetta; (*of box*) coperchio; (*beginning*) principio; (*of bottle*) imboccatura; (*of a bridge*) testata; (*of wagon*) mantice *m;* (*of car*) tetto; (*of wall*) coronamento; (*toy*) trottola; (naut) gabbia; **at the top of one's voice** a perdifiato; **from top to bottom** daccapo a piedi, dal principio alla fine; **on top of** in cima di; subito dopo; **the tops** (coll) il migliore, il fiore; **to blow one's top** (slang) dare in escandescenze; **to sleep like a top** dormire come un ghiro || *v* (*pret & pp* **topped;** *ger* **topping**) *tr* (*a tree*) svettare; coronare; superare
topaz ['topæz] *s* topazio
top' bil'ling *s*—**to get top billing** essere artista di cartello; (journ) ricevere il posto più importante
top' boot' *s* stivale *m* a tromba
top'coat' *s* soprabito di mezza stagione
toper ['topər] *s* ubriacone *m*
topgal'lant sail' [,tap'gælənt] *s* (naut) pappafico, veletta
top' hat' *s* cappello a staio or a cilindro
top'-heav'y *adj* troppo pesante in cima, sovraccarico in cima
topic ['tapɪk] *s* topica, tema *m*
top'knot' *s* crocchia
topless ['taplɪs] *adj* (*mountain*) di cui non si vede la vetta, eccelso; (*bathing suit*) topless
top'mast' *s* (naut) alberetto
top'most' *adj* il più alto
topogra·phy [tə'pagrəfi] *s* (**-phies**) topografia
topple ['tapəl] *tr* abbattere, rovesciare || *intr* rovesciarsi, cadere
top' prior'ity *s* priorità massima
topsail ['tapsəl] or ['tap,sel] *s* (naut) gabbia
top'-se'cret *adj* segretissimo
top'soil' *s* strato superiore del terreno
topsy-turvy ['tapsi'tʌrvi] *adj* rovesciato; confuso || *s* soqquadro || *adv* a soqquadro
torch [tɔrtʃ] *s* fiaccola, torcia; **to carry the torch for** (slang) amare disperatamente
torch'bear'er *s* portatore *m* di fiaccola; (fig) capo, guida *m*
torch'light' *s* luce *f* di fiaccola
torch' song' *s* canzone *f* triste d'amore non corrisposto
torment ['tɔrment] *s* tormento || [tɔr'ment] *tr* tormentare
torna·do [tɔr'nedo] *s* (**-dos** or **-does**) tornado, tromba d'aria
torpe·do [tɔr'pido] *s* (**-does**) siluro || *tr* silurare
torpe'do boat' *s* motosilurante *f*
torpe'do-boat destroy'er *s* torpediniera
torrent ['tarənt] or ['tɔrənt] *s* torrente *m*
torrid ['tarɪd] or ['tɔrɪd] *adj* torrido
torsion ['tɔrʃən] *s* torsione
tor'sion bar' *s* barra di torsione
tor·so ['tɔrso] *s* (**-sos**) torso
tortoise ['tɔrtəs] *s* tartaruga
tor'toise shell' *s* tartaruga
torture ['tɔrtʃər] *s* tortura || *tr* torturare
toss [tɔs] or [tas] *s* lancio, getto || *tr* lanciare, gettare; (*to fling about*) sballottare; (*one's head*) alzare sdegnosamente; agitare; rivoltare; (*an opinion*) avventare; **to toss off** fare rapidamente; (*e.g., a drink*) buttar giù; **to toss up** (*a coin*) gettar in aria, gettare a testa e croce; (coll) rigettare || *intr* agitarsi, dimenarsi; **to toss and turn** (*in bed*) girarsi; **to toss up** giocare a testa e croce
toss'up' *s* testa e croce; (coll) eguale probabilità *f*
tot [tat] *s* bambino, piccolo
to·tal ['totəl] *adj* totale; (*e.g., loss*) completo || *s* totale *m* || *v* (*pret & pp* **-taled** or **-talled;** *ger* **-taling** or **-talling**) *tr* ammontare a; (*to make a total of*) sommare
totalitarian [to,tælɪ'terɪ·ən] *adj* totalitario || *s* aderente *mf* al totalitarismo
totter ['tatər] *s* vacillamento || *intr* vacillare
touch [tʌtʃ] *s* (*act*) tocco; (*sense*) tatto; (*of an illness*) leggero attacco; (*slight amount*) punta; (*for money*) (slang) stoccata; **to get in touch with** mettersi in contatto con; **to lose one's touch** perdere il tocco personale || *tr* toccare; raggiungere; riguardare; (*for a loan*) (slang) dare una stoccata a; **to touch on** menzionare; **to touch up** ritoccare || *intr* toccare; **to touch down** (aer) atterrare
touching ['tʌtʃɪŋ] *adj* toccante, commovente || *prep* riguardo a
touch'stone' *s* pietra di paragone
touch' type'writing *s* dattilografia a tatto
touch·y ['tʌtʃi] *adj* (**-ier; -iest**) suscettibile, permaloso; delicato, precario, rischioso
tough [tʌf] *adj* duro; forte; (*luck*) cattivo; violento || *s* malvivente *m*
toughen ['tʌfən] *tr* indurire || *intr* indurirsi
tough' luck' *s* disdetta, sfortuna
tour [tur] *s* gita, viaggio; (sports) giro; (mil) turno; (theat) tournée *f* || *tr* girare; (theat) portare in tournée || *intr* girare; (theat) andare in tournée
tour'ing car' ['turɪŋ] *s* automobile *f* da turismo
tourist ['turɪst] *adj* turistico || *s* turista *mf*
tournament ['turnəmənt] or ['tʌrnəmənt] *s* torneo
tourney ['turni] or ['tʌrni] *s* torneo || *intr* giostrare
tourniquet ['turnɪ,ket] or ['tʌrnɪ,ke] *s* laccio emostatico
tousle ['tauzəl] *tr* spettinare
tow [to] *s* rimorchio; (*e.g., of hemp*) stoppa; **to take in tow** prendere a rimorchio || *tr* rimorchiare
toward(s) [tord(z)] or [tə'wɔrd(z)] *prep* (*in the direction of*) verso; (*in respect to*) per; (*near*) vicino a; (*a certain hour*) su, verso
tow'boat' *s* rimorchiatore *m*
tow' car' *s* rimorchiatore *m*
tow·el ['tau·əl] *s* asciugamano; (*of paper*) salvietta; **to throw in the**

towel (slang) gettare la spugna || *v* (*pret & pp* **-eled** or **-elled;** *ger* **-eling** or **-elling**) *tr* asciugare
tow'el rack' *s* portaasciugamani *m*
tower ['taʊ·ər] *s* torre *f* || *intr* torreggiare
towering ['taʊ·ərɪŋ] *adj* torreggiante; gigantesco; eccessivo
towline ['to,laɪn] *s* cavo di rimorchio
town [taʊn] *s* città *f;* (*townspeople*) cittadinanza; **in town** in città
town' clerk' *s* segretario municipale
town' coun'cil *s* consiglio comunale
town' cri'er *s* banditore *m* municipale
town' hall' *s* municipio
township ['taʊnʃɪp] *s* suddivisione di contea
towns'man *s* (**-men**) cittadino; concittadino
towns'peo'ple *spl* cittadini *mpl;* gente *f* di città
town' talk' *s* dicerie *fpl,* pettegolezzi *mpl*
tow'path' *s* strada d'alaggio
tow'rope' *s* corda da rimorchio
tow' truck' *s* autogru *f*
toxic ['tɑksɪk] *adj & s* tossico
toy [tɔɪ] *adj* giocattolo; di giocattoli || *s* giocattolo; (*trifle*) nonnulla *m;* (*trinket*) gingillo || *intr* giocare; **to toy with** (*to play with*) giocare con; (*to trifle, e.g., with food*) baloccarsi con; (*an idea*) accarezzare; (*to flirt with*) flirtare con
toy' bank' *s* salvadanaio
toy' sol'dier *s* soldatino di piombo
trace [tres] *s* traccia, vestigio; (*tracing*) tracciato; (*of harness*) tirella; (fig) ombra || *tr* tracciare; (*e.g., s.o.'s ancestry*) rintracciare; (*a pattern*) lucidare
trac'er bul'let ['tresər] *s* pallottola tracciante
trache·a ['trekɪ·ə] *s* (**-ae** [,i]) trachea
tracing ['tresɪŋ] *s* tracciato
track [træk] *s* (*of foot*) traccia, pesta; (*rut*) solco, rotaia; (*of boat*) scia; corso; (*course followed by boat*) rotta; (*of tape recorder*) pista; (*of tractor*) cingolo; (*of ideas*) successione; (*width of a vehicle measured from wheel to wheel*) (aut) carreggiata; (rr) binario; (*track and field*) (sports) atletica leggera; (*for horses*) (sports) galoppatoio; (*for running*) (sports) pista, corsia; **to keep track of** non perder di vista; **to lose track of** perder di vista; **to make tracks** (coll) affrettarsi; **to stop in one's tracks** (coll) fermarsi di colpo || *tr* rintracciare, seguire le tracce di; lasciare tracce su; **to track down** rintracciare
track'ing sta'tion ['trækɪŋ] *s* (rok) stazione di avvistamento
track'less trol'ley ['træklɪs] *s* filobus *m*
track' meet' *s* incontro di atletica leggera
track'walk'er *s* (rr) guardialinee *m*
tract [trækt] *s* tratto, opuscolo, trattatello; (anat) tubo, canale *m*
traction ['trækʃən] *s* trazione
trac'tion com'pany *s* società *f* di trasporti urbani
tractor ['træktər] *s* trattore *m;* (*of a tractor-trailer*) motrice *f*
trac'tor-trail'er *s* treno stradale
trade [tred] *s* commercio; affare *m;* occupazione, mestiere *m;* (*people*) commercianti *mpl,* professionisti *mpl;* mercato; (*customers*) clientela; (*in slaves*) tratta || *tr* mercanteggiare; cambiare; **to trade in** dare come pagamento parziale || *intr* trafficare, commerciare; comprare; **to trade in** lavorare in; **to trade on** approfittarsi di
trade'mark' *s* marca or marchio di fabbrica
trade' name' *s* ragione sociale
trader ['tredər] *s* trafficante *m*
trade' school' *s* scuola d'avviamento professionale, scuola d'arti e mestieri
trades'man *s* (**-men**) commerciante *m;* artigiano
trade' un'ion *s* sindacato di lavoratori
trade' un'ionist *s* sindacalista *mf*
trade' winds' *spl* alisei *mpl*
trad'ing post' *s* centro di scambi commerciali; (*in stock exchange*) posto delle compravendite
trad'ing stamp' *s* buono premio
tradition [trə'dɪʃən] *s* tradizione
traditional [trə'dɪʃənəl] *adj* tradizionale
traduce [trə'djus] or [trə'dus] *tr* calunniare
traf·fic ['træfɪk] *s* traffico, circolazione; commercio; comunicazione || *v* (*pret & pp* **-ficked;** *ger* **-ficking**) *intr* trafficare
traf'fic cir'cle *s* raccordo a circolazione rotatoria
traf'fic court' *s* tribunale *m* della polizia stradale
traf'fic is'land *s* isola spartitraffico
traf'fic jam' *s* intralcio del traffico, ingorgo stradale
traf'fic light' *s* semaforo
traf'fic man'ager *s* dirigente *m* del traffico; (rr) gestore *m* di stazione
traf'fic sign' *s* segnale *m* di circolazione stradale, cartello indicatore
traf'fic tick'et *s* contravvenzione per violazione del traffico
tragedian [trə'dʒidɪ·ən] *s* tragico
trage·dy ['trædʒɪdi] *s* (**-dies**) tragedia
tragic ['trædʒɪk] *adj* tragico
trail [trel] *s* sentiero; (*track*) traccia, pista; (*of robe*) strascico, coda; (*of smoke*) pennacchio; (*left by an airplane*) striscia; (*of people*) codazzo || *tr* strascicare; essere sulla fatta di; (*e.g., dust on the road*) sollevare; (*mud*) lasciar cadere || *intr* strascicare; (*said, e.g., of a snake*) strisciare; (*said of a plant*) arrampicarsi; **to trail off** mutare; (*to weaken*) affievolirsi
trailer ['trelər] *s* traino; (*to haul freight*) semirimorchio; (*for living*) carovana, roulotte *f;* (bot) rampicante *m*
train [tren] *s* (*of vehicles*) convoglio; (*of robe*) strascico; (*of thought*) or-

dine *m;* (*of people*) coda; (rr) treno || *tr* addestrare, impratichire; (*a weapon*) puntare, rivolgere; (*a horse*) scozzonare; (*e.g., a dog*) ammaestrare; (*a plant*) far crescere; (sports) allenare || *intr* addestrarsi; ammaestrarsi; (sports) allenarsi
trained' nurse' *s* infermiera diplomata
trainer ['trenər] *s* allenatore *m*
training ['trenɪŋ] *s* esercizio, esercitazione; (sports) allenamento
train'ing camp' *s* campo addestramento
train'ing school' *s* scuola di addestramento professionale; riformatorio
train'ing ship' *s* nave *f* scuola
trait [tret] *s* tratto, caratteristica
traitor ['tretər] *s* traditore *m*
traitress ['tretrɪs] *s* traditrice *f*
trajecto·ry [trə'dʒɛktəri] *s* (**-ries**) traiettoria
tramp [træmp] *s* lunga camminata; vagabondo; (*hussy*) sgualdrina || *tr* attraversare; calpestare || *intr* camminare a passi fermi; fare il vagabondo
trample ['træmpəl] *tr* calpestare; (fig) conculcare || *intr*—**to trample on** or **upon** calpestare
trampoline ['træmpə,lin] *s* trampolino di olona per salti mortali
tramp' steam'er *s* carretta
trance [træns] or [trɑns] *s* trance *f;* (*dazed condition*) estasi *f*
tranquil ['træŋkwɪl] *adj* tranquillo
tranquilize ['træŋkwɪ,laɪz] *tr* tranquillizzare || *intr* tranquillizzarsi
tranquilizer ['træŋkwɪ,laɪzər] *s* tranquillante *m*
tranquillity [træn'kwɪlɪti] *s* tranquillità *f*
transact [træn'zækt] or [træns'ækt] *tr* sbrigare, trattare
transaction [træn'zækʃən] or [træns'ækʃən] *s* disbrigo, operazione
transatlantic [,trænsət'læntɪk] *adj & s* transatlantico
transcend [træn'sɛnd] *tr* trascendere, sorpassare || *intr* eccellere
transcribe [træn'skraɪb] *tr* trascrivere
transcript ['trænskrɪpt] *s* copia; traduzione; (educ) copia ufficiale del certificato di studi
transcription [træn'skrɪpʃən] *s* trascrizione
transept ['trænsept] *s* transetto
trans·fer ['trænsfər] *s* trasferimento; passaggio; (*pattern*) rapporto; (*of funds*) giro; (*of real estate*) compravendita; (law) voltura || [træns'fʌr] or ['trænsfər] *v* (*pret & pp* **-ferred;** *ger* **-ferring**) *tr* trasferire, trasportare; (*funds*) stornare; (*a design*) rapportare; (*real estate*) compravendere || *intr* trasferirsi; cambiare di treno
trans'fer tax' *s* tassa di successione; tassa sulla compravendita
transfix [træns'fɪks] *tr* trafiggere; paralizzare, inchiodare
transform [træns'fɔrm] *tr* trasformare; (elec) trasformare || *intr* trasformarsi
transforma'tional gram'mar [,trænsfər'meʃənəl] *s* grammatica trasformativa
transformer [træns'fɔrmər] *s* trasformatore *m*
transfusion [træns'fjuʃən] *s* trasfusione
transgress [træns'grɛs] *tr* trasgredire; (*a limit or boundry*) oltrepassare || *intr* peccare
transgression [træns'grɛʃən] *s* trasgressione; peccato
transient ['trænʃənt] *adj* passeggero, temporaneo; di passaggio || *s* ospite *mf* di passaggio
transistor [træn'zɪstər] *s* transistore *m*
transit ['trænsɪt] or ['trænzɪt] *s* transito
transition [træn'zɪʃən] *s* transizione
transitional [træn'zɪʃənəl] *adj* di transizione
transitive ['trænsɪtɪv] *adj* transitivo || *s* verbo transitivo
transitory ['trænsɪ,tori] *adj* transitorio
translate [træns'let] or ['trænslet] *tr* tradurre; convertire; (*to transfer*) trasportare || *intr* tradursi
translation [træns'leʃən] *s* traduzione; trasformazione; (telg) ritrasmissione
translator [træns'letər] *s* traduttore *m*
transliterate [træns'lɪtə,ret] *tr* traslitterare
translucent [træns'lusənt] *adj* traslucido; (fig) chiaro
transmission [træns'mɪʃən] *s* trasmissione; (aut) trasmissione
trans·mit [træns'mɪt] *v* (*pret & pp* **-mitted;** *ger* **-mitting**) *tr & intr* trasmettere
transmitter [træns'mɪtər] *s* trasmettitore *m*
transmit'ting set' *s* emittente *f*
transmit'ting sta'tion *s* stazione trasmettitrice
transmute [træns'mjut] *tr & intr* trasmutare
transom ['trænsəm] *s* (*crosspiece*) traversa; (*window over door*) vasistas *m;* (naut) specchio di poppa
transparen·cy ['træns'perənsi] *s* (**-cies**) trasparenza; (*design on a translucent substance*) trasparente *m;* (phot) diapositiva
transparent [træns'perənt] *adj* trasparente
transpire [træns'paɪr] *intr* (*to happen*) avvenire; (*to perspire*) traspirare; (*to become known*) trapelare
transplant [træns'plænt] or [træns'plɑnt] *tr* trapiantare || *intr* trapiantarsi
transport ['trænsport] *s* trasporto; mezzo di trasporto || [træns'port] *tr* trasportare
transportation [,trænspor'teʃən] *s* trasporto; trasporti *mpl,* locomozione; biglietto di trasporto
trans'port work'er *s* ferrotranviere *m*
transpose [træns'poz] *tr* trasporre; (mus) trasportare
trans·ship [træns'ʃɪp] *v* (*pret & pp* **-shipped;** *ger* **-shipping**) *tr* trasbordare
trap [træp] *s* trappola, tranello;

(*double-curved pipe*) sifone *m;* (slang) bocca; (sports) congegno lanciapiattelli || *v* (*pret & pp* **trapped;** *ger* **trapping**) *tr* intrappolare, accalappiare
trap' door' *s* trabocchetto, botola; (theat) ribalta
trapeze [trə'piz] *s* (sports) trapezio
trapezoid ['træpɪ,zɔɪd] *s* (geom) trapezio, trapezoide *m*
trapper ['træpər] *s* cacciatore *m* di animali da pelliccia con trappole
trappings ['træpɪŋz] *spl* ornamenti *mpl;* (*for a horse*) gualdrappa
trap'shoot'ing *s* tiro al piattello
trash [træʃ] *s* immondizia, spazzatura; (*nonsense*) sciocchezze *fpl;* (*junk*) ciarpame *m;* (*worthless people*) gentaglia
trash' can' *s* portaimmondizie *m*
travail ['trævel] or [trə'vel] *s* travaglio; travaglio di parto
trav•el ['trævəl] *s* viaggio; traffico; (mach) corsa || *v* (*pret & pp* **-eled** or **-elled;** *ger* **-eling** or **-elling**) *tr* viaggiare per, percorrere || *intr* viaggiare; muoversi; (coll) andare
trav'el a'gency *s* ufficio turistico
traveler ['trævələr] *s* viaggiatore *m*
trav'eler's check' *s* assegno viaggiatori
trav'eling bag' *s* sacca da viaggio
trav'eling expens'es *spl* spese *fpl* di viaggio; (*per diem*) trasferta
trav'eling sales'man *s* (**-men**) commesso viaggiatore
traverse ['trævərs] or [trə'vʌrs] *tr* attraversare
traves•ty ['trævɪsti] *s* (**-ties**) parodia || *v* (*pret & pp* **-tied**) *tr* parodiare
trawl [trɔl] *s* (*fishing net*) rete *f* a strascico; (*fishing line*) lenza al traino || *tr & intr* pescare con la rete a strascico; pescare con la lenza al traino
trawling ['trɔlɪŋ] *s* pesca con la rete a strascico; pesca con la lenza al traino
tray [tre] *s* guantiera, vassoio; (chem, phot) bacinella
treacherous ['trɛtʃərəs] *adj* traditore, subdolo; incerto, pericoloso
treacher•y ['tretʃəri] *s* (**-ies**) tradimento
tread [trɛd] *s* (*step*) passo; (*of shoe*) suola; (*of tire*) battistrada *m;* (*of stairs*) pedata || *v* (*pret* **trod** [trɑd]; *pp* **trodden** ['trɑdən] or **trod**) *tr* calpestare; (*the boards*) calcare; accoppiarsi con || *intr* camminare; **to tread on** calpestare
treadle ['trɛdəl] *s* pedale *m*
tread'mill' *s* ruota azionata col camminare; (fig) lavoro ingrato
treason ['trizən] *s* tradimento
treasonable ['trizənəbəl] *adj* traditore
treasure ['trɛʒər] *s* tesoro || *tr* far tesoro di
treasurer ['trɛʒərər] *s* tesoriere *m*
treas'ure hunt' *s* caccia al tesoro
treasur•y ['trɛʒəri] *s* (**-ies**) tesoreria; tesoro, erario
treat [trit] *s* trattenimento; (*something affording pleasure*) piacere *m,* diletto || *tr* trattare; (*to cure*) curare, medicare; offrire un trattenimento a || *intr* trattare; pagare per il trattenimento
treatise ['tritɪs] *s* trattato
treatment ['tritmənt] *s* trattamento; (*of a theme*) trattazione
trea•ty ['triti] *s* (**-ties**) trattato
treble ['trɛbəl] *adj* (*threefold*) triplo; (mus) soprano || *s* (*person*) soprano *mf;* (*voice*) soprano || *tr* triplicare || *intr* triplicarsi
tree [tri] *s* albero
tree' farm' *s* bosco ceduo
tree' frog' *s* raganella
treeless ['trilɪs] *adj* spoglio, senza alberi
tree'top' *s* cima dell'albero
trellis ['trɛlɪs] *s* traliccio, graticcio
tremble ['trɛmbəl] *s* tremito || *intr* tremare
tremendous [trɪ'mɛndəs] *adj* tremendo
tremor ['trɛmər] or ['trimər] *s* tremito; (*of earth*) scossa
trench [trɛntʃ] *s* fosso, canale *m;* (mil) trincea
trenchant ['trɛntʃənt] *adj* mordace, caustico; vigoroso; incisivo
trench' coat' *s* trench *m*
trench' mor'tar *s* lanciabombe *m*
trend [trɛnd] *s* tendenza, orientamento || *intr* tendere, dirigersi
Trent [trɛnt] *s* Trento *f*
trespass ['trɛspəs] *s* (law) intrusione, violazione di proprietà || *intr* entrare senza diritto, intrudersi; peccare; **no trespassing** divieto di passaggio; **to trespass against** peccare contro; **to trespass on** entrare abusivamente in; (*e.g., s.o.'s time*) abusare di; violare
tress [trɛs] *s* treccia
trestle ['trɛsəl] *s* cavalletto; viadotto a cavalletti; ponte *m* a cavalletti
trial ['traɪ·əl] *s* tentativo, prova; tribolazione, croce *f;* (law) giudizio, processo; **on trial** in prova; (law) sotto processo; **to bring to trial** sottoporre a processo
tri'al and er'ror *s* metodo per tentativo; **by trial and error** a tastoni
tri'al balloon' *s* pallone *m* sonda
tri'al by ju'ry *s* processo con giuria
tri'al ju'ry *s* giuria civile or processuale
tri'al or'der *s* (com) ordine *m* di prova
tri'al run' *s* viaggio di prova
triangle ['traɪ,æŋgəl] *s* triangolo; (*in drafting*) quartabuono
tribe [traɪb] *s* tribù *f*
tribunal [trɪ'bjunəl] or [traɪ'bjunəl] *s* tribunale *m*
tribune ['trɪbjun] *s* tribuna
tributar•y ['trɪbjə,teri] *adj* tributario || *s* (**-ies**) tributario
tribute ['trɪbjut] *s* tributo; **to pay tribute to** (*e.g., beauty*) rendere omaggio a
trice [traɪs] *s* momento, istante *m;* **in a trice** in un batter d'occhio
trick [trɪk] *s* gherminella, inganno; trucco, tiro, scherzo; (*knack*) abilità *f;* (*feat*) atto; (*set of cards won*) presa; turno; (coll) piccola; **to be up to one's old tricks** farne una delle

sue; **to play a dirty trick on** fare un brutto tiro a|| *tr* giocare, ingannare
tricker•y ['trɪkəri] *s* (**-ies**) gherminella, inganno
trickle ['trɪkəl] *s* gocciolio, filo || *intr* gocciolare; (*said of people*) andare or venire alla spicciolata; (*said of news*) trapelare
trickster ['trɪkstər] *s* imbroglione *m*
trick•y ['trɪki] *adj* (**-ier; -iest**) ingannatore; (*machine*) complicato; (*ticklish to deal with*) delicato
tried [traɪd] *adj* fedele, provato
trifle ['traɪfəl] *s* bazzecola, bagattella; (*small amount of money*) piccolezza, miseria; **a trifle** un po' || *tr*—**to trifle away** sprecare || *intr* gingillarsi; **to trifle with** giocherellare con; scherzare con; divertirsi con
trifling ['traɪflɪŋ] *adj* futile; insignificante, trascurabile
trifocal [traɪ'fokəl] *adj* trifocale || **trifocals** *spl* occhiali *mpl* trifocali
trigger ['trɪgər] *s* (*of a firearm*) grilletto; (*of any device*) leva di sgancio || *tr* (*a gun*) far sparare; (fig) scatenare
trigonometry [,trɪgə'nɑmɪtri] *s* trigonometria
trill [trɪl] *s* trillo, gorgheggio; vibrazione; (*speech sound*) (phonet) vibrante *f* || *tr* gorgheggiare; pronunziare con vibrazione || *intr* trillare, gorgheggiare
trillion ['trɪljən] *s* trilione *m*
trilo•gy ['trɪlədʒi] *s* (**-gies**) trilogia
trim [trɪm] *adj* (**trimmer; trimmest**) lindo, azzimato || *s* condizione; buona condizione; (*dress*) vestito; (*of hair*) taglio, sfumatura; decorazione, ornamento; (*of sails*) orientamento; (aut) attrezzatura della carrozzeria || *v* (*pret & pp* **trimmed**; *ger* **trimming**) *tr* tagliare; (*an edge*) rifilare; adattare; arrangiare; (*Christmas tree*) decorare; (*hair*) sfumare; (*a tree*) potare; ordinare, assettare; (*a sail*) orientare; (aer) equilibrare; (mach) sbavare; (coll) rimproverare; (coll) bastonare; (*to defeat* (coll) battere, vincere
trimming ['trɪmɪŋ] *s* ornamento, guarnizione; (coll) battitura, batosta; **trimmings** guarnizioni *mpl;* (mach) sbavatura; (mach) rifilatura
trini•ty ['trɪnɪti] *s* (**-ties**) (*group of three*) triade *f* || **Trinity** *s* Trinità *f*
trinket ['trɪŋkɪt] *s* (*small ornament*) ninnolo, gingillo; **trinkets** (*trivial objects*) paccottiglia
tri•o ['tri•o] *s* (**-os**) terzetto
trip [trɪp] *s* viaggio; corsa; (*stumble*) inciampata; (*act of causing s.o. to stumble*) sgambetto; (*error*) passo falso; passo agile || *v* (*pret & pp* **tripped**; *ger* **tripping**) *tr* far inciampare, far cadere; fare lo sgambetto a; cogliere in fallo; (mach) far scattare || *intr* inciampare; fare un passo falso; avanzare saltellando, saltellare; **to trip over** inciampare in
tripartite [traɪ'pɑrtaɪt] *adj* tripartito
tripe [traɪp] *s* trippa; (slang) sciocchezze *fpl*
trip'ham'mer *s* maglio meccanico
triphthong ['trɪfθɔŋ] or ['trɪfθɑŋ] *s* trittongo
triple ['trɪpəl] *adj & s* triplo || *tr* triplicare || *intr* triplicarsi
triplet ['trɪplɪt] *s* (*offspring*) nato da un parto trigemino; (mus, poet) terzina
triplicate ['trɪplɪkɪt] *adj* triplicato || *s* triplice copia || ['trɪplɪ,ket] *tr* triplicare
tripod ['traɪpɑd] *s* (*e.g., for a camera*) treppiede *m;* (*stool with three legs*) tripode *m*
triptych ['trɪptɪk] *s* trittico
trite [traɪt] *adj* trito, ritrito
triumph ['traɪ•əmf] *s* trionfo || *intr* trionfare
trium'phal arch' [traɪ'ʌmfəl] *s* arco trionfale
trivia ['trɪvɪ•ə] *spl* banalità *f*, futilità *f*
trivial ['trɪvɪ•əl] *adj* insignificante, futile, banale
Trojan ['trodʒən] *adj & s* troiano
Tro'jan Horse' *s* cavallo di Troia
Tro'jan War' *s* guerra troiana
troll [trol] *tr & intr* pescare con la lenza al traino, pescare con il cucchiaino
trolley ['trɑli] *s* asta di presa, trolley *m;* carrozza tranviaria, tram *m*
trol'ley bus' *s* filobus *m*
trol'ley car' *s* vettura tranviaria, tram *m*
trol'ley pole' *s* trolley *m*
trollop ['trɑləp] *s* (*slovenly woman*) sciattona; (*hussy*) sgualdrina
trombone ['trɑmbon] *s* trombone *m*
troop [trup] *s* truppa, gruppo; (*of animals*) branco; (*of cavalry*) squadrone *m;* **troops** soldati *mpl* || *intr* raggrupparsi; marciare insieme
trooper ['trupər] *s* soldato di cavalleria; poliziotto a cavallo; **to swear like a trooper** bestemmiare come un turco
tro•phy ['trofi] *s* (**-phies**) trofeo; (*any memento*) ricordo
tropic ['trɑpɪk] *adj* tropicale || *s* tropico; **tropics** zona tropicale
tropical ['trɑpɪkəl] *adj* tropicale
troposphere ['trɑpə,sfɪr] *s* troposfera
trot [trɑt] *s* trotto || *v* (*pret & pp* **trotted**; *ger* **trotting**) *tr* far trottare; **to trot out** (coll) squadernare, esibire || *intr* trottare
troth [trəθ] or [troθ] *s* promessa di matrimonio; **by my troth** affé di Dio; **in troth** in verità; **to plight one's troth** impegnarsi; dare la parola
troubadour ['trubə,dor] or ['trubə,dur] *s* trovatore *m*
trouble ['trʌbəl] *s* disturbo, fastidio; inconveniente *m*, grattacapo; disordine *m*, conflitto; (*of a mechanical nature*) panna, guasto; **not to be worth the trouble** non valere la pena; **that's the trouble** questo è il male; **the trouble is that** il guaio è che; **to be in trouble** essere nei guai; **to be**

looking for trouble andare a cercarsi le grane; **to get into trouble** mettersi nei pasticci; **to have trouble in** + *ger* durar fatica a + *inf;* **to take the trouble** incomodarsi || *tr* molestare, disturbare; (*e.g., water*) intorbidare; dar del filo da torcere a; **to be troubled with** soffrire di; **to trouble oneself** scomodarsi
trouble' light' *s* lampada di soccorso
trou'ble•mak'er *s* mettimale *mf*
troubleshooter ['trʌbəl ˌʃutər] *s* localizzatore *m* di guasti; (*in disputes*) paciere *m,* conciliatore *m*
troubleshooting ['trʌbəl ˌʃutɪŋ] *s* localizzazione dei guasti; (*of disputes*) composizione
troublesome ['trʌbəlsəm] *adj* molesto; difficile
trouble' spot' *s* luogo di disordini, polveriera
trough [trɔf] or [trɑf] *s* (*to knead bread*) madia; (*for feeding pigs*) trogolo; (*for feeding animals*) mangiatoia; (*for watering animals*) abbeveratoio; (*gutter*) doccia; (*between two waves*) cavo
troupe [trup] *s* troupe *f*
trouper ['trupər] *s* membro della troupe; vecchio attore; tipo di cui ci si può fidare
trousers ['trauzərz] *spl* pantaloni *mpl*
trousseau [tru'so] or ['truso] *s* (**-seaux** or **-seaus**) corredo da sposa
trout [traut] *s* trota
trouvère [tru'vɛr] *s* troviero
trowel ['trau·əl] *s* cazzuola, mestola
Troy [trɔɪ] *s* Troia
truant ['tru·ənt] *s* fannullone *m;* **to play truant** marinare la scuola
truce [trus] *s* tregua
truck [trʌk] *s* autocarro, camion *m;* (*tractor-trailer*) autotreno; (*van*) furgone *m;* (*to be moved by hand*) carretto; verdura per il mercato; (mach, rr) carrello; (coll) robaccia; (coll) relazioni *fpl* || *tr* trasportare per autocarro, autotrasportare
truck'driv'er *s* camionista *m*
truck' farm' *s* fattoria agricola per la produzione degli ortaggi
truculent ['trʌkjələnt] or ['trukjələnt] *adj* truculento
trudge [trʌdʒ] *intr* camminare; **to trudge along** camminare laboriosamente, scarpinare
true [tru] *adj* vero; esatto, conforme; legittimo; infallibile; a livello; **to come true** verificarsi; **true to life** conforme alla realtà
true' cop'y *s* copia conforme
true-hearted ['tru ˌhɑrtɪd] *adj* fedele
true'love knot' *s* nodo d'amore
truffle ['trʌfəl] or ['trufəl] *s* tartufo
truism ['tru·ɪzəm] *s* truismo
truly ['truli] *adv* veramente; correttamente; **yours truly** distinti saluti
trump [trʌmp] *s* (cards) atout *m;* (Italian cards) briscola; **no trump** senza atout || *tr* superare; (cards) pigliare con un atout or con una briscola; **to trump up** inventare, fabbricare || *intr* giocare un atout or una briscola
trumpet ['trʌmpɪt] *s* tromba; (*toy*) trombetta; **to blow one's own trumpet** cantare le proprie lodi || *tr* strombazzare || *intr* sonar la tromba; strombazzare; (*said of an elephant*) barrire
truncheon ['trʌntʃən] *s* bastone *m* del comando; (Brit) manganello
trunk [trʌŋk] *s* (*of living body, tree, family, railroad*) tronco; (*for clothes*) baule *m;* (*of elephant*) tromba; (aut) bagagliaio; (archit) fusto; (telp) linea principale; **trunks** pantaloncini *mpl*
trunk' hose' *s* (hist) brache *fpl*
truss [trʌs] *s* (*to support a roof*) capriata, incavallatura; (*based on cantilever system*) intralicciatura; (*for reducing a hernia*) cinto, brachiere *m;* (bot) infiorescenza || *tr* legare, assicurare
trust [trʌst] *s* fede *f;* speranza; fiducia, custodia; (com) trust *m,* cartello; (law) fedecommesso; **in trust** in deposito; come fedecommesso; **on trust** a credito || *tr* fidarsi di; credere (with *dat*); (*to entrust*) dare in deposito a; dare a credito a || *intr* credere; fidarsi, prestar fede; **to trust in** (*e.g., a friend*) fidarsi di; (*God*) aver fede in
trust' com'pany *s* compagnia fedecommissaria; banca di deposito
trustee [trʌs'ti] *s* amministratore *m;* fiduciario; (*of a university*) curatore *m;* (*of an estate*) fedecommissario
trusteeship [trʌs'tiʃɪp] *s* amministrazione; (law) fedecommesso; (pol) amministrazione fiduciaria
trustful ['trʌstfəl] *adj* fiducioso
trust'wor'thy *adj* fidato, di fiducia
trust•y ['trʌsti] *adj* (**-ier; -iest**) fidato || *s* (**-ies**) carcerato degno di fiducia
truth [truθ] *s* verità *f;* **in truth** in verità
truthful ['truθfəl] *adj* verace, veritiero
try [traɪ] *s* (**tries**) tentativo, prova || *v* (*pret & pp* **tried**) *tr* provare; (*s.o.'s patience*) mettere a dura prova; (*a person*) (law) processare; (*a case*) (law) giudicare; **to try on** (*clothes*) provare; **to try out** provare; esperimentare || *intr* cercare, tentare; **to try out for** cercare di ottenere il posto di; (sports) cercare di farsi accettare in; **to try to** cercare di
trying ['traɪ·ɪŋ] *adj* duro, penoso, difficile
tryst [trɪst] or [traɪst] *s* appuntamento
T'-shirt' *s* maglietta
tub [tʌb] *s* tino, bigoncia; vasca da bagno; (*clumsy boat*) (slang) carretta; (*fat person*) (slang) bombolo
tube [tjub] or [tub] *s* tubo; (*e.g., for toothpaste*) tubetto; (*of tire*) camera d'aria; (anat) tuba, tromba; (coll) ferrovia sotterranea
tuber ['tjuber] or ['tubər] *s* tubero
tubercle ['tjubərkəl] or ['tubərkəl] *s* tubercolo

tuberculosis [tju ˌbʌrkjəˈlosɪs] or [tuˌbʌrkjəˈlosɪs] *s* tubercolosi *f*
tuck [tʌk] *s* basta || *tr* ripiegare; **to tuck away** nascondere; (slang) fare una scorpacciata di; **to tuck in** rincalzare; **to tuck up** rimboccare
tucker [ˈtʌkər] *s* collarino di merletto || *tr*—**to tucker out** (coll) stancare
Tuesday [ˈtjuzdi] or [ˈtuzdi] *s* martedì *m*
tuft [tʌft] *s* (*of feathers*) pennacchio; (*of hair*) cernecchio; (*of flowers*) cespo; (*fluffy threads*) fiocco, nappa || *tr* impuntire; adornare di fiocchi || *intr* crescere a cernecchi
tug [tʌg] *s* strattone *m*, strappata; (*struggle*) lotta; (*boat*) rimorchiatore *m* || *v* (*pret & pp* **tugged**; *ger* **tugging**) *tr* tirare; (*a boat*) rimorchiare || *intr* tirare con forza; lottare
tug'boat' *s* rimorchiatore *m*
tug' of war' *s* tiro alla fune
tuition [tjuˈɪʃən] or [tuˈɪʃən] *s* (*instruction*) insegnamento; tassa scolastica
tulip [ˈtjulɪp] or [ˈtulɪp] *s* tulipano
tumble [ˈtʌmbəl] *s* rotolone *m*, ruzzolone *m*; (*somersault*) salto mortale; caduta; disordine *m*, confusione; (*confused heap*) mucchio || *intr* rotolare, ruzzolare; cadere, capitombolare; gettarsi; rigirarsi; **to tumble down** cadere in rovina; **to tumble to** (coll) rendersi conto di
tum'ble-down' *adj* dilapidato
tumbler [ˈtʌmblər] *s* (*acrobat*) saltimbanco; (*glass*) bicchiere *m*; (*in a lock*) levetta; (*toy*) misirizzi *m*
tumor [ˈtjumər] or [ˈtumər] *s* tumore *m*
tumult [ˈtjumʌlt] or [ˈtumʌlt] *s* tumulto
tun [tʌn] *s* botte *f*, barile *m*
tuna [ˈtunə] *s* tonno
tune [tjun] or [tun] *s* (*air*) aria; (*manner of speaking*) tono; **in tune** intonato; **out of tune** stonato; **to change one's tune** cambiare di tono || *tr* intonare; **to tune in** (rad) sintonizzare; **to tune out** (rad) interrompere la sintonizzazione di; **to tune up** (*a motor*) mettere a punto; (mus) intonare
tuner [ˈtunər] or [ˈtjunər] *s* (rad) sintonizzatore *m*; (mus) accordatore *m*
tungsten [ˈtʌŋstən] *s* tungsteno
tunic [ˈtjunɪk] or [ˈtunɪk] *s* tunica
tun'ing coil' [ˈtunɪŋ] or [ˈtjunɪŋ] *s* bobina di sintonia
tun'ing fork' *s* diapason *m*, corista *m*
Tunis [ˈtjunɪs] or [ˈtunɪs] *s* Tunisi *f*
Tunisia [tjuˈniʒə] or [tuˈniʒə] *s* la Tunisia
Tunisian [tjuˈniʒən] or [tuˈniʒən] *adj & s* tunisino
tun·nel [ˈtʌnəl] *s* tunnel *m*, traforo, galleria; (min) galleria || *v* (*pret & pp* **-neled** or **-nelled**; *ger* **-neling** or **-nelling**) *tr* costruire un passaggio attraverso or sotto a
turban [ˈtʌrbən] *s* turbante *m*
turbid [ˈtʌrbɪd] *adj* turbido
turbine [ˈtʌrbɪn] or [ˈtʌrbaɪn] *s* turbina
turbojet [ˈtʌrbo ˌdʒɛt] *s* turboreattore *m*
turboprop [ˈtʌrbo ˌprɑp] *s* turboelica *m*
turbulent [ˈtʌrbjələnt] *adj* turbolento
tureen [tʊˈrin] or [tjʊˈrin] *s* terrina
turf [tʌrf] *s* zolla erbosa; (*peat*) torba; **the turf** il campo delle corse; le corse, il turf
turf'man *s* (**-men**) amatore *m* delle corse ippiche
Turk [tʌrk] *s* turco
turkey [ˈtʌrki] *s* tacchino || **Turkey** *s* la Turchia
turk'ey vul'ture *s* (*Cathartes aura*) avvoltoio americano
Turkish [ˈtʌrkɪʃ] *adj & s* turco
Turk'ish tow'el *s* asciugamano spugna
turmoil [ˈtʌrmɔɪl] *s* subbuglio
turn [tʌrn] *s* giro; (*time for action*) turno, volta; (*change of direction*) voltata; (*bend*) svolta, curva; (*of events*) piega; servizio; inclinazione, attitudine *f*; (*of key*) mandata; (*of coil*) spira; (coll) colpo, sussulto; (aer, naut) virata; **at every turn** a ogni piè sospinto; **in turn** a tua (Sua, vostra, etc.) volta; **to be one's turn** toccare a qlcu, e.g., **it's your turn** tocca a Lei; **to take turns** fare a turno || *tr* girare, voltare; (*soil*) rovesciare; cambiare; (*to make sour*) coagulare; (*to translate*) tradurre; (*e.g., ten years*) raggiungere; (*e.g., one's eyes*) volgere; (*on a lathe*) tornire; (*e.g., a coat*) rivoltare; (*to twist*) torcere; (*the wheel*) (aut) sterzare; **to turn against** mettere su contro; **to turn around** rigirare; (*s.o.'s words*) ritorcere; **to turn aside** sviare; **to turn away** cacciare via; **to turn back** ricacciare; restituire; (*the clock*) ritardare; **to turn down** ripiegare; (*the light*) abbassare; (*an offer*) rifiutare; **to turn in** ripiegare; denunziare; rassegnare; **to turn off** (*e.g., light*) spegnere, smorzare; (*gas, water, etc.*) tagliare; (*e.g., a faucet*) chiudere; **to turn on** (*e.g., light, radio, etc.*) accendere; (*e.g., a faucet*) aprire; **to turn out** mettere alla porta; (*animals*) fare uscire dalla stalla; rivoltare; (*light*) spegnere; produrre, fabbricare; **to turn up** ripiegare in su, rimboccare; (*on a lathe*) tornire; tirar su; (*a card*) scoprire; trovare; (*e.g., the radio*) alzare || *intr* girare; svoltare, e.g., **turn left at the corner** svolti a sinistra all'angolo; girarsi; cambiare; fermentare; cambiare di colore; diventare; (naut) virare; **to turn against** voltarsi contro; inimicarsi con; **to turn around** fare una giravolta; **to turn aside** or **away** sviarsi; **to turn back** ritornare; retrocedere; **to turn down** piegarsi in giù; rovesciarsi; **to turn in** piegarsi, ripiegarsi; tornare a casa; (coll) andare a dormire; **to turn into** sfogare in; trasformarsi in; **to turn on** voltarsi contro; girarsi su; dipendere da; occuparsi di; **to turn**

out riuscire; **to turn out to be** manifestarsi; riuscire ad essere; **to turn over** rotolarsi; rovesciarsi; **to turn up** voltarsi all'insù; alzarsi; apparire, farsi vedere
turn'buck'le *s* tenditore *m*
turn'coat' *s* voltagabbana *mf;* **to become a turncoat** voltar gabbano
turn'down' *adj* (*collar*) rovesciato || *s* rifiuto
turn'ing point' *s* punto decisivo
turnip ['tʌrnɪp] *s* rapa
turn'key' *s* secondino, carceriere *m*
turn' of life' *s* menopausa
turn' of mind' *s* disposizione naturale
turn'out' *s* (*gathering of people*) concorso; (*crowd*) folla; produzione; (*outfit*) vestito; stile *m*, moda; (*in a road*) slargo, piazzola; (*horse and carriage*) equipaggio; (rr) binario laterale
turn'over' *s* (*upset*) rovesciamento, ribaltamento; (*of customers*) movimento di clienti; (*of business*) giro d'affari; rotazione di lavoratori; (com) ciclo operativo
turn'pike' *s* autostrada a pedaggio
turn' sig'nal *s* (aut) indicatore *m* di direzione, lampeggiatore *m*
turnstile ['tʌrn ,staɪl] *s* tornello
turn'ta'ble *s* (*of phonograph*) piatto rotante; (rr) piattaforma girevole
turpentine ['tʌrpən ,taɪn] *s* trementina
turpitude ['tʌrpɪ ,tjud] or ['tʌrpɪ ,tud] *s* turpitudine *f*
turquoise ['tʌrkɔɪz] or ['tʌrkwɔɪz] *s* turchese *m*
turret ['tʌrɪt] *s* torretta
turtle ['tʌrtəl] *s* tartaruga; **to turn turtle** rovesciarsi, capovolgersi
tur'tle·dove' *s* tortora
Tuscan ['tʌskən] *adj & s* toscano
Tuscany ['tʌskəni] *s* la Toscana
tusk [tʌsk] *s* zanna
tussle ['tʌsəl] *s* lotta, zuffa || *intr* lottare, azzuffarsi
tutor ['tjutər] or ['tutər] *s* istitutore privato, ripetitore *m;* (*guardian*) tutore *m* || *tr* dare ripetizione a || *intr* dare ripetizioni; studiare con un ripetitore
tuxe·do [tʌk'sido] *s* (**-dos**) smoking *m*
twaddle ['twɑdəl] *s* sciocchezze *fpl* || *intr* dire sciocchezze
twang [twæŋ] *s* (*of musical instrument*) suono vibrato; (*of voice*) timbro nasale || *tr* pizzicare; dire con un timbro nasale || *intr* parlare con voce nasale
twang·y [twæŋi] *adj* (**-ier; -iest**) (*tone*) metallico; (*voice*) nasale
tweed [twid] *s* tweed *m;* **tweeds** abito di tweed
tweet [twit] *s* pigolio || *intr* pigolare
tweeter ['twitər] *s* altoparlante *m* per alte audiofrequenze, tweeter *m*
tweezers ['twizərz] *spl* pinzette *fpl*
twelfth [twɛlfθ] *adj, s & pron* dodicesimo || *s* (*in dates*) dodici *m*
Twelfth'-night' *s* vigilia dell'Epifania; sera dell'Epifania
twelve [twɛlv] *adj & pron* dodici || *s* dodici *m;* **twelve o'clock** le dodici
twentieth ['twɛntɪ·ɪθ] *adj, s & pron* ventesimo || *s* (*in dates*) venti *m*
twen·ty ['twɛnti] *adj & pron* venti || *s* (**-ties**) venti *m;* **the twenties** gli anni venti
twice [twaɪs] *adv* due volte
twice'-told' *adj* detto più di una volta; detto e ridetto
twiddle ['twɪdəl] *tr*—**to twiddle one's thumbs** rigirare i pollici, oziare
twig [twɪg] *s* ramoscello; **twigs** sterpi *mpl*
twilight ['twaɪ ,laɪt] *adj* crepuscolare || *s* crepuscolo
twill [twɪl] *s* diagonale *m* || *tr* tessere in diagonale
twin [twɪn] *adj & s* gemello
twine [twaɪn] *s* spago || *tr* intrecciare || *intr* intrecciarsi
twinge [twɪndʒ] *s* punta, dolore acuto
twinkle ['twɪŋkəl] *s* scintillio; batter *m* d'occhio || *intr* scintillare
twin'-screw' *adj* a due eliche
twirl [twʌrl] *s* giro, mulinello || *tr* girare; (slang) lanciare || *intr* girare rapidamente, frullare
twist [twɪst] *s* curva; giro; viluppo, intreccio; tendenza, inclinazione; (*yarn*) ritorno; (*e.g., of lemon*) fettina; (*dance*) twist *m* || *tr* intrecciare; torcere; (*e.g., the face*) contorcere; (*the meaning*) stravolgere, stiracchiare; girare || *intr* intrecciarsi; torcersi, divincolarsi; girare; serpeggiare; **to twist and turn** (*in bed*) girarsi e rigirarsi
twister ['twɪstər] *s* (coll) tromba d'aria
twit [twɪt] *v* (*pret & pp* **twitted;** *ger* **twitting**) *tr* ridicolizzare
twitch [twɪtʃ] *s* tic *m;* (*jerk*) strattone *m;* (*to restrain a horse*) torcinaso || *intr* contrarsi; tremare; **to twitch at** tirare
twitter ['twɪtər] *s* garrito, cinguettio; (*chatter*) chiacchierio; ansia, agitazione || *intr* garrire, cinguettare; chiacchierare; tremare d'ansia
two [tu] *adj & pron* due || *s* due *m;* **to put two and two together** arrivare alle logiche conclusioni; **two o'clock** le due
two'-cy'cle *adj* a due tempi
two'-cyl'inder *adj* a due cilindri
two-edged ['tu ,ɛdʒd] *adj* a doppio filo
two'fold' *adj* duplice, doppio
two' hun'dred *adj, s & pron* duecento
twosome ['tusəm] *s* coppia
two'-time' *tr* (slang) fare le corna a
two'-way ra'dio *s* ricetrasmettitore *m*
tycoon [taɪ'kun] *s* magnate *m*
type [taɪp] *s* tipo; (typ) carattere *m;* (*pieces collectively*) (typ) caratteri *mpl* || *tr* scrivere a macchina; simbolizzare || *intr* scrivere a macchina
type'face' *s* stile *m* di carattere
type'script' *s* dattiloscritto
typesetter ['taɪp ,sɛtər] *s* (*person*) compositore *m;* (*machine*) compositrice *f*

type'write' *v* (*pret* **-wrote;** *pp* **-written**) *tr* & *intr* dattilografare, scrivere a macchina
type'writ'er *s* (*machine*) macchina da scrivere; (*typist*) dattilografo
type'writ'ing *s* dattilografia, scrittura a macchina; lavoro battuto a macchina
ty'phoid fe'ver ['taɪfɔɪd] *s* febbre *f* tifoide
typhoon [taɪ'fun] *s* tifone *m*
typical ['tɪpɪkəl] *adj* tipico
typi·fy ['tɪpɪ,faɪ] *v* (*pret* & *pp* **-fied**) *tr* simbolizzare
typist ['taɪpɪst] *s* dattilografo
typographic(al) [,taɪpə'græfɪk(əl)] *adj* tipografico
typograph'ical er'ror *s* errore *m* di stampa
typography [taɪ'pɑgrəfi] *s* tipografia
tyrannic(al) [tɪ'rænɪk(əl)] or [taɪ'rænɪk(əl)] *adj* tirannico
tyrannous ['tɪrənəs] *adj* tiranno
tyrant ['taɪrənt] *s* tiranno
ty·ro ['taɪro] *s* (**-ros**) principiante *m*
Tyrrhe'nian Sea' [tɪ'rinɪ·ən] *s* Mare Tirreno

U

U, u [ju] *s* ventunesima lettera dell'alfabeto inglese
ubiquitous [ju'bɪkwɪtəs] *adj* ubiquo
udder ['ʌdər] *s* mammella
ugliness ['ʌglɪnɪs] *s* bruttezza
ug·ly ['ʌgli] *adj* (**-lier; -liest**) brutto
Ukraine, the ['jukren] or [ju'kren] *s* l'Ucraina *f*
Ukrainian [ju'krenɪ·ən] *adj* & *s* ucraino
ulcer ['ʌlsər] *s* piaga, ulcera; (*corrupting element*) (fig) piaga
ulcerate ['ʌlsə,ret] *tr* ulcerare || *intr* ulcerarsi
ulterior [ʌl'tɪrɪ·ər] *adj* ulteriore; (*motive*) nascosto, secondo
ultimate ['ʌltɪmɪt] *adj* ultimo
ultima·tum [,ʌltɪ'metəm] *s* (**-tums** or **-ta** [tə]) ultimato
ultimo ['ʌltɪ,mo] *adv* del mese scorso
ul'tra·high fre'quency ['ʌltrə'haɪ] *s* frequenza ultraelevata
ultrashort [,ʌltrə'ʃɔrt] *adj* ultracorto
ultraviolet [,ʌltrə'vaɪ·əlɪt] *adj* & *s* ultravioletto
umbil'ical cord' [ʌm'bɪlɪkəl] *s* cordone *m* ombelicale
umbrage ['ʌmbrɪdʒ] *s*—**to take umbrage at** adombrarsi per
umbrella [ʌm'brɛlə] *s* ombrello, paracqua *m;* (mil) ombrello
umbrel'la stand' *s* portaombrelli *m*
Umbrian ['ʌmbrɪ·ən] *adj* & *s* umbro
umlaut ['ʊmlaʊt] *s* metafonesi *f;* (*mark*) dieresi *f* || *tr* cambiare il timbro di; scrivere con dieresi
umpire ['ʌmpaɪr] *s* arbitro || *tr* arbitrare || *intr* fare l'arbitro
UN ['ju'en] *s* (letterword) (**United Nations**) ONU *f*
unable [ʌn'ebəl] *adj* incapace; **to be unable to** essere impossibilitato a, non potere
unabridged [,ʌnə'brɪdʒd] *adj* integrale, non abbreviato
unaccented [ʌn'æksɛntɪd] or [,ʌnæk'sɛntɪd] *adj* non accentato, atono
unacceptable [,ʌnək'sɛptəbəl] *adj* inaccettabile
unaccountable [,ʌnə'kaʊntəbəl] *adj* irresponsabile; inesplicabile
unaccounted-for [,ʌnə'kaʊntɪd,fɔr] *adj* (*e.g.*, *failure*) inesplicato; (*e.g.*, *soldier*) irreperibile, mancante
unaccustomed [,ʌnə'kʌstəmd] *adj* (*unusual*) insolito; non abituato
unafraid [,ʌnə'fred] *adj* impavido
unaligned [ʌnə'laɪnd] *adj* non impegnato
unanimity [,junə'nɪmɪti] *s* unanimità *f*
unanimous [jʊ'nænɪməs] *adj* unanime
unanswerable [ʌn'ænsərəbəl] *adj* per cui non vi è risposta; (*argument*) irrefutabile, incontestabile
unappreciative [,ʌnə'priʃɪ,etɪv] *adj* sconoscente, ingrato
unapproachable [,ʌnə'protʃəbəl] *adj* inabbordabile; incomparabile
unarmed [ʌn'ɑrmd] *adj* disarmato, inerme
unascertainable [ʌn,æsər'tenəbəl] *adj* non verificabile
unassailable [,ʌnə'seləbəl] *adj* inattaccabile
unassembled [,ʌnə'sɛmbəld] *adj* smontato
unassuming [,ʌnə'sumɪŋ] or [,ʌnə'sjumɪŋ] *adj* modesto, semplice
unattached [,ʌnə'tætʃt] *adj* indipendente; (*loose*) sciolto; non sposato; non fidanzato
unattainable [,ʌnə'tenəbəl] *adj* inarrivabile, irraggiungibile
unattractive [,ʌnə'træktɪv] *adj* poco attraente
unavailable [,ʌnə'veləbəl] *adj* non disponibile
unavailing [,ʌnə'velɪŋ] *adj* futile
unavoidable [,ʌnə'vɔɪdəbəl] *adj* inevitabile, ineluttabile
unaware [,ʌnə'wɛr] *adj* inconsapevole, ignaro || *adv* inaspettatamente; (*unknowingly*) inavvertitamente
unawares [,ʌnə'wɛrz] *adv* inaspettatamente; (*unknowingly*) inavvertitamente
unbalanced [ʌn'bælənst] *adj* sbilanciato, squilibrato
unbandage [ʌn'bændɪdʒ] *tr* sbendare
un·bar [ʌn'bɑr] *v* (*pret* & *pp* **-barred;** *ger* **-barring**) *tr* disserrare il chiavistello di
unbearable [ʌn'bɛrəbəl] *adj* insopportabile, insostenibile

unbeatable [ʌn'bitəbəl] *adj* imbattibile
unbecoming [ˌʌnbɪ'kʌmɪŋ] *adj* sconveniente, indegno; (*e.g., hat*) disadatto, che non sta bene
unbelievable [ˌʌnbɪ'livəbəl] *adj* incredibile
unbeliever [ˌʌnbɪ'livər] *s* miscredente *mf*
unbending [ʌn'bendɪŋ] *adj* inflessibile
unbiased [ʌn'baɪ·əst] *adj* imparziale, spassionato
un·bind [ʌn'baɪnd] *v* (*pret & pp* **-bound** ['baʊnd]) *tr* slegare
unbleached [ʌn'blitʃt] *adj* non candeggiato, al colore naturale
unbolt [ʌn'bolt] *tr* (*a door*) togliere il chiavistello a; sbullonare
unborn [ʌn'bɔrn] *adj* nascituro
unbosom [ʌn'bʊzəm] *tr* (*a secret*) rivelare; **to unbosom oneself** aprire il proprio animo, sfogarsi
unbound [ʌn'baʊnd] *adj* sciolto, libero; (*book*) non rilegato
unbreakable [ʌn'brekəbəl] *adj* infrangibile
unbridle [ʌn'braɪdəl] *tr* sbrigliare
unbuckle [ʌn'bʌkəl] *tr* sfibbiare
unburden [ʌn'bʌrdən] *tr* scaricare; **to unburden oneself (of)** vuotare il sacco (di)
unburied [ʌn'berid] *adj* insepolto
unbutton [ʌn'bʌtən] *tr* sbottonare
uncalled-for [ʌn'kɔld ˌfɔr] *adj* superfluo, gratuito; fuori di posto, sconveniente
uncanny [ʌn'kæni] *adj* misterioso, straordinario
uncared-for [ʌn'kerd ˌfɔr] *adj* negletto, trascurato
unceasing [ʌn'sisɪŋ] *adj* incessante
unceremonious [ˌʌnserɪ'monɪ·əs] *adj* senza cerimonie
uncertain [ʌn'sʌrtən] *adj* incerto
uncertain·ty [ʌn'sʌrtənti] *s* (**-ties**) incertezza
unchain [ʌn'tʃen] *tr* scatenare, sferrare
unchangeable [ʌn'tʃendʒəbəl] *adj* immutabile
uncharted [ʌn'tʃɑrtɪd] *adj* inesplorato
unchecked [ʌn'tʃekt] *adj* incontrollato
uncivilized [ʌn'sɪvɪ ˌlaɪzd] *adj* incivile
unclad [ʌn'klæd] *adj* svestito
unclaimed [ʌn'klemd] *adj* non reclamato; (*letter*) giacente
unclasp [ʌn'klæsp] or [ʌn'klɑsp] *tr* sfibbiare
unclassified [ʌn'klæsɪ ˌfaɪd] *adj* non classificato; non secreto
uncle ['ʌŋkəl] *s* zio
unclean [ʌn'klin] *adj* immondo
un·clog [ʌn'klɑg] *v* (*pret & pp* **-clogged**; *ger* **-clogging**) *tr* disintasare
unclouded [ʌn'klaʊdɪd] *adj* sereno, senza nubi
uncollectible [ˌʌnkə'lektɪbəl] *adj* inesigibile
uncomfortable [ʌn'kʌmfərtəbəl] *adj* scomodo, disagevole
uncommitted [ˌʌnkə'mɪtɪd] *adj* non impegnato
uncommon [ʌn'kɑmən] *adj* raro, straordinario
uncompromising [ʌn'kɑmprə ˌmaɪzɪŋ] *adj* intransigente
unconcerned [ˌʌnkən'sʌrnd] *adj* indifferente, noncurante
unconditional [ˌʌnkən'dɪʃənəl] *adj* incondizionato
uncongenial [ˌʌnkən'dʒinɪ·əl] *adj* antipatico, sgradito
unconquerable [ʌn'kɑŋkərəbəl] *adj* inconquistabile, inespugnabile
unconscionable [ʌn'kɑnʃənəbəl] *adj* senza scrupoli; eccessivo
unconscious [ʌn'kɑnʃəs] *adj* (*without awareness*) inconscio, inconsapevole; (*temporarily devoid of consciousness*) incosciente; (*unintentional*) involontario
unconsciousness [ʌn'kɑnʃəsnɪs] *s* incoscienza
unconstitutional [ˌʌnkɑnstɪ'tjuʃənəl] or [ˌʌnkɑnstɪ'tuʃənəl] *adj* incostituzionale
uncontrollable [ˌʌnkən'troləbəl] *adj* incontrollabile, ingovernabile
unconventional [ˌʌnkən'venʃənəl] *adj* non convenzionale, anticonformista
uncork [ʌn'kɔrk] *tr* stappare
uncouple [ʌn'kʌpəl] *tr* sganciare, disconnettere
uncouth [ʌn'kuθ] *adj* zotico, incivile, pacchiano
uncover [ʌn'kʌvər] *tr* scoprire
unction ['ʌŋkʃən] *s* unzione; (fig) untuosità *f*
unctuous ['ʌŋktʃʊ·əs] *adj* untuoso
uncultivated [ʌn'kʌltɪ ˌvetɪd] *adj* incolto
uncultured [ʌn'kʌltʃərd] *adj* incolto, rozzo
uncut [ʌn'kʌt] *adj* non tagliato; (*book*) intonso
undamaged [ʌn'dæmɪdʒd] *adj* indenne, illeso
undaunted [ʌn'dɔntɪd] *adj* imperterrito, impavido
undeceive [ˌʌndɪ'siv] *tr* disingannare
undecided [ˌʌndɪ'saɪdɪd] *adj* indeciso
undefeated [ˌʌndɪ'fitɪd] *adj* invitto
undefended [ˌʌndɪ'fendɪd] *adj* indifeso
undefensible [ˌʌndɪ'fensɪbəl] *adj* insostenibile
undefiled [ˌʌndɪ'faɪld] *adj* puro, immacolato
undeniable [ˌʌndɪ'naɪ·əbəl] *adj* innegabile, indubitato
under ['ʌndər] *adj* di sotto; (*lower*) inferiore; (*clothing*) intimo, personale ‖ *adv* sotto; più sotto; **to go under** affondare; cedere; (coll) fallire ‖ *prep* sotto; sotto a; (*e.g., 20 years old*) meno di; **under full sail** a vele spiegate; **under lock and key** sotto chiave; **under oath** sotto giuramento; **under penalty of death** sotto pena di morte; **under sail** a vela; **under separate cover** in plico separato; **under steam** sotto pressione; **under the hand and seal of** firmato di pugno di; **under the weather** (coll) un po' indisposto; **under way** già iniziato
un'der·age' *adj* minorenne
un'der-arm' pad' *s* sottoascella *m*

un'der·bid' *v* (*pret & pp* **-bid;** *ger* **-bidding)** *tr* fare un'offerta inferiore a quella di
un'der·brush' *s* sottobosco
un'der·car'riage *s* (aut) telaio; (aer) carrello d'atterraggio
un'der·clothes' *spl* biancheria intima
un'der·consump'tion *s* sottoconsumo
un'der·cov'er *adj* segreto
un'der·cur'rent *s* (*of water*) corrente subacquea; (*of air*) corrente *f* inferiore; (fig) controcorrente *f*
underdeveloped [ˌʌndərdɪˈvɛləpt] *adj* sottosviluppato
un'der·dog' *s* chi è destinato ad avere la peggio; vittima; **the underdogs** i diseredati
un'der·done' *adj* non cotto abbastanza
un'der·es'timate' *tr* sottovalutare
un'der·gar'ment *s* indumento intimo
un'der·go' *v* (*pret* **-went;** *pp* **-gone)** *tr* (*a test*) passare, sottostare (with *dat*); (*surgery*) subire, sottoporsi a; soffrire
un'der·grad'uate *adj* (*student*) non ancora laureato; (*course*) per studenti non ancora laureati ‖ *s* studente universitario che non ha ancora ricevuto il primo diploma
un'der·ground' *adj* sotterraneo; segreto ‖ *s* regione sotterranea; macchia, resistenza ‖ *adv* sottoterra; alla macchia, segretamente
un'der·growth' *s* sterpaglia
underhanded [ˈʌndərˈhændəd] *adj* subdolo, di sottomano
un'der·line' or **un'der·line'** *tr* sottolineare
underling [ˈʌndərlɪŋ] *s* tirapiedi *m*
un'der·mine' *tr* scalzare, minare
underneath [ˌʌndərˈniθ] *adj* inferiore ‖ *s* disotto ‖ *adv* sotto, di sotto ‖ *prep* sotto a, sotto
undernourished [ˌʌndərˈnʌrɪʃt] *adj* denutrito, malnutrito
un'der·pass' *s* sottopassaggio
un'der·pay' *s* (*pret & pp* **-paid)** *tr & intr* pagare insufficientemente
un'der·pin' *v* (*pret & pp* **-pinned;** *ger* **-pinning)** *tr* rincalzare
underprivileged [ˌʌndərˈprɪvɪlɪdʒd] *adj* derelitto, diseredato
un'der·rate' *tr* sottovalutare
un'der·score' *tr* sottolineare
un'der·sea' *adj* sottomarino ‖ *adv* sotto il mare
un'der·seas' *adv* sotto il mare
un'der·sec'retar'y *s* (**-ies**) sottosegretario
un'der·sell' *v* (*pret & pp* **-sold)** *tr* vendere a prezzo minore di; (*to sell for less than actual value*) svendere
un'der·shirt' *s* camiciola, canottiera
undersigned [ˈʌndərˌsaɪnd] *adj* sottoscritto
un'der·skirt' *s* sottogonna
un'der·stand' *v* (*pret & pp* **-stood)** *tr* capire, comprendere; sottintendere; (*to accept as true*) constare, e.g., **he understands that you are wrong** gli consta che Lei ha torto ‖ *intr* capire, comprendere
understandable [ˌʌndərˈstændəbəl] *adj* comprensibile
understanding [ˌʌndərˈstændɪŋ] *adj* comprensivo, tollerante ‖ *s* (*mind*) intelletto; (*knowledge*) conoscenza; comprensione, intendimento; (*agreement*) intesa, accordo
understatement [ˌʌndərˈstetmənt] *s* sottovalutazione
un'der·stud'y *s* (**-ies**) (theat) doppio, sostituto ‖ *v* (**-ied**) *tr* (*an actor*) fare il doppio di
un'der·take' *v* (*pret* **-took;** *ger* **-taken)** *tr* intraprendere; (*to promise*) promettere
undertaker [ˌʌnderˈtekər] or [ˈʌndərˌtekər] *s* impresario ‖ [ˈʌndərˌtekər] *s* impresario di pompe funebri
undertaking [ˌʌndərˈtekɪŋ] *s* (*task*) impresa; (*promise*) promessa ‖ [ˈʌndərˌtekɪŋ] *s* impresa di pompe funebri
un'der·tone' *s* bassa voce; (*background sound*) ronzio di fondo; tono; colore smorzato
un'der·tow' *s* (*on the beach*) risacca; (*countercurrent below surface*) controcorrente *f*
un'der·wa'ter *adj* subacqueo ‖ *adv* sottacqua
un'der·wear' *s* biancheria intima
un'der·world' *s* (*criminal world*) malavita, teppa; (*abode of spirits*) ade *m*, averno; mondo sotterraneo; mondo sottomarino; antipodi *mpl*
un'der·write' *v* (*pret* **-wrote;** *pp* **-written)** *tr* sottoscrivere; (*to insure*) assicurare
un'der·writ'er *s* sottoscrittore *m;* (ins) assicuratore *m*
undeserved [ˌʌndɪˈzʌrvd] *adj* immeritato
undesirable [ˌʌndɪˈzaɪrəbəl] *adj & s* indesiderabile *mf*
undetachable [ˌʌndɪˈtætʃəbəl] *adj* non movibile
undeveloped [ˌʌndɪˈvɛləpt] *adj* (*land*) non sfruttato; (*country*) sottosviluppato
undigested [ˌʌndɪˈdʒestɪd] *adj* non digerito
undignified [ʌnˈdɪgnɪˌfaɪd] *adj* poco decoroso
undiscernible [ˌʌndɪˈzʌrnɪbəl] or [ˌʌndɪˈsʌrnɪbəl] *adj* impercettibile
undisputed [ˌʌndɪˈspjutəd] *adj* indiscusso, incontrastato
un·do [ʌnˈdu] *v* (*pret* **-did;** *pp* **-done)** *tr* sfare, disfare; rovinare; (*a package*) aprire; (*a knot*) sciogliere
undoing [ʌnˈdu·ɪŋ] *s* rovina
undone [ʌnˈdʌn] *adj* non finito; **to come undone** disfarsi; **to leave nothing undone** non tralasciare di fare nulla
undoubtedly [ʌnˈdaʊtɪdli] *adv* indubbiamente, senza dubbio
undress [ˈʌnˌdres] or [ʌnˈdres] *s* vestaglia; vestito da ogni giorno ‖ [ʌnˈdres] *tr* spogliare, svestire; (*a*

wound) sbendare || *intr* spogliarsi, svestirsi
undrinkable [ʌn'drɪŋkəbəl] *adj* imbevibile, non potabile
undue [ʌn'dju] or [ʌn'du] *adj* indebito; immeritato; eccessivo
undulate ['ʌndjə,let] *intr* ondulare
unduly [ʌn'djuli] or [ʌn'duli] *adv* indebitamente, eccessivamente
unearned [ʌn'ʌrnd] *adj* non guadagnato col lavoro; immeritato; non ancora guadagnato
un'earned in'crement *s* plusvalenza
unearth [ʌn'ʌrθ] *tr* dissotterrare
unearthly [ʌn'ʌrθli] *adj* ultraterreno; spettrale; impossibile, straordinario
uneasy [ʌn'izi] *adj* (*worried*) preoccupato; (*constrained*) scomodo; (*not conducive to ease*) inquietante, a disagio
uneatable [ʌn'itəbəl] *adj* immangiabile
uneconomic(al) [,ʌnikə'nɑmɪk(əl)] or [,ʌnɛkə'nɑmɪk(əl)] *adj* antieconomico
uneducated [ʌn'ɛdjə,ketɪd] *adj* ineducato
unemployed [,ʌnɛm'plɔɪd] *adj* disoccupato, incollocato; improduttivo || **the unemployed** i disoccupati
unemployment [,ʌnɛm'plɔɪmənt] *s* disimpiego, disoccupazione
unemploy'ment compensa'tion *s* sussidio di disoccupazione
unending [ʌn'ɛndɪŋ] *adj* interminabile
unequal [ʌn'ikwəl] *adj* disuguale, impari; **to be unequal to** (*a task*) non essere all'altezza di
unequaled or **unequalled** [ʌn'ikwəld] *adj* ineguagliato
unerring [ʌn'ʌrɪŋ] or [ʌn'ɛrɪŋ] *adj* infallibile; corretto, preciso
unessential [,ʌnɛ'sɛnʃəl] *adj* non essenziale
uneven [ʌn'ivən] *adj* disuguale, ineguale; (*number*) dispari
uneventful [,ʌnɪ'vɛntfəl] *adj* senza avvenimenti importanti; (*life*) tranquillo
unexceptionable [,ʌnɛk'sɛpʃənəbəl] *adj* ineccepibile, irreprensibile
unexpected [,ʌnɛk'spɛktɪd] *adj* insospettato, imprevisto
unexplained [,ʌnɛk'splend] *adj* inesplicato
unexplored [,ʌnɛk'splord] *adj* inesplorato
unexposed [,ʌnɛk'spozd] *adj* (phot) non esposto alla luce
unfading [ʌn'fedɪŋ] *adj* immarcescibile; imperituro
unfailing [ʌn'felɪŋ] *adj* immancabile, infallibile; (*inexhaustible*) inesauribile; (*dependable*) sicuro
unfair [ʌn'fɛr] *adj* ingiusto; disonesto, sleale
unfaithful [ʌn'feθfəl] *adj* infedele
unfamiliar [,ʌnfə'mɪljər] *adj* poco pratico; poco abituale, strano; non conosciuto
unfasten [ʌn'fæsən] or [ʌn'fɑsən] *tr* sfibbiare, sciogliere
unfathomable [ʌn'fæðəməbəl] *adj* insondabile
unfavorable [ʌn'fevərəbəl] *adj* sfavorevole
unfeeling [ʌn'filɪŋ] *adj* insensibile
unfetter [ʌn'fɛtər] *tr* sciogliere dalle catene
unfinished [ʌn'fɪnɪʃt] *adj* incompiuto; grezzo, non rifinito; (*business*) inevaso
unfit [ʌn'fɪt] *adj* disadatto; inabile
unfledged [ʌn'flɛdʒd] *adj* implume
unfold [ʌn'fold] *tr* schiudere; (*e.g.*, *a newspaper*) spiegare || *intr* schiudersi; svolgersi
unforeseeable [,ʌnfor'si·əbəl] *adj* imprevedibile
unforeseen [,ʌnfor'sin] *adj* imprevisto
unforgettable [,ʌnfər'gɛtəbəl] *adj* indimenticabile
unforgivable [,ʌnfər'gɪvəbəl] *adj* imperdonabile
unfortunate [ʌn'fɔrtjənɪt] *adj* & *s* disgraziato, sfortunato
unfounded [ʌn'faʊndɪd] *adj* infondato
un·freeze [ʌn'friz] *v* (*pret* **-froze**; *pp* **-frozen**) *tr* disgelare; (*credit*) sbloccare
unfriend·ly [ʌn'frɛndli] *adj* (**-lier; -liest**) *adj* mal disposto, ostile; sfavorevole
unfruitful [ʌn'frutfəl] *adj* infruttuoso
unfulfilled [,ʌnfəl'fɪld] *adj* incompiuto
unfurl [ʌn'fʌrl] *tr* spiegare, dispiegare
unfurnished [ʌn'fʌrnɪʃt] *adj* smobiliato
ungainly [ʌn'genli] *adj* sgraziato, maldestro
ungentlemanly [ʌn'dʒɛntəlmənli] *adj* indegno di un gentleman
ungird [ʌn'gʌrd] *tr* discingere
ungodly [ʌn'gɑdli] *adj* irreligioso, empio; (*dreadful*) (coll) atroce
ungracious [ʌn'greʃəs] *adj* rude, scortese; (*task*) sgradevole
ungrammatical [,ʌngrə'mætɪkəl] *adj* sgrammaticato
ungrateful [ʌn'gretfəl] *adj* ingrato
ungrudgingly [ʌn'grʌdʒɪŋli] *adv* di buon grado, volentieri
unguarded [ʌn'gɑrdɪd] *adj* incustodito, indifeso; incauto, imprudente
unguent ['ʌŋgwənt] *s* unguento
unhappiness [ʌn'hæpɪnɪs] *s* infelicità *f*
unhap·py [ʌn'hæpi] *adj* (**-pier; -piest**) infelice, sfortunato
unharmed [ʌn'hɑrmd] *adj* illeso
unharness [ʌn'hɑrnɪs] *tr* togliere i finimenti a
unhealth·y [ʌn'hɛlθi] *adj* (**-ier; -iest**) malsano
unheard-of [ʌn'hʌrd,ɑv] *adj* (*unknown*) sconosciuto; inaudito
unhinge [ʌn'hɪndʒ] *tr* sgangherare; (fig) sconvolgere
unhitch [ʌn'hɪtʃ] *tr* sganciare; (*a horse*) staccare
unho·ly [ʌn'holi] *adj* (**-lier; -liest**) empio; terribile, atroce
unhook [ʌn'hʊk] *tr* sganciare
unhoped-for [ʌn'hopt,fɔr] *adj* insperato
unhorse [ʌn'hɔrs] *tr* disarcionare

unhurt [ʌn'hʌrt] *adj* incolume, illeso
unicorn ['junɪ ,kɔrn] *s* unicorno
unification [,junɪfɪ'keʃən] *s* unificazione
uniform ['junɪ ,fɔrm] *adj & s* uniforme *f* || *tr* uniformare
uni·fy ['junɪ ,faɪ] *v* (*pret & pp* **-fied**) *tr* unificare
unilateral [,junɪ'lætərəl] *adj* unilaterale
unimpeachable [,ʌnɪm'pitʃəbəl] *adj* irrefutabile; irreprensibile
unimportant [,ʌnɪm'pɔrtənt] *adj* poco importante
uninhabited [,ʌnɪn'hæbɪtɪd] *adj* inabitato, disabitato
uninspired [,ʌnɪn'spaɪrd] *adj* senza ispirazione, prosaico
unintelligent [,ʌnɪn'telɪdʒənt] *adj* non intelligente; stupido
unintelligible [,ʌnɪn'telɪdʒɪbəl] *adj* inintelligibile
uninterested [ʌn'ɪntrɪstɪd] or [ʌn'ɪntə ,restɪd] *adj* non interessato
uninteresting [ʌn'ɪntrɪstɪŋ] or [ʌn'ɪntə ,restɪŋ] *adj* poco interessante
uninterrupted [,ʌnɪntə'rʌptɪd] *adj* ininterrotto
union ['junjən] *s* unione; unione matrimoniale; (*of workers*) sindacato
unionize ['junjə ,naɪz] *tr* organizzare in un sindacato || *intr* organizzarsi in un sindacato
un'ion shop' *s* fabbrica che assume solo sindacalisti
un'ion suit' *s* combinazione
unique [jʊ'nik] *adj* unico
unison ['junɪsən] or ['junɪzən] *s* unisono; **in unison** all'unisono
unit ['junɪt] *adj* unitario || *s* unità *f*; (mach, elec) gruppo
unite [jʊ'naɪt] *tr* unire || *intr* unirsi
united [jʊ'naɪtɪd] *adj* unito
Unit'ed King'dom *s* Regno Unito
Unit'ed Na'tions *spl* Organizzazione delle Nazioni Unite
Unit'ed States' *adj* statunitense || **the United States** *ssg* gli Stati Uniti
uni·ty ['junɪti] *s* (**-ties**) unità *f*
universal [,junɪ'vʌrsəl] *adj* universale
u'niver'sal joint' *s* giunto cardanico
universe ['junɪ ,vʌrs] *s* universo
universi·ty [,junɪ'vʌrsɪti] *adj* universitario || *s* (**-ties**) università *f*
unjust [ʌn'dʒʌst] *adj* ingiusto
unjustified [ʌn'dʒʌstɪ ,faɪd] *adj* ingiustificato
unkempt [ʌn'kempt] *adj* spettinato; trascurato
unkind [ʌn'kaɪnd] *adj* scortese; duro, crudele
unknowable [ʌn'no·əbəl] *adj* inconoscibile
unknowingly [ʌn'no·ɪŋli] *adv* inconsapevolmente
unknown [ʌn'non] *adj* sconosciuto || *s* incognito; (math) incognita
Un'known Sol'dier *s* Milite Ignoto
unlace [ʌn'les] *tr* slacciare
unlatch [ʌn'lætʃ] *tr* tirare il saliscendi a
unlawful [ʌn'lɔfəl] *adj* illegale
unleash [ʌn'liʃ] *tr* sguinzagliare; (fig) scatenare
unleavened [ʌn'levənd] *adj* azzimo
unless [ʌn'les] *conj* se non che, salvo che
unlettered [ʌn'letərd] *adj* ignorante; (*illiterate*) analfabeta
unlike [ʌn'laɪk] *adj* dissimile, differente; dissimile da, e.g., **a copy unlike the original** una copia dissimile dall'originale; (elec) di segno contrario || *prep* diversamente da, a differenza di; **it was unlike him to arrive late** non era cosa normale per lui arrivare in ritardo
unlikely [ʌn'laɪkli] *adj* improbabile
unlimber [ʌn'lɪmbər] *tr* mettere in batteria || *intr* prepararsi a fare fuoco; (fig) prepararsi
unlimited [ʌn'lɪmɪtɪd] *adj* illimitato
unlined [ʌn'laɪnd] *adj* (*e.g., coat*) non foderato; (*paper*) non rigato
unload [ʌn'lod] *tr* scaricare; (*passengers*) sbarcare; (*to get rid of*) liberarsi di || *intr* scaricare; sbarcare
unloading [ʌn'lodɪŋ] *s* discarica; sbarco
unlock [ʌn'lɑk] *tr* aprire
unloose [ʌn'lus] *tr* rilasciare; sciogliere
unloved [ʌn'lʌvd] *adj* poco amato
unlovely [ʌn'lʌvli] *adj* poco attraente
unluck·y [ʌn'lʌki] *adj* (**-ier; -iest**) sfortunato, disgraziato
un·make [ʌn'mek] *v* (*pret & pp* **-made** ['med]) *tr* disfare; deporre
unmanageable [ʌn'mænɪdʒəbəl] *adj* incontrollabile
unmanly [ʌn'mænli] *adj* non virile, effemminato; codardo
unmannerly [ʌn'mænərli] *adj* scortese
unmarketable [ʌn'mɑrkɪtəbəl] *adj* invendibile
unmarriageable [ʌn'mærɪdʒəbəl] *adj* che non si può sposare; non adatto al matrimonio
unmarried [ʌn'mærid] *adj* scapolo; (*female*) nubile
unmask [ʌn'mæsk] or [ʌn'mɑsk] *tr* smascherare || *intr* smascherarsi
unmatchable [ʌn'mætʃəbəl] *adj* impareggiabile
unmatched [ʌn'mætʃd] *adj* impareggiabile; (*unpaired*) spaigliato
unmentionable [ʌn'menʃənəbəl] *adj* innominabile
unmerciful [ʌn'mʌrsɪfəl] *adj* spietato
unmesh [ʌn'meʃ] *tr* disingranare || *intr* disingranarsi
unmindful [ʌn'maɪndfəl] *adj* immemore; incurante
unmistakable [,ʌnmɪs'tekəbəl] *adj* inconfondibile
unmitigated [ʌn'mɪtɪ ,getɪd] *adj* completo; assoluto, perfetto
unmixed [ʌn'mɪkst] *adj* puro
unmoor [ʌn'mʊr] *tr* disormeggiare
unmoved [ʌn'muvd] *adj* immoto; fisso, immobile; (fig) impassibile
unmuzzle [ʌn'mʌzəl] *tr* togliere la museruola a
unnamed [ʌn'nemd] *adj* innominato
unnatural [ʌn'nætʃərəl] *adj* contro natura, snaturato; innaturale, affettato

unnecessary [ʌn'nesə ˌseri] *adj* inutile
unnerve [ʌn'nʌrv] *tr* snervare
unnoticeable [ʌn'notɪsəbəl] *adj* impercettibile
unnoticed [ʌn'notɪst] *adj* inosservato
unobserved [ˌʌnəb'zʌrvd] *adj* inosservato
unobtainable [ˌʌnəb'tenəbəl] *adj* non ottenibile, irraggiungibile
unobtrusive [ˌʌnəb'trusɪv] *adj* discreto, riservato
unoccupied [ʌn'ɑkjəˌpaɪd] *adj* libero, disponibile; (*not busy*) disoccupato
unofficial [ˌʌnə'fɪʃəl] *adj* non ufficiale, ufficioso
unopened [ʌn'opənd] *adj* non aperto, chiuso; (*letter*) non dissuggellato; (*book*) intonso
unorthodox [ʌn'ɔrθəˌdɑks] *adj* non ortodosso
unpack [ʌn'pæk] *tr* spaccare, sballare
unpalatable [ʌn'pælətəbəl] *adj* di gusto spiacevole
unparalleled [ʌn'pærəˌleld] *adj* incomparabile, senza pari
unpardonable [ʌn'pɑrdənəbəl] *adj* imperdonabile
unpatriotic [ˌʌnpetrɪ'ɑtɪk] or [ˌʌnpætrɪ'ɑtɪk] *adj* antipatriottico
unperceived [ˌʌnpər'sivd] *adj* inosservato
unperturbable [ˌʌnpər'tʌrbəbəl] *adj* imperterrito, imperturbato
unpleasant [ʌn'plesənt] *adj* spiacevole; (*person*) antipatico
unpopular [ʌn'pɑpjələr] *adj* impopolare
unpopularity [ʌnˌpɑpjə'lærɪti] *s* impopolarità *f*
unprecedented [ʌn'presɪˌdentɪd] *adj* senza precedenti, inaudito
unprejudiced [ʌn'predʒədɪst] *adj* senza pregiudizio, imparziale
unpremeditated [ˌʌnprɪ'medɪˌtetɪd] *adj* impremeditato
unprepared [ˌʌnprɪ'perd] *adj* impreparato
unprepossessing [ˌʌnpripə'zesɪŋ] *adj* poco attraente, antipatico
unpresentable [ˌʌnprɪ'zentəbəl] *adj* impresentabile
unpretentious [ˌʌnprɪ'tenʃəs] *adj* modesto, senza pretese
unprincipled [ʌn'prɪnsɪpəld] *adj* senza principi
unproductive [ˌʌnprə'dʌktɪv] *adj* improduttivo
unprofitable [ʌn'prɑfɪtəbəl] *adj* infruttuoso
unpronounceable [ˌʌnprə'naʊnsəbəl] *adj* impronunziabile
unpropitious [ˌʌnprə'pɪʃəs] *adj* inauspicato
unpublished [ʌn'pʌblɪʃt] *adj* inedito
unpunished [ʌn'pʌnɪʃt] *adj* impunito
unqualified [ʌn'kwɑlɪˌfaɪd] *adj* inabile, inidoneo; assoluto, completo
unquenchable [ʌn'kwentʃəbəl] *adj* inappagabile, inestinguibile
unquestionable [ʌn'kwestʃənəbəl] *adj* indiscutibile
unrav·el [ʌn'rævəl] *v* (*pret & pp* **-eled** or **-elled**; *ger* **-eling** or **-elling**) *tr* dipanare || *intr* districarsi; chiarirsi
unreachable [ʌn'ritʃəbəl] *adj* irraggiungibile
unreal [ʌn'ri·əl] *adj* irreale
unreali·ty [ˌʌnrɪ'ælɪti] *s* (**-ties**) irrealità *f*
unreasonable [ʌn'rizənəbəl] *adj* irragionevole
unrecognizable [ʌn'rekəgˌnaɪzəbəl] *adj* irriconoscibile
unreel [ʌn'ril] *tr* svolgere, srotolare || *intr* srotolarsi
unrefined [ˌʌnrɪ'faɪnd] *adj* non raffinato, greggio; volgare, ordinario
unrelenting [ˌʌnrɪ'lentɪŋ] *adj* inesorabile, inflessibile; indefesso
unreliable [ˌʌnrɪ'laɪ·əbəl] *adj* malfido; (*news*) inattendibile
unremitting [ˌʌnrɪ'mɪtɪŋ] *adj* incessante, costante
unrented [ʌn'rentɪd] *adj* da affittare
unrepeatable [ˌʌnrɪpitəbəl] *adj* irripetibile
unrepentant [ˌʌnrɪ'pentənt] *adj* impenitente
un'requit'ed love' [ˌʌnrɪ'kwaɪtɪd] *s* amore non corrisposto
unresponsive [ˌʌnrɪ'spɑnsɪv] *adj* apatico, insensibile
unrest [ʌn'rest] *s* agitazione
un·rig [ʌn'rɪg] *v* (*pret & pp* **-rigged**; *ger* **-rigging**) *tr* (naut) disarmare
unrighteous [ʌn'raɪtʃəs] *adj* ingiusto
unripe [ʌn'raɪp] *adj* immaturo
unrivaled or **unrivalled** [ʌn'raɪvəld] *adj* senza pari
unroll [ʌn'rol] *tr* srotolare
unromantic [ˌʌnro'mæntɪk] *adj* poco romantico
unruffled [ʌn'rʌfəld] *adj* calmo, imperturbabile
unruly [ʌn'ruli] *adj* turbolento; indisciplinato, insubordinato
unsaddle [ʌn'sædəl] *tr* (*a horse*) dissellare; (*a rider*) scavalcare
unsafe [ʌn'sef] *adj* malsicuro, pericolante
unsaid [ʌn'sed] *adj* non detto, taciuto; **to leave unsaid** passare sotto silenzio
unsalable [ʌn'seləbəl] *adj* invendibile
unsanitary [ʌn'sænɪˌteri] *adj* antigienico
unsatisfactory [ʌnˌsætɪs'fæktəri] *adj* poco soddisfacente
unsatisfied [ʌn'sætɪsˌfaɪd] *adj* insoddisfatto, inappagato
unsavory [ʌn'sevəri] *adj* insipido; (fig) disgustoso, nauseabondo
un·say [ʌn'se] *v* (*pret & pp* **-said** [sed']) *tr* disdire
unscathed [ʌn'skeðd] *adj* incolume
unscheduled [ʌn'skedjʊld] *adj* non in elenco; (*event*) fuori programma; (*e.g., flight*) fuori orario; (*phase of production*) non programmato
unscientific [ˌʌnsaɪ·ən'tɪfɪk] *adj* poco scientifico
unscrew [ʌn'skru] *tr* svitare || *intr* svitarsi
unscrupulous [ʌn'skrupjələs] *adj* senza scrupoli
unseal [ʌn'sil] *tr* dissigillare

unseasonable [ʌn'sizənəbəl] *adj* fuori stagione; inopportuno
unseasoned [ʌn'sizənd] *adj* scondito; (*crop*) immaturo; (*crew*) inesperto
unseat [ʌn'sit] *tr* (*a rider*) scavalcare, disarcionare; (*e.g.*, *a congressman*) far perdere il seggio a, defenestrare
unseemly [ʌn'simli] *adj* disdicevole, sconveniente
unseen [ʌn'sin] *adj* non visto, inosservato; nascosto, occulto; invisibile
unselfish [ʌn'selfɪʃ] *adj* disinteressato
unsettled [ʌn'sɛtəld] *adj* disabitato; disorganizzato; disordinato, erratico; indeciso; (*bill*) da pagare
unshackle [ʌn'ʃækəl] *tr* liberare
unshaken [ʌn'ʃekən] *adj* inconcusso
unshapely [ʌn'ʃepli] *adj* senza forma, deforme
unshaven [ʌn'ʃevən] *adj* non rasato
unshatterable [ʌn'ʃætərəbəl] *adj* infrangibile
unsheathe [ʌn'ʃið] *tr* sguainare
unshod [ʌn'ʃɑd] *adj* scalzo; (*horse*) sferrato
unshrinkable [ʌn'ʃrɪŋkəbəl] *adj* irrestringibile
unsightly [ʌn'saɪtli] *adj* ripugnante, brutto
unsinkable [ʌn'sɪŋkəbəl] *adj* insommergibile
unskilled [ʌn'skɪld] *adj* inesperto
un'skilled la'bor *s* lavoro manuale; mano d'opera non specializzata
unskillful [ʌn'skɪlfəl] *adj* maldestro
unsnarl [ʌn'snɑrl] *tr* sbrogliare
unsociable [ʌn'soʃəbəl] *adj* insocievole
unsold [ʌn'sold] *adj* invenduto
unsolder [ʌn'sɑdər] *tr* dissaldare
unsophisticated [,ʌnsə'fɪstɪ,ketɪd] *adj* semplice, puro
unsound [ʌn'saʊnd] *adj* malsano, malato; (*decayed*) guasto, imputridito; falso, fallace; (*sleep*) leggero
unsown [ʌn'son] *adj* incolto, non seminato
unspeakable [ʌn'spikəbəl] *adj* indicibile; (*atrocious*) innominabile, inqualificabile
unsportsmanlike [ʌn'sportsmən,laɪk] *adj* antisportivo
unstable [ʌn'stebəl] *adj* instabile
unsteady [ʌn'stɛdi] *adj* malfermo; incostante; irregolare
unstinted [ʌn'stɪntɪd] *adj* generoso, senza limiti
unstitch [ʌn'stɪtʃ] *tr* scucire
un•stop [ʌn'stɑp] *v* (*pret* & *pp* **-stopped**; *ger* **-stopping**) *tr* stasare
unstressed [ʌn'strest] *adj* non accentuato; (*e.g.*, *syllable*) non accentato
unstrung [ʌn'strʌŋ] *adj* (*beads*) sfilato; (*instrument*) allentato; (*person*) snervato
unsuccessful [,ʌnsək'sesfəl] *adj* (*person*) sfortunato; (*deal*) mancato; **to be unsuccessful** fallire
unsuitable [ʌn'sutəbəl] or [ʌn'sjutəbəl] *adj* inappropriato
unsurpassable [ʌnsər'pæsəbəl] or [,ʌnsər'pɑsəbəl] *adj* insuperabile
unsuspected [,ʌnsəs'pɛktɪd] *adj* insospettato
unswerving [ʌn'swʌrvɪŋ] *adj* diritto, fermo, costante
unsympathetic [,ʌnsɪmpə'θɛtɪk] *adj* indifferente, che non mostra comprensione
unsystematic(al) [,ʌnsɪstə'mætɪk(əl)] *adj* senza sistema
untactful [ʌn'tæktfəl] *adj* senza tatto
untamed [ʌn'temd] *adj* indomito
untangle [ʌn'tæŋgəl] *tr* sgrovigliare
unteachable [ʌn'titʃəbəl] *adj* indocile; refrattario agli studi
untenable [ʌn'tɛnəbəl] *adj* insostenibile
unthankful [ʌn'θæŋkfəl] *adj* ingrato
unthinkable [ʌn'θɪŋkəbəl] *adj* impensabile
unthinking [ʌn'θɪŋkɪŋ] *adj* irriflessivo
untidy [ʌn'taɪdi] *adj* disordinato
un•tie [ʌn'taɪ] *v* (*pret* & *pp* **-tied**; *ger* **-tying**) *tr* sciogliere; (*a knot*) slacciare, snodare || *intr* sciogliersi
until [ʌn'tɪl] *prep* fino, fino a || *conj* fino a che, finché
untillable [ʌn'tɪləbəl] *adj* incoltivabile
untimely [ʌn'taɪmli] *adj* intempestivo; (*death*) prematuro
untiring [ʌn'taɪrɪŋ] *adj* instancabile
untold [ʌn'told] *adj* non detto, non raccontato; incalcolabile; (*inexpressable*) indicibile
untouchable [ʌn'tʌtʃəbəl] *adj* & *s* intoccabile *mf*
untouched [ʌn'tʌtʃt] *adj* intatto; insensibile; non menzionato
untoward [ʌn'tord] *adj* sfavorevole; sconveniente, disdicevole
untrammeled or **untrammelled** [ʌn'træməld] *adj* non inceppato
untried [ʌn'traɪd] *adj* non provato
untroubled [ʌn'trʌbləd] *adj* tranquillo
untrue [ʌn'tru] *adj* falso
untrustworthy [ʌn'trʌst,wʌrði] *adj* infido, malfido
untruth [ʌn'truθ] *s* falsità *f*, menzogna
untruthful [ʌn'truθfəl] *adj* falso, menzognero
untwist [ʌn'twɪst] *tr* districare || *intr* districarsi
unusable [ʌn'juzəbəl] *adj* inservibile
unused [ʌn'juzd] *adj* inutilizzato; **unused to** [ʌn'justʊ] disavvezzo a
unusual [ʌn'juʒʊ·əl] *adj* insolito
unutterable [ʌn'ʌtərəbəl] *adj* impronunciabile; indicibile
unvanquished [ʌn'væŋkwɪʃt] *adj* invitto
unvarnished [ʌn'vɑrnɪʃt] *adj* non verniciato; puro, semplice
unveil [ʌn'vel] *tr* svelare; (*a statue*) scoprire, inaugurare || *intr* scoprirsi
unveiling [,ʌn'velɪŋ] *s* scoprimento
unvoiced [ʌn'vɔɪst] *adj* non espresso; (phonet) sordo
unwanted [ʌn'wɑntɪd] *adj* non desiderato
unwarranted [ʌn'wɑrəntɪd] *adj* ingiustificato
unwary [ʌn'wɛri] *adj* incauto
unwavering [ʌn'wevərɪŋ] *adj* fermo, incrollabile
unwelcome [ʌn'wɛlkəm] *adj* malaccetto, sgradito
unwell [ʌn'wɛl] *adj* poco bene; **to be**

unwell (*said of a woman*) (coll) avere le mestruazioni
unwholesome [ʌn'holsəm] *adj* malsano
unwieldy [ʌn'wildi] *adj* ingombrante
unwilling [ʌn'wɪlɪŋ] *adj* riluttante
unwillingly [ʌn'wɪlɪŋli] *adv* a malincuore, a controvoglia
un•wind [ʌn'waɪnd] *v* (*pret & pp* **-wound** ['waund]) *tr* svolgere ‖ *intr* svolgersi; (*said of a watch*) scaricarsi; (*said of a person*) rilasciarsi
unwise [ʌn'waɪz] *adj* malaccorto
unwished-for [ʌn'wɪʃt ˌfɔr] *adj* indesiderato, non augurato
unwitting [ʌn'wɪtɪŋ] *adj* involontario
unwonted [ʌn'wʌntɪd] *adj* insolito
unworldly [ʌn'wʌrdli] *adj* (*not of this world*) non terrestre; (*not interested in things of this world*) non mondano; (*naive*) semplice
unworthy [ʌn'wʌrði] *adj* indegno
un•wrap [ʌn'ræp] *v* (*pret & pp* **-wrapped**; *ger* **-wrapping**) *tr* scartare, svolgere, scartocciare
unwrinkled [ʌn'rɪŋkəld] *adj* senza una grinza
unwritten [ʌn'rɪtən] *adj* orale; non scritto; (*blank*) in bianco
unyielding [ʌn'jildɪŋ] *adj* inflessibile
unyoke [ʌn'yok] *tr* liberare dal giogo
up [ʌp] *adj* che va verso la città; diretto al nord; al corrente; finito, terminato; alto; su; (sports) pari; **to be up and about** essere in piedi ‖ *s* salita; vantaggio; aumento; **ups and downs** alti e bassi *mpl* ‖ *adv* su; in alto; alla pari; **to be up** essere alzato; (*in sports or games*) essere avanti; **to be up in arms** essere in armi; essere indignato; **to be up to a person** toccare a una persona; **to get up** alzarsi; **to go up** salire; **to keep up** mantenere; continuare; **to keep up with** mantenersi alla pari con; **up above** lassù; **up against** (coll) contro; **up against it** (coll) in una strettoia; **up to** fino a; (*capable of*) (coll) all'altezza di; (*scheming*) (coll) tramando; **what's up?** che succede? ‖ *prep* su; sopra; fino a; **to go up a river** risalire un fiume
up-and-coming ['ʌpən'kʌmɪŋ] *adj* promettente
up-and-doing ['ʌpən'du·ɪŋ] *adj* (coll) intraprendente; (coll) attivo
up-and-up ['ʌpən'ʌp] *s*—**on the up-and-up** (coll) aperto; (coll) apertamente; (coll) in ascesa
up•braid' *tr* rimproverare, strapazzare
upbringing ['ʌp ˌbrɪŋɪŋ] *s* educazione
up'coun'try *adj* all'interno ‖ *s* interno ‖ *adv* verso l'interno
up•date' *tr* aggiornare
upheaval [ʌp'hivəl] *s* sommovimento; (geol) sconvolgimento tellurico
up'hill' *adj* erto, scosceso; arduo, faticoso ‖ *adv* in salita, all'insù
up•hold' *v* (*pret & pp* **-held**) *tr* alzare; sostenere; difendere
upholster [ʌp'holstər] *tr* tappezzare
upholsterer [ʌp'holstərər] *s* tappezziere *m*
upholster•y [ʌp'holstəri] *s* (**-ies**) tappezzeria; (*e.g., of cushions*) imbottitura; (aut) selleria
up'keep' *s* manutenzione; spese *fpl* di manutenzione
upland ['ʌplənd] or ['ʌplænd] *adj* alto, elevato ‖ *s* terreno elevato
up'lift' *s* elevazione; miglioramento sociale; edificazione ‖ **up'lift'** *tr* elevare
upon [ʌ'pɑn] *prep* su, sopra, in; **upon** + *ger* non appena + *pp*, e.g., **upon arising** non appena alzato; **upon my word!** sulla mia parola!
upper ['ʌpər] *adj* superiore, disopra; (*town*) soprano; (*river*) alto ‖ *s* disopra *m*; (*of shoe*) tomaia; (rr) (coll) cuccetta; **on one's uppers** ridotto al verde
up'per berth' *s* cuccetta superiore
up'per case' *s* (typ) cassa delle maiuscole, cassa superiore
up'per-case' *adj* (typ) maiuscolo
up'per classes' *spl* classi *fpl* elevate
up'per hand' *s* vantaggio; **to have the upper hand** prendere il disopra
up'per•most' *adj* (il) più alto; principale ‖ *adv* principalmente, in primo luogo
uppish ['ʌpɪʃ] *adj* (coll) arrogante, snob
up•raise' *tr* alzare, tirare su
up'right' *adj* ritto, verticale; dabbene, onesto ‖ *s* staggio, montante *m* ‖ *adv* verticalmente
uprising [ʌp'raɪzɪŋ] or ['ʌp ˌraɪzɪŋ] *s* sollevazione, insurrezione
up'roar' *s* gazzarra, cagnara, fracasso
uproarious [ʌp'rorɪ·əs] *adj* tumultuoso; (*noisy*) rumoroso; (*funny*) comico
up•root' *tr* sradicare
up•set' *adj* rovesciato; scompigliato; (*emotionally*) scombussolato; (*stomach*) imbarazzato ‖ **up'set'** *s* (*overturn*) rovesciamento; (*defeat*) rovescio; (*disorder*) scompiglio; (*illness*) imbarazzo, disturbo ‖ **up•set'** *v* (*pret & pp* **-set**; *ger* **-setting**) *tr* rovesciare; scompigliare; indisporre ‖ *intr* rovesciarsi, ribaltarsi
upset' price' *s* prezzo minimo di vendita di un oggetto all'asta
upsetting [ʌp'setɪŋ] *adj* sconcertante
up'shot' *s* conclusione; essenziale *m*
up'side' *s* disopra *m*
up'side down' *adv* alla rovescia; a gambe all'aria; a soqquadro
up'stage' *adj* al fondo della scena; altiero, arrogante ‖ *adv* al fondo della scena ‖ *tr* trattare altezzosamente; (theat) rubare la scena a
up'stairs' *adj* del piano di sopra ‖ *s* piano di sopra ‖ *adv* su, al piano di sopra
upstanding [ʌp'stændɪŋ] *adj* diritto; forte; onorevole
up'start' *s* arrivato, nuovo ricco
up'stream' *adv* a monte, controcorrente
up'stroke' *s* (*in handwriting*) tratto ascendente; (mach) corsa ascendente
up'swing' *s* (*in prices*) ascesa; miglioramento; **to be on the upswing** migliorare

up'-to-date' *adj* recentissimo; moderno; dell'ultima ora
up'town' *adj* della parte più alta della città || *adv* nella parte più alta della città
up'trend' *s* tendenza al rialzo
up'turn' *s* rivolta; (com) rialzo
upturned [ʌp'tʌrnd] *adj* rivolto all'insù; (*upside down*) capovolto
upward ['ʌpwərd] *adj* ascendente || *adv* all'insù; **upward of** più di
U'ral Moun'tains ['jurəl] *spl* Urali *mpl*
uranium [jʊ'renɪ·əm] *s* uranio
urban ['ʌrbən] *adj* urbano
urbane [ʌr'ben] *adj* urbano
urbanite ['ʌrbə,naɪt] *s* abitante *mf* di una città
urbanity [ʌr'bænɪti] *s* urbanità *f*
urbanize ['ʌrbə,naɪz] *tr* urbanizzare
ur'ban renew'al *s* ricostruzione urbanistica
urchin ['ʌrtʃɪn] *s* monello, birichino
ure·thra [ju'riθrə] *s* (**-thras** or **-thrae** [θri]) uretra
urge [ʌrdʒ] *s* stimolo || *tr* urgere, sollecitare, spronare; (*to endeavor to persuade*) esortare; (*an enterprise*) accelerare || *intr*—**to urge against** opporsi a
urgen·cy ['ʌrdʒənsi] *s* (**-cies**) urgenza
urgent ['ʌrdʒənt] *adj* urgente; (*desire*) prepotente
urinal ['jʊrɪnəl] *s* (*receptacle*) orinale *m;* (*for a bedridden person*) pappagallo; (*place*) orinatoio, vespasiano
urinary ['jʊrɪ,neri] *adj* urinario
urinate ['jʊrɪ,net] *tr & intr* orinare
urine ['jʊrɪn] *s* urina
urn [ʌrn] *s* urna; (*for making coffee*) caffettiera; (*for making tea*) samovar *m*
urology [jʊ'rɑlədʒi] *s* urologia
Uruguay ['jʊrə,gwe] or ['jʊrə,gwaɪ] *s* l'Uruguai *m*
Uruguayan [,jʊrə'gwe·ən] or [,jʊrə'gwaɪ·ən] *adj & s* uruguaiano
us [ʌs] *pron pers* ci; noi; **to us** ci, a noi, per noi
U.S.A. ['ju'ɛs'e] *s* (letterword) (**United States of America**) S.U.A. *mpl*
usable ['juzəbəl] *adj* servibile, adoperabile
usage ['jusɪdʒ] or ['juzɪdʒ] *s* uso, usanza; (*of a language*) uso
use [jus] *s* uso, impiego, usanza; **in use** in uso, in servizio; **it's no use** non giova; **out of use** disusato; **to be of no use** non servire a nulla; **to have no use for** non aver bisogno di; non poter soffrire; **to make use of** servirsi di; **what's the use?** a che pro? || [juz] *tr* usare, impiegare, servirsi di; **to use badly** maltrattare; **to use up** consumare, esaurire || *intr*—**used to** translated in Italian in three ways: (1) by the imperfect indicative, e.g., **he used to go to church at seven o'clock** andava in chiesa alle sette; (2) by the imperfect indicative of **solere**, e.g., **he used to smoke all day** soleva fumare tutto il giorno; (3) by the imperfect indicative of **avere l'abitudine di**, e.g., **he used to go to the shore** aveva l'abitudine di andare alla spiaggia
used [juzd] *adj* uso, usato; **to get used to** ['juzdtʊ] or ['justʊ] fare la mano a, abituarsi a
useful ['jusfəl] *adj* utile
usefulness ['jusfəlnɪs] *s* utilità *f*
useless ['juslɪs] *adj* inutile, inservibile
user ['juzər] *s* utente *mf*
usher ['ʌʃər] *s* (*doorkeeper*) portiere *m;* (hist) cerimoniere *m;* (theat) maschera; (mov) lucciola || *tr* introdurre; **to usher in** annunciare, introdurre
U.S.S.R. ['ju'ɛs'ɛs'ɑr] *s* (letterword) (**Union of Soviet Socialist Republics**) U.R.S.S. *f*
usual ['juʒʊ·əl] *adj* usuale, abituale; **as usual** come il solito
usually ['juʒʊ·əli] *adj* usualmente
usurp [jʊ'zʌrp] *tr* usurpare
usu·ry [juʒəri] *s* (**-ries**) usura
utensil [jʊ'tensɪl] *s* utensile *m*
uter·us ['jutərəs] *s* (**-i** [,aɪ]) utero
utilitarian [,jutɪlɪ'terɪ·ən] *adj* utilitario
utili·ty [ju'tɪlɪti] *s* (**-ties**) utilità *f;* compagnia di servizi pubblici
utilize ['jutɪ,laɪz] *tr* utilizzare
utmost ['ʌt,most] *adj* sommo; estremo; massimo || *s*—**the utmost** il massimo; **to do one's utmost** fare tutto il possibile; **to the utmost** al massimo limite
utopia [ju'topɪ·ə] *s* utopia
utopian [ju'topɪ·ən] *adj* utopistico || *s* utopista *mf*
utter ['ʌtər] *adj* completo, totale || *tr* proferire, pronunziare; (*a sigh*) dare, fare
utterly ['ʌtərli] *adj* completamente
uxoricide [ʌk'sorɪ,saɪd] *s* (*husband*) uxoricida *m;* (*act*) uxoricidio
uxorious [ʌk'sorɪ·əs] *adj* eccessivamente innamorato della propria moglie; dominato dalla moglie

V

V, v [vi] *s* ventiduesima lettera dell'alfabeto inglese
vacan·cy ['vekənsi] *s* (**-cies**) (*emptiness*) vuoto; (*unfilled position*) vacanza; (*unfilled job*) posto vacante; (*in a building*) appartamento libero; (*in a hotel*) camera libera; **no vacancy** completo
vacant ['vekənt] *adj* (*empty*) vuoto; (*position*) vacante; (*expression of the face*) vago
vacate ['veket] *tr* sgombrare; (*a posi-*

tion) ritirarsi da; (law) annullare; **to vacate one's mind of worries** liberarsi dalle preoccupazioni || *intr* sloggiare; (coll) andarsene
vacation [ve'keʃən] *s* vacanza, villeggiatura; vacanze *fpl* || *intr* estivare, villeggiare
vacationer [ve'keʃənər] *s* villeggiante *mf*, vacanziere *m*
vacationist [ve'keʃənɪst] *s* villeggiante *mf*, vacanziere *m*
vaca'tion with pay' *s* vacanze *fpl* pagate
vaccinate ['væksɪ,net] *tr* vaccinare
vaccination [,væksɪ'neʃən] *s* vaccinazione
vaccine [væk'sin] *s* vaccino
vacillate ['væsɪ,let] *intr* vacillare
vacillating ['væsɪ,letɪŋ] *adj* vacillante
vacui•ty [væ'kjʊ·ɪti] *s* **(-ties)** vacuità *f*
vacu•um ['vækjʊ·əm] *s* **(-ums** or **-a** [ə]) vuoto; **in a vacuum** sotto vuoto || *tr* pulire con l'aspirapolvere
vac'uum clean'er *s* aspirapolvere *m*
vac'uum-pack'ed *adj* confezionato sotto vuoto
vac'uum tube' *s* tubo elettronico
vagabond ['vægə,bɑnd] *adj* & *s* vagabondo
vagar•y [və'geri] *s* **(-ies)** capriccio
vagran•cy ['vegrənsi] *s* **(-cies)** vagabondaggio
vagrant ['vegrənt] *adj* & *s* vagabondo
vague [veg] *adj* vago
va'gus nerve' ['vegəs] *s* (anat) vago
vain [ven] *adj* vano; (*conceited*) vanitoso; **in vain** in vano
vainglorious [ven'glorɪ·əs] *adj* vanaglorioso
valance ['væləns] *s* balza, mantovana
vale [vel] *s* valle *f*
valedictorian [,vælɪdɪk'torɪ·ən] *s* studente *m* che pronuncia il discorso di commiato
valence ['veləns] *s* (chem) valenza
valentine ['vælən,taɪn] *s* (*sweetheart*) valentino; (*card*) cartolina di San Valentino
valet ['vælɪt] or ['væle] *s* valletto
valiant ['væljənt] *adj* valoroso
valid ['vælɪd] *adj* valido
validate ['vælɪ,det] *tr* convalidare, vidimare; (sports) omologare
validation [,vælɪ'deʃən] *s* convalida, vidimazione; (sports) omologazione
validi•ty [və'lɪdɪti] *s* **(-ties)** validità *f*
valise [və'lis] *s* valigetta
valley ['væli] *s* valle *f*, vallata; (*of roof*) linea di compluvio
valor ['vælər] *s* valore *m*, coraggio
valorous ['vælərəs] *adj* valoroso
valuable ['væljʊ·əbəl] or ['væljəbəl] *adj* (*having monetary worth*) prezioso; pregevole, pregiato || **valuables** *spl* valori *mpl*
value ['væljʊ] *s* valore *m*; importanza; (com) valuta, valore *m*; **an excellent value** un acquisto eccellente || *tr* stimare, valutare
value'-added tax' *s* imposta sul valore aggiunto
valueless ['væljʊlɪs] *adj* senza valore
valve [vælv] *s* (anat, mach, rad, telv) valvola; (bot, zool) valva; (mus) pistone *m*
valve' gears' *spl* meccanismo di distribuzione
valve'-in-head' en'gine *s* motore *m* a valvole in testa
valve' lift'er ['lɪftər] *s* alzavalvole *m*
valve' seat' *s* sede *f* della valvola
valve' spring' *s* molla di valvola
valve' stem' *s* stelo di comando della valvola
vamp [væmp] *s* parte *f* anteriore della tomaia; (*patchwork*) rabberciatura; (*female*) vamp *f* || *tr* (*a shoe*) rimontare; rabberciare; (*to concoct*) inventare, raffazzonare; (*an accompaniment*) improvvisare; (*said of a female*) sedurre
vampire ['væmpaɪr] *s* vampiro; (*female*) vamp *f*
van [væn] *s* camionetta, autofurgone *m*; (*mil & fig*) avanguardia
vanadium [və'nedɪ·əm] *s* vanadio
vandal ['vændəl] *adj* & *s* vandalo || **Vandal** *adj* & *s* Vandalo
vandalism ['vændə,lɪzəm] *s* vandalismo
vane [ven] *s* (*weathervane*) banderuola; (*of windmill, of turbine*) pala; (*of feather*) barba
vanguard ['væn,gɑrd] *s* avanguardia; **in the vanguard** all'avanguardia
vanilla [və'nɪlə] *s* vaniglia
vanish ['vænɪʃ] *intr* svanire
van'ishing cream' ['vænɪʃɪŋ] *s* crema evanescente
vani•ty ['vænɪti] *s* **(-ties)** vanità *f*; (*table*) toletta; (*case*) astuccio di toletta
vanquish ['væŋkwɪʃ] *tr* superare, vincere
van'tage ground' ['væntɪdʒ] *s* posizione favorevole
vapid ['væpɪd] *adj* insipido
vapor ['vepər] *s* vapore *m*; (*visible vapor*) vapori *mpl*
vaporize ['vepə,raɪz] *tr* vaporizzare || *intr* vaporizzarsi
va'por lock' *s* tampone *m* di vapore
vaporous ['vepərəs] *adj* vaporoso
va'por trail' *s* scia di condensazione
variable ['verɪ·əbəl] *adj* & *s* variabile *f*
variance ['verɪ·əns] *s* divario, differenza; **at variance with** (*a thing*) differente da; differentemente da; (*a person*) in disaccordo con
variant ['verɪ·ənt] *adj* & *s* variante *f*
variation [,verɪ'eʃən] *s* variazione
varicose ['værɪ,kos] *adj* varicoso
varied ['verid] *adj* vario, svariato
variegated ['verɪ·ə,getɪd] or ['verɪ,getɪd] *adj* variegato, screziato
varie•ty [və'raɪ·ɪti] *s* **(-ties)** varietà *f*
vari'ety show' *s* spettacolo di varietà
varnish ['vɑrnɪʃ] *s* vernice *f* || *tr* verniciare; (fig) dare la vernice a
variola [və'raɪ·ələ] *s* (pathol) vaiolo
various ['verɪ·əs] *adj* vari; (*varicolored*) vario, variegato
varsi•ty ['vɑrsɪti] *adj* (sports) universitario || *s* **(-ties)** (sports) squadra numero uno

var·y ['vɛri] *v* (*pret & pp* **-ied**) *tr & intr* variare
vase [ves] or [vez] *s* vaso
vaseline ['væsə ,lin] *s* (trademark) vaselina
vassal ['væsəl] *adj & s* vassallo
vast [væst] or [vɑst] *adj* vasto
vastly ['væstli] or ['vɑstli] *adv* enormemente
vastness ['væstnɪs] or ['vɑstnɪs] *s* vastità *f*
vat [væt] *s* tino, bigoncia
Vatican ['vætɪkən] *adj* vaticano ‖ *s* Vaticano
Vat'ican Cit'y *s* Città *f* del Vaticano
vaudeville ['vodvɪl] or ['vɔdəvɪl] *s* spettacolo di varietà; (*theatrical piece*) vaudeville *m*, commedia musicale
vault [vɔlt] *s* volta; (*underground chamber*) cantina; (*of a bank*) camera di sicurezza; (*burial chamber*) cripta; (*of heaven*) cappa; (*leap*) salto ‖ *tr* formare a mo' di volta; saltare ‖ *intr* saltare
vaunt [vɔnt] or [vɑnt] *s* vanto, vanteria ‖ *tr* vantarsi di ‖ *intr* vantarsi
veal [vil] *s* vitello
veal' chop' *s* scaloppa, cotoletta di vitello
veal' cut'let *s* scaloppina
vedette [vɪ'dɛt] *s* (nav) vedetta; (mil) sentinella avanzata
veer [vɪr] *s* virata ‖ *tr* far cambiare di direzione a ‖ *intr* virare; (*said of the wind*) cambiare di direzione
vegetable ['vɛdʒɪtəbəl] *adj* vegetale ‖ *s* (*plant*) vegetale *m;* (*edible plant*) ortaggio; **vegetables** verdura, erbe *fpl*, erbaggi *mpl*, ortaggi *mpl*
veg'etable gar'den *s* orto
veg'etable soup' *s* minestra di verdura
vegetarian [,vɛdʒɪ'tɛrɪ·ən] *adj & s* vegetariano
vegetate ['vɛdʒɪ ,tet] *intr* vegetare
vehemence ['vi·ɪməns] *s* veemenza
vehement ['vi·ɪmənt] *adj* veemente
vehicle ['vi·ɪkəl] *s* veicolo
vehic'ular traf'fic [vɪ'hɪkjələr] *s* circolazione stradale
veil [vel] *s* velo; **to take the veil** prendere il velo ‖ *tr* velare
vein [ven] *s* vena; (*streak*) venatura; (*of ore*) filone *m* ‖ *tr* venare
velar ['vilər] *adj & s* velare *f*
vellum ['vɛləm] *s* pergamena
veloci·ty [vɪ'lɑsɪti] *s* (**-ties**) velocità *f*
velvet ['vɛlvɪt] *adj* di velluto ‖ *s* velluto; (slang) guadagno al gioco; (coll) situazione all'acqua di rose
velveteen [,vɛlvɪ'tin] *s* vellutino di cotone
velvety ['vɛlvɪti] *adj* vellutato
vend [vɛnd] *tr* vendere; (*to peddle*) fare il venditore ambulante di
vend'ing machine' *s* distributore automatico
vendor ['vɛndər] *s* venditore *m*
veneer [və'nɪr] *s* impiallacciatura, piallaccio; (fig) vernice *f* ‖ *tr* impiallacciare
venerable ['vɛnərəbəl] *adj* venerabile
venerate ['vɛnə ,ret] *tr* venerare
venereal [vɪ'nɪrɪ·əl] *adj* venereo
Venetia [vɪ'niʃɪ·ə] or [vɪ'niʃə] *s* (*province*) Venezia
Venetian [vɪ'niʃən] *adj & s* veneziano
Vene'tian blind' *s* veneziana, persiana avvolgibile
Venezuelan [,vɛnɪ'zwilən] *adj & s* venezolano
vengeance ['vɛndʒəns] *s* vendetta; **with a vengeance** violentemente; eccessivamente
vengeful ['vɛndʒfəl] *adj* vendicativo
Venice ['vɛnɪs] *s* Venezia
venire·man [vɪ'naɪrimən] *s* (**-men**) membro di un collegio di giurati
venison ['vɛnɪsən] or ['vɛnɪzən] *s* carne *f* di cervo
venom ['vɛnəm] *s* veleno
venomous ['vɛnəməs] *adj* velenoso
vent [vɛnt] *s* sfiatatoio; (*of jacket*) spacco; **to give vent to** dare sfogo a ‖ *tr* sfogare, sfuriare; mettere uno sfiatatoio a; **to vent one's spleen** sfogare la bile
vent' hole' *s* apertura di sfogo
ventilate ['vɛntɪ ,let] *tr* ventilare
ventilator ['vɛntɪ ,letər] *s* ventilatore *m*
ventricle ['vɛntrɪkəl] *s* ventricolo
ventriloquist [vɛn'trɪləkwɪst] *s* ventriloquo
venture ['vɛntʃər] *s* azzardo, avventura rischiosa; **at a venture** alla ventura ‖ *tr* avventurare ‖ *intr* avventurarsi, arrischiarsi
venturesome ['vɛntʃərsəm] *adj* (*risky*) rischioso; (*daring*) avventuroso
venturous ['vɛntʃərəs] *adj* avventuroso
vent' win'dow *s* (aut) deflettore *m*
venue ['vɛnju] *s* (law) posto dove ha avuto luogo il reato; (law) luogo dove si riunisce la corte; **change of venue** cambio di giurisdizione
Venus ['vinəs] *s* (*very beautiful woman*) venere *f;* (astr) Venere *m;* (myth) Venere *f*
veracious [vɪ'reʃəs] *adj* verace
veraci·ty [vɪ'ræsɪti] *s* (**-ties**) veridicità *f*
veranda or **verandah** [və'rændə] *s* veranda
verb [vʌrb] *adj* verbale ‖ *s* verbo
verbalize ['vʌrbə ,laɪz] *tr* esprimere con parole; (gram) convertire in forma verbale ‖ *intr* essere verboso
verbatim [vər'betɪm] *adj* letterale ‖ *adv* parola per parola, testualmente
verbena [vər'binə] *s* (bot) verbena
verbiage ['vʌrbɪ·ɪdʒ] *s* verbosità *f;* (*style of wording*) espressione
verbose [vər'bos] *adj* verboso
verdant ['vʌrdənt] *adj* verde, verdeggiante
verdict ['vʌrdɪkt] *s* verdetto
verdigris ['vʌrdɪ ,gris] *s* verderame *m*
verdure ['vʌrdʒər] *s* verde *m*
verge [vʌrdʒ] *s* orlo, limite *m;* bordo; (*of a column*) fusto; **on the verge of** al punto di; all'orlo di ‖ *intr*—**to verge on** costeggiare, rasentare
verification [,vɛrɪfɪ'keʃən] *s* verifica

veri·fy ['verɪ,faɪ] *v* (*pret & pp* **-fied**) *tr* verificare, confermare
verily ['verɪli] *adv* in verità
veritable ['verɪtəbəl] *adj* vero
vermilion [vər'mɪljən] *adj & s* vermiglio
vermin ['vʌrmɪn] *ssg* (*person*) persona abominevole || *spl* (*animals or persons*) insetti *mpl*
vermouth [vər'muθ] or ['vʌrmuθ] *s* vermut *m*
vernacular [vər'nækjələr] *adj* volgare || *s* volgare *m*, vernacolo; (*language peculiar to a class or profession*) gergo
versatile ['vʌrsətɪl] *adj* (*person*) versatile; (*tool or device*) a vari usi
verse [vʌrs] *s* verso; (Bib) versetto
versed [vʌrst] *adj* versato
versification [,vʌrsɪfɪ'keʃən] *s* versificazione
versi·fy ['vʌrsɪ,faɪ] *v* (*pret & pp* **-fied**) *tr & intr* versificare
version ['vʌrʒən] *s* versione
ver·so ['vʌrso] *s* (**-sos**) (*of coin*) rovescio; (*of page*) verso
versus ['vʌrsəs] *prep* contro; in confronto a
verte·bra ['vʌrtɪbrə] *s* (**-brae** [,bri] or **-bras**) vertebra
vertebrate ['vʌrtə,bret] *adj & s* vertebrato
ver·tex ['vʌrteks] *s* (**-texes** or **-tices** [tɪ,siz]) vertice *m*
vertical ['vʌrtɪkəl] *adj & s* verticale *f*
ver'tical hold' *s* (telv) regolatore *m* del sincronismo verticale
ver'tical sta'bilizer *s* (aer) deriva
verti·go ['vʌrtɪ,go] *s* (**-goes** or **-gos**) vertigine *f*
verve [vʌrv] *s* verve *f*, brio
very ['vɛri] *adj* (*utter*) grande, completo; (*precise*) vero e proprio; (*mere*) stesso, e.g., **his very brother** suo fratello stesso || *adv* molto, e.g., **to be very rich** essere molto ricco
vesicle ['vesɪkəl] *s* vescichetta
vesper ['vespər] *s* vespro; **vespers** vespri *mpl* || **Vesper** *s* Vespero
ves'per bell' *s* campana a vespro
vessel ['vesəl] *s* (*ship*) nave *f*, vascello; (*container*) vaso; (anat) vaso; (fig) vasello
vest [vest] *s* (*of man's suit*) panciotto, gilè *m*; (*of woman's garment*) corpino || *tr* vestire; **to vest** (*authority*) **in** concedere a; **to vest with** investire di || *intr* vestirisi; **to vest in** passare a
vest'ed in'terest *s* interesse acquisito
vestibule ['vestɪ,bjul] *s* vestibolo
vestige ['vestɪdʒ] *s* vestigio
vestment ['vestmənt] *s* (eccl) paramento
vest'-pock'et *adj* da tasca, tascabile
ves·try ['vestri] *s* (**-tries**) sagrestia; (*chapel*) cappella; giunta esecutiva della chiesa episcopaliana
ves'try·man *s* (**-men**) membro della giunta esecutiva della chiesa episcopaliana
Vesuvius [vɪ'suvɪ·əs] or [vɪ'sjuvɪ·əs] *s* il Vesuvio
vetch [vetʃ] *s* veccia; (*grass pea*) cicerchia
veteran ['vetərən] *adj & s* veterano
veterinarian [,vetərɪ'nerɪ·ən] *s* veterinario
veterinar·y ['vetərɪ,neri] *adj* veterinario || *s* (**-ies**) veterinario
ve·to ['vito] *s* (**-toes**) veto || *tr* porre il veto a
vex [veks] *tr* irritare, tormentare
vexation [vek'seʃən] *s* fastidio, contrarietà *f*
vexatious [vek'seʃəs] *adj* irritante, fastidioso; (law) vessatorio
vexing ['veksɪŋ] *adj* noioso, fastidioso, irritante
via ['vaɪ·ə] *prep* via, per via di
viaduct ['vaɪ·ə,dʌkt] *s* viadotto
vial ['vaɪ·əl] *s* fiala, boccetta
viand ['vaɪ·ənd] *s* vivanda, manicaretto
viati·cum [vaɪ'ætɪkəm] *s* (**-cums** or **-ca** [kə]) (eccl) viatico
vibrate ['vaɪbret] *tr & intr* vibrare
vibration [vaɪ'breʃən] *s* vibrazione
vicar ['vɪkər] *s* vicario
vicarage ['vɪkərɪdʒ] *s* residenza del vicario; (*office; duties*) vicariato
vicarious [vaɪ'kerɪ·əs] or [vɪ'kerɪ·əs] *adj* sostituto; (*punishment*) ricevuto in vece di altra persona; (*power*) delegato; (*enjoyment*) di riflesso
vice [vaɪs] *s* vizio
vice'-ad'miral *s* viceammiraglio, ammiraglio di squadra
vice'-pres'ident *s* vicepresidente *m*
viceroy ['vaɪsrɔɪ] *s* viceré *m*
vice versa ['vaɪsi 'vʌrsə] or ['vaɪsə 'vʌrsə] *adv* viceversa
vicini·ty [vɪ'sɪnɪti] *s* (**-ties**) vicinanze *fpl*, paraggi *mpl*
vicious ['vɪʃəs] *adj* vizioso; maligno, malvagio; (*dog*) cattivo, che morde; (*horse*) selvaggio; (*headache*) tremendo; (*reasoning; circle*) vizioso
victim ['vɪktɪm] *s* vittima
victimize ['vɪktɪ,maɪz] *tr* fare una vittima di; ingannare; (hist) sacrificare
victor ['vɪktər] *s* vincitore *m*
victorious [vɪk'torɪ·əs] *adj* vittorioso
victo·ry ['vɪktəri] *s* (**-ries**) vittoria
victuals ['vɪtəlz] *spl* vettovaglie *fpl*
vid'eo cassette' ['vɪdɪ,o] *s* videocassetta
vid'eo sig'nal *s* segnale *m* video
vid'eo tape' *s* nastro televisivo
vie [vaɪ] *v* (*pret & pp* **vied**; *ger* **vying**) *intr* gareggiare; **to vie for** disputarsi
Vien·nese [,vi·ə'niz] *adj* viennese || *s* (**-nese**) viennese *mf*
Vietnam [,viet'nɑm] *s* il Vietnam
Vietnam·ese [vɪ,etnə'miz] *adj* vietnamita || *s* (**-ese**) vietnamita *mf*; (*language*) vietnamita *m*
view [vju] *s* vista; (*picture*) veduta; prospetto; esame *m*; punto di vista; **to be on view** (*said of a corpse*) essere esposto; **to keep in view** non perdere di vista; **to take a dim view of** avere un'opinione scettica di; **with a view to** con lo scopo di || *tr* guardare, osservare; considerare

viewer ['vju·ər] *s* spettatore *m;* (telv) telespettatore *m;* (phot) visore *m;* (phot) proiettore *m* di diapositive
view'find'er *s* (phot) traguardo, visore *m*
view'point' *s* punto di vista
vigil ['vɪdʒɪl] *s* vigilia; **to keep vigil** vegliare
vigilance ['vɪdʒɪləns] *s* vigilanza
vigilant ['vɪdʒɪlənt] *adj* vigilante
vignette [vɪn'jet] *s* vignetta
vigor ['vɪgər] *s* vigore *m,* gagliardia
vigorous ['vɪgərəs] *adj* vigoroso
Viking ['vaɪkɪŋ] *s* vichingo
vile [vaɪl] *adj* vile, malvagio; (*wretchedly bad*) orribile; disgustoso, ripugnante; (*filthy*) sporco; (*poor*) povero, basso
vili·fy ['vɪlɪ,faɪ] *v* (*pret & pp* **-fied**) *tr* vilificare
villa ['vɪlə] *s* villa
village ['vɪlɪdʒ] *s* villaggio, paese *m*
villager ['vɪlɪdʒər] *s* paesano
villain ['vɪlən] *s* scellerato; (*of a play*) cattivo, anima nera
villainous ['vɪlənəs] *adj* vile, infame
villain·y ['vɪləni] *s* (**-ies**) scelleratezza, malvagità *f*
vim [vɪm] *s* vigore *m,* brio
vinaigrette [,vɪnə'gret] *s* boccetta dell'aceto aromatico
vinaigrette' sauce' *s* salsa verde
vindicate ['vɪndɪ,ket] *tr* scolpare; difendere, sostenere; (*e.g., a claim*) rivendicare
vindictive [vɪn'dɪktɪv] *adj* vendicativo
vine [vaɪn] *s* (*climber*) rampicante *f;* (*grape plant*) vite *f*
vine'dress'er *s* vignaiolo
vinegar ['vɪnɪgər] *s* aceto
vinegarish ['vɪnɪgərɪʃ] *adj* acetoso; (fig) acre, mordace
vinegary ['vɪnɪgəri] *adj* acetoso; (fig) irritabile, irascibile
vineyard ['vɪnjərd] *s* vigna, vigneto
vintage ['vɪntɪdʒ] *s* vendemmia; vino di annata eccezionale; (fig) edizione
vintager ['vɪntɪdʒər] *s* vendemmiatore *m*
vin'tage wine' *s* vino di marca
vin'tage year' *s* buona annata
vintner ['vɪntnər] *s* produttore *m* di vino; vinaio
vinyl ['vaɪnɪl] or ['vɪnɪl] *s* vinile *m*
violate ['vaɪ·ə,let] *tr* violare
violation [,vaɪ·ə'leʃən] *s* violazione
violence ['vaɪ·ələns] *s* violenza
violent ['vaɪ·ələnt] *adj* violento
violet ['vaɪ,əlɪt] *adj* violetto ‖ *s* (*color*) violetto, viola; (bot) violetta; (*Viola odorata*) viola mammola
violin [,vaɪ·ə'lɪn] *s* violino
violinist [,vaɪ·ə'lɪnɪst] *s* violinista *mf*
violoncellist [,vaɪ·ələn'tʃɛlɪst] or [,viələn'tʃɛlɪst] *s* violoncellista *mf*
violoncel·lo [,vaɪ·ələn'tʃɛlo] or [,viələn'tʃɛlo] *s* (**-los**) violoncello
VIP ['vi'aɪ'pi] *s* (letterword) (**Very Important Person**) persona di maggiore riguardo
viper ['vaɪpər] *s* vipera; (*any snake*) serpe *f;* (*spiteful person*) vipera
vira·go [vɪ'rego] *s* (**-goes** or **-gos**) megera, donna dal caratteraccio impossibile
virgin ['vʌrdʒɪn] *adj & s* vergine *f* ‖ **Virgin** *s* Vergine *f*
vir'gin birth' *s* parto verginale della Madonna; (zool) partenogenesi *f*
Virgin'ia creep'er [vər'dʒɪnɪ·ə] *s* vite *f* del Canada
virginity [vər'dʒɪnɪti] *s* virginità *f*
Virgo ['vʌrgo] *s* (astr) Vergine *f*
virility [vɪ'rɪlɪti] *s* virilità *f*
virology [vaɪ'rɑlədʒi] *s* virologia
virtual ['vʌrtʃʊ·əl] *adj* virtuale
virtue ['vʌrtʃʊ] *s* virtù *f*
virtuosi·ty [,vʌrtʃʊ'ɑsɪti] *s* (**-ties**) virtuosità *f,* virtuosismo
virtuo·so [,vʌrtʃʊ'oso] *s* (**-sos** or **-si** [si]) virtuoso
virtuous ['vʌrtʃʊ·əs] *adj* virtuoso
virulence ['vɪrjələns] *s* virulenza
virulent ['vɪrjələnt] *adj* virulento
virus ['vaɪrəs] *s* virus *m*
visa ['vizə] *s* visto ‖ *tr* vistare
visage ['vɪzɪdʒ] *s* faccia; apparenza
vis-à-vis [,vizə'vi] *adj* l'uno di fronte all'altro ‖ *adv* vis-à-vis ‖ *prep* di fronte a
viscera ['vɪsərə] *spl* visceri *mpl,* viscere *fpl*
viscount ['vaɪkaunt] *s* visconte *m*
viscountess ['vaɪkauntɪs] *s* viscontessa
viscous ['vɪskəs] *adj* viscoso
vise [vaɪs] *s* morsa
visé ['vize] or [vi'ze] *s & tr* var of **visa**
visible ['vɪzɪbəl] *adj* visibile
Visigoth ['vɪzɪ,gɑθ] *s* visigoto
vision ['vɪʒən] *s* visione; (*sense*) vista
visionar·y ['vɪʒə,nɛri] *adj* visionario ‖ *s* (**-ies**) visionario
visit ['vɪzɪt] *s* visitare; affliggere, colpire; (*a punishment*) far ricadere ‖ *intr* visitare; (*to chat*) fare un chiacchierata
visitation [,vɪzɪ'teʃən] *s* visitazione; punizione divina, visita del Signore
vis'iting card' *s* biglietto da visita
vis'iting hours' *spl* orario delle visite
vis'iting nurse' *s* infermiera che visita i pazienti a domicilio
visitor ['vɪsɪtər] *s* visitatore *m*
visor ['vaɪzər] *s* visiera; (fig) maschera
vista ['vɪstə] *s* vista, prospettiva
visual ['vɪʒʊ·əl] *adj* visivo, visuale
vis'ual acu'ity *s* acutezza visiva
visualize ['vɪʒʊ·ə,laɪz] *tr* formare l'immagine mentale di; (*to make visible*) visualizzare
vital ['vaɪtəl] *adj* vitale; (*deadly*) mortale ‖ **vitals** *spl* organi vitali
vitality [vaɪ'tælɪti] *s* vitalità *f*
vitalize ['vaɪtə,laɪz] *tr* animare, infondere vita a
vi'tal statis'tics *spl* statistiche *fpl* anagrafiche
vitamin ['vaɪtəmɪn] *s* vitamina
vitiate ['vɪʃɪ,et] *tr* viziare
vitreous ['vɪtrɪ·əs] *adj* vitreo, vetroso
vitriolic [,vɪtrɪ'ɑlɪk] *adj* di vetriolo; (fig) caustico
vituperate [vaɪ'tupə,ret] or [vaɪ'tjupə,ret] *tr* vituperare

viva ['vivə] *s* evviva || *interj* viva!
vivacious [vɪ'veʃəs] or [vaɪ'veʃəs] *adj* vivace
vivaci·ty [vɪ'væsɪti] or [vaɪ'væsɪti] *s* (**-ties**) vivacità *f*, gaiezza
viva voce ['vaɪvə 'vosi] *adv* a viva voce
vivid ['vɪvɪd] *adj* vivido
vivi·fy ['vɪvɪ,faɪ] *v* (*pret & pp* **-fied**) *tr* vivificare
vivisection [,vɪvɪ'sɛkʃən] *s* vivisezione
vixen ['vɪksən] *s* volpe femmina; (*ill-tempered woman*) megera
vizier [vɪ'zɪr] or ['vɪzjər] *s* visir *m*
vocabular·y [vo'kæbjə,lɛri] *s* (**-ies**) vocabolario
vocal ['vokəl] *adj* vocale; (*inclined to express oneself freely*) che si fa sentire, loquace; (*e.g., outburst*) verbale
vocalist ['vokəlɪst] *s* cantante *mf;* (*of jazz*) vocalist *mf*
vocalize ['vokə,laɪz] *tr* vocalizzare || *intr* vocalizzarsi
vocation [vo'keʃən] *s* vocazione; professione, impiego
voca'tional educa'tion *s* istruzione professionale
vocative ['vɑkətɪv] *s* vocativo
vociferate [vo'sɪfə,ret] *intr* vociferare
vociferous [vo'sɪfərəs] *adj* rumoroso, vociferante
vogue [vog] *s* voga, moda; **in vogue** in voga, di moda
voice [vɔɪs] *s* voce *f;* (*of animals*) verso; **in a loud voice** a voce alta; **in a low voice** a voce bassa; **to give voice to** esprimere; **with one voice** con una sola voce || *tr* esprimere; (phonet) sonorizzare || *intr* sonorizzarsi
voiced [vɔɪst] *adj* (phonet) sonoro
voiceless ['vɔɪslɪs] *adj* senza voce; muto; (phonet) sordo, duro
void [vɔɪd] *adj* (*useless*) inutile; (*empty*) vuoto; (law) invalido, nullo; **void of** sprovvisto di || *s* vuoto; (*gap*) buco || *tr* vuotare; (*the bowels*) evacuare; annullare || *intr* andare di corpo
volatile ['vɑlətɪl] *adj* volatile; instabile; (*disposition*) volubile, incostante
volatilize ['vɑlətɪ,laɪz] *tr* volatilizzare || *intr* volatilizzarsi
volcanic [vɑl'kænɪk] *adj* vulcanico
volca·no [vɑl'keno] *s* (**-noes** or **-nos**) vulcano
volition [və'lɪʃən] *s* volontà *f;* **of one's own volition** di propria volontà
volley ['vɑli] *s* (*e.g., of bullets*) scarica, sventagliata; (tennis) volata || *tr* colpire a volo || *intr* colpire la palla a volo
vol'ley·ball' *s* pallavolo *f*
volplane ['vɑl,plen] *s* planata || *intr* planare
volt [volt] *s* volt *m*
voltage ['voltɪdʒ] *s* voltaggio
volt'age divid'er [dɪ'vaɪdər] *s* divisore *m* del voltaggio
voltaic [vɑl'te·ɪk] *adj* voltaico
volte-face [vɔlt'fɑs] *s* voltafaccia *m*
volt'me'ter *s* voltmetro
voluble ['vɑljəbəl] *adj* locuace
volume ['vɑljəm] *s* volume *m;* **to speak volumes** avere molta importanza; essere molto espressivo
voluminous [və'lumɪnəs] *adj* voluminoso
voluntar·y ['vɑlən,tɛri] *adj* volontario || *s* (**-ies**) assolo di organo
volunteer [,vɑlən'tɪr] *adj & s* volontario || *tr* dare or dire volontariamente || *intr* offrirsi; arruolarsi come volontario; **to volunteer to** + *inf* offrirsi di + *inf*
voluptuar·y [və'lʌptʃu,ɛri] *adj* voluttuoso || *s* (**-ies**) sibarita *m*, epicureo
voluptuous [və'lʌptʃu·əs] *adj* voluttuoso
volute [və'lut] *s* voluta
vomit ['vɑmɪt] *s* vomito || *tr & intr* vomitare, rigettare
voodoo ['vudu] *adj* di vudù || *s* (*practice*) vudù *m;* (*person*) vuduista *mf*
voracious [və'reʃəs] *adj* vorace
voracity [və'ræsɪti] *s* voracità *f*
vor·tex ['vɔrtɛks] *s* (**-texes** or **-tices** [tɪ,siz]) vortice *m*
vota·ry ['votəri] *s* (**-ries**) persona legata da un voto; amante *mf*, appassionato
vote [vot] *s* voto; **to put to the vote** mettere ai voti; **to tally the votes** procedere allo scrutinio dei voti || *tr* votare; dichiarare; **to vote down** respingere; **to vote in** eleggere; **to vote out** scacciare || *intr* votare
vote' get'ter ['getər] *s* accaparratore *m* di voti; slogan *m* che conquista voti
voter ['votər] *s* elettore *m*
vot'ing machine' ['votɪŋ] *s* macchina per registrare lo scrutinio dei voti
votive ['votɪv] *adj* votivo
vo'tive of'fering *s* voto, ex voto, offerta votiva
vouch [vautʃ] *tr* garantire || *intr*—**to vouch for** (*s.th*) garantire; (*s.o.*) rendersi garante per, garantire per
voucher ['vautʃər] *s* garante *mf;* (*certificate*) ricevuta, pezza d'appoggio
vouch·safe' *tr* concedere, accordare || *intr*—**to vouchsafe to** + *inf* degnarsi di + *inf*
voussoir [vu'swɑr] *s* cuneo
vow [vau] *s* voto; **to take vows** pronunciare i voti || *tr* promettere; (*vengeance*) giurare || *intr* fare un voto
vowel ['vau·əl] *s* vocale *f*
voyage ['vɔɪ·ɪdʒ] *s* viaggio; (*by sea*) traversata || *tr* attraversare || *intr* viaggiare
voyager ['vɔɪ·ɪdʒər] *s* viaggiatore *m*, passeggero
vulcanize ['vʌlkə,naɪz] *tr* vulcanizzare
vulgar ['vʌlgər] *adj* volgare; comune, popolare
vulgari·ty [vʌl'gærɪti] *s* (**-ties**) volgarità *f*
Vul'gar Lat'in *s* latino volgare
Vulgate ['vʌlget] *s* Vulgata
vulnerable ['vʌlnərəbəl] *adj* vulnerabile
vulture ['vʌltʃər] *s* avvoltoio

W

W, w ['dʌbəl ˌju] *s* ventitreesima lettera dell'alfabeto inglese
wad [wɑd] *s* (*of cotton*) batuffolo, bioccolo; (*of money*) mazzetta, rotolo; (*of tobacco*) pallottola; (*in a gun*) stoppaccio || *v* (*pret & pp* **wadded;** *ger* **wadding**) *tr* arrotolare; (*shot*) comprimere; (fig) imbottire
waddle ['wɑdəl] *s* andatura a mo' di anitra || *intr* sculettare
wade [wed] *tr* guadare || *intr* guadare; avanzare faticosamente; sguazzare; **to wade into** (coll) attaccare violentemente; **to wade through** procedere a stento per; leggere con difficoltà
wad'ing bird' ['wedɪŋ] *s* trampoliere *m*
wafer ['wefər] *s* disco adesivo di carta per chiudere lettere; (*cake*) wafer *m*, cialda; (eccl, med) ostia
waffle ['wɑfəl] *s* cialda
waf'fle i'ron *s* schiacce *fpl*
waft [wæft] or [wɑft] *tr* portare leggermente or a volo || *intr* librarsi, spandersi
wag [wæg] *s* (*of head*) cenno; (*of tail*) scodinzolio; (*person*) burlone *m* || *v* (*pret & pp* **wagged;** *ger* **wagging**) *tr* (*the head*) scuotere; (*the tail*) dimenare || *intr* scodinzolare
wage [wedʒ] *s* salario, paga; **wages** salario, paga; ricompensa; prezzo, e.g., **the wages of sin is death** la morte è il prezzo del peccato || *tr* (*war*) fare
wage' earn'er ['ʌrnər] *s* salariato
wager ['wedʒər] *s* scommessa; **to lay a wager** fare una scommessa || *tr & intr* scommettere
wage'work'er *s* lavoratore salariato
waggish ['wægɪʃ] *adj* scherzoso, comico, burlone
Wagnerian [vɑg'nɪrɪ·ən] *adj & s* wagneriano
wagon ['wægən] *s* carro, carretto; (*e.g., Conestoga wagon*) carriaggio; furgone *m;* carrozzone *m;* **to be on the wagon** (slang) astenersi dal bere; **to hitch one's wagon to a star** avere altissime ambizioni
wag'tail' *s* (orn) ballerina, cutrettola
waif [wef] *s* (*foundling*) trovatello; abbandonato; animale smarrito
wail [wel] *s* gemito, lamento || *intr* gemere, lamentarsi
wain•scot ['wenskət] or ['wenskɑt] *s* pannello per rivestimenti || *v* (*pret & pp* **-scoted** or **-scotted;** *ger* **-scoting** or **-scotting**) *tr* rivestire di pannelli di legno
waist [west] *s* vita, cintura; blusa, camicetta, corpetto
waist'band' *s* cintola
waist'cloth' *s* perizoma *m*
waistcoat ['west ˌkot] or ['westkət] *s* corpetto, gilè *m*
waist'line' *s* vita, cintura; **to keep** or **watch one's waistline** conservare la linea
wait [wet] *s* attesa; **to lie in wait** attendere al varco || *tr* (*one's turn*) attendere || *intr* attendere, aspettare; **to wait for** attendere, aspettare; **to wait on** servire; **to wait up for** (coll) aspettare alzato
wait'-and-see' pol'icy *s* attendismo
waiter ['wetər] *s* cameriere *m;* (*tray*) vassoio
wait'ing list' *s* lista di aspettativa
wait'ing room' *s* sala d'aspetto
waitress ['wetrɪs] *s* cameriera
waive [wev] *tr* (*one's rights*) rinunciare (with *dat*); differire; mettere da parte
waiver ['wevər] *s* rinuncia
wake [wek] *s* (*any watch*) veglia; (*watch by a dead body*) veglia funebre; (*of a boat*) solco, scia; **in the wake of** come risultato di; nelle orme di || *v* (*pret* **waked** or **woke** [wok]; *pp* **waked**) *tr* svegliare || *intr* svegliarsi; **to wake to** darsi conto di; **to wake up** svegliarsi
wakeful ['wekfəl] *adj* sveglio; insonne
waken ['wekən] *tr* svegliare || *intr* svegliarsi
wale [wel] *s* segno lasciato da una frustata, vescica; (*in fabric*) riga, costa
Wales [welz] *s* la Galles
walk [wɔk] *s* (*act*) camminata; (*distance*) cammino; (*for pleasure*) passeggiata; (*gait*) andatura; (*line of work*) attività *f*, mestiere *m;* (*sidewalk*) marciapiede *m;* (*in a garden*) sentiero; (*yard for domestic animals to exercise in*) recinto; (sports) marcia; **to go for a walk** andare a fare una passeggiata || *tr* (*a street*) percorrere; (*a horse*) passeggiare; (*a patient*) far camminare; (*a heavy piece of furniture*) abbambinare; **to walk off** (*a headache*) far passare camminando || *intr* camminare; passeggiare; (*said of a horse*) andare al passo; (sports) marciare; **to walk away from** andarsene a piedi da; **to walk off with** rubare; vincere con facilità; **to walk out** uscire in segno di protesta; (coll) mettersi in sciopero; **to walk out on** (coll) piantare in asso
walkaway ['wɔkə ˌwe] *s* facile vittoria
walker ['wɔkər] *s* camminatore *m;* (*to teach a baby to walk*) girello
walkie-talkie ['wɔki'tɔki] *s* trasmettitore-ricevitore *m* portatile
walk'ing pa'pers *spl*—**to give s.o. his walking papers** (coll) dare gli otto giorni a qlcu
walk'-in refrig'erator *s* cella frigorifera
walk'ing stick' *s* bastone *m* da passeggio
walk'-on' *s* (*actor*) figurante *m*, comparsa; (*role*) particina
walk'out' *s* sciopero
walk'o'ver *s* facile vittoria, passeggiata
wall [wɔl] *s* muro; (*between rooms; of a vein*) parete *f;* (*rampart*) muraglia; **to drive to the wall** ridurre alla disperazione; **to go to the wall** per-

dere; fare fallimento || *tr* murare; **to wall up** circondare con muro
wall'board' *s* pannello da costruzione
wallet ['wɑlɪt] *s* portafoglio
wall'flow'er *s* violacciocca gialla; **to be a wallflower** fare tappezzeria
Walloon [wɑ'lun] *adj & s* vallone *mf*
wallop ['wɑləp] *s* (coll) colpo violento; (coll) effetto || *tr* (coll) dare un colpo violento a; (coll) battere completamente
wallow ['wɑlo] *s* diguazzamento; (*place*) brago, pantano || *intr* diguazzare; (*in wealth*) nuotare
wall'pa'per *s* tappezzeria || *tr* tappezzare
walnut ['wɔlnət] *s* (*tree; wood*) noce *m;* (*fruit*) noce *f*
walrus ['wɔlrəs] or ['wɑlrəs] *s* tricheco
Walter ['wɔltər] *s* Gualtiero
waltz [wɔlts] *s* valzer *m* || *tr* ballare il valzer con; (coll) condurre con disinvoltura || *intr* ballare il valzer
wan [wɑn] *adj* (**wanner; wannest**) (*face*) smunto, sparuto, smorto; (*light*) debole
wand [wɑnd] *s* bacchetta
wander ['wɑndər] *tr* vagare per || *intr* vagare, vagabondare; errare
wanderer ['wɑndərər] *s* vagabondo; pellegrino
Wan'dering Jew' *s* ebreo errante
wan'der•lust' *s* passione del vagabondaggio
wane [wen] *s* decadenza, declino; calare *m* della luna; **on the wane** in declino; (*moon*) calante || *intr* decadere, declinare; (*said of the moon*) calare
wangle ['wæŋgəl] *tr* (coll) ottenere con l'astuzia, rimediare; (coll) falsificare; **to wangle one's way out of** (coll) tirarsi fuori da . . . con l'astuzia || *intr* (coll) arrangiarsi
want [wɑnt] or [wɔnt] *s* bisogno, necessità *f;* domanda; miseria; **for want of** a causa della mancanza di; **to be in want** essere in miseria; **to be in want of** aver bisogno di || *tr* volere, desiderare; mancare; aver bisogno di || *intr* desiderare; **to be wanting** mancare, e.g., **three cards are wanting** mancano tre carte; **to want for** aver bisogno di
want' ad' *s* annunzio economico
wanton ['wɑntən] *adj* di proposito, deliberato; arbitrario; licenzioso, sfrenato; (*archaic*) lussureggiante
war [wɔr] *s* guerra; **to go to war** entrare in guerra; (*said of a soldier*) andare in guerra; **to wage war** fare la guerra || *v* (*pret & pp* **warred;** *ger* **warring**) *intr* guerreggiare; **to war on** fare la guerra a
warble ['wɔrbəl] *s* gorgheggio || *intr* gorgheggiare
warbler ['wɔrblər] *s* canterino; uccello canoro; (orn) beccafico
war' cloud' *s* minaccia di guerra
ward [wɔrd] *s* (*of city*) distretto; (*division of hospital*) corsia; (*separate building in hospital*) padiglione *m;* (*guardianship*) tutela; (*minor*) pupillo; (*of lock*) scontro || *tr*—**to ward off** stornare, schermirsi da
warden ['wɔrdən] *s* guardiano; (*of jail*) direttore *m;* (*in wartime*) capofabbricato
ward' heel'er *s* politicantuccio
ward'robe *s* guardaroba *m*
ward'robe trunk' *s* baule *m* armadio
ward'room' *s* (nav) quadrato
ware [wɛr] *s* vasellame *m;* **wares** merce *f*
war' ef'fort *s* sforzo bellico
ware'house' *s* deposito, magazzino
ware'house'man *s* (**-men**) magazziniere *m*
war'fare' *s* guerra
war'head' *s* (mil) testa
war'horse' *s* cavallo di battaglia; (coll) veterano
warily ['wɛrɪli] *adv* con cautela
wariness ['wɛrɪnɪs] *s* cautela
war'like' *adj* guerresco, guerriero
war' loan' *s* prestito di guerra
war' lord' *s* generalissimo
warm [wɔrm] *adj* caldo; (*lukewarm*) tiepido; (*clothes*) che tiene caldo; (*with anger*) acceso; **to be warm** (*said of a person*) avere caldo; (*said of the weather*) fare caldo || *tr* scaldare, riscaldare; (*s.o.'s heart*) slargare; **to warm up** riscaldare || *intr* scaldarsi, riscaldarsi; **to warm up** (*said, e.g., of a room*) riscaldarsi; (*with emotion*) eccitarsi, accalorarsi; **to warm up to** prender simpatia per
warm-blooded ['wɔrm'blʌdɪd] *adj* (*animal*) a sangue caldo; impetuoso, ardente
war' memo'rial *s* monumento ai caduti
warmer ['wɔrmər] *s* scaldino
warm-hearted ['wɔrm'hɑrtɪd] *adj* caloroso, cordiale
warm'ing pan' *s* scaldaletto
warmonger ['wɔr,mʌŋgər] *s* guerrafondaio
war' moth'er *s* madrina di guerra
warmth [wɔrmθ] *s* calore *m*, tepore *m;* foga, entusiasmo
warm'up' *s* preparazione; (*of radio, engine, etc.*) riscaldamento
warn [wɔrn] *tr* avvertire, mettere in guardia; (*to admonish*) ammonire; informare; **to warn off** intimare di allontanarsi (da)
warn'ing *adj* di avvertimento || *s* avvertimento, ammonimento; (law) diffida
war' nose' *s* acciarino, testa
war' of nerves' *s* guerra dei nervi
War' of the Roses' *s* Guerra delle due Rose
warp [wɔrp] *s* (*of a fabric*) ordito; (*of a board*) svergolamento, curvatura; aberrazione mentale; (naut) gherlino || *tr* curvare, svergolare; (*a fabric*) ordire; falsare, alterare; (naut) tirare col gherlino || *intr* curvarsi; falsarsi, alterarsi; (naut) alare
war'path' *s*—**to be on the warpath** essere sul sentiero della guerra, prepararsi alla guerra; (*to be angry*)

essere arrabiato, essere di cattivo umore
war'plane' *s* aeroplano da guerra
war' prof'iteer *s* pescecane *m*
warrant ['wɑrənt] or ['wɔrənt] *s* garanzia; certificato; ricevuta; (com) nota di pegno; (law) ordine *m*, mandato || *tr* garantire; autorizzare
warrantable ['wɑrəntəbəl] or ['wɔrəntəbəl] *adj* giustificabile, legittimo
war'rant of'ficer *s* sottufficiale *m*
warran·ty ['wɑrənti] or ['wɔrənti] *s* (**-ties**) garanzia; autorizzazione
warren ['wɑrən] or ['wɔrən] *s* conigliera; (fig) formicaio
warrior ['wɔrjər] or ['wɑrjər] *s* guerriero
Warsaw ['wɔrsɔ] *s* Varsavia
war'ship' *s* nave *f* da guerra
wart [wɔrt] *s* verruca
war'time' *s* tempo di guerra
war'-torn' *adj* devastato dalla guerra
war' to the death' *s* guerra a morte
war·y ['weri] *adj* (**-ier; -iest**) guardingo
wash [wɑʃ] or [wɔʃ] *s* lavata; (*clothes washed or to be washed*) bucato; (*rushing movement of water*) sciacquio; (*dirty water*) lavatura; (*painting*) mano *f* di colore; (aer, naut) scia || *tr* lavare; (*dishes*) rigovernare; (*said of sea or river*) bagnare; **to be washed up** essere finito; **to wash away** (*soil of river bank*) dilavare; portar via || *intr* lavarsi; fare il bucato; essere lavabile; (*said of waves*) battere
washable ['wɑʃəbəl] or ['wɔʃəbəl] *adj* lavabile
wash'-and-wear' *adj* non-stiro
wash'ba'sin *s* conca, catinella
wash'bas'ket *s* cesto del bucato
wash'board' *s* asse *m* da lavanda; (*baseboard*) battiscopa *m*
wash'bowl' *s* conca, catinella
wash'cloth' *s* pezzuola per lavarsi
wash'day' *s* giorno del bucato
washed-out ['wɑʃt ˌaʊt] or ['wɔʃt ˌaʊt] *adj* slavato; (coll) stanco; (coll) abbattuto, accasciato
washed-up ['wɑʃt'ʌp] or ['wɔʃt'ʌp] *adj* (coll) finito
washer ['wɑʃər] or ['wɔʃər] *s* (*person*) lavatore *m;* (*machine*) lavatrice *f;* (*under head of bolt*) rondella, rosetta; (*ring to prevent leakage*) guarnizione
wash'er·man *s* (**-men**) lavatore *m*
wash'er·wom'an *s* (**-wom'en**) lavatrice *f*, lavandaia
wash' goods' *spl* tessuti *mpl* lavabili
washing ['wɑʃɪŋ] or ['wɔʃɪŋ] *s* lavata, lavaggio, lavanda; (*of clothes*) bucato; **washings** lavaggio
wash'ing machine' *s* lavabiancheria, lavatrice *f*
wash'ing so'da *s* soda da lavare
wash'out' *s* erosione; (aer) svergolamento negativo; (coll) rovina completa
wash'rag' *s* pezzuola per lavarsi; straccio di cucina
wash'room' *s* gabinetto, toletta
wash'stand' *s* lavabo, lavamano
wash'tub' *s* mastello, lavatoio
wash' wa'ter *s* lavatura
wasp [wɑsp] *s* vespa
waste [west] *s* spreco; (*refuse*) scarico, rifiuto; (*desolate country*) landa; (*excess material*) scarto; (*for wiping machinery*) cascame *m* di cotone; **to go to waste** essere sciupato; **to lay waste** devastare || *tr* perdere, sciupare, sprecare || *intr*—**to waste away** intristire, consumarsi
waste'bas'ket *s* cestino della carta straccia
wasteful ['westfəl] *adj* dispendioso; distruttivo
waste'pa'per *s* cartastraccia
waste' pipe' *s* tubo di scarico
waste' prod'uct *s* scarto; (*body excretion*) escremento
wastrel ['westrəl] *s* sciupone *m;* spendaccione *m*, prodigo
watch [wɑtʃ] *s* orologio; (*lookout*) guardia; (mil) guardia; (naut) turno; **to be on the watch for** essere all'erta per; **to keep watch over** vegliare su || *tr* (*to look at*) osservare; (*to oversee*) vigilare; guardare; fare attenzione a || *intr* guardare; (*to keep awake*) vegliare; **to watch for** fare attenzione a; **to watch out** fare attenzione; **to watch out for** fare attenzione a; essere all'erta per; **to watch over** sorvegliare; **watch out!** attenzione!
watch'band' *s* cinturino dell'orologio
watch'case' *s* cassa dell'orologio
watch' charm' *s* ciondolo dell'orologio
watch' crys'tal *s* cristallo dell'orologio
watch'dog' *s* cane *m* da guardia; (fig) guardiano
watch'dog' commit'tee *s* comitato di sorveglianza
watchful ['wɑtʃfəl] *adj* vigile
watchfulness ['wɑtʃfəlnɪs] *s* vigilanza
watch'mak'er *s* orologiaio
watch'man *s* (**-men**) guardiano, sorvegliante *m;* (*at night*) guardia notturna, metronotte *m*
watch' night' *s* notte *f* di San Silvestro; ufficio religioso della vigilia di Capodanno
watch' pock'et *s* taschino dell'orologio
watch'tow'er *s* torre *f* d'osservazione
watch'word' *s* parola d'ordine, consegna; slogan *m*
water ['wɔtər] or ['wɑtər] *s* acqua; **of the first water** di prim'ordine; (*e.g., a thief*) della più bell'acqua; **to back water** retrocedere; **to be in deep water** essere in cattive acque; **to fish in troubled waters** pescare nel torbido; **to hold water** aver fondamento; **to keep above water** (fig) tenersi a galla; **to make water** (*to urinate*) urinare; (naut) fare acqua; **to throw cold water on** scoraggiare || *tr* bagnare; dare acqua a; (*cattle*) abbeverare; (*wine*) annacquare || *intr* abbeverarsi; (*said of the mouth*) aver l'acquolina; (*said, e.g., of a ship*) fare acqua; (*said of the eyes*) lacrimare

wa'ter bug' *s* bacherozzolo
wa'ter car'rier *s* acquaiolo
wa'ter·col'or *s* acquerello
wa'ter-cooled' *adj* a raffreddamento ad acqua
wa'ter·course' *s* corso d'acqua
wa'ter·cress' *s* crescione *m*
wa'ter cure' *s* cura delle acque
wa'ter·fall' *s* cascata
wa'ter·front' *s* riva, banchina
wa'ter gap' *s* gola, passo
wa'ter ham'mer *s* colpo d'ariete
wa'ter heat'er *s* scaldabagno, scalda-acqua *m*
wa'ter ice' *s* granita
wa'tering can' *s* annaffiatoio
wa'tering place' *s* stabilimento balneare; stazione termale; (*drinking place*) abbeveratoio
wa'tering pot' *s* annaffiatoio
wa'tering trough' *s* abbeveratoio
wa'ter jack'et *s* camicia d'acqua
wa'ter lil'y *s* nenufaro
wa'ter line' *s* linea di galleggiamento or d'acqua; linea di livello
wa'ter main' *s* tubo di flusso principale
wa'ter·mark' *s* linea di livello massimo; (*in paper*) filigrana
wa'ter·mel'on *s* cocomero, anguria
wa'ter me'ter *s* contatore *m* dell'acqua
wa'ter mill' *s* mulino ad acqua
wa'ter pipe' *s* tubo dell'acqua
wa'ter po'lo *s* pallanuoto *f*
wa'ter pow'er *s* forza idrica
wa'ter·proof' *adj & s* impermeabile *m*
wa'ter·repel'lent *adj* idroripellente
wa'ter·shed' *s* spartiacque *m*, displuvio
wa'ter ski' *s* idrosci *m*
wa'ter sof'tener *s* decalcificatore *m*
wa'ter·spout' *s* (*to carry water from roof*) pluviale *m*; (meteor) tromba marina
wa'ter sys'tem *s* (*of a river*) sistema *m* fluviale; (*of city*) conduttura dell'acqua, impianto idrico
wa'ter·tight' *adj* stagno, ermetico; (fig) perfetto, inconfutabile
wa'ter tow'er *s* torre *f* serbatoio
wa'ter wag'on *s* (mil) carro dell'acqua; **to be on the water wagon** (slang) astenersi dal bere
wa'ter·way' *s* via d'acqua, idrovia
wa'ter wheel' *s* ruota or turbina idraulica; (*of steamboat*) ruota a pale
wa'ter wings' *spl* galleggiante *m* per nuotare
wa'ter·works' *s* impianto idrico; (*pumping station*) impianto di pompaggio
watery ['wɔtəri] or ['wɑtəri] *adj* acquoso; lacrimoso; povero, insipido; umido, acquitrinoso
watt [wɑt] *s* watt *m*
watt'-hour' *s* (**-hours**) wattora *m*
wattle ['wɑtəl] *s* (*of bird*) bargiglio
watt'me'ter *s* wattmetro
wave [wev] *s* onda; (*of cold; of feeling*) ondata; (*of the hand*) cenno; (*of hair*) onda, ondulazione || *tr* (*a flag*) sventolare; (*the hair*) ondulare; (*the hand*) fare cenno con; **to wave aside** fare cenno di allontanarsi a; (*e.g., a proposal*) rifiutare || *intr* ondeggiare; fare cenni con la mano
wave'length' *s* lunghezza d'onda
wave' mo'tion *s* movimento ondulatorio
waver ['wevər] *intr* ondeggiare, oscillare; (*to hesitate*) titubare, tentennare; (*to totter*) pencolare
wav·y ['wevi] *adj* (**-ier; -iest**) (*sea*) ondoso; (*hair*) ondulato
wax [wæks] *s* cera; (fig) fantoccio || *tr* incerare; (*a recording*) (coll) registrare || *intr* aumentare; diventare; (*said of the moon*) crescere; **to wax indignant** indignarsi
wax' pa'per *s* carta cerata, carta oleata
wax'works' *s* museo di statue di cera
way [we] *s* maniera, modo; via; condizione; **across the way** di fronte; **a good way** un buon tratto; **all the way** fino alla fine della strada; completamente; **all the way to** fino a; **any way** ad ogni modo; **by the way** a proposito; **in a way** in un certo modo; fino a un certo punto; **in every way** per ogni verso; **in this way** in questa maniera; **one way** senso unico; **on the way to** andando a; **on the way out** uscendo; diminuendo, sparendo; **out of the way** eliminato; fuori mano; strano; irregolare; **that way** in quella direzione; per di lì; in quella maniera; **this way** in questa direzione; per di qui; in questa maniera; **to be in the way** essere d'impaccio; **to feel one's way** avanzare a tentoni; **to force one's way** aprirsi il passo a viva forza; **to get out of the way** togliersi di mezzo; **to give way** ritirarsi, cedere; (*said of a rope*) rompersi; **to give way to** cedere a, darsi a; **to go out of one's way** darsi da fare, disturbarsi; **to have one's way** vincerla; **to keep out of the way** stare fuori dai piedi; **to know one's way around** conoscere bene la via; (fig) sapere il fatto proprio; **to know one's way to** sapere andare a; **to lead the way** guidare, fare da guida; prendere l'iniziativa; **to lose one's way** perdersi; **to make one's way** avanzare; fare carriera; **to make way for** far largo a; **to mend one's ways** mettere la testa a partito; **to not know which way to turn** non sapere a che santo votarsi; **to put out of the way** togliere di mezzo; **to see one's way to** vedere la possibilità di; **to take one's way** andarsene; **to wind one's way through** andare a zig zag per; **to wing one's way** andare a volo; **under way** in moto; in cammino, avviato; **way in** entrata; **way out** uscita; **ways** modi *mpl*, maniere *fpl*; (naut) scalo; **which way?** da che parte?; in che modo?, per dove?
way'bill' *s* lettera di vettura
wayfarer ['we ˌferər] *s* viandante *m*
way'lay' *v* (*pret & pp* **-laid**) *tr* tendere un agguato a; fermare improvvisamente
way' of life' *s* tenore *m* di vita

way'side' *s* bordo della strada; **to fall by the wayside** cadere per istrada; (fig) fare fiasco
way' sta'tion *s* stazione con fermata facoltativa
way' train' *s* treno omnibus
wayward ['wewərd] *adj* indocile, caparbio; irregolare; capriccioso
we [wi] *pron pers* noi; noialtri, e.g., **we Italians** noialtri italiani
weak [wik] *adj* debole
weaken ['wikən] *tr* indebolire, infiacchire || *intr* indebolirsi, infiacchirsi
weakling ['wiklɪŋ] *s* debolino, rammollito
weak-minded ['wik'maɪndɪd] *adj* irresoluto; scemo
weakness ['wiknɪs] *s* debolezza, fiacchezza; (*liking*) debole *m*
wealth [wɛlθ] *s* ricchezza
wealth•y ['wɛlθi] *adj* (**-ier; -iest**) ricco
wean [win] *tr* svezzare, slattare; **to wean away from** disavvezzare da
weanling ['winlɪŋ] *adj* appena svezzato || *s* bambino or animale appena svezzato
weapon ['wepən] *s* arma
weaponry ['wɛpənri] *s* armi *fpl*, armamento
wear [wer] *s* uso, servizio; (*clothing*) vestiti *mpl*, indumenti *mpl*; (*wasting away from use*) consumo, logorio; (*lasting quality*) durata, durabilità *f*; **for everyday wear** per ogni giorno || *v* (*pret* **wore** [wor]; *pp* **worn** [worn]) *tr* portare, avere indosso; (*to cause to deteriorate*) logorare, consumare; (*to tire*) stancare; **to wear out** logorare, strusciare; (*a horse*) sfiancare; (*one's patience*) esaurire; (*s.o.'s hospitality*) abusare di || *intr* logorarsi, consumarsi; **to wear off** diminuire, sparire; **to wear out** logorarsi; stancarsi; esaurirsi; **to wear well** essere di ottima durata
wear' and tear' [ter] *s* logorio
weariness ['wɪrɪnɪs] *s* fatica, stanchezza
wear'ing appar'el ['werɪŋ] *s* abbigliamento, articoli *mpl* d'abbigliamento
wearisome ['wɪrɪsəm] *adj* affaticante; (*tedious*) noioso
wea•ry ['wɪri] *adj* (**-rier; -riest**) stanco || *v* (*pret & pp* **-ried**) *tr* stancare || *intr* stancarsi
weasel ['wizəl] *s* donnola
wea'sel words' *spl* parole *fpl* ambigue
weather ['weðər] *s* tempo; maltempo; **to be under the weather** (coll) non sentirsi bene; (*to be slightly drunk*) (coll) essere alticcio || *tr* (*lumber*) stagionare; (*adversities*) superare, resistere (with *dat*)
weather-beaten ['weðər,bitən] *adj* segnato dalle intemperie
weath'er bu'reau *s* servizio metereologico
weath'er•cock' *s* banderuola
weath'er fore'cast *s* previsioni *fpl* del tempo, bollettino metereologico
weath'er•man' *s* (**-men'**) metereologo
weath'er report' *s* bollettino metereologico
weath'er strip'ping ['strɪpɪŋ] *s* guarnizione a nastro per inzeppare
weath'er vane' *s* banderuola, ventarola
weave [wiv] *s* tessitura || *v* (*pret* **wove** [wov] or **weaved**; *pp* **wove** or **woven** ['wovən]) *tr* tessere; (fig) inserire; **to weave one's way** aprirsi un varco serpeggiando || *intr* tessere; serpeggiare
weaver ['wivər] *s* tessitore *m*
web [wɛb] *s* tessuto; (*of spider*) tela; (*of rail*) anima, gambo; (zool) membrana; (fig) rete *f*, maglia
web-footed ['web,futɪd] *adj* palmipede
wed [wed] *v* (*pret & pp* **wed** or **wedded**; *ger* **wedding**) *tr* sposare; (*said of the groom*) impalmare; (*said of the bride*) andare in sposa a || *intr* sposarsi
wedding ['wedɪŋ] *adj* nuziale || *s* sposalizio, nozze *fpl*, matrimonio
wed'ding cake' *s* torta nuziale
wed'ding day' *s* giorno di nozze
wed'ding invita'tion *s* invito a nozze
wed'ding march' *s* marcia nuziale
wed'ding ring' *s* fede *f*, vera
wedge [wedʒ] *s* cuneo; (*of pie*) spicchio; (*to split wood*) bietta; (*to hold a wheel*) scarpa || *tr* incuneare
wed'lock *s* matrimonio
Wednesday ['wenzdi] *s* mercoledì *m*
wee [wi] *adj* piccolo piccolo
weed [wid] *s* malerba, erbaccia; (coll) sigaretta; (slang) marijuana; **weeds** vestito da lutto, gramaglie *fpl* || *tr* sarchiare, mondare
weeder ['widər] *s* (agr) estirpatore *m*
weed'ing hoe' *s* sarchio, zappa
weed'-kill'er *s* diserbante *m*
week [wik] *s* settimana; **week in, week out** una settimana dopo l'altra
week'day' *s* giorno feriale
week'end' *s* fine-settimana *m*, fine *f* di settimana, week-end *m* || *intr* passare il fine-settimana
week•ly ['wikli] *adj* settimanale || *s* (**-lies**) settimanale *m* || *adv* settimanalmente
weep [wip] *v* (*pret & pp* **wept** [wept]) *tr* piangere; **to weep oneself to sleep** addormentarsi piangendo; **to weep one's eyes out** piangere a calde lacrime || *intr* piangere; **to weep for joy** piangere di gioia
weeper ['wipər] *s* piagnone *m*; (*hired mourner*) prefica
weep'ing wil'low *s* salice *m* piangente
weep•y ['wipi] *adj* (**-ier; -iest**) piangente, lacrimoso
weevil ['wivəl] *s* curculione *m*
weft [weft] *s* (*yarns running across warp*) trama; (*fabric*) tela, tessuto
weigh [we] *tr* pesare; (*anchor*) levare; (*to make heavy*) appesantire; (fig) soppesare, ponderare; **to weigh down** piegare || *intr* pesare; gravitare; **to weigh in** (sports) pesarsi; **to weigh upon** gravare a
weigh'bridge' *s* stadera
weight [wet] *s* peso; (fig) peso; **to carry weight** aver del peso; **to lose weight** diminuire di peso; **to put on weight** crescere di peso; **to throw**

one's weight around far sentire la propria importanza || *tr* appesantire; (*statistically*) ponderare, dare un certo peso a
weightless ['wetlɪs] *adj* senza peso, imponderabile
weightlessness ['wetlɪsnɪs] *s* imponderabilità *f*
weight·y ['weti] *adj* (**-ier; -iest**) pesante; importante
weir [wɪr] *s* sbarramento; (*for catching fish*) pescaia
weird [wɪrd] *adj* soprannaturale, misterioso; strano, bizzarro
welcome ['wɛlkəm] *adj* benvenuto; gradito; **you are welcome** (*i.e., gladly received*) sia il benvenuto; (*in answer to thanks*) prego; **you are welcome to it** è a Sua disposizione; **you are welcome to your opinion** pensi come la vuole || *s* benvenuto || *tr* dare il benvenuto a; accettare; gradire || *interj* benvenuto!
weld [wɛld] *s* saldatura autogena; (bot) guaderella || *tr* saldare || *intr* saldarsi
welder ['wɛldər] *s* saldatore *m;* (*machine*) saldatrice *f*
welding ['wɛldɪŋ] *s* saldatura autogena
wel'fare' *s* benessere *m;* (*effort to improve living conditions*) beneficenza, assistenza; **to be on welfare** ricevere assistenza pubblica
wel'fare state' *s* stato sociale or assistenziale
well [wɛl] *adj* bene; in buona salute || *s* pozzo; (*for ink*) pozzetto, serbatoio; (*spring*) sorgente *f;* (*shaft for stairs*) tromba || *adv* bene; **as well** pure; **as well . . . as** tanto . . . come; **as well as** tanto come, non meno che || *intr* **—to well up** sgorgare || *interj* beh!; bene!; allora!, dunque!
well-appointed ['wɛlə'pɔɪntɪd] *adj* ben ammobiliato
well-attended ['wɛlə'tɛndɪd] *adj* molto frequentato
well-behaved ['wɛlbɪ'hevd] *adj* beneducato; **to be well-behaved** comportarsi bene
well'-be'ing *s* benessere *m*
well'born' *adj* bennato
well-bred ['wɛl'brɛd] *adj* educato, costumato
well-disposed ['wɛldɪs'pozd] *adj* bendisposto
well-done ['wɛl'dʌn] *adj* benfatto; (*meat*) ben cotto
well-fixed ['wɛl'fɪkst] *adj* (coll) agiato, abbiente
well-formed ['wɛl'fɔrmd] *adj* benfatto
well-founded ['wɛl'faʊndɪd] *adj* fondato
well-groomed ['wɛl'grumd] *adj* (*person*) curato; (*horse*) ben governato
well-heeled ['wɛl'hild] *adj* (coll) agiato, benestante
well-informed ['wɛlɪn'fɔrmd] *adj* bene informato
well-intentioned ['wɛlɪn'tɛnʃənd] *adj* benintenzionato
well'-kept' *adj* ben conservato; (*person*) benportante; (*secret*) ben mantenuto
well-known ['wɛl'non] *adj* notorio, ben noto
well-meaning ['wɛl'minɪŋ] *adj* benevolo, benintenzionato
well-nigh ['wɛl'naɪ] *adv* quasi
well'-off' *adj* agiato, benestante
well-preserved ['wɛlprɪ'zʌrvd] *adj* ben conservato; (*person*) benportante
well-read ['wɛl'rɛd] *adj* colto, che ha letto molto
well-spoken ['wɛl'spokən] *adj* (*person*) raffinato nel parlare; (*word*) a proposito
well'spring' *s* sorgente *f*
well' sweep' *s* mazzacavallo del pozzo
well-tempered ['wɛl'tɛmpərd] *adj* ben temperato
well-thought-of ['wɛl'θɔt,ɑv] *adj* tenuto in alta considerazione
well-timed ['wɛl'taɪmd] *adj* opportuno
well-to-do ['wɛltə'du] *adj* benestante
well-wisher ['wɛl'wɪʃər] *s* amico, sostenitore *m*
well-worn ['wɛl'worn] *adj* (*clothing*) liso, consunto, trito; (*argument*) logoro, banale; portato con eleganza
welsh [wɛlʃ] *intr*—**to welsh on** (*a promise*) (slang) mancare a; (*a person*) (slang) fregare || **Welsh** *adj & s* gallese *mf;* **the Welsh** i gallesi
Welsh'man *s* (**-men**) gallese *m*
Welsh' rab'bit or **rare'bit** ['rɛrbɪt] *s* fonduta fatta con la birra servita su pane abbrustolito
welt [wɛlt] *s* (*finish along a seam*) costa; (*of shoe*) guardolo; (*wale from a blow*) riga, sferzata
welter ['wɛltər] *s* guazzabuglio; confusione; (*a tumbling about*) rotolio || *intr* rotolarsi, guazzare
wel'ter·weight' *s* (boxing) peso welter, peso medio-leggero
wench [wɛntʃ] *s* ragazza, giovane *f*
wend [wɛnd] *tr*—**to wend one's way** dirigere i propri passi
werewolf ['wɪr,wʊlf] *s* lupo mannaro
west [wɛst] *adj* occidentale || *s* ovest *m,* occidente *m* || *adv* verso l'ovest
western ['wɛstərn] *adj* occidentale || *s* western *m*
West' In'dies ['ɪndiz] *spl* Indie *fpl* Occidentali
westward ['wɛstwərd] *adv* verso l'ovest
wet [wɛt] *adj* (**wetter; wettest**) bagnato; (*paint*) fresco; (*damp*) umido; (*rainy*) piovoso; che permette la vendita delle bevande alcoliche || *s* umidità *f;* antiproibizionista *mf* || *v* (*pret & pp* **wet** or **wetted;** *ger* **wetting**) *tr* bagnare || *intr* bagnarsi
wet' blan'ket *s* guastafeste *mf*
wether ['wɛðər] *s* castrone *m*
wet' nurse' *s* nutrice *f*, balia
whack [hwæk] *s* (slang) colpo, percossa; (slang) prova, tentativo || *tr* (slang) percuotere
whale [hwel] *s* balena; **a whale of** (slang) gigantesco, e.g., **a whale of a lie** una bugia gigantesca; enorme, e.g., **a whale of a difference** una differenza enorme || *tr* (coll) battere || *intr* pescare balene
whale'bone' *s* osso di balena, fanone *m*

wharf [hwɔrf] *s* (**wharves** [hwɔrvz] or **wharfs**) molo
what [hwɑt] *adj interr* che; quale || *adj rel* quello . . . che; il . . . che, e.g., **wear what tie you prefer** mettiti la cravatta che preferisci || *pron interr* che; quale; **what else?** che altro?; **what if . . . ?** e se . . . ?; **what of it?** e che me ne importa? || *pron rel* quello che; **what's what** (coll) tutta la situazione || *interj* **what a . . . !** che . . . !, e.g., **what a beautiful day!** che splendida giornata!
what·ev'er *adj* qualsiasi; qualunque || *pron* quanto; che; quello che
what'not' *s* scaffaletto
wheal [hwil] *s* vescichetta
wheat [hwit] *s* grano, frumento
wheedle ['hwidəl] *tr* adulare; persuadere con lusinghe; (*money*) spillare
wheel [hwil] *s* ruota; (*of cheese*) forma; (coll) bicicletta; **at the wheel** al volante; in controllo || *tr* roteare; portare in carrozzella || *intr* girare
wheelbarrow ['hwil ,bæro] *s* carriola
wheel'base' *s* passo
wheel'chair' *s* carrozzella
wheel' col'umn *s* (aut) piantone *m* di guida
wheeler-dealer ['hwilər'dilər] *s* (slang) grande affarista *m*
wheel' horse' *s* cavallo di timone; lavoratore *m* di fiducia
wheelwright ['hwil ,raɪt] *s* carradore *m*
wheeze [hwiz] *s* affanno; (pathol) rantolo || *intr* respirare affannosamente; (pathol) rantolare
whelp [hwɛlp] *s* cucciolo || *tr & intr* figliare, partorire
when [hwen] *adv & conj* quando
whence [hwens] *adv* donde, di dove || *conj* donde; per che ragione
when·ev'er *conj* ogniqualvolta, qualora
where [hwɛr] *adv & conj* dove
whereabouts ['hwɛrə ,baʊts] *s* luogo dove uno si trova || *adv & conj* dove
whereas [hwɛr'æz] *conj* mentre; visto che, considerato che
where·by' *adv* per cui, col quale
wherever [hwɛr'ɛvər] *adv* dove mai || *conj* dovunque
wherefore ['hwɛrfor] *s* perché *m* || *adv* perché || *conj* per cui, percome
where·from' *adv* donde
where·in' *adv* dove; in che modo || *conj* dove; nel quale
where·of' *adv* di che || *conj* di che; del quale
where'upon' *adv* sul che; laonde, dopodiché
wherewithal ['hwɛrwɪð ,ɔl] *s* mezzi *mpl*
whet [hwɛt] *v* (*pret & pp* **whetted**; *ger* **whetting**) *tr* affilare; (*the appetite*) aguzzare
whether ['wɛðər] *conj* se; **whether or no** ad ogni modo, in ogni caso; **whether or not** che . . . o che non
whet'stone' *s* pietra da affilare
whey [hwe] *s* scotta
which [hwɪtʃ] *adj interr* quale || *adj rel* il (la, etc.) quale || *pron interr* che; quale; **which is which** qual'è l'uno e qual'è l'altro || *pron rel* che; il quale; quello che
which·ev'er *adj & pron rel* qualunque
whiff [hwɪf] *s* (*of air*) soffio; fiutata; (*trace of odor*) zaffata; **to get a whiff of** sentire l'odore di || *intr* soffiare; (*said of a smoker*) dare boccate
while [hwaɪl] *s* tempo; **a long while** un bel pezzo; **a while ago** un tratto fa; **to be worth one's while** valere la pena || *conj* mentre || *tr*—**to while away** passare piacevolmente
whim [hwɪm] *s* capriccio, estro
whimper ['hwɪmpər] *s* piagnucolio || *tr & intr* piagnucolare
whimsical ['hwɪmzɪkəl] *adj* capriccioso, estroso, stravagante
whine [hwaɪn] *s* (*of dog*) guaito; (*of person*) piagnucolio || *intr* (*said of a dog*) guaire, uggiolare; (*said of a person*) piagnucolare
whin·ny ['hwɪni] *s* (**-nies**) nitrito || *v* (*pret & pp* **-nied**) *intr* nitrire
whip [hwɪp] *s* frusta; uova *fpl* sbattute con frutta || *v* (*pret & pp* **whipped** or **whipt**; *ger* **whipping**) *tr* frustare, battere; (*eggs*) frullare; (coll) vincere, sconfiggere; **to whip off** (coll) buttar giù; **to whip out** tirar fuori rapidamente; **to whip up** (coll) preparare in quattro e quattr'otto; (coll) eccitare, incitare
whip'cord' *s* cordino della frusta; (*fabric*) saia a diagonale
whip' hand' *s* mano che tiene la frusta; vantaggio, posizione vantaggiosa
whip'lash' *s* scudisciata
whipped' cream' *s* panna montata
whipper-snapper ['hwɪpər ,snæpər] *s* pivello
whippet ['hwɪpɪt] *s* piccolo levriere
whip'ping boy' ['hwɪpɪŋ] *s* testa di turco
whip'ping post' *s* palo per la fustigazione
whippoorwill [,hwɪpər'wɪl] *s* caprimulgo, succiacapre *m*
whir [hwʌr] *s* ronzio || *v* (*pret & pp* **whirred**; *ger* **whirring**) *intr* ronzare; volare ronzando
whirl [hwʌrl] *s* giro improvviso; corsa; mulinello; (fig) successione || *tr & intr* mulinare; **my head whirls** mi gira la testa
whirligig ['hwʌrlɪ ,gɪg] *s* turbine *m;* (*carrousel*) giostra; (*toy*) girandola; (ent) ragno d'acqua
whirl'pool' *s* risucchio, mulinello
whirl'wind' *s* turbine *m*, tromba d'aria
whirlybird ['hwʌrli ,bʌrd] *s* (coll) elicottero
whish [hwɪʃ] *s* fruscio || *intr* frusciare
whisk [hwɪsk] *s* scopatina || *tr* scopare, spolverare; (*eggs*) sbattere; **to whisk out of sight** far sparire || *intr* guizzare
whisk' broom' *s* scopetta per i vestiti, spolverino
whiskers ['hwɪskərz] *spl* barba; (*on side of man's face*) basette *fpl;* (*of cat*) baffi *mpl*
whiskey ['hwɪski] *s* whisky *m*

whisper ['hwɪspər] *s* sussurro, bisbiglio, mormorio; **in a whisper** in un sussurro || *tr & intr* sussurrare, bisbigliare, mormorare
whisperer ['hwɪspərər] *s* sussurrone *m*
whispering ['hwɪspərɪŋ] *adj* di maldicenze || *s* sussurro; maldicenza
whistle ['hwɪsəl] *s* fischio; **to wet one's whistle** (coll) bagnarsi l'ugola || *tr* fischiare || *intr* fischiare, zufolare; **to whistle for** chiamare con un fischio; (*money*) aspettare in vano
whis'tle stop' s stazioncina, paesetto
whit [hwɪt] *s*—**not a whit** niente affatto
white [hwaɪt] *adj* bianco || *s* bianco; **whites** (pathol) leucorrea
white'cap' *s* frangente *m*, cavallone *m*, onda crespa
white' coal' *s* carbone bianco
white'-col'lar *adj* impiegatizio
white' feath'er *s*—**to show the white feather** mostrarsi vile
white' goods' *spl* biancheria da casa; articoli *mpl* di cotone; apparecchi *mpl* elettrodomestici
white-haired ['hwaɪt ,herd] *adj* dai capelli bianchi; (coll) favorito
white' heat' *s* calor bianco
white' lead' [lɛd] *s* biacca
white' lie' *s* bugia innocente
white' meat' *s* bianco, carne *f* del petto
whiten ['hwaɪtən] *tr* imbiancare, sbiancare || *intr* imbiancarsi, sbiancarsi; impallidire
whiteness ['hwaɪtnɪs] *s* bianchezza
white' plague' *s* tubercolosi *f*
white' slav'ery *s* tratta delle bianche
white' tie' *s* cravatta da frac; marsina, abito da cerimonia
white'wash' *s* imbiancatura; (fig) copertura || *tr* imbiancare, intonacare; (fig) coprire
white' wa'ter lil'y *s* ninfea
whither ['hwɪθər] *adv* dove, a che luogo || *conj* dove
whiting ['hwaɪtɪŋ] *s* (ichth) nasello; (ichth) merlango
whitish ['hwaɪtɪʃ] *adj* biancastro
whitlow ['hwɪtlo] *s* patereccio
Whitsuntide ['hwɪtsən ,taɪd] *s* settimana di Pentecoste
whittle ['hwɪtəl] *tr* digrossare; **to whittle away** or **down** ridurre gradualmente
whiz or **whizz** [hwɪz] *s* sibilo; (coll) asso || *v* (*pret & pp* **whizzed**; *ger* **whizzing**) *intr*—**to whiz by** passare sibilando; passare come una freccia
who [hu] *pron interr* chi; **who else?** chi altri?; **who goes there?** (mil) chi va là?; **who's who** chi è l'uno e chi è l'altro; chi è la gente importante || *pron rel* chi; il quale
whoa [hwo] or [wo] *interj* fermo!
who•ev'er *pron rel* chiunque
whole [hol] *adj* tutto, intero; sano, intatto; **made out of the whole cloth** completamente immaginario || *s* tutto; **as a whole** nell'insieme; **on the whole** in generale
wholehearted ['hol ,hɑrtɪd] *adj* molto sincero, generoso
whole' note' *s* (mus) semibreve *f*
whole'sale' *adj & adv* all'ingrosso || *s* ingrosso || *tr* vendere all'ingrosso || *intr* vendersi all'ingrosso
wholesaler ['hol ,selər] *s* grossista *mf*
wholesome ['holsəm] *adj* (*beneficial*) salutare; (*in good health*) sano
wholly ['holi] *adv* interamente
whom [hum] *pron interr* chi || *pron rel* che; il quale
whom•ev'er *pron rel* chiunque
whoop [hup] or [hwup] *s* urlo; (pathol) urlo della pertosse; **to not be worth a whoop** (coll) non valere un fico secco || *tr*—**to whoop it up** (slang) fare il diavolo a quattro || *intr* urlare
whoop'ing cough' ['hupɪŋ] or ['hupɪŋ] *s* pertosse *f*
whopper ['hwɑpər] *s* (coll) enormità *f*; (coll) fandonia, bugia enorme
whopping ['hwɑpɪŋ] *adj* (coll) enorme
whore [hor] *s* puttana || *intr*—**to whore around** puttaneggiare; andare a puttane
whortleber•ry ['hwʌrtəl ,bɛri] *s* (**-ries**) mirtillo
whose [huz] *pron interr* di chi || *pron rel* di chi; del quale; di cui
why [hwaɪ] *s* (**whys**) perché *m*; **the whys and the wherefores** il perché e il percome || *adv* perché || *interj* diamine!; **why, certainly!** certamente!; **why, yes!** evidentemente!
wick [wɪk] *s* stoppino, lucignolo
wicked ['wɪkɪd] *adj* malvagio; (*mischievous*) cattivo; (*dreadful*) terribile, bestiale
wicker ['wɪkər] *adj* di vimini || *s* vimine *m*
wicket ['wɪkɪt] *s* (*small door*) portello; (*ticket window*) sportello; (*of a canal*) chiusa; (cricket) porta; (croquet) archetto
wide [waɪd] *adj* largo; esteso; (*eyes*) aperto; (*sense of a word*) lato || *adv* largamente; completamente; lontano; **wide of the mark** lontano dal bersaglio
wide'-an'gle *adj* grandangolare
wide'-awake' *adj* sveglio
widen ['waɪdən] *tr* slargare, estendere || *intr* slargarsi, estendersi
wide'-o'pen *adj* spalancato; (*to a gambler*) accessibile
wide'-spread' *adj* (*e.g., arms*) aperto; diffuso
widow ['wɪdo] *s* vedova; (cards) morto || *tr* lasciar vedova
widower ['wɪdo•ər] *s* vedovo
widowhood ['wɪdo ,hud] *s* vedovanza
wid'ow's mite' *s* obolo della vedova
wid'ow's weeds' *spl* gramaglie *fpl* vedovili
width [wɪdθ] *s* larghezza
wield [wild] *tr* (*e.g., a sword*) brandire; (*e.g., a hammer*) maneggiare; (*power*) esercitare
wife [waɪf] *s* (**wives** [waɪvz]) moglie *f*
wig [wɪg] *s* parrucca
wiggle ['wɪgəl] *s* dimenio; (*of fish*)

guizzo || *tr* dimenare || *intr* dimenarsi; guizzare
wig'wag' *s* segnalazione con bandierine || *v* (*pret & pp* **-wagged**; *ger* **-wagging**) *tr & intr* segnalare con bandierine
wigwam ['wɪgwɑm] *s* tenda a cupola dei pellirosse, wigwam *m*
wild [waɪld] *adj* (*animal*) feroce; (*e.g., berry*) selvatico; (*barbarous*) selvaggio; (*violent*) furioso; (*mad*) pazzo; (*unruly*) discolo, indisciplinato; (*extravagant*) pazzesco; (*shot or throw*) lanciato all'impazzata; **wild about** pazzo per || *s* regione deserta; **the wild** la foresta; **wilds** regioni selvagge || *adv* pazzamente; **to go wild** andare in delirio; **to run wild** crescere all'impazzata; correre senza freno
wild' boar' *s* cinghiale *m*
wild' card' *s* matta
wild'cat' *s* gatto selvatico; lince *f*; impresa arrischiata || *v* (*pret & pp* **-catted**; *ger* **-catting**) *tr & intr* esplorare per conto proprio
wild'cat strike' *s* sciopero non autorizzato dal sindacato
wilderness ['wɪldərnɪs] *s* deserto
wild-eyed ['waɪld ,aɪd] *adj* stralunato; (*scheme*) pazzesco
wild'fire' *s* fuoco greco; fuoco fatuo; **to spread like wildfire** crescere come la gramigna; (*said of news*) spargersi come il baleno
wild' flow'er *s* fiore *m* di campo
wild' goose' *s* oca selvatica
wild'-goose' chase' *s* ricerca della luna nel pozzo
wild'life' *s* animali *spl* selvatici
wild' oat' *s* avena selvatica; **to sow one's wild oats** correre la cavallina
wild' ol'ive *s* olivastro, oleastro
wile [waɪl] *s* stratagemma *m*, inganno; (*cunning*) astuzia || *tr* allettare; **to wile away** passare piacevolmente
will [wɪl] *s* volontà *f*, volere *m*; (law) testamento; **at will** a volontà || *tr* volere; (law) legare || *intr* volere; **do as you will** faccia come vuole || *v* (*pret & cond* **would**) *aux* **she will leave tomorrow** partirà domani; **a cactus plant will live two months without water** una pianta grassa può vivere due mesi senz'acqua
willful ['wɪlfəl] *adj* volontario; ostinato
willfulness ['wɪlfəlnɪs] *s* volontarietà *f*; ostinatezza
William ['wɪljəm] *s* Guglielmo
willing ['wɪlɪŋ] *adj* volonteroso; **to be willing** essere disposto
willingly ['wɪlɪŋli] *adv* di buon grado, volentieri
willingness ['wɪlɪŋnɪs] *s* buona voglia, propensione
will-o'-the-wisp ['wɪləðə'wɪsp] *s* fuoco fatuo; (fig) illusione, chimera
willow ['wɪlo] *s* salice *m*
willowy ['wɪlo·i] *adj* pieghevole; (*slender*) snello; pieno di giunchi
will' pow'er *s* forza di volontà
willy-nilly ['wɪli'nɪli] *adv* volente o nolente
wilt [wɪlt] *tr* far appassire || *intr* appassire, avvizzire
wil·y ['waɪli] *adj* (**-ier**; **-iest**) astuto, scaltro
wimple ['wɪmpəl] *s* soggolo
win [wɪn] *s* vittoria, vincita || *v* (*pret & pp* **won** [wʌn]; *ger* **winning**) *tr & intr* guadagnare; **to win out** vincere, aver successo
wince [wɪns] *s* sussulto || *intr* sussultare
winch [wɪntʃ] *s* verricello; (*handle*) manovella; (naut) molinello
wind [wɪnd] *s* vento; (*gas in intestines*) vento; (*breath*) fiato, tenuta; **to break wind** scoreggiare; **to get wind of** subodorare; **to sail close to the wind** (naut) andare all'orza; **to take the wind out of the sails of** sconcertare; **winds** (mus) fiati *mpl* || *tr* far perdere il fiato a || [waɪnd] *v* (*pret & pp* **wound** [waʊnd]) *tr* (*to wrap up*) arrotolare; (*thread, wool*) dipanare, aggomitolare; (*a clock*) caricare; (*a handle*) far girare; **to wind one's way through** serpeggiare per; **to wind up** arrotolare; eccitare; finire, portare a termine || *intr* serpeggiare, snodarsi
windbag ['wɪnd ,bæg] *s* (*of a bagpipe*) otre *m*; (fig) parolaio, otre *m* di vento
windbreak ['wɪnd ,brek] *s* frangivento
wind' cone' [wɪnd] *s* manica a vento
winded ['wɪndɪd] *adj* senza fiato
windfall ['wɪnd ,fɔl] *s* frutta abbattuta dal vento; provvidenza, manna del cielo
wind'ing sheet' ['waɪndɪŋ] *s* lenzuolo funebre
wind'ing stairs' ['waɪndɪŋ] *spl* scala a chiocciola
wind' in'strument [wɪnd] *s* (mus) strumento a fiato
windlass ['wɪndləs] *s* verricello
windmill ['wɪnd ,mɪl] *s* mulino a vento; (*air turbine*) aeromotore *m*; **to tilt at windmills** combattere i mulini a vento
window ['wɪndo] *s* finestra; (*of ticket office*) sportello; (*of car or coach*) finestrino
win'dow dress'er *s* vetrinista *mf*
win'dow dress'ing *s* vetrinistica; (fig) facciata, apparenza
win'dow en'velope *s* busta a finestrella
win'dow frame' *s* intelaiatura della finestra
win'dow·pane' *s* vetro, invetriata
win'dow sash' *s* intelaiatura della finestra
win'dow screen' *s* zanzariera
win'dow shade' *s* tendina avvolgibile
win'dow-shop' *v* (*pret & pp* **-shopped**; *ger* **-shopping**) *intr* guardare nelle vetrine senza comprare
win'dow sill' *s* davanzale *m* della finestra
windpipe ['wɪnd ,paɪp] *s* trachea
windproof ['wɪnd ,pruf] *adj* resistente al vento
windshield ['wɪnd ,ʃild] *s* parabrezza *m*
wind'shield wash'er *s* lavacristallo

wind'shield wip'er *s* tergicristallo
windsock ['wɪnd,sɑk] *s* (aer) manica a vento
windstorm ['wɪnd,stɔrm] *s* bufera di vento
wind' tun'nel [wɪnd] *s* (aer) galleria aerodinamica
wind-up ['waɪnd,ʌp] *s* conclusione
windward ['wɪndwərd] *s* orza, sopravvento; **to turn to windward** mettersi al sopravvento
Wind'ward Is'lands *spl* Isole *fpl* Sopravvento
wind•y ['wɪndi] *adj* **(-ier; -iest)** ventoso; verboso, ampolloso; **it is windy** fa vento
wine [waɪn] *s* vino ‖ *tr* offrire vino a ‖ *intr* bere del vino
wine' cel'lar *s* cantina
wine'glass' *s* bicchiere da vino
winegrower ['waɪn,gro•ər] *s* vinificatore *m*, viticoltore *m*
wine' press' *s* torchio per l'uva
winer•y ['waɪnəri] *s* **(-ies)** stabilimento vinicolo
wine'shop' *s* fiaschetteria
wine'skin' *s* otre *m*
wine' stew'ard *s* sommelier *m*
winetaster ['waɪn,testər] *s* degustatore *m* di vini
wing [wɪŋ] *s* ala; (*unit of air force*) aerobrigata; (theat) quinta; **to take wing** levarsi a volo; **under one's wing** sotto la protezione di qlcu ‖ *tr* ferire nell'ala; **to wing one's way** volare, portarsi a volo
wing' chair' *s* poltrona a orecchioni
wing' col'lar *s* colletto per marsina
wing' nut' *s* (mach) galletto
wing'span' *s* (*of airplane*) apertura alare
wing'spread' *s* (*of bird*) apertura alare
wink [wɪŋk] *s* ammicco; **in a wink** in un batter d'occhio; **to not sleep a wink** non chiudere occhio; **to take forty winks** (coll) schiacciare un pisolino ‖ *tr* (*the eye*) strizzare ‖ *intr* ammiccare, strizzare l'occhio; (*to blink*) battere le ciglia; **to wink at** ammiccare a; far finta di non vedere
winner ['wɪnər] *s* vincitore *m*
winning ['wɪnɪŋ] *adj* vincente, vincitore; attraente, simpatico ‖ **winnings** *spl* vincita
winnow ['wɪno] *tr* ventilare, brezzare; (fig) vagliare ‖ *intr* svolazzare
winsome ['wɪnsəm] *adj* attraente
winter ['wɪntər] *adj* invernale ‖ *s* inverno ‖ *intr* svernare
win'ter•green' *s* tè *m* del Canadà; olio di gaulteria
win•try ['wɪntri] *adj* **(-trier; -triest)** invernale; freddo
wipe [waɪp] *tr* forbire, detergere; (*to dry*) asciugare; **to wipe away** (*tears*) asciugare; **to wipe off** pulire, forbire; **to wipe out** distruggere completamente; (coll) eliminare
wiper ['waɪpər] *s* strofinaccio; (mach) camma; (elec) contatto scorrevole
wire [waɪr] *s* filo metallico; telegramma *m;* (coll) telegrafo; **to pull wires** manovrare di dietro le quinte ‖ *tr* legare con filo metallico; attrezzare l'elettricità in; (coll) mandare per telegrafo; (coll) telegrafare ‖ *intr* (coll) telegrafare
wire' cut'ter *s* pinza tagliafili
wire' entan'glement *s* reticolato di filo spinato
wire' gauge' *s* calibro da fili
wire-haired ['waɪr,herd] *adj* a pelo ruvido
wireless ['waɪrlɪs] *adj* senza fili ‖ *s* telegrafo senza fili; telegrafia senza fili
wire' nail' *s* chiodo da falegname
wirepulling ['waɪr,pʊlɪŋ] *s* manovra dietro alle quinte
wire' record'er *s* magnetofono a filo
wire' screen' *s* rete metallica
wire'tap' *v* (*pret & pp* **-tapped;** *ger* **-tapping)** *tr* (*a conversation*) intercettare
wiring ['waɪrɪŋ] *s* sistema *m* di fili elettrici
wir•y ['waɪri] *adj* **(-ier; -iest)** fatto di filo; (*hair*) ispido; (*tone*) metallico, vibrante; (*sinewy*) segaligno
wisdom ['wɪzdəm] *s* senno, sapienza, saggezza
wis'dom tooth' *s* dente *m* del giudizio
wise [waɪz] *adj* saggio, sapiente; (*decision*) giudizioso; **to be wise to** (slang) accorgersi del gioco di; **to get wise** (slang) mangiare la foglia; (slang) diventare impertinente ‖ *s* modo, maniera; **in no wise** in nessun modo ‖ *tr*—**to wise up** (slang) avvertire ‖ *intr*—**to wise up** (slang) accorgersi
wiseacre ['waɪz,ekər] *s* sapientone *m*
wise'crack' *s* (coll) spiritosaggine *f* ‖ *intr* (coll) dire spiritosaggini
wise' guy' *s* (slang) sputasentenze *m*
wish [wɪʃ] *s* desiderio; augurio; **to make a wish** formulare un desiderio ‖ *tr* desiderare; augurare; **to wish s.o. a good day** dare il buon giorno a qlcu ‖ *intr* desiderare; **to wish for** desiderare
wish'bone' *s* forcella
wishful ['wɪʃəl] *adj* desideroso
wish'ful think'ing *s* pio desiderio
wistful ['wɪstfəl] *adj* melanconico, pensoso, meditabondo
wit [wɪt] *s* spirito; (*person*) bellospirito; (*understanding*) senso; **to be at one's wits' end** non sapere a che santo votarsi; **to have one's wits about one** avere presenza di spirito; **to live by one's wits** vivere di espedienti
witch [wɪtʃ] *s* strega
witch'craft' *s* stregoneria
witch' doc'tor *s* stregone *m*
witch'es' Sab'bath *s* sabba *m*
witch' ha'zel *s* (*shrub*) amamelide *f;* (*liquid*) estratto di amamelide
witch' hunt' *s* caccia alle streghe
with [wɪð] or [wɪθ] *prep* con; a, e.g., **with open arms** a braccia aperte; di, e.g., **covered with silk** coperto di seta; **to be satisfied with the performance** essere contento della rappresentazione; da, e.g., **with the In-**

dians dagli indiani; **to part with** separarsi da
with·draw' *v* (*pret* **-drew;** *pp* **-drawn**) *tr* ritirare || *intr* ritirarsi
withdrawal [wɪð'drɔ·əl] or [wɪθ'drɔ·əl] *s* ritiro, ritirata; (*of funds*) prelevamento
wither ['wɪðər] *tr* intisichire; (*with a glance*) incenerire || *intr* avvizzire, intisichire
with·hold' *v* (*pret & pp* **-held**) *tr* trattenere; (*information*) sottacere; (*payment*) defalcare; (*permission*) negare
withhold'ing tax' *s* imposta trattenuta
with·in' *adv* dentro, didentro || *prep* entro, entro di, dentro a, dentro di; fra; in; (*a time period*) nel giro di
with·out' *adv* fuori || *prep* senza; fuori, fuori di; **to do without** fare a meno di; **without** + *ger* senza + *inf*, e.g., **without saying a word** senza dire una parola; senza che + *subj*, e.g., **she fell without anyone helping her** cadde senza che nessuno l'aiutasse
with·stand' *v* (*pret & pp* **-stood**) *tr* resistere (with *dat*), reggere (with *dat*)
witness ['wɪtnɪs] *s* testimone *mf;* **in witness whereof** in fé di che; **to bear witness** far fede || *tr* (*to be present at*) presenziare; (*to attest*) testimoniare, firmare come testimone
wit'ness stand' *s* banco dei testimoni
witticism ['wɪtɪ,sɪzəm] *s* motto, battuta spiritosa, spiritosaggine *f*
wittingly ['wɪtɪŋli] *adv* consapevolmente
wit·ty ['wɪti] *adj* (**-tier; -tiest**) spiritoso, divertente
wizard ['wɪzərd] *s* mago
wizardry ['wɪzərdri] *s* magia
wizened ['wɪzənd] *adj* raggrinzito
woad [wod] *s* (bot) guado
wobble ['wɑbəl] *s* oscillazione, dondolio || *intr* oscillare, dondolare; (*said of a chair*) zoppicare; (fig) titubare
wob·bly ['wɑbli] *adj* (**-blier; -bliest**) oscillante, zoppo, malfermo
woe [wo] *s* disgrazia, afflizione, sventura; || *interj*—**woe is me!** ahimè!
woebegone ['wobɪ,gɔn] or ['wobɪ,gɑn] *adj* triste, abbattuto
woeful ['wofəl] *adj* sfortunato, disgraziato; (*of poor quality*) orribile
wolf [wulf] *s* (**wolves** [wulvz]) lupo; (coll) dongiovanni *m;* **to cry wolf** gridare al lupo; **to keep the wolf from the door** tener lontana la miseria || *tr & intr* mangiare come un lupo
wolf'hound' *s* cane *m* da pastore alsaziano
wolfram ['wulfrəm] *s* wolframio
wolf's-bane or **wolfsbane** ['wulfs,ben] *s* (bot) aconito
wolverine [,wulvə'rin] *s* (zool) ghiottone *m*
woman ['wumən] *s* (**women** ['wɪmɪn]) donna
womanhood ['wumən,hud] *s* (*quality*) femminilità *f;* (*women collectively*) donne *fpl*, sesso femminile
womanish ['wumənɪʃ] *adj* femminile; (*effeminate*) effeminato
wom'an·kind' *s* sesso femminile
womanly ['wumənli] *adj* (**-lier; -liest**) femminile, muliebre
wom'an suf'frage *s* suffragio alle donne
woman-suffragist ['wumən'sʌfrədʒɪst] *s* suffragista *mf*
womb [wum] *s* utero; (fig) seno
womenfolk ['wɪmɪn,fok] *spl* le donne
wonder ['wʌndər] *s* (*something strange and surprising*) meraviglia; (*feeling*) ammirazione; (*miracle*) prodigio, miracolo; **for a wonder** cosa strana; **no wonder that** non fa meraviglia che; **to work wonders** fare miracoli || *tr*—**to wonder that** meravigliarsi che; **to wonder how, if, when, where, who, why** domandarsi or chiedersi come, se, quando, dove, chi, perché || *intr* meravigliarsi; chiedersi; **to wonder at** ammirare
won'der drug' *s* medicina miracolosa
wonderful ['wʌndərfəl] *adj* meraviglioso
won'der·land' *s* paese *m* delle meraviglie
wonderment ['wʌndərmənt] *s* sorpresa, meraviglia, stupore *m*
won'der-work'er *s* taumaturgo
wont [wʌnt] or [wɔnt] *adj* abituato, solito || *s* abitudine *f*, costume *m*
wonted ['wʌntɪd] or ['wɔntɪd] *adj* solito, abituale
woo [wu] *tr* (*a woman*) corteggiare; (*to seek to win*) allettare; (*good or bad consequences*) andare in cerca di
wood [wud] *s* legno; (*firewood*) legna; (*keg*) barile *m;* **out of the woods** fuori pericolo; al sicuro; **woods** bosco, selva
woodbine ['wud,baɪn] *s* (*honeysuckle*) abbracciabosco; (*Virginia creeper*) vite *f* del Canadà
wood' carv'ing *s* intaglio in legno, statua in legno
wood'chuck' *s* marmotta americana
wood'cock' *s* beccaccia
wood'cut' *s* silografia
wood'cut'ter *s* boscaiolo
wooded ['wudɪd] *adj* legnoso, boschivo
wooden ['wudən] *adj* di legno; duro, rigido; inespressivo
wood' engrav'ing *s* silografia
wooden-headed ['wudən,hɛdɪd] *adj* (coll) dalla testa dura
wood'en leg' *s* gamba di legno
wood'en shoe' *s* zoccolo
wood' grouse' *s* gallo cedrone
woodland ['wudlənd] *adj* boschivo || *s* foresta, bosco
wood'man *s* (**-men**) boscaiolo
woodpecker ['wud,pɛkər] *s* picchio
wood'pile' *s* legnaia
wood' screw' *s* vite *f* per legno
wood'shed' *s* legnaia
woods'man *s* (**-men**) abitatore *m* dei boschi; boscaiolo
wood'wind' *s* strumento a fiato di legno
wood'work' *s* lavoro in legno; parti *fpl* di legno
wood'work'er *s* ebanista *m*, falegname *m*
wood'worm' *s* tarlo

wood•y ['wudi] *adj* **(-ier; -iest)** boscoso, alberato; (*like wood*) legnoso
wooer ['wu•ər] *s* corteggiatore *m*
woof [wuf] *s* (*yarns running across warp*) trama; (*fabric*) tessuto
woofer ['wufər] *s* altoparlante *m* per basse audiofrequenze, woofer *m*
wool [wul] *s* lana
woolen ['wulən] *adj* di lana || *s* tessuto di lana; **woolens** laneria
woolgrower ['wul,gro•ər] *s* allevatore *m* di pecore
wool•ly ['wuli] *adj* **(-lier; -liest)** di lana; lanoso; (coll) confuso
word [wʌrd] *s* parola; **by word of mouth** oralmente; **to be as good as one's word** essere di parola; **to have a word with** dire quattro parole a; **to have word from** aver notizie da; **to keep one's word** essere di parola; **to leave word** lasciar detto; **to send word that** mandare a dire che; **words** (*quarrel*) baruffa || *tr* esprimere, formulare || **Word** *s* (theol) Verbo
word' count' *s* conto lessicale
word' forma'tion *s* formazione delle parole
wording ['wʌrdɪŋ] *s* fraseologia, dicitura
word' or'der *s* disposizione delle parole in una frase
word'stock' *s* lessico
word•y ['wʌrdi] *adj* **(-ier; -iest)** verboso, parolaio
work [wʌrk] *s* lavoro; (*of art, fortification, etc.*) opera; **at work** al lavoro, in ufficio; (*in operation*) in servizio; **out of work** senza lavoro, disoccupato; **to give s.o. the works** (slang) trattare male; (slang) ammazzare; **to shoot the works** (slang) scialare; **works** opificio; meccanismo; (*of clock*) castello || *tr* far funzionare; lavorare, maneggiare; (*e.g., a miracle*) operare; (*e.g., iron*) trattare; **to work up** preparare; stimulare, eccitare || *intr* lavorare; (*said of a machine*) funzionare; (*said of a remedy*) avere effetto; **to work loose** sciogliersi; **to work out** andare a finire; (*said of a problem*) sciogliersi; (*said of a total*) ammontare; (sports) allenarsi
workable ['wʌrkəbəl] *adj* (*feasible*) praticabile; (*e.g., iron*) lavorabile
work'bench' *s* banco
work'book' *s* manuale *m* d'istruzioni; (*for students*) quaderno d'esercizi
work'box' *s* cassetta dei ferri del mestiere; (*for needlework*) cestino da lavoro
work'day' *adj* lavorativo; ordinario, di tutti i giorni || *s* (*working day*) giorno feriale, giornata lavorativa
worked-up ['wʌrkt'ʌp] *adj* sovreccitato
worker ['wʌrkər] *s* lavorante *m*, lavoratore *m*, operaio
work' force' *s* mano *f* d'opera
work'horse' *s* cavallo da tiro; (*tireless worker*) lavoratore indefesso
work'house' *s* carcere *m* con lavoro obbligatorio; (Brit) istituto dei poveri
work'ing class' *s* classe operaia
work'ing condi'tions *spl* trattamento, condizioni *fpl* di lavoro
work'ing girl' *s* ragazza lavoratrice
work'ing hours' *spl* orario di lavoro
working'man *s* **(-men)** lavoratore *m*
work'ing or'der *s* buone condizioni, efficienza
work'ing•wom'an *s* **(-wom'en)** operaia, lavoratrice *f*
work'man *s* **(-men)** lavoratore *m;* (*skilled worker*) operaio specializzato
workmanship ['wʌrkmən,ʃɪp] *s* fattura; (*work executed*) opera
work' of art' *s* opera d'arte
work'out' *s* (sports) esercizio, allenamento
work'room' *s* (*for manual work*) officina; (*study*) gabinetto, laboratorio
work'shop' *s* officina
work' stop'page *s* sospensione del lavoro
world [wʌrld] *adj* mondiale || *s* mondo; **a world of** un monte di; **for all the world** per tutto l'oro del mondo; **in the world** al mondo; **since the world began** da che mondo è mondo; **the other world** l'altro mondo; **to bring into the world** mettere al mondo; **to see the world** conoscere il mondo; **to think the world of** tenere in altissima considerazione
world' affairs' *spl* relazioni *fpl* internazionali
world•ly ['wʌrdli] *adj* **(-lier; -liest)** mondano, secolare
world'ly-wise' *adj* vissuto
world's' fair' *s* esposizione *f* mondiale
world' war' *s* guerra mondiale
world'-wide' *adj* mondiale
worm [wʌrm] *s* verme *m* || *tr* liberare dai vermi; **to worm a secret out of s.o.** carpire un segreto a qlcu; **to worm one's way into** insinuarsi in
worm-eaten ['wʌrm,itən] *adj* tarlato, bacato
worm' gear' *s* meccanismo a vite perpetua, ingranaggio elicoidale
worm'wood' *s* assenzio; (fig) amarezza
worm•y ['wʌrmi] *adj* **(-ier; -iest)** verminoso; (*worm-eaten*) bacato; (*groveling*) vile, strascicante
worn [worn] *adj* usato; (*look*) stanco, esausto
worn'-out' *adj* logoro, scalcinato; (*by illness*) consunto; (fig) trito
worrisome ['wʌrisəm] *adj* preoccupante; (*inclined to worry*) preoccupato
wor•ry ['wʌri] *s* **(-ries)** preoccupazione, inquietudine *f;* (*trouble*) fastidio || *v* (*pret & pp* **-ried**) *tr* preoccupare, inquietare; **to be worried** essere impensierito || *intr* preoccuparsi, inquietarsi; **don't worry!** non si preoccupi!
worse [wʌrs] *adj & s* peggiore *m*, peggio || *adv* peggio; **worse and worse** di male in peggio
worsen ['wʌrsən] *tr & intr* peggiorare
wor•ship ['wʌrʃɪp] *s* venerazione, adorazione; servizio religioso; **your Worship** La Signoria Vostra || *v* (*pret &*

pp **-shiped** or **-shipped;** *ger* **-shiping** or **-shipping)** *tr* venerare, adorare
worshiper or **worshipper** ['wʌrʃɪpər] *s* adoratore *m;* (*in church*) devoto, fedele *m*
worst [wʌrst] *adj* (il) peggiore; pessimo || *s* peggio, peggiore *m;* **at worst** alla peggio; **if worst comes to worst** alla peggio; **to get the worst** averne la peggio || *adv* peggio
worsted ['wʊstɪd] *adj* di lana pettinata || *s* tessuto di lana pettinata
wort [wʌrt] *s* mosto di malto; pianta, erba
worth [wʌrθ] *adj* che vale, da, e.g., **worth ten dollars** da dieci dollari; **to be worth** valere; essere di pregio; **to be worth** + *ger* valere la pena (di) + *inf*, e.g., **it is worth reading** vale la pena (di) leggerlo || *s* pregio, valore *m;* **a dollar's worth** un dollaro di
worthless ['wʌrθlɪs] *adj* senza valore; inutile; inservibile; (*person*) indegno
worth'while' *adj* meritevole, meritevole d'attenzione
wor·thy ['wʌrði] *adj* **(-thier; -thiest)** degno, meritevole || *s* **(-thies)** maggiorente *mf*
would [wʊd] *v aux* **they said they would come** dissero che sarebbero venuti; **he would buy it if he had the money** lo comprerebbe se avesse i soldi; **would you be so kind to** avrebbe la cortesia di; **he would spend every winter in Florida** passava tutti gli inverni in Florida; **would that . . . !** oh se . . . !, volesse il cielo che . . . !, magari . . . !
would'-be' *adj* preteso, sedicente; (*intended to be*) inteso
wound [wund] *s* ferita || *tr* ferire
wounded ['wundɪd] *adj* ferito || **the wounded** i feriti
wow [waʊ] *s* distorsione acustica di suono riprodotto; (slang) successone *m* || *tr* (slang) entusiasmare || *interj* (coll) accidenti!
wrack [ræk] *s* naufragio; vestigio; (*seaweed*) alghe marine gettate sulla spiaggia; **to go to wrack and ruin** andare completamente in rovina
wraith [reθ] *s* spettro, fantasma *m*
wrangle ['ræŋgəl] *s* baruffa, alterco || *intr* altercare, rissare
wrap [ræp] *s* sciarpa; mantello || *v* (*pret & pp* **wrapped;** *ger* **wrapping)** *tr* involgere; impaccare; **to be wrapped up in** essere assorto in; **to wrap up** avvolgere; (*in paper*) incartare; (*in clothing*) imbacuccare; (coll) concludere || *intr*—**to wrap up** imbacuccarsi, avvolgersi
wrapper ['ræpər] *s* veste *f* da camera, peignoir *m;* (*of newspaper*) fascia, fascetta; (*of cigars*) involto
wrap'ping pa'per ['ræpɪŋ] *s* carta d'impacco or d'imballaggio
wrath [ræθ] or [rɑθ] *s* ira; vendetta
wrathful ['ræθfəl] or ['rɑθfəl] *adj* collerico, iracondo
wreak [rik] *tr* (*vengeance*) infliggere; (*anger*) scaricare
wreath [riθ] *s* **(wreaths** [riðz]**)** ghirlanda; (*of laurel*) laurea; (*of smoke*) spirale *f*
wreathe [rið] *tr* inghirlandare; avviluppare; (*a garland*) intessere || *intr* (*said of smoke*) innalzarsi in spire
wreck [rɛk] *s* rottame *m*, relitto; naufragio; rovina; catastrofe *f*, disastro; (fig) rottame *m*, relitto || *tr* far naufragare; distruggere, rovinare; (*a train*) fare scontrare, fare deragliare; (*a building*) demolire
wreckage ['rɛkɪdʒ] *s* rottami *mpl*, relitti *mpl;* rovine *fpl*
wrecker ['rɛkər] *s* (*tow truck*) autogrù *f;* (*housewrecker*) demolitore *m*
wreck'ing ball' *s* martello demolitore
wreck'ing car' *s* autogrù *f*
wrecking' crane' *s* (rr) carro gru
wren [rɛn] *s* scricciolo
wrench [rɛntʃ] *s* chiave *f;* (*pull*) tiro; (*of a joint*) distorsione || *tr* torcere, distorcere; (*one's limb*) torcersi, distorcersi
wrest [rɛst] *tr* strappare, togliere a viva forza; (*to twist*) torcere
wrestle ['rɛsəl] *s* lotta, combattimento || *intr* fare la lotta, lottare
wrestler ['rɛstlər] *s* lottatore *m*
wrestling ['rɛslɪŋ] *s* lotta
wretch [rɛtʃ] *s* disgraziato, tapino
wretched ['rɛtʃɪd] *adj* (*pitiable*) misero, disgraziato, tapino; (*poor, worthless*) miserabile
wriggle ['rɪgəl] *s* (*e.g., of a snake*) guizzo; dondolio || *tr* dondolare, dimenare || *intr* guizzare; dimenarsi; **to wriggle out of** sgattaiolare da, divincolarsi da
wrig·gly ['rɪgli] *adj* **(-glier; -gliest)** che si contorce; (fig) evasivo
wring [rɪŋ] *v* (*pret & pp* **wrung** [rʌŋ]) *tr* torcere; (*wet clothing*) strizzare; (*one's heart*) stringersi; (*e.g., one's hands*) torcersi; **to wring the truth out of** strappare la verità a
wringer ['rɪŋər] *s* strizzatoio
wrinkle ['rɪŋkəl] *s* (*on skin*) ruga; (*on fabric*) crespa, grinza; (coll) trovata, espediente *m* || *tr* corrugare, raggrinzire; (*fabric*) increspare
wrin'kle-proof' *adj* antipiega, ingualcibile
wrin·kly ['rɪŋkli] *adj* **(-klier; -kliest)** rugoso, grinzoso
wrist [rɪst] *s* polso
wrist'band' *s* polso
wrist' pin' *s* spinotto
wrist' watch' *s* orologio da polso
writ [rɪt] *s* scritto; (law) ordine *m*
write [raɪt] *v* (*pret* **wrote** [rot]; *pp* **written** ['rɪtən]) *tr* scrivere; **to write down** mettere in iscritto; (*to disparage*) menomare; **to write off** (*a debt*) cancellare; (com) stornare; **to write up** redigere, scrivere in pieno; (*to ballyhoo*) scrivere le lodi di || *intr* scrivere; **to write back** rispondere per lettera
write'-in-vote' *s* voto per candidato il cui nome non è nella lista
writer ['raɪtər] *s* scrittore *m*

write'-up' *s* descrizione scritta, conto; stamburata, elogio; (com) valutazione eccesiva
writhe [raɪð] *intr* contorcersi, spasimare, dibattersi
writing ['raɪtɪŋ] *s* lo scrivere; (*something written*) scritto; (*characters written*) scrittura; professione di scrittore; **at this writing** scrivendo questa mia; **in one's own writing** di proprio pugno; **to put in writing** mettere in iscritto
writ'ing desk' *s* scrittoio
writ'ing mate'rials *spl* l'occorrente *m* per scrivere, oggetti *mpl* di cancelleria
writ'ing pa'per *s* carta da lettere
writ'ten ac'cent ['rɪtən] *s* accento grafico
wrong [rɔŋ] or [rɑŋ] *adj* sbagliato, erroneo; (*awry*) guasto; (*step*) falso; cattivo, ingiusto; **there is nothing wrong with him** non ha niente; **to be wrong** (*mistaken*) aver torto; (*guilty*) aver la colpa || *s* torto; **to be in the wrong** essere in errore; **to do wrong** fare del male; commettere un'ingiustizia || *adv* male; (*backward*) alla rovescia; **to go wrong** andare alla rovescia; andare per la cattiva strada || *tr* far torto a, offendere, maltrattare
wrongdoer ['rɔŋ,du·ər] or ['rɑn-,du·ər] *s* peccatore *m*, trasgressore *m*
wrongdoing ['rɔŋ,du·ɪŋ] or ['rɑn-,du·ɪŋ] *s* peccato, offesa, trasgressione
wrong' num'ber *s* (telp) numero sbagliato; **you have the wrong number** Lei si è sbagliato di numero
wrong' side' *s* rovescio; (*of street*) altra parte; **to get out of bed on the wrong side** alzarsi di malumore; **wrong side out** alla rovescia
wrought' i'ron [rɔt] *s* ferro battuto
wrought'-up' *adj* sovreccitato
wry [raɪ] *adj* (**wrier; wriest**) sbieco, storto; pervertito, alterato; ironico
wry'neck' *s* (orn & pathol) torcicollo

X

X, x [ɛks] *s* ventiquattresima lettera dell'alfabeto inglese
Xanthippe [zæn'tɪpi] *s* Santippe *f*
Xavier ['zævɪ·ər] or ['zevɪ·ər] *s* Saverio
xebec ['zibɛk] *s* (naut) sciabecco
xenon ['zinɑn] or ['zɛnɑn] *s* xeno
xenophobe ['zɛnə,fob] *s* xenofobo
Xenophon ['zɛnəfən] *s* Senofonte *m*
xerography [zɪ'rɑgrəfi] *s* xerografia
xerophyte [zɪrə,faɪt] *s* xerofito
Xerxes ['zʌrksɪs] *s* Serse *m*
Xmas ['krɪsməs] *s* Natale *m*
x-ray ['ɛks,re] *adj* radiografico || *s* raggio X; (*photograph*) radiogramma *m*, radiografia || *tr* radiografare
xylograph ['zaɪlə,græf] or ['zaɪlə-,grɑf] *s* silografia
xylophone ['zaɪlə,fon] *s* silofono

Y

Y, y [waɪ] s venticinquesima lettera dell'alfabeto inglese
yacht [jɑt] *s* yacht *m*, panfilo
yacht' club' *s* club *m* nautico, associazione velica
yak [jæk] *s* yak *m* || *v* (*pret & pp* **yakked;** *ger* **yakking**) *intr* (slang) ciarlare, chiacchierare
yam [jæm] *s* igname *m;* (*sweet potato*) patata dolce, batata
yank [jæŋk] *s* tiro, strattone *m* || *tr* dare uno strattone a, tirare || *intr* dare uno strattone, tirare
Yankee ['jæŋki] *adj & s* yankee *mf*
yap [jæp] *s* guaito; (slang) chiacchierio, ciancia || *v* (*pret & pp* **yapped;** *ger* **yapping**) *intr* latrare, guaire; (slang) chiacchierare, ciarlare
yard [jɑrd] *s* cortile *m;* recinto; yard *m*, iarda; (naut) pennone *m;* (rr) scalo smistamento
yard'arm' *s* estremità *f* del pennone
yard' goods' *spl* tessuti *mpl* in pezza
yard'mas'ter *s* (rr) capo dello scalo smistamento
yard'stick' *s* stecca di una iarda di lunghezza; (fig) metro
yarn [jɑrn] *s* filo, filato; (coll) storia
yarrow ['jæro] *s* millefoglie *m*
yaw [jɔ] *s* (naut) straorzata; (aer) imbardata || *intr* (naut) straorzare, guizzare; (aer) imbardare
yawl [jɔl] *s* barca a remi; (naut) iolla
yawn [jɔn] *s* sbadiglio || *intr* sbadigliare; (*said, e.g., of a hole*) vaneggiare, aprirsi
yea [je] *s & adv* sì *m*
yean [jin] *intr* (*said of sheep or goat*) partorire
year [jɪr] *s* anno; **to be . . . years old** avere . . . anni; **year in, year out** un anno dopo l'altro
year'book' *s* annuario
yearling ['jɪrlɪŋ] *adj* di un anno di età || *s* animale *m* di un anno di età

yearly [ˈjɪrli] *adj* annuale || *adv* annualmente
yearn [jʌrn] *intr* smaniare, sospirare; **to yearn for** anelare per
yearning [ˈjʌrnɪŋ] *s* anelo, sospiro ardente
yeast [jist] *s* lievito
yeast' cake' *s* compressa di lievito
yell [jɛl] *s* urlo || *tr* gridare || *intr* urlare
yellow [ˈjɛlo] *adj* giallo; (*newspaper*) sensazionale; (*cowardly*) (coll) vile || *s* giallo; giallo d'uovo || *intr* ingiallire
yellowish [ˈjɛlo·ɪʃ] *adj* giallastro
yel'low·jack'et *s* vespa, calabrone *m*
yel'low streak' *s* (coll) vena di codardia
yelp [jɛlp] *s* guaito || *intr* guaire
yeo'man *s* (**-men**) (naut) sottufficiale *m;* (Brit) piccolo proprietario terriero
yeo'man of the guard' *s* guardia del servizio reale
yeo'man's serv'ice *s* lavoro onesto
yes [jɛs] *s* sì *m;* **to say yes** dire di sì || *adv* sì || *v* (*pret & pp* **yessed;** *ger* **yessing**) *tr* dire di sì a || *intr* dire di sì
yes' man' *s* (coll) persona che approva sempre; (coll) leccapiedi *m*
yesterday [ˈjɛstərdi] or [ˈjɛstər ˌde] *s & adv* ieri *m*
yet [jɛt] *adv* ancora; tuttavia; **as yet** sinora; **nor yet** nemmeno; **not yet** non ancora || *conj* ma, però, pure
yew' tree' [ju] *s* tasso
Yiddish [ˈjɪdɪʃ] *adj & s* yiddish *m*
yield [jild] *s* rendimento, resa; (*crop*) raccolto; (com) reddito, gettito || *tr* rendere, fruttare || *intr* rendere, fruttare, produrre; (*to surrender*) cedere, arrendersi; sottomettersi; cedere il posto
yodeling or **yodelling** [ˈjodəlɪŋ] *s* tirolesa
yoke [jok] *s* (*contrivance*) giogo; (*pair, e.g., of oxen*) paio; (*of shirt*) sprone *m;* (naut) barra del timone; **to throw off the yoke** scuotere il giogo || *tr* aggiogare
yokel [ˈjokəl] *s* zoticone *m*
yolk [jok] *s* tuorlo
yonder [ˈjandər] *adj* situato lassù; situato laggiù || *adv* lassù; laggiù
yore [jor] *s*—**of yore** del tempo antico, del tempo in cui Berta filava
you [ju] *pron pers* Lei; tu; Le, La; te, ti; voi; vi; Loro || *pron indef* si, e.g., **you eat at noon** si mangia a mezzogiorno
young [jʌŋ] *adj* (**younger** [ˈjʌŋgər]; **youngest** [ˈjʌŋgɪst]) giovane || **the young** i giovani
young' hope'ful *s* giovane *m* di belle speranze
young' la'dy *s* giovane *f;* (*married*) giovane signora
young' man' *s* giovane *m*, giovanotto
young' peo'ple *s* i giovani
youngster [ˈjʌŋstər] *s* giovanetto; (*child*) bambino
your [jʊr] *adj* Suo, il Suo; tuo, il tuo; vostro, il vostro
yours [jʊrz] *pron poss* Suo, il Suo; tuo, il tuo; vostro, il vostro; **of yours** Suo; **very truly yours** distinti saluti
your·self [jʊrˈsɛlf] *pron pers* (**-selves** [ˈsɛlvz]) Lei stesso; sé stesso; si, e.g., **are your enjoying yourself?** si diverte?
youth [juθ] *s* (**youths** [juθs] or [juðz]) gioventù *f*, giovinezza; (*person*) giovane *mf;* i giovani
youthful [ˈjuθfəl] *adj* giovane, giovanile
yowl [jaʊl] *s* urlo || *intr* urlare
Yugoslav [ˈjugoˈslɑv] *adj & s* iugoslavo
Yugoslavia [ˈjugoˈslɑvɪ·ə] *s* la Iugoslavia
Yule [jul] *s* il Natale; le feste natalizie
Yule' log' *s* ceppo
Yuletide [ˈjul ˌtaɪd] *s* le feste natalizie

Z

Z, z [zi] *s* ventiseiesima lettera dell'alfabeto inglese
za·ny [ˈzeni] *adj* (**-nier; -niest**) comico, buffonesco || *s* (**-nies**) buffone *m*, pagliaccio
zeal [zil] *s* zelo, entusiasmo
zealot [ˈzɛlət] *s* zelante *mf*, fanatico
zealotry [ˈzɛlətri] *s* fanatismo
zealous [ˈzɛləs] *adj* zelante, volonteroso
zebra [ˈzibrə] *s* zebra
ze'bra cross'ing *s* zebre *fpl*
zebu [ˈzibju] *s* zebù *m*
zenith [ˈzinɪθ] *s* zenit *m*
zephyr [ˈzɛfər] *s* zefiro
ze·ro [ˈziro] *s* (**-roes**) zero || *tr*—**to zero in** (mil) aggiustare il mirino di || *intr*—**to zero in on** (mil) concentrare il fuoco su
ze'ro grav'ity *s* gravità *f* zero
ze'ro hour' *s* ora zero
zest [zɛst] *s* entusiasmo; (*flavor*) aroma *m*, sapore *m*
Zeus [zus] *s* Zeus *m*
zig-zag [ˈzɪg ˌzæg] *adj & adv* a zigzag || *s* zigzag *m;* serpentina || *v* (*pret & pp* **-zagged;** *ger* **-zagging**) *intr* zigzagare; serpeggiare
zinc [zɪŋk] *s* zinco
zinnia [ˈzɪnɪ·ə] *s* zinnia
Zionism [ˈzaɪ·ə ˌnɪzəm] *s* sionismo
zip [zɪp] *s* (coll) sibilo; (coll) energia, vigore *m* || *v* (*pret & pp* **zipped;** *ger* **zipping**) *tr* chiudere con cerniera lampo; aprire con cerniera lampo; (coll) portare rapidamente; **to zip up** (*to add zest to*) dare gusto a || *intr* aprirsi con cerniera lampo; sibilare; (coll) filare, correre; **to zip by** (coll) passare come un lampo

zip′ code′ *s* codice *m* di avviamento postale
zipper ['zɪpər] *s* cerniera or serratura lampo
zircon ['zʌrkɑn] *s* zircone *m*
zirconium [zər'konɪ·əm] *s* zirconio
zither ['zɪθər] *s* cetra tirolese
zodiac ['zodɪ ,æk] *s* zodiaco
zone [zon] *s* zona; distretto postale || *tr* dividere in zone
zoo [zu] *s* giardino zoologico
zoologic(al) [,zo·ə'lɑdʒɪk(əl)] *adj* zoologico
zoologist [zo'ɑlədʒɪst] *s* zoologo
zoology [zo'ɑlədʒi] *s* zoologia
zoom [zum] *s* ronzio; (aer) cabrata, impennata; (mov, telv) zumata || *tr* (aer) far cabrare, fare impennare; (mov, telv) zumare || *intr* ronzare; (aer) cabrare, impennarsi; (mov, telv) zumare
zoom′ lens′ *s* (phot) transfocatore *m*
zoophite ['zo·ə ,faɪt] *s* zoofito
Zu·lu ['zulu] *adj* zulù || *s* (**-lus**) zulù *mf*
Zurich ['zurɪk] *s* Zurigo *f*